FORMULAS FROM GEOMETRY

Triangle

$h = a \sin \theta$

$\text{Area} = \dfrac{1}{2}bh$

Laws of Cosines:
$c^2 = a^2 + b^2 - 2ab \cos \theta$

Circular Ring

$\text{Area} = \pi(R^2 - r^2)$

$\quad\quad = 2\pi pw$

(p = average radius,

$\quad w$ = width of ring)

 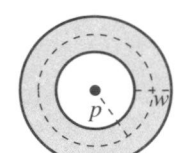

Right Triangle

Pythagorean Theorem:
$c^2 = a^2 + b^2$

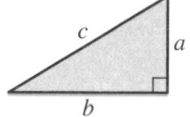

Ellipse

$\text{Area} = \pi ab$

$\text{Circumference} \approx 2\pi\sqrt{\dfrac{a^2 + b^2}{2}}$

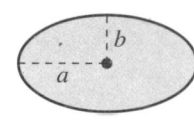

Equilateral Triangle

$h = \dfrac{\sqrt{3}s}{2}$

$\text{Area} = \dfrac{\sqrt{3}s^2}{4}$

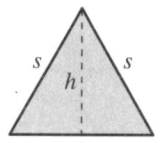

Cone

(A = area of base)

$\text{Volume} = \dfrac{Ah}{3}$

Parallelogram

$\text{Area} = bh$

Right Circular Cone

$\text{Volume} = \dfrac{\pi r^2 h}{3}$

$\text{Lateral Surface Area} = \pi r\sqrt{r^2 + h^2}$

Trapezoid

$\text{Area} = \dfrac{h}{2}(a + b)$

 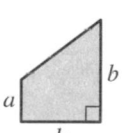

Frustum of Right Circular Cone

$\text{Volume} = \dfrac{\pi(r^2 + rR + R^2)h}{3}$

$\text{Lateral Surface Area} = \pi s(R + r)$

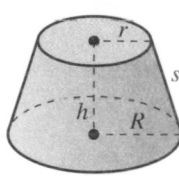

Circle

$\text{Area} = \pi r^2$

$\text{Circumference} = 2\pi r$

Right Circular Cylinder

$\text{Volume} = \pi r^2 h$

$\text{Lateral Surface Area} = 2\pi rh$

Sector of Circle

$\text{Area} = \dfrac{\theta r^2}{2}$

$s = r\theta$

(θ in radians)

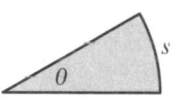

Sphere

$\text{Volume} = \dfrac{4}{3}\pi r^3$

$\text{Surface Area} = 4\pi r^2$

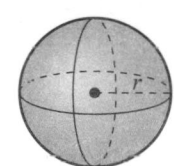

Definition of the Six Trigonometric Functions

Right triangle definitions, where $0 < \theta < \pi/2$

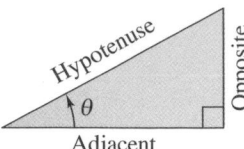

$$\sin \theta = \frac{\text{opp.}}{\text{hyp.}} \qquad \csc \theta = \frac{\text{hyp.}}{\text{opp.}}$$

$$\cos \theta = \frac{\text{adj.}}{\text{hyp.}} \qquad \sec \theta = \frac{\text{hyp.}}{\text{adj.}}$$

$$\tan \theta = \frac{\text{opp.}}{\text{adj.}} \qquad \cot \theta = \frac{\text{adj.}}{\text{opp.}}$$

Circular function definitions, where θ is any angle

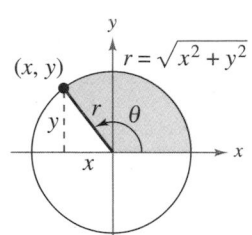

$$\sin \theta = \frac{y}{r} \qquad \csc \theta = \frac{r}{y}$$

$$\cos \theta = \frac{x}{r} \qquad \sec \theta = \frac{r}{x}$$

$$\tan \theta = \frac{y}{x} \qquad \cot \theta = \frac{x}{y}$$

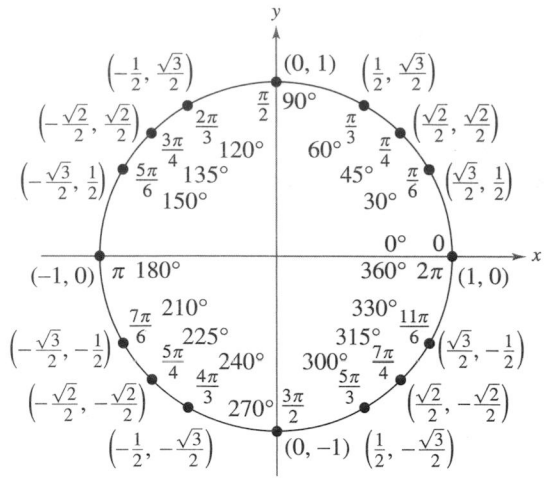

Reciprocal Identities

$$\sin u = \frac{1}{\csc u} \qquad \cos u = \frac{1}{\sec u} \qquad \tan u = \frac{1}{\cot u}$$

$$\csc u = \frac{1}{\sin u} \qquad \sec u = \frac{1}{\cos u} \qquad \cot u = \frac{1}{\tan u}$$

Quotient Identities

$$\tan u = \frac{\sin u}{\cos u} \qquad \cot u = \frac{\cos u}{\sin u}$$

Pythagorean Identities

$$\sin^2 u + \cos^2 u = 1$$
$$1 + \tan^2 u = \sec^2 u \qquad 1 + \cot^2 u = \csc^2 u$$

Cofunction Identities

$$\sin\left(\frac{\pi}{2} - u\right) = \cos u \qquad \cot\left(\frac{\pi}{2} - u\right) = \tan u$$

$$\cos\left(\frac{\pi}{2} - u\right) = \sin u \qquad \sec\left(\frac{\pi}{2} - u\right) = \csc u$$

$$\tan\left(\frac{\pi}{2} - u\right) = \cot u \qquad \csc\left(\frac{\pi}{2} - u\right) = \sec u$$

Even/Odd Identities

$$\sin(-u) = -\sin u \qquad \cot(-u) = -\cot u$$
$$\cos(-u) = \cos u \qquad \sec(-u) = \sec u$$
$$\tan(-u) = -\tan u \qquad \csc(-u) = -\csc u$$

Sum and Difference Formulas

$$\sin(u \pm v) = \sin u \cos v \pm \cos u \sin v$$
$$\cos(u \pm v) = \cos u \cos v \mp \sin u \sin v$$

$$\tan(u \pm v) = \frac{\tan u \pm \tan v}{1 \mp \tan u \tan v}$$

Double-Angle Formulas

$$\sin 2u = 2 \sin u \cos u$$
$$\cos 2u = \cos^2 u - \sin^2 u = 2 \cos^2 u - 1 = 1 - 2 \sin^2 u$$

$$\tan 2u = \frac{2 \tan u}{1 - \tan^2 u}$$

Power-Reducing Formulas

$$\sin^2 u = \frac{1 - \cos 2u}{2}$$

$$\cos^2 u = \frac{1 + \cos 2u}{2}$$

$$\tan^2 u = \frac{1 - \cos 2u}{1 + \cos 2u}$$

Sum-to-Product Formulas

$$\sin u + \sin v = 2 \sin\left(\frac{u + v}{2}\right) \cos\left(\frac{u - v}{2}\right)$$

$$\sin u - \sin v = 2 \cos\left(\frac{u + v}{2}\right) \sin\left(\frac{u - v}{2}\right)$$

$$\cos u + \cos v = 2 \cos\left(\frac{u + v}{2}\right) \cos\left(\frac{u - v}{2}\right)$$

$$\cos u - \cos v = -2 \sin\left(\frac{u + v}{2}\right) \sin\left(\frac{u - v}{2}\right)$$

Product-to-Sum Formulas

$$\sin u \sin v = \frac{1}{2}[\cos(u - v) - \cos(u + v)]$$

$$\cos u \cos v = \frac{1}{2}[\cos(u - v) + \cos(u + v)]$$

$$\sin u \cos v = \frac{1}{2}[\sin(u + v) + \sin(u - v)]$$

$$\cos u \sin v = \frac{1}{2}[\sin(u + v) - \sin(u - v)]$$

Precalculus with Limits
A Graphing Approach
Seventh Edition

Ron Larson

The Pennsylvania State University
The Behrend College

With the assistance of David C. Falvo

The Pennsylvania State University
The Behrend College

CENGAGE
Learning

Australia · Brazil · Mexico · Singapore · United Kingdom · United States

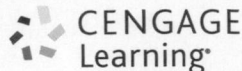
CENGAGE
Learning®

Precalculus with Limits: A Graphing Approach
Seventh Edition

Ron Larson

Senior Product Director: Richard Stratton
Product Manager: Gary Whalen
Senior Content Developer: Stacy Green
Associate Content Developer: Samantha Lugtu
Product Assistant: Katharine Werring
Media Developer: Lynh Pham
Senior Marketing Manager: Mark Linton
Content Project Manager: Jill Quinn
Manufacturing Planner: Doug Bertke
IP Analyst: Christina Ciaramella
IP Project Manager: John Sarantakis
VP, Director, Advanced and Elective Products Program:
    Alison Zetterquist
Associate Content Developer, Advanced and Elective Products
    Program: Ashley Bargende
Senior Media Developer, Advanced and Elective Products
    Program: Philip Lanza
Compositor: Larson Texts, Inc.
Text and Cover Designer: Larson Texts, Inc.
Cover Images: kentoh/Shutterstock.com;
    ecco/Shutterstock.com; Georgios Kollidas/Shutterstock.com;
    PureSolution/Shutterstock.com; mtkang/Shutterstock.com

Library of Congress Control Number: 2014947834

ISBN-13: 978-1-305-07171-1

Cengage Learning
20 Channel Center Street
Boston, MA 02210
USA

Cengage Learning is a leading provider of customized learning solutions with office locations around the globe, including Singapore, the United Kingdom, Australia, Mexico, Brazil, and Japan. Locate your local office at **www.cengage.com/global.**

Cengage Learning products are represented in Canada by Nelson Education, Ltd.

To learn more about Cengage Learning Solutions, visit **www.cengage.com.**

To find online supplements and other instructional support, please visit **www.cengagebrain.com.**

Instructors: Please visit **login.cengage.com** and log in to access instructor-specific resources.

Printed in the United States of America

Print Number: 01   Print Year: 2014

Contents

1 ▷ Functions and Their Graphs   **1**

     Introduction to Library of Parent Functions   2
1.1   Lines in the Plane   3
1.2   Functions   16
1.3   Graphs of Functions   29
1.4   Shifting, Reflecting, and Stretching Graphs   41
1.5   Combinations of Functions   50
1.6   Inverse Functions   60
1.7   Linear Models and Scatter Plots   71
     Chapter Summary   80
     Review Exercises   82
     Chapter Test   86
     Proofs in Mathematics   87

2 ▷ Polynomial and Rational Functions   **89**

2.1   Quadratic Functions   90
2.2   Polynomial Functions of Higher Degree   100
2.3   Real Zeros of Polynomial Functions   113
2.4   Complex Numbers   128
2.5   The Fundamental Theorem of Algebra   135
2.6   Rational Functions and Asymptotes   142
2.7   Graphs of Rational Functions   151
2.8   Quadratic Models   161
     Chapter Summary   168
     Review Exercises   170
     Chapter Test   175
     Proofs in Mathematics   176
     Progressive Summary (Chapters 1–2)   178

3 ▷ Exponential and Logarithmic Functions   **179**

3.1   Exponential Functions and Their Graphs   180
3.2   Logarithmic Functions and Their Graphs   192
3.3   Properties of Logarithms   203
3.4   Solving Exponential and Logarithmic Equations   210
3.5   Exponential and Logarithmic Models   221
3.6   Nonlinear Models   233
     Chapter Summary   242
     Review Exercises   244
     Chapter Test   248
     Cumulative Test: Chapters 1–3   249
     Proofs in Mathematics   251
     Progressive Summary (Chapters 1–3)   252

4 ▷ Trigonometric Functions   253

4.1   Radian and Degree Measure   254
4.2   Trigonometric Functions: The Unit Circle   265
4.3   Right Triangle Trigonometry   273
4.4   Trigonometric Functions of Any Angle   284
4.5   Graphs of Sine and Cosine Functions   292
4.6   Graphs of Other Trigonometric Functions   304
4.7   Inverse Trigonometric Functions   315
4.8   Applications and Models   326
Chapter Summary   338
Review Exercises   340
Chapter Test   345
Library of Parent Functions Review   346
Proofs in Mathematics   348

5 ▷ Analytic Trigonometry   349

5.1   Using Fundamental Identities   350
5.2   Verifying Trigonometric Identities   357
5.3   Solving Trigonometric Equations   365
5.4   Sum and Difference Formulas   377
5.5   Multiple-Angle and Product-to-Sum Formulas   384
Chapter Summary   394
Review Exercises   396
Chapter Test   399
Proofs in Mathematics   400

6 ▷ Additional Topics in Trigonometry   403

6.1   Law of Sines   404
6.2   Law of Cosines   413
6.3   Vectors in the Plane   420
6.4   Vectors and Dot Products   434
6.5   Trigonometric Form of a Complex Number   443
Chapter Summary   456
Review Exercises   458
Chapter Test   461
Cumulative Test: Chapters 4–6   462
Proofs in Mathematics   464
Progressive Summary (Chapters 1–6)   468

7 ▷ Linear Systems and Matrices   **469**

7.1   Solving Systems of Equations   470
7.2   Systems of Linear Equations in Two Variables   480
7.3   Multivariable Linear Systems   489
7.4   Matrices and Systems of Equations   504
7.5   Operations with Matrices   518
7.6   The Inverse of a Square Matrix   532
7.7   The Determinant of a Square Matrix   541
7.8   Applications of Matrices and Determinants   548
       Chapter Summary   558
       Review Exercises   560
       Chapter Test   566
       Proofs in Mathematics   567

8 ▷ Sequences, Series, and Probability   **569**

8.1   Sequences and Series   570
8.2   Arithmetic Sequences and Partial Sums   581
8.3   Geometric Sequences and Series   589
8.4   The Binomial Theorem   599
8.5   Counting Principles   607
8.6   Probability   616
       Chapter Summary   626
       Review Exercises   628
       Chapter Test   631
       Proofs in Mathematics   632

9 ▷ Topics in Analytic Geometry   **635**

9.1   Circles and Parabolas   636
9.2   Ellipses   647
9.3   Hyperbolas and Rotation of Conics   656
9.4   Parametric Equations   669
9.5   Polar Coordinates   677
9.6   Graphs of Polar Equations   683
9.7   Polar Equations of Conics   691
       Chapter Summary   698
       Review Exercises   700
       Chapter Test   704
       Cumulative Test: Chapters 7–9   705
       Proofs in Mathematics   707
       Progressive Summary (Chapters 3–9)   710

10 ▷ Analytic Geometry in Three Dimensions   **711**

10.1   The Three-Dimensional Coordinate System   712
10.2   Vectors in Space   719
10.3   The Cross Product of Two Vectors   726
10.4   Lines and Planes in Space   733
     Chapter Summary   742
     Review Exercises   744
     Chapter Test   746
     Proofs in Mathematics   747

11 ▷ Limits and an Introduction to Calculus   **749**

11.1   Introduction to Limits   750
11.2   Techniques for Evaluating Limits   760
11.3   The Tangent Line Problem   770
11.4   Limits at Infinity and Limits of Sequences   780
11.5   The Area Problem   789
     Chapter Summary   796
     Review Exercises   798
     Chapter Test   801
     Cumulative Test: Chapters 10–11   802
     Proofs in Mathematics   804
     Progressive Summary (Chapters 3–11)   805

Appendices

Appendix A   **Technology Support Guide**   A1
Appendix B   **Concepts in Statistics**   A25
     B.1   Representing Data Graphically   A25
     B.2   Measures of Central Tendency and Dispersion   A35
     B.3   Least Squares Regression   A44
Appendix C   **Review of Graphs, Equations, and Inequalities**   (web)
     C.1   The Cartesian Plane
     C.2   Graphs of Equations
     C.3   Solving Equations Algebraically and Graphically
     C.4   Solving Inequalities Algebraically and Graphically
Appendix D   **Variation**   (web)
Appendix E   **Solving Linear Equations and Inequalities**   (web)
Appendix F   **Systems of Inequalities**   (web)
     F.1   Solving Systems of Inequalities
     F.2   Linear Programming
Appendix G   **Mathematical Induction**   (web)

     Answers to Odd-Numbered Exercises and Tests   A47
     Index of Selected Applications   A157
     Index   A159

$$f(x) = \frac{2x}{x-3}$$

Preface

Welcome to *Precalculus with Limits: A Graphing Approach*, Seventh Edition. I am proud to present to you this new edition. As with all editions, I have been able to incorporate many useful comments from you, our user. And while much has changed in this revision, you will still find what you expect—a pedagogically sound, mathematically precise, and comprehensive textbook. While we need the mathematics of precalculus to master calculus, precalculus is not simply preliminary material for calculus. It stands alone as "real mathematics" in itself. In this book you will see how precalculus is used by real people to solve real-life problems and make real-life decisions.

In addition to providing real and relevant mathematics, I am pleased and excited to offer you something brand new—a companion website at **LarsonPrecalculus.com.** My goal is to provide students with the tools they need to master precalculus.

New To This Edition

NEW LarsonPrecalculus.com

This companion website offers multiple tools and resources to supplement your learning. Access to these features is free. View and listen to worked-out solutions of Checkpoint problems in English or Spanish, explore examples, download data sets, watch lesson videos, and much more.

NEW Checkpoints

Accompanying every example, the Checkpoint problems encourage immediate practice and check your understanding of the concepts presented in the example. View and listen to worked-out solutions of the Checkpoint problems in English or Spanish at LarsonPrecalculus.com.

130. HOW DO YOU SEE IT? Decide whether the two functions shown in each graph appear to be inverse functions of each other. Explain your reasoning.

(a)

(b)

(c)

(d)

NEW How Do You See It?

The How Do You See It? feature in each section presents an exercise that you will solve by visual inspection using the concepts learned in the lesson. This exercise is excellent for classroom discussion or test preparation.

NEW Data Spreadsheets

Download these editable spreadsheets from LarsonPrecalculus.com and use the data to solve exercises.

REVISED Exercise Sets

The exercise sets have been carefully and extensively examined to ensure they are rigorous and relevant and to include all topics our users have suggested. The exercises have been **reorganized and titled** so you can better see the connections between examples and exercises. Multi-step exercises reinforce problem-solving skills and mastery of concepts by giving you the opportunity to apply the concepts in real-life situations.

REVISED Remarks

These hints and tips reinforce or expand upon concepts, help you learn how to study mathematics, address special cases, or show alternative or additional steps to a solution of an example.

Trusted Features

Calc Chat

For the past several years, an independent website—CalcChat.com—has provided free solutions to all odd-numbered problems in the text. Thousands of students have visited the site for practice and help with their homework.

Side-By-Side Examples

Throughout the text, we present solutions to examples from multiple perspectives—algebraically, graphically, and numerically. The side-by-side format of this pedagogical feature helps you to see that a problem can be solved in more than one way and to see that different methods yield the same result. The side-by-side format also addresses different learning styles.

Why You Should Learn It Exercise

An engaging real-life application of the concepts in the section. This application exercise is typically described in the section opener as a motivator for the section.

Library of Parent Functions

To facilitate familiarity with the basic functions, several elementary and nonelementary functions have been compiled as a Library of Parent Functions. Each function is introduced at its first appearance in the text with a definition and description of basic characteristics. The Library of Parent Functions Examples are identified in the title of the example and there is a Review of Library of Parent Functions after Chapter 4. A summary of functions is presented on the inside cover of this text.

Make a Decision Exercises

The Make a Decision exercises at the end of selected sections involve in-depth applied exercises in which you will work with large, real-life data sets, often creating or analyzing models. These exercises are offered online at LarsonPrecalculus.com.

Chapter Openers

Each Chapter Opener highlights a real-life modeling problem, showing a graph of the data, a section reference, and a short description of the data.

Explore the Concept

Each Explore the Concept engages you in active discovery of mathematical concepts, strengthens critical thinking skills, and helps build intuition.

Explore the Concept

Complete the following:

$i^1 = i$ $i^7 = \boxed{}$

$i^2 = -1$ $i^8 = \boxed{}$

$i^3 = -i$ $i^9 = \boxed{}$

$i^4 = 1$ $i^{10} = \boxed{}$

$i^5 = \boxed{}$ $i^{11} = \boxed{}$

$i^6 = \boxed{}$ $i^{12} = \boxed{}$

What pattern do you see? Write a brief description of how you would find i raised to any positive integer power.

$$f(x) = \frac{2x}{x-3}$$

Technology Tip

Although a graphing utility can be useful in helping to verify an identity, you must use algebraic techniques to produce a valid proof. For example, graph the two functions $y_1 = \sin 50x$ and $y_2 = \sin 2x$ in a trigonometric viewing window. On some graphing utilities the graphs appear to be identical. However, $\sin 50x \neq \sin 2x$.

What's Wrong?

Each What's Wrong? points out common errors made using graphing utilities.

Technology Tip

Technology Tips provide graphing calculator tips or provide alternative methods of solving a problem using a graphing utility.

Algebra of Calculus

Throughout the text, special emphasis is given to the algebraic techniques used in calculus. Algebra of Calculus examples and exercises are integrated throughout the text and are identified by the symbol f.

Algebraic-Graphical-Numerical Exercises

These exercises allow you to solve a problem using multiple approaches—algebraic, graphical, and numerical. This helps you to see that a problem can be solved in more than one way and to see that different methods yield the same result.

Modeling Data Exercises

These multi-part applications that involve real-life data offer you the opportunity to generate and analyze mathematical models.

Vocabulary and Concept Check

The Vocabulary and Concept Check appears at the beginning of the exercise set for each section. Each of these checks asks fill-in-the-blank, matching, and non-computational questions designed to help you learn mathematical terminology and to test basic understanding of that section's concepts.

What you should learn/Why you should learn it

These summarize important topics in the section and why they are important in math and in life.

Chapter Summaries

The Chapter Summary includes explanations and examples of the objectives taught in the chapter.

Error Analysis Exercises

This exercise presents a sample solution that contains a common error which you are asked to identify.

ENHANCED WebAssign

Enhanced WebAssign combines exceptional Precalculus content with the most powerful online homework solution, WebAssign. Enhanced WebAssign engages you with immediate feedback, rich tutorial content and interactive, fully customizable eBooks (YouBook) helping you to develop a deeper conceptual understanding of the subject matter.

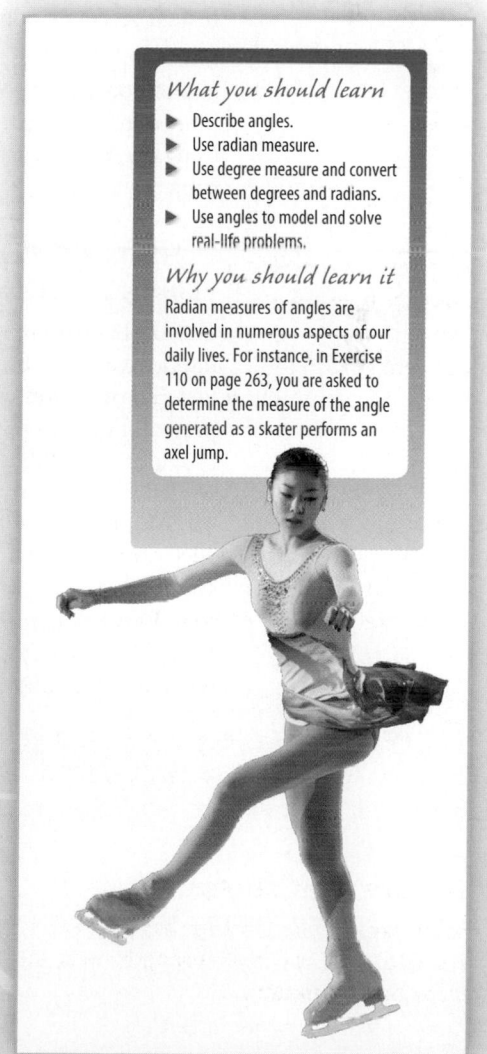

What you should learn
- ▶ Describe angles.
- ▶ Use radian measure.
- ▶ Use degree measure and convert between degrees and radians.
- ▶ Use angles to model and solve real-life problems.

Why you should learn it
Radian measures of angles are involved in numerous aspects of our daily lives. For instance, in Exercise 110 on page 263, you are asked to determine the measure of the angle generated as a skater performs an axel jump.

Complete Solutions Manual

• ISBN-13: 9781305117662

This manual contains solutions to all exercises from the text, including Chapter Review Exercises and Chapter Tests. This manual is found on the Instructors Companion Site.

Test Bank

• ISBN-13: 9781305117570

This supplement includes test forms for every chapter of the text, and is found on the instructor companion site.

Text-Specific DVDs

• ISBN-13: 9781305117143

These text-specific DVDs cover all sections of the text—providing explanations of key concepts as well as examples, exercises, and applications in a lecture-based format.

Enhanced WebAssign

Printed Access Card: 9781285858333
Instant Access Code: 9781285858319

Enhanced WebAssign combines exceptional mathematics content with the most powerful online homework solution, WebAssign. Enhanced WebAssign engages your students with immediate feedback, rich tutorial content, and an interactive, fully customizable eBook, Cengage YouBook helping students to develop a deeper conceptual understanding of the subject matter.

PowerLecture with ExamView

• ISBN-13: 9781305117600

The DVD provides you with dynamic media tools for teaching Precalculus while using an interactive white board, PowerPoint® lecture slides and art slides of the figures from the text. The algorithmic ExamView allows you to create, deliver, and customize tests (both print and online) in minutes with this easy-to-use assessment system. The DVD also provides you with a tutorial on integrating our instructor materials into your interactive whiteboard platform. Enhance how your students interact with you, your lecture, and each other.

Instructor Companion Site

Everything you need for your course in one place! This collection of book-specific lecture and class tools is available online via www.cengage.com/login. Access and download PowerPoint presentations, images, instructor's manual, and more.

Student Solutions Manual

• ISBN-13: 9781305117112

Contains fully worked-out solutions to all of the odd-numbered exercises in the text, giving you a way to check your answers and ensure that you took the correct steps to arrive at an answer.

K12HS Note Taking and Keystroke Guide: A Workbook for Students

• ISBN-13: 9781305117150

This study aid provides both a notebook organizer that helps you develop a section-by-section summary of key concepts and a graphing calculator keystroke guide that includes step-by-step instruction on how best to use a graphing calculator.

Enhanced WebAssign

Printed Access Card: 9781285858333
Instant Access Code: 9781285858319

Enhanced WebAssign combines exceptional mathematics content with the most powerful online homework solution, WebAssign. Enhanced WebAssign engages you with immediate feedback, rich tutorial content, and an interactive, fully customizable eBook, Cengage YouBook helping you to develop a deeper conceptual understanding of the subject matter.

CengageBrain.com

To access additional course materials, please visit www.cengagebrain.com. At the CengageBrain.com home page, search for the ISBN of your title (from the back cover of your book) using the search box at the top of the page. This will take you to the product page where these resources can be found.

Acknowledgments

I would like to thank my colleagues who have helped me develop this program. Their encouragement, criticisms, and suggestions have been invaluable to me.

Reviewers

Hugh Cornell, *University of North Florida*
Kewal Krishan, *Hudson County Community College*
Ferdinand Orock, *Hudson County Community College*
Marnie Phipps, *North Georgia College and State University*
Nancy Schendel, *Iowa Lakes Community College*
Ann Wheeler, *Texas Woman's University*

I would also like to thank the following reviewers, who have given me many useful insights to this and previous editions.

Tony Homayoon Akhlaghi, *Bellevue Community College;* Daniel D. Anderson, *University of Iowa;* Bruce Armbrust, *Lake Tahoe Community College;* Jamie Whitehead Ashby, *Texarkana College;* Teresa Barton, *Western New England College;* Kimberly Bennekin, *Georgia Perimeter College;* Charles M. Biles, *Humboldt State University;* Phyllis Barsch Bolin, *Oklahoma Christian University;* Khristo Boyadzhiev, *Ohio Northern University;* Dave Bregenzer, *Utah State University;* Anne E. Brown, *Indiana University-South Bend;* Diane Burleson, *Central Piedmont Community College;* Beth Burns, *Bowling Green State University;* Alexander Burstein, *University of Rhode Island;* Marilyn Carlson, *University of Kansas;* Victor M. Cornell, *Mesa Community College;* John Dersh, *Grand Rapids Community College;* Jennifer Dollar, *Grand Rapids Community College;* Marcia Drost, *Texas A & M University;* Cameron English, *Rio Hondo College;* Susan E. Enyart, *Otterbein College;* Patricia J. Ernst, *St. Cloud State University;* Eunice Everett, *Seminole Community College;* Kenny Fister, *Murray State University;* Susan C. Fleming, *Virginia Highlands Community College;* Jeff Frost, *Johnson County Community College;* James R. Fryxell, *College of Lake County;* Khadiga H. Gamgoum, *Northern Virginia Community College;* Nicholas E. Geller, *Collin County Community College;* Betty Givan, *Eastern Kentucky University;* Patricia K. Gramling, *Trident Technical College;* Michele Greenfield, *Middlesex County College;* Bernard Greenspan, *University of Akron;* Zenas Hartvigson, *University of Colorado at Denver;* Rodger Hergert, *Rock Valley College;* Allen Hesse, *Rochester Community College;* Rodney Holke-Farnam, *Hawkeye Community College;* Lynda Hollingsworth, *Northwest Missouri State University;* Jean M. Horn, *Northern Virginia Community College;* Spencer Hurd, *The Citadel;* Bill Huston, *Missouri Western State College;* Deborah Johnson, *Cambridge South Dorchester High School;* Francine Winston Johnson, *Howard Community College;* Luella Johnson, *State University of New York, College at Buffalo;* Susan Kellicut, *Seminole Community College;* John Kendall, *Shelby State Community College;* Donna M. Krawczyk, *University of Arizona;* Laura Lake, *Center for Advanced Technologies/ Lakewood High School;* Peter A. Lappan, *Michigan State University;* Charles G. Laws, *Cleveland State Community College;* JoAnn Lewin, *Edison Community College;* Richard J. Maher, *Loyola University;* Carl Main, *Florida College;* Marilyn McCollum, *North Carolina State University;* Judy McInerney, *Sandhills Community College;* David E. Meel, *Bowling Green University;* Beverly Michael, *University of Pittsburgh;* Wendy Morin, *Dwight D. Eisenhower High School;* Roger B. Nelsen, *Lewis and Clark College;* Stephen Nicoloff, *Paradise Valley Community College;* Jon Odell, *Richland Community College;* Paul Oswood, *Ridgewater College;* Wing M. Park, *College of Lake County;* Rupa M. Patel, *University of Portland;* Robert Pearce, *South Plains College;* David R. Peterson, *University of Central Arkansas;* Sandra Poinsett, *College of Southern Maryland;* James Pommersheim, *Reed College;* Antonio Quesada, *University of Akron;* Laura Reger, *Milwaukee Area Technical College;* Jennifer Rhinehart, *Mars Hill College;* Lila F. Roberts, *Georgia Southern University;* Keith Schwingendorf, *Purdue University North Central;* Abdallah Shuaibi, *Truman College;* George W. Shultz, *St. Petersburg Junior College;* Stephen Slack, *Kenyon College;*

$$f(x) = \dfrac{2x}{x-3}$$

Judith Smalling, *St. Petersburg Junior College;* Pamela K. M. Smith, *Fort Lewis College;* Cathryn U. Stark, *Collin County Community College;* Craig M. Steenberg, *Lewis-Clark State College;* Mary Jane Sterling, *Bradley University;* G. Bryan Stewart, *Tarrant County Junior College;* Diane Veneziale, *Burlington County College;* Mahbobeh Vezvaei, *Kent State University;* Ellen Vilas, *York Technical College;* Hayat Weiss, *Middlesex Community College;* Rich West, *Francis Marion University;* Vanessa White, *Southern University;* Howard L. Wilson, *Oregon State University;* Joel E. Wilson, *Eastern Kentucky University;* Michelle Wilson, *Franklin University;* Paul Winterbottom, *Montgomery County Community College;* Fred Worth, *Henderson State University;* Karl M. Zilm, *Lewis and Clark Community College;* Cathleen Zucco-Teveloff, *Rowan University*

I hope that you enjoy learning the mathematics presented in this text. More than that, I hope you gain a new appreciation for the relevance of mathematics to careers in science, technology, business, and medicine.

My thanks to Robert Hostetler, The Behrend College, The Pennsylvania State University, Bruce Edwards, University of Florida, and David Heyd, The Behrend College, The Pennsylvania State University, for their significant contributions to previous editions of this text.

I would also like to thank the staff of Larson Texts, Inc. who assisted in preparing the manuscript, rendering the art package, and typesetting and proofreading the pages and supplements.

On a personal level, I am grateful to my spouse, Deanna Gilbert Larson, for her love, patience, and support. Also, a special thanks goes to R. Scott O'Neil.

If you have suggestions for improving this text, please feel free to write me. Over the past two decades I have received many useful comments from both instructors and students, and I value these very much.

Ron Larson, Ph.D.
Professor of Mathematics
Penn State University
www.RonLarson.com

1 Functions and Their Graphs

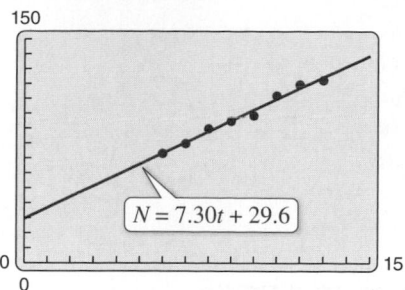

$N = 7.30t + 29.6$

Section 1.7, Example 4
e-Filed Tax Returns

1.1 Lines in the Plane

1.2 Functions

1.3 Graphs of Functions

1.4 Shifting, Reflecting, and Stretching Graphs

1.5 Combinations of Functions

1.6 Inverse Functions

1.7 Linear Models and Scatter Plots

Introduction to Library of Parent Functions

In Chapter 1, you will be introduced to the concept of a *function*. As you proceed through the text, you will see that functions play a primary role in modeling real-life situations.

There are three basic types of functions that have proven to be the most important in modeling real-life situations. These functions are algebraic functions, exponential and logarithmic functions, and trigonometric and inverse trigonometric functions. These three types of functions are referred to as the *elementary functions*, though they are often placed in the two categories of *algebraic functions* and *transcendental functions*. Each time a new type of function is studied in detail in this text, it will be highlighted in a box similar to those shown below. The graphs of these functions are shown on the inside covers of this text.

Algebraic Functions

These functions are formed by applying algebraic operations to the linear function $f(x) = x$.

Name	Function	Location
Linear	$f(x) = x$	Section 1.1
Quadratic	$f(x) = x^2$	Section 2.1
Cubic	$f(x) = x^3$	Section 2.2
Rational	$f(x) = \dfrac{1}{x}$	Section 2.7
Square root	$f(x) = \sqrt{x}$	Section 1.2

Transcendental Functions

These functions cannot be formed from the linear function by using algebraic operations.

Name	Function	Location
Exponential	$f(x) = a^x, a > 0, a \neq 1$	Section 3.1
Logarithmic	$f(x) = \log_a x, x > 0, a > 0, a \neq 1$	Section 3.2
Trigonometric	$f(x) = \sin x$	Section 4.5
	$f(x) = \cos x$	Section 4.5
	$f(x) = \tan x$	Section 4.6
	$f(x) = \csc x$	Section 4.6
	$f(x) = \sec x$	Section 4.6
	$f(x) = \cot x$	Section 4.6
Inverse trigonometric	$f(x) = \arcsin x$	Section 4.7
	$f(x) = \arccos x$	Section 4.7
	$f(x) = \arctan x$	Section 4.7

Nonelementary Functions

Some useful nonelementary functions include the following.

Name	Function	Location
Absolute value	$f(x) = |x|$	Section 1.2
Greatest integer	$f(x) = [\![x]\!]$	Section 1.3

1.1   Lines in the Plane

The Slope of a Line

In this section, you will study lines and their equations. The **slope** of a nonvertical line represents the number of units the line rises or falls vertically for each unit of horizontal change from left to right. For instance, consider the two points

$$(x_1, y_1) \qquad \text{and} \qquad (x_2, y_2)$$

on the line shown in Figure 1.1.

Figure 1.1

As you move from left to right along this line, a change of $(y_2 - y_1)$ units in the vertical direction corresponds to a change of $(x_2 - x_1)$ units in the horizontal direction. That is,

$$y_2 - y_1 = \text{the change in } y$$

and

$$x_2 - x_1 = \text{the change in } x.$$

The slope of the line is given by the ratio of these two changes.

Definition of the Slope of a Line

The **slope** m of the nonvertical line through (x_1, y_1) and (x_2, y_2) is

$$m = \frac{y_2 - y_1}{x_2 - x_1} = \frac{\text{change in } y}{\text{change in } x}$$

where $x_1 \neq x_2$.

When this formula for slope is used, the *order of subtraction* is important. Given two points on a line, you are free to label either one of them as (x_1, y_1) and the other as (x_2, y_2). Once you have done this, however, you must form the numerator and denominator using the same order of subtraction.

$$m = \frac{y_2 - y_1}{x_2 - x_1} \qquad m = \frac{y_1 - y_2}{x_1 - x_2} \qquad m = \frac{y_2 - y_1}{x_1 - x_2}$$

Correct   Correct   Incorrect

Throughout this text, the term *line* always means a *straight* line.

EXAMPLE 1   Finding the Slope of a Line

Find the slope of the line passing through each pair of points.

a. $(-2, 0)$ and $(3, 1)$ **b.** $(-1, 2)$ and $(2, 2)$ **c.** $(0, 4)$ and $(1, -1)$

Solution

Difference in y-values

a. $m = \dfrac{y_2 - y_1}{x_2 - x_1} = \dfrac{1 - 0}{3 - (-2)} = \dfrac{1}{3 + 2} = \dfrac{1}{5}$

Difference in x-values

b. $m = \dfrac{2 - 2}{2 - (-1)} = \dfrac{0}{3} = 0$

c. $m = \dfrac{-1 - 4}{1 - 0} = \dfrac{-5}{1} = -5$

The graphs of the three lines are shown in Figure 1.2. Note that the *square setting* gives the correct "steepness" of the lines.

(a)

(b)

(c)

Figure 1.2

✓ *Checkpoint* ◀))) *Audio-video solution in English & Spanish at LarsonPrecalculus.com.*

Find the slope of the line passing through each pair of points.

a. $(-5, -6)$ and $(2, 8)$ **b.** $(4, 2)$ and $(2, 5)$ **c.** $(0, -1)$ and $(3, -1)$

The definition of slope does not apply to vertical lines. For instance, consider the points $(3, 4)$ and $(3, 1)$ on the vertical line shown in Figure 1.3. Applying the formula for slope, you obtain

$$m = \frac{4 - 1}{3 - 3} = \frac{3}{0}. \qquad \text{Undefined}$$

Figure 1.3

Because division by zero is undefined, the slope of a vertical line is undefined.

From the lines shown in Figures 1.2 and 1.3, you can make the following generalizations about the slope of a line.

The Slope of a Line

1. A line with positive slope $(m > 0)$ *rises* from left to right.

2. A line with negative slope $(m < 0)$ *falls* from left to right.

3. A line with zero slope $(m = 0)$ is *horizontal*.

4. A line with undefined slope is *vertical*.

Explore the Concept

Use a graphing utility to compare the slopes of the lines $y = 0.5x$, $y = x$, $y = 2x$, and $y = 4x$. What do you observe about these lines? Compare the slopes of the lines $y = -0.5x$, $y = -x$, $y = -2x$, and $y = -4x$. What do you observe about these lines? (*Hint:* Use a *square setting* to obtain a true geometric perspective.)

The Point–Slope Form of the Equation of a Line

When you know the slope of a line *and* you also know the coordinates of one point on the line, you can find an equation of the line. For instance, in Figure 1.4, let (x_1, y_1) be a point on the line whose slope is m. When (x, y) is any *other* point on the line, it follows that

$$\frac{y - y_1}{x - x_1} = m.$$

This equation in the variables x and y can be rewritten in the **point-slope form** of the equation of a line.

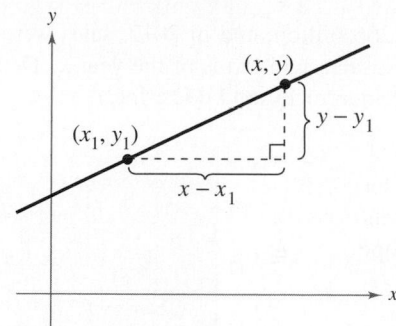

Figure 1.4

Point-Slope Form of the Equation of a Line

The **point-slope form** of the equation of the line that passes through the point (x_1, y_1) and has a slope of m is

$$y - y_1 = m(x - x_1).$$

EXAMPLE 2   The Point-Slope Form of the Equation of a Line

Find an equation of the line that passes through the point

$$(1, -2)$$

and has a slope of 3.

Solution

$$\begin{aligned} y - y_1 &= m(x - x_1) && \text{Point-slope form} \\ y - (-2) &= 3(x - 1) && \text{Substitute for } y_1, m, \text{ and } x_1. \\ y + 2 &= 3x - 3 && \text{Simplify.} \\ y &= 3x - 5 && \text{Solve for } y. \end{aligned}$$

The line is shown in Figure 1.5.

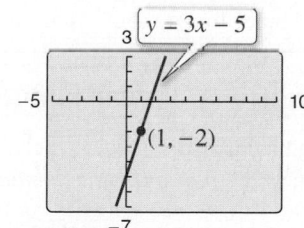

Figure 1.5

✓ **Checkpoint** ◀))) *Audio-video solution in English & Spanish at LarsonPrecalculus.com.*

Find an equation of the line that passes through the point $(3, -7)$ and has a slope of 2.

The point-slope form can be used to find an equation of a nonvertical line passing through two points

$$(x_1, y_1) \quad \text{and} \quad (x_2, y_2).$$

First, find the slope of the line.

$$m = \frac{y_2 - y_1}{x_2 - x_1}, \quad x_1 \neq x_2$$

Then use the point-slope form to obtain the equation

$$y - y_1 = \frac{y_2 - y_1}{x_2 - x_1}(x - x_1).$$

This is sometimes called the **two-point form** of the equation of a line.

Remark

When you find an equation of the line that passes through two given points, you need to substitute the coordinates of only one of the points into the point-slope form. It does not matter which point you choose because both points will yield the same result.

EXAMPLE 3 A Linear Model for Profits Prediction

In 2011, Tyson Foods had sales of $32.266 billion, and in 2012, sales were $33.278 billion. Write a linear equation giving the sales y in terms of the year x. Then use the equation to predict the sales for 2013. (Source: Tyson Foods, Inc.)

Solution

Let $x = 0$ represent 2000. In Figure 1.6, let (11, 32.266) and (12, 33.278) be two points on the line representing the sales. The slope of this line is

$$m = \frac{33.278 - 32.266}{12 - 11} = 1.012.$$

Next, use the point-slope form to find the equation of the line.

$$y - 32.266 = 1.012(x - 11)$$

$$y = 1.012x + 21.134$$

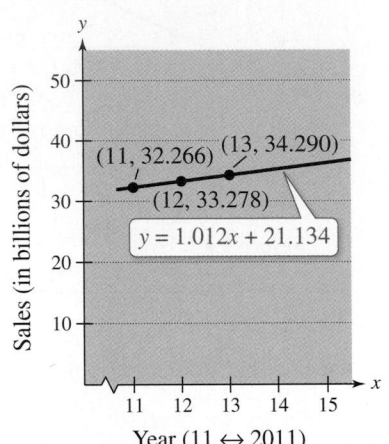

Now, using this equation, you can predict the 2013 sales ($x = 13$) to be

Figure 1.6

$$y = 1.012(13) + 21.134 = 13.156 + 21.134 = \$34.290 \text{ billion}.$$

(In this case, the prediction is quite good—the actual sales in 2013 were $34.374 billion.)

✓ **Checkpoint** ◀))) *Audio-video solution in English & Spanish at LarsonPrecalculus.com.*

In 2012, Apple had sales of $156.508 billion, and in 2013, sales were $170.910 billion. Write a linear equation giving the sales y in terms of the year x. Then use the equation to predict the sales for 2014. (Source: Apple, Inc.)

Library of Parent Functions: Linear Function

In the next section, you will be introduced to the precise meaning of the term *function*. The simplest type of function is the *parent linear function*

$$f(x) = x.$$

As its name implies, the graph of the parent linear function is a line. The basic characteristics of the parent linear function are summarized below and on the inside cover of this text. (Note that some of the terms below will be defined later in the text.)

Graph of $f(x) = x$

Domain: $(-\infty, \infty)$
Range: $(-\infty, \infty)$
Intercept: $(0, 0)$
Increasing

The function $f(x) = x$ is also referred to as the *identity function*. Later in this text, you will learn that the graph of the linear function $f(x) = mx + b$ is a line with slope m and y-intercept $(0, b)$. When $m = 0$, $f(x) = b$ is called a *constant function* and its graph is a horizontal line.

Sketching Graphs of Lines

Many problems in coordinate geometry can be classified in two categories.

1. Given a graph (or parts of it), find its equation.

2. Given an equation, sketch its graph.

For lines, the first problem can be solved by using the point-slope form. This formula, however, is not particularly useful for solving the second type of problem. The form that is better suited to graphing linear equations is the **slope-intercept form** of the equation of a line, $y = mx + b$.

Slope-Intercept Form of the Equation of a Line

The graph of the equation

$$y = mx + b$$

is a line whose slope is m and whose y-intercept is $(0, b)$.

EXAMPLE 4   Using the Slope-Intercept Form

See LarsonPrecalculus.com for an interactive version of this type of example.

Determine the slope and y-intercept of each linear equation. Then describe its graph.

a. $x + y = 2$ **b.** $y = 2$

Algebraic Solution

a. Begin by writing the equation in slope-intercept form.

$x + y = 2$	Write original equation.
$y = 2 - x$	Subtract x from each side.
$y = -x + 2$	Write in slope-intercept form.

From the slope-intercept form of the equation, the slope is -1 and the y-intercept is

$$(0, 2).$$

Because the slope is negative, you know that the graph of the equation is a line that falls one unit for every unit it moves to the right.

b. By writing the equation $y = 2$ in slope-intercept form

$$y = (0)x + 2$$

you can see that the slope is 0 and the y-intercept is

$$(0, 2).$$

A zero slope implies that the line is horizontal.

Graphical Solution

a.

b.

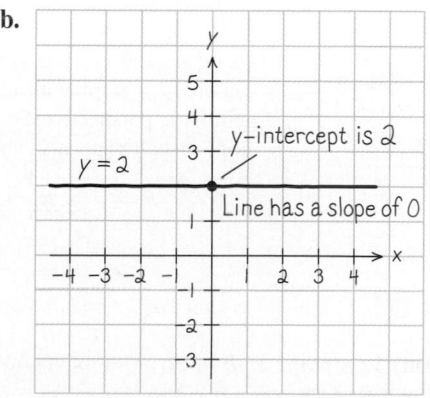

✓ **Checkpoint** ◀))) *Audio-video solution in English & Spanish at LarsonPrecalculus.com.*

Determine the slope and y-intercept of $x - 2y = 4$. Then describe its graph.

From the slope-intercept form of the equation of a line, you can see that a horizontal line ($m = 0$) has an equation of the form $y = b$. This is consistent with the fact that each point on a horizontal line through $(0, b)$ has a y-coordinate of b. Similarly, each point on a vertical line through $(a, 0)$ has an x-coordinate of a. So, a vertical line has an equation of the form $x = a$. This equation cannot be written in slope-intercept form because the slope of a vertical line is undefined. However, every line has an equation that can be written in the **general form**

$Ax + By + C = 0$ General form of the equation of a line

where A and B are not *both* zero.

Summary of Equations of Lines

1. General form: $Ax + By + C = 0$
2. Vertical line: $x = a$
3. Horizontal line: $y = b$
4. Slope-intercept form: $y = mx + b$
5. Point-slope form: $y - y_1 = m(x - x_1)$

EXAMPLE 5   Different Viewing Windows

When a graphing utility is used to graph a line, it is important to realize that the line may not visually appear to have the slope indicated by its equation. This occurs because of the viewing window used for the graph. For instance, Figure 1.7 shows graphs of $y = 2x + 1$ produced on a graphing utility using three different viewing windows. Notice that the slopes in Figures 1.7(a) and (b) do not visually appear to be equal to 2. When you use a *square setting*, as in Figure 1.7(c), the slope visually appears to be 2.

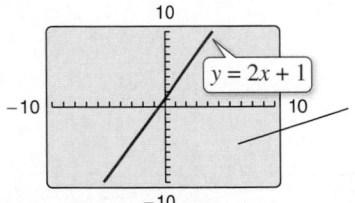

Using a *nonsquare setting*, you do *not* obtain a graph with a true geometric perspective. So, the slope does *not* visually appear to be 2.

(a) Nonsquare setting

(b) Nonsquare setting

Using a *square setting*, you can obtain a graph with a true geometric perspective. So, the slope visually appears to be 2.

(c) Square setting
Figure 1.7

✓ **Checkpoint** 🔊))) *Audio-video solution in English & Spanish at LarsonPrecalculus.com.*

Use a graphing utility to graph $y = 0.5x - 3$ using each viewing window. Describe the difference in the graphs.

a. Xmin = -5, Xmax = 10, Xscl = 1, Ymin = -1, Ymax = 10, Yscl = 1

b. Xmin = -2, Xmax = 10, Xscl = 1, Ymin = -4, Ymax = 1, Yscl = 1

c. Xmin = -5, Xmax = 10, Xscl = 1, Ymin = -7, Ymax = 3, Yscl = 1

Parallel and Perpendicular Lines

The slope of a line is a convenient tool for determining whether two lines are parallel or perpendicular.

> **Parallel Lines**
>
> Two distinct nonvertical lines are **parallel** if and only if their slopes are equal. That is, $m_1 = m_2$.

EXAMPLE 6   Equations of Parallel Lines

Find the slope-intercept form of the equation of the line that passes through the point $(2, -1)$ and is parallel to the line $2x - 3y = 5$.

Solution

Begin by writing the equation of the line in slope-intercept form.

$$2x - 3y = 5 \qquad \text{Write original equation.}$$

$$-2x + 3y = -5 \qquad \text{Multiply by } -1.$$

$$3y = 2x - 5 \qquad \text{Add } 2x \text{ to each side.}$$

$$y = \frac{2}{3}x - \frac{5}{3} \qquad \text{Write in slope-intercept form.}$$

Therefore, the given line has a slope of

$$m = \tfrac{2}{3}.$$

Any line parallel to the given line must also have a slope of $\frac{2}{3}$. So, the line through $(2, -1)$ has the following equation.

$$y - y_1 = m(x - x_1) \qquad \text{Point-slope form}$$

$$y - (-1) = \frac{2}{3}(x - 2) \qquad \text{Substitute for } y_1, m, \text{ and } x_1.$$

$$y + 1 = \frac{2}{3}x - \frac{4}{3} \qquad \text{Simplify.}$$

$$y = \frac{2}{3}x - \frac{7}{3} \qquad \text{Write in slope-intercept form.}$$

Notice the similarity between the slope-intercept form of the original equation and the slope-intercept form of the parallel equation. The graphs of both equations are shown in Figure 1.8.

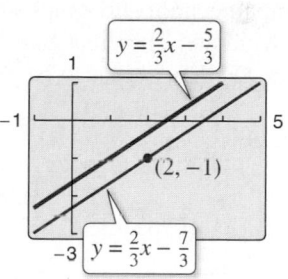

Figure 1.8

✓ **Checkpoint** ◀))) *Audio-video solution in English & Spanish at LarsonPrecalculus.com.*

Find the slope-intercept form of the equation of the line that passes through the point $(-4, 1)$ and is parallel to the line $5x - 3y = 8$. ■

> **Perpendicular Lines**
>
> Two nonvertical lines are **perpendicular** if and only if their slopes are negative reciprocals of each other. That is,
>
> $$m_1 = -\frac{1}{m_2}.$$

EXAMPLE 7   Equations of Perpendicular Lines

Find the slope-intercept form of the equation of the line that passes through the point $(2, -1)$ and is perpendicular to the line $2x - 3y = 5$.

Solution

From Example 6, you know that the equation can be written in the slope-intercept form $y = \frac{2}{3}x - \frac{5}{3}$. You can see that the line has a slope of $\frac{2}{3}$. So, any line perpendicular to this line must have a slope of $-\frac{3}{2}$ (because $-\frac{3}{2}$ is the negative reciprocal of $\frac{2}{3}$). So, the line through the point $(2, -1)$ has the following equation.

$$y - (-1) = -\frac{3}{2}(x - 2) \qquad \text{Write in point-slope form.}$$

$$y + 1 = -\frac{3}{2}x + 3 \qquad \text{Simplify.}$$

$$y = -\frac{3}{2}x + 2 \qquad \text{Write in slope-intercept form.}$$

The graphs of both equations are shown in the figure.

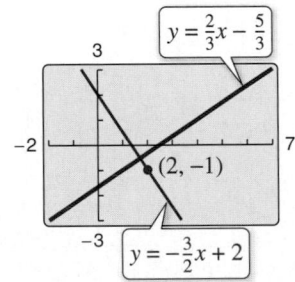

✓ **Checkpoint** ◀))) *Audio-video solution in English & Spanish at LarsonPrecalculus.com.*

Find the slope-intercept form of the equation of the line that passes through the point $(-4, 1)$ and is perpendicular to the line $5x - 3y = 8$.

EXAMPLE 8   Graphs of Perpendicular Lines

Use a graphing utility to graph the lines $y = x + 1$ and $y = -x + 3$ in the same viewing window. The lines are perpendicular (they have slopes of $m_1 = 1$ and $m_2 = -1$). Do they appear to be perpendicular on the display?

Solution

When the viewing window is nonsquare, as in Figure 1.9, the two lines will not appear perpendicular. When, however, the viewing window is square, as in Figure 1.10, the lines will appear perpendicular.

Figure 1.9

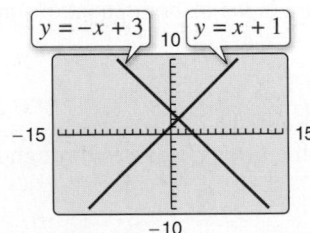

Figure 1.10

✓ **Checkpoint** ◀))) *Audio-video solution in English & Spanish at LarsonPrecalculus.com.*

Identify any relationships that exist among the lines $y = 2x$, $y = -2x$, and $y = \frac{1}{2}x$. Then use a graphing utility to graph the three equations in the same viewing window. Adjust the viewing window so that each slope appears visually correct. Use the slopes of the lines to verify your results. ∎

What's Wrong?

You use a graphing utility to graph $y_1 = 1.5x$ and $y_2 = -1.5x + 5$, as shown in the figure. You use the graph to conclude that the lines are perpendicular. What's wrong?

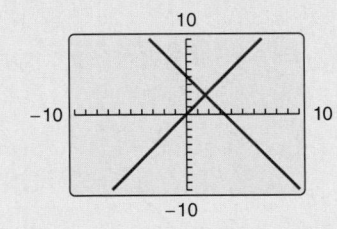

1.1 Exercises

See *CalcChat.com* for tutorial help and worked-out solutions to odd-numbered exercises.
For instructions on how to use a graphing utility, see Appendix A.

Vocabulary and Concept Check

1. Match each equation with its form.

(a) $Ax + By + C = 0$ (i) vertical line

(b) $x = a$ (ii) slope-intercept form

(c) $y = b$ (iii) general form

(d) $y = mx + b$ (iv) point-slope form

(e) $y - y_1 = m(x - x_1)$ (v) horizontal line

In Exercises 2 and 3, fill in the blank.

2. For a line, the ratio of the change in y to the change in x is called the _____ of the line.

3. Two lines are _____ if and only if their slopes are equal.

4. What is the relationship between two lines whose slopes are -3 and $\frac{1}{3}$?

5. What is the slope of a line that is perpendicular to the line represented by $x = 3$?

6. Give the coordinates of a point on the line whose equation in point-slope form is $y - (-1) = \frac{1}{4}(x - 8)$.

Procedures and Problem Solving

Using Slope   In Exercises 7 and 8, identify the line that has the indicated slope.

7. (a) $m = \frac{2}{3}$ (b) m is undefined.   (c) $m = -2$

8. (a) $m = 0$ (b) $m = -\frac{3}{4}$ (c) $m = 1$

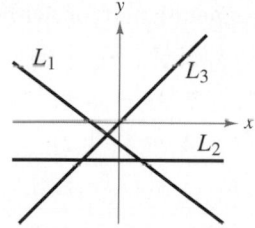

Estimating Slope   In Exercises 9 and 10, estimate the slope of the line.

9.

10.

Sketching Lines   In Exercises 11 and 12, sketch the lines through the point with the indicated slopes on the same set of coordinate axes.

	Point		Slopes		
11.	$(2, 3)$	(a) 0 (b) 1	(c) 2	(d) -3	
12.	$(-4, 1)$	(a) 4 (b) -2	(c) $\frac{1}{2}$	(d) Undefined	

Finding the Slope of a Line   In Exercises 13–16, find the slope of the line passing through the pair of points. Then use a graphing utility to plot the points and use the *draw* feature to graph the line segment connecting the two points. (Use a *square setting*.)

13. $(0, -10), (-4, 0)$ **14.** $(2, 4), (4, -4)$

15. $(-6, -1), (-6, 4)$ **16.** $(4, 9), (6, 12)$

Using Slope   In Exercises 17–24, use the point on the line and the slope of the line to find three additional points through which the line passes. (There are many correct answers.)

	Point	Slope
17.	$(2, 1)$	$m = 0$
18.	$(3, -2)$	$m = 0$
19.	$(1, 5)$	m is undefined.
20.	$(-4, 1)$	m is undefined.
21.	$(0, -9)$	$m = -2$
22.	$(-5, 4)$	$m = 4$
23.	$(7, -2)$	$m = \frac{1}{2}$
24.	$(-1, -6)$	$m = -\frac{1}{3}$

The Point-Slope Form of the Equation of a Line In Exercises 25–32, find an equation of the line that passes through the given point and has the indicated slope. Sketch the line by hand. Use a graphing utility to verify your sketch, if possible.

25. $(0, -2)$, $m = 3$

26. $(-3, 6)$, $m = -3$

27. $(2, -3)$, $m = -\frac{1}{2}$

28. $(-2, -5)$, $m = \frac{3}{4}$

29. $(6, -1)$, m is undefined.

30. $(-10, 4)$, m is undefined.

31. $\left(-\frac{1}{2}, \frac{3}{2}\right)$, $m = 0$

32. $(2.3, -8.5)$, $m = 0$

33. Finance   The median player salary for the New York Yankees was \$1.5 million in 2007 and \$1.7 million in 2013. Write a linear equation giving the median salary y in terms of the year x. Then use the equation to predict the median salary in 2020.

34. Finance   The median player salary for the Dallas Cowboys was \$348,000 in 2004 and \$555,000 in 2013. Write a linear equation giving the median salary y in terms of the year x. Then use the equation to predict the median salary in 2019.

Using the Slope-Intercept Form In Exercises 35–42, determine the slope and y-intercept (if possible) of the linear equation. Then describe its graph.

35. $2x - 3y = 9$

36. $3x + 4y = 1$

37. $2x - 5y + 10 = 0$

38. $4x - 3y - 9 = 0$

39. $x = -6$

40. $y = 12$

41. $3y + 2 = 0$

42. $2x - 5 = 0$

Using the Slope-Intercept Form In Exercises 43–48, (a) find the slope and y-intercept (if possible) of the equation of the line algebraically, and (b) sketch the line by hand. Use a graphing utility to verify your answers to parts (a) and (b).

43. $5x - y + 3 = 0$

44. $2x + 3y - 9 = 0$

45. $5x - 2 = 0$

46. $3x + 7 = 0$

47. $3y + 5 = 0$

48. $-11 - 4y = 0$

Finding the Slope-Intercept Form In Exercises 49 and 50, find the slope-intercept form of the equation of the line shown.

49.

50.

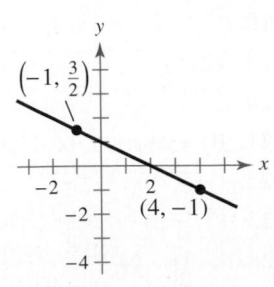

Finding the Slope-Intercept Form In Exercises 51–60, write an equation of the line that passes through the points. Use the slope-intercept form (if possible). If not possible, explain why and use the general form. Use a graphing utility to graph the line (if possible).

51. $(5, -1), (-5, 5)$

52. $(4, 3), (-4, -4)$

53. $(-8, 1), (-8, 7)$

54. $(-1, 6), (5, 6)$

55. $\left(2, \frac{1}{2}\right), \left(\frac{1}{2}, \frac{5}{4}\right)$

56. $(1, 1), \left(6, -\frac{2}{3}\right)$

57. $\left(-\frac{1}{10}, -\frac{3}{5}\right), \left(\frac{9}{10}, -\frac{9}{5}\right)$

58. $\left(\frac{3}{4}, \frac{3}{2}\right), \left(-\frac{4}{3}, \frac{7}{4}\right)$

59. $(1, 0.6), (-2, -0.6)$

60. $(-8, 0.6), (2, -2.4)$

Different Viewing Windows In Exercises 61 and 62, use a graphing utility to graph the equation using each viewing window. Describe the differences in the graphs.

61. $y = 0.25x - 2$

Xmin = -1	Xmin = -5	Xmin = -5
Xmax = 9	Xmax = 10	Xmax = 10
Xscl = 1	Xscl = 1	Xscl = 1
Ymin = -5	Ymin = -3	Ymin = -5
Ymax = 4	Ymax = 4	Ymax = 5
Yscl = 1	Yscl = 1	Yscl = 1

62. $y = -8x + 5$

Xmin = -5	Xmin = -5	Xmin = -5
Xmax = 5	Xmax = 10	Xmax = 13
Xscl = 1	Xscl = 1	Xscl = 1
Ymin = -10	Ymin = -80	Ymin = -2
Ymax = 10	Ymax = 80	Ymax = 10
Yscl = 1	Yscl = 20	Yscl = 1

Parallel and Perpendicular Lines In Exercises 63–66, determine whether the lines L_1 and L_2 passing through the pairs of points are parallel, perpendicular, or neither.

63. L_1: $(0, -1), (5, 9)$
L_2: $(0, 3), (4, 1)$

64. L_1: $(-2, -1), (1, 5)$
L_2: $(1, 3), (5, -5)$

65. L_1: $(3, 6), (-6, 0)$
L_2: $(0, -1), \left(5, \frac{7}{3}\right)$

66. L_1: $(4, 8), (-4, 2)$
L_2: $(3, -5), \left(-1, \frac{1}{3}\right)$

Equations of Parallel and Perpendicular Lines In Exercises 67–76, write the slope-intercept forms of the equations of the lines through the given point (a) parallel to the given line and (b) perpendicular to the given line.

67. $(2, 1)$, $4x - 2y = 3$

68. $(-3, 2)$, $x + y = 7$

69. $\left(-\frac{2}{3}, \frac{7}{8}\right)$, $3x + 4y = 7$

70. $\left(\frac{2}{5}, -1\right)$, $3x - 2y = 6$

71. $(-3.9, -1.4)$, $6x + 5y = 9$

72. $(-1.2, 2.4)$, $5x + 4y = 1$

73. $(3, -2)$, $x - 4 = 0$

74. $(3, -1)$, $y - 2 = 0$

75. $(-5, 1)$, $y + 2 = 0$

76. $(-2, 4)$, $x + 5 = 0$

Equations of Parallel Lines In Exercises 77 and 78, the lines are parallel. Find the slope-intercept form of the equation of line y_2.

77.

$y_1 = 2x + 4$

78.

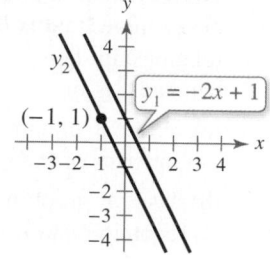

$y_1 = -2x + 1$

Equations of Perpendicular Lines In Exercises 79 and 80, the lines are perpendicular. Find the slope-intercept form of the equation of line y_2.

79.

$y_1 = 2x + 3$

80.

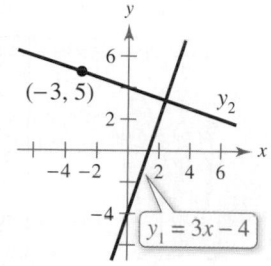

$y_1 = 3x - 4$

Graphs of Parallel and Perpendicular Lines In Exercises 81–84, identify any relationships that exist among the lines, and then use a graphing utility to graph the three equations in the same viewing window. Adjust the viewing window so that each slope appears visually correct. Use the slopes of the lines to verify your results.

81. (a) $y = 4x$ (b) $y = -4x$ (c) $y = \frac{1}{4}x$

82. (a) $y = \frac{2}{3}x$ (b) $y = -\frac{3}{2}x$ (c) $y = \frac{2}{3}x + 2$

83. (a) $y = -\frac{1}{2}x$ (b) $y = -\frac{1}{2}x + 3$ (c) $y = 2x - 4$

84. (a) $y = x - 8$ (b) $y = x + 1$ (c) $y = -x + 3$

85. **Architectural Design** The rise-to-run ratio of the roof of a house determines the steepness of the roof. The rise-to-run ratio of the roof in the figure is 3 to 4. Determine the maximum height in the attic of the house if the house is 32 feet wide.

attic height

32 ft

86. **Highway Engineering** When driving down a mountain road, you notice warning signs indicating that it is a "12% grade." This means that the slope of the road is $-\frac{12}{100}$. Approximate the amount of horizontal change in your position if you note from elevation markers that you have descended 2000 feet vertically.

©Andrey_Popov/Shutterstock.com   ©iStock.com/sykadelx

87. **MODELING DATA**

The graph shows the sales y (in billions of dollars) of the Coca-Cola Company each year x from 2005 through 2012, where $x = 5$ represents 2005. (Source: Coca-Cola Company)

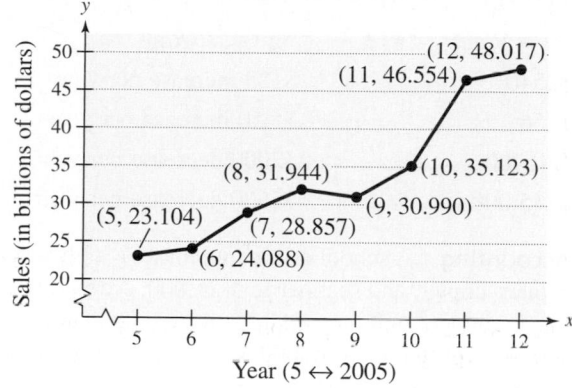

(a) Use the slopes to determine the years in which the sales showed the greatest increase and greatest decrease.

(b) Find the equation of the line between the years 2005 and 2012.

(c) Interpret the meaning of the slope of the line from part (b) in the context of the problem.

(d) Use the equation from part (b) to estimate the sales of the Coca-Cola Company in 2017. Do you think this is an accurate estimate? Explain.

88. **MODELING DATA**

The table shows the profits y (in millions of dollars) for Buffalo Wild Wings for each year x from 2007 through 2013, where $x = 7$ represents 2007. (Source: Buffalo Wild Wings, Inc.)

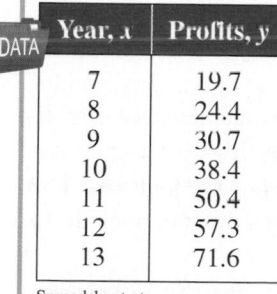

Year, x	Profits, y
7	19.7
8	24.4
9	30.7
10	38.4
11	50.4
12	57.3
13	71.6

Spreadsheet at
LarsonPrecalculus.com

(a) Sketch a graph of the data.

(b) Use the slopes to determine the years in which the profits showed the greatest and least increases.

(c) Find the equation of the line between the years 2007 and 2013.

(d) Interpret the meaning of the slope of the line from part (c) in the context of the problem.

(e) Use the equation from part (c) to estimate the profit for Buffalo Wild Wings in 2017. Do you think this is an accurate estimate? Explain.

Using a Rate of Change to Write an Equation In Exercises 89–92, you are given the dollar value of a product in 2015 and the rate at which the value of the product is expected to change during the next 5 years. Write a linear equation that gives the dollar value V of the product in terms of the year t. (Let $t = 15$ represent 2015.)

	2015 Value	Rate
89.	$2540	$125 increase per year
90.	$156	$5.50 increase per year
91.	$20,400	$2000 decrease per year
92.	$245,000	$5600 decrease per year

93. Accounting A school district purchases a high-volume printer, copier, and scanner for $25,000. After 10 years, the equipment will have to be replaced. Its value at that time is expected to be $2000.

(a) Write a linear equation giving the value V of the equipment for each year t during its 10 years of use.

(b) Use a graphing utility to graph the linear equation representing the depreciation of the equipment, and use the *value* or *trace* feature to complete the table. Verify your answers algebraically by using the equation you found in part (a).

t	0	1	2	3	4	5	6	7	8	9	10
V											

94. Meterology Recall that water freezes at 0°C (32°F) and boils at 100°C (212°F).

(a) Find an equation of the line that shows the relationship between the temperature in degrees Celsius C and degrees Fahrenheit F.

(b) Use the result of part (a) to complete the table.

C	−10°	10°			177°
F	0°			68°	90°	

95. Business A contractor purchases a bulldozer for $36,500. The bulldozer requires an average expenditure of $11.25 per hour for fuel and maintenance, and the operator is paid $19.50 per hour.

(a) Write a linear equation giving the total cost C of operating the bulldozer for t hours. (Include the purchase cost of the bulldozer.)

(b) Assuming that customers are charged $80 per hour of bulldozer use, write an equation for the revenue R derived from t hours of use.

(c) Use the profit formula ($P = R - C$) to write an equation for the profit gained from t hours of use.

(d) Use the result of part (c) to find the break-even point (the number of hours the bulldozer must be used to gain a profit of 0 dollars).

96. Real Estate A real estate office handles an apartment complex with 50 units. When the rent per unit is $580 per month, all 50 units are occupied. However, when the rent is $625 per month, the average number of occupied units drops to 47. Assume that the relationship between the monthly rent p and the demand x is linear.

(a) Write an equation of the line giving the demand x in terms of the rent p.

(b) Use a graphing utility to graph the demand equation and use the *trace* feature to estimate the number of units occupied when the rent is $655. Verify your answer algebraically.

(c) Use the demand equation to predict the number of units occupied when the rent is lowered to $595. Verify your answer graphically.

97. *Why you should learn it* (p. 3) In 1994, Penn State University had an enrollment of 73,500 students. By 2013, the enrollment had increased to 98,097. (Source: Penn State Fact Book)

(a) What was the average annual change in enrollment from 1994 to 2013?

(b) Use the average annual change in enrollment to estimate the enrollments in 1996, 2006, and 2011.

(c) Write an equation of a line that represents the given data. What is its slope? Interpret the slope in the context of the problem.

98. Writing Using the results of Exercise 97, write a short paragraph discussing the concepts of *slope* and *average rate of change*.

Conclusions

True or False? In Exercises 99 and 100, determine whether the statement is true or false. Justify your answer.

99. The line through $(-8, 2)$ and $(-1, 4)$ and the line through $(0, -4)$ and $(-7, 7)$ are parallel.

100. If the points $(10, -3)$ and $(2, -9)$ lie on the same line, then the point $\left(-12, -\frac{37}{2}\right)$ also lies on that line.

Exploration In Exercises 101–104, use a graphing utility to graph the equation of the line in the form

$$\frac{x}{a} + \frac{y}{b} = 1, \quad a \neq 0, b \neq 0.$$

Use the graphs to make a conjecture about what a and b represent. Verify your conjecture.

101. $\dfrac{x}{7} + \dfrac{y}{-3} = 1$

102. $\dfrac{x}{-6} + \dfrac{y}{2} = 1$

103. $\dfrac{x}{4} + \dfrac{y}{-\frac{2}{3}} = 1$

104. $\dfrac{x}{\frac{1}{2}} + \dfrac{y}{5} = 1$

Using Intercepts   **In Exercises 105–108, use the results of Exercises 101–104 to write an equation of the line that passes through the points.**

105. x-intercept: $(2, 0)$
   y-intercept: $(0, 9)$

106. x-intercept: $(-5, 0)$
   y-intercept: $(0, -4)$

107. x-intercept: $\left(-\frac{1}{6}, 0\right)$
   y-intercept: $\left(0, -\frac{2}{3}\right)$

108. x-intercept: $\left(\frac{3}{4}, 0\right)$
   y-intercept: $\left(0, \frac{4}{3}\right)$

Think About It   **In Exercises 109 and 110, determine which equation(s) may be represented by the graphs shown. (There may be more than one correct answer.)**

109.

(a) $2x - y = -10$
(b) $2x + y = 10$
(c) $x - 2y = 10$
(d) $x + 2y = 10$

110.

(a) $2x + y = 5$
(b) $2x + y = -5$
(c) $x - 2y = 5$
(d) $x - 2y = -5$

Think About It   **In Exercises 111 and 112, determine which pair of equations may be represented by the graphs shown.**

111.

(a) $2x - y = 5$
   $2x - y = 1$
(b) $2x + y = -5$
   $2x + y = 1$
(c) $2x - y = -5$
   $2x - y = 1$
(d) $x - 2y = -5$
   $x - 2y = -1$

112.

(a) $2x - y = 2$
   $x + 2y = 12$
(b) $x - y = 1$
   $x + y = 6$
(c) $2x + y = 2$
   $x - 2y = 12$
(d) $x - 2y = 2$
   $x + 2y = 12$

113. Think About It   Does every line have both an x-intercept and a y-intercept? Explain.

114. Think About It   Can every line be written in slope-intercept form? Explain.

115. Think About It   Does every line have an infinite number of lines that are parallel to it? Explain.

116. **HOW DO YOU SEE IT?**   Match the description with its graph. Determine the slope and y-intercept of each graph and interpret their meaning in the context of the problem. [The graphs are labeled (i), (ii), (iii), and (iv).]

(i)

(ii)

(iii)

(iv)

(a) You are paying $10 per week to repay a $100 loan.

(b) An employee is paid $13.50 per hour plus $2 for each unit produced per hour.

(c) A sales representative receives $35 per day for food plus $0.50 for each mile traveled.

(d) A tablet computer that was purchased for $600 depreciates $100 per year.

Cumulative Mixed Review

Identifying Polynomials   **In Exercises 117–122, determine whether the expression is a polynomial. If it is, write the polynomial in standard form.**

117. $x + 20$

118. $3x - 10x^2 + 1$

119. $4x^2 + x^{-1} - 3$

120. $2x^2 - 2x^4 - x^3 + \sqrt{2}$

121. $\dfrac{x^2 + 3x + 4}{x^2 - 9}$

122. $\sqrt{x^2 + 7x + 6}$

Factoring Trinomials   **In Exercises 123–126, factor the trinomial.**

123. $x^2 - 6x - 27$

124. $x^2 + 11x + 28$

125. $2x^2 + 11x - 40$

126. $3x^2 - 16x + 5$

127. Make a Decision   To work an extended application analyzing the numbers of bachelor's degrees earned by women in the United States from 2001 through 2012, visit this textbook's website at *LarsonPrecalculus.com*. (Data Source: National Center for Education Statistics)

The *Make a Decision* exercise indicates a multipart exercise using large data sets. Visit this textbook's website at *LarsonPrecalculus.com*.

1.2 Functions

Introduction to Functions

Many everyday phenomena involve two quantities that are related to each other by some rule of correspondence. The mathematical term for such a rule of correspondence is a **relation.** Here are two examples.

1. The simple interest I earned on an investment of \$1000 for 1 year is related to the annual interest rate r by the formula $I = 1000r$.

2. The area A of a circle is related to its radius r by the formula $A = \pi r^2$.

Not all relations have simple mathematical formulas. For instance, you can match NFL starting quarterbacks with touchdown passes and time of day with temperature. In each of these cases, there is some relation that matches each item from one set with exactly one item from a different set. Such a relation is called a **function.**

> **Definition of a Function**
>
> A **function** f from a set A to a set B is a relation that assigns to each element x in the set A exactly one element y in the set B. The set A is the **domain** (or set of inputs) of the function f, and the set B contains the **range** (or set of outputs).

To help understand this definition, look at the function that relates the time of day to the temperature in Figure 1.11.

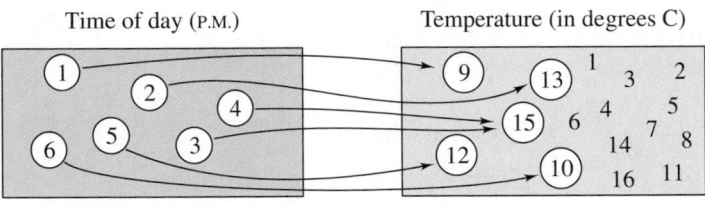

Time of day (P.M.)	Temperature (in degrees C)
Set A is the domain.	Set B contains the range.
Inputs: 1, 2, 3, 4, 5, 6	Outputs: 9, 10, 12, 13, 15

Figure 1.11

This function can be represented by the ordered pairs

$$\{(1, 9°), (2, 13°), (3, 15°), (4, 15°), (5, 12°), (6, 10°)\}.$$

In each ordered pair, the first coordinate (x-value) is the **input** and the second coordinate (y-value) is the **output.**

> **Characteristics of a Function from Set A to Set B**
>
> 1. Each element of A must be matched with an element of B.
>
> 2. Some elements of B may not be matched with any element of A.
>
> 3. Two or more elements of A may be matched with the same element of B.
>
> 4. An element of A (the domain) cannot be matched with two different elements of B.

To determine whether or not a relation is a function, you must decide whether each input value is matched with exactly one output value. When any input value is matched with two or more output values, the relation is not a function.

EXAMPLE 1 **Testing for Functions**

Determine whether each relation represents y as a function of x.

a.

Input, x	2	2	3	4	5
Output, y	11	10	8	5	1

b.

Solution

a. This table *does not* describe y as a function of x. The input value 2 is matched with two different y-values.

b. The graph *does* describe y as a function of x. Each input value is matched with exactly one output value.

✓ **Checkpoint** 🔊))) *Audio-video solution in English & Spanish at LarsonPrecalculus.com.*

Determine whether the relation represents y as a function of x.

Input, x	0	1	2	3	4
Output, y	−4	−2	0	2	4

In algebra, it is common to represent functions by equations or formulas involving two variables. For instance, $y = x^2$ represents the variable y as a function of the variable x. In this equation, x is the **independent variable** and y is the **dependent variable.** The domain of the function is the set of all values taken on by the independent variable x, and the range of the function is the set of all values taken on by the dependent variable y.

EXAMPLE 2 **Testing for Functions Represented Algebraically**

See LarsonPrecalculus.com for an interactive version of this type of example.

Determine whether each equation represents y as a function of x.

a. $x^2 + y = 1$ **b.** $-x + y^2 = 1$

Solution

To determine whether y is a function of x, try to solve for y in terms of x.

a. $x^2 + y = 1$ Write original equation.

$\quad\quad y = 1 - x^2$ Solve for y.

Each value of x corresponds to exactly one value of y. So, y is a function of x.

b. $-x + y^2 = 1$ Write original equation.

$\quad\quad y^2 = 1 + x$ Add x to each side.

$\quad\quad y = \pm\sqrt{1 + x}$ Solve for y.

The $\pm$ indicates that for a given value of x, there correspond two values of y. For instance, when $x = 3$, $y = 2$ or $y = -2$. So, y is not a function of x.

✓ **Checkpoint** 🔊))) *Audio-video solution in English & Spanish at LarsonPrecalculus.com.*

Determine whether each equation represents y as a function of x.

a. $x^2 + y^2 = 8$ **b.** $y - 4x^2 = 36$

Explore the Concept

Use a graphing utility to graph $x^2 + y = 1$. Then use the graph to write a convincing argument that each x-value corresponds to at most one y-value.

Use a graphing utility to graph $-x + y^2 = 1$. (*Hint:* You will need to use two equations.) Does the graph represent y as a function of x? Explain.

Function Notation

When an equation is used to represent a function, it is convenient to name the function so that it can be referenced easily. For example, you know that the equation $y = 1 - x^2$ describes y as a function of x. Suppose you give this function the name "f." Then you can use the following **function notation**.

Input	Output	Equation
x	$f(x)$	$f(x) = 1 - x^2$

The symbol $f(x)$ is read as the *value of f at x* or simply *f of x*. The symbol $f(x)$ corresponds to the y-value for a given x. So, you can write $y = f(x)$. Keep in mind that f is the *name* of the function, whereas $f(x)$ is the *output value* of the function at the *input value x*. In function notation, the *input* is the independent variable and the *output* is the dependent variable. For instance, the function $f(x) = 3 - 2x$ has *function values* denoted by $f(-1)$, $f(0)$, and so on. To find these values, substitute the specified input values into the given equation.

For $x = -1$, $f(-1) = 3 - 2(-1) = 3 + 2 = 5.$

For $x = 0$, $f(0) = 3 - 2(0) = 3 - 0 = 3.$

Although f is often used as a convenient function name and x is often used as the independent variable, you can use other letters. For instance,

$$f(x) = x^2 - 4x + 7, \quad f(t) = t^2 - 4t + 7, \quad \text{and} \quad g(s) = s^2 - 4s + 7$$

all define the same function. In fact, the role of the independent variable is that of a "placeholder." Consequently, the function could be written as

$$f(\;\;\;\;) = (\;\;\;\;)^2 - 4(\;\;\;\;) + 7.$$

EXAMPLE 3   Evaluating a Function

Let $g(x) = -x^2 + 4x + 1$. Find each value of the function.

a. $g(2)$ **b.** $g(t)$ **c.** $g(x + 2)$

Solution

a. Replacing x with 2 in $g(x) = -x^2 + 4x + 1$ yields the following.

$$g(2) = -(2)^2 + 4(2) + 1 = -4 + 8 + 1 = 5$$

b. Replacing x with t yields the following.

$$g(t) = -(t)^2 + 4(t) + 1 = -t^2 + 4t + 1$$

c. Replacing x with $x + 2$ yields the following.

$g(x + 2) = -(x + 2)^2 + 4(x + 2) + 1$	Substitute $x + 2$ for x.
$= -(x^2 + 4x + 4) + 4x + 8 + 1$	Multiply.
$= -x^2 - 4x - 4 + 4x + 8 + 1$	Distributive Property
$= -x^2 + 5$	Simplify.

✓ **Checkpoint** 🔊))) Audio-video solution in English & Spanish at LarsonPrecalculus.com.

Let $f(x) = 10 - 3x^2$. Find each function value.

a. $f(2)$ **b.** $f(-4)$ **c.** $f(x - 1)$

In part (c) of Example 3, note that $g(x + 2)$ is not equal to $g(x) + g(2)$. In general, $g(u + v) \neq g(u) + g(v)$.

Library of Parent Functions: Absolute Value Function

The *parent absolute value function* given by

$$f(x) = |x|$$

can be written as a piecewise-defined function. The basic characteristics of the parent absolute value function are summarized below and on the inside cover of this text.

Graph of $f(x) = |x| = \begin{cases} x, & x \geq 0 \\ -x, & x < 0 \end{cases}$

Domain: $(-\infty, \infty)$
Range: $[0, \infty)$
Intercept: $(0, 0)$
Decreasing on $(-\infty, 0)$
Increasing on $(0, \infty)$

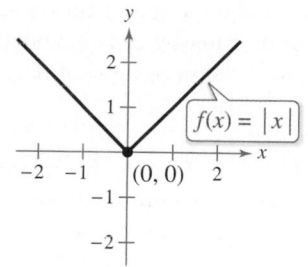

A function defined by two or more equations over a specified domain is called a **piecewise-defined function.**

EXAMPLE 4   A Piecewise–Defined Function

Evaluate the function when $x = -1, 0,$ and 1.

$$f(x) = \begin{cases} x^2 + 1, & x < 0 \\ x - 1, & x \geq 0 \end{cases}$$

Solution

Because $x = -1$ is less than 0, use $f(x) = x^2 + 1$ to obtain

$f(-1) = (-1)^2 + 1$ Substitute -1 for x.

    $-2.$ Simplify.

For $x = 0$, use $f(x) = x - 1$ to obtain

$f(0) = 0 - 1$ Substitute 0 for x.

    $= -1.$ Simplify.

For $x = 1$, use $f(x) = x - 1$ to obtain

$f(1) = 1 - 1$ Substitute 1 for x.

    $= 0.$ Simplify.

The graph of f is shown in the figure.

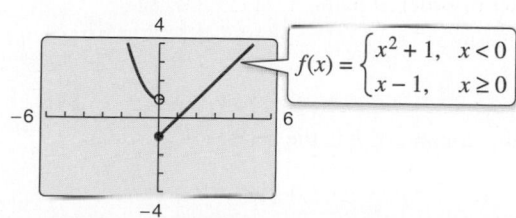

Technology Tip

Most graphing utilities can graph piecewise-defined functions. For instructions on how to enter a piecewise-defined function into your graphing utility, consult your user's manual. You may find it helpful to set your graphing utility to *dot mode* before graphing such functions.

✓ **Checkpoint** 🔊))) *Audio-video solution in English & Spanish at LarsonPrecalculus.com.*

Evaluate the function given in Example 4 when $x = -2, 2,$ and 3.

The Domain of a Function

The domain of a function can be described explicitly or it can be *implied* by the expression used to define the function. The **implied domain** is the set of all real numbers for which the expression is defined. For instance, the function

$$f(x) = \frac{1}{x^2 - 4} \qquad \text{Domain excludes } x\text{-values that result in division by zero.}$$

has an implied domain that consists of all real numbers x other than $x = \pm 2$. These two values are excluded from the domain because division by zero is undefined. Another common type of implied domain is that used to avoid even roots of negative numbers. For example, the function

$$(x) = \sqrt{x} \qquad \text{Domain excludes } x\text{-values that result in even roots of negative numbers.}$$

is defined only for $x \geq 0$. So, its implied domain is the interval $[0, \infty)$. In general, the domain of a function *excludes* values that would cause division by zero *or* result in the even root of a negative number.

Library of Parent Functions: Square Root Function

Radical functions arise from the use of rational exponents. The most common radical function is the *parent square root* function given by $f(x) = \sqrt{x}$. The basic characteristics of the parent square root function are summarized below and on the inside cover of this text.

Graph of $f(x) = \sqrt{x}$

Domain: $[0, \infty)$
Range: $[0, \infty)$
Intercept: $(0, 0)$
Increasing on $(0, \infty)$

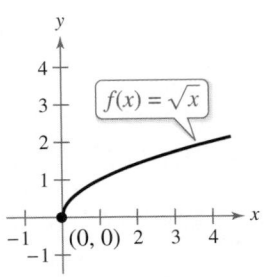

$f(x) = \sqrt{x}$

EXAMPLE 5   Finding the Domain of a Function

Find the domain of each function.

a. $f: \{(-3, 0), (-1, 4), (0, 2), (2, 2), (4, -1)\}$

b. $g(x) = -3x^2 + 4x + 5$

c. $h(x) = \dfrac{1}{x + 5}$

Solution

a. The domain of f consists of all first coordinates in the set of ordered pairs.

    Domain $= \{-3, -1, 0, 2, 4\}$

b. The domain of g is the set of all *real* numbers.

c. Excluding x-values that yield zero in the denominator, the domain of h is the set of all real numbers x except $x = -5$.

✓ **Checkpoint** ◄))) *Audio-video solution in English & Spanish at LarsonPrecalculus.com.*

Find the domain of each function.

a. $f: \{(-2, 2), (-1, 1), (0, 3), (1, 1), (2, 2)\}$ **b.** $g(x) = \dfrac{1}{3 - x}$ ∎

EXAMPLE 6   Finding the Domain of a Function

Find the domain of each function.

a. Volume of a sphere: $V = \frac{4}{3}\pi r^3$ **b.** $k(x) = \sqrt{4 - 3x}$

Solution

a. Because this function represents the volume of a sphere, the values of the radius r must be positive (see Figure 1.12). So, the domain is the set of all real numbers r such that $r > 0$.

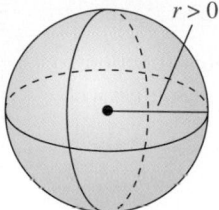

Figure 1.12

b. This function is defined only for x-values for which $4 - 3x \geq 0$. By solving this inequality, you will find that the domain of k is all real numbers that are less than or equal to $\frac{4}{3}$.

 ✔ **Checkpoint** 🔊))) *Audio-video solution in English & Spanish at LarsonPrecalculus.com.*

Find the domain of each function.

a. Circumference of a circle: $C = 2\pi r$ **b.** $h(x) = \sqrt{x - 16}$ ■

In Example 6(a), note that the *domain of a function may be implied by the physical context.* For instance, from the equation $V = \frac{4}{3}\pi r^3$, you would have no reason to restrict r to positive values, but the physical context implies that a sphere cannot have a negative or zero radius.

For some functions, it may be easier to find the domain and range of the function by examining its graph.

EXAMPLE 7   Finding the Domain and Range of a Function

Use a graphing utility to find the domain and range of the function $f(x) = \sqrt{9 - x^2}$.

Solution

Graph the function as $y = \sqrt{9 - x^2}$, as shown in Figure 1.13. Using the *trace* feature of a graphing utility, you can determine that the x-values extend from -3 to 3 and the y-values extend from 0 to 3. So, the domain of the function f is all real numbers such that $-3 \leq x \leq 3$, and the range of f is all real numbers such that $0 \leq y \leq 3$.

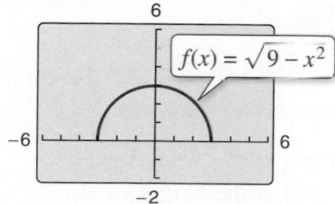

Figure 1.13

> **Remark**
>
> Be sure you see that the *range* of a function is not the same as the use of *range* relating to the viewing window of a graphing utility.

✔ **Checkpoint** 🔊))) *Audio-video solution in English & Spanish at LarsonPrecalculus.com.*

Use a graphing utility to find the domain and range of the function $f(x) = \sqrt{4 - x^2}$.

■

Applications

EXAMPLE 8   Interior Design Services Employees

The number N (in thousands) of employees in the interior design services industry in the United States decreased in a linear pattern from 2007 through 2010 (see Figure 1.14). In 2011, the number rose and increased through 2012 in a different linear pattern. These two patterns can be approximated by the function

$$N(t) = \begin{cases} -4.64t + 76.2, & 7 \leq t \leq 10 \\ 0.90t + 20.0, & 11 \leq t \leq 12 \end{cases}$$

where t represents the year, with $t = 7$ corresponding to 2007. Use this function to approximate the number of employees for the years 2007 and 2011.   (Source: U.S. Bureau of Labor Statistics)

Interior Design Services

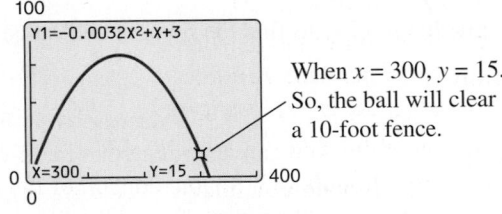

Figure 1.14

Solution

For 2007, $t = 7$, so use $N(t) = -4.64t + 76.2$.

$\qquad N(7) = -4.64(7) + 76.2 = -32.48 + 76.2 = 43.72$ thousand employees

For 2011, $t = 11$, so use $N(t) = 0.90t + 20.0$.

$\qquad N(11) = 0.90(11) + 20.0 = 9.9 + 20.0 = 29.9$ thousand employees

✔ **Checkpoint** 🔊))) *Audio-video solution in English & Spanish at LarsonPrecalculus.com.*

Use the function in Example 8 to approximate the number of employees for the years 2010 and 2012.

EXAMPLE 9   The Path of a Baseball

A baseball is hit at a point 3 feet above the ground at a velocity of 100 feet per second and an angle of 45°. The path of the baseball is given by $f(x) = -0.0032x^2 + x + 3$, where $f(x)$ is the height of the baseball (in feet) and x is the horizontal distance from home plate (in feet). Will the baseball clear a 10-foot fence located 300 feet from home plate?

Algebraic Solution

The height of the baseball is a function of the horizontal distance from home plate. When $x = 300$, you can find the height of the baseball as follows.

$\qquad f(x) = -0.0032x^2 + x + 3$ \hfill Write original function.

$\qquad f(300) = -0.0032(300)^2 + 300 + 3$ \hfill Substitute 300 for x.

$\qquad\qquad = 15$ \hfill Simplify.

When $x = 300$, the height of the baseball is 15 feet. So, the baseball will clear a 10-foot fence.

Graphical Solution

When $x = 300$, $y = 15$. So, the ball will clear a 10-foot fence.

✔ **Checkpoint** 🔊))) *Audio-video solution in English & Spanish at LarsonPrecalculus.com.*

A second baseman throws a baseball toward the first baseman 60 feet away. The path of the baseball is given by $f(x) = -0.004x^2 + 0.3x + 6$, where $f(x)$ is the height of the baseball (in feet) and x is the horizontal distance from the second baseman (in feet). The first baseman can reach 8 feet high. Can the first baseman catch the baseball without jumping?

Difference Quotients

One of the basic definitions in calculus employs the ratio

$$\frac{f(x+h)-f(x)}{h}, \quad h \neq 0.$$

This ratio is called a **difference quotient,** as illustrated in Example 10.

EXAMPLE 10   Evaluating a Difference Quotient

For $f(x) = x^2 - 4x + 7$, find $\dfrac{f(x+h)-f(x)}{h}$.

Solution

$$\frac{f(x+h)-f(x)}{h} = \frac{[(x+h)^2 - 4(x+h) + 7] - (x^2 - 4x + 7)}{h}$$

$$= \frac{x^2 + 2xh + h^2 - 4x - 4h + 7 - x^2 + 4x - 7}{h}$$

$$= \frac{2xh + h^2 - 4h}{h}$$

$$= \frac{h(2x + h - 4)}{h}$$

$$= 2x + h - 4, \quad h \neq 0$$

> **Remark**
>
> Notice in Example 10 that h cannot be zero in the original expression. Therefore, you must restrict the domain of the simplified expression by listing $h \neq 0$ so that the simplified expression is equivalent to the original expression.

✓ **Checkpoint** Audio-video solution in English & Spanish at LarsonPrecalculus.com.

For $f(x) = x^2 + 2x - 3$, evaluate the difference quotient in Example 10. ■

Summary of Function Terminology

Function: A **function** is a relationship between two variables such that to each value of the independent variable there corresponds exactly one value of the dependent variable.

Function Notation: $y = f(x)$

   f is the *name* of the function.
   y is the **dependent variable,** or output value.
   x is the **independent variable,** or input value.
   $f(x)$ is the *value of the function at x.*

Domain: The **domain** of a function is the set of all values (inputs) of the independent variable for which the function is defined. If x is in the domain of f, then f is said to be *defined* at x. If x is not in the domain of f, then f is said to be *undefined* at x.

Range: The **range** of a function is the set of all values (outputs) assumed by the dependent variable (that is, the set of all function values).

Implied Domain: If f is defined by an algebraic expression and the domain is not specified, then the **implied domain** consists of all real numbers for which the expression is defined.

The symbol ∫ indicates an example or exercise that highlights algebraic techniques specifically used in calculus.

See *CalcChat.com* for tutorial help and worked-out solutions to odd-numbered exercises.
For instructions on how to use a graphing utility, see Appendix A.

1.2 Exercises

Vocabulary and Concept Check

In Exercises 1 and 2, fill in the blanks.

1. A relation that assigns to each element x from a set of inputs, or _____ , exactly one element y in a set of outputs, or _____ , is called a _____ .

2. For an equation that represents y as a function of x, the _____ variable is the set of all x in the domain, and the _____ variable is the set of all y in the range.

3. Can the ordered pairs $(3, 0)$ and $(3, 5)$ represent a function?

4. To find $g(x + 1)$, what do you substitute for x in the function $g(x) = 3x - 2$?

5. Does the domain of the function $f(x) = \sqrt{1 + x}$ include $x = -2$?

6. Is the domain of a piecewise-defined function *implied* or *explicitly described*?

Procedures and Problem Solving

Testing for Functions In Exercises 7–10, does the relation describe a function? Explain your reasoning.

7. *Domain   Range*

8. *Domain   Range*

9. *Domain   Range*

10. *Domain   Range*

(State)   (Electoral votes 2010–2012)

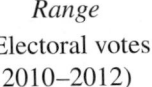

Testing for Functions In Exercises 11–14, determine whether the relation represents y as a function of x. Explain your reasoning.

11.

Input, x	-3	-1	0	1	3
Output, y	-9	-1	0	1	-9

12.

Input, x	0	1	2	1	0
Output, y	-4	-2	0	2	4

13.

14.

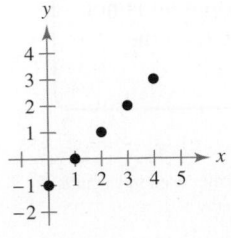

Testing for Functions In Exercises 15 and 16, which sets of ordered pairs represent functions from A to B? Explain.

15. $A = \{0, 1, 2, 3\}$ and $B = \{-2, -1, 0, 1, 2\}$
   (a) $\{(0, 1), (1, -2), (2, 0), (3, 2)\}$
   (b) $\{(0, -1), (2, 2), (1, -2), (3, 0), (1, 1)\}$
   (c) $\{(1, 0), (-2, 3), (-1, 3), (0, 0)\}$

16. $A = \{a, b, c\}$ and $B = \{0, 1, 2, 3\}$
   (a) $\{(a, 1), (c, 2), (c, 3), (b, 3)\}$
   (b) $\{(a, 1), (b, 2), (c, 3)\}$
   (c) $\{(1, a), (0, a), (2, c), (3, b)\}$

Pharmacology In Exercises 17 and 18, use the graph, which shows the average prices of name brand and generic drug prescriptions in the United States. (Source: National Association of Chain Drug Stores)

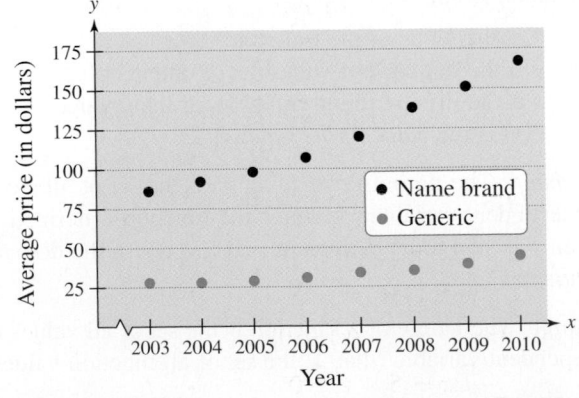

17. Is the average price of a name brand prescription a function of the year? Is the average price of a generic prescription a function of the year? Explain.

18. Let $b(t)$ and $g(t)$ represent the average prices of name brand and generic prescriptions, respectively, in year t. Find $b(2009)$ and $g(2006)$.

Testing for Functions Represented Algebraically In Exercises 19–30, determine whether the equation represents y as a function of x.

19. $x^2 + y^2 = 4$

20. $x = y^2 + 1$

21. $y = \sqrt{x^2 - 1}$

22. $y = \sqrt{x + 5}$

23. $2x + 3y = 4$

24. $x = -y + 5$

25. $y^2 = x^2 - 1$

26. $x + y^2 = 3$

27. $y = |4 - x|$

28. $|y| = 3 - 2x$

29. $x = -7$

30. $y = 8$

Evaluating a Function In Exercises 31–46, evaluate the function at each specified value of the independent variable and simplify.

31. $f(t) = 3t + 1$

  (a) $f(2)$ (b) $f(-4)$ (c) $f(t + 2)$

32. $g(y) = 7 - 3y$

  (a) $g(0)$ (b) $g\left(\frac{7}{3}\right)$ (c) $g(s + 5)$

33. $h(t) = t^2 - 2t$

  (a) $h(2)$ (b) $h(1.5)$ (c) $h(x - 4)$

34. $V(r) = \frac{4}{3}\pi r^3$

  (a) $V(3)$ (b) $V\left(\frac{3}{2}\right)$ (c) $V(2r)$

35. $f(y) = 3 - \sqrt{y}$

  (a) $f(4)$ (b) $f(0.25)$ (c) $f(4x^2)$

36. $f(x) = \sqrt{x + 8} + 2$

  (a) $f(-4)$ (b) $f(8)$ (c) $f(x - 8)$

37. $q(x) = \dfrac{1}{x^2 - 9}$

  (a) $q(-3)$ (b) $q(2)$ (c) $q(y + 3)$

38. $q(t) = \dfrac{2t^2 + 3}{t^2}$

  (a) $q(2)$ (b) $q(0)$ (c) $q(-x)$

39. $f(x) = \dfrac{|x|}{x}$

  (a) $f(9)$ (b) $f(-9)$ (c) $f(t)$

40. $f(x) = |x| + 4$

  (a) $f(5)$ (b) $f(-5)$ (c) $f(t)$

41. $f(x) = \begin{cases} 2x + 1, & x < 0 \\ 2x + 2, & x \geq 0 \end{cases}$

  (a) $f(-1)$ (b) $f(0)$ (c) $f(2)$

42. $f(x) = \begin{cases} 2x + 5, & x \leq 0 \\ 2 - x, & x > 0 \end{cases}$

  (a) $f(-2)$ (b) $f(0)$ (c) $f(1)$

43. $f(x) = \begin{cases} x^2 + 2, & x \leq 1 \\ 2x^2 + 2, & x > 1 \end{cases}$

  (a) $f(-2)$ (b) $f(1)$ (c) $f(2)$

44. $f(x) = \begin{cases} x^2 - 4, & x \leq 0 \\ 1 - 2x^2, & x > 0 \end{cases}$

  (a) $f(-2)$ (b) $f(0)$ (c) $f(1)$

45. $f(x) = \begin{cases} x + 2, & x < 0 \\ 4, & 0 \leq x < 2 \\ x^2 + 1, & x \geq 2 \end{cases}$

  (a) $f(-2)$ (b) $f(0)$ (c) $f(2)$

46. $f(x) = \begin{cases} 5 - 2x, & x < 0 \\ 5, & 0 \leq x < 1 \\ 4x + 1, & x \geq 1 \end{cases}$

  (a) $f(-4)$ (b) $f(0)$ (c) $f(1)$

Evaluating a Function In Exercises 47–50, assume that the domain of f is the set $A = \{-2, -1, 0, 1, 2\}$. Determine the set of ordered pairs representing the function f.

47. $f(x) = (x - 1)^2$

48. $f(x) = x^2 - 3$

49. $f(x) = |x| + 2$

50. $f(x) = |x + 1|$

Evaluating a Function In Exercises 51 and 52, complete the table.

51. $h(t) = \frac{1}{2}|t + 3|$

t	-5	-4	-3	-2	-1
$h(t)$					

52. $f(s) = \dfrac{|s - 2|}{s - 2}$

s	0	1	$\frac{3}{2}$	$\frac{5}{2}$	4
$f(s)$					

Finding the Inputs That Have Outputs of Zero In Exercises 53–56, find all values of x such that $f(x) = 0$.

53. $f(x) = 15 - 3x$

54. $f(x) = 5x + 1$

55. $f(x) = \dfrac{9x - 4}{5}$

56. $f(x) = \dfrac{2x - 3}{7}$

Finding the Domain of a Function In Exercises 57–66, find the domain of the function.

57. $f(x) = 5x^2 + 2x - 1$

58. $g(x) = 1 - 2x^2$

59. $h(t) = \dfrac{4}{t}$

60. $s(y) = \dfrac{3y}{y + 5}$

61. $f(x) = \sqrt[3]{x - 4}$

62. $f(x) = \sqrt[4]{x^2 + 3x}$

63. $g(x) = \dfrac{1}{x} - \dfrac{3}{x + 2}$

64. $h(x) = \dfrac{10}{x^2 - 2x}$

65. $g(y) = \dfrac{y + 2}{\sqrt{y - 10}}$

66. $f(x) = \dfrac{\sqrt{x + 6}}{6 + x}$

Finding the Domain and Range of a Function In Exercises 67–70, use a graphing utility to graph the function. Find the domain and range of the function.

67. $f(x) = \sqrt{16 - x^2}$ 68. $f(x) = \sqrt{x^2 + 1}$

69. $g(x) = |2x + 3|$ 70. $g(x) = |3x - 5|$

71. **Geometry** Write the area A of a circle as a function of its circumference C.

72. **Geometry** Write the area A of an equilateral triangle as a function of the length s of its sides.

73. **Exploration** An open box of maximum volume is to be made from a square piece of material, 24 centimeters on a side, by cutting equal squares from the corners and turning up the sides. (See figure.)

$x \mapsto 24 - 2x \mapsto x$

x

$24 - 2x$

(a) The table shows the volume V (in cubic centimeters) of the box for various heights x (in centimeters). Use the table to estimate the maximum volume.

Height, x	Volume, V
1	484
2	800
3	972
4	1024
5	980
6	864

(b) Plot the points (x, V) from the table in part (a). Does the relation defined by the ordered pairs represent V as a function of x?

(c) If V is a function of x, write the function and determine its domain.

(d) Use a graphing utility to plot the points from the table in part (a) with the function from part (c). How closely does the function represent the data? Explain.

74. **Geometry** A right triangle is formed in the first quadrant by the x- and y-axes and a line through the point $(2, 1)$, as shown in the figure. Write the area A of the triangle as a function of x and determine the domain of the function.

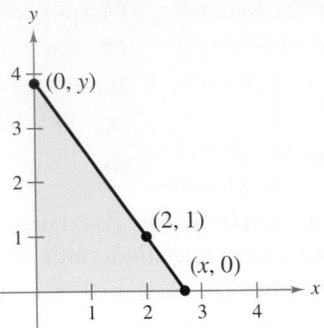

75. **Geometry** A rectangle is bounded by the x-axis and the semicircle $y = \sqrt{36 - x^2}$, as shown in the figure. Write the area A of the rectangle as a function of x and determine the domain of the function.

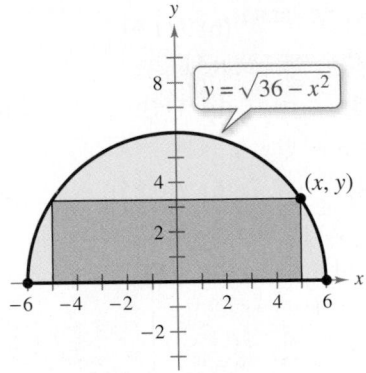

76. **Geometry** A rectangular package to be sent by the U.S. Postal Service can have a maximum combined length and girth (perimeter of a cross section) of 108 inches. (See figure.)

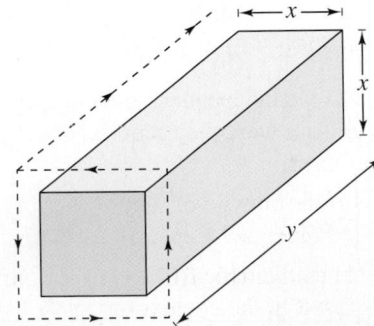

(a) Write the volume V of the package as a function of x. What is the domain of the function?

(b) Use a graphing utility to graph the function. Be sure to use an appropriate viewing window.

(c) What dimensions will maximize the volume of the package? Explain.

77. Business A company produces a product for which the variable cost is $68.75 per unit and the fixed costs are $248,000. The product sells for $99.99. Let x be the number of units produced and sold.

(a) The total cost for a business is the sum of the variable cost and the fixed costs. Write the total cost C as a function of the number of units produced.

(b) Write the revenue R as a function of the number of units sold.

(c) Write the profit P as a function of the number of units sold. (*Note*: $P = R - C$.)

(d) Use the model in part (c) to find $P(20,000)$. Interpret your result in the context of the situation.

(e) Use the model in part (c) to find $P(0)$. Interpret your result in the context of the situation.

78. MODELING DATA

The table shows the revenue y (in thousands of dollars) of a landscaping business for each month of 2015, with $x = 1$ representing January.

Month, x	Revenue, y
1	5.2
2	5.6
3	6.6
4	8.3
5	11.5
6	15.8
7	12.8
8	10.1
9	8.6
10	6.9
11	4.5
12	2.7

The mathematical model below represents the data.

$$f(x) = \begin{cases} -1.97x + 26.3 \\ 0.505x^2 - 1.47x + 6.3 \end{cases}$$

(a) Identify the independent and dependent variables and explain what they represent in the context of the problem.

(b) What is the domain of each part of the piecewise-defined function? Explain your reasoning.

(c) Use the mathematical model to find $f(5)$. Interpret your result in the context of the problem.

(d) Use the mathematical model to find $f(11)$. Interpret your result in the context of the problem.

(e) How do the values obtained from the models in parts (c) and (d) compare with the actual data values?

79. Civil Engineering The total numbers n (in millions) of miles for all public roadways in the United States from 2000 through 2011 can be approximated by the model

$$n(t) = \begin{cases} 0.0050t^2 + 0.005t + 3.95, & 0 \le t \le 2 \\ 0.013t + 3.95, & 2 < t \le 11 \end{cases}$$

where t represents the year, with $t = 0$ corresponding to 2000. The actual numbers are shown in the bar graph. (Source: U.S. Federal Highway Administration)

Year (0 ↔ 2000)

(a) Identify the independent and dependent variables and explain what they represent in the context of the problem.

(b) Use the *table* feature of a graphing utility to approximate the total number of miles for all public roadways each year from 2000 through 2011.

(c) Compare the values in part (b) with the actual values shown in the bar graph. How well does the model fit the data?

(d) Do you think the piecewise-defined function could be used to predict the total number of miles for all public roadways for years outside the domain? Explain your reasoning.

80. Why you should learn it (p. 16) The force F (in tons) of water against the face of a dam is estimated by the function

$$F(y) = 149.76\sqrt{10}y^{5/2}$$

where y is the depth of the water (in feet).

(a) Complete the table. What can you conclude?

y	5	10	20	30	40
$F(y)$					

(b) Use a graphing utility to graph the function. Describe your viewing window.

(c) Use the table to approximate the depth at which the force against the dam is 1,000,000 tons. Verify your answer graphically. How could you find a better estimate?

81. Projectile Motion   The height y (in feet) of a baseball thrown by a child is

$$y = -0.1x^2 + 3x + 6$$

where x is the horizontal distance (in feet) from where the ball was thrown. Will the ball fly over the glove of another child 30 feet away trying to catch the ball? Explain. (Assume that the child who is trying to catch the ball holds a baseball glove at a height of 5 feet.)

82. Business   The graph shows the sales (in millions of dollars) of Green Mountain Coffee Roasters from 2005 through 2013. Let $f(x)$ represent the sales in year x. (Source: Green Mountain Coffee Roasters, Inc.)

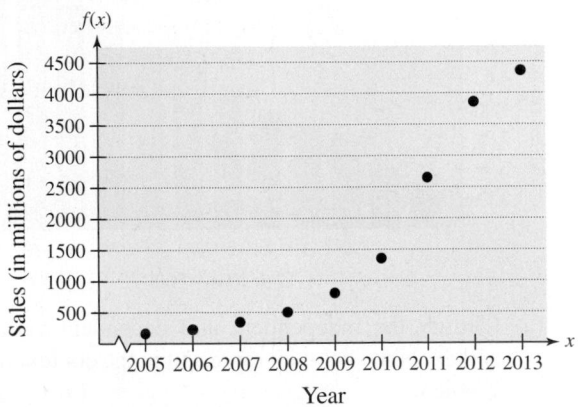

(a) Find $\dfrac{f(2013) - f(2005)}{2013 - 2005}$ and interpret the result in the context of the problem.

(b) An approximate model for the function is

$$S(t) = 90.442t^2 - 1075.25t + 3332.5, \quad 5 \le t \le 13$$

where S is the sales (in millions of dollars) and $t = 5$ represents 2005. Complete the table and compare the results with the data in the graph.

t	5	6	7	8	9	10	11	12	13
$S(t)$									

Evaluating a Difference Quotient   In Exercises 83–86, find the difference quotient and simplify your answer.

83. $f(x) = 2x$, $\quad \dfrac{f(x + c) - f(x)}{c}$, $\quad c \ne 0$

84. $g(x) = 3x - 1$, $\quad \dfrac{g(x + h) - g(x)}{h}$, $\quad h \ne 0$

85. $f(x) = x^2 - x + 1$, $\quad \dfrac{f(2 + h) - f(2)}{h}$, $\quad h \ne 0$

86. $f(x) = x^3 + x$, $\quad \dfrac{f(x + h) - f(x)}{h}$, $\quad h \ne 0$

Conclusions

True or False?   In Exercises 87 and 88, determine whether the statement is true or false. Justify your answer.

87. The domain of the function $f(x) = x^4 - 1$ is $(-\infty, \infty)$, and the range of f is $(0, \infty)$.

88. The set of ordered pairs $\{(-8, -2), (-6, 0), (-4, 0), (-2, 2), (0, 4), (2, -2)\}$ represents a function.

Think About It   In Exercises 89 and 90, write a square root function for the graph shown. Then identify the domain and range of the function.

89.

90.

91. Think About It   Given $f(x) = x^2$, is f the independent variable? Why or why not?

92. HOW DO YOU SEE IT?   The graph represents the height h of a projectile after t seconds.

Time (in seconds)

(a) Explain why h is a function of t.

(b) Approximate the height of the projectile after 0.5 second and after 1.25 seconds.

(c) Approximate the domain of h.

(d) Is t a function of h? Explain.

Cumulative Mixed Review

Operations with Rational Expressions   In Exercises 93–96, perform the operation and simplify.

93. $12 - \dfrac{4}{x + 2}$

94. $\dfrac{3}{x^2 + x - 20} + \dfrac{2x}{x^2 + 4x - 5}$

95. $\dfrac{x^5}{2x^3 + 4x^2} \cdot \dfrac{4x + 8}{3x}$

96. $\dfrac{x + 7}{2(x - 9)} \div \dfrac{x - 7}{2(x - 9)}$

The symbol **f** indicates an example or exercise that highlights algebraic techniques specifically used in calculus.

The Graph of a Function

In Section 1.2, some functions were represented graphically by points on a graph in a coordinate plane in which the input values are represented by the horizontal axis and the output values are represented by the vertical axis. The **graph of a function** f is the collection of ordered pairs $(x, f(x))$ such that x is in the domain of f. As you study this section, remember the geometric interpretations of x and $f(x)$.

x = the directed distance from the y-axis

$f(x)$ = the directed distance from the x-axis

Example 1 shows how to use the graph of a function to find the domain and range of the function.

EXAMPLE 1   Finding the Domain and Range of a Function

Use the graph of the function f to find
(a) the domain of f, (b) the function values
$f(-1)$ and $f(2)$, and (c) the range of f.

Solution

a. The closed dot at $(-1, -5)$ indicates that
$x = -1$ is in the domain of f, whereas the
open dot at $(4, 0)$ indicates that $x = 4$ is
not in the domain. So, the domain of f is
all x in the interval $[-1, 4)$.

b. Because $(-1, -5)$ is a point on the graph of
f, it follows that

$$f(-1) = -5.$$

Similarly, because $(2, 4)$ is a point on the graph of f, it follows that

$$f(2) = 4.$$

c. Because the graph does not extend below $f(-1) = -5$ or above $f(2) = 4$, the
range of f is the interval $[-5, 4]$.

✓ **Checkpoint** ◀))) *Audio-video solution in English & Spanish at LarsonPrecalculus.com.*

Use the graph of the function f to find
(a) the domain of f, (b) the function values
$f(0)$ and $f(3)$, and (c) the range of f.

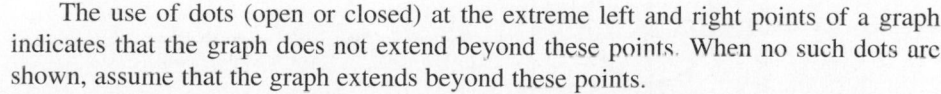

The use of dots (open or closed) at the extreme left and right points of a graph indicates that the graph does not extend beyond these points. When no such dots are shown, assume that the graph extends beyond these points.

What you should learn
- ▶ Find the domains and ranges of functions and use the Vertical Line Test for functions.
- ▶ Determine intervals on which functions are increasing, decreasing, or constant.
- ▶ Determine relative maximum and relative minimum values of functions.
- ▶ Identify and graph step functions and other piecewise-defined functions.
- ▶ Identify even and odd functions.

Why you should learn it
Graphs of functions provide visual relationships between two variables. For example, in Exercise 92 on page 39, you will use the graph of a step function to model the cost of sending a package.

EXAMPLE 2   Finding the Domain and Range of a Function

Find the domain and range of $f(x) = \sqrt{x - 4}$.

Algebraic Solution

Because the expression under a radical cannot be negative, the domain of $f(x) = \sqrt{x - 4}$ is the set of all real numbers such that $x - 4 \geq 0$. Solve this linear inequality for x as follows. (For help with solving linear inequalities, see Appendix E at this textbook's *Companion Website*.)

$x - 4 \geq 0$ Write original inequality.

$x \geq 4$ Add 4 to each side.

So, the domain is the set of all real numbers greater than or equal to 4. Because the value of a radical expression is never negative, the range of $f(x) = \sqrt{x - 4}$ is the set of all nonnegative real numbers.

Graphical Solution

The x-coordinates of points on the graph extend from 4 to the right. So, the domain is the set of all real numbers greater than or equal to 4.

The y-coordinates of points on the graph extend from 0 upwards. So, the range is the set of all nonnegative real numbers.

✓ **Checkpoint** *Audio-video solution in English & Spanish at LarsonPrecalculus.com.*

Find the domain and range of $f(x) = \sqrt{x - 1}$.

By the definition of a function, at most one y-value corresponds to a given x-value. It follows, then, that a vertical line can intersect the graph of a function at most once. This leads to the **Vertical Line Test** for functions.

> **Vertical Line Test for Functions**
>
> A set of points in a coordinate plane is the graph of y as a function of x if and only if no vertical line intersects the graph at more than one point.

EXAMPLE 3   Vertical Line Test for Functions

Use the Vertical Line Test to decide whether each graph represents y as a function of x.

a.

b.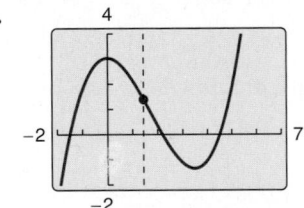

Solution

a. This is *not* a graph of y as a function of x because you can find a vertical line that intersects the graph twice.

b. This *is* a graph of y as a function of x because every vertical line intersects the graph at most once.

✓ **Checkpoint** *Audio-video solution in English & Spanish at LarsonPrecalculus.com.*

Use the Vertical Line Test to decide whether the graph at the right represents y as a function of x.

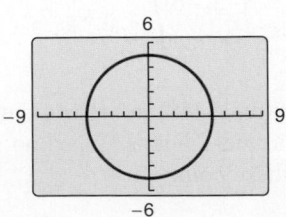

Technology Tip

Most graphing utilities are designed to graph functions of x more easily than other types of equations. For instance, the graph shown in Example 3(a) represents the equation $x - (y - 1)^2 = 0$. To use a graphing utility to duplicate this graph, you must first solve the equation for y to obtain $y = 1 \pm \sqrt{x}$, and then graph the two equations $y_1 = 1 + \sqrt{x}$ and $y_2 = 1 - \sqrt{x}$ in the same viewing window.

Increasing and Decreasing Functions

The more you know about the graph of a function, the more you know about the function itself. Consider the graph shown in Figure 1.15. Moving from *left to right,* this graph falls from $x = -2$ to $x = 0$, is constant from $x = 0$ to $x = 2$, and rises from $x = 2$ to $x = 4$.

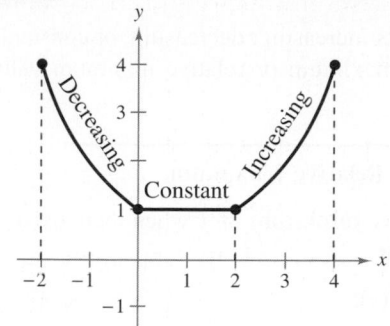

Figure 1.15

Increasing, Decreasing, and Constant Functions

A function f is **increasing** on an interval when, for any x_1 and x_2 in the interval,

$x_1 < x_2$ implies $f(x_1) < f(x_2)$.

A function f is **decreasing** on an interval when, for any x_1 and x_2 in the interval,

$x_1 < x_2$ implies $f(x_1) > f(x_2)$.

A function f is **constant** on an interval when, for any x_1 and x_2 in the interval,

$f(x_1) = f(x_2)$.

EXAMPLE 4   Increasing and Decreasing Functions

In Figure 1.16, determine the open intervals on which each function is increasing, decreasing, or constant.

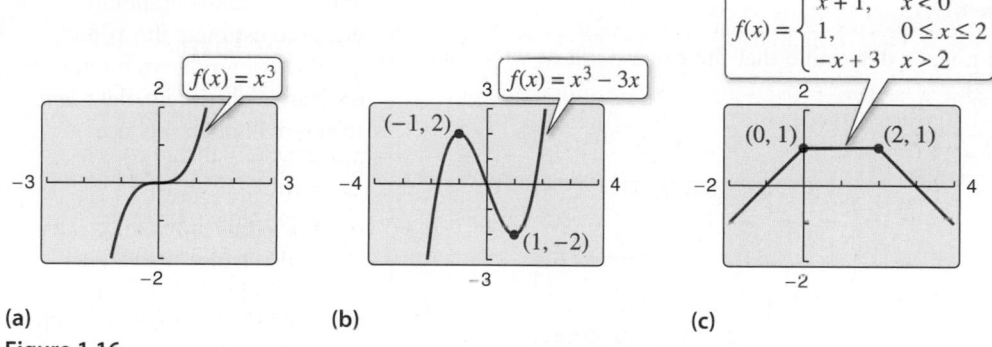

(a)   (b)   (c)

Figure 1.16

Solution

a. Although it might appear that there is an interval in which this function is constant, you can see that if $x_1 < x_2$, then $(x_1)^3 < (x_2)^3$, which implies that $f(x_1) < f(x_2)$. So, the function is increasing over the entire real line.

b. This function is increasing on the interval $(-\infty, -1)$, decreasing on the interval $(-1, 1)$, and increasing on the interval $(1, \infty)$.

c. This function is increasing on the interval $(-\infty, 0)$, constant on the interval $(0, 2)$, and decreasing on the interval $(2, \infty)$.

✓ *Checkpoint* 🔊))) *Audio-video solution in English & Spanish at LarsonPrecalculus.com.*

Graph the function $f(x) = x^3 + 3x^2 - 1$. Then use the graph to describe the increasing and decreasing behavior of the function. ∎

Relative Minimum and Maximum Values

The points at which a function changes its increasing, decreasing, or constant behavior are helpful in determining the relative maximum or relative minimum values of the function.

> **Definition of Relative Minimum and Relative Maximum**
>
> A function value $f(a)$ is called a **relative minimum** of f when there exists an interval (x_1, x_2) that contains a such that
>
> $$x_1 < x < x_2 \quad \text{implies} \quad f(a) \le f(x).$$
>
> A function value $f(a)$ is called a **relative maximum** of f when there exists an interval (x_1, x_2) that contains a such that
>
> $$x_1 < x < x_2 \quad \text{implies} \quad f(a) \ge f(x).$$

Figure 1.17

Figure 1.17 shows several different examples of relative minima and relative maxima. In Section 2.1, you will study a technique for finding the *exact points* at which a second-degree polynomial function has a relative minimum or relative maximum. For the time being, however, you can use a graphing utility to find reasonable approximations of these points.

EXAMPLE 5 **Approximating a Relative Minimum**

Use a graphing utility to approximate the relative minimum of the function given by $f(x) = 3x^2 - 4x - 2$.

Solution

The graph of f is shown in Figure 1.18. By using the *zoom* and *trace* features of a graphing utility, you can estimate that the function has a relative minimum at the point

$$(0.67, -3.33). \qquad \text{See Figure 1.19.}$$

Later, in Section 2.1, you will be able to determine that the exact point at which the relative minimum occurs is $\left(\frac{2}{3}, -\frac{10}{3}\right)$.

Figure 1.18

Figure 1.19

Technology Tip

When you use a graphing utility to estimate the *x*- and *y*-values of a relative minimum or relative maximum, the *zoom* feature will often produce graphs that are nearly flat, as shown in Figure 1.19. To overcome this problem, you can manually change the vertical setting of the viewing window. The graph will stretch vertically when the values of Ymin and Ymax are closer together.

✔ *Checkpoint* 🔊)) *Audio-video solution in English & Spanish at LarsonPrecalculus.com.*

Use a graphing utility to approximate the relative maximum of the function

$$f(x) = -4x^2 - 7x + 3.$$

You can also use the *table* feature of a graphing utility to numerically approximate the relative minimum of the function in Example 5. Using a table that begins at 0.6 and increments the value of x by 0.01, you can approximate that the minimum of f occurs at the point $(0.67, -3.33)$. Some graphing utilities have built-in programs that will find minimum or maximum values, as shown in Example 6.

EXAMPLE 6   Approximating Relative Minima and Maxima

Use a graphing utility to approximate the relative minimum and relative maximum of the function $f(x) = -x^3 + x$.

Solution

By using the *minimum* and *maximum* features of the graphing utility, you can estimate that the function has a relative minimum at the point

$(-0.58, -0.38)$ See Figure 1.20.

and a relative maximum at the point

$(0.58, 0.38)$.   See Figure 1.21.

If you take a course in calculus, you will learn a technique for finding the exact points at which this function has a relative minimum and a relative maximum.

Figure 1.20   **Figure 1.21**

✓ *Checkpoint* *Audio-video solution in English & Spanish at LarsonPrecalculus.com.*

Use a graphing utility to approximate the relative minimum and relative maximum of the function $f(x) = 2x^3 + 3x^2 - 12x$.

EXAMPLE 7   Temperature

During a 24-hour period, the temperature y (in degrees Fahrenheit) of a certain city can be approximated by the model

$$y = 0.026x^3 - 1.03x^2 + 10.2x + 34, \quad 0 \le x \le 24$$

where x represents the time of day, with $x = 0$ corresponding to 6 A.M. Approximate the maximum temperature during this 24-hour period.

Solution

Using the *maximum* feature of a graphing utility, you can determine that the maximum temperature during the 24-hour period was approximately 64°F. This temperature occurred at about 12:36 P.M. ($x \approx 6.6$), as shown in Figure 1.22.

Figure 1.22

✓ *Checkpoint* *Audio-video solution in English & Spanish at LarsonPrecalculus.com.*

In Example 7, approximate the minimum temperature during the 24-hour period. ■

Step Functions and Piecewise-Defined Functions

Library of Parent Functions: Greatest Integer Function

The *greatest integer function*, denoted by $[\![x]\!]$ and defined as the greatest integer less than or equal to x, has an infinite number of breaks or steps—one at each integer value in its domain. The basic characteristics of the greatest integer function are summarized below.

Graph of $f(x) = [\![x]\!]$

Domain: $(-\infty, \infty)$

Range: the set of integers

x-intercepts: in the interval $[0, 1)$

y-intercept: $(0, 0)$

Constant between each pair of consecutive integers

Jumps vertically one unit at each integer value

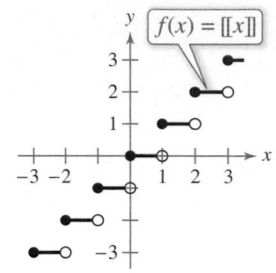

$f(x) = [\![x]\!]$

Technology Tip

Most graphing utilities display graphs in *connected mode*, which works well for graphs that do not have breaks. For graphs that do have breaks, such as the greatest integer function, it is better to use *dot mode*. Graph the greatest integer function [often called Int (x)] in *connected* and *dot* modes, and compare the two results.

Because of the vertical jumps described above, the greatest integer function is an example of a **step function** whose graph resembles a set of stairsteps. Some values of the greatest integer function are as follows.

$$[\![-1]\!] = (\text{greatest integer} \leq -1) = -1$$

$$\left[\!\!\left[-\tfrac{1}{2}\right]\!\!\right] = \left(\text{greatest integer} \leq -\tfrac{1}{2}\right) = -1$$

$$\left[\!\!\left[\tfrac{1}{10}\right]\!\!\right] = \left(\text{greatest integer} \leq \tfrac{1}{10}\right) = 0$$

$$[\![1.5]\!] = (\text{greatest integer} \leq 1.5) = 1$$

In Section 1.2, you learned that a piecewise-defined function is a function that is defined by two or more equations over a specified domain. To sketch the graph of a piecewise-defined function, you need to sketch the graph of each equation on the appropriate portion of the domain.

EXAMPLE 8   Sketching a Piecewise-Defined Function

Sketch the graph of

$$f(x) = \begin{cases} 2x + 3, & x \leq 1 \\ -x + 4, & x > 1 \end{cases}$$

by hand.

Solution

This piecewise-defined function is composed of two linear functions. At and to the left of $x = 1$, the graph is the line $y = 2x + 3$. To the right of $x = 1$, the graph is the line $y = -x + 4$, as shown in the figure. Notice that the point $(1, 5)$ is a solid dot and the point $(1, 3)$ is an open dot. This is because $f(1) = 5$.

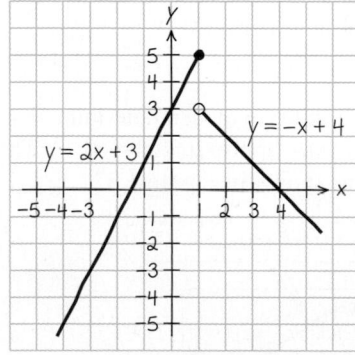

$y = 2x + 3$

$y = -x + 4$

What's Wrong?

You use a graphing utility to graph

$$f(x) = \begin{cases} x^2 + 1, & x \leq 0 \\ 4 - x, & x > 0 \end{cases}$$

by letting $y_1 = x^2 + 1$ and $y_2 = 4 - x$, as shown in the figure. You conclude that this is the graph of f. What's wrong?

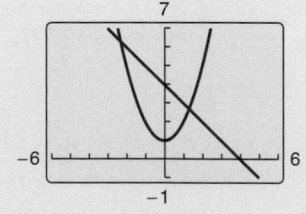

✔ **Checkpoint** 🔊))) *Audio-video solution in English & Spanish at LarsonPrecalculus.com.*

Sketch the graph of $f(x) = \begin{cases} -\tfrac{1}{2}x - 6, & x \leq -4 \\ x + 5, & x > -4 \end{cases}$ by hand.

∎

Even and Odd Functions

A graph has *symmetry with respect to the y-axis* if whenever (x, y) is on the graph, then so is the point $(-x, y)$. A graph has *symmetry with respect to the origin* if whenever (x, y) is on the graph, then so is the point $(-x, -y)$. A graph has *symmetry with respect to the x-axis* if whenever (x, y) is on the graph, then so is the point $(x, -y)$. A function whose graph is symmetric with respect to the y-axis is an **even function.** A function whose graph is symmetric with respect to the origin is an **odd function.** A graph that is symmetric with respect to the x-axis is not the graph of a function (except for the graph of $y = 0$). These three types of symmetry are illustrated in Figure 1.23.

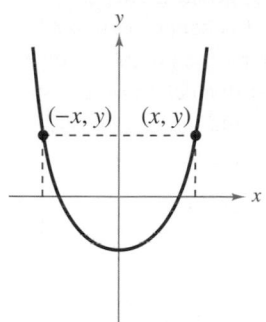

Symmetric to y-axis
Even function

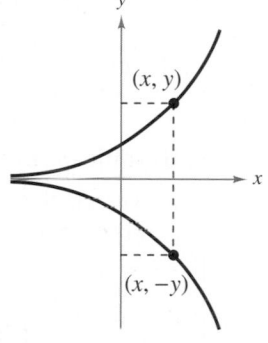

Symmetric to origin
Odd function

Symmetric to x-axis
Not a function

Figure 1.23

> ### Explore the Concept
>
> Graph each function with a graphing utility. Determine whether the function is *even*, *odd*, or *neither*.
>
> $f(x) = x^2 - x^4$
>
> $g(x) = 2x^3 + 1$
>
> $h(x) = x^5 - 2x^3 + x$
>
> $j(x) = 2 - x^6 - x^8$
>
> $k(x) = x^5 - 2x^4 + x - 2$
>
> $p(x) = x^9 + 3x^5 - x^3 + x$
>
> What do you notice about the equations of functions that are (a) odd and (b) even? Describe a way to identify a function as (c) odd, (d) even, or (e) neither odd nor even by inspecting the equation.

EXAMPLE 9   Even and Odd Functions

See LarsonPrecalculus.com for an interactive version of this type of example.

For each graph, determine whether the function is even, odd, or neither.

a.

b.

c.

d.

Solution

a. The graph is symmetric with respect to the y-axis. So, the function is even.

b. The graph is symmetric with respect to the origin. So, the function is odd.

c. The graph is neither symmetric with respect to the origin nor with respect to the y-axis. So, the function is neither even nor odd.

d. The graph is symmetric with respect to the y-axis. So, the function is even.

✓ **Checkpoint** 🔊))) *Audio-video solution in English & Spanish at LarsonPrecalculus.com.*

Use a graphing utility to graph $f(x) = x^2 - 4$ and determine whether it is even, odd, or neither.

> **Test for Even and Odd Functions**
>
> A function f is **even** when, for each x in the domain of f, $f(-x) = f(x)$.
> A function f is **odd** when, for each x in the domain of f, $f(-x) = -f(x)$.

EXAMPLE 10 Even and Odd Functions

Determine whether each function is even, odd, or neither.

a. $g(x) = x^3 - x$

b. $h(x) = x^2 + 1$

c. $f(x) = x^3 - 1$

Algebraic Solution

a. This function is odd because

$$g(-x) = (-x)^3 - (-x)$$

$$= -x^3 + x$$

$$= -(x^3 - x)$$

$$= -g(x).$$

b. This function is even because

$$h(-x) = (-x)^2 + 1$$

$$= x^2 + 1$$

$$= h(x).$$

c. Substituting $-x$ for x produces

$$f(-x) = (-x)^3 - 1$$

$$= -x^3 - 1.$$

Because

$$f(x) = x^3 - 1$$

and

$$-f(x) = -x^3 + 1$$

you can conclude that

$$f(-x) \neq f(x)$$

and

$$f(-x) \neq -f(x).$$

So, the function is neither even nor odd.

Graphical Solution

a. The graph is symmetric with respect to the origin. So, this function is odd.

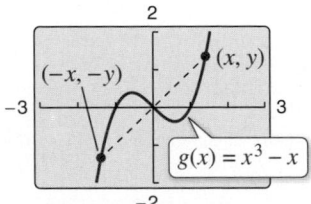

b. The graph is symmetric with respect to the y-axis. So, this function is even.

c. The graph is neither symmetric with respect to the origin nor with respect to the y-axis. So, this function is neither even nor odd.

✓ *Checkpoint* *Audio-video solution in English & Spanish at LarsonPrecalculus.com.*

Determine whether the function is even, odd, or neither. Then describe the symmetry.

a. $f(x) = 5 - 3x$ **b.** $g(x) = x^4 - x^2 - 1$ **c.** $h(x) = 2x^3 + 3x$ ∎

To help visualize symmetry with respect to the origin, place a pin at the origin of a graph and rotate the graph 180°. If the result after rotation coincides with the original graph, then the graph is symmetric with respect to the origin.

1.3   Exercises

See *CalcChat.com* for tutorial help and worked-out solutions to odd-numbered exercises. For instructions on how to use a graphing utility, see Appendix A.

Vocabulary and Concept Check

In Exercises 1 and 2, fill in the blank.

1. A function f is _____ on an interval when, for any x_1 and x_2 in the interval, $x_1 < x_2$ implies $f(x_1) > f(x_2)$.

2. A function f is _____ when, for each x in the domain of f, $f(-x) = f(x)$.

3. The graph of a function f is the segment from $(1, 2)$ to $(4, 5)$, including the endpoints. What is the domain of f?

4. A vertical line intersects a graph twice. Does the graph represent a function?

5. Let f be a function such that $f(2) \geq f(x)$ for all values of x in the interval $(0, 3)$. Does $f(2)$ represent a relative minimum or a relative maximum?

6. Given $f(x) = [\![x]\!]$, in what interval does $f(x) = 5$?

Procedures and Problem Solving

Finding the Domain and Range of a Function   In Exercises 7–10, use the graph of the function to find the domain and range of f. Then find $f(0)$.

7.

8.

9.

10.

Finding the Domain and Range of a Function   In Exercises 11–16, use a graphing utility to graph the function and estimate its domain and range. Then find the domain and range algebraically.

11. $f(x) = -2x^2 + 3$

12. $f(x) = x^2 - 1$

13. $f(x) = \sqrt{x + 2}$

14. $h(t) = \sqrt{4 - t^2}$

15. $f(x) = |x + 3|$

16. $f(x) = -\frac{1}{4}|x - 5|$

Analyzing a Graph   In Exercises 17 and 18, use the graph of the function to answer the questions.

(a) Determine the domain of the function.

(b) Determine the range of the function.

(c) Find the value(s) of x for which $f(x) = 0$.

(d) What are the values of x from part (c) referred to graphically?

(e) Find $f(0)$, if possible.

(f) What is the value from part (e) referred to graphically?

(g) What is the value of f at $x = 1$? What are the coordinates of the point?

(h) What is the value of f at $x = -1$? What are the coordinates of the point?

(i) The coordinates of the point on the graph of f at which $x = -3$ can be labeled $(-3, f(-3))$, or $(-3, \rule{1cm}{0.4pt})$.

17.
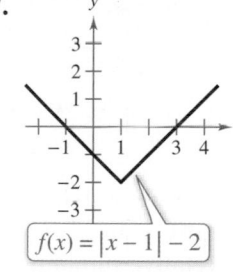

$f(x) = |x - 1| - 2$

18.
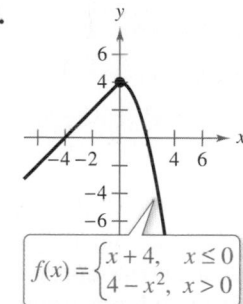

$f(x) = \begin{cases} x + 4, & x \leq 0 \\ 4 - x^2, & x > 0 \end{cases}$

Vertical Line Test for Functions   In Exercises 19–22, use the Vertical Line Test to determine whether y is a function of x. Describe how you can use a graphing utility to produce the given graph.

19. $y = \frac{1}{2}x^2$

20. $x - y^2 = 1$

21. $0.25x^2 + y^2 = 1$ **22.** $x^2 = 2xy - 1$

Increasing and Decreasing Functions   In Exercises 23–26, determine the open intervals on which the function is increasing, decreasing, or constant.

23. $f(x) = \frac{3}{2}x$ **24.** $f(x) = x^2 - 4x$

25. $f(x) = x^3 - 3x^2 + 2$ **26.** $f(x) = \sqrt{x^2 - 1}$

          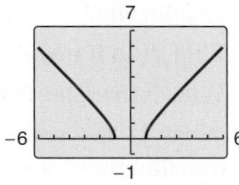

Increasing and Decreasing Functions   In Exercises 27–34, (a) use a graphing utility to graph the function and (b) determine the open intervals on which the function is increasing, decreasing, or constant.

27. $f(x) = 3$ **28.** $f(x) = x$

29. $f(x) = x^{2/3}$ **30.** $f(x) = -x^{3/4}$

31. $f(x) = x\sqrt{x + 3}$ **32.** $f(x) = x\sqrt{3 - x}$

33. $f(x) = |x + 1| + |x - 1|$

34. $f(x) = -|x + 4| - |x + 1|$

Approximating Relative Minima and Maxima   In Exercises 35–46, use a graphing utility to graph the function and to approximate any relative minimum or relative maximum values of the function.

35. $f(x) = x^2 - 6x$ **36.** $f(x) = 3x^2 - 2x - 5$

37. $y = -2x^3 - x^2 + 14x$ **38.** $y = x^3 - 6x^2 + 15$

39. $h(x) = (x - 1)\sqrt{x}$ **40.** $g(x) = x\sqrt{4 - x}$

41. $f(x) = x^2 - 4x - 5$ **42.** $f(x) = 3x^2 - 12x$

43. $f(x) = x^3 - 3x$ **44.** $f(x) = -x^3 + 3x^2$

45. $f(x) = 3x^2 - 6x + 1$ **46.** $f(x) = 8x - 4x^2$

Library of Parent Functions   In Exercises 47–52, sketch the graph of the function by hand. Then use a graphing utility to verify the graph.

47. $f(x) = [\![x]\!] + 2$ **48.** $f(x) = [\![x]\!] - 3$

49. $f(x) = [\![x - 1]\!] - 2$ **50.** $f(x) = [\![x + 2]\!] + 1$

51. $f(x) = 2[\![x]\!]$ **52.** $f(x) = [\![4x]\!]$

Describing a Step Function   In Exercises 53 and 54, use a graphing utility to graph the function. State the domain and range of the function. Describe the pattern of the graph.

53. $s(x) = 2\left(\frac{1}{4}x - [\![\frac{1}{4}x]\!]\right)$

54. $g(x) = 2\left(\frac{1}{4}x - [\![\frac{1}{4}x]\!]\right)^2$

Sketching a Piecewise-Defined Function   In Exercises 55–62, sketch the graph of the piecewise-defined function by hand.

55. $f(x) = \begin{cases} 2x + 3, & x < 0 \\ 3 - x, & x \geq 0 \end{cases}$

56. $f(x) = \begin{cases} x + 6, & x \leq -4 \\ 3x - 4, & x > -4 \end{cases}$

57. $f(x) = \begin{cases} \sqrt{4 + x}, & x < 0 \\ \sqrt{4 - x}, & x \geq 0 \end{cases}$

58. $f(x) = \begin{cases} 1 - (x - 1)^2, & x \leq 2 \\ \sqrt{x - 2}, & x > 2 \end{cases}$

59. $f(x) = \begin{cases} x + 3, & x \leq 0 \\ 3, & 0 < x \leq 2 \\ 2x - 1, & x > 2 \end{cases}$

60. $g(x) = \begin{cases} x + 5, & x \leq -3 \\ 5, & -3 < x < 1 \\ 5x - 4, & x \geq 1 \end{cases}$

61. $f(x) = \begin{cases} 2x + 1, & x \leq -1 \\ x^2 - 2, & x > -1 \end{cases}$

62. $h(x) = \begin{cases} 3 + x, & x < 0 \\ x^2 + 1, & x \geq 0 \end{cases}$

Even and Odd Functions   In Exercises 63–72, use a graphing utility to graph the function and determine whether it is even, odd, or neither.

63. $f(x) = 5$ **64.** $f(x) = -9$

65. $f(x) = 3x - 2$ **66.** $f(x) = 4 - 5x$

67. $h(x) = x^2 + 6$ **68.** $f(x) = -x^2 - 8$

69. $f(x) = \sqrt{1 - x}$ **70.** $g(t) = \sqrt[3]{t - 1}$

71. $f(x) = |x + 2|$ **72.** $f(x) = -|x - 5|$

Think About It   In Exercises 73–78, find the coordinates of a second point on the graph of a function f if the given point is on the graph and the function is (a) even and (b) odd.

73. $\left(\frac{3}{2}, 4\right)$ **74.** $\left(-\frac{5}{3}, -7\right)$

75. $(-2, -9)$ **76.** $(5, -1)$

77. $(x, -y)$ **78.** $(2a, 2c)$

Algebraic-Graphical-Numerical   In Exercises 79–86, determine whether the function is even, odd, or neither (a) algebraically, (b) graphically by using a graphing utility to graph the function, and (c) numerically by using the *table* feature of the graphing utility to compare $f(x)$ and $f(-x)$ for several values of x.

79. $f(t) = t^2 + 2t - 3$

80. $f(x) = x^6 - 2x^2 + 3$

81. $g(x) = x^3 - 5x$

82. $h(x) = x^5 - 4x^3$

83. $f(x) = x\sqrt{1 - x^2}$

84. $f(x) = x\sqrt{x + 5}$

85. $g(s) = 4s^{2/3}$

86. $f(s) = 4s^{3/5}$

Finding the Intervals Where a Function is Positive   In Exercises 87–90, graph the function and determine the interval(s) (if any) on the real axis for which $f(x) \geq 0$. Use a graphing utility to verify your results.

87. $f(x) = 4 - x$

88. $f(x) = 4x + 8$

89. $f(x) = x^2 - 9$

90. $f(x) = x^2 - 4x$

91. Business   The cost of parking in a metered lot is $1.00 for the first hour and $0.50 for each additional hour or portion of an hour.

(a) A customer needs a model for the cost C of parking in the metered lot for t hours. Which of the following is the appropriate model?

$C_1(t) = 1 + 0.50[\![t - 1]\!]$

$C_2(t) = 1 - 0.50[\![-(t - 1)]\!]$

(b) Use a graphing utility to graph the appropriate model. Estimate the cost of parking in the metered lot for 7 hours and 10 minutes.

92. *Why you should learn it*   (p. 29)   The cost of sending an overnight package from New York to Atlanta is $23.20 for a package weighing up to but not including 1 pound and $2.00 for each additional pound or portion of a pound. Use the greatest integer function to create a model for the cost C of overnight delivery of a package weighing x pounds, where $x > 0$. Sketch the graph of the function.

Using the Graph of a Function   In Exercises 93 and 94, write the height h of the rectangle as a function of x.

93.

$y = -x^2 + 4x - 1$

$(1, 2)$ $(3, 2)$

94.

$(1, 3)$

$y = 4x - x^2$

95. MODELING DATA

The number N (in thousands) of existing condominiums and cooperative homes sold each year from 2010 through 2013 in the United States is approximated by the model

$N = -24.83t^3 + 906t^2 - 10{,}928.2t + 44{,}114,$

$10 \leq t \leq 13$

where t represents the year, with $t = 10$ corresponding to 2010.   (Source: National Association of Realtors)

(a) Use a graphing utility to graph the model over the appropriate domain.

(b) Use the graph from part (a) to determine during which years the number of cooperative homes and condos was increasing. During which years was the number decreasing?

(c) Approximate the minimum number of cooperative homes and condos sold from 2010 through 2013.

96. Mechanical Engineering   The intake pipe of a 100-gallon tank has a flow rate of 10 gallons per minute, and two drain pipes have a flow rate of 5 gallons per minute each. The graph shows the volume V of fluid in the tank as a function of time t. Determine in which pipes the fluid is flowing in specific subintervals of the one-hour interval of time shown on the graph. (There are many correct answers.)

Conclusions

True or False? In Exercises 97 and 98, determine whether the statement is true or false. Justify your answer.

97. A function with a square root cannot have a domain that is the set of all real numbers.

98. It is possible for an odd function to have the interval $[0, \infty)$ as its domain.

Think About It   In Exercises 99–104, match the graph of the function with the description that best fits the situation.

(a) The air temperature at a beach on a sunny day

(b) The height of a football kicked in a field goal attempt

(c) The number of children in a family over time

(d) The population of California as a function of time

(e) The depth of the tide at a beach over a 24-hour period

(f) The number of cupcakes on a tray at a party

99.   **100.**

101.   **102.**

103.   **104.**

105. Think About It Does the graph in Exercise 19 represent x as a function of y? Explain.

106. Think About It Does the graph in Exercise 21 represent x as a function of y? Explain.

107. Think About It Can you represent the greatest integer function using a piecewise-defined function?

108. Think About It How does the graph of the greatest integer function differ from the graph of a line with a slope of zero?

109. Think About It Let f be an even function. Determine whether g is even, odd, or neither. Explain.

(a) $g(x) = -f(x)$ (b) $g(x) = f(-x)$

(c) $g(x) = f(x) - 2$ (d) $g(x) = -f(x + 3)$

110. **HOW DO YOU SEE IT?** Half of the graph of an odd function is shown.

(a) Sketch a complete graph of the function.

(b) Find the domain and range of the function.

(c) Identify the open intervals on which the function is increasing, decreasing, or constant.

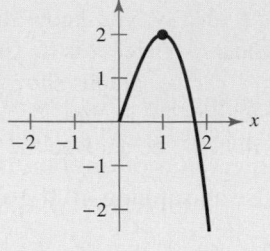

(d) Find any relative minimum and relative maximum values of the function.

111. Proof Prove that a function of the following form is odd.

$$y = a_{2n+1}x^{2n+1} + a_{2n-1}x^{2n-1} + \cdots + a_3x^3 + a_1x$$

112. Proof Prove that a function of the following form is even.

$$y = a_{2n}x^{2n} + a_{2n-2}x^{2n-2} + \cdots + a_2x^2 + a_0$$

Cumulative Mixed Review

Identifying Terms and Coefficients In Exercises 113–116, identify the terms. Then identify the coefficients of the variable terms of the expression.

113. $-2x^2 + 11x + 3$ **114.** $10 + 3x$

115. $\dfrac{x}{3} - 5x^2 + x^3$ **116.** $7x^4 + \sqrt{2}x^2 - x$

Evaluating a Function In Exercises 117 and 118, evaluate the function at each specified value of the independent variable and simplify.

117. $f(x) = -x^2 - x + 3$

(a) $f(4)$ (b) $f(-5)$ (c) $f(x - 2)$

118. $f(x) = x\sqrt{x - 3}$

(a) $f(3)$ (b) $f(12)$ (c) $f(6)$

Evaluating a Difference Quotient   In Exercises 119 and 120, find the difference quotient and simplify your answer.

119. $f(x) = x^2 - 2x + 9,\ \dfrac{f(3 + h) - f(3)}{h},\ h \neq 0$

120. $f(x) = 5 + 6x - x^2,\ \dfrac{f(6 + h) - f(6)}{h},\ h \neq 0$

1.4   Shifting, Reflecting, and Stretching Graphs

Summary of Graphs of Parent Functions

One of the goals of this text is to enable you to build your intuition for the basic shapes of the graphs of different types of functions. For instance, from your study of lines in Section 1.1, you can determine the basic shape of the graph of the parent linear function

$$f(x) = x.$$

Specifically, you know that the graph of this function is a line whose slope is 1 and whose y-intercept is $(0, 0)$.

The six graphs shown in Figure 1.24 represent the most commonly used types of functions in algebra. Familiarity with the basic characteristics of these parent graphs will help you analyze the shapes of more complicated graphs.

Library of Parent Functions: Commonly Used Functions

(a) *Linear Function*

(b) *Absolute Value Function*

(c) *Square Root Function*

(d) *Quadratic Function*

(e) *Cubic Function*

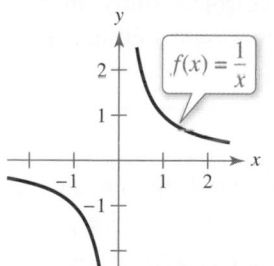

(f) *Rational Function*

Figure 1.24

Throughout this section, you will discover how many complicated graphs are derived by shifting, stretching, shrinking, or reflecting the parent graphs shown above. Shifts, stretches, shrinks, and reflections are called *transformations*. Many graphs of functions can be created from combinations of these transformations.

What you should learn

▶ Recognize graphs of parent functions.
▶ Use vertical and horizontal shifts to sketch graphs of functions.
▶ Use reflections to sketch graphs of functions.
▶ Use nonrigid transformations to sketch graphs of functions.

Why you should learn it

Recognizing the graphs of parent functions and knowing how to shift, reflect, and stretch graphs of functions can help you sketch or describe the graphs of a wide variety of simple functions. For example, in Exercise 66 on page 49, you are asked to describe a transformation that produces the graph of a model for the sales of the WD-40 Company.

Vertical and Horizontal Shifts

Many functions have graphs that are simple transformations of the graphs of parent functions summarized in Figure 1.24. For example, you can obtain the graph of

$$h(x) = x^2 + 2$$

by shifting the graph of $f(x) = x^2$ two units *upward*, as shown in Figure 1.25. In function notation, h and f are related as follows.

$$h(x) = x^2 + 2$$
$$\quad = f(x) + 2 \qquad \text{Upward shift of two units}$$

Similarly, you can obtain the graph of

$$g(x) = (x - 2)^2$$

by shifting the graph of $f(x) = x^2$ two units to the *right*, as shown in Figure 1.26. In this case, the functions g and f have the following relationship.

$$g(x) = (x - 2)^2$$
$$\quad = f(x - 2) \qquad \text{Right shift of two units}$$

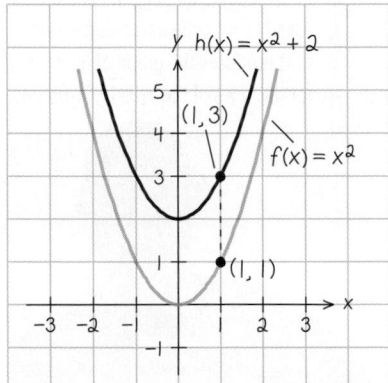

Vertical shift upward: two units
Figure 1.25

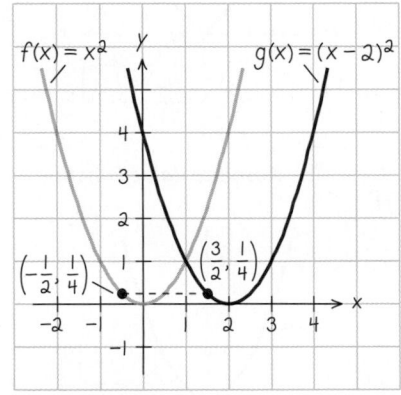

Horizontal shift to the right: two units
Figure 1.26

Explore the Concept

Use a graphing utility to display (in the same viewing window) the graphs of $y = x^2 + c$, where $c = -2, 0, 2,$ and 4. Use the results to describe the effect that c has on the graph.

Use a graphing utility to display (in the same viewing window) the graphs of $y = (x + c)^2$, where $c = -2, 0, 2,$ and 4. Use the results to describe the effect that c has on the graph.

The following list summarizes vertical and horizontal shifts. In items 3 and 4, be sure you see that $h(x) = f(x - c)$ corresponds to a *right* shift and $h(x) = f(x + c)$ corresponds to a *left* shift for $c > 0$.

Vertical and Horizontal Shifts

Let c be a positive real number. **Vertical and horizontal shifts** in the graph of $y = f(x)$ are represented as follows.

1. Vertical shift c units *upward*: $h(x) = f(x) + c$

2. Vertical shift c units *downward*: $h(x) = f(x) - c$

3. Horizontal shift c units to the *right*: $h(x) = f(x - c)$

4. Horizontal shift c units to the *left*: $h(x) = f(x + c)$

Some graphs can be obtained from combinations of vertical and horizontal shifts, as shown in Example 1(c) on the next page. Vertical and horizontal shifts generate a *family of functions*, each with a graph that has the same shape but at a different location in the plane.

EXAMPLE 1   Shifts in the Graph of a Function

a. To use the graph of $f(x) = x^3$ to sketch the graph of $g(x) = x^3 - 1$, shift the graph of f one unit downward.

b. To use the graph of $f(x) = x^3$ to sketch the graph of $h(x) = (x - 1)^3$, shift the graph of f one unit to the right.

c. To use the graph of $f(x) = x^3$ to sketch the graph of $k(x) = (x + 2)^3 + 1$, shift the graph of f two units to the left and then one unit upward.

  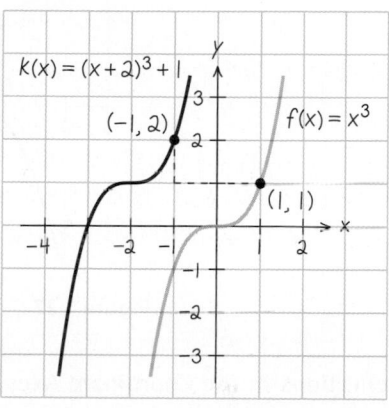

(a) *Vertical shift: one unit downward*   (b) *Horizontal shift: one unit right*   (c) *Two units left and one unit upward*

✓ **Checkpoint** 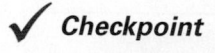 *Audio-video solution in English & Spanish at LarsonPrecalculus.com.*

Use the graph of $f(x) = x^3$ to sketch the graph of each function.

a. $h(x) = x^3 + 5$ **b.** $g(x) = (x - 3)^3 + 2$

EXAMPLE 2   Writing Equations from Graphs

Each graph is a transformation of the graph of $f(x) = x^2$. Write an equation for each function.

a. **b.**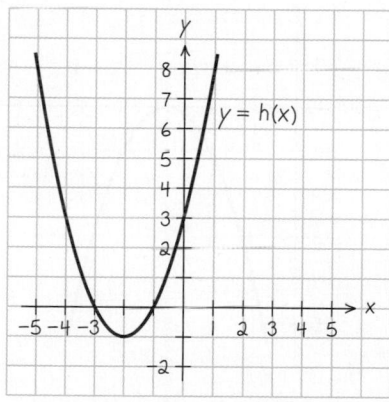

Solution

a. The graph of g is a vertical shift of four units upward of the graph of $f(x) = x^2$. So, the equation for g is $g(x) = x^2 + 4$.

b. The graph of h is a horizontal shift of two units to the left, and a vertical shift of one unit downward, of the graph of $f(x) = x^2$. So, the equation for h is $h(x) = (x + 2)^2 - 1$.

✓ **Checkpoint** *Audio-video solution in English & Spanish at LarsonPrecalculus.com.*

The graph at the right is a transformation of the graph of $f(x) = x^2$. Write an equation for the function.

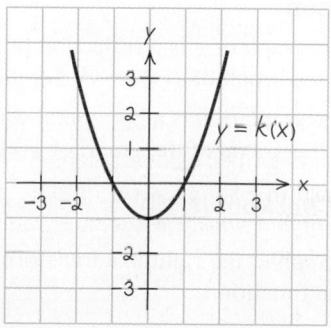

Reflecting Graphs

Another common type of transformation is called a **reflection.** For instance, when you consider the x-axis to be a mirror, the graph of $h(x) = -x^2$ is the mirror image (or reflection) of the graph of $f(x) = x^2$, as shown in Figure 1.27.

Figure 1.27

Reflections in the Coordinate Axes

Reflections in the coordinate axes of the graph of $y = f(x)$ are represented as follows.

1. Reflection in the x-axis: $h(x) = -f(x)$

2. Reflection in the y-axis: $h(x) = f(-x)$

EXAMPLE 3 Writing Equations from Graphs

Each graph is a transformation of the graph of $f(x) = x^2$. Write an equation for each function.

a.

b.

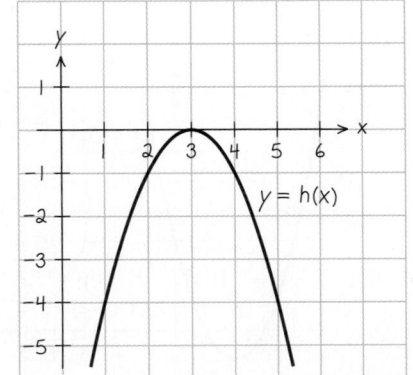

Solution

a. The graph of g is a reflection in the x-axis *followed by* an upward shift of two units of the graph of $f(x) = x^2$. So, the equation for g is $g(x) = -x^2 + 2$.

b. The graph of h is a horizontal shift of three units to the right *followed by* a reflection in the x-axis of the graph of $f(x) = x^2$. So, the equation for h is $h(x) = -(x - 3)^2$.

✓ **Checkpoint** 🔊))) *Audio-video solution in English & Spanish at LarsonPrecalculus.com.*

The graph at the right is a transformation of the graph of $f(x) = x^2$. Write an equation for the function. ■

EXAMPLE 4   Reflections and Shifts

Compare the graph of each function with the graph of

$$f(x) = \sqrt{x}.$$

a. $g(x) = -\sqrt{x}$

b. $h(x) = \sqrt{-x}$

c. $k(x) = -\sqrt{x + 2}$

Algebraic Solution

a. Relative to the graph of $f(x) = \sqrt{x}$, the graph of g is a reflection in the x-axis because

$$g(x) = -\sqrt{x}$$

$$= -f(x).$$

b. The graph of h is a reflection of the graph of $f(x) = \sqrt{x}$ in the y-axis because

$$h(x) = \sqrt{-x}$$

$$= f(-x).$$

c. From the equation

$$k(x) = -\sqrt{x + 2}$$

$$= -f(x + 2)$$

you can conclude that the graph of k is a left shift of two units, followed by a reflection in the x-axis, of the graph of $f(x) = \sqrt{x}$.

Graphical Solution

a. From the graph in Figure 1.28, you can see that the graph of g is a reflection of the graph of f in the x-axis. Note that the domain of g is $x \geq 0$.

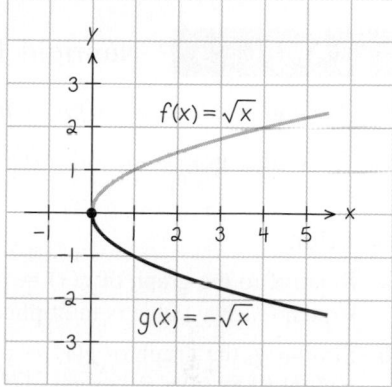

Figure 1.28

b. From the graph in Figure 1.29, you can see that the graph of h is a reflection of the graph of f in the y-axis. Note that the domain of h is $x \leq 0$.

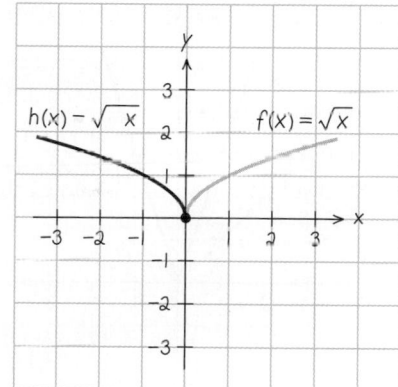

Figure 1.29

c. From the graph in Figure 1.30, you can see that the graph of k is a left shift of two units of the graph of f, followed by a reflection in the x-axis. Note that the domain of k is $x \geq -2$.

Figure 1.30

 Checkpoint))) Audio-video solution in English & Spanish at LarsonPrecalculus.com.

Compare the graph of $g(x) = -|x|$ with the graph of $f(x) = |x|$. ▪

Nonrigid Transformations

Horizontal shifts, vertical shifts, and reflections are called **rigid transformations** because the basic shape of the graph is unchanged. These transformations change only the *position* of the graph in the coordinate plane. **Nonrigid transformations** are those that cause a *distortion*—a change in the shape of the original graph. For instance, a nonrigid transformation of the graph of $y = f(x)$ is represented by $g(x) = cf(x)$, where the transformation is a **vertical stretch** when $c > 1$ and a **vertical shrink** when $0 < c < 1$. Another nonrigid transformation of the graph of $y = f(x)$ is represented by $h(x) = f(cx)$, where the transformation is a **horizontal shrink** when $c > 1$ and a **horizontal stretch** when $0 < c < 1$.

EXAMPLE 5   Nonrigid Transformations

See LarsonPrecalculus.com for an interactive version of this type of example.

Compare the graphs of (a) $h(x) = 3|x|$ and (b) $g(x) = \frac{1}{3}|x|$ with the graph of $f(x) = |x|$.

Solution

a. Relative to the graph of $f(x) = |x|$, the graph of $h(x) = 3|x| = 3f(x)$ is a vertical stretch (each y-value is multiplied by 3) of the graph of f. (See Figure 1.31.)

b. Similarly, the graph of $g(x) = \frac{1}{3}|x| = \frac{1}{3}f(x)$ is a vertical shrink $\left(\text{each } y\text{-value is multiplied by } \frac{1}{3}\right)$ of the graph of f. (See Figure 1.32.)

Figure 1.31

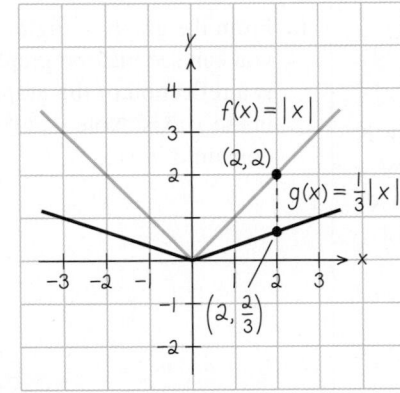

Figure 1.32

✓ **Checkpoint** 🔊)) *Audio-video solution in English & Spanish at LarsonPrecalculus.com.*

Compare the graphs of (a) $g(x) = 4x^2$ and (b) $h(x) = \frac{1}{4}x^2$ with the graph of $f(x) = x^2$.

EXAMPLE 6   Nonrigid Transformations

Compare the graph of $h(x) = f\left(\frac{1}{2}x\right)$ with the graph of $f(x) = 2 - x^3$.

Solution

Relative to the graph of $f(x) = 2 - x^3$, the graph of

$$h(x) = f\left(\tfrac{1}{2}x\right) = 2 - \left(\tfrac{1}{2}x\right)^3 = 2 - \tfrac{1}{8}x^3$$

is a horizontal stretch (each x-value is multiplied by 2) of the graph of f. (See Figure 1.33.)

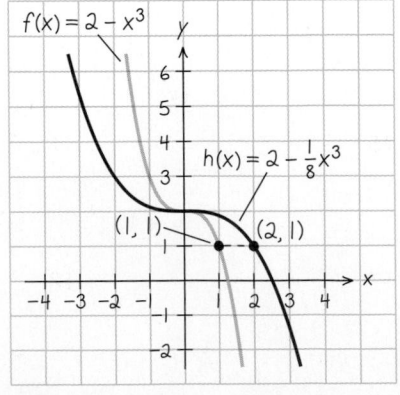

Figure 1.33

✓ **Checkpoint** 🔊)) *Audio-video solution in English & Spanish at LarsonPrecalculus.com.*

Compare the graphs of (a) $g(x) = f(2x)$ and (b) $h(x) = f\left(\frac{1}{2}x\right)$ with the graph of $f(x) = x^2 + 3$.

1.4   Exercises

See *CalcChat.com* for tutorial help and worked-out solutions to odd-numbered exercises.
For instructions on how to use a graphing utility, see Appendix A.

Vocabulary and Concept Check

1. Name three types of rigid transformations.

2. Match the rigid transformation of $y = f(x)$ with the correct representation, where $c > 0$.
   - (a) $h(x) = f(x) + c$
   - (b) $h(x) = f(x) - c$
   - (c) $h(x) = f(x - c)$
   - (d) $h(x) = f(x + c)$
   - (i) horizontal shift c units to the left
   - (ii) vertical shift c units upward
   - (iii) horizontal shift c units to the right
   - (iv) vertical shift c units downward

In Exercises 3 and 4, fill in the blanks.

3. A reflection in the x-axis of $y = f(x)$ is represented by $h(x) = $ _____ ,
   while a reflection in the y-axis of $y = f(x)$ is represented by $h(x) = $ _____ .

4. A nonrigid transformation of $y = f(x)$ represented by $cf(x)$ is a vertical stretch
   when _____ and a vertical shrink when _____ .

Procedures and Problem Solving

Sketching Transformations In Exercises 5–18, sketch the graphs of the three functions by hand on the same rectangular coordinate system. Verify your results with a graphing utility.

5. $f(x) = x$
   $g(x) = x - 4$
   $h(x) = 3x$

6. $f(x) = \frac{1}{2}x$
   $g(x) = \frac{1}{2}x + 2$
   $h(x) = 4(x - 2)$

7. $f(x) = x^2$
   $g(x) = x^2 + 2$
   $h(x) = (x - 2)^2$

8. $f(x) = x^2$
   $g(x) = 3x^2$
   $h(x) = (x + 2)^2 + 1$

9. $f(x) = -x^2$
   $g(x) = -x^2 + 1$
   $h(x) = -(x + 3)^2$

10. $f(x) = (x - 2)^2$
    $g(x) = (x + 2)^2 + 2$
    $h(x) = -(x - 2)^2 - 1$

11. $f(x) = x^2$
    $g(x) = \frac{1}{2}x^2$
    $h(x) = (2x)^2$

12. $f(x) = x^2$
    $g(x) = \frac{1}{4}x^2 + 2$
    $h(x) = -\frac{1}{4}x^2$

13. $f(x) = |x|$
    $g(x) = |x| - 1$
    $h(x) = 3|x - 3|$

14. $f(x) = |x|$
    $g(x) = |2x|$
    $h(x) = -2|x + 2| - 1$

15. $f(x) = -\sqrt{x}$
    $g(x) = \sqrt{x + 1}$
    $h(x) = \sqrt{x - 2} + 1$

16. $f(x) = \sqrt{x}$
    $g(x) = \frac{1}{2}\sqrt{x}$
    $h(x) = -\sqrt{x - 4}$

17. $f(x) = \dfrac{1}{x}$
    $g(x) = \dfrac{1}{x} - 2$
    $h(x) = \dfrac{1}{x - 1} + 2$

18. $f(x) = \dfrac{1}{x}$
    $g(x) = \dfrac{1}{x} - 4$
    $h(x) = \dfrac{1}{x + 3} - 1$

Sketching Transformations In Exercises 19 and 20, use the graph of f to sketch each graph. To print an enlarged copy of the graph, go to *MathGraphs.com*.

19. (a) $y = f(x) + 2$
    (b) $y = -f(x)$
    (c) $y = f(x - 2)$
    (d) $y = f(x + 3)$
    (e) $y = 2f(x)$
    (f) $y = f(-x)$
    (g) $y = f\left(\frac{1}{2}x\right)$

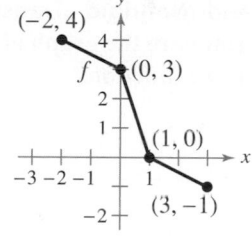

20. (a) $y = f(x) - 1$
    (b) $y = f(x + 2)$
    (c) $y = f(x - 1)$
    (d) $y = -f(x - 2)$
    (e) $y = f(-x)$
    (f) $y = \frac{1}{2}f(x)$
    (g) $y = f(2x)$

Error Analysis In Exercises 21 and 22, describe the error in graphing the function.

21. $f(x) = (x + 1)^2$

22. $f(x) = (x - 1)^2$

Library of Parent Functions In Exercises 23–28, compare the graph of the function with the graph of its parent function.

23. $y = \sqrt{x} + 2$

24. $y = \dfrac{1}{x} - 5$

25. $y = (x - 4)^3$

26. $y = |x + 5|$

27. $y = x^2 - 2$

28. $y = \sqrt{x - 2}$

Library of Parent Functions In Exercises 29–34, identify the parent function and describe the transformation shown in the graph. Write an equation for the graphed function.

29.

30.

31.

32.

33.

34.
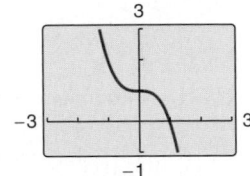

Rigid and Nonrigid Transformations In Exercises 35–46, compare the graph of the function with the graph of its parent function.

35. $y = -x$

36. $y = |-x|$

37. $y = (-x)^2$

38. $y = -x^3$

39. $y = \dfrac{1}{-x}$

40. $y = -\dfrac{1}{x}$

41. $h(x) = 4|x|$

42. $p(x) = \frac{1}{2}x^2$

43. $g(x) = \frac{1}{4}x^3$

44. $y = 2\sqrt{x}$

45. $f(x) = \sqrt{4x}$

46. $y = \left|\frac{1}{2}x\right|$

Rigid and Nonrigid Transformations In Exercises 47–50, use a graphing utility to graph the three functions in the same viewing window. Describe the graphs of g and h relative to the graph of f.

47. $f(x) = x^3 - 3x^2$
$g(x) = f(x + 2)$
$h(x) = \frac{1}{2}f(x)$

48. $f(x) = x^3 - 3x^2 + 2$
$g(x) = f(x - 1)$
$h(x) = f(3x)$

49. $f(x) = x^3 - 3x^2$
$g(x) = -\frac{1}{3}f(x)$
$h(x) = f(-x)$

50. $f(x) = x^3 - 3x^2 + 2$
$g(x) = -f(x)$
$h(x) = f(2x)$

Describing Transformations In Exercises 51–64, g is related to one of the six parent functions on page 41. (a) Identify the parent function f. (b) Describe the sequence of transformations from f to g. (c) Sketch the graph of g by hand. (d) Use function notation to write g in terms of the parent function f.

51. $g(x) = 2 - (x + 5)^2$

52. $g(x) = (x - 10)^2 + 5$

53. $g(x) = 3 + 2(x - 4)^2$

54. $g(x) = -\frac{1}{4}(x + 2)^2 - 2$

55. $g(x) = \frac{1}{3}(x - 2)^3$

56. $g(x) = \frac{1}{2}(x + 1)^3$

57. $g(x) = (x - 1)^3 + 2$

58. $g(x) = -(x + 3)^3 - 10$

59. $g(x) = \dfrac{1}{x + 8} - 9$

60. $g(x) = \dfrac{1}{x - 7} + 4$

61. $g(x) = -2|x - 1| - 4$

62. $g(x) = \frac{1}{2}|x - 2| - 3$

63. $g(x) = -\frac{1}{2}\sqrt{x + 3} - 1$

64. $g(x) = -3\sqrt{x + 1} - 6$

65. MODELING DATA

The numbers N (in millions) of households in the United States from 2000 through 2013 are given by the ordered pairs of the form $(t, N(t))$, where $t = 0$ represents 2000. A model for the data is

$$N(t) = -0.03(t - 26.17)^2 + 126.5.$$

(Source: U.S. Census Bureau)

(0, 104.7)
(1, 108.2)
(2, 109.3)
(3, 111.3)
(4, 112.0)
(5, 113.3)
(6, 114.4)
(7, 116.0)
(8, 116.8)
(9, 117.2)
(10, 117.5)
(11, 119.9)
(12, 121.1)
(13, 122.5)

(a) Describe the transformation of the parent function $f(t) = t^2$.

(b) Use a graphing utility to graph the model and the data in the same viewing window.

(c) Rewrite the function so that $t = 0$ represents 2009. Explain how you got your answer.

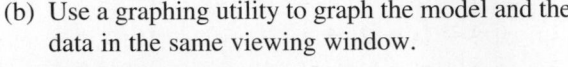

66. *Why you should learn it* (p. 41)   The depreciation D (in millions of dollars) of the WD-40 Company assets from 2009 through 2013 can be approximated by the function

$$D(t) = 1.9\sqrt{t} + 3.7$$

where $t = 0$ represents 2009.   (Source: WD-40 Company)

(a) Describe the transformation of the parent function $f(t) = \sqrt{t}$.

(b) Use a graphing utility to graph the model over the interval $0 \le t \le 4$.

(c) According to the model, in what year will the depreciation of WD-40 assets be approximately 6 million dollars?

(d) Rewrite the function so that $t = 0$ represents 2011. Explain how you got your answer.

Conclusions

True or False?   In Exercises 67 and 68, determine whether the statement is true or false. Justify your answer.

67. The graph of $y = f(-x)$ is a reflection of the graph of $y = f(x)$ in the x-axis.

68. The graphs of $f(x) = |x| + 6$ and $f(x) = |-x| + 6$ are identical.

Exploration   In Exercises 69–72, use the fact that the graph of $y = f(x)$ has x-intercepts at $x = 2$ and $x = -3$ to find the x-intercepts of the given graph. If not possible, state the reason.

69. $y = f(-x)$ **70.** $y = 2f(x)$

71. $y = f(x) + 2$ **72.** $y = f(x - 3)$

Library of Parent Functions   In Exercises 73–76, determine which equation(s) may be represented by the graph shown. (There may be more than one correct answer.)

73.

74.

(a) $f(x) = |x + 2| + 1$ (a) $f(x) = -\sqrt{x} - 4$

(b) $f(x) = |x - 1| + 2$ (b) $f(x) = -4 - \sqrt{x}$

(c) $f(x) = |x - 2| + 1$ (c) $f(x) = -4 - \sqrt{-x}$

(d) $f(x) = 2 + |x - 2|$ (d) $f(x) = \sqrt{-x} - 4$

(e) $f(x) = |(x - 2) + 1|$ (e) $f(x) = \sqrt{-x} + 4$

(f) $f(x) = 1 - |x - 2|$ (f) $f(x) = \sqrt{x} - 4$

75.

76.

(a) $f(x) = (x - 2)^2 - 2$ (a) $f(x) = -(x - 4)^3 + 2$

(b) $f(x) = (x + 4)^2 - 4$ (b) $f(x) = -(x + 4)^3 + 2$

(c) $f(x) = (x - 2)^2 - 4$ (c) $f(x) = -(x - 2)^3 + 4$

(d) $f(x) = (x + 2)^2 - 4$ (d) $f(x) = (-x - 4)^3 + 2$

(e) $f(x) = 4 - (x - 2)^2$ (e) $f(x) = (x + 4)^3 + 2$

(f) $f(x) = 4 - (x + 2)^2$ (f) $f(x) = (-x + 4)^3 + 2$

77. Think About It   You can use either of two methods to graph a function: plotting points, or translating a parent function as shown in this section. Which method do you prefer to use for each function? Explain.

(a) $f(x) = 3x^2 - 4x + 1$ (b) $f(x) = 2(x - 1)^2 - 6$

78. Think About It   The graph of $y = f(x)$ passes through the points $(0, 1)$, $(1, 2)$, and $(2, 3)$. Find the corresponding points on the graph of $y = f(x + 2) - 1$.

79. Think About It   Compare the graph of $g(x) = ax^2$ with the graph of $f(x) = x^2$ when (a) $0 < a < 1$ and (b) $a > 1$.

80.

HOW DO YOU SEE IT?   Use the graph of $y = f(x)$ to find the intervals on which each of the graphs in (a)–(c) is increasing and decreasing. If not possible, then state the reason.

(a) $y = -f(x)$

(b) $y = f(x) - 3$

(c) $y = f(x - 1)$

Cumulative Mixed Review

Parallel and Perpendicular Lines   In Exercises 81 and 82, determine whether the lines L_1 and L_2 passing through the pairs of points are parallel, perpendicular, or neither.

81. L_1: $(-2, -2)$, $(2, 10)$ **82.** L_1: $(-1, -7)$, $(4, 3)$

L_2: $(-1, 3)$, $(3, 9)$ L_2: $(1, 5)$, $(-2, -7)$

Finding the Domain of a Function   In Exercises 83–86, find the domain of the function.

83. $f(x) = \dfrac{4}{9 - x}$ **84.** $f(x) = \dfrac{\sqrt{x - 5}}{x - 7}$

85. $f(x) = \sqrt{100 - x^2}$ **86.** $f(x) = \sqrt[3]{16 - x^2}$

1.5 Combinations of Functions

Arithmetic Combinations of Functions

Just as two real numbers can be combined by the operations of addition, subtraction, multiplication, and division to form other real numbers, two *functions* can be combined to create new functions. When $f(x) = 2x - 3$ and $g(x) = x^2 - 1$, you can form the sum, difference, product, and quotient of f and g as follows.

$$f(x) + g(x) = (2x - 3) + (x^2 - 1) = x^2 + 2x - 4 \qquad \text{Sum}$$

$$f(x) - g(x) = (2x - 3) - (x^2 - 1) = -x^2 + 2x - 2 \qquad \text{Difference}$$

$$f(x) \cdot g(x) = (2x - 3)(x^2 - 1) = 2x^3 - 3x^2 - 2x + 3 \qquad \text{Product}$$

$$\frac{f(x)}{g(x)} = \frac{2x - 3}{x^2 - 1}, \quad x \neq \pm 1 \qquad \text{Quotient}$$

The domain of an **arithmetic combination** of functions f and g consists of all real numbers that are common to the domains of f and g. In the case of the quotient

$$\frac{f(x)}{g(x)}$$

there is the further restriction that $g(x) \neq 0$.

What you should learn

▶ Add, subtract, multiply, and divide functions.
▶ Find compositions of one function with another function.
▶ Use combinations of functions to model and solve real-life problems.

Why you should learn it

You can model some situations by combining functions. For instance, in Exercise 79 on page 57, you will model the stopping distance of a car by combining the driver's reaction time with the car's braking distance.

Sum, Difference, Product, and Quotient of Functions

Let f and g be two functions with overlapping domains. Then, for all x common to both domains, the sum, difference, product, and quotient of f and g are defined as follows.

1. Sum: $\qquad\qquad (f + g)(x) = f(x) + g(x)$

2. Difference: $(f - g)(x) = f(x) - g(x)$

3. Product: $\qquad (fg)(x) = f(x) \cdot g(x)$

4. Quotient: $\qquad \left(\dfrac{f}{g}\right)(x) = \dfrac{f(x)}{g(x)}, \quad g(x) \neq 0$

EXAMPLE 1   Finding the Sum of Two Functions

Given $f(x) = 2x + 1$ and $g(x) = x^2 + 2x - 1$, find $(f + g)(x)$. Then evaluate the sum when $x = 2$.

Solution

$$(f + g)(x) = f(x) + g(x)$$
$$= (2x + 1) + (x^2 + 2x - 1)$$
$$= x^2 + 4x$$

When $x = 2$, the value of this sum is $(f + g)(2) = 2^2 + 4(2) = 12$.

✓ **Checkpoint** ◀))) *Audio-video solution in English & Spanish at LarsonPrecalculus.com.*

Given $f(x) = x^2$ and $g(x) = 1 - x$, find $(f + g)(x)$. Then evaluate the sum when $x = 2$.

EXAMPLE 2   Finding the Difference of Two Functions

Given $f(x) = 2x + 1$ and $g(x) = x^2 + 2x - 1$, find $(f - g)(x)$. Then evaluate the difference when $x = 2$.

Algebraic Solution

The difference of the functions f and g is

$$(f - g)(x) = f(x) - g(x)$$

$$= (2x + 1) - (x^2 + 2x - 1)$$

$$= -x^2 + 2.$$

When $x = 2$, the value of this difference is

$$(f - g)(2) = -(2)^2 + 2$$

$$= -2.$$

Graphical Solution

Enter $y_1 = f(x)$, $y_2 = g(x)$, and $y_3 = f(x) - g(x)$. Then graph the difference of the two functions, y_3.

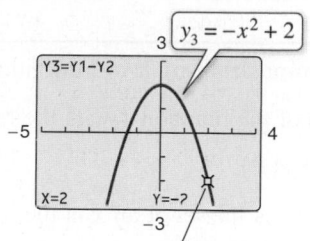

The value of $(f - g)(2)$ is -2.

✓ **Checkpoint** 🔊))) *Audio-video solution in English & Spanish at LarsonPrecalculus.com.*

Given $f(x) = x^2$ and $g(x) = 1 - x$, find $(f - g)(x)$. Then evaluate the difference when $x = 3$.

EXAMPLE 3   Finding the Product of Two Functions

Given $f(x) = x^2$ and $g(x) = x - 3$, find $(fg)(x)$. Then evaluate the product when $x = 4$.

Solution

$$(fg)(x) = f(x)g(x) = (x^2)(x - 3) = x^3 - 3x^2$$

When $x = 4$, the value of this product is $(fg)(4) = 4^3 - 3(4)^2 = 16$.

✓ **Checkpoint** 🔊))) *Audio-video solution in English & Spanish at LarsonPrecalculus.com.*

Given $f(x) = x^2$ and $g(x) = 1 - x$, find $(fg)(x)$. Then evaluate the product when $x = 3$.

In Examples 1–3, both f and g have domains that consist of all real numbers. So, the domains of $(f + g)$ and $(f - g)$ are also the set of all real numbers. Remember to consider any restrictions on the domains of f or g when forming the sum, difference, product, or quotient of f and g. For instance, the domain of $f(x) = 1/x$ is all $x \neq 0$, and the domain of $g(x) = \sqrt{x}$ is $[0, \infty)$. This implies that the domain of $(f + g)$ is $(0, \infty)$.

EXAMPLE 4   Finding the Quotient of Two Functions

Given $f(x) = \sqrt{x}$ and $g(x) = \sqrt{4 - x^2}$, find $(f/g)(x)$. Then find the domain of f/g.

Solution

$$\left(\frac{f}{g}\right)(x) = \frac{f(x)}{g(x)} = \frac{\sqrt{x}}{\sqrt{4 - x^2}}$$

The domain of f is $[0, \infty)$ and the domain of g is $[-2, 2]$. The intersection of these domains is $[0, 2]$. So, the domain of f/g is $[0, 2)$.

✓ **Checkpoint** 🔊))) *Audio-video solution in English & Spanish at LarsonPrecalculus.com.*

Find $(f/g)(x)$ and $(g/f)(x)$ for the functions $f(x) = \sqrt{x - 3}$ and $g(x) = \sqrt{16 - x^2}$. Then find the domains of f/g and g/f.

Compositions of Functions

Another way of combining two functions is to form the **composition** of one with the other. For instance, when $f(x) = x^2$ and $g(x) = x + 1$, the composition of f with g is

$$f(g(x)) = f(x + 1)$$
$$= (x + 1)^2.$$

This composition is denoted as $f \circ g$ and is read as "f composed with g."

Definition of Composition of Two Functions

The **composition** of the function f with the function g is

$$(f \circ g)(x) = f(g(x)).$$

The domain of $f \circ g$ is the set of all x in the domain of g such that $g(x)$ is in the domain of f. (See Figure 1.34.)

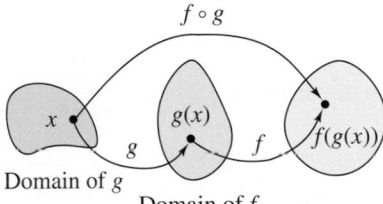

Domain of g

Domain of f

Figure 1.34

EXAMPLE 5   Forming the Composition of f with g

Find $(f \circ g)(x)$ for $f(x) = \sqrt{x}, x \geq 0$, and $g(x) = x - 1, x \geq 1$. If possible, find $(f \circ g)(2)$ and $(f \circ g)(0)$.

Solution

The composition of f with g is

$$(f \circ g)(x) = f(g(x)) \qquad \text{Definition of } f \circ g$$
$$= f(x - 1) \qquad \text{Definition of } g(x)$$
$$= \sqrt{x - 1}, \ x \geq 1. \qquad \text{Definition of } f(x)$$

The domain of $(f \circ g)$ is $[1, \infty)$ (see Figure 1.35). So,

$$(f \circ g)(2) = \sqrt{2 - 1} = 1$$

is defined, but $(f \circ g)(0)$ is not defined because 0 is not in the domain of $f \circ g$.

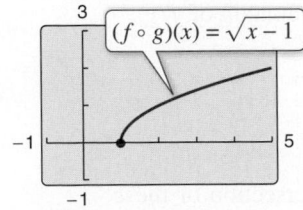

$(f \circ g)(x) = \sqrt{x - 1}$

Figure 1.35

Explore the Concept

Let $f(x) = x + 2$ and $g(x) = 4 - x^2$. Are the compositions $f \circ g$ and $g \circ f$ equal? You can use your graphing utility to answer this question by entering and graphing the following functions.

$$y_1 = (4 - x^2) + 2$$
$$y_2 = 4 - (x + 2)^2$$

What do you observe? Which function represents $f \circ g$ and which represents $g \circ f$?

✓ **Checkpoint** ◀))) *Audio-video solution in English & Spanish at LarsonPrecalculus.com.*

Find $(f \circ g)(x)$ for $f(x) = x^2$ and $g(x) = x - 1$. If possible, find $(f \circ g)(0)$.

The composition of f with g is generally not the same as the composition of g with f. This is illustrated in Example 6.

EXAMPLE 6   Compositions of Functions

See LarsonPrecalculus.com for an interactive version of this type of example.

Given $f(x) = x + 2$ and $g(x) = 4 - x^2$, evaluate (a) $(f \circ g)(x)$ and (b) $(g \circ f)(x)$ when $x = 0$ and 1.

Algebraic Solution

a. $(f \circ g)(x) = f(g(x))$ Definition of $f \circ g$

$\quad\quad\quad = f(4 - x^2)$ Definition of $g(x)$

$\quad\quad\quad = (4 - x^2) + 2$ Definition of $f(x)$

$\quad\quad\quad = -x^2 + 6$

$(f \circ g)(0) = -0^2 + 6 = 6$

$(f \circ g)(1) = -1^2 + 6 = 5$

b. $(g \circ f)(x) = g(f(x))$ Definition of $g \circ f$

$\quad\quad\quad = g(x + 2)$ Definition of $f(x)$

$\quad\quad\quad = 4 - (x + 2)^2$ Definition of $g(x)$

$\quad\quad\quad = 4 - (x^2 + 4x + 4)$

$\quad\quad\quad = -x^2 - 4x$

$(g \circ f)(0) = -0^2 - 4(0) = 0$

$(g \circ f)(1) = -1^2 - 4(1) = -5$

Note that $(f \circ g) \neq g \circ f$.

Numerical Solution

a. and b. Enter $y_1 = f(x)$, $y_2 = g(x)$, $y_3(f \circ g)(x)$, and $y_4 = (g \circ f)(x)$. Then use the *table* feature to find the desired function values.

X	Y3	Y4
0	6	0
1	5	-5

X=

From the table, you can see that $f \circ g \neq g \circ f$.

✓ **Checkpoint** 🔊)) Audio-video solution in English & Spanish at LarsonPrecalculus.com.

Given $f(x) = 2x + 5$ and $g(x) = 4x^2 + 1$, find the following.

a. $(f \circ g)(x)$ **b.** $(g \circ f)(x)$ **c.** $(f \circ g)\left(-\frac{1}{2}\right)$

EXAMPLE 7   Finding the Domain of a Composite Function

Find the domain of $f \circ g$ for the functions $f(x) = x^2 - 9$ and $g(x) = \sqrt{9 - x^2}$.

Algebraic Solution

The composition of the functions is as follows.

$\quad (f \circ g)(x) = f(g(x))$

$\quad\quad\quad\quad = f\left(\sqrt{9 - x^2}\right)$

$\quad\quad\quad\quad = \left(\sqrt{9 - x^2}\right)^2 - 9$

$\quad\quad\quad\quad = 9 - x^2 - 9$

$\quad\quad\quad\quad = -x^2$

From this, it might appear that the domain of the composition is the set of all real numbers. This, however, is not true. Because the domain of f is the set of all real numbers and the domain of g is $[-3, 3]$, the domain of $f \circ g$ is $[-3, 3]$.

Graphical Solution

The x-coordinates of points on the graph extend from -3 to 3. So, the domain of $f \circ g$ is $[-3, 3]$.

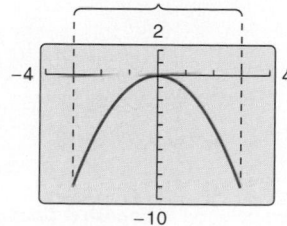

✓ **Checkpoint** 🔊)) Audio-video solution in English & Spanish at LarsonPrecalculus.com.

Find the domain of $(f \circ g)(x)$ for the functions $f(x) = \sqrt{x}$ and $g(x) = x^2 + 4$. ■

EXAMPLE 8   A Case in Which $f \circ g = g \circ f$

Given $f(x) = 2x + 3$ and $g(x) = \frac{1}{2}(x - 3)$, find (a) $(f \circ g)(x)$ and (b) $(g \circ f)(x)$.

Solution

a. $(f \circ g)(x) = f(g(x))$

$$= f\left(\frac{1}{2}(x - 3)\right)$$

$$= 2\left[\frac{1}{2}(x - 3)\right] + 3$$

$$= x - 3 + 3$$

$$= x$$

b. $(g \circ f)(x) = g(f(x))$

$$= g(2x + 3)$$

$$= \frac{1}{2}[(2x + 3) - 3]$$

$$= \frac{1}{2}(2x)$$

$$= x$$

> ### Remark
> In Example 8, note that the two composite functions $f \circ g$ and $g \circ f$ are equal, and both represent the identity function. That is, $(f \circ g)(x) = x$ and $(g \circ f)(x) = x$. You will study this special case in the next section.

✓ *Checkpoint* Audio-video solution in English & Spanish at LarsonPrecalculus.com.

Given $f(x) = x^{1/3}$ and $g(x) = x^6$, find (a) $(f \circ g)(x)$ and (b) $(g \circ f)(x)$.

In Examples 5–8, you formed the composition of two given functions. In calculus, it is also important to be able to identify two functions that make up a given composite function. Basically, to "decompose" a composite function, look for an "inner" and an "outer" function.

EXAMPLE 9   Identifying a Composite Function

Write the function

$$h(x) = \frac{1}{(x - 2)^2}$$

as a composition of two functions.

Solution

One way to write h as a composition of two functions is to take the inner function to be $g(x) = x - 2$ and the outer function to be

$$f(x) = \frac{1}{x^2} = x^{-2}.$$

Then you can write

$$h(x) = \frac{1}{(x - 2)^2} = (x - 2)^{-2} = f(x - 2) = f(g(x)).$$

✓ *Checkpoint* Audio-video solution in English & Spanish at LarsonPrecalculus.com.

Write the function

$$h(x) = \frac{\sqrt[3]{8 - x}}{5}$$

as a composition of two functions.

> ### Explore the Concept
> Write each function as a composition of two functions.
>
> **a.** $h(x) = |x^3 - 2|$
>
> **b.** $r(x) = |x^3| - 2$
>
> What do you notice about the inner and outer functions?

Application

EXAMPLE 10   Bacteria Count

The number N of bacteria in a refrigerated petri dish is given by

$$N(T) = 20T^2 - 80T + 500, \quad 2 \le T \le 14$$

where T is the temperature of the petri dish (in degrees Celsius). When the petri dish is removed from refrigeration, the temperature of the petri dish is given by

$$T(t) = 4t + 2, \quad 0 \le t \le 3$$

where t is the time (in hours).

a. Find the composition $N(T(t))$ and interpret its meaning in context.

b. Find the number of bacteria in the petri dish when $t = 2$ hours.

c. Find the time when the bacteria count reaches 2000.

Solution

a. $N(T(t)) = 20(4t + 2)^2 - 80(4t + 2) + 500$

$\qquad\qquad = 20(16t^2 + 16t + 4) - 320t - 160 + 500$

$\qquad\qquad = 320t^2 + 320t + 80 - 320t - 160 + 500$

$\qquad\qquad = 320t^2 + 420$

The composite function $N(T(t))$ represents the number of bacteria as a function of the amount of time the petri dish has been out of refrigeration.

b. When $t = 2$, the number of bacteria is

$$N = 320(2)^2 + 420 = 1280 + 420 = 1700.$$

c. The bacteria count will reach $N = 2000$ when $320t^2 + 420 = 2000$. You can solve this equation for t algebraically as follows.

$$320t^2 + 420 = 2000$$

$$320t^2 = 1580$$

$$t^2 = \frac{79}{16}$$

$$t = \frac{\sqrt{79}}{4} \quad \Longrightarrow \quad t \approx 2.22 \text{ hours}$$

So, the count will reach 2000 when $t \approx 2.22$ hours. Note that the negative value is rejected because it is not in the domain of the composite function. To confirm your solution, graph the equation $N = 320t^2 + 420$, as shown in Figure 1.36. Then use the *zoom* and *trace* features to approximate $N = 2000$ when $t \approx 2.22$, as shown in Figure 1.37.

Microbiologist

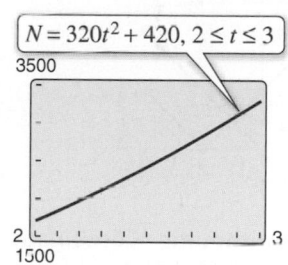

$N = 320t^2 + 420, \; 2 \le t \le 3$

Figure 1.36

Y1=320X²+420

X=2.2234043 Y=2001.9285

Figure 1.37

✓ **Checkpoint** ◀))) *Audio-video solution in English & Spanish at LarsonPrecalculus.com.*

The number N of bacteria in a refrigerated food is given by

$$N(T) = 8T^2 - 14T + 200, \quad 2 \le T \le 12$$

where T is the temperature of the food in degrees Celsius. When the food is removed from refrigeration, the temperature of the food is given by

$$T(t) = 2t + 2, \quad 0 \le t \le 5$$

where t is the time in hours. Find (a) $(N \circ T)(t)$ and (b) the time when the bacteria count reaches 1000.

1.5 Exercises

See *CalcChat.com* for tutorial help and worked-out solutions to odd-numbered exercises.
For instructions on how to use a graphing utility, see Appendix A.

Vocabulary and Concept Check

In Exercises 1–4, fill in the blank(s).

1. Two functions f and g can be combined by the arithmetic operations of _____ , _____ , _____ , and _____ to create new functions.

2. The _____ of the function f with the function g is $(f \circ g)(x) = f(g(x))$.

3. The domain of $f \circ g$ is the set of all x in the domain of g such that _____ is in the domain of f.

4. To decompose a composite function, look for an _____ and an _____ function.

5. Given $f(x) = x^2 + 1$ and $(fg)(x) = 2x(x^2 + 1)$, what is $g(x)$?

6. Given $(f \circ g)(x) = f(x^2 + 1)$, what is $g(x)$?

Procedures and Problem Solving

Graphing the Sum of Two Functions   In Exercises 7–10, use the graphs of f and g to graph $h(x) = (f + g)(x)$. To print an enlarged copy of the graph, go to *MathGraphs.com*.

7.

8.

9.

10.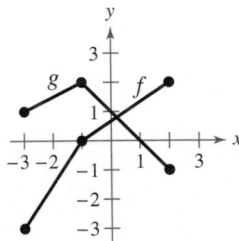

Finding Arithmetic Combinations of Functions   In Exercises 11–18, find (a) $(f + g)(x)$, (b) $(f - g)(x)$, (c) $(fg)(x)$, and (d) $(f/g)(x)$. What is the domain of f/g?

11. $f(x) = x + 3$, $g(x) = x - 3$

12. $f(x) = 2x - 5$, $g(x) = 1 - x$

13. $f(x) = 3x^2$, $g(x) = 6 - 5x$

14. $f(x) = 2x + 5$, $g(x) = x^2 - 9$

15. $f(x) = x^2 + 5$, $g(x) = \sqrt{1 - x}$

16. $f(x) = \sqrt{x^2 - 4}$, $g(x) = \dfrac{x^2}{x^2 + 1}$

17. $f(x) = \dfrac{1}{x}$, $g(x) = \dfrac{1}{x^2}$

18. $f(x) = \dfrac{x}{x + 1}$, $g(x) = \dfrac{1}{x^3}$

Evaluating an Arithmetic Combination of Functions   In Exercises 19–32, evaluate the indicated function for $f(x) = x^2 - 1$ and $g(x) = x - 2$ algebraically. If possible, use a graphing utility to verify your answer.

19. $(f + g)(3)$ 20. $(f - g)(-2)$

21. $(f - g)(0)$ 22. $(f + g)(1)$

23. $(fg)(-6)$ 24. $(fg)(4)$

25. $(f/g)(-5)$ 26. $(f/g)(0)$

27. $(f - g)(t + 1)$ 28. $(f + g)(t - 3)$

29. $(fg)(-5t)$ 30. $(fg)(3t^2)$

31. $(f/g)(t - 4)$ 32. $(f/g)(t + 2)$

Graphing an Arithmetic Combination of Functions   In Exercises 33–36, use a graphing utility to graph the functions f, g, and h in the same viewing window.

33. $f(x) = \frac{1}{2}x$, $g(x) = x - 1$, $h(x) = f(x) + g(x)$

34. $f(x) = \frac{1}{3}x$, $g(x) = -x + 4$, $h(x) = f(x) - g(x)$

35. $f(x) = x^2$, $g(x) = -2x + 5$, $h(x) = f(x) \cdot g(x)$

36. $f(x) = 4 - x^2$, $g(x) = x$, $h(x) = f(x)/g(x)$

Graphing a Sum of Functions   In Exercises 37–40, use a graphing utility to graph f, g, and $f + g$ in the same viewing window. Which function contributes most to the magnitude of the sum when $0 \le x \le 2$? Which function contributes most to the magnitude of the sum when $x > 6$?

37. $f(x) = 3x$, $g(x) = -\dfrac{x^3}{10}$

38. $f(x) = \dfrac{x}{2}$, $g(x) = \sqrt{x}$

39. $f(x) = 3x + 2$, $g(x) = -\sqrt{x + 5}$

40. $f(x) = x^2 - \frac{1}{2}$, $g(x) = -3x^2 - 1$

Compositions of Functions   In Exercises 41–44, find (a) $f \circ g$, (b) $g \circ f$, and, if possible, (c) $(f \circ g)(0)$.

41. $f(x) = 2x^2$, $g(x) = x + 4$

42. $f(x) = \sqrt[3]{x - 1}$, $g(x) = x^3 + 1$

43. $f(x) = 3x + 5$, $g(x) = 5 - x$

44. $f(x) = x^3$, $g(x) = \dfrac{1}{x}$

Finding the Domain of a Composite Function   In Exercises 45–54, determine the domains of (a) f, (b) g, and (c) $f \circ g$. Use a graphing utility to verify your results.

45. $f(x) = \sqrt{x - 7}$, $g(x) = 4x^2$

46. $f(x) = \sqrt{x + 3}$, $g(x) = \dfrac{x}{2}$

47. $f(x) = x^2 + 1$, $g(x) = \sqrt{x}$

48. $f(x) = x^{1/4}$, $g(x) = x^4$

49. $f(x) = \dfrac{1}{x}$, $g(x) = \dfrac{1}{x + 3}$

50. $f(x) = \dfrac{1}{x}$, $g(x) = \dfrac{1}{2x}$

51. $f(x) = |x - 4|$, $g(x) = 3 - x$

52. $f(x) = \dfrac{2}{|x|}$ $g(x) = x - 5$

53. $f(x) = x + 2$, $g(x) = \dfrac{1}{x^2 - 4}$

54. $f(x) = \dfrac{3}{x^2 - 1}$, $g(x) = x + 1$

Determining Whether $f \circ g = g \circ f$ In Exercises 55–60, (a) find $f \circ g$, $g \circ f$, and the domain of $f \circ g$. (b) Use a graphing utility to graph $f \circ g$ and $g \circ f$. Determine whether $f \circ g = g \circ f$.

55. $f(x) = \sqrt{x + 4}$, $g(x) = x^2$

56. $f(x) = \sqrt[3]{x + 1}$, $g(x) = x^3 - 1$

57. $f(x) = \frac{1}{3}x - 3$, $g(x) = 3x + 9$

58. $f(x) = \sqrt{x}$, $g(x) = \sqrt{x}$

59. $f(x) = x^{2/3}$, $g(x) = x^6$

60. $f(x) = |x|$, $g(x) = -x^2 + 1$

Determining Whether $f \circ g = g \circ f$ In Exercises 61–66, (a) find $(f \circ g)(x)$ and $(g \circ f)(x)$, (b) determine algebraically whether $(f \circ g)(x) = (g \circ f)(x)$, and (c) use a graphing utility to complete a table of values for the two compositions to confirm your answer to part (b).

61. $f(x) = 5x + 4$, $g(x) = \frac{1}{5}(x - 4)$

62. $f(x) = \frac{1}{4}(x - 1)$, $g(x) = 4x + 1$

63. $f(x) = \sqrt{x + 6}$, $g(x) = x^2 - 5$

64. $f(x) = x^3 - 4$, $g(x) = \sqrt[3]{x + 10}$

65. $f(x) = |x|$, $g(x) = 2x^3$

66. $f(x) = \dfrac{6}{3x - 5}$, $g(x) = -x$

Evaluating Combinations of Functions   In Exercises 67–70, use the graphs of f and g to evaluate the functions.

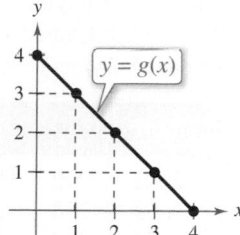

67. (a) $(f + g)(3)$ (b) $(f/g)(2)$

68. (a) $(f - g)(1)$ (b) $(fg)(4)$

69. (a) $(f \circ g)(3)$ (b) $(g \circ f)(2)$

70. (a) $(f \circ g)(1)$ (b) $(g \circ f)(3)$

Identifying a Composite Function   In Exercises 71–78, find two functions f and g such that $(f \circ g)(x) = h(x)$. (There are many correct answers.)

71. $h(x) = (2x + 1)^2$

72. $h(x) = (1 - x)^3$

73. $h(x) = \sqrt[3]{x^2 - 4}$

74. $h(x) = \sqrt{9 - x}$

75. $h(x) = \dfrac{1}{x + 2}$

76. $h(x) = \dfrac{4}{(5x + 2)^2}$

77. $h(x) = (x + 4)^2 + 2(x + 4)$

78. $h(x) = (x + 3)^{3/2} + 4(x + 3)^{1/2}$

79. *Why you should learn it* (p. 50) The research and development department of an automobile manufacturer has determined that when required to stop quickly to avoid an accident, the distance (in feet) a car travels during the driver's reaction time is given by

$$R(x) = \tfrac{3}{4}x$$

where x is the speed of the car in miles per hour. The distance (in feet) traveled while the driver is braking is given by

$$B(x) = \tfrac{1}{15}x^2.$$

(a) Find the function that represents the total stopping distance T.

(b) Use a graphing utility to graph the functions R, B, and T in the same viewing window for $0 \leq x \leq 60$.

(c) Which function contributes most to the magnitude of the sum at higher speeds? Explain.

80. MODELING DATA

The table shows the total amounts (in billions of dollars) of health consumption expenditures in the United States (including Puerto Rico) for the years 2002 through 2012. The variables y_1, y_2, and y_3 represent out-of-pocket payments, insurance premiums, and other types of payments, respectively.
(Source: U.S. Centers for Medicare and Medicaid Services)

Year	y_1	y_2	y_3
2002	222	1122	140
2003	238	1223	153
2004	252	1322	159
2005	267	1417	168
2006	277	1521	177
2007	294	1612	187
2008	301	1703	182
2009	301	1799	185
2010	306	1874	195
2011	316	1943	202
2012	328	2014	216

DATA — Spreadsheet at LarsonPrecalculus.com

The data are approximated by the following models, where t represents the year, with $t = 2$ corresponding to 2002.

$y_1 = -0.62t^2 + 18.7t + 188$

$y_2 = -1.86t^2 + 116.4t + 890$

$y_3 = -0.12t^2 + 8.3t + 128$

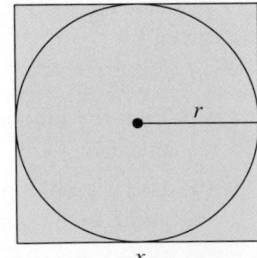

(a) Use the models and the *table* feature of a graphing utility to create a table showing the values of y_1, y_2, and y_3 for each year from 2002 through 2012. Compare these models with the original data. Are the models a good fit? Explain.

(b) Use the graphing utility to graph y_1, y_2, y_3, and $y_T = y_1 + y_2 + y_3$ in the same viewing window. What does the function y_T represent?

81. Geometry A square concrete foundation was prepared as a base for a large cylindrical gasoline tank (see figure).

(a) Write the radius r of the tank as a function of the length x of the sides of the square.

(b) Write the area A of the circular base of the tank as a function of the radius r.

(c) Find and interpret $(A \circ r)(x)$.

82. Geometry A pebble is dropped into a calm pond, causing ripples in the form of concentric circles. The radius (in feet) of the outermost ripple is given by $r(t) = 0.6t$, where t is the time (in seconds) after the pebble strikes the water. The area of the circle is given by $A(r) = \pi r t^2$. Find and interpret $(A \circ r)(t)$.

83. Business A company owns two retail stores. The annual sales (in thousands of dollars) of the stores each year from 2009 through 2015 can be approximated by the models

$$S_1 = 973 + 1.3t^2 \quad \text{and} \quad S_2 = 349 + 72.4t$$

where t is the year, with $t = 9$ corresponding to 2009.

(a) Write a function T that represents the total annual sales of the two stores.

(b) Use a graphing utility to graph S_1, S_2, and T in the same viewing window.

84. Business The annual cost C (in thousands of dollars) and revenue R (in thousands of dollars) for a company each year from 2009 through 2015 can be approximated by the models

$$C = 254 - 9t + 1.1t^2 \quad \text{and} \quad R = 341 + 3.2t$$

where t is the year, with $t = 9$ corresponding to 2009.

(a) Write a function P that represents the annual profits of the company.

(b) Use a graphing utility to graph C, R, and P in the same viewing window.

85. Biology The number of bacteria in a refrigerated food product is given by

$$N(T) = 10T^2 - 20T + 600, \quad 1 \le T \le 20$$

where T is the temperature of the food in degrees Celsius. When the food is removed from the refrigerator, the temperature of the food is given by

$$T(t) = 2t + 1$$

where t is the time in hours.

(a) Find the composite function $N(T(t))$ or $(N \circ T)(t)$ and interpret its meaning in the context of the situation.

(b) Find $(N \circ T)(12)$ and interpret its meaning.

(c) Find the time when the bacteria count reaches 1200.

86. Environmental Science The spread of a contaminant is increasing in a circular pattern on the surface of a lake. The radius of the contaminant can be modeled by $r(t) = 5.25\sqrt{t}$, where r is the radius in meters and t is time in hours since contamination.

(a) Find a function that gives the area A of the circular leak in terms of the time t since the spread began.

(b) Find the size of the contaminated area after 36 hours.

(c) Find when the size of the contaminated area is 6250 square meters.

87. Air Traffic Control An air traffic controller spots two planes flying at the same altitude. Their flight paths form a right angle at point P. One plane is 150 miles from point P and is moving at 450 miles per hour. The other plane is 200 miles from point P and is moving at 450 miles per hour. Write the distance s between the planes as a function of time t.

Distance (in miles)

88. Marketing The suggested retail price of a new car is p dollars. The dealership advertised a factory rebate of $2000 and a 9% discount.

(a) Write a function R in terms of p giving the cost of the car after receiving the rebate from the factory.

(b) Write a function S in terms of p giving the cost of the car after receiving the dealership discount.

(c) Form the composite functions $(R \circ S)(p)$ and $(S \circ R)(p)$ and interpret each.

(d) Find $(R \circ S)(24{,}795)$ and $(S \circ R)(24{,}795)$. Which yields the lower cost for the car? Explain.

Conclusions

True or False? In Exercises 89 and 90, determine whether the statement is true or false. Justify your answer.

89. A function that represents the graph of $f(x) = x^2$ shifted three units to the right is $f(g(x))$, where $g(x) = x + 3$.

90. Given two functions f and g, you can calculate $(f \circ g)(x)$ if and only if the range of g is a subset of the domain of f.

91. Exploration The function in Example 9 can be decomposed in other ways. For which of the following pairs of functions is $h(x) = \dfrac{1}{(x-2)^2}$ equal to $f(g(x))$?

(a) $g(x) = \dfrac{1}{x-2}$ and $f(x) = x^2$

(b) $g(x) = x^2$ and $f(x) = \dfrac{1}{x-2}$

(c) $g(x) = (x-2)^2$ and $f(x) = \dfrac{1}{x}$

92. Proof Prove that the product of two odd functions is an even function, and that the product of two even functions is an even function.

93. Proof Use examples to hypothesize whether the product of an odd function and an even function is even or odd. Then prove your hypothesis.

Exploration In Exercises 94 and 95, three siblings are of three different ages. The oldest is twice the age of the middle sibling, and the middle sibling is six years older than one-half the age of the youngest.

94. (a) Write a composite function that gives the oldest sibling's age in terms of the youngest. Explain how you arrived at your answer.

(b) The oldest sibling is 16 years old. Find the ages of the other two siblings.

95. (a) Write a composite function that gives the youngest sibling's age in terms of the oldest. Explain how you arrived at your answer.

(b) The youngest sibling is two years old. Find the ages of the other two siblings.

96. HOW DO YOU SEE IT? The graphs labeled L_1, L_2, L_3, and L_4 represent four different pricing discounts, where p is the original price (in dollars) and S is the sale price (in dollars). Match each function with its graph. Describe the situations in parts (c) and (d).

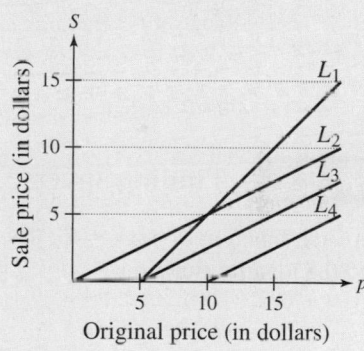

Original price (in dollars)

(a) $f(p)$: A 50% discount is applied.

(b) $g(p)$: A $5 discount is applied.

(c) $(g \circ f)(p)$

(d) $(f \circ g)(p)$

Cumulative Mixed Review

Evaluating an Equation In Exercises 97–100, find three points that lie on the graph of the equation. (There are many correct answers.)

97. $y = -x^2 + x - 5$

98. $y = \frac{1}{5}x^3 - 4x^2 + 1$

99. $x^2 + y^2 = 49$

100. $y = \dfrac{x}{x^2 - 5}$

1.6 Inverse Functions

Inverse Functions

Recall from Section 1.2 that a function can be represented by a set of ordered pairs. For instance, the function $f(x) = x + 4$ from the set $A = \{1, 2, 3, 4\}$ to the set $B = \{5, 6, 7, 8\}$ can be written as follows.

$$f(x) = x + 4: \{(1, 5), (2, 6), (3, 7), (4, 8)\}$$

In this case, by interchanging the first and second coordinates of each of these ordered pairs, you can form the **inverse function** of f, which is denoted by f^{-1}. It is a function from the set B to the set A, and can be written as follows.

$$f^{-1}(x) = x - 4: \{(5, 1), (6, 2), (7, 3), (8, 4)\}$$

Note that the domain of f is equal to the range of f^{-1}, and vice versa, as shown in Figure 1.38. Also note that the functions f and f^{-1} have the effect of "undoing" each other. In other words, when you form the composition of f with f^{-1} or the composition of f^{-1} with f, you obtain the identity function.

$$f(f^{-1}(x)) = f(x - 4) = (x - 4) + 4 = x$$

$$f^{-1}(f(x)) = f^{-1}(x + 4) = (x + 4) - 4 = x$$

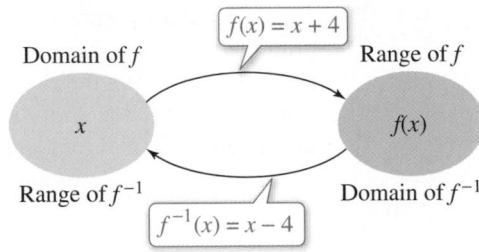

Domain of f $\boxed{f(x) = x + 4}$ Range of f

x $f(x)$

Range of f^{-1} Domain of f^{-1}

$\boxed{f^{-1}(x) = x - 4}$

Figure 1.38

EXAMPLE 1   **Finding Inverse Functions Informally**

Find the inverse function of $f(x) = 4x$. Then verify that both $f(f^{-1}(x))$ and $f^{-1}(f(x))$ are equal to the identity function.

Solution

The function f *multiplies* each input by 4. To "undo" this function, you need to *divide* each input by 4. So, the inverse function of $f(x) = 4x$ is given by

$$f^{-1}(x) = \frac{x}{4}.$$

You can verify that both $f(f^{-1}(x))$ and $f^{-1}(f(x))$ are equal to the identity function as follows.

$$f(f^{-1}(x)) = f\left(\frac{x}{4}\right) = 4\left(\frac{x}{4}\right) = x$$

$$f^{-1}(f(x)) = f^{-1}(4x) = \frac{4x}{4} = x$$

✓ **Checkpoint** ◀))) *Audio-video solution in English & Spanish at LarsonPrecalculus.com.*

Find the inverse function of $f(x) = \frac{1}{5}x$. Then verify that both $f(f^{-1}(x))$ and $f^{-1}(f(x))$ are equal to the identity function. ∎

Do not be confused by the use of the exponent -1 to denote the inverse function f^{-1}. In this text, whenever f^{-1} is written, it always refers to the inverse function of the function f and not to the reciprocal of $f(x)$, which is given by

$$\frac{1}{f(x)}.$$

EXAMPLE 2   Finding Inverse Functions Informally

Find the inverse function of $f(x) = x - 6$. Then verify that both $f(f^{-1}(x))$ and $f^{-1}(f(x))$ are equal to the identity function.

Solution

The function f *subtracts* 6 from each input. To "undo" this function, you need to *add* 6 to each input. So, the inverse function of $f(x) = x - 6$ is given by $f^{-1}(x) = x + 6$. You can verify that both $f(f^{-1}(x))$ and $f^{-1}(f(x))$ are equal to the identity function as follows.

$$f(f^{-1}(x)) = f(x + 6) = (x + 6) - 6 = x$$

$$f^{-1}(f(x)) = f^{-1}(x - 6) = (x - 6) + 6 = x$$

✓ **Checkpoint** ◀))) *Audio-video solution in English & Spanish at LarsonPrecalculus.com.*

Find the inverse function of $f(x) = x + 7$. Then verify that both $f(f^{-1}(x))$ and $f^{-1}(f(x))$ are equal to the identity function. ∎

A table of values can help you understand inverse functions. For instance, the first table below shows several values of the function in Example 2. Interchange the rows of this table to obtain values of the inverse function.

x	-2	-1	0	1	2
$f(x)$	-8	-7	-6	-5	-4

⟹

x	-8	-7	-6	-5	-4
$f^{-1}(x)$	-2	-1	0	1	2

In the table at the left, each output is 6 less than the input, and in the table at the right, each output is 6 more than the input.

The formal definition of an inverse function is as follows.

Definition of Inverse Function

Let f and g be two functions such that

$$f(g(x)) = x \qquad \text{for every } x \text{ in the domain of } g$$

and

$$g(f(x)) = x \qquad \text{for every } x \text{ in the domain of } f.$$

Under these conditions, the function g is the **inverse function** of the function f. The function g is denoted by f^{-1} (read "f-inverse"). So,

$$f(f^{-1}(x)) = x \quad \text{and} \quad f^{-1}(f(x)) = x.$$

The domain of f must be equal to the range of f^{-1}, and the range of f must be equal to the domain of f^{-1}.

If the function g is the inverse function of the function f, then it must also be true that the function f is the inverse function of the function g. For this reason, you can say that the functions f and g are *inverse functions of each other.*

EXAMPLE 3 Verifying Inverse Functions Algebraically

Show that the functions are inverse functions of each other.

$$f(x) = 2x^3 - 1 \quad \text{and} \quad g(x) = \sqrt[3]{\dfrac{x+1}{2}}$$

Solution

$$f(g(x)) = f\left(\sqrt[3]{\dfrac{x+1}{2}}\right)$$

$$= 2\left(\sqrt[3]{\dfrac{x+1}{2}}\right)^3 - 1$$

$$= 2\left(\dfrac{x+1}{2}\right) - 1$$

$$= x + 1 - 1$$

$$= x$$

$$g(f(x)) = g(2x^3 - 1)$$

$$= \sqrt[3]{\dfrac{(2x^3 - 1) + 1}{2}}$$

$$= \sqrt[3]{\dfrac{2x^3}{2}}$$

$$= \sqrt[3]{x^3}$$

$$= x$$

> **Technology Tip**
>
> Most graphing utilities can graph $y = x^{1/3}$ in two ways:
>
> $$y_1 = x \wedge (1/3) \text{ or}$$
>
> $$y_1 = \sqrt[3]{x}.$$
>
> On some graphing utilities, you may not be able to obtain the complete graph of $y = x^{2/3}$ by entering $y_1 = x \wedge (2/3)$. If not, you should use
>
> $$y_1 = (x \wedge (1/3))^2 \text{ or}$$
>
> $$y_1 = \sqrt[3]{x^2}.$$

✓ **Checkpoint** Audio-video solution in English & Spanish at LarsonPrecalculus.com.

Show that $f(x) = x^5$ and $g(x) = \sqrt[5]{x}$ are inverse functions of each other.

EXAMPLE 4 Verifying Inverse Functions Algebraically

Which of the functions is the inverse function of $f(x) = \dfrac{5}{x - 2}$?

$$g(x) = \dfrac{x - 2}{5} \quad \text{or} \quad h(x) = \dfrac{5}{x} + 2$$

Solution

By forming the composition of f with g, you have

$$f(g(x)) = f\left(\dfrac{x - 2}{5}\right) = \dfrac{5}{\left(\dfrac{x - 2}{5}\right) - 2} = \dfrac{25}{x - 12} \neq x.$$

Because this composition is not equal to the identity function x, it follows that g *is not* the inverse function of f. By forming the composition of f with h, you have

$$f(h(x)) = f\left(\dfrac{5}{x} + 2\right) = \dfrac{5}{\left(\dfrac{5}{x} + 2\right) - 2} = \dfrac{5}{\left(\dfrac{5}{x}\right)} = x.$$

So, it appears that h is the inverse function of f. You can confirm this by showing that the composition of h with f is also equal to the identity function.

$$h(f(x)) = h\left(\dfrac{5}{x - 2}\right) = \dfrac{5}{\left(\dfrac{5}{x - 2}\right)} + 2 = x - 2 + 2 = x$$

✓ **Checkpoint** Audio-video solution in English & Spanish at LarsonPrecalculus.com.

Which of the functions is the inverse function of $f(x) = \dfrac{x - 4}{7}$?

$$g(x) = 7x + 4 \qquad h(x) = \dfrac{7}{x - 4}$$

The Graph of an Inverse Function

The graphs of a function f and its inverse function f^{-1} are related to each other in the following way. If the point

(a, b)

lies on the graph of f, then the point

(b, a)

must lie on the graph of f^{-1}, and vice versa. This means that the graph of f^{-1} is a reflection of the graph of f in the line $y = x$, as shown in Figure 1.39.

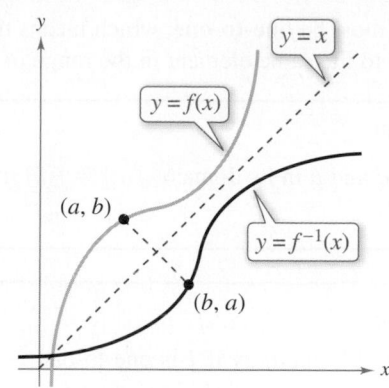

Figure 1.39

Technology Tip

Many graphing utilities have a built-in feature for drawing an inverse function. For instructions on how to use the *draw inverse* feature, see Appendix A; for specific keystrokes, go to this textbook's *Companion Website*.

EXAMPLE 5   Verifying Inverse Functions Graphically

Verify that the functions f and g from Example 3 are inverse functions of each other graphically.

Solution

From the figure, it appears that f and g are inverse functions of each other.

The graph of g is a reflection of the graph of f in the line $y = x$.

✓ **Checkpoint** 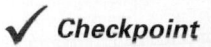 *Audio-video solution in English & Spanish at LarsonPrecalculus.com.*

Verify that $f(x) = x^5$ and $g(x) = \sqrt[5]{x}$ are inverse functions of each other graphically.

EXAMPLE 6   Verifying Inverse Functions Numerically

Verify that the functions $f(x) = \dfrac{x - 5}{2}$ and $g(x) = 2x + 5$ are inverse functions of each other numerically.

Solution

You can verify that f and g are inverse functions of each other *numerically* by using a graphing utility. Enter $y_1 = f(x)$, $y_2 = g(x)$, $y_3 = f(g(x))$, and $y_4 = g(f(x))$. Then use the *table* feature to create a table.

Plot1 Plot2 Plot3
\Y1=(X-5)/2
\Y2=2X+5
\Y3=Y1(Y2)
\Y4=Y2(Y1)
\Y5=
\Y6=
\Y7=

X	Y3	Y4
-2	-2	-2
-1	-1	-1
0	0	0
1	1	1
2	2	2
3	3	3
4	4	4

X=-2

Note that the entries for x, y_3, and y_4 are the same. So, it appears that $f(g(x)) = x$ and $g(f(x)) = x$, and that f and g are inverse functions of each other.

✓ **Checkpoint** 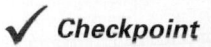 *Audio-video solution in English & Spanish at LarsonPrecalculus.com.*

Verify that $f(x) = x^5$ and $g(x) = \sqrt[5]{x}$ are inverse functions of each other numerically. ▪

The Existence of an Inverse Function

To have an inverse function, a function must be **one-to-one,** which means that no two elements in the domain of f correspond to the same element in the range of f.

> **Definition of a One-to-One Function**
>
> A function f is **one-to-one** when, for a and b in its domain, $f(a) = f(b)$ implies that $a = b$.

> **Existence of an Inverse Function**
>
> A function f has an inverse function f^{-1} if and only if f is one-to-one.

From its graph, it is easy to tell whether a function of x is one-to-one. Simply check to see that every horizontal line intersects the graph of the function at most once. This is called the **Horizontal Line Test.** For instance, Figure 1.40 shows the graph of $f(x) = x^2$. On the graph, you can find a horizontal line that intersects the graph twice. So, f is not one-to-one and does not have an inverse function.

Two special types of functions that pass the Horizontal Line Test are those that are increasing or decreasing on their entire domains. If f is *increasing* on its entire domain, then f is one-to-one. If f is *decreasing* on its entire domain, then f is one-to-one.

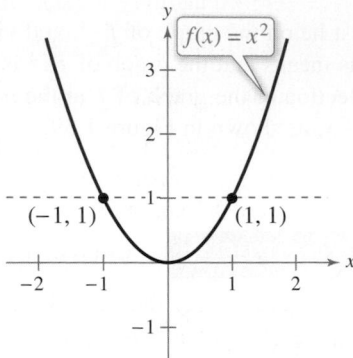

$f(x) = x^2$ is not one-to-one.
Figure 1.40

EXAMPLE 7 **Testing Whether a Function Is One-to-One**

Is the function $f(x) = \sqrt{x} + 1$ one-to-one?

Algebraic Solution

Let a and b be nonnegative real numbers with $f(a) = f(b)$.

$$\sqrt{a} + 1 = \sqrt{b} + 1 \qquad \text{Set } f(a) = f(b).$$
$$\sqrt{a} = \sqrt{b}$$
$$a = b$$

So, $f(a) = f(b)$ implies that $a = b$. You can conclude that f is one-to-one and *does* have an inverse function.

Graphical Solution

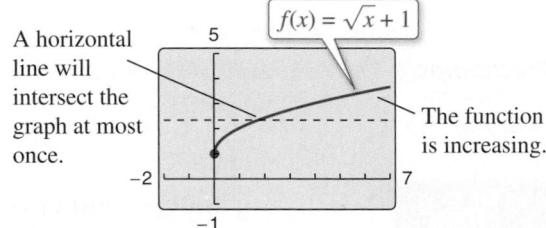

A horizontal line will intersect the graph at most once.

The function is increasing.

From the figure, you can conclude that f is one-to-one and *does* have an inverse function.

✓ **Checkpoint** ◀))) *Audio-video solution in English & Spanish at LarsonPrecalculus.com.*

Is the function $f(x) = \sqrt[3]{x}$ one-to-one?

EXAMPLE 8 **Testing Whether a Function Is One-to-One**

See LarsonPrecalculus.com for an interactive version of this type of example.

To determine whether $f(x) = x^2 - x$ is one-to-one, note that $f(-1) = (-1)^2 - (-1) = 2$ and $f(2) = 2^2 - 2 = 2$. Because you have two inputs matched with the same output, f *is not* one-to-one and *does not* have an inverse function. You can confirm this graphically by noticing that the horizontal line $y = 2$ intersects the graph of f twice, as shown in Figure 1.41.

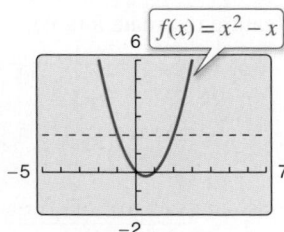

Figure 1.41

✓ **Checkpoint** ◀))) *Audio-video solution in English & Spanish at LarsonPrecalculus.com.*

Is the function $f(x) = |x|$ one-to-one? ∎

Finding Inverse Functions Algebraically

For relatively simple functions (such as the ones in Examples 1 and 2), you can find inverse functions by inspection. For more complicated functions, however, it is best to use the following guidelines.

Finding an Inverse Function

1. Use the Horizontal Line Test to decide whether f has an inverse function.

2. In the equation for $f(x)$, replace $f(x)$ with y.

3. Interchange the roles of x and y, and solve for y.

4. Replace y with $f^{-1}(x)$ in the new equation.

5. Verify that f and f^{-1} are inverse functions of each other by showing that the domain of f is equal to the range of f^{-1}, the range of f is equal to the domain of f^{-1}, and $f(f^{-1}(x)) = x$ and $f^{-1}(f(x)) = x$.

The key step in these guidelines is Step 3—interchanging the roles of x and y. This step corresponds to the fact that inverse functions have ordered pairs with the coordinates reversed.

What's Wrong?

You use a graphing utility to graph $y_1 = x^2$ and then use the *draw inverse* feature to conclude that $f(x) = x^2$ has an inverse function (see figure). What's wrong?

EXAMPLE 9   Finding an Inverse Function Algebraically

Find the inverse function of

$$f(x) = \frac{5 - 3x}{2}.$$

Solution

The graph of f in Figure 1.42 passes the Horizontal Line Test. So, you know that f is one-to-one and has an inverse function.

$$f(x) = \frac{5 - 3x}{2} \qquad \text{Write original function.}$$

$$y = \frac{5 - 3x}{2} \qquad \text{Replace } f(x) \text{ with } y.$$

$$x = \frac{5 - 3y}{2} \qquad \text{Interchange } x \text{ and } y.$$

$$2x = 5 - 3y \qquad \text{Multiply each side by 2.}$$

$$3y = 5 - 2x \qquad \text{Isolate the } y\text{-term.}$$

$$y = \frac{5 - 2x}{3} \qquad \text{Solve for } y.$$

$$f^{-1}(x) = \frac{5 - 2x}{3} \qquad \text{Replace } y \text{ with } f^{-1}(x).$$

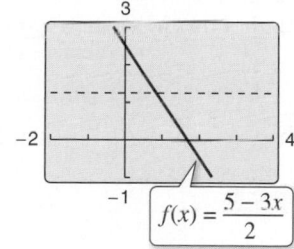

Figure 1.42

The domains and ranges of f and f^{-1} consist of all real numbers. Verify that $f(f^{-1}(x)) = x$ and $f^{-1}(f(x)) = x$.

✓ **Checkpoint**))) Audio-video solution in English & Spanish at LarsonPrecalculus.com.

Find the inverse function of $f(x) = 2x - 3$.

EXAMPLE 10 Finding an Inverse Function Algebraically

Find the inverse function of $f(x) = \sqrt{2x - 3}$.

Solution

The graph of f in Figure 1.43 passes the Horizontal Line Test. So, you know that f is one-to-one and has an inverse function.

$$f(x) = \sqrt{2x - 3} \qquad \text{Write original function.}$$

$$y = \sqrt{2x - 3} \qquad \text{Replace } f(x) \text{ with } y.$$

$$x = \sqrt{2y - 3} \qquad \text{Interchange } x \text{ and } y.$$

$$x^2 = 2y - 3 \qquad \text{Square each side.}$$

$$2y = x^2 + 3 \qquad \text{Isolate } y.$$

$$y = \frac{x^2 + 3}{2} \qquad \text{Solve for } y.$$

$$f^{-1}(x) = \frac{x^2 + 3}{2}, \ x \geq 0 \qquad \text{Replace } y \text{ with } f^{-1}(x).$$

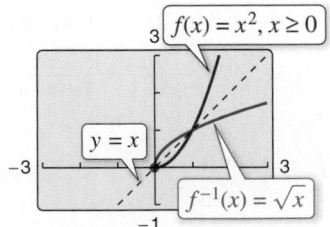

Figure 1.43

The range of f is the interval $[0, \infty)$, which implies that the domain of f^{-1} is the interval $[0, \infty)$. Moreover, the domain of f is the interval $\left[\frac{3}{2}, \infty\right)$, which implies that the range of f^{-1} is the interval $\left[\frac{3}{2}, \infty\right)$. Verify that $f(f^{-1}(x)) = x$ and $f^{-1}(f(x)) = x$.

✓ *Checkpoint* ◄))) *Audio-video solution in English & Spanish at LarsonPrecalculus.com.*

Find the inverse function of $f(x) = \sqrt[3]{x + 10}$. ■

A function f with an implied domain of all real numbers may not pass the Horizontal Line Test. In this case, the domain of f may be restricted so that f does have an inverse function. Recall from Figure 1.40 that $f(x) = x^2$ is not one-to-one. By restricting the domain of f to $x \geq 0$, the function is one-to-one and does have an inverse function (see Figure 1.44).

EXAMPLE 11 Restricting the Domain of a Function

Find the inverse function of $f(x) = x^2$, $x \geq 0$.

Solution

The graph of f in Figure 1.44 passes the Horizontal Line Test. So, you know that f is one-to-one and has an inverse function.

Figure 1.44

$$f(x) = x^2, \ x \geq 0 \qquad \text{Write original function with restricted domain.}$$

$$y = x^2 \qquad \text{Replace } f(x) \text{ with } y.$$

$$x = y^2, \ y \geq 0 \qquad \text{Interchange } x \text{ and } y.$$

$$y = \sqrt{x} \qquad \text{Solve for } y. \text{ Extract positive square root } (y \geq 0).$$

$$f^{-1}(x) = \sqrt{x} \qquad \text{Replace } y \text{ with } f^{-1}(x).$$

The graph of f^{-1} in Figure 1.45 is the reflection of the graph of f in the line $y = x$. The domains and ranges of f and f^{-1} consist of all nonnegative real numbers. Verify that $f(f^{-1}(x)) = x$ and $f^{-1}(f(x)) = x$.

Figure 1.45

✓ *Checkpoint* ◄))) *Audio-video solution in English & Spanish at LarsonPrecalculus.com.*

Find the inverse function of $f(x) = (x - 1)^2$, $x \geq 1$. ■

1.6   Exercises

Vocabulary and Concept Check

In Exercises 1–4, fill in the blank(s).

1. If f and g are functions such that $f(g(x)) = x$ and $g(f(x)) = x$, then the function g is the _____ function of f, and is denoted by _____ .

2. The domain of f is the _____ of f^{-1}, and the _____ of f^{-1} is the range of f.

3. The graphs of f and f^{-1} are reflections of each other in the line _____ .

4. To have an inverse function, a function f must be _____ ; that is, $f(a) = f(b)$ implies $a = b$.

5. How many times can a horizontal line intersect the graph of a function that is one-to-one?

6. Can $(1, 4)$ and $(2, 4)$ be two ordered pairs of a one-to-one function?

Procedures and Problem Solving

Finding Inverse Functions Informally   In Exercises 7–14, find the inverse function of f informally. Verify that $f(f^{-1}(x)) = x$ and $f^{-1}(f(x)) = x$.

7. $f(x) = 6x$

8. $f(x) = \frac{1}{3}x$

9. $f(x) = x + 11$

10. $f(x) = x + 3$

11. $f(x) = (x - 1)/2$

12. $f(x) = 4(x - 1)$

13. $f(x) = \sqrt[3]{x}$

14. $f(x) = x^7$

Identifying Graphs of Inverse Functions   In Exercises 15–18, match the graph of the function with the graph of its inverse function. [The graphs of the inverse functions are labeled (a), (b), (c), and (d).]

(a)

(b)

(c)

(d)

15.

16.

17.

18.

Verifying Inverse Functions Algebraically   In Exercises 19–24, show that f and g are inverse functions algebraically. Use a graphing utility to graph f and g in the same viewing window. Describe the relationship between the graphs.

19. $f(x) = x^3$, $g(x) = \sqrt[3]{x}$

20. $f(x) = \dfrac{1}{x}$, $g(x) = \dfrac{1}{x}$

21. $f(x) = \sqrt{x - 4}$; $g(x) = x^2 + 4$, $x \geq 0$

22. $f(x) = 9 - x^2, x \geq 0$; $g(x) = \sqrt{9 - x}$

23. $f(x) = 1 - x^3$, $g(x) = \sqrt[3]{1 - x}$

24. $f(x) = \dfrac{1}{1 + x}, x \geq 0$; $g(x) = \dfrac{1 - x}{x}, 0 < x \leq 1$

Algebraic-Graphical-Numerical   In Exercises 25–34, show that f and g are inverse functions (a) algebraically, (b) graphically, and (c) numerically.

25. $f(x) = -\dfrac{7}{2}x - 3$, $g(x) = -\dfrac{2x + 6}{7}$

26. $f(x) = \dfrac{x - 9}{4}$, $g(x) = 4x + 9$

27. $f(x) = x^3 + 5$, $g(x) = \sqrt[3]{x - 5}$

28. $f(x) = \dfrac{x^3}{2}$, $g(x) = \sqrt[3]{2x}$

29. $f(x) = -\sqrt{x - 8}$; $g(x) = 8 + x^2$, $x \leq 0$

30. $f(x) = \sqrt[4]{3x - 10}$; $g(x) = \dfrac{x^4 + 10}{3}$, $x \geq 0$

31. $f(x) = 2x$, $g(x) = \dfrac{x}{2}$

32. $f(x) = -3x + 5$, $g(x) = -\dfrac{x - 5}{3}$

33. $f(x) = \dfrac{x - 1}{x + 5}$, $g(x) = -\dfrac{5x + 1}{x - 1}$

34. $f(x) = \dfrac{x + 3}{x - 2}$, $g(x) = \dfrac{2x + 3}{x - 1}$

Identifying Whether Functions Have Inverses In Exercises 35–38, does the function have an inverse? Explain.

35. *Domain*   *Range*

1 can ⟶ $1
6 cans ⟶ $5
12 cans ⟶ $9
24 cans ⟶ $16

36. *Domain*   *Range*

1/2 hour ⟶ $40
1 hour ⟶ $70
2 hours ⟶ $120
4 hours

37. $\{(-3, 6), (-1, 5), (0, 6)\}$

38. $\{(2, 4), (3, 7), (7, 2)\}$

Recognizing One-to-One Functions In Exercises 39–44, determine whether the graph is that of a function. If so, determine whether the function is one-to-one.

39.

40.

41.

42.

43.

44.
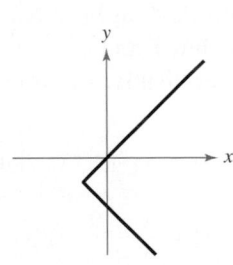

Using the Horizontal Line Test In Exercises 45–56, use a graphing utility to graph the function and use the Horizontal Line Test to determine whether the function is one-to-one and so has an inverse function.

45. $f(x) = 3 - \frac{1}{2}x$

46. $f(x) = 2x^{1/3} + 5$

47. $h(x) = \dfrac{x^2}{x^2 + 1}$

48. $g(x) = \dfrac{4 - x}{6x^2}$

49. $h(x) = \sqrt{16 - x^2}$

50. $f(x) = -2x\sqrt{16 - x^2}$

51. $f(x) = 10$

52. $f(x) = -0.65$

53. $g(x) = (x + 5)^3$

54. $f(x) = x^5 - 7$

55. $h(x) = |x| - |x - 4|$

56. $f(x) = -\dfrac{|x^2 - 9|}{|x^2 + 7|}$

Analyzing a Piecewise-Defined Function In Exercises 57 and 58, sketch the graph of the piecewise-defined function by hand and use the graph to determine whether an inverse function exists.

57. $f(x) = \begin{cases} x^2, & 0 \le x \le 1 \\ x, & x > 1 \end{cases}$

58. $f(x) = \begin{cases} (x - 2)^3, & x < 3 \\ (x - 4)^2, & x \ge 3 \end{cases}$

Testing Whether a Function Is One-to-One In Exercises 59–70, determine algebraically whether the function is one-to-one. Verify your answer graphically. If the function is one-to-one, find its inverse.

59. $f(x) = x^4$

60. $g(x) = x^2 - x^4$

61. $f(x) = \dfrac{3x + 4}{5}$

62. $f(x) = 3x + 5$

63. $f(x) = \dfrac{1}{x^2}$

64. $h(x) = \dfrac{4}{x^2}$

65. $f(x) = (x + 3)^2, \quad x \ge -3$

66. $q(x) = (x - 5)^2, \quad x \le 5$

67. $f(x) = \sqrt{2x + 3}$

68. $f(x) = \sqrt{x - 2}$

69. $f(x) = |x - 2|, \quad x \le 2$

70. $f(x) = \dfrac{x^2}{x^2 + 1}, \quad x \ge 0$

Finding an Inverse Function Algebraically In Exercises 71–80, find the inverse function of f algebraically. Use a graphing utility to graph both f and f^{-1} in the same viewing window. Describe the relationship between the graphs.

71. $f(x) = 4x - 9$

72. $f(x) = 3x$

73. $f(x) = x^5$

74. $f(x) = x^3 + 1$

75. $f(x) = x^4, \quad x \le 0$

76. $f(x) = x^2, \quad x \ge 0$

77. $f(x) = \sqrt{4 - x^2}, \quad 0 \le x \le 2$

78. $f(x) = \sqrt{16 - x^2}, \quad -4 \le x \le 0$

79. $f(x) = \dfrac{4}{x^3}$

80. $f(x) = \dfrac{6}{\sqrt{x}}$

Think About It In Exercises 81–90, restrict the domain of the function f so that the function is one-to-one and has an inverse function. Then find the inverse function f^{-1}. State the domains and ranges of f and f^{-1}. Explain your results. (There are many correct answers.)

81. $f(x) = (x - 2)^2$ **82.** $f(x) = x^4 + 1$

83. $f(x) = |x + 2|$ **84.** $f(x) = |x - 2|$

85. $f(x) = (x + 3)^2$

86. $f(x) = (x - 4)^2$

87. $f(x) = -2x^2 - 5$

88. $f(x) = \frac{1}{2}x^2 + 1$

89. $f(x) = |x - 4| + 1$

90. $f(x) = -|x - 1| - 2$

Using the Properties of Inverse Functions In Exercises 91 and 92, use the graph of the function f to complete the table and sketch the graph of f^{-1}.

91.

x	$f^{-1}(x)$
-4	
-2	
2	
3	

92.

x	$f^{-1}(x)$
-3	
-2	
0	
6	

Using Graphs to Evaluate a Function In Exercises 93–100, use the graphs of $y = f(x)$ and $y = g(x)$ to evaluate the function.

93. $f^{-1}(-4)$ **94.** $g^{-1}(0)$

95. $(f \circ g)(2)$ **96.** $g(f(-4))$

97. $f^{-1}(g(0))$ **98.** $(g^{-1} \circ f)(3)$

99. $(g \circ f^{-1})(2)$ **100.** $(f^{-1} \circ g^{-1})(6)$

Using the *Draw Inverse* Feature In Exercises 101–104, (a) use a graphing utility to graph the function f, (b) use the *draw inverse* feature of the graphing utility to draw the inverse relation of the function, and (c) determine whether the inverse relation is an inverse function. Explain your reasoning.

101. $f(x) = x^3 + x + 1$

102. $f(x) = x\sqrt{4 - x^2}$

103. $f(x) = \dfrac{3x^2}{x^2 + 1}$

104. $f(x) = \dfrac{4x}{\sqrt{x^2 + 15}}$

Evaluating a Composition of Functions In Exercises 105–110, use the functions $f(x) = \frac{1}{8}x - 3$ and $g(x) = x^3$ to find the indicated value or function.

105. $(f^{-1} \circ g^{-1})(1)$ **106.** $(g^{-1} \circ f^{-1})(-3)$

107. $(f^{-1} \circ f^{-1})(-6)$ **108.** $(g^{-1} \circ g^{-1})(4)$

109. $f^{-1} \circ g^{-1}$ **110.** $g^{-1} \circ f^{-1}$

Finding a Composition of Functions In Exercises 111–114, use the functions $f(x) = x + 4$ and $g(x) = 2x - 5$ to find the specified function.

111. $g^{-1} \circ f^{-1}$ **112.** $f^{-1} \circ g^{-1}$

113. $(f \circ g)^{-1}$ **114.** $(g \circ f)^{-1}$

115. *Why you should learn it* (p. 60) The table shows men's shoe sizes in the United States and the corresponding European shoe sizes. Let $y = f(x)$ represent the function that gives the men's European shoe size in terms of x, the men's U.S. size.

Men's U.S. shoe size	Men's European shoe size
8	41
9	42
10	43
11	44
12	45
13	46

(a) Is f one-to-one? Explain.

(b) Find $f(11)$.

(c) Find $f^{-1}(43)$, if possible.

(d) Find $f(f^{-1}(41))$.

(e) Find $f^{-1}(f(12))$.

116. Fashion Design Let $y = g(x)$ represent the function that gives the women's European shoe size in terms of x, the women's U.S. size. A women's U.S. size 6 shoe corresponds to a European size 37. Find $g^{-1}(g(6))$.

117. Military Science You can encode and decode messages using functions and their inverses. To code a message, first translate the letters to numbers using 1 for "A," 2 for "B," and so on. Use 0 for a space. So, "A ball" becomes

1 0 2 1 12 12.

Then, use a one-to-one function to convert to coded numbers. Using $f(x) = 2x - 1$, "A ball" becomes

1 -1 3 1 23 23.

(a) Encode "Call me later" using the function $f(x) = 5x + 4$.

(b) Find the inverse function of $f(x) = 5x + 4$ and use it to decode 119 44 9 104 4 104 49 69 29.

118. Production Management Your wage is $12.00 per hour plus $0.55 for each unit produced per hour. So, your hourly wage y in terms of the number of units produced x is $y = 12 + 0.55x$.

(a) Find the inverse function. What does each variable in the inverse function represent?

(b) Use a graphing utility to graph the function and its inverse function.

(c) Use the *trace* feature of the graphing utility to find the hourly wage when 9 units are produced per hour.

(d) Use the *trace* feature of the graphing utility to find the number of units produced per hour when your hourly wage is $21.35.

Conclusions

True or False? **In Exercises 119 and 120, determine whether the statement is true or false. Justify your answer.**

119. If f is an even function, then f^{-1} exists.

120. If the inverse function of f exists, and the graph of f has a y-intercept, then the y-intercept of f is an x-intercept of f^{-1}.

Think About It **In Exercises 121–124, determine whether the situation could be represented by a one-to-one function. If so, write a statement that describes the inverse function.**

121. The number of miles n a marathon runner has completed in terms of the time t in hours

122. The population p of a town in terms of the year t from 2005 through 2015 given that the population was greatest in 2012

123. The depth of the tide d at a beach in terms of the time t over a 24-hour period

124. The height h in inches of a human child from age 2 to age 14 in terms of his or her age n in years

125. Writing Describe the relationship between the graph of a function f and the graph of its inverse function f^{-1}.

126. Think About It The domain of a one-to-one function f is $[0, 9]$ and the range is $[-3, 3]$. Find the domain and range of f^{-1}.

127. Think About It The function $f(x) = \frac{9}{5}x + 32$ can be used to convert a temperature of x degrees Celsius to its corresponding temperature in degrees Fahrenheit.

(a) Using the expression for f, make a conceptual argument to show that f has an inverse function.

(b) What does $f^{-1}(50)$ represent?

128. Think About It A function f is increasing over its entire domain. Does f have an inverse function? Explain.

129. Think About It Describe a type of function that is *not* one-to-one on any interval of its domain.

130. **HOW DO YOU SEE IT?** Decide whether the two functions shown in each graph appear to be inverse functions of each other. Explain your reasoning.

131. Proof Prove that if f and g are one-to-one functions, then $(f \circ g)^{-1}(x) = (g^{-1} \circ f^{-1})(x)$.

132. Proof Prove that if f is a one-to-one odd function, then f^{-1} is an odd function.

Cumulative Mixed Review

Simplifying a Rational Expression **In Exercises 133–136, write the rational expression in simplest form.**

133. $\dfrac{27x^3}{3x^2}$

134. $\dfrac{5x^2y^2 + 25x^2y}{xy + 5x}$

135. $\dfrac{x^2 - 36}{6 - x}$

136. $\dfrac{x^2 + 3x - 40}{x^2 - 3x - 10}$

Testing for Functions **In Exercises 137–140, determine whether the equation represents y as a function of x.**

137. $x = 5$

138. $y - 7 = -3$

139. $x^2 + y = 5$

140. $x - y^2 = 0$

1.7   Linear Models and Scatter Plots

Scatter Plots and Correlation

Many real-life situations involve finding relationships between two variables, such as the year and the population of the United States. In a typical situation, data are collected and written as a set of ordered pairs. The graph of such a set is called a *scatter plot*. (For a brief discussion of scatter plots, see Appendix B.1.)

EXAMPLE 1   Constructing a Scatter Plot

The populations P (in millions) of the United States from 2008 through 2013 are shown in the table. Construct a scatter plot of the data.   (Source: U.S. Census Bureau)

Year	Population, P (in millions)
2008	304.1
2009	306.8
2010	309.3
2011	311.6
2012	313.9
2013	316.1

Spreadsheet at LarsonPrecalculus.com

Solution

Begin by representing the data with a set of ordered pairs. Let t represent the year, with $t = 8$ corresponding to 2008.

$(8, 304.1), (9, 306.8), (10, 309.3),$
$(11, 311.6), (12, 313.9), (13, 316.1)$

Then plot each point in a coordinate plane, as shown in the figure.

U.S. Population

✓ **Checkpoint** 🔊))) *Audio-video solution in English & Spanish at LarsonPrecalculus.com.*

The median sales prices (in thousands of dollars) of new homes sold in a neighborhood from 2006 through 2013 are given by the following ordered pairs. *(Spreadsheet at LarsonPrecalculus.com)* Construct a scatter plot of the data.

   $(2006, 179.4), (2007, 185.4), (2008, 191.0), (2009, 196.7),$
$(2010, 202.6), (2011, 208.7), (2012, 214.9), (2013, 221.4)$ ■

From the scatter plot in Example 1, it appears that the points describe a relationship that is nearly linear. The relationship is not *exactly* linear because the population did not increase by precisely the same amount each year.

A mathematical equation that approximates the relationship between t and P is a *mathematical model*. When developing a mathematical model to describe a set of data, you strive for two (often conflicting) goals—accuracy and simplicity. For the data above, a linear model of the form $P = at + b$ (where a and b are constants) appears to be best. It is simple and relatively accurate.

Consider a collection of ordered pairs of the form (x, y). If y tends to increase as x increases, then the collection is said to have a **positive correlation.** If y tends to decrease as x increases, then the collection is said to have a **negative correlation.** Figure 1.46 shows three examples: one with a positive correlation, one with a negative correlation, and one with no (discernible) correlation.

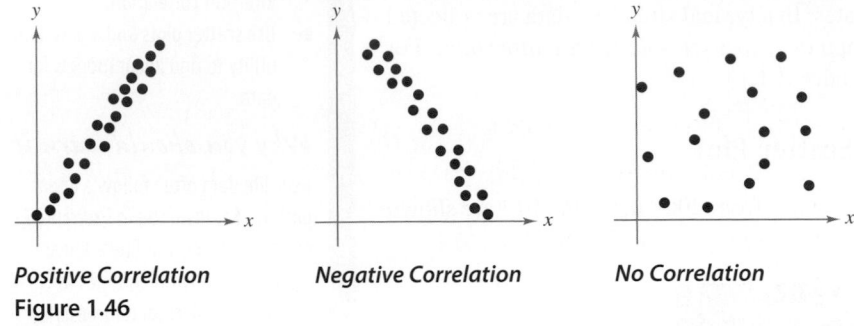

Positive Correlation   *Negative Correlation*   *No Correlation*
Figure 1.46

EXAMPLE 2   **Interpreting Correlation**

On a Friday, 22 students in a class were asked to record the numbers of hours they spent studying for a test on Monday. The results are shown below. The first coordinate is the number of hours and the second coordinate is the score obtained on the test. *(Spreadsheet at LarsonPrecalculus.com)*

 Study Hours: (0, 40), (1, 41), (2, 51), (3, 58), (3, 49), (4, 48), (4, 64), (5, 55), (5, 69), (5, 58), (5, 75), (6, 68), (6, 63), (6, 93), (7, 84), (7, 67), (8, 90), (8, 76), (9, 95), (9, 72), (9, 85), (10, 98)

a. Construct a scatter plot of the data.

b. Determine whether the points are positively correlated, are negatively correlated, or have no discernible correlation. What can you conclude?

Solution

a. The scatter plot is shown in the figure.

b. The scatter plot relating study hours and test scores has a positive correlation. This means that the more a student studied, the higher his or her score tended to be.

✓ *Checkpoint* *Audio-video solution in English & Spanish at LarsonPrecalculus.com.*

The students in Example 2 also recorded the numbers of hours they spent watching television. The results are shown below. The first coordinate is the number of hours and the second coordinate is the score obtained on the test. *(Spreadsheet at LarsonPrecalculus.com)*

 TV Hours: (0, 98), (1, 85), (2, 72), (2, 90), (3, 67), (3, 93), (3, 95), (4, 68), (4, 84), (5, 76), (7, 75), (7, 58), (9, 63), (9, 69), (11, 55), (12, 58), (14, 64), (16, 48), (17, 51), (18, 41), (19, 49), (20, 40)

a. Construct a scatter plot of the data.

b. Determine whether the points are positively correlated, are negatively correlated, or have no discernible correlation. What can you conclude?

Fitting a Line to Data

Finding a linear model to represent the relationship described by a scatter plot is called **fitting a line to data.** You can do this graphically by simply sketching the line that appears to fit the points, finding two points on the line, and then finding the equation of the line that passes through the two points.

EXAMPLE 3   Fitting a Line to Data

See LarsonPrecalculus.com for an interactive version of this type of example.

Find a linear model that relates the year to the population of the United States. (See Example 1.)

DATA Year	U.S. Population, P (in millions)
2008	304.1
2009	306.8
2010	309.3
2011	311.6
2012	313.9
2013	316.1

Spreadsheet at LarsonPrecalculus.com

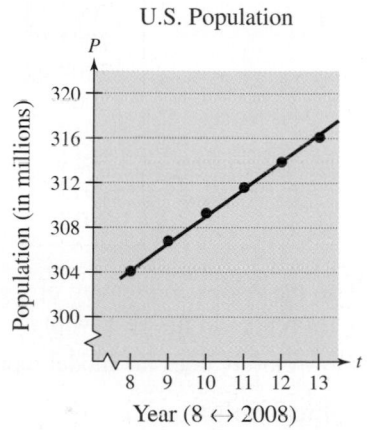

U.S. Population

Year (8 ↔ 2008)

Solution

Let t represent the year, with $t = 8$ corresponding to 2008. After plotting the data in the table, draw the line that you think best represents the data, as shown in the figure. Two points that lie on this line are (8, 304.1) and (12, 313.9). Using the point-slope form, you can find the equation of the line to be

$$P = 2.45(t - 8) + 304.1$$

$$= 2.45t + 284.5. \qquad \text{Linear model}$$

✓ **Checkpoint** 🔊))) *Audio-video solution in English & Spanish at LarsonPrecalculus.com.*

Find a linear model that relates the year to the median sales prices (in thousands of dollars) of new homes sold in a neighborhood from 2006 through 2013. (See Checkpoint for Example 1.) *(Spreadsheet at LarsonPrecalculus.com)*

DATA   (2006, 179.4), (2007, 185.4), (2008, 191.0), (2009, 196.7),
(2010, 202.6), (2011, 208.7), (2012, 214.9), (2013, 221.4)

After finding a model, you can measure how well the model fits the data by comparing the actual values with the values given by the model, as shown in the table.

	t	8	9	10	11	12	13
Actual ⇨	P	304.1	306.8	309.3	311.6	313.9	316.1
Model ⇨	P	304.1	306.6	309.0	311.5	313.9	316.4

The sum of the squares of the differences between the actual values and the model values is called the **sum of the squared differences.** The model that has the least sum is called the **least squares regression line** for the data. For the model in Example 3, the sum of the squared differences is 0.23. The least squares regression line for the data is

$$P = 2.39t + 285.2. \qquad \text{Best-fitting linear model}$$

Its sum of squared differences is 0.14. For more on the least squares regression line, see Appendix C.2 at this textbook's *Companion Website*.

Remark

The model in Example 3 is based on the two data points chosen. When different points are chosen, the model may change somewhat. For instance, when you choose (9, 306.8) and (12, 313.9), the new model is

$$P = 2.37(t - 9) + 306.8$$

$$= 2.37t + 285.5.$$

Another way to find a linear model to represent the relationship described by a scatter plot is to enter the data points into a graphing utility and use the *linear regression* feature. This method is demonstrated in Example 4.

Technology Tip

For instructions on how to use the *linear regression* feature, see Appendix A; for specific keystrokes, go to this textbook's *Companion Website*.

EXAMPLE 4   A Mathematical Model

The table shows the numbers N (in millions) of tax returns made through e-file from 2006 through 2013.   (Source: Internal Revenue Service)

DATA Year	Number of tax returns made through e-file, N (in millions)
2006	73.3
2007	80.0
2008	89.9
2009	95.0
2010	98.7
2011	112.2
2012	119.6
2013	122.5

Spreadsheet at LarsonPrecalculus.com

a. Use the *regression* feature of a graphing utility to find a linear model for the data. Let t represent the year, with $t = 6$ corresponding to 2006.

b. How closely does the model represent the data?

Graphical Solution

a. Use the *linear regression* feature of a graphing utility to obtain the model shown in the figure. You can approximate the model to be $N = 7.30t + 29.6$.

```
LinReg
 y=ax+b
 a=7.297619048
 b=29.57261905
```

b. Graph the actual data and the model. From the figure, it appears that the model is a good fit for the actual data.

$N = 7.30t + 29.6$

Numerical Solution

a. Using the *linear regression* feature of a graphing utility, you can find that a linear model for the data is $N = 7.30t + 29.6$.

b. You can see how well the model fits the data by comparing the actual values of N with the values of N given by the model, which are labeled $N*$ in the table below. From the table, you can see that the model appears to be a good fit for the actual data.

Year	N	$N*$
2006	73.3	73.4
2007	80.0	80.7
2008	89.9	88.0
2009	95.0	95.3
2010	98.7	102.6
2011	112.2	109.9
2012	119.6	117.2
2013	122.5	124.5

✓ **Checkpoint** ◀))) Audio-video solution in English & Spanish at LarsonPrecalculus.com.

The numbers N (in millions) of people unemployed in the U.S. from 2007 through 2013 are given by the following ordered pairs. *(Spreadsheet at LarsonPrecalculus.com)* (Source: U.S. Bureau of Labor Statistics)

(2007, 7.078), (2008, 8.924), (2009, 14.265), (2010, 14.825), (2011, 13.747), (2012, 12.506), (2013, 11.460)

a. Use the *regression* feature of a graphing utility to find a linear model for the data. Let t represent the year, with $t = 7$ corresponding to 2007.

b. How closely does the model represent the data?

When you use the *regression* feature of a graphing calculator or computer program to find a linear model for data, you will notice that the program may also output an "*r*-value." For instance, the *r*-value from Example 4 was $r \approx 0.992$. This *r*-value is the **correlation coefficient** of the data and gives a measure of how well the model fits the data. The correlation coefficient r varies between -1 and 1. Basically, the closer $|r|$ is to 1, the better the points can be described by a line. Three examples are shown in Figure 1.47.

$r = 0.972$

$r = -0.856$

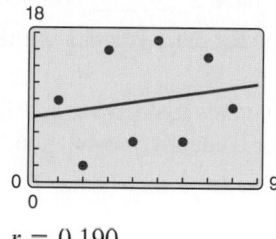
$r = 0.190$

Figure 1.47

EXAMPLE 5   Finding a Least Squares Regression Line

The ordered pairs (w, h) represent the shoe sizes w and the heights h (in inches) of 25 men. Use the *regression* feature of a graphing utility to find the least squares regression line for the data.

(10.0, 70.5)	(10.5, 71.0)	(9.5, 69.0)	(11.0, 72.0)	(12.0, 74.0)
(8.5, 67.0)	(9.0, 68.5)	(13.0, 76.0)	(10.5, 71.5)	(10.5, 70.5)
(10.0, 71.0)	(9.5, 70.0)	(10.0, 71.0)	(10.5, 71.0)	(11.0, 71.5)
(12.0, 73.5)	(12.5, 75.0)	(11.0, 72.0)	(9.0, 68.0)	(10.0, 70.0)
(13.0, 75.5)	(10.5, 72.0)	(10.5, 71.0)	(11.0, 73.0)	(8.5, 67.5)

Solution

After entering the data into a graphing utility (see Figure 1.48), you obtain the model shown in Figure 1.49. So, the least squares regression line for the data is

$h = 1.84w + 51.9.$

In Figure 1.50, this line is plotted with the data. Note that the plot does not have 25 points because some of the ordered pairs graph as the same point. The correlation coefficient for this model is $r \approx 0.981$, which implies that the model is a good fit for the data.

Figure 1.48

Figure 1.49

Figure 1.50

 Checkpoint 🔊))) *Audio-video solution in English & Spanish at LarsonPrecalculus.com.*

The ordered pairs (g, e) represent the gross domestic products g (in millions of U.S. dollars) and the carbon dioxide emissions e (in millions of metric tons) for seven countries. *(Spreadsheet at LarsonPrecalculus.com)* Use the *regression* feature of a graphing utility to find the least squares regression line for the data.   (Sources: World Bank and U.S. Energy Information Administration)

DATA   (14.99, 5491), (5.87, 1181), (3.6, 748), (2.77, 374),
(2.48, 475), (2.45, 497), (2.19, 401)

1.7   Exercises

See *CalcChat.com* for tutorial help and worked-out solutions to odd-numbered exercises.
For instructions on how to use a graphing utility, see Appendix A.

Vocabulary and Concept Check

In Exercises 1 and 2, fill in the blank.

1. Consider a collection of ordered pairs of the form (x, y). If y tends to increase as x increases, then the collection is said to have a _____ correlation.

2. To find the least squares regression line for data, you can use the _____ feature of a graphing utility.

3. In a collection of ordered pairs (x, y), y tends to decrease as x increases. Does the collection have a positive correlation or a negative correlation?

4. You find the least squares regression line for a set of data. The correlation coefficient is 0.114. Is the model a good fit?

Procedures and Problem Solving

5. **Constructing a Scatter Plot**   The following ordered pairs give the years of experience x for 15 sales representatives and the monthly sales y (in thousands of dollars).

   (1.5, 41.7), (1.0, 32.4), (0.3, 19.2), (3.0, 48.4),
   (4.0, 51.2), (0.5, 28.5), (2.5, 50.4), (1.8, 35.5),
   (2.0, 36.0), (1.5, 40.0), (3.5, 50.3), (4.0, 55.2),
   (0.5, 29.1), (2.2, 43.2), (2.0, 41.6)

   (a) Create a scatter plot of the data.

   (b) Does the relationship between x and y appear to be approximately linear? Explain.

6. **Constructing a Scatter Plot**   The following ordered pairs give the scores on two consecutive 15-point quizzes for a class of 18 students.

   (7, 13), (9, 7), (14, 14), (15, 15), (10, 15), (9, 7),
   (14, 11), (14, 15), (8, 10), (9, 10), (15, 9), (10, 11),
   (11, 14), (7, 14), (11, 10), (14, 11), (10, 15), (9, 6)

   (a) Create a scatter plot of the data.

   (b) Does the relationship between consecutive quiz scores appear to be approximately linear? If not, give some possible explanations.

Interpreting Correlation   **In Exercises 7–10, the scatter plot of a set of data is shown. Determine whether the points are positively correlated, are negatively correlated, or have no discernible correlation.**

7.

8.

9.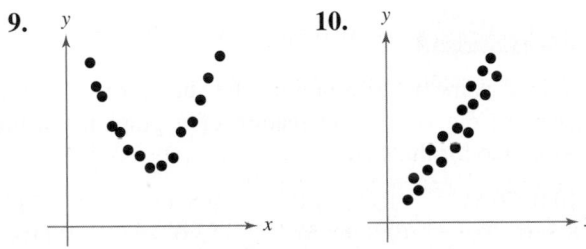

10.

Fitting a Line to Data   **In Exercises 11–16, (a) create a scatter plot of the data, (b) draw a line of fit that passes through two of the points, and (c) use the two points to find an equation of the line.**

11. $(-3, -3)$, $(3, 4)$, $(1, 1)$, $(3, 2)$, $(4, 4)$, $(-1, -1)$

12. $(-2, 3)$, $(-2, 4)$, $(-1, 2)$, $(1, -2)$, $(0, 0)$, $(0, 1)$

13. $(0, 2)$, $(-2, 1)$, $(3, 3)$, $(1, 3)$, $(4, 4)$

14. $(3, 2)$, $(2, 3)$, $(1, 5)$, $(4, 0)$, $(5, 0)$

15. $(0, 7)$, $(3, 2)$, $(6, 0)$, $(4, 3)$, $(2, 5)$

16. $(3, 4)$, $(2, 2)$, $(5, 6)$, $(1, 1)$, $(0, 2)$

A Mathematical Model   **In Exercises 17 and 18, use the *regression* feature of a graphing utility to find a linear model for the data. Then use the graphing utility to decide how closely the model fits the data (a) graphically and (b) numerically. To print an enlarged copy of the graph, go to *MathGraphs.com*.**

17.

18.

19. MODELING DATA

Hooke's Law states that the force F required to compress or stretch a spring (within its elastic limits) is proportional to the distance d that the spring is compressed or stretched from its original length. That is, $F = kd$, where k is the measure of the stiffness of the spring and is called the *spring constant*. The table shows the elongation d in centimeters of a spring when a force of F kilograms is applied.

Force, F	Elongation, d
20	1.4
40	2.5
60	4.0
80	5.3
100	6.6

(a) Sketch a scatter plot of the data.

(b) Find the equation of the line that seems to best fit the data.

(c) Use the *regression* feature of a graphing utility to find a linear model for the data.

(d) Use the model from part (c) to estimate the elongation of the spring when a force of 55 kilograms is applied.

20. MODELING DATA

The numbers of subscribers S (in millions) to wireless networks from 2006 through 2012 are shown in the table.   (Source: CTIA–The Wireless Association)

DATA Year	Subscribers, S (in millions)
2006	233.0
2007	255.4
2008	270.3
2009	285.6
2010	296.3
2011	316.0
2012	326.5

Spreadsheet at LarsonPrecalculus.com

(a) Use a graphing utility to create a scatter plot of the data, with $t = 6$ corresponding to 2006.

(b) Use the *regression* feature of the graphing utility to find a linear model for the data.

(c) Use the graphing utility to plot the data and graph the model in the same viewing window. Is the model a good fit? Explain.

(d) Use the model to predict the number of subscribers in 2020. Is your answer reasonable? Explain.

21. MODELING DATA

The total enterprise values V (in millions of dollars) for the Pittsburgh Penguins from 2008 through 2012 are shown in the table.   (Source: Forbes)

Year	Total enterprise value, V (in millions of dollars)
2008	195
2009	222
2010	235
2011	264
2012	288

(a) Use a graphing utility to create a scatter plot of the data, with $t = 8$ corresponding to 2008.

(b) Use the *regression* feature of the graphing utility to find a linear model for the data.

(c) Use the graphing utility to plot the data and graph the model in the same viewing window. Is the model a good fit? Explain.

(d) Use the model to predict the values in 2015 and 2020. Do the results seem reasonable? Explain.

(e) What is the slope of your model? What does it tell you about the enterprise value?

22. MODELING DATA

The mean salaries S (in thousands of dollars) of public school teachers in the United States from 2005 through 2011 are shown in the table.   (Source: National Education Association)

DATA Year	Mean salary, S (in thousands of dollars)
2005	47.5
2006	49.1
2007	51.1
2008	52.8
2009	54.3
2010	55.5
2011	57.2

Spreadsheet at LarsonPrecalculus.com

(a) Use a graphing utility to create a scatter plot of the data, with $t = 5$ corresponding to 2005.

(b) Use the *regression* feature of the graphing utility to find a linear model for the data.

(c) Use the graphing utility to plot the data and graph the model in the same viewing window. Is the model a good fit? Explain.

(d) Use the model to predict the mean salaries in 2020 and 2022. Do the results seem reasonable? Explain.

23. MODELING DATA

The populations P (in thousands) of New Jersey from 2008 through 2013 are shown in the table. (Source: U.S. Census Bureau)

DATA Year	Population, P (in thousands)
2008	8711
2009	8756
2010	8792
2011	8821
2012	8868
2013	8899

Spreadsheet at LarsonPrecalculus.com

(a) Use a graphing utility to create a scatter plot of the data, with $t = 8$ corresponding to 2008.

(b) Use the *regression* feature of the graphing utility to find a linear model for the data.

(c) Use the graphing utility to plot the data and graph the model in the same viewing window.

(d) Create a table showing the actual values of P and the values of P given by the model. How closely does the model fit the data?

(e) Use the model to predict the population of New Jersey in 2050. Does the result seem reasonable? Explain.

24. MODELING DATA

The populations P (in thousands) of Wyoming from 2009 through 2013 are shown in the table. (Source: U.S. Census Bureau)

Year	Population, P (in thousands)
2009	560
2010	564
2011	568
2012	577
2013	583

(a) Use a graphing utility to create a scatter plot of the data, with $t = 9$ corresponding to 2009.

(b) Use the *regression* feature of the graphing utility to find a linear model for the data.

(c) Use the graphing utility to plot the data and graph the model in the same viewing window.

(d) Create a table showing the actual values of P and the values of P given by the model. How closely does the model fit the data?

(e) Use the model to predict the population of Wyoming in 2050. Does the result seem reasonable? Explain.

25. MODELING DATA

The table shows the advertising expenditures x and sales volumes y for a company for nine randomly selected months. Both are measured in thousands of dollars.

DATA Month	Advertising expenditures, x	Sales volume, y
1	2.4	215
2	1.6	182
3	1.4	172
4	2.3	214
5	2.0	201
6	2.6	230
7	1.4	176
8	1.6	177
9	2.0	196

Spreadsheet at LarsonPrecalculus.com

(a) Use the *regression* feature of a graphing utility to find a linear model for the data.

(b) Use the graphing utility to plot the data and graph the model in the same viewing window.

(c) Interpret the slope of the model in the context of the problem.

(d) Use the model to estimate sales for advertising expenditures of $1500.

26. MODELING DATA

The table shows the numbers T of stores owned by the Target Corporation from 2006 through 2012. (Source: Target Corp.)

DATA Year	Number of stores, T
2006	1488
2007	1591
2008	1682
2009	1740
2010	1750
2011	1763
2012	1778

Spreadsheet at LarsonPrecalculus.com

(a) Use a graphing utility to make a scatter plot of the data, with $t = 6$ corresponding to 2006. Identify two sets of points in the scatter plot that are approximately linear.

(b) Use the *regression* feature of the graphing utility to find a linear model for each set of points.

(c) Write a piecewise-defined model for the data. Use the graphing utility to graph the piecewise-defined model.

(d) Describe a scenario that could be the cause of the break in the data.

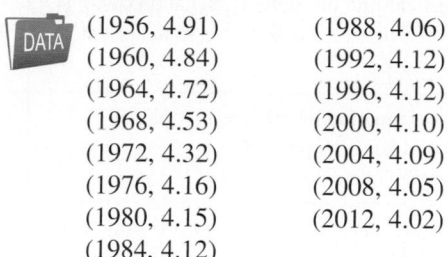

27. *Why you should learn it* *(p. 71)* The following ordered pairs (t, T) represent the Olympic year t and the winning time T (in minutes) in the women's 400-meter freestyle swimming event. (*Spreadsheet at LarsonPrecalculus.com*) (Source: International Olympic Committee)

(1956, 4.91)	(1988, 4.06)
(1960, 4.84)	(1992, 4.12)
(1964, 4.72)	(1996, 4.12)
(1968, 4.53)	(2000, 4.10)
(1972, 4.32)	(2004, 4.09)
(1976, 4.16)	(2008, 4.05)
(1980, 4.15)	(2012, 4.02)
(1984, 4.12)	

(a) Use the *regression* feature of a graphing utility to find a linear model for the data and to identify the correlation coefficient. Let t represent the year, with $t = 0$ corresponding to 1950.

(b) What information is given by the sign of the slope of the model?

(c) Use the graphing utility to plot the data and graph the model in the same viewing window.

(d) Create a table showing the actual values of y and the values of y given by the model. How closely does the model fit the data?

(e) How can you use the value of the correlation coefficient to help answer the question in part (d)?

(f) Would you use the model to predict the winning times in the future? Explain.

28. MODELING DATA

In a study, 60 colts were measured every 14 days from birth. The ordered pairs (d, l) represent the average length l (in centimeters) of the 60 colts d days after birth. (*Spreadsheet at LarsonPrecalculus.com*) (Source: American Society of Animal Science)

(14, 81.2)	(28, 87.1)	(42, 93.7)
(56, 98.3)	(70, 102.4)	(84, 106.2)
(98, 110.0)		

(a) Use the *regression* feature of a graphing utility to find a linear model for the data and to identify the correlation coefficient.

(b) According to the correlation coefficient, does the model represent the data well? Explain.

(c) Use the graphing utility to plot the data and graph the model in the same viewing window. How closely does the model fit the data?

(d) Use the model to predict the average length of a colt 112 days after birth.

Conclusions

True or False? In Exercises 29 and 30, determine whether the statement is true or false. Justify your answer.

29. A linear regression model with a positive correlation will have a slope that is greater than 0.

30. When the correlation coefficient for a linear regression model is close to -1, the regression line is a poor fit for the data.

31. Writing Use your school's library, the Internet, or some other reference source to locate data that you think describe a linear relationship. Create a scatter plot of the data and find the least squares regression line that represents the points. Interpret the slope and y-intercept in the context of the data. Write a summary of your findings.

32. HOW DO YOU SEE IT? Each graphing utility screen below shows the least squares regression line for a set of data. The equations and r-values for the models are given.

$y = 0.68x + 2.7$ (i)
$y = 0.41x + 2.7$
$y = -0.62x + 10.0$

$r = 0.973$
$r = -0.986$
$r = 0.624$

(ii)   (iii)

(a) Determine the equation and correlation coefficient (r-value) that represent each graph. Explain how you found your answers.

(b) According to the correlation coefficients, which model is the best fit for its data? Explain.

Cumulative Mixed Review

Evaluating a Function In Exercises 33 and 34, evaluate the function at each value of the independent variable and simplify.

33. $f(x) = 2x^2 - 3x + 5$ **34.** $g(x) = 5x^2 - 6x + 1$
   (a) $f(-1)$ (a) $g(-2)$
   (b) $f(w + 2)$ (b) $g(z - 2)$

Solving Equations In Exercises 35–38, solve the equation algebraically. Check your solution graphically.

35. $6x + 1 = -9x - 8$ **36.** $3(x - 3) = 7x + 2$
37. $8x^2 - 10x - 3 = 0$ **38.** $10x^2 - 23x - 5 = 0$

1 Chapter Summary

	What did you learn?	Explanation and Examples	Review Exercises
1.1	Find the slopes of lines (*p. 3*).	The slope m of the nonvertical line through (x_1, y_1) and (x_2, y_2) is $m = \dfrac{y_2 - y_1}{x_2 - x_1}$, $x_1 \neq x_2$.	1–8
	Write linear equations given points on lines and their slopes (*p. 5*).	The point-slope form of the equation of the line that passes through the point (x_1, y_1) and has a slope of m is $y - y_1 = m(x - x_1)$.	9–16
	Use slope-intercept forms of linear equations to sketch lines (*p. 7*).	The graph of the equation $y = mx + b$ is a line whose slope is m and whose y-intercept is $(0, b)$.	17–30
	Use slope to identify parallel and perpendicular lines (*p. 9*).	**Parallel lines:** Slopes are equal. **Perpendicular lines:** Slopes are negative reciprocals of each other.	31, 32
1.2	Decide whether a relation between two variables represents a function (*p. 16*).	A function f from a set A to a set B is a relation that assigns to each element x in the set A exactly one element y in the set B. The set A is the domain (or set of inputs) of the function f, and the set B contains the range (or set of outputs).	33–42
	Use function notation and evaluate functions (*p. 18*), and find the domains of functions (*p. 20*).	**Equation:** $f(x) = 5 - x^2$ **$f(2)$:** $f(2) = 5 - 2^2 = 1$ **Domain of $f(x) = 5 - x^2$:** All real numbers x	43–50
	Use functions to model and solve real-life problems (*p. 22*).	A function can be used to model the number of interior design services employees in the United States. (See Example 8.)	51, 52
	Evaluate difference quotients (*p. 23*).	**Difference quotient:** $\dfrac{f(x + h) - f(x)}{h}$, $h \neq 0$	53, 54
1.3	Find the domains and ranges of functions (*p. 29*).		55–62
	Use the Vertical Line Test for functions (*p. 30*).	A set of points in a coordinate plane is the graph of y as a function of x if and only if no *vertical* line intersects the graph at more than one point.	63–66
	Determine intervals on which functions are increasing, decreasing, or constant (*p. 31*).	A function f is increasing on an interval when, for any x_1 and x_2 in the interval, $x_1 < x_2$ implies $f(x_1) < f(x_2)$. A function f is decreasing on an interval when, for any x_1 and x_2 in the interval, $x_1 < x_2$ implies $f(x_1) > f(x_2)$. A function f is constant on an interval when, for any x_1 and x_2 in the interval, $f(x_1) = f(x_2)$.	67–70

	What did you learn?	Explanation and Examples	Review Exercises
1.3	**Determine relative maximum and relative minimum values of functions** (p. 32).	A function value $f(a)$ is called a relative minimum of f when there exists an interval (x_1, x_2) that contains a such that $x_1 < x < x_2$ implies $f(a) \leq f(x)$. A function value $f(a)$ is called a relative maximum of f when there exists an interval (x_1, x_2) that contains a such that $x_1 < x < x_2$ implies $f(a) \geq f(x)$.	71–74
	Identify and graph step functions and other piecewise-defined functions (p. 34).	**Greatest integer:** $f(x) = [\![x]\!]$	75–78
	Identify even and odd functions (p. 35).	**Even:** For each x in the domain of f, $f(-x) = f(x)$. **Odd:** For each x in the domain of f, $f(-x) = -f(x)$.	79–86
1.4	**Recognize graphs of parent functions** (p. 41).	**Linear:** $f(x) = x$; **Quadratic:** $f(x) = x^2$; **Cubic:** $f(x) = x^3$; **Absolute value:** $f(x) = |x|$; **Square root:** $f(x) = \sqrt{x}$; **Rational:** $f(x) = 1/x$ (See Figure 1.24, page 41.)	87–92
	Use vertical and horizontal shifts (p. 42), **reflections** (p. 44), **and nonrigid transformations** (p. 46) **to graph functions.**	**Vertical shifts:** $h(x) = f(x) + c$ or $h(x) = f(x) - c$ **Horizontal shifts:** $h(x) = f(x - c)$ or $h(x) = f(x + c)$ **Reflection in the x-axis:** $h(x) = -f(x)$ **Reflection in the y-axis:** $h(x) = f(-x)$ **Nonrigid transformations:** $h(x) = cf(x)$ or $h(x) = f(cx)$	93–106
1.5	**Add, subtract, multiply, and divide functions** (p. 50), **find the compositions of functions** (p. 52), **and write a function as a composition of two functions** (p. 54).	$(f + g)(x) = f(x) + g(x)$ $(f - g)(x) = f(x) - g(x)$ $(fg)(x) = f(x) \cdot g(x)$ $(f/g)(x) = f(x)/g(x), g(x) \neq 0$ **Composition of functions:** $(f \circ g)(x) = f(g(x))$	107–122
	Use combinations of functions to model and solve real-life problems (p. 55).	A composite function can be used to represent the number of bacteria in a petri dish as a function of the amount of time the petri dish has been out of refrigeration. (See Example 10.)	123, 124
1.6	**Find inverse functions informally and verify that two functions are inverse functions of each other** (p. 60).	Let f and g be two functions such that $f(g(x)) = x$ for every x in the domain of g and $g(f(x)) = x$ for every x in the domain of f. Under these conditions, the function g is the inverse function of the function f.	125–128
	Use graphs of functions to decide whether functions have inverse functions (p. 63).	If the point (a, b) lies on the graph of f, then the point (b, a) must lie on the graph of f^{-1}, and vice versa. In short, f^{-1} is a reflection of f in the line $y = x$.	129, 130
	Determine whether functions are one-to-one (p. 64).	A function f is one-to-one when, for a and b in its domain, $f(a) = f(b)$ implies $a = b$.	131–134
	Find inverse functions algebraically (p. 65).	To find inverse functions, replace $f(x)$ with y, interchange the roles of x and y, and solve for y. Replace y with $f^{-1}(x)$.	135–142
1.7	**Construct scatter plots** (p. 71) **and interpret correlation** (p. 72).	A scatter plot is a graphical representation of data written as a set of ordered pairs.	143–146
	Use scatter plots (p. 73) **and a graphing utility** (p. 74) **to find linear models for data.**	The best-fitting linear model can be found using the *linear regression* feature of a graphing utility or a computer program.	147, 148

1.1

Finding the Slope of a Line   In Exercises 1–8, plot the two points and find the slope of the line passing through the points.

1. $(-3, 2), (8, 2)$

2. $(3, -1), (-3, -1)$

3. $(-5, -1), (-5, 9)$

4. $(8, -1), (8, 2)$

5. $\left(\frac{3}{2}, 1\right), \left(5, \frac{5}{2}\right)$

6. $\left(-\frac{3}{4}, \frac{5}{6}\right), \left(\frac{1}{2}, -\frac{5}{2}\right)$

7. $(-4.5, 6), (2.1, 3)$

8. $(-2.7, -6.3), (0, 1.8)$

The Point-Slope Form of the Equation of a Line   In Exercises 9–16, (a) use the point on the line and the slope of the line to find an equation of the line, and (b) find three additional points through which the line passes. (There are many correct answers.)

Point	Slope
9. $(2, -1)$	$m = \frac{1}{4}$
10. $(-3, 5)$	$m = -\frac{3}{2}$
11. $(0, -5)$	$m = -\frac{3}{2}$
12. $(0, 1)$	$m = \frac{4}{5}$
13. $(-2, 6)$	$m = 0$
14. $(-8, 8)$	$m = 0$
15. $(10, -6)$	m is undefined.
16. $(-5, 4)$	m is undefined.

Finding the Slope-Intercept Form   In Exercises 17–24, write an equation of the line that passes through the points. Use the slope-intercept form, if possible. If not possible, explain why. Use a graphing utility to graph the line (if possible).

17. $(2, -1), (4, -1)$

18. $(0, 0), (0, 10)$

19. $\left(\frac{5}{6}, -1\right), \left(\frac{5}{6}, 3\right)$

20. $\left(7, \frac{4}{3}\right), \left(9, \frac{4}{3}\right)$

21. $(-1, 0), (6, 2)$

22. $(1, 6), (4, 2)$

23. $(3, -1), (-3, 2)$

24. $\left(-\frac{5}{2}, 1\right), \left(-4, \frac{2}{9}\right)$

Using a Rate of Change to Write an Equation   In Exercises 25–28, you are given the dollar value of a product in 2015 *and* the rate at which the value of the item is expected to change during the next 5 years. Use this information to write a linear equation that gives the dollar value V of the product in terms of the year t. (Let $t = 5$ represent 2015.)

2015 Value	Rate
25. $12,500	$850 increase per year
26. $4025	$275 decrease per year
27. $625.50	$42.70 increase per year
28. $72.95	$5.15 decrease per year

29. **Business**   During the second and third quarters of the year, an e-commerce business had sales of $170,000 and $195,000, respectively. The growth of sales follows a linear pattern. Estimate sales during the fourth quarter.

30. **Accounting**   The dollar value of an MP3 player in 2015 is $285. The product will decrease in value at an expected rate of $47.50 per year.

    (a) Write a linear equation that gives the dollar value V of the MP3 player in terms of the year t. (Let $t = 0$ represent 2015.)

    (b) Use a graphing utility to graph the equation found in part (a). Be sure to choose an appropriate viewing window. State the dimensions of your viewing window and explain why you chose the values that you did.

    (c) Use the *value* or *trace* feature of the graphing utility to estimate the dollar value of the MP3 player in 2019. Confirm your answer algebraically.

    (d) According to the model, when will the MP3 player have no value?

Equations of Parallel and Perpendicular Lines   In Exercises 31 and 32, write the slope-intercept forms of the equations of the lines through the given point (a) parallel to the given line and (b) perpendicular to the given line. Verify your results with a graphing utility (use a *square setting*).

Point	Line
31. $(3, -2)$	$5x - 4y = 8$
32. $(-8, 3)$	$2x + 3y = 5$

1.2

Testing for Functions   In Exercises 33 and 34, which set of ordered pairs represents a function from A to B? Explain.

33. $A = \{10, 20, 30, 40\}$ and $B = \{0, 2, 4, 6\}$

    (a) $\{(20, 4), (40, 0), (20, 6), (30, 2)\}$

    (b) $\{(10, 4), (20, 4), (30, 4), (40, 4)\}$

34. $A = \{u, v, w\}$ and $B = \{-2, -1, 0, 1, 2\}$

    (a) $\{(u, -2), (v, 2), (w, 1)\}$

    (b) $\{(w, -2), (v, 0), (w, 2)\}$

Testing for Functions Represented Algebraically   In Exercises 35–42, determine whether the equation represents y as a function of x.

35. $16x^2 - y^2 = 0$

36. $x^3 + y^2 = 64$

37. $2x - y - 3 = 0$

38. $2x + y = 10$

39. $y = \sqrt{1 - x}$

40. $y = \sqrt{x^2 + 4}$

41. $|y| = x + 2$

42. $16 - |y| - 4x = 0$

Evaluating a Function In Exercises 43–46, evaluate the function at each specified value of the independent variable, and simplify.

43. $f(x) = x^2 + 1$

   (a) $f(1)$ (b) $f(-3)$

   (c) $f(b^3)$ (d) $f(x - 1)$

44. $g(x) = \sqrt{x^2 + 1}$

   (a) $g(-1)$ (b) $g(3)$

   (c) $g(3x)$ (d) $g(x + 2)$

45. $h(x) = \begin{cases} 2x + 1, & x \le -1 \\ x^2 + 2, & x > -1 \end{cases}$

   (a) $h(-2)$ (b) $h(-1)$

   (c) $h(0)$ (d) $h(2)$

46. $f(x) = \dfrac{3}{2x - 5}$

   (a) $f(1)$ (b) $f(-2)$

   (c) $f(t)$ (d) $f(10)$

Finding the Domain of a Function In Exercises 47–50, find the domain of the function.

47. $f(x) = \dfrac{x - 1}{x + 2}$ **48.** $f(x) = \dfrac{x^2}{x^2 + 1}$

49. $f(x) = \sqrt{25 - x^2}$ **50.** $f(x) = \sqrt{x^2 - 16}$

51. Industrial Engineering A hand tool manufacturer produces a product for which the variable cost is $5.25 per unit and the fixed costs are $17,500. The company sells the product for $8.43 and can sell all that it produces.

   (a) Write the total cost C as a function of x, the number of units produced.

   (b) Write the profit P as a function of x.

52. Education The numbers n (in millions) of students enrolled in public schools in the United States from 2005 through 2012 can be approximated by

$$n(t) = \begin{cases} -0.35t^3 + 6.95t^2 - 44.8t + 158, & 5 \le t \le 8 \\ -0.35t^2 + 7.7t + 26, & 8 < t \le 12 \end{cases}$$

where t is the year, with $t = 5$ corresponding to 2005. (Source: U.S. Census Bureau)

   (a) Use the *table* feature of a graphing utility to approximate the enrollment from 2005 through 2012.

   (b) Use the graphing utility to graph the model and estimate the enrollment for the years 2013 through 2017. Do the values seem reasonable? Explain.

Evaluating a Difference Quotient In Exercises 53 and 54, find the difference quotient $\dfrac{f(x + h) - f(x)}{h}$ for the given function and simplify your answer.

53. $f(x) = 2x^2 + 3x - 1$ **54.** $f(x) = x^2 - 3x + 5$

Finding the Domain and Range of a Function In Exercises 55–62, use a graphing utility to graph the function and estimate its domain and range. Then find the domain and range algebraically.

55. $f(x) = 3 - 2x^2$ **56.** $f(x) = 2x^2 + 5$

57. $f(x) = \sqrt{x + 3} + 4$ **58.** $f(x) = 2 - \sqrt{x - 5}$

59. $h(x) = \sqrt{36 - x^2}$ **60.** $f(x) = \sqrt{x^2 - 9}$

61. $f(x) = |x - 5| + 2$ **62.** $f(x) = |x + 1| - 3$

Vertical Line Test for Functions In Exercises 63–66, use the Vertical Line Test to determine whether y is a function of x. Describe how to enter the equation into a graphing utility to produce the given graph.

63. $y - 4x = x^2$ **64.** $|x + 5| - 2y = 0$

65. $3x + y^2 - 2 = 0$ **66.** $x^2 + y^2 - 49 = 0$

 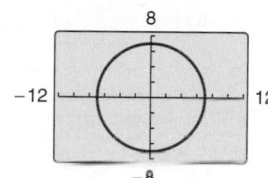

Increasing and Decreasing Functions In Exercises 67–70, (a) use a graphing utility to graph the function and (b) determine the open intervals on which the function is increasing, decreasing, or constant.

67. $f(x) = x^3 - 3x$ **68.** $f(x) = \sqrt{x^2 - 9}$

69. $f(x) = x\sqrt{x - 6}$ **70.** $f(x) = \dfrac{|x + 8|}{2}$

Approximating Relative Minima and Maxima In Exercises 71–74, use a graphing utility to approximate (to two decimal places) any relative minimum or relative maximum values of the function.

71. $f(x) = (x^2 - 4)^2$ **72.** $f(x) = x^2 + x$

73. $h(x) = x^3 + 4x^2 + 3$ **74.** $f(x) = x^3 - 4x^2 - 1$

Sketching Graphs In Exercises 75–78, sketch the graph of the function by hand.

75. $f(x) = \begin{cases} 3x + 5, & x < 0 \\ x - 4, & x \ge 0 \end{cases}$ **76.** $f(x) = \begin{cases} \frac{1}{2}x + 3, & x < 0 \\ 4 - x^2, & x \ge 0 \end{cases}$

77. $f(x) = \llbracket x \rrbracket - 3$ **78.** $f(x) = \llbracket x + 2 \rrbracket$

Even and Odd Functions In Exercises 79–86, determine algebraically whether the function is even, odd, or neither. Verify your answer using a graphing utility.

79. $f(x) = x^2 + 6$

80. $f(x) = x^2 - x - 1$

81. $f(x) = (x^2 - 8)^2$

82. $f(x) = 2x^3 - x$

83. $f(x) = 3x^{5/2}$

84. $f(x) = 3x^{2/5}$

85. $f(x) = 2x\sqrt{4 - x^2}$

86. $f(x) = x\sqrt{x^2 - 1}$

 1.4

Library of Parent Functions In Exercises 87–92, identify the parent function and describe the transformation shown in the graph. Write an equation for the graphed function.

87.

88.

89.

90.

91.

92.
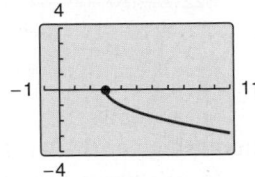

Sketching Transformations In Exercises 93–96, use the graph of $y = f(x)$ to graph the function.

93. $y = f(-x)$

94. $y = -f(x)$

95. $y = f(x) + 2$

96. $y = f(x - 1)$

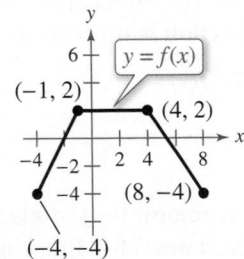

Describing Transformations In Exercises 97–106, h is related to one of the six parent functions on page 41. (a) Identify the parent function f. (b) Describe the sequence of transformations from f to h. (c) Sketch the graph of h by hand. (d) Use function notation to write h in terms of the parent function f.

97. $h(x) = \dfrac{1}{x} - 6$

98. $h(x) = -\dfrac{1}{x} + 3$

99. $h(x) = (x - 2)^3 + 5$

100. $h(x) = (-x)^2 - 8$

101. $h(x) = -\sqrt{x} - 6$

102. $h(x) = \sqrt{x - 1} + 4$

103. $h(x) = |3x| + 9$

104. $h(x) = |2x + 8| - 1$

105. $h(x) = \dfrac{-2}{x + 1} - 3$

106. $h(x) = \dfrac{5}{x + 2} - 4$

1.5

Evaluating a Combination of Functions In Exercises 107–116, let $f(x) = 3 - 2x$, $g(x) = \sqrt{x}$, and $h(x) = 3x^2 + 2$, and find the indicated values.

107. $(f - g)(4)$

108. $(f + h)(5)$

109. $(f + g)(25)$

110. $(g - h)(1)$

111. $(fh)(1)$

112. $\left(\dfrac{g}{h}\right)(1)$

113. $(h \circ g)(5)$

114. $(g \circ f)(-3)$

115. $(f \circ h)(-4)$

116. $(g \circ h)(6)$

Identifying a Composite Function In Exercises 117–122, find two functions f and g such that $(f \circ g)(x) = h(x)$. (There are many correct answers.)

117. $h(x) = (x + 3)^2$

118. $h(x) = (1 - 2x)^3$

119. $h(x) = \sqrt{4x + 2}$

120. $h(x) = \sqrt[3]{(x + 2)^2}$

121. $h(x) = \dfrac{4}{x + 2}$

122. $h(x) = \dfrac{6}{(3x + 1)^3}$

Education In Exercises 123 and 124, the numbers (in thousands) of students taking the SAT (y_1) and the ACT (y_2) for the years 2008 through 2013 can be modeled by

$$y_1 = -5.824t^3 + 182.05t^2 - 1832.8t + 7515 \text{ and}$$

$$y_2 = 3.398t^3 - 103.63t^2 + 1106.5t - 2543$$

where t represents the year, with $t = 8$ corresponding to 2008. (Sources: College Entrance Examination Board and ACT, Inc.)

123. Use a graphing utility to graph y_1, y_2, and $y_1 + y_2$ in the same viewing window.

124. Use the model $y_1 + y_2$ to estimate the total number of students taking the SAT and the ACT in 2017.

1.6

Finding Inverse Functions Informally In Exercises 125–128, find the inverse function of f informally. Verify that $f(f^{-1}(x)) = x$ and $f^{-1}(f(x)) = x$.

125. $f(x) = 6x$

126. $f(x) = x + 5$

127. $f(x) = \dfrac{1}{2}x + 3$

128. $f(x) = \dfrac{x - 4}{5}$

Algebraic-Graphical-Numerical In Exercises 129 and 130, show that f and g are inverse functions (a) algebraically, (b) graphically, and (c) numerically.

129. $f(x) = 3 - 4x$, $g(x) = \dfrac{3 - x}{4}$

130. $f(x) = \sqrt{x + 1}$; $g(x) = x^2 - 1$, $x \geq 0$

Using the Horizontal Line Test In Exercises 131–134, use a graphing utility to graph the function and use the Horizontal Line Test to determine whether the function is one-to-one and an inverse function exists.

131. $f(x) = \frac{1}{2}x - 3$

132. $f(x) = (x - 1)^2$

133. $h(t) = (t + 5)^{2/3}$

134. $g(x) = \dfrac{5}{x - 4}$

Finding an Inverse Function Algebraically In Exercises 135–142, find the inverse function of f algebraically.

135. $f(x) = \frac{1}{2}x - 5$ **136.** $f(x) = \dfrac{7x + 3}{8}$

137. $f(x) = -5x^3 - 3$ **138.** $f(x) = 5x^3 + 2$

139. $f(x) = \sqrt{x + 10}$ **140.** $f(x) = 4\sqrt{6 - x}$

141. $f(x) = \frac{1}{4}x^2 + 1, \quad x \geq 0$

142. $f(x) = 5 - \frac{1}{9}x^2, \quad x \leq 0$

 1.7

Interpreting Correlation In Exercises 143 and 144, the scatter plot of a set of data is shown. Determine whether the points are positively correlated, are negatively correlated, or have no discernible correlation.

143.

144.

145. Education The following ordered pairs give the entrance exam scores x and the grade-point averages y after 1 year of college for 10 students. *(Spreadsheet at LarsonPrecalculus.com)*

 (75, 2.3), (82, 3.0), (90, 3.6), (65, 2.0), (70, 2.1), (88, 3.5), (93, 3.9), (69, 2.0), (80, 2.8), (85, 3.3)

(a) Create a scatter plot of the data.

(b) Does the relationship between x and y appear to be approximately linear? Explain.

146. Industrial Engineering A machine part was tested by bending it x centimeters 10 times per minute until it failed (y equals the time to failure in hours). The results are given as the following ordered pairs. *(Spreadsheet at LarsonPrecalculus.com)*

 (3, 61), (6, 56), (9, 53), (12, 55), (15, 48), (18, 35), (21, 36), (24, 33), (27, 44), (30, 23)

(a) Create a scatter plot of the data.

(b) Does the relationship between x and y appear to be approximately linear? If not, give some possible explanations.

147. MODELING DATA

In an experiment, students measured the speed s (in meters per second) of a ball t seconds after it was released. The results are shown in the table.

Time, t	Speed, s
0	0
1	11.0
2	19.4
3	29.2
4	39.4

(a) Sketch a scatter plot of the data.

(b) Find an equation of a line that seems to fit the data best.

(c) Use the *regression* feature of a graphing utility to find a linear model for the data and identify the correlation coefficient.

(d) Use the model from part (c) to estimate the speed of the ball after 2.5 seconds.

148. MODELING DATA

The following ordered pairs (x, y) represent the Olympic year x and the winning time y (in minutes) in the men's 400-meter freestyle swimming event. *(Spreadsheet at LarsonPrecalculus.com)* (Source: International Olympic Committee)

(1968, 4.150) (1984, 3.854) (2000, 3.677)

(1972, 4.005) (1988, 3.783) (2004, 3.718)

(1976, 3.866) (1992, 3.750) (2008, 3.698)

(1980, 3.855) (1996, 3.800) (2012, 3.669)

(a) Use the *regression* feature of a graphing utility to find a linear model for the data. Let x represent the year, with $x = 8$ corresponding to 1968.

(b) Use the graphing utility to create a scatter plot of the data. Graph the model in the same viewing window.

(c) Is the model a good fit for the data? Explain.

(d) Is this model appropriate for predicting the winning times in future Olympics? Explain.

Conclusions

True or False? In Exercises 149–151, determine whether the statement is true or false. Justify your answer.

149. If the graph of the parent function $f(x) = x^2$ is moved six units to the right, moved three units upward, and reflected in the x-axis, then the point $(-1, 28)$ will lie on the graph of the transformation.

150. If $f(x) = x^n$ where n is odd, then f^{-1} exists.

151. There exists no function f such that $f = f^{-1}$.

1 Chapter Test

See *CalcChat.com* for tutorial help and worked-out solutions to odd-numbered exercises.
For instructions on how to use a graphing utility, see Appendix A.

Take this test as you would take a test in class. After you are finished, check your work against the answers given in the back of the book.

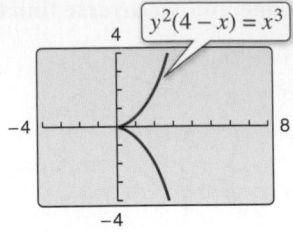

Figure for 3

1. Find the equations of the lines that pass through the point $(0, 4)$ and are (a) parallel to and (b) perpendicular to the line $5x + 2y = 3$.

2. Find the slope-intercept form of the equation of the line that passes through the points $(2, -1)$ and $(-3, 4)$.

3. Does the graph at the right represent y as a function of x? Explain.

4. Evaluate $f(x) = |x + 2| - 15$ at each value of the independent variable and simplify.

   (a) $f(-8)$ (b) $f(14)$ (c) $f(t - 6)$

5. Find the domain of $f(x) = 10 - \sqrt{3 - x}$.

6. An electronics company produces a car stereo for which the variable cost is \$24.60 per unit and the fixed costs are \$25,000. The product sells for \$101.50. Write the total cost C as a function of the number of units produced and sold, x. Write the profit P as a function of the number of units produced and sold, x.

In Exercises 7 and 8, determine algebraically whether the function is even, odd, or neither.

7. $f(x) = 2x^3 - 3x$ 8. $f(x) = 3x^4 + 5x^2$

In Exercises 9 and 10, determine the open intervals on which the function is increasing, decreasing, or constant.

9. $h(x) = \frac{1}{4}x^4 - 2x^2$ 10. $g(t) = |t + 2| - |t - 2|$

In Exercises 11 and 12, use a graphing utility to graph the functions and to approximate (to two decimal places) any relative minimum or relative maximum values of the function.

11. $f(x) = -x^3 - 5x^2 + 12$ 12. $f(x) = x^5 - 3x^3 + 4$

In Exercises 13–15, (a) identify the parent function f, (b) describe the sequence of transformations from f to g, and (c) sketch the graph of g.

13. $g(x) = -2(x - 5)^3 + 3$ 14. $g(x) = \sqrt{-7x - 14}$ 15. $g(x) = 4|-x| - 7$

16. Use the functions $f(x) = x^2$ and $g(x) = \sqrt{2 - x}$ to find the specified function and its domain.

   (a) $(f - g)(x)$ (b) $\left(\dfrac{f}{g}\right)(x)$ (c) $(f \circ g)(x)$ (d) $(g \circ f)(x)$

In Exercises 17–19, determine whether the function has an inverse function, and if so, find the inverse function.

17. $f(x) = x^3 + 8$ 18. $f(x) = x^2 + 6$ 19. $f(x) = \dfrac{3x\sqrt{x}}{8}$

Year, t	Average monthly cost, C (in dollars)
4	41.04
5	43.04
6	45.26
7	47.27
8	49.65
9	52.37
10	54.44
11	57.46
12	61.63

Spreadsheet at LarsonPrecalculus.com

Table for 20

20. The table shows the average monthly costs C of expanded basic cable television from 2004 through 2012, where t represents the year, with $t = 4$ corresponding to 2004. Use the *regression* feature of a graphing utility to find a linear model for the data. Use the model to estimate the year in which the average monthly cost reached \$85.   (Source: Federal Communications Commission)

Proofs in Mathematics

Conditional Statements

Many theorems are written in the **if-then form** "if p, then q," which is denoted by

$p \rightarrow q$ Conditional statement

where p is the **hypothesis** and q is the **conclusion.** Here are some other ways to express the conditional statement $p \rightarrow q$.

p implies q. p, only if q. p is sufficient for q.

Conditional statements can be either true or false. The conditional statement $p \rightarrow q$ is false only when p is true and q is false. To show that a conditional statement is true, you must prove that the conclusion follows for all cases that fulfill the hypothesis. To show that a conditional statement is false, you need to describe only a single **counterexample** that shows that the statement is not always true.

For instance, $x = -4$ is a counterexample that shows that the following statement is false.

If $x^2 = 16$, then $x = 4$.

The hypothesis "$x^2 = 16$" is true because $(-4)^2 = 16$. However, the conclusion "$x = 4$" is false. This implies that the given conditional statement is false.

For the conditional statement $p \rightarrow q$, there are three important associated conditional statements.

1. The **converse** of $p \rightarrow q$: $q \rightarrow p$

2. The **inverse** of $p \rightarrow q$: $\sim p \rightarrow \sim q$

3. The **contrapositive** of $p \rightarrow q$: $\sim q \rightarrow \sim p$

The symbol $\sim$ means the **negation** of a statement. For instance, the negation of "The engine is running" is "The engine is not running."

EXAMPLE 1   Writing the Converse, Inverse, and Contrapositive

Write the converse, inverse, and contrapositive of the conditional statement "If I get a B on my test, then I will pass the course."

Solution

a. *Converse:* If I pass the course, then I got a B on my test.

b. *Inverse:* If I do not get a B on my test, then I will not pass the course.

c. *Contrapositive:* If I do not pass the course, then I did not get a B on my test.

In the example above, notice that neither the converse nor the inverse is logically equivalent to the original conditional statement. On the other hand, the contrapositive is logically equivalent to the original conditional statement.

Biconditional Statements

Recall that a conditional statement is a statement of the form "if p, then q." A statement of the form "p if and only if q" is called a **biconditional statement.** A biconditional statement, denoted by

$$p \leftrightarrow q \qquad \text{Biconditional statement}$$

is the conjunction of the conditional statement $p \rightarrow q$ and its converse $q \rightarrow p$.

A biconditional statement can be either true or false. To be true, *both* the conditional statement and its converse must be true.

EXAMPLE 2   Analyzing a Biconditional Statement

Consider the statement $x = 3$ if and only if $x^2 = 9$.

a. Is the statement a biconditional statement?

b. Is the statement true?

Solution

a. The statement is a biconditional statement because it is of the form "p if and only if q."

b. The statement can be rewritten as the following conditional statement and its converse.

> *Conditional statement:* If $x = 3$, then $x^2 = 9$.

> *Converse:* If $x^2 = 9$, then $x = 3$.

The first of these statements is true, but the second is false because x could also equal -3. So, the biconditional statement is false. ■

Knowing how to use biconditional statements is an important tool for reasoning in mathematics.

EXAMPLE 3   Analyzing a Biconditional Statement

Determine whether the biconditional statement is true or false. If it is false, provide a counterexample.
    A number is divisible by 5 if and only if it ends in 0.

Solution

The biconditional statement can be rewritten as the following conditional statement and its converse.

> *Conditional statement:* If a number is divisible by 5, then it ends in 0.

> *Converse:* If a number ends in 0, then it is divisible by 5.

The conditional statement is false. A counterexample is the number 15, which is divisible by 5 but does not end in 0. So, the biconditional statement is false. ■

2 Polynomial and Rational Functions

$$y = 0.107x^2 - 0.16x + 74.6$$

Section 2.8, Example 4
People Not in the
U.S. Labor Force

2.1   Quadratic Functions

2.2   Polynomial Functions of Higher Degree

2.3   Real Zeros of Polynomial Functions

2.4   Complex Numbers

2.5   The Fundamental Theorem of Algebra

2.6   Rational Functions and Asymptotes

2.7   Graphs of Rational Functions

2.8   Quadratic Models

2.1 Quadratic Functions

The Graph of a Quadratic Function

In this and the next section, you will study the graphs of polynomial functions.

What you should learn
► Analyze graphs of quadratic functions.
► Write quadratic functions in standard form and use the results to sketch graphs of functions.
► Find minimum and maximum values of quadratic functions in real-life applications.

Why you should learn it
Quadratic functions can be used to model the design of a room. For instance, Exercise 63 on page 97 shows how the size of an indoor fitness room with a running track can be modeled.

> **Definition of Polynomial Function**
>
> Let n be a nonnegative integer and let $a_n, a_{n-1}, \ldots a_2, a_1, a_0$ be real numbers with $a_n \neq 0$. The function given by
>
> $$f(x) = a_n x^n + a_{n-1} x^{n-1} + \cdots + a_2 x^2 + a_1 x + a_0$$
>
> is called a **polynomial function of x with degree n.**

Polynomial functions are classified by degree. For instance, the polynomial function

$$f(x) = a, \quad a \neq 0 \qquad \text{Constant function}$$

has degree 0 and is called a **constant function.** In Chapter 1, you learned that the graph of this type of function is a horizontal line. The polynomial function

$$f(x) = mx + b, \quad m \neq 0 \qquad \text{Linear function}$$

has degree 1 and is called a **linear function.** You learned in Chapter 1 that the graph of $f(x) = mx + b$ is a line whose slope is m and whose y-intercept is $(0, b)$. In this section, you will study second-degree polynomial functions, which are called **quadratic functions.**

> **Definition of Quadratic Function**
>
> Let a, b, and c be real numbers with $a \neq 0$. The function given by
>
> $$f(x) = ax^2 + bx + c \qquad \text{Quadratic function}$$
>
> is called a **quadratic function.**

Often real-life data can be modeled by quadratic functions. For instance, the table at the right shows the height h (in feet) of a projectile fired from a height of 6 feet with an initial velocity of 256 feet per second at any time t (in seconds). A quadratic model for the data in the table is

$$h(t) = -16t^2 + 256t + 6 \quad \text{for} \quad 0 \leq t \leq 16.$$

Time, (in seconds) t	Height, (in feet) h
0	6
2	454
4	774
6	966
8	1030
10	966
12	774
14	454
16	6

The graph of a quadratic function is a special type of U-shaped curve called a **parabola.** Parabolas occur in many real-life applications, especially those involving reflective properties, such as satellite dishes or flashlight reflectors. You will study these properties in a later chapter.

All parabolas are symmetric with respect to a line called the **axis of symmetry,** or simply the **axis** of the parabola. The point where the axis intersects the parabola is called the **vertex** of the parabola. These and other basic characteristics of quadratic functions are summarized on the next page.

Basic Characteristics of Quadratic Functions

Graph of $f(x) = ax^2, a > 0$
Domain: $(-\infty, \infty)$
Range: $[0, \infty)$
Intercept: $(0, 0)$
Decreasing on $(-\infty, 0)$
Increasing on $(0, \infty)$
Even function
Axis of symmetry: $x = 0$
Relative minimum or vertex: $(0, 0)$

Graph of $f(x) = ax^2, a < 0$
Domain: $(-\infty, \infty)$
Range: $(-\infty, 0]$
Intercept: $(0, 0)$
Increasing on $(-\infty, 0)$
Decreasing on $(0, \infty)$
Even function
Axis of symmetry: $x = 0$
Relative maximum or vertex: $(0, 0)$

 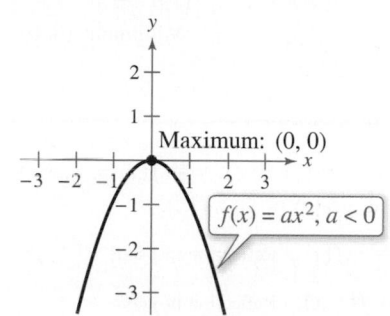

For the general quadratic form $f(x) = ax^2 + bx + c$, when the leading coefficient a is positive, the parabola opens upward; and when the leading coefficient a is negative, the parabola opens downward. Later in this section you will learn ways to find the coordinates of the vertex of a parabola.

 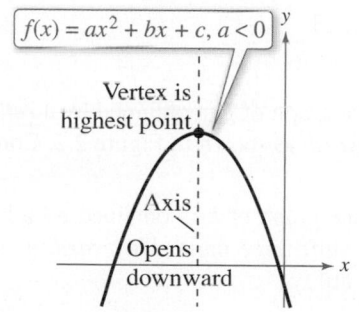

When sketching the graph of $f(x) = ax^2$, it is helpful to use the graph of $y = x^2$ as a reference, as discussed in Section 1.4. There you saw that when $a > 1$, the graph of $y = af(x)$ is a vertical stretch of the graph of $y = f(x)$. When $0 < a < 1$, the graph of $y = af(x)$ is a vertical shrink of the graph of $y = f(x)$. Notice in Figure 2.1 that the coefficient a determines how widely the parabola given by $f(x) = ax^2$ opens. When $|a|$ is small, the parabola opens more widely than when $|a|$ is large.

 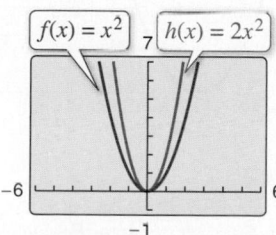

Vertical shrink
Figure 2.1

Vertical stretch

Library of Parent Functions: Quadratic Functions

The *parent quadratic function* is $f(x) = x^2$, also known as the *squaring function*. The basic characteristics of the parent quadratic function are summarized below and on the inside cover of this text.

Graph of $f(x) = x^2$

Domain: $(-\infty, \infty)$
Range: $[0, \infty)$
Intercept: $(0, 0)$
Decreasing on $(-\infty, 0)$
Increasing on $(0, \infty)$
Even function
Axis of symmetry: $x = 0$
Relative minimum or vertex: $(0, 0)$

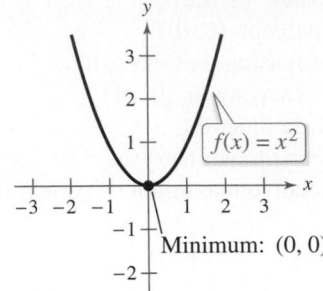

Recall from Section 1.4 that the graphs of $y = f(x \pm c)$, $y = f(x) \pm c$, $y = -f(x)$, and $y = f(-x)$ are rigid transformations of the graph of $y = f(x)$.

$y = f(x \pm c)$ Horizontal shift $y = -f(x)$ Reflection in x-axis

$y = f(x) \pm c$ Vertical shift $y = f(-x)$ Reflection in y-axis

EXAMPLE 1   Library of Parent Functions: $f(x) = x^2$

See LarsonPrecalculus.com for an interactive version of this type of example.

Sketch the graph of each function by hand and compare it with the graph of $f(x) = x^2$.

a. $g(x) = -x^2 + 1$ **b.** $h(x) = (x + 2)^2 - 3$

Solution

a. With respect to the graph of $f(x) = x^2$, the graph of g is obtained by a *reflection* in the x-axis and a vertical shift one unit *upward*, as shown in Figure 2.2. Confirm this with a graphing utility.

b. With respect to the graph of $f(x) = x^2$, the graph of h is obtained by a horizontal shift two units *to the left* and a vertical shift three units *downward*, as shown in Figure 2.3. Confirm this with a graphing utility.

Figure 2.2

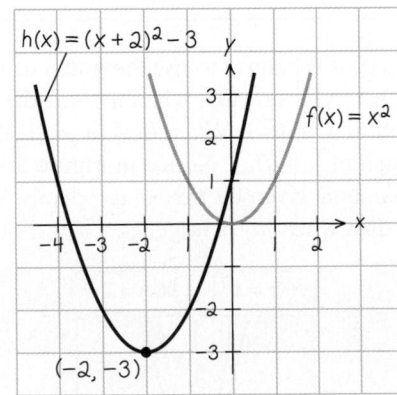

Figure 2.3

✓ *Checkpoint* 🔊))) Audio-video solution in English & Spanish at LarsonPrecalculus.com.

Sketch the graph of each function by hand and compare it with the graph of $f(x) = x^2$.

a. $g(x) = x^2 - 4$ **b.** $h(x) = (x - 3)^2 + 1$

The Standard Form of a Quadratic Function

The equation in Example 1(b) is written in the **standard form**

$$f(x) = a(x - h)^2 + k.$$

This form is especially convenient for sketching a parabola because it identifies the vertex of the parabola as (h, k).

> **Standard Form of a Quadratic Function**
>
> The quadratic function given by
>
> $$f(x) = a(x - h)^2 + k, \quad a \neq 0$$
>
> is in **standard form.** The graph of f is a parabola whose axis is the vertical line $x = h$ and whose vertex is the point (h, k). When $a > 0$, the parabola opens upward, and when $a < 0$, the parabola opens downward.

EXAMPLE 2   Identifying the Vertex of a Quadratic Function

Describe the graph of

$$f(x) = 2x^2 + 8x + 7$$

and identify the vertex.

Solution

Write the quadratic function in standard form by completing the square. Recall that the first step is to factor out any coefficient of x^2 that is not 1.

$$f(x) = 2x^2 + 8x + 7 \qquad \text{Write original function.}$$
$$= (2x^2 + 8x) + 7 \qquad \text{Group } x\text{-terms.}$$
$$= 2(x^2 + 4x) + 7 \qquad \text{Factor 2 out of } x\text{-terms.}$$
$$= 2(x^2 + 4x + 4 - 4) + 7 \qquad \begin{array}{l}\text{Add and subtract } (4/2)^2 = 4 \\ \text{within parentheses to complete} \\ \text{the square.}\end{array}$$

$$\underbrace{\qquad}_{(4/2)^2}$$

$$= 2(x^2 + 4x + 4) - 2(4) + 7 \qquad \text{Regroup terms.}$$
$$= 2(x + 2)^2 - 1 \qquad \text{Write in standard form.}$$

From the standard form, you can see that the graph of f is a parabola that opens upward with vertex

$$(-2, -1)$$

as shown in the figure. This corresponds to a left shift of two units and a downward shift of one unit relative to the graph of

$$y = 2x^2.$$

$f(x) = 2x^2 + 8x + 7$

$(-2, -1)$

✓ **Checkpoint** Audio-video solution in English & Spanish at LarsonPrecalculus.com.

Describe the graph of $f(x) = 3x^2 - 6x + 4$ and identify the vertex. ■

To find the x-intercepts of the graph of $f(x) = ax^2 + bx + c$, solve the equation $ax^2 + bx + c = 0$. When $ax^2 + bx + c$ does not factor, you can use the Quadratic Formula to find the x-intercepts, or a graphing utility to approximate the x-intercepts. Remember, however, that a parabola may not have x-intercepts.

Explore the Concept

Use a graphing utility to graph $y = ax^2$ with $a = -2, -1,$ $-0.5, 0.5, 1,$ and 2. How does changing the value of a affect the graph?

Use a graphing utility to graph $y = (x - h)^2$ with $h = -4, -2, 2,$ and 4. How does changing the value of h affect the graph?

Use a graphing utility to graph $y = x^2 + k$ with $k = -4, -2, 2,$ and 4. How does changing the value of k affect the graph?

EXAMPLE 3   Identifying *x*-Intercepts of a Quadratic Function

Describe the graph of $f(x) = -x^2 + 6x - 8$ and identify any *x*-intercepts.

Solution

$$f(x) = -x^2 + 6x - 8 \qquad \text{Write original function.}$$

$$= -(x^2 - 6x) - 8 \qquad \text{Factor } -1 \text{ out of } x\text{-terms.}$$

$$= -(x^2 - 6x + 9 - 9) - 8 \qquad \begin{array}{l}\text{Add and subtract } (-6/2)^2 = 9 \\ \text{within parentheses.}\end{array}$$

$$(-6/2)^2$$

$$= -(x^2 - 6x + 9) - (-9) - 8 \qquad \text{Regroup terms.}$$

$$= -(x - 3)^2 + 1 \qquad \text{Write in standard form.}$$

The graph of f is a parabola that opens downward with vertex $(3, 1)$, as shown in Figure 2.4. The *x*-intercepts are determined as follows.

$$-(x^2 - 6x + 8) = 0 \qquad \text{Factor out } -1.$$

$$-(x - 2)(x - 4) = 0 \qquad \text{Factor.}$$

$$x - 2 = 0 \implies x = 2 \qquad \text{Set 1st factor equal to 0.}$$

$$x - 4 = 0 \implies x = 4 \qquad \text{Set 2nd factor equal to 0.}$$

So, the *x*-intercepts are $(2, 0)$ and $(4, 0)$, as shown in Figure 2.4.

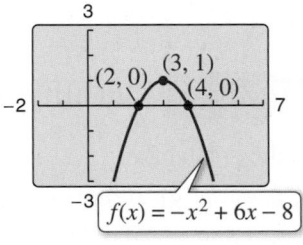

Figure 2.4

✓ *Checkpoint* ◀))) *Audio-video solution in English & Spanish at LarsonPrecalculus.com.*

Describe the graph of $f(x) = x^2 - 4x + 3$ and identify any *x*-intercepts.

EXAMPLE 4   Writing the Equation of a Parabola

Write the standard form of the equation of the parabola whose vertex is $(1, 2)$ and that passes through the point $(3, -6)$.

Solution

Because the vertex of the parabola is $(h, k) = (1, 2)$, the equation has the form

$$f(x) = a(x - 1)^2 + 2. \qquad \text{Substitute for } h \text{ and } k \text{ in standard form.}$$

Because the parabola passes through the point $(3, -6)$, it follows that $f(3) = -6$. So, you obtain

$$f(x) = a(x - 1)^2 + 2 \qquad \text{Write in standard form.}$$

$$-6 = a(3 - 1)^2 + 2 \qquad \text{Substitute } -6 \text{ for } f(x) \text{ and 3 for } x.$$

$$-6 = 4a + 2 \qquad \text{Simplify.}$$

$$-8 = 4a \qquad \text{Subtract 2 from each side.}$$

$$-2 = a. \qquad \text{Divide each side by 4.}$$

The equation in standard form is $f(x) = -2(x - 1)^2 + 2$. You can confirm this answer by graphing f with a graphing utility, as shown in Figure 2.5. Use the *zoom* and *trace* features or the *maximum* and *value* features to confirm that its vertex is $(1, 2)$ and that it passes through the point $(3, -6)$.

> **Remark**
>
> In Example 4, there are infinitely many different parabolas that have a vertex at $(1, 2)$. Of these, however, the only one that passes through the point $(3, -6)$ is the one given by
>
> $$f(x) = -2(x - 1)^2 + 2.$$

Figure 2.5

✓ *Checkpoint* ◀))) *Audio-video solution in English & Spanish at LarsonPrecalculus.com.*

Write the standard form of the equation of the parabola whose vertex is $(-4, 11)$ and that passes through the point $(-6, 15)$.

Finding Minimum and Maximum Values

Many applications involve finding the maximum or minimum value of a quadratic function. By completing the square of the quadratic function $f(x) = ax^2 + bx + c$, you can rewrite the function in standard form.

$$f(x) = a\left(x + \frac{b}{2a}\right)^2 + \left(c - \frac{b^2}{4a}\right) \qquad \text{Standard form}$$

So, the vertex of the graph of f is $\left(-\frac{b}{2a}, f\left(-\frac{b}{2a}\right)\right)$, which implies the following.

Minimum and Maximum Values of Quadratic Functions

Consider the function $f(x) = ax^2 + bx + c$ with vertex $\left(-\frac{b}{2a}, f\left(-\frac{b}{2a}\right)\right)$.

1. If $a > 0$, then f has a *minimum* at $x = -\frac{b}{2a}$.

   The minimum value is $f\left(-\frac{b}{2a}\right)$.

2. If $a < 0$, then f has a *maximum* at $x = -\frac{b}{2a}$.

   The maximum value is $f\left(-\frac{b}{2a}\right)$.

EXAMPLE 5   The Maximum Height of a Projectile

The path of a baseball is given by the function $f(x) = -0.0032x^2 + x + 3$, where $f(x)$ is the height of the baseball (in feet) and x is the horizontal distance from home plate (in feet). What is the maximum height reached by the baseball?

Algebraic Solution

For this quadratic function, you have

$$f(x) = ax^2 + bx + c = -0.0032x^2 + x + 3$$

which implies that $a = -0.0032$ and $b = 1$. Because the function has a maximum when $x = -b/(2a)$, you can conclude that the baseball reaches its maximum height when it is x feet from home plate, where x is

$$x = -\frac{b}{2a}$$

$$= -\frac{1}{2(-0.0032)}$$

$$= 156.25 \text{ feet.}$$

At this distance, the maximum height is

$$f(156.25) = -0.0032(156.25)^2 + 156.25 + 3$$

$$= 81.125 \text{ feet.}$$

Graphical Solution

The maximum height is $y \approx 81.125$ feet at $x \approx 156.25$ feet.

✓ **Checkpoint**))) *Audio-video solution in English & Spanish at LarsonPrecalculus.com.*

Rework Example 5 when the path of the baseball is given by the function

$$f(x) = -0.007x^2 + x + 4.$$

2.1   Exercises

See *CalcChat.com* for tutorial help and worked-out solutions to odd-numbered exercises.
For instructions on how to use a graphing utility, see Appendix A.

Vocabulary and Concept Check

In Exercises 1 and 2, fill in the blanks.

1. A polynomial function with degree n and leading coefficient a_n is a function of the form $f(x) = a_n x^n + a_{n-1} x^{n-1} + \cdots + a_2 x^2 + a_1 x + a_0,\ a_n \neq 0$, where n is a _____ and $a_n, a_{n-1}, \ldots, a_2, a_1, a_0$ are _____ numbers.

2. A _____ function is a second-degree polynomial function, and its graph is called a _____ .

3. Is the quadratic function $f(x) = (x - 2)^2 + 3$ written in standard form? Identify the vertex of the graph of f.

4. Does the graph of the quadratic function $f(x) = -3x^2 + 5x + 2$ have a relative minimum value at its vertex?

Procedures and Problem Solving

Graphs of Quadratic Functions   In Exercises 5–8, match the quadratic function with its graph. [The graphs are labeled (a), (b), (c), and (d).]

(a)

(b)

(c)

(d)

5. $f(x) = (x - 2)^2$

6. $f(x) = 3 - x^2$

7. $f(x) = x^2 + 3$

8. $f(x) = -(x - 4)^2$

Library of Parent Functions   In Exercises 9–16, sketch the graph of the function and compare it with the graph of $y = x^2$.

9. $y = -x^2$

10. $y = x^2 - 1$

11. $y = (x + 3)^2$

12. $y = -(x + 3)^2 - 1$

13. $y = (x + 1)^2$

14. $y = -x^2 + 2$

15. $y = (x - 3)^2$

16. $y = -(x - 3)^2 + 1$

Identifying the Vertex of a Quadratic Function   In Exercises 17–30, describe the graph of the function and identify the vertex. Use a graphing utility to verify your results.

17. $f(x) = 20 - x^2$

18. $f(x) = x^2 + 8$

19. $f(x) = \frac{1}{2}x^2 - 5$

20. $f(x) = -6 - \frac{1}{4}x^2$

21. $f(x) = (x + 3)^2 - 4$

22. $f(x) = (x - 7)^2 + 2$

23. $h(x) = x^2 - 2x + 1$

24. $g(x) = x^2 + 16x + 64$

25. $f(x) = x^2 - x + \frac{5}{4}$

26. $f(x) = x^2 + 3x + \frac{1}{4}$

27. $f(x) = -x^2 + 2x + 5$

28. $f(x) = -x^2 - 4x + 1$

29. $h(x) = 4x^2 - 4x + 21$

30. $f(x) = 2x^2 - x + 1$

Identifying x-Intercepts of a Quadratic Function   In Exercises 31–36, describe the graph of the quadratic function. Identify the vertex and x-intercept(s). Use a graphing utility to verify your results.

31. $g(x) = x^2 + 8x + 11$

32. $f(x) = x^2 + 10x + 14$

33. $f(x) = -(x^2 - 2x - 15)$

34. $f(x) = -(x^2 + 3x - 4)$

35. $f(x) = -2x^2 + 16x - 31$

36. $f(x) = -4x^2 + 24x - 41$

Writing the Equation of a Parabola in Standard Form   In Exercises 37 and 38, write an equation of the parabola in standard form. Use a graphing utility to graph the equation and verify your result.

37.

38.

Writing the Equation of a Parabola in Standard Form In Exercises 39–44, write the standard form of the quadratic function that has the indicated vertex and whose graph passes through the given point. Use a graphing utility to verify your result.

39. Vertex: $(-2, 5)$;   Point: $(0, 9)$

40. Vertex: $(4, 1)$;   Point: $(6, -7)$

41. Vertex: $(1, -2)$;   Point: $(-1, 14)$

42. Vertex: $(-4, -1)$;   Point: $(-2, 4)$

43. Vertex: $\left(\frac{1}{2}, 1\right)$;   Point: $\left(-2, -\frac{21}{5}\right)$

44. Vertex: $\left(-\frac{1}{4}, -1\right)$;   Point: $\left(0, -\frac{17}{16}\right)$

Using a Graph to Identify x-Intercepts In Exercises 45–48, determine the x-intercept(s) of the graph visually. Then find the x-intercept(s) algebraically to verify your answer.

45.

$y = x^2 - 4x - 5$

46.

$y = 2x^2 + 5x - 3$

47.

$y = x^2 + 8x + 16$

48.

$y = x^2 - 6x + 9$

Graphing to Identify x-Intercepts In Exercises 49–54, use a graphing utility to graph the quadratic function and find the x-intercepts of the graph. Then find the x-intercepts algebraically to verify your answer.

49. $y = x^2 - 4x$

50. $y = -2x^2 + 10x$

51. $y = 2x^2 - 7x - 30$

52. $y = 4x^2 + 25x - 21$

53. $y = -\frac{1}{2}(x^2 - 6x - 7)$

54. $y = \frac{7}{10}(x^2 + 12x - 45)$

Using the x-Intercepts to Write Equations In Exercises 55–58, find two quadratic functions, one that opens upward and one that opens downward, whose graphs have the given x-intercepts. (There are many correct answers.)

55. $(-1, 0), (3, 0)$

56. $(0, 0), (10, 0)$

57. $(-3, 0), \left(-\frac{1}{2}, 0\right)$

58. $\left(-\frac{5}{2}, 0\right), (2, 0)$

Maximizing a Product of Two Numbers In Exercises 59–62, find the two positive real numbers with the given sum whose product is a maximum.

59. The sum is 110.

60. The sum is 66.

61. The sum of the first and twice the second is 24.

62. The sum of the first and three times the second is 42.

63. *Why you should learn it* (p. 90) An indoor physical fitness room consists of a rectangular region with a semicircle on each end. The perimeter of the room is to be a 200-meter single-lane running track.

(a) Draw a diagram that illustrates the problem. Let x and y represent the length and width of the rectangular region, respectively.

(b) Determine the radius of the semicircular ends of the track. Determine the distance, in terms of y, around the inside edge of the two semicircular parts of the track.

(c) Use the result of part (b) to write an equation, in terms of x and y, for the distance traveled in one lap around the track. Solve for y.

(d) Use the result of part (c) to write the area A of the rectangular region as a function of x.

(e) Use a graphing utility to graph the area function from part (d). Use the graph to approximate the dimensions that will produce a rectangle of maximum area.

64. Algebraic-Graphical-Numerical A child-care center has 200 feet of fencing to enclose two adjacent rectangular safe play areas (see figure). Use the following methods to determine the dimensions that will produce a maximum enclosed area.

(a) Write the total area A of the play areas as a function of x.

(b) Use the *table* feature of a graphing utility to create a table showing possible values of x and the corresponding total area A of the play areas. Use the table to estimate the dimensions that will produce the maximum enclosed area.

(c) Use the graphing utility to graph the area function. Use the graph to approximate the dimensions that will produce the maximum enclosed area.

(d) Write the area function in standard form to find algebraically the dimensions that will produce the maximum enclosed area.

(e) Compare your results from parts (b), (c), and (d).

65. Height of a Projectile　The height y (in feet) of a punted football is approximated by

$$y = -\frac{16}{2025}x^2 + \frac{9}{5}x + \frac{3}{2}$$

where x is the horizontal distance (in feet) from where the football is punted. (See figure.)

Not drawn to scale

(a) Use a graphing utility to graph the path of the football.

(b) How high is the football when it is punted? (*Hint:* Find y when $x = 0$.)

(c) What is the maximum height of the football?

(d) How far from the punter does the football strike the ground?

66. Physics　The path of a diver is approximated by

$$y = -\frac{4}{9}x^2 + \frac{24}{9}x + 12$$

where y is the height (in feet) and x is the horizontal distance (in feet) from the end of the diving board (see figure). What is the maximum height of the diver?

67. Geometry　You have a steel wire that is 100 inches long. To make a sign holder, you bend the wire x inches from each end to form two right angles. To use the sign holder, you insert each end 6 inches into the ground. (See figure.)

(a) Write a function for the rectangular area A enclosed by the sign holder in terms of x.

(b) Use the *table* feature of a graphing utility to determine the value of x that maximizes the rectangular area enclosed by the sign holder.

68. Economics　The monthly revenue R (in thousands of dollars) from the sales of a digital picture frame is approximated by $R(p) = -10p^2 + 1580p$, where p is the price per unit (in dollars).

(a) Find the monthly revenues for unit prices of $50, $70, and $90.

(b) Find the unit price that will yield a maximum monthly revenue.

(c) What is the maximum monthly revenue?

69. Public Health　For selected years from 1955 through 2010, the annual per capita consumption C of cigarettes by Americans (ages 18 and older) can be modeled by

$$C(t) = -1.39t^2 + 36.5t + 3871, \quad 5 \le t \le 60$$

where t is the year, with $t = 5$ corresponding to 1955. (Sources: Centers for Disease Control and Prevention and U.S. Census Bureau)

(a) Use a graphing utility to graph the model.

(b) Use the graph of the model to approximate the year when the maximum annual consumption of cigarettes occurred. Approximate the maximum average annual consumption.

(c) Beginning in 1966, all cigarette packages were required by law to carry a health warning. Do you think the warning had any effect? Explain.

(d) In 2010, the U.S. population (ages 18 and older) was 234,564,000. Of those, about 45,271,000 were smokers. What was the average annual cigarette consumption *per smoker* in 2010? What was the average daily cigarette consumption *per smoker*?

70. Demography　The population P of Germany (in thousands) from 2000 through 2013 can be modeled by

$$P(t) = -14.82t^2 + 95.9t + 82,276, \quad 0 \le t \le 13$$

where t is the year, with $t = 0$ corresponding to 2000. (Source: U.S. Census Bureau)

(a) According to the model, in what year did Germany have its greatest population? What was the population?

(b) According to the model, what will Germany's population be in the year 2075? Is this result reasonable? Explain.

Conclusions

True or False?　In Exercises 71–74, determine whether the statement is true or false. Justify your answer.

71. The function $f(x) = -12x^2 - 1$ has no x-intercepts.

72. The function $f(x) = a(x - 5)^2$ has exactly one x-intercept for any nonzero value of a.

73. The functions $f(x) = 3x^2 + 6x + 7$ and $g(x) = 3x^2 + 6x - 1$ have the same vertex.

74. The graphs of $f(x) = -4x^2 - 10x + 7$ and $g(x) = 12x^2 + 30x + 1$ have the same axis of symmetry.

Library of Parent Functions   In Exercises 75 and 76, determine which equation(s) may be represented by the graph shown. (There may be more than one correct answer.)

75. (a) $f(x) = -(x - 4)^2 + 2$

    (b) $f(x) = -(x + 2)^2 + 4$

    (c) $f(x) = -(x + 2)^2 - 4$

    (d) $f(x) = -x^2 - 4x - 8$

    (e) $f(x) = -(x - 2)^2 - 4$

    (f) $f(x) = -x^2 + 4x - 8$

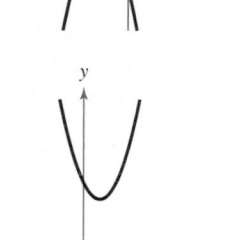

76. (a) $f(x) = (x - 1)^2 + 3$

    (b) $f(x) = (x + 1)^2 + 3$

    (c) $f(x) = (x - 3)^2 + 1$

    (d) $f(x) = x^2 + 2x + 4$

    (e) $f(x) = (x + 3)^2 + 1$

    (f) $f(x) = x^2 + 6x + 10$

Describing Parabolas   In Exercises 77–80, let z represent a positive real number. Describe how the family of parabolas represented by the given function compares with the graph of $g(x) = x^2$.

77. $f(x) = (x - z)^2$ 78. $f(x) = x^2 - z$

79. $f(x) = z(x - 3)^2$ 80. $f(x) = zx^2 + 4$

Think About It   In Exercises 81–84, find the value of b such that the function has the given maximum or minimum value.

81. $f(x) = -x^2 + bx - 75$; Maximum value: 25

82. $f(x) = -x^2 + bx - 16$; Maximum value: 48

83. $f(x) = x^2 + bx + 26$; Minimum value: 10

84. $f(x) = x^2 + bx - 25$; Minimum value: -50

85. **Proof**   Let x and y be two positive real numbers whose sum is S. Show that the maximum product of x and y occurs when x and y are both equal to $S/2$.

86. **Proof**   Assume that the function $f(x) = ax^2 + bx + c$, $a \neq 0$, has two real zeros. Show that the x-coordinate of the vertex of the graph is the average of the zeros of f. (*Hint:* Use the Quadratic Formula.)

87. **Writing**   The parabola in the figure has an equation of the form $y = ax^2 + bx - 4$. Find the equation of this parabola two different ways, by hand and with technology. Write a paragraph describing the methods you used and comparing the results.

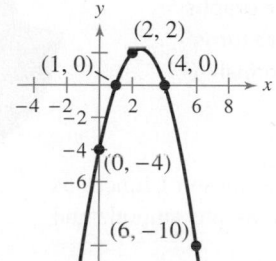

88. **HOW DO YOU SEE IT?**   The graph shows a quadratic function of the form $R(t) = at^2 + bt + c$, which represents the yearly revenues for a company, where $R(t)$ is the revenue in year t.

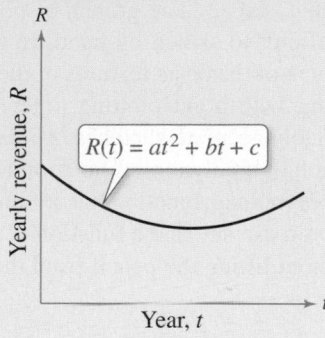

$R(t) = at^2 + bt + c$

(a) Is the value of a positive, negative, or zero?

(b) Write an expression in terms of a and b that represents the year t when the company had the least revenue.

(c) The company made the same yearly revenues in 2004 and 2014. Estimate the year in which the company had the least revenue.

(d) Assume that the model is still valid today. Are the yearly revenues currently increasing, decreasing, or constant? Explain.

89. **Think About It**   The annual profit P (in dollars) of a company is modeled by a function of the form $P = at^2 + bt + c$, where t represents the year. Discuss which of the following models the company might prefer.

(a) a is positive and $t \geq -b/(2a)$.

(b) a is positive and $t \leq -b/(2a)$.

(c) a is negative and $t \geq -b/(2a)$.

(d) a is negative and $t \leq -b/(2a)$.

Cumulative Mixed Review

Finding Points of Intersection   In Exercises 90–93, determine algebraically any point(s) of intersection of the graphs of the equations. Verify your results using the *intersect* feature of a graphing utility.

90. $x + y = 8$ 91. $y = 3x - 10$

     $-\frac{2}{3}x + y = 6$ $y = \frac{1}{4}x + 1$

92. $y = 9 - x^2$ 93. $y = x^3 + 2x - 1$

    $y = x + 3$ $y = -2x + 15$

94. *Make a Decision*   To work an extended application analyzing the heights of a softball after it has been dropped, visit this textbook's website at *LarsonPrecalculus.com*.

2.2   Polynomial Functions of Higher Degree

Graphs of Polynomial Functions

At this point, you should be able to sketch accurate graphs of polynomial functions of degrees 0, 1, and 2. The graphs of polynomial functions of degree greater than 2 are more difficult to sketch by hand. In this section, however, you will learn how to recognize some of the basic features of the graphs of polynomial functions. Using these features along with point plotting, intercepts, and symmetry, you should be able to make reasonably accurate sketches *by hand*.

The graph of a polynomial function is **continuous.** Essentially, this means that the graph of a polynomial function has no breaks, holes, or gaps, as shown in Figure 2.6. Informally, you can say that a function is continuous when its graph can be drawn with a pencil without lifting the pencil from the paper.

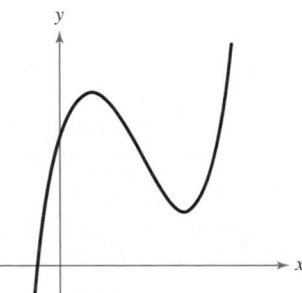

(a) **Polynomial functions have continuous graphs.**

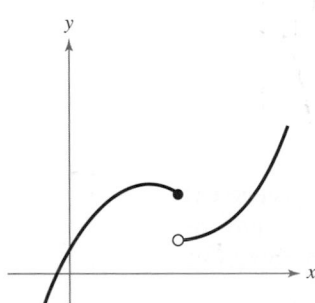

(b) **Functions with graphs that are not continuous are not polynomial functions.**

Figure 2.6

Another feature of the graph of a polynomial function is that it has only smooth, rounded turns, as shown in Figure 2.7(a). It cannot have a sharp turn, such as the one shown in Figure 2.7(b).

(a) **Polynomial functions have graphs with smooth, rounded turns.**

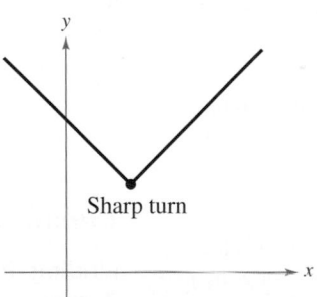

Sharp turn

(b) **Functions with graphs that have sharp turns are not polynomial functions.**

Figure 2.7

The graphs of polynomial functions of degree 1 are lines, and those of functions of degree 2 are parabolas. The graphs of all polynomial functions are smooth and continuous. A polynomial function of degree n has the form

$$f(x) = a_n x^n + a_{n-1} x^{n-1} + \cdots + a_2 x^2 + a_1 x + a_0$$

where n is a positive integer and $a_n \neq 0$.

What you should learn

► Use transformations to sketch graphs of polynomial functions.
► Use the Leading Coefficient Test to determine the end behavior of graphs of polynomial functions.
► Find and use zeros of polynomial functions as sketching aids.
► Use the Intermediate Value Theorem to help locate zeros of polynomial functions.

Why you should learn it

You can use polynomial functions to model various aspects of nature, such as the growth of a red oak tree, as shown in Exercise 112 on page 111.

The polynomial functions that have the simplest graphs are monomials of the form $f(x) = x^n$, where n is an integer greater than zero. The greater the value of n, the flatter the graph near the origin. When n is even, the graph is similar to the graph of $f(x) = x^2$ and touches the x-axis at the x-intercept. When n is odd, the graph is similar to the graph of $f(x) = x^3$ and crosses the x-axis at the x-intercept. Polynomial functions of the form $f(x) = x^n$ are often referred to as **power functions.**

Library of Parent Functions: Cubic Function

The basic characteristics of the *parent cubic function* $f(x) = x^3$ are summarized below and on the inside cover of this text.

Graph of $f(x) = x^3$

Domain: $(-\infty, \infty)$
Range: $(-\infty, \infty)$
Intercept: $(0, 0)$
Increasing on $(-\infty, \infty)$
Odd function
Origin symmetry

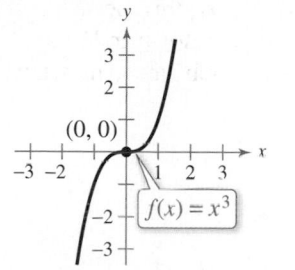

> **Explore the Concept**
>
> Use a graphing utility to graph $y = x^n$ for $n = 2$, 4, and 8. (Use the viewing window $-1.5 \le x \le 1.5$ and $-1 \le y \le 6$.) Compare the graphs. In the interval $(-1, 1)$, which graph is on the bottom? Outside the interval $(-1, 1)$, which graph is on the bottom?
>
> Use a graphing utility to graph $y = x^n$ for $n = 3$, 5, and 7. (Use the viewing window $-1.5 \le x \le 1.5$ and $-4 \le y \le 4$.) Compare the graphs. In the intervals $(-\infty, -1)$ and $(0, 1)$, which graph is on the bottom? In the intervals $(-1, 0)$ and $(1, \infty)$, which graph is on the bottom?

EXAMPLE 1 Library of Parent Functions: $f(x) = x^3$

See LarsonPrecalculus.com for an interactive version of this type of example.

Sketch the graphs of (a) $g(x) = -x^3$, (b) $h(x) = x^3 + 1$, and (c) $k(x) = (x - 1)^3$ by hand.

Solution

a. With respect to the graph of $f(x) = x^3$, the graph of g is obtained by a *reflection* in the x-axis, as shown in Figure 2.8.

b. With respect to the graph of $f(x) = x^3$, the graph of h is obtained by a vertical shift one unit *upward*, as shown in Figure 2.9.

c. With respect to the graph of $f(x) = x^3$, the graph of k is obtained by a horizontal shift one unit *to the right*, as shown in Figure 2.10.

Figure 2.8

Figure 2.9

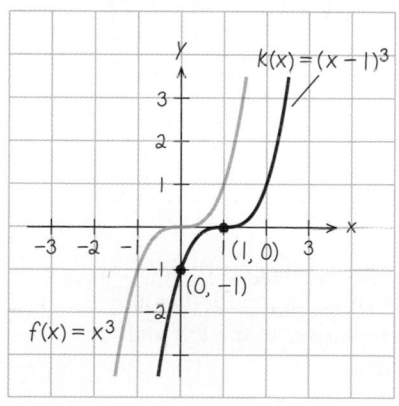

Figure 2.10

✓ **Checkpoint** 🔊))) *Audio-video solution in English & Spanish at LarsonPrecalculus.com.*

Sketch the graphs of (a) $g(x) = -x^3 + 2$, (b) $h(x) = x^3 - 5$, and (c) $k(x) = (x + 2)^3$ by hand. ∎

The Leading Coefficient Test

In Example 1, note that all three graphs eventually rise or fall without bound as x moves to the right. Whether the graph of a polynomial eventually rises or falls can be determined by the polynomial function's degree (even or odd) and by its leading coefficient, as indicated in the **Leading Coefficient Test.**

Leading Coefficient Test

As x moves without bound to the left or to the right, the graph of the polynomial function

$$f(x) = a_n x^n + \cdots + a_1 x + a_0, \quad a_n \neq 0$$

eventually rises or falls in the following manner.

1. When n is odd:

If the leading coefficient is positive ($a_n > 0$), then the graph falls to the left and rises to the right.

If the leading coefficient is negative ($a_n < 0$), then the graph rises to the left and falls to the right.

2. When n is even:

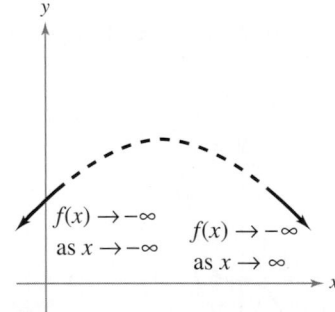

If the leading coefficient is positive ($a_n > 0$), then the graph rises to the left and right.

If the leading coefficient is negative ($a_n < 0$), then the graph falls to the left and right.

Note that the dashed portions of the graphs indicate that the test determines only the right-hand and left-hand behavior of the graph.

As you continue to study polynomial functions and their graphs, you will notice that the degree of a polynomial plays an important role in determining other characteristics of the polynomial function and its graph.

EXAMPLE 2   Applying the Leading Coefficient Test

Use the Leading Coefficient Test to describe the right-hand and left-hand behavior of the graph of $f(x) = -x^3 + 4x$.

Solution

Because the degree is odd and the leading coefficient is negative, the graph rises to the left and falls to the right, as shown in the figure.

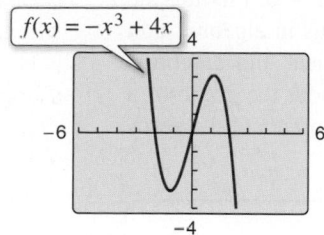

$f(x) = -x^3 + 4x$

✔ **Checkpoint** ◀))) *Audio-video solution in English & Spanish at LarsonPrecalculus.com.*

Use the Leading Coefficient Test to describe the right-hand and left-hand behavior of the graph of $f(x) = 2x^3 - 3x^2 + 5$.

EXAMPLE 3   Applying the Leading Coefficient Test

Use the Leading Coefficient Test to describe the right-hand and left-hand behavior of the graph of each polynomial function.

a. $f(x) = x^4 - 5x^2 + 4$ **b.** $f(x) = x^5 - x$

Solution

a. Because the degree is even and the leading coefficient is positive, the graph rises to the left and right, as shown in the figure.

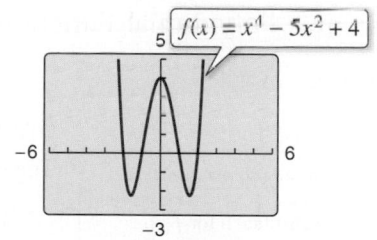

$f(x) = x^4 - 5x^2 + 4$

b. Because the degree is odd and the leading coefficient is positive, the graph falls to the left and rises to the right, as shown in the figure.

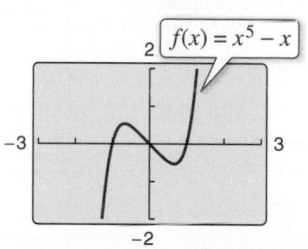

$f(x) = x^5 - x$

✔ **Checkpoint** ◀))) *Audio-video solution in English & Spanish at LarsonPrecalculus.com.*

Use the Leading Coefficient Test to describe the right-hand and left-hand behavior of the graph of each polynomial function.

a. $f(x) = -x^4 + 2x^2 + 6$ **b.** $f(x) = -x^5 + 3x^4 - x$ ◼

In Examples 2 and 3, note that the Leading Coefficient Test tells you only whether the graph *eventually* rises or falls to the right or left. Other characteristics of the graph, such as intercepts and minimum and maximum points, must be determined by other tests.

Explore the Concept

For each of the graphs in Examples 2 and 3, count the number of zeros of the polynomial function and the number of relative extrema, and compare these numbers with the degree of the polynomial. What do you observe?

Zeros of Polynomial Functions

It can be shown that for a polynomial function f of degree n, the following statements are true.

1. The function f has at most n real zeros. (You will study this result in detail in Section 2.5 on the Fundamental Theorem of Algebra.)

2. The graph of f has at most $n - 1$ relative **extrema** (relative minima or maxima).

Recall that a zero of a function f is a number x for which $f(x) = 0$. Finding the zeros of polynomial functions is one of the most important problems in algebra. You have already seen that there is a strong interplay between graphical and algebraic approaches to this problem. Sometimes you can use information about the graph of a function to help find its zeros. In other cases, you can use information about the zeros of a function to find a good viewing window.

Real Zeros of Polynomial Functions

When f is a polynomial function and a is a real number, the following statements are equivalent.

1. $x = a$ is a *zero* of the function f.

2. $x = a$ is a *solution* of the polynomial equation $f(x) = 0$.

3. $(x - a)$ is a *factor* of the polynomial $f(x)$.

4. $(a, 0)$ is an *x-intercept* of the graph of f.

Finding zeros of polynomial functions is closely related to factoring and finding x-intercepts, as demonstrated in Examples 4, 5, and 6.

EXAMPLE 4   Finding Zeros of a Polynomial Function

Find all real zeros of $f(x) = x^3 - x^2 - 2x$.

Algebraic Solution

$$f(x) = x^3 - x^2 - 2x \qquad \text{Write original function.}$$

$$0 = x^3 - x^2 - 2x \qquad \text{Substitute 0 for } f(x).$$

$$0 = x(x^2 - x - 2) \qquad \text{Remove common monomial factor.}$$

$$0 = x(x - 2)(x + 1) \qquad \text{Factor completely.}$$

So, the real zeros are $x = 0$, $x = 2$, and $x = -1$, and the corresponding x-intercepts are $(0, 0)$, $(2, 0)$, and $(-1, 0)$.

Check

$$(0)^3 - (0)^2 - 2(0) = 0 \qquad x = 0 \text{ is a zero. } \checkmark$$

$$(2)^3 - (2)^2 - 2(2) = 0 \qquad x = 2 \text{ is a zero. } \checkmark$$

$$(-1)^3 - (-1)^2 - 2(-1) = 0 \qquad x = -1 \text{ is a zero. } \checkmark$$

Graphical Solution

The graph of f has the x-intercepts

$$(0, 0), \quad (2, 0), \quad \text{and} \quad (-1, 0)$$

as shown in the figure. So, the real zeros of f are

$$x = 0, \quad x = 2, \quad \text{and} \quad x = -1.$$

Use the *zero* or *root* feature of a graphing utility to verify these zeros.

 Checkpoint *Audio-video solution in English & Spanish at LarsonPrecalculus.com.*

Find all real zeros of $f(x) = x^3 + x^2 - 6x$.

EXAMPLE 5   Analyzing a Polynomial Function

Find all real zeros and relative extrema of $f(x) = -2x^4 + 2x^2$.

Solution

$$0 = -2x^4 + 2x^2 \qquad \text{Substitute 0 for } f(x).$$

$$0 = -2x^2(x^2 - 1) \qquad \text{Remove common monomial factor.}$$

$$0 = -2x^2(x - 1)(x + 1) \qquad \text{Factor completely.}$$

So, the real zeros are $x = 0$, $x = 1$, and $x = -1$, and the corresponding x-intercepts are $(0, 0)$, $(1, 0)$, and $(-1, 0)$, as shown in Figure 2.11. Using the *minimum* and *maximum* features of a graphing utility, you can approximate the three relative extrema to be $(-0.71, 0.5)$, $(0, 0)$, and $(0.71, 0.5)$.

Figure 2.11

✓ **Checkpoint** *Audio-video solution in English & Spanish at LarsonPrecalculus.com.*

Find all real zeros and relative extrema of $f(x) = x^3 + 2x^2 - 3x$. ∎

Repeated Zeros

For a polynomial function, a factor of $(x - a)^k$, $k > 1$, yields a **repeated zero** $x = a$ of **multiplicity** k.

1. If k is odd, then the graph *crosses* the x-axis at $x = a$.

2. If k is even, then the graph *touches* the x-axis (but does not cross the x-axis) at $x = a$.

Remark

In Example 5, note that because k is even, the factor $-2x^2$ yields the repeated zero $x = 0$. The graph touches (but does not cross) the x-axis at $x = 0$, as shown in Figure 2.11.

EXAMPLE 6   Analyzing a Polynomial Function

To find all real zeros of $f(x) = x^5 - 3x^3 - x^2 - 4x - 1$, use the *zero* feature of a graphing utility. From Figure 2.12, the zeros are $x \approx -1.86$, $x \approx -0.25$, and $x \approx 2.11$. Note that this fifth-degree polynomial factors as

$$f(x) = x^5 - 3x^3 - x^2 - 4x - 1 = (x^2 + 1)(x^3 - 4x - 1).$$

The three zeros obtained above are the zeros of the cubic factor $x^3 - 4x - 1$. The quadratic factor $x^2 + 1$ has no real zeros but does have two *imaginary* zeros. You will learn more about imaginary zeros in Section 2.5.

Figure 2.12

✓ **Checkpoint** 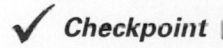 *Audio-video solution in English & Spanish at LarsonPrecalculus.com.*

Find all real zeros of $f(x) = x^5 - 2x^4 + x^3 - 2x^2$.

EXAMPLE 7   Finding a Polynomial Function with Given Zeros

Find a polynomial function with zeros $-\frac{1}{2}$, 3, and 3. (There are many correct solutions.)

Solution

Note that the zero $x = -\frac{1}{2}$ corresponds to either $\left(x + \frac{1}{2}\right)$ or $(2x + 1)$. To avoid fractions, choose the second factor and write

$$f(x) = (2x + 1)(x - 3)^2 = (2x + 1)(x^2 - 6x + 9) = 2x^3 - 11x^2 + 12x + 9.$$

✓ **Checkpoint** 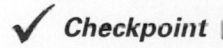 *Audio-video solution in English & Spanish at LarsonPrecalculus.com.*

Find a polynomial function with zeros -2, -1, 1, and 2. (There are many correct solutions.) ∎

Note in Example 7 that there are many polynomial functions with the indicated zeros. In fact, multiplying the function by any real number does not change the zeros of the function. For instance, multiply the function from Example 7 by $\frac{1}{2}$ to obtain

$$f(x) = x^3 - \tfrac{11}{2}x^2 + 6x + \tfrac{9}{2}.$$

Then find the zeros of the function. You will obtain the zeros $-\frac{1}{2}$, 3, and 3, as given in Example 7.

EXAMPLE 8   Sketching the Graph of a Polynomial Function

Sketch the graph of

$$f(x) = 3x^4 - 4x^3$$

by hand.

Solution

1. *Apply the Leading Coefficient Test.*   Because the leading coefficient is positive and the degree is even, you know that the graph eventually rises to the left and to the right (see Figure 2.13).

2. *Find the Real Zeros of the Polynomial.*   By factoring

$$f(x) = 3x^4 - 4x^3 = x^3(3x - 4)$$

you can see that the real zeros of f are $x = 0$ (of odd multiplicity 3) and $x = \frac{4}{3}$ (of odd multiplicity 1). So, the x-intercepts occur at $(0, 0)$ and $\left(\frac{4}{3}, 0\right)$. Add these points to your graph, as shown in Figure 2.13.

3. *Plot a Few Additional Points.*   To sketch the graph by hand, find a few additional points, as shown in the table. Be sure to choose points between the zeros and to the left and right of the zeros. Then plot the points (see Figure 2.14).

x	-1	0.5	1	1.5
$f(x)$	7	-0.31	-1	1.69

4. *Draw the Graph.*   Draw a continuous curve through the points, as shown in Figure 2.14. Because both zeros are of odd multiplicity, you know that the graph should cross the x-axis at $x = 0$ and $x = \frac{4}{3}$. When you are unsure of the shape of a portion of the graph, plot some additional points.

Figure 2.13

Figure 2.14

✓ **Checkpoint** ◀))) *Audio-video solution in English & Spanish at LarsonPrecalculus.com.*

Sketch the graph of $f(x) = 2x^3 - 6x^2$ by hand. ∎

Technology Tip

Because it is easy to make mistakes when entering functions into a graphing utility, it is important to understand the basic shapes of graphs and to be able to graph simple polynomials *by hand*. For instance, suppose you had entered the function in Example 8 as $y = 3x^5 - 4x^3$. From the graph, what mathematical principles would alert you to the fact that you had made a mistake?

EXAMPLE 9   Sketching the Graph of a Polynomial Function

Sketch the graph of

$$f(x) = -2x^3 + 6x^2 - \tfrac{9}{2}x.$$

Solution

1. *Apply the Leading Coefficient Test.*   Because the leading coefficient is negative and the degree is odd, you know that the graph eventually rises to the left and falls to the right (see Figure 2.15).

2. *Find the Real Zeros of the Polynomial.*   By factoring

$$f(x) = -2x^3 + 6x^2 - \tfrac{9}{2}x$$

$$= -\tfrac{1}{2}x(4x^2 - 12x + 9)$$

$$= -\tfrac{1}{2}x(2x - 3)^2$$

you can see that the real zeros of f are $x = 0$ (of odd multiplicity 1) and $x = \tfrac{3}{2}$ (of even multiplicity 2). So, the x-intercepts occur at $(0, 0)$ and $\left(\tfrac{3}{2}, 0\right)$. Add these points to your graph, as shown in Figure 2.15.

3. *Plot a Few Additional Points.*   To sketch the graph, find a few additional points, as shown in the table. Then plot the points (see Figure 2.16).

x	-0.5	0.5	1	2
$f(x)$	4	-1	-0.5	-1

4. *Draw the Graph.*   Draw a continuous curve through the points, as shown in Figure 2.16. As indicated by the multiplicities of the zeros, the graph crosses the x-axis at $(0, 0)$ and touches (but does not cross) the x-axis at $\left(\tfrac{3}{2}, 0\right)$.

Figure 2.15

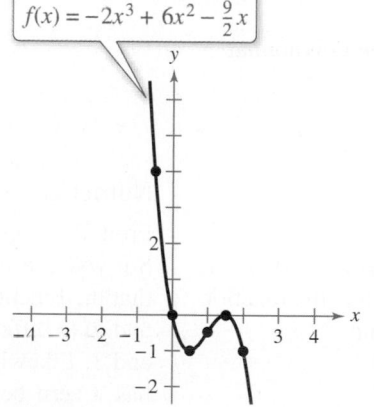

$$f(x) = -2x^3 + 6x^2 - \tfrac{9}{2}x$$

Figure 2.16

✓ **Checkpoint**))) *Audio-video solution in English & Spanish at LarsonPrecalculus.com.*

Sketch the graph of $f(x) = -\tfrac{1}{4}x^4 + \tfrac{3}{2}x^3 - \tfrac{9}{4}x^2$.

Remark

Observe in Example 9 that the sign of $f(x)$ is positive to the left of and negative to the right of the zero $x = 0$. Similarly, the sign of $f(x)$ is negative to the left and to the right of the zero $x = \tfrac{3}{2}$. This suggests that if a zero of a polynomial function is of *odd* multiplicity, then the sign of $f(x)$ changes from one side of the zero to the other side. If a zero is of *even* multiplicity, then the sign of $f(x)$ does not change from one side of the zero to the other side. The following table helps to illustrate this result.

x	-0.5	0	0.5
$f(x)$	4	0	-1
Sign	$+$		$-$

x	1	$\tfrac{3}{2}$	2
$f(x)$	-0.5	0	-1
Sign	$-$		$-$

This sign analysis may be helpful in graphing polynomial functions.

Technology Tip

Remember that when using a graphing utility to verify your graphs, you may need to adjust your viewing window in order to see all the features of the graph.

The Intermediate Value Theorem

The **Intermediate Value Theorem** implies that if $(a, f(a))$ and $(b, f(b))$ are two points on the graph of a polynomial function such that $f(a) \neq f(b)$, then for any number d between $f(a)$ and $f(b)$, there must be a number c between a and b such that $f(c) = d$. (See figure shown at the right.)

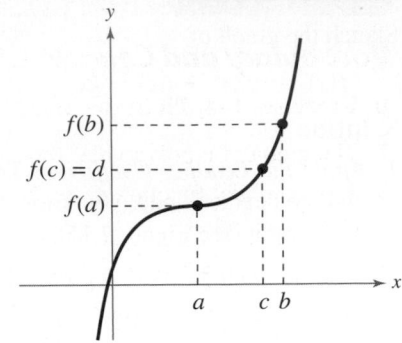

> **Intermediate Value Theorem**
>
> Let a and b be real numbers such that $a < b$. If f is a polynomial function such that $f(a) \neq f(b)$, then in the interval $[a, b]$, f takes on every value between $f(a)$ and $f(b)$.

This theorem helps you locate the real zeros of a polynomial function in the following way. If you can find a value $x = a$ at which a polynomial function is positive, and another value $x = b$ at which it is negative, then you can conclude that the function has at least one real zero between these two values. For example, the function $f(x) = x^3 + x^2 + 1$ is negative when $x = -2$ and positive when $x = -1$. So, it follows from the Intermediate Value Theorem that f must have a real zero somewhere between -2 and -1, as shown in the figure. By continuing this line of reasoning, you can approximate any real zeros of a polynomial function to any desired accuracy.

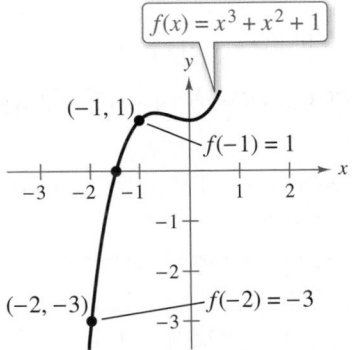

The function f must have a real zero somewhere between -2 and -1.

EXAMPLE 10　Approximating the Zeros of a Function

Find three intervals of length 1 in which the polynomial

$$f(x) = 12x^3 - 32x^2 + 3x + 5$$

is guaranteed to have a zero.

Graphical Solution

From the figure, you can see that the graph of f crosses the x-axis three times—between -1 and 0, between 0 and 1, and between 2 and 3. So, you can conclude that the function has zeros in the intervals $(-1, 0)$, $(0, 1)$, and $(2, 3)$.

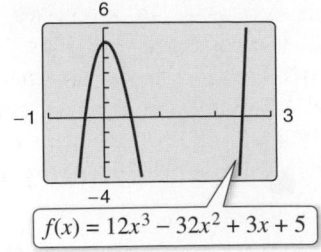

$$f(x) = 12x^3 - 32x^2 + 3x + 5$$

Numerical Solution

From the table, you can see that $f(-1)$ and $f(0)$ differ in sign. So, you can conclude from the Intermediate Value Theorem that the function has a zero between -1 and 0. Similarly, $f(0)$ and $f(1)$ differ in sign, so the function has a zero between 0 and 1. Likewise, $f(2)$ and $f(3)$ differ in sign, so the function has a zero between 2 and 3. So, you can conclude that the function has zeros in the intervals $(-1, 0)$, $(0, 1)$, and $(2, 3)$.

X	Y1
-2	-225
-1	-42
0	5
1	-12
2	-21
3	50
4	273
X=-1	

 Checkpoint 　*Audio-video solution in English & Spanish at LarsonPrecalculus.com.*

Find three intervals of length 1 in which the polynomial $f(x) = x^3 - 4x^2 + 1$ is guaranteed to have a zero.

2.2 Exercises

See *CalcChat.com* for tutorial help and worked-out solutions to odd-numbered exercises.
For instructions on how to use a graphing utility, see Appendix A.

Vocabulary and Concept Check

In Exercises 1–4, fill in the blank(s).

1. The graph of a polynomial function is _____ , so it has no breaks, holes, or gaps.

2. A polynomial function of degree n has at most _____ real zeros and at most _____ relative extrema.

3. When $x = a$ is a zero of a polynomial function f, the following statements are true.

(a) $x = a$ is a _____ of the polynomial equation $f(x) = 0$.

(b) _____ is a factor of the polynomial $f(x)$.

(c) The point _____ is an x-intercept of the graph of f.

4. If a zero of a polynomial function f is of even multiplicity, then the graph of f _____ the x-axis, and if the zero is of odd multiplicity, then the graph of f _____ the x-axis.

For Exercises 5–8, the graph shows the right-hand and left-hand behavior of a polynomial function f.

5. Can f be a fourth-degree polynomial function?

6. Can the leading coefficient of f be negative?

7. The graph shows that $f(x_1) < 0$. What other information shown in the graph allows you to apply the Intermediate Value Theorem to guarantee that f has a zero in the interval $[x_1, x_2]$?

8. Is the repeated zero of f in the interval $[x_3, x_4]$ of even or odd multiplicity?

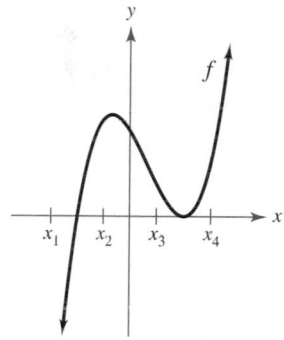

Procedures and Problem Solving

Identifying Graphs of Polynomial Functions In Exercises 9–16, match the polynomial function with its graph. [The graphs are labeled (a) through (h).]

9. $f(x) = -2x + 3$

10. $f(x) = x^2 - 4x$

11. $f(x) = -2x^2 - 5x$

12. $f(x) = 2x^3 - 3x + 1$

13. $f(x) = -\frac{1}{4}x^4 + 3x^2$

14. $f(x) = -\frac{1}{3}x^3 + x^2 - \frac{4}{3}$

15. $f(x) = x^4 + 2x^3$

16. $f(x) = \frac{1}{5}x^5 - 2x^3 + \frac{9}{5}x$

(a)

(b)

(c)

(d)

(e)

(f)

(g)

(h)

Library of Parent Functions In Exercises 17–22, sketch the graph of $f(x) = x^3$ and the graph of the function g. Describe the transformation from f to g.

17. $g(x) = (x - 3)^3$

18. $g(x) = x^3 - 3$

19. $g(x) = -x^3 + 4$

20. $g(x) = (x - 2)^3 - 3$

21. $g(x) = -(x - 3)^3$

22. $g(x) = (x + 4)^3 + 1$

Comparing End Behavior In Exercises 23–28, use a graphing utility to graph the functions f and g in the same viewing window. Zoom out far enough to see the right-hand and left-hand behavior of each graph. Do the graphs of f and g have the same right-hand and left-hand behavior? Explain why or why not.

23. $f(x) = 3x^3 - 9x + 1$, $g(x) = 3x^3$

24. $f(x) = -\frac{1}{3}(x^3 - 3x + 2)$, $g(x) = -\frac{1}{3}x^3$

25. $f(x) = -(x^4 - 4x^3 + 16x)$, $g(x) = -x^4$

26. $f(x) = 3x^4 - 6x^2$, $g(x) = 3x^4$

27. $f(x) = -2x^3 + 4x^2 - 1$, $g(x) = 2x^3$

28. $f(x) = -(x^4 - 6x^2 - x + 10)$, $g(x) = x^4$

Applying the Leading Coefficient Test In Exercises 29–36, use the Leading Coefficient Test to describe the right-hand and left-hand behavior of the graph of the polynomial function. Use a graphing utility to verify your results.

29. $f(x) = 2x^4 - 3x + 1$ 30. $h(x) = 1 - x^6$

31. $g(x) = 5 - \frac{7}{2}x - 3x^2$ 32. $f(x) = \frac{1}{3}x^3 + 5x$

33. $f(x) = \dfrac{6x^5 - 2x^4 + 4x^2 - 5x}{3}$

34. $f(x) = \dfrac{3x^7 - 2x^5 + 5x^3 + 6x^2}{4}$

35. $h(t) = -\frac{2}{3}(t^2 - 5t + 3)$

36. $f(s) = -\frac{7}{8}(s^3 + 5s^2 - 7s + 1)$

Finding Zeros of a Polynomial Function In Exercises 37–48, (a) find the zeros algebraically, (b) use a graphing utility to graph the function, and (c) use the graph to approximate any zeros and compare them with those from part (a).

37. $f(x) = 3x^2 - 12x + 3$ 38. $g(x) = 5x^2 - 10x - 5$

39. $g(t) = \frac{1}{2}t^4 - \frac{1}{2}$ 40. $y = \frac{1}{4}x^3(x^2 - 9)$

41. $f(x) = x^5 + x^3 - 6x$ 42. $g(t) = t^5 - 6t^3 + 9t$

43. $f(x) = 2x^4 - 2x^2 - 40$

44. $f(x) = 5x^4 + 15x^2 + 10$

45. $f(x) = x^3 - 4x^2 - 25x + 100$

46. $y = 4x^3 + 4x^2 - 7x + 2$

47. $y = 4x^3 - 20x^2 + 25x$

48. $y = x^5 - 5x^3 + 4x$

Finding Zeros and Their Multiplicities In Exercises 49–58, find all the real zeros of the polynomial function. Determine the multiplicity of each zero. Use a graphing utility to verify your results.

49. $f(x) = x^2 - 25$ 50. $f(x) = 49 - x^2$

51. $h(t) = t^2 - 6t + 9$ 52. $f(x) = x^2 + 10x + 25$

53. $f(x) = x^2 + x - 2$ 54. $f(x) = 2x^2 - 14x + 24$

55. $f(t) = t^3 - 4t^2 + 4t$ 56. $f(x) = x^4 - x^3 - 20x^2$

57. $f(x) = \frac{1}{2}x^2 + \frac{5}{2}x - \frac{3}{2}$ 58. $f(x) = \frac{5}{3}x^2 + \frac{8}{3}x - \frac{4}{3}$

Analyzing a Polynomial Function In Exercises 59–64, use a graphing utility to graph the function and approximate (accurate to three decimal places) any real zeros and relative extrema.

59. $f(x) = 2x^4 - 6x^2 + 1$

60. $f(x) = -\frac{3}{8}x^4 - x^3 + 2x^2 + 5$

61. $f(x) = x^5 + 3x^3 - x + 6$

62. $f(x) = -3x^3 - 4x^2 + x - 3$

63. $f(x) = -2x^4 + 5x^2 - x - 1$

64. $f(x) = 3x^5 - 2x^2 - x + 1$

Finding a Polynomial Function with Given Zeros In Exercises 65–74, find a polynomial function that has the given zeros. (There are many correct answers.)

65. $0, 7$ 66. $-2, 5$

67. $0, -2, -4$ 68. $0, 1, 6$

69. $4, -3, 3, 0$ 70. $-2, -1, 0, 1, 2$

71. $1 + \sqrt{2}, 1 - \sqrt{2}$ 72. $4 + \sqrt{3}, 4 - \sqrt{3}$

73. $2, 2 + \sqrt{5}, 2 - \sqrt{5}$ 74. $3, 2 + \sqrt{7}, 2 - \sqrt{7}$

Finding a Polynomial Function with Given Zeros In Exercises 75–80, find a polynomial function with the given zeros, multiplicities, and degree. (There are many correct answers.)

75. Zero: -2, multiplicity: 2   76. Zero: 3, multiplicity: 1
    Zero: -1, multiplicity: 1   Zero: 2, multiplicity: 3
    Degree: 3   Degree: 4

77. Zero: -4, multiplicity: 2   78. Zero: 5, multiplicity: 3
    Zero: 3, multiplicity: 2   Zero: 0, multiplicity: 2
    Degree: 4   Degree: 5

79. Zero: -1, multiplicity: 2   80. Zero: 1, multiplicity: 2
    Zero: -2, multiplicity: 1   Zero: 4, multiplicity: 2
    Degree: 3   Degree: 4
    Rises to the left,   Falls to the left,
    Falls to the right   Falls to the right

Sketching a Polynomial with Given Conditions In Exercises 81–84, sketch the graph of a polynomial function that satisfies the given conditions. If not possible, explain your reasoning. (There are many correct answers.)

81. Third-degree polynomial with two real zeros and a negative leading coefficient

82. Fourth-degree polynomial with three real zeros and a positive leading coefficient

83. Fifth-degree polynomial with three real zeros and a positive leading coefficient

84. Fourth-degree polynomial with two real zeros and a negative leading coefficient

Sketching the Graph of a Polynomial Function In Exercises 85–94, sketch the graph of the function by (a) applying the Leading Coefficient Test, (b) finding the zeros of the polynomial, (c) plotting sufficient solution points, and (d) drawing a continuous curve through the points.

85. $f(x) = x^3 - 9x$ 86. $g(x) = x^4 - 4x^2$

87. $f(x) = x^3 - 3x^2$ 88. $f(x) = 3x^3 - 24x^2$

89. $f(x) = -x^4 + 9x^2 - 20$

90. $f(x) = -x^6 + 7x^3 + 8$

91. $f(x) = x^3 + 3x^2 - 9x - 27$

92. $h(x) = x^5 - 4x^3 + 8x^2 - 32$

93. $g(t) = -\frac{1}{4}t^4 + 2t^2 - 4$

94. $g(x) = \frac{1}{10}(x^4 - 4x^3 - 2x^2 + 12x + 9)$

Approximating the Zeros of a Function In Exercises 95–100, (a) use the Intermediate Value Theorem and a graphing utility to find graphically any intervals of length 1 in which the polynomial function is guaranteed to have a zero, and (b) use the *zero* or *root* feature of the graphing utility to approximate the real zeros of the function. Verify your answers in part (a) by using the *table* feature of the graphing utility.

95. $f(x) = x^3 - 3x^2 + 3$ **96.** $f(x) = -2x^3 - 6x^2 + 3$

97. $g(x) = 3x^4 + 4x^3 - 3$ **98.** $h(x) = x^4 - 10x^2 + 2$

99. $f(x) = x^4 - 3x^3 - 4x - 3$

100. $f(x) = x^3 - 4x^2 - 2x + 10$

Identifying Symmetry and *x*-Intercepts In Exercises 101–108, use a graphing utility to graph the function. Identify any symmetry with respect to the *x*-axis, *y*-axis, or origin. Determine the number of *x*-intercepts of the graph.

101. $f(x) = x^2(x + 6)$ **102.** $h(x) = x^3(x - 3)^2$

103. $g(t) = -\frac{1}{2}(t - 4)^2(t + 4)^2$

104. $g(x) = \frac{1}{8}(x + 1)^2(x - 3)^3$

105. $f(x) = x^3 - 4x$ **106.** $f(x) = x^4 - 2x^2$

107. $g(x) = \frac{1}{5}(x + 1)^2(x - 3)(2x - 9)$

108. $h(x) = \frac{1}{5}(x + 2)^2(3x - 5)^2$

109. Geometry An open box is to be made from a square piece of material 36 centimeters on a side by cutting equal squares with sides of length x from the corners and turning up the sides (see figure).

$x \longmapsto 36 - 2x \longrightarrow x$

(a) Verify that the volume of the box is given by the function $V(x) = x(36 - 2x)^2$.

(b) Determine the domain of the function V.

(c) Use the *table* feature of a graphing utility to create a table that shows various box heights x and the corresponding volumes V. Use the table to estimate a range of dimensions within which the maximum volume is produced.

(d) Use the graphing utility to graph V and use the range of dimensions from part (c) to find the x-value for which $V(x)$ is maximum.

110. Geometry An open box with locking tabs is to be made from a square piece of material 24 inches on a side. This is done by cutting equal squares from the corners and folding along the dashed lines, as shown in the figure.

(a) Verify that the volume of the box is given by the function $V(x) = 8x(6 - x)(12 - x)$.

(b) Determine the domain of the function V.

(c) Sketch the graph of the function and estimate the value of x for which $V(x)$ is maximum.

111. Marketing The total revenue R (in millions of dollars) for a company is related to its advertising expense by the function

$$R = 0.00001(-x^3 + 600x^2), \quad 0 \le x \le 400$$

where x is the amount spent on advertising (in tens of thousands of dollars). Use the graph of the function shown in the figure to estimate the point on the graph at which the function is increasing most rapidly. This point is called the **point of diminishing returns** because any expense above this amount will yield less return per dollar invested in advertising.

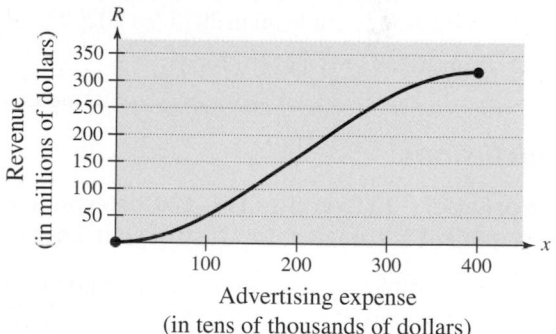

Advertising expense
(in tens of thousands of dollars)

112. Why you should learn it (*p. 100*) The growth of a red oak tree is approximated by the function

$$G = -0.003t^3 + 0.137t^2 + 0.458t - 0.839$$

where G is the height of the tree (in feet) and $t(2 \le t \le 32)$ is its age (in years). Use a graphing utility to graph the function and estimate the age of the tree when it is growing most rapidly. This point is called the **point of diminishing returns** because the increase in growth will be less with each additional year. (*Hint:* Use a viewing window in which $0 \le x \le 35$ and $0 \le y \le 60$.)

113. MODELING DATA

The U.S. production of crude oil y_1 (in quadrillions of British thermal units) and of solar and photovoltaic energy y_2 (in trillions of British thermal units) are shown in the table for the years 2004 through 2013, where t represents the year, with $t = 4$ corresponding to 2004. These data can be approximated by the models

$$y_1 = 0.00281t^4 - 0.0850t^3 + 1.027t^2 - 5.71t + 22.7$$

and

$$y_2 = 0.618t^3 - 10.80t^2 + 66.2t - 71.$$

(Source: Energy Information Administration)

Year, t	y_1	y_2
4	11.6	63
5	11.0	63
6	10.8	68
7	10.7	76
8	10.6	89
9	11.3	98
10	11.6	126
11	12.0	171
12	13.8	234
13	15.7	321

Spreadsheet at LarsonPrecalculus.com

(a) Use a graphing utility to plot the data and graph the model for y_1 in the same viewing window. How closely does the model represent the data?

(b) Extend the viewing window of the graphing utility to show the right-hand behavior of the model y_1. Would you use the model to estimate the production of crude oil in 2015? in 2020? Explain.

(c) Repeat parts (a) and (b) for y_2.

Conclusions

True or False? In Exercises 114–120, determine whether the statement is true or false. Justify your answer.

114. It is possible for a sixth-degree polynomial to have only one zero.

115. It is possible for a fifth-degree polynomial to have no real zeros.

116. It is possible for a polynomial with an even degree to have a range of $(-\infty, \infty)$.

117. The graph of the function $f(x) = x^6 - x^7$ rises to the left and falls to the right.

118. The graph of the function $f(x) = 2x(x - 1)^2(x + 3)^3$ crosses the x-axis at $x = 1$.

119. The graph of the function $f(x) = 2x(x - 1)^2(x + 3)^3$ touches, but does not cross, the x-axis.

120. The graph of the function $f(x) = 2x(x - 1)^2(x + 3)^3$ rises to the left and falls to the right.

121. Exploration Use a graphing utility to graph

$$y_1 = x + 2 \quad \text{and} \quad y_2 = (x + 2)(x - 1).$$

Predict the shape of the graph of

$$y_3 = (x + 2)(x - 1)(x - 3).$$

Use the graphing utility to verify your answer.

122. HOW DO YOU SEE IT? For each graph, describe a polynomial function that could represent the graph. (Indicate the degree of the function and the sign of its leading coefficient.)

(a)

(b)

(c)

(d)

Cumulative Mixed Review

Evaluating Combinations of Functions In Exercises 123–128, let $f(x) = 14x - 3$ and $g(x) = 8x^2$. Find the indicated value.

123. $(f + g)(-4)$

124. $(g - f)(3)$

125. $(fg)\left(-\dfrac{4}{7}\right)$

126. $\left(\dfrac{f}{g}\right)(-1.5)$

127. $(f \circ g)(-1)$

128. $(g \circ f)(0)$

Solving Inequalities In Exercises 129–132, solve the inequality and sketch the solution on the real number line. Use a graphing utility to verify your solution graphically.

129. $3(x - 5) < 4x - 7$

130. $2x^2 - x \geq 1$

131. $\dfrac{5x - 2}{x - 7} \leq 4$

132. $|x + 8| - 1 \geq 15$

2.3   Real Zeros of Polynomial Functions

Long Division of Polynomials

In the graph of $f(x) = 6x^3 - 19x^2 + 16x - 4$ shown in Figure 2.17, it appears that $x = 2$ is a zero of f. Because $f(2) = 0$, you know that $x = 2$ is a zero of the polynomial function f, and that $(x - 2)$ is a factor of $f(x)$. This means that there exists a second-degree polynomial $q(x)$ such that $f(x) = (x - 2) \cdot q(x)$. To find $q(x)$, you can use **long division of polynomials.**

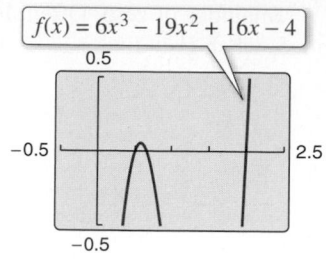

$f(x) = 6x^3 - 19x^2 + 16x - 4$

Figure 2.17

EXAMPLE 1   Long Division of Polynomials

Divide the polynomial $6x^3 - 19x^2 + 16x - 4$ by $x - 2$, and use the result to factor the polynomial completely.

Solution

Think $\dfrac{6x^3}{x} = 6x^2$.

Think $\dfrac{-7x^2}{x} = -7x$.

Think $\dfrac{2x}{x} = 2$.

$$
\begin{array}{r}
6x^2 - 7x + 2 \\
x - 2 \overline{)\, 6x^3 - 19x^2 + 16x - 4} \\
\underline{6x^3 - 12x^2} \qquad\qquad\qquad \\
-7x^2 + 16x \qquad\quad \\
\underline{-7x^2 + 14x} \qquad\quad \\
2x - 4 \\
\underline{2x - 4} \\
0
\end{array}
$$

Multiply: $6x^2(x - 2)$.
Subtract.
Multiply: $-7x(x - 2)$.
Subtract.
Multiply: $2(x - 2)$.
Subtract.

You can see that

$$6x^3 - 19x^2 + 16x - 4 = (x - 2)(6x^2 - 7x + 2)$$

$$= (x - 2)(2x - 1)(3x - 2).$$

Note that this factorization agrees with the graph of f (see Figure 2.17) in that the three x-intercepts occur at $x = 2$, $x = \frac{1}{2}$, and $x = \frac{2}{3}$.

✓ **Checkpoint** 🔊)) *Audio-video solution in English & Spanish at LarsonPrecalculus.com.*

Divide the polynomial $3x^2 + 19x + 28$ by $x + 4$, and use the result to factor the polynomial completely.

Note that in Example 1, the division process requires $-7x^2 + 14x$ to be subtracted from $-7x^2 + 16x$. So, it is implied that

$$
\begin{array}{r}
-7x^2 + 16x \\
\underline{-(-7x^2 + 14x)} \\
\end{array}
=
\begin{array}{r}
-7x^2 + 16x \\
\underline{7x^2 - 14x} \\
\end{array}
$$

and instead is written simply as

$$
\begin{array}{r}
-7x^2 + 16x \\
\underline{-7x^2 + 14x} \\
2x.
\end{array}
$$

In Example 1, $x - 2$ is a factor of the polynomial

$$6x^3 - 19x^2 + 16x - 4$$

and the long division process produces a remainder of zero. Often, long division will produce a nonzero remainder. For instance, when you divide $x^2 + 3x + 5$ by $x + 1$, you obtain the following.

$$
\begin{array}{r}
x + 2 \qquad \text{Quotient} \\
x + 1 \overline{)\, x^2 + 3x + 5} \qquad \text{Dividend} \\
\underline{x^2 + x} \\
2x + 5 \\
\underline{2x + 2} \\
3 \qquad \text{Remainder}
\end{array}
$$

In fractional form, you can write this result as follows.

$$\underbrace{\frac{x^2 + 3x + 5}{x + 1}}_{\text{Divisor}} = \overbrace{x + 2}^{\text{Quotient}} + \underbrace{\frac{\overset{\text{Remainder}}{3}}{x + 1}}_{\text{Divisor}}$$

This implies that

$$x^2 + 3x + 5 = (x + 1)(x + 2) + 3 \qquad \text{Multiply each side by } (x + 1).$$

which illustrates the following theorem, called the **Division Algorithm.**

The Division Algorithm

If $f(x)$ and $d(x)$ are polynomials such that $d(x) \neq 0$, and the degree of $d(x)$ is less than or equal to the degree of $f(x)$, then there exist unique polynomials $q(x)$ and $r(x)$ such that

$$\underset{\text{Dividend}}{f(x)} = \underset{\text{Divisor}}{d(x)} \, \underset{\text{Quotient}}{q(x)} + \underset{\text{Remainder}}{r(x)}$$

where $r(x) = 0$ *or* the degree of $r(x)$ is less than the degree of $d(x)$. If the remainder $r(x)$ is zero, then $d(x)$ *divides evenly* into $f(x)$.

The Division Algorithm can also be written as

$$\frac{f(x)}{d(x)} = q(x) + \frac{r(x)}{d(x)}.$$

In the Division Algorithm, the rational expression $f(x)/d(x)$ is **improper** because the degree of $f(x)$ is greater than or equal to the degree of $d(x)$. On the other hand, the rational expression $r(x)/d(x)$ is **proper** because the degree of $r(x)$ is less than the degree of $d(x)$.

Before you apply the Division Algorithm, follow these steps.

1. Write the dividend and divisor in descending powers of the variable.

2. Insert placeholders with zero coefficients for missing powers of the variable.

Note how these steps are applied in the next two examples.

EXAMPLE 2 Long Division of Polynomials

Divide $8x^3 - 1$ by $2x - 1$.

Solution

Because there is no x^2-term or x-term in the dividend, you need to line up the subtraction by using zero coefficients (or leaving spaces) for the missing terms.

$$
\begin{array}{r}
4x^2 + 2x + 1 \\
2x - 1 \overline{\smash{\big)}\, 8x^3 + 0x^2 + 0x - 1} \\
\underline{8x^3 - 4x^2} \\
4x^2 + 0x \\
\underline{4x^2 - 2x} \\
2x - 1 \\
\underline{2x - 1} \\
0
\end{array}
$$

So, $2x - 1$ divides evenly into $8x^3 - 1$, and you can write

$$
\frac{8x^3 - 1}{2x - 1} = 4x^2 + 2x + 1, \quad x \neq \frac{1}{2}.
$$

You can check this result by multiplying.

$$
(2x - 1)(4x^2 + 2x + 1) = 8x^3 + 4x^2 + 2x - 4x^2 - 2x - 1
$$
$$
= 8x^3 - 1
$$

✓ **Checkpoint** ◀))) *Audio-video solution in English & Spanish at LarsonPrecalculus.com.*

Divide $x^3 - 2x^2 - 9$ by $x - 3$.

In each of the long division examples presented so far, the divisor has been a first-degree polynomial. The long division algorithm works just as well with polynomial divisors of degree two or more, as shown in Example 3.

EXAMPLE 3 Long Division of Polynomials

Divide $-2 + 3x - 5x^2 + 4x^3 + 2x^4$ by $x^2 + 2x - 3$.

Solution

Begin by writing the dividend in descending powers of x.

$$
\begin{array}{r}
2x^2 \qquad\quad + 1 \\
x^2 + 2x - 3 \overline{\smash{\big)}\, 2x^4 + 4x^3 - 5x^2 + 3x - 2} \\
\underline{2x^4 + 4x^3 - 6x^2} \\
x^2 + 3x - 2 \\
\underline{x^2 + 2x - 3} \\
x + 1
\end{array}
$$

Note that the first subtraction eliminated two terms from the dividend. When this happens, the quotient skips a term. You can write the result as

$$
\frac{2x^4 + 4x^3 - 5x^2 + 3x - 2}{x^2 + 2x - 3} = 2x^2 + 1 + \frac{x + 1}{x^2 + 2x - 3}.
$$

✓ **Checkpoint** ◀))) *Audio-video solution in English & Spanish at LarsonPrecalculus.com.*

Divide $-x^3 + 9x + 6x^4 - x^2 - 3$ by $1 + 3x$.

Synthetic Division

There is a nice shortcut for long division of polynomials when dividing by divisors of the form

$$x - k.$$

The shortcut is called **synthetic division.** The pattern for synthetic division of a cubic polynomial is summarized as follows. (The pattern for higher-degree polynomials is similar.)

Synthetic Division (of a Cubic Polynomial)

To divide $ax^3 + bx^2 + cx + d$ by $x - k$, use the following pattern.

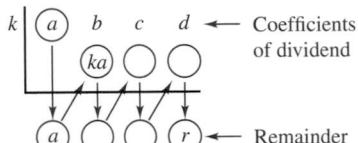

Vertical pattern: Add terms.
Diagonal pattern: Multiply by k.

This algorithm for synthetic division works *only* for divisors of the form $x - k$. Remember that

$$x + k = x - (-k).$$

EXAMPLE 4 Using Synthetic Division

Use synthetic division to divide

$$x^4 - 10x^2 - 2x + 4 \quad \text{by} \quad x + 3.$$

Solution

You should set up the array as follows. Note that a zero is included for the missing term in the dividend.

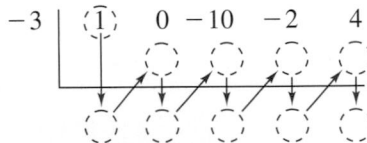

Then, use the synthetic division pattern by adding terms in columns and multiplying the results by -3.

Divisor: $x + 3$ Dividend: $x^4 - 10x^2 - 2x + 4$

$$
\begin{array}{r|rrrrr}
-3 & 1 & 0 & -10 & -2 & 4 \\
   &   & -3 & 9 & 3 & -3 \\
\hline
   & 1 & -3 & -1 & 1 & 1 \\
\end{array}
$$

← Remainder: 1

Quotient: $x^3 - 3x^2 - x + 1$

So, you have

$$\frac{x^4 - 10x^2 - 2x + 4}{x + 3} = x^3 - 3x^2 - x + 1 + \frac{1}{x + 3}.$$

✓ **Checkpoint** ◀))) *Audio-video solution in English & Spanish at LarsonPrecalculus.com.*

Use synthetic division to divide $5x^3 + 8x^2 - x + 6$ by $x + 2$. ■

> **Explore the Concept**
>
> Evaluate the polynomial $x^4 - 10x^2 - 2x + 4$ when $x = -3$. What do you observe?

The Remainder and Factor Theorems

The remainder obtained in the synthetic division process has an important interpretation, as described in the **Remainder Theorem.**

The Remainder Theorem   (See the proof on page 176.)

If a polynomial $f(x)$ is divided by $x - k$, then the remainder is

$r = f(k)$.

The Remainder Theorem tells you that synthetic division can be used to evaluate a polynomial function. That is, to evaluate a polynomial $f(x)$ when $x = k$, divide $f(x)$ by $x - k$. The remainder will be $f(k)$.

EXAMPLE 5   Using the Remainder Theorem

Use the Remainder Theorem to evaluate

$$f(x) = 3x^3 + 8x^2 + 5x - 7$$

when $x = -2$.

Solution

Using synthetic division, you obtain the following.

$$
\begin{array}{r|rrrr}
-2 & 3 & 8 & 5 & -7 \\
   &   & -6 & -4 & -2 \\
\hline
   & 3 & 2 & 1 & -9
\end{array}
$$

Because the remainder is $r = -9$, you can conclude that

$$f(-2) = -9. \qquad {\scriptstyle r\,=\,f(k)}$$

This means that $(-2, -9)$ is a point on the graph of f. You can check this by substituting $x = -2$ in the original function.

Check

$$f(-2) = 3(-2)^3 + 8(-2)^2 + 5(-2) - 7$$
$$= 3(-8) + 8(4) - 10 - 7$$
$$= -24 + 32 - 10 - 7$$
$$= -9$$

✓ **Checkpoint** ◀))) *Audio-video solution in English & Spanish at LarsonPrecalculus.com.*

Use the Remainder Theorem to find each function value given

$$f(x) = 4x^3 + 10x^2 - 3x - 8.$$

a. $f(-1)$ **b.** $f(4)$

c. $f\left(\frac{1}{2}\right)$ **d.** $f(-3)$ ■

Another important theorem is the **Factor Theorem.** This theorem states that you can test whether a polynomial has $(x - k)$ as a factor by evaluating the polynomial at $x = k$. If the result is 0, then $(x - k)$ is a factor.

The Factor Theorem   (See the proof on page 176.)

A polynomial $f(x)$ has a factor $(x - k)$ if and only if $f(k) = 0$.

EXAMPLE 6   Factoring a Polynomial: Repeated Division

Show that $(x - 2)$ and $(x + 3)$ are factors of

$$f(x) = 2x^4 + 7x^3 - 4x^2 - 27x - 18.$$

Then find the remaining factors of $f(x)$.

Algebraic Solution

Using synthetic division with the factor $(x - 2)$, you obtain the following.

$$\begin{array}{r|rrrrr} 2 & 2 & 7 & -4 & -27 & -18 \\ & & 4 & 22 & 36 & 18 \\ \hline & 2 & 11 & 18 & 9 & 0 \end{array}$$

⟶ 0 remainder;
$(x - 2)$ is
a factor.

Take the result of this division and perform synthetic division again using the factor $(x + 3)$.

$$\begin{array}{r|rrrr} -3 & 2 & 11 & 18 & 9 \\ & & -6 & -15 & -9 \\ \hline & 2 & 5 & 3 & 0 \end{array}$$

$\underbrace{\qquad\qquad}_{2x^2 + 5x + 3}$

⟶ 0 remainder;
$(x + 3)$ is
a factor.

Because the resulting quadratic factors as

$$2x^2 + 5x + 3 = (2x + 3)(x + 1)$$

the complete factorization of $f(x)$ is

$$f(x) = (x - 2)(x + 3)(2x + 3)(x + 1).$$

Graphical Solution

From the graph of

$$f(x) = 2x^4 + 7x^3 - 4x^2 - 27x - 18$$

you can see that there are four x-intercepts (see Figure 2.18). These occur at $x = -3$, $x = -\frac{3}{2}$, $x = -1$, and $x = 2$. (Check this algebraically.) This implies that $(x + 3)$, $\left(x + \frac{3}{2}\right)$, $(x + 1)$, and $(x - 2)$ are factors of $f(x)$. $\left[\text{Note that } \left(x + \frac{3}{2}\right) \text{ and } (2x + 3) \text{ are equivalent factors because they both yield the same zero, } x = -\frac{3}{2}.\right]$

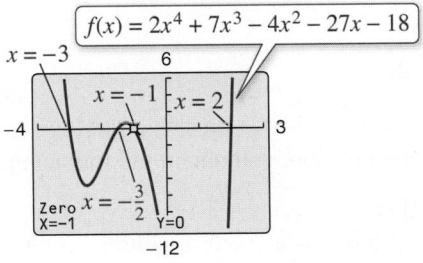

Figure 2.18

✓ **Checkpoint** 🔊))) *Audio-video solution in English & Spanish at LarsonPrecalculus.com.*

Show that $(x + 3)$ is a factor of $f(x) = x^3 - 19x - 30$. Then find the remaining factors of $f(x)$.

Note in Example 6 that the complete factorization of $f(x)$ implies that f has four real zeros:

$$x = 2, \quad x = -3, \quad x = -\tfrac{3}{2}, \quad \text{and} \quad x = -1.$$

This is confirmed by the graph of f, which is shown in Figure 2.18.

Using the Remainder in Synthetic Division

In summary, the remainder r, obtained in the synthetic division of a polynomial $f(x)$ by $x - k$, provides the following information.

1. The remainder r gives the *value* of f at $x = k$. That is, $r = f(k)$.

2. If $r = 0$, then $(x - k)$ is a *factor* of $f(x)$.

3. If $r = 0$, then $(k, 0)$ is an *x-intercept* of the graph of f.

Throughout this text, the importance of developing several problem-solving strategies is emphasized. In the exercises for this section, try using more than one strategy to solve several of the exercises. For instance, when you find that $x - k$ divides evenly into $f(x)$, try sketching the graph of f. You should find that $(k, 0)$ is an x-intercept of the graph.

The Rational Zero Test

The **Rational Zero Test** relates the possible rational zeros of a polynomial (having integer coefficients) to the leading coefficient and to the constant term of the polynomial.

The Rational Zero Test

If the polynomial

$$f(x) = a_n x^n + a_{n-1} x^{n-1} + \cdots + a_2 x^2 + a_1 x + a_0$$

has integer coefficients, then every rational zero of f has the form

$$\text{Rational zero} = \frac{p}{q}$$

where p and q have no common factors other than 1, p is a factor of the constant term a_0, and q is a factor of the leading coefficient a_n.

> **Remark**
>
> Use a graphing utility to graph the polynomial
>
> $$y = x^3 - 53x^2 + 103x - 51$$
>
> in a standard viewing window. From the graph alone, it appears that there is only one zero. From the Leading Coefficient Test, you know that because the degree of the polynomial is odd and the leading coefficient is positive, the graph falls to the left and rises to the right. So, the function must have another zero. From the Rational Zero Test, you know that ± 51 might be zeros of the function. When you zoom out several times, you will see a more complete picture of the graph. Your graph should confirm that $x = 51$ is a zero of f.

To use the Rational Zero Test, first list all rational numbers whose numerators are factors of the constant term and whose denominators are factors of the leading coefficient.

$$\text{Possible rational zeros} = \frac{\text{factors of constant term}}{\text{factors of leading coefficient}}$$

Now that you have formed this list of *possible rational zeros,* use a trial-and-error method to determine which, if any, are actual zeros of the polynomial. Note that when the leading coefficient is 1, the possible rational zeros are simply the factors of the constant term. This case is illustrated in Example 7.

EXAMPLE 7   **Rational Zero Test with Leading Coefficient of 1**

Find the rational zeros of $f(x) = x^3 + x + 1$.

Solution

Because the leading coefficient is 1, the possible rational zeros are simply the factors of the constant term.

Possible rational zeros: ± 1

By testing these possible zeros, you can see that neither works.

$$f(1) = (1)^3 + 1 + 1 = 3$$

$$f(-1) = (-1)^3 + (-1) + 1 = -1$$

So, you can conclude that the polynomial has *no* rational zeros. Note from the graph of f shown below that f does have one real zero between -1 and 0. However, by the Rational Zero Test, you know that this real zero is *not* a rational number.

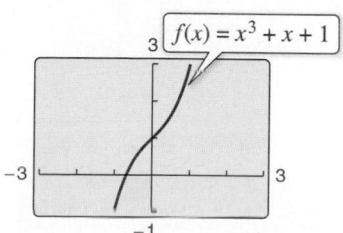

✓ *Checkpoint* 🔊))) *Audio-video solution in English & Spanish at LarsonPrecalculus.com.*

Find the rational zeros of $f(x) = x^3 - 5x^2 + 2x + 8$. ∎

When the leading coefficient of a polynomial is not 1, the list of possible rational zeros can increase dramatically. In such cases, the search can be shortened in several ways.

1. A graphing utility can be used to speed up the calculations.

2. A graph, drawn either by hand or with a graphing utility, can give good estimates of the locations of the zeros.

3. The Intermediate Value Theorem, along with a table generated by a graphing utility, can give approximations of zeros.

4. The Factor Theorem and synthetic division can be used to test the possible rational zeros.

Finding the first zero is often the most difficult part. After that, the search is simplified by working with the lower-degree polynomial obtained in synthetic division, as shown in Example 8.

EXAMPLE 8   Using the Rational Zero Test

Find the rational zeros of

$$f(x) = 2x^3 + 3x^2 - 8x + 3.$$

Solution

The leading coefficient is 2, and the constant term is 3.

$$\text{Possible rational zeros: } \frac{\text{Factors of 3}}{\text{Factors of 2}} = \frac{\pm 1, \pm 3}{\pm 1, \pm 2} = \pm 1, \pm 3, \pm \frac{1}{2}, \pm \frac{3}{2}$$

By synthetic division, you can determine that $x = 1$ is a rational zero.

$$
\begin{array}{r|rrrr}
1 & 2 & 3 & -8 & 3 \\
  &   & 2 & 5 & -3 \\
\hline
  & 2 & 5 & -3 & 0 \\
\end{array}
$$

So, $f(x)$ factors as

$$f(x) = (x - 1)(2x^2 + 5x - 3)$$
$$= (x - 1)(2x - 1)(x + 3)$$

and you can conclude that the rational zeros of f are $x = 1$, $x = \frac{1}{2}$, and $x = -3$, as shown in the figure.

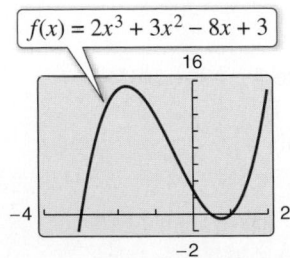

$f(x) = 2x^3 + 3x^2 - 8x + 3$

✓ **Checkpoint** ◀))) Audio-video solution in English & Spanish at LarsonPrecalculus.com.

Find the rational zeros of $f(x) = 2x^4 - 9x^3 - 18x^2 + 71x - 30$. ∎

Remember that when you try to find the rational zeros of a polynomial function with many possible rational zeros, as in Example 8, you must use trial and error. There is no quick algebraic method to determine which of the possibilities is an actual zero; however, sketching a graph may be helpful.

Other Tests for Zeros of Polynomials

You know that an nth-degree polynomial function can have *at most n* real zeros. Of course, many nth-degree polynomials do not have that many real zeros. For instance, $f(x) = x^2 + 1$ has no real zeros, and $f(x) = x^3 + 1$ has only one real zero. The following theorem, called **Descartes's Rule of Signs,** sheds more light on the number of real zeros of a polynomial.

Decartes's Rule of Signs

Let $f(x) = a_n x^n + a_{n-1} x^{n-1} + \cdots + a_2 x^2 + a_1 x + a_0$ be a polynomial with real coefficients and $a_0 \neq 0$.

1. The number of *positive real zeros* of f is either equal to the number of variations in sign of $f(x)$ or less than that number by an even integer.

2. The number of *negative real zeros* of f is either equal to the number of variations in sign of $f(-x)$ or less than that number by an even integer.

A **variation in sign** means that two consecutive coefficients have opposite signs. Missing terms (those with zero coefficients) can be ignored.

When using Descartes's Rule of Signs, a zero of multiplicity k should be counted as k zeros. For instance, the polynomial $x^3 - 3x + 2$ has two variations in sign, and so has either two positive or no positive real zeros. Because

$$x^3 - 3x + 2 = (x - 1)(x - 1)(x + 2)$$

you can see that the two positive real zeros are $x = 1$ of multiplicity 2.

EXAMPLE 9   Using Descartes's Rule of Signs

Determine the possible numbers of positive and negative real zeros of

$$f(x) = 3x^3 - 5x^2 + 6x - 4.$$

Solution

The original polynomial has *three* variations in sign.

$$
\begin{array}{c}
{\scriptsize +\text{ to }-\qquad\ +\text{ to }-} \\
{\downarrow\ \ \downarrow\quad\ \downarrow\ \ \downarrow} \\
f(x) = 3x^3 - 5x^2 + 6x - 4 \\
{\uparrow\qquad\ \uparrow} \\
{\scriptsize -\ \text{ to }\ +}
\end{array}
$$

The polynomial

$$
\begin{aligned}
f(-x) &= 3(-x)^3 - 5(-x)^2 + 6(-x) - 4 \\
&= -3x^3 - 5x^2 - 6x - 4
\end{aligned}
$$

has no variations in sign. So, from Descartes's Rule of Signs, the polynomial $f(x) = 3x^3 - 5x^2 + 6x - 4$ has either three positive real zeros or one positive real zero, and has no negative real zeros. By using the *trace* feature of a graphing utility, you can see that the function has only one real zero (it is a positive number near $x = 1$), as shown in the figure.

✓ *Checkpoint* ◀)))

Determine the possible numbers of positive and negative real zeros of

$$f(x) = -2x^3 + 5x^2 - x + 8. \qquad ■$$

Another test for zeros of a polynomial function is related to the sign pattern in the last row of the synthetic division array. This test can give you an upper or lower bound for the real zeros of f, which can help you eliminate possible real zeros. A real number c is an **upper bound** for the real zeros of f when no zeros are greater than c. Similarly, c is a **lower bound** when no real zeros of f are less than c.

Upper and Lower Bound Rules

Let $f(x)$ be a polynomial with real coefficients and a positive leading coefficient. Suppose $f(x)$ is divided by $x - c$, using synthetic division.

1. If $c > 0$ and each number in the last row is either positive or zero, then c is an **upper bound** for the real zeros of f.

2. If $c < 0$ and the numbers in the last row are alternately positive and negative (zero entries count as positive or negative), then c is a **lower bound** for the real zeros of f.

EXAMPLE 10   Finding the Zeros of a Polynomial Function

Find all real zeros of $f(x) = 6x^3 - 4x^2 + 3x - 2$.

Solution

The possible real zeros are as follows.

$$\frac{\text{Factors of } -2}{\text{Factors of } 6} = \frac{\pm 1, \pm 2}{\pm 1, \pm 2, \pm 3, \pm 6} = \pm 1, \pm \frac{1}{2}, \pm \frac{1}{3}, \pm \frac{1}{6}, \pm \frac{2}{3}, \pm 2$$

The original polynomial $f(x)$ has three variations in sign. The polynomial

$$f(-x) = 6(-x)^3 - 4(-x)^2 + 3(-x) - 2$$
$$= -6x^3 - 4x^2 - 3x - 2$$

has no variations in sign. So, you can apply Descartes's Rule of Signs to conclude that there are either three positive real zeros or one positive real zero, and no negative real zeros. Trying $x = 1$ produces the following.

$$
\begin{array}{r|rrrr}
1 & 6 & -4 & 3 & -2 \\
  &   & 6 & 2 & 5 \\
\hline
  & 6 & 2 & 5 & 3 \\
\end{array}
$$

So, $x = 1$ is not a zero, but because the last row has all positive entries, you know that $x = 1$ is an upper bound for the real zeros. Therefore, you can restrict the search to zeros between 0 and 1. By trial and error, you can determine that $x = \frac{2}{3}$ is a zero. So,

$$f(x) = \left(x - \frac{2}{3}\right)(6x^2 + 3).$$

Because $6x^2 + 3$ has no real zeros, it follows that $x = \frac{2}{3}$ is the only real zero, as shown in the figure.

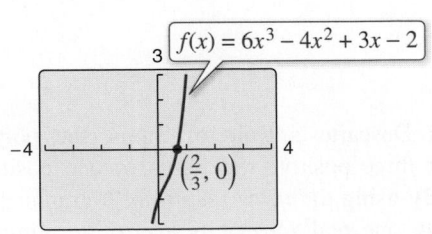

$f(x) = 6x^3 - 4x^2 + 3x - 2$

$\left(\frac{2}{3}, 0\right)$

✓ **Checkpoint** ◀))) Audio-video solution in English & Spanish at LarsonPrecalculus.com.

Find all real zeros of

$$f(x) = 8x^3 - 4x^2 + 6x - 3.$$

Explore the Concept

Use a graphing utility to graph the polynomial

$$y_1 = 6x^3 - 4x^2 + 3x - 2.$$

Notice that the graph intersects the x-axis at the point $\left(\frac{2}{3}, 0\right)$. How does this information relate to the real zero found in Example 10? Use the graphing utility to graph

$$y_2 = x^4 - 5x^3 + 3x^2 + x.$$

How many times does the graph intersect the x-axis? How many real zeros does y_2 have?

Here are two additional hints that can help you find the real zeros of a polynomial.

1. When the terms of $f(x)$ have a common monomial factor, it should be factored out before applying the tests in this section. For instance, by writing

$$f(x) = x^4 - 5x^3 + 3x^2 + x = x(x^3 - 5x^2 + 3x + 1)$$

you can see that $x = 0$ is a zero of f and that the remaining zeros can be obtained by analyzing the cubic factor.

2. When you are able to find all but two zeros of f, you can always use the Quadratic Formula on the remaining quadratic factor. For instance, after writing

$$f(x) = x^4 - 5x^3 + 3x^2 + x = x(x - 1)(x^2 - 4x - 1)$$

you can apply the Quadratic Formula to $x^2 - 4x - 1$ to conclude that the two remaining zeros are $x = 2 + \sqrt{5}$ and $x = 2 - \sqrt{5}$.

Note how these hints are applied in the next example.

EXAMPLE 11   **Finding the Zeros of a Polynomial Function**

See LarsonPrecalculus.com for an interactive version of this type of example.

Find all real zeros of $f(x) = 10x^4 - 15x^3 - 16x^2 + 12x$.

Solution

Remove the common monomial factor x to write

$$f(x) = 10x^4 - 15x^3 - 16x^2 + 12x = x(10x^3 - 15x^2 - 16x + 12).$$

So, $x = 0$ is a zero of f. You can find the remaining zeros of f by analyzing the cubic factor. Because the leading coefficient is 10 and the constant term is 12, there is a long list of possible rational zeros.

Possible rational zeros:

$$\frac{\text{Factors of } 12}{\text{Factors of } 10} = \frac{\pm 1, \pm 2, \pm 3, \pm 4, \pm 6, \pm 12}{\pm 1, \pm 2, \pm 5, \pm 10}$$

With so many possibilities (32, in fact), it is worth your time to use a graphing utility to focus on just a few. By using the *trace* feature of a graphing utility, it looks like three reasonable choices are $x = -\frac{6}{5}$, $x = \frac{1}{2}$, and $x = 2$ (see figure). Synthetic division shows that only $x = 2$ works. (You could also use the Factor Theorem to test these choices.)

$$\begin{array}{r|rrrr} 2 & 10 & -15 & -16 & 12 \\ & & 20 & 10 & -12 \\ \hline & 10 & 5 & -6 & 0 \end{array}$$

So, $x = 2$ is one zero and you have

$$f(x) = x(x - 2)(10x^2 + 5x - 6).$$

Using the Quadratic Formula, you find that the two additional zeros are irrational numbers.

$$x = \frac{-5 + \sqrt{265}}{20} \approx 0.56 \quad \text{and} \quad x = \frac{-5 - \sqrt{265}}{20} \approx -1.06$$

✓ Checkpoint Audio-video solution in English & Spanish at LarsonPrecalculus.com.

Find all real zeros of $f(x) = 3x^4 - 14x^2 - 4x$. ■

2.3 Exercises

See *CalcChat.com* for tutorial help and worked-out solutions to odd-numbered exercises.
For instructions on how to use a graphing utility, see Appendix A.

Vocabulary and Concept Check

1. Two forms of the Division Algorithm are shown below. Identify and label each part.

$$f(x) = d(x)q(x) + r(x) \qquad \frac{f(x)}{d(x)} = q(x) + \frac{r(x)}{d(x)}$$

In Exercises 2–5, fill in the blank(s).

2. The rational expression $p(x)/q(x)$ is called _____ when the degree of the numerator is greater than or equal to that of the denominator.

3. Every rational zero of a polynomial function with integer coefficients has the form p/q, where p is a factor of the _____ and q is a factor of the _____ .

4. The theorem that can be used to determine the possible numbers of positive real zeros and negative real zeros of a function is called _____ of _____ .

5. A real number c is a(n) _____ bound for the real zeros of f when no zeros are greater than c, and is a(n) _____ bound when no real zeros of f are less than c.

6. How many negative real zeros are possible for a polynomial function f, given that $f(-x)$ has 5 variations in sign?

7. You divide the polynomial $f(x)$ by $(x - 4)$ and obtain a remainder of 7. What is $f(4)$?

8. What value should you write in the circle to check whether $(x - 2)$ is a factor of $f(x) = x^3 + 6x^2 - 5x + 3$?

$$\bigcirc \, \underline{|\; 1 \quad 6 \quad -5 \quad 3}$$

Procedures and Problem Solving

Long Division of Polynomials In Exercises 9–12, use long division to divide and use the result to factor the dividend completely.

9. $(x^2 + 5x + 6) \div (x + 3)$

10. $(5x^2 - 17x - 12) \div (x - 4)$

11. $(x^3 + 5x^2 - 12x - 36) \div (x + 2)$

12. $(2x^3 - 3x^2 - 50x + 75) \div (2x - 3)$

Long Division of Polynomials In Exercises 13–22, use long division to divide.

13. $(x^3 - 4x^2 - 17x + 6) \div (x - 3)$

14. $(4x^3 - 7x^2 - 11x + 5) \div (4x + 5)$

15. $(7x^3 + 3) \div (x + 2)$ 16. $(8x^4 - 5) \div (2x + 1)$

17. $(5x - 1 + 10x^3 - 2x^2) \div (2x^2 + 1)$

18. $(1 + 3x^2 + x^4) \div (3 - 2x + x^2)$

19. $(x^3 - 9) \div (x^2 + 1)$ 20. $(x^5 + 7) \div (x^3 - 1)$

21. $\dfrac{2x^3 - 4x^2 - 15x + 5}{(x - 1)^2}$ 22. $\dfrac{x^4}{(x - 1)^3}$

Using Synthetic Division In Exercises 23–32, use synthetic division to divide.

23. $(3x^3 - 17x^2 + 15x - 25) \div (x - 5)$

24. $(5x^3 + 18x^2 + 7x - 6) \div (x + 3)$

25. $(6x^3 + 7x^2 - x + 26) \div (x - 3)$

26. $(2x^3 + 14x^2 - 20x + 7) \div (x + 6)$

27. $(9x^3 - 18x^2 - 16x + 32) \div (x - 2)$

28. $(5x^3 + 6x + 8) \div (x + 2)$

29. $(x^3 + 512) \div (x + 8)$ 30. $(x^3 - 729) \div (x - 9)$

31. $\dfrac{4x^3 + 16x^2 - 23x - 15}{x + \frac{1}{2}}$ 32. $\dfrac{3x^3 - 4x^2 + 5}{x - \frac{3}{2}}$

Verifying Quotients In Exercises 33–36, use a graphing utility to graph the two equations in the same viewing window. Use the graphs to verify that the expressions are equivalent. Verify the results algebraically.

33. $y_1 = \dfrac{x^2}{x + 2}, \quad y_2 = x - 2 + \dfrac{4}{x + 2}$

34. $y_1 = \dfrac{x^2 + 2x - 1}{x + 3}, \quad y_2 = x - 1 + \dfrac{2}{x + 3}$

35. $y_1 = \dfrac{x^4 - 3x^2 - 1}{x^2 + 5}, \quad y_2 = x^2 - 8 + \dfrac{39}{x^2 + 5}$

36. $y_1 = \dfrac{x^4 + x^2 - 1}{x^2 + 1}, \quad y_2 = x^2 - \dfrac{1}{x^2 + 1}$

Verifying the Remainder Theorem In Exercises 37–42, write the function in the form $f(x) = (x - k)q(x) + r(x)$ for the given value of k. Use a graphing utility to demonstrate that $f(k) = r$.

Function	Value of k
37. $f(x) = x^3 - x^2 - 14x + 11$	$k = 4$
38. $f(x) = 15x^4 + 10x^3 - 6x^2 + 14$	$k = -\frac{2}{3}$

Function	Value of k
39. $f(x) = x^3 + 3x^2 - 2x - 14$	$k = \sqrt{2}$
40. $f(x) = x^3 + 2x^2 - 5x - 4$	$k = -\sqrt{5}$
41. $f(x) = 4x^3 - 6x^2 - 12x - 4$	$k = 1 - \sqrt{3}$
42. $f(x) = -3x^3 + 8x^2 + 10x - 8$	$k = 2 + \sqrt{2}$

Using the Remainder Theorem   **In Exercises 43–46,** use the Remainder Theorem and synthetic division to evaluate the function at each given value. Use a graphing utility to verify your results.

43. $f(x) = 2x^3 - 7x + 3$

    (a) $f(1)$ (b) $f(-2)$ (c) $f\left(\tfrac{1}{2}\right)$ (d) $f(2)$

44. $g(x) = 2x^6 + 3x^4 - x^2 + 3$

    (a) $g(2)$ (b) $g(1)$ (c) $g(3)$ (d) $g(-1)$

45. $h(x) = x^3 - 5x^2 - 7x + 4$

    (a) $h(3)$ (b) $h(2)$ (c) $h(-2)$ (d) $h(-5)$

46. $f(x) = 4x^4 - 16x^3 + 7x^2 + 20$

    (a) $f(1)$ (b) $f(-2)$ (c) $f(5)$ (d) $f(-10)$

Using the Factor Theorem   **In Exercises 47–52,** use synthetic division to show that x is a solution of the third-degree polynomial equation, and use the result to factor the polynomial completely. List all the real solutions of the equation.

Polynomial Equation	Value of x
47. $x^3 - 13x - 12 = 0$	$x = 4$
48. $x^3 - 31x + 30 = 0$	$x = -6$
49. $2x^3 - 17x^2 + 12x + 63 = 0$	$x = -\tfrac{3}{2}$
50. $60x^3 - 89x^2 + 41x - 6 = 0$	$x = \tfrac{1}{3}$
51. $x^3 + 2x^2 - 3x - 6 = 0$	$x = \sqrt{3}$
52. $x^3 - x^2 - 13x - 3 = 0$	$x = 2 - \sqrt{5}$

Factoring a Polynomial   **In Exercises 53–58,** (a) verify the given factor(s) of the function f, (b) find the remaining factors of f, (c) use your results to write the complete factorization of f, and (d) list all real zeros of f. Confirm your results by using a graphing utility to graph the function.

Function	Factor(s)
53. $f(x) = 2x^3 + x^2 - 5x + 2$	$(x + 2)$
54. $f(x) = 3x^3 + 2x^2 - 19x + 6$	$(x + 3)$
55. $f(x) = x^4 - 4x^3 - 15x^2$ $+ 58x - 40$	$(x - 5), (x + 4)$
56. $f(x) = 8x^4 - 14x^3 - 71x^2$ $- 10x + 24$	$(x + 2), (x - 4)$
57. $f(x) = 6x^3 + 41x^2 - 9x - 14$	$(2x + 1)$
58. $f(x) = 2x^3 - x^2 - 10x + 5$	$(2x - 1)$

Using the Rational Zero Test   **In Exercises 59–62,** use the Rational Zero Test to list all possible rational zeros of f. Then find the rational zeros.

59. $f(x) = x^3 + 3x^2 - x - 3$

60. $f(x) = x^3 - 4x^2 - 4x + 16$

61. $f(x) = 2x^4 - 17x^3 + 35x^2 + 9x - 45$

62. $f(x) = 4x^5 - 8x^4 - 5x^3 + 10x^2 + x - 2$

Using Descartes's Rule of Signs   **In Exercises 63–66,** use Descartes's Rule of Signs to determine the possible numbers of positive and negative real zeros of the function.

63. $f(x) = 2x^4 - x^3 + 6x^2 - x + 5$

64. $f(x) = 3x^4 + 5x^3 - 6x^2 + 8x - 3$

65. $g(x) = 4x^3 - 5x + 8$

66. $g(x) = 2x^3 - 4x^2 - 5$

Finding the Zeros of a Polynomial Function   **In Exercises 67–72,** (a) use Descartes's Rule of Signs to determine the possible numbers of positive and negative real zeros of f, (b) list the possible rational zeros of f, (c) use a graphing utility to graph f so that some of the possible zeros in parts (a) and (b) can be disregarded, and (d) determine all the real zeros of f.

67. $f(x) = x^3 + x^2 - 4x - 4$

68. $f(x) = -3x^3 + 20x^2 - 36x + 16$

69. $f(x) = -2x^4 + 13x^3 - 21x^2 + 2x + 8$

70. $f(x) = 4x^4 - 17x^2 + 4$

71. $f(x) = 32x^3 - 52x^2 + 17x + 3$

72. $f(x) = x^4 - x^3 - 29x^2 - x - 30$

Finding the Zeros of a Polynomial Function   **In Exercises 73–76,** use synthetic division to verify the upper and lower bounds of the real zeros of f. Then find all real zeros of the function.

73. $f(x) = x^4 - 4x^3 + 15$

    Upper bound: $x = 4$

    Lower bound: $x = -1$

74. $f(x) = 2x^3 - 3x^2 - 12x + 8$

    Upper bound: $x = 4$

    Lower bound: $x = -3$

75. $f(x) = x^4 - 4x^3 + 16x - 16$

    Upper bound: $x = 5$

    Lower bound: $x = -3$

76. $f(x) = 2x^4 - 8x + 3$

    Upper bound: $x = 3$

    Lower bound: $x = -4$

Occasionally, throughout this text, you will be asked to round to a place value rather than to a number of decimal places.

Rewriting to Use the Rational Zero Test **In Exercises 77–80, find the rational zeros of the polynomial function.**

77. $P(x) = x^4 - \frac{25}{4}x^2 + 9 = \frac{1}{4}(4x^4 - 25x^2 + 36)$

78. $f(x) = x^3 - \frac{3}{2}x^2 - \frac{23}{2}x + 6 = \frac{1}{2}(2x^3 - 3x^2 - 23x + 12)$

79. $f(x) = x^3 - \frac{1}{4}x^2 - x + \frac{1}{4} = \frac{1}{4}(4x^3 - x^2 - 4x + 1)$

80. $f(z) = z^3 + \frac{11}{6}z^2 - \frac{1}{2}z - \frac{1}{3} = \frac{1}{6}(6z^3 + 11z^2 - 3z - 2)$

A Cubic Polynomial with Two Terms **In Exercises 81–84, match the cubic function with the correct number of rational and irrational zeros.**

(a) Rational zeros: 0; Irrational zeros: 1

(b) Rational zeros: 3; Irrational zeros: 0

(c) Rational zeros: 1; Irrational zeros: 2

(d) Rational zeros: 1; Irrational zeros: 0

81. $f(x) = x^3 - 1$ **82.** $f(x) = x^3 - 2$

83. $f(x) = x^3 - x$ **84.** $f(x) = x^3 - 2x$

Using a Graph to Help Find Zeros **In Exercises 85–88, the graph of $y = f(x)$ is shown. Use the graph as an aid to find all real zeros of the function.**

85. $y = 2x^4 - 9x^3 + 5x^2$ **86.** $y = x^4 - 5x^3 - 7x^2$
$\quad\quad + 3x - 1$ $\quad\quad + 13x - 2$

87. $y = -2x^4 + 17x^3$ **88.** $y = -x^4 + 5x^3$
$\quad\quad - 3x^2 - 25x - 3$ $\quad\quad - 10x - 4$

Finding the Zeros of a Polynomial Function **In Exercises 89–100, find all real zeros of the polynomial function.**

89. $f(x) = 5x^4 + 9x^3 - 19x^2 - 3x$

90. $g(x) = 4x^4 - 11x^3 - 22x^2 + 8x$

91. $f(z) = z^4 - z^3 - 2z - 4$

92. $f(x) = 4x^3 + 7x^2 - 11x - 18$

93. $g(y) = 2y^4 + 7y^3 - 26y^2 + 23y - 6$

94. $h(x) = x^5 - x^4 - 3x^3 + 5x^2 - 2x$

95. $f(x) = 4x^4 - 55x^2 - 45x + 36$

96. $z(x) = 6x^4 + 33x^3 - 69x + 30$

97. $g(x) = 8x^4 + 28x^3 + 9x^2 - 9x$

98. $h(x) = x^5 + 5x^4 - 5x^3 - 15x^2 - 6x$

99. $f(x) = 8x^5 + 6x^4 - 37x^3 - 36x^2 + 29x + 30$

100. $g(x) = 4x^5 + 8x^4 - 15x^3 - 23x^2 + 11x + 15$

Using a Rational Zero **In Exercises 101–104, (a) use the *zero* or *root* feature of a graphing utility to approximate (accurate to the nearest thousandth) the zeros of the function, (b) determine one of the exact zeros and use synthetic division to verify your result, and (c) factor the polynomial completely.**

101. $h(t) = t^3 - 2t^2 - 7t + 2$

102. $f(s) = s^3 - 12s^2 + 40s - 24$

103. $h(x) = x^5 - 7x^4 + 10x^3 + 14x^2 - 24x$

104. $g(x) = 6x^4 - 11x^3 - 51x^2 + 99x - 27$

105. MODELING DATA

The table shows the numbers S of cellular phone subscriptions per 100 people in the United States from 1995 through 2012. (Source: International Telecommunications Union)

Year	Subscriptions per 100 people, S
1995	12.6
1996	16.2
1997	20.1
1998	24.9
1999	30.6
2000	38.5
2001	44.7
2002	48.9
2003	54.9
2004	62.6
2005	68.3
2006	76.3
2007	82.1
2008	85.2
2009	88.6
2010	91.3
2011	94.7
2012	95.5

Spreadsheet at LarsonPrecalculus.com

The data can be approximated by the model

$S = -0.0223t^3 + 0.825t^2 - 3.58t + 12.6,$
$5 \le t \le 22$

where t represents the year, with $t = 5$ corresponding to 1995.

(a) Use a graphing utility to plot the data and graph the model in the same viewing window.

(b) How well does the model fit the data?

(c) Use the Remainder Theorem to evaluate the model for the year 2020. Is the value reasonable? Explain.

106. *Why you should learn it* (*p. 113*) The numbers of employees E (in thousands) in education and health services in the United States from 1960 through 2013 are approximated by $E = -0.088t^3 + 10.77t^2 + 14.6t + 3197$, $0 \le t \le 53$, where t is the year, with $t = 0$ corresponding to 1960. (Source: U.S. Bureau of Labor Statistics)

(a) Use a graphing utility to graph the model over the domain.

(b) Estimate the number of employees in education and health services in 1960. Use the Remainder Theorem to estimate the number in 2010.

(c) Is this a good model for making predictions in future years? Explain.

107. Geometry A rectangular package sent by a delivery service can have a maximum combined length and girth (perimeter of a cross section) of 120 inches (see figure).

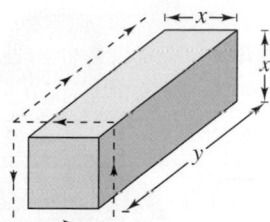

(a) Show that the volume of the package is given by the function $V(x) = 4x^2(30 - x)$.

(b) Use a graphing utility to graph the function and approximate the dimensions of the package that yield a maximum volume.

(c) Find values of x such that $V = 13,500$. Which of these values is a physical impossibility in the construction of the package? Explain.

108. Environmental Science The number of parts per million of nitric oxide emissions y from a car engine is approximated by $y = -5.05x^3 + 3857x - 38,411.25$, $13 \le x \le 18$, where x is the air-fuel ratio.

(a) Use a graphing utility to graph the model.

(b) There are two air-fuel ratios that produce 2400 parts per million of nitric oxide. One is $x = 15$. Use the graph to approximate the other.

(c) Find the second air-fuel ratio from part (b) algebraically. (*Hint:* Use the known value of $x = 15$ and synthetic division.)

Conclusions

True or False? In Exercises 109 and 110, determine whether the statement is true or false. Justify your answer.

109. If $(7x + 4)$ is a factor of some polynomial function f, then $\frac{4}{7}$ is a zero of f.

110. The value $x = \frac{1}{7}$ is a zero of the polynomial function $f(x) = 3x^5 - 2x^4 + x^3 - 16x^2 + 3x - 8$.

Think About It In Exercises 111 and 112, the graph of a cubic polynomial function $y = f(x)$ with integer zeros is shown. Find the factored form of f.

111. **112.**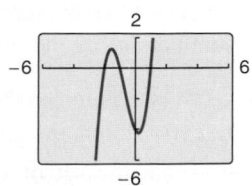

113. Think About It Let $y = f(x)$ be a fourth-degree polynomial with leading coefficient $a = -1$ and $f(\pm 1) = f(\pm 2) = 0$. Find the factored form of f.

114. Think About It Find the value of k such that $x - 3$ is a factor of $x^3 - kx^2 + 2kx - 12$.

115. Writing Complete each polynomial division. Write a brief description of the pattern that you obtain, and use your result to find a formula for the polynomial division $(x^n - 1)/(x - 1)$. Create a numerical example to test your formula.

(a) $\dfrac{x^2 - 1}{x - 1} = $ ▢   (b) $\dfrac{x^3 - 1}{x - 1} = $ ▢

(c) $\dfrac{x^4 - 1}{x - 1} = $ ▢

116. **HOW DO YOU SEE IT?** A graph of $y = f(x)$ is shown, where
$$f(x) = 2x^5 - 3x^4 + x^3 - 8x^2 + 5x + 3 \text{ and}$$
$$f(-x) = -2x^5 - 3x^4 - x^3 - 8x^2 - 5x + 3.$$

(a) How many negative real zeros does f have? Explain.

(b) How many positive real zeros are *possible* for f? Explain. What does this tell you about the eventual right-hand behavior of the graph?

(c) Is $x = -\frac{1}{3}$ a possible rational zero of f? Explain.

(d) Explain how to check whether $\left(x - \frac{3}{2}\right)$ is a factor of f and whether $x = \frac{3}{2}$ is an upper bound for the real zeros of f.

Cumulative Mixed Review

Solving a Quadratic Equation In Exercises 117–120, use any convenient method to solve the quadratic equation.

117. $4x^2 - 17 = 0$ **118.** $25x^2 - 1 = 0$

119. $3x^2 - 11x - 20 = 0$ **120.** $6x^2 + 4x - 3 = 0$

2.4 Complex Numbers

The Imaginary Unit i

Some quadratic equations have no real solutions. For instance, the quadratic equation $x^2 + 1 = 0$ has no real solution because there is no real number x that can be squared to produce -1. To overcome this deficiency, mathematicians created an expanded system of numbers using the **imaginary unit i,** defined as

$$i = \sqrt{-1} \qquad \text{Imaginary unit}$$

where $i^2 = -1$. By adding real numbers to real multiples of this imaginary unit, you obtain the set of **complex numbers.** Each complex number can be written in the **standard form** $a + bi$. For instance, the standard form of the complex number $\sqrt{-9} - 5$ is $-5 + 3i$ because

$$\sqrt{-9} - 5 = \sqrt{3^2(-1)} - 5$$
$$= 3\sqrt{-1} - 5$$
$$= 3i - 5$$
$$= -5 + 3i.$$

In the standard form $a + bi$, the real number a is called the **real part** of the **complex number $a + bi$,** and the number bi (where b is a real number) is called the **imaginary part** of the complex number.

Definition of a Complex Number

If a and b are real numbers, then the number $a + bi$ is a **complex number,** and it is said to be written in **standard form.** If $b = 0$, then the number $a + bi = a$ is a real number. If $b \neq 0$, then the number $a + bi$ is called an **imaginary number.** A number of the form bi, where $b \neq 0$, is called a **pure imaginary number.**

The set of real numbers is a subset of the set of complex numbers, as shown in Figure 2.19. This is true because every real number a can be written as a complex number using $b = 0$. That is, for every real number a, you can write $a = a + 0i$.

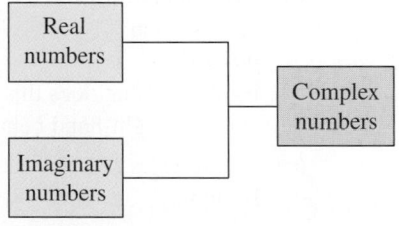

Figure 2.19

Equality of Complex Numbers

Two complex numbers $a + bi$ and $c + di$, written in standard form, are equal to each other

$$a + bi = c + di \qquad \text{Equality of two complex numbers}$$

if and only if $a = c$ and $b = d$.

What you should learn
- ▶ Use the imaginary unit i to write complex numbers.
- ▶ Add, subtract, and multiply complex numbers.
- ▶ Use complex conjugates to write the quotient of two complex numbers in standard form.
- ▶ Find complex solutions of quadratic equations.

Why you should learn it
Complex numbers are used to model numerous aspects of the natural world, such as the impedance of an electrical circuit, as shown in Exercise 89 on page 134.

Operations with Complex Numbers

To add (or subtract) two complex numbers, you add (or subtract) the real and imaginary parts of the numbers separately.

Addition and Subtraction of Complex Numbers

If $a + bi$ and $c + di$ are two complex numbers written in standard form, then their sum and difference are defined as follows.

Sum: $(a + bi) + (c + di) = (a + c) + (b + d)i$

Difference: $(a + bi) - (c + di) = (a - c) + (b - d)i$

The **additive identity** in the complex number system is zero (the same as in the real number system). Furthermore, the **additive inverse** of the complex number $a + bi$ is

$$-(a + bi) = -a - bi.$$ Additive inverse

So, you have

$$(a + bi) + (-a - bi) = 0 + 0i$$
$$= 0.$$

EXAMPLE 1   **Adding and Subtracting Complex Numbers**

a. $(3 - i) + (2 + 3i) = 3 - i + 2 + 3i$ Remove parentheses.
$$= (3 + 2) + (-i + 3i)$$ Group like terms.
$$= 5 + 2i$$ Write in standard form.

b. $(1 + 2i) - (4 + 2i) = 1 + 2i - 4 - 2i$ Remove parentheses.
$$= (1 - 4) + (2i - 2i)$$ Group like terms.
$$= -3 + 0i$$ Simplify.
$$= -3$$ Write in standard form.

c. $3 - (-2 + 3i) + (-5 + i) = 3 + 2 - 3i - 5 + i$
$$= (3 + 2 - 5) + (-3i + i)$$
$$= 0 - 2i$$
$$= -2i$$

d. $(3 + 2i) + (4 - i) - (7 + i) = 3 + 2i + 4 - i - 7 - i$
$$= (3 + 4 - 7) + (2i - i - i)$$
$$= 0 + 0i$$
$$= 0$$

✓ *Checkpoint* 🔊))) *Audio-video solution in English & Spanish at LarsonPrecalculus.com.*

Perform each operation and write the result in standard form.

a. $(7 + 3i) + (5 - 4i)$
b. $(3 + 4i) - (5 - 3i)$
c. $2i + (-3 - 4i) - (-3 - 3i)$
d. $(5 - 3i) + (3 + 5i) - (8 + 2i)$

In Examples 1(b) and 1(d), note that the sum of complex numbers can be a real number.

Many of the properties of real numbers are valid for complex numbers as well. Here are some examples.

    Associative Properties of Addition and Multiplication

    Commutative Properties of Addition and Multiplication

    Distributive Property of Multiplication over Addition

Notice how these properties are used when two complex numbers are multiplied.

$(a + bi)(c + di) = a(c + di) + bi(c + di)$	Distributive Property
$= ac + (ad)i + (bc)i + (bd)i^2$	Distributive Property
$= ac + (ad)i + (bc)i + (bd)(-1)$	$i^2 = -1$
$= ac - bd + (ad)i + (bc)i$	Commutative Property
$= (ac - bd) + (ad + bc)i$	Associative Property

The procedure above is similar to multiplying two polynomials and combining like terms, as in the FOIL Method.

> ### Explore the Concept
>
> Complete the following:
>
> $i^1 = i$ $i^7 =$ ▭
>
> $i^2 = -1$ $i^8 =$ ▭
>
> $i^3 = -i$ $i^9 =$ ▭
>
> $i^4 = 1$ $i^{10} =$ ▭
>
> $i^5 =$ ▭ $i^{11} =$ ▭
>
> $i^6 =$ ▭ $i^{12} =$ ▭
>
> What pattern do you see? Write a brief description of how you would find i raised to any positive integer power.

EXAMPLE 2   Multiplying Complex Numbers

a.
$5(-2 + 3i) = 5(-2) + 5(3i)$	Distributive Property
$= -10 + 15i$	Simplify.

b.
$(2 - i)(4 + 3i) = 2(4 + 3i) - i(4 + 3i)$	Distributive Property
$= 8 + 6i - 4i - 3i^2$	Distributive Property
$= 8 + 6i - 4i - 3(-1)$	$i^2 = -1$
$= 8 + 3 + 6i - 4i$	Group like terms.
$= 11 + 2i$	Write in standard form.

c.
$(3 + 2i)(3 - 2i) = 3(3 - 2i) + 2i(3 - 2i)$	Distributive Property
$= 9 - 6i + 6i - 4i^2$	Distributive Property
$= 9 - 4(-1)$	$i^2 = -1$
$= 9 + 4$	Simplify.
$= 13$	Write in standard form.

d.
$4i(-1 + 5i) = 4i(-1) + 4i(5i)$	Distributive Property
$= -4i + 20i^2$	Simplify.
$= -4i + 20(-1)$	$i^2 = -1$
$= -20 - 4i$	Write in standard form.

e.
$(3 + 2i)^2 = (3 + 2i)(3 + 2i)$	Property of exponents
$= 3(3 + 2i) + 2i(3 + 2i)$	Distributive Property
$= 9 + 6i + 6i + 4i^2$	Distributive Property
$= 9 + 6i + 6i + 4(-1)$	$i^2 = -1$
$= 9 + 12i - 4$	Simplify.
$= 5 + 12i$	Write in standard form.

✓ **Checkpoint** ◀))) *Audio-video solution in English & Spanish at LarsonPrecalculus.com.*

Perform each operation and write the result is standard form.

a. $(2 - 4i)(3 + 3i)$

b. $(4 + 5i)(4 - 5i)$

c. $(4 + 2i)^2$

Complex Conjugates

Notice in Example 2(c) that the product of two complex numbers can be a real number. This occurs with pairs of complex numbers of the forms $a + bi$ and $a - bi$, called **complex conjugates.**

$$(a + bi)(a - bi) = a^2 - abi + abi - b^2 i^2$$
$$= a^2 - b^2(-1)$$
$$= a^2 + b^2$$

EXAMPLE 3   Multiplying Conjugates

Multiply each complex number by its complex conjugate.

a. $1 + i$ **b.** $4 - 3i$

Solution

a. The complex conjugate of $1 + i$ is $1 - i$.

$$(1 + i)(1 - i) = 1^2 - i^2 = 1 - (-1) = 2$$

b. The complex conjugate of $4 - 3i$ is $4 + 3i$.

$$(4 - 3i)(4 + 3i) = 4^2 - (3i)^2 = 16 - 9i^2 = 16 - 9(-1) = 25$$

✓ **Checkpoint** 🔊 *Audio-video solution in English & Spanish at LarsonPrecalculus.com.*

Multiply each complex number by its complex conjugate.

a. $3 + 6i$ **b.** $2 - 5i$

To write the quotient of $a + bi$ and $c + di$ in standard form, where c and d are not both zero, multiply the numerator and denominator by the complex conjugate of the *denominator* to obtain

$$\frac{a + bi}{c + di} = \frac{a + bi}{c + di}\left(\frac{c - di}{c - di}\right) \qquad \text{Multiply numerator and denominator by complex conjugate of denominator.}$$

$$= \frac{ac + bd}{c^2 + d^2} + \left(\frac{bc - ad}{c^2 + d^2}\right)i. \qquad \text{Standard form}$$

EXAMPLE 4   Quotient of Complex Numbers in Standard Form

$$\frac{2 + 3i}{4 - 2i} = \frac{2 + 3i}{4 - 2i}\left(\frac{4 + 2i}{4 + 2i}\right) \qquad \text{Multiply numerator and denominator by complex conjugate of denominator.}$$

$$= \frac{8 + 4i + 12i + 6i^2}{16 - 4i^2} \qquad \text{Expand.}$$

$$= \frac{8 - 6 + 16i}{16 + 4} \qquad i^2 = -1$$

$$= \frac{2 + 16i}{20} \qquad \text{Simplify.}$$

$$= \frac{1}{10} + \frac{4}{5}i \qquad \text{Write in standard form.}$$

✓ **Checkpoint** 🔊 *Audio-video solution in English & Spanish at LarsonPrecalculus.com.*

Write $\dfrac{2 + i}{2 - i}$ in standard form.

©Edyta Pawlowska/Shutterstock.com

Technology Tip

Some graphing utilities can perform operations with complex numbers. For instance, on some graphing utilities, to divide $2 + 3i$ by $4 - 2i$, use the following keystrokes.

(2 + 3 *i*)) ÷
(4 − 2 *i*)) ENTER

(2+3i)/(4-2i)
                    .1+.8i
Ans▶Frac
                  1/10+4/5i

Complex Solutions of Quadratic Equations

When using the Quadratic Formula to solve a quadratic equation, you often obtain a result such as $\sqrt{-3}$, which you know is not a real number. By factoring out $i = \sqrt{-1}$, you can write this number in standard form.

$$\sqrt{-3} = \sqrt{3(-1)} = \sqrt{3}\sqrt{-1} = \sqrt{3}i$$

The number $\sqrt{3}i$ is called the *principal square root* of -3.

Principal Square Root of a Negative Number

If a is a positive number, then the **principal square root** of the negative number $-a$ is defined as

$$\sqrt{-a} = \sqrt{a}i.$$

Remark

The definition of principal square root uses the rule

$$\sqrt{ab} = \sqrt{a}\sqrt{b}$$

for $a > 0$ and $b < 0$. This rule is not valid when *both* a and b are negative. For example,

$$\sqrt{-5}\sqrt{-5} = \sqrt{5(-1)}\sqrt{5(-1)}$$
$$= \sqrt{5}i\sqrt{5}i$$
$$= \sqrt{25}i^2$$
$$= 5i^2$$
$$= -5$$

whereas

$$\sqrt{(-5)(-5)} = \sqrt{25} = 5.$$

To avoid problems with square roots of negative numbers, be sure to convert complex numbers to standard form *before* multiplying.

EXAMPLE 5 Writing Complex Numbers in Standard Form

a. $\sqrt{-3}\sqrt{-12} = \sqrt{3}i\sqrt{12}i = \sqrt{36}i^2 = 6(-1) = -6$

b. $\sqrt{-48} - \sqrt{-27} = \sqrt{48}i - \sqrt{27}i$
$$= 4\sqrt{3}i - 3\sqrt{3}i$$
$$= \sqrt{3}i$$

c. $\left(-1 + \sqrt{-3}\right)^2 = \left(-1 + \sqrt{3}i\right)^2$
$$= (-1)^2 - 2\sqrt{3}i + \left(\sqrt{3}\right)^2(i^2)$$
$$= 1 - 2\sqrt{3}i + 3(-1)$$
$$= -2 - 2\sqrt{3}i$$

✓ **Checkpoint** ◀))) *Audio-video solution in English & Spanish at LarsonPrecalculus.com.*

Write $\sqrt{-14}\sqrt{-2}$ in standard form.

EXAMPLE 6 Complex Solutions of a Quadratic Equation

See LarsonPrecalculus.com for an interactive version of this type of example.

Solve (a) $x^2 + 4 = 0$ and (b) $3x^2 - 2x + 5 = 0$.

Solution

a. $x^2 + 4 = 0$ Write original equation.

$\quad\quad x^2 = -4$ Subtract 4 from each side.

$\quad\quad\quad x = \pm 2i$ Extract square roots.

b. $3x^2 - 2x + 5 = 0$ Write original equation.

$$x = \frac{-(-2) \pm \sqrt{(-2)^2 - 4(3)(5)}}{2(3)}$$ Quadratic Formula

$$= \frac{2 \pm \sqrt{-56}}{6}$$ Simplify.

$$= \frac{2 \pm 2\sqrt{14}i}{6}$$ Write $\sqrt{-56}$ in standard form.

$$= \frac{1}{3} \pm \frac{\sqrt{14}}{3}i$$ Write in standard form.

✓ **Checkpoint** ◀))) *Audio-video solution in English & Spanish at LarsonPrecalculus.com.*

Solve $8x^2 + 14x + 9 = 0$.

2.4   Exercises

See *CalcChat.com* for tutorial help and worked-out solutions to odd-numbered exercises.
For instructions on how to use a graphing utility, see Appendix A.

Vocabulary and Concept Check

1. Match the type of complex number with its definition.

   (a) real number   (i) $a + bi, a = 0, b \neq 0$

   (b) imaginary number   (ii) $a + bi, b = 0$

   (c) pure imaginary number   (iii) $a + bi, a \neq 0, b \neq 0$

In Exercises 2 and 3, fill in the blanks.

2. The imaginary unit i is defined as $i =$ _____ , where $i^2 =$ _____ .

3. When you add $(7 + 6i)$ and $(8 + 5i)$, the real part of the sum is _____ and the imaginary part of the sum is _____ .

4. What method for multiplying two polynomials can you use when multiplying two complex numbers?

5. What is the additive inverse of the complex number $2 - 4i$?

6. What is the complex conjugate of the complex number $2 - 4i$?

Procedures and Problem Solving

Equality of Complex Numbers   In Exercises 7–10, find real numbers a and b such that the equation is true.

7. $a + bi = -9 + 4i$ 8. $a + bi = 12 + 5i$

9. $3a + (b + 3)i = 9 + 8i$ 10. $(a + 6) + 2bi = 6 - i$

Writing a Complex Number in Standard Form   In Exercises 11–20, write the complex number in standard form.

11. $4 + \sqrt{-9}$ 12. $7 - \sqrt{-25}$

13. 12 14. -3

15. $-8i - i^2$ 16. $2i^2 - 6i$

17. $\left(\sqrt{-16}\right)^2 + 5$ 18. $-i - \left(\sqrt{-23}\right)^2$

19. $\sqrt{-0.09}$ 20. $\sqrt{-0.0004}$

Adding and Subtracting Complex Numbers   In Exercises 21–30, perform the addition or subtraction and write the result in standard form.

21. $(4 + i) - (7 - 2i)$ 22. $(11 - 2i) - (-3 + 6i)$

23. $(-1 + 8i) + (8 - 5i)$ 24. $(7 + 6i) + (3 + 12i)$

25. $13i - (14 - 7i)$ 26. $22 + (-5 + 8i) - 9i$

27. $\left(\frac{3}{2} + \frac{5}{2}i\right) + \left(\frac{5}{3} + \frac{11}{3}i\right)$ 28. $\left(\frac{3}{4} + \frac{7}{5}i\right) - \left(\frac{5}{6} - \frac{1}{6}i\right)$

29. $(1.6 + 3.2i) + (-5.8 + 4.3i)$

30. $-(-3.7 - 12.8i) - (6.1 - 16.3i)$

Multiplying Complex Numbers   In Exercises 31–42, perform the operation(s) and write the result in standard form.

31. $4(3 + 5i)$ 32. $-6(5 - 3i)$

33. $(1 + i)(3 - 2i)$ 34. $(6 - 2i)(2 - 3i)$

35. $4i(8 + 5i)$ 36. $-3i(6 - i)$

37. $\left(\sqrt{14} + \sqrt{10}i\right)\left(\sqrt{14} - \sqrt{10}i\right)$

38. $\left(\sqrt{3} + \sqrt{15}i\right)\left(\sqrt{3} - \sqrt{15}i\right)$

39. $(6 + 7i)^2$ 40. $(5 - 4i)^2$

41. $(4 + 5i)^2 - (4 - 5i)^2$ 42. $(1 - 2i)^2 - (1 + 2i)^2$

Multiplying Conjugates   In Exercises 43–50, write the complex conjugate of the complex number. Then multiply the number by its complex conjugate.

43. $6 - 2i$ 44. $3 + 5i$

45. $-1 + \sqrt{7}i$ 46. $-4 - \sqrt{3}i$

47. $\sqrt{-29}$ 48. $\sqrt{-10}$

49. $9 - \sqrt{6}i$ 50. $-8 + \sqrt{15}i$

Writing a Quotient of Complex Numbers in Standard Form   In Exercises 51–58, write the quotient in standard form.

51. $\dfrac{6}{i}$ 52. $-\dfrac{5}{2i}$

53. $\dfrac{2}{4 - 5i}$ 54. $\dfrac{3}{1 - i}$

55. $\dfrac{2 + i}{2 - i}$ 56. $\dfrac{8 - 7i}{1 - 2i}$

57. $i/(4 - 5i)^2$ 58. $5i/(2 + 3i)^2$

Adding or Subtracting Quotients of Complex Numbers   In Exercises 59 and 60, perform the operation and write the result in standard form.

59. $\dfrac{2}{1 + i} - \dfrac{3}{1 - i}$ 60. $\dfrac{2i}{2 + i} + \dfrac{5}{2 - i}$

Writing Complex Numbers in Standard Form In Exercises 61–70, perform the operation and write the result in standard form.

61. $\sqrt{-18} - \sqrt{-54}$ 62. $\sqrt{-50} + \sqrt{-275}$

63. $\left(-3 + \sqrt{-24}\right) + \left(7 - \sqrt{-44}\right)$

64. $\left(-12 - \sqrt{-72}\right) + \left(9 + \sqrt{-108}\right)$

65. $\sqrt{-6}\sqrt{-2}$ 66. $\sqrt{-5}\sqrt{-10}$

67. $\left(\sqrt{-10}\right)^2$ 68. $\left(\sqrt{-75}\right)^2$

69. $\left(2 - \sqrt{-6}\right)^2$ 70. $\left(3 + \sqrt{-5}\right)\left(7 - \sqrt{-10}\right)$

Complex Solutions of a Quadratic Equation In Exercises 71–82, solve the quadratic equation.

71. $x^2 + 25 = 0$ 72. $x^2 + 32 = 0$

73. $x^2 - 2x + 2 = 0$ 74. $x^2 + 6x + 10 = 0$

75. $4x^2 + 16x + 17 = 0$ 76. $9x^2 - 6x + 37 = 0$

77. $16t^2 - 4t + 3 = 0$ 78. $4x^2 + 16x + 15 = 0$

79. $\frac{3}{2}x^2 - 6x + 9 = 0$ 80. $\frac{7}{8}x^2 - \frac{3}{4}x + \frac{5}{16} = 0$

81. $1.4x^2 - 2x - 10 = 0$ 82. $4.5x^2 - 3x + 12 = 0$

Expressions Involving Powers of i In Exercises 83–88, simplify the complex number and write the result in standard form.

83. $-6i^3 + i^2$ 84. $4i^2 - 2i^3$

85. $\left(\sqrt{-75}\right)^3$ 86. $\left(\sqrt{-2}\right)^6$

87. $\dfrac{1}{i^3}$ 88. $\dfrac{1}{(2i)^3}$

89. **Why you should learn it** (p. 128) The opposition to current in an electrical circuit is called its impedance. The impedance z in a parallel circuit with two pathways satisfies the equation $1/z = 1/z_1 + 1/z_2$, where z_1 is the impedance (in ohms) of pathway 1, and z_2 is the impedance (in ohms) of pathway 2. Use the table to determine the impedance of each parallel circuit. (*Hint:* You can find the impedance of each pathway in a parallel circuit by adding the impedances of all components in the pathway.)

	Resistor	Inductor	Capacitor
Symbol	$-\!\!\bigwedge\!\!\bigwedge\!\!-$ $a\,\Omega$	$-\!\!\overset{\frown\frown\frown}{}\!\!-$ $b\,\Omega$	$-\!|\!|\!-$ $c\,\Omega$
Impedance	a	bi	$-ci$

(a)   (b)

90. **Exploration** Consider the functions
$$f(x) = 2(x - 3)^2 - 4 \quad \text{and} \quad g(x) = -2(x - 3)^2 - 4.$$

(a) Without graphing either function, determine whether the graph of f and the graph of g have x-intercepts. Explain your reasoning.

(b) Solve $f(x) = 0$ and $g(x) = 0$.

(c) Explain how the zeros of f and g are related to whether their graphs have x-intercepts.

(d) For the function $f(x) = a(x - h)^2 + k$, make a general statement about how a, h, and k affect whether the graph of f has x-intercepts, and whether the zeros of f are real or complex.

Conclusions

True or False? In Exercises 91–94, determine whether the statement is true or false. Justify your answer.

91. No complex number is equal to its complex conjugate.

92. $i^{44} + i^{150} - i^{74} - i^{109} + i^{61} = -1$

93. The conjugate of the product of two complex numbers is equal to the product of the conjugates of the two complex numbers.

94. The conjugate of the sum of two complex numbers is equal to the sum of the conjugates of the two complex numbers.

95. **Error Analysis** Describe the error.

$$\sqrt{-6}\sqrt{-6} = \sqrt{(-6)(-6)} = \sqrt{36} = 6$$

96. **HOW DO YOU SEE IT?** The coordinate system shown below is called the *complex plane*. In the complex plane, the point that corresponds to the complex number $a + bi$ is (a, b).

Match each complex number with its corresponding point.

(i) 2   (ii) $2i$ (iii) $-2 + i$ (iv) $1 - 2i$

Cumulative Mixed Review

Multiplying Polynomials In Exercises 97–100, perform the operation and write the result in standard form.

97. $(4x - 5)(4x + 5)$ 98. $(x + 2)^3$

99. $\left(3x - \frac{1}{2}\right)(x + 4)$ 100. $(2x - 5)^2$

2.5   The Fundamental Theorem of Algebra

The Fundamental Theorem of Algebra

You know that an *n*th-degree polynomial can have at most *n* real zeros. In the complex number system, this statement can be improved. That is, in the complex number system, every *n*th-degree polynomial function has *precisely n zeros*. This important result is derived from the **Fundamental Theorem of Algebra,** first proved by the German mathematician Carl Friedrich Gauss (1777–1855).

> **The Fundamental Theorem of Algebra**
>
> If $f(x)$ is a polynomial of degree n, where $n > 0$, then f has at least one zero in the complex number system.

Using the Fundamental Theorem of Algebra and the equivalence of zeros and factors, you obtain the **Linear Factorization Theorem.**

> **Linear Factorization Theorem**   (See the proof on page 177.)
>
> If $f(x)$ is a polynomial of degree n, where $n > 0$, then f has precisely n linear factors
>
> $$f(x) = a_n(x - c_1)(x - c_2) \cdots (x - c_n)$$
>
> where $c_1, c_2, \ldots, c_n$ are complex numbers.

Note that the Fundamental Theorem of Algebra and the Linear Factorization Theorem tell you only that the zeros or factors of a polynomial exist, not how to find them. Such theorems are called *existence theorems*. To find the zeros of a polynomial function, you still must rely on other techniques.

EXAMPLE 1   Zeros of Polynomial Functions

See LarsonPrecalculus.com for an interactive version of this type of example.

a. The first-degree polynomial $f(x) = x - 2$ has exactly *one* zero: $x = 2$.

b. Counting multiplicity, the second-degree polynomial function

$$f(x) = x^2 - 6x + 9$$
$$= (x - 3)(x - 3)$$

has exactly *two* zeros: $x = 3$ and $x = 3$. (This is called a *repeated zero*.)

c. The third-degree polynomial function

$$f(x) = x^3 + 4x = x(x^2 + 4) = x(x - 2i)(x + 2i)$$

has exactly *three* zeros: $x = 0$, $x = 2i$, and $x = -2i$.

d. The fifth-degree polynomial function

$$f(x) = x^5 + 9x^3 = x^3(x^2 + 9) = x^3(x - 3i)(x + 3i)$$

has exactly *five* zeros: $x = 0$, $x = 0$, $x = 0$, $x = 3i$, and $x = -3i$.

✓ **Checkpoint** *Audio-video solution in English & Spanish at LarsonPrecalculus.com.*

Determine the number of zeros of the polynomial function $f(x) = x^4 - 1$. ■

Finding Zeros of a Polynomial Function

Remember that the n zeros of a polynomial function can be real or imaginary, and they may be repeated. Examples 2 and 3 illustrate several cases.

EXAMPLE 2   Complex Zeros of a Polynomial Function

Confirm that the third-degree polynomial function $f(x) = x^3 + 4x$ has exactly three zeros: $x = 0$, $x = 2i$, and $x = -2i$.

Solution

Factor the polynomial completely as $x(x - 2i)(x + 2i)$. So, the zeros are

$$x(x - 2i)(x + 2i) = 0$$

$$x = 0 \qquad\qquad \text{Set 1st factor equal to 0.}$$

$$x - 2i = 0 \implies x = 2i \qquad \text{Set 2nd factor equal to 0.}$$

$$x + 2i = 0 \implies x = -2i. \qquad \text{Set 3rd factor equal to 0.}$$

In Figure 2.20, only the real zero $x = 0$ appears as an x-intercept.

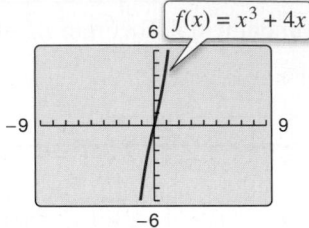

Figure 2.20

✔ **Checkpoint** 🔊))) *Audio-video solution in English & Spanish at LarsonPrecalculus.com.*

Confirm that the fourth-degree polynomial function $f(x) = x^4 - 1$ has exactly four zeros: $x = 1$, $x = -1$, $x = i$, and $x = -i$. ∎

The next example shows how to use the methods described in Sections 2.2 and 2.3 (the Rational Zero Test, synthetic division, and factoring) to find all the zeros of a polynomial function, including imaginary zeros.

EXAMPLE 3   Finding the Zeros of a Polynomial Function

Write $f(x) = x^5 + x^3 + 2x^2 - 12x + 8$ as the product of linear factors, and list all the zeros of f.

Solution

The possible rational zeros are ± 1, ± 2, ± 4, and ± 8. The graph shown in Figure 2.21 indicates that 1 and -2 are likely zeros, and that 1 is possibly a repeated zero because it appears that the graph touches (but does not cross) the x-axis at this point. Using synthetic division, you can determine that -2 is a zero and 1 is a repeated zero of f. So, you have

$$f(x) = x^5 + x^3 + 2x^2 - 12x + 8 = (x - 1)(x - 1)(x + 2)(x^2 + 4).$$

By factoring $x^2 + 4$ as

$$x^2 - (-4) = \left(x - \sqrt{-4}\right)\left(x + \sqrt{-4}\right) = (x - 2i)(x + 2i)$$

you obtain

$$f(x) = (x - 1)(x - 1)(x + 2)(x - 2i)(x + 2i)$$

which gives the following five zeros of f.

$$x = 1, \, x = 1, \, x = -2, \, x = 2i, \quad \text{and} \quad x = -2i$$

Note from the graph of f shown in Figure 2.21 that the *real* zeros are the only ones that appear as x-intercepts.

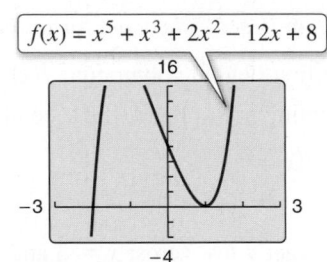

Figure 2.21

✔ **Checkpoint** 🔊))) *Audio-video solution in English & Spanish at LarsonPrecalculus.com.*

Write $f(x) = x^4 - 256$ as the product of linear factors, and list all the zeros of f. ∎

Conjugate Pairs

In Example 3, note that the two complex zeros $2i$ and $-2i$ are **conjugates.** That is, they are of the forms $a + bi$ and $a - bi$.

> **Complex Zeros Occur in Conjugate Pairs**
>
> Let f be a polynomial function that has *real coefficients*. If $a + bi$, where $b \neq 0$, is a zero of the function, then the conjugate $a - bi$ is also a zero of the function.

Be sure you see that this result is true only when the polynomial function has *real coefficients*. For instance, the result applies to the function $f(x) = x^2 + 1$, but not to the function $g(x) = x - i$.

EXAMPLE 4   Finding a Polynomial with Given Zeros

Find a *fourth-degree* polynomial function with real coefficients that has -1, -1, and $3i$ as zeros.

Solution

Because $3i$ is a zero *and* the polynomial is stated to have real coefficients, you know that the conjugate $-3i$ must also be a zero. So, from the Linear Factorization Theorem, $f(x)$ can be written as

$$f(x) = a(x + 1)(x + 1)(x - 3i)(x + 3i).$$

For simplicity, let $a = 1$ to obtain

$$f(x) = (x^2 + 2x + 1)(x^2 + 9) = x^4 + 2x^3 + 10x^2 + 18x + 9.$$

✓ **Checkpoint** ◀))) *Audio-video solution in English & Spanish at LarsonPrecalculus.com.*

Find a *fourth-degree* polynomial function with real coefficients that has 2, -2, and $7i$ as zeros.

EXAMPLE 5   Finding a Polynomial with Given Zeros

Find a *cubic* polynomial function f with real coefficients that has 2 and $1 - i$ as zeros, and $f(1) = 3$.

Solution

Because $1 - i$ is a zero of f, the conjugate $1 + i$ must also be a zero.

$$\begin{aligned}
f(x) &= a(x - 2)[x - (1 - i)][x - (1 + i)] \\
&= a(x - 2)[x^2 - x(1 + i) - x(1 - i) + 1 - i^2] \\
&= a(x - 2)(x^2 - 2x + 2) \\
&= a(x^3 - 4x^2 + 6x - 4)
\end{aligned}$$

To find the value of a, use the fact that $f(1) = 3$ to obtain

$$a[(1)^3 - 4(1)^2 + 6(1) - 4] = 3.$$

So, $a = -3$ and you can conclude that

$$f(x) = -3(x^3 - 4x^2 + 6x - 4) = -3x^3 + 12x^2 - 18x + 12.$$

✓ **Checkpoint** ◀))) *Audio-video solution in English & Spanish at LarsonPrecalculus.com.*

Find a *quartic* polynomial function f with real coefficients that has 1, -2, and $2i$ as zeros, and $f(-1) = 10$. ∎

Factoring a Polynomial

The Linear Factorization Theorem states that you can write any nth-degree polynomial as the product of n linear factors.

$$f(x) = a_n(x - c_1)(x - c_2)(x - c_3) \cdots (x - c_n)$$

This result, however, includes the possibility that some of the values of c_i are imaginary. The next theorem states that even when you do not want to get involved with "imaginary factors," you can still write $f(x)$ as the product of linear and quadratic factors.

> **Factors of a Polynomial** (See the proof on page 177.)
>
> Every polynomial of degree $n > 0$ with real coefficients can be written as the product of linear and quadratic factors with real coefficients, where the quadratic factors have no real zeros.

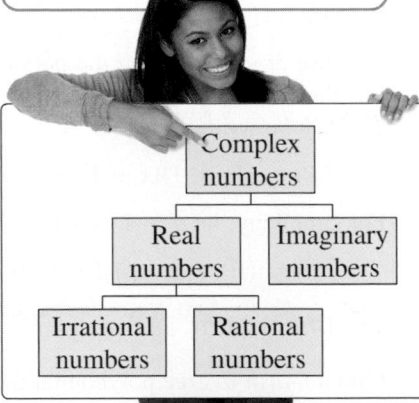

> **Remark**
>
> Recall that irrational and rational numbers are subsets of the set of real numbers, and the real numbers are a subset of the set of complex numbers.

A quadratic factor with no real zeros is said to be **prime** or **irreducible over the reals.** Be sure you see that this is not the same as being *irreducible over the rationals.* For example, the quadratic

$$x^2 + 1 = (x - i)(x + i)$$

is irreducible over the reals (and therefore over the rationals). On the other hand, the quadratic

$$x^2 - 2 = \left(x - \sqrt{2}\right)\left(x + \sqrt{2}\right)$$

is irreducible over the rationals, but *reducible* over the reals.

EXAMPLE 6 Factoring a Polynomial

Write the polynomial $f(x) = x^4 - x^2 - 20$

a. as the product of factors that are irreducible over the *rationals*,

b. as the product of linear factors and quadratic factors that are irreducible over the *reals*, and

c. in completely factored form.

Solution

a. Begin by factoring the polynomial as the product of two quadratic polynomials.

$$x^4 - x^2 - 20 = (x^2 - 5)(x^2 + 4)$$

Both of these factors are irreducible over the rationals.

b. By factoring over the reals, you have

$$x^4 - x^2 - 20 = \left(x + \sqrt{5}\right)\left(x - \sqrt{5}\right)(x^2 + 4)$$

where the quadratic factor is irreducible over the reals.

c. In completely factored form, you have

$$x^4 - x^2 - 20 = \left(x + \sqrt{5}\right)\left(x - \sqrt{5}\right)(x - 2i)(x + 2i).$$

✓ *Checkpoint* Audio-video solution in English & Spanish at LarsonPrecalculus.com.

Write the polynomial $f(x) = x^4 - 2x^2 - 3$ (a) as the product of factors that are irreducible over the *rationals*, (b) as the product of linear factors and quadratic factors that are irreducible over the *reals*, and (c) in completely factored form. ■

In Example 6, notice from the completely factored form that the *fourth*-degree polynomial has *four* zeros.

Throughout this chapter, the results and theorems have been stated in terms of zeros of polynomial functions. Be sure you see that the same results could have been stated in terms of solutions of polynomial equations. This is true because the zeros of the polynomial function

$$f(x) = a_n x^n + a_{n-1} x^{n-1} + \cdots + a_2 x^2 + a_1 x + a_0$$

are precisely the solutions of the polynomial equation

$$a_n x^n + a_{n-1} x^{n-1} + \cdots + a_2 x^2 + a_1 x + a_0 = 0.$$

EXAMPLE 7   Finding the Zeros of a Polynomial Function

Find all the zeros of

$$f(x) = x^4 - 3x^3 + 6x^2 + 2x - 60$$

given that $1 + 3i$ is a zero of f.

Algebraic Solution

Because complex zeros occur in conjugate pairs, you know that $1 - 3i$ is also a zero of f. This means that both

$$x - (1 + 3i) \quad \text{and} \quad x - (1 - 3i)$$

are factors of f. Multiplying these two factors produces

$$[x - (1 + 3i)][x - (1 - 3i)] = [(x - 1) - 3i][(x - 1) + 3i]$$

$$= (x - 1)^2 - 9i^2$$

$$= x^2 - 2x + 10.$$

Using long division, you can divide $x^2 - 2x + 10$ into f to obtain the following.

$$
\begin{array}{r}
x^2 - x - 6 \\
x^2 - 2x + 10 \overline{)\, x^4 - 3x^3 + 6x^2 + 2x - 60} \\
\underline{x^4 - 2x^3 + 10x^2} \\
-x^3 - 4x^2 + 2x \\
\underline{-x^3 + 2x^2 - 10x} \\
-6x^2 + 12x - 60 \\
\underline{-6x^2 + 12x - 60} \\
0
\end{array}
$$

So, you have

$$f(x) = (x^2 - 2x + 10)(x^2 - x - 6)$$

$$= (x^2 - 2x + 10)(x - 3)(x + 2)$$

and you can conclude that the zeros of f are

$$x = 1 + 3i, x = 1 - 3i, x = 3, \text{ and } x = -2.$$

Graphical Solution

Using the *zero* feature of a graphing utility, you can conclude that $x = -2$ and $x = 3$ are zeros of f. (See figure.)

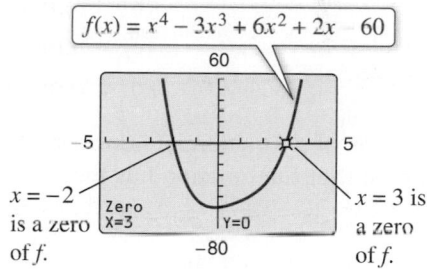

$x = -2$ is a zero of f.

$x = 3$ is a zero of f.

Because $1 + 3i$ is a zero of f, you know that the conjugate $1 - 3i$ must also be a zero. So, you can conclude that the zeros of f are

$$x = 1 + 3i, x = 1 - 3i, x = 3, \text{ and } x = -2.$$

✓ **Checkpoint** ◄))) *Audio-video solution in English & Spanish at LarsonPrecalculus.com.*

Find all the zeros of $f(x) = 3x^3 - 2x^2 + 48x - 32$ given that $4i$ is a zero of f. ■

In Example 7, if you were not told that $1 + 3i$ is a zero of f, you could still find all the zeros of the function by using synthetic division to find the real zeros -2 and 3. Then, you could factor the polynomial as $(x + 2)(x - 3)(x^2 - 2x + 10)$. Finally, by using the Quadratic Formula, you could determine that the zeros are $x = 1 + 3i$, $x = 1 - 3i$, $x = 3$, and $x = -2$.

2.5   Exercises

See *CalcChat.com* for tutorial help and worked-out solutions to odd-numbered exercises.
For instructions on how to use a graphing utility, see Appendix A.

Vocabulary and Concept Check

In Exercises 1 and 2, fill in the blanks.

1. The _____ of _____ states that if $f(x)$ is a polynomial of degree n $(n > 0)$, then f has at least one zero in the complex number system.

2. A quadratic factor that cannot be factored as a product of linear factors containing real numbers is said to be _____ over the _____ .

3. How many linear factors does a polynomial function f of degree n have, where $n > 0$?

4. Three of the zeros of a fourth-degree polynomial function f are -1, 3, and $2i$. What is the other zero of f?

Procedures and Problem Solving

Zeros of a Polynomial Function   In Exercises 5–8, match the function with its exact number of zeros.

5. $f(x) = -2x^4 + 32$ (a) 1 zero

6. $f(x) = x^5 - x^3$ (b) 3 zeros

7. $f(x) = x^3 + 3x^2 + 2x$ (c) 4 zeros

8. $f(x) = x - 14$ (d) 5 zeros

Complex Zeros of a Polynomial Function   In Exercises 9–12, confirm that the function has the indicated zeros.

9. $f(x) = x^2 + 5$; $-\sqrt{5}i$, $\sqrt{5}i$

10. $f(x) = x^3 + 9x$; 0, $-3i$, $3i$

11. $f(x) = 3x^4 - 48$; -2, 2, $-2i$, $2i$

12. $f(x) = 2x^5 - 2x$; 0, 1, -1, $-i$, i

Comparing the Zeros and the *x*-Intercepts   In Exercises 13–16, find all the zeros of the function. Is there a relationship between the number of real zeros and the number of *x*-intercepts of the graph? Explain.

13. $f(x) = x^3 - 4x^2$
    $+ x - 4$

14. $f(x) = x^3 - 4x^2$
    $- 4x + 16$

15. $f(x) = x^4 + 4x^2 + 4$

16. $f(x) = x^4 - 3x^2 - 4$

Finding the Zeros of a Polynomial Function   In Exercises 17–36, find all the zeros of the function and write the polynomial as a product of linear factors. Use a graphing utility to verify your results graphically. (If possible, use the graphing utility to verify the imaginary zeros.)

17. $h(x) = x^2 - 4x + 1$ 18. $g(x) = x^2 + 10x + 23$

19. $f(x) = x^2 - 12x + 26$ 20. $f(x) = x^2 + 6x - 2$

21. $f(x) = x^2 + 25$ 22. $f(x) = x^2 + 36$

23. $f(x) = 16x^4 - 81$ 24. $f(y) = 81y^4 - 625$

25. $f(z) = z^2 - z + 56$ 26. $h(x) = x^2 - 4x - 3$

27. $f(x) = x^4 + 10x^2 + 9$ 28. $f(x) = x^4 + 29x^2 + 100$

29. $f(x) = 3x^3 - 5x^2 + 48x - 80$

30. $f(x) = 3x^3 - 2x^2 + 75x - 50$

31. $f(t) = t^3 - 3t^2 - 15t + 125$

32. $f(x) = x^3 + 11x^2 + 39x + 29$

33. $f(x) = 5x^3 - 9x^2 + 28x + 6$

34. $f(s) = 3s^3 - 4s^2 + 8s + 8$

35. $g(x) = x^4 - 4x^3 + 8x^2 - 16x + 16$

36. $h(x) = x^4 + 6x^3 + 10x^2 + 6x + 9$

Using the Zeros to Find *x*-Intercepts   In Exercises 37–44, (a) find all zeros of the function, (b) write the polynomial as a product of linear factors, and (c) use your factorization to determine the *x*-intercepts of the graph of the function. Use a graphing utility to verify that the real zeros are the only *x*-intercepts.

37. $f(x) = x^2 - 14x + 46$ 38. $f(x) = x^2 - 12x + 34$

39. $f(x) = 2x^3 - 3x^2 + 8x - 12$

40. $f(x) = 2x^3 - 5x^2 + 18x - 45$

41. $f(x) = x^3 - 11x + 150$

42. $f(x) = x^3 + 10x^2 + 33x + 34$

43. $f(x) = x^4 + 25x^2 + 144$

44. $f(x) = x^4 - 8x^3 + 17x^2 - 8x + 16$

Finding a Polynomial with Given Zeros   **In Exercises 45–50, find a polynomial function with real coefficients that has the given zeros. (There are many correct answers.)**

45. $5, i, -i$

46. $3, 4i, -4i$

47. $1, 1, 2i$

48. $-3, -3, i$

49. $0, -5, 1 + \sqrt{2}i$

50. $0, 4, 1 + \sqrt{2}i$

Finding a Polynomial with Given Zeros   **In Exercises 51–54, a polynomial function f with real coefficients has the given degree, zeros, and solution point. Write the function (a) in completely factored form and (b) in polynomial form.**

	Degree	Zeros	Solution Point
51.	4	$-1, 2, i$	$f(1) = 8$
52.	4	$1, -4, \sqrt{3}i$	$f(0) = -6$
53.	3	$-1, 2 + \sqrt{5}i$	$f(2) = 45$
54.	3	$-2, 2 + 2\sqrt{2}i$	$f(-1) = -34$

Factoring a Polynomial   **In Exercises 55–58, write the polynomial (a) as the product of factors that are irreducible over the *rationals*, (b) as the product of linear and quadratic factors that are irreducible over the *reals*, and (c) in completely factored form.**

55. $f(x) = x^4 - 6x^2 - 7$ 56. $f(x) = x^4 + 6x^2 - 27$

57. $f(x) = x^4 - 2x^3 - 3x^2 + 12x - 18$

   (*Hint:* One factor is $x^2 - 6$.)

58. $f(x) = x^4 - 3x^3 - x^2 - 12x - 20$

   (*Hint:* One factor is $x^2 + 4$.)

Finding the Zeros of a Polynomial Function   **In Exercises 59–64, use the given zero to find all the zeros of the function.**

	Function	Zero
59.	$f(x) = 2x^3 + 3x^2 + 50x + 75$	$5i$
60.	$f(x) = x^3 + x^2 + 9x + 9$	$3i$
61.	$g(x) = x^3 - 7x^2 - x + 87$	$5 + 2i$
62.	$g(x) = 4x^3 + 23x^2 + 34x - 10$	$-3 + i$
63.	$h(x) = 3x^3 - 4x^2 + 8x + 8$	$1 - \sqrt{3}i$
64.	$f(x) = 25x^3 - 55x^2 - 54x - 18$	$\frac{1}{5}(-2 + \sqrt{2}i)$

Using a Graph to Locate the Real Zeros   **In Exercises 65–68, (a) use a graphing utility to find the real zeros of the function, and then (b) use the real zeros to find the exact values of the imaginary zeros.**

65. $f(x) = x^4 + 3x^3 - 5x^2 - 21x + 22$

66. $f(x) = x^3 + 4x^2 + 14x + 20$

67. $h(x) = 8x^3 - 14x^2 + 18x - 9$

68. $f(x) = 25x^3 - 55x^2 - 54x - 18$

69. ***Why you should learn it***   (*p. 135*) A football is kicked off the ground with an initial upward velocity of 48 feet per second. The football's height h (in feet) is given by

$$h(t) = -16t^2 + 48t, \quad 0 \le t \le 3$$

where t is the time (in seconds). Does the football reach a height of 50 feet? Explain.

70. **Marketing**   The demand equation for a microwave is $p = 140 - 0.001x$, where p is the unit price (in dollars) of the microwave and x is the number of units produced and sold. The cost equation for the microwave is $C = 40x + 150,000$, where C is the total cost (in dollars) and x is the number of units produced. The total profit P obtained by producing and selling x units is given by $P = R - C = xp - C$. Is there a price p that yields a profit of \$3 million? Explain.

Conclusions

True or False?   **In Exercises 71 and 72, decide whether the statement is true or false. Justify your answer.**

71. It is possible for a third-degree polynomial function with integer coefficients to have no real zeros.

72. If $[x + (4 + 3i)]$ is a factor of a polynomial function f with real coefficients, then $[x - (4 + 3i)]$ is also a factor of f.

73. **Writing**   Compile a list of all the various techniques for factoring a polynomial that have been covered so far in the text. Give an example illustrating each technique and write a paragraph discussing when the use of each technique is appropriate.

74. **HOW DO YOU SEE IT?**   Describe a translation of the graph that will result in a function with (a) four distinct real zeros, (b) two real zeros, each of multiplicity 2, (c) two real zeros and two imaginary zeros, and (d) four imaginary zeros.

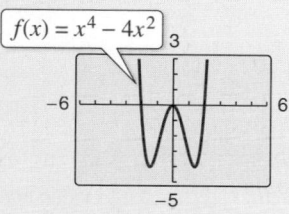

$f(x) = x^4 - 4x^2$

Cumulative Mixed Review

Identifying the Vertex of a Quadratic Function   **In Exercises 75–78, describe the graph of the function and identify the vertex.**

75. $f(x) = x^2 - 7x - 8$ 76. $f(x) = -x^2 + x + 6$

77. $f(x) = 6x^2 + 5x - 6$ 78. $f(x) = 4x^2 + 2x - 12$

2.6   Rational Functions and Asymptotes

Introduction to Rational Functions

A **rational function** can be written in the form

$$f(x) = \frac{N(x)}{D(x)}$$

where $N(x)$ and $D(x)$ are polynomials and $D(x)$ is not the zero polynomial.

   In general, the *domain* of a rational function of x includes all real numbers except x-values that make the denominator zero. Much of the discussion of rational functions will focus on their graphical behavior near these x-values.

What you should learn
▶ Find the domains of rational functions.
▶ Find vertical and horizontal asymptotes of graphs of rational functions.
▶ Use rational functions to model and solve real-life problems.

Why you should learn it
Rational functions are convenient in modeling a wide variety of real-life problems, such as environmental scenarios. For instance, Exercise 49 on page 150 shows how to determine the cost of supplying recycling bins to the population of a rural township.

| EXAMPLE 1 | Finding the Domain of a Rational Function |

See LarsonPrecalculus.com for an interactive version of this type of example.

Find the domain of $f(x) = 1/x$ and discuss the behavior of f near any excluded x-values.

Solution

Because the denominator is zero when $x = 0$, the domain of f is all real numbers except $x = 0$. To determine the behavior of f near this excluded value, evaluate $f(x)$ to the left and right of $x = 0$, as indicated in the following tables.

x	-1	-0.5	-0.1	-0.01	-0.001	$\to 0$
$f(x)$	-1	-2	-10	-100	-1000	$\to -\infty$

x	$0 \leftarrow$	0.001	0.01	0.1	0.5	1
$f(x)$	$\infty \leftarrow$	1000	100	10	2	1

From the table, note that as x approaches 0 *from the left*, $f(x)$ decreases without bound. In contrast, as x approaches 0 *from the right*, $f(x)$ increases without bound. Because $f(x)$ decreases without bound from the left and increases without bound from the right, you can conclude that f is not continuous. The graph of f is shown in the figure.

$$f(x) = \frac{1}{x}$$

 Checkpoint))) *Audio-video solution in English & Spanish at LarsonPrecalculus.com.*

Find the domain of $f(x) = \dfrac{3x}{x - 1}$ and discuss the behavior of f near any excluded x-values.

Explore the Concept

Use the *table* and *trace* features of a graphing utility to verify that the function $f(x) = 1/x$ in Example 1 is not continuous.

Vertical and Horizontal Asymptotes

In Example 1, the behavior of f near $x = 0$ is denoted as follows.

$f(x) \to -\infty$ as $x \to 0^-$ $f(x) \to \infty$ as $x \to 0^+$

$f(x)$ decreases without bound as $f(x)$ increases without bound as
x approaches 0 from the left. x approaches 0 from the right.

The line $x = 0$ is a **vertical asymptote** of the graph of f, as shown in Figure 2.22. From this figure, you can see that the graph of f also has a **horizontal asymptote**—the line $y = 0$. This means the values of $f(x) = 1/x$ approach zero as x increases or decreases without bound.

$f(x) \to 0$ as $x \to -\infty$ $f(x) \to 0$ as $x \to \infty$

$f(x)$ approaches 0 as x $f(x)$ approaches 0 as x
decreases without bound.   increases without bound.

Figure 2.22

Definition of Vertical and Horizontal Asymptotes

1. The line $x = a$ is a **vertical asymptote** of the graph of f when

$$f(x) \to \infty \quad \text{or} \quad f(x) \to -\infty$$

as $x \to a$, either from the right or from the left.

2. The line $y = b$ is a **horizontal asymptote** of the graph of f when

$$f(x) \to b$$

as $x \to \infty$ or $x \to -\infty$.

Figure 2.23 shows the vertical and horizontal asymptotes of the graphs of three rational functions. Note in Figure 2.23 that eventually (as $x \to \infty$ or $x \to -\infty$) the distance between the horizontal asymptote and the points on the graph must approach zero. [The graphs shown in Figures 2.22 and 2.23(a) are **hyperbolas.** You will study hyperbolas in Section 9.3.]

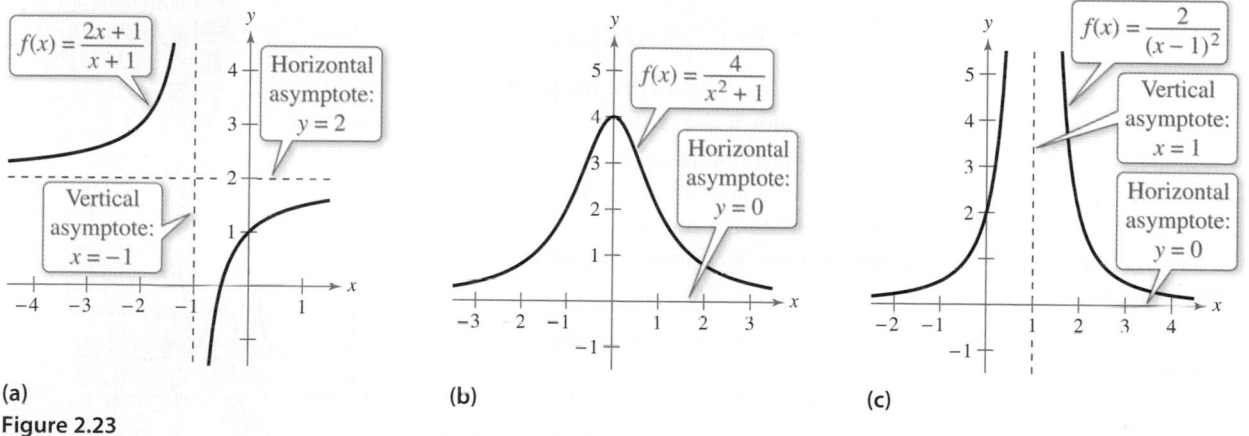

(a)   (b)   (c)

Figure 2.23

Explore the Concept

Use a table of values to determine whether the functions in Figure 2.23 are continuous. When the graph of a function has an asymptote, can you conclude that the function is not continuous? Explain.

Vertical and Horizontal Asymptotes of a Rational Function

Let f be the rational function

$$f(x) = \frac{N(x)}{D(x)} = \frac{a_n x^n + a_{n-1}x^{n-1} + \cdots + a_1 x + a_0}{b_m x^m + b_{m-1}x^{m-1} + \cdots + b_1 x + b_0}$$

where $N(x)$ and $D(x)$ have no common factors.

1. The graph of f has *vertical* asymptotes at the zeros of the denominator, $D(x)$.

2. The graph of f has at most one *horizontal* asymptote determined by comparing the degrees of $N(x)$ and $D(x)$.

   a. If $n < m$, then the graph of f has the line $y = 0$ (the x-axis) as a horizontal asymptote.

   b. If $n = m$, then the graph of f has the line

   $$y = \frac{a_n}{b_m}$$

   as a horizontal asymptote, where a_n is the leading coefficient of the numerator and b_m is the leading coefficient of the denominator.

   c. If $n > m$, then the graph of f has no horizontal asymptote.

What's Wrong?

You use a graphing utility to graph

$$y_1 = \frac{2x^3 + 1000x^2 + x}{x^3 + 1000x^2 + x + 1000}$$

as shown in the figure. You use the graph to conclude that the graph of y_1 has the line $y = 1$ as a horizontal asymptote. What's wrong?

EXAMPLE 2   Finding Vertical and Horizontal Asymptotes

Find all asymptotes of the graph of each rational function.

a. $f(x) = \dfrac{2x}{3x^2 + 1}$ **b.** $f(x) = \dfrac{2x^2}{x^2 - 1}$

Solution

a. For this rational function, the degree of the numerator is *less than* the degree of the denominator, so the graph has the line $y = 0$ as a horizontal asymptote. To find any vertical asymptotes, set the denominator equal to zero and solve the resulting equation for x.

$$3x^2 + 1 = 0 \qquad \text{Set denominator equal to zero.}$$

Because this equation has no real solutions, you can conclude that the graph has no vertical asymptote. The graph of the function is shown in Figure 2.24.

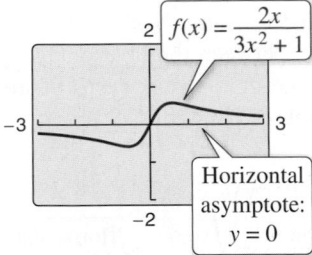

Figure 2.24

b. For this rational function, the degree of the numerator is *equal* to the degree of the denominator. The leading coefficient of the numerator is 2 and the leading coefficient of the denominator is 1, so the graph has the line $y = 2$ as a horizontal asymptote. To find any vertical asymptotes, set the denominator equal to zero and solve the resulting equation for x.

$$x^2 - 1 = 0 \qquad \text{Set denominator equal to zero.}$$

$$(x + 1)(x - 1) = 0 \qquad \text{Factor.}$$

$$x + 1 = 0 \ \Longrightarrow \ x = -1 \qquad \text{Set 1st factor equal to 0.}$$

$$x - 1 = 0 \ \Longrightarrow \ x = 1 \qquad \text{Set 2nd factor equal to 0.}$$

This equation has two real solutions, $x = -1$ and $x = 1$, so the graph has the lines $x = -1$ and $x = 1$ as vertical asymptotes, as shown in Figure 2.25.

Figure 2.25

 Checkpoint))) *Audio-video solution in English & Spanish at LarsonPrecalculus.com.*

Find all vertical and horizontal asymptotes of the graph of $f(x) = \dfrac{5x^2}{x^2 - 1}$. ∎

Values for which a rational function is undefined (the denominator is zero) result in a vertical asymptote or a hole in the graph, as shown in Example 3.

EXAMPLE 3   Finding Asymptotes and Holes

Find all asymptotes and holes in the graph of

$$f(x) = \frac{x^2 + x - 2}{x^2 - x - 6}.$$

Solution

For this rational function, the degree of the numerator is *equal* to the degree of the denominator. The leading coefficients of the numerator and denominator are both 1, so the graph has the line $y = 1$ as a horizontal asymptote. To find any vertical asymptotes, first factor the numerator and denominator as follows.

$$f(x) = \frac{x^2 + x - 2}{x^2 - x - 6} = \frac{(x - 1)(x + 2)}{(x + 2)(x - 3)} = \frac{x - 1}{x - 3}, \quad x \neq -2$$

By setting the denominator $x - 3$ (of the simplified function) equal to zero, you can determine that the graph has the line $x = 3$ as a vertical asymptote, as shown in the figure. To find any holes in the graph, note that the function is undefined at $x = -2$ and $x = 3$. Because $x = -2$ is not a vertical asymptote of the function, there is a hole in the graph at $x = -2$. To find the y-coordinate of the hole, substitute $x = -2$ into the simplified form of the function.

$$y = \frac{x - 1}{x - 3} = \frac{-2 - 1}{-2 - 3} = \frac{3}{5}$$

So, the graph of the rational function has a hole at $\left(-2, \frac{3}{5}\right)$.

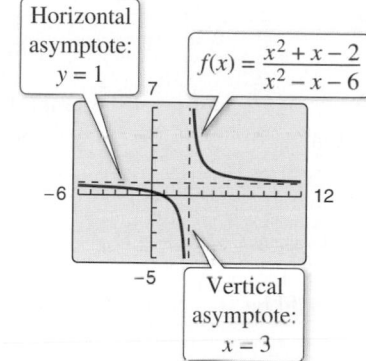

Horizontal asymptote: $y = 1$

$f(x) = \dfrac{x^2 + x - 2}{x^2 - x - 6}$

Vertical asymptote: $x = 3$

✓ **Checkpoint** ◀))) *Audio-video solution in English & Spanish at LarsonPrecalculus.com.*

Find all asymptotes and holes in the graph of $f(x) = \dfrac{x^2 - 25}{x^2 + 5x}.$

EXAMPLE 4   Finding a Function's Domain and Asymptotes

For the function f, find (a) the domain of f, (b) the vertical asymptote of f, and (c) the horizontal asymptote of f.

$$f(x) = \frac{3x^3 + 7x^2 + 2}{-2x^3 + 16}$$

Solution

a. Because the denominator is zero when $-2x^3 + 16 = 0$, solve this equation to determine that the domain of f is all real numbers except $x = 2$.

b. Because the denominator of f has a zero at $x = 2$, and 2 is not a zero of the numerator, the graph of f has the vertical asymptote $x = 2$.

c. Because the degrees of the numerator and denominator are the same, and the leading coefficient of the numerator is 3 and the leading coefficient of the denominator is -2, the horizontal asymptote of f is $y = -\frac{3}{2}$.

✓ **Checkpoint** ◀))) *Audio-video solution in English & Spanish at LarsonPrecalculus.com.*

Repeat Example 4 using the function $f(x) = \dfrac{3x^2 + x - 5}{x^2 + 1}.$

Application

There are many examples of asymptotic behavior in real life. For instance, Example 5 shows how a vertical asymptote can be used to analyze the cost of removing pollutants from smokestack emissions.

EXAMPLE 5   Cost-Benefit Model

A utility company burns coal to generate electricity. The cost C (in dollars) of removing $p\%$ of the smokestack pollutants is given by

$$C = \frac{80{,}000p}{100 - p}$$

for $0 \le p < 100$. Use a graphing utility to graph this function. You are a member of a state legislature that is considering a law that would require utility companies to remove 90% of the pollutants from their smokestack emissions. The current law requires 85% removal. How much additional cost would the utility company incur as a result of the new law?

Solution

The graph of this function is shown in Figure 2.26. Note that the graph has a vertical asymptote at $p = 100$. Because the current law requires 85% removal, the current cost to the utility company is

$$C = \frac{80{,}000(85)}{100 - 85} \approx \$453{,}333. \qquad \text{Evaluate } C \text{ when } p = 85.$$

The cost to remove 90% of the pollutants would be

$$C = \frac{80{,}000(90)}{100 - 90} \approx \$720{,}000. \qquad \text{Evaluate } C \text{ when } p = 90.$$

So, the new law would require the utility company to spend an additional

$$720{,}000 - 453{,}333 = \$266{,}667. \qquad \text{Subtract 85\% removal cost from 90\% removal cost.}$$

Figure 2.26

 Checkpoint ◀))) *Audio-video solution in English & Spanish at LarsonPrecalculus.com.*

The cost C (in millions of dollars) of removing $p\%$ of the industrial and municipal pollutants discharged into a river is given by

$$C = \frac{255p}{100 - p}, \quad 0 \le p < 100.$$

a. Find the costs of removing 20%, 45%, and 80% of the pollutants.

b. According to the model, would it be possible to remove 100% of the pollutants? Explain.

Explore the Concept

The *table* feature of a graphing utility can be used to estimate vertical and horizontal asymptotes of rational functions. Use the *table* feature to find any vertical or horizontal asymptotes of

$$f(x) = \frac{2x}{x + 1}.$$

Write a statement explaining how you found the asymptote(s) using the table.

2.6   Exercises

See *CalcChat.com* for tutorial help and worked-out solutions to odd-numbered exercises.
For instructions on how to use a graphing utility, see Appendix A.

Vocabulary and Concept Check

In Exercises 1 and 2, fill in the blank.

1. Functions of the form $f(x) = N(x)/D(x)$, where $N(x)$ and $D(x)$ are polynomials and $D(x)$ is not the zero polynomial, are called _____ .

2. If $f(x) \rightarrow \pm\infty$ as $x \rightarrow a$ from the left (or right), then $x = a$ is a _____ of the graph of f.

3. What feature of the graph of $y = \dfrac{9}{x - 3}$ can you find by solving $x - 3 = 0$?

4. Is $y = \dfrac{2}{3}$ a horizontal asymptote of the function $f(x) = \dfrac{2x}{3x^2 - 5}$?

Procedures and Problem Solving

Finding the Domain of a Rational Function   In Exercises 5–10, (a) find the domain of the function, (b) complete each table, and (c) discuss the behavior of f near any excluded x-values.

x	$f(x)$
0.5	
0.9	
0.99	
0.999	

x	$f(x)$
1.5	
1.1	
1.01	
1.001	

x	$f(x)$
5	
10	
100	
1000	

x	$f(x)$
-5	
-10	
-100	
-1000	

5. $f(x) = \dfrac{1}{x - 1}$

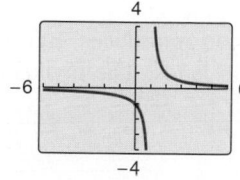

6. $f(x) = \dfrac{5x}{x - 1}$

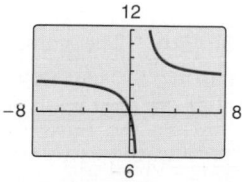

7. $f(x) = \dfrac{3x}{|x - 1|}$

8. $f(x) = \dfrac{3}{|x - 1|}$

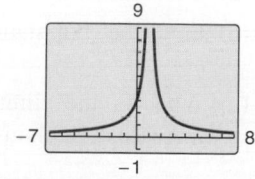

9. $f(x) = \dfrac{3x^2}{x^2 - 1}$

10. $f(x) = \dfrac{4x}{x^2 - 1}$

Identifying Graphs of Rational Functions   In Exercises 11–16, match the function with its graph. [The graphs are labeled (a), (b), (c), (d), (e), and (f).]

(a)

(b)

(c)

(d)

(e)

(f)

11. $f(x) = \dfrac{2}{x + 2}$

12. $f(x) = \dfrac{1}{x - 3}$

13. $f(x) = \dfrac{4x + 1}{x}$

14. $f(x) = \dfrac{1 - x}{x}$

15. $f(x) = \dfrac{x - 2}{x - 4}$

16. $f(x) = -\dfrac{x + 2}{x + 4}$

Finding Vertical and Horizontal Asymptotes In Exercises 17–20, find any asymptotes of the graph of the rational function. Verify your answers by using a graphing utility to graph the function.

17. $f(x) = \dfrac{1}{x^2}$ **18.** $f(x) = \dfrac{3}{(x-2)^3}$

19. $f(x) = \dfrac{2x^2}{x^2 + x - 6}$ **20.** $f(x) = \dfrac{x^2 - 4x}{x^2 - 4}$

Finding Asymptotes and Holes In Exercises 21–24, find any asymptotes and holes in the graph of the rational function. Verify your answers by using a graphing utility.

21. $f(x) = \dfrac{x(2 + x)}{2x - x^2}$ **22.** $f(x) = \dfrac{x^2 + 2x + 1}{2x^2 - x - 3}$

23. $f(x) = \dfrac{x^2 - 16}{x^2 + 8x}$ **24.** $f(x) = \dfrac{3 - 14x - 5x^2}{3 + 7x + 2x^2}$

Finding a Function's Domain and Asymptotes In Exercises 25–28, (a) find the domain of the function, (b) decide whether the function is continuous, and (c) identify any horizontal and vertical asymptotes. Verify your answer to part (a) both graphically by using a graphing utility and numerically by creating a table of values.

25. $f(x) = \dfrac{5x^2 - 2x - 6}{x^2 + 4}$ **26.** $f(x) = \dfrac{3x^2 + 1}{x^2 + x + 9}$

27. $f(x) = \dfrac{x^2 + 3x - 4}{-x^3 + 27}$ **28.** $f(x) = \dfrac{4x^3 - x^2 + 3}{3x^3 + 24}$

Algebraic-Graphical-Numerical In Exercises 29–32, (a) determine the domains of f and g, (b) find any vertical asymptotes and holes in the graphs of f and g, (c) compare f and g by completing the table, (d) use a graphing utility to graph f and g, and (e) explain why the differences in the domains of f and g are not shown in their graphs.

29. $f(x) = \dfrac{x^2 - 16}{x - 4}, \quad g(x) = x + 4$

x	1	2	3	4	5	6	7
$f(x)$							
$g(x)$							

30. $f(x) = \dfrac{x^2 - 9}{x - 3}, \quad g(x) = x + 3$

x	0	1	2	3	4	5	6
$f(x)$							
$g(x)$							

31. $f(x) = \dfrac{x^2 - 1}{x^2 - 2x - 3}, \quad g(x) = \dfrac{x - 1}{x - 3}$

x	-2	-1	0	1	2	3	4
$f(x)$							
$g(x)$							

32. $f(x) = \dfrac{x^2 - 4}{x^2 - 3x + 2}, \quad g(x) = \dfrac{x + 2}{x - 1}$

x	-3	-2	-1	0	1	2	3
$f(x)$							
$g(x)$							

Exploration In Exercises 33–36, determine the value that the function f approaches as the magnitude of x increases. Is $f(x)$ greater than or less than this value when x is positive and large in magnitude? What about when x is negative and large in magnitude?

33. $f(x) = 4 - \dfrac{1}{x}$ **34.** $f(x) = 2 + \dfrac{1}{x - 3}$

35. $f(x) = \dfrac{2x - 1}{x - 3}$ **36.** $f(x) = \dfrac{2x - 1}{x^2 + 1}$

Finding the Zeros of a Rational Function In Exercises 37–44, find the zeros (if any) of the rational function. Use a graphing utility to verify your answer.

37. $f(x) = \dfrac{x^2 - 9}{x^2 + 5}$ **38.** $h(x) = \dfrac{x^3 + 8}{x^2 - 11}$

39. $g(x) = 1 + \dfrac{6}{x - 3}$ **40.** $f(x) = 3 - \dfrac{-12}{x^2 + 2}$

41. $h(x) = \dfrac{x^2 - x - 20}{x^2 + 7}$ **42.** $g(x) = \dfrac{x^2 - 8x + 12}{x^2 + 4}$

43. $f(x) = \dfrac{x^2 + 4x - 21}{x^2 - 4x + 3}$ **44.** $h(x) = \dfrac{2x^2 + 11x + 5}{3x^2 + 13x - 10}$

45. Biology The game commission introduces 100 deer into newly acquired state game lands. The population N of the herd is given by

$$N = \dfrac{20(5 + 3t)}{1 + 0.04t}, \quad t \geq 0$$

where t is the time in years.

(a) Use a graphing utility to graph the model.

(b) Find the populations when $t = 5$, $t = 10$, and $t = 25$.

(c) What is the limiting size of the herd as time increases? Explain.

46. MODELING DATA

The endpoints of the interval over which distinct vision is possible are called the *near point* and *far point* of the eye (see figure). With increasing age, these points normally change. The table shows the approximate near points y (in inches) for various ages x (in years).

Age, x	Near point, y
16	3.0
32	4.7
44	9.8
50	19.7
60	39.7

(a) Find a rational model for the data. Take the reciprocals of the near points to generate the points

$$\left(x, \frac{1}{y}\right).$$

Use the *regression* feature of a graphing utility to find a linear model for the data. The resulting line has the form

$$\frac{1}{y} = ax + b.$$

Solve for y.

(b) Use the *table* feature of the graphing utility to create a table showing the predicted near point based on the model for each of the ages in the original table.

(c) Do you think the model can be used to predict the near point for a person who is 70 years old? Explain.

47. Physics

Consider a physics laboratory experiment designed to determine an unknown mass. A flexible metal meter stick is clamped to a table with 50 centimeters overhanging the edge (see figure). Known masses M ranging from 200 grams to 2000 grams are attached to the end of the meter stick. For each mass, the meter stick is displaced vertically and then allowed to oscillate. The average time t (in seconds) of one oscillation for each mass is recorded in the table.

Mass, M	Time, t
200	0.450
400	0.597
600	0.712
800	0.831
1000	0.906
1200	1.003
1400	1.088
1600	1.126
1800	1.218
2000	1.338

Spreadsheet at LarsonPrecalculus.com

A model for the data is given by

$$t = \frac{38M + 16{,}965}{10(M + 5000)}.$$

(a) Use the *table* feature of a graphing utility to create a table showing the estimated time based on the model for each of the masses shown in the table. What can you conclude?

(b) Use the model to approximate the mass of an object when the average time for one oscillation is 1.056 seconds.

48. Business

The sales S (in thousands of units) of a tablet computer during the nth week after the tablet is released are given by

$$S = \frac{150n}{n^2 + 100}, \quad n \geq 0.$$

(a) Use a graphing utility to graph the sales function.

(b) Find the sales in week 5, week 10, and week 20.

(c) According to this model, will sales ever drop to zero units? Explain.

49. *Why you should learn it* (p. 142) The cost C (in dollars) of supplying recycling bins to $p\%$ of the population of a rural township is given by

$$C = \frac{25{,}000p}{100 - p}, \quad 0 \le p < 100.$$

(a) Use a graphing utility to graph the cost function.

(b) Find the costs of supplying bins to 15%, 50%, and 90% of the population.

(c) According to the model, would it be possible to supply bins to 100% of the population? Explain.

Conclusions

True or False? In Exercises 50 and 51, determine whether the statement is true or false. Justify your answer.

50. A rational function can have infinitely many vertical asymptotes.

51. A rational function must have at least one vertical asymptote.

52. Writing a Rational Function Write a rational function f that has the specified characteristics. (There are many correct answers.)

(a) Vertical asymptote: $x = 2$

Horizontal asymptote: $y = 0$

Zero: $x = 1$

(b) Vertical asymptote: $x = -1$

Horizontal asymptote: $y = 0$

Zero: $x = 2$

(c) Vertical asymptotes: $x = -2$, $x = 1$

Horizontal asymptote: $y = 2$

Zeros: $x = 3$, $x = -3$

(d) Vertical asymptotes: $x = -1$, $x = 2$

Horizontal asymptote: $y = -2$

Zeros: $x = -2$, $x = 3$

(e) Vertical asymptotes: $x = 0$, $x = \pm 3$

Horizontal asymptote: $y = 3$

Zeros: $x = -1$, $x = 1$, $x = 2$

53. Think About It A real zero of the numerator of a rational function f is $x = c$. Must $x = c$ also be a zero of f? Explain.

54. Think About It When the graph of a rational function f has a vertical asymptote at $x = 4$, can f have a common factor of $(x - 4)$ in the numerator and denominator? Explain.

55. Exploration Use a graphing utility to compare the graphs of y_1 and y_2.

$$y_1 = \frac{3x^3 - 5x^2 + 4x - 5}{2x^2 - 6x + 7}, \quad y_2 = \frac{3x^3}{2x^2}$$

Start with a viewing window of $-5 \le x \le 5$ and $-10 \le y \le 10$, and then zoom out. Make a conjecture about how the graph of a rational function f is related to the graph of $y = a_n x^n / b_m x^m$, where $a_n x^n$ is the leading term of the numerator of f and $b_m x^m$ is the leading term of the denominator of f.

56. **HOW DO YOU SEE IT?** The graph of a rational function

$$f(x) = \frac{N(x)}{D(x)}$$

is shown below. Determine which of the statements about the function is false. Justify your answer.

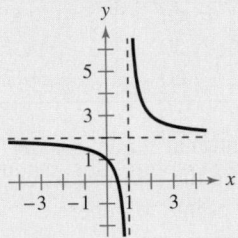

(a) $D(1) = 0$.

(b) The degrees of $N(x)$ and $D(x)$ are equal.

(c) The ratio of the leading coefficients of $N(x)$ and $D(x)$ is 1.

Cumulative Mixed Review

Finding the Equation of a Line In Exercises 57–60, write the general form of the equation of the line that passes through the points.

57. $(3, 2)$, $(0, -1)$ **58.** $(-6, 1)$, $(4, -5)$

59. $(2, 7)$, $(3, 10)$ **60.** $(0, 0)$, $(-9, 4)$

Long Division of Polynomials In Exercises 61–64, divide using long division.

61. $(x^2 + 5x + 6) \div (x - 4)$

62. $(x^2 - 10x + 15) \div (x - 3)$

63. $(2x^4 + x^2 - 11) \div (x^2 + 5)$

64. $(4x^5 + 3x^3 - 10) \div (2x + 3)$

2.7   Graphs of Rational Functions

The Graph of a Rational Function

To sketch the graph of a rational function, use the following guidelines.

Guidelines for Graphing Rational Functions

Let $f(x) = N(x)/D(x)$, where $N(x)$ and $D(x)$ are polynomials and $D(x)$ is not the zero polynomial.

1. Simplify f, if possible. Any restrictions on the domain of f not in the simplified function should be listed.

2. Find and plot the y-intercept (if any) by evaluating $f(0)$.

3. Find the zeros of the numerator (if any) by setting the numerator equal to zero. Then plot the corresponding x-intercepts.

4. Find the zeros of the denominator (if any) by setting the denominator equal to zero. Then sketch the corresponding vertical asymptotes using dashed vertical lines and plot the corresponding holes using open circles.

5. Find and sketch any other asymptotes of the graph using dashed lines.

6. Plot at least one point *between* and one point *beyond* each x-intercept and vertical asymptote.

7. Use smooth curves to complete the graph between and beyond the vertical asymptotes, excluding any points where f is not defined.

When graphing simple rational functions, testing for symmetry can be useful. For instance, the graph of $f(x) = 1/x$ is symmetrical with respect to the origin, and the graph of $g(x) = 1/x^2$ is symmetrical with respect to the y-axis.

Technology Tip

Some graphing utilities have difficulty graphing rational functions that have vertical asymptotes. Often, the utility will connect parts of the graph that are not supposed to be connected. Notice that the graph in Figure 2.27(a) should consist of two *unconnected* portions—one to the left of $x = 2$ and the other to the right of $x = 2$. To eliminate this problem, you can try changing the *mode* of the graphing utility to *dot mode*. The problem with this mode is that the graph is then represented as a collection of dots rather than as a smooth curve, as shown in Figure 2.27(b).

(a) Connected mode

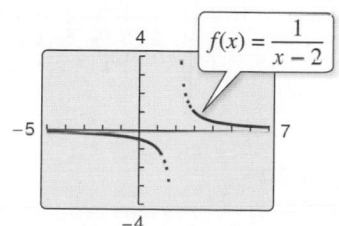

(b) Dot mode

Figure 2.27

Library of Parent Functions: Rational Function

The simplest type of rational function is the *parent rational function* $f(x) = 1/x$, also known as the *reciprocal function*. The basic characteristics of the parent rational function are summarized below and on the inside cover of this text.

Graph of $f(x) = \dfrac{1}{x}$

Domain: $(-\infty, 0) \cup (0, \infty)$
Range: $(-\infty, 0) \cup (0, \infty)$
No intercepts
Decreasing on $(-\infty, 0)$ and $(0, \infty)$
Odd function
Origin symmetry
Vertical asymptote: y-axis
Horizontal asymptote: x-axis

Vertical asymptote: y-axis

$f(x) = \dfrac{1}{x}$

Horizontal asymptote: x-axis

EXAMPLE 1   Library of Parent Functions: $f(x) = 1/x$

See LarsonPrecalculus.com for an interactive version of this type of example.

Sketch the graph of each function by hand and compare it with the graph of $f(x) = 1/x$.

a. $g(x) = \dfrac{-1}{x + 2}$

b. $h(x) = \dfrac{1}{x - 1} + 3$

Solution

a. With respect to the graph of $f(x) = 1/x$, the graph of g is obtained by a *reflection* in the y-axis and a horizontal shift two units *to the left*, as shown in Figure 2.28. Confirm this with a graphing utility.

b. With respect to the graph of $f(x) = 1/x$, the graph of h is obtained by a horizontal shift one unit *to the right* and a vertical shift three units *upward*, as shown in Figure 2.29. Confirm this with a graphing utility.

Figure 2.28

Figure 2.29

 Checkpoint *Audio-video solution in English & Spanish at LarsonPrecalculus.com.*

Sketch the graph of each function by hand and compare it with the graph of $f(x) = 1/x$.

a. $g(x) = \dfrac{1}{x - 4}$ **b.** $h(x) = \dfrac{1}{x + 3} - 1$

In Examples 2–6, note that the vertical asymptotes are included in the tables of additional points. This is done to emphasize numerically the behavior of the graph of the function.

EXAMPLE 2   Sketching the Graph of a Rational Function

Sketch the graph of $g(x) = \dfrac{3}{x - 2}$ by hand.

Solution

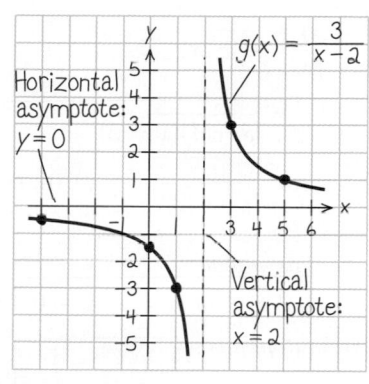

Figure 2.30

y-intercept:	$\left(0, -\dfrac{3}{2}\right)$, because $g(0) = -\dfrac{3}{2}$
x-intercept:	None, because $3 \neq 0$
Vertical asymptote:	$x = 2$, zero of denominator
Horizontal asymptote:	$y = 0$, because degree of $N(x) <$ degree of $D(x)$

Additional points:

x	-4	1	2	3	5
$g(x)$	-0.5	-3	Undefined	3	1

By plotting the intercept, asymptotes, and a few additional points, you can obtain the graph shown in Figure 2.30. Confirm this with a graphing utility.

✓ **Checkpoint** 🔊))) *Audio-video solution in English & Spanish at LarsonPrecalculus.com.*

Sketch the graph of $f(x) = \dfrac{1}{x + 3}$ by hand.

Note that the graph of g in Example 2 is a vertical stretch and a right shift of the graph of

$$f(x) = \frac{1}{x}$$

because

$$g(x) = \frac{3}{x - 2} = 3\left(\frac{1}{x - 2}\right) = 3f(x - 2).$$

EXAMPLE 3   Sketching the Graph of a Rational Function

Sketch the graph of $f(x) = \dfrac{2x - 1}{x}$ by hand.

Solution

Figure 2.31

y-intercept:	None, because $x = 0$ is not in the domain
x-intercept:	$\left(\dfrac{1}{2}, 0\right)$, because $2x - 1 = 0$ when $x = \dfrac{1}{2}$
Vertical asymptote:	$x = 0$, zero of denominator
Horizontal asymptote:	$y = 2$, because degree of $N(x) =$ degree of $D(x)$

Additional points:

x	-4	-1	0	$\dfrac{1}{4}$	4
$f(x)$	2.25	3	Undefined	-2	1.75

By plotting the intercept, asymptotes, and a few additional points, you can obtain the graph shown in Figure 2.31. Confirm this with a graphing utility.

✓ **Checkpoint** 🔊))) *Audio-video solution in English & Spanish at LarsonPrecalculus.com.*

Sketch the graph of $f(x) = \dfrac{2x + 3}{x + 1}$ by hand.

EXAMPLE 4   Sketching the Graph of a Rational Function

Sketch the graph of $f(x) = \dfrac{x}{x^2 - x - 2}$.

Solution

Factor the denominator to determine the zeros of the denominator.

$$f(x) = \frac{x}{x^2 - x - 2}$$

$$= \frac{x}{(x + 1)(x - 2)}$$

y-intercept: $(0, 0)$, because $f(0) = 0$

x-intercept: $(0, 0)$

Vertical asymptotes: $x = -1$, $x = 2$, zeros of denominator

Horizontal asymptote: $y = 0$, because degree of $N(x) <$ degree of $D(x)$

Additional points:

x	-3	-1	-0.5	1	2	3
$f(x)$	-0.3	Undefined	0.4	-0.5	Undefined	0.75

The graph is shown in Figure 2.32.

Figure 2.32

✓ **Checkpoint** 🔊))) *Audio-video solution in English & Spanish at LarsonPrecalculus.com.*

Sketch the graph of $f(x) = \dfrac{3x}{x^2 + x - 2}$.

EXAMPLE 5   Sketching the Graph of a Rational Function

Sketch the graph of $f(x) = \dfrac{x^2 - 9}{x^2 - 2x - 3}$.

Solution

By factoring the numerator and denominator, you have

$$f(x) = \frac{x^2 - 9}{x^2 - 2x - 3} = \frac{(x - 3)(x + 3)}{(x - 3)(x + 1)} = \frac{x + 3}{x + 1}, \quad x \neq 3.$$

y-intercept: $(0, 3)$, because $f(0) = 3$

x-intercept: $(-3, 0)$, because $x + 3 = 0$ when $x = -3$

Vertical asymptote: $x = -1$, zero of (simplified) denominator

Hole: $\left(3, \frac{3}{2}\right)$, f is not defined at $x = 3$

Horizontal asymptote: $y = 1$, because degree of $N(x) =$ degree of $D(x)$

Additional points:

x	-5	-2	-1	-0.5	1	3	4
$f(x)$	0.5	-1	Undefined	5	2	Undefined	1.4

The graph is shown in Figure 2.33.

Figure 2.33   *Hole at $x = 3$*

✓ **Checkpoint** 🔊))) *Audio-video solution in English & Spanish at LarsonPrecalculus.com.*

Sketch the graph of $f(x) = \dfrac{x^2 - 4}{x^2 - x - 6}$.

Slant Asymptotes

Consider a rational function whose denominator is of degree 1 or greater. If the degree of the numerator is exactly *one more* than the degree of the denominator, then the graph of the function has a **slant** (or **oblique**) **asymptote.** For example, the graph of

$$f(x) = \frac{x^2 - x}{x + 1}$$

has a slant asymptote, as shown in Figure 2.34. To find the equation of a slant asymptote, use long division. For instance, by dividing $x + 1$ into $x^2 - x$, you have

$$f(x) = \frac{x^2 - x}{x + 1} = \underbrace{x - 2}_{\substack{\text{Slant asymptote} \\ (y = x - 2)}} + \frac{2}{x + 1}.$$

As x increases or decreases without bound, the remainder term $2/(x + 1)$ approaches 0, so the graph of f approaches the line $y = x - 2$, as shown in Figure 2.34.

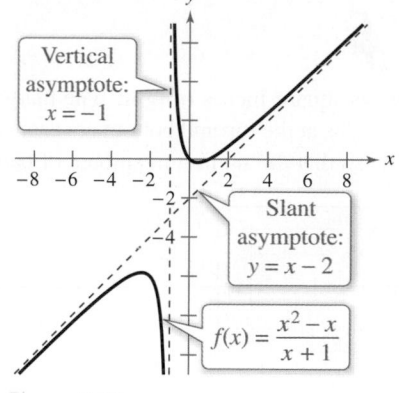

Figure 2.34

Explore the Concept

Do you think it is possible for the graph of a rational function to cross its horizontal asymptote or its slant asymptote? Use the graphs of the following functions to investigate this question. Write a summary of your conclusion. Explain your reasoning.

$$f(x) = \frac{x}{x^2 + 1}$$

$$g(x) = \frac{2x}{3x^2 - 2x + 1}$$

$$h(x) = \frac{x^3}{x^2 + 1}$$

EXAMPLE 6 A Rational Function with a Slant Asymptote

Sketch the graph of $f(x) = \dfrac{x^2 - x - 2}{x - 1}$.

Solution

First, write $f(x)$ in two different ways. Factoring the numerator

$$f(x) = \frac{x^2 - x - 2}{x - 1} = \frac{(x - 2)(x + 1)}{x - 1}$$

enables you to recognize the x-intercepts. Long division

$$f(x) = \frac{x^2 - x - 2}{x - 1} = x - \frac{2}{x - 1}$$

enables you to recognize that the line $y = x$ is a slant asymptote of the graph.

y-intercept: $(0, 2)$, because $f(0) = 2$

x-intercepts: $(-1, 0)$ and $(2, 0)$

Vertical asymptote: $x = 1$, zero of denominator

Horizontal asymptote: None, because degree of $N(x) >$ degree of $D(x)$

Slant asymptote: $y = x$

Additional points:

x	-2	0.5	1	1.5	3
$f(x)$	-1.33	4.5	Undefined	-2.5	2

The graph is shown in Figure 2.35.

Figure 2.35

 Checkpoint Audio-video solution in English & Spanish at LarsonPrecalculus.com.

Sketch the graph of $f(x) = \dfrac{3x^2 + 1}{x}$.

Application

 EXAMPLE 7 Publishing

A rectangular page is designed to contain 48 square inches of print. The margins on each side of the page are $1\frac{1}{2}$ inches wide. The margins at the top and bottom are each 1 inch deep. What should the dimensions of the page be so that the minimum amount of paper is used?

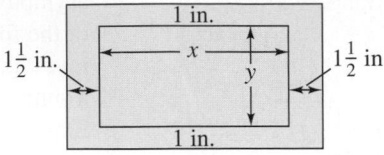

Figure 2.36

Graphical Solution

Let A be the area to be minimized. From Figure 2.36, you can write

$$A = (x + 3)(y + 2).$$

The printed area inside the margins is modeled by $48 = xy$ or $y = 48/x$. To find the minimum area, rewrite the equation for A in terms of just one variable by substituting $48/x$ for y.

$$A = (x + 3)\left(\frac{48}{x} + 2\right) = \frac{(x + 3)(48 + 2x)}{x}, \quad x > 0$$

The graph of this rational function is shown in Figure 2.37. Because x represents the width of the printed area, you need consider only the portion of the graph for which x is positive. Using the *minimum* feature of a graphing utility, you can approximate the minimum value of A to occur when $x \approx 8.5$ inches. The corresponding value of y is $48/8.5 \approx 5.6$ inches. So, the dimensions should be

$$x + 3 \approx 11.5 \text{ inches by } y + 2 \approx 7.6 \text{ inches.}$$

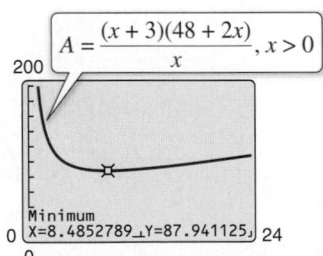

Figure 2.37

Numerical Solution

Let A be the area to be minimized. From Figure 2.36, you can write

$$A = (x + 3)(y + 2).$$

The printed area inside the margins is modeled by $48 = xy$ or $y = 48/x$. To find the minimum area, rewrite the equation for A in terms of just one variable by substituting $48/x$ for y.

$$A = (x + 3)\left(\frac{48}{x} + 2\right) = \frac{(x + 3)(48 + 2x)}{x}, \quad x > 0$$

Use the *table* feature of a graphing utility to create a table of values for the function

$$y_1 = \frac{(x + 3)(48 + 2x)}{x}$$

beginning at $x = 1$. From the table, you can see that the minimum value of y_1 occurs when x is somewhere between 8 and 9, as shown in Figure 2.38. To approximate the minimum value of y_1 to one decimal place, change the table to begin at $x = 8$ and set the table step to 0.1. The minimum value of y_1 occurs when $x \approx 8.5$, as shown in Figure 2.39. The corresponding value of y is $48/8.5 \approx 5.6$ inches. So, the dimensions should be

$$x + 3 \approx 11.5 \text{ inches by } y + 2 \approx 7.6 \text{ inches.}$$

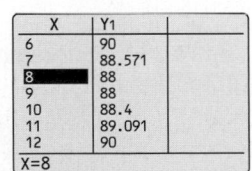

X	Y1
6	90
7	88.571
8	**88**
9	88
10	88.4
11	89.091
12	90
X=8	

X	Y1
8.2	87.961
8.3	87.949
8.4	87.943
8.5	**87.941**
8.6	87.944
8.7	87.952
8.8	87.964
X=8.5	

Figure 2.38   **Figure 2.39**

✔ **Checkpoint** Audio-video solution in English & Spanish at LarsonPrecalculus.com.

Rework Example 7 when the margins on each side are 2 inches wide and the page contains 40 square inches of print.

If you go on to take a course in calculus, you will learn an analytic technique for finding the exact value of x that produces a minimum area in Example 7. In this case, that value is $x = 6\sqrt{2} \approx 8.485$.

2.7 Exercises

See *CalcChat.com* for tutorial help and worked-out solutions to odd-numbered exercises.
For instructions on how to use a graphing utility, see Appendix A.

Vocabulary and Concept Check

In Exercises 1 and 2, fill in the blank(s).

1. For the rational function $f(x) = N(x)/D(x)$, if the degree of $N(x)$ is exactly one more than the degree of $D(x)$, then the graph of f has a _____ (or oblique) _____ .

2. The graph of $f(x) = 1/x$ has a _____ asymptote at $x = 0$.

3. Does the graph of $f(x) = \dfrac{x^3 - 1}{x^2 + 2}$ have a slant asymptote?

4. Using long division, you find that $f(x) = \dfrac{x^2 + 1}{x + 1} = x - 1 + \dfrac{2}{x + 1}$. What is the slant asymptote of the graph of f?

Procedures and Problem Solving

Library of Parent Functions: $f(x) = 1/x$ In Exercises 5–8, sketch the graph of the function g and describe how the graph is related to the graph of $f(x) = 1/x$.

5. $g(x) = \dfrac{-1}{x} + 2$

6. $g(x) = \dfrac{1}{x - 6}$

7. $g(x) = \dfrac{1}{x - 3} - 1$

8. $g(x) = \dfrac{-1}{x + 2} - 4$

Describing a Transformation of $f(x) = 2/x$ In Exercises 9–12, use a graphing utility to graph $f(x) = 2/x$ and the function g in the same viewing window. Describe the relationship between the two graphs.

9. $g(x) = f(x) + 1$

10. $g(x) = f(x - 1)$

11. $g(x) = -f(x)$

12. $g(x) = \frac{1}{2}f(x + 2)$

Describing a Transformation of $f(x) = 3/x^2$ In Exercises 13–16, use a graphing utility to graph $f(x) = 3/x^2$ and the function g in the same viewing window. Describe the relationship between the two graphs.

13. $g(x) = f(x) - 2$

14. $g(x) = -2f(x)$

15. $g(x) = f(x - 2)$

16. $g(x) = \frac{1}{4}f(x)$

Sketching the Graph of a Rational Function In Exercises 17–32, sketch the graph of the rational function by hand. As sketching aids, check for intercepts, vertical asymptotes, horizontal asymptotes, and holes. Use a graphing utility to verify your graph.

17. $f(x) = \dfrac{1}{x + 2}$

18. $f(x) = \dfrac{1}{x - 6}$

19. $C(x) = \dfrac{5 + 2x}{1 + x}$

20. $P(x) = \dfrac{1 - 3x}{1 - x}$

21. $f(t) = \dfrac{1 - 2t}{t}$

22. $g(x) = \dfrac{1}{x + 2} + 2$

23. $f(x) = \dfrac{x^2}{x^2 - 4}$

24. $g(x) = \dfrac{x}{x^2 - 9}$

25. $g(x) = \dfrac{4(x + 1)}{x(x - 4)}$

26. $h(x) = \dfrac{2}{x^2(x - 3)}$

27. $f(x) = \dfrac{3x}{x^2 - x - 2}$

28. $f(x) = \dfrac{2x}{x^2 + x - 2}$

29. $f(x) = \dfrac{x^2 + 3x}{x^2 + x - 6}$

30. $g(x) = \dfrac{5(x + 4)}{x^2 + x - 12}$

31. $f(x) = \dfrac{x^2 - 1}{x + 1}$

32. $f(x) = \dfrac{x^2 - 16}{x - 4}$

Finding the Domain and Asymptotes In Exercises 33–42, use a graphing utility to graph the function. Determine its domain and identify any vertical or horizontal asymptotes.

33. $f(x) = \dfrac{2 + x}{1 - x}$

34. $f(x) = \dfrac{3 - x}{2 - x}$

35. $g(x) = \dfrac{3x - 4}{-x}$

36. $h(x) = \dfrac{2x - 1}{x + 5}$

37. $g(x) = \dfrac{5}{x^2 + 1}$

38. $g(x) = -\dfrac{x}{(x - 2)^2}$

39. $f(x) = \dfrac{x + 1}{x^2 - x - 6}$

40. $f(x) = \dfrac{x + 4}{x^2 + x - 6}$

41. $f(x) = \dfrac{20x}{x^2 + 1} - \dfrac{1}{x}$

42. $f(x) = 5\left(\dfrac{1}{x - 4} - \dfrac{1}{x + 2}\right)$

Exploration In Exercises 43–48, use a graphing utility to graph the function. What do you observe about its asymptotes?

43. $h(x) = \dfrac{6x}{\sqrt{x^2 + 1}}$

44. $f(x) = -\dfrac{x}{\sqrt{9 + x^2}}$

45. $g(x) = \dfrac{4|x - 2|}{x + 1}$

46. $f(x) = \dfrac{8|3 + x|}{x - 2}$

47. $f(x) = \dfrac{4(x - 1)^2}{x^2 - 4x + 5}$

48. $g(x) = \dfrac{3x^4 - 5x + 3}{x^4 + 1}$

A Rational Function with a Slant Asymptote In Exercises 49–56, sketch the graph of the rational function by hand. As sketching aids, check for intercepts, vertical asymptotes, and slant asymptotes.

49. $f(x) = \dfrac{2x^2 + 1}{x}$

50. $g(x) = \dfrac{1 - x^2}{x}$

51. $h(x) = \dfrac{x^2}{x - 1}$

52. $f(x) = \dfrac{x^3}{x^2 - 1}$

53. $g(x) = \dfrac{x^3}{2x^2 - 8}$

54. $f(x) = \dfrac{x^3}{x^2 + 4}$

55. $f(x) = \dfrac{x^3 + 2x^2 + 4}{2x^2 + 1}$

56. $f(x) = \dfrac{2x^2 - 5x + 5}{x - 2}$

Finding the x-Intercepts In Exercises 57–60, use the graph to estimate any x-intercepts of the rational function. Set $y = 0$ and solve the resulting equation to confirm your result.

57. $y = \dfrac{x + 1}{x - 3}$

58. $y = \dfrac{2x}{x - 3}$

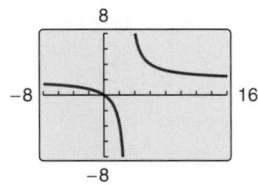

59. $y = \dfrac{1}{x} - x$

60. $y = x - 3 + \dfrac{2}{x}$

Finding the Domain and Asymptotes In Exercises 61–64, use a graphing utility to graph the rational function. Determine the domain of the function and identify any asymptotes.

61. $y = \dfrac{2x^2 + x}{x + 1}$

62. $y = \dfrac{x^2 + 5x + 8}{x + 3}$

63. $y = \dfrac{1 + 3x^2 - x^3}{x^2}$

64. $y = \dfrac{12 - 2x - x^2}{2(4 + x)}$

Finding Asymptotes and Holes In Exercises 65–70, find all vertical asymptotes, horizontal asymptotes, slant asymptotes, and holes in the graph of the function. Then use a graphing utility to verify your results.

65. $f(x) = \dfrac{x^2 - 5x + 4}{x^2 - 4}$

66. $f(x) = \dfrac{x^2 - 2x - 8}{x^2 - 9}$

67. $f(x) = \dfrac{2x^2 - 5x + 2}{2x^2 - x - 6}$

68. $f(x) = \dfrac{3x^2 - 8x + 4}{2x^2 - 3x - 2}$

69. $f(x) = \dfrac{2x^3 - x^2 - 2x + 1}{x^2 + 3x + 2}$

70. $f(x) = \dfrac{2x^3 + x^2 - 8x - 4}{x^2 - 3x + 2}$

Finding x-Intercepts Graphically In Exercises 71–82, use a graphing utility to graph the function and determine any x-intercepts. Set $y = 0$ and solve the resulting equation to confirm your result.

71. $y = \dfrac{1}{x + 5} + \dfrac{4}{x}$

72. $y = \dfrac{1}{x - 2} - \dfrac{5}{x}$

73. $y = \dfrac{2}{x + 2} - \dfrac{3}{x - 1}$

74. $y = \dfrac{6}{x + 3} - \dfrac{1}{x + 4}$

75. $y = x - \dfrac{2}{x + 1}$

76. $y = 2x - \dfrac{8}{x}$

77. $y = x + 2 - \dfrac{1}{x + 1}$

78. $y = 2x - 1 + \dfrac{1}{x - 2}$

79. $y = x + 1 + \dfrac{2}{x - 1}$

80. $y = x + 2 + \dfrac{2}{x + 2}$

81. $y = x + 3 - \dfrac{2}{2x - 1}$

82. $y = x - 1 - \dfrac{2}{2x - 3}$

83. Chemistry A 1000-liter tank contains 50 liters of a 25% brine solution. You add x liters of a 75% brine solution to the tank.

(a) Show that the concentration C (the ratio of brine to the total solution) of the final mixture is given by

$$C = \dfrac{3x + 50}{4(x + 50)}.$$

(b) Determine the domain of the function based on the physical constraints of the problem.

(c) Use a graphing utility to graph the function. As the tank is filled, what happens to the rate at which the concentration of brine increases? What percent does the concentration of brine appear to approach?

84. Geometry A rectangular region of length x and width y has an area of 500 square meters.

(a) Write the width y as a function of x.

(b) Determine the domain of the function based on the physical constraints of the problem.

(c) Sketch a graph of the function and determine the width of the rectangle when $x = 30$ meters.

85. Publishing   A page that is x inches wide and y inches high contains 30 square inches of print (see figure). The margins at the top and bottom are 2 inches deep and the margins on each side are 1 inch wide.

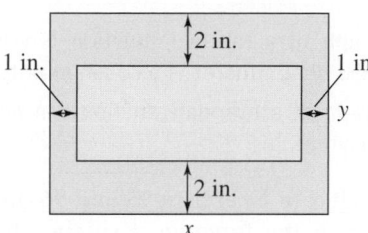

(a) Show that the total area A of the page is given by

$$A = \frac{2x(2x + 11)}{x - 2}.$$

(b) Determine the domain of the function based on the physical constraints of the problem.

(c) Use a graphing utility to graph the area function and approximate the page size such that the minimum amount of paper will be used. Verify your answer numerically using the *table* feature of the graphing utility.

86. Geometry   A right triangle is formed in the first quadrant by the x-axis, the y-axis, and a line segment through the point $(3, 2)$. (See figure.)

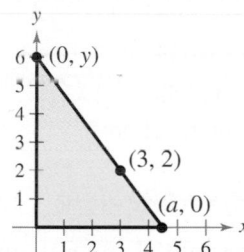

(a) Show that an equation of the line segment is given by

$$y = \frac{2(a - x)}{a - 3}, \quad 0 \le x \le a.$$

(b) Show that the area of the triangle is given by

$$A = \frac{a^2}{a - 3}.$$

(c) Use a graphing utility to graph the area function and estimate the value of a that yields a minimum area. Estimate the minimum area. Verify your answer numerically using the *table* feature of the graphing utility.

87. Cost Management   The ordering and transportation cost C (in thousands of dollars) for the components used in manufacturing a product is given by

$$C = 100\left(\frac{200}{x^2} + \frac{x}{x + 30}\right), \quad x \ge 1$$

where x is the order size (in hundreds). Use a graphing utility to graph the cost function. From the graph, estimate the order size that minimizes cost.

88. Cost Management   The cost C of producing x units of a product is given by $C = 0.2x^2 + 10x + 5$, and the average cost per unit is given by

$$\overline{C} = \frac{C}{x} = \frac{0.2x^2 + 10x + 5}{x}, \quad x > 0.$$

Sketch the graph of the average cost function, and estimate the number of units that should be produced to minimize the average cost per unit.

89. *Why you should learn it* *(p. 151)* The concentration

C of a chemical in the bloodstream t hours after injection into muscle tissue is given by

$$C = \frac{3t^2 + t}{t^3 + 50}, \quad t \ge 0.$$

(a) Determine the horizontal asymptote of the function and interpret its meaning in the context of the problem.

(b) Use a graphing utility to graph the function and approximate the time when the bloodstream concentration is greatest.

(c) Use the graphing utility to determine when the concentration is less than 0.345.

90. Algebraic-Graphical-Numerical   A driver averaged 50 miles per hour on the round trip between Baltimore, Maryland, and Philadelphia, Pennsylvania, 100 miles away. The average speeds for going and returning were x and y miles per hour, respectively.

(a) Show that $y = \dfrac{25x}{x - 25}$.

(b) Determine the vertical and horizontal asymptotes of the function.

(c) Use a graphing utility to complete the table. What do you observe?

x	30	35	40	45	50	55	60
y							

(d) Use the graphing utility to graph the function.

(e) Is it possible to average 20 miles per hour in one direction and still average 50 miles per hour on the round trip? Explain.

91. MODELING DATA

Data are recorded at 225 monitoring sites throughout the United States to study national trends in air quality. The table shows the mean amount A of carbon monoxide (in parts per million) recorded at these sites in each year from 2003 through 2012. (Source: EPA)

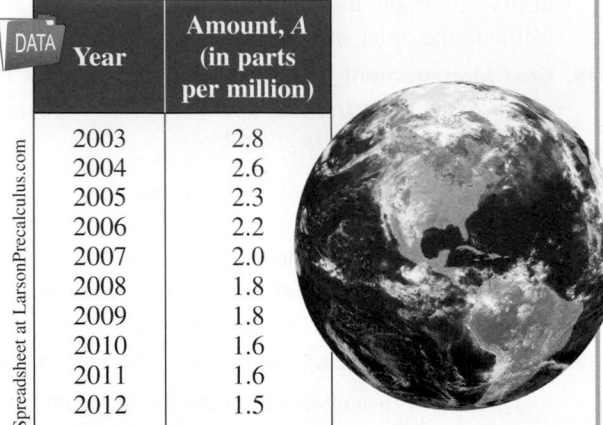

Year	Amount, A (in parts per million)
2003	2.8
2004	2.6
2005	2.3
2006	2.2
2007	2.0
2008	1.8
2009	1.8
2010	1.6
2011	1.6
2012	1.5

Spreadsheet at LarsonPrecalculus.com

(a) Use the *regression* feature of a graphing utility to find a linear model for the data. Let $t = 3$ represent 2003. Use the graphing utility to plot the data and graph the model in the same viewing window.

(b) Find a rational model for the data. Take the reciprocal of A to generate the points $(t, 1/A)$. Use the *regression* feature of the graphing utility to find a linear model for these data. The resulting line has the form $1/A = at + b$. Solve for A. Use the graphing utility to plot the data and graph the rational model in the same viewing window.

(c) Which model do you prefer? Why?

92. HOW DO YOU SEE IT?
A herd of elk is released onto state game lands. The graph shows the expected population P of the herd, where t is the time (in years) since the initial number of elk were released.

$$P = \frac{10 + 2.7t}{1 + 0.1t}$$

(a) Determine the domain of the function. Explain.

(b) Find the initial number of elk in the herd.

(c) Is there a limit to the size of the herd? If so, what is the expected population?

Conclusions

True or False? In Exercises 93 and 94, determine whether the statement is true or false. Justify your answer.

93. The graph of a rational function is continuous only when the denominator is a constant polynomial.

94. The graph of a rational function can never cross one of its asymptotes.

Think About It In Exercises 95 and 96, use a graphing utility to graph the function. Explain why there is no vertical asymptote when a superficial examination of the function might indicate that there should be one.

95. $h(x) = \dfrac{6 - 2x}{3 - x}$

96. $g(x) = \dfrac{x^2 + x - 2}{x - 1}$

97. **Writing** Write a set of guidelines for finding all the asymptotes of a rational function given that the degree of the numerator is not more than 1 greater than the degree of the denominator.

98. **Writing a Rational Function** Write a rational function that has the specified characteristics. (There are many correct answers.)

(a) Vertical asymptote: $x = -2$
    Slant asymptote: $y = x + 1$
    Zero of the function: $x = 2$

(b) Vertical asymptote: $x = -4$
    Slant asymptote: $y = x - 2$
    Zero of the function: $x = 3$

Cumulative Mixed Review

Simplifying Exponential Expressions In Exercises 99–102, simplify the expression.

99. $\left(\dfrac{x}{8}\right)^{-3}$

100. $(4x^2)^{-2}$

101. $\dfrac{3^{7/6}}{3^{1/6}}$

102. $\dfrac{(x^{-2})(x^{1/2})}{(x^{-1})(x^{5/2})}$

Finding the Domain and Range of a Function In Exercises 103–106, use a graphing utility to graph the function and find its domain and range.

103. $f(x) = \sqrt{6 + x^2}$

104. $f(x) = \sqrt{121 - x^2}$

105. $f(x) = -|x + 9|$

106. $f(x) = -x^2 + 9$

107. **Make a Decision** To work an extended application analyzing the median sales prices of existing one-family homes, visit this textbook's website at *LarsonPrecalculus.com*. (Data Source: National Association of Realtors)

2.8 Quadratic Models

Classifying Scatter Plots

In real life, many relationships between two variables are parabolic, as in Section 2.1, Example 5. A scatter plot can be used to give you an idea of which type of model will best fit a set of data.

EXAMPLE 1   Classifying Scatter Plots

See LarsonPrecalculus.com for an interactive version of this type of example.

Decide whether each set of data could be better modeled by a linear model,

$$y = ax + b$$

a quadratic model,

$$y = ax^2 + bc + c$$

or neither.

a. (0.9, 1.7), (1.2, 2.0), (1.3, 1.9), (1.4, 2.1), (1.6, 2.5), (1.8, 2.8), (2.1, 3.0), (2.5, 3.4), (2.9, 3.7), (3.2, 3.9), (3.3, 4.1), (3.6, 4.4), (4.0, 4.7), (4.2, 4.8), (4.3, 5.0)

b. (0.9, 3.2), (1.2, 4.0), (1.3, 4.1), (1.4, 4.4), (1.6, 5.1), (1.8, 6.0), (2.1, 7.6), (2.5, 9.8), (2.9, 12.4), (3.2, 14.3), (3.3, 15.2), (3.6, 18.1), (4.0, 22.7), (4.2, 24.9), (4.3, 27.2)

c. (0.9, 1.2), (1.2, 6.5), (1.3, 9.3), (1.4, 11.6), (1.6, 15.2), (1.8, 16.9), (2.1, 14.7), (2.5, 8.1), (2.9, 3.7), (3.2, 5.8), (3.3, 7.1), (3.6, 11.5), (4.0, 20.2), (4.2, 23.7), (4.3, 26.9)

Solution

a. Begin by entering the data into a graphing utility. Then display the scatter plot, as shown in Figure 2.40. From the scatter plot, it appears the data follow a linear pattern. So, the data can be better modeled by a linear function.

b. Enter the data into a graphing utility and then display the scatter plot (see Figure 2.41). From the scatter plot, it appears the data follow a parabolic pattern. So, the data can be better modeled by a quadratic function.

c. Enter the data into a graphing utility and then display the scatter plot (see Figure 2.42). From the scatter plot, it appears the data do not follow either a linear or a parabolic pattern. So, the data cannot be modeled by either a linear function or a quadratic function.

Figure 2.40

Figure 2.41

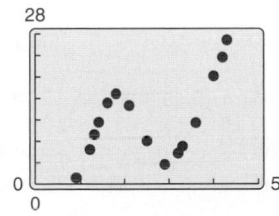

Figure 2.42

✓ **Checkpoint** 🔊))) *Audio-video solution in English & Spanish at LarsonPrecalculus.com.*

Decide whether the data could be better modeled by a linear model, $y = ax + b$, a quadratic model, $y = ax^2 + bx + c$, or neither.

(0, 3480), (5, 2235), (10, 1250), (15, 565), (20, 150), (25, 12), (30, 145), (35, 575), (40, 1275), (45, 2225), (50, 3500), (55, 5010)

What you should learn

▶ Classify scatter plots.
▶ Use scatter plots and a graphing utility to find quadratic models for data.
▶ Choose a model that best fits a set of data.

Why you should learn it

Many real-life situations can be modeled by quadratic equations. For instance, in Exercise 17 on page 165, a quadratic equation is used to model the monthly precipitation for San Francisco, California.

Fitting a Quadratic Model to Data

In Section 1.7, you created scatter plots of data and used a graphing utility to find the least squares regression lines for the data. You can use a similar procedure to find a model for nonlinear data. Once you have used a scatter plot to determine the type of model that would best fit a set of data, there are several ways that you can actually find the model. Each method is best used with a computer or calculator, rather than with hand calculations.

EXAMPLE 2   Fitting a Quadratic Model to Data

A study was done to compare the speed x (in miles per hour) with the mileage y (in miles per gallon) of an automobile. The results are shown in the table.

a. Use a graphing utility to create a scatter plot of the data.

b. Use the *regression* feature of the graphing utility to find a model that best fits the data.

c. Approximate the speed at which the mileage is the greatest.

Speed, x	Mileage, y
15	22.3
20	25.5
25	27.5
30	29.0
35	28.7
40	29.9
45	30.4
50	30.2
55	30.0
60	28.8
65	27.4
70	25.3
75	23.3

Spreadsheet at LarsonPrecalculus.com

Solution

a. Begin by entering the data into a graphing utility and displaying the scatter plot, as shown in Figure 2.43. From the scatter plot, you can see that the data appear to follow a parabolic pattern.

b. Using the *regression* feature of the graphing utility, you can find the quadratic model, as shown in Figure 2.44. So, the quadratic equation that best fits the data is given by

$$y = -0.0082x^2 + 0.75x + 13.5. \qquad \text{Quadratic model}$$

c. Graph the data and the model in the same viewing window, as shown in Figure 2.45. Use the *maximum* feature or the *zoom* and *trace* features of the graphing utility to approximate the speed at which the mileage is greatest. You should obtain a maximum of approximately $(46, 31)$, as shown in Figure 2.45. So, the speed at which the mileage is greatest is about 46 miles per hour.

Figure 2.43

Figure 2.44

Figure 2.45

✓ **Checkpoint** ◀))) *Audio-video solution in English & Spanish at LarsonPrecalculus.com.*

The time y (in seconds) required to attain a speed of x miles per hour from a standing start for an automobile is shown in the table.

Speed, x	0	20	30	40	50	60	70	80
Time, y	0	1.4	2.6	3.8	4.9	6.3	8.0	9.9

Spreadsheet at LarsonPrecalculus.com

a. Use a graphing utility to create a scatter plot of the data.

b. Use the *regression* feature of the graphing utility to find a model that best fits the data.

c. Use the model to estimate how long it takes the automobile, from a standing start, to reach a speed of 55 miles per hour.

EXAMPLE 3   Fitting a Quadratic Model to Data

A basketball is dropped from a height of about 5.25 feet. The height of the basketball is recorded 23 times at intervals of about 0.02 second. The results are shown in the table. Use a graphing utility to find a model that best fits the data. Then use the model to predict the time when the basketball will hit the ground.

Time, x	Height, y
0.0	5.23594
0.02	5.20353
0.04	5.16031
0.06	5.09910
0.08	5.02707
0.099996	4.95146
0.119996	4.85062
0.139992	4.74979
0.159988	4.63096
0.179988	4.50132
0.199984	4.35728
0.219984	4.19523
0.23998	4.02958
0.25993	3.84593
0.27998	3.65507
0.299976	3.44981
0.319972	3.23375
0.339961	3.01048
0.359961	2.76921
0.379951	2.52074
0.399941	2.25786
0.419941	1.98058
0.439941	1.63488

Spreadsheet at LarsonPrecalculus.com

Solution

Begin by entering the data into a graphing utility and displaying the scatter plot, as shown in Figure 2.46. From the scatter plot, you can see that the data show a parabolic trend. So, using the *regression* feature of the graphing utility, you can find the quadratic model, as shown in Figure 2.47. The quadratic model that best fits the data is given by $y = -15.449x^2 - 1.30x + 5.2$.

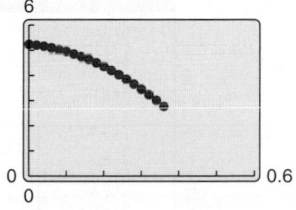

Figure 2.46   Figure 2.47

You can graph the data and the model in the same viewing window to see that the model fits the data well, as shown in the next figure.

Using this model, you can predict the time when the basketball will hit the ground by substituting 0 for y and solving the resulting equation for x.

$$y = -15.449x^2 - 1.30x + 5.2$$ 　　　　　Write original model.

$$0 = -15.449x^2 - 1.30x + 5.2$$ 　　　　　Substitute 0 for y.

$$x = \frac{-b \pm \sqrt{b^2 - 4ac}}{2a}$$ 　　　　　Quadratic Formula

$$= \frac{-(-1.30) \pm \sqrt{(-1.30)^2 - 4(-15.449)(5.2)}}{2(-15.449)}$$ 　　　　　Substitute for a, b, and c.

$$\approx 0.54$$ 　　　　　Choose positive solution.

So, the solution is about 0.54 second. In other words, the basketball will continue to fall for about $0.54 - 0.44 = 0.1$ second more before hitting the ground.

✓ **Checkpoint**   *Audio-video solution in English & Spanish at LarsonPrecalculus.com.*

The table shows the annual sales y (in millions of dollars) of a department store chain. Use a graphing utility to find a model that best fits the data. Then use the model to estimate the first year when the annual sales will be less than $190 million.

Year, x	1	2	3	4	5	6
Sales, y	221	222	220	219	216	211

Spreadsheet at LarsonPrecalculus.com

Choosing a Model

Sometimes it is not easy to distinguish from a scatter plot which type of model will best fit the data. You should first find several models for the data, using the *Library of Parent Functions*, and then choose the model that best fits the data by comparing the y-values of each model with the actual y-values.

EXAMPLE 4   Choosing a Model

The table shows the numbers y (in millions) of people ages 16 and older that were not in the U.S. labor force from 2003 through 2013. Use the *regression* feature of a graphing utility to find a linear model and a quadratic model for the data. Determine which model better fits the data.   (Source: U.S. Department of Labor)

DATA	Year	Number of people unemployed (in millions), y
	2003	74.7
	2004	76.0
	2005	76.8
	2006	77.4
	2007	78.7
	2008	79.5
	2009	81.7
	2010	83.9
	2011	86.0
	2012	88.3
	2013	90.3

Spreadsheet at LarsonPrecalculus.com

Solution

Let x represent the year, with $x = 3$ corresponding to 2003. Begin by entering the data into a graphing utility. Using the *regression* feature, a linear model for the data is

$$y = 1.55x + 68.8$$

and a quadratic model for the data is

$$y = 0.107x^2 - 0.16x + 74.6.$$

Plot the data and the linear model in the same viewing window, as shown in Figure 2.48. Then plot the data and the quadratic model in the same viewing window, as shown in Figure 2.49. To determine which model fits the data better, compare the y-values given by each model with the actual y-values. The model whose y-values are closest to the actual values is the better fit. In this case, the better-fitting model is the quadratic model.

Figure 2.48

Figure 2.49

 Checkpoint   Audio-video solution in English & Spanish at LarsonPrecalculus.com.

The table shows the numbers y (in thousands) of full-size, alternative fueled vehicles in use from 2005 through 2011. Use the *regression* feature of a graphing utility to find a linear model and a quadratic model for the data. Determine which model better fits the data.   (Source: U.S. Energy Information Administration)

DATA	Year	Number of alternative fueled vehicles (in thousands), y
	2005	19.2
	2006	31.3
	2007	44.9
	2008	59.8
	2009	64.2
	2010	72.1
	2011	81.3

Spreadsheet at LarsonPrecalculus.com

Technology Tip

When you use the *regression* feature of a graphing utility, the program may output an "r^2-value." This r^2-value is the **coefficient of determination** of the data and gives a measure of how well the model fits the data. The coefficient of determination for the linear model in Example 4 is $r^2 \approx 0.9608$, and the coefficient of determination for the quadratic model is $r^2 \approx 0.9962$. Because the coefficient of determination for the quadratic model is closer to 1, the quadratic model better fits the data.

2.8 Exercises

Vocabulary and Concept Check

1. What type of model best represents data that follow a parabolic pattern?
2. Which coefficient of determination indicates a better model for a set of data, $r^2 = 0.0365$ or $r^2 = 0.9688$?

Procedures and Problem Solving

Classifying Scatter Plots In Exercises 3–8, determine whether the scatter plot could best be modeled by a linear model, a quadratic model, or neither.

3.

4.

5.

6.

7.

8.

Choosing a Model In Exercises 9–16, (a) use a graphing utility to create a scatter plot of the data, (b) determine whether the data could be better modeled by a linear model or a quadratic model, (c) use the *regression* feature of the graphing utility to find a model for the data, (d) use the graphing utility to graph the model with the scatter plot from part (a), and (e) create a table comparing the original data with the data given by the model.

9. $(0, 2.1)$, $(1, 2.4)$, $(2, 2.5)$, $(3, 2.8)$, $(4, 2.9)$, $(5, 3.0)$, $(6, 3.0)$, $(7, 3.2)$, $(8, 3.4)$, $(9, 3.5)$, $(10, 3.6)$

10. $(-2, 11.0)$, $(-1, 10.7)$, $(0, 10.4)$, $(1, 10.3)$, $(2, 10.1)$, $(3, 9.9)$, $(4, 9.6)$, $(5, 9.4)$, $(6, 9.4)$, $(7, 9.2)$, $(8, 9.0)$

11. $(0, 2795)$, $(5, 1590)$, $(10, 650)$, $(15, -30)$, $(20, -450)$, $(25, -615)$, $(30, -520)$, $(35, -55)$, $(40, 625)$, $(45, 1630)$, $(50, 2845)$, $(55, 4350)$

12. $(0, 6140)$, $(2, 6815)$, $(4, 7335)$, $(6, 7710)$, $(8, 7915)$, $(10, 7590)$, $(12, 7975)$, $(14, 7700)$, $(16, 7325)$, $(18, 6820)$, $(20, 6125)$, $(22, 5325)$

13. $(1, 4.0)$, $(2, 6.5)$, $(3, 8.8)$, $(4, 10.6)$, $(5, 13.9)$, $(6, 15.0)$, $(7, 17.5)$, $(8, 20.1)$, $(9, 24.0)$, $(10, 27.1)$

14. $(-6, 10.7)$, $(-4, 9.0)$, $(-2, 7.0)$, $(0, 5.4)$, $(2, 3.5)$, $(4, 1.7)$, $(6, -0.1)$, $(8, -1.8)$, $(10, -3.6)$, $(12, -5.3)$

15. $(0, 587)$, $(5, 551)$, $(10, 512)$, $(15, 478)$, $(20, 436)$, $(25, 430)$, $(30, 424)$, $(35, 420)$, $(40, 423)$, $(45, 429)$, $(50, 444)$

16. $(2, 34.3)$, $(3, 33.8)$, $(4, 32.6)$, $(5, 30.1)$, $(6, 27.8)$, $(7, 22.5)$, $(8, 19.1)$, $(9, 14.8)$, $(10, 9.4)$, $(11, 3.7)$, $(12, -1.6)$

17. **Why you should learn it** *(p. 161)* The table shows the monthly normal precipitation P (in inches) for San Francisco, California. (Source: The Weather Channel)

Month	Precipitation, P
January	4.50
February	4.61
March	3.26
April	1.46
May	0.70
June	0.16
July	0.00
August	0.06
September	0.21
October	1.12
November	3.16
December	4.56

Spreadsheet at LarsonPrecalculus.com

(a) Use a graphing utility to create a scatter plot of the data. Let t represent the month, with $t = 1$ corresponding to January.

(b) Use the *regression* feature of the graphing utility to find a quadratic model for the data and identify the coefficient of determination.

(c) Use the graphing utility to graph the model with the scatter plot from part (a).

(d) Use the graph from part (c) to determine in which month the normal precipitation in San Francisco is the least.

(e) Use the table to determine the month in which the normal precipitation in San Francisco is the least. Compare your answer with that of part (d).

18. MODELING DATA

The table shows the annual sales S (in billions of dollars) of pharmacies and drug stores in the United States from 2007 through 2012. (Source: U.S. Census Bureau)

DATA Year	Sales, S (in billions of dollars)
2007	202.3
2008	211.0
2009	217.6
2010	222.8
2011	231.5
2012	233.4

Spreadsheet at LarsonPrecalculus.com

(a) Use a graphing utility to create a scatter plot of the data. Let t represent the year, with $t = 7$ corresponding to 2007.

(b) Use the *regression* feature of the graphing utility to find a quadratic model for the data.

(c) Use the graphing utility to graph the model with the scatter plot from part (a).

(d) Use the model to estimate the first year when the annual sales of pharmacies and drug stores will be less than \$200 billion. Is this a good model for predicting future sales? Explain.

19. MODELING DATA

The table shows the percents P of U.S. households with Internet access from 2007 through 2012. (Source: U.S. Census Bureau)

DATA Year	Percent, P
2007	54.7
2008	61.7
2009	68.7
2010	71.1
2011	71.7
2012	74.8

Spreadsheet at LarsonPrecalculus.com

(a) Use a graphing utility to create a scatter plot of the data. Let t represent the year, with $t = 7$ corresponding to 2007.

(b) Use the *regression* feature of the graphing utility to find a quadratic model for the data.

(c) Use the graphing utility to graph the model with the scatter plot from part (a).

(d) According to the model, in what year will the percent of U.S. households with Internet access be less than 60%? Is this a good model for making future predictions? Explain.

20. MODELING DATA

The table shows the estimated average numbers of hours H that adults in the United States spent reading newspapers each year from 2003 through 2012. (Source: Statista)

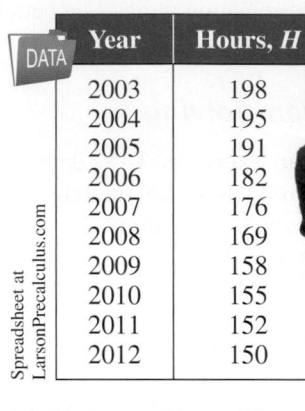

DATA Year	Hours, H
2003	198
2004	195
2005	191
2006	182
2007	176
2008	169
2009	158
2010	155
2011	152
2012	150

Spreadsheet at LarsonPrecalculus.com

(a) Use a graphing utility to create a scatter plot of the data. Let t represent the year, with $t = 3$ corresponding to 2003.

(b) A cubic model for the data is

$$H = 0.131t^3 - 2.81t^2 + 12.1t + 183$$

which has an r^2-value of 0.9962. Use the graphing utility to graph the model with the scatter plot from part (a). Is the cubic model a good fit for the data? Explain.

(c) Use the *regression* feature of the graphing utility to find a quadratic model for the data and identify the coefficient of determination.

(d) Use the graphing utility to graph the quadratic model with the scatter plot from part (a). Is the quadratic model a good fit for the data? Explain.

(e) Which model is a better fit for the data? Explain.

(f) A consumer research company makes projections about the average numbers of hours H^* that adults spent reading newspapers each year from 2013 through 2015. The company's projections are shown in the table. Use the models from parts (b) and (c) to *predict* the average numbers of hours for 2013 through 2015. Explain why your values may differ from those in the table.

Year	2013	2014	2015
H^*	145	143	139

21. MODELING DATA

The table shows the numbers of U.S. households with televisions (in millions) from 2000 through 2012. (Source: The Nielsen Company)

DATA Year	Televisions, T (in millions)
2000	100.8
2001	102.2
2002	105.5
2003	106.7
2004	108.4
2005	109.6
2006	110.2
2007	111.4
2008	112.8
2009	114.5
2010	114.9
2011	115.9
2012	114.7

Spreadsheet at LarsonPrecalculus.com

(a) Use a graphing utility to create a scatter plot of the data. Let t represent the year, with $t = 0$ corresponding to 2000.

(b) Use the *regression* feature of the graphing utility to find a linear model for the data and identify the coefficient of determination.

(c) Use the graphing utility to graph the linear model with the scatter plot from part (a).

(d) Use the *regression* feature of the graphing utility to find a quadratic model for the data and identify the coefficient of determination.

(e) Use the graphing utility to graph the quadratic model with the scatter plot from part (a).

(f) Which model is a better fit for the data? Explain.

(g) Use each model to approximate the year when the number of households with televisions will reach 120 million, if possible.

Conclusions

True or False? In Exercises 22–24, determine whether the statement is true or false. Justify your answer.

22. The graph of a quadratic model with a negative leading coefficient will have a maximum value at its vertex.

23. The graph of a quadratic model with a positive leading coefficient will have a minimum value at its vertex.

24. Data that are positively correlated are always better modeled by a linear equation than by a quadratic equation.

25. Writing Explain why the parabola shown in the figure is not a good fit for the data.

26. **HOW DO YOU SEE IT?** The r^2-values representing the coefficients of determination for the least squares linear model and the least squares quadratic model for the data shown are given below. Which is which? Explain your reasoning.

$$r^2 \approx 0.9995$$
$$r^2 \approx 0.9782$$

Cumulative Mixed Review

Compositions of Functions In Exercises 27–30, find (a) $f \circ g$ and (b) $g \circ f$.

27. $f(x) = 2x - 1$, $g(x) = x^2 + 3$

28. $f(x) = 5x + 8$, $g(x) = 2x^2 - 1$

29. $f(x) = x^3 - 1$, $g(x) = \sqrt[3]{x + 1}$

30. $f(x) = \sqrt[3]{x + 5}$, $g(x) = x^3 - 5$

Testing Whether a Function is One-to-One In Exercises 31–34, determine algebraically whether the function is one-to-one. If it is, find its inverse function. Verify your answer graphically.

31. $f(x) = 2x + 5$

32. $f(x) = \dfrac{x - 4}{5}$

33. $f(x) = x^2 + 5$, $x \geq 0$

34. $f(x) = 2x^2 - 3$, $x \geq 0$

Multiplying Complex Conjugates In Exercises 35–38, write the complex conjugate of the complex number. Then multiply the number by its complex conjugate.

35. $1 - 3i$

36. $-2 + 4i$

37. $-5i$

38. $8i$

2 Chapter Summary

		What did you learn?	Explanation and Examples	Review Exercises
2.1		**Analyze graphs of quadratic functions** *(p. 90)*.	Let a, b, and c be real numbers with $a \neq 0$. The function $f(x) = ax^2 + bx + c$ is called a quadratic function. Its graph is a "U-shaped" curve called a parabola.	1–6
		Write quadratic functions in standard form and use the results to sketch graphs of functions *(p. 93)*.	The quadratic function $f(x) = a(x - h)^2 + k$, $a \neq 0$, is in standard form. The graph of f is a parabola whose axis is the vertical line $x = h$ and whose vertex is the point (h, k). The parabola opens upward when $a > 0$ and opens downward when $a < 0$.	7–12
		Find minimum and maximum values of quadratic functions in real-life applications *(p. 95)*.	Consider $f(x) = ax^2 + bx + c$ with vertex $\left(-\dfrac{b}{2a}, f\left(-\dfrac{b}{2a}\right)\right)$. If $a > 0$, then f has a *minimum* at $x = -b/(2a)$. If $a < 0$, then f has a *maximum* at $x = -b/(2a)$.	13, 14
2.2		**Use transformations to sketch graphs of polynomial functions** *(p. 100)*.	The graph of a polynomial function is continuous (no breaks, holes, or gaps) and has only smooth, rounded turns.	15–20
		Use the Leading Coefficient Test to determine the end behavior of graphs of polynomial functions *(p. 102)*.	Consider $f(x) = a_n x^n + \cdots + a_1 x + a_0$, $a_n \neq 0$. ***n* is odd:** If $a_n > 0$, then the graph falls to the left and rises to the right. If $a_n < 0$, then the graph rises to the left and falls to the right. ***n* is even:** If $a_n > 0$, then the graph rises to the left and right. If $a_n < 0$, then the graph falls to the left and right.	21–26
		Find and use zeros of polynomial functions as sketching aids *(p. 104)*.	If f is a polynomial function and a is a real number, the following are equivalent: (1) $x = a$ is a *zero* of the function f, (2) $x = a$ is a *solution* of the polynomial equation $f(x) = 0$, (3) $(x - a)$ is a *factor* of the polynomial $f(x)$, and (4) $(a, 0)$ is an *x-intercept* of the graph of f.	27–38
		Use the Intermediate Value Theorem to help locate zeros of polynomial functions *(p. 108)*.	Let a and b be real numbers such that $a < b$. If f is a polynomial function such that $f(a) \neq f(b)$, then, in $[a, b]$, f takes on every value between $f(a)$ and $f(b)$.	39–42
2.3		**Use long division to divide polynomials by other polynomials** *(p. 113)*.	Dividend $\rightarrow$ $\dfrac{x^2 + 3x + 5}{x + 1}$ $\leftarrow$ Divisor, Quotient $x + 2$, Remainder $\dfrac{3}{x + 1}$ $\leftarrow$ Divisor $$\underbrace{\frac{x^2 + 3x + 5}{x + 1}}_{} = \overbrace{x + 2}^{} + \frac{3}{x + 1}$$	43–50
		Use synthetic division to divide polynomials by binomials of the form $x - k$ *(p. 116)*.	Divisor: $x + 3$ Dividend: $x^4 - 10x^2 - 2x + 4$ $$\begin{array}{r|rrrrr} -3 & 1 & 0 & -10 & -2 & 4 \\ & & -3 & 9 & 3 & -3 \\ \hline & 1 & -3 & -1 & 1 & 1 \end{array}$$ $\leftarrow$ Remainder: 1 Quotient: $x^3 - 3x^2 - x + 1$	51–56
		Use the Remainder Theorem and the Factor Theorem *(p. 117)*.	**The Remainder Theorem:** If a polynomial $f(x)$ is divided by $x - k$, then the remainder is $r = f(k)$. **The Factor Theorem:** A polynomial $f(x)$ has a factor $(x - k)$ if and only if $f(k) = 0$.	57–62
		Use the Rational Zero Test to determine possible rational zeros of polynomial functions *(p. 119)*.	The Rational Zero Test relates the possible rational zeros of a polynomial to the leading coefficient and to the constant term of the polynomial.	63, 64

	What did you learn?	Explanation and Examples	Review Exercises
2.3	Use Descartes's Rule of Signs (*p. 121*) and the Upper and Lower Bound Rules (*p. 122*) to find zeros of polynomials.	Example 9 shows how to use Descartes's Rule of Signs. Example 10 uses Descartes's Rule of Signs and the Upper and Lower Bound Rules.	65–72
2.4	Use the imaginary unit i to write complex numbers (*p. 128*).	The imaginary unit i is defined as $i = \sqrt{-1}$, where $i^2 = -1$. If a and b are real numbers, then the number $a + bi$ is a complex number, and it is written in standard form.	73–76
	Add, subtract, and multiply complex numbers (*p. 129*).	**Sum:** $(a + bi) + (c + di) = (a + c) + (b + d)i$ **Difference:** $(a + bi) - (c + di) = (a - c) + (b - d)i$	77–88
	Use complex conjugates to write the quotient of two complex numbers in standard form (*p. 131*).	Complex numbers of the forms $a + bi$ and $a - bi$ are complex conjugates. To write $(a + bi)/(c + di)$ in standard form, multiply by $(c - di)/(c - di)$.	89–92
	Find complex solutions of quadratic equations (*p. 132*).	If a is a positive number, then the principal square root of the negative number $-a$ is defined as $\sqrt{-a} = \sqrt{a}i$.	93–98
2.5	Use the Fundamental Theorem of Algebra to determine the number of zeros of a polynomial function (*p. 135*).	**The Fundamental Theorem of Algebra** If $f(x)$ is a polynomial of degree n, where $n > 0$, then f has at least one zero in the complex number system.	99–102
	Find all zeros of polynomial functions (*p. 136*) and find conjugate pairs of complex zeros (*p. 137*).	**Complex Zeros Occur in Conjugate Pairs** Let f be a polynomial function that has real coefficients. If $a + bi$ $(b \neq 0)$ is a zero of the function, the conjugate $a - bi$ is also a zero of the function.	103–120
	Find zeros of polynomials by factoring (*p. 138*).	Every polynomial of degree $n > 0$ with real coefficients can be written as the product of linear and quadratic factors with real coefficients, where the quadratic factors have no real zeros.	121–124
2.6	Find the domains (*p. 142*) and vertical and horizontal asymptotes (*p. 143*) of rational functions.	The domain of a rational function of x includes all real numbers except x-values that make the denominator zero.	125–136
	Use rational functions to model and solve real-life problems (*p. 146*).	A rational function can be used to model the cost of removing a given percent of smokestack pollutants at a utility company that burns coal. (See Example 5.)	137, 138
2.7	Analyze and sketch graphs of rational functions (*p. 151*), including functions with slant asymptotes (*p. 155*).	Consider a rational function whose denominator is of degree 1 or greater. If the degree of the numerator is exactly *one more* than the degree of the denominator, then the graph of the function has a slant asymptote.	139–152
	Use rational functions to model and solve real-life problems (*p. 156*).	A rational function can be used to model the area of a page. The model can be used to determine the dimensions of the page that use the minimum amount of paper. (See Example 7.)	153, 154
2.8	Classify scatter plots (*p. 161*), find quadratic models for data (*p. 162*), and choose a model that best fits a set of data (*p. 164*).	Sometimes it is not easy to distinguish from a scatter plot which type of model will best fit the data. You should first find several models for the data and then choose the model that best fits the data by comparing the y-values of each model with the actual y-values.	155–160

2   Review Exercises

2.1

Library of Parent Functions   In Exercises 1–6, sketch the graph of each function and compare it with the graph of $y = x^2$.

1. $y = x^2 + 1$

2. $y = -x^2 + 5$

3. $y = (x - 6)^2$

4. $y = -(x + 1)^2$

5. $y = -(x + 5)^2 - 1$

6. $y = -(x - 2)^2 + 2$

Identifying the Vertex of a Quadratic Function   In Exercises 7–10, describe the graph of the function and identify the vertex. Then, sketch the graph of the function. Identify any x-intercepts.

7. $f(x) = \left(x + \frac{3}{2}\right)^2 + 1$

8. $f(x) = (x - 4)^2 - 4$

9. $f(x) = \frac{1}{3}(x^2 + 5x - 4)$

10. $f(x) = 3x^2 - 12x + 11$

Writing the Equation of a Parabola in Standard Form   In Exercises 11 and 12, write the standard form of the quadratic function that has the indicated vertex and whose graph passes through the given point. Use a graphing utility to verify your result.

11. Vertex: $(-3, 4)$ Point: $(0, -5)$

12. Vertex: $(2, -1)$ Point: $(5, 2)$

13. Geometry   A rectangle is inscribed in the region bounded by the x-axis, the y-axis, and the graph of $x + 2y - 8 = 0$, as shown in the figure.

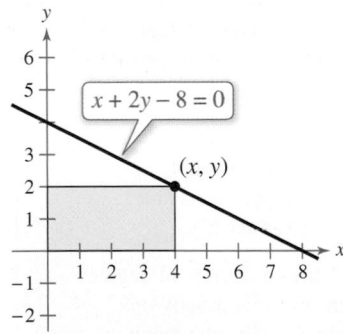

(a) Write the area A of the rectangle as a function of x. Determine the domain of the function in the context of the problem.

(b) Use a graphing utility to graph the area function. Use the graph to approximate the dimensions that will produce a maximum area.

(c) Write the area function in standard form to find algebraically the dimensions that will produce a maximum area. Compare your results with your answer from part (b).

14. Physical Education   A college has 1500 feet of portable rink boards to form three adjacent outdoor ice rinks, as shown in the figure. Determine the dimensions that will produce the maximum total area of ice surface.

2.2

Library of Parent Functions   In Exercises 15–20, sketch the graph of $f(x) = x^3$ and the graph of the function g. Describe the transformation from f to g.

15. $g(x) = (x - 5)^3$

16. $g(x) = x^3 - 2$

17. $g(x) = -(x + 4)^3$

18. $g(x) = (x + 4)^3 - 1$

19. $g(x) = -(x - 2)^3 + 6$

20. $g(x) = -(x - 1)^3 - 5$

Comparing End Behavior   In Exercises 21 and 22, use a graphing utility to graph the functions f and g in the same viewing window. Zoom out far enough to see the right-hand and left-hand behavior of each graph. Do the graphs of f and g have the same right-hand and left-hand behavior? Explain why or why not.

21. $f(x) = \frac{1}{2}x^3 - 2x + 1, \quad g(x) = \frac{1}{2}x^3$

22. $f(x) = -x^4 + 2x^3, \quad g(x) = -x^4$

Applying the Leading Coefficient Test   In Exercises 23–26, use the Leading Coefficient Test to describe the right-hand and left-hand behavior of the graph of the polynomial function.

23. $f(x) = x^2 - x - 6$

24. $g(x) = -3x^3 + 4x^2 - 1$

25. $h(x) = -\frac{2}{3}(x^4 - 7x^3 + 5)$

26. $f(x) = -x^2 + 4x^5 + 5 - 2x^4$

Finding Zeros of a Polynomial Function   In Exercises 27–32, (a) find the zeros algebraically, (b) use a graphing utility to graph the function, and (c) use the graph to approximate any zeros and compare them with those in part (a).

27. $g(x) = x^4 - x^3 - 2x^2$

28. $h(x) = -2x^3 - x^2 + x$

29. $f(t) = t^3 - 3t$

30. $f(x) = -(x + 6)^3 - 8$

31. $f(x) = x(x + 3)^2$

32. $f(t) = t^4 - 4t^2$

Finding a Polynomial Function with Given Zeros In Exercises 33–36, find a polynomial function that has the given zeros. (There are many correct answers.)

33. $4, -2, -2$

34. $-1, 0, 3, 5$

35. $3, 2 - \sqrt{3}, 2 + \sqrt{3}$

36. $-7, 4 - \sqrt{6}, 4 + \sqrt{6}$

Sketching the Graph of a Polynomial Function In Exercises 37 and 38, sketch the graph of the function by (a) applying the Leading Coefficient Test, (b) finding the zeros of the polynomial, (c) plotting sufficient solution points, and (d) drawing a continuous curve through the points.

37. $f(x) = x^4 - 2x^3 - 12x^2 + 18x + 27$

38. $f(x) = 18 + 27x - 2x^2 - 3x^3$

Approximating the Zeros of a Function In Exercises 39–42, (a) use the Intermediate Value Theorem and a graphing utility to find graphically any intervals of length 1 in which the polynomial function is guaranteed to have a zero, and (b) use the *zero* or *root* feature of the graphing utility to approximate the real zeros of the function. Verify your results in part (a) by using the *table* feature of the graphing utility.

39. $f(x) = x^3 + 2x^2 - x - 1$

40. $f(x) = x^4 - 6x^2 - 4$

41. $f(x) = 0.24x^3 - 2.6x - 1.4$

42. $f(x) = 2x^4 + \frac{7}{2}x^3 - 2$

2.3

Long Division of Polynomials In Exercises 43–50, use long division to divide.

43. $\dfrac{24x^2 - x - 8}{3x - 2}$

44. $\dfrac{4x^2 + 7}{3x - 2}$

45. $\dfrac{x^4 - 3x^2 + 2}{x^2 - 1}$

46. $\dfrac{3x^4 + x^2 - 1}{x^2 - 1}$

47. $(5x^3 - 13x^2 - x + 2) \div (x^2 - 3x + 1)$

48. $(x^4 + x^3 - x^2 + 2x) \div (x^2 + 2x)$

49. $\dfrac{6x^4 + 10x^3 + 13x^2 - 5x + 2}{2x^2 - 1}$

50. $\dfrac{x^4 - 3x^3 + 4x^2 - 6x + 3}{x^2 + 2}$

Using Synthetic Division In Exercises 51–56, use synthetic division to divide.

51. $(3x^3 - 10x^2 + 12x - 22) \div (x - 4)$

52. $(2x^3 + 6x^2 - 14x + 9) \div (x - 1)$

53. $(0.25x^4 - 4x^3) \div (x + 2)$

54. $(0.1x^3 + 0.3x^2 - 0.5) \div (x - 5)$

55. $(6x^4 - 4x^3 - 27x^2 + 18x) \div \left(x - \frac{2}{3}\right)$

56. $(2x^3 + 2x^2 - x + 2) \div \left(x - \frac{1}{2}\right)$

Using the Remainder Theorem In Exercises 57 and 58, use the Remainder Theorem and synthetic division to evaluate the function at each given value. Use a graphing utility to verify your results.

57. $f(x) = x^4 + 10x^3 - 24x^2 + 20x + 44$

   (a) $f(-3)$ (b) $f(-2)$

58. $g(t) = 2t^5 - 5t^4 - 8t + 20$

   (a) $g(-4)$ (b) $g(\sqrt{2})$

Factoring a Polynomial In Exercises 59–62, (a) verify the given factor(s) of the function f, (b) find the remaining factors of f, (c) use your results to write the complete factorization of f, and (d) list all real zeros of f. Confirm your results by using a graphing utility to graph the function.

	Function	*Factor(s)*
59.	$f(x) = x^3 + 4x^2 - 25x - 28$	$(x - 4)$
60.	$f(x) = 2x^3 + 11x^2 - 21x - 90$	$(x + 6)$
61.	$f(x) = x^4 - 4x^3 - 7x^2 + 22x + 24$	$(x + 2),$ $(x - 3)$
62.	$f(x) = x^4 - 11x^3 + 41x^2 - 61x + 30$	$(x - 2),$ $(x - 5)$

Using the Rational Zero Test In Exercises 63 and 64, use the Rational Zero Test to list all possible rational zeros of f. Use a graphing utility to verify that all the zeros of f are contained in the list.

63. $f(x) = 4x^3 - 11x^2 + 10x - 3$

64. $f(x) = 10x^3 + 21x^2 - x - 6$

Using Descartes's Rule of Signs In Exercises 65 and 66, use Descartes's Rule of Signs to determine the possible numbers of positive and negative real zeros of the function.

65. $g(x) = 5x^3 - 6x + 9$

66. $f(x) = 2x^5 - 3x^2 + 2x - 1$

Finding the Zeros of a Polynomial Function In Exercises 67 and 68, use synthetic division to verify the upper and lower bounds of the real zeros of f. Then find all real zeros of the function.

67. $f(x) = 4x^3 - 3x^2 + 4x - 3$

   Upper bound: $x = 1$; Lower bound: $x = -\frac{1}{4}$

68. $f(x) = 2x^3 - 5x^2 - 14x + 8$

   Upper bound: $x = 8$; Lower bound: $x = -4$

Finding the Zeros of a Polynomial Function In Exercises 69–72, find all real zeros of the polynomial function.

69. $f(x) = x^3 - 4x^2 + x + 6$

70. $f(x) = x^3 + x^2 - 28x - 10$

71. $f(x) = 6x^4 - 25x^3 + 14x^2 + 27x - 18$

72. $f(x) = 5x^4 + 126x^2 + 25$

2.4

Writing a Complex Number in Standard Form   In Exercises 73–76, write the complex number in standard form.

73. $3 - \sqrt{-16}$

74. $\sqrt{-50} + 8$

75. $-i + 4i^2$

76. $7i - 9i^2$

Operations with Complex Numbers   In Exercises 77–88, perform the operation(s) and write the result in standard form.

77. $(2 + 13i) + (6 - 5i)$

78. $\left(\dfrac{1}{2} + \dfrac{\sqrt{3}}{4}i\right) - \left(\dfrac{1}{2} - \dfrac{\sqrt{3}}{4}i\right)$

79. $5i(13 - 8i)$

80. $(1 + 6i)(5 - 2i)$

81. $(10 - 8i)(2 - 3i)$

82. $i(6 + i)(3 - 2i)$

83. $(3 + 7i)^2 + (3 - 7i)^2$

84. $(4 - i)^2 - (4 + i)^2$

85. $\left(\sqrt{-16} + 3\right)\left(\sqrt{-25} - 2\right)$

86. $\left(5 - \sqrt{-4}\right)\left(5 + \sqrt{-4}\right)$

87. $\sqrt{-9} + 3 + \sqrt{-36}$

88. $7 - \sqrt{-81} + \sqrt{-49}$

Writing a Quotient of Complex Numbers in Standard Form   In Exercises 89–92, write the quotient in standard form.

89. $\dfrac{6 + i}{i}$

90. $\dfrac{4}{-3i}$

91. $\dfrac{3 + 2i}{5 + i}$

92. $\dfrac{1 - 7i}{2 + 3i}$

Complex Solutions of a Quadratic Equation   In Exercises 93–98, solve the quadratic equation.

93. $x^2 + 16 = 0$

94. $x^2 + 48 = 0$

95. $x^2 + 3x + 6 = 0$

96. $x^2 + 4x + 8 = 0$

97. $3x^2 - 5x + 6 = 0$

98. $5x^2 - 2x + 4 = 0$

2.5

Zeros of a Polynomial Function   In Exercises 99–102, confirm that the function has the indicated zero(s).

99. $f(x) = x^2 + 6x + 9$;   Repeated zero: -3

100. $f(x) = x^2 - 10x + 25$;   Repeated zero: 5

101. $f(x) = x^3 + 16x$; $0, -4i, 4i$

102. $f(x) = x^3 + 144x$; $0, -12i, 12i$

Using the Factored Form of a Function   In Exercises 103 and 104, find all the zeros of the function.

103. $f(x) = -4x(x + 3)$

104. $f(x) = (x - 8)^3(x + 2)$

Finding the Zeros of a Polynomial Function   In Exercises 105–110, find all the zeros of the function and write the polynomial as a product of linear factors. Verify your results by using a graphing utility to graph the function.

105. $h(x) = x^3 - 7x^2 + 18x - 24$

106. $f(x) = 2x^3 - 5x^2 - 9x + 40$

107. $f(x) = 2x^4 - 5x^3 + 10x - 12$

108. $g(x) = 3x^4 - 4x^3 + 7x^2 + 10x - 4$

109. $f(x) = x^5 + x^4 + 5x^3 + 5x^2$

110. $f(x) = x^5 - 5x^3 + 4x$

Using the Zeros to Find the x-Intercepts   In Exercises 111–116, (a) find all the zeros of the function, (b) write the polynomial as a product of linear factors, and (c) use your factorization to determine the x-intercepts of the graph of the function. Use a graphing utility to verify that the real zeros are the only x-intercepts.

111. $f(x) = x^3 - 4x^2 + 6x - 4$

112. $f(x) = x^3 - 5x^2 - 7x + 51$

113. $f(x) = -3x^3 - 19x^2 - 4x + 12$

114. $f(x) = 2x^3 - 9x^2 + 22x - 30$

115. $f(x) = x^4 + 34x^2 + 225$

116. $f(x) = x^4 + 10x^3 + 26x^2 + 10x + 25$

Finding a Polynomial with Given Zeros   In Exercises 117–120, find a polynomial function with real coefficients that has the given zeros. (There are many correct answers.)

117. $5, 3i$

118. $-6, -i$

119. $-2, -2 - 4i$

120. $1, -5 + \sqrt{2}i$

Factoring a Polynomial   In Exercises 121 and 122, write the polynomial (a) as the product of factors that are irreducible over the *rationals*, (b) as the product of linear and quadratic factors that are irreducible over the *reals*, and (c) in completely factored form.

121. $f(x) = x^4 - 2x^3 + 8x^2 - 18x - 9$

(*Hint:* One factor is $x^2 + 9$.)

122. $f(x) = x^4 - 4x^3 + 3x^2 + 8x - 16$

(*Hint:* One factor is $x^2 - x - 4$.)

Finding the Zeros of a Polynomial Function   In Exercises 123 and 124, use the given zero to find all the zeros of the function.

	Function	*Zero*
123.	$f(x) = x^3 + 3x^2 + 4x + 12$	$-2i$
124.	$f(x) = 2x^3 - 7x^2 + 14x + 9$	$2 + \sqrt{5}i$

2.6

Finding a Function's Domain and Asymptotes In Exercises 125–136, (a) find the domain of the function, (b) decide whether the function is continuous, and (c) identify any horizontal and vertical asymptotes.

125. $f(x) = \dfrac{2 - x}{x + 3}$

126. $f(x) = \dfrac{4x}{x - 8}$

127. $f(x) = \dfrac{2}{x^2 - 3x - 18}$

128. $f(x) = \dfrac{2x^2 + 3}{x^2 + x + 3}$

129. $f(x) = \dfrac{7 + x}{7 - x}$

130. $f(x) = \dfrac{6x}{x^2 - 1}$

131. $f(x) = \dfrac{4x^2}{2x^2 - 3}$

132. $f(x) = \dfrac{3x^2 - 11x - 4}{x^2 + 2}$

133. $f(x) = \dfrac{2x - 10}{x^2 - 2x - 15}$

134. $f(x) = \dfrac{4 - x}{x^3 + 6x^2}$

135. $f(x) = \dfrac{3x^2 - 15}{x^3 - 5x^2 - 24x}$

136. $f(x) = \dfrac{x^2 + 3x + 2}{x^3 - 4x^2}$

137. Criminology The cost C (in millions of dollars) for the U.S. government to seize $p\%$ of an illegal drug as it enters the country is given by

$$C = \frac{528p}{100 - p}, \quad 0 \le p < 100.$$

(a) Find the costs of seizing 25%, 50%, and 75% of the illegal drug.

(b) Use a graphing utility to graph the function. Be sure to choose an appropriate viewing window. Explain why you chose the values you used in your viewing window.

(c) According to this model, would it be possible to seize 100% of the drug? Explain.

138. Biology A biology class performs an experiment comparing the quantity of food consumed by a certain kind of moth with the quantity supplied. The model for the experimental data is given by

$$y = \frac{1.568x - 0.001}{6.360x + 1}, \quad x > 0$$

where x is the quantity (in milligrams) of food supplied and y is the quantity (in milligrams) eaten (see figure). At what level of consumption will the moth become satiated?

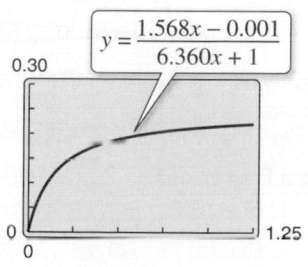

2.7

Finding Asymptotes and Holes In Exercises 139–142, find all of the vertical, horizontal, and slant asymptotes, and any holes in the graph of the function. Then use a graphing utility to verify your results.

139. $f(x) = \dfrac{x^2 - 5x + 4}{x^2 - 1}$

140. $f(x) = \dfrac{2x^2 - 7x + 3}{2x^2 - 3x - 9}$

141. $f(x) = \dfrac{3x^2 + 5x - 2}{x + 1}$

142. $f(x) = \dfrac{2x^2 + 5x + 3}{x - 2}$

Sketching the Graph of a Rational Function In Exercises 143–152, sketch the graph of the rational function by hand. As sketching aids, check for intercepts, vertical asymptotes, horizontal asymptotes, slant asymptotes, and holes.

143. $f(x) = \dfrac{1}{x} + 3$

144. $f(x) = \dfrac{-1}{x + 2}$

145. $f(x) = \dfrac{2x - 1}{x - 5}$

146. $f(x) = \dfrac{x - 3}{x - 2}$

147. $f(x) = \dfrac{2}{(x + 1)^2}$

148. $f(x) = \dfrac{4}{(x - 1)^2}$

149. $f(x) = \dfrac{2x^2}{x^2 - 4}$

150. $f(x) = \dfrac{5x}{x^2 + 1}$

151. $f(x) = \dfrac{x^2 - x + 1}{x - 3}$

152. $f(x) = \dfrac{2x^2 + 7x + 3}{x + 1}$

153. Biology A parks and wildlife commission releases 80,000 fish into a lake. After t years, the population N of the fish (in thousands) is given by

$$N = \frac{20(4 + 3t)}{1 + 0.05t}, \quad t \ge 0.$$

(a) Use a graphing utility to graph the function and find the populations when $t = 5$, $t = 10$, and $t = 25$.

(b) What is the maximum number of fish in the lake as time passes? Explain your reasoning.

154. Publishing A page that is x inches wide and y inches high contains 30 square inches of print. The top and bottom margins are 2 inches deep and the margins on each side are 2 inches wide.

(a) Draw a diagram that illustrates the problem.

(b) Show that the total area A of the page is given by

$$A = \frac{2x(2x + 7)}{x - 4}.$$

(c) Determine the domain of the function based on the physical constraints of the problem.

(d) Use a graphing utility to graph the area function and approximate the page size such that the minimum amount of paper will be used.

2.8

Classifying Scatter Plots In Exercises 155–158, determine whether the scatter plot could best be modeled by a linear model, a quadratic model, or neither.

155.   **156.**

157.   **158.**

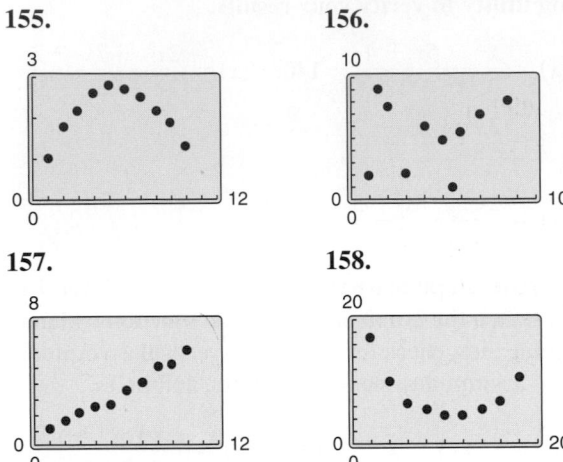

159. MODELING DATA

The table shows the numbers of commercial FM radio stations S in the United States from 2004 through 2013. (Source: Federal Communications Commission)

Year	FM Stations, S
2004	6218
2005	6231
2006	6266
2007	6309
2008	6427
2009	6479
2010	6526
2011	6542
2012	6598
2013	6612

Spreadsheet at LarsonPrecalculus.com

(a) Use a graphing utility to create a scatter plot of the data. Let t represent the year, with $t = 4$ corresponding to 2004.

(b) A cubic model for the data is
$$S = -1.088t^3 + 26.61t^2 - 150.9t + 6459$$
Use the graphing utility to graph this model with the scatter plot from part (a).

(c) Use the *regression* feature of the graphing utility to find a quadratic model for the data and identify the coefficient of determination.

(d) Use the graphing utility to graph the quadratic model with the scatter plot from part (a).

(e) Which model is a better fit for the data? Explain.

(f) Use the model you chose in part (e) to predict the number of commercial FM radio stations in 2015.

160. MODELING DATA

The table shows the sales S (in billions of dollars) of Office Depot for each of the years from 2007 through 2013. (Source: Office Depot, Inc.)

Year	Sales, S (in billions of dollars)
2007	15.528
2008	14.496
2009	12.144
2010	11.633
2011	11.489
2012	10.696
2013	11.242

Spreadsheet at LarsonPrecalculus.com

(a) Use a graphing utility to create a scatter plot of the data. Let t represent the year, with $t = 7$ corresponding to 2007.

(b) Use the *regression* feature of the graphing utility to find a quadratic model for the data.

(c) Use the graphing utility to graph the quadratic model with the scatter plot from part (a). Is the quadratic model a good fit for the data?

(d) According to the model, what is the first year when Office Depot will have sales greater than $14 billion?

(e) Is this a good model for predicting the sales of Office Depot in future years? Explain.

Conclusions

True or False? In Exercises 161–163, determine whether the statement is true or false. Justify your answer.

161. The graph of $f(x) = \dfrac{2x^3}{x + 1}$ has a slant asymptote.

162. A fourth-degree polynomial with real coefficients can have -5, $-8i$, $4i$, and 5 as its zeros.

163. The sum of two complex numbers cannot be a real number.

164. Think About It Describe the domain restrictions of a rational function when the denominator divides evenly into the numerator.

165. Writing Write a paragraph discussing whether every rational function has a vertical asymptote.

166. Error Analysis Describe the error.
$$\sqrt{-8}\sqrt{-8} = \sqrt{(-8)(-8)} = \sqrt{64} = 8$$

167. Error Analysis Describe the error.
$$-i(\sqrt{-4} - 1) = -i(4i - 1) = -4i^2 + i = 4 + i$$

168. Finding a Power of i Write each of the powers of i as i, $-i$, 1, or -1.
(a) i^{40} (b) i^{25} (c) i^{50} (d) i^{67}

See *CalcChat.com* for tutorial help and worked-out solutions to odd-numbered exercises.
For instructions on how to use a graphing utility, see Appendix A.

Take this test as you would take a test in class. After you are finished, check your work against the answers given in the back of the book.

1. Identify the vertex and intercepts of the graph of $y = x^2 + 5x + 6$.
2. Write an equation in standard form of the parabola shown at the right.
3. Find all the real zeros of $f(x) = 4x^3 - 12x^2 + 9x$. Determine the multiplicity of each zero.
4. Sketch the graph of the function $f(x) = -x^3 + 7x + 6$.
5. Divide using long division: $(2x^3 + 5x - 3) \div (x^2 + 2)$.
6. Divide using synthetic division: $(2x^4 - 5x^2 - 3) \div (x - 2)$.
7. Use synthetic division to evaluate $f(-2)$ for $f(x) = 3x^4 - 6x^2 + 5x - 1$.

Figure for 2

In Exercises 8 and 9, list all the possible rational zeros of the function. Use a graphing utility to graph the function and find all the rational zeros.

8. $g(t) = 2t^4 - 3t^3 + 16t - 24$
9. $h(x) = 3x^5 + 2x^4 - 3x - 2$

10. Find all the zeros of the function $f(x) = x^3 - 7x^2 + 11x + 19$ and write the polynomial as a product of linear factors.

In Exercises 11–14, perform the operation(s) and write the result in standard form.

11. $(-8 - 3i) + (-1 - 15i)$
12. $\left(10 + \sqrt{-20}\right) - \left(4 - \sqrt{-14}\right)$
13. $(2 + i)(6 - i)$
14. $(4 + 3i)^2 - (5 + i)^2$

In Exercises 15–17, write the quotient in standard form.

15. $\dfrac{8 + 5i}{i}$
16. $\dfrac{5i}{2 - i}$
17. $(2i - 1) \div (3i + 2)$

In Exercises 18 and 19, solve the quadratic equation.

18. $x^2 + 54 = 0$
19. $x^2 - 2x + 8 = 0$

In Exercises 20–22, sketch the graph of the rational function. As sketching aids, check for intercepts, vertical asymptotes, horizontal asymptotes, and slant asymptotes.

20. $h(x) = \dfrac{4}{x^2} - 1$
21. $g(x) = \dfrac{x^2 + 2}{x - 1}$
22. $f(x) = \dfrac{2x^2 + 9}{5x^2 + 2}$

23. The table shows the amounts A (in billions of dollars) spent on national defense by the United States for the years 2007 through 2013. (Source: U.S. Office of Management and Budget)

(a) Use a graphing utility to create a scatter plot of the data. Let t represent the year, with $t = 7$ corresponding to 2007.

(b) Use the *regression* feature of the graphing utility to find a quadratic model for the data.

(c) Use the graphing utility to graph the quadratic model with the scatter plot from part (a). Is the quadratic model a good fit for the data?

(d) Use the model to estimate the amounts spent on national defense in 2015 and 2020.

(e) Do you believe the model is useful for predicting the amounts spent on national defense for years beyond 2013? Explain.

Year	National defense, A (in billions of dollars)
2007	551.3
2008	616.1
2009	661.0
2010	693.5
2011	705.6
2012	677.9
2013	633.4

Table for 23

Proofs in Mathematics

These two pages contain proofs of four important theorems about polynomial functions. The first two theorems are from Section 2.3, and the second two theorems are from Section 2.5.

The Remainder Theorem   (p. 117)

If a polynomial $f(x)$ is divided by $x - k$, then the remainder is

$$r = f(k).$$

Proof

From the Division Algorithm, you have

$$f(x) = (x - k)q(x) + r(x)$$

and because either $r(x) = 0$ or the degree of $r(x)$ is less than the degree of $x - k$, you know that $r(x)$ must be a constant. That is, $r(x) = r$. Now, by evaluating $f(x)$ at $x = k$, you have

$$f(k) = (k - k)q(k) + r$$

$$= (0)q(k) + r$$

$$= r.$$

To be successful in algebra, it is important that you understand the connection among the *factors* of a polynomial, the *zeros* of a polynomial function, and the *solutions* or *roots* of a polynomial equation. The Factor Theorem is the basis for this connection.

The Factor Theorem   (p. 117)

A polynomial $f(x)$ has a factor $(x - k)$ if and only if $f(k) = 0$.

Proof

Using the Division Algorithm with the factor $(x - k)$, you have

$$f(x) = (x - k)q(x) + r(x).$$

By the Remainder Theorem, $r(x) = r = f(k)$, and you have

$$f(x) = (x - k)q(x) + f(k)$$

where $q(x)$ is a polynomial of lesser degree than $f(x)$. If $f(k) = 0$, then

$$f(x) = (x - k)q(x)$$

and you see that $(x - k)$ is a factor of $f(x)$. Conversely, if $(x - k)$ is a factor of $f(x)$, then division of $f(x)$ by $(x - k)$ yields a remainder of 0. So, by the Remainder Theorem, you have $f(k) = 0$.

Linear Factorization Theorem (p. 135)

If $f(x)$ is a polynomial of degree n, where $n > 0$, then f has precisely n linear factors

$$f(x) = a_n(x - c_1)(x - c_2) \cdots (x - c_n)$$

where $c_1, c_2, \ldots, c_n$ are complex numbers.

Proof

Using the Fundamental Theorem of Algebra, you know that f must have at least one zero, c_1. Consequently, $(x - c_1)$ is a factor of $f(x)$, and you have

$$f(x) = (x - c_1)f_1(x).$$

If the degree of $f_1(x)$ is greater than zero, then apply the Fundamental Theorem again to conclude that f_1 must have a zero c_2, which implies that

$$f(x) = (x - c_1)(x - c_2)f_2(x).$$

It is clear that the degree of $f_1(x)$ is $n - 1$, that the degree of $f_2(x)$ is $n - 2$, and that you can repeatedly apply the Fundamental Theorem n times until you obtain

$$f(x) = a_n(x - c_1)(x - c_2) \cdots (x - c_n)$$

where a_n is the leading coefficient of the polynomial $f(x)$. ■

Factors of a Polynomial (p. 138)

Every polynomial of degree $n > 0$ with real coefficients can be written as the product of linear and quadratic factors with real coefficients, where the quadratic factors have no real zeros.

Proof

To begin, you use the Linear Factorization Theorem to conclude that $f(x)$ can be *completely* factored in the form

$$f(x) = d(x - c_1)(x - c_2)(x - c_3) \ldots (x - c_n).$$

If each c_i is real, then there is nothing more to prove. If any c_i is complex ($c_i = a + bi$, $b \neq 0$), then, because the coefficients of $f(x)$ are real, you know that the conjugate $c_j = a - bi$ is also a zero. By multiplying the corresponding factors, you obtain

$$(x - c_i)(x - c_j) = [x - (a + bi)][x - (a - bi)]$$
$$= x^2 - 2ax + (a^2 + b^2)$$

where each coefficient is real. ■

The Fundamental Theorem of Algebra

The Linear Factorization Theorem is closely related to the Fundamental Theorem of Algebra. The Fundamental Theorem of Algebra has a long and interesting history. In the early work with polynomial equations, the Fundamental Theorem of Algebra was thought to have been not true, because imaginary solutions were not considered. In fact, in the very early work by mathematicians such as Abu al-Khwarizmi (c. 800 A.D.), negative solutions were also not considered.

Once imaginary numbers were accepted, several mathematicians attempted to give a general proof of the Fundamental Theorem of Algebra. These included Gottfried von Leibniz (1702), Jean d'Alembert (1746), Leonhard Euler (1749), Joseph-Louis Lagrange (1772), and Pierre Simon Laplace (1795). The mathematician usually credited with the first correct proof of the Fundamental Theorem of Algebra is Carl Friedrich Gauss, who published the proof in his doctoral thesis in 1799.

Progressive Summary (Chapters 1–2)

This chart outlines the topics that have been covered so far in this text. Progressive Summary charts appear after Chapters 2, 3, 6, and 9. In each Progressive Summary, new topics encountered for the first time appear in blue.

Algebraic Functions

Polynomial, Rational, Radical

■ **Rewriting**

Polynomial form ↔ Factored form
Operations with polynomials
Rationalize denominators
Simplify rational expressions
Operations with complex numbers

■ **Solving**

Equation	Strategy
Linear	Isolate variable
Quadratic.	Factor, set to zero
	Extract square roots
	Complete the square
	Quadratic Formula
Polynomial	Factor, set to zero
	Rational Zero Test
Rational.	Multiply by LCD
Radical	Isolate, raise to power
Absolute value . . .	Isolate, form two equations

■ **Analyzing**

Graphically	Algebraically
Intercepts	Domain, Range
Symmetry	Transformations
Slope	Composition
Asymptotes	Standard forms
End behavior	of equations
Minimum values	Leading Coefficient
Maximum values	Test
	Synthetic division
	Descartes's Rule of Signs

Numerically
Table of values

Transcendental Functions

■ **Rewriting**

■ **Solving**

■ **Analyzing**

Other Topics

■ **Rewriting**

■ **Solving**

■ **Analyzing**

3 Exponential and Logarithmic Functions

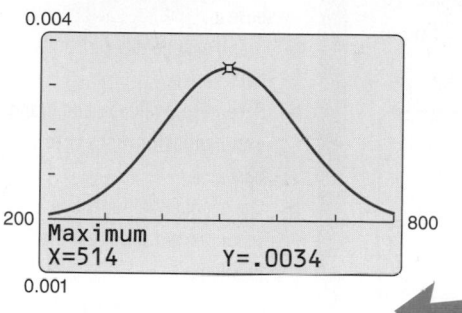

Maximum
X=514   Y=.0034

Section 3.5, Example 4
SAT Scores

3.1   Exponential Functions and Their Graphs
3.2   Logarithmic Functions and Their Graphs
3.3   Properties of Logarithms
3.4   Solving Exponential and Logarithmic Equations
3.5   Exponential and Logarithmic Models
3.6   Nonlinear Models

3.1   Exponential Functions and Their Graphs

Exponential Functions

So far, this text has dealt mainly with **algebraic functions,** which include polynomial functions and rational functions. In this chapter, you will study two types of nonalgebraic functions—*exponential functions* and *logarithmic functions*. These functions are examples of **transcendental functions.**

> **Definition of Exponential Function**
>
> The **exponential function** f with base a is denoted by
>
> $$f(x) = a^x$$
>
> where $a > 0$, $a \neq 1$, and x is any real number.

Note that in the definition of an exponential function, the base $a = 1$ is excluded because it yields

$$f(x) = 1^x = 1. \qquad \text{Constant function}$$

This is a constant function, not an exponential function.

You have already evaluated a^x for integer and rational values of x. For example, you know that

$$4^3 = 64 \qquad \text{and} \qquad 4^{1/2} = 2.$$

However, to evaluate 4^x for any real number x, you need to interpret forms with *irrational* exponents. For the purposes of this text, it is sufficient to think of $a^{\sqrt{2}}$ (where $\sqrt{2} \approx 1.41421356$) as the number that has the successively closer approximations

$$a^{1.4}, a^{1.41}, a^{1.414}, a^{1.4142}, a^{1.41421}, \ldots .$$

Example 1 shows how to use a calculator to evaluate exponential functions.

What you should learn
► Recognize and evaluate exponential functions with base a.
► Graph exponential functions with base a.
► Recognize, evaluate, and graph exponential functions with base e.
► Use exponential functions to model and solve real-life problems.

Why you should learn it
Exponential functions are useful in modeling data that represent quantities that increase or decrease quickly. For instance, Exercise 82 on page 191 shows how an exponential function is used to model the depreciation of a new vehicle.

EXAMPLE 1   **Evaluating Exponential Functions**

Use a calculator to evaluate each function at the indicated value of x.

Function	*Value*
a. $f(x) = 2^x$	$x = -3.1$
b. $f(x) = 2^{-x}$	$x = \pi$
c. $f(x) = 0.6^x$	$x = \frac{3}{2}$
d. $f(x) = 1.05^{2x}$	$x = 12$

Solution

Function Value	*Graphing Calculator Keystrokes*	*Display*
a. $f(-3.1) = 2^{-3.1}$	2 [^] [(-)] 3.1 [ENTER]	0.1166291
b. $f(\pi) = 2^{-\pi}$	2 [^] [(-)] π [ENTER]	0.1133147
c. $f\left(\frac{3}{2}\right) = (0.6)^{3/2}$	.6 [^] [(] 3 [÷] 2 [)] [ENTER]	0.4647580
d. $f(12) = (1.05)^{2(12)}$	1.05 [^] [(] 2 [×] 12 [)] [ENTER]	3.2250999

✓ **Checkpoint** Audio-video solution in English & Spanish at LarsonPrecalculus.com.

Use a calculator to evaluate $f(x) = 8^{-x}$ at $x = \sqrt{2}$.   ∎

Technology Tip

When evaluating exponential functions with a calculator, remember to enclose fractional exponents in parentheses. Because the calculator follows the order of operations, parentheses are crucial in order to obtain the correct result.

Graphs of Exponential Functions

The graphs of all exponential functions have similar characteristics, as shown in Examples 2, 3, and 4.

EXAMPLE 2   Graphs of $y = a^x$

In the same coordinate plane, sketch the graphs of $f(x) = 2^x$ and $g(x) = 4^x$.

Solution

The table below lists some values for each function. By plotting these points and connecting them with smooth curves, you obtain the graphs shown in Figure 3.1. Note that both graphs are increasing. Moreover, the graph of $g(x) = 4^x$ is increasing more rapidly than the graph of $f(x) = 2^x$.

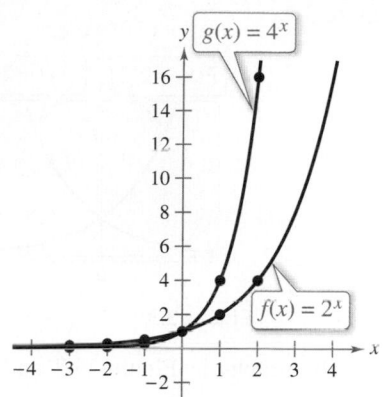

x	-3	-2	-1	0	1	2
2^x	$\frac{1}{8}$	$\frac{1}{4}$	$\frac{1}{2}$	1	2	4
4^x	$\frac{1}{64}$	$\frac{1}{16}$	$\frac{1}{4}$	1	4	16

Figure 3.1

✓ **Checkpoint** ◀))) *Audio-video solution in English & Spanish at LarsonPrecalculus.com.*

In the same coordinate plane, sketch the graphs of $f(x) = 3^x$ and $g(x) = 9^x$.

EXAMPLE 3   Graphs of $y = a^{-x}$

In the same coordinate plane, sketch the graphs of $F(x) = 2^{-x}$ and $G(x) = 4^{-x}$.

Solution

The table below lists some values for each function. By plotting these points and connecting them with smooth curves, you obtain the graphs shown in Figure 3.2. Note that both graphs are decreasing. Moreover, the graph of $G(x) = 4^{-x}$ is decreasing more rapidly than the graph of $F(x) = 2^{-x}$.

x	-2	-1	0	1	2	3
2^{-x}	4	2	1	$\frac{1}{2}$	$\frac{1}{4}$	$\frac{1}{8}$
4^{-x}	16	4	1	$\frac{1}{4}$	$\frac{1}{16}$	$\frac{1}{64}$

Figure 3.2

✓ **Checkpoint** ◀))) *Audio-video solution in English & Spanish at LarsonPrecalculus.com.*

In the same coordinate plane, sketch the graphs of $f(x) = 3^{-x}$ and $g(x) = 9^{-x}$. ■

The properties of exponents can also be applied to real-number exponents. For review, these properties are listed below.

1. $a^x a^y = a^{x+y}$ **2.** $\dfrac{a^x}{a^y} = a^{x-y}$ **3.** $a^{-x} = \dfrac{1}{a^x} = \left(\dfrac{1}{a}\right)^x$ **4.** $a^0 = 1$

5. $(ab)^x = a^x b^x$ **6.** $(a^x)^y = a^{xy}$ **7.** $\left(\dfrac{a}{b}\right)^x = \dfrac{a^x}{b^x}$ **8.** $|a^2| = |a|^2 = a^2$

In Example 3, note that the functions $F(x) = 2^{-x}$ and $G(x) = 4^{-x}$ can be rewritten with positive exponents as

$$F(x) = 2^{-x} = \left(\frac{1}{2}\right)^x \quad \text{and} \quad G(x) = 4^{-x} = \left(\frac{1}{4}\right)^x.$$

Comparing the functions in Examples 2 and 3, observe that

$$F(x) = 2^{-x} = f(-x) \quad \text{and} \quad G(x) = 4^{-x} = g(-x).$$

Consequently, the graph of F is a reflection (in the y-axis) of the graph of f, as shown in Figure 3.3. The graphs of G and g have the same relationship, as shown in Figure 3.4.

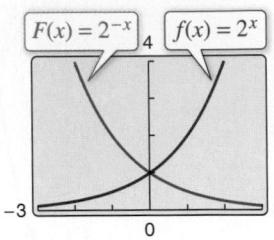

Figure 3.3   **Figure 3.4**

The graphs in Figures 3.3 and 3.4 are typical of the graphs of the exponential functions

$$f(x) = a^x \quad \text{and} \quad f(x) = a^{-x}.$$

They have one y-intercept and one horizontal asymptote (the x-axis), and they are continuous. The basic characteristics of these exponential functions are summarized below.

Library of Parent Functions: Exponential Function

The *parent exponential function*

$$f(x) = a^x, \ a > 0, \ a \neq 1$$

is different from all the functions you have studied so far because the variable x is an *exponent*. A distinguishing characteristic of an exponential function is its rapid increase as x increases (for $a > 1$). Many real-life phenomena with patterns of rapid growth (or decline) can be modeled by exponential functions. The basic characteristics of the exponential function are summarized below and on the inside cover of this text.

Graph of $f(x) = a^x, \ a > 1$

Domain: $(-\infty, \infty)$

Range: $(0, \infty)$

Intercept: $(0, 1)$

Increasing on $(-\infty, \infty)$

x-axis is a horizontal asymptote

$(a^x \to 0$ as $x \to -\infty)$

Continuous

Graph of $f(x) = a^{-x}, \ a > 1$

Domain: $(-\infty, \infty)$

Range: $(0, \infty)$

Intercept: $(0, 1)$

Decreasing on $(-\infty, \infty)$

x-axis is a horizontal asymptote

$(a^{-x} \to 0$ as $x \to \infty)$

Continuous

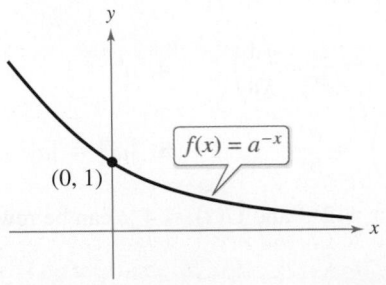

Explore the Concept

Use a graphing utility to graph $y = a^x$ for $a = 3, 5,$ and 7 in the same viewing window. (Use a viewing window in which $-2 \leq x \leq 1$ and $0 \leq y \leq 2$.) How do the graphs compare with each other? Which graph is on the top in the interval $(-\infty, 0)$? Which is on the bottom? Which graph is on the top in the interval $(0, \infty)$? Which is on the bottom? Repeat this experiment with the graphs of $y = b^x$ for $b = \frac{1}{3}, \frac{1}{5},$ and $\frac{1}{7}$. (Use a viewing window in which $-1 \leq x \leq 2$ and $0 \leq y \leq 2$.) What can you conclude about the shape of the graph of $y = b^x$ and the value of b?

In the next example, notice how the graph of $y = a^x$ can be used to sketch the graphs of functions of the form $f(x) = b \pm a^{x+c}$.

EXAMPLE 4   **Library of Parent Functions: $f(x) = a^x$**

See LarsonPrecalculus.com for an interactive version of this type of example.

Each of the following graphs is a transformation of the graph of $f(x) = 3^x$.

a. Because $g(x) = 3^{x+1} = f(x + 1)$, the graph of g can be obtained by shifting the graph of f one unit to the *left*, as shown in Figure 3.5.

b. Because $h(x) = 3^x - 2 = f(x) - 2$, the graph of h can be obtained by shifting the graph of f *downward* two units, as shown in Figure 3.6.

c. Because $k(x) = -3^x = -f(x)$, the graph of k can be obtained by *reflecting* the graph of f in the x-axis, as shown in Figure 3.7.

d. Because $j(x) = 3^{-x} = f(-x)$, the graph of j can be obtained by *reflecting* the graph of f in the y-axis, as shown in Figure 3.8.

Figure 3.5

Figure 3.6

Figure 3.7

Figure 3.8

✓ **Checkpoint** 🔊))) *Audio-video solution in English & Spanish at LarsonPrecalculus.com.*

Use the graph of $f(x) = 4^x$ to describe the transformation that yields the graph of each function.

a. $g(x) = 4^{x-2}$ **b.** $h(x) = 4^x + 3$ **c.** $k(x) = 4^{-x} - 3$ ◼

Notice that the transformations in Figures 3.5, 3.7, and 3.8 keep the x-axis ($y = 0$) as a horizontal asymptote, but the transformation in Figure 3.6 yields a new horizontal asymptote of $y = -2$. Also, be sure to note how the y-intercept is affected by each transformation.

What's Wrong?

You use a graphing utility to graph $f(x) = 3^x$ and $g(x) = 3^{x+2}$, as shown in the figure. You use the graph to conclude that the graph of g can be obtained by shifting the graph of f upward two units. What's wrong?

Explore the Concept

The following table shows some points on the graphs in Figure 3.5, where $Y_1 = f(x)$ and $Y_2 = g(x)$. Explain how you can use the table to describe the transformation.

X	Y₁	Y₂
-3	.03704	.11111
-2	.11111	.33333
-1	.33333	1
0	1	3
1	3	9
2	9	27
3	27	81

X=-3

The Natural Base e

For many applications, the convenient choice for a base is the irrational number

$$e = 2.71828128 \ldots .$$

This number is called the **natural base.** The function $f(x) = e^x$ is called the **natural exponential function,** and its graph is shown in Figure 3.9. The graph of the natural exponential function has the same basic characteristics as the graph of the function $f(x) = a^x$ (see page 182). Be sure you see that for the natural exponential function $f(x) = e^x$, e is the constant 2.718281828 . . . , whereas x is the variable.

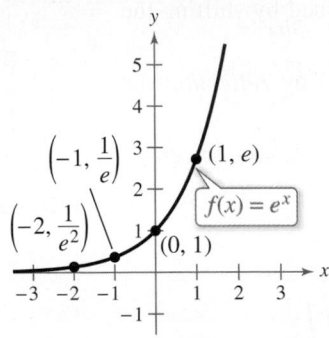

Figure 3.9   *The Natural Exponential Function*

In Example 5, you will see that, for large values of x, the number e can be approximated by the expression

$$\left(1 + \frac{1}{x}\right)^x.$$

Explore the Concept

Use your graphing utility to graph the functions

$$y_1 = 2^x$$

$$y_2 = e^x$$

$$y_3 = 3^x$$

in the same viewing window. From the relative positions of these graphs, make a guess as to the value of the real number e. Then try to find a number a such that the graphs of $y_2 = e^x$ and $y_4 = a^x$ are as close to each other as possible.

EXAMPLE 5   Approximation of the Number e

Evaluate the expression

$$\left(1 + \frac{1}{x}\right)^x$$

for several large values of x to see that the values approach $e \approx 2.718281828$ as x increases without bound.

Graphical Solution

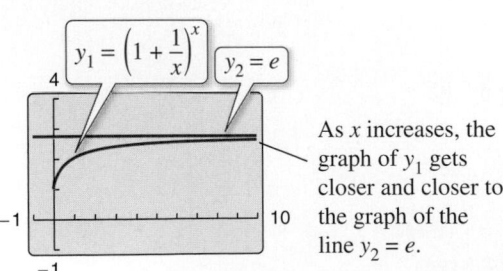

As x increases, the graph of y_1 gets closer and closer to the graph of the line $y_2 = e$.

Numerical Solution

Enter $y_1 = [1 + (1/x)]^x$.

Use the *table* feature (in *ask* mode) to evaluate y_1 for increasing values of x.

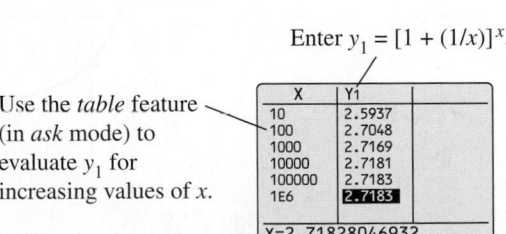

From the table, it seems reasonable to conclude that

$$\left(1 + \frac{1}{x}\right)^x \to e \text{ as } x \to \infty.$$

✓ **Checkpoint** 🔊)) *Audio-video solution in English & Spanish at LarsonPrecalculus.com.*

Evaluate the expression $\left(1 + \frac{2}{x}\right)^x$ for several large values of x to see that the values approach $e^2 \approx 7.389056099$.

EXAMPLE 6   Evaluating the Natural Exponential Function

Use a calculator to evaluate the function $f(x) = e^x$ at each indicated value of x.

a. $x = -2$

b. $x = 0.25$

c. $x = -0.4$

d. $x = \frac{2}{3}$

Solution

Function Value	Graphing Calculator Keystrokes	Display
a. $f(-2) = e^{-2}$	e^x $(-)$ 2 ENTER	0.1353353
b. $f(0.25) = e^{0.25}$	e^x .25 ENTER	1.2840254
c. $f(-0.4) = e^{-0.4}$	e^x $(-)$ .4 ENTER	0.6703200
d. $f(\frac{2}{3}) = e^{2/3}$	e^x $($ 2 $\div$ 3 $)$ ENTER	1.9477340

✓ **Checkpoint** 🔊)) Audio-video solution in English & Spanish at LarsonPrecalculus.com.

Use a calculator to evaluate the function $f(x) = e^x$ at each value of x.

a. $x = 0.3$ b. $x = -1.2$ c. $x = 6.2$

EXAMPLE 7   Graphing Natural Exponential Functions

Sketch the graphs of $f(x) = 2e^{0.24x}$ and $g(x) = \frac{1}{2}e^{-0.58x}$.

Solution

To sketch these two graphs, you can use a calculator to construct a table of values, as shown below.

x	-3	-2	-1	0	1	2	3
$f(x)$	0.974	1.238	1.573	2.000	2.542	3.232	4.109
$g(x)$	2.849	1.595	0.893	0.500	0.280	0.157	0.088

After constructing the table, plot the points and connect them with smooth curves. Note that the graph in Figure 3.10 is increasing, whereas the graph in Figure 3.11 is decreasing. Use a graphing calculator to verify these graphs.

Figure 3.10

Figure 3.11

✓ **Checkpoint** 🔊)) Audio-video solution in English & Spanish at LarsonPrecalculus.com.

Sketch the graph of $f(x) = 5e^{0.17x}$.

Explore the Concept

Use a graphing utility to graph $y = (1 + x)^{1/x}$. Describe the behavior of the graph near $x = 0$. Is there a y-intercept? How does the behavior of the graph near $x = 0$ relate to the result of Example 5? Use the *table* feature of the graphing utility to create a table that shows values of y for values of x near $x = 0$ to help you describe the behavior of the graph near this point.

Applications

One of the most familiar examples of exponential growth is an investment earning *continuously compounded interest.* Suppose a principal P is invested at an annual interest rate r, compounded once a year. If the interest is added to the principal at the end of the year, then the new balance P_1 is

$$P_1 = P + Pr = P(1 + r).$$

This pattern of multiplying the previous principal by $1 + r$ is then repeated each successive year, as shown in the table.

Time in years	Balance after each compounding
0	$P = P$
1	$P_1 = P(1 + r)$
2	$P_2 = P_1(1 + r) = P(1 + r)(1 + r) = P(1 + r)^2$
$\vdots$	$\vdots$
t	$P_t = P(1 + r)^t$

Explore the Concept

Use the formula

$$A = P\left(1 + \frac{r}{n}\right)^{nt}$$

to calculate the amount in an account when $P = \$3000$, $r = 6\%$, $t = 10$ years, and the interest is compounded (a) by the day, (b) by the hour, (c) by the minute, and (d) by the second. Does increasing the number of compoundings per year result in unlimited growth of the amount in the account? Explain.

To accommodate more frequent (quarterly, monthly, or daily) compounding of interest, let n be the number of compoundings per year and let t be the number of years. (The product nt represents the total number of times the interest will be compounded.) Then the interest rate per compounding period is r/n, and the account balance after t years is

$$A = P\left(1 + \frac{r}{n}\right)^{nt}.$$ Amount (balance) with n compoundings per year

When the number of compoundings n increases without bound, the process approaches what is called **continuous compounding.** In the formula for n compoundings per year, let $m = n/r$. This produces

$$A = P\left(1 + \frac{r}{n}\right)^{nt} = P\left(1 + \frac{1}{m}\right)^{mrt} = P\left[\left(1 + \frac{1}{m}\right)^m\right]^{rt}.$$

As m increases without bound, you know from Example 5 that

$$\left(1 + \frac{1}{m}\right)^m$$

approaches e. So, for continuous compounding, it follows that

$$P\left[\left(1 + \frac{1}{m}\right)^m\right]^{rt} \implies P[e]^{rt}$$

and you can write $A = Pe^{rt}$. This result is part of the reason that e is the "natural" choice for a base of an exponential function.

Formulas for Compound Interest

After t years, the balance A in an account with principal P and annual interest rate r (in decimal form) is given by the following formulas.

1. For n compoundings per year: $A = P\left(1 + \dfrac{r}{n}\right)^{nt}$

2. For continuous compounding: $A = Pe^{rt}$

Remark

The interest rate r in the formulas for compound interest should be written as a decimal. For example, an interest rate of 2.5% would be written as $r = 0.025$.

EXAMPLE 8　Finding the Balance for Compound Interest

A total of $9000 is invested at an annual interest rate of 2.5%, compounded annually. Find the balance in the account after 5 years.

Algebraic Solution

In this case, $P = 9000$, $r = 2.5\% = 0.025$, $n = 1$, and $t = 5$. Using the formula for compound interest with n compoundings per year, you have

$$A = P\left(1 + \frac{r}{n}\right)^{nt}$$ 　Formula for compound interest

$$= 9000\left(1 + \frac{0.025}{1}\right)^{1(5)}$$ 　Substitute for P, r, n, and t.

$$= 9000(1.025)^5$$ 　Simplify.

$$\approx \$10{,}182.67.$$ 　Use a calculator.

So, the balance in the account after 5 years is $10,182.67.

Graphical Solution

Substitute the values for P, r, and n into the formula for compound interest with n compoundings per year and simplify to obtain $A = 9000(1.025)^t$. Use a graphing utility to graph $A = 9000(1.025)^t$. Then use the *value* feature to approximate the value of A when $t = 5$, as shown in the figure.

The balance in the account after 5 years is $10,182.67.

✓ **Checkpoint** Audio-video solution in English & Spanish at LarsonPrecalculus.com.

For the account in Example 8, find the balance after 10 years.

EXAMPLE 9　Finding Compound Interest

A total of $12,000 is invested at an annual interest rate of 3%. Find the balance after 4 years when the interest is compounded (a) quarterly and (b) continuously.

Solution

a. For quarterly compoundings, $n = 4$. So, after 4 years at 3%, the balance is

$$A = P\left(1 + \frac{r}{n}\right)^{nt}$$ 　Formula for compound interest

$$= 12{,}000\left(1 + \frac{0.03}{4}\right)^{4(4)}$$ 　Substitute for P, r, n, and t.

$$\approx \$13{,}523.91.$$ 　Use a calculator.

b. For continuous compounding, the balance is

$$A = Pe^{rt}$$ 　Formula for continuous compounding

$$= 12{,}000e^{0.03(4)}$$ 　Substitute for P, r, and t.

$$\approx \$13{,}529.96.$$ 　Use a calculator.

Note that a continuous-compounding account yields more than a quarterly-compounding account.

Financial Analyst

✓ **Checkpoint** Audio-video solution in English & Spanish at LarsonPrecalculus.com.

You invest $6000 at an annual rate of 4%. Find the balance after 7 years when the interest is compounded (a) quarterly, (b) monthly, and (c) continuously.

Example 9 illustrates the following general rule. For a given principal, interest rate, and time, the more often the interest is compounded per year, the greater the balance will be. Moreover, the balance obtained by continuous compounding is greater than the balance obtained by compounding n times per year.

EXAMPLE 10   Radioactive Decay

Let y represent a mass, in grams, of radioactive strontium (^{90}Sr), whose half-life is about 29 years. The quantity of strontium present after t years is $y = 10\left(\frac{1}{2}\right)^{t/29}$.

a. What is the initial mass (when $t = 0$)?

b. How much of the initial mass is present after 80 years?

Algebraic Solution

a. $y = 10\left(\frac{1}{2}\right)^{t/29}$ Write original equation.

$= 10\left(\frac{1}{2}\right)^{0/29}$ Substitute 0 for t.

$= 10$ Simplify.

So, the initial mass is 10 grams.

b. $y = 10\left(\frac{1}{2}\right)^{t/29}$ Write original equation.

$= 10\left(\frac{1}{2}\right)^{80/29}$ Substitute 80 for t.

$\approx 10\left(\frac{1}{2}\right)^{2.759}$ Simplify.

≈ 1.48 Use a calculator.

So, about 1.48 grams are present after 80 years.

Graphical Solution

a.

When $t = 0$, $y = 10$. So, the initial mass is 10 grams.

b.

When $t = 80$, $y \approx 1.48$. So, about 1.48 grams are present after 80 years.

✓ **Checkpoint** 🔊))) Audio-video solution in English & Spanish at LarsonPrecalculus.com.

In Example 10, how much of the initial mass is present after 160 years?

EXAMPLE 11   Population Growth

The approximate number of fruit flies in an experimental population after t hours is given by $Q(t) = 20e^{0.03t}$, where $t \geq 0$.

a. Find the initial number of fruit flies in the population.

b. How large is the population of fruit flies after 72 hours?

c. Graph Q.

Solution

a. To find the initial population, evaluate $Q(t)$ when $t = 0$.

$$Q(0) = 20e^{0.03(0)} = 20e^0 = 20(1) = 20 \text{ flies}$$

b. After 72 hours, the population size is

$$Q(72) = 20e^{0.03(72)} = 20e^{2.16} \approx 173 \text{ flies}.$$

c. The graph of Q is shown in the figure.

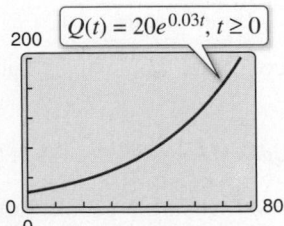

✓ **Checkpoint** 🔊))) Audio-video solution in English & Spanish at LarsonPrecalculus.com.

Rework Example 11 when the approximate number of fruit flies in the experimental population after t hours is given by $Q(t) = 10e^{0.02t}$.

3.1   Exercises

See *CalcChat.com* for tutorial help and worked-out solutions to odd-numbered exercises.
For instructions on how to use a graphing utility, see Appendix A.

Vocabulary and Concept Check

In Exercises 1 and 2, fill in the blank(s).

1. Exponential and logarithmic functions are examples of nonalgebraic functions, also called _____ functions.

2. The exponential function $f(x) = e^x$ is called the _____ function, and the base e is called the _____ base.

3. What type of transformation of the graph of $f(x) = 5^x$ is the graph of $f(x + 1)$?

4. The formula $A = Pe^{rt}$ gives the balance A of an account earning what type of interest?

Procedures and Problem Solving

Evaluating Exponential Functions   In Exercises 5–8, use a calculator to evaluate the function at the indicated value of x. Round your result to three decimal places.

Function	Value
5. $f(x) = 3.4^x$	$x = 6.8$
6. $f(x) = 1.2^x$	$x = \frac{1}{3}$
7. $g(x) = 5^x$	$x = -\pi$
8. $h(x) = 8.6^{-3x}$	$x = -\sqrt{2}$

Graphs of $y = a^x$ and $y = a^{-x}$ In Exercises 9–16, graph the exponential function by hand. Identify any asymptotes and intercepts and determine whether the graph of the function is increasing or decreasing.

9. $g(x) = 5^x$
10. $f(x) = 10^x$
11. $f(x) = 5^{-x}$
12. $h(x) = 10^{-x}$
13. $h(x) = \left(\frac{5}{4}\right)^x$
14. $g(x) = \left(\frac{3}{2}\right)^x$
15. $g(x) = \left(\frac{5}{4}\right)^{-x}$
16. $f(x) = \left(\frac{3}{2}\right)^{-x}$

Library of Parent Functions   In Exercises 17–20, use the graph of $y = 2^x$ to match the function with its graph. [The graphs are labeled (a), (b), (c), and (d).]

(a)

(b)

(c)

(d)

17. $f(x) = 2^{x-2}$
18. $f(x) = 2^{-x}$
19. $f(x) = 2^x - 4$
20. $f(x) = 2^x + 1$

Library of Parent Functions   In Exercises 21–30, use the graph of f to describe the transformation that yields the graph of g. Then sketch the graphs of f and g by hand.

21. $f(x) = 3^x$, $g(x) = 3^{x-5}$
22. $f(x) = 10^x$, $g(x) = 10^{x+4}$
23. $f(x) = 6^x$, $g(x) = 6^x + 5$
24. $f(x) = -2^x$, $g(x) = 5 - 2^x$
25. $f(x) = \left(\frac{3}{5}\right)^x$, $g(x) = -\left(\frac{3}{5}\right)^{x+4}$
26. $f(x) = 0.3^x$, $g(x) = -0.3^x + 5$
27. $f(x) = 0.4^x$, $g(x) = 0.4^{x-2} - 3$
28. $f(x) = \left(\frac{2}{3}\right)^x$, $g(x) = \left(\frac{2}{3}\right)^{x+2} - 3$
29. $f(x) = \left(\frac{1}{4}\right)^x$, $g(x) = \left(\frac{1}{4}\right)^{-x} + 2$
30. $f(x) = \left(\frac{1}{2}\right)^x$, $g(x) = \left(\frac{1}{2}\right)^{-(x+4)}$

Approximation of a Power with Base e In Exercises 31 and 32, show that the value of $f(x)$ approaches the value of $g(x)$ as x increases without bound (a) graphically and (b) numerically.

31. $f(x) = 1 + \left(\dfrac{0.5}{x}\right)^x$, $g(x) = e^{0.5}$

32. $f(x) = 1 + \left(\dfrac{3}{x}\right)^x$, $g(x) = e^3$

Evaluating the Natural Exponential Function   In Exercises 33–36, use a calculator to evaluate the function at the indicated value of x. Round your result to the nearest thousandth.

Function	Value
33. $f(x) = e^x$	$x = 9.2$
34. $f(x) = e^{-x}$	$x = -\frac{3}{4}$
35. $g(x) = 50e^{4x}$	$x = 0.02$
36. $h(x) = -5.5e^{-x}$	$x = 200$

Graphing an Exponential Function In Exercises 37–52, use a graphing utility to construct a table of values for the function. Then sketch the graph of the function. Identify any asymptotes of the graph.

37. $f(x) = \left(\frac{5}{2}\right)^x$

38. $f(x) = \left(\frac{5}{2}\right)^{-x}$

39. $f(x) = 6^x$

40. $f(x) = 2^{x-1}$

41. $f(x) = 3^{x+2}$

42. $y = 2^{-x^2}$

43. $y = 3^{x-2} + 1$

44. $y = 4^{x+1} - 2$

45. $f(x) = e^{-x}$

46. $s(t) = 3e^{-0.2t}$

47. $f(x) = 3e^{x+4}$

48. $f(x) = 2e^{x-3}$

49. $f(x) = 2 + e^{x-5}$

50. $g(x) = e^{x+1} + 2$

51. $s(t) = 2e^{-0.12t}$

52. $g(x) = e^{0.5x} - 1$

Finding Asymptotes In Exercises 53–56, use a graphing utility to (a) graph the function and (b) find any asymptotes numerically by creating a table of values for the function.

53. $f(x) = \dfrac{8}{1 + e^{-0.5x}}$

54. $g(x) = \dfrac{8}{1 + e^{-0.5/x}}$

55. $f(x) = -\dfrac{6}{2 - e^{0.2x}}$

56. $f(x) = \dfrac{6}{2 - e^{0.2/x}}$

Finding Points of Intersection In Exercises 57–60, use a graphing utility to find the point(s) of intersection, if any, of the graphs of the functions. Round your result to three decimal places.

57. $y = 20e^{0.05x}$
$y = 1500$

58. $y = 100e^{0.01x}$
$y = 12{,}500$

59. $y = 2.5e^{0.3x}$
$y = 0.2$

60. $y = 3.2e^{0.5x}$
$y = 0.9$

Approximating Relative Extrema In Exercises 61–64, (a) use a graphing utility to graph the function, (b) use the graph to find the open intervals on which the function is increasing and decreasing, and (c) approximate any relative maximum or minimum values.

61. $f(x) = x^2 e^{-x}$

62. $f(x) = 2x^2 e^{x+1}$

63. $f(x) = x^3 e^x$

64. $f(x) = x^3 e^{-x+2}$

Finding the Balance for Compound Interest In Exercises 65–68, complete the table to determine the balance A for $2500 invested at rate r for t years and compounded n times per year.

n	1	2	4	12	365	Continuous
A						

65. $r = 2\%$, $t = 10$ years

66. $r = 6\%$, $t = 10$ years

67. $r = 4\%$, $t = 20$ years

68. $r = 3\%$, $t = 40$ years

Finding the Balance for Compound Interest In Exercises 69–72, complete the table to determine the balance A for $12,000 invested at rate r for t years, compounded continuously.

t	1	10	20	30	40	50
A						

69. $r = 4\%$

70. $r = 6\%$

71. $r = 3.5\%$

72. $r = 2.5\%$

Finding the Amount of an Annuity In Exercises 73–76, you build an annuity by investing P dollars every month at interest rate r, compounded monthly. Find the amount A accrued after n months using the formula

$$A = P\left[\frac{(1 + r/12)^n - 1}{r/12}\right], \text{ where } r \text{ is in decimal form.}$$

73. $P = \$25$, $r = 0.12$, $n = 48$ months

74. $P = \$100$, $r = 0.09$, $n = 60$ months

75. $P = \$200$, $r = 0.06$, $n = 72$ months

76. $P = \$75$, $r = 0.03$, $n = 24$ months

77. MODELING DATA

There are three options for investing $500. The first earns 7% compounded annually, the second earns 7% compounded quarterly, and the third earns 7% compounded continuously.

(a) Find equations that model the growth of each investment and use a graphing utility to graph each model in the same viewing window over a 20-year period.

(b) Use the graph from part (a) to determine which investment yields the highest return after 20 years. What are the differences in earnings among the three investments?

78. Radioactive Decay Let Q represent a mass, in grams, of radioactive radium (^{226}Ra), whose half-life is 1600 years. The quantity of radium present after t years is given by $Q = 25\left(\frac{1}{2}\right)^{t/1600}$.

(a) Determine the initial quantity (when $t = 0$).

(b) Determine the quantity present after 1000 years.

(c) Use a graphing utility to graph the function over the interval $t = 0$ to $t = 5000$.

(d) When will the quantity of radium be 0 grams? Explain.

79. Radioactive Decay Let Q represent a mass, in grams, of carbon 14 (^{14}C), whose half-life is 5700 years. The quantity present after t years is given by $Q = 10\left(\frac{1}{2}\right)^{t/5700}$.

(a) Determine the initial quantity (when $t = 0$).

(b) Determine the quantity present after 2000 years.

(c) Sketch the graph of the function over the interval $t = 0$ to $t = 10,000$.

80. Algebraic-Graphical-Numerical Assume the annual rate of inflation is 4% for the next 10 years. The approximate cost C of goods or services during these years is $C(t) = P(1.04)^t$, where t is the time (in years) and P is the present cost. An oil change for your car presently costs $26.88. Use the following methods to approximate the cost 10 years from now.

(a) Use a graphing utility to graph the function and then use the *value* feature.

(b) Use the *table* feature of the graphing utility to find a numerical approximation.

(c) Use a calculator to evaluate the cost function algebraically.

81. Population Growth The projected populations of California for the years 2020 through 2060 can be modeled by $P = 36.308e^{0.0065t}$, where P is the population (in millions) and t is the time (in years), with $t = 20$ corresponding to 2020. (Source: California Department of Finance)

(a) Use a graphing utility to graph the function for the years 2020 through 2060.

(b) Use the *table* feature of the graphing utility to create a table of values for the same time period as in part (a).

(c) According to the model, in what year will the population of California exceed 51 million?

82. *Why you should learn it* (p. 180) In early 2014, a new sedan had a manufacturer's suggested retail price of $31,340. After t years, the sedan's value is given by
$$V(t) = 31,340\left(\tfrac{4}{5}\right)^t.$$

(a) Use a graphing utility to graph the function.

(b) Use the graphing utility to create a table of values that shows the value V for $t = 1$ to $t = 10$ years.

(c) According to the model, when will the sedan have no value?

Conclusions

True or False? In Exercises 83 and 84, determine whether the statement is true or false. Justify your answer.

83. $f(x) = 1^x$ is not an exponential function.

84. $e = \dfrac{271,801}{99,990}$

85. Library of Parent Functions Determine which equation(s) may be represented by the graph shown. (There may be more than one correct answer.)

(a) $y = e^x + 1$

(b) $y = -e^{-x} + 1$

(c) $y = e^{-x} - 1$

(d) $y = e^{-x} + 1$

86. Exploration Use a graphing utility to graph $y_1 = e^x$ and each of the functions $y_2 = x^2$, $y_3 = x^3$, $y_4 = \sqrt{x}$, and $y_5 = |x|$ in the same viewing window.

(a) Which function increases at the fastest rate for "large" values of x?

(b) Use the result of part (a) to make a conjecture about the rates of growth of $y_1 = e^x$ and $y = x^n$, where n is a natural number and x is "large."

(c) Use the results of parts (a) and (b) to describe what is implied when it is stated that a quantity is growing exponentially.

87. Think About It Graph $y = 3^x$ and $y = 4^x$. Use the graph to solve the inequality $3^x < 4^x$.

88. HOW DO YOU SEE IT? The figure shows the graphs of $y = 2^x$, $y = e^x$, $y = 10^x$, $y = 2^{-x}$, $y = e^{-x}$, and $y = 10^{-x}$. Match each function with its graph. [The graphs are labeled (a) through (f).] Explain.

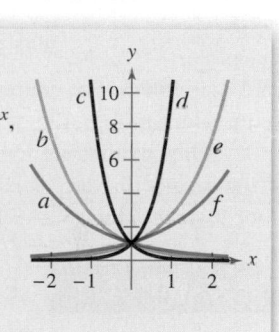

Think About It In Exercises 89–92, place the correct symbol ($<$ or $>$) between the two numbers.

89. e^{π} ____ π^e

90. 2^{10} ____ 10^2

91. 5^{-3} ____ 3^{-5}

92. $4^{1/2}$ ____ $\left(\tfrac{1}{2}\right)^4$

Cumulative Mixed Review

Inverse Functions In Exercises 93–96, determine whether the function has an inverse function. If it does, find f^{-1}.

93. $f(x) = 5x - 7$

94. $f(x) = -\tfrac{2}{3}x + \tfrac{5}{2}$

95. $f(x) = \sqrt[3]{x + 8}$

96. $f(x) = \sqrt{x^2 + 6}$

97. *Make a Decision* To work an extended application analyzing the population per square mile in the United States, visit this textbook's website at *LarsonPrecalculus.com*. (Data Source: U.S. Census Bureau)

3.2 Logarithmic Functions and Their Graphs

Logarithmic Functions

In Section 1.6, you studied the concept of an inverse function. There, you learned that when a function is one-to-one—that is, when the function has the property that no horizontal line intersects its graph more than once—the function must have an inverse function. By looking back at the graphs of the exponential functions introduced in Section 3.1, you will see that every function of the form $f(x) = a^x$, where $a > 0$ and $a \neq 1$, passes the Horizontal Line Test and therefore must have an inverse function. This inverse function is called the **logarithmic function with base a**.

> **Definition of Logarithmic Function**
>
> For $x > 0$, $a > 0$, and $a \neq 1$,
>
> $y = \log_a x$ if and only if $x = a^y$.
>
> The function given by
>
> $f(x) = \log_a x$ Read as "log base a of x."
>
> is called the **logarithmic function with base a.**

From the definition above, you can see that every logarithmic equation can be written in an equivalent exponential form and every exponential equation can be written in logarithmic form. So, the equations

$y = \log_a x$ and $x = a^y$

are equivalent. For example, $2 = \log_3 9$ is equivalent to $9 = 3^2$, and $5^3 = 125$ is equivalent to $\log_5 125 = 3$.

When evaluating logarithms, remember that *a logarithm is an exponent*. This means that $\log_a x$ is the exponent to which a must be raised to obtain x. For instance, $\log_2 8 = 3$ because 2 must be raised to the third power to get 8.

EXAMPLE 1   Evaluating Logarithms

Evaluate each logarithm at the indicated value of x.

a. $f(x) = \log_2 x$, $x = 32$

b. $f(x) = \log_3 x$, $x = 1$

c. $f(x) = \log_4 x$, $x = 2$

d. $f(x) = \log_{10} x$, $x = \frac{1}{100}$

Solution

a. $f(32) = \log_2 32 = 5$ because $2^5 = 32$.

b. $f(1) = \log_3 1 = 0$ because $3^0 = 1$.

c. $f(2) = \log_4 2 = \frac{1}{2}$ because $4^{1/2} = \sqrt{4} = 2$.

d. $f\left(\dfrac{1}{100}\right) = \log_{10} \dfrac{1}{100} = -2$ because $10^{-2} = \dfrac{1}{10^2} = \dfrac{1}{100}$.

✔ **Checkpoint** 🔊))) *Audio-video solution in English & Spanish at LarsonPrecalculus.com.*

Evaluate each logarithm at the indicated value of x.

a. $f(x) = \log_6 x, x = 1$ **b.** $f(x) = \log_5 x, x = \frac{1}{125}$ **c.** $f(x) = \log_{10} x, x = 10{,}000$

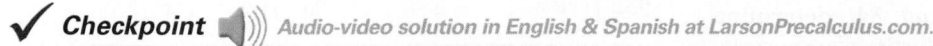

©Kjpargeter/Shutterstock.com

What you should learn

▶ Recognize and evaluate logarithmic functions with base a.
▶ Graph logarithmic functions with base a.
▶ Recognize, evaluate, and graph natural logarithmic functions.
▶ Use logarithmic functions to model and solve real-life problems.

Why you should learn it

Logarithmic functions are useful in modeling data that represent quantities that increase or decrease slowly. For instance, Exercise 114 on page 201 shows how to use a logarithmic function to model the minimum required ventilation rates in public school classrooms.

Remark

In this text, the parentheses in $\log_a(u)$ are sometimes omitted when u is an expression involving exponents, radicals, products, or quotients. For instance, $\log_{10}(2x)$ can be written as $\log_{10} 2x$. To evaluate $\log_{10} 2x$, find the logarithm of the product $2x$.

The logarithmic function with base 10 is called the **common logarithmic function.** On most calculators, this function is denoted by $\boxed{\text{LOG}}$. Example 2 shows how to use a calculator to evaluate common logarithmic functions. You will learn how to use a calculator to calculate logarithms to any base in the next section.

EXAMPLE 2 Evaluating Common Logarithms on a Calculator

Use a calculator to evaluate the function $f(x) = \log_{10} x$ at each value of x.

a. $x = 10$ **b.** $x = \frac{1}{3}$ **c.** $x = 2.5$ **d.** $x = -2$

Solution

Function Value	Graphing Calculator Keystrokes	Display
a. $f(10) = \log_{10} 10$	$\boxed{\text{LOG}}$ 10 $\boxed{\text{ENTER}}$	1
b. $f(\frac{1}{3}) = \log_{10}\frac{1}{3}$	$\boxed{\text{LOG}}$ $\boxed{(}$ 1 $\boxed{\div}$ 3 $\boxed{)}$ $\boxed{\text{ENTER}}$	-0.4771213
c. $f(2.5) = \log_{10} 2.5$	$\boxed{\text{LOG}}$ 2.5 $\boxed{\text{ENTER}}$	0.3979400
d. $f(-2) = \log_{10}(-2)$	$\boxed{\text{LOG}}$ $\boxed{(-)}$ 2 $\boxed{\text{ENTER}}$	ERROR

Note that the calculator displays an error message when you try to evaluate $\log_{10}(-2)$. In this case, there is no *real* power to which 10 can be raised to obtain -2.

✓ **Checkpoint** *Audio-video solution in English & Spanish at LarsonPrecalculus.com.*

Use a calculator to evaluate the function $f(x) = \log_{10} x$ at each value of x.

a. $x = 275$ **b.** $x = 0.275$ **c.** $x = -\frac{1}{2}$ **d.** $x = \frac{1}{2}$ ■

> **Technology Tip**
>
> Some graphing utilities do not give an error message for $\log_{10}(-2)$. Instead, the graphing utility will display a complex number. For the purpose of this text, however, the domain of a logarithmic function is the set of positive *real* numbers.

The properties of logarithms listed below follow directly from the definition of the logarithmic function with base a.

> **Properties of Logarithms**
>
> **1.** $\log_a 1 = 0$ because $a^0 = 1$.
>
> **2.** $\log_a a = 1$ because $a^1 = a$.
>
> **3.** $\log_a a^x = x$ and $a^{\log_a x} = x$.   Inverse Properties
>
> **4.** If $\log_a x = \log_a y$, then $x = y$.   One-to-One Property

EXAMPLE 3 Using Properties of Logarithms

a. Solve for x: $\log_2 x = \log_2 3$

b. Solve for x: $\log_4 4 = x$

c. Simplify: $\log_5 5^x$

d. Simplify: $7^{\log_7 14}$

Solution

a. Using the One-to-One Property (Property 4), you can conclude that $x = 3$.

b. Using Property 2, you can conclude that $x = 1$.

c. Using the Inverse Property (Property 3), it follows that $\log_5 5^x = x$.

d. Using the Inverse Property (Property 3), it follows that $7^{\log_7 14} = 14$.

✓ **Checkpoint** *Audio-video solution in English & Spanish at LarsonPrecalculus.com.*

a. Solve for x: $\log_{10} x = \log_{10} 2$ **b.** Simplify: $20^{\log_{20} 3}$ ■

Graphs of Logarithmic Functions

To sketch the graph of $y = \log_a x$, you can use the fact that the graphs of inverse functions are reflections of each other in the line $y = x$.

EXAMPLE 4   Graphs of Exponential and Logarithmic Functions

In the same coordinate plane, sketch the graph of each function by hand.

a. $f(x) = 2^x$

b. $g(x) = \log_2 x$

Solution

a. For $f(x) = 2^x$, construct a table of values. By plotting these points and connecting them with a smooth curve, you obtain the graph of f shown in Figure 3.12.

Figure 3.12

x	-2	-1	0	1	2	3
$f(x) = 2^x$	$\frac{1}{4}$	$\frac{1}{2}$	1	2	4	8

b. Because $g(x) = \log_2 x$ is the inverse function of $f(x) = 2^x$, the graph of g is obtained by plotting the points $(f(x), x)$ and connecting them with a smooth curve. The graph of g is a reflection of the graph of f in the line $y = x$, as shown in Figure 3.12.

✓ **Checkpoint** *Audio-video solution in English & Spanish at LarsonPrecalculus.com.*

In the same coordinate plane, sketch the graphs of (a) $f(x) = 8^x$ and (b) $g(x) = \log_8 x$.

Before you can confirm the result of Example 4 using a graphing utility, you need to know how to enter $\log_2 x$. You will learn how to do this using the *change-of-base formula* discussed in the next section.

EXAMPLE 5   Sketching the Graph of a Logarithmic Function

Sketch the graph of the common logarithmic function $f(x) = \log_{10} x$ by hand.

Solution

Begin by constructing a table of values. Note that some of the values can be obtained without a calculator by using the Inverse Property of Logarithms. Others require a calculator. Next, plot the points and connect them with a smooth curve, as shown in Figure 3.13. Note that $x = 0$ (the y-axis) is a vertical asymptote of the graph.

Figure 3.13

x	Without calculator				With calculator		
	$\frac{1}{100}$	$\frac{1}{10}$	1	10	2	5	8
$f(x) = \log_{10} x$	-2	-1	0	1	0.301	0.699	0.903

✓ **Checkpoint** *Audio-video solution in English & Spanish at LarsonPrecalculus.com.*

Without using a calculator, sketch the graph of $f(x) = \log_3 x$ by hand.

The nature of the graph in Figure 3.13 is typical of functions of the form $f(x) = \log_a x$, $a > 1$. They have one x-intercept and one vertical asymptote. Notice how slowly the graph rises for $x > 1$.

Library of Parent Functions: Logarithmic Function

The *parent logarithmic function* $f(x) = \log_a x$, $a > 0, a \neq 1$ is the inverse function of the exponential function. Its domain is the set of positive real numbers and its range is the set of all real numbers. This is the opposite of the exponential function. Moreover, the logarithmic function has the y-axis as a vertical asymptote, whereas the exponential function has the x-axis as a horizontal asymptote. Many real-life phenomena with slow rates of growth can be modeled by logarithmic functions. The basic characteristics of the logarithmic function are summarized below and on the inside cover of this text.

Graph of $f(x) = \log_a x$, $a > 1$

Domain: $(0, \infty)$

Range: $(-\infty, \infty)$

Intercept: $(1, 0)$

Increasing on $(0, \infty)$

y-axis is a vertical asymptote
$(\log_a x \to -\infty$ as $x \to 0^+)$

Continuous

Reflection of graph of $f(x) = a^x$
in the line $y = x$

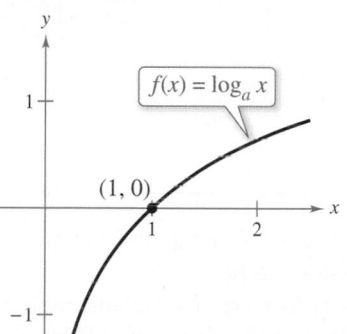

Explore the Concept

Use a graphing utility to graph $y = \log_{10} x$ and $y = 8$ in the same viewing window. Find a viewing window that shows the point of intersection. What is the point of intersection? Use the point of intersection to complete the equation $\log_{10}$ ▢ $= 8$.

EXAMPLE 6   Library of Parent Functions $f(x) = \log_a x$

See LarsonPrecalculus.com for an interactive version of this type of example.

Each of the following functions is a transformation of the graph of $f(x) = \log_{10} x$.

a. Because $g(x) = \log_{10}(x - 1) = f(x - 1)$, the graph of g can be obtained by shifting the graph of f one unit to the *right*, as shown in Figure 3.14.

b. Because $h(x) = 2 + \log_{10} x = 2 + f(x)$, the graph of h can be obtained by shifting the graph of f two units *upward*, as shown in Figure 3.15.

Figure 3.14

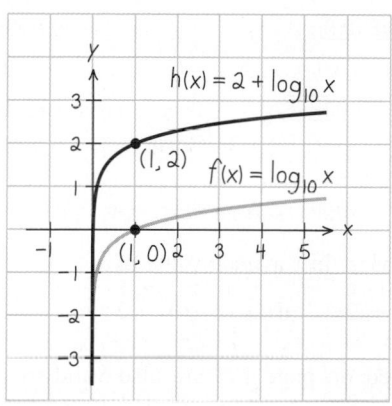

Figure 3.15

Notice that the transformation in Figure 3.15 keeps the y-axis as a vertical asymptote, but the transformation in Figure 3.14 yields the new vertical asymptote $x - 1$.

✓ **Checkpoint** ◀))) *Audio-video solution in English & Spanish at LarsonPrecalculus.com.*

Use the graph of $f(x) = \log_{10} x$ to sketch the graph of each function by hand.

a. $g(x) = -1 + \log_{10} x$ **b.** $h(x) = \log_{10}(x + 3)$

The Natural Logarithmic Function

By looking back at the graph of the natural exponential function introduced in Section 3.1, you will see that $f(x) = e^x$ is one-to-one and so has an inverse function. This inverse function is called the **natural logarithmic function** and is denoted by the special symbol $\ln x$, read as "the natural log of x" or "el en of x."

The Natural Logarithmic Function

For $x > 0$,

$$y = \ln x \quad \text{if and only if} \quad x = e^y.$$

The function given by

$$f(x) = \log_e x = \ln x$$

is called the **natural logarithmic function.**

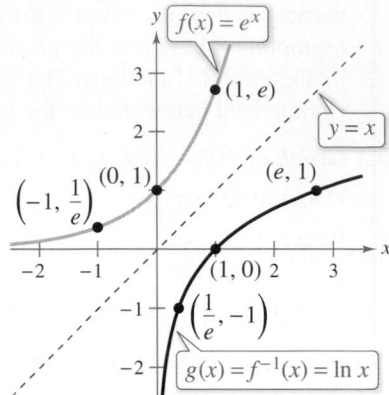

Reflection of graph of $f(x) = e^x$ in the line $y = x$

Figure 3.16

The equations $y = \ln x$ and $x = e^y$ are equivalent. Note that the natural logarithm $\ln x$ is written without a base. The base is understood to be e.

Because the functions $f(x) = e^x$ and $g(x) = \ln x$ are inverse functions of each other, their graphs are reflections of each other in the line $y = x$. This reflective property is illustrated in Figure 3.16.

EXAMPLE 7   Evaluating the Natural Logarithmic Function

Use a calculator to evaluate the function $f(x) = \ln x$ at each value of x.

a. $x = 2$

b. $x = 0.3$

c. $x = -1$

d. $x = 1 + \sqrt{2}$

Solution

	Function Value	Graphing Calculator Keystrokes	Display
a.	$f(2) = \ln 2$	LN 2 ENTER	0.6931472
b.	$f(0.3) = \ln 0.3$	LN .3 ENTER	-1.2039728
c.	$f(-1) = \ln(-1)$	LN (−) 1 ENTER	ERROR
d.	$f(1 + \sqrt{2}) = \ln(1 + \sqrt{2})$	LN (1 + √ 2) ENTER	0.8813736

✓ **Checkpoint**))) *Audio-video solution in English & Spanish at LarsonPrecalculus.com.*

Use a calculator to evaluate the function $f(x) = \ln x$ at each value of x.

a. $x = 0.01$ **b.** $x = 4$ **c.** $x = \sqrt{3} + 2$ **d.** $x = \sqrt{3} - 2$

The four properties of logarithms listed on page 193 are also valid for natural logarithms.

Properties of Natural Logarithms

1. $\ln 1 = 0$ because $e^0 = 1$.

2. $\ln e = 1$ because $e^1 = e$.

3. $\ln e^x = x$ and $e^{\ln x} = x$.   Inverse Properties

4. If $\ln x = \ln y$, then $x = y$.   One-to-One Property

Technology Tip

On most calculators, the natural logarithm is denoted by LN, as illustrated in Example 7.

Remark

In Example 7(c), be sure you see that $\ln(-1)$ gives an error message on most calculators. This occurs because the domain of $\ln x$ is the set of *positive* real numbers (see Figure 3.16). So, $\ln(-1)$ is undefined.

EXAMPLE 8   Using Properties of Natural Logarithms

Use the properties of natural logarithms to rewrite each expression.

a. $\ln\dfrac{1}{e}$ **b.** $e^{\ln 5}$ **c.** $4 \ln 1$ **d.** $2 \ln e$

Solution

a. $\ln\dfrac{1}{e} = \ln e^{-1} = -1$ Inverse Property

b. $e^{\ln 5} = 5$ Inverse Property

c. $4 \ln 1 = 4(0) = 0$ Property 1

d. $2 \ln e = 2(1) = 2$ Property 2

✓ **Checkpoint** ◀))) *Audio-video solution in English & Spanish at LarsonPrecalculus.com.*

Use the properties of natural logarithms to simplify each expression.

a. $\ln e^{1/3}$ **b.** $5 \ln 1$ **c.** $\frac{3}{4} \ln e$ **d.** $e^{\ln 7}$

EXAMPLE 9   Finding the Domains of Logarithmic Functions

Find the domain of each function.

a. $f(x) = \ln(x - 2)$ **b.** $g(x) = \ln(2 - x)$ **c.** $h(x) = \ln x^2$

Algebraic Solution

a. Because $\ln(x - 2)$ is defined only when

$$x - 2 > 0$$

it follows that the domain of f is $(2, \infty)$.

b. Because $\ln(2 - x)$ is defined only when

$$2 - x > 0$$

it follows that the domain of g is $(-\infty, 2)$.

c. Because $\ln x^2$ is defined only when

$$x^2 > 0$$

it follows that the domain of h is all real numbers except $x = 0$.

Graphical Solution

a.

The x-coordinates of points on the graph appear to extend from the right of 2 to ∞. So, you can estimate the domain to be $(2, \infty)$.

b.

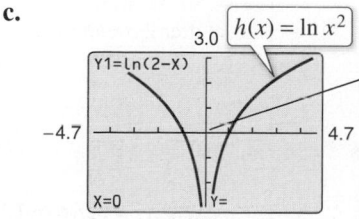

The x-coordinates of points on the graph appear to extend from $-\infty$ to the left of 2. So, you can estimate the domain to be $(-\infty, 2)$.

c.

The x-coordinates of points on the graph appear to include all real numbers except 0. So, you can estimate the domain to be all real numbers except $x = 0$.

✓ **Checkpoint** ◀))) *Audio-video solution in English & Spanish at LarsonPrecalculus.com.*

Find the domain of $f(x) = \ln(x + 3)$.

In Example 9, suppose you had been asked to analyze the function $h(x) = \ln|x - 2|$. How would the domain of this function compare with the domains of the functions given in parts (a) and (b) of the example?

Application

EXAMPLE 10   Psychology

Students participating in a psychology experiment attended several lectures on a subject and were given an exam. Every month for a year after the exam, the students were retested to see how much of the material they remembered. The average scores for the group are given by the *human memory model*

$$f(t) = 75 - 6 \ln(t + 1), \quad 0 \le t \le 12$$

where t is the time in months. The graph of f is shown in Figure 3.17.

a. What was the average score on the original exam ($t = 0$)?

b. What was the average score at the end of $t = 2$ months?

c. What was the average score at the end of $t = 6$ months?

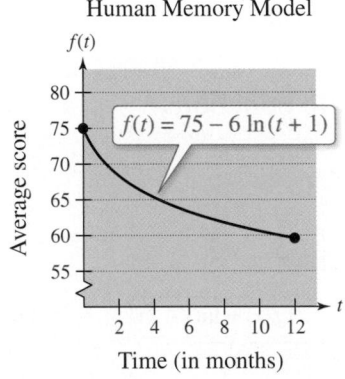

Human Memory Model

$f(t) = 75 - 6 \ln(t + 1)$

Average score

Time (in months)

Figure 3.17

Psychologist

Algebraic Solution

a. The original average score was

$$f(0) = 75 - 6 \ln(0 + 1)$$
$$= 75 - 6 \ln 1$$
$$= 75 - 6(0)$$
$$= 75.$$

b. After 2 months, the average score was

$$f(2) = 75 - 6 \ln(2 + 1)$$
$$= 75 - 6 \ln 3$$
$$\approx 75 - 6(1.0986)$$
$$\approx 68.41.$$

c. After 6 months, the average score was

$$f(6) = 75 - 6 \ln(6 + 1)$$
$$= 75 - 6 \ln 7$$
$$\approx 75 - 6(1.9459)$$
$$\approx 63.32.$$

Graphical Solution

a.

When $t = 0$, $f(0) = 75$. So, the original average score was 75.

b.

When $t = 2$, $f(2) \approx 68.41$. So, the average score after 2 months was about 68.41.

c.

When $t = 6$, $f(6) \approx 63.32$. So, the average score after 6 months was about 63.32.

✓ **Checkpoint** 🔊))) *Audio-video solution in English & Spanish at LarsonPrecalculus.com.*

In Example 10, find the average score at the end of (a) $t = 1$ month, (b) $t = 9$ months, and (c) $t = 12$ months.

©iStock.com/stocknroll

3.2   Exercises

See *CalcChat.com* for tutorial help and worked-out solutions to odd-numbered exercises.
For instructions on how to use a graphing utility, see Appendix A.

Vocabulary and Concept Check

In Exercises 1–4, fill in the blank(s).

1. The inverse function of the exponential function $f(x) = a^x$ is called the _____ with base a.

2. The base of the _____ logarithmic function is 10, and the base of the _____ logarithmic function is e.

3. The inverse properties of logarithms are $\log_a a^x = x$ and _____ .

4. If $x = e^y$, then $y = $ _____ .

5. What exponential equation is equivalent to the logarithmic equation $\log_a b = c$?

6. For what value(s) of x is $\ln x = \ln 7$?

Procedures and Problem Solving

Rewriting Logarithmic Equations   In Exercises 7–14, write the logarithmic equation in exponential form. For example, the exponential form of $\log_5 25 = 2$ is $5^2 = 25$.

7. $\log_4 64 = 3$

8. $\log_3 81 = 4$

9. $\log_7 \frac{1}{49} = -2$

10. $\log_{10} \frac{1}{1000} = -3$

11. $\log_{32} 4 = \frac{2}{5}$

12. $\log_{16} 8 = \frac{3}{4}$

13. $\log_2 \sqrt{2} = \frac{1}{2}$

14. $\log_5 \sqrt[3]{25} = \frac{2}{3}$

Rewriting Exponential Equations   In Exercises 15–22, write the exponential equation in logarithmic form. For example, the logarithmic form of $2^3 = 8$ is $\log_2 8 = 3$.

15. $5^3 = 125$

16. $8^2 = 64$

17. $81^{1/4} = 3$

18. $9^{3/2} = 27$

19. $6^{-2} = \frac{1}{36}$

20. $10^{-3} = 0.001$

21. $g^a = 4$

22. $n^t = 10$

Evaluating Logarithms   In Exercises 23–26, use the definition of logarithmic function to evaluate the function at the indicated value of x without using a calculator.

Function	Value
23. $f(x) = \log_2 x$	$x = 16$
24. $f(x) = \log_{16} x$	$x = \frac{1}{4}$
25. $g(x) = \log_{10} x$	$x = \frac{1}{1000}$
26. $g(x) = \log_{10} x$	$x = 100{,}000$

Evaluating Common Logarithms on a Calculator   In Exercises 27–30, use a calculator to evaluate the function at the indicated value of x. Round your result to three decimal places.

Function	Value
27. $f(x) = \log_{10} x$	$x = 345$
28. $f(x) = \log_{10} x$	$x = \frac{4}{5}$
29. $h(x) = 6 \log_{10} x$	$x = 14.8$
30. $h(x) = 1.9 \log_{10} x$	$x = 4.3$

Using Properties of Logarithms   In Exercises 31–36, solve the equation for x.

31. $\log_7 x = \log_7 9$

32. $\log_5 5 = \log_5 x$

33. $\log_4 4^2 = x$

34. $\log_3 3^{-5} = x$

35. $\log_8 x = \log_8 10^{-1}$

36. $\log_4 4^3 = \log_4 x$

Using Properties of Logarithms   In Exercises 37–40, use the properties of logarithms to simplify the expression.

37. $\log_4 4^{3x}$

38. $6^{\log_6 36x}$

39. $3 \log_2 \frac{1}{2}$

40. $\frac{1}{4} \log_4 16$

Graphs of Exponential and Logarithmic Functions   In Exercises 41–44, sketch the graph of f. Then use the graph of f to sketch the graph of g.

41. $f(x) = 6^x$
   $g(x) = \log_6 x$

42. $f(x) = 5^x$
   $g(x) = \log_5 x$

43. $f(x) = 15^x$
   $g(x) = \log_{15} x$

44. $f(x) = 4^x$
   $g(x) = \log_4 x$

Sketching the Graph of a Logarithmic Function   In Exercises 45–50, find the domain, vertical asymptote, and x-intercept of the logarithmic function, and sketch its graph by hand.

45. $y = \log_{10}(x + 2)$

46. $y = \log_{10}(x - 1)$

47. $y = 1 + \log_{10} x$

48. $y = 2 - \log_{10} x$

49. $y = 1 + \log_{10}(x - 2)$

50. $y = 2 + \log_{10}(x + 1)$

Library of Parent Functions In Exercises 51–54, use the graph of $y = \log_3 x$ to match the function with its graph. [The graphs are labeled (a), (b), (c), and (d).]

(a)

(b)

(c)

(d)
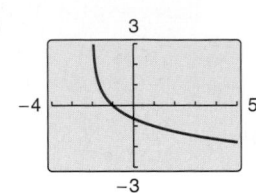

51. $f(x) = \log_3 x + 2$

52. $f(x) = -\log_3 x$

53. $f(x) = -\log_3(x + 2)$

54. $f(x) = \log_3(1 - x)$

Library of Parent Functions In Exercises 55–60, describe the transformation of the graph of f that yields the graph of g.

55. $f(x) = \log_{10} x$, $g(x) = \log_{10}(-x)$

56. $f(x) = \log_{10} x$, $g(x) = \log_{10}(x + 7)$

57. $f(x) = \log_2 x$, $g(x) = 4 - \log_2 x$

58. $f(x) = \log_2 x$, $g(x) = -3 + \log_2 x$

59. $f(x) = \log_8 x$, $g(x) = -2 + \log_8(x - 3)$

60. $f(x) = \log_8 x$, $g(x) = 4 + \log_8(x - 1)$

Rewriting Logarithmic Equations In Exercises 61–68, write the logarithmic equation in exponential form. For example, the exponential form of $\ln 5 = 1.6094\ldots$ is $e^{1.6094\ldots} = 5$.

61. $\ln 6 = 1.7917\ldots$

62. $\ln 4 = 1.3862\ldots$

63. $\ln e = 1$

64. $\ln e^3 = 3$

65. $\ln \sqrt{e} = \dfrac{1}{2}$

66. $\ln \dfrac{1}{e^2} = -2$

67. $\ln 9 = 2.1972\ldots$

68. $\ln \sqrt[3]{e} = \frac{1}{3}$

Rewriting Exponential Equations In Exercises 69–76, write the exponential equation in logarithmic form. For example, the logarithmic form of $e^2 = 7.3890\ldots$ is $\ln 7.3890\ldots = 2$.

69. $e^3 = 20.0855\ldots$

70. $e^0 = 1$

71. $e^{1.3} = 3.6692\ldots$

72. $e^{2.5} = 12.1824\ldots$

73. $\sqrt[3]{e} = 1.3956\ldots$

74. $\dfrac{1}{e^4} = 0.0183\ldots$

75. $\sqrt{e^3} = 4.4816\ldots$

76. $e^{3/4} = 2.1170\ldots$

Evaluating the Natural Logarithmic Function In Exercises 77–80, use a calculator to evaluate the function at the indicated value of x. Round your result to three decimal places.

Function	Value
77. $f(x) = \ln x$	$x = 11$
78. $f(x) = \ln x$	$x = 18.31$
79. $f(x) = -\ln x$	$x = \frac{1}{2}$
80. $f(x) = 3 \ln x$	$x = \sqrt{0.65}$

Using Properties of Natural Logarithms In Exercises 81–88, use the properties of natural logarithms to rewrite the expression.

81. $\ln e^2$

82. $-\ln e$

83. $e^{\ln 1.8}$

84. $7 \ln e^0$

85. $e \ln 1$

86. $e^{\ln 22}$

87. $\ln e^{\ln e}$

88. $\ln \dfrac{1}{e^4}$

Library of Parent Functions In Exercises 89–92, find the domain, vertical asymptote, and x-intercept of the logarithmic function, and sketch its graph by hand. Verify using a graphing utility.

89. $f(x) = \ln(x - 1)$

90. $h(x) = \ln(x + 1)$

91. $g(x) = \ln(-x)$

92. $f(x) = \ln(3 - x)$

Library of Parent Functions In Exercises 93–98, use the graph of $f(x) = \ln x$ to describe the transformation that yields the graph of g.

93. $g(x) = \ln(x + 8)$

94. $g(x) = \ln(x - 4)$

95. $g(x) = \ln x - 5$

96. $g(x) = \ln x + 4$

97. $g(x) = \ln(x - 1) + 2$

98. $g(x) = \ln(x + 2) - 5$

Analyzing Graphs of Functions In Exercises 99–108, (a) use a graphing utility to graph the function, (b) find the domain, (c) use the graph to find the open intervals on which the function is increasing and decreasing, and (d) approximate any relative maximum or minimum values of the function. Round your results to three decimal places.

99. $f(x) = \dfrac{x}{2} - \ln \dfrac{x}{4}$

100. $g(x) = 6x \ln x$

101. $h(x) = \dfrac{14 \ln x}{x}$

102. $f(x) = \dfrac{x}{\ln x}$

103. $f(x) = \ln \dfrac{x + 2}{x - 1}$

104. $f(x) = \ln \dfrac{2x}{x + 2}$

105. $f(x) = \ln \dfrac{x^2}{10}$

106. $f(x) = \ln \dfrac{x}{x^2 + 1}$

107. $f(x) = \sqrt{\ln x}$

108. $f(x) = (\ln x)^2$

109. Psychology Students in a mathematics class were given an exam and then tested monthly with an equivalent exam. The average scores for the class are given by the human memory model

$$f(t) = 80 - 17 \log_{10}(t + 1), \quad 0 \le t \le 12$$

where t is the time in months.

(a) What was the average score on the original exam $(t = 0)$?

(b) What was the average score after 2 months?

(c) What was the average score after 11 months?

Verify your answers in parts (a), (b), and (c) using a graphing utility.

110. MODELING DATA

The table shows the temperatures T (in degrees Fahrenheit) at which water boils at selected pressures p (in pounds per square inch). (Source: Standard Handbook of Mechanical Engineers)

DATA Pressure, p	Temperature, T
5	162.24°
10	193.21°
14.696 (1 atm)	212.00°
20	227.96°
30	250.33°
40	267.25°
60	292.71°
80	312.03°
100	327.81°

Spreadsheet at LarsonPrecalculus.com

A model that approximates the data is

$$T = 87.97 + 34.96 \ln p + 7.91 \sqrt{p}.$$

(a) Use a graphing utility to plot the data and graph the model in the same viewing window. How well does the model fit the data?

(b) Use the graph to estimate the pressure at which the boiling point of water is 300°F.

(c) Calculate T when the pressure is 74 pounds per square inch. Verify your answer graphically.

111. Finance A principal P, invested at $3\frac{1}{2}\%$ and compounded continuously, increases to an amount K times the original principal after t years, where $T = (\ln K)/0.035$.

(a) Complete the table and interpret your results.

K	1	2	4	6	8	10	12
t							

(b) Use a graphing utility to graph the function.

112. Audiology The relationship between the number of decibels β and the intensity of a sound I in watts per square meter is given by

$$\beta = 10 \log_{10}\left(\frac{I}{10^{-12}}\right).$$

(a) Determine the number of decibels of a sound with an intensity of 1 watt per square meter.

(b) Determine the number of decibels of a sound with an intensity of 10^{-2} watt per square meter.

(c) The intensity of the sound in part (a) is 100 times as great as that in part (b). Is the number of decibels 100 times as great? Explain.

113. Real Estate The model

$$t = 16.625 \ln \frac{x}{x - 750}, \quad x > 750$$

approximates the length of a home mortgage of $150,000 at 6% in terms of the monthly payment. In the model, t is the length of the mortgage in years and x is the monthly payment in dollars.

(a) Use the model to approximate the lengths of a $150,000 mortgage at 6% when the monthly payment is $897.72 and when the monthly payment is $1659.24.

(b) Approximate the total amounts paid over the term of the mortgage with a monthly payment of $897.72 and with a monthly payment of $1659.24. What amount of the total is interest costs for each payment?

114. *Why you should learn it* (p. 192) The rate of ventilation required in a public school classroom depends on the volume of air space per child. The model

$$y = 80.4 - 11 \ln x, \quad 100 \le x \le 1500$$

approximates the minimum required rate of ventilation y (in cubic feet per minute per child) in a classroom with x cubic feet of air space per child.

(a) Use a graphing utility to graph the function and approximate the required rate of ventilation in a room with 300 cubic feet of air space per child.

(b) A classroom of 30 students has an air conditioning system that moves 450 cubic feet of air per minute. Determine the rate of ventilation per child.

(c) Use the graph in part (a) to estimate the minimum required air space per child for the classroom in part (b).

(d) The classroom in part (b) has 960 square feet of floor space and a ceiling that is 12 feet high. Is the rate of ventilation for this classroom adequate? Explain.

Conclusions

True or False? In Exercises 115 and 116, determine whether the statement is true or false. Justify your answer.

115. You can determine the graph of $f(x) = \log_6 x$ by graphing $g(x) = 6^x$ and reflecting it about the x-axis.

116. The graph of $f(x) = \log_3 x$ contains the point $(27, 3)$.

Think About It In Exercises 117–120, find the value of the base b so that the graph of $f(x) = \log_b x$ contains the given point.

117. $(32, 5)$ **118.** $(81, 4)$

119. $\left(\frac{1}{81}, 2\right)$ **120.** $\left(\frac{1}{64}, 3\right)$

Library of Parent Functions In Exercises 121 and 122, determine which equation(s) may be represented by the graph shown. (There may be more than one correct answer.)

121.

122.

(a) $y = \log_2(x + 1) + 2$ (a) $y = \ln(x - 1) + 2$
(b) $y = \log_2(x - 1) + 2$ (b) $y = \ln(x + 2) - 1$
(c) $y = 2 - \log_2(x - 1)$ (c) $y = 2 - \ln(x - 1)$
(d) $y = \log_2(x + 2) + 1$ (d) $y = \ln(x - 2) + 1$

123. Writing Explain why $\log_a x$ is defined only for $0 < a < 1$ and $a > 1$.

124. Exploration Let $f(x) = \ln x$ and $g(x) = x^{1/n}$.

(a) Use a graphing utility to graph g (for $n = 2$) and f in the same viewing window.

(b) Determine which function is increasing at a greater rate as x approaches infinity.

(c) Repeat parts (a) and (b) for $n = 3$, 4, and 5. What do you notice?

125. Exploration

(a) Use a graphing utility to compare the graph of the function $y = \ln x$ with the graph of each function.

$$y_1 = x - 1, \quad y_2 = (x - 1) - \tfrac{1}{2}(x - 1)^2,$$

$$y_3 = (x - 1) - \tfrac{1}{2}(x - 1)^2 + \tfrac{1}{3}(x - 1)^3$$

(b) Identify the pattern of successive polynomials given in part (a). Extend the pattern one more term and compare the graph of the resulting polynomial function with the graph of $y = \ln x$. What do you think the pattern implies?

126. **HOW DO YOU SEE IT?** The figure shows the graphs of $f(x) = 3^x$ and $g(x) = \log_3 x$. [The graphs are labeled m and n.]

(a) Match each function with its graph.

(b) Given that $f(a) = b$, what is $g(b)$? Explain.

127. Exploration

(a) Use a graphing utility to complete the table for the function $f(x) = (\ln x)/x$.

x	1	5	10	10^2	10^4	10^6
$f(x)$						

(b) Use the table in part (a) to determine what value $f(x)$ approaches as x increases without bound. Use the graphing utility to confirm your result.

128. Writing Use a graphing utility to determine how many months it would take for the average score in Example 10 to decrease to 60. Explain your method of solving the problem. Describe another way that you can use the graphing utility to determine the answer. Also, based on the shape of the graph, does the rate at which a student forgets information *increase* or *decrease* with time? Explain.

Cumulative Mixed Review

Factoring a Polynomial In Exercises 129–136, factor the polynomial.

129. $x^2 + 2x - 3$ **130.** $x^2 + 4x - 5$

131. $12x^2 + 5x - 3$ **132.** $16x^2 - 54x - 7$

133. $16x^2 - 25$ **134.** $36x^2 - 49$

135. $2x^3 + x^2 - 45x$ **136.** $3x^3 - 5x^2 - 12x$

Evaluating an Arithmetic Combination of Functions In Exercises 137 and 138, evaluate the function for $f(x) = 3x + 2$ and $g(x) = x^3 - 1$.

137. $(f + g)(2)$ **138.** $(f - g)(-1)$

Using Graphs In Exercises 139–142, solve the equation graphically.

139. $5x - 7 = 7 + 5x$ **140.** $-2x + 3 = 8x$

141. $\sqrt{3x - 2} = 9$ **142.** $\sqrt{x - 11} = x + 2$

3.3   Properties of Logarithms

Change of Base

Most calculators have only two types of log keys, one for common logarithms (base 10) and one for natural logarithms (base e). Although common logs and natural logs are the most frequently used, you may occasionally need to evaluate logarithms to other bases. To do this, you can use the following **change-of-base formula.**

> **Change-of-Base Formula**
>
> Let a, b, and x be positive real numbers such that $a \neq 1$ and $b \neq 1$. Then $\log_a x$ can be converted to a different base using any of the following formulas.
>
> Base b Base 10   Base e
>
> $$\log_a x = \frac{\log_b x}{\log_b a} \qquad \log_a x = \frac{\log_{10} x}{\log_{10} a} \qquad \log_a x = \frac{\ln x}{\ln a}$$

One way to look at the change-of-base formula is that logarithms to base a are simply *constant multiples* of logarithms to base b. The constant multiplier is $1/(\log_b a)$.

EXAMPLE 1   **Changing Bases Using Common Logarithms**

a. $\log_4 25 = \dfrac{\log_{10} 25}{\log_{10} 4}$ $\qquad \log_a x = \dfrac{\log_{10} x}{\log_{10} a}$

$\qquad \approx \dfrac{1.39794}{0.60206}$ $\qquad$ Use a calculator.

$\qquad \approx 2.32$ $\qquad$ Simplify.

b. $\log_3 17 = \dfrac{\log_{10} 17}{\log_{10} 3} \approx \dfrac{1.23045}{0.47712} \approx 2.58$

 ✓ **Checkpoint** 🔊))) *Audio-video solution in English & Spanish at LarsonPrecalculus.com.*

Evaluate $\log_2 12$ using the change-of-base formula and common logarithms.

EXAMPLE 2   **Changing Bases Using Natural Logarithms**

a. $\log_4 25 = \dfrac{\ln 25}{\ln 4}$ $\qquad \log_a x = \dfrac{\ln x}{\ln a}$

$\qquad \approx \dfrac{3.21888}{1.38629}$ $\qquad$ Use a calculator.

$\qquad \approx 2.32$ $\qquad$ Simplify.

b. $\log_3 17 = \dfrac{\ln 17}{\ln 3} \approx \dfrac{2.83321}{1.09861} \approx 2.58$

 ✓ **Checkpoint** 🔊))) *Audio-video solution in English & Spanish at LarsonPrecalculus.com.*

Evaluate $\log_2 12$ using the change-of-base formula and natural logarithms.

Notice in Examples 1 and 2 that the result is the same whether common logarithms or natural logarithms are used in the change-of-base formula.

What you should learn
- ▶ Rewrite logarithms with different bases.
- ▶ Use properties of logarithms to evaluate or rewrite logarithmic expressions.
- ▶ Use properties of logarithms to expand or condense logarithmic expressions.
- ▶ Use logarithmic functions to model and solve real-life problems.

Why you should learn it
Logarithmic functions can be used to model and solve real-life problems, such as the model for the number of decibels of a sound in Exercise 107 on page 208.

Properties of Logarithms

You know from the previous section that the logarithmic function with base a is the *inverse function* of the exponential function with base a. So, it makes sense that the properties of exponents (see Section 3.1) should have corresponding properties involving logarithms. For instance, the exponential property

$$a^0 = 1$$

has the corresponding logarithmic property

$$\log_a 1 = 0.$$

Properties of Logarithms   (See the proof on page 251.)

Let a be a positive real number such that $a \neq 1$, and let n be a real number. If u and v are positive real numbers, then the following properties are true.

	Logarithm with Base a	*Natural Logarithm*
1. Product Property:	$\log_a(uv) = \log_a u + \log_a v$	$\ln(uv) = \ln u + \ln v$
2. Quotient Property:	$\log_a \dfrac{u}{v} = \log_a u - \log_a v$	$\ln \dfrac{u}{v} = \ln u - \ln v$
3. Power Property:	$\log_a u^n = n \log_a u$	$\ln u^n = n \ln u$

Remark

There is no general property that can be used to rewrite $\log_a(u \pm v)$. Specifically, $\log_a(x + y)$ is *not* equal to $\log_a x + \log_a y$.

EXAMPLE 3   Using Properties of Logarithms

Write each logarithm in terms of $\ln 2$ and $\ln 3$.

a. $\ln 6$ **b.** $\ln \dfrac{2}{27}$

Solution

a. $\ln 6 = \ln(2 \cdot 3)$ Rewrite 6 as $2 \cdot 3$.

         $= \ln 2 + \ln 3$ Product Property

b. $\ln \dfrac{2}{27} = \ln 2 - \ln 27$ Quotient Property

         $= \ln 2 - \ln 3^3$ Rewrite 27 as 3^3.

         $= \ln 2 - 3 \ln 3$ Power Property

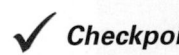 **Checkpoint** ◀))) *Audio-video solution in English & Spanish at LarsonPrecalculus.com.*

Write each logarithm in terms of $\log_{10} 3$ and $\log_{10} 5$.

a. $\log_{10} 75$ **b.** $\log_{10} \dfrac{9}{125}$

EXAMPLE 4   Using Properties of Logarithms

Use the properties of logarithms to verify that $-\log_{10} \frac{1}{100} = \log_{10} 100$.

Solution

    $-\log_{10} \frac{1}{100} = -\log_{10}(100^{-1})$ Rewrite $\frac{1}{100}$ as 100^{-1}.

            $= -(-1) \log_{10} 100$ Power Property

            $= \log_{10} 100$ Simplify.

Use the properties of logarithms to verify that $\ln e^5 = 5$.

Rewriting Logarithmic Expressions

The properties of logarithms are useful for rewriting logarithmic expressions in forms that simplify the operations of algebra. This is true because they convert complicated products, quotients, and exponential forms into simpler sums, differences, and products, respectively.

EXAMPLE 5   Expanding Logarithmic Expressions

Use the properties of logarithms to expand each expression.

a. $\log_4 5x^3y$ **b.** $\ln \dfrac{\sqrt{3x-5}}{7}$

Solution

a. $\log_4 5x^3y = \log_4 5 + \log_4 x^3 + \log_4 y$ Product Property

$\qquad\qquad = \log_4 5 + 3\log_4 x + \log_4 y$ Power Property

b. $\ln \dfrac{\sqrt{3x-5}}{7} = \ln \dfrac{(3x-5)^{1/2}}{7}$ Rewrite radical using rational exponent.

$\qquad\qquad = \ln(3x-5)^{1/2} - \ln 7$ Quotient Property

$\qquad\qquad = \dfrac{1}{2}\ln(3x-5) - \ln 7$ Power Property

✔ **Checkpoint** Audio-video solution in English & Spanish at LarsonPrecalculus.com.

Use the properties of logarithms to expand the expression $\log_3 \dfrac{4x^2}{\sqrt{y}}$.

In Example 5, the properties of logarithms were used to *expand* logarithmic expressions. In Example 6, this procedure is reversed and the properties of logarithms are used to *condense* logarithmic expressions.

EXAMPLE 6   Condensing Logarithmic Expressions

See LarsonPrecalculus.com for an interactive version of this type of example.

Use the properties of logarithms to condense each expression.

a. $\frac{1}{2}\log_{10} x + 3\log_{10}(x+1)$

b. $2\ln(x+2) - \ln x$

c. $\frac{1}{3}[\log_2 x + \log_2(x-4)]$

Solution

a. $\frac{1}{2}\log_{10} x + 3\log_{10}(x+1) = \log_{10} x^{1/2} + \log_{10}(x+1)^3$ Power Property

$\qquad\qquad\qquad = \log_{10}\left[\sqrt{x}(x+1)^3\right]$ Product Property

b. $2\ln(x+2) - \ln x = \ln(x+2)^2 - \ln x$ Power Property

$\qquad\qquad = \ln \dfrac{(x+2)^2}{x}$ Quotient Property

c. $\frac{1}{3}[\log_2 x + \log_2(x-4)] = \frac{1}{3}\{\log_2[x(x-4)]\}$ Product Property

$\qquad\qquad\qquad = \log_2[x(x-4)]^{1/3}$ Power Property

$\qquad\qquad\qquad = \log_2 \sqrt[3]{x(x-4)}$ Rewrite with a radical.

✔ **Checkpoint** Audio-video solution in English & Spanish at LarsonPrecalculus.com.

Use the properties of logarithms to condense the expression

$2[\log_{10}(x+3) - 2\log_{10}(x-2)]$.

Explore the Concept

Use a graphing utility to graph the functions

$$y = \ln x - \ln(x-3)$$

and

$$y = \ln \frac{x}{x-3}$$

in the same viewing window. Does the graphing utility show the functions with the same domain? Should it? Explain your reasoning.

Application

| EXAMPLE 7 | Finding a Mathematical Model |

The table shows the mean distance x from the sun and the period y (the time it takes a planet to orbit the sun) for each of the six planets that are closest to the sun. In the table, the mean distance is given in astronomical units (where the Earth's mean distance is defined as 1.0), and the period is given in years. The points in the table are plotted in Figure 3.18. Find an equation that relates y and x.

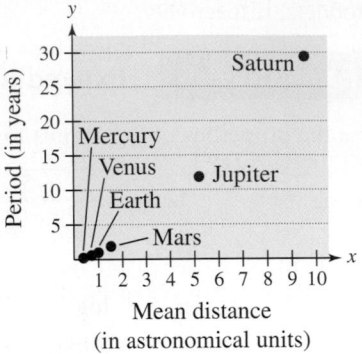

Figure 3.18

	Planet	Mercury	Venus	Earth	Mars	Jupiter	Saturn
DATA	Mean distance, x	0.387	0.723	1.000	1.524	5.203	9.537
	Period, y	0.241	0.615	1.000	1.881	11.863	29.447

Spreadsheet at LarsonPrecalculus.com

Solution

From Figure 3.18, it is not clear how to find an equation that relates y and x. To solve this problem, take the natural log of each of the x- and y-values in the table. This produces the following results.

Planet	Mercury	Venus	Earth	Mars	Jupiter	Saturn
$\ln x = X$	-0.949	-0.324	0.000	0.421	1.649	2.255
$\ln y = Y$	-1.423	-0.486	0.000	0.632	2.473	3.383

Now, by plotting the points in the table, you can see that all six of the points appear to lie in a line, as shown in Figure 3.19. To find an equation of the line through these points, you can use one of the following methods.

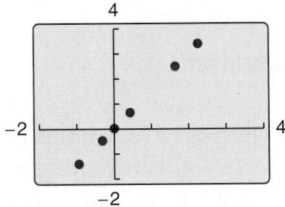

Figure 3.19

Method 1: Algebraic

Choose any two points to determine the slope of the line. Using the two points $(0.421, 0.632)$ and $(0, 0)$, you can determine that the slope of the line is

$$m = \frac{0.632 - 0}{0.421 - 0} \approx 1.5 = \frac{3}{2}.$$

By the point-slope form, the equation of the line is

$$Y = \tfrac{3}{2}X$$

where $Y = \ln y$ and $X = \ln x$. You can therefore conclude that

$$\ln y = \frac{3}{2} \ln x.$$

Method 2: Graphical

Using the *linear regression* feature of a graphing utility, you can find a linear model for the data, as shown in Figure 3.20. You can approximate this model to be $Y = 1.5X$, where $Y = \ln y$ and $X = \ln x$. From the model, you can see that the slope of the line is $\tfrac{3}{2}$. So, you can conclude that $\ln y = \tfrac{3}{2} \ln x$.

```
LinReg
 y=ax+b
 a=1.499936827
 b=1.9880074E-4
 r²=.999999952
 r=.999999976
```

Figure 3.20

✓ **Checkpoint** 🔊))) *Audio-video solution in English & Spanish at LarsonPrecalculus.com.*

Find a logarithmic equation that relates y and x for the following ordered pairs.

$(0.37, 0.51)$, $(1.00, 1.00)$, $(2.72, 1.95)$, $(7.39, 3.79)$, $(20.09, 7.39)$

In Example 7, try to convert the final equation to $y = f(x)$ form. You will get a function of the form $y = ax^b$, which is called a *power model*.

3.3   Exercises

See *CalcChat.com* for tutorial help and worked-out solutions to odd-numbered exercises.
For instructions on how to use a graphing utility, see Appendix A.

Vocabulary and Concept Check

In Exercises 1 and 2, fill in the blank(s).

1. You can evaluate logarithms to any base using the _____ formula.
2. Two properties of logarithms are _____ $= n \log_a u$ and $\ln(uv) =$ _____ .

3. Is $\log_3 24 = \dfrac{\ln 3}{\ln 24}$ or $\log_3 24 = \dfrac{\ln 24}{\ln 3}$ correct?

4. Which property of logarithms can you use to condense the expression $\ln x - \ln 2$?

Procedures and Problem Solving

Changing the Base In Exercises 5–12, rewrite the logarithm as a ratio of (a) common logarithms and (b) natural logarithms.

5. $\log_5 x$
6. $\log_3 x$
7. $\log_{1/6} x$
8. $\log_{1/4} x$
9. $\log_a \frac{3}{10}$
10. $\log_{8a} \frac{4}{5}$
11. $\log_{2.6} x$
12. $\log_{7.1} x$

Changing the Base In Exercises 13–20, evaluate the logarithm using the change-of-base formula. Round your result to three decimal places.

13. $\log_3 7$
14. $\log_9 4$
15. $\log_{1/2} 16$
16. $\log_{1/8} 64$
17. $\log_6 0.9$
18. $\log_4 0.045$
19. $\log_{15} 1460$
20. $\log_{20} 175$

Using Properties of Logarithms In Exercises 21–24, rewrite the expression in terms of $\ln 4$ and $\ln 5$.

21. $\ln 20$
22. $\ln 500$
23. $\ln \frac{25}{4}$
24. $\ln \frac{5}{2}$

Using Properties to Evaluate Logarithms In Exercises 25–28, approximate the logarithm using the properties of logarithms, given the values $\log_b 2 \approx 0.3562$, $\log_b 3 \approx 0.5646$, and $\log_b 5 \approx 0.8271$. Round your result to four decimal places.

25. $\log_b 8$
26. $\log_b 30$
27. $\log_b \frac{16}{25}$
28. $\log_b \sqrt{3}$

Graphing a Logarithm with Any Base In Exercises 29–36, use the change-of-base formula $\log_a x = (\ln x)/(\ln a)$ and a graphing utility to graph the function.

29. $f(x) = \log_3(x + 1)$
30. $f(x) = \log_2(x - 1)$
31. $f(x) = \log_{1/2}(x - 2)$
32. $f(x) = \log_{1/3}(x + 2)$
33. $f(x) = \log_{1/4} x^2$
34. $f(x) = \log_3 \sqrt{x}$
35. $f(x) = \log_5\left(\frac{x}{2}\right)$
36. $f(x) = \log_{1/3}\left(\frac{x}{3}\right)$

Simplifying a Logarithm In Exercises 37–44, use the properties of logarithms to rewrite and simplify the logarithmic expression.

37. $\log_4 8$
38. $\log_9 243$
39. $\log_2 4^2 \cdot 3^4$
40. $\log_3 9^2 \cdot 2^4$
41. $\ln 5e^6$
42. $\ln 8e^3$
43. $\ln \dfrac{6}{e^2}$
44. $\ln \dfrac{e^5}{7}$

Using Properties of Logarithms In Exercises 45 and 46, use the properties of logarithms to verify the equation.

45. $\log_5 \frac{1}{250} = -3 - \log_5 2$
46. $-\ln 24 = -(3 \ln 2 + \ln 3)$

Expanding Logarithmic Expressions In Exercises 47–64, use the properties of logarithms to expand the expression as a sum, difference, and/or constant multiple of logarithms. (Assume all variables are positive.)

47. $\log_{10} 10x$
48. $\log_{10} 100x$
49. $\log_{10} \dfrac{t}{8}$
50. $\log_{10} \dfrac{7}{z}$
51. $\log_8 x^4$
52. $\log_6 z^{-3}$
53. $\ln \sqrt{z}$
54. $\ln \sqrt[3]{t}$
55. $\ln xyz$
56. $\ln \dfrac{xy}{z}$
57. $\log_6 ab^3 c^{-2}$
58. $\log_4 xy^6 z^4$
59. $\ln \sqrt[3]{\dfrac{x^4}{y^3}}$
60. $\ln \sqrt{\dfrac{x^2}{y^3}}$
61. $\ln \dfrac{x^2 - 1}{x^3}, \quad x > 1$
62. $\ln \dfrac{x}{\sqrt{x^2 + 1}}$
63. $\log_b \dfrac{x^4 \sqrt{y}}{z^5}$
64. $\log_b \dfrac{\sqrt{xy^4}}{z^4}$

Algebraic-Graphical-Numerical In Exercises 65–68, (a) use a graphing utility to graph the two equations in the same viewing window and (b) use the *table* feature of the graphing utility to create a table of values for each equation. (c) What do the graphs and tables suggest? Verify your conclusion algebraically.

65. $y_1 = \ln[x^2(x-4)]$

   $y_2 = 2\ln x + \ln(x-4)$

66. $y_1 = \ln 9x^3$

   $y_2 = \ln 9 + 3\ln x$

67. $y_1 = \ln\left(\dfrac{x^4}{x-2}\right)$

   $y_2 = 4\ln x - \ln(x-2)$

68. $y_1 = \ln\left(\dfrac{\sqrt{x}}{x+3}\right)$

   $y_2 = \dfrac{1}{2}\ln x - \ln(x+3)$

Condensing Logarithmic Expressions In Exercises 69–84, use the properties of logarithms to condense the expression.

69. $\ln x + \ln 4$

70. $\ln y + \ln z$

71. $\log_4 z - \log_4 y$

72. $\log_5 8 - \log_5 t$

73. $4\log_3(x+2)$

74. $\dfrac{5}{2}\log_7(z-4)$

75. $\dfrac{1}{2}\ln(x^2+4) + \ln x$

76. $2\ln x + \ln(x+1)$

77. $\ln x - 3\ln(x+1)$

78. $\ln x - 2\ln(x+2)$

79. $\ln(x-2) + \ln 2 - 3\ln y$

80. $3\ln x + 2\ln y - 4\ln z$

81. $\ln x - 2[\ln(x+2) + \ln(x-2)]$

82. $4[\ln z + \ln(z+5)] - 2\ln(z-5)$

83. $\dfrac{1}{3}[2\ln(x+3) + \ln x - \ln(x^2-1)]$

84. $2[\ln x - \ln(x+1) - \ln(x-1)]$

Algebraic-Graphical-Numerical In Exercises 85–88, (a) use a graphing utility to graph the two equations in the same viewing window and (b) use the *table* feature of the graphing utility to create a table of values for each equation. (c) What do the graphs and tables suggest? Verify your conclusion algebraically.

85. $y_1 = 2[\ln 8 - \ln(x^2+1)]$, $y_2 = \ln\left[\dfrac{64}{(x^2+1)^2}\right]$

86. $y_1 = 2[\ln 6 + \ln(x^2+1)]$, $y_2 = \ln[36(x^2+1)^2]$

87. $y_1 = \ln x + \dfrac{1}{2}\ln(x+1)$, $y_2 = \ln(x\sqrt{x+1})$

88. $y_1 = \dfrac{1}{2}\ln x - \ln(x+2)$, $y_2 = \ln\left(\dfrac{\sqrt{x}}{x+2}\right)$

Using Properties to Evaluate Logarithms In Exercises 89–102, find the exact value of the logarithm without using a calculator. If this is not possible, state the reason.

89. $\log_3 9$

90. $\log_6 6$

91. $\log_4 16^{3.4}$

92. $\log_5\left(\dfrac{1}{125}\right)$

93. $\log_2(-4)$

94. $\log_4(-16)$

95. $\log_5 375 - \log_5 3$

96. $\log_4 2 + \log_4 32$

97. $\ln e^3 - \ln e^7$

98. $\ln e^6 - 2\ln e^7$

99. $2\ln e^4$

100. $3\ln e^5$

101. $\ln\dfrac{1}{\sqrt{e}}$

102. $\ln\sqrt[5]{e^3}$

Algebraic-Graphical-Numerical In Exercises 103–106, (a) use a graphing utility to graph the two equations in the same viewing window and (b) use the *table* feature of the graphing utility to create a table of values for each equation. (c) Are the expressions equivalent? Explain. Verify your conclusion algebraically.

103. $y_1 = \ln x^2$, $y_2 = 2\ln x$

104. $y_1 = 2(\ln 2 + \ln x)$, $y_2 = \ln 4x^2$

105. $y_1 = \ln(x-2) + \ln(x+2)$, $y_2 = \ln(x^2-4)$

106. $y_1 = \dfrac{1}{4}\ln[x^4(x^2+1)]$, $y_2 = \ln x + \dfrac{1}{4}\ln(x^2+1)$

107. *Why you should learn it* (p. 203) The relationship between the number of decibels β and the intensity of a sound I in watts per square meter is given by

$$\beta = 10\log_{10}\left(\dfrac{I}{10^{-12}}\right).$$

   (a) Use the properties of logarithms to write the formula in a simpler form.

   (b) Use a graphing utility to complete the table. Verify your answers algebraically.

I	10^{-4}	10^{-6}	10^{-8}	10^{-10}	10^{-12}	10^{-14}
β						

108. Nail Length The table shows the approximate lengths and diameters (in inches) of common nails. Find a logarithmic equation that relates the diameter y of a common nail to its length x.

Length, x	Diameter, y
1	0.072
2	0.120
3	0.148
4	0.203
5	0.238
6	0.284

Spreadsheet at LarsonPrecalculus.com

109. MODELING DATA

A beaker of liquid at an initial temperature of 78°C is placed in a room at a constant temperature of 21°C. The temperature of the liquid is measured every 5 minutes during a half-hour period. The results are recorded as ordered pairs of the form (t, T), where t is the time (in minutes) and T is the temperature (in degrees Celsius). *(Spreadsheet at LarsonPrecalculus.com)*

 (0, 78.0°), (5, 66.0°), (10, 57.5°), (15, 51.2°), (20, 46.3°), (25, 42.5°), (30, 39.6°)

(a) The graph of the temperature of the room should be an asymptote of the graph of the model for the data. Subtract the room temperature from each of the temperatures in the ordered pairs. Use a graphing utility to plot the data points (t, T) and $(t, T - 21)$.

(b) An exponential model for the data $(t, T - 21)$ is given by

$$T - 21 = 54.4(0.964)^t.$$

Solve for T and graph the model. Compare the result with the plot of the original data.

(c) Take the natural logarithms of the revised temperatures. Use the graphing utility to plot the points $(t, \ln(T - 21))$ and observe that the points appear linear. Use the *regression* feature of the graphing utility to fit a line to the data. The resulting line has the form

$$ln(T - 21) = at + b.$$

Use the properties of logarithms to solve for T. Verify that the result is equivalent to the model in part (b).

(d) Fit a rational model to the data. Take the reciprocals of the y-coordinates of the revised data points to generate the points

$$\left(t, \frac{1}{T - 21}\right).$$

Use the graphing utility to plot these points and observe that they appear linear. Use the *regression* feature of the graphing utility to fit a line to the data. The resulting line has the form

$$\frac{1}{T - 21} = at + b.$$

Solve for T and use the graphing utility to graph the rational function and the original data points.

110. Writing
Write a short paragraph explaining why the transformations of the data in Exercise 109 were necessary to obtain the models. Why did taking the logarithms of the temperatures lead to a linear scatter plot? Why did taking the reciprocals of the temperatures lead to a linear scatter plot?

Conclusions

True or False? In Exercises 111–116, determine whether the statement is true or false given that $f(x) = \ln x$, where $x > 0$. Justify your answer.

111. $f(ax) = f(a) + f(x)$, $a > 0$

112. $f(x - a) = f(x) - f(a)$, $x > a$

113. $\sqrt{f(x)} = \frac{1}{2}f(x)$

114. $[f(x)]^n = nf(x)$

115. If $f(x) < 0$, then $0 < x < 1$.

116. If $f(x) > 0$, then $x > e$.

117. Error Analysis Describe the error.

118. Think About It Consider the functions below.

$$f(x) = \ln \frac{x}{2}, \quad g(x) = \frac{\ln x}{\ln 2}, \quad h(x) = \ln x - \ln 2$$

Which two functions have identical graphs? Verify your answer by using a graphing utility to graph all three functions in the same viewing window.

119. Exploration For how many integers between 1 and 20 can the natural logarithms be approximated given that $\ln 2 \approx 0.6931$, $\ln 3 \approx 1.0986$, and $\ln 5 \approx 1.6094$? Approximate these logarithms without a calculator.

120. HOW DO YOU SEE IT? The figure shows the graphs of $y = \ln x$, $y = \ln x^2$, $y = \ln 2x$, and $y = \ln 2$. Match each function with its graph. (The graphs are labeled A through D.) Explain your reasoning.

121. Think About It Does $y_1 = \ln[x(x - 2)]$ have the same domain as $y_2 = \ln x + \ln(x - 2)$? Explain.

122. Proof Prove that $\dfrac{\log_a x}{\log_{a/b} x} = 1 + \log_a \dfrac{1}{b}$.

Cumulative Mixed Review

Using Properties of Exponents In Exercises 123–126, simplify the expression.

123. $(64x^3y^4)^{-3}(8x^3y^2)^4$

124. $xy(x^{-1} + y^{-1})^{-1}$

125. $\dfrac{24xy^{-2}}{16x^{-3}y}$

126. $\left(\dfrac{2x^3}{3y}\right)^{-3}$

3.4 Solving Exponential and Logarithmic Equations

Introduction

So far in this chapter, you have studied the definitions, graphs, and properties of exponential and logarithmic functions. In this section, you will study procedures for *solving equations* involving exponential and logarithmic functions.

There are two basic strategies for solving exponential or logarithmic equations. The first is based on the One-to-One Properties and the second is based on the Inverse Properties. For $a > 0$ and $a \neq 1$, the following properties are true for all x and y for which $\log_a x$ and $\log_a y$ are defined.

One-to-One Properties

$a^x = a^y$ if and only if $x = y$.

$\log_a x = \log_a y$ if and only if $x = y$.

Inverse Properties

$a^{\log_a x} = x$

$\log_a a^x = x$

EXAMPLE 1   Solving Simple Equations

	Original Equation	Rewritten Equation	Solution	Property
a.	$2^x = 32$	$2^x = 2^5$	$x = 5$	One-to-One
b.	$\log_4 x - \log_4 8 = 0$	$\log_4 x = \log_4 8$	$x = 8$	One-to-One
c.	$\ln x - \ln 3 = 0$	$\ln x = \ln 3$	$x = 3$	One-to-One
d.	$\left(\frac{1}{3}\right)^x = 9$	$3^{-x} = 3^2$	$x = -2$	One-to-One
e.	$e^x = 7$	$\ln e^x = \ln 7$	$x = \ln 7$	Inverse
f.	$\ln x = -3$	$e^{\ln x} = e^{-3}$	$x = e^{-3}$	Inverse
g.	$\log_{10} x = -1$	$10^{\log_{10} x} = 10^{-1}$	$x = 10^{-1} = \frac{1}{10}$	Inverse
h.	$\log_3 x = 4$	$3^{\log_3 x} = 3^4$	$x = 81$	Inverse

✓ **Checkpoint** Audio-video solution in English & Spanish at *LarsonPrecalculus.com*.

Solve each equation for x.

a. $2^x = 512$ **b.** $\log_6 x = 3$ **c.** $5 - e^x = 0$ **d.** $9^x = \frac{1}{3}$

The strategies used in Example 1 are summarized as follows.

Strategies for Solving Exponential and Logarithmic Equations

1. Rewrite the original equation in a form that allows the use of the One-to-One Properties of exponential or logarithmic functions.

2. Rewrite an *exponential* equation in logarithmic form and apply the Inverse Property of logarithmic functions.

3. Rewrite a *logarithmic* equation in exponential form and apply the Inverse Property of exponential functions.

Solving Exponential Equations

EXAMPLE 2 Solving Exponential Equations

Solve each equation.

a. $e^x = 72$

b. $3(2^x) = 42$

Algebraic Solution

a.

$e^x = 72$	Write original equation.
$\ln e^x = \ln 72$	Take natural log of each side.
$x = \ln 72$	Inverse Property
$x \approx 4.28$	Use a calculator.

The solution is $x = \ln 72 \approx 4.28$. Check this in the original equation.

b.

$3(2^x) = 42$	Write original equation.
$2^x = 14$	Divide each side by 3.
$\log_2 2^x = \log_2 14$	Take log (base 2) of each side.
$x = \log_2 14$	Inverse Property
$x = \dfrac{\ln 14}{\ln 2}$	Change-of-base formula
$x \approx 3.81$	Use a calculator.

The solution is $x = \log_2 14 \approx 3.81$. Check this in the original equation.

Graphical Solution

To solve an equation using a graphing utility, you can graph the left- and right-hand sides of the equation and use the *intersect* feature.

a.

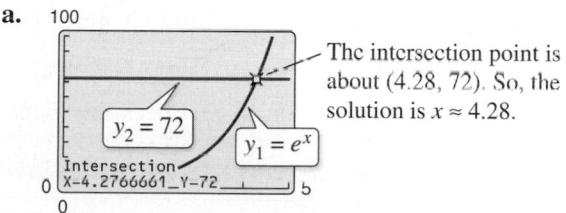

The intersection point is about (4.28, 72). So, the solution is $x \approx 4.28$.

b.

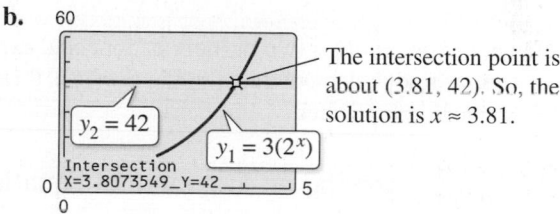

The intersection point is about (3.81, 42). So, the solution is $x \approx 3.81$.

✓ **Checkpoint** ◀))) *Audio-video solution in English & Spanish at LarsonPrecalculus.com.*

Solve (a) $e^x = 10$ and (b) $2(5^x) = 32$.

EXAMPLE 3 Solving an Exponential Equation

Solve $4e^{2x} - 3 = 2$.

Algebraic Solution

$4e^{2x} - 3 = 2$	Write original equation.
$4e^{2x} = 5$	Add 3 to each side.
$e^{2x} = \dfrac{5}{4}$	Divide each side by 4.
$\ln e^{2x} = \ln \dfrac{5}{4}$	Take natural log of each side.
$2x = \ln \dfrac{5}{4}$	Inverse Property
$x = \dfrac{1}{2} \ln \dfrac{5}{4}$	Divide each side by 2.
$x \approx 0.11$	Use a calculator.

The solution is $x = \frac{1}{2} \ln \frac{5}{4} \approx 0.11$. Check this in the original equation.

Graphical Solution

Rather than using the procedure in Example 2, another way to solve the equation graphically is first to rewrite the equation as $4e^{2x} - 5 = 0$, and then use a graphing utility to graph $y = 4e^{2x} - 5$. Use the *zero* or *root* feature of the graphing utility to approximate the value of x for which $y = 0$, as shown in the figure.

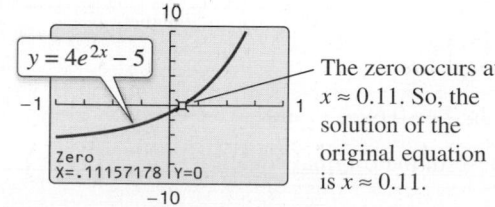

The zero occurs at $x \approx 0.11$. So, the solution of the original equation is $x \approx 0.11$.

✓ **Checkpoint** ◀))) *Audio-video solution in English & Spanish at LarsonPrecalculus.com.*

Solve $2e^{3x} + 5 = 29$.

EXAMPLE 4   Solving an Exponential Equation

Solve $2(3^{2t-5}) - 4 = 11$.

Solution

$2(3^{2t-5}) - 4 = 11$	Write original equation.
$2(3^{2t-5}) = 15$	Add 4 to each side.
$3^{2t-5} = \frac{15}{2}$	Divide each side by 2.
$\log_3 3^{2t-5} = \log_3 \frac{15}{2}$	Take log (base 3) of each side.
$2t - 5 = \log_3 \frac{15}{2}$	Inverse Property
$2t = 5 + \log_3 7.5$	Add 5 to each side.
$t = \frac{5}{2} + \frac{1}{2}\log_3 7.5$	Divide each side by 2.
$t \approx 3.42$	Use a calculator.

The solution is $t = \frac{5}{2} + \frac{1}{2}\log_3 7.5 \approx 3.42$. Check this in the original equation.

✓ **Checkpoint** Audio-video solution in English & Spanish at LarsonPrecalculus.com.

Solve $6(2^{t+5}) + 4 = 11$.

> **Remark**
>
> Remember that to evaluate a logarithm such as $\log_3 7.5$, you need to use the change-of-base formula.
>
> $$\log_3 7.5 = \frac{\ln 7.5}{\ln 3} \approx 1.834$$

When an equation involves two or more exponential expressions, you can still use a procedure similar to that demonstrated in the previous three examples. However, the algebra is a bit more complicated.

EXAMPLE 5   Solving an Exponential Equation in Quadratic Form

Solve $e^{2x} - 3e^x + 2 = 0$.

Algebraic Solution

$e^{2x} - 3e^x + 2 = 0$	Write original equation.
$(e^x)^2 - 3e^x + 2 = 0$	Write in quadratic form.
$(e^x - 2)(e^x - 1) = 0$	Factor.
$e^x - 2 = 0$	Set 1st factor equal to 0.
$e^x = 2$	Add 2 to each side.
$x = \ln 2$	Solution
$e^x - 1 = 0$	Set 2nd factor equal to 0.
$e^x = 1$	Add 1 to each side.
$x = \ln 1$	Inverse Property
$x = 0$	Solution

The solutions are

$$x = \ln 2 \approx 0.69 \quad \text{and} \quad x = 0.$$

Check these in the original equation.

Graphical Solution

Use a graphing utility to graph $y = e^{2x} - 3e^x + 2$ and then find the zeros.

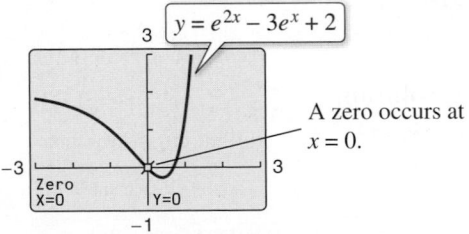

A zero occurs at $x = 0$.

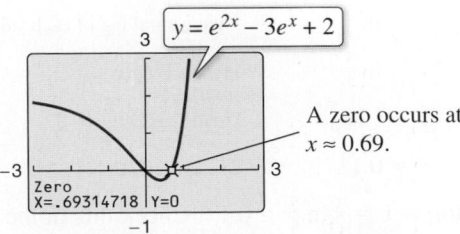

A zero occurs at $x \approx 0.69$.

From the figures, you can conclude that the solutions are $x = 0$ and $x \approx 0.69$.

✓ **Checkpoint** Audio-video solution in English & Spanish at LarsonPrecalculus.com.

Solve $e^{2x} - 7e^x + 12 = 0$.

Solving Logarithmic Equations

To solve a logarithmic equation, you can write it in exponential form.

$\ln x = 3$ Logarithmic form

$e^{\ln x} = e^3$ Exponentiate each side.

$x = e^3$ Exponential form

This procedure is called *exponentiating* each side of an equation. It is applied after the logarithmic expression has been isolated.

EXAMPLE 6   Solving Logarithmic Equations

Solve each logarithmic equation.

a. $\ln 3x = 2$

b. $\log_3(5x - 1) = \log_3(x + 7)$

Solution

a.
$\ln 3x = 2$	Write original equation.
$e^{\ln 3x} = e^2$	Exponentiate each side.
$3x = e^2$	Inverse Property
$x = \frac{1}{3}e^2$	Multiply each side by $\frac{1}{3}$.
$x \approx 2.46$	Use a calculator.

The solution is $x = \frac{1}{3}e^2 \approx 2.46$. Check this in the original equation.

b.
$\log_3(5x - 1) = \log_3(x + 7)$	Write original equation.
$5x - 1 = x + 7$	One-to-One Property
$x = 2$	Solve for x.

The solution is $x = 2$. Check this in the original equation.

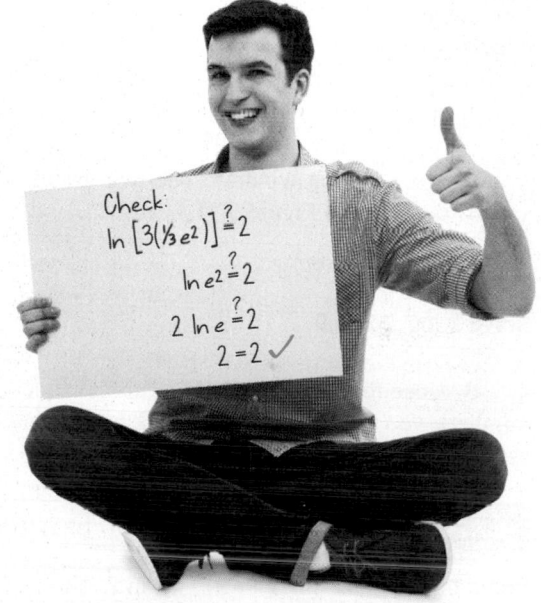

Check:
$$\ln\left[3\left(\tfrac{1}{3}e^2\right)\right] \overset{?}{=} 2$$
$$\ln e^2 \overset{?}{=} 2$$
$$2 \ln e \overset{?}{=} 2$$
$$2 = 2 \checkmark$$

✓ **Checkpoint** 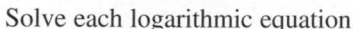 *Audio-video solution in English & Spanish at LarsonPrecalculus.com.*

Solve each logarithmic equation.

a. $\ln x = \frac{2}{3}$ **b.** $\log_2(2x - 3) = \log_2(x + 4)$

EXAMPLE 7   Solving a Logarithmic Equation

Solve $5 + 2 \ln x = 4$.

Algebraic Solution

$5 + 2 \ln x = 4$	Write original equation.
$2 \ln x = -1$	Subtract 5 from each side.
$\ln x = -\frac{1}{2}$	Divide each side by 2.
$e^{\ln x} = e^{-1/2}$	Exponentiate each side.
$x = e^{-1/2}$	Inverse Property
$x \approx 0.61$	Use a calculator.

The solution is $x = e^{-1/2} \approx 0.61$. Check this in the original equation.

Graphical Solution

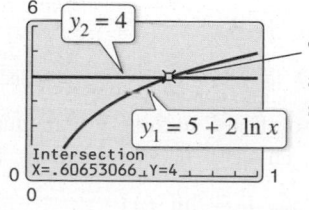

The intersection point is about (0.61, 4). So, the solution is $x \approx 0.61$.

✓ **Checkpoint** *Audio-video solution in English & Spanish at LarsonPrecalculus.com.*

Solve $7 + 3 \ln x = 5$.

EXAMPLE 8   Solving a Logarithmic Equation

Solve $2 \log_5 3x = 4$.

Solution

$2 \log_5 3x = 4$	Write original equation.
$\log_5 3x = 2$	Divide each side by 2.
$5^{\log_5 3x} = 5^2$	Exponentiate each side (base 5).
$3x = 25$	Inverse Property
$x = \frac{25}{3}$	Divide each side by 3.

The solution is $x = \frac{25}{3}$. Check this in the original equation. Or, perform a graphical check by graphing

$$y_1 = 2 \log_5 3x = 2\left(\frac{\log_{10} 3x}{\log_{10} 5}\right) \quad \text{and} \quad y_2 = 4$$

in the same viewing window. The two graphs should intersect at $x = \frac{25}{3} \approx 8.33$ and $y = 4$, as shown in Figure 3.21.

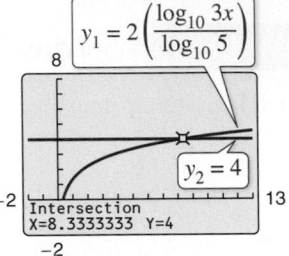

Figure 3.21

✓ **Checkpoint** ◀))) Audio-video solution in English & Spanish at LarsonPrecalculus.com.

Solve $3 \log_4 6x = 9$.

Because the domain of a logarithmic function generally does not include all real numbers, you should be sure to check for extraneous solutions of logarithmic equations, as shown in the next example.

EXAMPLE 9   Checking for Extraneous Solutions

Solve $\ln(x - 2) + \ln(2x - 3) = 2 \ln x$.

Algebraic Solution

$\ln(x - 2) + \ln(2x - 3) = 2 \ln x$	Write original equation.
$\ln[(x - 2)(2x - 3)] = \ln x^2$	Use properties of logarithms.
$\ln(2x^2 - 7x + 6) = \ln x^2$	Multiply binomials.
$2x^2 - 7x + 6 = x^2$	One-to-One Property
$x^2 - 7x + 6 = 0$	Write in general form.
$(x - 6)(x - 1) = 0$	Factor.
$x - 6 = 0 \implies x = 6$	Set 1st factor equal to 0.
$x - 1 = 0 \implies x = 1$	Set 2nd factor equal to 0.

Finally, by checking these two "solutions" in the original equation, you can conclude that $x = 1$ is not valid. This is because when $x = 1$,

$$\ln(x - 2) + \ln(2x - 3) = \ln(-1) + \ln(-1)$$

which is invalid because -1 is not in the domain of the natural logarithmic function. So, the only solution is $x = 6$.

Graphical Solution

First, rewrite the original equation as

$$\ln(x - 2) + \ln(2x - 3) - 2 \ln x = 0.$$

Then, use a graphing utility to graph the equation

$$y = \ln(x - 2) + \ln(2x - 3) - 2 \ln x$$

and find the zeros, as shown in the figure.

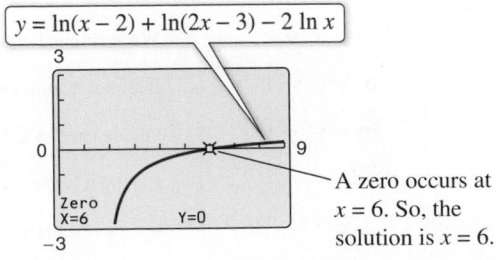

A zero occurs at $x = 6$. So, the solution is $x = 6$.

✓ **Checkpoint** ◀))) Audio-video solution in English & Spanish at LarsonPrecalculus.com.

Solve $\log_{10} x + \log_{10}(x - 9) = 1$.

EXAMPLE 10   The Change-of-Base Formula

Prove the change-of-base formula: $\log_a x = \dfrac{\log_b x}{\log_b a}$.

Solution

Begin by letting $y = \log_a x$ and writing the equivalent exponential form

$$a^y = x.$$

Now, taking the logarithms *with base b* of each side produces the following.

$$\log_b a^y = \log_b x$$

$$y \log_b a = \log_b x \qquad \text{Power Property}$$

$$y = \frac{\log_b x}{\log_b a} \qquad \text{Divide each side by } \log_b a.$$

$$\log_a x = \frac{\log_b x}{\log_b a} \qquad \text{Replace } y \text{ with } \log_a x.$$

✓ **Checkpoint** Audio-video solution in English & Spanish at LarsonPrecalculus.com.

Prove that $\log_a \dfrac{1}{x} = -\log_a x$. ■

Equations that involve combinations of algebraic functions, exponential functions, and logarithmic functions can be very difficult to solve by algebraic procedures. Here again, you can take advantage of a graphing utility.

EXAMPLE 11   Approximating the Solution of an Equation

Approximate (to three decimal places) the solution of $\ln x = x^2 - 2$.

Solution

First, rewrite the equation as

$$\ln x - x^2 + 2 = 0.$$

Then, use a graphing utility to graph

$$y = -x^2 + 2 + \ln x$$

as shown in Figure 3.22. From this graph, you can see that the equation has two solutions. Next, using the *zero* or *root* feature, you can approximate the two solutions to be $x \approx 0.138$ and $x \approx 1.564$.

Figure 3.22

Check

$$\ln x = x^2 - 2 \qquad \text{Write original equation.}$$

$$\ln(0.138) \overset{?}{\approx} (0.138)^2 - 2 \qquad \text{Substitute 0.138 for } x.$$

$$-1.9805 \approx -1.9810 \qquad \text{Solution checks. ✓}$$

$$\ln(1.564) \overset{?}{\approx} (1.564)^2 - 2 \qquad \text{Substitute 1.564 for } x.$$

$$0.4472 \approx 0.4461 \qquad \text{Solution checks. ✓}$$

So, the two solutions $x \approx 0.138$ and $x \approx 1.564$ seem reasonable.

✓ **Checkpoint** Audio-video solution in English & Spanish at LarsonPrecalculus.com.

Approximate (to three decimal places) the solution of $5e^{0.3x} = 17$. ■

Applications

EXAMPLE 12 Doubling an Investment

See LarsonPrecalculus.com for an interactive version of this type of example.

You have deposited $500 in an account that pays 6.75% interest, compounded continuously. How long will it take your money to double?

Solution

Using the formula for continuous compounding, you can find that the balance in the account is $A = Pe^{rt} = 500e^{0.0675t}$. To find the time required for the balance to double, let $A = 1000$ and solve the resulting equation for t.

$500e^{0.0675t} = 1000$	Substitute 1000 for A.
$e^{0.0675t} = 2$	Divide each side by 500.
$\ln e^{0.0675t} = \ln 2$	Take natural log of each side.
$0.0675t = \ln 2$	Inverse Property
$t = \dfrac{\ln 2}{0.0675}$	Divide each side by 0.0675.
$t \approx 10.27$	Use a calculator.

The balance in the account will double after approximately 10.27 years. This result is demonstrated graphically in Figure 3.23.

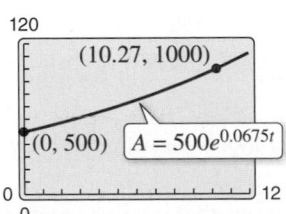

Figure 3.23

✓ **Checkpoint** 🔊 *Audio-video solution in English & Spanish at LarsonPrecalculus.com.*

You invest $500 at an annual interest rate of 5.25%, compounded continuously. How long will it take your money to double? Compare your result with that of Example 12.

EXAMPLE 13 Average Salary for Public School Teachers

From 2004 through 2013, the average salary y (in thousands of dollars) for public school teachers for the year t can be modeled by the equation $y = 33.374 + 9.162 \ln t$, where $t = 4$ represents 2004. During which year did the average salary for public school teachers reach $50 thousand? (Source: National Center for Education Statistics)

Solution

$33.374 + 9.162 \ln t = y$	Write original equation.
$33.374 + 9.162 \ln t = 50$	Substitute 50 for y.
$9.162 \ln t = 16.626$	Subtract 33.374 from each side.
$\ln t = \dfrac{16.626}{9.162}$	Divide each side by 9.162.
$e^{\ln t} = e^{16.626/9.162}$	Exponentiate each side.
$t = e^{16.626/9.162}$	Inverse Property
$t \approx 6.14$	Use a calculator.

The solution is $t \approx 6.14$ years. Because $t = 4$ represents 2004, it follows that the average salary for public school teachers reached $50 thousand in 2006.

✓ **Checkpoint** 🔊 *Audio-video solution in English & Spanish at LarsonPrecalculus.com.*

In Example 13, during which year did the average salary reach $52.5 thousand? ■

Teacher

3.4   Exercises

See *CalcChat.com* for tutorial help and worked-out solutions to odd-numbered exercises.
For instructions on how to use a graphing utility, see Appendix A.

Vocabulary and Concept Check

In Exercises 1 and 2, fill in the blank.

1. To solve exponential and logarithmic equations, you can use the following One-to-One and Inverse Properties.

  (a) $a^x = a^y$ if and only if _____ .   (b) $\log_a x = \log_a y$ if and only if _____ .

  (c) $a^{\log_a x} =$ _____   (d) $\log_a a^x =$ _____

2. A(n) _____ solution does not satisfy the original equation.

3. What is the value of $\ln e^7$?

4. Can you solve $5^x = 125$ using a One-to-One Property?

5. What is the first step in solving the equation $3 + \ln x = 10$?

6. Do you solve $\log_4 x = 2$ by using a One-to-One Property or an Inverse Property?

Procedures and Problem Solving

Checking Solutions   In Exercises 7–14, determine whether each x-value is a solution of the equation.

7. $4^{2x-7} = 64$
  (a) $x = 5$
  (b) $x = 2$

8. $2^{3x+1} = 128$
  (a) $x = -1$
  (b) $x = 2$

9. $3e^{x+2} = 75$
  (a) $x = -2 + e^{25}$
  (b) $x = -2 + \ln 25$
  (c) $x \approx 1.2189$

10. $4e^{x-1} = 60$
  (a) $x = 1 + \ln 15$
  (b) $x \approx 3.7081$
  (c) $x = \ln 16$

11. $\log_4(3x) = 3$
  (a) $x \approx 21.3560$
  (b) $x = -4$
  (c) $x = \frac{64}{3}$

12. $\log_6\left(\frac{5}{3}x\right) = 2$
  (a) $x \approx 20.2882$
  (b) $x = \frac{108}{5}$
  (c) $x = 21.6$

13. $\ln(x - 1) = 3.8$
  (a) $x = 1 + e^{3.8}$
  (b) $x \approx 45.7012$
  (c) $x = 1 + \ln 3.8$

14. $\ln(2 + x) = 2.5$
  (a) $x = e^{2.5} - 2$
  (b) $x \approx \frac{4073}{400}$
  (c) $x = \frac{1}{2}$

Solving Equations Graphically   In Exercises 15–22, use a graphing utility to graph f and g in the same viewing window. Approximate the point of intersection of the graphs of f and g. Then solve the equation $f(x) = g(x)$ algebraically.

15. $f(x) = 64^x$
  $g(x) = 8$

16. $f(x) = 27^x$
  $g(x) = 9$

17. $f(x) = 5^{x-2} - 15$
  $g(x) = 10$

18. $f(x) = 2^{-x+1} - 3$
  $g(x) = 13$

19. $f(x) = 4 \log_3 x$
  $g(x) = 20$

20. $f(x) = 3 \log_5 x$
  $g(x) = 6$

21. $f(x) = \ln e^{x+1}$
  $g(x) = 2x + 5$

22. $f(x) = \ln e^{x-2}$
  $g(x) = 3x + 2$

Solving an Exponential Equation   In Exercises 23–36, solve the exponential equation.

23. $4^x = 16$

24. $3^x = 243$

25. $5^x = \frac{1}{625}$

26. $7^x = \frac{1}{49}$

27. $\left(\frac{1}{8}\right)^x = 64$

28. $\left(\frac{1}{2}\right)^x = 32$

29. $\left(\frac{2}{3}\right)^x = \frac{81}{16}$

30. $\left(\frac{3}{4}\right)^x = \frac{64}{27}$

31. $e^x = 14$

32. $e^x = 66$

33. $6(10^x) = 216$

34. $5(8^x) = 325$

35. $2^{x+3} = 256$

36. $4^{x-1} = 256$

Solving a Logarithmic Equation   In Exercises 37–46, solve the logarithmic equation.

37. $\ln x - \ln 5 = 0$

38. $\ln x - \ln 2 = 0$

39. $\ln x = -9$

40. $\ln x = -14$

41. $\log_x 625 = 4$

42. $\log_x 81 = 2$

43. $\log_{11} x = -1$

44. $\log_{10} x = -\frac{1}{4}$

45. $\ln(2x - 1) = 5$

46. $\ln(3x + 5) = 8$

Using Inverse Properties   In Exercises 47–54, simplify the expression.

47. $\ln e^{x^2}$

48. $\ln e^{2x-1}$

49. $e^{\ln(x^2-3)}$

50. $e^{\ln x^2}$

51. $-1 + \ln e^{2x}$

52. $-4 + e^{\ln x^4}$

53. $5 - e^{\ln(x^2+1)}$

54. $3 - \ln(e^{x^2+2})$

Solving an Exponential Equation In Exercises 55–80, solve the exponential equation algebraically. Round your result to three decimal places. Use a graphing utility to verify your answer.

55. $8^{3x} = 360$

56. $6^{5x} = 3000$

57. $5^{-t/2} = 0.20$

58. $4^{-2t} = 0.0625$

59. $250e^{0.02x} = 10,000$

60. $100e^{0.005x} = 125,000$

61. $500e^{-x} = 300$

62. $1000e^{-4x} = 75$

63. $7 - 2e^x = 1$

64. $-14 + 3e^x = 11$

65. $5(2^{3-x}) - 13 = 100$

66. $6(8^{-2-x}) + 15 = 2601$

67. $\left(1 + \dfrac{0.10}{12}\right)^{12t} = 2$

68. $\left(16 + \dfrac{0.878}{26}\right)^{3t} = 30$

69. $5000\left[\dfrac{(1 + 0.005)^x}{0.005}\right] = 250,000$

70. $250\left[\dfrac{(1 + 0.01)^x}{0.01}\right] = 150,000$

71. $e^{2x} - 4e^x - 5 = 0$

72. $e^{2x} - e^x - 6 = 0$

73. $e^x = e^{x^2 - 2}$

74. $e^{2x} = e^{x^2 - 8}$

75. $e^{x^2 - 3x} = e^{x - 2}$

76. $e^{-x^2} = e^{x^2 - 2x}$

77. $\dfrac{400}{1 + e^{-x}} = 350$

78. $\dfrac{525}{1 + e^{-x}} = 275$

79. $\dfrac{40}{1 - 5e^{-0.01x}} = 200$

80. $\dfrac{50}{1 - 2e^{-0.001x}} = 1000$

Algebraic-Graphical-Numerical In Exercises 81–84, (a) complete the table to find an interval containing the solution of the equation, (b) use a graphing utility to graph both sides of the equation to estimate the solution, and (c) solve the equation algebraically. Round your results to three decimal places.

81. $e^{3x} = 12$

x	0.6	0.7	0.8	0.9	1.0
e^{3x}					

82. $4e^{5x} = 24$

x	0.1	0.2	0.3	0.4	0.5
$4e^{5x}$					

83. $20(100 - e^{x/2}) = 500$

x	5	6	7	8	9
$20(100 - e^{x/2})$					

84. $11(77 - e^{x-4}) = 264$

x	5	6	7	8	9
$11(77 - e^{x-4})$					

Solving an Exponential Equation Graphically In Exercises 85–88, use the *zero* or *root* feature or the *zoom* and *trace* features of a graphing utility to approximate the solution of the exponential equation accurate to three decimal places.

85. $\left(1 + \dfrac{0.065}{365}\right)^{365t} = 4$

86. $\left(4 - \dfrac{2.471}{40}\right)^{9t} = 21$

87. $\dfrac{7000}{5 + e^{3x}} = 2$

88. $\dfrac{119}{e^{6x} - 14} = 7$

Finding the Zero of a Function In Exercises 89–92, use a graphing utility to graph the function and approximate its zero accurate to three decimal places.

89. $g(x) = 6e^{1-x} - 25$

90. $f(x) = 3e^{3x/2} - 962$

91. $g(t) = e^{0.09t} - 3$

92. $h(t) = e^{-0.125t} - 8$

Solving a Logarithmic Equation In Exercises 93–114, solve the logarithmic equation algebraically. Round the result to three decimal places. Verify your answer(s) using a graphing utility.

93. $\ln x = -3$

94. $\ln x = -4$

95. $\ln 4x = 2.1$

96. $\ln 2x = 1.5$

97. $\log_5(3x + 2) = \log_5(-x)$

98. $\log_9(4 + x) = \log_9 2x$

99. $-2 + 2\ln 3x = 17$

100. $3 + 2\ln x = 10$

101. $7\log_4(0.6x) = 12$

102. $4\log_{10}(x - 6) = 11$

103. $\log_{10}(z^2 + 19) = 2$

104. $\log_{12} x^2 = 6$

105. $\ln \sqrt{x + 2} = 1$

106. $\ln \sqrt{x - 8} = 5$

107. $\ln(x + 1)^2 = 2$

108. $\ln(x - 4)^2 = 5$

109. $\log_4 x - \log_4(x - 1) = \frac{1}{2}$

110. $\log_3 x + \log_3(x - 8) = 2$

111. $\ln(x + 5) = \ln(x - 1) + \ln(x + 1)$

112. $\ln(x + 1) - \ln(x - 2) = \ln x$

113. $\log_{10} 8x - \log_{10}\left(1 + \sqrt{x}\right) = 2$

114. $\log_{10} 4x - \log_{10}\left(12 + \sqrt{x}\right) = 2$

Algebraic-Graphical-Numerical In Exercises 115–118, (a) complete the table to find an interval containing the solution of the equation, (b) use a graphing utility to graph both sides of the equation to estimate the solution, and (c) solve the equation algebraically. Round your results to three decimal places.

115. $\ln 2x = 2.4$

x	2	3	4	5	6
$\ln 2x$					

116. $3\ln 5x = 10$

x	4	5	6	7	8
$3\ln 5x$					

117. $6 \log_3(0.5x) = 11$

x	12	13	14	15	16
$6 \log_3(0.5x)$					

118. $5 \log_{10}(x - 2) = 11$

x	150	155	160	165	170
$5 \log_{10}(x - 2)$					

Approximating the Solution of an Equation   In Exercises 119–124, use the *zero* or *root* feature of a graphing utility to approximate the solution of the logarithmic equation.

119. $\log_{10} x = x^3 - 3$ **120.** $\log_{10} x = (x - 3)^2$

121. $\log_{10} x + e^{0.5x} = 6$ **122.** $e^x \log_{10} x = 7$

123. $\ln(x + 2) - 3^{x-2} + 10 = 5$

124. $\ln x^2 - e^x = -3$ $\ln x^2$

Finding the Point of Intersection   In Exercises 125–130, use a graphing utility to approximate the point of intersection of the graphs. Round your result to three decimal places.

125. $y_1 = 7$
$y_2 = 2^{x-1} - 5$

126. $y_1 = 4$
$y_2 = 3^{x+1} - 2$

127. $y_1 = 80$
$y_2 = 4e^{-0.2x}$

128. $y_1 = 500$
$y_2 = 1500e^{-x/2}$

129. $y_1 = 3.25$
$y_2 = \frac{1}{2} \ln(x + 2)$

130. $y_1 = 1.05$
$y_2 = \ln \sqrt{x - 2}$

Solving Exponential and Logarithmic Equations   In Exercises 131–138, solve the equation algebraically. Round the result to three decimal places. Verify your answer using a graphing utility.

131. $2x^2 e^{2x} + 2x e^{2x} = 0$ **132.** $-x^2 e^{-x} + 2x e^{-x} = 0$

133. $-xe^{-x} + e^{-x} = 0$ **134.** $e^{-2x} - 2xe^{-2x} = 0$

135. $2x \ln x + x = 0$ **136.** $\frac{1 - \ln x}{x^2} = 0$

137. $\frac{1 + \ln x}{2} = 0$ **138.** $3x \ln\left(\frac{1}{x}\right) - x = 0$

Solving a Model for x In Exercises 139–142, the equation represents the given type of model, which you will use in Section 3.5. Solve the equation for x.

Model Type	*Equation*
139. Exponential growth	$y = ae^{bx}$
140. Exponential decay	$y = ae^{-bx}$
141. Gaussian	$y = ae^{-(x-b)^2/c}$
142. Logarithmic	$y = a + b \ln x$

Doubling and Tripling an Investment   In Exercises 143–146, find the time required for a $1000 investment to (a) double at interest rate r, compounded continuously, and (b) triple at interest rate r, compounded continuously. Round your results to two decimal places.

143. $r = 7\%$ **144.** $r = 6\%$

145. $r = 2.5\%$ **146.** $r = 3.75\%$

147. Economics   The percent p (in decimal form) of the United States population who own a smartphone is given by

$$p = \frac{1}{1 + e^{-(t-93)/22.5}}$$

where t is the number of months after smartphones were available on the market. Find the number of months t when the percent of the population owning smartphones is (a) 50% and (b) 80%.

148. *Why you should learn it* *(p. 210)* The percent m of American males between the ages of 18 and 24 who are no more than x inches tall is modeled by

$$m(x) = \frac{100}{1 + e^{-0.6114(x - 69.71)}}$$

and the percent f of American females between the ages of 18 and 24 who are no more than x inches tall is modeled by

$$f(x) = \frac{100}{1 + e^{-0.66607(x - 64.51)}}.$$

(Source: U.S. National Center for Health Statistics)

(a) Use a graphing utility to graph the two functions in the same viewing window.

(b) Use the graphs in part (a) to determine the horizontal asymptotes of the functions. Interpret their meanings in the context of the problem.

(c) What is the average height for each sex?

149. Finance   The numbers y of commercial banks in the United States from 2007 through 2013 can be modeled by

$$y = 11{,}912 - 2340.1 \ln t, \quad 7 \le t \le 13$$

where t represents the year, with $t = 7$ corresponding to 2007. In what year were there about 6300 commercial banks?   (Source: Federal Deposit Insurance Corp.)

150. Forestry   The yield V (in millions of cubic feet per acre) for a forest at age t years is given by $V = 6.7e^{-48.1/t}$.

(a) Use a graphing utility to graph the function.

(b) Determine the horizontal asymptote of the function. Interpret its meaning in the context of the problem.

(c) Find the time necessary to obtain a yield of 1.3 million cubic feet.

151. Science An object at a temperature of 160°C was removed from a furnace and placed in a room at 20°C. The temperature T (in degrees Celsius) of the object was measured after each hour h and recorded in the table. A model for the data is given by $T = 20[1 + 7(2^{-h})]$.

Hour, h	Temperature, T
0	160°
1	90°
2	56°
3	38°
4	29°
5	24°

DATA

Spreadsheet at LarsonPrecalculus.com

(a) Use a graphing utility to plot the data and graph the model in the same viewing window.

(b) Identify the horizontal asymptote of the graph. Interpret its meaning in the context of the problem.

(c) Approximate the time when the temperature of the object is 100°C.

(d) How long does it take the object to cool to 80°C, one-half the initial temperature?

152. MODELING DATA

The table shows the numbers N of college-bound seniors intending to major in engineering who took the SAT exam from 2008 through 2013. The data can be modeled by the logarithmic function

$N = -152,656 + 111,959.9 \ln t$

where t represents the year, with $t = 8$ corresponding to 2008.   (Source: The College Board)

Year	Number, N
2008	81,338
2009	88,719
2010	108,389
2011	116,746
2012	127,061
2013	132,275

DATA

Spreadsheet at LarsonPrecalculus.com

(a) According to the model, in what year would 150,537 seniors intending to major in engineering take the SAT exam?

(b) Use a graphing utility to graph the model with the data, and use the graph to verify your answer in part (a).

(c) Do you think this is a good model for predicting future values? Explain.

Conclusions

True or False? In Exercises 153 and 154, determine whether the statement is true or false. Justify your answer.

153. An exponential equation must have at least one solution.

154. A logarithmic equation can have at most one extraneous solution.

155. Error Analysis Describe the error.

$2e^x = 10$
$\ln(2e^x) = \ln 10$
$2x = \ln 10$
$x = \frac{1}{2} \ln 10$

156. HOW DO YOU SEE IT? Solving $\log_3 x + \log_3(x - 8) = 2$ algebraically, the solutions appear to be $x = 9$ and $x = -1$. Use the graph of $y = \log_3 x + \log_3(x - 8) - 2$ to determine whether each value is an actual solution of the equation. Explain your reasoning.

157. Exploration Let $f(x) = \log_a x$ and $g(x) = a^x$, where $a > 1$.

(a) Let $a = 1.2$ and use a graphing utility to graph the two functions in the same viewing window. What do you observe? Approximate any points of intersection of the two graphs.

(b) Determine the value(s) of a for which the two graphs have one point of intersection.

(c) Determine the value(s) of a for which the two graphs have two points of intersection.

158. Think About It Is the time required for a continuously compounded investment to quadruple twice as long as the time required for it to double? Give a reason for your answer and verify your answer algebraically.

Cumulative Mixed Review

Sketching Graphs In Exercises 159–162, sketch the graph of the function.

159. $f(x) = 3x^3 - 4$

160. $f(x) = |x - 2| - 8$

161. $f(x) = \begin{cases} 2x + 1, & x < 0 \\ -x^2, & x \geq 0 \end{cases}$

162. $f(x) = \begin{cases} x - 9, & x \leq 1 \\ x^2 + 1, & x > 1 \end{cases}$

3.5 Exponential and Logarithmic Models

Introduction

There are many examples of exponential and logarithmic models in real life. In Section 3.1, you used the formula

$$A = Pe^{rt} \qquad \text{Exponential model}$$

to find the balance in an account when the interest was compounded continuously. In Section 3.2, Example 10, you used the human memory model

$$f(t) = 75 - 6\ln(t + 1). \qquad \text{Logarithmic model}$$

The five most common types of mathematical models involving exponential functions or logarithmic functions are listed below.

1. **Exponential growth model:** $y = ae^{bx}, \quad b > 0$

2. **Exponential decay model:** $y = ae^{-bx}, \quad b > 0$

3. **Gaussian model:** $y = ae^{-(x-b)^2/c}$

4. **Logistic growth model:** $y = \dfrac{a}{1 + be^{-rx}}$

5. **Logarithmic models:** $y = a + b\ln x, \quad y = a + b\log_{10} x$

The basic shapes of the graphs of these models are shown in Figure 3.24.

What you should learn

▶ Recognize the five most common types of models involving exponential or logarithmic functions.
▶ Use exponential growth and decay functions to model and solve real-life problems.
▶ Use Gaussian functions to model and solve real-life problems.
▶ Use logistic growth functions to model and solve real-life problems.
▶ Use logarithmic functions to model and solve real-life problems.

Why you should learn it

Exponential decay models are used in carbon dating. For instance, in Exercise 39 on page 230, you will use an exponential decay model to estimate the age of a piece of ancient charcoal.

Exponential Growth Model

Exponential Decay Model

Gaussian Model

Logistic Growth Model

Natural Logarithmic Model

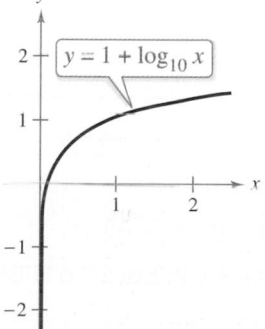

Common Logarithmic Model

Figure 3.24

You can often gain quite a bit of insight into a situation modeled by an exponential or logarithmic function by identifying and interpreting the function's asymptotes.

Exponential Growth and Decay

EXAMPLE 1   Demography

See LarsonPrecalculus.com for an interactive version of this type of example.

The table shows estimates of the world population (in millions) from 2007 through 2013. A scatter plot of the data is shown in the figure at the right. (Source: U.S. Census Bureau)

Year	Population, P
2007	6631
2008	6710
2009	6788
2010	6866
2011	6943
2012	7021
2013	7098

DATA

Spreadsheet at LarsonPrecalculus.com

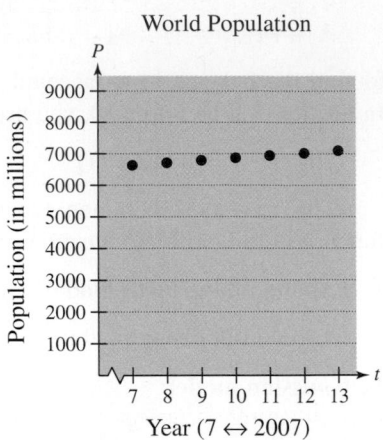

World Population

An exponential growth model that approximates these data is given by

$$P = 6128e^{0.0113t}$$

where P is the population (in millions) and $t = 7$ represents 2007. Compare the values given by the model with the estimates shown in the table. According to this model, when will the world population reach 7.6 billion?

Algebraic Solution

The following table compares the two sets of population figures.

Year	2007	2008	2009	2010	2011	2012	2013
Population	6631	6710	6788	6866	6943	7021	7098
Model	6632	6708	6784	6861	6939	7018	7098

From the table, it appears that the model is a good fit for the data. To find when the world population will reach 7.6 billion, let $P = 7600$ in the model and solve for t.

$6128e^{0.0113t} = P$	Write original equation.
$6128e^{0.0113t} = 7600$	Substitute 7600 for P.
$e^{0.0113t} \approx 1.24021$	Divide each side by 6128.
$\ln e^{0.0113t} \approx \ln 1.24021$	Take natural log of each side.
$0.0113t \approx 0.21528$	Inverse Property
$t \approx 19.1$	Divide each side by 0.0113.

According to the model, the world population will reach 7.6 billion in 2019.

Graphical Solution

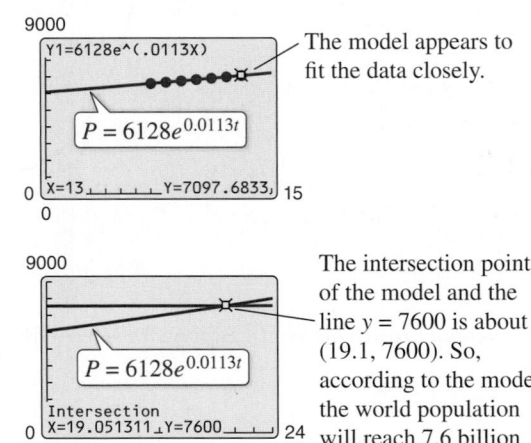

The model appears to fit the data closely.

$P = 6128e^{0.0113t}$

The intersection point of the model and the line $y = 7600$ is about $(19.1, 7600)$. So, according to the model, the world population will reach 7.6 billion in 2019.

✓ **Checkpoint** *Audio-video solution in English & Spanish at LarsonPrecalculus.com.*

In Example 1, when will the world population reach 9 billion?

An exponential model increases (or decreases) by the same percent each year. What is the annual percent increase for the model in Example 1?

In Example 1, you were given the exponential growth model. Sometimes you must find such a model. One technique for doing this is shown in Example 2.

EXAMPLE 2 Modeling Population Growth

In a research experiment, a population of fruit flies is increasing according to the law of exponential growth. After 2 days there are 100 flies, and after 4 days there are 300 flies. How many flies will there be after 5 days?

Solution

Let y be the number of flies at time t (in days). From the given information, you know that $y = 100$ when $t = 2$ and $y = 300$ when $t = 4$. Substituting this information into the model $y = ae^{bt}$ produces

$$100 = ae^{2b} \quad \text{and} \quad 300 = ae^{4b}.$$

To solve for b, solve for a in the first equation.

$$100 = ae^{2b} \implies a = \frac{100}{e^{2b}} \qquad \text{Solve for } a \text{ in the first equation.}$$

Then substitute the result into the second equation.

$$300 = ae^{4b} \qquad \text{Write second equation.}$$

$$300 = \left(\frac{100}{e^{2b}}\right)e^{4b} \qquad \text{Substitute } \frac{100}{e^{2b}} \text{ for } a.$$

$$300 = 100e^{2b} \qquad \text{Simplify.}$$

$$3 = e^{2b} \qquad \text{Divide each side by 100.}$$

$$\ln 3 = \ln e^{2b} \qquad \text{Take natural log of each side.}$$

$$\ln 3 = 2b \qquad \text{Inverse Property}$$

$$\frac{1}{2}\ln 3 = b \qquad \text{Solve for } b.$$

Using $b = \frac{1}{2}\ln 3$ and the equation you found for a, you can determine that

$$a = \frac{100}{e^{2[(1/2)\ln 3]}} \qquad \text{Substitute } \frac{1}{2}\ln 3 \text{ for } b.$$

$$= \frac{100}{e^{\ln 3}} \qquad \text{Simplify.}$$

$$= \frac{100}{3} \qquad \text{Inverse Property}$$

$$\approx 33.33. \qquad \text{Simplify.}$$

So, with $a \approx 33.33$ and $b = \frac{1}{2}\ln 3 \approx 0.5493$, the exponential growth model is

$$y = 33.33e^{0.5493t}$$

as shown in Figure 3.25. After 5 days, the population will be

$$y = 33.33e^{0.5493(5)} \approx 520 \text{ flies.}$$

Figure 3.25

✓ **Checkpoint** 🔊))) *Audio-video solution in English & Spanish at LarsonPrecalculus.com.*

The number of bacteria in a culture is increasing according to the law of exponential growth. After 1 hour there are 100 bacteria, and after 2 hours there are 200 bacteria. How many bacteria will there be after 3 hours? ■

Entomologist

In living organic material, the ratio of the content of radioactive carbon isotopes (carbon 14) to the content of nonradioactive carbon isotopes (carbon 12) is about 1 to 10^{12}. When organic material dies, its carbon 12 content remains fixed, whereas its radioactive carbon 14 begins to decay with a half-life of about 5700 years. To estimate the age of dead organic material, scientists use the following formula, which denotes the ratio of carbon 14 to carbon 12 present at any time t (in years).

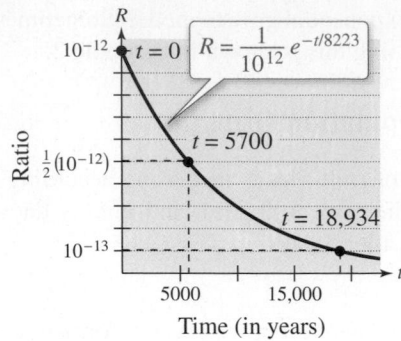

Figure 3.26

$$R = \frac{1}{10^{12}}e^{-t/8223} \qquad \text{Carbon dating model}$$

The graph of R is shown in Figure 3.26. Note that R decreases as t increases.

EXAMPLE 3 Carbon Dating

The ratio of carbon 14 to carbon 12 in a newly discovered fossil is

$$R = \frac{1}{10^{13}}.$$

Estimate the age of the fossil.

Algebraic Solution

In the carbon dating model, substitute the given value of R and solve for t.

$\dfrac{1}{10^{12}}e^{-t/8223} = R$	Write original model.
$\dfrac{e^{-t/8223}}{10^{12}} = \dfrac{1}{10^{13}}$	Substitute $\dfrac{1}{10^{13}}$ for R.
$e^{-t/8223} = \dfrac{1}{10}$	Multiply each side by 10^{12}.
$\ln e^{-t/8223} = \ln \dfrac{1}{10}$	Take natural log of each side.
$-\dfrac{t}{8223} \approx -2.3026$	Inverse Property
$t \approx 18{,}934$	Multiply each side by -8223.

So, to the nearest thousand years, you can estimate the age of the fossil to be 19,000 years.

Graphical Solution

Use a graphing utility to graph the formula for the ratio of carbon 14 to carbon 12 at any time t as

$$y_1 = \frac{1}{10^{12}}e^{-x/8223}.$$

In the same viewing window, graph $y_2 = 1/(10^{13})$, as shown in the figure.

Use the *intersect* feature to estimate that $x \approx 18{,}934$ when $y = 1/(10^{13})$.

So, to the nearest thousand years, you can estimate the age of the fossil to be 19,000 years.

✓ **Checkpoint** 🔊))) *Audio-video solution in English & Spanish at LarsonPrecalculus.com.*

Estimate the age of a newly discovered fossil for which the ratio of carbon 14 to carbon 12 is $R = 1/10^{14}$. ∎

The carbon dating model in Example 3 assumed that the carbon 14 to carbon 12 ratio was one part in 10,000,000,000,000. Suppose an error in measurement occurred and the actual ratio was only one part in 8,000,000,000,000. The fossil age corresponding to the actual ratio would then be approximately 17,000 years. Try checking this result.

Gaussian Models

As mentioned at the beginning of this section, Gaussian models are of the form

$$y = ae^{-(x-b)^2/c}.$$

This type of model is commonly used in probability and statistics to represent populations that are **normally distributed.** For *standard* normal distributions, the model takes the form

$$y = \frac{1}{\sqrt{2\pi}}e^{-x^2/2}.$$

The graph of a Gaussian model is called a **bell-shaped curve.** Try graphing the standard normal distribution curve with a graphing utility. Can you see why it is called a bell-shaped curve?

The average value for a population can be found from the bell-shaped curve by observing where the maximum y-value of the function occurs. The x-value corresponding to the maximum y-value of the function represents the average value of the independent variable—in this case, x.

EXAMPLE 4   SAT Scores

In 2013, the Scholastic Aptitude Test (SAT) mathematics scores for college-bound seniors roughly followed the normal distribution

$$y = 0.0034e^{-(x-514)^2/27,848}, \qquad 200 \le x \le 800$$

where x is the SAT score for mathematics. Use a graphing utility to graph this function and estimate the average SAT mathematics score.   (Source: College Board)

Solution

The graph of the function is shown in Figure 3.27. On this bell-shaped curve, the maximum value of the curve represents the average score. Using the *maximum* feature of the graphing utility, you can see that the average mathematics score for college-bound seniors in 2013 was 514.

Figure 3.27

✔ **Checkpoint** ◀))) *Audio-video solution in English & Spanish at LarsonPrecalculus.com.*

In 2013, the Scholastic Aptitude Test (SAT) critical reading scores for college-bound seniors roughly followed the normal distribution

$$y = 0.0035e^{-(x-496)^2/26,450}$$

where x is the SAT score for critical reading. Use a graphing utility to graph this function and estimate the average SAT critical reading score.   (Source: College Board) ■

In Example 4, note that 50% of the seniors who took the test received scores lower than 514 (see Figure 3.28).

SAT Mathematics Scores

Figure 3.28

Logistic Growth Models

Some populations initially have rapid growth, followed by a declining rate of growth, as indicated by the graph in Figure 3.29. One model for describing this type of growth pattern is the **logistic curve** given by the function

$$y = \frac{a}{1 + be^{-rx}}$$

where y is the population size and x is the time. An example is a bacteria culture that is initially allowed to grow under ideal conditions, and then under less favorable conditions that inhibit growth. A logistic growth curve is also called a **sigmoidal curve**.

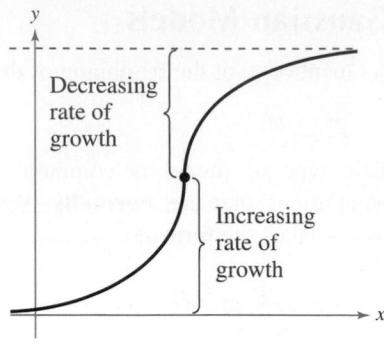

Figure 3.29   Logistic Curve

EXAMPLE 5   Spread of a Virus

On a college campus of 5000 students, one student returns from vacation with a contagious flu virus. The spread of the virus is modeled by

$$y = \frac{5000}{1 + 4999e^{-0.8t}}, \quad t \geq 0$$

where y is the total number of students infected after t days. The college will cancel classes when 40% or more of the students are infected.

a. How many students are infected after 5 days?

b. After how many days will the college cancel classes?

Algebraic Solution

a. After 5 days, the number of students infected is

$$y = \frac{5000}{1 + 4999e^{-0.8(5)}} = \frac{5000}{1 + 4999e^{-4}} \approx 54.$$

b. Classes are canceled when the number of infected students is $(0.40)(5000) = 2000$.

$$2000 = \frac{5000}{1 + 4999e^{-0.8t}}$$

$$1 + 4999e^{-0.8t} = 2.5$$

$$e^{-0.8t} = \frac{1.5}{4999}$$

$$\ln e^{-0.8t} = \ln \frac{1.5}{4999}$$

$$-0.8t = \ln \frac{1.5}{4999}$$

$$t = -\frac{1}{0.8} \ln \frac{1.5}{4999}$$

$$t \approx 10.14$$

So, after about 10 days, at least 40% of the students will be infected, and classes will be canceled.

Graphical Solution

a.

Use the *value* feature to estimate that $y \approx 54$ when $x = 5$. So, after 5 days, about 54 students will be infected.

b. Classes are canceled when the number of infected students is $(0.40)(5000) = 2000$. Use a graphing utility to graph

$$y_1 = \frac{5000}{1 + 4999e^{-0.8x}} \quad \text{and} \quad y_2 = 2000$$

in the same viewing window. Use the *intersect* feature of the graphing utility to find the point of intersection of the graphs, as shown in the figure.

The intersection point occurs near $x \approx 10.14$. So, after about 10 days, at least 40% of the students will be infected, and classes will be canceled.

✓ **Checkpoint**   *Audio-video solution in English & Spanish at LarsonPrecalculus.com.*

In Example 5, after how many days are 250 students infected?

Logarithmic Models

On the Richter scale, the magnitude R of an earthquake of intensity I is given by

$$R = \log_{10} \frac{I}{I_0}$$

where $I_0 = 1$ is the minimum intensity used for comparison. Intensity is a measure of the wave energy of an earthquake.

EXAMPLE 6   Magnitudes of Earthquakes

In 2014, Edgefield, South Carolina, experienced an earthquake that measured 4.1 on the Richter scale. Also in 2014, Nago, Japan, experienced an earthquake that measured 6.5 on the Richter scale. (Source: U.S. Geological Survey)

a. Find the intensity of each earthquake.

b. Compare the two intensities.

Solution

a. Because $I_0 = 1$ and $R = 4.1$, the intensity of the earthquake in South Carolina can be found as shown.

$$R = \log_{10} \frac{I}{I_0} \qquad \text{Write original model.}$$

$$4.1 = \log_{10} \frac{I}{1} \qquad \text{Substitute 1 for } I_0 \text{ and 4.1 for } R.$$

$$10^{4.1} = 10^{\log_{10} I} \qquad \text{Exponentiate each side.}$$

$$10^{4.1} = I \qquad \text{Inverse Property}$$

So, the intensity was about $10^{4.1} \approx 12{,}589$. For the earthquake in Japan, $R = 6.5$. The intensity of this earthquake was

$$R = \log_{10} \frac{I}{I_0} \qquad \text{Write original model.}$$

$$6.5 = \log_{10} \frac{I}{1} \qquad \text{Substitute 1 for } I_0 \text{ and 6.5 for } R.$$

$$10^{6.5} = 10^{\log_{10} I} \qquad \text{Exponentiate each side.}$$

$$10^{6.5} = I. \qquad \text{Inverse Property}$$

So, the intensity was about $10^{6.5} \approx 3{,}162{,}278$.

b. Note that an increase of 2.4 units on the Richter scale (from 4.1 to 6.5) represents an increase in intensity by a factor of

$$\frac{10^{6.5}}{10^{4.1}} = 10^{2.4}$$

$$\approx 251$$

In other words, the intensity of the earthquake in Japan was about 251 times as great as the intensity of the earthquake in South Carolina.

Seismologist

✓ **Checkpoint** ◀))) Audio-video solution in English & Spanish at LarsonPrecalculus.com.

Find the intensities of earthquakes whose magnitudes are (a) $R = 6.0$ and (b) $R = 7.9$.

3.5   Exercises

See *CalcChat.com* for tutorial help and worked-out solutions to odd-numbered exercises.
For instructions on how to use a graphing utility, see Appendix A.

Vocabulary and Concept Check

1. Match each equation with its model.

  (a) Exponential growth model   (i) $y = ae^{-bx}, b > 0$

  (b) Exponential decay model   (ii) $y = a + b \ln x$

  (c) Logistic growth model   (iii) $y = \dfrac{a}{1 + be^{-rx}}$

  (d) Gaussian model   (iv) $y = ae^{bx}, b > 0$

  (e) Natural logarithmic model   (v) $y = a + b \log_{10} x$

  (f) Common logarithmic model   (vi) $y = ae^{-(x-b)^2/c}$

In Exercises 2 and 3, fill in the blank.

2. Gaussian models are commonly used in probability and statistics to represent populations that are _____ distributed.

3. Logistic growth curves are also called _____ curves.

4. Which model in Exercise 1 has a graph called a bell-shaped curve?

5. Does the model $y = 120e^{-0.25x}$ represent exponential growth or exponential decay?

6. Which model in Exercise 1 has a graph with two horizontal asymptotes?

Procedures and Problem Solving

Identifying Graphs of Models   **In Exercises 7–12, match the function with its graph. [The graphs are labeled (a), (b), (c), (d), (e), and (f).]**

7. $y = 2e^{x/4}$ **8.** $y = 6e^{-x/4}$

9. $y = 6 + \log_{10}(x + 2)$ **10.** $y = 3e^{-(x-2)^2/5}$

11. $y = \ln(x + 1)$ **12.** $y = \dfrac{4}{1 + e^{-2x}}$

(a)

(b)

(c)

(d)

(e)

(f)

Using a Compound Interest Formula   **In Exercises 13–20, complete the table for a savings account in which interest is compounded continuously.**

	Initial Investment	Annual % Rate	Time to Double	Amount After 10 Years
13.	$10,000	4%		
14.	$2000	2%		
15.	$7500		21 years	
16.	$1000		12 years	
17.	$5000			$5665.74
18.	$300			$385.21
19.		4.5%		$100,000.00
20.		3.5%		$2500.00

21. Tripling an Investment   Complete the table for the time t (in years) necessary for P dollars to triple when interest is compounded continuously at rate r. Create a scatter plot of the data.

r	2%	4%	6%	8%	10%	12%
t						

22. Tripling an Investment Complete the table for the time t (in years) necessary for P dollars to triple when interest is compounded annually at rate r. Create a scatter plot of the data.

r	2%	4%	6%	8%	10%	12%
t						

23. Finance When $1 is invested in an account over a 10-year period, the amount A in the account after t years is given by

$$A = 1 + 0.075t \quad \text{or} \quad A = e^{0.07t}$$

depending on whether the account pays simple interest at $7\frac{1}{2}\%$ or continuous compound interest at 7%. Use a graphing utility to graph each function in the same viewing window. Which grows at a greater rate?

24. Finance When $1 is invested in an account over a 10-year period, the amount A in the account after t years is given by

$$A = 1 + 0.06t \quad \text{or} \quad A = \left(1 + \frac{0.055}{365}\right)^{365t}$$

depending on whether the account pays simple interest at 6% or compound interest at $5\frac{1}{2}\%$ compounded daily. Use a graphing utility to graph each function in the same viewing window. Which grows at a greater rate?

Radioactive Decay   In Exercises 25–30, complete the table for the radioactive isotope.

Isotope	Half-Life (years)	Initial Quantity	Amount After 1000 Years
25. ^{226}Ra	1600	10 g	
26. ^{14}C	5730	3 g	
27. ^{231}Pa	32,800		1.5 g
28. ^{239}Pu	24,100		0.4 g
29. ^{241}Am	432.2	26.4 g	
30. ^{238}Pu	87.74		0.1 g

Writing a Model   In Exercises 31–34, find the exponential model $y = ae^{bx}$ that fits the points shown in the graph or table.

31.

32.

33.

34.

35. Demography The populations P (in thousands) of Antioch, California, from 2006 through 2012 can be modeled by $P = 90e^{0.013t}$, where t is the year, with $t = 6$ corresponding to 2006.   (Source: U.S. Census Bureau)

(a) According to the model, was the population of Antioch increasing or decreasing from 2006 through 2012? Explain your reasoning.

(b) What were the populations of Antioch in 2006, 2009, and 2012?

(c) According to the model, when will the population of Antioch be approximately 116,000?

36. MODELING DATA

The table shows the populations (in millions) of five countries in 2013 and the projected populations (in millions) for 2025.   (Source: U.S. Census Bureau)

Country	2013	2025
Australia	22.3	25.1
Canada	34.6	37.6
Hungary	9.9	9.6
Philippines	105.7	128.9
Turkey	80.7	90.5

(a) Find the exponential growth or decay model, $y = ae^{bt}$ or $y = ae^{-bt}$, for the population of each country, where t is the year, with $t = 13$ corresponding to 2013. Use the model to predict the population of each country in 2040.

(b) You can see that the populations of Canada and the Philippines are growing at different rates. What constant in the equation $y = ae^{bt}$ is determined by these different growth rates? Discuss the relationship between the different growth rates and the magnitude of the constant.

(c) The population of Turkey is increasing while the population of Hungary is decreasing. What constant in the equation $y = ae^{bt}$ reflects this difference? Explain.

37. Demography The populations P (in thousands) of Cameron County, Texas, from 2006 through 2012 can be modeled by

$$P = 339.2e^{kt}$$

where t is the year, with $t = 6$ corresponding to 2006. In 2011, the population was 412,600.   (Source: U.S. Census Bureau)

(a) Find the value of k for the model. Round your result to four decimal places.

(b) Use your model to predict the population in 2018.

38. Demography The populations P (in thousands) of Pineville, North Carolina, from 2006 through 2012 can be modeled by $P = 5.4e^{kt}$, where t is the year, with $t = 6$ corresponding to 2006. In 2008, the population was 7000. (Source: U.S. Census Bureau)

(a) Find the value of k for the model. Round your result to four decimal places.

(b) Use your model to predict the population in 2018.

39. *Why you should learn it* (p. 221) Carbon 14 (^{14}C) dating assumes that the carbon dioxide on Earth today has the same radioactive content as it did centuries ago. If this is true, then the amount of ^{14}C absorbed by a tree that grew several centuries ago should be the same as the amount of ^{14}C absorbed by a tree growing today. A piece of ancient charcoal contains only 15% as much radioactive carbon as a piece of modern charcoal. How long ago was the tree burned to make the ancient charcoal, given that the half-life of ^{14}C is about 5700 years?

40. Radioactive Decay The half-life of radioactive radium (^{226}Ra) is 1600 years. What percent of a present amount of radioactive radium will remain after 100 years?

41. MODELING DATA

A new 2014 luxury sedan that sold for $39,780 has a book value V of $25,459 after 2 years.

(a) Find a linear model for the value V of the sedan.

(b) Find an exponential model for the value V of the sedan. Round the numbers in the model to four decimal places.

(c) Use a graphing utility to graph the two models in the same viewing window.

(d) Which model represents a greater depreciation rate in the first year?

(e) For what years is the value of the sedan greater using the linear model? the exponential model?

42. MODELING DATA

A new laptop computer that sold for $1200 in 2014 has a book value V of $650 after 2 years.

(a) Find a linear model for the value V of the laptop.

(b) Find an exponential model for the value V of the laptop. Round the numbers in the model to four decimal places.

(c) Use a graphing utility to graph the two models in the same viewing window.

(d) Which model represents a greater depreciation rate in the first year?

(e) For what years is the value of the laptop greater using the linear model? the exponential model?

43. Psychology The IQ scores for adults roughly follow the normal distribution $y = 0.0266e^{-(x-100)^2/450}$, $70 \le x \le 115$, where x is the IQ score.

(a) Use a graphing utility to graph the function.

(b) Use the graph in part (a) to estimate the average IQ score.

44. Marketing The sales S (in thousands of units) of a cleaning solution after x hundred dollars is spent on advertising are given by $S = 10(1 - e^{kx})$. When $500 is spent on advertising, 2500 units are sold.

(a) Complete the model by solving for k.

(b) Estimate the number of units that will be sold when advertising expenditures are raised to $700.

45. Forestry A conservation organization releases 100 animals of an endangered species into a game preserve. The organization believes that the preserve has a carrying capacity of 1000 animals and that the growth of the herd will follow the logistic curve

$$p(t) = \frac{1000}{1 + 9e^{-0.1656t}}$$

where t is measured in months.

(a) What is the population after 5 months?

(b) After how many months will the population reach 500?

(c) Use a graphing utility to graph the function. Use the graph to determine the values of p at which the horizontal asymptotes occur. Identify the asymptote that is most relevant in the context of the problem and interpret its meaning.

46. Biology The number Y of yeast organisms in a culture is given by the model

$$Y = \frac{663}{1 + 72e^{-0.547t}}$$

where t represents the time (in hours).

(a) Use a graphing utility to graph the model.

(b) Use the model to predict the populations for the 19th hour and the 30th hour.

(c) According to this model, what is the limiting value of the population?

(d) Why do you think this population of yeast follows a logistic growth model instead of an exponential growth model?

Geology In Exercises 47 and 48, use the Richter scale (see page 227) for measuring the magnitudes of earthquakes.

47. Find the intensities I of the following earthquakes measuring R on the Richter scale (let $I_0 = 1$). (Source: U.S. Geological Survey)

(a) Falkland Islands in 2013, $R = 7.0$

(b) Sea of Okhotsk in 2013, $R = 8.3$

(c) Kunisaki-shi, Japan in 2014, $R = 6.3$

48. Find the magnitudes R of the following earthquakes of intensity I (let $I_0 = 1$).

    (a) $I = 39,811,000$

    (b) $I = 12,589,000$

    (c) $I = 251,200$

Audiology **In Exercises 49–52, use the following information for determining sound intensity. The level of sound β (in decibels) with an intensity I is**

$$\beta = 10 \log_{10} \frac{I}{I_0}$$

where I_0 is an intensity of 10^{-12} watt per square meter, corresponding roughly to the faintest sound that can be heard by the human ear. In Exercises 49 and 50, find the level of each sound β.

49. (a) $I = 10^{-10}$ watt per m² (quiet room)

    (b) $I = 10^{-5}$ watt per m² (busy street corner)

    (c) $I \approx 10^{0}$ watt per m² (threshold of pain)

50. (a) $I = 10^{-4}$ watt per m² (door slamming)

    (b) $I = 10^{-3}$ watt per m² (loud car horn)

    (c) $I = 10^{-2}$ watt per m² (siren at 30 meters)

51. As a result of the installation of a muffler, the noise level of an engine was reduced from 88 to 72 decibels. Find the percent decrease in the intensity level of the noise due to the installation of the muffler.

52. As a result of the installation of noise suppression materials, the noise level in an auditorium was reduced from 93 to 80 decibels. Find the percent decrease in the intensity level of the noise due to the installation of these materials.

Chemistry **In Exercises 53–56, use the acidity model**

$$pH = -\log[H^+]$$

where acidity (pH) is a measure of the hydrogen ion concentration $[H^+]$ (in moles of hydrogen per liter) of a solution.

53. Find the pH when $[H^+] = 2.3 \times 10^{-5}$.

54. Compute $[H^+]$ for a solution for which pH $= 5.8$.

55. A grape has a pH of 3.5, and baking soda has a pH of 8.0. The hydrogen ion concentration of the grape is how many times that of the baking soda?

56. The pH of a solution is decreased by one unit. The hydrogen ion concentration is increased by what factor?

57. Finance The total interest u paid on a home mortgage of P dollars at interest rate r for t years is given by

$$u = P\left[\frac{rt}{1 - \left(\dfrac{1}{1 + r/12}\right)^{12t}} - 1\right].$$

Consider a $230,000 home mortgage at 3%.

    (a) Use a graphing utility to graph the total interest function.

    (b) Approximate the length of the mortgage when the total interest paid is the same as the amount of the mortgage. Is it possible that a person could pay twice as much in interest charges as the amount of the mortgage?

58. Finance A $200,000 home mortgage for 30 years at 4.25% has a monthly payment of $983.88. Part of the monthly payment goes toward the interest charge on the unpaid balance, and the remainder of the payment is used to reduce the principal. The amount that goes toward the interest is given by

$$u = M - \left(M - \frac{Pr}{12}\right)\left(1 + \frac{r}{12}\right)^{12t}$$

and the amount that goes toward reduction of the principal is given by

$$v = \left(M - \frac{Pr}{12}\right)\left(1 + \frac{r}{12}\right)^{12t}.$$

In these formulas, P is the amount of the mortgage, r is the interest rate, M is the monthly payment, and t is the time (in years).

    (a) Use a graphing utility to graph each function in the same viewing window. (The viewing window should show all 30 years of mortgage payments.)

    (b) In the early years of the mortgage, the larger part of the monthly payment goes for what purpose? Approximate the time when the monthly payment is evenly divided between interest and principal reduction.

    (c) Repeat parts (a) and (b) for a repayment period of 20 years ($M = \$1238.47$). What can you conclude?

59. Forensics At 8:30 A.M., a coroner was called to the home of a person who had died during the night. In order to estimate the time of death, the coroner took the person's temperature twice. At 9:00 A.M. the temperature was 85.7°F, and at 11:00 A.M. the temperature was 82.8°F. From these two temperatures the coroner was able to determine that the time elapsed since death and the body temperature were related by the formula

$$t = -10 \ln \frac{T - 70}{98.6 - 70}$$

where t is the time (in hours elapsed since the person died) and T is the temperature (in degrees Fahrenheit) of the person's body. Assume that the person had a normal body temperature of 98.6°F at death and that the room temperature was a constant 70°F. Use the formula to estimate the time of death of the person. (This formula is derived from a general cooling principle called Newton's Law of Cooling.)

60. Culinary Arts You take a five-pound package of steaks out of a freezer at 11 A.M. and place it in a refrigerator. Will the steaks be thawed in time to be grilled at 6 P.M.? Assume that the refrigerator temperature is 40°F and the freezer temperature is 0°F. Use the formula (derived from Newton's Law of Cooling)

$$t = -5.05 \ln \frac{T - 40}{0 - 40}$$

where t is the time in hours (with $t = 0$ corresponding to 11 A.M.) and T is the temperature of the package of steaks (in degrees Fahrenheit).

Conclusions

True or False? In Exercises 61 and 62, determine whether the statement is true or false. Justify your answer.

61. The domain of a logistic growth function cannot be the set of real numbers.

62. The graph of a logistic growth function will always have an x-intercept.

63. Think About It Can the graph of a Gaussian model ever have an x-intercept? Explain.

64. HOW DO YOU SEE IT? For each graph, state whether an exponential, Gaussian, logarithmic, logistic, or quadratic model will fit the data best. Explain your reasoning. Then describe a real-life situation that could be represented by the data.

(a)

(b)

(c)

(d)

(e)

(f)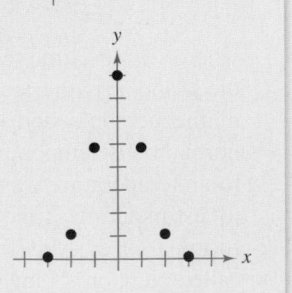

Identifying Models In Exercises 65–68, identify the type of model you studied in this section that has the given characteristic.

65. The maximum value of the function occurs at the average value of the independent variable.

66. A horizontal asymptote of its graph represents the limiting value of a population.

67. Its graph shows a steadily increasing rate of growth.

68. The only asymptote of its graph is a vertical asymptote.

Cumulative Mixed Review

Identifying Graphs of Linear Equations In Exercises 69–72, match the equation with its graph and identify any intercepts. [The graphs are labeled (a), (b), (c), and (d).]

(a)

(b)

(c)

(d)

69. $4x - 3y - 9 = 0$

70. $2x + 5y - 10 = 0$

71. $y = 25 - 2.25x$

72. $\dfrac{x}{2} + \dfrac{y}{4} = 1$

Applying the Leading Coefficient Test In Exercises 73–76, use the Leading Coefficient Test to determine the right-hand and left-hand behavior of the graph of the polynomial function.

73. $f(x) = 2x^3 - 3x^2 + x - 1$

74. $f(x) = 5 - x^2 - 4x^4$

75. $g(x) = -1.6x^5 + 4x^2 - 2$

76. $g(x) = 7x^6 + 9.1x^5 - 3.2x^4 + 25x^3$

Using Synthetic Division In Exercises 77 and 78, divide using synthetic division.

77. $(2x^3 - 8x^2 + 3x - 9) \div (x - 4)$

78. $(x^4 - 3x + 1) \div (x + 5)$

79. *Make a Decision* To work an extended application analyzing the sales per share for Kohl's Corporation from 1995 through 2012, visit this textbook's website at *LarsonPrecalculus.com*. (Data Source: Kohl's Corp.)

3.6   Nonlinear Models

Classifying Scatter Plots

In Section 1.7, you saw how to fit linear models to data, and in Section 2.8, you saw how to fit quadratic models to data. In real life, many relationships between two variables are represented by different types of growth patterns. You can use a scatter plot to get an idea of which type of model will best fit a set of data.

EXAMPLE 1   **Classifying Scatter Plots**

See LarsonPrecalculus.com for an interactive version of this type of example.

Decide whether each set of data could best be modeled by a linear model, $y = ax + b$, an exponential model, $y = ab^x$, or a logarithmic model, $y = a + b \ln x$.

a. (2, 1), (2.5, 1.2), (3, 1.3), (3.5, 1.5), (4, 1.8), (4.5, 2),
 (5, 2.4), (5.5, 2.5), (6, 3.1), (6.5, 3.8), (7, 4.5), (7.5, 5),
 (8, 6.5), (8.5, 7.8), (9, 9), (9.5, 10)

b. (2, 2), (2.5, 3.1), (3, 3.8), (3.5, 4.3), (4, 4.6), (4.5, 5.3),
 (5, 5.6), (5.5, 5.9), (6, 6.2), (6.5, 6.4), (7, 6.9), (7.5, 7.2),
 (8, 7.6), (8.5, 7.9), (9, 8), (9.5, 8.2)

c. (2, 1.9), (2.5, 2.5), (3, 3.2), (3.5, 3.6), (4, 4.3), (4.5, 4.7),
 (5, 5.2), (5.5, 5.7), (6, 6.4), (6.5, 6.8), (7, 7.2), (7.5, 7.9),
 (8, 8.6), (8.5, 8.9), (9, 9.5), (9.5, 9.9)

Solution

a. From the figure, it appears that the data can best be modeled by an exponential function.

b. From the figure, it appears that the data can best be modeled by a logarithmic function.

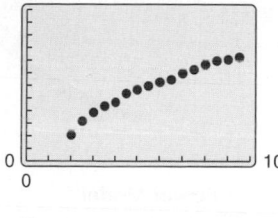

c. From the figure, it appears that the data can best be modeled by a linear function.

 Checkpoint *Audio-video solution in English & Spanish at LarsonPrecalculus.com.*

Decide whether the set of data could best be modeled by a linear model, $y = ax + b$, an exponential model, $y = ab^x$, or a logarithmic model, $y = a + b \ln x$.

 (0.5, 12), (1, 8), (1.5, 5.7), (2, 4), (2.5, 3.1), (3, 2), (3.5, 1.4), (4, 1), (4.5, 0.8),
 (5, 0.6), (5.5, 0.4), (6, 0.25), (6.5, 0.18), (7, 0.13), (7.5, 0.09), (8, 0.06)

What you should learn

▶ Classify scatter plots.
▶ Use scatter plots and a graphing utility to find models for data and choose the model that best fits a set of data.
▶ Use a graphing utility to find exponential and logistic models for data.

Why you should learn it

Many real-life applications can be modeled by nonlinear equations. For instance, in Exercise 34 on page 240, you are asked to find a nonlinear model that relates air pressure to altitude.

Fitting Nonlinear Models to Data

Once you have used a scatter plot to determine the type of model that would best fit a set of data, there are several ways that you can actually find the model. Each method is best used with a computer or calculator, rather than with hand calculations.

EXAMPLE 2 Fitting a Model to Data

Fit the data from Example 1(a) to an exponential model and a power model. Identify the coefficient of determination and determine which model fits the data better.

(2, 1), (2.5, 1.2), (3, 1.3), (3.5, 1.5), (4, 1.8), (4.5, 2), (5, 2.4), (5.5, 2.5),
(6, 3.1), (6.5, 3.8), (7, 4.5), (7.5, 5), (8, 6.5), (8.5, 7.8), (9, 9), (9.5, 10)

Solution

Begin by entering the data into a graphing utility. Then use the *regression* feature of the graphing utility to find exponential and power models for the data, as shown in Figure 3.30.

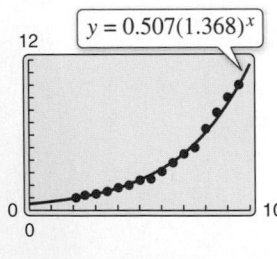

```
ExpReg
 y=a*b^x
 a=.5068515281
 b=1.367597236
 r²=.9944719477
 r=.9972321434
```
Exponential Model

```
PwrReg
 y=a*x^b
 a=.2492030149
 b=1.517901806
 r²=.9314968981
 r=.9651408696
```
Power Model

Figure 3.30

So, an exponential model for the data is $y = 0.507(1.368)^x$, and a power model for the data is $y = 0.249x^{1.518}$. Plot the data and each model in the same viewing window, as shown in Figure 3.31. To determine which model fits the data better, compare the coefficients of determination for each model. The model whose r^2-value is closest to 1 is the model that better fits the data. In this case, the better-fitting model is the exponential model.

$y = 0.507(1.368)^x$

Exponential Model

$y = 0.249x^{1.518}$

Power Model

Figure 3.31

✓ *Checkpoint* ◀))) *Audio-video solution in English & Spanish at LarsonPrecalculus.com.*

Fit the data from the Checkpoint for Example 1 to an exponential model and a power model. Identify the coefficient of determination and determine which model fits the data better.

(0.5, 12), (1, 8), (1.5, 5.7), (2, 4), (2.5, 3.1), (3, 2), (3.5, 1.4), (4, 1), (4.5, 0.8),
(5, 0.6), (5.5, 0.4), (6, 0.25), (6.5, 0.18), (7, 0.13), (7.5, 0.09), (8, 0.06)

Deciding which model best fits a set of data is a question that is studied in detail in statistics. Recall from Section 1.7 that the model that best fits a set of data is the one whose *sum of squared differences* is the least. In Example 2, the sums of squared differences are 0.90 for the exponential model and 14.30 for the power model.

EXAMPLE 3   Fitting a Model to Data

The table shows the yield y (in milligrams) of a chemical reaction after x minutes. Use a graphing utility to find a logarithmic model and a linear model for the data and identify the coefficient of determination for each model. Determine which model fits the data better.

DATA	Minutes, x	Yield, y
	1	1.5
	2	7.4
	3	10.2
	4	13.4
	5	15.8
	6	16.3
	7	18.2
	8	18.3

Spreadsheet at LarsonPrecalculus.com

Solution

Begin by entering the data into a graphing utility. Then use the *regression* feature of the graphing utility to find logarithmic and linear models for the data, as shown in Figure 3.32.

```
LnReg
 y=a+blnx
 a=1.537949373
 b=8.373383316
 r²=.9934905682
 r=.9967399702
```

Logarithmic Model

```
LinReg
 y=ax+b
 a=2.289285714
 b=2.335714286
 r²=.9005643856
 r=.9489807088
```

Linear Model

Figure 3.32

So, a logarithmic model for the data is $y = 1.538 + 8.373 \ln x$, and a linear model for the data is $y = 2.29x + 2.3$. Plot the data and each model in the same viewing window, as shown in Figure 3.33. To determine which model fits the data better, compare the coefficients of determination for each model. The model whose coefficient of determination is closer to 1 is the model that better fits the data. In this case, the better-fitting model is the logarithmic model.

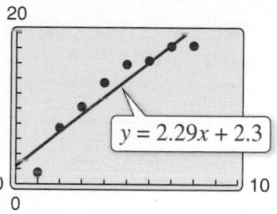

$y = 1.538 + 8.373 \ln x$

Logarithmic Model
Figure 3.33

$y = 2.29x + 2.3$

Linear Model

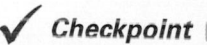

✓ **Checkpoint**))) *Audio-video solution in English & Spanish at LarsonPrecalculus.com.*

Use a graphing utility to find a logarithmic model and a linear model for the set of data. Identify the coefficient of determination for each model and determine which model fits the data better.

(0.5, 1.7), (1, 2.5), (1.5, 3), (2, 3.2), (2.5, 3.5), (3, 3.7),
(3.5, 3.8), (4, 3.9), (4.5, 3.9), (5, 4.1), (5.5, 4.2), (6, 4.3),
(6.5, 4.5), (7, 4.6), (7.5, 4.8), (8, 5)

In Example 3, the sum of the squared differences for the logarithmic model is 1.59 and the sum of the squared differences for the linear model is 24.31.

Modeling With Exponential and Logistic Functions

 EXAMPLE 4 Fitting an Exponential Model to Data

The table shows the amount y (in grams) of a radioactive substance remaining after x days. Use a graphing utility to find a model for the data. How much of the substance remains after 15 days?

Solution

Begin by entering the data into a graphing utility and displaying the scatter plot, as shown in Figure 3.34.

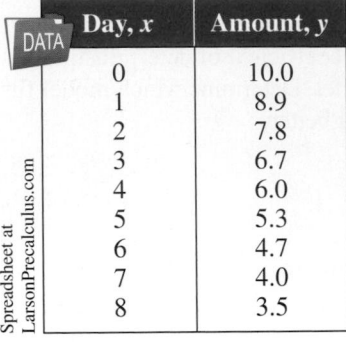

Day, x	Amount, y
0	10.0
1	8.9
2	7.8
3	6.7
4	6.0
5	5.3
6	4.7
7	4.0
8	3.5

Spreadsheet at LarsonPrecalculus.com

```
ExpReg
y=a*b^x
a=10.08405951
b=.8774212774
r²=.9988231047
r=.9994113791
```

Figure 3.34   **Figure 3.35**

From the scatter plot, it appears that an exponential model is a good fit. Use the *regression* feature of the graphing utility to find the exponential model, as shown in Figure 3.35. Change the model to a natural exponential model, as follows.

$$y = 10.08(0.877)^x \qquad \text{Write original model.}$$
$$= 10.08e^{(\ln 0.877)x} \qquad b = e^{\ln b}$$
$$\approx 10.08e^{-0.131x} \qquad \text{Simplify.}$$

Graph the data and the natural exponential model

$$y = 10.08e^{-0.131x}$$

in the same viewing window, as shown in Figure 3.36. From the model, you can see that the amount of the substance decreases by about 13% each day. Also, the amount of the substance remaining after 15 days is

$$y = 10.08e^{-0.131x} \qquad \text{Write natural exponential model.}$$
$$= 10.08e^{-0.131(15)} \qquad \text{Substitute 15 for } x.$$
$$\approx 1.4 \text{ grams.} \qquad \text{Use a calculator.}$$

You can also use the *value* feature of the graphing utility to approximate the amount remaining after 15 days, as shown in Figure 3.37.

Figure 3.36   **Figure 3.37**

> **Remark**
>
> You can change an exponential model of the form
>
> $$y = ab^x$$
>
> to one of the form
>
> $$y = ae^{cx}$$
>
> by rewriting b in the form
>
> $$b = e^{\ln b}.$$
>
> For instance,
>
> $$y = 3(2^x)$$
>
> can be written as
>
> $$y = 3(2^x)$$
> $$= 3e^{(\ln 2)x}$$
> $$\approx 3e^{0.693x}.$$

 Checkpoint Audio-video solution in English & Spanish at LarsonPrecalculus.com.

In Example 4, the initial amount of the substance is 10 grams. According to the natural exponential model, after how many days is the amount of the substance 5 grams? Interpret this value in the context of the problem.

The next example demonstrates how to use a graphing utility to fit a logistic model to data.

EXAMPLE 5   Fitting a Logistic Model to Data

To estimate the amount of defoliation caused by the gypsy moth during a given year, a forester counts the number x of egg masses on $\frac{1}{40}$ of an acre (circle of radius 18.6 feet) in the fall. The percent of defoliation y the next spring is shown in the table.   (Source: USDA, Forest Service)

Egg masses, x	Percent of defoliation, y
0	12
25	44
50	81
75	96
100	99

Forester

a. Use the *regression* feature of a graphing utility to find a logistic model for the data.

b. How closely does the model represent the data?

Graphical Solution

a. Enter the data into a graphing utility. Using the *regression* feature of the graphing utility, you can find the logistic model, as shown in the figure.

```
Logistic
 y=c/(1+ae^(-bx))
 a=7.163373551
 b=.0689483064
 c=99.74649743
```

You can approximate this model to be

$$y = \frac{100}{1 + 7e^{-0.069x}}.$$

b. You can use the graphing utility to graph the actual data and the model in the same viewing window. In the figure, it appears that the model is a good fit for the actual data.

Numerical Solution

a. Enter the data into a graphing utility. Using the *regression* feature of the graphing utility, you can approximate the logistic model to be

$$y = \frac{100}{1 + 7e^{-0.069x}}.$$

b. You can see how well the model fits the data by comparing the actual values of y with the values of y given by the model, which are labeled y^* in the table below.

x	0	25	50	75	100
y	12	44	81	96	99
y^*	12.5	44.5	81.8	96.2	99.3

In the table, you can see that the model appears to be a good fit for the actual data.

✓ **Checkpoint**))) *Audio-video solution in English & Spanish at LarsonPrecalculus.com.*

Use a graphing utility to graph the logistic model in Example 5. Use the graph to determine the horizontal asymptotes. Interpret the asymptotes in the context of the real-life situation. ∎

3.6   Exercises

See *CalcChat.com* for tutorial help and worked-out solutions to odd-numbered exercises.
For instructions on how to use a graphing utility, see Appendix A.

Vocabulary and Concept Check

In Exercises 1 and 2, fill in the blank.

1. A power model has the form _____ .

2. An exponential model of the form $y = ab^x$ can be rewritten as a natural exponential model of the form _____ .

3. What type of visual display can you create to get an idea of which type of model will best fit the data set?

4. A power model for a set of data has a coefficient of determination of $r^2 \approx 0.901$ and an exponential model for the data has a coefficient of determination of $r^2 \approx 0.967$. Which model fits the data better?

Procedures and Problem Solving

Classifying Scatter Plots   In Exercises 5–12, determine whether the scatter plot could best be modeled by a linear model, a quadratic model, an exponential model, a logarithmic model, or a logistic model.

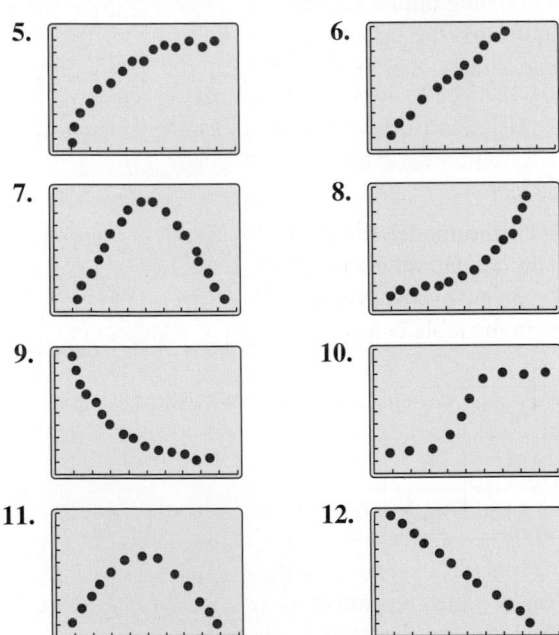

Classifying Scatter Plots   In Exercises 13–18, use a graphing utility to create a scatter plot of the data. Decide whether the data could best be modeled by a linear model, an exponential model, or a logarithmic model.

13. $(1, 2.0), (1.5, 3.5), (2, 4.0), (4, 5.8), (6, 7.0), (8, 7.8)$

14. $(1, 5.8), (1.5, 6.0), (2, 6.5), (4, 7.6), (6, 8.9), (8, 10.0)$

15. $(1, 4.4), (1.5, 4.7), (2, 5.5), (4, 9.9), (6, 18.1), (8, 33.0)$

16. $(1, 11.0), (1.5, 9.6), (2, 8.2), (4, 4.5), (6, 2.5), (8, 1.4)$

17. $(1, 7.5), (1.5, 7.0), (2, 6.8), (4, 5.0), (6, 3.5), (8, 2.0)$

18. $(1, 5.0), (1.5, 6.0), (2, 6.4), (4, 7.8), (6, 8.6), (8, 9.0)$

Finding an Exponential Model   In Exercises 19–22, use the *regression* feature of a graphing utility to find an exponential model $y = ab^x$ for the data and identify the coefficient of determination. Use the graphing utility to plot the data and graph the model in the same viewing window.

19. $(0, 5), (1, 6), (2, 7), (3, 9), (4, 13)$

20. $(0, 4.0), (2, 6.9), (4, 18.0), (6, 32.3), (8, 59.1),$
    $(10, 118.5)$

21. $(0, 8.3), (1, 6.1), (2, 4.6), (3, 3.8), (4, 3.6)$

22. $(-3, 102.2), (0, 80.5), (3, 67.8), (6, 58.2), (10, 55.0)$

Finding a Logarithmic Model   In Exercises 23–26, use the *regression* feature of a graphing utility to find a logarithmic model $y = a + b \ln x$ for the data and identify the coefficient of determination. Use the graphing utility to plot the data and graph the model in the same viewing window.

23. $(1, 2.0), (2, 3.0), (3, 3.5), (4, 4.0), (5, 4.1), (6, 4.2),$
    $(7, 4.5)$

24. $(1, 8.5), (2, 11.4), (4, 12.8), (6, 13.6), (8, 14.2),$
    $(10, 14.6)$

25. $(1, 11), (2, 6), (3, 5), (4, 4), (5, 3), (6, 2)$

26. $(3, 14.6), (6, 11.0), (9, 9.0), (12, 7.6), (15, 6.5)$

Finding a Power Model   In Exercises 27–30, use the *regression* feature of a graphing utility to find a power model $y = ax^b$ for the data and identify the coefficient of determination. Use the graphing utility to plot the data and graph the model in the same viewing window.

27. $(1, 2.0), (2, 3.4), (5, 6.7), (6, 7.3), (10, 12.0)$

28. $(0.5, 1.0), (2, 12.5), (4, 33.2), (6, 65.7), (8, 98.5),$
    $(10, 150.0)$

29. $(1, 10.0), (2, 4.0), (3, 0.7), (4, 0.1)$

30. $(2, 450), (4, 385), (6, 345), (8, 332), (10, 312)$

31. MODELING DATA

The table shows the yearly sales S (in millions of dollars) of Whole Foods Market for the years 2006 through 2013.   (Source: Whole Foods Market)

Year	Sales, S
2006	5,607.4
2007	6,591.8
2008	7,953.9
2009	8,031.6
2010	9,005.8
2011	10,108.0
2012	11,699.0
2013	12,917.0

Spreadsheet at LarsonPrecalculus.com

(a) Use the *regression* feature of a graphing utility to find an exponential model and a power model for the data and identify the coefficient of determination for each model. Let t represent the year, with $t = 6$ corresponding to 2006.

(b) Use the graphing utility to graph each model with the data.

(c) Use the coefficients of determination to determine which model fits the data better.

32. MODELING DATA

The table shows the numbers of single beds B (in thousands) on North American cruise ships from 2007 through 2012.   (Source: Cruise Lines International Association)

Year	Beds, B
2007	260.0
2008	270.7
2009	284.8
2010	307.7
2011	321.2
2012	333.7

Spreadsheet at LarsonPrecalculus.com

(a) Use the *regression* feature of a graphing utility to find a linear model, an exponential model, and a logarithmic model for the data and identify the coefficient of determination for each model. Let t represent the year, with $t = 7$ corresponding to 2007.

(b) Which model is the best fit for the data? Explain.

(c) Use the model you chose in part (b) to predict the number of beds in 2017. Is the number reasonable?

33. MODELING DATA

The populations P (in thousands) of Luxembourg for the years 1999 through 2013 are shown in the table, where t represents the year, with $t = 9$ corresponding to 1999.   (Source: European Commission Eurostat)

Year	Population, P
1999	427.4
2000	433.6
2001	439.0
2002	444.1
2003	448.3
2004	455.0
2005	461.2
2006	469.1
2007	476.2
2008	483.8
2009	493.5
2010	502.1
2011	511.8
2012	524.9
2013	537.0

Spreadsheet at LarsonPrecalculus.com

(a) Use the *regression* feature of a graphing utility to find a linear model for the data and to identify the coefficient of determination. Plot the model and the data in the same viewing window.

(b) Use the *regression* feature of the graphing utility to find a power model for the data and to identify the coefficient of determination. Plot the model and the data in the same viewing window.

(c) Use the *regression* feature of the graphing utility to find an exponential model for the data and to identify the coefficient of determination. Plot the model and the data in the same viewing window.

(d) Use the *regression* feature of the graphing utility to find a logarithmic model for the data and to identify the coefficient of determination. Plot the model and the data in the same viewing window.

(e) Which model is the best fit for the data? Explain.

(f) Use each model to predict the populations of Luxembourg for the years 2014 through 2018.

(g) Which model is the best choice for predicting the future population of Luxembourg? Explain.

(h) Were your choices of models the same for parts (e) and (g)? If not, explain why your choices were different.

34. *Why you should learn it* (p. 233) The atmospheric
pressure decreases with increasing altitude. At sea
level, the average air pressure is approximately
1.03323 kilograms per square centimeter, and this
pressure is called one atmosphere. Variations in
weather conditions cause changes in the atmospheric
pressure of up to ±5 percent. The ordered pairs
(h, p) give the pressures p (in atmospheres) for
various altitudes h (in kilometers). *(Spreadsheet
at LarsonPrecalculus.com)*

DATA   (0, 1), (10, 0.25), (20, 0.06), (5, 0.55),
(15, 0.12), (25, 0.02)

(a) Use the *regression* feature of a graphing
utility to attempt to find the logarithmic model
$p = a + b \ln h$ for the data. Explain why the result
is an error message.

(b) Use the *regression* feature of the graphing utility to
find the logarithmic model $h = a + b \ln p$ for the
data.

(c) Use the graphing utility to plot the data and
graph the logarithmic model in the same viewing
window.

(d) Use the model to estimate the altitude at which the
pressure is 0.75 atmosphere.

(e) Use the graph in part (c) to estimate the pressure at
an altitude of 13 kilometers.

35. MODELING DATA

The table shows the annual sales S (in billions of
dollars) of Starbucks for the years from 2009 through
2013.   (Source: Starbucks Corp.)

Year	Sales, S
2009	9.77
2010	10.71
2011	11.70
2012	13.30
2013	14.89

(a) Use the *regression* feature of a graphing utility
to find an exponential model for the data. Let t
represent the year, with $t = 9$ corresponding to
2009.

(b) Rewrite the model from part (a) as a natural
exponential model.

(c) Use the natural exponential model to predict the
annual sales of Starbucks in 2018. Is the value
reasonable?

36. MODELING DATA

A beaker of liquid at an initial temperature of 78°C is
placed in a room at a constant temperature of 21°C.
The temperature of the liquid is measured every
5 minutes for a period of $\frac{1}{2}$ hour. The results are
recorded in the table, where t is the time (in minutes)
and T is the temperature (in degrees Celsius).

Time, t	Temperature, T
0	78.0°
5	66.0°
10	57.5°
15	51.2°
20	46.3°
25	42.5°
30	39.6°

Spreadsheet at
LarsonPrecalculus.com

(a) Use the *regression* feature
of a graphing utility to find
a linear model for the data.
Use the graphing utility to
plot the data and graph the
model in the same viewing
window. Do the data
appear linear? Explain.

(b) Use the *regression* feature of
the graphing utility to find a
quadratic model for the data.
Use the graphing utility to
plot the data and graph the
model in the same viewing
window. Do the data appear
quadratic? Even though the
quadratic model appears to be
a good fit, explain why it might
not be a good model for predicting
the temperature of the liquid when $t = 60$.

(c) The graph of the temperature of the room
should be an asymptote of the graph of the
model. Subtract the room temperature from
each of the temperatures in the table. Use
the *regression* feature of the graphing utility
to find an exponential model for the revised
data. Add the room temperature to this model.
Use the graphing utility to plot the original
data and graph the model in the same viewing
window.

(d) Explain why the procedure in part (c) was
necessary for finding the exponential model.

37. MODELING DATA

The table shows the percents P of women in different age groups (in years) who have been married at least once. (Source: U.S. Census Bureau)

DATA Age group	Percent, P
18–24	14.6
25–29	49.0
30–34	70.3
35–39	79.9
40–44	85.0
45–49	87.0
50–54	89.5
55–59	91.1

Spreadsheet at LarsonPrecalculus.com

(a) Use the *regression* feature of a graphing utility to find a logistic model for the data. Let x represent the midpoint of the age group.

(b) Use the graphing utility to graph the model with the original data. How closely does the model represent the data?

38. MODELING DATA

The table shows the lengths y (in centimeters) of yellowtail snappers caught off the coast of Brazil for different ages (in years). (Source: Brazilian Journal of Oceanography)

DATA Age, x	Length, y
1	11.21
2	20.77
3	28.94
4	35.92
5	41.87
6	46.96
7	51.30
8	55.01
9	58.17
10	60.87
11	63.18
12	65.15
13	66.84
14	68.27
15	69.50

Spreadsheet at LarsonPrecalculus.com

(a) Use the *regression* feature of a graphing utility to find a logistic model and a power model for the data.

(b) Use the graphing utility to graph each model from part (a) with the data. Use the graphs to determine which model better fits the data.

(c) Use the model from part (b) to predict the length of a 17-year-old yellowtail snapper.

Conclusions

True or False? In Exercises 39 and 40, determine whether the statement is true or false. Justify your answer.

39. The exponential model $y = ae^{bx}$ represents a growth model when $b > 0$.

40. To change an exponential model of the form $y = ab^x$ to one of the form $y = ae^{cx}$, rewrite b as $b = \ln e^b$.

41. **Writing** In your own words, explain how to fit a model to a set of data using a graphing utility.

42. **HOW DO YOU SEE IT?** Each graphing utility screen below shows a model that fits the set of data. The equations and r^2-values for the models are given. Determine the equation and coefficient of determination that represents each graph. Explain how you found your result.

$y = 1.05e^{0.02288x}$ $r^2 = 0.968$
$y = 1.06 \ln x + 0.96$ $r^2 = 0.9991$

Cumulative Mixed Review

Using the Slope-Intercept Form In Exercises 43–46, find the slope and y-intercept of the equation of the line. Then sketch the line by hand.

43. $2x + 5y = 10$ 44. $3x - 2y = 9$

45. $0.4x - 2.5y = 12.5$ 46. $1.2x + 3.5y = 10.5$

Writing the Equation of a Parabola in Standard Form In Exercises 47–50, write an equation of the parabola in standard form.

3   Chapter Summary

What did you learn?	Explanation and Examples	Review Exercises
Recognize and evaluate exponential functions with base *a* (p. 180).	The exponential function f with base a is denoted by $f(x) = a^x$, where $a > 0$, $a \neq 1$, and x is any real number.	1–4
Graph exponential functions with base *a* (p. 181).		5–12
Recognize, evaluate, and graph exponential functions with base *e* (p. 184).	The function $f(x) = e^x$ is called the natural exponential function.	13–18
Use exponential functions to model and solve real-life problems (p. 186).	Exponential functions are used in compound interest formulas (see Example 8) and in radioactive decay models (see Example 10).	19–22
Recognize and evaluate logarithmic functions with base *a* (p. 192).	For $x > 0$, $a > 0$, and $a \neq 1$, $y = \log_a x$ if and only if $x = a^y$. The function $f(x) = \log_a x$ is called the logarithmic function with base a.	23–36
Graph logarithmic functions with base *a* (p. 194), and recognize, evaluate, and graph natural logarithmic functions (p. 196).	The graphs of $g(x) = \log_a x$ and $f(x) = a^x$ are reflections of each other in the line $y = x$. The function defined by $g(x) = \ln x$, $x > 0$, is called the natural logarithmic function.	37–48
Use logarithmic functions to model and solve real-life problems (p. 198).	A logarithmic function is used in the human memory model. (See Example 10.)	49, 50
Rewrite logarithms with different bases (p. 203).	Let a, b, and x be positive real numbers such that $a \neq 1$ and $b \neq 1$. Then $\log_a x$ can be converted to a different base as follows. *Base b* *Base 10* *Base e* $\log_a x = \dfrac{\log_b x}{\log_b a}$ $\log_a x = \dfrac{\log_{10} x}{\log_{10} a}$ $\log_a x = \dfrac{\ln x}{\ln a}$	51–58

Section markers: 3.1, 3.2, 3.3

	What did you learn?	Explanation and Examples	Review Exercises
3.3	Use properties of logarithms to evaluate, rewrite, expand, or condense logarithmic expressions (*p. 204*).	Let a be a real positive number ($a \neq 1$), n be a real number, and u and v be positive real numbers. **1. Product Property:** $\log_a(uv) = \log_a u + \log_a v$ $\ln(uv) = \ln u + \ln v$ **2. Quotient Property:** $\log_a(u/v) = \log_a u - \log_a v$ $\ln(u/v) = \ln u - \ln v$ **3. Power Property:** $\log_a u^n = n \log_a u, \quad \ln u^n = n \ln u$	59–78
	Use logarithmic functions to model and solve real-life problems (*p. 206*).	Logarithmic functions can be used to find an equation that relates the periods of several planets and their distances from the sun. (See Example 7.)	79, 80
3.4	Solve simple exponential and logarithmic equations (*p. 210*).	Solve simple exponential or logarithmic equations using the One-to-One Properties and Inverse Properties of exponential and logarithmic functions.	81–94
	Solve more complicated exponential (*p. 211*) and logarithmic (*p. 213*) equations.	To solve more complicated equations, rewrite the equations so that the One-to-One Properties and Inverse Properties of exponential and logarithmic functions can be used. (See Examples 2–9.)	95–118
	Use exponential and logarithmic equations to model and solve real-life problems (*p. 216*).	Exponential and logarithmic equations can be used to find how long it will take to double an investment (see Example 12) and to find the year in which the average salary for public school teachers reached $50,000 (see Example 13).	119, 120
3.5	Recognize the five most common types of models involving exponential or logarithmic functions (*p. 221*).	**1. Exponential growth model:** $y = ae^{bx}, \quad b > 0$ **2. Exponential decay model:** $y = ae^{-bx}, \quad b > 0$ **3. Gaussian model:** $y = ae^{-(x-b)^2/c}$ **4. Logistic growth model:** $y = \dfrac{a}{1 + be^{-rx}}$ **5. Logarithmic models:** $y = a + b \ln x,$ $y = a + b \log_{10} x$	121–126
	Use exponential growth and decay functions to model and solve real-life problems (*p. 222*).	An exponential growth function can be used to model the world population (see Example 1) and an exponential decay function can be used to estimate the age of a fossil (see Example 3).	127
	Use Gaussian functions (*p. 225*), logistic growth functions (*p. 226*), and logarithmic functions (*p. 227*) to model and solve real-life problems.	A Gaussian function can be used to model SAT mathematics scores for college-bound seniors (see Example 4). A logistic growth function can be used to model the spread of a flu virus (see Example 5). A logarithmic function can be used to find the intensity of an earthquake using its magnitude (see Example 6).	128–130
3.6	Classify scatter plots (*p. 233*), and use scatter plots and a graphing utility to find models for data and choose the model that best fits a set of data (*p. 234*).	You can use a scatter plot and a graphing utility to choose a model that best fits a set of data that represents the yield of a chemical reaction. (See Example 3.)	131, 132
	Use a graphing utility to find exponential and logistic models for data (*p. 236*).	An exponential model can be used to estimate the amount of a radioactive substance remaining after a given day (see Example 4), and a logistic model can be used to estimate the percent of defoliation caused by the gypsy moth (see Example 5).	133, 134

3 Review Exercises

See *CalcChat.com* for tutorial help and worked-out solutions to odd-numbered exercises. For instructions on how to use a graphing utility, see Appendix A.

3.1

Evaluating Exponential Functions In Exercises 1–4, use a calculator to evaluate the function at the indicated value of x. Round your result to four decimal places.

1. $f(x) = 1.45^x$, $x = 2\pi$
2. $f(x) = 7^x$, $x = \sqrt{11}$
3. $g(x) = 60^{2x}$, $x = -0.5$
4. $g(x) = 25^{-3x}$, $x = \frac{3}{2}$

Library of Parent Functions In Exercises 5–8, use the graph of $y = 4^x$ to match the function with its graph. [The graphs are labeled (a), (b), (c), and (d).]

(a)

(b)

(c)

(d)

5. $f(x) = 4^{x-3}$
6. $f(x) = 4^{-x}$
7. $f(x) = -4^x$
8. $f(x) = 4^x + 1$

Graphs of $y = a^x$ and $y = a^{-x}$ In Exercises 9–12, graph the exponential function by hand. Identify any asymptotes and intercepts and determine whether the graph of the function is increasing or decreasing.

9. $f(x) = 8^x$
10. $f(x) = 0.3^x$
11. $g(x) = 8^{-x}$
12. $g(x) = 0.3^{-x}$

Graphing Natural Exponential Functions In Exercises 13–18, use a graphing utility to construct a table of values for the function. Then sketch the graph of the function. Identify any asymptotes of the graph.

13. $h(x) = e^{x-1}$
14. $f(x) = e^{x+2}$
15. $h(x) = -e^x + 3$
16. $f(x) = -2e^{-x}$
17. $f(x) = 4e^{-0.5x}$
18. $f(x) = 2 + e^{x-3}$

Finding the Balance for Compound Interest In Exercises 19 and 20, complete the table to determine the balance A for $10,000 invested at rate r for t years, compounded continuously.

t	1	10	20	30	40	50
A						

19. $r = 8\%$
20. $r = 3\%$

21. Economics A new SUV costs $30,795. The value V of the SUV after t years is modeled by $V(t) = 30,795\left(\frac{4}{5}\right)^t$.
(a) Use a graphing utility to graph the function.
(b) Find the value of the SUV after 2 years.
(c) According to the model, when does the SUV depreciate most rapidly? Is this realistic? Explain.

22. Radioactive Decay Let Q represent the mass, in grams, of a quantity of plutonium 241 (^{241}Pu), whose half-life is about 14 years. The quantity of plutonium present after t years is given by $Q = 50\left(\frac{1}{2}\right)^{t/14}$.
(a) Determine the initial quantity (when $t = 0$).
(b) Determine the quantity present after 10 years.
(c) Use a graphing utility to graph the function over the interval $t = 0$ to $t = 50$.

3.2

Rewriting Equations In Exercises 23–32, write the logarithmic equation in exponential form, or write the exponential equation in logarithmic form.

23. $\log_5 625 = 4$
24. $\log_9 81 = 2$
25. $\log_{64} 2 = \frac{1}{6}$
26. $\log_{10}\left(\frac{1}{100}\right) = -2$
27. $4^3 = 64$
28. $3^5 = 243$
29. $e^{3.2} = 24.532\ldots$
30. $\ln 5 = 1.6094\ldots$
31. $\left(\frac{1}{2}\right)^{-3} = 8$
32. $\left(\frac{2}{3}\right)^{-2} = \frac{9}{4}$

Evaluating Logarithms In Exercises 33–36, use the definition of a logarithmic function to evaluate the function at the indicated value of x without using a calculator.

	Function	Value
33.	$f(x) = \log_6 x$	$x = 216$
34.	$f(x) = \log_7 x$	$x = 1$
35.	$f(x) = \log_4 x$	$x = \frac{1}{4}$
36.	$f(x) = \log_{10} x$	$x = 0.00001$

Sketching the Graph of a Logarithmic Function In Exercises 37–40, find the domain, vertical asymptote, and x-intercept of the logarithmic function, and sketch its graph by hand.

37. $g(x) = -\log_{10} x + 5$
38. $g(x) = \log_{10}(x - 3)$
39. $f(x) = \log_{10}(x - 1) + 6$
40. $f(x) = \log_{10}(x + 2) - 3$

Evaluating the Natural Logarithmic Function In Exercises 41–44, use a calculator to evaluate the function $f(x) = \ln x$ at the indicated value of x. Round your result to three decimal places.

41. $x = 21.5$
42. $x = 0.46$
43. $x = \sqrt{6}$
44. $x = \frac{5}{6}$

Analyzing Graphs of Functions   In Exercises 45–48, use a graphing utility to graph the logarithmic function. Determine the domain and identify any vertical asymptote and x-intercept.

45. $f(x) = \ln x + 3$
46. $f(x) = \ln(x - 3)$
47. $h(x) = \frac{1}{2} \ln x$
48. $f(x) = 4 \ln x$

49. Aeronautics   The time t (in minutes) for a small plane to climb to an altitude of h feet is given by

$$t = 50 \log_{10}[18{,}000/(18{,}000 - h)]$$

where 18,000 feet is the plane's absolute ceiling.

(a) Determine the domain of the function appropriate for the context of the problem.

(b) Use a graphing utility to graph the function and identify any asymptotes.

(c) As the plane approaches its absolute ceiling, what can be said about the time required to further increase its altitude?

(d) Find the amount of time it will take for the plane to climb to an altitude of 4000 feet.

50. Real Estate   The model

$$t = 12.542 \ln[x/(x - 1000)], \quad x > 1000$$

approximates the length of a home mortgage of $150,000 at 8% in terms of the monthly payment. In the model, t is the length of the mortgage in years and x is the monthly payment in dollars.

(a) Use the model to approximate the length of a $150,000 mortgage at 8% when the monthly payment is $1254.68.

(b) Approximate the total amount paid over the term of the mortgage with a monthly payment of $1254.68. What amount of the total is interest costs?

3.3

Changing the Base   In Exercises 51–54, evaluate the logarithm using the change-of-base formula. Do each problem twice, once with common logarithms and once with natural logarithms. Round your results to three decimal places.

51. $\log_4 9$
52. $\log_{1/2} 10$
53. $\log_{14} 15.6$
54. $\log_3 0.28$

Graphing a Logarithm with Any Base   In Exercises 55–58, use the change-of-base formula and a graphing utility to graph the function.

55. $f(x) = \log_2(x - 2)$
56. $f(x) = 2 - \log_3 x$
57. $f(x) = -\log_{1/2}(x - 2)$
58. $f(x) = \log_{1/3}(x - 1) + 1$

Using Properties to Evaluate Logarithms   In Exercises 59–62, approximate the logarithm using the properties of logarithms, given the values $\log_b 2 \approx 0.3562$, $\log_b 3 \approx 0.5646$, and $\log_b 5 \approx 0.8271$.

59. $\log_b 9$
60. $\log_b \frac{4}{9}$
61. $\log_b \sqrt{5}$
62. $\log_b 50$

Simplifying a Logarithm   In Exercises 63–66, use the properties of logarithms to rewrite and simplify the logarithmic expression.

63. $\ln(5e^{-2})$
64. $\ln \sqrt{e^5}$
65. $\log_{10} 200$
66. $\log_{10} 0.002$

Expanding Logarithmic Expressions   In Exercises 67–72, use the properties of logarithms to expand the expression as a sum, difference, and/or constant multiple of logarithms. (Assume all variables are positive.)

67. $\log_5 5x^2$
68. $\log_4 16xy^2$
69. $\log_{10} \dfrac{5\sqrt{y}}{x^2}$
70. $\ln \dfrac{\sqrt{x}}{4}$
71. $\ln \dfrac{x + 3}{xy}$
72. $\ln \dfrac{xy^5}{\sqrt{z}}$

Condensing Logarithmic Expressions   In Exercises 73–78, condense the expression to the logarithm of a single quantity.

73. $\log_2 9 + \log_2 x$
74. $\log_6 y - 2 \log_6 z$
75. $\frac{1}{2} \ln(2x - 1) - 2 \ln(x + 1)$
76. $5 \ln(x - 2) - \ln(x + 2) + 3 \ln x$
77. $\ln 3 + \frac{1}{3} \ln(4 - x^2) - \ln x$
78. $3[\ln x - 2 \ln(x^2 + 1)] + 2 \ln 5$

79. Public Service   The number of miles s of roads cleared of snow in 1 hour is approximated by the model

$$s = 25 - \frac{13 \ln(h/12)}{\ln 3}, \quad 2 \le h \le 15$$

where h is the depth of the snow (in inches).

(a) Use a graphing utility to graph the function.

(b) Complete the table.

h	4	6	8	10	12	14
s						

(c) Using the graph of the function and the table, what conclusion can you make about the number of miles of roads cleared as the depth of the snow increases?

80. Psychology Students in a sociology class were given an exam and then retested monthly with an equivalent exam. The average scores for the class are given by the human memory model $f(t) = 85 - 17 \log_{10}(t + 1)$, where t is the time in months and $0 \le t \le 10$. When will the average score decrease to 68?

3.4

Solving an Exponential or Logarithmic Equation In Exercises 81–94, solve the equation without using a calculator.

81. $10^x = 10,000$

82. $7^x = 343$

83. $6^x = \frac{1}{216}$

84. $6^{x-2} = \frac{1}{1296}$

85. $2^{x+1} = \frac{1}{16}$

86. $4^{x/2} = 64$

87. $\log_8 x = 4$

88. $\log_x 729 = 6$

89. $\log_2(x - 1) = 3$

90. $\log_5(2x + 27) = 2$

91. $\ln x = 4$

92. $\ln x = -3$

93. $\ln(x - 1) = 2$

94. $\ln(2x + 1) = -4$

Solving an Exponential Equation In Exercises 95–104, solve the exponential equation algebraically. Round your result to three decimal places.

95. $3e^{-5x} = 132$

96. $14e^{3x+2} = 560$

97. $2^x + 13 = 35$

98. $6^x - 28 = -8$

99. $-4(5^x) = -68$

100. $2(12^x) = 190$

101. $2e^{x-3} - 1 = 4$

102. $-e^{x/2} + 1 = \frac{1}{2}$

103. $e^{2x} - 7e^x + 10 = 0$

104. $e^{2x} - 6e^x + 8 = 0$

Solving a Logarithmic Equation In Exercises 105–114, solve the logarithmic equation algebraically. Round your result to three decimal places.

105. $\ln 3x = 6.4$

106. $\ln 5x = 4.5$

107. $\ln x - \ln 5 = 2$

108. $\ln x - \ln 3 = 4$

109. $\ln \sqrt{x + 1} = 2$

110. $\ln \sqrt{x + 40} = 3$

111. $\log_4(x + 5) = \log_4(13 - x) - \log_4(x - 3)$

112. $\log_5(x + 2) - \log_5 x = \log_5(x + 5)$

113. $\log_{10}(1 - x) = -1$

114. $\log_{10}(-x - 4) = 2$

Solving an Exponential or Logarithmic Equation In Exercises 115–118, solve the equation algebraically. Round your result to three decimal places.

115. $xe^x + e^x = 0$

116. $2xe^{2x} + e^{2x} = 0$

117. $x \ln x + x = 0$

118. $\frac{1 + \ln x}{x^2} = 0$

119. Finance You deposit $7550 in an account that pays 6.9% interest, compounded continuously. How long will it take for the money to double?

120. Economics The demand x for a 32-inch plasma television is modeled by

$$p = 5000\left(1 - \frac{4}{4 + e^{-0.0005x}}\right).$$

Find the demands x for prices of (a) $p = \$500$ and (b) $p = \$350$.

3.5

Identifying Graphs of Models In Exercises 121–126, match the function with its graph. [The graphs are labeled (a), (b), (c), (d), (e), and (f).]

(a)

(b)

(c)

(d)

(e)

(f)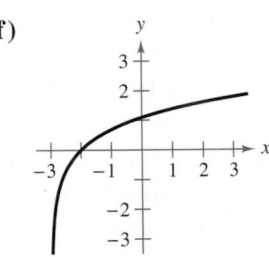

121. $y = 3e^{-2x/3}$

122. $y = 4e^{2x/3}$

123. $y = \ln(x + 3)$

124. $y = 7 - \log_{10}(x + 3)$

125. $y = 2e^{-(x+4)^2/3}$

126. $y = \frac{6}{1 + 2e^{-2x}}$

127. Demography The populations P (in millions) of North Carolina from 2000 through 2012 can be modeled by $P = 8.06e^{kt}$, where t is the year, with $t = 0$ corresponding to 2000. In 2001, the population was about 8,210,000. Find the value of k and use the result to predict the population in the year 2020. (Source: U.S. Census Bureau)

128. Education The scores for a biology test follow a normal distribution modeled by $y = 0.0499e^{-(x-74)^2/128}$, where x is the test score and $40 \le x \le 100$.

(a) Use a graphing utility to graph the function.

(b) Use the graph to estimate the average test score.

129. Education The average number N of words per minute that the students in a first grade class could read orally after t weeks of school is modeled by

$$N = \frac{62}{1 + 5.4e^{-0.24t}}.$$

Find the numbers of weeks it took the class to read at average rates of (a) 45 words per minute and (b) 61 words per minute.

130. Geology On the Richter scale, the magnitude R of an earthquake of intensity I is modeled by

$$R = \log_{10} \frac{I}{I_0}$$

where $I_0 = 1$ is the minimum intensity used for comparison. Find the intensities I of the following earthquakes measuring R on the Richter scale.

(a) $R = 7.1$ (b) $R = 9.2$ (c) $R = 3.8$

3.6

Classifying Scatter Plots In Exercises 131 and 132, determine whether the scatter plot could best be modeled by a linear model, an exponential model, a logarithmic model, or a logistic model.

131.

132.

133. MODELING DATA

Each ordered pair (t, N) represents the year t and the number N (in thousands) of female participants in high school athletic programs during 13 school years, with $t = 1$ corresponding to the 2000–2001 school year. *(Spreadsheet at LarsonPrecalculus.com)* (Source: National Federation of State High School Associations)

 (1, 2784), (2, 2807), (3, 2856), (4, 2865), (5, 2908), (6, 2953), (7, 3022), (8, 3057), (9, 3114), (10, 3173), (11, 3174), (12, 3208), (13, 3223)

(a) Use the *regression* feature of a graphing utility to find a linear model, an exponential model, and a power model for the data and identify the coefficient of determination for each model.

(b) Use the graphing utility to graph each model with the original data.

(c) Determine which model best fits the data. Explain.

(d) Use the model you chose in part (c) to predict the school year in which about 3,697,000 girls will participate.

134. MODELING DATA

You plant a tree when it is 1 meter tall and check its height h (in meters) every 10 years, as shown in the table.

Year	Height, h
0	1
10	3
20	7.5
30	14.5
40	19
50	20.5
60	21

Spreadsheet at LarsonPrecalculus.com

(a) Use the *regression* feature of a graphing utility to find a logistic model for the data. Let x represent the year.

(b) Use the graphing utility to graph the model with the original data.

(c) How closely does the model represent the data?

(d) What is the limiting height of the tree?

Conclusions

True or False? In Exercises 135–138, determine whether the equation or statement is true or false. Justify your answer.

135. $e^{x-1} = \dfrac{e^x}{e}$ **136.** $\ln(x + y) = \ln(xy)$

137. The domain of the function $f(x) = \ln x$ is the set of all real numbers.

138. The logarithm of the quotient of two numbers is equal to the difference of the logarithms of the numbers.

139. Think About It Without using a calculator, explain why you know that $2^{\sqrt{2}}$ is greater than 2, but less than 4.

140. Exploration

(a) Use a graphing utility to compare the graph of the function $y = e^x$ with the graph of each function below. [$n!$ (read as "n factorial") is defined as $n! = 1 \cdot 2 \cdot 3 \cdots (n-1) \cdot n$.]

$$y_1 = 1 + \frac{x}{1!}, \; y_2 = 1 + \frac{x}{1!} + \frac{x^2}{2!},$$

$$y_3 = 1 + \frac{x}{1!} + \frac{x^2}{2!} + \frac{x^3}{3!}$$

(b) Identify the pattern of successive polynomials given in part (a). Extend the pattern one more term and compare the graph of the resulting polynomial function with the graph of $y = e^x$. What do you think this pattern implies?

See *CalcChat.com* for tutorial help and worked-out solutions to odd-numbered exercises.
For instructions on how to use a graphing utility, see Appendix A.

3   Chapter Test

Take this test as you would take a test in class. After you are finished, check your
work against the answers given in the back of the book.

In Exercises 1–3, use a graphing utility to construct a table of values for the function.
Then sketch a graph of the function. Identify any asymptotes and intercepts.

1. $f(x) = 10^{-x}$ **2.** $f(x) = -6^{x-2}$ **3.** $f(x) = 1 - e^{2x}$

In Exercises 4–6, evaluate the expression.

4. $\log_7 7^{-0.89}$ **5.** $4.6 \ln e^2$ **6.** $5 - \log_{10} 1000$

In Exercises 7–9, find the domain, vertical asymptote, and x-intercept of the
logarithmic function, and sketch its graph by hand.

7. $f(x) = -\log_{10} x - 6$ **8.** $f(x) = \ln(x + 4)$ **9.** $f(x) = 1 + \ln(x - 6)$

In Exercises 10–12, evaluate the logarithm using the change-of-base formula.
Round your result to three decimal places.

10. $\log_7 44$ **11.** $\log_{2/5} 1.3$ **12.** $\log_{12} 64$

In Exercises 13–15, use the properties of logarithms to expand the expression as a
sum, difference, and/or multiple of logarithms.

13. $\log_2 3a^4$ **14.** $\ln \dfrac{5\sqrt{x}}{6}$ **15.** $\ln \dfrac{x\sqrt{x+1}}{2e^4}$

In Exercises 16–18, condense the expression.

16. $\log_3 13 + \log_3 y$ **17.** $4 \ln x - 4 \ln y$

18. $\ln x - \ln(x + 2) + \ln(2x - 3)$

In Exercises 19–22, solve the equation.

19. $3^x = 81$ **20.** $5^{2x} = 2500$

21. $\log_7 x = 6$ **22.** $\log_{10}(x - 4) = 5$

In Exercises 23–26, solve the equation algebraically. Round your result to three
decimal places.

23. $\dfrac{1025}{8 + e^{4x}} = 5$ **24.** $-xe^{-x} + e^{-x} = 0$

25. $\log_{10} x - \log_{10}(8 - 5x) = 2$ **26.** $2x \ln x - x = 0$

27. The half-life of radioactive actinium (^{227}Ac) is about 22 years. What percent of a
present amount of radioactive actinium will remain after 15 years?

28. The table shows the annual revenues R (in billions of dollars) for Amazon.com
from 2006 through 2013.   (Source: Amazon.com)

   (a) Use the *regression* feature of a graphing utility to find a logarithmic model, an
   exponential model, and a power model for the data. Let t represent the year,
   with $t = 6$ corresponding to 2006.

   (b) Use the graphing utility to graph each model with the original data.

   (c) Determine which model best fits the data. Use the model to predict the revenue
   of Amazon.com in 2019.

Year	Revenue, R
2006	10.711
2007	14.836
2008	19.166
2009	24.509
2010	34.204
2011	48.077
2012	61.093
2013	74.452

Table for 28

Spreadsheet at
LarsonPrecalculus.com

1-3   Cumulative Test

See *CalcChat.com* for tutorial help and worked-out solutions to odd-numbered exercises. For instructions on how to use a graphing utility, see Appendix A.

Take this test to review the material in Chapters 1–3. After you are finished, check your work against the answers given in the back of the book.

In Exercises 1–3, (a) write the slope-intercept form of the equation of the line that satisfies the given conditions and (b) find three additional points through which the line passes.

1. The line passes through the points $(-5, 8)$ and $(-1, 4)$.

2. The line passes through the point $\left(-\frac{1}{2}, 1\right)$ and has a slope of -2.

3. The line has an undefined slope and passes through the point $\left(\frac{3}{7}, \frac{1}{8}\right)$.

In Exercises 4 and 5, evaluate the function at each value of the independent variable and simplify.

4. $f(x) = \dfrac{x}{x - 2}$

   (a) $f(5)$ (b) $f(2)$ (c) $f(5 + 4s)$

5. $f(x) = \begin{cases} 3x - 8, & x < 0 \\ x^2 + 4, & x \geq 0 \end{cases}$

   (a) $f(-8)$ (b) $f(0)$ (c) $f(4)$

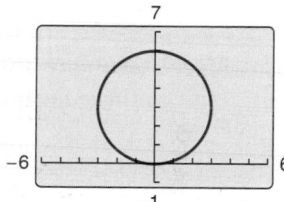

Figure for 6

6. Does the graph at the right represent y as a function of x? Explain.

7. Use a graphing utility to graph the function $f(x) = 2|x - 5| - |x + 5|$. Then determine the open intervals over which the function is increasing, decreasing, or constant.

8. Compare the graph of each function with the graph of $f(x) = \sqrt{x}$.

   (a) $r(x) = \dfrac{1}{4}\sqrt{x}$ (b) $h(x) = \sqrt{x} - 3$ (c) $g(x) = -\sqrt{x + 3}$

In Exercises 9–12, evaluate the indicated function for

$$f(x) = -x^2 + 3x - 10 \quad \text{and} \quad g(x) = 4x + 1.$$

9. $(f + g)(-4)$

10. $(g - f)\left(\frac{3}{4}\right)$

11. $(g \circ f)(2)$

12. $(fg)(-1)$

13. Determine whether $h(x) = 5x - 2$ has an inverse function. If so, find it.

In Exercises 14–16, sketch the graph of the function. Use a graphing utility to verify the graph.

14. $f(x) = -(x - 2)^2 + 5$

15. $f(x) = x^2 - 6x + 5$

16. $f(x) = x^3 + 3x^2 - 4x - 12$

17. Find all the zeros of $f(x) = x^3 + 2x^2 + 4x + 8$.

18. Use a graphing utility to approximate any real zeros of $g(x) = x^3 + 5x^2 + 4$ accurate to three decimal places.

19. Divide $(4x^2 + 14x - 9)$ by $(x + 3)$ using long division.

20. Divide $(2x^3 - 5x^2 + 6x - 20)$ by $(x - 6)$ using synthetic division.

21. Multiply the complex number $-8 + 3i$ by its complex conjugate.

22. Find a polynomial function with real coefficients that has the zeros 0, -3, and $1 + \sqrt{5}i$.

In Exercises 23–26, sketch the graph of the rational function. Identify any asymptotes. Use a graphing utility to verify your graph.

23. $f(x) = \dfrac{2x}{x - 3}$

24. $f(x) = \dfrac{5x}{x^2 + x - 6}$

25. $f(x) = \dfrac{x^2 - 3x + 8}{x - 2}$

26. $f(x) = \dfrac{4x^3}{x^3 + 5x}$

In Exercises 27–30, use a calculator to evaluate the expression. Round your answer to three decimal places.

27. $(1.49)^{3.1}$

28. $58^{\sqrt{5}}$

29. $e^{-8/5}$

30. $4e^{2.56}$

In Exercises 31–34, sketch the graph of the function by hand. Use a graphing utility to verify your graph.

31. $f(x) = -3^{x+4} - 5$

32. $f(x) = -\left(\frac{1}{2}\right)^{-x} + 3$

33. $f(x) = 4 + \log_{10}(x - 3)$

34. $f(x) = \ln(4 - x)$

In Exercises 35–37, evaluate the logarithm using the change-of-base formula. Round your result to three decimal places.

35. $\log_5 16$

36. $\log_9 7.3$

37. $\log_2\left(\frac{3}{2}\right)$

38. Use the properties of logarithms to expand $\ln \dfrac{x^2 - 4}{x^2 + 1}$.

39. Write $2 \ln x - \ln(x - 1) + \ln(x + 1)$ as a logarithm of a single quantity.

In Exercises 40–45, solve the equation algebraically. Round your result to three decimal places and verify your result graphically.

40. $6e^{2x} = 72$

41. $4^{x-5} + 21 = 30$

42. $\log_2 x + \log_2 5 = 6$

43. $2500e^{0.05x} = 500{,}000$

44. $2x^2 e^{2x} - 2x e^{2x} = 0$

45. $\ln(2x - 5) - \ln x = 1$

46. A rectangular plot of land with a perimeter of 546 feet has a width of x.

(a) Write the area A of the plot as a function of x.

(b) Use a graphing utility to graph the area function. What is the domain of the function?

(c) Approximate the dimensions of the plot when the area is 15,000 square feet.

47. The table shows the annual sales S (in billions of dollars) for Wal-Mart from 2003 through 2012.   (Source: Wal-Mart Stores, Inc.)

(a) Use the *regression* feature of a graphing utility to find a quadratic model, an exponential model, and a power model for the data and identify the coefficient of determination for each model. Let t represent the year, with $t = 3$ corresponding to 2003.

(b) Use the graphing utility to graph each model with the original data.

(c) Determine which model best fits the data. Explain.

(d) Use the model you chose in part (c) to predict the annual sales of Wal-Mart in 2020. Is your answer reasonable? Explain.

DATA

Year	Sales, S
2003	258.681
2004	287.989
2005	315.654
2006	348.650
2007	378.799
2008	405.607
2009	408.214
2010	421.849
2011	446.950
2012	469.162

Spreadsheet at LarsonPrecalculus.com

Table for 47

Proofs in Mathematics

Proofs in Mathematics

Each of the following three properties of logarithms can be proved by using properties of exponential functions.

Properties of Logarithms   (p. 204)

Let a be a positive real number such that $a \neq 1$, and let n be a real number. If u and v are positive real numbers, then the following properties are true.

	Logarithm with Base a	*Natural Logarithm*
1. Product Property:	$\log_a(uv) = \log_a u + \log_a v$	$\ln(uv) = \ln u + \ln v$
2. Quotient Property:	$\log_a \dfrac{u}{v} = \log_a u - \log_a v$	$\ln \dfrac{u}{v} = \ln u - \ln v$
3. Power Property:	$\log_a u^n = n \log_a u$	$\ln u^n = n \ln u$

Proof

Let

$$x = \log_a u \qquad \text{and} \qquad y = \log_a v.$$

The corresponding exponential forms of these two equations are

$$a^x = u \qquad \text{and} \qquad a^y = v.$$

To prove the Product Property, multiply u and v to obtain

$$uv = a^x a^y = a^{x+y}.$$

The corresponding logarithmic form of $uv = a^{x+y}$ is

$$\log_a(uv) = x + y.$$

So,

$$\log_a(uv) = \log_a u + \log_a v.$$

To prove the Quotient Property, divide u by v to obtain

$$\frac{u}{v} = \frac{a^x}{a^y} = a^{x-y}.$$

The corresponding logarithmic form of $u/v = a^{x-y}$ is

$$\log_a \frac{u}{v} = x - y.$$

So,

$$\log_a \frac{u}{v} = \log_a u - \log_a v.$$

To prove the Power Property, substitute a^x for u in the expression $\log_a u^n$, as follows.

$$\log_a u^n = \log_a(a^x)^n \qquad \text{Substitute } a^x \text{ for } u.$$
$$= \log_a a^{nx} \qquad \text{Property of exponents}$$
$$= nx \qquad \text{Inverse Property of logarithms}$$
$$= n \log_a u \qquad \text{Substitute } \log_a u \text{ for } x.$$

So, $\log_a u^n = n \log_a u.$

Slide Rules

The slide rule was invented by William Oughtred (1574–1660) in 1625. The slide rule is a computational device with a sliding portion and a fixed portion. A slide rule enables you to perform multiplication by using the Product Property of logarithms. There are other slide rules that allow for the calculation of roots and trigonometric functions. Slide rules were used by mathematicians and engineers until the invention of the handheld calculator in 1972.

Progressive Summary (Chapters 1–3)

This chart outlines the topics that have been covered so far in this text. Progressive Summary charts appear after Chapters 2, 3, 6, and 9. In each Progressive Summary, new topics encountered for the first time appear in blue.

Algebraic Functions

Polynomial, Rational, Radical

■ Rewriting
Polynomial form ↔ Factored form
Operations with polynomials
Rationalize denominators
Simplify rational expressions
Operations with complex numbers

■ Solving

Equation	*Strategy*
Linear	Isolate variable
Quadratic.	Factor, set to zero
	Extract square roots
	Complete the square
	Quadratic Formula
Polynomial	Factor, set to zero
	Rational Zero Test
Rational.	Multiply by LCD
Radical	Isolate, raise to power
Absolute value . . .	Isolate, form two equations

■ Analyzing

Graphically	*Algebraically*
Intercepts	Domain, Range
Symmetry	Transformations
Slope	Composition
Asymptotes	Standard forms
End behavior	of equations
Minimum values	Leading Coefficient
Maximum values	Test
	Synthetic division
	Descartes's Rule of Signs

Numerically
Table of values

Transcendental Functions

Exponential, Logarithmic

■ Rewriting
Exponential form ↔ Logarithmic form
Condense/expand logarithmic expressions

■ Solving

Equation	*Strategy*
Exponential	Take logarithm of each side
Logarithmic.	Exponentiate each side

■ Analyzing

Graphically	*Algebraically*
Intercepts	Domain, Range
Asymptotes	Transformations
	Composition
	Inverse Properties

Numerically
Table of values

Other Topics

■ Rewriting

■ Solving

■ Analyzing

4 Trigonometric Functions

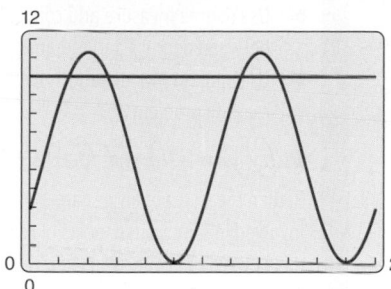

Section 4.5, Example 8
A Depth of at Least 10 Feet

4.1   Radian and Degree Measure

4.2   Trigonometric Functions: The Unit Circle

4.3   Right Triangle Trigonometry

4.4   Trigonometric Functions of Any Angle

4.5   Graphs of Sine and Cosine Functions

4.6   Graphs of Other Trigonometric Functions

4.7   Inverse Trigonometric Functions

4.8   Applications and Models

4.1   Radian and Degree Measure

Angles

As derived from the Greek language, the word **trigonometry** means "measurement of triangles." Initially, trigonometry dealt with relationships among the sides and angles of triangles and was used in the development of astronomy, navigation, and surveying. With the development of calculus and the physical sciences in the seventeenth century, a different perspective arose—one that viewed the classic trigonometric relationships as *functions* with the set of real numbers as their domains. Consequently, the applications of trigonometry expanded to include a vast number of physical phenomena involving rotations and vibrations, including the following.

- sound waves
- light rays
- planetary orbits
- vibrating strings
- pendulums
- orbits of atomic particles

The approach in this text incorporates *both* perspectives, starting with angles and their measure.

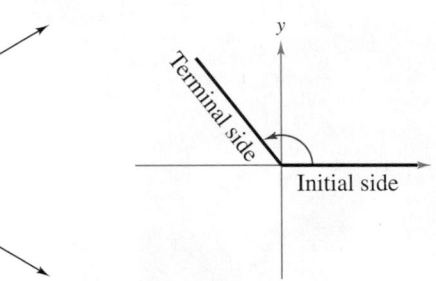

Figure 4.1   **Figure 4.2**

An **angle** is determined by rotating a ray (half-line) about its endpoint. The starting position of the ray is the **initial side** of the angle, and the position after rotation is the **terminal side,** as shown in Figure 4.1. The endpoint of the ray is the **vertex** of the angle. This perception of an angle fits a coordinate system in which the origin is the vertex and the initial side coincides with the positive *x*-axis. Such an angle is in **standard position,** as shown in Figure 4.2. **Positive angles** are generated by counterclockwise rotation, and **negative angles** by clockwise rotation, as shown in Figure 4.3. Angles are labeled with Greek letters such as α (alpha), β (beta), and θ (theta), as well as uppercase letters such as A, B, and C. In Figure 4.4, note that angles α and β have the same initial and terminal sides. Such angles are **coterminal.**

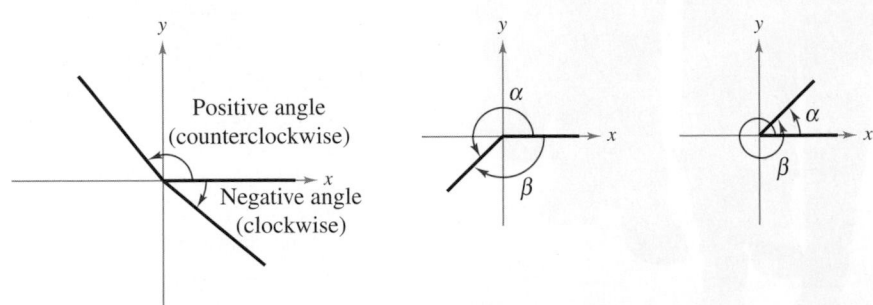

Figure 4.3   **Figure 4.4**

Radian Measure

The **measure of an angle** is determined by the amount of rotation from the initial side to the terminal side. One way to measure angles is in *radians*. This type of measure is especially useful in calculus. To define a radian, you can use a **central angle** of a circle, one whose vertex is the center of the circle, as shown in Figure 4.5.

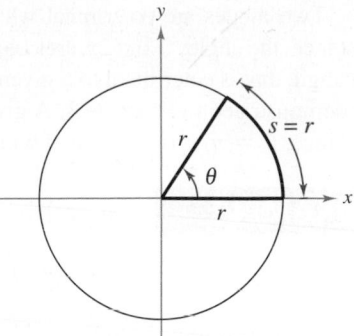

Arc length = radius when $\theta = 1$ radian.

Figure 4.5

Definition of Radian

One **radian** (rad) is the measure of a central angle θ that intercepts an arc s equal in length to the radius r of the circle. (See Figure 4.5.) Algebraically this means that

$$\theta = \frac{s}{r}$$

where θ is measured in radians.

Because the circumference of a circle is $2\pi r$ units, it follows that a central angle of one full revolution (counterclockwise) corresponds to an arc length of $s = 2\pi r$. Moreover, because $2\pi \approx 6.28$, there are just over six radius lengths in a full circle, as shown in Figure 4.6. Because the units of measure for s and r are the same, the ratio s/r has no units—it is simply a real number.

Because the radian measure of an angle of one full revolution is 2π, you can obtain the following.

$$\frac{1}{2}\text{ revolution} = \frac{2\pi}{2} = \pi \text{ radians} \qquad \frac{1}{4}\text{ revolution} = \frac{2\pi}{4} = \frac{\pi}{2}\text{ radians}$$

$$\frac{1}{6}\text{ revolution} = \frac{2\pi}{6} = \frac{\pi}{3}\text{ radians} \qquad \frac{1}{8}\text{ revolution} = \frac{2\pi}{8} = \frac{\pi}{4}\text{ radian}$$

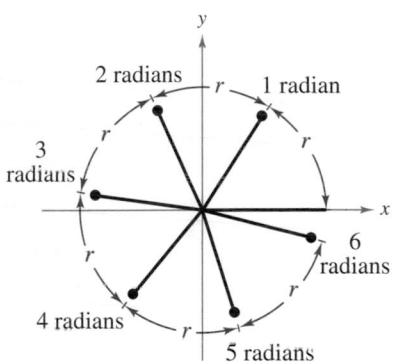

Figure 4.6

These and other common angles are shown below.

Recall that the four quadrants in a coordinate system are numbered I, II, III, and IV. The figure below shows which angles between 0 and 2π lie in each of the four quadrants. Note that angles between 0 and $\pi/2$ are **acute** and that angles between $\pi/2$ and π are **obtuse**.

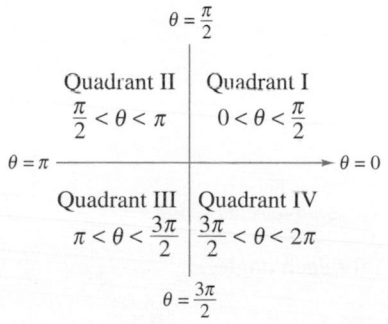

Remark

The phrase "the terminal side of θ lies in a quadrant" is often abbreviated by simply saying that "θ lies in a quadrant." The terminal sides of the "quadrant angles" 0, $\pi/2$, π, and $3\pi/2$ do not lie within quadrants.

Two angles are coterminal when they have the same initial and terminal sides. For instance, the angles 0 and 2π are coterminal, as are the angles $\pi/6$ and $13\pi/6$. You can find an angle that is coterminal to a given angle θ by adding or subtracting 2π (one revolution), as demonstrated in Example 1. A given angle θ has infinitely many coterminal angles. For instance, $\theta = \pi/6$ is coterminal with $\pi/6 + 2n\pi$, where n is an integer.

EXAMPLE 1   Sketching and Finding Coterminal Angles

See LarsonPrecalculus.com for an interactive version of this type of example.

a. For the positive angle $\theta = \dfrac{13\pi}{6}$, subtract 2π to obtain a coterminal angle.

$$\frac{13\pi}{6} - 2\pi = \frac{\pi}{6} \qquad \text{See figure.}$$

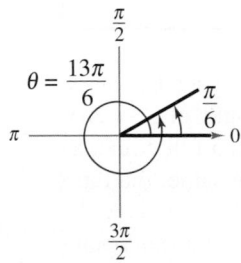

b. For the positive angle $\theta = \dfrac{3\pi}{4}$, subtract 2π to obtain a coterminal angle.

$$\frac{3\pi}{4} - 2\pi = -\frac{5\pi}{4} \qquad \text{See figure.}$$

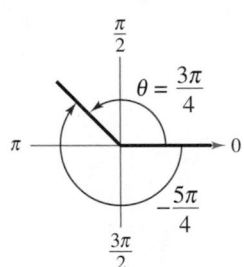

c. For the negative angle $\theta = -\dfrac{2\pi}{3}$, add 2π to obtain a coterminal angle.

$$-\frac{2\pi}{3} + 2\pi = \frac{4\pi}{3} \qquad \text{See figure.}$$

✓ **Checkpoint** Audio-video solution in English & Spanish at LarsonPrecalculus.com.

Determine two coterminal angles (one positive and one negative) for each angle.

a. $\theta = \dfrac{9\pi}{4}$ **b.** $\theta = -\dfrac{\pi}{3}$

Degree Measure

A second way to measure angles is in terms of **degrees,** denoted by the symbol °. A measure of one degree (1°) is equivalent to a rotation of $\frac{1}{360}$ of a complete revolution about the vertex. To measure angles, it is convenient to mark degrees on the circumference of a circle, as shown in Figure 4.7. So, a full revolution (counterclockwise) corresponds to 360°, a half revolution to 180°, a quarter revolution to 90°, and so on.

Because 2π radians corresponds to one complete revolution, degrees and radians are related by the equations

$$360° = 2\pi \text{ rad} \qquad \text{and} \qquad 180° = \pi \text{ rad}.$$

From the second equation, you obtain

$$1° = \frac{\pi}{180} \text{ rad} \qquad \text{and} \qquad 1 \text{ rad} = \frac{180°}{\pi}$$

which lead to the conversion rules below.

Figure 4.7

Conversions Between Degrees and Radians

1. To convert degrees to radians, multiply degrees by $\dfrac{\pi \text{ rad}}{180°}$.

2. To convert radians to degrees, multiply radians by $\dfrac{180°}{\pi \text{ rad}}$.

To apply these two conversion rules, use the basic relationship π rad = 180°. (See Figure 4.8.)

Figure 4.8

When no units of angle measure are specified, *radian measure is implied.* For instance, $\theta = 2$ implies that $\theta = 2$ radians.

EXAMPLE 2   Converting from Degrees to Radians

a. $135° = (135 \text{ deg})\left(\dfrac{\pi \text{ rad}}{180 \text{ deg}}\right) - \dfrac{3\pi}{4}$ radians   Multiply by $\frac{\pi}{180}$.

b. $540° = (540 \text{ deg})\left(\dfrac{\pi \text{ rad}}{180 \text{ deg}}\right) = 3\pi$ radians   Multiply by $\frac{\pi}{180}$.

✓ *Checkpoint*))) *Audio-video solution in English & Spanish at LarsonPrecalculus.com.*

Rewrite each angle in radian measure as a multiple of π. (Do not use a calculator.)

a. $\theta = 75°$

b. $\theta = 320°$

EXAMPLE 3   Converting from Radians to Degrees

a. $-\dfrac{\pi}{2}$ rad $= \left(-\dfrac{\pi}{2}\text{ rad}\right)\left(\dfrac{180\text{ deg}}{\pi\text{ rad}}\right) = -90°$ Multiply by $\dfrac{180}{\pi}$.

b. 2 rad $= (2\text{ rad})\left(\dfrac{180\text{ deg}}{\pi\text{ rad}}\right) = \dfrac{360}{\pi} \approx 114.59°$ Multiply by $\dfrac{180}{\pi}$.

✔ **Checkpoint**)))) *Audio-video solution in English & Spanish at LarsonPrecalculus.com.*

Rewrite each angle in degree measure. (Do not use a calculator.)

a. $\dfrac{\pi}{6}$ **b.** $\dfrac{5\pi}{3}$

Two positive angles α and β are **complementary** (complements of each other) when their sum is 90° (or $\pi/2$). Two positive angles are **supplementary** (supplements of each other) when their sum is 180° (or π). (See Figure 4.9.)

    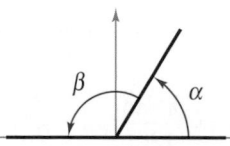

Complementary angles   *Supplementary angles*
Figure 4.9

EXAMPLE 4   Complementary and Supplementary Angles

If possible, find the complement and supplement of each angle.

a. 72°   **b.** 148°   **c.** $\dfrac{2\pi}{5}$ **d.** $\dfrac{4\pi}{5}$

Solution

a. The complement is $90° - 72° = 18°$. The supplement is $180° - 72° = 108°$.

b. Because 148° is greater than 90°, it has no complement. (Remember that complements are *positive* angles.) The supplement is

$$180° - 148° = 32°.$$

c. The complement is

$$\dfrac{\pi}{2} - \dfrac{2\pi}{5} = \dfrac{5\pi}{10} - \dfrac{4\pi}{10} = \dfrac{\pi}{10}.$$

The supplement is

$$\pi - \dfrac{2\pi}{5} = \dfrac{5\pi}{5} - \dfrac{2\pi}{5} = \dfrac{3\pi}{5}.$$

d. Because $4\pi/5$ is greater than $\pi/2$, it has no complement. The supplement is

$$\pi - \dfrac{4\pi}{5} = \dfrac{5\pi}{5} - \dfrac{4\pi}{5} = \dfrac{\pi}{5}.$$

✔ **Checkpoint**)))) *Audio-video solution in English & Spanish at LarsonPrecalculus.com.*

If possible, find the complement and supplement of each angle.

a. 36°   **b.** 91°   **c.** $\dfrac{\pi}{6}$ **d.** $\dfrac{5\pi}{6}$

Technology Tip

Historically, fractional parts of degrees were expressed in *minutes* and *seconds*, using the prime (′) and double prime (″) notations, respectively. That is,

$$1' = \text{one minute} = \tfrac{1}{60}(1°)$$

$$1'' = \text{one second} = \tfrac{1}{3600}(1°).$$

Many calculators have special keys for converting angles in degrees, minutes, and seconds (D° M′S″) to decimal degree form, and vice versa.

Linear and Angular Speed

The *radian measure* formula, $\theta = s/r$, can be used to measure arc length along a circle.

Arc Length

For a circle of radius r, a central angle θ intercepts an arc of length s given by

$$s = r\theta \qquad \text{Length of circular arc}$$

where θ is measured in radians. Note that if $r = 1$, then $s = \theta$, and the radian measure of θ equals the arc length.

EXAMPLE 5   Finding Arc Length

A circle has a radius of 4 inches. Find the length of the arc intercepted by a central angle of 240°, as shown in Figure 4.10.

Solution

To use the formula

$$s = r\theta$$

first convert 240° to radian measure.

$$240° = (240 \text{ deg})\left(\frac{\pi \text{ rad}}{180 \text{ deg}}\right) = \frac{4\pi}{3} \text{ radians}$$

Then, using a radius of $r = 4$ inches, you can find the arc length to be

$$s = r\theta = 4\left(\frac{4\pi}{3}\right) - \frac{16\pi}{3} \approx 16.76 \text{ inches.}$$

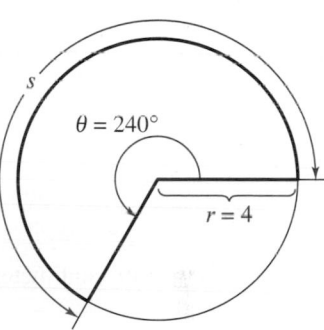

Figure 4.10

Note that the units for $r\theta$ are determined by the units for r because θ is given in radian measure and therefore has no units.

✔ **Checkpoint** 🔊))) *Audio-video solution in English & Spanish at LarsonPrecalculus.com.*

A circle has a radius of 27 inches. Find the length of the arc intercepted by a central angle of 160°. ■

The formula for the length of a circular arc can be used to analyze the motion of a particle moving at a *constant speed* along a circular path.

Linear and Angular Speed

Consider a particle moving at a constant speed along a circular arc of radius r. If s is the length of the arc traveled in time t, then the **linear speed** of the particle is

$$\text{Linear speed} = \frac{\text{arc length}}{\text{time}} = \frac{s}{t}.$$

Moreover, if θ is the angle (in radian measure) corresponding to the arc length s, then the **angular speed** of the particle is

$$\text{Angular speed} = \frac{\text{central angle}}{\text{time}} = \frac{\theta}{t}.$$

Linear speed measures how fast the particle moves, and angular speed measures how fast the angle changes.

EXAMPLE 6   Finding Linear Speed

The second hand of a clock is 10.2 centimeters long, as shown in Figure 4.11. Find the linear speed of the tip of this second hand.

Solution

In one revolution, the arc length traveled is

$s = 2\pi r$

$\quad = 2\pi(10.2)$ Substitute for r.

$\quad = 20.4\pi$ centimeters.

The time required for the second hand to travel this distance is

$t = 1$ minute $= 60$ seconds.

So, the linear speed of the tip of the second hand is

$$\text{Linear speed} = \frac{s}{t}$$

$$= \frac{20.4\pi \text{ centimeters}}{60 \text{ seconds}}$$

$$\approx 1.07 \text{ centimeters per second.}$$

Figure 4.11

✓ **Checkpoint** Audio-video solution in English & Spanish at LarsonPrecalculus.com.

The second hand of a clock is 8 centimeters long. Find the linear speed of the tip of this second hand as it passes around the clock face.

EXAMPLE 7   Finding Angular and Linear Speed

The blades of a wind turbine are 116 feet long (see Figure 4.12). The propeller rotates at 15 revolutions per minute.

a. Find the angular speed of the propeller in radians per minute.

b. Find the linear speed of the tips of the blades.

Solution

a. Because each revolution generates 2π radians, it follows that the propeller turns

$(15)(2\pi) = 30\pi$ radians per minute.

In other words, the angular speed is

$$\text{Angular speed} = \frac{\theta}{t} = \frac{30\pi \text{ radians}}{1 \text{ minute}} = 30\pi \text{ radians per minute.}$$

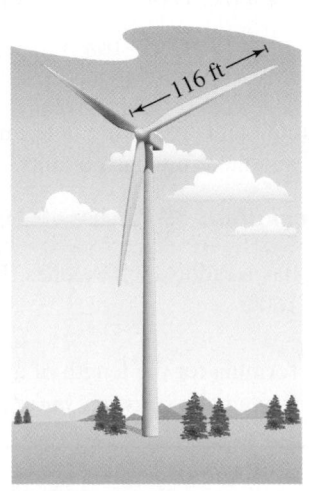

Figure 4.12

b. The linear speed is

$$\text{Linear speed} = \frac{s}{t} = \frac{r\theta}{t} = \frac{(116)(30\pi) \text{ feet}}{1 \text{ minute}} \approx 10,933 \text{ feet per minute.}$$

✓ **Checkpoint** Audio-video solution in English & Spanish at LarsonPrecalculus.com.

The circular blade on a saw rotates at 2400 revolutions per minute.

a. Find the angular speed of the blade in radians per minute.

b. The blade has a radius of 4 inches. Find the linear speed of a blade tip.

4.1   Exercises

See *CalcChat.com* for tutorial help and worked-out solutions to odd-numbered exercises.
For instructions on how to use a graphing utility, see Appendix A.

Vocabulary and Concept Check

In Exercises 1–6, fill in the blank.

1. _____ means "measurement of triangles."

2. A(n) _____ is determined by rotating a ray about its endpoint.

3. An angle with its initial side coinciding with the positive *x*-axis and the origin as its vertex is said to be in _____ .

4. Two angles that have the same initial and terminal sides are _____ .

5. One _____ is the measure of a central angle that intercepts an arc equal in length to the radius of the circle.

6. The _____ speed of a particle is a ratio of the change in the central angle to the time.

7. Is one-half revolution of a circle equal to $90°$ or $180°$?

8. What is the sum of two complementary angles?

9. Are the angles $315°$ and $-225°$ coterminal?

10. Is the angle $\dfrac{2\pi}{3}$ acute or obtuse?

Procedures and Problem Solving

Estimating an Angle   In Exercises 11 and 12, estimate the angle to the nearest one-half radian.

11.

12.

Determining Quadrants   In Exercises 13–18, determine the quadrant in which each angle lies. (The angle measure is given in radians.)

13. (a) $\dfrac{\pi}{6}$ (b) $\dfrac{5\pi}{4}$

14. (a) $\dfrac{5\pi}{6}$ (b) $-\dfrac{5\pi}{3}$

15. (a) $\dfrac{7\pi}{4}$ (b) $\dfrac{11\pi}{4}$

16. (a) $-\dfrac{5\pi}{12}$ (b) $-\dfrac{13\pi}{9}$

17. (a) -1 (b) -2

18. (a) 3.5 (b) 2.25

Sketching Angles   In Exercises 19–24, sketch each angle in standard position.

19. (a) $\dfrac{3\pi}{2}$ (b) $-\dfrac{\pi}{2}$

20. (a) $\dfrac{3\pi}{4}$ (b) $\dfrac{4\pi}{3}$

21. (a) $-\dfrac{7\pi}{4}$ (b) $-\dfrac{5\pi}{2}$

22. (a) $\dfrac{11\pi}{6}$ (b) $-\dfrac{2\pi}{3}$

23. (a) 5π (b) -4

24. (a) 2 (b) -3π

Finding Coterminal Angles   In Exercises 25–28, determine two coterminal angles in radian measure (one positive and one negative) for each angle. (There are many correct answers).

25. (a)   (b)

26. (a)   (b)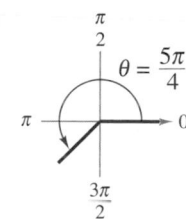

27. (a) $\dfrac{9\pi}{4}$ (b) $-\dfrac{2\pi}{15}$

28. (a) $-\dfrac{7\pi}{8}$ (b) $\dfrac{\pi}{12}$

Estimating an Angle   In Exercises 29 and 30, estimate the number of degrees in the angle.

29.   30.

Determining Quadrants In Exercises 31–36, determine the quadrant in which each angle lies.

31. (a) 55°   (b) 215°
32. (a) 121°   (b) 181°
33. (a) −150°   (b) 282°
34. (a) 87.9°   (b) −8.5°
35. (a) 132° 50′   (b) −336° 30′
36. (a) −245.25°   (b) 12.35°

Sketching Angles In Exercises 37–42, sketch each angle in standard position.

37. (a) 45°   (b) 90°   **38.** (a) 60°   (b) 180°
39. (a) −30° (b) 150°   **40.** (a) 270° (b) −120°
41. (a) 405° (b) −780°   **42.** (a) −450° (b) 600°

Finding Coterminal Angles In Exercises 43–46, determine two coterminal angles in degree measure (one positive and one negative) for each angle. (There are many correct answers.)

43. (a)   (b)

44. (a)   (b)

45. (a) −300°   (b) 230°
46. (a) 445°   (b) −740°

Converting From Degrees to Radians In Exercises 47–50, rewrite each angle in radian measure as a multiple of π. (Do not use a calculator.)

47. (a) 30°   (b) 150°
48. (a) 315°   (b) 120°
49. (a) 18°   (b) −240°
50. (a) −270°   (b) 144°

Converting From Radians to Degrees In Exercises 51–54, rewrite each angle in degree measure. (Do not use a calculator.)

51. (a) $\dfrac{3\pi}{2}$ (b) $-\dfrac{7\pi}{6}$
52. (a) -4π (b) 3π
53. (a) $\dfrac{7\pi}{3}$ (b) $-\dfrac{13\pi}{60}$
54. (a) $-\dfrac{15\pi}{6}$ (b) $\dfrac{28\pi}{15}$

Converting From Degrees to Radians In Exercises 55–60, convert the angle measure from degrees to radians. Round your answer to three decimal places.

55. 115°   **56.** 83.7°
57. −216.35°   **58.** −46.52°
59. −0.78°   **60.** 395°

Converting From Radians to Degrees In Exercises 61–66, convert the angle measure from radians to degrees. Round your answer to three decimal places.

61. $\dfrac{\pi}{7}$ **62.** $\dfrac{5\pi}{11}$
63. 6.5π **64.** -4.2π
65. -2 **66.** -0.57

Converting to Decimal Degree Form In Exercises 67–72, use the angle-conversion capabilities of a graphing utility to convert the angle measure to decimal degree form. Round your answer to three decimal places, if necessary.

67. 64° 45′   **68.** −124° 30′
69. 85° 18′30″   **70.** −408° 16′25″
71. −125° 36″   **72.** 330° 25″

Finding an Angle Difference In Exercises 73–76, find the difference of the angles. Write your answer in D° M′S″ form.

73. 51° 22′30″ and 38° 17′15″
74. 120° 45′29″ and 12° 36′3″
75. 48° 18′ and 25° 16′59″
76. 36° 8′43″ and 81° 17″

Converting to D° M′S″ Form In Exercises 77–82, use the angle-conversion capabilities of a graphing utility to convert the angle measure to D° M′S″ form.

77. 280.6°   **78.** −115.8°
79. −345.12°   **80.** 490.75°
81. −0.355   **82.** 0.7865

Complementary and Supplementary Angles In Exercises 83–92, find (if possible) the complement and supplement of the angle.

83. 24°   **84.** 129°
85. 167°   **86.** 87°
87. $\dfrac{\pi}{3}$ **88.** $\dfrac{3\pi}{4}$
89. $\dfrac{2\pi}{3}$ **90.** $\dfrac{\pi}{6}$
91. $\dfrac{3\pi}{2}$ **92.** $\dfrac{12\pi}{5}$

Finding the Central Angle   **In Exercises 93–96, find the radian measure of the central angle of a circle of radius r that intercepts an arc of length s.**

Radius r	Arc Length s
93. 15 inches	8 inches
94. 22 feet	10 feet
95. 14.5 centimeters	35 centimeters
96. 80 kilometers	160 kilometers

Finding Arc Length   **In Exercises 97–100, find the length of the arc on a circle of radius r intercepted by a central angle θ.**

Radius r	Central Angle θ
97. 14 inches	π radians
98. 9 feet	$\dfrac{\pi}{3}$ radians
99. 27 meters	$120°$
100. 12 centimeters	$135°$

Finding the Radius   **In Exercises 101–104, find the radius r of a circle with an arc length s and a central angle θ.**

Arc Length s	Central Angle θ
101. 36 feet	$\dfrac{\pi}{2}$ radians
102. 3 meters	$\dfrac{4\pi}{3}$ radians
103. 82 miles	$135°$
104. 8 inches	$330°$

Earth-Space Science   **In Exercises 105 and 106, find the distance between the cities. Assume that Earth is a sphere of radius 4000 miles and the cities are on the same longitude (one city is due north of the other).**

City	Latitude
105. Dallas, Texas	$32°\,47'39''$N
Omaha, Nebraska	$41°\,15'50''$N
106. San Francisco, California	$37°\,47'36''$N
Seattle, Washington	$47°\,37'18''$N

107. Earth-Space Science   Assuming that Earth is a sphere of radius 6378 kilometers, what is the difference in the latitudes of Syracuse, New York, and Annapolis, Maryland, where Syracuse is 450 kilometers due north of Annapolis?

108. Electrical Engineering   A voltmeter's pointer is 6 centimeters in length (see figure). Find the number of degrees through which it rotates when it moves 2.5 centimeters on the scale.

Figure for 108   Figure for 109

109. Mechanical Engineering   An electric hoist is used to lift a piece of equipment 2 feet. The diameter of the drum on the hoist is 10 inches (see figure). Find the number of degrees through which the drum must rotate.

110. *Why you should learn it*   (p. 254) The number of revolutions made by a figure skater for each type of axel jump is given. Determine the measure of the angle generated as the skater performs each jump. Give the answer in both degrees and radians.

(a) Single axel: $1\frac{1}{2}$ revolutions

(b) Double axel: $2\frac{1}{2}$ revolutions

(c) Triple axel: $3\frac{1}{2}$ revolutions

111. Linear Speed   A satellite in a circular orbit 1250 kilometers above Earth makes one complete revolution every 110 minutes. What is its linear speed? Assume that Earth is a sphere of radius 6378 kilometers.

112. Mechanical Engineering   The circular blade on a saw has a diameter of 7.25 inches and rotates at 4800 revolutions per minute.

(a) Find the angular speed of the blade in radians per minute.

(b) Find the linear speed of the saw teeth (in inches per minute) as they contact the wood being cut.

113. Mechanical Engineering   A motorcycle wheel has a diameter of 19.5 inches (see figure) and rotates at 1050 revolutions per minute.

(a) Find the angular speed in radians per minute.

(b) Find the linear speed of the motorcycle (in inches per minute).

114. Angular Speed A computerized spin balance machine rotates a 25-inch diameter tire at 480 revolutions per minute.

(a) Find the road speed (in miles per hour) at which the tire is being balanced.

(b) At what rate should the spin balance machine be set so that the tire is being tested for 70 miles per hour?

115. Mechanical Engineering A Blu-ray disc is approximately 12 centimeters in diameter. The drive motor of the Blu-ray player is able to rotate up to 10,000 revolutions per minute, depending on what track is being read.

(a) Find the maximum angular speed (in radians per second) of a Blu-ray disc as it rotates.

(b) Find the maximum linear speed (in meters per second) of a point on the outermost track as the disc rotates.

116. MODELING DATA

The radii of the pedal sprocket, the wheel sprocket, and the wheel of the bicycle in the figure are 4 inches, 2 inches, and 14 inches, respectively. A cyclist is pedaling at a rate of 1 revolution per second.

(a) Find the speed of the bicycle in feet per second and miles per hour.

(b) Use your result from part (a) to write a function for the distance d (in miles) a cyclist travels in terms of the number n of revolutions of the pedal sprocket.

(c) Write a function for the distance d (in miles) a cyclist travels in terms of time t (in seconds). Compare this function with the function from part (b).

Conclusions

True or False? In Exercises 117–119, determine whether the statement is true or false. Justify your answer.

117. A degree is a larger unit of measure than a radian.

118. An angle that measures $-1260°$ lies in Quadrant III.

119. The angles of a triangle can have radian measures of $2\pi/3$, $\pi/4$, and $\pi/12$.

120. Proof Prove that the area of a circular sector of radius r with central angle θ is $A = \frac{1}{2}r^2\theta$, where θ is measured in radians.

Geometry In Exercises 121 and 122, use the result of Exercise 120 to find the area of the sector.

121.
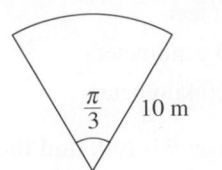
$\frac{\pi}{3}$ 10 m

122.   12 ft
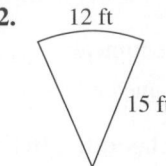
15 ft

123. Think About It The formulas for the area of a circular sector and arc length are $A = \frac{1}{2}r^2\theta$ and $s = r\theta$, respectively. (r is the radius and θ is the angle measured in radians.)

(a) Let $\theta = 0.8$. Write the area and arc length as functions of r. What is the domain of each function? Use a graphing utility to graph the functions. Use the graphs to determine which function changes more rapidly as r increases. Explain.

(b) Let $r = 10$ centimeters. Write the area and arc length as functions of θ. What is the domain of each function? Use a graphing utility to graph and identify the functions.

124. **HOW DO YOU SEE IT?** Determine which angles in the figure are coterminal angles with angle A. Explain your reasoning.

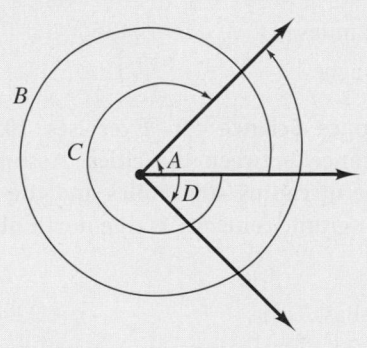

125. Writing In your own words, write a definition of 1 radian.

126. Writing In your own words, explain the difference between 1 radian and 1 degree.

Cumulative Mixed Review

Library of Parent Functions In Exercises 127–132, sketch the graph of $f(x) = x^3$ and the graph of the function g. Describe the transformation from f to g.

127. $g(x) = (x - 1)^3$ **128.** $g(x) = x^3 - 4$

129. $g(x) = 2 - x^3$ **130.** $g(x) = -(x + 3)^3$

131. $g(x) = (x + 1)^3 - 3$ **132.** $g(x) = (x - 5)^3 + 1$

4.2   Trigonometric Functions: The Unit Circle

The Unit Circle

The two historical perspectives of trigonometry incorporate different methods of introducing the trigonometric functions. One such perspective is based on the unit circle.

Consider the **unit circle** given by

$$x^2 + y^2 = 1 \qquad \text{Unit circle}$$

as shown in the figure.

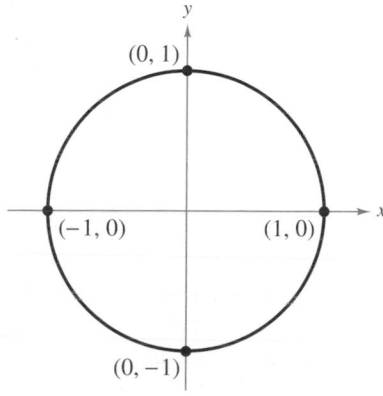

Imagine wrapping the real number line around this circle, with positive numbers corresponding to a counterclockwise wrapping and negative numbers corresponding to a clockwise wrapping, as shown below.

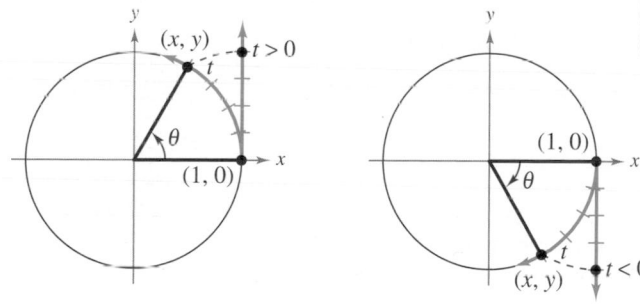

As the real number line wraps around the unit circle, each real number t corresponds to a point

$$(x, y)$$

on the circle. For example, the real number 0 corresponds to the point $(1, 0)$. Moreover, because the unit circle has a circumference of 2π, the real number 2π also corresponds to the point $(1, 0)$.

In general, each real number t also corresponds to a central angle θ (in standard position) whose radian measure is t. With this interpretation of t, the arc length formula

$$s = r\theta$$

(with $r = 1$) indicates that the real number t is the (directional) length of the arc intercepted by the angle θ, given in radians.

What you should learn

▶ Identify the unit circle and describe its relationship to real numbers.

▶ Evaluate trigonometric functions using the unit circle.

▶ Use domain and period to evaluate sine and cosine functions and use a calculator to evaluate trigonometric functions.

Why you should learn it

Trigonometric functions are used to model the movement of an oscillating weight. For instance, in Exercise 75 on page 271, the displacement from equilibrium of an oscillating weight suspended by a spring is modeled as a function of time.

The Trigonometric Functions

From the preceding discussion, it follows that the coordinates x and y are two functions of the real variable t. You can use these coordinates to define the six trigonometric functions of t.

sine	**cosine**	**tangent**
cosecant	**secant**	**cotangent**

These six functions are normally abbreviated sin, cos, tan, csc, sec, and cot, respectively.

Definitions of Trigonometric Functions

Let t be a real number and let (x, y) be the point on the unit circle corresponding to t.

$$\sin t = y \qquad \cos t = x \qquad \tan t = \frac{y}{x}, \quad x \neq 0$$

$$\csc t = \frac{1}{y}, \quad y \neq 0 \qquad \sec t = \frac{1}{x}, \quad x \neq 0 \qquad \cot t = \frac{x}{y}, \quad y \neq 0$$

Remark

Note in the definitions at the left that the functions in the second row are the *reciprocals* of the corresponding functions in the first row.

In the definitions of the trigonometric functions, note that the tangent and secant are not defined when $x = 0$. For instance, because $t = \pi/2$ corresponds to $(x, y) = (0, 1)$, it follows that $\tan(\pi/2)$ and $\sec(\pi/2)$ are *undefined*. Similarly, the cotangent and cosecant are not defined when $y = 0$. For instance, because $t = 0$ corresponds to $(x, y) = (1, 0)$, cot 0 and csc 0 are *undefined*.

In Figure 4.13, the unit circle is divided into eight equal arcs, corresponding to t-values of

$$0, \frac{\pi}{4}, \frac{\pi}{2}, \frac{3\pi}{4}, \pi, \frac{5\pi}{4}, \frac{3\pi}{2}, \frac{7\pi}{4}, \text{ and } 2\pi.$$

Similarly, in Figure 4.14, the unit circle is divided into 12 equal arcs, corresponding to t-values of

$$0, \frac{\pi}{6}, \frac{\pi}{3}, \frac{\pi}{2}, \frac{2\pi}{3}, \frac{5\pi}{6}, \pi, \frac{7\pi}{6}, \frac{4\pi}{3}, \frac{3\pi}{2}, \frac{5\pi}{3}, \frac{11\pi}{6}, \text{ and } 2\pi.$$

Using the (x, y) coordinates in Figures 4.13 and 4.14, you can evaluate the exact values of trigonometric functions for common t-values. Example 1 demonstrates this procedure. You should study and learn these exact values for common t-values because they will help you to perform calculations in later sections.

Figure 4.13

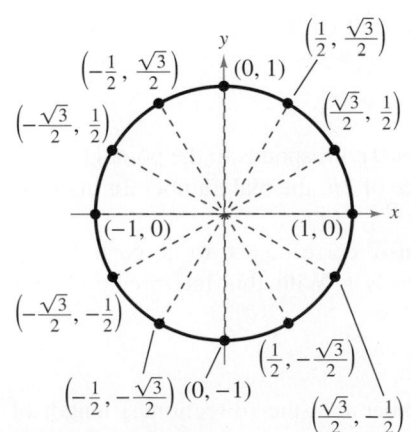

Figure 4.14

| EXAMPLE 1 | Evaluating Trigonometric Functions |

See LarsonPrecalculus.com for an interactive version of this type of example.

Evaluate the six trigonometric functions at each real number.

a. $t = \dfrac{\pi}{6}$ **b.** $t = \dfrac{5\pi}{4}$ **c.** $t = \pi$ **d.** $t = -\dfrac{\pi}{3}$

Solution

For each t-value, begin by finding the corresponding point (x, y) on the unit circle. Then use the definitions of trigonometric functions listed on page 266.

a. $t = \pi/6$ corresponds to the point $(x, y) = \left(\sqrt{3}/2,\, 1/2\right)$.

$$\sin \frac{\pi}{6} = y = \frac{1}{2} \qquad\qquad \csc \frac{\pi}{6} = \frac{1}{y} = \frac{1}{1/2} = 2$$

$$\cos \frac{\pi}{6} = x = \frac{\sqrt{3}}{2} \qquad\qquad \sec \frac{\pi}{6} = \frac{1}{x} = \frac{2}{\sqrt{3}} = \frac{2\sqrt{3}}{3}$$

$$\tan \frac{\pi}{6} = \frac{y}{x} = \frac{1/2}{\sqrt{3}/2} = \frac{1}{\sqrt{3}} = \frac{\sqrt{3}}{3} \qquad\qquad \cot \frac{\pi}{6} = \frac{x}{y} = \frac{\sqrt{3}/2}{1/2} = \sqrt{3}$$

b. $t = 5\pi/4$ corresponds to the point $(x, y) = \left(-\sqrt{2}/2,\, -\sqrt{2}/2\right)$.

$$\sin \frac{5\pi}{4} = y = -\frac{\sqrt{2}}{2} \qquad\qquad \csc \frac{5\pi}{4} = \frac{1}{y} = -\frac{2}{\sqrt{2}} = -\sqrt{2}$$

$$\cos \frac{5\pi}{4} = x = -\frac{\sqrt{2}}{2} \qquad\qquad \sec \frac{5\pi}{4} = \frac{1}{x} = -\frac{2}{\sqrt{2}} = -\sqrt{2}$$

$$\tan \frac{5\pi}{4} = \frac{y}{x} = \frac{-\sqrt{2}/2}{-\sqrt{2}/2} = 1 \qquad\qquad \cot \frac{5\pi}{4} = \frac{x}{y} = \frac{-\sqrt{2}/2}{-\sqrt{2}/2} = 1$$

c. $t = \pi$ corresponds to the point $(x, y) = (-1, 0)$.

$$\sin \pi = y = 0 \qquad\qquad \csc \pi = \frac{1}{y} \text{ is undefined.}$$

$$\cos \pi = x = -1 \qquad\qquad \sec \pi = \frac{1}{x} = \frac{1}{-1} = -1$$

$$\tan \pi = \frac{y}{x} = \frac{0}{-1} = 0 \qquad\qquad \cot \pi = \frac{x}{y} \text{ is undefined.}$$

d. Moving *clockwise* around the unit circle, it follows that $t = -\pi/3$ corresponds to the point $(x, y) = \left(1/2,\, -\sqrt{3}/2\right)$.

$$\sin\left(-\frac{\pi}{3}\right) = y = -\frac{\sqrt{3}}{2} \qquad\qquad \csc\left(-\frac{\pi}{3}\right) = \frac{1}{y} = -\frac{2}{\sqrt{3}} = -\frac{2\sqrt{3}}{3}$$

$$\cos\left(-\frac{\pi}{3}\right) = x = \frac{1}{2} \qquad\qquad \sec\left(-\frac{\pi}{3}\right) = \frac{1}{x} = \frac{1}{1/2} = 2$$

$$\tan\left(-\frac{\pi}{3}\right) = \frac{y}{x} = \frac{-\sqrt{3}/2}{1/2} = -\sqrt{3}$$

$$\cot\left(-\frac{\pi}{3}\right) = \frac{x}{y} = \frac{1/2}{-\sqrt{3}/2} = -\frac{1}{\sqrt{3}} = -\frac{\sqrt{3}}{3}$$

✓ **Checkpoint** *Audio-video solution in English & Spanish at LarsonPrecalculus.com.*

Evaluate the six trigonometric functions at each real number.

a. $t = \pi/2$ **b.** $t = 0$ **c.** $t = -5\pi/6$ **d.** $t = -3\pi/4$

Explore the Concept

With your graphing utility in *radian* and *parametric* modes, enter X1T = cos T and Y1T = sin T and use the following settings.

Tmin = 0, Tmax = 6.3,
Tstep = 0.1
Xmin = −1.5, Xmax = 1.5,
Xscl = 1
Ymin = −1, Ymax = 1,
Yscl = 1

1. Graph the entered equations and describe the graph.
2. Use the *trace* feature to move the cursor around the graph. What do the t-values represent? What do the x- and y-values represent?
3. What are the least and greatest values of x and y?

Domain and Period of Sine and Cosine

The *domain* of the sine and cosine functions is the set of all real numbers. To determine the *range* of these two functions, consider the unit circle shown in the figure. By definition, $\sin t = y$ and $\cos t = x$. Because (x, y) is on the unit circle, you know that $-1 \leq y \leq 1$ and $-1 \leq x \leq 1$. So, the values of sine and cosine also range between -1 and 1.

$$\begin{array}{ccc} -1 \leq & y & \leq 1 \\ -1 \leq & \sin t & \leq 1 \end{array} \quad \text{and} \quad \begin{array}{ccc} -1 \leq & x & \leq 1 \\ -1 \leq & \cos t & \leq 1 \end{array}$$

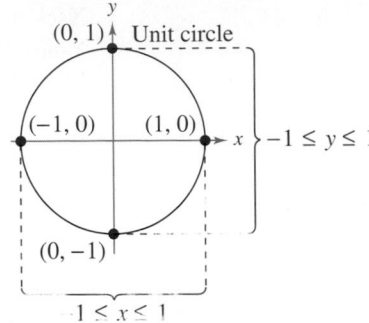

Adding 2π to each value of t in the interval $[0, 2\pi]$ completes a second revolution around the unit circle, as shown in the figure below.

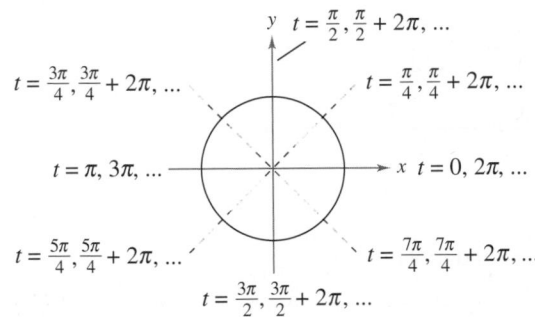

The values of $\sin(t + 2\pi)$ and $\cos(t + 2\pi)$ correspond to those of $\sin t$ and $\cos t$. Similar results can be obtained for repeated revolutions (positive or negative) around the unit circle. This leads to the general result

$$\sin(t + 2\pi n) = \sin t \quad \text{and} \quad \cos(t + 2\pi n) = \cos t$$

for any integer n and real number t. Functions that behave in such a repetitive (or cyclic) manner are called **periodic.**

Definition of Periodic Function

A function f is **periodic** when there exists a positive real number c such that

$$f(t + c) = f(t)$$

for all t in the domain of f. The least number c for which f is periodic is called the **period** of f.

From this definition, it follows that the sine and cosine functions are periodic and have a period of 2π. The other four trigonometric functions are also periodic and will be discussed further in Section 4.6.

Recall from Section 1.3 that a function f is *even* when $f(-t) = f(t)$ and is *odd* when $f(-t) = -f(t)$.

Even and Odd Trigonometric Functions

The cosine and secant functions are *even*.

$$\cos(-t) = \cos t \qquad \sec(-t) = \sec t$$

The sine, cosecant, tangent, and cotangent functions are *odd*.

$$\sin(-t) = -\sin t \qquad \csc(-t) = -\csc t$$

$$\tan(-t) = -\tan t \qquad \cot(-t) = -\cot t$$

Remark

In this text, the parentheses in $\sin(u)$ are sometimes omitted when u is an expression involving exponents, radicals, products, or quotients. For instance, $\sin(3\pi)$ can be written as $\sin 3\pi$. To evaluate $\sin 3\pi$, find the sine of the product 3π. The other trigonometric functions can be written and evaluated in the same manner.

EXAMPLE 2 Using the Period to Evaluate Sine and Cosine

a. Because $\dfrac{13\pi}{6} = 2\pi + \dfrac{\pi}{6}$, you have $\sin\dfrac{13\pi}{6} = \sin\left(2\pi + \dfrac{\pi}{6}\right) = \sin\dfrac{\pi}{6} = \dfrac{1}{2}.$

b. Because $-\dfrac{7\pi}{2} = -4\pi + \dfrac{\pi}{2}$, you have

$$\cos\left(-\dfrac{7\pi}{2}\right) = \cos\left(-4\pi + \dfrac{\pi}{2}\right) = \cos\dfrac{\pi}{2} = 0.$$

c. For $\sin t = \dfrac{4}{5}$, $\sin(-t) = -\dfrac{4}{5}$ because the function is odd.

✓ **Checkpoint**))) *Audio-video solution in English & Spanish at LarsonPrecalculus.com.*

a. Use the period of the cosine function to evaluate $\cos(9\pi/2)$.

b. Use the period of the sine function to evaluate $\sin(-7\pi/3)$.

c. Evaluate $\cos t$ given that $\cos(-t) = 0.3$.

When evaluating a trigonometric function with a calculator, you need to set the calculator to the desired *mode* of measurement (degrees or radians). Most calculators do not have keys for the cosecant, secant, and cotangent functions. To evaluate these functions, you can use the $\boxed{x^{-1}}$ key with their respective reciprocal functions sine, cosine, and tangent. For example, to evaluate $\csc(\pi/8)$, use the fact that

$$\csc\dfrac{\pi}{8} = \dfrac{1}{\sin(\pi/8)}$$

and enter the following keystroke sequence in *radian* mode.

$\boxed{(}\,\boxed{\text{SIN}}\,\boxed{(}\,\pi\,\boxed{\div}\,8\,\boxed{)}\,\boxed{)}\,\boxed{x^{-1}}\,\boxed{\text{ENTER}}$ Display 2.6131259

Technology Tip

When evaluating trigonometric functions with a calculator, remember to enclose all fractional angle measures in parentheses. For instance, to evaluate $\sin t$ for $t = \pi/6$, you should enter

$\boxed{\text{SIN}}\,\boxed{(}\,\boxed{\pi}\,\boxed{\div}\,6\,\boxed{)}\,\boxed{\text{ENTER}}$

to obtain 0.5.

EXAMPLE 3 Using a Calculator

Function	Mode	Graphing Calculator Keystrokes	Display
a. $\sin\dfrac{2\pi}{3}$	Radian	$\boxed{\text{SIN}}\,\boxed{(}\,2\,\boxed{\pi}\,\boxed{\div}\,3\,\boxed{)}\,\boxed{\text{ENTER}}$	0.8660254
b. $\cot 1.5$	Radian	$\boxed{(}\,\boxed{\text{TAN}}\,\boxed{(}\,1.5\,\boxed{)}\,\boxed{)}\,\boxed{x^{-1}}\,\boxed{\text{ENTER}}$	0.0709148

✓ **Checkpoint**))) *Audio-video solution in English & Spanish at LarsonPrecalculus.com.*

Use a calculator to evaluate (a) $\sin(5\pi/7)$ and (b) $\csc 2.0$.

4.2   Exercises

See *CalcChat.com* for tutorial help and worked-out solutions to odd-numbered exercises.
For instructions on how to use a graphing utility, see Appendix A.

Vocabulary and Concept Check

In Exercises 1–3, fill in the blank(s).

1. Each real number t corresponds to a point (x, y) on the _____ .

2. A function f is _____ if there exists a positive real number c such that $f(t + c) = f(t)$ for all t in the domain of f.

3. A function f is _____ if $f(-t) = -f(t)$ and _____ if $f(-t) = f(t)$.

4. List the names and abbreviations of the six trigonometric functions.

5. Which trigonometric functions are even? odd?

6. Which trigonometric functions are undefined when $x = 0$?

7. How many equal arcs can you divide the unit circle into using t-values that are multiples of $\pi/4$?

8. How many times is $\tan t = y/x$ undefined on the unit circle?

Procedures and Problem Solving

Determining Values of Trigonometric Functions   In Exercises 9–12, determine the exact values of the six trigonometric functions of the angle θ.

9.

$\left(-\frac{8}{17}, \frac{15}{17}\right)$

10.

$\left(\frac{12}{13}, \frac{5}{13}\right)$

11.

$\left(\frac{12}{13}, -\frac{5}{13}\right)$

12.
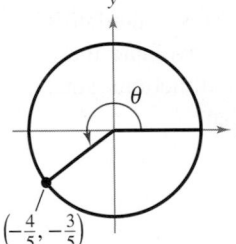
$\left(-\frac{4}{5}, -\frac{3}{5}\right)$

Finding a Point on the Unit Circle   In Exercises 13–22, find the point (x, y) on the unit circle that corresponds to the real number t.

13. $t = \dfrac{\pi}{4}$

14. $t = \dfrac{\pi}{3}$

15. $t = \dfrac{7\pi}{6}$

16. $t = \dfrac{5\pi}{4}$

17. $t = \dfrac{3\pi}{2}$

18. $t = \pi$

19. $t = -\dfrac{7\pi}{4}$

20. $t = -\dfrac{4\pi}{3}$

21. 4π

22. $\dfrac{11\pi}{3}$

Evaluating Sine, Cosine, and Tangent   In Exercises 23–32, evaluate (if possible) the sine, cosine, and tangent of the real number.

23. $t = \dfrac{\pi}{4}$

24. $t = \dfrac{\pi}{3}$

25. $t = -\dfrac{7\pi}{4}$

26. $t = -\dfrac{5\pi}{4}$

27. $t = \dfrac{2\pi}{3}$

28. $t = \dfrac{5\pi}{3}$

29. $t = -\dfrac{\pi}{2}$

30. $t = \dfrac{11\pi}{6}$

31. $t = -\dfrac{\pi}{6}$

32. $t = -\dfrac{3\pi}{2}$

Evaluating Trigonometric Functions   In Exercises 33–38, evaluate (if possible) the six trigonometric functions of the real number.

33. $t = 3\pi/4$

34. $t = 5\pi/6$

35. $t = 2\pi$

36. $t = 3\pi/2$

37. $t = -4\pi/3$

38. $t = 7\pi/4$

Using the Period to Evaluate Sine and Cosine   In Exercises 39–46, evaluate the trigonometric function using its period as an aid.

39. $\sin 5\pi$

40. $\cos 5\pi$

41. $\cos \dfrac{8\pi}{3}$

42. $\sin \dfrac{9\pi}{4}$

43. $\cos\left(-\dfrac{13\pi}{6}\right)$

44. $\sin\left(-\dfrac{19\pi}{6}\right)$

45. $\sin\left(-\dfrac{9\pi}{4}\right)$

46. $\cos\left(-\dfrac{8\pi}{3}\right)$

Using the Value of a Trigonometric Function In Exercises 47–52, use the value of the trigonometric function to evaluate each function.

47. $\sin t = \frac{1}{3}$
  (a) $\sin(-t)$
  (b) $\csc(-t)$

48. $\cos t = -\frac{3}{4}$
  (a) $\cos(-t)$
  (b) $\sec(-t)$

49. $\cos(-t) = -\frac{1}{5}$
  (a) $\cos t$
  (b) $\sec(-t)$

50. $\sin(-t) = \frac{3}{8}$
  (a) $\sin t$
  (b) $\csc t$

51. $\tan t = \frac{4}{5}$
  (a) $\tan(-t)$
  (b) $\cot t$

52. $\cot t = -\frac{1}{4}$
  (a) $\cot(-t)$
  (b) $\tan(-t)$

Using a Calculator In Exercises 53–68, use a calculator to evaluate the trigonometric expression. Round your answer to four decimal places. (Be sure the calculator is in the correct angle mode.)

53. $\sin \dfrac{\pi}{7}$

54. $\tan \dfrac{3\pi}{5}$

55. $\cos \dfrac{11\pi}{5}$

56. $\sin \dfrac{11\pi}{9}$

57. $\tan 100°$

58. $\cos 135°$

59. $\cos(-1.7)$

60. $\sin(-13.4)$

61. $\tan(-229°)$

62. $\cos(-96°)$

63. $\sec \dfrac{5\pi}{6}$

64. $\cot \dfrac{4\pi}{3}$

65. $\cot 32°$

66. $\csc 75°$

67. $\csc(-5.2)$

68. $\sec(-4.9)$

Approximating the Value of a Trigonometric Function In Exercises 69 and 70, use the figure and a straightedge to approximate the value of each trigonometric function. Check your approximation using a graphing utility. To print an enlarged copy of the graph, go to *MathGraphs.com*.

69. (a) $\sin 5$ (b) $\cos 2$

70. (a) $\sin 0.75$ (b) $\cos 2.5$

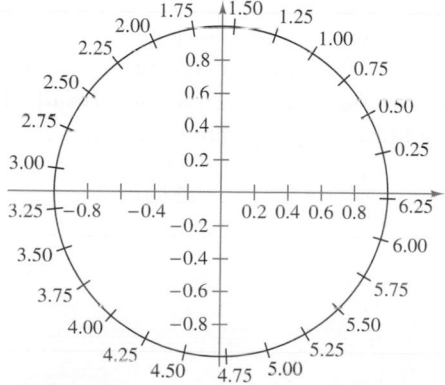

Figure for 69–72

Fotosenmeer.nl/Fotolia LLC

Approximating the Solution of an Equation In Exercises 71 and 72, use the figure and a straightedge to approximate the solution of each equation, where $0 \le t < 2\pi$. Check your approximation using a graphing utility. To print an enlarged copy of the graph, go to *MathGraphs.com*.

71. (a) $\sin t = 0.25$ (b) $\cos t = -0.25$

72. (a) $\sin t = -0.75$ (b) $\cos t = 0.75$

73. Electrical Engineering The initial current and charge of an electrical circuit are zero. The current I (in amperes) t seconds after 100 volts is applied to the circuit is given by $I = 5e^{-2t}\sin t$, where the resistance, inductance, and capacitance are 80 ohms, 20 henrys, and 0.01 farad, respectively. Approximate the current 0.7 second after the voltage is applied.

74. Physics The horizontal distance D (in feet) traveled by a projectile launched at an angle a with level ground is given by

$$D = \frac{100 \sin 2a}{9.8}$$

where the initial velocity is 10 meters per second. Approximate the horizontal distance traveled by a projectile launched at an angle of $\pi/3$ radians.

75. *Why you should learn it* *(p. 265)* The displacement from equilibrium of an oscillating weight suspended by a spring is given by

$$y(t) = \frac{1}{4}\cos 6t$$

where y is the displacement (in feet) and t is the time (in seconds) (see figure). Find the displacement when (a) $t = 0$, (b) $t = \frac{1}{4}$, and (c) $t = \frac{1}{2}$.

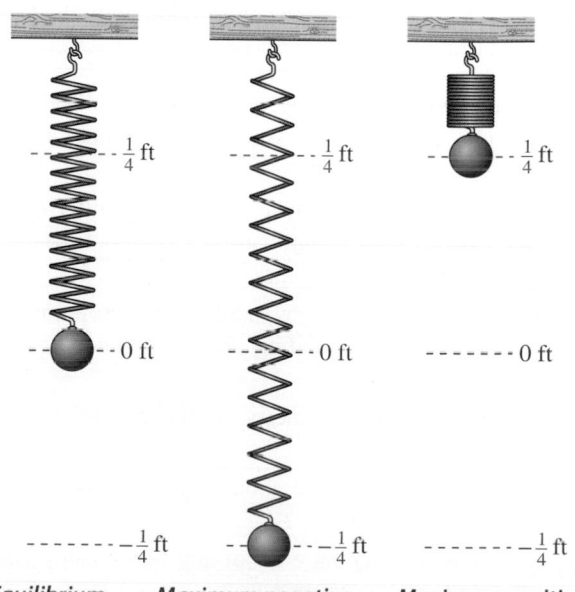

Equilibrium   *Maximum negative displacement*   *Maximum positive displacement*

Simple Harmonic Motion

76. MODELING DATA

The displacement from equilibrium of an oscillating weight suspended by a spring and subject to the damping effect of friction is given by

$$y(t) = \tfrac{1}{4}e^{-t} \cos 6t$$

where y is the displacement (in feet) and t is the time (in seconds).

(a) What is the initial displacement $(t = 0)$?

(b) Use a graphing utility to complete the table.

t	0.50	1.02	1.54	2.07	2.59
y					

(c) The approximate times when the weight is at its maximum distance from equilibrium are shown in the table in part (b). Explain why the magnitude of the maximum displacement is decreasing. What causes this decrease in maximum displacement in the physical system? What factor in the model measures this decrease?

(d) Find the first two times when the weight is at the equilibrium point $(y = 0)$.

Conclusions

True or False? In Exercises 77–80, determine whether the statement is true or false. Justify your answer.

77. Because $\sin(-t) = -\sin t$, it can be said that the sine of a negative angle is a negative number.

78. $\sin a = \sin(a - 6\pi)$

79. $\tan a = \tan(a - 6\pi)$

80. The real number 0 corresponds to the point $(0, 1)$ on the unit circle.

81. Think About It Because $f(t) = \sin t$ is an odd function and $g(t) = \cos t$ is an even function, what can be said about the function $h(t) = f(t)g(t)$?

82. Think About It Because $f(t) = \sin t$ and $g(t) = \tan t$ are odd functions, what can be said about the function $h(t) = f(t)g(t)$?

83. Exploration Let (x_1, y_1) and (x_2, y_2) be points on the unit circle corresponding to $t = t_1$ and $t = \pi - t_1$, respectively.

(a) Identify the symmetry of the points (x_1, y_1) and (x_2, y_2).

(b) Make a conjecture about any relationship between $\sin t_1$ and $\sin(\pi - t_1)$.

(c) Make a conjecture about any relationship between $\cos t_1$ and $\cos(\pi - t_1)$.

84. Exploration Let (x_1, y_1) and (x_2, y_2) be points on the unit circle corresponding to $t = t_1$ and $t = t_1 + \pi$, respectively.

(a) Identify the symmetry of the points (x_1, y_1) and (x_2, y_2).

(b) Make a conjecture about any relationship between $\sin t_1$ and $\sin(t_1 + \pi)$.

(c) Make a conjecture about any relationship between $\cos t_1$ and $\cos(t_1 + \pi)$.

Using the Value of a Trigonometric Function In Exercises 85 and 86, use the value of the trigonometric function to evaluate the indicated functions.

85. $\sin t = \tfrac{2}{3}$

(a) $\sin(\pi - t)$

(b) $\sin(t + \pi)$

86. $\cos t = -\tfrac{1}{7}$

(a) $\cos(\pi - t)$

(b) $\cos(t + \pi)$

87. Proof Verify that $\cos 2t = 2 \cos t$ is a false statement by providing a counterexample.

88. HOW DO YOU SEE IT? Use the figure below.

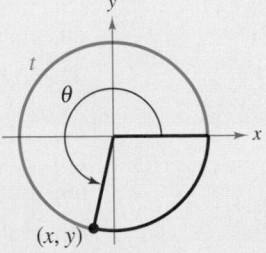

(a) Do all of the trigonometric functions of t exist? Explain your reasoning.

(b) For those trigonometric functions that exist, determine whether the sign of the trigonometric function is positive or negative. Explain your reasoning.

Cumulative Mixed Review

Finding Vertical and Horizontal Asymptotes In Exercises 89–92, find any asymptotes of the graph of the rational function. Verify your results by using a graphing utility to graph the function.

89. $f(x) = \dfrac{2x}{x - 3}$

90. $f(x) = \dfrac{5x}{x^2 + x - 6}$

91. $f(x) = \dfrac{x^2 + 3x - 10}{2x^2 - 8}$

92. $f(x) = \dfrac{x^3 - 6x^2 + x - 1}{2x^2 - 5x - 8}$

4.3   Right Triangle Trigonometry

The Six Trigonometric Functions

This section introduces the trigonometric functions from a *right triangle* perspective. Consider a right triangle with one acute angle labeled θ, as shown in the figure. Relative to the angle θ, the three sides of the triangle are the **hypotenuse,** the **opposite side** (the side opposite the angle θ), and the **adjacent side** (the side adjacent to the angle θ).

Side adjacent to θ

Using the lengths of these three sides, you can form six ratios that define the six trigonometric functions of the acute angle θ.

sine	**cosecant**
cosine	**secant**
tangent	**cotangent**

In the definitions below, it is important to see that

$$0° < \theta < 90°$$ θ lies in the first quadrant

and that for such angles, the value of each trigonometric function is *positive*.

Right Triangle Definitions of Trigonometric Functions

Let θ be an *acute* angle of a right triangle. Then the six trigonometric functions *of the angle* θ are defined as follows. (Note that the functions in the second column are the *reciprocals* of the corresponding functions in the first column.)

$$\sin \theta = \frac{\text{opp}}{\text{hyp}} \qquad \csc \theta = \frac{\text{hyp}}{\text{opp}}$$

$$\cos \theta = \frac{\text{adj}}{\text{hyp}} \qquad \sec \theta = \frac{\text{hyp}}{\text{adj}}$$

$$\tan \theta = \frac{\text{opp}}{\text{adj}} \qquad \cot \theta = \frac{\text{adj}}{\text{opp}}$$

The abbreviations

"opp," "adj," and "hyp"

represent the lengths of the three sides of a right triangle.

opp = the length of the side *opposite* θ

adj = the length of the side *adjacent* to θ

hyp = the length of the *hypotenuse*

EXAMPLE 1   Evaluating Trigonometric Functions

See LarsonPrecalculus.com for an interactive version of this type of example.

Use the triangle in Figure 4.15 to find the exact values of the six trigonometric functions of θ.

Solution

By the Pythagorean Theorem, $(\text{hyp})^2 = (\text{opp})^2 + (\text{adj})^2$, it follows that

$$\text{hyp} = \sqrt{4^2 + 3^2} = \sqrt{25} = 5.$$

So, the six trigonometric functions of θ are

$$\sin \theta = \frac{\text{opp}}{\text{hyp}} = \frac{4}{5} \qquad \csc \theta = \frac{\text{hyp}}{\text{opp}} = \frac{5}{4}$$

$$\cos \theta = \frac{\text{adj}}{\text{hyp}} = \frac{3}{5} \qquad \sec \theta = \frac{\text{hyp}}{\text{adj}} = \frac{5}{3}$$

$$\tan \theta = \frac{\text{opp}}{\text{adj}} = \frac{4}{3} \qquad \cot \theta = \frac{\text{adj}}{\text{opp}} = \frac{3}{4}.$$

Figure 4.15

✓ **Checkpoint** 🔊))) *Audio-video solution in English & Spanish at LarsonPrecalculus.com.*

Use the triangle to find the exact values of the six trigonometric functions of θ.

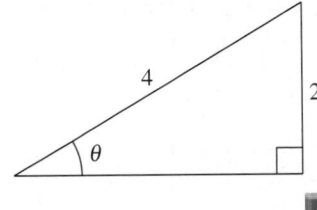

In Example 1, you were given the lengths of two sides of the right triangle but not the angle θ. Often, you will be asked to find the trigonometric functions for a *given* acute angle θ. To do this, you can construct a right triangle having θ as one of its angles.

EXAMPLE 2   Evaluating Trigonometric Functions of 45°

Find the exact values of sin 45°, cos 45°, and tan 45°.

Solution

Construct a right triangle having 45° as one of its acute angles, as shown in Figure 4.16. Choose 1 as the length of the adjacent side. From geometry, you know that the other acute angle is also 45°. So, the triangle is isosceles and the length of the opposite side is also 1. Using the Pythagorean Theorem, you can find the length of the hypotenuse to be $\sqrt{2}$.

Figure 4.16

$$\sin 45° = \frac{\text{opp}}{\text{hyp}} = \frac{1}{\sqrt{2}} = \frac{\sqrt{2}}{2}$$

$$\cos 45° = \frac{\text{adj}}{\text{hyp}} = \frac{1}{\sqrt{2}} = \frac{\sqrt{2}}{2}$$

$$\tan 45° = \frac{\text{opp}}{\text{adj}} = \frac{1}{1} = 1$$

✓ **Checkpoint** 🔊))) *Audio-video solution in English & Spanish at LarsonPrecalculus.com.*

Find the exact values of cot 45°, sec 45°, and csc 45°.

Technology Tip

You can use a calculator to convert the answers in Example 2 to decimals. However, the radical form is the exact value and, in most cases, the exact value is preferred.

EXAMPLE 3   **Evaluating Trigonometric Functions of 30° and 60°**

Use the equilateral triangle shown in Figure 4.17 to find the exact values of sin 60°, cos 60°, sin 30°, and cos 30°.

Solution

For $\theta = 60°$, you have adj $= 1$, opp $= \sqrt{3}$, and hyp $= 2$. So,

$$\sin 60° = \frac{\text{opp}}{\text{hyp}} = \frac{\sqrt{3}}{2} \quad \text{and} \quad \cos 60° = \frac{\text{adj}}{\text{hyp}} = \frac{1}{2}.$$

For $\theta = 30°$, adj $= \sqrt{3}$, opp $= 1$, and hyp $= 2$. So,

$$\sin 30° = \frac{\text{opp}}{\text{hyp}} = \frac{1}{2} \quad \text{and} \quad \cos 30° = \frac{\text{adj}}{\text{hyp}} = \frac{\sqrt{3}}{2}.$$

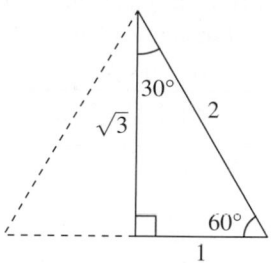

Figure 4.17

✓ **Checkpoint** ◀))) *Audio-video solution in English & Spanish at LarsonPrecalculus.com.*

Use the equilateral triangle shown in Figure 4.17 to find the exact values of tan 60° and tan 30°.

Sines, Cosines, and Tangents of Special Angles

$$\sin 30° = \sin \frac{\pi}{6} = \frac{1}{2} \qquad \cos 30° = \cos \frac{\pi}{6} = \frac{\sqrt{3}}{2} \qquad \tan 30° = \tan \frac{\pi}{6} = \frac{\sqrt{3}}{3}$$

$$\sin 45° = \sin \frac{\pi}{4} = \frac{\sqrt{2}}{2} \qquad \cos 45° = \cos \frac{\pi}{4} = \frac{\sqrt{2}}{2} \qquad \tan 45° = \tan \frac{\pi}{4} = 1$$

$$\sin 60° = \sin \frac{\pi}{3} = \frac{\sqrt{3}}{2} \qquad \cos 60° = \cos \frac{\pi}{3} = \frac{1}{2} \qquad \tan 60° = \tan \frac{\pi}{3} = \sqrt{3}$$

Remark

Because the angles 30°, 45°, and 60° ($\pi/6$, $\pi/4$, and $\pi/3$, respectively) occur frequently in trigonometry, you should learn to construct the triangles shown in Figures 4.16 and 4.17.

Note that $\sin 30° = \frac{1}{2} = \cos 60°$. This occurs because 30° and 60° are complementary angles. In general, it can be shown from the right triangle definitions that *cofunctions of complementary angles are equal*. That is, if θ is an acute angle, then the relationships below are true.

$$\sin(90° - \theta) = \cos \theta \qquad \cos(90° - \theta) = \sin \theta \qquad \tan(90° - \theta) = \cot \theta$$

$$\cot(90° - \theta) = \tan \theta \qquad \sec(90° - \theta) = \csc \theta \qquad \csc(90° - \theta) = \sec \theta$$

To use a calculator to evaluate trigonometric functions of angles measured in degrees, set the calculator to *degree* mode and then proceed as demonstrated in Section 4.2.

EXAMPLE 4   **Using a Calculator**

To evaluate $\cos(5° \, 40' \, 12'')$, begin by converting to decimal degree form.

$$5° \, 40' \, 12'' = 5° + \left(\frac{40}{60}\right)° + \left(\frac{12}{3600}\right)° = 5.67°$$

Then use a calculator to evaluate cos 5.67°.

Function	Graphing Calculator Keystrokes	Display
$\cos(5° \, 40' \, 12'') = \cos 5.67°$	(COS) ⦗ 5.67 ⦘ (ENTER)	0.9951074

✓ **Checkpoint** ◀))) *Audio-video solution in English & Spanish at LarsonPrecalculus.com.*

Use a calculator to evaluate sin 34° 30′36″.

Trigonometric Identities

In trigonometry, a great deal of time is spent studying relationships between trigonometric functions (identities).

Fundamental Trigonometric Identities

Reciprocal Identities

$$\sin \theta = \frac{1}{\csc \theta} \qquad \cos \theta = \frac{1}{\sec \theta} \qquad \tan \theta = \frac{1}{\cot \theta}$$

$$\csc \theta = \frac{1}{\sin \theta} \qquad \sec \theta = \frac{1}{\cos \theta} \qquad \cot \theta = \frac{1}{\tan \theta}$$

Quotient Identities

$$\tan \theta = \frac{\sin \theta}{\cos \theta} \qquad \cot \theta = \frac{\cos \theta}{\sin \theta}$$

Pythagorean Identities

$$\sin^2 \theta + \cos^2 \theta = 1$$

$$1 + \tan^2 \theta = \sec^2 \theta$$

$$1 + \cot^2 \theta = \csc^2 \theta$$

Note that $\sin^2 \theta$ represents $(\sin \theta)^2$, $\cos^2 \theta$ represents $(\cos \theta)^2$, and so on.

EXAMPLE 5   Applying Trigonometric Identities

Let θ be an acute angle such that $\cos \theta = 0.8$. Find the values of (a) $\sin \theta$ and (b) $\tan \theta$ using trigonometric identities.

Solution

a. To find the value of $\sin \theta$, use the Pythagorean identity

$$\sin^2 \theta + \cos^2 \theta = 1.$$

So, you have

$\sin^2 \theta + (0.8)^2 = 1$	Substitute 0.8 for $\cos \theta$.
$\sin^2 \theta = 1 - (0.8)^2$	Subtract $(0.8)^2$ from each side.
$\sin^2 \theta = 0.36$	Simplify.
$\sin \theta = \sqrt{0.36}$	Extract positive square root.
$\sin \theta = 0.6$	Simplify.

b. Now, knowing the sine and cosine of θ, you can find the tangent of θ to be

$$\tan \theta = \frac{\sin \theta}{\cos \theta} = \frac{0.6}{0.8} = 0.75.$$

Use the definitions of $\sin \theta$ and $\tan \theta$ and the triangle shown in Figure 4.18 to check these results.

Figure 4.18

✓ **Checkpoint** Audio-video solution in English & Spanish at LarsonPrecalculus.com.

Let θ be an acute angle such that $\sin \theta = 0.28$. Find the values of (a) $\cos \theta$ and (b) $\tan \theta$ using trigonometric identities.

EXAMPLE 6   **Applying Trigonometric Identities**

Let θ be an acute angle such that $\tan \theta = \frac{1}{3}$. Find the values of (a) $\cot \theta$ and (b) $\sec \theta$ using trigonometric identities.

Solution

a. $\cot \theta = \dfrac{1}{\tan \theta}$ Reciprocal identity

$\qquad = \dfrac{1}{1/3}$

$\qquad = 3$

b. $\sec^2 \theta = 1 + \tan^2 \theta$ Pythagorean identity

$\quad \sec^2 \theta = 1 + \left(\dfrac{1}{3}\right)^2$

$\quad \sec^2 \theta = \dfrac{10}{9}$

$\quad \sec \theta = \dfrac{\sqrt{10}}{3}$

Use the definitions of $\cot \theta$ and $\sec \theta$ and the triangle to check these results.

✓ **Checkpoint** ◀))) *Audio-video solution in English & Spanish at LarsonPrecalculus.com.*

Let θ be an acute angle such that $\tan \theta = 2$. Find the values of (a) $\cot \theta$ and (b) $\sec \theta$ using trigonometric identities.

EXAMPLE 7   **Using Trigonometric Identities**

Use trigonometric identities to transform one side of the equation into the other $(0 < \theta < \pi/2)$.

a. $\cos \theta \sec \theta = 1$ **b.** $(\sec \theta + \tan \theta)(\sec \theta - \tan \theta) = 1$

Solution

Simplify the expression on the left-hand side of the equation until you obtain the right-hand side.

a. $\cos \theta \sec \theta = \left(\dfrac{1}{\sec \theta}\right) \sec \theta$ Reciprocal identity

$\qquad\qquad\quad = 1$ Divide out common factor.

b. $(\sec \theta + \tan \theta)(\sec \theta - \tan \theta)$

$\qquad = \sec^2 \theta - \sec \theta \tan \theta + \sec \theta \tan \theta - \tan^2 \theta$ Distributive Property

$\qquad = \sec^2 \theta - \tan^2 \theta$ Simplify.

$\qquad = 1$ Pythagorean identity

✓ **Checkpoint** ◀))) *Audio-video solution in English & Spanish at LarsonPrecalculus.com.*

Use trigonometric identities to transform one side of the equation into the other $(0 < \theta < \pi/2)$.

a. $\tan \theta \csc \theta = \sec \theta$ **b.** $(\csc \theta + 1)(\csc \theta - 1) = \cot^2 \theta$

Applications

Many applications of trigonometry involve a process called **solving right triangles.** In this type of application, you are usually given one side of a right triangle and one of the acute angles and are asked to find one of the other sides, *or* you are given two sides and are asked to find one of the acute angles.

In Example 8, you are given the **angle of elevation,** which represents the angle from the horizontal upward to the object. In other applications you may be given the **angle of depression,** which represents the angle from the horizontal downward to the object. (See Figure 4.19.)

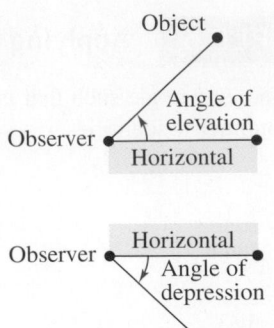

Figure 4.19

EXAMPLE 8   Using Trigonometry to Solve a Right Triangle

A surveyor is standing 50 feet from the base of a large tree, as shown in Figure 4.20. The surveyor measures the angle of elevation to the top of the tree as 71.5°. How tall is the tree?

Solution

From Figure 4.20, you can see that

$$\tan 71.5° = \frac{\text{opp}}{\text{adj}} = \frac{y}{x}$$

where $x = 50$ and y is the height of the tree. So, the height of the tree is

$$y = x \tan 71.5° = 50 \tan 71.5° \approx 149.43 \text{ feet.}$$

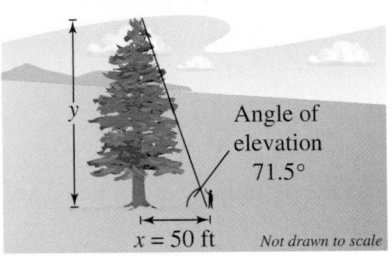

Figure 4.20

✓ **Checkpoint** 🔊))) *Audio-video solution in English & Spanish at LarsonPrecalculus.com.*

At a distance of 19 feet from its base, the angle of elevation to the top of a flagpole is 64.6°. (See figure.) How tall is the flagpole?

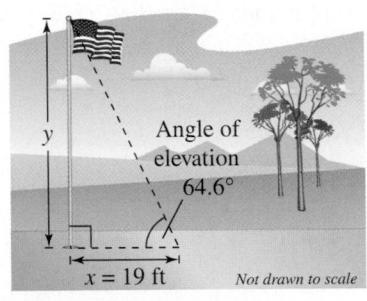

EXAMPLE 9   Using Trigonometry to Solve a Right Triangle

You are 200 yards from a river. Rather than walking directly to the river, you walk 400 yards along a straight path to the river's edge. Find the acute angle θ between this path and the river's edge, as illustrated in Figure 4.21.

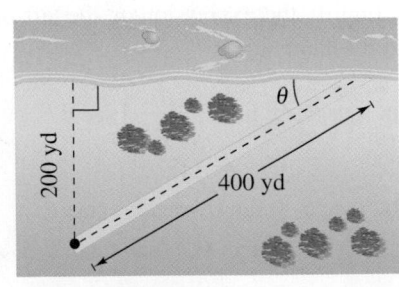

Figure 4.21

Solution

From Figure 4.21, you can see that the sine of the angle θ is

$$\sin \theta = \frac{\text{opp}}{\text{hyp}} = \frac{200}{400} = \frac{1}{2}.$$

Now you should recognize that $\theta = 30°$.

✓ **Checkpoint** 🔊))) *Audio-video solution in English & Spanish at LarsonPrecalculus.com.*

In Example 9, find the acute angle θ when you are $200\sqrt{3}$ yards from the river and you walk 400 yards along a straight path to the river's edge.

In Example 9, you were able to recognize that $\theta = 30°$ is the acute angle that satisfies the equation $\sin\theta = \frac{1}{2}$. Consider, however, the equation $\sin\theta = 0.6$. To find the acute angle θ, note that

$$\sin 30° = \frac{1}{2} = 0.5000$$

and

$$\sin 45° = \frac{1}{\sqrt{2}} \approx 0.7071.$$

So, you might guess that θ lies somewhere between $30°$ and $45°$. In a later section, you will study a method by which a more precise value of θ can be determined.

EXAMPLE 10   Solving a Right Triangle

Find the length c of the skateboard ramp shown in the figure below. Find the horizontal length a of the ramp.

Solution

From the figure, you can see that

$$\sin 18.4° = \frac{\text{opp}}{\text{hyp}} = \frac{4}{c}.$$

So, the length of the skateboard ramp is

$$c = \frac{4}{\sin 18.4°} \approx \frac{4}{0.3156} \approx 12.7 \text{ feet.}$$

Also from the figure, you can see that

$$\tan 18.4° = \frac{\text{opp}}{\text{adj}} = \frac{4}{a}.$$

So, the horizontal length is

$$a = \frac{4}{\tan 18.4°} \approx 12.0 \text{ feet.}$$

✓ **Checkpoint** 🔊))) *Audio-video solution in English & Spanish at LarsonPrecalculus.com.*

Find the length c of the loading ramp shown in the figure below. Find the horizontal length a of the ramp.

What's Wrong?

You use a graphing utility to check the answers to Example 10 and obtain the screen shown below. What's wrong?

```
4/sin(18.4)
               -9.20459373
4/tan(18.4)
              -8.290026883
```

Technology Tip

Calculators and graphing utilities have both *degree* and *radian* modes. As you progress through this chapter, be sure you use the correct mode.

4.3 Exercises

See *CalcChat.com* for tutorial help and worked-out solutions to odd-numbered exercises. For instructions on how to use a graphing utility, see Appendix A.

Vocabulary and Concept Check

1. Match each trigonometric function with its right triangle definition.

   (a) sine   (b) cosine   (c) tangent

   (d) cosecant   (e) secant   (f) cotangent

   (i) $\dfrac{\text{hyp}}{\text{adj}}$ (ii) $\dfrac{\text{opp}}{\text{adj}}$ (iii) $\dfrac{\text{opp}}{\text{hyp}}$ (iv) $\dfrac{\text{adj}}{\text{opp}}$ (v) $\dfrac{\text{hyp}}{\text{opp}}$ (vi) $\dfrac{\text{adj}}{\text{hyp}}$

In Exercises 2 and 3, fill in the blanks.

2. Relative to the acute angle θ, the three sides of a right triangle are the _____ , the _____ side, and the _____ side.

3. An angle that measures from the horizontal upward to an object is called the angle of _____ , whereas an angle that measures from the horizontal downward to an object is called the angle of _____ .

In Exercises 4–6, use the figure to answer the question.

4. What is the length of the side opposite the angle θ?

5. What is the length of the side adjacent to the angle θ?

6. What is the length of the hypotenuse?

Figure for 4–6

Procedures and Problem Solving

Evaluating Trigonometric Functions In Exercises 7–10, find the exact values of the six trigonometric functions of the angle θ shown in the figure. (Use the Pythagorean Theorem to find the third side of the triangle.)

7.

8.

9.

10.

Evaluating Trigonometric Functions In Exercises 11 and 12, find the exact values of the six trigonometric functions of the angle θ for each of the triangles. Explain why the function values are the same.

11.

12.

Evaluating Trigonometric Functions In Exercises 13–20, sketch a right triangle corresponding to the trigonometric function of the acute angle θ. Use the Pythagorean Theorem to determine the third side of the triangle and then find the values of the other five trigonometric functions of θ.

13. $\sin\theta = \frac{5}{6}$ 14. $\cot\theta = 5$

15. $\sec\theta = 4$ 16. $\cos\theta = \frac{3}{7}$

17. $\tan\theta = 3$ 18. $\csc\theta = \frac{17}{4}$

19. $\cot\theta = \frac{3}{2}$ 20. $\sin\theta = \frac{3}{8}$

Evaluating Trigonometric Functions of 30°, 45°, and 60°
In Exercises 21–30, construct an appropriate triangle to complete the table. ($0° \le \theta \le 90°$, $0 \le \theta \le \pi/2$)

	Function	θ (deg)	θ (rad)	Function Value
21.	sin	30°		
22.	cos	60°		
23.	tan		$\dfrac{\pi}{3}$	
24.	sec		$\dfrac{\pi}{4}$	
25.	csc			$\sqrt{2}$
26.	cot			$\dfrac{\sqrt{3}}{3}$

Function	θ (deg)	θ (rad)	Function Value
27. cos		$\dfrac{\pi}{6}$	
28. sin		$\dfrac{\pi}{4}$	
29. cot			1
30. tan			$\dfrac{1}{\sqrt{3}}$

Using a Calculator   In Exercises 31–36, use a calculator to evaluate each function. Round your answers to four decimal places. (Be sure the calculator is in the correct angle mode.)

31. (a) $\sin 10°$ 　　(b) $\cos 80°$

32. (a) $\tan 18.5°$ 　　(b) $\cot 71.5°$

33. (a) $\sec 42° \, 12'$ 　　(b) $\csc 48° \, 7'30''$

34. (a) $\cos 8° \, 50'25''$ 　　(b) $\sec 56° \, 10''$

35. (a) $\cot \dfrac{\pi}{16}$ 　　(b) $\tan \dfrac{\pi}{8}$

36. (a) $\sec 1.54$ 　　(b) $\cos 1.25$

Fundamental Trigonometric Identities   In Exercises 37–52, complete the identity.

37. $\sin \theta = \dfrac{1}{\rule{1cm}{0.4pt}}$ 　　**38.** $\cos \theta = \dfrac{1}{\rule{1cm}{0.4pt}}$

39. $\tan \theta = \dfrac{1}{\rule{1cm}{0.4pt}}$ 　　**40.** $\csc \theta = \dfrac{1}{\rule{1cm}{0.4pt}}$

41. $\sec \theta = \dfrac{1}{\rule{1cm}{0.4pt}}$ 　　**42.** $\cot \theta = \dfrac{1}{\rule{1cm}{0.4pt}}$

43. $\tan \theta = \dfrac{\rule{1cm}{0.4pt}}{\rule{1cm}{0.4pt}}$ 　　**44.** $\cot \theta = \dfrac{\rule{1cm}{0.4pt}}{\rule{1cm}{0.4pt}}$

45. $\sin^2 \theta + \cos^2 \theta = \rule{1cm}{0.4pt}$

46. $1 + \tan^2 \theta = \rule{1cm}{0.4pt}$

47. $\sin(90° - \theta) = \rule{1cm}{0.4pt}$

48. $\cos(90° - \theta) = \rule{1cm}{0.4pt}$

49. $\tan(90° - \theta) = \rule{1cm}{0.4pt}$

50. $\cot(90° - \theta) = \rule{1cm}{0.4pt}$

51. $\sec(90° - \theta) = \rule{1cm}{0.4pt}$

52. $\csc(90° - \theta) = \rule{1cm}{0.4pt}$

Applying Trigonometric Identities   In Exercises 53–58, use the function value(s) and the trigonometric identities to evaluate each trigonometric function.

53. $\sin 60° = \dfrac{\sqrt{3}}{2}$, $\cos 60° = \dfrac{1}{2}$

(a) $\tan 60°$ 　　(b) $\sin 30°$

(c) $\cos 30°$ 　　(d) $\cot 60°$

54. $\sin 30° = \dfrac{1}{2}$, $\tan 30° = \dfrac{\sqrt{3}}{3}$

(a) $\csc 30°$ 　　(b) $\cot 60°$

(c) $\cos 30°$ 　　(d) $\cot 30°$

55. $\csc \theta = 3$, $\sec \theta = \dfrac{3\sqrt{2}}{4}$

(a) $\sin \theta$ 　　(b) $\cos \theta$

(c) $\tan \theta$ 　　(d) $\sec(90° - \theta)$

56. $\sec \theta = 5$, $\tan \theta = 2\sqrt{6}$

(a) $\cos \theta$ 　　(b) $\cot \theta$

(c) $\cot(90° - \theta)$ 　　(d) $\sin \theta$

57. $\cot \alpha = 4$

(a) $\tan \alpha$ 　　(b) $\csc \alpha$

(c) $\sec \alpha$ 　　(d) $\tan(90° - \alpha)$

58. $\tan \beta = 3$

(a) $\cot \beta$ 　　(b) $\cos \beta$

(c) $\tan(90° - \beta)$ 　　(d) $\csc \beta$

Using Trigonometric Identities   In Exercises 59–66, use trigonometric identities to transform one side of the equation into the other $(0 < \theta < \pi/2)$.

59. $\tan \theta \cot \theta = 1$

60. $\csc^2 \theta \sin^2 \theta = 1$

61. $\csc \theta \tan \theta = \sec \theta$

62. $\cot \theta \sin \theta = \cos \theta$

63. $(1 + \cos \theta)(1 - \cos \theta) = \sin^2 \theta$

64. $(\csc \theta + \cot \theta)(\csc \theta - \cot \theta) = 1$

65. $\dfrac{\sec \theta - \cos \theta}{\sec \theta} = \sin^2 \theta$

66. $\dfrac{\tan \theta + \cot \theta}{\tan \theta} = \csc^2 \theta$

Finding Special Angles of a Triangle   In Exercises 67–72, find each value of θ in degrees $(0° < \theta < 90°)$ and radians $(0 < \theta < \pi/2)$ without using a calculator.

67. (a) $\sin \theta = \frac{1}{2}$ 　　(b) $\csc \theta = 2$

68. (a) $\cos \theta = \dfrac{\sqrt{2}}{2}$ 　　(b) $\tan \theta = 1$

69. (a) $\sec \theta = 2$ 　　(b) $\cot \theta = 1$

70. (a) $\csc \theta = \dfrac{2\sqrt{3}}{3}$ 　　(b) $\sin \theta = \dfrac{1}{2}$

71. (a) $\tan \theta = \sqrt{3}$ 　　(b) $\cos \theta = \dfrac{\sqrt{2}}{2}$

72. (a) $\cot \theta = \dfrac{\sqrt{3}}{3}$ 　　(b) $\sec \theta = \sqrt{2}$

Finding Side Lengths of a Triangle In Exercises 73–76, find the exact values of the indicated variables.

73. Find y and r.

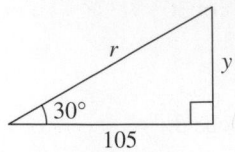

74. Find x and y.

75. Find x and y.

76. Find x and r.

77. Geomatics The Johnstown Inclined Plane in Pennsylvania is one of the longest and steepest hoists in the world. The railway cars travel a distance of 896.5 feet at an angle of approximately 35.4°, rising to a height of 1693.5 feet above sea level. (See figure.)

Not drawn to scale

(a) Find the vertical rise of the inclined plane.

(b) Find the elevation of the lower end of the inclined plane.

(c) The cars move up the mountain at a rate of 300 feet per minute. Find the rate at which they rise vertically.

78. *Why you should learn it* (p. 273) A zip line steel cable is being constructed for a reality television competition show. The high end of the zip line is attached to the top of a 50-foot pole, while the lower end is anchored at ground level to a stake 50 feet from the base of the pole. (See figure.)

(a) Find the angle of elevation of the zip line.

(b) Find the number of feet of steel cable needed for the zip line.

(c) A contestant takes 6 seconds to reach the ground from the top of the zip line. At what rate is the contestant moving down the line? At what rate is the contestant dropping vertically?

79. Biology A biologist wants to know the width w of a river in order to properly set instruments for studying the pollutants in the water. From point A, the biologist walks upstream 100 feet and sights to point C. From this sighting, it is determined that $\theta = 58°$ (see figure). How wide is the river? Verify your result numerically.

80. Geomatics In traveling across flat land, you notice a mountain directly in front of you. Its angle of elevation (to the peak) is 3.5°. After you drive 13 miles closer to the mountain, the angle of elevation is 9° (see figure). Approximate the height of the mountain.

Not drawn to scale

81. Mechanical Engineering A steel plate has the form of one-fourth of a circle with a radius of 60 centimeters. Two 2-centimeter holes are to be drilled in the plate, positioned as shown in the figure. Find the coordinates of the center of each hole.

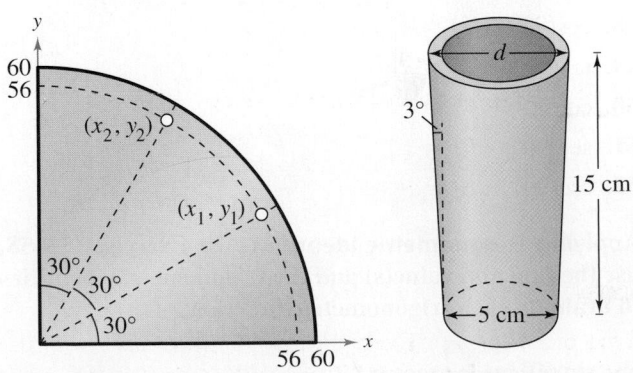

Figure for 81   Figure for 82

82. Mechanical Engineering A tapered shaft has a diameter of 5 centimeters at the small end and is 15 centimeters long. The taper is 3° (see figure). Find the diameter d of the large end of the shaft.

83. Geometry   A six-foot person walks from the base of a streetlight directly toward the tip of the shadow cast by the streetlight. When the person is 16 feet from the streetlight and 5 feet from the tip of the streetlight's shadow, the person's shadow starts to appear beyond the streetlight's shadow.

(a) Draw a right triangle that gives a visual representation of the problem. Show the known quantities and use a variable to indicate the height of the streetlight.

(b) Use a trigonometric function to write an equation involving the unknown quantity.

(c) What is the height of the streetlight?

---

84. MODELING DATA

A 20-meter line is used to tether a helium-filled balloon. Because of a breeze, the line makes an angle of approximately 85° with the ground.

(a) Draw a right triangle that gives a visual representation of the problem. Show the known quantities of the triangle and use a variable to indicate the height of the balloon.

(b) Use a trigonometric function to write an equation involving the unknown quantity.

(c) What is the height of the balloon?

(d) The breeze becomes stronger, and the angle the balloon makes with the ground decreases. How does this affect your triangle from part (a)?

(e) Complete the table, which shows the heights (in meters) of the balloon for decreasing angle measures θ.

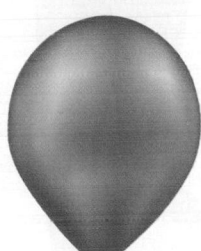

Angle, θ	80°	70°	60°	50°
Height				

Angle, θ	40°	30°	20°	10°
Height				

(f) As the angle the balloon makes with the ground approaches 0°, how does this affect the height of the balloon? Draw a right triangle to explain your reasoning.

Conclusions

True or False?   In Exercises 85–90, determine whether the statement is true or false. Justify your answer.

85. $\sin 60° \csc 60° = 1$ **86.** $\sec 30° = \csc 60°$

87. $\sin 45° + \cos 45° = 1$ **88.** $\cot^2 10° - \csc^2 10° = -1$

89. $\dfrac{\sin 60°}{\sin 30°} = \sin 2°$ **90.** $\tan[(5°)^2] = \tan^2 5°$

91. Think About It   You are given the value of $\tan \theta$. Is it possible to find the value of $\sec \theta$ without finding the measure of θ? Explain.

92.   HOW DO YOU SEE IT?   Use the figure to answer each question.

(a) Which side is opposite θ?

(b) Which side is adjacent to $90° - \theta$?

(c) Explain why $\sin \theta = \cos(90° - \theta)$.

93. Exploration

(a) Use a graphing utility to complete the table. Round your results to four decimal places.

θ	0°	20°	40°	60°	80°
$\sin \theta$					
$\cos \theta$					
$\tan \theta$					

(b) Classify each of the three trigonometric functions as increasing or decreasing for the table values.

(c) From the values in the table, verify that the tangent function is the quotient of the sine and cosine functions.

Cumulative Mixed Review

Graphing an Exponential Function   In Exercises 94–97, use a graphing utility to construct a table of values for the function. Then sketch the graph of the function. Identify any asymptote of the graph.

94. $f(x) = e^{3x}$ **95.** $f(x) = -e^{3x}$

96. $f(x) = 2 + e^{3x}$ **97.** $f(x) = -4 + e^{3x}$

Graphing a Logarithmic Function   In Exercises 98–101, use a graphing utility to graph the logarithmic function. Find the domain, vertical asymptote, and x-intercept of the logarithmic function.

98. $f(x) = \log_3 x$ **99.** $f(x) = \log_3 x + 1$

100. $f(x) = -\log_3 x$ **101.** $f(x) = \log_3(x - 4)$

4.4   Trigonometric Functions of Any Angle

Introduction

In Section 4.3, the definitions of trigonometric functions were restricted to acute angles. In this section, the definitions are extended to cover *any* angle. When θ is an *acute* angle, the definitions here coincide with those given in the preceding section.

Definitions of Trigonometric Functions of Any Angle

Let θ be an angle in standard position with (x, y) a point on the terminal side of θ and $r = \sqrt{x^2 + y^2} \neq 0$.

$$\sin \theta = \frac{y}{r} \qquad\qquad \cos \theta = \frac{x}{r}$$

$$\tan \theta = \frac{y}{x}, \quad x \neq 0 \qquad \cot \theta = \frac{x}{y}, \quad y \neq 0$$

$$\sec \theta = \frac{r}{x}, \quad x \neq 0 \qquad \csc \theta = \frac{r}{y}, \quad y \neq 0$$

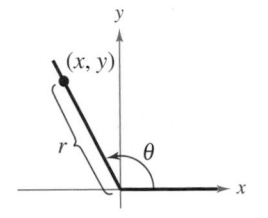

Because $r = \sqrt{x^2 + y^2}$ cannot be zero, it follows that the sine and cosine functions are defined for any real value of θ. However, when $x = 0$, the tangent and secant of θ are undefined. For example, the tangent of $90°$ is undefined. Similarly, when $y = 0$, the cotangent and cosecant of θ are undefined.

EXAMPLE 1   Evaluating Trigonometric Functions

Let $(-3, 4)$ be a point on the terminal side of θ. (See figure.) Find the sine, cosine, and tangent of θ.

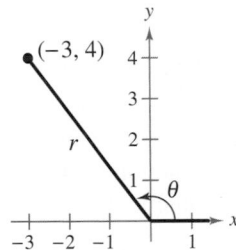

Solution

Referring to the figure, you can see that $x = -3$, $y = 4$, and

$$r = \sqrt{x^2 + y^2}$$

$$= \sqrt{(-3)^2 + 4^2}$$

$$= \sqrt{25}$$

$$= 5.$$

So, you have $\sin \theta = \dfrac{y}{r} = \dfrac{4}{5}$, $\cos \theta = \dfrac{x}{r} = -\dfrac{3}{5}$, and $\tan \theta = \dfrac{y}{x} = -\dfrac{4}{3}$.

✓ **Checkpoint** *Audio-video solution in English & Spanish at LarsonPrecalculus.com.*

Let $(-2, 3)$ be a point on the terminal side of θ. Find the sine, cosine, and tangent of θ.

The *signs* of the trigonometric functions in the four quadrants can be determined from the definitions of the functions. For instance, because $\cos \theta = x/r$, it follows that $\cos \theta$ is positive wherever $x > 0$, which is in Quadrants I and IV. (Remember, r is always positive.) In a similar manner, you can verify the other results shown in Figure 4.22.

Quadrant II	Quadrant I
$\sin \theta$: + $\cos \theta$: − $\tan \theta$: −	$\sin \theta$: + $\cos \theta$: + $\tan \theta$: +
Quadrant III	Quadrant IV
$\sin \theta$: − $\cos \theta$: − $\tan \theta$: +	$\sin \theta$: − $\cos \theta$: + $\tan \theta$: −

EXAMPLE 2   Evaluating Trigonometric Functions

Given $\sin \theta = -\frac{2}{3}$ and $\tan \theta > 0$, find $\cos \theta$ and $\cot \theta$.

Solution

Note that θ lies in Quadrant III because that is the only quadrant in which the sine is negative and the tangent is positive. Moreover, using

$$\sin \theta = \frac{y}{r} = -\frac{2}{3}$$

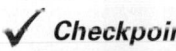

and the fact that y is negative in Quadrant III, you can let $y = -2$ and $r = 3$. Because x is negative in Quadrant III,

$$x = -\sqrt{9-4} = -\sqrt{5}$$

and you have the following.

$$\cos \theta = \frac{x}{r} = \frac{-\sqrt{5}}{3} \qquad \text{Exact value}$$

$$\approx -0.75 \qquad \text{Approximate value}$$

$$\cot \theta = \frac{x}{y} = \frac{-\sqrt{5}}{-2} \qquad \text{Exact value}$$

$$\approx 1.12 \qquad \text{Approximate value}$$

✓ **Checkpoint**))) *Audio-video solution in English & Spanish at LarsonPrecalculus.com.*

Given $\sin \theta = \frac{4}{5}$ and $\tan \theta < 0$, find $\cos \theta$ and $\tan \theta$.

$\frac{\pi}{2} < \theta < \pi$ $0 < \theta < \frac{\pi}{2}$

$x < 0$ $y > 0$ $x > 0$ $y > 0$

$x < 0$ $y < 0$ $x > 0$ $y < 0$

$\pi < \theta < \frac{3\pi}{2}$ $\frac{3\pi}{2} < \theta < 2\pi$

Figure 4.22

EXAMPLE 3   Trigonometric Functions of Quadrant Angles

Evaluate the sine and cosine functions at the angles 0, $\frac{\pi}{2}$, π, and $\frac{3\pi}{2}$.

Solution

To begin, choose a point on the terminal side of each angle, as shown in Figure 4.23. For each of the four points, $r = 1$, and you have the following.

$$\sin 0 = \frac{y}{r} = \frac{0}{1} = 0 \qquad\qquad \cos 0 = \frac{x}{r} = \frac{1}{1} = 1 \qquad\qquad (x, y) = (1, 0)$$

$$\sin \frac{\pi}{2} = \frac{y}{r} = \frac{1}{1} = 1 \qquad\qquad \cos \frac{\pi}{2} = \frac{x}{r} = \frac{0}{1} = 0 \qquad\qquad (x, y) = (0, 1)$$

$$\sin \pi = \frac{y}{r} = \frac{0}{1} = 0 \qquad\qquad \cos \pi = \frac{x}{r} = \frac{-1}{1} = -1 \qquad\qquad (x, y) = (-1, 0)$$

$$\sin \frac{3\pi}{2} = \frac{y}{r} = \frac{-1}{1} = -1 \qquad \cos \frac{3\pi}{2} = \frac{x}{r} = \frac{0}{1} = 0 \qquad\qquad (x, y) = (0, -1)$$

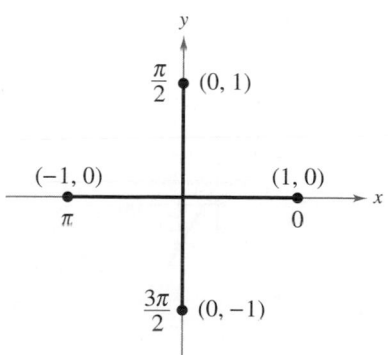

Figure 4.23

✓ **Checkpoint**))) *Audio-video solution in English & Spanish at LarsonPrecalculus.com.*

Evaluate the tangent and cotangent functions at the angle $\frac{3\pi}{2}$.

Reference Angles

The values of the trigonometric functions of angles greater than 90° (or less than 0°) can be determined from their values at corresponding acute angles called **reference angles.**

> **Definition of Reference Angle**
>
> Let θ be an angle in standard position. Its **reference angle** is the acute angle θ' formed by the terminal side of θ and the horizontal axis.

The reference angles for θ in Quadrants II, III, and IV are shown below.

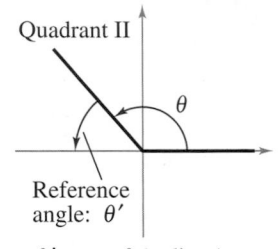

Quadrant II

Reference angle: θ'

$\theta' = \pi - \theta$ (radians)
$\theta' = 180° - \theta$ (degrees)

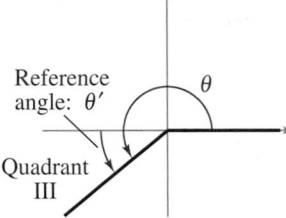

Reference angle: θ'

Quadrant III

$\theta' = \theta - \pi$ (radians)
$\theta' = \theta - 180°$ (degrees)

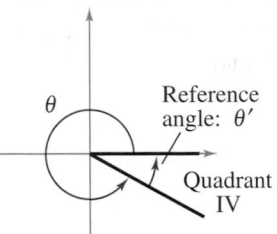

Reference angle: θ'

Quadrant IV

$\theta' = 2\pi - \theta$ (radians)
$\theta' = 360° - \theta$ (degrees)

EXAMPLE 4   Finding Reference Angles

Find the reference angle θ' for each value of θ.

a. $\theta = 300°$ **b.** $\theta = 2.3$ **c.** $\theta = -135°$

Solution

a. Because 300° lies in Quadrant IV, the angle it makes with the x-axis is

$\theta' = 360° - 300° = 60°.$ Degrees

b. Because 2.3 lies between $\pi/2 \approx 1.5708$ and $\pi \approx 3.1416$, it follows that it is in Quadrant II and its reference angle is

$\theta' = \pi - 2.3 \approx 0.8416.$ Radians

c. First, determine that $-135°$ is coterminal with 225°, which lies in Quadrant III. So, the reference angle is

$\theta' = 225° - 180° = 45°.$ Degrees

The figure shows each angle θ and its reference angle θ'.

(a)   (b)   (c)

✓ **Checkpoint** ◀))) Audio-video solution in English & Spanish at *LarsonPrecalculus.com.*

Find the reference angle θ'.

a. $\theta = 213°$ **b.** $\theta = \dfrac{14\pi}{9}$ **c.** $\theta = \dfrac{4\pi}{5}$

Trigonometric Functions of Real Numbers

To see how a reference angle is used to evaluate a trigonometric function, consider the point (x, y) on the terminal side of θ, as shown in the figure. By definition, you know that

$$\sin \theta = \frac{y}{r}$$

and

$$\tan \theta = \frac{y}{x}.$$

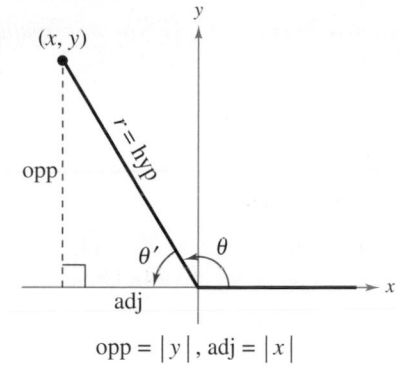

$$\text{opp} = |y|, \text{adj} = |x|$$

For the right triangle with acute angle θ' and sides of lengths $|x|$ and $|y|$, you have

$$\sin \theta' = \frac{\text{opp}}{\text{hyp}} = \frac{|y|}{r}$$

and

$$\tan \theta' = \frac{\text{opp}}{\text{adj}} = \frac{|y|}{|x|}.$$

So, it follows that $\sin \theta$ and $\sin \theta'$ are equal, *except possibly in sign*. The same is true for $\tan \theta$ and $\tan \theta'$ and for the other four trigonometric functions. In all cases, the sign of the function value can be determined by the quadrant in which θ lies.

Evaluating Trigonometric Functions of Any Angle

To find the value of a trigonometric function of any angle θ:

1. Determine the function value of the associated reference angle θ'.

2. Depending on the quadrant in which θ lies, affix the appropriate sign to the function value.

By using reference angles and the special angles discussed in the previous section, you can greatly extend the scope of *exact* trigonometric values. For instance, knowing the function values of $30°$ means that you know the function values of all angles for which $30°$ is a reference angle. For convenience, the table below shows the exact values of the sine, cosine, and tangent functions of special angles and quadrant angles.

Trigonometric Values of Common Angles

θ (degrees)	$0°$	$30°$	$45°$	$60°$	$90°$	$180°$	$270°$
θ (radians)	0	$\dfrac{\pi}{6}$	$\dfrac{\pi}{4}$	$\dfrac{\pi}{3}$	$\dfrac{\pi}{2}$	π	$\dfrac{3\pi}{2}$
$\sin \theta$	0	$\dfrac{1}{2}$	$\dfrac{\sqrt{2}}{2}$	$\dfrac{\sqrt{3}}{2}$	1	0	-1
$\cos \theta$	1	$\dfrac{\sqrt{3}}{2}$	$\dfrac{\sqrt{2}}{2}$	$\dfrac{1}{2}$	0	-1	0
$\tan \theta$	0	$\dfrac{\sqrt{3}}{3}$	1	$\sqrt{3}$	Undef.	0	Undef.

Remark

Learning the trigonometric values of common angles in the table at the left is worth the effort because doing so will increase both your efficiency and your confidence. Below is a pattern for the sine function that may help you remember the values. Reverse the order to get cosine values of the same angles.

θ	$0°$	$30°$	$45°$	$60°$	$90°$
$\sin \theta$	$\dfrac{\sqrt{0}}{2}$	$\dfrac{\sqrt{1}}{2}$	$\dfrac{\sqrt{2}}{2}$	$\dfrac{\sqrt{3}}{2}$	$\dfrac{\sqrt{4}}{2}$

EXAMPLE 5 Trigonometric Functions of Nonacute Angles

See LarsonPrecalculus.com for an interactive version of this type of example.

Evaluate each trigonometric function.

a. $\cos \dfrac{4\pi}{3}$ **b.** $\tan(-210°)$ **c.** $\csc \dfrac{11\pi}{4}$

Solution

Figure 4.24

a. Because $\theta = 4\pi/3$ lies in Quadrant III, the reference angle is $\theta' = (4\pi/3) - \pi = \pi/3$, as shown in Figure 4.24. Moreover, the cosine is negative in Quadrant III, so

$$\cos \frac{4\pi}{3} = (-)\cos \frac{\pi}{3} = -\frac{1}{2}.$$

b. Because $-210° + 360° = 150°$, it follows that $-210°$ is coterminal with the second-quadrant angle 150°. So, the reference angle is $\theta' = 180° - 150° = 30°$, as shown in Figure 4.25. Finally, because the tangent is negative in Quadrant II, you have

$$\tan(-210°) = (-)\tan 30° = -\frac{\sqrt{3}}{3}.$$

Figure 4.25

c. Because $(11\pi/4) - 2\pi = 3\pi/4$, it follows that $11\pi/4$ is coterminal with the second-quadrant angle $3\pi/4$. So, the reference angle is $\theta' = \pi - (3\pi/4) = \pi/4$, as shown in Figure 4.26. Because the cosecant is positive in Quadrant II, you have

$$\csc \frac{11\pi}{4} = (+)\csc \frac{\pi}{4} = \frac{1}{\sin(\pi/4)} = \sqrt{2}.$$

 Checkpoint ◀))) *Audio-video solution in English & Spanish at LarsonPrecalculus.com.*

Evaluate each trigonometric function.

a. $\sin \dfrac{7\pi}{4}$ **b.** $\cos(-120°)$ **c.** $\tan \dfrac{11\pi}{6}$

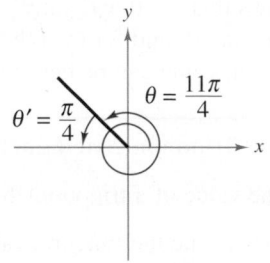

Figure 4.26

The fundamental trigonometric identities listed in the preceding section (for an acute angle θ) are also valid when θ is any angle in the domain of the function.

EXAMPLE 6 Using Trigonometric Identities

Let θ be an angle in Quadrant II such that $\sin \theta = \frac{1}{3}$. Find $\cos \theta$ by using trigonometric identities.

Solution

Using the Pythagorean identity $\sin^2 \theta + \cos^2 \theta = 1$, you obtain

$$\left(\tfrac{1}{3}\right)^2 + \cos^2 \theta = 1$$

$$\cos^2 \theta = 1 - \tfrac{1}{9}$$

$$\cos^2 \theta = \tfrac{8}{9}.$$

Because $\cos \theta < 0$ in Quadrant II, you can use the negative root to obtain

$$\cos \theta = -\frac{\sqrt{8}}{\sqrt{9}} = -\frac{2\sqrt{2}}{3}.$$

 Checkpoint ◀))) *Audio-video solution in English & Spanish at LarsonPrecalculus.com.*

Let θ be an angle in Quadrant III such that $\sin \theta = -\frac{4}{5}$. Find $\cos \theta$ by using trigonometric identities.

4.4   Exercises

See *CalcChat.com* for tutorial help and worked-out solutions to odd-numbered exercises.
For instructions on how to use a graphing utility, see Appendix A.

Vocabulary and Concept Check

In Exercises 1–6, let θ be an angle in standard position with (x, y) a point on the terminal side of θ and $r = \sqrt{x^2 + y^2} \neq 0$. Fill in the blank.

1. $\sin \theta = $ _____
2. $\dfrac{r}{y} = $ _____
3. $\tan \theta = $ _____
4. $\sec \theta = $ _____
5. $\dfrac{x}{r} = $ _____
6. $\dfrac{x}{y} = $ _____

7. What do you call the acute angle formed by the terminal side of an angle θ in standard position and the horizontal axis?

8. In which quadrants is $\cos \theta$ positive?

9. For which of the quadrant angles 0, $\pi/2$, π, and $3\pi/2$ is the sine function equal to 0?

10. Is the value of $\cos 170°$ equal to the value of $\cos 10°$?

Procedures and Problem Solving

Evaluating Trigonometric Functions   In Exercises 11–14, determine the exact values of the six trigonometric functions of the angle θ.

11. (a)   (b)

12. (a)   (b)

13. (a)   (b)

14. (a)   (b)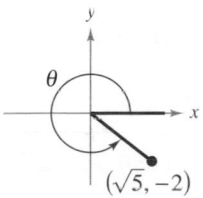

Evaluating Trigonometric Functions   In Exercises 15–22, the point is on the terminal side of an angle in standard position. Determine the exact values of the six trigonometric functions of the angle.

15. $(7, 24)$
16. $(8, 15)$
17. $(5, -12)$
18. $(-24, 10)$
19. $\left(-\sqrt{21}, 2\right)$
20. $\left(-3, -\sqrt{7}\right)$
21. $(-10, -8)$
22. $(3, -9)$

Determining a Quadrant   In Exercises 23–26, state the quadrant in which θ lies.

23. $\sin \theta < 0$ and $\cos \theta < 0$
24. $\sec \theta > 0$ and $\cot \theta < 0$
25. $\cot \theta > 0$ and $\cos \theta > 0$
26. $\tan \theta > 0$ and $\csc \theta < 0$

Evaluating Trigonometric Functions   In Exercises 27–34, find the values of the six trigonometric functions of θ.

	Function Value	*Constraint*
27.	$\sin \theta = \frac{3}{5}$	θ lies in Quadrant II.
28.	$\cos \theta = -\frac{4}{5}$	θ lies in Quadrant III.
29.	$\tan \theta = -\frac{15}{8}$	$\sin \theta < 0$
30.	$\csc \theta = 4$	$\cot \theta < 0$
31.	$\sec \theta = -2$	$0 \leq \theta \leq \pi$
32.	$\sin \theta = 0$	$\dfrac{\pi}{2} \leq \theta \leq \dfrac{3\pi}{2}$
33.	$\cot \theta$ is undefined.	$\dfrac{\pi}{2} \leq \theta \leq \dfrac{3\pi}{2}$
34.	$\tan \theta$ is undefined.	$\pi \leq \theta \leq 2\pi$

An Angle Formed by a Line Through the Origin In Exercises 35–38, the terminal side of θ lies on the given line in the specified quadrant. Find the values of the six trigonometric functions of θ by finding a point on the line.

Line	Quadrant
35. $y = -x$	II
36. $y = \frac{1}{3}x$	I
37. $2x - y = 0$	III
38. $4x + 3y = 0$	IV

Trigonometric Function of a Quadrant Angle In Exercises 39–46, evaluate the trigonometric function of the quadrant angle.

39. $\sec \pi$
40. $\tan \dfrac{\pi}{2}$

41. $\sec \dfrac{3\pi}{2}$
42. $\csc 0$

43. $\csc \dfrac{3\pi}{2}$
44. $\sec 0$

45. $\cot \pi$
46. $\csc \dfrac{\pi}{2}$

Finding a Reference Angle In Exercises 47–58, find the reference angle θ' for the special angle θ. Sketch θ in standard position and label θ'.

47. $\theta = 120°$
48. $\theta = 225°$
49. $\theta = 150°$
50. $\theta = 315°$
51. $\theta = -45°$
52. $\theta = -330°$
53. $\theta = \dfrac{5\pi}{3}$
54. $\theta = \dfrac{3\pi}{4}$
55. $\theta = -\dfrac{5\pi}{6}$
56. $\theta = \dfrac{7\pi}{6}$
57. $\theta = \dfrac{11\pi}{6}$
58. $\theta = -\dfrac{5\pi}{3}$

Finding a Reference Angle In Exercises 59–66, find the reference angle θ'. Sketch θ in standard position and label θ'.

59. $\theta = 208°$
60. $\theta = 322°$
61. $\theta = -292°$
62. $\theta = -165°$
63. $\theta = -\dfrac{11\pi}{5}$
64. $\theta = \dfrac{10\pi}{3}$
65. $\theta = 1.8$
66. $\theta = -6.5$

Trigonometric Functions of a Nonacute Angle In Exercises 67–78, evaluate the sine, cosine, and tangent of the angle without using a calculator.

67. $225°$
68. $300°$
69. $-750°$
70. $-495°$

71. $5\pi/3$
72. $3\pi/4$
73. $-5\pi/6$
74. $-4\pi/3$
75. $11\pi/4$
76. $10\pi/3$
77. $-17\pi/6$
78. $-20\pi/3$

Using Trigonometric Identities In Exercises 79–84, find the indicated trigonometric value in the specified quadrant.

Function	Quadrant	Trigonometric Value
79. $\sin \theta = -\frac{3}{5}$	IV	$\cos \theta$
80. $\cot \theta = -3$	II	$\sin \theta$
81. $\csc \theta = -2$	IV	$\cot \theta$
82. $\cos \theta = \frac{5}{8}$	I	$\sec \theta$
83. $\sec \theta = -\frac{9}{4}$	III	$\tan \theta$
84. $\tan \theta = -\frac{5}{4}$	IV	$\csc \theta$

Using Trigonometric Identities In Exercises 85–90, use the given value and the trigonometric identities to find the remaining trigonometric functions of the angle.

85. $\sin \theta = \frac{2}{5}$, $\cos \theta > 0$
86. $\cos \theta = -\frac{3}{7}$, $\sin \theta < 0$
87. $\tan \theta = -4$, $\cos \theta < 0$
88. $\cot \theta = 5$, $\sin \theta > 0$
89. $\csc \theta = -\frac{3}{2}$, $\tan \theta < 0$
90. $\sec \theta = -\frac{4}{3}$, $\cot \theta > 0$

Using a Calculator In Exercises 91–102, use a calculator to evaluate the trigonometric function. Round your answer to four decimal places. (Be sure the calculator is set in the correct angle mode.)

91. $\sin 10°$
92. $\tan 245°$
93. $\sec 235°$
94. $\csc 320°$
95. $\cos(-110°)$
96. $\sin(-220°)$
97. $\cot 4.82$
98. $\sec 0.33$
99. $\tan \dfrac{2\pi}{9}$
100. $\cos \dfrac{11\pi}{9}$
101. $\csc\left(-\dfrac{8\pi}{9}\right)$
102. $\cot\left(-\dfrac{15\pi}{14}\right)$

Solving for θ In Exercises 103–108, find two solutions of each equation. Give your solutions in both degrees $(0° \leq \theta < 360°)$ and radians $(0 \leq \theta < 2\pi)$. Do not use a calculator.

103. (a) $\sin \theta = \frac{1}{2}$ (b) $\sin \theta = -\frac{1}{2}$
104. (a) $\cos \theta = \dfrac{\sqrt{2}}{2}$ (b) $\cos \theta = -\dfrac{\sqrt{2}}{2}$
105. (a) $\csc \theta = \dfrac{2\sqrt{3}}{3}$ (b) $\cot \theta = -1$
106. (a) $\cot \theta = -\sqrt{3}$ (b) $\csc \theta = 2$
107. (a) $\sec \theta = -\dfrac{2\sqrt{3}}{3}$ (b) $\tan \theta = -\dfrac{\sqrt{3}}{3}$
108. (a) $\tan \theta = 1$ (b) $\sec \theta = \sqrt{2}$

Evaluating Trigonometric Functions In Exercises 109–122, find the exact value of each function for the given angle for $f(\theta) = \sin\theta$ and $g(\theta) = \cos\theta$. Do not use a calculator.

(a) $(f + g)(\theta)$ (b) $(g - f)(\theta)$ (c) $[g(\theta)]^2$

(d) $(fg)(\theta)$ (e) $f(2\theta)$ (f) $g(-\theta)$

109. $\theta = 30°$ **110.** $\theta = 60°$

111. $\theta = 315°$ **112.** $\theta = 225°$

113. $\theta = -150°$ **114.** $\theta = -300°$

115. $\theta = 7\pi/6$ **116.** $\theta = 5\pi/6$

117. $\theta = 4\pi/3$ **118.** $\theta = -5\pi/3$

119. $\theta = -270°$ **120.** $\theta = 180°$

121. $\theta = 7\pi/2$ **122.** $\theta = 5\pi/2$

123. Meteorology The normal daily high temperature T (in degrees Fahrenheit) in Savannah, Georgia, can be approximated by

$$T = 76.4 + 16\cos\left(\frac{\pi t}{6} - \frac{7\pi}{6}\right)$$

where t is the time (in months), with $t = 1$ corresponding to January. Find the normal daily high temperature for each month. (Source: National Climatic Data Center)

(a) January   (b) July   (c) October

124. *Why you should learn it* (p. 284) A company that produces wakeboards forecasts monthly sales S over a two-year period to be

$$S = 2.7 + 0.142t + 2.2\sin\left(\frac{\pi t}{6} - \frac{\pi}{2}\right)$$

where S is measured in hundreds of units and t is the time (in months), with $t = 1$ corresponding to January 2014. Estimate sales for each month.

(a) January 2014   (b) February 2015

(c) May 2014   (d) June 2015

125. Aeronautics An airplane flying at an altitude of 6 miles is on a flight path that passes directly over an observer (see figure). Let θ be the angle of elevation from the observer to the plane. Find the distance from the observer to the plane when (a) $\theta = 30°$, (b) $\theta = 90°$, and (c) $\theta = 120°$.

Not drawn to scale

126. **HOW DO YOU SEE IT?** Consider an angle in standard position with $r = 12$ centimeters, as shown in the figure. Describe the changes in the values of x, y, $\sin\theta$, $\cos\theta$, and $\tan\theta$ as θ increases continuously from $0°$ to $90°$.

Conclusions

True or False? In Exercises 127–130, determine whether the statement is true or false. Justify your answer.

127. $\sin\theta < \tan\theta$ in Quadrant I

128. $\sin\theta < \cos\theta$ for $0° < \theta < 45°$

129. $\sin\theta = -\sqrt{1 - \cos^2\theta}$ for $90° < \theta < 180°$

130. $\cos\theta = -\sqrt{1 - \sin^2\theta}$ for $90° < \theta < 180°$

131. Exploration Use a graphing utility to complete the table. Then make a conjecture about the relationship between $\sin\theta$ and $\sin(180° - \theta)$.

θ	$0°$	$20°$	$40°$	$60°$	$80°$
$\sin\theta$					
$\sin(180° - \theta)$					

132. Exploration Use the procedure in Exercise 131 and a graphing utility to create a table of values and make a conjecture about the relationship between $\cos\theta$ and $\cos(180° - \theta)$ for an acute angle θ.

133. Error Analysis Your classmate uses a calculator to evaluate $\tan(\pi/2)$ and gets a result of 0.0274224385. Describe the error.

134. Writing Write a study sheet that will help you remember how to evaluate the six trigonometric functions of any angle θ in standard position. Include figures and diagrams as needed.

Cumulative Mixed Review

Solving an Equation In Exercises 135–140, solve the equation. Round your answer to three decimal places, if necessary.

135. $3x - 7 = 14$ **136.** $44 - 9x = 61$

137. $x^2 - 2x - 5 = 0$ **138.** $2x^2 + x - 4 = 0$

139. $\dfrac{3}{x - 1} = \dfrac{x + 2}{9}$ **140.** $\dfrac{5}{x} = \dfrac{x + 4}{2x}$

4.5 Graphs of Sine and Cosine Functions

Basic Sine and Cosine Curves

In this section, you will study techniques for sketching the graphs of the sine and cosine functions. The graph of the sine function is a **sine curve.** In Figure 4.27, the black portion of the graph represents one period of the function and is called **one cycle** of the sine curve. The gray portion of the graph indicates that the basic sine wave repeats indefinitely to the right and left. The graph of the cosine function is shown in Figure 4.28. To produce these graphs with a graphing utility, make sure you set the graphing utility to *radian* mode.

Recall from Section 4.2 that the domain of the sine and cosine functions is the set of all real numbers. Moreover, the range of each function is the interval

$$[-1, 1]$$

and each function has a period of 2π. Do you see how this information is consistent with the basic graphs shown in Figures 4.27 and 4.28?

Figure 4.27

Figure 4.28

To sketch the graphs of the basic sine and cosine functions by hand, it helps to note five *key points* in one period of each graph: the *intercepts*, the *maximum points*, and the *minimum points*. The table below lists the five key points on the graphs of

$y = \sin x$ and $y = \cos x$.

x	0	$\dfrac{\pi}{2}$	π	$\dfrac{3\pi}{2}$	2π
$\sin x$	0	1	0	-1	0
$\cos x$	1	0	-1	0	1

Note in Figures 4.27 and 4.28 that the sine curve is symmetric with respect to the *origin*, whereas the cosine curve is symmetric with respect to the *y-axis*. These properties of symmetry follow from the fact that the sine function is odd, whereas the cosine function is even.

Library of Parent Functions: Sine and Cosine Functions

The basic characteristics of the parent sine function and parent cosine function are listed below and summarized on the inside cover of this text.

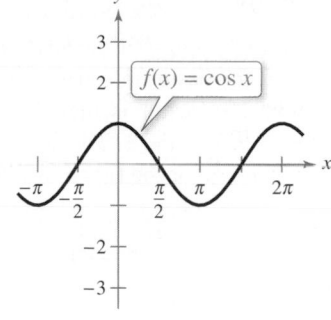

Domain: $(-\infty, \infty)$
Range: $[-1, 1]$
Period: 2π
x-intercepts: $(n\pi, 0)$
y-intercept: $(0, 0)$
Odd function
Origin symmetry

Domain: $(-\infty, \infty)$
Range: $[-1, 1]$
Period: 2π
x-intercepts: $(\pi/2 + n\pi, 0)$
y-intercept: $(0, 1)$
Even function
y-axis symmetry

EXAMPLE 1   Library of Parent Functions: $f(x) = \sin x$

See LarsonPrecalculus.com for an interactive version of this type of example.

Sketch the graph of $g(x) = 2 \sin x$ by hand on the interval $[-\pi, 4\pi]$.

Solution

Note that $g(x) = 2 \sin x = 2(\sin x)$ indicates that the y-values of the key points will have twice the magnitude of those on the graph of $f(x) = \sin x$. Divide the period 2π into four equal parts to get the key points

Intercept	*Maximum*	*Intercept*	*Minimum*		*Intercept*
$(0, 0)$,	$(\pi/2, 2)$,	$(\pi, 0)$,	$(3\pi/2, -2)$,	and	$(2\pi, 0)$.

By connecting these key points with a smooth curve and extending the curve in both directions over the interval $[-\pi, 4\pi]$, you obtain the graph shown below. Use a graphing utility to confirm this graph. Be sure to set the graphing utility to *radian* mode.

Sketch the graph of $y = 2 \cos x$ by hand on the interval $[-\pi/2, 9\pi/2]$. ■

Explore the Concept

Enter the Graphing a Sine Function Program, found at this textbook's *Companion Website*, into your graphing utility. This program simultaneously draws the unit circle and the corresponding points on the sine curve, as shown below. After the circle and sine curve are drawn, you can connect the points on the unit circle with their corresponding points on the sine curve by pressing ENTER. Discuss the relationship that is illustrated.

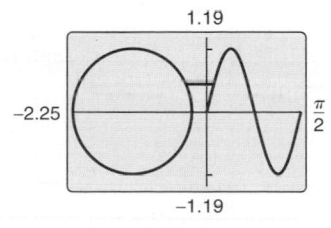

Amplitude and Period of Sine and Cosine Curves

In the rest of this section, you will study the graphic effect of each of the constants a, b, c, and d in equations of the forms

$$y = d + a\sin(bx - c) \quad \text{and} \quad y = d + a\cos(bx - c).$$

The constant factor a in $y = a\sin x$ acts as a *scaling factor*—a *vertical stretch* or *vertical shrink* of the basic sine curve. When $|a| > 1$, the basic sine curve is stretched, and when $|a| < 1$, the basic sine curve is shrunk. The result is that the graph of $y = a\sin x$ ranges between $-a$ and a instead of between -1 and 1. The absolute value of a is the **amplitude** of the function $y = a\sin x$. The range of the function $y = a\sin x$ for $a > 0$ is $-a \le y \le a$.

> **Definition of Amplitude of Sine and Cosine Curves**
>
> The **amplitude** of $y = a\sin x$ and $y = a\cos x$ represents half the distance between the maximum and minimum values of the function and is given by
>
> $$\text{Amplitude} = |a|.$$

EXAMPLE 2   Scaling: Vertical Shrinking and Stretching

On the same set of coordinate axes, sketch the graph of each function by hand.

a. $y = \frac{1}{2}\cos x$

b. $y = 3\cos x$

Solution

a. Because the amplitude of $y = \frac{1}{2}\cos x$ is $\frac{1}{2}$, the maximum value is $\frac{1}{2}$ and the minimum value is $-\frac{1}{2}$. Divide one cycle, $0 \le x \le 2\pi$, into four equal parts to get the key points

Maximum	*Intercept*	*Minimum*	*Intercept*		*Maximum*
$\left(0, \frac{1}{2}\right)$,	$\left(\frac{\pi}{2}, 0\right)$,	$\left(\pi, -\frac{1}{2}\right)$,	$\left(\frac{3\pi}{2}, 0\right)$,	and	$\left(2\pi, \frac{1}{2}\right)$.

b. A similar analysis shows that the amplitude of $y = 3\cos x$ is 3, and the key points are

Maximum	*Intercept*	*Minimum*	*Intercept*		*Maximum*
$(0, 3)$,	$\left(\frac{\pi}{2}, 0\right)$,	$(\pi, -3)$,	$\left(\frac{3\pi}{2}, 0\right)$,	and	$(2\pi, 3)$.

The graphs of these two functions are shown in the figure. Notice that the graph of

$$y = \frac{1}{2}\cos x$$

is a vertical shrink of the graph of $y = \cos x$ and the graph of

$$y = 3\cos x$$

is a vertical stretch of the graph of $y = \cos x$. Use a graphing utility to confirm these graphs.

✓ *Checkpoint* *Audio-video solution in English & Spanish at LarsonPrecalculus.com.*

On the same set of coordinate axes, sketch the graph of each function by hand.

a. $y = \frac{1}{3}\sin x$ **b.** $y = 3\sin x$

You know from Section 1.4 that the graph of $y = -f(x)$ is a *reflection* in the *x*-axis of the graph of $y = f(x)$. For instance, the graph of $y = -3 \cos x$ is a reflection of the graph of $y = 3 \cos x$, as shown in Figure 4.29.

Next, consider the effect of the *positive* real number b on the graphs of $y = a \sin bx$ and $y = a \cos bx$. Because $y = a \sin x$ completes one cycle from $x = 0$ to $x = 2\pi$, it follows that $y = a \sin bx$ completes one cycle from $x = 0$ to $x = 2\pi/b$.

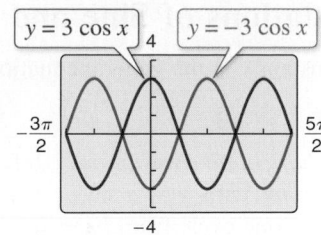

Figure 4.29

Period of Sine and Cosine Functions

Let b be a positive real number. The **period** of

$$y = a \sin\ bx \qquad \text{and} \qquad y = a \cos bx$$

is given by

$$\text{Period} = \frac{2\pi}{b}.$$

Note that when $0 < b < 1$, the period of $y = a \sin bx$ is greater than 2π and represents a *horizontal stretching* of the graph of $y = a \sin x$. Similarly, when $b > 1$, the period of $y = a \sin bx$ is less than 2π and represents a *horizontal shrinking* of the graph of $y = a \sin x$. When b is negative, the identities

$$\sin(-x) = -\sin x \qquad \text{and} \qquad \cos(-x) = \cos x$$

are used to rewrite the function.

EXAMPLE 3   Scaling: Horizontal Stretching

Sketch the graph of $y = \sin \dfrac{x}{2}$ by hand.

Solution

The amplitude is 1. Moreover, because $b = \frac{1}{2}$, the period is

$$\frac{2\pi}{b} = \frac{2\pi}{\frac{1}{2}} = 4\pi. \qquad \text{Substitute for } b.$$

Now, divide the period-interval $[0, 4\pi]$ into four equal parts using the values π, 2π, and 3π to obtain the key points on the graph

Intercept	*Maximum*	*Intercept*	*Minimum*		*Intercept*
$(0, 0)$,	$(\pi, 1)$,	$(2\pi, 0)$,	$(3\pi, -1)$,	and	$(4\pi, 0)$.

The graph is shown below. Use a graphing utility to confirm this graph.

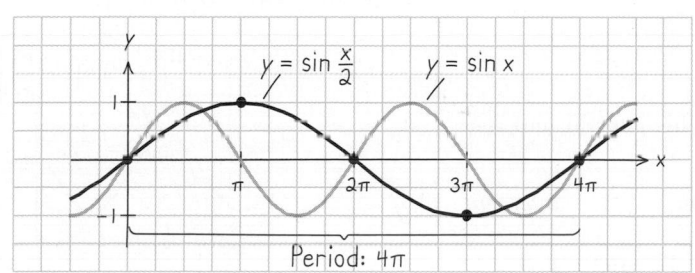

✓ **Checkpoint** 🔊 *Audio-video solution in English & Spanish at LarsonPrecalculus.com.*

Sketch the graph of $y = \cos \dfrac{x}{3}$ by hand.

Remark

In general, to divide a period-interval into four equal parts, successively add "period/4," starting with the left endpoint of the interval. For instance, for the period-interval $[-\pi/6, \pi/2]$ of length $2\pi/3$, you would successively add

$$\frac{2\pi/3}{4} = \frac{\pi}{6}$$

to get $-\pi/6$, 0, $\pi/6$, $\pi/3$, and $\pi/2$ as the *x*-values of the key points on the graph.

Translations of Sine and Cosine Curves

The constant c in the general equations

$$y = a \sin(bx - c) \qquad \text{and} \qquad y = a \cos(bx - c)$$

creates *horizontal translations* (shifts) of the basic sine and cosine curves. Comparing $y = a \sin bx$ with $y = a \sin(bx - c)$, you find that the graph of $y = a \sin(bx - c)$ completes one cycle from $bx - c = 0$ to $bx - c = 2\pi$. By solving for x, you can find the interval for one cycle to be

$$\overbrace{\frac{c}{b}}^{\text{Left endpoint}} \leq x \leq \overbrace{\frac{c}{b}}^{\text{Right endpoint}} + \underbrace{\frac{2\pi}{b}}_{\text{Period}}.$$

This implies that the period of $y = a \sin(bx - c)$ is $2\pi/b$, and the graph of $y = a \sin bx$ is shifted by an amount c/b. The number c/b is the **phase shift.**

Graphs of Sine and Cosine Functions

The graphs of $y = a \sin(bx - c)$ and $y = a \cos(bx - c)$ have the following characteristics. (Assume $b > 0$.)

$$\text{Amplitude} = |a| \qquad \text{Period} = \frac{2\pi}{b}$$

The left and right endpoints of a one-cycle interval can be determined by solving the equations $bx - c = 0$ and $bx - c = 2\pi$ for x.

EXAMPLE 4 **Horizontal Translation**

Analyze the graph of $y = \dfrac{1}{2} \sin\left(x - \dfrac{\pi}{3}\right)$.

Algebraic Solution

The amplitude is $\frac{1}{2}$ and the period is 2π. By solving the equations

$$x - \frac{\pi}{3} = 0 \qquad \text{and} \qquad x - \frac{\pi}{3} = 2\pi$$

$$x = \frac{\pi}{3} \qquad\qquad x = \frac{7\pi}{3}$$

you see that the interval

$$\left[\frac{\pi}{3}, \frac{7\pi}{3}\right]$$

corresponds to one cycle of the graph. Dividing this interval into four equal parts produces the key points

Intercept	*Maximum*	*Intercept*	*Minimum*	*Intercept*
$\left(\dfrac{\pi}{3}, 0\right),$	$\left(\dfrac{5\pi}{6}, \dfrac{1}{2}\right),$	$\left(\dfrac{4\pi}{3}, 0\right),$	$\left(\dfrac{11\pi}{6}, -\dfrac{1}{2}\right),$ and	$\left(\dfrac{7\pi}{3}, 0\right).$

Graphical Solution

Use a graphing utility set in *radian* mode to graph

$$y = \left(\frac{1}{2}\right) \sin\left(x - \frac{\pi}{3}\right)$$

as shown below. Use the *minimum*, *maximum*, and *zero* or *root* features of the graphing utility to approximate the key points $(1.05, 0)$, $(2.62, 0.5)$, $(4.19, 0)$, $(5.76, -0.5)$, and $(7.33, 0)$.

$y = \dfrac{1}{2} \sin\left(x - \dfrac{\pi}{3}\right)$

Zero
X=1.0471976 Y=0

✓ *Checkpoint* ◀))) *Audio-video solution in English & Spanish at LarsonPrecalculus.com.*

Analyze the graph of $y = 2 \cos\left(x - \dfrac{\pi}{2}\right)$.

EXAMPLE 5   Horizontal Translation

Analyze the graph of $y = -3\cos(2\pi x + 4\pi)$.

Algebraic Solution

The amplitude is 3 and the period is

$$\frac{2\pi}{2\pi} = 1.$$

By solving the equations

$$2\pi x + 4\pi = 0 \qquad \text{and} \qquad 2\pi x + 4\pi = 2\pi$$
$$2\pi x = -4\pi \qquad\qquad\qquad 2\pi x = -2\pi$$
$$x = -2 \qquad\qquad\qquad\quad x = -1$$

you see that the interval $[-2, -1]$ corresponds to one cycle of the graph. Dividing this interval into four equal parts produces the key points

Minimum	Intercept	Maximum	Intercept		Minimum
$(-2, -3)$,	$(-7/4, 0)$,	$(-3/2, 3)$,	$(-5/4, 0)$,	and	$(-1, -3)$.

Graphical Solution

Use a graphing utility set in *radian* mode to graph $y = -3\cos(2\pi x + 4\pi)$, as shown below. Use the *minimum*, *maximum*, and *zero* or *root* features of the graphing utility to approximate the key points $(-2, -3)$, $(-1.75, 0)$, $(-1.5, 3)$, $(-1.25, 0)$, and $(-1, -3)$.

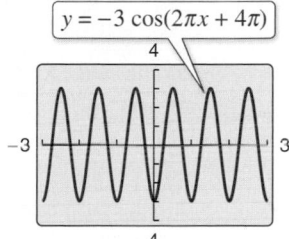

✓ **Checkpoint** 🔊))) *Audio-video solution in English & Spanish at LarsonPrecalculus.com.*

Analyze the graph of $y = -\frac{1}{2}\sin(\pi x + \pi)$.

The final type of transformation is the *vertical translation* caused by the constant d in the equations $y = d + a\sin(bx - c)$ and $y = d + a\cos(bx - c)$. The shift is d units upward for $d > 0$ and d units downward for $d < 0$. In other words, the graph oscillates about the horizontal line $y = d$ instead of about the x-axis.

EXAMPLE 6   Vertical Translation

Use a graphing utility to analyze the graph of $y = 2 + 3\cos 2x$.

Solution

The amplitude is 3 and the period is π. The key points over the interval $[0, \pi]$ are

$$(0, 5), \qquad (\pi/4, 2), \qquad (\pi/2, -1), \qquad (3\pi/4, 2), \qquad \text{and} \qquad (\pi, 5).$$

The graph is shown in Figure 4.30. Compared with the graph of $f(x) = 3\cos 2x$, the graph of $y = 2 + 3\cos 2x$ is shifted upward two units.

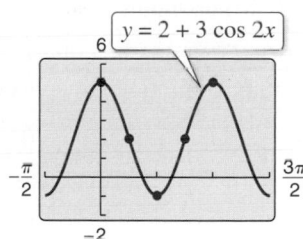

Figure 4.30

✓ **Checkpoint** 🔊))) *Audio-video solution in English & Spanish at LarsonPrecalculus.com.*

Use a graphing utility to analyze the graph of $y = 2\cos x - 5$.

EXAMPLE 7   Finding an Equation of a Graph

Find the amplitude, period, and phase shift of the function whose graph is shown in Figure 4.31. Write an equation of this graph in terms of a sine function.

Solution

The amplitude of this sine curve is 2. The period is 2π, and there is a right phase shift of $\pi/2$. So, you can write $y = 2\sin(x - \pi/2)$.

Figure 4.31

✓ **Checkpoint** 🔊))) *Audio-video solution in English & Spanish at LarsonPrecalculus.com.*

In Example 7, write an equation of the graph in terms of a cosine function.

Mathematical Modeling

Sine and cosine functions can be used to model many real-life situations, including electric currents, musical tones, radio waves, tides, and weather patterns.

EXAMPLE 8 Finding a Trigonometric Model

Throughout the day, the depth of the water at the end of a dock varies with the tides. The table shows the depths y (in feet) at various times during the morning.

DATA	Time	Depth, y
	Midnight	3.4
	2 A.M.	8.7
	4 A.M.	11.3
	6 A.M.	9.1
	8 A.M.	3.8
	10 A.M.	0.1
	Noon	1.2

Spreadsheet at LarsonPrecalculus.com

a. Use a trigonometric function to model the data. Let t be the time, with $t = 0$ corresponding to midnight.

b. A boat needs at least 10 feet of water to moor at the dock. During what times in the afternoon can it safely dock?

Solution

a. Begin by graphing the data, as shown in Figure 4.32. You can use either a sine or cosine model. So, use a cosine model of the form

$$y = a \cos(bt - c) + d.$$

The difference between the maximum value and minimum value is twice the amplitude of the function. So, the amplitude is

$$a = \tfrac{1}{2}[(\text{maximum depth}) - (\text{minimum depth})] = \tfrac{1}{2}(11.3 - 0.1) = 5.6.$$

The cosine function completes one half of a cycle between the times at which the maximum and minimum depths occur. So, the period p is

$$p = 2[(\text{time of min. depth}) - (\text{time of max. depth})] = 2(10 - 4) = 12$$

which implies that $b = 2\pi/p \approx 0.524$. Because high tide occurs 4 hours after midnight, consider the left endpoint to be $c/b = 4$, so $c \approx 2.094$. Moreover, because the average depth is

$$\tfrac{1}{2}(11.3 + 0.1) = 5.7$$

it follows that $d = 5.7$. So, you can model the depth with the function

$$y = 5.6 \cos(0.524t - 2.094) + 5.7.$$

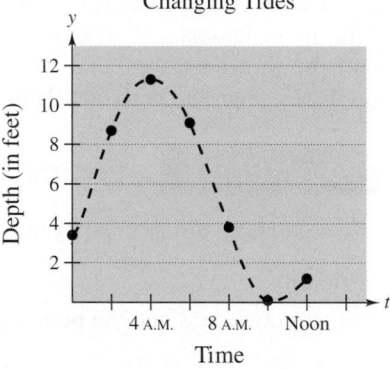

Changing Tides

Depth (in feet) vs. Time

Figure 4.32

b. Using a graphing utility, graph the model with the line $y = 10$. Using the *intersect* feature, you can determine that the depth is at least 10 feet between 2:42 P.M. ($t \approx 14.7$) and 5:18 P.M. ($t \approx 17.3$), as shown at the right.

(14.7, 10) (17.3, 10)

$y = 10$

$y = 5.6 \cos(0.524t - 2.094) + 5.7$

 Checkpoint Audio-video solution in English & Spanish at LarsonPrecalculus.com.

Find a sine model for the data in Example 8.

4.5   Exercises

See *CalcChat.com* for tutorial help and worked-out solutions to odd-numbered exercises.
For instructions on how to use a graphing utility, see Appendix A.

Vocabulary and Concept Check

In Exercises 1–4, fill in the blank.

1. The _____ of a sine or cosine curve represents half the distance between the maximum and minimum values of the function.

2. One period of a sine function is called _____ of the sine curve.

3. The period of a sine or cosine function is given by _____ .

4. For the equation $y = a \sin(bx - c)$, $\dfrac{c}{b}$ is the _____ of the graph of the equation.

5. What is the period of the sine function $y = \sin x$?

6. How do you find the period of a cosine function of the form $y = \cos bx$?

7. Describe the effect of the constant d on the graph of $y = \sin x + d$.

8. What is the amplitude of $y = -4.5 \sin x$?

Procedures and Problem Solving

Library of Parent Functions   In Exercises 9 and 10, use the graph of the function to answer each question.

(a) Find the x-intercepts of the graph of $y = f(x)$.

(b) Find the y-intercept of the graph of $y = f(x)$.

(c) Find the intervals on which the graph of $y = f(x)$ is increasing and the intervals on which the graph of $y = f(x)$ is decreasing.

(d) Find the relative extrema of the graph of $y = f(x)$.

9. $f(x) = \sin x$ **10.** $f(x) = \cos x$

Finding the Period and Amplitude   In Exercises 11–20, find the period and amplitude.

11. $y = 3 \sin 2x$ **12.** $y = 2 \cos 3x$

13. $y = 5 \cos \dfrac{x}{2}$ **14.** $y = -3 \sin \dfrac{x}{3}$

15. $y = \dfrac{2}{3} \sin \pi x$ **16.** $y = \dfrac{3}{2} \cos \dfrac{\pi x}{2}$

17. $y = -2 \sin x$ **18.** $y = -\cos \dfrac{2x}{5}$

19. $y = \dfrac{1}{4} \cos \dfrac{4x}{3}$ **20.** $y = \dfrac{5}{2} \cos \dfrac{x}{4}$

Describing the Relationship Between Graphs   In Exercises 21–28, describe the relationship between the graphs of f and g. Consider amplitudes, periods, and shifts.

21. $f(x) = \sin x$ **22.** $f(x) = \cos x$

$g(x) = \sin(x - \pi)$ $g(x) = \cos(x + \pi)$

23. $f(x) = \cos 2x$ **24.** $f(x) = \sin 3x$

$g(x) = -\cos 2x$ $g(x) = \sin(-3x)$

25. $f(x) = \cos 2x$ **26.** $f(x) = \cos 4x$

$g(x) = 3 + \cos 2x$ $g(x) = -2 + \cos 4x$

27. $f(x) = \sin x$ **28.** $f(x) = \sin x$

$g(x) = 5 \sin(-x)$ $g(x) = -\dfrac{1}{2} \sin x$

Describing the Relationship Between Graphs   In Exercises 29–32, describe the relationship between the graphs of f and g. Consider amplitudes, periods, and shifts.

29.   **30.**

31.   **32.**

Sketching Graphs of Sine or Cosine Functions In Exercises 33–38, sketch the graphs of f and g in the same coordinate plane. (Include two full periods.)

33. $f(x) = \sin x$

$g(x) = -4 \sin x$

34. $f(x) = \sin x$

$g(x) = \sin \dfrac{x}{3}$

35. $f(x) = \cos \pi x$

$g(x) = 1 + \cos \pi x$

36. $f(x) = 4 \sin x$

$g(x) = 4 \sin x - 1$

37. $f(x) = -\dfrac{1}{2} \sin \dfrac{x}{2}$

$g(x) = 2 \sin \dfrac{x}{4}$

38. $f(x) = 2 \cos 2x$

$g(x) = -\cos 4x$

Using Graphs to Compare Functions In Exercises 39–42, use a graphing utility to graph f and g in the same viewing window. (Include two full periods.) Make a conjecture about the functions.

39. $f(x) = \sin x$

$g(x) = \cos\left(x - \dfrac{\pi}{2}\right)$

40. $f(x) = \sin x$

$g(x) = \cos\left(x + \dfrac{3\pi}{2}\right)$

41. $f(x) = \cos x$

$g(x) = -\sin\left(x - \dfrac{\pi}{2}\right)$

42. $f(x) = \cos x$

$g(x) = -\cos(x - \pi)$

Sketching a Sine or Cosine Function In Exercises 43–56, sketch the graph of the function. Use a graphing utility to verify your sketch. (Include two full periods.)

43. $y = 4 \sin x$

44. $y = 5 \sin x$

45. $y = \dfrac{1}{4} \cos x$

46. $y = \dfrac{3}{4} \cos x$

47. $y = \cos \dfrac{x}{2}$

48. $y = \sin \dfrac{x}{4}$

49. $y = \sin\left(x - \dfrac{\pi}{4}\right)$

50. $y = \sin(x - \pi)$

51. $y = -8 \cos(x + \pi)$

52. $y = 3 \cos\left(x + \dfrac{\pi}{2}\right)$

53. $y = 1 - \sin \dfrac{2\pi x}{3}$

54. $y = 2 \cos x - 3$

55. $y = \dfrac{2}{3} \cos\left(\dfrac{x}{2} - \dfrac{\pi}{4}\right)$

56. $y = -2 \cos(4\pi x + 1)$

Analyzing Graphs of Sine or Cosine Functions In Exercises 57–70, use a graphing utility to graph the function. (Include two full periods.) Identify the amplitude and period of the graph.

57. $y = -2 \sin \dfrac{2\pi x}{3}$

58. $y = -10 \cos \dfrac{\pi x}{6}$

59. $y = -4 + 5 \cos \dfrac{\pi t}{12}$

60. $y = 2 - 2 \sin \dfrac{2\pi x}{3}$

61. $y = -\dfrac{2}{3} \cos\left(\dfrac{x}{2} - \dfrac{\pi}{4}\right)$

62. $y = \dfrac{5}{2} \cos(6x + \pi)$

63. $y = -2 \sin(4x + \pi)$

64. $y = -4 \sin\left(\dfrac{2}{3}x - \dfrac{\pi}{3}\right)$

65. $y = \cos\left(2\pi x - \dfrac{\pi}{2}\right) + 1$

66. $y = 3 \cos\left(\dfrac{\pi x}{2} + \dfrac{\pi}{2}\right) - 2$

67. $y = 5 \sin(\pi - 2x) + 10$

68. $y = 5 \cos(\pi - 2x) + 6$

69. $y = \dfrac{1}{100} \sin 120\pi t$

70. $y = \dfrac{1}{100} \cos 50\pi t$

Finding an Equation of a Graph In Exercises 71–74, find a and d for the function $f(x) = a \cos x + d$ such that the graph of f matches the figure.

71.

72.

73.

74.

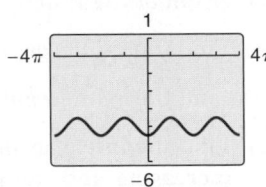

Finding an Equation of a Graph In Exercises 75–78, find a, b, and c for the function $f(x) = a \sin(bx - c)$ such that the graph of f matches the graph shown.

75.

76.

77.

78.

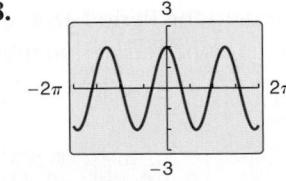

Solving a Trigonometric Equation Graphically In Exercises 79 and 80, use a graphing utility to graph y_1 and y_2 for all real numbers x in the interval $[-2\pi, 2\pi]$. Use the graphs to find the real numbers x such that $y_1 = y_2$.

79. $y_1 = \sin x$

$y_2 = -\dfrac{1}{2}$

80. $y_1 = \cos x$

$y_2 = \dfrac{1}{2}$

81. Health The pressure P (in millimeters of mercury) against the walls of the blood vessels of a person is modeled by

$$P = 100 - 20 \cos \frac{8\pi t}{3}$$

where t is the time (in seconds). Use a graphing utility to graph the model. One cycle is equivalent to one heartbeat. What is the person's pulse rate in heartbeats per minute?

82. Health For a person at rest, the velocity v (in liters per second) of air flow during a respiratory cycle (the time from the beginning of one breath to the beginning of the next) is given by

$$v = 0.85 \sin \frac{\pi t}{3}$$

where t is the time (in seconds). (Inhalation occurs when $v > 0$, and exhalation occurs when $v < 0$.)

(a) Use a graphing utility to graph v.

(b) Find the time for one full respiratory cycle.

(c) Find the number of cycles per minute.

(d) The model is for a person at rest. How might the model change for a person who is exercising? Explain.

83. Economics A company that produces snowboards, which are seasonal products, forecasts monthly sales for one year to be

$$S = 74.50 + 43.75 \cos \frac{\pi t}{6}$$

where S is the sales in thousands of units and t is the time in months, with $t = 1$ corresponding to January.

(a) Use a graphing utility to graph the sales function over the one-year period.

(b) Use the graph in part (a) to determine the months of maximum and minimum sales.

84. Agriculture The daily consumption C (in gallons) of diesel fuel on a farm is modeled by

$$C = 30.3 + 21.6 \sin\left(\frac{2\pi t}{365} + 10.9\right)$$

where t is the time in days, with $t = 1$ corresponding to January 1.

(a) What is the period of the model? Is it what you expected? Explain.

(b) What is the average daily fuel consumption? Which term of the model did you use? Explain.

(c) Use a graphing utility to graph the model. Use the graph to approximate the time of the year when consumption exceeds 40 gallons per day.

85. Physics You are riding a Ferris wheel. Your height h (in feet) above the ground at any time t (in seconds) can be modeled by

$$h = 25 \sin \frac{\pi}{15}(t - 75) + 30.$$

The Ferris wheel turns for 135 seconds before it stops to let the first passengers off.

(a) Use a graphing utility to graph the model.

(b) What are the minimum and maximum heights above the ground?

86. Physics The motion of an oscillating weight suspended from a spring was measured by a motion detector. The data were collected, and the approximate maximum displacements from equilibrium ($y = 2$) are labeled in the figure. The distance y from the motion detector is measured in centimeters, and the time t is measured in seconds.

(a) Is y a function of t? Explain.

(b) Approximate the amplitude and period.

(c) Find a model for the data.

(d) Use a graphing utility to graph the model in part (c). Compare the result with the data in the figure.

87. *Why you should learn it* (p. 292) The table shows the percent y (in decimal form) of the moon's face that is illuminated on day x of the year 2016, where $x = 1$ represents January 1. (Source: U.S. Naval Observatory)

Day, x	Percent, y
10	0.0
16	0.5
24	1.0
32	0.5
39	0.0
46	0.5

spreadsheet at LarsonPrecalculus.com

(a) Create a scatter plot of the data.

(b) Find a trigonometric model for the data.

(c) Add the graph of your model in part (b) to the scatter plot. How well does the model fit the data?

(d) What is the period of the model?

(e) Estimate the percent illumination of the moon on June 21, 2017. (Assume there are 366 days in 2016.)

88. MODELING DATA

The table shows the average daily high temperatures (in degrees Fahrenheit) for Quillayute, Washington, Q and Chicago, Illinois, C for month t, with $t = 1$ corresponding to January. (Source: U.S. Weather Bureau and the National Weather Service)

Month, t	Quillayute, Q	Chicago, C
1	47.1	31.0
2	49.1	35.3
3	51.4	46.6
4	54.8	59.0
5	59.5	70.0
6	63.1	79.7
7	67.4	84.1
8	68.6	81.9
9	66.2	74.8
10	58.2	62.3
11	50.3	48.2
12	46.0	34.8

(a) A model for the temperature in Quillayute is given by

$$Q(t) = 57.5 + 10.6 \sin(0.566x - 2.568)$$

Find a trigonometric model for Chicago.

(b) Use a graphing utility to graph the data and the model for the temperatures in Quillayute in the same viewing window. How well does the model fit the data?

(c) Use the graphing utility to graph the data and the model for the temperatures in Chicago in the same viewing window. How well does the model fit the data?

(d) Use the models to estimate the average daily high temperature in each city. Which term of the models did you use? Explain.

(e) What is the period of each model? Are the periods what you expected? Explain.

(f) Which city has the greater variability in temperature throughout the year? Which factor of the models determines this variability? Explain.

Conclusions

True or False? In Exercises 89–92, determine whether the statement is true or false. Justify your answer.

89. The graph of the function given by $g(x) = \sin(x + 2\pi)$ translates the graph of $f(x) = \sin x$ one period to the right.

90. The graph of $y = 6 - \dfrac{3}{4} \sin \dfrac{3x}{10}$ has a period of $\dfrac{20\pi}{3}$.

91. The function $y = \frac{1}{2} \cos 2x$ has an amplitude that is twice that of the function $y = \cos x$.

92. The graph of $y = -\cos x$ is a reflection of the graph of $y = \sin\left(x + \dfrac{\pi}{2}\right)$ in the x-axis.

93. Writing Sketch the graph of $y = \cos bx$ for $b = \frac{1}{2}, 2$, and 3. How does the value of b affect the graph? How many complete cycles of the graph of y occur between 0 and 2π for each value of b?

94. Writing Use a graphing utility to graph the function given by $y = d + a \sin(bx - c)$ for several different values of $a, b, c,$ and d. Write a paragraph describing how the values of $a, b, c,$ and d affect the graph.

Library of Parent Functions In Exercises 95 and 96, determine which function is represented by the graph. Do not use a calculator.

95.

96.
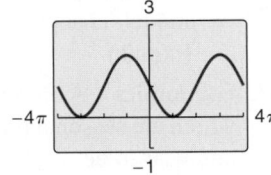

(a) $f(x) = 4 \cos(x + \pi)$ (a) $f(x) = 1 + \sin \dfrac{x}{2}$

(b) $f(x) = 4 \cos 4x$ (b) $f(x) = 1 + \cos \dfrac{x}{2}$

(c) $f(x) = 4 \sin(x - \pi)$ (c) $f(x) = 1 - \sin \dfrac{x}{2}$

(d) $f(x) = -4 \cos(x + \pi)$ (d) $f(x) = 1 - \cos 2x$

(e) $f(x) = 1 - \sin \dfrac{x}{2}$ (e) $f(x) = 1 - \sin 2x$

97. Exploration In Section 4.2, it was shown that $f(x) = \cos x$ is an even function and $g(x) = \sin x$ is an odd function. Use a graphing utility to graph h and use the graph to determine whether h is even, odd, or neither.

(a) $h(x) = \cos^2 x$

(b) $h(x) = \sin^2 x$

(c) $h(x) = \sin x \cos x$

98. Conjecture If f is an even function and g is an odd function, use the results of Exercise 97 to make a conjecture about whether h is even, odd, or neither.

(a) $h(x) = [f(x)]^2$

(b) $h(x) = [g(x)]^2$

(c) $h(x) = f(x)g(x)$

99. Exploration Use a graphing utility to explore the ratio $(\sin x)/x$, which appears in calculus.

(a) Complete the table. Round your results to four decimal places.

x	-1	-0.1	-0.01	-0.001
$\dfrac{\sin x}{x}$				

x	0	0.001	0.01	0.1	1
$\dfrac{\sin x}{x}$					

(b) Use the graphing utility to graph the function

$$f(x) = \frac{\sin x}{x}.$$

Use the *zoom* and *trace* features to describe the behavior of the graph as x approaches 0.

(c) Write a brief statement regarding the value of the ratio based on your results in parts (a) and (b).

100. Exploration Use a graphing utility to explore the ratio $(1 - \cos x)/x$, which appears in calculus.

(a) Complete the table. Round your results to four decimal places.

x	-1	-0.1	-0.01	-0.001
$\dfrac{1 - \cos x}{x}$				

x	0	0.001	0.01	0.1	1
$\dfrac{1 - \cos x}{x}$					

(b) Use the graphing utility to graph the function

$$f(x) = \frac{1 - \cos x}{x}.$$

Use the *zoom* and *trace* features to describe the behavior of the graph as x approaches 0.

(c) Write a brief statement regarding the value of the ratio based on your results in parts (a) and (b).

101. Exploration Using calculus, it can be shown that the sine and cosine functions can be approximated by the polynomials

$$\sin x \approx x - \frac{x^3}{3!} + \frac{x^5}{5!} \quad \text{and} \quad \cos x \approx 1 - \frac{x^2}{2!} + \frac{x^4}{4!}$$

where x is in radians.

(a) Use a graphing utility to graph the sine function and its polynomial approximation in the same viewing window. How do the graphs compare?

(b) Use the graphing utility to graph the cosine function and its polynomial approximation in the same viewing window. How do the graphs compare?

(c) Study the patterns in the polynomial approximations of the sine and cosine functions and predict the next term in each. Then repeat parts (a) and (b). How did the accuracy of the approximations change when an additional term was added?

102. HOW DO YOU SEE IT? The figure below shows the graph of $y = \sin(x - c)$ for

$$c = -\frac{\pi}{4}, \quad 0, \quad \text{and} \quad \frac{\pi}{4}.$$

(a) How does the value of c affect the graph?

(b) Which graph is equivalent to that of

$$y = -\cos\!\left(x + \frac{\pi}{4}\right)?$$

Cumulative Mixed Review

Finding the Slope of a Line In Exercises 103 and 104, plot the points and find the slope of the line passing through the points.

103. $(0, 1), (2, 5)$ **104.** $(-1, 4), (3, -2)$

Converting from Radians to Degrees In Exercises 105 and 106, convert the angle measure from radians to degrees. Round your answer to three decimal places.

105. 8.5 **106.** -0.48

107. Make a Decision To work an extended application analyzing the mean monthly high temperature and normal precipitation in Cheyenne, Wyoming, visit this textbook's website at *LarsonPrecalculus.com*. (Data Source: NOAA)

4.6   Graphs of Other Trigonometric Functions

Graph of the Tangent Function

Recall that the tangent function is odd. That is, $\tan(-x) = -\tan x$. Consequently, the graph of $y = \tan x$ is symmetric with respect to the origin. You also know from the identity $\tan x = \sin x / \cos x$ that the tangent function is undefined when $\cos x = 0$. Two such values are $x = \pm\pi/2 \approx \pm 1.5708$.

x	$-\dfrac{\pi}{2}$	-1.57	-1.5	$-\dfrac{\pi}{4}$	0	$\dfrac{\pi}{4}$	1.5	1.57	$\dfrac{\pi}{2}$
$\tan x$	Undef.	-1255.8	-14.1	-1	0	1	14.1	1255.8	Undef.

> $\tan x$ approaches $-\infty$ as x approaches $-\pi/2$ from the right.

> $\tan x$ approaches ∞ as x approaches $\pi/2$ from the left.

As indicated in the table, $\tan x$ increases without bound as x approaches $\pi/2$ from the left, and decreases without bound as x approaches $-\pi/2$ from the right. So, the graph of $y = \tan x$ has *vertical asymptotes* at $x = \pi/2$ and $x = -\pi/2$, as shown in Figure 4.33. Moreover, because the period of the tangent function is π, vertical asymptotes also occur at $x = \pi/2 + n\pi$, where n is an integer. The domain of the tangent function is the set of all real numbers other than $x = \pi/2 + n\pi$, and the range is the set of all real numbers.

Library of Parent Functions: Tangent Function

The basic characteristics of the parent tangent function are summarized below and on the inside cover of this text.

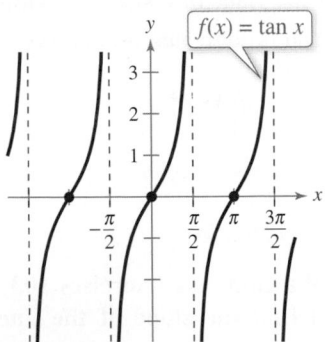

Domain: all real numbers x,
$$x \neq \frac{\pi}{2} + n\pi$$
Range: $(-\infty, \infty)$
Period: π
x-intercepts: $(n\pi, 0)$
y-intercept: $(0, 0)$
Vertical asymptotes: $x = \dfrac{\pi}{2} + n\pi$
Odd function
Origin symmetry

Figure 4.33

Sketching the graph of $y = a\tan(bx - c)$ is similar to sketching the graph of $y = a\sin(bx - c)$ in that you locate key points that identify the intercepts and asymptotes. Two consecutive asymptotes can be found by solving the equations $bx - c = -\pi/2$ and $bx - c = \pi/2$ for x. The midpoint between two consecutive asymptotes is an x-intercept of the graph. The period of the function $y = a\tan(bx - c)$ is the distance between two consecutive asymptotes. The amplitude of a tangent function is not defined. After plotting the asymptotes and the x-intercept, plot a few additional points between the two asymptotes and sketch one cycle. Finally, sketch one or two additional cycles to the left and right.

EXAMPLE 1   **Library of Parent Functions:** $f(x) = \tan x$

Sketch the graph of $y = \tan \dfrac{x}{2}$ by hand.

Solution

By solving the equations $x/2 = -\pi/2$ and $x/2 = \pi/2$, you can see that two consecutive asymptotes occur at $x = -\pi$ and $x = \pi$. Between these two asymptotes, plot a few points, including the x-intercept, as shown in the table. Three cycles of the graph are shown in Figure 4.34. Use a graphing utility to confirm this graph.

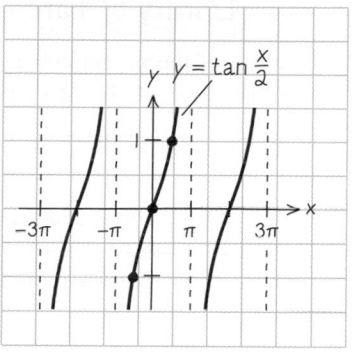

Figure 4.34

x	$-\pi$	$-\dfrac{\pi}{2}$	0	$\dfrac{\pi}{2}$	π
$\tan \dfrac{x}{2}$	Undef.	-1	0	1	Undef.

 Checkpoint Audio-video solution in English & Spanish at LarsonPrecalculus.com.

Sketch the graph of $y = \tan x/4$ by hand.

EXAMPLE 2   **Library of Parent Functions:** $f(x) = \tan x$

Sketch the graph of $y = -3 \tan 2x$ by hand.

Solution

By solving the equations $2x = -\pi/2$ and $2x = \pi/2$, you can see that two consecutive asymptotes occur at $x = -\pi/4$ and $x = \pi/4$. Between these two asymptotes, plot a few points, including the x-intercept, as shown in the table. Three cycles of the graph are shown in Figure 4.35. Use a graphing utility to confirm this graph, as shown in Figure 4.36.

Figure 4.36

x	$-\dfrac{\pi}{4}$	$-\dfrac{\pi}{8}$	0	$\dfrac{\pi}{8}$	$\dfrac{\pi}{4}$
$-3 \tan 2x$	Undef.	3	0	-3	Undef.

Figure 4.35

 Checkpoint Audio-video solution in English & Spanish at LarsonPrecalculus.com.

Sketch the graph of $y = \tan 2x$ by hand.

By comparing the graphs in Examples 1 and 2, you can see that the graph of $y = a \tan(bx - c)$ increases between consecutive vertical asymptotes when $a > 0$ and decreases between consecutive vertical asymptotes when $a < 0$. In other words, the graph for $a < 0$ is a reflection in the x-axis of the graph for $a > 0$.

Graph of the Cotangent Function

Library of Parent Functions: Cotangent Function

The graph of the parent cotangent function is similar to the graph of the parent tangent function. It also has a period of π. However, from the identity

$$f(x) = \cot x = \frac{\cos x}{\sin x}$$

you can see that the cotangent function has vertical asymptotes when $\sin x$ is zero, which occurs at $x = n\pi$, where n is an integer. The basic characteristics of the parent cotangent function are summarized below and on the inside cover of this text.

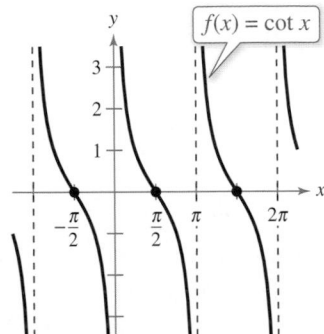

Domain: all real numbers x, $x \neq n\pi$
Range: $(-\infty, \infty)$
Period: π

x-intercepts: $\left(\frac{\pi}{2} + n\pi, 0\right)$

Vertical asymptotes: $x = n\pi$
Odd function
Origin symmetry

EXAMPLE 3   Library of Parent Functions: $f(x) = \cot x$

Sketch the graph of $y = 2\cot\frac{x}{3}$ by hand.

Solution

To locate two consecutive vertical asymptotes of the graph, solve the equations $x/3 = 0$ and $x/3 = \pi$ to see that two consecutive asymptotes occur at $x = 0$ and $x = 3\pi$. Then, between these two asymptotes, plot a few points, including the x-intercept, as shown in the table. Three cycles of the graph are shown in the figure. Use a graphing utility to confirm this graph. [Enter the function as $y = 2/\tan(x/3)$.] Note that the period is 3π, the distance between consecutive asymptotes.

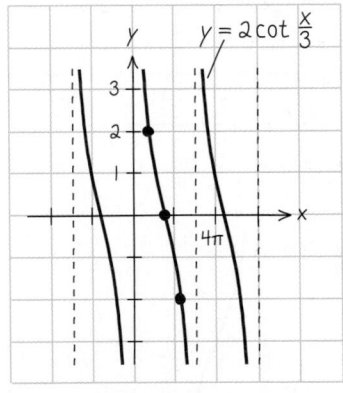

x	0	$\frac{3\pi}{4}$	$\frac{3\pi}{2}$	$\frac{9\pi}{4}$	3π
$2\cot\frac{x}{3}$	Undef.	2	0	-2	Undef.

✓ **Checkpoint**   *Audio-video solution in English & Spanish at LarsonPrecalculus.com.*

Sketch the graph of $y = \cot\frac{x}{4}$ by hand.

Graphs of the Reciprocal Functions

The graphs of the two remaining trigonometric functions can be obtained from the graphs of the sine and cosine functions using the reciprocal identities

$$\csc x = \frac{1}{\sin x} \quad \text{and} \quad \sec x = \frac{1}{\cos x}.$$

For instance, at a given value of x, the y-coordinate of $\sec x$ is the reciprocal of the y-coordinate of $\cos x$. Of course, when $\cos x = 0$, the reciprocal does not exist. Near such values of x, the behavior of the secant function is similar to that of the tangent function. In other words, the graphs of

$$\tan x = \frac{\sin x}{\cos x} \quad \text{and} \quad \sec x = \frac{1}{\cos x}$$

have vertical asymptotes where $\cos x = 0$—that is, at $x = \pi/2 + n\pi$, where n is an integer. Similarly,

$$\cot x = \frac{\cos x}{\sin x} \quad \text{and} \quad \csc x = \frac{1}{\sin x}$$

have vertical asymptotes where $\sin x = 0$—that is, at $x = n\pi$, where n is an integer.

To sketch the graph of a secant or cosecant function, you should first make a sketch of its reciprocal function. For instance, to sketch the graph of $y = \csc x$, first sketch the graph of $y = \sin x$. Then take the reciprocals of the y-coordinates to obtain points on the graph of $y = \csc x$. You can use this procedure to obtain the graphs shown in Figure 4.37.

Explore the Concept

Use a graphing utility to graph the functions $y_1 = \cos x$ and $y_2 = \sec x = 1/\cos x$ in the same viewing window. How are the graphs related? What happens to the graph of the secant function as x approaches the zeros of the cosine function?

Library of Parent Functions: Cosecant and Secant Functions

The basic characteristics of the parent cosecant and secant functions are summarized below and on the inside cover of this text.

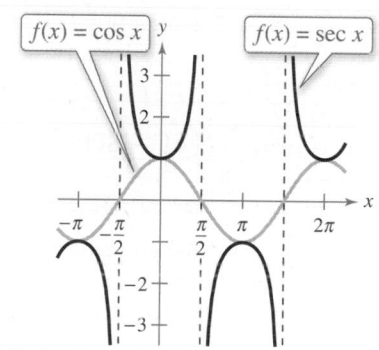

Domain: all real numbers x, $x \neq n\pi$

Range: $(-\infty, -1] \cup [1, \infty)$
Period: 2π
No intercepts

Vertical asymptotes: $x = n\pi$

Odd function
Origin symmetry

Domain: all real numbers x, $x \neq \dfrac{\pi}{2} + n\pi$

Range: $(-\infty, -1] \cup [1, \infty)$
Period: 2π
y-intercept: $(0, 1)$

Vertical asymptotes: $x = \dfrac{\pi}{2} + n\pi$

Even function
y-axis symmetry

Figure 4.37

In comparing the graphs of the cosecant and secant functions with those of the sine and cosine functions, note that the "hills" and "valleys" are interchanged. For instance, a hill (or maximum point) on the sine curve corresponds to a valley (a relative minimum) on the cosecant curve, and a valley (or minimum point) on the sine curve corresponds to a hill (a relative maximum) on the cosecant curve, as shown in Figure 4.38. Additionally, x-intercepts of the sine and cosine functions become vertical asymptotes of the cosecant and secant functions, respectively (see Figure 4.38).

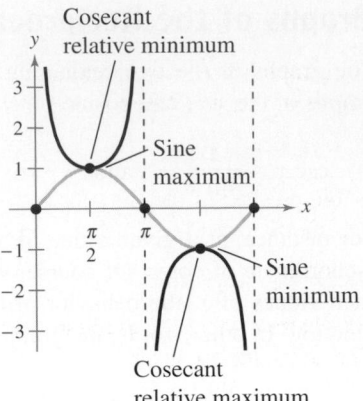

Figure 4.38

EXAMPLE 4   Library of Parent Functions: $f(x) = \csc x$

Sketch the graph of $y = 2\csc\left(x + \dfrac{\pi}{4}\right)$ by hand.

Solution

Begin by sketching the graph of $y = 2\sin\left(x + \dfrac{\pi}{4}\right)$. For this function, the amplitude is 2 and the period is 2π. By solving the equations

$$x + \frac{\pi}{4} = 0 \qquad \text{and} \qquad x + \frac{\pi}{4} = 2\pi$$

you can see that one cycle of the sine function corresponds to the interval from $x = -\pi/4$ to $x = 7\pi/4$. The graph of this sine function is represented by the gray curve in Figure 4.39. Because the sine function is zero at the midpoint and endpoints of this interval, the corresponding cosecant function

$$y = 2\csc\left(x + \frac{\pi}{4}\right) = 2\left(\frac{1}{\sin[x + (x/4)]}\right)$$

has vertical asymptotes at $x = -\dfrac{\pi}{4}$, $x = \dfrac{3\pi}{4}$, $x = \dfrac{7\pi}{4}$, and so on. The graph of the cosecant function is represented by the black curve in Figure 4.39.

Figure 4.39

✔ **Checkpoint** *Audio-video solution in English & Spanish at LarsonPrecalculus.com.*

Sketch the graph of $y = 2\csc\left(x + \dfrac{\pi}{2}\right)$ by hand.

EXAMPLE 5   Library of Parent Functions: $f(x) = \sec x$

See LarsonPrecalculus.com for an interactive version of this type of example.

To sketch the graph of $y = \sec 2x$ by hand, begin by sketching the graph of $y = \cos 2x$, as indicated by the gray curve in Figure 4.40. Then, form the graph of $y = \sec 2x$, as indicated by the black curve in the figure. Note that the x-intercepts of $y = \cos 2x$

$$\left(-\frac{\pi}{4}, 0\right), \qquad \left(\frac{\pi}{4}, 0\right), \qquad \left(\frac{3\pi}{4}, 0\right), \dots$$

correspond to the vertical asymptotes

$$x = -\frac{\pi}{4}, \qquad x = \frac{\pi}{4}, \qquad x = \frac{3\pi}{4}, \dots$$

of the graph of $y = \sec 2x$. Moreover, notice that the period of $y = \cos 2x$ and $y = \sec 2x$ is π.

Figure 4.40

✔ **Checkpoint** *Audio-video solution in English & Spanish at LarsonPrecalculus.com.*

Sketch the graph of $y = \sec \dfrac{x}{2}$ by hand.

Damped Trigonometric Graphs

A *product* of two functions can be graphed using properties of the individual functions. For instance, consider the function

$$f(x) = x \sin x$$

as the product of the functions $y = x$ and $y = \sin x$. Using properties of absolute value and the fact that $|\sin x| \le 1$, you have $0 \le |x||\sin x| \le |x|$. Consequently,

$$-|x| \le x \sin x \le |x|$$

which means that the graph of $f(x) = x \sin x$ lies between the lines $y = -x$ and $y = x$. Furthermore, because

$$f(x) = x \sin x = \pm x \qquad \text{at} \qquad x = \frac{\pi}{2} + n\pi$$

and

$$f(x) = x \sin x = 0 \qquad \text{at} \qquad x = n\pi$$

where n is an integer, the graph of f touches the line $y = -x$ or the line $y = x$ at $x = \pi/2 + n\pi$ and has x-intercepts at $x = n\pi$. A sketch of f is shown in Figure 4.41. In the function $f(x) = x \sin x$, the factor x is called the **damping factor.**

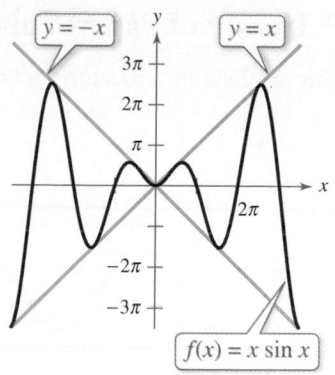

Figure 4.41

EXAMPLE 6   Analyzing a Damped Sine Curve

Analyze the graph of $f(x) = e^{-x} \sin 3x$.

Solution

Consider $f(x)$ as the product of the two functions

$$y = e^{-x} \qquad \text{and} \qquad y = \sin 3x$$

each of which has the set of real numbers as its domain. For any real number x, you know that $e^{-x} > 0$ and $|\sin 3x| \le 1$. So, $e^{-x}|\sin 3x| \le e^{-x}$, which means that

$$-e^{-x} \le e^{-x} \sin 3x \le e^{-x}.$$

Furthermore, because

$$f(x) = e^{-x} \sin 3x = \pm e^{-x} \qquad \text{at} \qquad x = \frac{\pi}{6} + \frac{n\pi}{3}$$

and

$$f(x) = e^{-x} \sin 3x = 0 \qquad \text{at} \qquad x = \frac{n\pi}{3}$$

the graph of f touches the curves $y = -e^{-x}$ and $y = e^{-x}$ at $x = \pi/6 + n\pi/3$ and has intercepts at $x = n\pi/3$. The graph is shown below.

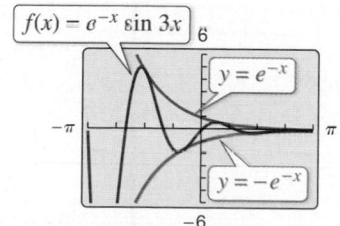

> ## Remark
>
> Do you see why the graph of $f(x) = x \sin x$ touches the lines $y = \pm x$ at $x = \pi/2 + n\pi$ and why the graph has x-intercepts at $x = n\pi$? Recall that the sine function is equal to ± 1 at $\pi/2, 3\pi/2, 5\pi/2, \ldots$ (odd multiples of $\pi/2$) and is equal to 0 at $\pi, 2\pi, 3\pi, \ldots$ (multiples of π).

✓ *Checkpoint* 🔊)) *Audio-video solution in English & Spanish at LarsonPrecalculus.com.*

Analyze the graph of $f(x) = e^x \sin 4x$.

Library of Parent Functions: Trigonometric Functions

Figure 4.42 summarizes the six basic trigonometric functions.

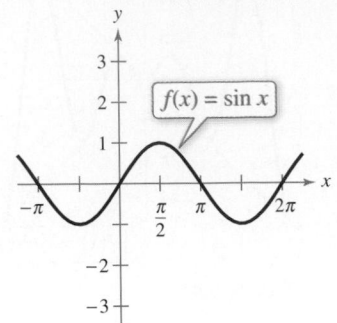

Domain: all real numbers x
Range: $[-1, 1]$
Period: 2π

Domain: all real numbers x
Range: $[-1, 1]$
Period: 2π

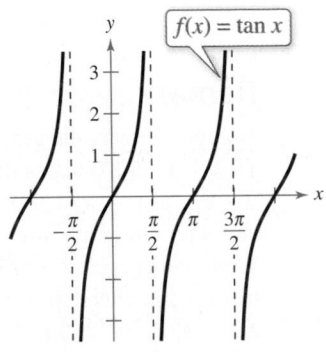

Domain: all real numbers x,

$$x \neq \frac{\pi}{2} + n\pi$$

Range: $(-\infty, \infty)$
Period: π

Domain: all real numbers x,
$$x \neq n\pi$$
Range: $(-\infty, \infty)$
Period: π

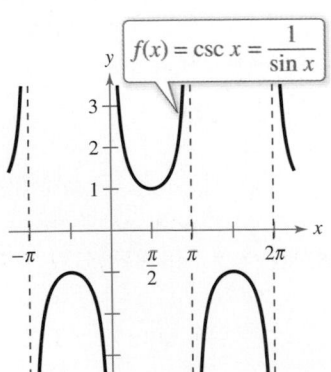

Domain: all real numbers x,
$$x \neq n\pi$$
Range: $(-\infty, -1] \cup [1, \infty)$
Period: 2π

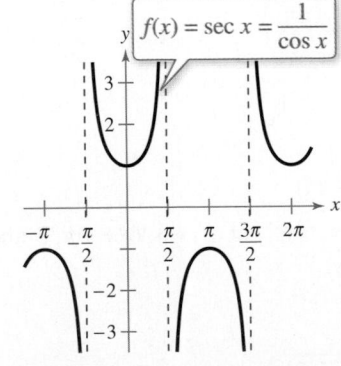

Domain: all real numbers x,

$$x \neq \frac{\pi}{2} + n\pi$$

Range: $(-\infty, -1] \cup [1, \infty)$
Period: 2π

Figure 4.42

4.6   Exercises

See *CalcChat.com* for tutorial help and worked-out solutions to odd-numbered exercises.
For instructions on how to use a graphing utility, see Appendix A.

Vocabulary and Concept Check

In Exercises 1 and 2, fill in the blank.

1. The graphs of the tangent, cotangent, secant, and cosecant functions have _____ asymptotes.

2. To sketch the graph of a secant or cosecant function, first make a sketch of its _____ function.

3. Which two parent trigonometric functions have a period of π and a range that consists of the set of all real numbers?

4. What is the damping factor of the function $f(x) = e^{2x} \sin x$?

Procedures and Problem Solving

Library of Parent Functions   In Exercises 5–8, use the graph of the function to answer each question.

(a) Find any x-intercepts of the graph of $y = f(x)$.

(b) Find any y-intercepts of the graph of $y = f(x)$.

(c) Find the intervals on which the graph of $y = f(x)$ is increasing and the intervals on which the graph of $y = f(x)$ is decreasing.

(d) Find all relative extrema, if any, of the graph of $y = f(x)$.

(e) Find all vertical asymptotes, if any, of the graph of $y = f(x)$.

5. $f(x) = \tan x$

6. $f(x) = \cot x$

7. $f(x) = \sec x$

8. $f(x) = \csc x$

 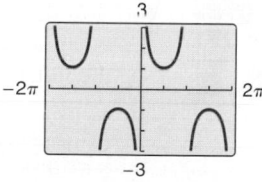

Library of Parent Functions   In Exercises 9–28, sketch the graph of the function. (Include two full periods.) Use a graphing utility to verify your result.

9. $y = \tan \dfrac{x}{5}$

10. $y = \tan 3x$

11. $y = -2 \tan 2x$

12. $y = -4 \tan \dfrac{x}{3}$

13. $y = \dfrac{1}{2} \cot \dfrac{x}{2}$

14. $y = 3 \cot \pi x$

15. $y = -\dfrac{1}{2} \sec x$

16. $y = \dfrac{1}{4} \sec x$

17. $y = 3 \csc \dfrac{x}{2}$

18. $y = -\csc \dfrac{x}{3}$

19. $y = \sec \pi x - 3$

20. $y = 2 \sec 4x + 2$

21. $y = 2 \tan \dfrac{\pi x}{4}$

22. $y = \dfrac{1}{2} \tan \pi x$

23. $y = -\csc(\pi - x)$

24. $y = -\sec(x + \pi)$

25. $y = \dfrac{1}{2} \sec(2x - \pi)$

26. $y = \csc(2x - \pi)$

27. $y = 2 \cot\left(x + \dfrac{\pi}{2}\right)$

28. $y = \dfrac{1}{4} \cot(x + \pi)$

Comparing Trigonometric Graphs   In Exercises 29–34, use a graphing utility to graph the function (include two full periods). Graph the corresponding reciprocal function in the same viewing window. Describe and compare the graphs.

29. $y = 2 \csc 3x$

30. $y = -\csc 4x$

31. $y = -2 \sec 4x$

32. $y = \dfrac{1}{4} \sec \pi x$

33. $y = \dfrac{1}{3} \sec\left(\dfrac{\pi x}{2} + \dfrac{\pi}{2}\right)$

34. $y = \dfrac{1}{2} \csc(2x - \pi)$

Solving a Trigonometric Equation Graphically   In Exercises 35–40, use a graph of the function to approximate the solution of the equation on the interval $[-2\pi, 2\pi]$.

35. $\tan x = 1$

36. $\cot x = -1$

37. $\sec x = 2$

38. $\csc x = \sqrt{2}$

39. $\cot x = -\sqrt{3}$

40. $\sec x = -\sqrt{2}$

Even and Odd Trigonometric Functions   In Exercises 41–46, use the graph of the function to determine whether the function is even, odd, or neither.

41. $f(x) = \sec x$

42. $f(x) = \tan x$

43. $f(x) = \csc 2x$

44. $f(x) = \cot 2x$

45. $f(x) = \tan\left(x - \dfrac{\pi}{2}\right)$

46. $f(x) = \sec(x + \pi)$

Using Graphs to Compare Functions **In Exercises 47–50, use a graphing utility to graph the two equations in the same viewing window. Use the graphs to determine whether the expressions are equivalent. Verify the results algebraically.**

47. $y_1 = \sin x \sec x,\quad y_2 = \tan x$

48. $y_1 = \dfrac{\cos x}{\sin x},\quad y_2 = \cot x$

49. $y_1 = 1 + \cot^2 x,\quad y_2 = \csc^2 x$

50. $y_1 = \sec^2 x - 1,\quad y_2 = \tan^2 x$

Identifying Damped Trigonometric Graphs **In Exercises 51–54, match the function with its graph. Describe the behavior of the function as x approaches zero. [The graphs are labeled (a), (b), (c), and (d).]**

(a)

(b)

(c)

(d)

51. $f(x) = x \cos x$

52. $f(x) = |x \sin x|$

53. $g(x) = |x| \sin x$

54. $g(x) = |x| \cos x$

Analyzing a Damped Trigonometric Graph **In Exercises 55–58, use a graphing utility to graph the function and the damping factor of the function in the same viewing window. Then analyze the graph of the function using the method in Example 6.**

55. $f(x) = e^{-x} \cos x$

56. $f(x) = e^{-2x} \sin x$

57. $h(x) = 2^{-x^2/4} \sin x$

58. $g(x) = 2^{-x^2/2} \cos x$

Exploration **In Exercises 59 and 60, use a graphing utility to graph the function. Use the graph to determine the behavior of the function as $x \to c$.**

(a) $x \to \dfrac{\pi}{2}^+ \left(\text{as } x \text{ approaches } \dfrac{\pi}{2} \text{ from the right}\right)$

(b) $x \to \dfrac{\pi}{2}^- \left(\text{as } x \text{ approaches } \dfrac{\pi}{2} \text{ from the left}\right)$

(c) $x \to -\dfrac{\pi}{2}^+ \left(\text{as } x \text{ approaches } -\dfrac{\pi}{2} \text{ from the right}\right)$

(d) $x \to -\dfrac{\pi}{2}^- \left(\text{as } x \text{ approaches } -\dfrac{\pi}{2} \text{ from the left}\right)$

59. $f(x) = \tan x$

60. $f(x) = \sec x$

Exploration **In Exercises 61 and 62, use a graphing utility to graph the function. Use the graph to determine the behavior of the function as $x \to c$.**

(a) As $x \to 0^+$, the value of $f(x) \to$ ▢.

(b) As $x \to 0^-$, the value of $f(x) \to$ ▢.

(c) As $x \to \pi^+$, the value of $f(x) \to$ ▢.

(d) As $x \to \pi^-$, the value of $f(x) \to$ ▢.

61. $f(x) = \csc x$

62. $f(x) = \cot x$

63. **Aviation** A plane flying at an altitude of 7 miles over level ground will pass directly over a radar antenna. Let d be the ground distance from the antenna to the point directly under the plane and let x be the angle of elevation to the plane from the antenna (see figure). Write d as a function of x and graph the function over the interval $0 < x < \pi$. (Consider d as positive when the plane approaches the antenna.)

7 mi

Not drawn to scale

64. ***Why you should learn it*** *(p. 304)* A television camera is on a reviewing platform 27 meters from the street on which a parade will be passing from left to right (see figure). Write the distance d from the camera to a particular unit in the parade as a function of the angle x, and graph the function over the interval $-\pi/2 < x < \pi/2$. (Consider x as negative when a unit in the parade approaches from the left.)

Not drawn to scale

27 m

d

x

Camera

65. Harmonic Motion An object weighing W pounds is suspended from a ceiling by a steel spring. The weight is pulled downward (positive direction) from its equilibrium position and released (see figure). The resulting motion of the weight is described by the function $y = \frac{1}{2}e^{-t/4}\cos 4t$, where y is the distance in feet and t is the time in seconds ($t > 0$).

(a) Use a graphing utility to graph the function.

(b) Describe the behavior of the displacement function for increasing values of time t.

66. Mechanical Engineering A crossed belt connects a 10-centimeter pulley on an electric motor with a 20-centimeter pulley on a saw arbor (see figure). The electric motor runs at 1700 revolutions per minute.

(a) Determine the number of revolutions per minute of the saw.

(b) How does crossing the belt affect the saw in relation to the motor?

(c) Let L be the total length of the belt. Write L as a function of ϕ, where ϕ is measured in radians. What is the domain of the function? (*Hint:* Add the lengths of the straight sections of the belt and the length of the belt around each pulley.)

(d) Use a graphing utility to complete the table.

ϕ	0.3	0.6	0.9	1.2	1.5
L					

(e) As ϕ increases, do the lengths of the straight sections of the belt change faster or slower than the lengths of the belts around each pulley?

(f) Use the graphing utility to graph the function over the appropriate domain.

67. MODELING DATA

The motion of an oscillating weight suspended by a spring was measured by a motion detector. The data were collected, and the approximate maximum (positive and negative) displacements from equilibrium are shown in the graph. The displacement y is measured in centimeters and the time t is measured in seconds.

(a) Is y a function of t? Explain.

(b) Approximate the frequency of the oscillations.

(c) Fit a model of the form $y = ab^t \cos ct$ to the data. Use the result of part (b) to approximate c. Use the *regression* feature of a graphing utility to fit an exponential model to the positive maximum displacements of the weight.

(d) Rewrite the model in the form $y = ae^{kt}\cos ct$.

(e) Use the graphing utility to graph the model. Compare the result with the data in the graph above.

Conclusions

True or False? In Exercises 68–71, determine whether the statement is true or false. Justify your answer.

68. The graph of $y = -\dfrac{1}{8}\tan\left(\dfrac{x}{2} + \pi\right)$ has an asymptote at $x = -7\pi$.

69. For the graph of $y = 2^x \sin x$, as x approaches $-\infty$, y approaches 0.

70. The graph of $y = \csc x$ can be obtained on a calculator by graphing the reciprocal of $y = \sin x$.

71. The graph of $y = \sec x$ can be obtained on a calculator by graphing a translation of the reciprocal of $y = \sin x$.

72. Exploration Consider the functions

$$f(x) = 2\sin x \qquad \text{and} \qquad g(x) = \tfrac{1}{2}\csc x$$

on the interval $(0, \pi)$.

(a) Use a graphing utility to graph f and g in the same viewing window.

(b) Approximate the interval in which $f(x) > g(x)$.

(c) Describe the behavior of each of the functions as x approaches π. How is the behavior of g related to the behavior of f as x approaches π?

73. Exploration Consider the functions given by

$$f(x) = \tan \frac{\pi x}{2} \quad \text{and} \quad g(x) = \frac{1}{2} \sec \frac{\pi x}{2}$$

on the interval $(-1, 1)$,

(a) Use a graphing utility to graph f and g in the same viewing window.

(b) Approximate the interval in which $f(x) < g(x)$.

(c) Approximate the interval in which $2f(x) < 2g(x)$. How does the result compare with that of part (b)? Explain.

74. Exploration

(a) Use a graphing utility to graph each function.

$$y_1 = \frac{4}{\pi}\left(\sin \pi x + \frac{1}{3}\sin 3\pi x\right)$$

$$y_2 = \frac{4}{\pi}\left(\sin \pi x + \frac{1}{3}\sin 3\pi x + \frac{1}{5}\sin 5\pi x\right)$$

(b) Identify the pattern in part (a) and find a function y_3 that continues the pattern one more term. Use the graphing utility to graph y_3.

(c) The graphs in parts (a) and (b) approximate the periodic function in the figure. Find a function y_4 that is a better approximation.

Exploration In Exercises 75 and 76, use a graphing utility to explore the ratio $f(x)$, which appears in calculus.

(a) **Complete the table. Round your results to four decimal places.**

x	-1	-0.1	-0.01	-0.001
$f(x)$				

x	0	0.001	0.01	0.1	1
$f(x)$					

(b) **Use the graphing utility to graph f. Use the *zoom* and *trace* features to describe the behavior of the graph as x approaches 0.**

(c) **Write a brief statement regarding the value of the ratio based on your results in parts (a) and (b).**

75. $f(x) = \dfrac{\tan x}{x}$ **76.** $f(x) = \dfrac{\tan 3x}{3x}$

77. Exploration Using calculus, it can be shown that the tangent function can be approximated by the polynomial

$$\tan x \approx x + \frac{2x^3}{3!} + \frac{16x^5}{5!}$$

where x is in radians. Use a graphing utility to graph the tangent function and its polynomial approximation in the same viewing window. How do the graphs compare?

78. HOW DO YOU SEE IT? Determine which function is represented by each graph. Do not use a calculator.

(a) (b)

(i) $f(x) = \tan 2x$ (i) $f(x) = \sec 4x$

(ii) $f(x) = \tan \dfrac{x}{2}$ (ii) $f(x) = \csc 4x$

(iii) $f(x) = 2 \tan x$ (iii) $f(x) = \csc \dfrac{x}{4}$

(iv) $f(x) = -\tan 2x$ (iv) $f(x) = \sec \dfrac{x}{4}$

(v) $f(x) = -\tan \dfrac{x}{2}$ (v) $f(x) = \csc(4x - \pi)$

Cumulative Mixed Review

Properties of Real Numbers In Exercises 79–82, identify the rule of algebra illustrated by the statement.

79. $5(a - 9) = 5a - 45$

80. $7\left(\frac{1}{7}\right) = 1$

81. $(3 + x) + 0 = 3 + x$

82. $(a + b) + 10 = a + (b + 10)$

Finding an Inverse Function In Exercises 83–86, determine whether the function is one-to-one. If it is, find its inverse function.

83. $f(x) = -10$ **84.** $f(x) = (x - 7)^2 + 3$

85. $f(x) = \sqrt{3x - 14}$ **86.** $f(x) = \sqrt[4]{x - 5}$

Finding the Domain, Intercepts, and Asymptotes of a Function In Exercises 87–90, identify the domain, any intercepts, and any asymptotes of the function.

87. $y = x^2 + 3x - 4$ **88.** $y = \ln x^4$

89. $f(x) = 3^{x+1} + 2$ **90.** $f(x) = \dfrac{x - 7}{x^2 + 4x + 4}$

4.7   Inverse Trigonometric Functions

Inverse Sine Function

Recall from Section 1.6 that for a function to have an inverse function, it must be one-to-one—that is, it must pass the Horizontal Line Test. Notice from Figure 4.43 that $y = \sin x$ does not pass the test because different values of x yield the same y-value.

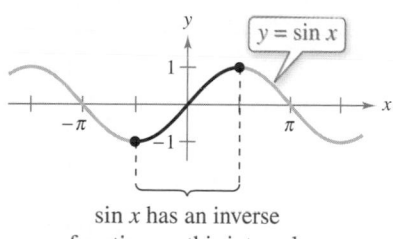

sin x has an inverse
function on this interval.

Figure 4.43

However, when you restrict the domain to the interval $-\pi/2 \leq x \leq \pi/2$ (corresponding to the black portion of the graph in Figure 4.43), the properties listed below hold.

1. On the interval $[-\pi/2, \pi/2]$, the function $y = \sin x$ is increasing.

2. On the interval $[-\pi/2, \pi/2]$, $y = \sin x$ takes on its full range of values, $-1 \leq \sin x \leq 1$.

3. On the interval $[-\pi/2, \pi/2]$, $y = \sin x$ is one-to-one.

So, on the restricted domain $-\pi/2 \leq x \leq \pi/2$, $y = \sin x$ has a unique inverse function called the **inverse sine function.** It is denoted by

$$y = \arcsin x \qquad \text{or} \qquad y = \sin^{-1} x.$$

The notation $\sin^{-1} x$ is consistent with the inverse function notation $f^{-1}(x)$. The arcsin x notation (read as "the arcsine of x") comes from the association of a central angle with its intercepted *arc length* on a unit circle. So, arcsin x means the angle (or arc) whose sine is x. Both notations, arcsin x and $\sin^{-1} x$, are commonly used in mathematics, so remember that $\sin^{-1} x$ denotes the *inverse* sine function rather than $1/\sin x$. The values of arcsin x lie in the interval

$$-\frac{\pi}{2} \leq \arcsin x \leq \frac{\pi}{2}.$$

The graph of $y = \arcsin x$ is shown in Example 2.

Definition of Inverse Sine Function

The **inverse sine function** is defined by

$$y = \arcsin x \qquad \text{if and only if} \qquad \sin y = x$$

where $-1 \leq x \leq 1$ and $-\pi/2 \leq y \leq \pi/2$. The domain of $y = \arcsin x$ is $[-1, 1]$ and the range is $[-\pi/2, \pi/2]$.

When evaluating the inverse sine function, it helps to remember the phrase "the arcsine of x is the angle (or number) whose sine is x."

EXAMPLE 1   Evaluating the Inverse Sine Function

If possible, find the exact value.

a. $\arcsin\left(-\dfrac{1}{2}\right)$ **b.** $\sin^{-1}\dfrac{\sqrt{3}}{2}$ **c.** $\sin^{-1}2$

Solution

a. Because $\sin\left(-\dfrac{\pi}{6}\right) = -\dfrac{1}{2}$, and $-\dfrac{\pi}{6}$ lies in $\left[-\dfrac{\pi}{2}, \dfrac{\pi}{2}\right]$, it follows that

$$\arcsin\left(-\frac{1}{2}\right) = -\frac{\pi}{6}. \qquad \text{Angle whose sine is } -\tfrac{1}{2}$$

b. Because $\sin\dfrac{\pi}{3} = \dfrac{\sqrt{3}}{2}$, and $\dfrac{\pi}{3}$ lies in $\left[-\dfrac{\pi}{2}, \dfrac{\pi}{2}\right]$, it follows that

$$\sin^{-1}\frac{\sqrt{3}}{2} = \frac{\pi}{3}. \qquad \text{Angle whose sine is } \sqrt{3}/2$$

c. It is not possible to evaluate $y = \sin^{-1}x$ at $x = 2$ because there is no angle whose sine is 2. Remember that the domain of the inverse sine function is $[-1, 1]$.

✓ **Checkpoint** Audio-video solution in English & Spanish at LarsonPrecalculus.com.

If possible, find the exact value.

a. $\arcsin 1$ **b.** $\sin^{-1}(-2)$

> **Remark**
>
> As with the trigonometric functions, much of the work with the inverse trigonometric functions can be done by *exact* calculations rather than by calculator approximations. Exact calculations help to increase your understanding of the inverse functions by relating them to the triangle definitions of the trigonometric functions.

EXAMPLE 2   Graphing the Arcsine Function

Sketch a graph of $y = \arcsin x$ by hand.

Solution

By definition, the equations

$$y = \arcsin x \qquad \text{and} \qquad \sin y = x$$

are equivalent for $-\pi/2 \le y \le \pi/2$. So, their graphs are the same. For the interval $[-\pi/2, \pi/2]$, you can assign values to y in the equation $\sin y = x$ to make a table of values.

y	$-\dfrac{\pi}{2}$	$-\dfrac{\pi}{4}$	$-\dfrac{\pi}{6}$	0	$\dfrac{\pi}{6}$	$\dfrac{\pi}{4}$	$\dfrac{\pi}{2}$
$x = \sin y$	-1	$-\dfrac{\sqrt{2}}{2}$	$-\dfrac{1}{2}$	0	$\dfrac{1}{2}$	$\dfrac{\sqrt{2}}{2}$	1

Then plot the points and connect them with a smooth curve. The resulting graph of $y = \arcsin x$ is shown in Figure 4.44. Note that it is the reflection (in the line $y = x$) of the black portion of the graph in Figure 4.43. Be sure you see that Figure 4.44 shows the *entire* graph of the inverse sine function. Remember that the domain of $y = \arcsin x$ is the closed interval $[-1, 1]$ and the range is the closed interval $[-\pi/2, \pi/2]$.

✓ **Checkpoint** Audio-video solution in English & Spanish at LarsonPrecalculus.com.

Use a graphing utility to graph $f(x) = \sin x$, $g(x) = \arcsin x$, and $y = x$ in the same viewing window to verify geometrically that g is the inverse function of f. (Be sure to restrict the domain of f properly.) ∎

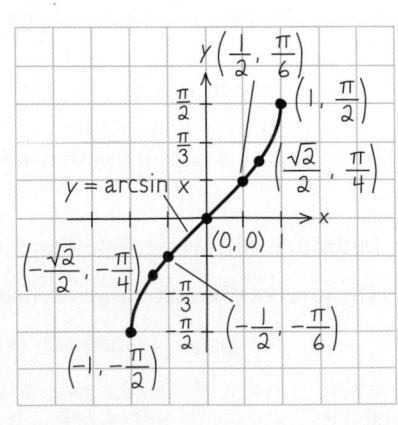

Figure 4.44

Other Inverse Trigonometric Functions

The cosine function is decreasing and one-to-one on the interval $0 \le x \le \pi$, as shown in the figure.

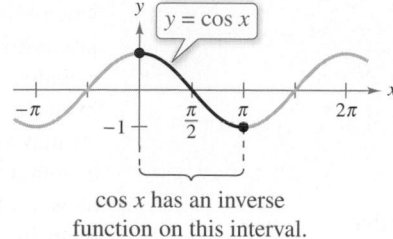

cos x has an inverse
function on this interval.

Consequently, on this interval the cosine function has an inverse function—the **inverse cosine function**—denoted by

$$y = \arccos x \qquad \text{or} \qquad y = \cos^{-1} x.$$

Because $y = \arccos x$ and $x = \cos y$ are equivalent for $0 \le y \le \pi$, their graphs are the same and can be confirmed by the table of values below.

y	0	$\dfrac{\pi}{6}$	$\dfrac{\pi}{3}$	$\dfrac{\pi}{2}$	$\dfrac{2\pi}{3}$	$\dfrac{5\pi}{6}$	π
$x = \cos y$	1	$\dfrac{\sqrt{3}}{2}$	$\dfrac{1}{2}$	0	$-\dfrac{1}{2}$	$-\dfrac{\sqrt{3}}{2}$	-1

Similarly, you can define an **inverse tangent function** by restricting the domain of $y = \tan x$ to the interval $(-\pi/2, \pi/2)$. The inverse tangent function is denoted by

$$y = \arctan x \qquad \text{or} \qquad y = \tan^{-1} x.$$

Because $y = \arctan x$ and $x = \tan y$ are equivalent for $-\pi/2 < y < \pi/2$, their graphs are the same and can be confirmed by the table of values below.

y	$-\dfrac{\pi}{4}$	$-\dfrac{\pi}{6}$	0	$\dfrac{\pi}{6}$	$\dfrac{\pi}{4}$
$x = \tan y$	-1	$-\dfrac{\sqrt{3}}{3}$	0	$\dfrac{\sqrt{3}}{3}$	1

The list below summarizes the definitions of the three most common inverse trigonometric functions. (Their graphs are shown on page 319.) The remaining three are defined in Exercises 107–109.

Definitions of the Inverse Trigonometric Functions

Function	*Domain*	*Range*
$y = \arcsin x$ if and only if $\sin y = x$	$-1 \le x \le 1$	$-\dfrac{\pi}{2} \le y \le \dfrac{\pi}{2}$
$y = \arccos x$ if and only if $\cos y = x$	$-1 \le x \le 1$	$0 \le y \le \pi$
$y = \arctan x$ if and only if $\tan y = x$	$-\infty < x < \infty$	$-\dfrac{\pi}{2} < y < \dfrac{\pi}{2}$

EXAMPLE 3   Evaluating Inverse Trigonometric Functions

Find the exact value.

a. $\arccos \dfrac{\sqrt{2}}{2}$

b. $\cos^{-1}(-1)$

c. $\arctan 0$

d. $\tan^{-1}(-1)$

Solution

a. Because $\cos(\pi/4) = \sqrt{2}/2$, and $\pi/4$ lies in $[0, \pi]$, it follows that

$$\arccos \frac{\sqrt{2}}{2} = \frac{\pi}{4}. \qquad \text{Angle whose cosine is } \frac{\sqrt{2}}{2}$$

b. Because $\cos \pi = -1$, and π lies in $[0, \pi]$, it follows that

$$\cos^{-1}(-1) = \pi. \qquad \text{Angle whose cosine is } -1$$

c. Because $\tan 0 = 0$, and 0 lies in $(-\pi/2, \pi/2)$, it follows that

$$\arctan 0 = 0. \qquad \text{Angle whose tangent is } 0$$

d. Because $\tan(-\pi/4) = -1$, and $-\pi/4$ lies in $(-\pi/2, \pi/2)$, it follows that

$$\tan^{-1}(-1) = -\frac{\pi}{4}. \qquad \text{Angle whose tangent is } -1$$

✓ **Checkpoint** *Audio-video solution in English & Spanish at LarsonPrecalculus.com.*

Find the exact value.

a. $\cos^{-1}\left(-\dfrac{\sqrt{2}}{2}\right)$ **b.** $\arctan \sqrt{3}$

EXAMPLE 4   Calculators and Inverse Trigonometric Functions

Use a calculator to approximate the value, if possible.

a. $\arctan(-8.45)$ **b.** $\sin^{-1} 0.2447$ **c.** $\arccos 2$

Solution

Function	Mode	Graphing Calculator Keystrokes
a. $\arctan(-8.45)$	Radian	TAN⁻¹ ((-) 8.45) ENTER

From the display, it follows that $\arctan(-8.45) \approx -1.4530010$.

b. $\sin^{-1} 0.2447$	Radian	SIN⁻¹ (0.2447) ENTER

From the display, it follows that $\sin^{-1} 0.2447 \approx 0.2472103$.

c. $\arccos 2$	Radian	COS⁻¹ (2) ENTER

The calculator should display an *error message*, because the domain of the inverse cosine function is $[-1, 1]$.

✓ **Checkpoint** *Audio-video solution in English & Spanish at LarsonPrecalculus.com.*

Use a calculator to approximate the value, if possible.

a. $\arctan 4.84$ **b.** $\arcsin(-1.1)$ **c.** $\arccos(-0.349)$

Remember that the domain of the inverse sine function and the inverse cosine function is $[-1, 1]$, as indicated in Example 4(c).

Library of Parent Functions: Inverse Trigonometric Functions

The parent inverse sine function, parent inverse cosine function, and parent inverse tangent function are summarized below and on the inside cover of this text.

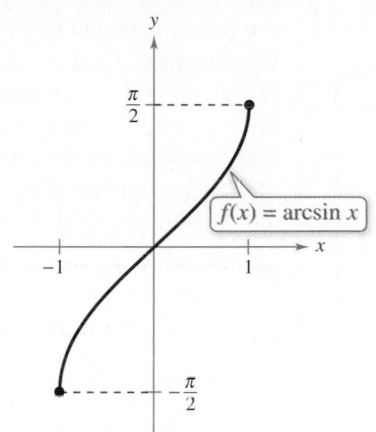

Domain: $[-1, 1]$

Range: $\left[-\dfrac{\pi}{2}, \dfrac{\pi}{2}\right]$

Intercept: $(0, 0)$

Odd function

Origin symmetry

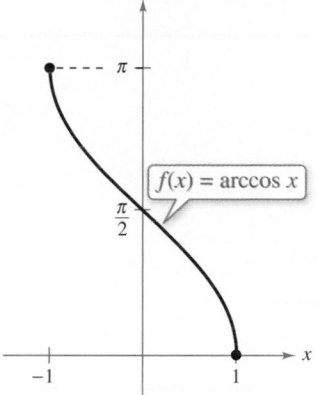

Domain: $[-1, 1]$

Range: $[0, \pi]$

y-intercept: $\left(0, \dfrac{\pi}{2}\right)$

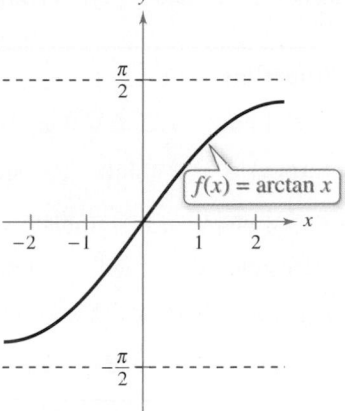

Domain: $(-\infty, \infty)$

Range: $\left(-\dfrac{\pi}{2}, \dfrac{\pi}{2}\right)$

Intercept: $(0, 0)$

Horizontal asymptotes: $y = \pm\dfrac{\pi}{2}$

Odd function

Origin symmetry

EXAMPLE 5   Library of Parent Functions: $f(x) = \arccos x$

See LarsonPrecalculus.com for an interactive version of this type of example.

Note that the graphs of $g(x) = \arccos(x - 2)$ and $h(x) = \arccos(-x)$ are transformations of the graph of $f(x) = \arccos x$.

a. Because $g(x) = \arccos(x - 2) = f(x - 2)$, the graph of g can be obtained by shifting the graph of f two units to the *right*, as shown in Figure 4.45.

b. Because $h(x) = \arccos(-x) = f(-x)$, the graph of h can be obtained by *reflecting* the graph of f in the *y*-axis, as shown in Figure 4.46.

Figure 4.45

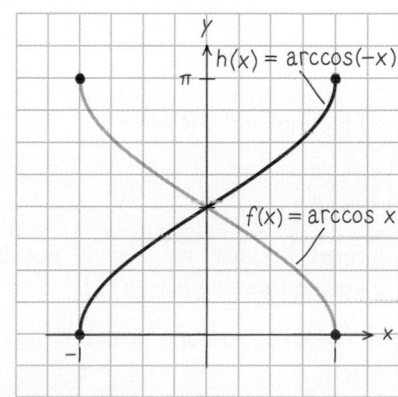

Figure 4.46

✓ *Checkpoint* 🔊))) Audio-video solution in English & Spanish at LarsonPrecalculus.com.

Compare the graph of $g(x) = \arccos(x + 1)$ with the graph of $f(x) = \arccos x$.   ◼

Compositions of Functions

Recall from Section 1.6 that for all x in the domains of f and f^{-1}, inverse functions have the properties

$$f(f^{-1}(x)) = x \qquad \text{and} \qquad f^{-1}(f(x)) = x.$$

Inverse Properties

If $-1 \le x \le 1$ and $-\pi/2 \le y \le \pi/2$, then

$$\sin(\arcsin x) = x \qquad \text{and} \qquad \arcsin(\sin y) = y.$$

If $-1 \le x \le 1$ and $0 \le y \le \pi$, then

$$\cos(\arccos x) = x \qquad \text{and} \qquad \arccos(\cos y) = y.$$

If x is a real number and $-\pi/2 < y < \pi/2$, then

$$\tan(\arctan x) = x \qquad \text{and} \qquad \arctan(\tan y) = y.$$

Keep in mind that these properties do not apply for arbitrary values of x and y. For instance,

$$\arcsin\left(\sin \frac{3\pi}{2}\right) = \arcsin(-1) = -\frac{\pi}{2} \ne \frac{3\pi}{2}.$$

In other words, the property $\arcsin(\sin y) = y$ is not valid for values of y outside the interval $[-\pi/2, \pi/2]$.

EXAMPLE 6 Using Inverse Properties

If possible, find the exact value.

a. $\tan[\arctan(-5)]$ **b.** $\arcsin\left(\sin \dfrac{5\pi}{3}\right)$ **c.** $\cos(\cos^{-1}\pi)$

Solution

a. Because -5 lies in the domain of the arctangent function, the inverse property applies, and you have

$$\tan[\arctan(-5)] = -5.$$

b. In this case, $5\pi/3$ does not lie within the range of the arcsine function, $-\pi/2 \le y \le \pi/2$. However, $5\pi/3$ is coterminal with

$$\frac{5\pi}{3} - 2\pi = -\frac{\pi}{3}$$

which does lie in the range of the arcsine function, and you have

$$\arcsin\left(\sin \frac{5\pi}{3}\right) = \arcsin\left[\sin\left(-\frac{\pi}{3}\right)\right] = -\frac{\pi}{3}.$$

c. The expression $\cos(\cos^{-1}\pi)$ is not defined because $\cos^{-1}\pi$ is not defined. Remember that the domain of the inverse cosine function is $[-1, 1]$.

✓ **Checkpoint** 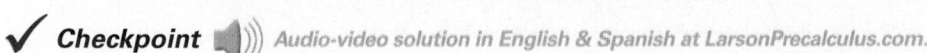 Audio-video solution in English & Spanish at LarsonPrecalculus.com.

If possible, find the exact value.

a. $\tan[\tan^{-1}(-14)]$ **b.** $\sin^{-1}\left(\sin \dfrac{7\pi}{4}\right)$ **c.** $\cos(\arccos 0.54)$ ∎

Explore the Concept

Use a graphing utility to graph $y = \arcsin(\sin x)$. What are the domain and range of this function? Explain why $\arcsin(\sin 4)$ does not equal 4. Now graph $y = \sin(\arcsin x)$ and determine the domain and range. Explain why $\sin(\arcsin 4)$ is not defined.

The algebraic solution of Example 7 shows how to use right triangles to find exact values of compositions of inverse functions.

EXAMPLE 7 Evaluating Compositions of Functions

Find the exact value.

a. $\tan\left(\arccos\dfrac{2}{3}\right)$ **b.** $\cos\left[\arcsin\left(-\dfrac{3}{5}\right)\right]$

Algebraic Solution

a. If you let $u = \arccos\frac{2}{3}$, then $\cos u = \frac{2}{3}$. Because the range of the arccosine function is $[0, \pi]$ and $\cos u$ is positive, u is a first-quadrant angle. You can sketch and label angle u as shown in Figure 4.47. Consequently,

$$\tan\left(\arccos\frac{2}{3}\right) = \tan u = \frac{\text{opp}}{\text{adj}} = \frac{\sqrt{5}}{2}.$$

b. If you let $u = \arcsin\left(-\frac{3}{5}\right)$, then $\sin u = -\frac{3}{5}$. Because the range of the arcsine function is $[-\pi/2, \pi/2]$ and $\sin u$ is negative, u is a fourth-quadrant angle. You can sketch and label angle u as shown in Figure 4.48. Consequently,

$$\cos\left[\arcsin\left(-\frac{3}{5}\right)\right] = \cos u = \frac{\text{adj}}{\text{hyp}} = \frac{4}{5}.$$

Figure 4.47

Figure 4.48

Graphical Solution

a. Use a graphing utility set in *radian* mode to graph $y = \tan(\arccos x)$, as shown below.

When $x = \frac{2}{3} \approx 0.667$, $y \approx 1.118 \approx \frac{\sqrt{5}}{2}$.

b. Use the graphing utility set in *radian* mode to graph $y = \cos(\arcsin x)$, as shown below.

When $x = -\frac{3}{5} = -0.6$, $y - 0.8 = \frac{4}{5}$.

Find the exact value of $\cos\left[\arctan\left(-\frac{3}{4}\right)\right]$.

EXAMPLE 8 Some Problems from Calculus

Write each of the following as an algebraic expression in x.

a. $\sin(\arccos 3x), \quad 0 \le x \le \frac{1}{3}$ **b.** $\cot(\arccos 3x), \quad 0 \le x < \frac{1}{3}$

Solution

If you let $u = \arccos 3x$, then $\cos u = 3x$, where $-1 \le 3x \le 1$. Because $\cos u = \text{adj}/\text{hyp} = (3x)/1$, you can sketch a right triangle with acute angle u, as shown in Figure 4.49. From this triangle, you can convert each expression to algebraic form.

a. $\sin(\arccos 3x) = \sin u = \dfrac{\text{opp}}{\text{hyp}} = \sqrt{1 - 9x^2}, \quad 0 \le x \le \dfrac{1}{3}$

b. $\cot(\arccos 3x) = \cot u = \dfrac{\text{adj}}{\text{opp}} = \dfrac{3x}{\sqrt{1 - 9x^2}}, \quad 0 \le x < \dfrac{1}{3}$

Figure 4.49

Write $\sec(\arctan x)$ as an algebraic expression in x.

4.7   Exercises

See *CalcChat.com* for tutorial help and worked-out solutions to odd-numbered exercises.
For instructions on how to use a graphing utility, see Appendix A.

Vocabulary and Concept Check

In Exercises 1 and 2, fill in the blanks.

Function	Alternative Notation	Domain	Range

1. $y = \arcsin x$ _____ _____ $-\dfrac{\pi}{2} \le y \le \dfrac{\pi}{2}$

2. _____ $y = \cos^{-1} x$ $-1 \le x \le 1$ _____

3. What notation can you use to represent the inverse sine function?

4. Does $\arccos x = \dfrac{1}{\cos x}$?

Procedures and Problem Solving

Evaluating an Inverse Trigonometric Function In Exercises 5–13, find the exact value of each expression, if possible, without using a calculator.

5. (a) $\arcsin \frac{1}{2}$ (b) $\arcsin 0$

6. (a) $\arccos \frac{1}{2}$ (b) $\arccos 0$

7. (a) $\arcsin(-1)$ (b) $\arccos 1$

8. (a) $\arctan 1$ (b) $\arccos(-1)$

9. (a) $\arctan \dfrac{\sqrt{3}}{3}$ (b) $\arcsin \dfrac{3}{2}$

10. (a) $\cos^{-1}(-2)$ (b) $\sin^{-1}\left(-\dfrac{\sqrt{2}}{2}\right)$

11. (a) $\arctan\left(-\sqrt{3}\right)$ (b) $\arccos \dfrac{\sqrt{3}}{2}$

12. (a) $\arccos\left(-\sqrt{3}\right)$ (b) $\arcsin \dfrac{\sqrt{2}}{2}$

13. (a) $\sin^{-1} \dfrac{\sqrt{5}}{2}$ (b) $\tan^{-1}\left(-\dfrac{\sqrt{3}}{3}\right)$

14. Graphing the Arccosine Function Consider the function $y = \arccos x$.

(a) Use a graphing utility to complete the table.

x	-1	-0.8	-0.6	-0.4	-0.2
y					

x	0	0.2	0.4	0.6	0.8	1
y						

(b) Plot the points from the table in part (a) and graph the function. (Do not use a graphing utility.)

(c) Use the graphing utility to graph the inverse cosine function and compare the result with your hand-drawn graph in part (b).

(d) Determine any intercepts and symmetry of the graph.

15. Graphing the Arcsine Function Consider the function $y = \arcsin x$.

(a) Use a graphing utility to complete the table.

x	-1	-0.8	-0.6	-0.4	-0.2
y					

x	0	0.2	0.4	0.6	0.8	1
y						

(b) Plot the points from the table in part (a) and graph the function. (Do not use a graphing utility.)

(c) Use the graphing utility to graph the inverse sine function and compare the result with your hand-drawn graph in part (b).

(d) Determine any intercepts and symmetry of the graph.

16. Graphing the Arctangent Function Consider the function $y = \arctan x$.

(a) Use a graphing utility to complete the table.

x	-10	-8	-6	-4	-2
y					

x	0	2	4	6	8	10
y						

(b) Plot the points from the table in part (a) and graph the function. (Do not use a graphing utility.)

(c) Use the graphing utility to graph the inverse tangent function and compare the result with your hand-drawn graph in part (b).

(d) Determine the horizontal asymptotes of the graph.

Finding Missing Coordinates   In Exercises 17 and 18, determine the missing coordinates of the points on the graph of the function.

17.   **18.**

Calculators and Inverse Trigonometric Functions   In Exercises 19–32, use a calculator to approximate the value of the expression, if possible. Round your answer to the nearest hundredth.

19. $\arcsin 0.45$	**20.** $\cos^{-1} 0.28$
21. $\tan^{-1} 0.75$	**22.** $\arctan 15$
23. $\cos^{-1} 3.5$	**24.** $\sin^{-1} 0.56$
25. $\arccos(-0.9)$	**26.** $\arcsin(-1.3)$
27. $\arctan(-6)$	**28.** $\tan^{-1} 5.9$
29. $\sin^{-1}\left(-\dfrac{3}{4}\right)$	**30.** $\arccos \dfrac{5}{3}$
31. $\arctan \dfrac{7}{2}$	**32.** $\tan^{-1}\left(-\dfrac{95}{7}\right)$

Library of Parent Functions: $f(x) = \arcsin x$ In Exercises 33–36, compare the graph of the function with the graph of $f(x) = \arcsin x$.

33. $g(x) = \arcsin(x + 3)$

34. $g(x) = \arcsin(x - 4)$

35. $g(x) = \arcsin(-x)$

36. $g(x) = -\arcsin x$

Library of Parent Functions: $f(x) = \arccos x$ In Exercises 37–40, compare the graph of the function with the graph of $f(x) = \arccos x$.

37. $g(x) = \arccos(x + \pi)$

38. $g(x) = \arccos x - 5$

39. $g(x) = \arccos(-x - 2)$

40. $g(x) = \arccos(-x) - 3$

Library of Parent Functions: $f(x) = \arctan x$ In Exercises 41–44, compare the graph of the function with the graph of $f(x) = \arctan x$.

41. $g(x) = \arctan x + 1$

42. $g(x) = \arctan(x - 2)$

43. $g(x) = -\arctan x - 3$

44. $g(x) = \arctan(-x) + 4$

Using an Inverse Trigonometric Function   In Exercises 45–48, use an inverse trigonometric function to write θ as a function of x.

45.   **46.**

47.   **48.**

   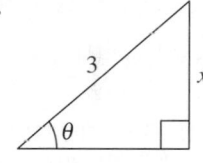

Using an Inverse Trigonometric Function   In Exercises 49–52, find the length of the third side of the triangle in terms of x. Then find θ in terms of x for all three inverse trigonometric functions.

49.   **50.**

51.   **52.**

   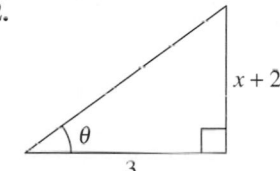

Using Inverse Properties   In Exercises 53–64, use the properties of inverse functions to find the exact value of the expression, if possible.

53. $\cos(\arccos 0.3)$ **54.** $\tan(\arctan 25)$

55. $\sin(\arcsin 1.7)$ **56.** $\sin[\arcsin(-0.1)]$

57. $\tan[\tan^{-1}(-0.5)]$ **58.** $\cos[\cos^{-1}(-2)]$

59. $\arctan\left(\tan \dfrac{11\pi}{6}\right)$ **60.** $\arcsin\left(\sin \dfrac{4\pi}{3}\right)$

61. $\sin^{-1}\left(\sin \dfrac{5\pi}{2}\right)$ **62.** $\cos^{-1}\left(\cos \dfrac{3\pi}{2}\right)$

63. $\sin^{-1}\left(\tan \dfrac{5\pi}{4}\right)$ **64.** $\cos^{-1}\left(\tan \dfrac{3\pi}{4}\right)$

Evaluating a Composition of Functions   In Exercises 65–72, find the exact value of the expression. Use a graphing utility to verify your result. (*Hint:* Make a sketch of a right triangle.)

65. $\sin\left(\arctan \dfrac{4}{3}\right)$ **66.** $\cos\left(\arcsin \dfrac{24}{25}\right)$

67. $\sec\left(\arcsin \dfrac{4}{5}\right)$ **68.** $\csc\left[\arctan\left(-\dfrac{12}{5}\right)\right]$

69. $\sin\left[\arccos\left(-\dfrac{2}{3}\right)\right]$ **70.** $\sec\left[\arctan\left(-\dfrac{3}{5}\right)\right]$

71. $\tan\left[\arcsin\left(-\dfrac{3}{4}\right)\right]$ **72.** $\cot\left(\arctan \dfrac{5}{8}\right)$

Writing an Algebraic Expression In Exercises 73–80, write an algebraic expression that is equivalent to the expression. (*Hint:* Sketch a right triangle, as demonstrated in Example 8.)

73. $\cot(\arctan x)$

74. $\sin(\arctan x)$

75. $\sin[\arccos(x + 2)]$

76. $\sec[\arcsin(x - 1)]$

77. $\tan\left(\arccos \dfrac{x}{5}\right)$

78. $\cot\left(\arctan \dfrac{4}{x}\right)$

79. $\csc\left(\arctan \dfrac{x}{\sqrt{7}}\right)$

80. $\cos\left(\arcsin \dfrac{x - h}{r}\right)$

Completing an Equation In Exercises 81–84, complete the equation.

81. $\arctan \dfrac{14}{x} = \arcsin(\ \ \ ), \quad x > 0$

82. $\arcsin \dfrac{\sqrt{36 - x^2}}{6} = \arccos(\ \ \ ), \quad 0 \le x \le 6$

83. $\arccos \dfrac{3}{\sqrt{x^2 - 2x + 10}} = \arcsin(\ \ \ )$

84. $\arccos \dfrac{x - 2}{2} = \arctan(\ \ \ ), \quad 2 < x < 4$

Graphing an Inverse Trigonometric Function In Exercises 85–90, use a graphing utility to graph the function.

85. $y = 2 \arccos x$

86. $y = \arcsin \dfrac{x}{2}$

87. $f(x) = \arcsin(x - 2)$

88. $g(t) = \arccos(t + 2)$

89. $f(x) = \arctan \dfrac{x}{4}$

90. $f(x) = \arctan 3x$

Using a Trigonometric Identity In Exercises 91 and 92, write the function in terms of the sine function by using the identity

$$A \cos \omega t + B \sin \omega t = \sqrt{A^2 + B^2} \sin\left(\omega t + \arctan \dfrac{A}{B}\right).$$

Use a graphing utility to graph both forms of the function. What does the graph imply?

91. $f(t) = 3 \cos 2t + 3 \sin 2t$

92. $f(t) = 4 \cos \pi t + 3 \sin \pi t$

Analyzing an Inverse Trigonometric Function In Exercises 93–98, find the value. If not possible, state the reason.

93. As $x \to 1^-$, the value of $\arcsin x \to$ ▢ .

94. As $x \to 1^-$, the value of $\arccos x \to$ ▢ .

95. As $x \to \infty$, the value of $\arctan x \to$ ▢ .

96. As $x \to -1^+$, the value of $\arcsin x \to$ ▢ .

97. As $x \to -1^+$, the value of $\arccos x \to$ ▢ .

98. As $x \to -\infty$, the value of $\arctan x \to$ ▢ .

99. *Why you should learn it* (p. 315) Different types of granular substances naturally settle at different angles when stored in cone-shaped piles. This angle θ is called the *angle of repose*. When rock salt is stored in a cone-shaped pile 5.5 meters high, the diameter of the pile's base is about 17 meters. (Source: Bulk-Store Structures, Inc.)

(a) Draw a diagram that gives a visual representation of the problem. Label all quantities.

(b) Find the angle of repose for rock salt.

(c) How tall is a pile of rock salt that has a base diameter of 25 meters?

100. MODELING DATA

A photographer takes a picture of a three-foot painting hanging in an art gallery. The camera lens is 1 foot below the lower edge of the painting (see figure). The angle β subtended by the camera lens x feet from the painting is $\beta = \arctan[3x/(x^2 + 4)]$, $x > 0$.

Not drawn to scale

(a) Use a graphing utility to graph β as a function of x.

(b) Use the *trace* feature to approximate the distance from the picture when β is maximum.

(c) Identify the asymptote of the graph and discuss its meaning in the context of the problem.

101. Angle of Elevation An airplane flies at an altitude of 6 miles toward a point directly over an observer. Consider θ and x as shown in the figure.

Not drawn to scale

(a) Write θ as a function of x.

(b) Find θ when $x = 10$ miles and $x = 3$ miles.

102. Criminal Justice A police car with its spotlight on is parked 20 meters from a warehouse. Consider θ and x as shown in the figure.

Not drawn to scale

(a) Write θ as a function of x.

(b) Find θ when $x = 5$ meters and $x = 12$ meters.

Conclusions

True or False?   In Exercises 103–105, determine whether the statement is true or false. Justify your answer.

103. $\sin \dfrac{5\pi}{6} = \dfrac{1}{2}$ ⟹ $\arcsin \dfrac{1}{2} = \dfrac{5\pi}{6}$

104. $\tan \dfrac{5\pi}{4} = 1$ ⟹ $\arctan 1 = \dfrac{5\pi}{4}$

105. $\arctan x = \dfrac{\arcsin x}{\arccos x}$

106. HOW DO YOU SEE IT? Use the figure below to determine the value(s) of x for which each statement is true.

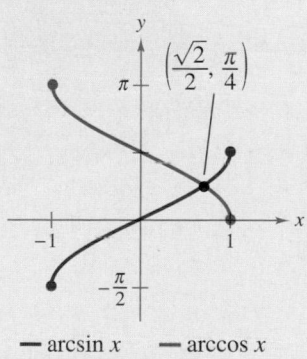

— arcsin x — arccos x

(a) $\arcsin x < \arccos x$

(b) $\arcsin x = \arccos x$

(c) $\arcsin x > \arccos x$

107. Inverse Cotangent Function Define the inverse cotangent function by restricting the domain of the cotangent function to the interval $(0, \pi)$, and sketch the graph of the inverse function.

108. Inverse Secant Function Define the inverse secant function by restricting the domain of the secant function to the intervals $[0, \pi/2)$ and $(\pi/2, \pi]$, and sketch the graph of the inverse function.

109. Inverse Cosecant Function Define the inverse cosecant function by restricting the domain of the cosecant function to the intervals $[-\pi/2, 0)$ and $(0, \pi/2]$, and sketch the graph of the inverse function.

110. Writing Use the results of Exercises 107–109 to explain how to graph (a) the inverse cotangent function, (b) the inverse secant function, and (c) the inverse cosecant function on a graphing utility.

Evaluating an Inverse Trigonometric Function In Exercises 111–114, use the results of Exercises 107–109 to evaluate the expression without using a calculator.

111. $\operatorname{arcsec} \sqrt{2}$

112. $\operatorname{arcsec} 1$

113. $\operatorname{arccot}\left(-\sqrt{3}\right)$

114. $\operatorname{arccsc} 2$

Proof   In Exercises 115–117, prove the identity.

115. $\arcsin(-x) = -\arcsin x$

116. $\arctan(-x) = -\arctan x$

117. $\arcsin x + \arccos x = \dfrac{\pi}{2}$

118. Finding the Area of a Plane Region In calculus, it is shown that the area of the region bounded by the graphs of $y = 0$, $y = 1/(x^2 + 1)$, $x = a$, and $x = b$ is given by

$$\text{Area} = \arctan b - \arctan a$$

(see figure). Find the area for each value of a and b.

(a) $a = 0, b = 1$

(b) $a = -1, b = 1$

(c) $a = 0, b = 3$

(d) $a = -1, b = 3$

Cumulative Mixed Review

Simplifying a Radical Expression   In Exercises 119–122, simplify the radical expression.

119. $\dfrac{4}{4\sqrt{2}}$

120. $\dfrac{2}{\sqrt{3}}$

121. $\dfrac{2\sqrt{3}}{6}$

122. $\dfrac{5\sqrt{5}}{2\sqrt{10}}$

Evaluating Trigonometric Functions In Exercises 123–126, sketch a right triangle corresponding to the trigonometric function of the acute angle θ. Use the Pythagorean Theorem to determine the third side and then find the values of the other five trigonometric functions of θ.

123. $\sin \theta = \frac{5}{6}$

124. $\tan \theta = 2$

125. $\cos \theta = \frac{3}{4}$

126. $\sec \theta = 3$

4.8   Applications and Models

Applications Involving Right Triangles

In this section, the three angles of a right triangle are denoted by A, B, and C (where C is the right angle), and the lengths of the sides opposite these angles by a, b, and c, respectively (where c is the hypotenuse).

EXAMPLE 1   Solving a Right Triangle

See LarsonPrecalculus.com for an interactive version of this type of example.

Solve the right triangle for all unknown sides and angles.

Solution

Because $C = 90°$, it follows that

$$A + B = 90°$$

and

$$B = 90° - 34.2° = 55.8°.$$

To solve for a, use the fact that

$$\tan A = \frac{\text{opp}}{\text{adj}} = \frac{a}{b} \quad \Longrightarrow \quad a = b \tan A.$$

So, $a = 19.4 \tan 34.2° \approx 13.18$. Similarly, to solve for c, use the fact that

$$\cos A = \frac{\text{adj}}{\text{hyp}} = \frac{b}{c} \quad \Longrightarrow \quad c = \frac{b}{\cos A}.$$

So, $c = \dfrac{19.4}{\cos 34.2°} \approx 23.46$.

✓ **Checkpoint** *Audio-video solution in English & Spanish at LarsonPrecalculus.com.*

Solve the right triangle for all unknown sides and angles.

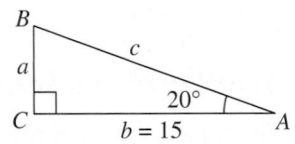

EXAMPLE 2   Finding a Side of a Right Triangle

A safety regulation states that the maximum angle of elevation for a rescue ladder is 72°. A fire department's longest ladder is 110 feet. What is the maximum safe rescue height?

Solution

A sketch is shown in Figure 4.50. From the equation $\sin A = a/c$, it follows that

$$a = c \sin A = 110 \sin 72° \approx 104.6.$$

So, the maximum safe rescue height is about 104.6 feet above the height of the fire truck.

✓ **Checkpoint** *Audio-video solution in English & Spanish at LarsonPrecalculus.com.*

A ladder that is 16 feet long leans against the side of a house. The angle of elevation of the ladder is 80°. Find the height from the top of the ladder to the ground.

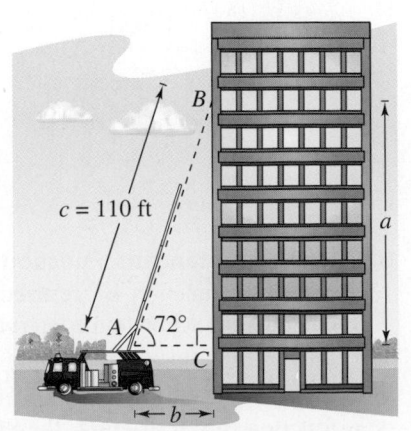

Figure 4.50

EXAMPLE 3   Finding a Side of a Right Triangle

At a point 200 feet from the base of a building, the angle of elevation to the *bottom* of a smokestack is 35°, and the angle of elevation to the *top* is 53°, as shown in Figure 4.51. Find the height *s* of the smokestack alone.

Figure 4.51

Solution

This problem involves two right triangles. For the smaller right triangle, use the fact that

$$\tan 35° = \frac{a}{200}$$

to conclude that the height of the building is

$$a = 200 \tan 35°.$$

For the larger right triangle, use the equation

$$\tan 53° = \frac{a + s}{200}$$

to conclude that

$$a + s = 200 \tan 53°.$$

So, the height of the smokestack is

$$s = 200 \tan 53° - a$$

$$= 200 \tan 53° - 200 \tan 35°$$

$$\approx 125.4 \text{ feet.}$$

✓ **Checkpoint** 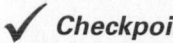 *Audio-video solution in English & Spanish at LarsonPrecalculus.com.*

At a point 65 feet from the base of a church, the angles of elevation to the bottom of the steeple and the top of the steeple are 35° and 43°, respectively. Find the height of the steeple.

EXAMPLE 4   Finding an Angle of Depression

A swimming pool is 20 meters long and 12 meters wide. The bottom of the pool is slanted so that the water depth is 1.3 meters at the shallow end and 4 meters at the deep end, as shown in Figure 4.52. Find the angle of depression (in degrees) of the bottom of the pool.

Figure 4.52

Solution

Using the tangent function, you see that

$$\tan A = \frac{\text{opp}}{\text{adj}}$$

$$= \frac{2.7}{20}$$

$$= 0.135.$$

So, the angle of depression is

$$A = \arctan 0.135 \approx 0.13419 \text{ radian} \approx 7.69°.$$

✓ **Checkpoint** *Audio-video solution in English & Spanish at LarsonPrecalculus.com.*

From the time a small airplane is 100 feet high and 1600 ground feet from its landing runway, the plane descends in a straight line to the runway. Determine the angle of descent (in degrees) of the plane.

Trigonometry and Bearings

In surveying and navigation, directions are generally given in terms of **bearings.** A bearing measures the acute angle that a path or line of sight makes with a fixed north-south line, as shown in Figure 4.53. For instance, the bearing S 35° E in Figure 4.53(a) means 35 degrees east of south.

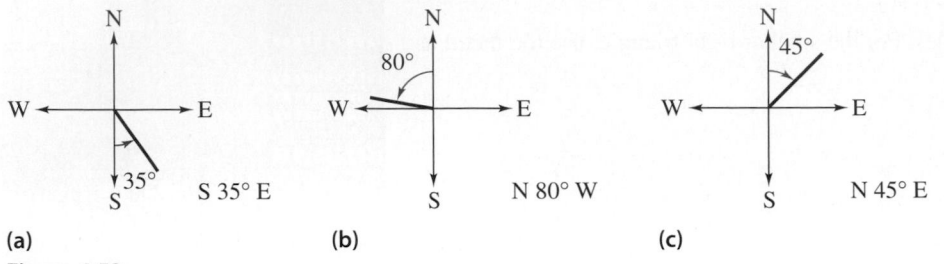

(a)   (b)   (c)

Figure 4.53

Remark

In *air navigation*, bearings are measured in degrees *clockwise* from north. Examples of air navigation bearings are shown below.

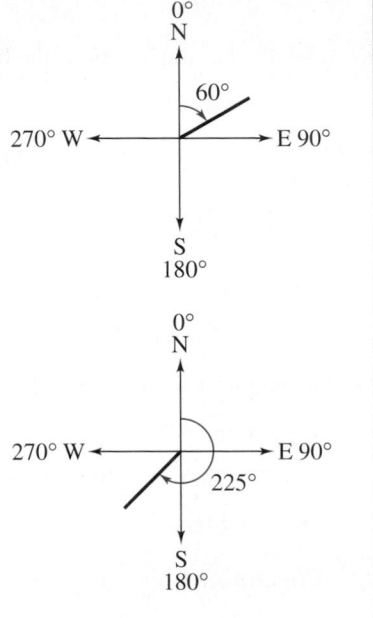

EXAMPLE 5   Finding Directions in Terms of Bearings

A ship leaves port at noon and heads due west at 20 knots, or 20 nautical miles (nm) per hour. At 2 P.M. the ship changes course to N 54° W, as shown in the figure. Find the ship's bearing and distance from the port of departure at 3 P.M.

Solution

For triangle *BCD*, you have

$$B = 90° - 54° = 36°.$$

The two sides of this triangle can be determined to be

$$b = 20 \sin 36° \qquad \text{and} \qquad d = 20 \cos 36°.$$

In triangle *ACD*, you can find angle *A* as follows.

$$\tan A = \frac{b}{d + 40} = \frac{20 \sin 36°}{20 \cos 36° + 40} \approx 0.2092494$$

$$A \approx \arctan 0.2092494 \approx 0.2062732 \text{ radian} \approx 11.82°$$

The angle with the north-south line is $90° - 11.82° = 78.18°$. So, the bearing of the ship is N 78.18° W. Finally, from triangle *ACD*, you have

$$\sin A = \frac{b}{c}$$

which yields

$$c = \frac{b}{\sin A} = \frac{20 \sin 36°}{\sin 11.82°} \approx 57.39 \text{ nautical miles.} \qquad \text{Distance from port}$$

✓ **Checkpoint** ◀))) *Audio-video solution in English & Spanish at LarsonPrecalculus.com.*

A sailboat leaves a pier heading due west at 8 knots. After 15 minutes, the sailboat changes its course to N 16° W and changes its speed to 10 knots. Find the sailboat's bearing and distance from the pier after 12 minutes on this course. ■

Harmonic Motion

The periodic nature of the trigonometric functions is useful for describing the motion of a point on an object that vibrates, oscillates, rotates, or is moved by wave motion.

For example, consider a ball that is bobbing up and down on the end of a spring, as shown in Figure 4.54. Assume that 10 centimeters is the maximum distance the ball moves vertically upward or downward from its equilibrium (at rest) position. Assume further that the time it takes for the ball to move from its maximum displacement above zero to its maximum displacement below zero and back again is

$t = 4$ seconds.

With the ideal conditions of perfect elasticity and no friction or air resistance, the ball would continue to move up and down in a uniform and regular manner.

| *Equilibrium* | *Maximum negative displacement* | *Maximum positive displacement* | **Physics Professor** |

Figure 4.54

From this spring, you can conclude that the period (time for one complete cycle) of the motion is

Period = 4 seconds

its amplitude (maximum displacement from equilibrium) is

Amplitude = 10 centimeters

and its **frequency** (number of cycles per second) is

Frequency = $\dfrac{1}{4}$ cycle per second.

Motion of this nature can be described by a sine or cosine function and is called **simple harmonic motion.**

Definition of Simple Harmonic Motion

A point that moves on a coordinate line is in **simple harmonic motion** when its distance d from the origin at time t is given by either

$$d = a \sin \omega t \quad \text{or} \quad d = a \cos \omega t$$

where a and ω are real numbers such that $\omega > 0$. The motion has amplitude $|a|$, period $2\pi/\omega$, and frequency $\omega/(2\pi)$.

EXAMPLE 6   Simple Harmonic Motion

Write an equation for the simple harmonic motion of the ball described in Figure 4.54, where the period is 4 seconds. What is the frequency of this motion?

Solution

Because the spring is at equilibrium $(d = 0)$ when $t = 0$, use the equation

$$d = a \sin \omega t.$$

Moreover, because the maximum displacement from zero is 10 and the period is 4, you have the following.

$$\text{Amplitude} = |a| = 10$$

$$\text{Period} = \frac{2\pi}{\omega} = 4 \quad \Longrightarrow \quad \omega = \frac{\pi}{2}$$

Consequently, an equation of motion is

$$d = 10 \sin \frac{\pi}{2} t.$$

Note that the choice of $a = 10$ or $a = -10$ depends on whether the ball initially moves up or down. The frequency is

$$\text{Frequency} = \frac{\omega}{2\pi} = \frac{\pi/2}{2\pi} = \frac{1}{4} \text{ cycle per second.}$$

 ✓ **Checkpoint** ◀))) *Audio-video solution in English & Spanish at LarsonPrecalculus.com.*

Find a model for simple harmonic motion that satisfies the following conditions: $d = 0$ when $t = 0$, the amplitude is 6 centimeters, and the period is 3 seconds. Then find the frequency. ■

One illustration of the relationship between sine waves and harmonic motion is the wave motion that results when a stone is dropped into a calm pool of water. The waves move outward in roughly the shape of sine (or cosine) waves, as shown in Figure 4.55. As an example, assume you are fishing and your fishing bobber is attached so that it does not move horizontally. As the waves move outward from the dropped stone, your fishing bobber will move up and down in simple harmonic motion, as shown in Figure 4.56.

Figure 4.55

Figure 4.56

EXAMPLE 7   Simple Harmonic Motion

Consider the equation for simple harmonic motion

$$d = 6 \cos \frac{3\pi}{4} t.$$

Find (a) the maximum displacement, (b) the frequency, (c) the value of d when $t = 4$, and (d) the least positive value of t for which $d = 0$.

Algebraic Solution

The equation has the form $d = a \cos \omega t$, with

$$a = 6 \quad \text{and} \quad \omega = \frac{3\pi}{4}.$$

a. The maximum displacement (from the point of equilibrium) is the amplitude. So, the maximum displacement is 6.

b. Frequency $= \dfrac{\omega}{2\pi}$

$$= \frac{3\pi/4}{2\pi}$$

$$= \frac{3}{8} \text{ cycle per unit of time}$$

c. $d = 6 \cos \left[\dfrac{3\pi}{4}(4) \right]$

$$= 6 \cos 3\pi$$

$$= 6(-1)$$

$$= -6$$

d. To find the least positive value of t for which $d = 0$, solve the equation

$$6 \cos \frac{3\pi}{4} t = 0.$$

First, divide each side by 6 to obtain

$$\cos \frac{3\pi}{4} t = 0.$$

This equation is satisfied when

$$\frac{3\pi}{4} t = \frac{\pi}{2}, \frac{3\pi}{2}, \frac{5\pi}{2}, \dots .$$

Multiply these values by

$$\frac{4}{3\pi}$$

to obtain

$$t = \tfrac{2}{3}, 2, \tfrac{10}{3}, \dots .$$

So, the least positive value of t is $t = \tfrac{2}{3}$.

Graphical Solution

Use a graphing utility in *radian* mode to graph

$$d = 6 \cos \frac{3\pi}{4} t.$$

a.

The maximum displacement from the point of equilibrium ($d = 0$) is 6.

Maximum
X=2.6666688 Y=6

b.

Y1=6cos((3π/4)x)

X=2.6666667 Y=6

The period is the time for the graph to complete one cycle, which is $t \approx 2.67$.

You can estimate the frequency as follows.

$$\text{Frequency} \approx \frac{1}{2.67} \approx 0.37 \text{ cycle per unit of time}$$

c.

Y1=6cos((3π/4)x)

X=4   Y=-6

The value of d when $t = 4$ is $d = -6$.

d.   The least positive value of t for which $d = 0$ is $t \approx 0.67$.

Zero
X=.66666667 Y=-6

✓ *Checkpoint* 🔊)) *Audio-video solution in English & Spanish at LarsonPrecalculus.com.*

Rework Example 7 for the equation $d = 4 \cos 6\pi t$.

4.8   Exercises

See *CalcChat.com* for tutorial help and worked-out solutions to odd-numbered exercises.
For instructions on how to use a graphing utility, see Appendix A.

Vocabulary and Concept Check

In Exercises 1 and 2, fill in the blank.

1. A point that moves on a coordinate line is said to be in simple _____ when its distance from the origin at time t is given by either $d = a \sin \omega t$ or $d = a \cos \omega t$.

2. A _____ measures the acute angle a path or line of sight makes with a fixed north-south line.

3. Does the bearing of N 20° E mean 20 degrees north of east?

4. What is the amplitude of the simple harmonic motion described by $d = 3 \sin \frac{\pi}{2} t$?

Procedures and Problem Solving

Solving a Right Triangle   In Exercises 5–14, solve the right triangle shown in the figure.

5. $A = 30°$, $b = 10$
6. $B = 60°$, $c = 15$
7. $B = 71°$, $b = 14$
8. $A = 7.4°$, $a = 20.5$
9. $a = 6$, $b = 12$
10. $a = 25$, $b = 37$
11. $a = 16$, $c = 54$
12. $b = 1.32$, $c = 18.9$
13. $A = 12°\ 15'$, $c = 430.5$
14. $B = 65°\ 12'$, $a = 145.5$

Finding an Altitude   In Exercises 15–18, find the altitude of the isosceles triangle shown in the figure.

15. $\theta = 52°$, $b = 8$ inches
16. $\theta = 48.5°$, $b = 13$ feet
17. $\theta = 71°\ 38'$, $b = 16$ meters
18. $\theta = 62°\ 23'45''$, $b = 3.1$ centimeters

19. **Home Maintenance**   A ladder that is 20 feet long leans against the side of a house. The angle of elevation of the ladder is 75°. Find the height from the top of the ladder to the ground.

20. **Electrical Maintenance**   An electrician is running wire from the electric box on a house to a utility pole 75 feet away. The angle of elevation to the connection on the pole is 16°. How much wire does the electrician need?

21. **ROTC**   A cadet rappelling down a cliff on a rope needs help. A cadet on the ground pulls tight on the end of the rope that hangs down from the rappelling cadet to lock the cadet in place. The length of the rope between the two cadets is 120 feet, and the angle of elevation of the rope is 66°. The cadet on the ground is holding the rope at a height of 4 feet. How high above the ground is the cadet on the rope?

22. **Architecture**   The front of an A-frame cottage has the shape of an isosceles triangle. It stands 28 feet high and the angle of elevation of its roof is 70°. What is the width of the cottage at its base?

23. **Angle of Depression**   The sonar of a navy cruiser detects a submarine that is 4000 feet from the cruiser. The angle between the water level and the submarine is 31.5° (see figure). How deep is the submarine?

24. **Topography**   A sign on the roadway at the top of a mountain indicates that for the next 4 miles the grade is 9.5° (see figure). Find the change in elevation for a car descending the 4-mile stretch.

25. Finding a Height From a point 100 feet in front of a public library, the angles of elevation to the base of the flagpole and the top of the flagpole are 28° and 39° 45', respectively (see figure). Find the height of the flagpole.

26. Architecture From a point 50 feet in front of a church, the angles of elevation to the base of the steeple and the top of the steeple are 37° and 49° 40', respectively.

(a) Draw right triangles that give a visual representation of the problem. Label the known and unknown quantities.

(b) Use a trigonometric function to write an equation involving the unknown quantity.

(c) Find the height of the steeple.

27. Marine Transportation An observer in a lighthouse 350 feet above sea level observes two ships in the same vertical plane as the lighthouse. The angles of depression to the ships are 4° and 6.5° (see figure). How far apart are the ships?

Not drawn to scale

28. Aviation A passenger in an airplane flying at an altitude of 10 kilometers sees two towns due east of the plane. The angles of depression to the towns are 28° and 55° (see figure). How far apart are the towns?

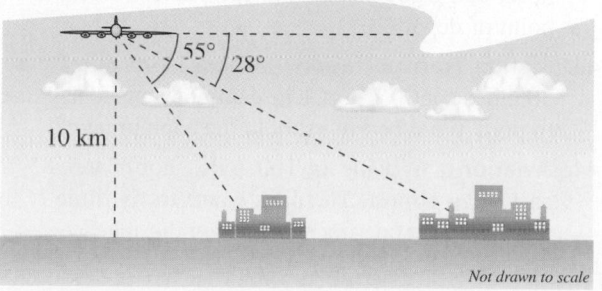

Not drawn to scale

©Andrew Zarivny/Shutterstock.com

29. Aviation The angle of elevation to a plane approaching your home is 16°. One minute later, it is 57°. You assume that the speed of the plane is 550 miles per hour. Approximate the altitude of the plane.

30. Topography While traveling across flat land, you notice a mountain directly in front of you. The angle of elevation to the peak is 2.5°. After you drive 18 miles closer to the mountain, the angle of elevation is 10°. Approximate the height of the mountain.

31. Communications A Global Positioning System satellite orbits 12,500 miles above Earth's surface (see figure). Find the angle of depression from the satellite to the horizon. Assume the radius of Earth is 4000 miles.

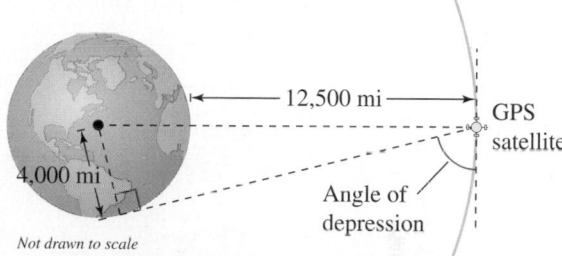

Not drawn to scale

32. Marine Transportation Find the angle of depression from the top of a lighthouse 250 feet above water level to the water line of a ship $2\frac{1}{2}$ miles offshore.

33. Aviation When an airplane leaves the runway, its angle of climb is 18° and its speed is 275 feet per second. Find the plane's altitude after 1 minute.

34. Aviation How long will it take the plane in Exercise 33 to climb to an altitude of 10,000 feet? 16,000 feet?

35. *Why you should learn it* (p. 326) The Sundial Bridge in Redding, California, is supported by cables attached to a 217-foot sundial that leans backward at a 42° angle. (See figure.)

(a) Determine the height h of the sundial.

(b) The distance d shows how far the shadow extends horizontally from the tip of the sundial. Draw the right triangle formed by d and h. Label the angle of elevation of the sun as θ.

(c) Write d as a function of θ.

(d) Find d when $\theta = 10°$, $\theta = 20°$, $\theta = 30°$, $\theta = 40°$, and $\theta = 50°$.

(e) As the angle measure increases in equal increments, does the distance also increase in equal increments? Explain.

36. Parks and Recreation The height of an outdoor basketball backboard is $12\frac{1}{2}$ feet, and the backboard casts a shadow $17\frac{1}{3}$ feet long.

(a) Draw a right triangle that gives a visual representation of the problem. Label the known and unknown quantities.

(b) Use a trigonometric function to write an equation involving the unknown angle of elevation.

(c) Find the angle of elevation of the sun.

37. Finding a Height Before a parade, you are holding one of the tethers attached to the top of a character balloon that will be in the parade. The balloon is upright, and the bottom is floating approximately 20 feet above ground level. You are standing approximately 100 feet from the balloon. (See figure.)

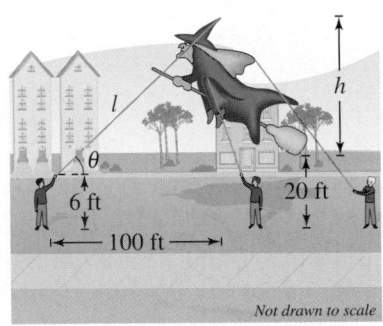

(a) Find an expression for the length l of the tether in terms of h, the height of the balloon from top to bottom.

(b) Find an expression for the angle of elevation θ from you to the top of the balloon.

(c) The angle of elevation to the top of the balloon is 35°. Find the height h.

38. Parks and Recreation The designers of a park are creating a water slide and have sketched a preliminary drawing. The length of the stairs is 30 feet, and its angle of elevation is 45°. (See figure.)

(a) Find the height h of the slide.

(b) Find the angle of depression θ from the top of the slide to the end of the slide at the ground in terms of the horizontal distance d a rider travels.

(c) The designers want the angle of depression of the slide to be at least 25° and at most 30°. Find an interval for how far a rider travels horizontally.

39. Cinema A park is showing a movie on the lawn. The base of the screen is 6 feet off the ground and the screen is 22 feet high. (See figure.)

(a) Find the angles of elevation to the top of the screen from distances of 15 feet and 100 feet.

(b) You are lying on the ground and the angle of elevation to the top of the screen is 42°. How far are you from the screen?

40. Speed Enforcement A police department has set up a speed enforcement zone on a straight length of highway. A patrol car is parked parallel to the zone, 200 feet from one end and 150 feet from the other end. (See figure.)

(a) Find the length l of the zone and the measures of the angles A and B (in degrees).

(b) Find the minimum amount of time (in seconds) it takes for a vehicle to pass through the zone without exceeding the posted speed limit of 35 miles per hour.

41. Marine Transportation A ship leaves port at noon and has a bearing of S 29° W. The ship sails at 20 knots. How many nautical miles south and how many nautical miles west does the ship travel by 6:00 P.M.?

42. Aviation An airplane flying at 600 miles per hour has a bearing of 52°. After flying for 1.5 hours, how far north and how far east has the plane traveled from its point of departure?

43. Marine Transportation A ship is 45 miles east and 30 miles south of port. The captain wants to sail directly to port. What bearing should the captain take?

44. Aviation A plane is 160 miles north and 85 miles east of an airport. The pilot wants to fly directly to the airport. What bearing should the pilot take?

45. Geomatics A surveyor wants to find the distance across a pond. The bearing from A to B is N 32° W. The surveyor walks 50 meters from A to C. At C, the bearing to B is N 68° W. (See figure.)

(a) Find the bearing from A to C.

(b) Find the distance from A to B.

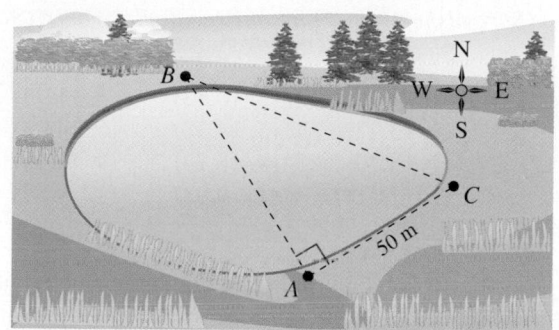

46. Forestry Fire tower A is 30 kilometers due west of fire tower B. A fire is spotted from the towers, and the bearings to the fire from A and B are N 14° E and N 34° W, respectively (see figure). Find the distance d of the fire from the line segment AB.

Geometry   In Exercises 47 and 48, find the angle α between the two nonvertical lines L_1 and L_2 (assume L_1 and L_2 are not perpendicular). The angle α satisfies the equation

$$\tan \alpha = \left| \frac{m_2 - m_1}{1 + m_2 m_1} \right|$$

where m_1 and m_2 are the slopes of L_1 and L_2, respectively.

47. L_1: $3x - 2y = 5$
   L_2: $x + y = 1$

48. L_1: $2x + y = 8$
   L_2: $x - 5y = -4$

49. Geometry Determine the angle between the diagonal of a cube and the diagonal of its base, as shown in the figure.

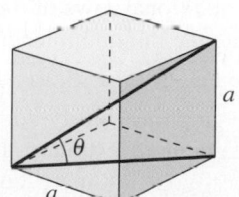

50. Geometry Determine the angle between the diagonal of a cube and its edge, as shown in the figure.

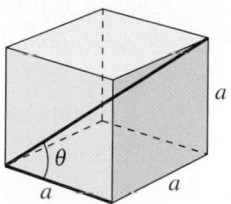

51. Mechanical Engineering Write the distance y from one side of a hexagonal nut to the opposite side as a function of r, as shown in the figure.

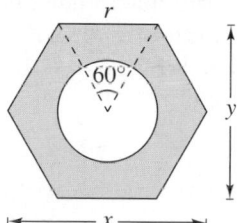

52. Mechanical Engineering The figure shows a circular piece of sheet metal of diameter 40 centimeters. The piece contains 12 equally spaced bolt holes. Determine the straight-line distance between the centers of two consecutive bolt holes.

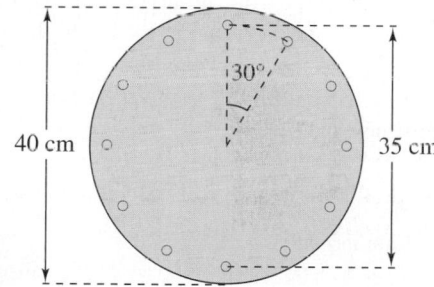

Trusses   In Exercises 53 and 54, find the lengths of the indicated members of the truss.

53. Find a and b.

54. Find a, b, and c.

Harmonic Motion In Exercises 55–58, find a model for simple harmonic motion satisfying the specified conditions.

	Displacement ($t = 0$)	Amplitude	Period
55.	0	8 centimeters	2 seconds
56.	0	3 meters	6 seconds
57.	3 inches	3 inches	1.5 seconds
58.	-2 feet	2 feet	10 seconds

Harmonic Motion In Exercises 59–62, for the simple harmonic motion described by the trigonometric function, find (a) the maximum displacement, (b) the frequency, (c) the value of d when $t = 5$, and (d) the least positive value of t for which $d = 0$. Use a graphing utility to verify your results.

59. $d = 4 \cos 8\pi t$

60. $d = \frac{1}{2} \cos 20\pi t$

61. $d = -\frac{1}{16} \sin 140\pi t$

62. $d = \frac{1}{64} \sin 792\pi t$

63. Music A point on the end of a tuning fork moves in the simple harmonic motion described by $d = a \sin \omega t$. A tuning fork for middle C has a frequency of 264 vibrations per second. Find ω.

64. Harmonic Motion A buoy oscillates in simple harmonic motion as waves go past. The buoy moves a total of 3.5 feet from its high point to its low point (see figure), and it returns to its high point every 10 seconds. Write an equation that describes the motion of the buoy, where the high point corresponds to the time $t = 0$.

65. Harmonic Motion A ball that is bobbing up and down on the end of a spring has a maximum displacement of 3 inches. Its motion (in ideal conditions) is modeled by

$$y = \tfrac{1}{4} \cos 16t, \quad t > 0$$

where y is measured in feet and t is the time in seconds.

(a) Use a graphing utility to graph the function.

(b) What is the period of the oscillations?

(c) Determine the first time the ball passes the point of equilibrium ($y = 0$).

66. Climatology The numbers of hours H of daylight in Denver, Colorado, on the 15th of each month are given by ordered pairs of the form $(t, H(t))$, where $t = 1$ represents January. A model for the data is

$$H(t) = 12.18 + 2.81 \sin\!\left(\frac{\pi t}{6} - \frac{\pi}{2}\right).$$

(Spreadsheet at LarsonPrecalculus.com) (Source: United States Navy)

(1, 9.68)	(2, 10.73)	(3, 11.93)
(4, 13.27)	(5, 14.38)	(6, 14.98)
(7, 14.70)	(8, 13.73)	(9, 12.45)
(10, 11.18)	(11, 9.98)	(12, 9.37)

(a) Use a graphing utility to graph the data points and the model in the same viewing window.

(b) What is the period of the model? Is it what you expected? Explain.

(c) What is the amplitude of the model? What does it represent in the context of the problem? Explain.

67. Home Maintenance You are washing your house. Use the following steps to find the shortest ladder that will reach over the greenhouse to the side of the house. (See figure.)

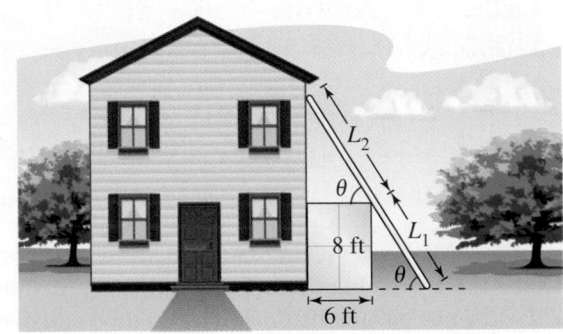

(a) Complete four rows of the table.

θ	L_1	L_2	$L_1 + L_2$
0.1	$\dfrac{8}{\sin 0.1}$	$\dfrac{6}{\cos 0.1}$	86.16
0.2	$\dfrac{8}{\sin 0.2}$	$\dfrac{6}{\cos 0.2}$	46.39

(b) Use the *table* feature of a graphing utility to generate additional rows of the table. Use the table to estimate the minimum length of the ladder.

(c) Write the length $L_1 + L_2$ as a function of θ.

(d) Use the graphing utility to graph the function. Use the graph to estimate the minimum length. How does your estimate compare with that in part (b)?

68. Irrigation Engineering The cross sections of an irrigation canal are isosceles trapezoids, where the lengths of three of the sides are 8 feet (see figure). The objective is to find the angle θ that maximizes the area of the cross sections. [*Hint:* The area of a trapezoid is given by $(h/2)(b_1 + b_2)$.]

(a) Complete seven rows of the table.

Base 1	Base 2	Altitude	Area
8	$8 + 16 \cos 10°$	$8 \sin 10°$	22.06
8	$8 + 16 \cos 20°$	$8 \sin 20°$	42.46

(b) Use the *table* feature of a graphing utility to generate additional rows of the table. Use the table to estimate the maximum cross-sectional area.

(c) Write the area A as a function of θ.

(d) Use the graphing utility to graph the function. Use the graph to estimate the maximum cross-sectional area. How does your estimate compare with that in part (b)?

69. MODELING DATA

The table shows the average sales S (in millions of dollars) of an outerwear manufacturer for each month t, where $t = 1$ represents January.

Month, t	Sales, S	Month, t	Sales, S
1	6.73	7	1.27
2	5.58	8	2.43
3	4.00	9	4.00
4	2.43	10	5.58
5	1.27	11	6.73
6	0.85	12	7.15

(a) Create a scatter plot of the data.

(b) Find a trigonometric model that fits the data. Graph the model on your scatter plot. How well does the model fit the data?

(c) What is the period of the model? Do you think it is reasonable given the context? Explain.

(d) Interpret the meaning of the model's amplitude in the context of the problem.

Conclusions

True or False? In Exercises 70–72, determine whether the statement is true or false. Justify your answer.

70. Simple harmonic motion does not involve a damping factor.

71. The tangent function can be used to model harmonic motion.

72. An example of a bearing used in aviation is S 25° W.

73. Writing Find two bearings perpendicular to N 32° E and explain how you found them.

74. HOW DO YOU SEE IT? The figure shows the displacement of an object in simple harmonic motion.

(a) What is the amplitude?

(b) What is the period?

(c) Is the equation of the simple harmonic motion of the form $d = a \sin \omega t$ or $d = a \cos \omega t$?

Cumulative Mixed Review

Equation of a Line in Standard Form In Exercises 75–78, write the standard form of the equation of the line that has the specified characteristics.

75. $m = 4$, passes through $(-1, 2)$

76. $m = -\frac{1}{2}$, passes through $\left(\frac{1}{3}, 0\right)$

77. Passes through $(-2, 6)$ and $(3, 2)$

78. Passes through $\left(\frac{1}{4}, -\frac{2}{3}\right)$ and $\left(-\frac{1}{2}, \frac{1}{3}\right)$

Finding the Domain of a Function In Exercises 79–84, find the domain of the function.

79. $f(x) = 3x + 8$ **80.** $f(x) = -x^2 - 1$

81. $g(x) = \sqrt[3]{x + 2}$

82. $g(x) = \sqrt{7 - x}$

83. $h(x) = \dfrac{1}{\sqrt{x - 6}}$

84. $h(x) = \dfrac{x}{x^2 - 9}$

4   Chapter Summary

	What did you learn?	Explanation and Examples	Review Exercises
4.1	**Describe angles** *(p. 254)*.		1, 2
	Use radian *(p. 255)* **and degree** *(p. 257)* **measure, and convert between degree and radian measure** *(p. 257)*.	To convert degrees to radians, multiply degrees by $(\pi\ \text{rad})/180°$. To convert radians to degrees, multiply radians by $180°/(\pi\ \text{rad})$.	3–34
	Use angles to model and solve real-life problems *(p. 259)*.	Angles can help you find the length of a circular arc. (See Example 5.)	35–40
4.2	**Identify the unit circle and describe its relationship to real numbers** *(p. 265)*.		41–48
	Evaluate trigonometric functions using the unit circle *(p. 266)*.	$t = \dfrac{2\pi}{3}$ corresponds to $(x, y) = \left(-\dfrac{1}{2}, \dfrac{\sqrt{3}}{2}\right)$. So, $$\cos \frac{2\pi}{3} = -\frac{1}{2},\ \sin \frac{2\pi}{3} = \frac{\sqrt{3}}{2},\ \text{and } \tan \frac{2\pi}{3} = -\sqrt{3}.$$	49–56
	Use domain and period to evaluate sine and cosine functions *(p. 268)*, **and use a calculator to evaluate trigonometric functions** *(p. 269)*.	Because $\dfrac{9\pi}{4} = 2\pi + \dfrac{\pi}{4}$, $$\sin \frac{9\pi}{4} = \sin\left(2\pi + \frac{\pi}{4}\right) = \sin \frac{\pi}{4} = \frac{\sqrt{2}}{2}.$$	57–68
4.3	**Evaluate trigonometric functions of acute angles** *(p. 273)* **and use a calculator to evaluate trigonometric functions** *(p. 275)*.	$\sin \theta = \dfrac{\text{opp}}{\text{hyp}},\quad \cos \theta = \dfrac{\text{adj}}{\text{hyp}},\quad \tan \theta = \dfrac{\text{opp}}{\text{adj}}$ $\csc \theta = \dfrac{\text{hyp}}{\text{opp}},\quad \sec \theta = \dfrac{\text{hyp}}{\text{adj}},\quad \cot \theta = \dfrac{\text{adj}}{\text{opp}}$	69–80
	Use fundamental trigonometric identities *(p. 276)*.	$\sin \theta = \dfrac{1}{\csc \theta},\quad \cos \theta = \dfrac{1}{\sec \theta},\quad \tan \theta = \dfrac{\sin \theta}{\cos \theta}$ $\sin^2 \theta + \cos^2 \theta = 1,\quad 1 + \tan^2 \theta = \sec^2 \theta$	81, 82
	Use trigonometric functions to model and solve real-life problems *(p. 278)*.	Trigonometric functions can help you find the height of a tree, the angle between a path and a river, and the length of a ramp. (See Examples 8–10.)	83, 84
4.4	**Evaluate trigonometric functions of any angle** *(p. 284)*.	Let $(3, 4)$ be a point on the terminal side of angle θ in standard position. Then $\sin \theta = \frac{4}{5}$, $\cos \theta = \frac{3}{5}$, and $\tan \theta = \frac{4}{3}$.	85–94

	What did you learn?	Explanation and Examples	Review Exercises
4.4	**Find reference angles** *(p. 286)*.	Let θ be an angle in standard position. Its reference angle is the acute angle θ' formed by the terminal side of θ and the horizontal axis.	95–102
	Evaluate trigonometric functions of real numbers *(p. 287)*.	For $\cos \frac{7\pi}{3}$, $\theta = \frac{7\pi}{3}$ lies in Quadrant I and the reference angle is $\theta' = \frac{7\pi}{3} - 2\pi = \frac{\pi}{3}$. So, $$\cos \frac{7\pi}{3} = (+)\cos \frac{\pi}{3} = \frac{1}{2}.$$	103–114
4.5	**Sketch the graphs of sine and cosine functions using amplitude and period** *(p. 292)*.		115–128
	Sketch translations of graphs of sine and cosine functions *(p. 296)*.	For $y = d + a\sin(bx - c)$ and $y = d + a\cos(bx - c)$, the constant c creates a horizontal translation, and the constant d creates a vertical translation. (See Examples 4–6.)	129–138
	Use sine and cosine functions to model real-life data *(p. 298)*.	A cosine function can help you model the depth of the water at the end of a dock at various times. (See Example 8.)	139, 140
4.6	**Sketch the graphs of tangent** *(p. 304)*, **cotangent** *(p. 306)*, **secant** *(p. 307)*, **and cosecant** *(p. 307)* **functions.**		141–162
	Sketch the graphs of damped trigonometric functions *(p. 309)*.	For $f(x) = x\cos 2x$ and $g(x) = e^{-x}\sin 4x$, the factors x and e^{-x} are called damping factors.	163–166
4.7	**Evaluate and graph inverse trigonometric functions** *(p. 315)*.	$\sin^{-1}\frac{1}{2} = \frac{\pi}{6}$, $\cos^{-1}\left(-\frac{\sqrt{2}}{2}\right) = \frac{3\pi}{4}$, $\tan^{-1}\sqrt{3} = \frac{\pi}{3}$	167–180
	Evaluate compositions of trigonometric functions *(p. 320)*.	$\cos\left(\arctan\frac{5}{12}\right) = \frac{12}{13}$ $\sin(\sin^{-1} 0.4) = 0.4$	181–184
4.8	**Solve real-life problems involving right triangles** *(p. 326)*.	A trigonometric function can help you find the height of a smokestack on top of a building. (See Example 3.)	185–187
	Solve real-life problems involving directional bearings *(p. 328)*.	Trigonometric functions can help you to find a ship's bearing and distance from a port at a given time. (See Example 5.)	188
	Solve real-life problems involving harmonic motion *(p. 329)*.	Sine or cosine functions can help you describe the motion of an object that vibrates, oscillates, rotates, or is moved by wave motion. (See Examples 6 and 7.)	189, 190

4   Review Exercises

See *CalcChat.com* for tutorial help and worked-out solutions to odd-numbered exercises. For instructions on how to use a graphing utility, see Appendix A.

4.1

Estimating an Angle   In Exercises 1 and 2, estimate the angle to the nearest one-half radian.

1.

2.

Using Radian Measure   In Exercises 3–6, (a) sketch the angle in standard position, (b) determine the quadrant in which the angle lies, and (c) list one positive and one negative coterminal angle.

3. $\dfrac{4\pi}{3}$

4. $\dfrac{11\pi}{6}$

5. $-\dfrac{5\pi}{6}$

6. $-\dfrac{9\pi}{4}$

Using Degree Measure   In Exercises 7–10, (a) sketch the angle in standard position, (b) determine the quadrant in which the angle lies, and (c) list one positive and one negative coterminal angle.

7. $45°$

8. $210°$

9. $-405°$

10. $-135°$

Converting from Degrees to Radians   In Exercises 11–14, convert the angle measure from degrees to radians. Round your answer to three decimal places.

11. $-90°$

12. $225°$

13. $478°$

14. $-151°$

Converting from Radians to Degrees   In Exercises 15–18, convert the angle measure from radians to degrees. Round your answer to three decimal places.

15. $\dfrac{5\pi}{7}$

16. $-\dfrac{3\pi}{5}$

17. -3.5

18. 1.55

Converting to Decimal Degree Form   In Exercises 19–22, use the angle-conversion capabilities of a graphing utility to convert the angle measure to decimal degree form. Round your answer to three decimal places.

19. $135°\,16'45''$

20. $-234°\,40''$

21. $-6°\,34'19''$

22. $242°\,24'9''$

Converting to D° M′ S″ Form   In Exercises 23–26, use the angle-conversion capabilities of a graphing utility to convert the angle measure to D° M′ S″ form.

23. $135.29°$

24. $25.8°$

25. $-85.36°$

26. $-327.93°$

Complementary and Supplementary Angles   In Exercises 27–34, find (if possible) the complement and supplement of the angle.

27. $\dfrac{\pi}{8}$

28. $\dfrac{\pi}{12}$

29. $\dfrac{7\pi}{10}$

30. $\dfrac{8\pi}{5}$

31. $5°$

32. $84°$

33. $253°$

34. $108°$

Finding an Angle   In Exercises 35 and 36, find the angle in radians.

35.

36.

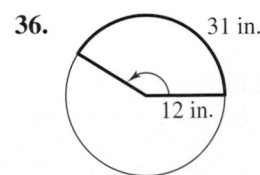

37. Finding Arc Length   Find the length of the arc on a circle with a radius of 20 meters intercepted by a central angle of $138°$.

38. Finding Arc Length   Find the length of the arc on a circle with a radius of 15 centimeters intercepted by a central angle of $60°$.

39. Finding Linear Speed   The radius of a compact disc is 6 centimeters. Find the linear speed of a point on the circumference of the disc when it is rotating at a speed of 500 revolutions per minute.

40. Finding Angular Speed   A car is moving at a rate of 28 miles per hour, and the diameter of its wheels is about $2\frac{1}{3}$ feet.

  (a) Find the number of revolutions per minute the wheels are rotating.

  (b) Find the angular speed of the wheels in radians per minute.

4.2

Finding a Point on the Unit Circle   In Exercises 41–48, find the point (x, y) on the unit circle that corresponds to the real number t.

41. $t = \dfrac{7\pi}{4}$

42. $t = \dfrac{3\pi}{4}$

43. $t = \dfrac{5\pi}{6}$

44. $t = \dfrac{4\pi}{3}$

45. $t = -\dfrac{2\pi}{3}$

46. $t = -\dfrac{7\pi}{6}$

47. $t = -\dfrac{5\pi}{4}$

48. $t = -\dfrac{5\pi}{6}$

Evaluating Trigonometric Functions In Exercises 49–56, evaluate (if possible) the six trigonometric functions of the real number.

49. $t = 4\pi/3$

50. $t = 7\pi/6$

51. $t = 4\pi$

52. $t = -\pi$

53. $t = -11\pi/6$

54. $t = -2\pi/3$

55. $t = -5\pi/3$

56. $t = -\pi/4$

Using the Period to Evaluate Sine and Cosine In Exercises 57–60, evaluate the trigonometric function using its period as an aid.

57. $\cos 6\pi$

58. $\sin \dfrac{11\pi}{4}$

59. $\sin\left(-\dfrac{17\pi}{6}\right)$

60. $\cos\left(-\dfrac{13\pi}{3}\right)$

Using the Value of a Trigonometric Function In Exercises 61–64, use the value of the trigonometric function to evaluate the indicated functions.

61. $\sin t = \frac{3}{5}$
   (a) $\sin(-t)$
   (b) $\csc(-t)$

62. $\cos t = \frac{5}{13}$
   (a) $\cos(-t)$
   (b) $\sec(-t)$

63. $\sin(-t) = -\frac{2}{3}$
   (a) $\sin t$
   (b) $\csc t$

64. $\cos(-t) = \frac{5}{8}$
   (a) $\cos t$
   (b) $\sec(-t)$

Using a Calculator In Exercises 65–68, use a calculator to evaluate the expression. Round your answer to four decimal places.

65. $\cos \dfrac{5\pi}{3}$

66. $\tan\left(-\dfrac{11\pi}{6}\right)$

67. $\cot 2.3$

68. $\sec 4.5$

 4.3

Evaluating Trigonometric Functions In Exercises 69–76, find the exact values of the six trigonometric functions of the angle θ.

69.

70.

71.

72.
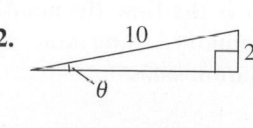

73. $\sin \theta = \frac{7}{10}$

74. $\cos \theta = \frac{2}{3}$

75. $\tan \theta = \frac{1}{4}$

76. $\cot \theta = \frac{9}{40}$

Using a Calculator In Exercises 77–80, use a calculator to evaluate each function. Round your answers to four decimal places.

77. (a) $\cos 84°$

   (b) $\sin 6°$

78. (a) $\csc 52° \, 12'$

   (b) $\sec 66° \, 7'$

79. (a) $\cos \dfrac{\pi}{4}$

   (b) $\sec \dfrac{\pi}{4}$

80. (a) $\tan \dfrac{3\pi}{20}$

   (b) $\cot \dfrac{3\pi}{20}$

Using Trigonometric Identities In Exercises 81 and 82, use trigonometric identities to transform one side of the equation into the other.

81. $\cos \theta \sec \theta = 1$

82. $\dfrac{\cot \theta + \tan \theta}{\cot \theta} = \sec^2 \theta$

83. **Surveying** A surveyor is trying to determine the width of a river. From point P, the surveyor walks downstream 125 feet and sights to point Q. From this sighting, it is determined that $\theta = 62°$ (see figure). How wide is the river?

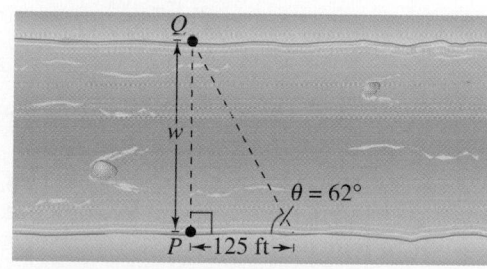

84. **Architecture** An escalator 152 feet in length rises to a platform and makes a 30° angle with the ground.

   (a) Draw a right triangle that gives a visual representation of the problem. Show the known quantities and use a variable to indicate the height of the platform above the ground.

   (b) Use a trigonometric function to write an equation involving the unknown quantity.

   (c) Find the height of the platform above the ground.

4.4

Evaluating Trigonometric Functions In Exercises 85–90, the point is on the terminal side of an angle in standard position. Determine the exact values of the six trigonometric functions of the angle.

85. $(12, 16)$

86. $(2, 10)$

87. $(-7, 2)$

88. $(3, -7)$

89. $\left(\frac{2}{3}, \frac{5}{8}\right)$

90. $\left(-\frac{10}{3}, -\frac{2}{3}\right)$

Evaluating Trigonometric Functions In Exercises 91–94, find the values of the other five trigonometric functions of θ satisfying the given conditions.

91. $\sec \theta = \frac{6}{5}$, $\tan \theta < 0$

92. $\sin \theta = \frac{3}{8}$, $\cos \theta < 0$

93. $\cos \theta = -\frac{2}{5}$, $\sin \theta > 0$

94. $\tan \theta = -\frac{12}{5}$, $\sin \theta > 0$

Finding a Reference Angle In Exercises 95–102, find the reference angle θ'. Sketch θ in standard position and label θ'.

95. $\theta = 330°$ **96.** $\theta = 210°$

97. $\theta = \dfrac{5\pi}{4}$ **98.** $\theta = \dfrac{9\pi}{4}$

99. $\theta = -264°$ **100.** $\theta = -635°$

101. $\theta = -\dfrac{6\pi}{5}$ **102.** $\theta = -\dfrac{17\pi}{3}$

Trigonometric Functions of a Nonacute Angle In Exercises 103–110, evaluate the sine, cosine, and tangent of the angle without using a calculator.

103. $240°$ **104.** $315°$

105. $-225°$ **106.** $-315°$

107. 4π **108.** $\dfrac{7\pi}{3}$

109. $-\dfrac{9\pi}{4}$ **110.** -3π

Using a Calculator In Exercises 111–114, use a calculator to evaluate the trigonometric function. Round your answer to four decimal places.

111. $\tan 33°$ **112.** $\csc 105°$

113. $\sec \dfrac{12\pi}{5}$ **114.** $\sin\left(-\dfrac{\pi}{9}\right)$

4.5

Sketching Graphs of Sine and Cosine Functions In Exercises 115–118, sketch the graph of the function.

115. $f(x) = 6 \sin x$ **116.** $f(x) = 7 \cos x$

117. $f(x) = \frac{1}{5} \cos x$ **118.** $f(x) = \frac{3}{5} \sin x$

Finding the Period and Amplitude In Exercises 119–122, find the period and amplitude.

119. $\boxed{y = 5 \cos \pi x}$ **120.** $\boxed{y = -\dfrac{3}{2} \sin \dfrac{x}{2}}$

          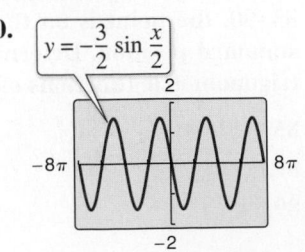

121. $\boxed{y = -3.4 \sin 2x}$ **122.** $\boxed{y = 4 \cos \dfrac{\pi x}{2}}$

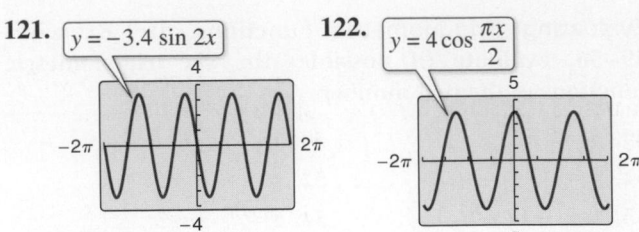

Graphing Sine and Cosine Functions In Exercises 123–134, sketch the graph of the function. (Include two full periods.)

123. $f(x) = 3 \cos 2\pi x$ **124.** $f(x) = -2 \sin \pi x$

125. $f(x) = 5 \sin\left(-\dfrac{2x}{5}\right)$ **126.** $f(x) = 8 \cos\left(-\dfrac{x}{4}\right)$

127. $f(x) = -\dfrac{5}{2} \cos \dfrac{x}{4}$ **128.** $f(x) = -\dfrac{1}{2} \sin \dfrac{\pi x}{4}$

129. $f(x) = \frac{5}{2} \sin(x - \pi)$

130. $f(x) = 3 \cos(x + \pi)$

131. $f(x) = 2 - \cos \dfrac{\pi x}{2}$

132. $f(x) = \frac{1}{2} \sin \pi x - 3$

133. $f(x) = -3 \sin\left(2x - \dfrac{\pi}{4}\right) - 1$

134. $f(x) = 4 - 2 \cos(4x + \pi)$

Finding an Equation of a Graph In Exercises 135–138, find a, b, and c for the function $f(x) = a \cos(bx - c)$ such that the graph of f matches the graph shown.

135.   **136.**

137.   **138.**

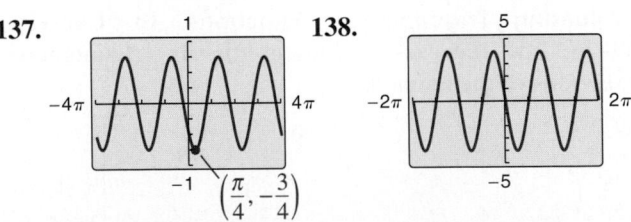

$\left(\dfrac{\pi}{4}, -\dfrac{3}{4}\right)$

Economics In Exercises 139 and 140, use a graphing utility to graph the sales function over 1 year, where S is the sales (in thousands of units) of a seasonal product, and t is the time (in months), with $t = 1$ corresponding to January. Determine the months of maximum and minimum sales.

139. $S = 48.4 - 6.1 \cos \dfrac{\pi t}{6}$

140. $S = 56.25 + 9.50 \sin \dfrac{\pi t}{6}$

4.6

Library of Parent Functions In Exercises 141–154, sketch the graph of the function. (Include two full periods.)

141. $f(x) = -\tan\dfrac{\pi x}{4}$

142. $f(x) = 4\tan \pi x$

143. $f(x) = \dfrac{1}{4}\tan 2x - 1$

144. $f(x) = 2 + 2\tan\dfrac{x}{3}$

145. $f(x) = 3\cot\dfrac{x}{2}$

146. $f(x) = \dfrac{1}{2}\cot\dfrac{\pi x}{2}$

147. $f(x) = \dfrac{1}{2}\cot\left(x - \dfrac{\pi}{2}\right)$

148. $f(x) = 4\cot\left(x + \dfrac{\pi}{4}\right)$

149. $f(x) = 4\sec x$

150. $f(x) = -\dfrac{1}{2}\csc x$

151. $f(x) = \dfrac{1}{4}\csc 2x$

152. $f(x) = \dfrac{1}{2}\sec 2\pi x$

153. $f(x) = \sec\left(x + \dfrac{\pi}{4}\right)$

154. $f(x) = \dfrac{1}{2}\csc(2x - \pi)$

Comparing Trigonometric Graphs In Exercises 155–162, use a graphing utility to graph the function. (Include two full periods.) Graph the corresponding reciprocal function in the same viewing window. Compare the graphs.

155. $f(x) = \dfrac{1}{4}\sec\dfrac{\pi x}{2}$

156. $f(x) = \csc\left(x + \dfrac{\pi}{4}\right)$

157. $f(x) = 4\csc(2x - \pi)$

158. $f(x) = -2\sec(4x + \pi)$

159. $f(x) = 2\sec(x - \pi)$

160. $f(x) = 2\csc(x - \pi)$

161. $f(x) = -\csc\left(3x - \dfrac{\pi}{2}\right)$

162. $f(x) = \dfrac{1}{3}\sec\left(2x - \dfrac{\pi}{4}\right)$

Analyzing a Damped Trigonometric Graph In Exercises 163–166, use a graphing utility to graph the function and the damping factor of the function in the same viewing window. Then, analyze the graph of the function using the method in Example 6 in Section 4.6.

163. $f(x) = e^x \sin 2x$

164. $f(x) = e^x \cos x$

165. $f(x) = 2x \cos x$

166. $f(x) = x \sin \pi x$

4.7

Evaluating an Inverse Trigonometric Function In Exercises 167–170, find the exact value of each expression without using a calculator.

167. (a) $\arcsin\left(-\dfrac{1}{2}\right)$ (b) $\arccos\left(-\dfrac{\sqrt{3}}{2}\right)$

168. (a) $\arcsin\left(-\dfrac{\sqrt{3}}{2}\right)$ (b) $\arccos\left(-\dfrac{1}{2}\right)$

169. (a) $\cos^{-1} 0$ (b) $\tan^{-1}(-1)$

170. (a) $\cos^{-1} 1$ (b) $\tan^{-1}\left(-\sqrt{3}\right)$

Calculators and Inverse Trigonometric Functions In Exercises 171–178, use a calculator to approximate the value of the expression. Round your answer to the nearest hundredth.

171. $\arccos 0.42$ **172.** $\arcsin 0.63$

173. $\sin^{-1}(-0.94)$ **174.** $\cos^{-1}(-0.12)$

175. $\arctan 21$ **176.** $\arctan(-12)$

177. $\tan^{-1} 0.81$ **178.** $\tan^{-1} 6.4$

Using an Inverse Trigonometric Function In Exercises 179 and 180, use an inverse trigonometric function to write θ as a function of x.

179.

180.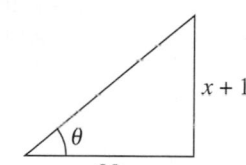

Writing an Algebraic Expression In Exercises 181–184, write an algebraic expression that is equivalent to the expression.

181. $\sec(\arcsin x)$

182. $\csc(\arcsin 10x)$

183. $\sin\left(\arccos\dfrac{x^2}{4 - x^2}\right)$

184. $\tan\left(\arccos\dfrac{x}{2}\right)$

4.8

185. Topography A train travels 3.5 kilometers on a straight track with a grade of $1°\,10'$ (see figure). What is the vertical rise of the train in that distance?

186. Topography A road sign at the top of a mountain indicates that for the next 4 miles the grade is 12%. Find the angle of the grade and the change in elevation for a car descending the 4-mile stretch.

187. Aviation A passenger in an airplane flying at an altitude of 37,000 feet sees two towns due west of the airplane. The angles of depression to the towns are 32° and 76° (see figure). How far apart are the towns?

32°
76°
37,000 ft
Not drawn to scale

188. Aviation From city A to city B, a plane flies 650 miles at a bearing of 48°. From city B to city C, the plane flies 810 miles at a bearing of 115°. Find the distance from A to C and the bearing from A to C.

189. Harmonic Motion A buoy oscillates in simple harmonic motion as waves go past. The buoy moves a total of 6 feet from its high point to its low point, returning to its high point every 15 seconds (see figure). Write an equation that describes the motion of the buoy, where the high point corresponds to the time $t = 0$.

High point
Equilibrium
6 ft
Low point

190. Harmonic Motion Your fishing bobber is oscillating in simple harmonic motion caused by waves. Your bobber moves a total of 7 inches from its high point to its low point and returns to its high point every 2 seconds. Write an equation modeling the motion of your bobber, where the high point corresponds to the time $t = 0$.

Conclusions

True or False? **In Exercises 191–194, determine whether the statement is true or false. Justify your answer.**

191. $y = \sin \theta$ is not a function because $\sin 30° = \sin 150°$.

192. The equation $y = \cos x$ does not have an inverse function on the interval $-\dfrac{\pi}{2} \le x \le \dfrac{\pi}{2}$.

193. You can use the cotangent function to model simple harmonic motion.

194. The sine of any nonacute angle θ is equal to the sine of the reference angle for θ.

195. Numerical Analysis A 3000-pound automobile is negotiating a circular interchange of radius 300 feet at a speed of s miles per hour (see figure). The relationship between the speed and the angle θ (in degrees) at which the roadway should be banked so that no lateral frictional force is exerted on the tires is $\tan \theta = 0.672s^2/3000$.

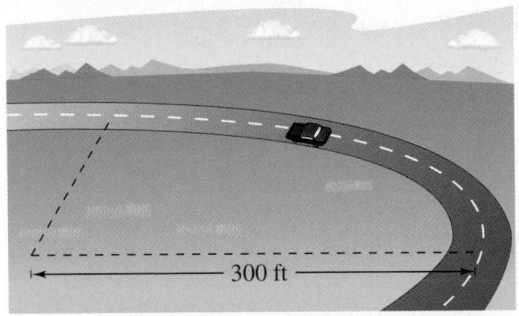

300 ft

(a) Use a graphing utility to complete the table.

s	10	20	30	40	50	60
θ						

(b) In the table, s is incremented by 10, but θ does not increase by equal increments. Explain.

196. Exploration Using calculus, it can be shown that the secant function can be approximated by the polynomial

$$\sec x \approx 1 + \frac{x^2}{2!} + \frac{5x^4}{4!}$$

where x is in radians. Use a graphing utility to graph the secant function and its polynomial approximation in the same viewing window. How do the graphs compare?

197. Exploration Using calculus, it can be shown that the arctangent function can be approximated by the polynomial

$$\arctan x \approx x - \frac{x^3}{3} + \frac{x^5}{5} - \frac{x^7}{7}$$

where x is in radians.

(a) Use a graphing utility to graph the arctangent function and its polynomial approximation in the same viewing window. How do the graphs compare?

(b) Study the pattern in the polynomial approximation of the arctangent function and predict the next term. Then repeat part (a). How does the accuracy of the approximation change when an additional term is added?

4 Chapter Test

See *CalcChat.com* for tutorial help and worked-out solutions to odd-numbered exercises. For instructions on how to use a graphing utility, see Appendix A.

Take this test as you would take a test in class. After you are finished, check your work against the answers given in the back of the book.

1. Consider an angle that measures $\dfrac{5\pi}{3}$ radians.

    (a) Sketch the angle in standard position.

    (b) Determine two coterminal angles (one positive and one negative).

    (c) Convert the angle to degree measure.

2. A truck is moving at a rate of 100 kilometers per hour, and the diameter of its wheels is 1.25 meters. Find the angular speed of the wheels in radians per second.

3. Find the exact values of the six trigonometric functions of the angle θ shown in the figure.

4. Given that $\tan \theta = \frac{7}{2}$ and θ is an acute angle, find the other five trigonometric functions of θ.

5. Determine the reference angle θ' of the angle $\theta = 255°$. Sketch θ in standard position and label θ'.

6. Determine the quadrant in which θ lies when $\sec \theta < 0$ and $\tan \theta > 0$.

7. Find two exact values of θ in degrees $(0 \le \theta < 360°)$ when $\cos \theta = -\sqrt{3}/2$.

8. Use a calculator to approximate two values of θ in radians $(0 \le \theta < 2\pi)$ for which $\csc \theta = 1.030$. Round your answer to two decimal places.

9. Find the five remaining trigonometric functions of θ, given that $\cos \theta = -\frac{3}{5}$ and $\sin \theta > 0$.

Figure for 3

In Exercises 10–15, sketch the graph of the function. (Include two full periods.)

10. $g(x) = -2 \sin \dfrac{2x}{3}$

11. $f(x) = \dfrac{1}{2} \tan 4x$

12. $f(x) = \frac{1}{2} \sec(x - \pi) - 4$

13. $f(x) = 2 \cos(-2x) + 3$

14. $f(x) = 2 \cot\left(x - \dfrac{\pi}{2}\right)$

15. $f(x) = 2 \csc\left(x + \dfrac{\pi}{2}\right)$

In Exercises 16 and 17, use a graphing utility to graph the function. If the function is periodic, find its period.

16. $y = \sin 2\pi x + 2 \cos \pi x$

17. $y = 6e^{-0.12t} \cos(0.25t), \quad 0 \le t \le 32$

18. Find a, b, and c for the function $f(x) = a \cos(bx - c)$ such that the graph of f matches the graph at the right.

19. Find the exact value of $\tan\left(\arccos \frac{2}{3}\right)$ without using a calculator.

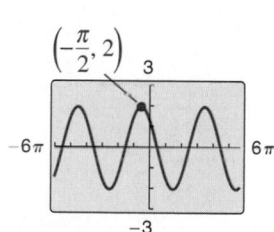

Figure for 18

In Exercises 20–22, use a graphing utility to graph the function.

20. $f(x) = 2 \arcsin \dfrac{x}{2}$

21. $f(x) = 2 \arccos x$

22. $f(x) = \arctan \dfrac{x}{2}$

23. A plane is 64 miles north and 80 miles east of an airport. What bearing should the pilot take to fly directly to the airport?

24. Write an equation for the simple harmonic motion of a ball on a spring that starts at its lowest point of 6 inches below equilibrium, bounces to its maximum height of 6 inches above equilibrium, and returns to its lowest point in a total of 2 seconds.

Library of Parent Functions Review

In Exercises 1–12, fill in the blank to identify the parent function represented by the graph.

1. $f(x) =$ _____

2. $f(x) =$ _____

3. $f(x) =$ _____

4. $f(x) =$ _____

5. $f(x) =$ _____

6. $f(x) =$ _____

7. $f(x) =$ _____

8. $f(x) =$ _____

9. $f(x) =$ _____

10. $f(x) =$ _____

11. $f(x) =$ _____

12. $f(x) =$ _____

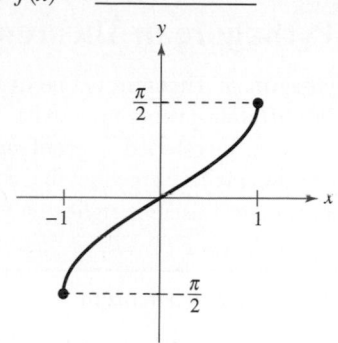

In Exercises 13–18, identify the parent function and describe the transformation shown in the graph. Write an equation for the graphed function. (There may be more than one correct answer.)

13.

14.

15.

16.

17.

18.

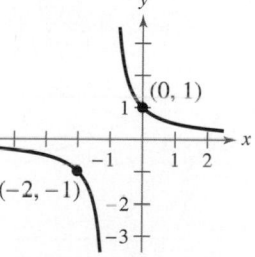

In Exercises 19 and 20, determine which function is represented by the graph. Do not use a calculator.

19. (a) $y = -\dfrac{3}{2}\sin x$

(b) $y = -\dfrac{3}{2}\cos x$

(c) $y = -\sin\dfrac{3}{2}x$

(d) $y = \cos\dfrac{3}{2}x$

20. (a) $y = \dfrac{1}{2}\tan x$

(b) $y = \dfrac{1}{2}\cot x$

(c) $y = \tan\dfrac{x}{2}$

(d) $y = \cot\dfrac{x}{2}$

In Exercises 21–24, sketch the graph of the function by hand.

21. $y = (x - 1)^2 - 4$

22. $y = -(x - 4)^3$

23. $y = |x + 1| - 3$

24. $y = -2\cos 2x$

Proofs in Mathematics

The Pythagorean Theorem

The Pythagorean Theorem is one of the most famous theorems in mathematics. More than 100 different proofs now exist. James A. Garfield, the twentieth president of the United States, developed a proof of the Pythagorean Theorem in 1876. His proof, shown below, involves the fact that a trapezoid can be formed from two congruent right triangles and an isosceles right triangle.

The Pythagorean Theorem

In a right triangle, the sum of the squares of the lengths of the legs is equal to the square of the length of the hypotenuse, where a and b are the legs and c is the hypotenuse.

$$a^2 + b^2 = c^2$$

Proof

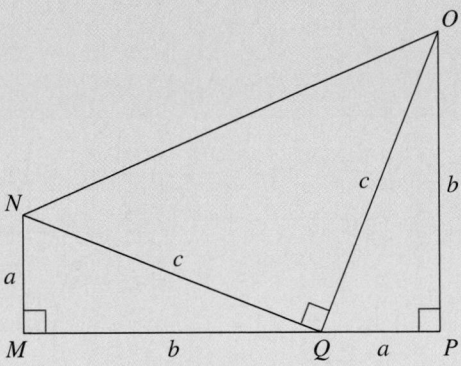

$$\begin{array}{c} \text{Area of} \\ \text{trapezoid } MNOP \end{array} = \begin{array}{c} \text{Area of} \\ \triangle MNQ \end{array} + \begin{array}{c} \text{Area of} \\ \triangle PQO \end{array} + \begin{array}{c} \text{Area of} \\ \triangle NOQ \end{array}$$

$$\frac{1}{2}(a + b)(a + b) = \frac{1}{2}ab + \frac{1}{2}ab + \frac{1}{2}c^2$$

$$\frac{1}{2}(a + b)(a + b) = ab + \frac{1}{2}c^2$$

$$(a + b)(a + b) = 2ab + c^2$$

$$a^2 + 2ab + b^2 = 2ab + c^2$$

$$a^2 + b^2 = c^2$$

5 Analytic Trigonometry

Section 5.3, Example 12
Minimum Surface Area
of a Honeycomb

5.1   Using Fundamental Identities

5.2   Verifying Trigonometric Identities

5.3   Solving Trigonometric Equations

5.4   Sum and Difference Formulas

5.5   Multiple-Angle and Product-to-Sum Formulas

©iStockphoto.com/skodonnell

5.1   Using Fundamental Identities

Introduction

In Chapter 4, you studied the basic definitions, properties, graphs, and applications of the individual trigonometric functions. In this chapter, you will learn how to use the fundamental identities to do the following.

1. Evaluate trigonometric functions.

2. Simplify trigonometric expressions.

3. Develop additional trigonometric identities.

4. Solve trigonometric equations.

Fundamental Trigonometric Identities

Reciprocal Identities

$$\sin u = \frac{1}{\csc u} \qquad \cos u = \frac{1}{\sec u} \qquad \tan u = \frac{1}{\cot u}$$

$$\csc u = \frac{1}{\sin u} \qquad \sec u = \frac{1}{\cos u} \qquad \cot u = \frac{1}{\tan u}$$

Quotient Identities

$$\tan u = \frac{\sin u}{\cos u} \qquad \cot u = \frac{\cos u}{\sin u}$$

Pythagorean Identities

$$\sin^2 u + \cos^2 u = 1$$

$$1 + \tan^2 u = \sec^2 u$$

$$1 + \cot^2 u = \csc^2 u$$

Cofunction Identities

$$\sin\left(\frac{\pi}{2} - u\right) = \cos u \qquad \cos\left(\frac{\pi}{2} - u\right) = \sin u$$

$$\tan\left(\frac{\pi}{2} - u\right) = \cot u \qquad \cot\left(\frac{\pi}{2} - u\right) = \tan u$$

$$\sec\left(\frac{\pi}{2} - u\right) = \csc u \qquad \csc\left(\frac{\pi}{2} - u\right) = \sec u$$

Even/Odd Identities

$$\sin(-u) = -\sin u \qquad \csc(-u) = -\csc u$$

$$\cos(-u) = \cos u \qquad \sec(-u) = \sec u$$

$$\tan(-u) = -\tan u \qquad \cot(-u) = -\cot u$$

Pythagorean identities are sometimes used in radical form such as

$$\sin u = \pm\sqrt{1 - \cos^2 u}$$

or

$$\tan u = \pm\sqrt{\sec^2 u - 1}$$

where the sign depends on the choice of u.

Using the Fundamental Identities

One common use of trigonometric identities is to use given values of trigonometric functions to evaluate other trigonometric functions.

EXAMPLE 1   Using Identities to Evaluate Functions

Use the values $\sec u = -\frac{3}{2}$ and $\tan u > 0$ to find the values of all six trigonometric functions.

Solution

Using a reciprocal identity, you have

$$\cos u = \frac{1}{\sec u} = \frac{1}{-3/2} = -\frac{2}{3}.$$

Using a Pythagorean identity, you have

$$\sin^2 u = 1 - \cos^2 u \qquad \text{Pythagorean identity}$$

$$= 1 - \left(-\frac{2}{3}\right)^2 \qquad \text{Substitute } -\frac{2}{3} \text{ for } \cos u.$$

$$= 1 - \frac{4}{9} \qquad \text{Evaluate power.}$$

$$= \frac{5}{9}. \qquad \text{Simplify.}$$

Because $\sec u < 0$ and $\tan u > 0$, it follows that u lies in Quadrant III. Moreover, because $\sin u$ is negative when u is in Quadrant III, choose the negative root to obtain $\sin u = -\sqrt{5}/3$. Now, knowing the values of the sine and cosine, you can find the values of all six trigonometric functions.

$$\sin u = -\frac{\sqrt{5}}{3} \qquad\qquad \csc u = \frac{1}{\sin u} = -\frac{3}{\sqrt{5}} = -\frac{3\sqrt{5}}{5}$$

$$\cos u = -\frac{2}{3} \qquad\qquad \sec u = \frac{1}{\cos u} = -\frac{3}{2}$$

$$\tan u = \frac{\sin u}{\cos u} = \frac{-\sqrt{5}/3}{-2/3} = \frac{\sqrt{5}}{2} \qquad \cot u = \frac{1}{\tan u} = \frac{2}{\sqrt{5}} = \frac{2\sqrt{5}}{5}$$

✓ **Checkpoint** Audio-video solution in English & Spanish at LarsonPrecalculus.com.

Use the values $\tan x = \frac{1}{3}$ and $\cos x < 0$ to find the values of all six trigonometric functions.

EXAMPLE 2   Simplifying a Trigonometric Expression

To simplify $\sin x \cos^2 x - \sin x$, factor out the common monomial factor $\sin x$ and then use a fundamental identity.

$$\sin x \cos^2 x - \sin x = \sin x(\cos^2 x - 1) \qquad \text{Factor out monomial factor.}$$

$$= -\sin x(1 - \cos^2 x) \qquad \text{Factor out } -1.$$

$$= -\sin x(\sin^2 x) \qquad \text{Pythagorean identity}$$

$$= -\sin^3 x \qquad \text{Multiply.}$$

✓ **Checkpoint** Audio-video solution in English & Spanish at LarsonPrecalculus.com.

Simplify $\cos^2 x \csc x - \csc x$.

Technology Tip

You can use a graphing utility to check the result of Example 2. To do this, enter

$$y_1 = \sin x \cos^2 x - \sin x$$

and

$$y_2 = -\sin^3 x.$$

Select the *line* style for y_1 and the *path* style for y_2. Now, graph both equations in the same viewing window. The two graphs *appear* to coincide, so the expressions *appear* to be equivalent. Remember that in order to be certain that two expressions are equivalent, you need to show their equivalence algebraically, as in Example 2.

When factoring trigonometric expressions, it is helpful to find a polynomial form that fits the expression, as shown in Example 3.

EXAMPLE 3   Factoring Trigonometric Expressions

Factor (a) $\sec^2 \theta - 1$ and (b) $4 \tan^2 \theta + \tan \theta - 3$.

Solution

a. This expression is a difference of two squares, which factors as

$$\sec^2 \theta - 1 = (\sec \theta - 1)(\sec \theta + 1).$$

b. This expression has the polynomial form $ax^2 + bx + c$, and it factors as

$$4 \tan^2 \theta + \tan \theta - 3 = (4 \tan \theta - 3)(\tan \theta + 1).$$

✓ **Checkpoint** Audio-video solution in English & Spanish at LarsonPrecalculus.com.

Factor (a) $1 - \cos^2 \theta$ and (b) $2 \csc^2 \theta - 7 \csc \theta + 6$.

On occasion, factoring or simplifying can best be done by first rewriting the expression in terms of just *one* trigonometric function or in terms of *sine or cosine alone*. These strategies are illustrated in Examples 4 and 5.

EXAMPLE 4   Factoring a Trigonometric Expression

Factor $\csc^2 x - \cot x - 3$.

Solution

Use the identity $\csc^2 x = 1 + \cot^2 x$ to rewrite the expression in terms of the cotangent.

$$\csc^2 x - \cot x - 3 = (1 + \cot^2 x) - \cot x - 3 \qquad \text{Pythagorean identity}$$

$$= \cot^2 x - \cot x - 2 \qquad \text{Combine like terms.}$$

$$= (\cot x - 2)(\cot x + 1) \qquad \text{Factor.}$$

✓ **Checkpoint** Audio-video solution in English & Spanish at LarsonPrecalculus.com.

Factor $\sec^2 x + 3 \tan x + 1$.

EXAMPLE 5   Simplifying a Trigonometric Expression

See LarsonPrecalculus.com for an interactive version of this type of example.

Simplify $\sin t + \cot t \cos t$.

Solution

Begin by rewriting $\cot t$ in terms of sine and cosine.

$$\sin t + \cot t \cos t = \sin t + \left(\frac{\cos t}{\sin t} \right) \cos t \qquad \text{Quotient identity}$$

$$= \frac{\sin^2 t + \cos^2 t}{\sin t} \qquad \text{Add fractions.}$$

$$= \frac{1}{\sin t} \qquad \text{Pythagorean identity}$$

$$= \csc t \qquad \text{Reciprocal identity}$$

✓ **Checkpoint** Audio-video solution in English & Spanish at LarsonPrecalculus.com.

Simplify $\csc x - \cos x \cot x$.

Technology Tip

You can use the *table* feature of a graphing utility to check the result of Example 5. To do this, enter

$$y_1 = \sin x + \left(\frac{\cos x}{\sin x} \right) \cos x$$

and

$$y_2 = \frac{1}{\sin x}.$$

Now, create a table that shows the values of y_1 and y_2 for different values of x. The values of y_1 and y_2 *appear* to be identical, so the expressions *appear* to be equivalent. To show that the expressions are equivalent, you need to show their equivalence algebraically, as in Example 5.

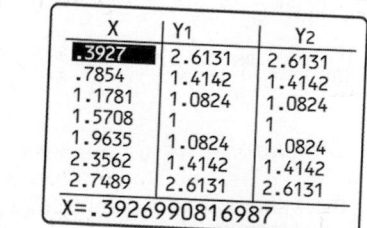

X	Y1	Y2
.3927	2.6131	2.6131
.7854	1.4142	1.4142
1.1781	1.0824	1.0824
1.5708	1	1
1.9635	1.0824	1.0824
2.3562	1.4142	1.4142
2.7489	2.6131	2.6131

X=.3926990816987

The next two examples involve techniques for rewriting expressions in forms that are used in calculus.

EXAMPLE 6   Rewriting a Trigonometric Expression

Rewrite $\dfrac{1}{1 + \sin x}$ so that it is *not* in fractional form.

Solution

From the Pythagorean identity

$$\cos^2 x = 1 - \sin^2 x = (1 - \sin x)(1 + \sin x)$$

you can see that multiplying both the numerator and the denominator by $(1 - \sin x)$ will produce a monomial denominator.

$$\frac{1}{1 + \sin x} = \frac{1}{1 + \sin x} \cdot \frac{1 - \sin x}{1 - \sin x} \qquad \text{Multiply numerator and denominator by } (1 - \sin x).$$

$$= \frac{1 - \sin x}{1 - \sin^2 x} \qquad \text{Multiply.}$$

$$= \frac{1 - \sin x}{\cos^2 x} \qquad \text{Pythagorean identity}$$

$$= \frac{1}{\cos^2 x} - \frac{\sin x}{\cos^2 x} \qquad \text{Write as separate fractions.}$$

$$= \frac{1}{\cos^2 x} - \frac{\sin x}{\cos x} \cdot \frac{1}{\cos x} \qquad \text{Product of fractions}$$

$$= \sec^2 x - \tan x \sec x \qquad \text{Reciprocal and quotient identities}$$

✓ **Checkpoint** *Audio-video solution in English & Spanish at LarsonPrecalculus.com.*

Rewrite $\dfrac{\cos^2 \theta}{1 - \sin \theta}$ so that it is *not* in fractional form.

EXAMPLE 7   Trigonometric Substitution

Use the substitution $x = 2 \tan \theta, 0 < \theta < \pi/2$, to write $\sqrt{4 + x^2}$ as a trigonometric function of θ.

Solution

Begin by letting $x = 2 \tan \theta$. Then you can obtain

$$\sqrt{4 + x^2} = \sqrt{4 + (2 \tan \theta)^2} \qquad \text{Substitute } 2 \tan \theta \text{ for } x.$$

$$= \sqrt{4(1 + \tan^2 \theta)} \qquad \text{Property of exponents and factor out 4.}$$

$$= \sqrt{4 \sec^2 \theta} \qquad \text{Pythagorean identity}$$

$$= 2 \sec \theta. \qquad \sec \theta > 0 \text{ for } 0 < \theta < \frac{\pi}{2}$$

✓ **Checkpoint** *Audio-video solution in English & Spanish at LarsonPrecalculus.com.*

Use the substitution $x = 3 \sin \theta, 0 < \theta < \pi/2$, to write $\sqrt{9 - x^2}$ as a trigonometric function of θ.

Figure 5.1 shows the right triangle illustration of the trigonometric substitution $x = 2 \tan \theta$ in Example 7. For $0 < \theta < \pi/2$, you have

$$\text{opp} = x, \text{ adj} = 2, \text{ and hyp} = \sqrt{4 + x^2}.$$

Try using these expressions to obtain the result shown in Example 7.

$$\theta = \arctan \frac{x}{2}$$

$$\tan \theta = \frac{x}{2}$$

Figure 5.1

5.1   Exercises

See *CalcChat.com* for tutorial help and worked-out solutions to odd-numbered exercises.
For instructions on how to use a graphing utility, see Appendix A.

Vocabulary and Concept Check

1. Match each function with an equivalent expression.

(a) $\sin u$ (i) $\dfrac{1}{\sec u}$

(b) $\cos u$ (ii) $\dfrac{1}{\cot u}$

(c) $\tan u$ (iii) $\dfrac{1}{\csc u}$

2. Match each expression with an equivalent expression.

(a) $\sin^2 u$ (i) $1 + \cot^2 u$

(b) $\sec^2 u$ (ii) $1 - \cos^2 u$

(c) $\csc^2 u$ (iii) $1 + \tan^2 u$

In Exercises 3–6, fill in the blank to complete the trigonometric identity.

3. $\cos\left(\dfrac{\pi}{2} - u\right) = $ _____

4. $\csc\left(\dfrac{\pi}{2} - u\right) = $ _____

5. $\sec(-u) = $ _____

6. $\tan(-u) = $ _____

Procedures and Problem Solving

Using Identities to Evaluate Functions In Exercises 7–20, use the values to evaluate (if possible) all six trigonometric functions.

7. $\sin x = \dfrac{1}{2}, \quad \cos x = \dfrac{\sqrt{3}}{2}$

8. $\cos \theta = \dfrac{1}{2}, \quad \sin \theta = \dfrac{\sqrt{3}}{2}$

9. $\cot \theta = -1, \quad \sin \theta = -\dfrac{\sqrt{2}}{2}$

10. $\tan x = \dfrac{\sqrt{3}}{3}, \quad \csc x = -2$

11. $\tan x = \dfrac{7}{24}, \quad \sec x = -\dfrac{25}{24}$

12. $\cot \phi = -5, \quad \sin \phi = \dfrac{\sqrt{26}}{26}$

13. $\sec \phi = -\dfrac{17}{15}, \quad \sin \phi = \dfrac{8}{17}$

14. $\cos\left(\dfrac{\pi}{2} - x\right) = \dfrac{3}{5}, \quad \cos x = \dfrac{4}{5}$

15. $\sin(-x) = -\dfrac{2}{3}, \quad \tan x = -\dfrac{2\sqrt{5}}{5}$

16. $\csc(-x) = -5, \quad \cos x = \dfrac{\sqrt{24}}{5}$

17. $\tan \theta = 2, \quad \sin \theta < 0$

18. $\sec \theta = 4, \quad \tan \theta < 0$

19. $\csc \theta$ is undefined, $\quad \cos \theta < 0$

20. $\tan \theta$ is undefined, $\quad \sin \theta > 0$

Matching Trigonometric Expressions In Exercises 21–26, match the trigonometric expression with its simplified form.

(a) $\sec x$ (b) -1 (c) $\cot x$

(d) 1 (e) $-\tan x$ (f) $\sin x$

21. $\sec x \cos x$

22. $\tan x \csc x$

23. $\cot^2 x - \csc^2 x$

24. $(1 - \cos^2 x)(\csc x)$

25. $\dfrac{\sin(-x)}{\cos(-x)}$

26. $\dfrac{\sin[(\pi/2) - x]}{\cos[(\pi/2) - x]}$

Matching Trigonometric Expressions In Exercises 27–32, match the trigonometric expression with its simplified form.

(a) $\csc x$ (b) $\tan x$ (c) $\sin^2 x$

(d) $\sin x \tan x$ (e) $\sec^2 x$ (f) $\sec^2 x + \tan^2 x$

27. $\sin x \sec x$

28. $\cos^2 x(\sec^2 x - 1)$

29. $\sec^4 x - \tan^4 x$

30. $\cot x \sec x$

31. $\dfrac{\sec^2 x - 1}{\sin^2 x}$

32. $\dfrac{\cos^2[(\pi/2) - x]}{\cos x}$

Simplifying a Trigonometric Expression In Exercises 33–44, use the fundamental identities to simplify the expression. Use the *table* feature of a graphing utility to check your result numerically.

33. $\cot x \sin x$

34. $\cos \beta \tan \beta$

35. $\sin \phi(\csc \phi - \sin \phi)$

36. $\cos x(1 + \tan^2 x)$

37. $\dfrac{\csc x}{\cot x}$

38. $\dfrac{\sec \theta}{\csc \theta}$

39. $\sec \alpha \cdot \dfrac{\sin \alpha}{\tan \alpha}$

40. $\dfrac{1 + \tan^2 \theta}{\sec^2 \theta}$

41. $\sin\!\left(\dfrac{\pi}{2} - x\right)\csc x$

42. $\cot\!\left(\dfrac{\pi}{2} - x\right)\cos x$

43. $\dfrac{\cos^2 y}{1 - \sin y}$

44. $\dfrac{1}{\cot^2 x + 1}$

Factoring Trigonometric Expressions **In Exercises 45–54, factor the expression and use the fundamental identities to simplify. Use a graphing utility to check your result graphically.**

45. $\cot^2 x - \cot^2 x \cos^2 x$

46. $\sec^2 x \tan^2 x + \sec^2 x$

47. $\dfrac{\cos^2 x - 4}{\cos x - 2}$

48. $\dfrac{\csc^2 x - 1}{\csc x - 1}$

49. $\tan^4 x + 2 \tan^2 x + 1$

50. $1 - 2 \sin^2 x + \sin^4 x$

51. $\sin^4 x - \cos^4 x$

52. $\sec^4 x - \tan^4 x$

53. $\csc^3 x - \csc^2 x - \csc x + 1$

54. $\sec^3 x - \sec^2 x - \sec x + 1$

Multiplying Trigonometric Expressions **In Exercises 55–58, perform the multiplication and use the fundamental identities to simplify.**

55. $(\sin x + \cos x)^2$

56. $(1 + \tan x)^2$

57. $(\csc x + 1)(\csc x - 1)$

58. $(5 - 5 \sin x)(5 + 5 \sin x)$

Adding or Subtracting Trigonometric Expressions **In Exercises 59–64, perform the addition or subtraction and use the fundamental identities to simplify.**

59. $\dfrac{1}{1 + \cos x} + \dfrac{1}{1 - \cos x}$

60. $\dfrac{1}{\sec x + 1} - \dfrac{1}{\sec x - 1}$

61. $\tan x - \dfrac{\sec^2 x}{\tan x}$

62. $\tan x + \dfrac{\cos x}{1 + \sin x}$

63. $\dfrac{\cos x}{1 + \sin x} + \dfrac{1 + \sin x}{\cos x}$

64. $\dfrac{\tan x}{1 + \sec x} + \dfrac{1 + \sec x}{\tan x}$

Rewriting a Trigonometric Expression **In Exercises 65–70, rewrite the expression so that it is *not* in fractional form.**

65. $\dfrac{\sin x}{\tan x}$

66. $\dfrac{\csc y}{\cot y}$

67. $\dfrac{\sin^2 y}{1 - \cos y}$

68. $\dfrac{\tan^2 x}{\csc x + 1}$

69. $\dfrac{3}{\sec x - \tan x}$

70. $\dfrac{5}{\tan x + \sec x}$

Graphing Trigonometric Functions **In Exercises 71–74, use a graphing utility to complete the table and graph the functions in the same viewing window. Make a conjecture about y_1 and y_2.**

x	0.2	0.4	0.6	0.8	1.0	1.2	1.4
y_1							
y_2							

71. $y_1 = \cos\!\left(\dfrac{\pi}{2} - x\right), \quad y_2 = \sin x$

72. $y_1 = \cos x + \sin x \tan x, \quad y_2 = \sec x$

73. $y_1 = \dfrac{\cos x}{1 - \sin x}, \quad y_2 = \dfrac{1 + \sin x}{\cos x}$

74. $y_1 = \sec^4 x - \sec^2 x, \quad y_2 = \tan^2 x + \tan^4 x$

Graphing Trigonometric Functions **In Exercises 75–78, use a graphing utility to determine which of the six trigonometric functions is equal to the expression. Verify your answer algebraically.**

75. $\cos x \cot x + \sin x$

76. $\sin x(\cot x + \tan x)$

77. $\dfrac{1}{\sin x}\!\left(\dfrac{1}{\cos x} - \cos x\right)$

78. $\dfrac{1}{2}\!\left(\dfrac{1 + \sin \theta}{\cos \theta} + \dfrac{\cos \theta}{1 + \sin \theta}\right)$

Trigonometric Substitution **In Exercises 79–90, use the trigonometric substitution to write the algebraic expression as a trigonometric function of θ, where $0 < \theta < \pi/2$.**

79. $\sqrt{25 - x^2}, \quad x = 5 \sin \theta$

80. $\sqrt{4 - x^2}, \quad x = 2 \cos \theta$

81. $\sqrt{x^2 + 9}, \quad x = 3 \tan \theta$

82. $\sqrt{x^2 + 100}, \quad x = 10 \tan \theta$

83. $\sqrt{49 - x^2}, \quad x = 7 \sin \theta$

84. $\sqrt{64 - x^2}, \quad x = 8 \cos \theta$

85. $\sqrt{4x^2 + 9}, \quad 2x = 3 \tan \theta$

86. $\sqrt{9x^2 + 4}, \quad 3x = 2 \tan \theta$

87. $\sqrt{2 - x^2}, \quad x = \sqrt{2} \sin \theta$

88. $\sqrt{5 - x^2}, \quad x = \sqrt{5} \cos \theta$

89. $\sqrt{(9 + x^2)^3}, \quad x = 3 \tan \theta$

90. $\sqrt{(x^2 - 16)^3}, \quad x = 4 \sec \theta$

Solving a Trigonometric Equation **In Exercises 91–94, use a graphing utility to solve the equation for θ, where $0 \le \theta < 2\pi$.**

91. $\sin \theta = \sqrt{1 - \cos^2 \theta}$

92. $\cos \theta = -\sqrt{1 - \sin^2 \theta}$

93. $\sec \theta = \sqrt{1 + \tan^2 \theta}$

94. $\tan \theta = \sqrt{\sec^2 \theta - 1}$

Rewriting Expressions In Exercises 95–100, rewrite the expression as a single logarithm and simplify the result. (*Hint*: Begin by using the properties of logarithms.)

95. $\ln|\cos\theta| - \ln|\sin\theta|$ **96.** $\ln|\cot\theta| + \ln|\sin\theta|$

97. $\ln|\sec x| + \ln|\sin x|$ **98.** $\ln|\tan x| - \ln|\sin x|$

99. $\ln(1 + \sin x) - \ln|\sec x|$

100. $\ln|\cot t| + \ln(1 + \tan^2 t)$

Demonstrating an Identity Numerically In Exercises 101–104, use the *table* feature of a graphing utility to demonstrate the identity for each value of θ.

101. $\csc^2\theta - \cot^2\theta = 1$,   (a) $\theta = 132°$ (b) $\theta = \dfrac{2\pi}{7}$

102. $\tan^2\theta + 1 = \sec^2\theta$,   (a) $\theta = 346°$ (b) $\theta = 3.1$

103. $\cos\!\left(\dfrac{\pi}{2} - \theta\right) = \sin\theta$,   (a) $\theta = 80°$ (b) $\theta = 0.8$

104. $\sin(-\theta) = -\sin\theta$,   (a) $\theta = 250°$ (b) $\theta = \dfrac{\pi}{4}$

105. *Why you should learn it* (p. 350) The forces acting on an object weighing W units on an inclined plane positioned at an angle of θ with the horizontal are modeled by

$$\mu W \cos\theta = W \sin\theta$$

where μ is the coefficient of friction (see figure). Solve the equation for μ and simplify the result.

106. Rate of Change The rate of change of the function $f(x) = \tan x + \cot x$ is given by the expression $\sec^2 x - \csc^2 x$. Show that this expression can also be written as $\tan^2 x - \cot^2 x$.

107. Rate of Change The rate of change of the function $f(x) = \sec x + \cos x$ is given by the expression $\sec x \tan x - \sin x$. Show that this expression can also be written as $\sin x \tan^2 x$.

Conclusions

True or False? In Exercises 108 and 109, determine whether the statement is true or false. Justify your answer.

108. $\sin\theta\csc\theta = 1$ **109.** $\cos\theta\sec\phi = 1$

110. HOW DO YOU SEE IT?

Explain how to use the figure to derive the Pythagorean identities

$$\sin^2\theta + \cos^2\theta = 1,$$

$$1 + \tan^2\theta = \sec^2\theta,$$

and $1 + \cot^2\theta = \csc^2\theta$.

Discuss how to remember these identities and other fundamental trigonometric identities.

Analyzing Trigonometric Functions In Exercises 111–114, fill in the blanks. (*Note*: $x \to c^+$ indicates that x approaches c from the right, and $x \to c^-$ indicates that x approaches c from the left.)

111. As $x \to \dfrac{\pi^-}{2}$, $\sin x \to$ ▨ and $\csc x \to$ ▨.

112. As $x \to 0^+$, $\cos x \to$ ▨ and $\sec x \to$ ▨.

113. As $x \to \dfrac{\pi^+}{2}$, $\tan x \to$ ▨ and $\cot x \to$ ▨.

114. As $x \to \pi^-$, $\sin x \to$ ▨ and $\csc x \to$ ▨.

115. Rewriting Trigonometric Functions Rewrite each trigonometric function of θ in terms of $\sin\theta$.

116. Rewriting Trigonometric Functions Rewrite each trigonometric function of θ in terms of $\cos\theta$.

Rewriting a Trigonometric Expression In Exercises 117 and 118, rewrite the expression in terms of $\sin\theta$ and $\cos\theta$.

117. $\dfrac{\sec\theta(1 + \tan\theta)}{\sec\theta + \csc\theta}$ **118.** $\dfrac{\csc\theta(1 + \cot\theta)}{\tan\theta + \cot\theta}$

Cumulative Mixed Review

Adding or Subtracting Rational Expressions In Exercises 119–122, perform the addition or subtraction and simplify.

119. $\dfrac{1}{x + 5} + \dfrac{x}{x - 8}$ **120.** $\dfrac{6x}{x - 4} - \dfrac{3}{4 - x}$

121. $\dfrac{4x}{x^2 - 25} - \dfrac{x^2}{x - 5}$ **122.** $\dfrac{2x}{x^2 - 4} + \dfrac{5}{x + 4}$

Graphing Trigonometric Functions In Exercises 123–126, sketch the graph of the function. (Include two full periods.)

123. $f(x) = -\sin\pi x - 1$ **124.** $f(x) = -2\tan\dfrac{\pi x}{2}$

125. $f(x) = \dfrac{1}{2}\cot\!\left(x + \dfrac{\pi}{4}\right)$ **126.** $f(x) = \cos(x - \pi) + 3$

In Example 2, you needed to write the Pythagorean identity $\sin^2 u + \cos^2 u = 1$ in the equivalent form $\cos^2 u = 1 - \sin^2 u$. When verifying identities, you may find it useful to write Pythagorean identities in one of these equivalent forms.

Pythagorean Identities	Equivalent Forms

$\sin^2 u + \cos^2 u = 1$ ⟨ $\sin^2 u = 1 - \cos^2 u$
$\cos^2 u = 1 - \sin^2 u$

$1 + \tan^2 u = \sec^2 u$ ⟨ $1 = \sec^2 u - \tan^2 u$
$\tan^2 u = \sec^2 u - 1$

$1 + \cot^2 u = \csc^2 u$ ⟨ $1 = \csc^2 u - \cot^2 u$
$\cot^2 u = \csc^2 u - 1$

EXAMPLE 3   Verifying a Trigonometric Identity

Verify the identity $(\tan^2 x + 1)(\cos^2 x - 1) = -\tan^2 x$.

Algebraic Solution

By applying identities before multiplying, you obtain the following.

$(\tan^2 x + 1)(\cos^2 x - 1) = (\sec^2 x)(-\sin^2 x)$ Pythagorean identities

$\qquad = -\dfrac{\sin^2 x}{\cos^2 x}$ Reciprocal identity

$\qquad = -\left(\dfrac{\sin x}{\cos x}\right)^2$ Property of exponents

$\qquad = -\tan^2 x$ Quotient identity

Graphical Solution

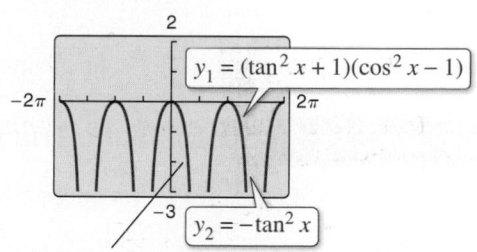

Because the graphs appear to coincide, the given equation appears to be an identity.

✓ **Checkpoint** 🔊))) *Audio-video solution in English & Spanish at LarsonPrecalculus.com.*

Verify the identity $(\sec^2 x - 1)(\sin^2 x - 1) = -\sin^2 x$.

EXAMPLE 4   Converting to Sines and Cosines

Verify the identity $\tan x + \cot x = \sec x \csc x$.

Solution

In this case there appear to be no fractions to add, no products to find, and no opportunities to use the Pythagorean identities. So, try converting the left side to sines and cosines.

$\tan x + \cot x = \dfrac{\sin x}{\cos x} + \dfrac{\cos x}{\sin x}$ Quotient identities

$\qquad = \dfrac{\sin^2 x + \cos^2 x}{\cos x \sin x}$ Add fractions.

$\qquad = \dfrac{1}{\cos x \sin x}$ Pythagorean identity

$\qquad = \dfrac{1}{\cos x} \cdot \dfrac{1}{\sin x}$ Product of fractions

$\qquad = \sec x \csc x$ Reciprocal identities

✓ **Checkpoint** 🔊))) *Audio-video solution in English & Spanish at LarsonPrecalculus.com.*

Verify the identity $\csc x - \sin x = \cos x \cot x$.

Recall from algebra that *rationalizing the denominator* using conjugates is, on occasion, a powerful simplification technique. A related form of this technique works for simplifying trigonometric expressions as well. For instance, to simplify

$$\frac{1}{1 - \cos x}$$

multiply the numerator and the denominator by $(1 + \cos x)$.

$$\frac{1}{1 - \cos x} = \frac{1}{1 - \cos x}\left(\frac{1 + \cos x}{1 + \cos x}\right)$$

$$= \frac{1 + \cos x}{1 - \cos^2 x}$$

$$= \frac{1 + \cos x}{\sin^2 x}$$

$$= \csc^2 x(1 + \cos x)$$

The expression $\csc^2 x(1 + \cos x)$ is considered a simplified form of

$$\frac{1}{1 - \cos x}$$

because the expression does not contain any fractions.

EXAMPLE 5   Verifying a Trigonometric Identity

See LarsonPrecalculus.com for an interactive version of this type of example.

Verify the identity.

$$\sec x + \tan x = \frac{\cos x}{1 - \sin x}$$

Algebraic Solution

Begin with the *right* side because you can create a monomial denominator by multiplying the numerator and denominator by $(1 + \sin x)$.

$$\frac{\cos x}{1 - \sin x} = \frac{\cos x}{1 - \sin x}\left(\frac{1 + \sin x}{1 + \sin x}\right) \qquad \text{Multiply numerator and denominator by } (1 + \sin x).$$

$$= \frac{\cos x + \cos x \sin x}{1 - \sin^2 x} \qquad \text{Multiply.}$$

$$= \frac{\cos x + \cos x \sin x}{\cos^2 x} \qquad \text{Pythagorean identity}$$

$$= \frac{\cos x}{\cos^2 x} + \frac{\cos x \sin x}{\cos^2 x} \qquad \text{Write as separate fractions.}$$

$$= \frac{1}{\cos x} + \frac{\sin x}{\cos x} \qquad \text{Simplify.}$$

$$= \sec x + \tan x \qquad \text{Identities}$$

Graphical Solution

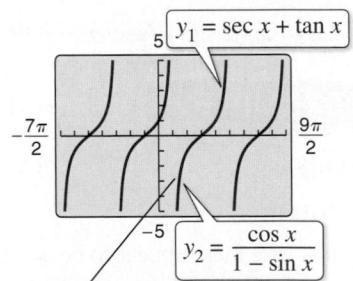

Because the graphs appear to coincide, the given equation appears to be an identity.

✓ *Checkpoint* 🔊))) *Audio-video solution in English & Spanish at LarsonPrecalculus.com.*

Verify the identity $\csc x + \cot x = \dfrac{\sin x}{1 - \cos x}$. ∎

In Examples 1 through 5, you have been verifying trigonometric identities by working with one side of the equation and converting it to the form given on the other side. On occasion, it is practical to work with each side *separately* to obtain one common form equivalent to both sides. This is illustrated in Example 6.

EXAMPLE 6   **Working with Each Side Separately**

Verify the identity $\dfrac{\cot^2 \theta}{1 + \csc \theta} = \dfrac{1 - \sin \theta}{\sin \theta}$.

Algebraic Solution

Working with the left side, you have

$$\dfrac{\cot^2 \theta}{1 + \csc \theta} = \dfrac{\csc^2 \theta - 1}{1 + \csc \theta} \qquad \text{Pythagorean identity}$$

$$= \dfrac{(\csc \theta - 1)(\csc \theta + 1)}{1 + \csc \theta} \qquad \text{Factor.}$$

$$= \csc \theta - 1. \qquad \text{Simplify.}$$

Now, simplifying the right side, you have

$$\dfrac{1 - \sin \theta}{\sin \theta} = \dfrac{1}{\sin \theta} - \dfrac{\sin \theta}{\sin \theta} \qquad \text{Write as separate fractions.}$$

$$= \csc \theta - 1. \qquad \text{Reciprocal identity}$$

The identity is verified because both sides are equal to $\csc \theta - 1$.

Numerical Solution

Use a graphing utility to create a table that shows the values of

$$y_1 = \dfrac{\cot^2 x}{1 + \csc x}$$

and

$$y_2 = \dfrac{1 - \sin x}{\sin x}$$

for different values of x, as shown in the figure.

X	Y1	Y2
-.5	-3.086	-3.086
-.25	-5.042	-5.042
0	ERROR	ERROR
.25	3.042	3.042
.5	1.0858	1.0858
.75	.46705	.46705
1	.1884	.1884

X=1

The values for y_1 and y_2 appear to be identical, so the equation appears to be an identity.

✓ **Checkpoint** ◀))) *Audio-video solution in English & Spanish at LarsonPrecalculus.com.*

Verify the identity $\dfrac{\tan^2 \theta}{1 + \sec \theta} = \dfrac{1 - \cos \theta}{\cos \theta}$.

In Example 7, powers of trigonometric functions are rewritten as more complicated sums of products of trigonometric functions. This is a common procedure used in calculus.

EXAMPLE 7   **Examples from Calculus** ∫

Verify each identity.

a. $\tan^4 x = \tan^2 x \sec^2 x - \tan^2 x$

b. $\sin^3 x \cos^4 x = (\cos^4 x - \cos^6 x)\sin x$

c. $\csc^4 x \cot x = \csc^2 x(\cot x + \cot^3 x)$

Solution

a. $\tan^4 x = (\tan^2 x)(\tan^2 x) \qquad$ Write as separate factors.

$\quad = \tan^2 x(\sec^2 x - 1) \qquad$ Pythagorean identity

$\quad = \tan^2 x \sec^2 x - \tan^2 x \qquad$ Multiply.

b. $\sin^3 x \cos^4 x = \sin^2 x \cos^4 x \sin x \qquad$ Write as separate factors.

$\quad = (1 - \cos^2 x)\cos^4 x \sin x \qquad$ Pythagorean identity

$\quad = (\cos^4 x - \cos^6 x)\sin x \qquad$ Multiply.

c. $\csc^4 x \cot x = \csc^2 x \csc^2 x \cot x \qquad$ Write as separate factors.

$\quad = \csc^2 x(1 + \cot^2 x)\cot x \qquad$ Pythagorean identity

$\quad = \csc^2 x(\cot x + \cot^3 x) \qquad$ Multiply.

What's Wrong?

To determine the validity of the statement $\tan^2 x \sin^2 x \overset{?}{=} \dfrac{5}{6} \tan^2 x$, you use a graphing utility to graph $y_1 = \tan^2 x \sin^2 x$ and $y_2 = \dfrac{5}{6} \tan^2 x$, as shown in the figure. You use the graph to conclude that the statement is an identity. What's wrong?

✓ **Checkpoint** ◀))) *Audio-video solution in English & Spanish at LarsonPrecalculus.com.*

Verify the identity $\tan^3 x = \tan x \sec^2 x - \tan x$.

5.2 Exercises

See *CalcChat.com* for tutorial help and worked-out solutions to odd-numbered exercises.
For instructions on how to use a graphing utility, see Appendix A.

Vocabulary and Concept Check

In Exercises 1–8, fill in the blank to complete the trigonometric identity.

1. $\dfrac{1}{\tan u} = $ _____   **2.** $\dfrac{1}{\csc u} = $ _____

3. $\dfrac{\sin u}{\cos u} = $ _____   **4.** $\dfrac{1}{\sec u} = $ _____

5. $\sin^2 u + $ _____ $= 1$ **6.** $\tan\left(\dfrac{\pi}{2} - u\right) = $ _____

7. $\cos(-u) = $ _____   **8.** $\csc(-u) = $ _____

9. Is a graphical solution sufficient to verify a trigonometric identity?

10. Is a conditional equation true for all real values in its domain?

Procedures and Problem Solving

Verifying a Trigonometric Identity   In Exercises 11–20, verify the identity.

11. $\sin t \csc t = 1$

12. $\sec y \cos y = 1$

13. $\dfrac{\csc^2 x}{\cot x} = \csc x \sec x$

14. $\dfrac{\sin^2 t}{\tan^2 t} = \cos^2 t$

15. $\cos^2 \beta - \sin^2 \beta = 1 - 2\sin^2 \beta$

16. $\cot^2 \beta + \csc^2 \beta = 2\csc^2 \beta - 1$

17. $\tan^2 \theta + 6 = \sec^2 \theta + 5$

18. $3 + \sin^2 z = 4 - \cos^2 z$

19. $(1 + \sin x)(1 - \sin x) = \cos^2 x$

20. $\tan^2 y(\csc^2 y - 1) = 1$

Algebraic-Graphical-Numerical   In Exercises 21–30, use a graphing utility to complete the table and graph the functions in the same viewing window. Use both the table and the graph as evidence that $y_1 = y_2$. Then verify the identity algebraically.

x	0.2	0.4	0.6	0.8	1.0	1.2	1.4
y_1							
y_2							

21. $y_1 = \dfrac{\sec\theta - 1}{1 - \cos\theta}$, $y_2 = \sec\theta$

22. $y_1 = \dfrac{\csc x - 1}{1 - \sin x}$, $y_2 = \csc x$

23. $y_1 = (1 + \cot^2 x)\cos^2 x$, $y_2 = \cot^2 x$

24. $y_1 = (1 + \tan^2 x)\sin^2 x$, $y_2 = \tan^2 x$

25. $y_1 = \csc x - \sin x$, $y_2 = \cos x \cot x$

26. $y_1 = \sec x - \cos x$, $y_2 = \sin x \tan x$

27. $y_1 = \sin x + \cos x \cot x$, $y_2 = \csc x$

28. $y_1 = \cos x + \sin x \tan x$, $y_2 = \sec x$

29. $y_1 = \dfrac{1}{\tan x} + \dfrac{1}{\cot x}$, $y_2 = \tan x + \cot x$

30. $y_1 = \dfrac{1}{\sin x} - \dfrac{1}{\csc x}$, $y_2 = \csc x - \sin x$

Error Analysis   In Exercises 31 and 32, describe the error.

31. $(1 + \tan x)[1 + \cot(-x)]$
$= (1 + \tan x)(1 + \cot x)$
$= 1 + \cot x + \tan x + \tan x \cot x$
$= 1 + \cot x + \tan x + 1$
$= 2 + \cot x + \tan x$

32. $\dfrac{1 + \sec(-\theta)}{\sin(-\theta) + \tan(-\theta)} = \dfrac{1 - \sec\theta}{\sin\theta - \tan\theta}$

$= \dfrac{1 - \sec\theta}{\sin\theta - \dfrac{\sin\theta}{\cos\theta}}$

$= \dfrac{1 - \sec\theta}{(\sin\theta)\left[1 - \left(\dfrac{1}{\cos\theta}\right)\right]}$

$= \dfrac{1 - \sec\theta}{\sin\theta(1 - \sec\theta)}$

$= \dfrac{1}{\sin\theta}$

$= \csc\theta$

Verifying a Trigonometric Identity In Exercises 33 and 34, fill in the missing step(s).

33. $\sec^4 x - 2 \sec^2 x + 1 = (\sec^2 x - 1)^2$

$$= \boxed{}$$

$$= \tan^4 x$$

34. $\dfrac{\tan x - \cot x}{\tan x + \cot x} = \dfrac{\dfrac{\sin x}{\cos x} - \dfrac{\cos x}{\sin x}}{\dfrac{\sin x}{\cos x} + \dfrac{\cos x}{\sin x}}$

$$= \boxed{}$$

$$= \dfrac{\sin^2 x - \cos^2 x}{1}$$

$$- \sin^2 x - \cos^2 x$$

$$= \boxed{}$$

$$= 1 - 2 \cos^2 x$$

Verifying a Trigonometric Identity In Exercises 35–40, verify the identity.

35. $\cot\left(\dfrac{\pi}{2} - x\right)\csc x = \sec x$

36. $\dfrac{\cos\left[\left(\dfrac{\pi}{2}\right) - x\right]}{\sin\left[\left(\dfrac{\pi}{2}\right) - x\right]} = \tan x$

37. $\dfrac{\csc(-x)}{\sec(-x)} = -\cot x$

38. $(1 + \sin y)[1 + \sin(-y)] = \cos^2 y$

39. $\sin^{1/2} x \cos x - \sin^{5/2} x \cos x = \cos^3 x \sqrt{\sin x}$

40. $\sec^6 x(\sec x \tan x) - \sec^4 x(\sec x \tan x) = \sec^5 x \tan^3 x$

Verifying a Trigonometric Identity In Exercises 41–48, verify the identity algebraically. Use the *table* feature of a graphing utility to check your result numerically.

41. $\dfrac{\cos x - \cos y}{\sin x + \sin y} + \dfrac{\sin x - \sin y}{\cos x + \cos y} = 0$

42. $\dfrac{\tan x + \cot y}{\tan x \cot y} = \tan y + \cot x$

43. $\dfrac{\cos \theta}{1 - \sin \theta} = \sec \theta + \tan \theta$

44. $(\sec \theta - \tan \theta)(\csc \theta + 1) = \cot \theta$

45. $\sin^2\left(\dfrac{\pi}{2} - x\right) + \sin^2 x = 1$

46. $\sec^2 y - \cot^2\left(\dfrac{\pi}{2} - y\right) = 1$

47. $\sin x \csc x\left(\dfrac{\pi}{2} - x\right) = \tan x$

48. $\sec^2\left(\dfrac{\pi}{2} - x\right) - 1 = \cot^2 x$

Verifying a Trigonometric Identity In Exercises 49–60, verify the identity algebraically. Use a graphing utility to check your result graphically.

49. $2 \sec^2 x - 2 \sec^2 x \sin^2 x - \sin^2 x - \cos^2 x = 1$

50. $\csc x(\csc x - \sin x) + \dfrac{\sin x - \cos x}{\sin x} + \cot x = \csc^2 x$

51. $\dfrac{\cot x \tan x}{\cos x} = \sec x$

52. $\dfrac{1 + \csc \theta}{\sec \theta} - \cot \theta = \cos \theta$

53. $\sec \theta \cot \theta = \csc \theta$

54. $\sin \theta \csc \theta - \sin^2 \theta = \cos^2 \theta$

55. $\dfrac{1 + \sin \theta}{\cos \theta} + \dfrac{\cos \theta}{1 + \sin \theta} = 2 \sec \theta$

56. $\dfrac{\tan \theta}{1 + \sec \theta} + \dfrac{1 + \sec \theta}{\tan \theta} = 2 \csc \theta$

57. $\dfrac{\sin \beta}{1 - \cos \beta} = \dfrac{1 + \cos \beta}{\sin \beta}$

58. $\dfrac{\cot \alpha}{\csc \alpha - 1} = \dfrac{\csc \alpha + 1}{\cot \alpha}$

59. $\sqrt{\dfrac{1 + \sin \alpha}{1 - \sin \alpha}} = \dfrac{1 + \sin \alpha}{|\cos \alpha|}$

60. $\sqrt{\dfrac{1 - \cos \beta}{1 + \cos \beta}} = \dfrac{1 - \cos \beta}{|\sin \beta|}$

Graphing a Trigonometric Function In Exercises 61–64, use a graphing utility to graph the trigonometric function. Use the graph to make a conjecture about a simplification of the expression. Verify the resulting identity algebraically.

61. $y = \dfrac{1}{\cot x + 1} + \dfrac{1}{\tan x + 1}$

62. $y = \dfrac{\cos x}{1 - \tan x} + \dfrac{\sin x \cos x}{\sin x - \cos x}$

63. $y = \dfrac{1}{\sin x} - \dfrac{\cos^2 x}{\sin x}$ **64.** $y = \sin t + \dfrac{\cot^2 t}{\csc t}$

Verifying an Identity Involving Logarithms In Exercises 65 and 66, use the properties of logarithms and trigonometric identities to verify the identity.

65. $\ln|\cot \theta| = \ln|\cos \theta| - \ln|\sin \theta|$

66. $\ln|\sec \theta| = -\ln|\cos \theta|$

Using Cofunction Identities In Exercises 67–70, use the cofunction identities to evaluate the expression without using a calculator.

67. $\sin^2 25° + \sin^2 65°$ **68.** $\cos^2 18° + \cos^2 72°$

69. $\cos^2 20° + \cos^2 52° + \cos^2 38° + \cos^2 70°$

70. $\sin^2 18° + \sin^2 40° + \sin^2 50° + \sin^2 72°$

Examples from Calculus In Exercises 71–74, powers of trigonometric functions are rewritten to be useful in calculus. Verify the identity.

71. $\cot^6 x = \cot^4 x \csc^2 x - \cot^4 x$

72. $\sec^4 x \tan^2 x = (\tan^2 x + \tan^4 x)\sec^2 x$

73. $\cos^3 x \sin^2 x = (\sin^2 x - \sin^4 x)\cos x$

74. $\sin^4 x + \cos^4 x = 1 - 2\cos^2 x + 2\cos^4 x$

Verifying a Trigonometric Identity In Exercises 75–78, verify the identity.

75. $\tan(\sin^{-1} x) = \dfrac{x}{\sqrt{1 - x^2}}$　**76.** $\cos(\sin^{-1} x) = \sqrt{1 - x^2}$

77. $\tan\left(\sin^{-1}\dfrac{x - 1}{4}\right) = \dfrac{x - 1}{\sqrt{16 - (x - 1)^2}}$

78. $\tan\left(\cos^{-1}\dfrac{x + 1}{2}\right) = \dfrac{\sqrt{4 - (x + 1)^2}}{x + 1}$

79. *Why you should learn it* (p. 357) The length s of a shadow cast by a vertical gnomon (a device used to tell time) of height h when the angle of the sun above the horizon is θ (see figure) can be modeled by

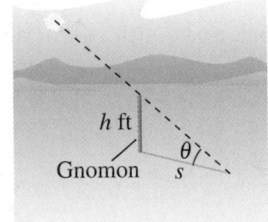

$$s = \frac{h \sin(90° - \theta)}{\sin \theta}.$$

Gnomon　s

(a) Verify that the expression for s is equivalent to $h \cot \theta$.

(b) Use a graphing utility to complete the table. Let $h = 5$ feet.

θ	15°	30°	45°	60°	75°	90°
s						

(c) Use your table from part (b) to determine the angles of the sun that result in the maximum and minimum lengths of the shadow.

(d) Based on your results from part (c), what time of day do you think it is when the angle of the sun above the horizon is 90°?

80. Rate of Change The rate of change of the function $f(x) = \sin x + \csc x$ is given by $\cos x - \csc x \cot x$. Show that the expression for the rate of change can also be given by $-\cos x \cot^2 x$.

Conclusions

True or False? In Exercises 81 and 82, determine whether the statement is true or false. Justify your answer.

81. The equation $\sin^2 \theta + \cos^2 \theta = 1 + \tan^2 \theta$ is an identity, because $\sin^2(0) + \cos^2(0) = 1$ and $1 + \tan^2(0) = 1$.

82. $\sin(x^2) = \sin^2(x)$

Verifying a Trigonometric Identity In Exercises 83 and 84, (a) verify the identity and (b) determine whether the identity is true for the given value of x. Explain.

83. $\dfrac{\sin x}{1 + \cos x} = \dfrac{1 - \cos x}{\sin x}$,　$x = 0$

84. $\dfrac{\sec x}{\tan x} = \dfrac{\tan x}{\sec x - \cos x}$,　$x = \pi$

Using Trigonometric Substitution In Exercises 85–88, use the trigonometric substitution to write the algebraic expression as a trigonometric function of θ, where $0 < \theta < \pi/2$. Assume $a > 0$.

85. $\sqrt{a^2 - u^2}$,　$u = a \sin \theta$

86. $\sqrt{a^2 - u^2}$,　$u = a \cos \theta$

87. $\sqrt{a^2 + u^2}$,　$u = a \tan \theta$

88. $\sqrt{u^2 - a^2}$,　$u = a \sec \theta$

Think About It In Exercises 89–92, explain why the equation is not an identity and find one value of the variable for which the equation is not true.

89. $\sqrt{\sec^2 x - 1} = \tan x$　**90.** $\sin \theta = \sqrt{1 - \cos^2 \theta}$

91. $1 - \cos \theta = \sin \theta$　**92.** $1 + \tan x = \sec x$

93. Verifying a Trigonometric Identity Verify that for all integers n, $\sin\left[\dfrac{(12n + 1)\pi}{6}\right] = \dfrac{1}{2}$.

94. HOW DO YOU SEE IT? Explain how to use the figure to derive the identity

$$\frac{\sec^2 \theta - 1}{\sec^2 \theta} = \sin^2 \theta$$

given in Example 1.

Cumulative Mixed Review

Graphing an Exponential Function In Exercises 95–98, use a graphing utility to construct a table of values for the function. Then sketch the graph of the function. Identify any asymptotes of the graph.

95. $f(x) = 2^x + 3$　**96.** $f(x) = -2^{x-3}$

97. $f(x) = 2^{-x} - 1$　**98.** $f(x) = 2^{x+1} + 5$

5.3   Solving Trigonometric Equations

Introduction

To solve a trigonometric equation, use standard algebraic techniques such as collecting like terms and factoring. Your preliminary goal is to isolate the trigonometric function involved in the equation.

EXAMPLE 1   **Solving a Trigonometric Equation**

Solve $2 \sin x - 1 = 0$.

Solution

$2 \sin x - 1 = 0$	Write original equation.
$2 \sin x = 1$	Add 1 to each side.
$\sin x = \frac{1}{2}$	Divide each side by 2.

To solve for x, note in Figure 5.2 that the equation $\sin x = \frac{1}{2}$ has solutions $x = \pi/6$ and $x = 5\pi/6$ in the interval $[0, 2\pi)$. Moreover, because $\sin x$ has a period of 2π, there are infinitely many other solutions, which can be written as

$$x = \frac{\pi}{6} + 2n\pi \quad \text{and} \quad x = \frac{5\pi}{6} + 2n\pi \qquad \text{General solution}$$

where n is an integer, as shown in Figure 5.2.

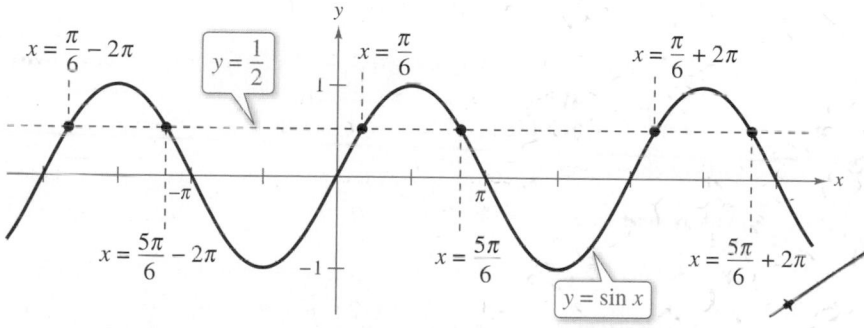

Figure 5.2

✓ **Checkpoint** 🔊)) *Audio-video solution in English & Spanish at LarsonPrecalculus.com.*

Solve $\sin x + 1 = 0$.

Another way to show that the equation $\sin x = \frac{1}{2}$ has infinitely many solutions is indicated in Figure 5.3. Any angles that are coterminal with $\pi/6$ or $5\pi/6$ are also solutions of the equation.

Figure 5.3

©Kesu/Shutterstock.com

EXAMPLE 2   Collecting Like Terms

Find all solutions of

$$\sin x + \sqrt{2} = -\sin x$$

in the interval $[0, 2\pi)$.

Algebraic Solution

Rewrite the equation so that $\sin x$ is isolated on one side of the equation.

$\sin x + \sqrt{2} = -\sin x$	Write original equation.
$\sin x + \sin x = -\sqrt{2}$	Add $\sin x$ to and subtract $\sqrt{2}$ from each side.
$2 \sin x = -\sqrt{2}$	Combine like terms.
$\sin x = -\dfrac{\sqrt{2}}{2}$	Divide each side by 2.

The solutions in the interval $[0, 2\pi)$ are

$$x = \frac{5\pi}{4} \quad \text{and} \quad x = \frac{7\pi}{4}.$$

Numerical Solution

Use a graphing utility set in *radian* mode to create a table that shows the values of $y_1 = \sin x + \sqrt{2}$ and $y_2 = -\sin x$ for different values of x. Your table should go from $x = 0$ to $x = 2\pi$ using increments of $\pi/8$, as shown in the figure.

X	Y1	Y2
3.1416	1.4142	0
3.5343	1.0315	.38268
3.927	.70711	.70711
4.3197	.49033	.92388
4.7124	.41421	1
5.1051	.49033	.92388
5.4978	.70711	.70711

X=5.497787143782

The values of y_1 and y_2 appear to be identical when $x \approx 3.927 \approx 5\pi/4$ and $x \approx 5.4978 \approx 7\pi/4$. These values are the approximate solutions of $\sin x + \sqrt{2} = -\sin x$.

✓ **Checkpoint** ◀))) *Audio-video solution in English & Spanish at LarsonPrecalculus.com.*

Solve $\sin x - \sqrt{2} = -\sin x$ in the interval $[0, 2\pi)$.

EXAMPLE 3   Extracting Square Roots

Solve $3 \tan^2 x - 1 = 0$.

Solution

Rewrite the equation so that $\tan x$ is isolated on one side of the equation.

$3 \tan^2 x - 1 = 0$	Write original equation.
$3 \tan^2 x = 1$	Add 1 to each side.
$\tan^2 x = \dfrac{1}{3}$	Divide each side by 3.
$\tan x = \pm \dfrac{1}{\sqrt{3}}$	Extract square roots.
$\tan x = \pm \dfrac{\sqrt{3}}{3}$	Rationalize the denominator.

Because $\tan x$ has a period of π, first find all solutions in the interval $[0, \pi)$. These are

$$x = \frac{\pi}{6} \quad \text{and} \quad x = \frac{5\pi}{6}.$$

Finally, add multiples of π to each of these solutions to get the general form

$$x = \frac{\pi}{6} + n\pi \quad \text{and} \quad x = \frac{5\pi}{6} + n\pi \qquad \text{General solution}$$

where n is an integer. You can confirm this answer by graphing $y = 3 \tan^2 x - 1$ with a graphing utility, as shown in Figure 5.4. The graph has x-intercepts at $\pi/6, 5\pi/6, 7\pi/6$, and so on. These x-intercepts correspond to the solutions of $3 \tan^2 x - 1 = 0$.

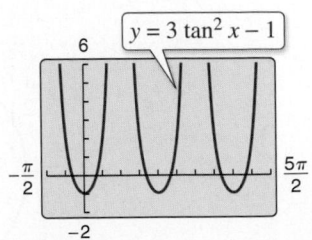

Figure 5.4

✓ **Checkpoint** ◀))) *Audio-video solution in English & Spanish at LarsonPrecalculus.com.*

Solve $4 \sin^2 x - 3 = 0$.

The equations in Examples 1–3 involved only one trigonometric function. When two or more functions occur in the same equation, collect all terms on one side and try to separate the functions by factoring or by using appropriate identities. This may produce factors that yield no solutions, as illustrated in Example 4.

EXAMPLE 4   Factoring

Solve $\cot x \cos^2 x = 2 \cot x$.

Solution

Begin by rewriting the equation so that all terms are collected on one side of the equation.

$$\cot x \cos^2 x = 2 \cot x \qquad \text{Write original equation.}$$

$$\cot x \cos^2 x - 2 \cot x = 0 \qquad \text{Subtract } 2 \cot x \text{ from each side.}$$

$$\cot x(\cos^2 x - 2) = 0 \qquad \text{Factor.}$$

By setting each of these factors equal to zero, you obtain the following.

$$\cot x = 0 \qquad \text{and} \qquad \cos^2 x - 2 = 0$$

$$\cos^2 x = 2$$

$$\cos x = \pm\sqrt{2}$$

In the interval $(0, \pi)$, the equation $\cot x = 0$ has the solution

$$x = \frac{\pi}{2}.$$

No solution is obtained for

$$\cos x = \pm\sqrt{2}$$

because $\pm\sqrt{2}$ are outside the range of the cosine function. Because $\cot x$ has a period of π, the general form of the solution is obtained by adding multiples of π to $x = \pi/2$, to get

$$x = \frac{\pi}{2} + n\pi \qquad \text{General solution}$$

where n is an integer. The graph of $y = \cot x \cos^2 x - 2 \cot x$, shown in Figure 5.5, confirms this result. From the graph, you can see that the x-intercepts occur at

$$-\frac{\pi}{2}, \frac{\pi}{2}, \frac{3\pi}{2}, \frac{5\pi}{2}$$

and so on. These x-intercepts correspond to the solutions of

$$\cot x \cos^2 x = 2 \cot x.$$

Figure 5.5

> ### Explore the Concept
> Using the equation in Example 4, explain what happens when each side of the equation is divided by $\cot x$. Why is this an incorrect method to use when solving an equation?

 Checkpoint ◀))) *Audio-video solution in English & Spanish at LarsonPrecalculus.com.*

Solve $\sin^2 x = 2 \sin x$.

Equations of Quadratic Type

Many trigonometric equations are of quadratic type $ax^2 + bx + c = 0$, as shown below. To solve equations of this type, factor the quadratic or, when factoring is not possible, use the Quadratic Formula.

Quadratic in sin x	*Quadratic in sec x*
$2 \sin^2 x - \sin x - 1 = 0$	$\sec^2 x - 3 \sec x - 2 = 0$
$2(\sin x)^2 - \sin x - 1 = 0$	$(\sec x)^2 - 3(\sec x) - 2 = 0$

EXAMPLE 5 Factoring an Equation of Quadratic Type

Find all solutions of $2 \sin^2 x - \sin x - 1 = 0$ in the interval $[0, 2\pi)$.

Algebraic Solution

Treat the equation as a quadratic in $\sin x$ and factor.

$2 \sin^2 x - \sin x - 1 = 0$ Write original equation.

$(2 \sin x + 1)(\sin x - 1) = 0$ Factor.

Setting each factor equal to zero, you obtain the following solutions in the interval $[0, 2\pi)$.

$2 \sin x + 1 = 0$ and $\sin x - 1 = 0$

$\sin x = -\dfrac{1}{2}$ $\sin x = 1$

$x = \dfrac{7\pi}{6}, \dfrac{11\pi}{6}$ $x = \dfrac{\pi}{2}$

Graphical Solution

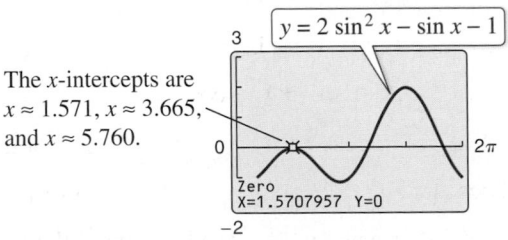

The x-intercepts are $x \approx 1.571$, $x \approx 3.665$, and $x \approx 5.760$.

From the figure, you can conclude that the approximate solutions of $2 \sin^2 x - \sin x - 1 = 0$ in the interval $[0, 2\pi)$ are

$x \approx 1.571 \approx \dfrac{\pi}{2}$, $x \approx 3.665 \approx \dfrac{7\pi}{6}$, and $x \approx 5.760 \approx \dfrac{11\pi}{6}$.

✓ **Checkpoint** ◀))) Audio-video solution in English & Spanish at LarsonPrecalculus.com.

Find all solutions of $2 \sin^2 x - 3 \sin x + 1 = 0$ in the interval $[0, 2\pi)$. ■

When working with an equation of quadratic type, be sure that the equation involves a *single* trigonometric function, as shown in the next example.

EXAMPLE 6 Rewriting with a Single Trigonometric Function

To solve $2 \sin^2 x + 3 \cos x - 3 = 0$, begin by rewriting the equation so that it has only cosine functions.

$2 \sin^2 x + 3 \cos x - 3 = 0$ Write original equation.

$2(1 - \cos^2 x) + 3 \cos x - 3 = 0$ Pythagorean identity

$2 \cos^2 x - 3 \cos x + 1 = 0$ Combine like terms and multiply each side by -1.

$(2 \cos x - 1)(\cos x - 1) = 0$ Factor.

By setting each factor equal to zero, you can find the solutions in the interval $[0, 2\pi)$ to be $x = 0$, $x = \pi/3$, and $x = 5\pi/3$. Because $\cos x$ has a period of 2π, the general solution is

$$x = 2n\pi, \quad x = \dfrac{\pi}{3} + 2n\pi, \quad x = \dfrac{5\pi}{3} + 2n\pi \qquad \text{General solution}$$

where n is an integer. The graph of $y = 2 \sin^2 x + 3 \cos x - 3$, shown in Figure 5.6, confirms this result.

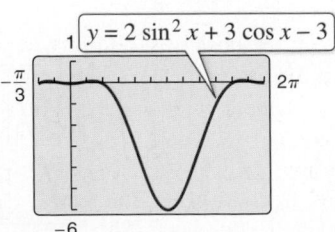

Figure 5.6

✓ **Checkpoint** ◀))) Audio-video solution in English & Spanish at LarsonPrecalculus.com.

Solve $3 \sec^2 x - 2 \tan^2 x - 4 = 0$. ■

Sometimes you must square each side of an equation to obtain a quadratic. Because this procedure can introduce extraneous solutions, you should check any solutions in the original equation to see whether they are valid or extraneous.

EXAMPLE 7   Squaring and Converting to Quadratic Type

See LarsonPrecalculus.com for an interactive version of this type of example.

Find all solutions of $\cos x + 1 = \sin x$ in the interval $[0, 2\pi)$.

Solution

It is not clear how to rewrite this equation in terms of a single trigonometric function. Because the squares of the sine and cosine functions are related by a Pythagorean identity, try squaring each side of the equation and then rewriting the equation so that it has only cosine functions.

$\cos x + 1 = \sin x$	Write original equation.
$\cos^2 x + 2 \cos x + 1 = \sin^2 x$	Square each side.
$\cos^2 x + 2 \cos x + 1 = 1 - \cos^2 x$	Pythagorean identity
$2 \cos^2 x + 2 \cos x = 0$	Combine like terms.
$2 \cos x(\cos x + 1) = 0$	Factor.

Setting each factor equal to zero produces the following.

$$2 \cos x = 0 \quad \text{and} \quad \cos x + 1 = 0$$

$$\cos x = 0 \qquad\qquad\qquad \cos x = -1$$

$$x = \frac{\pi}{2}, \frac{3\pi}{2} \qquad\qquad\qquad x = \pi$$

Because you squared the original equation, check for extraneous solutions.

Check

$\cos \dfrac{\pi}{2} + 1 \overset{?}{=} \sin \dfrac{\pi}{2}$	Substitute $\pi/2$ for x.
$0 + 1 = 1$	Solution checks. ✓
$\cos \dfrac{3\pi}{2} + 1 \overset{?}{=} \sin \dfrac{3\pi}{2}$	Substitute $3\pi/2$ for x.
$0 + 1 \neq -1$	Solution does not check.
$\cos \pi + 1 \overset{?}{=} \sin \pi$	Substitute π for x.
$-1 + 1 = 0$	Solution checks. ✓

Of the three possible solutions, $x = 3\pi/2$ is extraneous. So, in the interval $[0, 2\pi)$, the only solutions are $x = \pi/2$ and $x = \pi$. At the right, the graph of $y = \cos x + 1 - \sin x$ confirms this result because the graph has two x-intercepts (at $x = \pi/2$ and $x = \pi$) in the interval $[0, 2\pi)$.

Explore the Concept

Use a graphing utility to confirm the solutions found in Example 7 in two different ways. Do both methods produce the same x-values? Which method do you prefer? Why?

1. Graph both sides of the equation and find the x-coordinates of the points at which the graphs intersect.

   Left side: $y = \cos x + 1$

   Right side: $y = \sin x$

2. Graph the equation $y = \cos x + 1 - \sin x$ and find the x-intercepts of the graph.

✓ **Checkpoint**))) *Audio-video solution in English & Spanish at LarsonPrecalculus.com.*

Find all solutions of $\sin x + 1 = \cos x$ in the interval $[0, 2\pi)$.

Functions Involving Multiple Angles

The next two examples involve trigonometric functions of multiple angles of the forms $\sin ku$ and $\cos ku$. To solve equations of these forms, first solve the equation for ku, then divide your result by k.

EXAMPLE 8   Functions of Multiple Angles

Solve $2 \cos 3t - 1 = 0$.

Solution

$2 \cos 3t - 1 = 0$	Write original equation.
$2 \cos 3t = 1$	Add 1 to each side.
$\cos 3t = \dfrac{1}{2}$	Divide each side by 2.

In the interval $[0, 2\pi)$, you know that $3t = \pi/3$ and $3t = 5\pi/3$ are the only solutions. So in general, you have $3t = \pi/3 + 2n\pi$ and $3t = 5\pi/3 + 2n\pi$. Dividing this result by 3, you obtain the general solution

$$t = \frac{\pi}{9} + \frac{2n\pi}{3} \quad \text{and} \quad t = \frac{5\pi}{9} + \frac{2n\pi}{3} \qquad \text{General solution}$$

where n is an integer. This solution is confirmed graphically in Figure 5.7.

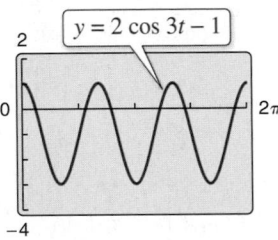

Figure 5.7

✓ **Checkpoint** 🔊))) *Audio-video solution in English & Spanish at LarsonPrecalculus.com.*

Solve $2 \sin 2t - \sqrt{3} = 0$.

EXAMPLE 9   Functions of Multiple Angles

$3 \tan \dfrac{x}{2} + 3 = 0$	Original equation
$3 \tan \dfrac{x}{2} = -3$	Subtract 3 from each side.
$\tan \dfrac{x}{2} = -1$	Divide each side by 3.

In the interval $[0, \pi)$, you know that $x/2 = 3\pi/4$ is the only solution. So in general, you have $x/2 = 3\pi/4 + n\pi$. Multiplying this result by 2, you obtain the general solution

$$x = \frac{3\pi}{2} + 2n\pi \qquad \text{General solution}$$

where n is an integer. This solution is confirmed graphically in Figure 5.8.

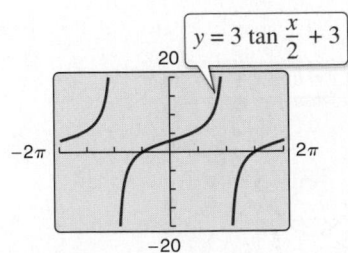

Figure 5.8

✓ **Checkpoint** 🔊))) *Audio-video solution in English & Spanish at LarsonPrecalculus.com.*

Solve $2 \tan \dfrac{x}{2} - 2 = 0$.

Using Inverse Functions

EXAMPLE 10 **Using Inverse Functions**

Solve $\sec^2 x - 2 \tan x = 4$.

Solution

$\sec^2 x - 2 \tan x = 4$	Write original equation.
$1 + \tan^2 x - 2 \tan x - 4 = 0$	Pythagorean identity
$\tan^2 x - 2 \tan x - 3 = 0$	Combine like terms.
$(\tan x - 3)(\tan x + 1) = 0$	Factor.

Setting each factor equal to zero, you obtain two solutions in the interval $(-\pi/2, \pi/2)$. [Recall that the range of the inverse tangent function is $(-\pi/2, \pi/2)$.]

$$\tan x = 3 \qquad \text{and} \qquad \tan x = -1$$

$$x = \arctan 3 \qquad\qquad x = \arctan(-1) = -\frac{\pi}{4}$$

Finally, because $\tan x$ has a period of π, add multiples of π to obtain

$$x = \arctan 3 + n\pi \qquad \text{and} \qquad x = -\frac{\pi}{4} + n\pi \qquad \text{General solution}$$

where n is an integer. This solution is confirmed graphically in Figure 5.9.

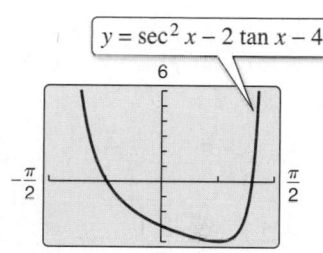

Figure 5.9

✓ **Checkpoint** ◀))) Audio-video solution in English & Spanish at LarsonPrecalculus.com.

Solve $4 \tan^2 x + 5 \tan x - 6 = 0$.   ◼

   With some trigonometric equations, there is no reasonable way to find the solutions algebraically. In such cases, you can still use a graphing utility to approximate the solutions.

EXAMPLE 11 **Approximating Solutions**

Approximate the solutions of

$$x = 2 \sin x$$

in the interval $[-\pi, \pi]$.

Solution

Use a graphing utility to graph $y = x - 2 \sin x$ in the interval $[-\pi, \pi]$. Using the *zero* or *root* feature, you can see that the solutions are

$$x \approx -1.8955, \quad x = 0, \quad \text{and} \quad x \approx 1.8955. \qquad \text{See Figure 5.10.}$$

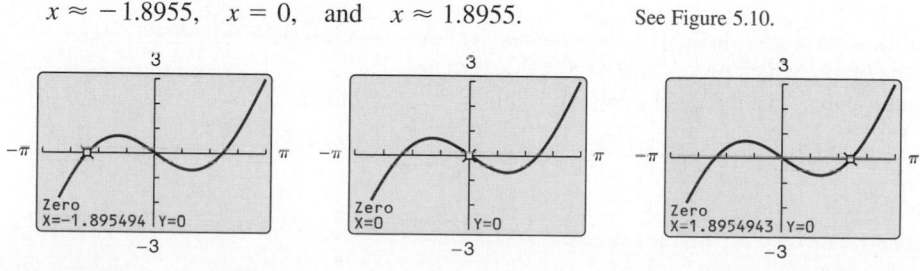

Figure 5.10 $y = x - 2 \sin x$

✓ **Checkpoint** ◀))) Audio-video solution in English & Spanish at LarsonPrecalculus.com.

Approximate the solutions of $x = -4 \sin 2x$ in the interval $[-\pi, \pi]$.   ◼

EXAMPLE 12   Surface Area of a Honeycomb

The surface area S (in square inches) of a honeycomb is given by

$$S = 6hs + \frac{3}{2}s^2\left(\frac{\sqrt{3} - \cos\theta}{\sin\theta}\right), \qquad 0 < \theta \le 90°$$

where $h = 2.4$ inches, $s = 0.75$ inch, and θ is the angle indicated in Figure 5.11.

a. For what value(s) of θ is the surface area 12 square inches?

b. What value of θ gives the minimum surface area?

$h = 2.4$ in.

$s = 0.75$ in.

Figure 5.11

Solution

a. Let $h = 2.4$, $s = 0.75$, and $S = 12$.

$$S = 6hs + \frac{3}{2}s^2\left(\frac{\sqrt{3} - \cos\theta}{\sin\theta}\right)$$

$$12 = 6(2.4)(0.75) + \frac{3}{2}(0.75)^2\left(\frac{\sqrt{3} - \cos\theta}{\sin\theta}\right)$$

$$12 = 10.8 + 0.84375\left(\frac{\sqrt{3} - \cos\theta}{\sin\theta}\right)$$

$$0 = 0.84375\left(\frac{\sqrt{3} - \cos\theta}{\sin\theta}\right) - 1.2$$

Using a graphing utility set in *degree* mode, you can graph the function

$$y = 0.84375\left(\frac{\sqrt{3} - \cos x}{\sin x}\right) - 1.2.$$

Using the *zero* or *root* feature, you can determine that

$$\theta \approx 49.9° \qquad \text{and} \qquad \theta \approx 59.9°. \qquad \text{See Figure 5.12.}$$

Figure 5.12 $y = 0.84375\left(\dfrac{\sqrt{3} - \cos x}{\sin x}\right) - 1.2$

b. From part (a), let $h = 2.4$ and $s = 0.75$ to obtain

$$S = 10.8 + 0.84375\left(\frac{\sqrt{3} - \cos\theta}{\sin\theta}\right).$$

Graph this function using a graphing utility set in *degree* mode. Use the *minimum* feature to approximate the minimum point on the graph, which occurs at $\theta \approx 54.7°$, as shown in Figure 5.13. By using calculus, it can be shown that the exact minimum value is

$$\theta = \arccos\left(\frac{1}{\sqrt{3}}\right) \approx 54.7356°.$$

$y = 10.8 + 0.84375\left(\dfrac{\sqrt{3} - \cos x}{\sin x}\right)$

Figure 5.13

✓ **Checkpoint** *Audio-video solution in English & Spanish at LarsonPrecalculus.com.*

Use the equation for the surface area of a honeycomb given in Example 12 with $h = 3.2$ inches and $s = 0.75$ inch to answer each question.

a. For what value(s) of θ is the surface area 15.8 square inches?

b. What value of θ gives the minimum surface area?

5.3   Exercises

See *CalcChat.com* for tutorial help and worked-out solutions to odd-numbered exercises.
For instructions on how to use a graphing utility, see Appendix A.

Vocabulary and Concept Check

In Exercises 1 and 2, fill in the blank.

1. The _____ solution of the equation $2 \cos x - 1 = 0$ is given by

$x = \dfrac{\pi}{3} + 2n\pi$ and $x = \dfrac{5\pi}{3} + 2n\pi$, where n is an integer.

2. The equation $\tan^2 x - 5 \tan x + 6 = 0$ is an equation of _____ type.

3. Is $x = 0$ a solution of the equation $\cos x = 0$?

4. To solve $\sec x \sin^2 x = \sec x$, do you divide each side by $\sec x$?

Procedures and Problem Solving

Verifying Solutions   In Exercises 5–10, verify that each x-value is a solution of the equation.

5. $\tan x - \sqrt{3} = 0$

   (a) $x = \dfrac{\pi}{3}$ (b) $x = \dfrac{4\pi}{3}$

6. $\sec x - 2 = 0$

   (a) $x = \dfrac{\pi}{3}$ (b) $x = \dfrac{5\pi}{3}$

7. $3 \tan^2 2x - 1 = 0$

   (a) $x = \dfrac{\pi}{12}$ (b) $x = \dfrac{5\pi}{12}$

8. $2 \cos^2 4x - 1 = 0$

   (a) $x = \dfrac{\pi}{16}$ (b) $x = \dfrac{3\pi}{16}$

9. $2 \sin^2 x - \sin x - 1 = 0$

   (a) $x = \dfrac{\pi}{2}$ (b) $x = \dfrac{7\pi}{6}$

10. $\csc^4 x - 4 \csc^2 x = 0$

   (a) $x = \dfrac{\pi}{6}$ (b) $x = \dfrac{5\pi}{6}$

Solving a Trigonometric Equation   In Exercises 11–16, find all solutions of the equation in the interval $[0°, 360°)$.

11. $\sin x = 0$ **12.** $\cos x = -1$

13. $\cos x = -\dfrac{\sqrt{2}}{2}$ **14.** $\cos x = \dfrac{\sqrt{3}}{2}$

15. $\tan x = 1$ **16.** $\tan x = -\sqrt{3}$

Solving a Trigonometric Equation   In Exercises 17–28, find all solutions of the equation in the interval $[0, 2\pi)$.

17. $\cos x = -\dfrac{\sqrt{3}}{2}$ **18.** $\sin x = -\dfrac{1}{2}$

19. $\cot x = -1$ **20.** $\sin x = \dfrac{\sqrt{3}}{2}$

21. $\tan x = -\dfrac{\sqrt{3}}{3}$ **22.** $\cos x = \dfrac{\sqrt{2}}{2}$

23. $\csc x = -2$ **24.** $\sec x = \sqrt{2}$

25. $\cot x = \sqrt{3}$ **26.** $\sec x = 2$

27. $\tan x = -1$ **28.** $\csc x = -\sqrt{2}$

Solving a Trigonometric Equation   In Exercises 29–36, solve the equation.

29. $2 \sin x + 1 = 0$ **30.** $\sqrt{2} \sin x + 1 = 0$

31. $\sqrt{3} \csc x - 2 = 0$ **32.** $\cot x + 1 = 0$

33. $3 \sec^2 x - 4 = 0$ **34.** $3 \cot^2 x - 1 = 0$

35. $\sin x(\sin x + 1) = 0$ **36.** $\cos x(\cos x - 1) = 0$

Solving a Trigonometric Equation   In Exercises 37–48, find all solutions of the equation in the interval $[0, 2\pi)$ algebraically. Use the *table* feature of a graphing utility to check your answers numerically.

37. $\cos x + 1 = -\cos x$ **38.** $3 \sin x + 1 = \sin x$

39. $\csc^2 x - 2 = 0$ **40.** $\tan^2 x - 1 = 0$

41. $\cos^3 x = \cos x$ **42.** $3 \tan^3 x = \tan x$

43. $\sin x \cos x = 3 \cos x$ **44.** $\sec x \csc x = 2 \csc x$

45. $2 \sin x + \csc x = 0$ **46.** $\sec x + \tan x = 1$

47. $\sec^2 x + \tan^2 x - 1 = 0$

48. $\sin^2 x + \cos x + 1 = 0$

Approximating Solutions   In Exercises 49–56, use a graphing utility to approximate the solutions of the equation in the interval $[0, 2\pi)$ by collecting all terms on one side, graphing the new equation, and using the *zero* or *root* feature to approximate the x-intercepts of the graph.

49. $2 \sin^2 x + 3 \sin x = -1$ **50.** $2 \sec^2 x + \tan^2 x = 3$

51. $4 \sin^2 x = 2 \cos x + 1$ **52.** $\csc^2 x - 3 \csc x = 4$

53. $\csc x + \cot x = 1$ **54.** $4 \sin x = \cos x - 2$

55. $\dfrac{\cos x \cot x}{1 - \sin x} = 3$ **56.** $\dfrac{1 + \sin x}{\cos^2 x} = 2$

Graphing a Trigonometric Function   In Exercises 57–60, (a) use a graphing utility to graph each function in the interval $[0, 2\pi)$, (b) write an equation whose solutions are the points of intersection of the graphs, and (c) use the *intersect* feature of the graphing utility to find the points of intersection (to four decimal places).

57. $y = \sin 2x, \quad y = x^2 - 2x$

58. $y = \cos x, \quad y = x + x^2$

59. $y = \sin^2 x, \quad y = e^x - 4x$

60. $y = \cos^2 x, \quad y = e^{-x} + x - 1$

Functions of Multiple Angles   In Exercises 61–68, solve the multiple-angle equation.

61. $\cos \dfrac{x}{4} = 0$

62. $\sin \dfrac{x}{2} = 0$

63. $\tan 4x = 1$

64. $\tan 2x = -1$

65. $\sec 4x = 2$

66. $\sin 2x = -\dfrac{\sqrt{3}}{2}$

67. $\cos \dfrac{x}{2} = \dfrac{\sqrt{2}}{2}$

68. $\csc \dfrac{x}{4} = \sqrt{2}$

Approximating x-Intercepts   In Exercises 69–72, approximate the x-intercepts of the graph. Use a graphing utility to check your solutions.

69. $y = \sin \dfrac{\pi x}{2} + 1$

70. $y = \sin \pi x + \cos \pi x$

71. $y = \tan^2\left(\dfrac{\pi x}{6}\right) - 3$

72. $y = \sec^4\left(\dfrac{\pi x}{8}\right) - 4$

     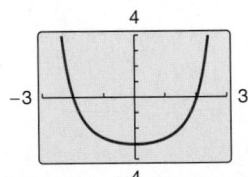

Approximating Solutions   In Exercises 73–80, use a graphing utility to approximate the solutions of the equation in the interval $[0, 2\pi)$.

73. $2 \cos x - \sin x = 0$

74. $2 \sin x + \cos x = 0$

75. $x \tan x - 1 = 0$

76. $2x \sin x - 2 = 0$

77. $\sec^2 x + 0.5 \tan x = 1$

78. $\csc^2 x + 0.5 \cot x = 5$

79. $6 \sin^2 x - 7 \sin x + 2 = 0$

80. $2 \tan^2 x + 7 \tan x - 15 = 0$

Using Inverse Functions   In Exercises 81–86, use inverse functions where necessary to solve the equation.

81. $\tan^2 x + \tan x - 12 = 0$

82. $\tan^2 x - \tan x - 2 = 0$

83. $\sec^2 x - 6 \tan x + 4 = 0$

84. $\sec^2 x + \tan x - 3 = 0$

85. $2 \sin^2 x + 5 \cos x = 4$

86. $2 \cos^2 x + 7 \sin x = 5$

Approximating Solutions   In Exercises 87–90, use a graphing utility to approximate the solutions (to three decimal places) of the equation in the given interval.

87. $3 \tan^2 x + 5 \tan x - 4 = 0, \quad \left(-\dfrac{\pi}{2}, \dfrac{\pi}{2}\right)$

88. $\cos^2 x - 2 \cos x - 1 = 0, \quad [0, \pi]$

89. $4 \cos^2 x - 2 \sin x + 1 = 0, \quad \left[-\dfrac{\pi}{2}, \dfrac{\pi}{2}\right]$

90. $2 \sec^2 x + \tan x - 6 = 0, \quad \left(-\dfrac{\pi}{2}, \dfrac{\pi}{2}\right)$

Approximating Maximum and Minimum Points   In Exercises 91–96, (a) use a graphing utility to graph the function and approximate the maximum and minimum points (to four decimal places) of the graph in the interval $[0, 2\pi]$, and (b) solve the trigonometric equation and verify that the x-coordinates of the maximum and minimum points of f are among its solutions. (The trigonometric equation is found using calculus.)

	Function	*Trigonometric Equation*
91.	$f(x) = \sin 2x$	$2 \cos 2x = 0$
92.	$f(x) = \cos 2x$	$-2 \sin 2x = 0$
93.	$f(x) = \sin^2 x + \cos x$	$2 \sin x \cos x - \sin x = 0$
94.	$f(x) = \cos^2 x - \sin x$	$-2 \sin x \cos x - \cos x = 0$
95.	$f(x) = \sin x + \cos x$	$\cos x - \sin x = 0$
96.	$f(x) = 2 \sin x + \cos 2x$	$2 \cos x - 4 \sin x \cos x = 0$

Finding a Fixed Point   In Exercises 97 and 98, find the smallest positive fixed point of the function f. [A *fixed point* of a function f is a real number c such that $f(c) = c$.]

97. $f(x) = \tan \dfrac{\pi x}{4}$

98. $f(x) = \cos x$

99. Economics   The monthly unit sales U (in thousands) of lawn mowers are approximated by

$$U = 74.50 - 43.75 \cos \dfrac{\pi t}{6}$$

where t is the time (in months), with $t = 1$ corresponding to January. Determine the months in which unit sales exceed 100,000.

100. Why you should learn it *(p. 365)* The monthly unit sales U (in hundreds) of skis for a chain of sports stores are approximated by

$$U = 58.3 + 32.5 \cos \frac{\pi t}{6}$$

where t is the time (in months), with $t = 1$ corresponding to January. Determine the months in which unit sales exceed 7500.

101. Graphical Reasoning Consider the function

$$f(x) = \cos \frac{1}{x}$$

and its graph shown in the figure.

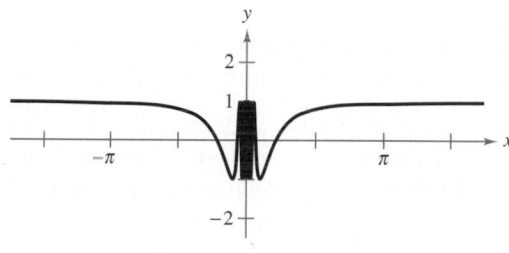

(a) What is the domain of the function?

(b) Identify any symmetry and asymptotes of the graph.

(c) Describe the behavior of the function as $x \to 0$.

(d) How many solutions does the equation $\cos(1/x) = 0$ have in the interval $[-1, 1]$? Find the solutions.

(e) Does the equation $\cos(1/x) = 0$ have a greatest solution? If so, approximate the solution. If not, explain why.

102. Graphical Reasoning Consider the function

$$f(x) = \frac{\sin x}{x}$$

and its graph shown in the figure.

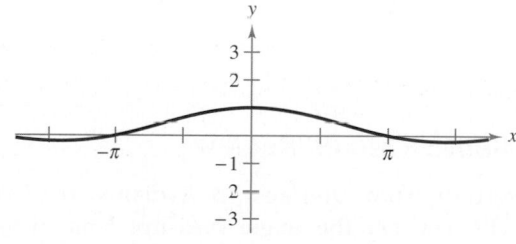

(a) What is the domain of the function?

(b) Identify any symmetry and asymptotes of the graph.

(c) Describe the behavior of the function as $x \to 0$.

(d) How many solutions does the equation $(\sin x)/x = 0$ have in the interval $[-8, 8]$? Find the solutions.

103. Harmonic Motion A weight is oscillating on the end of a spring (see figure). The position of the weight relative to the point of equilibrium is given by

$$y = \frac{1}{4}(\cos 8t - 3 \sin 8t)$$

where y is the displacement (in meters) and t is the time (in seconds). Find the times at which the weight is at the point of equilibrium ($y = 0$) for $0 \le t \le 1$.

Equilibrium

104. Damped Harmonic Motion The displacement from equilibrium of a weight oscillating on the end of a spring is given by $y = 1.56e^{-0.22t} \cos 4.9t$, where y is the displacement (in feet) and t is the time (in seconds). Use a graphing utility to graph the displacement function for $0 \le t \le 10$. Find the time beyond which the displacement does not exceed 1 foot from equilibrium.

105. Projectile Motion A batted baseball leaves the bat at an angle of θ with the horizontal and an initial velocity of $v_0 = 100$ feet per second. The ball is caught by an outfielder 310 feet from home plate (see figure). Find θ where the range r of a projectile is given by

$$r = \frac{1}{32}v_0^2 \sin 2\theta.$$

$r = 310$ ft

Not drawn to scale

106. Exploration Consider the function

$$f(x) = 3 \sin(0.6x - 2).$$

(a) Find the zero of f in the interval $[0, 6]$.

(b) A quadratic approximation of f near $x = 4$ is

$$g(x) = -0.45x^2 + 5.52x - 13.70.$$

Use a graphing utility to graph f and g in the same viewing window. Describe the result.

(c) Use the Quadratic Formula to approximate the zeros of g. Compare the zero in the interval $[0, 6]$ with the result of part (a).

107. Geometry The area of a rectangle inscribed in one arc of the graph of $y = \cos x$ (see figure) is given by

$$A = 2x \cos x, \quad 0 \le x \le \frac{\pi}{2}.$$

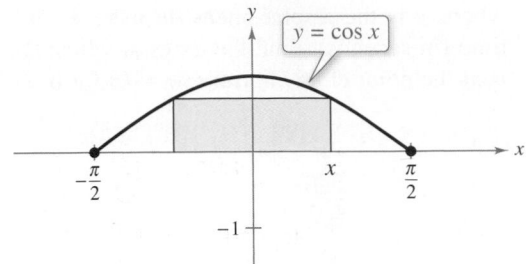

(a) Use a graphing utility to graph the area function and approximate the area of the largest inscribed rectangle.

(b) Determine the values of x for which $A \ge 1$.

108. MODELING DATA

The table shows the normal daily high temperatures in Honolulu, Hawaii, T (in degrees Fahrenheit) for month t, with $t = 1$ corresponding to January. (Source: NOAA)

Month, t	Temperature, T
1	80.1
2	80.2
3	81.2
4	82.7
5	84.6
6	87.0
7	87.9
8	88.7
9	88.6
10	86.7
11	83.9
12	81.2

Spreadsheet at LarsonPrecalulus.com

(a) Use a graphing utility to create a scatter plot of the data.

(b) Find a sine model for the temperatures.

(c) Use a graphing utility to plot the data and graph the model in the same viewing window. How well does the model fit the data?

(d) What term in the model you found in part (b) gives the average normal daily high temperature? What is the temperature?

(e) Use a graphing utility to describe the months in which the normal daily high temperature is above 86°F.

Points of Intersection In Exercises 109 and 110, use the graph to approximate the number of points of intersection of the graphs of y_1 and y_2.

109. $y_1 = 2 \sin x$
$y_2 = 3x + 1$

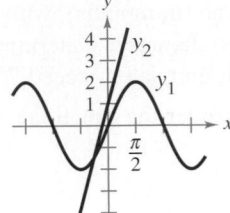

110. $y_1 = 2 \sin x$
$y_2 = \frac{1}{2}x + 1$

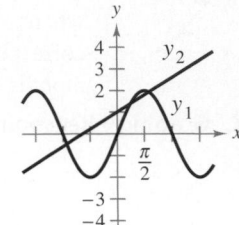

Conclusions

True or False? In Exercises 111 and 112, determine whether the statement is true or false. Justify your answer.

111. If you correctly solve a trigonometric equation down to the statement $\sin x = 3.4$, then you can finish solving the equation by using an inverse trigonometric function.

112. The equation $2 \sin 4t - 1 = 0$ has four times the number of solutions in the interval $[0, 2\pi)$ as the equation $2 \sin t - 1 = 0$.

113. Writing Describe the difference between verifying an identity and solving an equation.

114. HOW DO YOU SEE IT? Explain how to use the figure to solve the equation $2 \cos x - 1 = 0$.

Cumulative Mixed Review

Converting from Degrees to Radians In Exercises 115–118, convert the angle measure from degrees to radians. Round your answer to three decimal places.

115. $124°$ **116.** $486°$

117. $-215.63°$ **118.** $-0.46°$

119. Make a Decision To work an extended application analyzing the normal daily high temperatures in Phoenix and in Yakima, visit this textbook's website at *LarsonPrecalulus.com*. (Data Source: NOAA)

5.4   Sum and Difference Formulas

Using Sum and Difference Formulas

In this section and the following section, you will study the uses of several trigonometric identities and formulas.

Sum and Difference Formulas   (See proofs on page 400.)

$$\sin(u + v) = \sin u \cos v + \cos u \sin v$$

$$\sin(u - v) = \sin u \cos v - \cos u \sin v$$

$$\cos(u + v) = \cos u \cos v - \sin u \sin v$$

$$\cos(u - v) = \cos u \cos v + \sin u \sin v$$

$$\tan(u + v) = \frac{\tan u + \tan v}{1 - \tan u \tan v}$$

$$\tan(u - v) = \frac{\tan u - \tan v}{1 + \tan u \tan v}$$

What you should learn

▶ Use sum and difference formulas to evaluate trigonometric functions, verify trigonometric identities, and solve trigonometric equations.

Why you should learn it

You can use sum and difference formulas to rewrite trigonometric expressions. For instance, Exercise 77 on page 382 shows how to use sum and difference formulas to rewrite a trigonometric expression in a form that helps you find the equation of a standing wave.

Example 1 shows how **sum and difference formulas** can be used to find exact values of trigonometric functions involving sums or differences of special angles.

EXAMPLE 1   Evaluating a Trigonometric Function

See LarsonPrecalculus.com for an interactive version of this type of example.

Find the exact value of (a) $\cos 75°$ and (b) $\sin \dfrac{\pi}{12}$.

Solution

a. Using the fact that $75° = 30° + 45°$ with the formula for $\cos(u + v)$ yields

$$\cos 75° = \cos(30° + 45°)$$

$$= \cos 30° \cos 45° - \sin 30° \sin 45°$$

$$= \frac{\sqrt{3}}{2}\left(\frac{\sqrt{2}}{2}\right) - \frac{1}{2}\left(\frac{\sqrt{2}}{2}\right)$$

$$= \frac{\sqrt{6} - \sqrt{2}}{4}.$$

Try checking this result on your calculator. You will find that $\cos 75° \approx 0.259$.

b. Using the fact that

$$\frac{\pi}{12} = \frac{\pi}{3} - \frac{\pi}{4}$$

with the formula for $\sin(u - v)$ yields

$$\sin \frac{\pi}{12} = \sin\left(\frac{\pi}{3} - \frac{\pi}{4}\right)$$

$$= \sin \frac{\pi}{3} \cos \frac{\pi}{4} - \cos \frac{\pi}{3} \sin \frac{\pi}{4}$$

$$= \frac{\sqrt{3}}{2}\left(\frac{\sqrt{2}}{2}\right) - \frac{1}{2}\left(\frac{\sqrt{2}}{2}\right)$$

$$= \frac{\sqrt{6} - \sqrt{2}}{4}.$$

✓ *Checkpoint* 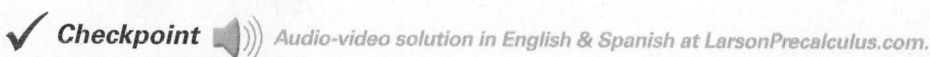 Audio-video solution in English & Spanish at LarsonPrecalculus.com.

Find the exact value of (a) $\cos(\pi/12)$ and (b) $\sin 75°$.

EXAMPLE 2 Evaluating a Trigonometric Expression

Find the exact value of $\sin(u + v)$ given $\sin u = 4/5$, where $0 < u < \pi/2$, and $\cos v = -12/13$, where $\pi/2 < v < \pi$.

Solution

Because $\sin u = 4/5$ and u is in Quadrant I, $\cos u = 3/5$, as shown in Figure 5.14. Because $\cos v = -12/13$ and v is in Quadrant II, $\sin v = 5/13$, as shown in Figure 5.15. You can find $\sin(u + v)$ as follows.

$$\sin(u + v) = \sin u \cos v + \cos u \sin v$$

$$= \left(\frac{4}{5}\right)\left(-\frac{12}{13}\right) + \left(\frac{3}{5}\right)\left(\frac{5}{13}\right) = -\frac{48}{65} + \frac{15}{65} = -\frac{33}{65}$$

Figure 5.14

Figure 5.15

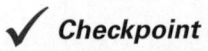 **Checkpoint** ◀))) Audio-video solution in English & Spanish at LarsonPrecalculus.com.

Find the exact value of $\cos(u + v)$ given $\sin u = 12/13$, where $0 < u < \pi/2$, and $\cos v = -3/5$, where $\pi/2 < v < \pi$.

EXAMPLE 3 An Application of a Sum Formula

Write $\cos(\arctan 1 + \arccos x)$ as an algebraic expression.

Solution

This expression fits the formula for $\cos(u + v)$. Angles $u = \arctan 1$ and $v = \arccos x$ are shown in Figures 5.16 and 5.17, respectively.

$$\cos(u + v) = \cos(\arctan 1)\cos(\arccos x) - \sin(\arctan 1)\sin(\arccos x)$$

$$= \frac{1}{\sqrt{2}} \cdot x - \frac{1}{\sqrt{2}} \cdot \sqrt{1 - x^2}$$

$$= \frac{x - \sqrt{1 - x^2}}{\sqrt{2}}.$$

Figure 5.16

Figure 5.17

 Checkpoint ◀))) Audio-video solution in English & Spanish at LarsonPrecalculus.com.

Write $\sin(\arctan 1 + \arccos x)$ as an algebraic expression.

Explore the Concept

Use a graphing utility to graph $y_1 = \cos(x + 2)$ and $y_2 = \cos x + \cos 2$ in the same viewing window. What can you conclude about the graphs? Is it true that

$$\cos(x + 2) = \cos x + \cos 2?$$

Use the graphing utility to graph

$$y_1 = \sin(x + 4)$$

and

$$y_2 = \sin x + \sin 4$$

in the same viewing window. What can you conclude about the graphs? Is it true that

$$\sin(x + 4) = \sin x + \sin 4?$$

EXAMPLE 4   Proving a Cofunction Identity

Prove the cofunction identity $\cos\left(\dfrac{\pi}{2} - x\right) = \sin x$.

Solution

Using the formula for $\cos(u - v)$, you have

$$\cos\left(\frac{\pi}{2} - x\right) = \cos\frac{\pi}{2}\cos x + \sin\frac{\pi}{2}\sin x$$

$$= (0)(\cos x) + (1)(\sin x)$$

$$= \sin x.$$

✓ **Checkpoint** ◀))) *Audio-video solution in English & Spanish at LarsonPrecalculus.com.*

Use a difference formula to prove the cofunction identity $\sin\left(x - \dfrac{\pi}{2}\right) = -\cos x$. ■

Sum and difference formulas can be used to derive **reduction formulas** involving expressions such as

$$\sin\left(\theta + \frac{n\pi}{2}\right) \quad \text{and} \quad \cos\left(\theta + \frac{n\pi}{2}\right)$$

where n is an integer.

EXAMPLE 5   Deriving Reduction Formulas

Simplify each expression.

a. $\cos\left(\theta - \dfrac{3\pi}{2}\right)$ **b.** $\tan(\theta + 3\pi)$

Solution

a. Using the formula for $\cos(u - v)$, you have

$$\cos\left(\theta - \frac{3\pi}{2}\right) = \cos\theta\cos\frac{3\pi}{2} + \sin\theta\sin\frac{3\pi}{2}$$

$$= (\cos\theta)(0) + (\sin\theta)(-1)$$

$$= -\sin\theta.$$

b. Using the formula for $\tan(u + v)$, you have

$$\tan(\theta + 3\pi) = \frac{\tan\theta + \tan 3\pi}{1 - \tan\theta\tan 3\pi}$$

$$= \frac{\tan\theta + 0}{1 - (\tan\theta)(0)}$$

$$= \tan\theta.$$

Note that the period of $\tan\theta$ is π, so the period of $\tan(\theta + 3\pi)$ is the same as the period of $\tan\theta$.

✓ **Checkpoint** ◀))) *Audio-video solution in English & Spanish at LarsonPrecalculus.com.*

Simplify each expression.

a. $\sin\left(\dfrac{3\pi}{2} - \theta\right)$ **b.** $\tan\left(\theta - \dfrac{\pi}{4}\right)$

■

EXAMPLE 6 **Solving a Trigonometric Equation**

Find all solutions of

$$\sin\left(x + \frac{\pi}{4}\right) + \sin\left(x - \frac{\pi}{4}\right) = -1$$

in the interval $[0, 2\pi)$.

Algebraic Solution

Using sum and difference formulas, rewrite the equation as

$$\sin x \cos \frac{\pi}{4} + \cos x \sin \frac{\pi}{4} + \sin x \cos \frac{\pi}{4} - \cos x \sin \frac{\pi}{4} = -1$$

$$2 \sin x \cos \frac{\pi}{4} = -1$$

$$2(\sin x)\left(\frac{\sqrt{2}}{2}\right) = -1$$

$$\sin x = -\frac{1}{\sqrt{2}}$$

$$\sin x = -\frac{\sqrt{2}}{2}.$$

So, the only solutions in the interval $[0, 2\pi)$ are

$$x = \frac{5\pi}{4} \quad \text{and} \quad x = \frac{7\pi}{4}.$$

Graphical Solution

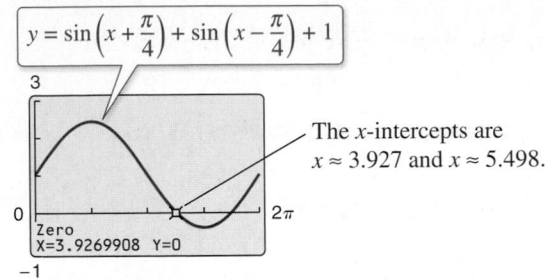

$$y = \sin\left(x + \frac{\pi}{4}\right) + \sin\left(x - \frac{\pi}{4}\right) + 1$$

The x-intercepts are $x \approx 3.927$ and $x \approx 5.498$.

From the figure, you can conclude that the approximate solutions in the interval $[0, 2\pi)$ are

$$x \approx 3.927 \approx \frac{5\pi}{4} \quad \text{and} \quad x \approx 5.498 \approx \frac{7\pi}{4}.$$

✓ **Checkpoint** ◀))) *Audio-video solution in English & Spanish at LarsonPrecalculus.com.*

Find all solutions of $\sin\left(x + \frac{\pi}{2}\right) + \sin\left(x - \frac{3\pi}{2}\right) = 1$ in the interval $[0, 2\pi)$. ■

The next example was taken from calculus. It is used to derive the formula for the derivative of the cosine function.

EXAMPLE 7 **An Application from Calculus** ∫

Verify that $\dfrac{\sin(x + h) - \sin x}{h} = (\cos x)\left(\dfrac{\sin h}{h}\right) - (\sin x)\left(\dfrac{1 - \cos h}{h}\right)$, where $h \neq 0$.

Solution

Using the formula for $\sin(u + v)$, you have

$$\frac{\sin(x + h) - \sin x}{h} = \frac{\sin x \cos h + \cos x \sin h - \sin x}{h}$$

$$= \frac{\cos x \sin h - \sin x(1 - \cos h)}{h}$$

$$= (\cos x)\left(\frac{\sin h}{h}\right) - (\sin x)\left(\frac{1 - \cos h}{h}\right).$$

✓ **Checkpoint** ◀))) *Audio-video solution in English & Spanish at LarsonPrecalculus.com.*

Verify that $\dfrac{\cos(x + h) - \cos x}{h} = (\cos x)\left(\dfrac{\cos h - 1}{h}\right) - (\sin x)\left(\dfrac{\sin h}{h}\right)$, where $h \neq 0$. ■

5.4 Exercises

See *CalcChat.com* for tutorial help and worked-out solutions to odd-numbered exercises.
For instructions on how to use a graphing utility, see Appendix A.

Vocabulary and Concept Check

In Exercises 1–6, fill in the blank to complete the trigonometric formula.

1. $\sin(u - v) = $ _____
2. $\cos(u + v) = $ _____
3. $\tan(u + v) = $ _____
4. $\sin(u + v) = $ _____
5. $\cos(u - v) = $ _____
6. $\tan(u - v) = $ _____

7. Rewrite $\sin 195°$ so that you can use a sum formula.

8. Rewrite $\cos \dfrac{\pi}{12}$ so that you can use a difference formula.

Procedures and Problem Solving

Evaluating Trigonometric Expressions In Exercises 9–12, find the exact value of each expression.

9. (a) $\cos(240° - 0°)$ (b) $\cos 240° - \cos 0°$
10. (a) $\sin(405° + 120°)$ (b) $\sin 405° + \sin 120°$
11. (a) $\sin\left(\dfrac{2\pi}{3} + \dfrac{5\pi}{6}\right)$ (b) $\sin\dfrac{2\pi}{3} + \sin\dfrac{5\pi}{6}$
12. (a) $\cos\left(\dfrac{\pi}{4} + \dfrac{\pi}{3}\right)$ (b) $\cos\dfrac{\pi}{4} + \cos\dfrac{\pi}{3}$

Evaluating Trigonometric Functions In Exercises 13–26, find the exact values of the sine, cosine, and tangent of the angle.

13. $105° = 60° + 45°$
14. $165° = 135° + 30°$
15. $195° = 225° - 30°$
16. $255° = 300° - 45°$
17. $-\dfrac{11\pi}{12} = \dfrac{\pi}{4} - \dfrac{7\pi}{6}$
18. $-\dfrac{19\pi}{12} = \dfrac{2\pi}{3} - \dfrac{9\pi}{4}$
19. $285°$
20. $15°$
21. $-105°$
22. $-165°$
23. $\dfrac{13\pi}{12}$
24. $\dfrac{5\pi}{12}$
25. $-\dfrac{7\pi}{12}$
26. $-\dfrac{23\pi}{12}$

Rewriting a Trigonometric Expression In Exercises 27–34, write the expression as the sine, cosine, or tangent of an angle.

27. $\sin 60° \cos 10° - \cos 60° \sin 10°$
28. $\sin 110° \cos 80° + \cos 110° \sin 80°$
29. $\dfrac{\tan 325° - \tan 116°}{1 + \tan 325° \tan 116°}$
30. $\dfrac{\tan 154° - \tan 49°}{1 + \tan 154° \tan 49°}$
31. $\cos\dfrac{\pi}{9} \cos\dfrac{\pi}{7} - \sin\dfrac{\pi}{9} \sin\dfrac{\pi}{7}$
32. $\sin\dfrac{4\pi}{9} \cos\dfrac{\pi}{8} + \cos\dfrac{4\pi}{9} \sin\dfrac{\pi}{8}$
33. $\sin 3.5x \cos 1.2y + \cos 3.5x \sin 1.2y$
34. $\cos 0.96y \cos 0.42z - \sin 0.96y \sin 0.42z$

Evaluating a Trigonometric Expression In Exercises 35–40, find the exact value of the expression.

35. $\sin\dfrac{\pi}{12} \cos\dfrac{\pi}{4} + \cos\dfrac{\pi}{12} \sin\dfrac{\pi}{4}$
36. $\cos\dfrac{\pi}{16} \cos\dfrac{3\pi}{16} - \sin\dfrac{\pi}{16} \sin\dfrac{3\pi}{16}$
37. $\sin 120° \cos 60° - \cos 120° \sin 60°$
38. $\cos 120° \cos 30° + \sin 120° \sin 30°$
39. $\dfrac{\tan(5\pi/6) - \tan(\pi/6)}{1 + \tan(5\pi/6) \tan(\pi/6)}$
40. $\dfrac{\tan 25° + \tan 110°}{1 - \tan 25° \tan 110°}$

Algebraic-Graphical-Numerical In Exercises 41 and 42, use a graphing utility to complete the table and graph the two functions in the same viewing window. Use both the table and the graph as evidence that $y_1 = y_2$. Then verify the identity algebraically.

x	0.2	0.4	0.6	0.8	1.0	1.2	1.4
y_1							
y_2							

41. $y_1 = \cos(x + \pi) \cos(x - \pi)$, $y_2 = \cos^2 x$
42. $y_1 = \sin(x + \pi) \sin(x - \pi)$, $y_2 = \sin^2 x$

Evaluating a Trigonometric Expression In Exercises 43–46, find the exact value of the trigonometric expression when $\sin u = \dfrac{5}{13}$ and $\cos v = -\dfrac{3}{5}$. (Both u and v are in Quadrant II.)

43. $\sin(u + v)$
44. $\tan(u + v)$
45. $\cos(u - v)$
46. $\sin(u - v)$

Evaluating a Trigonometric Expression In Exercises 47–50, find the exact value of the trigonometric expression when $\sin u = -\dfrac{7}{25}$ and $\cos v = -\dfrac{4}{5}$. (Both u and v are in Quadrant III.)

47. $\tan(u + v)$
48. $\cos(u + v)$
49. $\sin(v - u)$
50. $\cos(v - u)$

An Application of a Sum or Difference Formula In Exercises 51–54, write the trigonometric expression as an algebraic expression.

51. $\sin(\arcsin x + \arccos x)$ 52. $\cos(\arccos x - \arcsin x)$

53. $\sin(\arctan 2x - \arccos x)$

54. $\cos(\arcsin x - \arctan 2x)$

Evaluating a Trigonometric Expression In Exercises 55–58, find the value of the expression without using a calculator.

55. $\sin\left[\dfrac{\pi}{2} + \sin^{-1}(-1)\right]$ 56. $\sin[\cos^{-1}(-1) + \pi]$

57. $\sin(\sin^{-1} 1 + \cos^{-1} 1)$ 58. $\cos(\sin^{-1} 1 + \cos^{-1} 0)$

Evaluating a Trigonometric Expression In Exercises 59 and 60, use right triangles to evaluate the expression.

59. $\sin\left(\cos^{-1}\dfrac{4}{5} + \sin^{-1}\dfrac{3}{5}\right)$

60. $\sin\left(\cos^{-1}\dfrac{3}{5} - \sin^{-1}\dfrac{5}{13}\right)$

Verifying a Trigonometric Identity In Exercises 61–68, verify the identity.

61. $\sin\left(\dfrac{\pi}{2} + x\right) = \cos x$ 62. $\sin(3\pi - x) = \sin x$

63. $\tan(x + \pi) - \tan(\pi - x) = 2 \tan x$

64. $\tan\left(\dfrac{\pi}{4} - \theta\right) = \dfrac{1 - \tan\theta}{1 + \tan\theta}$

65. $\sin(x + y) + \sin(x - y) = 2 \sin x \cos y$

66. $\cos(x + y) + \cos(x - y) = 2 \cos x \cos y$

67. $\cos(x + y)\cos(x - y) = \cos^2 x - \sin^2 y$

68. $\sin(x + y)\sin(x - y) = \sin^2 x - \sin^2 y$

Solving a Trigonometric Equation In Exercises 69–72, find the solution(s) of the equation in the interval $[0, 2\pi)$. Use a graphing utility to verify your results.

69. $\sin\left(x + \dfrac{\pi}{3}\right) + \sin\left(x - \dfrac{\pi}{3}\right) = 1$

70. $\cos\left(x + \dfrac{\pi}{6}\right) - \cos\left(x - \dfrac{\pi}{6}\right) = 1$

71. $\tan(x + \pi) + 2 \sin(x + \pi) = 0$

72. $2 \sin\left(x + \dfrac{\pi}{2}\right) + 3 \tan(\pi - x) = 0$

Approximating Solutions Graphically In Exercises 73–76, use a graphing utility to approximate the solutions of the equation in the interval $[0, 2\pi)$.

73. $\cos\left(x + \dfrac{\pi}{4}\right) + \cos\left(x - \dfrac{\pi}{4}\right) = 1$

74. $\sin\left(x + \dfrac{\pi}{2}\right) - \cos\left(x + \dfrac{3\pi}{2}\right) = 1$

75. $\sin\left(x + \dfrac{\pi}{2}\right) = -\cos^2 x$

76. $\cos\left(x - \dfrac{\pi}{2}\right) = \sin^2 x$

77. **Why you should learn it** (p. 377) The equation of a standing wave is obtained by adding the displacements of two waves traveling in opposite directions (see figure). Assume that each wave has amplitude A, period T, and wavelength λ. The models for two such waves are

$$y_1 = A \cos 2\pi\left(\dfrac{t}{T} - \dfrac{x}{\lambda}\right) \text{ and } y_2 = A \cos 2\pi\left(\dfrac{t}{T} + \dfrac{x}{\lambda}\right).$$

Show that $y_1 + y_2 = 2A \cos\dfrac{2\pi t}{T} \cos\dfrac{2\pi x}{\lambda}$.

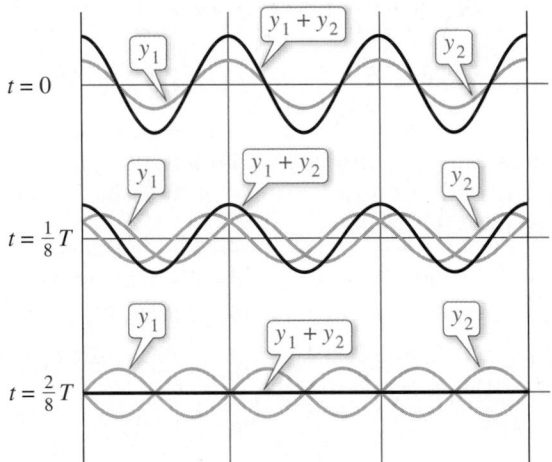

78. **Harmonic Motion** A weight is attached to a spring suspended vertically from a ceiling. When a driving force is applied to the system, the weight moves vertically from its equilibrium position, and this motion is modeled by

$$y = \dfrac{1}{3} \sin 2t + \dfrac{1}{4} \cos 2t$$

where y is the distance from equilibrium (in feet) and t is the time (in seconds).

(a) Use a graphing utility to graph the model.

(b) Use the identity

$$a \sin B\theta + b \cos B\theta = \sqrt{a^2 + b^2} \sin(B\theta + C)$$

where $C = \arctan(b/a)$, $a > 0$, to write the model in the form $y = \sqrt{a^2 + b^2} \sin(Bt + C)$. Use the graphing utility to verify your result.

(c) Find the amplitude of the oscillations of the weight.

(d) Find the frequency of the oscillations of the weight.

Conclusions

True or False? In Exercises 79 and 80, determine whether the statement is true or false. Justify your answer.

79. $\cos(u \pm v) = \cos u \pm \cos v$

80. $\sin\left(x - \dfrac{11\pi}{2}\right) = \cos x$

81. An Application from Calculus Let $x = \pi/3$ in the identity in Example 7 and define the functions f and g as follows.

$$f(h) = \frac{\sin[(\pi/3) + h] - \sin(\pi/3)}{h}$$

$$g(h) = \cos\frac{\pi}{3}\left(\frac{\sin h}{h}\right) - \sin\frac{\pi}{3}\left(\frac{1 - \cos h}{h}\right)$$

(a) What are the domains of the functions f and g?

(b) Use a graphing utility to complete the table.

h	0.01	0.02	0.05	0.1	0.2	0.5
$f(h)$						
$g(h)$						

(c) Use the graphing utility to graph the functions f and g.

(d) Use the table and graph to make a conjecture about the values of the functions f and g as $h \to 0^+$.

82. HOW DO YOU SEE IT? Explain how to use the figure to justify each statement.

(a) $\sin(u + v) \neq \sin u + \sin v$

(b) $\sin(u - v) \neq \sin u - \sin v$

Verifying an Identity In Exercises 83–86, verify the identity.

83. $\cos(n\pi + \theta) = (-1)^n \cos \theta$, $\quad n$ is an integer.

84. $\sin(n\pi + \theta) = (-1)^n \sin \theta$, $\quad n$ is an integer.

85. $a \sin B\theta + b \cos B\theta = \sqrt{a^2 + b^2} \sin(B\theta + C)$, where $C = \arctan(b/a)$ and $a > 0$.

86. $a \sin B\theta + b \cos B\theta = \sqrt{a^2 + b^2} \cos(B\theta - C)$, where $C = \arctan(a/b)$ and $b > 0$.

Rewriting a Trigonometric Expression In Exercises 87–90, use the formulas given in Exercises 85 and 86 to write the expression in the following forms. Use a graphing utility to verify your results.

(a) $\sqrt{a^2 + b^2} \sin(B\theta + C)$ (b) $\sqrt{a^2 + b^2} \cos(B\theta - C)$

87. $\sin \theta + \cos \theta$ **88.** $\sin 2\theta + \cos 2\theta$

89. $12 \sin 3\theta + 5 \cos 3\theta$ **90.** $3 \sin 2\theta + 4 \cos 2\theta$

Rewriting a Trigonometric Expression In Exercises 91 and 92, use the formulas given in Exercises 85 and 86 to write the trigonometric expression in the form $a \sin B\theta + b \cos B\theta$.

91. $2 \sin\left(\theta + \dfrac{\pi}{2}\right)$ **92.** $5 \cos\left(\theta + \dfrac{\pi}{4}\right)$

Angle Between Two Lines In Exercises 93 and 94, use the figure, which shows two lines whose equations are $y_1 = m_1 x + b_1$ and $y_2 = m_2 x + b_2$. Assume that both lines have positive slopes. Derive a formula for the angle between the two lines. Then use your formula to find the angle between the given pair of lines.

93. $y = x$,

$\quad\;\; y = \sqrt{3}x$

94. $y = x$,

$\quad\;\; y = \dfrac{1}{\sqrt{3}}x$

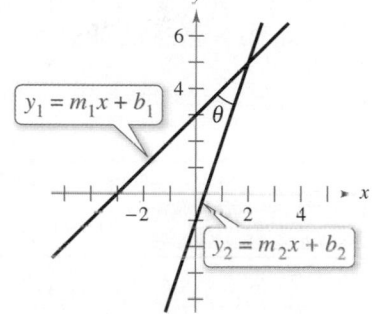

95. Proof Three squares of side s are placed side by side (see figure). Make a conjecture about the relationship between the sum $u + v$ and w. Prove your conjecture by using the formula for $\tan(u + v)$.

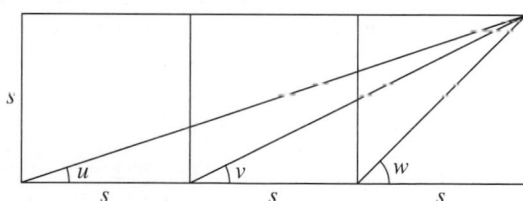

96. Writing a Formula Write a sum formula for $\cos(u + v + w)$.

Cumulative Mixed Review

Finding Intercepts In Exercises 97–100, find the x- and y-intercepts of the graph of the equation. Use a graphing utility to verify your results.

97. $y = -\frac{1}{2}(x - 10) + 14$ **98.** $y = x^2 - 3x - 40$

99. $y = |2x - 9| - 5$ **100.** $y - 2x\sqrt{x + 7}$

5.5 Multiple-Angle and Product-to-Sum Formulas

Multiple-Angle Formulas

In this section, you will study four additional categories of trigonometric identities.

1. The first category involves *functions of multiple angles* such as

$$\sin ku \quad \text{and} \quad \cos ku.$$

2. The second category involves *squares of trigonometric functions* such as

$$\sin^2 u.$$

3. The third category involves *functions of half-angles* such as

$$\sin \frac{u}{2}.$$

4. The fourth category involves *products of trigonometric functions* such as

$$\sin u \cos v.$$

You should learn the **double-angle formulas** below because they are used often in trigonometry and calculus.

Double-Angle Formulas (See the proofs on page 401.)

$$\sin 2u = 2 \sin u \cos u \qquad \cos 2u = \cos^2 u - \sin^2 u$$
$$\tan 2u = \frac{2 \tan u}{1 - \tan^2 u} \qquad \qquad = 2 \cos^2 u - 1$$
$$\qquad \qquad \qquad \qquad \qquad = 1 - 2 \sin^2 u$$

What you should learn

▶ Use multiple-angle formulas to rewrite and evaluate trigonometric functions.
▶ Use power-reducing formulas to rewrite and evaluate trigonometric functions.
▶ Use half-angle formulas to rewrite and evaluate trigonometric functions.
▶ Use product-to-sum and sum-to-product formulas to rewrite and evaluate trigonometric functions.

Why you should learn it

You can use a variety of trigonometric formulas to rewrite trigonometric functions in more convenient forms. For instance, Exercise 126 on page 393 shows you how to use a half-angle formula to determine the apex angle of a sound wave cone caused by the speed of an airplane.

EXAMPLE 1 Solving a Multiple-Angle Equation

Solve $2 \cos x + \sin 2x = 0$.

Solution

Begin by rewriting the equation so that it involves functions of x (rather than $2x$). Then factor and solve as usual.

$2 \cos x + \sin 2x = 0$	Write original equation.
$2 \cos x + 2 \sin x \cos x = 0$	Double-angle formula
$2 \cos x(1 + \sin x) = 0$	Factor.
$2 \cos x = 0 \qquad 1 + \sin x = 0$	Set factors equal to zero.
$\cos x = 0 \qquad \sin x = -1$	Isolate trigonometric functions.
$x = \dfrac{\pi}{2}, \dfrac{3\pi}{2} \qquad x = \dfrac{3\pi}{2}$	Solutions in $[0, 2\pi)$

So, the general solution is

$$x = \frac{\pi}{2} + 2n\pi \quad \text{and} \quad x = \frac{3\pi}{2} + 2n\pi \qquad \text{General solution}$$

where n is an integer. Try verifying this solution graphically.

✔ *Checkpoint* *Audio-video solution in English & Spanish at LarsonPrecalculus.com.*

Solve $\cos 2x + \cos x = 0$.

EXAMPLE 2   Evaluating Functions Involving Double Angles

Use the following to find $\sin 2\theta$, $\cos 2\theta$, and $\tan 2\theta$.

$$\cos \theta = \frac{5}{13}, \quad \frac{3\pi}{2} < \theta < 2\pi$$

Solution

In Figure 5.18, you can see that

$$\sin \theta = \frac{y}{r} = -\frac{12}{13} \quad \text{and} \quad \tan \theta = \frac{y}{x} = -\frac{12}{5}.$$

Consequently, using each of the double-angle formulas, you can write

$$\sin 2\theta = 2 \sin \theta \cos \theta = 2\left(-\frac{12}{13}\right)\left(\frac{5}{13}\right) = -\frac{120}{169}$$

$$\cos 2\theta = 2 \cos^2 \theta - 1 = 2\left(\frac{25}{169}\right) - 1 = -\frac{119}{169}$$

$$\tan 2\theta = \frac{2 \tan \theta}{1 - \tan^2 \theta} = \frac{2\left(-\frac{12}{5}\right)}{1 - \left(-\frac{12}{5}\right)^2} = \frac{120}{119}.$$

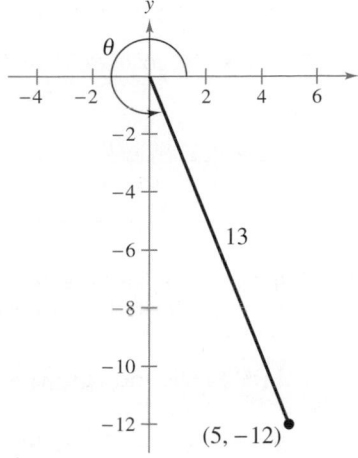

Figure 5.18

✓ **Checkpoint** 🔊))) *Audio-video solution in English & Spanish at LarsonPrecalculus.com.*

Use the following to find $\sin 2\theta$, $\cos 2\theta$, and $\tan 2\theta$.

$$\sin \theta = \frac{3}{5}, \quad 0 < \theta < \frac{\pi}{2}$$

The double-angle formulas are not restricted to the angles 2θ and θ. Other *double* combinations, such as 4θ and 2θ or 6θ and 3θ, are also valid. Here are two examples.

$$\sin 4\theta = 2 \sin 2\theta \cos 2\theta \quad \text{and} \quad \cos 6\theta = \cos^2 3\theta - \sin^2 3\theta$$

By using double-angle formulas together with the sum formulas derived in the preceding section, you can form other multiple-angle formulas.

EXAMPLE 3   Deriving a Triple-Angle Formula

Rewrite $\sin 3x$ in terms of $\sin x$.

Solution

$$\sin 3x = \sin(2x + x) \qquad \text{Rewrite as a sum.}$$

$$= \sin 2x \cos x + \cos 2x \sin x \qquad \text{Sum formula}$$

$$= 2 \sin x \cos x \cos x + (1 - 2 \sin^2 x) \sin x \qquad \text{Double-angle formulas}$$

$$= 2 \sin x \cos^2 x + \sin x - 2 \sin^3 x \qquad \text{Multiply.}$$

$$= 2 \sin x(1 - \sin^2 x) + \sin x - 2 \sin^3 x \qquad \text{Pythagorean identity}$$

$$= 2 \sin x - 2 \sin^3 x + \sin x - 2 \sin^3 x \qquad \text{Multiply.}$$

$$= 3 \sin x - 4 \sin^3 x \qquad \text{Simplify.}$$

✓ **Checkpoint** 🔊))) *Audio-video solution in English & Spanish at LarsonPrecalculus.com.*

Rewrite $\cos 3x$ in terms of $\cos x$.

Power–Reducing Formulas

The double-angle formulas can be used to obtain the following **power-reducing formulas.**

Power–Reducing Formulas   (See the proofs on page 401.)

$$\sin^2 u = \frac{1 - \cos 2u}{2}$$

$$\cos^2 u = \frac{1 + \cos 2u}{2}$$

$$\tan^2 u = \frac{1 - \cos 2u}{1 + \cos 2u}$$

Example 4 shows a typical power reduction that is used in calculus. Note the repeated use of power-reducing formulas.

EXAMPLE 4   Reducing a Power

Rewrite $\sin^4 x$ as a sum of first powers of the cosines of multiple angles.

Solution

$$\sin^4 x = (\sin^2 x)^2 \qquad\qquad \text{Property of exponents}$$

$$= \left(\frac{1 - \cos 2x}{2}\right)^2 \qquad \text{Power-reducing formula}$$

$$= \frac{1}{4}(1 - 2\cos 2x + \cos^2 2x) \qquad \text{Expand binomial.}$$

$$= \frac{1}{4}\left(1 - 2\cos 2x + \frac{1 + \cos 4x}{2}\right) \qquad \text{Power-reducing formula}$$

$$= \frac{1}{4} - \frac{1}{2}\cos 2x + \frac{1}{8} + \frac{1}{8}\cos 4x \qquad \text{Distributive Property}$$

$$= \frac{3}{8} - \frac{1}{2}\cos 2x + \frac{1}{8}\cos 4x \qquad \text{Simplify.}$$

$$= \frac{1}{8}(3 - 4\cos 2x + \cos 4x) \qquad \text{Factor.}$$

You can use a graphing utility to check this result, as shown in Figure 5.19. Notice that the graphs coincide.

Figure 5.19

✓ *Checkpoint* *Audio-video solution in English & Spanish at LarsonPrecalculus.com.*

Rewrite $\tan^4 x$ in terms of first powers of the cosines of multiple angles.

Half-Angle Formulas

You can derive some useful alternative forms of the power-reducing formulas by replacing u with $u/2$. The results are called **half-angle formulas.**

Half-Angle Formulas

$$\sin \frac{u}{2} = \pm \sqrt{\frac{1 - \cos u}{2}} \qquad \cos \frac{u}{2} = \pm \sqrt{\frac{1 + \cos u}{2}}$$

$$\tan \frac{u}{2} = \frac{1 - \cos u}{\sin u} = \frac{\sin u}{1 + \cos u}$$

The signs of $\sin \dfrac{u}{2}$ and $\cos \dfrac{u}{2}$ depend on the quadrant in which $\dfrac{u}{2}$ lies.

Remark

To find the exact value of a trigonometric function with an angle in D° M′S″ form using a half-angle formula, first convert the angle measure to decimal degree form. Then multiply the angle measure by 2.

EXAMPLE 5   Using a Half-Angle Formula

Find the exact value of $\sin 105°$.

Solution

Begin by noting that $105°$ is half of $210°$. Then, using the half-angle formula for $\sin(u/2)$ and the fact that $105°$ lies in Quadrant II, you have

$$\sin 105° = \sqrt{\frac{1 - \cos 210°}{2}} = \sqrt{\frac{1 + \left(\sqrt{3}/2\right)}{2}} = \frac{\sqrt{2 + \sqrt{3}}}{2}.$$

The positive square root is chosen because $\sin \theta$ is positive in Quadrant II.

Technology Tip

Use your calculator to verify the result obtained in Example 5. That is, evaluate $\sin 105°$ and $\left(\sqrt{2 + \sqrt{3}}\right)/2$. You will notice that both expressions yield the same result.

✓ **Checkpoint** ◀))) Audio-video solution in English & Spanish at LarsonPrecalculus.com.

Find the exact value of $\cos 105°$.

EXAMPLE 6   Solving a Trigonometric Equation

Find all solutions of $1 + \cos^2 x = 2 \cos^2 \dfrac{x}{2}$ in the interval $[0, 2\pi)$.

Algebraic Solution

$$1 + \cos^2 x = 2 \cos^2 \frac{x}{2} \qquad \text{Write original equation.}$$

$$1 + \cos^2 x = 2\left(\pm \sqrt{\frac{1 + \cos x}{2}}\right)^2 \qquad \text{Half-angle formula}$$

$$1 + \cos^2 x = 1 + \cos x \qquad \text{Simplify.}$$

$$\cos^2 x - \cos x = 0 \qquad \text{Simplify.}$$

$$\cos x(\cos x - 1) = 0 \qquad \text{Factor.}$$

By setting the factors $\cos x$ and $\cos x - 1$ equal to zero, you find that the solutions in the interval $[0, 2\pi)$ are $x = \pi/2$, $x = 3\pi/2$, and $x = 0$.

Graphical Solution

The x-intercepts are $x = 0$, $x \approx 1.571$, and $x \approx 4.712$.

$$y = 1 + \cos^2 x - 2 \cos^2 \frac{x}{2}$$

From the figure, you can conclude that the approximate solutions of $1 + \cos^2 x = 2 \cos^2 \dfrac{x}{2}$ in the interval $[0, 2\pi)$ are $x = 0$, $x \approx 1.571 \approx \dfrac{\pi}{2}$, and $x \approx 4.712 \approx \dfrac{3\pi}{2}$.

✓ **Checkpoint** ◀))) Audio-video solution in English & Spanish at LarsonPrecalculus.com.

Find all solutions of $\cos^2 x = \sin^2 \dfrac{x}{2}$ in the interval $[0, 2\pi)$.

Product–to–Sum Formulas

Each of the following **product-to-sum formulas** is easily verified using the sum and difference formulas discussed in the preceding section.

Product-to-Sum Formulas

$$\sin u \sin v = \frac{1}{2}[\cos(u - v) - \cos(u + v)]$$

$$\cos u \cos v = \frac{1}{2}[\cos(u - v) + \cos(u + v)]$$

$$\sin u \cos v = \frac{1}{2}[\sin(u + v) + \sin(u - v)]$$

$$\cos u \sin v = \frac{1}{2}[\sin(u + v) - \sin(u - v)]$$

Product-to-sum formulas are used in calculus to evaluate integrals involving the products of sines and cosines of two different angles.

EXAMPLE 7   Writing Products as Sums

Rewrite the product as a sum or difference.

$$\cos 5x \sin 4x$$

Solution

Using the appropriate product-to-sum formula, you obtain

$$\cos 5x \sin 4x = \frac{1}{2}[\sin(5x + 4x) - \sin(5x - 4x)]$$

$$= \frac{1}{2}\sin 9x - \frac{1}{2}\sin x.$$

✓ *Checkpoint*   *Audio-video solution in English & Spanish at LarsonPrecalculus.com.*

Rewrite the product $\sin 5x \cos 3x$ as a sum or difference.

Occasionally, it is useful to reverse the procedure and write a sum of trigonometric functions as a product. This can be accomplished with the following **sum-to-product formulas.**

Sum-to-Product Formulas   (See proof on page 402.)

$$\sin u + \sin v = 2 \sin\left(\frac{u + v}{2}\right) \cos\left(\frac{u - v}{2}\right)$$

$$\sin u - \sin v = 2 \cos\left(\frac{u + v}{2}\right) \sin\left(\frac{u - v}{2}\right)$$

$$\cos u + \cos v = 2 \cos\left(\frac{u + v}{2}\right) \cos\left(\frac{u - v}{2}\right)$$

$$\cos u - \cos v = -2 \sin\left(\frac{u + v}{2}\right) \sin\left(\frac{u - v}{2}\right)$$

Technology Tip

You can use a graphing utility to verify the solution to Example 7. Graph $y_1 = \cos 5x \sin 4x$ and $y_2 = \frac{1}{2}\sin 9x - \frac{1}{2}\sin x$ in the same viewing window. Notice that the graphs coincide. So, you can conclude that the two expressions are equivalent.

EXAMPLE 8   Using a Sum-to-Product Formula

Find the exact value of $\cos 195° + \cos 105°$.

Solution

Using the appropriate sum-to-product formula, you obtain

$$\cos 195° + \cos 105° = 2 \cos\left(\frac{195° + 105°}{2}\right) \cos\left(\frac{195° - 105°}{2}\right)$$

$$= 2 \cos 150° \cos 45°$$

$$= 2\left(-\frac{\sqrt{3}}{2}\right)\left(\frac{\sqrt{2}}{2}\right)$$

$$= -\frac{\sqrt{6}}{2}.$$

✓ **Checkpoint** ◄))) *Audio-video solution in English & Spanish at LarsonPrecalculus.com.*

Find the exact value of $\sin 195° + \sin 105°$.

EXAMPLE 9   Solving a Trigonometric Equation

See LarsonPrecalculus.com for an interactive version of this type of example.

Find all solutions of $\sin 5x + \sin 3x = 0$ in the interval $[0, 2\pi)$.

Solution

$$\sin 5x + \sin 3x = 0 \qquad \text{Write original equation.}$$

$$2 \sin\left(\frac{5x + 3x}{2}\right) \cos\left(\frac{5x - 3x}{2}\right) = 0 \qquad \text{Sum-to-product formula}$$

$$2 \sin 4x \cos x = 0 \qquad \text{Simplify.}$$

By setting the factor $\sin 4x$ equal to zero, you can find that the solutions in the interval $[0, 2\pi)$ are

$$x = 0, \frac{\pi}{4}, \frac{\pi}{2}, \frac{3\pi}{4}, \pi, \frac{5\pi}{4}, \frac{3\pi}{2}, \frac{7\pi}{4}.$$

The equation $\cos x = 0$ yields no additional solutions. You can use a graphing utility to confirm the solutions, as shown in the figure.

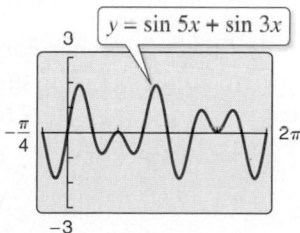

Notice that the general solution is

$$x = \frac{n\pi}{4}$$

where n is an integer.

✓ **Checkpoint** ◄))) *Audio-video solution in English & Spanish at LarsonPrecalculus.com.*

Solve $\sin 4x - \sin 2x = 0$ in the interval $[0, 2\pi)$.   ◼

5.5   Exercises

See *CalcChat.com* for tutorial help and worked-out solutions to odd-numbered exercises.
For instructions on how to use a graphing utility, see Appendix A.

Vocabulary and Concept Check

In Exercises 1–6, fill in the blank to complete the trigonometric formula.

1. $\cos^2 u = $ _____

2. $\sin u \sin v = $ _____

3. $\cos u - \cos v = $ _____

4. $\sin \dfrac{u}{2} = $ _____

5. _____ $= \dfrac{\sin u}{1 + \cos u}$

6. _____ $= \dfrac{1 - \cos 2u}{1 + \cos 2u}$

7. Match each function with its double-angle formula.

   (a) $\sin 2u$ (i) $1 - 2\sin^2 u$

   (b) $\cos 2u$ (ii) $2\sin u \cos u$

   (c) $\tan 2u$ (iii) $\dfrac{2 \tan u}{1 - \tan^2 u}$

8. Match each expression with its product-to-sum formula.

   (a) $\sin u \cos v$ (i) $\frac{1}{2}[\cos(u - v) + \cos(u + v)]$

   (b) $\cos u \sin v$ (ii) $\frac{1}{2}[\sin(u + v) + \sin(u - v)]$

   (c) $\cos u \cos v$ (iii) $\frac{1}{2}[\sin(u + v) - \sin(u - v)]$

Procedures and Problem Solving

Finding Exact Values of Trigonometric Functions   In Exercises 9 and 10, use the figure to find the exact value of each trigonometric function.

9.

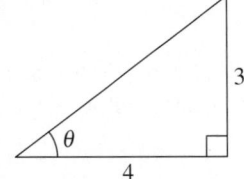

   (a) $\sin \theta$ (b) $\cos \theta$

   (c) $\tan \theta$ (d) $\sin 2\theta$

   (e) $\cos 2\theta$ (f) $\sec 2\theta$

   (g) $\csc 2\theta$ (h) $\cot 2\theta$

10.

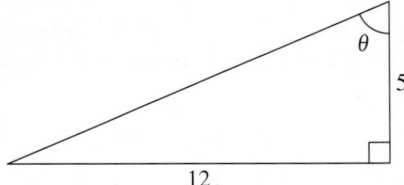

   (a) $\sin \theta$ (b) $\cos \theta$

   (c) $\tan \theta$ (d) $\cos 2\theta$

   (e) $\tan 2\theta$ (f) $\cot 2\theta$

   (g) $\sec 2\theta$ (h) $\csc 2\theta$

Solving a Multiple-Angle Equation   In Exercises 11–20, use a graphing utility to approximate the solutions of the equation in the interval $[0, 2\pi)$. If possible, find the exact solutions algebraically.

11. $\sin 2x - \sin x = 0$

12. $\sin 2x + \cos x = 0$

13. $4 \sin x \cos x = 1$

14. $\sin 2x \sin x = \cos x$

15. $\cos 2x - \cos x = 0$

16. $\cos 2x + \sin x = 0$

17. $\sin 4x = -2 \sin 2x$

18. $(\sin 2x + \cos 2x)^2 = 1$

19. $\tan 2x - \cot x = 0$

20. $\tan 2x - 2 \cos x = 0$

Evaluating Functions Involving Double Angles   In Exercises 21–26, find the exact values of $\sin 2u$, $\cos 2u$, and $\tan 2u$ using the double-angle formulas.

21. $\sin u = -\frac{3}{5}, \quad 3\pi/2 < u < 2\pi$

22. $\cos u = -\frac{2}{3}, \quad \pi/2 < u < \pi$

23. $\tan u = \frac{1}{2}, \quad \pi < u < 3\pi/2$

24. $\cot u = -6, \quad 3\pi/2 < u < 2\pi$

25. $\sec u = -2, \quad \pi/2 < u < \pi$

26. $\csc u = 3, \quad 0 < u < \pi/2$

Using a Double-Angle Formula   In Exercises 27–30, use a double-angle formula to rewrite the expression. Use a graphing utility to graph both expressions to verify that both forms are the same.

27. $6 \sin x \cos x$

28. $14 \sin x \cos x$

29. $\cos^2 x - \frac{1}{2}$

30. $10 \sin^2 x - 5$

Using a Power-Reducing Formula   In Exercises 31–34, rewrite the function using the power-reducing formulas. Then use a graphing utility to graph the function.

31. $f(x) = \sin^2 x$ **32.** $f(x) = \cos^2 x$

33. $f(x) = \cos^3 x$ **34.** $f(x) = \sin^3 x$

Reducing a Power   In Exercises 35–48, rewrite the expression in terms of the first power of the cosine. Use a graphing utility to graph both expressions to verify that both forms are the same.

35. $\cos^4 x$ **36.** $\sin^2 x \cos^2 x$

37. $\sin^8 x$ **38.** $\cos^8 x$

39. $\sin^2 x \cos^4 x$ **40.** $\sin^4 x \cos^2 x$

41. $\sin^2 2x$ **42.** $\cos^2 2x$

43. $\cos^2 \dfrac{x}{2}$ **44.** $\sin^2 \dfrac{x}{2}$

45. $\cos^2 x \tan^2 x$ **46.** $\sin^2 x \tan^2 x$

47. $\sin^4 \dfrac{x}{2}$ **48.** $\cos^4 \dfrac{x}{2}$

Finding Exact Values of Trigonometric Functions In Exercises 49 and 50, use the figure to find the exact value of each trigonometric function.

49.

(a) $\cos \dfrac{\theta}{2}$ (b) $\sin \dfrac{\theta}{2}$

(c) $\tan \dfrac{\theta}{2}$ (d) $\sec \dfrac{\theta}{2}$

(e) $\csc \dfrac{\theta}{2}$ (f) $\cot \dfrac{\theta}{2}$

(g) $2 \sin \dfrac{\theta}{2} \cos \dfrac{\theta}{2}$ (h) $2 \cos \dfrac{\theta}{2} \tan \dfrac{\theta}{2}$

50.

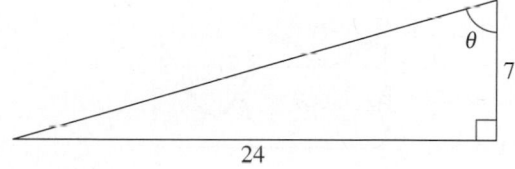

(a) $\sin \dfrac{\theta}{2}$ (b) $\cos \dfrac{\theta}{2}$

(c) $\tan \dfrac{\theta}{2}$ (d) $\cot \dfrac{\theta}{2}$

(e) $\sec \dfrac{\theta}{2}$ (f) $\csc \dfrac{\theta}{2}$

(g) $2 \sin \dfrac{\theta}{2} \cos \dfrac{\theta}{2}$ (h) $2 \cos \dfrac{\theta}{2} \tan \dfrac{\theta}{2}$

Using a Half-Angle Formula In Exercises 51–58, use the half-angle formulas to determine the exact values of the sine, cosine, and tangent of the angle.

51. $75°$ **52.** $165°$

53. $112° 30'$ **54.** $67° 30'$

55. $\dfrac{\pi}{8}$ **56.** $\dfrac{\pi}{12}$

57. $\dfrac{7\pi}{12}$ **58.** $\dfrac{5\pi}{8}$

Using a Half-Angle Formula In Exercises 59–64, find the exact values of $\sin(u/2)$, $\cos(u/2)$, and $\tan(u/2)$ using the half-angle formulas.

59. $\cos u = \dfrac{7}{25}, \quad 0 < u < \pi/2$

60. $\sin u = \dfrac{5}{13}, \quad \pi/2 < u < \pi$

61. $\cot u = 3, \quad \pi < u < 3\pi/2$

62. $\tan u = -\dfrac{5}{12}, \quad 3\pi/2 < u < 2\pi$

63. $\csc u = -\dfrac{5}{3}, \quad \pi < u < 3\pi/2$

64. $\sec u = \dfrac{7}{2}, \quad 0 < u < \pi/2$

Using a Half-Angle Formula In Exercises 65–68, use the half-angle formulas to simplify the expression.

65. $\sqrt{\dfrac{1 - \cos 6x}{2}}$ **66.** $\sqrt{\dfrac{1 + \cos 4x}{2}}$

67. $-\sqrt{\dfrac{1 - \cos 8x}{1 + \cos 8x}}$ **68.** $-\sqrt{\dfrac{1 - \cos(x - 1)}{2}}$

Solving a Trigonometric Equation In Exercises 69–72, find the solutions of the equation in the interval $[0, 2\pi)$. Use a graphing utility to verify your answers.

69. $\sin \dfrac{x}{2} + \cos x = 0$ **70.** $\sin \dfrac{x}{2} + \cos x - 1 = 0$

71. $\cos \dfrac{x}{2} - \sin x = 0$ **72.** $\tan \dfrac{x}{2} - \sin x = 0$

Writing Products as Sums In Exercises 73–80, use the product-to-sum formulas to write the product as a sum or difference.

73. $10 \cos 75° \cos 15°$ **74.** $6 \sin 45° \cos 15°$

75. $6 \sin \dfrac{\pi}{3} \cos \dfrac{\pi}{3}$ **76.** $4 \cos \dfrac{\pi}{3} \sin \dfrac{5\pi}{6}$

77. $5 \sin \theta \sin 3\theta$ **78.** $3 \sin 2\alpha \sin 3\alpha$

79. $\sin(x + y) \cos(x - y)$ **80.** $\sin(x + y) \sin(x - y)$

Writing Sums as Products In Exercises 81–88, use the sum-to-product formulas to write the sum or difference as a product.

81. $\sin 5\theta - \sin \theta$ **82.** $\sin 3\theta - \sin \theta$

83. $\cos 6x + \cos 2x$ **84.** $\sin x + \sin 5x$

85. $\sin(\alpha + \beta) - \sin(\alpha - \beta)$

86. $\cos(\phi + \alpha) - \cos(\phi - \alpha)$

87. $\cos\left(\theta + \dfrac{\pi}{2}\right) - \cos\left(\theta - \dfrac{\pi}{2}\right)$

88. $\sin\left(x + \dfrac{\pi}{2}\right) + \sin\left(x - \dfrac{\pi}{2}\right)$

Using a Sum-to-Product Formula In Exercises 89–92, use the sum-to-product formulas to find the exact value of the expression.

89. $\sin 75° + \sin 15°$ **90.** $\cos 120° + \cos 60°$

91. $\cos \dfrac{3\pi}{4} - \cos \dfrac{\pi}{4}$ **92.** $\sin \dfrac{5\pi}{4} - \sin \dfrac{3\pi}{4}$

Solving a Trigonometric Equation In Exercises 93–96, find the solutions of the equation in the interval $[0, 2\pi)$. Use a graphing utility to verify your answers.

93. $\sin 6x + \sin 2x = 0$ **94.** $\cos 2x - \cos 6x = 0$

95. $\dfrac{\cos 2x}{\sin 3x - \sin x} - 1 = 0$ **96.** $\sin^2 3x - \sin^2 x = 0$

Using Trigonometric Identities In Exercises 97–100, use the figure and trigonometric identities to find the exact value of the trigonometric function in two ways.

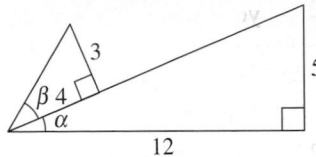

97. $\sin^2 \alpha$ **98.** $\cos^2 \alpha$

99. $\sin \alpha \cos \beta$ **100.** $\cos \alpha \sin \beta$

Verifying a Trigonometric Identity In Exercises 101–114, verify the identity algebraically. Use a graphing utility to check your result graphically.

101. $\csc 2\theta = \dfrac{\csc \theta}{2 \cos \theta}$ **102.** $\tan \dfrac{u}{2} = \csc u - \cot u$

103. $\cos^2 2\alpha - \sin^2 2\alpha = \cos 4\alpha$

104. $\cos^4 x - \sin^4 x = \cos 2x$

105. $(\sin x + \cos x)^2 = 1 + \sin 2x$

106. $\sin \dfrac{\alpha}{3} \cos \dfrac{\alpha}{3} = \dfrac{1}{2} \sin \dfrac{2\alpha}{3}$

107. $\dfrac{\sin 3y}{\sin y} = 1 - 2 \sin^2 y + 2 \cos^2 y$

108. $\dfrac{\cos 3\beta}{\cos \beta} = 1 - 4 \sin^2 \beta$

109. $\csc \dfrac{u}{2} = \pm \sqrt{\dfrac{2 \csc u}{\csc u - \cot u}}$

110. $\sec \dfrac{u}{2} = \pm \sqrt{\dfrac{2 \tan u}{\tan u + \sin u}}$

111. $\cos 3\beta = \cos^3 \beta - 3 \sin^2 \beta \cos \beta$

112. $\sin 4\beta = 4 \sin \beta \cos \beta (1 - 2 \sin^2 \beta)$

113. $\dfrac{\sin x \pm \sin y}{\cos x + \cos y} = \tan \dfrac{x \pm y}{2}$

114. $\dfrac{\sin x + \sin y}{\cos x - \cos y} = -\cot \dfrac{x - y}{2}$

Rewriting a Trigonometric Expression In Exercises 115–120, write the trigonometric expression as an algebraic expression.

115. $\sin(2 \arcsin x)$ **116.** $\cos(2 \arccos x)$

117. $\cos(2 \arcsin x)$ **118.** $\sin(2 \arccos x)$

119. $\sin(2 \arctan x)$ **120.** $\cos(2 \arctan x)$

ƒ **An Application from Calculus** In Exercises 121 and 122, the graph of a function f is shown over the interval $[0, 2\pi]$. **(a)** Find the x-intercepts of the graph of f algebraically. Verify your solutions by using the *zero* or *root* feature of a graphing utility. **(b)** The x-coordinates of the extrema of f are solutions of the trigonometric equation. (Calculus is required to find the trigonometric equation.) Find the solutions of the equation algebraically. Verify these solutions using the *maximum* and *minimum* features of the graphing utility.

121. *Function:* $f(x) = \sin 2x - \sin x$

Trigonometric Equation: $2 \cos 2x - \cos x = 0$

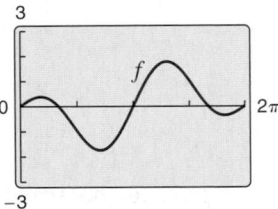

122. *Function:* $f(x) = \cos 2x + \sin x$

Trigonometric Equation: $-2 \sin 2x + \cos x = 0$

123. Projectile Motion The range of a projectile fired at an angle θ with the horizontal and with an initial velocity of v_0 feet per second is given by

$$r = \dfrac{1}{32} v_0^2 \sin 2\theta$$

where r is measured in feet. An athlete throws a javelin at 75 feet per second. At what angle must the athlete throw the javelin so that the javelin travels 130 feet?

124. Geometry The length of each of the two equal sides of an isosceles triangle is 10 meters (see figure). The angle between the two sides is θ.

10 m   10 m

(a) Write the area of the triangle as a function of $\theta/2$.

(b) Write the area of the triangle as a function of θ and determine the value of θ such that the area is a maximum.

125. Mechanical Engineering When two railroad tracks merge, the overlapping portions of the tracks are in the shape of a circular arc (see figure). The radius of each arc r (in feet) and the angle θ are related by

$$\frac{x}{2} = 2r \sin^2 \frac{\theta}{2}.$$

Write a formula for x in terms of $\cos \theta$.

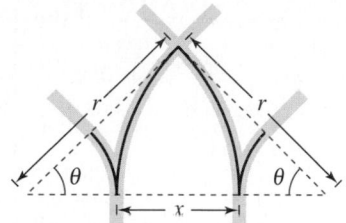

126. *Why you should learn it* (p. 384) The Mach number M of an airplane is the ratio of its speed to the speed of sound. When an airplane travels faster than the speed of sound, the sound waves form a cone behind the airplane (see figure). The Mach number is related to the apex angle θ of the cone by

$$\sin \frac{\theta}{2} = \frac{1}{M}.$$

(a) Find the angle θ that corresponds to a Mach number of 1.

(b) Find the angle θ that corresponds to a Mach number of 4.5.

(c) The speed of sound is about 760 miles per hour. Determine the speed of an object having the Mach numbers in parts (a) and (b).

(d) Rewrite the equation as a trigonometric function of θ.

Conclusions

True or False? In Exercises 127 and 128, determine whether the statement is true or false. Justify your answer.

127. $\sin \dfrac{x}{2} = -\sqrt{\dfrac{1 - \cos x}{2}}, \quad \pi \le x \le 2\pi$

128. The graph of $y = 4 - 8 \sin^2 x$ has a maximum at $(\pi, 4)$.

129. Exploration Consider the function

$$f(x) = \sin^4 x + \cos^4 x.$$

(a) Use the power-reducing formulas to write the function in terms of cosine to the first power.

(b) Determine another way of rewriting the function. Use a graphing utility to rule out incorrectly rewritten functions.

(c) Add a trigonometric term to the function so that it becomes a perfect square trinomial. Rewrite the function as a perfect square trinomial minus the term that you added. Use the graphing utility to rule out incorrectly rewritten functions.

(d) Rewrite the result of part (c) in terms of the sine of a double angle. Use the graphing utility to rule out incorrectly rewritten functions.

(e) When you rewrite a trigonometric expression, your result may not be the same as a friend's. Does this mean that one of you is wrong? Explain.

130. **HOW DO YOU SEE IT?** Explain how to use the figure to verify each double-angle formula.

(a) $\sin 2u = 2 \sin u \cos u$

(b) $\cos 2u = \cos^2 u - \sin^2 u$

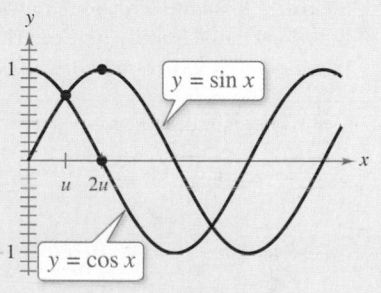

Cumulative Mixed Review

Finding the Midpoint of a Line Segment In Exercises 131–134, (a) plot the points, (b) find the distance between the points, and (c) find the midpoint of the line segment connecting the points.

131. $(5, 2), (-1, 4)$ **132.** $(-4, -3), (6, 10)$

133. $\left(-1, \frac{1}{2}\right), \left(\frac{4}{3}, \frac{5}{2}\right)$ **134.** $\left(\frac{1}{3}, \frac{2}{3}\right), \left(-1, -\frac{3}{2}\right)$

Finding the Complement and Supplement of Angles In Exercises 135–138, find (if possible) the complement and supplement of each angle.

135. (a) $55°$ (b) $162°$ **136.** (a) $109°$ (b) $78°$

137. (a) $\dfrac{\pi}{18}$ (b) $\dfrac{9\pi}{20}$ **138.** (a) $\dfrac{2\pi}{7}$ (b) $\dfrac{11\pi}{15}$

Finding an Arc Length In Exercises 139 and 140, find the length of the arc on a circle of radius r intercepted by a central angle θ.

139. $r = 21$ cm, $\theta = 35°$ **140.** $r = 15$ in., $\theta = 110°$

5 Chapter Summary

What did you learn?	Explanation and Examples	Review Exercises
5.1 Recognize and write the fundamental trigonometric identities *(p. 350)*.	**Reciprocal Identities** $\sin u = 1/\csc u \qquad \cos u = 1/\sec u \qquad \tan u = 1/\cot u$ $\csc u = 1/\sin u \qquad \sec u = 1/\cos u \qquad \cot u = 1/\tan u$ **Quotient Identities** $\qquad \tan u = \dfrac{\sin u}{\cos u} \qquad \cot u = \dfrac{\cos u}{\sin u}$ **Pythagorean Identities** $\sin^2 u + \cos^2 u = 1 \qquad\qquad 1 + \tan^2 u = \sec^2 u$ $1 + \cot^2 u = \csc^2 u$ **Cofunction Identities** $\sin[(\pi/2) - u] = \cos u \qquad \cos[(\pi/2) - u] = \sin u$ $\tan[(\pi/2) - u] = \cot u \qquad \cot[(\pi/2) - u] = \tan u$ $\sec[(\pi/2) - u] = \csc u \qquad \csc[(\pi/2) - u] = \sec u$ **Even/Odd Identities** $\sin(-u) = -\sin u \qquad \cos(-u) = \cos u \qquad \tan(-u) = -\tan u$ $\csc(-u) = -\csc u \qquad \sec(-u) = \sec u \qquad \cot(-u) = -\cot u$	1–10
Use the fundamental trigonometric identities to evaluate trigonometric functions, and simplify and rewrite trigonometric expressions *(p. 351)*.	On occasion, factoring or simplifying trigonometric expressions can best be done by first rewriting the expression in terms of just *one* trigonometric function or in terms of *sine or cosine alone*.	11–26
5.2 Verify trigonometric identities *(p. 357)*.	**Guidelines for Verifying Trigonometric Identities** 1. Work with one side of the equation at a time. 2. Look to factor an expression, add fractions, square a binomial, or create a monomial denominator. 3. Look to use the fundamental identities. Note which functions are in the final expression you want. Sines and cosines pair up well, as do secants and tangents, and cosecants and cotangents. 4. When the preceding guidelines do not help, try converting all terms to sines and cosines. 5. Always try *something*.	27–38
5.3 Use standard algebraic techniques to solve trigonometric equations *(p. 365)*.	Use standard algebraic techniques such as collecting like terms, extracting square roots, and factoring to solve trigonometric equations.	39–50
Solve trigonometric equations of quadratic type *(p. 368)*.	To solve trigonometric equations of quadratic type $ax^2 + bx + c = 0$, factor the quadratic or, when factoring is not possible, use the Quadratic Formula.	51–54
Solve trigonometric equations involving multiple angles *(p. 370)*.	To solve equations that contain forms such as $\sin ku$ or $\cos ku$, first solve the equation for ku, then divide your result by k.	55–62
Use inverse trigonometric functions to solve trigonometric equations *(p. 371)*.	After factoring an equation and setting the factors equal to 0, you may obtain an equation such as $\tan x - 3 = 0$. In this case, use inverse trigonometric functions to solve. (See Example 10.)	63–66

What did you learn?	Explanation and Examples	Review Exercises
5.4 Use sum and difference formulas to evaluate trigonometric functions, verify trigonometric identities, and solve trigonometric equations (*p. 377*).	**Sum and Difference Formulas** $\sin(u + v) = \sin u \cos v + \cos u \sin v$ $\sin(u - v) = \sin u \cos v - \cos u \sin v$ $\cos(u + v) = \cos u \cos v - \sin u \sin v$ $\cos(u - v) = \cos u \cos v + \sin u \sin v$ $\tan(u + v) = \dfrac{\tan u + \tan v}{1 - \tan u \tan v}$ $\tan(u - v) = \dfrac{\tan u - \tan v}{1 + \tan u \tan v}$	67–88
Use multiple-angle formulas to rewrite and evaluate trigonometric functions (*p. 384*).	**Double-Angle Formulas** $\sin 2u = 2 \sin u \cos u$ $\tan 2u = \dfrac{2 \tan u}{1 - \tan^2 u}$ $\cos 2u = \cos^2 u - \sin^2 u$ $ = 2 \cos^2 u - 1$ $ = 1 - 2 \sin^2 u$	89–98
Use power-reducing formulas to rewrite and evaluate trigonometric functions (*p. 386*).	**Power-Reducing Formulas** $\sin^2 u = \dfrac{1 - \cos 2u}{2}$ $\cos^2 u = \dfrac{1 + \cos 2u}{2}$ $\tan^2 u = \dfrac{1 - \cos 2u}{1 + \cos 2u}$	99–104
5.5 Use half-angle formulas to rewrite and evaluate trigonometric functions (*p. 387*).	**Half-Angle Formulas** $\sin \dfrac{u}{2} = \pm \sqrt{\dfrac{1 - \cos u}{2}}$ $\cos \dfrac{u}{2} = \pm \sqrt{\dfrac{1 + \cos u}{2}}$ $\tan \dfrac{u}{2} = \dfrac{1 - \cos u}{\sin u} = \dfrac{\sin u}{1 + \cos u}$ The signs of $\sin \dfrac{u}{2}$ and $\cos \dfrac{u}{2}$ depend on the quadrant in which $\dfrac{u}{2}$ lies.	105–118
Use product-to-sum formulas and sum-to-product formulas to rewrite and evaluate trigonometric functions (*p. 388*).	**Product-to-Sum Formulas** $\sin u \sin v = (1/2)[\cos(u - v) - \cos(u + v)]$ $\cos u \cos v = (1/2)[\cos(u - v) + \cos(u + v)]$ $\sin u \cos v = (1/2)[\sin(u + v) + \sin(u - v)]$ $\cos u \sin v = (1/2)[\sin(u + v) - \sin(u - v)]$ **Sum-to-Product Formulas** $\sin u + \sin v = 2 \sin\left(\dfrac{u + v}{2}\right) \cos\left(\dfrac{u - v}{2}\right)$ $\sin u - \sin v = 2 \cos\left(\dfrac{u + v}{2}\right) \sin\left(\dfrac{u - v}{2}\right)$ $\cos u + \cos v = 2 \cos\left(\dfrac{u + v}{2}\right) \cos\left(\dfrac{u - v}{2}\right)$ $\cos u - \cos v = -2 \sin\left(\dfrac{u + v}{2}\right) \sin\left(\dfrac{u - v}{2}\right)$	119–130

5   Review Exercises

See *CalcChat.com* for tutorial help and worked-out solutions to odd-numbered exercises.
For instructions on how to use a graphing utility, see Appendix A.

5.1

Recognizing a Fundamental Identity   In Exercises 1–10, name the trigonometric function that is equivalent to the expression.

1. $\dfrac{1}{\cos x}$

2. $\dfrac{1}{\sin x}$

3. $\dfrac{1}{\sec x}$

4. $\dfrac{1}{\csc x}$

5. $\sqrt{1 - \cos^2 x}$

6. $\sqrt{\csc^2 x - 1}$

7. $\cot\left(\dfrac{\pi}{2} - x\right)$

8. $\sec\left(\dfrac{\pi}{2} - x\right)$

9. $\sec(-x)$

10. $\tan(-x)$

Using Identities to Evaluate Functions   In Exercises 11–14, use the values to evaluate (if possible) the remaining trigonometric functions of the angle.

11. $\sin x = \dfrac{4}{5}, \quad \cos x = \dfrac{3}{5}$

12. $\tan \theta = \dfrac{2}{3}, \quad \sec \theta = \dfrac{\sqrt{13}}{3}$

13. $\sin\left(\dfrac{\pi}{2} - x\right) = \dfrac{1}{\sqrt{2}}, \quad \sin x = -\dfrac{1}{\sqrt{2}}$

14. $\csc\left(\dfrac{\pi}{2} - \theta\right) = -3, \quad \sin \theta = \dfrac{2\sqrt{2}}{3}$

Simplifying a Trigonometric Expression   In Exercises 15–24, use the fundamental identities to simplify the expression. Use the *table* feature of a graphing utility to check your result numerically.

15. $\dfrac{1}{\tan^2 x + 1}$

16. $\dfrac{\sin^2 \theta + \cos^2 \theta}{\sin \theta}$

17. $\dfrac{\tan(-\theta)}{\sec \theta}$

18. $\dfrac{\sec^2(-\theta)}{\csc^2 \theta}$

19. $\tan^2 \theta(\csc^2 \theta - 1)$

20. $\csc^2 x(1 - \cos^2 x)$

21. $\tan\left(\dfrac{\pi}{2} - x\right)\sec x$

22. $\dfrac{\sin x \cot x}{\sin\left(\dfrac{\pi}{2} - x\right)}$

23. $\dfrac{\sec^2 x - 1}{\sec x - 1}$

24. $\dfrac{\sin^2 \alpha - \cos^2 \alpha}{\sin^2 \alpha - \sin \alpha \cos \alpha}$

25. **Rate of Change** The rate of change of the function $f(x) = 2\sqrt{\sin x}$ is given by $\sin^{-1/2} x \cos x$. Show that the rate of change can also be written as $\cot x \sqrt{\sin x}$.

26. **Rate of Change** The rate of change of the function $f(x) = \csc x - \cot x$ is given by $\csc^2 x - \csc x \cot x$. Show that the rate of change can also be written as $(1 - \cos x)/\sin^2 x$.

5.2

Verifying a Trigonometric Identity   In Exercises 27–38, verify the identity.

27. $\cos x(\tan^2 x + 1) = \sec x$

28. $\sec^2 x \cot x - \cot x = \tan x$

29. $\sin^3 \theta + \sin \theta \cos^2 \theta = \sin \theta$

30. $\cot^2 x - \cos^2 x = \cot^2 x \cos^2 x$

31. $\csc^2\left(\dfrac{\pi}{2} - x\right) - 1 = \tan^2 x$

32. $\tan\left(\dfrac{\pi}{2} - x\right)\sec x = \csc x$

33. $\sin^4 x \cos^2 x = \cos^2 x - 2\cos^4 x + \cos^6 x$

34. $\cos^4 x \csc^2 x = \csc^2 x + \sin^2 x - 2$

35. $\sqrt{\dfrac{1 - \sin \theta}{1 + \sin \theta}} = \dfrac{1 - \sin \theta}{|\cos \theta|}$

36. $\sqrt{1 - \cos x} = \dfrac{|\sin x|}{\sqrt{1 + \cos x}}$

37. $\dfrac{\csc(-x)}{\sec(-x)} = -\cot x$

38. $\dfrac{1 + \sec(-x)}{\sin(-x) + \tan(-x)} = -\csc x$

5.3

Solving a Trigonometric Equation   In Exercises 39–50, solve the equation.

39. $2 \sin x - 1 = 0$

40. $\tan x + 1 = 0$

41. $\sin x = \sqrt{3} - \sin x$

42. $4 \cos x = 1 + 2 \cos x$

43. $3\sqrt{3} \cot x = 3$

44. $\frac{1}{2} \sec x - 1 = 0$

45. $3 \csc^2 x = 4$

46. $4 \tan^2 x - 1 = \tan^2 x$

47. $2 \cos^2 x - \cos x = 0$

48. $\sin^2 x + \sin x = 0$

49. $\sin x - \tan x = 0$

50. $\csc x - 2 \cot x = 0$

Solving a Trigonometric Equation   In Exercises 51–54, find all solutions of the equation in the interval $[0, 2\pi)$. Use a graphing utility to check your answers.

51. $2 \cos^2 x - \cos x = 1$

52. $2 \sin^2 x - 3 \sin x = -1$

53. $\cos^2 x + \sin x = 1$

54. $\sin^2 x + 2 \cos x = 2$

Functions of Multiple Angles   In Exercises 55–58, find all solutions of the multiple-angle equation in the interval $[0, 2\pi)$.

55. $2 \sin 2x = \sqrt{2}$

56. $\sqrt{3} \tan 3x = 1$

57. $2 \sin \dfrac{x}{2} = 1$

58. $\cos \dfrac{x}{3} = 0$

Functions of Multiple Angles   **In Exercises 59–62, solve the multiple-angle equation.**

59. $2 \sin 2x + 1 = 0$ **60.** $2 \cos 4x + \sqrt{3} = 0$

61. $2 \sin^2 3x - 1 = 0$ **62.** $4 \cos^2 2x - 3 = 0$

Using Inverse Functions   **In Exercises 63–66, use inverse functions where necessary to solve the equation.**

63. $\tan^2 x - 2 \tan x = 0$ **64.** $3 \cos^2 x + 5 \cos x = 0$

65. $3 \cos^2 x - \sin x - 1 = 0$

66. $\sec^2 x + 6 \tan x + 4 = 0$

5.4

Evaluating Trigonometric Functions   **In Exercises 67–70, find the exact values of the sine, cosine, and tangent of the angle.**

67. $285° = 315° - 30°$ **68.** $345° = 300° + 45°$

69. $\dfrac{31\pi}{12} = \dfrac{11\pi}{6} + \dfrac{3\pi}{4}$ **70.** $\dfrac{17\pi}{12} = \dfrac{7\pi}{4} - \dfrac{\pi}{3}$

Rewriting a Trigonometric Expression   **In Exercises 71–74, write the expression as the sine, cosine, or tangent of an angle.**

71. $\sin 45° \cos 60° - \cos 45° \sin 60°$

72. $\cos 45° \cos 120° - \sin 45° \sin 120°$

73. $\dfrac{\tan 25° + \tan 50°}{1 - \tan 25° \tan 50°}$ **74.** $\dfrac{\tan 63° - \tan 112°}{1 + \tan 63° \tan 112°}$

Evaluating a Trigonometric Expression   **In Exercises 75–80, find the exact value of the trigonometric function when $\sin u = \frac{4}{5}$ and $\cos v = -\frac{7}{25}$. (u is in Quadrant I and v is in Quadrant III.)**

75. $\sin(u + v)$ **76.** $\tan(u + v)$

77. $\tan(u - v)$ **78.** $\sin(u - v)$

79. $\cos(u + v)$ **80.** $\cos(u - v)$

Verifying a Trigonometric Identity   **In Exercises 81–86, verify the identity.**

81. $\cos\left(x + \dfrac{\pi}{2}\right) = -\sin x$ **82.** $\sin\left(x - \dfrac{3\pi}{2}\right) = \cos x$

83. $\cos(5\pi - x) = -\cos x$ **84.** $\sin(\pi - x) = \sin x$

85. $\cos 3x = 4 \cos^3 x - 3 \cos x$

86. $\dfrac{\sin(\alpha + \beta)}{\cos \alpha \cos \beta} = \tan \alpha + \tan \beta$

Solving a Trigonometric Equation   **In Exercises 87 and 88, find the solutions of the equation in the interval $[0, 2\pi)$.**

87. $\sin\left(x + \dfrac{\pi}{2}\right) - \sin\left(x - \dfrac{\pi}{2}\right) = \sqrt{2}$

88. $\cos\left(x + \dfrac{\pi}{4}\right) - \cos\left(x - \dfrac{\pi}{4}\right) = 1$

5.5

Evaluating Functions Involving Double Angles   **In Exercises 89–92, find the exact values of $\sin 2u$, $\cos 2u$, and $\tan 2u$ using the double-angle formulas.**

89. $\sin u = \dfrac{5}{7}, \quad 0 < u < \dfrac{\pi}{2}$

90. $\cos u = \dfrac{4}{5}, \quad \dfrac{3\pi}{2} < u < 2\pi$

91. $\tan u = -\dfrac{2}{9}, \quad \dfrac{\pi}{2} < u < \pi$

92. $\cos u = -\dfrac{2}{\sqrt{5}}, \quad \pi < u < \dfrac{3\pi}{2}$

Verifying a Trigonometric Identity   **In Exercises 93–96, use double-angle formulas to verify the identity algebraically. Use a graphing utility to check your result graphically.**

93. $6 \sin x \cos x = 3 \sin 2x$

94. $4 \sin x \cos x + 2 = 2 \sin 2x + 2$

95. $1 - 4 \sin^2 x \cos^2 x = \cos^2 2x$

96. $\sin 4x = 8 \cos^3 x \sin x - 4 \cos x \sin x$

97. Projectile Motion   A baseball leaves the hand of a player at first base at an angle of θ with the horizontal and at an initial velocity of $v_0 = 80$ feet per second. A player at second base 100 feet away catches the ball. Find θ when the range r of a projectile is

$$r = \dfrac{1}{32} v_0^2 \sin 2\theta.$$

98. Projectile Motion   Use the equation in Exercise 97 to find θ when a golf ball is hit with an initial velocity of $v_0 = 50$ feet per second and lands 77 feet away.

Reducing a Power   **In Exercises 99–104, use the power-reducing formulas to rewrite the expression in terms of the first power of the cosine.**

99. $\tan^2 4x$ **100.** $\sin^6 x$

101. $\cos^4 2x$ **102.** $\sin^4 2x$

103. $\cos^4 x \sin^4 x$

104. $\sin^2 2x \tan^2 2x$

Using a Half-Angle Formula   **In Exercises 105–108, use the half-angle formulas to determine the exact values of the sine, cosine, and tangent of the angle.**

105. $15°$ **106.** $157° \, 30'$

107. $\dfrac{7\pi}{8}$ **108.** $\dfrac{11\pi}{12}$

Using a Half-Angle Formula   In Exercises 109–112, find the exact values of $\sin(u/2)$, $\cos(u/2)$, and $\tan(u/2)$ using the half-angle formulas.

109. $\sin u = \dfrac{12}{13}$, $0 < u < \dfrac{\pi}{2}$

110. $\cos u = -\dfrac{3}{5}$, $\pi < u < \dfrac{3\pi}{2}$

111. $\tan u = -\dfrac{\sqrt{45}}{2}$, $\dfrac{\pi}{2} < u < \pi$

112. $\sec u = 6$, $\dfrac{3\pi}{2} < u < 2\pi$

Using a Half-Angle Formula   In Exercises 113–116, use the half-angle formulas to simplify the expression.

113. $-\sqrt{\dfrac{1 + \cos 8x}{2}}$ 114. $\sqrt{\dfrac{1 - \cos 6x}{2}}$

115. $\dfrac{\sin 10x}{1 + \cos 10x}$ 116. $\dfrac{1 - \cos 12x}{\sin 12x}$

Agriculture   In Exercises 117 and 118, a trough for feeding cattle is 4 meters long and its cross sections are isosceles triangles with two equal sides of $\frac{1}{2}$ meter (see figure). The angle between the equal sides is θ.

117. Write the trough's volume as a function of $\theta/2$.

118. Write the volume of the trough as a function of θ and determine the value of θ such that the volume is maximum.

Writing Products as Sums   In Exercises 119–122, use the product-to-sum formulas to write the product as a sum or difference.

119. $6 \sin \dfrac{\pi}{4} \cos \dfrac{\pi}{4}$ 120. $4 \sin 15° \sin 45°$

121. $\sin 5\alpha \sin 4\alpha$ 122. $\cos 6\theta \sin 8\theta$

Writing Sums as Products   In Exercises 123–126, use the sum-to-product formulas to write the sum or difference as a product.

123. $\cos 5\theta + \cos 4\theta$ 124. $\sin 3\theta + \sin 2\theta$

125. $\sin\left(x + \dfrac{\pi}{4}\right) - \sin\left(x - \dfrac{\pi}{4}\right)$

126. $\cos\left(x + \dfrac{\pi}{6}\right) - \cos\left(x - \dfrac{\pi}{6}\right)$

Harmonic Motion   In Exercises 127–130, a weight is attached to a spring suspended vertically from a ceiling. When a driving force is applied to the system, the weight moves vertically from its equilibrium position. This motion is described by the model

$$y = 1.5 \sin 8t - 0.5 \cos 8t$$

where y is the distance from equilibrium in feet and t is the time in seconds.

127. Write the model in the form

$$y = \sqrt{a^2 + b^2} \sin(Bt + C).$$

128. Use a graphing utility to graph the model.

129. Find the amplitude of the oscillations of the weight.

130. Find the frequency of the oscillations of the weight.

Conclusions

True or False?   In Exercises 131–134, determine whether the statement is true or false. Justify your answer.

131. If $\dfrac{\pi}{2} < \theta < \pi$, then $\cos \dfrac{\theta}{2} < 0$.

132. $\sin(x + y) = \sin x + \sin y$

133. $4 \sin(-x) \cos(-x) = -2 \sin 2x$

134. $4 \sin 45° \cos 15° = 1 + \sqrt{3}$

135. **Think About It**   List the reciprocal identities, quotient identities, and Pythagorean identities from memory.

136. **Think About It**   Is $\cos \theta = \sqrt{1 - \sin^2 \theta}$ an identity? Explain.

137. **Think About It**   Is any trigonometric equation with an infinite number of solutions an identity? Explain.

138. **Think About It**   Does the equation $a \sin x - b = 0$ have a solution when $|a| < |b|$? Explain.

Think About It   In Exercises 139 and 140, use the graphs of y_1 and y_2 to determine how to change y_2 to a new function y_3 such that $y_1 = y_3$.

139. $y_1 = \sec^2\left(\dfrac{\pi}{2} - x\right)$ 140. $y_1 = \dfrac{\cos 3x}{\cos x}$

$y_2 = \cot^2 x$ $y_2 = (2 \sin x)^2$

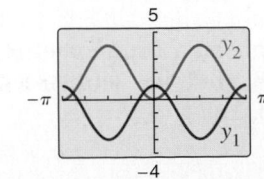

5 Chapter Test

See *CalcChat.com* for tutorial help and worked-out solutions to odd-numbered exercises. For instructions on how to use a graphing utility, see Appendix A.

Take this test as you would take a test in class. After you are finished, check your work against the answers given in the back of the book.

1. Given $\tan \theta = \frac{3}{2}$ and $\cos \theta < 0$, use the fundamental identities to evaluate the other five trigonometric functions of θ.

2. Use the fundamental identities to simplify $\csc^2 \beta (1 - \cos^2 \beta)$.

3. Factor and simplify $\dfrac{\sec^4 x - \tan^4 x}{\sec^2 x + \tan^2 x}$.

4. Add and simplify $\dfrac{\cos \theta}{\sin \theta} + \dfrac{\sin \theta}{\cos \theta}$.

5. Determine the values of $\theta, 0 \le \theta < 2\pi$, for which $\tan \theta = -\sqrt{\sec^2 \theta - 1}$ is true.

6. Use a graphing utility to graph the functions $y_1 = \sin x + \cos x \cot x$ and $y_2 = \csc x$. Make a conjecture about y_1 and y_2. Verify your result algebraically.

In Exercises 7–12, verify the identity.

7. $\sin \theta \sec \theta = \tan \theta$

8. $\sec^2 x \tan^2 x + \sec^2 x = \sec^4 x$

9. $\dfrac{\csc \alpha + \sec \alpha}{\sin \alpha + \cos \alpha} = \cot \alpha + \tan \alpha$

10. $\sin\left(x - \dfrac{3\pi}{2}\right) + \sin\left(\dfrac{\pi}{2} + x\right) = 2 \cos x$

11. $\sin(n\pi + \theta) = (-1)^n \sin \theta$, n is an integer.

12. $(\sin x + \cos x)^2 = 1 + \sin 2x$

13. Find the exact value of $\cos 255°$.

14. Rewrite $\sin^4 x \tan^2 x$ in terms of the first power of the cosine.

15. Use a half-angle formula to simplify the expression $\dfrac{\sin 4\theta}{1 + \cos 4\theta}$.

16. Write $4 \cos 2\theta \sin 4\theta$ as a sum or difference.

17. Write $\cos 3\theta - \cos \theta$ as a product.

In Exercises 18–21, find all solutions of the equation in the interval $[0, 2\pi)$.

18. $\tan^2 x + \tan x = 0$

19. $\sin 2\alpha - \cos \alpha = 0$

20. $4 \cos^2 x - 3 = 0$

21. $\csc^2 x - \csc x - 2 = 0$

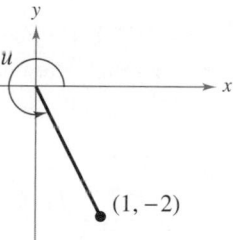

Figure for 23

22. Use a graphing utility to approximate the solutions of the equation $5 \sin x - x = 0$ accurate to three decimal places.

23. Use the figure to find the exact values of $\sin 2u$, $\cos 2u$, and $\tan 2u$.

24. The *index of refraction n* of a transparent material is the ratio of the speed of light in a vacuum to the speed of light in the material. For the triangular glass prism in the figure, $n = 1.5$ and $\alpha = 60°$. Find the angle θ for the glass prism given that

$$n = \dfrac{\sin\left(\dfrac{\theta}{2} + \dfrac{\alpha}{2}\right)}{\sin \dfrac{\theta}{2}}.$$

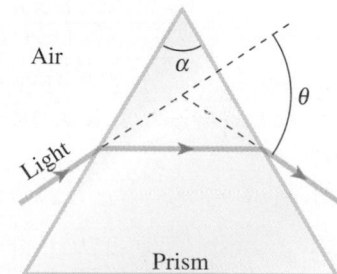

Figure for 24

Proofs in Mathematics

Sum and Difference Formulas (p. 377)

$$\sin(u + v) = \sin u \cos v + \cos u \sin v$$

$$\sin(u - v) = \sin u \cos v - \cos u \sin v$$

$$\cos(u + v) = \cos u \cos v - \sin u \sin v$$

$$\cos(u - v) = \cos u \cos v + \sin u \sin v$$

$$\tan(u + v) = \frac{\tan u + \tan v}{1 - \tan u \tan v}$$

$$\tan(u - v) = \frac{\tan u - \tan v}{1 + \tan u \tan v}$$

Proof

You can use the figures at the right for the proofs of the formulas for $\cos(u \pm v)$. In the top figure, let A be the point $(1, 0)$ and then use u and v to locate the points $B(x_1, y_1)$, $C(x_2, y_2)$, and $D(x_3, y_3)$ on the unit circle. So, $x_i^2 + y_i^2 = 1$ for $i = 1, 2,$ and 3. For convenience, assume that $0 < v < u < 2\pi$. In the bottom figure, note that arcs AC and BD have the same length. So, line segments AC and BD are also equal in length, which implies that

$$\sqrt{(x_2 - 1)^2 + (y_2 - 0)^2} = \sqrt{(x_3 - x_1)^2 + (y_3 - y_1)^2}$$

$$x_2^2 - 2x_2 + 1 + y_2^2 = x_3^2 - 2x_1x_3 + x_1^2 + y_3^2 - 2y_1y_3 + y_1^2$$

$$(x_2^2 + y_2^2) + 1 - 2x_2 = (x_3^2 + y_3^2) + (x_1^2 + y_1^2) - 2x_1x_3 - 2y_1y_3$$

$$1 + 1 - 2x_2 = 1 + 1 - 2x_1x_3 - 2y_1y_3$$

$$x_2 = x_3x_1 + y_3y_1.$$

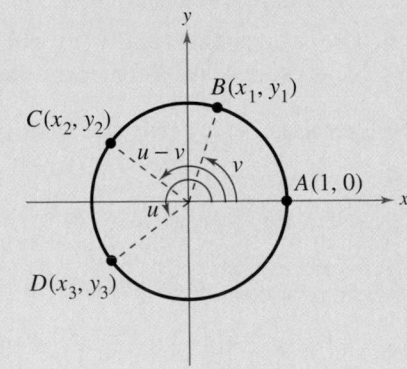

Finally, by substituting the values $x_2 = \cos(u - v)$, $x_3 = \cos u$, $x_1 = \cos v$, $y_3 = \sin u$, and $y_1 = \sin v$, you obtain $\cos(u - v) = \cos u \cos v + \sin u \sin v$. The formula for $\cos(u + v)$ can be established by considering $u + v = u - (-v)$ and using the formula just derived to obtain

$$\cos(u + v) = \cos[u - (-v)] = \cos u \cos(-v) + \sin u \sin(-v)$$

$$= \cos u \cos v - \sin u \sin v.$$

You can use the sum and difference formulas for sine and cosine to prove the formulas for $\tan(u \pm v)$.

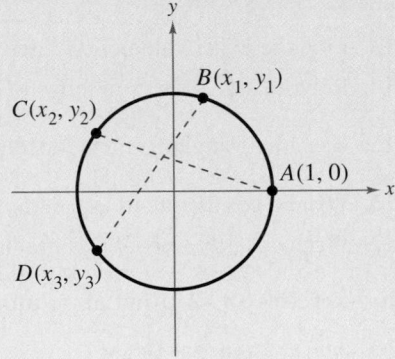

$$\tan(u \pm v) = \frac{\sin(u \pm v)}{\cos(u \pm v)} \qquad \text{Quotient identity}$$

$$= \frac{\sin u \cos v \pm \cos u \sin v}{\cos u \cos v \mp \sin u \sin v} \qquad \text{Sum and difference formulas}$$

$$= \frac{\dfrac{\sin u \cos v \pm \cos u \sin v}{\cos u \cos v}}{\dfrac{\cos u \cos v \mp \sin u \sin v}{\cos u \cos v}} \qquad \begin{array}{l}\text{Divide numerator and denominator} \\ \text{by } \cos u \cos v.\end{array}$$

$$= \dfrac{\dfrac{\sin u \cos v}{\cos u \cos v} \pm \dfrac{\cos u \sin v}{\cos u \cos v}}{\dfrac{\cos u \cos v}{\cos u \cos v} \mp \dfrac{\sin u \sin v}{\cos u \cos v}}$$ Write as separate fractions.

$$= \dfrac{\dfrac{\sin u}{\cos u} \pm \dfrac{\sin v}{\cos v}}{1 \mp \dfrac{\sin u}{\cos u} \cdot \dfrac{\sin v}{\cos v}}$$ Product of fractions

$$= \dfrac{\tan u \pm \tan v}{1 \mp \tan u \tan v}$$ Quotient identity   ■

Double-Angle Formulas   (p. 384)

$$\sin 2u = 2 \sin u \cos u \qquad \cos 2u = \cos^2 u - \sin^2 u$$

$$\tan 2u = \dfrac{2 \tan u}{1 - \tan^2 u} \qquad\quad = 2 \cos^2 u - 1$$

$$\qquad\qquad\qquad\qquad\qquad = 1 - 2 \sin^2 u$$

Proof

To prove all three formulas, let $v = u$ in the corresponding sum formulas.

$$\sin 2u = \sin(u + u) = \sin u \cos u + \cos u \sin u = 2 \sin u \cos u$$

$$\cos 2u = \cos(u + u) = \cos u \cos u - \sin u \sin u = \cos^2 u - \sin^2 u$$

$$\tan 2u = \tan(u + u) = \dfrac{\tan u + \tan u}{1 - \tan u \tan u} = \dfrac{2 \tan u}{1 - \tan^2 u}$$ ■

Power-Reducing Formulas   (p. 386)

$$\sin^2 u = \dfrac{1 - \cos 2u}{2} \qquad \cos^2 u = \dfrac{1 + \cos 2u}{2} \qquad \tan^2 u = \dfrac{1 - \cos 2u}{1 + \cos 2u}$$

Proof

To prove the first formula, solve for $\sin^2 u$ in the double-angle formula $\cos 2u = 1 - 2 \sin^2 u$, as follows.

$$\cos 2u = 1 - 2 \sin^2 u$$ Write double-angle formula.

$$2 \sin^2 u = 1 - \cos 2u$$ Subtract cos $2u$ from and add 2 sin^2 u to each side.

$$\sin^2 u = \dfrac{1 - \cos 2u}{2}$$ Divide each side by 2.

Trigonometry and Astronomy

Trigonometry was used by early astronomers to calculate measurements in the universe. Trigonometry was used to calculate the circumference of Earth and the distance from Earth to the moon. Another major accomplishment in astronomy using trigonometry was computing distances to stars.

In a similar way, you can prove the second formula by solving for $\cos^2 u$ in the double-angle formula

$$\cos 2u = 2\cos^2 u - 1.$$

To prove the third formula, use a quotient identity, as follows.

$$\tan^2 u = \frac{\sin^2 u}{\cos^2 u}$$

$$= \frac{\dfrac{1 - \cos 2u}{2}}{\dfrac{1 + \cos 2u}{2}}$$

$$= \frac{1 - \cos 2u}{1 + \cos 2u} \qquad\blacksquare$$

Sum-to-Product Formulas (p.388)

$$\sin u + \sin v = 2 \sin\!\left(\frac{u + v}{2}\right) \cos\!\left(\frac{u - v}{2}\right)$$

$$\sin u - \sin v = 2 \cos\!\left(\frac{u + v}{2}\right) \sin\!\left(\frac{u - v}{2}\right)$$

$$\cos u + \cos v = 2 \cos\!\left(\frac{u + v}{2}\right) \cos\!\left(\frac{u - v}{2}\right)$$

$$\cos u - \cos v = -2 \sin\!\left(\frac{u + v}{2}\right) \sin\!\left(\frac{u - v}{2}\right)$$

Proof

To prove the first formula, let $x = u + v$ and $y = u - v$. Then substitute $u = (x + y)/2$ and $v = (x - y)/2$ in the product-to-sum formula.

$$\sin u \cos v = \frac{1}{2}[\sin(u + v) + \sin(u - v)]$$

$$\sin\!\left(\frac{x + y}{2}\right) \cos\!\left(\frac{x - y}{2}\right) = \frac{1}{2}(\sin x + \sin y)$$

$$2 \sin\!\left(\frac{x + y}{2}\right) \cos\!\left(\frac{x - y}{2}\right) = \sin x + \sin y$$

The other sum-to-product formulas can be proved in a similar manner. $\qquad\blacksquare$

6 Additional Topics in Trigonometry

6.1 Law of Sines

6.2 Law of Cosines

6.3 Vectors in the Plane

6.4 Vectors and Dot Products

6.5 Trigonometric Form of a Complex Number

```
180-abs(tan-1(-2.4065))
            112.5648997
```

Section 6.3, Example 10
Direction of an Airplane

©Andresr/Shutterstock.com

403

6.1 Law of Sines

Introduction

In Chapter 4, you studied techniques for solving right triangles. In this section and the next, you will solve **oblique triangles**—triangles that have no right angles. As standard notation, the angles of a triangle are labeled

A, B, and C

and their opposite sides are labeled

a, b, and c

as shown in the figure.

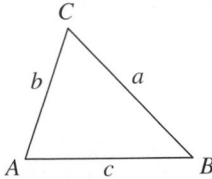

To solve an oblique triangle, you need to know the measure of at least one side and the measures of any two other parts of the triangle—two sides, two angles, or one angle and one side. This breaks down into the following four cases.

1. Two angles and any side (AAS or ASA)

2. Two sides and an angle opposite one of them (SSA)

3. Three sides (SSS)

4. Two sides and their included angle (SAS)

The first two cases can be solved using the **Law of Sines,** whereas the last two cases can be solved using the Law of Cosines (see Section 6.2).

What you should learn

▶ Use the Law of Sines to solve oblique triangles (AAS or ASA).
▶ Use the Law of Sines to solve oblique triangles (SSA).
▶ Find areas of oblique triangles and use the Law of Sines to model and solve real-life problems.

Why you should learn it

You can use the Law of Sines to solve real-life problems involving oblique triangles. For instance, Exercise 48 on page 411 shows how the Law of Sines can be used to help determine the distance from a boat to the shoreline.

Law of Sines   (See the proof on page 464.)

If ABC is a triangle with sides a, b, and c, then

$$\frac{a}{\sin A} = \frac{b}{\sin B} = \frac{c}{\sin C}.$$

Oblique Triangles

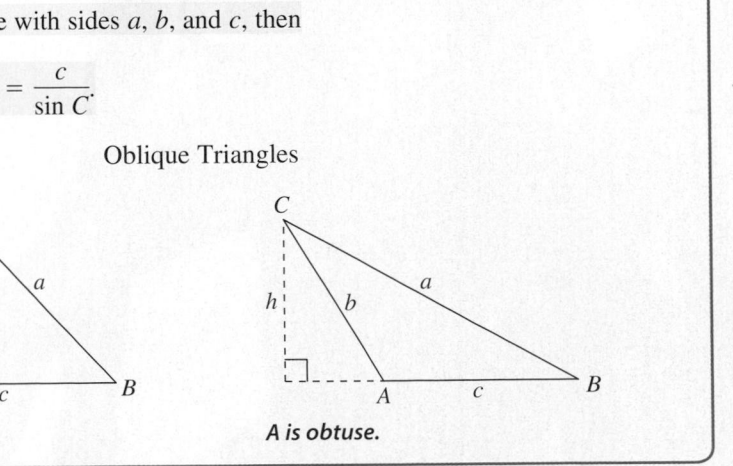

A is acute.   A is obtuse.

Remark

Notice that the height h of each triangle can be found using the formula

$$\frac{h}{b} = \sin A$$

or

$$h = b \sin A.$$

The Law of Sines can also be written in the reciprocal form

$$\frac{\sin A}{a} = \frac{\sin B}{b} = \frac{\sin C}{c}.$$

EXAMPLE 1   Given Two Angles and One Side—AAS

For the triangle shown,

$C = 102.3°, B = 28.7°,$ and $b = 27.4$ feet.

Find the remaining angle and sides.

Solution

The third angle of the triangle is

$A = 180° - B - C$

$= 180° - 28.7° - 102.3°$

$= 49.0°.$

By the Law of Sines, you have

$$\frac{a}{\sin A} = \frac{b}{\sin B} = \frac{c}{\sin C}.$$

Using $b = 27.4$ produces

$$a = \frac{b}{\sin B}(\sin A) = \frac{27.4}{\sin 28.7°}(\sin 49.0°) \approx 43.06 \text{ feet}$$

and

$$c = \frac{b}{\sin B}(\sin C) = \frac{27.4}{\sin 28.7°}(\sin 102.3°) \approx 55.75 \text{ feet}.$$

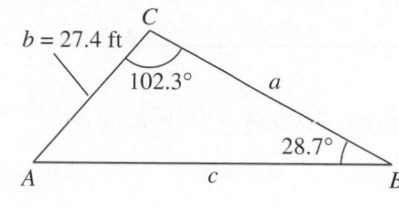

Remark

When you are solving a triangle, a careful sketch is useful as a quick test for the feasibility of an answer. Remember that the longest side lies opposite the largest angle, and the shortest side lies opposite the smallest angle.

✓ **Checkpoint** 🔊))) *Audio-video solution in English & Spanish at LarsonPrecalculus.com.*

For the triangle shown, $A = 30°, B = 45°,$ and $a = 32.$ Find the remaining angle and sides.

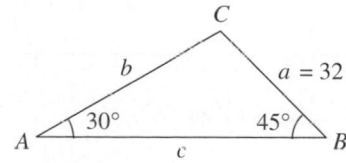

EXAMPLE 2   Given Two Angles and One Side—ASA

A pole tilts *toward* the sun at an 8° angle from the vertical, and it casts a 22-foot shadow. (See Figure 6.1.) The angle of elevation from the tip of the shadow to the top of the pole is 43°. How tall is the pole?

Solution

In Figure 6.1, $A = 43°$ and $B = 90° + 8° = 98°.$ So, the third angle is

$C = 180° - A - B = 180° - 43° - 98° = 39°.$

By the Law of Sines, you have

$$\frac{a}{\sin A} = \frac{c}{\sin C}.$$

Because $c = 22$ feet, the length of the pole is

$$a = \frac{c}{\sin C}(\sin A) = \frac{22}{\sin 39°}(\sin 43°) \approx 23.84 \text{ feet}.$$

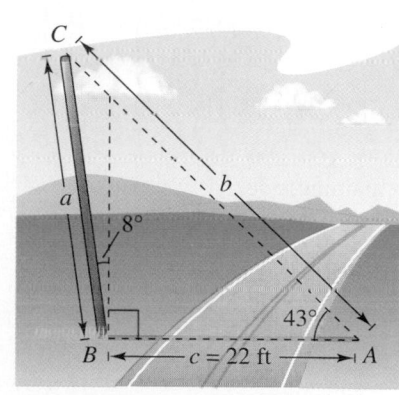

Figure 6.1

✓ **Checkpoint** 🔊))) *Audio-video solution in English & Spanish at LarsonPrecalculus.com.*

Rework Example 2 for a pole that tilts *away from* the sun under the same conditions.

The Ambiguous Case (SSA)

In Examples 1 and 2, you saw that two angles and one side determine a unique triangle. However, if two sides and one opposite angle are given, then three possible situations can occur: (1) no such triangle exists, (2) one such triangle exists, or (3) two distinct triangles satisfy the conditions.

The Ambiguous Case (SSA)

Consider a triangle in which you are given a, b, and A. ($h = b \sin A$)

	A is acute.	A is acute.	A is acute.	A is acute.	A is obtuse.	A is obtuse.
Sketch					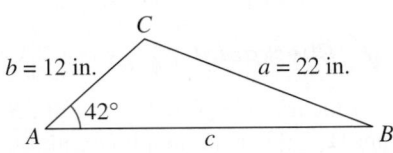	
Necessary condition	$a < h$	$a = h$	$a \geq b$	$h < a < b$	$a \leq b$	$a > b$
Possible triangles	None	One	One	Two	None	One

Single-Solution Case—SSA

See LarsonPrecalculus.com for an interactive version of this type of example.

For the triangle in Figure 6.2, $a = 22$ inches, $b = 12$ inches, and $A = 42°$. Find the remaining side and angles.

Solution

By the Law of Sines, you have

$$\frac{\sin B}{b} = \frac{\sin A}{a} \qquad \text{Reciprocal form}$$

$$\sin B = b\left(\frac{\sin A}{a}\right) \qquad \text{Multiply each side by } b.$$

$$\sin B = 12\left(\frac{\sin 42°}{22}\right) \qquad \text{Substitute for } A, a, \text{ and } b.$$

$$B \approx 21.41°. \qquad \text{Solve for acute angle } B.$$

Now you can determine that $C \approx 180° - 42° - 21.41° = 116.59°$. Then find the remaining side.

$$\frac{c}{\sin C} = \frac{a}{\sin A} \qquad \text{Law of Sines}$$

$$c = \frac{a}{\sin A}(\sin C) \qquad \text{Multiply each side by } \sin C.$$

$$c \approx \frac{22}{\sin 42°}(\sin 116.59°) \qquad \text{Substitute for } a, A, \text{ and } C.$$

$$c \approx 29.40 \text{ inches} \qquad \text{Simplify.}$$

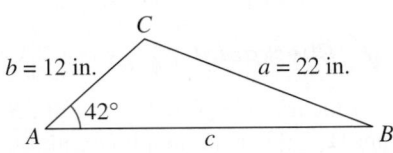

One solution: $a \geq b$

Figure 6.2

✓ **Checkpoint**))) *Audio-video solution in English & Spanish at LarsonPrecalculus.com.*

Given $A = 31°$, $a = 12$, and $b = 5$, find the remaining side and angles of the triangle.

Figure 6.3   No solution: $a < h$

   No-Solution Case–SSA

Show that there is no triangle for which $a = 15$, $b = 25$, and $A = 85°$.

Solution

Begin by making a sketch, as shown in Figure 6.3. From this figure, it appears that no triangle is formed. You can verify this by using the Law of Sines.

$$\frac{\sin B}{b} = \frac{\sin A}{a} \qquad \text{Reciprocal form}$$

$$\sin B = b\left(\frac{\sin A}{a}\right) = 25\left(\frac{\sin 85°}{15}\right) \approx 1.6603 > 1$$

This contradicts the fact that $|\sin B| \leq 1$. So, no triangle can be formed having sides $a = 15$ and $b = 25$ and an angle of $A = 85°$.

✓ **Checkpoint**)))) Audio-video solution in English & Spanish at LarsonPrecalculus.com.

Show that there is no triangle for which $a = 4$, $b = 14$, and $A = 60°$.

EXAMPLE 5   Two-Solution Case–SSA

Find two triangles for which $a = 12$ meters, $b = 31$ meters, and $A = 20.5°$.

Solution

Because $h = b \sin A = 31(\sin 20.5°) \approx 10.86$ meters and $h < a < b$, you can conclude that there are two possible triangles. By the Law of Sines, you have

$$\frac{\sin B}{b} = \frac{\sin A}{a} \qquad \text{Reciprocal form}$$

$$\sin B = b\left(\frac{\sin A}{a}\right) = 31\left(\frac{\sin 20.5°}{12}\right) \approx 0.9047.$$

There are two angles

$$B_1 \approx 64.8° \text{ and } B_2 \approx 180° - 64.8° = 115.2°$$

between $0°$ and $180°$ whose sine is 0.9047. For $B_1 \approx 64.8°$, you obtain

$$C \approx 180° - 20.5° - 64.8° = 94.7°$$

$$c = \frac{a}{\sin A}(\sin C) \approx \frac{12}{\sin 20.5°}(\sin 94.7°) \approx 34.15 \text{ meters.}$$

For $B_2 \approx 115.2°$, you obtain

$$C \approx 180° - 20.5° - 115.2° = 44.3°$$

$$c = \frac{a}{\sin A}(\sin C) \approx \frac{12}{\sin 20.5°}(\sin 44.3°) \approx 23.93 \text{ meters.}$$

The resulting triangles are shown in Figure 6.4.

Figure 6.4   Two solutions: $h < a < b$

✓ **Checkpoint**)))) Audio-video solution in English & Spanish at LarsonPrecalculus.com.

Find two triangles for which $a = 4.5$ feet, $b = 5$ feet, and $A = 58°$.

Remark

When using the Law of Sines, choose the form so that the unknown variable is in the numerator.

Known: A, B, b
To find: a

Choose:
$$\frac{a}{\sin A} = \frac{b}{\sin B}$$

Known: b, c, B
To find: C

Choose:
$$\frac{\sin C}{c} = \frac{\sin B}{b}$$

Area of an Oblique Triangle

The procedure used to prove the Law of Sines leads to a formula for the area of an oblique triangle. Referring to Figure 6.5, note that each triangle has a height of

$$h = b \sin A.$$

To see this when A is obtuse, substitute the reference angle $180° - A$ for A. Now the height of the triangle is given by

$$h = b \sin(180° - A).$$

Using the difference formula for sine, the height is given by

$$h = b(\sin 180° \cos A - \cos 180° \sin A) \qquad \sin(u - v) = \sin u \cos v - \cos u \sin v$$

$$= b[0 \cdot \cos A - (-1) \cdot \sin A]$$

$$= b \sin A.$$

Consequently, the area of each triangle is

$$\text{Area} = \frac{1}{2}(\text{base})(\text{height})$$

$$= \frac{1}{2}(c)(b \sin A)$$

$$= \frac{1}{2}bc \sin A.$$

By similar arguments, you can develop the formulas

$$\text{Area} = \frac{1}{2}ab \sin C = \frac{1}{2}ac \sin B.$$

A is acute.

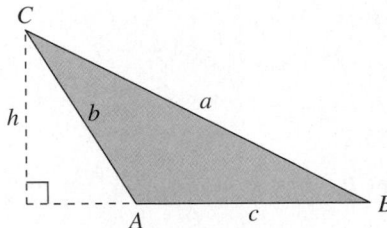

A is obtuse.

Figure 6.5

Area of an Oblique Triangle

The area of any triangle is one-half the product of the lengths of two sides times the sine of their included angle. That is,

$$\text{Area} = \frac{1}{2}bc \sin A = \frac{1}{2}ab \sin C = \frac{1}{2}ac \sin B.$$

Note that when angle A is 90°, the formula gives the area of a right triangle as

$$\text{Area} = \frac{1}{2}bc$$

$$= \frac{1}{2}(\text{base})(\text{height}).$$

Similar results are obtained for angles C and B equal to 90°.

EXAMPLE 6   Finding the Area of an Oblique Triangle

Find the area of a triangular lot having two sides of lengths 90 meters and 52 meters and an included angle of 102°.

Solution

Consider $a = 90$ meters, $b = 52$ meters, and $C = 102°$, as shown in Figure 6.6. Then the area of the triangle is

$$\text{Area} = \frac{1}{2}ab \sin C \qquad \text{Formula for area}$$

$$= \frac{1}{2}(90)(52)(\sin 102°) \qquad \text{Substitute for } a, b, \text{ and } C.$$

$$\approx 2288.87 \text{ square meters.} \qquad \text{Simplify.}$$

Figure 6.6

✓ **Checkpoint** ◀))) *Audio-video solution in English & Spanish at LarsonPrecalculus.com.*

Find the area of a triangular lot having two sides of lengths 24 yards and 18 yards and an included angle of 80°.

EXAMPLE 7   An Application of the Law of Sines

The course for a boat race starts at point A and proceeds in the direction S 52° W to point B, then in the direction S 40° E to point C, and finally back to point A, as shown in Figure 6.7. Point C lies 8 kilometers directly south of point A. Approximate the total distance of the race course.

Solution

Because lines BD and AC are parallel, it follows that

$$\angle BCA \cong \angle DBC.$$

Consequently, triangle ABC has the measures shown in Figure 6.8. For angle B, you have

$$B = 180° - 52° - 40° = 88°.$$

Using the Law of Sines

$$\frac{a}{\sin 52°} = \frac{b}{\sin 88°} = \frac{c}{\sin 40°}$$

with $b = 8$, you obtain

$$a = \frac{8}{\sin 88°}(\sin 52°) \approx 6.31$$

and

$$c = \frac{8}{\sin 88°}(\sin 40°) \approx 5.15.$$

The total distance of the course is approximately

$$8 + 6.31 + 5.15 = 19.46 \text{ kilometers.}$$

Figure 6.7

Figure 6.8

✓ **Checkpoint** ◀))) *Audio-video solution in English & Spanish at LarsonPrecalculus.com.*

On a small lake, you swim from point A to point B at a bearing of N 28° E, then to point C at a bearing of N 58° W, and finally back to point A. Point C lies 800 meters directly north of point A. Draw a diagram to represent this situation. Then approximate the total distance that you swim.

See *CalcChat.com* for tutorial help and worked-out solutions to odd-numbered exercises.
For instructions on how to use a graphing utility, see Appendix A.

6.1 Exercises

Vocabulary and Concept Check

In Exercises 1–4, fill in the blank(s).

1. A(n) _____ triangle has no right angles.

2. Law of Sines: $\dfrac{a}{\sin A} =$ _____ $= \dfrac{c}{\sin C}$

3. To find the area of any triangle, use one of the three formulas:
   Area = _____ , _____ , or _____ .

4. Two _____ and one _____ determine a unique triangle.

5. Which two cases can be solved using the Law of Sines?

6. Is the longest side of an oblique triangle always opposite the largest angle of the triangle?

Procedures and Problem Solving

Using the Law of Sines   In Exercises 7–24, use the Law of Sines to solve the triangle.

7.

8.

9.

10.

11.

12.

13. $A = 36°, \quad a = 8, \quad b = 5$

14. $A = 76°, \quad a = 34, \quad b = 21$

15. $A = 35°, \quad B = 40°, \quad c = 10$

16. $A = 120°, \quad B = 45°, \quad c = 16$

17. $A = 110°, \quad a = 125, \quad b = 100$

18. $A = 145°, \quad a = 14, \quad b = 4$

19. $A = 102.4°, \quad C = 16.7°, \quad a = 21.6$

20. $A = 24.3°, \quad C = 54.6°, \quad c = 2.68$

21. $B = 28°, \quad C = 104°, \quad a = 3\frac{5}{8}$

22. $A = 55°, \quad B = 42°, \quad c = \frac{3}{4}$

23. $A = 110° \ 15', \quad a = 48, \quad b = 16$

24. $B = 2° \ 45', \quad b = 6.2, \quad c = 5.8$

Using the Law of Sines   In Exercises 25–30, use the Law of Sines to solve the triangle. If two solutions exist, find both.

25. $A = 76°, \quad a = 18, \quad b = 20$

26. $A = 110°, \quad a = 125, \quad b = 200$

27. $A = 120°, \quad a = b = 25$

28. $A = 60°, \quad a = 9, \quad c = 10$

29. $A = 58°, \quad a = 11.4, \quad b = 12.8$

30. $A = 58°, \quad a = 4.5, \quad b = 12.8$

Using the Law of Sines   In Exercises 31–34, find the value(s) of b such that the triangle has (a) one solution, (b) two solutions, and (c) no solution.

31. $A = 36°, \quad a = 5$

32. $A = 60°, \quad a = 10$

33. $A = 10°, \quad a = 10.8$

34. $A = 88°, \quad a = 315.6$

Finding the Area of an Oblique Triangle   In Exercises 35–40, find the area of the triangle having the indicated angle and sides.

35. $C = 110°, \quad a = 6, \quad b = 10$

36. $B = 130°, \quad a = 92, \quad c = 30$

37. $A = 150°, \quad b = 8, \quad c = 10$

38. $C = 120°, \quad a = 4, \quad b = 6$

39. $B = 75° \ 15', \quad a = 103, \quad c = 58$

40. $C = 85° \ 45', \quad a = 16, \quad b = 20$

41. Height Because of prevailing winds, a tree grew so that it is leaning 4° from the vertical. At a point 40 meters from the tree, the angle of elevation to the top of the tree is 30° (see figure). Find the height *h* of the tree.

42. Architecture A bridge is to be built across a small lake from a gazebo to a dock. The bearing from the gazebo to the dock is S 41° W. From a tree 100 meters from the gazebo, the bearings to the gazebo and the dock are S 74° E and S 28° E, respectively (see figure). Find the distance from the gazebo to the dock.

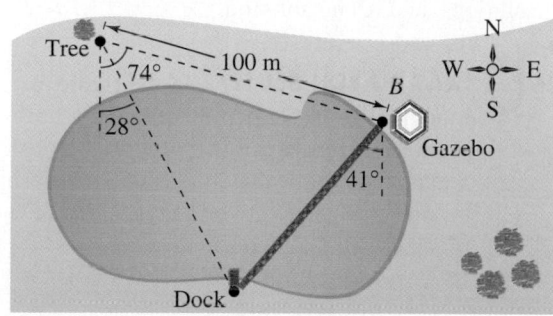

43. Aviation A plane flies 500 kilometers with a bearing of 316° (clockwise from north) from Naples to Elgin. The plane then flies 720 kilometers from Elgin to Canton (see figure). Canton is due west of Naples. Find the bearing of the flight from Elgin to Canton.

44. Physics A flagpole at a right angle to the horizontal is located on a slope that makes an angle of 12° with the horizontal. The flagpole casts a 16-meter shadow up the slope when the angle of elevation from the tip of the shadow to the sun is 20°.

(a) Draw a triangle that represents the problem. Show the known quantities on the triangle and use a variable to indicate the height of the flagpole.

(b) Write an equation involving the unknown quantity.

(c) Find the height of the flagpole.

45. Aviation The angles of elevation θ and ϕ to an airplane are being continuously monitored at two observation points *A* and *B*, respectively, which are 2 miles apart, and the airplane is east of both points in the same vertical plane.

(a) Draw a diagram that illustrates the problem.

(b) Write an equation giving the distance *d* between the plane and point *B* in terms of θ and ϕ.

(c) Use the equation from part (b) to find the distance between the plane and point *B* when $\theta = 40°$ and $\phi = 60°$.

46. Environmental Science The bearing from the Pine Knob fire tower to the Colt Station fire tower is N 65° E, and the two towers are 30 kilometers apart. A fire spotted by rangers in each tower has a bearing of N 80° E from Pine Knob and S 70° E from Colt Station (see figure). Find the distance of the fire from each tower.

47. Angle of Elevation A 10-meter telephone pole casts a 17-meter shadow directly down a slope when the angle of elevation of the sun is 42° (see figure). Find θ, the angle of elevation of the ground.

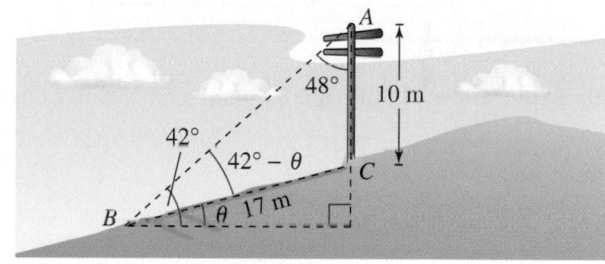

48. *Why you should learn it* (p. 404) A boat is sailing due east parallel to the shoreline at a speed of 10 miles per hour. At a given time, the bearing to a lighthouse is S 70° E, and 15 minutes later, the bearing is S 63° E (see figure). The lighthouse is located at the shoreline. Find the distance *d* from the boat to the shoreline.

49. MODELING DATA

The Leaning Tower of Pisa in Italy leans because it was built on unstable soil—a mixture of clay, sand, and water. The tower is approximately 58.36 meters tall from its foundation. The top of the tower leans about 5.45 meters off center. (See figure.)

(a) Find the angle of lean α of the tower.

(b) Write β as a function of d and θ, where θ is the angle of elevation to the sun.

(c) Use the Law of Sines to write an equation for the length d of the shadow cast by the tower in terms of θ.

(d) Use a graphing utility to complete the table.

θ	10°	20°	30°	40°	50°	60°
d						

50. Exploration   In the figure, α and β are positive angles.

(a) Write α as a function of β.

(b) Use a graphing utility to graph the function. Determine its domain and range.

(c) Use the result of part (a) to write c as a function of β.

(d) Use the graphing utility to graph the function in part (c). Determine its domain and range.

(e) Use the graphing utility to complete the table. What can you conclude?

β	0.4	0.8	1.2	1.6	2.0	2.4	2.8
α							
c							

Conclusions

True or False?   In Exercises 51–53, determine whether the statement is true or false. Justify your answer.

51. If any three sides or angles of an oblique triangle are known, then the triangle can be solved.

52. If a triangle contains an obtuse angle, then it must be oblique.

53. Two angles and one side of a triangle do not necessarily determine a unique triangle.

54. Writing   Can the Law of Sines be used to solve a right triangle? If so, write a short paragraph explaining how to use the Law of Sines to solve the following triangle. Is there an easier way to solve the triangle? Explain.

$$B = 50°, \quad C = 90°, \quad a = 10$$

55. Think About It   Given $A = 36°$ and $a = 5$, find values of b such that the triangle has (a) one solution, (b) two solutions, and (c) no solution.

56. HOW DO YOU SEE IT?   In the figure, a triangle is to be formed by drawing a line segment of length a from $(4, 3)$ to the positive x-axis. For what value(s) of a can you form (a) one triangle, (b) two triangles, and (c) no triangles? Explain your reasoning.

Cumulative Mixed Review

Evaluating Trigonometric Functions   In Exercises 57 and 58, use the given values to find the values of the remaining four trigonometric functions of θ.

57. $\cos \theta = \frac{5}{13}, \quad \sin \theta = -\frac{12}{13}$

58. $\tan \theta = -\frac{8}{15}, \quad \csc \theta = \frac{17}{8}$

Writing Products as Sums or Differences   In Exercises 59–62, write the product as a sum or difference.

59. $6 \sin 8\theta \cos 3\theta$

60. $2 \cos 2\theta \cos 5\theta$

61. $\frac{1}{3} \cos \frac{\pi}{6} \sin \frac{5\pi}{3}$

62. $\frac{5}{2} \sin \frac{3\pi}{4} \sin \frac{5\pi}{6}$

6.2   Law of Cosines

Introduction

Two cases remain in the list of conditions needed to solve an oblique triangle—SSS and SAS. When you are given three sides (SSS) or two sides and their included angle (SAS), none of the ratios in the Law of Sines would be complete. In such cases you can use the **Law of Cosines.**

Law of Cosines   (See the proof on page 465.)

Standard Form	*Alternative Form*
$a^2 = b^2 + c^2 - 2bc \cos A$	$\cos A = \dfrac{b^2 + c^2 - a^2}{2bc}$
$b^2 = a^2 + c^2 - 2ac \cos B$	$\cos B = \dfrac{a^2 + c^2 - b^2}{2ac}$
$c^2 = a^2 + b^2 - 2ab \cos C$	$\cos C = \dfrac{a^2 + b^2 - c^2}{2ab}$

EXAMPLE 1   **Three Sides of a Triangle—SSS**

Find the three angles of the triangle shown in the figure.

Solution

It is a good idea first to find the angle opposite the longest side—side b in this case. Using the alternative form of the Law of Cosines, you find that

$$\cos B = \frac{a^2 + c^2 - b^2}{2ac} \qquad \text{Alternative form}$$

$$= \frac{8^2 + 14^2 - 19^2}{2(8)(14)} \qquad \text{Substitute for } a, b, \text{ and } c.$$

$$\approx -0.45089. \qquad \text{Simplify.}$$

Because $\cos B$ is negative, you know that B is an *obtuse* angle given by $B \approx 116.80°$. At this point, it is simpler to use the Law of Sines to determine A.

$$\sin A = a\left(\frac{\sin B}{b}\right) \approx 8\left(\frac{\sin 116.80°}{19}\right) \approx 0.37583$$

Because B is obtuse and a triangle can have at most one obtuse angle, you know that A must be acute. So, $A \approx 22.08°$ and

$$C \approx 180° - 22.08° - 116.80°$$

$$= 41.12°.$$

✓ **Checkpoint** 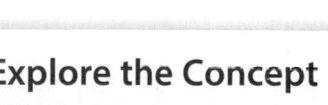 Audio-video solution in English & Spanish at *LarsonPrecalculus.com*.

Find the three angles of the triangle whose sides have lengths $a = 6$, $b = 8$, and $c = 12$. ∎

What you should learn

▶ Use the Law of Cosines to solve oblique triangles (SSS or SAS).
▶ Use the Law of Cosines to model and solve real-life problems.
▶ Use Heron's Area Formula to find areas of triangles.

Why you should learn it

You can use the Law of Cosines to solve real-life problems involving oblique triangles. For instance, Exercise 53 on page 418 shows you how the Law of Cosines can be used to determine the lengths of the guy wires that anchor a tower.

Surveyor

Explore the Concept

What familiar formula do you obtain when you use the third form of the Law of Cosines

$$c^2 = a^2 + b^2 - 2ab \cos C$$

and you let $C = 90°$? What is the relationship between the Law of Cosines and this formula?

Do you see why it was wise to find the largest angle *first* in Example 1? Knowing the cosine of an angle, you can determine whether the angle is acute or obtuse. That is,

$\cos \theta > 0$ for $0° < \theta < 90°$ Acute

$\cos \theta < 0$ for $90° < \theta < 180°.$ Obtuse

So, in Example 1, once you found that angle B was obtuse, you knew that angles A and C were both acute. Furthermore, if the largest angle is acute, then the remaining two angles are also acute.

EXAMPLE 2   Two Sides and the Included Angle—SAS

See LarsonPrecalculus.com for an interactive version of this type of example.

Find the remaining angles and side of the triangle shown below.

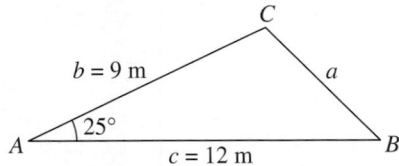

Solution

Use the Law of Cosines to find the unknown side a in the figure.

$a^2 = b^2 + c^2 - 2bc \cos A$

$a^2 = 9^2 + 12^2 - 2(9)(12) \cos 25°$

$a^2 \approx 29.2375$

$a \approx 5.4072$

Because $a \approx 5.4072$ meters, you now know the ratio $(\sin A)/a$, and you can use the reciprocal form of the Law of Sines to solve for B.

$\dfrac{\sin B}{b} = \dfrac{\sin A}{a}$ Reciprocal form

$\sin B = b\left(\dfrac{\sin A}{a}\right)$ Multiply each side by b.

$\sin B \approx 9\left(\dfrac{\sin 25°}{5.4072}\right)$ Substitute for A, a, and b.

$\sin B \approx 0.7034$ Use a calculator.

There are two angles between $0°$ and $180°$ whose sine is 0.7034,

$B_1 \approx 44.7°$ and $B_2 \approx 180° - 44.7° = 135.3°.$

For $B_1 \approx 44.7°$,

$C_1 \approx 180° - 25° - 44.7° = 110.3°.$

For $B_2 \approx 135.3°$,

$C_2 \approx 180° - 25° - 135.3° = 19.7°.$

Because side c is the longest side of the triangle, C must be the largest angle of the triangle. So, $B \approx 44.7°$ and $C \approx 110.3°$.

✓ *Checkpoint* 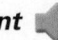 *Audio-video solution in English & Spanish at LarsonPrecalculus.com.*

Given $A = 80°$, $b = 16$, and $c = 12$, find the remaining angles and side of the triangle. ■

Remark

When solving an oblique triangle given two sides and their included angle, you use the standard form of the Law of Cosines to solve for the unknown side. When solving an oblique triangle given three sides, you use the alternative form of the Law of Cosines to solve for an angle.

Explore the Concept

In Example 2, suppose $A = 115°$. After solving for a, which angle would you solve for next, B or C? Are there two possible solutions for that angle? If so, how can you determine which angle is the correct measure?

Applications

EXAMPLE 3   An Application of the Law of Cosines

The pitcher's mound on a softball field is 43 feet from home plate. The distance between the bases is 60 feet, as shown in Figure 6.9. (The pitcher's mound is *not* halfway between home plate and second base.) How far is the pitcher's mound from first base?

Solution

In triangle *HPF*, $H = 45°$ (line segment *HP* bisects the right angle at *H*), $f = 43$, and $p = 60$. Using the Law of Cosines for this SAS case, you have

$$h^2 = f^2 + p^2 - 2fp \cos H \qquad \text{Law of Cosines}$$

$$= 43^2 + 60^2 - 2(43)(60) \cos 45° \qquad \text{Substitute for } H, f, \text{ and } p.$$

$$\approx 1800.33. \qquad \text{Simplify.}$$

So, the approximate distance from the pitcher's mound to first base is

$$h \approx \sqrt{1800.33} \approx 42.43 \text{ feet.}$$

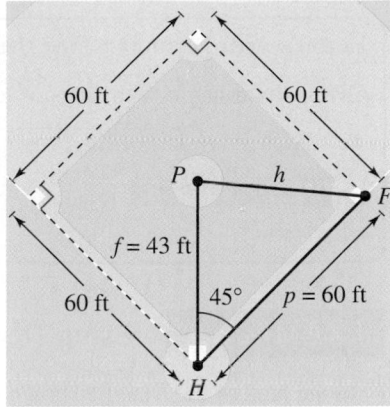

Figure 6.9

✓ **Checkpoint** 🔊))) *Audio-video solution in English & Spanish at LarsonPrecalculus.com.*

In a softball game, a batter hits a ball to dead center field, a distance of 240 feet from home plate. The center fielder then throws the ball to third base and gets a runner out. The distance between the bases is 60 feet. How far is the center fielder from third base?

EXAMPLE 4   An Application of the Law of Cosines

A ship travels 60 miles due east and then changes direction, as shown in the figure. After traveling 80 miles in this new direction, the ship is 139 miles from its point of departure. Describe the bearing from point *B* to point *C*.

Solution

Using the alternative form of the Law of Cosines, you have

$$\cos B = \frac{a^2 + c^2 - b^2}{2ac} \qquad \text{Alternative form}$$

$$= \frac{80^2 + 60^2 - 139^2}{2(80)(60)} \qquad \text{Substitute for } a, b, \text{ and } c.$$

$$\approx -0.97094. \qquad \text{Simplify.}$$

So, $B \approx \arccos(-0.97094) \approx 166.15°$, and the bearing measured from due north from point *B* to point *C* is approximately $166.15° - 90° = 76.15°$, or N 76.15° E.

✓ **Checkpoint** 🔊))) *Audio-video solution in English & Spanish at LarsonPrecalculus.com.*

A ship travels 40 miles due east and then changes direction, as shown in Figure 6.10. After traveling 30 miles in this new direction, the ship is 56 miles from its point of departure. Describe the bearing from point *B* to point *C*.

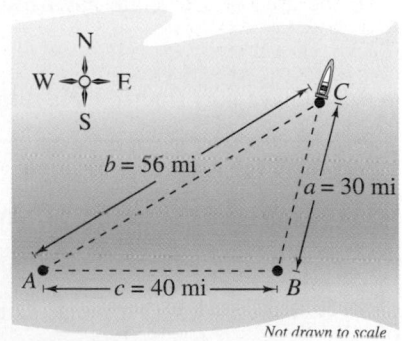

Figure 6.10

Heron's Area Formula

The Law of Cosines can be used to establish the following formula for the area of a triangle. This formula is called **Heron's Area Formula** after the Greek mathematician Heron (ca. 100 B.C.).

Heron's Area Formula   (See the proof on page 466.)

Given any triangle with sides of lengths a, b, and c, the area of the triangle is

$$\text{Area} = \sqrt{s(s-a)(s-b)(s-c)}$$

where $s = \dfrac{a+b+c}{2}$.

> **EXAMPLE 5**   Using Heron's Area Formula

Find the area of the triangle shown below.

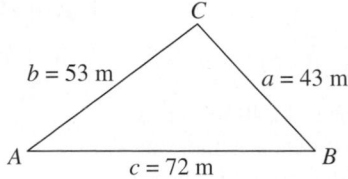

Solution

Because

$$s = \frac{a+b+c}{2}$$

$$= \frac{168}{2}$$

$$= 84$$

Heron's Area Formula yields

$$\text{Area} = \sqrt{s(s-a)(s-b)(s-c)}$$

$$= \sqrt{84(84-43)(84-53)(84-72)}$$

$$= \sqrt{84(41)(31)(12)}$$

$$\approx 1131.89 \text{ square meters.}$$

✓ **Checkpoint** ◀)) *Audio-video solution in English & Spanish at LarsonPrecalculus.com.*

Find the area of a triangle having sides of lengths $a = 5$ feet, $b = 9$ feet, and $c = 8$ feet.

You have now studied three different formulas for the area of a triangle.

Formulas for Area of a Triangle

1. **Standard Formula:** $\text{Area} = \frac{1}{2}bh$

2. **Oblique Triangle:** $\text{Area} = \frac{1}{2}bc \sin A = \frac{1}{2}ab \sin C = \frac{1}{2}ac \sin B$

3. **Heron's Area Formula:** $\text{Area} = \sqrt{s(s-a)(s-b)(s-c)}$

Explore the Concept

Can the formulas at the bottom of the page be used to find the area of any type of triangle? Explain the advantages and disadvantages of using one formula over another.

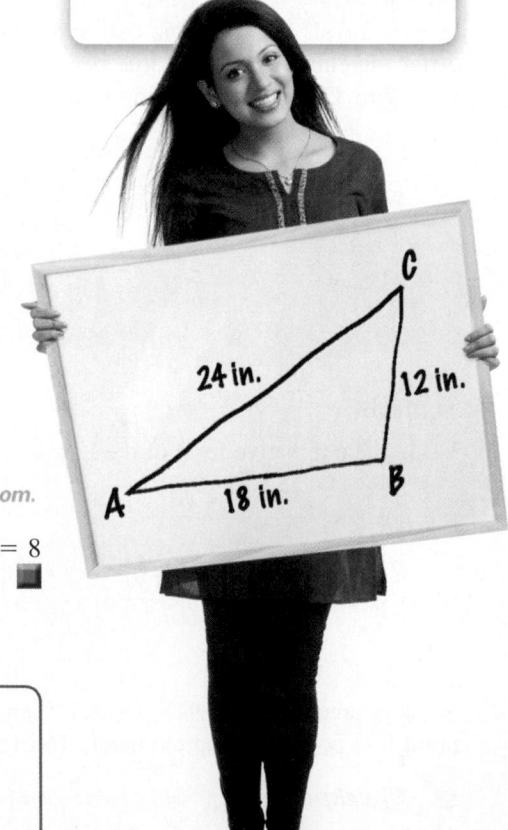

6.2   Exercises

See *CalcChat.com* for tutorial help and worked-out solutions to odd-numbered exercises.
For instructions on how to use a graphing utility, see Appendix A.

Vocabulary and Concept Check

In Exercises 1 and 2, fill in the blank(s).

1. The standard form of the Law of Cosines for $\cos C = \dfrac{a^2 + b^2 - c^2}{2ab}$ is _____ .

2. Three different formulas for the area of a triangle are Area = _____,
    Area = $\frac{1}{2}bc \sin A = \frac{1}{2}ab \sin C = \frac{1}{2}ac \sin B$, and Area = _____ .

In Exercises 3–6, one of the cases for the known measures of an oblique triangle is given. State whether the Law of Cosines can be used to solve the triangle.

3. ASA   4. SAS   5. SSS   6. AAS

Procedures and Problem Solving

Using the Law of Cosines   In Exercises 7–24, use the Law of Cosines to solve the triangle.

7.

8.

9.

10.

11.

12.

13. $a = 11$, $b = 15$, $c = 21$
14. $a = 9$, $b = 3$, $c = 11$
15. $A = 50°$, $b = 15$, $c = 30$
16. $C = 108°$, $a = 10$, $b = 7$
17. $A = 120°$, $b = 6$, $c = 7$
18. $A = 48°$, $b = 3$, $c = 14$
19. $a = 75.4$, $b = 48$, $c = 48$
20. $a = 1.42$, $b = 0.75$, $c = 1.25$
21. $B = 8° 15'$, $a = 26$, $c = 18$
22. $B = 10° 35'$, $a = 40$, $c = 30$
23. $C = 43°$, $a = \frac{4}{9}$, $b = \frac{7}{9}$
24. $C = 101°$, $a = \frac{3}{8}$, $b = \frac{3}{4}$

Finding Measures in a Parallelogram   In Exercises 25–30, complete the table by solving the parallelogram shown in the figure. (The lengths of the diagonals are given by c and d.)

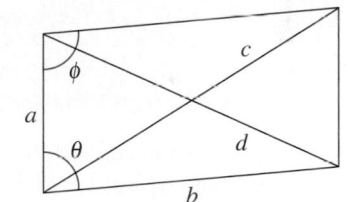

	a	b	c	d	θ	ϕ
25.	4	8			30°	
26.	25	35				120°
27.	10	14	20			
28.	40	60		80		
29.	15		25	20		
30.		25	50	35		

Solving a Triangle   In Exercises 31–38, determine whether the Law of Sines or the Law of Cosines can be used to find another measure of the triangle. Then solve the triangle.

31.

32.

33. $a = 8$, $c = 5$, $B = 40°$
34. $a = 10$, $b = 12$, $C = 70°$
35. $A = 24°$, $a = 4$, $b = 18$
36. $a = 11$, $b = 13$, $c = 7$
37. $A = 42°$, $B = 35°$, $c = 1.2$
38. $C = 95°$, $b = 19$, $c = 25$

Using Heron's Area Formula **In Exercises 39–46, use Heron's Area Formula to find the area of the triangle.**

39. $a = 12$, $b = 24$, $c = 18$

40. $a = 25$, $b = 35$, $c = 32$

41. $a = 5$, $b = 8$, $c = 10$

42. $a = 12$, $b = 17$, $c = 8$

43. $a = 1.24$, $b = 2.45$, $c = 1.25$

44. $a = 2.4$, $b = 2.75$, $c = 2.25$

45. $a = 1$, $b = \frac{1}{2}$, $c = \frac{3}{4}$

46. $a = \frac{3}{5}$, $b = \frac{5}{8}$, $c = \frac{3}{8}$

47. Surveying To approximate the length of a marsh, a surveyor walks 380 meters from point A to point B. Then, the surveyor turns 80° and walks 240 meters to point C (see figure). Approximate the length AC of the marsh.

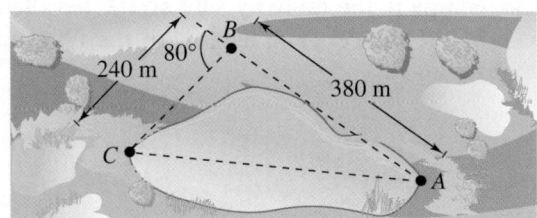

48. Geometry Determine the angle θ in the design of the streetlight shown in the figure.

49. Geography On a map, Minneapolis is 165 millimeters due west of Albany, Phoenix is 216 millimeters from Minneapolis, and Phoenix is 368 millimeters from Albany. (See figure.)

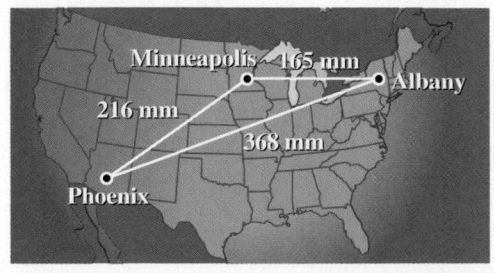

(a) Find the bearing of Minneapolis from Phoenix.

(b) Find the bearing of Albany from Phoenix.

50. Marine Transportation Two ships leave a port at 9 A.M. One travels at a bearing of N 53° W at 12 miles per hour, and the other travels at a bearing of S 67° W at 16 miles per hour. Approximate how far apart the ships are at noon.

51. Surveying A triangular parcel of ground has sides of lengths 725 feet, 650 feet, and 575 feet. Find the measure of the largest angle.

52. Structural Engineering Q is the midpoint of the line segment $\overline{PR}$ in the truss rafter shown in the figure. What are the lengths of the line segments $\overline{PQ}$, $\overline{QS}$, and $\overline{RS}$?

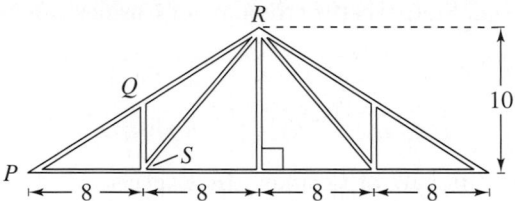

53. *Why you should learn it* (p. 413) A 100-foot vertical tower is to be erected on the side of a hill that makes a 6° angle with the horizontal. Find the length of each of the two guy wires that will be anchored 75 feet uphill and downhill from the base of the tower (see figure).

54. Architecture A retractable awning above a patio lowers at an angle of 50° from the exterior wall at a height of 10 feet above the ground. No direct sunlight is to enter the door when the angle of elevation of the sun is greater than 70° (see figure). What is the length of the awning?

55. Geometry The lengths of the sides of a triangular garden at a university are approximately 160 feet, 150 feet, and 140 feet. Approximate the area of the garden.

56. Geometry A parking lot has the shape of a parallelogram. The lengths of two adjacent sides are 70 meters and 100 meters. The angle between the two sides is 70° (see figure). What is the area of the parking lot?

70 m

70°

100 m

57. Mechanical Engineering An engine has a seven-inch connecting rod fastened to a crank. (See figure.)

(a) Use the Law of Cosines to write an equation giving the relationship between x and θ.

(b) Write x as a function of θ (Select the sign that yields positive values of x.)

(c) Use a graphing utility to graph the function in part (b).

(d) Use the graph in part (c) to determine the total distance the piston moves in one cycle.

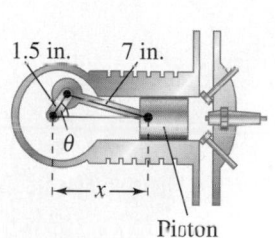

1.5 in.   7 in.

θ

x

Piston

Figure for 57

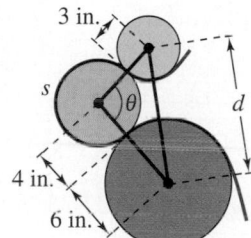

3 in.

s

θ

d

4 in.

6 in.

Figure for 58

58. MODELING DATA

In a process with continuous paper, the paper passes across three rollers of radii 3 inches, 4 inches, and 6 inches. The centers of the three-inch and six-inch rollers are d inches apart, and the length of the arc in contact with the paper on the four-inch roller is s inches. (See figure.)

(a) Use the Law of Cosines to write an equation giving the relationship between d and θ.

(b) Write θ as a function of d.

(c) Write s as a function of θ.

(d) Complete the table.

d (inches)	9	10	12	13	14	15	16
θ (degrees)							
s (inches)							

Conclusions

True or False? **In Exercises 59 and 60, determine whether the statement is true or false. Justify your answer.**

59. Two sides and their included angle determine a unique triangle.

60. In Heron's Area Formula, s is the average of the lengths of the three sides of the triangle.

61. Proof Use the Law of Cosines to prove each identity.

(a) $\dfrac{1}{2}bc(1 + \cos A) = \left(\dfrac{a + b + c}{2}\right)\left(\dfrac{-a + b + c}{2}\right)$

(b) $\dfrac{1}{2}bc(1 - \cos A) = \left(\dfrac{a - b + c}{2}\right)\left(\dfrac{a + b - c}{2}\right)$

62. HOW DO YOU SEE IT? To solve the triangle, would you begin by using the Law of Sines or the Law of Cosines? Explain.

(a)

C

$b = 16$ $a - 12$

A $c = 18$ B

(b)

A

35°   c

b

55°

C $a = 18$ B

63. Writing Describe how the Law of Cosines can be used to solve the ambiguous case of the oblique triangle ABC, where $a = 12$ feet, $b = 30$ feet, and $A = 20°$. Is the result the same as when the Law of Sines is used to solve the triangle? Describe the advantages and the disadvantages of each method.

64. Proof Use a half-angle formula and the Law of Cosines to show that, for any triangle,

(a) $\cos\dfrac{C}{2} = \sqrt{\dfrac{s(s - c)}{ab}}$ and

(b) $\sin\dfrac{C}{2} = \sqrt{\dfrac{(s - a)(s - b)}{ab}}$

where $s = \frac{1}{2}(a + b + c)$.

Cumulative Mixed Review

Evaluating an Inverse Trigonometric Function In Exercises 65–68, evaluate the expression without using a calculator.

65. $\arcsin(-1)$

66. $\arccos\left(-\dfrac{\sqrt{3}}{2}\right)$

67. $\tan^{-1}\dfrac{\sqrt{3}}{3}$

68. $\tan^{-1}\sqrt{3}$

6.3   Vectors in the Plane

Introduction

Many quantities in geometry and physics, such as area, time, and temperature, can be represented by a single real number. Other quantities, such as force and velocity, involve both *magnitude* and *direction* and cannot be completely characterized by a single real number. To represent such a quantity, you can use a **directed line segment,** as shown in Figure 6.11. The directed line segment $\overrightarrow{PQ}$ has **initial point** P and **terminal point** Q. Its **magnitude**, or **length**, is denoted by $\|\overrightarrow{PQ}\|$ and can be found by using the Distance Formula.

Figure 6.11

Figure 6.12

Two directed line segments that have the same magnitude and direction are *equivalent*. For example, the directed line segments in Figure 6.12 are all equivalent. The set of all directed line segments that are equivalent to a given directed line segment $\overrightarrow{PQ}$ is a **vector v in the plane,** written $\mathbf{v} = \overrightarrow{PQ}$. Vectors are denoted by lowercase, boldface letters such as $\mathbf{u}$, $\mathbf{v}$, and $\mathbf{w}$.

EXAMPLE 1   Showing That Two Vectors Are Equivalent

Show that $\mathbf{u}$ and $\mathbf{v}$ in the figure at the right are equivalent.

Solution

From the Distance Formula, it follows that $\overrightarrow{PQ}$ and $\overrightarrow{RS}$ have the *same magnitude*.

$$\|\overrightarrow{PQ}\| = \sqrt{(3-0)^2 + (2-0)^2} = \sqrt{13}$$

$$\|\overrightarrow{RS}\| = \sqrt{(4-1)^2 + (4-2)^2} = \sqrt{13}$$

Moreover, both line segments have the *same direction*, because they are both directed toward the upper right on lines having the same slope.

$$\text{Slope of } \overrightarrow{PQ} = \frac{2-0}{3-0} = \frac{2}{3}$$

$$\text{Slope of } \overrightarrow{RS} = \frac{4-2}{4-1} = \frac{2}{3}$$

Because $\overrightarrow{PQ}$ and $\overrightarrow{RS}$ have the same magnitude and direction, $\mathbf{u}$ and $\mathbf{v}$ are equivalent.

✓ **Checkpoint** ◄))) *Audio-video solution in English & Spanish at LarsonPrecalculus.com.*

Show that $\mathbf{u}$ and $\mathbf{v}$ in the figure at the right are equivalent.

Component Form of a Vector

The directed line segment whose initial point is the origin is often the most convenient representative of a set of equivalent directed line segments. This representative of the vector **v** is in **standard position.**

A vector whose initial point is at the origin $(0, 0)$ can be uniquely represented by the coordinates of its terminal point (v_1, v_2). This is the **component form of a vector v,** written as

$$\mathbf{v} = \langle v_1, v_2 \rangle.$$

The coordinates v_1 and v_2 are the *components* of **v**. If both the initial point and the terminal point lie at the origin, then **v** is the **zero vector** and is denoted by $\mathbf{0} = \langle 0, 0 \rangle$.

Component Form of a Vector

The component form of the vector with initial point $P(p_1, p_2)$ and terminal point $Q(q_1, q_2)$ is given by

$$\overrightarrow{PQ} = \langle q_1 - p_1, q_2 - p_2 \rangle = \langle v_1, v_2 \rangle = \mathbf{v}.$$

The **magnitude** (or **length**) of **v** is given by

$$\|\mathbf{v}\| = \sqrt{(q_1 - p_1)^2 + (q_2 - p_2)^2} = \sqrt{v_1^2 + v_2^2}.$$

If $\|\mathbf{v}\| = 1$, then **v** is a **unit vector.** Moreover, $\|\mathbf{v}\| = 0$ if and only if **v** is the zero vector **0**.

Two vectors $\mathbf{u} = \langle u_1, u_2 \rangle$ and $\mathbf{v} = \langle v_1, v_2 \rangle$ are *equal* if and only if $u_1 = v_1$ and $u_2 = v_2$. For instance, in Example 1, the vector **u** from $P(0, 0)$ to $Q(3, 2)$ is

$$\mathbf{u} = \overrightarrow{PQ} = \langle 3 - 0, 2 - 0 \rangle = \langle 3, 2 \rangle$$

and the vector **v** from $R(1, 2)$ to $S(4, 4)$ is

$$\mathbf{v} = \overrightarrow{RS} = \langle 4 - 1, 4 - 2 \rangle = \langle 3, 2 \rangle.$$

> **Technology Tip**
>
> You can graph vectors with a graphing utility by graphing directed line segments. Consult the user's guide for your graphing utility for specific instructions.

EXAMPLE 2   Finding the Component Form of a Vector

Find the component form and magnitude of the vector **v** represented by the directed line segment that has initial point $(4, -7)$ and terminal point $(-1, 5)$.

Algebraic Solution

Let

$$P(4, -7) = (p_1, p_2)$$

and

$$Q(-1, 5) = (q_1, q_2).$$

Then, the components of $\mathbf{v} = \langle v_1, v_2 \rangle$ are

$$v_1 = q_1 - p_1 = -1 - 4 = -5$$
$$v_2 = q_2 - p_2 = 5 - (-7) = 12.$$

So, $\mathbf{v} = \langle -5, 12 \rangle$ and the magnitude of **v** is

$$\|\mathbf{v}\| = \sqrt{(-5)^2 + 12^2} = \sqrt{169} = 13.$$

Graphical Solution

Use centimeter graph paper to plot the points $P(4, -7)$ and $Q(-1, 5)$. Carefully sketch the vector **v**. Use the sketch to find the components of $\mathbf{v} = \langle v_1, v_2 \rangle$. Then use a centimeter ruler to find the magnitude of **v**. The figure at the right shows that the components of **v** are $v_1 = -5$ and $v_2 = 12$, so $\mathbf{v} = \langle -5, 12 \rangle$. The figure also shows that the magnitude of **v** is $\|\mathbf{v}\| = 13$.

✓ **Checkpoint** ◀))) *Audio-video solution in English & Spanish at LarsonPrecalculus.com.*

Find the component form and magnitude of the vector **v** represented by the directed line segment that has initial point $(-2, 3)$ and terminal point $(-7, 9)$. ∎

Vector Operations

The two basic vector operations are **scalar multiplication** and **vector addition.** In operations with vectors, numbers are usually referred to as **scalars.** In this text, scalars will always be real numbers. Geometrically, the product of a vector **v** and a scalar k is the vector that is $|k|$ times as long as **v**. If k is positive, then $k\mathbf{v}$ has the same direction as **v**, and if k is negative, then $k\mathbf{v}$ has the opposite direction of **v**, as shown in Figure 6.13.

To add two vectors **u** and **v** geometrically, first position them (without changing their lengths or directions) so that the initial point of the second vector **v** coincides with the terminal point of the first vector **u**. The sum

$$\mathbf{u} + \mathbf{v}$$

is the vector formed by joining the initial point of the first vector **u** with the terminal point of the second vector **v**, as shown in the figures below. This technique is called the **parallelogram law** for vector addition because the vector **u** + **v**, often called the **resultant** of vector addition, is the diagonal of a parallelogram having adjacent sides **u** and **v**.

Figure 6.13

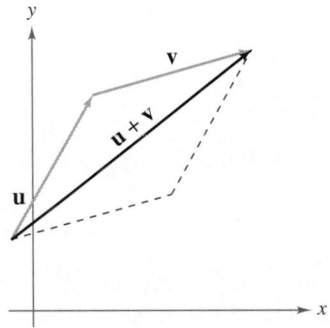

Definitions of Vector Addition and Scalar Multiplication

Let $\mathbf{u} = \langle u_1, u_2 \rangle$ and $\mathbf{v} = \langle v_1\ v_2 \rangle$ be vectors and let k be a scalar (a real number). Then the **sum** of **u** and **v** is the vector

$$\mathbf{u} + \mathbf{v} = \langle u_1 + v_1, u_2 + v_2 \rangle \qquad \text{Sum}$$

and the **scalar multiple** of k times **u** is the vector

$$k\mathbf{u} = k\langle u_1, u_2 \rangle = \langle ku_1, ku_2 \rangle. \qquad \text{Scalar multiple}$$

The **negative** of $\mathbf{v} = \langle v_1, v_2 \rangle$ is

$$-\mathbf{v} = (-1)\mathbf{v}$$

$$= \langle -v_1, -v_2 \rangle \qquad \text{Negative}$$

and the **difference** of **u** and **v** is

$$\mathbf{u} - \mathbf{v} = \mathbf{u} + (-\mathbf{v}) \qquad \text{Add } (-\mathbf{v}). \text{ See Figure 6.14.}$$

$$= \langle u_1 - v_1, u_2 - v_2 \rangle. \qquad \text{Difference}$$

To represent **u** − **v** geometrically, you can use directed line segments with the *same* initial point. The difference

$$\mathbf{u} - \mathbf{v}$$

is the vector from the terminal point of **v** to the terminal point of **u**, which is equal to

$$\mathbf{u} + (-\mathbf{v})$$

as shown in Figure 6.14.

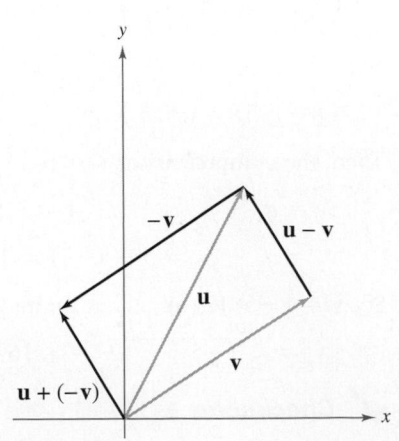

Figure 6.14

Example 3 illustrates the component definitions of vector addition and scalar multiplication. In this example, notice that each of the vector operations can be interpreted geometrically.

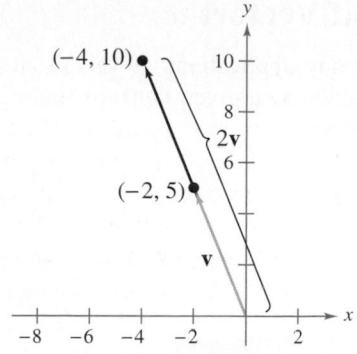

Figure 6.15

EXAMPLE 3   Vector Operations

See LarsonPrecalculus.com for an interactive version of this type of example.

Let $\mathbf{v} = \langle -2, 5 \rangle$ and $\mathbf{w} = \langle 3, 4 \rangle$. Find each of the following vectors.

a. $2\mathbf{v}$ **b.** $\mathbf{w} - \mathbf{v}$ **c.** $\mathbf{v} + 2\mathbf{w}$

Solution

a. Because $\mathbf{v} = \langle -2, 5 \rangle$, you have

$$2\mathbf{v} = 2\langle -2, 5 \rangle$$
$$= \langle 2(-2), 2(5) \rangle$$
$$= \langle -4, 10 \rangle.$$

A sketch of $2\mathbf{v}$ is shown in Figure 6.15.

b. The difference of $\mathbf{w}$ and $\mathbf{v}$ is

$$\mathbf{w} - \mathbf{v} = \langle 3, 4 \rangle - \langle -2, 5 \rangle$$
$$= \langle 3 - (-2), 4 - 5 \rangle$$
$$= \langle 5, -1 \rangle.$$

A sketch of $\mathbf{w} - \mathbf{v}$ is shown in Figure 6.16. Note that the figure shows the vector difference $\mathbf{w} - \mathbf{v}$ as the sum $\mathbf{w} + (-\mathbf{v})$.

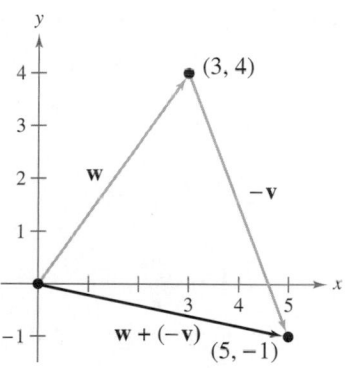

Figure 6.16

c. The sum of $\mathbf{v}$ and $2\mathbf{w}$ is

$$\mathbf{v} + 2\mathbf{w} = \langle -2, 5 \rangle + 2\langle 3, 4 \rangle$$
$$= \langle -2, 5 \rangle + \langle 6, 8 \rangle$$
$$= \langle 4, 13 \rangle.$$

A sketch of $\mathbf{v} + 2\mathbf{w}$ is shown in Figure 6.17.

✓ **Checkpoint** ◀))) Audio-video solution in English & Spanish at LarsonPrecalculus.com

Let $\mathbf{u} = \langle 1, 4 \rangle$ and $\mathbf{v} = \langle 3, 2 \rangle$. Find each of the following vectors.

a. $\mathbf{u} + \mathbf{v}$ **b.** $\mathbf{u} - \mathbf{v}$ **c.** $2\mathbf{u} - 3\mathbf{v}$

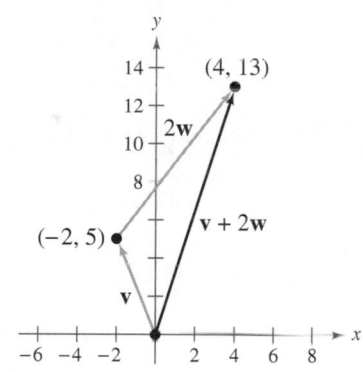

Figure 6.17

Vector addition and scalar multiplication share many of the properties of ordinary arithmetic.

Properties of Vector Addition and Scalar Multiplication

Let $\mathbf{u}$, $\mathbf{v}$, and $\mathbf{w}$ be vectors and let c and d be scalars. Then the following properties are true.

1. $\mathbf{u} + \mathbf{v} = \mathbf{v} + \mathbf{u}$ **2.** $(\mathbf{u} + \mathbf{v}) + \mathbf{w} = \mathbf{u} + (\mathbf{v} + \mathbf{w})$

3. $\mathbf{u} + \mathbf{0} = \mathbf{u}$ **4.** $\mathbf{u} + (-\mathbf{u}) = \mathbf{0}$

5. $c(d\mathbf{u}) = (cd)\mathbf{u}$ **6.** $(c + d)\mathbf{u} = c\mathbf{u} + d\mathbf{u}$

7. $c(\mathbf{u} + \mathbf{v}) = c\mathbf{u} + c\mathbf{v}$ **8.** $1(\mathbf{u}) = \mathbf{u}, 0(\mathbf{u}) = \mathbf{0}$

9. $\|c\mathbf{v}\| = |c|\,\|\mathbf{v}\|$

◁ **Remark**

Property 9 can be stated as follows: The magnitude of the vector $c\mathbf{v}$ is the absolute value of c times the magnitude of $\mathbf{v}$.

Unit Vectors

In many applications of vectors, it is useful to find a unit vector that has the same direction as a given nonzero vector **v**. To do this, you can divide **v** by its magnitude to obtain

$$\mathbf{u} = \text{unit vector} = \frac{\mathbf{v}}{\|\mathbf{v}\|} = \left(\frac{1}{\|\mathbf{v}\|}\right)\mathbf{v}. \qquad \text{Unit vector in direction of } \mathbf{v}$$

Note that **u** is a scalar multiple of **v**. The vector **u** has a magnitude of 1 and the same direction as **v**. The vector **u** is called a **unit vector in the direction of v.**

EXAMPLE 4   Finding a Unit Vector

Find a unit vector in the direction of $\mathbf{v} = \langle -2, 5 \rangle$ and verify that the result has a magnitude of 1.

Solution

The unit vector in the direction of **v** is

$$\frac{\mathbf{v}}{\|\mathbf{v}\|} = \frac{\langle -2, 5 \rangle}{\sqrt{(-2)^2 + 5^2}}$$

$$= \frac{1}{\sqrt{4 + 25}} \langle -2, 5 \rangle$$

$$= \frac{1}{\sqrt{29}} \langle -2, 5 \rangle$$

$$= \left\langle \frac{-2}{\sqrt{29}}, \frac{5}{\sqrt{29}} \right\rangle$$

$$= \left\langle \frac{-2\sqrt{29}}{29}, \frac{5\sqrt{29}}{29} \right\rangle.$$

This vector has a magnitude of 1 because

$$\sqrt{\left(\frac{-2\sqrt{29}}{29}\right)^2 + \left(\frac{5\sqrt{29}}{29}\right)^2} = \sqrt{\frac{116}{841} + \frac{725}{841}} = \sqrt{\frac{841}{841}} = 1.$$

✓ **Checkpoint** 🔊))) *Audio-video solution in English & Spanish at LarsonPrecalculus.com.*

Find a unit vector **u** in the direction of $\mathbf{v} = \langle 6, -1 \rangle$ and verify that the result has a magnitude of 1. ■

The unit vectors $\langle 1, 0 \rangle$ and $\langle 0, 1 \rangle$ are called the **standard unit vectors** and are denoted by

$$\mathbf{i} = \langle 1, 0 \rangle \qquad \text{and} \qquad \mathbf{j} = \langle 0, 1 \rangle$$

as shown in Figure 6.18. (Note that the lowercase letter **i** is written in boldface to distinguish it from the imaginary unit $i = \sqrt{-1}$.) These vectors can be used to represent any vector $\mathbf{v} = \langle v_1, v_2 \rangle$ as follows.

$$\mathbf{v} = \langle v_1, v_2 \rangle = v_1 \langle 1, 0 \rangle + v_2 \langle 0, 1 \rangle = v_1 \mathbf{i} + v_2 \mathbf{j}$$

The scalars v_1 and v_2 are called the **horizontal** and **vertical components of v,** respectively. The vector sum

$$v_1 \mathbf{i} + v_2 \mathbf{j}$$

is called a **linear combination** of the vectors **i** and **j**. Any vector in the plane can be written as a linear combination of the standard unit vectors **i** and **j**.

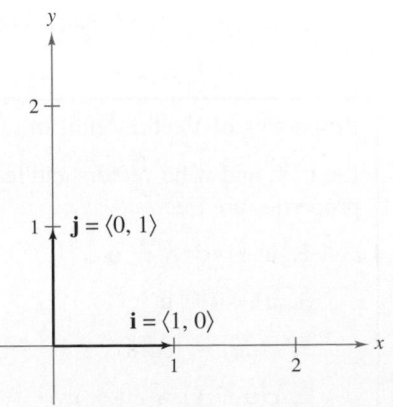

Figure 6.18

EXAMPLE 5   Writing a Linear Combination of Unit Vectors

Let **u** be the vector with initial point $(2, -5)$ and terminal point $(-1, 3)$. Write **u** as a linear combination of the standard unit vectors **i** and **j**.

Solution

Begin by writing the component form of the vector **u**.

$$\mathbf{u} = \langle -1 - 2, 3 - (-5) \rangle = \langle -3, 8 \rangle = -3\mathbf{i} + 8\mathbf{j}$$

This result is shown graphically in the figure.

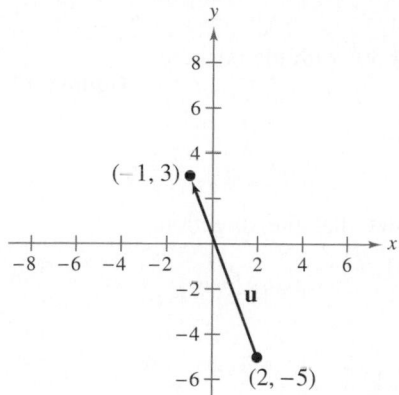

✓ **Checkpoint** 🔊))) Audio-video solution in English & Spanish at LarsonPrecalculus.com.

Let **u** be the vector with initial point $(-2, 6)$ and terminal point $(-8, 3)$. Write **u** as a linear combination of the standard unit vectors **i** and **j**.

EXAMPLE 6   Vector Operations

Let $\mathbf{u} = -3\mathbf{i} + 8\mathbf{j}$ and $\mathbf{v} = 2\mathbf{i} - \mathbf{j}$. Find $2\mathbf{u} - 3\mathbf{v}$.

Solution

You could solve this problem by converting **u** and **v** to component form. This, however, is not necessary. Performing the operations in unit vector form gives the same results.

$$\begin{aligned}
2\mathbf{u} - 3\mathbf{v} &= 2(-3\mathbf{i} + 8\mathbf{j}) - 3(2\mathbf{i} - \mathbf{j}) \\
&= -6\mathbf{i} + 16\mathbf{j} - 6\mathbf{i} + 3\mathbf{j} \\
&= -12\mathbf{i} + 19\mathbf{j}
\end{aligned}$$

✓ **Checkpoint** 🔊))) Audio-video solution in English & Spanish at LarsonPrecalculus.com.

Let $\mathbf{u} = \mathbf{i} - 2\mathbf{j}$ and $\mathbf{v} = -3\mathbf{i} + 2\mathbf{j}$. Find $5\mathbf{u} - 2\mathbf{v}$.   ■

In Example 6, to perform the operations in component form, write

$$\mathbf{u} = -3\mathbf{i} + 8\mathbf{j} = \langle -3, 8 \rangle \quad \text{and} \quad \mathbf{v} = 2\mathbf{i} - \mathbf{j} = \langle 2, -1 \rangle.$$

The difference of $2\mathbf{u}$ and $3\mathbf{v}$ is

$$\begin{aligned}
2\mathbf{u} - 3\mathbf{v} &= 2\langle -3, 8 \rangle - 3\langle 2, -1 \rangle \\
&= \langle -6, 16 \rangle - \langle 6, -3 \rangle \\
&= \langle -6 - 6, 16 - (-3) \rangle \\
&= \langle -12, 19 \rangle.
\end{aligned}$$

Compare this result with the solution to Example 6.

Direction Angles

If **u** is a *unit vector* such that θ is the angle (measured counterclockwise) from the positive x-axis to **u**, then the terminal point of **u** lies on the unit circle and you have

$$\mathbf{u} = \langle x, y \rangle = \langle \cos\theta, \sin\theta \rangle = (\cos\theta)\mathbf{i} + (\sin\theta)\mathbf{j}$$

as shown in Figure 6.19. The angle θ is the **direction angle** of the vector **u**.

Assume that **u** is a unit vector with direction angle θ. If $\mathbf{v} = a\mathbf{i} + b\mathbf{j}$ is any vector that makes an angle θ with the positive x-axis, then it has the same direction as **u** and you can write

$$\mathbf{v} = \|\mathbf{v}\|\langle \cos\theta, \sin\theta \rangle = \|\mathbf{v}\|(\cos\theta)\mathbf{i} + \|\mathbf{v}\|(\sin\theta)\mathbf{j}.$$

For instance, the vector **v** of magnitude 3 that makes an angle of 30° with the positive x-axis is

$$\mathbf{v} = 3(\cos 30°)\mathbf{i} + 3(\sin 30°)\mathbf{j} = \frac{3\sqrt{3}}{2}\mathbf{i} + \frac{3}{2}\mathbf{j}.$$

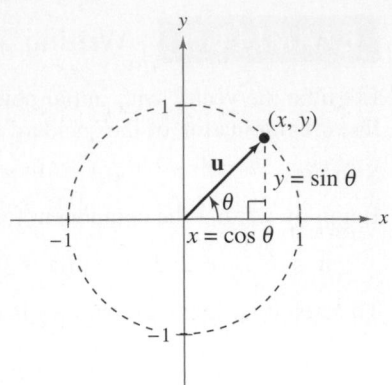

Figure 6.19

Because $\mathbf{v} = a\mathbf{i} + b\mathbf{j} = \|\mathbf{v}\|(\cos\theta)\mathbf{i} + \|\mathbf{v}\|(\sin\theta)\mathbf{j}$, it follows that the direction angle θ for **v** is determined from

$$\tan\theta = \frac{\sin\theta}{\cos\theta} \qquad \text{Quotient identity}$$

$$= \frac{\|\mathbf{v}\|\sin\theta}{\|\mathbf{v}\|\cos\theta} \qquad \text{Multiply numerator and denominator by } \|\mathbf{v}\|.$$

$$= \frac{b}{a}. \qquad \text{Simplify.}$$

EXAMPLE 7   Finding Direction Angles of Vectors

Find the direction angle of each vector.

a. $\mathbf{u} = 3\mathbf{i} + 3\mathbf{j}$ **b.** $\mathbf{v} = 3\mathbf{i} - 4\mathbf{j}$

Solution

a. The direction angle is determined from

$$\tan\theta = \frac{b}{a} = \frac{3}{3} = 1.$$

So, $\theta = 45°$, as shown in Figure 6.20.

b. The direction angle is determined from

$$\tan\theta = \frac{b}{a} = \frac{-4}{3}.$$

Moreover, because $\mathbf{v} = 3\mathbf{i} - 4\mathbf{j}$ lies in Quadrant IV, θ lies in Quadrant IV and its reference angle is

$$\theta' = \left|\arctan\left(-\frac{4}{3}\right)\right| \approx |-53.13°| = 53.13°.$$

So, it follows that $\theta \approx 360° - 53.13° = 306.87°$, as shown in Figure 6.21.

Figure 6.20

Figure 6.21

✓ **Checkpoint** ◀))) *Audio-video solution in English & Spanish at LarsonPrecalculus.com.*

Find the direction angle of each vector.

a. $\mathbf{v} = -6\mathbf{i} + 6\mathbf{j}$

b. $\mathbf{v} = -7\mathbf{i} - 4\mathbf{j}$

Applications

| EXAMPLE 8 | Finding the Component Form of a Vector

Find the component form of the vector that represents the velocity of an airplane descending at a speed of 100 miles per hour at an angle of 30° below the horizontal, as shown in Figure 6.22.

Solution

The velocity vector $\mathbf{v}$ has a magnitude of 100 and a direction angle of $\theta = 210°$.

$$\mathbf{v} = \|\mathbf{v}\|(\cos \theta)\mathbf{i} + \|\mathbf{v}\|(\sin \theta)\mathbf{j}$$

$$= 100(\cos 210°)\mathbf{i} + 100(\sin 210°)\mathbf{j}$$

$$= 100\left(-\frac{\sqrt{3}}{2}\right)\mathbf{i} + 100\left(-\frac{1}{2}\right)\mathbf{j}$$

$$= -50\sqrt{3}\mathbf{i} - 50\mathbf{j}$$

$$= \langle -50\sqrt{3}, -50 \rangle$$

Figure 6.22

You can check that $\mathbf{v}$ has a magnitude of 100 as follows.

$$\|\mathbf{v}\| = \sqrt{(-50\sqrt{3})^2 + (-50)^2} = \sqrt{7500 + 2500} = \sqrt{10{,}000} = 100 \quad \text{Solution checks.} \checkmark$$

✓ **Checkpoint** ◀))) *Audio-video solution in English & Spanish at LarsonPrecalculus.com.*

Rework Example 8 when the airplane descends at an angle 45° below the horizontal under the same conditions.

| EXAMPLE 9 | Using Vectors to Determine Weight

A force of 600 pounds is required to pull a boat and trailer up a ramp inclined at 15° from the horizontal. Find the combined weight of the boat and trailer.

Solution

Based on Figure 6.23, you can make the following observations.

$\|\overrightarrow{DA}\|$ = force of gravity = combined weight of boat and trailer

$\|\overrightarrow{BC}\|$ = force against ramp

$\|\overrightarrow{AC}\|$ = force required to move boat up ramp = 600 pounds

By construction, triangles BWD and ABC are similar. So, angle ABC is 15°. In triangle ABC you have

$$\sin 15° = \frac{\|\overrightarrow{AC}\|}{\|\overrightarrow{BA}\|}$$

$$\sin 15° = \frac{600}{\|\overrightarrow{BA}\|}$$

$$\|\overrightarrow{BA}\| = \frac{600}{\sin 15°}$$

$$\|\overrightarrow{BA}\| \approx 2318.$$

Figure 6.23

So, the combined weight is approximately 2318 pounds. (In Figure 6.23, note that $\overrightarrow{AC}$ is parallel to the ramp.)

✓ **Checkpoint** ◀))) *Audio-video solution in English & Spanish at LarsonPrecalculus.com.*

A force of 500 pounds is required to pull a boat and trailer up a ramp inclined at 12° from the horizontal. Find the combined weight of the boat and trailer. ■

EXAMPLE 10   Using Vectors to Find Speed and Direction

An airplane is traveling at a speed of 500 miles per hour with a bearing of 330° at a fixed altitude with a negligible wind velocity, as shown in Figure 6.24(a). (Note that a bearing of 330° corresponds to a direction angle of 120°.) The airplane encounters a wind blowing with a velocity of 70 miles per hour in the direction N 45° E, as shown in Figure 6.24(b). What are the resultant speed and direction of the airplane?

(a)   (b)

Figure 6.24

Solution

Using Figure 6.24, the velocity of the airplane (alone) is

$$\mathbf{v}_1 = 500\langle\cos 120°, \sin 120°\rangle = \langle-250, 250\sqrt{3}\rangle$$

and the velocity of the wind is

$$\mathbf{v}_2 = 70\langle\cos 45°, \sin 45°\rangle = \langle 35\sqrt{2}, 35\sqrt{2}\rangle.$$

So, the velocity of the airplane (in the wind) is

$$\mathbf{v} = \mathbf{v}_1 + \mathbf{v}_2$$
$$= \langle-250 + 35\sqrt{2}, 250\sqrt{3} + 35\sqrt{2}\rangle$$
$$\approx \langle-200.5, 482.5\rangle$$

and the resultant speed of the airplane is

$$\|\mathbf{v}\| \approx \sqrt{(-200.5)^2 + (482.5)^2} \approx 522.5 \text{ miles per hour.}$$

To find θ, the direction angle of the flight path, note that

$$\tan\theta \approx \frac{482.5}{-200.5} \approx -2.4065.$$

The flight path lies in Quadrant II, so θ lies in Quadrant II and its reference angle is

$$\theta = |\arctan(-2.4065)| \approx 67.4°.$$

So, the direction angle is

$$\theta \approx 180° - 67.4° = 112.6°.$$

You can use a graphing utility in *degree* mode to check this calculation, as shown in the figure. So, the true direction of the airplane is approximately 337.4°.

```
180-abs(tan⁻¹(-2.4065))
              112.5648997
```

> **Remark**
> Recall from Section 4.8 that in air navigation, bearings are measured in degrees clockwise from north. In Figure 6.24, north is in the positive *y*-direction.

Airplane Pilot

✓ **Checkpoint** 🔊))) *Audio-video solution in English & Spanish at LarsonPrecalculus.com.*

Repeat Example 10 for an airplane traveling at a speed of 450 miles per hour with a bearing of 300° that encounters a wind with a velocity of 40 miles per hour in the direction N 30° E. ∎

6.3   Exercises

See *CalcChat.com* for tutorial help and worked-out solutions to odd-numbered exercises.
For instructions on how to use a graphing utility, see Appendix A.

Vocabulary and Concept Check

In Exercises 1–8, fill in the blank(s).

1. A _____ can be used to represent a quantity that involves both magnitude and direction.

2. The directed line segment $\overrightarrow{PQ}$ has _____ point P and _____ point Q.

3. The _____ of the directed line segment $\overrightarrow{PQ}$ is denoted by $\|\overrightarrow{PQ}\|$.

4. The set of all directed line segments that are equivalent to a given directed line segment $\overrightarrow{PQ}$ is a _____ **v** in the plane.

5. The directed line segment whose initial point is the origin is said to be in _____ .

6. The two basic vector operations are scalar _____ and vector _____ .

7. The vector **u** + **v** is called the _____ of vector addition.

8. The vector sum $v_1\mathbf{i} + v_2\mathbf{j}$ is called a _____ of the vectors **i** and **j**, and the scalars v_1 and v_2 are called the _____ and _____ components of **v**, respectively.

9. What two characteristics determine whether two directed line segments are equivalent?

10. What do you call a vector that has a magnitude of 1?

Procedures and Problem Solving

Showing That Two Vectors Are Equivalent   In Exercises 11 and 12, show that u and v are equivalent.

11.

12.

Finding the Component Form of a Vector   In Exercises 13–24, find the component form and the magnitude of the vector v.

13.

14.

15.

16.

17.

18.
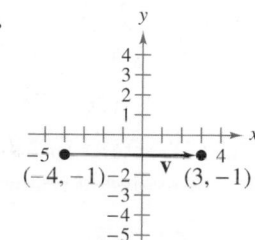

	Initial Point	Terminal Point
19.	$(-3, -5)$	$(5, 1)$
20.	$(-2, 7)$	$(5, -17)$
21.	$(0.6, 3)$	$(-3, -0.6)$
22.	$(-4.5, -2)$	$(2, 4.5)$
23.	$\left(-\frac{2}{3}, -1\right)$	$\left(\frac{1}{2}, \frac{4}{5}\right)$
24.	$\left(\frac{5}{2}, -2\right)$	$\left(1, \frac{2}{5}\right)$

Sketching the Graph of a Vector   In Exercises 25–30, use the figure to sketch a graph of the specified vector. To print an enlarged copy of the graph, go to *MathGraphs.com*.

25. $-\mathbf{v}$

26. $3\mathbf{u}$

27. $\mathbf{u} + \mathbf{v}$

28. $\mathbf{u} - \mathbf{v}$

29. $2\mathbf{v} - \mathbf{u}$

30. $\mathbf{v} + \frac{1}{2}\mathbf{u}$

Sketching the Graph of a Vector In Exercises 31–36, use the figure to sketch a graph of the specified vector. To print an enlarged copy of the graph, go to *MathGraphs.com.*

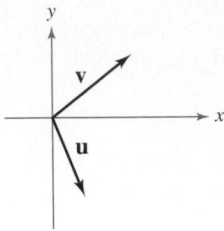

31. $2\mathbf{u}$

32. $-3\mathbf{v}$

33. $\mathbf{u} + 2\mathbf{v}$

34. $\mathbf{u} + \frac{1}{2}\mathbf{v}$

35. $2\mathbf{v} - \frac{1}{2}\mathbf{u}$

36. $3\mathbf{v} + 2\mathbf{u}$

Vector Operations In Exercises 37–42, find (a) $\mathbf{u} + \mathbf{v}$, (b) $\mathbf{u} - \mathbf{v}$, (c) $2\mathbf{u} - 3\mathbf{v}$, and (d) $\frac{1}{2}\mathbf{v} + 4\mathbf{u}$. Then sketch each resultant vector.

37. $\mathbf{u} = \langle 4, 2 \rangle$, $\mathbf{v} = \langle 8, 0 \rangle$

38. $\mathbf{u} = \langle 5, 3 \rangle$, $\mathbf{v} = \langle -4, 0 \rangle$

39. $\mathbf{u} = \langle -6, -8 \rangle$, $\mathbf{v} = \langle 2, 4 \rangle$

40. $\mathbf{u} = \langle 0, -5 \rangle$, $\mathbf{v} = \langle -4, 10 \rangle$

41. $\mathbf{u} = \mathbf{i} + \mathbf{j}$, $\mathbf{v} = 2\mathbf{i} - 3\mathbf{j}$

42. $\mathbf{u} = 2\mathbf{i} - \mathbf{j}$, $\mathbf{v} = -\mathbf{i} + \mathbf{j}$

Writing a Vector In Exercises 43–46, use the figure to write the vector in terms of the other two vectors.

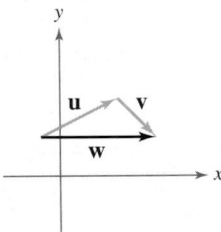

43. $\mathbf{w}$

44. $\mathbf{v}$

45. $\mathbf{u}$

46. $2\mathbf{v}$

Finding a Unit Vector In Exercises 47–56, find a unit vector in the direction of the given vector. Verify that the result has a magnitude of 1.

47. $\mathbf{u} = \langle 6, 0 \rangle$

48. $\mathbf{u} = \langle 0, -2 \rangle$

49. $\mathbf{v} = \langle -1, 1 \rangle$

50. $\mathbf{v} = \langle -2, 2 \rangle$

51. $\mathbf{v} = \langle -24, -7 \rangle$

52. $\mathbf{v} = \langle -9, 12 \rangle$

53. $\mathbf{v} = 4\mathbf{i} - 3\mathbf{j}$

54. $\mathbf{w} = \mathbf{i} - 2\mathbf{j}$

55. $\mathbf{w} = 2\mathbf{j}$

56. $\mathbf{w} = -3\mathbf{i}$

Finding a Vector In Exercises 57–62, find the vector $\mathbf{v}$ with the given magnitude and the same direction as $\mathbf{u}$.

Magnitude	Direction
57. $\|\mathbf{v}\| = 10$	$\mathbf{u} = \langle -3, 4 \rangle$
58. $\|\mathbf{v}\| = 3$	$\mathbf{u} = \langle -12, -5 \rangle$
59. $\|\mathbf{v}\| = 8$	$\mathbf{u} = \langle 5, 6 \rangle$
60. $\|\mathbf{v}\| = 3$	$\mathbf{u} = \langle 4, -4 \rangle$
61. $\|\mathbf{v}\| = 7$	$\mathbf{u} = 3\mathbf{i} + 4\mathbf{j}$
62. $\|\mathbf{v}\| = 10$	$\mathbf{u} = 2\mathbf{i} - 3\mathbf{j}$

Writing a Linear Combination of Unit Vectors In Exercises 63–66, the initial and terminal points of a vector are given. Write the vector as a linear combination of the standard unit vectors $\mathbf{i}$ and $\mathbf{j}$.

Initial Point	Terminal Point
63. $(-3, 1)$	$(4, 5)$
64. $(0, -2)$	$(3, 6)$
65. $(-6, 4)$	$(0, 1)$
66. $(-1, -5)$	$(2, 3)$

Vector Operations In Exercises 67–72, find the component form of $\mathbf{v}$ and sketch the specified vector operations geometrically, where $\mathbf{u} = 2\mathbf{i} - \mathbf{j}$ and $\mathbf{w} = \mathbf{i} + 2\mathbf{j}$.

67. $\mathbf{v} = \frac{3}{2}\mathbf{u}$

68. $\mathbf{v} = \frac{3}{4}\mathbf{w}$

69. $\mathbf{v} = \mathbf{u} + 2\mathbf{w}$

70. $\mathbf{v} = -\mathbf{u} + \mathbf{w}$

71. $\mathbf{v} = \frac{1}{2}(3\mathbf{u} + \mathbf{w})$

72. $\mathbf{v} = 2(\mathbf{u} - \mathbf{w})$

Finding Direction Angles of Vectors In Exercises 73–78, find the magnitude and direction angle of the vector $\mathbf{v}$.

73. $\mathbf{v} = 5(\cos 60°\mathbf{i} + \sin 60°\mathbf{j})$

74. $\mathbf{v} = 8(\cos 135°\mathbf{i} + \sin 135°\mathbf{j})$

75. $\mathbf{v} = 12\mathbf{i} + 15\mathbf{j}$

76. $\mathbf{v} = 8\mathbf{i} - 3\mathbf{j}$

77. $\mathbf{v} = -2\mathbf{i} + 5\mathbf{j}$

78. $\mathbf{v} = -7\mathbf{i} - 6\mathbf{j}$

Finding the Component Form of a Vector In Exercises 79–86, find the component form of $\mathbf{v}$ given its magnitude and the angle it makes with the positive x-axis. Sketch $\mathbf{v}$.

Magnitude	Angle
79. $\|\mathbf{v}\| = 3$	$\theta = 0°$
80. $\|\mathbf{v}\| = 1$	$\theta = 45°$
81. $\|\mathbf{v}\| = \frac{7}{2}$	$\theta = 120°$
82. $\|\mathbf{v}\| = \frac{5}{2}$	$\theta = 135°$
83. $\|\mathbf{v}\| = 3\sqrt{2}$	$\theta = 150°$
84. $\|\mathbf{v}\| = 4\sqrt{3}$	$\theta = 90°$
85. $\|\mathbf{v}\| = 2$	$\mathbf{v}$ in the direction $\mathbf{i} + 3\mathbf{j}$
86. $\|\mathbf{v}\| = 3$	$\mathbf{v}$ in the direction $3\mathbf{i} + 4\mathbf{j}$

Finding the Component Form of a Vector **In Exercises 87–90, find the component form of the sum of u and v with direction angles θ_u and θ_v.**

Magnitude	Angle
87. $\|\mathbf{u}\| = 5$	$\theta_u = 0°$
$\|\mathbf{v}\| = 5$	$\theta_v = 90°$
88. $\|\mathbf{u}\| = 4$	$\theta_u = 60°$
$\|\mathbf{v}\| = 4$	$\theta_v = 90°$
89. $\|\mathbf{u}\| = 20$	$\theta_u = 45°$
$\|\mathbf{v}\| = 50$	$\theta_v = 160°$
90. $\|\mathbf{u}\| = 35$	$\theta_u = 25°$
$\|\mathbf{v}\| = 50$	$\theta_v = 120°$

Using the Law of Cosines **In Exercises 91 and 92, use the Law of Cosines to find the angle α between the vectors. (Assume $0° \le \alpha \le 180°$.)**

91. $\mathbf{v} = \mathbf{i} + \mathbf{j}, \quad \mathbf{w} = 2(\mathbf{i} - \mathbf{j})$

92. $\mathbf{v} = 3\mathbf{i} + \mathbf{j}, \quad \mathbf{w} = 2\mathbf{i} - \mathbf{j}$

Graphing Vectors **In Exercises 93 and 94, graph the vectors and the resultant of the vectors. Find the magnitude and direction of the resultant.**

93.

94.

Resultant Force **In Exercises 95 and 96, find the angle between the forces given the magnitude of their resultant. (*Hint*: Write force 1 as a vector in the direction of the positive x-axis and force 2 as a vector at an angle θ with the positive x-axis.)**

Force 1	Force 2	Resultant Force
95. 45 pounds	60 pounds	90 pounds
96. 3000 pounds	1000 pounds	3750 pounds

97. Physical Education A ball is thrown with an initial velocity of 70 feet per second, at an angle of 40° with the horizontal (see figure). Find the vertical and horizontal components of the velocity.

98. Velocity A gun with a muzzle velocity of 1200 feet per second is fired at an angle of 6° above the horizontal. Find the vertical and horizontal components of the velocity.

99. *Why you should learn it* (*p. 420*) The cranes shown in the figure are lifting an object that weighs 20,240 pounds. Find the tension in the cable of each crane.

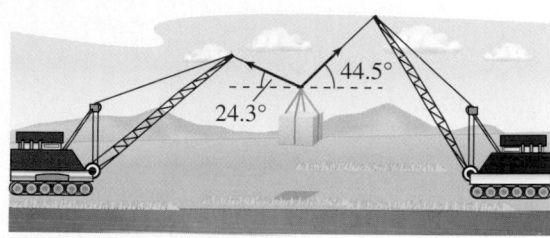

100. Physics Use the figure to determine the tension in each cable supporting the load.

101. MODELING DATA

A loaded barge is being towed by two tugboats, and the magnitude of the resultant is 6000 pounds directed along the axis of the barge. Each tow line makes an angle of θ degrees with the axis of the barge. (See figure.)

(a) Write the resultant tension T of each tow line as a function of θ. Determine the domain of the function.

(b) Use a graphing utility to complete the table.

θ	10°	20°	30°	40°	50°	60°
T						

(c) Use the graphing utility to graph the tension function.

(d) Explain why the tension increases as θ increases.

102. MODELING DATA

To carry a 100-pound cylindrical weight, two people lift on the ends of short ropes that are tied to an eyelet on the top center of the cylinder. Each rope makes an angle of θ degrees with the vertical. (See figure.)

(a) Write the tension T of each rope as a function of θ. Determine the domain of the function.

(b) Use a graphing utility to complete the table.

θ	10°	20°	30°	40°	50°	60°
T						

(c) Use the graphing utility to graph the tension function.

(d) Explain why the tension increases as θ increases.

103. MODELING DATA

Forces with magnitudes of 150 newtons and 220 newtons act on a hook, as shown in the figure.

(a) Find the direction and magnitude of the resultant of the forces when $\theta = 30°$.

(b) Write the magnitude M of the resultant and the direction α of the resultant as functions of θ, where $0° \le \theta \le 180°$.

(c) Use a graphing utility to complete the table.

θ	0°	30°	60°	90°	120°	150°	180°
M							
α							

(d) Use the graphing utility to graph the two functions.

(e) Explain why one function decreases for increasing θ, whereas the other does not.

104. MODELING DATA

A tetherball weighing 1 pound is pulled outward from the pole by a horizontal force **u** until the rope makes an angle of θ degrees with the pole. (See figure.)

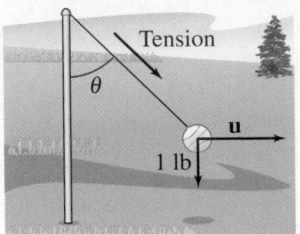

(a) Write the tension T in the rope and the magnitude of **u** as functions of θ. Determine the domain of each function.

(b) Use a graphing utility to graph the two functions for $0° \le \theta \le 60°$.

(c) Compare T and $\|\mathbf{u}\|$ as θ increases.

105. Aviation
An airplane is flying in the direction 148° with an airspeed of 860 kilometers per hour. Because of the wind, its groundspeed and direction are 800 kilometers per hour and 140°, respectively (see figure). Find the direction and speed of the wind.

106. MODELING DATA

A commercial jet is flying from Miami to Seattle. The jet's velocity with respect to the air is 580 miles per hour, and its bearing is 332°. The wind, at the altitude of the jet, is blowing from the southwest with a velocity of 60 miles per hour.

(a) Draw a figure that gives a visual representation of the problem.

(b) Write the velocity of the wind as a vector in component form.

(c) Write the velocity of the jet relative to the air as a vector in component form.

(d) What is the speed of the jet with respect to the ground?

(e) What is the true direction of the jet?

Conclusions

True or False?   In Exercises 107–110, determine whether the statement is true or false. Justify your answer.

107. If **u** and **v** have the same magnitude and direction, then **u** = **v**.

108. If **u** is a unit vector in the direction of **v**, then $\mathbf{v} = \|\mathbf{v}\|\mathbf{u}$.

109. If $\mathbf{v} = a\mathbf{i} + b\mathbf{j} = 0$, then $a = -b$.

110. If $\mathbf{u} = a\mathbf{i} + b\mathbf{j}$ is a unit vector, then $a^2 + b^2 = 1$.

111. Think About It   Consider two forces of equal magnitude acting on a point.

(a) If the magnitude of the resultant is the sum of the magnitudes of the two forces, make a conjecture about the angle between the forces.

(b) If the resultant of the forces is 0, make a conjecture about the angle between the forces.

(c) Can the magnitude of the resultant be greater than the sum of the magnitudes of the two forces? Explain.

112. Exploration   Consider two forces

$$\mathbf{F}_1 = \langle 10, 0 \rangle \quad \text{and} \quad \mathbf{F}_2 = 5\langle \cos\theta, \sin\theta \rangle.$$

(a) Write $\|\mathbf{F}_1 + \mathbf{F}_2\|$ as a function of θ.

(b) Use a graphing utility to graph the function for $0 \le \theta < 2\pi$.

(c) Use the graph in part (b) to determine the range of the function. What is its maximum, and for what value of θ does it occur? What is its minimum, and for what value of θ does it occur?

(d) Explain why the magnitude of the resultant is never 0.

113. Writing   Give geometric descriptions of (a) vector addition and (b) scalar multiplication.

114.   HOW DO YOU SEE IT?   Use the figure to determine whether each statement is true or false. Justify your answer.

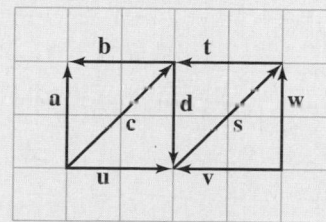

(a) **a** = −**d**   (b) **c** = **s**
(c) **a** + **u** = **c**   (d) **v** + **w** = −**s**
(e) **a** + **w** = −2**d**   (f) **a** + **d** = 0
(g) **u** − **v** = −2(**b** + **t**)   (h) **t** − **w** = **b** − **a**

115. Proof   Prove that $(\cos\theta)\mathbf{i} + (\sin\theta)\mathbf{j}$ is a unit vector for any value of θ.

116. Programming   Write a program for a graphing utility that graphs two vectors and their difference given the vectors in component form.

Finding the Difference of Two Vectors   In Exercises 117 and 118, use the program in Exercise 116 to find the difference of the vectors shown in the graph.

117.   118.

119. Think About It   Identify each quantity as either a scalar or a vector. Explain.

(a) muzzle velocity of a bullet

(b) price of a company's stock

(c) air temperature of a room

(d) weight of an automobile

(e) volume of a fish tank

(f) current of a river

Cumulative Mixed Review

Simplifying an Expression   In Exercises 120–125, simplify the expression.

120. $\left(\dfrac{6x^4}{7y^{-2}}\right)(14x^{-1}y^5)$ **121.** $(5s^5t^{-5})\left(\dfrac{3s^{-2}}{50t^{-1}}\right)$

122. $(18x)^0(4xy)^2(3x^{-1})$

123. $(5ab^2)(a^{-3}b^0)(2a^0b)^{-2}$

124. $(2.1 \times 10^9)(3.4 \times 10^{-4})$

125. $(6.5 \times 10^{-6})(3.8 \times 10^4)$

Solving an Equation   In Exercises 126–129, solve the equation.

126. $\cos x(\cos x + 1) = 0$

127. $\sin x(2\sin x + \sqrt{2}) = 0$

128. $3\sec x + 4 = 10$

129. $7\csc x + 18 = 4$

Trigonometric Substitution   In Exercises 130 and 131, use the trigonometric substitution to write the algebraic expression as a trigonometric function of θ, where $0 < \theta < \pi/2$.

130. $\sqrt{x^2 + 100}$, $x = 10\cot\theta$

131. $\sqrt{x^2 - 49}$, $x = 7\sec\theta$

6.4   Vectors and Dot Products

The Dot Product of Two Vectors

So far, you have studied two vector operations—vector addition and multiplication by a scalar—each of which yields another vector. In this section, you will study a third vector operation, the **dot product.** This product yields a scalar, rather than a vector.

Definition of Dot Product

The **dot product** of $\mathbf{u} = \langle u_1, u_2 \rangle$ and $\mathbf{v} = \langle v_1, v_2 \rangle$ is $\mathbf{u} \cdot \mathbf{v} = u_1 v_1 + u_2 v_2$.

Properties of the Dot Product   (See the proofs on page 467.)

Let $\mathbf{u}$, $\mathbf{v}$, and $\mathbf{w}$ be vectors in the plane or in space and let c be a scalar.

1. $\mathbf{u} \cdot \mathbf{v} = \mathbf{v} \cdot \mathbf{u}$
2. $\mathbf{0} \cdot \mathbf{v} = 0$
3. $\mathbf{u} \cdot (\mathbf{v} + \mathbf{w}) = \mathbf{u} \cdot \mathbf{v} + \mathbf{u} \cdot \mathbf{w}$
4. $\mathbf{v} \cdot \mathbf{v} = \|\mathbf{v}\|^2$
5. $c(\mathbf{u} \cdot \mathbf{v}) = c\mathbf{u} \cdot \mathbf{v} = \mathbf{u} \cdot c\mathbf{v}$

EXAMPLE 1   Finding Dot Products

a. $\langle 4, 5 \rangle \cdot \langle 2, 3 \rangle = 4(2) + 5(3) = 8 + 15 = 23$

b. $\langle 2, -1 \rangle \cdot \langle 1, 2 \rangle = 2(1) + (-1)(2) = 2 - 2 = 0$

c. $\langle 0, 3 \rangle \cdot \langle 4, -2 \rangle = 0(4) + 3(-2) = 0 - 6 = -6$

 ✔ **Checkpoint** 🔊))) *Audio-video solution in English & Spanish at LarsonPrecalculus.com.*

Find the dot product of $\mathbf{u} = \langle 3, 4 \rangle$ and $\mathbf{v} = \langle 2, -3 \rangle$.

In Example 1, be sure you see that the dot product of two vectors is a scalar (a real number), not a vector. Moreover, notice that the dot product can be positive, zero, or negative.

EXAMPLE 2   Using Properties of Dot Products

Let $\mathbf{u} = \langle -1, 3 \rangle$, $\mathbf{v} = \langle 2, -4 \rangle$, and $\mathbf{w} = \langle 1, -2 \rangle$. Use the vectors and the properties of the dot product to find (a) $(\mathbf{u} \cdot \mathbf{v})\mathbf{w}$, (b) $\mathbf{u} \cdot 2\mathbf{v}$, and (c) $\|\mathbf{u}\|$.

Solution

Begin by finding the dot product of $\mathbf{u}$ and $\mathbf{v}$ and the dot product of $\mathbf{u}$ and $\mathbf{u}$.

$$\mathbf{u} \cdot \mathbf{v} = \langle -1, 3 \rangle \cdot \langle 2, -4 \rangle = -1(2) + 3(-4) = -14$$

$$\mathbf{u} \cdot \mathbf{u} = \langle -1, 3 \rangle \cdot \langle -1, 3 \rangle = -1(-1) + 3(3) = 10$$

a. $(\mathbf{u} \cdot \mathbf{v})\mathbf{w} = -14\langle 1, -2 \rangle = \langle -14, 28 \rangle$

b. $\mathbf{u} \cdot 2\mathbf{v} = 2(\mathbf{u} \cdot \mathbf{v}) = -28$

c. Because $\|\mathbf{u}\|^2 = \mathbf{u} \cdot \mathbf{u} = 10$, it follows that $\|\mathbf{u}\| = \sqrt{\mathbf{u} \cdot \mathbf{u}} = \sqrt{10}$.

 ✔ **Checkpoint** 🔊))) *Audio-video solution in English & Spanish at LarsonPrecalculus.com.*

Let $\mathbf{u} = \langle 3, 4 \rangle$ and $\mathbf{v} = \langle -2, 6 \rangle$. Use the vectors and the properties of the dot product to find (a) $(\mathbf{u} \cdot \mathbf{v})\mathbf{v}$, (b) $\mathbf{u} \cdot (\mathbf{u} + \mathbf{v})$, and (c) $\|\mathbf{v}\|$.

What you should learn

▶ Find the dot product of two vectors and use the properties of the dot product.
▶ Find the angle between two vectors and determine whether two vectors are orthogonal.
▶ Write vectors as the sums of two vector components.
▶ Use vectors to find the work done by a force.

Why you should learn it

You can use the dot product of two vectors to solve real-life problems involving two vector quantities. For instance, Exercise 73 on page 441 shows you how the dot product can be used to find the force necessary to keep a truck from rolling down a hill.

Remark

In Example 2, notice that the product in part (a) is a vector, whereas the product in part (b) is a scalar. Can you see why?

The Angle Between Two Vectors

The **angle between two nonzero vectors** is the angle θ, $0 \le \theta \le \pi$, between their respective standard position vectors, as shown in the figure. This angle can be found using the dot product. (Note that the angle between the zero vector and another vector is not defined.)

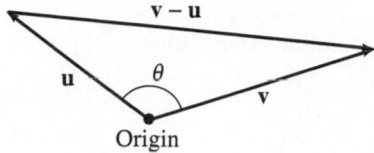

Origin

Angle Between Two Vectors (See the proof on page 467.)

If θ is the angle between two nonzero vectors **u** and **v**, then

$$\cos \theta = \frac{\mathbf{u} \cdot \mathbf{v}}{\|\mathbf{u}\| \|\mathbf{v}\|}.$$

EXAMPLE 3   Finding the Angle Between Two Vectors

See LarsonPrecalculus.com for an interactive version of this type of example.

Find the angle θ between

$$\mathbf{u} = \langle 4, 3 \rangle \text{ and } \mathbf{v} = \langle 3, 5 \rangle.$$

Solution

$$\cos \theta = \frac{\mathbf{u} \cdot \mathbf{v}}{\|\mathbf{u}\| \|\mathbf{v}\|}$$

$$= \frac{\langle 4, 3 \rangle \cdot \langle 3, 5 \rangle}{\|\langle 4, 3 \rangle\| \|\langle 3, 5 \rangle\|}$$

$$= \frac{27}{5\sqrt{34}}$$

This implies that the angle between the two vectors is

$$\theta = \arccos \frac{27}{5\sqrt{34}} \approx 22.2°$$

as shown below.

✓ **Checkpoint** 🔊))) *Audio-video solution in English & Spanish at LarsonPrecalculus.com.*

Find the angle θ between $\mathbf{u} = \langle 2, 1 \rangle$ and $\mathbf{v} = \langle 1, 3 \rangle$.

Rewriting the expression for the angle between two vectors in the form

$$\mathbf{u} \cdot \mathbf{v} = \|\mathbf{u}\| \, \|\mathbf{v}\| \cos \theta \qquad \text{Alternative form of dot product}$$

produces an alternative way to calculate the dot product. From this form, you can see that because $\|\mathbf{u}\|$ and $\|\mathbf{v}\|$ are always positive,

$$\mathbf{u} \cdot \mathbf{v} \text{ and } \cos \theta$$

will always have the same sign. The figures below show the five possible orientations of two vectors.

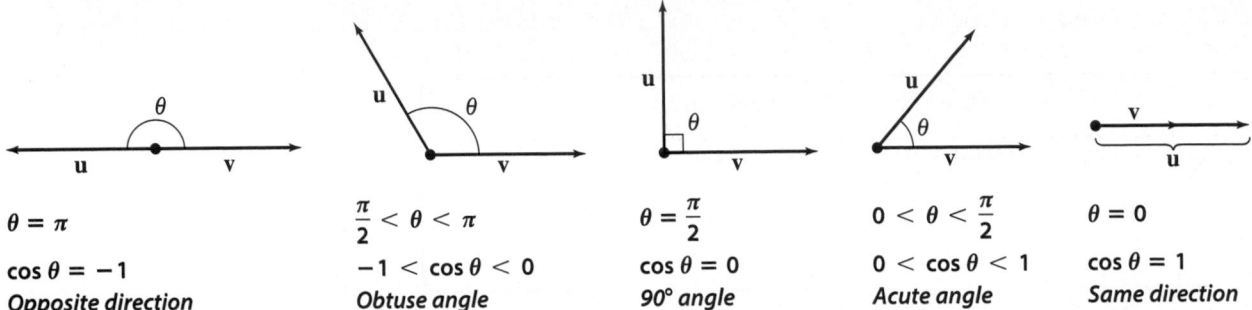

$\theta = \pi$	$\dfrac{\pi}{2} < \theta < \pi$	$\theta = \dfrac{\pi}{2}$	$0 < \theta < \dfrac{\pi}{2}$	$\theta = 0$
$\cos \theta = -1$	$-1 < \cos \theta < 0$	$\cos \theta = 0$	$0 < \cos \theta < 1$	$\cos \theta = 1$
Opposite direction	**Obtuse angle**	**90° angle**	**Acute angle**	**Same direction**

Definition of Orthogonal Vectors

The vectors $\mathbf{u}$ and $\mathbf{v}$ are **orthogonal** when $\mathbf{u} \cdot \mathbf{v} = 0$.

The terms *orthogonal* and *perpendicular* mean essentially the same thing—meeting at right angles. Even though the angle between the zero vector and another vector is not defined, it is convenient to extend the definition of orthogonality to include the zero vector. In other words, the zero vector is orthogonal to every vector $\mathbf{u}$ because $\mathbf{0} \cdot \mathbf{u} = 0$.

EXAMPLE 4 Determining Orthogonal Vectors

Are the vectors

$$\mathbf{u} = \langle 2, -3 \rangle \text{ and } \mathbf{v} = \langle 6, 4 \rangle$$

orthogonal?

Solution

Find the dot product of the two vectors.

$$\mathbf{u} \cdot \mathbf{v} = \langle 2, -3 \rangle \cdot \langle 6, 4 \rangle = 2(6) + (-3)(4) = 0$$

Because the dot product is 0, the two vectors are orthogonal, as shown below.

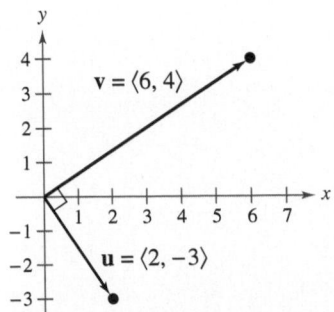

✓ **Checkpoint**))) *Audio-video solution in English & Spanish at LarsonPrecalculus.com.*

Are the vectors $\mathbf{u} = \langle 6, 10 \rangle$ and $\mathbf{v} = \left\langle -\frac{1}{3}, \frac{1}{5} \right\rangle$ orthogonal?

Technology Tip

The graphing utility program Finding the Angle Between Two Vectors, found at this textbook's *Companion Website*, graphs two vectors $\mathbf{u} = \langle a, b \rangle$ and $\mathbf{v} = \langle c, d \rangle$ in standard position and finds the measure of the angle between them. Use the program to verify the solutions to Examples 3 and 4.

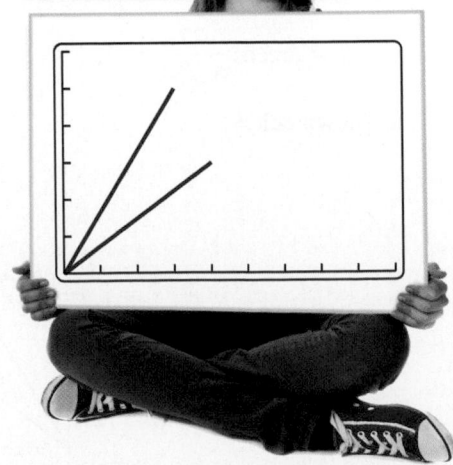

Finding Vector Components

You have already seen applications in which two vectors are added to produce a resultant vector. Many applications in physics and engineering pose the reverse problem—decomposing a given vector into the sum of two **vector components.**

Consider a boat on an inclined ramp, as shown in Figure 6.25. The force **F** due to gravity pulls the boat *down* the ramp and *against* the ramp. These two orthogonal forces, $\mathbf{w}_1$ and $\mathbf{w}_2$, are vector components of **F**. That is,

$$\mathbf{F} = \mathbf{w}_1 + \mathbf{w}_2. \qquad \text{Vector components of } \mathbf{F}$$

The negative of component $\mathbf{w}_1$ represents the force needed to keep the boat from rolling down the ramp, and $\mathbf{w}_2$ represents the force that the tires must withstand against the ramp. A procedure for finding $\mathbf{w}_1$ and $\mathbf{w}_2$ is shown below.

Figure 6.25

Definition of Vector Components

Let **u** and **v** be nonzero vectors such that

$$\mathbf{u} = \mathbf{w}_1 + \mathbf{w}_2$$

where $\mathbf{w}_1$ and $\mathbf{w}_2$ are orthogonal and $\mathbf{w}_1$ is parallel to (or a scalar multiple of) **v**, as shown in Figure 6.26. The vectors $\mathbf{w}_1$ and $\mathbf{w}_2$ are called **vector components** of **u**. The vector $\mathbf{w}_1$ is the **projection** of **u** onto **v** and is denoted by

$$\mathbf{w}_1 = \text{proj}_{\mathbf{v}}\mathbf{u}.$$

The vector $\mathbf{w}_2$ is given by

$$\mathbf{w}_2 = \mathbf{u} - \mathbf{w}_1.$$

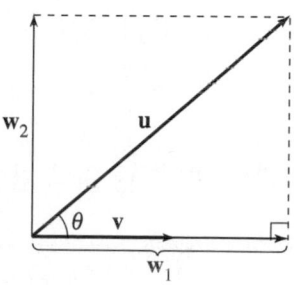

θ *is acute.*

From the definition of vector components, notice that you can find the component $\mathbf{w}_2$ once you have found the projection of **u** onto **v**. To find the projection, you can use the dot product, as follows.

$$\mathbf{u} = \mathbf{w}_1 + \mathbf{w}_2$$
$$\mathbf{u} = c\mathbf{v} + \mathbf{w}_2 \qquad \text{$\mathbf{w}_1$ is a scalar multiple of } \mathbf{v}.$$
$$\mathbf{u} \cdot \mathbf{v} = (c\mathbf{v} + \mathbf{w}_2) \cdot \mathbf{v} \qquad \text{Take dot product of each side with } \mathbf{v}.$$
$$\mathbf{u} \cdot \mathbf{v} = c\mathbf{v} \cdot \mathbf{v} + \mathbf{w}_2 \cdot \mathbf{v}$$
$$\mathbf{u} \cdot \mathbf{v} = c\|\mathbf{v}\|^2 + 0 \qquad \text{$\mathbf{w}_2$ and $\mathbf{v}$ are orthogonal.}$$

So,

$$c = \frac{\mathbf{u} \cdot \mathbf{v}}{\|\mathbf{v}\|^2}$$

and

$$\mathbf{w}_1 = \text{proj}_{\mathbf{v}}\mathbf{u} = c\mathbf{v} = \left(\frac{\mathbf{u} \cdot \mathbf{v}}{\|\mathbf{v}\|^2}\right)\mathbf{v}.$$

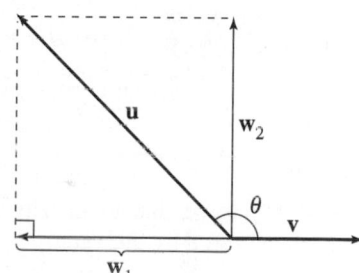

θ *is obtuse.*
Figure 6.26

Projection of u onto v

Let **u** and **v** be nonzero vectors. The projection of **u** onto **v** is given by

$$\text{proj}_{\mathbf{v}}\mathbf{u} = \left(\frac{\mathbf{u} \cdot \mathbf{v}}{\|\mathbf{v}\|^2}\right)\mathbf{v}.$$

EXAMPLE 5 Decomposing a Vector into Components

Find the projection of

$$\mathbf{u} = \langle 3, -5 \rangle \quad \text{onto} \quad \mathbf{v} = \langle 6, 2 \rangle.$$

Then write $\mathbf{u}$ as the sum of two orthogonal vectors, one of which is $\text{proj}_{\mathbf{v}}\mathbf{u}$.

Solution

The projection of $\mathbf{u}$ onto $\mathbf{v}$ is

$$\mathbf{w}_1 = \text{proj}_{\mathbf{v}}\mathbf{u} = \left(\frac{\mathbf{u} \cdot \mathbf{v}}{\|\mathbf{v}\|^2}\right)\mathbf{v} = \left(\frac{8}{40}\right)\langle 6, 2 \rangle = \left\langle \frac{6}{5}, \frac{2}{5} \right\rangle$$

as shown in Figure 6.27. The other component, $\mathbf{w}_2$, is

$$\mathbf{w}_2 = \mathbf{u} - \mathbf{w}_1 = \langle 3, -5 \rangle - \left\langle \frac{6}{5}, \frac{2}{5} \right\rangle = \left\langle \frac{9}{5}, -\frac{27}{5} \right\rangle.$$

So,

$$\mathbf{u} = \mathbf{w}_1 + \mathbf{w}_2 = \left\langle \frac{6}{5}, \frac{2}{5} \right\rangle + \left\langle \frac{9}{5}, -\frac{27}{5} \right\rangle = \langle 3, -5 \rangle.$$

Figure 6.27

✓ **Checkpoint** *Audio-video solution in English & Spanish at LarsonPrecalculus.com.*

Find the projection of $\mathbf{u} = \langle 3, 4 \rangle$ onto $\mathbf{v} = \langle 8, 2 \rangle$. Then write $\mathbf{u}$ as the sum of two orthogonal vectors, one of which is $\text{proj}_{\mathbf{v}}\mathbf{u}$.

EXAMPLE 6 Finding a Force

A 200-pound cart sits on a ramp inclined at 30°, as shown in Figure 6.28. What force is required to keep the cart from rolling down the ramp?

Solution

Because the force due to gravity is vertical and downward, you can represent the gravitational force by the vector

$$\mathbf{F} = -200\mathbf{j}. \qquad \text{Force due to gravity}$$

To find the force required to keep the cart from rolling down the ramp, project $\mathbf{F}$ onto a unit vector $\mathbf{v}$ in the direction of the ramp, as follows.

$$\mathbf{v} = (\cos 30°)\mathbf{i} + (\sin 30°)\mathbf{j} = \frac{\sqrt{3}}{2}\mathbf{i} + \frac{1}{2}\mathbf{j} \qquad \text{Unit vector along ramp}$$

Figure 6.28

So, the projection of $\mathbf{F}$ onto $\mathbf{v}$ is

$$\begin{aligned}
\mathbf{w}_1 = \text{proj}_{\mathbf{v}}\mathbf{F} &= \left(\frac{\mathbf{F} \cdot \mathbf{v}}{\|\mathbf{v}\|^2}\right)\mathbf{v} \\
&= (\mathbf{F} \cdot \mathbf{v})\mathbf{v} \\
&= (-200)\left(\frac{1}{2}\right)\mathbf{v} \\
&= -100\left(\frac{\sqrt{3}}{2}\mathbf{i} + \frac{1}{2}\mathbf{j}\right).
\end{aligned}$$

The magnitude of this force is 100, so a force of 100 pounds is required to keep the cart from rolling down the ramp.

✓ **Checkpoint** *Audio-video solution in English & Spanish at LarsonPrecalculus.com.*

Rework Example 6 for a 150-pound cart sitting on a ramp inclined at 15°.

Work

The work W done by a constant force $\mathbf{F}$ acting along the line of motion of an object is given by

$$W = (\text{magnitude of force})(\text{distance})$$

$$= \|\mathbf{F}\|\,\|\overrightarrow{PQ}\|$$

as shown in Figure 6.29. If the constant force $\mathbf{F}$ is not directed along the line of motion (see Figure 6.30), then the work W done by the force is given by

$$W = \|\text{proj}_{\overrightarrow{PQ}}\mathbf{F}\|\,\|\overrightarrow{PQ}\| \qquad \text{Projection form for work}$$

$$= (\cos\theta)\,\|\mathbf{F}\|\,\|\overrightarrow{PQ}\| \qquad \|\text{proj}_{\overrightarrow{PQ}}\mathbf{F}\| = (\cos\theta)\|\mathbf{F}\|$$

$$= \mathbf{F}\cdot\overrightarrow{PQ}. \qquad \text{Dot product form for work}$$

Force acts along the line of motion.
Figure 6.29

Force acts at angle θ with the line of motion.
Figure 6.30

This notion of work is summarized in the definition below.

> **Definition of Work**
>
> The **work** W done by a constant force $\mathbf{F}$ as its point of application moves along the vector $\overrightarrow{PQ}$ is given by either of the following.
>
> **1.** $W = \|\text{proj}_{\overrightarrow{PQ}}\mathbf{F}\|\,\|\overrightarrow{PQ}\|$ Projection form
>
> **2.** $W = \mathbf{F}\cdot\overrightarrow{PQ}$ Dot product form

---

EXAMPLE 7   Finding the Work Done

To close a barn's sliding door, a person pulls on a rope with a constant force of 50 pounds at a constant angle of 60°, as shown in Figure 6.31. Find the work done in moving the door 12 feet to its closed position.

Solution

Using a projection, you can calculate the work as follows.

$$W = \|\text{proj}_{\overrightarrow{PQ}}\mathbf{F}\|\,\|\overrightarrow{PQ}\| \qquad \text{Projection form for work}$$

$$= (\cos 60°)\,\|\mathbf{F}\|\,\|\overrightarrow{PQ}\| \qquad \|\text{proj}_{\overrightarrow{PQ}}\mathbf{F}\| = (\cos\theta)\|\mathbf{F}\|$$

$$= \frac{1}{2}(50)(12)$$

$$= 300 \text{ foot-pounds}$$

So, the work done is 300 foot-pounds. You can verify this result by finding the vectors $\mathbf{F}$ and $\overrightarrow{PQ}$ and calculating their dot product.

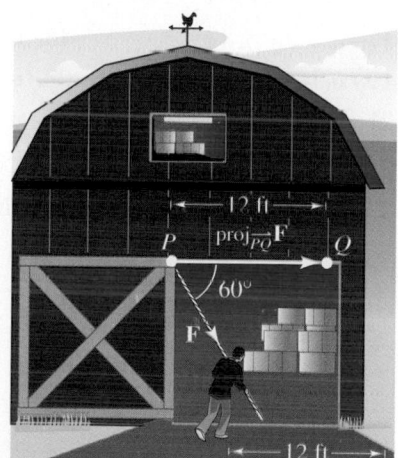

Figure 6.31

✓ **Checkpoint** 🔊))) *Audio-video solution in English & Spanish at LarsonPrecalculus.com.*

A wagon is pulled by exerting a force of 35 pounds on a handle that makes a 30° angle with the horizontal. Find the work done in pulling the wagon 40 feet.

6.4   Exercises

See *CalcChat.com* for tutorial help and worked-out solutions to odd-numbered exercises.
For instructions on how to use a graphing utility, see Appendix A.

Vocabulary and Concept Check

1. For two vectors **u** and **v**, does $\mathbf{u} \cdot \mathbf{v} = \mathbf{v} \cdot \mathbf{u}$?

2. What is the dot product of two orthogonal vectors?

3. Is the dot product of two vectors an angle, a vector, or a scalar?

In Exercises 4–6, fill in the blank(s).

4. If θ is the angle between two nonzero vectors **u** and **v**, then $\cos \theta =$ _____ .

5. The projection of **u** onto **v** is given by $\text{proj}_\mathbf{v} \mathbf{u} =$ _____ .

6. The work W done by a constant force **F** as its point of application moves along the vector $\overrightarrow{PQ}$ is given by either $W =$ _____ or $W =$ _____ .

Procedures and Problem Solving

Finding the Dot Product   **In Exercises 7–10, find the dot product of u and v.**

7. $\mathbf{u} = \langle 6, 3 \rangle$
   $\mathbf{v} = \langle 2, -4 \rangle$

8. $\mathbf{u} = \langle -4, 1 \rangle$
   $\mathbf{v} = \langle 5, -4 \rangle$

9. $\mathbf{u} = 5\mathbf{i} + \mathbf{j}$
   $\mathbf{v} = 3\mathbf{i} - \mathbf{j}$

10. $\mathbf{u} = 2\mathbf{i} + 6\mathbf{j}$
    $\mathbf{v} = -3\mathbf{i} + 7\mathbf{j}$

Using Properties of Dot Products   **In Exercises 11–16, use the vectors $\mathbf{u} = \langle 2, 2 \rangle$, $\mathbf{v} = \langle -5, 3 \rangle$, and $\mathbf{w} = \langle 1, -4 \rangle$ to find the indicated quantity. State whether the result is a vector or a scalar.**

11. $\mathbf{u} \cdot \mathbf{u}$

12. $\mathbf{v} \cdot \mathbf{w}$

13. $\mathbf{u} \cdot 2\mathbf{v}$

14. $4\mathbf{u} \cdot \mathbf{v}$

15. $(3\mathbf{w} \cdot \mathbf{v})\mathbf{u}$

16. $(\mathbf{u} \cdot 2\mathbf{v})\mathbf{w}$

Finding the Magnitude of a Vector   **In Exercises 17–22, use the dot product to find the magnitude of u.**

17. $\mathbf{u} = \langle -5, 12 \rangle$

18. $\mathbf{u} = \langle -8, 15 \rangle$

19. $\mathbf{u} = 20\mathbf{i} + 25\mathbf{j}$

20. $\mathbf{u} = 6\mathbf{i} - 10\mathbf{j}$

21. $\mathbf{u} = -4\mathbf{j}$

22. $\mathbf{u} = 9\mathbf{i}$

Finding the Angle Between Two Vectors   **In Exercises 23–30, find the angle θ between the vectors.**

23. $\mathbf{u} = \langle -1, 0 \rangle$
    $\mathbf{v} = \langle 0, 2 \rangle$

24. $\mathbf{u} = \langle 4, 4 \rangle$
    $\mathbf{v} = \langle -2, 0 \rangle$

25. $\mathbf{u} = 2\mathbf{i} + 6\mathbf{j}$
    $\mathbf{v} = -5\mathbf{i} + 2\mathbf{j}$

26. $\mathbf{u} = 7\mathbf{i} - 2\mathbf{j}$
    $\mathbf{v} = -8\mathbf{i} + 6\mathbf{j}$

27. $\mathbf{u} = 2\mathbf{i}$
    $\mathbf{v} = -3\mathbf{j}$

28. $\mathbf{u} = 4\mathbf{j}$
    $\mathbf{v} = -9\mathbf{i}$

29. $\mathbf{u} = \cos\left(\dfrac{\pi}{3}\right)\mathbf{i} + \sin\left(\dfrac{\pi}{3}\right)\mathbf{j}$

    $\mathbf{v} = \cos\left(\dfrac{3\pi}{4}\right)\mathbf{i} + \sin\left(\dfrac{3\pi}{4}\right)\mathbf{j}$

30. $\mathbf{u} = \cos\left(\dfrac{\pi}{4}\right)\mathbf{i} + \sin\left(\dfrac{\pi}{4}\right)\mathbf{j}$

    $\mathbf{v} = \cos\left(\dfrac{2\pi}{3}\right)\mathbf{i} + \sin\left(\dfrac{2\pi}{3}\right)\mathbf{j}$

Finding the Angle Between Two Vectors   **In Exercises 31–34, graph the vectors and find the degree measure of the angle between the vectors.**

31. $\mathbf{u} = 2\mathbf{i} - 4\mathbf{j}$
    $\mathbf{v} = 3\mathbf{i} - 5\mathbf{j}$

32. $\mathbf{u} = 6\mathbf{i} - 2\mathbf{j}$
    $\mathbf{v} = 8\mathbf{i} - 5\mathbf{j}$

33. $\mathbf{u} = -6\mathbf{i} - 3\mathbf{j}$
    $\mathbf{v} = -8\mathbf{i} + 4\mathbf{j}$

34. $\mathbf{u} = -7\mathbf{i} - 4\mathbf{j}$
    $\mathbf{v} = -8\mathbf{i} + 2\mathbf{j}$

Finding the Angles in a Triangle   **In Exercises 35–38, use vectors to find the interior angles of the triangle with the given vertices.**

35. $(1, 2), (3, 4), (2, 5)$

36. $(-3, -4), (1, 7), (8, 2)$

37. $(-3, 0), (2, 2), (0, 6)$

38. $(-3, 5), (-1, 9), (7, 9)$

Using the Angle Between Two Vectors   **In Exercises 39–42, find $\mathbf{u} \cdot \mathbf{v}$, where θ is the angle between u and v.**

39. $\|\mathbf{u}\| = 9, \|\mathbf{v}\| = 36, \theta = \dfrac{3\pi}{4}$

40. $\|\mathbf{u}\| = 4, \|\mathbf{v}\| = 12, \theta = \dfrac{\pi}{3}$

41. $\|\mathbf{u}\| = 4, \|\mathbf{v}\| = 10, \theta = \dfrac{2\pi}{3}$

42. $\|\mathbf{u}\| = 100, \|\mathbf{v}\| = 250, \theta = \dfrac{\pi}{6}$

Determining Orthogonal Vectors   **In Exercises 43–46, determine whether u and v are orthogonal.**

43. $\mathbf{u} = \langle 10, -6 \rangle$
    $\mathbf{v} = \langle 9, 15 \rangle$

44. $\mathbf{u} = \langle 12, 4 \rangle$
    $\mathbf{v} = \langle \frac{1}{4}, -\frac{1}{3} \rangle$

45. $u = j$
   $v = i - j$

46. $u = 2i - 2j$
   $v = -i - j$

A Relationship of Two Vectors   **In Exercises 47–50, determine whether u and v are orthogonal, parallel, or neither.**

47. $u = \langle 10, 20 \rangle$
   $v = \langle -18, 9 \rangle$

48. $u = \langle 15, 9 \rangle$
   $v = \langle -5, -3 \rangle$

49. $u = -\frac{3}{5}i + \frac{7}{10}j$
   $v = 12i - 14j$

50. $u = -\frac{9}{10}i + 3j$
   $v = -5i + \frac{3}{2}j$

Finding an Unknown Vector Component   **In Exercises 51–56, find the value of k such that the vectors u and v are orthogonal.**

51. $u = 2i - kj$
   $v = 3i + 2j$

52. $u = 8i + 4j$
   $v = 2i - kj$

53. $u = i + 4j$
   $v = 7ki - 5j$

54. $u = -3ki + 5j$
   $v = 2i - 4j$

55. $u = -3ki + 2j$
   $v = -6i$

56. $u = 4i - 4kj$
   $v = 3j$

Decomposing a Vector into Components   **In Exercises 57–60, find the projection of u onto v. Then write u as the sum of two orthogonal vectors, one of which is proj$_v$u.**

57. $u = \langle 2, 2 \rangle$
   $v = \langle 6, 1 \rangle$

58. $u = \langle 4, 2 \rangle$
   $v = \langle 1, -2 \rangle$

59. $u = \langle 0, 3 \rangle$
   $v = \langle 2, 15 \rangle$

60. $u = \langle -5, -1 \rangle$
   $v = \langle -1, 1 \rangle$

Finding the Projection of u onto v Mentally   **In Exercises 61–64, use the graph to determine mentally the projection of u onto v. (The coordinates of the terminal points of the vectors in standard position are given.) Use the formula for the projection of u onto v to verify your result.**

61.

62.

63.

64.

Finding Orthogonal Vectors   **In Exercises 65–68, find two vectors in opposite directions that are orthogonal to the vector u. (There are many correct answers.)**

65. $u = \langle 2, 6 \rangle$

66. $u = \langle -7, 5 \rangle$

67. $u = \frac{1}{2}i - \frac{3}{4}j$

68. $u = -\frac{5}{2}i - 3j$

Finding the Work Done   **In Exercises 69 and 70, find the work done in moving a particle from P to Q when the magnitude and direction of the force are given by v.**

69. $P = (0, 0)$, $Q = (4, 7)$, $v = \langle 1, 4 \rangle$

70. $P = (1, 3)$, $Q = (-3, 5)$, $v = -2i + 3j$

71. Business   The vector $u = \langle 1225, 2445 \rangle$ gives the numbers of hours worked by employees of a temp agency at two pay levels. The vector $v = \langle 12.00, 10.25 \rangle$ gives the hourly wage (in dollars) paid at each level, respectively. (a) Find the dot product $u \cdot v$ and explain its meaning in the context of the problem. (b) Identify the vector operation used to increase wages by 2 percent.

72. Business   The vector $u = \langle 3240, 2450 \rangle$ gives the numbers of hamburgers and hot dogs, respectively, sold at a fast food stand in one week. The vector $v = \langle 3.25, 3.50 \rangle$ gives the prices in dollars of the food items. (a) Find the dot product $u \cdot v$ and explain its meaning in the context of the problem. (b) Identify the vector operation used to increase prices by $2\frac{1}{2}$ percent.

73. *Why you should learn it*   (p. 434) A truck with a gross weight of 30,000 pounds is parked on a slope of $d°$ (see figure). Assume that the only force to overcome is the force of gravity.

Weight = 30,000 lb

(a) Find the force required to keep the truck from rolling down the hill in terms of the slope d.

(b) Use a graphing utility to complete the table.

d	0°	1°	2°	3°	4°	5°
Force						

d	6°	7°	8°	9°	10°
Force					

(c) Find the force perpendicular to the hill when $d = 5°$.

74. Physics A sport utility vehicle with a gross weight of 5400 pounds is parked on a slope of 10°. Assume that the only force to overcome is the force of gravity. Find the force required to keep the vehicle from rolling down the hill. Find the force perpendicular to the hill.

75. MODELING DATA

One of the events in a local strongman contest is to drag a concrete block. One competitor drags the block with a constant force of 250 pounds at a constant angle of 30° with the horizontal. (See figure.)

(a) Find the work done in terms of the distance d.

(b) Use a graphing utility to complete the table.

d (in feet)	25	50	100
Work			

76. Public Safety A ski patroller pulls a rescue toboggan across a flat snow surface by exerting a constant force of 35 pounds on a handle that makes a constant angle of 22° with the horizontal (see figure). Find the work done in pulling the toboggan 200 feet.

77. Work A force of 50 pounds, exerted at an angle of 25° with the horizontal, is required to slide a desk across a floor. Determine the work done in sliding the desk 15 feet.

78. Work A mover exerts a horizontal force of 25 pounds on a crate as it is pushed up a ramp that is 12 feet long and inclined at an angle of 20° above the horizontal. Find the work done in pushing the crate up the ramp.

Conclusions

True or False? In Exercises 79 and 80, determine whether the statement is true or false. Justify your answer.

79. The vectors $\mathbf{u} = \langle 0, 0 \rangle$ and $\mathbf{v} = \langle -12, 6 \rangle$ are orthogonal.

80. The work W done by a constant force $\mathbf{F}$ acting along the line of motion of an object is represented by a vector.

81. Think About It If $\mathbf{u} = \langle \cos \theta, \sin \theta \rangle$ and $\mathbf{v} = \langle \sin \theta, -\cos \theta \rangle$, are $\mathbf{u}$ and $\mathbf{v}$ orthogonal, parallel, or neither? Explain.

82. Error Analysis Describe the error.

$$\langle 5, 8 \rangle \cdot \langle -2, 7 \rangle = \langle -10, 56 \rangle$$

83. Think About It Let $\mathbf{u}$ be a unit vector. What is the value of $\mathbf{u} \cdot \mathbf{u}$? Explain.

84. HOW DO YOU SEE IT? What is known about θ, the angle between two nonzero vectors $\mathbf{u}$ and $\mathbf{v}$ (see figure) under each condition?

(a) $\mathbf{u} \cdot \mathbf{v} = 0$ (b) $\mathbf{u} \cdot \mathbf{v} > 0$ (c) $\mathbf{u} \cdot \mathbf{v} < 0$

85. Think About It What can be said about the vectors $\mathbf{u}$ and $\mathbf{v}$ under each condition?

(a) The projection of $\mathbf{u}$ onto $\mathbf{v}$ equals $\mathbf{u}$.

(b) The projection of $\mathbf{u}$ onto $\mathbf{v}$ equals 0.

86. Proof Use vectors to prove that the diagonals of a rhombus are perpendicular.

87. Proof Prove the following.

$$\|\mathbf{u} - \mathbf{v}\|^2 = \|\mathbf{u}\|^2 + \|\mathbf{v}\|^2 - 2\mathbf{u} \cdot \mathbf{v}$$

88. Proof Prove that if $\mathbf{u}$ is orthogonal to $\mathbf{v}$ and $\mathbf{w}$, then $\mathbf{u}$ is orthogonal to $c\mathbf{v} + d\mathbf{w}$ for any scalars c and d.

89. Proof Prove that if $\mathbf{u}$ is a unit vector and θ is the angle between $\mathbf{u}$ and $\mathbf{i}$, then $\mathbf{u} = \cos \theta \mathbf{i} + \sin \theta \mathbf{j}$.

90. Proof Prove that if $\mathbf{u}$ is a unit vector and θ is the angle between $\mathbf{u}$ and $\mathbf{j}$, then

$$\mathbf{u} = \cos\left(\frac{\pi}{2} - \theta\right)\mathbf{i} + \sin\left(\frac{\pi}{2} - \theta\right)\mathbf{j}.$$

Cumulative Mixed Review

Transformation of a Graph In Exercises 91–94, describe how the graph of g is related to the graph of f.

91. $g(x) = f(x - 4)$ **92.** $g(x) = -f(x)$

93. $g(x) = f(x) + 6$ **94.** $g(x) = f(2x)$

Operations with Complex Numbers In Exercises 95–100, perform the operation and write the result in standard form.

95. $3i(4 - 5i)$ **96.** $-2i(1 + 6i)$

97. $(1 + 3i)(1 - 3i)$ **98.** $(7 - 4i)(7 + 4i)$

99. $\dfrac{3}{1 + i} + \dfrac{2}{2 - 3i}$ **100.** $\dfrac{6}{4 - i} - \dfrac{3}{1 + i}$

6.5   Trigonometric Form of a Complex Number

The Complex Plane

Just as real numbers can be represented by points on the real number line, you can represent a complex number $z = a + bi$ as the point (a, b) in a coordinate plane (the **complex plane**). The horizontal axis is called the **real axis** and the vertical axis is called the **imaginary axis,** as shown in the figure.

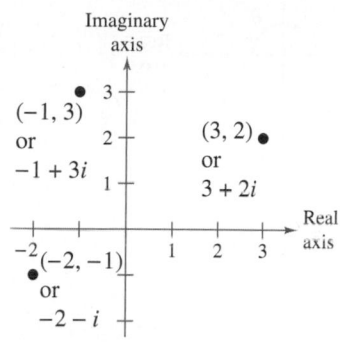

The **absolute value of a complex number** $a + bi$ is defined as the distance between the origin $(0, 0)$ and the point (a, b).

Definition of the Absolute Value of a Complex Number

The **absolute value** of the complex number $z = a + bi$ is given by

$$|a + bi| = \sqrt{a^2 + b^2}.$$

When the complex number $a + bi$ is a real number (that is, when $b = 0$), this definition agrees with that given for the absolute value of a real number

$$|a + 0i| = \sqrt{a^2 + 0^2} = |a|.$$

EXAMPLE 1   Finding the Absolute Value of a Complex Number

See LarsonPrecalculus.com for an interactive version of this type of example.

Plot

$$z = -2 + 5i$$

and find its absolute value.

Solution

The complex number

$$z = -2 + 5i$$

is plotted in the figure. The absolute value of z is

$$|z| = \sqrt{(-2)^2 + 5^2}$$

$$= \sqrt{29}.$$

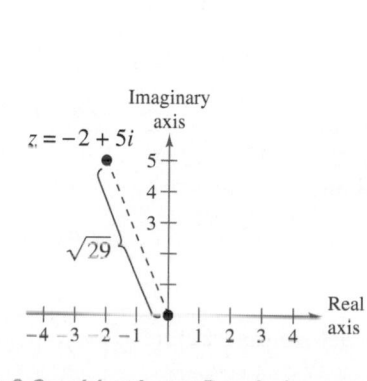

✓ **Checkpoint** 🔊))) *Audio-video solution in English & Spanish at LarsonPrecalculus.com.*

Plot $z = 3 - 4i$ and find its absolute value.

What you should learn

▶ Plot complex numbers in the complex plane and find absolute values of complex numbers.
▶ Write trigonometric forms of complex numbers.
▶ Multiply and divide complex numbers written in trigonometric form.
▶ Use DeMoivre's Theorem to find powers of complex numbers.
▶ Find nth roots of complex numbers.

Why you should learn it

You can use the trigonometric form of a complex number to perform operations with complex numbers. For instance, in Exercises 161–166 on page 455, you will use the trigonometric forms of complex numbers to find voltage, current, or impedance for given conditions.

Trigonometric Form of a Complex Number

In Section 2.4, you learned how to add, subtract, multiply, and divide complex numbers. To work effectively with *powers* and *roots* of complex numbers, it is helpful to write complex numbers in trigonometric form. Consider the nonzero complex number $a + bi$, plotted at the right. By letting θ be the angle from the positive real axis (measured counterclockwise) to the line segment connecting the origin and the point (a, b), you can write

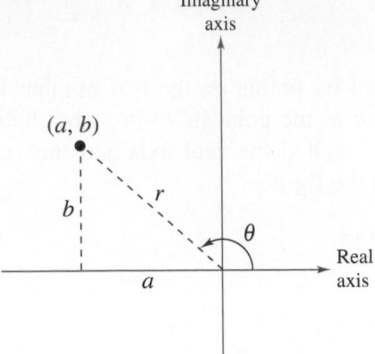

$$a = r \cos \theta \quad \text{and} \quad b = r \sin \theta$$

where

$$r = \sqrt{a^2 + b^2}.$$

Consequently, you have

$$a + bi = (r \cos \theta) + (r \sin \theta)i$$

from which you can obtain the **trigonometric form of a complex number.**

Trigonometric Form of a Complex Number

The **trigonometric form** of the complex number $z = a + bi$ is given by

$$z = r(\cos \theta + i \sin \theta)$$

where $a = r \cos \theta$, $b = r \sin \theta$, $r = \sqrt{a^2 + b^2}$, and $\tan \theta = b/a$. The number r is the **modulus** of z, and θ is called an **argument** of z.

The trigonometric form of a complex number is also called the *polar form*. Because there are infinitely many choices for θ, the trigonometric form of a complex number is not unique. Normally, θ is restricted to the interval $0 \le \theta < 2\pi$, although on occasion it is convenient to use $\theta < 0$.

EXAMPLE 2   Trigonometric Form of a Complex Number

Write the complex number $z = -2i$ in trigonometric form.

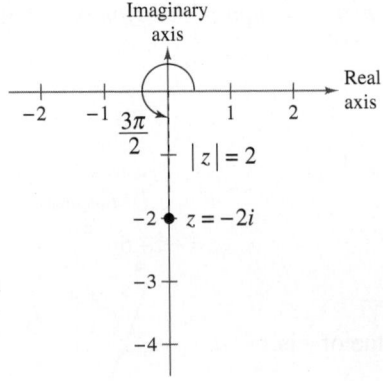

Solution

The absolute value of z is

$$r = |-2i| = \sqrt{0^2 + (-2)^2} = \sqrt{4} = 2.$$

With $a = 0$, you cannot use $\tan \theta = b/a$ to find θ. Because $z = -2i$ lies on the negative imaginary axis (see figure), choose $\theta = 3\pi/2$. So, the trigonometric form is

$$z = r(\cos \theta + i \sin \theta)$$

$$= 2\left(\cos \frac{3\pi}{2} + i \sin \frac{3\pi}{2} \right).$$

✓ *Checkpoint* ◀))) *Audio-video solution in English & Spanish at LarsonPrecalculus.com.*

Write the complex number $z = 3i$ in trigonometric form.

EXAMPLE 3   **Trigonometric Form of a Complex Number**

Write the complex number $z = -2 - 2\sqrt{3}i$ in trigonometric form.

Solution

The absolute value of z is

$$r = |-2 - 2\sqrt{3}i| = \sqrt{(-2)^2 + (-2\sqrt{3})^2} = \sqrt{16} = 4$$

and the angle θ is determined from

$$\tan \theta = \frac{b}{a} = \frac{-2\sqrt{3}}{-2} = \sqrt{3}.$$

Because $\tan(\pi/3) = \sqrt{3}$ and $z = -2 - 2\sqrt{3}i$ lies in Quadrant III, $\theta = \pi + \pi/3 = 4\pi/3$. So, the trigonometric form is

$$z = r(\cos \theta + i \sin \theta) = 4\left(\cos \frac{4\pi}{3} + i \sin \frac{4\pi}{3}\right).$$

See the figure below.

 ✓ Checkpoint Audio-video solution in English & Spanish at LarsonPrecalculus.com.

Write the complex number $z = 6 - 6i$ in trigonometric form.

EXAMPLE 4   **Writing a Complex Number in Standard Form**

Write the complex number in standard form $a + bi$.

$$z = \sqrt{8}\left[\cos\left(-\frac{\pi}{3}\right) + i \sin\left(-\frac{\pi}{3}\right)\right]$$

Solution

Because $\cos(-\pi/3) = 1/2$ and $\sin(-\pi/3) - -\sqrt{3}/2$, you can write

$$z = \sqrt{8}\left[\cos\left(-\frac{\pi}{3}\right) + i \sin\left(-\frac{\pi}{3}\right)\right]$$

$$= \sqrt{8}\left[\frac{1}{2} - \frac{\sqrt{3}}{2}i\right]$$

$$= 2\sqrt{2}\left[\frac{1}{2} - \frac{\sqrt{3}}{2}i\right]$$

$$= \sqrt{2} - \sqrt{6}i.$$

✓ Checkpoint Audio-video solution in English & Spanish at LarsonPrecalculus.com.

Write $z = 8[\cos(2\pi/3) + i \sin(2\pi/3)]$ in standard form $a + bi$.

What's Wrong?

You use a graphing utility to check the answer to Example 3, as shown in the figure. You determine that $r = 4$ and $\theta \approx 1.047 \approx \pi/3$. Your value for θ does not agree with the value found in the example. What's wrong?

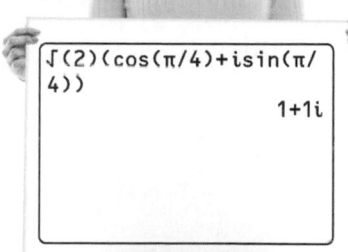

Technology Tip

A graphing utility can be used to convert a complex number in trigonometric form to standard form. For instance, enter the complex number $\sqrt{2}(\cos \pi/4 + i \sin \pi/4)$ in your graphing utility and press ENTER. You should obtain the standard form $1 + i$, as shown below.

Multiplication and Division of Complex Numbers

The trigonometric form adapts nicely to multiplication and division of complex numbers. For two complex numbers

$$z_1 = r_1(\cos \theta_1 + i \sin \theta_1) \quad \text{and} \quad z_2 = r_2(\cos \theta_2 + i \sin \theta_2)$$

the product of z_1 and z_2 is

$$
\begin{aligned}
z_1 z_2 &= r_1 r_2(\cos \theta_1 + i \sin \theta_1)(\cos \theta_2 + i \sin \theta_2) \\
&= r_1 r_2[(\cos \theta_1 \cos \theta_2 - \sin \theta_1 \sin \theta_2) + i(\sin \theta_1 \cos \theta_2 + \cos \theta_1 \sin \theta_2)] \\
&= r_1 r_2[\cos(\theta_1 + \theta_2) + i \sin(\theta_1 + \theta_2)]. \qquad \text{Sum and difference formulas}
\end{aligned}
$$

This establishes the first part of the following rule. The second part is left for you to verify (see Exercise 171).

Product and Quotient of Two Complex Numbers

Let $z_1 = r_1(\cos \theta_1 + i \sin \theta_1)$ and $z_2 = r_2(\cos \theta_2 + i \sin \theta_2)$ be complex numbers.

$$z_1 z_2 = r_1 r_2[\cos(\theta_1 + \theta_2) + i \sin(\theta_1 + \theta_2)] \qquad \text{Product}$$

$$\frac{z_1}{z_2} = \frac{r_1}{r_2}[\cos(\theta_1 - \theta_2) + i \sin(\theta_1 - \theta_2)], \ z_2 \neq 0 \qquad \text{Quotient}$$

Note that this rule says that to *multiply* two complex numbers you multiply moduli and add arguments, whereas to *divide* two complex numbers you divide moduli and subtract arguments.

EXAMPLE 5   Multiplying Complex Numbers

Find the product $z_1 z_2$ of the complex numbers.

$$z_1 = 3\left(\cos \frac{\pi}{4} + i \sin \frac{\pi}{4}\right)$$

$$z_2 = 2\left(\cos \frac{3\pi}{4} + i \sin \frac{3\pi}{4}\right)$$

Solution

$$
\begin{aligned}
z_1 z_2 &= 3\left(\cos \frac{\pi}{4} + i \sin \frac{\pi}{4}\right) \cdot 2\left(\cos \frac{3\pi}{4} + i \sin \frac{3\pi}{4}\right) \\
&= 6\left[\cos\left(\frac{\pi}{4} + \frac{3\pi}{4}\right) + i \sin\left(\frac{\pi}{4} + \frac{3\pi}{4}\right)\right] \\
&= 6(\cos \pi + i \sin \pi) \\
&= 6[-1 + i(0)] \\
&= -6
\end{aligned}
$$

The numbers z_1, z_2, and $z_1 z_2$ are plotted in the figure.

✓ **Checkpoint** ◀))) *Audio-video solution in English & Spanish at LarsonPrecalculus.com.*

Find the product $z_1 z_2$ of $z_1 = 2\left(\cos \frac{5\pi}{6} + i \sin \frac{5\pi}{6}\right)$ and $z_2 = 5\left(\cos \frac{7\pi}{6} + i \sin \frac{7\pi}{6}\right)$.

EXAMPLE 6   Multiplying Complex Numbers

Find the product z_1z_2 of the complex numbers.

$$z_1 = 2\left(\cos\frac{2\pi}{3} + i\sin\frac{2\pi}{3}\right) \qquad z_2 = 8\left(\cos\frac{11\pi}{6} + i\sin\frac{11\pi}{6}\right)$$

Solution

$$z_1z_2 = 2\left(\cos\frac{2\pi}{3} + i\sin\frac{2\pi}{3}\right) \cdot 8\left(\cos\frac{11\pi}{6} + i\sin\frac{11\pi}{6}\right)$$

$$= 16\left[\cos\left(\frac{2\pi}{3} + \frac{11\pi}{6}\right) + i\sin\left(\frac{2\pi}{3} + \frac{11\pi}{6}\right)\right]$$

$$= 16\left(\cos\frac{5\pi}{2} + i\sin\frac{5\pi}{2}\right)$$

$$= 16\left(\cos\frac{\pi}{2} + i\sin\frac{\pi}{2}\right) \qquad \frac{5\pi}{2} \text{ and } \frac{\pi}{2} \text{ are coterminal.}$$

$$= 16[0 + i(1)]$$

$$= 16i$$

You can check this result by first converting to the standard forms

$$z_1 = -1 + \sqrt{3}i \quad \text{and} \quad z_2 = 4\sqrt{3} - 4i$$

and then multiplying algebraically.

$$z_1z_2 = \left(-1 + \sqrt{3}i\right)\left(4\sqrt{3} - 4i\right) = -4\sqrt{3} + 4i + 12i + 4\sqrt{3} = 16i$$

✓ **Checkpoint** ◀))) *Audio-video solution in English & Spanish at LarsonPrecalculus.com.*

Find the product z_1z_2 of the complex numbers.

$$z_1 = 3\left(\cos\frac{\pi}{3} + i\sin\frac{\pi}{3}\right) \qquad z_2 = 4\left(\cos\frac{\pi}{6} + i\sin\frac{\pi}{6}\right)$$

EXAMPLE 7   Dividing Complex Numbers

Find the quotient z_1/z_2 of the complex numbers.

$$z_1 = 24(\cos 300° + i\sin 300°) \qquad z_2 = 8(\cos 75° + i\sin 75°)$$

Solution

$$\frac{z_1}{z_2} = \frac{24(\cos 300° + i\sin 300°)}{8(\cos 75° + i\sin 75°)}$$

$$= \frac{24}{8}[\cos(300° - 75°) + i\sin(300° - 75°)]$$

$$= 3(\cos 225° + i\sin 225°)$$

$$= 3\left[-\frac{\sqrt{2}}{2} + i\left(-\frac{\sqrt{2}}{2}\right)\right]$$

$$= -\frac{3\sqrt{2}}{2} - \frac{3\sqrt{2}}{2}i$$

✓ **Checkpoint** ◀))) *Audio-video solution in English & Spanish at LarsonPrecalculus.com.*

Find the quotient z_1/z_2 of the complex numbers.

$$z_1 = \cos 40° + i\sin 40° \qquad z_2 = \cos 10° + i\sin 10°$$

Technology Tip

Some graphing utilities can multiply and divide complex numbers in trigonometric form. If you have access to such a graphing utility, use it to find z_1z_2 and z_1/z_2 in Examples 6 and 7.

```
2(cos(2π/3)+isin(2π/3)
)*8(cos(11π/6)+isin(11
π/6))
                    16i
```

Powers of Complex Numbers

The trigonometric form of a complex number can be used to raise a complex number to a power. To accomplish this, consider repeated use of the multiplication rule.

$$z = r(\cos \theta + i \sin \theta)$$

$$z^2 = r(\cos \theta + i \sin \theta)r(\cos \theta + i \sin \theta) = r^2(\cos 2\theta + i \sin 2\theta)$$

$$z^3 = r^2(\cos 2\theta + i \sin 2\theta)r(\cos \theta + i \sin \theta) = r^3(\cos 3\theta + i \sin 3\theta)$$

$$z^4 = r^4(\cos 4\theta + i \sin 4\theta)$$

$$z^5 = r^5(\cos 5\theta + i \sin 5\theta)$$

$$\vdots$$

This pattern leads to **DeMoivre's Theorem,** which is named after the French mathematician Abraham DeMoivre (1667–1754).

DeMoivre's Theorem

If $z = r(\cos \theta + i \sin \theta)$ is a complex number and n is a positive integer, then

$$z^n = [r(\cos \theta + i \sin \theta)]^n$$

$$= r^n(\cos n\theta + i \sin n\theta).$$

Explore the Concept

Plot the numbers i, i^2, i^3, i^4, and i^5 in the complex plane. Write each number in trigonometric form and describe what happens to the angle θ as you form higher powers of i.

EXAMPLE 8   Finding a Power of a Complex Number

Use DeMoivre's Theorem to find $\left(1 + \sqrt{3}i\right)^{12}$.

Solution

First, convert the complex number to trigonometric form using

$$r = \sqrt{(1)^2 + \left(\sqrt{3}\right)^2} = 2$$

and

$$\theta = \arctan \frac{\sqrt{3}}{1} = \frac{\pi}{3}.$$

So, the trigonometric form is

$$1 + \sqrt{3}i = 2\left(\cos \frac{\pi}{3} + i \sin \frac{\pi}{3}\right).$$

Then, by DeMoivre's Theorem, you have

$$\left(1 + \sqrt{3}i\right)^{12} = \left[2\left(\cos \frac{\pi}{3} + i \sin \frac{\pi}{3}\right)\right]^{12}$$

$$= 2^{12}\left(\cos \frac{12\pi}{3} + i \sin \frac{12\pi}{3}\right)$$

$$= 4096(\cos 4\pi + i \sin 4\pi)$$

$$= 4096(1 + 0)$$

$$= 4096.$$

✓ **Checkpoint** 🔊))) *Audio-video solution in English & Spanish at LarsonPrecalculus.com.*

Use DeMoivre's Theorem to find $(-1 - i)^4$.

Roots of Complex Numbers

Recall that a consequence of the Fundamental Theorem of Algebra is that a polynomial equation of degree n has n solutions in the complex number system. So, an equation such as $x^6 = 1$ has six solutions, and in this particular case you can find the six solutions by factoring and using the Quadratic Formula.

$$x^6 - 1 = 0$$

$$(x^3 - 1)(x^3 + 1) = 0$$

$$(x - 1)(x^2 + x + 1)(x + 1)(x^2 - x + 1) = 0$$

Consequently, the solutions are

$$x = \pm 1, \quad x = \frac{-1 \pm \sqrt{3}i}{2}, \quad \text{and} \quad x = \frac{1 \pm \sqrt{3}i}{2}.$$

Each of these numbers is a sixth root of 1. In general, the **nth root of a complex number** is defined as follows.

Definition of an nth Root of a Complex Number

The complex number $u = a + bi$ is an **nth root** of the complex number z when

$$z = u^n = (a + bi)^n.$$

To find a formula for an nth root of a complex number, let u be an nth root of z, where $u = s(\cos \beta + i \sin \beta)$ and $z = r(\cos \theta + i \sin \theta)$. By DeMoivre's Theorem and the fact that $u^n = z$, you have

$$s^n(\cos n\beta + i \sin n\beta) = r(\cos \theta + i \sin \theta).$$

Taking the absolute value of each side of this equation, it follows that $s^n = r$. Substituting back into the previous equation and dividing by r, you get

$$\cos n\beta + i \sin n\beta = \cos \theta + i \sin \theta.$$

So, it follows that

$$\cos n\beta = \cos \theta \quad \text{and} \quad \sin n\beta = \sin \theta.$$

Because both sine and cosine have a period of 2π, these last two equations have solutions if and only if the angles differ by a multiple of 2π. Consequently, there must exist an integer k such that

$$n\beta = \theta + 2\pi k$$

$$\beta = \frac{\theta + 2\pi k}{n}.$$

By substituting this value of β into the trigonometric form of u, you get the result stated in the theorem on the next page.

Explore the Concept

The nth roots of a complex number are useful for solving some polynomial equations. For instance, explain how you can use DeMoivre's Theorem to solve the polynomial equation $x^4 + 16 = 0$. [*Hint:* Write -16 as $16(\cos \pi + i \sin \pi)$.]

> **nth Roots of a Complex Number**
>
> For a positive integer n, the complex number $z = r(\cos\theta + i\sin\theta)$ has exactly n distinct nth roots given by
>
> $$z_k = \sqrt[n]{r}\left(\cos\frac{\theta + 2\pi k}{n} + i\sin\frac{\theta + 2\pi k}{n}\right)$$
>
> where $k = 0, 1, 2, \ldots, n - 1$.

When $k > n - 1$, the roots begin to repeat. For instance, when $k = n$, the angle

$$\frac{\theta + 2\pi n}{n} = \frac{\theta}{n} + 2\pi$$

is coterminal with θ/n, which is also obtained when $k = 0$.

The formula for the nth roots of a complex number z has a nice geometrical interpretation, as shown in Figure 6.32. Note that because the nth roots of z all have the same magnitude $\sqrt[n]{r}$, they all lie on a circle of radius $\sqrt[n]{r}$ with center at the origin. Furthermore, because successive nth roots have arguments that differ by

$$\frac{2\pi}{n}$$

the nth roots are equally spaced around the circle.

You have already found the sixth roots of 1 by factoring and by using the Quadratic Formula. Example 9 shows how you can solve the same problem with the formula for nth roots.

Figure 6.32

EXAMPLE 9   Finding the nth Roots of a Real Number

Find all the sixth roots of 1.

Solution

First, write 1 in the trigonometric form $1 = 1(\cos 0 + i\sin 0)$. Then, by the nth root formula with $n = 6$ and $r = 1$, the roots have the form

$$z_k = \sqrt[6]{1}\left(\cos\frac{0 + 2\pi k}{6} + i\sin\frac{0 + 2\pi k}{6}\right) = \cos\frac{\pi k}{3} + i\sin\frac{\pi k}{3}.$$

So, for $k = 0, 1, 2, 3, 4,$ and 5, the sixth roots are as follows. (See Figure 6.33.)

$$z_0 = \cos 0 + i\sin 0 = 1$$

$$z_1 = \cos\frac{\pi}{3} + i\sin\frac{\pi}{3} = \frac{1}{2} + \frac{\sqrt{3}}{2}i \qquad \text{Incremented by } \frac{2\pi}{n} = \frac{2\pi}{6} = \frac{\pi}{3}$$

$$z_2 = \cos\frac{2\pi}{3} + i\sin\frac{2\pi}{3} = -\frac{1}{2} + \frac{\sqrt{3}}{2}i$$

$$z_3 = \cos\pi + i\sin\pi = -1$$

$$z_4 = \cos\frac{4\pi}{3} + i\sin\frac{4\pi}{3} = -\frac{1}{2} - \frac{\sqrt{3}}{2}i$$

$$z_5 = \cos\frac{5\pi}{3} + i\sin\frac{5\pi}{3} = \frac{1}{2} - \frac{\sqrt{3}}{2}i$$

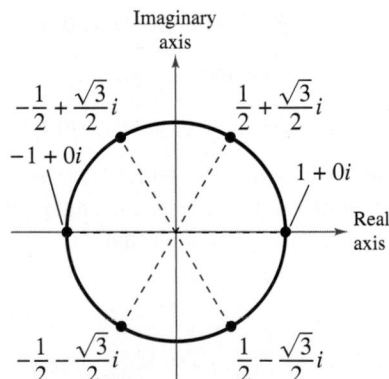

Figure 6.33

✓ **Checkpoint**))) *Audio-video solution in English & Spanish at LarsonPrecalculus.com.*

Find all fourth roots of 1.

In Figure 6.33, notice that the roots obtained in Example 9 all have a magnitude of 1 and are equally spaced around the unit circle. Also notice that the complex roots occur in conjugate pairs, as discussed in Section 2.5. The n distinct nth roots of 1 are called the **nth roots of unity.**

EXAMPLE 10   Finding the nth Roots of a Complex Number

Find the three cube roots of $z = -2 + 2i$.

Solution

The absolute value of z is $r = |-2 + 2i| = \sqrt{(-2)^2 + 2^2} = \sqrt{8}$, and the angle θ is determined from

$$\tan \theta = \frac{b}{a} = \frac{2}{-2} = -1.$$

Because z lies in Quadrant II, the trigonometric form of z is

$$z = -2 + 2i = \sqrt{8}(\cos 135° + i \sin 135°).$$

By the formula for nth roots, the cube roots have the form

$$z_k = \sqrt[6]{8}\left(\cos \frac{135° + 360°k}{3} + i \sin \frac{135° + 360°k}{3}\right).$$

Finally, for $k = 0$, 1, and 2, you obtain the roots

$$z_0 = \sqrt[6]{8}\left(\cos \frac{135° + 360°(0)}{3} + i \sin \frac{135° + 360°(0)}{3}\right)$$

$$= \sqrt{2}(\cos 45° + i \sin 45°)$$

$$= 1 + i$$

$$z_1 = \sqrt[6]{8}\left(\cos \frac{135° + 360°(1)}{3} + i \sin \frac{135° + 360°(1)}{3}\right)$$

$$= \sqrt{2}(\cos 165° + i \sin 165°)$$

$$\approx -1.3660 + 0.3660i$$

$$z_2 = \sqrt[6]{8}\left(\cos \frac{135° + 360°(2)}{3} + i \sin \frac{135° + 360°(2)}{3}\right)$$

$$= \sqrt{2}(\cos 285° + i \sin 285°)$$

$$\approx 0.3660 - 1.3660i$$

See Figure 6.34.

✓ **Checkpoint** 🔊))) Audio-video solution in English & Spanish at LarsonPrecalculus.com.

Find the three cube roots of $z = -6 + 6i$.   ◼

Remark

In Example 10, because $r = \sqrt{8}$, it follows that

$$\sqrt[n]{r} = \sqrt[3]{\sqrt{8}}$$

$$= (8^{1/2})^{1/3}$$

$$= 8^{1/6}$$

$$= \sqrt[6]{8}.$$

Figure 6.34

Explore the Concept

Use a graphing utility set in *parametric* and *radian* modes to display the graphs of $X1T = \cos T$ and $Y1T = \sin T$. Set the viewing window so that $-1.5 \le X \le 1.5$ and $-1 \le Y \le 1$. Then, using $0 \le T \le 2\pi$, set the "Tstep" to $2\pi/n$ for various values of n. Explain how the graphing utility can be used to obtain the nth roots of unity.

6.5   Exercises

Vocabulary and Concept Check

In Exercises 1–3, fill in the blank.

1. The _____ of a complex number $a + bi$ is the distance between the origin $(0, 0)$ and the point (a, b).

2. _____ Theorem states that if $z = r(\cos \theta + i \sin \theta)$ is a complex number and n is a positive integer, then $z^n = r^n(\cos n\theta + i \sin n\theta)$.

3. The complex number $u = a + bi$ is an _____ of the complex number z when $z = u^n = (a + bi)^n$.

4. What is the trigonometric form of the complex number $z = a + bi$?

5. When a complex number is written in trigonometric form, what does r represent?

6. When a complex number is written in trigonometric form, what does θ represent?

Procedures and Problem Solving

Finding the Absolute Value of a Complex Number   In Exercises 7–14, plot the complex number and find its absolute value.

7. $9 + 7i$

8. $10 - 3i$

9. $-5 - 12i$

10. $-4 + 6i$

11. $9i$

12. $-2i$

13. -5

14. 8

Trigonometric Form of a Complex Number   In Exercises 15–22, write the complex number in trigonometric form without using a calculator.

15.

16.

17.

18.

19.

20.

21.

22.

Trigonometric Form of a Complex Number   In Exercises 23–46, represent the complex number graphically, and find the trigonometric form of the number.

23. $-8i$

24. $4i$

25. $5i$

26. $-10i$

27. $7 - 7i$

28. $2 + 2i$

29. $\sqrt{3} + i$

30. $1 - \sqrt{3}i$

31. $1 + i$

32. $4 - 4i$

33. $-2(1 + \sqrt{3}i)$

34. $-\frac{5}{2}(\sqrt{3} + i)$

35. $-7 + 4i$

36. $5 - 3i$

37. 3

38. 6

39. $3 + \sqrt{3}i$

40. $-2\sqrt{2} + i$

41. $-1 - 5i$

42. $1 + 3i$

43. $5 - 2i$

44. $-3 + i$

45. $3\sqrt{2} - 7i$

46. $-8 - 5\sqrt{3}i$

Writing a Complex Number in Standard Form **In Exercises 47–58, represent the complex number graphically, and find the standard form of the number.**

47. $6\left(\cos\dfrac{\pi}{3} + i\sin\dfrac{\pi}{3}\right)$

48. $8\left(\cos\dfrac{5\pi}{6} + i\sin\dfrac{5\pi}{6}\right)$

49. $3.75\left(\cos\dfrac{3\pi}{4} + i\sin\dfrac{3\pi}{4}\right)$

50. $1.5\left(\cos\dfrac{\pi}{2} + i\sin\dfrac{\pi}{2}\right)$

51. $2(\cos 120° + i\sin 120°)$

52. $5(\cos 135° + i\sin 135°)$

53. $\frac{5}{2}[\cos(-30°) + i\sin(-30°)]$

54. $\frac{1}{4}[\cos(-45°) + i\sin(-45°)]$

55. $\sqrt{12}\left(\cos\dfrac{3\pi}{2} + i\sin\dfrac{3\pi}{2}\right)$

56. $\sqrt{48}(\cos 0 + i\sin 0)$

57. $3[\cos(18° \, 45') + i\sin(18° \, 45')]$

58. $6[\cos(230° \, 30') + i\sin(230° \, 30')]$

Writing a Complex Number in Standard Form **In Exercises 59–62, use a graphing utility to represent the complex number in standard form.**

59. $5\left(\cos\dfrac{7\pi}{9} + i\sin\dfrac{7\pi}{9}\right)$ 60. $12\left(\cos\dfrac{3\pi}{5} + i\sin\dfrac{3\pi}{5}\right)$

61. $9(\cos 58° + i\sin 58°)$ 62. $2(\cos 73° + i\sin 73°)$

Multiplying or Dividing Complex Numbers **In Exercises 63–76, perform the operation and leave the result in trigonometric form.**

63. $\left[3\left(\cos\dfrac{\pi}{2} + i\sin\dfrac{\pi}{2}\right)\right]\left[9\left(\cos\dfrac{3\pi}{2} + i\sin\dfrac{3\pi}{2}\right)\right]$

64. $\left[4\left(\cos\dfrac{\pi}{12} + i\sin\dfrac{\pi}{12}\right)\right]\left[5\left(\cos\dfrac{7\pi}{12} + i\sin\dfrac{7\pi}{12}\right)\right]$

65. $\left[\dfrac{2}{3}\left(\cos\dfrac{6\pi}{7} + i\sin\dfrac{6\pi}{7}\right)\right]\left[9\left(\cos\dfrac{9\pi}{14} + i\sin\dfrac{9\pi}{14}\right)\right]$

66. $\left[\dfrac{3}{2}\left(\cos\dfrac{\pi}{6} + i\sin\dfrac{\pi}{6}\right)\right]\left[6\left(\cos\dfrac{\pi}{4} + i\sin\dfrac{\pi}{4}\right)\right]$

67. $[\frac{5}{3}(\cos 140° + i\sin 140°)][\frac{2}{3}(\cos 60° + i\sin 60°)]$

68. $[\frac{1}{2}(\cos 115° + i\sin 115°)][\frac{4}{5}(\cos 300° + i\sin 300°)]$

69. $(\cos 290° + i\sin 290°)(\cos 200° + i\sin 200°)$

70. $(\cos 5° + i\sin 5°)(\cos 20° + i\sin 20°)$

71. $\dfrac{\cos 50° + i\sin 50°}{\cos 20° + i\sin 20°}$

72. $\dfrac{2(\cos 120° + i\sin 120°)}{4(\cos 40° + i\sin 40°)}$

73. $\dfrac{5(\cos 2\pi + i\sin 2\pi)}{4(\cos \pi + i\sin \pi)}$

74. $\dfrac{\cos\left(\dfrac{7\pi}{4}\right) + i\sin\left(\dfrac{7\pi}{4}\right)}{\cos \pi + i\sin \pi}$

75. $\dfrac{18(\cos 54° + i\sin 54°)}{3(\cos 102° + i\sin 102°)}$

76. $\dfrac{9(\cos 20° + i\sin 20°)}{5(\cos 75° + i\sin 75°)}$

Operations with Complex Numbers **In Exercises 77–92, (a) write the trigonometric forms of the complex numbers, (b) perform the indicated operation using the trigonometric forms, and (c) perform the indicated operation using the standard forms and check your result with that of part (b).**

77. $(2 - 2i)(1 + i)$

78. $(3 - 3i)(1 - i)$

79. $(2 + 2i)(1 - i)$

80. $(3 + 3i)(1 + i)$

81. $-2i(1 + i)$

82. $3i(1 + \sqrt{2}i)$

83. $-2i(\sqrt{3} - i)$

84. $-i(1 + \sqrt{3}i)$

85. $2(1 - i)$

86. $-4(1 + i)$

87. $\dfrac{3 + 4i}{1 - \sqrt{3}i}$

88. $\dfrac{2 + 2i}{1 + \sqrt{3}i}$

89. $\dfrac{5}{2 + 2i}$

90. $\dfrac{2}{\sqrt{3} - i}$

91. $\dfrac{4i}{-1 + i}$

92. $\dfrac{2i}{1 - \sqrt{3}i}$

Representing a Power **In Exercises 93 and 94, represent the powers z, z^2, z^3, and z^4 graphically. Describe the pattern.**

93. $z = \dfrac{\sqrt{2}}{2}(1 + i)$

94. $z = \dfrac{1}{2}(1 + \sqrt{3}i)$

Sketching the Graph of Complex Numbers   **In Exercises 95–106, sketch the graph of all complex numbers z satisfying the given condition.**

95. $|z| = 3$

96. $|z| = 5$

97. $|z| = 4$

98. $|z| = 6$

99. $|z| = 7$

100. $|z| = 8$

101. $\theta = \dfrac{\pi}{6}$

102. $\theta = \dfrac{\pi}{4}$

103. $\theta = \dfrac{\pi}{3}$

104. $\theta = \dfrac{\pi}{2}$

105. $\theta = \dfrac{2\pi}{3}$

106. $\theta = \dfrac{3\pi}{4}$

Finding a Power of a Complex Number   **In Exercises 107–126, use DeMoivre's Theorem to find the indicated power of the complex number. Write the result in standard form.**

107. $(1 + i)^3$

108. $(2 + 2i)^6$

109. $(-1 + i)^6$

110. $(3 - 3i)^8$

111. $2(\sqrt{3} - i)^5$

112. $4(1 - \sqrt{3}i)^3$

113. $[5(\cos 140° + i \sin 140°)]^3$

114. $[3(\cos 150° + i \sin 150°)]^4$

115. $\left(\cos \dfrac{5\pi}{4} + i \sin \dfrac{5\pi}{4} \right)^{10}$

116. $\left[2\left(\cos \dfrac{\pi}{2} + i \sin \dfrac{\pi}{2} \right) \right]^{12}$

117. $[2(\cos \pi + i \sin \pi)]^{14}$

118. $(\cos 0 + i \sin 0)^{20}$

119. $[4(\cos 10° + i \sin 10°)]^6$

120. $[6(\cos 15° + i \sin 15°)]^4$

121. $\left[3\left(\cos \dfrac{\pi}{8} + i \sin \dfrac{\pi}{8} \right) \right]^2$

122. $\left[2\left(\cos \dfrac{\pi}{10} + i \sin \dfrac{\pi}{10} \right) \right]^5$

123. $(3 - 2i)^5$

124. $\left(\sqrt{5} - 4i \right)^4$

125. $[2(\cos 1.25 + i \sin 1.25)]^4$

126. $[4(\cos 2.8 + i \sin 2.8)]^5$

Verifying nth Roots   **In Exercises 127 and 128, use DeMoivre's Theorem to verify the indicated root of the real number.**

127. $-\frac{1}{2}\left(1 + \sqrt{3}i\right)$ is a sixth root of 1.

128. $2^{-1/4}(1 - i)$ is a fourth root of -2.

Finding Square Roots of a Complex Number   **In Exercises 129–136, find the square roots of the complex number.**

129. $2i$

130. $5i$

131. $-3i$

132. $-6i$

133. $2 - 2i$

134. $2 + 2i$

135. $1 + \sqrt{3}i$

136. $1 - \sqrt{3}i$

Finding the nth Roots of a Complex Number   **In Exercises 137–152, (a) use the theorem on page 450 to find the indicated roots of the complex number, (b) represent each of the roots graphically, and (c) write each of the roots in standard form.**

137. Square roots of $5(\cos 120° + i \sin 120°)$

138. Square roots of $16(\cos 60° + i \sin 60°)$

139. Fourth roots of $81\left(\cos \dfrac{2\pi}{3} + i \sin \dfrac{2\pi}{3} \right)$

140. Fifth roots of $32\left(\cos \dfrac{5\pi}{6} + i \sin \dfrac{5\pi}{6} \right)$

141. Cube roots of $-25i$

142. Fourth roots of $625i$

143. Cube roots of $-\frac{125}{2}\left(1 + \sqrt{3}i\right)$

144. Cube roots of $-4\sqrt{2}(1 - i)$

145. Fourth roots of $256i$

146. Fourth roots of i

147. Fifth roots of 1

148. Cube roots of 1000

149. Cube roots of -125

150. Fourth roots of -4

151. Fifth roots of $128(-1 + i)$

152. Fifth roots of $4(1 - i)$

Solving an Equation   **In Exercises 153–160, use the theorem on page 450 to find all the solutions of the equation, and represent the solutions graphically.**

153. $x^4 - i = 0$

154. $x^3 + 1 = 0$

155. $x^5 + 243 = 0$

156. $x^3 - 27 = 0$

157. $x^4 + 16i = 0$

158. $x^6 - 64i = 0$

159. $x^3 - (1 - i) = 0$

160. $x^4 + (1 + i) = 0$

Why you should learn it *(p. 443)* **The formula $E = IZ$, where E represents voltage, I represents current, and Z represents impedance (a measure of opposition to a sinusoidal electric current), is used in electrcal engineering. Each variable is a complex number.**

In Exercises 161–166, use the formula to find the missing quantity for the given conditions. Then convert the given conditions to trigonometric form and check your result.

161. $I = 10 + 2i$
   $Z = 4 + 3i$

162. $I = 12 + 2i$
   $Z = 3 + 5i$

163. $I = 2 + 4i$
   $E = 5 + 5i$

164. $I = 10 + 2i$
   $E = 4 + 5i$

165. $E = 12 + 24i$
   $Z = 12 + 20i$

166. $E = 15 + 12i$
   $Z = 25 + 24i$

Conclusions

True or False?   In Exercises 167–170, determine whether the statement is true or false. Justify your answer.

167. $\frac{1}{2}(1 - \sqrt{3}i)$ is a ninth root of -1.

168. $\sqrt{3} + i$ is a solution of the equation $x^2 - 8i = 0$.

169. The product of two complex numbers is 0 only when the modulus of one (or both) of the complex numbers is 0.

170. Geometrically, the nth roots of any complex number z are equally spaced around the unit circle centered at the origin.

171. Quotient of Two Complex Numbers   Given two complex numbers $z_1 = r_1(\cos \theta_1 + i \sin \theta_1)$ and $z_2 = r_2(\cos \theta_2 + i \sin \theta_2)$, $z_2 \neq 0$, show that

$$\frac{z_1}{z_2} = \frac{r_1}{r_2}[\cos(\theta_1 - \theta_2) + i \sin(\theta_1 - \theta_2)].$$

172. Complex Conjugates   Show that

$$\bar{z} = r[\cos(-\theta) + i \sin(-\theta)]$$

is the complex conjugate of

$$z = r(\cos \theta + i \sin \theta).$$

173. Complex Conjugates   Use trigonometric forms of z and $\bar{z}$ in Exercise 172 to find the following.

(a) $z\bar{z}$

(b) $\frac{z}{\bar{z}}, \bar{z} \neq 0$

174. Think About It   Show that the negative of $z = r(\cos \theta + i \sin \theta)$ is

$$-z = r[\cos(\theta + \pi) + i \sin(\theta + \pi)].$$

175. Writing   The famous formula

$$e^{a + bi} = e^a(\cos b + i \sin b)$$

is called Euler's Formula, after the Swiss mathematician Leonhard Euler (1707–1783). This formula gives rise to the equation

$$e^{\pi i} + 1 = 0.$$

This equation relates the five most famous numbers in mathematics—0, 1, π, e, and i—in a single equation. Show how Euler's Formula can be used to derive this equation. Write a short paragraph summarizing your work.

176. **HOW DO YOU SEE IT?**   One of the fourth roots of a complex number z is shown in the figure.

(a) How many roots are not shown?

(b) Describe the other roots.

Cumulative Mixed Review

Harmonic Motion   In Exercises 177–180, for the simple harmonic motion described by the trigonometric function, find the maximum displacement from equilibrium and the lowest possible positive value of t for which $d = 0$.

177. $d = 16 \cos \frac{\pi}{4}t$

178. $d = \frac{1}{7} \sin \frac{5\pi}{4}t$

179. $d = \frac{1}{8} \cos 12\pi t$

180. $d = \frac{1}{12} \sin 60 \pi t$

6   Chapter Summary

What did you learn?	Explanation and Examples	Review Exercises
6.1 **Use the Law of Sines to solve oblique triangles (AAS or ASA)** *(p. 404)*.	**Law of Sines** If ABC is a triangle with sides a, b, and c, then $$\frac{a}{\sin A} = \frac{b}{\sin B} = \frac{c}{\sin C}.$$ A is acute. A is obtuse.	1–6
Use the Law of Sines to solve oblique triangles (SSA) *(p. 406)*.	If two sides and one opposite angle are given, then three possible situations can occur: (1) no such triangle exists (see Example 4), (2) one such triangle exists (see Example 3), or (3) two distinct triangles satisfy the conditions (see Example 5).	7–10
Find areas of oblique triangles *(p. 408)*, **and use the Law of Sines to model and solve real-life problems** *(p. 409)*.	The area of any triangle is one-half the product of the lengths of two sides times the sine of their included angle. That is, Area $= \frac{1}{2} bc \sin A = \frac{1}{2} ab \sin C = \frac{1}{2} ac \sin B$. The Law of Sines can be used to approximate the total distance of a boat race course. (See Example 7.)	11–16
6.2 **Use the Law of Cosines to solve oblique triangles (SSS or SAS)** *(p. 413)*.	**Law of Cosines** *Standard Form* *Alternative Form* $a^2 = b^2 + c^2 - 2bc \cos A$ $\cos A = \dfrac{b^2 + c^2 - a^2}{2bc}$ $b^2 = a^2 + c^2 - 2ac \cos B$ $\cos B = \dfrac{a^2 + c^2 - b^2}{2ac}$ $c^2 = a^2 + b^2 - 2ab \cos C$ $\cos C = \dfrac{a^2 + b^2 - c^2}{2ab}$	17–22
Use the Law of Cosines to model and solve real-life problems *(p. 415)*.	The Law of Cosines can be used to find the distance between the pitcher's mound and first base on a softball field. (See Example 3.)	23, 24
Use Heron's Area Formula to find areas of triangles *(p. 416)*.	**Heron's Area Formula:** For any triangle with sides of lengths a, b, and c, the area of the triangle is Area $= \sqrt{s(s-a)(s-b)(s-c)}$, where $s = (a+b+c)/2$.	25–28
6.3 **Represent vectors as directed line segments** *(p. 420)*.		29, 30
Write the component forms of vectors *(p. 421)*.	The component form of the vector with initial point $P(p_1, p_2)$ and terminal point $Q(q_1, q_2)$ is given by $\overrightarrow{PQ} = \langle q_1 - p_1, q_2 - p_2 \rangle = \langle v_1, v_2 \rangle = \mathbf{v}$.	31–34
Perform basic vector operations and represent vectors graphically *(p. 422)*.	Let $\mathbf{u} = \langle u_1, u_2 \rangle$ and $\mathbf{v} = \langle v_1, v_2 \rangle$ be vectors and let k be a scalar (a real number). $\mathbf{u} + \mathbf{v} = \langle u_1 + v_1, u_2 + v_2 \rangle$ $k\mathbf{u} = \langle ku_1, ku_2 \rangle$ $-\mathbf{v} = \langle -v_1, -v_2 \rangle$ $\mathbf{u} - \mathbf{v} = \langle u_1 - v_1, u_2 - v_2 \rangle$	35–44

	What did you learn?	Explanation and Examples	Review Exercises
6.3	**Write vectors as linear combinations of unit vectors** *(p. 424)*.	$\mathbf{v} = \langle v_1, v_2 \rangle = v_1\langle 1, 0\rangle + v_2\langle 0, 1\rangle = v_1\mathbf{i} + v_2\mathbf{j}$ The scalars v_1 and v_2 are the horizontal and vertical components of $\mathbf{v}$, respectively. The vector sum $v_1\mathbf{i} + v_2\mathbf{j}$ is a linear combination of the vectors $\mathbf{i}$ and $\mathbf{j}$.	45–50
	Find the direction angles of vectors *(p. 426)*.	If $\mathbf{u} = 2\mathbf{i} + 2\mathbf{j}$, then the direction angle is determined from $\tan \theta = 2/2 = 1$. So, $\theta = 45°$.	51–56
	Use vectors to model and solve real-life problems *(p. 427)*.	Vectors can be used to find the resultant speed and direction of an airplane. (See Example 10.)	57–60
6.4	**Find the dot product of two vectors and use the properties of the dot product** *(p. 434)*.	The dot product of $\mathbf{u} = \langle u_1, u_2\rangle$ and $\mathbf{v} = \langle v_1, v_2\rangle$ is $\mathbf{u} \cdot \mathbf{v} = u_1 v_1 + u_2 v_2$.	61–68
	Find the angle between two vectors and determine whether two vectors are orthogonal *(p. 435)*.	If θ is the angle between two nonzero vectors $\mathbf{u}$ and $\mathbf{v}$, then $\cos\theta = \dfrac{\mathbf{u} \cdot \mathbf{v}}{\|\mathbf{u}\|\,\|\mathbf{v}\|}$. Vectors $\mathbf{u}$ and $\mathbf{v}$ are orthogonal when $\mathbf{u} \cdot \mathbf{v} = 0$.	69–84
	Write vectors as the sums of two vector components *(p. 437)*.	Many applications in physics and engineering require the decomposition of a given vector into the sum of two vector components. (See Example 6.)	85–88
	Use vectors to find the work done by a force *(p. 439)*.	The work W done by a constant force $\mathbf{F}$ as its point of application moves along the vector $\overrightarrow{PQ}$ is given by either of the following. **1.** $W = \|\operatorname{proj}_{\overrightarrow{PQ}}\mathbf{F}\|\,\|\overrightarrow{PQ}\|$ Projection form **2.** $W = \mathbf{F} \cdot \overrightarrow{PQ}$ Dot product form	89, 90
6.5	**Plot complex numbers in the complex plane and find absolute values of complex numbers** *(p. 443)*.	A complex number $z = a + bi$ can be represented as the point (a, b) in the complex plane. The horizontal axis is the real axis and the vertical axis is the imaginary axis. The absolute value of $z = a + bi$ is $|a + bi| = \sqrt{a^2 + b^2}$.	91–94
	Write trigonometric forms of complex numbers *(p. 444)*.	The trigonometric form of the complex number $z = a + bi$ is $z = r(\cos\theta + i\sin\theta)$, where $a = r\cos\theta$, $b = r\sin\theta$, $r = \sqrt{a^2 + b^2}$, and $\tan\theta = b/a$.	95–98
	Multiply and divide complex numbers written in trigonometric form *(p. 446)*.	Let $z_1 = r_1(\cos\theta_1 + i\sin\theta_1)$ and $z_2 = r_2(\cos\theta_2 + i\sin\theta_2)$. $z_1 z_2 = r_1 r_2[\cos(\theta_1 + \theta_2) + i\sin(\theta_1 + \theta_2)]$ $\dfrac{z_1}{z_2} = \dfrac{r_1}{r_2}[\cos(\theta_1 - \theta_2) + i\sin(\theta_1 - \theta_2)]$, $z_2 \neq 0$	99–106
	Use DeMoivre's Theorem to find powers of complex numbers *(p. 448)*.	**DeMoivre's Theorem:** If $z = r(\cos\theta + i\sin\theta)$ is a complex number and n is a positive integer, then $z^n = [r(\cos\theta + i\sin\theta)]^n = r^n(\cos n\theta + i\sin n\theta)$.	107–110
	Find nth roots of complex numbers *(p. 449)*.	The complex number $u = a + bi$ is an nth root of the complex number z when $z = u^n = (a + bi)^n$.	111–122

6   Review Exercises

See *CalcChat.com* for tutorial help and worked-out solutions to odd-numbered exercises.
For instructions on how to use a graphing utility, see Appendix A.

6.1

Using the Law of Sines   In Exercises 1–10, use the Law of Sines to solve the triangle. If two solutions exist, find both.

1. $A = 32°$, $B = 50°$, $a = 16$
2. $A = 38°$, $B = 58°$, $a = 12$
3. $B = 16°$, $C = 98°$, $a = 8.4$
4. $B = 95°$, $C = 45°$, $a = 104.8$
5. $A = 60° 15'$, $B = 45° 30'$, $b = 4.8$
6. $A = 82° 45'$, $B = 28° 45'$, $b = 40.2$
7. $A = 75°$, $a = 51.2$, $b = 33.7$
8. $A = 15°$, $a = 5$, $b = 10$
9. $B = 25°$, $a = 6.2$, $b = 4$
10. $B = 150°$, $a = 10$, $b = 3$

Finding the Area of an Oblique Triangle   In Exercises 11–14, find the area of the triangle having the indicated angle and sides.

11. $A = 33°$, $b = 7$, $c = 10$
12. $B = 80°$, $a = 4$, $c = 8$
13. $C = 122°$, $b = 18$, $a = 29$
14. $C = 100°$, $a = 120$, $b = 74$

15. **Height**   A tree stands on a hillside of slope 28° from the horizontal. From a point 75 feet down the hill, the angle of elevation to the top of the tree is 45° (see figure). Find the height of the tree.

16. **Surveying**   A surveyor finds that a tree on the opposite bank of a river has a bearing of N 22° 30′ E from a certain point and a bearing of N 15° W from a point 400 feet downstream. Find the width of the river.

6.2

Using the Law of Cosines   In Exercises 17–22, use the Law of Cosines to solve the triangle.

17. $a = 9$, $b = 12$, $c = 20$
18. $a = 7$, $b = 15$, $c = 19$
19. $A = 150°$, $b = 10$, $c = 20$
20. $a = 6.2$, $b = 6.4$, $c = 2.1$
21. $C = 65°$, $a = 25$, $b = 12$
22. $B = 48°$, $a = 18$, $c = 12$

23. **Geometry**   The lengths of the diagonals of a parallelogram are 10 feet and 16 feet. Find the lengths of the sides of the parallelogram when the diagonals intersect at an angle of 28°.

24. **Surveying**   To approximate the length of a marsh, a surveyor walks 425 meters from point A to point B. Then the surveyor turns 65° and walks 300 meters to point C (see figure). Approximate the length AC of the marsh.

Using Heron's Area Formula   In Exercises 25–28, use Heron's Area Formula to find the area of the triangle.

25. $a = 3$, $b = 6$, $c = 8$
26. $a = 15$, $b = 8$, $c = 10$
27. $a = 64.8$, $b = 49.2$, $c = 24.1$
28. $a = 8.55$, $b = 5.14$, $c = 12.73$

6.3

Showing That Two Vectors Are Equivalent   In Exercises 29 and 30, show that **u** and **v** are equivalent.

29.

30.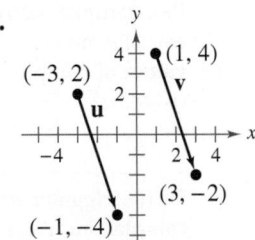

Finding the Component Form of a Vector   In Exercises 31–34, find the component form and the magnitude of the vector **v**.

31.   32.

33. Initial point: $(0, 10)$; terminal point: $(7, 3)$
34. Initial point: $(1, 5)$; terminal point: $(15, 9)$

Vector Operations In Exercises 35–40, find (a) u + v, (b) u − v, (c) 3u, and (d) 2v + 5u. Then sketch each resultant vector.

35. $u = \langle -1, -3 \rangle$, $v = \langle -3, 6 \rangle$
36. $u = \langle 4, 5 \rangle$, $v = \langle 0, -1 \rangle$
37. $u = \langle -5, 2 \rangle$, $v = \langle 4, 4 \rangle$
38. $u = \langle 1, -8 \rangle$, $v = \langle 3, -2 \rangle$
39. $u = 2i - j$, $v = 5i + 3j$
40. $u = -7i - 3j$, $v = 4i - j$

Vector Operations In Exercises 41–44, find the component form of w and sketch the specified vector operations geometrically, where $u = 6i - 5j$ and $v = 10i + 3j$.

41. $w = \frac{1}{3}v$
42. $w = \frac{1}{2}v$
43. $w = 4u + 5v$
44. $w = 3v - 2u$

Finding a Unit Vector In Exercises 45–48, find a unit vector in the direction of the given vector. Verify that the result has a magnitude of 1.

45. $u = \langle 0, -6 \rangle$
46. $v = \langle -12, -5 \rangle$
47. $v = 8i - 15j$
48. $w = -7i$

Writing a Linear Combination of Unit Vectors In Exercises 49 and 50, the initial and terminal points of a vector are given. Write the vector as a linear combination of the standard unit vectors i and j.

49. Initial point: $(-8, 3)$
    Terminal point: $(1, -5)$
50. Initial point: $(-2, 7)$
    Terminal point: $(5, -9)$

Finding Direction Angles of Vectors In Exercises 51–56, find the magnitude and the direction angle of the vector v.

51. $v = 7(\cos 120°i + \sin 120°j)$
52. $v = 3(\cos 150°i + \sin 150°j)$
53. $v = 5i + 4j$
54. $v = -3i - 3j$
55. $v = -4i + 7j$
56. $v = 8i - j$

57. **Resultant Force** Forces with magnitudes of 85 pounds and 50 pounds act on a single point. The angle between the forces is 15°. Describe the resultant force.

58. **Physics** A 180-pound weight is supported by two ropes, as shown in the figure. Find the tension in each rope.

59. **Physics** In a manufacturing process, an electric hoist lifts 200-pound ingots. Find the tension in the supporting cables. (See figure.)

60. **Aviation** An airplane has an airspeed of 430 miles per hour at a bearing of 135°. The wind velocity is 35 miles per hour in the direction N 30° E. Find the resultant speed and direction of the plane.

6.4

Finding the Dot Product In Exercises 61–64, find the dot product of u and v.

61. $u = \langle -6, 7 \rangle$
    $v = \langle -3, -5 \rangle$
62. $u = \langle -7, 12 \rangle$
    $v = \langle -4, -14 \rangle$
63. $u = 6i - j$
    $v = 2i + 5j$
64. $u = 8i - 7j$
    $v = 3i - 4j$

Using Properties of Dot Products In Exercises 65–68, use the vectors $u = \langle 6, -4 \rangle$ and $v = \langle 2, 1 \rangle$ to find the indicated quantity. State whether the result is a vector or a scalar.

65. $u \cdot u$
66. $\|v\| - 3$
67. $(u \cdot v)v$
68. $(u \cdot v)u$

Finding the Angle Between Two Vectors In Exercises 69–72, find the angle θ between the vectors.

69. $u = \langle 2\sqrt{2}, -4 \rangle$, $v = \langle -\sqrt{2}, 1 \rangle$
70. $u = \langle 3, \sqrt{3} \rangle$, $v = \langle 4, 3\sqrt{3} \rangle$
71. $u = \cos \frac{7\pi}{4}i + \sin \frac{7\pi}{4}j$
    $v = \cos \frac{5\pi}{6}i + \sin \frac{5\pi}{6}j$
72. $u = \cos 45°i + \sin 45°j$
    $v = \cos 300°i + \sin 300°j$

Finding the Angle Between Two Vectors In Exercises 73–76, graph the vectors and find the degree measure of the angle between the vectors.

73. $u = 4i + j$
    $v = i - 4j$
74. $u = 6i + 2j$
    $v = -3i - j$
75. $u = 7.2i - 5.6j$
    $v = 10i + 3.1j$
76. $u = -5.3i + 2.8j$
    $v = -8.1i - 4j$

A Relationship of Two Vectors In Exercises 77–80, determine whether u and v are orthogonal, parallel, or neither.

77. $u = \langle 12, -8 \rangle$
    $v = \langle 6, 9 \rangle$

78. $u = \langle 8, -4 \rangle$
    $v = \langle 5, 10 \rangle$

79. $u = \langle 8, 5 \rangle$
    $v = \langle -2, 4 \rangle$

80. $u = \langle -15, 51 \rangle$
    $v = \langle 20, -68 \rangle$

Finding an Unknown Vector Component In Exercises 81–84, find the value of k such that the vectors u and v are orthogonal.

81. $u = i - kj$
    $v = i + 2j$

82. $u = -2i + 4j$
    $v = 6i - kj$

83. $u = ki - j$
    $v = 2i - 2j$

84. $u = ki - 2j$
    $v = i + 4j$

Decomposing a Vector into Components In Exercises 85–88, find the projection of u onto v. Then write u as the sum of two orthogonal vectors, one of which is $proj_v u$.

85. $u = \langle -4, 3 \rangle$, $v = \langle -8, -2 \rangle$
86. $u = \langle 5, 6 \rangle$, $v = \langle 10, 0 \rangle$
87. $u = \langle 2, 7 \rangle$, $v = \langle 1, -1 \rangle$
88. $u = \langle -3, 5 \rangle$, $v = \langle -5, 2 \rangle$

89. **Work** Determine the work done by a crane lifting an 18,000-pound truck 48 inches.

90. **Physics** A 500-pound motorcycle is stopped on a hill inclined at 12°. What force is required to keep the motorcycle from rolling back down the hill?

6.5

Finding the Absolute Value of a Complex Number In Exercises 91–94, plot the complex number and find its absolute value.

91. $5 + 3i$
92. $-10 - 4i$
93. $-7i$
94. $6i$

Trigonometric Form of a Complex Number In Exercises 95–98, write the complex number in trigonometric form without using a calculator.

95. $4i$
96. -9
97. $-\sqrt{3} - i$
98. $-3\sqrt{3} + 3i$

Multiplying or Dividing Complex Numbers In Exercises 99–102, perform the operation and leave the result in trigonometric form.

99. $\left[\frac{5}{2}\left(\cos\frac{\pi}{2} + i\sin\frac{\pi}{2}\right)\right]\left[4\left(\cos\frac{\pi}{4} + i\sin\frac{\pi}{4}\right)\right]$

100. $\left[2\left(\cos\frac{2\pi}{3} + i\sin\frac{2\pi}{3}\right)\right]\left[3\left(\cos\frac{\pi}{6} + i\sin\frac{\pi}{6}\right)\right]$

101. $\dfrac{20(\cos 320° + i\sin 320°)}{5(\cos 80° + i\sin 80°)}$

102. $\dfrac{3(\cos 230° + i\sin 230°)}{9(\cos 95° + i\sin 95°)}$

Operations with Complex Numbers In Exercises 103–106, (a) write the trigonometric forms of the complex numbers, (b) perform the indicated operation using the trigonometric forms, and (c) perform the indicated operation using the standard forms and check your result with that of part (b).

103. $(2 - 2i)(3 + 3i)$
104. $(4 + 4i)(-1 - i)$
105. $\dfrac{3 - 3i}{2 + 2i}$
106. $\dfrac{-1 - i}{-2 - 2i}$

Finding a Power In Exercises 107–110, use DeMoivre's Theorem to find the indicated power of the complex number. Write the result in standard form.

107. $\left[5\left(\cos\frac{\pi}{12} + i\sin\frac{\pi}{12}\right)\right]^4$

108. $\left[2\left(\cos\frac{4\pi}{15} + i\sin\frac{4\pi}{15}\right)\right]^5$

109. $(2 + 3i)^6$
110. $(1 - i)^8$

Finding Square Roots In Exercises 111–114, find the square roots of the complex number.

111. $-\sqrt{3} + i$
112. $\sqrt{3} - i$
113. $-4i$
114. $-9i$

Finding the nth Roots of a Complex Number In Exercises 115–118, (a) use the theorem on page 450 to find the indicated roots of the complex number, (b) represent each of the roots graphically, and (c) write each of the roots in standard form.

115. Sixth roots of $-729i$
116. Fourth roots of $256i$
117. Cube roots of 8
118. Fifth roots of -1024

Solving an Equation In Exercises 119–122, use the theorem on page 450 to find all solutions of the equation, and represent the solutions graphically.

119. $x^4 + 256 = 0$
120. $x^5 - 32i = 0$
121. $x^3 + 8i = 0$
122. $x^4 + 81 = 0$

Conclusions

True or False? In Exercises 123 and 124, determine whether the statement is true or false. Justify your answer.

123. The Law of Sines is true if one of the angles in the triangle is a right angle.

124. When the Law of Sines is used, the solution is always unique.

6 Chapter Test

Take this test as you would take a test in class. After you are finished, check your work against the answers given in the back of the book.

In Exercises 1–6, use the given information to solve the triangle. If two solutions exist, find both solutions.

1. $A = 36°$, $B = 98°$, $c = 16$

2. $a = 2$, $b = 4$, $c = 5$

3. $A = 35°$, $b = 8$, $c = 12$

4. $B = 24°$, $C = 68°$, $b = 12.2$

5. $A = 25°$, $b = 28$, $a = 18$

6. $B = 130°$, $c = 10.1$, $b = 5.2$

7. Find the length of the pond shown at the right.

Figure for 7

8. A triangular parcel of land has borders of lengths 55 meters, 85 meters, and 100 meters. Find the area of the parcel of land.

9. Find the component form and magnitude of the vector **w** that has initial point $(-8, -12)$ and terminal point $(4, 1)$.

In Exercises 10–13, find (a) $2\mathbf{v} + \mathbf{u}$, (b) $\mathbf{u} - 3\mathbf{v}$, and (c) $5\mathbf{u} - 4\mathbf{v}$.

10. $\mathbf{u} = \langle -7, -4 \rangle$, $\mathbf{v} = \langle 4, 6 \rangle$

11. $\mathbf{u} = \langle -5, 2 \rangle$, $\mathbf{v} = \langle -1, -10 \rangle$

12. $\mathbf{u} = \mathbf{i} - \mathbf{j}$, $\mathbf{v} = 6\mathbf{i} + 9\mathbf{j}$

13. $\mathbf{u} = 2\mathbf{i} + 3\mathbf{j}$, $\mathbf{v} = -\mathbf{i} - 2\mathbf{j}$

14. Find a unit vector in the direction of $\mathbf{v} = 24\mathbf{i} - 7\mathbf{j}$.

15. Find the component form of the vector **v** with $\|\mathbf{v}\| = 12$, in the same direction as $\mathbf{u} = \langle 3, -5 \rangle$.

16. Forces with magnitudes of 250 pounds and 130 pounds act on an object at angles of $45°$ and $-60°$, respectively, with the positive x-axis. Find the direction and magnitude of the resultant of these forces.

17. Find the dot product of $\mathbf{u} = \langle -9, 4 \rangle$ and $\mathbf{v} = \langle 1, 2 \rangle$.

18. Find the angle between the vectors $\mathbf{u} = 7\mathbf{i} + 2\mathbf{j}$ and $\mathbf{v} = -4\mathbf{j}$.

19. Are the vectors $\mathbf{u} = \langle 6, 10 \rangle$ and $\mathbf{v} = \langle -5, -3 \rangle$ orthogonal? Explain.

20. Find the projection of $\mathbf{u} = \langle 6, 7 \rangle$ onto $\mathbf{v} = \langle -5, -1 \rangle$. Then write **u** as the sum of two orthogonal vectors, one of which is proj$_\mathbf{v}\mathbf{u}$.

21. Write the complex number $z = -6 + 6i$ in trigonometric form.

22. Write the complex number $100(\cos 240° + i \sin 240°)$ in standard form.

In Exercises 23 and 24, use DeMoivre's Theorem to find the indicated power of the complex number. Write the result in standard form.

23. $\left[3\left(\cos \dfrac{5\pi}{6} + i \sin \dfrac{5\pi}{6} \right) \right]^8$ 24. $(3 - 3i)^6$

25. Find the fourth roots of $128\left(1 + \sqrt{3}i\right)$.

26. Find all solutions of the equation $x^4 - 625i = 0$ and represent the solutions graphically.

Take this test to review the material in Chapters 4–6. After you are finished, check
your work against the answers given in the back of the book.

1. Consider the angle $\theta = -150°$.
   (a) Sketch the angle in standard position.
   (b) Determine a coterminal angle in the interval $[0°, 360°)$.
   (c) Convert the angle to radian measure.
   (d) Find the reference angle θ'.
   (e) Find the exact values of the six trigonometric functions of θ.

2. Convert the angle $\theta = 2.55$ radians to degrees. Round your answer to one decimal place.

3. Find $\cos \theta$ when $\tan \theta = -\frac{21}{20}$ and $\sin \theta < 0$.

In Exercises 4–6, sketch the graph of the function by hand. (Include two full periods.) Use a graphing utility to verify your graph.

4. $f(x) = 3 - 2 \sin \pi x$ 5. $f(x) = \dfrac{1}{2} \tan\left(x - \dfrac{\pi}{2}\right)$ 6. $f(x) = \sec(x + \pi) - 2$

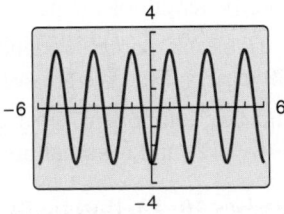

7. Find values of a, b, and c such that the graph of the function $h(x) = a\cos(bx - c)$ matches the graph in the figure at the right.

Figure for 7

In Exercises 8 and 9, find the exact value of the expression, if possible, without using a calculator.

8. $\cos(\arccos 3.6)$

9. $\sin\left(\arctan \frac{3}{4}\right)$

10. Write an algebraic expression equivalent to $\sin(\arccos 2x)$.

11. Subtract and simplify: $\dfrac{\sin \theta - 1}{\cos \theta} - \dfrac{\cos \theta}{\sin \theta - 1}$.

In Exercises 12–14, verify the identity.

12. $\cot^2 \alpha (\sec^2 \alpha - 1) = 1$

13. $\sin(x + y) \sin(x - y) = \sin^2 x - \sin^2 y$

14. $\sin^2 x \cos^2 x = \frac{1}{8}(1 - \cos 4x)$

In Exercises 15 and 16, solve the equation.

15. $\sin^2 x + 2 \sin x + 1 = 0$

16. $3 \tan \theta - \cot \theta = 0$

17. Approximate the solutions of the equation $\cos^2 x - 5 \cos x - 1 = 0$ in the interval $[0, 2\pi)$.

In Exercises 18 and 19, use a graphing utility to graph the function and approximate its zeros in the interval $[0, 2\pi)$. If possible, find the exact values of the zeros algebraically.

18. $y = \dfrac{1 + \sin x}{\cos x} + \dfrac{\cos x}{1 + \sin x} - 4$

19. $y = \tan^3 x - \tan^2 x + 3 \tan x - 3$

20. Given that $\sin u = \frac{12}{13}$, $\cos v = \frac{3}{5}$, and angles u and v are both in Quadrant I, find $\tan(u - v)$.

21. If $\tan \theta = \frac{1}{2}$, find the exact value of $\tan 2\theta$, $0 < \theta < \frac{\pi}{2}$.

22. If $\tan \theta = \frac{4}{3}$, find the exact value of $\sin \frac{\theta}{2}$, $\pi < \theta < \frac{3\pi}{2}$.

23. Write $\cos 8x + \cos 4x$ as a product.

In Exercises 24–27, verify the identity.

24. $\tan x(1 - \sin^2 x) = \frac{1}{2} \sin 2x$

25. $\sin 3\theta \sin \theta = \frac{1}{2}(\cos 2\theta - \cos 4\theta)$

26. $\sin 3x \cos 2x = \frac{1}{2}(\sin 5x + \sin x)$

27. $\dfrac{2 \cos 3x}{\sin 4x - \sin 2x} = \csc x$

In Exercises 28–31, use the information to solve the triangle shown at the right.

28. $A = 46°$, $a = 14$, $b = 5$ **29.** $A = 32°$, $b = 8$, $c = 10$

30. $A = 24°$, $C = 101°$, $a = 10$ **31.** $a = 24$, $b = 30$, $c = 47$

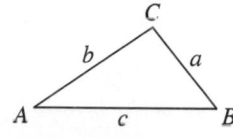

Figure for 28–31

32. Two sides of a triangle have lengths 14 inches and 19 inches. Their included angle measures 82°. Find the area of the triangle.

33. Find the area of a triangle with sides of lengths 30 meters, 41 meters, and 45 meters.

34. Write the vector $\mathbf{u} = \langle 3, 5 \rangle$ as a linear combination of the standard unit vectors $\mathbf{i}$ and $\mathbf{j}$.

35. Find a unit vector in the direction of $\mathbf{v} = 4\mathbf{i} - 2\mathbf{j}$.

36. Find $\mathbf{u} \cdot \mathbf{v}$ for $\mathbf{u} = 3\mathbf{i} + 4\mathbf{j}$ and $\mathbf{v} = 6\mathbf{i} - 9\mathbf{j}$.

37. Find k such that $\mathbf{u} = \mathbf{i} + 2k\mathbf{j}$ and $\mathbf{v} = 2\mathbf{i} - \mathbf{j}$ are orthogonal.

38. Find the projection of $\mathbf{u} = \langle 8, -2 \rangle$ onto $\mathbf{v} = \langle 1, 5 \rangle$. Then write $\mathbf{u}$ as the sum of two orthogonal vectors, one of which is $\text{proj}_{\mathbf{v}}\mathbf{u}$.

39. Find the trigonometric form of the complex number plotted at the right.

Figure for 39

40. Write the complex number $6\sqrt{3}\left(\cos \dfrac{5\pi}{6} + i \sin \dfrac{5\pi}{6}\right)$ in standard form.

41. Find the product $[4(\cos 30° + i \sin 30°)][6(\cos 120° + i \sin 120°)]$. Write the answer in standard form.

42. Find the square roots of $2 + i$.

43. Find the three cube roots of 1.

44. Write all the solutions of the equation $x^4 + 1296 = 0$.

45. From a point 200 feet from a flagpole, the angles of elevation to the bottom and top of the flag are 16° 45′ and 18°, respectively. Approximate the height of the flag to the nearest foot.

46. Write a model for a particle in simple harmonic motion with a maximum displacement of 7 inches when $t = 0$, an amplitude of 7 inches, and a period of 8 seconds.

47. An airplane's velocity with respect to the air is 500 kilometers per hour, with a bearing of 30°. The airplane is in a steady wind blowing from the northwest with a velocity of 50 kilometers per hour. What is the true direction of the airplane? What is its speed relative to the ground?

48. Forces of 60 pounds and 100 pounds have a resultant force of 125 pounds. Find the angle between the two forces.

Proofs in Mathematics

Law of Sines   (p. 404)

If ABC is a triangle with sides a, b, and c, then

$$\frac{a}{\sin A} = \frac{b}{\sin B} = \frac{c}{\sin C}.$$

Oblique Triangles

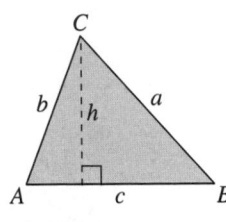

A is acute.   A is obtuse.

Law of Tangents

Besides the Law of Sines and the Law of Cosines, there is also a Law of Tangents, which was developed by Francois Viète (1540–1603). The Law of Tangents follows from the Law of Sines and the sum-to-product formulas for sine and is defined as follows.

$$\frac{a + b}{a - b} = \frac{\tan[(A + B)/2]}{\tan[(A - B)/2]}$$

The Law of Tangents can be used to solve a triangle when two sides and the included angle are given (SAS). Before calculators were invented, the Law of Tangents was used to solve the SAS case instead of the Law of Cosines, because computation with a table of tangent values was easier.

Proof

Let h be the altitude of either triangle shown in the figure above. Then you have

$$\sin A = \frac{h}{b} \qquad \text{or} \qquad h = b \sin A$$

$$\sin B = \frac{h}{a} \qquad \text{or} \qquad h = a \sin B.$$

Equating these two values of h, you have

$$a \sin B = b \sin A \qquad \text{or} \qquad \frac{a}{\sin A} = \frac{b}{\sin B}.$$

Note that $\sin A \neq 0$ and $\sin B \neq 0$ because no angle of a triangle can have a measure of $0°$ or $180°$. In a similar manner, construct an altitude from vertex B to side AC (extended in the obtuse triangle), as shown at the right. Then you have

$$\sin A = \frac{h}{c} \qquad \text{or} \qquad h = c \sin A$$

$$\sin C = \frac{h}{a} \qquad \text{or} \qquad h = a \sin C.$$

Equating these two values of h, you have

$$a \sin C = c \sin A \qquad \text{or} \qquad \frac{a}{\sin A} = \frac{c}{\sin C}.$$

By the Transitive Property of Equality, you know that

$$\frac{a}{\sin A} = \frac{b}{\sin B} = \frac{c}{\sin C}.$$

So, the Law of Sines is established.

A is acute.

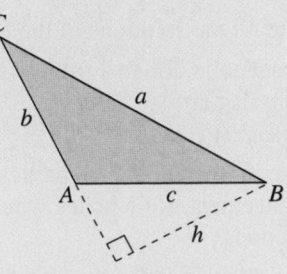

A is obtuse.

Law of Cosines   (p. 413)

Standard Form	Alternative Form
$a^2 = b^2 + c^2 - 2bc \cos A$	$\cos A = \dfrac{b^2 + c^2 - a^2}{2bc}$
$b^2 = a^2 + c^2 - 2ac \cos B$	$\cos B = \dfrac{a^2 + c^2 - b^2}{2ac}$
$c^2 = a^2 + b^2 - 2ab \cos C$	$\cos C = \dfrac{a^2 + b^2 - c^2}{2ab}$

Proof

To prove the first formula, consider the top triangle at the right, which has three acute angles. Note that vertex B has coordinates $(c, 0)$. Furthermore, C has coordinates (x, y), where

$$x = b \cos A \quad \text{and} \quad y = b \sin A.$$

Because a is the distance from vertex C to vertex B, it follows that

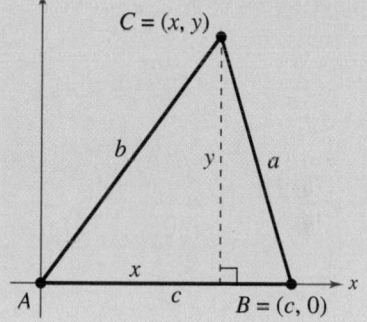

$a = \sqrt{(x - c)^2 + (y - 0)^2}$	Distance Formula
$a^2 = (x - c)^2 + (y - 0)^2$	Square each side.
$a^2 = (b \cos A - c)^2 + (b \sin A)^2$	Substitute for x and y.
$a^2 = b^2 \cos^2 A - 2bc \cos A + c^2 + b^2 \sin^2 A$	Expand.
$a^2 = b^2(\sin^2 A + \cos^2 A) + c^2 - 2bc \cos A$	Factor out b^2.
$a^2 = b^2 + c^2 - 2bc \cos A.$	$\sin^2 A + \cos^2 A = 1$

To prove the second formula, consider the bottom triangle at the right, which also has three acute angles. Note that vertex A has coordinates $(c, 0)$. Furthermore, C has coordinates (x, y), where

$$x = a \cos B \quad \text{and} \quad y = a \sin B.$$

Because b is the distance from vertex C to vertex A, it follows that

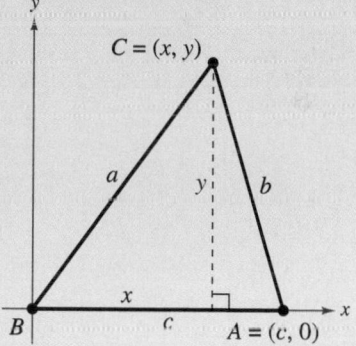

$b = \sqrt{(x - c)^2 + (y - 0)^2}$	Distance Formula
$b^2 = (x - c)^2 + (y - 0)^2$	Square each side.
$b^2 = (a \cos B - c)^2 + (a \sin B)^2$	Substitute for x and y.
$b^2 = a^2 \cos^2 B - 2ac \cos B + c^2 + a^2 \sin^2 B$	Expand.
$b^2 = a^2(\sin^2 B + \cos^2 B) + c^2 - 2ac \cos B$	Factor out a^2.
$b^2 = a^2 + c^2 - 2ac \cos B.$	$\sin^2 B + \cos^2 B = 1$

A similar argument is used to establish the third formula.

Heron's Area Formula   (p. 416)

For any triangle with sides of lengths a, b, and c, the area of the triangle is

$$\text{Area} = \sqrt{s(s-a)(s-b)(s-c)}$$

where $s = \dfrac{a+b+c}{2}$.

Proof

From Section 6.1, you know that

$$\text{Area} = \frac{1}{2}bc\sin A \qquad \text{Formula for the area of an oblique triangle}$$

$$(\text{Area})^2 = \frac{1}{4}b^2c^2\sin^2 A \qquad \text{Square each side.}$$

$$\text{Area} = \sqrt{\frac{1}{4}b^2c^2\sin^2 A} \qquad \text{Take the square root of each side.}$$

$$= \sqrt{\frac{1}{4}b^2c^2(1-\cos^2 A)} \qquad \text{Pythagorean identity}$$

$$= \sqrt{\left[\frac{1}{2}bc(1+\cos A)\right]\left[\frac{1}{2}bc(1-\cos A)\right]}. \qquad \text{Factor.}$$

Using the alternative form of the Law of Cosines,

$$\frac{1}{2}bc(1+\cos A) = \frac{a+b+c}{2}\cdot\frac{-a+b+c}{2}.$$

Similarly,

$$\frac{1}{2}bc(1-\cos A) = \frac{a-b+c}{2}\cdot\frac{a+b-c}{2}.$$

Letting

$$s = \frac{a+b+c}{2}$$

these two equations can be rewritten as

$$\frac{1}{2}bc(1+\cos A) = s(s-a)$$

and

$$\frac{1}{2}bc(1-\cos A) = (s-b)(s-c).$$

By substituting into the last formula for area, you can conclude that

$$\text{Area} = \sqrt{s(s-a)(s-b)(s-c)}.$$

Remark

$$\frac{1}{2}bc(1+\cos A)$$

$$= \frac{1}{2}bc\left(1 + \frac{b^2+c^2-a^2}{2bc}\right)$$

$$= \frac{1}{2}bc\left(\frac{2bc+b^2+c^2-a^2}{2bc}\right)$$

$$= \frac{1}{4}(2bc+b^2+c^2-a^2)$$

$$= \frac{1}{4}(b^2+2bc+c^2-a^2)$$

$$= \frac{1}{4}\left[(b+c)^2-a^2\right]$$

$$= \frac{1}{4}(b+c+a)(b+c-a)$$

$$= \frac{a+b+c}{2}\cdot\frac{-a+b+c}{2}$$

Properties of the Dot Product   (p. 434)

Let **u**, **v**, and **w** be vectors in the plane or in space and let c be a scalar.

1. $\mathbf{u} \cdot \mathbf{v} = \mathbf{v} \cdot \mathbf{u}$ **2.** $\mathbf{0} \cdot \mathbf{v} = 0$

3. $\mathbf{u} \cdot (\mathbf{v} + \mathbf{w}) = \mathbf{u} \cdot \mathbf{v} + \mathbf{u} \cdot \mathbf{w}$ **4.** $\mathbf{v} \cdot \mathbf{v} = \|\mathbf{v}\|^2$

5. $c(\mathbf{u} \cdot \mathbf{v}) = c\mathbf{u} \cdot \mathbf{v} = \mathbf{u} \cdot c\mathbf{v}$

Proof

Let $\mathbf{u} = \langle u_1, u_2 \rangle$, $\mathbf{v} = \langle v_1, v_2 \rangle$, $\mathbf{w} = \langle w_1, w_2 \rangle$, $\mathbf{0} = \langle 0, 0 \rangle$, and let c be a scalar.

1. $\mathbf{u} \cdot \mathbf{v} = u_1 v_1 + u_2 v_2 = v_1 u_1 + v_2 u_2 = \mathbf{v} \cdot \mathbf{u}$

2. $\mathbf{0} \cdot \mathbf{v} = 0 \cdot v_1 + 0 \cdot v_2 = 0$

3. $\mathbf{u} \cdot (\mathbf{v} + \mathbf{w}) = \mathbf{u} \cdot \langle v_1 + w_1, v_2 + w_2 \rangle$

$\qquad\qquad = u_1(v_1 + w_1) + u_2(v_2 + w_2)$

$\qquad\qquad = u_1 v_1 + u_1 w_1 + u_2 v_2 + u_2 w_2$

$\qquad\qquad = (u_1 v_1 + u_2 v_2) + (u_1 w_1 + u_2 w_2) = \mathbf{u} \cdot \mathbf{v} + \mathbf{u} \cdot \mathbf{w}$

4. $\mathbf{v} \cdot \mathbf{v} = v_1^2 + v_2^2 = \left(\sqrt{v_1^2 + v_2^2} \right)^2 = \|\mathbf{v}\|^2$

5. $c(\mathbf{u} \cdot \mathbf{v}) = c(\langle u_1, u_2 \rangle \cdot \langle v_1, v_2 \rangle)$

$\qquad\qquad = c(u_1 v_1 + u_2 v_2)$

$\qquad\qquad = (cu_1)v_1 + (cu_2)v_2$

$\qquad\qquad = \langle cu_1, cu_2 \rangle \cdot \langle v_1, v_2 \rangle$

$\qquad\qquad = c\mathbf{u} \cdot \mathbf{v}$

Angle Between Two Vectors   (p. 435)

If θ is the angle between two nonzero vectors **u** and **v**, then

$$\cos \theta = \frac{\mathbf{u} \cdot \mathbf{v}}{\|\mathbf{u}\| \, \|\mathbf{v}\|}.$$

Proof

Consider the triangle determined by vectors **u**, **v**, and $\mathbf{v} - \mathbf{u}$, as shown in the figure. By the Law of Cosines, you can write

$$\|\mathbf{v} - \mathbf{u}\|^2 = \|\mathbf{u}\|^2 + \|\mathbf{v}\|^2 - 2\|\mathbf{u}\| \, \|\mathbf{v}\| \cos \theta$$

$$(\mathbf{v} - \mathbf{u}) \cdot (\mathbf{v} - \mathbf{u}) = \|\mathbf{u}\|^2 + \|\mathbf{v}\|^2 - 2\|\mathbf{u}\| \, \|\mathbf{v}\| \cos \theta$$

$$(\mathbf{v} - \mathbf{u}) \cdot \mathbf{v} - (\mathbf{v} - \mathbf{u}) \cdot \mathbf{u} = \|\mathbf{u}\|^2 + \|\mathbf{v}\|^2 - 2\|\mathbf{u}\| \, \|\mathbf{v}\| \cos \theta$$

$$\mathbf{v} \cdot \mathbf{v} - \mathbf{u} \cdot \mathbf{v} - \mathbf{v} \cdot \mathbf{u} + \mathbf{u} \cdot \mathbf{u} = \|\mathbf{u}\|^2 + \|\mathbf{v}\|^2 - 2\|\mathbf{u}\| \, \|\mathbf{v}\| \cos \theta$$

$$\|\mathbf{v}\|^2 - 2\mathbf{u} \cdot \mathbf{v} + \|\mathbf{u}\|^2 = \|\mathbf{u}\|^2 + \|\mathbf{v}\|^2 - 2\|\mathbf{u}\| \, \|\mathbf{v}\| \cos \theta$$

$$\cos \theta = \frac{\mathbf{u} \cdot \mathbf{v}}{\|\mathbf{u}\| \, \|\mathbf{v}\|}.$$

Progressive Summary (Chapters 1–6)

This chart outlines the topics that have been covered so far in this text. Progressive Summary charts appear after Chapters 2, 3, 6, and 9. In each Progressive Summary, new topics encountered for the first time appear in blue.

Algebraic Functions

Polynomial, Rational, Radical

■ Rewriting
Polynomial form ↔ Factored form
Operations with polynomials
Rationalize denominators
Simplify rational expressions
Operations with complex numbers

■ Solving

Equation	Strategy
Linear	Isolate variable
Quadratic........	Factor, set to zero
	Extract square roots
	Complete the square
	Quadratic Formula
Polynomial	Factor, set to zero
	Rational Zero Test
Rational........	Multiply by LCD
Radical	Isolate, raise to power
Absolute value ...	Isolate, form two equations

■ Analyzing

Graphically	Algebraically
Intercepts	Domain, Range
Symmetry	Transformations
Slope	Composition
Asymptotes	Standard forms
End behavior	of equations
Minimum values	Leading Coefficient
Maximum values	Test
	Synthetic division
	Descartes's Rule of Signs

Numerically
Table of values

Transcendental Functions

Exponential, Logarithmic
Trigonometric, Inverse Trigonometric

■ Rewriting
Exponential form ↔ Logarithmic form
Condense/expand logarithmic expressions
Simplify trigonometric expressions
Prove trigonometric identities
Use conversion formulas
Operations with vectors
Powers and roots of complex numbers

■ Solving

Equation	Strategy
Exponential......	Take logarithm of each side
Logarithmic......	Exponentiate each side
Trigonometric....	Isolate function
	Factor, use inverse function
Multiple angle.... or high powers	Use trigonometric identities

■ Analyzing

Graphically	Algebraically
Intercepts	Domain, Range
Asymptotes	Transformations
Minimum values	Composition
Maximum values	Inverse Properties
	Amplitude, Period
	Reference angles

Numerically
Table of values

Other Topics

■ Rewriting

■ Solving

■ Analyzing

7 Linear Systems and Matrices

[C][E]

[[2250 2598]]

Section 7.5, Example 11
Softball Team Expenses

7.1 Solving Systems of Equations

7.2 Systems of Linear Equations in Two Variables

7.3 Multivariable Linear Systems

7.4 Matrices and Systems of Equations

7.5 Operations with Matrices

7.6 The Inverse of a Square Matrix

7.7 The Determinant of a Square Matrix

7.8 Applications of Matrices and Determinants

7.1 Solving Systems of Equations

The Methods of Substitution and Graphing

So far in this text, most problems have involved either a function of one variable or a single equation in two variables. However, many problems in science, business, and engineering involve two or more equations in two or more variables. To solve such problems, you need to find solutions of **systems of equations**. Here is an example of a system of two equations in two unknowns, x and y.

$$\begin{cases} 2x + y = 5 & \text{Equation 1} \\ 3x - 2y = 4 & \text{Equation 2} \end{cases}$$

A **solution** of this system is an ordered pair that satisfies each equation in the system. Finding the set of all such solutions is called **solving the system of equations.** For instance, the ordered pair $(2, 1)$ is a solution of this system. To check this, you can substitute 2 for x and 1 for y in *each* equation.

Check $(2, 1)$ *in Equation 1:*

$$2x + y = 5$$
$$2(2) + 1 \stackrel{?}{=} 5$$
$$5 = 5 \checkmark$$

Check $(2, 1)$ *in Equation 2:*

$$3x - 2y = 4$$
$$3(2) - 2(1) \stackrel{?}{=} 4$$
$$4 = 4 \checkmark$$

In this section, you will study two ways to solve systems of equations, beginning with the **method of substitution.**

The Method of Substitution

To use the **method of substitution** to solve a system of two equations in x and y, perform the following steps.

1. Solve one of the equations for one variable in terms of the other.

2. Substitute the expression found in Step 1 into the other equation to obtain an equation in one variable.

3. Solve the equation obtained in Step 2.

4. Back-substitute the value(s) obtained in Step 3 into the expression obtained in Step 1 to find the value(s) of the other variable.

5. Check that each solution satisfies *both* of the original equations.

Another method is the **method of graphing.** When using this method, note that the solution of the system corresponds to the **point(s) of intersection** of the graphs.

Remark

When using the method of substitution, it does not matter which variable you choose to solve for first. Whether you solve for y first or x first, you will obtain the same solution. When making your choice, you should choose the variable and equation that are easier to work with.

The Method of Graphing

To use the **method of graphing** to solve a system of two equations in x and y, perform the following steps.

1. Solve both equations for y in terms of x.

2. Use a graphing utility to graph both equations in the same viewing window.

3. Use the *intersect* feature or the *zoom* and *trace* features of the graphing utility to approximate the point(s) of intersection of the graphs.

4. Check that each solution satisfies *both* of the original equations.

EXAMPLE 1 Solving a System of Equations

Solve the system of equations.

$$\begin{cases} x + y = 4 & \text{Equation 1} \\ x - y = 2 & \text{Equation 2} \end{cases}$$

Algebraic Solution

Begin by solving for y in Equation 1.

$y = 4 - x$ Solve for y in Equation 1.

Next, substitute this expression for y into Equation 2 and solve the resulting single-variable equation for x.

$x - y = 2$	Write Equation 2.
$x - (4 - x) = 2$	Substitute $4 - x$ for y.
$x - 4 + x = 2$	Distributive Property
$2x - 4 = 2$	Combine like terms.
$2x = 6$	Add 4 to each side.
$x = 3$	Divide each side by 2.

Finally, you can solve for y by *back-substituting* $x = 3$ into the equation $y = 4 - x$ to obtain

$y = 4 - x$	Write revised Equation 1.
$y = 4 - 3$	Substitute 3 for x.
$y = 1.$	Solve for y.

The solution is the ordered pair $(3, 1)$. Check this as follows.

Check $(3, 1)$ *in Equation 1:*

$x + y = 4$	Write Equation 1.
$3 + 1 \stackrel{?}{=} 4$	Substitute for x and y.
$4 = 4$	Solution checks in Equation 1. ✓

Check $(3, 1)$ *in Equation 2:*

$x - y = 2$	Write Equation 2.
$3 - 1 \stackrel{?}{=} 2$	Substitute for x and y.
$2 = 2$	Solution checks in Equation 2. ✓

Because $(3, 1)$ satisfies both equations in the system, it is a solution of the system of equations.

Graphical Solution

Begin by solving both equations for y. Then use a graphing utility to graph the equations

$$y_1 = 4 - x$$

and

$$y_2 = x - 2$$

in the same viewing window. Use the *intersect* feature (see figure) to approximate the point of intersection of the graphs.

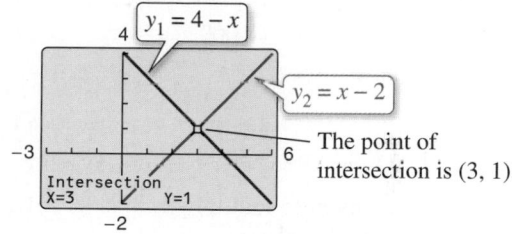

The point of intersection is $(3, 1)$.

Check that $(3, 1)$ is the exact solution as follows.

Check $(3, 1)$ *in Equation 1:*

$x + y = 4$	Write Equation 1.
$3 + 1 \stackrel{?}{=} 4$	Substitute for x and y.
$4 = 4$	Solution checks in Equation 1. ✓

Check $(3, 1)$ *in Equation 2:*

$x - y = 2$	Write Equation 2.
$3 - 1 \stackrel{?}{=} 2$	Substitute for x and y.
$2 = 2$	Solution checks in Equation 2. ✓

Because $(3, 1)$ satisfies both equations in the system, it is a solution of the system of equations.

✓ **Checkpoint** 🔊))) *Audio-video solution in English & Spanish at LarsonPrecalculus.com.*

Solve the system of equations by the method of substitution.

$$\begin{cases} x - y = 0 \\ 5x - 3y = 6 \end{cases}$$

In the algebraic solution to Example 1, note that the term *back-substitution* implies that you work *backwards*. First you solve for one of the variables, and then you substitute that value *back* into one of the equations in the system to find the value of the other variable.

EXAMPLE 2   Solving a System by Substitution

A total of $12,000 is invested in two funds paying 5% and 3% simple interest. The yearly interest is $500. How much is invested at each rate?

Solution

Verbal Model:

| Amount in 5% fund | + | Amount in 3% fund | = | Total investment |

| Interest for 5% fund | + | Interest for 3% fund | = | Total interest |

Labels:

Amount in 5% fund $= x$	(dollars)
Interest for 5% fund $= 0.05x$	(dollars)
Amount in 3% fund $= y$	(dollars)
Interest for 3% fund $= 0.03y$	(dollars)
Total investment $= 12,000$	(dollars)
Total interest $= 500$	(dollars)

System:
$$\begin{cases} x + y = 12,000 & \text{Equation 1} \\ 0.05x + 0.03y = 500 & \text{Equation 2} \end{cases}$$

To begin, it is convenient to multiply each side of Equation 2 by 100. This eliminates the need to work with decimals.

$5x + 3y = 50,000$ Revised Equation 2

To solve this system, you can solve for x in Equation 1.

$x = 12,000 - y$ Revised Equation 1

Next, substitute this expression for x into revised Equation 2 and solve the resulting equation for y.

$5x + 3y = 50,000$	Write revised Equation 2.
$5(12,000 - y) + 3y = 50,000$	Substitute $12,000 - y$ for x.
$60,000 - 5y + 3y = 50,000$	Distributive Property
$-2y = -10,000$	Combine like terms.
$y = 5000$	Divide each side by -2.

Finally, back-substitute the value $y = 5000$ to solve for x.

$x = 12,000 - y$	Write revised Equation 1.
$x = 12,000 - 5000$	Substitute 5000 for y.
$x = 7000$	Simplify.

The solution is $(7000, 5000)$. So, $7000 is invested at 5% and $5000 is invested at 3% to yield yearly interest of $500. Check this in the original system.

✓ **Checkpoint**   Audio-video solution in English & Spanish at LarsonPrecalculus.com.

A total of $25,000 is invested in two funds paying 6.5% and 8.5% simple interest. The yearly interest is $2000. How much is invested at each rate? ◼

The equations in Examples 1 and 2 are linear. Substitution and graphing can also be used to solve systems in which one or both of the equations are nonlinear.

Technology Tip

Remember that a good way to check the answers you obtain in this section is to use a graphing utility. For instance, enter the two equations in Example 2

$$y_1 = 12,000 - x$$

$$y_2 = \frac{500 - 0.05x}{0.03}$$

and find an appropriate viewing window that shows where the lines intersect. Then use the *intersect* feature or the *zoom* and *trace* features to find the point of intersection.

Intersection
X=7000   Y=5000

EXAMPLE 3   Substitution: Two-Solution Case

Solve the system of equations.

$$\begin{cases} x^2 + 4x - y = 7 & \text{Equation 1} \\ 2x - y = -1 & \text{Equation 2} \end{cases}$$

Algebraic Solution

Begin by solving for y in Equation 2 to obtain

$$y = 2x + 1. \qquad \text{Solve for } y \text{ in Equation 2.}$$

Next, substitute this expression for y into Equation 1 and solve for x.

$x^2 + 4x - y = 7$	Write Equation 1.
$x^2 + 4x - (2x + 1) = 7$	Substitute $2x + 1$ for y.
$x^2 + 4x - 2x - 1 = 7$	Distributive Property
$x^2 + 2x - 8 = 0$	Write in general form.
$(x + 4)(x - 2) = 0$	Factor.
$x + 4 = 0 \quad\Longrightarrow\quad x = -4$	Set 1st factor equal to 0.
$x - 2 = 0 \quad\Longrightarrow\quad x = 2$	Set 2nd factor equal to 0.

Back-substituting these values of x into revised Equation 2 produces

$$y = 2(-4) + 1 = -7 \quad \text{and} \quad y = 2(2) + 1 = 5.$$

So, the solutions are $(-4, -7)$ and $(2, 5)$. Check these in the original system.

Graphical Solution

Solve each equation for y and use a graphing utility to graph the equations in the same viewing window. From the figures below, the solutions are $(-4, -7)$ and $(2, 5)$. Check these in the original system.

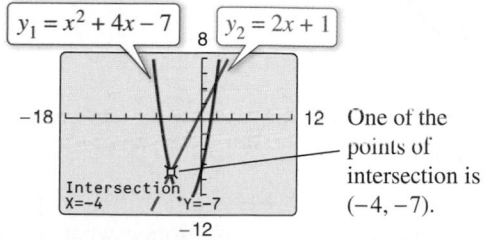

One of the points of intersection is $(-4, -7)$.

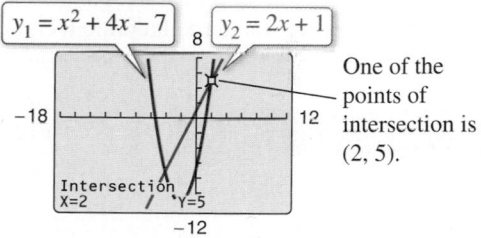

One of the points of intersection is $(2, 5)$.

✔ **Checkpoint** ◀))) *Audio-video solution in English & Spanish at LarsonPrecalculus.com.*

Solve the system of equations.

$$\begin{cases} -2x + y = 5 \\ x^2 - y + 3x = 1 \end{cases}$$

EXAMPLE 4   Substitution: No-Solution Case

To solve the system of equations

$$\begin{cases} -x + y = 4 & \text{Equation 1} \\ x^2 + y = 3 & \text{Equation 2} \end{cases}$$

begin by solving for y in Equation 1 to obtain $y = x + 4$. Next, substitute this expression for y into Equation 2 and solve for x.

$x^2 + (x + 4) = 3$	Substitute $x + 4$ for y in Equation 2.
$x^2 + x + 1 = 0$	Write in general form.
$x = \dfrac{-1 \pm \sqrt{3}i}{2}$	Quadratic Formula

Because this yields two imaginary values, the equation $x^2 + x + 1 = 0$ has no *real* solution. So, the original system of equations has no *real* solution.

Explore the Concept

Graph the system of equations in Example 4. Do the graphs of the equations intersect? Why or why not?

✔ **Checkpoint** ◀))) *Audio-video solution in English & Spanish at LarsonPrecalculus.com.*

Solve $\begin{cases} 2x - y = -3 \\ 2x^2 + 4x - y^2 = 0 \end{cases}$

From Examples 1, 3, and 4, you can see that a system of two equations in two unknowns can have exactly one solution, more than one solution, or no solution. For instance, in Figure 7.1, the two equations in Example 1 graph as two lines with a *single point* of intersection. The two equations in Example 3 graph as a parabola and a line with *two points* of intersection, as shown in Figure 7.2. The two equations in Example 4 graph as a line and a parabola that have *no points* of intersection, as shown in Figure 7.3.

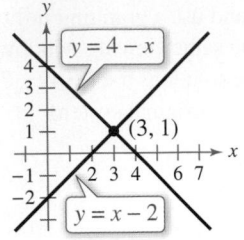

One Intersection Point
Figure 7.1

Two Intersection Points
Figure 7.2

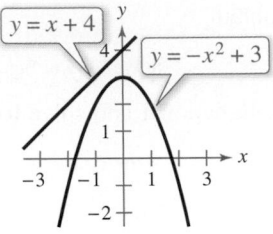

No Intersection Points
Figure 7.3

Example 5 shows the benefit of a graphical approach to solving systems of equations in two variables. Notice what happens when you try only the substitution method in Example 5. You obtain the equation $x + \ln x = 1$. It is difficult to solve this equation for x using standard algebraic techniques. In such cases, a graphical approach to solving systems of equations is more convenient.

EXAMPLE 5   Solving a System of Equations Graphically

See LarsonPrecalculus.com for an interactive version of this type of example.

Solve the system of equations.

$$\begin{cases} y = \ln x & \text{Equation 1} \\ x + y = 1 & \text{Equation 2} \end{cases}$$

Solution

From the graphs of these equations, it is clear that there is only one point of intersection. Use the *intersect* feature of a graphing utility to approximate the solution point as $(1, 0)$, as shown in the figure.

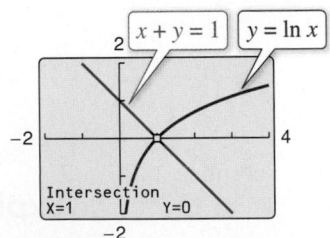

You can confirm this by substituting $(1, 0)$ into *both* equations.

Check $(1, 0)$ in Equation 1:

$y = \ln x$ Write Equation 1.

$0 = \ln 1$ Equation 1 checks. ✓

Check $(1, 0)$ in Equation 2:

$x + y = 1$ Write Equation 2.

$1 + 0 = 1$ Equation 2 checks. ✓

✓ **Checkpoint** Audio-video solution in English & Spanish at LarsonPrecalculus.com.

Solve the system of equations.

$$\begin{cases} y = 3 - \log_{10} x \\ -2x + y = 1 \end{cases}$$

Application

The total cost C of producing x units of a product typically has two components: the initial cost and the cost per unit. When enough units have been sold so that the total revenue R equals the total cost C, the sales are said to have reached the **break-even point.** You will find that the break-even point corresponds to the point of intersection of the cost and revenue curves.

EXAMPLE 6   Break–Even Analysis

A small business invests $10,000 in equipment to produce a new soft drink. Each bottle of the soft drink costs $0.65 to produce and is sold for $1.20. How many bottles must be sold before the business breaks even?

Solution

The total cost of producing x bottles is

$$\boxed{\begin{array}{c}\text{Total}\\\text{cost}\end{array}} = \boxed{\begin{array}{c}\text{Cost per}\\\text{bottle}\end{array}} \cdot \boxed{\begin{array}{c}\text{Number}\\\text{of bottles}\end{array}} + \boxed{\begin{array}{c}\text{Initial}\\\text{cost}\end{array}}$$

$$C = 0.65x + 10,000. \qquad \text{Equation 1}$$

The revenue obtained by selling x bottles is

$$\boxed{\begin{array}{c}\text{Total}\\\text{revenue}\end{array}} = \boxed{\begin{array}{c}\text{Price per}\\\text{bottle}\end{array}} \cdot \boxed{\begin{array}{c}\text{Number}\\\text{of bottles}\end{array}}$$

$$R = 1.20x. \qquad \text{Equation 2}$$

Because the break-even point occurs when $R = C$, you have

$$C = 1.20x$$

and the system of equations to solve is

$$\begin{cases} C = 0.65x + 10,000 \\ C = 1.20x \end{cases}.$$

Now you can solve by substitution.

$C = 0.65x + 10,000$	Write Equation 1.
$1.20x = 0.65x + 10,000$	Substitute $1.20x$ for C.
$0.55x = 10,000$	Subtract $0.65x$ from each side.
$x = \dfrac{10,0000}{0.55}$	Divide each side by 0.55.
$x \approx 18,182$ bottles	Use a calculator.

So, the business must sell about 18,182 bottles to break even. Note in Figure 7.4 that revenue less than the break-even point corresponds to an overall loss, whereas revenue greater than the break-even point corresponds to a profit. Verify the break-even point using the *intersect* feature or the *zoom* and *trace* features of a graphing utility.

Break-Even Analysis

Figure 7.4

✓ **Checkpoint** 🔊))) *Audio-video solution in English & Spanish at LarsonPrecalculus.com.*

In Example 6, each bottle of the soft drink costs $0.50 to produce. How many bottles must be sold before the business breaks even?

Another way to view the solution in Example 6 is to consider the profit function $P = R - C$. The break-even point occurs when the profit is 0, which is the same as saying that $R = C$.

7.1   Exercises

See *CalcChat.com* for tutorial help and worked-out solutions to odd-numbered exercises.
For instructions on how to use a graphing utility, see Appendix A.

Vocabulary and Concept Check

In Exercises 1–4, fill in the blank(s).

1. A set of two or more equations in two or more unknowns is called a _____ of _____ .

2. A _____ of a system of equations is an ordered pair that satisfies each equation in the system.

3. The first step in solving a system of two equations in x and y by the method of _____ is to solve one of the equations for one variable in terms of the other.

4. A point of intersection of the graphs of the equations of a system is a _____ of the system.

5. What is the point of intersection of the graphs of the cost and revenue functions called?

6. The graphs of the equations of a system do not intersect. What can you conclude about the system?

Procedures and Problem Solving

Checking Solutions   In Exercises 7–10, determine whether each ordered pair is a solution of the system of equations.

7. $\begin{cases} 4x - y = 1 \\ 6x + y = -6 \end{cases}$
   (a) $(0, -3)$ (b) $(-1, -5)$
   (c) $\left(-\frac{3}{2}, 3\right)$ (d) $\left(-\frac{1}{2}, -3\right)$

8. $\begin{cases} 4x^2 + y = 3 \\ -x - y = 11 \end{cases}$
   (a) $(2, -13)$ (b) $(-2, -9)$
   (c) $\left(-\frac{3}{2}, 6\right)$ (d) $\left(-\frac{7}{4}, -\frac{37}{4}\right)$

9. $\begin{cases} y = -2e^x \\ 3x - y = 2 \end{cases}$
   (a) $(-2, 0)$ (b) $(0, -2)$
   (c) $(0, -3)$ (d) $(-1, -5)$

10. $\begin{cases} -\log_{10} x + 3 = y \\ \frac{1}{9}x + y = \frac{28}{9} \end{cases}$
    (a) $(100, 1)$ (b) $(10, 2)$
    (c) $(1, 3)$ (d) $(1, 1)$

Solving a System by Substitution   In Exercises 11–18, solve the system by the method of substitution. Check your solution graphically.

11. $\begin{cases} 2x + y = 6 \\ -x + y = 0 \end{cases}$

12. $\begin{cases} x - y = -4 \\ x + 2y = 5 \end{cases}$

13. $\begin{cases} x - y = -4 \\ x^2 - y = -2 \end{cases}$

14. $\begin{cases} -2x + y = -5 \\ x^2 + y^2 = 25 \end{cases}$

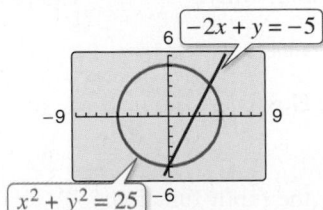

15. $\begin{cases} 3x + y = 2 \\ x^3 - 2 + y = 0 \end{cases}$

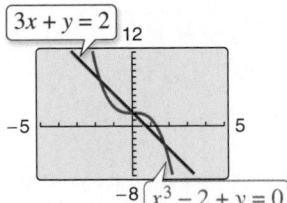

16. $\begin{cases} x + y = 0 \\ x^3 - 5x - y = 0 \end{cases}$

17. $\begin{cases} -\frac{7}{2}x - y = -18 \\ 8x^2 - 2y^3 = 0 \end{cases}$

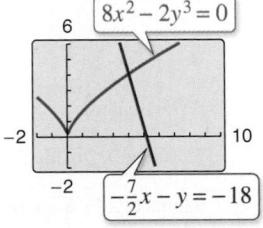

18. $\begin{cases} y = x^3 - 3x^2 + 4 \\ y = -2x + 4 \end{cases}$

Solving a System of Equations   In Exercises 19–28, solve the system by the method of substitution. Use a graphing utility to verify your results.

19. $\begin{cases} x + y = 0 \\ 4x + 3y = 10 \end{cases}$

20. $\begin{cases} x + 2y = 1 \\ 5x - 4y = -23 \end{cases}$

21. $\begin{cases} 2x - y + 2 = 0 \\ 4x + y - 5 = 0 \end{cases}$

22. $\begin{cases} 6x - 3y - 4 = 0 \\ x + 2y - 4 = 0 \end{cases}$

23. $\begin{cases} 1.5x + 0.8y = 2.3 \\ 0.3x - 0.2y = 0.1 \end{cases}$

24. $\begin{cases} -0.5x + 4y = 7.8 \\ 0.2x - 1.6y = -3.6 \end{cases}$

25. $\begin{cases} \frac{1}{5}x + \frac{1}{2}y = 8 \\ x + y = 20 \end{cases}$

26. $\begin{cases} \frac{1}{2}x + \frac{3}{4}y = 10 \\ \frac{3}{4}x - y = 4 \end{cases}$

27. $\begin{cases} -\frac{5}{3}x + y = 5 \\ -5x + 3y = 6 \end{cases}$ **28.** $\begin{cases} -\frac{2}{3}x + y = 2 \\ 3x - \frac{1}{2}y = 4 \end{cases}$

Solving a System by Substitution   In Exercises 29–32, you are given the yearly interest earned from a total of $18,000 invested in two funds paying the given rates of simple interest. Write and solve a system of equations to find the amount invested at each rate.

	Yearly Interest	Rate 1	Rate 2
29.	$400	4%	2%
30.	$840	6%	3%
31.	$1182	5.6%	6.8%
32.	$684	2.75%	4.25%

Solving a System with a Nonlinear Equation   In Exercises 33–38, solve the system by the method of substitution. Use a graphing utility to verify your results.

33. $\begin{cases} x^2 - 2x + y = 8 \\ x - y = -2 \end{cases}$ **34.** $\begin{cases} 2x^2 - 2x - y = 14 \\ 2x - y = -2 \end{cases}$

35. $\begin{cases} 2x^2 - y = 1 \\ x - y = 2 \end{cases}$ **36.** $\begin{cases} 2x^2 + y = 3 \\ x + y = 4 \end{cases}$

37. $\begin{cases} x^3 - y = 0 \\ x - y = 0 \end{cases}$ **38.** $\begin{cases} y = -x \\ y = x^3 + 3x^2 + 2x \end{cases}$

Solving a System of Equations Graphically   In Exercises 39–46, solve the system graphically. Verify your solutions algebraically.

39. $\begin{cases} -2x + y = 7 \\ x + 3y = 0 \end{cases}$ **40.** $\begin{cases} x + y = 8 \\ 4x + 4y = 0 \end{cases}$

41. $\begin{cases} x - 2y = -3 \\ 5x + 6y = 17 \end{cases}$ **42.** $\begin{cases} -5x + 2y = -2 \\ x - 2y = 6 \end{cases}$

43. $\begin{cases} x^2 + y = -1 \\ -x + 2y = 5 \end{cases}$ **44.** $\begin{cases} x^2 - y = 3 \\ x - y = 1 \end{cases}$

45. $\begin{cases} -x - y = 3 \\ x^2 + y^2 - 4x - 21 = 0 \end{cases}$

46. $\begin{cases} y^2 - x^2 + 9 = 0 \\ -\frac{1}{2}x + y = \frac{3}{2} \end{cases}$

Solving a System of Equations Graphically   In Exercises 47–60, use a graphing utility to approximate all points of intersection of the graphs of equations in the system. Round your results to three decimal places. Verify your solutions by checking them in the original system.

47. $\begin{cases} 7x + 8y = 24 \\ x - 8y = 8 \end{cases}$ **48.** $\begin{cases} x - y = 0 \\ 5x - 2y = 6 \end{cases}$

49. $\begin{cases} x - y^2 = -1 \\ x - y = 5 \end{cases}$ **50.** $\begin{cases} x - y^2 = -2 \\ x - 2y = 6 \end{cases}$

51. $\begin{cases} x^2 + y^2 = 8 \\ y = x^2 \end{cases}$ **52.** $\begin{cases} x^2 + y^2 = 25 \\ (x - 8)^2 + y^2 = 41 \end{cases}$

53. $\begin{cases} y = e^x \\ x - y + 1 = 0 \end{cases}$ **54.** $\begin{cases} y = -4e^{-x} \\ y + 3x + 8 = 0 \end{cases}$

55. $\begin{cases} x + 2y = 8 \\ y = 2 + \ln x \end{cases}$

56. $\begin{cases} 3y + 2x = 9 \\ y = -2 + \ln(x - 1) \end{cases}$

57. $\begin{cases} y = \sqrt{x} + 4 \\ y = 2x + 1 \end{cases}$ **58.** $\begin{cases} x - y = 3 \\ \sqrt{x} - y = 1 \end{cases}$

59. $\begin{cases} x^2 + y^2 = 169 \\ x^2 - 8y = 104 \end{cases}$ **60.** $\begin{cases} x^2 + y^2 = 4 \\ 2x^2 - y = 2 \end{cases}$

Choosing a Solution Method   In Exercises 61–74, solve the system graphically or algebraically. Explain your choice of method.

61. $\begin{cases} 2x - y = 0 \\ x^2 - y = -1 \end{cases}$ **62.** $\begin{cases} x + y = 4 \\ x^2 + y = 2 \end{cases}$

63. $\begin{cases} 3x - 7y = -6 \\ x^2 - y^2 = 4 \end{cases}$ **64.** $\begin{cases} x^2 + y^2 = 25 \\ 2x + y = 10 \end{cases}$

65. $\begin{cases} x^2 + y^2 = 1 \\ x + y = 4 \end{cases}$ **66.** $\begin{cases} x^2 + y^2 = 4 \\ x - y = 5 \end{cases}$

67. $\begin{cases} y = 2x + 1 \\ y = \sqrt{x + 2} \end{cases}$ **68.** $\begin{cases} y = 2x - 1 \\ y = \sqrt{x + 1} \end{cases}$

69. $\begin{cases} y - e^{-x} = 1 \\ y - \ln x = 3 \end{cases}$ **70.** $\begin{cases} 2\ln x + y = 4 \\ e^x - y = 0 \end{cases}$

71. $\begin{cases} y = x^3 - 2x^2 + 1 \\ y = 1 - x^2 \end{cases}$ **72.** $\begin{cases} y = x^3 - 2x^2 + x - 1 \\ y = -x^2 + 3x - 1 \end{cases}$

73. $\begin{cases} xy - 1 = 0 \\ -5x - 2y + 1 = 0 \end{cases}$

74. $\begin{cases} xy - 2 = 0 \\ 3x - 2y + 4 = 0 \end{cases}$

Break-Even Analysis   In Exercises 75–78, use a graphing utility to graph the cost and revenue functions in the same viewing window. Find the sales x necessary to break even $(R = C)$ and the corresponding revenue R obtained by selling x units. (Round to the nearest whole unit.)

	Cost	Revenue
75.	$C = 8650x + 250{,}000$	$R = 9950x$
76.	$C = 2.65x + 350{,}000$	$R = 4.15x$
77.	$C = 5.5\sqrt{x} + 10{,}000$	$R = 3.29x$
78.	$C = 7.8\sqrt{x} + 18{,}500$	$R = 12.84x$

Geometry   In Exercises 79 and 80, find the dimensions of the rectangle meeting the specified conditions.

79. The perimeter is 30 meters and the length is 3 meters greater than the width.

80. The perimeter is 280 centimeters and the width is 20 centimeters less than the length.

81. Marketing Research The daily DVD rentals of a newly released animated film and a newly released horror film from a movie rental store can be modeled by the equations

$$\begin{cases} N = 360 - 24x & \text{Animated film} \\ N = 24 + 18x & \text{Horror film} \end{cases}$$

where N is the number of DVDs rented and x represents the week, with $x = 1$ corresponding to the first week of release.

(a) Use the *table* feature of a graphing utility to find the numbers of rentals of each movie for each of the first 12 weeks of release.

(b) Use the results of part (a) to determine the solution to the system of equations.

(c) Solve the system of equations algebraically.

(d) Compare your results from parts (b) and (c).

(e) Interpret the results in the context of the situation.

82. Economics You want to buy either a wood pellet stove or an electric furnace. The pellet stove costs $3650 and produces heat at a cost of $19.15 per 1 million Btu (British thermal units). The electric furnace costs $2780 and produces heat at a cost of $33.25 per 1 million Btu.

(a) Write a function for the total cost y of buying the pellet stove and producing x million Btu of heat.

(b) Write a function for the total cost y of buying the electric furnace and producing x million Btu of heat.

(c) Use a graphing utility to graph and solve the system of equations formed by the two cost functions.

(d) Solve the system of equations algebraically.

(e) Interpret the results in the context of the situation.

83. Break-Even Analysis A small software company invests $16,000 to produce a software package that will sell for $55.95. Each unit can be produced for $9.45.

(a) Write the cost and revenue functions for x units produced and sold.

(b) Use a graphing utility to graph the cost and revenue functions in the same viewing window. Use the graph to approximate the number of units that must be sold to break even and verify the result algebraically.

84. Professional Sales You are offered two jobs selling college textbooks. One company offers an annual salary of $33,000 plus a year-end bonus of 1% of your total sales. The other company offers an annual salary of $30,000 plus a year-end bonus of 2.5% of your total sales. How much would you have to sell in a year to make the second offer the better offer?

85. Geometry What are the dimensions of a rectangular tract of land with a perimeter of 40 miles and an area of 96 square miles?

86. Geometry What are the dimensions of an isosceles right triangle with a two-inch hypotenuse and an area of 1 square inch?

87. Finance You are deciding how to invest a total of $20,000 in two funds paying 5.5% and 7.5% simple interest. You want to earn a total of $1300 in interest from the investments each year.

(a) Write a system of equations in which one equation represents the total amount invested and the other equation represents the $1300 yearly interest. Let x and y represent the amounts invested at 5.5% and 7.5%, respectively.

(b) Use a graphing utility to graph the two equations in the same viewing window.

(c) How much of the $20,000 should you invest at 5.5% to earn $1300 in interest per year? Explain your reasoning.

88. *Why you should learn it* *(p. 470)* You are offered two different rules for estimating the number of board feet in a 16-foot log. (A board foot is a unit of measure for lumber equal to a board 1 foot square and 1 inch thick.) One rule is the Doyle Log Rule modeled by

$$V = (D - 4)^2, \quad 5 \le D \le 40$$

where D is the diameter (in inches) of the log and V is its volume (in board feet). The other rule is the Scribner Log Rule modeled by

$$V = 0.79D^2 - 2D - 4, \quad 5 \le D \le 40.$$

(a) Use a graphing utility to graph the two log rules in the same viewing window.

(b) For what diameter do the two rules agree?

(c) You are selling large logs by the board foot. Which rule would you use? Explain your reasoning.

89. Algebraic-Graphical-Numerical The populations (in thousands) of Colorado C and Minnesota M from 2008 through 2012 can be modeled by the system

$$\begin{array}{ll} C = 74.0t + 4303 & \text{Colorado} \\ M = 33.0t + 4988 & \text{Minnesota} \end{array}$$

where t is the year, with $t = 8$ corresponding to 2008. (Source: U.S. Census Bureau)

(a) Record in a table the populations predicted by the models for the two states in the years 2013 through 2020.

(b) According to the table, in what year(s) will the population of Colorado be greater than that of Minnesota?

(c) Use a graphing utility to graph the models in the same viewing window. Estimate the point of intersection of the models.

(d) Find the point of intersection algebraically.

(e) Summarize your findings of parts (b) through (d).

90. MODELING DATA

The table shows the yearly revenues (in millions of dollars) of the online travel companies Expedia and Priceline.com from 2008 through 2013.   (Sources: Expedia and Priceline.com)

Year	Expedia	Priceline.com
2008	2937	1885
2009	2955	2338
2010	3348	3085
2011	3449	4356
2012	4030	5261
2013	4771	6793

Spreadsheet at LarsonPrecalculus.com

(a) Use the *regression* feature of a graphing utility to find a quadratic model for the yearly revenue E of Expedia and a linear model for the yearly revenue P of Priceline.com. Let x represent the year, with $x = 8$ corresponding to 2008.

(b) Use the graphing utility to graph the models with the original data in the same viewing window.

(c) Use the graph in part (b) to approximate the first year when the revenues of Priceline.com will be greater than the revenues of Expedia.

(d) Algebraically approximate the first year when the revenues of Priceline.com will be greater than the revenues of Expedia.

(e) Compare your results from parts (c) and (d).

Conclusions

True or False?   In Exercises 91 and 92, determine whether the statement is true or false. Justify your answer.

91. In order to solve a system of equations by substitution, you must always solve for y in one of the two equations and then back-substitute.

92. If a system consists of a parabola and a circle, then it can have at most two solutions.

93. **Think About It**   When solving a system of equations by substitution, how do you recognize that the system has no solution?

94. **Exploration**   Find equations of lines whose graphs intersect the graph of the parabola $y = x^2$ at (a) two points, (b) one point, and (c) no points. (There are many correct answers.)

95. **Exploration**   Create systems of two linear equations in two variables that have (a) no solution, (b) one distinct solution, and (c) infinitely many solutions. (There are many correct answers.)

96. **Exploration**   Create a system of linear equations in two variables that has the solution $(2, -1)$ as its only solution. (There are many correct answers.)

97. **Exploration**   Consider the system of equations.

$$\begin{cases} y = b^x \\ y = x^b \end{cases}$$

(a) Use a graphing utility to graph the system of equations for $b = 2$ and $b = 4$.

(b) For a fixed value of $b > 1$, make a conjecture about the number of points of intersection of the graphs in part (a).

98. **HOW DO YOU SEE IT?**   The cost C of producing x units and the revenue R obtained by selling x units are shown in the figure.

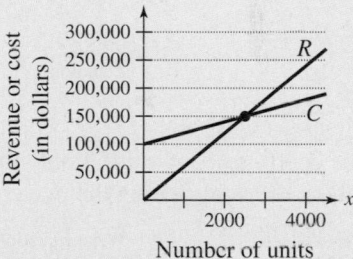

(a) Estimate the point of intersection. What does this point represent?

(b) Use the figure to identify the x-values that correspond to (i) an overall loss and (ii) a profit. Explain your reasoning.

Cumulative Mixed Review

Finding the Slope-Intercept Form   In Exercises 99–102, write an equation of the line passing through the two points. Use the slope-intercept form, if possible. If not possible, explain why.

99. $(3, 4)$, $(10, 6)$

100. $(6, 3)$, $(10, 3)$

101. $(4, -2)$, $(4, 5)$

102. $\left(\frac{3}{5}, 0\right)$, $(4, 6)$

Finding the Domain and Asymptotes of a Function   In Exercises 103–108, find the domain of the function and identify any horizontal or vertical asymptotes.

103. $f(x) = \dfrac{5}{x - 6}$

104. $f(x) = \dfrac{2x - 7}{3x + 2}$

105. $f(x) = \dfrac{x^2 + 2}{x^2 - 16}$

106. $f(x) = 3 - \dfrac{2}{x^2}$

107. $f(x) = \dfrac{x + 1}{x^2 + 1}$

108. $f(x) = \dfrac{x - 4}{x^2 + 16}$

7.2   Systems of Linear Equations in Two Variables

The Method of Elimination

In Section 7.1, you studied two methods for solving a system of equations: substitution and graphing. Now you will study the **method of elimination.** The key step in this method is to obtain, for one of the variables, coefficients that differ only in sign so that *adding* the equations eliminates the variable.

$$
\begin{array}{ll}
3x + 5y = 7 & \text{Equation 1} \\
\underline{-3x - 2y = -1} & \text{Equation 2} \\
3y = 6 & \text{Add equations.}
\end{array}
$$

Note that by adding the two equations, you eliminate the x-terms and obtain a single equation in y. Solving this equation for y produces

$$y = 2$$

which you can then back-substitute into one of the original equations to solve for x.

EXAMPLE 1   Solving a System by Elimination

Solve the system of linear equations.

$$
\begin{cases}
3x + 2y = 4 & \text{Equation 1} \\
5x - 2y = 8 & \text{Equation 2}
\end{cases}
$$

Solution

Because the coefficients of y differ only in sign, you can eliminate the y-terms by adding the two equations.

$$
\begin{array}{ll}
3x + 2y = 4 & \text{Write Equation 1.} \\
\underline{5x - 2y = 8} & \text{Write Equation 2.} \\
8x = 12 & \text{Add equations.} \\
x = \tfrac{3}{2} & \text{Solve for } x.
\end{array}
$$

So, $x = \tfrac{3}{2}$. By back-substituting into Equation 1, you can solve for y.

$$
\begin{array}{ll}
3x + 2y = 4 & \text{Write Equation 1.} \\
3\left(\tfrac{3}{2}\right) + 2y = 4 & \text{Substitute } \tfrac{3}{2} \text{ for } x. \\
y = -\tfrac{1}{4} & \text{Solve for } y.
\end{array}
$$

The solution is $\left(\tfrac{3}{2}, -\tfrac{1}{4}\right)$. You can check the solution *algebraically* by substituting into the original system, or graphically, as shown in Section 7.1.

Check

$$
\begin{array}{ll}
3\left(\tfrac{3}{2}\right) + 2\left(-\tfrac{1}{4}\right) \overset{?}{=} 4 & \text{Substitute into Equation 1.} \\
\tfrac{9}{2} - \tfrac{1}{2} = 4 & \text{Equation 1 checks. } \checkmark \\
5\left(\tfrac{3}{2}\right) - 2\left(-\tfrac{1}{4}\right) \overset{?}{=} 8 & \text{Substitute into Equation 2.} \\
\tfrac{15}{2} + \tfrac{1}{2} = 8 & \text{Equation 2 checks. } \checkmark
\end{array}
$$

✓ *Checkpoint* 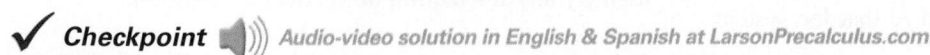 Audio-video solution in English & Spanish at LarsonPrecalculus.com.

Solve the system of linear equations.

$$
\begin{cases}
2x + y = 4 \\
2x - y = -1
\end{cases}
$$

What you should learn

▶ Use the method of elimination to solve systems of linear equations in two variables.
▶ Graphically interpret the number of solutions of a system of linear equations in two variables.
▶ Use systems of linear equations in two variables to model and solve real-life problems.

Why you should learn it

You can use systems of linear equations to model many business applications. For instance, Exercise 84 on page 487 shows how to use a system of linear equations to determine the number of running shoes sold.

Explore the Concept

Use the method of substitution to solve the system given in Example 1. Which method is easier?

> **The Method of Elimination**
>
> To use the **method of elimination** to solve a system of two linear equations in x and y, perform the following steps.
>
> **1.** Obtain coefficients for x (or y) that differ only in sign by multiplying all terms of one or both equations by suitably chosen constants.
>
> **2.** Add the equations to eliminate one variable; solve the resulting equation.
>
> **3.** Back-substitute the value obtained in Step 2 into either of the original equations and solve for the other variable.
>
> **4.** Check your solution in both of the original equations.

EXAMPLE 2   Solving a System by Elimination

Solve the system of linear equations.

$$\begin{cases} 5x + 3y = 9 & \text{Equation 1} \\ 2x - 4y = 14 & \text{Equation 2} \end{cases}$$

Algebraic Solution

You can obtain coefficients of y that differ only in sign by multiplying Equation 1 by 4 and multiplying Equation 2 by 3.

$$
\begin{array}{lll}
5x + 3y = 9 & \Longrightarrow & 20x + 12y = 36 \qquad \text{Multiply Equation 1 by 4.} \\
2x - 4y = 14 & \Longrightarrow & \underline{6x - 12y = 42} \qquad \text{Multiply Equation 2 by 3.} \\
& & 26x = 78 \qquad\ \text{Add equations.}
\end{array}
$$

From this equation, you can see that $x = 3$. By back-substituting this value of x into Equation 2, you can solve for y.

$$
\begin{array}{ll}
2x - 4y = 14 & \text{Write Equation 2.} \\
2(3) - 4y = 14 & \text{Substitute 3 for } x. \\
-4y = 8 & \text{Combine like terms.} \\
y = -2 & \text{Solve for } y.
\end{array}
$$

The solution is $(3, -2)$. You can check the solution algebraically by substituting into the original system.

Graphical Solution

Solve each equation for y and use a graphing utility to graph the equations in the same viewing window. From the figure, the solution is $(3, -2)$. Check this in the original system.

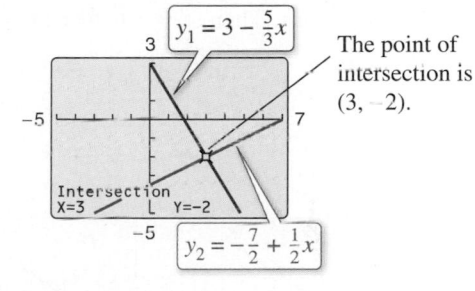

$y_1 = 3 - \frac{5}{3}x$

The point of intersection is $(3, -2)$.

$y_2 = -\frac{7}{2} + \frac{1}{2}x$

Intersection
X=3   Y=-2

✓ **Checkpoint** 🔊))) *Audio-video solution in English & Spanish at LarsonPrecalculus.com.*

Solve the system of linear equations.

$$\begin{cases} 3x + 2y = 7 \\ 2x + 5y = 1 \end{cases}$$

In Example 2, the two systems of linear equations (the original system and the system obtained by multiplying by constants)

$$\begin{cases} 5x + 3y = 9 \\ 2x - 4y = 14 \end{cases} \quad \text{and} \quad \begin{cases} 20x + 12y = 36 \\ 6x - 12y = 42 \end{cases}$$

are called **equivalent systems** because they have precisely the same solution set. The operations that can be performed on a system of linear equations to produce an equivalent system are (1) interchanging any two equations, (2) multiplying an equation by a nonzero constant, and (3) adding a multiple of one equation to any other equation in the system.

Graphical Interpretation of Two-Variable Systems

It is possible for any system of equations to have exactly one solution, two or more solutions, or no solution. If a system of *linear* equations has two different solutions, then it must have an *infinite* number of solutions. To see why this is true, consider the following graphical interpretations of a system of two linear equations in two variables.

> **Graphical Interpretations of Solutions**
>
> For a system of two linear equations in two variables, the number of solutions is one of the following.
>
> | *Number of Solutions* | *Graphical Interpretation* |
> |---|---|
> | **1.** Exactly one solution | The two lines intersect at one point. |
> | **2.** Infinitely many solutions | The two lines are coincident (identical). |
> | **3.** No solution | The two lines are parallel. |

A system of linear equations is **consistent** when it has at least one solution. It is **inconsistent** when it has no solution.

EXAMPLE 3   Recognizing Graphs of Linear Systems

See LarsonPrecalculus.com for an interactive version of this type of example.

Match each system of linear equations (a, b, c) with its graph (i, ii, iii). Describe the number of solutions. Then state whether the system is consistent or inconsistent.

a. $\begin{cases} 2x - 3y = 3 \\ -4x + 6y = 6 \end{cases}$ **b.** $\begin{cases} 2x - 3y = 3 \\ x + 2y = 5 \end{cases}$ **c.** $\begin{cases} 2x - 3y = 3 \\ -4x + 6y = -6 \end{cases}$

i.   **ii.**   **iii.**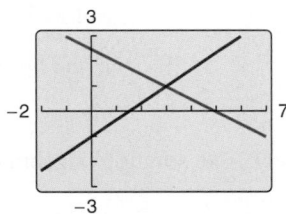

Solution

a. The graph of system (a) is a pair of parallel lines (ii). The lines have no point of intersection, so the system has no solution. The system is inconsistent.

b. The graph of system (b) is a pair of intersecting lines (iii). The lines have one point of intersection, so the system has exactly one solution. The system is consistent.

c. The graph of system (c) is a pair of lines that coincide (i). The lines have infinitely many points of intersection, so the system has infinitely many solutions. The system is consistent.

 Checkpoint *Audio-video solution in English & Spanish at LarsonPrecalculus.com.*

Sketch the graph of the system of linear equations. Then describe the number of solutions and state whether the system is consistent or inconsistent.

$$\begin{cases} -2x + 3y = 6 \\ 4x - 6y = -9 \end{cases}$$

Explore the Concept

Rewrite each system of equations in slope-intercept form and use a graphing utility to graph each system. What is the relationship between the slopes of the two lines and the number of points of intersection?

a. $\begin{cases} y = 5x + 1 \\ y - x = -5 \end{cases}$

b. $\begin{cases} 3y = 4x - 1 \\ -8x + 2 = -6y \end{cases}$

c. $\begin{cases} 2y = -x + 3 \\ -4 = y + \frac{1}{2}x \end{cases}$

In Examples 4 and 5, note how you can use the method of elimination to determine that a system of linear equations has no solution or infinitely many solutions.

EXAMPLE 4   Method of Elimination: No Solution

Solve the system of linear equations.

$$\begin{cases} x - 2y = 3 & \text{Equation 1} \\ -2x + 4y = 1 & \text{Equation 2} \end{cases}$$

Algebraic Solution

To obtain coefficients that differ only in sign, multiply Equation 1 by 2.

$$\begin{aligned} x - 2y &= 3 \quad\Longrightarrow\quad 2x - 4y = 6 \\ -2x + 4y &= 1 \quad\Longrightarrow\quad \underline{-2x + 4y = 1} \\ & \qquad\qquad\qquad\qquad\quad 0 = 7 \end{aligned}$$

By adding the equations, you obtain $0 = 7$. Because there are no values of x and y for which

$$0 = 7 \qquad \text{False statement}$$

this is a false statement. So, you can conclude that the system is inconsistent and has no solution.

Graphical Solution

Solve each equation for y and use a graphing utility to graph the equations in the same viewing window. From the figure, it appears that the system has no solution. When you use the *intersect* feature, the graphing utility cannot find a point of intersection and you will get an error message.

The lines have the same slope but different y-intercepts, so they are parallel.

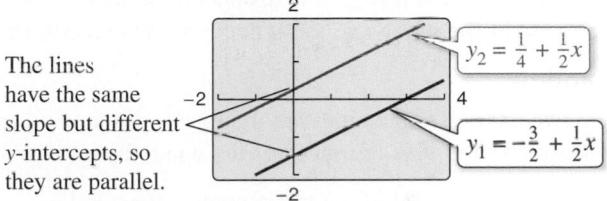

✓ **Checkpoint** 🔊))) *Audio-video solution in English & Spanish at LarsonPrecalculus.com.*

Solve the system of linear equations.

$$\begin{cases} 6x - 5y = 3 \\ -12x + 10y = 5 \end{cases}$$

EXAMPLE 5   Method of Elimination: Infinitely Many Solutions

Solve the system of linear equations.

$$\begin{cases} 2x - y = 1 & \text{Equation 1} \\ 4x - 2y = 2 & \text{Equation 2} \end{cases}$$

Solution

To obtain coefficients that differ only in sign, multiply Equation 1 by -2.

$$\begin{aligned} 2x - y &= 1 \quad\Longrightarrow\quad -4x + 2y = -2 \qquad \text{Multiply Equation 1 by } -2. \\ 4x - 2y &= 2 \quad\Longrightarrow\quad \underline{4x - 2y = 2} \qquad \text{Write Equation 2.} \\ & \qquad\qquad\qquad\qquad\quad 0 = 0 \qquad \text{Add equations.} \end{aligned}$$

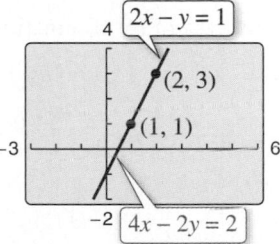

Because $0 = 0$ for all values of x and y, the two equations turn out to be equivalent (have the same solution set). You can conclude that the system has infinitely many solutions. The solution set consists of all points (x, y) lying on the line $2x - y = 1$, as shown in Figure 7.5.

Figure 7.5

✓ **Checkpoint** 🔊))) *Audio-video solution in English & Spanish at LarsonPrecalculus.com.*

Solve the system of linear equations.

$$\begin{cases} \frac{1}{2}x - \frac{1}{8}y = -\frac{3}{8} \\ -4x + y = 3 \end{cases}$$

In Example 4, note that the occurrence of the false statement $0 = 7$ indicates that the system has no solution. In Example 5, note that the occurrence of a statement that is true for all values of the variables—in this case, $0 = 0$—indicates that the system has infinitely many solutions.

Application

At this point, you may be asking the question "How can I tell which application problems can be solved using a system of linear equations?" The answer comes from the following considerations.

1. Does the problem involve more than one unknown quantity?

2. Are there two (or more) equations or conditions to be satisfied?

When one or both of these conditions are met, the appropriate mathematical model for the problem may be a system of linear equations.

EXAMPLE 6 Aviation

An airplane flying into a headwind travels the 2000-mile flying distance between Cleveland, Ohio, and Fresno, California, in 4 hours and 24 minutes. On the return flight, the airplane travels this distance in 4 hours. Find the airspeed of the plane and the speed of the wind, assuming that both remain constant.

Solution

The two unknown quantities are the speeds of the wind and the plane. If r_1 is the speed of the plane and r_2 is the speed of the wind, then

$$r_1 - r_2 = \text{speed of the plane } against \text{ the wind}$$

$$r_1 + r_2 = \text{speed of the plane } with \text{ the wind}$$

as shown in Figure 7.6. Using the formula

$$\text{distance} = (\text{rate})(\text{time})$$

for these two speeds, you obtain the following equations.

$$2000 = (r_1 - r_2)\left(4 + \frac{24}{60}\right)$$

$$2000 = (r_1 + r_2)(4)$$

These two equations simplify as follows.

$$\begin{cases} 5000 = 11r_1 - 11r_2 & \text{Equation 1} \\ 500 = r_1 + r_2 & \text{Equation 2} \end{cases}$$

To solve this system by elimination, multiply Equation 2 by 11.

$$
\begin{array}{ll}
5000 = 11r_1 - 11r_2 & \Rightarrow \quad 5000 = 11r_1 - 11r_2 \qquad \text{Write Equation 1.} \\
\underline{500 = r_1 + r_2} & \Rightarrow \quad \underline{5500 = 11r_1 + 11r_2} \qquad \begin{array}{l}\text{Multiply Equation 2} \\ \text{by 11.}\end{array} \\
& \qquad\qquad 10{,}500 = 22r_1 \qquad\quad \text{Add equations.}
\end{array}
$$

So,

$$r_1 = \frac{10{,}500}{22} = \frac{5250}{11} \approx 477.27 \text{ miles per hour} \qquad \text{Speed of plane}$$

and

$$r_2 = 500 - \frac{5250}{11} = \frac{250}{11} \approx 22.73 \text{ miles per hour} \qquad \text{Speed of wind}$$

Check this solution in the original statement of the problem.

✓ **Checkpoint** Audio-video solution in English & Spanish at LarsonPrecalculus.com.

In Example 6, the return flight takes 4 hours and 6 minutes. Find the airspeed of the plane and the speed of the wind, assuming that both remain constant. ◼

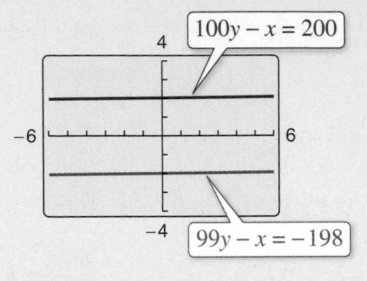

What's Wrong?

You use a graphing utility to graph the system

$$\begin{cases} 100y - x = 200 \\ 99y - x = -198 \end{cases}$$

as shown in the figure. You use the graph to conclude that the system has no solution. What's wrong?

Original flight

Return flight

Figure 7.6

7.2 Exercises

See *CalcChat.com* for tutorial help and worked-out solutions to odd-numbered exercises. For instructions on how to use a graphing utility, see Appendix A.

Vocabulary and Concept Check

In Exercises 1 and 2, fill in the blank(s).

1. The first step in solving a system of equations by the _____ of _____ is to obtain coefficients for x (or y) that differ only in sign.

2. Two systems of equations that have the same solution set are called _____ systems.

3. Is a system of linear equations with no solution consistent or inconsistent?

4. Is a system of linear equations with at least one solution consistent or inconsistent?

5. Is a system of two linear equations consistent when the lines are coincident?

6. When a system of linear equations has no solution, do the lines intersect?

Procedures and Problem Solving

Solving a System by Elimination In Exercises 7–12, solve the system by the method of elimination. Label each line with its equation.

7. $\begin{cases} 2x + y = 5 \\ x - y = 1 \end{cases}$

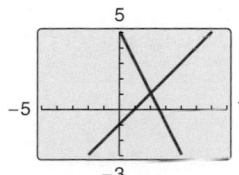

8. $\begin{cases} x + 3y = 1 \\ -x + 2y = 4 \end{cases}$

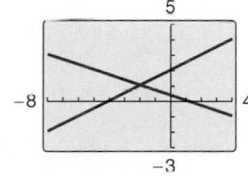

9. $\begin{cases} x + y = 0 \\ 3x + 2y = 1 \end{cases}$

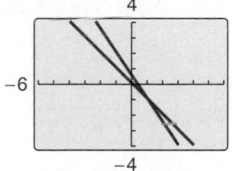

10. $\begin{cases} 2x - y = 3 \\ 4x + 3y = 21 \end{cases}$

11. $\begin{cases} x - y = 2 \\ -2x + 2y = 5 \end{cases}$

12. $\begin{cases} 3x - 2y = 5 \\ -6x + 4y = -10 \end{cases}$

Solving a System by Elimination In Exercises 13–26, solve the system by the method of elimination and check any solutions algebraically.

13. $\begin{cases} x + 2y = 3 \\ x - 2y = 1 \end{cases}$

14. $\begin{cases} 3x - 5y = 2 \\ 2x + 5y = 13 \end{cases}$

15. $\begin{cases} 2x + 3y = 18 \\ 5x - y = 11 \end{cases}$

16. $\begin{cases} x + 7y = 12 \\ 3x - 5y = 10 \end{cases}$

17. $\begin{cases} 3r + 2s = -6 \\ 2r + 6s = 3 \end{cases}$

18. $\begin{cases} 8r + 16s = 20 \\ 16r + 50s = 55 \end{cases}$

19. $\begin{cases} 5u + 6v = 24 \\ 3u + 5v = 18 \end{cases}$

20. $\begin{cases} 3u + 11v = 4 \\ -2u - 5v = 9 \end{cases}$

21. $\begin{cases} -6x + 5y = -15 \\ 4x + 12y = 10 \end{cases}$

22. $\begin{cases} 9x + 3y = 18 \\ 2x - 7y = -19 \end{cases}$

23. $\begin{cases} 1.8x + 1.2y = 4 \\ 9x + 6y = 3 \end{cases}$

24. $\begin{cases} 3.1x - 2.9y = -10.2 \\ 31x - 12y = 34 \end{cases}$

25. $\begin{cases} 3x + \frac{1}{4}y = 1 \\ 2x - \frac{1}{3}y = 0 \end{cases}$

26. $\begin{cases} \frac{1}{2}x - 2y = -\frac{5}{2} \\ -x + 4y = 5 \end{cases}$

Recognizing Graphs of Linear Systems In Exercises 27–30, match the system of linear equations with its graph. State the number of solutions. Then state whether the system is consistent or inconsistent. [The graphs are labeled (a), (b), (c), and (d).]

(a)

(b)

(c)

(d)

27. $\begin{cases} 2x - 5y = 0 \\ x - y = 3 \end{cases}$

28. $\begin{cases} -7x + 6y = -4 \\ 14x - 12y = 8 \end{cases}$

29. $\begin{cases} 7x - 6y = -6 \\ -7x + 6y = -4 \end{cases}$

30. $\begin{cases} 2x - 5y = 0 \\ 2x - 3y = -4 \end{cases}$

Solving a System by Elimination   In Exercises 31–46, solve the system by the method of elimination and check any solutions using a graphing utility.

31. $\begin{cases} 5x + 3y = 6 \\ 3x - y = 5 \end{cases}$

32. $\begin{cases} x + 5y = 10 \\ 3x - 10y = -5 \end{cases}$

33. $\begin{cases} \frac{2}{5}x - \frac{3}{2}y = 4 \\ \frac{1}{5}x - \frac{3}{4}y = -2 \end{cases}$

34. $\begin{cases} \frac{2}{3}x + \frac{1}{6}y = \frac{2}{3} \\ 4x + y = 4 \end{cases}$

35. $\begin{cases} \frac{3}{4}x + y = \frac{1}{8} \\ \frac{9}{4}x + 3y = \frac{3}{8} \end{cases}$

36. $\begin{cases} \frac{1}{4}x + \frac{1}{6}y = 1 \\ -3x - 2y = 0 \end{cases}$

37. $\begin{cases} \dfrac{x+2}{4} + \dfrac{y-1}{4} = 1 \\ x - y = 4 \end{cases}$

38. $\begin{cases} \dfrac{2x+5}{2} + \dfrac{y-1}{3} = -1 \\ 2x - y = 12 \end{cases}$

39. $\begin{cases} -5x + 6y = -3 \\ 20x - 24y = 12 \end{cases}$

40. $\begin{cases} 7x + 8y = 16 \\ -14x - 16y = -4 \end{cases}$

41. $\begin{cases} 2.5x - 3y = 1.5 \\ x - 1.2y = -3.6 \end{cases}$

42. $\begin{cases} 6.3x + 7.2y = 5.4 \\ 5.6x + 6.4y = 4.8 \end{cases}$

43. $\begin{cases} 0.2x - 0.5y = -27.8 \\ 0.3x + 0.4y = 68.7 \end{cases}$

44. $\begin{cases} 0.2x + 0.6y = -1 \\ x - 0.5y = 2 \end{cases}$

45. $\begin{cases} \dfrac{1}{x} + \dfrac{3}{y} = 2 \\ \dfrac{4}{x} - \dfrac{1}{y} = -5 \end{cases}$

46. $\begin{cases} \dfrac{2}{x} - \dfrac{1}{y} = 5 \\ \dfrac{6}{x} + \dfrac{1}{y} = 11 \end{cases}$

Solving a System Graphically   In Exercises 47–52, use a graphing utility to graph the lines in the system. Use the graphs to determine whether the system is consistent or inconsistent. If the system is consistent, determine the solution. Verify your results algebraically.

47. $\begin{cases} 3x + 5y = -2 \\ 4x - y = 5 \end{cases}$

48. $\begin{cases} -x + 3y = 0 \\ 3x - 9y = 14 \end{cases}$

49. $\begin{cases} 6x + 3y = -8 \\ -x - \frac{1}{2}y = \frac{4}{3} \end{cases}$

50. $\begin{cases} -\frac{1}{4}x - \frac{1}{2}y = 1 \\ 5x + y = 1 \end{cases}$

51. $\begin{cases} 3.2x - 16y = 7.5 \\ x - 5y = -9 \end{cases}$

52. $\begin{cases} -6x + 4y = -9 \\ 4.5x - 3y = 6.75 \end{cases}$

Solving a System Graphically   In Exercises 53–60, use a graphing utility to graph the two equations. Use the graphs to approximate the solution of the system. Round your results to three decimal places.

53. $\begin{cases} 6y = 42 \\ 6x - y = 16 \end{cases}$

54. $\begin{cases} 4y = -8 \\ 7x - 2y = 25 \end{cases}$

55. $\begin{cases} \frac{3}{2}x - \frac{1}{5}y = 8 \\ -2x + 3y = 3 \end{cases}$

56. $\begin{cases} \frac{3}{4}x - \frac{5}{2}y = -9 \\ -x + 6y = 28 \end{cases}$

57. $\begin{cases} \frac{1}{3}x + y = -\frac{1}{3} \\ 5x - 3y = 7 \end{cases}$

58. $\begin{cases} 5x - y = -4 \\ 2x + \frac{3}{5}y = \frac{2}{5} \end{cases}$

59. $\begin{cases} 0.5x + 2.2y = 9 \\ 6x + 0.4y = -22 \end{cases}$

60. $\begin{cases} 2.4x + 3.8y = -17.6 \\ 4x - 0.2y = -3.2 \end{cases}$

Solving a System   In Exercises 61–68, use any method to solve the system.

61. $\begin{cases} 3x - 5y = 7 \\ 2x + y = 9 \end{cases}$

62. $\begin{cases} -x + 3y = 17 \\ 4x + 3y = 7 \end{cases}$

63. $\begin{cases} y = 2x - 5 \\ y = 5x - 11 \end{cases}$

64. $\begin{cases} 7x + 3y = 16 \\ y = x + 2 \end{cases}$

65. $\begin{cases} x - 5y = 21 \\ 6x + 5y = 21 \end{cases}$

66. $\begin{cases} y = -2x - 17 \\ y = 2 - 3x \end{cases}$

67. $\begin{cases} -5x + 9y = 13 \\ y = x - 4 \end{cases}$

68. $\begin{cases} 4x - 3y = 6 \\ -5x + 7y = -1 \end{cases}$

Finding a System   In Exercises 69–72, find a system of linear equations that has the given solution. (There are many correct answers.)

69. $(5, 0)$

70. $(-6, 1)$

71. $(2.5, -4)$

72. $\left(-\frac{3}{4}, 12\right)$

Economics   In Exercises 73–76, find the *point of* *equilibrium* of the demand and supply equations. The point of equilibrium is the price p and the number of units x that satisfy both the demand and supply equations.

	Demand	Supply
73.	$p = 500 - 0.4x$	$p = 380 + 0.1x$
74.	$p = 100 - 0.05x$	$p = 25 + 0.1x$
75.	$p = 140 - 0.00002x$	$p = 80 + 0.00001x$
76.	$p = 400 - 0.0002x$	$p = 225 + 0.0005x$

77. **Aviation**   An airplane flying into a headwind travels the 1800-mile flying distance between New York City and Albuquerque, New Mexico, in 3 hours and 36 minutes. On the return flight, the same distance is traveled in 3 hours. Find the airspeed of the plane and the speed of the wind, assuming that both remain constant.

78. **Navigation**   A motorboat traveling with the current takes 40 minutes to travel 20 miles downstream. The return trip takes 60 minutes. Find the speed of the current and the speed of the boat relative to the current, assuming that both remain constant.

79. **Business**   A minor league baseball team had a total attendance one evening of 1175. The tickets for adults and children sold for $15 and $12, respectively. The ticket revenue that night was $16,275.

(a) Create a system of linear equations to find the numbers of adults A and children C at the game.

(b) Solve your system of equations by elimination or by substitution. Explain your choice.

(c) Use the *intersect* feature or the *zoom* and *trace* features of a graphing utility to solve your system.

80. Chemistry Thirty liters of a 40% acid solution is obtained by mixing a 25% solution with a 50% solution.

(a) Write a system of equations in which one equation represents the amount of final mixture required and the other represents the percent of acid in the final mixture. Let x and y represent the amounts of the 25% and 50% solutions, respectively.

(b) Use a graphing utility to graph the two equations in part (a) in the same viewing window.

(c) As the amount of the 25% solution increases, how does the amount of the 50% solution change?

(d) How much of each solution is required to obtain the specified concentration of the final mixture?

81. Business A grocer sells oranges for $0.95 each and grapefruits for $1.05 each. You purchased a mix of 16 oranges and grapefruits and paid $15.90. How many of each type of fruit did you buy?

82. Nutrition Two cheeseburgers and one small order of french fries from a fast-food restaurant contain a total of 830 calories. Three cheeseburgers and two small orders of french fries contain a total of 1360 calories. Find the number of calories in each item.

83. Sales The projected sales S (in millions of dollars) of two clothing retailers from 2015 through 2020 can be modeled by

$$\begin{cases} S - 149.9t = 415.5 & \text{Retailer A} \\ S - 183.1t = 117.3 & \text{Retailer B} \end{cases}$$

where t is the year, with $t = 5$ corresponding to 2015.

(a) Solve the system of equations using the method of your choice. Explain why you chose that method.

(b) Interpret the meaning of the solution in the context of the problem.

(c) Interpret the meaning of the coefficient of the t-term in each model.

(d) Suppose the coefficients of t were equal and the models remained the same otherwise. How would this affect your answers in parts (a) and (b)?

84. *Why you should learn it* (p. 480) On a Saturday night, the manager of a shoe store evaluates the receipts of the previous week's sales. Two hundred fifty pairs of two different styles of running shoes were sold. One style sold for $79.50 and the other sold for $89.95. The receipts totaled $20,713.40. The cash register that was supposed to record the number of each type of shoe sold malfunctioned. Can you recover the information? If so, how many shoes of each type were sold?

Fitting a Line to Data **To find the least squares regression line** $y = ax + b$ **for a set of points**

$$(x_1, y_1), (x_2, y_2), \ldots, (x_n, y_n)$$

you can solve the following system for a **and** b.

$$\begin{cases} nb + \left(\displaystyle\sum_{i=1}^{n} x_i\right)a = \left(\displaystyle\sum_{i=1}^{n} y_i\right) \\ \left(\displaystyle\sum_{i=1}^{n} x_i\right)b + \left(\displaystyle\sum_{i=1}^{n} x_i^2\right)a = \left(\displaystyle\sum_{i=1}^{n} x_i y_i\right) \end{cases}$$

In Exercises 85–88, the sums have been evaluated. Solve the given system for a **and** b **to find the least squares regression line for the points. Use a graphing utility to confirm the results.**

85. $\begin{cases} 5b + 10a = 20.2 \\ 10b + 30a = 50.1 \end{cases}$ **86.** $\begin{cases} 5b + 10a = 11.7 \\ 10b + 30a = 25.6 \end{cases}$

87. $\begin{cases} 6b + 15a = 23.6 \\ 15b + 55a = 48.8 \end{cases}$ **88.** $\begin{cases} 7b + 21a = 13.1 \\ 21b + 91a = -2.8 \end{cases}$

89. MODELING DATA

Four test plots were used to explore the relationship between wheat yield y (in bushels per acre) and amount of fertilizer applied x (in hundreds of pounds per acre). The results are given by the ordered pairs (1.0, 32), (1.5, 41), (2.0, 48), and (2.5, 53).

(a) Find the least squares regression line $y = ax + b$ for the data by solving the system for a and b.

$$\begin{cases} 4b + 7.0a = 174 \\ 7b + 13.5a = 322 \end{cases}$$

(b) Use the *regression* feature of a graphing utility to confirm the result in part (a).

(c) Use the graphing utility to plot the data and graph the linear model from part (a) in the same viewing window.

(d) Use the linear model from part (a) to predict the yield for a fertilizer application of 160 pounds per acre.

90. MODELING DATA

A candy store manager wants to know the demand for a candy bar as a function of the price. The daily sales for different prices of the product are shown in the table.

Price, x	Demand, y
$1.00	45
$1.20	37
$1.50	23

(a) Find the least squares regression line $y = ax + b$ for the data by solving the system for a and b.

$$\begin{cases} 3.00b + 3.70a = 105.00 \\ 3.70b + 4.69a = 123.90 \end{cases}$$

(b) Use the *regression* feature of a graphing utility to confirm the result in part (a).

(c) Use the graphing utility to plot the data and graph the linear model from part (a) in the same viewing window.

(d) Use the linear model from part (a) to predict the demand when the price is $1.75.

Conclusions

True or False? In Exercises 91–93, determine whether the statement is true or false. Justify your answer.

91. If a system of linear equations has two distinct solutions, then it has an infinite number of solutions.

92. If a system of linear equations has no solution, then the lines must be parallel.

93. Solving a system of equations graphically using a graphing utility always yields an exact solution.

94. **Writing** Briefly explain whether or not it is possible for a consistent system of linear equations to have exactly two solutions.

95. **Think About It** Find all value(s) of k for which the system of linear equations

$$\begin{cases} x + 3y = 9 \\ 2x + 6y = k \end{cases}$$

has (a) infinitely many solutions and (b) no solution.

96. **HOW DO YOU SEE IT?** Use the graphs of the two equations shown below.

(a) Describe the graphs of the two equations.

(b) Can you conclude that the system of equations shown in the graph is inconsistent? Explain.

Solving a System In Exercises 97 and 98, solve the system of equations for u and v. While solving for these variables, consider the transcendental functions as constants. (Systems of this type are found in a course in differential equations.)

97. $\begin{cases} u \sin x + v \cos x = 0 \\ u \cos x - v \sin x = \sec x \end{cases}$

98. $\begin{cases} u \cos 2x + v \sin 2x = 0 \\ u(-2 \sin 2x) + v(2 \cos 2x) = \csc 2x \end{cases}$

Cumulative Mixed Review

Solving an Inequality In Exercises 99–104, solve the inequality and graph the solution on a real number line.

99. $-11 - 6x \geq 33$

100. $-6 \leq 3x - 10 < 6$

101. $|x - 8| < 10$

102. $|x + 10| \geq -3$

103. $2x^2 + 3x - 35 < 0$

104. $3x^2 + 12x > 0$

Rewriting a Logarithmic Expression In Exercises 105–110, write the expression as the logarithm of a single quantity.

105. $\ln x + \ln 6$

106. $\ln x - 5 \ln(x + 3)$

107. $\log_9 12 - \log_9 x$

108. $\frac{1}{4} \log_6 3 + \frac{1}{4} \log_6 x$

109. $2 \ln x - \ln(x + 2)$

110. $\frac{1}{2} \ln(x^2 + 4) - \ln x$

111. **Make a Decision** To work an extended application analyzing the average undergraduate tuition, room, and board charges at private degree-granting institutions in the United States from 1990 through 2012, visit this textbook's website at *LarsonPrecalculus.com*. (Data Source: U.S. Department of Education)

7.3   Multivariable Linear Systems

Row–Echelon Form and Back-Substitution

The method of elimination can be applied to a system of linear equations in more than two variables. When elimination is used to solve a system of linear equations, the goal is to rewrite the system in a form to which back-substitution can be applied. To see how this works, consider the following two systems of linear equations.

System of Three Linear Equations in Three Variables (See Example 2):

$$\begin{cases} x - 2y + 3z = 9 \\ -x + 3y + z = -2 \\ 2x - 5y + 5z = 17 \end{cases}$$

Equivalent System in Row-Echelon Form (See Example 1):

$$\begin{cases} x - 2y + 3z = 9 \\ y + 4z = 7 \\ z = 2 \end{cases}$$

The second system is said to be in **row-echelon form,** which means that it has a "stair-step" pattern with leading coefficients of 1. After comparing the two systems, it should be clear that it is easier to solve the system in row-echelon form, using back-substitution.

EXAMPLE 1   Using Back-Substitution in Row-Echelon Form

Solve the system of linear equations.

$$\begin{cases} x - 2y + 3z = 9 & \text{Equation 1} \\ y + 4z = 7 & \text{Equation 2} \\ z = 2 & \text{Equation 3} \end{cases}$$

Solution

From Equation 3, you know the value of z. To solve for y, substitute $z = 2$ into Equation 2 to obtain

$$y + 4(2) = 7 \qquad \text{Substitute 2 for } z.$$

$$y = -1. \qquad \text{Solve for } y.$$

Next, substitute $y = -1$ and $z = 2$ into Equation 1 to obtain

$$x - 2(-1) + 3(2) = 9 \qquad \text{Substitute } -1 \text{ for } y \text{ and 2 for } z.$$

$$x = 1. \qquad \text{Solve for } x.$$

The solution is

$$x = 1, \ y = -1, \text{ and } z = 2$$

which can be written as the **ordered triple**

$$(1, -1, 2).$$

Check this in the original system of equations.

✓ **Checkpoint** Audio-video solution in English & Spanish at LarsonPrecalculus.com.

Solve the system of linear equations.

$$\begin{cases} 2x - y + 5z = 22 \\ y + 3z = 6 \\ z = 3 \end{cases}$$

What you should learn

▶ Use back-substitution to solve linear systems in row-echelon form.
▶ Use Gaussian elimination to solve systems of linear equations.
▶ Solve nonsquare systems of linear equations.
▶ Graphically interpret three-variable linear systems.
▶ Use systems of linear equations to write partial fraction decompositions of rational expressions.
▶ Use systems of linear equations in three or more variables to model and solve real-life problems.

Why you should learn it

Systems of linear equations in three or more variables can be used to model and solve real-life problems. For instance, Exercise 94 on page 501 shows how to use a system of linear equations to analyze the numbers of par-3, par-4, and par-5 holes on a golf course.

Gaussian Elimination

Two systems of equations are *equivalent* when they have the same solution set. To solve a system that is not in row-echelon form, first convert it to an *equivalent* system that *is* in row-echelon form by using one or more of the elementary row operations shown below. This process is called **Gaussian elimination,** after the German mathematician Carl Friedrich Gauss (1777–1855).

> **Elementary Row Operations for Systems of Equations**
>
> **1.** Interchange two equations.
>
> **2.** Multiply one of the equations by a nonzero constant.
>
> **3.** Add a multiple of one equation to another equation.

EXAMPLE 2   Using Gaussian Elimination to Solve a System

Solve the system of linear equations.

$$\begin{cases} x - 2y + 3z = 9 & \text{Equation 1} \\ -x + 3y + z = -2 & \text{Equation 2} \\ 2x - 5y + 5z = 17 & \text{Equation 3} \end{cases}$$

Solution

Because the leading coefficient of the first equation is 1, you can begin by saving the x at the upper left and eliminating the other x-terms from the first column.

$$\begin{cases} x - 2y + 3z = 9 \\ y + 4z = 7 \\ 2x - 5y + 5z = 17 \end{cases}$$

> Adding the first equation to the second equation produces a new second equation.

$$\begin{cases} x - 2y + 3z = 9 \\ y + 4z = 7 \\ -y - z = -1 \end{cases}$$

> Adding -2 times the first equation to the third equation produces a new third equation.

Now that all but the first x have been eliminated from the first column, go to work on the second column. (You need to eliminate y from the third equation.)

$$\begin{cases} x - 2y + 3z = 9 \\ y + 4z = 7 \\ 3z = 6 \end{cases}$$

> Adding the second equation to the third equation produces a new third equation.

Finally, you need a coefficient of 1 for z in the third equation.

$$\begin{cases} x - 2y + 3z = 9 \\ y + 4z = 7 \\ z = 2 \end{cases}$$

> Multiplying the third equation by $\frac{1}{3}$ produces a new third equation.

This is the same system that was solved in Example 1. So, the solution is $x = 1$, $y = -1$, and $z = 2$.

Remark

Arithmetic errors are often made when elementary row operations are performed. You should note the operation performed in each step so that you can go back and check your work.

✓ **Checkpoint** ◀))) *Audio-video solution in English & Spanish at LarsonPrecalculus.com.*

Solve the system of linear equations.

$$\begin{cases} x + y + z = 6 \\ 2x - y + z = 3 \\ 3x + y - z = 2 \end{cases}$$

The goal of Gaussian elimination is to use elementary row operations on a system in order to isolate one variable. You can then solve for the value of the variable and use back-substitution to find the values of the remaining variables.

The next example involves an inconsistent system—one that has no solution. The key to recognizing an inconsistent system is that at some stage in the elimination process, you obtain a false statement such as $0 = -2$.

EXAMPLE 3   An Inconsistent System

Solve the system of linear equations.

$$\begin{cases} x - 3y + z = 1 & \text{Equation 1} \\ 2x - y - 2z = 2 & \text{Equation 2} \\ x + 2y - 3z = -1 & \text{Equation 3} \end{cases}$$

Solution

$$\begin{cases} x - 3y + z = 1 \\ 5y - 4z = 0 \\ x + 2y - 3z = -1 \end{cases}$$

Adding -2 times the first equation to the second equation produces a new second equation.

$$\begin{cases} x - 3y + z = 1 \\ 5y - 4z = 0 \\ 5y - 4z = -2 \end{cases}$$

Adding -1 times the first equation to the third equation produces a new third equation.

$$\begin{cases} x - 3y + z = 1 \\ 5y - 4z = 0 \\ 0 = -2 \end{cases}$$

Adding -1 times the second equation to the third equation produces a new third equation.

Because $0 = -2$ is a false statement, you can conclude that this system is inconsistent and has no solution. Moreover, because this system is equivalent to the original system, you can conclude that the original system also has no solution.

✓ **Checkpoint** ◀))) *Audio-video solution in English & Spanish at LarsonPrecalculus.com.*

Solve the system of linear equations.

$$\begin{cases} x + y - 2z = 3 \\ 3x - 2y + 4z = 1 \\ 2x - 3y + 6z = 8 \end{cases}$$

As with a system of linear equations in two variables, the number of solutions of a system of linear equations in more than two variables must fall into one of three categories.

The Number of Solutions of a Linear System

For a system of linear equations, exactly one of the following is true.

1. There is exactly one solution.

2. There are infinitely many solutions.

3. There is no solution.

A system of linear equations is called *consistent* when it has at least one solution. A consistent system with exactly one solution is **independent**. A consistent system with infinitely many solutions is **dependent**. A system of linear equations is called *inconsistent* when it has no solution.

EXAMPLE 4   A System with Infinitely Many Solutions

Solve the system of linear equations.

$$\begin{cases} x + y - 3z = -1 & \text{Equation 1} \\ \quad\quad y - z = 0 & \text{Equation 2} \\ -x + 2y = 1 & \text{Equation 3} \end{cases}$$

Solution

$$\begin{cases} x + y - 3z = -1 \\ \quad\quad y - z = 0 \\ \quad\quad 3y - 3z = 0 \end{cases}$$

Adding the first equation to the third equation produces a new third equation.

$$\begin{cases} x + y - 3z = -1 \\ \quad\quad y - z = 0 \\ \quad\quad\quad 0 = 0 \end{cases}$$

Adding -3 times the second equation to the third equation produces a new third equation.

This result means that Equation 3 depends on Equations 1 and 2 in the sense that it gives no additional information about the variables. So, the original system is equivalent to

$$\begin{cases} x + y - 3z = -1 \\ \quad\quad y - z = 0 \end{cases}.$$

In the last equation, solve for y in terms of z to obtain $y = z$. Back-substituting for y in the previous equation produces

$$x = 2z - 1.$$

Finally, letting $z = a$, where a is a real number, the solutions of the original system are all of the form

$$x = 2a - 1, \quad y = a, \quad \text{and} \quad z = a.$$

So, every ordered triple of the form

$$(2a - 1, a, a) \qquad \text{\textit{a} is a real number.}$$

is a solution of the system.

✓ **Checkpoint** 🔊))) *Audio-video solution in English & Spanish at LarsonPrecalculus.com.*

Solve the system of linear equations.

$$\begin{cases} x + 2y - 7z = -4 \\ 2x + 3y + z = 5 \\ 3x + 7y - 36z = -25 \end{cases}$$

In Example 4, there are other ways to write the same infinite set of solutions. For instance, the solutions could have been written as

$$\left(b, \tfrac{1}{2}(b + 1), \tfrac{1}{2}(b + 1)\right). \qquad \text{\textit{b} is a real number.}$$

This description produces the same set of solutions, as shown below.

Substitution	Solution	
$a = 0$	$(2(0) - 1, 0, 0) = (-1, 0, 0)$	Same solution
$b = -1$	$\left(-1, \tfrac{1}{2}(-1 + 1), \tfrac{1}{2}(-1 + 1)\right) = (-1, 0, 0)$	
$a = 1$	$(2(1) - 1, 1, 1) = (1, 1, 1)$	Same solution
$b = 1$	$\left(1, \tfrac{1}{2}(1 + 1), \tfrac{1}{2}(1 + 1)\right) = (1, 1, 1)$	
$a = 3$	$(2(3) - 1, 3, 3) = (5, 3, 3)$	Same solution
$b = 5$	$\left(5, \tfrac{1}{2}(5 + 1), \tfrac{1}{2}(5 + 1)\right) = (5, 3, 3)$	

Remark

There are an infinite number of solutions to Example 4, but they are all of a specific form. By selecting, for instance, a-values of 0, 1, and 3, you can verify that $(-1, 0, 0)$, $(1, 1, 1)$, and $(5, 3, 3)$ are specific solutions. It is incorrect to say simply that the solution to Example 4 is "infinite." You must also specify the form of the solutions.

Nonsquare Systems

So far, each system of linear equations you have looked at has been *square*, which means that the number of equations is equal to the number of variables. In a **nonsquare system of equations,** the number of equations differs from the number of variables. A system of linear equations cannot have a unique solution unless there are at least as many equations as there are variables in the system.

EXAMPLE 5   A System with Fewer Equations than Variables

See LarsonPrecalculus.com for an interactive version of this type of example.

Solve the system of linear equations.

$$\begin{cases} x - 2y + z = 2 & \text{Equation 1} \\ 2x - y - z = 1 & \text{Equation 2} \end{cases}$$

Solution

Begin by rewriting the system in row-echelon form.

$$\begin{cases} x - 2y + z = 2 \\ 3y - 3z = -3 \end{cases}$$

> Adding -2 times the first equation to the second equation produces a new second equation.

$$\begin{cases} x - 2y + z = 2 \\ y - z = -1 \end{cases}$$

> Multiplying the second equation by $\frac{1}{3}$ produces a new second equation.

Solve for y in terms of z to obtain

$$y = z - 1.$$

By back-substituting into Equation 1, you can solve for x as follows.

$x - 2y + z = 2$	Write Equation 1.
$x - 2(z - 1) + z = 2$	Substitute $z - 1$ for y.
$x - 2z + 2 + z = 2$	Distributive Property
$x = z$	Solve for x.

Finally, by letting $z = a$, where a is a real number, you have the solution

$$x = a, \quad y = a - 1, \quad \text{and} \quad z = a.$$

So, every ordered triple of the form

$$(a, a - 1, a) \qquad a \text{ is a real number.}$$

is a solution of the system.

✓ **Checkpoint**))) *Audio-video solution in English & Spanish at LarsonPrecalculus.com.*

Solve the system of linear equations.

$$\begin{cases} x - y + 4z = 3 \\ 4x - z = 0 \end{cases}$$

In Example 5, try choosing some values of a to obtain different solutions of the system, such as

$$(1, 0, 1), \quad (2, 1, 2), \quad \text{and} \quad (3, 2, 3).$$

Then check each ordered triple in the original system to verify that it is a solution of the system.

Check: $(1, 0, 1)$

$1 - 2(0) + 1 \overset{?}{=} 2$

$2 = 2 \checkmark$

$2(1) - 0 - 1 \overset{?}{=} 1$

$1 = 1 \checkmark$

Check: $(2, 1, 2)$

$2 - 2(1) + 2 \overset{?}{=} 2$

$2 = 2 \checkmark$

$2(2) - 1 - 2 \overset{?}{=} 1$

$1 = 1 \checkmark$

Graphical Interpretation of Three-Variable Systems

Solutions of equations in three variables can be represented graphically using a **three-dimensional coordinate system.** To construct such a system, begin with the xy-coordinate plane in a horizontal position. Then draw the z-axis as a vertical line through the origin.

Every ordered triple (x, y, z) corresponds to a point on the three-dimensional coordinate system. For instance, the points corresponding to $(-2, 5, 4)$, $(2, -5, 3)$, and $(3, 3, -2)$ are shown in Figure 7.7.

The **graph of an equation in three variables** consists of all points (x, y, z) that are solutions of the equation. The graph of a linear equation in three variables is a *plane*. Sketching graphs on a three-dimensional coordinate system is difficult because the sketch itself is only two-dimensional.

One technique for sketching a plane is to find the three points at which the plane intersects the axes. For instance, the plane

$$3x + 2y + 4z = 12$$

intersects the x-axis at the point $(4, 0, 0)$, the y-axis at the point $(0, 6, 0)$, and the z-axis at the point $(0, 0, 3)$. By plotting these three points, connecting them with line segments, and shading the resulting triangular region, you can sketch a portion of the graph, as shown in Figure 7.8.

The graph of a system of three linear equations in three variables consists of *three* planes. When these planes intersect in a single point, the system has exactly one solution (see Figure 7.9). When the three planes have no point in common, the system has no solution (see Figures 7.10 and 7.11). When the three planes intersect in a line or a plane, the system has infinitely many solutions (see Figures 7.12 and 7.13).

Figure 7.7

Figure 7.8

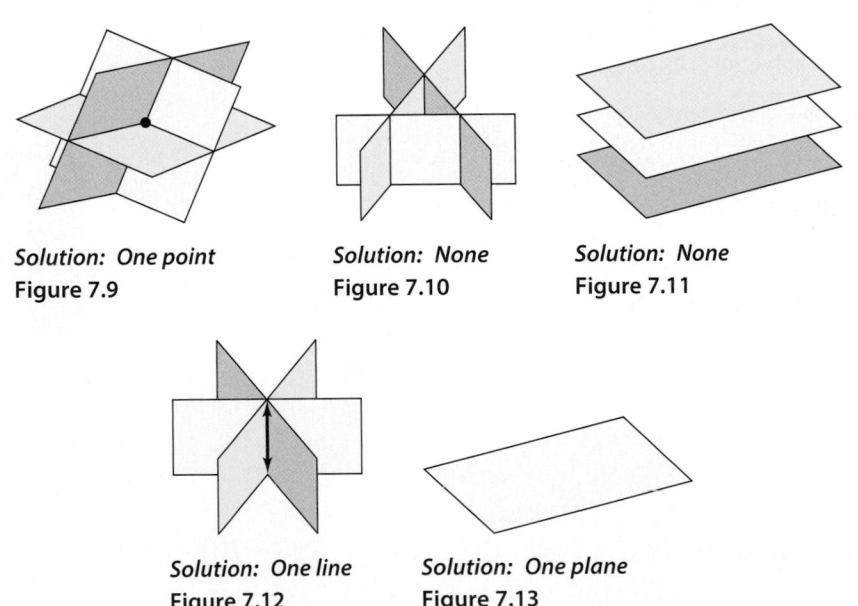

Solution: One point
Figure 7.9

Solution: None
Figure 7.10

Solution: None
Figure 7.11

Solution: One line
Figure 7.12

Solution: One plane
Figure 7.13

Technology Tip

Three-dimensional graphing utilities and computer algebra systems, such as *Maple* and *Mathematica*, are very efficient in producing three-dimensional graphs. They are good tools to use while studying calculus. If you have access to such a utility, try reproducing the plane shown in Figure 7.8.

Partial Fraction Decomposition

A rational expression can often be written as the sum of two or more simpler rational expressions. For example, the rational expression

$$\frac{x + 7}{x^2 - x - 6}$$

can be written as the sum of two fractions with linear denominators. That is,

Partial fraction decomposition

of $\dfrac{x + 7}{x^2 - x - 6}$

$$\frac{x + 7}{x^2 - x - 6} = \overbrace{\frac{2}{x - 3}}^{} + \overbrace{\frac{-1}{x + 2}}^{}.$$

Partial Partial
fraction fraction

Each fraction on the right side of the equation is a **partial fraction,** and together they make up the **partial fraction decomposition** of the left side.

Decomposition of N(x)/D(x) into Partial Fractions

1. *Divide when improper:* When $N(x)/D(x)$ is an improper fraction [degree of $N(x) \geq$ degree of $D(x)$], divide the denominator into the numerator to obtain

$$\frac{N(x)}{D(x)} = (\text{polynomial}) + \frac{N_1(x)}{D(x)}$$

   and apply Steps 2, 3, and 4 (below) to the proper rational expression

$$\frac{N_1(x)}{D(x)}.$$

2. *Factor the denominator:* Completely factor the denominator into factors of the form

$$(px + q)^m \quad \text{and} \quad (ax^2 + bx + c)^n$$

   where $(ax^2 + bx + c)$ is irreducible over the reals.

3. *Linear factors:* For *each* factor of the form

$$(px + q)^m$$

   the partial fraction decomposition must include the following sum of m fractions.

$$\frac{A_1}{(px + q)} + \frac{A_2}{(px + q)^2} + \cdots + \frac{A_m}{(px + q)^m}$$

4. *Quadratic factors:* For *each* factor of the form

$$(ax^2 + bx + c)^n$$

   the partial fraction decomposition must include the following sum of n fractions.

$$\frac{B_1x + C_1}{ax^2 + bx + c} + \frac{B_2x + C_2}{(ax^2 + bx + c)^2} + \cdots + \frac{B_nx + C_n}{(ax^2 + bx + c)^n}$$

One of the most important applications of partial fractions is in calculus. Partial fractions can be used in a calculus operation called antidifferentiation.

EXAMPLE 6   Distinct Linear Factors

Write the partial fraction decomposition of

$$\frac{x + 7}{x^2 - x - 6}.$$

Solution

The expression is proper, so factor the denominator. Because

$$x^2 - x - 6 = (x - 3)(x + 2)$$

you should include one partial fraction with a constant numerator for each linear factor of the denominator and write

$$\frac{x + 7}{x^2 - x - 6} = \frac{A}{x - 3} + \frac{B}{x + 2}.$$

Multiplying each side of this equation by $(x - 3)(x + 2)$, the least common denominator (LCD), leads to the basic equation

$$
\begin{aligned}
x + 7 &= A(x + 2) + B(x - 3) &&\text{Basic equation}\\
&= Ax + 2A + Bx - 3B &&\text{Distributive Property}\\
&= (A + B)x + 2A - 3B. &&\text{Write in polynomial form.}
\end{aligned}
$$

Because two polynomials are equal if and only if the coefficients of like terms are equal, you can equate the coefficients of like terms to opposite sides of the equation.

$$x + 7 = (A + B)x + (2A - 3B) \qquad \text{Equate coefficients of like terms.}$$

You can now write the following system of linear equations.

$$
\begin{cases}
A + B = 1 & \text{Equation 1}\\
2A - 3B = 7 & \text{Equation 2}
\end{cases}
$$

You can solve the system of linear equations as follows.

$$
\begin{array}{lll}
A + B = 1 & \Longrightarrow & 3A + 3B = 3 \qquad \text{Multiply Equation 1 by 3.}\\
2A - 3B = 7 & \Longrightarrow & \underline{2A - 3B = 7} \qquad \text{Write Equation 2.}\\
& & 5A \phantom{{} - 3B} = 10 \qquad \text{Add equations.}
\end{array}
$$

From this equation, you can see that $A = 2$. By back-substituting this value of A into Equation 1, you can solve for B as follows.

$$
\begin{aligned}
A + B &= 1 &&\text{Write Equation 1.}\\
2 + B &= 1 &&\text{Substitute 2 for } A.\\
B &= -1 &&\text{Solve for } B.
\end{aligned}
$$

So, the partial fraction decomposition is

$$\frac{x + 7}{x^2 - x - 6} = \frac{2}{x - 3} - \frac{1}{x + 2}.$$

Check this result by combining the two partial fractions on the right side of the equation, or by using a graphing utility.

✓ **Checkpoint**)))   *Audio-video solution in English & Spanish at LarsonPrecalculus.com.*

Write the partial fraction decomposition of

$$\frac{x + 5}{2x^2 - x - 1}.$$

Technology Tip

You can graphically check the decomposition found in Example 6. To do this, use a graphing utility to graph

$$y_1 = \frac{x + 7}{x^2 - x - 6} \quad \text{and}$$

$$y_2 = \frac{2}{x - 3} - \frac{1}{x + 2}$$

in the same viewing window. The graphs should be identical.

The next example shows how to find the partial fraction decomposition for a rational function whose denominator has a repeated linear factor.

EXAMPLE 7   Repeated Linear Factors

Write the partial fraction decomposition of

$$\frac{5x^2 + 20x + 6}{x^3 + 2x^2 + x}.$$

Solution

The expression is proper, so factor the denominator. Because the denominator factors as

$$x^3 + 2x^2 + x = x(x^2 + 2x + 1) = x(x + 1)^2$$

you should include one partial fraction with a constant numerator for each power of x and $(x + 1)$ and write

$$\frac{5x^2 + 20x + 6}{x^3 + 2x^2 + x} = \frac{A}{x} + \frac{B}{x + 1} + \frac{C}{(x + 1)^2}.$$

Multiplying by the LCD $x(x + 1)^2$ leads to the basic equation

$$
\begin{aligned}
5x^2 + 20x + 6 &= A(x + 1)^2 + Bx(x + 1) + Cx && \text{Basic equation}\\
&= Ax^2 + 2Ax + A + Bx^2 + Bx + Cx && \text{Expand.}\\
&= (A + B)x^2 + (2A + B + C)x + A. && \text{Polynomial form}
\end{aligned}
$$

Equating coefficients of like terms on opposite sides of the equation

$$5x^2 + 20x + 6 = (A + B)x^2 + (2A + B + C)x + A$$

produces the following system of linear equations.

$$
\begin{cases}
A + B & = 5 & \text{Equation 1}\\
2A + B + C & = 20 & \text{Equation 2}\\
A & = 6 & \text{Equation 3}
\end{cases}
$$

Substituting 6 for A in Equation 1 yields

$$6 + B = 5$$

$$B = -1.$$

Substituting 6 for A and -1 for B in Equation 2 yields

$$2(6) + (-1) + C = 20$$

$$C = 9.$$

So, the partial fraction decomposition is

$$\frac{5x^2 + 20x + 6}{x^3 + 2x^2 + x} = \frac{6}{x} - \frac{1}{x + 1} + \frac{9}{(x + 1)^2}.$$

Check this result by combining the three partial fractions on the right side of the equation, or by using a graphing utility.

✓ **Checkpoint** ◀))) *Audio-video solution in English & Spanish at LarsonPrecalculus.com.*

Write the partial fraction decomposition of

$$\frac{x + 4}{x^3 + x^2}.$$

Explore the Concept

Partial fraction decomposition is practical only for rational functions whose denominators factor "nicely." For example, the factorization of the expression $x^2 - x - 5$ is

$$\left(x - \frac{1 - \sqrt{21}}{2}\right)\left(x - \frac{1 + \sqrt{21}}{2}\right).$$

Write the basic equation and try to complete the decomposition for

$$\frac{x + 7}{x^2 - x - 5}.$$

What problems do you encounter?

Applications

| EXAMPLE 8 | Vertical Motion |

The height at time t of an object that is moving in a (vertical) line with constant acceleration a is given by the *position equation* $s = \frac{1}{2}at^2 + v_0t + s_0$. The height s is measured in feet, the acceleration a is measured in feet per second squared, t is measured in seconds, v_0 is the initial velocity (in feet per second) at $t = 0$, and s_0 is the initial height (in feet). Find the values of a, v_0, and s_0 when

$$s = 52 \text{ at } t = 1, \quad s = 52 \text{ at } t = 2, \quad \text{and } s = 20 \text{ at } t = 3$$

and interpret the result. (See Figure 7.14.)

Solution

You can obtain three linear equations in a, v_0, and s_0 as follows.

When $t = 1$: $\frac{1}{2}a(1)^2 + v_0(1) + s_0 = 52$ $\Longrightarrow$ $a + 2v_0 + 2s_0 = 104$

When $t = 2$: $\frac{1}{2}a(2)^2 + v_0(2) + s_0 = 52$ $\Longrightarrow$ $2a + 2v_0 + s_0 = 52$

When $t = 3$: $\frac{1}{2}a(3)^2 + v_0(3) + s_0 = 20$ $\Longrightarrow$ $9a + 6v_0 + 2s_0 = 40$

Solving this system yields $a = -32$, $v_0 = 48$, and $s_0 = 20$. This solution results in a position equation of

$$s = -16t^2 + 48t + 20$$

Figure 7.14

and implies that the object was thrown upward at a velocity of 48 feet per second from a height of 20 feet.

✓ **Checkpoint** ◀))) *Audio-video solution in English & Spanish at LarsonPrecalculus.com.*

For the position equation $s = \frac{1}{2}at^2 + v_0t + s_0$ given in Example 8, find the values of a, v_0, and s_0 when $s = 104$ at $t = 1$, $s = 76$ at $t = 2$, and $s = 16$ at $t = 3$, and interpret the result.

| EXAMPLE 9 | Data Analysis: Curve-Fitting |

Find a quadratic equation $y = ax^2 + bx + c$ whose graph passes through the points $(-1, 3)$, $(1, 1)$, and $(2, 6)$.

Solution

Because the graph of $y = ax^2 + bx + c$ passes through the points $(-1, 3)$, $(1, 1)$, and $(2, 6)$, you can write the following.

When $x = -1$, $y = 3$: $a(-1)^2 + b(-1) + c = 3$

When $x = 1$, $y = 1$: $a(1)^2 + b(1) + c = 1$

When $x = 2$, $y = 6$: $a(2)^2 + b(2) + c = 6$

This produces the following system of linear equations.

$$\begin{cases} a - b + c = 3 & \text{Equation 1} \\ a + b + c = 1 & \text{Equation 2} \\ 4a + 2b + c = 6 & \text{Equation 3} \end{cases}$$

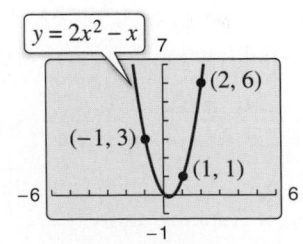

The solution of this system is $a = 2$, $b = -1$, and $c = 0$. So, the equation of the parabola is $y = 2x^2 - x$, and its graph is shown in Figure 7.15.

Figure 7.15

✓ **Checkpoint** ◀))) *Audio-video solution in English & Spanish at LarsonPrecalculus.com.*

Find a quadratic equation $y = ax^2 + bx + c$ whose graph passes through the points $(0, 0)$, $(3, -3)$, and $(6, 0)$.

7.3   Exercises

See *CalcChat.com* for tutorial help and worked-out solutions to odd-numbered exercises.
For instructions on how to use a graphing utility, see Appendix A.

Vocabulary and Concept Check

In Exercises 1–6, fill in the blank.

1. A system of equations that is in _____ form has a "stair-step" pattern with leading coefficients of 1.

2. A solution of a system of three linear equations in three unknowns can be written as an _____ , which has the form (x, y, z).

3. The process used to write a system of equations in row-echelon form is called _____ elimination.

4. A system of equations is called _____ when the number of equations differs from the number of variables in the system.

5. Solutions of equations in three variables can be pictured using a _____ coordinate system.

6. The process of writing a rational expression as the sum of two or more simpler rational expressions is called _____ .

7. Is a consistent system with exactly one solution *independent* or *dependent*?

8. Is a consistent system with infinitely many solutions *independent* or *dependent*?

Procedures and Problem Solving

Checking Solutions In Exercises 9–12, determine whether each ordered triple is a solution of the system of equations.

9. $\begin{cases} 3x - y + z = 1 \\ 2x - 3z = -14 \\ 5y + 2z = 8 \end{cases}$

(a) $(3, 5, -3)$ (b) $(-1, 0, 4)$
(c) $(0, -1, 3)$ (d) $(1, 0, 4)$

10. $\begin{cases} 3x + 4y - z = 17 \\ 5x - y + 2z = -2 \\ 2x - 3y + 7z = -21 \end{cases}$

(a) $(1, 5, 6)$ (b) $(-2, -4, 2)$
(c) $(1, 3, -2)$ (d) $(0, 7, 0)$

11. $\begin{cases} 4x + y - z = 0 \\ -8x - 6y + z = -\frac{7}{4} \\ 3x - y = -\frac{9}{4} \end{cases}$

(a) $(0, 1, 1)$ (b) $\left(-\frac{3}{2}, \frac{5}{4}, -\frac{5}{4}\right)$
(c) $\left(-\frac{1}{2}, \frac{3}{4}, -\frac{5}{4}\right)$ (d) $\left(-\frac{1}{2}, \frac{1}{6}, -\frac{3}{4}\right)$

12. $\begin{cases} -4x - y - 8z = -6 \\ y + z = 0 \\ 4x - 7y = 6 \end{cases}$

(a) $(-2, -2, 2)$ (b) $\left(-\frac{33}{2}, -10, 10\right)$
(c) $\left(\frac{1}{8}, -\frac{1}{2}, \frac{1}{2}\right)$ (d) $\left(-\frac{11}{2}, -4, 4\right)$

Using Back-Substitution In Exercises 13–18, use back-substitution to solve the system of linear equations.

13. $\begin{cases} 2x - y + 5z = 16 \\ y + 2z = 2 \\ z = 2 \end{cases}$

14. $\begin{cases} 4x - 3y - 2z = 21 \\ 6y - 5z = -8 \\ z = -2 \end{cases}$

15. $\begin{cases} 2x + y - 3z = 10 \\ y + z = 12 \\ z = 2 \end{cases}$

16. $\begin{cases} x - y + 2z = 22 \\ 3y - 8z = -9 \\ z = -3 \end{cases}$

17. $\begin{cases} 4x - 2y + z = 8 \\ -y + z = 4 \\ z = 11 \end{cases}$

18. $\begin{cases} 5x - 8z = 22 \\ 3y - 5z = 10 \\ z = -4 \end{cases}$

Performing Row Operations In Exercises 19 and 20, perform the row operation and write the equivalent system. What did the operation accomplish?

19. Add Equation 1 to Equation 2.

$\begin{cases} x - 2y + 3z = 5 & \text{Equation 1} \\ -x + 3y - 5z = 4 & \text{Equation 2} \\ 2x - 3z = 0 & \text{Equation 3} \end{cases}$

20. Add -2 times Equation 1 to Equation 3.

$\begin{cases} x - 2y + 3z = 5 & \text{Equation 1} \\ -x + 3y - 5z = 4 & \text{Equation 2} \\ 2x - 3z = 0 & \text{Equation 3} \end{cases}$

Solving a System of Linear Equations In Exercises 21–42, solve the system of linear equations and check any solution algebraically.

21. $\begin{cases} x + y + z = 6 \\ 2x - y + z = 3 \\ 3x \qquad - z = 0 \end{cases}$ 22. $\begin{cases} x + y + z = 5 \\ x - 2y + 4z = -1 \\ 3y + 4z = -1 \end{cases}$

23. $\begin{cases} 2x \qquad + 2z = 2 \\ 5x + 3y \qquad = 4 \\ 3y - 4z = 4 \end{cases}$ 24. $\begin{cases} 2x + 4y + z = 2 \\ - 2y - 3z = -8 \\ x \qquad - z = -1 \end{cases}$

25. $\begin{cases} 4x + y - 3z = 11 \\ 2x - 3y + 2z = 9 \\ x + y + z = -3 \end{cases}$ 26. $\begin{cases} 5x - 3y + 2z = 3 \\ 2x + 4y - z = 7 \\ x - 11y + 4z = 3 \end{cases}$

27. $\begin{cases} 3x - 2y + 4z = 1 \\ x + y - 2z = 3 \\ 2x - 3y + 6z = 8 \end{cases}$ 28. $\begin{cases} 2x + 4y + z = -4 \\ 2x - 4y + 6z = 13 \\ 4x - 2y + z = 6 \end{cases}$

29. $\begin{cases} 3x + 3y + 5z = 1 \\ 3x + 5y + 9z = 0 \\ 5x + 9y + 17z = 0 \end{cases}$ 30. $\begin{cases} 2x + y + 3z = 1 \\ 2x + 6y + 8z = 3 \\ 6x + 8y + 18z = 5 \end{cases}$

31. $\begin{cases} 3x - 3y + 6z = 6 \\ x + 2y - z = 5 \\ 5x - 8y + 13z = 7 \end{cases}$ 32. $\begin{cases} -x + 3y + z = 4 \\ 4x - 2y - 5z = -7 \\ 2x + 4y - 3z = 12 \end{cases}$

33. $\begin{cases} x - 2y + 3z = 4 \\ 3x - y + 2z = 0 \\ x + 3y - 4z = -2 \end{cases}$ 34. $\begin{cases} x \qquad + 4z = 13 \\ 4x - 2y + z = 7 \\ 2x - 2y - 7z = -19 \end{cases}$

35. $\begin{cases} x + 2y + z = 1 \\ x - 2y + 3z = -3 \\ 2x + y + z = -1 \end{cases}$ 36. $\begin{cases} 3x - 2y - 6z = -4 \\ -3x + 2y + 6z = 1 \\ x - y - 5z = -3 \end{cases}$

37. $\begin{cases} x \qquad + 4z = 1 \\ x + y + 10z = 10 \\ 2x - y + 2z = -5 \end{cases}$ 38. $\begin{cases} x - 2y + z = 2 \\ 2x + 2y - 3z = -4 \\ 5x \qquad + z = 1 \end{cases}$

39. $\begin{cases} x - 2y + 5z = 2 \\ 4x \qquad - z = 0 \end{cases}$ 40. $\begin{cases} 2x - 3y + z = -2 \\ -4x + 9y \qquad = 7 \end{cases}$

41. $\begin{cases} 12x + 5y + z = 0 \\ 23x + 4y - z = 0 \end{cases}$ 42. $\begin{cases} 10x - 3y + 2z = 0 \\ 19x - 5y - z = 0 \end{cases}$

Finding a System In Exercises 43–48, find a system of linear equations that has the given solution. (There are many correct answers.)

43. $(3, -4, 2)$ 44. $(-5, -2, 1)$
45. $\left(-6, -\frac{1}{2}, -\frac{7}{4}\right)$ 46. $\left(-\frac{3}{2}, 4, -7\right)$
47. $(a, a + 4, a)$, where a is a real number
48. $(3a, a, a + 2)$, where a is a real number

Sketching a Plane In Exercises 49–52, sketch the plane represented by the linear equation. Then list four points that lie in the plane.

49. $x + y + z = 8$ 50. $x + 2y + z = 4$
51. $3x + 2y + 2z = 12$ 52. $5x + y + 3z = 15$

Writing the Partial Fraction Decomposition In Exercises 53–60, write the form of the partial fraction decomposition of the rational expression. Do not solve for the constants.

53. $\dfrac{7}{x^2 - 14x}$ 54. $\dfrac{x - 2}{x^2 + 4x + 3}$

55. $\dfrac{12}{x^3 - 10x^2}$ 56. $\dfrac{x^2 - 3x + 2}{4x^3 + 11x^2}$

57. $\dfrac{4x^2 + 3}{(x - 5)^3}$ 58. $\dfrac{6x + 5}{(x + 2)^4}$

59. $\dfrac{x - 1}{x(x^2 + 1)^2}$ 60. $\dfrac{x + 4}{x^2(3x - 1)^2}$

Partial Fraction Decomposition In Exercises 61–74, write the partial fraction decomposition for the rational expression. Check your result algebraically by combining fractions, and check your result graphically by using a graphing utility to graph the rational expression and the partial fractions in the same viewing window.

61. $\dfrac{1}{x^2 + x}$ 62. $\dfrac{1}{4x^2 - 9}$

63. $\dfrac{5 - x}{2x^2 + x - 1}$ 64. $\dfrac{x - 2}{x^2 + 4x + 3}$

65. $\dfrac{x^2 + 12x + 12}{x^3 - 4x}$ 66. $\dfrac{x^2 + 12x - 9}{x^3 - 9x}$

67. $\dfrac{4x^2 + 2x - 1}{x^2(x + 1)}$ 68. $\dfrac{2x - 3}{(x - 1)^2}$

69. $\dfrac{2x^3 - x^2 + x + 5}{x^2 + 3x + 2}$ 70. $\dfrac{x^3 + 2x^2 - x + 1}{x^2 + 3x - 4}$

71. $\dfrac{x^4}{(x - 1)^3}$ 72. $\dfrac{4x^4}{(2x - 1)^3}$

73. $\dfrac{x}{x^3 - x^2 - 2x + 2}$ 74. $\dfrac{2x^2 + x + 8}{x^4 + 8x^2 + 16}$

Writing the Partial Fraction Decomposition In Exercises 75 and 76, write the partial fraction decomposition for the rational function. Identify the graph of the rational function and the graph of each term of its decomposition. State any relationship between the vertical asymptotes of the rational function and the vertical asymptotes of the terms of the decomposition.

75. $y = \dfrac{x - 12}{x(x - 4)}$ 76. $y = \dfrac{2(4x - 3)}{x^2 - 9}$

Vertical Motion   In Exercises 77–80, an object moving vertically is at the given heights at the specified times. Find the position equation $s = \frac{1}{2}at^2 + v_0 t + s_0$ for the object.

77. At $t = 1$ second, $s = 128$ feet.

At $t = 2$ seconds, $s = 80$ feet.

At $t = 3$ seconds, $s = 0$ feet.

78. At $t = 1$ second, $s = 32$ feet.

At $t = 2$ seconds, $s = 32$ feet.

At $t = 3$ seconds, $s = 0$ feet.

79. At $t = 1$ second, $s = 352$ feet.

At $t = 2$ seconds, $s = 272$ feet.

At $t = 3$ seconds, $s = 160$ feet.

80. At $t = 1$ second, $s = 132$ feet.

At $t = 2$ seconds, $s = 100$ feet.

At $t = 3$ seconds, $s = 36$ feet.

Data Analysis: Curve-Fitting   In Exercises 81–84, find the equation of the parabola

$$y = ax^2 + bx + c$$

that passes through the points. To verify your result, use a graphing utility to plot the points and graph the parabola.

81. $(0, 0), (3, 0), (4, 4)$ **82.** $(0, 5), (1, 6), (2, 5)$

83. $(-1, 1), (0, -4), (1, -13)$

84. $(-2, 9), (-1, 0), (1, 6)$

Finding the Equation of a Circle   In Exercises 85–88, find the equation of the circle

$$x^2 + y^2 + Dx + Ey + F = 0$$

that passes through the points. To verify your result, use a graphing utility to plot the points and graph the circle.

85. $(0, 0), (5, 5), (10, 0)$ **86.** $(0, 0), (0, 6), (3, 3)$

87. $(-3, -1), (2, 4), (-6, 8)$

88. $(0, 0), (0, -2), (3, 0)$

89. Finance   A college student borrowed $30,000 to pay for tuition, room, and board. Some of the money was borrowed at 4%, some at 6%, and some at 8%. How much was borrowed at each rate, given that the annual interest was $1550 and the amount borrowed at 8% was three times the amount borrowed at 6%?

90. Finance   A small corporation borrowed $775,000 to expand its software line. Some of the money was borrowed at 8%, some at 9%, and some at 10%. How much was borrowed at each rate, given that the annual interest was $67,500 and the amount borrowed at 8% was four times the amount borrowed at 10%?

Investment Portfolio   In Exercises 91 and 92, consider an investor with a portfolio totaling $500,000 that is invested in certificates of deposit, municipal bonds, blue-chip stocks, and growth or speculative stocks. How much is invested in each type of investment?

91. The certificates of deposit pay 3% annually, and the municipal bonds pay 5% annually. Over a five-year period, the investor expects the blue-chip stocks to return 8% annually and the growth stocks to return 10% annually. The investor wants a combined annual return of 5% and also wants to have only one-fourth of the portfolio invested in stocks.

92. The certificates of deposit pay 2% annually, and the municipal bonds pay 4% annually. Over a five-year period, the investor expects the blue-chip stocks to return 10% annually and the growth stocks to return 14% annually. The investor wants a combined annual return of 6% and also wants to have only one-fourth of the portfolio invested in stocks.

93. Physical Education   In the 2013 Women's NCAA Championship basketball game, the University of Connecticut defeated Louisville University by a score of 93 to 60. Connecticut won by scoring a combination of two-point baskets, three-point baskets, and one-point free throws. The number of two-point baskets was 12 more than the number of free throws. The number of free throws was three less than the number of three-point baskets. What combination of scoring accounted for Connecticut's 93 points?   (Source: NCAA)

94. Why you should learn it   (p. 489) The Augusta National Golf Club in Augusta, Georgia, is an 18-hole course that consists of par-3 holes, par-4 holes, and par-5 holes. A golfer who shoots par has a total of 72 strokes for the entire course. There are two more par-4 holes than twice the number of par-5 holes, and the number of par-3 holes is equal to the number of par-5 holes. Find the numbers of par-3, par-4, and par-5 holes on the course.   (Source: Augusta National, Inc.)

95. Electrical Engineering   When Kirchhoff's Laws are applied to the electrical network in the figure, the currents I_1, I_2, and I_3 (in amperes) are the solution of the system

$$\begin{cases} I_1 - I_2 + I_3 = 0 \\ 3I_1 + 2I_2 \quad\quad = 7. \\ \quad\quad 2I_2 + 4I_3 = 8 \end{cases}$$

Find the currents.

96. Physics A system of pulleys is loaded with 128-pound and 32-pound weights (see figure). The tensions t_1 and t_2 in the ropes and the acceleration a of the 32-pound weight are modeled by the following system, where t_1 and t_2 are measured in pounds and a is in feet per second squared. Solve the system.

$$\begin{cases} t_1 - 2t_2 & = 0 \\ t_1 & -2a = 128 \\ t_2 + a & = 32 \end{cases}$$

32 lb

128 lb

Fitting a Parabola To find the least squares regression parabola $y = ax^2 + bx + c$ for a set of points (x_1, y_1), $(x_2, y_2), \ldots, (x_n, y_n)$ you can solve the following system of linear equations for a, b, and c.

$$\begin{cases} nc + \left(\sum_{i=1}^{n} x_i\right)b + \left(\sum_{i=1}^{n} x_i^2\right)a = \sum_{i=1}^{n} y_i \\ \left(\sum_{i=1}^{n} x_i\right)c + \left(\sum_{i=1}^{n} x_i^2\right)b + \left(\sum_{i=1}^{n} x_i^3\right)a = \sum_{i=1}^{n} x_i y_i \\ \left(\sum_{i=1}^{n} x_i^2\right)c + \left(\sum_{i=1}^{n} x_i^3\right)b + \left(\sum_{i=1}^{n} x_i^4\right)a = \sum_{i=1}^{n} x_i^2 y_i \end{cases}$$

In Exercises 97–100, the sums have been evaluated. Solve the given system for a, b, and c to find the least squares regression parabola for the points. Use a graphing utility to confirm the result.

97. $\begin{cases} 4c & + 40a = 19 \\ 40b & = -12 \\ 40c & + 544a = 160 \end{cases}$

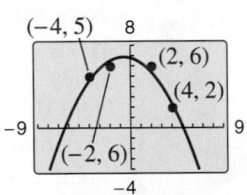

98. $\begin{cases} 5c & + 10a = 8 \\ 10b & = 12 \\ 10c & + 34a = 22 \end{cases}$

99. $\begin{cases} 4c + 9b + 29a = 20 \\ 9c + 29b + 99a = 70 \\ 29c + 99b + 353a = 254 \end{cases}$

100. $\begin{cases} 4c + 6b + 14a = 25 \\ 6c + 14b + 36a = 21 \\ 14c + 36b + 98a = 33 \end{cases}$

101. MODELING DATA

During the testing of a new automobile braking system, the speeds x (in miles per hour) and the stopping distances y (in feet) were recorded in the table.

Speed, x	Stopping distance, y
30	55
40	105
50	188

(a) Use the data to create a system of linear equations. Then find the least squares regression parabola for the data by solving the system.

(b) Use a graphing utility to graph the parabola and the data in the same viewing window.

(c) Use the model to estimate the stopping distance for a speed of 70 miles per hour.

102. MODELING DATA

A wildlife management team studied the reproduction rates of deer in three five-acre tracts of a wildlife preserve. In each tract, the number of females x and the percent of females y that had offspring the following year were recorded. The results are shown in the table.

Number, x	Percent, y
120	68
140	55
160	30

(a) Use the data to create a system of linear equations. Then find the least squares regression parabola for the data by solving the system.

(b) Use a graphing utility to graph the parabola and the data in the same viewing window.

(c) Use the model to predict the percent of females that had offspring when there were 170 females.

103. Environment The predicted cost C (in thousands of dollars) for a company to remove $p\%$ of a chemical from its wastewater is given by the model

$$C = \frac{120p}{10{,}000 - p^2}, \quad 0 \le p < 100.$$

Write the partial fraction decomposition of the rational function. Verify your result by using the *table* feature of a graphing utility to create a table comparing the original function with the partial fractions.

104. Thermodynamics The magnitude of the range R of exhaust temperatures (in degrees Fahrenheit) in an experimental diesel engine is approximated by the model

$$R = \frac{2000(4 - 3x)}{(11 - 7x)(7 - 4x)}, \quad 0 \le x \le 1$$

where x is the relative load (in foot-pounds).

(a) Write the partial fraction decomposition of the rational function.

(b) The decomposition in part (a) is the difference of two fractions. The absolute values of the terms give the expected maximum and minimum temperatures of the exhaust gases. Use a graphing utility to graph each term.

Conclusions

True or False? In Exercises 105 and 106, determine whether the statement is true or false. Justify your answer.

105. The system

$$\begin{cases} x + 4y - 5z = 8 \\ \quad\; 2y + \; z = 5 \\ \qquad\qquad z = 1 \end{cases}$$

is in row-echelon form.

106. If a system of three linear equations is inconsistent, then its graph has no points common to all three equations.

107. Error Analysis You are tutoring a student in algebra. In trying to find a partial fraction decomposition, your student writes the following.

$$\frac{x^2 + 1}{x(x - 1)} = \frac{A}{x} + \frac{B}{x - 1}$$

$$x^2 + 1 = A(x - 1) + Bx \qquad \text{Basic equation}$$

$$x^2 + 1 = (A + B)x - A$$

Your student then forms the following system of linear equations.

$$\begin{cases} \;\; A + B = 0 \\ -A \qquad = 1 \end{cases}$$

Solve the system and check the partial fraction decomposition it yields. Has your student worked the problem correctly? If not, what went wrong?

108. Think About It Find values of a, b, and c (if possible) such that the system of linear equations has (a) a unique solution, (b) no solution, and (c) an infinite number of solutions.

$$\begin{cases} x + y \qquad\;\; = 2 \\ \quad\; y + z = 2 \\ x \qquad + z = 2 \\ ax + by + cz = 0 \end{cases}$$

109. Think About It Are the two systems of equations equivalent? Give reasons for your answer.

$$\begin{cases} x + 3y - \;\; z = 6 \\ 2x - \;\; y + 2z = 1 \\ 3x + 2y - \;\; z = 2 \end{cases} \qquad \begin{cases} x + 3y - \;\; z = \;\;\;\; 6 \\ \quad\; -7y + 4z = \;\;\;\; 1 \\ \quad\; -7y - 4z = -16 \end{cases}$$

110. **HOW DO YOU SEE IT?** The number of sides x and the combined number of sides and diagonals y for each of three regular polygons are shown below. Write a system of linear equations to find an equation of the form $y = ax^2 + bx + c$ that represents the relationship between x and y for the three polygons.

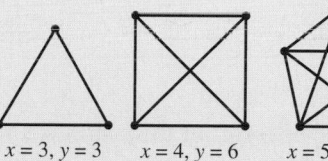

$$x = 3, y = 3 \qquad x = 4, y = 6 \qquad x = 5, y = 10$$

111. Exploration Find a system of equations in three variables that has exactly two equations and no solution.

112. Writing When using Gaussian elimination to solve a system of linear equations, explain how you can recognize that the system has no solution. Give an example that illustrates your answer.

Lagrange Multiplier In Exercises 113 and 114, find values of x, y, and λ that satisfy the system. These systems arise in certain optimization problems in calculus. (λ is called a *Lagrange multiplier*.)

113.
$$\begin{cases} \qquad y + \;\; \lambda = 0 \\ x \qquad + \;\; \lambda = 0 \\ x + y - 10 = 0 \end{cases}$$

114.
$$\begin{cases} 2x \qquad\quad + \lambda = 0 \\ \quad\; 2y + \lambda = 0 \\ \quad\; x + \;\; y - 4 = 0 \end{cases}$$

Cumulative Mixed Review

Finding Zeros In Exercises 115–118, (a) determine the real zeros of f and (b) sketch the graph of f.

115. $f(x) = x^3 + x^2 - 12x$ 　**116.** $f(x) = -8x^4 + 32x^2$

117. $f(x) = 2x^3 + 5x^2 - 21x - 36$

118. $f(x) = 6x^3 - 29x^2 + 6x + 5$

Solving a Trigonometric Equation In Exercises 119 and 120, solve the equation.

119. $4\sqrt{3} \tan \theta - 3 = 1$ 　**120.** $6 \cos x - 2 = 1$

121. *Make a Decision* To work an extended application analyzing the earnings per share for Wal-Mart Stores, Inc. from 1990 through 2012, visit this textbook's website at *LarsonPrecalculus.com*. (Data Source: Wal-Mart Stores, Inc.)

7.4 Matrices and Systems of Equations

Matrices

In this section, you will study a streamlined technique for solving systems of linear equations. This technique involves the use of a rectangular array of real numbers called a **matrix.** The plural of matrix is *matrices.*

Definition of Matrix

If m and n are positive integers, then an $m \times n$ (read "m by n") matrix is a rectangular array

$$
\begin{array}{c}
\quad \text{Column 1} \quad \text{Column 2} \quad \text{Column 3} \quad \cdots \quad \text{Column } n \\
\begin{array}{c}
\text{Row 1} \\
\text{Row 2} \\
\text{Row 3} \\
\vdots \\
\text{Row } m
\end{array}
\begin{bmatrix}
a_{11} & a_{12} & a_{13} & \cdots & a_{1n} \\
a_{21} & a_{22} & a_{23} & \cdots & a_{2n} \\
a_{31} & a_{32} & a_{33} & \cdots & a_{3n} \\
\vdots & \vdots & \vdots & & \vdots \\
a_{m1} & a_{m2} & a_{m3} & \cdots & a_{mn}
\end{bmatrix}
\end{array}
$$

in which each **entry** a_{ij} of the matrix is a real number. An $m \times n$ matrix has m rows and n columns.

The entry in the ith row and jth column of a matrix is denoted by the *double subscript* notation a_{ij}. For instance, the entry a_{23} is the entry in the second row and third column. A matrix having m rows and n columns is said to be of **dimension** $m \times n$. If $m = n$, then the matrix is **square** of dimension $m \times m$ (or $n \times n$). For a square matrix, the entries

$$a_{11}, a_{22}, a_{33}, \ldots$$

are the **main diagonal** entries.

EXAMPLE 1 Dimension of a Matrix

Determine the dimension of each matrix.

a. $\begin{bmatrix} 2 \end{bmatrix}$ **b.** $\begin{bmatrix} 1 & -3 & 0 & \frac{1}{2} \end{bmatrix}$ **c.** $\begin{bmatrix} 0 & 0 \\ 0 & 0 \end{bmatrix}$ **d.** $\begin{bmatrix} 5 & 0 \\ 2 & -2 \\ -7 & 4 \end{bmatrix}$ **e.** $\begin{bmatrix} -2 \\ 0 \\ 1 \end{bmatrix}$

Solution

a. This matrix has *one* row and *one* column. The dimension of the matrix is 1×1.

b. This matrix has *one* row and *four* columns. The dimension of the matrix is 1×4.

c. This matrix has *two* rows and *two* columns. The dimension of the matrix is 2×2.

d. This matrix has *three* rows and *two* columns. The dimension of the matrix is 3×2.

e. This matrix has *three* rows and *one* column. The dimension of the matrix is 3×1.

✓ **Checkpoint** ◀))) Audio-video solution in English & Spanish at LarsonPrecalculus.com.

Determine the dimension of the matrix $\begin{bmatrix} 14 & 7 & 10 \\ -2 & -3 & -8 \end{bmatrix}$. ■

A matrix that has only one row [such as the matrix in Example 1(b)] is called a **row matrix,** and a matrix that has only one column [such as the matrix in Example 1(e)] is called a **column matrix.**

What you should learn

▶ Write matrices and identify their dimensions.
▶ Perform elementary row operations on matrices.
▶ Use matrices and Gaussian elimination to solve systems of linear equations.
▶ Use matrices and Gauss-Jordan elimination to solve systems of linear equations.

Why you should learn it

Matrices can be used to solve systems of linear equations in two or more variables. For instance, Exercise 95 on page 516 shows how a matrix can be used to help model an equation for the average annual consumer costs for health insurance.

Physician

A matrix derived from a system of linear equations (each written in standard form with the constant term on the right) is the **augmented matrix** of the system. Moreover, the matrix derived from the coefficients of the system (but not including the constant terms) is the **coefficient matrix** of the system.

System:
$$\begin{cases} x - 4y + 3z = 5 \\ -x + 3y - z = -3 \\ 2x \qquad - 4z = 6 \end{cases}$$

Augmented Matrix:
$$\begin{bmatrix} 1 & -4 & 3 & \vdots & 5 \\ -1 & 3 & -1 & \vdots & -3 \\ 2 & 0 & -4 & \vdots & 6 \end{bmatrix}$$

Coefficient Matrix:
$$\begin{bmatrix} 1 & -4 & 3 \\ -1 & 3 & -1 \\ 2 & 0 & -4 \end{bmatrix}$$

> **Remark**
>
> The optional dotted line in the augmented matrix helps to separate the coefficients of the linear system from the constant terms.

Note the use of 0 for the missing coefficient of the y-variable in the third equation, and also note the fourth column (of constant terms) in the augmented matrix.

When forming either the coefficient matrix or the augmented matrix of a system, you should begin by vertically aligning the variables in the equations and using 0's for any missing coefficients of variables.

EXAMPLE 2   Writing an Augmented Matrix

Write the augmented matrix for the system of linear equations. What is the dimension of the augmented matrix?

$$\begin{cases} x + 3y = 9 \\ -y + 4z = -2 \\ x - 5z = 0 \end{cases}$$

Solution

Begin by writing the linear system and aligning the variables.

$$\begin{cases} x + 3y \qquad = 9 \\ \qquad -y + 4z = -2 \\ x \qquad - 5z = 0 \end{cases}$$

Next, use the coefficients and constant terms as the matrix entries. Include zeros for the coefficients of the missing variables.

$$\begin{matrix} R_1 \\ R_2 \\ R_3 \end{matrix} \begin{bmatrix} 1 & 3 & 0 & \vdots & 9 \\ 0 & -1 & 4 & \vdots & -2 \\ 1 & 0 & -5 & \vdots & 0 \end{bmatrix}$$

The augmented matrix has three rows and four columns, so it is a 3×4 matrix. The notation R_n is used to designate each row in the matrix. For instance, Row 1 is represented by R_1.

✓ **Checkpoint** �))) *Audio-video solution in English & Spanish at LarsonPrecalculus.com.*

Write the augmented matrix for the system of linear equations. What is the dimension of the augmented matrix?

$$\begin{cases} x + y + z = 2 \\ 2x - y + 3z = -1 \\ -x + 2y - z = 4 \end{cases}$$

Elementary Row Operations

In Section 7.3, you studied three operations that can be used on a system of linear equations to produce an equivalent system. Recall that the operations are (1) interchanging any two equations, (2) multiplying one of the equations by a nonzero constant, and (3) adding a multiple of one equation to another equation.

In matrix terminology, these three operations correspond to **elementary row operations.** An elementary row operation on an augmented matrix of a given system of linear equations produces a new augmented matrix corresponding to a new (but equivalent) system of linear equations. Two matrices are **row-equivalent** when one can be obtained from the other by a sequence of elementary row operations.

Elementary Row Operations for Matrices

   1. Interchange two rows.

   2. Multiply one of the rows by a nonzero constant.

   3. Add a multiple of one row to another row.

Although elementary row operations are simple to perform, they involve a lot of arithmetic. Because it is easy to make a mistake, you should get in the habit of noting the elementary row operations performed in each step so that you can go back and check your work. Example 3 demonstrates the elementary row operations described above.

EXAMPLE 3   Elementary Row Operations

a. Interchange the first and second rows of the original matrix.

Original Matrix

$$\begin{bmatrix} 0 & 1 & 3 & 4 \\ -1 & 2 & 0 & 3 \\ 2 & -3 & 4 & 1 \end{bmatrix}$$

New Row-Equivalent Matrix

$$\begin{matrix} R_2 \\ R_1 \end{matrix} \begin{bmatrix} -1 & 2 & 0 & 3 \\ 0 & 1 & 3 & 4 \\ 2 & -3 & 4 & 1 \end{bmatrix}$$

b. Multiply the first row of the original matrix by $\frac{1}{2}$.

Original Matrix

$$\begin{bmatrix} 2 & -4 & 6 & -2 \\ 1 & 3 & -3 & 0 \\ 5 & -2 & 1 & 2 \end{bmatrix}$$

New Row-Equivalent Matrix

$$\frac{1}{2}R_1 \rightarrow \begin{bmatrix} 1 & -2 & 3 & -1 \\ 1 & 3 & -3 & 0 \\ 5 & -2 & 1 & 2 \end{bmatrix}$$

c. Add -2 times the first row of the original matrix to the third row.

Original Matrix

$$\begin{bmatrix} 1 & 2 & -4 & 3 \\ 0 & 3 & -2 & -1 \\ 2 & 1 & 5 & -2 \end{bmatrix}$$

New Row-Equivalent Matrix

$$\begin{matrix} \\ \\ -2R_1 + R_3 \rightarrow \end{matrix} \begin{bmatrix} 1 & 2 & -4 & 3 \\ 0 & 3 & -2 & -1 \\ 0 & -3 & 13 & -8 \end{bmatrix}$$

Note that the elementary row operation is written beside the row that is *changed*.

✓ **Checkpoint** 🔊)) *Audio-video solution in English & Spanish at LarsonPrecalculus.com.*

Fill in the blank using an elementary row operation to form a row-equivalent matrix.

$$\begin{bmatrix} 1 & 2 & 3 \\ 3 & 12 & 5 \end{bmatrix} \qquad \begin{bmatrix} 1 & 2 & 3 \\ 0 & & -4 \end{bmatrix}$$

Technology Tip

Most graphing utilities can perform elementary row operations on matrices. For instructions on how to use the *matrix* feature and the elementary row operations features of a graphing utility, see Appendix A; for specific keystrokes, go to this textbook's *Companion Website*.

Gaussian Elimination with Back-Substitution

In Example 2 of Section 7.3, you used Gaussian elimination with back-substitution to solve a system of linear equations. The next example demonstrates the matrix version of Gaussian elimination. The basic difference between the two methods is that with matrices you do not need to keep writing the variables.

EXAMPLE 4   Comparing Linear Systems and Matrix Operations

Linear System   *Associated Augmented Matrix*

$$\begin{cases} x - 2y + 3z = 9 \\ -x + 3y + z = -2 \\ 2x - 5y + 5z = 17 \end{cases}$$
$$\left[\begin{array}{ccc:c} 1 & -2 & 3 & 9 \\ -1 & 3 & 1 & -2 \\ 2 & -5 & 5 & 17 \end{array}\right]$$

Add the first equation to the second equation.

Add the first row to the second row: $R_1 + R_2$.

$$\begin{cases} x - 2y + 3z = 9 \\ y + 4z = 7 \\ 2x - 5y + 5z = 17 \end{cases}$$
$$R_1 + R_2 \rightarrow \left[\begin{array}{ccc:c} 1 & -2 & 3 & 9 \\ 0 & 1 & 4 & 7 \\ 2 & -5 & 5 & 17 \end{array}\right]$$

Add -2 times the first equation to the third equation.

Add -2 times the first row to the third row: $-2R_1 + R_3$.

$$\begin{cases} x - 2y + 3z = 9 \\ y + 4z = 7 \\ -y - z = -1 \end{cases}$$
$$-2R_1 + R_3 \rightarrow \left[\begin{array}{ccc:c} 1 & -2 & 3 & 9 \\ 0 & 1 & 4 & 7 \\ 0 & -1 & -1 & -1 \end{array}\right]$$

Add the second equation to the third equation.

Add the second row to the third row: $R_2 + R_3$.

$$\begin{cases} x - 2y + 3z = 9 \\ y + 4z = 7 \\ 3z = 6 \end{cases}$$
$$R_2 + R_3 \rightarrow \left[\begin{array}{ccc:c} 1 & -2 & 3 & 9 \\ 0 & 1 & 4 & 7 \\ 0 & 0 & 3 & 6 \end{array}\right]$$

Multiply the third equation by $\frac{1}{3}$.

Multiply the third row by $\frac{1}{3}$: $\frac{1}{3}R_3$.

$$\begin{cases} x - 2y + 3z = 9 \\ y + 4z = 7 \\ z = 2 \end{cases}$$
$$\tfrac{1}{3}R_3 \rightarrow \left[\begin{array}{ccc:c} 1 & -2 & 3 & 9 \\ 0 & 1 & 4 & 7 \\ 0 & 0 & 1 & 2 \end{array}\right]$$

At this point, you can use back-substitution to find x and y.

$$y + 4(2) = 7 \qquad \text{Substitute 2 for } z.$$
$$y = -1 \qquad \text{Solve for } y.$$
$$x - 2(-1) + 3(2) = 9 \qquad \text{Substitute } -1 \text{ for } y \text{ and 2 for } z.$$
$$x = 1 \qquad \text{Solve for } x.$$

The solution is $x = 1$, $y = -1$, and $z = 2$.

✓ **Checkpoint** 🔊)) *Audio-video solution in English & Spanish at LarsonPrecalculus.com.*

Compare solving the linear system to solving it using its associated augmented matrix.

$$\begin{cases} 2x + y - z = -3 \\ 4x - 2y + 2z = -2 \\ -6x + 5y + 4z = 10 \end{cases}$$

> **Remark**
>
> Remember that you should check a solution by substituting the values of x, y, and z into each equation of the original system. For instance, you can check the solution to Example 4 as shown.
>
> Equation 1:
> $1 - 2(-1) + 3(2) = 9$ ✓
>
> Equation 2:
> $-1 + 3(-1) + 2 = -2$ ✓
>
> Equation 3:
> $2(1) - 5(-1) + 5(2) = 17$ ✓

The last matrix in Example 4 is in **row-echelon form.** The term *echelon* refers to the stair-step pattern formed by the nonzero elements of the matrix. To be in this form, a matrix must have the following properties.

Row-Echelon Form and Reduced Row-Echelon Form

A matrix in **row-echelon form** has the following properties.

1. Any rows consisting entirely of zeros occur at the bottom of the matrix.

2. For each row that does not consist entirely of zeros, the first nonzero entry is 1 (called a **leading 1**).

3. For two successive (nonzero) rows, the leading 1 in the higher row is farther to the left than the leading 1 in the lower row.

A matrix in *row-echelon form* is in **reduced row-echelon form** when every column that has a leading 1 has zeros in every position above and below its leading 1.

It is worth mentioning that the row-echelon form of a matrix is not unique. That is, two different sequences of elementary row operations may yield different row-echelon forms. The *reduced* row-echelon form of a given matrix, however, is unique.

Technology Tip

Some graphing utilities can automatically transform a matrix to row-echelon form and reduced row-echelon form. For instructions on how to use the *row-echelon form* feature and the *reduced row-echelon form* feature of a graphing utility, see Appendix A; for specific keystrokes, go to this textbook's *Companion Website.*

EXAMPLE 5   Row-Echelon Form

Determine whether each matrix is in row-echelon form. If it is, determine whether the matrix is in reduced row-echelon form.

a. $\begin{bmatrix} 1 & 2 & -1 & 4 \\ 0 & 1 & 0 & 3 \\ 0 & 0 & 1 & -2 \end{bmatrix}$
  b. $\begin{bmatrix} 1 & 2 & -1 & 2 \\ 0 & 0 & 0 & 0 \\ 0 & 1 & 2 & -4 \end{bmatrix}$

c. $\begin{bmatrix} 1 & -5 & 2 & -1 & 3 \\ 0 & 0 & 1 & 3 & -2 \\ 0 & 0 & 0 & 1 & 4 \\ 0 & 0 & 0 & 0 & 1 \end{bmatrix}$
  d. $\begin{bmatrix} 1 & 0 & 0 & -1 \\ 0 & 1 & 0 & 2 \\ 0 & 0 & 1 & 3 \\ 0 & 0 & 0 & 0 \end{bmatrix}$

e. $\begin{bmatrix} 1 & 2 & -3 & 4 \\ 0 & 2 & 1 & -1 \\ 0 & 0 & 1 & -3 \end{bmatrix}$
  f. $\begin{bmatrix} 0 & 1 & 0 & 5 \\ 0 & 0 & 1 & 3 \\ 0 & 0 & 0 & 0 \end{bmatrix}$

Solution

The matrices in (a), (c), (d), and (f) are in row-echelon form. The matrices in (d) and (f) are in *reduced* row-echelon form because every column that has a leading 1 has zeros in every position above and below its leading 1. The matrix in (b) is not in row-echelon form because the row of all zeros does not occur at the bottom of the matrix. The matrix in (e) is not in row-echelon form because the first nonzero entry in Row 2 is not a leading 1.

✔ **Checkpoint** Audio-video solution in English & Spanish at LarsonPrecalculus.com.

Determine whether the matrix is in row-echelon form. If it is, determine whether it is in reduced row-echelon form.
$\begin{bmatrix} 1 & 0 & -2 & 4 \\ 0 & 1 & 11 & 3 \\ 0 & 0 & 0 & 0 \end{bmatrix}$ ■

Every matrix is row-equivalent to a matrix in row-echelon form. For instance, in Example 5, you can change the matrix in part (e) to row-echelon form by multiplying its second row by $\frac{1}{2}$.

Gaussian elimination with back-substitution works well for solving systems of linear equations by hand or with a computer. For this algorithm, the order in which the elementary row operations are performed is important. You should operate *from left to right by columns*, using elementary row operations to obtain zeros in all entries directly below the leading 1's.

EXAMPLE 6   Gaussian Elimination with Back-Substitution

Solve the system of equations.

$$\begin{cases} y + z - 2w = -3 \\ x + 2y - z = 2 \\ 2x + 4y + z - 3w = -2 \\ x - 4y - 7z - w = -19 \end{cases}$$

Solution

$$\begin{bmatrix} 0 & 1 & 1 & -2 & \vdots & -3 \\ 1 & 2 & -1 & 0 & \vdots & 2 \\ 2 & 4 & 1 & -3 & \vdots & -2 \\ 1 & -4 & -7 & -1 & \vdots & -19 \end{bmatrix}$$ Write augmented matrix.

$$\begin{matrix} R_2 \\ R_1 \end{matrix} \begin{bmatrix} 1 & 2 & -1 & 0 & \vdots & 2 \\ 0 & 1 & 1 & -2 & \vdots & -3 \\ 2 & 4 & 1 & -3 & \vdots & -2 \\ 1 & -4 & -7 & -1 & \vdots & -19 \end{bmatrix}$$ Interchange R_1 and R_2 so first column has leading 1 in upper left corner.

$$\begin{matrix} \\ \\ -2R_1 + R_3 \to \\ -R_1 + R_4 \to \end{matrix} \begin{bmatrix} 1 & 2 & -1 & 0 & \vdots & 2 \\ 0 & 1 & 1 & -2 & \vdots & -3 \\ 0 & 0 & 3 & -3 & \vdots & -6 \\ 0 & -6 & -6 & -1 & \vdots & -21 \end{bmatrix}$$ Perform operations on R_3 and R_4 so first column has zeros below its leading 1.

$$\begin{matrix} \\ \\ \\ 6R_2 + R_4 \to \end{matrix} \begin{bmatrix} 1 & 2 & -1 & 0 & \vdots & 2 \\ 0 & 1 & 1 & -2 & \vdots & -3 \\ 0 & 0 & 3 & -3 & \vdots & -6 \\ 0 & 0 & 0 & -13 & \vdots & -39 \end{bmatrix}$$ Perform operations on R_4 so second column has zeros below its leading 1.

$$\begin{matrix} \\ \\ \frac{1}{3}R_3 \to \\ -\frac{1}{13}R_4 \to \end{matrix} \begin{bmatrix} 1 & 2 & -1 & 0 & \vdots & 2 \\ 0 & 1 & 1 & -2 & \vdots & -3 \\ 0 & 0 & 1 & -1 & \vdots & -2 \\ 0 & 0 & 0 & 1 & \vdots & 3 \end{bmatrix}$$ Perform operations on R_3 and R_4 so third and fourth columns have leading 1's.

The matrix is now in row-echelon form, and the corresponding system is

$$\begin{cases} x + 2y - z = 2 \\ y + z - 2w = -3 \\ z - w = -2 \\ w = 3 \end{cases}.$$

Using back-substitution, you can determine that the solution is

$$x = -1, \quad y = 2, \quad z = 1, \quad \text{and} \quad w = 3.$$

✓ *Checkpoint* 🔊 *Audio-video solution in English & Spanish at LarsonPrecalculus.com.*

Solve the system of equations.

$$\begin{cases} -3x + 5y + 3z = -19 \\ 3x + 4y + 4z = 8 \\ 4x - 8y - 6z = 26 \end{cases}$$

The following steps summarize the procedure used in Example 6.

> **Gaussian Elimination with Back-Substitution**
>
> **1.** Write the augmented matrix of the system of linear equations.
>
> **2.** Use elementary row operations to rewrite the augmented matrix in row-echelon form.
>
> **3.** Write the system of linear equations corresponding to the matrix in row-echelon form and use back-substitution to find the solution.

Remember that it is possible for a system to have no solution. If, in the elimination process, you obtain a row with zeros except for the last entry, then you can conclude that the system is inconsistent.

EXAMPLE 7   A System with No Solution

Solve the system of equations.

$$\begin{cases} x - y + 2z = 4 \\ x \quad\;\; + z = 6 \\ 2x - 3y + 5z = 4 \\ 3x + 2y - z = 1 \end{cases}$$

Solution

$$\begin{bmatrix} 1 & -1 & 2 & \vdots & 4 \\ 1 & 0 & 1 & \vdots & 6 \\ 2 & -3 & 5 & \vdots & 4 \\ 3 & 2 & -1 & \vdots & 1 \end{bmatrix}$$ Write augmented matrix.

$$\begin{matrix} \\ -R_1 + R_2 \to \\ -2R_1 + R_3 \to \\ -3R_1 + R_4 \to \end{matrix} \begin{bmatrix} 1 & -1 & 2 & \vdots & 4 \\ 0 & 1 & -1 & \vdots & 2 \\ 0 & -1 & 1 & \vdots & -4 \\ 0 & 5 & -7 & \vdots & -11 \end{bmatrix}$$ Perform row operations.

$$\begin{matrix} \\ \\ R_2 + R_3 \to \\ \\ \end{matrix} \begin{bmatrix} 1 & -1 & 2 & \vdots & 4 \\ 0 & 1 & -1 & \vdots & 2 \\ 0 & 0 & 0 & \vdots & -2 \\ 0 & 5 & -7 & \vdots & -11 \end{bmatrix}$$ Perform row operations.

Note that the third row of this matrix consists of zeros except for the last entry. This means that the original system of linear equations is *inconsistent*. You can see why this is true by converting back to a system of linear equations. Because the third equation is not possible, the system has no solution.

$$\begin{cases} x - y + 2z = \quad 4 \\ y - z = \quad 2 \\ 0 = -2 \\ 5y - 7z = -11 \end{cases}$$

✓ **Checkpoint** Audio-video solution in English & Spanish at LarsonPrecalculus.com.

Solve the system of equations.

$$\begin{cases} x + y + z = 1 \\ x + 2y + 2z = 2 \\ x - y - z = 1 \end{cases}$$

Gauss–Jordan Elimination

With Gaussian elimination, elementary row operations are applied to a matrix to obtain a (row-equivalent) row-echelon form of the matrix. A second method of elimination, called **Gauss-Jordan elimination** after Carl Friedrich Gauss (1777–1855) and Wilhelm Jordan (1842–1899), continues the reduction process until a *reduced* row-echelon form is obtained. This procedure is demonstrated in Example 8.

EXAMPLE 8   Gauss–Jordan Elimination

See LarsonPrecalculus.com for an interactive version of this type of example.

Use Gauss-Jordan elimination to solve the system.

$$\begin{cases} x - 2y + 3z = 9 \\ -x + 3y + z = -2 \\ 2x - 5y + 5z - 17 \end{cases}$$

Solution

In Example 4, Gaussian elimination was used to obtain the row-echelon form

$$\begin{bmatrix} 1 & -2 & 3 & \vdots & 9 \\ 0 & 1 & 4 & \vdots & 7 \\ 0 & 0 & 1 & \vdots & 2 \end{bmatrix}.$$

Now, rather than using back-substitution, apply additional elementary row operations until you obtain a matrix in *reduced* row-echelon form. To do this, you must produce zeros above each of the leading 1's, as follows.

$$2R_2 + R_1 \rightarrow \begin{bmatrix} 1 & 0 & 11 & \vdots & 23 \\ 0 & 1 & 4 & \vdots & 7 \\ 0 & 0 & 1 & \vdots & 2 \end{bmatrix}$$

Perform operations on R_1 so second column has a zero above its leading 1.

$$\begin{matrix} -11R_3 + R_1 \rightarrow \\ -4R_3 + R_2 \rightarrow \end{matrix} \begin{bmatrix} 1 & 0 & 0 & \vdots & 1 \\ 0 & 1 & 0 & \vdots & -1 \\ 0 & 0 & 1 & \vdots & 2 \end{bmatrix}$$

Perform operations on R_1 and R_2 so third column has zeros above its leading 1.

The matrix is now in reduced row-echelon form. Converting back to a system of linear equations, you have

$$\begin{cases} x = 1 \\ y = -1. \\ z = 2 \end{cases}$$

Now you can simply read the solution, $x = 1$, $y = -1$, and $z = 2$, which can be written as the ordered triple $(1, -1, 2)$. You can check this result using the *reduced row-echelon form* feature of a graphing utility, as shown in Figure 7.16.

 ✓ **Checkpoint**))) *Audio-video solution in English & Spanish at LarsonPrecalculus.com.*

Use Gauss-Jordan elimination to solve the system.

$$\begin{cases} -3x + 7y + 2z = 1 \\ -5x + 3y - 5z = -8 \\ 2x - 2y - 3z = 15 \end{cases}$$

In Example 8, note that the solution is the same as the one obtained using Gaussian elimination in Example 4. The advantage of Gauss-Jordan elimination is that, from the reduced row-echelon form, you can simply read the solution without the need for back-substitution.

Technology Tip

For a demonstration of a graphical approach to Gauss-Jordan elimination on a 2 × 3 matrix, see the Visualizing Row Operations Program, available for several models of graphing calculators at this textbook's *Companion Website*.

```
prgmROWOPS
ENTER A
2 BY 3 MATRIX:
A B C
D E F
A=?1
B=?4
C=?
```

```
rref(LAJ)
       [[1 0 0 1 ]
        [0 1 0 -1]
        [0 0 1 2 ]]
```

Figure 7.16

The elimination procedures described in this section employ an algorithmic approach that is easily adapted to computer programs. However, the procedure makes no effort to avoid fractional coefficients. For instance, in the elimination procedure for the system

$$\begin{cases} 2x - 5y + 5z = 17 \\ 3x - 2y + 3z = 11 \\ -3x + 3y \quad\;\; = -6 \end{cases}$$

you may be inclined to multiply the first row by $\frac{1}{2}$ to produce a leading 1, which will result in working with fractional coefficients. For hand computations, you can sometimes avoid fractions by judiciously choosing the order in which you apply elementary row operations.

EXAMPLE 9   A System with an Infinite Number of Solutions

Solve the system.

$$\begin{cases} 2x + 4y - 2z = 0 \\ 3x + 5y \quad\;\; = 1 \end{cases}$$

Solution

$$\begin{bmatrix} 2 & 4 & -2 & \vdots & 0 \\ 3 & 5 & 0 & \vdots & 1 \end{bmatrix}$$

$$\tfrac{1}{2}R_1 \rightarrow \begin{bmatrix} 1 & 2 & -1 & \vdots & 0 \\ 3 & 5 & 0 & \vdots & 1 \end{bmatrix}$$

$$-3R_1 + R_2 \rightarrow \begin{bmatrix} 1 & 2 & -1 & \vdots & 0 \\ 0 & -1 & 3 & \vdots & 1 \end{bmatrix}$$

$$-R_2 \rightarrow \begin{bmatrix} 1 & 2 & -1 & \vdots & 0 \\ 0 & 1 & -3 & \vdots & -1 \end{bmatrix}$$

$$-2R_2 + R_1 \rightarrow \begin{bmatrix} 1 & 0 & 5 & \vdots & 2 \\ 0 & 1 & -3 & \vdots & -1 \end{bmatrix}$$

The corresponding system of equations is

$$\begin{cases} x + 5z = \quad 2 \\ y - 3z = -1 \end{cases}.$$

Solving for x and y in terms of z, you have

$$x = -5z + 2 \quad \text{and} \quad y = 3z - 1.$$

To write a solution of the system that does not use any of the three variables of the system, let a represent any real number and let $z = a$. Now substitute a for z in the equations for x and y.

$$x = -5z + 2 = -5a + 2 \quad \text{and} \quad y = 3z - 1 = 3a - 1$$

So, the solution set has the form $(-5a + 2, 3a - 1, a)$. Recall from Section 7.3 that a solution set of this form represents an infinite number of solutions. Try substituting values for a to obtain a few solutions. Then check each solution in the original system of equations.

✓ **Checkpoint** Audio-video solution in English & Spanish at LarsonPrecalculus.com.

Solve the system.

$$\begin{cases} 2x - 6y + 6z = 46 \\ 2x - 3y \quad\;\; = 31 \end{cases}$$

7.4   Exercises

See *CalcChat.com* for tutorial help and worked-out solutions to odd-numbered exercises.
For instructions on how to use a graphing utility, see Appendix A.

Vocabulary and Concept Check

In Exercises 1–3, fill in the blank.

1. A rectangular array of real numbers that can be used to solve a system of linear equations is called a _____ .

2. A matrix in row-echelon form is in _____ when every column that has a leading 1 has zeros in every position above and below its leading 1.

3. The process of using row operations to write a matrix in reduced row-echelon form is called _____ .

In Exercises 4–6, refer to the system of linear equations $\begin{cases} -2x + 3y = 5 \\ 6x + 7y = 4 \end{cases}$.

4. Is the coefficient matrix for the system a *square* matrix?

5. Is the augmented matrix for the system of dimension 3×2?

6. Is the augmented matrix row-equivalent to its reduced row-echelon form?

Procedures and Problem Solving

Dimension of a Matrix   In Exercises 7–12, determine the dimension of the matrix.

7. $\begin{bmatrix} 7 & 0 \end{bmatrix}$

8. $\begin{bmatrix} 3 & -1 & 2 & 6 \end{bmatrix}$

9. $\begin{bmatrix} 4 \\ 32 \\ 3 \end{bmatrix}$

10. $\begin{bmatrix} 5 & 4 & 2 \\ 3 & -5 & 1 \\ 7 & -2 & 9 \end{bmatrix}$

11. $\begin{bmatrix} 33 & 45 \\ -9 & 20 \end{bmatrix}$

12. $\begin{bmatrix} 3 & -1 & 6 & 4 \\ -2 & 5 & 7 & 7 \end{bmatrix}$

Writing an Augmented Matrix   In Exercises 13–18, write the augmented matrix for the system of linear equations. What is the dimension of the augmented matrix?

13. $\begin{cases} 4x - 3y = -5 \\ -x + 3y = 12 \end{cases}$

14. $\begin{cases} 7x + 4y = 22 \\ 5x - 9y = 15 \end{cases}$

15. $\begin{cases} x + 10y - 2z = 2 \\ 5x - 3y + 4z = 0 \\ 2x + y = 6 \end{cases}$

16. $\begin{cases} x - 3y + z = 1 \\ 4y = 0 \\ 7z = -5 \end{cases}$

17. $\begin{cases} 7x - 5y + z = 13 \\ 19x - 8z = 10 \end{cases}$

18. $\begin{cases} 9x + 2y - 3z = 20 \\ -25y + 11z = -5 \end{cases}$

Writing a System of Equations   In Exercises 19–22, write the system of linear equations represented by the augmented matrix. (Use the variables x, y, z, and w, if applicable.)

19. $\begin{bmatrix} 3 & 4 & \vdots & 0 \\ 1 & -1 & \vdots & 7 \end{bmatrix}$

20. $\begin{bmatrix} 7 & -5 & \vdots & 2 \\ 8 & 0 & \vdots & -2 \end{bmatrix}$

21. $\begin{bmatrix} 0 & 12 & 3 & \vdots & 0 \\ -2 & 18 & 0 & \vdots & 10 \\ 1 & 7 & -8 & \vdots & 43 \end{bmatrix}$

22. $\begin{bmatrix} 6 & 2 & -1 & -5 & \vdots & -25 \\ -1 & 0 & 7 & 3 & \vdots & 7 \\ 4 & -1 & -10 & 6 & \vdots & 23 \\ 0 & 8 & 1 & 11 & \vdots & -21 \end{bmatrix}$

Identifying an Elementary Row Operation   In Exercises 23–26, identify the elementary row operation performed to obtain the new row-equivalent matrix.

	Original Matrix	*New Row-Equivalent Matrix*

23. $\begin{bmatrix} -4 & 8 & -20 \\ -2 & 6 & 7 \end{bmatrix}$ $\begin{bmatrix} 1 & -2 & 5 \\ -2 & 6 & 7 \end{bmatrix}$

24. $\begin{bmatrix} -3 & 6 & 0 \\ 5 & 2 & -2 \end{bmatrix}$ $\begin{bmatrix} -18 & 0 & 6 \\ 5 & 2 & -2 \end{bmatrix}$

25. $\begin{bmatrix} -1 & -2 & 3 & -2 \\ 2 & -5 & 1 & -7 \\ 5 & 4 & -7 & 6 \end{bmatrix}$ $\begin{bmatrix} -1 & -2 & 3 & -2 \\ 2 & -5 & 1 & -7 \\ 0 & -6 & 8 & -4 \end{bmatrix}$

26. $\begin{bmatrix} 0 & -1 & -5 & 5 \\ -1 & 3 & -7 & 6 \\ 4 & -5 & 1 & 3 \end{bmatrix}$ $\begin{bmatrix} -1 & 3 & -7 & 6 \\ 0 & -1 & -5 & 5 \\ 4 & -5 & 1 & 3 \end{bmatrix}$

Elementary Row Operations   In Exercises 27–30, fill in the blank(s) using elementary row operations to form a row-equivalent matrix.

27. $\begin{bmatrix} 1 & 4 & 3 \\ 2 & 10 & 5 \end{bmatrix}$

$\begin{bmatrix} 1 & 4 & 3 \\ 0 & & -1 \end{bmatrix}$

28. $\begin{bmatrix} 3 & 6 & 8 \\ 4 & -3 & 6 \end{bmatrix}$

$\begin{bmatrix} 1 & & \frac{8}{3} \\ 4 & -3 & 6 \end{bmatrix}$

29. $\begin{bmatrix} 1 & 1 & 4 & -1 \\ 3 & 8 & 10 & 3 \\ -2 & 1 & 12 & 6 \end{bmatrix}$ **30.** $\begin{bmatrix} 2 & 4 & 8 & 3 \\ 1 & -1 & -3 & 2 \\ 2 & 6 & 4 & 9 \end{bmatrix}$

$\begin{bmatrix} 1 & 1 & 4 & -1 \\ 0 & 5 & \blacksquare & \blacksquare \\ 0 & 3 & \blacksquare & \blacksquare \end{bmatrix}$ $\begin{bmatrix} 1 & -1 & -3 & 2 \\ 2 & \blacksquare & \blacksquare & \blacksquare \\ 2 & 6 & 4 & 9 \end{bmatrix}$

$\begin{bmatrix} 1 & 1 & 4 & -1 \\ 0 & 1 & \blacksquare & \blacksquare \\ 0 & 3 & \blacksquare & \blacksquare \end{bmatrix}$ $\begin{bmatrix} 1 & -1 & -3 & 2 \\ 0 & 6 & \blacksquare & \blacksquare \\ 0 & 8 & \blacksquare & \blacksquare \end{bmatrix}$

Comparing Linear Systems and Matrix Operations In Exercises 31 and 32, (a) perform the row operations to solve the augmented matrix, (b) write and solve the system of linear equations represented by the augmented matrix, and (c) compare the two solution methods. Which do you prefer?

31. $\begin{bmatrix} -3 & 4 & \vdots & 22 \\ 6 & -4 & \vdots & -28 \end{bmatrix}$

(i) Add R_2 to R_1.

(ii) Add -2 times R_1 to R_2.

(iii) Multiply R_2 by $-\frac{1}{4}$.

(iv) Multiply R_1 by $\frac{1}{3}$.

32. $\begin{bmatrix} 7 & 13 & 1 & \vdots & -4 \\ -3 & -5 & -1 & \vdots & -4 \\ 3 & 6 & 1 & \vdots & -2 \end{bmatrix}$

(i) Add R_2 to R_1.

(ii) Multiply R_1 by $\frac{1}{4}$.

(iii) Add R_3 to R_2.

(iv) Add -3 times R_1 to R_3.

(v) Add -2 times R_2 to R_1.

33. Repeat steps (i) through (iv) for the matrix in Exercise 31 using a graphing utility.

34. Repeat steps (i) through (v) for the matrix in Exercise 32 using a graphing utility.

Row-Echelon Form In Exercises 35–40, determine whether the matrix is in row-echelon form. If it is, determine if it is also in reduced row-echelon form.

35. $\begin{bmatrix} 1 & 0 & 0 & 0 \\ 0 & 1 & 1 & 5 \\ 0 & 0 & 0 & 0 \end{bmatrix}$ **36.** $\begin{bmatrix} 1 & 0 & 1 & 0 \\ 0 & 1 & 0 & 2 \\ 0 & 0 & 1 & 0 \end{bmatrix}$

37. $\begin{bmatrix} 3 & 0 & 3 & 7 \\ 0 & -2 & 0 & 4 \\ 0 & 0 & 1 & 5 \end{bmatrix}$ **38.** $\begin{bmatrix} 1 & 3 & 0 & 0 \\ 0 & 0 & 1 & 8 \\ 0 & 0 & 0 & 0 \end{bmatrix}$

39. $\begin{bmatrix} 1 & 0 & 2 & 1 \\ 0 & 1 & -3 & 10 \\ 0 & 0 & 1 & 0 \end{bmatrix}$ **40.** $\begin{bmatrix} 1 & 0 & 0 & 1 \\ 0 & 1 & 0 & -1 \\ 0 & 0 & 0 & 2 \end{bmatrix}$

Using Gaussian Elimination In Exercises 41–44, write the matrix in row-echelon form. Remember that the row-echelon form of a matrix is not unique.

41. $\begin{bmatrix} 1 & -4 & 5 \\ -2 & 6 & -6 \end{bmatrix}$ **42.** $\begin{bmatrix} 1 & -3 & 2 \\ 5 & 0 & 7 \end{bmatrix}$

43. $\begin{bmatrix} 1 & 2 & -1 & 3 \\ 3 & 7 & -5 & 14 \\ -2 & -1 & -3 & 8 \end{bmatrix}$

44. $\begin{bmatrix} 1 & -3 & 0 & -7 \\ -3 & 10 & 1 & 23 \\ 4 & -10 & 2 & -24 \end{bmatrix}$

Using a Graphing Utility In Exercises 45–48, use the matrix capabilities of a graphing utility to write the matrix in reduced row-echelon form.

45. $\begin{bmatrix} 3 & 3 & 3 \\ -1 & 0 & -4 \\ 2 & 4 & -2 \end{bmatrix}$ **46.** $\begin{bmatrix} 1 & 3 & 2 \\ 5 & 15 & 9 \\ 2 & 6 & 10 \end{bmatrix}$

47. $\begin{bmatrix} -4 & 1 & 0 & 6 \\ 1 & -2 & 3 & -4 \end{bmatrix}$

48. $\begin{bmatrix} 5 & 1 & 2 & 4 \\ -1 & 5 & 10 & -32 \end{bmatrix}$

Using Back-Substitution In Exercises 49–52, write the system of linear equations represented by the augmented matrix. Then use back-substitution to find the solution. (Use the variables x, y, and z, if applicable.)

49. $\begin{bmatrix} 1 & -2 & \vdots & 4 \\ 0 & 1 & \vdots & -3 \end{bmatrix}$ **50.** $\begin{bmatrix} 1 & 8 & \vdots & 12 \\ 0 & 1 & \vdots & 3 \end{bmatrix}$

51. $\begin{bmatrix} 1 & -1 & 4 & \vdots & 0 \\ 0 & 1 & -1 & \vdots & 2 \\ 0 & 0 & 1 & \vdots & -2 \end{bmatrix}$

52. $\begin{bmatrix} 1 & 0 & -2 & \vdots & -7 \\ 0 & 1 & 1 & \vdots & 9 \\ 0 & 0 & 1 & \vdots & -3 \end{bmatrix}$

Interpreting Reduced Row-Echelon Form In Exercises 53–56, an augmented matrix that represents a system of linear equations (in the variables x and y or x, y, and z) has been reduced using Gauss-Jordan elimination. Write the solution represented by the augmented matrix.

53. $\begin{bmatrix} 1 & 0 & \vdots & 7 \\ 0 & 1 & \vdots & -5 \end{bmatrix}$ **54.** $\begin{bmatrix} 1 & 0 & \vdots & -2 \\ 0 & 1 & \vdots & 4 \end{bmatrix}$

55. $\begin{bmatrix} 1 & 0 & 0 & \vdots & -4 \\ 0 & 1 & 0 & \vdots & -8 \\ 0 & 0 & 1 & \vdots & 2 \end{bmatrix}$

56. $\begin{bmatrix} 1 & 0 & 0 & \vdots & 3 \\ 0 & 1 & 0 & \vdots & -1 \\ 0 & 0 & 1 & \vdots & 0 \end{bmatrix}$

Gaussian Elimination with Back-Substitution In Exercises 57–64, use matrices to solve the system of equations, if possible. Use Gaussian elimination with back-substitution.

57. $\begin{cases} x + 2y = 7 \\ 2x + y = 8 \end{cases}$

58. $\begin{cases} 2x + 6y = 16 \\ 2x + 3y = 7 \end{cases}$

59. $\begin{cases} -x + y = -22 \\ 3x + 4y = 4 \\ 4x - 8y = 32 \end{cases}$

60. $\begin{cases} x + 2y = 0 \\ x + y = 6 \\ 3x - 2y = 8 \end{cases}$

61. $\begin{cases} x + 2y - 3z = -28 \\ 4y + 2z = 0 \\ -x + y - z = -5 \end{cases}$

62. $\begin{cases} -x + y - 2z = -4 \\ 4x + 2y - 3z = 8 \\ 2x + 4y - 7z = 1 \end{cases}$

63. $\begin{cases} 3x + 2y - z + w = 0 \\ x - y + 4z + 2w = 25 \\ -2x + y + 2z - w = 2 \\ x + y + z + w = 6 \end{cases}$

64. $\begin{cases} x - 4y + 3z - 2w = 9 \\ 3x - 2y + z - 4w = -13 \\ -4x + 3y - 2z + w = -4 \\ -2x + y - 4z + 3w = -10 \end{cases}$

Gauss-Jordan Elimination In Exercises 65–72, use matrices to solve the system of equations, if possible. Use Gauss-Jordan elimination.

65. $\begin{cases} x - 3z = -2 \\ 3x + y - 2z = 5 \\ 2x + 2y + z = 4 \end{cases}$

66. $\begin{cases} 2x - y + 3z = 24 \\ 2y - z = 14 \\ 7x - 5y = 6 \end{cases}$

67. $\begin{cases} -x - y - 3z = -12 \\ 2x - y - 4z = 6 \\ -2x + 4y + 14z = 19 \end{cases}$

68. $\begin{cases} 2x + 3z = 3 \\ 4x - 3y + 7z = 5 \\ 8x - 9y + 15z = 9 \end{cases}$

69. $\begin{cases} x + y - 5z = 3 \\ x - 2z = 1 \\ 2x - y - z = 0 \end{cases}$

70. $\begin{cases} 2x + 2y - z = 2 \\ x - 3y + z = 28 \\ -x + y = 14 \end{cases}$

71. $\begin{cases} x + 2y + z = 8 \\ 3x + 7y + 6z = 26 \end{cases}$

72. $\begin{cases} x + y + 4z = 5 \\ 2x + y - z = 9 \end{cases}$

Using a Graphing Utility In Exercises 73–76, use the matrix capabilities of a graphing utility to reduce the augmented matrix corresponding to the system of equations, and solve the system.

73. $\begin{cases} x + y + 4z = 2 \\ 2x + 5y + 20z = 10 \\ -x + 3y + 8z = -2 \end{cases}$

74. $\begin{cases} x + y + z = 0 \\ 2x + 3y + z = 0 \\ 3x + 5y + z = 0 \end{cases}$

75. $\begin{cases} 2x + 10y + 2z = 6 \\ x + 5y + 2z = 6 \\ x + 5y + z = 3 \\ -3x - 15y - 3z = -9 \end{cases}$

76. $\begin{cases} 2x + y - z + 2w = -6 \\ 3x + 4y + w = 1 \\ x + 5y + 2z + 6w = -3 \\ 5x + 2y - z - w = 3 \end{cases}$

Comparing Solutions of Two Systems In Exercises 77–80, determine whether the two systems of linear equations yield the same solution. If so, find the solution.

77. (a) $\begin{cases} x - 2y + z = -6 \\ y - 5z = 16 \\ z = -3 \end{cases}$
(b) $\begin{cases} x + y - 2z = 6 \\ y + 3z = -8 \\ z = -3 \end{cases}$

78. (a) $\begin{cases} x - 3y + 4z = -11 \\ y - z = -4 \\ z = 2 \end{cases}$
(b) $\begin{cases} x + 4y = -11 \\ y + 3z = 4 \\ z = 2 \end{cases}$

79. (a) $\begin{cases} x - 4y + 5z = 27 \\ y - 7z = -54 \\ z = 8 \end{cases}$
(b) $\begin{cases} x - 6y + z = 15 \\ y + 5z = 42 \\ z = 8 \end{cases}$

80. (a) $\begin{cases} x + 3y - z = 19 \\ y + 6z = -18 \\ z = -4 \end{cases}$
(b) $\begin{cases} x - y + 3z = -21 \\ y - 2z = 14 \\ z = -4 \end{cases}$

Data Analysis: Curve Fitting In Exercises 81–84, use a system of equations to find the equation of the parabola $y = ax^2 + bx + c$ that passes through the points. Solve the system using matrices. Use a graphing utility to verify your result.

81.

82.

83.

84.

Curve Fitting In Exercises 85 and 86, use a system of equations to find the quadratic function $f(x) = ax^2 + bx + c$ that satisfies the equations. Solve the system using matrices.

85. $f(-2) = -15$
    $f(-1) = 7$
    $f(1) = -3$

86. $f(-2) = -3$
    $f(1) = -3$
    $f(2) = -11$

Curve Fitting In Exercises 87 and 88, use a system of equations to find the cubic function $f(x) = ax^3 + bx^2 + cx + d$ that satisfies the equations. Solve the system using matrices.

87. $f(-2) = -7$
    $f(-1) = 2$
    $f(1) = -4$
    $f(2) = -7$

88. $f(-2) = -17$
    $f(-1) = -5$
    $f(1) = 1$
    $f(2) = 7$

89. **Electrical Engineering** The currents in an electrical network are given by the solution of the system

$$\begin{cases} I_1 - I_2 + I_3 = 0 \\ 2I_1 + 2I_2 \quad\quad = 7 \\ \quad\quad 2I_2 + 4I_3 = 8 \end{cases}$$

where I_1, I_2, and I_3 are measured in amperes. Solve the system of equations using matrices.

90. **Finance** A corporation borrowed $1,500,000 to expand its line of shoes. Some of the money was borrowed at 3%, some at 4%, and some at 6%. Use a system of equations to determine how much was borrowed at each rate, given that the annual interest was $74,000 and the amount borrowed at 6% was four times the amount borrowed at 3%. Solve the system using matrices.

91. **Using Matrices** A food server examines the amount of money earned in tips after working an 8-hour shift. The server has a total of $95 in denominations of $1, $5, $10, and $20 bills. The total number of paper bills is 26. The number of $5 bills is 4 times the number of $10 bills, and the number of $1 bills is 1 less than twice the number of $5 bills. Write a system of linear equations to represent the situation. Then use matrices to find the number of each denomination.

92. **Marketing** A wholesale paper company sells a 100-pound package of computer paper that consists of three grades, glossy, semi-gloss, and matte, for printing photographs. Glossy costs $5.50 per pound, semi-gloss costs $4.25 per pound, and matte costs $3.75 per pound. One half of the 100-pound package consists of the two less expensive grades. The cost of the 100-pound package is $480. Set up and solve a system of equations, using matrices, to find the number of pounds of each grade of paper in a 100-pound package.

93. **Partial Fractions** Use a system of equations to write the partial fraction decomposition of the rational expression. Solve the system using matrices.

$$\frac{8x^2}{(x-1)^2(x+1)} = \frac{A}{x+1} + \frac{B}{x-1} + \frac{C}{(x-1)^2}$$

94. **MODELING DATA**

A video of the path of a ball thrown by a baseball player was analyzed with a grid covering the TV screen. The video was paused three times, and the position of the ball was measured each time. The coordinates obtained are shown in the table (x and y are measured in feet).

Horizontal distance, x	Height, y
0	5.0
15	9.6
30	12.4

(a) Use a system of equations to find the equation of the parabola $y = ax^2 + bx + c$ that passes through the points. Solve the system using matrices.

(b) Use a graphing utility to graph the parabola.

(c) Graphically approximate the maximum height of the ball and the point at which the ball strikes the ground.

(d) Algebraically approximate the maximum height of the ball and the point at which the ball strikes the ground.

95. ***Why you should learn it*** *(p. 504)* The table shows the average annual consumer costs y (in dollars) for health insurance from 2010 to 2012. (Source: U.S. Bureau of Labor Statistics)

Year	Cost, y
2010	1831
2011	1922
2012	2061

(a) Use a system of equations to find the equation of the parabola $y = at^2 + bt + c$ that passes through the points. Let t represent the year, with $t = 0$ corresponding to 2010. Solve the system using matrices.

(b) Use a graphing utility to graph the parabola and plot the data points.

(c) Use the equation in part (a) to estimate the average consumer costs in 2015, 2020, and 2025.

(d) Are your estimates in part (c) reasonable? Explain.

96. MODELING DATA

The table shows the average annual salaries y (in thousands of dollars) for public school classroom teachers in the United States from 2011 through 2013. (Source: National Education Association)

Year	Annual salary, y
2011	55.5
2012	55.4
2013	56.4

(a) Use a system of equations to find the equation of the parabola $y = at^2 + bt + c$ that passes through the points. Let t represent the year, with $t = 1$ corresponding to 2011. Solve the system using matrices.

(b) Use a graphing utility to graph the parabola and plot the data points.

(c) Use the equation in part (a) to estimate the average annual salaries in 2015, 2020, and 2025.

(d) Are your estimates in part (c) reasonable? Explain.

97. **Network Analysis** Water flowing through a network of pipes (in thousands of cubic meters per hour) is shown below.

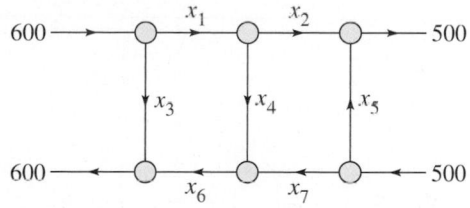

(a) Use matrices to solve this system for the water flow represented by x_i, $i = 1, 2, 3, 4, 5, 6,$ and 7.

(b) Find the network flow pattern when $x_6 = 0$ and $x_7 = 0$.

(c) Find the network flow pattern when $x_5 = 400$ and $x_6 = 500$.

98. **Network Analysis** The flow of water (in thousands of cubic meters per hour) into and out of the right side of the network of pipes in Exercise 97 is increased from 500 to 700.

(a) Draw a diagram of the new network.

(b) Use matrices to solve this system for the water flow represented by x_i, $i = 1, 2, 3, 4, 5, 6,$ and 7.

(c) Find the network flow pattern when $x_1 = 600$ and $x_7 = 200$.

(d) Find the network flow pattern when $x_4 = 150$ and $x_5 = 350$.

Conclusions

True or False? In Exercises 99 and 100, determine whether the statement is true or false. Justify your answer.

99. When using Gaussian elimination to solve a system of linear equations, you may conclude that the system is inconsistent before you complete the process of rewriting the augmented matrix in row-echelon form.

100. You cannot write an augmented matrix for a dependent system of linear equations in reduced row-echelon form.

101. **Think About It** The augmented matrix represents a system of linear equations (in the variables x, y, and z) that has been reduced using Gauss-Jordan elimination. Write a system of three equations in three variables with *nonzero* coefficients that is represented by the reduced matrix. (There are many correct answers.)

$$\begin{bmatrix} 1 & 0 & 3 & \vdots & -2 \\ 0 & 1 & 4 & \vdots & 1 \\ 0 & 0 & 0 & \vdots & 0 \end{bmatrix}$$

102. **HOW DO YOU SEE IT?** Determine whether the matrix below is in row-echelon form, reduced row-echelon form, or neither when it satisfies the given conditions.

$$\begin{bmatrix} 1 & b \\ c & 1 \end{bmatrix}$$

(a) $b = 0, c = 0$ (b) $b \neq 0, c = 0$

(c) $b = 0, c \neq 0$ (d) $b \neq 0, c \neq 0$

103. **Think About It** Can a 2×4 augmented matrix whose entries are all nonzero real numbers represent an independent system of linear equations? Explain.

104. **Think About It** Determine all values of a and b for which the augmented matrix has each given number of solutions.

$$\begin{bmatrix} 1 & 2 & \vdots & -4 \\ 0 & a & \vdots & b \end{bmatrix}$$

(a) Exactly one solution

(b) Infinitely many solutions

(c) No solution

Cumulative Mixed Review

Graphing a Rational Function In Exercises 105–108, sketch the graph of the function. Identify any asymptotes.

105. $f(x) = \dfrac{7}{-x-1}$

106. $f(x) = \dfrac{4x}{5x^2 + 2}$

107. $f(x) = \dfrac{x^2 - 2x - 3}{x - 4}$

108. $f(x) = \dfrac{x^2 - 36}{x + 1}$

7.5 Operations with Matrices

Equality of Matrices

In Section 7.4, you used matrices to solve systems of linear equations. There is a rich mathematical theory of matrices, and its applications are numerous. This section and the next two introduce some fundamentals of matrix theory. It is standard mathematical convention to represent matrices in any of the following three ways.

> **Representation of Matrices**
>
> 1. A matrix can be denoted by an uppercase letter such as A, B, or C.
>
> 2. A matrix can be denoted by a representative element enclosed in brackets, such as
>
> $[a_{ij}]$, $[b_{ij}]$, or $[c_{ij}]$.
>
> 3. A matrix can be denoted by a rectangular array of numbers such as
>
> $$A = [a_{ij}] = \begin{bmatrix} a_{11} & a_{12} & a_{13} & \cdots & a_{1n} \\ a_{21} & a_{22} & a_{23} & \cdots & a_{2n} \\ a_{31} & a_{32} & a_{33} & \cdots & a_{3n} \\ \vdots & \vdots & \vdots & & \vdots \\ a_{m1} & a_{m2} & a_{m3} & \cdots & a_{mn} \end{bmatrix}.$$

Two matrices

$$A = [a_{ij}] \quad \text{and} \quad B = [b_{ij}]$$

are **equal** when they have the same dimension $(m \times n)$ and all of their corresponding entries are equal.

EXAMPLE 1 Equality of Matrices

Solve for a_{11}, a_{12}, a_{21}, and a_{22} in the following matrix equation.

$$\begin{bmatrix} a_{11} & a_{12} \\ a_{21} & a_{22} \end{bmatrix} = \begin{bmatrix} 2 & -1 \\ -3 & 0 \end{bmatrix}$$

Solution

Because two matrices are equal only when their corresponding entries are equal, you can conclude that

$$a_{11} = 2, \quad a_{12} = -1, \quad a_{21} = -3, \quad \text{and} \quad a_{22} = 0.$$

✓ **Checkpoint** *Audio-video solution in English & Spanish at LarsonPrecalculus.com.*

Solve for a_{11}, a_{12}, a_{21}, and a_{22} in the following matrix equation.

$$\begin{bmatrix} a_{11} & a_{12} \\ a_{21} & a_{22} \end{bmatrix} = \begin{bmatrix} 6 & 3 \\ -2 & 4 \end{bmatrix}$$

Be sure you see that for two matrices to be equal, they must have the same dimension *and* their corresponding entries must be equal. For instance,

$$\begin{bmatrix} 2 & -1 \\ \sqrt{4} & \frac{1}{2} \end{bmatrix} = \begin{bmatrix} 2 & -1 \\ 2 & 0.5 \end{bmatrix} \quad \text{but} \quad \begin{bmatrix} 2 & -1 \\ 3 & 4 \\ 0 & 0 \end{bmatrix} \neq \begin{bmatrix} 2 & -1 \\ 3 & 4 \end{bmatrix}.$$

What you should learn

▶ Decide whether two matrices are equal.
▶ Add and subtract matrices and multiply matrices by scalars.
▶ Multiply two matrices.
▶ Use matrix operations to model and solve real-life problems.

Why you should learn it

Matrix algebra provides a systematic way of performing mathematical operations on large arrays of numbers. In Exercise 89 on page 530, you will use matrix multiplication to help analyze the labor and wage requirements for a boat manufacturer.

Matrix Addition and Scalar Multiplication

Definition of Matrix Addition

If $A = [a_{ij}]$ and $B = [b_{ij}]$ are matrices of dimension $m \times n$, then their sum is the $m \times n$ matrix given by $A + B = [a_{ij} + b_{ij}]$. The sum of two matrices of different dimensions is undefined.

Remark

With matrix addition, you can add two matrices (of the same dimension) by adding their corresponding entries.

EXAMPLE 2   Addition of Matrices

a. $\begin{bmatrix} -1 & 2 \\ 0 & 1 \end{bmatrix} + \begin{bmatrix} 1 & 3 \\ -1 & 2 \end{bmatrix} = \begin{bmatrix} -1 + 1 & 2 + 3 \\ 0 + (-1) & 1 + 2 \end{bmatrix} = \begin{bmatrix} 0 & 5 \\ -1 & 3 \end{bmatrix}$

b. $\begin{bmatrix} 1 \\ -3 \\ -2 \end{bmatrix} + \begin{bmatrix} -1 \\ 3 \\ 2 \end{bmatrix} = \begin{bmatrix} 0 \\ 0 \\ 0 \end{bmatrix}$

c. The sum of

$$A = \begin{bmatrix} 2 & 1 & 0 \\ 4 & 0 & -1 \end{bmatrix} \quad \text{and} \quad B = \begin{bmatrix} 0 & 1 \\ -1 & 3 \end{bmatrix}$$

is undefined because A is of dimension 2×3 and B is of dimension 2×2.

✓ **Checkpoint** �))) *Audio-video solution in English & Spanish at LarsonPrecalculus.com.*

Evaluate the expression.

$$\begin{bmatrix} 4 & -1 \\ 2 & -3 \end{bmatrix} + \begin{bmatrix} 2 & -1 \\ 0 & 6 \end{bmatrix}$$

In operations with matrices, numbers are usually referred to as **scalars.** In this text, scalars will always be real numbers. You can multiply a matrix A by a scalar c by multiplying each entry in A by c.

Technology Tip

Try using a graphing utility to find the sum of the two matrices in Example 2(c). Your graphing utility should display an error message similar to the one shown below.

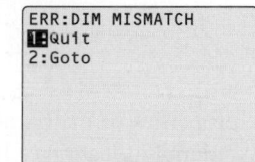

```
ERR:DIM MISMATCH
1▪Quit
2:Goto
```

Definition of Scalar Multiplication

If $A = [a_{ij}]$ is an $m \times n$ matrix and c is a scalar, then the **scalar multiple** of A by c is the $m \times n$ matrix given by $cA = [ca_{ij}]$.

EXAMPLE 3   Scalar Multiplication

Find $3A$ using $A = \begin{bmatrix} 2 & 2 & 4 \\ -3 & 0 & -1 \\ 2 & 1 & 2 \end{bmatrix}$.

Solution

$$3A = 3\begin{bmatrix} 2 & 2 & 4 \\ -3 & 0 & -1 \\ 2 & 1 & 2 \end{bmatrix} = \begin{bmatrix} 3(2) & 3(2) & 3(4) \\ 3(-3) & 3(0) & 3(-1) \\ 3(2) & 3(1) & 3(2) \end{bmatrix} = \begin{bmatrix} 6 & 6 & 12 \\ -9 & 0 & -3 \\ 6 & 3 & 6 \end{bmatrix}$$

✓ **Checkpoint** ◍))) *Audio-video solution in English & Spanish at LarsonPrecalculus.com.*

Find $3A$ using $A = \begin{bmatrix} 4 & -1 \\ 0 & 4 \\ -3 & 8 \end{bmatrix}$.

The symbol $-A$ represents the negation of A, which is the scalar product $(-1)A$. Moreover, if A and B are of the same dimension, then $A - B$ represents the sum of A and $(-1)B$. That is,

$$A - B = A + (-1)B.$$

The order of operations for matrix expressions is similar to that for real numbers. In particular, you perform scalar multiplication before matrix addition and subtraction, as shown in Example 4.

EXAMPLE 4   Scalar Multiplication and Matrix Subtraction

Find $3A - B$ using $A = \begin{bmatrix} 2 & 2 & 4 \\ -3 & 0 & -1 \\ 2 & 1 & 2 \end{bmatrix}$ and $B = \begin{bmatrix} 2 & 0 & 0 \\ 1 & -4 & 3 \\ -1 & 3 & 2 \end{bmatrix}$.

Solution

Note that A is the same matrix from Example 3, where you found $3A$.

$$3A - B = \begin{bmatrix} 6 & 6 & 12 \\ -9 & 0 & -3 \\ 6 & 3 & 6 \end{bmatrix} - \begin{bmatrix} 2 & 0 & 0 \\ 1 & -4 & 3 \\ -1 & 3 & 2 \end{bmatrix} \qquad \text{Perform scalar multiplication first.}$$

$$= \begin{bmatrix} 4 & 6 & 12 \\ -10 & 4 & -6 \\ 7 & 0 & 4 \end{bmatrix} \qquad \text{Subtract corresponding entries.}$$

✓ *Checkpoint* 🔊)) *Audio-video solution in English & Spanish at LarsonPrecalculus.com.*

Find $3A - 2B$ using $A = \begin{bmatrix} 4 & -1 \\ 0 & 4 \\ -3 & 8 \end{bmatrix}$ and $B = \begin{bmatrix} 0 & 4 \\ -1 & 3 \\ 1 & 7 \end{bmatrix}$. ■

The properties of matrix addition and scalar multiplication are similar to those of addition and multiplication of real numbers. One important property of addition of real numbers is that the number 0 is the additive identity. That is, $c + 0 = c$ for any real number c. For matrices, a similar property holds. That is, if A is an $m \times n$ matrix and O is the $m \times n$ **zero matrix** consisting entirely of zeros, then $A + O = A$. In other words, O is the **additive identity** for the set of all $m \times n$ matrices. For example, the following matrices are the additive identities for the sets of all 2×3 and 2×2 matrices.

$$O = \begin{bmatrix} 0 & 0 & 0 \\ 0 & 0 & 0 \end{bmatrix} \qquad \text{and} \qquad O = \begin{bmatrix} 0 & 0 \\ 0 & 0 \end{bmatrix}$$

$$\underbrace{\hspace{3cm}}_{2 \times 3 \text{ zero matrix}} \qquad \qquad \underbrace{\hspace{2cm}}_{2 \times 2 \text{ zero matrix}}$$

Properties of Matrix Addition and Scalar Multiplication

Let A, B, and C be $m \times n$ matrices and let c and d be scalars.

1. $A + B = B + A$		Commutative Property of Matrix Addition
2. $A + (B + C) = (A + B) + C$		Associative Property of Matrix Addition
3. $(cd)A = c(dA)$		Associative Property of Scalar Multiplication
4. $1A = A$		Scalar Identity
5. $A + O = A$		Additive Identity
6. $c(A + B) = cA + cB$		Distributive Property
7. $(c + d)A = cA + dA$		Distributive Property

Explore the Concept

What do you observe about the relationship between the corresponding entries of A and B below? Use a graphing utility to find $A + B$. What conclusion can you make about the entries of A and B and the sum $A + B$?

$$A = \begin{bmatrix} -1 & 5 \\ 2 & -6 \end{bmatrix}$$

$$B = \begin{bmatrix} 1 & -5 \\ -2 & 6 \end{bmatrix}$$

Remark

Note that the Associative Property of Matrix Addition allows you to write expressions such as $A + B + C$ without ambiguity because the same sum occurs no matter how the matrices are grouped. This same reasoning applies to sums of four or more matrices.

EXAMPLE 5 Using the Distributive Property

$$3\left(\begin{bmatrix} -2 & 0 \\ 4 & 1 \end{bmatrix} + \begin{bmatrix} 4 & -2 \\ 3 & 7 \end{bmatrix}\right) = 3\begin{bmatrix} -2 & 0 \\ 4 & 1 \end{bmatrix} + 3\begin{bmatrix} 4 & -2 \\ 3 & 7 \end{bmatrix}$$

$$= \begin{bmatrix} -6 & 0 \\ 12 & 3 \end{bmatrix} + \begin{bmatrix} 12 & -6 \\ 9 & 21 \end{bmatrix}$$

$$= \begin{bmatrix} 6 & -6 \\ 21 & 24 \end{bmatrix}$$

Remark

In Example 5, you could add the two matrices first and then multiply the resulting matrix by 3. The result would be the same.

✓ **Checkpoint**))) *Audio-video solution in English & Spanish at LarsonPrecalculus.com.*

Evaluate the expression using the Distributive Property.

$$2\left(\begin{bmatrix} 1 & 3 \\ -2 & 2 \end{bmatrix} + \begin{bmatrix} -4 & 0 \\ -3 & 1 \end{bmatrix}\right)$$

The algebra of real numbers and the algebra of matrices have many similarities. For example, compare the following solutions.

Real Numbers (Solve for x.)	m × n Matrices (Solve for X.)
$x + a = b$	$X + A = B$
$x + a + (-a) = b + (-a)$	$X + A + (-A) = B + (-A)$
$x + 0 = b - a$	$X + O = B - A$
$x = b - a$	$X = B - A$

The algebra of real numbers and the algebra of matrices also have important differences, which will be discussed later.

EXAMPLE 6 Solving a Matrix Equation

Solve for X in the equation $3X + A = B$, where

$$A = \begin{bmatrix} 1 & -2 \\ 0 & 3 \end{bmatrix} \quad \text{and} \quad B = \begin{bmatrix} -3 & 4 \\ 2 & 1 \end{bmatrix}.$$

Solution

Begin by solving the matrix equation for X.

$$3X + A = B \quad \Longrightarrow \quad 3X = B - A \quad \Longrightarrow \quad X = \tfrac{1}{3}(B - A)$$

Now, using the matrices A and B, you have

$$X = \frac{1}{3}\left(\begin{bmatrix} -3 & 4 \\ 2 & 1 \end{bmatrix} - \begin{bmatrix} 1 & -2 \\ 0 & 3 \end{bmatrix}\right) \qquad \text{Substitute the matrices.}$$

$$= \frac{1}{3}\begin{bmatrix} -4 & 6 \\ 2 & -2 \end{bmatrix} \qquad \text{Subtract matrix } A \text{ from matrix } B.$$

$$= \begin{bmatrix} -\frac{4}{3} & 2 \\ \frac{2}{3} & -\frac{2}{3} \end{bmatrix}. \qquad \text{Multiply the resulting matrix by } \tfrac{1}{3}.$$

✓ **Checkpoint**))) *Audio-video solution in English & Spanish at LarsonPrecalculus.com.*

Solve for X in the equation $2X - A = B$, where

$$A = \begin{bmatrix} 6 & 1 \\ 0 & 3 \end{bmatrix} \quad \text{and} \quad B = \begin{bmatrix} 4 & -1 \\ -2 & 5 \end{bmatrix}.$$

Matrix Multiplication

Another basic matrix operation is **matrix multiplication.**

> **Definition of Matrix Multiplication**
>
> If $A = [a_{ij}]$ is an $m \times n$ matrix and $B = [b_{ij}]$ is an $n \times p$ matrix, then the product AB is an $m \times p$ matrix given by
>
> $$AB = [c_{ij}]$$
>
> where
>
> $$c_{ij} = a_{i1}b_{1j} + a_{i2}b_{2j} + a_{i3}b_{3j} + \cdots + a_{in}b_{nj}.$$

Remark

At first glance, this definition may seem unusual. You will see later, however, that the definition of the product of two matrices has many practical applications.

The definition of matrix multiplication indicates a *row-by-column* multiplication, where the entry in the ith row and jth column of the product AB is obtained by multiplying the entries in the ith row of A by the corresponding entries in the jth column of B and then adding the results. The general pattern for matrix multiplication is as follows.

$$
\begin{bmatrix}
a_{11} & a_{12} & a_{13} & \cdots & a_{1n} \\
a_{21} & a_{22} & a_{23} & \cdots & a_{2n} \\
a_{31} & a_{32} & a_{33} & \cdots & a_{3n} \\
\vdots & \vdots & \vdots & & \vdots \\
a_{i1} & a_{i2} & a_{i3} & \cdots & a_{in} \\
\vdots & \vdots & \vdots & & \vdots \\
a_{m1} & a_{m2} & a_{m3} & \cdots & a_{mn}
\end{bmatrix}
\begin{bmatrix}
b_{11} & b_{12} & \cdots & b_{1j} & \cdots & b_{1p} \\
b_{21} & b_{22} & \cdots & b_{2j} & \cdots & b_{2p} \\
b_{31} & b_{32} & \cdots & b_{3j} & \cdots & b_{3p} \\
\vdots & \vdots & & \vdots & & \vdots \\
b_{n1} & b_{n2} & \cdots & b_{nj} & \cdots & b_{np}
\end{bmatrix}
=
\begin{bmatrix}
c_{11} & c_{12} & \cdots & c_{1j} & \cdots & c_{1p} \\
c_{21} & c_{22} & \cdots & c_{2j} & \cdots & c_{2p} \\
\vdots & \vdots & & \vdots & & \vdots \\
c_{i1} & c_{i2} & \cdots & c_{ij} & \cdots & c_{ip} \\
\vdots & \vdots & & \vdots & & \vdots \\
c_{m1} & c_{m2} & \cdots & c_{mj} & \cdots & c_{mp}
\end{bmatrix}
$$

$$a_{i1}b_{1j} + a_{i2}b_{2j} + a_{i3}b_{3j} + \cdots + a_{in}b_{nj} = c_{ij}$$

EXAMPLE 7 Finding the Product of Two Matrices

Find the product AB using $A = \begin{bmatrix} -1 & 3 \\ 4 & -2 \\ 5 & 0 \end{bmatrix}$ and $B = \begin{bmatrix} -3 & 2 \\ -4 & 1 \end{bmatrix}$.

Solution

First, note that the product AB is defined because the number of columns of A is equal to the number of rows of B. Moreover, the product AB has dimension 3×2. To find the entries of the product, multiply each row of A by each column of B.

$$
\begin{aligned}
AB &= \begin{bmatrix} -1 & 3 \\ 4 & -2 \\ 5 & 0 \end{bmatrix} \begin{bmatrix} -3 & 2 \\ -4 & 1 \end{bmatrix} \\[2mm]
&= \begin{bmatrix} (-1)(-3) + (3)(-4) & (-1)(2) + (3)(1) \\ (4)(-3) + (-2)(-4) & (4)(2) + (-2)(1) \\ (5)(-3) + (0)(-4) & (5)(2) + (0)(1) \end{bmatrix} \\[2mm]
&= \begin{bmatrix} -9 & 1 \\ -4 & 6 \\ -15 & 10 \end{bmatrix}
\end{aligned}
$$

✓ **Checkpoint** 🔊 *Audio-video solution in English & Spanish at LarsonPrecalculus.com.*

Find the product AB using $A = \begin{bmatrix} -1 & 4 \\ 2 & 0 \\ 1 & 2 \end{bmatrix}$ and $B = \begin{bmatrix} 1 & -2 \\ 0 & 7 \end{bmatrix}$.

Be sure you understand that for the product of two matrices to be defined, the number of *columns* of the first matrix must equal the number of *rows* of the second matrix. That is, the middle two indices must be the same. The outside two indices give the dimension of the product, as shown in the following diagram.

$$A \quad \times \quad B \quad = \quad AB$$
$$m \times n \qquad n \times p \qquad m \times p$$

Equal

Dimension of AB

EXAMPLE 8   Matrix Multiplication

See LarsonPrecalculus.com for an interactive version of this type of example.

a. $\begin{bmatrix} 1 & 0 & 3 \\ 2 & -1 & -2 \end{bmatrix} \begin{bmatrix} -2 & 4 & 2 \\ 1 & 0 & 0 \\ -1 & 1 & -1 \end{bmatrix} = \begin{bmatrix} -5 & 7 & -1 \\ -3 & 6 & 6 \end{bmatrix}$

$\qquad 2 \times 3 \qquad\qquad 3 \times 3 \qquad\qquad 2 \times 3$

b. $\begin{bmatrix} 3 & 4 \\ -2 & 5 \end{bmatrix} \begin{bmatrix} 1 & 0 \\ 0 & 1 \end{bmatrix} = \begin{bmatrix} 3 & 4 \\ -2 & 5 \end{bmatrix}$

$\qquad 2 \times 2 \qquad 2 \times 2 \qquad 2 \times 2$

c. $\begin{bmatrix} 1 & 2 \\ 1 & 1 \end{bmatrix} \begin{bmatrix} -1 & 2 \\ 1 & -1 \end{bmatrix} = \begin{bmatrix} 1 & 0 \\ 0 & 1 \end{bmatrix}$

$\qquad 2 \times 2 \qquad 2 \times 2 \qquad 2 \times 2$

d. $\begin{bmatrix} 1 & -2 & -3 \end{bmatrix} \begin{bmatrix} 2 \\ -1 \\ 1 \end{bmatrix} = \begin{bmatrix} 1 \end{bmatrix}$

$\qquad 1 \times 3 \qquad 3 \times 1 \quad 1 \times 1$

e. $\begin{bmatrix} 2 \\ -1 \\ 1 \end{bmatrix} \begin{bmatrix} 1 & -2 & -3 \end{bmatrix} = \begin{bmatrix} 2 & -4 & -6 \\ -1 & 2 & 3 \\ 1 & -2 & -3 \end{bmatrix}$

$\quad 3 \times 1 \qquad 1 \times 3 \qquad\qquad 3 \times 3$

f. The product AB for the following matrices is not defined.

$$A = \begin{bmatrix} -2 & 1 \\ 1 & -3 \\ 1 & 4 \end{bmatrix} \quad \text{and} \quad B = \begin{bmatrix} -2 & 3 & 1 & 4 \\ 0 & 1 & -1 & 2 \\ 2 & -1 & 0 & 1 \end{bmatrix}$$

$$\qquad\quad 3 \times 2 \qquad\qquad\qquad 3 \times 4$$

✓ **Checkpoint**))) *Audio-video solution in English & Spanish at LarsonPrecalculus.com.*

Find the product AB using $A = \begin{bmatrix} 0 & 4 & -3 \\ 2 & 1 & 7 \\ 3 & -2 & 1 \end{bmatrix}$ and $B = \begin{bmatrix} -2 & 0 \\ 0 & -4 \\ 1 & 2 \end{bmatrix}$.

In parts (d) and (e) of Example 8, note that the two products are different. Even when both AB and BA are defined, matrix multiplication is not, in general, commutative. That is, for most matrices,

$$AB \neq BA.$$

This is one way in which the algebra of real numbers and the algebra of matrices differ.

Explore the Concept

Use the following matrices to find AB, BA, $(AB)C$, and $A(BC)$. What do your results tell you about matrix multiplication and commutativity and associativity?

$$A = \begin{bmatrix} 1 & 2 \\ 3 & 4 \end{bmatrix}$$

$$B = \begin{bmatrix} 0 & 1 \\ 2 & 3 \end{bmatrix}$$

$$C = \begin{bmatrix} 3 & 0 \\ 0 & 1 \end{bmatrix}$$

[A] [B]

[[4 7]
 [8 15]]

EXAMPLE 9 Matrix Multiplication

Use a graphing utility to find the product AB using

$$A = \begin{bmatrix} 1 & 2 & 3 \\ 2 & -5 & 1 \end{bmatrix} \quad \text{and} \quad B = \begin{bmatrix} -3 & 2 & 1 \\ 4 & -2 & 0 \\ 1 & 2 & 3 \end{bmatrix}.$$

Solution

Note that the dimension of A is 2×3 and the dimension of B is 3×3. So, the product will have dimension 2×3. Use the *matrix editor* to enter A and B into the graphing utility. Then, find the product, as shown in Figure 7.17.

Figure 7.17

✓ *Checkpoint* 🔊))) *Audio-video solution in English & Spanish at LarsonPrecalculus.com.*

Find the product AB using $A = \begin{bmatrix} 7 & 5 & -4 \\ -2 & 5 & 1 \\ 10 & -4 & -7 \end{bmatrix}$ and $B = \begin{bmatrix} 2 & -2 & 3 \\ 8 & 1 & 4 \\ -4 & 2 & -8 \end{bmatrix}$. ■

Properties of Matrix Multiplication

Let A, B, and C be matrices and let c be a scalar.

1. $A(BC) = (AB)C$ Associative Property of Matrix Multiplication

2. $A(B + C) = AB + AC$ Left Distributive Property

3. $(A + B)C = AC + BC$ Right Distributive Property

4. $c(AB) = (cA)B = A(cB)$ Associative Property of Scalar Multiplication

---

Definition of Identity Matrix

The $n \times n$ matrix that consists of 1's on its main diagonal and 0's elsewhere is called the **identity matrix of dimension $n \times n$** and is denoted by

$$I_n = \begin{bmatrix} 1 & 0 & 0 & \ldots & 0 \\ 0 & 1 & 0 & \ldots & 0 \\ 0 & 0 & 1 & \ldots & 0 \\ \vdots & \vdots & \vdots & & \vdots \\ 0 & 0 & 0 & \ldots & 1 \end{bmatrix}. \quad \text{Identity matrix}$$

Note that an identity matrix must be *square*. When the dimension is understood to be $n \times n$, you can denote I_n simply by I.

If A is an $n \times n$ matrix, then the identity matrix has the property that $AI_n = A$ and $I_n A = A$. For example,

$$\begin{bmatrix} 3 & -2 & 5 \\ 1 & 0 & 4 \\ -1 & 2 & -3 \end{bmatrix} \begin{bmatrix} 1 & 0 & 0 \\ 0 & 1 & 0 \\ 0 & 0 & 1 \end{bmatrix} = \begin{bmatrix} 3 & -2 & 5 \\ 1 & 0 & 4 \\ -1 & 2 & -3 \end{bmatrix} \quad AI = A$$

and

$$\begin{bmatrix} 1 & 0 & 0 \\ 0 & 1 & 0 \\ 0 & 0 & 1 \end{bmatrix} \begin{bmatrix} 3 & -2 & 5 \\ 1 & 0 & 4 \\ -1 & 2 & -3 \end{bmatrix} = \begin{bmatrix} 3 & -2 & 5 \\ 1 & 0 & 4 \\ -1 & 2 & -3 \end{bmatrix}. \quad IA = A$$

Applications

Matrix multiplication can be used to represent a system of linear equations. Note how the system

$$\begin{cases} a_{11}x_1 + a_{12}x_2 + a_{13}x_3 = b_1 \\ a_{21}x_1 + a_{22}x_2 + a_{23}x_3 = b_2 \\ a_{31}x_1 + a_{32}x_2 + a_{33}x_3 = b_3 \end{cases}$$

can be written as the matrix equation $AX = B$, where A is the *coefficient matrix* of the system, and X and B are column matrices. The column matrix B is also called a *constant matrix*. Its entries are the constant terms in the system of equations.

$$\underbrace{\begin{bmatrix} a_{11} & a_{12} & a_{13} \\ a_{21} & a_{22} & a_{23} \\ a_{31} & a_{32} & a_{33} \end{bmatrix}}_{A} \times \underbrace{\begin{bmatrix} x_1 \\ x_2 \\ x_3 \end{bmatrix}}_{X} = \underbrace{\begin{bmatrix} b_1 \\ b_2 \\ b_3 \end{bmatrix}}_{B}$$

EXAMPLE 10   Solving a System of Linear Equations

For the system of linear equations, (a) write the system as a matrix equation $AX = B$ and (b) use Gauss-Jordan elimination on $[A \vdots B]$ to solve for the matrix X.

$$\begin{cases} x_1 - 2x_2 + x_3 = -4 \\ x_2 + 2x_3 = 4 \\ 2x_1 + 3x_2 - 2x_3 = 2 \end{cases}$$

Solution

a. In matrix form $AX = B$, the system can be written as follows.

$$\begin{bmatrix} 1 & -2 & 1 \\ 0 & 1 & 2 \\ 2 & 3 & -2 \end{bmatrix} \begin{bmatrix} x_1 \\ x_2 \\ x_3 \end{bmatrix} = \begin{bmatrix} -4 \\ 4 \\ 2 \end{bmatrix}$$

b. The augmented matrix is

$$[A \vdots B] = \begin{bmatrix} 1 & -2 & 1 & \vdots & -4 \\ 0 & 1 & 2 & \vdots & 4 \\ 2 & 3 & -2 & \vdots & 2 \end{bmatrix}.$$

Using Gauss-Jordan elimination, you can rewrite this equation as

$$[I \vdots X] = \begin{bmatrix} 1 & 0 & 0 & \vdots & -1 \\ 0 & 1 & 0 & \vdots & 2 \\ 0 & 0 & 1 & \vdots & 1 \end{bmatrix}.$$

So, the solution of the system of linear equations is $x_1 = -1$, $x_2 = 2$, and $x_3 = 1$. The solution of the matrix equation is

$$X = \begin{bmatrix} x_1 \\ x_2 \\ x_3 \end{bmatrix} = \begin{bmatrix} -1 \\ 2 \\ 1 \end{bmatrix}.$$

Technology Tip

Most graphing utilities can be used to obtain the reduced row-echelon form of a matrix. The screen below shows how one graphing utility displays the reduced row-echelon form of the augmented matrix in Example 10.

```
rref([C])
            [[1 0 0 -1]
             [0 1 0 2 ]
             [0 0 1 1 ]]
```

✓ *Checkpoint* �))) Audio-video solution in English & Spanish at LarsonPrecalculus.com.

For the system of linear equations, (a) write the system as a matrix equation $AX = B$ and (b) use Gauss-Jordan elimination on $[A \vdots B]$ to solve for the matrix X.

$$\begin{cases} -2x_1 - 3x_2 = -4 \\ 6x_1 + x_2 = -36 \end{cases}$$

EXAMPLE 11   Softball Team Expenses

Two softball teams submit equipment lists to their sponsors, as shown in the table.

Equipment	Women's team	Men's team
Bats	12	15
Balls	45	38
Gloves	15	17

The equipment costs are as follows.

Bats: $90 per bat

Balls: $6 per ball

Gloves: $60 per glove

Use matrices to find the total cost of equipment for each team.

Solution

The equipment list E can be written in matrix form as

$$E = \begin{bmatrix} 12 & 15 \\ 45 & 38 \\ 15 & 17 \end{bmatrix}.$$

The costs per item C can be written in matrix form as

$$C = \begin{bmatrix} 90 & 6 & 60 \end{bmatrix}.$$

You can find the total cost of the equipment for each team using the product CE because the number of columns of C (3 columns) equals the number of rows of E (3 rows). Therefore, the total cost of equipment for each team is given by

$$CE = \begin{bmatrix} 90 & 6 & 60 \end{bmatrix} \begin{bmatrix} 12 & 15 \\ 45 & 38 \\ 15 & 17 \end{bmatrix}$$

$$= \begin{bmatrix} 90(12) + 6(45) + 60(15) & 90(15) + 6(38) + 60(17) \end{bmatrix}$$

$$= \begin{bmatrix} 2250 & 2598 \end{bmatrix}.$$

Remark

Notice in Example 11 that you cannot find the total cost using the product EC because EC is not defined. That is, the number of columns of E (2 columns) does not equal the number of rows of C (1 row).

So, the total cost of equipment for the women's team is $2250, and the total cost of equipment for the men's team is $2598. You can use a graphing utility to check this result, as shown in Figure 7.18.

```
[C][E]
         [[2250 2598]]
```

Figure 7.18

✔ *Checkpoint* 🔊 *Audio-video solution in English & Spanish at LarsonPrecalculus.com.*

Repeat Example 11 when each bat costs $100, each ball costs $7, and each glove costs $65.

7.5   Exercises

See *CalcChat.com* for tutorial help and worked-out solutions to odd-numbered exercises.
For instructions on how to use a graphing utility, see Appendix A.

Vocabulary and Concept Check

In Exercises 1–4, fill in the blank(s).

1. Two matrices are _____ when they have the same dimension and all of their corresponding entries are equal.

2. When working with matrices, real numbers are often referred to as _____ .

3. A matrix consisting entirely of zeros is called a _____ matrix and is denoted by _____ .

4. The $n \times n$ matrix consisting of 1's on its main diagonal and 0's elsewhere is called the _____ matrix of dimension n.

In Exercises 5 and 6, match the matrix property with the correct form. A, B, and C are matrices, and c and d are scalars.

5. (a) $(cd)A = c(dA)$ (i) Commutative Property of Matrix Addition
   (b) $A + B = B + A$ (ii) Associative Property of Matrix Addition
   (c) $1A = A$ (iii) Associative Property of Scalar Multiplication
   (d) $c(A + B) = cA + cB$ (iv) Scalar Identity
   (e) $A + (B + C) = (A + B) + C$ (v) Distributive Property

6. (a) $A(B + C) = AB + AC$ (i) Associative Property of Matrix Multiplication
   (b) $c(AB) = (cA)B = A(cB)$ (ii) Left Distributive Property
   (c) $A(BC) = (AB)C$ (iii) Right Distributive Property
   (d) $(A + B)C = AC + BC$ (iv) Associative Property of Scalar Multiplication

7. In general, when multiplying matrices A and B, does $AB = BA$?

8. What is the dimension of AB when A is a 2×3 matrix and B is a 3×4 matrix?

Procedures and Problem Solving

Equality of Matrices   In Exercises 9–12, find x and y or x, y, and z.

9. $\begin{bmatrix} x & -7 \\ 9 & y \end{bmatrix} = \begin{bmatrix} 5 & -7 \\ 9 & -8 \end{bmatrix}$

10. $\begin{bmatrix} -5 & x \\ y & 8 \end{bmatrix} = \begin{bmatrix} -5 & 13 \\ 12 & 8 \end{bmatrix}$

11. $\begin{bmatrix} 4 & 5 & 4 \\ 13 & 15 & 3y \\ 2 & 2z - 6 & 0 \end{bmatrix} = \begin{bmatrix} 4 & 2x + 7 & 4 \\ 13 & 15 & 12 \\ 2 & 3z - 14 & 0 \end{bmatrix}$

12. $\begin{bmatrix} x + 4 & 8 & -3 \\ 1 & 22 & 2y \\ 7 & -2 & z + 2 \end{bmatrix} = \begin{bmatrix} 2x + 9 & 8 & -3 \\ 1 & 22 & -8 \\ 7 & -2 & 11 \end{bmatrix}$

Operations with Matrices   In Exercises 13–20, find, if possible, (a) $A + B$, (b) $A - B$, (c) $3A$, and (d) $3A - 2B$. Use the matrix capabilities of a graphing utility to verify your results.

13. $A = \begin{bmatrix} 5 & -2 \\ 3 & 1 \end{bmatrix}$, $B = \begin{bmatrix} 3 & 1 \\ -2 & 6 \end{bmatrix}$

14. $A = \begin{bmatrix} 1 & 2 \\ 2 & 1 \end{bmatrix}$, $B = \begin{bmatrix} -3 & -2 \\ 4 & 2 \end{bmatrix}$

15. $A = \begin{bmatrix} 8 & -1 \\ 2 & 3 \\ -4 & 5 \end{bmatrix}$, $B = \begin{bmatrix} 1 & 6 \\ -1 & -5 \\ 1 & 10 \end{bmatrix}$

16. $A = \begin{bmatrix} 1 & -1 & 3 \\ 0 & 6 & 9 \end{bmatrix}$, $B = \begin{bmatrix} -2 & 0 & -5 \\ -3 & 4 & -7 \end{bmatrix}$

17. $A = \begin{bmatrix} 4 & 5 & 1 & 3 & 4 \\ 1 & 2 & -2 & -1 & 0 \end{bmatrix}$, $B = \begin{bmatrix} 1 & 0 & -1 & 1 & 0 \\ -6 & 8 & 2 & -3 & -7 \end{bmatrix}$

18. $A = \begin{bmatrix} -1 & 4 & 0 \\ 3 & -2 & 2 \\ 5 & 4 & -1 \\ 0 & 8 & -6 \\ -4 & -1 & 0 \end{bmatrix}$, $B = \begin{bmatrix} -3 & 5 & 1 \\ 2 & -4 & -7 \\ 10 & -9 & -1 \\ 3 & 2 & -4 \\ 0 & 1 & -2 \end{bmatrix}$

19. $A = \begin{bmatrix} 6 & 0 & 3 \\ -1 & -4 & 0 \end{bmatrix}$, $B = \begin{bmatrix} 8 & -1 \\ 4 & -3 \end{bmatrix}$

20. $A = \begin{bmatrix} 3 \\ 2 \\ -1 \end{bmatrix}$, $B = \begin{bmatrix} -4 & 6 & 2 \end{bmatrix}$

Evaluating an Expression In Exercises 21–24, evaluate the expression.

21. $\begin{bmatrix} -5 & 0 \\ 3 & -6 \end{bmatrix} + \begin{bmatrix} 7 & 1 \\ -2 & -1 \end{bmatrix} + \begin{bmatrix} -10 & -8 \\ 14 & 6 \end{bmatrix}$

22. $\begin{bmatrix} 6 & 9 \\ -1 & 0 \\ 7 & 1 \end{bmatrix} + \begin{bmatrix} 0 & 5 \\ -2 & -1 \\ 3 & -6 \end{bmatrix} + \begin{bmatrix} -13 & -7 \\ 4 & -1 \\ -6 & 0 \end{bmatrix}$

23. $\frac{1}{3}\left(\begin{bmatrix} -4 & 0 & 1 \\ 0 & 2 & -12 \end{bmatrix} - \begin{bmatrix} 5 & 1 & -2 \\ 12 & -6 & 3 \end{bmatrix} \right)$

24. $\frac{1}{2}([3 \quad -2 \quad 4 \quad 0] - [10 \quad -6 \quad -18 \quad 9])$

Operations with Matrices In Exercises 25–28, use the matrix capabilities of a graphing utility to evaluate the expression. Round your results to the nearest thousandths, if necessary.

25. $\frac{3}{7}\begin{bmatrix} 2 & 5 \\ -1 & -4 \end{bmatrix} + 6\begin{bmatrix} -3 & 0 \\ 2 & 2 \end{bmatrix}$

26. $\frac{4}{5}\begin{bmatrix} 14 & -11 \\ -22 & 19 \end{bmatrix} + 7\begin{bmatrix} -22 & 20 \\ 13 & 6 \end{bmatrix}$

27. $-5\begin{bmatrix} 3.211 & 6.829 \\ -1.004 & 4.914 \\ 0.055 & -3.889 \end{bmatrix} - \frac{1}{4}\begin{bmatrix} 1.630 & -3.090 \\ 5.256 & 8.335 \\ -9.768 & 4.251 \end{bmatrix}$

28. $-3\begin{bmatrix} 10 & 15 \\ -20 & 10 \\ 12 & 4 \end{bmatrix} - \frac{1}{8}\left(\begin{bmatrix} 12 & 11 \\ 7 & 0 \\ 6 & 9 \end{bmatrix} + \begin{bmatrix} -3 & 13 \\ -3 & 8 \\ -14 & 15 \end{bmatrix} \right)$

Solving a Matrix Equation In Exercises 29–32, solve for X when

$$A = \begin{bmatrix} -2 & -1 \\ 1 & 0 \\ 3 & -4 \end{bmatrix} \quad \text{and} \quad B = \begin{bmatrix} 0 & 3 \\ 2 & 0 \\ -4 & -1 \end{bmatrix}.$$

29. $3X = A + 3B$
30. $2X = 2A + B$
31. $2A + 4B = -2X$
32. $-3X - 3A = 9B$

Finding the Product of Two Matrices In Exercises 33–40, find AB, if possible.

33. $A = \begin{bmatrix} 3 & -1 \\ 4 & -5 \\ 2 & 6 \end{bmatrix}$, $B = \begin{bmatrix} 6 & 0 \\ 7 & -1 \end{bmatrix}$

34. $A = \begin{bmatrix} -1 & 6 \\ -4 & 5 \\ 0 & 3 \end{bmatrix}$, $B = \begin{bmatrix} 2 & 3 \\ 0 & 9 \end{bmatrix}$

35. $A = \begin{bmatrix} 2 & 1 \\ -3 & 4 \\ -1 & 6 \end{bmatrix}$, $B = \begin{bmatrix} 0 & -3 & 0 \\ 4 & 0 & 2 \\ 8 & -2 & 7 \end{bmatrix}$

36. $A = \begin{bmatrix} 1 & 0 & 3 & -2 \\ 6 & 13 & 8 & -17 \end{bmatrix}$, $B = \begin{bmatrix} 1 & 6 \\ 4 & 2 \end{bmatrix}$

37. $A = \begin{bmatrix} 6 & 0 & 0 \\ 0 & 4 & 0 \\ 0 & 0 & -2 \end{bmatrix}$, $B = \begin{bmatrix} \frac{1}{3} & 0 & 0 \\ 0 & -\frac{1}{4} & 0 \\ 0 & 0 & \frac{1}{6} \end{bmatrix}$

38. $A = \begin{bmatrix} 5 & 0 & 0 \\ 0 & -8 & 0 \\ 0 & 0 & 7 \end{bmatrix}$, $B = \begin{bmatrix} \frac{1}{5} & 0 & 0 \\ 0 & -\frac{1}{8} & 0 \\ 0 & 0 & \frac{1}{2} \end{bmatrix}$

39. $A = \begin{bmatrix} 5 \\ -3 \\ 4 \end{bmatrix}$, $B = [2 \quad -8 \quad 4]$

40. $A = \begin{bmatrix} 5 \\ 6 \end{bmatrix}$, $B = [-3 \quad -1 \quad -5 \quad -9]$

Operations with Matrices In Exercises 41–46, find, if possible, (a) AB, (b) BA, and (c) A^2. (*Note:* $A^2 = AA$.) Use the matrix capabilities of a graphing utility to verify your results.

41. $A = \begin{bmatrix} 1 & 2 \\ 4 & 2 \end{bmatrix}$, $B = \begin{bmatrix} 2 & -1 \\ -1 & 8 \end{bmatrix}$

42. $A = \begin{bmatrix} 6 & 3 \\ -2 & -4 \end{bmatrix}$, $B = \begin{bmatrix} -2 & 0 \\ 2 & 4 \end{bmatrix}$

43. $A = \begin{bmatrix} 3 & -1 \\ 1 & 3 \end{bmatrix}$, $B = \begin{bmatrix} 1 & -3 \\ 3 & 1 \end{bmatrix}$

44. $A = \begin{bmatrix} 1 & -1 \\ 1 & 1 \end{bmatrix}$, $B = \begin{bmatrix} 1 & 3 \\ -3 & 1 \end{bmatrix}$

45. $A = \begin{bmatrix} 7 \\ 8 \\ -1 \end{bmatrix}$, $B = [1 \quad 1 \quad 2]$

46. $A = [3 \quad 2 \quad 1]$, $B = \begin{bmatrix} 2 \\ 3 \\ 0 \end{bmatrix}$

Matrix Multiplication In Exercises 47–50, use the matrix capabilities of a graphing utility to find AB, if possible.

47. $A = \begin{bmatrix} 1 & -12 & 4 \\ 14 & 10 & 12 \\ 6 & -15 & 3 \end{bmatrix}$, $B = \begin{bmatrix} 12 & 10 \\ -6 & 12 \\ 10 & 16 \end{bmatrix}$

48. $A = \begin{bmatrix} -3 & 8 & -6 & 8 \\ -12 & 15 & 9 & 6 \\ 5 & -1 & 1 & 5 \end{bmatrix}$, $B = \begin{bmatrix} 3 & 1 & 6 \\ 24 & 15 & 14 \\ 16 & 10 & 21 \\ 8 & -4 & 10 \end{bmatrix}$

49. $A = \begin{bmatrix} 7 & 6 & 9 & -4 \\ 3 & -4 & 11 & -2 \\ -5 & -8 & 1 & 12 \end{bmatrix}$, $B = \begin{bmatrix} 15 & 8 \\ 23 & -17 \\ 9 & 10 \end{bmatrix}$

50. $A = \begin{bmatrix} -2 & 6 & 12 \\ 21 & -5 & 6 \\ 13 & -2 & 9 \end{bmatrix}$, $B = \begin{bmatrix} 3 & 0 \\ -7 & 18 \\ 34 & 14 \\ 0.5 & 1.4 \end{bmatrix}$

Operations with Matrices   In Exercises 51–54, use the matrix capabilities of a graphing utility to evaluate the expression.

51. $\begin{bmatrix} 3 & 1 \\ 0 & -2 \end{bmatrix}\begin{bmatrix} 1 & 0 \\ -2 & 2 \end{bmatrix}\begin{bmatrix} 1 & 0 \\ 2 & 4 \end{bmatrix}$

52. $\begin{bmatrix} 6 & 5 & -1 \\ 1 & -2 & 0 \end{bmatrix}\begin{bmatrix} 0 & 3 \\ -1 & -3 \\ 4 & 1 \end{bmatrix}\begin{bmatrix} -2 & 2 \\ 0 & -1 \end{bmatrix}$

53. $\begin{bmatrix} 0 & 2 & -2 \\ 4 & 1 & 2 \end{bmatrix}\left(\begin{bmatrix} 4 & 0 \\ 0 & -1 \\ -1 & 2 \end{bmatrix}+\begin{bmatrix} -2 & 3 \\ -3 & 5 \\ 0 & -3 \end{bmatrix}\right)$

54. $\begin{bmatrix} 3 \\ -1 \\ 5 \\ 7 \end{bmatrix}([5 \quad 6] + [7 \quad -1] + [-8 \quad 9])$

Matrix Multiplication   In Exercises 55–58, use matrix multiplication to determine whether each matrix is a solution of the system of equations. Use a graphing utility to verify your results.

55. $\begin{cases} x + 2y = 4 \\ 3x + 2y = 0 \end{cases}$

(a) $\begin{bmatrix} 2 \\ 1 \end{bmatrix}$ (b) $\begin{bmatrix} -2 \\ 3 \end{bmatrix}$ (c) $\begin{bmatrix} -4 \\ 4 \end{bmatrix}$ (d) $\begin{bmatrix} 2 \\ -3 \end{bmatrix}$

56. $\begin{cases} 6x + 2y = 0 \\ -x + 5y = 16 \end{cases}$

(a) $\begin{bmatrix} -1 \\ 3 \end{bmatrix}$ (b) $\begin{bmatrix} 2 \\ -6 \end{bmatrix}$ (c) $\begin{bmatrix} 3 \\ -9 \end{bmatrix}$ (d) $\begin{bmatrix} -3 \\ 9 \end{bmatrix}$

57. $\begin{cases} -2x - 3y = -6 \\ 4x + 2y = 20 \end{cases}$

(a) $\begin{bmatrix} 3 \\ 0 \end{bmatrix}$ (b) $\begin{bmatrix} 4 \\ 2 \end{bmatrix}$ (c) $\begin{bmatrix} -6 \\ 6 \end{bmatrix}$ (d) $\begin{bmatrix} 6 \\ -2 \end{bmatrix}$

58. $\begin{cases} 5x - 7y = -15 \\ 3x + y = 17 \end{cases}$

(a) $\begin{bmatrix} -4 \\ -5 \end{bmatrix}$ (b) $\begin{bmatrix} 5 \\ 2 \end{bmatrix}$ (c) $\begin{bmatrix} 4 \\ 5 \end{bmatrix}$ (d) $\begin{bmatrix} 2 \\ 11 \end{bmatrix}$

Solving a System of Linear Equations   In Exercises 59–66, (a) write the system of equations as a matrix equation $AX = B$ and (b) use Gauss-Jordan elimination on the augmented matrix $\lfloor A \vdots B \rfloor$ to solve for the matrix X. Use a graphing utility to check your solution.

59. $\begin{cases} -x_1 + x_2 = 4 \\ -2x_1 + x_2 = 0 \end{cases}$ 60. $\begin{cases} 2x_1 + 3x_2 = 5 \\ x_1 + 4x_2 = 10 \end{cases}$

61. $\begin{cases} -2x_1 - 3x_2 = -4 \\ 6x_1 + x_2 = -36 \end{cases}$

62. $\begin{cases} -4x_1 + 9x_2 = -13 \\ x_1 - 3x_2 = 12 \end{cases}$

63. $\begin{cases} x_1 - 2x_2 + 3x_3 = 9 \\ -x_1 + 3x_2 - x_3 = -6 \\ 2x_1 - 5x_2 + 5x_3 = 17 \end{cases}$

64. $\begin{cases} x_1 + x_2 - 3x_3 = 9 \\ -x_1 + 2x_2 = 6 \\ x_1 - x_2 + x_3 = -5 \end{cases}$

65. $\begin{cases} x_1 - 5x_2 + 2x_3 = -20 \\ -3x_1 + x_2 - x_3 = 8 \\ -2x_2 + 5x_3 = -16 \end{cases}$

66. $\begin{cases} x_1 - x_2 + 4x_3 = 17 \\ x_1 + 3x_2 = -11 \\ -6x_2 + 5x_3 = 40 \end{cases}$

Operations with Matrices   In Exercises 67–72, use a graphing utility to perform the operations for the matrices A, B, and C and the scalar c. Write a brief statement comparing the results of parts (a) and (b).

$A = \begin{bmatrix} 1 & 2 & -1 \\ 0 & -2 & 3 \\ 4 & -3 & 2 \end{bmatrix}$, $B = \begin{bmatrix} 2 & 3 & 0 \\ 4 & 1 & -2 \\ -1 & 2 & 0 \end{bmatrix}$,

$C = \begin{bmatrix} 3 & -2 & 1 \\ -4 & 0 & 3 \\ -1 & 3 & -2 \end{bmatrix}$, and $c = 3$

67. (a) $A(B + C)$ (b) $AB + AC$
68. (a) $(B + C)A$ (b) $BA + CA$
69. (a) $A(BC)$ (b) $(AB)C$
70. (a) $c(AB)$ (b) $(cA)B$
71. (a) $(A + B)^2$ (b) $A^2 + AB + BA + B^2$
72. (a) $(A - B)^2$ (b) $A^2 - AB - BA + B^2$

Operations with Matrices   In Exercises 73–80, perform the operations (a) using a graphing utility and (b) by hand algebraically. If it is not possible to perform the operation(s), state the reason.

$A = \begin{bmatrix} 1 & 2 & -2 \\ -1 & 1 & 0 \end{bmatrix}$, $B = \begin{bmatrix} -1 & 4 & -1 \\ -2 & -1 & 0 \end{bmatrix}$,

$C = \begin{bmatrix} 1 & 2 \\ -2 & 3 \\ 1 & 0 \end{bmatrix}$, $c = -2$, and $d = -3$

73. $A + cB$ 74. $B + dA$
75. $c(AB)$ 76. $A(B + C)$
77. $CA - BC$ 78. dAB^2
79. $cdA + B$ 80. $cA + dB$

Operations with Matrices   In Exercises 81 and 82, use a graphing utility to perform the indicated operations.

$A = \begin{bmatrix} 2 & 0 \\ 4 & 5 \end{bmatrix}$ and $B = \begin{bmatrix} 5 & 3 \\ 1 & 4 \end{bmatrix}$

81. $A^2 - 5A + 2I_2$ 82. $B^2 - 7B + 6I_2$

83. Manufacturing A corporation that makes sunglasses has four factories, each of which manufactures standard and designer sunglasses. The production levels are represented by A.

$$A = \begin{matrix} & \overbrace{\begin{matrix} 1 & 2 & 3 & 4 \end{matrix}}^{\text{Factory}} & \\ \begin{bmatrix} 100 & 120 & 60 & 40 \\ 140 & 160 & 200 & 80 \end{bmatrix} & \begin{matrix} \text{Standard} \\ \text{Designer} \end{matrix} \left.\rule{0pt}{18pt}\right\} \text{Sunglass type} \end{matrix}$$

Find the production levels when production is decreased by 15%.

84. Manufacturing A corporation has four factories, each of which manufactures sport utility vehicles and pickup trucks. The production levels are represented by A.

$$A = \begin{matrix} & \overbrace{\begin{matrix} 1 & 2 & 3 & 4 \end{matrix}}^{\text{Factory}} & \\ \begin{bmatrix} 100 & 90 & 70 & 30 \\ 40 & 20 & 60 & 60 \end{bmatrix} & \begin{matrix} \text{SUV} \\ \text{Pickup} \end{matrix} \left.\rule{0pt}{18pt}\right\} \text{Vehicle type} \end{matrix}$$

Find the production levels when production is decreased by 10%.

85. Manufacturing A corporation has three factories, each of which manufactures acoustic guitars and electric guitars. The production levels are represented by A.

$$A = \begin{matrix} & \overbrace{\begin{matrix} A & B & C \end{matrix}}^{\text{Factory}} & \\ \begin{bmatrix} 70 & 50 & 25 \\ 35 & 100 & 70 \end{bmatrix} & \begin{matrix} \text{Acoustic} \\ \text{Electric} \end{matrix} \left.\rule{0pt}{18pt}\right\} \text{Guitar type} \end{matrix}$$

Find the production levels when production is increased by 20%.

86. Tourism A vacation service has identified four resort hotels with a special all-inclusive package (room and meals included) at a popular travel destination. The quoted room rates are for double and family (maximum of four people) occupancy for 5 days and 4 nights. The current rates for the two types of rooms at the four hotels are represented by matrix A.

$$A = \begin{matrix} & \overbrace{\begin{matrix} w & x & y & z \end{matrix}}^{\text{Hotel}} & \\ \begin{bmatrix} 668 & 2666 & 973 & 918 \\ 1214 & 4637 & 1656 & 1699 \end{bmatrix} & \begin{matrix} \text{Double} \\ \text{Family} \end{matrix} \left.\rule{0pt}{18pt}\right\} \text{Occupancy} \end{matrix}$$

Room rates are guaranteed not to increase by more than 12%. What is the maximum rate per package per hotel during the next year?

87. Agriculture A fruit grower raises two crops, apples and peaches. Each of these crops is shipped to three different outlets. The shipment levels are represented by A.

$$A = \begin{matrix} & \overbrace{\begin{matrix} 1 & 2 & 3 \end{matrix}}^{\text{Outlet}} & \\ \begin{bmatrix} 125 & 100 & 75 \\ 100 & 175 & 125 \end{bmatrix} & \begin{matrix} \text{Apples} \\ \text{Peaches} \end{matrix} \left.\rule{0pt}{18pt}\right\} \text{Crop} \end{matrix}$$

(a) The grower earns a $3.50 profit per unit of apples and a $6.00 profit per unit of peaches. Organize the profit per unit of each crop in a matrix B.

(b) Find the product BA and interpret the result.

88. Physical Education The numbers of calories burned per hour by individuals of different weights performing different types of aerobic exercises are shown in the matrix.

$$B = \begin{matrix} \overbrace{\begin{matrix} \text{130-lb} & \text{155-lb} \\ \text{person} & \text{person} \end{matrix}}^{} & \\ \begin{bmatrix} 325 & 387 \\ 236 & 281 \\ 354 & 422 \end{bmatrix} & \begin{matrix} \text{Bicycling} \\ \text{Jogging} \\ \text{Swimming} \end{matrix} \end{matrix}$$

(a) A 130-pound person and a 155-pound person bicycle for 30 minutes, jog for 15 minutes, and swim for 60 minutes. Organize the time spent exercising in a matrix A.

(b) Find the product AB and interpret the result.

89. *Why you should learn it* *(p. 518)* A company manufactures boats. Its labor-hour and wage requirements are represented by L and W, respectively. Compute LW and interpret the result.

$$L = \begin{matrix} & \overbrace{\begin{matrix} \text{Cutting} & \text{Assembly} & \text{Packaging} \end{matrix}}^{\text{Department}} & \\ \begin{bmatrix} 1.0 \text{ h} & 0.5 \text{ h} & 0.2 \text{ h} \\ 1.6 \text{ h} & 1.0 \text{ h} & 0.2 \text{ h} \\ 2.5 \text{ h} & 2.0 \text{ h} & 1.4 \text{ h} \end{bmatrix} & \begin{matrix} \text{Small} \\ \text{Medium} \\ \text{Large} \end{matrix} \left.\rule{0pt}{22pt}\right\} \text{Boat size} \end{matrix}$$

$$W = \begin{matrix} & \overbrace{\begin{matrix} A & B \end{matrix}}^{\text{Plant}} & \\ \begin{bmatrix} \$15 & \$13 \\ \$12 & \$11 \\ \$11 & \$10 \end{bmatrix} & \begin{matrix} \text{Cutting} \\ \text{Assembly} \\ \text{Packaging} \end{matrix} \left.\rule{0pt}{22pt}\right\} \text{Department} \end{matrix}$$

90. Inventory Control A company sells five models of computers through three retail outlets. The inventories are represented by S. The wholesale and retail prices are represented by T. Compute ST and interpret the result.

$$S = \begin{matrix} & \overbrace{\begin{matrix} A & B & C & D & E \end{matrix}}^{\text{Model}} & \\ \begin{bmatrix} 3 & 2 & 2 & 3 & 0 \\ 0 & 2 & 3 & 4 & 3 \\ 4 & 2 & 1 & 3 & 2 \end{bmatrix} & \begin{matrix} 1 \\ 2 \\ 3 \end{matrix} \left.\rule{0pt}{22pt}\right\} \text{Outlet} \end{matrix}$$

$$T = \begin{matrix} & \overbrace{\begin{matrix} \text{Wholesale} & \text{Retail} \end{matrix}}^{\text{Price}} & \\ \begin{bmatrix} \$840 & \$1100 \\ \$1200 & \$1350 \\ \$1450 & \$1650 \\ \$2650 & \$3000 \\ \$3050 & \$3200 \end{bmatrix} & \begin{matrix} A \\ B \\ C \\ D \\ E \end{matrix} \left.\rule{0pt}{30pt}\right\} \text{Model} \end{matrix}$$

91. Politics The matrix

From

$$P = \begin{bmatrix} 0.6 & 0.1 & 0.1 \\ 0.2 & 0.7 & 0.1 \\ 0.2 & 0.2 & 0.8 \end{bmatrix} \begin{matrix} 1 \\ 2 \\ 3 \end{matrix} \Bigg\} \text{To}$$

$$\begin{matrix} \text{R} & \text{D} & \text{I} \end{matrix}$$

is called a *stochastic matrix*. Each entry $p_{ij} (i \neq j)$ represents the proportion of the voting population that changes from party i to party j, and p_{ii} represents the proportion that remains loyal to the party from one election to the next. Compute and interpret P^2.

92. Politics Use a graphing utility to find P^3, P^4, P^5, P^6, P^7, and P^8 for the matrix given in Exercise 91. Can you detect a pattern as P is raised to higher powers?

Conclusions

True or False? **In Exercises 93 and 94, determine whether the statement is true or false. Justify your answer.**

93. Two matrices can be added only when they have the same dimension.

94. $\begin{bmatrix} -6 & -2 \\ 2 & -6 \end{bmatrix}\begin{bmatrix} 4 & 0 \\ 0 & -1 \end{bmatrix} = \begin{bmatrix} 4 & 0 \\ 0 & -1 \end{bmatrix}\begin{bmatrix} -6 & -2 \\ 2 & -6 \end{bmatrix}$

Think About It **In Exercises 95–102, let matrices A, B, C, and D be of dimensions 2×3, 2×3, 3×2, and 2×2, respectively. Determine whether the matrices are of proper dimension to perform the operation(s). If so, give the dimension of the answer.**

95. $A + 2C$ **96.** $B - 3C$

97. CD **98.** BC

99. $CA - D$ **100.** $CB - D$

101. $D(A - 3B)$ **102.** $C(A + 2B)$

Think About It **In Exercises 103–106, use the matrices**

$$A = \begin{bmatrix} 2 & -1 \\ 1 & 3 \end{bmatrix} \quad \text{and} \quad B = \begin{bmatrix} -1 & 1 \\ 0 & -2 \end{bmatrix}.$$

103. Show that $(A + B)^2 \neq A^2 + 2AB + B^2$.

104. Show that $(A - B)^2 \neq A^2 - 2AB + B^2$.

105. Show that $(A + B)(A - B) \neq A^2 - B^2$.

106. Show that $(A + B)^2 = A^2 + AB + BA + B^2$.

107. Think About It If a, b, and c are real numbers such that $c \neq 0$ and $ac = bc$, then $a = b$. However, if A, B, and C are nonzero matrices such that $AC = BC$, then A is *not necessarily* equal to B. Illustrate this using the following matrices.

$$A = \begin{bmatrix} 0 & 1 \\ 0 & 1 \end{bmatrix}, \quad B = \begin{bmatrix} 1 & 0 \\ 1 & 0 \end{bmatrix}, \quad C = \begin{bmatrix} 2 & 3 \\ 2 & 3 \end{bmatrix}$$

108. Think About It If a and b are real numbers such that $ab = 0$, then $a = 0$ or $b = 0$. However, if A and B are matrices such that $AB = O$, it is *not necessarily* true that $A = O$ or $B = O$. Illustrate this using the following matrices.

$$A = \begin{bmatrix} 3 & 3 \\ 4 & 4 \end{bmatrix}, \quad B = \begin{bmatrix} 1 & -1 \\ -1 & 1 \end{bmatrix}$$

109. Exploration Let $i = \sqrt{-1}$ and let

$$A = \begin{bmatrix} i & 0 \\ 0 & i \end{bmatrix} \quad \text{and} \quad B = \begin{bmatrix} 0 & -i \\ i & 0 \end{bmatrix}.$$

(a) Find A^2, A^3, and A^4. Identify any similarities with i^2, i^3, and i^4.

(b) Find and identify B^2.

110. Exploration Let A and B be unequal diagonal matrices of the same dimension. (A **diagonal matrix** is a square matrix in which each entry not on the main diagonal is zero.) Determine the products AB for several pairs of such matrices. Make a conjecture about a quick rule for such products.

111. Think About It Let matrices A and B be of dimensions 3×2 and 2×2, respectively. Answer the following questions and explain your reasoning.

(a) Is it possible that $A = B$?

(b) Is $A + B$ defined?

(c) Is AB defined?

112. **HOW DO YOU SEE IT?** An electronics manufacturer produces two models of LCD televisions, which are shipped to three warehouses. The shipment levels are represented by A.

Warehouse

$$A = \begin{bmatrix} 5,000 & 4,000 & 8,000 \\ 6,000 & 10,000 & 5,000 \end{bmatrix} \begin{matrix} \text{A} \\ \text{B} \end{matrix} \Bigg\} \text{Model}$$

$$\begin{matrix} 1 & 2 & 3 \end{matrix}$$

(a) Interpret the value of a_{21}.

(b) How could you find the shipment levels when the shipments are increased by 15%?

(c) Each model A television sells for $700 and each model B television sells for $900. How could you use matrices to find the cost of the two models of LCD televisions at each warehouse?

Cumulative Mixed Review

Condensing a Logarithmic Expression **In Exercises 113 and 114, condense the expression to the logarithm of a single quantity.**

113. $3 \ln 4 - \frac{1}{3} \ln(x^2 + 3)$ **114.** $2 \ln 7t^4 - \frac{3}{5} \ln t^5$

7.6 The Inverse of a Square Matrix

The Inverse of a Matrix

This section further develops the algebra of matrices. To begin, consider the real number equation $ax = b$. To solve this equation for x, multiply each side of the equation by a^{-1} (provided that $a \neq 0$).

$$ax = b$$
$$(a^{-1}a)x = a^{-1}b$$
$$(1)x = a^{-1}b$$
$$x = a^{-1}b$$

The number a^{-1} is called the *multiplicative inverse* of a because $a^{-1}a = 1$. The definition of the multiplicative **inverse of a matrix** is similar.

> **Definition of the Inverse of a Square Matrix**
>
> Let A be an $n \times n$ matrix and let I_n be the $n \times n$ identity matrix. If there exists a matrix A^{-1} such that
>
> $$AA^{-1} = I_n = A^{-1}A$$
>
> then A^{-1} is called the **inverse** of A. The symbol A^{-1} is read "A inverse."

EXAMPLE 1 The Inverse of a Matrix

Show that B is the inverse of A, where

$$A = \begin{bmatrix} -1 & 2 \\ -1 & 1 \end{bmatrix} \quad \text{and} \quad B = \begin{bmatrix} 1 & -2 \\ 1 & -1 \end{bmatrix}.$$

Solution

To show that B is the inverse of A, show that $AB = I = BA$, as follows.

$$AB = \begin{bmatrix} -1 & 2 \\ -1 & 1 \end{bmatrix}\begin{bmatrix} 1 & -2 \\ 1 & -1 \end{bmatrix} = \begin{bmatrix} -1+2 & 2-2 \\ -1+1 & 2-1 \end{bmatrix} = \begin{bmatrix} 1 & 0 \\ 0 & 1 \end{bmatrix}$$

$$BA = \begin{bmatrix} 1 & -2 \\ 1 & -1 \end{bmatrix}\begin{bmatrix} -1 & 2 \\ -1 & 1 \end{bmatrix} = \begin{bmatrix} -1+2 & 2-2 \\ -1+1 & 2-1 \end{bmatrix} = \begin{bmatrix} 1 & 0 \\ 0 & 1 \end{bmatrix}$$

As you can see,

$$AB = I = BA.$$

This is an example of a square matrix that has an inverse. Note that not all square matrices have inverses.

 ✓ **Checkpoint** ◀))) *Audio-video solution in English & Spanish at LarsonPrecalculus.com.*

Show that B is the inverse of A, where

$$A = \begin{bmatrix} 2 & -1 \\ -3 & 1 \end{bmatrix} \quad \text{and} \quad B = \begin{bmatrix} -1 & -1 \\ -3 & -2 \end{bmatrix}.$$

Recall that it is not always true that $AB = BA$, even when both products are defined. However, if A and B are both square matrices and $AB = I_n$, then it can be shown that $BA = I_n$. So, in Example 1, you need only check that $AB = I_2$.

What you should learn
- ▶ Verify that two matrices are inverses of each other.
- ▶ Use Gauss-Jordan elimination to find inverses of matrices.
- ▶ Use a formula to find inverses of 2×2 matrices.
- ▶ Use inverse matrices to solve systems of linear equations.

Why you should learn it

A system of equations can be solved using the inverse of the coefficient matrix. This method is particularly useful when the coefficients are the same for several systems, but the constants are different. Exercise 66 on page 540 shows how to use an inverse matrix to find a model for the number of international travelers to the United States from South America.

Finding Inverse Matrices

When a matrix A has an inverse, A is called **invertible** (or **nonsingular**); otherwise, A is called **singular.** A nonsquare matrix cannot have an inverse. To see this, note that if A is of dimension $m \times n$ and B is of dimension $n \times m$ (where $m \neq n$), then the products AB and BA are of different dimensions and so cannot be equal to each other. Not all square matrices have inverses, as you will see later in this section. When a matrix does have an inverse, however, that inverse is unique. Example 2 shows how to use systems of equations to find the inverse of a matrix.

EXAMPLE 2   Finding the Inverse of a Matrix

See LarsonPrecalculus.com for an interactive version of this type of example.

Find the inverse of

$$A = \begin{bmatrix} 1 & 4 \\ -1 & -3 \end{bmatrix}.$$

Solution

To find the inverse of A, try to solve the matrix equation $AX = I$ for X.

$$\begin{array}{ccc} A & X & I \end{array}$$
$$\begin{bmatrix} 1 & 4 \\ -1 & -3 \end{bmatrix}\begin{bmatrix} x_{11} & x_{12} \\ x_{21} & x_{22} \end{bmatrix} = \begin{bmatrix} 1 & 0 \\ 0 & 1 \end{bmatrix}$$

$$\begin{bmatrix} x_{11} + 4x_{21} & x_{12} + 4x_{22} \\ -x_{11} - 3x_{21} & -x_{12} - 3x_{22} \end{bmatrix} = \begin{bmatrix} 1 & 0 \\ 0 & 1 \end{bmatrix}$$

Equating corresponding entries, you obtain the following two systems of linear equations.

$$\begin{cases} x_{11} + 4x_{21} = 1 \\ -x_{11} - 3x_{21} = 0 \end{cases} \quad \text{Linear system with two variables, } x_{11} \text{ and } x_{21}.$$

$$\begin{cases} x_{12} + 4x_{22} = 0 \\ -x_{12} - 3x_{22} = 1 \end{cases} \quad \text{Linear system with two variables, } x_{12} \text{ and } x_{22}.$$

Solve the first system using elementary row operations to determine that $x_{11} = -3$ and $x_{21} = 1$. From the second system you can determine that $x_{12} = -4$ and $x_{22} = 1$. Therefore, the inverse of A is

$$A^{-1} = X$$

$$= \begin{bmatrix} -3 & -4 \\ 1 & 1 \end{bmatrix}.$$

You can use matrix multiplication to check this result.

Check

$$AA^{-1} = \begin{bmatrix} 1 & 4 \\ -1 & -3 \end{bmatrix}\begin{bmatrix} -3 & -4 \\ 1 & 1 \end{bmatrix} = \begin{bmatrix} 1 & 0 \\ 0 & 1 \end{bmatrix} \checkmark$$

$$A^{-1}A = \begin{bmatrix} -3 & -4 \\ 1 & 1 \end{bmatrix}\begin{bmatrix} 1 & 4 \\ -1 & -3 \end{bmatrix} = \begin{bmatrix} 1 & 0 \\ 0 & 1 \end{bmatrix} \checkmark$$

✓ **Checkpoint** Audio-video solution in English & Spanish at LarsonPrecalculus.com.

Find the inverse of

$$A = \begin{bmatrix} 1 & -2 \\ -1 & 3 \end{bmatrix}.$$

Explore the Concept

Most graphing utilities are capable of finding the inverse of a square matrix. Try using a graphing utility to find the inverse of the matrix

$$A = \begin{bmatrix} 2 & -3 & 1 \\ -1 & 2 & -1 \\ -2 & 0 & 1 \end{bmatrix}.$$

After you find A^{-1}, store it as $[B]$ and use the graphing utility to find $[A] \times [B]$ and $[B] \times [A]$. What can you conclude?

In Example 2, note that the two systems of linear equations have the *same coefficient matrix A*. Rather than solve the two systems represented by

$$\begin{bmatrix} 1 & 4 & \vdots & 1 \\ -1 & -3 & \vdots & 0 \end{bmatrix}$$

and

$$\begin{bmatrix} 1 & 4 & \vdots & 0 \\ -1 & -3 & \vdots & 1 \end{bmatrix}$$

separately, you can solve them *simultaneously* by *adjoining* the identity matrix to the coefficient matrix to obtain

$$\begin{matrix} A & & I \\ \begin{bmatrix} 1 & 4 & \vdots & 1 & 0 \\ -1 & -3 & \vdots & 0 & 1 \end{bmatrix} \end{matrix}.$$

This "doubly augmented" matrix can be represented as

$$[A \; \vdots \; I].$$

By applying Gauss-Jordan elimination to this matrix, you can solve *both* systems with a single elimination process.

$$\begin{bmatrix} 1 & 4 & \vdots & 1 & 0 \\ -1 & -3 & \vdots & 0 & 1 \end{bmatrix}$$

$$R_1 + R_2 \to \begin{bmatrix} 1 & 4 & \vdots & 1 & 0 \\ 0 & 1 & \vdots & 1 & 1 \end{bmatrix}$$

$$-4R_2 + R_1 \to \begin{bmatrix} 1 & 0 & \vdots & -3 & -4 \\ 0 & 1 & \vdots & 1 & 1 \end{bmatrix}$$

So, from the "doubly augmented" matrix $[A \; \vdots \; I]$, you obtained the matrix $[I \; \vdots \; A^{-1}]$.

$$\begin{matrix} A & & I \\ \begin{bmatrix} 1 & 4 & \vdots & 1 & 0 \\ -1 & -3 & \vdots & 0 & 1 \end{bmatrix} \end{matrix} \implies \begin{matrix} I & & A^{-1} \\ \begin{bmatrix} 1 & 0 & \vdots & -3 & -4 \\ 0 & 1 & \vdots & 1 & 1 \end{bmatrix} \end{matrix}$$

This procedure (or algorithm) works for any square matrix that has an inverse.

> ## Explore the Concept
>
> Select two 2×2 matrices A and B that have inverses. Enter them into your graphing utility and calculate $(AB)^{-1}$. Then calculate $B^{-1}A^{-1}$ and $A^{-1}B^{-1}$. Make a conjecture about the inverse of the product of two invertible matrices.

Finding an Inverse Matrix

Let A be a square matrix of dimension $n \times n$.

1. Write the $n \times 2n$ matrix that consists of the given matrix A on the left and the $n \times n$ identity matrix I on the right to obtain

   $$[A \; \vdots \; I].$$

2. If possible, row reduce A to I using elementary row operations on the *entire* matrix

   $$[A \; \vdots \; I].$$

   The result will be the matrix

   $$[I \; \vdots \; A^{-1}].$$

   If this is not possible, then A is not invertible.

3. Check your work by multiplying to see that

   $$AA^{-1} = I = A^{-1}A.$$

EXAMPLE 3   Finding the Inverse of a Matrix

Find the inverse of $A = \begin{bmatrix} 1 & -1 & 0 \\ 1 & 0 & -1 \\ 6 & -2 & -3 \end{bmatrix}$.

Solution

Begin by adjoining the identity matrix to A to form the matrix

$$[A \;\vdots\; I] = \begin{bmatrix} 1 & -1 & 0 & \vdots & 1 & 0 & 0 \\ 1 & 0 & -1 & \vdots & 0 & 1 & 0 \\ 6 & -2 & -3 & \vdots & 0 & 0 & 1 \end{bmatrix}.$$

Use elementary row operations to obtain the form $[I \;\vdots\; A^{-1}]$, as follows.

$$\begin{bmatrix} 1 & 0 & 0 & \vdots & -2 & -3 & 1 \\ 0 & 1 & 0 & \vdots & -3 & -3 & 1 \\ 0 & 0 & 1 & \vdots & -2 & -4 & 1 \end{bmatrix}$$

Therefore, the matrix A is invertible and its inverse is

$$A^{-1} = \begin{bmatrix} -2 & -3 & 1 \\ -3 & -3 & 1 \\ -2 & -4 & 1 \end{bmatrix}.$$

Confirm this result by multiplying A by A^{-1} to obtain I as follows.

Check

$$AA^{-1} = \begin{bmatrix} 1 & -1 & 0 \\ 1 & 0 & -1 \\ 6 & -2 & -3 \end{bmatrix}\begin{bmatrix} -2 & -3 & 1 \\ -3 & -3 & 1 \\ -2 & -4 & 1 \end{bmatrix} = \begin{bmatrix} 1 & 0 & 0 \\ 0 & 1 & 0 \\ 0 & 0 & 1 \end{bmatrix} = I$$

✓ **Checkpoint** 🔊))) *Audio-video solution in English & Spanish at LarsonPrecalculus.com.*

Find the inverse of $A = \begin{bmatrix} 1 & -2 & -1 \\ 0 & -1 & 2 \\ 1 & -2 & 0 \end{bmatrix}$.   ■

The algorithm shown in Example 3 applies to any $n \times n$ matrix A. When using this algorithm, if the matrix A does not reduce to the identity matrix, then A does not have an inverse. For instance, the following matrix has no inverse.

$$A = \begin{bmatrix} 1 & 2 & 0 \\ 3 & -1 & 2 \\ -2 & 3 & -2 \end{bmatrix}$$

To see why matrix A above has no inverse, begin by adjoining the identity matrix to A to form

$$[A \;\vdots\; I] = \begin{bmatrix} 1 & 2 & 0 & \vdots & 1 & 0 & 0 \\ 3 & -1 & 2 & \vdots & 0 & 1 & 0 \\ -2 & 3 & -2 & \vdots & 0 & 0 & 1 \end{bmatrix}.$$

Then, use elementary row operations to obtain

$$\begin{bmatrix} 1 & 2 & 0 & \vdots & 1 & 0 & 0 \\ 0 & -7 & 2 & \vdots & -3 & 1 & 0 \\ 0 & 0 & 0 & \vdots & -1 & 1 & 1 \end{bmatrix}.$$

At this point in the elimination process, you can see that it is impossible to obtain the identity matrix I on the left. Therefore, A is not invertible.

Technology Tip

Most graphing utilities can find the inverse of a matrix by using the inverse key $\boxed{x^{-1}}$. For instructions on how to use the inverse key to find the inverse of a matrix, see Appendix A; for specific keystrokes, go to this textbook's *Companion Website*.

[A]

[[1   4]
 [-1 -3]]

[A]⁻¹

[[-3 -4]
 [1   1]]

The Inverse of a 2 × 2 Matrix

Using Gauss-Jordan elimination to find the inverse of a matrix works well (even as a computer technique) for matrices of dimension 3×3 or greater. For 2×2 matrices, however, many people prefer to use a formula for the inverse rather than Gauss-Jordan elimination. This simple formula, which works *only* for 2×2 matrices, is explained as follows. If A is the 2×2 matrix given by

$$A = \begin{bmatrix} a & b \\ c & d \end{bmatrix}$$

then A is invertible if and only if

$$ad - bc \neq 0.$$

If $ad - bc \neq 0$, then the inverse is given by

$$A^{-1} = \frac{1}{ad - bc} \begin{bmatrix} d & -b \\ -c & a \end{bmatrix}. \qquad \text{Formula for the inverse of a } 2 \times 2 \text{ matrix}$$

The denominator

$$ad - bc$$

is called the *determinant* of the 2×2 matrix A. You will study determinants in the next section.

EXAMPLE 4   Finding the Inverse of a 2 × 2 Matrix

If possible, find the inverse of each matrix.

a. $A = \begin{bmatrix} 3 & -1 \\ -2 & 2 \end{bmatrix}$

b. $B = \begin{bmatrix} 3 & -1 \\ -6 & 2 \end{bmatrix}$

Solution

a. For the matrix A, apply the formula for the inverse of a 2×2 matrix to obtain

$$ad - bc = (3)(2) - (-1)(-2)$$

$$= 4.$$

Because this quantity is not zero, the inverse is formed by interchanging the entries on the main diagonal, changing the signs of the other two entries, and multiplying by the scalar $\frac{1}{4}$, as follows.

$$A^{-1} = \frac{1}{4} \begin{bmatrix} 2 & 1 \\ 2 & 3 \end{bmatrix} \qquad \text{Substitute for } a, b, c, d, \text{ and the determinant.}$$

$$= \begin{bmatrix} \frac{1}{2} & \frac{1}{4} \\ \frac{1}{2} & \frac{3}{4} \end{bmatrix} \qquad \text{Multiply by the scalar } \frac{1}{4}.$$

b. For the matrix B, you have

$$ad - bc = (3)(2) - (-1)(-6)$$

$$= 0$$

which means that B is not invertible.

✓ **Checkpoint** ◀))) *Audio-video solution in English & Spanish at LarsonPrecalculus.com.*

If possible, find the inverse of $A = \begin{bmatrix} 5 & -1 \\ 3 & 4 \end{bmatrix}$. ∎

Explore the Concept

Use a graphing utility to find the inverse of the matrix

$$A = \begin{bmatrix} 1 & -3 \\ -2 & 6 \end{bmatrix}.$$

What message appears on the screen? Why does the graphing utility display this message?

Systems of Linear Equations

You know that a system of linear equations can have exactly one solution, infinitely many solutions, or no solution. If the coefficient matrix A of a *square* system (a system that has the same number of equations as variables) is invertible, then the system has a unique solution, which is defined as follows.

A System of Equations with a Unique Solution

If A is an invertible matrix, then the system of linear equations represented by $AX = B$ has a unique solution given by

$$X = A^{-1}B.$$

The formula $X = A^{-1}B$ is used on most graphing utilities to solve linear systems that have invertible coefficient matrices. That is, you enter the $n \times n$ coefficient matrix $[A]$ and the $n \times 1$ column matrix $[B]$. The solution X is given by $[A]^{-1}[B]$.

EXAMPLE 5   Solving a System of Equations Using an Inverse

Use an inverse matrix to solve the system.

$$\begin{cases} 2x + 3y + z = -1 \\ 3x + 3y + z = 1 \\ 2x + 4y + z = -2 \end{cases}$$

Solution

Begin by writing the system as $AX = B$.

$$\begin{bmatrix} 2 & 3 & 1 \\ 3 & 3 & 1 \\ 2 & 4 & 1 \end{bmatrix} \begin{bmatrix} x \\ y \\ z \end{bmatrix} = \begin{bmatrix} -1 \\ 1 \\ -2 \end{bmatrix}$$

Then, use Gauss-Jordan elimination to find A^{-1}.

$$A^{-1} = \begin{bmatrix} -1 & 1 & 0 \\ -1 & 0 & 1 \\ 6 & -2 & -3 \end{bmatrix}$$

Finally, multiply B by A^{-1} on the left to obtain the solution.

$$X = A^{-1}B$$

$$= \begin{bmatrix} -1 & 1 & 0 \\ -1 & 0 & 1 \\ 6 & -2 & -3 \end{bmatrix} \begin{bmatrix} -1 \\ 1 \\ -2 \end{bmatrix}$$

$$= \begin{bmatrix} 2 \\ -1 \\ -2 \end{bmatrix}$$

So, the solution is $x = 2$, $y = -1$, and $z = -2$. Use a graphing utility to verify A^{-1} for the system of equations.

Remark

Remember that matrix multiplication is not commutative. So, you must multiply matrices in the correct order. For instance, in Example 5, you must multiply B by A^{-1} on the left.

✓ **Checkpoint** 🔊))) *Audio-video solution in English & Spanish at LarsonPrecalculus.com.*

Use an inverse matrix to solve the system.

$$\begin{cases} x + y + z = 6 \\ 3x + 5y + 4z = 27 \\ 3x + 6y + 5z = 35 \end{cases}$$

7.6   Exercises

Vocabulary and Concept Check

In Exercises 1 and 2, fill in the blank(s).

1. If there exists an $n \times n$ matrix A^{-1} such that $AA^{-1} = I_n = A^{-1}A$, then A^{-1} is called the _____ of A.

2. If a matrix A has an inverse, then it is called invertible or _____ ; if it does not have an inverse, then it is called _____ .

3. Do all square matrices have inverses?

4. Given that A and B are square matrices and $AB = I_n$, does $BA = I_n$?

Procedures and Problem Solving

The Inverse of a Matrix   In Exercises 5–10, show that B is the inverse of A.

5. $A = \begin{bmatrix} 1 & 3 \\ -1 & -2 \end{bmatrix}$, $B = \begin{bmatrix} -2 & -3 \\ 1 & 1 \end{bmatrix}$

6. $A = \begin{bmatrix} -4 & 3 \\ 3 & -2 \end{bmatrix}$, $B = \begin{bmatrix} 2 & 3 \\ 3 & 4 \end{bmatrix}$

7. $A = \begin{bmatrix} 5 & 4 \\ 3 & 2 \end{bmatrix}$, $B = \begin{bmatrix} -1 & 2 \\ \frac{3}{2} & -\frac{5}{2} \end{bmatrix}$

8. $A = \begin{bmatrix} -\frac{1}{2} & -\frac{5}{4} \\ 1 & 2 \end{bmatrix}$, $B = \begin{bmatrix} 8 & 5 \\ -4 & -2 \end{bmatrix}$

9. $A = \begin{bmatrix} 2 & -17 & 11 \\ -1 & 11 & -7 \\ 0 & 3 & -2 \end{bmatrix}$, $B = \begin{bmatrix} 1 & 1 & 2 \\ 2 & 4 & -3 \\ 3 & 6 & -5 \end{bmatrix}$

10. $A = \begin{bmatrix} -4 & 1 & 5 \\ -1 & 2 & 4 \\ 0 & -1 & -1 \end{bmatrix}$, $B = \frac{1}{4}\begin{bmatrix} -2 & 4 & 6 \\ 1 & -4 & -11 \\ -1 & 4 & 7 \end{bmatrix}$

Finding the Inverse of a Matrix   In Exercises 11–20, find the inverse of the matrix (if it exists).

11. $\begin{bmatrix} 2 & 0 \\ 0 & 3 \end{bmatrix}$

12. $\begin{bmatrix} 1 & 2 \\ 3 & 7 \end{bmatrix}$

13. $\begin{bmatrix} 1 & -2 \\ 2 & -3 \end{bmatrix}$

14. $\begin{bmatrix} -2 & 5 \\ 6 & -15 \\ 0 & 1 \end{bmatrix}$

15. $\begin{bmatrix} 2 & 7 & 1 \\ -3 & -9 & 2 \end{bmatrix}$

16. $\begin{bmatrix} -7 & 33 \\ 4 & -19 \end{bmatrix}$

17. $\begin{bmatrix} 1 & 0 & 0 \\ 3 & 5 & 0 \\ 2 & 5 & 0 \end{bmatrix}$

18. $\begin{bmatrix} 1 & 2 & 2 \\ 3 & 7 & 9 \\ -1 & -4 & -7 \end{bmatrix}$

19. $\begin{bmatrix} 1 & 1 & 1 \\ 3 & 5 & 4 \\ 3 & 6 & 5 \end{bmatrix}$

20. $\begin{bmatrix} 1 & 6 & 10 \\ 3 & 4 & 0 \\ 2 & 5 & 5 \end{bmatrix}$

Finding the Inverse of a Matrix   In Exercises 21–28, use the matrix capabilities of a graphing utility to find the inverse of the matrix (if it exists).

21. $\begin{bmatrix} 1 & 1 & 2 \\ 3 & 1 & 0 \\ -2 & 0 & 3 \end{bmatrix}$

22. $\begin{bmatrix} 1 & 2 & -1 \\ 3 & 7 & -10 \\ -5 & -7 & -15 \end{bmatrix}$

23. $\begin{bmatrix} -\frac{1}{2} & \frac{3}{4} & \frac{1}{4} \\ 1 & 0 & -\frac{3}{2} \\ 0 & -1 & \frac{1}{2} \end{bmatrix}$

24. $\begin{bmatrix} -\frac{5}{6} & \frac{1}{3} & \frac{11}{6} \\ 0 & \frac{2}{3} & 2 \\ 1 & -\frac{1}{2} & -\frac{5}{2} \end{bmatrix}$

25. $\begin{bmatrix} 0.1 & 0.2 & 0.3 \\ -0.3 & 0.2 & 0.2 \\ 0.5 & 0.4 & 0.4 \end{bmatrix}$

26. $\begin{bmatrix} 0.6 & 0 & -0.3 \\ 0.7 & -1 & 0.2 \\ 1 & 0 & -0.9 \end{bmatrix}$

27. $\begin{bmatrix} -1 & 0 & 1 & 0 \\ 0 & 2 & 0 & -2 \\ 2 & 0 & -1 & 0 \\ 0 & -1 & 0 & 1 \end{bmatrix}$

28. $\begin{bmatrix} 1 & -2 & -1 & -2 \\ 3 & -5 & -2 & -3 \\ 2 & -5 & -2 & -5 \\ -1 & 4 & 4 & 11 \end{bmatrix}$

Finding the Inverse of a 2 × 2 Matrix   In Exercises 29–34, use the formula on page 536 to find the inverse of the 2 × 2 matrix (if it exists).

29. $\begin{bmatrix} 4 & -3 \\ 8 & -6 \end{bmatrix}$

30. $\begin{bmatrix} 1 & -2 \\ -3 & 2 \end{bmatrix}$

31. $\begin{bmatrix} \frac{7}{2} & -\frac{3}{4} \\ \frac{1}{5} & \frac{4}{5} \end{bmatrix}$

32. $\begin{bmatrix} -\frac{1}{4} & -\frac{2}{3} \\ \frac{1}{3} & \frac{8}{9} \end{bmatrix}$

33. $\begin{bmatrix} 2 & 3 \\ -1 & 5 \end{bmatrix}$

34. $\begin{bmatrix} 7 & 12 \\ -8 & -5 \end{bmatrix}$

Finding a Matrix Entry   In Exercises 35 and 36, find the value of the constant k such that $B = A^{-1}$.

35. $A = \begin{bmatrix} 1 & 2 \\ -2 & 0 \end{bmatrix}$, $B = \begin{bmatrix} k & -\frac{1}{2} \\ \frac{1}{2} & \frac{1}{4} \end{bmatrix}$

36. $A = \begin{bmatrix} -1 & 1 \\ 2 & 1 \end{bmatrix}$, $B = \begin{bmatrix} -\frac{1}{3} & \frac{1}{3} \\ k & \frac{1}{3} \end{bmatrix}$

Solving a System of Linear Equations In Exercises 37–40, use the inverse matrix found in Exercise 13 to solve the system of linear equations.

37. $\begin{cases} x - 2y = 5 \\ 2x - 3y = 10 \end{cases}$ 38. $\begin{cases} x - 2y = 0 \\ 2x - 3y = 3 \end{cases}$

39. $\begin{cases} x - 2y = 4 \\ 2x - 3y = 2 \end{cases}$ 40. $\begin{cases} x - 2y = 1 \\ 2x - 3y = -2 \end{cases}$

Solving a System of Linear Equations In Exercises 41 and 42, use the inverse matrix found in Exercise 19 to solve the system of linear equations.

41. $\begin{cases} x + y + z = 0 \\ 3x + 5y + 4z = 5 \\ 3x + 6y + 5z = 2 \end{cases}$ 42. $\begin{cases} x + y + z = -1 \\ 3x + 5y + 4z = 2 \\ 3x + 6y + 5z = 0 \end{cases}$

Solving a System of Linear Equations In Exercises 43 and 44, use the inverse matrix found in Exercise 28 and the matrix capabilities of a graphing utility to solve the system of linear equations.

43. $\begin{cases} x_1 - 2x_2 - x_3 - 2x_4 = 0 \\ 3x_1 - 5x_2 - 2x_3 - 3x_4 = 1 \\ 2x_1 - 5x_2 - 2x_3 - 5x_4 = -1 \\ -x_1 + 4x_2 + 4x_3 + 11x_4 = 2 \end{cases}$

44. $\begin{cases} x_1 - 2x_2 - x_3 - 2x_4 = 1 \\ 3x_1 - 5x_2 - 2x_3 - 3x_4 = -2 \\ 2x_1 - 5x_2 - 2x_3 - 5x_4 = 0 \\ -x_1 + 4x_2 + 4x_3 + 11x_4 = -3 \end{cases}$

Solving a System of Equations Using an Inverse In Exercises 45–52, use an inverse matrix to solve (if possible) the system of linear equations.

45. $\begin{cases} 3x + 4y = -2 \\ 5x + 3y = 4 \end{cases}$ 46. $\begin{cases} 18x + 12y = 13 \\ 30x + 24y - 23 \end{cases}$

47. $\begin{cases} -0.4x + 0.8y = 1.6 \\ 2x - 4y = 5 \end{cases}$ 48. $\begin{cases} 0.2x - 0.6y = 2.4 \\ -x + 1.4y = -8.8 \end{cases}$

49. $\begin{cases} -\frac{1}{4}x + \frac{3}{8}y = -2 \\ \frac{3}{2}x + \frac{3}{4}y = -12 \end{cases}$ 50. $\begin{cases} \frac{5}{6}x - y = -10 \\ -\frac{5}{4}x + \frac{3}{2}y = -2 \end{cases}$

51. $\begin{cases} 4x - y + z = -5 \\ 2x + 2y + 3z = 10 \\ 5x - 2y + 6z = 1 \end{cases}$ 52. $\begin{cases} 4x - 2y + 3z = -2 \\ 2x + 2y + 5z = 16 \\ 8x - 5y - 2z = 4 \end{cases}$

Solving a System of Linear Equations In Exercises 53–56, use the matrix capabilities of a graphing utility to solve (if possible) the system of linear equations.

53. $\begin{cases} 5x - 3y + 2z = 2 \\ 2x + 2y - 3z = 3 \\ -x + 7y - 8z = 4 \end{cases}$ 54. $\begin{cases} 2x + 3y + 5z = 4 \\ 3x + 5y - 9z = 7 \\ 5x + 9y + 17z = 13 \end{cases}$

55. $\begin{cases} 7x - 3y + 2w = 41 \\ -2x + y - w = -13 \\ 4x + z - 2w = 12 \\ -x + y - w = -8 \end{cases}$

56. $\begin{cases} 2x + 5y + w = 11 \\ x + 4y + 2z - 2w = -7 \\ 2x - 2y + 5z + w = 3 \\ x - 3w = -1 \end{cases}$

Investment Portfolio In Exercises 57–60, consider a person who invests in AAA-rated bonds, A-rated bonds, and B-rated bonds. The average yields are 4.5% on AAA bonds, 5% on A bonds, and 7% on B bonds. The person invests twice as much in B bonds as in A bonds. Let x, y, and z represent the amounts (in dollars) invested in AAA, A, and B bonds, respectively.

$\begin{cases} x + y + z = \text{(total investment)} \\ 0.045x + 0.05y + 0.07z = \text{(annual return)} \\ 2y - z = 0 \end{cases}$

Use the inverse of the coefficient matrix of this system to find the amount invested in each type of bond.

	Total Investment	Annual Return
57.	$10,000	$560
58.	$20,000	$955
59.	$300,000	$18,450
60.	$500,000	$28,000

Electrical Engineering In Exercises 61 and 62, consider the circuit in the figure. The currents I_1, I_2, and I_3, in amperes, are given by the solution of the system of linear equations

$\begin{cases} 2I_1 + 4I_3 - E_1 \\ I_2 + 4I_3 = E_2 \\ I_1 + I_2 - I_3 = 0 \end{cases}$

where E_1 and E_2 are voltages. Use the inverse of the coefficient matrix of this system to find the unknown currents for the given voltages.

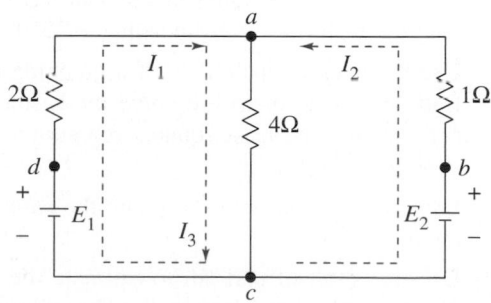

61. $E_1 = 15$ volts, $E_2 = 17$ volts
62. $E_1 = 10$ volts, $E_2 = 10$ volts

Horticulture In Exercises 63 and 64, consider a company that specializes in potting soil. Each bag of potting soil for seedlings requires 2 units of sand, 1 unit of loam, and 1 unit of peat moss. Each bag of potting soil for general potting requires 1 unit of sand, 2 units of loam, and 1 unit of peat moss. Each bag of potting soil for hardwood plants requires 2 units of sand, 2 units of loam, and 2 units of peat moss. Find the numbers of bags of the three types of potting soil that the company can produce with the given amounts of raw materials.

63. 500 units of sand
    500 units of loam
    400 units of peat moss

64. 500 units of sand
    750 units of loam
    450 units of peat moss

65. **Floral Design** A florist is creating 10 centerpieces for the tables at a wedding reception. Roses cost $2.50 each, lilies cost $4 each, and irises cost $2 each. The customer has a budget of $300 for the centerpieces and wants each centerpiece to contain 12 flowers, with twice as many roses as the number of irises and lilies combined.

(a) Write a linear system that represents the situation.

(b) Write a matrix equation that corresponds to your system.

(c) Solve your linear system using an inverse matrix. Find the number of flowers of each type that the florist can use to create the 10 centerpieces.

66. *Why you should learn it* (p. 532) The table shows the numbers of international travelers y (in thousands) to the United States from South America from 2010 through 2012. (Source: U.S. Department of Commerce)

Year	Travelers, y (in thousands)
2010	3250
2011	3757
2012	4416

(a) The data can be approximated by a parabola. Create a system of linear equations for the data. Let t represent the year, with $t = 0$ corresponding to 2010.

(b) Use the matrix capabilities of a graphing utility to find an inverse matrix to solve the system in part (a) and find the least squares regression parabola $y = at^2 + bt + c$.

(c) Use the graphing utility to graph the parabola with the data points.

(d) Use the result of part (b) to estimate the numbers of international travelers to the United States from South America in 2013, 2014, and 2015.

(e) Are your estimates from part (d) reasonable? Explain.

Conclusions

True or False? In Exercises 67–69, determine whether the statement is true or false. Justify your answer.

67. Multiplication of an invertible matrix and its inverse is commutative.

68. When the product of two square matrices is the identity matrix, the matrices are inverses of one another.

69. A nonsingular matrix can have dimension 2×3.

70. **Writing** Explain how to determine whether the inverse of a 2×2 matrix exists. If so, explain how to find the inverse.

71. **Writing** Explain in your own words how to write a system of three linear equations in three variables as a matrix equation $AX = B$, as well as how to solve the system using an inverse matrix.

72. **The Inverse of a 2 × 2 Matrix** If A is a 2×2 matrix given by $A = \begin{bmatrix} a & b \\ c & d \end{bmatrix}$, then A is invertible if and only if $ad - bc \neq 0$. If $ad - bc \neq 0$, verify that the inverse is $A^{-1} = \dfrac{1}{ad - bc} \begin{bmatrix} d & -b \\ -c & a \end{bmatrix}$.

73. **Exploration** Consider matrices of the form

$$A = \begin{bmatrix} a_{11} & 0 & 0 & 0 & \cdots & 0 \\ 0 & a_{22} & 0 & 0 & \cdots & 0 \\ 0 & 0 & a_{33} & 0 & \cdots & 0 \\ \vdots & \vdots & \vdots & \vdots & \cdots & \vdots \\ 0 & 0 & 0 & 0 & \cdots & a_{nn} \end{bmatrix}.$$

(a) Write a 2×2 matrix and a 3×3 matrix in the form of A. Find the inverse of each.

(b) Use the result of part (a) to make a conjecture about the inverse of a matrix in the form of A.

74. **HOW DO YOU SEE IT?** Let A be a 2×2 matrix given by

$$A = \begin{bmatrix} x & 0 \\ 0 & y \end{bmatrix}.$$

Use the determinant of A to determine the conditions under which A^{-1} exists.

Cumulative Mixed Review

Solving an Equation In Exercises 75–78, solve the equation algebraically. Round your result to three decimal places.

75. $e^{2x} + 2e^x - 15 = 0$

76. $e^{2x} - 10e^x + 24 = 0$

77. $7 \ln 3x = 12$

78. $\ln(x + 9) = 2$

7.7 The Determinant of a Square Matrix

The Determinant of a 2 × 2 Matrix

Every *square* matrix can be associated with a real number called its **determinant.** Determinants have many uses, and several will be discussed in this and the next section. Historically, the use of determinants arose from special number patterns that occur when systems of linear equations are solved. For instance, the system

$$\begin{cases} a_1 x + b_1 y = c_1 \\ a_2 x + b_2 y = c_2 \end{cases}$$

has a solution

$$x = \frac{c_1 b_2 - c_2 b_1}{a_1 b_2 - a_2 b_1}$$

and

$$y = \frac{a_1 c_2 - a_2 c_1}{a_1 b_2 - a_2 b_1}$$

provided that $a_1 b_2 - a_2 b_1 \neq 0$. Note that each fraction has the same denominator. This denominator is called the *determinant* of the coefficient matrix of the system.

Coefficient Matrix   *Determinant*

$$A = \begin{bmatrix} a_1 & b_1 \\ a_2 & b_2 \end{bmatrix} \qquad \det(A) = a_1 b_2 - a_2 b_1$$

The determinant of the matrix A can also be denoted by vertical bars on both sides of the matrix, as indicated in the following definition.

> **Definition of the Determinant of a 2 × 2 Matrix**
>
> The **determinant** of the matrix
>
> $$A = \begin{bmatrix} a_1 & b_1 \\ a_2 & b_2 \end{bmatrix}$$
>
> is given by
>
> $$\det(A) = |A|$$
> $$= \begin{vmatrix} a_1 & b_1 \\ a_2 & b_2 \end{vmatrix}$$
> $$= a_1 b_2 - a_2 b_1.$$

In this text, $\det(A)$ and $|A|$ are used interchangeably to represent the determinant of A. Although vertical bars are also used to denote the absolute value of a real number, the context will show which use is intended.

A convenient method for remembering the formula for the determinant of a 2 × 2 matrix is shown in the following diagram.

$$\det(A) = \begin{vmatrix} a_1 & b_1 \\ a_2 & b_2 \end{vmatrix} = a_1 b_2 - a_2 b_1$$

Note that the determinant is the difference of the products of the two diagonals of the matrix.

EXAMPLE 1   The Determinant of a 2×2 Matrix

Find the determinant of each matrix.

a. $A = \begin{bmatrix} 2 & -3 \\ 1 & 2 \end{bmatrix}$

b. $B = \begin{bmatrix} 2 & 1 \\ 4 & 2 \end{bmatrix}$

c. $C = \begin{bmatrix} 0 & \frac{3}{2} \\ 2 & 4 \end{bmatrix}$

Solution

a. $\det(A) = \begin{vmatrix} 2 & -3 \\ 1 & 2 \end{vmatrix} = 2(2) - 1(-3) = 4 + 3 = 7$

b. $\det(B) = \begin{vmatrix} 2 & 1 \\ 4 & 2 \end{vmatrix} = 2(2) - 4(1) = 4 - 4 = 0$

c. $\det(C) = \begin{vmatrix} 0 & \frac{3}{2} \\ 2 & 4 \end{vmatrix} = 0(4) - 2\left(\frac{3}{2}\right) = 0 - 3 = -3$

✓ **Checkpoint** Audio-video solution in English & Spanish at LarsonPrecalculus.com.

Find the determinant of each matrix.

a. $A = \begin{bmatrix} 1 & 2 \\ 3 & -1 \end{bmatrix}$ **b.** $B = \begin{bmatrix} 5 & 0 \\ -4 & 2 \end{bmatrix}$ **c.** $C = \begin{bmatrix} 3 & 6 \\ 2 & 4 \end{bmatrix}$

Notice in Example 1 that the determinant of a matrix can be positive, zero, or negative.

The determinant of a matrix of dimension 1×1 is defined simply as the entry of the matrix. For instance, if $A = [-2]$, then $\det(A) = -2$.

EXAMPLE 2   Using a Graphing Utility

Use the matrix capabilities of a graphing utility to find the determinant of the matrix.

$$A = \begin{bmatrix} 1.4 & 0.7 \\ -0.3 & -2.5 \end{bmatrix}$$

Solution

Use the *matrix editor* to enter the matrix as $[A]$, as shown in Figure 7.19. Then choose the *determinant* feature. From Figure 7.20, $\det(A) = -3.29$.

```
MATRIX[A] 2 X2
[1.4    .7      ]
[-.3    -2.5    ]



2,2=-2.5
```

```
[A]
        [1.4   .7  ]
        [-.3 -2.5  ]
det([A])
              -3.29
```

Figure 7.19   **Figure 7.20**

✓ **Checkpoint** Audio-video solution in English & Spanish at LarsonPrecalculus.com.

Use the matrix capabilities of a graphing utility to find the determinant of the matrix.

$$A = \begin{bmatrix} 0.1 & -0.7 \\ 0.8 & 0.8 \end{bmatrix}$$

Explore the Concept

Try using a graphing utility to find the determinant of

$$A = \begin{bmatrix} 3 & -1 & 1 \\ 0 & 2 & 1 \end{bmatrix}.$$

What message appears on the screen? Why does the graphing utility display this message?

```
ERR:INVALID DIM
1:Quit
2:Goto
```

Minors and Cofactors

To define the determinant of a square matrix of dimension 3×3 or greater, it is helpful to introduce the concepts of **minors** and **cofactors**.

Minors and Cofactors of a Square Matrix

If A is a square matrix, then the **minor** M_{ij} of the entry a_{ij} is the determinant of the matrix obtained by deleting the ith row and jth column of A. The **cofactor** C_{ij} of the entry a_{ij} is given by $C_{ij} = (-1)^{i+j} M_{ij}$.

In the sign patterns for cofactors at the right, notice that *odd* positions (where $i + j$ is odd) have negative signs and *even* positions (where $i + j$ is even) have positive signs.

Sign Patterns for Cofactors

$$\begin{bmatrix} + & - & + \\ - & + & - \\ + & - & + \end{bmatrix}$$

3×3 matrix

$$\begin{bmatrix} + & - & + & - \\ - & + & - & + \\ + & - & + & - \\ - & + & - & + \end{bmatrix}$$

4×4 matrix

$$\begin{bmatrix} + & - & + & - & + & \cdots \\ - & + & - & + & - & \cdots \\ + & - & + & - & + & \cdots \\ - & + & - & + & - & \cdots \\ + & - & + & - & + & \cdots \\ \vdots & \vdots & \vdots & \vdots & \vdots \end{bmatrix}$$

$n \times n$ matrix

EXAMPLE 3   Finding the Minors and Cofactors of a Matrix

Find all the minors and cofactors of

$$A = \begin{bmatrix} 0 & 2 & 1 \\ 3 & -1 & 2 \\ 4 & 0 & 1 \end{bmatrix}.$$

Solution

To find the minor M_{11}, delete the first row and first column of A and evaluate the determinant of the resulting matrix.

$$\begin{bmatrix} 0 & 2 & 1 \\ 3 & -1 & 2 \\ 4 & 0 & 1 \end{bmatrix}, \quad M_{11} = \begin{vmatrix} -1 & 2 \\ 0 & 1 \end{vmatrix} = -1(1) - 0(2) = -1$$

Similarly, to find the minor M_{12}, delete the first row and second column.

$$\begin{bmatrix} 0 & 2 & 1 \\ 3 & -1 & 2 \\ 4 & 0 & 1 \end{bmatrix}, \quad M_{12} = \begin{vmatrix} 3 & 2 \\ 4 & 1 \end{vmatrix} = 3(1) - 4(2) = -5$$

Continuing this pattern, you obtain all the minors.

$$\begin{array}{lll} M_{11} = -1 & M_{12} = -5 & M_{13} = 4 \\ M_{21} = 2 & M_{22} = -4 & M_{23} = -8 \\ M_{31} = 5 & M_{32} = -3 & M_{33} = -6 \end{array}$$

Now, to find the cofactors, combine these minors with the checkerboard pattern of signs for a 3×3 matrix shown at the upper right.

$$\begin{array}{lll} C_{11} = -1 & C_{12} = 5 & C_{13} = 4 \\ C_{21} = -2 & C_{22} = -4 & C_{23} = 8 \\ C_{31} = 5 & C_{32} = 3 & C_{33} = -6 \end{array}$$

✓ **Checkpoint** ◀))) *Audio-video solution in English & Spanish at LarsonPrecalculus.com.*

Find all the minors and cofactors of

$$A = \begin{bmatrix} 1 & 2 & 3 \\ 0 & -1 & 5 \\ 2 & 1 & 4 \end{bmatrix}.$$

The Determinant of a Square Matrix

The following definition is called *inductive* because it uses determinants of matrices of dimension $(n - 1) \times (n - 1)$ to define determinants of matrices of dimension $n \times n$.

Determinant of a Square Matrix

If A is a square matrix (of dimension 2×2 or greater), then the determinant of A is the sum of the entries in any row (or column) of A multiplied by their respective cofactors. For instance, expanding along the first row yields

$$|A| = a_{11}C_{11} + a_{12}C_{12} + \cdots + a_{1n}C_{1n}.$$

Applying this definition to find a determinant is called **expanding by cofactors.**

Try checking that for a 2×2 matrix

$$A = \begin{bmatrix} a_1 & b_1 \\ a_2 & b_2 \end{bmatrix}$$

this definition of the determinant yields $|A| = a_1b_2 - a_2b_1$, as previously defined.

EXAMPLE 4   The Determinant of a 3 × 3 Matrix

See LarsonPrecalculus.com for an interactive version of this type of example.

Find the determinant of $A = \begin{bmatrix} 0 & 2 & 1 \\ 3 & -1 & 2 \\ 4 & 0 & 1 \end{bmatrix}$.

Solution

Note that this is the same matrix that was in Example 3. There you found the cofactors of the entries in the first row to be

$$C_{11} = -1, \quad C_{12} = 5, \quad \text{and} \quad C_{13} = 4.$$

So, by the definition of the determinant of a square matrix, you have

$$\begin{aligned} |A| &= a_{11}C_{11} + a_{12}C_{12} + a_{13}C_{13} && \text{First-row expansion} \\ &= 0(-1) + 2(5) + 1(4) \\ &= 14. \end{aligned}$$

✓ **Checkpoint** ◀))) *Audio-video solution in English & Spanish at LarsonPrecalculus.com.*

Find the determinant of $A = \begin{bmatrix} 3 & 4 & -2 \\ 3 & 5 & 0 \\ -1 & 4 & 1 \end{bmatrix}$.   ■

In Example 4, the determinant was found by expanding by the cofactors in the first row. You could have used any row or column. For instance, you could have expanded along the second row to obtain

$$\begin{aligned} |A| &= a_{21}C_{21} + a_{22}C_{22} + a_{23}C_{23} && \text{Second-row expansion} \\ &= 3(-2) + (-1)(-4) + 2(8) \\ &= 14. \end{aligned}$$

When expanding by cofactors, you do not need to find cofactors of zero entries, because when $a_{ij} = 0$, you have $a_{ij}C_{ij} = (0)C_{ij} = 0$. So, the row (or column) containing the most zeros is usually the best choice for expansion by cofactors.

7.7   Exercises

See *CalcChat.com* for tutorial help and worked-out solutions to odd-numbered exercises.
For instructions on how to use a graphing utility, see Appendix A.

Vocabulary and Concept Check

In Exercises 1 and 2, fill in the blank.

1. Both det(A) and $|A|$ represent the _____ of the matrix A.

2. The determinant of the matrix obtained by deleting the ith row and jth column of a square matrix A is called the _____ of the entry a_{ij}.

3. For a square matrix B, the minor $M_{23} = 5$. What is the cofactor C_{23} of matrix B?

4. To find the determinant of a matrix using expanding by cofactors, do you need to find all the cofactors?

Procedures and Problem Solving

The Determinant of a Matrix   In Exercises 5–12, find the determinant of the matrix.

5. $[4]$

6. $[-12]$

7. $\begin{bmatrix} 8 & 4 \\ -2 & 3 \end{bmatrix}$

8. $\begin{bmatrix} -5 & 2 \\ 6 & 3 \end{bmatrix}$

9. $\begin{bmatrix} -7 & 6 \\ \frac{1}{2} & 3 \end{bmatrix}$

10. $\begin{bmatrix} 4 & -3 \\ 0 & 0 \end{bmatrix}$

11. $\begin{bmatrix} \sqrt{3} & 3 \\ 4 & \sqrt{3} \end{bmatrix}$

12. $\begin{bmatrix} 9 & \sqrt{5} \\ \sqrt{5} & 4 \end{bmatrix}$

Using a Graphing Utility   In Exercises 13–16, use the matrix capabilities of a graphing utility to find the determinant of the matrix.

13. $\begin{bmatrix} 1.9 & -0.3 \\ 5.6 & 3.2 \end{bmatrix}$

14. $\begin{bmatrix} 7.2 & 0.8 \\ 3.6 & -0.4 \end{bmatrix}$

15. $\begin{bmatrix} 1.3 & 0.2 & 3.2 \\ 0.2 & 6.2 & 0.2 \\ -0.4 & 4.4 & 0.3 \end{bmatrix}$

16. $\begin{bmatrix} 5.1 & 0.2 & 7.3 \\ -6.3 & 0.2 & 0.2 \\ 0.5 & 3.4 & 0.4 \end{bmatrix}$

Finding the Minors and Cofactors of a Matrix   In Exercises 17–20, find all (a) minors and (b) cofactors of the matrix.

17. $\begin{bmatrix} 3 & 4 \\ 2 & -5 \end{bmatrix}$

18. $\begin{bmatrix} 11 & 6 \\ -3 & 2 \end{bmatrix}$

19. $\begin{bmatrix} -4 & 6 & 3 \\ 7 & -2 & 8 \\ 1 & 0 & -5 \end{bmatrix}$

20. $\begin{bmatrix} -2 & 9 & 4 \\ 7 & -6 & 0 \\ 6 & 7 & -6 \end{bmatrix}$

Finding a Determinant   In Exercises 21–24, find the determinant of the matrix. Expand by cofactors on each indicated row or column.

21. $\begin{bmatrix} -3 & 2 & 1 \\ 4 & 5 & 6 \\ 2 & -3 & 1 \end{bmatrix}$

   (a) Row 1
   (b) Column 2

22. $\begin{bmatrix} -3 & 4 & 2 \\ 6 & 3 & 1 \\ 4 & -7 & -8 \end{bmatrix}$

   (a) Row 2
   (b) Column 3

23. $\begin{bmatrix} 6 & 0 & -3 & 5 \\ 4 & 13 & 6 & -8 \\ -1 & 0 & 7 & 4 \\ 8 & 6 & 0 & 2 \end{bmatrix}$

   (a) Row 2
   (b) Column 2

24. $\begin{bmatrix} 10 & 8 & 3 & -7 \\ 4 & 0 & 5 & -6 \\ 0 & 3 & 2 & 7 \\ 1 & 0 & -3 & 2 \end{bmatrix}$

   (a) Row 3
   (b) Column 1

Finding a Determinant   In Exercises 25–34, find the determinant of the matrix. Expand by cofactors on the row or column that appears to make the computations easiest.

25. $\begin{bmatrix} 1 & 4 & -2 \\ 3 & 2 & 0 \\ -1 & 4 & 3 \end{bmatrix}$

26. $\begin{bmatrix} -3 & 1 & 0 \\ 7 & 11 & 5 \\ 1 & 2 & 2 \end{bmatrix}$

27. $\begin{bmatrix} 6 & 3 & -7 \\ 0 & 0 & 0 \\ 4 & -6 & 3 \end{bmatrix}$

28. $\begin{bmatrix} 1 & 1 & 2 \\ 3 & -5 & 9 \\ 0 & 0 & 0 \end{bmatrix}$

29. $\begin{bmatrix} -1 & 2 & -5 \\ 0 & 3 & -4 \\ 0 & 0 & 3 \end{bmatrix}$

30. $\begin{bmatrix} 1 & 0 & 0 \\ -1 & -1 & 0 \\ 4 & 1 & 5 \end{bmatrix}$

31. $\begin{bmatrix} 2 & 6 & 6 & 2 \\ 2 & 7 & 3 & 6 \\ 1 & 5 & 0 & 1 \\ 3 & 7 & 0 & 7 \end{bmatrix}$

32. $\begin{bmatrix} 3 & 6 & -5 & 4 \\ -2 & 2 & 6 & 0 \\ 1 & 1 & 2 & 0 \\ 0 & 3 & -1 & -1 \end{bmatrix}$

33. $\begin{bmatrix} 3 & 2 & 4 & -1 & 5 \\ -2 & 0 & 1 & 3 & 2 \\ 1 & 0 & 0 & 4 & 0 \\ 6 & 0 & 2 & -1 & 0 \\ 3 & 0 & 5 & 1 & 0 \end{bmatrix}$

34. $\begin{bmatrix} 5 & 2 & 0 & 0 & -2 \\ 0 & 1 & 4 & 3 & 2 \\ 0 & 0 & 2 & 6 & 3 \\ 0 & 0 & 3 & 4 & 1 \\ 0 & 0 & 0 & 0 & 2 \end{bmatrix}$

Using a Graphing Utility   In Exercises 35–38, use the matrix capabilities of a graphing utility to evaluate the determinant.

35. $\begin{vmatrix} 1 & -1 & 8 & 4 \\ 2 & 6 & 0 & -4 \\ 2 & 0 & 2 & 6 \\ 0 & 2 & 8 & 0 \end{vmatrix}$ 36. $\begin{vmatrix} 0 & -3 & 8 & 2 \\ 8 & 1 & -1 & 6 \\ -4 & 6 & 0 & 9 \\ -7 & 0 & 0 & 14 \end{vmatrix}$

37. $\begin{vmatrix} 3 & -2 & 4 & 3 & 1 & 3 \\ -1 & 0 & 2 & 1 & 0 & 0 \\ 5 & -1 & 0 & 3 & 2 & 1 \\ 4 & 7 & -8 & 0 & 0 & -2 \\ 1 & 2 & 3 & 0 & 2 & 4 \\ 3 & -5 & 1 & 2 & 3 & 1 \end{vmatrix}$

38. $\begin{vmatrix} -2 & 0 & 1 & 4 & 3 & -2 \\ -3 & 3 & 0 & -2 & 1 & -1 \\ 4 & 5 & -1 & 0 & 7 & 3 \\ 2 & 4 & 3 & 2 & 0 & 1 \\ 1 & 3 & 4 & 2 & -4 & 0 \\ -5 & 2 & -1 & 3 & 2 & -3 \end{vmatrix}$

The Determinant of a Matrix Product   In Exercises 39–42, find (a) $|A|$, (b) $|B|$, (c) AB, and (d) $|AB|$. What do you notice about $|AB|$?

39. $A = \begin{bmatrix} -2 & 1 \\ 4 & -2 \end{bmatrix}$, $B = \begin{bmatrix} 1 & 2 \\ 0 & -1 \end{bmatrix}$

40. $A = \begin{bmatrix} 4 & 0 \\ 3 & -2 \end{bmatrix}$, $B = \begin{bmatrix} -1 & 1 \\ -2 & 2 \end{bmatrix}$

41. $A = \begin{bmatrix} 3 & 2 & 0 \\ -1 & -3 & 4 \\ -2 & 0 & 1 \end{bmatrix}$, $B = \begin{bmatrix} -3 & 0 & 1 \\ 0 & 2 & -1 \\ -2 & -1 & 1 \end{bmatrix}$

42. $A = \begin{bmatrix} 2 & 0 & 1 \\ 1 & -4 & 2 \\ 3 & 1 & 0 \end{bmatrix}$, $B = \begin{bmatrix} 2 & -1 & 4 \\ 0 & 1 & 0 \\ 3 & -2 & 1 \end{bmatrix}$

Using a Graphing Utility   In Exercises 43 and 44, use the matrix capabilities of a graphing utility to find (a) $|A|$, (b) $|B|$, (c) AB, and (d) $|AB|$. What do you notice about $|AB|$?

43. $A = \begin{bmatrix} 6 & 4 & 0 & 1 \\ 2 & -3 & -2 & -4 \\ 0 & 1 & 5 & 0 \\ -1 & 0 & -1 & 1 \end{bmatrix}$, $B = \begin{bmatrix} 0 & -5 & 0 & -2 \\ -2 & 4 & -1 & -4 \\ 3 & 0 & 1 & 0 \\ 1 & -2 & 3 & 0 \end{bmatrix}$

44. $A = \begin{bmatrix} -1 & 5 & 2 & 0 \\ 0 & 0 & 1 & 1 \\ 3 & -3 & -1 & 0 \\ 4 & 2 & 4 & -1 \end{bmatrix}$, $B = \begin{bmatrix} 1 & 5 & 0 & 0 \\ 10 & -1 & 2 & 4 \\ 2 & 0 & 0 & 1 \\ -3 & 2 & 5 & 0 \end{bmatrix}$

Verifying an Equation   In Exercises 45–50, evaluate the determinants to verify the equation.

45. $\begin{vmatrix} w & x \\ y & z \end{vmatrix} = -\begin{vmatrix} y & z \\ w & x \end{vmatrix}$

46. $\begin{vmatrix} w & cx \\ y & cz \end{vmatrix} = c\begin{vmatrix} w & x \\ y & z \end{vmatrix}$

47. $\begin{vmatrix} w & x \\ y & z \end{vmatrix} = \begin{vmatrix} w & x + cw \\ y & z + cy \end{vmatrix}$

48. $\begin{vmatrix} w & x \\ cw & cx \end{vmatrix} = 0$

49. $\begin{vmatrix} 1 & x & x^2 \\ 1 & y & y^2 \\ 1 & z & z^2 \end{vmatrix} = (y - x)(z - x)(z - y)$

50. $\begin{vmatrix} a + b & a & a \\ a & a + b & a \\ a & a & a + b \end{vmatrix} = b^2(3a + b)$

Solving an Equation   In Exercises 51–62, solve for x.

51. $\begin{vmatrix} x & 2 \\ 1 & x \end{vmatrix} = 2$ 52. $\begin{vmatrix} x & 4 \\ -1 & x \end{vmatrix} = 20$

53. $\begin{vmatrix} 2x & -3 \\ -2 & 2x \end{vmatrix} = 3$ 54. $\begin{vmatrix} x & 2 \\ 4 & 9x \end{vmatrix} = 8$

55. $\begin{vmatrix} x & 2 \\ 2 & x - 2 \end{vmatrix} = -1$ 56. $\begin{vmatrix} x + 1 & 2 \\ -1 & x \end{vmatrix} = 4$

57. $\begin{vmatrix} x + 3 & 2 \\ 1 & x + 2 \end{vmatrix} = 0$ 58. $\begin{vmatrix} x - 1 & 2 \\ 3 & x - 2 \end{vmatrix} = 0$

59. $\begin{vmatrix} 2x & 1 \\ -1 & x - 1 \end{vmatrix} = x$ 60. $\begin{vmatrix} x - 1 & x \\ x + 1 & 2 \end{vmatrix} = -8$

61. $\begin{vmatrix} 1 & 2 & x \\ -1 & 3 & 2 \\ 3 & -2 & 1 \end{vmatrix} = 0$ 62. $\begin{vmatrix} 1 & x & -2 \\ 1 & 3 & 3 \\ 0 & 2 & -2 \end{vmatrix} = 0$

∫ Entries Involving Expressions   In Exercises 63–68, evaluate the determinant, in which the entries are functions. Determinants of this type occur when changes of variables are made in calculus.

63. $\begin{vmatrix} 4u & -1 \\ -1 & 2v \end{vmatrix}$

64. $\begin{vmatrix} 3x^2 & -3y^2 \\ 1 & 1 \end{vmatrix}$

65. $\begin{vmatrix} e^{2x} & e^{3x} \\ 2e^{2x} & 3e^{3x} \end{vmatrix}$

66. $\begin{vmatrix} e^{-x} & xe^{-x} \\ -e^{-x} & (1 - x)e^{-x} \end{vmatrix}$

67. $\begin{vmatrix} x & \ln x \\ 1 & 1/x \end{vmatrix}$

68. $\begin{vmatrix} x & x \ln x \\ 1 & 1 + \ln x \end{vmatrix}$

Conclusions

True or False? In Exercises 69 and 70, determine whether the statement is true or false. Justify your answer.

69. If a square matrix has an entire row of zeros, then the determinant will always be zero.

70. If two columns of a square matrix are the same, then the determinant of the matrix will be zero.

71. Exploration Find a pair of 3×3 matrices A and B to demonstrate that $|A + B| \neq |A| + |B|$.

72. Think About It Let A be a 3×3 matrix such that $|A| = 5$. Can you use this information to find $|2A|$? Explain.

Exploration In Exercises 73–76, (a) find the determinant of A, (b) find A^{-1}, (c) find $\det(A^{-1})$, and (d) compare your results from parts (a) and (c). Make a conjecture based on your results.

73. $A = \begin{bmatrix} 1 & 2 \\ -2 & 2 \end{bmatrix}$ **74.** $A = \begin{bmatrix} 5 & -1 \\ 2 & -1 \end{bmatrix}$

75. $A = \begin{bmatrix} 1 & 3 & -2 \\ -1 & 3 & 1 \\ 0 & 2 & -2 \end{bmatrix}$ **76.** $A = \begin{bmatrix} -1 & 3 & 2 \\ 1 & 3 & -1 \\ 1 & 1 & 2 \end{bmatrix}$

Properties of Determinants In Exercises 77–79, a property of determinants is given (A and B are square matrices). State how the property has been applied to the given determinants and use a graphing utility to verify the results.

77. If B is obtained from A by interchanging two rows of A or by interchanging two columns of A, then $|B| = -|A|$.

(a) $\begin{vmatrix} 1 & 3 & 4 \\ -7 & 2 & -5 \\ 6 & 1 & 2 \end{vmatrix} = -\begin{vmatrix} 1 & 4 & 3 \\ -7 & -5 & 2 \\ 6 & 2 & 1 \end{vmatrix}$

(b) $\begin{vmatrix} 1 & 3 & 4 \\ -2 & 2 & 0 \\ 1 & 6 & 2 \end{vmatrix} = -\begin{vmatrix} 1 & 6 & 2 \\ -2 & 2 & 0 \\ 1 & 3 & 4 \end{vmatrix}$

78. If B is obtained from A by adding a multiple of a row of A to another row of A or by adding a multiple of a column of A to another column of A, then $|B| = |A|$.

(a) $\begin{vmatrix} 1 & -3 \\ 5 & 2 \end{vmatrix} = \begin{vmatrix} 1 & -3 \\ 0 & 17 \end{vmatrix}$

(b) $\begin{vmatrix} 5 & 4 & 2 \\ 2 & -3 & 4 \\ 7 & 6 & 3 \end{vmatrix} = \begin{vmatrix} 1 & 10 & -6 \\ 2 & -3 & 4 \\ 7 & 6 & 3 \end{vmatrix}$

79. If B is obtained from A by multiplying a row of A by a nonzero constant c or by multiplying a column of A by a nonzero constant c, then $|B| = c|A|$.

(a) $\begin{vmatrix} 1 & 5 \\ 6 & 9 \end{vmatrix} = 3\begin{vmatrix} 1 & 5 \\ 2 & 3 \end{vmatrix}$ (b) $\begin{vmatrix} 2 & 8 \\ 6 & 8 \end{vmatrix} = 8\begin{vmatrix} 1 & 2 \\ 3 & 2 \end{vmatrix}$

80. Exploration A **diagonal matrix** is a square matrix with all zero entries above and below its main diagonal. Evaluate the determinant of each diagonal matrix. Make a conjecture based on your results.

(a) $\begin{bmatrix} 7 & 0 \\ 0 & 4 \end{bmatrix}$ (b) $\begin{bmatrix} -1 & 0 & 0 \\ 0 & 5 & 0 \\ 0 & 0 & 2 \end{bmatrix}$ (c) $\begin{bmatrix} 2 & 0 & 0 & 0 \\ 0 & -2 & 0 & 0 \\ 0 & 0 & 1 & 0 \\ 0 & 0 & 0 & 3 \end{bmatrix}$

81. Exploration A **triangular matrix** is a square matrix with all zero entries either above or below its main diagonal. Such a matrix is **upper triangular** when it has all zeros below the main diagonal and **lower triangular** when it has all zeros above the main diagonal. A diagonal matrix is both upper and lower triangular. Evaluate the determinant of each triangular matrix. Make a conjecture based on your results.

(a) $\begin{bmatrix} 3 & -2 \\ 0 & 5 \end{bmatrix}$ (b) $\begin{bmatrix} 3 & -7 & 1 \\ 0 & -5 & -9 \\ 0 & 0 & 5 \end{bmatrix}$ (c) $\begin{bmatrix} 4 & 0 & 0 & 0 \\ 3 & -3 & 0 & 0 \\ 3 & 6 & 5 & 0 \\ 2 & -2 & 1 & 2 \end{bmatrix}$

82. **HOW DO YOU SEE IT?** Explain why the determinant of the matrix is equal to zero.

$$\begin{bmatrix} 2 & -4 & 5 \\ 1 & -2 & 3 \\ 0 & 0 & 0 \end{bmatrix}$$

83. Writing Describe the different methods you have learned for finding the determinant of a square matrix.

84. Exploration Consider square matrices in which the entries are consecutive integers. An example of such a matrix is shown below. Use a graphing utility to evaluate four determinants of this type. Make a conjecture based on the results. Then verify your conjecture.

$$\begin{bmatrix} 4 & 5 & 6 \\ 7 & 8 & 9 \\ 10 & 11 & 12 \end{bmatrix}$$

Cumulative Mixed Review

Factoring a Quadratic Expression In Exercises 85 and 86, factor the expression.

85. $4y^2 - 12y + 9$ **86.** $4y^2 - 28y + 49$

Solving a System of Equations In Exercises 87 and 88, solve the system of equations using the method of substitution or the method of elimination.

87. $\begin{cases} 3x - 10y = 46 \\ x + y = -2 \end{cases}$ **88.** $\begin{cases} 5x + 7y = 23 \\ -4x - 2y = -4 \end{cases}$

7.8   Applications of Matrices and Determinants

Area of a Triangle

In this section, you will study some additional applications of matrices and determinants. The first involves a formula for finding the area of a triangle whose vertices are given by three points on a rectangular coordinate system.

> **Area of a Triangle**
>
> The area of a triangle with vertices (x_1, y_1), (x_2, y_2), and (x_3, y_3) is
>
> $$\text{Area} = \pm \frac{1}{2} \begin{vmatrix} x_1 & y_1 & 1 \\ x_2 & y_2 & 1 \\ x_3 & y_3 & 1 \end{vmatrix}$$
>
> where the symbol $(\pm)$ indicates that the appropriate sign should be chosen to yield a positive area.

EXAMPLE 1   Finding the Area of a Triangle

See LarsonPrecalculus.com for an interactive version of this type of example.

Find the area of the triangle whose vertices are $(1, 0)$, $(2, 2)$, and $(4, 3)$, as shown in the figure.

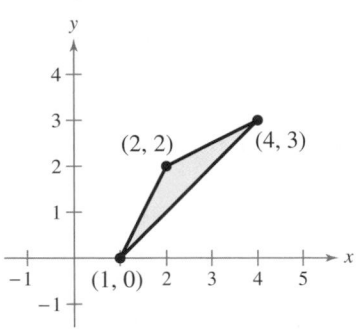

Solution

Begin by letting $(x_1, y_1) = (1, 0)$, $(x_2, y_2) = (2, 2)$, and $(x_3, y_3) = (4, 3)$. Then, to find the area of the triangle, evaluate the determinant by expanding along row 1.

$$\begin{vmatrix} x_1 & y_1 & 1 \\ x_2 & y_2 & 1 \\ x_3 & y_3 & 1 \end{vmatrix} = \begin{vmatrix} 1 & 0 & 1 \\ 2 & 2 & 1 \\ 4 & 3 & 1 \end{vmatrix}$$

$$= 1(-1)^2 \begin{vmatrix} 2 & 1 \\ 3 & 1 \end{vmatrix} + 0(-1)^3 \begin{vmatrix} 2 & 1 \\ 4 & 1 \end{vmatrix} + 1(-1)^4 \begin{vmatrix} 2 & 2 \\ 4 & 3 \end{vmatrix}$$

$$= 1(-1) + 0 + 1(-2)$$

$$= -3$$

Using this value, you can conclude that the area of the triangle is

$$\text{Area} = -\frac{1}{2} \begin{vmatrix} 1 & 0 & 1 \\ 2 & 2 & 1 \\ 4 & 3 & 1 \end{vmatrix} = -\frac{1}{2}(-3) = \frac{3}{2} \text{ square units.}$$

✓ *Checkpoint* *Audio-video solution in English & Spanish at LarsonPrecalculus.com.*

Find the area of a triangle whose vertices are $(0, 0)$, $(4, 1)$, and $(2, 5)$.

Collinear Points

What if the three points in Example 1 had been on the same line? What would have happened had the area formula been applied to three such points? The answer is that the determinant would have been zero. Consider, for instance, the three collinear points $(0, 1)$, $(2, 2)$, and $(4, 3)$, as shown in Figure 7.21. The area of the "triangle" that has these three points as vertices is

$$\frac{1}{2}\begin{vmatrix} 0 & 1 & 1 \\ 2 & 2 & 1 \\ 4 & 3 & 1 \end{vmatrix} = \frac{1}{2}\left[0(-1)^2\begin{vmatrix} 2 & 1 \\ 3 & 1 \end{vmatrix} + 1(-1)^3\begin{vmatrix} 2 & 1 \\ 4 & 1 \end{vmatrix} + 1(-1)^4\begin{vmatrix} 2 & 2 \\ 4 & 3 \end{vmatrix} \right]$$

$$= \frac{1}{2}[0 - 1(-2) + 1(-2)]$$

$$= 0$$

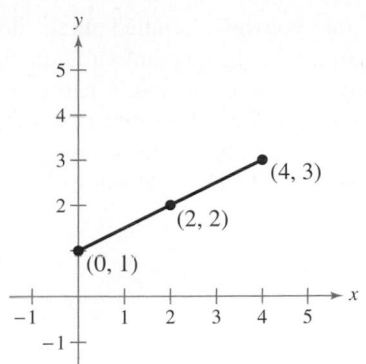

Figure 7.21

This result is generalized as follows.

Test for Collinear Points

Three points (x_1, y_1), (x_2, y_2), and (x_3, y_3) are **collinear** (lie on the same line) if and only if

$$\begin{vmatrix} x_1 & y_1 & 1 \\ x_2 & y_2 & 1 \\ x_3 & y_3 & 1 \end{vmatrix} = 0.$$

EXAMPLE 2 Testing for Collinear Points

Determine whether the points

$$(-2, -2), \quad (1, 1), \quad \text{and} \quad (7, 5)$$

are collinear. (See Figure 7.22.)

Solution

Begin by letting $(x_1, y_1) = (-2, -2)$, $(x_2, y_2) = (1, 1)$, and $(x_3, y_3) = (7, 5)$. Then by expanding along row 1, you have

$$\begin{vmatrix} x_1 & y_1 & 1 \\ x_2 & y_2 & 1 \\ x_3 & y_3 & 1 \end{vmatrix} = \begin{vmatrix} -2 & -2 & 1 \\ 1 & 1 & 1 \\ 7 & 5 & 1 \end{vmatrix}$$

$$= -2(-1)^2\begin{vmatrix} 1 & 1 \\ 5 & 1 \end{vmatrix} + (-2)(-1)^3\begin{vmatrix} 1 & 1 \\ 7 & 1 \end{vmatrix} + 1(-1)^4\begin{vmatrix} 1 & 1 \\ 7 & 5 \end{vmatrix}$$

$$= -2(-4) + 2(-6) + 1(-2)$$

$$= -6.$$

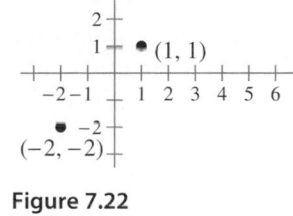

Figure 7.22

Because the value of this determinant is *not* zero, you can conclude that the three points are not collinear.

✓ **Checkpoint** ◀))) *Audio-video solution in English & Spanish at LarsonPrecalculus.com.*

Determine whether the points

$$(-2, 4), \quad (3, -1), \quad \text{and} \quad (6, -4)$$

are collinear.

Cramer's Rule

So far, you have studied three methods for solving a system of linear equations: substitution, elimination with equations, and elimination with matrices. You will now study one more method, **Cramer's Rule,** named after Gabriel Cramer (1704–1752). This rule uses determinants to write the solution of a system of linear equations. To see how Cramer's Rule works, take another look at the solution described at the beginning of Section 7.7. There, it was pointed out that the system

$$\begin{cases} a_1x + b_1y = c_1 \\ a_2x + b_2y = c_2 \end{cases}$$

has a solution

$$x = \frac{c_1b_2 - c_2b_1}{a_1b_2 - a_2b_1}$$

and

$$y = \frac{a_1c_2 - a_2c_1}{a_1b_2 - a_2b_1}$$

provided that

$$a_1b_2 - a_2b_1 \neq 0.$$

Each numerator and denominator in this solution can be expressed as a determinant, as follows.

$$x = \frac{c_1b_2 - c_2b_1}{a_1b_2 - a_2b_1} = \frac{\begin{vmatrix} c_1 & b_1 \\ c_2 & b_2 \end{vmatrix}}{\begin{vmatrix} a_1 & b_1 \\ a_2 & b_2 \end{vmatrix}}$$

$$y = \frac{a_1c_2 - a_2c_1}{a_1b_2 - a_2b_1} = \frac{\begin{vmatrix} a_1 & c_1 \\ a_2 & c_2 \end{vmatrix}}{\begin{vmatrix} a_1 & b_1 \\ a_2 & b_2 \end{vmatrix}}$$

Relative to the original system, the denominators of x and y are simply the determinant of the *coefficient* matrix of the system. This determinant is denoted by D. The numerators of x and y are denoted by D_x and D_y, respectively. They are formed by using the column of constants as replacements for the coefficients of x and y, as follows.

Coefficient Matrix	D	D_x	D_y
$\begin{bmatrix} a_1 & b_1 \\ a_2 & b_2 \end{bmatrix}$	$\begin{vmatrix} a_1 & b_1 \\ a_2 & b_2 \end{vmatrix}$	$\begin{vmatrix} c_1 & b_1 \\ c_2 & b_2 \end{vmatrix}$	$\begin{vmatrix} a_1 & c_1 \\ a_2 & c_2 \end{vmatrix}$

For example, given the system

$$\begin{cases} 2x - 5y = 3 \\ -4x + 3y = 8 \end{cases}$$

the coefficient matrix, D, D_x, and D_y are as follows.

Coefficient Matrix	D	D_x	D_y
$\begin{bmatrix} 2 & -5 \\ -4 & 3 \end{bmatrix}$	$\begin{vmatrix} 2 & -5 \\ -4 & 3 \end{vmatrix}$	$\begin{vmatrix} 3 & -5 \\ 8 & 3 \end{vmatrix}$	$\begin{vmatrix} 2 & 3 \\ -4 & 8 \end{vmatrix}$

Cramer's Rule generalizes easily to systems of n equations in n variables. The value of each variable is given as the quotient of two determinants. The denominator is the determinant of the coefficient matrix, and the numerator is the determinant of the matrix formed by replacing the column corresponding to the variable being solved for with the column representing the constants. For instance, the solution for x_3 in the following system is shown.

$$\begin{cases} a_{11}x_1 + a_{12}x_2 + a_{13}x_3 = b_1 \\ a_{21}x_1 + a_{22}x_2 + a_{23}x_3 = b_2 \\ a_{31}x_1 + a_{32}x_2 + a_{33}x_3 = b_3 \end{cases} \qquad x_3 = \frac{|A_3|}{|A|} = \frac{\begin{vmatrix} a_{11} & a_{12} & b_1 \\ a_{21} & a_{22} & b_2 \\ a_{31} & a_{32} & b_3 \end{vmatrix}}{\begin{vmatrix} a_{11} & a_{12} & a_{13} \\ a_{21} & a_{22} & a_{23} \\ a_{31} & a_{32} & a_{33} \end{vmatrix}}$$

Cramer's Rule

If a system of n linear equations in n variables has a coefficient matrix A with a *nonzero* determinant $|A|$, then the solution of the system is

$$x_1 = \frac{|A_1|}{|A|}, \quad x_2 = \frac{|A_2|}{|A|}, \dots, \quad x_n = \frac{|A_n|}{|A|}$$

where the ith column of A_i is the column of constants in the system of equations. If the determinant of the coefficient matrix is zero, then the system has either no solution or infinitely many solutions.

EXAMPLE 3   Using Cramer's Rule for a 2 × 2 System

Use Cramer's Rule to solve the system.

$$\begin{cases} 4x - 2y = 10 \\ 3x - 5y = 11 \end{cases}$$

Solution

To begin, find the determinant of the coefficient matrix.

$$D = \begin{vmatrix} 4 & -2 \\ 3 & -5 \end{vmatrix} = -20 - (-6) = -14$$

Because this determinant is not zero, apply Cramer's Rule.

$$x = \frac{D_x}{D} = \frac{\begin{vmatrix} 10 & -2 \\ 11 & -5 \end{vmatrix}}{-14} = \frac{(-50) - (-22)}{-14} = \frac{-28}{-14} = 2$$

$$y = \frac{D_y}{D} = \frac{\begin{vmatrix} 4 & 10 \\ 3 & 11 \end{vmatrix}}{-14} = \frac{44 - 30}{-14} = \frac{14}{-14} = -1$$

So, the solution is $x = 2$ and $y = -1$. Check this in the original system.

✓ **Checkpoint** ◄))) *Audio-video solution in English & Spanish at LarsonPrecalculus.com.*

Use Cramer's Rule to solve the system.

$$\begin{cases} 3x + 4y = 1 \\ 5x + 3y = 9 \end{cases}$$

EXAMPLE 4   Using Cramer's Rule for a 3×3 System

Use Cramer's Rule, if possible, to solve the system of linear equations.

Coefficient Matrix

$$\begin{cases} -x + 2y - 3z = 1 \\ 2x \quad\quad + z = 0 \\ 3x - 4y + 4z = 2 \end{cases} \implies \begin{bmatrix} -1 & 2 & -3 \\ 2 & 0 & 1 \\ 3 & -4 & 4 \end{bmatrix}$$

Solution

The coefficient matrix above can be expanded along the second row, as follows.

$$D = 2(-1)^3 \begin{vmatrix} 2 & -3 \\ -4 & 4 \end{vmatrix} + 0(-1)^4 \begin{vmatrix} -1 & -3 \\ 3 & 4 \end{vmatrix} + 1(-1)^5 \begin{vmatrix} -1 & 2 \\ 3 & -4 \end{vmatrix}$$

$$= -2(-4) + 0 - 1(-2)$$

$$= 10$$

Because this determinant is not zero, you can apply Cramer's Rule.

$$x = \frac{D_x}{D} = \frac{\begin{vmatrix} 1 & 2 & -3 \\ 0 & 0 & 1 \\ 2 & -4 & 4 \end{vmatrix}}{10} = \frac{8}{10} = \frac{4}{5}$$

$$y = \frac{D_y}{D} = \frac{\begin{vmatrix} -1 & 1 & -3 \\ 2 & 0 & 1 \\ 3 & 2 & 4 \end{vmatrix}}{10} = \frac{-15}{10} = -\frac{3}{2}$$

$$z = \frac{D_z}{D} = \frac{\begin{vmatrix} -1 & 2 & 1 \\ 2 & 0 & 0 \\ 3 & -4 & 2 \end{vmatrix}}{10} = \frac{-16}{10} = -\frac{8}{5}$$

The solution is

$$\left(\tfrac{4}{5}, -\tfrac{3}{2}, -\tfrac{8}{5} \right).$$

Check this in the original system.

✓ **Checkpoint** 🔊)) *Audio-video solution in English & Spanish at LarsonPrecalculus.com.*

Use Cramer's Rule to solve the system.

$$\begin{cases} 4x - y + z = 12 \\ 2x + 2y + 3z = 1 \\ 5x - 2y + 6z = 22 \end{cases}$$

Remember that Cramer's Rule does not apply when the determinant of the coefficient matrix is zero. This would create division by zero, which is undefined. For example, consider this system of linear equations.

$$\begin{cases} -x \quad\quad + z = 4 \\ 2x - y + z = -3 \\ \quad\quad y - 3z = 1 \end{cases}$$

Using a graphing utility to evaluate the determinant of the coefficient matrix A, you find that Cramer's Rule cannot be applied because $|A| = 0$.

Technology Tip

Try using a graphing utility to evaluate D_x/D for the system of linear equations shown at the lower left. You should obtain an error message similar to the one shown below.

```
ERR:DIVIDE BY 0
1:Quit
2:Goto
```

Cryptography

A **cryptogram** is a message written according to a secret code. (The Greek word *kryptos* means "hidden.") Matrix multiplication can be used to encode and decode messages. To begin, you need to assign a number to each letter in the alphabet (with 0 assigned to a blank space), as follows.

0 = _	9 = I	18 = R
1 = A	10 = J	19 = S
2 = B	11 = K	20 = T
3 = C	12 = L	21 = U
4 = D	13 = M	22 = V
5 = E	14 = N	23 = W
6 = F	15 = O	24 = X
7 = G	16 = P	25 = Y
8 = H	17 = Q	26 = Z

Then the message is converted to numbers and partitioned into **uncoded row matrices,** each having n entries, as demonstrated in Example 5.

EXAMPLE 5   Forming Uncoded Row Matrices

Write the uncoded row matrices of dimension 1×3 for the message

    MEET ME MONDAY.

Solution

Partitioning the message (including blank spaces, but ignoring punctuation) into groups of three produces the following uncoded row matrices.

$$[13 \quad 5 \quad 5] \quad [20 \quad 0 \quad 13] \quad [5 \quad 0 \quad 13] \quad [15 \quad 14 \quad 4] \quad [1 \quad 25 \quad 0]$$
$$\ \ \text{M} \quad \text{E} \quad \text{E} \quad \quad \text{T} \quad \quad \text{M} \quad \text{E} \quad \quad \text{M} \quad \text{O} \quad \text{N} \quad \quad \text{D} \quad \text{A} \quad \text{Y}$$

Note that a blank space is used to fill out the last uncoded row matrix.

✓ *Checkpoint* *Audio-video solution in English & Spanish at LarsonPrecalculus.com.*

Write the uncoded row matrices of order 1×3 for the message

    OWLS ARE NOCTURNAL.

To encode a message, use the techniques demonstrated in Section 7.6 to choose an $n \times n$ invertible matrix such as

$$A = \begin{bmatrix} 1 & -2 & 2 \\ -1 & 1 & 3 \\ 1 & -1 & -4 \end{bmatrix}$$

and multiply the uncoded row matrices by A (on the right) to obtain **coded row matrices.** Here is an example.

Uncoded Matrix   *Encoding Matrix A*   *Coded Matrix*

$$[13 \quad 5 \quad 5] \begin{bmatrix} 1 & -2 & 2 \\ -1 & 1 & 3 \\ 1 & -1 & -4 \end{bmatrix} = [13 \quad -26 \quad 21]$$

This technique is further illustrated in Example 6.

Applied Cryptography Researcher

EXAMPLE 6 Encoding a Message

Use the matrix A to encode the message MEET ME MONDAY.

$$A = \begin{bmatrix} 1 & -2 & 2 \\ -1 & 1 & 3 \\ 1 & -1 & -4 \end{bmatrix}$$

Solution

The coded row matrices are obtained by multiplying each of the uncoded row matrices found in Example 5 by the matrix A, as follows.

Uncoded Matrix   Encoding Matrix A   Coded Matrix

$$\begin{bmatrix} 13 & 5 & 5 \end{bmatrix} \begin{bmatrix} 1 & -2 & 2 \\ -1 & 1 & 3 \\ 1 & -1 & -4 \end{bmatrix} = \begin{bmatrix} 13 & -26 & 21 \end{bmatrix}$$

$$\begin{bmatrix} 20 & 0 & 13 \end{bmatrix} \begin{bmatrix} 1 & -2 & 2 \\ -1 & 1 & 3 \\ 1 & -1 & -4 \end{bmatrix} = \begin{bmatrix} 33 & -53 & -12 \end{bmatrix}$$

$$\begin{bmatrix} 5 & 0 & 13 \end{bmatrix} \begin{bmatrix} 1 & -2 & 2 \\ -1 & 1 & 3 \\ 1 & -1 & -4 \end{bmatrix} = \begin{bmatrix} 18 & -23 & -42 \end{bmatrix}$$

$$\begin{bmatrix} 15 & 14 & 4 \end{bmatrix} \begin{bmatrix} 1 & -2 & 2 \\ -1 & 1 & 3 \\ 1 & -1 & -4 \end{bmatrix} = \begin{bmatrix} 5 & -20 & 56 \end{bmatrix}$$

$$\begin{bmatrix} 1 & 25 & 0 \end{bmatrix} \begin{bmatrix} 1 & -2 & 2 \\ -1 & 1 & 3 \\ 1 & -1 & -4 \end{bmatrix} = \begin{bmatrix} -24 & 23 & 77 \end{bmatrix}$$

So, the sequence of coded row matrices is

$$\begin{bmatrix} 13 & -26 & 21 \end{bmatrix} \begin{bmatrix} 33 & -53 & -12 \end{bmatrix} \begin{bmatrix} 18 & -23 & -42 \end{bmatrix} \begin{bmatrix} 5 & -20 & 56 \end{bmatrix} \begin{bmatrix} -24 & 23 & 77 \end{bmatrix}.$$

Finally, removing the matrix notation produces the following cryptogram.

13 −26 21 33 −53 −12 18 −23 −42 5 −20 56 −24 23 77

✓ **Checkpoint** Audio-video solution in English & Spanish at LarsonPrecalculus.com.

Use the following invertible matrix to encode the message OWLS ARE NOCTURNAL.

$$A = \begin{bmatrix} 1 & -1 & 0 \\ 1 & 0 & -1 \\ 6 & -2 & -3 \end{bmatrix}$$

For those who do not know the encoding matrix A, decoding the cryptogram found in Example 6 is difficult. But for an authorized receiver who knows the encoding matrix A, decoding is simple. The receiver need only multiply the coded row matrices by A^{-1} (on the right) to retrieve the uncoded row matrices. Here is an example.

$$\underbrace{\begin{bmatrix} 13 & -26 & 21 \end{bmatrix}}_{\text{Coded}} \underbrace{\begin{bmatrix} -1 & -10 & -8 \\ -1 & -6 & -5 \\ 0 & -1 & -1 \end{bmatrix}}_{A^{-1}} = \underbrace{\begin{bmatrix} 13 & 5 & 5 \end{bmatrix}}_{\text{Uncoded}}$$

This technique is further illustrated in Example 7.

Technology Tip

An efficient method for encoding the message at the left with your graphing utility is to enter A as a 3×3 matrix. Let B be the 5×3 matrix whose rows are the uncoded row matrices

$$B = \begin{bmatrix} 13 & 5 & 5 \\ 20 & 0 & 13 \\ 5 & 0 & 13 \\ 15 & 14 & 4 \\ 1 & 25 & 0 \end{bmatrix}.$$

The product BA gives the coded row matrices.

EXAMPLE 7   Decoding a Message

Use the inverse of the matrix A in Example 6 to decode the cryptogram.

13 −26 21 33 −53 −12 18 −23 −42 5 −20 56 −24 23 77

Solution

First, find the decoding matrix A^{-1} by using the techniques demonstrated in Section 7.6. Next partition the message into groups of three to form the coded row matrices. Then multiply each coded row matrix by A^{-1} (on the right).

Coded Matrix Decoding Matrix A^{-1} Decoded Matrix

$$[13 \ -26 \ \ \ 21]\begin{bmatrix} -1 & -10 & -8 \\ -1 & -6 & -5 \\ 0 & -1 & -1 \end{bmatrix} = [13 \ \ \ 5 \ \ \ 5]$$

$$[33 \ -53 \ -12]\begin{bmatrix} -1 & -10 & -8 \\ -1 & -6 & -5 \\ 0 & -1 & -1 \end{bmatrix} = [20 \ \ \ 0 \ \ \ 13]$$

$$[18 \ -23 \ -42]\begin{bmatrix} -1 & -10 & -8 \\ -1 & -6 & -5 \\ 0 & -1 & -1 \end{bmatrix} = [5 \ \ \ 0 \ \ \ 13]$$

$$[5 \ -20 \ \ \ 56]\begin{bmatrix} -1 & -10 & -8 \\ -1 & -6 & -5 \\ 0 & -1 & -1 \end{bmatrix} - [15 \ \ \ 14 \ \ \ 4]$$

$$[-24 \ \ \ 23 \ \ \ 77]\begin{bmatrix} -1 & -10 & -8 \\ -1 & -6 & -5 \\ 0 & -1 & -1 \end{bmatrix} = [1 \ \ \ 25 \ \ \ 0]$$

So, the message is as follows.

[13 5 5] [20 0 13] [5 0 13] [15 14 4] [1 25 0]

  M E E T   M E   M O N D A Y

✓ **Checkpoint** *Audio-video solution in English & Spanish at LarsonPrecalculus.com.*

Use the inverse of the matrix A in the Checkpoint with Example 6 to decode the cryptogram.

110   39 −59 25 −21 −3 23 −18 −5 47 −20 −24
149 −56 −75 87 −38 −37.

Technology Tip

An efficient method for decoding the cryptogram in Example 7 with your graphing utility is to enter A as a 3×3 matrix and then find A^{-1}. Let B be the 5×3 matrix whose rows are the coded row matrices, as shown below. The product BA^{-1} gives the decoded row matrices.

$$B = \begin{bmatrix} 13 & -26 & 21 \\ 33 & -53 & -12 \\ 18 & -23 & -42 \\ 5 & -20 & 56 \\ -24 & 23 & 77 \end{bmatrix}$$

7.8   Exercises

See *CalcChat.com* for tutorial help and worked-out solutions to odd-numbered exercises.
For instructions on how to use a graphing utility, see Appendix A.

Vocabulary and Concept Check

In Exercises 1 and 2, fill in the blank.

1. _____ is a method for using determinants to solve a system of linear equations.

2. A message written according to a secret code is called a _____ .

In Exercises 3 and 4, consider three points (x_1, y_1), (x_2, y_2), and (x_3, y_3), and the determinant shown at the right.

$$\begin{vmatrix} x_1 & y_1 & 1 \\ x_2 & y_2 & 1 \\ x_3 & y_3 & 1 \end{vmatrix}$$

3. Suppose the three points are vertices of a triangle and the value of the determinant is -6. What number do you multiply -6 by to find the area of the triangle?

4. Suppose the value of the determinant is 0. What can you conclude?

Procedures and Problem Solving

Finding an Area   In Exercises 5–10, use a determinant to find the area of the figure with the given vertices.

5. $(-2, 4)$, $(2, 3)$, $(-1, 5)$

6. $(-3, 5)$, $(2, 6)$, $(3, -5)$

7. $\left(0, \frac{1}{2}\right)$, $\left(\frac{5}{2}, 0\right)$, $(4, 3)$

8. $\left(\frac{9}{2}, 0\right)$, $(2, 6)$, $\left(0, -\frac{3}{2}\right)$

9.

10.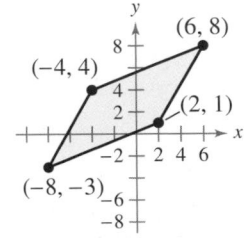

Finding a Coordinate   In Exercises 11 and 12, find x or y such that the triangle has an area of 4 square units.

11. $(-1, 5)$, $(-2, 0)$, $(x, 2)$

12. $(-4, 2)$, $(-3, 5)$, $(-1, y)$

Testing for Collinear Points   In Exercises 13–16, use a determinant to determine whether the points are collinear.

13. $(3, -1)$, $(0, -3)$, $(12, 5)$

14. $(3, -5)$, $(6, 1)$, $(4, 2)$

15. $\left(2, -\frac{1}{2}\right)$, $(-4, 4)$, $(6, -3)$

16. $\left(0, \frac{1}{2}\right)$, $(2, -1)$, $\left(-4, \frac{7}{2}\right)$

Finding a Coordinate   In Exercises 17 and 18, find x or y such that the points are collinear.

17. $(1, -2)$, $(x, 2)$, $(5, 6)$

18. $(-6, 2)$, $(-5, y)$, $(-3, 5)$

Using Cramer's Rule   In Exercises 19–24, use Cramer's Rule to solve (if possible) the system of equations.

19. $\begin{cases} -7x + 11y = -1 \\ 3x - 9y = 9 \end{cases}$

20. $\begin{cases} 3x + 2y = -2 \\ 6x + 4y = 4 \end{cases}$

21. $\begin{cases} 4x - 3y = -10 \\ 6x + 9y = 12 \end{cases}$

22. $\begin{cases} 6x - 5y = 17 \\ -13x + 3y = -76 \end{cases}$

23. $\begin{cases} 4x - y + z = -5 \\ 2x + 2y + 3z = 10 \\ 6x + y + 4z = -5 \end{cases}$

24. $\begin{cases} 4x - 2y + 3z = -2 \\ 2x + 2y + 5z = 16 \\ 8x - 5y - 2z = 4 \end{cases}$

Comparing Solution Methods   In Exercises 25 and 26, solve the system of equations using (a) Gaussian elimination and (b) Cramer's Rule. Which method do you prefer, and why?

25. $\begin{cases} 3x + 3y + 5z = 1 \\ 3x + 5y + 9z = 2 \\ 5x + 9y + 17z = 4 \end{cases}$

26. $\begin{cases} 2x + 3y - 5z = 1 \\ 3x + 5y + 9z = -16 \\ 5x + 9y + 17z = -30 \end{cases}$

27. **Why you should learn it**   (*p. 541*) The retail sales of family clothing stores in the United States from 2009 through 2013 are shown in the table.   (Source: U.S. Census Bureau)

Year	Sales (in billions of dollars)
2009	81.4
2010	85.3
2011	89.9
2012	94.7
2013	99.5

The coefficients of the least squares regression parabola $y = at^2 + bt + c$, where y represents the retail sales (in billions of dollars) and t represents the year, with $t = 9$ corresponding to 2009, can be found by solving the system

$$\begin{cases} 80{,}499a + 6985b + 615c = 56{,}453.6 \\ 6985a + 615b + 55c = 5004.4. \\ 615a + 55b + 5c = 450.8 \end{cases}$$

(a) Use Cramer's Rule to solve the system and write the least squares regression parabola for the data.

(b) Use a graphing utility to graph the parabola with the data. How well does the model fit the data?

(c) Use the model to predict the retail sales of family clothing stores in the U.S. in the year 2015.

28. MODELING DATA

The retail sales y (in billions of dollars) of stores selling auto parts, accessories, and tires in the United States from 2009 through 2013 are given by the ordered pairs of the form $(t, y(t))$, where $t = 9$ represents 2009. (Source: U.S. Census Bureau)

(9, 74.1)   (10, 77.7)   (11, 82.7)

(12, 83.9)   (13, 82.8)

The coefficients of the least squares regression parabola $y = at^2 + bt + c$ can be found by solving the system

$$\begin{cases} 80{,}499a + 6985b + 615c = 49{,}853.8 \\ 6985a + 615b + 55c = 4436.8. \\ 615a + 55b + 5c = 401.2 \end{cases}$$

(a) Use Cramer's Rule to solve the system and write the least squares regression parabola for the data.

(b) Use a graphing utility to graph the parabola with the data. How well does the model fit the data?

(c) Is this a good model for predicting retail sales in future years? Explain.

Encoding a Message In Exercises 29 and 30, (a) write the uncoded 1×2 row matrices for the message, and then (b) encode the message using the encoding matrix.

Message	Encoding Matrix
29. COME HOME SOON	$\begin{bmatrix} 1 & 2 \\ 3 & 5 \end{bmatrix}$
30. HELP IS ON THE WAY	$\begin{bmatrix} -2 & 3 \\ -1 & 1 \end{bmatrix}$

Encoding a Message In Exercises 31 and 32, (a) write the uncoded 1×3 row matrices for the message, and then (b) encode the message using the encoding matrix.

Message	Encoding Matrix
31. CALL ME TOMORROW	$\begin{bmatrix} 1 & -1 & 0 \\ 1 & 0 & -1 \\ -6 & 2 & 3 \end{bmatrix}$
32. HAPPY BIRTHDAY	$\begin{bmatrix} 1 & 2 & 2 \\ 3 & 7 & 9 \\ -1 & -4 & -7 \end{bmatrix}$

Decoding a Message In Exercises 33 and 34, use A^{-1} to decode the cryptogram.

33. $A = \begin{bmatrix} 1 & 2 \\ 3 & 5 \end{bmatrix}$ 11 21 64 112 25 50 29
53 23 46 40 75 55 92

34. $A = \begin{bmatrix} 3 & -4 & 2 \\ 0 & 2 & 1 \\ 4 & -5 & 3 \end{bmatrix}$ 112 -140 83 19 -25 13 72
-76 61 95 -118 71 20 21
38 35 -23 36 42 -48 32

35. Decoding a Message The following cryptogram was encoded with a 2×2 matrix.

5 2 25 11 -2 -7 -15 -15 32 14 -8 -13 38
19 -19 -19 37 16

The last word of the message is _SUE. What is the message?

36. Why you should learn it (p. 548) The following cryptogram was encoded with a 2×2 matrix.

8 21 -15 -10 -13 -13 5 10 5 25
5 19 -1 6 20 40 -18 -18 1 16

The last word of the message is _RON. What is the message?

Conclusions

True or False? In Exercises 37 and 38, determine whether the statement is true or false. Justify your answer.

37. Cramer's Rule cannot be used to solve a system of linear equations when the determinant of the coefficient matrix is zero.

38. In a system of linear equations, when the determinant of the coefficient matrix is zero, the system has no solution.

39. **Writing** Describe a way to use an invertible $n \times n$ matrix to encode a message that is converted to numbers and partitioned into uncoded column matrices.

40. **HOW DO YOU SEE IT?** At this point in the text, you have learned several methods for finding an equation of a line that passes through two given points. Briefly describe these methods and discuss the advantages and disadvantages of each.

Cumulative Mixed Review

Equation of a Line In Exercises 41–44, find the general form of the equation of the line that passes through the two points.

41. $(-1, 5), (7, 3)$ 42. $(0, -6), (-2, 10)$

43. $(3, -3), (10, -1)$ 44. $(-4, 12), (4, 2)$

7   Chapter Summary

	What did you learn?	Explanation and Examples	Review Exercises
7.1	Use the methods of substitution and graphing to solve systems of equations in two variables (*p. 470*), and use systems of equations to model and solve real-life problems (*p. 475*).	**Substitution:** (1) Solve one of the equations for one variable in terms of the other. (2) Substitute the expression found in Step 1 into the other equation to obtain an equation in one variable and (3) solve the equation. (4) Back-substitute the value(s) obtained in Step 3 into the expression obtained in Step 1 to find the value(s) of the other variable. (5) Check the solution(s). **Graphing:** (1) Solve both equations for *y* in terms of *x*. (2) Use a graphing utility to graph both equations. (3) Use the *intersect* feature or the *zoom* and *trace* features of the graphing utility to approximate the point(s) of intersection of the graphs. (4) Check the solution(s).	1–20
7.2	Use the method of elimination to solve systems of linear equations in two variables (*p. 480*), and graphically interpret the number of solutions of a system of linear equations in two variables (*p. 482*).	**Elimination:** (1) Obtain coefficients for *x* (or *y*) that differ only in sign by multiplying all terms of one or both equations by suitably chosen constants. (2) Add the equations to eliminate one variable and solve the resulting equation. (3) Back-substitute the value obtained in Step 2 into either of the original equations and solve for the other variable. (4) Check the solution(s).	21–36
	Use systems of linear equations in two variables to model and solve real-life problems (*p. 484*).	A system of linear equations in two variables can be used to find the airspeed of an airplane and the speed of the wind. (See Example 6.)	37–40
7.3	Use back-substitution to solve linear systems in row-echelon form (*p. 489*).	$\begin{cases} x - 2y + 3z = 9 \\ -x + 3y = -4 \\ 2x - 5y + 5z = 17 \end{cases} \rightarrow \begin{cases} x - 2y + 3z = 9 \\ y + 3z = 5 \\ z = 2 \end{cases}$	41, 42
	Use Gaussian elimination to solve systems of linear equations (*p. 490*).	Use elementary row operations to convert a system of linear equations to row-echelon form. (1) Interchange two equations. (2) Multiply one of the equations by a nonzero constant. (3) Add a multiple of one equation to another equation.	43–48
	Solve nonsquare systems of linear equations (*p. 493*).	In a nonsquare system, the number of equations differs from the number of variables. A system of linear equations cannot have a unique solution unless there are at least as many equations as there are variables.	49, 50
	Graphically interpret three-variable linear systems (*p. 494*).	The graph of a system of three linear equations in three variables consists of three planes. When they intersect in a single point, the system has exactly one solution. When they have no point in common, the system has no solution. When they intersect in a line or a plane, the system has infinitely many solutions (see Figures 7.9–7.13).	51, 52
	Use systems of linear equations to write partial fraction decompositions of rational expressions (*p. 495*).	$\dfrac{9}{x^3 - 6x^2} = \dfrac{9}{x^2(x - 6)} = \dfrac{A}{x} + \dfrac{B}{x^2} + \dfrac{C}{x - 6}$	53–58
	Use systems of linear equations in three or more variables to model and solve real-life problems (*p. 498*).	A system of linear equations in three variables can be used to find the position equation of an object that is moving in a (vertical) line with constant acceleration. (See Example 8.)	59–62

What did you learn?		Explanation and Examples	Review Exercises
7.4	Write matrices and identify their dimensions (*p. 504*), and perform elementary row operations on matrices (*p. 506*).	**Elementary Row Operations** 1. Interchange two rows. 2. Multiply a row by a nonzero constant. 3. Add a multiple of a row to another row.	63–80
	Use matrices and Gaussian elimination to solve systems of linear equations (*p. 507*).	Write the augmented matrix of the system. Use elementary row operations to rewrite the augmented matrix in row-echelon form. Write the system of linear equations corresponding to the matrix in row-echelon form and use back-substitution to find the solution.	81–88
	Use matrices and Gauss-Jordan elimination to solve systems of linear equations (*p. 511*).	Gauss-Jordan elimination continues the reduction process on a matrix in row-echelon form until a reduced row-echelon form is obtained. (See Example 8.)	89–100
7.5	Decide whether two matrices are equal (*p. 518*).	Two matrices are equal when they have the same dimension and all of their corresponding entries are equal.	101–104
	Add and subtract matrices and multiply matrices by scalars (*p. 519*), multiply two matrices (*p. 522*), and use matrix operations to model and solve real-life problems (*p. 525*).	1. Let $A = [a_{ij}]$ and $B = [b_{ij}]$ be matrices of dimension $m \times n$ and let c be a scalar. $A + B = [a_{ij} + b_{ij}] \qquad cA = [ca_{ij}]$ 2. Let $A = [a_{ij}]$ be an $m \times n$ matrix and let $B = [b_{ij}]$ be an $n \times p$ matrix. The product AB is an $m \times p$ matrix given by $AB = [c_{ij}]$, where $c_{ij} = a_{i1}b_{1j} + a_{i2}b_{2j} + a_{i3}b_{3j} + \cdots + a_{in}b_{nj}.$	105–128
7.6	Verify that two matrices are inverses of each other (*p. 532*), and use Gauss-Jordan elimination to find inverses of matrices (*p. 533*).	Write the $n \times 2n$ matrix $[A \vdots I]$. Row reduce A to I using elementary row operations. The result will be the matrix $[I \vdots A^{-1}]$.	129–140
	Use a formula to find inverses of 2×2 matrices (*p. 536*).	If $A = \begin{bmatrix} a & b \\ c & d \end{bmatrix}$ and $ad - bc \neq 0$, then $A^{-1} = \dfrac{1}{ad - bc}\begin{bmatrix} d & -b \\ -c & a \end{bmatrix}.$	141–146
	Use inverse matrices to solve systems of linear equations (*p. 537*).	If A is an invertible matrix, then the system of linear equations represented by $AX = B$ has a unique solution given by $X = A^{-1}B$.	147–156
7.7	Find the determinants of 2×2 matrices (*p. 541*).	$\det(A) = |A| = \begin{vmatrix} a_1 & b_1 \\ a_2 & b_2 \end{vmatrix} = a_1b_2 - a_2b_1$	157–162
	Find minors and cofactors of square matrices (*p. 543*), and find the determinants of square matrices (*p. 544*).	The determinant of a square matrix A (of dimension 2×2 or greater) is the sum of the entries in any row (or column) of A multiplied by their respective cofactors.	163–174
7.8	Use determinants to find areas of triangles (*p. 548*) and to determine whether points are collinear (*p. 549*), use Cramer's Rule to solve systems of linear equations (*p. 550*), and use matrices to encode and decode messages (*p. 553*).	If a system of n linear equations in n variables has a coefficient matrix A with a *nonzero* determinant $|A|$, then the solution of the system is $x_1 = \dfrac{|A_1|}{|A|}, x_2 = \dfrac{|A_2|}{|A|}, \ldots, x_n = \dfrac{|A_n|}{|A|}$ where the ith column of A_i is the column of constants in the system of equations.	175–201

7.1

Solving a System by Substitution   In Exercises 1–10, solve the system by the method of substitution.

1. $\begin{cases} x + y = 2 \\ x - y = 0 \end{cases}$

2. $\begin{cases} 2x - 3y = 3 \\ x - y = 0 \end{cases}$

3. $\begin{cases} 4x - y = 1 \\ -8x + 2y = 5 \end{cases}$

4. $\begin{cases} 10x + 6y = -14 \\ x + 9y = -7 \end{cases}$

5. $\begin{cases} 0.5x + y = 0.75 \\ 1.25x - 4.5y = -2.5 \end{cases}$

6. $\begin{cases} -x + \frac{2}{5}y = \frac{3}{5} \\ -x + \frac{1}{5}y = -\frac{4}{5} \end{cases}$

7. $\begin{cases} x^2 - y^2 = 9 \\ x - y = 1 \end{cases}$

8. $\begin{cases} x^2 + y^2 = 169 \\ 3x + 2y = 39 \end{cases}$

9. $\begin{cases} y = 2x^2 \\ y = x^4 - 2x^2 \end{cases}$

10. $\begin{cases} x = y + 3 \\ x = y^2 + 7 \end{cases}$

Solving a System of Equations Graphically   In Exercises 11–16, use a graphing utility to approximate all points of intersection of the graphs of the equations in the system. Verify your solutions by checking them in the original system.

11. $\begin{cases} 5x + 6y = 7 \\ -x - 4y = 0 \end{cases}$

12. $\begin{cases} 8x - 3y = -3 \\ 2x + 5y = 28 \end{cases}$

13. $\begin{cases} y^2 - 4x = 0 \\ x + y = 0 \end{cases}$

14. $\begin{cases} y = 2x^2 - 4x + 1 \\ y = x^2 - 4x + 3 \end{cases}$

15. $\begin{cases} y = 2(6 - x) \\ y = 2^{x-2} \end{cases}$

16. $\begin{cases} y = \ln(x + 2) + 1 \\ x + y = 0 \end{cases}$

17. **Finance** You invest $5000 in a greenhouse. The planter, potting soil, and seed for each plant cost $6.43, and the selling price of each plant is $12.68. How many plants must you sell to break even?

18. **Finance** You are offered two sales jobs. One company offers an annual salary of $55,000 plus a year-end bonus of 1.5% of your total sales. The other company offers an annual salary of $52,000 plus a year-end bonus of 2% of your total sales. How much would you have to sell in a year to make the second offer the better offer?

19. **Geometry** The perimeter of a rectangle is 480 meters and its length is 1.5 times its width. Find the dimensions of the rectangle.

20. **Geometry** The perimeter of a rectangle is 68 feet and its width is $\frac{8}{9}$ times its length. Find the dimensions of the rectangle.

7.2

Solving a System by Elimination   In Exercises 21–30, solve the system by the method of elimination.

21. $\begin{cases} x + 3y = -5 \\ -x - 8y = 0 \end{cases}$

22. $\begin{cases} 7x + 2y = 12 \\ x - 2y = -4 \end{cases}$

23. $\begin{cases} 2x - y = 2 \\ 6x + 8y = 39 \end{cases}$

24. $\begin{cases} 7x + 12y = 63 \\ 2x + 3y = 15 \end{cases}$

25. $\begin{cases} \frac{1}{5}x + \frac{3}{10}y = 7 \\ \frac{2}{5}x + \frac{3}{5}y = 14 \end{cases}$

26. $\begin{cases} 0.2x + 0.3y = 0.14 \\ 0.4x + 0.5y = 0.20 \end{cases}$

27. $\begin{cases} 3x - 2y = 0 \\ 3x + 2(y + 5) = 10 \end{cases}$

28. $\begin{cases} 6x - 4(y - 1) = 19 \\ -3x + 2y = 3 \end{cases}$

29. $\begin{cases} 1.5x + 2.5y = 8.5 \\ 6x + 10y = 24 \end{cases}$

30. $\begin{cases} 1.25x - 2y = 3.5 \\ 5x - 8y = 14 \end{cases}$

Solving a System Graphically   In Exercises 31–36, use a graphing utility to graph the lines in the system. Use the graphs to determine whether the system is consistent or inconsistent. If the system is consistent, determine the solution. Verify your results algebraically.

31. $\begin{cases} 3x + 2y = 0 \\ x - y = 4 \end{cases}$

32. $\begin{cases} x + y = 6 \\ -2x - 2y = -12 \end{cases}$

33. $\begin{cases} \frac{1}{4}x - \frac{1}{5}y = 2 \\ -5x + 4y = 8 \end{cases}$

34. $\begin{cases} \frac{7}{2}x - 7y = -1 \\ -x + 2y = 4 \end{cases}$

35. $\begin{cases} 8x - 2y = 10 \\ -6x + 1.5y = -7.5 \end{cases}$

36. $\begin{cases} -x + 3.2y = 10.4 \\ -2x - 9.6y = 6.4 \end{cases}$

Supply and Demand   In Exercises 37 and 38, find the point of equilibrium of the demand and supply equations.

	Demand	*Supply*
37.	$p = 37 - 0.0002x$	$p = 22 + 0.00001x$
38.	$p = 120 - 0.0001x$	$p = 45 + 0.0002x$

39. **Aviation** Two planes leave Pittsburgh and Philadelphia at the same time, each going to the other city. One plane flies 25 miles per hour faster than the other. Find the airspeed of each plane given that the cities are 275 miles apart and the planes pass each other after 40 minutes of flying time.

40. **Economics** A total of $46,000 is invested in two corporate bonds that pay 6.75% and 7.25% simple interest. The investor wants an annual interest income of $3245 from the investments. What is the most that can be invested in the 6.75% bond?

7.3

Using Back-Substitution   In Exercises 41 and 42, use back-substitution to solve the system of linear equations.

41. $\begin{cases} x - 4y + 3z = 3 \\ -y + z = -1 \\ z = -5 \end{cases}$

42. $\begin{cases} x - 7y + 8z = -14 \\ y - 9z = 26 \\ z = -3 \end{cases}$

Solving a System of Linear Equations In Exercises 43–50, solve the system of linear equations and check any solution algebraically.

43. $\begin{cases} x - 2y + 5z = -12 \\ 2x + 6z = -28 \\ x + y + 18z = -4 \end{cases}$

44. $\begin{cases} x + y + z = 2 \\ -x + 3y + 2z = 8 \\ 4x + y = 4 \end{cases}$

45. $\begin{cases} x - 2y + z = -6 \\ 2x - 3y = -7 \\ -x + 3y - 3z = 11 \end{cases}$

46. $\begin{cases} 2x + 6z = -9 \\ 3x - 2y + 11z = -16 \\ 3x - y + 7z = -11 \end{cases}$

47. $\begin{cases} x - 2y + 3z = -5 \\ 2x + 4y + 5z = 1 \\ x + 2y + z = 0 \end{cases}$

48. $\begin{cases} x - 2y + z = 5 \\ 2x + 3y + z = 5 \\ x + y + 2z = 3 \end{cases}$

49. $\begin{cases} 5x - 12y + 7z = 16 \\ 3x - 7y + 4z = 9 \end{cases}$

50. $\begin{cases} 2x + 5y - 19z = 34 \\ 3x + 8y - 31z = 54 \end{cases}$

Sketching a Plane In Exercises 51 and 52, sketch the plane represented by the linear equation. Then list four points that lie in the plane.

51. $x + 5y + z = 10$ 52. $2x + 3y + 4z = 12$

Partial Fraction Decomposition In Exercises 53–58, write the partial fraction decomposition for the rational expression. Check your result algebraically by combining the fractions, and check your result graphically by using a graphing utility to graph the rational expression and the partial fractions in the same viewing window.

53. $\dfrac{4 - x}{x^2 + 6x + 8}$

54. $\dfrac{-x}{x^2 + 3x + 2}$

55. $\dfrac{9}{x^2 - 9}$

56. $\dfrac{x^2}{x^2 + 2x - 15}$

57. $\dfrac{x^2 + 2x}{x^3 - x^2 + x - 1}$

58. $\dfrac{2x^2 - x + 7}{x^4 + 8x^2 + 16}$

Data Analysis: Curve-Fitting In Exercises 59 and 60, find the equation of the parabola $y = ax^2 + bx + c$ that passes through the points. To verify your result, use a graphing utility to plot the points and graph the parabola.

59. $(-1, -4), (1, -2), (2, 5)$ 60. $(-1, 0) (1, 4), (2, 3)$

61. **Physical Education** Pebble Beach Golf Links in Pebble Beach, California, is an 18-hole course that consists of par-3 holes, par-4 holes, and par-5 holes. There are two more par-4 holes than twice the number of par-5 holes, and the number of par-3 holes is equal to the number of par-5 holes. Find the number of par-3, par-4, and par-5 holes on the course. (Source: Pebble Beach Resorts)

62. **Economics** An inheritance of $40,000 is divided among three investments yielding $3500 in interest per year. The interest rates for the three investments are 7%, 9%, and 11%. Find the amount of each investment when the second and third are $3000 and $5000 less than the first, respectively.

7.4

Dimension of a Matrix In Exercises 63–66, determine the dimension of the matrix.

63. $\begin{bmatrix} -3 \\ 1 \\ 10 \end{bmatrix}$

64. $\begin{bmatrix} 3 & -1 & 0 & 6 \\ -2 & 7 & 1 & 4 \end{bmatrix}$

65. $[3]$

66. $\begin{bmatrix} 6 & 7 & -5 & 0 & -8 \end{bmatrix}$

Writing an Augmented Matrix In Exercises 67–70, write the augmented matrix for the system of linear equations.

67. $\begin{cases} 6x - 7y = 11 \\ -2x + 5y = -1 \end{cases}$

68. $\begin{cases} -x + y = 12 \\ 10x = -90 \end{cases}$

69. $\begin{cases} 3x - 5y + z = 25 \\ -4x - 2z = -14 \\ 6x + y = 15 \end{cases}$

70. $\begin{cases} 8x - 7y + 4z = 12 \\ 3x - 5y + 2z = 20 \\ 5x + 3y - 3z = 26 \end{cases}$

Writing a System of Equations In Exercises 71 and 72, write the system of linear equations represented by the augmented matrix. (Use the variables x, y, z, and w, if applicable.)

71. $\begin{bmatrix} 5 & 1 & 7 & \vdots & -9 \\ 4 & 2 & 0 & \vdots & 10 \\ 9 & 4 & 2 & \vdots & 3 \end{bmatrix}$

72. $\begin{bmatrix} 13 & 16 & 7 & 3 & \vdots & 0 \\ 0 & 21 & 0 & 5 & \vdots & 12 \\ 4 & 10 & -4 & 3 & \vdots & -1 \end{bmatrix}$

Using Gaussian Elimination In Exercises 73–76, write the matrix in row-echelon form. Remember that the row-echelon form of a matrix is not unique.

73. $\begin{bmatrix} -1 & 4 & 0 \\ 3 & -5 & 9 \end{bmatrix}$

74. $\begin{bmatrix} 0 & -2 & 7 \\ 2 & 6 & 14 \end{bmatrix}$

75. $\begin{bmatrix} 0 & 1 & 1 \\ 1 & 2 & 3 \\ 2 & 2 & 2 \end{bmatrix}$

76. $\begin{bmatrix} 4 & 8 & 16 & -4 \\ 3 & -1 & 2 & 0 \\ -2 & 10 & 12 & 3 \end{bmatrix}$

Using a Graphing Utility In Exercises 77–80, use the matrix capabilities of a graphing utility to write the matrix in reduced row-echelon form.

77. $\begin{bmatrix} 3 & -2 \\ 4 & -3 \end{bmatrix}$

78. $\begin{bmatrix} 1 & 1 & 2 \\ -1 & 0 & 3 \\ 1 & 2 & 8 \end{bmatrix}$

79. $\begin{bmatrix} 1.5 & 3.6 & 4.2 \\ 0.2 & 1.4 & 1.8 \\ 2.0 & 4.4 & 6.4 \end{bmatrix}$

80. $\begin{bmatrix} 4.1 & 8.3 & 1.6 \\ 3.2 & -1.7 & 2.4 \\ -2.3 & 1.0 & 1.2 \end{bmatrix}$

Gaussian Elimination with Back-Substitution In Exercises 81–88, use matrices to solve the system of equations, if possible. Use Gaussian elimination with back-substitution.

81. $\begin{cases} 5x + 4y = 2 \\ -x + y = -22 \end{cases}$ 82. $\begin{cases} 2x - 5y = 2 \\ 3x - 7y = 1 \end{cases}$

83. $\begin{cases} 0.6x - 0.9y = -0.3 \\ 0.4x - 0.6y = 0.3 \end{cases}$ 84. $\begin{cases} 0.2x - 0.1y = 0.07 \\ 0.4x - 0.5y = -0.01 \end{cases}$

85. $\begin{cases} 2x + 3y + 3z = 3 \\ 6x + 6y + 12z = 13 \\ 12x + 9y - z = 2 \end{cases}$ 86. $\begin{cases} x + 2y + 6z = 1 \\ 2x + 5y + 15z = 4 \\ 3x + y + 3z = -6 \end{cases}$

87. $\begin{cases} x + 2y - z = 1 \\ y + z = 0 \end{cases}$

88. $\begin{cases} x - y + 4z - w = 4 \\ x + 3y - 2z + w = -4 \\ y - z + w = -3 \\ 2x + z + w = 0 \end{cases}$

Gauss-Jordan Elimination In Exercises 89–96, use matrices to solve the system of equations, if possible. Use Gauss-Jordan elimination.

89. $\begin{cases} x + y + z = -3 \\ 4x + y - 2z = -12 \end{cases}$ 90. $\begin{cases} 2x + 2y = 4 \\ -3x - y = -16 \end{cases}$

91. $\begin{cases} -x + y + 2z = 1 \\ 2x + 3y + z = -2 \\ 5x + 4y + 2z = 4 \end{cases}$ 92. $\begin{cases} 4x + 4y + 4z = 5 \\ 4x - 2y - 8z = 1 \\ 5x + 3y + 8z = 6 \end{cases}$

93. $\begin{cases} x + y + 2z = 4 \\ x - y + 4z = 1 \\ x + 3z = -5 \end{cases}$ 94. $\begin{cases} x + y + 4z = 0 \\ 2x + y + 2z = 0 \\ -x + y - 2z = -1 \end{cases}$

95. $\begin{cases} x + 2y - z = 3 \\ x - y - z = -3 \\ 2x + y + 3z = 10 \end{cases}$ 96. $\begin{cases} x - 3y + z = 2 \\ 3x - y - z = -6 \\ -x - 5y + 3z = 10 \end{cases}$

Using a Graphing Utility In Exercises 97–100, use the matrix capabilities of a graphing utility to reduce the augmented matrix corresponding to the system of equations and solve the system.

97. $\begin{cases} x + 2y - z = 7 \\ - y - z = 4 \\ 4x - z = 16 \end{cases}$ 98. $\begin{cases} 3x + 6z = 0 \\ -2x + y = 5 \\ y + 2z = 3 \end{cases}$

99. $\begin{cases} 4x + 12y + 2z = 20 \\ x + 6y + 4z = 12 \\ 5x + 6y - 8z = -4 \end{cases}$

100. $\begin{cases} 3x - y + 5z - 2w = -44 \\ x + 6y + 4z - w = 1 \\ 5x - y + z + 3w = -15 \\ 4y - z - 8w = 58 \end{cases}$

Equality of Matrices In Exercises 101–104, find x and y.

101. $\begin{bmatrix} -1 & x \\ y & 9 \end{bmatrix} = \begin{bmatrix} -1 & 12 \\ -7 & 9 \end{bmatrix}$

102. $\begin{bmatrix} -1 & 0 \\ x & 5 \\ -4 & y \end{bmatrix} = \begin{bmatrix} -1 & 0 \\ 8 & 5 \\ -4 & 0 \end{bmatrix}$

103. $\begin{bmatrix} x+3 & 4 & -4y \\ 0 & -3 & 2 \\ -2 & y+5 & 6x \end{bmatrix} = \begin{bmatrix} 5x-1 & 4 & -44 \\ 0 & -3 & 2 \\ -2 & 16 & 6 \end{bmatrix}$

104. $\begin{bmatrix} -9 & 4 & 2x & -5 \\ 0 & -3 & 7 & -4 \\ -5 & -2 & 1 & 0 \end{bmatrix} = \begin{bmatrix} -9 & 4 & x-10 & -5 \\ 0 & -3 & 7 & 2y \\ \frac{1}{2}x & y & 1 & 0 \end{bmatrix}$

Operations with Matrices In Exercises 105–108, find, if possible, (a) $A + B$, (b) $A - B$, (c) $2A$, and (d) $A + 3B$.

105. $A = \begin{bmatrix} 7 & 3 \\ -1 & 5 \end{bmatrix}$, $B = \begin{bmatrix} 10 & -20 \\ 14 & -3 \end{bmatrix}$

106. $A = \begin{bmatrix} 6 & 0 & 7 \\ 5 & -1 & 2 \\ 3 & 2 & 3 \end{bmatrix}$, $B = \begin{bmatrix} 0 & 5 & 1 \\ -4 & 8 & 6 \\ 2 & -1 & 1 \end{bmatrix}$

107. $A = \begin{bmatrix} -11 & 16 & 19 \\ -7 & -2 & 1 \end{bmatrix}$, $B = \begin{bmatrix} 6 & 0 \\ 8 & -4 \\ -2 & 10 \end{bmatrix}$

108. $A = \begin{bmatrix} 6 & 5 & 8 \\ -1 & 2 & 4 \\ 3 & 9 & -2 \end{bmatrix}$, $B = \begin{bmatrix} -8 \\ 3 \\ 7 \end{bmatrix}$

Evaluating an Expression In Exercises 109–112, evaluate the expression.

109. $\begin{bmatrix} 2 & 1 & 0 \\ 0 & 5 & -4 \end{bmatrix} - 3\begin{bmatrix} 5 & 3 & -6 \\ 0 & -2 & 5 \end{bmatrix}$

110. $-4\begin{bmatrix} 1 & 2 \\ 5 & -4 \\ 6 & 0 \end{bmatrix} + 8\begin{bmatrix} 7 & 1 \\ 1 & 2 \\ 1 & 4 \end{bmatrix}$

111. $-1\begin{bmatrix} 8 & -1 \\ -2 & 4 \end{bmatrix} + 5\left(\begin{bmatrix} -2 & 0 \\ 3 & -1 \end{bmatrix} + \begin{bmatrix} 7 & -8 \\ 4 & 3 \end{bmatrix}\right)$

112. $6\left(\begin{bmatrix} -4 & -1 & -3 & 4 \\ 2 & -5 & 7 & -10 \end{bmatrix} - \begin{bmatrix} -1 & 1 & 13 & -7 \\ 14 & -3 & 8 & -1 \end{bmatrix}\right)$

Operations with Matrices In Exercises 113 and 114, use the matrix capabilities of a graphing utility to evaluate the expression.

113. $-\frac{3}{8}\begin{bmatrix} 8 & -2 & 5 \\ 1 & 3 & -1 \end{bmatrix} + 6\begin{bmatrix} 4 & -2 & -3 \\ 2 & 7 & 6 \end{bmatrix}$

114. $-5\begin{bmatrix} 2.7 & 0.2 \\ 7.3 & -2.9 \\ 8.6 & 2.1 \end{bmatrix} + \frac{7}{4}\begin{bmatrix} 4.4 & -2.3 \\ 6.6 & 11.6 \\ -1.5 & 3.9 \end{bmatrix}$

Solving a Matrix Equation In Exercises 115–118, solve for X when

$$A = \begin{bmatrix} -4 & 0 \\ 1 & -5 \\ -3 & 2 \end{bmatrix} \quad \text{and} \quad B = \begin{bmatrix} -2 & 2 \\ -2 & 1 \\ 4 & 4 \end{bmatrix}.$$

115. $2X = 3A - 2B$

116. $6X = 6A + 3B$

117. $3X + 2A = B$

118. $2A = 3X + 5B$

Finding the Product of Two Matrices In Exercises 119–122, find AB, if possible.

119. $A = \begin{bmatrix} 1 & 2 \\ 5 & -4 \\ 6 & 0 \end{bmatrix}, \quad B = \begin{bmatrix} 6 & -2 & 8 \\ 4 & 0 & 0 \end{bmatrix}$

120. $A = \begin{bmatrix} 6 & -5 & 7 \end{bmatrix}, \quad B = \begin{bmatrix} -1 & 2 & 1 \\ 4 & -3 & 0 \\ 8 & 1 & 1 \end{bmatrix}$

121. $A = \begin{bmatrix} 1 & 5 & 6 \\ 2 & -4 & 0 \end{bmatrix}, \quad B = \begin{bmatrix} 7 & 5 & 2 \\ 0 & 1 & 0 \end{bmatrix}$

122. $A = \begin{bmatrix} 3 & 2 \\ 2 & -4 \\ -1 & 3 \end{bmatrix}, \quad B = \begin{bmatrix} 4 & -3 & 2 \\ 0 & 3 & -1 \\ 0 & 6 & 2 \end{bmatrix}$

Operations with Matrices In Exercises 123–126, use the matrix capabilities of a graphing utility to evaluate the expression.

123. $\begin{bmatrix} 4 & 1 \\ 11 & -7 \\ 12 & 3 \end{bmatrix} \begin{bmatrix} 3 & -5 & 6 \\ 2 & -2 & -2 \end{bmatrix}$

124. $\begin{bmatrix} -2 & 3 & 10 \\ 4 & -2 & 2 \end{bmatrix} \begin{bmatrix} 1 & 1 \\ -5 & 2 \\ 3 & 2 \end{bmatrix}$

125. $\begin{bmatrix} 2 & 1 \\ 6 & 0 \end{bmatrix} \left(\begin{bmatrix} 4 & 2 \\ -3 & 1 \end{bmatrix} + \begin{bmatrix} -2 & 4 \\ 0 & 4 \end{bmatrix} \right)$

126. $\begin{bmatrix} 1 & -1 \\ 4 & 2 \end{bmatrix} \begin{bmatrix} 0 & 3 \\ 1 & 2 \end{bmatrix} \begin{bmatrix} 1 & 0 \\ 5 & -3 \end{bmatrix}$

127. Manufacturing A tire corporation has three factories, each of which manufactures two models of tires. The production levels are represented by A.

Factory

$$A = \begin{matrix} & 1 & 2 & 3 \\ & \begin{bmatrix} 80 & 120 & 140 \\ 40 & 100 & 80 \end{bmatrix} & \begin{matrix} A \\ B \end{matrix} \end{matrix} \right\} \text{Model}$$

(a) The price per unit for a model A tire is \$99 and the price per unit for a model B tire is \$112. Organize the price per unit of each tire in a matrix B.

(b) Find the product BA and interpret the result.

128. Manufacturing An electronics manufacturing company produces three different models of headphones that are shipped to two warehouses. The shipment levels are represented by A.

Warehouse

$$A = \begin{matrix} & 1 & 2 \\ & \begin{bmatrix} 8200 & 7400 \\ 6500 & 9800 \\ 5400 & 4800 \end{bmatrix} & \begin{matrix} A \\ B \\ C \end{matrix} \end{matrix} \right\} \text{Model}$$

(a) The price per unit is \$79.99 for model A headphones, \$109.95 for model B headphones, and \$189.99 for model C headphones. Organize the price per unit of the headphones in a matrix B.

(b) Find the product BA and interpret the result.

7.6

The Inverse of a Matrix In Exercises 129 and 130, show that B is the inverse of A.

129. $A = \begin{bmatrix} -4 & -1 \\ 7 & 2 \end{bmatrix}, \quad B = \begin{bmatrix} -2 & -1 \\ 7 & 4 \end{bmatrix}$

130. $A = \begin{bmatrix} 1 & 1 & 0 \\ 1 & 0 & 1 \\ 6 & 2 & 3 \end{bmatrix}, \quad B = \begin{bmatrix} -2 & -3 & 1 \\ 3 & 3 & -1 \\ 2 & 4 & -1 \end{bmatrix}$

Finding the Inverse of a Matrix In Exercises 131–134, find the inverse of the matrix (if it exists).

131. $\begin{bmatrix} -6 & 5 \\ -5 & 4 \end{bmatrix}$

132. $\begin{bmatrix} -3 & -9 \\ 4 & 12 \end{bmatrix}$

133. $\begin{bmatrix} 2 & 0 & 3 \\ -1 & 1 & 1 \\ 2 & -2 & 1 \end{bmatrix}$

134. $\begin{bmatrix} 0 & -2 & 1 \\ -5 & -2 & -3 \\ 7 & 3 & 4 \end{bmatrix}$

Finding the Inverse of a Matrix In Exercises 135–140, use the matrix capabilities of a graphing utility to find the inverse of the matrix (if it exists).

135. $\begin{bmatrix} 2 & 6 \\ 3 & -6 \end{bmatrix}$

136. $\begin{bmatrix} 3 & -10 \\ 4 & 2 \end{bmatrix}$

137. $\begin{bmatrix} 1 & -1 & -2 \\ 0 & 3 & -2 \\ 1 & 2 & -4 \end{bmatrix}$

138. $\begin{bmatrix} 1 & 2 & 0 \\ -1 & 1 & 1 \\ 0 & -1 & 0 \end{bmatrix}$

139. $\begin{bmatrix} 1 & 3 & 1 & 6 \\ 4 & 4 & 2 & 6 \\ 3 & 4 & 1 & 2 \\ -1 & 2 & -1 & -2 \end{bmatrix}$

140. $\begin{bmatrix} 8 & 0 & 2 & 8 \\ 4 & -2 & 0 & -2 \\ 1 & 2 & 1 & 4 \\ -1 & 4 & 1 & 1 \end{bmatrix}$

Finding the Inverse of a 2 × 2 Matrix In Exercises 141–146, use the formula on page 536 to find the inverse of the 2 × 2 matrix (if it exists).

141. $\begin{bmatrix} -7 & 2 \\ -8 & 2 \end{bmatrix}$ 142. $\begin{bmatrix} 10 & 4 \\ 7 & 3 \end{bmatrix}$

143. $\begin{bmatrix} -1 & 10 \\ 2 & -20 \end{bmatrix}$ 144. $\begin{bmatrix} -6 & -5 \\ 3 & 3 \end{bmatrix}$

145. $\begin{bmatrix} -\frac{1}{2} & 20 \\ \frac{3}{10} & -6 \end{bmatrix}$ 146. $\begin{bmatrix} -\frac{3}{4} & \frac{5}{2} \\ -\frac{4}{5} & -\frac{8}{3} \end{bmatrix}$

Solving a System of Equations Using an Inverse In Exercises 147–152, use an inverse matrix to solve (if possible) the system of linear equations.

147. $\begin{cases} -x + 4y = 8 \\ 2x - 7y = -5 \end{cases}$ 148. $\begin{cases} 2x + 3y = -10 \\ 4x - y = 1 \end{cases}$

149. $\begin{cases} 3x + 2y - z = 6 \\ x - y + 2z = -1 \\ 5x + y + z = 7 \end{cases}$

150. $\begin{cases} -x + 4y - 2z = 12 \\ 2x - 9y + 5z = -25 \\ -x + 5y - 4z = 10 \end{cases}$

151. $\begin{cases} x + 2y + z - w = -2 \\ 2x + y + z + w = 1 \\ x - y + 2w = -4 \\ z + w = 1 \end{cases}$

152. $\begin{cases} x + y + z + w = 1 \\ x - y + 2z + w = -3 \\ y + w = 2 \\ x + w = 2 \end{cases}$

Solving a System of Linear Equations In Exercises 153–156, use the matrix capabilities of a graphing utility to solve (if possible) the system of linear equations.

153. $\begin{cases} x + 2y = -1 \\ 3x + 4y = -5 \end{cases}$ 154. $\begin{cases} x + 3y = 23 \\ -6x + 2y = -18 \end{cases}$

155. $\begin{cases} -3x - 3y - 4z = 2 \\ y + z = -1 \\ 4x + 3y + 4z = -1 \end{cases}$

156. $\begin{cases} 2x + 3y - 4z = 1 \\ x - y + 2z = -4 \\ 3x + 7y - 10z = 0 \end{cases}$

7.7

The Determinant of a Matrix In Exercises 157–162, find the determinant of the matrix.

157. $\begin{bmatrix} -23 \end{bmatrix}$ 158. $\begin{bmatrix} 0 \end{bmatrix}$

159. $\begin{bmatrix} 8 & 5 \\ 2 & -4 \end{bmatrix}$ 160. $\begin{bmatrix} -9 & 11 \\ 7 & -4 \end{bmatrix}$

161. $\begin{bmatrix} 50 & -30 \\ 10 & 5 \end{bmatrix}$ 162. $\begin{bmatrix} 14 & -24 \\ 12 & -15 \end{bmatrix}$

Finding the Minors and Cofactors of a Matrix In Exercises 163–166, find all (a) minors and (b) cofactors of the matrix.

163. $\begin{bmatrix} 2 & -1 \\ 7 & 4 \end{bmatrix}$ 164. $\begin{bmatrix} 3 & 6 \\ 5 & -4 \end{bmatrix}$

165. $\begin{bmatrix} 3 & 2 & -1 \\ -2 & 5 & 0 \\ 1 & 8 & 6 \end{bmatrix}$ 166. $\begin{bmatrix} 8 & 3 & 4 \\ 6 & 5 & -9 \\ -4 & 1 & 2 \end{bmatrix}$

Finding a Determinant In Exercises 167–174, find the determinant of the matrix. Expand by cofactors on the row or column that appears to make the computations easiest.

167. $\begin{bmatrix} -2 & 4 & 1 \\ -6 & 0 & 2 \\ 5 & 3 & 4 \end{bmatrix}$ 168. $\begin{bmatrix} 4 & 7 & -1 \\ 2 & -3 & 4 \\ -5 & 0 & -1 \end{bmatrix}$

169. $\begin{bmatrix} -2 & 5 & 0 \\ 2 & -1 & 0 \\ -1 & 1 & 3 \end{bmatrix}$ 170. $\begin{bmatrix} 0 & 1 & -2 \\ 0 & 1 & 2 \\ -1 & -1 & 3 \end{bmatrix}$

171. $\begin{bmatrix} 1 & 4 & -2 \\ 3 & 1 & 0 \\ -2 & 2 & 1 \end{bmatrix}$ 172. $\begin{bmatrix} 0 & 3 & 1 \\ 5 & -2 & 1 \\ 1 & 6 & 1 \end{bmatrix}$

173. $\begin{bmatrix} 3 & 0 & -4 & 0 \\ 0 & 8 & 1 & 2 \\ 6 & 1 & 8 & 2 \\ 0 & 3 & -4 & 1 \end{bmatrix}$ 174. $\begin{bmatrix} -5 & 6 & 0 & 0 \\ 0 & 1 & -1 & 2 \\ -3 & 4 & -5 & 1 \\ 1 & 6 & 0 & 3 \end{bmatrix}$

7.8

Finding an Area In Exercises 175–180, use a determinant to find the area of the figure with the given vertices.

175. $(1, 0), (5, 0), (5, 8)$ 176. $(-4, 0), (4, 0), (0, 6)$
177. $\left(\frac{1}{2}, 1\right), \left(2, -\frac{5}{2}\right) \left(\frac{3}{2}, 1\right)$ 178. $\left(\frac{3}{2}, 1\right), \left(4, -\frac{1}{2}\right), (4, 2)$
179. $(-2, -1), (4, 9), (-2, -9), (4, 1)$
180. $(-4, 8), (4, 0), (-4, 0), (4, -8)$

Testing for Collinear Points In Exercises 181–184, use a determinant to determine whether the points are collinear.

181. $(2, 4), (5, 6), (4, 1)$ 182. $(0, -5), (2, 1), (4, 7)$
183. $(-1, 7), (3, -9), (-3, 15)$
184. $(-3, 2), (2, -3), (-4, -4)$

Using Cramer's Rule In Exercises 185–192, use Cramer's Rule to solve (if possible) the system of equations.

185. $\begin{cases} x + 2y = 5 \\ -x + y = 1 \end{cases}$ 186. $\begin{cases} 2x - y = -10 \\ 3x + 2y = -1 \end{cases}$

187. $\begin{cases} 8x - 4y = 3 \\ -12x + 6y = -15 \end{cases}$ **188.** $\begin{cases} 3x + 8y = -7 \\ 9x - 5y = 37 \end{cases}$

189. $\begin{cases} -2x + 3y - 5z = -11 \\ 4x - y + z = -3 \\ -x - 4y + 6z = 15 \end{cases}$

190. $\begin{cases} 5x - 2y + z = 15 \\ -8x + 3y - 9z = -39 \\ 2x - y - 7z = -3 \end{cases}$

191. $\begin{cases} x - 3y + 2z = 2 \\ 2x + 2y - 3z = 3 \\ x - 7y + 8z = -4 \end{cases}$ **192.** $\begin{cases} 14x - 21y - 7z = 10 \\ -4x + 2y - 2z = 4 \\ 56x - 21y + 7z = 5 \end{cases}$

Comparing Solution Methods In Exercises 193 and 194, solve the system of equations using (a) Gaussian elimination and (b) Cramer's Rule. Which method do you prefer, and why?

193. $\begin{cases} x - 3y + 2z = 5 \\ 2x + y - 4z = -1 \\ 2x + 4y + 2z = 3 \end{cases}$ **194.** $\begin{cases} x + 2y - z = -3 \\ 2x - y + z = -1 \\ 4x - 2y - z = 5 \end{cases}$

Encoding a Message In Exercises 195 and 196, (a) write the uncoded 1×3 row matrices for the message, and then (b) encode the message using the encoding matrix.

	Message	Encoding Matrix

195. LOOK OUT BELOW $\begin{bmatrix} 2 & -2 & 0 \\ 3 & 0 & -3 \\ -6 & 2 & 3 \end{bmatrix}$

196. JUST DO IT $\begin{bmatrix} 2 & 1 & 0 \\ -6 & -6 & -2 \\ 3 & 2 & 1 \end{bmatrix}$

Decoding a Message In Exercises 197–199, use A^{-1} to decode the cryptogram.

197. $A = \begin{bmatrix} 1 & 0 & -1 \\ 1 & -2 & 0 \\ 1 & -2 & 2 \end{bmatrix}$

32 −46 37 9 −48 15 3 −14
10 −1 −6 2 −8 −22 −3

198. $A = \begin{bmatrix} 1 & 2 & 0 \\ -1 & 1 & 2 \\ 2 & -1 & 2 \end{bmatrix}$

30 −7 30 5 10 80 37 34 16 40 −7
38 −3 8 36 16 −1 58 23 46 0

199. $A = \begin{bmatrix} 1 & -1 & 0 \\ 0 & 1 & 2 \\ 1 & 1 & -2 \end{bmatrix}$

21 −11 14 29 −11 −18 32 −6 −26 31 −19
−12 10 6 26 13 −11 −2 37 28 −8 5 13 36

200. MODELING DATA

The populations (in millions) of Florida for the years 2010 through 2013 are shown in the table.   (Source: U.S. Census Bureau)

Year	Population (in millions)
2010	18.8
2011	18.9
2012	19.0
2013	19.2

The coefficients of the least squares regression line $y = at + b$, where y is the population (in millions) and t is the year, with $t = 10$ corresponding to 2010, can be found by solving the system

$\begin{cases} 4b + 46a = 75.9 \\ 46b + 534a = 873.5 \end{cases}$

(a) Use Cramer's Rule to solve the system and find the least squares regression line.

(b) Use a graphing utility to graph the line from part (a).

(c) Use the graph from part (b) to estimate when the population of Florida will exceed 20 million.

(d) Use your regression equation to find algebraically when the population will exceed 20 million.

Conclusions

True or False? In Exercises 201 and 202, determine whether the statement is true or false. Justify your answer.

201. Solving a system of equations graphically will always give an exact solution.

202. $\begin{vmatrix} a_{11} & a_{12} & a_{13} \\ a_{21} & a_{22} & a_{23} \\ a_{31} + c_1 & a_{32} + c_2 & a_{33} + c_3 \end{vmatrix} =$

$\begin{vmatrix} a_{11} & a_{12} & a_{13} \\ a_{21} & a_{22} & a_{23} \\ a_{31} & a_{32} & a_{33} \end{vmatrix} + \begin{vmatrix} a_{11} & a_{12} & a_{13} \\ a_{21} & a_{22} & a_{23} \\ c_1 & c_2 & c_3 \end{vmatrix}$

203. Writing What is the relationship between the three elementary row operations performed on an augmented matrix and the operations that lead to equivalent systems of equations?

204. Think About It Under what conditions does a matrix have an inverse?

7   Chapter Test

See *CalcChat.com* for tutorial help and worked-out solutions to odd-numbered exercises. For instructions on how to use a graphing utility, see Appendix A.

Take this test as you would take a test in class. After you are finished, check your work against the answers given in the back of the book.

In Exercises 1–3, solve the system by the method of substitution. Check your solution graphically.

1. $\begin{cases} x - y = 6 \\ 3x + 5y = 2 \end{cases}$

2. $\begin{cases} y = x - 1 \\ y = (x - 1)^3 \end{cases}$

3. $\begin{cases} 4x - y^2 = 7 \\ x - y = -3 \end{cases}$

In Exercises 4–6, solve the system by the method of elimination.

4. $\begin{cases} 3x + 5y = -11 \\ 5x - y = 19 \end{cases}$

5. $\begin{cases} 1.5x + 3y = -9 \\ 2x - 1.2y = 5 \end{cases}$

6. $\begin{cases} x - 4y - z = 3 \\ 2x - 5y + z = 0 \\ 3x - 3y + 2z = -1 \end{cases}$

7. Find the equation of the parabola $y = ax^2 + bx + c$ that passes through the points $(0, 6)$, $(-2, 2)$, and $\left(3, \frac{9}{2}\right)$.

In Exercises 8 and 9, write the partial fraction decomposition for the rational expression.

8. $\dfrac{5x - 2}{(x - 1)^2}$

9. $\dfrac{x^3 + x^2 + x + 2}{x^4 + x^2}$

In Exercises 10 and 11, use matrices to solve the system of equations, if possible.

10. $\begin{cases} 2x + y + 2z = 4 \\ 2x + 2y = 5 \\ 2x - y + 6z = 2 \end{cases}$

11. $\begin{cases} 2x + 3y + z = 10 \\ 2x - 3y - 3z = 22 \\ 4x - 2y + 3z = -2 \end{cases}$

12. If possible, find (a) $A - B$, (b) $3A$, (c) $3A - 2B$, and (d) AB.

$$A = \begin{bmatrix} 5 & 4 & 4 \\ -4 & -4 & 0 \\ 1 & 2 & 0 \end{bmatrix}, \quad B = \begin{bmatrix} 4 & 4 & 0 \\ 3 & 2 & 1 \\ 1 & -2 & 0 \end{bmatrix}$$

13. Use the inverse of $A = \begin{bmatrix} -2 & 2 & 3 \\ 1 & -1 & 0 \\ 0 & 1 & 4 \end{bmatrix}$ to solve the system shown below.

$$\begin{cases} -2x + 2y + 3z = 7 \\ x - y = -5 \\ y + 4z = -1 \end{cases}$$

In Exercises 14 and 15, find the determinant of the matrix.

14. $\begin{bmatrix} -25 & 18 \\ 6 & -7 \end{bmatrix}$

15. $\begin{bmatrix} 4 & 0 & 3 \\ 1 & -8 & 2 \\ 3 & 2 & 2 \end{bmatrix}$

16. Use determinants to find the area of the parallelogram shown at the right.

17. Use Cramer's Rule to solve (if possible) $\begin{cases} 2x - 2y = 3 \\ x + 4y = -1 \end{cases}$.

18. The flow of traffic (in vehicles per hour) through a network of streets is shown at the right. Solve the system for the traffic flow represented by x_i, $i = 1, 2, 3, 4$, and 5.

Figure for 16

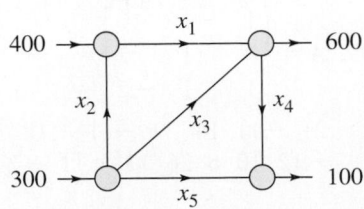

Figure for 18

Proofs in Mathematics

An **indirect proof** can be useful in proving statements of the form "p implies q." Recall that the conditional statement $p \rightarrow q$ is false only when p is true and q is false. To prove a conditional statement indirectly, assume that p is true and q is false. If this assumption leads to an impossibility, then you have proved that the conditional statement is true. An indirect proof is also called a **proof by contradiction.**

You can use an indirect proof to prove the conditional statement

"If a is a positive integer and a^2 is divisible by 2, then a is divisible by 2"

as follows. First, assume that p, "a is a positive integer and a^2 is divisible by 2," is true and q, "a is divisible by 2," is false. This means that a is not divisible by 2. If so, then a is odd and can be written as

$$a = 2n + 1$$

where n is an integer.

$a = 2n + 1$	Definition of an odd integer
$a^2 = 4n^2 + 4n + 1$	Square each side.
$a^2 = 2(2n^2 + 2n) + 1$	Distributive Property

So, by the definition of an odd integer, a^2 is odd. This contradicts the assumption, and you can conclude that a is divisible by 2.

EXAMPLE   Using an Indirect Proof

Use an indirect proof to prove that $\sqrt{2}$ is an irrational number.

Solution

Begin by assuming that $\sqrt{2}$ is *not* an irrational number. Then $\sqrt{2}$ can be written as the quotient of two integers a and b ($b \neq 0$) that have no common factors.

$\sqrt{2} = \dfrac{a}{b}$	Assume that $\sqrt{2}$ is a rational number.
$2 = \dfrac{a^2}{b^2}$	Square each side.
$2b^2 = a^2$	Multiply each side by b^2.

This implies that 2 is a factor of a^2. So, 2 is also a factor of a, and a can be written as $2c$, where c is an integer.

$2b^2 = (2c)^2$	Substitute $2c$ for a.
$2b^2 = 4c^2$	Simplify.
$b^2 = 2c^2$	Divide each side by 2.

This implies that 2 is a factor of b^2 and also a factor of b. So, 2 is a factor of both a and b. This contradicts the assumption that a and b have no common factors. So, you can conclude that $\sqrt{2}$ is an irrational number.

Proofs without words are pictures or diagrams that give a visual understanding of why a theorem or statement is true. They can also provide a starting point for writing a formal proof. The following proof shows that a 2×2 determinant is the area of a parallelogram.

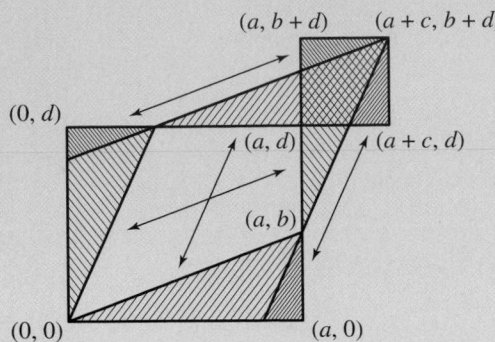

$$\begin{vmatrix} a & b \\ c & d \end{vmatrix} = ad - bc = \| \square \| - \| \square \| = \| \square \|$$

The following is a color-coded version of the proof along with a brief explanation of why this proof works.

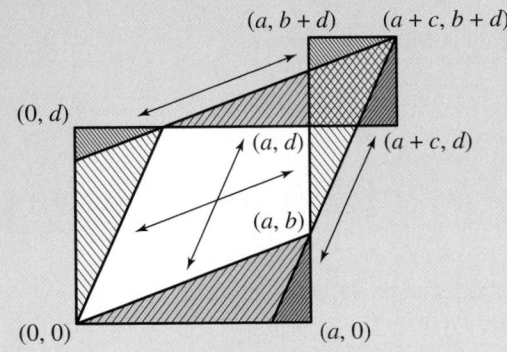

$$\begin{vmatrix} a & b \\ c & d \end{vmatrix} = ad - bc = \| \square \| - \| \square \| = \| \square \|$$

Area of $\square$ = Area of orange $\triangle$ + Area of yellow $\triangle$ + Area of blue $\triangle$ +
        Area of pink $\triangle$ + Area of white quadrilateral

Area of $\square$ = Area of orange $\triangle$ + Area of pink $\triangle$ + Area of green quadrilateral

Area of $\square$ = Area of white quadrilateral + Area of blue $\triangle$ + Area of yellow $\triangle$ −
        Area of green quadrilateral

      = Area of $\square$ − Area of $\square$

From "Proof Without Words" by Solomon W. Golomb, *Mathematics Magazine*, March 1985. Vol. 58, No. 2, pg. 107.

8 Sequences, Series, and Probability

```
sum(seq(50(1.0025)^n,n,1
,24))
                1238.228737
```

Section 8.3, Example 8
Increasing Annuity

8.1 **Sequences and Series**

8.2 **Arithmetic Sequences and Partial Sums**

8.3 Geometric Sequences and Series

8.4 **The Binomial Theorem**

8.5 **Counting Principles**

8.6 **Probability**

8.1   Sequences and Series

Sequences

In mathematics, the word *sequence* is used in much the same way as in ordinary English. Saying that a collection is listed in *sequence* means that it is ordered so that it has a first member, a second member, a third member, and so on.

Mathematically, you can think of a sequence as a *function* whose domain is the set of positive integers. Instead of using function notation, sequences are usually written using subscript notation, as shown in the following definition.

What you should learn
▶ Use sequence notation to write the terms of sequences.
▶ Use factorial notation.
▶ Use summation notation to write sums.
▶ Find sums of infinite series.
▶ Use sequences and series to model and solve real-life problems.

Why you should learn it
Sequences and series are useful in modeling sets of values in order to identify patterns. For instance, Exercise 123 on page 579 shows how a sequence can be used to model the population of trout in a lake.

Definition of Sequence

An **infinite sequence** is a function whose domain is the set of positive integers. The function values

$$a_1, a_2, a_3, a_4, \ldots, a_n, \ldots$$

are the **terms** of the sequence. If the domain of a function consists of the first n positive integers only, then the sequence is a **finite sequence.**

On occasion, it is convenient to begin subscripting a sequence with 0 instead of 1 so that the terms of the sequence become

$$a_0, a_1, a_2, a_3, \ldots.$$

The domain of the function is the set of nonnegative integers.

EXAMPLE 1   Writing the Terms of a Sequence

Write the first four terms of each sequence.

a. $a_n = 3n - 2$

b. $a_n = 3 + (-1)^n$

Solution

a. The first four terms of the sequence given by $a_n = 3n - 2$ are

$a_1 = 3(1) - 2 = 1$ 1st term

$a_2 = 3(2) - 2 = 4$ 2nd term

$a_3 = 3(3) - 2 = 7$ 3rd term

$a_4 = 3(4) - 2 = 10.$ 4th term

b. The first four terms of the sequence given by $a_n = 3 + (-1)^n$ are

$a_1 = 3 + (-1)^1 = 3 - 1 = 2$ 1st term

$a_2 = 3 + (-1)^2 = 3 + 1 = 4$ 2nd term

$a_3 = 3 + (-1)^3 = 3 - 1 = 2$ 3rd term

$a_4 = 3 + (-1)^4 = 3 + 1 = 4.$ 4th term

✓ *Checkpoint* 🔊))) *Audio-video solution in English & Spanish at LarsonPrecalculus.com.*

Write the first four terms of the sequence given by $a_n = 2n + 1.$

EXAMPLE 2   Writing the Terms of a Sequence

Write the first five terms of the sequence given by $a_n = \dfrac{(-1)^n}{2n - 1}$.

Algebraic Solution

The first five terms of the sequence are as follows.

$$a_1 = \frac{(-1)^1}{2(1) - 1} = \frac{-1}{2 - 1} = -1 \qquad \text{1st term}$$

$$a_2 = \frac{(-1)^2}{2(2) - 1} = \frac{1}{4 - 1} = \frac{1}{3} \qquad \text{2nd term}$$

$$a_3 = \frac{(-1)^3}{2(3) - 1} = \frac{-1}{6 - 1} = -\frac{1}{5} \qquad \text{3rd term}$$

$$a_4 = \frac{(-1)^4}{2(4) - 1} = \frac{1}{8 - 1} = \frac{1}{7} \qquad \text{4th term}$$

$$a_5 = \frac{(-1)^5}{2(5) - 1} = \frac{-1}{10 - 1} = -\frac{1}{9} \qquad \text{5th term}$$

Numerical Solution

Set your graphing utility to *sequence* mode and enter the sequence. Use the *table* feature to create a table showing the terms of the sequence, as shown in the figure.

Use the *table* feature in *ask* mode.

n	u(n)
1	-1
2	.33333
3	-.2
4	.14286
5	-.1111

n=1

So, you can estimate the first five terms of the sequence as follows.

$$u_1 = -1, \qquad u_2 = 0.33333 \approx \tfrac{1}{3}, \qquad u_3 = -0.2 = -\tfrac{1}{5},$$

$$u_4 = 0.14286 \approx \tfrac{1}{7}, \qquad \text{and} \qquad u_5 = -0.1111 \approx -\tfrac{1}{9}$$

✓ **Checkpoint** 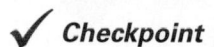 Audio-video solution in English & Spanish at LarsonPrecalculus.com.

Write the first four terms of the sequence given by $a_n = \dfrac{2 + (-1)^n}{n}$.

Simply listing the first few terms is not sufficient to define a unique sequence—the *n*th term *must be given*. To see this, consider the following sequences, both of which have the same first three terms.

$$\frac{1}{2}, \frac{1}{4}, \frac{1}{8}, \frac{1}{16}, \cdots \cdot \frac{1}{2^n}, \cdots$$

$$\frac{1}{2}, \frac{1}{4}, \frac{1}{8}, \frac{1}{15}, \cdots \cdot \frac{6}{(n + 1)(n^2 - n + 6)}, \cdots$$

EXAMPLE 3   Finding the *n*th Term of a Sequence

Write an expression for the apparent *n*th term a_n of each sequence.

a. $1, 3, 5, 7, \ldots$ **b.** $2, 5, 10, 17, \ldots$

Solution

a.   *n*: 1 2 3 4 . . . *n*

  Terms: 1 3 5 7 . . . a_n

  Apparent Pattern: Each term is 1 less than twice *n*. So, the apparent *n*th term is $a_n = 2n - 1$.

b.   *n*: 1 2   3   4 . . . *n*

  Terms: 2 5 10 17 . . . a_n

  Apparent Pattern: Each term is 1 more than the square of *n*. So, the apparent *n*th term is $a_n = n^2 + 1$.

✓ **Checkpoint** Audio-video solution in English & Spanish at LarsonPrecalculus.com.

Write an expression for the apparent *n*th term a_n of each sequence.

a. $1, 5, 9, 13, 17, \ldots$ **b.** $3, 5, 7, 9, 11, \ldots$

Some sequences are defined **recursively.** To define a sequence recursively, you need to be given one or more of the first few terms. All other terms of the sequence are then defined using previous terms.

Technology Tip

To graph a sequence using a graphing utility, set the mode to *dot* and *sequence* and enter the sequence. Try graphing the sequence in Example 4 and using the *trace* feature to identify the terms. For instructions on how to use the sequence mode, see Appendix A; for specific keystrokes, go to this textbook's *Companion Website.*

EXAMPLE 4   A Recursive Sequence

Write the first five terms of the sequence defined recursively as

$$a_1 = 3, \, a_k = 2a_{k-1} + 1, \quad \text{where} \quad k \geq 2.$$

Solution

$a_1 = 3$	1st term is given.
$a_2 = 2a_{2-1} + 1 = 2a_1 + 1 = 2(3) + 1 = 7$	Use recursion formula.
$a_3 = 2a_{3-1} + 1 = 2a_2 + 1 = 2(7) + 1 = 15$	Use recursion formula.
$a_4 = 2a_{4-1} + 1 = 2a_3 + 1 = 2(15) + 1 = 31$	Use recursion formula.
$a_5 = 2a_{5-1} + 1 = 2a_4 + 1 = 2(31) + 1 = 63$	Use recursion formula.

✓ *Checkpoint* Audio-video solution in English & Spanish at LarsonPrecalculus.com.

Write the first five terms of the sequence defined recursively as

$$a_1 = 6, \quad a_{k+1} = a_k + 1, \quad \text{where} \quad k \geq 2.$$

In the next example you will study a well-known recursive sequence, the Fibonacci sequence.

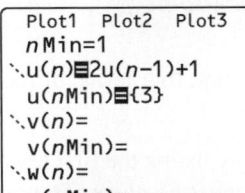

```
Plot1  Plot2  Plot3
 nMin=1
\.u(n)⊟2u(n−1)+1
  u(nMin)⊟{3}
\.v(n)=
  v(nMin)=
\.w(n)=
  w(nMin)=
```

EXAMPLE 5   The Fibonacci Sequence: A Recursive Sequence

The Fibonacci sequence is defined recursively as follows.

$$a_0 = 1, \, a_1 = 1, \, a_k = a_{k-2} + a_{k-1}, \quad \text{where } k \geq 2$$

Write the first six terms of this sequence.

Solution

$a_0 = 1$	0th term is given.
$a_1 = 1$	1st term is given.
$a_2 = a_{2-2} + a_{2-1} = a_0 + a_1 = 1 + 1 = 2$	Use recursion formula.
$a_3 = a_{3-2} + a_{3-1} = a_1 + a_2 = 1 + 2 = 3$	Use recursion formula.
$a_4 = a_{4-2} + a_{4-1} = a_2 + a_3 = 2 + 3 = 5$	Use recursion formula.
$a_5 = a_{5-2} + a_{5-1} = a_3 + a_4 = 3 + 5 = 8$	Use recursion formula.

You can check this result using the *table* feature of a graphing utility, as shown below.

n	$u(n)$	
0	1	
1	1	
2	2	
3	3	
4	5	
5	8	

$n=$

✓ *Checkpoint* Audio-video solution in English & Spanish at LarsonPrecalculus.com.

Write the first five terms of the sequence defined recursively as

$$a_0 = 1, \quad a_1 = 3, \quad a_k = a_{k-2} + a_{k-1}, \quad \text{where} \quad k \geq 2.$$

Factorial Notation

Some very important sequences in mathematics involve terms that are defined with special types of products called **factorials**.

> **Definition of Factorial**
>
> If n is a positive integer, then n **factorial** is defined as
>
> $$n! = 1 \cdot 2 \cdot 3 \cdot 4 \cdots (n-1) \cdot n.$$
>
> As a special case, zero factorial is defined as
>
> $$0! = 1.$$

Explore the Concept

Most graphing utilities have the capability to compute $n!$. Use your graphing utility to compare $3 \cdot 5!$ and $(3 \cdot 5)!$. How do they differ? Notice that the value of n does not have to be very large before the value of $n!$ becomes huge. How large a value of n will your graphing utility allow you to compute?

Notice that $0! = 1$ and $1! = 1$. Here are some other values of $n!$.

$$2! = 1 \cdot 2 = 2 \quad 3! = 1 \cdot 2 \cdot 3 = 6 \quad 4! = 1 \cdot 2 \cdot 3 \cdot 4 = 24$$

Factorials follow the same conventions for order of operations as do exponents. For instance,

$$2n! = 2(n!) = 2(1 \cdot 2 \cdot 3 \cdot 4 \cdots n), \quad \text{whereas} \quad (2n)! = 1 \cdot 2 \cdot 3 \cdot 4 \cdots 2n.$$

EXAMPLE 6   Writing the Terms of a Sequence Involving Factorials

Write the first five terms of the sequence given by $a_n = \dfrac{2^n}{n!}$. Begin with $n = 0$.

Algebraic Solution

$$a_0 = \frac{2^0}{0!} = \frac{1}{1} = 1 \qquad \text{0th term}$$

$$a_1 = \frac{2^1}{1!} = \frac{2}{1} = 2 \qquad \text{1st term}$$

$$a_2 = \frac{2^2}{2!} = \frac{4}{2} = 2 \qquad \text{2nd term}$$

$$a_3 = \frac{2^3}{3!} = \frac{8}{6} = \frac{4}{3} \qquad \text{3rd term}$$

$$a_4 = \frac{2^4}{4!} = \frac{16}{24} = \frac{2}{3} \qquad \text{4th term}$$

Graphical Solution

Using a graphing utility set to *dot* and *sequence* modes, enter the sequence. Next, graph the sequence, as shown in the figure.

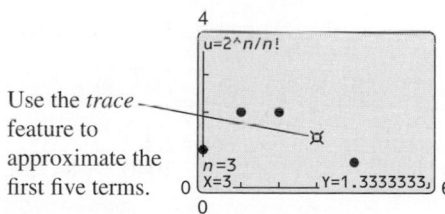

Use the *trace* feature to approximate the first five terms.

The first five terms are $u_0 = 1$, $u_1 = 2$, $u_2 = 2$, $u_3 \approx 1.333 \approx \frac{4}{3}$, and $u_4 \approx 0.667 \approx \frac{2}{3}$.

✓ **Checkpoint**))) *Audio-video solution in English & Spanish at LarsonPrecalculus.com.*

Write the first five terms of the sequence given by $a_n = \dfrac{3^n + 1}{n!}$. Begin with $n = 0$.

EXAMPLE 7   Simplifying Factorial Expressions

a. $\dfrac{8!}{2! \cdot 6!} = \dfrac{1 \cdot 2 \cdot 3 \cdot 4 \cdot 5 \cdot 6 \cdot 7 \cdot 8}{1 \cdot 2 \cdot 1 \cdot 2 \cdot 3 \cdot 4 \cdot 5 \cdot 6} = \dfrac{7 \cdot 8}{2} = 28$

b. $\dfrac{n!}{(n-1)!} = \dfrac{1 \cdot 2 \cdot 3 \cdots (n-1) \cdot n}{1 \cdot 2 \cdot 3 \cdots (n-1)} = n$

✓ **Checkpoint**))) *Audio-video solution in English & Spanish at LarsonPrecalculus.com.*

Simplify the factorial expression $\dfrac{4!(n+1)!}{3!n!}$.

Remark

In Example 7(a), you can also simplify the computation as

$$\frac{8!}{2! \cdot 6!} = \frac{8 \cdot 7 \cdot 6!}{2! \cdot 6!} = 28.$$

■

Summation Notation

There is a convenient notation for the sum of the terms of a finite sequence. It is called **summation notation** or **sigma notation** because it involves the use of the uppercase Greek letter sigma, written as Σ.

Definition of Summation Notation

The sum of the first n terms of a sequence is represented by

$$\sum_{i=1}^{n} a_i = a_1 + a_2 + a_3 + a_4 + \cdots + a_n$$

where i is called the **index of summation**, n is the **upper limit of summation,** and 1 is the **lower limit of summation.**

Remark

Summation notation is an instruction to add the terms of a sequence. From the definition at the left, the upper limit of summation tells you where to end the sum. Summation notation helps you generate the appropriate terms of the sequence prior to finding the actual sum.

EXAMPLE 8   Sigma Notation for Sums

a. $\displaystyle\sum_{i=1}^{5} 3i = 3(1) + 3(2) + 3(3) + 3(4) + 3(5)$

$\qquad\quad = 3(1 + 2 + 3 + 4 + 5)$

$\qquad\quad = 3(15)$

$\qquad\quad = 45$

b. $\displaystyle\sum_{k=3}^{6} (1 + k^2) = (1 + 3^2) + (1 + 4^2) + (1 + 5^2) + (1 + 6^2)$

$\qquad\qquad\quad = 10 + 17 + 26 + 37$

$\qquad\qquad\quad = 90$

c. $\displaystyle\sum_{n=0}^{8} \frac{1}{n!} = \frac{1}{0!} + \frac{1}{1!} + \frac{1}{2!} + \frac{1}{3!} + \frac{1}{4!} + \frac{1}{5!} + \frac{1}{6!} + \frac{1}{7!} + \frac{1}{8!}$

$\qquad\quad = 1 + 1 + \frac{1}{2} + \frac{1}{6} + \frac{1}{24} + \frac{1}{120} + \frac{1}{720} + \frac{1}{5040} + \frac{1}{40{,}320}$

$\qquad\quad \approx 2.71828$

For the summation in part (c), note that the sum is very close to the irrational number $e \approx 2.718281828$. It can be shown that as more terms of the sequence whose nth term is $1/n!$ are added, the sum becomes closer and closer to e.

✓ **Checkpoint** 🔊))) *Audio-video solution in English & Spanish at LarsonPrecalculus.com.*

Find the sum $\displaystyle\sum_{i=1}^{4} (4i + 1)$.   ■

In Example 8, note that the lower limit of a summation does not have to be 1. Also note that the index of summation does not have to be the letter i. For instance, in part (b), the letter k is the index of summation.

Properties of Sums   (See the proofs on page 632.)

1. $\displaystyle\sum_{i=1}^{n} c = cn,\quad c$ is a constant.   **2.** $\displaystyle\sum_{i=1}^{n} ca_i = c\sum_{i=1}^{n} a_i,\quad c$ is a constant.

3. $\displaystyle\sum_{i=1}^{n} (a_i + b_i) = \sum_{i=1}^{n} a_i + \sum_{i=1}^{n} b_i$ **4.** $\displaystyle\sum_{i=1}^{n} (a_i - b_i) = \sum_{i=1}^{n} a_i - \sum_{i=1}^{n} b_i$

Series

Many applications involve the sum of the terms of a finite or an infinite sequence. Such a sum is called a **series**.

Definition of a Series

Consider the infinite sequence $a_1, a_2, a_3, \ldots, a_i, \ldots$.

1. The sum of the first n terms of the sequence is called a **finite series** or the **nth partial sum** of the sequence and is denoted by

$$a_1 + a_2 + a_3 + \cdots + a_n = \sum_{i=1}^{n} a_i.$$

2. The sum of all the terms of the infinite sequence is called an **infinite series** and is denoted by

$$a_1 + a_2 + a_3 + \cdots + a_i + \cdots = \sum_{i=1}^{\infty} a_i.$$

EXAMPLE 9   Finding the Sum of a Series

See LarsonPrecalculus.com for an interactive version of this type of example.

For the series

$$\sum_{i=1}^{\infty} \frac{3}{10^i}$$

find (a) the third partial sum and (b) the sum.

Solution

a. The third partial sum is

$$\sum_{i=1}^{3} \frac{3}{10^i} = \frac{3}{10^1} + \frac{3}{10^2} + \frac{3}{10^3}$$

$$= 0.3 + 0.03 + 0.003$$

$$= 0.333.$$

b. The sum of the series is

$$\sum_{i=1}^{\infty} \frac{3}{10^i} = \frac{3}{10^1} + \frac{3}{10^2} + \frac{3}{10^3} + \frac{3}{10^4} + \frac{3}{10^5} + \cdots$$

$$= 0.3 + 0.03 + 0.003 + 0.0003 + 0.00003 + \cdots$$

$$= 0.33333 \ldots$$

$$= \frac{1}{3}.$$

✓ **Checkpoint** Audio-video solution in English & Spanish at LarsonPrecalculus.com.

For the series

$$\sum_{i=1}^{\infty} \frac{5}{10^i}$$

find (a) the fourth partial sum and (b) the sum.

Notice in Example 9(b) that the sum of an infinite series can be a finite number.

Technology Tip

Most graphing utilities are able to sum the first n terms of a sequence. Try using a graphing utility to confirm the results in Example 8 and Example 9(a).

```
sum(seq(1/n!,n,0,8))
              2.71827877
```

Application

EXAMPLE 10   Compound Interest

An investor deposits $5000 in an account that earns 3% interest compounded quarterly. The balance in the account after n quarters is given by

$$A_n = 5000\left(1 + \frac{0.03}{4}\right)^n, \quad n = 0, 1, 2, \ldots$$

Use this information to (a) write the first three terms of the sequence and (b) find the balance in the account after 10 years by computing the 40th term of the sequence.

Solution

a. The first three terms of the sequence are as follows.

$$A_0 = 5000\left(1 + \frac{0.03}{4}\right)^0 = \$5000.00 \qquad \text{Original deposit}$$

$$A_1 = 5000\left(1 + \frac{0.03}{4}\right)^1 = \$5037.50 \qquad \text{First-quarter balance}$$

$$A_2 = 5000\left(1 + \frac{0.03}{4}\right)^2 \approx \$5075.28 \qquad \text{Second-quarter balance}$$

b. The 40th term of the sequence is

$$A_{40} = 5000\left(1 + \frac{0.03}{4}\right)^{40} \approx \$6741.74. \qquad \text{Ten-year balance}$$

✓ **Checkpoint**))) *Audio-video solution in English & Spanish at LarsonPrecalculus.com.*

An investor deposits $1000 in an account that earns 3% interest compounded monthly. The balance in the account after n months is given by

$$A_n = 1000\left(1 + \frac{0.03}{12}\right)^n, \quad n = 0, 1, 2, \ldots$$

Use this information to (a) write the first three terms of the sequence and (b) find the balance in the account after 4 years by computing the 48th term of the sequence. ∎

Explore the Concept

A $3 \times 3 \times 3$ cube is created using 27 unit cubes (a unit cube has a length, width, and height of 1 unit), and only the faces of the cubes that are visible are painted blue (see the figure at the right). Complete the table below to determine how many unit cubes of the $3 \times 3 \times 3$ cube have no blue faces, one blue face, two blue faces, and three blue faces. Do the same for a $4 \times 4 \times 4$ cube, a

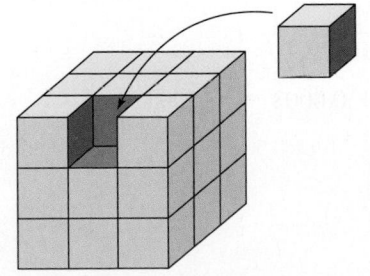

$5 \times 5 \times 5$ cube, and a $6 \times 6 \times 6$ cube, and record your results in the table below. What type of pattern do you observe in the table? Write a formula you could use to determine the column values for an $n \times n \times n$ cube.

Cube \ Number of blue faces	0	1	2	3
$3 \times 3 \times 3$				

8.1 Exercises

See *CalcChat.com* for tutorial help and worked-out solutions to odd-numbered exercises.
For instructions on how to use a graphing utility, see Appendix A.

Vocabulary and Concept Check

In Exercises 1–4, fill in the blank(s).

1. The function values $a_1, a_2, a_3, a_4, \ldots, a_n, \ldots$ are called the _____ of a sequence.

2. If you are given one or more of the first few terms of a sequence, and all other terms of the sequence are defined using previous terms, then the sequence is defined _____ .

3. For the sum $\sum\limits_{i=1}^{n} a_i$, i is called the _____ of summation, n is the _____ of summation, and 1 is the _____ of summation.

4. The sum of the terms of a finite or an infinite sequence is called a _____ .

5. Which describes an infinite sequence? a finite sequence?
   (a) The domain consists of the first n positive integers.
   (b) The domain consists of the set of positive integers.

6. Write $1 \cdot 2 \cdot 3 \cdot 4 \cdot 5 \cdot 6$ in factorial notation.

Procedures and Problem Solving

Writing the Terms of a Sequence   In Exercises 7–16, write the first five terms of the sequence. (Assume n begins with 1.)

7. $a_n = 2n - 5$

8. $a_n = 4n - 7$

9. $a_n = 3^n$

10. $a_n = \left(\frac{1}{2}\right)^n$

11. $a_n = \left(-\frac{1}{2}\right)^n$

12. $a_n = (-2)^n$

13. $a_n = \dfrac{n + 1}{n}$

14. $a_n = \dfrac{n}{n + 1}$

15. $a_n = \dfrac{n}{n^2 + 1}$

16. $a_n = \dfrac{2n}{n + 1}$

Writing the Terms of a Sequence   In Exercises 17–26, write the first five terms of the sequence (a) using the *table* feature of a graphing utility and (b) algebraically. (Assume n begins with 1.)

17. $a_n = \dfrac{1 + (-1)^n}{n}$

18. $a_n = \dfrac{1 + (-1)^n}{2n}$

19. $a_n - 1 - \dfrac{1}{2^n}$

20. $a_n = \dfrac{3^n}{4^n}$

21. $a_n = \dfrac{1}{n^{3/2}}$

22. $a_n = \dfrac{1}{\sqrt{n}}$

23. $a_n = \dfrac{(-1)^n}{n^2}$

24. $a_n = (-1)^n\left(\dfrac{n}{n + 1}\right)$

25. $a_n = (2n - 1)(2n + 1)$

26. $a_n = n(n - 1)(n - 2)$

Using a Graphing Utility   In Exercises 27–32, use the *table* feature of a graphing utility to find the first 10 terms of the sequences. (Assume n begins with 1.)

27. $a_n = 2(3n - 1) + 5$

28. $a_n = 2n(n + 1) - 7$

29. $a_n = 1 + \dfrac{n + 1}{n}$

30. $a_n = \dfrac{4n^2}{n + 2}$

31. $a_n = (-1)^n + 1$

32. $a_n = (-1)^{n+1} + 8$

Finding a Term of a Sequence   In Exercises 33–38, find the indicated term of the sequence.

33. $a_n = \dfrac{n^2}{n^2 + 1}$

$a_{10} = $ ▢

34. $a_n = \dfrac{n^2}{2n + 1}$

$a_5 = $ ▢

35. $a_n = (-1)^n(3n - 2)$

$a_{25} = $ ▢

36. $a_n = (-1)^{n-1}[n(n - 1)]$

$a_{16} = $ ▢

37. $a_n = \dfrac{2^{n+1}}{2^n + 1}$

$a_7 = $ ▢

38. $a_n = \dfrac{3^n}{3^n + 1}$

$a_6 = $ ▢

Finding the nth Term of a Sequence   In Exercises 39–52, write an expression for the apparent nth term of the sequence. (Assume n begins with 1.)

39. $3, 8, 13, 18, 23, \ldots$

40. $3, 7, 11, 15, 19, \ldots$

41. $7, 13, 19, 25, 31, \ldots$

42. $9, 11, 13, 15, 17, \ldots$

43. $0, 3, 8, 15, 24, \ldots$

44. $4, 7, 12, 19, 28, \ldots$

45. $\dfrac{2}{3}, \dfrac{3}{4}, \dfrac{4}{5}, \dfrac{5}{6}, \dfrac{6}{7}, \ldots$

46. $\dfrac{2}{1}, \dfrac{3}{3}, \dfrac{4}{5}, \dfrac{5}{7}, \dfrac{6}{9}, \ldots$

47. $\dfrac{1}{2}, \dfrac{-1}{4}, \dfrac{1}{8}, \dfrac{-1}{16}, \ldots$

48. $\dfrac{1}{3}, -\dfrac{2}{9}, \dfrac{4}{27}, -\dfrac{8}{81}, \ldots$

49. $1 + \dfrac{1}{1}, 1 + \dfrac{1}{2}, 1 + \dfrac{1}{3}, 1 + \dfrac{1}{4}, 1 + \dfrac{1}{5}, \ldots$

50. $1 + \dfrac{1}{3}, 1 + \dfrac{1}{6}, 1 + \dfrac{1}{11}, 1 + \dfrac{1}{18}, 1 + \dfrac{1}{27}, \ldots$

51. $1, 3, 1, 3, 1, \ldots$

52. $1, -1, 1, -1, 1, \ldots$

A Recursive Sequence   In Exercises 53–58, write the first five terms of the sequence defined recursively.

53. $a_1 = 28, a_k = a_{k-1} - 4$

54. $a_1 = 15, a_k = a_{k-1} + 3$

55. $a_1 = 3, a_{k+1} = 2(a_k - 1)$

56. $a_1 = 32, a_{k+1} = \frac{1}{2}a_k$

57. $a_0 = 1, a_1 = 3, a_k = a_{k-2} + a_{k-1}$

58. $a_0 = -1, a_1 = 5, a_k = a_{k-2} + a_{k-1}$

Finding the *n*th Term of a Recursive Sequence   In Exercises 59–62, write the first five terms of the sequence defined recursively. Use the pattern to write the *n*th term of the sequence as a function of *n*. (Assume *n* begins with 1.)

59. $a_1 = 6, a_{k+1} = a_k + 2$

60. $a_1 = 25, a_{k+1} = a_k - 5$

61. $a_1 = 81, a_{k+1} = \frac{1}{3}a_k$

62. $a_1 = 14, a_{k+1} = -2a_k$

Writing the Terms of a Sequence Involving Factorials   In Exercises 63–68, write the first five terms of the sequence (a) using the *table* feature of a graphing utility and (b) algebraically. (Assume *n* begins with 0.)

63. $a_n = \dfrac{1}{n!}$

64. $a_n = \dfrac{1}{(n+1)!}$

65. $a_n = \dfrac{n^2}{(n+1)!}$

66. $a_n = \dfrac{n^3}{(n+2)!}$

67. $a_n = \dfrac{(-1)^{2n}}{(2n)!}$

68. $a_n = \dfrac{(-1)^{2n+1}}{(2n+1)!}$

Simplifying Factorial Expressions   In Exercises 69–76, simplify the factorial expression.

69. $\dfrac{2!}{4!}$

70. $\dfrac{5!}{7!}$

71. $\dfrac{12!}{4! \cdot 8!}$

72. $\dfrac{10!}{5! \cdot 3!}$

73. $\dfrac{(n+3)!}{n!}$

74. $\dfrac{(n+2)!}{n!}$

75. $\dfrac{(2n-1)!}{(2n+1)!}$

76. $\dfrac{(2n-2)!}{(2n)!}$

Identifying a Graph of a Sequence   In Exercises 77–80, match the sequence with its graph. [The graphs are labeled (a), (b), (c), and (d).]

(a)

(b)

(c)

(d)

77. $a_n = \dfrac{8}{n+1}$

78. $a_n = \dfrac{8n}{n+1}$

79. $a_n = \dfrac{2^{n+2}}{2n!}$

80. $a_n = \dfrac{4^n}{n!}$

Graphing the Terms of a Sequence   In Exercises 81–86, use a graphing utility to graph the first 10 terms of the sequence. (Assume *n* begins with 1.)

81. $a_n = \frac{2}{3}n$

82. $a_n = \frac{1}{2}n + 3$

83. $a_n = 16(-0.5)^{n-1}$

84. $a_n = 8(-0.75)^{n-1}$

85. $a_n = \dfrac{2n}{n+1}$

86. $a_n = \dfrac{3n^2}{n^2+1}$

Sigma Notation for Sums   In Exercises 87–98, find the sum.

87. $\sum_{i=1}^{5} (2i+1)$

88. $\sum_{i=1}^{6} (3i-1)$

89. $\sum_{i=0}^{6} 4i^2$

90. $\sum_{i=0}^{5} 3i^2$

91. $\sum_{j=3}^{5} \dfrac{1}{j^2-3}$

92. $\sum_{j=3}^{5} \dfrac{1}{j+1}$

93. $\sum_{k=1}^{4} 10$

94. $\sum_{k=1}^{5} 4$

95. $\sum_{i=2}^{5} [(i-1)^3 + (i+1)^2]$

96. $\sum_{k=2}^{7} [(k+1) + (k-3)^2]$

97. $\sum_{i=0}^{4} 2^i$

98. $\sum_{j=0}^{4} (-2)^j$

Using a Graphing Utility   In Exercises 99–102, use a graphing utility to find the sum.

99. $\sum_{j=1}^{6} (24-3j)$

100. $\sum_{j=1}^{10} \dfrac{6}{3j+1}$

101. $\sum_{k=0}^{4} \dfrac{(-1)^k}{(k+1)!}$

102. $\sum_{k=0}^{4} \dfrac{(-1)^k}{k!}$

Writing a Sum Using Sigma Notation   In Exercises 103–112, use sigma notation to write the sum. Then use a graphing utility to find the sum.

103. $\dfrac{1}{3(1)} + \dfrac{1}{3(2)} + \dfrac{1}{3(3)} + \cdots + \dfrac{1}{3(9)}$

104. $\dfrac{5}{1+1} + \dfrac{5}{1+2} + \dfrac{5}{1+3} + \cdots + \dfrac{5}{1+15}$

105. $\left[2\left(\frac{1}{8}\right) + 3\right] + \left[2\left(\frac{2}{8}\right) + 3\right] + \cdots + \left[2\left(\frac{8}{8}\right) + 3\right]$

106. $\left[1 - \left(\frac{1}{6}\right)^2\right] + \left[1 - \left(\frac{2}{6}\right)^2\right] + \cdots + \left[1 - \left(\frac{6}{6}\right)^2\right]$

107. $-3 + 9 - 27 + 81 - 243 + 729$

108. $1 - \frac{1}{2} + \frac{1}{4} - \frac{1}{8} + \cdots - \frac{1}{128}$

109. $\frac{1}{1^2} - \frac{1}{2^2} + \frac{1}{3^2} - \frac{1}{4^2} + \cdots - \frac{1}{20^2}$

110. $\frac{1}{1 \cdot 3} - \frac{1}{2 \cdot 4} + \frac{1}{3 \cdot 5} - \frac{1}{4 \cdot 6} + \cdots - \frac{1}{10 \cdot 12}$

111. $\frac{1}{4} + \frac{3}{8} + \frac{7}{16} + \frac{15}{32} + \frac{31}{64}$

112. $\frac{1}{2} + \frac{2}{4} + \frac{6}{8} + \frac{24}{16} + \frac{120}{32} + \frac{720}{64}$

Finding a Partial Sum In Exercises 113–116, find the indicated partial sum of the series.

113. $\displaystyle\sum_{i=1}^{\infty} \frac{7}{5^i}$

Fourth partial sum

114. $\displaystyle\sum_{i=1}^{\infty} \frac{2}{3^i}$

Fifth partial sum

115. $\displaystyle\sum_{n=1}^{\infty} 4\left(-\frac{1}{2}\right)^n$

Third partial sum

116. $\displaystyle\sum_{n=1}^{\infty} 8\left(-\frac{1}{4}\right)^n$

Fourth partial sum

Finding the Sum of a Series In Exercises 117–120, find (a) the fourth partial sum and (b) the sum of the infinite series.

117. $\displaystyle\sum_{i=1}^{\infty} \frac{6}{10^i}$

118. $\displaystyle\sum_{k=1}^{\infty} \frac{4}{10^k}$

119. $\displaystyle\sum_{k=1}^{\infty} 7\left(\frac{1}{10}\right)^k$

120. $\displaystyle\sum_{i=1}^{\infty} 2\left(\frac{1}{10}\right)^i$

121. Compound Interest A deposit of $5000 is made in an account that earns 3% interest compounded quarterly. The balance in the account after n quarters is given by

$$A_n = 5000\left(1 + \frac{0.03}{4}\right)^n, \quad n = 1, 2, 3, \ldots.$$

(a) Compute the first eight terms of this sequence.

(b) Find the balance in this account after 10 years by computing the 40th term of the sequence.

122. Compound Interest An investor deposits $10,000 in an account that earns 3.5% interest compounded monthly. The balance in the account after n months is given by

$$A_n = 10,000\left(1 + \frac{0.035}{12}\right)^n, \quad n = 1, 2, 3, \ldots.$$

(a) Write the first eight terms of the sequence.

(b) Find the balance in the account after 5 years by computing the 60th term of the sequence.

(c) Is the balance after 10 years twice the balance after 5 years? Explain.

123. *Why you should learn it* (p. 570) A landlocked lake has been selected to be stocked in the year 2015 with 5500 trout, and to be restocked each year thereafter with 500 trout. Each year the fish population declines 25% due to harvesting and other natural causes.

(a) Write a recursive sequence that gives the population p_n of trout in the lake in terms of the year n, with $n = 0$ corresponding to 2015.

(b) Use the recursion formula from part (a) to find the numbers of trout in the lake for $n = 1, 2, 3,$ and 4. Interpret these values in the context of the situation.

(c) Use a graphing utility to find the number of trout in the lake as time passes infinitely. Explain your result.

124. MODELING DATA

The revenues R_n (in millions of dollars) of Netflix from 2008 through 2013 are shown in the table. (Source: Netflix, Inc.)

DATA Year	Revenue, R_n (in millions of dollars)
2008	1364.7
2009	1670.3
2010	2162.6
2011	3204.6
2012	3609.3
2013	4374.6

Spreadsheet at LarsonPrecalculus.com

(a) Use a graphing utility to graph the data. Let n represent the year, with $n = 8$ corresponding to 2008.

(b) Use the *regression* feature of the graphing utility to find a linear sequence and a quadratic sequence that model the data. Identify the coefficient of determination for each model.

(c) Graph each model with the data. Decide which model is a better fit for the data. Explain.

(d) Use the model you chose in part (c) to predict the revenue of Netflix in 2017. Does your answer seem reasonable? Explain.

(e) Use your model from part (c) to find when the revenue will reach 15 billion dollars.

(f) Use the model you chose in part (c) to approximate the total revenue from 2008 through 2013. Compare this sum with the result of adding the revenues shown in the table.

Conclusions

True or False?   In Exercises 125 and 126, determine whether the statement is true or false. Justify your answer.

125. $\sum_{i=1}^{4} (i^2 + 2i) = \sum_{i=1}^{4} i^2 + 2\sum_{i=1}^{4} i$

126. $\sum_{j=1}^{4} 2^j = \sum_{j=3}^{6} 2^{j-2}$

Fibonacci Sequence   In Exercises 127 and 128, use the Fibonacci sequence. (See Example 5.)

127. Write the first 12 terms of the Fibonacci sequence a_n and the first 10 terms of the sequence given by

$$b_n = \frac{a_{n+1}}{a_n}, \quad n > 0.$$

128. Using the definition of b_n given in Exercise 127, show that b_n can be defined recursively by

$$b_n = 1 + \frac{1}{b_{n-1}}.$$

Exploration   In Exercises 129–132, let

$$a_n = \frac{\left(1 + \sqrt{5}\right)^n - \left(1 - \sqrt{5}\right)^n}{2^n \sqrt{5}}$$

be a sequence with nth term a_n.

129. Use the *table* feature of a graphing utility to find the first five terms of the sequence.

130. Do you recognize the terms of the sequence in Exercise 129? What sequence is it?

131. Find expressions for a_{n+1} and a_{n+2} in terms of n.

132. Use the result from Exercise 131 to show that $a_{n+2} = a_{n+1} + a_n$. Is this result the same as your answer to Exercise 129? Explain.

A Sequence Involving x   In Exercises 133–142, write the first five terms of the sequence.

133. $a_n = \dfrac{x^n}{n!}$ **134.** $a_n = \dfrac{x^2}{n^2}$

135. $a_n = \dfrac{(-1)^n x^{2n+1}}{2n + 1}$ **136.** $a_n = \dfrac{(-1)^n x^{n+1}}{n + 1}$

137. $a_n = \dfrac{(-1)^n x^{2n}}{(2n)!}$ **138.** $a_n = \dfrac{(-1)^n x^{2n+1}}{(2n + 1)!}$

139. $a_n = \dfrac{(-1)^n x^n}{n!}$ **140.** $a_n = \dfrac{(-1)^n x^{n+1}}{(n + 1)!}$

141. $a_n = \dfrac{(-1)^{n+1}(x + 1)^n}{n!}$

142. $a_n = \dfrac{(-1)^n (x - 1)^n}{(n + 1)!}$

Writing Partial Sums   In Exercises 143–146, write the first five terms of the sequence. Then find an expression for the nth partial sum.

143. $a_n = \dfrac{1}{2n} - \dfrac{1}{2n + 2}$

144. $a_n = \dfrac{1}{n} - \dfrac{1}{n + 1}$

145. $a_n = \dfrac{1}{n + 1} - \dfrac{1}{n + 2}$

146. $a_n = \dfrac{1}{n} - \dfrac{1}{n + 2}$

147. Think About It   Does every finite series whose terms are integers have a finite sum? Explain.

148. **HOW DO YOU SEE IT?**   The graph represents the first six terms of a sequence.

(a) Write the first six terms of the sequence.

(b) Write an expression for the apparent nth term a_n of the sequence.

(c) Use sigma notation to represent the partial sum of the first 50 terms of the sequence.

Cumulative Mixed Review

Operations with Matrices   In Exercises 149–152, find, if possible, (a) $A - B$, (b) $2B - 3A$, (c) AB, and (d) BA.

149. $A = \begin{bmatrix} 6 \\ 3 \end{bmatrix}$, $B = \begin{bmatrix} 4 \\ -3 \end{bmatrix}$

150. $A = \begin{bmatrix} 10 & 7 \\ -4 & 6 \end{bmatrix}$, $B = \begin{bmatrix} 0 & -12 \\ 8 & 11 \end{bmatrix}$

151. $A = \begin{bmatrix} -2 & -3 & 6 \\ 4 & 5 & 7 \\ 1 & 7 & 4 \end{bmatrix}$, $B = \begin{bmatrix} 1 & 4 & 2 \\ 0 & 1 & 6 \\ 0 & 3 & 1 \end{bmatrix}$

152. $A = \begin{bmatrix} -1 & 4 \\ 5 & 1 \\ 0 & -1 \end{bmatrix}$, $B = \begin{bmatrix} 0 & 4 & 0 \\ 3 & 1 & -2 \end{bmatrix}$

8.2   Arithmetic Sequences and Partial Sums

Arithmetic Sequences

A sequence whose consecutive terms have a common difference is called an **arithmetic sequence.**

> **Definition of Arithmetic Sequence**
>
> A sequence is **arithmetic** when the differences between consecutive terms are the same. So, the sequence
>
> $$a_1, a_2, a_3, a_4, \ldots, a_n, \ldots$$
>
> is arithmetic when there is a number d such that
>
> $$a_2 - a_1 = a_3 - a_2 = a_4 - a_3 = \cdots = d.$$
>
> The number d is the **common difference** of the sequence.

EXAMPLE 1   Examples of Arithmetic Sequences

a. The sequence whose nth term is

$$4n + 3$$

is arithmetic. The common difference between consecutive terms is 4.

$$\underbrace{7, 11,}_{11 - 7 = 4} 15, 19, \ldots, 4n + 3, \ldots \qquad \text{Begin with } n = 1.$$

b. The sequence whose nth term is

$$7 - 5n$$

is arithmetic. The common difference between consecutive terms is -5.

$$\underbrace{2, -3,}_{-3 - 2 = -5} -8, -13, \ldots, 7 - 5n, \ldots \qquad \text{Begin with } n = 1.$$

c. The sequence whose nth term is

$$\tfrac{1}{4}(n + 3)$$

is arithmetic. The common difference between consecutive terms is $\tfrac{1}{4}$.

$$\underbrace{1, \tfrac{5}{4},}_{\frac{5}{4} - 1 = \frac{1}{4}} \tfrac{3}{2}, \tfrac{7}{4}, \ldots, \frac{n + 3}{4}, \ldots \qquad \text{Begin with } n = 1.$$

✓ **Checkpoint** *Audio-video solution in English & Spanish at LarsonPrecalculus.com.*

Write the first four terms of the arithmetic sequence whose nth term is $3n - 1$. Then find the common difference between consecutive terms. ■

The sequence 1, 4, 9, 16, . . . , whose nth term is n^2, is *not* arithmetic. The difference between the first two terms is

$$a_2 - a_1 = 4 - 1 = 3$$

but the difference between the second and third terms is

$$a_3 - a_2 = 9 - 4 = 5.$$

The nth term of an arithmetic sequence can be derived from the pattern below.

$$a_1 = a_1 \qquad \text{1st term}$$
$$a_2 = a_1 + d \qquad \text{2nd term}$$
$$a_3 = a_1 + 2d \qquad \text{3rd term}$$
$$a_4 = a_1 + 3d \qquad \text{4th term}$$
$$a_5 = a_1 + 4d \qquad \text{5th term}$$

1 less

$$\vdots$$

$$a_n = a_1 + (n-1)d \qquad n\text{th term}$$

1 less

The result is summarized in the following definition.

The nth Term of an Arithmetic Sequence

The nth term of an arithmetic sequence has the form

$$a_n = a_1 + (n-1)d$$

where d is the common difference between consecutive terms of the sequence and a_1 is the first term of the sequence.

EXAMPLE 2   Finding the nth Term of an Arithmetic Sequence

Find a formula for the nth term of the arithmetic sequence whose common difference is 3 and whose first term is 2.

Solution

You know that the formula for the nth term is of the form $a_n = a_1 + (n-1)d$. Moreover, because the common difference is $d = 3$ and the first term is $a_1 = 2$, the formula must have the form

$$a_n = 2 + 3(n-1) \qquad \text{Substitute 2 for } a_1 \text{ and 3 for } d.$$

or $a_n = 3n - 1$. The sequence therefore has the following form.

$$2, 5, 8, 11, 14, \ldots, 3n - 1, \ldots$$

The figure below shows a graph of the first 15 terms of the sequence. Notice that the points lie on a line. This makes sense because a_n is a linear function of n. In other words, the terms "arithmetic" and "linear" are closely connected.

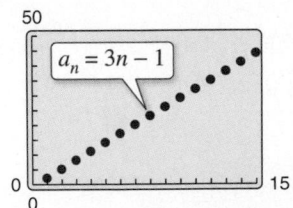

$a_n = 3n - 1$

✓ **Checkpoint**))) *Audio-video solution in English & Spanish at LarsonPrecalculus.com.*

Find a formula for the nth term of the arithmetic sequence whose common difference is 5 and whose first term is -1.

EXAMPLE 3 Writing the Terms of an Arithmetic Sequence

The fourth term of an arithmetic sequence is 20, and the 13th term is 65. Write the first 13 terms of this sequence.

Solution

You know that $a_4 = 20$ and $a_{13} = 65$. So, you must add the common difference d nine times to the fourth term to obtain the 13th term. Therefore, the fourth and 13th terms of the sequence are related by

$$a_{13} = a_4 + 9d. \qquad \text{\small a_4 and a_{13} are nine terms apart.}$$

Using $a_4 = 20$ and $a_{13} = 65$, you have

$$65 = 20 + 9d.$$

So, you can conclude that $d = 5$, which implies that the sequence is as follows.

a_1,	a_2	a_3	a_4	a_5	a_6	a_7	a_8	a_9	a_{10}	a_{11}	a_{12}	a_{13}	$\ldots$
5,	10,	15,	20,	25,	30,	35,	40,	45,	50,	55,	60,	65,	$\ldots$

✓ **Checkpoint** Audio-video solution in English & Spanish at LarsonPrecalculus.com.

The eighth term of an arithmetic sequence is 25, and the 12th term is 41. Write the first 11 terms of this sequence.

When you know the nth term of an arithmetic sequence *and* you know the common difference of the sequence, you can find the $(n + 1)$th term by using the *recursion formula*

$$a_{n+1} = a_n + d. \qquad \text{\small Recursion formula}$$

With this formula, you can find any term of an arithmetic sequence, *provided* that you know the preceding term. For instance, when you know the first term, you can find the second term. Then, knowing the second term, you can find the third term, and so on.

EXAMPLE 4 Using a Recursion Formula

Find the ninth term of the arithmetic sequence whose first two terms are 2 and 9.

Solution

You know that the sequence is arithmetic. Also, $a_1 = 2$ and $a_2 = 9$. So, the common difference for this sequence is

$$d = 9 - 2 = 7.$$

There are two ways to find the ninth term. One way is simply to write out the first nine terms (by repeatedly adding 7),

2, 9, 16, 23, 30, 37, 44, 51, 58

Another way to find the ninth term is to first find a formula for the nth term. Because the common difference is $d = 7$ and the first term is $a_1 = 2$, the formula must have the form

$$a_n = 2 + 7(n - 1). \qquad \text{\small Substitute 2 for a_1 and 7 for d.}$$

So, a formula for the nth term is $a_n = 7n - 5$, which implies that the ninth term is

$$a_9 = 7(9) - 5 = 58.$$

✓ **Checkpoint** Audio-video solution in English & Spanish at LarsonPrecalculus.com.

Find the tenth term of the arithmetic sequence that begins with 7 and 15.

> **Technology Tip**
>
> Most graphing utilities have a built-in function that will display the terms of an arithmetic sequence. For instructions on how to use the *sequence* feature, see Appendix A; for specific keystrokes, go to this textbook's *Companion Website*.

seq(2+7(n−1),n,1,9)
...30   37   44   51   58}

The Sum of a Finite Arithmetic Sequence

There is a simple formula for the *sum* of a finite arithmetic sequence.

The Sum of a Finite Arithmetic Sequence   (See the proof on page 633.)

The sum of a finite arithmetic sequence with *n* terms is given by $S_n = \frac{n}{2}(a_1 + a_n)$.

Remark

Note that this formula works only for *arithmetic* sequences.

EXAMPLE 5   Sum of a Finite Arithmetic Sequence

Find the sum: $1 + 3 + 5 + 7 + 9 + 11 + 13 + 15 + 17 + 19$.

Solution

To begin, notice that the sequence is arithmetic (with a common difference of 2). Moreover, the sequence has 10 terms. So, the sum of the sequence is

$$S_n = 1 + 3 + 5 + 7 + 9 + 11 + 13 + 15 + 17 + 19$$

$$= \frac{n}{2}(a_1 + a_n) \qquad \text{Formula for sum of an arithmetic sequence}$$

$$= \frac{10}{2}(1 + 19) \qquad \text{Substitute 10 for } n, 1 \text{ for } a_1, \text{ and 19 for } a_n.$$

$$= 5(20) \qquad \text{Simplify.}$$

$$= 100. \qquad \text{Sum of the sequence}$$

✓ **Checkpoint** 🔊))) *Audio-video solution in English & Spanish at LarsonPrecalculus.com.*

Find the sum: $40 + 37 + 34 + 31 + 28 + 25 + 22$.

The sum of the first *n* terms of an infinite sequence is called the **nth partial sum.** The *n*th partial sum of an arithmetic sequence can be found by using the formula for the sum of a finite arithmetic sequence.

Remark

If you go on to take a course in calculus, you will study sequences and series in detail. You will learn that sequences and series play a major role in the study of calculus.

EXAMPLE 6   Partial Sum of an Arithmetic Sequence

Find the 150th partial sum of the arithmetic sequence 5, 16, 27, 38, 49, ...

Solution

For this arithmetic sequence, you have $a_1 = 5$ and $d = 16 - 5 = 11$. So,

$$a_n = 5 + 11(n - 1)$$

and the *n*th term is $a_n = 11n - 6$. Therefore, $a_{150} = 11(150) - 6 = 1644$, and the sum of the first 150 terms is

$$S_n = \frac{n}{2}(a_1 + a_n) \qquad n\text{th partial sum formula}$$

$$= \frac{150}{2}(5 + 1644) \qquad \text{Substitute 150 for } n, 5 \text{ for } a_1, \text{ and 1644 for } a_n.$$

$$= 75(1649) \qquad \text{Simplify.}$$

$$= 123{,}675. \qquad n\text{th partial sum}$$

✓ **Checkpoint** 🔊))) *Audio-video solution in English & Spanish at LarsonPrecalculus.com.*

Find the 120th partial sum of the arithmetic sequence

$$6, 12, 18, 24, 30, \ldots .$$

Application

EXAMPLE 7   Total Sales

See LarsonPrecalculus.com for an interactive version of this type of example.

A small business sells $20,000 worth of sports memorabilia during its first year. The owner of the business has set a goal of increasing annual sales by $15,000 each year for 19 years. Assuming that this goal is met, find the total sales during the first 20 years this business is in operation.

Algebraic Solution

The annual sales form an arithmetic sequence in which $a_1 = 20{,}000$ and $d = 15{,}000$. So,

$$a_n = 20{,}000 + 15{,}000(n - 1)$$

and the *n*th term of the sequence is

$$a_n = 15{,}000n + 5000.$$

This implies that the 20th term of the sequence is

$$a_{20} = 15{,}000(20) + 5000$$

$$= 300{,}000 + 5000$$

$$= 305{,}000.$$

The sum of the first 20 terms of the sequence is

$$S_n = \frac{n}{2}(a_1 + a_n)$$ *n*th partial sum formula

$$= \frac{20}{2}(20{,}000 + 305{,}000)$$ Substitute 20 for *n*, 20,000 for a_1, and 305,000 for a_n.

$$= 10(325{,}000)$$ Simplify.

$$= 3{,}250{,}000.$$ Simplify.

So, the total sales for the first 20 years are $3,250,000.

Numerical Solution

The annual sales form an arithmetic sequence in which $a_1 = 20{,}000$ and $d = 15{,}000$. So,

$$a_n = 20{,}000 + 15{,}000(n - 1)$$

and the *n*th term of the sequence is

$$a_n = 15{,}000n + 5000.$$

Use the *list editor* of a graphing utility to create a table that shows the sales for each of the first 20 years and the total sales for the first 20 years, as shown in the figure.

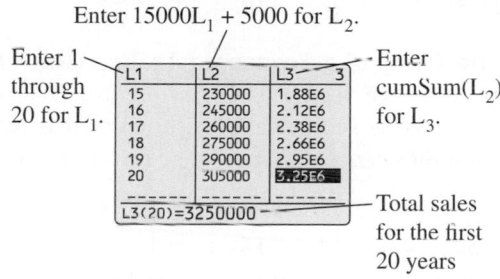

Enter $15000L_1 + 5000$ for L_2.

Enter 1 through 20 for L_1.

Enter cumSum(L_2) for L_3.

Total sales for the first 20 years

So, the total sales for the first 20 years are $3,250,000.

✔ **Checkpoint** 🔊)) *Audio-video solution in English & Spanish at LarsonPrecalculus.com.*

A company sells $160,000 worth of printing paper during its first year. The sales manager has set a goal of increasing annual sales of printing paper by $20,000 each year for 9 years. Assuming that this goal is met, find the total sales of printing paper during the first 10 years this company is in operation. ■

The figure below shows the annual sales for the business in Example 7. Notice that the annual sales for the business follow a *linear growth* pattern. In other words, saying that a quantity increases arithmetically is the same as saying that it increases linearly.

8.2 Exercises

See *CalcChat.com* for tutorial help and worked-out solutions to odd-numbered exercises.
For instructions on how to use a graphing utility, see Appendix A.

Vocabulary and Concept Check

In Exercises 1 and 2, fill in the blank.

1. The nth term of an arithmetic sequence has the form _____ .

2. The formula $S_n = \dfrac{n}{2}(a_1 + a_n)$ can be used to find the sum of the first n terms of an arithmetic sequence, called the _____ .

3. How do you know when a sequence is arithmetic?

4. Is 4 or 1 the common difference of the arithmetic sequence $a_n = 4n + 1$?

Procedures and Problem Solving

Identifying an Arithmetic Sequence In Exercises 5–10, determine whether or not the sequence is arithmetic. If it is, find the common difference.

5. $10, 12, 14, 16, 18, \ldots$
6. $4, 9, 14, 19, 24, \ldots$
7. $3, \frac{5}{2}, 2, \frac{3}{2}, 1, \ldots$
8. $3.7, 3.1, 2.5, 1.9, 1.3, \ldots$
9. $1^2, 2^2, 3^2, 4^2, 5^2, \ldots$
10. $\frac{1}{3}, \frac{2}{3}, \frac{4}{3}, \frac{8}{3}, \frac{16}{3}, \ldots$

Writing the Terms of a Sequence In Exercises 11–20, write the first five terms of the sequence. Determine whether or not the sequence is arithmetic. If it is, find the common difference. (Assume n begins with 1.)

11. $a_n = 8 + 13n$
12. $a_n = 150 - 7n$
13. $a_n = 53 - 4(n + 6)$
14. $a_n = 1 + (n - 1)4$
15. $a_n = 2^n + n$
16. $a_n = 2^{n-1}$
17. $a_n = 3 + 2(-1)^n$
18. $a_n = (-1)^n$
19. $a_n = \dfrac{(-1)^{2n}}{4}$
20. $a_n = (-1)^{2n+1}$

Finding the nth Term of an Arithmetic Sequence In Exercises 21–30, find a formula for a_n for the arithmetic sequence.

21. $a_1 = 1, d = 6$
22. $a_1 = 15, d = 4$
23. $a_1 = 43, d = -7$
24. $a_1 = 100, d = -8$
25. $3, \frac{9}{4}, \frac{3}{2}, \frac{3}{4}, 0, \ldots$
26. $4, \frac{3}{2}, -1, -\frac{7}{2}, \ldots$
27. $a_1 = -5, a_4 = 22$
28. $a_1 = -4, a_5 = 16$
29. $a_3 = 94, a_6 = 85$
30. $a_5 = 190, a_{10} = 115$

Writing the Terms of an Arithmetic Sequence In Exercises 31–38, write the first five terms of the arithmetic sequence. Use the *table* feature of a graphing utility to verify your results.

31. $a_1 = 5, d = 6$
32. $a_1 = 5, d = -\frac{3}{4}$
33. $a_1 = -2.6, d = 0.2$
34. $a_1 = -10, d = 9$
35. $a_8 = 26, a_{12} = 42$
36. $a_6 = -38, a_{11} = -73$
37. $a_3 = 19, a_{15} = -1.7$
38. $a_5 = 16, a_{14} = 38.5$

Writing the Terms of an Arithmetic Sequence In Exercises 39–42, write the first five terms of the arithmetic sequence. Find the common difference and write the nth term of the sequence as a function of n.

39. $a_1 = 15, \; a_{k+1} = a_k + 4$
40. $a_1 = 6, \; a_{k+1} = a_k + 5$
41. $a_1 = \frac{3}{5}, \; a_{k+1} = -\frac{1}{10} + a_k$
42. $a_1 = 1.5, \; a_{k+1} = a_k - 2.5$

Using a Recursion Formula In Exercises 43–46, the first two terms of the arithmetic sequence are given. Find the missing term. Use the *table* feature of a graphing utility to verify your results.

43. $a_1 = 5, \; a_2 = 11, \; a_{10} = $
44. $a_1 = 3, \; a_2 = 13, \; a_9 = $
45. $a_1 = 4.2, \; a_2 = 1.8, \; a_7 = $
46. $a_1 = -0.7, \; a_2 = -13.8, \; a_8 = $

Graphing the Terms of a Sequence In Exercises 47–50, use a graphing utility to graph the first 10 terms of the sequence. (Assume n begins with 1.)

47. $a_n = 15 - \frac{3}{2}n$
48. $a_n = -5 + 2n$
49. $a_n = 0.4n - 2$
50. $a_n = -1.3n + 7$

Finding the Terms of a Sequence In Exercises 51–56, use the *table* feature of a graphing utility to find the first 10 terms of the sequence. (Assume n begins with 1.)

51. $a_n = 4n - 5$
52. $a_n = 17 + 3n$
53. $a_n = 20 - \frac{3}{4}n$
54. $a_n = \frac{4}{5}n - 3$
55. $a_n = 1.5 + 0.05n$
56. $a_n = 8 - 12.5n$

Finding the Sum of a Finite Arithmetic Sequence In Exercises 57–64, find the sum of the finite arithmetic sequence.

57. $2 + 4 + 6 + 8 + 10 + 12 + 14 + 16 + 18 + 20$
58. $1 + 4 + 7 + 10 + 13 + 16 + 19$

59. $-1 + (-3) + (-5) + (-7) + (-9)$

60. $-2 + (-5) + (-8) + (-11) + (-14) + (-17)$

61. Sum of the first 100 positive integers

62. Sum of the first 50 negative integers

63. Sum of the integers from -100 to 30

64. Sum of the integers from -10 to 50

Finding a Partial Sum of an Arithmetic Sequence In Exercises 65–70, find the indicated nth partial sum of the arithmetic sequence.

65. $8, 20, 32, 44, \ldots; \; n = 10$

66. $2, 8, 14, 20, \ldots; \; n = 25$

67. $7.2, 6.4, 5.6, 4.8, \ldots; \; n = 10$

68. $4.2, 3.7, 3.2, 2.7, \ldots; \; n = 12$

69. $a_1 = 100, \; a_{25} = 220, \; n = 25$

70. $a_1 = 15, \; a_{100} = 307, \; n = 100$

Finding a Partial Sum of an Arithmetic Sequence In Exercises 71–76, find the partial sum without using a graphing utility.

71. $\displaystyle\sum_{n=1}^{50} n$

72. $\displaystyle\sum_{n=1}^{100} 2n$

73. $\displaystyle\sum_{n=11}^{30} n - \sum_{n=1}^{10} n$

74. $\displaystyle\sum_{n=51}^{100} n - \sum_{n=1}^{50} n$

75. $\displaystyle\sum_{n=1}^{500} (n + 8)$

76. $\displaystyle\sum_{n=1}^{250} (1000 - n)$

Finding a Partial Sum Using a Graphing Utility In Exercises 77–82, use a graphing utility to find the partial sum.

77. $\displaystyle\sum_{n=1}^{20} (2n + 1)$

78. $\displaystyle\sum_{n=1}^{50} (40 - 2n)$

79. $\displaystyle\sum_{n=0}^{100} \frac{n + 5}{2}$

80. $\displaystyle\sum_{n=0}^{100} \frac{4 - n}{4}$

81. $\displaystyle\sum_{i=1}^{60} \left(250 - \tfrac{2}{5}i\right)$

82. $\displaystyle\sum_{j=1}^{200} (10.5 + 0.025j)$

83. *Why you should learn it* (p. 581) A brick patio has the approximate shape of a trapezoid, as shown in the figure. The patio has 18 rows of bricks. The first row has 14 bricks and the 18th row has 31 bricks. How many bricks are in the patio?

31

14

84. Performing Arts An auditorium has 20 rows of seats. There are 20 seats in the first row, 21 seats in the second row, 22 seats in the third row, and so on (see figure). How many seats are there in all 20 rows?

20

85. Business A hardware store makes a profit of $30,000 during its first year. The store owner sets a goal of increasing profits by $5000 each year for 4 years. Assuming that this goal is met, find the total profit during the first 5 years of business.

86. Physics An object with negligible air resistance is dropped from a plane. During the first second of fall, the object falls 16 feet; during the second second, it falls 48 feet; during the third second, it falls 80 feet; and during the fourth second, it falls 112 feet. Assume this pattern continues. How many feet will the object fall in 8 seconds?

87. MODELING DATA

The table shows the sales a_n (in billions of dollars) for PetSmart from 2006 through 2013. (Source: PetSmart, Inc.)

Year	Sales, a_n (in billions of dollars)
2006	4.23
2007	4.67
2008	5.07
2009	5.34
2010	5.69
2011	6.11
2012	6.76
2013	6.92

Spreadsheet at LarsonPrecalculus.com

(a) Use the *regression* feature of a graphing utility to find an arithmetic sequence for the data. Let n represent the year, with $n = 6$ corresponding to 2006.

(b) Use the sequence from part (a) to approximate the annual sales for PetSmart for the years 2006 through 2013. How well does the model fit the data?

(c) Use the sequence to find the total sales for PetSmart during the period from 2006 through 2013.

(d) Use the sequence to predict the total sales during the period from 2014 through 2021. Is your total reasonable? Explain.

88. MODELING DATA

The table shows the numbers a_n (in thousands) of master's degrees conferred in the United States from 2005 through 2012.   (Source: U.S. National Center for Education Statistics)

DATA Year	Master's degrees conferred, a_n (in thousands)
2005	580
2006	600
2007	611
2008	631
2009	662
2010	693
2011	731
2012	754

Spreadsheet at LarsonPrecalculus.com

(a) Use the *regression* feature of a graphing utility to find an arithmetic sequence for the data. Let n represent the year, with $n = 5$ corresponding to 2005.

(b) Use the sequence from part (a) to approximate the numbers of master's degrees conferred for the years 2005 through 2012. How well does the model fit the data?

(c) Use the sequence to find the total number of master's degrees conferred during the period from 2005 through 2012.

(d) Use the sequence to predict the total number of master's degrees conferred during the period from 2013 through 2023. Is your total reasonable? Explain.

Conclusions

True or False?   In Exercises 89 and 90, determine whether the statement is true or false. Justify your answer.

89. Given the nth term and the common difference of an arithmetic sequence, it is possible to find the $(n + 1)$th term.

90. If the only known information about a finite arithmetic sequence is its first term and its last term, then it is possible to find the sum of the sequence.

Finding the Terms of a Sequence   In Exercises 91 and 92, find the first 10 terms of the sequence.

91. $a_1 = x, d = 2x$ **92.** $a_1 = -y, d = 5y$

93. Writing   Explain how to use the first two terms of an arithmetic sequence to find the nth term.

94. Think About It   The sum of the first 20 terms of an arithmetic sequence with a common difference of 3 is 650. Find the first term.

95. Think About It   The sum of the first n terms of an arithmetic sequence with first term a_1 and common difference d is S_n. Determine the sum when each term is increased by 5. Explain.

96. Think About It   In each sequence, decide whether it is possible to fill in the blanks to form an arithmetic sequence. If so, find a recursion formula for the sequence. Explain how you found your answers.

(a) -7, ▢, ▢, ▢, ▢, ▢, 11

(b) $2, 6$, ▢, ▢, 162

(c) $4, 7.5$, ▢, ▢, ▢, ▢, ▢, 28.5

97. Writing   Carl Friedrich Gauss, a famous nineteenth century mathematician, was a child prodigy. It was said that when Gauss was 10, he was asked by his teacher to add the numbers from 1 to 100. Almost immediately, Gauss found the answer by mentally finding the summation. Write an explanation of how he arrived at his conclusion, and then find the formula for the sum of the first n natural numbers.

98. **HOW DO YOU SEE IT?**   The graph of a sequence is shown below. Determine which of the statements about the sequence is false. Justify your answer.

(a) The sequence is arithmetic.

(b) The common difference is 2.

(c) $a_1 = 3$.

Cumulative Mixed Review

Gauss-Jordan Elimination   In Exercises 99 and 100, use Gauss-Jordan elimination to solve the system of equations.

99. $\begin{cases} 2x - y + 7z = -10 \\ 3x + 2y - 4z = 17 \\ 6x - 5y + z = -20 \end{cases}$

100. $\begin{cases} -x + 4y + 10z = 4 \\ 5x - 3y + z = 31 \\ 8x + 2y - 3z = -5 \end{cases}$

101. *Make a Decision* To work an extended application analyzing the net sales of Dollar Tree from 2001 through 2013, visit this textbook's website at *LarsonPrecalculus.com*. (Data Source: Dollar Tree, Inc.)

8.3   Geometric Sequences and Series

Geometric Sequences

In Section 8.2, you learned that a sequence whose consecutive terms have a common *difference* is an arithmetic sequence. In this section, you will study another important type of sequence called a **geometric sequence.** Consecutive terms of a geometric sequence have a common *ratio.*

> **Definition of Geometric Sequence**
>
> A sequence is **geometric** when the ratios of consecutive terms are the same. So, the sequence $u_1, a_2, a_3, a_4, \ldots, a_n, \ldots$ is geometric when there is a number r such that
>
> $$\frac{a_2}{a_1} = \frac{a_3}{a_2} = \frac{a_4}{a_3} = \cdots = r, \quad r \neq 0.$$
>
> The number r is the **common ratio** of the sequence.

| EXAMPLE 1 | Examples of Geometric Sequences |

a. The sequence whose nth term is 2^n is geometric. For this sequence, the common ratio between consecutive terms is 2.

$$\underbrace{2, 4, 8, 16, \ldots, 2^n, \ldots}_{} \qquad \text{Begin with } n = 1.$$
$$\frac{4}{2} = 2$$

b. The sequence whose nth term is $4(3^n)$ is geometric. For this sequence, the common ratio between consecutive terms is 3.

$$\underbrace{12, 36, 108, 324, \ldots, 4(3^n), \ldots}_{} \qquad \text{Begin with } n = 1.$$
$$\frac{36}{12} = 3$$

c. The sequence whose nth term is $\left(-\frac{1}{3}\right)^n$ is geometric. For this sequence, the common ratio between consecutive terms is $-\frac{1}{3}$.

$$\underbrace{-\frac{1}{3}, \frac{1}{9}, -\frac{1}{27}, \frac{1}{81}, \ldots, \left(-\frac{1}{3}\right)^n, \ldots}_{} \qquad \text{Begin with } n = 1$$
$$\frac{1/9}{-1/3} = -\frac{1}{3}$$

In parts (a), (b), and (c), notice that each of the geometric sequences has an nth term of the form ar^n, where r is the common ratio of the sequence.

 ✔ **Checkpoint** ◀))) *Audio-video solution in English & Spanish at LarsonPrecalculus.com.*

Write the first four terms of the geometric sequence whose nth term is $6(-2)^n$. Then find the common ratio of the consecutive terms. ■

The sequence 1, 4, 9, 16, . . . , whose nth term is n^2, is *not* geometric. The ratio of the second term to the first term is

$$\frac{a_2}{a_1} = \frac{4}{1} = 4$$

but the ratio of the third term to the second term is

$$\frac{a_3}{a_2} = \frac{9}{4}.$$

What you should learn

▶ Recognize, write, and find the nth terms of geometric sequences.
▶ Find nth partial sums of geometric sequences.
▶ Find sums of infinite geometric series.
▶ Use geometric sequences to model and solve real-life problems.

Why you should learn it

Geometric sequences can reduce the amount of time it takes to find the sum of a sequence of numbers with a common ratio. For instance, Exercise 111 on page 598 shows how to use a geometric sequence to find the total vertical distance traveled by a bouncing ball.

The nth Term of a Geometric Sequence

The nth term of a geometric sequence has the form

$$a_n = a_1 r^{n-1}$$

where r is the common ratio of consecutive terms of the sequence. So, every geometric sequence can be written in the following form.

$$a_1, \quad a_2, \quad a_3, \quad a_4, \quad a_5, \quad \ldots, \quad a_n, \quad \ldots$$

$$a_1, a_1 r, a_1 r^2, a_1 r^3, a_1 r^4, \ldots, a_1 r^{n-1}, \ldots$$

When you know the nth term of a geometric sequence, you can find the $(n + 1)$th term by multiplying by r. That is, $a_{n+1} = a_n r$.

EXAMPLE 2   Writing the Terms of a Geometric Sequence

Write the first five terms of the geometric sequence whose first term is $a_1 = 3$ and whose common ratio is $r = 2$.

Solution

Starting with 3, repeatedly multiply by 2 to obtain the following.

$a_1 = 3$	1st term
$a_2 = 3(2^1) = 6$	2nd term
$a_3 = 3(2^2) = 12$	3rd term
$a_4 = 3(2^3) = 24$	4th term
$a_5 = 3(2^4) = 48$	5th term

✓ **Checkpoint** 🔊))) *Audio-video solution in English & Spanish at LarsonPrecalculus.com.*

Write the first five terms of the geometric sequence whose first term is $a_1 = 2$ and whose common ratio is $r = 4$.

EXAMPLE 3   Finding a Term of a Geometric Sequence

Find the 15th term of the geometric sequence whose first term is 20 and whose common ratio is 1.05.

Algebraic Solution

$a_n = a_1 r^{n-1}$	Formula for a geometric sequence
$a_{15} = 20(1.05)^{15-1}$	Substitute 20 for a_1, 1.05 for r, and 15 for n.
≈ 39.60	Use a calculator.

Numerical Solution

For this sequence, $r = 1.05$ and $a_1 = 20$. So, $a_n = 20(1.05)^{n-1}$. Use the *table* feature of a graphing utility to create a table that shows the terms of the sequence, as shown in the figure.

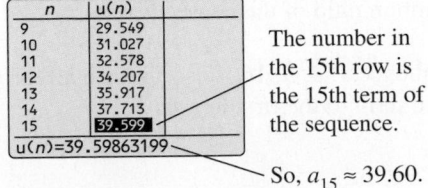

The number in the 15th row is the 15th term of the sequence.

So, $a_{15} \approx 39.60$.

✓ **Checkpoint** 🔊))) *Audio-video solution in English & Spanish at LarsonPrecalculus.com.*

Find the 12th term of the geometric sequence whose first term is 14 and whose common ratio is 1.2.

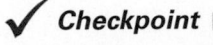

Technology Tip

You can use a graphing utility to generate the geometric sequence in Example 2 by using the following steps.

3 ENTER

2 × ANS

Now press the *enter* key repeatedly to generate the terms of the sequence.

EXAMPLE 4   Finding a Term of a Geometric Sequence

Find a formula for the nth term of the geometric sequence 5, 15, 45, ... What is the ninth term of the sequence?

Solution

The common ratio of this sequence is $r = 15/3 = 3$. Because the first term is $a_1 = 5$, the formula must have the form

$$a_n = a_1 r^{n-1} = 5(3)^{n-1}.$$

You can determine the ninth term $(n = 9)$ to be

$$a_9 = 5(3)^{9-1} \qquad \text{Substitute 9 for } n.$$

$$= 5(6561) \qquad \text{Use a calculator.}$$

$$= 32,805. \qquad \text{Simplify.}$$

A graph of the first nine terms of the sequence is shown in the figure. Notice that the points lie on an exponential curve. This makes sense because a_n is an exponential function of n.

> **Technology Tip**
>
> Most graphing utilities have a built-in function that will display the terms of a geometric sequence. For instructions on how to use the *sequence* feature, see Appendix A; for specific keystrokes, go to this textbook's *Companion Website*.
>
> ```
> seq(5*3^(n-1),n,1,9)
> ...45   10935   32805}
> ```

✓ **Checkpoint** ◀))) *Audio-video solution in English & Spanish at LarsonPrecalculus.com.*

Find a formula for the nth term of the geometric sequence 4, 20, 100, ... What is the 12th term of the sequence? ▪

When you know *any* two terms of a geometric sequence, you can use that information to find *any other* term of the sequence.

EXAMPLE 5   Finding a Term of a Geometric Sequence

The fourth term of a geometric sequence is 125, and the 10th term is 125/64. Find the 14th term. (Assume that the terms of the sequence are positive.)

Solution

The 10th term is related to the fourth term by the equation

$$a_{10} = a_4 r^6. \qquad \text{Multiply 4th term by } r^{10-4}.$$

Because $a_{10} = 125/64$ and $a_4 = 125$, you can solve for r as follows.

$$\frac{125}{64} = 125r^6 \qquad \text{Substitute } \tfrac{125}{64} \text{ for } a_{10} \text{ and } 125 \text{ for } a_4.$$

$$\frac{1}{64} = r^6 \qquad \text{Divide each side by 125.}$$

$$\frac{1}{2} = r \qquad \text{Take the sixth root of each side.}$$

You can obtain the 14th term by multiplying the 10th term by $r^{14-10} = r^4$.

$$a_{14} = a_{10}r^4 = \frac{125}{64}\left(\frac{1}{2}\right)^4 = \frac{125}{1024}$$

> **Remark**
>
> Remember that r is the common ratio of consecutive terms of a geometric sequence. So, in Example 5,
>
> $$a_{10} = a_1 r^9$$
>
> $$= a_1 \cdot r \cdot r \cdot r \cdot r^6$$
>
> $$= a_1 \cdot \frac{a_2}{a_1} \cdot \frac{a_3}{a_2} \cdot \frac{a_4}{a_3} \cdot r^6$$
>
> $$= a_4 r^6.$$

✓ **Checkpoint** ◀))) *Audio-video solution in English & Spanish at LarsonPrecalculus.com.*

The second term of a geometric sequence is 6, and the fifth term is 81/4. Find the eighth term. (Assume that the terms of the sequence are positive.) ▪

The Sum of a Finite Geometric Sequence

The formula for the sum of a *finite* geometric sequence is as follows.

The Sum of a Finite Geometric Sequence   (See the proof on page 633.)

The sum of the finite geometric sequence

$$a_1, a_1r, a_1r^2, a_1r^3, a_1r^4, \ldots, a_1r^{n-1}$$

with common ratio $r \neq 1$ is given by

$$S_n = \sum_{i=1}^{n} a_1 r^{i-1} = a_1 \left(\frac{1-r^n}{1-r} \right).$$

EXAMPLE 6   Sum of a Finite Geometric Sequence

Find the following sum.

$$\sum_{n=1}^{12} 4(0.3)^n$$

Solution

By writing out a few terms, you have

$$\sum_{n=1}^{12} 4(0.3)^n = 4(0.3)^1 + 4(0.3)^2 + 4(0.3)^3 + \cdots + 4(0.3)^{12}.$$

Now, because

$$a_1 = 4(0.3), \qquad r = 0.3, \qquad \text{and} \qquad n = 12$$

you can apply the formula for the sum of a finite geometric sequence to obtain

$$\sum_{n=1}^{12} 4(0.3)^n = a_1 \left(\frac{1-r^n}{1-r} \right) \qquad \text{Formula for sum of a finite geometric sequence}$$

$$= 4(0.3) \left[\frac{1-(0.3)^{12}}{1-0.3} \right] \qquad \text{Substitute } 4(0.3) \text{ for } a_1, 0.3 \text{ for } r, \text{ and } 12 \text{ for } n.$$

$$\approx 1.71. \qquad \text{Use a calculator.}$$

✓ **Checkpoint** 🔊))) *Audio-video solution in English & Spanish at LarsonPrecalculus.com.*

Find the sum $\displaystyle\sum_{i=1}^{10} 2(0.25)^{i-1}$. ■

When using the formula for the sum of a geometric sequence, be careful to check that the index begins at $i = 1$. For an index that begins at $i = 0$, you must adjust the formula for the nth partial sum. For instance, if the index in Example 6 had begun with $n = 0$, then the sum would have been

$$\sum_{n=0}^{12} 4(0.3)^n = 4(0.3)^0 + \sum_{n=1}^{12} 4(0.3)^n$$

$$= 4 + \sum_{n=1}^{12} 4(0.3)^n$$

$$\approx 4 + 1.71$$

$$= 5.71.$$

Technology Tip

Using the *sum sequence* feature of a graphing utility, you can calculate the sum of the sequence in Example 6 to be about 1.7142848, as shown below.

```
sum(seq(4*0.3^n,n,1,12
))
              1.714284803
```

Calculate the sum beginning at $n = 0$. You should obtain a sum of about 5.7142848.

What's Wrong?

You use a graphing utility to find the sum

$$\sum_{n=1}^{6} 7(0.5)^n$$

as shown in the figure. What's wrong?

```
7*(1-.5^6)/(1-.5)
              13.78125
```

Geometric Series

The sum of the terms of an infinite geometric sequence is called an **infinite geometric series** or simply a **geometric series.**

The formula for the sum of a *finite geometric sequence* can, depending on the value of r, be extended to produce a formula for the sum of an *infinite geometric series*. Specifically, if the common ratio r has the property that $|r| < 1$, then it can be shown that r^n becomes arbitrarily close to zero as n increases without bound. Consequently,

$$a_1\left(\frac{1 - r^n}{1 - r}\right) \longrightarrow a_1\left(\frac{1 - 0}{1 - r}\right) \qquad \text{as} \qquad n \longrightarrow \infty.$$

This result is summarized as follows.

The Sum of an Infinite Geometric Sequence

If $|r| < 1$, then the infinite geometric series

$$a_1 + a_1 r + a_1 r^2 + a_1 r^3 + \cdots + a_1 r^{n-1} + \cdots$$

has the sum

$$S = \sum_{i=0}^{\infty} a_1 r^i = \frac{a_1}{1 - r}.$$

Note that when $|r| \geq 1$, the series does not have a sum.

Explore the Concept

Notice that the formula for the sum of an infinite geometric series requires that $|r| < 1$. What happens when $r = 1$ or $r = -1$? Give examples of infinite geometric series for which $|r| > 1$ and convince yourself that they do not have finite sums.

EXAMPLE 7   **Finding the Sum of an Infinite Geometric Series**

Find each sum.

a. $\displaystyle\sum_{n=0}^{\infty} 4(0.6)^n$

b. $3 + 0.3 + 0.03 + 0.003 + \cdots$

Solution

a. $\displaystyle\sum_{n=0}^{\infty} 4(0.6)^n = 4 + 4(0.6) + 4(0.6)^2 + 4(0.6)^3 + \cdots + 4(0.6)^n + \cdots$

$$= \frac{4}{1 - 0.6} \qquad\qquad \frac{a_1}{a - r}$$

$$= 10$$

b. $3 + 0.3 + 0.03 + 0.003 + \cdots = 3 + 3(0.1) + 3(0.1)^2 + 3(0.1)^3 + \cdots$

$$= \frac{3}{1 - 0.1} \qquad\qquad \frac{a_1}{a - r}$$

$$= \frac{10}{3}$$

$$\approx 3.33$$

✓ **Checkpoint** 🔊)) *Audio-video solution in English & Spanish at LarsonPrecalculus.com.*

Find each sum.

a. $\displaystyle\sum_{n=0}^{\infty} 5(0.5)^n$

b. $5 + 1 + 0.2 + 0.04 + \cdots$

Application

EXAMPLE 8   Increasing Annuity

See LarsonPrecalculus.com for an interactive version of this type of example.

A deposit of $50 is made on the first day of each month in an account that pays 3% compounded monthly. What is the balance at the end of 2 years? (This type of savings plan is called an **increasing annuity.**)

Solution

Recall from Section 3.1 that the compound interest formula is

$$A = P\left(1 + \frac{r}{n}\right)^{nt}. \qquad \text{Formula for compound interest}$$

To find the balance in the account after 24 months, consider each of the 24 deposits separately. The first deposit will gain interest for 24 months, and its balance will be

$$A_{24} = 50\left(1 + \frac{0.03}{12}\right)^{24}$$

$$= 50(1.0025)^{24}.$$

The second deposit will gain interest for 23 months, and its balance will be

$$A_{23} = 50\left(1 + \frac{0.03}{12}\right)^{23}$$

$$= 50(1.0025)^{23}.$$

The last deposit will gain interest for only 1 month, and its balance will be

$$A_1 = 50\left(1 + \frac{0.03}{12}\right)^{1}$$

$$= 50(1.0025).$$

Personal Financial Advisor

The total balance in the annuity will be the sum of the balances of the 24 deposits. Using the formula for the sum of a finite geometric sequence, with $a_1 = 50(1.0025)$, $r = 1.0025$, and $n = 24$, you have

$$S_n = a_1\left(\frac{1 - r^n}{1 - r}\right) \qquad \begin{array}{l}\text{Formula for sum of a finite}\\\text{geometric sequence}\end{array}$$

$$S_{24} = 50(1.0025)\left[\frac{1 - (1.0025)^{24}}{1 - 1.0025}\right] \qquad \begin{array}{l}\text{Substitute } 50(1.0025) \text{ for } a_1,\\ 1.0025 \text{ for } r, \text{ and } 24 \text{ for } n.\end{array}$$

$$\approx \$1238.23. \qquad \text{Use a calculator.}$$

You can use the *sum sequence* feature of a graphing utility to verify this result, as shown in the figure.

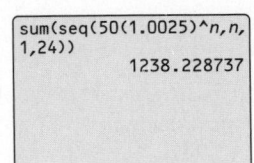

```
sum(seq(50(1.0025)^n,n,
1,24))
            1238.228737
```

✓ *Checkpoint* �))) *Audio-video solution in English & Spanish at LarsonPrecalculus.com.*

An investor deposits $70 on the first day of each month in an account that pays 2% interest, compounded monthly. What is the balance at the end of 4 years? ■

8.3   Exercises

See *CalcChat.com* for tutorial help and worked-out solutions to odd-numbered exercises.
For instructions on how to use a graphing utility, see Appendix A.

Vocabulary and Concept Check

In Exercises 1–3, fill in the blank(s).

1. A sequence is called a _____ sequence if the ratios of consecutive terms are the same. This ratio is called the _____ ratio.

2. The nth term of a geometric sequence has the form $a_n =$ _____ .

3. The sum of the terms of an infinite geometric sequence is called a _____ .

4. Can a geometric sequence have a common ratio of 0?

5. For what values of the common ratio r is it possible to find the sum of an infinite geometric series?

6. Which formula represents the sum of a *finite geometric sequence*? an *infinite geometric series*?

   (a) $S = \dfrac{a_1}{1 - r}$, $|r| < 1$ (b) $S_n = a_1\left(\dfrac{1 - r^n}{1 - r}\right)$

Procedures and Problem Solving

Identifying a Geometric Sequence   In Exercises 7–16, determine whether or not the sequence is geometric. If it is, find the common ratio.

7. $5, 15, 45, 135, \ldots$

8. $3, 12, 48, 192, \ldots$

9. $6, 18, 30, 42, \ldots$

10. $4, 19, 34, 49, \ldots$

11. $1, -\frac{1}{2}, \frac{1}{4}, -\frac{1}{8}, \ldots$

12. $9, -6, 4, -\frac{8}{3}, \ldots$

13. $20, 2, 0.2, 0.02, \ldots$

14. $5, 1, 0.2, 0.04, \ldots$

15. $1, \frac{1}{2}, \frac{1}{3}, \frac{1}{4}, \ldots$

16. $\frac{1}{5}, \frac{2}{7}, \frac{3}{9}, \frac{4}{11}, \ldots$

Writing the Terms of a Geometric Sequence   In Exercises 17–24, write the first five terms of the geometric sequence.

17. $a_1 = 6$, $r = 3$

18. $a_1 = 4$, $r = 2$

19. $a_1 = 1$, $r = \frac{1}{2}$

20. $a_1 = 2$, $r = \frac{1}{3}$

21. $a_1 = 5$, $r = -\frac{1}{10}$

22. $a_1 = 6$, $r = -\frac{1}{4}$

23. $a_1 = 9$, $r = e$

24. $a_1 = 7$, $r = \sqrt{5}$

Finding the nth Term of a Geometric Sequence   In Exercises 25–30, write the first five terms of the geometric sequence. Find the common ratio and write the nth term of the sequence as a function of n.

25. $a_1 = 64$, $a_{k+1} = \frac{1}{2}a_k$

26. $a_1 = 81$, $a_{k+1} = \frac{1}{3}a_k$

27. $a_1 = 9$, $a_{k+1} = 2a_k$

28. $a_1 = 5$, $a_{k+1} = 3a_k$

29. $a_1 = 6$, $a_{k+1} = -\frac{3}{2}a_k$

30. $a_1 = 30$, $a_{k+1} = -\frac{2}{3}a_k$

Finding a Term of a Geometric Sequence   In Exercises 31–38, find the indicated term of the geometric sequence (a) using the *table* feature of a graphing utility and (b) algebraically.

31. $a_1 = 11$, $r = 1.03$, 12th term

32. $a_1 = 24$, $r = 2.6$, 8th term

33. $a_1 = 8$, $r = -\frac{4}{3}$, 7th term

34. $a_1 = 8$, $r = -\frac{3}{4}$, 9th term

35. $a_1 = -\frac{1}{4}$, $r = 8$, 6th term

36. $a_1 = -\frac{1}{128}$, $r = 2$, 12th term

37. $a_1 = 7$, $r = \sqrt{2}$, 14th term

38. $a_1 = 2$, $r = \sqrt{3}$, 11th term

Finding a Term of a Geometric Sequence   In Exercises 39–42, find a formula for the nth term of the geometric sequence. Then find the indicated term of the geometric sequence.

39. 9th term: $7, 21, 63, \ldots$

40. 7th term: $3, 36, 432, \ldots$

41. 10th term: $5, 30, 180, \ldots$

42. 22nd term: $4, 8, 16, \ldots$

Finding a Term of a Geometric Sequence   In Exercises 43–46, find the indicated term of the geometric sequence.

43. $a_1 = 4$, $a_4 = \frac{1}{2}$, 10th term

44. $a_1 = 5$, $a_3 = \frac{45}{4}$, 8th term

45. $a_2 = -18$, $a_5 = \frac{2}{3}$, 6th term

46. $a_2 = -8$, $a_5 = \frac{64}{27}$, 6th term

Graphing the Terms of a Sequence   In Exercises 47–50, use a graphing utility to graph the first 10 terms of the sequence.

47. $a_n = 12(-0.75)^{n-1}$

48. $a_n = 20(0.85)^{n-1}$

49. $a_n = 2(1.3)^{n-1}$

50. $a_n = 10(-1.2)^{n-1}$

Finding a Sequence of Partial Sums In Exercises 51 and 52, find the sequence of the first five partial sums S_1, S_2, S_3, S_4, and S_5 of the geometric sequence by adding terms.

51. $8, -4, 2, -1, \frac{1}{2}, \ldots$ **52.** $8, 12, 18, 27, \frac{81}{2}, \ldots$

Finding a Sequence of Partial Sums In Exercises 53 and 54, use a graphing utility to create a table showing the sequence of the first 10 partial sums S_1, S_2, S_3, $\ldots$, and S_{10} for the series.

53. $\displaystyle\sum_{n=1}^{\infty} 16\left(\frac{1}{2}\right)^{n-1}$ **54.** $\displaystyle\sum_{n=1}^{\infty} 4(0.2)^{n-1}$

Finding the Sum of a Finite Geometric Sequence In Exercises 55–64, find the sum. Use a graphing utility to verify your result.

55. $\displaystyle\sum_{n=1}^{9} 2^{n-1}$ **56.** $\displaystyle\sum_{n=1}^{9} (-2)^{n-1}$

57. $\displaystyle\sum_{i=1}^{7} 64\left(-\frac{1}{2}\right)^{i-1}$ **58.** $\displaystyle\sum_{i=1}^{6} 32\left(\frac{1}{4}\right)^{i-1}$

59. $\displaystyle\sum_{n=0}^{20} 12\left(\frac{6}{5}\right)^{n}$ **60.** $\displaystyle\sum_{n=0}^{15} 10\left(\frac{7}{6}\right)^{n}$

61. $\displaystyle\sum_{i=1}^{10} 8\left(-\frac{1}{4}\right)^{i-1}$ **62.** $\displaystyle\sum_{i=1}^{10} 5\left(-\frac{1}{3}\right)^{i-1}$

63. $\displaystyle\sum_{n=0}^{5} 300(1.06)^{n}$ **64.** $\displaystyle\sum_{n=0}^{6} 500(1.04)^{n}$

Using Summation Notation In Exercises 65–68, use summation notation to write the sum.

65. $5 + 15 + 45 + \cdots + 3645$

66. $7 + 14 + 28 + \cdots + 896$

67. $2 - \frac{1}{2} + \frac{1}{8} - \cdots + \frac{1}{2048}$

68. $15 - 3 + \frac{3}{5} - \cdots - \frac{3}{625}$

Finding the Sum of an Infinite Geometric Series In Exercises 69–84, find the sum of the infinite geometric series, if possible. If not possible, explain why.

69. $\displaystyle\sum_{n=0}^{\infty} 10\left(\frac{4}{5}\right)^{n}$ **70.** $\displaystyle\sum_{n=0}^{\infty} 6\left(\frac{2}{3}\right)^{n}$

71. $\displaystyle\sum_{n=0}^{\infty} 5\left(-\frac{1}{2}\right)^{n}$ **72.** $\displaystyle\sum_{n=0}^{\infty} 5\left(-\frac{1}{4}\right)^{n}$

73. $\displaystyle\sum_{n=1}^{\infty} 2\left(\frac{7}{3}\right)^{n-1}$ **74.** $\displaystyle\sum_{n=1}^{\infty} 8\left(\frac{5}{3}\right)^{n-1}$

75. $\displaystyle\sum_{n=0}^{\infty} 10(0.11)^{n}$ **76.** $\displaystyle\sum_{n=0}^{\infty} 5(0.45)^{n}$

77. $\displaystyle\sum_{n=0}^{\infty} [-3(-0.9)^{n}]$ **78.** $\displaystyle\sum_{n=0}^{\infty} [-10(-0.2)^{n}]$

79. $9 + 6 + 4 + \frac{8}{3} + \cdots$

80. $8 + 6 + \frac{9}{2} + \frac{27}{8} + \cdots$

81. $3 + \frac{15}{2} + \frac{75}{4} + \frac{375}{8} + \cdots$

82. $2 + \frac{7}{3} + \frac{49}{18} + \frac{343}{108} + \cdots$

83. $-7 + 2 - \frac{4}{7} + \frac{8}{49} - \cdots$

84. $-6 + 5 - \frac{25}{6} + \frac{125}{36} - \cdots$

Writing a Repeating Decimal as a Rational Number In Exercises 85–88, find the rational number representation of the repeating decimal.

85. $0.\overline{36}$ **86.** $0.\overline{297}$

87. $1.2\overline{5}$ **88.** $1.3\overline{8}$

Identifying a Sequence In Exercises 89–96, determine whether the sequence associated with the series is arithmetic or geometric. Find the common difference or ratio and find the sum of the first 15 terms.

89. $8 + 16 + 32 + 64 + \cdots$

90. $17 + 14 + 11 + 8 + \cdots$

91. $90 + 30 + 10 + \frac{10}{3} + \cdots$

92. $\frac{5}{4} + \frac{7}{4} + \frac{9}{4} + \frac{11}{4} + \cdots$

93. $\displaystyle\sum_{n=1}^{\infty} 6n$ **94.** $\displaystyle\sum_{n=1}^{\infty} 3^{n-1}$

95. $\displaystyle\sum_{n=0}^{\infty} 6(0.8)^{n}$ **96.** $\displaystyle\sum_{n=0}^{\infty} \frac{n+8}{8}$

97. Annuity A deposit of $100 is made at the beginning of each month in an account that pays 3% interest, compounded monthly. The balance A in the account at the end of 5 years is given by

$$A = 100\left(1 + \frac{0.03}{12}\right)^{1} + \cdots + 100\left(1 + \frac{0.03}{12}\right)^{60}.$$

Find A.

98. Annuity A deposit of $50 is made at the beginning of each month in an account that pays 2% interest, compounded monthly. The balance A in the account at the end of 6 years is given by

$$A = 50\left(1 + \frac{0.02}{12}\right)^{1} + \cdots + 50\left(1 + \frac{0.02}{12}\right)^{72}.$$

Find A.

99. Annuity A deposit of P dollars is made at the beginning of each month in an account earning an annual interest rate r, compounded monthly. The balance A after t years is given by

$$A = P\left(1 + \frac{r}{12}\right) + P\left(1 + \frac{r}{12}\right)^{2} + \cdots$$
$$+ P\left(1 + \frac{r}{12}\right)^{12t}.$$

Show that the balance is given by

$$A = P\left[\left(1 + \frac{r}{12}\right)^{12t} - 1\right]\left(1 + \frac{12}{r}\right).$$

100. Annuity A deposit of P dollars is made at the beginning of each month in an account earning an annual interest rate r, compounded continuously. The balance A after t years is given by $A = Pe^{r/12} + Pe^{2r/12} + \cdots + Pe^{12tr/12}$. Show that the balance is given by

$$A = \frac{Pe^{r/12}(e^{rt} - 1)}{e^{r/12} - 1}.$$

Annuities In Exercises 101–104, consider making monthly deposits of P dollars in a savings account earning an annual interest rate r. Use the results of Exercises 99 and 100 to find the balances A after t years when the interest is compounded (a) monthly and (b) continuously.

101. $P = \$50$, $r = 7\%$, $t = 20$ years

102. $P = \$75$, $r = 4\%$, $t = 25$ years

103. $P = \$100$, $r = 5\%$, $t = 40$ years

104. $P = \$20$, $r = 6\%$, $t = 50$ years

105. Geometry The sides of a square are 16 inches in length. A new square is formed by connecting the midpoints of the sides of the original square, and two of the resulting triangles are shaded (see figure). After this process is repeated five more times, determine the total area of the shaded region.

106. Geometry The sides of a square are 27 inches in length. New squares are formed by dividing the original square into nine squares. The center square is then shaded (see figure). After this process is repeated three more times, determine the total area of the shaded region.

107. Physics The temperature of water in an ice cube tray is 70°F when it is placed in a freezer. Its temperature n hours after being placed in the freezer is 20% less than 1 hour earlier.

(a) Find a formula for the nth term of the geometric sequence that gives the temperature of the water n hours after it is placed in the freezer.

(b) Find the temperatures of the water 6 hours and 12 hours after it is placed in the freezer.

(c) Use a graphing utility to graph the sequence to approximate the time required for the water to freeze.

108. MODELING DATA

The mid-year populations a_n of China (in millions) from 2007 through 2013 are given by ordered pairs of the form (n, a_n), with $n = 7$ corresponding to 2007. (*Spreadsheet at LarsonPrecalculus.com*) (Source: U.S. Census Bureau)

 (7, 1310.6)   (8, 1317.1)   (9, 1323.6)
(10, 1330.1)   (11, 1336.7)   (12, 1343.2)
(13, 1349.6)

(a) Use the *exponential regression* feature of a graphing utility to find a geometric sequence that models the data.

(b) Use the sequence from part (a) to describe the rate at which the population of China is growing.

(c) Use the sequence from part (a) to predict the population of China in 2018. The U.S. Census Bureau predicts that the population of China will be 1376.7 million in 2018. How does this value compare with your prediction?

(d) Use the sequence from part (a) to determine when the population of China will reach 1.40 billion.

109. Fractals In a *fractal*, a geometric figure is repeated at smaller and smaller scales. The sphereflake shown is a computer-generated fractal that was created by Eric Haines. The radius of the large sphere is 1. Attached to the large sphere are nine spheres of radius $\frac{1}{3}$. Attached to each of the smaller spheres are nine spheres of radius $\frac{1}{9}$. This process is continued infinitely.

(a) Write a formula in series notation that gives the surface area of the sphereflake.

(b) Write a formula in series notation that gives the volume of the sphereflake.

(c) Is the surface area of the sphereflake finite or infinite? Is the volume finite or infinite? If either is finite, find the value.

110. Manufacturing The manufacturer of a new food processor plans to produce and sell 8000 units per year. Each year, 10% of all units sold become inoperative. So, 8000 units will be in use after 1 year, $[8000 + 0.9(8000)]$ units will be in use after 2 years, and so on.

(a) Write a formula in series notation for the number of units that will be operative after n years.

(b) Find the numbers of units that will be operative after 10 years, 15 years, and 20 years.

(c) If this trend continues indefinitely, will the number of units that will be operative be finite? If so, how many? If not, explain your reasoning.

111. *Why you should learn it* (p. 589) A ball is dropped from a height of 6 feet and begins bouncing, as shown in the figure. The height of each bounce is three-fourths the height of the previous bounce. Find the total vertical distance the ball travels before coming to rest.

Conclusions

True or False? In Exercises 112–114, determine whether the statement is true or false. Justify your answer.

112. For a geometric sequence in which the quotient of term a_7 and term a_5 is 16, the common ratio is 8.

113. The first n terms of a geometric sequence with a common ratio of 1 are the same as the first n terms of an arithmetic sequence with a common difference of 0 if both sequences have the same first term.

114. You can find the nth term of a geometric sequence by multiplying its common ratio by the first term of the sequence raised to the $(n-1)$th power.

Writing the Terms of a Geometric Sequence In Exercises 115 and 116, write the first five terms of the geometric sequence.

115. $a_1 = 3, r = \dfrac{x}{2}$

116. $a_1 = \frac{1}{4}, r = 7x$

Finding a Term of a Geometric Sequence In Exercises 117 and 118, find the indicated term of the geometric sequence.

117. $a_1 = 100, r = e^x$, 9th term

118. $a_1 = 4, r = (4x)/3$, 6th term

119. Exploration Use a graphing utility to graph each function. Identify the horizontal asymptote of the graph and determine its relationship to the sum.

(a) $f(x) = 6\left[\dfrac{1-(0.5)^x}{1-(0.5)}\right]$, $\displaystyle\sum_{n=0}^{\infty} 6\left(\dfrac{1}{2}\right)^n$

(b) $f(x) = 2\left[\dfrac{1-(0.8)^x}{1-(0.8)}\right]$, $\displaystyle\sum_{n=0}^{\infty} 2\left(\dfrac{4}{5}\right)^n$

120. Writing Write a brief paragraph explaining why the terms of a geometric sequence decrease in magnitude when $-1 < r < 1$.

121. Writing Write a brief paragraph explaining how to use the first two terms of a geometric sequence to find the nth term.

122. HOW DO YOU SEE IT? Use the figures shown below.

(a) Without performing any calculations, determine which figure shows the terms of the sequence $a_n = 20\left(\frac{4}{3}\right)^{n-1}$, and which shows the terms of $a_n = 20\left(\frac{3}{4}\right)^{n-1}$. Explain your reasoning,

(b) Which sequence has terms that can be summed? Explain your reasoning.

Cumulative Mixed Review

Finding a Determinant In Exercises 123 and 124, find the determinant of the matrix.

123. $\begin{bmatrix} -1 & 3 & 4 \\ -2 & 8 & 0 \\ 0 & 5 & -1 \end{bmatrix}$
    124. $\begin{bmatrix} -1 & 0 & 4 \\ -4 & 3 & 5 \\ 0 & 2 & -3 \end{bmatrix}$

125. *Make a Decision* To work an extended application analyzing the monthly profits of a clothing manufacturer during a period of 36 months, visit the textbook's website at *LarsonPrecalculus.com*.

8.4   The Binomial Theorem

Binomial Coefficients

Recall that a *binomial* is a polynomial that has two terms. In this section, you will study a formula that provides a quick method of raising a binomial to a power. To begin, look at the expansion of

$$(x + y)^n$$

for several values of n.

$$(x + y)^0 = 1$$

$$(x + y)^1 = x + y$$

$$(x + y)^2 = x^2 + 2xy + y^2$$

$$(x + y)^3 = x^3 + 3x^2y + 3xy^2 + y^3$$

$$(x + y)^4 = x^4 + 4x^3y + 6x^2y^2 + 4xy^3 + y^4$$

$$(x + y)^5 = x^5 + 5x^4y + 10x^3y^2 + 10x^2y^3 + 5xy^4 + y^5$$

$$(x + y)^6 = x^6 + 6x^5y + 15x^4y^2 + 20x^3y^3 + 15x^2y^4 + 6xy^5 + y^6$$

There are several observations you can make about these expansions.

1. In each expansion, there are $n + 1$ terms.

2. In each expansion, x and y have symmetric roles. The powers of x decrease by 1 in successive terms, whereas the powers of y increase by 1.

3. The sum of the powers of each term is n. For instance, in the expansion of

$$(x + y)^5$$

the sum of the powers of each term is 5.

$$4 + 1 = 5 \quad 3 + 2 = 5$$

$$(x + y)^5 = x^5 + 5x^4y^1 + 10x^3y^2 + 10x^2y^3 + 5x^1y^4 + y^5$$

4. The coefficients increase and then decrease in a symmetric pattern.

The coefficients of a binomial expansion are called **binomial coefficients.** To find them, you can use the **Binomial Theorem.**

The Binomial Theorem   (See the proof on page 634.)

In the expansion of $(x + y)^n$

$$(x + y)^n = x^n + nx^{n-1}y + \cdots + {}_nC_r x^{n-r}y^r + \cdots + nxy^{n-1} + y^n$$

the coefficient of $x^{n-r}y^r$ is

$${}_nC_r = \frac{n!}{(n-r)!r!}.$$

The symbol

$$\binom{n}{r}$$

is sometimes used in place of ${}_nC_r$ to denote binomial coefficients.

EXAMPLE 1   Finding Binomial Coefficients

Find each binomial coefficient.

a. $_8C_2$ **b.** $\binom{10}{3}$ **c.** $_7C_0$ **d.** $\binom{8}{8}$

Solution

a. $_8C_2 = \dfrac{8!}{6! \cdot 2!} = \dfrac{(8 \cdot 7) \cdot \cancel{6!}}{\cancel{6!} \cdot 2!} = \dfrac{8 \cdot 7}{2 \cdot 1} = 28$

b. $\binom{10}{3} = \dfrac{10!}{7! \cdot 3!} = \dfrac{(10 \cdot 9 \cdot 8) \cdot \cancel{7!}}{\cancel{7!} \cdot 3!} = \dfrac{10 \cdot 9 \cdot 8}{3 \cdot 2 \cdot 1} = 120$

c. $_7C_0 = \dfrac{\cancel{7!}}{\cancel{7!} \cdot 0!} = 1$

d. $\binom{8}{8} = \dfrac{\cancel{8!}}{0! \cdot \cancel{8!}} = 1$

✓ *Checkpoint* Audio-video solution in English & Spanish at LarsonPrecalculus.com.

Find each binomial coefficient.

a. $\binom{11}{5}$ **b.** $_9C_2$ **c.** $\binom{5}{0}$ **d.** $_{15}C_{15}$

When $r \neq 0$ and $r \neq n$, as in parts (a) and (b) of Example 1, there is a simple pattern for evaluating binomial coefficients that works because there will always be factorial terms that divide out from the expression.

$$_8C_2 = \frac{\overbrace{8 \cdot 7}^{2 \text{ factors}}}{\underbrace{2 \cdot 1}_{2 \text{ factorial}}} \quad \text{and} \quad \binom{10}{3} = \frac{\overbrace{10 \cdot 9 \cdot 8}^{3 \text{ factors}}}{\underbrace{3 \cdot 2 \cdot 1}_{3 \text{ factorial}}}$$

EXAMPLE 2   Finding Binomial Coefficients

Notice how the pattern shown above is used in parts (a) and (b).

a. $_7C_3 = \dfrac{7 \cdot 6 \cdot 5}{3 \cdot 2 \cdot 1} = 35$

b. $_7C_4 = \dfrac{7 \cdot 6 \cdot 5 \cdot 4}{4 \cdot 3 \cdot 2 \cdot 1} = 35$

c. $_{12}C_1 = \dfrac{12}{1} = 12$

d. $_{12}C_{11} = \dfrac{12!}{1! \cdot 11!} = \dfrac{(12) \cdot \cancel{11!}}{1! \cdot \cancel{11!}} = \dfrac{12}{1} = 12$

✓ *Checkpoint* Audio-video solution in English & Spanish at LarsonPrecalculus.com.

Find each binomial coefficient.

a. $_7C_5$ **b.** $\binom{7}{2}$ **c.** $_{14}C_{13}$ **d.** $\binom{14}{1}$

It is not a coincidence that the results in parts (a) and (b) of Example 2 are the same and that the results in parts (c) and (d) are the same. In general, it is true that $_nC_r = {}_nC_{n-r}$.

Technology Tip

Most graphing utilities are programmed to evaluate $_nC_r$. For instructions on how to use the $_nC_r$ feature, see Appendix A; for specific keystrokes, go to this textbook's *Companion Website*.

8 nCr 2	28
10 nCr 3	120
7 nCr 0	1

Explore the Concept

Find each pair of binomial coefficients.

a. $_7C_0, \, _7C_7$ **d.** $_7C_1, \, _7C_6$

b. $_8C_0, \, _8C_8$ **e.** $_8C_1, \, _8C_7$

c. $_{10}C_0, \, _{10}C_{10}$ **f.** $_{10}C_1, \, _{10}C_9$

What do you observe about the pairs in (a), (b), and (c)? What do you observe about the pairs in (d), (e), and (f)? Write two conjectures from your observations. Develop a convincing argument for your two conjectures.

Binomial Expansions

As mentioned at the beginning of this section, when you write out the coefficients for a binomial that is raised to a power, you are **expanding a binomial.** The formula for binomial coefficients gives you a way to expand binomials.

EXAMPLE 3   Expanding a Binomial

Write the expansion of the expression $(x + 1)^3$.

Solution

The binomial coefficients are $_3C_0 = 1$, $_3C_1 = 3$, $_3C_2 = 3$, and $_3C_3 = 1$. So, the expansion is as follows.

$$(x + 1)^3 = (1)x^3 + (3)x^2(1) + (3)x(1^2) + (1)(1^3)$$

$$= x^3 + 3x^2 + 3x + 1$$

✓ **Checkpoint**))) *Audio-video solution in English & Spanish at LarsonPrecalculus.com.*

Write the expansion of the expression $(x + 1)^4$.

To expand binomials representing *differences*, rather than sums, you alternate signs, as shown in the next example.

EXAMPLE 4   Expanding a Binomial

Write the expansion of the expression $(x - 1)^3$.

Solution

Expand using the binomial coefficients from Example 3.

$$(x - 1)^3 = [x + (-1)]^3$$

$$= (1)x^3 + (3)x^2(-1) + (3)x(-1)^2 + (1)(-1)^3$$

$$= x^3 - 3x^2 + 3x - 1$$

✓ **Checkpoint**))) *Audio-video solution in English & Spanish at LarsonPrecalculus.com.*

Write the expansion of the expression $(x - 1)^4$.

EXAMPLE 5   Expanding Binomial Expressions

See LarsonPrecalculus.com for an interactive version of this type of example.

Write the expansion of (a) $(2x - 3)^4$ and (b) $(x - 2y)^4$.

Solution

The binomial coefficients are $_4C_0 = 1$, $_4C_1 = 4$, $_4C_2 = 6$, $_4C_3 = 4$, and $_4C_4 = 1$. So, the expansions are as follows.

a. $(2x - 3)^4 = (1)(2x)^4 - (4)(2x)^3(3) + (6)(2x)^2(3^2) - (4)(2x)(3^3) + (1)(3^4)$

$$= 16x^4 - 96x^3 + 216x^2 - 216x + 81$$

b. $(x - 2y)^4 = (1)x^4 - (4)x^3(2y) + (6)x^2(2y)^2 - (4)x(2y)^3 + (1)(2y)^4$

$$= x^4 - 8x^3y + 24x^2y^2 - 32xy^3 + 16y^4$$

✓ **Checkpoint**))) *Audio-video solution in English & Spanish at LarsonPrecalculus.com.*

Write the expansion of (a) $(3y - 1)^4$ and (b) $(2x - y)^5$.

Technology Tip

You can use a graphing utility to check the expansion in Example 5(a) by graphing the original binomial expression and the expansion in the same viewing window. The graphs should coincide, as shown below.

EXAMPLE 6   Expanding a Binomial

Write the expansion of the expression

$(x^2 + 4)^3$.

Solution

Expand using the binomial coefficients from Example 3.

$(x^2 + 4)^3 = (1)(x^2)^3 + (3)(x^2)^2(4) + (3)x^2(4^2) + (1)(4^3)$

$\qquad\qquad = x^6 + 12x^4 + 48x^2 + 64$

✓ *Checkpoint* *Audio-video solution in English & Spanish at LarsonPrecalculus.com.*

Write the expansion of the expression $(5 + y^2)^3$.

Sometimes you will need to find a specific term in a binomial expansion. Instead of writing out the entire expansion, you can use the fact that, from the Binomial Theorem, the $(r + 1)$th term is

$_nC_r x^{n-r}y^r$.

For instance, to find the third term of the expression in Example 6, you could use the formula above with $n = 3$ and $r = 2$ to obtain

$_3C_2(x^2)^{3-2} \cdot 4^2 = 3(x^2) \cdot 16 = 48x^2$.

EXAMPLE 7   Finding a Term or Coefficient

a. Find the sixth term of $(a + 2b)^8$.

b. Find the coefficient of the term a^6b^5 in the expansion of $(2a - 5b)^{11}$.

Solution

a. Because the formula is for the $(r + 1)$th term, r is one less than the number of the term you need. So, to find the sixth term in this binomial expansion, use $r = 5$, $n = 8$, $x = a$, and $y = 2b$.

$_nC_r x^{n-r}y^r = {_8C_5}a^{8-5}(2b)^5$

$\qquad\qquad = 56 \cdot a^3 \cdot (2b)^5$

$\qquad\qquad = 56(2^5)a^3b^5$

$\qquad\qquad = 1792a^3b^5$

b. Note that

$(2a - 5b)^{11} = [2a + (-5b)]^{11}$.

So, $n = 11, r = 5, x = 2a$, and $y = -5b$. Substitute these values to obtain

$_nC_r x^{n-r}y^r = {_{11}C_5}(2a)^6(-5b)^5$

$\qquad\qquad = (462)(64a^6)(-3125b^5)$

$\qquad\qquad = -92,400,000a^6b^5$.

So, the coefficient is $-92,400,000$.

✓ *Checkpoint* *Audio-video solution in English & Spanish at LarsonPrecalculus.com.*

a. Find the fifth term of $(a + 2b)^8$.

b. Find the coefficient of the term a^4b^7 in the expansion of $(2a - 5b)^{11}$.

Pascal's Triangle

There is a convenient way to remember the pattern for binomial coefficients. By arranging the coefficients in a triangular pattern, you obtain the following array, which is called **Pascal's Triangle.** This triangle is named after the famous French mathematician Blaise Pascal (1623–1662).

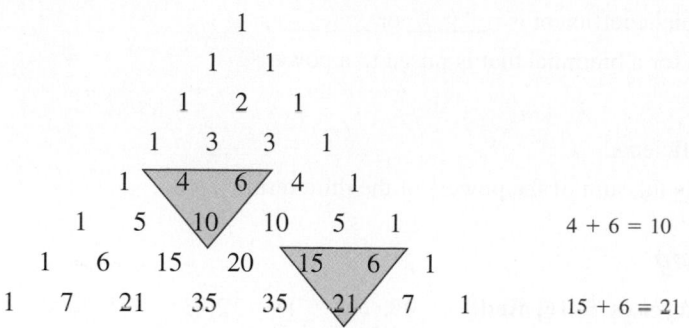

$4 + 6 = 10$

$15 + 6 = 21$

The first and last number in each row of Pascal's Triangle is 1. Every other number in each row is formed by adding the two numbers immediately above the number. Pascal noticed that the numbers in this triangle are precisely the same numbers as the coefficients of binomial expansions, as follows.

$$
\begin{aligned}
(x + y)^0 &= 1 & \text{0th row}\\
(x + y)^1 &= 1x + 1y & \text{1st row}\\
(x + y)^2 &= 1x^2 + 2xy + 1y^2 & \text{2nd row}\\
(x + y)^3 &= 1x^3 + 3x^2y + 3xy^2 + 1y^3 & \text{3rd row}\\
(x + y)^4 &= 1x^4 + 4x^3y + 6x^2y^2 + 4xy^3 + 1y^4 & \vdots\\
(x + y)^5 &= 1x^5 + 5x^4y + 10x^3y^2 + 10x^2y^3 + 5xy^4 + 1y^5\\
(x + y)^6 &= 1x^6 + 6x^5y + 15x^4y^2 + 20x^3y^3 + 15x^2y^4 + 6xy^5 + 1y^6\\
(x + y)^7 &= 1x^7 + 7x^6y + 21x^5y^2 + 35x^4y^3 + 35x^3y^4 + 21x^2y^5 + 7xy^6 + 1y^7
\end{aligned}
$$

The top row of Pascal's Triangle is called the *zeroth row* because it corresponds to the binomial expansion $(x + y)^0 = 1$. Similarly, the next row is called the *first row* because it corresponds to the binomial expansion

$$(x + y)^1 = 1(x) + 1(y).$$

In general, the *nth row* of Pascal's Triangle gives the coefficients of $(x + y)^n$.

EXAMPLE 8   Using Pascal's Triangle

Use the seventh row of Pascal's Triangle to find the binomial coefficients.

$$_8C_0 \quad _8C_1 \quad _8C_2 \quad _8C_3 \quad _8C_4 \quad _8C_5 \quad _8C_6 \quad _8C_7 \quad _8C_8$$

Solution

✓ **Checkpoint** 🔊))) *Audio-video solution in English & Spanish at LarsonPrecalculus.com.*

Use the eighth row of Pascal's Triangle (see Example 8) to find the binomial coefficients.

$$_9C_0 \quad _9C_1 \quad _9C_2 \quad _9C_3 \quad _9C_4 \quad _9C_5 \quad _9C_6 \quad _9C_7 \quad _9C_8 \quad _9C_9$$

Vocabulary and Concept Check

In Exercises 1 and 2, fill in the blanks.

1. The notation used to denote a binomial coefficient is _____ or _____ .

2. When you write out the coefficients for a binomial that is raised to a power, you are _____ a _____ .

3. List two ways to find binomial coefficients.

4. In the expression of $(x + y)^3$, what is the sum of the powers of the third term?

Procedures and Problem Solving

Finding Binomial Coefficients   In Exercises 5–16, find the binomial coefficient.

5. $_7C_5$

6. $_8C_6$

7. $_{20}C_{15}$

8. $_{19}C_{12}$

9. $_{14}C_1$

10. $_{18}C_2$

11. $\binom{12}{0}$

12. $\binom{20}{20}$

13. $\binom{10}{4}$

14. $\binom{10}{6}$

15. $\binom{100}{98}$

16. $\binom{100}{2}$

Finding Binomial Coefficients   In Exercises 17–22, use a graphing utility to find $_nC_r$.

17. $_{41}C_{36}$

18. $_{34}C_4$

19. $_{50}C_{46}$

20. $_{500}C_{498}$

21. $_{250}C_2$

22. $_{1000}C_2$

Expanding a Binomial   In Exercises 23–54, use the Binomial Theorem to expand and simplify the expression.

23. $(x + 1)^5$

24. $(x + 1)^6$

25. $(a + 3)^3$

26. $(a + 2)^4$

27. $(y - 4)^3$

28. $(y - 5)^4$

29. $(x + y)^5$

30. $(x + y)^6$

31. $(2x - y)^5$

32. $(5x - y)^4$

33. $(4y - 3)^3$

34. $(2y - 5)^3$

35. $(2r - 3s)^6$

36. $(4x - 3y)^4$

37. $(x^2 + 2)^4$

38. $(y^2 + 2)^6$

39. $(5 - x^2)^5$

40. $(3 - y^2)^3$

41. $(x^2 + y^2)^4$

42. $(x^2 + y^2)^6$

43. $(3x^3 - y)^6$

44. $(2x^3 - y)^5$

45. $\left(\frac{1}{x} + y\right)^5$

46. $\left(\frac{1}{x} + y\right)^6$

47. $\left(\frac{2}{x} - 2y\right)^4$

48. $\left(\frac{2}{x} - 3y\right)^5$

49. $(4x - 1)^3 - 2(4x - 1)^4$

50. $(x + 3)^5 - 4(x + 3)^4$

51. $3(x + 1)^5 + 4(x + 1)^3$

52. $2(x - 3)^4 + 5(x - 3)^2$

53. $-3(x - 2)^3 - 4(x + 1)^6$

54. $-5(x + 2)^5 - 2(x - 1)^2$

Finding a Term in a Binomial Expansion   In Exercises 55–62, find the specified nth term in the expansion of the binomial.

55. $(x + 8)^{10}$, $n = 4$

56. $(x + 6)^6$, $n = 7$

57. $(x - 6y)^5$, $n = 3$

58. $(x - 10z)^7$, $n = 4$

59. $(4x + 3y)^9$, $n = 8$

60. $(5a + 6b)^5$, $n = 5$

61. $(10x - 3y)^{12}$, $n = 10$

62. $(7x - 2y)^{15}$, $n = 7$

Finding a Coefficient in a Binomial Expansion   In Exercises 63–70, find the coefficient a of the given term in the expansion of the binomial.

	Binomial	Term
63.	$(x + 3)^{12}$	ax^5
64.	$(x + 4)^{12}$	ax^4
65.	$(x - 2y)^{10}$	ax^8y^2
66.	$(4x - y)^{10}$	ax^2y^8
67.	$(3x - 2y)^9$	ax^6y^3
68.	$(2x - 3y)^8$	ax^4y^4
69.	$(x^2 + y)^{10}$	ax^8y^6
70.	$(z^2 + y)^{12}$	$az^{14}y^5$

Using Pascal's Triangle   In Exercises 71–74, use Pascal's Triangle to find the binomial coefficient.

71. $_7C_4$

72. $_6C_3$

73. $_6C_5$

74. $_5C_2$

Using Pascal's Triangle   In Exercises 75–80, expand the binomial by using Pascal's Triangle to determine the coefficients.

75. $(5y + 2)^5$

76. $(2v + 3)^6$

77. $(2x + 3y)^5$

78. $(3x + 4y)^5$

79. $(3t - 2v)^4$

80. $(5v - 2z)^4$

Using the Binomial Theorem   In Exercises 81–84, use the Binomial Theorem to expand and simplify the expression.

81. $\left(3\sqrt{x} + 5\right)^3$

82. $\left(2\sqrt{t} - 7\right)^3$

83. $(x^{2/3} - y^{1/3})^3$

84. $(u^{3/5} + v^{1/5})^5$

∫ Expanding an Expression   In Exercises 85–88, expand the expression in the difference quotient and simplify.

$$\frac{f(x + h) - f(x)}{h}, \quad h \neq 0$$

85. $f(x) = x^3$

86. $f(x) = x^4$

87. $f(x) = x^6$

88. $f(x) = x^8$

Expanding a Complex Number   In Exercises 89–102, use the Binomial Theorem to expand the complex number. Simplify your result. $\left(\text{Remember that } i = \sqrt{-1}.\right)$

89. $(1 + i)^4$

90. $(1 - i)^6$

91. $(4 + i)^4$

92. $(2 + i)^5$

93. $(2 - 3i)^6$

94. $(3 - 2i)^6$

95. $\left(5 + \sqrt{-16}\right)^3$

96. $\left(5 + \sqrt{-9}\right)^3$

97. $\left(4 + \sqrt{3}i\right)^4$

98. $\left(5 - \sqrt{3}i\right)^4$

99. $\left(-\frac{1}{2} + \frac{\sqrt{3}}{2}i\right)^3$

100. $\left(-\frac{1}{3} + \frac{\sqrt{3}}{3}i\right)^3$

101. $\left(\frac{1}{4} - \frac{\sqrt{3}}{4}i\right)^3$

102. $\left(\frac{1}{2} - \frac{\sqrt{3}}{2}i\right)^3$

Using the Binomial Theorem to Approximate   In Exercises 103–106, use the Binomial Theorem to approximate the quantity accurate to three decimal places. For example, in Exercise 103, use the expansion

$$(1.02)^8 = (1 + 0.02)^8$$
$$= 1 + 8(0.02) + 28(0.02)^2 + \cdots.$$

103. $(1.02)^8$

104. $(2.005)^{10}$

105. $(2.99)^{12}$

106. $(1.98)^9$

Using the Binomial Theorem   In Exercises 107–110, use a graphing utility to graph f and g in the same viewing window. What is the relationship between the two graphs? Use the Binomial Theorem to write the polynomial function g in standard form.

107. $f(x) = x^4 - 5x^2$
$g(x) = f(x - 2)$

108. $f(x) = x^3 - 4x$
$g(x) = f(x + 4)$

109. $f(x) = -x^3 + 3x^2 - 4$
$g(x) = f(x + 5)$

110. $f(x) = -x^4 + 4x^2 - 1$
$g(x) = f(x - 3)$

Using a Graphing Utility   In Exercises 111 and 112, use a graphing utility to graph the functions in the given order and in the same viewing window. Compare the graphs. Which two functions have identical graphs, and why?

111. (a) $f(x) = (1 - x)^3$

(b) $g(x) = 1 - 3x$

(c) $h(x) = 1 - 3x + 3x^2$

(d) $p(x) = 1 - 3x + 3x^2 - x^3$

112. (a) $f(x) = \left(1 - \frac{1}{2}x\right)^4$

(b) $g(x) = 1 - 2x + \frac{3}{2}x^2$

(c) $h(x) = 1 - 2x + \frac{3}{2}x^2 - \frac{1}{2}x^3$

(d) $p(x) = 1 - 2x + \frac{3}{2}x^2 - \frac{1}{2}x^3 + \frac{1}{16}x^4$

Finding a Probability   In Exercises 113–116, consider n independent trials of an experiment in which each trial has two possible outcomes, success or failure. The probability of a success on each trial is p and the probability of a failure is $q = 1 - p$. In this context, the term $_nC_k p^k q^{n-k}$ in the expansion of $(p + q)^n$ gives the probability of k successes in the n trials of the experiment.

113. A fair coin is tossed seven times. To find the probability of obtaining four heads, evaluate the term

$$_7C_4\left(\tfrac{1}{2}\right)^4\left(\tfrac{1}{2}\right)^3$$

in the expansion of $\left(\tfrac{1}{2} + \tfrac{1}{2}\right)^7$.

114. The probability of a baseball player getting a hit during any given time at bat is $\tfrac{1}{4}$. To find the probability that the player gets three hits during the next 10 times at bat, evaluate the term

$$_{10}C_3\left(\tfrac{1}{4}\right)^3\left(\tfrac{3}{4}\right)^7$$

in the expansion of $\left(\tfrac{1}{4} + \tfrac{3}{4}\right)^{10}$.

115. The probability of a sales representative making a sale to any one customer is $\tfrac{1}{3}$. The sales representative makes eight contacts a day. To find the probability of making four sales, evaluate the term

$$_8C_4\left(\tfrac{1}{3}\right)^4\left(\tfrac{2}{3}\right)^4$$

in the expansion of $\left(\tfrac{1}{3} + \tfrac{2}{3}\right)^8$.

116. To find the probability that the sales representative in Exercise 115 makes four sales when the probability of a sale to any one customer is $\tfrac{1}{2}$, evaluate the term

$$_8C_4\left(\tfrac{1}{2}\right)^4\left(\tfrac{1}{2}\right)^4$$

in the expansion of $\left(\tfrac{1}{2} + \tfrac{1}{2}\right)^8$.

117. MODELING DATA

The per capita consumptions of milk f (in gallons) in the United States from 1990 through 2012 can be approximated by the model

$f(t) = 0.005t^2 - 0.37t + 25.7, \quad 0 \le t \le 22$

where t represents the year, with $t = 0$ corresponding to 1990 (see figure). (Source: Economic Research Service, U.S. Department of Agriculture)

(a) Adjust the model so that $t = 0$ corresponds to 2000 rather than 1990. To do this, shift the graph of f 10 units to the left and obtain $g(t) = f(t + 10)$. Write $g(t)$ in standard form.

(b) Use a graphing utility to graph f and g in the same viewing window.

118. Why you should learn it (p. 599) The amounts f (in billions of dollars) of child support collected in the United States from 2000 through 2013 can be approximated by the model

$f(t) = -0.039t^2 + 1.30t + 17.7,$

$0 \le t \le 13$

where t represents the year, with $t = 0$ corresponding to 2000 (see figure). (Source: U.S. Department of Health and Human Services)

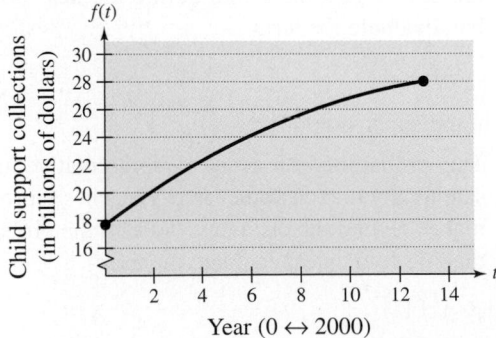

(a) Adjust the model so that $t = 0$ corresponds to 2005 rather than 2000. To do this, shift the graph of f five units to the left and obtain $g(t) = f(t + 5)$. Write $g(t)$ in standard form.

(b) Use a graphing utility to graph f and g in the same viewing window.

Conclusions

True or False? **In Exercises 119 and 120, determine whether the statement is true or false. Justify your answer.**

119. The Binomial Theorem can be used to produce each row of Pascal's Triangle.

120. A binomial that represents a difference cannot always be accurately expanded using the Binomial Theorem.

121. Writing In your own words, explain how to form the rows of Pascal's Triangle. Then form rows 8–10 of Pascal's Triangle.

122. **HOW DO YOU SEE IT?** The expansions of $(x + y)^4$, $(x + y)^5$, and $(x + y)^6$ are as follows.

$(x + y)^4 = 1x^4 + 4x^3y + 6x^2y^2 + 4xy^3 + 1y^4$

$(x + y)^5 = 1x^5 + 5x^4y + 10x^3y^2 + 10x^2y^3$
$\qquad\qquad\qquad + 5xy^4 + 1y^5$

$(x + y)^6 = 1x^6 + 6x^5y + 15x^4y^2 + 20x^3y^3 + 15x^2y^4$
$\qquad\qquad\qquad + 6xy^5 + 1y^6$

(a) Explain how the exponent of a binomial is related to the number of terms in its expansion.

(b) How many terms are in the expansion of $(x + y)^n$?

Proof **In Exercises 123–126, prove the property for all integers r and n, where $0 \le r \le n$.**

123. $_nC_r = {_nC_{n-r}}$

124. $_nC_0 - {_nC_1} + {_nC_2} - \cdots \pm {_nC_n} = 0$

125. $_{n+1}C_r = {_nC_r} + {_nC_r} + {_nC_{r-1}}$

126. The sum of the numbers in the nth row of Pascal's Triangle is 2^n.

127. Error Analysis You are a math instructor and receive the following solution from one of your students on a quiz. Find the error(s) in the solution and write a short paragraph discussing ways that your student could avoid the error(s) in the future. Find the second term in the expansion of $(2x - 3y)^5$.

$\overline{5(2x)^4(3y)^2 = 720x^4y^2}$

Cumulative Mixed Review

Finding the Inverse of a Matrix **In Exercises 128 and 129, find the inverse of the matrix.**

128. $\begin{bmatrix} -1 & -4 \\ 1 & 2 \end{bmatrix}$ **129.** $\begin{bmatrix} 11 & -12 \\ 2 & -2 \end{bmatrix}$

8.5   Counting Principles

Simple Counting Problems

The last two sections of this chapter present a brief introduction to some of the basic counting principles and their application to probability. In the next section, you will see that much of probability has to do with counting the number of ways an event can occur.

EXAMPLE 1   Selecting Pairs of Numbers at Random

You place eight pieces of paper, numbered from 1 to 8, in a box. You draw one piece of paper at random from the box, record its number, and *replace* the paper in the box. Then, you draw a second piece of paper at random from the box and record its number. Finally, you add the two numbers. How many different ways can you obtain a sum of 12?

Solution

To solve this problem, count the number of different ways that a sum of 12 can be obtained using two numbers from 1 to 8. As shown below, a sum of 12 can occur in five different ways.

First number | 4 | 5 | 6 | 7 | 8 |

Second number | 8 | 7 | 6 | 5 | 4 |

 Checkpoint ◀))) *Audio-video solution in English & Spanish at LarsonPrecalculus.com.*

In Example 1, how many different ways can you obtain a sum of 14?

EXAMPLE 2   Selecting Pairs of Numbers at Random

You place eight pieces of paper, numbered from 1 to 8, in a box. You draw one piece of paper at random from the box, record its number, and *do not* replace the paper in the box. Then, you draw a second piece of paper at random from the box and record its number. Finally, you add the two numbers. How many different ways can you obtain a sum of 12?

Solution

To solve this problem, count the number of different ways that a sum of 12 can be obtained using two *different* numbers from 1 to 8. As shown below, a sum of 12 can occur in four different ways.

First number | 4 | 5 | 7 | 8 |

Second number | 8 | 7 | 5 | 4 |

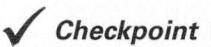 **Checkpoint** ◀))) *Audio-video solution in English & Spanish at LarsonPrecalculus.com.*

Repeat Example 2 for drawing *three* pieces of paper. ◼

The difference between the counting problems in Examples 1 and 2 can be described by saying that the random selection in Example 1 occurs **with replacement,** whereas the random selection in Example 2 occurs **without replacement,** which eliminates the possibility of choosing two 6's.

What you should learn

▶ Solve simple counting problems.
▶ Use the Fundamental Counting Principle to solve more complicated counting problems.
▶ Use permutations to solve counting problems.
▶ Use combinations to solve counting problems.

Why you should learn it

You can use counting principles to solve counting problems that occur in real life. For instance, in Exercise 67 on page 615, you are asked to use counting principles to determine in how many ways a player can select six numbers in a Powerball lottery.

The Fundamental Counting Principle

Examples 1 and 2 describe simple counting problems in which you can *list* each possible way that an event can occur. When it is possible, this is always the best way to solve a counting problem. However, some events can occur in so many different ways that it is not feasible to write out the entire list. In such cases, you must rely on formulas and counting principles. The most important of these is the **Fundamental Counting Principle.**

Fundamental Counting Principle

Let E_1 and E_2 be two events. The first event E_1 can occur in m_1 different ways. After E_1 has occurred, E_2 can occur in m_2 different ways. The number of ways that the two events can occur is $m_1 \cdot m_2$.

The Fundamental Counting Principle can be extended to three or more events. For instance, the number of ways that three events E_1, E_2, and E_3 can occur is $m_1 \cdot m_2 \cdot m_3$.

EXAMPLE 3   Using the Fundamental Counting Principle

How many different pairs of letters from the English alphabet are possible?

Solution

There are two events in this situation. The first event is the choice of the first letter, and the second event is the choice of the second letter. Because the English alphabet contains 26 letters, it follows that the number of two-letter pairs is

$$26 \cdot 26 = 676.$$

✓ **Checkpoint** ◀))) *Audio-video solution in English & Spanish at LarsonPrecalculus.com.*

A combination lock will open when you select the right choice of three numbers (from 1 to 30, inclusive). How many different lock combinations are possible?

EXAMPLE 4   Using the Fundamental Counting Principle

Telephone numbers in the United States currently have 10 digits. The first three are the *area code* and the next seven are the *local telephone number*. How many different telephone numbers are possible within each area code? (Note that at this time, a local telephone number cannot begin with 0 or 1.)

Solution

Because the first digit of a local number cannot be 0 or 1, there are only eight choices for the first digit. For each of the other six digits, there are 10 choices.

So, the number of local telephone numbers that are possible within each area code is

$$8 \cdot 10 \cdot 10 \cdot 10 \cdot 10 \cdot 10 \cdot 10 = 8{,}000{,}000.$$

✓ **Checkpoint** ◀))) *Audio-video solution in English & Spanish at LarsonPrecalculus.com.*

A product's catalog number is made up of one letter from the English alphabet followed by a five-digit number. How many different catalog numbers are possible? ■

Permutations

One important application of the Fundamental Counting Principle is in determining the number of ways that n elements can be arranged (in order). An ordering of n elements is called a **permutation** of the elements.

Definition of Permutation

A **permutation** of n different elements is an ordering of the elements such that one element is first, one is second, one is third, and so on.

EXAMPLE 5   Finding the Number of Permutations

How many permutations of the letters

Α, Β, C, D, E, and F

are possible?

Solution

Consider the following reasoning.

First position: Any of the *six* letters
Second position: Any of the remaining *five* letters
Third position: Any of the remaining *four* letters
Fourth position: Any of the remaining *three* letters
Fifth position: Either of the remaining *two* letters
Sixth position: The *one* remaining letter

So, the numbers of choices for the six positions are as follows.

Permutations of six letters

The total number of permutations of the six letters is

$$6! = 6 \cdot 5 \cdot 4 \cdot 3 \cdot 2 \cdot 1 = 720.$$

✓ **Checkpoint**))) *Audio-video solution in English & Spanish at LarsonPrecalculus.com.*

How many permutations of the letters

W, X, Y, and Z

are possible?

The result obtained in Example 5 can be generalized to conclude that the number of permutations of n different elements is $n!$.

Number of Permutations of n Elements

The number of permutations of n elements is given by

$$n \cdot (n-1) \cdots 4 \cdot 3 \cdot 2 \cdot 1 = n!.$$

In other words, there are $n!$ different ways that n elements can be ordered.

It is useful, on occasion, to order a *subset* of a collection of elements rather than the entire collection. For instance, you might want to order r elements out of a collection of n elements. Such an ordering is called a **permutation of n elements taken r at a time.** This ordering is demonstrated in the next example.

EXAMPLE 6   Counting Horse Race Finishes

Eight horses are running in a race. In how many different ways can these horses come in first, second, and third? (Assume that there are no ties.)

Solution

Here are the different possibilities.

Win (first position):	*Eight* choices
Place (second position):	*Seven* choices
Show (third position):	*Six* choices

The numbers of choices for the three positions are as follows.

Different orders of horses

$$8 \quad 7 \quad 6$$

So, using the Fundamental Counting Principle, you can determine that there are

$$8 \cdot 7 \cdot 6 = 336$$

different ways in which the eight horses can come in first, second, and third.

✓ **Checkpoint** 🔊))) *Audio-video solution in English & Spanish at LarsonPrecalculus.com.*

A coin club has five members. In how many ways can there be a president and a vice-president? ▪

The result obtained in Example 6 can be generalized to the formula in the following definition.

Permutations of n Elements Taken r at a Time

The number of **permutations of n elements taken r at a time** is given by

$$_nP_r = \frac{n!}{(n - r)!} = n(n - 1)(n - 2) \cdots (n - r + 1).$$

Using this formula, you can rework Example 6 to find that the number of permutations of eight horses taken three at a time is

$$_8P_3 = \frac{8!}{(8 - 3)!}$$

$$= \frac{8!}{5!}$$

$$= \frac{8 \cdot 7 \cdot 6 \cdot \cancel{5!}}{\cancel{5!}}$$

$$= 336$$

which is the same answer obtained in the example.

Technology Tip

Most graphing utilities are programmed to evaluate $_nP_r$. The figure below shows how one graphing utility evaluates the permutation $_8P_3$. For instructions on how to use the $_nP_r$ feature, see Appendix A; for specific keystrokes, go to this textbook's *Companion Website.*

Remember that for permutations, order is important. So, to find the possible permutations of the letters A, B, C, and D taken three at a time, you count the permutations (A, B, D) and (B, A, D) as different because the *order* of the elements is different.

Consider, however, the possible permutations of the letters A, A, B, and C. The total number of permutations of the four letters would be

$$_4P_4 = 4!.$$

However, not all of these arrangements would be *distinguishable* because there are two A's in the list. To find the number of distinguishable permutations, you can use the following formula.

Distinguishable Permutations

Suppose a set of n objects has n_1 of one kind of object, n_2 of a second kind, n_3 of a third kind, and so on, with

$$n = n_1 + n_2 + n_3 + \cdots + n_k.$$

The number of **distinguishable permutations** of the n objects is given by

$$\frac{n!}{n_1! \cdot n_2! \cdot n_3! \cdot \cdots \cdot n_k!}.$$

EXAMPLE 7   Distinguishable Permutations

See LarsonPrecalculus.com for an interactive version of this type of example.

In how many distinguishable ways can the letters in BANANA be written?

Solution

This word has six letters, of which three are A's, two are N's, and one is a B. So, the number of distinguishable ways in which the letters can be written is

$$\frac{6!}{3! \cdot 2! \cdot 1!} = \frac{6 \cdot 5 \cdot 4 \cdot 3!}{3! \cdot 2!} = 60.$$

The 60 different distinguishable permutations are as follows.

AAABNN	AAANBN	AAANNB	AABANN
AABNAN	AABNNA	AANABN	AANANB
AANBAN	AANBNA	AANNAB	AANNBA
ABAANN	ABANAN	ABANNA	ABNAAN
ABNANA	ABNNAA	ANAABN	ANAANB
ANABAN	ANABNA	ANANAB	ANANBA
ANBAAN	ANBANA	ANBNAA	ANNAAB
ANNABA	ANNBAA	BAAANN	BAANAN
BAANNA	BANAAN	BANANA	BANNAA
BNAAAN	BNAANA	BNANAA	BNNAAA
NAAABN	NAAANB	NAABAN	NAABNA
NAANAB	NAANBA	NABAAN	NABANA
NABNAA	NANAAB	NANABA	NANBAA
NBAAAN	NBAANA	NBANAA	NBNAAA
NNAAAB	NNAABA	NNABAA	NNBAAA

✓ *Checkpoint*   Audio-video solution in English & Spanish at LarsonPrecalculus.com.

In how many distinguishable ways can the letters in MITOSIS be written?   ◼

Combinations

When you count the number of possible permutations of a set of elements, order is important. As a final topic in this section, you will look at a method for selecting subsets of a larger set in which order *is not* important. Such subsets are called **combinations of *n* elements taken *r* at a time.** For instance, the combinations {A, B, C} and {B, A, C} are equivalent because both sets contain the same three elements, and the order in which the elements are listed is not important. So, you would count only one of the two sets. A common example of a combination is a card game in which the player is free to reorder the cards after they have been dealt.

> **Combinations of *n* Elements Taken *r* at a Time**
>
> The number of **combinations of *n* elements taken *r* at a time** is given by
>
> $$_nC_r = \frac{n!}{(n-r)!r!}.$$

Note that the formula for $_nC_r$ is the same one given for binomial coefficients.

EXAMPLE 8   Combinations of *n* Elements Taken *r* at a Time

a. In how many different ways can three letters be chosen from the letters A, B, C, D, and E? (The order of the three letters is not important.)

b. A standard poker hand consists of five cards dealt from a deck of 52. How many different poker hands are possible? (After the cards are dealt, the player may reorder them, so order is not important.)

Solution

a. You can find the number of different ways in which the letters can be chosen by using the formula for the number of combinations of five elements taken three at a time, as follows.

$$_5C_3 = \frac{5!}{2!3!} = \frac{5 \cdot \overset{2}{\cancel{4}} \cdot \cancel{3!}}{\cancel{2} \cdot 1 \cdot \cancel{3!}} = 10$$

b. You can find the number of different poker hands by using the formula for the number of combinations of 52 elements taken five at a time, as follows.

$$_{52}C_5 = \frac{52!}{47!5!} = \frac{52 \cdot 51 \cdot 50 \cdot 49 \cdot 48 \cdot \cancel{47!}}{5 \cdot 4 \cdot 3 \cdot 2 \cdot 1 \cdot \cancel{47!}} = 2{,}598{,}960$$

✓ **Checkpoint** *Audio-video solution in English & Spanish at LarsonPrecalculus.com.*

In how many different ways can two letters be chosen from the letters A, B, C, D, E, F, and G? (The order of the two letters is not important.) ∎

When solving problems involving counting principles, you need to be able to distinguish among the various counting principles in order to determine which is necessary to solve the problem correctly. To do this, ask yourself the following questions.

1. Is the order of the elements important? *Permutation*

2. Are the chosen elements a subset of a larger set in which order is not important? *Combination*

3. Are there two or more separate events? *Fundamental Counting Principle*

Remark

In Example 8(a), you could also make a list of the different combinations of three letters chosen from five letters.

{A, B, C}	{A, B, D}
{A, B, E}	{A, C, D}
{A, C, E}	{A, D, E}
{B, C, D}	{B, C, E}
{B, D, E}	{C, D, E}

From this list, you can conclude that there are 10 different ways in which three letters can be chosen from five letters, which is the same answer obtained in Example 8(a).

8.5 Exercises

See *CalcChat.com* for tutorial help and worked-out solutions to odd-numbered exercises. For instructions on how to use a graphing utility, see Appendix A.

Vocabulary and Concept Check

In Exercises 1 and 2, fill in the blank.

1. The _____ states that if there are m_1 ways for one event to occur and m_2 ways for a second event to occur, then there are $m_1 \cdot m_2$ ways for both events to occur.

2. The number of _____ of n objects is given by $\dfrac{n!}{n_1! \cdot n_2! \cdot n_3! \cdot \cdots \cdot n_k!}$.

3. Is the ordering of n elements called a *permutation* or a *combination* of the elements?

4. What do n and r represent in the formula $_nP_r = \dfrac{n!}{(n-r)!}$?

Procedures and Problem Solving

Selecting Numbers at Random In Exercises 5–12, determine the number of ways in which a computer can randomly generate one or more such integers, or pairs of integers, from 1 through 15.

5. An odd integer

6. An even integer

7. A prime integer

8. An integer that is greater than 11

9. A pair of integers whose sum is 20

10. A pair of integers whose sum is 22

11. A pair of distinct integers whose sum is 8

12. A pair of distinct integers whose sum is 24

13. **Audio Engineering** A customer can choose one of four amplifiers, one of ten stereo receivers, and one of five speaker models for an entertainment system. Determine the number of possible system configurations.

14. **Education** A college student is preparing a course schedule for the next semester. The student must select one of two mathematics courses, one of three science courses, and one of five courses from the social sciences and humanities. How many schedules are possible?

15. **Education** In how many ways can a 10-question true-false exam be answered? (Assume that no questions are omitted.)

16. **Physiology** In a physiology class, a student must dissect three different specimens. The student can select one of nine earthworms, one of four frogs, and one of seven fetal pigs. In how many ways can the student select the specimens?

17. **Fundamental Counting Principle** How many three-digit numbers can be formed under each condition?

    (a) The leading digit cannot be 0.

    (b) The leading digit cannot be 0 and no repetition of digits is allowed.

    (c) The leading digit cannot be 0 and the number must be a multiple of 5.

18. **Fundamental Counting Principle** How many four-digit numbers can be formed under each condition?

    (a) The leading digit cannot be 0 and the number must be less than 5000.

    (b) The leading digit cannot be 0 and the number must be even.

19. **Telecommunication** In 2014, the state of Nevada added a third area code. Using the information about telephone numbers given in Example 4, how many telephone numbers can Nevada's phone system accommodate?

20. **Transportation** In Pennsylvania, each standard automobile license plate number consists of three letters followed by a four-digit number. How many distinct Pennsylvania license plate numbers can be formed?

21. **Operations Research** In 1963, the United States Postal Service launched the Zoning Improvement Plan (ZIP) Code to streamline the mail-delivery system. A ZIP code consists of a five-digit sequence of numbers.

    (a) Find the number of ZIP codes consisting of five digits.

    (b) Find the number of ZIP codes consisting of five digits when the first digit is 1 or 2.

22. **Operations Research** In 1983, in order to identify small geographic segments within a delivery code, the post office began to use an expanded ZIP code called ZIP+4, which is composed of the original five-digit code plus a four-digit add-on code.

    (a) Find the number of ZIP codes consisting of five digits followed by the four additional digits.

    (b) Find the number of ZIP codes consisting of five digits followed by the four additional digits when the first number of the five-digit code is 1 or 2.

23. **Banking** ATM personal identification number (PIN) codes typically consist of four-digit sequences of numbers.

    (a) Find the total number of ATM codes possible.

    (b) Find the total number of ATM codes possible when the first digit is not 0.

24. Radio Broadcasting Typically, radio stations are identified by four "call letters." Radio stations east of the Mississippi River have call letters that start with the letter W, and radio stations west of the Mississippi River have call letters that start with the letter K.

(a) Find the number of different sets of radio station call letters that are possible in the United States.

(b) Find the number of different sets of radio station call letters that are possible when the call letters must include a Q.

25. Finding Permutations Three couples have reserved seats in a row for a concert. In how many different ways can they be seated when (a) there are no seating restrictions? (b) each couple sits together?

26. Finding Permutations In how many orders can five girls and three boys walk through a doorway single file when (a) there are no restrictions? (b) the girls walk through before the boys?

27. Photography In how many ways can five children posing for a photograph line up in a row?

28. Transportation Design In how many ways can eight people sit in an eight-passenger vehicle?

29. Politics The nine justices of the U.S. Supreme Court pose for a photograph while standing in a straight line, as opposed to the typical pose of two rows. How many different orders of the justices are possible for this photograph?

30. Manufacturing Four processes are involved in assembling a product, and they can be performed in any order. The management wants to test each order to determine which is the least time-consuming. How many different orders will have to be tested?

Evaluating a Permutation   In Exercises 31–36, evaluate $_nP_r$ **using the formula from this section.**

31. $_4P_4$ **32.** $_5P_5$

33. $_8P_3$ **34.** $_{20}P_2$

35. $_6P_5$ **36.** $_7P_4$

Evaluating a Permutation Using a Graphing Utility   In Exercises 37–40, evaluate $_nP_r$ **using a graphing utility.**

37. $_{30}P_6$

38. $_{10}P_8$

39. $_{120}P_4$

40. $_{100}P_5$

41. Politics From a pool of 12 candidates, the offices of president, vice-president, secretary, and treasurer will be filled. In how many ways can the offices be filled?

42. Physical Education How many different batting orders can a baseball coach create from a team of 15 players when there are nine positions to fill?

43. Education The graphic design department is holding a contest in which it will award scholarships of different values to those who finish in first place, second place, and third place. The department receives 104 entries. How many different orders of the top three places are possible?

44. Athletics Eight sprinters have qualified for the finals in the 100-meter dash at the NCAA national track meet. How many different orders of the top three finishes are possible? (Assume there are no ties.)

Writing Permutations   In Exercises 45 and 46, use the letters **A, B, C, and D.**

45. Write all permutations of the letters.

46. Write all permutations of the letters when the letters B and C must remain between the letters A and D.

Distinguishable Permutations   In Exercises 47–50, find the number of distinguishable permutations of the group of letters.

47. A, A, G, E, E, E, M

48. B, B, B, T, T, T, T, T

49. A, L, G, E, B, R, A

50. M, I, S, S, I, S, S, I, P, P, I

Evaluating a Combination   In Exercises 51–56, evaluate $_nC_r$ **using the formula from this section.**

51. $_5C_2$ **52.** $_6C_3$

53. $_4C_1$ **54.** $_7C_1$

55. $_{25}C_0$ **56.** $_{20}C_0$

Evaluating a Combination Using a Graphing Utility   In Exercises 57–60, evaluate $_nC_r$ **using a graphing utility.**

57. $_{33}C_4$ **58.** $_{10}C_7$

59. $_{42}C_5$ **60.** $_{50}C_6$

Writing Combinations   In Exercises 61 and 62, use the letters **A, B, C, D, E, and F.**

61. Write all possible selections of two letters that can be formed from the letters. (The order of the two letters is not important.)

62. Write all possible selections of three letters that can be formed from the letters. (The order of the three letters is not important.)

63. Politics As of May 2014, the U.S. Senate Committee on Indian Affairs had 14 members. Party affiliation is not a factor in selection. How many different committees are possible from the 100 U.S. senators?

64. Education You can answer any 18 questions from a total of 20 questions on an exam. In how many different ways can you select the questions?

65. Jury Selection   In how many different ways can a jury of 12 people be randomly selected from a group of 40 people?

66. Geometry   Three points that are not collinear determine three lines. How many lines are determined by nine points, of which no three are collinear?

67. *Why you should learn it*   (p. 607)   Powerball is played with 59 white balls, numbered 1 through 59, and 35 red balls, numbered 1 through 35. Five white balls and one red ball, the Powerball, are drawn. In how many ways can a player select the six numbers?

68. Law   A law office interviews paralegals for 10 openings. There are 13 paralegals with two years of experience and 20 paralegals with one year of experience. How many combinations of seven paralegals with two years of experience and three paralegals with one year of experience are possible?

69. Forming a Committee   A six-member research committee is to be formed having one administrator, three faculty members, and two students. There are seven administrators, 12 faculty members, and 25 students in contention for the committee. How many six-member committees are possible?

70. Sociology   The number of possible interpersonal relationships increases dramatically as the size of a group increases. Determine the numbers of different two-person relationships that are possible in groups of people of sizes (a) 3, (b) 8, (c) 12, and (d) 20.

71. Game Theory   You are dealt five cards from an ordinary deck of 52 playing cards. In how many ways can you get a full house? (A full house consists of three of one kind and two of another. For example, 8-8-8-5-5 and K-K-K-10-10 are full houses.)

72. Quality Engineering   A shipment of 30 flat screen televisions contains three defective units. In how many ways can a vending company purchase four of these units and receive (a) all good units, (b) two good units, and (c) at least two good units?

Geometry   **In Exercises 73–76, find the number of diagonals of the polygon. (A line segment connecting any two nonadjacent vertices is called a *diagonal* of a polygon.)**

73. Pentagon   **74.** Hexagon

75. Octagon   **76.** Decagon (10 sides)

Solving an Equation   **In Exercises 77–84, solve for n.**

77. $14 \cdot {}_nP_3 = {}_{n+2}P_4$ **78.** $ {}_nP_5 = 18 \cdot {}_{n-2}P_4$

79. $ {}_nP_4 = 10 \cdot {}_{n-1}P_3$ **80.** $ {}_nP_6 = 12 \cdot {}_{n-1}P_5$

81. $ {}_{n+1}P_3 = 4 \cdot {}_nP_2$ **82.** $ {}_{n+2}P_3 = 6 \cdot {}_{n+2}P_1$

83. $4 \cdot {}_{n+1}P_2 = {}_{n+2}P_3$ **84.** $5 \cdot {}_{n-1}P_1 = {}_nP_2$

Conclusions

True or False?   **In Exercises 85 and 86, determine whether the statement is true or false. Justify your answer.**

85. The number of pairs of letters that can be formed from any of the first 13 letters in the alphabet (A–M), where repetitions are allowed, is an example of a permutation.

86. The number of permutations of n elements can be derived by using the Fundamental Counting Principle.

87. Think About It   Can your calculator evaluate ${}_{100}P_{80}$? If not, explain why.

88. Think About It   Decide whether each scenario should be counted using permutations or combinations. Explain your reasoning. (Do not calculate.)

(a) Number of ways 10 people can line up in a row for concert tickets

(b) Number of different arrangements of three types of flowers from an array of 20 types

89. Writing   Explain in your own words the meaning of ${}_nP_r$.

90.   **HOW DO YOU SEE IT?**   Without calculating, determine whether the value of ${}_nP_r$ is greater than the value of ${}_nC_r$ for the values of n and r given in the table. Complete the table using yes (Y) or no (N). Is the value of ${}_nP_r$ always greater than the value of ${}_nC_r$? Explain.

n \ r	0	1	2	3	4	5
1						
2						
3						
4						
5						

Proof   **In Exercises 91–94, prove the identity.**

91. $ {}_nP_{n-1} = {}_nP_n$ **92.** $ {}_nC_n = {}_nC_0$

93. $ {}_nC_{n-1} = {}_nC_1$ **94.** $ {}_nC_r = \dfrac{{}_nP_r}{r!}$

Cumulative Mixed Review

Using Cramer's Rule   **In Exercises 95 and 96, use Cramer's Rule to solve the system of equations.**

95. $\begin{cases} -5x + 3y = -14 \\ 7x - 2y = 2 \end{cases}$ **96.** $\begin{cases} -3x - 4y = -1 \\ 9x + 5y = -4 \end{cases}$

8.6   Probability

The Probability of an Event

Any happening whose result is uncertain is called an **experiment.** The possible results of the experiment are **outcomes,** the set of all possible outcomes of the experiment is the **sample space** of the experiment, and any subcollection of a sample space is an **event.**

For instance, when a six-sided die is tossed, the sample space can be represented by the numbers 1 through 6. For the experiment to be fair, each of the outcomes must be *equally likely.*

To describe a sample space in such a way that each outcome is equally likely, you must sometimes distinguish between or among various outcomes in ways that appear artificial. Example 1 illustrates such a situation.

What you should learn
▶ Find probabilities of events.
▶ Find probabilities of mutually exclusive events.
▶ Find probabilities of independent events.

Why you should learn it
You can use probability to solve a variety of problems that occur in real life. For instance, in Exercise 58 on page 623, you are asked to use probability to help analyze the age distribution of unemployed workers.

EXAMPLE 1   Finding the Sample Space

Find the sample space for each experiment.

a. One coin is tossed.

b. Two coins are tossed.

c. Three coins are tossed.

Solution

a. Because the coin will land either heads up (denoted by H) or tails up (denoted by T), the sample space is $S = \{H, T\}$.

b. Because either coin can land heads up or tails up, the possible outcomes are as follows.

HH = heads up on both coins

HT = heads up on first coin and tails up on second coin

TH = tails up on first coin and heads up on second coin

TT = tails up on both coins

So, the sample space is $S = \{HH, HT, TH, TT\}$.

Note that this list distinguishes between the two cases

HT and TH

even though these two outcomes appear to be similar.

c. Following the notation in part (b), the sample space is

$S = \{HHH, HHT, HTH, HTT, THH, THT, TTH, TTT\}$.

Note that this list distinguishes among the cases

HHT, HTH,   and THH

and among the cases

HTT, THT,   and TTH.

✓ **Checkpoint** 🔊))) *Audio-video solution in English & Spanish at LarsonPrecalculus.com.*

Find the sample space for the following experiment.

You toss a coin twice and a six-sided die once.

To calculate the probability of an event, count the number of outcomes in the event and in the sample space. The *number of equally likely outcomes* in event E is denoted by $n(E)$, and the number of equally likely outcomes in the sample space S is denoted by $n(S)$. The probability that event E will occur is given by $n(E)/n(S)$.

The Probability of an Event

If an event E has $n(E)$ equally likely outcomes and its sample space S has $n(S)$ equally likely outcomes, then the **probability** of event E is given by

$$P(E) = \frac{n(E)}{n(S)}.$$

Because the number of outcomes in an event must be less than or equal to the number of outcomes in the sample space, the probability of an event must be a number from 0 to 1, inclusive. That is,

$$0 \le P(E) \le 1$$

as shown in the figure. If $P(E) = 0$, then event E *cannot occur,* and E is called an **impossible event.** If $P(E) = 1$, then event E *must occur,* and E is called a **certain event.**

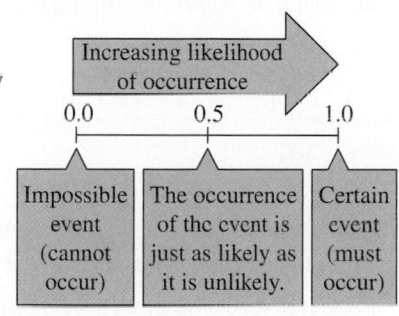

Explore the Concept
Toss two coins 40 times and write down the number of heads that occur on each toss (0, 1, or 2). How many times did two heads occur? Without performing the experiment, how many times would you expect two heads to occur when two coins are tossed 1000 times?

EXAMPLE 2   Finding the Probability of an Event

See LarsonPrecalculus.com for an interactive version of this type of example.

a. Two coins are tossed. What is the probability that both land heads up?

b. A card is drawn at random from a standard deck of playing cards. What is the probability that it is an ace?

Solution

a. Following the procedure in Example 1(b), let

$$E = \{HH\} \quad \text{and} \quad S = \{HH, HT, TH, TT\}.$$

The probability of getting two heads is

$$P(E) = \frac{n(E)}{n(S)} = \frac{1}{4}.$$

b. Because there are 52 cards in a standard deck of playing cards and there are four aces (one of each suit), the probability of drawing an ace is

$$P(E) = \frac{n(E)}{n(S)} = \frac{4}{52} = \frac{1}{13}.$$

✓ Checkpoint *Audio-video solution in English & Spanish at LarsonPrecalculus.com.*

a. You toss three coins. What is the probability that all three land tails up?

b. You draw one card at random from a standard deck of playing cards. What is the probability that it is a diamond? ◼

You could have written out the sample space in Example 2(b) and simply counted the outcomes in the desired event. For larger sample spaces, however, using the counting principles discussed in Section 8.5 should save you time.

Remark

Note that a probability can be written as a fraction, a decimal, or a percent. For instance, in Example 2(a), the probability of getting two heads can be written as $\frac{1}{4}$, 0.25, or 25%.

EXAMPLE 3   Finding the Probability of an Event

Twelve-sided dice, as shown in the figure at the right, can be constructed (in the shape of regular dodecahedrons) such that each of the numbers from 1 to 6 appears twice on each die. Show that these dice can be used in any game requiring ordinary six-sided dice without changing the probabilities of the various events.

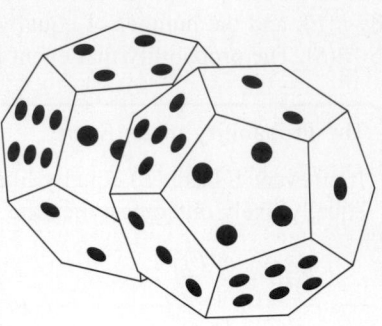

Solution

For an ordinary six-sided die, each of the numbers 1, 2, 3, 4, 5, and 6 occurs only once, so the probability of rolling any particular number is

$$P(E) = \frac{n(E)}{n(S)} = \frac{1}{6}.$$

For a 12-sided die, each number occurs twice, so the probability of rolling any particular number is

$$P(E) = \frac{n(E)}{n(S)} = \frac{2}{12} = \frac{1}{6}.$$

✓ **Checkpoint** Audio-video solution in English & Spanish at LarsonPrecalculus.com.

Show that the probability of drawing a club at random from a standard deck of playing cards is the same as the probability of drawing the ace of hearts at random from a set consisting of the aces of hearts, diamonds, clubs, and spades.

EXAMPLE 4   Random Selection

The numbers of colleges and universities in various regions of the United States in 2012 are shown in the figure. One institution is selected at random. What is the probability that the institution is in one of the three southern regions?   (Source: U.S. National Center for Education Statistics)

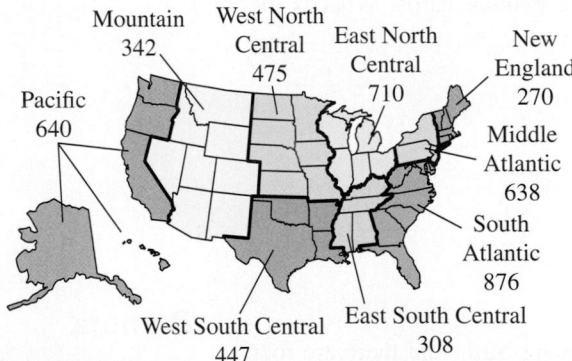

Solution

From the figure, the total number of colleges and universities is 4706. Because there are

$$447 + 308 + 876 = 1631$$

colleges and universities in the three southern regions, the probability that the institution is in one of these regions is

$$P(E) = \frac{n(E)}{n(S)} = \frac{1631}{4706} \approx 0.347.$$

✓ **Checkpoint** Audio-video solution in English & Spanish at LarsonPrecalculus.com.

In Example 4, what is the probability that the randomly selected institution is in the Pacific region?

Mutually Exclusive Events

Two events A and B (from the same sample space) are **mutually exclusive** when A and B have no outcomes in common. In the terminology of sets, the intersection of A and B is the empty set, which implies that

$$P(A \cap B) = 0.$$

For instance, when two dice are tossed, the event A of rolling a sum of 6 and the event B of rolling a sum of 9 are mutually exclusive. To find the probability that one or the other of two mutually exclusive events will occur, you can *add* their individual probabilities.

Probability of the Union of Two Events

If A and B are events in the same sample space, then the probability of A or B occurring is given by

$$P(A \cup B) = P(A) + P(B) - P(A \cap B).$$

If A and B are mutually exclusive, then

$$P(A \cup B) = P(A) + P(B).$$

EXAMPLE 5   The Probability of a Union

One card is selected at random from a standard deck of 52 playing cards. What is the probability that the card is either a heart or a face card?

Solution

Because the deck has 13 hearts, the probability of selecting a heart (event A) is

$$P(A) = \frac{13}{52}.$$

Similarly, because the deck has 12 face cards, the probability of selecting a face card (event B) is

$$P(B) = \frac{12}{52}.$$

Because three of the cards are hearts and face cards (see Figure 8.1), it follows that

$$P(A \cap B) = \frac{3}{52}.$$

Finally, applying the formula for the probability of the union of two events, you can conclude that the probability of selecting either a heart or a face card is

$$P(A \cup B) = P(A) + P(B) - P(A \cap B)$$

$$= \frac{13}{52} + \frac{12}{52} - \frac{3}{52}$$

$$= \frac{22}{52}$$

$$\approx 0.423.$$

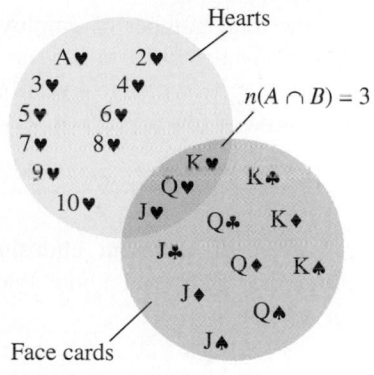

Figure 8.1

✓ **Checkpoint** 🔊 *Audio-video solution in English & Spanish at LarsonPrecalculus.com.*

You draw one card at random from a standard deck of 52 playing cards. What is the probability that the card is either an ace or a spade?

Human Resources Manager

EXAMPLE 6   Probability of Mutually Exclusive Events

The human resources department of a company has compiled data on the numbers of employees who have been with the company for various periods of time. The results are shown in the table.

DATA	Years of service	Number of employees
	0–4	157
	5–9	89
	10–14	74
	15–19	63
	20–24	42
	25–29	38
	30–34	37
	35–39	21
	40–44	8

Spreadsheet at LarsonPrecalculus.com

An employee is chosen at random. What is the probability that the employee has

a. 4 or fewer years of service?

b. 9 or fewer years of service?

Solution

a. To begin, add the numbers of employees.

$$157 + 89 + 74 + 63 + 42 + 38 + 37 + 21 + 8 = 529$$

So, the total number of employees is 529. Next, let event A represent choosing an employee with 0 to 4 years of service. From the table, you know there are 157 employees with 0 to 4 years of service. The probability of choosing an employee who has 4 or fewer years of service is

$$P(A) = \frac{157}{529} \approx 0.297.$$

b. Let event B represent choosing an employee with 5 to 9 years of service. From the table, you know that there are 89 employees with 5 to 9 years of service. Then

$$P(B) = \frac{89}{529}.$$

Because event A from part (a) and event B have no outcomes in common, you can conclude that these two events are mutually exclusive and that

$$P(A \cup B) = P(A) + P(B)$$

$$= \frac{157}{529} + \frac{89}{529}$$

$$= \frac{246}{529}$$

$$\approx 0.465.$$

So, the probability of choosing an employee who has 9 or fewer years of service is about 0.465.

✓ **Checkpoint** Audio-video solution in English & Spanish at LarsonPrecalculus.com.

In Example 6, what is the probability that an employee chosen at random has 30 or more years of service? ◼

Independent Events

Two events are **independent** when the occurrence of one has no effect on the occurrence of the other. For instance, rolling a total of 12 with two six-sided dice has no effect on the outcome of future rolls of the dice. To find the probability that two independent events will occur, *multiply* the probabilities of each.

Probability of Independent Events

If A and B are **independent events,** then the probability that both A and B will occur is given by

$$P(A \text{ and } B) = P(A) \cdot P(B).$$

This rule can be extended to any number of independent events.

EXAMPLE 7   Probability of Independent Events

A random number generator on a computer selects three integers from 1 to 20. What is the probability that all three numbers are less than or equal to 5?

Solution

The probability of selecting a number from 1 to 5 is

$$P(A) = \frac{5}{20} = \frac{1}{4}.$$

So, the probability that all three numbers are less than or equal to 5 is

$$P(A) \cdot P(A) \cdot P(A) = \left(\frac{1}{4}\right)\left(\frac{1}{4}\right)\left(\frac{1}{4}\right) = \frac{1}{64}.$$

✓ **Checkpoint** ◀))) *Audio-video solution in English & Spanish at LarsonPrecalculus.com.*

A random number generator on a computer selects two integers from 1 to 30. What is the probability that both numbers are less than 12?

EXAMPLE 8   Probability of Independent Events

In 2014, approximately 44% of the adult population in the United States said their cell phone would be very hard to give up. In a survey, 10 people were chosen at random from the adult population. What is the probability that all 10 say their cell phone would be very hard to give up?   (Source: Pew Research Center)

Solution

Let A represent choosing an adult who says his or her cell phone would be very hard to give up. The probability of choosing an adult who says his or her cell phone would be very hard to give up is 0.44, the probability of choosing a second adult who says his or her cell phone would be very hard to give up is 0.44, and so on. Because these events are independent, the probability that all 10 people say their cell phone would be very hard to give up is

$$[P(A)]^{10} = (0.44)^{10} \approx 0.000272.$$

✓ **Checkpoint** ◀))) *Audio-video solution in English & Spanish at LarsonPrecalculus.com.*

In 2014, approximately 35% of the adult population in the United States said their television would be very hard to give up. In a survey, eight people were chosen at random from the adult population. What is the probability that all eight say their television would be very hard to give up?   (Source: Pew Research Center)   ■

8.6   Exercises

Vocabulary and Concept Check

In Exercises 1–4, fill in the blank(s).

1. The set of all possible outcomes of an experiment is called the _____ .

2. To determine the probability of an event, use the formula $P(E) = \dfrac{n(E)}{n(S)}$, where

   $n(E)$ is _____ and $n(S)$ is _____ .

3. If two events from the same sample space have no outcomes in common, then the two events are _____ .

4. If the occurrence of one event has no effect on the occurrence of a second event, then the events are _____ .

5. Write an inequality that represents the possible values of the probability $P(E)$ of an event.

6. What is the probability of an impossible event?

7. What is the probability of a certain event?

8. Match the probability formula with the correct probability name.

   (a) Probability of the union of two events   (i) $P(A \cup B) = P(A) + P(B)$

   (b) Probability of mutually exclusive events   (ii) $P(A \cup B) = P(A) + P(B) - P(A \cap B)$

   (c) Probability of independent events   (iii) $P(A \text{ and } B) = P(A) \cdot P(B)$

Procedures and Problem Solving

Finding the Sample Space   In Exercises 9–12, determine the sample space for the experiment.

9. A coin and a six-sided die are tossed.

10. A six-sided die is tossed twice and the results of roll 1 and roll 2 are recorded.

11. A taste tester has to rank three varieties of orange juice, A, B, and C, according to preference.

12. Two county supervisors are selected from five supervisors, A, B, C, D, and E, to study a recycling plan.

Finding the Probability of an Event   In Exercises 13–16, find the probability for the experiment of tossing a coin three times. Use the sample space

$S = \{HHH, HHT, HTH, HTT, THH, THT, TTH, TTT\}.$

13. The probability of getting exactly two tails

14. The probability of getting a head on the first toss

15. The probability of getting at least one head

16. The probability of getting at least two heads

Finding the Probability of an Event   In Exercises 17–20, find the probability for the experiment of selecting one card at random from a standard deck of 52 playing cards.

17. The card is a face card.   **18.** The card is a black card.

19. The card is a red face card.

20. The card is a numbered card (2–10).

Finding the Probability of an Event   In Exercises 21–24, use the sample space from Exercise 10 to find the probability for the experiment of tossing a six-sided die twice.

21. The sum is 6.   **22.** The sum is at least 8.

23. The sum is less than 5.

24. The sum is odd or prime.

Random Selection   In Exercises 25–28, one of a team's 2200 season ticket holders is selected at random to win a prize. The circle graph shows the ages of the season ticket holders. Find the probability of the event.

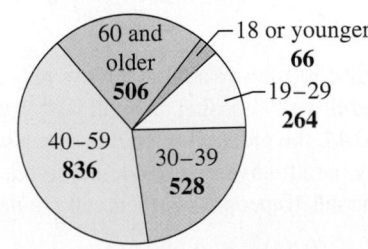

Ages of Season Ticket Holders

25. The winner is younger than 19 years old.

26. The winner is older than 39 years old.

27. The winner is 19 to 39 years old.

28. The winner is younger than 19 years old or older than 59 years old.

Using Combinations In Exercises 29–32, find the probability for the experiment of drawing two marbles at random (without replacement) from a bag containing one green, two yellow, and three red marbles. (*Hint:* Use combinations to find the numbers of outcomes for the given event and sample space.)

29. Both marbles are red.

30. Both marbles are yellow.

31. Neither marble is yellow.

32. The marbles are of different colors.

Finding the Probability of a Complement The *complement of an event A* is the collection of all outcomes in the sample space that are *not* in *A*. If the probability of *A* is $P(A)$, then the probability of the complement A' is given by $P(A') = 1 - P(A)$. In Exercises 33–36, you are given the probability that an event *will* happen. Find the probability that the event *will not* happen.

33. $P(E) = 0.75$ 34. $P(E) = 0.36$

35. $P(E) = \frac{2}{3}$ 36. $P(E) = \frac{7}{8}$

Using the Probability of a Complement In Exercises 37–40, you are given the probability that an event *will not* happen. Find the probability that the event *will* happen.

37. $P(E') = 0.12$ 38. $P(E') = 0.84$

39. $P(E') = \frac{13}{20}$ 40. $P(E') = \frac{61}{100}$

The Probability of a Union In Exercises 41–44, one card is selected at random from a standard deck of 52 playing cards. Use a formula to find the probability of the union of the two events.

41. The card is a club or a king.

42. The card is a face card or a black card.

43. The card is a 5 or a 2.

44. The card is a heart or a spade.

Probability of Mutually Exclusive Events In Exercises 45–50, use the table, which shows the age groups of students in a college sociology class.

Age	Number of students
18–19	11
20–21	18
22–30	2
31–40	1

A student from the class is randomly chosen for a project. Find the probability that the student is the given age.

45. 18 or 19 years old

46. 22 to 30 years old

47. 20 to 30 years old

48. 18 to 21 years old

49. Older than 21 years old

50. Younger than 31 years old

Probability of Independent Events In Exercises 51–56, a random number generator selects three numbers from 1 through 10. Find the probability of the event.

51. All three numbers are even.

52. All three numbers are a factor of 8.

53. All three numbers are less than or equal to 3.

54. All three numbers are greater than or equal to 9.

55. Two numbers are less than 5 and the other number is 10.

56. One number is 2, 4, or 6, and the other two numbers are odd.

57. **Political Science** Taylor, Moore, and Perez are candidates for public office. It is estimated that Moore and Perez have about the same probability of winning, and Taylor is believed to be twice as likely to win as either of the others. Find the probability of each candidate's winning the election.

58. **Why you should learn it** (*p. 616*) In 2013, there were 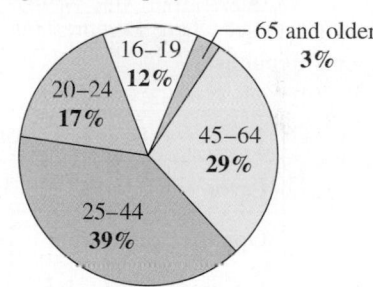 approximately 11.46 million unemployed workers in the United States. The circle graph shows the age profile of these unemployed workers. (Source: U.S. Bureau of Labor Statistics)

Ages of Unemployed Workers

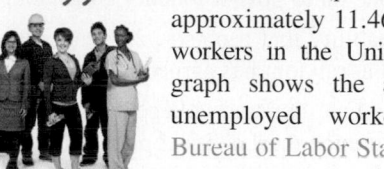

(a) Estimate the number of unemployed workers in the 16–19 age group.

(b) Estimate the number of unemployed workers who are 45 years or older.

(c) What is the probability that a person selected at random from the population of unemployed workers is in the 25–44 age group?

(d) What is the probability that a person selected at random from the population of unemployed workers is 25 to 64 years old?

(e) What is the probability that a person selected at random from the population of unemployed workers is 45 or older?

59. Education The levels of educational attainment of the United States population age 25 years or older in 2013 are shown in the circle graph. Use the fact that the population of people 25 years or older was 206.9 million in 2013.   (Source: U.S. Census Bureau)

Educational Attainment

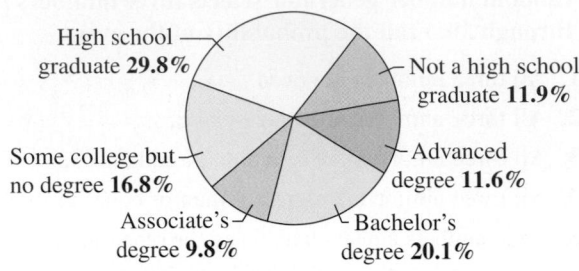

(a) Estimate the number of people 25 years old or older who have advanced degrees.

(b) Find the probability that a person 25 years old or older selected at random has earned a Bachelor's degree or higher.

(c) Find the probability that a person 25 years old or older selected at random has earned a high school diploma or gone on to post-secondary education.

(d) Find the probability that a person 25 years old or older selected at random has earned a degree.

60. Political Science One hundred college students were interviewed to determine their political party affiliations and whether they favored a balanced budget amendment to the U.S. Constitution. The results of the study are listed in the table, where D represents Democrat and R represents Republican.

	D	R	Total
Favor	23	32	55
Oppose	25	9	34
Unsure	7	4	11
Total	55	45	100

A person is selected at random from the sample. Find the probability that the person selected is (a) a person who does not favor the amendment, (b) a Republican, and (c) a Democrat who favors the amendment.

In Exercises 61–64, the sample spaces are large and you should use the counting principles discussed in Section 8.5.

61. Using Counting Principles On a game show, you are given five digits to arrange in the proper order to form the price of a car. If you are correct, you win the car. What is the probability of winning when you (a) randomly guess the position of each digit and (b) know the first digit and randomly guess the others?

62. Using Counting Principles The deck for a card game is made up of 108 cards. Twenty-five each are red, yellow, blue, and green, and eight are wild cards. Each player is randomly dealt a seven-card hand. What is the probability that a hand will contain (a) exactly two wild cards, and (b) two wild cards, two red cards, and three blue cards?

63. Using Counting Principles A shipment of 12 microwave ovens contains three defective units. A vending company has ordered four of these units, and because all are packaged identically, the selection will be random. What is the probability that (a) all four units are good, (b) exactly two units are good, and (c) at least two units are good?

64. Using Counting Principles Two integers from 1 through 40 are chosen by a random number generator. What is the probability that (a) the numbers are both even, (b) one number is even and one is odd, (c) both numbers are less than 30, and (d) the same number is chosen twice?

65. Marketing The circle graph shows the methods used by shoppers to pay for merchandise. Two shoppers are chosen at random. What is the probability that (a) both shoppers paid for their purchases only in cash, (b) at least one shopper paid only in cash, and (c) neither shopper paid only in cash?

How Shoppers Pay for Merchandise

66. Aerospace Engineering A space vehicle has an independent backup system for one of its communication networks. The probability that either system will function satisfactorily for the duration of a flight is 0.985. What is the probability that during a given flight (a) both systems function satisfactorily, (b) at least one system functions satisfactorily, and (c) both systems fail?

67. Marketing A sales representative makes sales on approximately one-fifth of all calls. On a given day, the representative contacts six potential clients. What is the probability that a sale will be made with (a) all six contacts, (b) none of the contacts, and (c) at least one contact?

68. Genetics Assume that the probability of the birth of a child of a particular sex is 50%. In a family with four children, what is the probability that (a) all the children are boys, (b) all the children are the same sex, and (c) there is at least one boy?

69. Estimating π A coin of diameter d is randomly dropped onto a paper that contains a grid of squares d units on a side. (See figure.)

(a) Find the probability that the coin covers a vertex of one of the squares on the grid.

(b) Perform the experiment 100 times and use the results to approximate π.

70. Geometry You and a friend agree to meet at your favorite fast food restaurant between 5:00 and 6:00 P.M. The one who arrives first will wait 15 minutes for the other, after which the first person will leave (see figure). What is the probability that the two of you will actually meet, assuming that your arrival times are random within the hour?

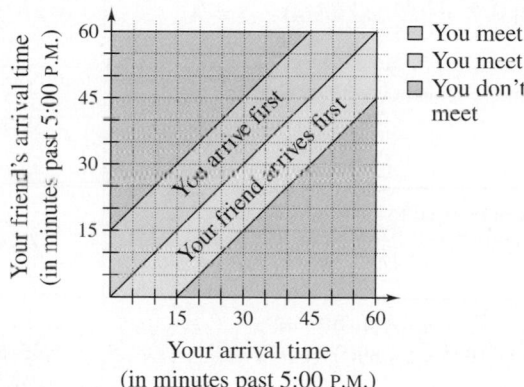

Your arrival time
(in minutes past 5:00 P.M.)

Conclusions

True or False? In Exercises 71 and 72, determine whether the statement is true or false. Justify your answer.

71. If the probability of an outcome in a sample space is 1, then the probability of the other outcomes in the sample space is 0.

72. If A and B are independent events with nonzero probabilities, then A can occur when B occurs.

73. Exploration Consider a group of n people.

(a) Explain why the following pattern gives the probability that the n people have distinct birthdays.

$$n = 2: \quad \frac{365}{365} \cdot \frac{364}{365} = \frac{365 \cdot 364}{365^2}$$

$$n = 3: \quad \frac{365}{365} \cdot \frac{364}{365} \cdot \frac{363}{365} = \frac{365 \cdot 364 \cdot 363}{365^3}$$

(b) Use the pattern in part (a) to write an expression for the probability that four people $(n = 4)$ have distinct birthdays.

(c) Let P_n be the probability that the n people have distinct birthdays. Verify that this probability can be obtained recursively by

$$P_1 = 1 \quad \text{and} \quad P_n = \frac{365 - (n - 1)}{365} P_{n-1}.$$

(d) Explain why $Q_n = 1 - P_n$ gives the probability that at least two people in a group of n people have the same birthday.

(e) Use the results of parts (c) and (d) to complete the table.

n	10	15	20	23	30	40	50
P_n							
Q_n							

(f) How many people must be in a group so that the probability of at least two of them having the same birthday is greater than $\frac{1}{2}$? Explain.

74. Writing Write a paragraph describing in your own words the difference between mutually exclusive events and independent events.

75. Think About It Let A and B be two events from the same sample space such that $P(A) = 0.76$ and $P(B) = 0.58$.

(a) Is it possible that A and B are mutually exclusive? Explain. Draw a diagram to support your answer.

(b) Is it possible that A' and B' are mutually exclusive? Explain. Draw a diagram to support your answer.

(c) Determine the possible range of $P(A \cup B)$.

76. HOW DO YOU SEE IT? Use the figure to determine whether events A and B are mutually exclusive. Explain your reasoning.

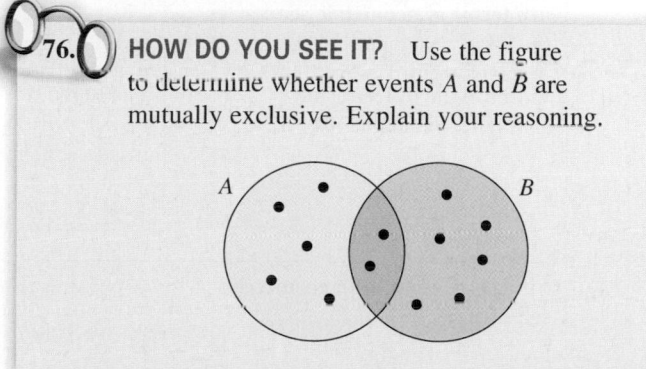

Cumulative Mixed Review

Evaluating a Combination In Exercises 77–80, evaluate $_nC_r$. Verify your result using a graphing utility.

77. $_8C_4$

78. $_9C_5$

79. $_{11}C_8$

80. $_{16}C_{13}$

8   Chapter Summary

	What did you learn?	Explanation and Examples	Review Exercises
8.1	Use sequence notation to write the terms of sequences (*p. 570*).	$a_n = 7n - 4$; $a_1 = 7(1) - 4 = 3$, $a_2 = 7(2) - 4 = 10$, $a_3 = 7(3) - 4 = 17$, $a_4 = 7(4) - 4 = 24$	1–8
	Use factorial notation (*p. 573*).	If n is a positive integer, then $n! = 1 \cdot 2 \cdot 3 \cdot 4 \cdots (n - 1) \cdot n$.	9–12
	Use summation notation to write sums (*p. 574*).	The sum of the first n terms of a sequence is represented by $$\sum_{i=1}^{n} a_i = a_1 + a_2 + a_3 + a_4 + \cdots + a_n.$$	13–20
	Find sums of infinite series (*p. 575*).	$$\sum_{i=1}^{\infty} \frac{5}{10^i} = \frac{5}{10^1} + \frac{5}{10^2} + \frac{5}{10^3} + \frac{5}{10^4} + \frac{5}{10^5} + \cdots$$ $$= 0.5 + 0.05 + 0.005 + 0.0005 + 0.00005 + \cdots$$ $$= 0.55555\ldots$$ $$= \tfrac{5}{9}$$	21–24
	Use sequences and series to model and solve real-life problems (*p. 576*).	A sequence can be used to model the balance in an account that earns compound interest. (See Example 10.)	25, 26
8.2	Recognize, write, and find the *n*th terms of arithmetic sequences (*p. 581*).	$a_n = 9n + 5$; $a_1 = 9(1) + 5 = 14$, $a_2 = 9(2) + 5 = 23$, $a_3 = 9(3) + 5 = 32$, $a_4 = 9(4) + 5 = 41$	27–38
	Find *n*th partial sums of arithmetic sequences (*p. 584*).	The sum of a finite arithmetic sequence with n terms is $$S_n = \frac{n}{2}(a_1 + a_n).$$	39–42
	Use arithmetic sequences to model and solve real-life problems (*p. 585*).	An arithmetic sequence can be used to find the total sales of a small business. (See Example 7.)	43, 44
8.3	Recognize, write, and find the *n*th terms of geometric sequences (*p. 589*).	$a_n = 3(4^n)$; $a_1 = 3(4^1) = 12$, $a_2 = 3(4^2) = 48$, $a_3 = 3(4^3) = 192$, $a_4 = 3(4^4) = 768$	45–56
	Find *n*th partial sums of geometric sequences (*p. 592*).	The sum of the finite geometric sequence $a_1, a_1 r, a_1 r^2, \ldots, a_1 r^{n-1}$ with common ratio $r \neq 1$ is given by $$S_n = \sum_{i=1}^{n} a_1 r^{i-1} = a_1 \left(\frac{1 - r^n}{1 - r} \right).$$	57–60
	Find sums of infinite geometric series (*p. 593*).	If $|r| < 1$, then the infinite geometric series $$a_1 + a_1 r + a_1 r^2 + \cdots + a_1 r^{n-1} + \cdots$$ has the sum $$S = \sum_{i=0}^{\infty} a_1 r^i = \frac{a_1}{1 - r}.$$	61–64
	Use geometric sequences to model and solve real-life problems (*p. 594*).	A finite geometric sequence can be used to find the balance in an annuity at the end of 2 years. (See Example 8.)	65, 66

What did you learn?	Explanation and Examples	Review Exercises
8.4 **Use the Binomial Theorem to calculate binomial coefficients** *(p. 599).*	**The Binomial Theorem:** In the expansion of $(x + y)^n = x^n + nx^{n-1}y + \cdots + {}_nC_r x^{n-r}y^r + \cdots + nxy^{n-1} + y^n$, the coefficient of $x^{n-r}y^r$ is $${}_nC_r = \frac{n!}{(n-r)!r!}.$$	67–70
Use binomial coefficients to write binomial expansions *(p. 601).*	$(x + 1)^3 = x^3 + 3x^2 + 3x + 1$ $(x - 1)^4 = x^4 - 4x^3 + 6x^2 - 4x + 1$	71–74
Use Pascal's Triangle to calculate binomial coefficients *(p. 603).*	First several rows of Pascal's triangle: 1 1 1 1 2 1 1 3 3 1 1 4 6 4 1	75–78
8.5 **Solve simple counting problems** *(p. 607).*	A computer randomly generates an integer from 1 through 15. The computer can generate an integer that is divisible by 3 in five ways (3, 6, 9, 12, and 15).	79, 80
Use the Fundamental Counting Principle to solve more complicated counting problems *(p. 608).*	**Fundamental Counting Principle:** Let E_1 and E_2 be two events. The first event E_1 can occur in m_1 different ways. After E_1 has occurred, E_2 can occur in m_2 different ways. The number of ways that the two events can occur is $m_1 \cdot m_2$.	81, 82
Use permutations to solve counting problems *(p. 609).*	A permutation of n different elements is an ordering of the elements such that one element is first, one is second, one is third, and so on. The number of permutations of n elements is given by $$n \cdot (n - 1) \cdots 4 \cdot 3 \cdot 2 \cdot 1 = n!.$$ In other words, there are $n!$ different ways that n elements can be ordered. The number of permutations of n elements taken r at a time is $${}_nP_r = \frac{n!}{(n-r)!}.$$	83–88, 91
Use combinations to solve counting problems *(p. 612).*	The number of combinations of n elements taken r at a time is $${}_nC_r = \frac{n!}{(n-r)!r!}.$$	89, 90, 92
8.6 **Find probabilities of events** *(p. 616).*	If an event E has $n(E)$ equally likely outcomes and its sample space S has $n(S)$ equally likely outcomes, then the probability of event E is $$P(E) = \frac{n(E)}{n(S)}.$$	93, 94
Find probabilities of mutually exclusive events *(p. 619).*	If A and B are events in the same sample space, then the probability of A *or* B occurring is $$P(A \cup B) = P(A) + P(B) - P(A \cap B).$$ If A and B are mutually exclusive, then $$P(A \cup B) = P(A) + P(B).$$	95
Find probabilities of independent events *(p. 621).*	If A and B are independent events, then the probability that both A and B will occur is $P(A \text{ and } B) = P(A) \cdot P(B)$.	96

8.1

Writing the Terms of a Sequence In Exercises 1 and 2, write the first five terms of the sequence. (Assume n begins with 1.)

1. $a_n = \dfrac{2^n}{2^n + 1}$

2. $a_n = \dfrac{(-1)^n 5n}{2n - 1}$

Finding the nth Term of a Sequence In Exercises 3–6, write an expression for the apparent nth term of the sequence. (Assume n begins with 1.)

3. 7, 12, 17, 22, 27, . . .

4. 50, 48, 46, 44, 42, . . .

5. $2, \frac{2}{3}, \frac{2}{5}, \frac{2}{7}, \frac{2}{9}, \ldots$

6. $\frac{3}{2}, \frac{4}{3}, \frac{5}{4}, \frac{6}{5}, \frac{7}{6}, \ldots$

A Recursive Sequence In Exercises 7 and 8, write the first five terms of the sequence defined recursively.

7. $a_1 = 9, \; a_{k+1} = \frac{1}{3}a_k$

8. $a_1 = 49, \; a_{k+1} = a_k + 6$

Simplifying Factorial Expressions In Exercises 9–12, simplify the factorial expression.

9. $\dfrac{18!}{20!}$

10. $\dfrac{10!}{8!}$

11. $\dfrac{(n+1)!}{(n-1)!}$

12. $\dfrac{2n!}{(n+1)!}$

Sigma Notation for Sums In Exercises 13–16, find the sum.

13. $\displaystyle\sum_{i=1}^{6} 5$

14. $\displaystyle\sum_{k=2}^{5} 4k$

15. $\displaystyle\sum_{j=1}^{4} \frac{6}{j^2}$

16. $\displaystyle\sum_{i=1}^{8} \frac{i}{i+1}$

Writing a Sum Using Sigma Notation In Exercises 17–20, use sigma notation to write the sum. Then use a graphing utility to find the sum.

17. $\dfrac{1}{2(1)} + \dfrac{1}{2(2)} + \dfrac{1}{2(3)} + \cdots + \dfrac{1}{2(20)}$

18. $3(1^2) + 3(2^2) + 3(3^2) + \cdots + 3(9^2)$

19. $\dfrac{1}{2} + \dfrac{2}{3} + \dfrac{3}{4} + \cdots + \dfrac{9}{10}$

20. $1 - \dfrac{1}{3} + \dfrac{1}{9} - \dfrac{1}{27} + \cdots$

Finding the Sum of a Series In Exercises 21–24, find (a) the fourth partial sum and (b) the sum of the infinite series.

21. $\displaystyle\sum_{j=1}^{\infty} \frac{8}{10^j}$

22. $\displaystyle\sum_{j=1}^{\infty} \frac{3}{100^j}$

23. $\displaystyle\sum_{k=1}^{\infty} 4(0.01)^k$

24. $\displaystyle\sum_{k=1}^{\infty} 2(0.1)^k$

25. Compound Interest A deposit of \$3000 is made in an account that earns 2% interest compounded quarterly. The balance in the account after n quarters is given by

$$a_n = 3000\left(1 + \frac{0.02}{4}\right)^n; \quad n = 1, 2, 3, \ldots$$

(a) Compute the first eight terms of this sequence.

(b) Find the balance in this account after 10 years by computing the 40th term of the sequence.

26. Education The average salaries a_n (in thousands of dollars) of college faculty members in the United States from 2001 through 2012 can be approximated by the model

$$a_n = -0.028n^2 + 2.31n + 56.7; \quad n = 1, 2, 3, \ldots, 12$$

where n is the year, with $n = 1$ corresponding to 2001. (Source: American Association of University Professors)

(a) Find the terms of this finite sequence for the given values of n.

(b) Use a graphing utility to graph the sequence for the given values of n.

(c) Use the sequence to predict the average salaries of college faculty members for the years 2013 through 2019. Do your results seem reasonable? Explain.

8.2

Identifying an Arithmetic Sequence In Exercises 27–30, determine whether or not the sequence is arithmetic. If it is, find the common difference.

27. $5, 3, 1, -1, -3, \ldots$

28. $0, 1, 3, 6, 10, \ldots$

29. $\frac{1}{4}, \frac{1}{8}, \frac{1}{16}, \frac{1}{32}, \ldots$

30. $\frac{9}{9}, \frac{8}{9}, \frac{7}{9}, \frac{6}{9}, \frac{5}{9}, \ldots$

Writing the Terms of an Arithmetic Sequence In Exercises 31–34, write the first five terms of the arithmetic sequence. Use the *table* feature of a graphing utility to verify your results.

31. $a_1 = 3, \quad d = 4$

32. $a_1 = 8, \quad d = -2$

33. $a_4 = 10, \quad a_{10} = 28$

34. $a_2 = 14, \quad a_6 = 22$

Writing the Terms of an Arithmetic Sequence In Exercises 35 and 36, write the first five terms of the arithmetic sequence. Find the common difference and write the nth term of the sequence as a function of n.

35. $a_1 = 35, \quad a_{k+1} = a_k - 3$

36. $a_1 = 15, \quad a_{k+1} = a_k + \frac{5}{2}$

Finding the nth Term of an Arithmetic Sequence In Exercises 37 and 38, find a formula for a_n for the arithmetic sequence and find the sum of the first 25 terms of the sequence.

37. $a_1 = 100, \quad d = -3$ 38. $a_1 = 10, \quad a_3 = 28$

Finding the Sum of a Finite Arithmetic Sequence In Exercises 39–42, find the sum of the finite arithmetic sequence. Use a graphing utility to verify your result.

39. $\sum_{j=1}^{11} (2.5j - 5)$ 40. $\sum_{k=1}^{11} \left(\frac{2}{3}k + 4\right)$

41. Sum of the first 50 positive multiples of 5

42. Sum of the integers from 10 to 70

43. **Accounting** The starting salary for an accountant is $53,300 with a guaranteed salary increase of $1066 per year. Determine (a) the salary during the fifth year and (b) the total compensation through 5 full years of employment.

44. **Agriculture** In his first trip around a field, a farmer makes 123 bales. In his second trip, he makes 11 fewer bales. Because each trip is shorter than the preceding trip, the farmer estimates that the same pattern will continue. Estimate the total number of bales made when there are another five trips around the field.

8.3

Identifying a Geometric Sequence In Exercises 45–48, determine whether or not the sequence is geometric. If it is, find the common ratio.

45. $5, 10, 20, 40, \ldots$

46. $54, -18, 6, -2, \ldots$

47. $\frac{1}{2}, \frac{2}{3}, \frac{3}{4}, \frac{4}{5}, \ldots$

48. $\frac{1}{3}, \frac{2}{3}, 1, \frac{4}{3}, \ldots$

Writing the Terms of a Geometric Sequence In Exercises 49–52, write the first five terms of the geometric sequence.

49. $a_1 = 4, \quad r = -\frac{1}{4}$ 50. $a_1 = 2, \quad r = \frac{3}{2}$

51. $a_1 = 9, \quad a_2 = 6$ 52. $a_1 = 2, \quad a_2 = 12$

Finding the nth Term of a Geometric Sequence In Exercises 53 and 54, write the first five terms of the geometric sequence. Find the common ratio and write the nth term of the sequence as a function of n.

53. $a_1 = 120, a_{k+1} = \frac{1}{3}a_k$ 54. $a_1 = 200, a_{k+1} = 0.1a_k$

Finding a Term of a Geometric Sequence In Exercises 55 and 56, find the indicated term of the geometric sequence (a) algebraically and (b) using the *table* feature of a graphing utility.

55. $a_1 = 16, \quad a_2 = -8, \quad$ 6th term

56. $a_3 = 6, \quad a_4 = 1, \quad$ 9th term

Finding the Sum of a Finite Geometric Sequence In Exercises 57–60, find the sum. Use a graphing utility to verify your result.

57. $\sum_{i=1}^{7} 5^{i-1}$ 58. $\sum_{i=1}^{5} 3^{i-1}$

59. $\sum_{n=1}^{7} 3(-4)^{n-1}$ 60. $\sum_{n=1}^{4} 12\left(-\frac{1}{2}\right)^{n-1}$

Finding the Sum of an Infinite Geometric Series In Exercises 61–64, find the sum of the infinite geometric series, if possible. If not possible, explain why.

61. $\sum_{i=1}^{\infty} 4\left(\frac{7}{8}\right)^{i-1}$ 62. $\sum_{i=1}^{\infty} 6\left(\frac{1}{3}\right)^{i-1}$

63. $\sum_{k=1}^{\infty} 4\left(\frac{3}{2}\right)^{k-1}$ 64. $\sum_{k=1}^{\infty} 1.3\left(\frac{1}{10}\right)^{k-1}$

65. **Finance** A company buys a fleet of six vans for $130,000. During the next 5 years, the fleet will depreciate at a rate of 30% per year. (That is, at the end of each year, the depreciated value will be 70% of the value at the beginning of the year.)

 (a) Find the formula for the nth term of a geometric sequence that gives the value of the fleet t full years after it was purchased.

 (b) Find the depreciated value of the fleet at the end of 5 full years.

66. **Finance** A deposit of $80 is made at the beginning of each month in an account that pays 4% interest, compounded monthly. The balance A in the account at the end of 4 years is given by

$$A = 80\left(1 + \frac{0.04}{12}\right)^1 + \cdots + 80\left(1 + \frac{0.04}{12}\right)^{48}.$$

Find A.

8.4

Finding Binomial Coefficients In Exercises 67–70, find the binomial coefficient. Use a graphing utility to verify your result.

67. $_{10}C_8$ 68. $_{12}C_5$

69. $_9C_4$ 70. $_{14}C_{12}$

Expanding a Binomial In Exercises 71–74, use the Binomial Theorem to expand and simplify the expression.

71. $(x + 5)^4$ 72. $(y - 3)^3$

73. $(a - 4b)^5$ 74. $(3x + y)^7$

Using Pascal's Triangle In Exercises 75–78, use Pascal's Triangle to find the binomial coefficient.

75. $_7C_2$ 76. $_9C_7$

77. $_8C_4$ 78. $_{10}C_5$

8.5

79. Probability Slips of paper numbered 1 through 15 are placed in a hat. In how many ways can two numbers be drawn so that the sum of the numbers is 12? Assume the random selection is without replacement.

80. Fundamental Counting Principle A customer can choose one of six speaker systems, one of five DVD players, and one of six flat screen televisions to design a home entertainment system. Determine the number of possible system configurations.

81. Education A college student is preparing a course schedule of four classes for the next semester. The student can choose from the open sections shown in the table.

Course	Sections
Math 100	001–004
Economics 110	001–003
English 105	001–006
Humanities 101	001–003

(a) Find the number of possible schedules that the student can create from the offerings.

(b) Find the number of possible schedules that the student can create from the offerings when two of the Math 100 sections are closed.

(c) Find the number of possible schedules that the student can create from the offerings when two of the Math 100 sections and four of the English 105 sections are closed.

82. Marketing A telemarketing firm is making calls to prospective customers by randomly dialing seven-digit phone numbers within an area code.

(a) Find the number of possible calls that the telemarketer can make.

(b) The telemarketing firm is calling only within exchanges that begin with a "7" or a "6." How many different calls are possible?

Evaluating a Permutation In Exercises 83 and 84, evaluate $_nP_r$ using the formula from Section 8.5. Use a graphing utility to verify your result.

83. $_{12}P_5$

84. $_6P_4$

Distinguishable Permutations In Exercises 85 and 86, find the number of distinguishable permutations of the group of letters.

85. C, A, L, C, U, L, U, S **86.** I, N, T, E, G, R, A, T, E

Solving an Equation In Exercises 87 and 88, solve for n.

87. $_{n+1}P_2 = 4 \cdot {_nP_1}$ **88.** $8 \cdot {_nP_2} = {_{n+1}P_3}$

Evaluating a Combination In Exercises 89 and 90, evaluate $_nC_r$ using the formula from Section 8.5. Use a graphing utility to verify your result.

89. $_8C_6$ **90.** $_{50}C_{48}$

91. Athletics There are 12 bicyclists entered in a race. In how many different orders could the 12 bicyclists finish? (Assume there are no ties.)

92. Athletics From a pool of seven juniors and eleven seniors, four co-captains will be chosen for the football team. How many different combinations are possible if two juniors and two seniors are to be chosen?

8.6

93. Random Selection A man has five pairs of socks (no two pairs are the same color). He randomly selects two socks from a drawer. What is the probability that he gets a matched pair?

94. Library Science A child returns a five-volume set of books to a bookshelf. The child is not able to read and so cannot distinguish one volume from another. What is the probability that the books are shelved in the correct order?

95. Education A sample of college students, faculty members, and administrators were asked whether they favored a proposed increase in the annual activity fee to enhance student life on campus. The results of the study are shown in the table.

	Favor	Oppose	Total
Students	237	163	400
Faculty	37	38	75
Admin.	18	7	25
Total	292	208	500

A person is selected at random from the sample. Find the probability that the person selected is (a) a person who does not favor the proposal, (b) a student, and (c) a faculty member who favors the proposal.

96. Probability A six-sided die is rolled six times. What is the probability that each side appears exactly once?

Conclusions

True or False? In Exercises 97 and 98, determine whether the statement is true or false. Justify your answer.

97. $\dfrac{(n+2)!}{n!} = (n+2)(n+1)$ **98.** $\displaystyle\sum_{j=1}^{6} 3^j = \sum_{j=3}^{8} 3^{j-2}$

99. Writing In your own words, explain what makes a sequence (a) arithmetic and (b) geometric.

Take this test as you would take a test in class. After you are finished, check your work against the answers given in the back of the book.

In Exercises 1–4, write the first five terms of the sequence.

1. $a_n = 3\left(\frac{2}{3}\right)^{n-1}$ (Begin with $n = 1$.)   **2.** $a_1 = 12$ and $a_{k+1} = a_k + 4$

3. $b_n = \dfrac{(-1)^n x^n}{n}$ (Begin with $n = 1$.)

4. $b_n = \dfrac{(-1)^{2n+1} x^{2n+1}}{n!}$ (Begin with $n = 1$.)

In Exercises 5–7, simplify the factorial expression.

5. $\dfrac{11! \cdot 4!}{4! \cdot 7!}$ **6.** $\dfrac{n!}{(n+1)!}$ **7.** $\dfrac{2n!}{(n-1)!}$

8. Write an expression for the apparent nth term of the sequence

$2, 5, 10, 17, 26, \ldots$ (Assume n begins with 1.)

In Exercises 9 and 10, find a formula for the nth term of the sequence.

9. Arithmetic: $a_1 = 5000, d = 100$ **10.** Geometric: $a_1 = 4, a_{k+1} = \frac{1}{2}a_k$

11. Use sigma notation to write $\dfrac{2}{3(1)+1} + \dfrac{2}{3(2)+1} + \cdots + \dfrac{2}{3(12)+1}$.

12. Use sigma notation to write $2 + \frac{1}{2} + \frac{1}{8} + \frac{1}{32} + \frac{1}{128} + \cdots$.

In Exercises 13–15, find the sum.

13. $\displaystyle\sum_{n=1}^{8} 49\left(\frac{1}{7}\right)^{n-1}$ **14.** $\displaystyle\sum_{n=1}^{7} (8n - 5)$

15. $5 - 2 + \frac{4}{5} - \frac{8}{25} + \frac{16}{125} - \cdots$

16. Use the Binomial Theorem to expand and simplify $(3a - 5b)^4$.

In Exercises 17–20, evaluate the expression.

17. $_9C_3$ **18.** $_{20}C_3$ **19.** $_{70}P_3$ **20.** $_9P_2$

21. Solve for n in $4 \cdot {}_nP_3 = {}_{n+1}P_4$.

22. How many distinct license plates can be issued consisting of one letter followed by a three-digit number?

23. Four students are randomly selected from a class of 25 to answer questions from a reading assignment. In how many ways can the four be selected?

24. A card is drawn from a standard deck of 52 playing cards. Find the probability that it is a face card in the suit of hearts.

25. In 2014, six of the twelve men's basketball teams in the Big Ten Conference participated in the NCAA Men's Basketball Championship Tournament. What is the probability that a random selection of six teams from the Big Ten Conference will be the same as the six teams that participated in the tournament?

26. Two integers from 1 to 60 are chosen by a random number generator. What is the probability that (a) both numbers are odd, (b) both numbers are less than 12, and (c) the same number is chosen twice?

Proofs in Mathematics

Properties of Sums   (p. 574)

1. $\displaystyle\sum_{i=1}^{n} c = cn,$ c is a constant.

2. $\displaystyle\sum_{i=1}^{n} ca_i = c\sum_{i=1}^{n} a_i,$ c is a constant.

3. $\displaystyle\sum_{i=1}^{n} (a_i + b_i) = \sum_{i=1}^{n} a_i + \sum_{i=1}^{n} b_i$

4. $\displaystyle\sum_{i=1}^{n} (a_i - b_i) = \sum_{i=1}^{n} a_i - \sum_{i=1}^{n} b_i$

Proof

Each of these properties follows directly from the properties of real numbers.

1. $\displaystyle\sum_{i=1}^{n} c = c + c + c + \cdots + c = cn$ n terms

The Distributive Property is used in the proof of Property 2.

2. $\displaystyle\sum_{i=1}^{n} ca_i = ca_1 + ca_2 + ca_3 + \cdots + ca_n$

$= c(a_1 + a_2 + a_3 + \cdots + a_n)$

$= c\displaystyle\sum_{i=1}^{n} a_i$

The proof of Property 3 uses the Commutative and Associative Properties of Addition.

3. $\displaystyle\sum_{i=1}^{n} (a_i + b_i) = (a_1 + b_1) + (a_2 + b_2) + (a_3 + b_3) + \cdots + (a_n + b_n)$

$= (a_1 + a_2 + a_3 + \cdots + a_n) + (b_1 + b_2 + b_3 + \cdots + b_n)$

$= \displaystyle\sum_{i=1}^{n} a_i + \sum_{i=1}^{n} b_i$

The proof of Property 4 uses the Commutative and Associative Properties of Addition and the Distributive Property.

4. $\displaystyle\sum_{i=1}^{n} (a_i - b_i) = (a_1 - b_1) + (a_2 - b_2) + (a_3 - b_3) + \cdots + (a_n - b_n)$

$= (a_1 + a_2 + a_3 + \cdots + a_n) + (-b_1 - b_2 - b_3 - \cdots - b_n)$

$= (a_1 + a_2 + a_3 + \cdots + a_n) - (b_1 + b_2 + b_3 + \cdots + b_n)$

$= \displaystyle\sum_{i=1}^{n} a_i - \sum_{i=1}^{n} b_i$

Infinite Series

The study of infinite series was considered a novelty in the fourteenth century. Logician Richard Suiseth, whose nickname was Calculator, solved this problem.

If throughout the first half of a given time interval a variation continues at a certain intensity; throughout the next quarter of the interval at double the intensity; throughout the following eighth at triple the intensity and so ad infinitum; The average intensity for the whole interval will be the intensity of the variation during the second subinterval (or double the intensity).

This is the same as saying that the sum of the infinite series

$$\frac{1}{2} + \frac{2}{4} + \frac{3}{8} + \cdots + \frac{n}{2^n} + \cdots$$

is 2.

The Sum of a Finite Arithmetic Sequence   (p. 584)

The sum of a finite arithmetic sequence with n terms is given by

$$S_n = \frac{n}{2}(a_1 + a_n).$$

Proof

Begin by generating the terms of the arithmetic sequence in two ways. In the first way, repeatedly add d to the first term to obtain

$$S_n = a_1 + a_2 + a_3 + \cdots + a_{n-2} + a_{n-1} + a_n$$
$$= a_1 + [a_1 + d] + [a_1 + 2d] + \cdots + [a_1 + (n-1)d].$$

In the second way, repeatedly subtract d from the nth term to obtain

$$S_n = a_n + a_{n-1} + a_{n-2} + \cdots + a_3 + a_2 + a_1$$
$$= a_n + [a_n - d] + [a_n - 2d] + \cdots + [a_n - (n-1)d].$$

When you add these two versions of S_n, the multiples of d subtract out and you obtain

$$2S_n = (a_1 + a_n) + (a_1 + a_n) + (a_1 + a_n) + \cdots + (a_1 + a_n) \qquad n \text{ terms}$$
$$2S_n = n(a_1 + a_n)$$
$$S_n = \frac{n}{2}(a_1 + a_n). \qquad\blacksquare$$

The Sum of a Finite Geometric Sequence   (p. 592)

The sum of the finite geometric sequence

$$a_1, \quad a_1 r, \quad a_1 r^2, \quad a_1 r^3, \quad a_1 r^4, \quad \ldots, \quad a_1 r^{n-1}$$

with common ratio $r \neq 1$ is given by

$$S_n = \sum_{i=1}^{n} a_1 r^{i-1} = a_1 \left(\frac{1 - r^n}{1 - r} \right).$$

Proof

$$S_n = a_1 + a_1 r + a_1 r^2 + \cdots + a_1 r^{n-2} + a_1 r^{n-1}$$
$$rS_n = a_1 r + a_1 r^2 + a_1 r^3 + \cdots + a_1 r^{n-1} + a_1 r^n \qquad \text{Multiply by } r.$$

Subtracting the second equation from the first yields

$$S_n - rS_n = a_1 - a_1 r^n.$$

So, $S_n(1 - r) = a_1(1 - r^n)$, and, because $r \neq 1$, you have

$$S_n = a_1 \left(\frac{1 - r^n}{1 - r} \right). \qquad\blacksquare$$

The Binomial Theorem   (p. 599)

In the expansion of $(x + y)^n$

$$(x + y)^n = x^n + nx^{n-1}y + \cdots + {}_nC_r x^{n-r}y^r + \cdots + nxy^{n-1} + y^n$$

the coefficient of $x^{n-r}y^r$ is

$${}_nC_r = \frac{n!}{(n-r)!r!}.$$

Proof

The Binomial Theorem can be proved quite nicely using **mathematical induction.** (For information about mathematical induction, see Appendix G at this textbook's *Companion Website.*) The steps are straightforward but look a little messy, so only an outline of the proof is presented.

1. For $n = 1$, you have

$$(x + y)^1 = x^1 + y^1 = {}_1C_0 x + {}_1C_1 y$$

and the formula is valid.

2. Assuming that the formula is true for $n = k$, the coefficient of $x^{k-r}y^r$ is

$${}_kC_r = \frac{k!}{(k-r)!r!} = \frac{k(k-1)(k-2)\cdots(k-r+1)}{r!}.$$

To show that the formula is true for $n = k + 1$, look at the coefficient of $x^{k+1-r}y^r$ in the expansion of

$$(x + y)^{k+1} = (x + y)^k(x + y).$$

From the right-hand side, you can determine that the term involving $x^{k+1-r}y^r$ is the sum of two products.

$$({}_kC_r x^{k-r}y^r)(x) + ({}_kC_{r-1}x^{k+1-r}y^{r-1})(y)$$

$$= \left[\frac{k!}{(k-r)!r!} + \frac{k!}{(k+1-r)!(r-1)!}\right]x^{k+1-r}y^r$$

$$= \left[\frac{(k+1-r)k!}{(k+1-r)!r!} + \frac{k!r}{(k+1-r)!r!}\right]x^{k+1-r}y^r$$

$$= \left[\frac{k!(k+1-r+r)}{(k+1-r)!r!}\right]x^{k+1-r}y^r$$

$$= \left[\frac{(k+1)!}{(k+1-r)!r!}\right]x^{k+1-r}y^r$$

$$= {}_{k+1}C_r x^{k+1-r}y^r$$

So, by mathematical induction, the Binomial Theorem is valid for all positive integers n.

The Principle of Mathematical Induction

Let P_n be a statement involving the positive integer n. If

1. P_1 is true, and

2. the truth of P_k implies the truth of P_{k+1} for every positive integer k,

then P_n must be true for all positive integers n.

9 Topics in Analytic Geometry

Section 9.2, Example 5
Orbit of the Moon

9.1   Circles and Parabolas

9.2   Ellipses

9.3   Hyperbolas and Rotation of Conics

9.4   Parametric Equations

9.5   Polar Coordinates

9.6   Graphs of Polar Equations

9.7   Polar Equations of Conics

9.1 Circles and Parabolas

Conics

Conic sections were discovered during the classical Greek period, 600 to 300 B.C. The early Greek studies were largely concerned with the geometric properties of conics. It was not until the early seventeenth century that the broad applicability of conics became apparent and played a prominent role in the early development of calculus.

A **conic section** (or simply **conic**) is the intersection of a plane and a double-napped cone. Notice in Figure 9.1 that in the formation of the four basic conics, the intersecting plane does not pass through the vertex of the cone.

What you should learn

▶ Recognize a conic as the intersection of a plane and a double-napped cone.
▶ Write equations of circles in standard form.
▶ Write equations of parabolas in standard form.
▶ Use the reflective property of parabolas to solve real-life problems.

Why you should learn it

Parabolas can be used to model and solve many types of real-life problems. For instance, in Exercise 100 on page 645, a parabola is used to design an entrance ramp for a highway.

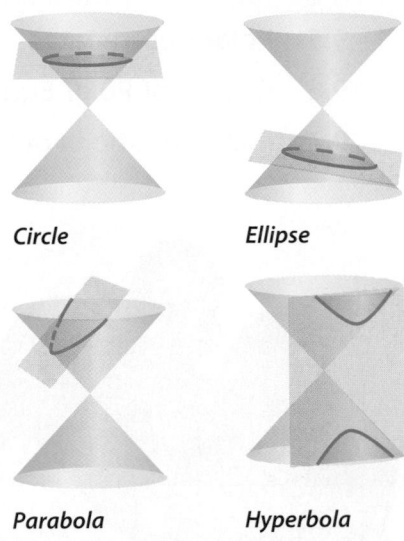

Circle   *Ellipse*

Parabola   *Hyperbola*
Figure 9.1   *Basic Conics*

When the plane does pass through the vertex, the resulting figure is a **degenerate conic,** as shown in Figure 9.2.

Point   *Line*   *Two intersecting lines*
Figure 9.2   *Degenerate Conics*

There are several ways to approach the study of conics. You could begin by defining conics in terms of the intersections of planes and cones, as the Greeks did, or you could define them algebraically, in terms of the general second-degree equation

$$Ax^2 + Bxy + Cy^2 + Dx + Ey + F = 0.$$

However, you will study a third approach, in which each of the conics is defined as a **locus** (collection) of points satisfying a certain geometric property. For example, the definition of a circle as *the collection of all points* (x, y) *that are equidistant from a fixed point* (h, k) leads to the standard equation of a circle

$$(x - h)^2 + (y - k)^2 = r^2. \qquad \text{Equation of circle}$$

Circles

The definition of a circle as a locus of points is a more general definition of a circle as it applies to conics.

> **Definition of a Circle**
>
> A **circle** is the set of all points (x, y) in a plane that are equidistant from a fixed point (h, k), called the **center** of the circle. (See Figure 9.3.) The distance r between the center and any point (x, y) on the circle is the **radius.**

The Distance Formula can be used to obtain an equation of a circle whose center is (h, k) and whose radius is r.

$$\sqrt{(x - h)^2 + (y - k)^2} = r \qquad \text{Distance Formula}$$

$$(x - h)^2 + (y - k)^2 = r^2 \qquad \text{Square each side.}$$

> **Standard Form of the Equation of a Circle**
>
> The **standard form of the equation of a circle** is
>
> $$(x - h)^2 + (y - k)^2 = r^2.$$
>
> The point (h, k) is the center of the circle, and the positive number r is the radius of the circle. The standard form of the equation of a circle whose center is the origin, $(h, k) = (0, 0)$, is $x^2 + y^2 = r^2$.

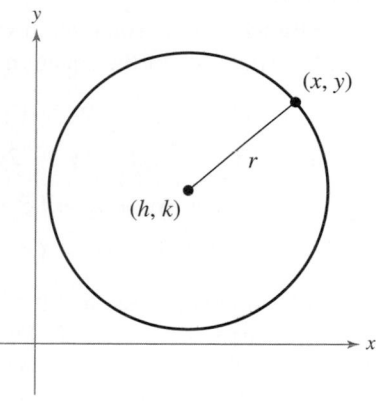

Figure 9.3

EXAMPLE 1   Finding the Standard Equation of a Circle

The point $(1, 4)$ is on a circle whose center is at $(-2, -3)$, as shown in Figure 9.4. Write the standard form of the equation of the circle.

Solution

The radius of the circle is the distance between $(-2, -3)$ and $(1, 4)$.

$$r = \sqrt{[1 - (-2)]^2 + [4 - (-3)]^2} \qquad \text{Use Distance Formula.}$$

$$= \sqrt{3^2 + 7^2} \qquad \text{Simplify.}$$

$$= \sqrt{58} \qquad \text{Radius}$$

The equation of the circle with center $(h, k) = (-2, -3)$ and radius $r = \sqrt{58}$ is

$$(x - h)^2 + (y - k)^2 = r^2 \qquad \text{Equation of a circle}$$

$$[x - (-2)]^2 + [y - (-3)]^2 = \left(\sqrt{58}\right)^2 \qquad \text{Substitute for } h, k, \text{ and } r.$$

$$(x + 2)^2 + (y + 3)^2 = 58. \qquad \text{Write in standard form.}$$

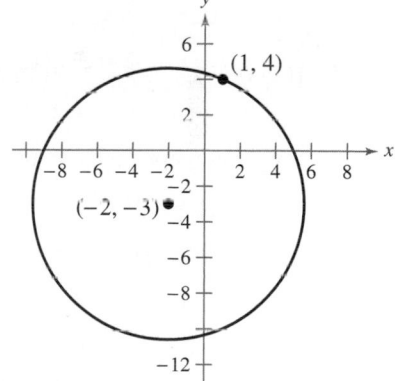

Figure 9.4

✓ **Checkpoint**))) *Audio-video solution in English & Spanish at LarsonPrecalculus.com.*

The point $(3, 1)$ is on a circle whose center is at $(1, -1)$. Write the standard form of the equation of the circle. ■

Be careful when you are finding h and k from the standard equation of a circle. For instance, to find the correct h and k from the equation of the circle in Example 1, rewrite the quantities $(x + 2)^2$ and $(y + 3)^2$ using subtraction.

$$(x + 2)^2 = [x - (-2)]^2 \implies h = -2$$

$$(y + 3)^2 = [y - (-3)]^2 \implies k = -3$$

EXAMPLE 2   Sketching a Circle

Sketch the circle given by $x^2 - 6x + y^2 - 2y + 6 = 0$ and identify its center and radius.

Solution

Begin by writing the equation in standard form. In the third step, note that 9 and 1 are added to *each* side of the equation when completing the squares.

$$x^2 - 6x + y^2 - 2y + 6 = 0 \qquad \text{Write original equation.}$$

$$\left(x^2 - 6x + \right) + \left(y^2 - 2y + \right) = -6 \qquad \text{Group terms.}$$

$$(x^2 - 6x + 9) + (y^2 - 2y + 1) = -6 + 9 + 1 \qquad \text{Complete the squares.}$$

$$(x - 3)^2 + (y - 1)^2 = 4 \qquad \text{Write in standard form.}$$

In this form, you can see that the graph is a circle whose center is the point $(3, 1)$ and whose radius is $r = \sqrt{4} = 2$. Plot several points that are two units from the center. The points $(5, 1)$, $(3, 3)$, $(1, 1)$, and $(3, -1)$ are convenient. Draw a circle that passes through the four points, as shown in Figure 9.5.

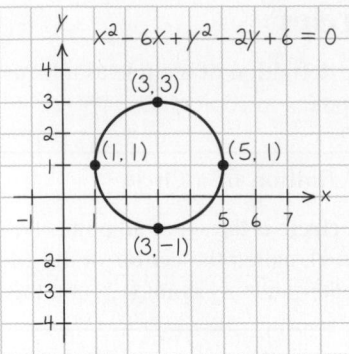

Figure 9.5

✓ **Checkpoint** ◀))) *Audio-video solution in English & Spanish at LarsonPrecalculus.com.*

Sketch the circle given by $x^2 + 4x + y^2 + 4y - 1 = 0$ and identify its center and radius.

EXAMPLE 3   Finding the Intercepts of a Circle

Find the x- and y-intercepts of the graph of the circle $(x - 4)^2 + (y - 2)^2 = 16$.

Solution

To find any x-intercepts, let $y = 0$.

$$(x - 4)^2 + (0 - 2)^2 = 16 \qquad \text{Substitute 0 for } y.$$

$$(x - 4)^2 = 12 \qquad \text{Simplify.}$$

$$x - 4 = \pm\sqrt{12} \qquad \text{Extract square roots.}$$

$$x = 4 \pm 2\sqrt{3} \qquad \text{Add 4 to each side.}$$

To find any y-intercepts, let $x = 0$.

$$(0 - 4)^2 + (y - 2)^2 = 16 \qquad \text{Substitute 0 for } x.$$

$$(y - 2)^2 = 0 \qquad \text{Simplify.}$$

$$y - 2 = 0 \qquad \text{Extract square roots.}$$

$$y = 2 \qquad \text{Add 2 to each side.}$$

So, the x-intercepts are $\left(4 + 2\sqrt{3}, 0\right)$ and $\left(4 - 2\sqrt{3}, 0\right)$, and the y-intercept is $(0, 2)$, as shown in the figure.

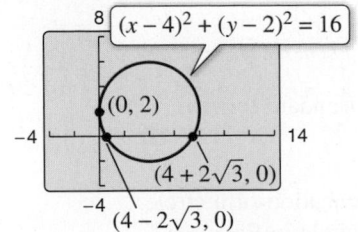

✓ **Checkpoint** ◀))) *Audio-video solution in English & Spanish at LarsonPrecalculus.com.*

Find the x- and y-intercepts of the graph of the circle $(x - 2)^2 + (y + 3)^2 = 9$. ∎

Technology Tip

You can use a graphing utility to confirm the result in Example 2 by graphing the upper and lower portions in the same viewing window. First, solve for y to obtain

$$y_1 = 1 + \sqrt{4 - (x - 3)^2}$$

and

$$y_2 = 1 - \sqrt{4 - (x - 3)^2}.$$

Then use a square setting, such as $-1 \le x \le 8$ and $-2 \le y \le 4$, to graph both equations.

Parabolas

In Section 2.1, you learned that the graph of the quadratic function $f(x) = ax^2 + bx + c$ is a parabola that opens upward or downward. The following definition of a parabola is more general in the sense that it is independent of the orientation of the parabola.

Definition of a Parabola

A **parabola** is the set of all points (x, y) in a plane that are equidistant from a fixed line, the **directrix,** and a fixed point, the **focus,** not on the line. (See Figure 9.6.) The midpoint between the focus and the directrix is the **vertex,** and the line passing through the focus and the vertex is the **axis** of the parabola.

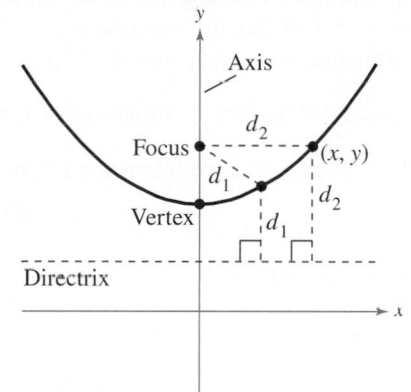

Figure 9.6

Note in Figure 9.6 that a parabola is symmetric with respect to its axis. Using the definition of a parabola, you can derive the following **standard form of the equation of a parabola** whose directrix is parallel to the x-axis or to the y-axis.

Standard Equation of a Parabola   (See the proof on page 707.)

The **standard form of the equation of a parabola** with vertex at (h, k) is as follows.

$$(x - h)^2 = 4p(y - k), \quad p \neq 0 \qquad \text{Vertical axis; directrix: } y = k - p$$

$$(y - k)^2 = 4p(x - h), \quad p \neq 0 \qquad \text{Horizontal axis; directrix: } x = h - p$$

The focus lies on the axis p units (*directed distance*) from the vertex. If the vertex is at the origin $(0, 0)$, then the equation takes one of the following forms.

$$x^2 = 4py \qquad \text{Vertical axis}$$

$$y^2 = 4px \qquad \text{Horizontal axis}$$

See Figure 9.7.

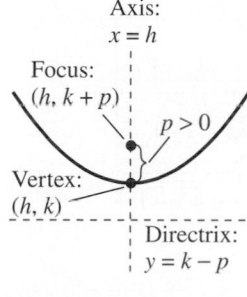

$$(x - h)^2 = 4p(y - k)$$

(a) *Vertical axis:* $p > 0$
Figure 9.7

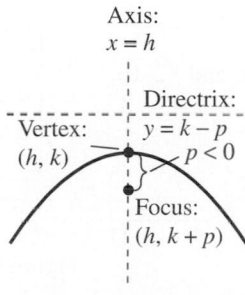

$$(x - h)^2 = 4p(y - k)$$

(b) *Vertical axis:* $p < 0$

$$(y - k)^2 = 4p(x - h)$$

(c) *Horizontal axis:* $p > 0$

$$(y - k)^2 = 4p(x - h)$$

(d) *Horizontal axis:* $p < 0$

EXAMPLE 4 Finding the Standard Equation of a Parabola

Find the standard form of the equation of the parabola with vertex at the origin and focus $(0, 4)$.

Solution

The axis of the parabola is vertical, passing through $(0, 0)$ and $(0, 4)$, as shown in Figure 9.8. The standard form is $x^2 = 4py$, where $p = 4$. So, the equation is $x^2 = 16y$. To check this on a graphing utility, solve the equation for y and graph $y = \frac{1}{16}x^2$.

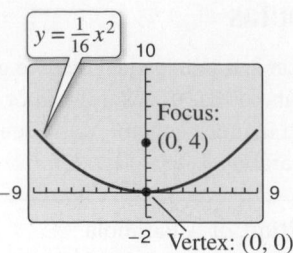

Figure 9.8

✓ **Checkpoint** ◀))) *Audio-video solution in English & Spanish at LarsonPrecalculus.com.*

Find the standard form of the equation of the parabola with vertex at the origin and focus $\left(0, \frac{3}{8}\right)$.

EXAMPLE 5 Finding the Focus of a Parabola

Find the focus of the parabola given by $y = -\frac{1}{2}x^2 - x + \frac{1}{2}$.

Solution

To find the focus, convert to standard form by completing the square.

$$y = -\tfrac{1}{2}x^2 - x + \tfrac{1}{2} \qquad \text{Write original equation.}$$
$$-2y = x^2 + 2x - 1 \qquad \text{Multiply each side by } -2.$$
$$1 - 2y = x^2 + 2x \qquad \text{Add 1 to each side.}$$
$$1 + 1 - 2y = x^2 + 2x + 1 \qquad \text{Complete the square.}$$
$$2 - 2y = x^2 + 2x + 1 \qquad \text{Combine like terms.}$$
$$-2(y - 1) = (x + 1)^2 \qquad \text{Write in standard form.}$$

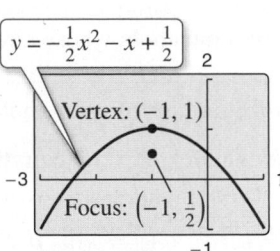

Figure 9.9

Comparing this equation with $(x - h)^2 = 4p(y - k)$, you can conclude that $h = -1$, $k = 1$, and $p = -\frac{1}{2}$. Because p is negative, the parabola opens downward, as shown in Figure 9.9. So, the focus of the parabola is $(h, k + p) = \left(-1, \frac{1}{2}\right)$.

✓ **Checkpoint** ◀))) *Audio-video solution in English & Spanish at LarsonPrecalculus.com.*

Find the focus of the parabola $x = \frac{1}{4}y^2 + \frac{3}{2}y + \frac{13}{4}$.

EXAMPLE 6 Finding the Standard Equation of a Parabola

See LarsonPrecalculus.com for an interactive version of this type of example.

Find the standard form of the equation of the parabola with vertex $(1, 0)$ and focus $(2, 0)$.

Solution

Because the axis of the parabola is horizontal, passing through $(1, 0)$ and $(2, 0)$, consider the equation $(y - k)^2 = 4p(x - h)$, where $h = 1$, $k = 0$, and $p = 2 - 1 = 1$. So, the standard form is

$$(y - 0)^2 = 4(1)(x - 1) \implies y^2 = 4(x - 1).$$

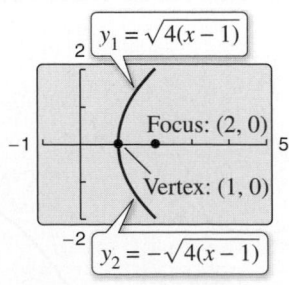

Figure 9.10

You can use a graphing utility to confirm this equation. To do this, let $y_1 = \sqrt{4(x - 1)}$ and $y_2 = -\sqrt{4(x - 1)}$, as shown in Figure 9.10.

✓ **Checkpoint** ◀))) *Audio-video solution in English & Spanish at LarsonPrecalculus.com.*

Find the standard form of the equation of the parabola with vertex $(2, -3)$ and focus $(4, -3)$. ∎

Reflective Property of Parabolas

A line segment that passes through the focus of a parabola and has endpoints on the parabola is called a **focal chord.** The specific focal chord perpendicular to the axis of the parabola is called the **latus rectum.**

Parabolas occur in a wide variety of applications. For instance, a parabolic reflector can be formed by revolving a parabola about its axis. The resulting surface has the property that all incoming rays parallel to the axis are reflected through the focus of the parabola. This is the principle behind the construction of the parabolic mirrors used in reflecting telescopes. Conversely, the light rays emanating from the focus of a parabolic reflector used in a flashlight are all parallel to one another, as shown in Figure 9.11.

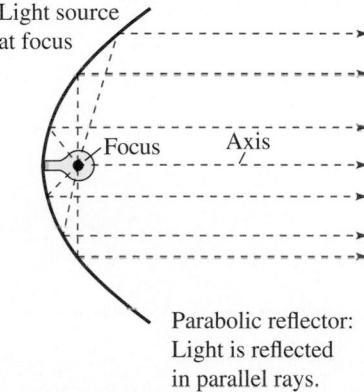

Figure 9.11

A line is **tangent** to a parabola at a point on the parabola when the line intersects, but does not cross, the parabola at the point. Tangent lines to parabolas have special properties related to the use of parabolas in constructing reflective surfaces.

Reflective Property of a Parabola

The tangent line to a parabola at a point P makes equal angles with the following two lines (see Figure 9.12).

   1. The line passing through P and the focus

   2. The axis of the parabola

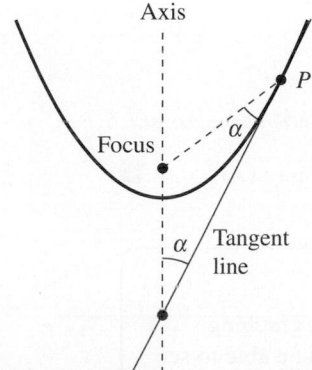

Figure 9.12

EXAMPLE 7 Finding the Tangent Line at a Point on a Parabola

Find an equation of the tangent line to the parabola given by $y = x^2$ at the point $(1, 1)$.

Solution

For this parabola, $p = \frac{1}{4}$ and the focus is $\left(0, \frac{1}{4}\right)$, as shown in Figure 9.13. You can find the y-intercept $(0, b)$ of the tangent line by equating the lengths of the two sides of the isosceles triangle shown in Figure 9.13:

$$d_1 = \frac{1}{4} - b$$

and

$$d_2 = \sqrt{(1 - 0)^2 + \left(1 - \frac{1}{4}\right)^2} = \frac{5}{4}.$$

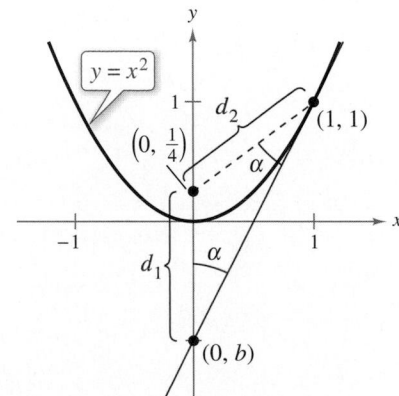

Figure 9.13

Note that $d_1 = \frac{1}{4} - b$ rather than $b - \frac{1}{4}$. The order of subtraction for the distance is important because the distance must be positive. Setting $d_1 = d_2$ produces

$$\frac{1}{4} - b = \frac{5}{4}$$

$$b = -1.$$

So, the slope of the tangent line is

$$m = \frac{1 - (-1)}{1 - 0} = 2$$

and the equation of the tangent line in slope-intercept form is

$$y = 2x - 1.$$

✓ **Checkpoint** 🔊 *Audio-video solution in English & Spanish at LarsonPrecalculus.com.*

Find an equation of the tangent line to the parabola $y = 3x^2$ at the point $(1, 3)$. ∎

Technology Tip

Try using a graphing utility to confirm the result of Example 7. By graphing $y_1 = x^2$ and $y_2 = 2x - 1$ in the same viewing window, you should be able to see that the line touches the parabola at the point $(1, 1)$.

Vocabulary and Concept Check

In Exercises 1–4, fill in the blank(s).

1. A _____ is the intersection of a plane and a double-napped cone.

2. A collection of points satisfying a geometric property can also be referred to as a _____ of points.

3. A _____ is the set of all points (x, y) in a plane that are equidistant from a fixed point, called the _____ .

4. A _____ is the set of all points (x, y) in a plane that are equidistant from a fixed line, called the _____ , and a fixed point, called the _____ , not on the line.

5. What does the equation $(x - h)^2 + (y - k)^2 = r^2$ represent? What do h, k, and r represent?

6. The tangent line to a parabola at a point P makes equal angles with what two lines?

Procedures and Problem Solving

Finding the Standard Equation of a Circle   In Exercises 7–12, find the standard form of the equation of the circle with the given characteristics.

7. Center at origin; radius: 4

8. Center at origin; radius: $\sqrt{11}$

9. Center: $(3, 7)$; point on circle: $(1, 0)$

10. Center: $(6, -3)$; point on circle: $(-2, 4)$

11. Endpoints of a diameter: $(-6, 0)$ and $(0, -2)$

12. Endpoints of a diameter: $(1, -7)$ and $(9, -5)$

Identifying the Center and Radius of a Circle   In Exercises 13–18, identify the center and radius of the circle.

13. $x^2 + y^2 = 36$ **14.** $x^2 + y^2 = 121$

15. $(x - 5)^2 + y^2 = 9$ **16.** $x^2 + (y + 8)^2 = 25$

17. $(x + 1)^2 + (y + 6)^2 = 19$

18. $(x + 7)^2 + (y - 3)^2 = 32$

Writing the Equation of a Circle in Standard Form   In Exercises 19–26, write the equation of the circle in standard form. Then identify its center and radius.

19. $\frac{1}{4}x^2 + \frac{1}{4}y^2 = 1$ **20.** $\frac{1}{9}x^2 + \frac{1}{9}y^2 = 1$

21. $\frac{4}{3}x^2 + \frac{4}{3}y^2 = 1$ **22.** $\frac{9}{2}x^2 + \frac{9}{2}y^2 = 1$

23. $x^2 + y^2 - 2x + 6y + 9 = 0$

24. $x^2 + y^2 - 10x - 6y + 25 = 0$

25. $4x^2 + 4y^2 + 12x - 24y + 41 = 0$

26. $9x^2 + 9y^2 + 54x - 36y + 17 = 0$

Sketching a Circle   In Exercises 27–34, sketch the circle. Identify its center and radius.

27. $x^2 = 16 - y^2$ **28.** $y^2 = 81 - x^2$

29. $x^2 + 8x + y^2 + 2y + 8 = 0$

30. $x^2 - 6x + y^2 + 6y + 14 = 0$

31. $x^2 - 14x + y^2 + 8y + 40 = 0$

32. $x^2 + 6x + y^2 - 12y + 41 = 0$

33. $x^2 + 2x + y^2 - 35 = 0$

34. $x^2 + y^2 + 10y + 9 = 0$

Finding the Intercepts of a Circle   In Exercises 35–40, find the x- and y-intercepts of the graph of the circle.

35. $(x + 5)^2 + (y - 3)^2 = 25$

36. $(x - 1)^2 + (y + 4)^2 = 16$

37. $(x - 6)^2 + (y + 3)^2 = 16$

38. $(x + 7)^2 + (y - 8)^2 = 4$

39. $x^2 - 2x + y^2 - 6y - 27 = 0$

40. $x^2 + 8x + y^2 + 2y + 9 = 0$

41. Seismology An earthquake was felt up to 52 miles from its epicenter. You were located 40 miles west and 30 miles south of the epicenter.

(a) Let the epicenter be at the point $(0, 0)$. Find the standard equation that describes the outer boundary of the earthquake.

(b) Would you have felt the earthquake?

(c) Verify your answer to part (b) by graphing the equation of the outer boundary of the earthquake and plotting your location. How far were you from the outer boundary of the earthquake?

42. Landscape Design A landscaper has installed a circular sprinkler that covers an area of 2000 square feet.

(a) Find the radius of the region covered by the sprinkler. Round your answer to three decimal places.

(b) The landscaper increases the area covered to 2500 square feet by increasing the water pressure. How much longer is the radius?

Matching an Equation with a Graph In Exercises 43–48, match the equation with its graph. [The graphs are labeled (a), (b), (c), (d), (e), and (f).]

(a)

(b)

(c)

(d)

(e)

(f)
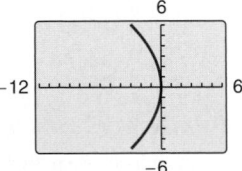

43. $y^2 = -4x$

44. $x^2 = 2y$

45. $x^2 = -8y$

46. $y^2 = -12x$

47. $(y - 1)^2 = 4(x - 3)$

48. $(x + 3)^2 = -2(y - 1)$

Finding the Standard Equation of a Parabola In Exercises 49–60, find the standard form of the equation of the parabola with the given characteristic(s) and vertex at the origin.

49.

50.
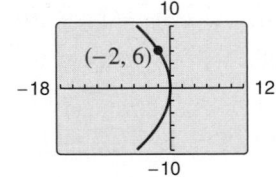

51. Focus: $(0, 2)$

52. Focus: $(0, 3)$

53. Focus: $\left(-\frac{1}{2}, 0\right)$

54. Focus: $\left(-\frac{3}{2}, 0\right)$

55. Directrix: $y = 4$

56. Directrix: $y = -1$

57. Directrix: $x = -2$

58. Directrix: $x = 5$

59. Horizontal axis and passes through the point $(3, 3)$

60. Vertical axis and passes through the point $(-8, -2)$

Finding the Vertex, Focus, and Directrix of a Parabola In Exercises 61–78, find the vertex, focus, and directrix of the parabola and sketch its graph. Use a graphing utility to verify your graph.

61. $y = \frac{1}{2}x^2$

62. $y = -2x^2$

63. $y^2 = -6x$

64. $y^2 = 3x$

65. $x^2 + 6y = 0$

66. $x + y^2 = 0$

67. $(x + 1)^2 - 8(y + 2) = 0$

68. $(x - 5) + (y + 4)^2 = 0$

69. $\left(x + \frac{3}{2}\right)^2 = 4(y - 2)$ **70.** $\left(x + \frac{1}{2}\right)^2 = 4(y - 1)$

71. $y^2 + 6y + 8x + 25 = 0$

72. $y^2 - 4y - 4x = 0$

73. $x^2 + 4x + 6y - 2 = 0$

74. $x^2 - 2x + 8y + 9 = 0$

75. $y^2 + x + y = 0$

76. $y^2 - 4x - 4 = 0$

77. $y = \frac{1}{4}(x^2 - 2x + 5)$

78. $x = \frac{1}{4}(y^2 + 2y + 33)$

Finding the Standard Equation of a Parabola In Exercises 79–90, find the standard form of the equation of the parabola with the given characteristics.

79.

80.

81.

82.
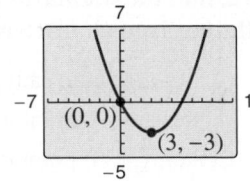

83. Vertex: $(-2, 0)$; focus: $\left(-\frac{3}{2}, 0\right)$

84. Vertex: $(3, -3)$; focus: $\left(3, -\frac{9}{4}\right)$

85. Vertex: $(5, 2)$; focus: $(3, 2)$

86. Vertex: $(-1, 2)$; focus: $(-1, 0)$

87. Vertex: $(0, 4)$; directrix: $y = 2$

88. Vertex: $(-2, 1)$; directrix: $x = 1$

89. Focus: $(2, 2)$; directrix: $x = -2$

90. Focus: $(0, 0)$; directrix: $y = 8$

Determining the Point of Tangency In Exercises 91 and 92, the equations of a parabola and a tangent line to the parabola are given. Use a graphing utility to graph both equations in the same viewing window. Determine the coordinates of the point of tangency.

Parabola	*Tangent Line*
91. $y^2 - 8x = 0$	$x - y + 2 = 0$
92. $x^2 + 12y = 0$	$x + y - 3 = 0$

Finding the Tangent Line at a Point on a Parabola In Exercises 93–96, find an equation of the tangent line to the parabola at the given point.

93. $x^2 = 2y$, $(4, 8)$

94. $x^2 = 2y$, $\left(-3, \frac{9}{2}\right)$

95. $x = -2y^2$, $(-2, -1)$

96. $x = -2y^2$, $(-8, 2)$

97. Window Design   A church window is bounded above by a parabola (see figure). Find the equation of the parabola.

Figure for 97   Figure for 98

98. Lattice Arch   A parabolic lattice arch is 8 feet high at the vertex. At a height of 4 feet, the width of the lattice arch is 4 feet (see figure). How wide is the lattice arch at ground level?

99. Environmental Science   Water is flowing from a horizontal pipe 48 feet above the ground. The falling stream of water has the shape of a parabola whose vertex $(0, 48)$ is at the end of the pipe (see figure). The stream of water strikes the ocean at the point $(10\sqrt{3}, 0)$. Find the equation of the path taken by the water.

100. *Why you should learn it* (p. 636) Road engineers design a parabolic entrance ramp from a straight street to an interstate highway (see figure). Find an equation of the parabola.

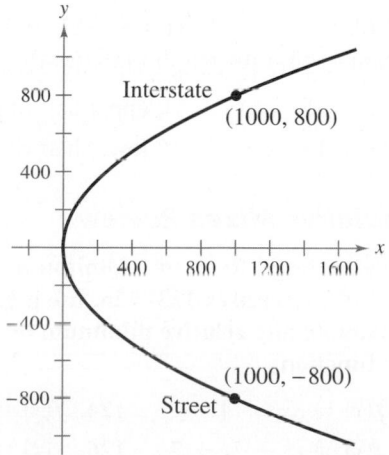

101. MODELING DATA

A cable of the Golden Gate Bridge is suspended (in the shape of a parabola) between two towers that are 1280 meters apart. The top of each tower is 152 meters above the roadway. The cable touches the roadway midway between the towers.

(a) Draw a sketch of the cable. Locate the origin of a rectangular coordinate system at the center of the roadway. Label the coordinates of the known points.

(b) Write an equation that models the cable.

(c) Complete the table by finding the height y of the suspension cable over the roadway at a distance of x meters from the center of the bridge.

x	0	200	400	500	600
y					

102. Transportation Design   Roads are often designed with parabolic surfaces to allow rain to drain off. A particular road that is 32 feet wide is 0.4 foot higher in the center than it is on the sides. (See figure.)

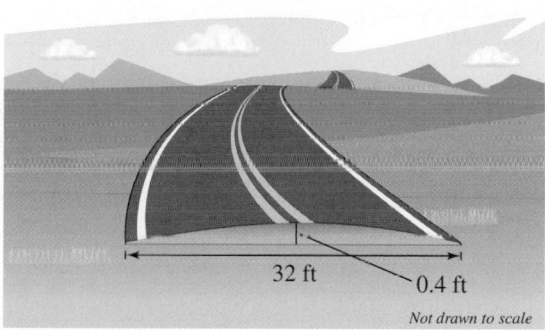

32 ft   0.4 ft

Not drawn to scale

(a) Find an equation of the parabola with its vertex at the origin that models the road surface.

(b) How far from the center of the road is the road surface 0.1 foot lower than in the middle?

103. Mechanical Engineering   The filament of an automobile headlight is at the focus of a parabolic reflector, which sends light out in a straight beam. (See figure.)

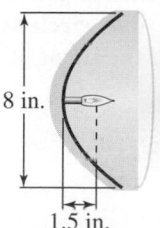

8 in.

1.5 in.

(a) The filament of the headlight is 1.5 inches from the vertex. Find an equation for the cross section of the reflector.

(b) The reflector is 8 inches wide. Find the depth of the reflector.

104. Astronomy A satellite in a 100-mile-high circular orbit around Earth has a velocity of approximately 17,500 miles per hour. When this velocity is multiplied by $\sqrt{2}$, the satellite has the minimum velocity necessary to escape Earth's gravity and follows a parabolic path with the center of Earth as the focus. (See figure.)

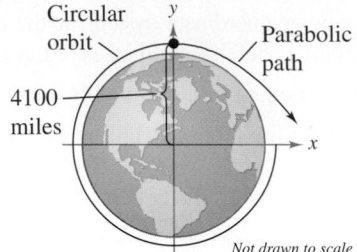

Circular orbit

Parabolic path

4100 miles

Not drawn to scale

(a) Find the escape velocity of the satellite.

(b) Find an equation of its path (assume the radius of Earth is 4000 miles).

Projectile Motion In Exercises 105 and 106, consider the path of a projectile projected horizontally with a velocity of v feet per second at a height of s feet, where the model for the path is

$$x^2 = -\frac{v^2}{16}(y - s).$$

In this model (in which air resistance is disregarded), y is the height (in feet) of the projectile and x is the horizontal distance (in feet) the projectile travels.

105. A ball is thrown from the top of a 100-foot tower with a velocity of 28 feet per second.

(a) Find the equation of the parabolic path.

(b) How far does the ball travel horizontally before striking the ground?

106. A cargo plane is flying at an altitude of 30,000 feet and a speed of 540 miles per hour. A supply crate is dropped from the plane. How many *feet* will the crate travel horizontally before it hits the ground?

Finding the Tangent Line at a Point on a Circle In Exercises 107–112, find an equation of the tangent line to the circle at the indicated point. Recall from geometry that the tangent line to a circle is perpendicular to the radius of the circle at the point of tangency.

	Circle	Point
107.	$x^2 + y^2 = 25$	$(3, -4)$
108.	$x^2 + y^2 = 169$	$(-5, 12)$
109.	$x^2 + y^2 = 12$	$(2, -2\sqrt{2})$
110.	$x^2 + y^2 = 24$	$(-2\sqrt{5}, 2)$
111.	$(x + 2)^2 + (y - 1)^2 = 100$	$(4, 9)$
112.	$x^2 + (y - 3)^2 = 16$	$(\sqrt{7}, 0)$

Conclusions

True or False? In Exercises 113–118, determine whether the statement is true or false. Justify your answer.

113. The equation $x^2 + (y + 5)^2 = 25$ represents a circle with its center at the origin and a radius of 5.

114. The graph of the equation $x^2 + y^2 = r^2$ will have x-intercepts $(\pm r, 0)$ and y-intercepts $(0, \pm r)$.

115. A circle is a degenerate conic.

116. The point which lies on the graph of a parabola closest to its focus is the vertex of the parabola.

117. The directrix of the parabola $x^2 = y$ intersects or is tangent to the graph of the parabola at its vertex, $(0, 0)$.

118. If the vertex and focus of a parabola are on a horizontal line, then the directrix of the parabola is a vertical line.

119. Think About It The equation $x^2 + y^2 = 0$ is a degenerate conic. Sketch the graph of this equation and identify the degenerate conic. Describe the intersection of the plane with the double-napped cone for this particular conic.

120. HOW DO YOU SEE IT? In parts (a)–(d), describe in words how a plane could intersect the double-napped cone to form the conic section (see figure).

(a) Circle   (b) Ellipse

(c) Parabola   (d) Hyperbola

Think About It In Exercises 121 and 122, change the equation so that its graph matches the description.

121. $(y - 3)^2 = 6(x + 1)$; upper half of parabola

122. $(y + 1)^2 = 2(x - 2)$; lower half of parabola

Cumulative Mixed Review

Approximating Relative Minimum and Maximum Values In Exercises 123–126, use a graphing utility to approximate any relative minimum or maximum values of the function.

123. $f(x) = 3x^3 - 4x + 2$ **124.** $f(x) = 2x^2 + 3x$

125. $f(x) = x^4 + 2x + 2$ **126.** $f(x) = x^5 - 3x - 1$

9.2   Ellipses

Introduction

The third type of conic is called an **ellipse.** It is defined as follows.

> #### Definition of an Ellipse
>
> An **ellipse** is the set of all points (x, y) in a plane, the sum of whose distances from two distinct fixed points **(foci)** is constant. (See Figure 9.14.)

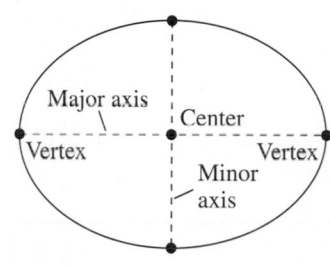

$d_1 + d_2$ is constant.

Figure 9.14   **Figure 9.15**

The line through the foci intersects the ellipse at two points called **vertices.** The chord joining the vertices is the **major axis,** and its midpoint is the **center** of the ellipse. The chord perpendicular to the major axis at the center is the **minor axis.** (See Figure 9.15.)

You can visualize the definition of an ellipse by imagining two thumbtacks placed at the foci, as shown in Figure 9.16. If the ends of a fixed length of string are fastened to the thumbtacks and the string is drawn taut with a pencil, then the path traced by the pencil will be an ellipse.

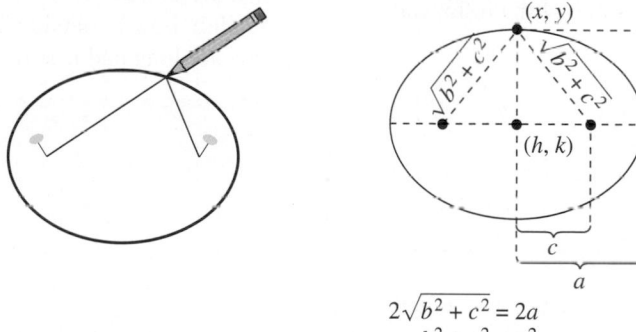

$$2\sqrt{b^2 + c^2} = 2a$$
$$b^2 + c^2 = a^2$$

Figure 9.16   **Figure 9.17**

Urologist

To derive the standard form of the equation of an ellipse, consider the ellipse in Figure 9.17 with the following points.

Center: (h, k) Vertices: $(h \pm a, k)$ Foci: $(h \pm c, k)$

Note that the center is the midpoint of the segment joining the foci.

The sum of the distances from any point on the ellipse to the two foci is constant. Using a vertex point, this constant sum is

$(a + c) + (a - c) = 2a$ Length of major axis

or simply the length of the major axis.

Now, if you let (x, y) be *any* point on the ellipse, then the sum of the distances between (x, y) and the two foci must also be $2a$. That is,

$$\sqrt{[x - (h - c)]^2 + (y - k)^2} + \sqrt{[x - (h + c)]^2 + (y - k)^2} = 2a$$

which, after expanding and regrouping, reduces to

$$(a^2 - c^2)(x - h)^2 + a^2(y - k)^2 = a^2(a^2 - c^2).$$

Finally, in Figure 9.17, you can see that

$$b^2 = a^2 - c^2$$

which implies that the equation of the ellipse is

$$b^2(x - h)^2 + a^2(y - k)^2 = a^2 b^2$$

$$\frac{(x - h)^2}{a^2} + \frac{(y - k)^2}{b^2} = 1.$$

You would obtain a similar equation in the derivation by starting with a vertical major axis. Both results are summarized as follows.

Standard Equation of an Ellipse

The **standard form of the equation of an ellipse** with center (h, k) and major and minor axes of lengths $2a$ and $2b$, respectively, where $0 < b < a$, is

$$\frac{(x - h)^2}{a^2} + \frac{(y - k)^2}{b^2} = 1 \qquad \text{Major axis is horizontal.}$$

$$\frac{(x - h)^2}{b^2} + \frac{(y - k)^2}{a^2} = 1. \qquad \text{Major axis is vertical.}$$

The foci lie on the major axis, c units from the center, with

$$c^2 = a^2 - b^2.$$

If the center is at the origin $(0, 0)$, then the equation takes one of the following forms.

$$\frac{x^2}{a^2} + \frac{y^2}{b^2} = 1 \qquad \text{Major axis is horizontal.}$$

$$\frac{x^2}{b^2} + \frac{y^2}{a^2} = 1 \qquad \text{Major axis is vertical.}$$

Explore the Concept

On page 647, it was noted that an ellipse can be drawn using two thumbtacks, a string of fixed length (greater than the distance between the two tacks), and a pencil. Try doing this. Vary the length of the string and the distance between the thumbtacks. Explain how to obtain ellipses that are almost circular. Explain how to obtain ellipses that are long and narrow.

Figure 9.18 shows both the vertical and horizontal orientations for an ellipse.

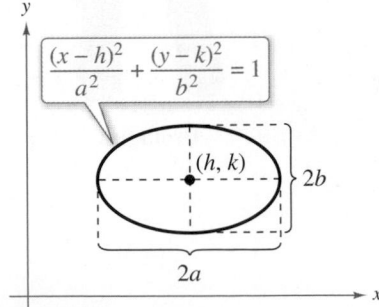

Major axis is horizontal.
Figure 9.18

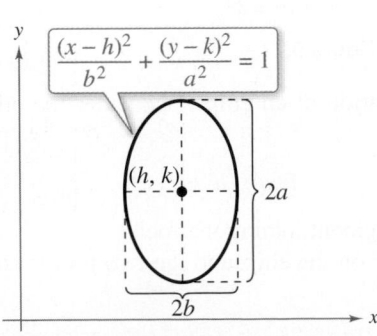

Major axis is vertical.

EXAMPLE 1   Finding the Standard Equation of an Ellipse

Find the standard form of the equation of the ellipse having foci at

$$(0, 1) \quad \text{and} \quad (4, 1)$$

and a major axis of length 6, as shown in Figure 9.19.

Figure 9.19

Solution

By the Midpoint Formula, the center of the ellipse is $(2, 1)$ and the distance from the center to one of the foci is $c = 2$. Because $2a = 6$, you know that $a = 3$. Now, from $c^2 = a^2 - b^2$, you have

$$b = \sqrt{a^2 - c^2} = \sqrt{9 - 4} = \sqrt{5}.$$

Because the major axis is horizontal, the standard equation is

$$\frac{(x - 2)^2}{3^2} + \frac{(y - 1)^2}{\left(\sqrt{5}\right)^2} = 1 \quad \text{or} \quad \frac{(x - 2)^2}{9} + \frac{(y - 1)^2}{5} = 1.$$

✓ **Checkpoint** ◀))) *Audio-video solution in English & Spanish at LarsonPrecalculus.com.*

Find the standard form of the equation of the ellipse having foci $(2, 0)$ and $(2, 6)$ and a major axis of length 8.

EXAMPLE 2   Sketching an Ellipse

Sketch the ellipse given by $4x^2 + y^2 = 36$ and identify the center and vertices.

Algebraic Solution

$$4x^2 + y^2 = 36 \qquad \text{Write original equation.}$$

$$\frac{4x^2}{36} + \frac{y^2}{36} = \frac{36}{36} \qquad \text{Divide each side by 36.}$$

$$\frac{x^2}{3^2} + \frac{y^2}{6^2} = 1 \qquad \text{Write in standard form.}$$

The center of the ellipse is $(0, 0)$. Because the denominator of the y^2-term is greater than the denominator of the x^2-term, you can conclude that the major axis is vertical. Moreover, because $a = 6$, the vertices are $(0, -6)$ and $(0, 6)$. Finally, because $b = 3$, the endpoints of the minor axis are $(-3, 0)$ and $(3, 0)$, as shown in the figure.

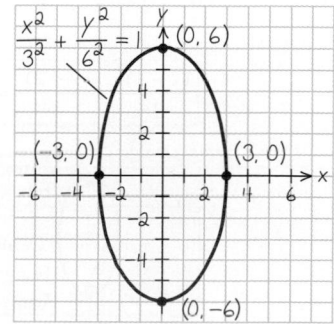

Graphical Solution

Solve the equation of the ellipse for y as follows.

$$4x^2 + y^2 = 36$$

$$y^2 = 36 - 4x^2$$

$$y = \pm\sqrt{36 - 4x^2}$$

Then use a graphing utility to graph

$$y_1 = \sqrt{36 - 4x^2}$$

and

$$y_2 = -\sqrt{36 - 4x^2}$$

in the same viewing window, as shown in the figure. Be sure to use a square setting.

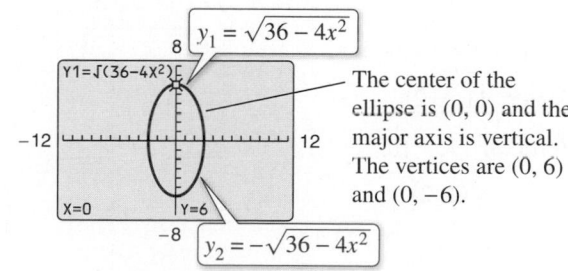

$y_1 = \sqrt{36 - 4x^2}$

The center of the ellipse is $(0, 0)$ and the major axis is vertical. The vertices are $(0, 6)$ and $(0, -6)$.

$y_2 = -\sqrt{36 - 4x^2}$

✓ **Checkpoint** ◀))) *Audio-video solution in English & Spanish at LarsonPrecalculus.com.*

Sketch the ellipse given by $x^2 + 4y^2 = 16$ and identify the center and vertices. ∎

EXAMPLE 3 Graphing an Ellipse

Graph the ellipse given by $x^2 + 4y^2 + 6x - 8y + 9 = 0$.

Solution

Begin by writing the original equation in standard form.

$$x^2 + 4y^2 + 6x - 8y + 9 = 0 \qquad \text{Write original equation.}$$

$$\left(x^2 + 6x + \boxed{}\right) + 4\left(y^2 - 2y + \boxed{}\right) = -9 \qquad \begin{array}{l}\text{Group terms and factor}\\ \text{4 out of } y\text{-terms.}\end{array}$$

$$(x^2 + 6x + 9) + 4(y^2 - 2y + 1) = -9 + 9 + 4(1) \qquad \text{Complete the squares.}$$

$$(x + 3)^2 + 4(y - 1)^2 = 4 \qquad \begin{array}{l}\text{Write in completed}\\ \text{square form.}\end{array}$$

$$\frac{(x + 3)^2}{2^2} + \frac{(y - 1)^2}{1^2} = 1 \qquad \text{Write in standard form.}$$

Now you see that the center is $(h, k) = (-3, 1)$. Because the denominator of the x-term is $a^2 = 2^2$, the endpoints of the major axis lie two units to the right and left of the center. Similarly, because the denominator of the y-term is $b^2 = 1^2$, the endpoints of the minor axis lie one unit up and down from the center. The ellipse is shown in Figure 9.20.

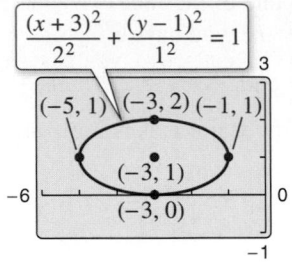

Figure 9.20

✓ **Checkpoint** ◀))) *Audio-video solution in English & Spanish at LarsonPrecalculus.com.*

Graph the ellipse given by $9x^2 + 4y^2 + 36x - 8y + 4 = 0$.

EXAMPLE 4 Analyzing an Ellipse

See LarsonPrecalculus.com for an interactive version of this type of example.

Find the center, vertices, and foci of the ellipse $4x^2 + y^2 - 8x + 4y - 8 = 0$.

Solution

By completing the square, you can write the original equation in standard form.

$$4x^2 + y^2 - 8x + 4y - 8 = 0 \qquad \text{Write original equation.}$$

$$4\left(x^2 - 2x + \boxed{}\right) + \left(y^2 + 4y + \boxed{}\right) = 8 \qquad \begin{array}{l}\text{Group terms and factor}\\ \text{4 out of } x\text{-terms.}\end{array}$$

$$4(x^2 - 2x + 1) + (y^2 + 4y + 4) = 8 + 4(1) + 4 \qquad \text{Complete the squares.}$$

$$4(x - 1)^2 + (y + 2)^2 = 16 \qquad \begin{array}{l}\text{Write in completed}\\ \text{square form.}\end{array}$$

$$\frac{(x - 1)^2}{2^2} + \frac{(y + 2)^2}{4^2} = 1 \qquad \text{Write in standard form.}$$

So, the major axis is vertical, where $h = 1$, $k = -2$, $a = 4$, $b = 2$, and

$$c = \sqrt{a^2 - b^2} = \sqrt{16 - 4} = \sqrt{12} = 2\sqrt{3}.$$

So, you have the following.

Center: $(1, -2)$

Vertices: $(1, -6)$

$(1, 2)$

Foci: $\left(1, -2 - 2\sqrt{3}\right)$

$\left(1, -2 + 2\sqrt{3}\right)$

The ellipse is shown in Figure 9.21.

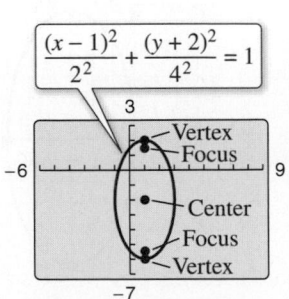

Figure 9.21

✓ **Checkpoint** ◀))) *Audio-video solution in English & Spanish at LarsonPrecalculus.com.*

Find the center, vertices, and foci of the ellipse $5x^2 + 9y^2 + 10x - 54y + 41 = 0$. ■

Application

Ellipses have many practical and aesthetic uses. For instance, machine gears, supporting arches, and acoustic designs often involve elliptical shapes. The orbits of satellites and planets are also ellipses. Example 5 investigates the elliptical orbit of the moon about Earth.

EXAMPLE 5   An Application Involving an Elliptical Orbit

The moon travels about Earth in an elliptical orbit with Earth at one focus, as shown in the figure. The major and minor axes of the orbit have lengths of 768,800 kilometers and 767,619 kilometers, respectively. Find the greatest and least distances (the *apogee* and *perigee*) from Earth's center to the moon's center. Then graph the orbit of the moon on a graphing utility.

> **Remark**
>
> Note in Example 5 and the figure that Earth *is not* the center of the moon's orbit.

Solution

Because $2a = 768,800$ and $2b = 767,619$, you have

$$a = 384,400 \quad \text{and} \quad b = 383,809.5$$

which implies that

$$c = \sqrt{a^2 - b^2} = \sqrt{384,400^2 - 383,809.5^2} \approx 21,299.$$

So, the greatest distance between the center of Earth and the center of the moon is

$$a + c \approx 384,400 + 21,299 = 405,699 \text{ kilometers}$$

and the least distance is

$$a - c \approx 384,400 - 21,299 = 363,101 \text{ kilometers}.$$

To graph the orbit of the moon on a graphing utility, first let $a = 384,400$ and $b = 383,809.5$ in the standard form of an equation of an ellipse centered at the origin, and then solve for y.

$$\frac{x^2}{384,400^2} + \frac{y^2}{383,809.5^2} = 1 \quad \Longrightarrow \quad y = \pm 383,809.5\sqrt{1 - \frac{x^2}{384,400^2}}$$

Graph the upper and lower portions in the same viewing window, as shown in Figure 9.22.

Astronaut

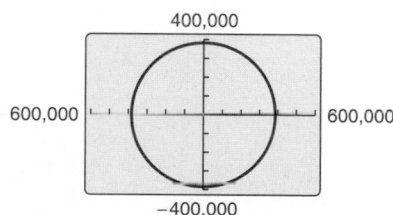

Figure 9.22

✓ **Checkpoint** 🔊))) *Audio-video solution in English & Spanish at LarsonPrecalculus.com.*

Encke's comet travels about the sun in an elliptical orbit with the sun at one focus. The major and minor axes of the orbit have lengths of approximately 4.429 astronomical units and 2.345 astronomical units, respectively. (An astronomical unit is about 93 million miles.) Find the greatest (*aphelion*) and least (*perihelion*) distances from the sun's center to the comet's center. ∎

Eccentricity

One of the reasons it was difficult for early astronomers to detect that the orbits of the planets are ellipses is that the foci of the planetary orbits are relatively close to their centers, and so the orbits are nearly circular. To measure the ovalness of an ellipse, you can use the concept of **eccentricity.**

Definition of Eccentricity

The **eccentricity** e of an ellipse is given by the ratio $e = \dfrac{c}{a}$.

Note that $0 < e < 1$ for *every* ellipse.

To see how this ratio is used to describe the shape of an ellipse, note that because the foci of an ellipse are located along the major axis between the vertices and the center, it follows that

$$0 < c < a.$$

For an ellipse that is nearly circular, the foci are close to the center and the ratio c/a is close to 0, as shown in Figure 9.23. On the other hand, for an elongated ellipse, the foci are close to the vertices and the ratio c/a is close to 1, as shown in Figure 9.24.

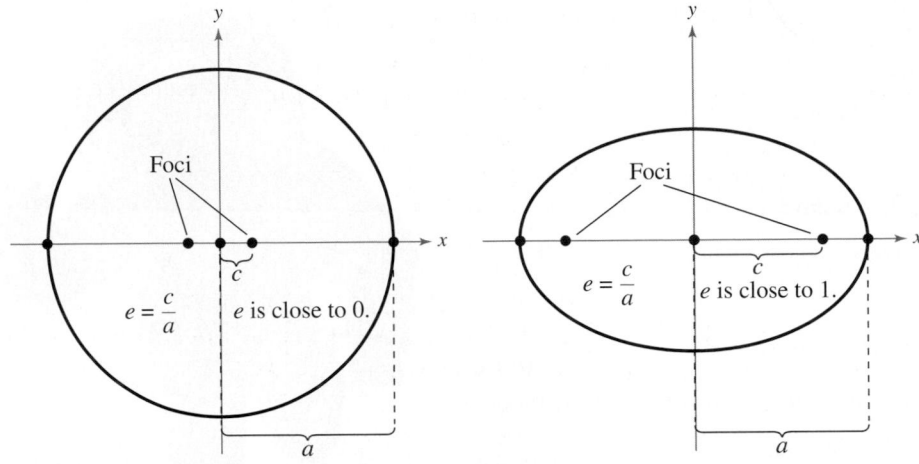

Figure 9.23   **Figure 9.24**

The orbit of the moon has an eccentricity of

$$e \approx 0.0554 \qquad \text{Eccentricity of the moon}$$

and the eccentricities of the eight planetary orbits are as follows.

Planet	Eccentricity, e
Mercury	0.2056
Venus	0.0068
Earth	0.0167
Mars	0.0934
Jupiter	0.0484
Saturn	0.0539
Uranus	0.0473
Neptune	0.0086

9.2 Exercises

Vocabulary and Concept Check

In Exercises 1–4, fill in the blank(s).

1. An _____ is the set of all points (x, y) in a plane, the sum of whose distances from two distinct fixed points called _____ is constant.

2. The chord joining the vertices of an ellipse is called the _____ , and its midpoint is the _____ of the ellipse.

3. The chord perpendicular to the major axis at the center of an ellipse is called the _____ of the ellipse.

4. The eccentricity e of an ellipse is given by the ratio $e =$ _____.

In Exercises 5–8, consider the ellipse given by $\dfrac{x^2}{2^2} + \dfrac{y^2}{8^2} = 1$.

5. Is the major axis horizontal or vertical?

6. What is the length of the major axis?

7. What is the length of the minor axis?

8. Is the ellipse elongated or nearly circular?

Procedures and Problem Solving

Matching an Equation with a Graph   In Exercises 9–12, match the equation with its graph. [The graphs are labeled (a), (b), (c), and (d).]

(a)

(b)

(c)

(d)

9. $\dfrac{x^2}{4} + \dfrac{y^2}{9} = 1$

10. $\dfrac{x^2}{9} + \dfrac{y^2}{4} = 1$

11. $\dfrac{(x - 2)^2}{4} + \dfrac{(y + 1)^2}{9} = 1$

12. $\dfrac{(x + 2)^2}{9} + \dfrac{(y + 2)^2}{4} = 1$

An Ellipse Centered at the Origin   In Exercises 13–20, find the standard form of the equation of the ellipse with the given characteristics and center at the origin.

13.

14.
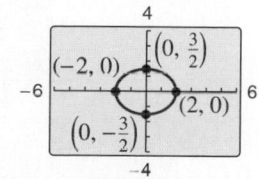

15. Vertices: $(\pm 3, 0)$; foci: $(\pm 2, 0)$

16. Vertices: $(0, \pm 8)$; foci: $(0, +4)$

17. Foci: $(0, \pm 5)$; major axis of length 14

18. Foci: $(\pm 2, 0)$; major axis of length 10

19. Vertices: $(0, \pm 4)$;
    passes through the point $(3, 1)$

20. Vertices: $(\pm 8, 0)$;
    passes through the point $(5, -3)$

Finding the Standard Equation of an Ellipse   In Exercises 21–28, find the standard form of the equation of the ellipse with the given characteristics.

21.

22.

23. Vertices: $(0, 2)$, $(8, 2)$; minor axis of length 2

24. Vertices: $(3, 1)$, $(3, 9)$; minor axis of length 6

25. Foci: $(0, 0)$, $(0, 8)$; major axis of length 36

26. Foci: $(0, 0)$, $(4, 0)$; major axis of length 6

27. Center: $(3, 2)$; $a = 3c$; foci: $(1, 2)$, $(5, 2)$

28. Center: $(0, 4)$, $a = 5c$; vertices: $(0, -1)$, $(0, 9)$

Sketching an Ellipse　In Exercises 29–34, find the center, vertices, foci, and eccentricity of the ellipse, and sketch its graph. Use a graphing utility to verify your graph.

29. $\dfrac{x^2}{64} + \dfrac{y^2}{9} = 1$　　　　30. $\dfrac{x^2}{16} + \dfrac{y^2}{81} = 1$

31. $\dfrac{(x-4)^2}{16} + \dfrac{(y+1)^2}{25} = 1$

32. $\dfrac{(x+3)^2}{12} + \dfrac{(y-2)^2}{16} = 1$

33. $\dfrac{(x+5)^2}{\frac{9}{4}} + (y-1)^2 = 1$

34. $(x+2)^2 + \dfrac{(y+4)^2}{\frac{1}{4}} = 1$

Analyzing an Ellipse　In Exercises 35–44, (a) find the standard form of the equation of the ellipse, (b) find the center, vertices, foci, and eccentricity of the ellipse, and (c) sketch the ellipse. Use a graphing utility to verify your graph.

35. $x^2 + 9y^2 = 36$　　　　36. $16x^2 + y^2 = 16$

37. $49x^2 + 4y^2 - 196 = 0$

38. $4x^2 + 49y^2 - 196 = 0$

39. $9x^2 + 4y^2 + 36x - 24y + 36 = 0$

40. $9x^2 + 4y^2 - 54x + 40y + 37 = 0$

41. $6x^2 + 2y^2 + 18x - 10y + 2 = 0$

42. $x^2 + 4y^2 - 6x + 20y - 2 = 0$

43. $12x^2 + 20y^2 - 12x + 40y - 37 = 0$

44. $36x^2 + 9y^2 + 48x - 36y + 43 = 0$

Finding Eccentricity　In Exercises 45–48, find the eccentricity of the ellipse.

45. $\dfrac{x^2}{4} + \dfrac{y^2}{9} = 1$　　　　46. $\dfrac{x^2}{25} + \dfrac{y^2}{49} = 1$

47. $x^2 + 9y^2 - 10x + 36y + 52 = 0$

48. $4x^2 + 3y^2 - 8x + 18y + 19 = 0$

Using Eccentricity　In Exercises 49–52, find an equation of the ellipse with the given characteristics.

49. Vertices: $(\pm 5, 0)$; eccentricity: $\frac{3}{5}$

50. Vertices: $(0, \pm 8)$; eccentricity: $\frac{1}{2}$

51. Foci: $(1, 1), (1, 13)$; eccentricity: $\frac{2}{3}$

52. Foci: $(-6, 5), (2, 5)$; eccentricity: $\frac{4}{5}$

53. **Astronomy**　Halley's comet has an elliptical orbit with the sun at one focus. The eccentricity of the orbit is approximately 0.97. The length of the major axis of the orbit is about 35.67 astronomical units. (An astronomical unit is about 93 million miles.) Find the standard form of the equation of the orbit. Place the center of the orbit at the origin and place the major axis on the x-axis.

54. **Architecture**　A fireplace arch is to be constructed in the shape of a semiellipse. The opening is to have a height of 2 feet at the center and a width of 6 feet along the base (see figure). The contractor draws the outline of the ellipse on the wall by the method discussed on page 647.

(a) What are the required positions of the tacks?

(b) What is the length of the string?

55. ***Why you should learn it***　(p. 647)　A lithotripter machine uses an elliptical reflector to break up kidney stones nonsurgically. A spark plug in the reflector generates energy waves at one focus of an ellipse. The reflector directs these waves toward the kidney stone positioned at the other focus of the ellipse with enough energy to break up the stone, as shown in the figure. The lengths of the major and minor axes of the ellipse are 280 millimeters and 160 millimeters, respectively. How far is the spark from the kidney stone?

Spark plug

Kidney stone

Elliptical reflector

56. **Aeronautics**　The first artificial satellite to orbit Earth was Sputnik I (launched by the former Soviet Union in 1957). Its highest point above Earth's surface was 947 kilometers, and its lowest point was 228 kilometers. The center of Earth was a focus of the elliptical orbit, and the radius of Earth is 6378 kilometers (see figure). Find the eccentricity of the orbit.

Focus

228 km　　　　　　　　　　　947 km

57. Geometry The area of the ellipse in the figure is twice the area of the circle. How long is the major axis? (*Hint:* The area of an ellipse is given by $A = \pi ab$.)

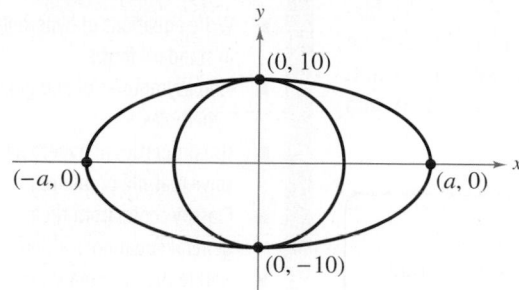

58. Geometry A line segment through a focus with endpoints on an ellipse, perpendicular to the major axis, is called a **latus rectum** of the ellipse. So, an ellipse has two latera recta. Knowing the length of the latera recta is helpful in sketching an ellipse because this information yields other points on the curve (see figure). Show that the length of each latus rectum is $2b^2/a$.

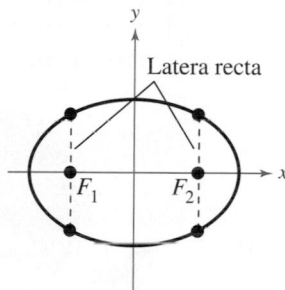

Using Latera Recta In Exercises 59–62, sketch the ellipse using the latera recta (see Exercise 58).

59. $\dfrac{x^2}{9} + \dfrac{y^2}{1} = 1$ **60.** $\dfrac{x^2}{4} + \dfrac{y^2}{25} = 1$

61. $16x^2 + 4y^2 = 64$

62. $6x^2 + 3y^2 = 12$

Conclusions

True or False? In Exercises 63 and 64, determine whether the statement is true or false. Justify your answer.

63. It is easier to distinguish the graph of an ellipse from the graph of a circle when the eccentricity of the ellipse is large (close to 1).

64. The area of a circle with diameter $d = 2r = 8$ is greater than the area of an ellipse with major axis $2a = 8$.

Identifying Degenerate Conics In Exercises 65 and 66, determine whether the equation represents a degenerate conic. Explain.

65. $16x^2 + 25y^2 - 32x + 50y + 16 = 0$

66. $9x^2 + 25y^2 - 36x - 50y + 61 = 0$

67. Think About It Is the ellipse $\dfrac{x^2}{328} + \dfrac{y^2}{327} = 1$ better described as *elongated* or *nearly circular*? Explain your reasoning.

68. HOW DO YOU SEE IT? Without performing any calculations, order the eccentricities of the ellipses from least to greatest.

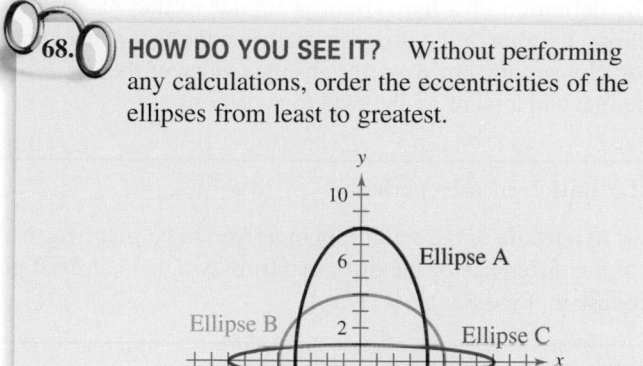

69. Think About It At the beginning of this section, it was noted that an ellipse can be drawn using two thumbtacks, a string of fixed length (greater than the distance between the two tacks), and a pencil (see Figure 9.16). When the ends of the string are fastened at the tacks and the string is drawn taut with a pencil, the path traced by the pencil is an ellipse.

(a) What is the length of the string in terms of a?

(b) Explain why the path is an ellipse.

70. Think About It Find the equation of an ellipse such that for any point on the ellipse, the sum of the distances from the points $(2, 2)$ and $(10, 2)$ is 36.

71. Proof Show that $a^2 = b^2 + c^2$ for the ellipse

$$\frac{x^2}{a^2} + \frac{y^2}{b^2} = 1$$

where $a > 0$, $b > 0$, and the distance from the center of the ellipse $(0, 0)$ to a focus is c.

Cumulative Mixed Review

Identifying a Sequence In Exercises 72–75, determine whether the sequence is arithmetic, geometric, or neither.

72. $66, 55, 44, 33, 22, \ldots$

73. $80, 40, 20, 10, 5, \ldots$

74. $\dfrac{1}{4}, \dfrac{1}{2}, 1, 2, 4, \ldots$ **75.** $-\dfrac{1}{2}, \dfrac{1}{2}, \dfrac{3}{2}, \dfrac{5}{2}, \dfrac{7}{2}, \ldots$

Finding the Sum of a Finite Geometric Sequence In Exercises 76 and 77, find the sum.

76. $\displaystyle\sum_{n=0}^{6} 3^n$ **77.** $\displaystyle\sum_{n=1}^{10} 4\left(\dfrac{3}{4}\right)^{n-1}$

9.3   Hyperbolas and Rotation of Conics

Introduction

The definition of a **hyperbola** is similar to that of an ellipse. You know that for an ellipse, the *sum* of the distances between the foci and a point on the ellipse is constant. For a hyperbola, however, the absolute value of the *difference* of the distances between the foci and a point on the hyperbola is constant.

What you should learn
- ▶ Write equations of hyperbolas in standard form.
- ▶ Find asymptotes of and graph hyperbolas.
- ▶ Use properties of hyperbolas to solve real-life problems.
- ▶ Classify conics from their general equations.
- ▶ Rotate the coordinate axes to eliminate the *xy*-term in equations of conics.

Why you should learn it
Hyperbolas can be used to model and solve many types of real-life problems. For instance, in Exercise 52 on page 666, hyperbolas are used to locate the position of an explosion that was recorded by three listening stations.

> **Definition of a Hyperbola**
>
> A **hyperbola** is the set of all points (x, y) in a plane for which the absolute value of the difference of the distances from two distinct fixed points, called **foci,** is constant. [See Figure 9.25(a).]

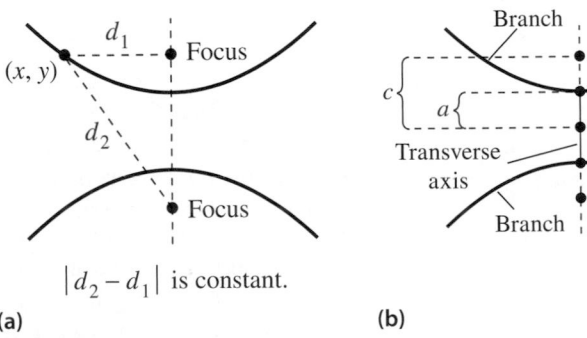

(a)

(b)

Figure 9.25

The graph of a hyperbola has two disconnected parts called the **branches.** The line through the two foci intersects the hyperbola at two points called the **vertices.** The line segment connecting the vertices is the **transverse axis,** and the midpoint of the transverse axis is the **center** of the hyperbola [see Figure 9.25(b)]. The development of the **standard form of the equation of a hyperbola** is similar to that of an ellipse. Note, however, that a, b, and c are related differently for hyperbolas than for ellipses. For a hyperbola, the distance between the foci and the center is greater than the distance between the vertices and the center.

> **Standard Equation of a Hyperbola**
>
> The **standard form of the equation of a hyperbola** with center at (h, k) is
>
> $$\frac{(x - h)^2}{a^2} - \frac{(y - k)^2}{b^2} = 1 \qquad \text{Transverse axis is horizontal.}$$
>
> $$\frac{(y - k)^2}{a^2} - \frac{(x - h)^2}{b^2} = 1. \qquad \text{Transverse axis is vertical.}$$
>
> The vertices are a units from the center, and the foci are c units from the center. Moreover, $c^2 = a^2 + b^2$. If the center of the hyperbola is at the origin $(0, 0)$, then the equation takes one of the following forms.
>
> $$\frac{x^2}{a^2} - \frac{y^2}{b^2} = 1 \qquad \text{Transverse axis is horizontal.}$$
>
> $$\frac{y^2}{a^2} - \frac{x^2}{b^2} = 1 \qquad \text{Transverse axis is vertical.}$$

Figure 9.26 shows both the horizontal and vertical orientations for a hyperbola.

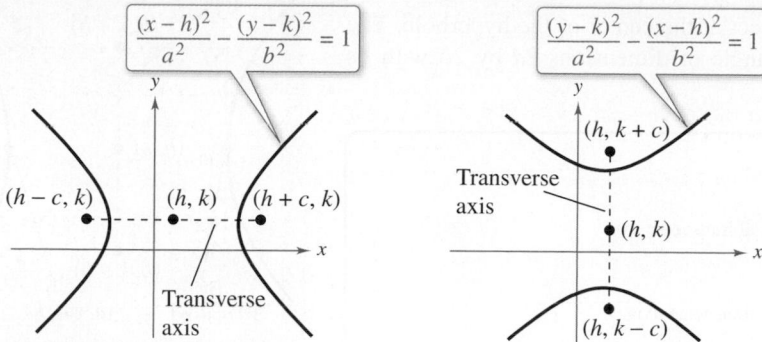

Transverse axis is horizontal.

Figure 9.26

Transverse axis is vertical.

EXAMPLE 1   Finding the Standard Equation of a Hyperbola

Find the standard form of the equation of the hyperbola with foci $(-1, 2)$ and $(5, 2)$ and vertices $(0, 2)$ and $(4, 2)$.

Solution

By the Midpoint Formula, the center of the hyperbola occurs at the point $(2, 2)$. Furthermore, $c = 3$ and $a = 2$, and it follows that

$$b = \sqrt{c^2 - a^2}$$
$$= \sqrt{3^2 - 2^2}$$
$$= \sqrt{9 - 4}$$
$$= \sqrt{5}.$$

So, the hyperbola has a horizontal transverse axis, and the standard form of the equation of the hyperbola is

$$\frac{(x - 2)^2}{2^2} - \frac{(y - 2)^2}{\left(\sqrt{5}\right)^2} = 1.$$

This equation simplifies to

$$\frac{(x - 2)^2}{4} - \frac{(y - 2)^2}{5} = 1.$$

The hyperbola is shown in the figure.

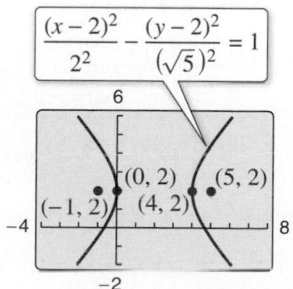

$$\frac{(x - 2)^2}{2^2} - \frac{(y - 2)^2}{(\sqrt{5})^2} = 1$$

✓ **Checkpoint** ◀))) *Audio-video solution in English & Spanish at LarsonPrecalculus.com.*

Find the standard form of the equation of the hyperbola with foci $(2, -5)$ and $(2, 3)$ and vertices $(2, -4)$ and $(2, 2)$.

> **Technology Tip**
>
> You can use a graphing utility to graph a hyperbola by graphing the upper and lower portions in the same viewing window. To do this, you must solve the equation for y before entering it into the graphing utility. When graphing equations of conics, it can be difficult to solve for y, which is why it is very important to know the algebra used to solve equations for y.

Asymptotes of a Hyperbola

Each hyperbola has two **asymptotes** that intersect at the center of the hyperbola. The asymptotes pass through the corners of a rectangle of dimensions $2a$ by $2b$ with its center at (h, k), as shown in Figure 9.27.

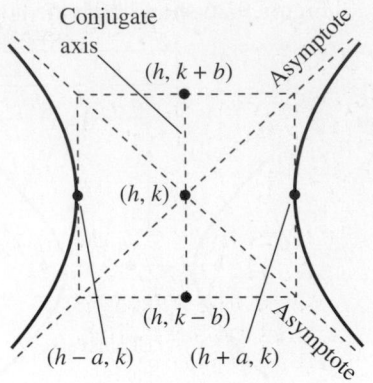

Figure 9.27

Asymptotes of a Hyperbola

$$y = k \pm \frac{b}{a}(x - h) \qquad \text{Asymptotes for horizontal transverse axis}$$

$$y = k \pm \frac{a}{b}(x - h) \qquad \text{Asymptotes for vertical transverse axis}$$

The **conjugate axis** of a hyperbola is the line segment of length $2b$ joining $(h, k + b)$ and $(h, k - b)$ when the transverse axis is horizontal, and the line segment of length $2b$ joining $(h + b, k)$ and $(h - b, k)$ when the transverse axis is vertical.

EXAMPLE 2   Sketching a Hyperbola

Sketch the hyperbola $4x^2 - y^2 = 16$.

Algebraic Solution

$$4x^2 - y^2 = 16 \qquad \text{Write original equation.}$$

$$\frac{4x^2}{16} - \frac{y^2}{16} = \frac{16}{16} \qquad \text{Divide each side by 16.}$$

$$\frac{x^2}{2^2} - \frac{y^2}{4^2} = 1 \qquad \text{Write in standard form.}$$

Because the x^2-term is positive, you can conclude that the transverse axis is horizontal. So, the vertices occur at $(-2, 0)$ and $(2, 0)$, the endpoints of the conjugate axis occur at $(0, -4)$ and $(0, 4)$, and you can sketch the rectangle shown in Figure 9.28. Finally, by drawing the asymptotes $y = 2x$ and $y = -2x$ through the corners of this rectangle, you can complete the sketch, as shown in Figure 9.29.

Graphical Solution

Solve the equation of the hyperbola for y, as follows.

$$4x^2 - y^2 = 16$$

$$4x^2 - 16 = y^2$$

$$\pm\sqrt{4x^2 - 16} = y$$

Then use a graphing utility to graph

$$y_1 = \sqrt{4x^2 - 16} \quad \text{and} \quad y_2 = -\sqrt{4x^2 - 16}$$

in the same viewing window, as shown in the figure. Be sure to use a square setting.

From the graph, you can see that the transverse axis is horizontal and the vertices are $(-2, 0)$ and $(2, 0)$.

Figure 9.28

Figure 9.29

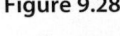 **Checkpoint** 🔊)) *Audio-video solution in English & Spanish at LarsonPrecalculus.com.*

Sketch the hyperbola $4y^2 - 9x^2 = 36$.

EXAMPLE 3   Finding the Asymptotes of a Hyperbola

Sketch the hyperbola $4x^2 - 3y^2 + 8x + 16 = 0$, find the equations of its asymptotes, and find the foci.

Solution

$4x^2 - 3y^2 + 8x + 16 = 0$	Write original equation.
$4(x^2 + 2x) - 3y^2 = -16$	Subtract 16 from each side and factor.
$4(x^2 + 2x + 1) - 3y^2 = -16 + 4(1)$	Complete the square.
$4(x + 1)^2 - 3y^2 = -12$	Write in completed square form.
$\dfrac{y^2}{2^2} - \dfrac{(x + 1)^2}{\left(\sqrt{3}\right)^2} = 1$	Write in standard form.

From this equation, you can conclude that the hyperbola has a vertical transverse axis, is centered at $(-1, 0)$, has vertices $(-1, 2)$ and $(-1, -2)$, and has a conjugate axis with endpoints $\left(-1 - \sqrt{3}, 0\right)$ and $\left(-1 + \sqrt{3}, 0\right)$. To sketch the hyperbola, draw a rectangle through these four points. The asymptotes are the lines passing through the corners of the rectangle. Using $a = 2$ and $b = \sqrt{3}$, you can conclude that the equations of the asymptotes are

$$y = \frac{2}{\sqrt{3}}(x + 1) \quad \text{and} \quad y = -\frac{2}{\sqrt{3}}(x + 1).$$

Finally, you can determine the foci by using the equation $c^2 = a^2 + b^2$. So, you have $c = \sqrt{2^2 + \left(\sqrt{3}\right)^2} = \sqrt{7}$, and the foci are $\left(-1, \sqrt{7}\right)$ and $\left(-1, -\sqrt{7}\right)$. The hyperbola is shown in the figure.

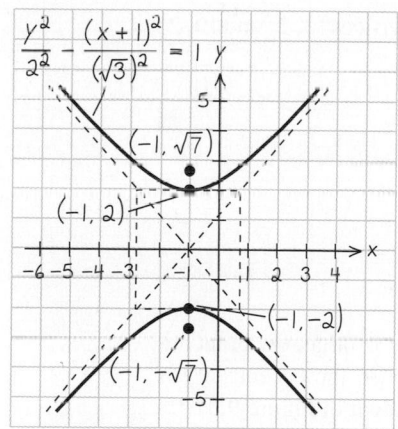

You can verify your sketch using a graphing utility, as shown in the figure. Notice that the graphing utility does not draw the asymptotes. When you trace along the branches, however, you will see that the values of the hyperbola approach the asymptotes.

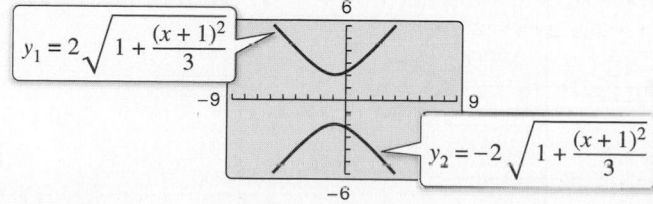

✓ **Checkpoint** ◀))) Audio-video solution in English & Spanish at LarsonPrecalculus.com.

Sketch the hyperbola $9x^2 - 4y^2 + 8y - 40 = 0$, find the equations of its asymptotes, and find the foci.

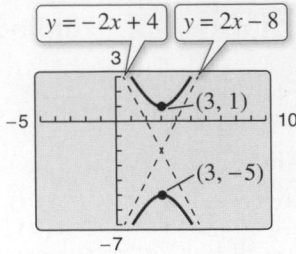

EXAMPLE 4 Using Asymptotes to Find the Standard Equation

See LarsonPrecalculus.com for an interactive version of this type of example.

Find the standard form of the equation of the hyperbola having vertices $(3, -5)$ and $(3, 1)$ and having asymptotes

$$y = 2x - 8 \quad \text{and} \quad y = -2x + 4$$

as shown in Figure 9.30.

Figure 9.30

Solution

By the Midpoint Formula, the center of the hyperbola is $(3, -2)$. Furthermore, the hyperbola has a vertical transverse axis with $a = 3$. From the original equations, you can determine the slopes of the asymptotes to be

$$m_1 = 2 = \frac{a}{b} \quad \text{and} \quad m_2 = -2 = -\frac{a}{b}$$

and because $a = 3$, you can conclude that

$$2 = \frac{a}{b} \implies 2 = \frac{3}{b} \implies b = \frac{3}{2}.$$

So, the standard form of the equation of the hyperbola is

$$\frac{(y + 2)^2}{3^2} - \frac{(x - 3)^2}{\left(\dfrac{3}{2}\right)^2} = 1.$$

 Checkpoint ◀)) *Audio-video solution in English & Spanish at LarsonPrecalculus.com.*

Find the standard form of the equation of the hyperbola having vertices $(3, 2)$ and $(9, 2)$ and having asymptotes

$$y = -2 + \frac{2}{3}x \quad \text{and} \quad y = 6 - \frac{2}{3}x.$$

As with ellipses, the *eccentricity* of a hyperbola is

$$e = \frac{c}{a} \qquad \text{Eccentricity}$$

and because $c > a$, it follows that $e > 1$. When the eccentricity is large, the branches of the hyperbola are nearly flat, as shown in Figure 9.31(a). When the eccentricity is close to 1, the branches of the hyperbola are more pointed, as shown in Figure 9.31(b).

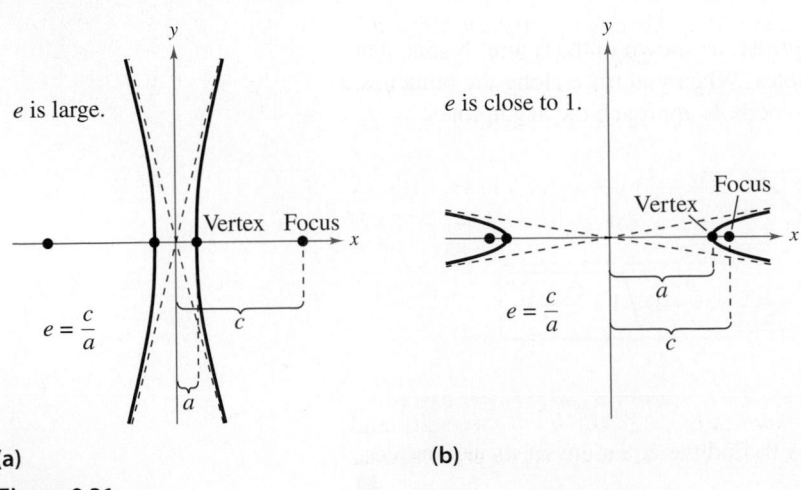

(a)

(b)

Figure 9.31

Applications

The following application was developed during World War II. It shows how the properties of hyperbolas can be used in radar and other detection systems.

EXAMPLE 5   An Application Involving Hyperbolas

Two microphones, 1 mile apart, record an explosion. Microphone A receives the sound 2 seconds before microphone B. Where did the explosion occur?

Solution

Assuming sound travels at 1100 feet per second, you know that the explosion took place 2200 feet farther from B than from A, as shown in the figure. The locus of all points that are 2200 feet closer to A than to B is one branch of the hyperbola

$$\frac{x^2}{a^2} - \frac{y^2}{b^2} = 1$$

where

$$c = \frac{5280}{2} = 2640$$

and

$$a = \frac{2200}{2} = 1100.$$

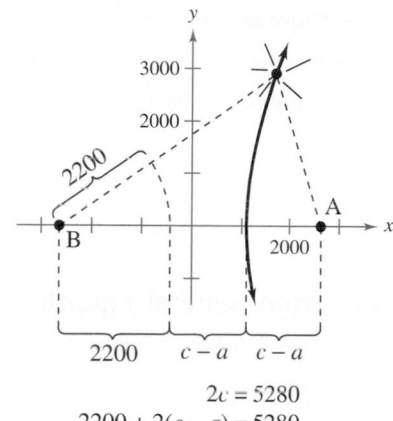

$$2c = 5280$$
$$2200 + 2(c - a) = 5280$$

So, $b^2 = c^2 - a^2 = 2640^2 - 1100^2 = 5,759,600$, and you can conclude that the explosion occurred somewhere on the right branch of the hyperbola

$$\frac{x^2}{1,210,000} - \frac{y^2}{5,759,600} = 1.$$

✓ **Checkpoint** 🔊))) *Audio-video solution in English & Spanish at LarsonPrecalculus.com.*

Repeat Example 5 when microphone A receives the sound 4 seconds before microphone B.

Another interesting application of conic sections involves the orbits of comets in our solar system. Of the 610 comets identified prior to 1970, 245 have elliptical orbits, 295 have parabolic orbits, and 70 have hyperbolic orbits. The center of the sun is a focus of each of these orbits, and each orbit has a vertex at the point where the comet is closest to the sun, as shown in Figure 9.32. Undoubtedly, there are many comets with parabolic or hyperbolic orbits that have not been identified. You get to see such comets only *once*. Comets with elliptical orbits, such as Halley's comet, are the only ones that remain in our solar system.

If p is the distance between the vertex and the focus in meters, and v is the velocity of the comet at the vertex in meters per second, then the type of orbit is determined as follows.

1. **Ellipse:** $v < \sqrt{2GM/p}$
2. **Parabola:** $v = \sqrt{2GM/p}$
3. **Hyperbola:** $v > \sqrt{2GM/p}$

In each of the above, $M \approx 1.989 \times 10^{30}$ kilograms (the mass of the sun) and $G \approx 6.67 \times 10^{-11}$ cubic meter per kilogram-second squared (the universal gravitational constant).

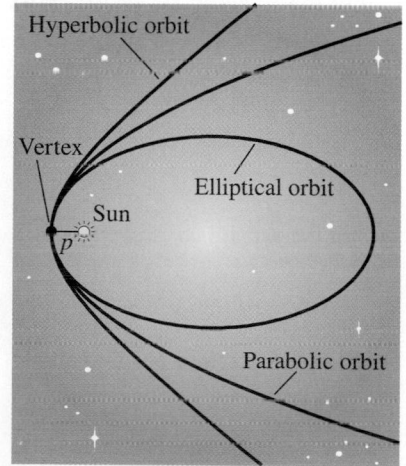

Figure 9.32

General Equations of Conics

> **Classifying a Conic from Its General Equation**
>
> The graph of $Ax^2 + Cy^2 + Dx + Ey + F = 0$ is one of the following.
>
> **1.** Circle: $A = C$ $A \neq 0$
>
> **2.** Parabola: $AC = 0$ $A = 0$ or $C = 0$, but not both.
>
> **3.** Ellipse: $AC > 0$ A and C have like signs.
>
> **4.** Hyperbola: $AC < 0$ A and C have unlike signs.

The test above is valid when the graph is a *conic*. The test does not apply to equations such as

$$x^2 + y^2 = -1$$

whose graphs are not conics.

EXAMPLE 6   Classifying Conics from General Equations

Classify the graph of each equation.

a. $4x^2 - 9x + y - 5 = 0$

b. $4x^2 - y^2 + 8x - 6y + 4 = 0$

c. $2x^2 + 4y^2 - 4x + 12y = 0$

d. $2x^2 + 2y^2 - 8x + 12y + 2 = 0$

Solution

a. For the equation $4x^2 - 9x + y - 5 = 0$, you have

$$AC = 4(0) = 0. \qquad \text{Parabola}$$

So, the graph is a parabola.

b. For the equation $4x^2 - y^2 + 8x - 6y + 4 = 0$, you have

$$AC = 4(-1) < 0. \qquad \text{Hyperbola}$$

So, the graph is a hyperbola.

c. For the equation $2x^2 + 4y^2 - 4x + 12y = 0$, you have

$$AC = 2(4) > 0. \qquad \text{Ellipse}$$

So, the graph is an ellipse.

d. For the equation $2x^2 + 2y^2 - 8x + 12y + 2 = 0$, you have

$$A = C = 2. \qquad \text{Circle}$$

So, the graph is a circle.

> **Remark**
>
> Notice in Example 6(a) that there is no y^2-term in the equation. So, $C = 0$.

✓ **Checkpoint** 🔊 *Audio-video solution in English & Spanish at LarsonPrecalculus.com.*

Classify the graph of each equation.

a. $3x^2 + 3y^2 - 6x + 6y + 5 = 0$

b. $2x^2 - 4y^2 + 4x + 8y - 3 = 0$

c. $3x^2 + y^2 + 6x - 2y + 3 = 0$

d. $2x^2 + 4x + y - 2 = 0$

Rotation

The equation of a conic with axes parallel to one of the coordinate axes has a standard form that can be written in the general form

$$Ax^2 + Cy^2 + Dx + Ey + F = 0. \qquad \text{Horizontal or vertical axis}$$

You will now study the equations of conics whose axes are rotated so that they are not parallel to either the x-axis or the y-axis. The general equation for such conics contains an xy-term.

$$Ax^2 + Bxy + Cy^2 + Dx + Ey + F = 0 \qquad \text{Equation in } xy\text{-plane}$$

To eliminate this xy-term, you can use a procedure called **rotation of axes.** The objective is to rotate the x- and y-axes until they are parallel to the axes of the conic. The rotated axes are denoted as the x'-axis and the y'-axis, as shown in Figure 9.33.

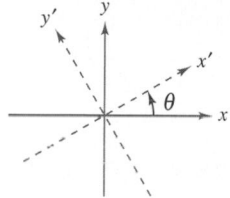

Figure 9.33

After the rotation, the equation of the conic in the new $x'y'$-plane will have the form

$$A'(x')^2 + C'(y')^2 + D'x' + E'y' + F' = 0. \qquad \text{Equation in } x'y'\text{-plane}$$

Because this equation has no xy-term, you can obtain a standard form by completing the square. The following theorem identifies how much to rotate the axes to eliminate the xy-term and also the equations for determining the new coefficients A', C', D', E', and F'.

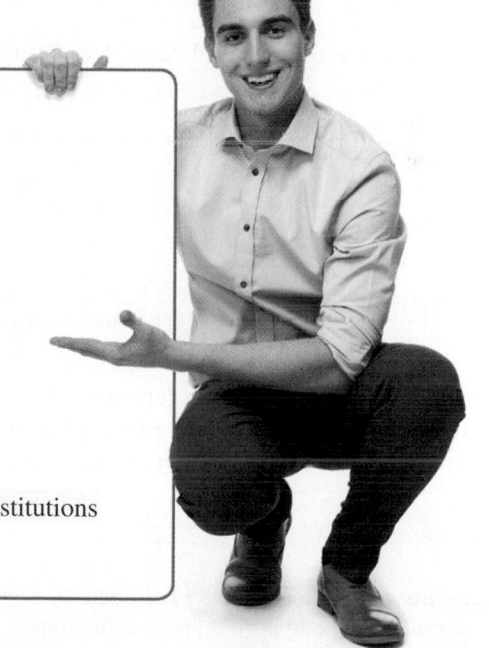

Rotation of Axes to Eliminate an xy-Term   (See the proof on page 708.)

The general second-degree equation

$$Ax^2 + Bxy + Cy^2 + Dx + Ey + F = 0$$

can be rewritten as

$$A'(x')^2 + C'(y')^2 + D'x' + E'y' + F' = 0$$

by rotating the coordinate axes through an angle θ, where

$$\cot 2\theta = \frac{A - C}{B}.$$

The coefficients of the new equation are obtained by making the substitutions

$$x = x' \cos \theta - y' \sin \theta \quad \text{and} \quad y = x' \sin \theta + y' \cos \theta.$$

Note that the substitutions

$$x = x' \cos \theta - y' \sin \theta \quad \text{and} \quad y = x' \sin \theta + y' \cos \theta$$

were developed to eliminate the $x'y'$-term in the rotated system. You can use this to check your work. In other words, when your final equation contains an $x'y'$-term, you know that you have made a mistake.

EXAMPLE 7   Rotation of Axes for a Hyperbola

Rotate the axes to eliminate the xy-term in the equation $xy - 1 = 0$. Then write the equation in standard form and sketch its graph.

Solution

Because $A = 0$, $B = 1$, and $C = 0$, you have

$$\cot 2\theta = \frac{A - C}{B} = 0$$

which implies that $2\theta = \pi/2$, or $\theta = \pi/4$. The equation in the $x'y'$-system is obtained by making the substitutions

$$x = x' \cos \frac{\pi}{4} - y' \sin \frac{\pi}{4}$$

$$= x'\left(\frac{1}{\sqrt{2}}\right) - y'\left(\frac{1}{\sqrt{2}}\right)$$

$$= \frac{x' - y'}{\sqrt{2}}$$

and

$$y = x' \sin \frac{\pi}{4} + y' \cos \frac{\pi}{4}$$

$$= x'\left(\frac{1}{\sqrt{2}}\right) + y'\left(\frac{1}{\sqrt{2}}\right)$$

$$= \frac{x' + y'}{\sqrt{2}}.$$

The equation in the $x'y'$-system is obtained by substituting these expressions into the equation $xy - 1 = 0$.

$$\left(\frac{x' - y'}{\sqrt{2}}\right)\left(\frac{x' + y'}{\sqrt{2}}\right) - 1 = 0$$

$$\frac{(x')^2 - (y')^2}{2} - 1 = 0$$

$$\frac{(x')^2}{(\sqrt{2})^2} - \frac{(y')^2}{(\sqrt{2})^2} = 1 \qquad \text{Write in standard form.}$$

In the $x'y'$-system, this is a hyperbola centered at the origin with vertices at $(\pm\sqrt{2}, 0)$, as shown in Figure 9.34. To find the coordinates of the vertices in the xy-system, substitute the coordinates $(\pm\sqrt{2}, 0)$ into the equations

$$x = \frac{x' - y'}{\sqrt{2}} \qquad \text{and} \qquad y = \frac{x' + y'}{\sqrt{2}}.$$

This substitution yields the vertices $(1, 1)$ and $(-1, -1)$ in the xy-system. Note also that the asymptotes of the hyperbola have equations

$$y' = \pm x'$$

which correspond to the original x- and y-axes.

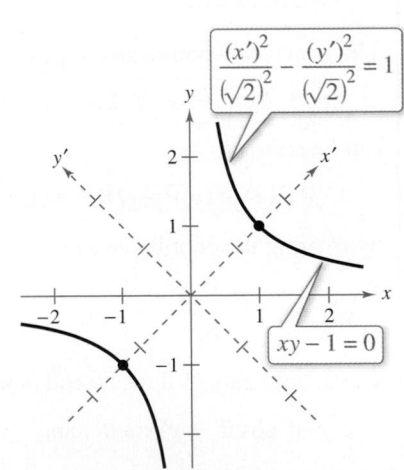

Vertices:
In $x'y'$-system: $\left(\sqrt{2}, 0\right), \left(-\sqrt{2}, 0\right)$
In xy-system: $(1, 1), (-1, -1)$
Figure 9.34

✔ **Checkpoint** 🔊 *Audio-video solution in English & Spanish at LarsonPrecalculus.com.*

Rotate the axes to eliminate the xy-term in the equation $xy + 6 = 0$. Then write the equation in standard form and sketch its graph. ■

9.3   Exercises

See *CalcChat.com* for tutorial help and worked-out solutions to odd-numbered exercises.
For instructions on how to use a graphing utility, see Appendix A.

Vocabulary and Concept Check

In Exercises 1–4, fill in the blank(s).

1. A _____ is the set of all points (x, y) in a plane for which the absolute value of the difference of the distances from two distinct fixed points, called foci, is constant.

2. The line segment connecting the vertices of a hyperbola is called the _____ , and the midpoint of the line segment is the _____ of the hyperbola.

3. The general form of the equation of a conic is given by _____ .

4. The procedure used to eliminate the xy-term in a general second-degree equation is called _____ of _____ .

5. Which of the following equations of a hyperbola have a horizontal transverse axis? a vertical transverse axis?

   (a) $\dfrac{(x - h)^2}{a^2} - \dfrac{(y - k)^2}{b^2} = 1$ (b) $\dfrac{(y - k)^2}{a^2} - \dfrac{(x - h)^2}{b^2} = 1$

   (c) $\dfrac{y^2}{a^2} - \dfrac{x^2}{b^2} = 1$ (d) $\dfrac{x^2}{a^2} - \dfrac{y^2}{b^2} = 1$

6. How many asymptotes does a hyperbola have? Where do these asymptotes intersect?

Procedures and Problem Solving

Matching an Equation with a Graph   In Exercises 7–10, match the equation with its graph. [The graphs are labeled (a), (b), (c), and (d).]

(a)

(b)

(c)

(d)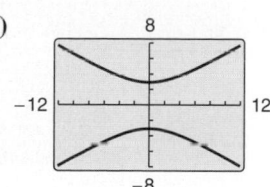

7. $\dfrac{x^2}{25} - \dfrac{y^2}{9} = 1$ 8. $\dfrac{y^2}{9} - \dfrac{x^2}{25} = 1$

9. $\dfrac{x^2}{4} - \dfrac{(y + 3)^2}{9} = 1$ 10. $\dfrac{(y - 2)^2}{4} - \dfrac{(x - 2)^2}{9} = 1$

Finding the Standard Equation of a Hyperbola   In Exercises 11–20, find the standard form of the equation of the hyperbola with the given characteristics.

11. Vertices: $(0, \pm 2)$; foci: $(0, \pm 4)$

12. Vertices: $(\pm 3, 0)$; foci: $(\pm 6, 0)$

13. Vertices: $(2, 0)$, $(6, 0)$; foci: $(0, 0)$, $(8, 0)$

14. Vertices: $(2, 3)$, $(2, -3)$; foci: $(2, 5)$, $(2, -5)$

15. Vertices: $(4, 1)$, $(4, 9)$; foci: $(4, 0)$, $(4, 10)$

16. Vertices: $(-2, 1)$, $(2, 1)$; foci: $(-3, 1)$, $(3, 1)$

17. Vertices: $(2, 3)$, $(2, -3)$; passes through the point $(0, 5)$

18. Vertices: $(-2, 1)$, $(2, 1)$; passes through the point $(5, 4)$

19. Vertices: $(0, 4)$, $(0, 0)$;
    passes through the point $\left(\sqrt{5}, -1\right)$

20. Vertices: $(1, 2)$, $(1, -2)$;
    passes through the point $\left(0, \sqrt{5}\right)$

Sketching a Hyperbola   In Exercises 21–30, find the center, vertices, foci, and asymptotes of the hyperbola, and sketch its graph using the asymptotes as an aid. Use a graphing utility to verify your graph.

21. $x^2 - y^2 = 1$ 22. $y^2 - x^2 = 1$

23. $\dfrac{y^2}{1} - \dfrac{x^2}{16} = 1$ 24. $\dfrac{x^2}{9} - \dfrac{y^2}{1} = 1$

25. $\dfrac{y^2}{16} - \dfrac{x^2}{4} = 1$

26. $\dfrac{x^2}{25} - \dfrac{y^2}{36} = 1$

27. $\dfrac{(x - 3)^2}{9} - \dfrac{(y - 1)^2}{1} = 1$

28. $\dfrac{(x - 2)^2}{4} - \dfrac{(y + 5)^2}{25} = 1$

29. $\dfrac{(y + 6)^2}{1} - \dfrac{(x - 2)^2}{\frac{1}{16}} = 1$

30. $\dfrac{(y + 4)^2}{\frac{1}{9}} - \dfrac{(x + 3)^2}{\frac{1}{4}} = 1$

Analyzing a Hyperbola In Exercises 31–40, (a) find the standard form of the equation of the hyperbola, (b) find the center, vertices, foci, and asymptotes of the hyperbola, and (c) sketch the hyperbola. Use a graphing utility to verify your graph.

31. $4x^2 - 9y^2 = 36$ **32.** $25x^2 - 4y^2 = 100$

33. $6y^2 - 3x^2 = 24$ **34.** $3x^2 - 2y^2 = 18$

35. $9x^2 - y^2 - 36x - 6y + 18 = 0$

36. $x^2 - 9y^2 + 36y - 72 = 0$

37. $2x^2 - 7y^2 + 16x + 18 = 0$

38. $3y^2 - 5x^2 + 6y - 60x - 192 = 0$

39. $9y^2 - x^2 + 2x + 54y + 62 = 0$

40. $9x^2 - y^2 + 54x + 10y + 55 = 0$

Using Asymptotes to Find the Standard Equation In Exercises 41–50, find the standard form of the equation of the hyperbola with the given characteristics.

41. Vertices: $(\pm 1, 0)$; asymptotes: $y = \pm 5x$

42. Vertices: $(0, \pm 3)$; asymptotes: $y = \pm 3x$

43. Foci: $(0, \pm 8)$; asymptotes: $y = \pm 4x$

44. Foci: $(\pm 10, 0)$; asymptotes: $y = \pm \frac{3}{4}x$

45. Vertices: $(1, 2)$, $(3, 2)$; asymptotes: $y = x$, $y = 4 - x$

46. Vertices: $(3, 0)$, $(3, -6)$;
    asymptotes: $y = x - 6$, $y = -x$

47. Vertices: $(0, 2)$, $(6, 2)$;
    asymptotes: $y = \frac{2}{3}x$, $y = 4 - \frac{2}{3}x$

48. Vertices: $(3, 0)$, $(3, 4)$;
    asymptotes: $y = \frac{2}{3}x$, $y = 4 - \frac{2}{3}x$

49. Foci: $(-1, 3)$, $(9, 3)$;
    asymptotes: $y = \frac{3}{4}x$, $y = 6 - \frac{3}{4}x$

50. Foci: $(1, 2)$, $(1, 6)$;
    asymptotes: $y = 2 + 2x$, $y = 6 - 2x$

51. Meteorology You and a friend live 4 miles apart (on the same "east-west" street) and are talking on the phone. You hear a clap of thunder from lightning in a storm, and 18 seconds later your friend hears the thunder. Find an equation that gives the possible places where the lightning could have occurred. (Assume that the coordinate system is measured in feet and that sound travels at 1100 feet per second.)

52. *Why you should learn it* *(p. 656)* Three listening stations located at $(3300, 0)$, $(3300, 1100)$, and $(-3300, 0)$ monitor an explosion. The last two stations detect the explosion 1 second and 4 seconds after the first, respectively. Determine the coordinates of the explosion. (Assume that the coordinate system is measured in feet and that sound travels at 1100 feet per second.)

53. Art and Design The base for the pendulum of a clock has the shape of a hyperbola. (See figure.)

(a) Write an equation of the cross section of the base.

(b) Each unit in the coordinate plane represents $\frac{1}{2}$ foot. Find the width of the base 4 inches from the bottom.

54. MODELING DATA

Long distance radio navigation for aircraft and ships uses synchronized pulses transmitted by widely separated transmitting stations. These pulses travel at the speed of light (186,000 miles per second). The difference in the times of arrival of these pulses at an aircraft or ship is constant on a hyperbola having the transmitting stations as foci. Assume that two stations, 300 miles apart, are positioned on a rectangular coordinate system at coordinates $(-150, 0)$ and $(150, 0)$, and that a ship is traveling on a hyperbolic path with coordinates $(x, 75)$. (See figure.)

(a) Find the x-coordinate of the position of the ship when the time difference between the pulses from the transmitting stations is 1000 microseconds (0.001 second).

(b) Determine the distance between the ship and station 1 when the ship reaches the shore.

(c) The captain of the ship wants to enter a bay located between the two stations. The bay is 30 miles from station 1. What should be the time difference between the pulses?

(d) The ship is 60 miles offshore when the time difference in part (c) is obtained. What is the position of the ship?

55. Hyperbolic Mirror A hyperbolic mirror (used in some telescopes) has the property that a light ray directed at a focus will be reflected to the other focus. The focus of a hyperbolic mirror (see figure) has coordinates (24, 0). Find the vertex of the mirror given that the mount at the top edge of the mirror has coordinates (24, 24).

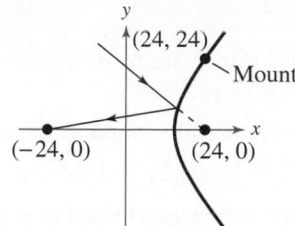

56. Photography A panoramic photo can be taken using a hyperbolic mirror. The camera is pointed toward the vertex of the mirror, and the camera's optical center is positioned at one focus of the mirror (see figure). An equation for the cross-section of the mirror is

$$\frac{x^2}{25} - \frac{y^2}{16} = 1.$$

Find the distance from the camera's optical center to the mirror.

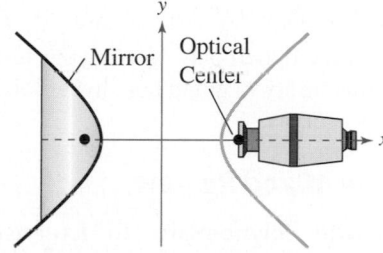

Classifying a Conic from a General Equation In Exercises 57–64, classify the graph of the equation as a circle, a parabola, an ellipse, or a hyperbola.

57. $9x^2 + 4y^2 - 18x + 16y - 119 = 0$

58. $x^2 + y^2 - 4x - 6y - 23 = 0$

59. $16x^2 - 9y^2 + 32x + 54y - 209 = 0$

60. $x^2 + 4x - 8y + 20 = 0$

61. $y^2 + 12x + 4y + 28 = 0$

62. $4x^2 + 25y^2 + 16x + 250y + 541 = 0$

63. $x^2 + y^2 + 2x - 6y = 0$

64. $y^2 - x^2 + 2x - 6y - 8 = 0$

Finding a Point in a Rotated Coordinate System In Exercises 65 and 66, the $x'y'$-coordinate system has been rotated θ degrees from the xy-coordinate system. The coordinates of a point in the xy-coordinate system are given. Find the coordinates of the point in the rotated coordinate system.

65. $\theta = 90°$, $(0, 3)$ 66. $\theta = 45°$, $(3, 3)$

Matching an Equation with a Graph In Exercises 67–72, match the graph with its equation. [The graphs are labeled (a), (b), (c), (d), (e), and (f).]

(a)

(b)

(c)

(d)

(e)

(f)
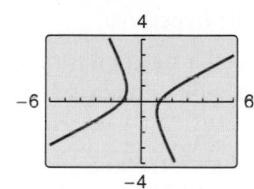

67. $xy + 4 = 0$ 68. $x^2 + 2xy + y^2 = 0$

69. $-2x^2 + 3xy + 2y^2 + 3 = 0$

70. $x^2 - xy + 3y^2 - 5 = 0$

71. $3x^2 + 2xy + y^2 - 10 = 0$

72. $x^2 - 4xy + 4y^2 + 10x - 30 = 0$

Rotation of Axes In Exercises 73–82, rotate the axes to eliminate the xy-term in the equation. Then write the equation in standard form. Sketch the graph of the resulting equation, showing both sets of axes.

73. $xy + 1 = 0$ 74. $xy - 2 = 0$

75. $x^2 - 4xy + y^2 + 1 = 0$

76. $xy + x - 2y + 3 = 0$

77. $5x^2 - 6xy + 5y^2 - 12 = 0$

78. $13x^2 + 6\sqrt{3}xy + 7y^2 - 16 = 0$

79. $3x^2 - 2\sqrt{3}xy + y^2 + 2x + 2\sqrt{3}y = 0$

80. $2x^2 + xy + 2y^2 - 8 = 0$

81. $16x^2 - 24xy + 9y^2 - 60x - 80y + 100 = 0$

82. $9x^2 + 24xy + 16y^2 + 80x - 60y = 0$

Graphing a Conic In Exercises 83–86, use a graphing utility to graph the conic. Determine the angle θ through which the axes are rotated. Explain how you used the graphing utility to obtain the graph.

83. $x^2 + 3xy + y^2 = 20$

84. $x^2 - 4xy + 2y^2 = 8$

85. $17x^2 + 32xy - 7y^2 = 75$

86. $40x^2 + 36xy + 25y^2 = 52$

Sketching the Graph of a Degenerate Conic In Exercises 87–92, sketch (if possible) the graph of the degenerate conic.

87. $y^2 - 16x^2 = 0$ 88. $x^2 - 10xy + y^2 = 0$

89. $x^2 + 2xy + y^2 - 1 = 0$

90. $x^2 + y^2 - 2x + 6y + 10 = 0$

91. $x^2 + y^2 + 2x - 4y + 5 = 0$

92. $4x^2 + 4xy + y^2 - 1 = 0$

Conclusions

True or False? In Exercises 93–97, determine whether the statement is true or false. Justify your answer.

93. In the standard form of the equation of a hyperbola, the larger the ratio of b to a, the larger the eccentricity of the hyperbola.

94. In the standard form of the equation of a hyperbola, the trivial solution of two intersecting lines occurs when $b = 0$.

95. If $D \neq 0$ and $E \neq 0$, then the graph of

$$x^2 - y^2 + Dx + Ey = 0$$

is a hyperbola.

96. If the asymptotes of the hyperbola

$$\frac{x^2}{a^2} - \frac{y^2}{b^2} = 1, \text{ where } a, b > 0$$

intersect at right angles, then $a = b$.

97. After using a rotation of axes to eliminate the xy-term from an equation of the form

$$Ax^2 + Bxy + Cy^2 + Dx + Ey + F = 0$$

the coefficients of the x^2- and y^2-terms remain A and C, respectively.

98. **Think About It** Consider a hyperbola centered at the origin with a horizontal transverse axis. Use the definition of a hyperbola to derive its standard form.

99. **Writing** Explain how the central rectangle of a hyperbola can be used to sketch its asymptotes.

100. **HOW DO YOU SEE IT?** Use the figure to explain why $|d_2 - d_1| = 2a$.

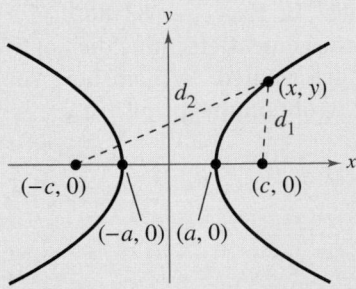

101. **Think About It** Find the equation of the hyperbola for any point at which the difference between its distances from the points $(2, 2)$ and $(10, 2)$ is 6.

102. **Proof** Show that $c^2 = a^2 + b^2$ for the equation of the hyperbola

$$\frac{x^2}{a^2} - \frac{y^2}{b^2} = 1$$

where the distance from the center of the hyperbola $(0, 0)$ to a focus is c.

103. **Proof** Prove that the graph of the equation

$$Ax^2 + Cy^2 + Dx + Ey + F = 0$$

is one of the following (except in degenerate cases).

Conic	Condition
(a) Circle	$A = C$
(b) Parabola	$A = 0$ or $C = 0$ (but not both)
(c) Ellipse	$AC > 0$
(d) Hyperbola	$AC < 0$

104. **Comparing Hyperbolas** Given the hyperbolas

$$\frac{x^2}{16} - \frac{y^2}{9} = 1 \quad \text{and} \quad \frac{y^2}{9} - \frac{x^2}{16} = 1$$

describe any common characteristics that the hyperbolas share, as well as any differences in the graphs of the hyperbolas. Verify your results by using a graphing utility to graph both hyperbolas in the same viewing window.

Cumulative Mixed Review

Operations with Polynomials In Exercises 105–108, perform the indicated operation.

105. Subtract: $(x^3 - 3x^2) - (6 - 2x - 4x^2)$

106. Multiply: $\left(3x - \frac{1}{2}\right)(x + 4)$

107. Divide: $\dfrac{x^3 - 3x + 4}{x + 2}$

108. Expand: $[(x + y) + 3]^2$

Factoring a Polynomial In Exercises 109–114, factor the polynomial completely.

109. $x^3 - 16x$ 110. $x^2 + 14x + 49$

111. $2x^3 - 24x^2 + 72x$ 112. $6x^3 - 11x^2 - 10x$

113. $16x^3 + 54$ 114. $4 - x + 4x^2 - x^3$

Graphing a Function In Exercises 115–122, graph the function.

115. $f(x) = |x + 3|$ 116. $f(x) = |x - 4| + 1$

117. $g(x) = \sqrt{4 - x^2}$ 118. $g(x) = \sqrt{3x - 2}$

119. $h(t) = -(t - 2)^3 + 3$ 120. $h(t) = \frac{1}{2}(t + 4)^3$

121. $f(t) = [\![t - 5]\!] + 1$ 122. $f(t) = -2[\![t]\!] + 3$

9.4   Parametric Equations

Plane Curves

Up to this point, you have been representing a graph by a single equation involving *two* variables such as x and y. In this section, you will study situations in which it is useful to introduce a *third* variable to represent a curve in the plane.

To see the usefulness of this procedure, consider the path of an object that is propelled into the air at an angle of 45°. When the initial velocity of the object is 48 feet per second, it can be shown that the object follows the parabolic path

$$y = -\frac{x^2}{72} + x \qquad \text{Rectangular equation}$$

as shown in Figure 9.35. However, this equation does not tell the whole story. Although it does tell you *where* the object has been, it does not tell you *when* the object was at a given point (x, y) on the path. To determine this time, you can introduce a third variable t, called a **parameter.** It is possible to write both x and y as functions of t to obtain the **parametric equations**

$$x = 24\sqrt{2}t \qquad \text{Parametric equation for } x$$

$$y = -16t^2 + 24\sqrt{2}t. \qquad \text{Parametric equation for } y$$

From this set of equations, you can determine that at time $t = 0$, the object is at the point $(0, 0)$. Similarly, at time $t = 1$, the object is at the point

$$\left(24\sqrt{2}, 24\sqrt{2} - 16\right)$$

and so on.

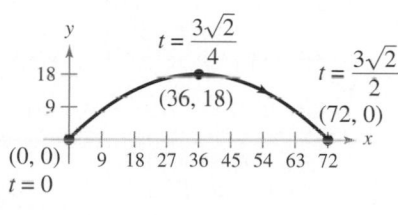

Rectangular equation:
$$y = -\frac{x^2}{72} + x$$

Parametric equations:
$$x = 24\sqrt{2}t$$
$$y = -16t^2 + 24\sqrt{2}t$$

Curvilinear motion: two variables for position, one variable for time
Figure 9.35

For this particular motion problem, x and y are continuous functions of t, and the resulting path is a **plane curve.** (Recall that a *continuous function* is one whose graph has no breaks, holes, or gaps.)

Definition of a Plane Curve

If f and g are continuous functions of t on an interval I, then the set of ordered pairs

$$(f(t), g(t))$$

is a **plane curve** C. The equations

$$x = f(t) \qquad \text{and} \qquad y = g(t)$$

are **parametric equations** for C, and t is the **parameter.**

What you should learn
- Evaluate sets of parametric equations for given values of the parameter.
- Graph curves that are represented by sets of parametric equations.
- Rewrite sets of parametric equations as single rectangular equations by eliminating the parameter.
- Find sets of parametric equations for graphs.

Why you should learn it
Parametric equations are useful for modeling the path of an object. For instance, in Exercise 64 on page 676, a set of parametric equations is used to model the path of an arrow.

Graphs of Plane Curves

One way to sketch a curve represented by a pair of parametric equations is to plot points in the xy-plane. Each set of coordinates (x, y) is determined from a value chosen for the parameter t. By plotting the resulting points in the order of *increasing* values of t, you trace the curve in a specific direction. This is called the **orientation** of the curve.

EXAMPLE 1   Sketching a Plane Curve

See LarsonPrecalculus.com for an interactive version of this type of example.

Sketch the curve given by the parametric equations

$$x = t^2 - 4 \quad \text{and} \quad y = \frac{t}{2}, \quad -2 \le t \le 3.$$

Describe the orientation of the curve.

Solution

Using values of t in the interval, the parametric equations yield the points (x, y) shown in the table.

t	-2	-1	0	1	2	3
x	0	-3	-4	-3	0	5
y	-1	$-\frac{1}{2}$	0	$\frac{1}{2}$	1	$\frac{3}{2}$

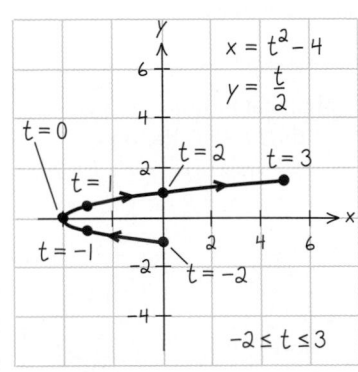

By plotting these points in the order of increasing t, you obtain the curve shown in Figure 9.36. The arrows on the curve indicate its orientation as t increases from -2 to 3. So, when a particle moves on this curve, it would start at $(0, -1)$ and then move along the curve to the point $\left(5, \frac{3}{2}\right)$.

Figure 9.36

✓ **Checkpoint** 🔊))) *Audio-video solution in English & Spanish at LarsonPrecalculus.com.*

Sketch the curve given by the parametric equations

$$x = 2t \quad \text{and} \quad y = 4t^2 + 2, \quad -2 \le t \le 2.$$

Note that the graph shown in Figure 9.36 does not define y as a function of x. This points out one benefit of parametric equations—they can be used to represent graphs that are more general than graphs of functions.

Two different sets of parametric equations can have the same graph. For example, the set of parametric equations

$$x = 4t^2 - 4 \quad \text{and} \quad y = t, \quad -1 \le t \le \tfrac{3}{2}$$

has the same graph as the set given in Example 1. However, by comparing the values of t in Figures 9.36 and 9.37, you can see that this second graph is traced out more *rapidly* (considering t as time) than the first graph. So, in applications, different parametric representations can be used to represent various *speeds* at which objects travel along a given path.

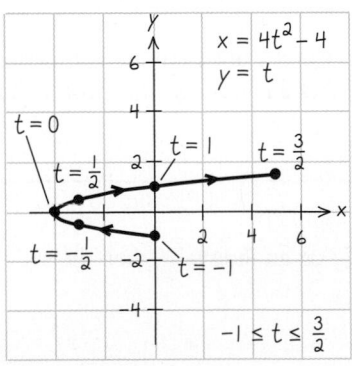

Figure 9.37

Technology Tip

Most graphing utilities have a *parametric* mode. So, another way to graph a curve represented by a pair of parametric equations is to use a graphing utility, as shown in Example 2. For instructions on how to use the *parametric* mode, see Appendix A; for specific keystrokes, go to this textbook's *Companion Website*.

EXAMPLE 2   Using a Graphing Utility in Parametric Mode

Use a graphing utility to graph the curves represented by the parametric equations. Use the graph and the Vertical Line Test to determine whether y is a function of x.

a. $x = t^2, y = t^3$

b. $x = t, y = t^3$

c. $x = t^2, y = t$

Solution

Begin by setting the graphing utility to *parametric* mode. When choosing a viewing window, you must set not only minimum and maximum values of x and y, but also minimum and maximum values of t.

a. Enter the parametric equations for x and y, as shown in Figure 9.38. Use the viewing window shown in Figure 9.39. The curve is shown in Figure 9.40. From the graph, you can see that y *is not* a function of x.

Figure 9.38   **Figure 9.39**   **Figure 9.40**

b. Enter the parametric equations for x and y, as shown in Figure 9.41. Use the viewing window shown in Figure 9.42. The curve is shown in Figure 9.43. From the graph, you can see that y *is* a function of x.

Figure 9.41   **Figure 9.42**   **Figure 9.43**

c. Enter the parametric equations for x and y, as shown in Figure 9.44. Use the viewing window shown in Figure 9.45. The curve is shown in Figure 9.46. From the graph, you can see that y *is not* a function of x.

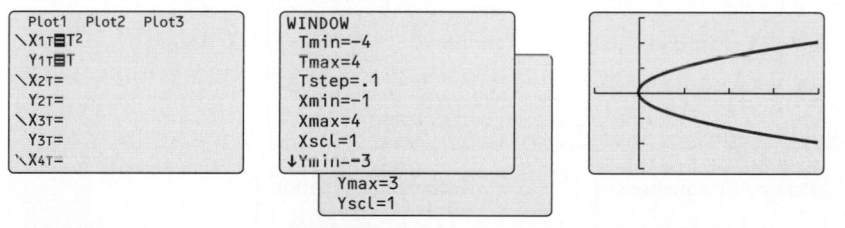

Figure 9.44   **Figure 9.45**   **Figure 9.46**

✓ *Checkpoint* 🔊)) *Audio-video solution in English & Spanish at LarsonPrecalculus.com.*

Use a graphing utility to graph the curve represented by the equations $x = (t - 2)^2$ and $y = 3t^2$. Use the graph and the Vertical Line Test to determine whether y is a function of x. ◼

Explore the Concept

Use a graphing utility set in *parametric* mode to graph the curve

$$x = t \quad \text{and} \quad y = 1 - t^2.$$

Set the viewing window so that $-4 \le x \le 4$ and $-12 \le y \le 2$. Then graph the curve using each of the following t settings.

a. $0 \le t \le 3$

b. $-3 \le t \le 0$

c. $-3 \le t \le 3$

Compare the curves given by the different t settings. Repeat this experiment using $x = -t$. How does this change the results?

Technology Tip

Notice in Example 2 that to set the viewing windows of parametric graphs, you have to scroll down to enter the Ymax and Yscl values.

Eliminating the Parameter

Many curves that are represented by sets of parametric equations have graphs that can also be represented by rectangular equations (in x and y). The process of finding the rectangular equation is called **eliminating the parameter.**

$$y = t^2 - 4 \qquad t = 2y \qquad x = (2y)^2 - 4 \qquad x = 4y^2 - 4$$
$$y = \tfrac{1}{2}t$$

Now, you can recognize that the equation $x = 4y^2 - 4$ represents a parabola with a horizontal axis and vertex at $(-4, 0)$. When converting equations from parametric to rectangular form, you may need to alter the domain of the rectangular equation so that its graph matches the graph of the parametric equations.

Remark

It is important to realize that eliminating the parameter is primarily an aid to curve sketching. When the parametric equations represent the path of a moving object, the graph alone is not sufficient to describe the object's motion. You still need the parametric equations to determine the *position, direction,* and *speed* at a given time.

EXAMPLE 3   **Eliminating the Parameter**

Identify the curve represented by the equations $x = \dfrac{1}{\sqrt{t+1}}$ and $y = \dfrac{t}{t+1}$.

Solution

Solving for t in the equation for x produces

$$x^2 = \frac{1}{t+1} \quad \Longrightarrow \quad \frac{1}{x^2} = t + 1 \quad \Longrightarrow \quad \frac{1}{x^2} - 1 = t.$$

Substituting in the equation for y, you obtain the rectangular equation

$$y = \frac{t}{t+1} = \frac{\dfrac{1}{x^2} - 1}{\dfrac{1}{x^2} - 1 + 1} = \frac{\dfrac{1 - x^2}{x^2}}{\dfrac{1}{x^2}} \cdot \frac{x^2}{x^2} = 1 - x^2.$$

From the rectangular equation, you can recognize that the curve is a parabola that opens downward and has its vertex at $(0, 1)$, as shown in Figure 9.47. The rectangular equation is defined for all values of x. The parametric equation for x, however, is defined only when $t > -1$. From the graph of the parametric equations, you can see that x is always positive, as shown in Figure 9.48. So, you should restrict the domain of x to positive values, as shown in Figure 9.49.

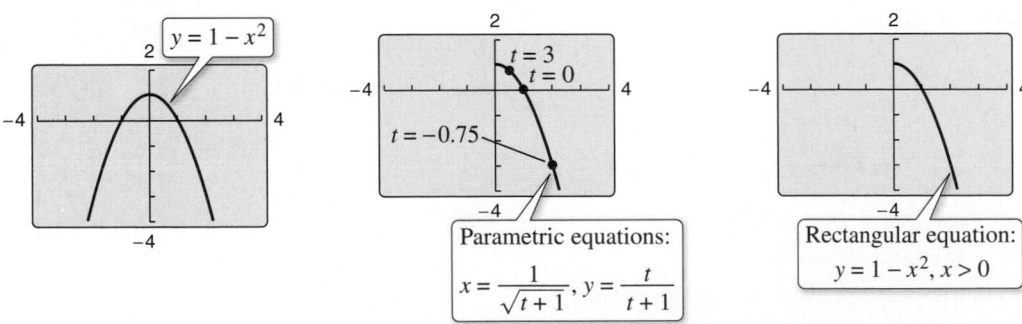

Figure 9.47   Figure 9.48   Figure 9.49

✔ **Checkpoint** ◀))) *Audio-video solution in English & Spanish at LarsonPrecalculus.com.*

Identify the curve represented by the equations $x = \dfrac{1}{\sqrt{t-1}}$ and $y = \dfrac{t+1}{t-1}$.   ■

Finding Parametric Equations for a Graph

You have been studying techniques for sketching the graph represented by a set of parametric equations. Now consider the *reverse* problem—that is, how can you find a set of parametric equations for a given graph or a given physical description? From the discussion following Example 1, you know that such a representation is not unique. That is, the equations

$$x = 4t^2 - 4 \quad \text{and} \quad y = t, \quad -1 \le t \le \frac{3}{2}$$

produced the same graph as the equations

$$x = t^2 - 4 \quad \text{and} \quad y = \frac{t}{2}, \quad -2 \le t \le 3.$$

This is further demonstrated in Example 4.

EXAMPLE 4   Finding Parametric Equations for a Graph

Find a set of parametric equations to represent the graph of $y = 1 - x^2$ using the parameters (a) $t = x$ and (b) $t = 1 - x$.

Solution

a. Letting $t = x$, you obtain the following parametric equations.

$$x = t \qquad \text{Parametric equation for } x$$

$$y = 1 - t^2 \qquad \text{Parametric equation for } y$$

The graph of these equations is shown in the figure.

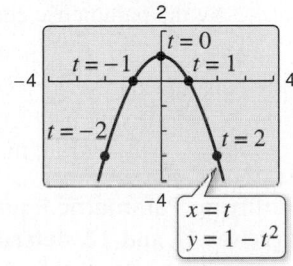

b. Letting $t = 1 - x$, you obtain the following parametric equations.

$$x = 1 - t \qquad \text{Parametric equation for } x$$

$$y = 1 - (1 - t)^2 = 2t - t^2 \qquad \text{Parametric equation for } y$$

The graph of these equations is shown in the figure. Note that the graph in this figure has the opposite orientation of the graph in part (a).

✓ **Checkpoint** 🔊 *Audio-video solution in English & Spanish at LarsonPrecalculus.com.*

Find a set of parametric equations to represent the graph of $y = x^2 + 2$ using the parameters (a) $t = x$ and (b) $t = 1 - x$.

9.4   Exercises

See *CalcChat.com* for tutorial help and worked-out solutions to odd-numbered exercises. For instructions on how to use a graphing utility, see Appendix A.

Vocabulary and Concept Check

In Exercises 1 and 2, fill in the blank(s).

1. If f and g are continuous functions of t on an interval I, then the set of ordered pairs $(f(t), g(t))$ is a _____ C. The equations given by $x = f(t)$ and $y = g(t)$ are _____ for C, and t is the _____ .

2. The _____ of a curve is the direction in which the curve is traced out for increasing values of the parameter.

3. Given a set of parametric equations, how do you find the corresponding rectangular equation?

4. What point on the plane curve represented by the parametric equations $x = t$ and $y = t$ corresponds to $t = 3$?

Procedures and Problem Solving

Identifying the Graph of Parametric Equations   In Exercises 5–8, match the set of parametric equations with its graph. [The graphs are labeled (a), (b), (c), and (d).]

(a)

(b)

(c)

(d)

5. $x = t, y = t + 2$

6. $x = t^2, y = t - 2$

7. $x = \sqrt{t}, y = t$

8. $x = \dfrac{1}{t}, y = t + 2$

9. **Using Parametric Equations**   Consider the parametric equations $x = \sqrt{t}$ and $y = 2 - t$.

   (a) Create a table of x- and y-values using $t = 0, 1, 2, 3,$ and 4.

   (b) Plot the points (x, y) generated in part (a) and sketch a graph of the parametric equations for $0 \le t \le 4$. Describe the orientation of the curve.

   (c) Use a graphing utility to graph the curve represented by the parametric equations.

   (d) Find the rectangular equation by eliminating the parameter. Sketch its graph. How does the graph differ from those in parts (b) and (c)?

10. **Using Parametric Equations**   Consider the parametric equations $x = 4 \cos^2 t$ and $y = 4 \sin t$.

    (a) Create a table of x- and y-values using $t = -\pi/2, -\pi/4, 0, \pi/4,$ and $\pi/2$.

    (b) Plot the points (x, y) generated in part (a) and sketch a graph of the parametric equations for $-\dfrac{\pi}{2} \le t \le \dfrac{\pi}{2}$. Describe the orientation of the curve.

    (c) Use a graphing utility to graph the curve represented by the parametric equations.

    (d) Find the rectangular equation by eliminating the parameter. (*Hint:* Use the trigonometric identity $\cos^2 t + \sin^2 t = 1$.) Sketch its graph. How does the graph differ from those in parts (b) and (c)?

Identifying Parametric Equations for a Plane Curve   In Exercises 11 and 12, determine which set of parametric equations represents the graph shown.

11. (a) $x = t^2$
        $y = 2t + 1$
    (b) $x = 2t + 1$
        $y = t^2$
    (c) $x = 2t - 1$
        $y = t^2$
    (d) $x = -2t + 1$
        $y = t^2$

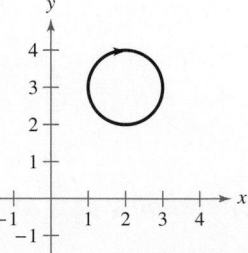

12. (a) $x = 2 - \cos \theta$
        $y = 3 - \sin \theta$
    (b) $x = 3 - \cos \theta$
        $y = 2 + \sin \theta$
    (c) $x = 2 + \cos \theta$
        $y = 3 - \sin \theta$
    (d) $x = 3 + \cos \theta$
        $y = 2 - \sin \theta$

Sketching a Plane Curve and Eliminating the Parameter
In Exercises 13–28, (a) sketch the curve represented by the parametric equations (indicate the orientation of the curve). Use a graphing utility to confirm your result. (b) Eliminate the parameter and write the corresponding rectangular equation whose graph represents the curve. Adjust the domain of the resulting rectangular equation, if necessary.

13. $x = t, y = -4t$

14. $x = t, y = \frac{1}{2}t$

15. $x = 3t - 3, y = 2t + 1$ **16.** $x = 3 - 2t, y = 2 + 3t$

17. $x = \frac{1}{4}t, y = t^2$

18. $x = t, y = t^3$

19. $x = t + 2, y = t^2$

20. $x = \sqrt{t}, y = 1 - t$

21. $x = 2t, y = |t - 2|$

22. $x = |t - 1|, y = t + 2$

23. $x = 2 \cos \theta, y = 3 \sin \theta$ **24.** $x = \cos \theta, y = 4 \sin \theta$

25. $x = e^{-t}, y = e^{3t}$

26. $x = e^{2t}, y = e^{t}$

27. $x = t^3, y = 3 \ln t$

28. $x = \ln 2t, y = 2t^2$

Using a Graphing Utility in Parametric Mode In Exercises 29–34, use a graphing utility to graph the curve represented by the parametric equations. Use the graph and the Vertical Line Test to determine whether y is a function of x.

29. $x = 4 + 3 \cos \theta$

$y = -2 + \sin \theta$

30. $x = 4 + 3 \cos \theta$

$y = -2 + 2 \sin \theta$

31. $x = 4 \sec \theta$

$y = 2 \tan \theta$

32. $x = \sec \theta$

$y = \tan \theta$

33. $x = t/2$

$y = \ln(t^2 + 1)$

34. $x = 10 - 0.01e^{t}$

$y = 0.4t^2$

Comparing Plane Curves In Exercises 35 and 36, determine how the plane curves differ from each other.

35. (a) $x = t$

$y = 2t + 1$

(b) $x = \cos \theta$

$y = 2 \cos \theta + 1$

(c) $x = e^{-t}$

$y = 2e^{-t} + 1$

(d) $x = e^{t}$

$y = 2e^{t} + 1$

36. (a) $x = 2\sqrt{t}$

$y = 4 - \sqrt{t}$

(b) $x = 2\sqrt[3]{t}$

$y = 4 - \sqrt[3]{t}$

(c) $x = 2(t + 1)$

$y = 3 - t$

(d) $x = -2t^2$

$y = 4 + t^2$

Eliminating the Parameter In Exercises 37–40, eliminate the parameter and obtain the standard form of the rectangular equation.

37. Line through (x_1, y_1) and (x_2, y_2):

$x = x_1 + t(x_2 - x_1)$

$y = y_1 + t(y_2 - y_1)$

38. Circle: $x = h + r \cos \theta, y = k + r \sin \theta$

39. Ellipse: $x = h + a \cos \theta, y = k + b \sin \theta$

40. Hyperbola: $x = h + a \sec \theta, y = k + b \tan \theta$

Finding Parametric Equations for a Graph In Exercises 41–44, use the results of Exercises 37–40 to find a set of parametric equations for the line or conic.

41. Line: passes through $(1, -1)$ and $(4, 8)$

42. Circle: center: $(-2, -5)$; radius: 7

43. Ellipse: vertices: $(\pm 5, 0)$; foci: $(\pm 4, 0)$

44. Hyperbola: vertices: $(\pm 2, 0)$; foci: $(\pm 3, 0)$

Finding Parametric Equations for a Graph In Exercises 45–52, find a set of parametric equations to represent the graph of the given rectangular equation using the parameters (a) $t = x$ and (b) $t = 2 - x$.

45. $y = -2x + 1$

46. $y = 4x - 9$

47. $y = \dfrac{3}{x}$

48. $y = \dfrac{1}{x^2}$

49. $y = 4x^2 + 5$

50. $y = x^3 - x^2$

51. $y = e^{-x}$

52. $y = \ln(x + 2)$

Using a Graphing Utility In Exercises 53–58, use a graphing utility to graph the curve represented by the parametric equations.

53. Hypocycloid: $x = 3 \cos^3 \theta, y = 3 \sin^3 \theta$

54. Curtate cycloid: $x = 8\theta - 4 \sin \theta, y = 8 - 4 \cos \theta$

55. Witch of Agnesi: $x = 2 \cot \theta, y = 2 \sin^2 \theta$

56. Folium of Descartes: $x = \dfrac{3t}{1 + t^3}, y = \dfrac{3t^2}{1 + t^3}$

57. Cycloid: $x = \theta + \sin \theta, y = 1 - \cos \theta$

58. Prolate cycloid: $x = 2\theta - 4 \sin \theta, y = 2 - 4 \cos \theta$

Identifying a Graph In Exercises 59–62, match the parametric equations with the correct graph. [The graphs are labeled (a), (b), (c), and (d).]

(a)

(b)

(c)

(d)
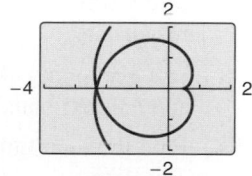

59. Lissajous curve: $x = 2 \cos \theta, y = \sin 2\theta$

60. Evolute of ellipse: $x = 2 \cos^3 \theta, y = 4 \sin^3 \theta$

61. Involute of circle: $x = \frac{1}{2}(\cos \theta + \theta \sin \theta)$

$y = \frac{1}{2}(\sin \theta - \theta \cos \theta)$

62. Serpentine curve: $x = \frac{1}{2} \cot \theta, y = 4 \sin \theta \cos \theta$

Projectile Motion   In Exercises 63 and 64, consider a projectile launched at a height of h feet above the ground at an angle of θ with the horizontal. The initial velocity is v_0 feet per second, and the path of the projectile is modeled by the parametric equations

$$x = (v_0 \cos \theta)t \quad \text{and} \quad y = h + (v_0 \sin \theta)t - 16t^2.$$

63. MODELING DATA

The center field fence in a baseball stadium is 7 feet high and 408 feet from home plate. A baseball is hit at a point 3 feet above the ground. It leaves the bat at an angle of θ degrees with the horizontal at a speed of 100 miles per hour (see figure).

Not drawn to scale

(a) Write a set of parametric equations that model the path of the baseball.

(b) Use a graphing utility to graph the path of the baseball when $\theta = 15°$. Is the hit a home run?

(c) Use the graphing utility to graph the path of the baseball when $\theta = 23°$. Is the hit a home run?

(d) Find the minimum angle required for the hit to be a home run.

64. *Why you should learn it* (p. 669)   An archer releases an arrow from a bow at a point 5 feet above the ground. The arrow leaves the bow at an angle of 15° with the horizontal and at an initial speed of 225 feet per second.

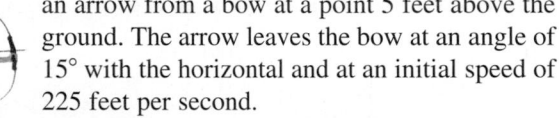

(a) Write a set of parametric equations that model the path of the arrow.

(b) Assuming the ground is level, find the distance the arrow travels before it hits the ground. (Ignore air resistance.)

(c) Use a graphing utility to graph the path of the arrow and approximate its maximum height.

(d) Find the total time the arrow is in the air.

Conclusions

True or False?   In Exercises 65–68, determine whether the statement is true or false. Justify your answer.

65. The two sets of parametric equations $x = t$, $y = t^2 + 1$ and $x = 3t$, $y = 9t^2 + 1$ correspond to the same rectangular equation.

66. Because the graphs of the parametric equations $x = t^2$, $y = t^2$ and $x = t$, $y = t$ both represent the line $y = x$, they are the same plane curve.

67. If y is a function of t and x is a function of t, then y must be a function of x.

68. The parametric equations $x = at + h$ and $y = bt + k$, where $a \neq 0$ and $b \neq 0$, represent a circle centered at (h, k) when $a = b$.

69. Think About It   The curve shown is represented by the parametric equations

$$x = 6 \cos \theta \quad \text{and} \quad y = 6 \sin \theta, \quad 0 \leq \theta \leq 6.$$

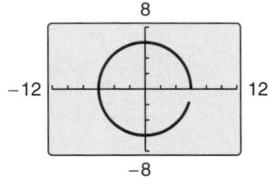

(a) Describe the orientation of the curve.

(b) Determine a range of θ that gives the graph of a circle.

(c) Write a set of parametric equations representing the curve so that the curve traces from the same point as the original curve but in the opposite direction.

(d) How does the original curve change when cosine and sine are interchanged?

70. **HOW DO YOU SEE IT?**   The graph of the parametric equations $x = t$ and $y = t^2$ is shown below. Determine whether the graph would change for each set of parametric equations. If so, how would it change?

(a) $x = -t$, $y = t^2$

(b) $x = t + 1$, $y = t^2$

(c) $x = t$, $y = t^2 + 1$

Cumulative Mixed Review

Even and Odd Functions   In Exercises 71–74, check for symmetry with respect to both axes and to the origin. Then determine whether the function is even, odd, or neither.

71. $f(x) = \dfrac{4x^2}{x^2 + 1}$

72. $f(x) = \sqrt{x}$

73. $y = e^x$

74. $(x - 2)^2 = y + 4$

9.5   Polar Coordinates

Introduction

So far, you have been representing graphs of equations as collections of points (x, y) in the rectangular coordinate system, where x and y represent the directed distances from the coordinate axes to the point (x, y). In this section, you will study a second coordinate system called the **polar coordinate system.**

To form the polar coordinate system in the plane, fix a point O, called the **pole** (or **origin**), and construct from O an initial ray called the **polar axis,** as shown in the figure. Then each point P in the plane can be assigned **polar coordinates** (r, θ), as follows.

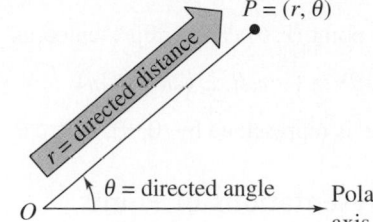

1. $r = $ *directed distance* from O to P

2. $\theta = $ *directed angle*, counterclockwise from the polar axis to segment $\overline{OP}$

EXAMPLE 1   Plotting Points in the Polar Coordinate System

Plot the points (a) $\left(2, \dfrac{\pi}{3}\right)$, (b) $\left(3, -\dfrac{\pi}{6}\right)$, and (c) $\left(3, \dfrac{11\pi}{6}\right)$ given in polar coordinates.

Solution

a. The point $(r, \theta) = \left(2, \dfrac{\pi}{3}\right)$ lies two units from the pole on the terminal side of the angle $\theta = \dfrac{\pi}{3}$, as shown in Figure 9.50.

b. The point $(r, \theta) = \left(3, -\dfrac{\pi}{6}\right)$ lies three units from the pole on the terminal side of the angle $\theta = -\dfrac{\pi}{6}$, as shown in Figure 9.51.

c. The point $(r, \theta) = \left(3, \dfrac{11\pi}{6}\right)$ coincides with the point $\left(3, -\dfrac{\pi}{6}\right)$, as shown in Figure 9.52.

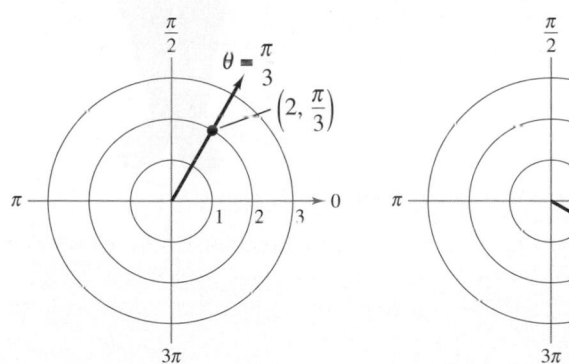

Figure 9.50   **Figure 9.51**   **Figure 9.52**

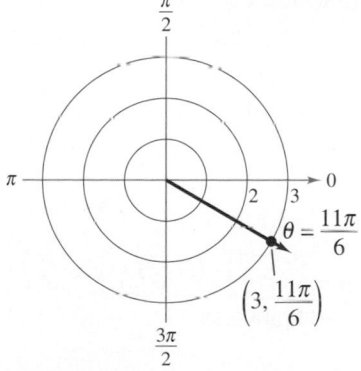

✓ **Checkpoint** 🔊)) *Audio-video solution in English & Spanish at LarsonPrecalculus.com.*

Plot the points (a) $\left(3, \dfrac{\pi}{4}\right)$, (b) $\left(2, -\dfrac{\pi}{3}\right)$, and (c) $\left(2, \dfrac{5\pi}{3}\right)$ given in polar coordinates. ◼

In rectangular coordinates, each point (x, y) has a unique representation. This is not true for polar coordinates. For instance, the coordinates

$$(r, \theta) \quad \text{and} \quad (r, \theta + 2\pi)$$

represent the same point, as illustrated in Example 1. Another way to obtain multiple representations of a point is to use negative values for r. Because r is a *directed distance*, the coordinates

$$(r, \theta) \quad \text{and} \quad (-r, \theta + \pi)$$

represent the same point. In general, the point (r, θ) can be represented as

$$(r, \theta) = (r, \theta \pm 2n\pi) \quad \text{or} \quad (r, \theta) = (-r, \theta \pm (2n + 1)\pi)$$

where n is any integer. Moreover, the pole is represented by $(0, \theta)$, where θ is any angle.

EXAMPLE 2 Multiple Representations of Points

Plot the point

$$\left(3, -\frac{3\pi}{4}\right)$$

and find three additional polar representations of this point, using

$$-2\pi < \theta < 2\pi.$$

Solution

The point is shown in Figure 9.53. Three other representations are as follows.

$$\left(3, -\frac{3\pi}{4} + 2\pi\right) = \left(3, \frac{5\pi}{4}\right) \qquad \text{Add } 2\pi \text{ to } \theta.$$

$$\left(-3, -\frac{3\pi}{4} - \pi\right) = \left(-3, -\frac{7\pi}{4}\right) \qquad \text{Replace } r \text{ by } -r, \text{ subtract } \pi \text{ from } \theta.$$

$$\left(-3, -\frac{3\pi}{4} + \pi\right) = \left(-3, \frac{\pi}{4}\right) \qquad \text{Replace } r \text{ by } -r, \text{ add } \pi \text{ to } \theta.$$

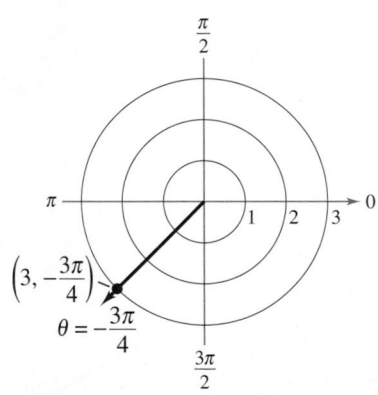

$$\left(3, -\tfrac{3\pi}{4}\right) = \left(3, \tfrac{5\pi}{4}\right) = \left(-3, -\tfrac{7\pi}{4}\right) = \left(-3, \tfrac{\pi}{4}\right) = \dots$$

Figure 9.53

Plot each point and find three additional polar representations of the point, using $-2\pi < \theta < 2\pi$.

a. $\left(3, \frac{4\pi}{3}\right)$ **b.** $\left(2, -\frac{5\pi}{6}\right)$ **c.** $\left(-1, \frac{3\pi}{4}\right)$

Explore the Concept

Set your graphing utility to *polar* mode. Then graph the equation $r = 3$. (Use a viewing window in which $0 \le \theta \le 2\pi$, $-6 \le x \le 6$, and $-4 \le y \le 4$.) You should obtain a circle of radius 3.

a. Use the *trace* feature to cursor around the circle. Can you locate the point $(3, 5\pi/4)$?

b. Can you locate other representations of the point $(3, 5\pi/4)$? If so, explain how you did it.

Coordinate Conversion

To establish the relationship between polar and rectangular coordinates, let the polar axis coincide with the positive x-axis and the pole with the origin, as shown in Figure 9.54. Because (x, y) lies on a circle of radius r, it follows that $r^2 = x^2 + y^2$. Moreover, for $r > 0$, the definitions of the trigonometric functions imply that

$$\tan \theta = \frac{y}{x}, \quad \cos \theta = \frac{x}{r}, \quad \text{and} \quad \sin \theta = \frac{y}{r}.$$

You can show that the same relationships hold for $r < 0$.

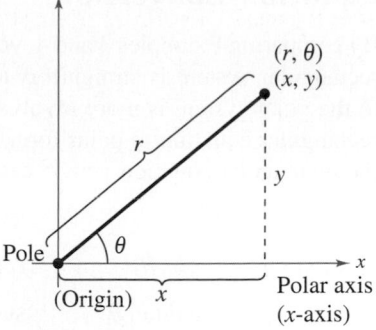

Figure 9.54

Coordinate Conversion

The polar coordinates (r, θ) are related to the rectangular coordinates (x, y), as follows.

Polar-to-Rectangular	*Rectangular-to-Polar*
$x = r \cos \theta$	$\tan \theta = \dfrac{y}{x}$
$y = r \sin \theta$	$r^2 = x^2 + y^2$

EXAMPLE 3   Polar-to-Rectangular Conversion

Convert the point $(2, \pi)$ to rectangular coordinates.

Solution

For the point $(r, \theta) = (2, \pi)$, you have the following.

$$x = r \cos \theta = 2 \cos \pi = -2$$

$$y = r \sin \theta = 2 \sin \pi = 0$$

The rectangular coordinates are $(x, y) = (-2, 0)$. (See Figure 9.55.)

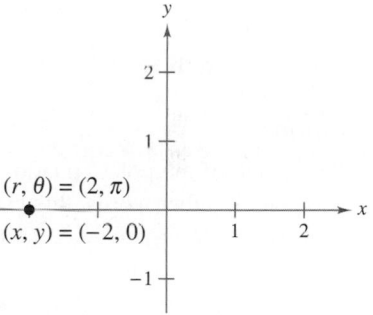

Figure 9.55

✓ **Checkpoint**))) *Audio-video solution in English & Spanish at LarsonPrecalculus.com.*

Convert the point $\left(4, \dfrac{\pi}{3}\right)$ to rectangular coordinates.

EXAMPLE 4   Rectangular-to-Polar Conversion

Convert the point $(-1, 1)$ to polar coordinates.

Solution

For the second-quadrant point $(x, y) = (-1, 1)$, you have

$$\tan \theta = \frac{y}{x} = \frac{1}{-1} = -1 \quad \Longrightarrow \quad \theta = \frac{3\pi}{4}.$$

Because θ lies in the same quadrant as (x, y), use positive r.

$$r = \sqrt{x^2 + y^2} = \sqrt{(-1)^2 + (1)^2} = \sqrt{2}$$

So, *one* set of polar coordinates is

$$(r, \theta) = \left(\sqrt{2}, \frac{3\pi}{4}\right). \qquad \text{See Figure 9.56.}$$

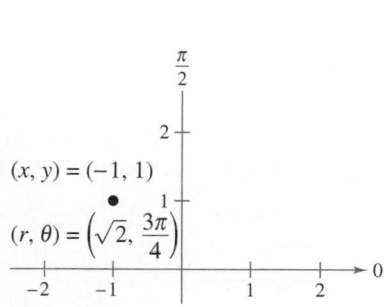

Figure 9.56

✓ **Checkpoint**))) *Audio-video solution in English & Spanish at LarsonPrecalculus.com.*

Convert the point $(0, 2)$ to polar coordinates.

Equation Conversion

By comparing Examples 3 and 4, you can see that point conversion from the polar to the rectangular system is straightforward, whereas point conversion from the rectangular to the polar system is more involved. For equations, the opposite is true. To convert a rectangular equation to polar form, replace x by $r \cos \theta$ and y by $r \sin \theta$. For instance, the rectangular equation $y = x^2$ can be written in polar form, as follows.

$$y = x^2 \qquad \text{Rectangular equation}$$

$$r \sin \theta = (r \cos \theta)^2 \qquad \text{Polar equation}$$

$$r = \sec \theta \tan \theta \qquad \text{Simplest form}$$

On the other hand, converting a polar equation to rectangular form requires considerable ingenuity. Example 5 demonstrates several polar-to-rectangular conversions that enable you to sketch the graphs of some polar equations.

EXAMPLE 5   Converting Polar Equations to Rectangular Form

See LarsonPrecalculus.com for an interactive version of this type of example.

Describe the graph of each polar equation and find the corresponding rectangular equation.

a. $r = 2$ **b.** $\theta = \dfrac{\pi}{3}$ **c.** $r = \sec \theta$

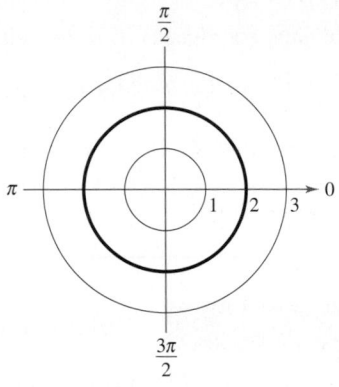

Figure 9.57

Solution

a. The graph of the polar equation $r = 2$ consists of all points that are two units from the pole. In other words, this graph is a circle centered at the origin with a radius of 2, as shown in Figure 9.57. You can confirm this by converting to rectangular form, using the relationship $r^2 = x^2 + y^2$.

$$r = 2 \implies r^2 = 2^2 \implies x^2 + y^2 = 2^2$$

Polar equation   Rectangular equation

b. The graph of the polar equation

$$\theta = \frac{\pi}{3}$$

consists of all points on the line that makes an angle of $\pi/3$ with the positive x-axis, as shown in Figure 9.58. To convert to rectangular form, you make use of the relationship $\tan \theta = y/x$.

Figure 9.58

$$\theta = \frac{\pi}{3} \implies \tan \theta = \sqrt{3} \implies y = \sqrt{3}x$$

Polar equation   Rectangular equation

c. The graph of the polar equation $r = \sec \theta$ is not evident by simple inspection, so you convert to rectangular form by using the relationship $r \cos \theta = x$.

$$r = \sec \theta \implies r \cos \theta = 1 \implies x = 1$$

Polar equation   Rectangular equation

Now you can see that the graph is a vertical line, as shown in Figure 9.59.

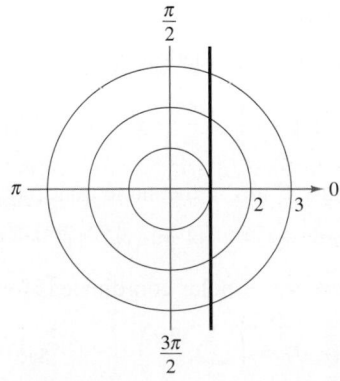

Figure 9.59

✓ **Checkpoint** ◀))) Audio-video solution in English & Spanish at LarsonPrecalculus.com.

Describe the graph of $r = 6 \sin \theta$ and find the corresponding rectangular equation. ∎

9.5   Exercises

See *CalcChat.com* for tutorial help and worked-out solutions to odd-numbered exercises.
For instructions on how to use a graphing utility, see Appendix A.

Vocabulary and Concept Check

In Exercises 1 and 2, fill in the blank(s).

1. The origin of the polar coordinate system is called the _____ .
2. For the point (r, θ), r is the _____ from O to P and θ is the _____ counterclockwise from the polar axis to segment $\overline{OP}$.

3. How are the rectangular coordinates (x, y) related to the polar coordinates (r, θ)?
4. Do the polar coordinates $(1, \pi)$ and the rectangular coordinates $(-1, 0)$ represent the same point?

Procedures and Problem Solving

Matching Polar Coordinates   In Exercises 5–8, match the polar coordinates with the point on the graph. Then find the rectangular coordinates of the point.

5. $\left(2, \dfrac{\pi}{2}\right)$

6. $\left(2, \dfrac{3\pi}{2}\right)$

7. $(0, 0)$

8. $\left(-2, \dfrac{5\pi}{4}\right)$

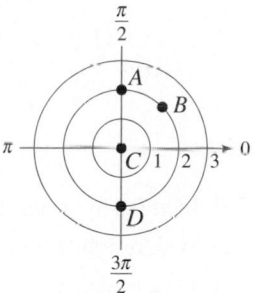

Plotting Points in the Polar Coordinate System   In Exercises 9–18, plot the point given in polar coordinates and find three additional polar representations of the point, using $-2\pi < \theta < 2\pi$.

9. $\left(3, \dfrac{5\pi}{6}\right)$

10. $\left(2, \dfrac{3\pi}{4}\right)$

11. $\left(1, -\dfrac{\pi}{3}\right)$

12. $\left(3, -\dfrac{7\pi}{6}\right)$

13. $\left(-4, \dfrac{5\pi}{6}\right)$

14. $\left(-5, -\dfrac{11\pi}{6}\right)$

15. $\left(-\dfrac{3}{2}, -\dfrac{7\pi}{4}\right)$

16. $\left(-5\sqrt{2}, \dfrac{2\pi}{3}\right)$

17. $(0, -\pi/2)$

18. $(0, \pi/6)$

Polar-to-Rectangular Conversion   In Exercises 19–26, plot the point given in polar coordinates and find the corresponding rectangular coordinates for the point.

19. $(3, \pi)$

20. $(2, 0)$

21. $\left(1, -\dfrac{3\pi}{4}\right)$

22. $\left(-16, \dfrac{5\pi}{2}\right)$

23. $\left(0, -\dfrac{7\pi}{6}\right)$

24. $\left(0, \dfrac{5\pi}{4}\right)$

25. $\left(-5, \dfrac{3\pi}{2}\right)$

26. $\left(-3, -\dfrac{\pi}{6}\right)$

Using a Graphing Utility to Find Rectangular Coordinates   In Exercises 27–32, use a graphing utility to find the rectangular coordinates of the point given in polar coordinates. Round your results to two decimal places.

27. $(2, 2\pi/9)$

28. $(4, 11\pi/9)$

29. $(-4.5, 1.3)$

30. $(8.25, 3.5)$

31. $(1.5, -2.82)$

32. $(-5.3, -0.78)$

Rectangular-to-Polar Conversion   In Exercises 33–40, plot the point given in rectangular coordinates and find two sets of polar coordinates for the point for $0 \le \theta < 2\pi$.

33. $(-7, 0)$

34. $(0, -5)$

35. $(1, 1)$

36. $(-3, -3)$

37. $\left(-\sqrt{3}, -\sqrt{3}\right)$

38. $\left(\sqrt{3}, -1\right)$

39. $(-3, 4)$

40. $(3, -1)$

Using a Graphing Utility to Find Polar Coordinates   In Exercises 41–46, use a graphing utility to find one set of polar coordinates for the point given in rectangular coordinates. (There are many correct answers.)

41. $(3, -2)$

42. $(-5, 2)$

43. $\left(-\sqrt{3}, 2\right)$

44. $\left(3\sqrt{2}, 3\sqrt{2}\right)$

45. $\left(\dfrac{5}{2}, \dfrac{4}{3}\right)$

46. $\left(-\dfrac{7}{4}, -\dfrac{3}{2}\right)$

Converting a Rectangular Equation to Polar Form   In Exercises 47–64, convert the rectangular equation to polar form. Assume $a < 0$.

47. $x^2 + y^2 = 9$

48. $x^2 + y^2 = 16$

49. $y = x$

50. $y = -\sqrt{3}x$

51. $y = a$

52. $x = a$

53. $3x - y + 2 = 0$

54. $3x + 5y - 2 = 0$

55. $xy = 4$

56. $2xy = 1$

57. $(x^2 + y^2)^2 = 9(x^2 - y^2)$

58. $y^2 - 8x - 16 = 0$

59. $x^2 + y^2 - 6x = 0$

60. $x^2 + y^2 - 8y = 0$

61. $x^2 + y^2 - 2ax = 0$

62. $x^2 + y^2 - 2ay = 0$

63. $y^2 = x^3$

64. $x^2 = y^3$

Converting a Polar Equation to Rectangular Form In Exercises 65–80, convert the polar equation to rectangular form.

65. $r = 4 \sin \theta$

66. $r = 2 \cos \theta$

67. $\theta = \dfrac{5\pi}{6}$

68. $\theta = \dfrac{11\pi}{6}$

69. $\theta = \pi/2$

70. $\theta = \pi$

71. $r = -3 \csc \theta$

72. $r = 2 \sec \theta$

73. $r^2 = \cos \theta$

74. $r^2 = \sin 2\theta$

75. $r = 2 \sin 3\theta$

76. $r = -3 \cos 2\theta$

77. $r = \dfrac{1}{1 - \cos \theta}$

78. $r = \dfrac{2}{1 + \sin \theta}$

79. $r = \dfrac{6}{2 - 3 \sin \theta}$

80. $r = \dfrac{6}{2 \cos \theta - 3 \sin \theta}$

Converting a Polar Equation to Rectangular Form In Exercises 81–86, describe the graph of the polar equation and find the corresponding rectangular equation. Sketch its graph.

81. $r = 6$

82. $r = 8$

83. $\theta = \dfrac{\pi}{4}$

84. $\theta = \dfrac{7\pi}{6}$

85. $r = 3 \sec \theta$

86. $r = 2 \csc \theta$

87. *Why you should learn it* (p. 677) The center of a Ferris wheel lies at the pole of the polar coordinate system, where the distances are in feet. Passengers enter a car at $(30, -\pi/2)$. It takes 45 seconds for the wheel to complete one clockwise revolution.

(a) Write a polar equation that models the possible positions of a passenger car.

(b) Passengers enter a car. Find and interpret their coordinates after 15 seconds of rotation.

(c) Convert the point in part (b) to rectangular coordinates. Interpret the coordinates.

88. Ferris Wheel Repeat Exercise 87 when the distance from a passenger car to the center is 35 feet and it takes 60 seconds to complete one clockwise revolution.

Conclusions

True or False?   In Exercises 89 and 90, determine whether the statement is true or false. Justify your answer.

89. If (r_1, θ_1) and (r_2, θ_2) represent the same point in the polar coordinate system, then $|r_1| = |r_2|$.

90. If (r, θ_1) and (r, θ_2) represent the same point in the polar coordinate system, then $\theta_1 = \theta_2 + 2\pi n$ for some integer n.

91. Think About It

(a) Show that the distance between the points (r_1, θ_1) and (r_2, θ_2) is $\sqrt{r_1^2 + r_2^2 - 2r_1 r_2 \cos(\theta_1 - \theta_2)}$.

(b) Simplify the Distance Formula for $\theta_1 = \theta_2$. Is the simplification what you expected? Explain.

(c) Simplify the Distance Formula for $\theta_1 - \theta_2 = 90°$. Is the simplification what you expected? Explain.

92. HOW DO YOU SEE IT?   Use the polar coordinate system shown below.

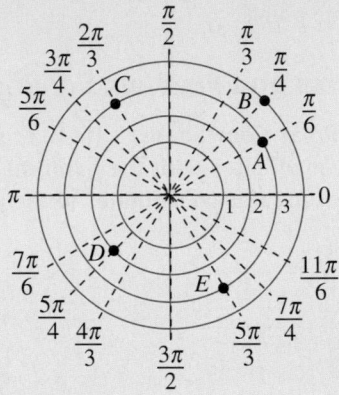

(a) Identify the polar coordinates of the points.

(b) Which points lie on the graph of $r = 3$?

(c) Which points lie on the graph of $\theta = \pi/4$?

93. Writing   In the rectangular coordinate system, each point (x, y) has a unique representation. Explain why this is not true for a point (r, θ) in the polar coordinate system.

94. Think About It Convert the polar equation $r = \cos \theta + 3 \sin \theta$ to rectangular form and identify the graph.

95. Think About It Convert the polar equation $r = 2(h \cos \theta + k \sin \theta)$ to rectangular form and verify that it is the equation of a circle. Find the radius of the circle and the rectangular coordinates of the center of the circle.

Cumulative Mixed Review

Solving a Triangle Using the Law of Sines or Cosines   In Exercises 96–99, use the Law of Sines or the Law of Cosines to solve the triangle.

96. $a = 13, b = 19, c = 25$

97. $A = 24°, a = 10, b = 6$

98. $A = 56°, C = 38°, c = 12$

99. $B = 71°, a = 21, c = 29$

9.6   Graphs of Polar Equations

Introduction

In previous chapters, you sketched graphs in rectangular coordinate systems. You began with the basic point-plotting method. Then you used sketching aids such as a graphing utility, symmetry, intercepts, asymptotes, periods, and shifts to further investigate the natures of the graphs. This section approaches curve sketching in the polar coordinate system similarly.

EXAMPLE 1   Graphing a Polar Equation by Point Plotting

Sketch the graph of the polar equation $r = 4 \sin \theta$ by hand.

Solution

The sine function is periodic, so you can get a full range of r-values by considering values of θ in the interval $0 \le \theta \le 2\pi$, as shown in the table.

θ	0	$\frac{\pi}{6}$	$\frac{\pi}{3}$	$\frac{\pi}{2}$	$\frac{2\pi}{3}$	$\frac{5\pi}{6}$	π	$\frac{7\pi}{6}$	$\frac{3\pi}{2}$	$\frac{11\pi}{6}$	2π
r	0	2	$2\sqrt{3}$	4	$2\sqrt{3}$	2	0	-2	-4	-2	0

By plotting these points, as shown in the figure, it appears that the graph is a circle of radius 2 whose center is the point $(x, y) = (0, 2)$.

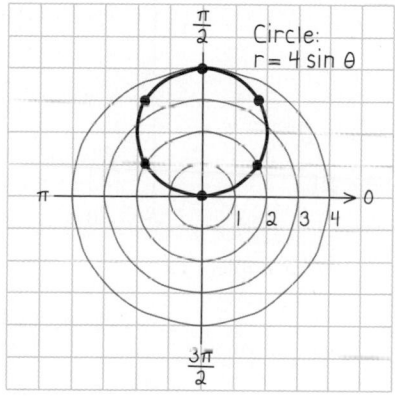

✓ Checkpoint 🔊))) *Audio-video solution in English & Spanish at LarsonPrecalculus.com.*

Sketch the graph of the polar equation $r = 6 \cos \theta$.

You can confirm the graph found in Example 1 in three ways.

1. *Convert to Rectangular Form*   Multiply each side of the polar equation by r and convert the result to rectangular form.

2. *Use a Polar Coordinate Mode*   Set your graphing utility to *polar* mode and graph the polar equation. (Use $0 \le \theta \le \pi$, $-6 \le x \le 6$, and $-4 \le y \le 4$.)

3. *Use a Parametric Mode*   Set your graphing utility to *parametric* mode and graph $x = (4 \sin t) \cos t$ and $y = (4 \sin t) \sin t$.

Most graphing utilities have a *polar* graphing mode. If yours does not, you can rewrite the polar equation $r = f(\theta)$ in parametric form, using t as a parameter with the equations $x = f(t) \cos t$ and $y = f(t) \sin t$.

Symmetry and Zeros

In Example 1, note in the graph of $r = 4 \sin \theta$ that as θ increases from 0 to 2π, the graph is traced out twice. Moreover, note that the graph is *symmetric with respect to the line* $\theta = \pi/2$. Had you known about this symmetry and retracing ahead of time, you could have used fewer points. The three important types of symmetry to consider in polar curve sketching are shown in Figure 9.60.

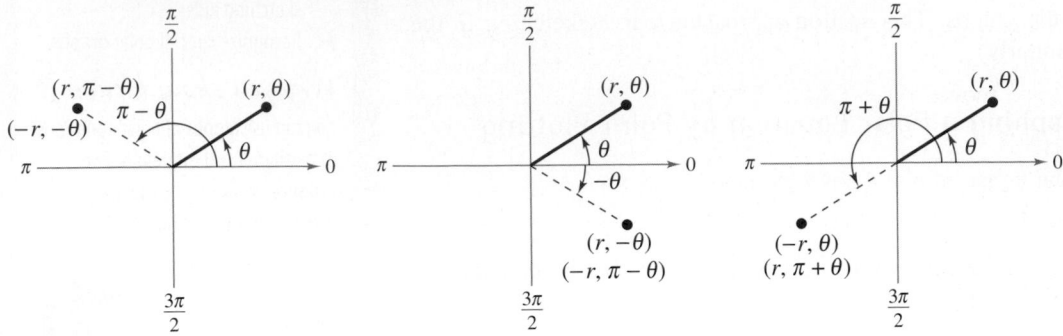

Symmetry with Respect to the Line $\theta = \dfrac{\pi}{2}$

Symmetry with Respect to the Polar Axis

Symmetry with Respect to the Pole

Figure 9.60

Testing for Symmetry in Polar Coordinates

The graph of a polar equation is symmetric with respect to the following when the given substitution yields an equivalent equation.

1. The line $\theta = \dfrac{\pi}{2}$: Replace (r, θ) by $(r, \pi - \theta)$ or $(-r, -\theta)$.

2. The polar axis: Replace (r, θ) by $(r, -\theta)$ or $(-r, \pi - \theta)$.

3. The pole: Replace (r, θ) by $(r, \pi + \theta)$ or $(-r, \theta)$.

You can determine the symmetry of the graph of $r = 4 \sin \theta$ (see Example 1) as follows.

1. Replace (r, θ) by $(-r, -\theta)$:

$$-r = 4 \sin(-\theta)$$
$$r = -4 \sin(-\theta)$$
$$r = 4 \sin \theta$$

2. Replace (r, θ) by $(r, -\theta)$:

$$r = 4 \sin(-\theta)$$
$$r = -4 \sin \theta$$

3. Replace (r, θ) by $(-r, \theta)$:

$$-r = 4 \sin \theta$$
$$r = -4 \sin \theta$$

So, the graph of $r = 4 \sin \theta$ is symmetric with respect to the line $\theta = \pi/2$. Recall from Section 4.2 that the sine function is odd. That is,

$$\sin(-\theta) = -\sin \theta.$$

EXAMPLE 2 Using Symmetry to Sketch a Polar Graph

Use symmetry to sketch the graph of $r = 3 + 2 \cos \theta$.

Solution

Replacing (r, θ) by $(r, -\theta)$ produces

$$r = 3 + 2 \cos(-\theta) = 3 + 2 \cos \theta. \qquad \cos(-u) = \cos u$$

So, by using the even trigonometric identity, you can conclude that the curve is symmetric with respect to the polar axis. Plotting the points in the table and using polar axis symmetry, you obtain the graph shown in Figure 9.61. This graph is called a **limaçon.**

θ	0	$\dfrac{\pi}{6}$	$\dfrac{\pi}{3}$	$\dfrac{\pi}{2}$	$\dfrac{2\pi}{3}$	$\dfrac{5\pi}{6}$	π
r	5	$3 + \sqrt{3}$	4	3	2	$3 - \sqrt{3}$	1

Use a graphing utility to confirm this graph.

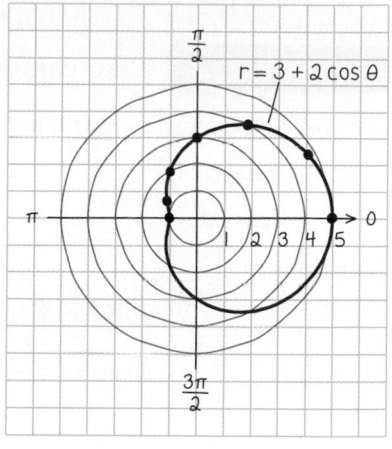

Figure 9.61

✓ **Checkpoint** ◀))) *Audio-video solution in English & Spanish at LarsonPrecalculus.com.*

Use symmetry to sketch the graph of $r = 3 + 2 \sin \theta$. ■

The three tests for symmetry in polar coordinates on page 684 are sufficient to guarantee symmetry, but they are not necessary. For instance, the figure at the right shows the graph of

$$r = \theta + 2\pi. \qquad \text{Spiral of Archimedes}$$

From the figure, you can see that the graph is symmetric with respect to the line $\theta = \pi/2$. Yet the tests on page 684 fail to indicate symmetry because neither of the following replacements yields an equivalent equation.

Spiral of Archimedes:
$r = \theta + 2\pi, -4\pi \le \theta \le 0$

Original Equation	*Replacement*	*New Equation*
$r = \theta + 2\pi$	(r, θ) by $(-r, -\theta)$	$-r = -\theta + 2\pi$
$r = \theta + 2\pi$	(r, θ) by $(r, \pi - \theta)$	$r = -\theta + 3\pi$

The equations discussed in Examples 1 and 2 are of the form

$$r = f(\sin \theta) \qquad \text{Example 1}$$

and

$$r = g(\cos \theta). \qquad \text{Example 2}$$

The graph of the first equation is symmetric with respect to the line $\theta = \pi/2$, and the graph of the second equation is symmetric with respect to the polar axis. This observation can be generalized to yield the following *quick tests for symmetry.*

Quick Tests for Symmetry in Polar Coordinates

1. The graph of $r = f(\sin \theta)$ is symmetric with respect to the line $\theta = \dfrac{\pi}{2}$.

2. The graph of $r = g(\cos \theta)$ is symmetric with respect to the polar axis.

An additional aid to sketching graphs of polar equations involves knowing the θ-values for which $r = 0$. In Example 1, $r = 0$ when $\theta = 0$. Some curves reach their zeros at more than one point, as shown in Example 3.

EXAMPLE 3 Sketching a Polar Graph

See LarsonPrecalculus.com for an interactive version of this type of example.

Sketch the graph of

$r = 2 \cos 3\theta$.

Solution

Symmetry: With respect to the polar axis

Zeros of r: $r = 0$ when $3\theta = \dfrac{\pi}{2}, \dfrac{3\pi}{2}, \dfrac{5\pi}{2}$

or $\theta = \dfrac{\pi}{6}, \dfrac{\pi}{2}, \dfrac{5\pi}{6}$

θ	0	$\dfrac{\pi}{12}$	$\dfrac{\pi}{6}$	$\dfrac{\pi}{4}$	$\dfrac{\pi}{3}$	$\dfrac{5\pi}{12}$	$\dfrac{\pi}{2}$
r	2	$\sqrt{2}$	0	$-\sqrt{2}$	-2	$-\sqrt{2}$	0

By plotting these points and using the specified symmetry and zeros, you can obtain the graph shown in Figure 9.62. This graph is called a **rose curve,** and each loop on the graph is called a *petal*. Note how the entire curve is generated as θ increases from 0 to π.

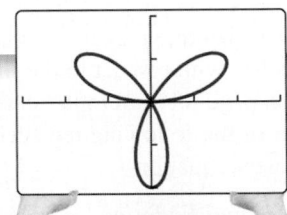

$0 \le \theta \le \dfrac{\pi}{6}$

$0 \le \theta \le \dfrac{\pi}{3}$

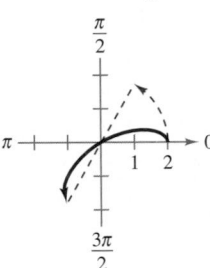

$0 \le \theta \le \dfrac{\pi}{2}$

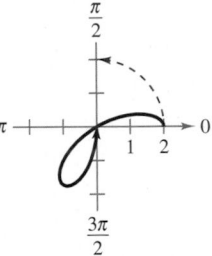

$0 \le \theta \le \dfrac{2\pi}{3}$

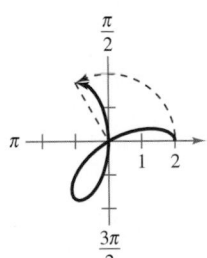

$0 \le \theta \le \dfrac{5\pi}{6}$

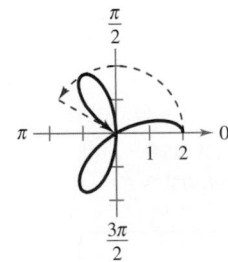

$0 \le \theta \le \pi$

Figure 9.62

✓ **Checkpoint** 🔊))) *Audio-video solution in English & Spanish at LarsonPrecalculus.com.*

Sketch the graph of $r = 4 \sin 2\theta$.

Special Polar Graphs

Several important types of graphs have equations that are simpler in polar form than in rectangular form. For example, the circle

$$r = 4 \sin \theta$$

in Example 1 has the more complicated rectangular equation

$$x^2 + (y - 2)^2 = 4.$$

Several other types of graphs that have simple polar equations are shown below.

Limaçons

$r = a \pm b \cos \theta, r = a \pm b \sin \theta \quad (a > 0, b > 0)$

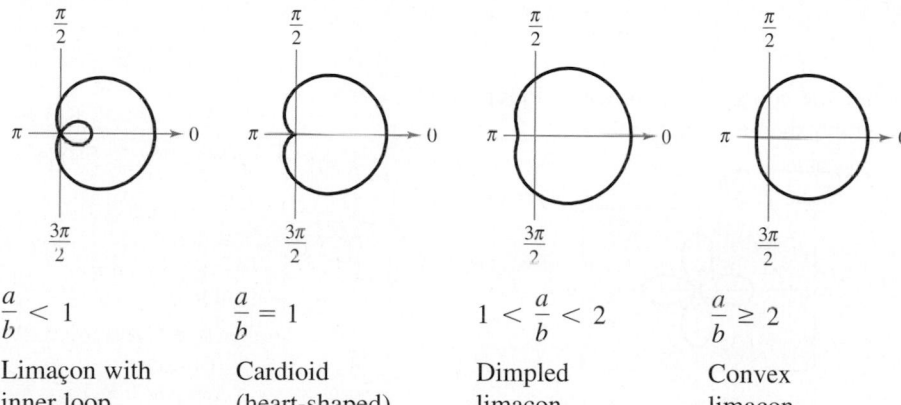

$\dfrac{a}{b} < 1$	$\dfrac{a}{b} = 1$	$1 < \dfrac{a}{b} < 2$	$\dfrac{a}{b} \geq 2$
Limaçon with inner loop	Cardioid (heart-shaped)	Dimpled limaçon	Convex limaçon

Rose Curves

n petals when n is odd, $2n$ petals when n is even $(n \geq 2)$

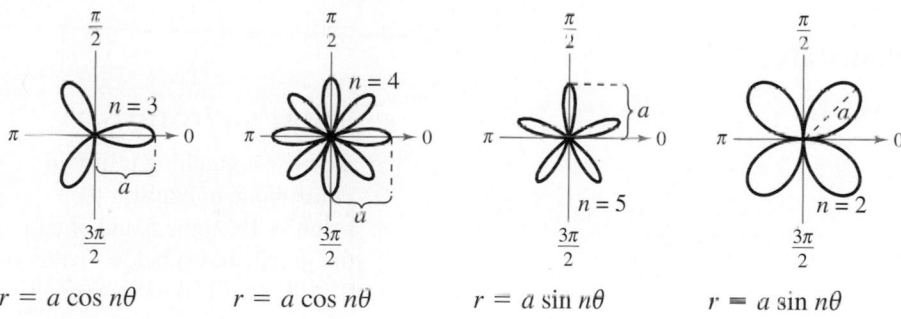

$r = a \cos n\theta$	$r = a \cos n\theta$	$r = a \sin n\theta$	$r = a \sin n\theta$

Circles and Lemniscates

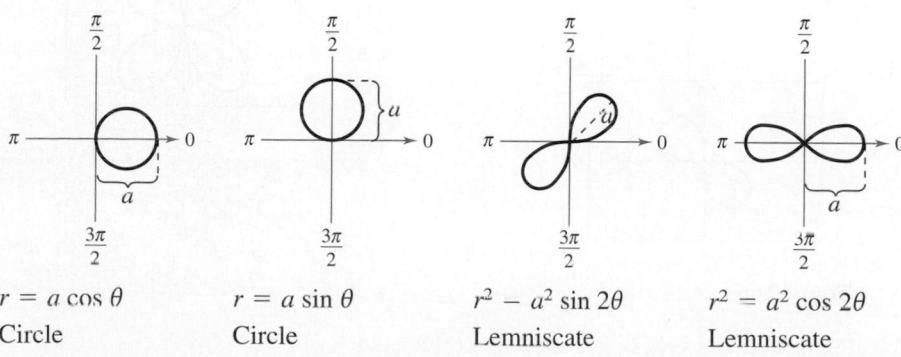

$r = a \cos \theta$	$r = a \sin \theta$	$r^2 = a^2 \sin 2\theta$	$r^2 = a^2 \cos 2\theta$
Circle	Circle	Lemniscate	Lemniscate

The quick tests for symmetry presented on page 685 are especially useful when graphing rose curves. Because rose curves have the form $r = f(\sin \theta)$ or the form $r = g(\cos \theta)$, you know that a rose curve will be either symmetric with respect to the line $\theta = \pi/2$ or symmetric with respect to the polar axis.

EXAMPLE 4   Graphing a Rose Curve

Use a graphing utility to graph $r = 3 \cos 2\theta$.

Solution

Type of curve: Rose curve with $2n = 4$ petals

Symmetry: With respect to the polar axis, the line $\theta = \dfrac{\pi}{2}$, and the pole

Zeros of r: $r = 0$ when $\theta = \dfrac{\pi}{4}, \dfrac{3\pi}{4}$

Using a graphing utility in *polar* mode, enter the equation, as shown in Figure 9.63 (with $0 \le \theta \le 2\pi$). You should obtain the graph shown in Figure 9.64.

Figure 9.63   Figure 9.64

 Checkpoint 🔊))) *Audio-video solution in English & Spanish at LarsonPrecalculus.com.*

Use a graphing utility to graph $r = 3 \sin 3\theta$.

EXAMPLE 5   Graphing a Lemniscate

Use a graphing utility to graph $r^2 = 9 \sin 2\theta$.

Solution

Type of curve: Lemniscate

Symmetry: With respect to the pole

Zeros of r: $r = 0$ when $\theta = 0, \dfrac{\pi}{2}$

Using a graphing utility in *polar* mode, enter the equation, as shown in Figure 9.65 (with $0 \le \theta \le 2\pi$). You should obtain the graph shown in Figure 9.66.

Figure 9.65   Figure 9.66

 Checkpoint 🔊))) *Audio-video solution in English & Spanish at LarsonPrecalculus.com.*

Use a graphing utility to graph $r^2 = 4 \cos 2\theta$.

What's Wrong?

You use a graphing utility in *polar* mode to confirm the result in Example 5 and obtain the graph shown below (with $0 \le \theta \le 2\pi$). What's wrong?

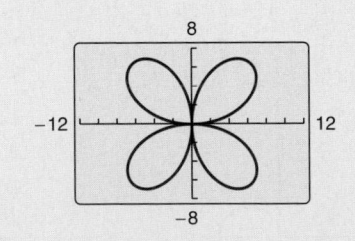

9.6   Exercises

See *CalcChat.com* for tutorial help and worked-out solutions to odd-numbered exercises. For instructions on how to use a graphing utility, see Appendix A.

Vocabulary and Concept Check

In Exercises 1–4, fill in the blank.

1. The equation $r = 2 + \cos \theta$ represents a _____ .

2. The equation $r = 2 \cos \theta$ represents a _____ .

3. The equation $r^2 = 4 \sin 2\theta$ represents a _____ .

4. The equation $r = 1 + \sin \theta$ represents a _____ .

5. How can you test whether the graph of a polar equation is symmetric with respect to the line $\theta = \dfrac{\pi}{2}$?

6. Is the graph of $r = 3 + 4 \cos \theta$ symmetric with respect to the line $\theta = \dfrac{\pi}{2}$ or to the polar axis?

Procedures and Problem Solving

Identifying Types of Polar Graphs **In Exercises 7–10, identify the type of polar graph.**

7. $r = 3 \cos 2\theta$

8. $r = 5 - 5 \sin \theta$

9. $r^2 = 9 \cos 2\theta$

10. $r = 1 + 4 \cos \theta$

Finding the Equation of a Polar Curve **In Exercises 11–14, determine the equation of the polar curve whose graph is shown.**

11.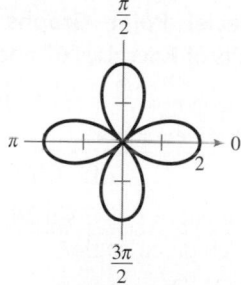

(a) $r = 2 \cos 4\theta$

(b) $r = \cos 4\theta$

(c) $r = 2 \cos 2\theta$

(d) $r = 2 \cos \dfrac{\theta}{2}$

12.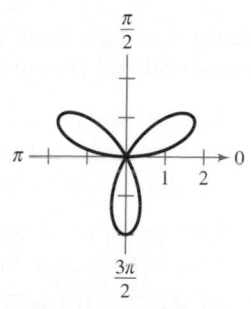

(a) $r = 2 \sin 6\theta$

(b) $r = 2 \cos\left(\dfrac{3\theta}{2}\right)$

(c) $r = 2 \sin\left(\dfrac{3\theta}{2}\right)$

(d) $r = 2 \sin 3\theta$

13.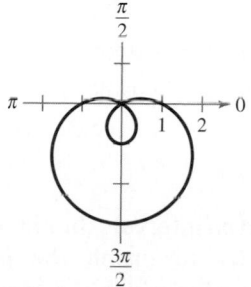

(a) $r = 1 - 2 \sin \theta$

(b) $r = 1 + 2 \sin \theta$

(c) $r = 1 + 2 \cos \theta$

(d) $r = 1 - 2 \cos \theta$

14.

(a) $r = 2 - \cos \theta$

(b) $r = 2 - \sin \theta$

(c) $r = 2 + \cos \theta$

(d) $r = 2 + \sin \theta$

Testing for Symmetry **In Exercises 15–22, test for symmetry with respect to the line $\theta = \pi/2$, the polar axis, and the pole.**

15. $r = 3$

16. $r = 5 + 4 \cos \theta$

17. $r = \dfrac{2}{1 - \cos \theta}$

18. $r = \dfrac{2}{1 + \sin \theta}$

19. $r = 6 \sin \theta$

20. $r = 4 \csc \theta \cos \theta$

21. $r^2 = 16 \sin 2\theta$

22. $r^2 = 36 \sin 2\theta$

Using Symmetry to Sketch a Polar Graph **In Exercises 23–30, use symmetry to sketch the graph of the polar equation. Use a graphing utility to verify your graph.**

23. $r = 5$

24. $\theta = -5\pi/3$

25. $r = 3 \sin \theta$

26. $r = 2 \cos \theta$

27. $r = 3(1 - \cos \theta)$

28. $r = 4(1 + \sin \theta)$

29. $r = 4 + 5 \sin \theta$

30. $r = 3 + 6 \cos \theta$

Sketching a Polar Graph In Exercises 31–36, identify and sketch the graph of the polar equation. Identify any symmetry and zeros of r. Use a graphing utility to verify your results.

31. $r = 5 \cos 3\theta$

32. $r = \sin 5\theta$

33. $r = -7 \sin 2\theta$

34. $r = 3 \cos 4\theta$

35. $r = 1 + 2 \sin \theta$

36. $r = \sqrt{3} - 2 \cos \theta$

Using a Graphing Utility to Graph a Polar Equation In Exercises 37–50, use a graphing utility to graph the polar equation. Describe your viewing window.

37. $r = 8 \cos 2\theta$

38. $r = -\cos 2\theta$

39. $r = 2(5 - \sin \theta)$

40. $r = 6 - 4 \sin \theta$

41. $r = \dfrac{3}{\sin \theta - 2 \cos \theta}$

42. $r = \dfrac{6}{2 \sin \theta - 3 \cos \theta}$

43. $r^2 = \sin 2\theta$

44. $r^2 = 4 \cos 3\theta$

45. $r = 8 \sin \theta \cos^2 \theta$

46. $r = 2 \cos(3\theta - 2)$

47. $r = 2 \csc \theta + 6$

48. $r = 4 - \sec \theta$

49. $r = e^\theta$

50. $r = e^{\theta/2}$

Using a Graphing Utility to Find an Interval In Exercises 51–56, use a graphing utility to graph the polar equation. Find an interval for θ for which the graph is traced *only once*.

51. $r = 3 - 4 \cos \theta$

52. $r = 2(1 - 2 \sin \theta)$

53. $r = 2 \cos \dfrac{3\theta}{2}$

54. $r = 3 \sin \dfrac{5\theta}{2}$

55. $r = 9 \sin \theta$

56. $r^2 = 25 \cos 2\theta$

Using a Graphing Utility to Graph a Polar Equation In Exercises 57–60, use a graphing utility to graph the polar equation and show that the indicated line is an asymptote of the graph.

	Name of Graph	Polar Equation	Asymptote
57.	Conchoid	$r = 2 - \sec \theta$	$x = -1$
58.	Conchoid	$r = 2 + \csc \theta$	$y = 1$
59.	Hyperbolic spiral	$r = 3/\theta$	$y = 3$
60.	Strophoid	$r = 2 \cos 2\theta \sec \theta$	$x = -2$

61. *Why you should learn it* (p. 683) The sound pickup pattern of a microphone is modeled by the polar equation $r = 5 + 5 \cos \theta$, where $|r|$ measures how sensitive the microphone is to sounds coming from the angle θ.

(a) Sketch the graph of the model and identify the type of polar graph.

(b) At what angle is the microphone most sensitive to sound?

62. Geometry The area of the lemniscate $r^2 = a^2 \cos 2\theta$ is a^2. Sketch the graph of $r^2 = 16 \cos 2\theta$. Then find the area of one loop of the graph.

Conclusions

True or False? In Exercises 63–65, determine whether the statement is true or false. Justify your answer.

63. The graph of $r = 6 \sin 5\theta$ is a rose curve with five petals.

64. The graph of $r = 4 + 2 \cos \theta$ is a dimpled limaçon.

65. A rose curve will always have symmetry with respect to the line $\theta = \pi/2$.

66. HOW DO YOU SEE IT? Determine which graph matches each polar equation.

(a) $r = 5 \sin \theta$ (b) $r = 2 + 5 \sin \theta$

(c) $r = 5 \cos 2\theta$

67. Exploration The graph of $r = f(\theta)$ is rotated about the pole through an angle ϕ. Show that the equation of the rotated graph is $r = f(\theta - \phi)$.

68. Exploration Consider the graph of $r = f(\sin \theta)$.

(a) Show that when the graph is rotated counterclockwise $\pi/2$ radians about the pole, the equation of the rotated graph is $r = f(-\cos \theta)$.

(b) Show that when the graph is rotated counterclockwise π radians about the pole, the equation of the rotated graph is $r = f(-\sin \theta)$.

(c) Show that when the graph is rotated counterclockwise $3\pi/2$ radians about the pole, the equation of the rotated graph is $r = f(\cos \theta)$.

Writing an Equation for Special Polar Graphs In Exercises 69 and 70, use the results of Exercises 67 and 68.

69. Write an equation for the limaçon $r = 2 - \sin \theta$ after it has been rotated through each given angle.

(a) $\pi/4$ (b) $\pi/2$ (c) π (d) $3\pi/2$

70. Write an equation for the rose curve $r = 2 \sin 2\theta$ after it has been rotated through each given angle.

(a) $\pi/6$ (b) $\pi/2$ (c) $2\pi/3$ (d) π

Cumulative Mixed Review

Finding the Zeros of a Rational Function In Exercises 71–74, find the zeros (if any) of the rational function.

71. $f(x) = \dfrac{x^2 - 9}{x + 1}$

72. $f(x) = 6 + \dfrac{4}{x^2 + 4}$

73. $f(x) = 5 - \dfrac{3}{x - 2}$

74. $f(x) = \dfrac{x^3 - 27}{x^2 + 4}$

9.7 Polar Equations of Conics

Alternative Definition of Conics and Polar Equations

In Sections 9.2 and 9.3, you learned that the rectangular equations of ellipses and hyperbolas take simple forms when the origin lies at the *center*. As it happens, there are many important applications of conics in which it is more convenient to use one of the *foci* as the origin. In this section, you will learn that polar equations of conics take simple forms when one of the foci lies at the pole.

To begin, consider the following alternative definition of a conic that uses the concept of eccentricity (a measure of the flatness of the conic).

Alternative Definition of a Conic

The locus of a point in the plane that moves such that its distance from a fixed point (focus) is in a constant ratio to its distance from a fixed line (directrix) is a **conic.** The constant ratio is the **eccentricity** of the conic and is denoted by e. Moreover, the conic is an **ellipse** when $0 < e < 1$, a **parabola** when $e = 1$, and a **hyperbola** when $e > 1$. (See Figure 9.67.)

In Figure 9.67, note that for each type of conic, the focus is at the pole.

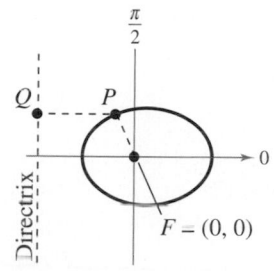

Ellipse: $0 < e < 1$

$$\frac{PF}{PQ} < 1$$

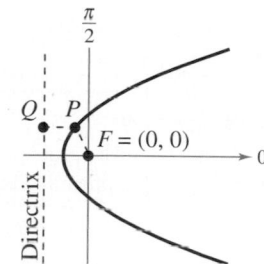

Parabola: $e = 1$

$$\frac{PF}{PQ} = 1$$

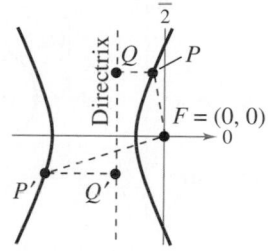

Hyperbola: $e > 1$

$$\frac{PF}{PQ} = \frac{P'F}{P'Q'} > 1$$

Figure 9.67

The benefit of locating a focus of a conic at the pole is that the equation of the conic becomes simpler.

Polar Equations of Conics (See the proof on page 709.)

The graph of a polar equation of the form

1. $r = \dfrac{ep}{1 \pm e \cos \theta}$

or

2. $r = \dfrac{ep}{1 \pm e \sin \theta}$

is a conic, where $e > 0$ is the eccentricity and $|p|$ is the distance between the focus (pole) and the directrix.

What you should learn
- ▶ Define conics in terms of eccentricities, and write and graph equations of conics in polar form.
- ▶ Use equations of conics in polar form to model real-life problems.

Why you should learn it
The orbits of planets and satellites can be modeled by polar equations. For instance, in Exercise 64 on page 697, you will use a polar equation to model the orbit of a satellite.

Jupiter

An equation of the form

$$r = \frac{ep}{1 \pm e \cos \theta} \qquad \text{Vertical directrix}$$

corresponds to a conic with a vertical directrix and symmetry with respect to the polar axis. An equation of the form

$$r = \frac{ep}{1 \pm e \sin \theta} \qquad \text{Horizontal directrix}$$

corresponds to a conic with a horizontal directrix and symmetry with respect to the line $\theta = \pi/2$. Moreover, the converse is also true—that is, any conic with a focus at the pole and having a horizontal or vertical directrix can be represented by one of these equations.

EXAMPLE 1 Identifying a Conic from Its Equation

See LarsonPrecalculus.com for an interactive version of this type of example.

Identify the type of conic represented by the equation $r = \dfrac{15}{3 - 2 \cos \theta}$.

Algebraic Solution

To identify the type of conic, rewrite the equation in the form $r = ep/(1 \pm e \cos \theta)$.

$$r = \frac{15}{3 - 2 \cos \theta}$$

$$= \frac{5}{1 - (2/3) \cos \theta} \qquad \begin{array}{l}\text{Divide numerator and}\\ \text{denominator by 3.}\end{array}$$

Because $e = \frac{2}{3} < 1$, you can conclude that the graph is an ellipse.

Graphical Solution

Use a graphing utility in *polar* mode and be sure to use a square setting, as shown in the figure.

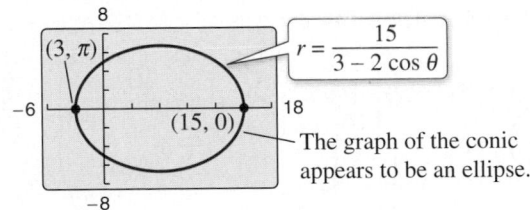

The graph of the conic appears to be an ellipse.

✓ **Checkpoint** ◀))) *Audio-video solution in English & Spanish at LarsonPrecalculus.com.*

Identify the type of conic represented by the equation $r = \dfrac{8}{2 - 3 \sin \theta}$. ■

For the ellipse in Example 1, the major axis is horizontal and the vertices lie at $(r, \theta) = (15, 0)$ and $(r, \theta) = (3, \pi)$. So, the length of the *major* axis is $2a = 18$. To find the length of the *minor* axis, you can use the equations $e = c/a$ and $b^2 = a^2 - c^2$ to conclude that

$$b^2 = a^2 - c^2$$

$$= a^2 - (ea)^2$$

$$= a^2(1 - e^2). \qquad \text{Ellipse}$$

Because $e = \frac{2}{3}$, you have $b^2 = 9^2\left[1 - \left(\frac{2}{3}\right)^2\right] = 45$, which implies that

$$b = \sqrt{45} = 3\sqrt{5}.$$

So, the length of the minor axis is $2b = 6\sqrt{5}$. A similar analysis for hyperbolas yields

$$b^2 = c^2 - a^2$$

$$= (ea)^2 - a^2$$

$$= a^2(e^2 - 1). \qquad \text{Hyperbola}$$

EXAMPLE 2   Analyzing the Graph of a Polar Equation

Analyze the graph of the polar equation $r = \dfrac{32}{3 + 5 \sin \theta}$.

Solution

Dividing the numerator and denominator by 3 produces

$$r = \frac{32/3}{1 + (5/3) \sin \theta}.$$

Because $e = \frac{5}{3} > 1$, the graph is a hyperbola. The transverse axis of the hyperbola lies on the line $\theta = \pi/2$, and the vertices occur at $(r, \theta) = (4, \pi/2)$ and $(r, \theta) = (-16, 3\pi/2)$. Because the length of the transverse axis is 12, you can see that $a = 6$. To find b, write

$$b^2 = a^2(e^2 - 1) = 6^2\left[\left(\frac{5}{3}\right)^2 - 1\right] = 64.$$

So, $b = 8$. You can use a and b to determine that the asymptotes are $y = 10 \pm \frac{3}{4}x$, as shown in Figure 9.68.

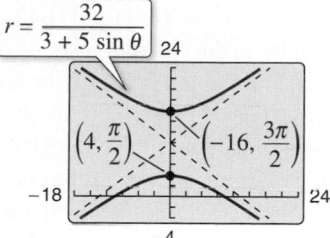

Figure 9.68

✔ **Checkpoint**))) *Audio-video solution in English & Spanish at LarsonPrecalculus.com.*

Identify the conic $r = \dfrac{3}{2 - 4 \sin \theta}$ and sketch its graph.   ■

   In the next example, you are asked to find a polar equation for a specified conic. To do this, let p be the distance between the pole and the directrix.

1. Horizontal directrix above the pole: $r = \dfrac{ep}{1 + e \sin \theta}$

2. Horizontal directrix below the pole: $r = \dfrac{ep}{1 - e \sin \theta}$

3. Vertical directrix to the right of the pole: $r = \dfrac{ep}{1 + e \cos \theta}$

4. Vertical directrix to the left of the pole: $r = \dfrac{ep}{1 - e \cos \theta}$

> ## Explore the Concept
>
> Try using a graphing utility in *polar* mode to verify the four orientations shown at the left.

EXAMPLE 3   Finding the Polar Equation of a Conic

Find the polar equation of the parabola whose focus is the pole and whose directrix is the line $y = 3$.

Solution

Because the directrix is horizontal and above the pole, use an equation of the form

$$r = \frac{ep}{1 + e \sin \theta}.$$

Moreover, because the eccentricity of a parabola is $e = 1$ and the distance between the pole and the directrix is $p = 3$, you have the equation

$$r = \frac{3}{1 + \sin \theta}. \qquad \text{See Figure 9.69.}$$

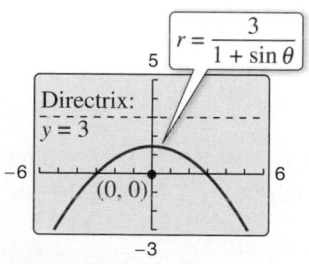

Figure 9.69

✔ **Checkpoint**))) *Audio-video solution in English & Spanish at LarsonPrecalculus.com.*

Find a polar equation of the parabola whose focus is the pole and whose directrix is the line $x = -2$.   ■

Application

Kepler's Laws (listed below), named after the German astronomer Johannes Kepler (1571–1630), can be used to describe the orbits of the planets about the sun.

1. Each planet moves in an elliptical orbit with the sun as a focus.

2. A ray from the sun to the planet sweeps out equal areas of the ellipse in equal times.

3. The square of the period (the time it takes for a planet to orbit the sun) is proportional to the cube of the mean distance between the planet and the sun.

Although Kepler simply stated these laws on the basis of observation, they were later validated by Isaac Newton (1642–1727). In fact, Newton was able to show that each law can be deduced from a set of universal laws of motion and gravitation that govern the movement of all heavenly bodies, including comets and satellites. This is illustrated in the next example, which involves the comet named after the English mathematician and physicist Edmund Halley (1656–1742).

If you use Earth as a reference with a period of 1 year and a distance of 1 astronomical unit (an *astronomical unit* is defined as the mean distance between Earth and the sun, or about 93 million miles), then the proportionality constant in Kepler's third law is 1. For example, because Mars has a mean distance to the sun of $d \approx 1.524$ astronomical units, its period P is given by

$$d^3 = P^2.$$

So, the period of Mars is $P \approx 1.88$ years.

Astronomer

EXAMPLE 4   Halley's Comet

Halley's comet has an elliptical orbit with an eccentricity of $e \approx 0.967$. The length of the major axis of the orbit is approximately 35.67 astronomical units. Find a polar equation for the orbit. How close does Halley's comet come to the sun?

Solution

Using a vertical major axis, as shown in Figure 9.70, choose an equation of the form

$$r = \frac{ep}{1 + e \sin \theta}.$$

Because the vertices of the ellipse occur at $\theta = \pi/2$ and $\theta = 3\pi/2$, you can determine the length of the major axis to be the sum of the r-values of the vertices. That is,

$$2a = \frac{0.967p}{1 + 0.967} + \frac{0.967p}{1 - 0.967} \implies 35.67 \approx 29.79p.$$

So, $p \approx 1.197$ and $ep \approx (0.967)(1.197) \approx 1.157$. Using this value of ep in the equation, you have

$$r = \frac{1.157}{1 + 0.967 \sin \theta}$$

where r is measured in astronomical units. To find the closest point to the sun (the focus), substitute $\theta = \pi/2$ into this equation to obtain

$$r = \frac{1.157}{1 + 0.967 \sin(\pi/2)} \approx 0.59 \text{ astronomical unit} \approx 55{,}000{,}000 \text{ miles.}$$

✓ **Checkpoint** ◀))) *Audio-video solution in English & Spanish at LarsonPrecalculus.com.*

Encke's comet has an elliptical orbit with an eccentricity of $e \approx 0.848$. The length of the major axis of the orbit is approximately 4.429 astronomical units. Find a polar equation for the orbit. How close does Encke's comet come to the sun?

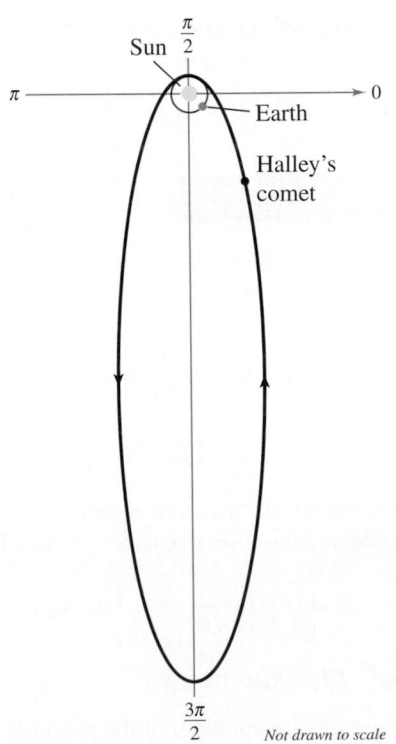

Figure 9.70

9.7   Exercises

See *CalcChat.com* for tutorial help and worked-out solutions to odd-numbered exercises. For instructions on how to use a graphing utility, see Appendix A.

Vocabulary and Concept Check

1. Fill in the blank: The locus of a point in the plane that moves such that its distance from a fixed point (focus) is in a constant ratio to its distance from a fixed line (directrix) is a _____ .

2. Match the conic with its eccentricity.

   (a) $0 < e < 1$ (i) ellipse

   (b) $e = 1$ (ii) hyperbola

   (c) $e > 1$ (iii) parabola

3. A conic has a polar equation of the form $r = \dfrac{ep}{1 + e \cos \theta}$. Is the directrix vertical or horizontal?

4. A conic with a horizontal directrix has a polar equation of the form $r = \dfrac{ep}{1 - e \sin \theta}$. Is the directrix above or below the pole?

Procedures and Problem Solving

Identifying a Conic   In Exercises 5–8, use a graphing utility to graph the polar equation for (a) $e = 1$, (b) $e = 0.5$, and (c) $e = 1.5$. Identify the conic for each equation.

5. $r = \dfrac{2e}{1 + e \cos \theta}$

6. $r = \dfrac{2e}{1 - e \cos \theta}$

7. $r = \dfrac{2e}{1 - e \sin \theta}$

8. $r = \dfrac{2e}{1 + e \sin \theta}$

Identifying the Polar Equation of a Conic   In Exercises 9–14, match the polar equation with its graph. [The graphs are labeled (a), (b), (c), (d), (e), and (f).]

(a)

(b)

(c)

(d)

(e)

(f)

9. $r = \dfrac{4}{1 - \cos \theta}$

10. $r = \dfrac{3}{2 - \cos \theta}$

11. $r = \dfrac{3}{2 + \cos \theta}$

12. $r = \dfrac{4}{1 - 3 \sin \theta}$

13. $r = \dfrac{3}{1 + 2 \sin \theta}$

14. $r = \dfrac{4}{1 + \sin \theta}$

Identifying a Conic from Its Equation   In Exercises 15–24, identify the type of conic represented by the equation. Use a graphing utility to confirm your result.

15. $r = \dfrac{3}{1 - \cos \theta}$

16. $r = \dfrac{2}{4 + \sin \theta}$

17. $r = \dfrac{4}{1 - 5 \cos \theta}$

18. $r = \dfrac{7}{1 + \sin \theta}$

19. $r = \dfrac{8}{4 + 3 \sin \theta}$

20. $r = \dfrac{9}{3 - 2 \cos \theta}$

21. $r = \dfrac{6}{2 + \sin \theta}$

22. $r = \dfrac{5}{-1 + \cos \theta}$

23. $r = \dfrac{3}{-4 - 8 \cos \theta}$

24. $r = \dfrac{10}{3 + 9 \sin \theta}$

Analyzing the Graph of a Polar Equation   In Exercises 25–30, identify the type of conic represented by the polar equation and analyze its graph. Then use a graphing utility to graph the polar equation.

25. $r = \dfrac{5}{1 - \sin \theta}$

26. $r = \dfrac{-1}{2 + 4 \sin \theta}$

27. $r = \dfrac{14}{14 + 17 \sin \theta}$

28. $r = \dfrac{12}{2 - \cos \theta}$

29. $r = \dfrac{-3}{-4 + 2 \cos \theta}$

30. $r = \dfrac{-4}{-1 + \cos \theta}$

Graphing a Rotated Conic   In Exercises 31–36, use a graphing utility to graph the rotated conic.

31. $r = \dfrac{3}{1 - \cos(\theta - \pi/4)}$ (See Exercise 15.)

32. $r = \dfrac{7}{1 + \sin(\theta - \pi/3)}$ (See Exercise 18.)

33. $r = \dfrac{4}{1 - 5\cos(\theta + 3\pi/4)}$ (See Exercise 17.)

34. $r = \dfrac{9}{3 - 2\cos(\theta + \pi/2)}$ (See Exercise 20.)

35. $r = \dfrac{8}{4 + 3\sin(\theta + \pi/6)}$ (See Exercise 19.)

36. $r = \dfrac{10}{3 + 9\sin(\theta + 2\pi/3)}$ (See Exercise 24.)

Finding the Polar Equation of a Conic   In Exercises 37–54, find a polar equation of the conic with its focus at the pole.

Conic	Eccentricity	Directrix
37. Parabola	$e = 1$	$x = -1$
38. Parabola	$e = 1$	$y = -4$
39. Ellipse	$e = \frac{1}{2}$	$y = 1$
40. Ellipse	$e = \frac{3}{4}$	$y = -4$
41. Hyperbola	$e = 2$	$x = 1$
42. Hyperbola	$e = \frac{3}{2}$	$x = -1$

Conic	Vertex or Vertices
43. Parabola	$\left(1, -\dfrac{\pi}{2}\right)$
44. Parabola	$(8, 0)$
45. Parabola	$(5, \pi)$
46. Parabola	$\left(10, \dfrac{\pi}{2}\right)$
47. Ellipse	$(2, 0), (10, \pi)$
48. Ellipse	$\left(2, \dfrac{\pi}{2}\right), \left(4, \dfrac{3\pi}{2}\right)$
49. Ellipse	$\left(1, \dfrac{3\pi}{2}\right), \left(11, \dfrac{\pi}{2}\right)$
50. Ellipse	$(20, 0), (4, \pi)$
51. Hyperbola	$\left(1, \dfrac{3\pi}{2}\right), \left(-9, \dfrac{\pi}{2}\right)$
52. Hyperbola	$(2, 0), (-8, \pi)$
53. Hyperbola	$\left(\dfrac{3}{5}, \pi\right), (-1, 0)$
54. Hyperbola	$\left(-4, \dfrac{3\pi}{2}\right), \left(1, \dfrac{\pi}{2}\right)$

55. Astronomy   The planets travel in elliptical orbits with the sun at one focus. Assume that the focus is at the pole, the major axis lies on the polar axis, and the length of the major axis is $2a$ (see figure). Show that the polar equation of the orbit of a planet is

$$r = \frac{(1 - e^2)a}{1 - e\cos\theta}$$

where e is the eccentricity.

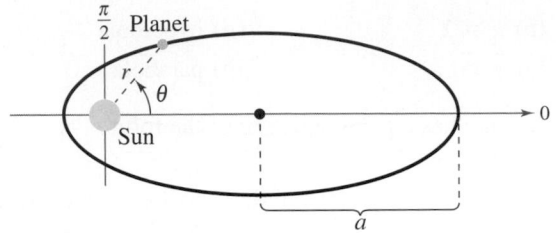

56. Astronomy   Use the result of Exercise 55 to show that the minimum distance (*perihelion*) from the sun to a planet is

$$r = a(1 - e)$$

and that the maximum distance (*aphelion*) is

$$r = a(1 + e).$$

Astronomy   In Exercises 57–62, use the results of Exercises 55 and 56 to find the polar equation of the orbit of the planet and the perihelion and aphelion distances.

57. Earth $a \approx 9.2956 \times 10^7$ miles, $e \approx 0.0167$

58. Mercury $a \approx 3.5983 \times 10^7$ miles, $e \approx 0.2056$

59. Mars $a \approx 1.4164 \times 10^8$ miles, $e \approx 0.0934$

60. Saturn $a \approx 1.4267 \times 10^9$ kilometers, $e \approx 0.0539$

61. Venus $a \approx 1.0821 \times 10^8$ kilometers, $e \approx 0.0068$

62. Jupiter $a \approx 7.7834 \times 10^8$ kilometers, $e \approx 0.0484$

63. Astronomy   Use the results of Exercises 55 and 56, where for the planet Neptune, $a = 4.498 \times 10^9$ kilometers and $e = 0.0086$ and for the dwarf planet Pluto, $a = 5.906 \times 10^9$ kilometers and $e = 0.2488$.

(a) Find the polar equation of the orbit of each planet.

(b) Find the perihelion and aphelion distances for each planet.

(c) Use a graphing utility to graph both Neptune's and Pluto's equations of orbit in the same viewing window.

(d) Is Pluto ever closer to the sun than Neptune? Until recently, Pluto was considered the ninth planet. Why was Pluto called the ninth planet and Neptune the eighth planet?

(e) Do the orbits of Neptune and Pluto intersect? Will Neptune and Pluto ever collide? Why or why not?

64. *Why you should learn it* (*p. 691*) On November 27, 1963, the United States launched a satellite named *Explorer 18*. Its low and high points above the surface of Earth were about 119 miles and 122,800 miles, respectively (see figure). The center of Earth is at one focus of the orbit.

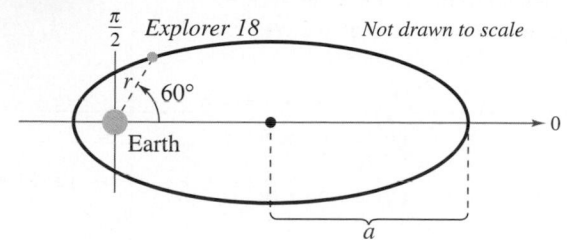

(a) Find the polar equation of the orbit (assume the radius of Earth is 4000 miles).

(b) Find the distance between the surface of Earth and the satellite when $\theta = 60°$.

(c) Find the distance between the surface of Earth and the satellite when $\theta = 30°$.

Conclusions

True or False?   In Exercises 65–68, determine whether the statement is true or false. Justify your answer.

65. The graph of $r = 4/(-3 - 3\sin\theta)$ has a horizontal directrix above the pole.

66. The conic represented by the following equation is an ellipse.

$$r^2 = \frac{16}{9 - 4\cos\left(\theta + \dfrac{\pi}{4}\right)}$$

67. For values of $e > 1$ and $0 \le \theta \le 2\pi$, the graphs of the following equations are the same.

$$r = \frac{ex}{1 - e\cos\theta} \quad \text{and} \quad r = \frac{e(-x)}{1 + e\cos\theta}$$

68. The graph of $r = \dfrac{5}{1 - \sin[\theta - (\pi/4)]}$ can be obtained by rotating the graph of $r = \dfrac{5}{1 + \sin\theta}$ about the pole.

69. Verifying a Polar Equation   Show that the polar equation of the ellipse

$$\frac{x^2}{a^2} + \frac{y^2}{b^2} = 1 \quad \text{is} \quad r^2 = \frac{b^2}{1 - e^2\cos^2\theta}.$$

70. Verifying a Polar Equation   Show that the polar equation of the hyperbola

$$\frac{x^2}{a^2} - \frac{y^2}{b^2} = 1 \quad \text{is} \quad r^2 = \frac{-b^2}{1 - e^2\cos^2\theta}.$$

Writing a Polar Equation   In Exercises 71–76, use the results of Exercises 69 and 70 to write the polar form of the equation of the conic.

71. $\dfrac{x^2}{169} + \dfrac{y^2}{144} = 1$ **72.** $\dfrac{x^2}{9} - \dfrac{y^2}{16} = 1$

73. $\dfrac{x^2}{25} + \dfrac{y^2}{16} = 1$ **74.** $\dfrac{x^2}{36} - \dfrac{y^2}{4} = 1$

75. Hyperbola   One focus: $(5, 0)$

Vertices: $(4, 0), (4, \pi)$

76. Ellipse   One focus: $(4, 0)$

Vertices: $(5, 0), (5, \pi)$

77. Think About It   What conic does the polar equation $r = a\sin\theta + b\cos\theta$ represent?

78. HOW DO YOU SEE IT?   The graph of $r = \dfrac{e}{1 - e\sin\theta}$ is shown for different values of e. Determine which graph matches each value of e.

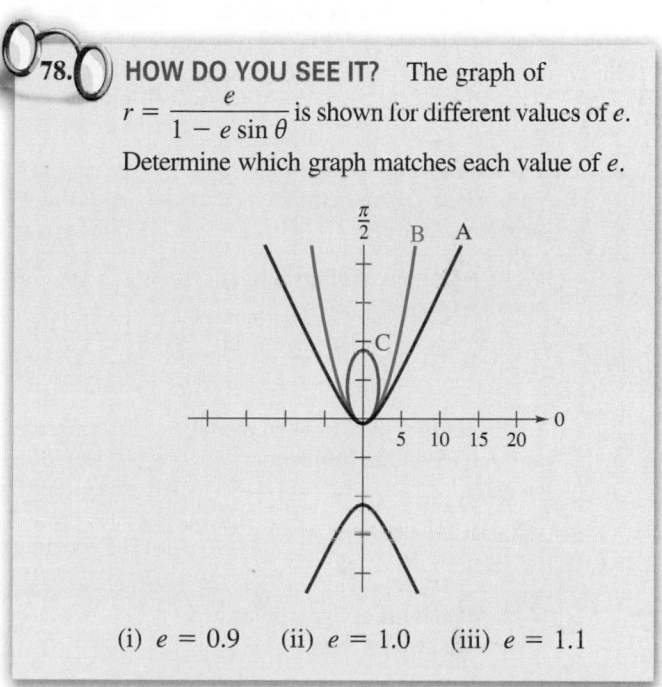

(i) $e = 0.9$ (ii) $e = 1.0$ (iii) $e = 1.1$

79. Writing   In your own words, define the term *eccentricity* and explain how it can be used to classify conics. Then explain how you can use the values of b and c to determine whether a polar equation of the form

$$r = \frac{a}{b + c\sin\theta}$$

represents an ellipse, a parabola, or a hyperbola.

Cumulative Mixed Review

Evaluating a Trigonometric Expression   In Exercises 80–83, find the exact value of the trigonometric expression when u and v are in Quadrant IV and $\sin u = -\frac{3}{5}$ and $\cos v = 1/\sqrt{2}$.

80. $\cos(u + v)$ **81.** $\sin(u + v)$

82. $\sin(u - v)$ **83.** $\cos(u - v)$

9 Chapter Summary

	What did you learn?	Explanation and Examples	Review Exercises
9.1	**Recognize a conic as the intersection of a plane and a double-napped cone** (*p. 636*).	In the formation of the four basic conics, the intersecting plane does not pass through the vertex of the cone. (See Figure 9.1.) When the plane does pass through the vertex, the resulting figure is a degenerate conic, such as a point or a line. (See Figure 9.2.)	1, 2
	Write equations of circles in standard form (*p. 637*).	The standard form of the equation of a circle with center at (h, k) is $(x - h)^2 + (y - k)^2 = r^2$. The standard form of the equation of a circle whose center is the origin, $(h, k) = (0, 0)$, is $x^2 + y^2 = r^2$.	3–14
	Write equations of parabolas in standard form (*p. 639*).	The standard form of the equation of a parabola with vertex at (h, k) is as follows. $(x - h)^2 = 4p(y - k),\ p \neq 0$ Vertical axis $(y - k)^2 = 4p(x - h),\ p \neq 0$ Horizontal axis	15–24
	Use the reflective property of parabolas to solve real-life problems (*p. 641*).	The tangent line to a parabola at a point P makes equal angles with (1) the line passing through P and the focus, and (2) the axis of the parabola. (See Figure 9.12.)	25, 26
9.2	**Write equations of ellipses in standard form** (*p. 647*).	$\dfrac{(x - h)^2}{a^2} + \dfrac{(y - k)^2}{b^2} = 1$ Horizontal major axis $\dfrac{(x - h)^2}{b^2} + \dfrac{(y - k)^2}{a^2} = 1$ Vertical major axis	27–38
	Use properties of ellipses to model and solve real-life problems (*p. 651*).	The properties of ellipses can be used to find the greatest and least distances from Earth's center to the moon's center. (See Example 5.)	39, 40
	Find eccentricities of ellipses (*p. 652*).	The eccentricity e of an ellipse is given by $e = \dfrac{c}{a}$.	41, 42
9.3	**Write equations of hyperbolas in standard form** (*p. 656*).	$\dfrac{(x - h)^2}{a^2} - \dfrac{(y - k)^2}{b^2} = 1$ Horizontal transverse axis $\dfrac{(y - k)^2}{a^2} - \dfrac{(x - h)^2}{b^2} = 1$ Vertical transverse axis	43–46
	Find asymptotes of and graph hyperbolas (*p. 658*).	$y = k \pm \dfrac{b}{a}(x - h)$ Horizontal transverse axis $y = k \pm \dfrac{a}{b}(x - h)$ Vertical transverse axis	47–52
	Use properties of hyperbolas to solve real-life problems (*p. 661*).	The properties of hyperbolas can be used in radar and other detection systems. (See Example 5.)	53, 54
	Classify conics from their general equations (*p. 662*).	The graph of $Ax^2 + Cy^2 + Dx + Ey + F = 0$ is • a circle when $A = C$, with $A \neq 0$. • a parabola when $AC = 0$, with $A = 0$ or $C = 0$ (but not both). • an ellipse when $AC > 0$. • a hyperbola when $AC < 0$.	55–58
	Rotate the coordinate axes to eliminate the xy-term in equations of conics (*p. 663*).	The equation $Ax^2 + Bxy + Cy^2 + Dx + Ey + F = 0$ can be rewritten as $A'(x')^2 + C'(y')^2 + D'x' + E'y' + F' = 0$ by rotating the coordinate axes through an angle θ, where $\cot 2\theta = (A - C)/B$.	59–62

What did you learn?		Explanation and Examples	Review Exercises
9.4	Evaluate sets of parametric equations for given values of the parameter *(p. 669)*.	If *f* and *g* are continuous functions of *t* on an interval *I*, then the set of ordered pairs $(f(t), g(t))$ is a plane curve *C*. The equations $x = f(t)$ and $y = g(t)$ are parametric equations for *C*, and *t* is the parameter.	63, 64
	Graph curves that are represented by sets of parametric equations *(p. 670)*, and rewrite sets of parametric equations as single rectangular equations by eliminating the parameter *(p. 672)*.	One way to sketch a curve represented by parametric equations is to plot points in the *xy*-plane. Each set of coordinates (x, y) is determined from a value chosen for the parameter *t*. To eliminate the parameter in a pair of parametric equations, solve for *t* in one equation, and substitute that value of *t* into the other equation. The result is the corresponding rectangular equation.	65–82
	Find sets of parametric equations for graphs *(p. 673)*.	When finding a set of parametric equations for a given graph, remember that the parametric equations are not unique.	83–94
9.5	Plot points and find multiple representations of points in the polar coordinate system *(p. 677)*.		95–100
	Convert points from rectangular to polar form and vice versa *(p. 679)*.	The polar coordinates (r, θ) are related to the rectangular coordinates (x, y), as follows. Polar-to-Rectangular: $x = r \cos \theta$, $y = r \sin \theta$ Rectangular-to-Polar: $\tan \theta = \dfrac{y}{x}$, $r^2 = x^2 + y^2$	101–110
	Convert equations from rectangular to polar form and vice versa *(p. 680)*.	To convert a rectangular equation to polar form, replace *x* by $r \cos \theta$ and *y* by $r \sin \theta$. Converting a polar equation to rectangular form is more complex.	111–126
9.6	Graph polar equations by point plotting *(p. 683)*, and use symmetry and zeros as sketching aids *(p. 684)*.	The graph of a polar equation is symmetric with respect to the following when the given substitution yields an equivalent equation. **1.** Line $\theta = \pi/2$: Replace (r, θ) by $(r, \pi - \theta)$ or $(-r, -\theta)$. **2.** Polar axis: Replace (r, θ) by $(r, -\theta)$ or $(-r, \pi - \theta)$. **3.** Pole: Replace (r, θ) by $(r, \pi + \theta)$ or $(-r, \theta)$.	127–140
	Recognize special polar graphs *(p. 687)*.	Several types of graphs, such as limaçons, rose curves, circles, and lemniscates, have equations that are simpler in polar form than in rectangular form. (See page 687.)	133–140
9.7	Define conics in terms of eccentricities, and write and graph equations of conics in polar form *(p. 691)*.	The eccentricity of a conic is denoted by *e*. The conic is an ellipse when $0 < e < 1$, a parabola when $e = 1$, and a hyperbola when $e > 1$. The graph of a polar equation of the form **1.** $r = (ep)/(1 \pm e \cos \theta)$ or **2.** $r = (ep)/(1 \pm e \sin \theta)$ is a conic, where $e > 0$ is the eccentricity and $|p|$ is the distance between the focus (pole) and the directrix.	141–150
	Use equations of conics in polar form to model real-life problems *(p. 694)*.	An equation of a conic in polar form can be used to model the orbit of Halley's comet. (See Example 4.)	151, 152

9.1

Forming a Conic Section   In Exercises 1 and 2, state the type of conic formed by the intersection of the plane and the double-napped cone.

1.   **2.**

Finding the Standard Equation of a Circle   In Exercises 3–6, find the standard form of the equation of the circle with the given characteristics.

3. Center at origin; point on the circle: $(-3, -4)$

4. Center at origin; point on the circle: $(8, -15)$

5. Center: $(2, 4)$; diameter: $2\sqrt{13}$

6. Center: $(-1, 2)$; diameter: $8\sqrt{2}$

Writing the Equation of a Circle in Standard Form   In Exercises 7–10, write the equation of the circle in standard form. Then identify its center and radius.

7. $\frac{1}{2}x^2 + \frac{1}{2}y^2 = 18$

8. $\frac{3}{4}x^2 + \frac{3}{4}y^2 = 1$

9. $16x^2 + 16y^2 - 16x + 24y - 3 = 0$

10. $4x^2 + 4y^2 + 32x - 24y + 51 = 0$

Sketching a Circle   In Exercises 11 and 12, sketch the circle. Identify its center and radius.

11. $x^2 + y^2 + 4x + 6y - 3 = 0$

12. $x^2 + y^2 + 8x - 10y - 8 = 0$

Finding the Intercepts of a Circle   In Exercises 13 and 14, find the x- and y-intercepts of the graph of the circle.

13. $(x - 2)^2 + (y + 4)^2 = 9$

14. $(x + 8)^2 + (y + 5)^2 = 25$

Finding the Vertex, Focus, and Directrix of a Parabola   In Exercises 15–18, find the vertex, focus, and directrix of the parabola, and sketch its graph.

15. $y = -\frac{1}{8}x^2$ **16.** $4x - y^2 = 0$

17. $\frac{1}{2}y^2 + 18x = 0$ **18.** $\frac{1}{4}y - 8x^2 = 0$

Finding the Standard Equation of a Parabola   In Exercises 19–22, find the standard form of the equation of the parabola with the given characteristics.

19. Vertex: $(0, 0)$ **20.** Vertex: $(-3, 0)$

Focus: $(0, 5)$ Focus: $(0, 0)$

21.   **22.**

Finding the Tangent Line at a Point on a Parabola   In Exercises 23 and 24, find an equation of the tangent line to the parabola at the given point.

23. $x^2 = -2y$, $(2, -2)$ **24.** $y^2 = -2x$, $(-8, -4)$

25. Architecture   A parabolic archway is 12 meters high at the vertex. At a height of 10 meters, the width of the archway is 8 meters (see figure). How wide is the archway at ground level?

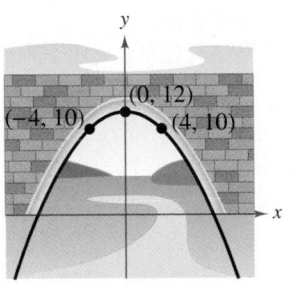

Figure for 25

26. Architecture   A church window is bounded on top by a parabola and below by the arc of a circle. (See figure.)

Figure for 26

(a) Find equations of the parabola and the circle.

(b) Use a graphing utility to create a table showing the vertical distances d between the circle and the parabola for various values of x.

x	0	1	2	3	4
d					

9.2

Sketching an Ellipse   In Exercises 27–30, find the center, vertices, foci, and eccentricity of the ellipse, and sketch its graph. Use a graphing utility to verify your graph.

27. $\dfrac{x^2}{25} + \dfrac{y^2}{36} = 1$

28. $\dfrac{y^2}{49} + \dfrac{x^2}{2} = 1$

29. $\dfrac{(x - 3)^2}{36} + \dfrac{(y - 2)^2}{4} = 1$

30. $\dfrac{(x + 5)^2}{1} + \dfrac{(y - 1)^2}{9} = 1$

Analyzing an Ellipse In Exercises 31–34, (a) find the standard form of the equation of the ellipse, (b) find the center, vertices, foci, and eccentricity of the ellipse, and (c) sketch the ellipse. Use a graphing utility to verify your graph.

31. $16x^2 + 9y^2 - 32x + 72y + 16 = 0$

32. $4x^2 + 25y^2 + 16x - 150y + 141 = 0$

33. $3x^2 + 8y^2 + 12x - 112y + 403 = 0$

34. $15x^2 + y^2 - 90x + 5y - 140 = 0$

Finding the Standard Equation of an Ellipse In Exercises 35–38, find the standard form of the equation of the ellipse with the given characteristics.

35. Vertices: $(\pm 5, 0)$; foci: $(\pm 4, 0)$

36. Vertices: $(0, \pm 6)$; passes through the point $(2, 2)$

37. Vertices: $(-3, 0), (7, 0)$; foci: $(0, 0), (4, 0)$

38. Vertices: $(2, 0), (2, 4)$; foci: $(2, 1), (2, 3)$

39. Architecture A semielliptical archway is to be formed over the entrance to an estate. The arch is to be set on pillars that are 10 feet apart and is to have a height (atop the pillars) of 4 feet. Where should the foci be placed in order to sketch the arch?

40. Architecture You are building a wading pool that is in the shape of an ellipse. Your plans give an equation for the elliptical shape of the pool measured in feet as

$$\frac{x^2}{324} + \frac{y^2}{196} = 1.$$

Find the longest distance across the pool, the shortest distance, and the distance between the foci.

41. Astronomy Saturn moves in an elliptical orbit with the sun at one focus. The least distance and the greatest distance of the planet from the sun are 1.3498×10^9 and 1.5035×10^9 kilometers, respectively. Find the eccentricity of the orbit, defined by $e = c/a$.

42. Astronomy Mercury moves in an elliptical orbit with the sun at one focus. The eccentricity of Mercury's orbit is $e \approx 0.2056$. The length of the major axis is 72 million miles. Find the standard equation of Mercury's orbit. Place the center of the orbit at the origin and the major axis on the x-axis.

9.3

Finding the Standard Equation of a Hyperbola In Exercises 43–46, find the standard form of the equation of the hyperbola with the given characteristics.

43. Vertices: $(\pm 4, 0)$; foci: $(\pm 6, 0)$

44. Vertices: $(0, \pm 1)$; foci: $(0, \pm 2)$

45. Foci: $(3, \pm 2)$; asymptotes: $y = \pm 2(x - 3)$

46. Foci: $(0, 0), (8, 0)$; asymptotes: $y = \pm 2(x - 4)$

Analyzing a Hyperbola In Exercises 47–52, (a) find the standard form of the equation of the hyperbola, (b) find the center, vertices, foci, and eccentricity of the hyperbola, and (c) sketch the hyperbola.

47. $5y^2 - 4x^2 = 20$

48. $x^2 - y^2 = \frac{9}{4}$

49. $9x^2 - 16y^2 - 18x - 32y - 151 = 0$

50. $-4x^2 + 25y^2 - 8x + 150y + 121 = 0$

51. $y^2 - 4x^2 - 2y - 48x + 59 = 0$

52. $9x^2 - y^2 - 72x + 8y + 119 = 0$

53. Marine Navigation Radio transmitting station A is located 200 miles east of transmitting station B. A ship is in an area to the north and 40 miles west of station A. Synchronized radio pulses transmitted to the ship at 186,000 miles per second by the two stations are received 0.0005 second sooner from station A than from station B. How far north is the ship?

54. Physics Two of your friends live 4 miles apart on the same "east-west" street, and you live halfway between them. You are having a three-way phone conversation when you hear an explosion. Six seconds later, your friend to the east hears the explosion, and your friend to the west hears it 8 seconds after you do. Find equations of two hyperbolas that would locate the explosion. (Assume that the coordinate system is measured in feet and that sound travels at 1100 feet per second.)

Classifying a Conic from a General Equation In Exercises 55–58, classify the graph of the equation as a circle, a parabola, an ellipse, or a hyperbola.

55. $6x^2 - x - 2y + 13 = 0$

56. $3x^2 + 5y^2 - 10x - 8y - 90 = 0$

57. $8x^2 + 8y^2 - 7x + 14y + 1 = 0$

58. $-x^2 + 4y^2 + 4x + 3y + 12 = 0$

Rotation of Axes In Exercises 59–62, rotate the axes to eliminate the xy-term in the equation. Then write the equation in standard form. Sketch the graph of the resulting equation, showing both sets of axes.

59. $xy - 3 = 0$

60. $x^2 - 4xy + y^2 + 9 = 0$

61. $5x^2 - 2xy + 5y^2 - 12 = 0$

62. $4x^2 + 8xy + 4y^2 + 7\sqrt{2}x + 9\sqrt{2}y = 0$

9.4

Using Parametric Equations In Exercises 63 and 64, complete the table for the set of parametric equations. Plot the points (x, y) and sketch a graph of the parametric equations.

63. $x = 3t - 2$
$\quad y = 7 - 4t$

t	-2	-1	0	1	2	3
x						
y						

64. $x = \sqrt{t}$
$y = 8 - t$

t	0	1	2	3	4
x					
y					

Sketching a Plane Curve and Eliminating the Parameter In Exercises 65–70, sketch the curve represented by the parametric equations (indicate the orientation of the curve). Then eliminate the parameter and write the corresponding rectangular equation whose graph represents the curve. Adjust the domain of the resulting rectangular equation, if necessary.

65. $x = 2t$
$y = 4t$

66. $x = 4t + 1$
$y = 2 - 3t$

67. $x = t^2 + 2$
$y = 4t^2 - 3$

68. $x = 5t$
$y = t^2$

69. $x = t^3$
$y = \dfrac{1}{2}t^2$

70. $x = \dfrac{4}{t}$
$y = t^2 - 1$

Using a Graphing Utility in Parametric Mode In Exercises 71–82, use a graphing utility to graph the curve represented by the parametric equations. Use the graph and the Vertical Line Test to determine whether y is a function of x.

71. $x = 3, y = t$

72. $x = t, y = 2$

73. $x = 2t, y = 4t$

74. $x = 1 + 4t, y = 2 - 3t$

75. $x = t^2, y = \sqrt{t}$

76. $x = t + 4, y = t^2$

77. $x = \sqrt[3]{t}, y = t$

78. $x = t, y = \sqrt[3]{t}$

79. $x = \dfrac{1}{t}, y = t$

80. $x = t, y = \dfrac{1}{t}$

81. $x = 6 \cos \theta$
$y = 6 \sin \theta$

82. $x = 3 + 3 \cos \theta$
$y = 2 + 5 \sin \theta$

Finding Parametric Equations for a Graph In Exercises 83–86, find a set of parametric equations to represent the graph of the given rectangular equation using the parameters (a) $t = x$ and (b) $t = 1 - x$.

83. $y = 6x + 2$

84. $y = 10 - x$

85. $y = x^2 + 2$

86. $y = 2x^3 + 5x$

Finding Parametric Equations for a Line In Exercises 87–90, find a set of parametric equations for the line that passes through the given points. (There are many correct answers.)

87. $(3, -6), (3, 1)$

88. $(-2, 0), (-8, 0)$

89. $(0, 4), (-5, 7)$

90. $(-3, -1), (2, 9)$

Athletics In Exercises 91–94, the quarterback of a football team releases a pass at a height of 7 feet above the playing field, and the football is caught at a height of 5 feet, 20 yards directly downfield. The pass is released at an angle of 30° with the horizontal.

91. Write a set of parametric equations for the path of the ball of the form

$x = v_0(\cos \theta)t$ and $y = h + (v_0 \sin \theta)t - 16t^2$

where the ball is thrown from a height of h feet at an angle of θ degrees with the horizontal and at an initial speed of v_0 feet per second.

92. Find the speed of the football when it is released.

93. Use a graphing utility to graph the path of the ball and approximate its maximum height.

94. Find the amount of time the receiver has to position himself after the quarterback releases the ball.

9.5

Plotting Points in the Polar Coordinate System In Exercises 95–100, plot the point given in polar coordinates and find three additional polar representations of the point, using $-2\pi < \theta < 2\pi$.

95. $\left(2, \dfrac{\pi}{4}\right)$

96. $\left(4, -\dfrac{\pi}{3}\right)$

97. $\left(-2, -\dfrac{11\pi}{6}\right)$

98. $\left(-3, \dfrac{5\pi}{6}\right)$

99. $\left(7, -\dfrac{4\pi}{3}\right)$

100. $\left(-3, -\dfrac{5\pi}{6}\right)$

Polar-to-Rectangular Conversion In Exercises 101–106, plot the point given in polar coordinates and find the corresponding rectangular coordinates for the point.

101. $\left(3, \dfrac{\pi}{2}\right)$

102. $\left(5, \dfrac{7\pi}{4}\right)$

103. $\left(-4, \dfrac{2\pi}{3}\right)$

104. $\left(1, -\dfrac{5\pi}{6}\right)$

105. $\left(0, -\dfrac{11\pi}{6}\right)$

106. $\left(-2, \dfrac{5\pi}{3}\right)$

Rectangular-to-Polar Conversion In Exercises 107–110, plot the point given in rectangular coordinates and find two sets of polar coordinates for the point for $0 \le \theta < 2\pi$.

107. $(0, -9)$

108. $(-3, 4)$

109. $(5, -5)$

110. $\left(-3, -\sqrt{3}\right)$

Converting a Rectangular Equation to Polar Form In Exercises 111–118, convert the rectangular equation to polar form.

111. $x^2 + y^2 = 81$

112. $x^2 + y^2 = 48$

113. $x^2 + y^2 - 4x = 0$

114. $x^2 + y^2 - 6y = 0$

115. $xy = 5$ **116.** $xy = -2$

117. $4x^2 + y^2 = 1$ **118.** $2x^2 + 3y^2 = 1$

Converting a Polar Equation to Rectangular Form In Exercises 119–126, convert the polar equation to rectangular form.

119. $r = 5$ **120.** $r = 12$

121. $r = 3 \cos \theta$ **122.** $r = 8 \sin \theta$

123. $r^2 = \cos 2\theta$ **124.** $r^2 = \sin \theta$

125. $\theta = \dfrac{5\pi}{4}$ **126.** $\theta = \dfrac{4\pi}{3}$

9.6

Using Symmetry to Sketch a Polar Graph In Exercises 127–132, use symmetry to sketch the graph of the polar equation. Then use a graphing utility to verify your graph.

127. $r = 5$ **128.** $r = 3$

129. $\theta = \dfrac{\pi}{2}$ **130.** $\theta = -\dfrac{5\pi}{6}$

131. $r = -5 \cos \theta$ **132.** $r = 2 \sin \theta$

Sketching a Polar Graph In Exercises 133–140, identify and then sketch the graph of the polar equation. Identify any symmetry and zeros of r. Use a graphing utility to verify your graph.

133. $r = 5 + 2 \cos \theta$ **134.** $r = 1 + 4 \sin \theta$

135. $r = 3 - 5 \sin \theta$ **136.** $r = 6 - 6 \cos \theta$

137. $r = -3 \cos 2\theta$ **138.** $r = \cos 5\theta$

139. $r^2 = 5 \sin 2\theta$ **140.** $r^2 = \cos 2\theta$

9.7

Identifying a Conic from Its Equation In Exercises 141–146, identify the type of conic represented by the equation. Then use a graphing utility to graph the polar equation.

141. $r = \dfrac{1}{1 + 2 \sin \theta}$ **142.** $r = \dfrac{6}{1 + \sin \theta}$

143. $r = \dfrac{4}{5 - 3 \cos \theta}$ **144.** $r = \dfrac{6}{-1 + 4 \cos \theta}$

145. $r = \dfrac{3}{4 - 4 \cos \theta}$ **146.** $r = \dfrac{5}{6 + 2 \sin \theta}$

Finding the Polar Equation of a Conic In Exercises 147–150, find a polar equation of the conic with its focus at the pole.

147. Parabola; vertex: $(3, \pi)$

148. Parabola; vertex: $(2, \pi/2)$

149. Ellipse; vertices: $(5, \pi/2)$, $(1, 3\pi/2)$

150. Hyperbola; vertices: $(1, 0)$, $(-7, \pi)$

151. Astronomy The planet Mars has an elliptical orbit with an eccentricity of $e \approx 0.093$. The length of the major axis of the orbit is approximately 3.05 astronomical units. Find a polar equation for the orbit and its perihelion and aphelion distances.

152. Astronomy An asteroid takes a parabolic path with Earth as its focus. It is about 6,000,000 miles from Earth at its closest approach. Write the polar equation of the path of the asteroid with its vertex at $\theta = -\pi/2$. Find the distance between the asteroid and Earth when $\theta = -\pi/3$.

Conclusions

True or False? In Exercises 153 and 154, determine whether the statement is true or false. Justify your answer.

153. The graph of $\frac{1}{4}x^2 - y^4 = 1$ represents the equation of a hyperbola.

154. There is only one set of parametric equations that represents the line $y = 3 - 2x$.

Writing In Exercises 155 and 156, an equation and four variations are given. In your own words, describe how the graph of each of the variations differs from the graph of the original equation.

155. $y^2 = 8x$

  (a) $(y - 2)^2 = 8x$ (b) $y^2 = 8(x + 1)$

  (c) $y^2 = -8x$ (d) $y^2 = 4x$

156. $\dfrac{x^2}{4} + \dfrac{y^2}{9} = 1$

  (a) $\dfrac{x^2}{9} + \dfrac{y^2}{4} = 1$ (b) $\dfrac{x^2}{4} + \dfrac{y^2}{4} = 1$

  (c) $\dfrac{x^2}{4} + \dfrac{y^2}{25} = 1$ (d) $\dfrac{(x - 3)^2}{4} + \dfrac{y^2}{9} = 1$

157. Think About It The graph of the parametric equations $x = 2 \sec t$ and $y = 3 \tan t$ is shown in the figure. Would the graph change for the equations $x = 2 \sec(-t)$ and $y = 3 \tan(-t)$? If so, how would it change?

    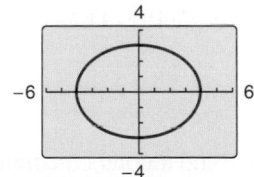

Figure for 157   Figure for 158

158. Think About It The path of a moving object is modeled by the parametric equations $x = 4 \cos t$ and $y = 3 \sin t$, where t is time (see figure). How would the path change for each of the following?

  (a) $x = 4 \cos 2t$, $y = 3 \sin 2t$

  (b) $x = 5 \cos t$, $y = 3 \sin t$

9 | Chapter Test

See *CalcChat.com* for tutorial help and worked-out solutions to odd-numbered exercises. For instructions on how to use a graphing utility, see Appendix A.

Take this test as you would take a test in class. After you are finished, check your work against the answers given in the back of the book.

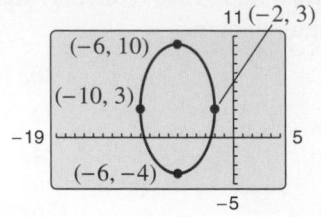

Figure for 5

In Exercises 1–3, graph the conic and identify any vertices and foci.

1. $y^2 - 8x = 0$ 2. $x^2 + 4y^2 - 24x + 32 = 0$ 3. $x^2 - 4y^2 - 4x = 0$

4. Find the standard form of the equation of the parabola with focus $(8, -2)$ and directrix $x = 4$, and sketch the parabola.

5. Find the standard form of the equation of the ellipse shown at the right.

6. Find the standard form of the equation of the hyperbola with vertices $(0, \pm 3)$ and asymptotes $y = \pm\frac{3}{2}x$.

7. Use a graphing utility to graph the conic $x^2 - \dfrac{y^2}{4} = 1$. Describe your viewing window.

8. (a) Determine the number of degrees the axis must be rotated to eliminate the xy-term of the conic $x^2 + 6xy + y^2 - 6 = 0$.

   (b) Graph the conic in part (a) and use a graphing utility to confirm your result.

In Exercises 9–11, sketch the curve represented by the parametric equations. Then eliminate the parameter and write the corresponding rectangular equation whose graph represents the curve.

9. $x = 1 - t$ 10. $x = \sqrt{t^2 + 2}$ 11. $x = 2 + 3\cos\theta$

   $y = 5t$ $y = \dfrac{t}{4}$ $y = 2\sin\theta$

In Exercises 12–14, find a set of parametric equations to represent the graph of the given rectangular equation using the parameters (a) $t = x$ and (b) $t = 2 - x$.

12. $y = -3x + 5$ 13. $xy = 8$ 14. $x^2 + 2y = 4$

15. Convert the polar coordinates $\left(-2, \dfrac{5\pi}{6}\right)$ to rectangular form.

16. Convert the rectangular coordinates $(2, -2)$ to polar form and find two additional polar representations of this point. (There are many correct answers.)

17. Convert the rectangular equation $x^2 + y^2 - 3x = 0$ to polar form.

18. Convert the polar equation $r = 2\sin\theta$ to rectangular form.

In Exercises 19–21, identify the conic represented by the polar equation algebraically. Then use a graphing utility to graph the polar equation.

19. $r = 2 + 3\sin\theta$ 20. $r = \dfrac{1}{1 - \cos\theta}$ 21. $r = \dfrac{4}{2 + 3\sin\theta}$

22. Find a polar equation that represents a rose curve that is symmetric with respect to the line $\theta = \pi/2$ and has 7 petals.

23. Sketch a graph of the polar equation $r = 8\cos 3\theta$. Identify any symmetry and zeros of the graph.

24. Find a polar equation of an ellipse with its focus at the pole, an eccentricity of $e = \frac{1}{4}$, and directrix at $y = 4$.

25. Find a polar equation of a hyperbola with its focus at the pole, an eccentricity of $e = \frac{5}{4}$, and directrix at $y = 2$.

7–9   Cumulative Test

See *CalcChat.com* for tutorial help and worked-out solutions to odd-numbered exercises.
For instructions on how to use a graphing utility, see Appendix A.

Take this test to review the material in Chapters 7–9. After you are finished, check your work against the answers given in the back of the book.

In Exercises 1–4, use any method to solve the system of equations.

1. $\begin{cases} -x - 3y = 5 \\ 4x + 2y = 10 \end{cases}$

2. $\begin{cases} 2x - y^2 = 0 \\ x - y = 4 \end{cases}$

3. $\begin{cases} 2x - 3y + z = 13 \\ -4x + y - 2z = -6 \\ x - 3y + 3z = 12 \end{cases}$

4. $\begin{cases} x + y - 5z = 3 \\ 4x + y - 11z = 6 \\ -x \quad\quad - 2z = -1 \end{cases}$

In Exercises 5–8, perform the matrix operations given

$$A = \begin{bmatrix} -3 & 0 & -4 \\ 2 & 4 & 5 \\ -4 & 8 & 1 \end{bmatrix} \quad \text{and} \quad B = \begin{bmatrix} -1 & 5 & 2 \\ 6 & -3 & 3 \\ 0 & 4 & -2 \end{bmatrix}.$$

5. $3A - 2B$ 6. $5A + 3B$ 7. AB 8. BA

9. Find (a) the inverse of A (if it exists) and (b) the determinant of A.

$$A = \begin{bmatrix} 1 & 2 & -1 \\ 3 & 7 & -10 \\ -5 & -7 & -15 \end{bmatrix}$$

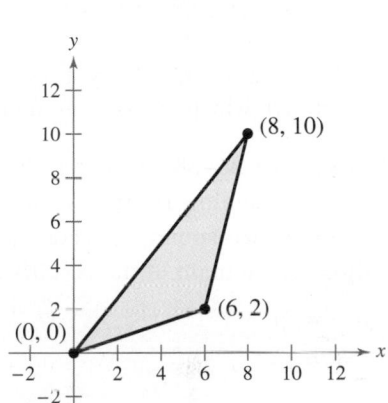

Figure for 10

10. Use a determinant to find the area of the figure shown at the right.

11. Write the first five terms of each sequence a_n. (Assume that n begins with 1.)

(a) $a_n = \dfrac{(-1)^{n+1}}{2n + 3}$

(b) $a_n = 3(2)^{n-1}$

In Exercises 12–15, find the sum. Use a graphing utility to verify your result.

12. $\displaystyle\sum_{k=1}^{6} (7k - 2)$ 13. $\displaystyle\sum_{k=1}^{4} \dfrac{2}{k^2 + 4}$ 14. $\displaystyle\sum_{n=0}^{10} 9\left(\dfrac{3}{4}\right)^n$ 15. $\displaystyle\sum_{n=0}^{50} 100\left(-\dfrac{1}{2}\right)^n$

In Exercises 16–18, find the sum of the infinite geometric series.

16. $\displaystyle\sum_{n=0}^{\infty} 3\left(-\dfrac{3}{5}\right)^n$ 17. $\displaystyle\sum_{n=1}^{\infty} 5(-0.02)^n$ 18. $4 - 2 + 1 - \dfrac{1}{2} + \dfrac{1}{4} - \cdots$

19. Find each binomial coefficient.

(a) $_{20}C_{18}$

(b) $\dbinom{20}{2}$

In Exercises 20–23, use the Binomial Theorem to expand and simplify the expression.

20. $(x + 3)^4$

21. $(2x + y^2)^5$

22. $(x - 2y)^6$

23. $(3a - 4b)^8$

In Exercises 24–27, find the number of distinguishable permutations of the group of letters.

24. C, O, U, N, T

25. P, R, I, N, C, I, P, L, E

26. A, T, L, A, N, T, A

27. C, I, N, C, I, N, N, A, T, I

In Exercises 28–31, identify the conic and sketch its graph.

28. $\dfrac{(y+3)^2}{36} - \dfrac{(x-5)^2}{121} = 1$

29. $\dfrac{(x-2)^2}{4} + \dfrac{(y+1)^2}{9} = 1$

30. $x^2 - y^2 = 25$

31. $x^2 + y^2 - 2x - 4y + 1 = 0$

In Exercises 32–34, find the standard form of the equation of the conic.

32.

33.

34.

35. Use a graphing utility to graph $x^2 - 4xy + 2y^2 = 6$. Determine the angle θ through which the axes are rotated.

In Exercises 36–38, (a) sketch the curve represented by the parametric equations, (b) use a graphing utility to verify your graph, and (c) eliminate the parameter and write the corresponding rectangular equation whose graph represents the curve. Adjust the domain of the resulting rectangular equation, if necessary.

36. $x = 2t + 1$
    $y = t^2$

37. $x = \cos\theta$
    $y = 2\sin^2\theta$

38. $x = 4\ln t$
    $y = \tfrac{1}{2}t^2$

In Exercises 39–42, find a set of parametric equations to represent the graph of the given rectangular equation using the parameters (a) $t = x$ and (b) $t = x/2$.

39. $y = 3x - 2$

40. $x^2 - y = 16$

41. $y = \dfrac{2}{x}$

42. $y = \dfrac{e^{2x}}{e^{2x}+1}$

In Exercises 43–46, plot the point given in polar coordinates and find three additional polar representations of the point, using $-2\pi < \theta < 2\pi$.

43. $\left(8, \dfrac{5\pi}{6}\right)$

44. $\left(5, -\dfrac{\pi}{2}\right)$

45. $\left(-2, \dfrac{5\pi}{4}\right)$

46. $\left(-3, -\dfrac{11\pi}{6}\right)$

47. Convert the rectangular equation $4x + 4y + 1 = 0$ to polar form.

48. Convert the polar equation $r = 4\cos\theta$ to rectangular form.

49. Convert the polar equation $r = \dfrac{2}{4 - 5\cos\theta}$ to rectangular form.

In Exercises 50–52, identify the type of polar graph represented by the polar equation. Then use a graphing utility to graph the polar equation.

50. $r = -4$

51. $r = 3 - \cos\theta$

52. $r = \dfrac{5}{6 + 2\sin\theta}$

53. The salary for the first year of a job is \$32,500. During the next 14 years, the salary increases by 3% each year. Determine the total compensation for the 15-year period.

54. On a game show, the digits 5, 6, and 7 must be arranged in the proper order to form the price of an appliance. If they are arranged correctly, then the contestant wins the appliance. What is the probability of winning when the contestant knows that the price is at least \$600?

55. A parabolic archway is 16 meters high at the vertex. At a height of 14 meters, the width of the archway is 12 meters, as shown in the figure at the right. How wide is the archway at ground level?

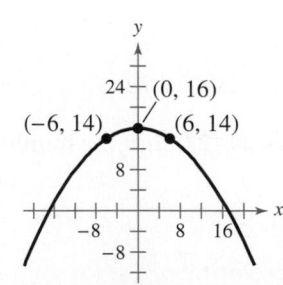

Figure for 55

Proofs in Mathematics

Standard Equation of a Parabola   (p. 639)

The standard form of the equation of a parabola with vertex at (h, k) is as follows.

$(x - h)^2 = 4p(y - k), \quad p \neq 0$ Vertical axis; directrix: $y = k - p$

$(y - k)^2 = 4p(x - h), \quad p \neq 0$ Horizontal axis; directrix: $x = h - p$

The focus lies on the axis p units (*directed distance*) from the vertex. If the vertex is at the origin $(0, 0)$, then the equation takes one of the following forms.

$x^2 = 4py$ Vertical axis

$y^2 = 4px$ Horizontal axis

Parabolic Paths

There are many natural occurrences of parabolas in real life. For instance, the famous astronomer Galileo discovered in the seventeenth century that an object that is projected upward and obliquely to the pull of gravity travels in a parabolic path. Examples of this are the center of gravity of a jumping dolphin and the path of water molecules in a drinking fountain.

Proof

For the case in which the directrix is parallel to the x-axis and the focus lies above the vertex, as shown in the top figure, if (x, y) is any point on the parabola, then, by definition, it is equidistant from the focus

$(h, k + p)$

and the directrix

$y = k - p.$

So, you have

$$\sqrt{(x - h)^2 + [y - (k + p)]^2} = y - (k - p)$$

$$(x - h)^2 + [y - (k + p)]^2 = [y - (k - p)]^2$$

$$(x - h)^2 + y^2 - 2y(k + p) + (k + p)^2 = y^2 - 2y(k - p) + (k - p)^2$$

$$(x - h)^2 + y^2 - 2ky - 2py + k^2 + 2pk + p^2 = y^2 - 2ky + 2py + k^2 - 2pk + p^2$$

$$(x - h)^2 - 2py + 2pk = 2py - 2pk$$

$$(x - h)^2 = 4p(y - k).$$

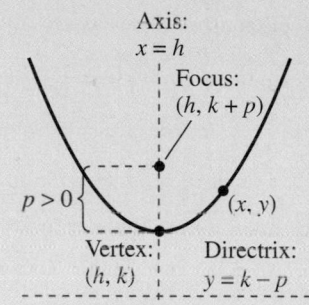

Parabola with vertical axis

For the case in which the directrix is parallel to the y-axis and the focus lies to the right of the vertex, as shown in the bottom figure, if (x, y) is any point on the parabola, then, by definition, it is equidistant from the focus

$(h + p, k)$

and the directrix

$x = h - p.$

So, you have

$$\sqrt{[x - (h + p)]^2 + (y - k)^2} = x - (h - p)$$

$$[x - (h + p)]^2 + (y - k)^2 = [x - (h - p)]^2$$

$$x^2 - 2x(h + p) + (h + p)^2 + (y - k)^2 = x^2 - 2x(h - p) + (h - p)^2$$

$$x^2 - 2hx - 2px + h^2 + 2ph + p^2 + (y - k)^2 = x^2 - 2hx + 2px + h^2 - 2ph + p^2$$

$$-2px + 2ph + (y - k)^2 = 2px - 2ph$$

$$(y - k)^2 = 4p(x - h).$$

Parabola with horizontal axis

Note that when the vertex of a parabola is at the origin, the two equations above simplify to $x^2 = 4py$ and $y^2 = 4px$, respectively. ∎

Rotation of Axes to Eliminate an xy-Term (p. 663)

The general second-degree equation $Ax^2 + Bxy + Cy^2 + Dx + Ey + F = 0$ can be rewritten as

$$A'(x')^2 + C'(y')^2 + D'x' + E'y' + F' = 0$$

by rotating the coordinate axes through an angle θ, where

$$\cot 2\theta = \frac{A - C}{B}.$$

The coefficients of the new equation are obtained by making the substitutions $x = x' \cos \theta - y' \sin \theta$ and $y = x' \sin \theta + y' \cos \theta$.

Proof

You need to discover how the coordinates in the xy-system are related to the coordinates in the $x'y'$-system. To do this, choose a point $P(x, y)$ in the original system and attempt to find its coordinates (x', y') in the rotated system. In either system, the distance r between the point P and the origin is the same. So, the equations for x, y, x', and y' are those given in the figures. Using the formulas for the sine and cosine of the difference of two angles, you have the following.

$$x' = r \cos(\alpha - \theta)$$
$$= r(\cos \alpha \cos \theta + \sin \alpha \sin \theta)$$
$$= r \cos \alpha \cos \theta + r \sin \alpha \sin \theta$$
$$= x \cos \theta + y \sin \theta$$

$$y' = r \sin(\alpha - \theta)$$
$$= r(\sin \alpha \cos \theta - \cos \alpha \sin \theta)$$
$$= r \sin \alpha \cos \theta - r \cos \alpha \sin \theta$$
$$= y \cos \theta - x \sin \theta$$

Rotated: $x' = r \cos(\alpha - \theta)$
$y' = r \sin(\alpha - \theta)$

Solving this system for x and y yields

$$x = x' \cos \theta - y' \sin \theta \quad \text{and} \quad y = x' \sin \theta + y' \cos \theta.$$

Finally, by substituting these values for x and y into the original equation and collecting terms, you obtain

$$A' = A \cos^2 \theta + B \cos \theta \sin \theta + C \sin^2 \theta$$
$$C' = A \sin^2 \theta - B \cos \theta \sin \theta + C \cos^2 \theta$$
$$D' = D \cos \theta + E \sin \theta$$
$$E' = -D \sin \theta + E \cos \theta$$
$$F' = F.$$

Original: $x = r \cos \alpha$
$y = r \sin \alpha$

To eliminate the $x'y'$-term, you must select θ such that $B' = 0$.

$$B' = 2(C - A) \sin \theta \cos \theta + B(\cos^2 \theta - \sin^2 \theta)$$
$$= (C - A) \sin 2\theta + B \cos 2\theta$$
$$= B(\sin 2\theta)\left(\frac{C - A}{B} + \cot 2\theta\right) = 0, \quad \sin 2\theta \neq 0$$

When $B = 0$, no rotation is necessary because the xy-term is not present in the original equation. When $B \neq 0$, the only way to make $B' = 0$ is to let

$$\cot 2\theta = \frac{A - C}{B}, \quad B \neq 0.$$

So, you have established the desired results.   ■

Polar Equations of Conics   (p. 691)

The graph of a polar equation of the form

    1. $r = \dfrac{ep}{1 \pm e \cos \theta}$ or   **2.** $r = \dfrac{ep}{1 \pm e \sin \theta}$

is a conic, where $e > 0$ is the eccentricity and $|p|$ is the distance between the focus (pole) and the directrix.

Proof

A proof for

$$r = \frac{ep}{1 + e \cos \theta}$$

with $p > 0$ is shown here. The proofs of the other cases are similar. In the figure, consider a vertical directrix, p units to the right of the focus $F(0, 0)$. If $P(r, \theta)$ is a point on the graph of

$$r = \frac{ep}{1 + e \cos \theta}$$

then the distance between P and the directrix is

$$PQ = |p - x|$$

$$= |p - r \cos \theta|$$

$$= \left| p - \left(\frac{ep}{1 + e \cos \theta} \right) \cos \theta \right|$$

$$= \left| p \left(1 - \frac{e \cos \theta}{1 + e \cos \theta} \right) \right|$$

$$= \left| \frac{p}{1 + e \cos \theta} \right|$$

$$= \left| \frac{r}{e} \right|.$$

Moreover, because the distance between P and the pole is simply $PF = |r|$, the ratio of PF to PQ is

$$\frac{PF}{PQ} = \frac{|r|}{\left| \dfrac{r}{e} \right|} = |e| = e$$

and, by definition, the graph of the equation must be a conic.   ■

Progressive Summary (Chapters 3–9)

This chart outlines the topics that have been covered so far in this text. Progressive Summary charts appear after Chapters 2, 3, 6, and 9. In each Progressive Summary, new topics encountered for the first time appear in blue.

Transcendental Functions

Exponential, Logarithmic, Trigonometric, Inverse Trigonometric

■ Rewriting

Exponential form $\leftrightarrow$ Logarithmic form
Condense/expand logarithmic
  expressions
Simplify trigonometric expressions
Prove trigonometric identities
Use conversion formulas
Operations with vectors
Powers and roots of complex numbers

■ Solving

Equation	*Strategy*
Exponential	Take logarithm of each side
Logarithmic	Exponentiate each side
Trigonometric	Isolate function Factor, use inverse function
Multiple angle . . . . or high powers	Use trigonometric identities

■ Analyzing

Graphically	*Algebraically*
Intercepts	Domain, Range
Asymptotes	Transformations
Minimum values	Composition
Maximum values	Inverse Properties
	Amplitude, Period
	Reference angles

Numerically
Table of values

Systems and Series

Systems, Sequences, Series

■ Rewriting

Row operations for systems of equations
Partial fraction decomposition
Operations with matrices
Matrix form of a system of equations
nth term of a sequence
Summation form of a series

■ Solving

Equation	*Strategy*
System of . . . . linear equations	Substitution
	Elimination
	Gaussian
	Gauss-Jordan
	Inverse matrices
	Cramer's Rule

■ Analyzing

Systems:
  Intersecting, parallel, and coincident
  lines, determinants
Sequences:
  Graphing utility in *dot* mode, nth term,
  partial sums, summation formulas

Other Topics

Conics, Parametric and Polar Equations

■ Rewriting

Standard forms of conics
Eliminate parameters
Rectangular form $\leftrightarrow$ Parametric form
Rectangular form $\leftrightarrow$ Polar form

■ Solving

Equation	*Strategy*
Conics	Convert to standard form
	Convert to polar form

■ Analyzing

Conics:
  Table of values, vertices, foci, axes,
  symmetry, asymptotes, translations,
  eccentricity, rotations
Parametric forms:
  Point plotting, eliminate parameters
Polar forms:
  Point plotting, special equations,
  symmetry, zeros, eccentricity,
  directrix

10 Analytic Geometry in Three Dimensions

10.1 The Three-Dimensional Coordinate System

10.2 Vectors in Space

10.3 The Cross Product of Two Vectors

10.4 Lines and Planes in Space

Section 10.3, Example 5
Volume of a Parallelepiped

10.1   The Three-Dimensional Coordinate System

The Three-Dimensional Coordinate System

Recall that the Cartesian plane is determined by two perpendicular number lines called the x-axis and the y-axis. These axes, together with their point of intersection (the origin), allow you to develop a two-dimensional coordinate system for identifying points in a plane. To identify a point in space, you must introduce a third dimension to the model. The geometry of this three-dimensional model is called **solid analytic geometry.**

You can construct a **three-dimensional coordinate system** by passing a z-axis perpendicular to both the x- and y-axes at the origin. Figure 10.1 shows the positive portion of each coordinate axis. Taken as pairs, the axes determine three **coordinate planes:** the **xy-plane,** the **xz-plane,** and the **yz-plane.** These three coordinate planes separate the three-dimensional coordinate system into eight **octants.** The first octant is the one in which all three coordinates are positive. In this three-dimensional system, a point P in space is determined by an ordered triple (x, y, z), where x, y, and z are as follows.

x = directed distance from yz-plane to P
y = directed distance from xz-plane to P
z = directed distance from xy-plane to P

Why you should learn it... as shown in Exercise 88 on page 718.

What you should learn

► Plot points in the three-dimensional coordinate system.
► Find distances between points in space and find midpoints of line segments joining points in space.
► Write equations of spheres in standard form and find traces of surfaces in space.

Why you should learn it

The three-dimensional coordinate system can be used to graph equations that model surfaces in space, such as the spherical shape of Earth, as shown in Exercise 88 on page 718.

Figure 10.1

Figure 10.2

A three-dimensional coordinate system can have either a **left-handed** or a **right-handed** orientation. In this text, you will work exclusively with right-handed systems, as illustrated in Figure 10.2. In a right-handed system, Octants II, III, and IV are found by rotating counterclockwise around the positive z-axis. Octant V is below Octant I. Octants VI, VII, and VIII are then found by rotating counterclockwise around the negative z-axis.

EXAMPLE 1   Plotting Points in Space

Plot the points (a) $(2, -3, 3)$, (b) $(-2, 6, 2)$, (c) $(1, 4, 0)$, and (d) $(2, 2, -3)$ in space.

Solution

To plot the point $(2, -3, 3)$, notice that $x = 2$, $y = -3$, and $z = 3$. To help visualize the point, locate the point $(2, -3)$ in the xy-plane (denoted by a cross in the figure). The point $(2, -3, 3)$ lies three units above the cross. You can plot the other points in a similar manner, as shown in the figure.

✓ **Checkpoint**   Audio-video solution in English & Spanish at LarsonPrecalculus.com.

Plot the points (a) $(-1, 2, -2)$, (b) $(3, -1, -1)$, (c) $(-1, -2, -1)$, and (d) $(-3, -2, 1)$ in space.

The Distance and Midpoint Formulas

Many of the formulas established for the two-dimensional coordinate system can be extended to three dimensions. For example, to find the distance between two points in space, you can use the Pythagorean Theorem twice, as shown in Figure 10.3.

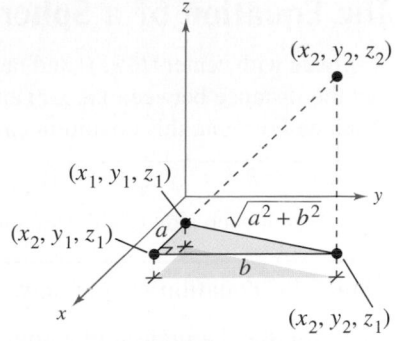

> **Distance Formula in Space**
>
> The distance between the points (x_1, y_1, z_1) and (x_2, y_2, z_2) given by the **Distance Formula in Space** is
>
> $$d = \sqrt{(x_2 - x_1)^2 + (y_2 - y_1)^2 + (z_2 - z_1)^2}.$$

EXAMPLE 2   Finding the Distance Between Two Points in Space

Find the distance between

$$(1, 0, 2) \quad \text{and} \quad (2, 4, -3).$$

Solution

$$
\begin{aligned}
d &= \sqrt{(x_2 - x_1)^2 + (y_2 - y_1)^2 + (z_2 - z_1)^2} && \text{Distance Formula in Space} \\
&= \sqrt{(2 - 1)^2 + (4 - 0)^2 + (-3 - 2)^2} && \text{Substitute.} \\
&= \sqrt{1 + 16 + 25} && \text{Simplify.} \\
&= \sqrt{42} && \text{Simplify.}
\end{aligned}
$$

✓ Checkpoint ◀))) *Audio-video solution in English & Spanish at LarsonPrecalculus.com.*

Find the distance between $(0, 1, 3)$ and $(1, 4, -2)$.

Figure 10.3

Notice the similarity between the Distance Formulas in the plane and in space. The Midpoint Formulas in the plane and in space are also similar.

> **Midpoint Formula in Space**
>
> The midpoint of the line segment joining the points (x_1, y_1, z_1) and (x_2, y_2, z_2) given by the **Midpoint Formula in Space** is
>
> $$\left(\frac{x_1 + x_2}{2}, \frac{y_1 + y_2}{2}, \frac{z_1 + z_2}{2} \right).$$

EXAMPLE 3   Using the Midpoint Formula in Space

Find the midpoint of the line segment joining

$$(5, -2, 3) \quad \text{and} \quad (0, 4, 4).$$

Solution

Using the Midpoint Formula in Space, the midpoint is

$$\left(\frac{5 + 0}{2}, \frac{-2 + 4}{2}, \frac{3 + 4}{2} \right) = \left(\frac{5}{2}, 1, \frac{7}{2} \right)$$

as shown in Figure 10.4.

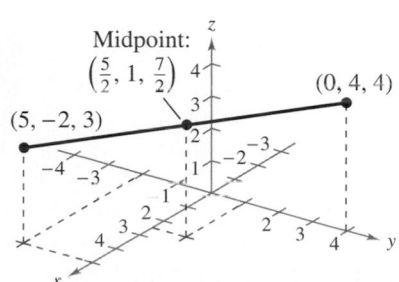

Figure 10.4

✓ Checkpoint ◀))) *Audio-video solution in English & Spanish at LarsonPrecalculus.com.*

Find the midpoint of the line segment joining $(7, -1, -2)$ and $(3, -5, 4)$.

The Equation of a Sphere

A **sphere** with center (h, k, j) and radius r is defined as the set of all points (x, y, z) such that the distance between (x, y, z) and (h, k, j) is r, as shown in Figure 10.5. Using the Distance Formula, this condition can be written as

$$\sqrt{(x - h)^2 + (y - k)^2 + (z - j)^2} = r.$$

By squaring each side of this equation, you obtain the standard equation of a sphere.

> **Standard Equation of a Sphere**
>
> The **standard equation of a sphere** with center (h, k, j) and radius r is given by
>
> $$(x - h)^2 + (y - k)^2 + (z - j)^2 = r^2.$$

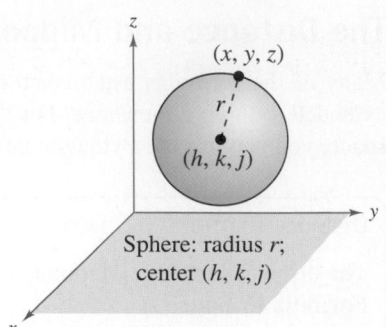

Figure 10.5

Sphere: radius r; center (h, k, j)

Notice the similarity of this formula to the equation of a circle in the plane.

$(x - h)^2 + (y - k)^2 + (z - j)^2 = r^2$ Equation of sphere in space

$(x - h)^2 + (y - k)^2 = r^2$ Equation of circle in the plane

As is true with the equation of a circle, the equation of a sphere is simplified when the center lies at the origin. In this case, the equation is

$x^2 + y^2 + z^2 = r^2.$ Sphere with center at origin

EXAMPLE 4   Finding the Equation of a Sphere

See LarsonPrecalculus.com for an interactive version of this type of example.

Find the standard equation of the sphere with center $(2, 4, 3)$ and radius 3. Does this sphere intersect the xy-plane?

Solution

The equation of the sphere with center $(h, k, j) = (2, 4, 3)$ and radius $r = 3$ is

$(x - h)^2 + (y - k)^2 + (z - j)^2 = r^2$ Standard equation

$(x - 2)^2 + (y - 4)^2 + (z - 3)^2 = 3^2.$ Substitute.

From the graph shown in Figure 10.6, you can see that the center of the sphere lies three units above the xy-plane. Because the sphere has a radius of 3, you can conclude that it does intersect the xy-plane—at the point $(2, 4, 0)$.

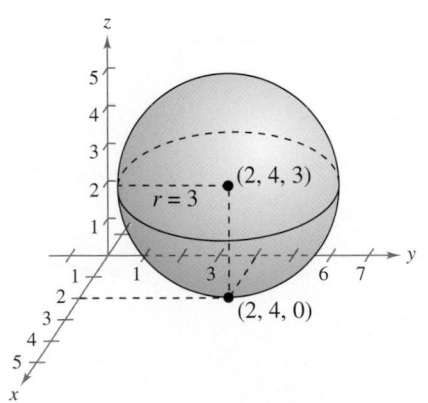

Figure 10.6

> ### Explore the Concept
>
> Find the equation of the sphere that has the points $(3, -2, 6)$ and $(-1, 4, 2)$ as endpoints of a diameter. Explain how this problem gives you a chance to use all three formulas discussed so far in this section: the Distance Formula in Space, the Midpoint Formula in Space, and the standard equation of a sphere.

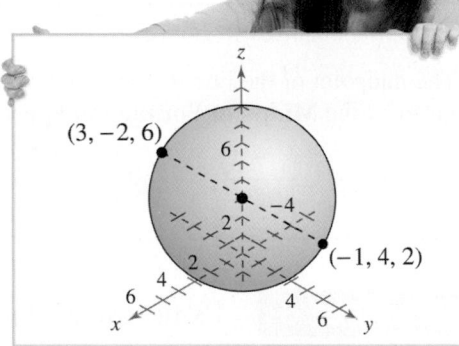

✓ Checkpoint 🔊)) *Audio-video solution in English & Spanish at LarsonPrecalculus.com.*

Find the standard equation of the sphere with center $(1, 3, 2)$ and radius 4.   ◼

©photomak/Shutterstock.com

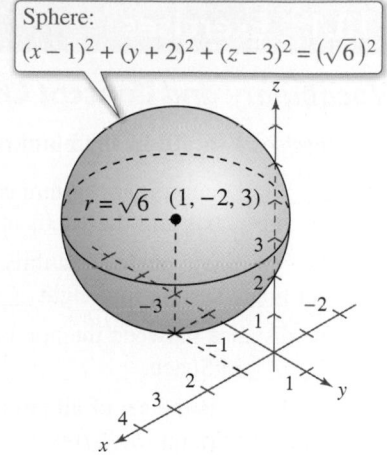

Sphere:
$(x - 1)^2 + (y + 2)^2 + (z - 3)^2 = (\sqrt{6})^2$

Figure 10.7

EXAMPLE 5 Finding the Center and Radius of a Sphere

Find the center and radius of the sphere $x^2 + y^2 + z^2 - 2x + 4y - 6z + 8 = 0$.

Solution

To obtain the standard equation of this sphere, complete the squares as follows.

$$x^2 + y^2 + z^2 - 2x + 4y - 6z + 8 = 0$$

$$\left(x^2 - 2x + \boxed{}\right) + \left(y^2 + 4y + \boxed{}\right) + \left(z^2 - 6z + \boxed{}\right) = -8$$

$$(x^2 - 2x + 1) + (y^2 + 4y + 4) + (z^2 - 6z + 9) = -8 + 1 + 4 + 9$$

$$(x - 1)^2 + (y + 2)^2 + (z - 3)^2 = \left(\sqrt{6}\right)^2$$

So, the center of the sphere is $(1, -2, 3)$, and its radius is $\sqrt{6}$. See Figure 10.7.

✓ **Checkpoint** 🔊)) *Audio-video solution in English & Spanish at LarsonPrecalculus.com.*

Find the center and radius of the sphere $x^2 + y^2 + z^2 + 6x - 4y + 8z - 7 = 0$.

Note in Example 5 that the points satisfying the equation of the sphere are "surface points," not "interior points." In general, the collection of points satisfying an equation involving x, y, and z is called a **surface in space.**

Finding the intersection of a surface with one of the three coordinate planes (or with a plane parallel to one of the three coordinate planes) helps one visualize the surface. Such an intersection is called a **trace** of the surface. For example, the xy-trace of a surface consists of all points that are common to both the surface *and* the xy-plane.

EXAMPLE 6 Finding a Trace of a Surface

Sketch the xy-trace of the sphere $(x - 3)^2 + (y - 2)^2 + (z + 4)^2 = 5^2$.

Solution

To find the xy-trace of this surface, use the fact that every point in the xy-plane has a z-coordinate of zero. By substituting $z = 0$ into the original equation, the resulting equation will represent the intersection of the surface with the plane.

$(x - 3)^2 + (y - 2)^2 + (z + 4)^2 = 5^2$	Write original equation.
$(x - 3)^2 + (y - 2)^2 + (0 + 4)^2 = 5^2$	Substitute 0 for z.
$(x - 3)^2 + (y - 2)^2 + 16 = 25$	Simplify.
$(x - 3)^2 + (y - 2)^2 = 9$	Subtract 16 from each side.
$(x - 3)^2 + (y - 2)^2 = 3^2$	Equation of circle

From this form, you can see that the xy-trace is a circle of radius 3, as shown in the figure.

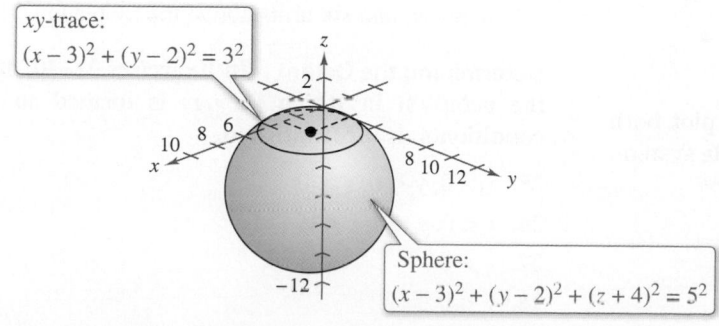

xy-trace:
$(x - 3)^2 + (y - 2)^2 = 3^2$

Sphere:
$(x - 3)^2 + (y - 2)^2 + (z + 4)^2 = 5^2$

✓ **Checkpoint** 🔊)) *Audio-video solution in English & Spanish at LarsonPrecalculus.com.*

Sketch the xz-trace of the sphere $(x - 1)^2 + (y - 3)^2 + (z - 8)^2 = 10^2$.

10.1   Exercises

See *CalcChat.com* for tutorial help and worked-out solutions to odd-numbered exercises.
For instructions on how to use a graphing utility, see Appendix A.

Vocabulary and Concept Check

In Exercises 1–6, fill in the blank(s).

1. A _____ coordinate system can be formed by passing a z-axis perpendicular to both the x-axis and the y-axis at the origin.

2. The coordinate planes of a three-dimensional coordinate system separate the coordinate system into eight _____ .

3. The distance between the points (x_1, y_1, z_1) and (x_2, y_2, z_2) can be found using the _____ in Space.

4. A _____ is the set of all points (x, y, z) such that the distance between (x, y, z) and a fixed point (h, k, j) is r.

5. A _____ in _____ is the collection of points satisfying an equation involving x, y, and z.

6. The intersection of a surface with one of the three coordinate planes is called a _____ of the surface.

7. What does the equation $(x - h)^2 + (y - k)^2 + (z - j)^2 = r^2$ represent? What do h, k, j, and r represent?

8. How do you find the yz-trace of the sphere given by $(x - 2)^2 + (y + 1)^2 + (z - 2)^2 = 7^2$?

Procedures and Problem Solving

Approximating the Coordinates of a Point   In Exercises 9–12, approximate the coordinates of the points.

9.

10.

11.

12.
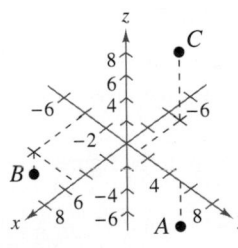

Plotting Points in Space   In Exercises 13–18, plot both points in the same three-dimensional coordinate system.

13. (a) $(0, 0, 2)$
    (b) $(1, -1, -2)$

14. (a) $(3, 0, 0)$
    (b) $(-3, -2, -1)$

15. (a) $(3, -1, 0)$
    (b) $(-4, 2, 2)$

16. (a) $(0, 4, -3)$
    (b) $(4, -2, 4)$

17. (a) $(3, -2, 5)$
    (b) $\left(\frac{3}{2}, 4, -2\right)$

18. (a) $(5, -2, 2)$
    (b) $\left(5, \frac{7}{2}, -2\right)$

Finding the Coordinates of a Point   In Exercises 19–24, find the coordinates of the point.

19. The point is located three units behind the yz-plane, three units to the right of the xz-plane, and five units above the xy-plane.

20. The point is located six units in front of the yz-plane, two units to the left of the xz-plane, and one unit below the xy-plane.

21. The point is located on the x-axis and 11 units in front of the yz-plane.

22. The point is located on the y-axis, nine units to the left of the xz-plane.

23. The point is located in the yz-plane, two units to the right of the xz-plane, and seven units above the xy-plane.

24. The point is located in the xz-plane, one unit behind the yz-plane, and six units above the xy-plane.

Determining the Octant   In Exercises 25–30, determine the octant(s) in which (x, y, z) is located so that the condition(s) is (are) satisfied.

25. $x > 0, y < 0, z > 0$

26. $x < 0, y > 0, z < 0$

27. $z > 0$

28. $y < 0$

29. $xy < 0$

30. $yz > 0$

Finding the Distance Between Two Points in Space In Exercises 31–38, find the distance between the points.

31.

32.

33. $(3, 0, 0)$, $(5, 2, 6)$

34. $(1, 0, 0)$, $(7, 0, 4)$

35. $(1, 0, -10)$, $(0, -3, 2)$

36. $(2, -4, 0)$, $(0, 6, -3)$

37. $(6, -9, 1)$, $(-2, -1, 5)$

38. $(1, 1, -7)$, $(-2, -3, -7)$

Using the Pythagorean Theorem In Exercises 39–42, find the lengths of the sides of the right triangle. Show that these lengths satisfy the Pythagorean Theorem.

39.

40.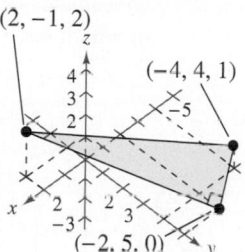

41. $(0, 0, 0)$, $(2, 2, 1)$, $(2, -4, 4)$

42. $(1, 0, 1)$, $(1, 3, 1)$, $(1, 0, 3)$

Finding the Side Lengths of a Triangle In Exercises 43–46, find the lengths of the sides of the triangle with the indicated vertices, and determine whether the triangle is a right triangle, an isosceles triangle, or neither.

43. $(1, -3, -2)$, $(5, -1, 2)$, $(-1, 1, 2)$

44. $(5, 3, 4)$, $(7, 1, 3)$, $(3, 5, 3)$

45. $(5, 0, 0)$, $(1, 3, -2)$, $(-2, -1, 4)$

46. $(1, -2, -1)$, $(3, 0, 0)$, $(3, -6, 3)$

Using the Midpoint Formula in Space In Exercises 47–52, find the midpoint of the line segment joining the points.

47. $(3, -6, 10)$, $(-3, 4, 4)$

48. $(6, -2, 5)$, $(-4, 2, 7)$

49. $(1, 5, -1)$, $(2, 2, 2)$

50. $(-3, 5, 5)$, $(-6, 4, 8)$

51. $(-2, 8, 10)$, $(7, -4, 2)$

52. $(9, -5, 1)$, $(9, -2, -4)$

Finding the Equation of a Sphere In Exercises 53–62, find the standard form of the equation of the sphere with the given characteristics.

53.

54.

55.

56.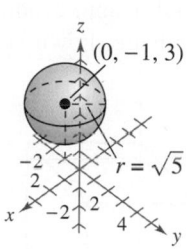

57. Center: $(0, 4, 3)$; radius: 4

58. Center: $(2, -1, 8)$; radius: 7

59. Center: $(-3, 7, 5)$; diameter: 10

60. Center: $(0, 5, -9)$; diameter: 8

61. Endpoints of a diameter: $(3, 0, 0)$, $(0, 0, 6)$

62. Endpoints of a diameter: $(1, 0, 0)$, $(0, 5, 0)$

Finding the Center and Radius of a Sphere In Exercises 63–74, find the center and radius of the sphere.

63. $x^2 + y^2 + z^2 - 6x = 0$

64. $x^2 + y^2 + z^2 - 10y = 0$

65. $x^2 + y^2 + z^2 - 4x + 2y = 0$

66. $x^2 + y^2 + z^2 + 2y - 14z = 0$

67. $x^2 + y^2 + z^2 + 4x - 8z + 19 = 0$

68. $x^2 + y^2 + z^2 - 8y - 6z + 13 = 0$

69. $x^2 + y^2 + z^2 - 4x + 2y - 6z + 10 = 0$

70. $x^2 + y^2 + z^2 - 6x + 4y - 8z + 4 = 0$

71. $4x^2 + 4y^2 + 4z^2 - 8x + 16y - 1 = 0$

72. $9x^2 + 9y^2 + 9z^2 - 6x + 18y + 1 = 0$

73. $4x^2 + 4y^2 + 4z^2 - 4x - 32y + 8z + 33 = 0$

74. $9x^2 + 9y^2 + 9z^2 - 18x + 36y + 54z - 126 = 0$

Finding a Trace of a Surface In Exercises 75–80, sketch the graph of the equation and sketch the specified trace.

75. $(x - 1)^2 + y^2 + z^2 = 36$; xz-trace

76. $x^2 + (y + 3)^2 + z^2 = 25$; yz-trace

77. $(x + 2)^2 + (y - 3)^2 + z^2 = 9$; yz-trace

78. $x^2 + (y - 1)^2 + (z + 1)^2 = 4$; xy-trace

79. $x^2 + y^2 + z^2 - 2x - 4z + 1 = 0$; yz-trace

80. $x^2 + y^2 + z^2 - 4y - 6z - 12 = 0$; xz-trace

Graphing a Sphere In Exercises 81–84, use a three-dimensional graphing utility to graph the sphere.

81. $x^2 + y^2 + z^2 - 6x - 8y - 10z + 46 = 0$

82. $x^2 + y^2 + z^2 + 6y - 8z + 21 = 0$

83. $4x^2 + 4y^2 + 4z^2 - 8x - 16y + 8z - 25 = 0$

84. $9x^2 + 9y^2 + 9z^2 + 18x - 18y + 36z + 35 = 0$

85. **Crystallography** Crystals are classified according to their symmetry. Crystals shaped like cubes are classified as isometric. The vertices of an isometric crystal mapped onto a three-dimensional coordinate system are shown in the figure. Determine (x, y, z).

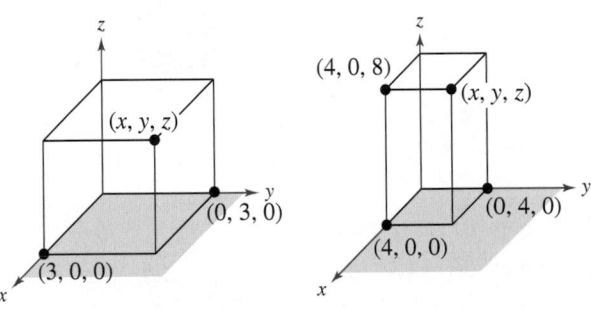

Figure for 85   Figure for 86

86. **Crystallography** Crystals shaped like rectangular prisms are classified as tetragonal. The vertices of a tetragonal crystal mapped onto a three-dimensional coordinate system are shown in the figure. Determine (x, y, z).

87. **Architecture** A spherical building has a diameter of 205 feet. The center of the building is placed at the origin of a three-dimensional coordinate system. What is the equation of the sphere?

88. *Why you should learn it* (p. 712) Assume that Earth is a sphere with a radius of 4000 miles. The center of Earth is placed at the origin of a three-dimensional coordinate system. (See figure.)

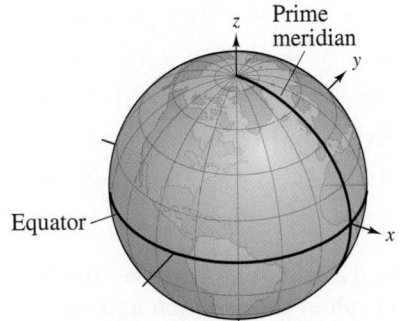

(a) What is the equation of the sphere?

(b) Lines of longitude that run north-south could be represented by what trace(s)? What shape would each of these traces form?

(c) Lines of latitude that run east-west could be represented by what trace(s)? What shape would each of these traces form?

(d) The prime meridian would represent what trace of the equation of the sphere from part (a)?

(e) The equator would represent what trace of the equation of the sphere from part (a)?

Conclusions

True or False? In Exercises 89 and 90, determine whether the statement is true or false. Justify your answer.

89. In the ordered triple (x, y, z) that represents point P in space, x is the directed distance from the xy-plane to P.

90. The surface consisting of all points (x, y, z) in space that are the same distance r from the point (h, k, j) has a circle as its xy-trace.

91. **Think About It** What is the z-coordinate of any point in the xy-plane? What is the y-coordinate of any point in the xz-plane? What is the x-coordinate of any point in the yz-plane?

92. **HOW DO YOU SEE IT?** Approximate the coordinates of each point, and state the octant in which each point lies.

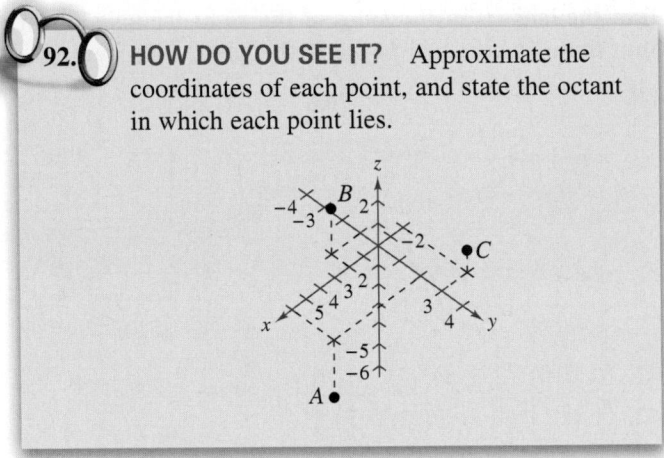

93. **Finding an Endpoint** A line segment has (x_1, y_1, z_1) as one endpoint and (x_m, y_m, z_m) as its midpoint. Find the other endpoint (x_2, y_2, z_2) of the line segment in terms of $x_1, y_1, z_1, x_m, y_m,$ and z_m.

94. **Finding an Endpoint** Use the result of Exercise 93 to find the coordinates of one endpoint of a line segment when the coordinates of the other endpoint and the midpoint are $(3, 0, 2)$ and $(5, 8, 7)$, respectively.

Cumulative Mixed Review

Completing the Square In Exercises 95–100, solve the quadratic equation by completing the square.

95. $v^2 + 3v - 2 = 0$ 96. $z^2 - 7z - 19 = 0$

97. $x^2 - 5x + 5 = 0$ 98. $x^2 + 3x - 1 = 0$

99. $4y^2 + 4y - 9 = 0$ 100. $2x^2 + 5x - 8 = 0$

Finding the Dot Product In Exercises 101 and 102, find the dot product of u and v.

101. $\mathbf{u} = \langle -4, 1 \rangle$ 102. $\mathbf{u} = \langle -1, 3 \rangle$

$\mathbf{v} = \langle 3, 5 \rangle$ $\mathbf{v} = \langle -2, -6 \rangle$

10.2   Vectors in Space

Vectors in Space

Physical forces and velocities are not confined to the plane, so it is natural to extend the concept of vectors from two-dimensional space to three-dimensional space. In space, vectors are denoted by ordered triples

$$\mathbf{v} = \langle v_1, v_2, v_3 \rangle. \qquad \text{Component form}$$

The **zero vector** is denoted by

$$\mathbf{0} = \langle 0, 0, 0 \rangle. \qquad \text{Zero vector}$$

Using the unit vectors $\mathbf{i} = \langle 1, 0, 0 \rangle$, $\mathbf{j} = \langle 0, 1, 0 \rangle$, and $\mathbf{k} = \langle 0, 0, 1 \rangle$ in the direction of the positive z-axis, the **standard unit vector notation** for $\mathbf{v}$ is

$$\mathbf{v} = v_1 \mathbf{i} + v_2 \mathbf{j} + v_3 \mathbf{k} \qquad \text{Unit vector form}$$

as shown in Figure 10.8. If $\mathbf{v}$ is represented by the directed line segment from $P(p_1, p_2, p_3)$ to $Q(q_1, q_2, q_3)$, as shown in Figure 10.9, then the **component form** of $\mathbf{v}$ is produced by subtracting the coordinates of the initial point from the coordinates of the terminal point

$$\mathbf{v} = \langle v_1, v_2, v_3 \rangle = \langle q_1 - p_1, q_2 - p_2, q_3 - p_3 \rangle.$$

Figure 10.8

Figure 10.9

What you should learn

▶ Find the component forms of, the unit vectors in the same direction of, the magnitudes of, the dot products of, and the angles between vectors in space.
▶ Determine whether vectors in space are parallel.
▶ Use vectors in space to solve real-life problems.

Why you should learn it

Vectors in space can be used to represent many physical forces, such as tension in the chains used to support a birdbath, as shown in Exercise 73 on page 725.

Vectors in Space

1. Two vectors are **equal** if and only if their corresponding components are equal.

2. The **magnitude** (or **length**) of $\mathbf{u} = \langle u_1, u_2, u_3 \rangle$ is

$$\|\mathbf{u}\| = \sqrt{u_1^2 + u_2^2 + u_3^2}.$$

3. A **unit vector** $\mathbf{u}$ in the direction of $\mathbf{v}$ is

$$\mathbf{u} = \frac{\mathbf{v}}{\|\mathbf{v}\|}, \quad \mathbf{v} \neq 0.$$

4. The **sum** of $\mathbf{u} = \langle u_1, u_2, u_3 \rangle$ and $\mathbf{v} = \langle v_1, v_2, v_3 \rangle$ is

$$\mathbf{u} + \mathbf{v} = \langle u_1 + v_1, u_2 + v_2, u_3 + v_3 \rangle. \qquad \text{Vector addition}$$

5. The **scalar multiple** of the real number c and $\mathbf{u} = \langle u_1, u_2, u_3 \rangle$ is

$$c\mathbf{u} = \langle cu_1, cu_2, cu_3 \rangle. \qquad \text{Scalar multiplication}$$

6. The **dot product** of $\mathbf{u} = \langle u_1, u_2, u_3 \rangle$ and $\mathbf{v} = \langle v_1, v_2, v_3 \rangle$ is

$$\mathbf{u} \cdot \mathbf{v} = u_1 v_1 + u_2 v_2 + u_3 v_3. \qquad \text{Dot product}$$

EXAMPLE 1 Finding the Component Form of a Vector

See LarsonPrecalculus.com for an interactive version of this type of example.

Find the component form and magnitude of the vector **v** having initial point $(3, 4, 2)$ and terminal point $(3, 6, 4)$. Then find a unit vector in the direction of **v**.

Solution

The component form of **v** is $\mathbf{v} = \langle 3 - 3, 6 - 4, 4 - 2 \rangle = \langle 0, 2, 2 \rangle$, which implies that its magnitude is $\|\mathbf{v}\| = \sqrt{0^2 + 2^2 + 2^2} = \sqrt{8} = 2\sqrt{2}$. The unit vector in the direction of **v** is

$$\mathbf{u} = \frac{\mathbf{v}}{\|\mathbf{v}\|} = \frac{1}{2\sqrt{2}} \langle 0, 2, 2 \rangle = \left\langle 0, \frac{1}{\sqrt{2}}, \frac{1}{\sqrt{2}} \right\rangle = \left\langle 0, \frac{\sqrt{2}}{2}, \frac{\sqrt{2}}{2} \right\rangle.$$

✓ **Checkpoint** ◀))) *Audio-video solution in English & Spanish at LarsonPrecalculus.com.*

Find the component form and magnitude of the vector **v** having initial point $(1, -4, 3)$ and terminal point $(2, 2, -1)$. Then find a unit vector in the direction of **v**.

EXAMPLE 2 Finding the Dot Product of Two Vectors

The dot product of $\langle 0, 3, -2 \rangle$ and $\langle 4, -2, 3 \rangle$ is

$$\langle 0, 3, -2 \rangle \cdot \langle 4, -2, 3 \rangle = 0(4) + 3(-2) + (-2)(3) = 0 - 6 - 6 = -12.$$

Note that the dot product of two vectors is a real number, not a vector.

✓ **Checkpoint** ◀))) *Audio-video solution in English & Spanish at LarsonPrecalculus.com.*

Find the dot product of $\langle 4, 0, 1 \rangle$ and $\langle -1, 3, 2 \rangle$.

As was discussed in Section 6.4, the **angle between two nonzero vectors** is the angle θ, $0 \le \theta \le \pi$, between their respective standard position vectors, as shown in Figure 10.10. This angle can be found using the dot product. (Note that the angle between the zero vector and another vector is not defined.)

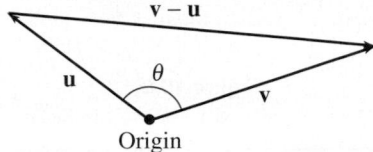

Figure 10.10

Angle Between Two Vectors

If θ is the angle between two nonzero vectors **u** and **v**, then $\cos \theta = \dfrac{\mathbf{u} \cdot \mathbf{v}}{\|\mathbf{u}\| \|\mathbf{v}\|}$.

If the dot product of two nonzero vectors is zero, then the angle between the vectors is 90°. Such vectors are called **orthogonal**. For instance, the standard unit vectors **i**, **j**, and **k** are orthogonal to each other.

EXAMPLE 3 Finding the Angle Between Two Vectors

Find the angle between $\mathbf{u} = \langle 1, 0, 2 \rangle$ and $\mathbf{v} = \langle 3, 1, 0 \rangle$.

Solution

$$\cos \theta = \frac{\mathbf{u} \cdot \mathbf{v}}{\|\mathbf{u}\| \|\mathbf{v}\|} = \frac{\langle 1, 0, 2 \rangle \cdot \langle 3, 1, 0 \rangle}{\|\langle 1, 0, 2 \rangle\| \|\langle 3, 1, 0 \rangle\|} = \frac{3}{\sqrt{50}}$$

So, the angle between **u** and **v** is $\theta = \arccos(3/\sqrt{50}) \approx 64.9°$. (See Figure 10.11.)

✓ **Checkpoint** ◀))) *Audio-video solution in English & Spanish at LarsonPrecalculus.com.*

Find the angle between $\mathbf{u} = \langle 1, -2, 4 \rangle$ and $\mathbf{v} = \langle 2, -3, -1 \rangle$.

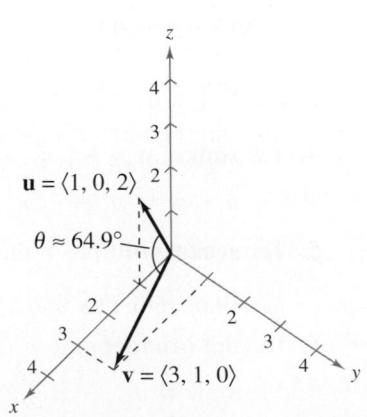

Figure 10.11

Parallel Vectors

Recall from the definition of scalar multiplication that positive scalar multiples of a nonzero vector **v** have the same direction as **v**, whereas negative multiples have the direction opposite that of **v**. In general, two nonzero vectors **u** and **v** are **parallel** when there is some scalar c such that $\mathbf{u} = c\mathbf{v}$. For instance, in Figure 10.12, the vectors **u**, **v**, and **w** are parallel because $\mathbf{u} = 2\mathbf{v}$ and $\mathbf{w} = -\mathbf{v}$.

Figure 10.12

EXAMPLE 4   Parallel Vectors

Vector **w** has initial point $(1, -2, 0)$ and terminal point $(3, 2, 1)$. Determine whether each vector is parallel to **w**.

a. $\mathbf{u} = \langle 4, 8, 2 \rangle$
b. $\mathbf{v} = \left\langle -1, -2, -\frac{1}{2} \right\rangle$
c. $\mathbf{z} = \langle 4, 8, 4 \rangle$

Solution

Begin by writing **w** in component form.

$$\mathbf{w} = \langle 3 - 1, 2 - (-2), 1 - 0 \rangle = \langle 2, 4, 1 \rangle$$

a. Because

$$\mathbf{u} = \langle 4, 8, 2 \rangle = 2 \langle 2, 4, 1 \rangle = 2\mathbf{w}$$

you can conclude that **u** *is* parallel to **w**.

b. Because

$$\mathbf{v} = \left\langle -1, -2, -\tfrac{1}{2} \right\rangle = -\tfrac{1}{2} \langle 2, 4, 1 \rangle = -\tfrac{1}{2}\mathbf{w}$$

you can conclude that **v** *is* parallel to **w**.

c. In this case, you need to find a scalar c such that $\langle 4, 8, 4 \rangle = c \langle 2, 4, 1 \rangle$. However, equating corresponding components produces $c = 2$ for the first two components and $c = 4$ for the third. So, the equation has no solution, and the vectors **z** and **w** are *not* parallel.

✓ **Checkpoint** 🔊)) *Audio-video solution in English & Spanish at LarsonPrecalculus.com.*

Vector **w** has initial point $(2, -2, 1)$ and terminal point $(0, 4, -3)$. Determine whether each vector is parallel to **w**.

a. $\mathbf{u} = \langle -1, 3, -2 \rangle$
b. $\mathbf{v} = \langle -2, 6, -5 \rangle$
c. $\mathbf{z} = \langle 3, -9, 6 \rangle$

You can use vectors to determine whether three points are collinear (lie on the same line). The points P, Q, and R are **collinear** if and only if the vectors $\overrightarrow{PQ}$ and $\overrightarrow{PR}$ are parallel.

EXAMPLE 5 Using Vectors to Determine Collinear Points

Determine whether the points $P(2, -1, 4)$, $Q(5, 4, 6)$, and $R(-4, -11, 0)$ are collinear.

Solution

The component forms of $\overrightarrow{PQ}$ and $\overrightarrow{PR}$ are

$$\overrightarrow{PQ} = \langle 5 - 2, 4 - (-1), 6 - 4 \rangle = \langle 3, 5, 2 \rangle$$

and

$$\overrightarrow{PR} = \langle -4 - 2, -11 - (-1), 0 - 4 \rangle = \langle -6, -10, -4 \rangle.$$

Because $\overrightarrow{PR} = -2\overrightarrow{PQ}$, you can conclude that the vectors are parallel. So, the points P, Q, and R lie on the same line, as shown in the figure.

✓ **Checkpoint** ◀))) *Audio-video solution in English & Spanish at LarsonPrecalculus.com.*

Determine whether the points $P(-2, 7, -3)$, $Q(1, 4, 3)$, and $R(3, 2, 7)$ are collinear.

EXAMPLE 6 Finding the Terminal Point of a Vector

The initial point of the vector $\mathbf{v} = \langle 4, 2, -1 \rangle$ is $P(3, -1, 6)$. What is the terminal point of this vector?

Solution

Using the component form of the vector whose initial point is $P(3, -1, 6)$ and whose terminal point is $Q(q_1, q_2, q_3)$, you can write

$$\overrightarrow{PQ} = \langle q_1 - p_1, q_2 - p_2, q_3 - p_3 \rangle = \langle q_1 - 3, q_2 + 1, q_3 - 6 \rangle = \langle 4, 2, -1 \rangle.$$

This implies that

$$q_1 - 3 = 4, \quad q_2 + 1 = 2, \quad \text{and} \quad q_3 - 6 = -1.$$

The solutions of these three equations are

$$q_1 = 7, \quad q_2 = 1, \quad \text{and} \quad q_3 = 5.$$

So, the terminal point is $Q(7, 1, 5)$.

✓ **Checkpoint** ◀))) *Audio-video solution in English & Spanish at LarsonPrecalculus.com.*

The initial point of the vector $\mathbf{v} = \langle 2, -3, 6 \rangle$ is $P(1, -2, -5)$. What is the terminal point of this vector?

Application

The next example shows how to use vectors to solve an equilibrium problem in space.

EXAMPLE 7   Solving an Equilibrium Problem

A weight of 480 pounds is supported by three ropes. As shown in Figure 10.13, the weight is located at $S(0, 2, -1)$. The ropes are tied to the points

$P(2, 0, 0), \quad Q(0, 4, 0), \quad$ and $\quad R(-2, 0, 0).$

Find the force (or tension) on each rope.

Solution

The (downward) force of the weight is represented by the vector

$\mathbf{w} = \langle 0, 0, -480 \rangle.$

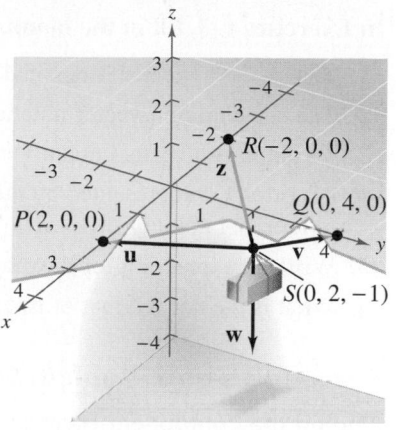

Figure 10.13

The force vectors corresponding to the ropes are as follows.

$$\mathbf{u} = \|\mathbf{u}\| \frac{\overrightarrow{SP}}{\|\overrightarrow{SP}\|} = \|\mathbf{u}\| \frac{\langle 2 - 0, 0 - 2, 0 - (-1) \rangle}{3} = \|\mathbf{u}\| \left\langle \frac{2}{3}, -\frac{2}{3}, \frac{1}{3} \right\rangle$$

$$\mathbf{v} = \|\mathbf{v}\| \frac{\overrightarrow{SQ}}{\|\overrightarrow{SQ}\|} = \|\mathbf{v}\| \frac{\langle 0 - 0, 4 - 2, 0 - (-1) \rangle}{\sqrt{5}} = \|\mathbf{v}\| \left\langle 0, \frac{2}{\sqrt{5}}, \frac{1}{\sqrt{5}} \right\rangle$$

$$\mathbf{z} = \|\mathbf{z}\| \frac{\overrightarrow{SR}}{\|\overrightarrow{SR}\|} = \|\mathbf{z}\| \frac{\langle -2 - 0, 0 - 2, 0 - (-1) \rangle}{3} = \|\mathbf{z}\| \left\langle -\frac{2}{3}, -\frac{2}{3}, \frac{1}{3} \right\rangle$$

For the system to be in equilibrium, it must be true that

$\mathbf{u} + \mathbf{v} + \mathbf{z} + \mathbf{w} = 0$

or

$\mathbf{u} + \mathbf{v} + \mathbf{z} = -\mathbf{w}.$

This yields the following system of linear equations.

$$\begin{cases} \dfrac{2}{3}\|\mathbf{u}\| & -\dfrac{2}{3}\|\mathbf{z}\| = & 0 \\[2mm] -\dfrac{2}{3}\|\mathbf{u}\| + \dfrac{2}{\sqrt{5}}\|\mathbf{v}\| - \dfrac{2}{3}\|\mathbf{z}\| = & 0 \\[2mm] \dfrac{1}{3}\|\mathbf{u}\| + \dfrac{1}{\sqrt{5}}\|\mathbf{v}\| + \dfrac{1}{3}\|\mathbf{z}\| = & 480 \end{cases}$$

Using the techniques demonstrated in Chapter 7, you can find the solution of the system to be

$\|\mathbf{u}\| = 360.0$

$\|\mathbf{v}\| \approx 536.7$

$\|\mathbf{z}\| = 360.0.$

So, the rope attached at point P has 360 pounds of tension, the rope attached at point Q has about 536.7 pounds of tension, and the rope attached at point R has 360 pounds of tension.

✓ **Checkpoint** ◀))) *Audio-video solution in English & Spanish at LarsonPrecalculus.com.*

A weight of 240 pounds, located at $S(0, 3, -2)$, is supported by ropes tied to the points $P(3, 0, 0)$, $Q(0, 6, 0)$, and $R(-3, 0, 0)$. Find the force (or tension) on each rope. ■

10.2   Exercises

See *CalcChat.com* for tutorial help and worked-out solutions to odd-numbered exercises.
For instructions on how to use a graphing utility, see Appendix A.

Vocabulary and Concept Check

In Exercises 1–3, fill in the blank.

1. The _____ vector is denoted by $\mathbf{0} = \langle 0, 0, 0 \rangle$.
2. The standard unit vector notation for a vector $\mathbf{v}$ in space is given by _____ .
3. Two nonzero vectors $\mathbf{u}$ and $\mathbf{v}$ are _____ when there is some scalar c such that $\mathbf{u} = c\mathbf{v}$.
4. A vector $\mathbf{v}$ is represented by the directed line segment from initial point $P(p_1, p_2, p_3)$ to terminal point $Q(q_1, q_2, q_3)$. What does $\langle q_1 - p_1, q_2 - p_2, q_3 - p_3 \rangle$ represent?
5. Write an expression for the magnitude of vector $\mathbf{v}$, $\|\mathbf{v}\|$, where $\mathbf{v} = \langle v_1, v_2, v_3 \rangle$.
6. What is the dot product of two vectors that are orthogonal?

Procedures and Problem Solving

Finding the Component Form of a Vector   In Exercises 7–10, (a) find the component form of the vector v and (b) sketch the vector with its initial point at the origin.

7.

8.

9.

10.
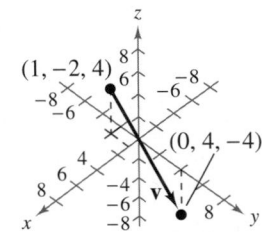

Finding the Component Form of a Vector   In Exercises 11–14, (a) write the component form of the vector v, (b) find the magnitude of v, and (c) find a unit vector in the direction of v.

	Initial Point	Terminal Point
11.	$(-7, 3, 5)$	$(0, 0, 2)$
12.	$(0, -1, 0)$	$(0, 2, 1)$
13.	$(-6, 4, -2)$	$(1, -1, 3)$
14.	$(-5, 3, 1)$	$(-7, -1, 6)$

Sketching Vectors   In Exercises 15–18, sketch each scalar multiple of v.

15. $\mathbf{v} = \langle 1, 1, 3 \rangle$
   (a) $2\mathbf{v}$ (b) $-\mathbf{v}$ (c) $\frac{3}{2}\mathbf{v}$ (d) $0\mathbf{v}$

16. $\mathbf{v} = \langle 1, 2, 3 \rangle$
   (a) $-\mathbf{v}$ (b) $2\mathbf{v}$ (c) $\frac{1}{2}\mathbf{v}$ (d) $\frac{5}{2}\mathbf{v}$

17. $\mathbf{v} = 2\mathbf{i} + 2\mathbf{j} - \mathbf{k}$
   (a) $3\mathbf{v}$ (b) $-2\mathbf{v}$ (c) $\frac{5}{2}\mathbf{v}$ (d) $\frac{3}{2}\mathbf{v}$

18. $\mathbf{v} = \mathbf{i} - 2\mathbf{j} + \mathbf{k}$
   (a) $4\mathbf{v}$ (b) $-2\mathbf{v}$ (c) $\frac{1}{2}\mathbf{v}$ (d) $0\mathbf{v}$

Using Vector Operations   In Exercises 19–24, find the vector z, given $\mathbf{u} = \langle -1, 3, 2 \rangle$, $\mathbf{v} = \langle 1, -2, -2 \rangle$, and $\mathbf{w} = \langle 5, 0, -5 \rangle$. Use a graphing utility to verify your answer.

19. $\mathbf{z} = \mathbf{u} - 2\mathbf{v}$ 20. $\mathbf{z} = 3\mathbf{w} - 2\mathbf{v} + \mathbf{u}$
21. $\mathbf{z} = 2\mathbf{u} - 3\mathbf{v} + \frac{1}{2}\mathbf{w}$ 22. $\mathbf{z} = 7\mathbf{u} + \mathbf{v} - \frac{1}{5}\mathbf{w}$
23. $2\mathbf{z} - 4\mathbf{u} = \mathbf{w}$ 24. $\mathbf{u} + \mathbf{v} - 2\mathbf{z} = \mathbf{0}$

Finding the Magnitude of a Vector   In Exercises 25–32, find the magnitude of v.

25. $\mathbf{v} = \langle 7, 8, 7 \rangle$ 26. $\mathbf{v} = \langle -5, 3, -4 \rangle$
27. $\mathbf{v} = \langle 1, -2, 4 \rangle$ 28. $\mathbf{v} = \langle -1, 0, 3 \rangle$
29. $\mathbf{v} = 6\mathbf{i} - \mathbf{j} + 8\mathbf{k}$ 30. $\mathbf{v} = 3\mathbf{i} + 7\mathbf{j} - \mathbf{k}$
31. Initial point: $(1, -3, 4)$; terminal point: $(1, 0, -1)$
32. Initial point: $(0, -1, 0)$; terminal point: $(1, 2, -2)$

Finding Unit Vectors   In Exercises 33–36, find a unit vector (a) in the direction of u and (b) in the direction opposite of u.

33. $\mathbf{u} = 5\mathbf{i} - 12\mathbf{k}$ 34. $\mathbf{u} = 3\mathbf{i} - 4\mathbf{k}$
35. $\mathbf{u} = 8\mathbf{i} + 3\mathbf{j} - \mathbf{k}$ 36. $\mathbf{u} = -3\mathbf{i} + 5\mathbf{j} + 10\mathbf{k}$

Using a Graphing Utility   In Exercises 37–42, use a graphing utility to determine the specified quantity, where $\mathbf{u} = \langle -1, 3, 4 \rangle$ and $\mathbf{v} = \langle 5, 4.5, -6 \rangle$.

37. $6\mathbf{u} - 4\mathbf{v}$ 38. $2\mathbf{u} + \frac{5}{2}\mathbf{v}$
39. $\|\mathbf{u} + \mathbf{v}\|$ 40. $\|\mathbf{u} - \mathbf{v}\|$
41. $\dfrac{\mathbf{v}}{\|\mathbf{v}\|}$ 42. $\|\mathbf{u}\| + \|\mathbf{v}\|$

Finding the Dot Product of Two Vectors   In Exercises 43–46, find the dot product of u and v.

43. $u = \langle 4, 4, -1 \rangle$
    $v = \langle 2, -5, -8 \rangle$

44. $u = \langle 3, -1, 6 \rangle$
    $v = \langle 4, -10, 1 \rangle$

45. $u = 2i - 5j + 3k$
    $v = 9i + 3j - k$

46. $u = 8i + 9j - 3k$
    $v = 3i - j + 5k$

Finding the Angle Between Two Vectors   In Exercises 47–50, find the angle θ between the vectors.

47. $u = \langle 0, 2, 2 \rangle$
    $v = \langle 3, 0, -4 \rangle$

48. $u = \langle -1, 3, 0 \rangle$
    $v = \langle 1, 2, -1 \rangle$

49. $u = 10i + 40j$
    $v = -3j + 8k$

50. $u = 8j - 20k$
    $v = 10i - 5k$

The Relationship of Two Vectors   In Exercises 51–56, determine whether u and v are orthogonal, parallel, or neither.

51. $u = \langle -12, 6, 15 \rangle$
    $v = \langle 8, -4, -10 \rangle$

52. $u = \langle -8, 16, 4 \rangle$
    $v = \langle 10, -20, -5 \rangle$

53. $u = \langle 0, 1, 6 \rangle$
    $v = \langle 1, -1, -2 \rangle$

54. $u = \langle 0, 4, -1 \rangle$
    $v = \langle -3, -5, 9 \rangle$

55. $u = -2i + 3j - k$
    $v = 2i + j - k$

56. $u = 2i - 3j + k$
    $v = -i - j - k$

Using Vectors to Determine Collinear Points   In Exercises 57–60, use vectors to determine whether the points are collinear.

57. $(1, 3, 2), (-1, 2, 5), (3, 4, -1)$
58. $(-2, 7, 4), (-4, 8, 1), (0, 6, 7)$
59. $(0, 4, 4), (-1, 5, 6), (-2, 6, 7)$
60. $(5, 4, 1), (7, 3, -1), (4, 5, 3)$

Using Vectors to Classify a Triangle   In Exercises 61–64, the vertices of a triangle are given. Determine whether the triangle is an acute triangle, an obtuse triangle, or a right triangle. Explain your reasoning.

61. $(1, 2, 0), (0, 0, 0), (-2, 1, 0)$
62. $(-3, 0, 0), (0, 0, 0), (1, 2, 3)$
63. $(2, -3, 4), (0, 1, 2), (-1, 2, 0)$
64. $(1, 1, 3), (-4, 5, 9), (3, -1, 6)$

Finding the Terminal Point of a Vector   In Exercises 65–68, the vector v and its initial point are given. Find the terminal point.

65. $v = \langle 2, -4, 7 \rangle$
    Initial point: $(1, 5, 0)$

66. $v = \langle -2, 15, -8 \rangle$
    Initial point: $(5, -6, 0)$

67. $v = \langle 4, \frac{3}{2}, -\frac{1}{4} \rangle$
    Initial point: $\left(2, 1, -\frac{3}{2} \right)$

68. $v = \langle \frac{5}{2}, -\frac{1}{2}, 4 \rangle$
    Initial point: $\left(3, 2, -\frac{1}{2} \right)$

Finding a Scalar   In Exercises 69 and 70, determine the values of c that satisfy the given conditions.

69. $\|cu\| = 3, u = i + 2j + 3k$
70. $\|cu\| = 12, u = -2i + 2j - 4k$

Finding a Vector   In Exercises 71 and 72, write the component form of v.

71. Vector **v** lies in the yz-plane, has magnitude 4, and makes an angle of 45° with the positive y-axis.

72. Vector **v** lies in the xz-plane, has magnitude 10, and makes an angle of 60° with the positive z-axis.

73. *Why you should learn it* (p. 719) A round birdbath weighs 8 pounds and has a radius of 6 inches. It is supported by three equally-spaced 24-inch chains attached to a tree branch (see figure). Find the tension in each chain.

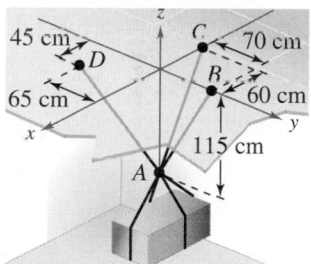

Figure for 73   Figure for 74

74. **Forces in Equilibrium** The weight of a crate is 500 newtons. Find the tension in each of the supporting cables shown in the figure.

Conclusions

True or False?   In Exercises 75 and 76, determine whether the statement is true or false. Justify your answer.

75. If the dot product of two nonzero vectors is zero, then the angle between the vectors is a right angle.

76. If $\overrightarrow{AB}$ and $\overrightarrow{AC}$ represent parallel vectors, then points A, B, and C are collinear.

77. **Think About It** The initial and terminal points of **v** are (x_1, y_1, z_1) and (x, y, z), respectively. Describe the set of all points (x, y, z) such that $\|v\| = 4$.

78. **HOW DO YOU SEE IT?**
Use the graph to determine whether the vectors **u** and **v** are orthogonal. Explain.

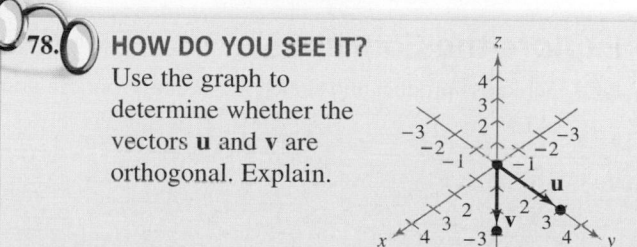

10.3   The Cross Product of Two Vectors

The Cross Product

Many applications in physics, engineering, and geometry involve finding a vector in space that is orthogonal to two given vectors. In this section, you will study a product that will yield such a vector. It is called the **cross product,** and it is most conveniently defined and calculated using the standard unit vector form.

Definition of Cross Product of Two Vectors in Space

Let

$$\mathbf{u} = u_1\mathbf{i} + u_2\mathbf{j} + u_3\mathbf{k} \qquad \text{and} \qquad \mathbf{v} = v_1\mathbf{i} + v_2\mathbf{j} + v_3\mathbf{k}$$

be vectors in space. The **cross product** of $\mathbf{u}$ and $\mathbf{v}$ is the vector

$$\mathbf{u} \times \mathbf{v} = (u_2v_3 - u_3v_2)\mathbf{i} - (u_1v_3 - u_3v_1)\mathbf{j} + (u_1v_2 - u_2v_1)\mathbf{k}.$$

It is important to note that this definition applies only to three-dimensional vectors. The cross product is not defined for two-dimensional vectors.

A convenient way to calculate $\mathbf{u} \times \mathbf{v}$ is to use the following *determinant form* with cofactor expansion. (This 3×3 determinant form is used simply to help remember the formula for the cross product—it is technically not a determinant because the entries of the corresponding matrix are not all real numbers.)

$$\mathbf{u} \times \mathbf{v} = \begin{vmatrix} \mathbf{i} & \mathbf{j} & \mathbf{k} \\ u_1 & u_2 & u_3 \\ v_1 & v_2 & v_3 \end{vmatrix} \qquad \begin{array}{l} \text{Put } \mathbf{u} \text{ in Row 2.} \\ \text{Put } \mathbf{v} \text{ in Row 3.} \end{array}$$

$$= \begin{vmatrix} \mathbf{i} & \mathbf{j} & \mathbf{k} \\ u_1 & u_2 & u_3 \\ v_1 & v_2 & v_3 \end{vmatrix}\mathbf{i} - \begin{vmatrix} \mathbf{i} & \mathbf{j} & \mathbf{k} \\ u_1 & u_2 & u_3 \\ v_1 & v_2 & v_3 \end{vmatrix}\mathbf{j} + \begin{vmatrix} \mathbf{i} & \mathbf{j} & \mathbf{k} \\ u_1 & u_2 & u_3 \\ v_1 & v_2 & v_3 \end{vmatrix}\mathbf{k}$$

$$= \begin{vmatrix} u_2 & u_3 \\ v_2 & v_3 \end{vmatrix}\mathbf{i} - \begin{vmatrix} u_1 & u_3 \\ v_1 & v_3 \end{vmatrix}\mathbf{j} + \begin{vmatrix} u_1 & u_2 \\ v_1 & v_2 \end{vmatrix}\mathbf{k}$$

$$= (u_2v_3 - u_3v_2)\mathbf{i} - (u_1v_3 - u_3v_1)\mathbf{j} + (u_1v_2 - u_2v_1)\mathbf{k}$$

Note the minus sign in front of the **j**-component. Recall from Section 7.7 that each of the three 2×2 determinants can be evaluated by using the following pattern.

$$\begin{vmatrix} a_1 & b_1 \\ a_2 & b_2 \end{vmatrix} = a_1b_2 - a_2b_1$$

Here is an example.

$$\begin{vmatrix} 2 & 4 \\ 3 & -1 \end{vmatrix} = 2(-1) - 4(3) = -2 - 12 = -14$$

Explore the Concept

Find each cross product and sketch the result. What can you conclude?

a. $\mathbf{i} \times \mathbf{j}$

b. $\mathbf{i} \times \mathbf{k}$

c. $\mathbf{j} \times \mathbf{k}$

What you should learn
▶ Find cross products of vectors in space.
▶ Use geometric properties of cross products of vectors in space.
▶ Use triple scalar products to find volumes of parallelepipeds.

Why you should learn it
The cross product of two vectors in space has many applications in physics and engineering. For instance, in Exercise 63 on page 732, the cross product is used to find the torque on the crank of a bicycle's brake.

EXAMPLE 1   Finding Cross Products

Given $\mathbf{u} = \mathbf{i} + 2\mathbf{j} + \mathbf{k}$ and $\mathbf{v} = 3\mathbf{i} + \mathbf{j} + 2\mathbf{k}$, find each cross product.

a. $\mathbf{u} \times \mathbf{v}$ **b. $\mathbf{v} \times \mathbf{u}$**   **c. $\mathbf{v} \times \mathbf{v}$**

Solution

a. $\mathbf{u} \times \mathbf{v} = \begin{vmatrix} \mathbf{i} & \mathbf{j} & \mathbf{k} \\ 1 & 2 & 1 \\ 3 & 1 & 2 \end{vmatrix}$

$= \begin{vmatrix} 2 & 1 \\ 1 & 2 \end{vmatrix} \mathbf{i} - \begin{vmatrix} 1 & 1 \\ 3 & 2 \end{vmatrix} \mathbf{j} + \begin{vmatrix} 1 & 2 \\ 3 & 1 \end{vmatrix} \mathbf{k}$

$= (4 - 1)\mathbf{i} - (2 - 3)\mathbf{j} + (1 - 6)\mathbf{k}$

$= 3\mathbf{i} + \mathbf{j} - 5\mathbf{k}$

b. $\mathbf{v} \times \mathbf{u} = \begin{vmatrix} \mathbf{i} & \mathbf{j} & \mathbf{k} \\ 3 & 1 & 2 \\ 1 & 2 & 1 \end{vmatrix}$

$= \begin{vmatrix} 1 & 2 \\ 2 & 1 \end{vmatrix} \mathbf{i} - \begin{vmatrix} 3 & 2 \\ 1 & 1 \end{vmatrix} \mathbf{j} + \begin{vmatrix} 3 & 1 \\ 1 & 2 \end{vmatrix} \mathbf{k}$

$= (1 - 4)\mathbf{i} - (3 - 2)\mathbf{j} + (6 - 1)\mathbf{k}$

$= -3\mathbf{i} - \mathbf{j} + 5\mathbf{k}$

Note that this result is the negative of that in part (a).

c. $\mathbf{v} \times \mathbf{v} = \begin{vmatrix} \mathbf{i} & \mathbf{j} & \mathbf{k} \\ 3 & 1 & 2 \\ 3 & 1 & 2 \end{vmatrix} = 0$

✓ **Checkpoint** ◀))) *Audio-video solution in English & Spanish at LarsonPrecalculus.com.*

Given $\mathbf{u} = \mathbf{i} - 3\mathbf{j} + 2\mathbf{k}$ and $\mathbf{v} = 2\mathbf{i} - \mathbf{j} + 2\mathbf{k}$, find each cross product.

a. $\mathbf{u} \times \mathbf{v}$ **b. $\mathbf{v} \times \mathbf{u}$**   **c. $\mathbf{v} \times \mathbf{v}$**

The results obtained in Example 1 suggest some interesting algebraic properties of the cross product. For instance,

$$\mathbf{u} \times \mathbf{v} = -(\mathbf{v} \times \mathbf{u}) \quad \text{and} \quad \mathbf{v} \times \mathbf{v} = 0.$$

These properties, and several others, are summarized in the following list.

Algebraic Properties of the Cross Product   (See the proof on page 747.)

Let $\mathbf{u}$, $\mathbf{v}$, and $\mathbf{w}$ be vectors in space, and let c be a scalar.

1. $\mathbf{u} \times \mathbf{v} = -(\mathbf{v} \times \mathbf{u})$

2. $\mathbf{u} \times (\mathbf{v} + \mathbf{w}) = (\mathbf{u} \times \mathbf{v}) + (\mathbf{u} \times \mathbf{w})$

3. $c(\mathbf{u} \times \mathbf{v}) = (c\mathbf{u}) \times \mathbf{v} = \mathbf{u} \times (c\mathbf{v})$

4. $\mathbf{u} \times \mathbf{0} = \mathbf{0} \times \mathbf{u} = \mathbf{0}$

5. $\mathbf{u} \times \mathbf{u} = \mathbf{0}$

6. $\mathbf{u} \cdot (\mathbf{v} \times \mathbf{w}) = (\mathbf{u} \times \mathbf{v}) \cdot \mathbf{w}$

Technology Tip

Some graphing utilities have the capability of performing vector operations, such as the cross product. Consult the user's guide for your graphing utility for specific instructions.

Explore the Concept

Calculate $\mathbf{u} \times \mathbf{v}$ and $-(\mathbf{v} \times \mathbf{u})$ for several values of $\mathbf{u}$ and $\mathbf{v}$. What do your results imply? Interpret your results geometrically.

Geometric Properties of the Cross Product

The first property listed on the preceding page indicates that the cross product is *not commutative*. In particular, this property indicates that the vectors $\mathbf{u} \times \mathbf{v}$ and $\mathbf{v} \times \mathbf{u}$ have equal lengths but opposite directions. The following list gives some other *geometric* properties of the cross product of two vectors.

Geometric Properties of the Cross Product   (See the proof on page 748.)

Let $\mathbf{u}$ and $\mathbf{v}$ be nonzero vectors in space, and let θ be the angle between $\mathbf{u}$ and $\mathbf{v}$.

1. $\mathbf{u} \times \mathbf{v}$ is orthogonal to both $\mathbf{u}$ and $\mathbf{v}$.

2. $\|\mathbf{u} \times \mathbf{v}\| = \|\mathbf{u}\|\|\mathbf{v}\| \sin \theta$

3. $\mathbf{u} \times \mathbf{v} = \mathbf{0}$ if and only if $\mathbf{u}$ and $\mathbf{v}$ are scalar multiples of each other.

4. $\|\mathbf{u} \times \mathbf{v}\|$ = area of parallelogram having $\mathbf{u}$ and $\mathbf{v}$ as adjacent sides.

Both $\mathbf{u} \times \mathbf{v}$ and $\mathbf{v} \times \mathbf{u}$ are perpendicular to the plane determined by $\mathbf{u}$ and $\mathbf{v}$. One way to remember the orientations of the vectors $\mathbf{u}$, $\mathbf{v}$, and $\mathbf{u} \times \mathbf{v}$ is to compare them with the unit vectors $\mathbf{i}$, $\mathbf{j}$, and $\mathbf{k} = \mathbf{i} \times \mathbf{j}$, as shown in Figure 10.14. The three vectors $\mathbf{u}$, $\mathbf{v}$, and $\mathbf{u} \times \mathbf{v}$ form a *right-handed system*.

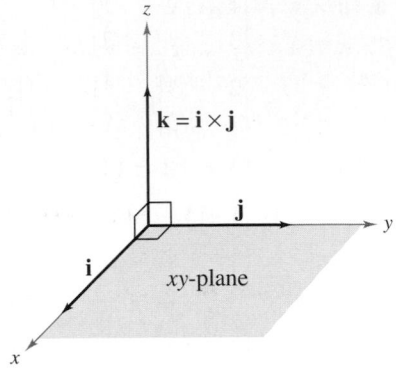

Figure 10.14

EXAMPLE 2   Using the Cross Product

See LarsonPrecalculus.com for an interactive version of this type of example.

Find a unit vector that is orthogonal to both

$$\mathbf{u} = 3\mathbf{i} - 4\mathbf{j} + \mathbf{k} \quad \text{and} \quad \mathbf{v} = -3\mathbf{i} + 6\mathbf{j}.$$

Solution

The cross product $\mathbf{u} \times \mathbf{v}$, as shown in the figure, is orthogonal to both $\mathbf{u}$ and $\mathbf{v}$.

$$\mathbf{u} \times \mathbf{v} = \begin{vmatrix} \mathbf{i} & \mathbf{j} & \mathbf{k} \\ 3 & -4 & 1 \\ -3 & 6 & 0 \end{vmatrix}$$

$$= -6\mathbf{i} - 3\mathbf{j} + 6\mathbf{k}$$

Because

$$\|\mathbf{u} \times \mathbf{v}\| = \sqrt{(-6)^2 + (-3)^2 + 6^2}$$

$$= \sqrt{81}$$

$$= 9$$

a unit vector orthogonal to both $\mathbf{u}$ and $\mathbf{v}$ is

$$\frac{\mathbf{u} \times \mathbf{v}}{\|\mathbf{u} \times \mathbf{v}\|} = -\frac{2}{3}\mathbf{i} - \frac{1}{3}\mathbf{j} + \frac{2}{3}\mathbf{k}.$$

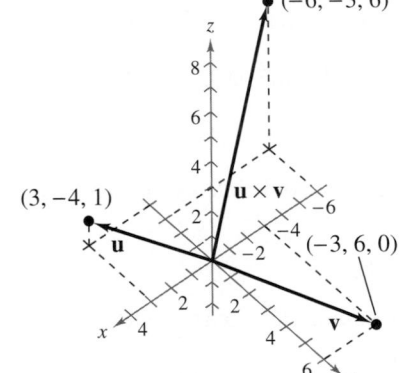

✔ **Checkpoint**))) *Audio-video solution in English & Spanish at LarsonPrecalculus.com.*

Find a unit vector that is orthogonal to both

$$\mathbf{u} = 2\mathbf{i} + 4\mathbf{j} - 3\mathbf{k}$$

and

$$\mathbf{v} = -2\mathbf{i} - 3\mathbf{j} + 2\mathbf{k}.$$

What's Wrong?

You use a graphing utility to find $\mathbf{u} \times \mathbf{v}$ for

$$\mathbf{u} = -\mathbf{i} + 4\mathbf{j} + 3\mathbf{k}$$

and

$$\mathbf{v} = \mathbf{i} - 2\mathbf{k}$$

as shown in the figure. You conclude that

$$\mathbf{w} = -8\mathbf{i} + \mathbf{j} - 4\mathbf{k}$$

is a unit vector orthogonal to both $\mathbf{u}$ and $\mathbf{v}$. What's wrong?

In Example 2, note that you could have used the cross product $\mathbf{v} \times \mathbf{u}$ to form a unit vector that is orthogonal to both $\mathbf{u}$ and $\mathbf{v}$. With that choice, you would have obtained the *negative* of the unit vector found in the example.

The fourth geometric property of the cross product states that $\|\mathbf{u} \times \mathbf{v}\|$ is the area of the parallelogram that has $\mathbf{u}$ and $\mathbf{v}$ as adjacent sides. It follows that the area of a triangle having vectors $\mathbf{u}$ and $\mathbf{v}$ as adjacent sides is $\frac{1}{2}\|\mathbf{u} \times \mathbf{v}\|$.

EXAMPLE 3   Geometric Application of the Cross Product

Show that the quadrilateral with the following vertices is a parallelogram. Then find the area of the parallelogram.

$A(5, 2, 0)$, $B(2, 6, 1)$, $C(2, 4, 7)$, $D(5, 0, 6)$

Solution

From Figure 10.15, you can see that the sides of the quadrilateral correspond to the following four vectors.

$$\overrightarrow{AB} = -3\mathbf{i} + 4\mathbf{j} + \mathbf{k} \qquad \overrightarrow{CD} = 3\mathbf{i} - 4\mathbf{j} - \mathbf{k} = -\overrightarrow{AB}$$
$$\overrightarrow{AD} = 0\mathbf{i} - 2\mathbf{j} + 6\mathbf{k} \qquad \overrightarrow{CB} = 0\mathbf{i} + 2\mathbf{j} - 6\mathbf{k} = -\overrightarrow{AD}$$

Because $\overrightarrow{CD} = -\overrightarrow{AB}$ and $\overrightarrow{CB} = -\overrightarrow{AD}$, you can conclude that $\overrightarrow{AB}$ is parallel to $\overrightarrow{CD}$ and $\overrightarrow{AD}$ is parallel to $\overrightarrow{CB}$. It follows that the quadrilateral is a parallelogram with $\overrightarrow{AB}$ and $\overrightarrow{AD}$ as adjacent sides. Moreover, because

$$\overrightarrow{AB} \times \overrightarrow{AD} = \begin{vmatrix} \mathbf{i} & \mathbf{j} & \mathbf{k} \\ -3 & 4 & 1 \\ 0 & -2 & 6 \end{vmatrix} = 26\mathbf{i} + 18\mathbf{j} + 6\mathbf{k}$$

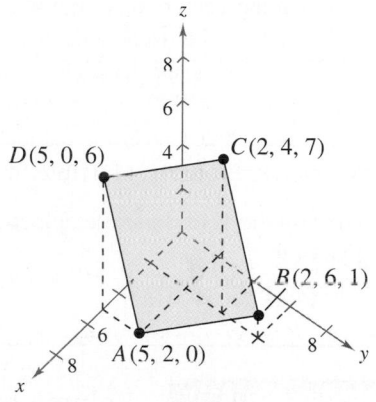

Figure 10.15

the area of the parallelogram is

$$\|\overrightarrow{AB} \times \overrightarrow{AD}\| = \sqrt{26^2 + 18^2 + 6^2} = \sqrt{1036} \approx 32.19 \text{ square units.}$$

✓ **Checkpoint** ◀))) *Audio-video solution in English & Spanish at LarsonPrecalculus.com.*

Show that the quadrilateral with the following vertices is a parallelogram. Then find the area of the parallelogram.

$A(4, 3, 0)$, $B(3, 4, 2)$, $C(3, 2, 6)$, $D(4, 1, 4)$

EXAMPLE 4   Finding the Area of a Triangle

Find the area of the triangle with vertices $A(4, 3, 0)$, $B(5, 4, 6)$, and $C(4, 1, 5)$.

Solution

The triangle is shown in Figure 10.16. The cross product of $\overrightarrow{AB} = \mathbf{i} + \mathbf{j} + 6\mathbf{k}$ and $\overrightarrow{AC} = 0\mathbf{i} - 2\mathbf{j} + 5\mathbf{k}$ is

$$\overrightarrow{AB} \times \overrightarrow{AC} = \begin{vmatrix} \mathbf{i} & \mathbf{j} & \mathbf{k} \\ 1 & 1 & 6 \\ 0 & -2 & 5 \end{vmatrix} = 17\mathbf{i} - 5\mathbf{j} - 2\mathbf{k}.$$

So, the area of the triangle is

$$A = \tfrac{1}{2}\|\overrightarrow{AB} \times \overrightarrow{AC}\| = \tfrac{1}{2}\sqrt{17^2 + (-5)^2 + (-2)^2} = \tfrac{1}{2}\sqrt{318} \approx 8.9 \text{ square units.}$$

✓ **Checkpoint** ◀))) *Audio-video solution in English & Spanish at LarsonPrecalculus.com.*

Find the area of the triangle with vertices

$A(3, 2, 1)$, $B(3, 1, 7)$, and $C(5, 2, 6)$.

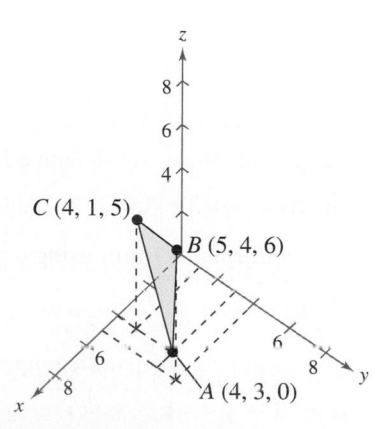

Figure 10.16

The Triple Scalar Product

For the vectors **u**, **v**, and **w** in space, the dot product of **u** and **v** × **w** is called the **triple scalar product** of **u**, **v**, and **w**.

The Triple Scalar Product

For $\mathbf{u} = u_1\mathbf{i} + u_2\mathbf{j} + u_3\mathbf{k}$, $\mathbf{v} = v_1\mathbf{i} + v_2\mathbf{j} + v_3\mathbf{k}$, and $\mathbf{w} = w_1\mathbf{i} + w_2\mathbf{j} + w_3\mathbf{k}$, the triple scalar product is given by

$$\mathbf{u} \cdot (\mathbf{v} \times \mathbf{w}) = \begin{vmatrix} u_1 & u_2 & u_3 \\ v_1 & v_2 & v_3 \\ w_1 & w_2 & w_3 \end{vmatrix}.$$

When the vectors **u**, **v**, and **w** do not lie in the same plane, the triple scalar product **u** · (**v** × **w**) can be used to determine the volume of the parallelepiped (a polyhedron, all of whose faces are parallelograms) with **u**, **v**, and **w** as adjacent edges, as shown in Figure 10.17.

Area of base $= \|\mathbf{v} \times \mathbf{w}\|$
Volume of
parallelepiped $= |\mathbf{u} \cdot (\mathbf{v} \times \mathbf{w})|$
Figure 10.17

Geometric Property of Triple Scalar Product

The volume V of a parallelepiped with vectors **u**, **v**, and **w** as adjacent edges is given by

$$V = |\mathbf{u} \cdot (\mathbf{v} \times \mathbf{w})|.$$

EXAMPLE 5 Volume by the Triple Scalar Product

Find the volume of the parallelepiped having

$$\mathbf{u} = 3\mathbf{i} - 5\mathbf{j} + \mathbf{k}, \quad \mathbf{v} = 2\mathbf{j} - 2\mathbf{k}, \quad \text{and} \quad \mathbf{w} = 3\mathbf{i} + \mathbf{j} + \mathbf{k}$$

as adjacent edges, as shown in Figure 10.18.

Solution

The value of the triple scalar product is

$$\mathbf{u} \cdot (\mathbf{v} \times \mathbf{w}) = \begin{vmatrix} 3 & -5 & 1 \\ 0 & 2 & -2 \\ 3 & 1 & 1 \end{vmatrix}$$

$$= 3\begin{vmatrix} 2 & -2 \\ 1 & 1 \end{vmatrix} - (-5)\begin{vmatrix} 0 & -2 \\ 3 & 1 \end{vmatrix} + 1\begin{vmatrix} 0 & 2 \\ 3 & 1 \end{vmatrix}$$

$$= 3(4) + 5(6) + 1(-6)$$

$$= 36.$$

So, the volume of the parallelepiped is

$$|\mathbf{u} \cdot (\mathbf{v} \times \mathbf{w})| = |36| = 36 \text{ cubic units.}$$

You can confirm this result using a graphing utility, as shown in Figure 10.19.

Figure 10.18

Figure 10.19

✓ **Checkpoint** 🔊))) *Audio-video solution in English & Spanish at LarsonPrecalculus.com.*

Find the volume of the parallelepiped having

$$\mathbf{u} = 2\mathbf{i} - \mathbf{j} + 4\mathbf{k}, \quad \mathbf{v} = \mathbf{i} + 3\mathbf{j} - 2\mathbf{k}, \quad \text{and} \quad \mathbf{w} = 2\mathbf{i} - 2\mathbf{j} + 3\mathbf{k}$$

as adjacent edges.

10.3   Exercises

See *CalcChat.com* for tutorial help and worked-out solutions to odd-numbered exercises.
For instructions on how to use a graphing utility, see Appendix A.

Vocabulary and Concept Check

In Exercises 1–4, fill in the blank.

1. To find a vector in space that is orthogonal to two given vectors, find the _____ of the two vectors.

2. $\mathbf{u} \times \mathbf{u} = $ _____

3. $\|\mathbf{u} \times \mathbf{v}\| = $ _____

4. The dot product of $\mathbf{u}$ and $\mathbf{v} \times \mathbf{w}$ is called the _____ of $\mathbf{u}$, $\mathbf{v}$, and $\mathbf{w}$.

5. Given $\mathbf{u} \times \mathbf{v} = \langle 1, 0, -2 \rangle$, what is $\mathbf{v} \times \mathbf{u}$?

6. Given $\mathbf{u}$ and $\mathbf{v}$ are nonzero vectors in space, when is $\mathbf{u} \times \mathbf{v} = \mathbf{0}$?

Procedures and Problem Solving

Finding the Cross Product   In Exercises 7–20, find $\mathbf{u} \times \mathbf{v}$ and show that it is orthogonal to both $\mathbf{u}$ and $\mathbf{v}$.

7. $\mathbf{u} = \langle 1, -1, 0 \rangle$
   $\mathbf{v} = \langle 0, 1, -1 \rangle$

8. $\mathbf{u} = \langle -1, 1, 0 \rangle$
   $\mathbf{v} = \langle 1, 0, -1 \rangle$

9. $\mathbf{u} = \langle -9, 4, 7 \rangle$
   $\mathbf{v} = \langle 6, 3, 2 \rangle$

10. $\mathbf{u} = \langle -5, 5, 11 \rangle$
    $\mathbf{v} = \langle 2, 2, 3 \rangle$

11. $\mathbf{u} = 6\mathbf{i} + 2\mathbf{j} + \mathbf{k}$
    $\mathbf{v} = \mathbf{i} + 3\mathbf{j} - 2\mathbf{k}$

12. $\mathbf{u} = 4\mathbf{i} + 2\mathbf{j} + \mathbf{k}$
    $\mathbf{v} = -5\mathbf{i} - \mathbf{j} + 3\mathbf{k}$

13. $\mathbf{u} = 2\mathbf{i} + 4\mathbf{j} + 3\mathbf{k}$
    $\mathbf{v} = -\mathbf{i} + 3\mathbf{j} - 2\mathbf{k}$

14. $\mathbf{u} = 3\mathbf{i} - 2\mathbf{j} + \mathbf{k}$
    $\mathbf{v} = -2\mathbf{i} + \mathbf{j} + 2\mathbf{k}$

15. $\mathbf{u} = \frac{1}{2}\mathbf{i} - \frac{2}{3}\mathbf{j} + \mathbf{k}$
    $\mathbf{v} = -\frac{3}{4}\mathbf{i} + \mathbf{j} + \frac{1}{4}\mathbf{k}$

16. $\mathbf{u} = \frac{2}{5}\mathbf{i} - \frac{1}{4}\mathbf{j} + \frac{1}{2}\mathbf{k}$
    $\mathbf{v} = -\frac{3}{5}\mathbf{i} + \mathbf{j} + \frac{1}{5}\mathbf{k}$

17. $\mathbf{u} = \frac{1}{6}\mathbf{k}$
    $\mathbf{v} = -6\mathbf{i} - \frac{1}{3}\mathbf{j}$

18. $\mathbf{u} = \frac{2}{3}\mathbf{i}$
    $\mathbf{v} = \frac{1}{3}\mathbf{j} - 3\mathbf{k}$

19. $\mathbf{u} = -\mathbf{i} + \mathbf{k}$
    $\mathbf{v} = \mathbf{j} - 2\mathbf{k}$

20. $\mathbf{u} = \mathbf{i} - \mathbf{k}$
    $\mathbf{v} = -\mathbf{j} + 8\mathbf{k}$

Using a Graphing Utility to Find the Cross Product   In Exercises 21–26, use a graphing utility to find $\mathbf{u} \times \mathbf{v}$.

21. $\mathbf{u} = \langle 2, 4, 3 \rangle$
    $\mathbf{v} = \langle 0, -2, 1 \rangle$

22. $\mathbf{u} = \langle 4, -2, 6 \rangle$
    $\mathbf{v} = \langle -1, 5, 7 \rangle$

23. $\mathbf{u} = \mathbf{i} - 2\mathbf{j} + 4\mathbf{k}$
    $\mathbf{v} = -4\mathbf{i} + 2\mathbf{j} - \mathbf{k}$

24. $\mathbf{u} = 2\mathbf{i} - \mathbf{j} + 3\mathbf{k}$
    $\mathbf{v} = -\mathbf{i} + \mathbf{j} - 4\mathbf{k}$

25. $\mathbf{u} = 6\mathbf{i} - 5\mathbf{j} + \mathbf{k}$
    $\mathbf{v} = \frac{1}{2}\mathbf{i} - \frac{3}{4}\mathbf{j} + \frac{2}{10}\mathbf{k}$

26. $\mathbf{u} = 8\mathbf{i} - 4\mathbf{j} + 2\mathbf{k}$
    $\mathbf{v} = \frac{1}{2}\mathbf{i} + \frac{3}{4}\mathbf{j} - \frac{1}{4}\mathbf{k}$

Vector Operations   In Exercises 27–32, evaluate the expression, where $\mathbf{u} = 3\mathbf{i} - \mathbf{j} + 4\mathbf{k}$ and $\mathbf{v} = 2\mathbf{i} + 2\mathbf{j} - \mathbf{k}$.

27. $\mathbf{u} \times (\mathbf{v} \times \mathbf{v})$

28. $\mathbf{v} \times (\mathbf{u} \times \mathbf{u})$

29. $\mathbf{u} \times (-3\mathbf{v})$

30. $(-2\mathbf{u}) \times \mathbf{v}$

31. $\mathbf{u} \cdot (\mathbf{u} \times \mathbf{v})$

32. $\mathbf{v} \cdot (\mathbf{v} \times \mathbf{u})$

Using the Cross Product   In Exercises 33–40, find a unit vector orthogonal to $\mathbf{u}$ and $\mathbf{v}$.

33. $\mathbf{u} = \langle 2, -3, 4 \rangle$
    $\mathbf{v} = \langle 0, -1, 1 \rangle$

34. $\mathbf{u} = \langle 2, -1, 3 \rangle$
    $\mathbf{v} = \langle 1, 0, -2 \rangle$

35. $\mathbf{u} = 3\mathbf{i} + \mathbf{j}$
    $\mathbf{v} = \mathbf{j} + \mathbf{k}$

36. $\mathbf{u} = \mathbf{i} + 2\mathbf{j}$
    $\mathbf{v} = \mathbf{i} - 3\mathbf{k}$

37. $\mathbf{u} = -3\mathbf{i} + 2\mathbf{j} - 5\mathbf{k}$
    $\mathbf{v} = 2\mathbf{i} - 6\mathbf{j} + 7\mathbf{k}$

38. $\mathbf{u} = 7\mathbf{i} - 14\mathbf{j} + 5\mathbf{k}$
    $\mathbf{v} = 14\mathbf{i} + 28\mathbf{j} - 15\mathbf{k}$

39. $\mathbf{u} = \mathbf{i} + \mathbf{j} - \mathbf{k}$
    $\mathbf{v} = \mathbf{i} + \mathbf{j} + \mathbf{k}$

40. $\mathbf{u} = \mathbf{i} - 2\mathbf{j} + 2\mathbf{k}$
    $\mathbf{v} = 2\mathbf{i} - \mathbf{j} - 2\mathbf{k}$

Finding the Area of a Parallelogram   In Exercises 41–46, find the area of the parallelogram that has the vectors as adjacent sides.

41. $\mathbf{u} = \mathbf{k}$
    $\mathbf{v} = \mathbf{i} + \mathbf{k}$

42. $\mathbf{u} = 3\mathbf{j}$
    $\mathbf{v} = 2\mathbf{i} + \mathbf{k}$

43. $\mathbf{u} = 3\mathbf{i} + 4\mathbf{j} + 6\mathbf{k}$
    $\mathbf{v} = 2\mathbf{i} - \mathbf{j} + 5\mathbf{k}$

44. $\mathbf{u} = -2\mathbf{i} + 3\mathbf{j} + 2\mathbf{k}$
    $\mathbf{v} = \mathbf{i} + 2\mathbf{j} + 4\mathbf{k}$

45. $\mathbf{u} = \langle 4, 4, -6 \rangle$
    $\mathbf{v} = \langle 0, 4, 6 \rangle$

46. $\mathbf{u} = \langle 4, -3, 2 \rangle$
    $\mathbf{v} = \langle 5, 0, 1 \rangle$

Geometric Application of the Cross Product   In Exercises 47 and 48, (a) verify that the points are the vertices of a parallelogram and (b) find its area.

47. $A(2, -1, 4)$, $B(3, 1, 2)$, $C(0, 5, 6)$, $D(-1, 3, 8)$

48. $A(1, 1, 1)$, $B(6, 5, 2)$, $C(7, 7, 5)$, $D(2, 3, 4)$

Finding the Area of a Triangle   In Exercises 49–52, find the area of the triangle with the given vertices.

49. $(0, 0, 0)$, $(1, 2, 3)$, $(-3, 0, 0)$

50. $(2, 4, 0)$, $(-2, -4, 0)$, $(0, 0, 4)$

51. $(1, -4, 3)$, $(2, 0, 2)$, $(-2, 2, 0)$

52. $(2, 3, -5)$, $(-2, -2, 0)$, $(3, 0, 6)$

Finding the Triple Scalar Product **In Exercises 53–56, find the triple scalar product.**

53. $\mathbf{u} = \langle 2, 3, 3 \rangle$, $\mathbf{v} = \langle 4, 4, 0 \rangle$, $\mathbf{w} = \langle 0, 0, 4 \rangle$

54. $\mathbf{u} = \langle 4, 8, 3 \rangle$, $\mathbf{v} = \langle 2, 3, 0 \rangle$, $\mathbf{w} = \langle 0, 0, 1 \rangle$

55. $\mathbf{u} = 2\mathbf{i} + 3\mathbf{j} + \mathbf{k}$, $\mathbf{v} = \mathbf{i} - \mathbf{j}$, $\mathbf{w} = 4\mathbf{i} + 3\mathbf{j} + \mathbf{k}$

56. $\mathbf{u} = \mathbf{i} + 4\mathbf{j} - 7\mathbf{k}$, $\mathbf{v} = 2\mathbf{i} + 4\mathbf{k}$, $\mathbf{w} = -3\mathbf{j} + 6\mathbf{k}$

Volume by the Triple Scalar Product **In Exercises 57–60, use the triple scalar product to find the volume of the parallelepiped having adjacent edges u, v, and w.**

57. $\mathbf{u} = \mathbf{i} + \mathbf{j}$
$\mathbf{v} = \mathbf{j} + \mathbf{k}$
$\mathbf{w} = \mathbf{i} + \mathbf{k}$

58. $\mathbf{u} = \mathbf{i} + \mathbf{j} + 3\mathbf{k}$
$\mathbf{v} = 3\mathbf{j} + 3\mathbf{k}$
$\mathbf{w} = 3\mathbf{i} + 3\mathbf{k}$

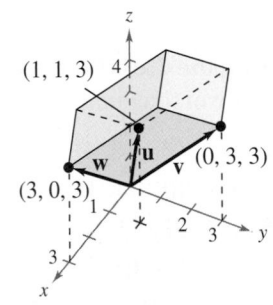

59. $\mathbf{u} = \langle 0, 2, 2 \rangle$
$\mathbf{v} = \langle 0, 0, -2 \rangle$
$\mathbf{w} = \langle 3, 0, 2 \rangle$

60. $\mathbf{u} = \langle 1, 2, -1 \rangle$
$\mathbf{v} = \langle -1, 2, 2 \rangle$
$\mathbf{w} = \langle 2, 0, 1 \rangle$

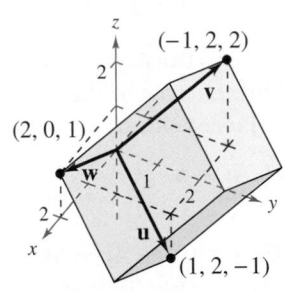

Finding the Volume of a Parallelepiped **In Exercises 61 and 62, find the volume of the parallelepiped with the given vertices.**

61. $A(0, 0, 0)$, $B(4, 0, 0)$, $C(4, -2, 3)$, $D(0, -2, 3)$,
$E(4, 5, 3)$, $F(0, 5, 3)$, $G(0, 3, 6)$, $H(4, 3, 6)$

62. $A(0, 0, 0)$, $B(1, 1, 0)$, $C(1, 0, 2)$, $D(0, 1, 1)$,
$E(2, 1, 2)$, $F(1, 1, 3)$, $G(1, 2, 1)$, $H(2, 2, 3)$

63. *Why you should learn it* (p. 726) The brakes on a bicycle are applied by using a downward force of p pounds on the pedal when the six-inch crank makes a 40° angle with the horizontal (see figure). Vectors representing the position of the crank and the force are $\mathbf{V} = \frac{1}{2}(\cos 40° \mathbf{j} + \sin 40° \mathbf{k})$ and $\mathbf{F} = -p\mathbf{k}$, respectively.

(a) The magnitude of the torque on the crank is given by $\|\mathbf{V} \times \mathbf{F}\|$. Using the given information, write the torque T on the crank as a function of p.

(b) Use the function from part (a) to complete the table.

p	15	20	25	30	35	40	45
T							

Figure for 63　　　　　Figure for 64

64. **Mechanical Engineering** Both the magnitude and direction of the force on a crankshaft rotates. Use the technique given in Exercise 63 to find the magnitude of the torque on the crankshaft shown in the figure.

Conclusions

True or False? **In Exercises 65 and 66, determine whether the statement is true or false. Justify your answer.**

65. The cross product is not defined for vectors in the plane.

66. If $\mathbf{u}$ and $\mathbf{v}$ are vectors in space that are nonzero and not parallel, then $\mathbf{u} \times \mathbf{v} = \mathbf{v} \times \mathbf{u}$.

67. **Proof** Prove that $\|\mathbf{u} \times \mathbf{v}\| = \|\mathbf{u}\| \|\mathbf{v}\|$ if $\mathbf{u}$ and $\mathbf{v}$ are orthogonal.

68. **Think About It** When the magnitudes of two vectors are doubled, how will the magnitude of the cross product of the vectors change?

69. **Proof** Consider the vectors $\mathbf{u} = \langle \cos \alpha, \sin \alpha, 0 \rangle$ and $\mathbf{v} = \langle \cos \beta, \sin \beta, 0 \rangle$, where $\alpha > \beta$. Find the cross product of the vectors and use the result to prove the identity $\sin(\alpha - \beta) = \sin \alpha \cos \beta - \cos \alpha \sin \beta$.

70. **HOW DO YOU SEE IT?**
The figure shows the two vectors $\mathbf{u}$ and $\mathbf{v}$. Sketch the cross products $\mathbf{u} \times \mathbf{v}$ and $\mathbf{v} \times \mathbf{u}$.

Cumulative Mixed Review

Evaluating a Trigonometric Expression **In Exercises 71 and 72, evaluate the expression without using a calculator.**

71. $\cos 480°$

72. $\sin 690°$

Lines in Space

In the plane, *slope* is used to determine an equation of a line. In space, it is more convenient to use *vectors* to determine the equation of a line.

In Figure 10.20, consider the line L through the point

$$P(x_1, y_1, z_1)$$

and parallel to the vector

$\mathbf{v} = \langle a, b, c \rangle.$ Direction vector for L

Figure 10.20

The vector $\mathbf{v}$ is the **direction vector** for the line L, and a, b, and c are the **direction numbers.** One way of describing the line L is to say that it consists of all points $Q(x, y, z)$ for which the vector $\overrightarrow{PQ}$ is parallel to $\mathbf{v}$. This means that $\overrightarrow{PQ}$ is a scalar multiple of $\mathbf{v}$, and you can write

$$\overrightarrow{PQ} = t\mathbf{v}$$

where t is a scalar.

$$\begin{aligned}
\overrightarrow{PQ} &= \langle x - x_1, y - y_1, z - z_1 \rangle \\
&= \langle at, bt, ct \rangle \\
&= t\mathbf{v}
\end{aligned}$$

By equating corresponding components, you can obtain the **parametric equations of a line in space.**

Parametric Equations of a Line in Space

A line L parallel to the nonzero vector

$$\mathbf{v} = \langle a, b, c \rangle$$

and passing through the point

$$P(x_1, y_1, z_1)$$

is represented by the parametric equations

$$x = x_1 + at, \quad y = y_1 + bt, \quad \text{and} \quad z = z_1 + ct.$$

When the direction numbers a, b, and c are all nonzero, you can eliminate the parameter t to obtain the **symmetric equations** of a line.

$$\frac{x - x_1}{a} = \frac{y - y_1}{b} = \frac{z - z_1}{c} \qquad \text{Symmetric equations}$$

EXAMPLE 1   Finding Parametric and Symmetric Equations

Find parametric and symmetric equations of the line L that passes through the point $(1, -2, 4)$ and is parallel to $\mathbf{v} = \langle 2, 4, -4 \rangle$.

Solution

To find a set of parametric equations of the line, use the coordinates $x_1 = 1$, $y_1 = -2$, and $z_1 = 4$ and direction numbers $a = 2$, $b = 4$, and $c = -4$. (See Figure 10.21.)

$$x = 1 + 2t, \quad y = -2 + 4t, \quad z = 4 - 4t \qquad \text{Parametric equations}$$

Because a, b, and c are all nonzero, a set of symmetric equations is

$$\frac{x - 1}{2} = \frac{y + 2}{4} = \frac{z - 4}{-4}. \qquad \text{Symmetric equations}$$

✓ **Checkpoint** Audio-video solution in English & Spanish at LarsonPrecalculus.com.

Figure 10.21

Find parametric and symmetric equations of the line L that passes through the point $(2, 1, -3)$ and is parallel to $\mathbf{v} = \langle 4, -2, 7 \rangle$.

Neither the parametric equations nor the symmetric equations of a given line are unique. For instance, in Example 1, by letting $t = 1$ in the parametric equations, you would obtain the point $(3, 2, 0)$. Using this point with the direction numbers

$$a = 2, \quad b = 4, \quad \text{and} \quad c = -4$$

produces the parametric equations

$$x = 3 + 2t, \quad y = 2 + 4t, \quad \text{and} \quad z = -4t.$$

EXAMPLE 2   A Line Through Two Points

Find a set of parametric and symmetric equations of the line that passes through the points $(-2, 1, 0)$ and $(1, 3, 5)$.

Solution

Begin by using the points $P = (-2, 1, 0)$ and $Q = (1, 3, 5)$. Then a direction vector for the line passing through P and Q is

$$\begin{aligned}
\mathbf{v} &= \overrightarrow{PQ} \\
&= \langle 1 - (-2), 3 - 1, 5 - 0 \rangle \\
&= \langle 3, 2, 5 \rangle \\
&= \langle a, b, c \rangle.
\end{aligned}$$

Using the direction numbers

$$a = 3, \quad b = 2, \quad \text{and} \quad c = 5$$

with the point $P(-2, 1, 0)$, you can obtain the parametric equations

$$x = -2 + 3t, \quad y = 1 + 2t, \quad \text{and} \quad z = 5t. \qquad \text{Parametric equations}$$

Because a, b, and c are all nonzero, a set of symmetric equations is

$$\frac{x + 2}{3} = \frac{y - 1}{2} = \frac{z}{5}. \qquad \text{Symmetric equations}$$

✓ **Checkpoint** Audio-video solution in English & Spanish at LarsonPrecalculus.com.

Find parametric and symmetric equations of the line that passes through the points $(1, -6, 3)$ and $(3, 5, 8)$.

Planes in Space

You have seen how an equation of a line in space can be obtained from a point on the line and a vector *parallel* to it. You will now see that an equation of a plane in space can be obtained from a point in the plane and a vector *normal* (perpendicular) to the plane.

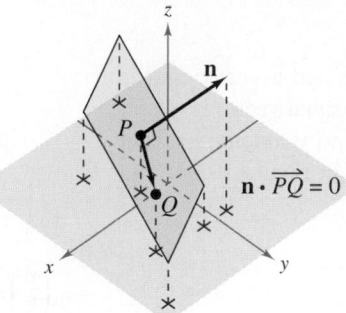

Figure 10.22

Consider the plane containing the point $P(x_1, y_1, z_1)$ having a nonzero normal vector $\mathbf{n} = \langle a, b, c \rangle$, as shown in Figure 10.22. This plane consists of all points $Q(x, y, z)$ for which the vector $\overrightarrow{PQ}$ is orthogonal to $\mathbf{n}$. Using the dot product, you can write the following.

$$\mathbf{n} \cdot \overrightarrow{PQ} = 0$$

$$\langle a, b, c \rangle \cdot \langle x - x_1, y - y_1, z - z_1 \rangle = 0$$

$$a(x - x_1) + b(y - y_1) + c(z - z_1) = 0$$

The third equation of the plane is said to be in **standard form.**

Standard Equation of a Plane in Space

The plane containing the point (x_1, y_1, z_1) and having nonzero normal vector $\mathbf{n} = \langle a, b, c \rangle$ can be represented by the **standard form of the equation of a plane**

$$a(x - x_1) + b(y - y_1) + c(z - z_1) = 0. \qquad \text{Standard form of equation of plane}$$

Regrouping terms yields the **general form of the equation of a plane** in space

$$ax + by + cz + d = 0. \qquad \text{General form of equation of plane}$$

Given the general form of the equation of a plane, it is easy to find a normal vector to the plane. Use the coefficients of x, y, and z to write $\mathbf{n} = \langle a, b, c \rangle$.

Explore the Concept

Consider the following four planes.

$$2x + 3y - z = 2$$

$$-2x - 3y + z = -2$$

$$4x + 6y - 2z = 5$$

$$-6x - 9y + 3z = 11$$

What are the normal vectors to each plane? What can you say about the relative positions of these planes in space?

EXAMPLE 3   Finding an Equation of a Plane in Three-Space

See LarsonPrecalculus.com for an interactive version of this type of example.

Find the general equation of the plane passing through the points $(2, 1, 1)$, $(0, 4, 1)$, and $(-2, 1, 4)$.

Solution

To find the equation of the plane, you need a point in the plane and a vector that is normal to the plane. There are three choices for the point, but no normal vector is given. To obtain a normal vector, use the cross product of vectors $\mathbf{u}$ and $\mathbf{v}$ extending from the point $(2, 1, 1)$ to the points $(0, 4, 1)$ and $(-2, 1, 4)$, as shown in Figure 10.23. The component forms of $\mathbf{u}$ and $\mathbf{v}$ are

$$\mathbf{u} = \langle 0 - 2, 4 - 1, 1 - 1 \rangle = \langle -2, 3, 0 \rangle$$

$$\mathbf{v} = \langle -2 - 2, 1 - 1, 4 - 1 \rangle = \langle -4, 0, 3 \rangle$$

and it follows that

$$\mathbf{n} = \mathbf{u} \times \mathbf{v} = \begin{vmatrix} \mathbf{i} & \mathbf{j} & \mathbf{k} \\ -2 & 3 & 0 \\ -4 & 0 & 3 \end{vmatrix}$$

$$= 9\mathbf{i} + 6\mathbf{j} + 12\mathbf{k}$$

$$= \langle a, b, c \rangle$$

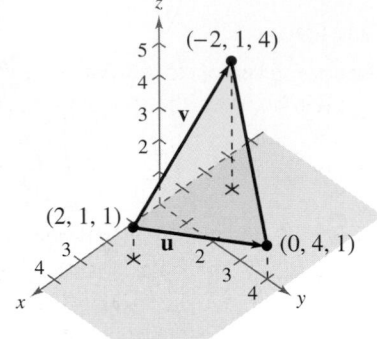

Figure 10.23

is normal to the given plane. Using the direction numbers for $\mathbf{n}$ and the point $(x_1, y_1, z_1) = (2, 1, 1)$, you can determine an equation of the plane to be

$$a(x - x_1) + b(y - y_1) + c(z - z_1) = 0$$

$$9(x - 2) + 6(y - 1) + 12(z - 1) = 0 \qquad \text{Standard form}$$

$$9x + 6y + 12z - 36 = 0$$

$$3x + 2y + 4z - 12 = 0. \qquad \text{General form}$$

Check that each of the three points satisfies the equation $3x + 2y + 4z - 12 = 0$.

✔ **Checkpoint** Audio-video solution in English & Spanish at LarsonPrecalculus.com.

Find the general form of the equation of the plane passing through the points $(1, 0, 5)$, $(-1, -2, 9)$, and $(2, 3, 2)$.

Two distinct planes in three-space either are parallel or intersect in a line. When they intersect, you can determine the angle θ $(0 \le \theta \le 90°)$ between them from the angle between their normal vectors, as shown in the figure. Specifically, if vectors $\mathbf{n}_1$ and $\mathbf{n}_2$ are normal to two intersecting planes, then the angle θ between the normal vectors is equal to the **angle between the two planes** and is given by

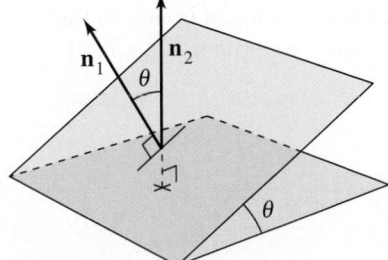

$$\cos \theta = \frac{|\mathbf{n}_1 \cdot \mathbf{n}_2|}{\|\mathbf{n}_1\| \|\mathbf{n}_2\|}. \qquad \text{Angle between two planes}$$

Consequently, two planes with normal vectors $\mathbf{n}_1$ and $\mathbf{n}_2$ are

1. *perpendicular* when $\mathbf{n}_1 \cdot \mathbf{n}_2 = 0$.

2. *parallel* when $\mathbf{n}_1$ is a scalar multiple of $\mathbf{n}_2$.

EXAMPLE 4   Finding the Line of Intersection of Two Planes

Find the angle between the two planes given by

$x - 2y + z = 0$ Equation for plane 1

$2x + 3y - 2z = 0$ Equation for plane 2

and find parametric equations of their line of intersection.

Solution

The normal vectors to the planes are $\mathbf{n}_1 = \langle 1, -2, 1 \rangle$ and $\mathbf{n}_2 = \langle 2, 3, -2 \rangle$. Consequently, the angle between the two planes is determined as follows.

$$\cos \theta = \frac{|\mathbf{n}_1 \cdot \mathbf{n}_2|}{\|\mathbf{n}_1\|\|\mathbf{n}_2\|} = \frac{|-6|}{\sqrt{6}\sqrt{17}} = \frac{6}{\sqrt{102}} \approx 0.59409$$

This implies that the angle between the two planes is $\theta \approx 53.55°$, as shown in Figure 10.24. You can find the line of intersection of the two planes by simultaneously solving the two linear equations representing the planes. One way to do this is to multiply the first equation by -2 and add the result to the second equation.

$$\begin{array}{l} x - 2y + z = 0 \\ 2x + 3y - 2z = 0 \end{array} \implies \begin{array}{l} -2x + 4y - 2z = 0 \\ \underline{2x + 3y - 2z = 0} \end{array}$$

$$7y - 4z = 0 \implies y = \frac{4z}{7}$$

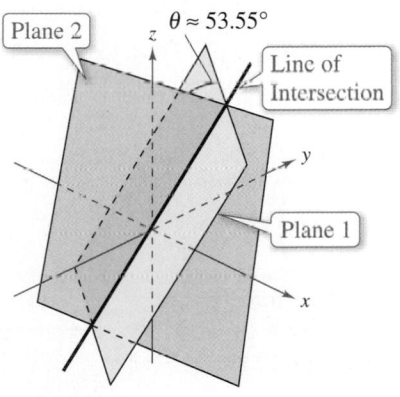

Figure 10.24

Substituting $y = 4z/7$ back into one of the original equations, you can determine that $x = z/7$. Finally, by letting $t = z/7$, you obtain the parametric equations

$x = t = x_1 + at$ Parametric equation for x

$y = 4t = y_1 + bt$ Parametric equation for y

$z = 7t = z_1 + ct.$ Parametric equation for z

Because $(x_1, y_1, z_1) = (0, 0, 0)$ lies in both planes, you can substitute for x_1, y_1, and z_1 in these parametric equations, which indicates that $a = 1$, $b = 4$, and $c = 7$ are direction numbers for the line of intersection.

✓ **Checkpoint** *Audio-video solution in English & Spanish at LarsonPrecalculus.com.*

Find the angle between the two planes given by

$2x + y + 3z = 0$ Equation for plane 1

$4x - 2y - 2z = 0$ Equation for plane 2

and find parametric equations of their line of intersection. ◼

Note that the direction numbers in Example 4 can be obtained from the cross product of the two normal vectors as follows.

$$\mathbf{n}_1 \times \mathbf{n}_2 = \begin{vmatrix} \mathbf{i} & \mathbf{j} & \mathbf{k} \\ 1 & -2 & 1 \\ 2 & 3 & -2 \end{vmatrix}$$

$$= \begin{vmatrix} -2 & 1 \\ 3 & -2 \end{vmatrix} \mathbf{i} - \begin{vmatrix} 1 & 1 \\ 2 & -2 \end{vmatrix} \mathbf{j} + \begin{vmatrix} 1 & -2 \\ 2 & 3 \end{vmatrix} \mathbf{k}$$

$$= \mathbf{i} + 4\mathbf{j} + 7\mathbf{k}$$

This means that the *line of intersection of the two planes is parallel to the cross product of their normal vectors.*

Sketching Planes in Space

As discussed in Section 10.1, when a plane in space intersects one of the coordinate planes, the line of intersection is called the *trace* of the given plane in the coordinate plane. To sketch a plane in space, it is helpful to find its points of intersection with the coordinate axes and its traces in the coordinate planes. For example, consider the plane

$$3x + 2y + 4z = 12. \qquad \text{Equation of plane}$$

You can find the *xy*-trace by letting $z = 0$ and sketching the line

$$3x + 2y = 12 \qquad \text{xy-trace}$$

in the *xy*-plane. This line intersects the *x*-axis at $(4, 0, 0)$ and the *y*-axis at $(0, 6, 0)$. In Figure 10.25, this process is continued by finding the *yz*-trace and the *xz*-trace and then shading the triangular region lying in the first octant.

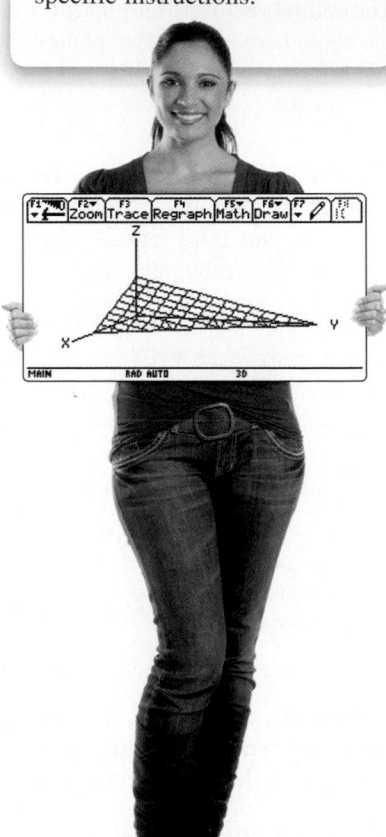

(a) *xy-trace* $(z = 0)$:
$3x + 2y = 12$

(b) *yz-trace* $(x = 0)$:
$2y + 4z = 12$

(c) *xz-trace* $(y = 0)$
$3x + 4z = 12$

Figure 10.25

If the equation of a plane has a missing variable, such as

$$2x + z = 1$$

then the plane must be *parallel to the axis* represented by the missing variable, as shown in Figure 10.26.

If two variables are missing from the equation of a plane, then it is *parallel to the coordinate plane* represented by the missing variables, as shown in Figure 10.27. For instance, the graph of

$$z + 2 = 0$$

is parallel to the *xy*-plane. Try confirming this using a three-dimensional graphing utility.

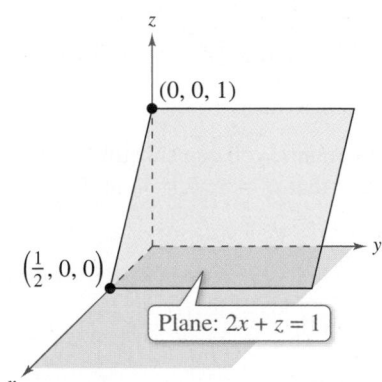

Plane is parallel to y-axis
Figure 10.26

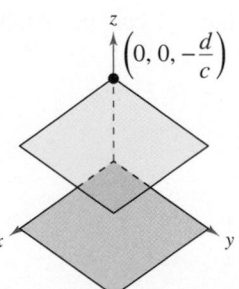

(a) *Plane* $ax + d = 0$
is parallel to yz-plane.

(b) *Plane* $by + d = 0$
is parallel to xz-plane.

(c) *Plane* $cz + d = 0$
is parallel to xy-plane.

Figure 10.27

Distance Between a Point and a Plane

The distance D between a point Q and a plane is the length of the shortest line segment connecting Q to the plane, as shown in Figure 10.28. When P is *any* point in the plane, you can find this distance by projecting the vector

$$\overrightarrow{PQ}$$

onto the normal vector $\mathbf{n}$. The length of this projection is the desired distance.

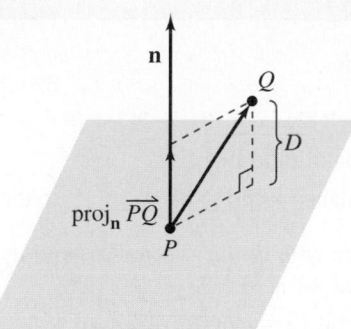

$$D = \|\mathrm{proj}_n\overrightarrow{PQ}\|$$
Figure 10.28

Distance Between a Point and a Plane

The **distance between a plane and a point** Q (not in the plane) is

$$D = \|\mathrm{proj}_\mathbf{n}\overrightarrow{PQ}\| = \frac{|\overrightarrow{PQ} \cdot \mathbf{n}|}{\|\mathbf{n}\|}$$

where P is a point in the plane and $\mathbf{n}$ is normal to the plane.

To find a point in the plane given by $ax + by + cz + d = 0$, where $a \neq 0$, let $y = 0$ and $z = 0$. Then, from the equation $ax + d = 0$, you can conclude that the point $(-d/a, 0, 0)$ lies in the plane.

EXAMPLE 5   Finding the Distance Between a Point and a Plane

Find the distance between the point $Q(1, 5, -4)$ and the plane $3x - y + 2z = 6$.

Solution

You know that $\mathbf{n} = \langle 3, -1, 2 \rangle$ is normal to the given plane. To find a point in the plane, let $y = 0$ and $z = 0$, and obtain the point $P(2, 0, 0)$. The vector from P to Q is

$$\overrightarrow{PQ} = \langle 1 - 2, 5 - 0, -4 - 0 \rangle = \langle -1, 5, -4 \rangle.$$

The formula for the distance between a point and a plane produces

$$\begin{aligned}
D &= \frac{|\overrightarrow{PQ} \cdot \mathbf{n}|}{\|\mathbf{n}\|} \\
&= \frac{|\langle -1, 5, -4 \rangle \cdot \langle 3, -1, 2 \rangle|}{\sqrt{9 + 1 + 4}} \\
&= \frac{|-3 - 5 - 8|}{\sqrt{14}} \\
&= \frac{16}{\sqrt{14}}.
\end{aligned}$$

✓ **Checkpoint**))) *Audio-video solution in English & Spanish at LarsonPrecalculus.com.*

Find the distance between the point $Q(-6, 2, 1)$ and the plane $2x + 5y - z = 3$. ■

The choice of the point P in Example 5 is arbitrary. Try choosing a different point to verify that you obtain the same distance.

10.4   Exercises

Vocabulary and Concept Check

In Exercises 1 and 2, fill in the blank.

1. The _____ vector for a line L is parallel to line L.

2. A vector that is perpendicular to a plane is said to be _____ to the plane.

3. For two distinct planes in three-space with normal vectors $\mathbf{n}_1$ and $\mathbf{n}_2$, $\mathbf{n}_1 \cdot \mathbf{n}_2 = 0$. Are the planes parallel, perpendicular, or neither?

4. Write the component form of a normal vector to the plane $ax + by + cz + d = 0$.

5. Which coordinate plane is parallel to the plane $x = 2$?

6. Which coordinate axis is parallel to the plane $y + z = 3$?

Procedures and Problem Solving

Finding Parametric and Symmetric Equations In Exercises 7–12, find (a) a set of parametric equations and (b) if possible, a set of symmetric equations for the line through the point and parallel to the specified vector or line. (There are many correct answers.)

Point	Parallel to
7. $(0, 0, 0)$	$\mathbf{v} = \langle 1, 2, 3 \rangle$
8. $(3, -5, 1)$	$\mathbf{v} = \langle 3, -7, -10 \rangle$
9. $(-4, 1, 0)$	$\mathbf{v} = 6\mathbf{j} - 5\mathbf{k}$
10. $(5, 0, 10)$	$\mathbf{v} = 4\mathbf{i} + 3\mathbf{k}$
11. $(3, 6, -5)$	$x = 5 + 2t, y = 7 - 3t, z = -2 + t$
12. $(7, -8, 2)$	$x = 3 + 3t, y = 5 - 2t, z = -7 + t$

A Line Through Two Points In Exercises 13–20, find (a) a set of parametric equations and (b) if possible, a set of symmetric equations of the line that passes through the two points. (There are many correct answers.)

13. $(2, 0, 2), (1, 4, -3)$ 14. $(6, 8, 0), (3, -2, 12)$

15. $(-3, 8, 15), (1, -2, 16)$ 16. $(2, 3, -1), (1, -5, 3)$

17. $(3, 1, 2), (-1, 1, 5)$ 18. $(2, -1, 5), (2, 1, -3)$

19. $\left(-\frac{1}{2}, 2, \frac{1}{2}\right), \left(1, -\frac{1}{2}, 0\right)$ 20. $\left(-\frac{3}{2}, \frac{3}{2}, 2\right), \left(0, -5, \frac{3}{2}\right)$

Using Parametric Equations In Exercises 21 and 22, sketch a graph of the line.

21. $x = 3 + 2t, y = 2 + t, z = 1 + \frac{1}{2}t$

22. $x = 5 - 2t, y = 1 + t, z = 5 - \frac{1}{2}t$

Finding an Equation of a Plane in Three-Space In Exercises 23–28, find the general form of the equation of the plane passing through the point and perpendicular to the specified vector or line.

Point	Perpendicular to
23. $(2, 1, 2)$	$\mathbf{n} = \mathbf{i}$
24. $(1, 0, -3)$	$\mathbf{n} = \mathbf{k}$
25. $(5, 6, 3)$	$\mathbf{n} = -2\mathbf{i} + \mathbf{j} - 2\mathbf{k}$
26. $(0, 0, 0)$	$\mathbf{n} = 9\mathbf{i} - 3\mathbf{j} + 5\mathbf{k}$
27. $(2, 0, 0)$	$x = 3 - t, y = 2 - 2t, z = 4 + t$
28. $(0, 0, 6)$	$x = 1 - t, y = 2 + t, z = 4 - 2t$

Finding an Equation of a Plane in Three-Space In Exercises 29–32, find the general form of the equation of the plane passing through the three points.

29. $(0, 0, 0), (1, 2, 3), (-2, 3, 3)$

30. $(4, -1, 3), (2, 5, 1), (-1, 2, 1)$

31. $(2, 3, -2), (3, 4, 2), (1, -1, 0)$

32. $(5, -1, 4), (1, -1, 2), (2, 1, -3)$

Finding an Equation of a Plane in Three-Space In Exercises 33–38, find the general form of the equation of the plane with the given characteristics.

33. Passes through $(2, 5, 3)$ and is parallel to the xz-plane

34. Passes through $(1, 2, 3)$ and is parallel to the yz-plane

35. Passes through $(0, 2, 4)$ and $(-1, -2, 0)$ and is perpendicular to the yz-plane

36. Passes through $(1, -2, 4)$ and $(4, 0, -1)$ and is perpendicular to the xz-plane

37. Passes through $(2, 2, 1)$ and $(-1, 1, -1)$ and is perpendicular to $2x - 3y + z = 3$

38. Passes through $(1, 2, 0)$ and $(-1, -1, 2)$ and is perpendicular to $2x - 3y + z = 6$

Finding Parametric Equations of a Line In Exercises 39–44, find a set of parametric equations of the line. (There are many correct answers.)

39. Passes through $(2, 3, 4)$ and is perpendicular to the plane given by $3x + 2y - z = 6$

40. Passes through $(-4, 5, 2)$ and is perpendicular to the plane given by $-x + 2y + z = 5$

41. Passes through $(5, -3, -4)$ and is parallel to $\mathbf{v} = 2\mathbf{j} - 6\mathbf{k}$

42. Passes through $(-1, 4, -3)$ and is parallel to $\mathbf{v} = 5\mathbf{i} - \mathbf{j}$

43. Passes through $(-2, 7, 4)$ and is parallel to $x = -t$, $y = 3 + 4t, z = -2 + 5t$

44. Passes through $(6, -3, 8)$ and is parallel to $x = 5 - 2t$, $y = -4 + 9t, z = 12t$

Parallel or Orthogonal Planes   In Exercises 45–48, determine whether the planes are parallel, orthogonal, or neither. If they are neither parallel nor orthogonal, find the angle of intersection.

45. $5x - 3y + z = 4$
$x + 4y + 7z = 1$

46. $3x + y - 4z = 3$
$-9x - 3y + 12z = 4$

47. $x - 5y - z = 1$
$5x - 25y - 5z = -3$

48. $-6x - y + 4z = 1$
$3x - 6y + 3z = -8$

Finding the Line of Intersection of Two Planes   In Exercises 49–52, (a) find the angle between the two planes and (b) find parametric equations of their line of intersection.

49. $x + y - 2z = 0$
$-4x - y + 3z = 0$

50. $x - 3y + 2z = 0$
$3x + 2y - 5z = 0$

51. $x + y - z = 0$
$2x - 5y - z = 1$

52. $3x - 4y + 5z = 6$
$x + y - z = 2$

Sketching a Plane in Space   In Exercises 53–56, plot the intercepts and sketch a graph of the plane.

53. $x + 2y + 3z = 6$

54. $2x - y + 4z = 4$

55. $x + 2y = 4$

56. $y + z = 5$

Finding the Distance Between a Point and a Plane   In Exercises 57–60, find the distance between the point and the plane.

57. $(1, 3, 4)$
$4x - 5y + 2z = 6$

58. $(3, 2, 1)$
$x - y + 2z = 4$

59. $(4, -2, -2)$
$2x - y + z = 4$

60. $(-1, 2, 5)$
$2x + 3y + z = 12$

61. Mechanical Engineering   A company that produces after-market machine parts is designing a reproduction of a fuel tank with the shape and dimensions shown in the figure. Find the angle between two adjacent sides of the tank.

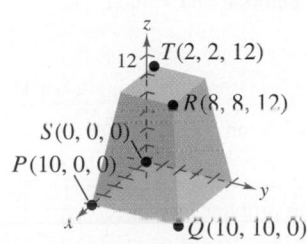

62. *Why you should learn it*   *(p. 733)*   A bread pan is tapered so that a loaf of bread can be easily removed. The shape and dimensions of the pan are shown in the figure. Find the angle between two adjacent sides of the pan.

Conclusions

True or False?   In Exercises 63 and 64, determine whether the statement is true or false. Justify your answer.

63. Two lines in space are either parallel or they intersect.

64. Two nonparallel planes in space will always intersect.

65. Error Analysis   Find the error in writing symmetric equations of the line that passes through $(1, 2, 6)$ and is parallel to $\mathbf{v} = \langle 3, 5, 4 \rangle$.

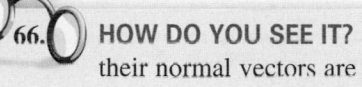

66. HOW DO YOU SEE IT?   Two planes and their normal vectors are shown below.

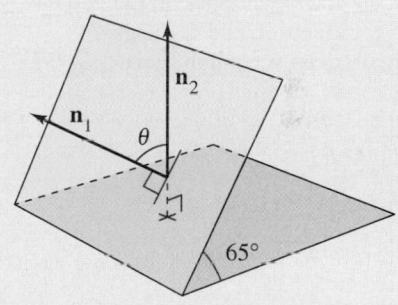

(a) What is the angle between the normal vectors? Explain your reasoning.

(b) A third plane is parallel to $\mathbf{n}_1$. What is the angle between this plane and the blue plane? Explain your reasoning.

(c) A third plane is parallel to $\mathbf{n}_2$. Explain how to find the angle between this plane and the blue plane.

67. Think About It   The direction numbers of two distinct lines in space are $10, -18, 20$, and $-15, 27, -30$. What is the relationship between the lines? Explain.

10   Chapter Summary

What did you learn?	Explanation and Examples	Review Exercises
10.1 Plot points in the three-dimensional coordinate system *(p. 712)*.		1–4
Find distances between points in space and find midpoints of line segments joining points in space *(p. 713)*.	The distance between the points (x_1, y_1, z_1) and (x_2, y_2, z_2) given by the Distance Formula in Space is $$d = \sqrt{(x_2 - x_1)^2 + (y_2 - y_1)^2 + (z_2 - z_1)^2}.$$ The midpoint of the line segment joining the points (x_1, y_1, z_1) and (x_2, y_2, z_2) given by the Midpoint Formula in Space is $$\left(\frac{x_1 + x_2}{2}, \frac{y_1 + y_2}{2}, \frac{z_1 + z_2}{2} \right).$$	5–12
Write equations of spheres in standard form and find traces of surfaces in space *(p. 714)*.	**Standard Equation of a Sphere** The standard equation of a sphere with center (h, k, j) and radius r is given by $$(x - h)^2 + (y - k)^2 + (z - j)^2 = r^2.$$	13–20
10.2 Find the component forms of, the unit vectors in the same direction of, the magnitudes of, the dot products of, and the angles between vectors in space *(p. 719)*.	**Vectors in Space** **1.** Two vectors are equal if and only if their corresponding components are equal. **2.** Magnitude of $\mathbf{u} = \langle u_1, u_2, u_3 \rangle$: $$\|\mathbf{u}\| = \sqrt{u_1^2 + u_2^2 + u_3^2}$$ **3.** A unit vector $\mathbf{u}$ in the direction of $\mathbf{v}$ is $$\mathbf{u} = \frac{\mathbf{v}}{\|\mathbf{v}\|}, \ \mathbf{v} \neq \mathbf{0}.$$ **4.** The sum of $\mathbf{u} = \langle u_1, u_2, u_3 \rangle$ and $\mathbf{v} = \langle v_1, v_2, v_3 \rangle$ is $\mathbf{u} + \mathbf{v} = \langle u_1 + v_1, u_2 + v_2, u_3 + v_3 \rangle$. **5.** The scalar multiple of the real number c and $\mathbf{u} = \langle u_1, u_2, u_3 \rangle$ is $c\mathbf{u} = \langle cu_1, cu_2, cu_3 \rangle$. **6.** The dot product of $\mathbf{u} = \langle u_1, u_2, u_3 \rangle$ and $\mathbf{v} = \langle v_1, v_2, v_3 \rangle$ is $\mathbf{u} \cdot \mathbf{v} = u_1 v_1 + u_2 v_2 + u_3 v_3$. **Angle Between Two Vectors** If θ is the angle between two nonzero vectors $\mathbf{u}$ and $\mathbf{v}$, then $$\cos \theta = \frac{\mathbf{u} \cdot \mathbf{v}}{\|\mathbf{u}\| \|\mathbf{v}\|}.$$	21–32
Determine whether vectors in space are parallel *(p. 721)*.	Two nonzero vectors $\mathbf{u}$ and $\mathbf{v}$ are parallel when there is some scalar c such that $\mathbf{u} = c\mathbf{v}$.	33–40
Use vectors in space to solve real-life problems *(p. 723)*.	Vectors can be used to solve equilibrium problems in space. (See Example 7.)	41, 42

What did you learn?	Explanation and Examples	Review Exercises
10.3 Find cross products of vectors in space *(p. 726)*.	**Definition of Cross Product of Two Vectors in Space** Let $\mathbf{u} = u_1\mathbf{i} + u_2\mathbf{j} + u_3\mathbf{k}$ and $\mathbf{v} = v_1\mathbf{i} + v_2\mathbf{j} + v_3\mathbf{k}$ be vectors in space. The cross product of $\mathbf{u}$ and $\mathbf{v}$, $\mathbf{u} \times \mathbf{v}$, is the vector $$(u_2v_3 - u_3v_2)\mathbf{i} - (u_1v_3 - u_3v_1)\mathbf{j} + (u_1v_2 - u_2v_1)\mathbf{k}.$$	43–46
Use geometric properties of cross products of vectors in space *(p. 728)*.	**Geometric Properties of the Cross Product** Let $\mathbf{u}$ and $\mathbf{v}$ be nonzero vectors in space, and let θ be the angle between $\mathbf{u}$ and $\mathbf{v}$. 1. $\mathbf{u} \times \mathbf{v}$ is orthogonal to both $\mathbf{u}$ and $\mathbf{v}$. 2. $\|\mathbf{u} \times \mathbf{v}\| = \|\mathbf{u}\|\|\mathbf{v}\| \sin \theta$ 3. $\mathbf{u} \times \mathbf{v} = \mathbf{0}$ if and only if $\mathbf{u}$ and $\mathbf{v}$ are scalar multiples of each other. 4. $\|\mathbf{u} \times \mathbf{v}\|$ = area of parallelogram having $\mathbf{u}$ and $\mathbf{v}$ as adjacent sides.	47–50
Use triple scalar products to find volumes of parallelepipeds *(p. 730)*.	**The Triple Scalar Product** For $\mathbf{u} = u_1\mathbf{i} + u_2\mathbf{j} + u_3\mathbf{k}$, $\mathbf{v} = v_1\mathbf{i} + v_2\mathbf{j} + v_3\mathbf{k}$, and $\mathbf{w} = w_1\mathbf{i} + w_2\mathbf{j} + w_3\mathbf{k}$, the triple scalar product is given by $$\mathbf{u} \cdot (\mathbf{v} \times \mathbf{w}) = \begin{vmatrix} u_1 & u_2 & u_3 \\ v_1 & v_2 & v_3 \\ w_1 & w_2 & w_3 \end{vmatrix}.$$ **Geometric Property of Triple Scalar Product** The volume V of a parallelepiped with vectors $\mathbf{u}$, $\mathbf{v}$, and $\mathbf{w}$ as adjacent edges is given by $$V = |\mathbf{u} \cdot (\mathbf{v} \times \mathbf{w})|.$$	51, 52
10.4 Find parametric and symmetric equations of lines in space *(p. 733)*.	**Parametric Equations of a Line in Space** A line L parallel to the nonzero vector $\mathbf{v} = \langle a, b, c \rangle$ and passing through the point $P(x_1, y_1, z_1)$ is represented by the parametric equations $$x = x_1 + at, \quad y = y_1 + bt, \quad \text{and} \quad z = z_1 + ct.$$	53–58
Find equations of planes in space *(p. 735)*.	**Standard Equation of a Plane in Space** The plane containing the point (x_1, y_1, z_1) and having nonzero normal vector $\mathbf{n} = \langle a, b, c \rangle$ can be represented by the standard form of the equation of a plane $$a(x - x_1) + b(y - y_1) + c(z - z_1) = 0.$$	59–62
Sketch planes in space *(p. 738)*.	See Figure 10.25, which shows how to sketch the plane $3x + 2y + 4z = 12$.	63–66
Find distances between points and planes in space *(p. 739)*.	**Distance Between a Point and a Plane** The distance between a plane and a point Q (not in the plane) is $$D = \|\text{proj}_{\mathbf{n}} \overrightarrow{PQ}\| = \frac{|\overrightarrow{PQ} \cdot \mathbf{n}|}{\|\mathbf{n}\|}$$ where P is a point in the plane and $\mathbf{n}$ is normal to the plane.	67–70

10.1

Plotting Points in Space   In Exercises 1 and 2, plot both points in the same three-dimensional coordinate system.

1. (a) $(5, -1, 3)$ **2.** (a) $(2, 4, -1)$
   (b) $(-3, 3, 0)$ (b) $(0, -1, 2)$

Finding the Coordinates of a Point   In Exercises 3 and 4, find the coordinates of the point.

3. The point is located in the *xy*-plane, nine units to the right of the *xz*-plane, and ten units behind the *yz*-plane.

4. The point is located on the *y*-axis and six units to the left of the *xz*-plane.

Finding the Distance Between Two Points in Space   In Exercises 5 and 6, find the distance between the points.

5. $(4, 0, -6), (5, -2, 1)$ **6.** $(2, 3, -4), (-1, -2, 0)$

Using the Pythagorean Theorem   In Exercises 7 and 8, find the lengths of the sides of the right triangle. Show that these lengths satisfy the Pythagorean Theorem.

7.

8.

Using the Midpoint Formula in Space   In Exercises 9–12, find the midpoint of the line segment joining the points.

9. $(-2, 3, 2), (2, -5, 4)$
10. $(7, 1, -4), (3, -1, 2)$
11. $(10, 6, -12), (-8, -4, -6)$
12. $(-5, -3, 1), (-9, -9, -5)$

Finding the Equation of a Sphere   In Exercises 13–16, find the standard form of the equation of the sphere with the given characteristics.

13. Center: $(2, 3, 5)$; radius: 1
14. Center: $(3, -2, 4)$; radius: 4
15. Center: $(-4, 0, 1)$; diameter: 17
16. Center: $(0, 4, -1)$; diameter: 15

Finding the Center and Radius of a Sphere   In Exercises 17 and 18, find the center and radius of the sphere.

17. $x^2 + y^2 + z^2 - 4x - 6y + 2z + 6 = 0$
18. $x^2 + y^2 + z^2 - 10x + 6y - 4z + 34 = 0$

Finding a Trace of a Surface   In Exercises 19 and 20, sketch the graph of the equation and sketch the specified trace.

19. $x^2 + (y - 3)^2 + z^2 = 16$
   (a) *xz*-trace   (b) *yz*-trace
20. $(x + 2)^2 + (y - 1)^2 + z^2 = 9$
   (a) *xy*-trace   (b) *yz*-trace

10.2

Finding the Component Form of a Vector   In Exercises 21–24, (a) write the component form of the vector **v**, (b) find the magnitude of **v**, and (c) find a unit vector in the direction of **v**.

	Initial Point	*Terminal Point*
21.	$(4, -2, 1)$	$(-1, 5, 0)$
22.	$(2, -1, 2)$	$(-3, 2, 3)$
23.	$(7, -4, 3)$	$(-3, 2, 10)$
24.	$(0, 3, -1)$	$(5, -6, 6)$

Finding the Dot Product of Two Vectors   In Exercises 25–28, find the dot product of **u** and **v**.

25. $\mathbf{u} = \langle -1, 4, 3 \rangle$ **26.** $\mathbf{u} = \langle 8, -4, 2 \rangle$
     $\mathbf{v} = \langle 0, -6, 5 \rangle$ $\mathbf{v} = \langle 2, 5, 2 \rangle$
27. $\mathbf{u} = 2\mathbf{i} + \mathbf{j} - 2\mathbf{k}$ **28.** $\mathbf{u} = 7\mathbf{i} + 4\mathbf{j} - 2\mathbf{k}$
     $\mathbf{v} = \mathbf{i} - 3\mathbf{j} + 2\mathbf{k}$ $\mathbf{v} = -5\mathbf{i} - 9\mathbf{k}$

Finding the Angle Between Two Vectors   In Exercises 29–32, find the angle θ between the vectors.

29. $\mathbf{u} = \langle 2, -1, 0 \rangle$ **30.** $\mathbf{u} = \langle 3, 1, -1 \rangle$
     $\mathbf{v} = \langle 1, 2, 1 \rangle$ $\mathbf{v} = \langle 4, 5, 2 \rangle$
31. $\mathbf{u} = \langle \sqrt{3}, -1, 3 \rangle$ **32.** $\mathbf{u} = \langle 2\sqrt{2}, -4, 4 \rangle$
     $\mathbf{v} = \langle -\sqrt{3}, 6, 7 \rangle$ $\mathbf{v} = \langle -\sqrt{2}, 1, 2 \rangle$

The Relationship of Two Vectors   In Exercises 33–36, determine whether **u** and **v** are orthogonal, parallel, or neither.

33. $\mathbf{u} = \langle 7, -2, 3 \rangle$ **34.** $\mathbf{u} = \langle -4, 3, -6 \rangle$
     $\mathbf{v} = \langle -1, 4, 5 \rangle$ $\mathbf{v} = \langle 16, -12, 24 \rangle$
35. $\mathbf{u} = 6\mathbf{i} + 5\mathbf{j} + 9\mathbf{k}$ **36.** $\mathbf{u} = 3\mathbf{j} + 2\mathbf{k}$
     $\mathbf{v} = 5\mathbf{i} + 3\mathbf{j} - 5\mathbf{k}$ $\mathbf{v} = 12\mathbf{i} - 18\mathbf{k}$

Using Vectors to Determine Collinear Points   In Exercises 37–40, use vectors to determine whether the points are collinear.

37. $(5, 2, 0), (2, 6, 1), (2, 4, 7)$
38. $(6, 3, -1), (5, 8, 3), (7, -2, -5)$

39. $(3, 4, -1), (-1, 6, 9), (5, 3, -6)$

40. $(5, -4, 7), (8, -5, 5), (11, 6, 3)$

41. Forces in Equilibrium   A load of 300 pounds is supported by three cables, as shown in the figure. Find the tension in each of the supporting cables.

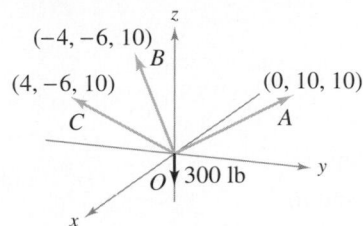

42. Forces in Equilibrium   Determine the tension in each of the supporting cables in Exercise 41 when the load is 200 pounds.

10.3

Finding the Cross Product   In Exercises 43–46, find $\mathbf{u} \times \mathbf{v}$.

43. $\mathbf{u} = \langle 0, -2, 8 \rangle$ **44.** $\mathbf{u} = \langle 10, 15, 5 \rangle$

  $\mathbf{v} = \langle 3, -1, 5 \rangle$ $\mathbf{v} = \langle 5, -3, 0 \rangle$

45. $\mathbf{u} = \mathbf{i} - 2\mathbf{j} + 12\mathbf{k}$ **46.** $\mathbf{u} = 3\mathbf{i} + 4\mathbf{j} - 9\mathbf{k}$

  $\mathbf{v} = 3\mathbf{i} + 5\mathbf{j} - 4\mathbf{k}$ $\mathbf{v} = 8\mathbf{i} - \mathbf{j} + 6\mathbf{k}$

Using the Cross Product   In Exercises 47 and 48, find a unit vector orthogonal to $\mathbf{u}$ and $\mathbf{v}$.

47. $\mathbf{u} = -3\mathbf{i} + 2\mathbf{j} - 5\mathbf{k}$ **48.** $\mathbf{u} = 2\mathbf{i} - \mathbf{j} + \mathbf{k}$

  $\mathbf{v} = 10\mathbf{i} - 15\mathbf{j} + 2\mathbf{k}$ $\mathbf{v} = -\mathbf{i} - \mathbf{j} - 2\mathbf{k}$

Geometric Application of the Cross Product   In Exercises 49 and 50, (a) verify that the points are the vertices of a parallelogram and (b) find its area.

49. $A(2, -1, 1), B(5, 1, 4), C(0, 1, 1), D(3, 3, 4)$

50. $A(0, 4, 0), B(1, 4, 1), C(0, 6, 0), D(1, 6, 1)$

Finding the Volume of a Parallelepiped   In Exercises 51 and 52, find the volume of the parallelepiped with the given vertices.

51. $A(0, 0, 0), B(3, 0, 0), C(0, 5, 1), D(3, 5, 1),$

  $E(2, 0, 5), F(5, 0, 5), G(2, 5, 6), H(5, 5, 6)$

52. $A(0, 0, 0), B(2, 0, 0), C(2, 4, 0), D(0, 4, 0),$

  $F(0, 0, 6), F(2, 0, 6), G(2, 4, 6), H(0, 4, 6)$

10.4

A Line Through Two Points   In Exercises 53 and 54, find (a) a set of parametric equations and (b) if possible, a set of symmetric equations for the line that passes through the two points. (There are many correct answers.)

53. $(3, 0, 2), (9, 11, 16)$ **54.** $(-1, 4, 3), (8, 10, 5)$

Finding Parametric and Symmetric Equations   In Exercises 55–58, find (a) a set of parametric equations and (b) if possible, a set of symmetric equations for the specified line. (There are many correct answers.)

55. Passes through $(0, -10, 3)$ and is parallel to $\mathbf{v} = \langle -5, 2, 3 \rangle$

56. Passes through $(0, 1, 7)$ and is parallel to $\mathbf{v} = \langle -2, \frac{5}{2}, 1 \rangle$

57. Passes through $(-1, 3, 5)$ and is parallel to $x = 1 + 2t$, $y = 2 - t$, and $z = 1 + 3t$

58. Passes through $(3, 2, 1)$ and is parallel to $x = y = z$

Finding an Equation of a Plane in Three-Space   In Exercises 59–62, find the general form of the equation of the plane with the given characteristics.

59. Passes through $(0, 0, 4), (5, 0, 2),$ and $(2, 3, 8)$

60. Passes through $(-1, 3, 4), (4, -2, 2),$ and $(2, 8, 6)$

61. Passes through $(5, 3, 2)$ and is parallel to the xy-plane

62. Passes through $(6, -3, 4)$ and is perpendicular to $x = 1 - t, y = 2 + t,$ and $z = 4 - 2t$

Sketching a Plane in Space   In Exercises 63–66, plot the intercepts and sketch a graph of the plane.

63. $3x - 2y + 3z = 6$ **64.** $5x - 5y - 2z = 10$

65. $2x - 3z = 6$ **66.** $-4x - 3z = 12$

Finding the Distance Between a Point and a Plane   In Exercises 67–70, find the distance between the point and the plane.

67. $(2, 3, 10)$ **68.** $(1, 2, 3)$

  $2x - 20y + 6z = 6$ $2x - y + z = 4$

69. $(0, 0, 0)$ **70.** $(0, 0, 0)$

  $x - 10y + 3z = 2$ $2x + 3y + z = 12$

Conclusions

True or False?   In Exercises 71 and 72, determine whether the statement is true or false. Justify your answer.

71. The cross product is commutative.

72. The triple scalar product of three vectors in space is a scalar.

Verifying Properties   In Exercises 73–76, let $\mathbf{u} = \langle 3, -2, 1 \rangle$, $\mathbf{v} = \langle 2, -4, -3 \rangle$, and $\mathbf{w} = \langle -1, 2, 2 \rangle$.

73. Show that $\mathbf{u} \cdot \mathbf{u} = \|\mathbf{u}\|^2$.

74. Show that $\mathbf{u} \times \mathbf{v} = -(\mathbf{v} \times \mathbf{u})$.

75. Show that $\mathbf{u} \cdot (\mathbf{v} + \mathbf{w}) = \mathbf{u} \cdot \mathbf{v} + \mathbf{u} \cdot \mathbf{w}$.

76. Show that $\mathbf{u} \times (\mathbf{v} + \mathbf{w}) = (\mathbf{u} \times \mathbf{v}) + (\mathbf{u} \times \mathbf{w})$.

77. Writing   Define the cross product of vectors $\mathbf{u}$ and $\mathbf{v}$.

78. Writing   The vertices of a triangle in space are $(x_1, y_1, z_1), (x_2, y_2, z_2),$ and (x_3, y_3, z_3). Explain how to find a vector perpendicular to the triangle.

10   Chapter Test

See *CalcChat.com* for tutorial help and worked-out solutions to odd-numbered exercises.
For instructions on how to use a graphing utility, see Appendix A.

Take this test as you would take a test in class. After you are finished, check your work against the answers given in the back of the book.

1. Plot each point in the same three-dimensional coordinate system.
   (a) $(5, -2, 3)$ (b) $(-3, 4, 2)$ (c) $(2, 1, -1)$

In Exercises 2–4, use the points $A(8, -2, 5)$, $B(6, 4, -1)$, and $C(-4, 3, 0)$ to solve the problem.

2. Consider the triangle with vertices A, B, and C. Is it a right triangle? Explain.

3. Find the coordinates of the midpoint of the line segment joining points A and B.

4. Find the standard form of the equation of the sphere for which A and B are the endpoints of a diameter. Sketch the sphere and its xz-trace.

In Exercises 5 and 6, find the component form and the magnitude of the vector v.

5. Initial point: $(2, -1, 3)$
   Terminal point: $(4, 4, -7)$

6. Initial point: $(6, 2, -5)$
   Terminal point: $(3, -4, 8)$

In Exercises 7–10, let u and v be the vectors from $A(8, -2, 5)$ to $B(6, 4, -1)$ and from A to $C(-4, 3, 0)$, respectively.

7. Write **u** and **v** in component form.

8. Find (a) $\|\mathbf{v}\|$, (b) $\mathbf{u} \cdot \mathbf{v}$, and (c) $\mathbf{u} \times \mathbf{v}$.

9. Find the angle between **u** and **v**.

10. Find a set of (a) parametric equations and (b) symmetric equations for the line through points A and B.

In Exercises 11–13, determine whether u and v are orthogonal, parallel, or neither.

11. $\mathbf{u} = \mathbf{i} - 2\mathbf{j} - \mathbf{k}$
    $\mathbf{v} = \mathbf{j} + 6\mathbf{k}$

12. $\mathbf{u} = -3\mathbf{i} + 2\mathbf{j} - \mathbf{k}$
    $\mathbf{v} = \mathbf{i} + \mathbf{j} - \mathbf{k}$

13. $\mathbf{u} = \langle 4, -1, 6 \rangle$
    $\mathbf{v} = \langle -2, \frac{1}{2}, -3 \rangle$

14. Verify that the points $A(2, -3, 1)$, $B(6, 5, -1)$, $C(3, -6, 4)$, and $D(7, 2, 2)$ are the vertices of a parallelogram, and find its area.

15. Find the general form of the equation of the plane passing through the points $(-3, -4, 2)$, $(-3, 4, 1)$, and $(1, 1, -2)$.

16. Find the volume of the parallelepiped at the right with the given vertices.
    $A(0, 0, 5)$, $B(0, 10, 5)$, $C(4, 10, 5)$, $D(4, 0, 5)$,
    $E(0, 1, 0)$, $F(0, 11, 0)$, $G(4, 11, 0)$, $H(4, 1, 0)$

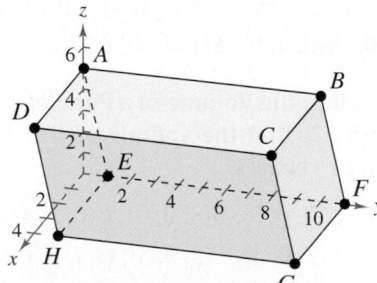

Figure for 16

In Exercises 17 and 18, label the intercepts and sketch a graph of the plane.

17. $3x + 6y + 2z = 18$

18. $4x - 5z = 20$

19. Find the distance between the point $(2, -1, 6)$ and the plane $3x - 2y + z = 6$.

Proofs in Mathematics

Algebraic Properties of the Cross Product   (p. 727)

Let $\mathbf{u}$, $\mathbf{v}$, and $\mathbf{w}$ be vectors in space, and let c be a scalar.

1. $\mathbf{u} \times \mathbf{v} = -(\mathbf{v} \times \mathbf{u})$ 2. $\mathbf{u} \times (\mathbf{v} + \mathbf{w}) = (\mathbf{u} \times \mathbf{v}) + (\mathbf{u} \times \mathbf{w})$

3. $c(\mathbf{u} \times \mathbf{v}) = (c\mathbf{u}) \times \mathbf{v} = \mathbf{u} \times (c\mathbf{v})$ 4. $\mathbf{u} \times \mathbf{0} = \mathbf{0} \times \mathbf{u} = \mathbf{0}$

5. $\mathbf{u} \times \mathbf{u} = \mathbf{0}$ 6. $\mathbf{u} \cdot (\mathbf{v} \times \mathbf{w}) = (\mathbf{u} \times \mathbf{v}) \cdot \mathbf{w}$

Notation for Dot and Cross Products

The notation for the dot products and cross products of vectors was first introduced by the American physicist Josiah Willard Gibbs (1839–1903). In the early 1880s, Gibbs built a system to represent physical quantities called *vector analysis*. The system was a departure from William Hamilton's theory of quaternions.

Proof

Let $\mathbf{u} = u_1\mathbf{i} + u_2\mathbf{j} + u_3\mathbf{k}$, $\mathbf{v} = v_1\mathbf{i} + v_2\mathbf{j} + v_3\mathbf{k}$, $\mathbf{w} = w_1\mathbf{i} + w_2\mathbf{j} + w_3\mathbf{k}$, $\mathbf{0} = 0\mathbf{i} + 0\mathbf{j} + 0\mathbf{k}$, and let c be a scalar.

1. $\mathbf{u} \times \mathbf{v} = (u_2v_3 - u_3v_2)\mathbf{i} - (u_1v_3 - u_3v_1)\mathbf{j} + (u_1v_2 - u_2v_1)\mathbf{k}$

   $\mathbf{v} \times \mathbf{u} = (v_2u_3 - v_3u_2)\mathbf{i} - (v_1u_3 - v_3u_1)\mathbf{j} + (v_1u_2 - v_2u_1)\mathbf{k}$

   So, this implies $\mathbf{u} \times \mathbf{v} = -(\mathbf{v} \times \mathbf{u})$.

2. $\mathbf{u} \times (\mathbf{v} + \mathbf{w}) = [u_2(v_3 + w_3) - u_3(v_2 + w_2)]\mathbf{i} - [u_1(v_3 + w_3) -$

   $\qquad u_3(v_1 + w_1)]\mathbf{j} + [u_1(v_2 + w_2) - u_2(v_1 + w_1)\mathbf{k}$

   $= (u_2v_3 - u_3v_2)\mathbf{i} - (u_1v_3 - u_3v_1)\mathbf{j} + (u_1v_2 - u_2v_1)\mathbf{k} +$

   $\qquad (u_2w_3 - u_3w_2)\mathbf{i} - (u_1w_3 - u_3w_1)\mathbf{j} + (u_1w_2 - u_2w_1)\mathbf{k}$

   $= (\mathbf{u} \times \mathbf{v}) + (\mathbf{u} \times \mathbf{w})$

3. $(c\mathbf{u}) \times \mathbf{v} = (cu_2v_3 - cu_3v_2)\mathbf{i} - (cu_1v_3 - cu_3v_1)\mathbf{j} + (cu_1v_2 - cu_2v_1)\mathbf{k}$

   $= c[(u_2v_3 - u_3v_2)\mathbf{i} - (u_1v_3 - u_3v_1)\mathbf{j} + (u_1v_2 - u_2v_1)\mathbf{k}]$

   $= c(\mathbf{u} \times \mathbf{v})$

4. $\mathbf{u} \times \mathbf{0} = (u_2 \cdot 0 - u_3 \cdot 0)\mathbf{i} - (u_1 \cdot 0 - u_3 \cdot 0)\mathbf{j} + (u_1 \cdot 0 - u_2 \cdot 0)\mathbf{k}$

   $\qquad = 0\mathbf{i} + 0\mathbf{j} + 0\mathbf{k} = \mathbf{0}$

   $\mathbf{0} \times \mathbf{u} = (0 \cdot u_3 - 0 \cdot u_2)\mathbf{i} - (0 \cdot u_3 - 0 \cdot u_1)\mathbf{j} + (0 \cdot u_2 - 0 \cdot u_1)\mathbf{k}$

   $\qquad = 0\mathbf{i} + 0\mathbf{j} + 0\mathbf{k} = \mathbf{0}$

   So, this implies $\mathbf{u} \times \mathbf{0} = \mathbf{0} \times \mathbf{u} = \mathbf{0}$.

5. $\mathbf{u} \times \mathbf{u} = (u_2u_3 - u_3u_2)\mathbf{i} - (u_1u_3 - u_3u_1)\mathbf{j} + (u_1u_2 - u_2u_1)\mathbf{k} = \mathbf{0}$

6. $\mathbf{u} \cdot (\mathbf{v} \times \mathbf{w}) = \begin{vmatrix} u_1 & u_2 & u_3 \\ v_1 & v_2 & v_3 \\ w_1 & w_2 & w_3 \end{vmatrix}$ and $(\mathbf{u} \times \mathbf{v}) \cdot \mathbf{w} = \mathbf{w} \cdot (\mathbf{u} \times \mathbf{v}) = \begin{vmatrix} w_1 & w_2 & w_3 \\ u_1 & u_2 & u_3 \\ v_1 & v_2 & v_3 \end{vmatrix}$

   $\mathbf{u} \cdot (\mathbf{v} \times \mathbf{w}) = u_1(v_2w_3 - w_2v_3) - u_2(v_1w_3 - w_1v_3) + u_3(v_1w_2 - w_1v_2)$

   $\qquad = u_1v_2w_3 - u_1w_2v_3 - u_2v_1w_3 + u_2w_1v_3 + u_3v_1w_2 - u_3w_1v_2$

   $\qquad = u_2w_1v_3 - u_3w_1v_2 - u_1w_2v_3 + u_3v_1w_2 + u_1v_2w_3 - u_2v_1w_3$

   $\qquad = w_1(u_2v_3 - v_2u_3) - w_2(u_1v_3 - v_1u_3) + w_3(u_1v_2 - v_1u_2)$

   $\qquad = (\mathbf{u} \times \mathbf{v}) \cdot \mathbf{w}$

> ### Geometric Properties of the Cross Product   (p. 728)
>
> Let **u** and **v** be nonzero vectors in space, and let θ be the angle between **u** and **v**.
>
> 1. $\mathbf{u} \times \mathbf{v}$ is orthogonal to both **u** and **v**.
>
> 2. $\|\mathbf{u} \times \mathbf{v}\| = \|\mathbf{u}\|\|\mathbf{v}\| \sin \theta$
>
> 3. $\mathbf{u} \times \mathbf{v} = \mathbf{0}$ if and only if **u** and **v** are scalar multiples of each other.
>
> 4. $\|\mathbf{u} \times \mathbf{v}\|$ = area of parallelogram having **u** and **v** as adjacent sides.

Proof

Let $\mathbf{u} = u_1\mathbf{i} + u_2\mathbf{j} + u_3\mathbf{k}$, $\mathbf{v} = v_1\mathbf{i} + v_2\mathbf{j} + v_3\mathbf{k}$, and $\mathbf{0} = 0\mathbf{i} + 0\mathbf{j} + 0\mathbf{k}$.

1.

$$\mathbf{u} \times \mathbf{v} = (u_2v_3 - u_3v_2)\mathbf{i} - (u_1v_3 - u_3v_1)\mathbf{j} + (u_1v_2 - u_2v_1)\mathbf{k}$$

$$(\mathbf{u} \times \mathbf{v}) \cdot \mathbf{u} = (u_2v_3 - u_3v_2)u_1 - (u_1v_3 - u_3v_1)u_2 + (u_1v_2 - u_2v_1)u_3$$

$$= u_1u_2v_3 - u_1u_3v_2 - u_1u_2v_3 + u_2u_3v_1 + u_1u_3v_2 - u_2u_3v_1$$

$$= 0$$

$$(\mathbf{u} \times \mathbf{v}) \cdot \mathbf{v} = (u_2v_3 - u_3v_2)v_1 - (u_1v_3 - u_3v_1)v_2 + (u_1v_2 - u_2v_1)v_3$$

$$= u_2v_1v_3 - u_3v_1v_2 - u_1v_2v_3 + u_3v_1v_2 + u_1v_2v_3 - u_2v_1v_3$$

$$= 0$$

Because two vectors are orthogonal when their dot product is zero, it follows that $\mathbf{u} \times \mathbf{v}$ is orthogonal to both **u** and **v**.

2. Note that $\cos \theta = \dfrac{\mathbf{u} \cdot \mathbf{v}}{\|\mathbf{u}\|\|\mathbf{v}\|}$. Therefore,

$$\|\mathbf{u}\|\|\mathbf{v}\| \sin \theta = \|\mathbf{u}\|\|\mathbf{v}\|\sqrt{1 - \cos^2 \theta}$$

$$= \|\mathbf{u}\|\|\mathbf{v}\|\sqrt{1 - \frac{(\mathbf{u} \cdot \mathbf{v})^2}{\|\mathbf{u}\|^2\|\mathbf{v}\|^2}}$$

$$= \sqrt{\|\mathbf{u}\|^2\|\mathbf{v}\|^2 - (\mathbf{u} \cdot \mathbf{v})^2}$$

$$= \sqrt{(u_1^2 + u_2^2 + u_3^2)(v_1^2 + v_2^2 + v_3^2) - (u_1v_1 + u_2v_2 + u_3v_3)^2}$$

$$= \sqrt{(u_2v_3 - u_3v_2)^2 + (u_1v_3 - u_3v_1)^2 + (u_1v_2 - u_2v_1)^2}$$

$$= \|\mathbf{u} \times \mathbf{v}\|.$$

3. If **u** and **v** are scalar multiples of each other, then $\mathbf{u} = c\mathbf{v}$ for some scalar c.

$$\mathbf{u} \times \mathbf{v} = (c\mathbf{v}) \times \mathbf{v} = c(\mathbf{v} \times \mathbf{v}) = c(\mathbf{0}) = \mathbf{0}$$

If $\mathbf{u} \times \mathbf{v} = \mathbf{0}$, then $\|\mathbf{u}\|\|\mathbf{v}\|\sin \theta = 0$. (Assume $\mathbf{u} \neq \mathbf{0}$ and $\mathbf{v} \neq \mathbf{0}$.) So, $\sin \theta = 0$, and $\theta = 0$ or $\theta = \pi$. In either case, because θ is the angle between the vectors, **u** and **v** are parallel. Therefore, $\mathbf{u} = c\mathbf{v}$ for some scalar c.

4. The figure at the right is a parallelogram having **v** and **u** as adjacent sides. Because the height of the parallelogram is $\|\mathbf{v}\| \sin \theta$, the area is

$$\text{Area} = (\text{base})(\text{height})$$

$$= \|\mathbf{u}\|\|\mathbf{v}\| \sin \theta$$

$$= \|\mathbf{u} \times \mathbf{v}\|.$$

11 Limits and an Introduction to Calculus

Section 11.4, Example 3
Average Cost

11.1   Introduction to Limits

11.2   Techniques for Evaluating Limits

11.3   The Tangent Line Problem

11.4   Limits at Infinity and Limits of Sequences

11.5   The Area Problem

11.1 Introduction to Limits

The Limit Concept

The notion of a limit is a *fundamental* concept of calculus. In this chapter, you will learn how to evaluate limits and how they are used in the two basic problems of calculus: the tangent line problem and the area problem.

EXAMPLE 1   Finding a Rectangle of Maximum Area

Find the dimensions of a rectangle that has a perimeter of 24 inches and a maximum area.

Solution

Let w represent the width of the rectangle and let l represent the length of the rectangle. Because

$$2w + 2l = 24 \qquad \text{Perimeter is 24.}$$

it follows that

$$l = 12 - w$$

as shown in Figure 11.1. So, the area of the rectangle is

$$
\begin{aligned}
A &= lw & &\text{Formula for area} \\
&= (12 - w)w & &\text{Substitute } 12 - w \text{ for } l. \\
&= 12w - w^2. & &\text{Simplify.}
\end{aligned}
$$

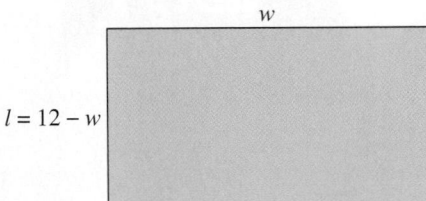

Figure 11.1

Using this model for area, you can experiment with different values of w to see how to obtain the maximum area. After trying several values, it appears that the maximum area occurs when $w = 6$, as shown in the table.

Width, w	5.0	5.5	5.9	6.0	6.1	6.5	7.0
Area, A	35.00	35.75	35.99	36.00	35.99	35.75	35.00

In limit terminology, you can say that "the limit of A as w approaches 6 is 36." This is written as

$$\lim_{w \to 6} A = \lim_{w \to 6} (12w - w^2) = 36.$$

So, the dimensions of a rectangle that has a perimeter of 24 inches and a maximum area are $w = 6$ inches and $l = 12 - 6 = 6$ inches, or 6×6 inches.

✓ **Checkpoint** ◀))) *Audio-video solution in English & Spanish at LarsonPrecalculus.com.*

Find the dimensions of a rectangle that has a perimeter of 52 inches and a maximum area.

What you should learn
- ▶ Understand the limit concept.
- ▶ Use the definition of a limit to estimate limits.
- ▶ Determine whether limits of functions exist.
- ▶ Use properties of limits to evaluate limits.

Why you should learn it
The concept of a limit is useful in applications involving maximization. For instance, in Exercise 5 on page 757, the concept of a limit is used to verify the maximum volume of an open box.

Definition of Limit

> **Definition of Limit**
>
> If $f(x)$ becomes arbitrarily close to a unique number L as x approaches c from either side, then the **limit** of $f(x)$ as x approaches c is L. This is written as
>
> $$\lim_{x \to c} f(x) = L.$$

EXAMPLE 2 **Estimating a Limit Numerically**

Use a table to estimate the limit: $\lim_{x \to 2} (3x - 2)$.

Solution

Let $f(x) = 3x - 2$. Then construct a table that shows values of $f(x)$ for two sets of x-values—one set that approaches 2 from the left and one that approaches 2 from the right.

x	1.9	1.99	1.999	2.0	2.001	2.01	2.1
$f(x)$	3.700	3.970	3.997	?	4.003	4.030	4.300

From the table, it appears that the closer x gets to 2, the closer $f(x)$ gets to 4. So, you can estimate the limit to be 4. Figure 11.2 adds further support to this conclusion.

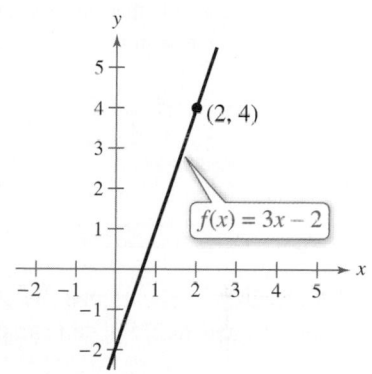

Figure 11.2

✓ **Checkpoint** ◀))) *Audio-video solution in English & Spanish at LarsonPrecalculus.com.*

Use a table to estimate the limit: $\lim_{x \to 3} (3 - 2x)$.

In Figure 11.2, note that the graph of $f(x) = 3x - 2$ is continuous. For graphs that are not continuous, finding a limit can be more difficult.

EXAMPLE 3 **Estimating a Limit Numerically**

Use a table to estimate the limit: $\lim_{x \to 0} \dfrac{x}{\sqrt{x+1} - 1}$.

Solution

Let $f(x) = x/\left(\sqrt{x+1} - 1\right)$. Then construct a table that shows values of $f(x)$ for two sets of x-values—one set that approaches 0 from the left and one that approaches 0 from the right.

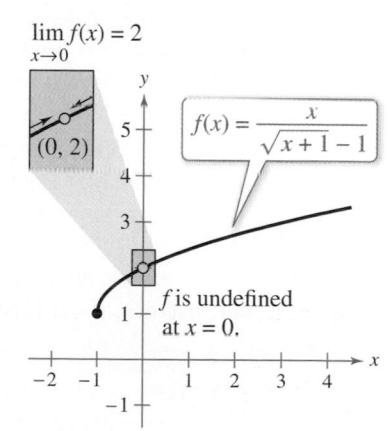

$$\lim_{x \to 0} f(x) = 2$$

f is undefined at $x = 0$.

Figure 11.3

x	-0.01	-0.001	-0.0001	0	0.0001	0.001	0.01
$f(x)$	1.99499	1.99949	1.99995	?	2.00005	2.00050	2.00499

From the table, it appears that the limit is 2. This limit is reinforced by the graph of f (see Figure 11.3).

✓ **Checkpoint** ◀))) *Audio-video solution in English & Spanish at LarsonPrecalculus.com.*

Use a table to estimate the limit: $\lim_{x \to 1} \dfrac{x - 1}{x^2 + 3x - 4}$.

In Example 3, note that $f(x)$ has a limit as x approaches 0 even though the function is not defined at $x = 0$. This often happens, and it is important to realize that *the existence or nonexistence of $f(x)$ at $x = c$ has no bearing on the existence of the limit of $f(x)$ as x approaches c.*

EXAMPLE 4   Using a Graphing Utility to Estimate a Limit

Estimate the limit: $\lim\limits_{x \to 1} \dfrac{x^3 - x^2 + x - 1}{x - 1}$.

Numerical Solution

Let $f(x) = (x^3 - x^2 + x - 1)/(x - 1)$.

Create a table that shows values of $f(x)$ for several x-values near 1.

X	Y1
.997	1.994
.998	1.996
.999	1.998
1	ERROR
1.001	2.002
1.002	2.004
1.003	2.006

X=1

From the figure, it appears that the closer x gets to 1, the closer $f(x)$ gets to 2. So, you can estimate the limit to be 2.

Graphical Solution

Use a graphing utility to graph

$$f(x) = (x^3 - x^2 + x - 1)/(x - 1)$$

using a *decimal* setting, as shown in the figure.

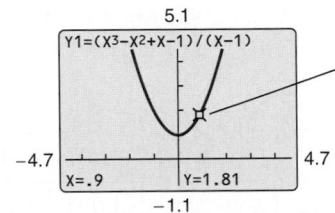

Y1=(X3-X2+X-1)/(X-1)

Use the *trace* feature to determine that as x gets closer and closer to 1, $f(x)$ gets closer and closer to 2 from the left and from the right.

From the figure, you can estimate the limit to be 2. As you use the *trace* feature, notice that there is no value given for y when $x = 1$, and that there is a hole or break in the graph at $x = 1$.

✓ **Checkpoint** ◀))) Audio-video solution in English & Spanish at LarsonPrecalculus.com.

Estimate the limit: $\lim\limits_{x \to 2} \dfrac{x^3 - 2x^2 + 3x - 6}{x - 2}$.

EXAMPLE 5   Using a Graph to Find a Limit

Find the limit of $f(x)$ as x approaches 3, where

$$f(x) = \begin{cases} 2, & x \neq 3 \\ 0, & x = 3 \end{cases}.$$

Solution

Because $f(x) = 2$ for all x other than $x = 3$ and because the value of $f(3)$ is immaterial, it follows that the limit is 2 (see Figure 11.4). So, you can write

$$\lim\limits_{x \to 3} f(x) = 2.$$

The fact that $f(3) = 0$ has no bearing on the existence or value of the limit as x approaches 3. For instance, if the function were defined as

$$f(x) = \begin{cases} 2, & x \neq 3 \\ 4, & x = 3 \end{cases}$$

then the limit as x approaches 3 would be the same.

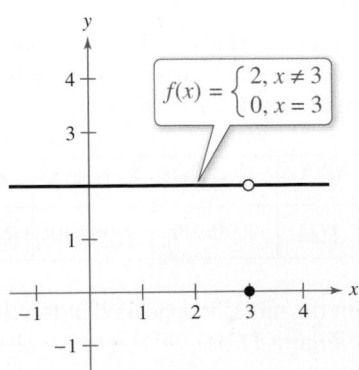

$$f(x) = \begin{cases} 2, x \neq 3 \\ 0, x = 3 \end{cases}$$

Figure 11.4

✓ **Checkpoint** ◀))) Audio-video solution in English & Spanish at LarsonPrecalculus.com.

Find the limit of $f(x)$ as x approaches 2, where

$$f(x) = \begin{cases} -3, & x \neq 2 \\ 0, & x = 2 \end{cases}.$$

Limits That Fail to Exist

In the next three examples, you will examine some limits that fail to exist.

EXAMPLE 6   **Comparing Left and Right Behavior**

Show that the limit does not exist.

$$\lim_{x \to 0} \frac{|x|}{x}$$

Solution

Consider the graph of the function given by $f(x) = |x|/x$. In the figure, you can see that for positive x-values

$$\frac{|x|}{x} = 1, \quad x > 0$$

and for negative x-values

$$\frac{|x|}{x} = -1, \quad x < 0.$$

This means that no matter how close x gets to 0, there will be both positive and negative x-values that yield $f(x) = 1$ and $f(x) = -1$. This implies that the limit does not exist.

✓ **Checkpoint** ◀))) *Audio-video solution in English & Spanish at LarsonPrecalculus.com.*

Show that the limit does not exist: $\displaystyle\lim_{x \to 1} \frac{2|x - 1|}{x - 1}$.

EXAMPLE 7   **Unbounded Behavior**

Discuss the existence of the limit: $\displaystyle\lim_{x \to 0} \frac{1}{x^2}$.

Solution

Let $f(x) = 1/x^2$. In Figure 11.5, note that as x approaches 0 from either the right or the left, $f(x)$ increases without bound. This means that by choosing x close enough to 0, you can force $f(x)$ to be as large as you want. For instance, $f(x)$ will be larger than 100 when you choose x that is within $\frac{1}{10}$ of 0. That is,

$$0 < |x| < \frac{1}{10} \implies f(x) = \frac{1}{x^2} > 100.$$

Similarly, you can force $f(x)$ to be larger than 1,000,000, as follows.

$$0 < |x| < \frac{1}{1000} \implies f(x) = \frac{1}{x^2} > 1,000,000$$

Because $f(x)$ is not approaching a unique real number L as x approaches 0, you can conclude that the limit does not exist.

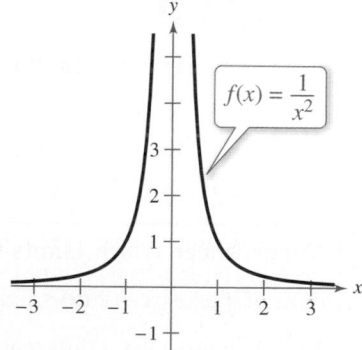

Figure 11.5

✓ **Checkpoint** ◀))) *Audio-video solution in English & Spanish at LarsonPrecalculus.com.*

Discuss the existence of the limit: $\displaystyle\lim_{x \to 0} \left(-\frac{1}{x^2} \right)$.

∎

EXAMPLE 8   Oscillating Behavior

See LarsonPrecalculus.com for an interactive version of this type of example.

Discuss the existence of the limit: $\lim\limits_{x \to 0} \sin \dfrac{1}{x}$.

Solution

Let $f(x) = \sin(1/x)$. In the figure, you can see that as x approaches 0, $f(x)$ oscillates between -1 and 1.

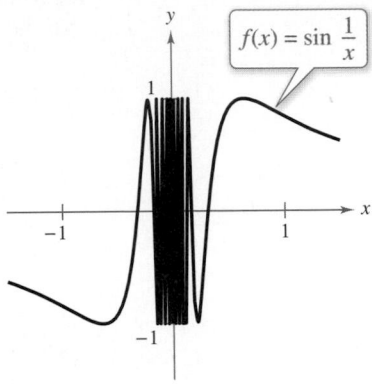

So, the limit does not exist because no matter how close you are to 0, it is possible to choose values of x_1 and x_2 such that

$$\sin \dfrac{1}{x_1} = 1 \quad \text{and} \quad \sin \dfrac{1}{x_2} = -1$$

as indicated in the table.

x	$\dfrac{2}{\pi}$	$\dfrac{2}{3\pi}$	$\dfrac{2}{5\pi}$	$\dfrac{2}{7\pi}$	$\dfrac{2}{9\pi}$	$\dfrac{2}{11\pi}$	$x \to 0$
$\sin \dfrac{1}{x}$	1	-1	1	-1	1	-1	Limit does not exist.

✓ **Checkpoint** 🔊))) *Audio-video solution in English & Spanish at LarsonPrecalculus.com.*

Discuss the existence of the limit: $\lim\limits_{x \to 1} \cos \dfrac{1}{x - 1}$.   ◼

Examples 6, 7, and 8 show three of the most common types of behavior associated with the *nonexistence* of a limit.

Conditions Under Which Limits Do Not Exist

The limit of $f(x)$ as $x \to c$ does not exist under any of the following conditions.

    1. $f(x)$ approaches a different number from the right   Example 6
        side of c than it approaches from the left side of c.

    2. $f(x)$ increases or decreases without bound as   Example 7
        x approaches c.

    3. $f(x)$ oscillates between two fixed values as   Example 8
        x approaches c.

Technology Tip

When using a graphing utility to investigate the behavior of a function near the x-value at which you are trying to evaluate a limit, remember that you cannot always trust the graphs that the graphing utility displays. For instance, consider the incorrect graph shown in Figure 11.6. The graphing utility cannot show the correct graph because $f(x) = \sin(1/x)$ has infinitely many oscillations over any interval that contains 0.

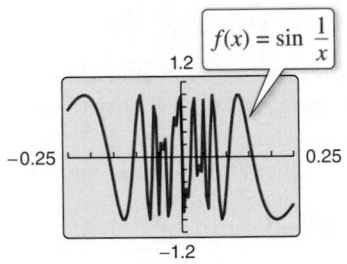

Figure 11.6

Properties of Limits

Sometimes, as in Example 2, the limit of $f(x)$ as $x \to c$ is simply $f(c)$. In such cases, it is said that the limit can be evaluated by **direct substitution.** That is,

$$\lim_{x \to c} f(x) = f(c). \qquad \text{Substitute } c \text{ for } x.$$

There are many "well-behaved" functions, such as polynomial functions and rational functions with nonzero denominators, that have this property. Some of the basic ones are included in the following list.

> ### Basic Limits
>
> Let b and c be real numbers and let n be a positive integer.
>
> 1. $\displaystyle\lim_{x \to c} b = b$
>
> 2. $\displaystyle\lim_{x \to c} x = c$
>
> 3. $\displaystyle\lim_{x \to c} x^n = c^n$ (See the proof on page 804.)
>
> 4. $\displaystyle\lim_{x \to c} \sqrt[n]{x} = \sqrt[n]{c},$ valid for all c when n is odd and valid for $c > 0$ when n is even

Trigonometric functions can also be included in this list. For instance,

$$\lim_{x \to \pi} \sin x = \sin \pi = 0 \quad \text{and} \quad \lim_{x \to 0} \cos x = \cos 0 = 1.$$

By combining the basic limits with the following operations, you can find limits for a wide variety of functions.

> ### Properties of Limits
>
> Let b and c be real numbers, let n be a positive integer, and let f and g be functions with the following limits.
>
> $$\lim_{x \to c} f(x) = L \quad \text{and} \quad \lim_{x \to c} g(x) = K$$
>
> 1. Scalar multiple: $\displaystyle\lim_{x \to c} [b\, f(x)] = bL$
>
> 2. Sum or difference: $\displaystyle\lim_{x \to c} [f(x) \pm g(x)] = L \pm K$
>
> 3. Product: $\displaystyle\lim_{x \to c} [f(x)g(x)] = LK$
>
> 4. Quotient: $\displaystyle\lim_{x \to c} \frac{f(x)}{g(x)} = \frac{L}{K},$ provided $K \neq 0$
>
> 5. Power: $\displaystyle\lim_{x \to c} [f(x)]^n = L^n$

Explore the Concept

Use a graphing utility to graph the tangent function. What are $\lim_{x \to 0} \tan x$ and $\lim_{x \to \pi/4} \tan x$? What can you say about the existence of the limit $\lim_{x \to \pi/2} \tan x$?

Technology Tip

When evaluating limits, remember that there are several ways to solve most problems. Often, a problem can be solved *numerically*, *graphically*, or *algebraically*. You can use a graphing utility to confirm the limits in the examples and in the exercise set numerically using the *table* feature or graphically using the *zoom* and *trace* features.

EXAMPLE 9   Basic Limits and Properties of Limits

a. $\lim\limits_{x \to 4} x^2 = (4)^2 = 16$ Use direct substitution.

b. $\lim\limits_{x \to 4} 5x = 5 \lim\limits_{x \to 4} x = 5(4) = 20$ Scalar Multiple Property

c. $\lim\limits_{x \to \pi} \dfrac{\tan x}{x} = \dfrac{\lim\limits_{x \to \pi} \tan x}{\lim\limits_{x \to \pi} x} = \dfrac{0}{\pi} = 0$ Quotient Property

d. $\lim\limits_{x \to 9} \sqrt{x} = \sqrt{9} = 3$ Use direct substitution.

e. $\lim\limits_{x \to \pi} (x \cos x) = (\lim\limits_{x \to \pi} x)(\lim\limits_{x \to \pi} \cos x) = \pi(\cos \pi) = -\pi$ Product Property

f. $\lim\limits_{x \to 3} (x + 4)^2 = \left[(\lim\limits_{x \to 3} x) + (\lim\limits_{x \to 3} 4) \right]^2$ Sum and Power Properties

$= (3 + 4)^2$

$= 49$

✓ **Checkpoint**))) *Audio-video solution in English & Spanish at LarsonPrecalculus.com.*

Find (a) $\lim\limits_{x \to 3} \dfrac{1}{4}$, (b) $\lim\limits_{x \to 3} x^3$, and (c) $\lim\limits_{x \to \pi} \dfrac{\cos x}{x}$. ■

The results of using direct substitution to evaluate limits of polynomial and rational functions are summarized as follows.

Limits of Polynomial and Rational Functions

1. If p is a polynomial function and c is a real number, then

$$\lim_{x \to c} p(x) = p(c).$$ (See the proof on page 804.)

2. If r is a rational function given by $r(x) = p(x)/q(x)$, and c is a real number such that $q(c) \neq 0$, then

$$\lim_{x \to c} r(x) = r(c) = \frac{p(c)}{q(c)}.$$

EXAMPLE 10   Limits of Polynomial and Rational Functions

Find (a) $\lim\limits_{x \to -1} (x^2 + x - 6)$ and (b) $\lim\limits_{x \to -1} \dfrac{x^2 + x - 6}{x + 3}$.

Solution

a. To evaluate the limit of a polynomial function, use direct substitution.

$$\lim_{x \to -1} (x^2 + x - 6) = (-1)^2 + (-1) - 6 = -6$$

b. The denominator is not 0 when $x = -1$, so you can evaluate the limit of the rational function using direct substitution.

$$\lim_{x \to -1} \frac{x^2 + x - 6}{x + 3} = \frac{(-1)^2 + (-1) - 6}{-1 + 3} = -\frac{6}{2} = -3$$

✓ **Checkpoint**))) *Audio-video solution in English & Spanish at LarsonPrecalculus.com.*

Find (a) $\lim\limits_{x \to 3} (x^2 - 3x + 7)$ and (b) $\lim\limits_{x \to 3} \dfrac{x^2 - 3x + 7}{x}$. ■

Explore the Concept

Sketch the graph of each function. Then find the limits of each function as x approaches 1 and as x approaches 2. What conclusions can you make?

a. $f(x) = x + 1$

b. $g(x) = \dfrac{x^2 - 1}{x - 1}$

c. $h(x) = \dfrac{x^3 - 2x^2 - x + 2}{x^2 - 3x + 2}$

Use a graphing utility to graph each function. Does the graphing utility distinguish among the three graphs? Write a short explanation of your findings.

Explore the Concept

Use a graphing utility to graph the function

$$f(x) = \frac{x^2 - 3x - 10}{x - 5}.$$

Use the *trace* feature to approximate $\lim\limits_{x \to 4} f(x)$. What do you think $\lim\limits_{x \to 5} f(x)$ equals? Is f defined at $x = 5$? Does this affect the existence of the limit as x approaches 5?

11.1 Exercises

See *CalcChat.com* for tutorial help and worked-out solutions to odd-numbered exercises.
For instructions on how to use a graphing utility, see Appendix A.

Vocabulary and Concept Check

In Exercises 1 and 2, fill in the blank.

1. If $f(x)$ becomes arbitrarily close to a unique number L as x approaches c from either side, then the _____ of $f(x)$ as x approaches c is L.

2. To find a limit of a polynomial function, use _____ .

3. Find the limit: $\lim\limits_{x \to 0} 3$.

4. List three conditions under which limits do not exist.

Procedures and Problem Solving

5. *Why you should learn it* (p. 750) You create an open box from a square piece of material, 24 centimeters on a side. You cut equal squares with sides of length x from the corners and turn up the sides.

   (a) Draw and label a diagram that represents the box.

   (b) Verify that the volume V of the box is given by $V = 4x(12 - x)^2$.

   (c) The box has a maximum volume when $x = 4$. Use a graphing utility to complete the table and observe the behavior of the function as x approaches 4. Use the table to find $\lim\limits_{x \to 4} V$.

x	3	3.5	3.9	4	4.1	4.5	5
V							

   (d) Use the graphing utility to graph the volume function. Verify that the volume is maximum when $x = 4$.

6. **Landscape Design** A landscaper arranges bricks to cover a region shaped like a right triangle with a hypotenuse of $\sqrt{18}$ meters and an area as large as possible.

   (a) Draw and label a diagram that shows the base x and height y of the triangle.

   (b) Verify that the area A of the triangle is given by $A = \frac{1}{2}x\sqrt{18 - x^2}$.

   (c) The triangle has a maximum area when $x = 3$ meters. Use a graphing utility to complete the table and observe the behavior of the function as x approaches 3. Use the table to find $\lim\limits_{x \to 3} A$.

x	2	2.5	2.9	3	3.1	3.5	4
A							

   (d) Use the graphing utility to graph the area function. Verify that the area is maximum when $x = 3$ meters.

Estimating a Limit Numerically In Exercises 7–10, complete the table and use the result to estimate the limit numerically. Determine whether the limit can be reached.

7. $\lim\limits_{x \to 2} (5x + 4)$

x	1.9	1.99	1.999	2	2.001	2.01	2.1
$f(x)$				?			

8. $\lim\limits_{x \to 0} (2x^2 + x - 4)$

x	-0.1	-0.01	-0.001	0	0.001
$f(x)$				?	

x	0.01	0.1
$f(x)$		

9. $\lim\limits_{x \to -1} \dfrac{x + 1}{x^2 - x - 2}$

x	-1.1	-1.01	-1.001	-1	-0.999
$f(x)$				?	

x	-0.99	-0.9
$f(x)$		

10. $\lim\limits_{x \to -2} \dfrac{x + 2}{x^2 - 4}$

x	-2.1	-2.01	-2.001	-2	-1.999
$f(x)$				?	

x	-1.99	-1.9
$f(x)$		

Using a Graphing Utility to Estimate a Limit In Exercises 11–26, use the *table* feature of a graphing utility to create a table for the function and use the result to estimate the limit numerically. Use the graphing utility to graph the corresponding function to confirm your result graphically.

11. $\lim\limits_{x \to -1} \dfrac{x^2 - 1}{x + 1}$

12. $\lim\limits_{x \to 2} \dfrac{4 - x^2}{x - 2}$

13. $\lim\limits_{x \to 1} \dfrac{x - 1}{x^2 + 2x - 3}$

14. $\lim\limits_{x \to -3} \dfrac{x + 3}{x^2 + x - 6}$

15. $\lim\limits_{x \to 6} \dfrac{\sqrt{x + 3} - 3}{x - 6}$

16. $\lim\limits_{x \to -3} \dfrac{\sqrt{1 - x} - 2}{x + 3}$

17. $\lim\limits_{x \to -4} \dfrac{\dfrac{x}{x + 2} - 2}{x + 4}$

18. $\lim\limits_{x \to 2} \dfrac{\dfrac{1}{x + 2} - \dfrac{1}{4}}{x - 2}$

19. $\lim\limits_{x \to 0} \dfrac{\sin x}{x}$

20. $\lim\limits_{x \to 0} \dfrac{\cos x - 1}{x}$

21. $\lim\limits_{x \to 0} \dfrac{\sin^2 x}{x}$

22. $\lim\limits_{x \to 0} \dfrac{-x}{\tan x}$

23. $\lim\limits_{x \to 0} \dfrac{e^{2x} - 1}{2x}$

24. $\lim\limits_{x \to 0} \dfrac{1 - e^{-4x}}{x}$

25. $\lim\limits_{x \to 2} \dfrac{\ln(2x - 3)}{x - 2}$

26. $\lim\limits_{x \to 1} \dfrac{\ln x^2}{x - 1}$

Using a Graph to Find a Limit In Exercises 27–32, graph the function and find the limit (if it exists) as x approaches 2.

27. $f(x) = \begin{cases} 3, & x \neq 2 \\ 1, & x = 2 \end{cases}$

28. $f(x) = \begin{cases} 5, & x \neq 2 \\ -4, & x = 2 \end{cases}$

29. $f(x) = \begin{cases} 2x + 1, & x < 2 \\ x + 3, & x \geq 2 \end{cases}$

30. $f(x) = \begin{cases} 2x - 3, & x < 2 \\ x^2 - 4x + 5, & x \geq 2 \end{cases}$

31. $f(x) = \begin{cases} -2x, & x \leq 2 \\ x^2 - 4x + 1, & x > 2 \end{cases}$

32. $f(x) = \begin{cases} -4x + 5, & x < 2 \\ x - 7, & x \geq 2 \end{cases}$

Using a Graph to Find a Limit In Exercises 33–42, use the graph to find the limit (if it exists). If the limit does not exist, explain why.

33. $\lim\limits_{x \to 0} (2 - x^2)$

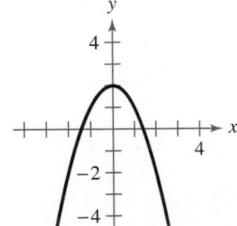

34. $\lim\limits_{x \to -2} \dfrac{x^2 - 4}{x + 2}$

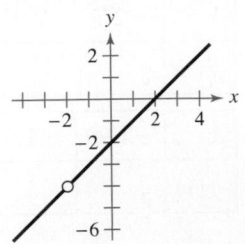

35. $\lim\limits_{x \to -2} \dfrac{|x + 2|}{x + 2}$

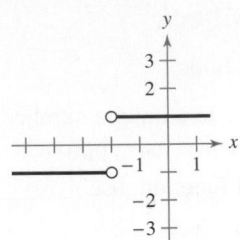

36. $\lim\limits_{x \to 3} \dfrac{x - 3}{|x - 3|}$

37. $\lim\limits_{x \to 1} \dfrac{1}{x - 1}$

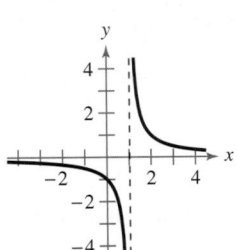

38. $\lim\limits_{x \to \pi/2} \sec x$

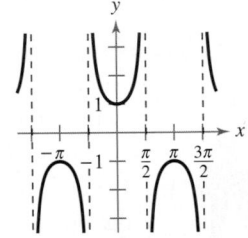

39. $\lim\limits_{x \to -1} \sin \dfrac{\pi x}{2}$

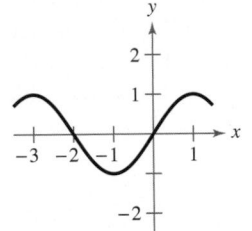

40. $\lim\limits_{x \to 1} \cos \pi x$

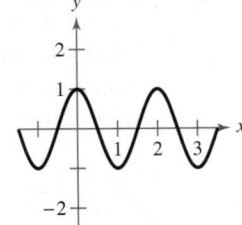

41. $\lim\limits_{x \to 0} 2 \cos \dfrac{\pi}{x}$

42. $\lim\limits_{x \to 0} \sin \dfrac{\pi}{x} + 1$

Determining Whether a Limit Exists In Exercises 43–50, use a graphing utility to graph the function and use the graph to determine whether the limit exists. If the limit does not exist, explain why.

43. $f(x) = \dfrac{5}{2 + e^{1/x}}$, $\lim\limits_{x \to 0} f(x)$

44. $f(x) = \dfrac{e^x - 1}{x}$, $\lim\limits_{x \to 0} f(x)$

45. $f(x) = \sin \pi x$, $\lim\limits_{x \to -1} f(x)$

46. $f(x) = \cos \dfrac{1}{x}$, $\lim\limits_{x \to 0} f(x)$

47. $f(x) = \dfrac{\sqrt{x+3}-1}{x-4}$, $\displaystyle\lim_{x\to 4} f(x)$

48. $f(x) = \dfrac{\sqrt{x+5}-4}{x-2}$, $\displaystyle\lim_{x\to 2} f(x)$

49. $f(x) = \ln(x+3)$, $\displaystyle\lim_{x\to 4} f(x)$

50. $f(x) = \ln(7-x)$, $\displaystyle\lim_{x\to -1} f(x)$

Using Properties of Limits **In Exercises 51 and 52, use the given information to evaluate each limit.**

51. $\displaystyle\lim_{x\to c} f(x) = 4$, $\displaystyle\lim_{x\to c} g(x) = 8$

  (a) $\displaystyle\lim_{x\to c} [-2g(x)]$ (b) $\displaystyle\lim_{x\to c} [f(x) + g(x)]$

  (c) $\displaystyle\lim_{x\to c} \dfrac{f(x)}{g(x)}$ (d) $\displaystyle\lim_{x\to c} \sqrt{f(x)}$

52. $\displaystyle\lim_{x\to c} f(x) = 3$, $\displaystyle\lim_{x\to c} g(x) = -1$

  (a) $\displaystyle\lim_{x\to c} [f(x) + g(x)]^2$ (b) $\displaystyle\lim_{x\to c} [6f(x)g(x)]$

  (c) $\displaystyle\lim_{x\to c} \dfrac{5g(x)}{4f(x)}$ (d) $\displaystyle\lim_{x\to c} \dfrac{1}{\sqrt{f(x)}}$

Evaluating Limits **In Exercises 53 and 54, find**
(a) $\displaystyle\lim_{x\to 2} f(x)$, **(b)** $\displaystyle\lim_{x\to 2} g(x)$, **(c)** $\displaystyle\lim_{x\to 2} [f(x)g(x)]$, **and**
(d) $\displaystyle\lim_{x\to 2} [g(x) - f(x)]$.

53. $f(x) = x^4$, $g(x) = \dfrac{\sqrt{x^2+5}}{2x^2}$

54. $f(x) = \dfrac{x}{3-x}$, $g(x) = \sin \pi x$

Evaluating a Limit by Direct Substitution **In Exercises 55–74, find the limit by direct substitution.**

55. $\displaystyle\lim_{x\to 5} (10 - x^2)$ **56.** $\displaystyle\lim_{x\to -2} \left(\tfrac{1}{2}x^3 - 5x\right)$

57. $\displaystyle\lim_{x\to -3} (2x^2 + 4x + 1)$ **58.** $\displaystyle\lim_{x\to -2} (x^3 - 6x + 5)$

59. $\displaystyle\lim_{x\to 4} \left(-\dfrac{8}{x}\right)$ **60.** $\displaystyle\lim_{x\to -5} \dfrac{6}{x+4}$

61. $\displaystyle\lim_{x\to -3} \dfrac{3x}{x^2+1}$ **62.** $\displaystyle\lim_{x\to 4} \dfrac{x-1}{x^2+2x+3}$

63. $\displaystyle\lim_{x\to -2} \dfrac{5x+3}{2x-9}$ **64.** $\displaystyle\lim_{x\to 3} \dfrac{x^2+1}{x}$

65. $\displaystyle\lim_{x\to -1} \sqrt{x+2}$ **66.** $\displaystyle\lim_{x\to 3} \sqrt[3]{x^2-1}$

67. $\displaystyle\lim_{x\to 0} \dfrac{2x+3}{\sqrt{x+16}}$ **68.** $\displaystyle\lim_{x\to 0} \dfrac{\sqrt{x+1}}{x-5}$

69. $\displaystyle\lim_{x\to 3} e^x$ **70.** $\displaystyle\lim_{x\to e} \ln x$

71. $\displaystyle\lim_{x\to \pi} \sin 2x$ **72.** $\displaystyle\lim_{x\to \pi} \tan x$

73. $\displaystyle\lim_{x\to 1/2} \arcsin x$ **74.** $\displaystyle\lim_{x\to 1/4} \arccos 2x$

Conclusions

True or False? **In Exercises 75 and 76, determine whether the statement is true or false. Justify your answer.**

75. The limit of a function as x approaches c does not exist when the function approaches -3 from the left of c and 3 from the right of c.

76. If f is a rational function, then the limit of $f(x)$ as x approaches c is $f(c)$.

77. Think About It From Exercises 7 to 10, select a limit that can be reached and one that cannot be reached.

  (a) Use a graphing utility to graph the corresponding functions using a standard viewing window. Do the graphs reveal whether the limit can be reached? Explain.

  (b) Use the graphing utility to graph the corresponding functions using a *decimal* setting. Do the graphs reveal whether the limit can be reached? Explain.

78. Think About It Use the results of Exercise 77 to draw a conclusion as to whether you can use the graph generated by a graphing utility to determine reliably when a limit can be reached.

79. Think About It

  (a) Given $f(2) = 4$, can you conclude anything about $\displaystyle\lim_{x\to 2} f(x)$? Explain your reasoning.

  (b) Given $\displaystyle\lim_{x\to 2} f(x) = 4$, can you conclude anything about $f(2)$? Explain your reasoning.

80. **HOW DO YOU SEE IT?** Use the graph of the function f to decide whether the value of the given quantity exists. If it does, find it. If not, explain why.

  (a) $f(0)$

  (b) $\displaystyle\lim_{x\to 0} f(x)$

  (c) $f(2)$

  (d) $\displaystyle\lim_{x\to 2} f(x)$

Cumulative Mixed Review

Simplifying Rational Expressions **In Exercises 81–86, simplify the rational expression.**

81. $\dfrac{5-x}{3x-15}$ **82.** $\dfrac{x^2-81}{9-x}$

83. $\dfrac{15x^2+7x-4}{15x^2+x-2}$ **84.** $\dfrac{x^2-12x+36}{x^2-7x+6}$

85. $\dfrac{x^3+27}{x^2+x-6}$ **86.** $\dfrac{x^3-8}{x^2-4}$

11.2 Techniques for Evaluating Limits

Dividing Out Technique

In Section 11.1, you studied several types of functions whose limits can be evaluated by direct substitution. In this section, you will study several techniques for evaluating limits of functions for which direct substitution fails. For instance, consider using direct substitution to find the limit

$$\lim_{x \to -3} \frac{x^2 + x - 6}{x + 3}.$$

The numerator and denominator are both 0 when $x = -3$, so direct substitution fails. By using a table, however, it appears that the limit of the function as x approaches -3 is -5.

x	-3.01	-3.001	-3.0001	-3	-2.9999	-2.999	-2.99
$\dfrac{x^2 + x - 6}{x + 3}$	-5.01	-5.001	-5.0001	?	-4.9999	-4.999	-4.99

Another way to find the limit of this function is shown in Example 1.

EXAMPLE 1 Dividing Out Technique

See LarsonPrecalculus.com for an interactive version of this type of example.

Find the limit.

$$\lim_{x \to -3} \frac{x^2 + x - 6}{x + 3}$$

Solution

Begin by factoring the numerator and dividing out any common factors.

$$\lim_{x \to -3} \frac{x^2 + x - 6}{x + 3} = \lim_{x \to -3} \frac{(x - 2)(x + 3)}{x + 3} \qquad \text{Factor numerator.}$$

$$= \lim_{x \to -3} \frac{(x - 2)\cancel{(x + 3)}}{\cancel{x + 3}} \qquad \text{Divide out common factor.}$$

$$= \lim_{x \to -3} (x - 2) \qquad \text{Simplify.}$$

$$= -3 - 2 \qquad \text{Direct substitution}$$

$$= -5 \qquad \text{Simplify.}$$

✓ **Checkpoint** *Audio-video solution in English & Spanish at LarsonPrecalculus.com.*

Find the limit: $\displaystyle \lim_{x \to 4} \frac{x^2 - 7x + 12}{x - 4}$.

The procedure for evaluating the limit shown in Example 1 is called the **dividing out technique.** The validity of this technique stems from the fact that when two functions agree at all but a single number c, they must have identical limit behavior at $x = c$. In Example 1, the functions given by

$$f(x) = \frac{x^2 + x - 6}{x + 3} \qquad \text{and} \qquad g(x) = x - 2$$

agree at all values of x other than $x = -3$. So, you can use $g(x)$ to find the limit of $f(x)$.

What you should learn

▶ Use the dividing out technique to evaluate limits of functions.
▶ Use the rationalizing technique to evaluate limits of functions.
▶ Use technology to approximate limits of functions graphically and numerically.
▶ Evaluate one-sided limits of functions.
▶ Evaluate limits of difference quotients from calculus.

Why you should learn it

Many definitions in calculus involve the limit of a function. For instance, in Exercises 61 and 62 on page 768, the definition of the velocity of a free-falling object at any instant in time involves finding the limit of a position function.

The dividing out technique should be applied only when direct substitution produces 0 in both the numerator *and* the denominator. An expression such as $\frac{0}{0}$ has no meaning as a real number. It is called an **indeterminate form** because you cannot, from the form alone, determine the limit. When you try to evaluate a limit of a rational function by direct substitution and encounter this form, you can conclude that the numerator and denominator must have a common factor. After factoring and dividing out, you should try direct substitution again.

EXAMPLE 2   Dividing Out Technique

Find the limit: $\displaystyle\lim_{x \to 1} \frac{x - 1}{x^3 - x^2 + x - 1}$.

Solution

Begin by substituting $x = 1$ into the numerator and denominator.

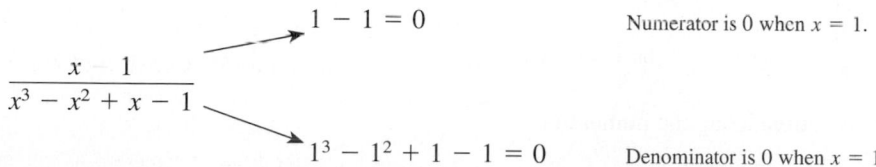

$1 - 1 = 0$ Numerator is 0 when $x = 1$.

$$\frac{x - 1}{x^3 - x^2 + x - 1}$$

$1^3 - 1^2 + 1 - 1 = 0$ Denominator is 0 when $x = 1$.

Because both the numerator and denominator are zero when $x = 1$, direct substitution will not yield the limit. To find the limit, you should factor the numerator and denominator, divide out any common factors, and then try direct substitution again.

$$\lim_{x \to 1} \frac{x - 1}{x^3 - x^2 + x - 1} = \lim_{x \to 1} \frac{x - 1}{(x - 1)(x^2 + 1)}$$ Factor denominator.

$$= \lim_{x \to 1} \frac{x - 1}{(x - 1)(x^2 + 1)}$$ Divide out common factor.

$$= \lim_{x \to 1} \frac{1}{x^2 + 1}$$ Simplify.

$$= \frac{1}{1^2 + 1}$$ Direct substitution

$$= \frac{1}{2}$$ Simplify.

This result is reinforced by the figure.

> ### Remark
>
> In Example 2, the factorization of the denominator can be obtained by dividing by $(x - 1)$ or by grouping as follows.
>
> $x^3 - x^2 + x - 1$
>
> $\qquad = x^2(x - 1) + (x - 1)$
>
> $\qquad = (x - 1)(x^2 + 1)$

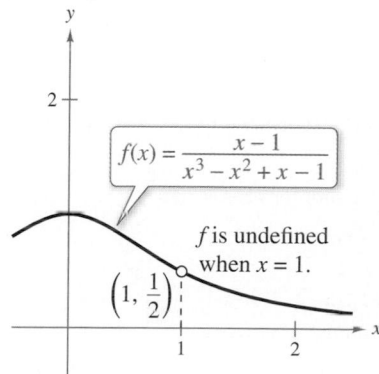

$f(x) = \dfrac{x - 1}{x^3 - x^2 + x - 1}$

f is undefined when $x = 1$.

$\left(1, \dfrac{1}{2}\right)$

✓ *Checkpoint*))) *Audio-video solution in English & Spanish at LarsonPrecalculus.com.*

Find the limit: $\displaystyle\lim_{x \to 7} \frac{x - 7}{x^3 - 7x^2 + 7x - 49}$.

Rationalizing Technique

Another way to find the limits of some functions is first to rationalize the numerator of the function. This is called the **rationalizing technique.** Recall that rationalizing the numerator means multiplying the numerator and denominator by the conjugate of the numerator. For instance, the conjugate of $\sqrt{x} + 4$ is $\sqrt{x} - 4$.

EXAMPLE 3   Rationalizing Technique

Find the limit.

$$\lim_{x \to 0} \frac{\sqrt{x+1} - 1}{x}$$

Solution

By direct substitution, you obtain the indeterminate form $\frac{0}{0}$.

$$\lim_{x \to 0} \frac{\sqrt{x+1} - 1}{x} = \frac{\sqrt{0+1} - 1}{0} = \frac{0}{0} \qquad \text{Indeterminate form}$$

In this case, you can rewrite the fraction by rationalizing the numerator.

$$\frac{\sqrt{x+1} - 1}{x} = \left(\frac{\sqrt{x+1} - 1}{x} \right) \left(\frac{\sqrt{x+1} + 1}{\sqrt{x+1} + 1} \right)$$

$$= \frac{(x+1) - 1}{x\left(\sqrt{x+1} + 1\right)} \qquad \text{Multiply.}$$

$$= \frac{x}{x\left(\sqrt{x+1} + 1\right)} \qquad \text{Simplify.}$$

$$= \frac{\cancel{x}}{\cancel{x}\left(\sqrt{x+1} + 1\right)} \qquad \text{Divide out common factor.}$$

$$= \frac{1}{\sqrt{x+1} + 1}, \quad x \neq 0 \qquad \text{Simplify.}$$

Now you can evaluate the limit by direct substitution.

$$\lim_{x \to 0} \frac{\sqrt{x+1} - 1}{x} = \lim_{x \to 0} \frac{1}{\sqrt{x+1} + 1} = \frac{1}{\sqrt{0+1} + 1} = \frac{1}{1+1} = \frac{1}{2}$$

You can reinforce your conclusion that the limit is $\frac{1}{2}$ by constructing a table, as shown below, or by sketching a graph, as shown in Figure 11.7.

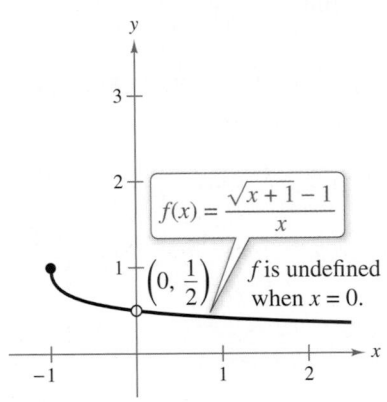

Figure 11.7

x	-0.1	-0.01	-0.001	0	0.001	0.01	0.1
$f(x)$	0.5132	0.5013	0.5001	?	0.4999	0.4988	0.4881

✔ **Checkpoint** 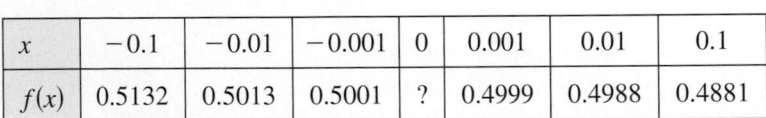 *Audio-video solution in English & Spanish at LarsonPrecalculus.com.*

Find the limit.

$$\lim_{x \to 0} \frac{1 - \sqrt{1 - x}}{x}$$

∎

The rationalizing technique for evaluating limits is based on multiplication by a convenient form of 1. In Example 3, the convenient form is

$$1 = \frac{\sqrt{x+1} + 1}{\sqrt{x+1} + 1}.$$

Using Technology

The dividing out and rationalizing techniques may not work well for finding limits of nonalgebraic functions. You often need to use more sophisticated analytic techniques to find limits of these types of functions.

EXAMPLE 4   Approximating a Limit Numerically

Approximate the limit: $\lim_{x \to 0} (1 + x)^{1/x}$.

Solution

Let $f(x) = (1 + x)^{1/x}$.

Create a table that shows values of f for several x-values near 0.

X	Y1
-.003	2.7224
-.002	2.721
-.001	2.7196
0	ERROR
.001	2.7169
.002	2.7156
.003	2.7142

X=0

Figure 11.8

Because 0 is halfway between -0.001 and 0.001 (see Figure 11.8), use the average of the values of f at these two x-values to estimate the limit.

$$\lim_{x \to 0} (1 + x)^{1/x} \approx \frac{2.7196 + 2.7169}{2} = 2.71825$$

The actual limit can be found algebraically to be

$e \approx 2.71828$.

✓ **Checkpoint** Audio-video solution in English & Spanish at LarsonPrecalculus.com.

Approximate the limit: $\lim_{x \to 0} \dfrac{e^x - 1}{x}$.

EXAMPLE 5   Approximating a Limit Graphically

Approximate the limit: $\lim_{x \to 0} \dfrac{\sin x}{x}$.

Solution

Direct substitution produces the indeterminate form $\frac{0}{0}$. To approximate the limit, begin by using a graphing utility to graph $f(x) = (\sin x)/x$, as shown in Figure 11.9. Then use the *zoom* and *trace* features of the graphing utility to choose a point on each side of 0, such as $(-0.0012467, 0.9999997)$ and $(0.0012467, 0.9999997)$. Because 0 is halfway between -0.0012467 and 0.0012467, use the average of the values of f at these two x-coordinates to estimate the limit.

$$\lim_{x \to 0} \frac{\sin x}{x} \approx \frac{0.9999997 + 0.9999997}{2} = 0.9999997$$

It can be shown algebraically that this limit is exactly 1.

✓ **Checkpoint** Audio-video solution in English & Spanish at LarsonPrecalculus.com.

Approximate the limit: $\lim_{x \to 0} \dfrac{1 - \cos x}{x}$.

Technology Tip

In Example 4, a graph of $f(x) = (1 + x)^{1/x}$ on a graphing utility would appear continuous at $x = 0$ (see below). But when you try to use the *trace* feature of a graphing utility to determine $f(0)$, no value is given. Some graphing utilities can show breaks or holes in a graph when an appropriate viewing window is used. Because the hole in the graph of f occurs on the y-axis, the hole is not visible.

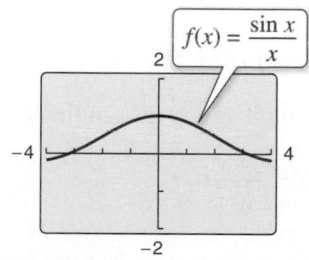
Y1=(1+X)^(1/X)
X=0   Y=

$f(x) = \dfrac{\sin x}{x}$

Figure 11.9

One–Sided Limits

In Section 11.1, you saw that one way in which a limit can fail to exist is when a function approaches a different value from the left side of c than it approaches from the right side of c. This type of behavior can be described more concisely with the concept of a **one-sided limit.**

$$\lim_{x \to c^-} f(x) = L_1 \text{ or } f(x) \to L_1 \text{ as } x \to c^- \qquad \text{Limit from the left}$$

$$\lim_{x \to c^+} f(x) = L_2 \text{ or } f(x) \to L_2 \text{ as } x \to c^+ \qquad \text{Limit from the right}$$

EXAMPLE 6   Evaluating One-Sided Limits

Find the limit as $x \to 0$ from the left and the limit as $x \to 0$ from the right for

$$f(x) = \frac{|2x|}{x}.$$

Solution

From the graph of f shown in the figure, you can see that $f(x) = -2$ for all $x < 0$.

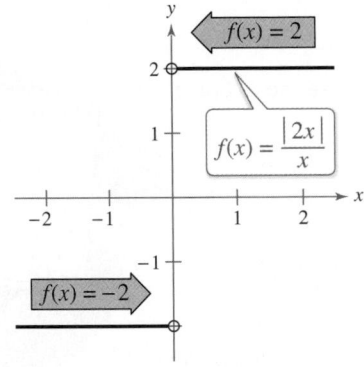

So, the limit from the left is

$$\lim_{x \to 0^-} \frac{|2x|}{x} = -2. \qquad \text{Limit from the left}$$

Because $f(x) = 2$ for all $x > 0$, the limit from the right is

$$\lim_{x \to 0^+} \frac{|2x|}{x} = 2. \qquad \text{Limit from the right}$$

✓ **Checkpoint** ◀))) *Audio-video solution in English & Spanish at LarsonPrecalculus.com.*

Find the limit as $x \to 3$ from the left and the limit as $x \to 3$ from the right for

$$f(x) = \frac{|x - 3|}{x - 3}.$$

In Example 6, note that the function approaches different limits from the left and from the right. In such cases, the limit of $f(x)$ as $x \to c$ does not exist. For the limit of a function to exist as $x \to c$, it must be true that both one-sided limits exist and are equal.

Existence of a Limit

If f is a function and c and L are real numbers, then $\lim_{x \to c} f(x) = L$ if and only if both the left and right limits *exist* and are *equal* to L.

EXAMPLE 7   Finding One-Sided Limits

Find the limit of $f(x)$ as x approaches 1.

$$f(x) = \begin{cases} 4 - x, & x < 1 \\ 4x - x^2, & x > 1 \end{cases}$$

Solution

Remember that you are concerned about the value of f *near* $x = 1$ rather than *at* $x = 1$. So, for $x < 1$, $f(x)$ is given by $4 - x$, and you can use direct substitution to obtain

$$\lim_{x \to 1^-} f(x) = \lim_{x \to 1^-} (4 - x) = 4 - 1 = 3.$$

For $x > 1$, $f(x)$ is given by $4x - x^2$, and you can use direct substitution to obtain

$$\lim_{x \to 1^+} f(x) = \lim_{x \to 1^+} (4x - x^2) = 4(1) - 1^2 = 3.$$

Because the one-sided limits both exist and are equal to 3, it follows that

$$\lim_{x \to 1} f(x) = 3.$$

The graph in Figure 11.10 confirms this conclusion.

Figure 11.10

✓ **Checkpoint** Audio-video solution in English & Spanish at LarsonPrecalculus.com.

Find the limit of $f(x)$ as x approaches -1.

$$f(x) = \begin{cases} -x^2 - 3x, & x < -1 \\ x + 3, & x > -1 \end{cases}$$

EXAMPLE 8   Comparing Limits from the Left and Right

To ship a package overnight, a delivery service charges \$24 for the first pound and \$4 for each additional pound or portion of a pound. Let x represent the weight of a package and let $f(x)$ represent the shipping cost. Show that the limit of $f(x)$ as $x \to 2$ does not exist.

$$f(x) = \begin{cases} 24, & 0 < x \le 1 \\ 28, & 1 < x \le 2 \\ 32, & 2 < x \le 3 \end{cases}$$

Solution

The graph of f is shown in the figure. The limit of $f(x)$ as x approaches 2 from the left is

$$\lim_{x \to 2^-} f(x) = 28$$

whereas the limit of $f(x)$ as x approaches 2 from the right is

$$\lim_{x \to 2^+} f(x) = 32.$$

Because these one-sided limits are not equal, the limit of $f(x)$ as $x \to 2$ does not exist.

✓ **Checkpoint** Audio-video solution in English & Spanish at LarsonPrecalculus.com.

In Example 8, show that the limit of $f(x)$ as $x \to 1$ does not exist.

A Limit from Calculus

In the next section, you will study an important type of limit from calculus—the limit of a *difference quotient*.

EXAMPLE 9 Evaluating a Limit from Calculus

For the function $f(x) = x^2 - 1$, find $\lim\limits_{h \to 0} \dfrac{f(3 + h) - f(3)}{h}$.

Solution

Direct substitution produces an indeterminate form.

$$\lim_{h \to 0} \frac{f(3 + h) - f(3)}{h} = \lim_{h \to 0} \frac{[(3 + h)^2 - 1] - [(3)^2 - 1]}{h}$$

$$= \lim_{h \to 0} \frac{9 + 6h + h^2 - 1 - 9 + 1}{h}$$

$$= \lim_{h \to 0} \frac{6h + h^2}{h}$$

$$= \frac{0}{0}$$

By factoring and dividing out, you obtain the following.

$$\lim_{h \to 0} \frac{f(3 + h) - f(3)}{h} = \lim_{h \to 0} \frac{6h + h^2}{h}$$

$$= \lim_{h \to 0} \frac{h(6 + h)}{h}$$

$$= \lim_{h \to 0} (6 + h)$$

$$= 6 + 0$$

$$= 6$$

So, the limit is 6.

✓ **Checkpoint** ◀))) *Audio-video solution in English & Spanish at LarsonPrecalculus.com.*

For the function $f(x) = 4x - x^2$, find $\lim\limits_{h \to 0} \dfrac{f(2 + h) - f(2)}{h}$.   ■

Note that for any *x*-value, the limit of a difference quotient is an expression of the form

$$\lim_{h \to 0} \frac{f(x + h) - f(x)}{h}.$$

Direct substitution into the difference quotient always produces the indeterminate form $\frac{0}{0}$. For instance,

$$\lim_{h \to 0} \frac{f(x + h) - f(x)}{h} = \frac{f(x + 0) - f(x)}{0}$$

$$= \frac{f(x) - f(x)}{0}$$

$$= \frac{0}{0}.$$

11.2 Exercises

See *CalcChat.com* for tutorial help and worked-out solutions to odd-numbered exercises. For instructions on how to use a graphing utility, see Appendix A.

Vocabulary and Concept Check

In Exercises 1 and 2, fill in the blank.

1. To find a limit of a rational function that has common factors in its numerator and denominator, use the _____ .

2. The expression $\frac{0}{0}$ has no meaning as a real number and is called an _____ because you cannot, from the form alone, determine the limit.

3. Which algebraic technique can you use to find $\lim\limits_{x \to 0} \dfrac{\sqrt{x+4}-2}{x}$?

4. Describe in words what is meant by $\lim\limits_{x \to 0^+} f(x) = -2$.

Procedures and Problem Solving

Using a Graph to Find Limits In Exercises 5–8, use the graph to find each limit (if it exists). Then identify another function that agrees with the given function at all but one point.

5. $g(x) = \dfrac{-2x^2 + x}{x}$

(a) $\lim\limits_{x \to 0} g(x)$

(b) $\lim\limits_{x \to -1} g(x)$

(c) $\lim\limits_{x \to -2} g(x)$

(d) $\lim\limits_{x \to 1} g(x)$

6. $h(x) = \dfrac{x^2 - 3x}{x}$

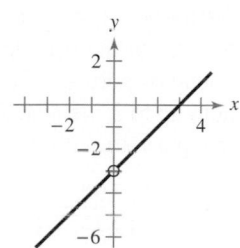

(a) $\lim\limits_{x \to -2} h(x)$

(b) $\lim\limits_{x \to 0} h(x)$

(c) $\lim\limits_{x \to 3} h(x)$

(d) $\lim\limits_{x \to 4} h(x)$

7. $g(x) = \dfrac{x^3 - x}{x - 1}$

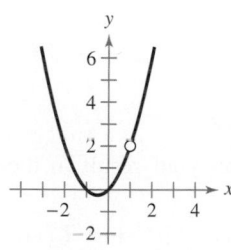

(a) $\lim\limits_{x \to 1} g(x)$

(b) $\lim\limits_{x \to -1} g(x)$

(c) $\lim\limits_{x \to 0} g(x)$

(d) $\lim\limits_{x \to -3} g(x)$

8. $f(x) = \dfrac{x^3 - 4x}{x + 2}$

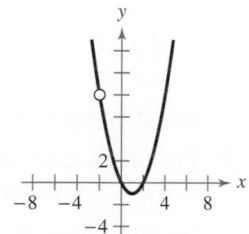

(a) $\lim\limits_{x \to 0} f(x)$

(b) $\lim\limits_{x \to -2} f(x)$

(c) $\lim\limits_{x \to 1} f(x)$

(d) $\lim\limits_{x \to 2} f(x)$

Finding a Limit In Exercises 9–36, find the limit (if it exists). Use a graphing utility to confirm your result graphically.

9. $\lim\limits_{x \to 6} \dfrac{x - 6}{x^2 - 36}$

10. $\lim\limits_{x \to 9} \dfrac{x - 9}{x^2 - 81}$

11. $\lim\limits_{x \to 2} \dfrac{x^2 - x - 2}{x - 2}$

12. $\lim\limits_{x \to -1} \dfrac{x^2 + 6x + 5}{x + 1}$

13. $\lim\limits_{x \to -1} \dfrac{1 - 2x - 3x^2}{1 + x}$

14. $\lim\limits_{x \to -3} \dfrac{3 - 5x - 2x^2}{3 + x}$

15. $\lim\limits_{t \to 2} \dfrac{t^3 - 8}{t - 2}$

16. $\lim\limits_{a \to -4} \dfrac{a^3 + 64}{a + 4}$

17. $\lim\limits_{x \to 2} \dfrac{x^5 - 32}{x - 2}$

18. $\lim\limits_{x \to 1} \dfrac{x^5 - 1}{x - 1}$

19. $\lim\limits_{x \to -4} \dfrac{x^2 + x - 12}{x^2 + 6x + 8}$

20. $\lim\limits_{x \to 3} \dfrac{x^2 - 8x + 15}{x^2 - 2x - 3}$

21. $\lim\limits_{x \to -1} \dfrac{x^3 + 2x^2 - x - 2}{x^3 + 4x^2 - x - 4}$

22. $\lim\limits_{x \to -3} \dfrac{x^3 + 2x^2 - 9x - 18}{x^3 + x^2 - 9x - 9}$

23. $\lim\limits_{y \to 0} \dfrac{\sqrt{5 + y} - \sqrt{5}}{y}$

24. $\lim\limits_{z \to 0} \dfrac{\sqrt{7 - z} - \sqrt{7}}{z}$

25. $\lim\limits_{x \to -3} \dfrac{\sqrt{x + 7} - 2}{x + 3}$

26. $\lim\limits_{x \to 2} \dfrac{4 - \sqrt{18 - x}}{x - 2}$

27. $\lim\limits_{x \to 0} \dfrac{\dfrac{1}{x + 1} - 1}{x}$

28. $\lim\limits_{x \to 0} \dfrac{\dfrac{1}{x - 8} + \dfrac{1}{8}}{x}$

29. $\lim\limits_{x \to 0} \dfrac{\dfrac{1}{x + 4} - \dfrac{1}{4}}{x}$

30. $\lim\limits_{x \to 0} \dfrac{\dfrac{1}{2 + x} - \dfrac{1}{2}}{x}$

31. $\lim\limits_{x \to \pi/2} \dfrac{1 - \sin x}{\cos x}$

32. $\lim\limits_{x \to 0} \dfrac{\cos x - 1}{\sin x}$

33. $\lim\limits_{x \to 0} \dfrac{\cos 2x}{\cot 2x}$

34. $\lim\limits_{x \to \pi} \dfrac{\sin x}{\csc x}$

35. $\lim\limits_{x \to \pi/2} \dfrac{\sin x - 1}{x}$

36. $\lim\limits_{x \to \pi} \dfrac{1 + \cos x}{x}$

Approximating a Limit Numerically In Exercises 37–42, use the *table* feature of a graphing utility to create a table for the function and use the result to approximate the limit numerically. Write an approximation that is accurate to three decimal places.

37. $\lim\limits_{x \to 0} \dfrac{e^{2x} - 1}{x}$

38. $\lim\limits_{x \to 0} \dfrac{1 - e^{-x}}{x}$

39. $\lim\limits_{x \to 1} \dfrac{x - 1}{\ln x}$

40. $\lim\limits_{x \to 2} \dfrac{-\ln(x - 1)}{x - 2}$

41. $\lim\limits_{x \to 0} (1 + x)^{3/x}$

42. $\lim\limits_{x \to 0} (1 + 2x)^{1/x}$

Approximating a Limit Graphically In Exercises 43–48, use a graphing utility to graph the function and approximate the limit. Write an approximation that is accurate to three decimal places.

43. $\lim\limits_{x \to 0} \dfrac{\sin 2x}{x}$

44. $\lim\limits_{x \to 0} \dfrac{\sin 3x}{x}$

45. $\lim\limits_{x \to 0} \dfrac{\tan x}{x}$

46. $\lim\limits_{x \to 0} \dfrac{1 - \cos 2x}{x}$

47. $\lim\limits_{x \to 1} \dfrac{1 - \sqrt[3]{x}}{1 - x}$

48. $\lim\limits_{x \to 1} \dfrac{\sqrt[3]{x} - x}{x - 1}$

Evaluating One-Sided Limits In Exercises 49–56, graph the function. Determine the limit (if it exists) by evaluating the corresponding one-sided limits.

49. $\lim\limits_{x \to 6} \dfrac{|x - 6|}{x - 6}$

50. $\lim\limits_{x \to 2} \dfrac{|x - 2|}{x - 2}$

51. $\lim\limits_{x \to -1} \dfrac{1}{x^3 + 1}$

52. $\lim\limits_{x \to 1} \dfrac{1}{x^2 - 1}$

53. $\lim\limits_{x \to 2} f(x)$ where $f(x) = \begin{cases} x - 1, & x \le 2 \\ 2x - 3, & x > 2 \end{cases}$

54. $\lim\limits_{x \to 1} f(x)$ where $f(x) = \begin{cases} 2x + 1, & x < 1 \\ x + 2, & x \ge 1 \end{cases}$

55. $\lim\limits_{x \to 1} f(x)$ where $f(x) = \begin{cases} 4 - x^2, & x \le 1 \\ 3 - x, & x > 1 \end{cases}$

56. $\lim\limits_{x \to 0} f(x)$ where $f(x) = \begin{cases} x^2 + 3, & x \le 0 \\ x + 5, & x > 0 \end{cases}$

Algebraic-Graphical-Numerical In Exercises 57–60, (a) graphically approximate the limit (if it exists) by using a graphing utility to graph the function, (b) numerically approximate the limit (if it exists) by using the *table* feature of the graphing utility to create a table, and (c) algebraically evaluate the limit (if it exists) by the appropriate technique(s).

57. $\lim\limits_{x \to 1^-} \dfrac{x - 1}{x^2 - 1}$

58. $\lim\limits_{x \to 5^+} \dfrac{5 - x}{25 - x^2}$

59. $\lim\limits_{x \to 16^+} \dfrac{4 - \sqrt{x}}{x - 16}$

60. $\lim\limits_{x \to 0^-} \dfrac{\sqrt{x + 2} - \sqrt{2}}{x}$

Why you should learn it (p. 760) In Exercises 61 and 62, use the position function

$$s(t) = -16t^2 + 128$$

which gives the height (in feet) of a free-falling object. The velocity at time $t = a$ seconds is given by

$$\lim\limits_{t \to a} \dfrac{s(a) - s(t)}{a - t}.$$

61. Find the velocity when $t = 1$ second.

62. Find the velocity when $t = 2$ seconds.

63. **Human Resources** A union contract guarantees a 3% salary increase yearly for 3 years. For a current salary of \$40,000, the salaries $f(t)$ (in thousands of dollars) for the next 3 years are given by

$$f(t) = \begin{cases} 40.000, & 0 < t \le 1 \\ 41.200, & 1 < t \le 2 \\ 42.436, & 2 < t \le 3 \end{cases}$$

where t represents the time in years. Show that the limit of f as $t \to 2$ does not exist.

64. **Business** The cost of sending a package overnight is \$17.95 for the first pound and \$1.20 for each additional pound or portion of a pound. A plastic mailing bag can hold up to 3 pounds. The cost $f(x)$ of sending a package in a plastic mailing bag is given by

$$f(x) = \begin{cases} 17.95, & 0 < x \le 1 \\ 19.15, & 1 < x \le 2 \\ 20.35, & 2 < x \le 3 \end{cases}$$

where x represents the weight of the package (in pounds). Show that the limit of f as $x \to 1$ does not exist.

65. **MODELING DATA**

The cost C (in dollars) of making x photocopies at a copy shop is given by the function

$$C(x) = \begin{cases} 0.20x, & 0 < x \le 9 \\ 0.15x, & 9 < x \le 99 \\ 0.10x, & 99 < x \le 999 \\ 0.08x, & x > 999 \end{cases}$$

(a) Sketch a graph of the function.

(b) Find each limit and interpret your result in the context of the situation.

   (i) $\lim\limits_{x \to 15} C(x)$ (ii) $\lim\limits_{x \to 98} C(x)$ (iii) $\lim\limits_{x \to 405} C(x)$

(c) Create a table of values to show numerically that each limit does not exist.

   (i) $\lim\limits_{x \to 9} C(x)$ (ii) $\lim\limits_{x \to 99} C(x)$ (iii) $\lim\limits_{x \to 999} C(x)$

(d) Explain how you can use the graph in part (a) to verify that the limits in part (c) do not exist.

66. MODELING DATA

The cost of hooking up and towing a car is $80 for the first mile and $3 for each additional mile or portion of a mile. A model for the cost C (in dollars) is $C(x) = 80 - 3[\![-(x - 1)]\!]$, where x is the distance in miles. (Recall from Section 1.3 that $f(x) = [\![x]\!] = $ the greatest integer less than or equal to x.)

(a) Use a graphing utility to graph C for $0 < x \le 10$.

(b) Complete the table and observe the behavior of C as x approaches 5.5. Use the graph from part (a) and the table to find $\lim\limits_{x \to 5.5} C(x)$.

x	5	5.3	5.4	5.5	5.6	5.7	6
$C(x)$				?			

(c) Complete the table and observe the behavior of C as x approaches 5. Does the limit of $C(x)$ as x approaches 5 exist? Explain.

x	4	4.5	4.9	5	5.1	5.5	6
$C(x)$				?			

Evaluating a Limit from Calculus In Exercises 67–74, find
$$\lim_{h \to 0} \frac{f(x + h) - f(x)}{h}.$$

67. $f(x) = 3x - 1$ **68.** $f(x) = 5 + 7x$

69. $f(x) = \sqrt{x}$ **70.** $f(x) = \sqrt{x - 2}$

71. $f(x) = x^2 - 3x - 6$ **72.** $f(x) = 4 - 2x - x^2$

73. $f(x) = \dfrac{1}{x + 2}$ **74.** $f(x) = \dfrac{1}{x - 1}$

Finding Limits In Exercises 75 and 76, state which limit can be evaluated by using direct substitution. Then evaluate or approximate each limit.

75. (a) $\lim\limits_{x \to 0} x^2 \sin x^2$ (b) $\lim\limits_{x \to 0} \dfrac{\sin x^2}{x^2}$

76. (a) $\lim\limits_{x \to 0} \dfrac{x}{\cos x}$ (b) $\lim\limits_{x \to 0} \dfrac{1 - \cos x}{x}$

Using Graphs to Find a Limit In Exercises 77–82, use a graphing utility to graph the function and the equations $y = |x|$ and $y = -|x|$ in the same viewing window. Use the graphs to find $\lim\limits_{x \to 0} f(x)$.

77. $f(x) = x \cos x$ **78.** $f(x) = |x \sin x|$

79. $f(x) = |x| \sin x$ **80.** $f(x) = |x| \cos x$

81. $f(x) = x \sin \dfrac{1}{x}$ **82.** $f(x) = x \cos \dfrac{1}{x}$

Conclusions

True or False? In Exercises 83 and 84, determine whether the statement is true or false. Justify your answer.

83. When your attempt to find the limit of a rational function yields the indeterminate form $\frac{0}{0}$, the numerator and denominator of the rational function have a common factor.

84. If $f(c) = L$, then $\lim\limits_{x \to c} f(c) = L$.

85. Think About It Sketch the graph of a function for which $f(2)$ is defined but the limit of $f(x)$ as x approaches 2 does not exist.

86. Think About It Sketch the graph of a function for which the limit of $f(x)$ as x approaches 1 is 4 but $f(1) \ne 4$.

87. Writing Consider the limit of the rational function $p(x)/q(x)$. What conclusion can you make when direct substitution produces each expression? Write a short paragraph explaining your reasoning.

(a) $\lim\limits_{x \to c} \dfrac{p(x)}{q(x)} = \dfrac{0}{1}$ (b) $\lim\limits_{x \to c} \dfrac{p(x)}{q(x)} = \dfrac{1}{1}$

(c) $\lim\limits_{x \to c} \dfrac{p(x)}{q(x)} = \dfrac{1}{0}$ (d) $\lim\limits_{x \to c} \dfrac{p(x)}{q(x)} = \dfrac{0}{0}$

88. HOW DO YOU SEE IT? For the function
$$f(x) = \begin{cases} 2x, & x \le 0 \\ x^2 + 1, & x > 0 \end{cases}$$
shown at the right, find each of the following limits. If the limit does not exist, then explain why.

(a) $\lim\limits_{x \to 0^-} f(x)$

(b) $\lim\limits_{x \to 0^+} f(x)$

(c) $\lim\limits_{x \to 0} f(x)$

Cumulative Mixed Review

Identifying a Conic from Its Equation In Exercises 89–92, identify the type of conic represented by the equation. Use a graphing utility to confirm your result.

89. $r = \dfrac{3}{1 + \cos \theta}$ **90.** $r = \dfrac{12}{3 + 2 \sin \theta}$

91. $r = \dfrac{6}{3 - 4 \sin \theta}$

92. $r = \dfrac{4}{4 + \cos \theta}$

11.3   The Tangent Line Problem

Tangent Line to a Graph

Calculus is a branch of mathematics that studies rates of change of functions. If you go on to take a course in calculus, you will learn that rates of change have many applications in real life.

Earlier in the text, you learned how the slope of a line indicates the rate at which a line rises or falls. For a line, this rate (or slope) is the same at every point on the line. For graphs other than lines, the rate at which the graph rises or falls changes from point to point. For instance, in Figure 11.11, the parabola is rising more quickly at the point (x_1, y_1) than it is at the point (x_2, y_2). At the vertex (x_3, y_3), the graph levels off, and at the point (x_4, y_4), the graph is falling.

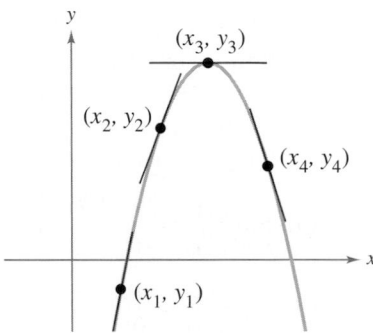

Figure 11.11

To determine the rate at which a graph rises or falls at a *single point,* you can find the slope of the tangent line at that point. In simple terms, the **tangent line** to the graph of a function f at a point

$$P(x_1, y_1)$$

is the line that best approximates the slope of the graph at the point. Figure 11.12 shows other examples of tangent lines.

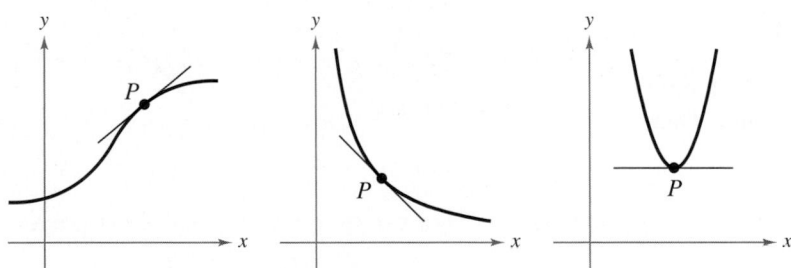

Figure 11.12

From geometry, you know that a line is tangent to a circle when the line intersects the circle at only one point (see Figure 11.13). Tangent lines to noncircular graphs, however, can intersect the graph at more than one point. For instance, in the first graph in Figure 11.12, if the tangent line were extended, then it would intersect the graph at a point other than the point of tangency.

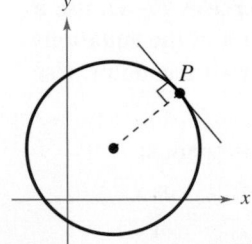

Figure 11.13

What you should learn
▶ Understand the tangent line problem.
▶ Use a tangent line to approximate the slope of a graph at a point.
▶ Use the limit definition of slope to find exact slopes of graphs.
▶ Find derivatives of functions and use derivatives to find slopes of graphs.

Why you should learn it
The derivative, or the slope of the tangent line to the graph of a function at a point, can be used to analyze rates of change. For instance, in Exercise 69 on page 779, the derivative is used to analyze the rate of change of the volume of a spherical balloon.

Slope of a Graph

Because a tangent line approximates the slope of a graph at a point, the problem of finding the slope of a graph at a point is the same as finding the slope of the tangent line at the point.

EXAMPLE 1 Visually Approximating the Slope of a Graph

Use Figure 11.14 to approximate the slope of the graph of $f(x) = x^2$ at the point $(1, 1)$.

Solution

From the graph of $f(x) = x^2$, you can see that the tangent line at $(1, 1)$ rises approximately two units for each unit change in x. So, you can estimate the slope of the tangent line at $(1, 1)$ to be

$$\text{Slope} = \frac{\text{change in } y}{\text{change in } x}$$

$$\approx \frac{2}{1}$$

$$= 2.$$

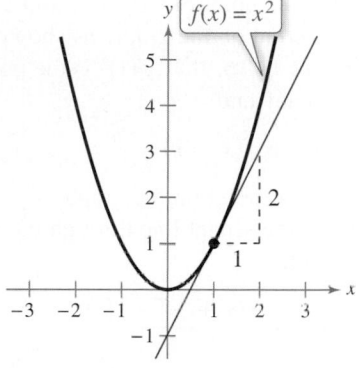

Figure 11.14

Because the tangent line at the point $(1, 1)$ has a slope of about 2, you can conclude that the graph of f has a slope of about 2 at the point $(1, 1)$.

✓ **Checkpoint** 🔊))) *Audio-video solution in English & Spanish at LarsonPrecalculus.com.*

Use Figure 11.14 to approximate the slope of the graph of $f(x) = x^2$ at the point $(2, 4)$.

▪

When you are visually approximating the slope of a graph, remember that the scales on the horizontal and vertical axes may differ. When this happens (as it frequently does in applications), the slope of the tangent line is distorted, and you must be careful to account for the difference in the scales.

EXAMPLE 2 Approximating the Slope of a Graph

Figure 11.15 graphically depicts the monthly normal temperatures (in degrees Fahrenheit) for Dallas, Texas. Approximate the slope of this graph at the indicated point and give a physical interpretation of the result.   (Source: National Climatic Data Center)

Solution

From the graph, you can see that the tangent line at the given point falls approximately 10 units for each one-unit change in x. So, you can estimate the slope at the given point to be

$$\text{Slope} = \frac{\text{change in } y}{\text{change in } x}$$

$$\approx \frac{-10}{1}$$

$$= -10 \text{ degrees per month.}$$

This means that you can expect the monthly normal temperature in November to be about 10 degrees lower than the normal temperature in October.

Monthly Normal Temperatures

Figure 11.15

✓ **Checkpoint** 🔊))) *Audio-video solution in English & Spanish at LarsonPrecalculus.com.*

In Example 2, approximate the slope of the graph at the point $(4, 65)$ and give a physical interpretation of the result.

▪

Slope and the Limit Process

In Examples 1 and 2, you approximated
the slope of a graph at a point by creating
a graph and then "eyeballing" the tangent
line at the point of tangency. A more
systematic method of approximating
tangent lines makes use of a **secant line**
through the point of tangency and a
second point on the graph, as shown
in Figure 11.16. If $(x, f(x))$ is the point
of tangency and

$$(x + h, f(x + h))$$

is a second point on the graph of f, then the
slope of the secant line through the two points
is given by

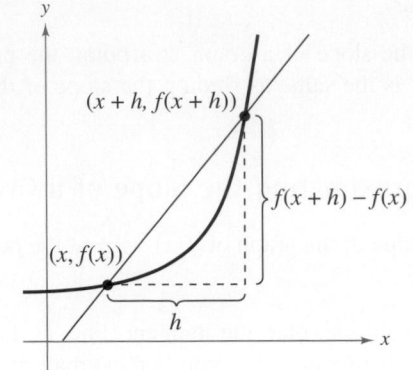

Figure 11.16

$$m_{\text{sec}} = \frac{f(x + h) - f(x)}{h}. \qquad \text{Slope of secant line}$$

The right side of this equation is called the **difference quotient.** The denominator h is
the *change in x*, and the numerator is the *change in y*. The beauty of this procedure is
that you obtain more and more accurate approximations of the slope of the tangent line
by choosing points closer and closer to the point of tangency, as shown in Figure 11.17.

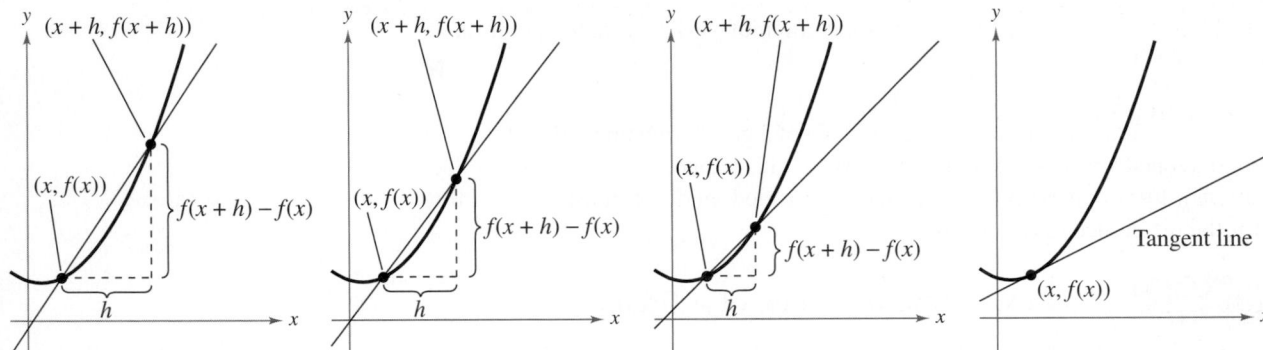

As h approaches 0, the secant line approaches the tangent line.
Figure 11.17

Using the limit process, you can find the *exact* slope of the tangent line at $(x, f(x))$.

Definition of the Slope of a Graph

The **slope** m of the graph of f at the point $(x, f(x))$ is equal to the slope of its
tangent line at $(x, f(x))$, and is given by

$$m = \lim_{h \to 0} m_{\text{sec}}$$

$$= \lim_{h \to 0} \frac{f(x + h) - f(x)}{h}$$

provided this limit exists.

From the definition above and from Section 11.2, you can see that the difference
quotient is used frequently in calculus. Using the difference quotient to find the slope
of a tangent line to a graph is a major concept of calculus.

EXAMPLE 3   Finding the Slope of a Graph

Find the slope of the graph of $f(x) = x^2$ at the point $(-2, 4)$.

Solution

Find an expression that represents the slope of a secant line at $(-2, 4)$.

$$m_{\text{sec}} = \frac{f(-2 + h) - f(-2)}{h} \qquad \text{Set up difference quotient.}$$

$$= \frac{(-2 + h)^2 - (-2)^2}{h} \qquad \text{Substitute into } f(x) = x^2.$$

$$= \frac{4 - 4h + h^2 - 4}{h} \qquad \text{Expand terms.}$$

$$= \frac{-4h + h^2}{h} \qquad \text{Simplify.}$$

$$= \frac{\cancel{h}(-4 + h)}{\cancel{h}} \qquad \text{Factor and divide out.}$$

$$= 4 + h, \quad h \neq 0 \qquad \text{Simplify.}$$

Next, take the limit of m_{sec} as h approaches 0.

$$m = \lim_{h \to 0} m_{\text{sec}} = \lim_{h \to 0} (-4 + h) = -4 + 0 = -4$$

The graph has a slope of -4 at the point $(-2, 4)$, as shown in Figure 11.18.

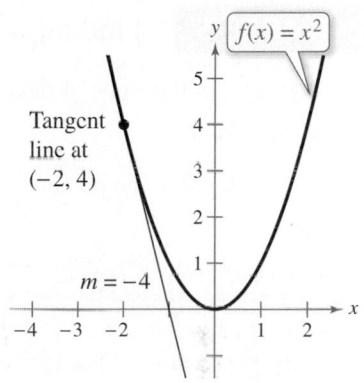

Figure 11.18

✓ **Checkpoint** ◀))) *Audio-video solution in English & Spanish at LarsonPrecalculus.com.*

Find the slope of the graph of $g(x) = x^2 - 2x$ at the point $(3, 3)$.

EXAMPLE 4   Finding the Slope of a Graph

Find the slope of $f(x) = -2x + 4$.

Solution

$$m = \lim_{h \to 0} \frac{f(x + h) - f(x)}{h} \qquad \text{Set up difference quotient.}$$

$$= \lim_{h \to 0} \frac{[-2(x + h) + 4] - (-2x + 4)}{h} \qquad \text{Substitute into } f(x) = -2x + 4.$$

$$= \lim_{h \to 0} \frac{-2x - 2h + 4 + 2x - 4}{h} \qquad \text{Expand terms.}$$

$$= \lim_{h \to 0} \frac{-2\cancel{h}}{\cancel{h}} \qquad \text{Divide out.}$$

$$= -2 \qquad \text{Simplify.}$$

You know from your study of linear functions that the line given by

$$f(x) = -2x + 4$$

has a slope of -2, as shown in Figure 11.19. This conclusion is consistent with that obtained by the limit definition of slope, as shown above.

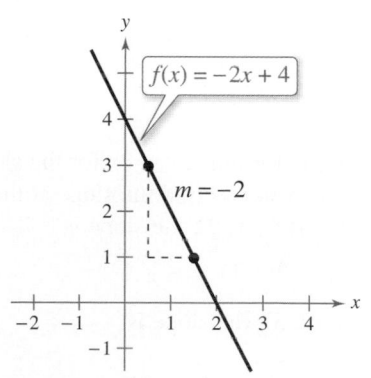

Figure 11.19

✓ **Checkpoint** ◀))) *Audio-video solution in English & Spanish at LarsonPrecalculus.com.*

Find the slope of $f(x) = -3x + 4$.

It is important that you see the difference between the ways the difference quotients were set up in Examples 3 and 4. In Example 3, you were finding the slope of a graph at a specific point $(c, f(c))$. To find the slope in such a case, you can use the following form of the difference quotient.

$$m = \lim_{h \to 0} \frac{f(c + h) - f(c)}{h}$$ Slope at specific point

In Example 4, however, you were finding a *formula* for the slope at *any* point on the graph. In such cases, you should use x, rather than c, in the difference quotient.

$$m = \lim_{h \to 0} \frac{f(x + h) - f(x)}{h}$$ Formula for slope

EXAMPLE 5   Finding a Formula for the Slope of a Graph

Find a formula for the slope of the graph of

$$f(x) = x^2 + 1.$$

What are the slopes at the points $(-1, 2)$ and $(2, 5)$?

Solution

$$m_{\text{sec}} = \frac{f(x + h) - f(x)}{h}$$ Set up difference quotient.

$$= \frac{[(x + h)^2 + 1] - (x^2 + 1)}{h}$$ Substitute into $f(x) = x^2 + 1$.

$$= \frac{x^2 + 2xh + h^2 + 1 - x^2 - 1}{h}$$ Expand terms.

$$= \frac{2xh + h^2}{h}$$ Simplify.

$$= \frac{\cancel{h}(2x + h)}{\cancel{h}}$$ Factor and divide out.

$$= 2x + h, \quad h \neq 0$$ Simplify.

Next, take the limit of m_{sec} as h approaches 0.

$$m = \lim_{h \to 0} m_{\text{sec}}$$

$$= \lim_{h \to 0} (2x + h)$$

$$= 2x + 0$$

$$= 2x$$

Using the formula $m = 2x$ for the slope at $(x, f(x))$, you can find the slope at the specified points. At $(-1, 2)$, the slope is

$$m = 2(-1) = -2$$

and at $(2, 5)$, the slope is

$$m = 2(2) = 4.$$

The graph of f is shown in the figure.

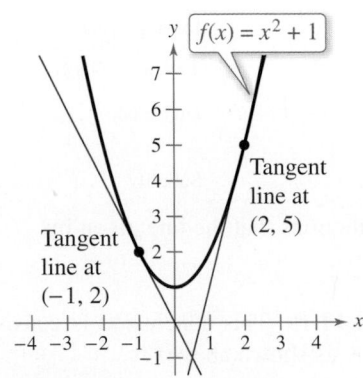

✓ *Checkpoint* 🔊))) *Audio-video solution in English & Spanish at LarsonPrecalculus.com.*

Find a formula for the slope of the graph of $f(x) = 2x^2 - 3$. What is the slope at the points $(-3, 15)$ and $(2, 5)$?

Technology Tip

To verify the result in Example 5, first use the point-slope form to find the tangent lines at $(-1, 2)$ and $(2, 5)$, which are $y = -2x$ and $y = 4x - 3$, respectively. Then use a graphing utility to graph the function and the tangent lines

$$y_1 = x^2 + 1$$

$$y_2 = -2x$$

$$y_3 = 4x - 3$$

in the same viewing window. You can also verify the result using the *tangent* feature. For instructions on how to use the *tangent* feature, see Appendix A; for specific keystrokes, go to this textbook's *Companion Website*.

The Derivative of a Function

In Example 5, you started with the function $f(x) = x^2 + 1$ and used the limit process to derive another function, $m = 2x$, that represents the slope of the graph of f at the point $(x, f(x))$. This derived function is called the **derivative** of f at x. It is denoted by $f'(x)$, which is read as "f prime of x."

Definition of the Derivative

The **derivative** of f at x is given by

$$f'(x) = \lim_{h \to 0} \frac{f(x + h) - f(x)}{h}$$

provided this limit exists.

Remember that the derivative $f'(x)$ is a formula for the slope of the tangent line to the graph of f at the point $(x, f(x))$.

> **Remark**
>
> In Section 1.1, you studied the slope of a line, which represents the *average rate of change* over an interval. The derivative of a function is a formula which represents the *instantaneous rate of change* at a point.

EXAMPLE 6   Finding a Derivative

See LarsonPrecalculus.com for an interactive version of this type of example.

Find the derivative of $f(x) = 3x^2 - 2x$.

Solution

$$f'(x) = \lim_{h \to 0} \frac{f(x + h) - f(x)}{h}$$

$$= \lim_{h \to 0} \frac{[3(x + h)^2 - 2(x + h)] - (3x^2 - 2x)}{h}$$

$$= \lim_{h \to 0} \frac{3x^2 + 6xh + 3h^2 - 2x - 2h - 3x^2 + 2x}{h}$$

$$= \lim_{h \to 0} \frac{6xh + 3h^2 - 2h}{h}$$

$$= \lim_{h \to 0} \frac{\cancel{h}(6x + 3h - 2)}{\cancel{h}}$$

$$= \lim_{h \to 0} (6x + 3h - 2)$$

$$= 6x + 3(0) - 2$$

$$= 6x - 2$$

So, the derivative of $f(x) = 3x^2 - 2x$ is

$$f'(x) = 6x - 2. \qquad \text{Derivative of } f \text{ at } x$$

✔ **Checkpoint** *Audio-video solution in English & Spanish at LarsonPrecalculus.com.*

Find the derivative of

$$f(x) = x^3 + 2x.$$

Note that in addition to $f'(x)$, other notations can be used to denote the derivative of $y = f(x)$. The most common are

$$\frac{dy}{dx}, \quad y', \quad \frac{d}{dx}[f(x)], \quad \text{and} \quad D_x[y].$$

> **Explore the Concept**
>
> Use a graphing utility to graph the function $f(x) = 3x^2 - 2x$. Use the *trace* feature to approximate the coordinates of the vertex of this parabola. Then use the derivative of $f(x) = 3x^2 - 2x$ to find the slope of the tangent line at the vertex. Make a conjecture about the slope of the tangent line at the vertex of an arbitrary parabola.

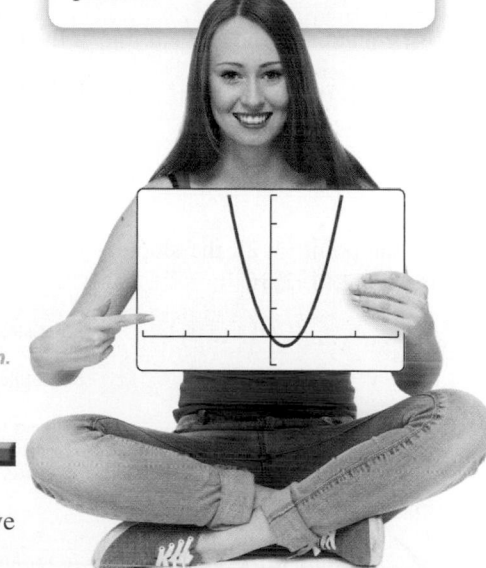

EXAMPLE 7   **Using the Derivative** ∫

See LarsonPrecalculus.com for an interactive version of this type of example.

Find $f'(x)$ for $f(x) = \sqrt{x}$. Then find the slopes of the graph of f at the points $(1, 1)$ and $(4, 2)$ and equations of the tangent lines to the graph at the points.

Solution

$$f'(x) = \lim_{h \to 0} \frac{f(x + h) - f(x)}{h}$$

$$= \lim_{h \to 0} \frac{\sqrt{x + h} - \sqrt{x}}{h}$$

Because direct substitution yields the indeterminate form $\frac{0}{0}$, you should use the rationalizing technique discussed in Section 11.2 to find the limit.

$$f'(x) = \lim_{h \to 0} \left(\frac{\sqrt{x + h} - \sqrt{x}}{h} \right) \left(\frac{\sqrt{x + h} + \sqrt{x}}{\sqrt{x + h} + \sqrt{x}} \right)$$

$$= \lim_{h \to 0} \frac{(x + h) - x}{h \left(\sqrt{x + h} + \sqrt{x} \right)}$$

$$= \lim_{h \to 0} \frac{h}{h \left(\sqrt{x + h} + \sqrt{x} \right)}$$

$$= \lim_{h \to 0} \frac{1}{\sqrt{x + h} + \sqrt{x}}$$

$$= \frac{1}{\sqrt{x + 0} + \sqrt{x}}$$

$$= \frac{1}{2\sqrt{x}}$$

> **Remark**
>
> Remember that to rationalize the numerator of an expression, you must multiply the numerator and denominator by the conjugate of the numerator.

At the point $(1, 1)$, the slope is

$$f'(1) = \frac{1}{2\sqrt{1}} = \frac{1}{2}.$$

An equation of the tangent line at the point $(1, 1)$ is

$$y - y_1 = m(x - x_1) \qquad \text{Point-slope form}$$

$$y - 1 = \tfrac{1}{2}(x - 1) \qquad \text{Substitute } \tfrac{1}{2} \text{ for } m, 1 \text{ for } x_1, \text{ and } 1 \text{ for } y_1.$$

$$y = \tfrac{1}{2}x + \tfrac{1}{2}. \qquad \text{Tangent line}$$

At the point $(4, 2)$, the slope is $f'(4) = \dfrac{1}{2\sqrt{4}} = \dfrac{1}{4}$. An equation of the tangent line at the point $(4, 2)$ is

$$y - y_1 = m(x - x_1) \qquad \text{Point-slope form}$$

$$y - 2 = \tfrac{1}{4}(x - 4) \qquad \text{Substitute } \tfrac{1}{4} \text{ for } m, 4 \text{ for } x_1, \text{ and } 2 \text{ for } y_1.$$

$$y = \tfrac{1}{4}x + 1. \qquad \text{Tangent line}$$

The graphs of f and the tangent lines at the points $(1, 1)$ and $(4, 2)$ are shown in Figure 11.20.

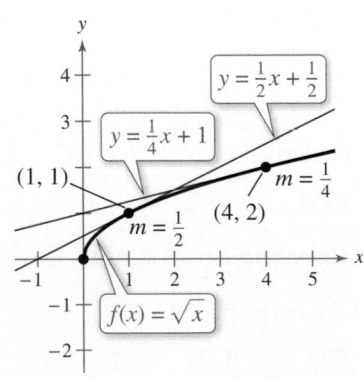

Figure 11.20

✓ **Checkpoint** ◄))) *Audio-video solution in English & Spanish at LarsonPrecalculus.com.*

Find the derivative of $f(x) = \sqrt{x - 1}$. Then find the slopes of the graph of f at the points $(2, 1)$ and $(10, 3)$ and equations of the tangent lines to the graph at the points.

11.3 Exercises

See *CalcChat.com* for tutorial help and worked-out solutions to odd-numbered exercises.
For instructions on how to use a graphing utility, see Appendix A.

Vocabulary and Concept Check

In Exercises 1–4, fill in the blank.

1. _____ is the study of the rates of change of functions.

2. The _____ to the graph of a function at a point is the line that best approximates the slope of the graph at the point.

3. To approximate a tangent line to a graph, you can make use of a _____ through the point of tangency and a second point on the graph.

4. The _____ of a function f at x represents the slope of the graph of f at the point $(x, f(x))$.

5. The slope of the tangent line to the graph of f at the point $(1, 5)$ is 2. What is the slope of the graph of f at the point $(1, 5)$?

6. Given $f(1) = 2$ and $f'(1) = -4$, what is the slope of the graph of f at the point $(1, 2)$?

Procedures and Problem Solving

Approximating the Slope of a Graph   In Exercises 7–10, use the figure to approximate the slope of the graph at the point (x, y).

7.

8.

9.

10.

Finding the Slope of a Graph   In Exercises 11–18, use the limit process to find the slope of the graph of the function at the specified point. Use a graphing utility to confirm your result.

11. $g(x) = x^2 - 4x$, $(3, -3)$

12. $f(x) = 10x - 2x^2$, $(3, 12)$

13. $g(x) = 11 - 6x$, $(1, 5)$

14. $h(x) = 5x + 9$, $(-1, 4)$

15. $g(x) = \dfrac{3}{x}$, $\left(2, \dfrac{3}{2}\right)$

16. $g(x) = \dfrac{1}{x - 2}$, $\left(4, \dfrac{1}{2}\right)$

17. $h(x) = \sqrt{x + 2}$, $(14, 4)$

18. $h(x) = \sqrt{x + 10}$, $(-1, 3)$

Finding a Formula for the Slope of a Graph   In Exercises 19–24, find a formula for the slope of the graph of f at the point $(x, f(x))$. Then use it to find the slopes at the two specified points.

19. $f(x) = 4 - x^2$
   (a) $(2, 0)$
   (b) $(-4, -12)$

20. $f(x) = x^3 + 1$
   (a) $(-1, 0)$
   (b) $(2, 9)$

21. $f(x) = \dfrac{1}{x + 4}$
   (a) $\left(0, \dfrac{1}{4}\right)$
   (b) $\left(-2, \dfrac{1}{2}\right)$

22. $f(x) = \dfrac{1}{x + 2}$
   (a) $\left(0, \dfrac{1}{2}\right)$
   (b) $(-3, -1)$

23. $f(x) = \sqrt{x - 3}$
   (a) $(4, 1)$
   (b) $(12, 3)$

24. $f(x) = \sqrt{x - 4}$
   (a) $(5, 1)$
   (b) $(8, 2)$

Approximating the Slope of a Tangent Line   In Exercises 25–28, use a graphing utility to graph the function and the tangent line at the point $(1, f(1))$. Use the graph to approximate the slope of the tangent line.

25. $f(x) = x^2 - 3$

26. $f(x) = x^2 - 2x + 1$

27. $f(x) = \sqrt{2 - x}$

28. $f(x) = \sqrt{x + 3}$

Finding a Derivative   In Exercises 29–40, find the derivative of the function.

29. $f(x) = 9 - \dfrac{1}{3}x$

30. $f(x) = 6 - \dfrac{1}{2}x$

31. $f(x) = 2x^2 - 7x$

32. $f(x) = x^2 - 3x + 4$

33. $f(x) = 5$

34. $f(x) = -1$

35. $f(x) = \dfrac{1}{x^2}$

36. $f(x) = \dfrac{1}{x^3}$

37. $f(x) = \sqrt{x + 4}$

38. $f(x) = \sqrt{x + 1}$

39. $f(x) = \dfrac{1}{\sqrt{x - 9}}$

40. $f(x) = \dfrac{1}{\sqrt{x + 1}}$

Using the Derivative In Exercises 41–50, (a) find the slope of the graph of f at the given point, (b) find an equation of the tangent line to the graph at the point, and (c) graph the function and the tangent line.

41. $f(x) = x^2 - 1$, $(2, 3)$ **42.** $f(x) = x^2 + 3$, $(2, 7)$

43. $f(x) = x^3 - 2x$, $(1, -1)$

44. $f(x) = x^3 - 5x$, $(2, -2)$

45. $f(x) = x^2 + 5x + 6$, $(-4, 2)$

46. $f(x) = x^2 + 2x + 1$, $(-3, 4)$

47. $f(x) = \sqrt{x + 3}$, $(6, 3)$ **48.** $f(x) = \sqrt{x - 2}$, $(3, 1)$

49. $f(x) = \dfrac{1}{x + 5}$, $(-4, 1)$ **50.** $f(x) = \dfrac{1}{x - 3}$, $(4, 1)$

Graphing a Function Over an Interval In Exercises 51–54, use a graphing utility to graph f over the interval $[-2, 2]$ and complete the table. Compare the value of the derivative with a visual approximation of the slope of the graph.

x	-2	-1.5	-1	-0.5	0	0.5	1	1.5	2
$f(x)$									
$f'(x)$									

51. $f(x) = \frac{1}{2}x^2$ **52.** $f(x) = \frac{1}{4}x^3$

53. $f(x) = \sqrt{x + 3}$ **54.** $f(x) = \dfrac{x^2 - 4}{x + 4}$

Using the Derivative In Exercises 55–58, find the derivative of f. Use the derivative to determine any points on the graph of f at which the tangent line is horizontal. Use a graphing utility to verify your results.

55. $f(x) = x^2 - 4x + 3$ **56.** $f(x) = x^2 - 6x + 4$

57. $f(x) = 2x^3 - 8x$ **58.** $f(x) = x^3 + 3x$

Using the Derivative In Exercises 59–66, use the function and its derivative to determine any points on the graph of f at which the tangent line is horizontal. Use a graphing utility to verify your results.

59. $f(x) = x^4 - 2x^2$, $f'(x) = 4x^3 - 4x$

60. $f(x) = 3x^4 + 4x^3$, $f'(x) = 12x^3 + 12x^2$

61. $f(x) = 2\cos x + x$, $f'(x) = -2\sin x + 1$, over the interval $(0, 2\pi)$

62. $f(x) = x - 2\sin x$, $f'(x) = 1 - 2\cos x$, over the interval $(0, 2\pi)$

63. $f(x) = x^2 e^x$, $f'(x) = x^2 e^x + 2xe^x$

64. $f(x) = xe^{-x}$, $f'(x) = e^{-x} - xe^{-x}$

65. $f(x) = x \ln x$, $f'(x) = \ln x + 1$

66. $f(x) = \dfrac{\ln x}{x}$, $f'(x) = \dfrac{1 - \ln x}{x^2}$

67. MODELING DATA

The table shows the revenues y (in billions of dollars) for eBay from 2007 through 2013.   (Source: eBay, Inc.)

Year	Revenue, y (in billions of dollars)
2007	7.67
2008	8.54
2009	8.73
2010	9.16
2011	11.65
2012	14.07
2013	16.05

DATA — Spreadsheet at LarsonPrecalculus.com

(a) Use the *regression* feature of a graphing utility to find a quadratic model for the data. Let t represent the year, with $t = 7$ corresponding to 2007.

(b) Use the graphing utility to graph the model found in part (a). Estimate the slope of the graph when $t = 12$ and interpret the result.

(c) Find the derivative of the model in part (a). Then evaluate the derivative for $t = 12$.

(d) Write a brief statement regarding your results for parts (a) through (c).

68. MODELING DATA

The table shows the numbers N (in thousands) of books sold when the price per book is p (in dollars).

Price, p	Number of books, n (in thousands)
$10	900
$15	630
$20	396
$25	227
$30	102
$35	36

DATA — Spreadsheet at LarsonPrecalculus.com

(a) Use the *regression* feature of a graphing utility to find a quadratic model for the data.

(b) Use the graphing utility to graph the model found in part (a). Estimate the slopes of the graph when $p = \$15$ and $p = \$30$.

(c) Use the graphing utility to graph the tangent lines to the model when $p = \$15$ and $p = \$30$. Compare the slopes given by the graphing utility with your estimates in part (b).

(d) The slopes of the tangent lines at $p = \$15$ and $p = \$30$ are not the same. Explain what this means to the company selling the books.

69. *Why you should learn it* (p. 770) A spherical balloon is inflated. The volume V is approximated by the formula $V(r) = \frac{4}{3}\pi r^3$, where r is the radius.

(a) Find the derivative of V with respect to r.

(b) Evaluate the derivative when the radius is 4 inches.

(c) What type of unit would be applied to your answer in part (b). Explain.

70. Rate of Change An approximately spherical benign tumor is reducing in size. The surface area S is given by the formula $S(r) = 4\pi r^2$, where r is the radius.

(a) Find the derivative of S with respect to r.

(b) Evaluate the derivative when the radius is 3 millimeters.

(c) What type of unit would be applied to your answer in part (b)? Explain.

71. Vertical Motion A water balloon is thrown upward from the top of an 80-foot building with an initial velocity of 64 feet per second. The height or displacement s (in feet) of the balloon can be modeled by the position function $s(t) = -16t^2 + 64t + 80$, where t is the time in seconds since it was thrown.

(a) Find a formula for the instantaneous rate of change of the balloon.

(b) Find the average rate of change of the balloon after the first three seconds of flight. Explain your results.

(c) Find the time at which the balloon reaches its maximum height. Explain your method.

(d) Velocity is given by the derivative of the position function. Find the velocity of the balloon as it impacts the ground.

(e) Use a graphing utility to graph the model and verify your results for parts (a)–(d).

72. Vertical Motion A coin is dropped from the top of a 120-foot building. The height or displacement s (in feet) of the coin can be modeled by the position function $s(t) = -16t^2 + 120$, where t is the time in seconds since it was dropped.

(a) Find a formula for the instantaneous rate of change of the coin.

(b) Find the average rate of change of the coin after the first two seconds of free fall. Explain your results.

(c) Velocity is given by the derivative of the position function. Find the velocity of the coin as it impacts the ground.

(d) Find the time when the coin's velocity is -70 feet per second.

(e) Use a graphing utility to graph the model and verify your results for parts (a)–(d).

Conclusions

True or False? In Exercises 73 and 74, determine whether the statement is true or false. Justify your answer.

73. The slope of the graph of $y = x^2$ is different at every point on the graph of f.

74. A tangent line to a graph can intersect the graph only at the point of tangency.

75. Writing Consider the graph of a function f.

(a) Explain how you can use a secant line to approximate the tangent line at $(x, f(x))$.

(b) Explain how you can use the limit process to find the exact slope of the tangent line at $(x, f(x))$.

76. HOW DO YOU SEE IT? Match the function with the graph of its *derivative*. Explain your reasoning. [The graphs are labeled (i), (ii), (iii), and (iv).]

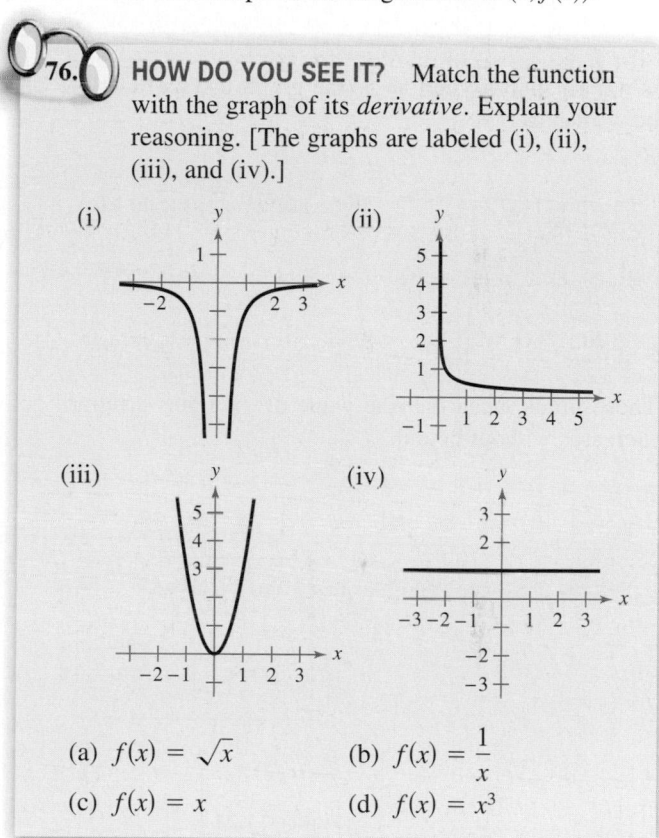

(a) $f(x) = \sqrt{x}$ (b) $f(x) = \dfrac{1}{x}$

(c) $f(x) = x$ (d) $f(x) = x^3$

77. Think About It Sketch the graph of a function whose derivative is always positive.

78. Think About It Sketch the graph of a function for which $f'(x) < 0$ for $x < 1$, $f'(x) \geq 0$ for $x > 1$, and $f'(1) = 0$.

Cumulative Mixed Review

Sketching the Graph of a Rational Function In Exercises 79 and 80, sketch the graph of the rational function.

79. $f(x) = \dfrac{1}{x^2 - x - 2}$ **80.** $f(x) = \dfrac{x - 2}{x^2 - 4x + 3}$

11.4   Limits at Infinity and Limits of Sequences

Limits at Infinity and Horizontal Asymptotes

As pointed out at the beginning of this chapter, there are two basic problems in calculus: finding **tangent lines** and finding the **area** of a region. In Section 11.3, you saw how limits can be used to solve the tangent line problem. In this section and the next, you will see how a different type of limit, a *limit at infinity*, can be used to solve the area problem. To get an idea of what is meant by a limit at infinity, consider the function

$$f(x) = \frac{x + 1}{2x}.$$

The graph of f is shown in Figure 11.21. From earlier work, you know that

$$y = \frac{1}{2}$$

is a horizontal asymptote of the graph of this function. Using limit notation, this can be written as

$$\lim_{x \to -\infty} f(x) = \frac{1}{2} \qquad \text{Horizontal asymptote to the left}$$

and

$$\lim_{x \to \infty} f(x) = \frac{1}{2}. \qquad \text{Horizontal asymptote to the right}$$

These limits mean that the value of $f(x)$ gets arbitrarily close to $\frac{1}{2}$ as x decreases or increases without bound.

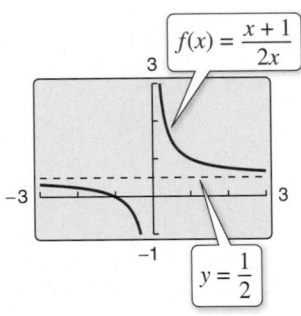

Figure 11.21

Definition of Limits at Infinity

If f is a function and L_1 and L_2 are real numbers, then the statements

$$\lim_{x \to -\infty} f(x) = L_1 \qquad \text{Limit as } x \text{ approaches } -\infty$$

and

$$\lim_{x \to \infty} f(x) = L_2 \qquad \text{Limit as } x \text{ approaches } \infty$$

denote the **limits at infinity.** The first statement is read *"the limit of $f(x)$ as x approaches $-\infty$ is L_1,"* and the second is read *"the limit of $f(x)$ as x approaches ∞ is L_2."*

To help evaluate limits at infinity, you can use the following definition.

> **Limits at Infinity**
>
> If r is a positive real number, then
>
> $$\lim_{x \to \infty} \frac{1}{x^r} = 0. \qquad \text{Limit toward the right}$$
>
> Furthermore, if x^r is defined when $x < 0$, then
>
> $$\lim_{x \to -\infty} \frac{1}{x^r} = 0. \qquad \text{Limit toward the left}$$

Explore the Concept

Use a graphing utility to graph the two functions given by

$$y_1 = \frac{1}{\sqrt{x}} \quad \text{and} \quad y_2 = \frac{1}{\sqrt[3]{x}}$$

in the same viewing window. Why doesn't y_1 appear to the left of the y-axis? How does this relate to the statement at the left about the infinite limit

$$\lim_{x \to -\infty} \frac{1}{x^r}?$$

Limits at infinity share many of the properties of limits listed in Section 11.1. Some of these properties are demonstrated in the next example.

EXAMPLE 1 Evaluating a Limit at Infinity

Find the limit: $\displaystyle \lim_{x \to \infty} \left(4 - \frac{3}{x^2} \right)$.

Algebraic Solution

Use the properties of limits listed in Section 11.1.

$$\lim_{x \to \infty} \left(4 - \frac{3}{x^2} \right) = \lim_{x \to \infty} 4 - \lim_{x \to \infty} \frac{3}{x^2}$$

$$= \lim_{x \to \infty} 4 - 3 \left(\lim_{x \to \infty} \frac{1}{x^2} \right)$$

$$= 4 - 3(0)$$

$$= 4$$

So, the limit of

$$f(x) = 4 - \frac{3}{x^2}$$

as x approaches ∞ is 4.

Graphical Solution

Use a graphing utility to graph

$$y = 4 - \frac{3}{x^2}.$$

Use the *trace* feature to determine that as x increases, y gets closer to 4.

Figure 11.22

From Figure 11.22, you can estimate the limit to be 4. Note in the figure that the line $y = 4$ is a horizontal asymptote to the right.

✓ **Checkpoint** ◀))) *Audio-video solution in English & Spanish at LarsonPrecalculus.com.*

Find the limit: $\displaystyle \lim_{x \to \infty} \frac{2}{x^2}$. ∎

In Figure 11.22, it appears that the line $y = 4$ is also a horizontal asymptote *to the left*. You can verify this by showing that

$$\lim_{x \to -\infty} \left(4 - \frac{3}{x^2} \right) = 4.$$

The graph of a rational function does not need to have a horizontal asymptote. When it does, however, its left and right asymptotes must be the same.

When evaluating limits at infinity for more complicated rational functions, divide the numerator and denominator by the *highest-powered term* in the denominator. This enables you to evaluate each limit using the limits at infinity at the top of this page.

EXAMPLE 2   Comparing Limits at Infinity

See LarsonPrecalculus.com for an interactive version of this type of example.

Find the limit as x approaches ∞ (if possible) for each function.

a. $f(x) = \dfrac{-2x + 3}{3x^2 + 1}$

b. $f(x) = \dfrac{-2x^2 + 3}{3x^2 + 1}$

c. $f(x) = \dfrac{-2x^3 + 3}{3x^2 + 1}$

Solution

In each case, begin by dividing both the numerator and denominator by x^2, the highest-powered term in the denominator.

a. $\displaystyle\lim_{x\to\infty} \frac{-2x + 3}{3x^2 + 1} = \lim_{x\to\infty} \frac{-\dfrac{2}{x} + \dfrac{3}{x^2}}{3 + \dfrac{1}{x^2}}$

$\qquad = \dfrac{-0 + 0}{3 + 0}$

$\qquad = 0$

b. $\displaystyle\lim_{x\to\infty} \frac{-2x^2 + 3}{3x^2 + 1} = \lim_{x\to\infty} \frac{-2 + \dfrac{3}{x^2}}{3 + \dfrac{1}{x^2}}$

$\qquad = \dfrac{-2 + 0}{3 + 0}$

$\qquad = -\dfrac{2}{3}$

c. $\displaystyle\lim_{x\to\infty} \frac{-2x^3 + 3}{3x^2 + 1} = \lim_{x\to\infty} \frac{-2x + \dfrac{3}{x^2}}{3 + \dfrac{1}{x^2}}$

In this case, you can conclude that the limit does not exist because the numerator decreases without bound as the denominator approaches 3.

✓ **Checkpoint** *Audio-video solution in English & Spanish at LarsonPrecalculus.com.*

Find the limit as x approaches ∞ (if possible) for each function.

a. $f(x) = \dfrac{2x}{1 - x^2}$ **b.** $f(x) = \dfrac{2x}{1 - x}$ **c.** $f(x) = \dfrac{2x^2}{1 - x}$ ■

In Example 2, observe that when the degree of the numerator is less than the degree of the denominator, as in part (a), the limit is 0. When the degrees of the numerator and denominator are equal, as in part (b), the limit is the ratio of the coefficients of the highest-powered terms. When the degree of the numerator is greater than the degree of the denominator, as in part (c), the limit does not exist. These results seem reasonable when you realize that for large values of x, the highest-powered term of a polynomial is the most "influential" term. That is, a polynomial tends to behave as its highest-powered term behaves as x approaches positive or negative infinity.

Explore the Concept

Use a graphing utility to complete the table below to verify that

$$\lim_{x\to\infty} \frac{1}{x} = 0.$$

x	10^0	10^1	10^2
$\dfrac{1}{x}$			

x	10^3	10^4	10^5
$\dfrac{1}{x}$			

Make a conjecture about

$$\lim_{x\to 0} \frac{1}{x}.$$

Limits at Infinity for Rational Functions

Consider the rational function

$$f(x) = \frac{N(x)}{D(x)}$$

where

$$N(x) = a_n x^n + \cdots + a_0 \quad \text{and} \quad D(x) = b_m x^m + \cdots + b_0.$$

The limit of $f(x)$ as x approaches positive or negative infinity is as follows.

$$\lim_{x \to \pm\infty} f(x) = \begin{cases} 0, & n < m \\ \dfrac{a_n}{b_m}, & n = m \end{cases}$$

If $n > m$, then the limit does not exist.

EXAMPLE 3   Finding the Average Cost

You are manufacturing greeting cards that cost \$0.50 per card to produce. Your initial investment is \$5000, which implies that the total cost C of producing x cards is given by $C = 0.50x + 5000$. The average cost $\overline{C}$ per card is given by

$$\overline{C} = \frac{C}{x} = \frac{0.50x + 5000}{x}.$$

Find the average cost per card when (a) $x = 1000$, (b) $x = 10{,}000$, and (c) $x = 100{,}000$. (d) What is the limit of $\overline{C}$ as x approaches infinity?

Solution

a. When $x = 1000$, the average cost per card is

$$\overline{C} = \frac{0.50(1000) + 5000}{1000} \qquad x = 1000$$

$$= \$5.50.$$

b. When $x = 10{,}000$, the average cost per card is

$$\overline{C} = \frac{0.50(10{,}000) + 5000}{10{,}000} \qquad x = 10{,}000$$

$$= \$1.00.$$

c. When $x = 100{,}000$, the average cost per card is

$$\overline{C} = \frac{0.50(100{,}000) + 5000}{100{,}000} \qquad x = 100{,}000$$

$$= \$0.55$$

d. As x approaches infinity, the limit of $\overline{C}$ is

$$\lim_{x \to \infty} \frac{0.50x + 5000}{x} = \$0.50. \qquad x \to \infty$$

The graph of $\overline{C}$ is shown in Figure 11.23.

As $x \to \infty$, the average cost per card approaches \$0.50.
Figure 11.23

✓ **Checkpoint** ◀))) *Audio-video solution in English & Spanish at LarsonPrecalculus.com.*

Repeat Example 3 when the greeting cards cost \$0.75 per card to produce.

Limits of Sequences

Limits of sequences have many of the same properties as limits of functions. For instance, consider the sequence whose nth term is $a_n = 1/2^n$.

$$\frac{1}{2}, \frac{1}{4}, \frac{1}{8}, \frac{1}{16}, \frac{1}{32}, \dots$$

As n increases without bound, the terms of this sequence get closer and closer to 0, and the sequence is said to **converge** to 0. Using limit notation, you can write

$$\lim_{n \to \infty} \frac{1}{2^n} = 0.$$

The following relationship shows how limits of functions of x can be used to evaluate the limit of a sequence.

Limit of a Sequence

Let L be a real number. Let f be a function of a real variable such that

$$\lim_{x \to \infty} f(x) = L.$$

If $\{a_n\}$ is a sequence such that $f(n) = a_n$ for every positive integer n, then

$$\lim_{n \to \infty} a_n = L.$$

A sequence that does not converge is said to **diverge.** For instance, the terms of the sequence $1, -1, 1, -1, 1, \dots$ oscillate between 1 and -1. This sequence diverges because it does not approach a unique number.

EXAMPLE 4   Finding the Limit of a Sequence

Find the limit of each sequence. (Assume n begins with 1.)

a. $a_n = \dfrac{2n + 1}{n + 4}$

b. $b_n = \dfrac{2n + 1}{n^2 + 4}$

c. $c_n = \dfrac{2n^2 + 1}{4n^2}$

Solution

a. $\displaystyle\lim_{n \to \infty} \frac{2n + 1}{n + 4} = 2$ $\dfrac{3}{5}, \dfrac{5}{6}, \dfrac{7}{7}, \dfrac{9}{8}, \dfrac{11}{9}, \dfrac{13}{10}, \dots \to 2$

b. $\displaystyle\lim_{n \to \infty} \frac{2n + 1}{n^2 + 4} = 0$ $\dfrac{3}{5}, \dfrac{5}{8}, \dfrac{7}{13}, \dfrac{9}{20}, \dfrac{11}{29}, \dfrac{13}{40}, \dots \to 0$

c. $\displaystyle\lim_{n \to \infty} \frac{2n^2 + 1}{4n^2} = \frac{1}{2}$ $\dfrac{3}{4}, \dfrac{9}{16}, \dfrac{19}{36}, \dfrac{33}{64}, \dfrac{51}{100}, \dfrac{73}{144}, \dots \to \dfrac{1}{2}$

> **Remark**
>
> You can use the definition of limits at infinity for rational functions on page 783 to verify the limits of the sequences in Example 4.

✓ **Checkpoint** ◁))) Audio-video solution in English & Spanish at LarsonPrecalculus.com.

Find the limit of each sequence. (Assume that n begins with 1.)

a. $a_n = \dfrac{n + 2}{2n - 1}$ **b.** $a_n = \dfrac{n^3 + 2}{3n^3}$ **c.** $a_n = \dfrac{n + 2}{3n^2}$

In the next section, you will encounter limits of sequences, such as that shown in Example 5. A strategy for evaluating such limits is to begin by writing the nth term in standard rational function form. Then you can determine the limit by comparing the degrees of the numerator and denominator, as shown on page 783.

EXAMPLE 5   Finding the Limit of a Sequence

Find the limit of the sequence whose nth term is

$$a_n = \frac{8}{n^3}\left[\frac{n(n+1)(2n+1)}{6}\right].$$

Algebraic Solution

Begin by writing the nth term in standard rational function form— as the ratio of two polynomials.

$$a_n = \frac{8}{n^3}\left[\frac{n(n+1)(2n+1)}{6}\right]$$ Write original nth term.

$$= \frac{8(n)(n+1)(2n+1)}{6n^3}$$ Multiply fractions.

$$= \frac{8n^3 + 12n^2 + 4n}{3n^3}$$ Write in standard rational form.

From this form, you can see that the degree of the numerator is equal to the degree of the denominator. So, the limit of the sequence is the ratio of the coefficients of the highest-powered terms.

$$\lim_{n\to\infty} \frac{8n^3 + 12n^2 + 4n}{3n^3} = \frac{8}{3}$$

Numerical Solution

Set your graphing utility to *sequence* mode and enter the sequence. Use the *table* feature to create a table that shows the value of a_n as n becomes larger and larger, as shown in Figure 11.24.

As n increases, a_n approaches 2.667.

Figure 11.24

So, you can estimate that as n approaches ∞, a_n gets closer and closer to $2.667 \approx \frac{8}{3}$.

✓ **Checkpoint** 🔊))) *Audio-video solution in English & Spanish at LarsonPrecalculus.com.*

Find the limit of each sequence.

a. $a_n = \frac{5}{n^3}\left[\frac{(n+1)(n-1)(2n)}{7}\right]$ **b.** $a_n = \frac{2}{n}\left(n - \frac{2}{n}\left[\frac{n(n-1)}{4}\right]\right)$ ■

The result of Example 5 is supported by the figure, which shows the graph of the sequence a_n and $y = 8/3$.

Explore the Concept

In Figure 11.24, the value of a_n approaches its limit of $\frac{8}{3}$ rather slowly. (The first term to be accurate to three decimal places is $a_{4801} \approx 2.667$.) Each of the following sequences converges to 0. Which converges the quickest? Which converges the slowest? Why? Write a short paragraph discussing your conclusions.

a. $a_n = \frac{1}{n}$ **b.** $b_n = \frac{1}{n^2}$ **c.** $c_n = \frac{1}{2^n}$ **d.** $d_n = \frac{1}{n!}$ **e.** $h_n = \frac{2^n}{n!}$

11.4   Exercises

See *CalcChat.com* for tutorial help and worked-out solutions to odd-numbered exercises.
For instructions on how to use a graphing utility, see Appendix A.

Vocabulary and Concept Check

1. The line $y = 5$ is a horizontal asymptote to the right of the graph of a function f. What is the limit of f as x approaches infinity?

2. Given $\lim\limits_{x \to \infty} f(x) = 2$ for a rational function f, how does the degree of the numerator compare with the degree of the denominator?

In Exercises 3 and 4, fill in the blank.

3. A sequence that has a limit is said to _____ .

4. A sequence that does not have a limit is said to _____ .

Procedures and Problem Solving

Identifying the Graph of an Equation   In Exercises 5–12, match the function with its graph, using horizontal asymptotes as aids. [The graphs are labeled (a), (b), (c), (d), (e), (f), (g), and (h).]

(a)

(b)

(c)

(d)

(e)

(f)

(g)

(h)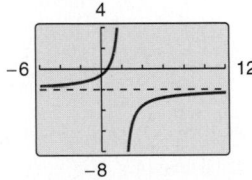

5. $f(x) = \dfrac{4x^2}{x^2 + 1}$

6. $f(x) = \dfrac{x^2}{x^2 + 1}$

7. $f(x) = 4 - \dfrac{1}{x^2}$

8. $f(x) = x + \dfrac{1}{x}$

9. $f(x) = \dfrac{x^2}{x^2 - 1}$

10. $f(x) = \dfrac{2x + 1}{x - 2}$

11. $f(x) = \dfrac{1 - 2x}{x - 2}$

12. $f(x) = \dfrac{1 - 4x^2}{x^2 - 4}$

Evaluating a Limit at Infinity   In Exercises 13–32, find the limit (if it exists). If the limit does not exist, explain why. Use a graphing utility to verify your result graphically.

13. $\lim\limits_{x \to \infty} \left(\dfrac{4}{x^2} + 2 \right)$

14. $\lim\limits_{x \to \infty} \left(\dfrac{5}{2x^6} - 6 \right)$

15. $\lim\limits_{x \to \infty} \dfrac{1 + 9x}{1 - 4x}$

16. $\lim\limits_{x \to \infty} \dfrac{2 - 7x}{2 + 3x}$

17. $\lim\limits_{x \to -\infty} \dfrac{12x + 5}{6x + 1}$

18. $\lim\limits_{x \to -\infty} \dfrac{8x + 7}{4x + 9}$

19. $\lim\limits_{x \to -\infty} \dfrac{4x^2 - 3}{2 - x^2}$

20. $\lim\limits_{x \to -\infty} \dfrac{x^2 + 3}{5x^2 - 4}$

21. $\lim\limits_{t \to \infty} \dfrac{t^2}{t + 3}$

22. $\lim\limits_{y \to \infty} \dfrac{4y^4}{y^2 + 3}$

23. $\lim\limits_{t \to \infty} \dfrac{4t^2 + 3t - 1}{3t^2 + 2t - 5}$

24. $\lim\limits_{x \to \infty} \dfrac{5 - 6x - 3x^2}{2x^2 + x + 4}$

25. $\lim\limits_{y \to -\infty} \dfrac{3 + 8y - 4y^2}{3 - y - 2y^2}$

26. $\lim\limits_{t \to -\infty} \dfrac{t^2 + 9t - 10}{2 + 4t - 3t^2}$

27. $\lim\limits_{x \to -\infty} \dfrac{-(x^2 + 3)}{(2 - x)^2}$

28. $\lim\limits_{x \to \infty} \dfrac{-(2x^2 - 6)}{(x - 1)^2}$

29. $\lim\limits_{x \to -\infty} \left[\dfrac{6x^2}{(x + 1)^2} - 4 \right]$

30. $\lim\limits_{x \to \infty} \left[7 + \dfrac{2x^2}{(x + 3)^2} \right]$

31. $\lim\limits_{t \to \infty} \left(\dfrac{1}{3t^2} - \dfrac{5t}{t + 2} \right)$

32. $\lim\limits_{x \to \infty} \left[\dfrac{4}{2x + 1} + \dfrac{3x^2}{(x - 3)^2} \right]$

Algebraic-Graphical-Numerical   In Exercises 33–38, (a) complete the table and numerically estimate the limit as x approaches infinity, (b) use a graphing utility to graph the function and estimate the limit graphically, and (c) find the limit algebraically.

x	10^0	10^1	10^2	10^3	10^4	10^5	10^6
$f(x)$							

33. $f(x) = \dfrac{2x}{3 - x}$

34. $f(x) = \dfrac{x^2}{x^2 + 4}$

35. $f(x) = \dfrac{7x}{1 - x^2}$ **36.** $f(x) = \dfrac{2x + 1}{x^2 - 1}$

37. $f(x) = 1 - \dfrac{3}{x^2}$ **38.** $f(x) = \dfrac{1}{x} - 2$

Estimating the Limit at Infinity   In Exercises 39–42, (a) complete the table and numerically estimate the limit as x approaches infinity and (b) use a graphing utility to graph the function and estimate the limit graphically.

x	10^0	10^1	10^2	10^3	10^4	10^5	10^6
$f(x)$							

39. $f(x) = x - \sqrt{x^2 + 2}$

40. $f(x) = 3x - \sqrt{9x^2 + 1}$

41. $f(x) = 3\left(2x - \sqrt{4x^2 + x}\right)$

42. $f(x) = 4\left(4x - \sqrt{16x^2 - x}\right)$

Finding the Limit of a Sequence   In Exercises 43–52, write the first five terms of the sequence and find the limit of the sequence (if it exists). If the limit does not exist, explain why. Assume n begins with 1.

43. $a_n = \dfrac{n + 1}{n^2 + 1}$ **44.** $a_n = \dfrac{n}{n^2 + 1}$

45. $a_n = \dfrac{6n - 2}{2n + 1}$ **46.** $a_n = \dfrac{4n - 1}{n + 3}$

47. $a_n = \dfrac{n^2}{3n + 2}$ **48.** $a_n = \dfrac{4n^2 + 1}{2n}$

49. $a_n = \dfrac{(n + 1)!}{n!}$ **50.** $a_n = \dfrac{(3n - 2)!}{(3n + 1)!}$

51. $a_n = \dfrac{(-1)^n}{n}$ **52.** $a_n = \dfrac{(-1)^{n+1}}{n^2}$

Finding the Limit of a Sequence   In Exercises 53–56, use a graphing utility to complete the table and estimate the limit of the sequence as n approaches infinity. Then find the limit algebraically.

n	10^0	10^1	10^2	10^3
a_n				

53. $a_n = \dfrac{1}{n}\left(n + \dfrac{1}{n}\left[\dfrac{n(n + 1)}{2}\right]\right)$

54. $a_n = \dfrac{4}{n}\left(n + \dfrac{4}{n}\left[\dfrac{n(n + 1)}{2}\right]\right)$

55. $a_n = \dfrac{10}{n^3}\left[\dfrac{n(n + 1)(3n + 1)}{6}\right]$

56. $a_n = \dfrac{3n(n + 1)}{n^2} - \dfrac{4}{n^4}\left[\dfrac{n(n + 1)}{2}\right]^2$

57. Average Cost   The cost function for a certain model of MP3 player is given by $C = 73x + 25{,}000$, where C is the cost (in dollars) and x is the number of MP3 players produced.

(a) Write a model for the average cost per unit produced.

(b) Find the average costs per unit when $x = 1000$ and $x = 5000$.

(c) Determine the limit of the average cost function as x approaches infinity. Explain the meaning of the limit in the context of the problem.

58. Average Cost   The cost function for a new supermarket to recycle x tons of organic material is given by $C = 50x + 2700$, where C is the cost (in dollars).

(a) Write a model for the average cost per ton of organic material recycled.

(b) Find the average costs of recycling 100 tons and 1000 tons of organic material.

(c) Determine the limit of the average cost function as x approaches infinity. Explain the meaning of the limit in the context of the problem.

59. MODELING DATA

The table shows the numbers R (in millions) of ready reserve personnel in the United States military for the years 2006 through 2012.   (Source: U.S. Dept. of Defense)

DATA Year	Ready reserves, R (in millions)
2006	1.102
2007	1.089
2008	1.081
2009	1.080
2010	1.079
2011	1.079
2012	1.086

Spreadsheet at LarsonPrecalculus.com

A model for the data is given by

$$R(t) = \dfrac{1.786 + 0.4583t}{1 + 0.5626t - 0.00721t^2}, \quad 6 \le t \le 12$$

where t represents the year, with $t = 6$ corresponding to 2006.

(a) Use a graphing utility to create a scatter plot of the data and graph the model in the same viewing window. How do they compare?

(b) Use the model to predict the numbers of ready reserves in 2013 and 2014.

(c) Find the limit of the model as $t \to \infty$ and interpret its meaning in the context of the situation.

(d) Is this a good model for predicting future numbers of ready reserves? Explain.

60. *Why you should learn it* (p. 780) The table shows the mean annual salaries S (in thousands of dollars) of a financial manager in the United States for the years 2006 through 2013. (Source: U.S. Bureau of Labor Statistics)

DATA Year	Salary, S (in thousands of dollars)
2006	101.45
2007	106.20
2008	110.64
2009	113.73
2010	116.97
2011	120.45
2012	123.26
2013	126.66

Spreadsheet at LarsonPrecalculus.com

A model for the data is given by

$$S(t) = \frac{11.67 + 47.505t - 2.6441t^2}{1 + 0.276t - 0.0186t^2}, \quad 6 \le t \le 13$$

where t represents the year, with $t = 6$ corresponding to 2006.

(a) Use a graphing utility to create a scatter plot of the data and graph the model in the same viewing window. How do they compare?

(b) Use the model to predict the mean salaries in 2014 and 2015.

(c) Find the limit of the model as $t \to \infty$ and interpret its meaning in the context of the situation.

(d) Is this a good model for predicting the mean annual salaries in future years? Explain.

Conclusions

True or False? In Exercises 61–64, determine whether the statement is true or false. Justify your answer.

61. Every rational function has a horizontal asymptote.

62. If a rational function f has a horizontal asymptote to the right, then the limit of $f(x)$ as x approaches $-\infty$ exists.

63. If a sequence converges, then it has a limit.

64. When the degrees of the numerator and denominator of a rational function are equal, the limit as x approaches infinity does not exist.

65. Think About It Find functions f and g such that both $f(x)$ and $g(x)$ increase without bound as x approaches ∞, but $\lim\limits_{x \to \infty} [f(x) - g(x)] \ne \infty$.

66. Think About It Use a graphing utility to graph the function

$$f(x) = \frac{x}{\sqrt{x^2 + 1}}.$$

How many horizontal asymptotes does the function appear to have? What are the horizontal asymptotes?

Finding the Limit of a Sequence In Exercises 67–70, use a graphing utility to create a scatter plot of the terms of the sequence. Determine whether the sequence converges or diverges. If it converges, estimate its limit.

67. $a_n = 4\left(\frac{2}{3}\right)^n$

68. $a_n = 3\left(\frac{3}{2}\right)^n$

69. $a_n = \dfrac{3[1 - (1.5)^n]}{1 - 1.5}$

70. $a_n = \dfrac{3[1 - (0.5)^n]}{1 - 0.5}$

71. Error Analysis Describe the error in finding the limit.

$$\lim_{x \to \infty} \frac{1 - 2x - x^2}{4x^2 + 1} = 0$$

72. **HOW DO YOU SEE IT?** Use the graph to estimate (a) $\lim\limits_{x \to \infty} f(x)$, (b) $\lim\limits_{x \to -\infty} f(x)$, and (c) the horizontal aysmptote of the graph of f.

(i)

(ii)

Cumulative Mixed Review

Sketching Transformations In Exercises 73 and 74, sketch the graphs of y and each transformation on the same rectangular coordinate system.

73. $y = x^4$

(a) $f(x) = (x + 3)^4$ (b) $f(x) = x^4 - 1$

(c) $f(x) = 2 - 4x^4$ (d) $f(x) = \frac{1}{2}(x - 4)^4$

74. $y = x^3$

(a) $f(x) = (x - 2)^3$ (b) $f(x) = x^3 - 3$

(c) $f(x) = 2 - \frac{1}{4}x^3$ (d) $f(x) = 3(x + 1)^3$

Using Sigma Notation In Exercises 75–78, find the sum.

75. $\sum\limits_{i=1}^{6} (2i + 3)$

76. $\sum\limits_{i=0}^{4} 5i^2$

77. $\sum\limits_{k=1}^{11} 16$

78. $\sum\limits_{k=0}^{8} \dfrac{3}{k^2 + 1}$

11.5   The Area Problem

Limits of Summations

Earlier in the text, you used the concept of a limit to obtain a formula for the sum S of an infinite geometric series

$$S = a_1 + a_1r + a_1r^2 + \cdots = \sum_{i=1}^{\infty} a_1r^{i-1} = \frac{a_1}{1-r}, \quad |r| < 1.$$

Using limit notation, this sum can be written as

$$S = \lim_{n \to \infty} \sum_{i=1}^{n} a_1 r^{i-1}$$

$$= \lim_{n \to \infty} \frac{a_1(1 - r^n)}{1 - r} \qquad \sum_{i=1}^{n} a_1 r^{i-1} = a_1 \left(\frac{1 - r^n}{1 - r}\right)$$

$$= \frac{a_1}{1 - r}\left[\lim_{n \to \infty}(1 - r^n)\right] \qquad \text{Scalar Multiple Property}$$

$$= \frac{a_1}{1 - r}. \qquad \lim_{n \to \infty} r^n = 0 \text{ for } |r| < 1$$

The following summation formulas and properties are used to evaluate finite and infinite summations.

Summation Formulas and Properties

1. $\displaystyle\sum_{i=1}^{n} c = cn$, c is a constant.

2. $\displaystyle\sum_{i=1}^{n} i = \frac{n(n+1)}{2}$

3. $\displaystyle\sum_{i=1}^{n} i^2 = \frac{n(n+1)(2n+1)}{6}$

4. $\displaystyle\sum_{i=1}^{n} i^3 = \frac{n^2(n+1)^2}{4}$

5. $\displaystyle\sum_{i=1}^{n} (a_i \pm b_i) = \sum_{i=1}^{n} a_i + \sum_{i=1}^{n} b_i$

6. $\displaystyle\sum_{i=1}^{n} ka_i = k\sum_{i=1}^{n} a_i$, k is a constant.

EXAMPLE 1   Evaluating a Summation

Evaluate the summation.

$$\sum_{i=1}^{200} i = 1 + 2 + 3 + 4 + \cdots + 200$$

Solution

Using Formula 2 with $n = 200$, you can write

$$\sum_{i=1}^{200} i = \frac{200(200 + 1)}{2} \qquad \sum_{i=1}^{n} i = \frac{n(n+1)}{2}$$

$$= \frac{40{,}200}{2}$$

$$= 20{,}100.$$

✓ **Checkpoint** Audio-video solution in English & Spanish at LarsonPrecalculus.com.

Evaluate the summation: $\displaystyle\sum_{i=1}^{10} i^2$.

EXAMPLE 2   Evaluating a Summation

Evaluate the summation

$$S = \sum_{i=1}^{n} \frac{i+2}{n^2} = \frac{3}{n^2} + \frac{4}{n^2} + \frac{5}{n^2} + \cdots + \frac{n+2}{n^2}$$

for $n = 10, 100, 1000,$ and $10,000$.

Solution

Begin by applying summation formulas and properties to simplify S. In the second line of the solution, note that

$$\frac{1}{n^2}$$

can be factored out of the sum because n is considered to be constant. You could not factor i out of the summation because i is the (variable) index of summation.

$S = \displaystyle\sum_{i=1}^{n} \frac{i+2}{n^2}$ Write original form of summation.

$= \dfrac{1}{n^2} \displaystyle\sum_{i=1}^{n} (i+2)$ Factor constant $1/n^2$ out of sum.

$= \dfrac{1}{n^2} \left(\displaystyle\sum_{i=1}^{n} i + \displaystyle\sum_{i=1}^{n} 2 \right)$ Write as two sums.

$= \dfrac{1}{n^2} \left[\dfrac{n(n+1)}{2} + 2n \right]$ Apply Formulas 1 and 2.

$= \dfrac{1}{n^2} \left(\dfrac{n^2 + 5n}{2} \right)$ Add fractions.

$= \dfrac{n+5}{2n}$ Simplify.

Now, evaluate the sum by substituting the appropriate values of n, as shown in the table.

n	10	100	1000	10,000
$\displaystyle\sum_{i=1}^{n} \dfrac{i+2}{n^2} = \dfrac{n+5}{2n}$	0.75	0.525	0.5025	0.50025

✓ **Checkpoint**))) *Audio-video solution in English & Spanish at LarsonPrecalculus.com.*

Evaluate the summation

$$S = \sum_{i=1}^{n} \frac{3i+2}{n^2} = \frac{5}{n^2} + \frac{8}{n^2} + \frac{11}{n^2} + \cdots + \frac{3n+2}{n^2}$$

for $n = 10, 100, 1000,$ and $10,000$.

In Example 2, note that the sum appears to approach a limit as n increases. To find the limit of

$$\frac{n+5}{2n}$$

as n approaches infinity, you can use the techniques from Section 11.4 to write

$$\lim_{n \to \infty} \frac{n+5}{2n} = \frac{1}{2}.$$

Technology Tip

Some graphing utilities have a *sum sequence* feature that is useful for computing summations. For instructions on how to use the *sum sequence* feature, see Appendix A; for specific keystrokes, go to this textbook's *Companion Website*.

```
10→n
                    10
sum(seq((I+2)/n²,I,1,
n))
                   .75
(n+5)/(2n)
                   .75
```

Be sure you notice the strategy used in Example 2. Rather than separately evaluating the sums

$$\sum_{i=1}^{10} \frac{i+2}{n^2}, \quad \sum_{i=1}^{100} \frac{i+2}{n^2}, \quad \sum_{i=1}^{1000} \frac{i+2}{n^2}, \quad \sum_{i=1}^{10,000} \frac{i+2}{n^2}$$

it was more efficient first to convert to rational form using the summation formulas and properties listed on page 789.

$$S = \underbrace{\sum_{i=1}^{n} \frac{i+2}{n^2}}_{\substack{\text{Summation} \\ \text{form}}} = \underbrace{\frac{n+5}{2n}}_{\substack{\text{Rational} \\ \text{form}}}$$

With this rational form, each sum can be evaluated by simply substituting appropriate values of n.

EXAMPLE 3   Finding the Limit of a Summation

Find the limit of $S(n)$ as $n \to \infty$.

$$S(n) = \sum_{i=1}^{n} \left(1 + \frac{i}{n}\right)^2 \left(\frac{1}{n}\right)$$

Solution

Begin by rewriting the summation in rational form.

$$S(n) = \sum_{i=1}^{n} \left(1 + \frac{i}{n}\right)^2 \left(\frac{1}{n}\right) \qquad \text{Write original form of summation.}$$

$$= \sum_{i=1}^{n} \left(\frac{n^2 + 2ni + i^2}{n^2}\right)\left(\frac{1}{n}\right) \qquad \text{Square } (1 + i/n) \text{ and write as a single fraction.}$$

$$= \frac{1}{n^3} \sum_{i=1}^{n} (n^2 + 2ni + i^2) \qquad \text{Factor constant } 1/n^3 \text{ out of the sum.}$$

$$= \frac{1}{n^3}\left(\sum_{i=1}^{n} n^2 + \sum_{i=1}^{n} 2ni + \sum_{i=1}^{n} i^2\right) \qquad \text{Write as three sums.}$$

$$= \frac{1}{n^3}\left\{n^3 + 2n\left[\frac{n(n+1)}{2}\right] + \frac{n(n+1)(2n+1)}{6}\right\} \qquad \text{Use summation formulas.}$$

$$= \frac{14n^3 + 9n^2 + n}{6n^3} \qquad \text{Simplify.}$$

> **Remark**
>
> As you can see from Example 3, there is a lot of algebra involved in rewriting a summation in rational form. You may want to review simplifying rational expressions if you are having difficulty with this procedure.

In this rational form, you can now find the limit as $n \to \infty$.

$$\lim_{n \to \infty} S(n) = \lim_{n \to \infty} \frac{14n^3 + 9n^2 + n}{6n^3}$$

$$= \frac{14}{6}$$

$$= \frac{7}{3}$$

✓ **Checkpoint** 🔊))) *Audio-video solution in English & Spanish at LarsonPrecalculus.com.*

Find the limit of $S(n)$ as $n \to \infty$.

$$S(n) = \sum_{i=1}^{n} \left(\frac{2}{n} + \frac{i}{n^2}\right)\left(\frac{1}{n}\right)$$

∎

The Area Problem

You now have the tools needed to solve the second basic problem of calculus: the area problem. The problem is to find the *area* of the region R bounded by the graph of a nonnegative, continuous function f, the x-axis, and the vertical lines $x = a$ and $x = b$, as shown in Figure 11.25.

When the region R is a square, a triangle, a trapezoid, or a semicircle, you can find its area by using a geometric formula. For more general regions, however, you must use a different approach—one that involves the limit of a summation. The basic strategy is to use a collection of rectangles of equal width that approximates the region R, as illustrated in Example 4.

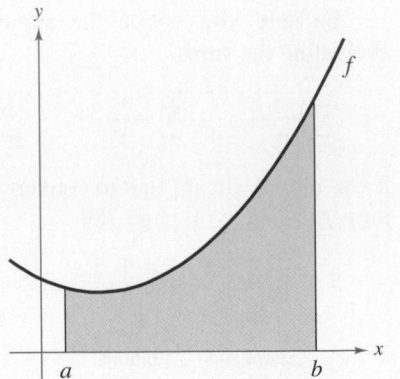

Figure 11.25

EXAMPLE 4   Approximating the Area of a Region

See LarsonPrecalculus.com for an interactive version of this type of example.

Use the five rectangles in Figure 11.26 to approximate the area of the region bounded by the graph of $f(x) = 6 - x^2$, the x-axis, and the lines $x = 0$ and $x = 2$.

Solution

Because the length of the interval along the x-axis is 2 and there are five rectangles, the width of each rectangle is $\frac{2}{5}$. The height of each rectangle can be obtained by evaluating f at the right endpoint of each interval. The five intervals are as follows.

$$\left[0, \frac{2}{5}\right], \quad \left[\frac{2}{5}, \frac{4}{5}\right], \quad \left[\frac{4}{5}, \frac{6}{5}\right], \quad \left[\frac{6}{5}, \frac{8}{5}\right], \quad \left[\frac{8}{5}, \frac{10}{5}\right]$$

Notice that the right endpoint of each interval is $\frac{2}{5}i$ for $i = 1, 2, 3, 4,$ and 5. The sum of the areas of the five rectangles is

Figure 11.26

$$\overset{\text{Height}}{\overbrace{}}\;\overset{\text{Width}}{\overbrace{}}$$

$$\sum_{i=1}^{5} f\left(\frac{2i}{5}\right)\left(\frac{2}{5}\right) = \sum_{i=1}^{5}\left[6 - \left(\frac{2i}{5}\right)^2\right]\left(\frac{2}{5}\right)$$

$$= \frac{2}{5}\left(\sum_{i=1}^{5} 6 - \frac{4}{25}\sum_{i=1}^{5} i^2\right)$$

$$= \frac{2}{5}\left(30 - \frac{44}{5}\right)$$

$$= \frac{212}{25}$$

$$= 8.48.$$

So, the area of R is approximately 8.48 square units.

✓ **Checkpoint**))) Audio-video solution in English & Spanish at LarsonPrecalculus.com.

Use the four rectangles in Figure 11.27 to approximate the area of the region bounded by the graph of $f(x) = x + 1$, the x-axis, and the lines $x = 0$ and $x = 2$.

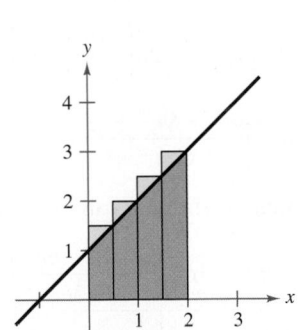

Figure 11.27

By increasing the number of rectangles used in Example 4, you can obtain closer and closer approximations of the area of the region. For instance, using 25 rectangles of width $\frac{2}{25}$ each, you can approximate the area to be $A \approx 9.17$ square units. The table shows even better approximations.

n	5	25	100	1000	5000
Approximate area	8.48	9.17	9.29	9.33	9.33

Based on the procedure illustrated in Example 4, the *exact* **area of a plane region** *R* is given by the limit of the sum of *n* rectangles as *n* approaches ∞.

> **Area of a Plane Region**
>
> Let f be continuous and nonnegative on the interval $[a, b]$. The **area** A of the region bounded by the graph of f, the x-axis, and the vertical lines $x = a$ and $x = b$ is given by
>
> $$A = \lim_{n \to \infty} \sum_{i=1}^{n} \underbrace{f\left(a + \frac{(b-a)i}{n}\right)}_{\text{Height}} \underbrace{\left(\frac{b-a}{n}\right)}_{\text{Width}}.$$

EXAMPLE 5   Finding the Area of a Region

Find the area of the region bounded by the graph of

$$f(x) = x^2$$

and the x-axis between

$$x = 0 \quad \text{and} \quad x = 1$$

as shown in Figure 11.28.

Solution

Begin by finding the dimensions of the rectangles.

$$\text{Width: } \frac{b-a}{n} = \frac{1-0}{n} = \frac{1}{n}$$

$$\text{Height: } f\left(a + \frac{(b-a)i}{n}\right) = f\left(0 + \frac{(1-0)i}{n}\right) = f\left(\frac{i}{n}\right) = \frac{i^2}{n^2}$$

Next, approximate the area as the sum of the areas of n rectangles.

$$A \approx \sum_{i=1}^{n} f\left(a + \frac{(b-a)i}{n}\right)\left(\frac{b-a}{n}\right)$$

$$= \sum_{i=1}^{n} \left(\frac{i^2}{n^2}\right)\left(\frac{1}{n}\right)$$

$$= \sum_{i=1}^{n} \frac{i^2}{n^3}$$

$$= \frac{1}{n^3} \sum_{i=1}^{n} i^2$$

$$= \frac{1}{n^3} \left[\frac{n(n+1)(2n+1)}{6}\right]$$

$$= \frac{2n^3 + 3n^2 + n}{6n^3}$$

Finally, find the exact area by taking the limit as n approaches ∞.

$$A = \lim_{n \to \infty} \frac{2n^3 + 3n^2 + n}{6n^3} = \frac{1}{3}$$

Figure 11.28

✓ **Checkpoint** *Audio-video solution in English & Spanish at LarsonPrecalculus.com.*

Find the area of the region bounded by the graph of $f(x) = 3x$ and the x-axis between $x = 0$ and $x = 1$. ∎

11.5   Exercises

Vocabulary and Concept Check

In Exercises 1 and 2, fill in the blank.

1. $\displaystyle\sum_{i=1}^{n} i =$ _____

2. $\displaystyle\sum_{i=1}^{n} i^3 =$ _____

3. Can you obtain a better approximation of the area of the shaded region shown using 10 rectangles of equal width or 100 rectangles of equal width?

4. Does the limit of the sum of n rectangles as n approaches infinity represent the *exact* area of a plane region or an *approximation* of the area?

Figure for 3

Procedures and Problem Solving

Evaluating a Summation   In Exercises 5–12, evaluate the sum using the summation formulas and properties.

5. $\displaystyle\sum_{i=1}^{60} 7$

6. $\displaystyle\sum_{i=1}^{45} 3$

7. $\displaystyle\sum_{i=1}^{20} i^3$

8. $\displaystyle\sum_{i=1}^{30} i^2$

9. $\displaystyle\sum_{k=1}^{20} (3k^3 - 16)$

10. $\displaystyle\sum_{k=1}^{50} (2k + 1)$

11. $\displaystyle\sum_{j=1}^{25} (j^2 + 2j)$

12. $\displaystyle\sum_{j=1}^{10} (j^3 - 3j^2)$

Finding the Limit of a Summation   In Exercises 13–18, (a) rewrite the sum as a rational function $S(n)$. (b) Use $S(n)$ to complete the table. (c) Find $\displaystyle\lim_{n\to\infty} S(n)$.

n	10^0	10^1	10^2	10^3	10^4
$S(n)$					

13. $\displaystyle\sum_{i=1}^{n} \frac{i^3}{n^4}$

14. $\displaystyle\sum_{i=1}^{n} \frac{i}{n^2}$

15. $\displaystyle\sum_{i=1}^{n} \frac{5 + 6i^2}{n^3}$

16. $\displaystyle\sum_{i=1}^{n} \frac{2i + 3}{n^2}$

17. $\displaystyle\sum_{i=1}^{n} \left(\frac{i^2}{n^3} + \frac{2}{n}\right)\left(\frac{1}{n}\right)$

18. $\displaystyle\sum_{i=1}^{n} \left(\frac{5}{n} + \frac{4i^3}{n^3}\right)\left(\frac{1}{n}\right)$

Approximating the Area of a Region   In Exercises 19–22, approximate the area of the region using the indicated number of rectangles of equal width.

19. $f(x) = x + 4$

20. $f(x) = 2 - x^2$

21. $f(x) = \frac{1}{4}x^3$
(8 rectangles)

22. $f(x) = \frac{1}{2}(x - 1)^3$
(4 rectangles)

Approximating the Area of a Region   In Exercises 23–26, complete the table to show the approximate area of the region using the indicated numbers n of rectangles of equal width.

n	4	8	20	50
Approximate area				

23. $f(x) = -\frac{1}{3}x + 4$

24. $f(x) = 9 - x^2$

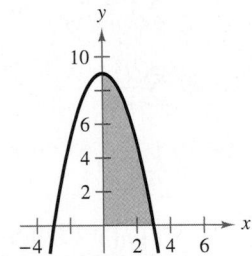

25. $f(x) = \frac{1}{9}x^3$

26. $f(x) = 3 - \frac{1}{4}x^3$

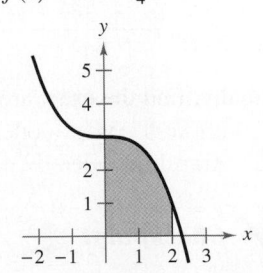

Finding the Area of a Region In Exercises 27–32, complete the table for each finite value of n to approximate the area of the region bounded by the graph of f and the x-axis over the specified interval using the given expression for the sum of the areas of n rectangles. Then find the exact area as $n \to \infty$.

n	4	8	20	50	100	∞
Area						

	Function	Interval	Sum of Areas of n Rectangles
27.	$f(x) = 2x + 5$	$[0, 4]$	$\dfrac{36n^2 + 16n}{n^2}$
28.	$f(x) = 3x + 1$	$[0, 4]$	$\dfrac{28n^2 + 24n}{n^2}$
29.	$f(x) = 9 - x^2$	$[0, 2]$	$\dfrac{46n^3 - 12n^2 - 4n}{3n^3}$
30.	$f(x) = x^2 + 1$	$[4, 6]$	$\dfrac{158n^3 + 60n^2 + 4n}{3n^3}$
31.	$f(x) = \frac{1}{2}x + 4$	$[-1, 3]$	$\dfrac{18n^2 + 4n}{n^2}$
32.	$f(x) = \frac{1}{2}x + 1$	$[-2, 2]$	$\dfrac{4n^2 + 4n}{n^2}$

Finding the Area of a Region In Exercises 33–44, use the limit process to find the area of the region bounded by the graph of the function and the x-axis over the specified interval.

	Function	Interval
33.	$f(x) = x + 1$	$[0, 1]$
34.	$f(x) = x + 2$	$[0, 2]$
35.	$f(x) = 2x - 8$	$[4, 7]$
36.	$f(x) = 3x - 6$	$[2, 5]$
37.	$f(x) = 16 - x^2$	$[-2, 1]$
38.	$f(x) = x^2 + 2$	$[-1, 2]$
39.	$g(x) = 8 - x^3$	$[0, 2]$
40.	$g(x) = 64 - x^3$	$[0, 3]$
41.	$g(x) = 2x - x^3$	$[0, 1]$
42.	$g(x) = 4x - x^3$	$[0, 2]$
43.	$f(x) = x^2 + 4x$	$[0, 6]$
44.	$f(x) = x^2 - x^3$	$[0, 1]$

45. Civil Engineering The boundaries of a parcel of land are two edges modeled by the coordinate axes and a stream modeled by the equation

$$y = (-3.0 \times 10^{-6})x^3 + 0.002x^2 - 1.05x + 400.$$

Use a graphing utility to graph the equation. Find the area of the property. (All distances are measured in feet.)

©Andrey_Popov/Shutterstock.com

46. *Why you should learn it* *(p. 789)* The table shows the measurements (in feet) of a lot bounded by a stream and two straight roads that meet at right angles. (See figure.)

x	0	50	100	150
y	450	362	305	268

x	200	250	300
y	245	156	0

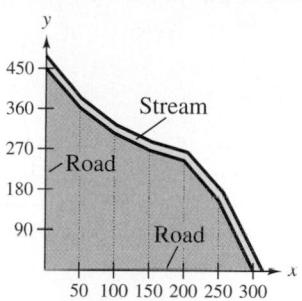

(a) Use the *regression* feature of a graphing utility to find a model of the form $y = ax^3 + bx^2 + cx + d$.

(b) Use the graphing utility to plot the data and graph the model in the same viewing window.

(c) Use the model in part (a) to estimate the area of the lot.

Conclusions

True or False? In Exercises 47 and 48, determine whether the statement is true or false. Justify your answer.

47. The sum of the first n positive integers is $n(n + 1)/2$.

48. The exact area of a region is given by the limit of the sum of n rectangles as n approaches 0.

49. Writing Describe the process of finding the areas of a region bounded by the graph of a nonnegative, continuous function f, the x-axis, and the vertical lines $x = a$ and $x = b$.

50. HOW DO YOU SEE IT? Without performing any calculations, choose the value that best approximates the area of the region shown in the graph. [The choices are labeled (a), (b), (c), (d), and (e).]

(a) -2

(b) 1

(c) 4

(d) 6

(e) 9

11 Chapter Summary

	What did you learn?	Explanation and Examples	Review Exercises
11.1	Understand the limit concept (*p. 750*) and use the definition of a limit to estimate limits (*p. 751*).	If $f(x)$ becomes arbitrarily close to a unique number L as x approaches c from either side, then the limit of $f(x)$ as x approaches c is L. This is written as $\lim\limits_{x \to c} f(x) = L$.	1–4
	Determine whether limits of functions exist (*p. 753*).	**Conditions Under Which Limits Do Not Exist** The limit of $f(x)$ as $x \to c$ does not exist under any of the following conditions. 1. $f(x)$ approaches a different number from the right side of c than it approaches from the left side of c. 2. $f(x)$ increases or decreases without bound as x approaches c. 3. $f(x)$ oscillates between two fixed values as x approaches c.	5–8
	Use properties of limits to evaluate limits (*p. 755*).	Let b and c be real numbers and let n be a positive integer. 1. $\lim\limits_{x \to c} b = b$ 2. $\lim\limits_{x \to c} x = c$ 3. $\lim\limits_{x \to c} x^n = c^n$ 4. $\lim\limits_{x \to c} \sqrt[n]{x} = \sqrt[n]{c}$, valid for all c when n is odd and valid for $c > 0$ when n is even **Properties of Limits** Let b and c be real numbers, let n be a positive integer, and let f and g be functions where $\lim\limits_{x \to c} f(x) = L$ and $\lim\limits_{x \to c} g(x) = K.$ 1. $\lim\limits_{x \to c} [bf(x)] = bL$ 2. $\lim\limits_{x \to c} [f(x) \pm g(x)] = L \pm K$ 3. $\lim\limits_{x \to c} [f(x)g(x)] = LK$ 4. $\lim\limits_{x \to c} \dfrac{f(x)}{g(x)} = \dfrac{L}{K}, \quad K \neq 0$ 5. $\lim\limits_{x \to c} [f(x)]^n = L^n$	9–22
11.2	Use the dividing out technique to evaluate limits of functions (*p. 760*).	When evaluating a limit of a rational function by direct substitution, you may encounter the indeterminate form 0/0. In this case, factor and divide out any common factors, then try direct substitution again. (See Examples 1 and 2.)	23–30
	Use the rationalizing technique to evaluate limits of functions (*p. 762*).	The rationalizing technique involves rationalizing the numerator of the function when finding a limit. (See Example 3.)	31, 32
	Use technology to approximate limits of functions graphically and numerically (*p. 763*).	The *table* feature or *zoom* and *trace* features of a graphing utility can be used to approximate limits. (See Examples 4 and 5.)	33–40
	Evaluate one-sided limits of functions (*p. 764*).	**Limit from left:** $\lim\limits_{x \to c^-} f(x) = L_1$ or $f(x) \to L_1$ as $x \to c^-$ **Limit from right:** $\lim\limits_{x \to c^+} f(x) = L_2$ or $f(x) \to L_2$ as $x \to c^+$	41–48
	Evaluate limits of difference quotients from calculus (*p. 766*).	For any x-value, the limit of a difference quotient is an expression of the form $\lim\limits_{h \to 0} \dfrac{f(x + h) - f(x)}{h}$.	49, 50

What did you learn?	Explanation and Examples	Review Exercises
11.3 Understand the tangent line problem *(p. 770)* and use a tangent line to approximate the slope of a graph at a point *(p. 771)*.	The tangent line to the graph of a function f at a point $P(x_1, y_1)$ is the line that best approximates the slope of the graph at the point.	51–58
Use the limit definition of slope to find exact slopes of graphs *(p. 772)*.	**Definition of the Slope of a Graph** The slope m of the graph of f at the point $(x, f(x))$ is equal to the slope of its tangent line at $(x, f(x))$, and is given by $$m = \lim_{h \to 0} m_{\text{sec}} = \lim_{h \to 0} \frac{f(x + h) - f(x)}{h}$$ provided this limit exists.	59–62
Find derivatives of functions and use derivatives to find slopes of graphs *(p. 775)*.	The derivative of f at x is given by $$f'(x) = \lim_{h \to 0} \frac{f(x + h) - f(x)}{h}$$ provided this limit exists. The derivative $f'(x)$ is a formula for the slope of the tangent line to the graph of f at the point $(x, f(x))$.	63–78
11.4 Evaluate limits of functions at infinity *(p. 780)*.	If f is a function and L_1 and L_2 are real numbers, then the statements $\lim_{x \to -\infty} f(x) = L_1$ and $\lim_{x \to \infty} f(x) = L_2$ denote the limits at infinity.	79–86
Find limits of sequences *(p. 784)*.	**Limit of a Sequence** Let L be a real number. Let f be a function of a real variable such that $\lim_{x \to \infty} f(x) = L$. If $\{a_n\}$ is a sequence such that $f(n) = a_n$ for every positive integer n, then $\lim_{n \to \infty} a_n = L$.	87–92
11.5 Find limits of summations *(p. 789)*.	**Summation Formulas and Properties** 1. $\sum_{i=1}^{n} c = cn$, c is a constant. 2. $\sum_{i=1}^{n} i = \frac{n(n + 1)}{2}$ 3. $\sum_{i=1}^{n} i^2 = \frac{n(n + 1)(2n + 1)}{6}$ 4. $\sum_{i=1}^{n} i^3 = \frac{n^2(n + 1)^2}{4}$ 5. $\sum_{i=1}^{n} (a_i \pm b_i) = \sum_{i=1}^{n} a_i \pm \sum_{i=1}^{n} b_i$ 6. $\sum_{i=1}^{n} ka_i = k \sum_{i=1}^{n} a_i$, k is a constant.	93, 94
Use rectangles to approximate and limits of summations to find areas of plane regions *(p. 792)*.	A collection of rectangles of equal width can be used to approximate the area of a region. Increasing the number of rectangles gives a closer approximation. (See Example 4.) **Area of a Plane Region** Let f be continuous and nonnegative on $[a, b]$. The area A of the region bounded by the graph of f, the x-axis, and the vertical lines $x = a$ and $x = b$ is given by $$A = \lim_{n \to \infty} \sum_{i=1}^{n} f\left(a + \frac{(b - a)i}{n}\right)\left(\frac{b - a}{n}\right).$$	95–105

11   Review Exercises

11.1

Estimating a Limit Numerically   In Exercises 1–4, complete the table and use the result to estimate the limit numerically. Determine whether the limit can be reached.

1. $\lim\limits_{x \to 3} (6x - 1)$

x	2.9	2.99	2.999	3	3.001	3.01	3.1
$f(x)$				?			

2. $\lim\limits_{x \to 1} (3x^2 - 4x - 4)$

x	0.9	0.99	0.999	1	1.001	1.01	1.1
$f(x)$				?			

3. $\lim\limits_{x \to 0} \dfrac{\tan x}{2x}$

x	-0.1	-0.01	-0.001	0	0.001	0.01	0.1
$f(x)$				?			

4. $\lim\limits_{x \to 0} \dfrac{\ln(1 - x)}{x}$

x	-0.1	-0.01	-0.001	0	0.001	0.01	0.1
$f(x)$				?			

Using a Graph to Find a Limit   In Exercises 5–8, use the graph to find the limit (if it exists). If the limit does not exist, explain why.

5. $\lim\limits_{x \to 1} (3 - x)$

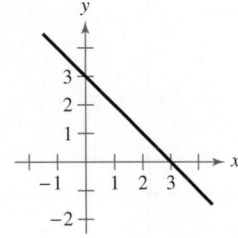

6. $\lim\limits_{x \to 2} \dfrac{1}{x - 2}$

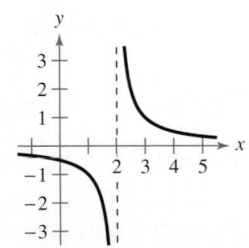

7. $\lim\limits_{x \to -3} \dfrac{|x + 3|}{x + 3}$

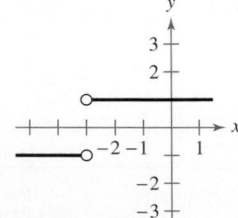

8. $\lim\limits_{x \to 1} \dfrac{x^2 - 1}{x - 1}$

Using Properties of Limits   In Exercises 9 and 10, use the given information to evaluate each limit.

9. $\lim\limits_{x \to c} f(x) = 2$, $\lim\limits_{x \to c} g(x) = 5$

   (a) $\lim\limits_{x \to c} [f(x)]^3$
   (b) $\lim\limits_{x \to c} [3f(x) - g(x)]$
   (c) $\lim\limits_{x \to c} [f(x)g(x)]$
   (d) $\lim\limits_{x \to c} \dfrac{f(x)}{g(x)}$

10. $\lim\limits_{x \to c} f(x) = 8$, $\lim\limits_{x \to c} g(x) = 3$

   (a) $\lim\limits_{x \to c} \sqrt[3]{f(x)}$
   (b) $\lim\limits_{x \to c} \dfrac{f(x)}{18}$
   (c) $\lim\limits_{x \to c} [f(x)g(x)]$
   (d) $\lim\limits_{x \to c} [f(x) - 2g(x)]$

Evaluating a Limit by Direct Substitution   In Exercises 11–22, find the limit by direct substitution.

11. $\lim\limits_{x \to 4} \left(\tfrac{1}{2}x + 3\right)$
12. $\lim\limits_{x \to -2} (5 - 2x - x^2)$
13. $\lim\limits_{t \to 3} \dfrac{t^2 + 1}{t}$
14. $\lim\limits_{x \to 2} \dfrac{3x + 5}{5x - 3}$
15. $\lim\limits_{x \to -2} \sqrt[3]{4x}$
16. $\lim\limits_{x \to -1} \sqrt{5 - x}$
17. $\lim\limits_{x \to \pi} \sin 3x$
18. $\lim\limits_{x \to 0} \cos x$
19. $\lim\limits_{x \to -1} e^{-x}$
20. $\lim\limits_{x \to 3} 2 \ln x$
21. $\lim\limits_{x \to 0} \arccos x$
22. $\lim\limits_{x \to 1} \arctan x$

11.2

Finding a Limit   In Exercises 23–32, find the limit (if it exists). Use a graphing utility to confirm your result graphically.

23. $\lim\limits_{t \to -2} \dfrac{t + 2}{t^2 - 4}$
24. $\lim\limits_{t \to 3} \dfrac{t^2 - 9}{t - 3}$
25. $\lim\limits_{x \to 5} \dfrac{x - 5}{x^2 + 5x - 50}$
26. $\lim\limits_{x \to -1} \dfrac{x + 1}{x^2 - 5x - 6}$
27. $\lim\limits_{x \to 1} \dfrac{x^2 + 7x - 8}{x^2 - 3x + 2}$
28. $\lim\limits_{x \to -2} \dfrac{x^2 + 8x + 12}{x^2 - 3x - 10}$
29. $\lim\limits_{x \to -1} \dfrac{\dfrac{1}{x + 2} - 1}{x + 1}$
30. $\lim\limits_{x \to 2} \dfrac{\dfrac{1}{x - 3} + 1}{x - 2}$
31. $\lim\limits_{u \to 0} \dfrac{\sqrt{4 + u} - 2}{u}$
32. $\lim\limits_{v \to 0} \dfrac{\sqrt{v + 9} - 3}{v}$

Approximating a Limit   In Exercises 33–40, (a) graphically approximate the limit (if it exists) by using a graphing utility to graph the function and (b) numerically approximate the limit (if it exists) by using the *table* feature of the graphing utility to create a table.

33. $\lim\limits_{x \to 3} \dfrac{x - 3}{x^2 - 9}$
34. $\lim\limits_{x \to 4} \dfrac{4 - x}{16 - x^2}$

35. $\displaystyle\lim_{x\to 0} e^{-2/x}$

36. $\displaystyle\lim_{x\to 0} e^{-4/x^2}$

37. $\displaystyle\lim_{x\to 0} \frac{\sin 4x}{2x}$

38. $\displaystyle\lim_{x\to 0} \frac{\tan 2x}{x}$

39. $\displaystyle\lim_{x\to 1^+} \frac{\sqrt{2x+1}-\sqrt{3}}{x-1}$

40. $\displaystyle\lim_{x\to 1^+} \frac{1-\sqrt{x}}{x-1}$

Evaluating One-Sided Limits In Exercises 41–48, graph the function. Determine the limit (if it exists) by evaluating the corresponding one-sided limits.

41. $\displaystyle\lim_{x\to 0} \frac{|3x|}{x}$

42. $\displaystyle\lim_{x\to 0} \frac{|x|}{2x}$

43. $\displaystyle\lim_{x\to 2} \frac{2}{x^2-4}$

44. $\displaystyle\lim_{x\to 3} \frac{1}{x^2-9}$

45. $\displaystyle\lim_{x\to 5} \frac{|x-5|}{x-5}$

46. $\displaystyle\lim_{x\to -2} \frac{|x+2|}{x+2}$

47. $\displaystyle\lim_{x\to -2} f(x)$ where $f(x) = \begin{cases} 4-x, & x \le -2 \\ x^2-3, & x > -2 \end{cases}$

48. $\displaystyle\lim_{x\to 0} f(x)$ where $f(x) = \begin{cases} x-6, & x \ge 0 \\ x^2-4, & x < 0 \end{cases}$

Evaluating a Limit from Calculus In Exercises 49 and 50, find $\displaystyle\lim_{h\to 0} \frac{f(x+h)-f(x)}{h}$.

49. $f(x) = 3x - x^2$

50. $f(x) = x^2 - 5x - 2$

11.3

Approximating the Slope of a Graph In Exercises 51 and 52, use the figure to approximate the slope of the graph at the point (x, y).

51.

52.

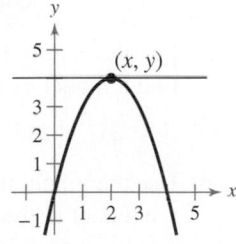

Approximating the Slope of a Tangent Line In Exercises 53–58, use a graphing utility to graph the function and the tangent line at the point $(2, f(2))$. Use the graph to approximate the slope of the tangent line.

53. $f(x) = 2x - x^2$

54. $f(x) = 6 - x^2$

55. $f(x) = \sqrt{x+2}$

56. $f(x) = \sqrt{x^2+5}$

57. $f(x) = \dfrac{6}{x-4}$

58. $f(x) = \dfrac{1}{3-x}$

Finding a Formula for the Slope of a Graph In Exercises 59–62, find a formula for the slope of the graph of f at the point $(x, f(x))$. Then use it to find the slopes at the two specified points.

59. $f(x) = x^2 - 4x$
  (a) $(4, 0)$
  (b) $(-1, 5)$

60. $f(x) = \frac{1}{4}x^4$
  (a) $(-2, 4)$
  (b) $\left(1, \frac{1}{4}\right)$

61. $f(x) = \dfrac{4}{x-6}$
  (a) $\left(9, \frac{4}{3}\right)$
  (b) $(8, 2)$

62. $f(x) = \sqrt{x}$
  (a) $(1, 1)$
  (b) $(4, 2)$

Finding a Derivative In Exercises 63–74, find the derivative of the function.

63. $f(x) = 9$

64. $g(x) = -3$

65. $h(x) = 7 - 6x$

66. $f(x) = 3x$

67. $g(x) = 2x^2 + x - 3$

68. $f(x) = -x^3 + 4x$

69. $f(t) = \sqrt{t+5}$

70. $g(t) = \sqrt{t-6}$

71. $g(s) = \dfrac{4}{s+5}$

72. $g(t) = \dfrac{6}{5-t}$

73. $g(x) = \dfrac{1}{\sqrt{x+4}}$

74. $f(x) = \dfrac{1}{\sqrt{12-x}}$

Using the Derivative In Exercises 75–78, (a) find the slope of the graph of f at the given point, (b) find an equation of the tangent line to the graph at the point, and (c) graph the function and the tangent line.

75. $f(x) = 2x^2 - 1$, $(3, 17)$

76. $f(x) = x^2 + 10$, $(2, 14)$

77. $f(x) = x^3 + 1$, $(1, 2)$ **78.** $f(x) = x^3 - x$, $(2, 6)$

11.4

Evaluating a Limit at Infinity In Exercises 79–86, find the limit (if it exists). If the limit does not exist, explain why. Use a graphing utility to verify your result graphically.

79. $\displaystyle\lim_{x\to\infty} \frac{4x}{2x-3}$

80. $\displaystyle\lim_{x\to\infty} \frac{7x}{14x+2}$

81. $\displaystyle\lim_{x\to -\infty} \frac{x+3}{3-x}$

82. $\displaystyle\lim_{x\to -\infty} \frac{1-2x}{x+2}$

83. $\displaystyle\lim_{x\to\infty} \frac{x^2}{2x+3}$

84. $\displaystyle\lim_{y\to\infty} \frac{3y^4}{y^2+1}$

85. $\displaystyle\lim_{x\to\infty} \left[\frac{x}{(x-2)^2} + 3 \right]$

86. $\displaystyle\lim_{x\to\infty} \left[2 - \frac{2x^2}{(x+1)^2} \right]$

Finding the Limit of a Sequence In Exercises 87–92, write the first five terms of the sequence and find the limit of the sequence (if it exists). If the limit does not exist, explain why. Assume n begins with 1.

87. $a_n = \dfrac{2n - 3}{5n + 4}$

88. $a_n = \dfrac{2n}{n^2 + 1}$

89. $a_n = \dfrac{(-1)^n}{n^3}$

90. $a_n = \dfrac{(-1)^{n+1}}{n}$

91. $a_n = \dfrac{1}{2n^2}[3 - 2n(n + 1)]$

92. $a_n = \dfrac{3}{n}\left\{ n + \dfrac{2}{n}\left[\dfrac{n(n - 1)}{2} \right] \right\}$

11.5

Finding the Limit of a Summation In Exercises 93 and 94, (a) rewrite the sum as a rational function $S(n)$. (b) Use $S(n)$ to complete the table. (c) Find $\lim\limits_{n \to \infty} S(n)$.

n	10^0	10^1	10^2	10^3	10^4
$S(n)$					

93. $\displaystyle\sum_{i=1}^{n} \left(\dfrac{4i^2}{n^2} - \dfrac{i}{n} \right)\left(\dfrac{1}{n} \right)$

94. $\displaystyle\sum_{i=1}^{n} \left[4 - \left(\dfrac{3i}{n} \right)^2 \right]\left(\dfrac{3i}{n^2} \right)$

Approximating the Area of a Region In Exercises 95 and 96, approximate the area of the region using the indicated number of rectangles of equal width.

95. $f(x) = 4 - x$

96. $f(x) = 4 - x^2$

Approximating the Area of a Region In Exercises 97 and 98, complete the table to show the approximate area of the region using the indicated numbers n of rectangles of equal width.

n	4	8	20	50
Approximate area				

97. $f(x) = \tfrac{1}{4}x^2$

98. $f(x) = 4x - x^2$

Finding the Area of a Region In Exercises 99–104, use the limit process to find the area of the region bounded by the graph of the function and the x-axis over the specified interval.

	Function	Interval
99.	$f(x) = 10 - x$	$[4, 6]$
100.	$f(x) = 2x - 6$	$[3, 6]$
101.	$f(x) = x^2 + 4$	$[0, 3]$
102.	$f(x) = 6(x - x^2)$	$[0, 1]$
103.	$f(x) = x^3 + 1$	$[0, 4]$
104.	$f(x) = 8 - x^3$	$[0, 2]$

105. **Civil Engineering** The table shows the measurements (in feet) of a lot bounded by a stream and two straight roads that meet at right angles. (See figure.)

x	0	100	200	300	400	500
y	125	125	120	112	90	90

x	600	700	800	900	1000
y	95	88	75	35	0

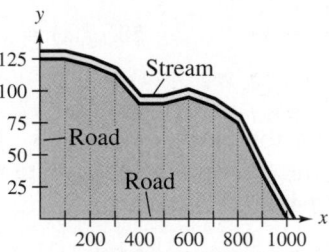

(a) Use the *regression* feature of a graphing utility to find a model of the form

$$y = ax^3 + bx^2 + cx + d.$$

(b) Use the graphing utility to plot the data and graph the model in the same viewing window.

(c) Use the model in part (a) to estimate the area of the lot.

Conclusions

True or False? In Exercises 106 and 107, determine whether the statement is true or false. Justify your answer.

106. If the degree of the numerator $N(x)$ of a rational function $f(x) = N(x)/D(x)$ is greater than the degree of its denominator $D(x)$, then the limit of the rational function as x approaches ∞ is 0.

107. The expression $f'(z)$ gives the slope of the tangent line to the graph of f at the point $(z, f(z))$.

108. **Writing** Write a short paragraph explaining several reasons why the limit of a function may not exist.

11　Chapter Test

Take this test as you would take a test in class. After you are finished, check your work against the answers given in the back of the book.

In Exercises 1–3, use a graphing utility to graph the function and approximate the limit (if it exists). Then find the limit (if it exists) algebraically by using appropriate techniques.

1. $\lim\limits_{x \to -2} \dfrac{x^2 - 1}{2x}$

2. $\lim\limits_{x \to 1} \dfrac{5 - 4x - x^2}{1 - x}$

3. $\lim\limits_{x \to 5} \dfrac{\sqrt{x} - 2}{x - 5}$

In Exercises 4 and 5, use a graphing utility to graph the function and approximate the limit. Write an approximation that is accurate to four decimal places. Then create a table to verify your limit numerically.

4. $\lim\limits_{x \to 0} \dfrac{\sin 5x}{3x}$

5. $\lim\limits_{x \to 0} \dfrac{e^{3x} - 1}{x}$

6. Find a formula for the slope of the graph of f at the point $(x, f(x))$. Then use it to find the slope at the specified point.

   (a) $f(x) = 3x^2 - 5x - 2, \ (2, 0)$

   (b) $f(x) = 2x^3 + 6x, \ (-1, -8)$

In Exercises 7–9, find the derivative of the function.

7. $f(x) = 3 - \dfrac{2}{5}x$

8. $f(x) = 2x^2 + 4x - 1$

9. $f(x) = \dfrac{1}{x + 1}$

In Exercises 10–12, find the limit (if it exists). If the limit does not exist, explain why. Use a graphing utility to verify your result graphically.

10. $\lim\limits_{x \to \infty} \dfrac{6}{5x - 1}$

11. $\lim\limits_{x \to \infty} \dfrac{1 - 3x^2}{x^2 - 5}$

12. $\lim\limits_{x \to -\infty} \dfrac{x^2}{3x + 2}$

In Exercises 13 and 14, write the first five terms of the sequence and find the limit of the sequence (if it exists). If the limit does not exist, explain why. Assume n begins with 1.

13. $a_n = \dfrac{n^2 + 3n - 4}{2n^2 + n - 2}$

14. $a_n = \dfrac{1 + (-1)^n}{n}$

15. Approximate the area of the region bounded by the graph of $f(x) = 8 - 2x^2$ shown at the right using the indicated number of rectangles of equal width.

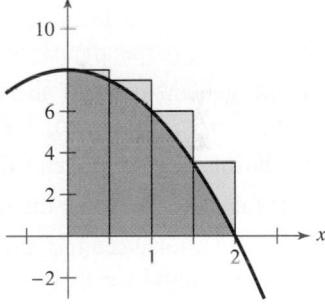

Figure for 15

In Exercises 16 and 17, use the limit process to find the area of the region bounded by the graph of the function and the *x*-axis over the specified interval.

16. $f(x) = x + 3$; interval: $[-2, 2]$

17. $f(x) = 7 - x^2$; interval: $[0, 2]$

18. The table shows the height of a space shuttle during its first 5 seconds of motion.

    (a) Use the *regression* feature of a graphing utility to find a quadratic model $y = ax^2 + bx + c$ for the data.

    (b) The value of the derivative of the model is the rate of change of height with respect to time, or the velocity, at that instant. Find the velocity of the shuttle after 5 seconds.

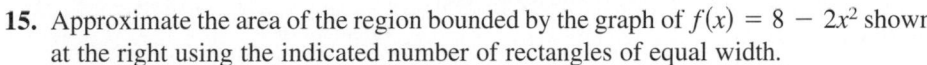

DATA	Time, x (in seconds)	Height, y (in feet)
	0	0
	1	1
	2	23
	3	60
	4	115
	5	188

Spreadsheet at LarsonPrecalculus.com

Table for 18

10–11   Cumulative Test

See *CalcChat.com* for tutorial help and worked-out solutions to odd-numbered exercises.
For instructions on how to use a graphing utility, see Appendix A.

Take this test to review the material in Chapters 10 and 11. After you are finished, check your work against the answers given in the back of the book.

In Exercises 1 and 2, find the coordinates of the point.

1. The point is located seven units behind the yz-plane, eight units to the right of the xz-plane, and nine units above the xy-plane.

2. The point is located on the z-axis, five units below the xy-plane.

3. Find the distance between the points $(-2, 3, -6)$ and $(4, -5, 1)$.

4. Find the lengths of the sides of the right triangle at the right. Show that these lengths satisfy the Pythagorean Theorem.

5. Find the midpoint of the line segment joining $(3, 4, -1)$ and $(-5, 0, 2)$.

6. Find the standard form of the equation of the sphere for which the endpoints of a diameter are $(0, 0, 0)$ and $(4, 4, 8)$.

7. Sketch the graph of the equation $(x - 2)^2 + (y + 1)^2 + z^2 = 4$, and then sketch the xy-trace and the yz-trace.

8. For the vectors $\mathbf{u} = \langle 2, -6, 0 \rangle$ and $\mathbf{v} = \langle -4, 5, 3 \rangle$, find $\mathbf{u} \cdot \mathbf{v}$ and $\mathbf{u} \times \mathbf{v}$.

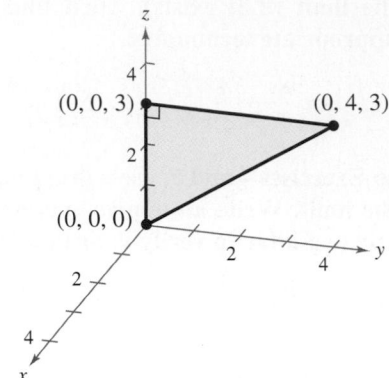

Figure for 4

In Exercises 9–11, determine whether u and v are orthogonal, parallel, or neither.

9. $\mathbf{u} = \langle 4, 4, 0 \rangle$
   $\mathbf{v} = \langle 0, -8, 6 \rangle$

10. $\mathbf{u} = \langle 4, -2, 10 \rangle$
    $\mathbf{v} = \langle -2, 6, 2 \rangle$

11. $\mathbf{u} = \langle -1, 6, -3 \rangle$
    $\mathbf{v} = \langle 3, -18, 9 \rangle$

12. Find the volume of the parallelepiped with the vertices $A(1, 3, 2)$, $B(3, 4, 2)$, $C(3, 2, 2)$, $D(1, 1, 2)$, $E(1, 3, 5)$, $F(3, 4, 5)$, $G(3, 2, 5)$, and $H(1, 1, 5)$.

13. Find sets of (a) parametric equations and (b) symmetric equations for the line passing through the points $(-2, 3, 0)$ and $(5, 8, 25)$.

14. Find the parametric form of the equation of the line passing through the point $(-1, 2, 0)$ and perpendicular to $2x - 4y + z = 8$.

15. Find the general form of the equation of the plane passing through the points $(0, 0, 0)$, $(-2, 3, 0)$, and $(5, 8, 25)$.

16. Label the intercepts and sketch the graph of the plane given by $3x - 6y - 12z = 24$.

17. Find the distance between the point $(0, 0, 25)$ and the plane $2x - 5y + z = 10$.

18. A plastic wastebasket has the shape and dimensions shown in the figure. In fabricating a mold for making the wastebasket, it is necessary to know the angle between two adjacent sides. Find the angle.

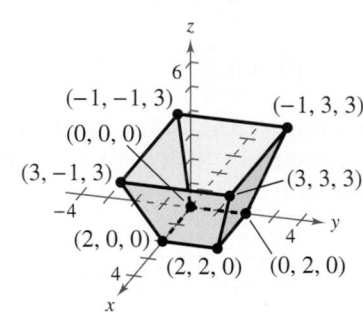

Figure for 18

In Exercises 19–27, find the limit (if it exists). If the limit does not exist, explain why. Use a graphing utility to verify your result graphically.

19. $\lim\limits_{x \to 4} (5x - x^2)$

20. $\lim\limits_{x \to -2} \dfrac{x - 1}{x^2 + x - 2}$

21. $\lim\limits_{x \to 7} \dfrac{x - 7}{x^2 - 49}$

22. $\lim\limits_{x \to -3} \dfrac{4|x + 3|}{x + 3}$

23. $\lim\limits_{x \to 4^-} \dfrac{|x - 4|}{x - 4}$

24. $\lim\limits_{x \to 0} \sin\left(\dfrac{\pi}{x}\right)$

25. $\lim\limits_{x \to 0} \dfrac{\dfrac{1}{x + 3} - \dfrac{1}{3}}{x}$

26. $\lim\limits_{x \to 0} \dfrac{\sqrt{x + 16} - 4}{x}$

27. $\lim\limits_{x \to 2} \dfrac{x - 2}{x^2 - 4}$

In Exercises 28–31, find a formula for the slope of the graph of f at the point $(x, f(x))$. Then use it to find the slope at the specified point.

28. $f(x) = 7 - x^2,$ $(-2, 3)$

29. $f(x) = \sqrt{x + 6},$ $(10, 4)$

30. $f(x) = \dfrac{1}{x + 3},$ $\left(1, \dfrac{1}{4}\right)$

31. $f(x) = x^2 - x,$ $(1, 0)$

In Exercises 32–37, find the limit (if it exists). If the limit does not exist, explain why. Use a graphing utility to verify your result graphically.

32. $\displaystyle\lim_{x \to \infty} \frac{x^3}{x^2 - 9}$

33. $\displaystyle\lim_{x \to \infty} \left(\frac{7}{x^3} - 8\right)$

34. $\displaystyle\lim_{x \to \infty} \frac{3x^2 + 1}{x^2 + 4}$

35. $\displaystyle\lim_{x \to \infty} \frac{2x}{x^2 + 3x - 2}$

36. $\displaystyle\lim_{x \to \infty} \frac{3 - x}{x^2 + 1}$

37. $\displaystyle\lim_{x \to \infty} \frac{3 + 4x - x^3}{2x^2 + 3}$

In Exercises 38–40, evaluate the sum using the summation formulas and properties.

38. $\displaystyle\sum_{i=1}^{50} (1 - i^2)$ **39.** $\displaystyle\sum_{k=1}^{20} (3k^2 - 2k)$ **40.** $\displaystyle\sum_{i=1}^{40} (12 + i^3)$

In Exercises 41–44, approximate the area of the region using the indicated number of rectangles of equal width.

41.

42.

43.

44.

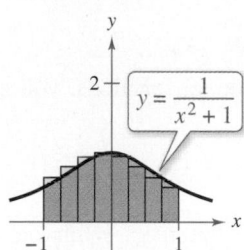

In Exercises 45–48, use the limit process to find the area of the region bounded by the graph of the function and the x-axis over the specified interval.

45. $f(x) = x^2 + 3$

Interval: $[0, 2]$

46. $f(x) = x + 5$

Interval: $[1, 5]$

47. $f(x) = 6 - x^2$

Interval: $[-1, 1]$

48. $f(x) = 1 - x^3$

Interval: $[0, 1]$

Proofs in Mathematics

Many of the proofs of the definitions and properties presented in this chapter are beyond the scope of this text. Included below are simple proofs for the limit of a power function and the limit of a polynomial function.

> **Limit of a Power Function (p. 755)**
>
> $\lim\limits_{x \to c} x^n = c^n$, where c is a real number and n is a positive integer.

Proving Limits

To prove most of the definitions and properties from this chapter, you must use the *formal definition of a limit*. This definition is called the *epsilon-delta definition* and was first introduced by Karl Weierstrass (1815–1897). If you go on to take a course in calculus, you will use this definition of a limit extensively.

Proof

$$\lim_{x \to c} x^n = \lim_{x \to c} (\underbrace{x \cdot x \cdot x \cdot \cdots \cdot x}_{n \text{ factors}})$$

$$= \underbrace{\lim_{x \to c} x \cdot \lim_{x \to c} x \cdot \lim_{x \to c} x \cdot \cdots \cdot \lim_{x \to c} x}_{n \text{ factors}} \qquad \text{Product Property of Limits}$$

$$= \underbrace{c \cdot c \cdot c \cdot \cdots \cdot c}_{n \text{ factors}} \qquad \text{Limit of the identity function}$$

$$= c^n \qquad \text{Exponential form} \quad \blacksquare$$

> **Limit of a Polynomial Function (p. 756)**
>
> If p is a polynomial function and c is a real number, then
>
> $$\lim_{x \to c} p(x) = p(c).$$

Proof

Let p be a polynomial function such that

$$p(x) = a_n x^n + a_{n-1} x^{n-1} + \cdots + a_2 x^2 + a_1 x + a_0.$$

Because a polynomial function is the sum of monomial functions, you can write the following.

$$\lim_{x \to c} p(x) = \lim_{x \to c} (a_n x^n + a_{n-1} x^{n-1} + \cdots + a_2 x^2 + a_1 x + a_0)$$

$$= \lim_{x \to c} a_n x^n + \lim_{x \to c} a_{n-1} x^{n-1} + \cdots + \lim_{x \to c} a_2 x^2 + \lim_{x \to c} a_1 x + \lim_{x \to c} a_0$$

$$\qquad \text{Scalar Multiple Property of}$$

$$= a_n c^n + a_{n-1} c^{n-1} + \cdots + a_2 c^2 + a_1 c + a_0 \qquad \text{Limits and limit of a power}$$

$$\qquad \text{function}$$

$$= p(c) \qquad p \text{ evaluated at } c \quad \blacksquare$$

Progressive Summary (Chapters 3–11)

This chart outlines the topics that have been covered so far in this text. Progressive Summary charts appear after Chapters 2, 3, 6, 9, and 11. In each Progressive Summary, new topics encountered for the first time appear in blue.

Transcendental Functions

Exponential, Logarithmic, Trigonometric, Inverse Trigonometric

■ Rewriting
Exponential form $\leftrightarrow$ Logarithmic form
Condense/expand logarithmic
  expressions
Simplify trigonometric expressions
Prove trigonometric identities
Use conversion formulas
Operations with vectors
Powers and roots of complex numbers

■ Solving

Equation	*Strategy*
Exponential	Take logarithm of each side
Logarithmic	Exponentiate each side
Trigonometric	Isolate function Factor, use inverse function
Multiple angle . . . . or high powers	Use trigonometric identities

■ Analyzing

Graphically	*Algebraically*
Intercepts	Domain, Range
Asymptotes	Transformations
Minimum values	Composition
Maximum values	Inverse Properties
	Amplitude, Period
	Reference angles

Numerically
Table of values

Systems and Series

Systems, Sequences, Series

■ Rewriting
Row operations for systems of equations
Partial fraction decomposition
Operations with matrices
Matrix form of a system of equations
nth term of a sequence
Summation form of a series

■ Solving

Equation	*Strategy*
System of . . . . linear equations	Substitution
	Elimination
	Gaussian
	Gauss-Jordan
	Inverse matrices
	Cramer's Rule

■ Analyzing
Systems:
  Intersecting, parallel, and coincident lines, determinants
Sequences:
  Graphing utility in *dot* mode, nth term, partial sums, summation formulas

Other Topics

Conics, Parametric and Polar Equations 3-space, Limits

■ Rewriting
Standard forms of conics
Eliminate parameters
Rectangular form $\leftrightarrow$ Parametric form
Rectangular form $\leftrightarrow$ Polar form
Rationalize numerator
Difference quotient

■ Solving

Equation	*Strategy*
Conics	Convert to standard form
	Convert to polar form
3-space	Equation of plane
	Equation of line
	Cross-product of vectors
Limits	Direct substitution
	One-sided limits
	Limits at infinity

■ Analyzing
Conics:
  Table of values, vertices, foci, axes, symmetry, asymptotes, translations, eccentricity
Parametric forms:
  Point plotting, eliminate parameters
Polar forms:
  Point plotting, special equations, symmetry, zeros, eccentricity, directrix
3-space:
  Point plotting, intercepts, traces, vectors

Appendix A: Technology Support

Introduction

Graphing utilities, such as graphing calculators and computers with graphing software, are very valuable tools for visualizing mathematical principles, verifying solutions of equations, exploring mathematical ideas, and developing mathematical models. Although graphing utilities are extremely helpful in learning mathematics, their use does not mean that learning algebra is any less important. In fact, the combination of knowledge of mathematics and the use of graphing utilities enables you to explore mathematics more easily and to a greater depth. If you are using a graphing utility in this course, it is up to you to learn its capabilities and to practice using this tool to enhance your mathematical learning.

In this text, there are many opportunities to use a graphing utility, some of which are described below.

Uses of a Graphing Utility

1. Check or validate answers to problems obtained using algebraic methods.

2. Discover and explore algebraic properties, rules, and concepts.

3. Graph functions, and approximate solutions of equations involving functions.

4. Efficiently perform complicated mathematical procedures, such as those found in many real-life applications.

5. Find mathematical models for sets of data.

In this appendix, the features of graphing utilities are discussed from a generic perspective and are listed in alphabetical order. To learn how to use the features of a specific graphing utility, consult your user's manual or go to this textbook's *Companion Website*. Additional keystroke guides are available for most graphing utilities, and your college library may have a resource on how to use your graphing utility.

Many graphing utilities are designed to act as "function graphers." In this course, functions and their graphs are studied in detail. You may recall from previous courses that a function can be thought of as a rule that describes the relationship between two variables. These rules are frequently written in terms of x and y. For instance, the equation

$$y = 3x + 5$$

represents y as a function of x.

Many graphing utilities have an *equation editor* feature that requires that an equation be written in "$y =$" form in order to be entered, as shown in Figure A.1. (You should note that your *equation editor* screen may not look like the screen shown in Figure A.1.)

```
Plot1  Plot2  Plot3
\Y1■3X+5
\Y2=
\Y3=
\Y4=
\Y5=
\Y6=
\Y7=
```

Figure A.1

Cumulative Sum Feature

The *cumulative sum* feature finds partial sums of a series. For instance, to find the first four partial sums of the series

$$\sum_{k=1}^{4} 2(0.1)^k$$

choose the *cumulative sum* feature, which is found in the *operations* menu of the *list* feature (see Figure A.2). To use this feature, you will also have to use the *sequence* feature (see Figure A.2 and page A15). You must enter an expression for the sequence, a variable, the lower limit of summation, and the upper limit of summation, as shown in Figure A.3. After pressing ENTER, you can see that the first four partial sums are 0.2, 0.22, 0.222, and 0.2222. You may have to scroll to the right in order to see all the partial sums.

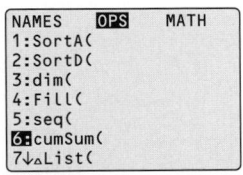

Figure A.2   Figure A.3

Technology Tip

As you use your graphing utility, be aware of how parentheses are inserted in an expression. Some graphing utilities automatically insert the left parenthesis when certain calculator buttons are pressed. The placement of parentheses can make a difference between a correct answer and an incorrect answer.

Determinant Feature

The *determinant* feature evaluates the determinant of a square matrix. For instance, to evaluate the determinant of

$$A = \begin{bmatrix} 7 & -1 & 0 \\ 2 & 2 & 3 \\ -6 & 4 & 1 \end{bmatrix}$$

enter the 3×3 matrix in the graphing utility using the *matrix editor*, as shown in Figure A.4. Then choose the *determinant* feature from the *math* menu of the *matrix* feature, as shown in Figure A.5. Once you choose the matrix name, A, press ENTER and you should obtain a determinant of -50, as shown in Figure A.6.

Figure A.4   Figure A.5   Figure A.6

Draw Inverse Feature

The *draw inverse* feature graphs the inverse function of a *one-to-one* function. For instance, to graph the inverse function of $f(x) = x^3 + 4$, first enter the function in the *equation editor* (see Figure A.7) and graph the function (using a square viewing window), as shown in Figure A.8. Then choose the *draw inverse* feature from the *draw* feature menu, as shown in Figure A.9. You must enter the function you want to graph the inverse function of, as shown in Figure A.10. Finally, press ENTER to obtain the graph of the inverse function of $f(x) = x^3 + 4$, as shown in Figure A.11. This feature can be used only when the graphing utility is in *function* mode.

Figure A.7

Figure A.8

Figure A.9

Figure A.10

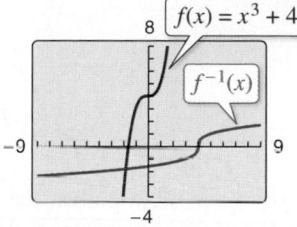

Figure A.11

Elementary Row Operations Features

Most graphing utilities can perform elementary row operations on matrices.

Row Swap Feature

The *row swap* feature interchanges two rows of a matrix. To interchange rows 1 and 3 of the matrix

$$A = \begin{bmatrix} -1 & -2 & 1 & 2 \\ 2 & -4 & 6 & -2 \\ 1 & 3 & -3 & 0 \end{bmatrix}$$

first enter the matrix in the graphing utility using the *matrix editor*, as shown in Figure A.12. Then choose the *row swap* feature from the *math* menu of the *matrix* feature, as shown in Figure A.13. When using this feature, you must enter the name of the matrix and the two rows that are to be interchanged. After pressing (ENTER), you should obtain the matrix shown in Figure A.14. Because the resulting matrix will be used to demonstrate the other elementary row operation features, use the *store* feature to copy the resulting matrix to [A], as shown in Figure A.15.

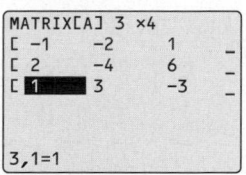

Figure A.12

Figure A.13

Figure A.14

Figure A.15

Technology Tip

The *store* feature of a graphing utility is used to store a value in a variable or to copy one matrix to another matrix. For instance, as shown at the left, after performing a row operation on a matrix, you can copy the answer to another matrix (see Figure A.15). You can then perform another row operation on the copied matrix. To continue performing row operations to obtain a matrix in row-echelon form or reduced row-echelon form, you must copy the resulting matrix to a new matrix before each operation.

Row Addition and Row Multiplication and Addition Features

The *row addition* and *row multiplication and addition* features add a row or a multiple of a row of a matrix to another row of the same matrix. To add row 1 to row 3 of the matrix stored in [A], choose the *row addition* feature from the *math* menu of the *matrix* feature, as shown in Figure A.16. When using this feature, you must enter the name of the matrix and the two rows that are to be added. After pressing (ENTER), you should obtain the matrix shown in Figure A.17. Copy the resulting matrix to [A].

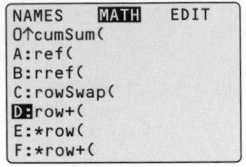

Figure A.16	**Figure A.17**

To add -2 times row 1 to row 2 of the matrix stored in [A], choose the *row multiplication and addition* feature from the *math* menu of the *matrix* feature, as shown in Figure A.18. When using this feature, you must enter the constant, the name of the matrix, the row the constant is multiplied by, and the row to be added to. After pressing (ENTER), you should obtain the matrix shown in Figure A.19. Copy the resulting matrix to [A].

Figure A.18	**Figure A.19**

Row Multiplication Feature

The *row multiplication* feature multiplies a row of a matrix by a nonzero constant. To multiply row 2 of the matrix stored in [A] by

$$-\frac{1}{10}$$

choose the *row multiplication* feature from the *math* menu of the *matrix* feature, as shown in Figure A.20. When using this feature, you must enter the constant, the name of the matrix, and the row to be multiplied. After pressing (ENTER), you should obtain the matrix shown in Figure A.21.

Figure A.20	**Figure A.21**

Intersect Feature

The *intersect* feature finds the point(s) of intersection of two graphs. The *intersect* feature is found in the *calculate* menu (see Figure A.22).

Figure A.22

To find the point(s) of intersection of the graphs of $y_1 = -x + 2$ and $y_2 = x + 4$, first enter the equations in the *equation editor*, as shown in Figure A.23. Then graph the equations, as shown in Figure A.24. Next, use the *intersect* feature to find the point of intersection. Trace the cursor along the graph of y_1 near the intersection and press (ENTER) (see Figure A.25). Then trace the cursor along the graph of y^2 near the intersection and press (ENTER) (see Figure A.26). Marks are then placed on the graph at these points (see Figure A.27). Finally, move the cursor near the point of intersection and press (ENTER). In Figure A.28, you can see that the coordinates of the point of intersection are displayed at the bottom of the window. So, the point of intersection is $(-1, 3)$.

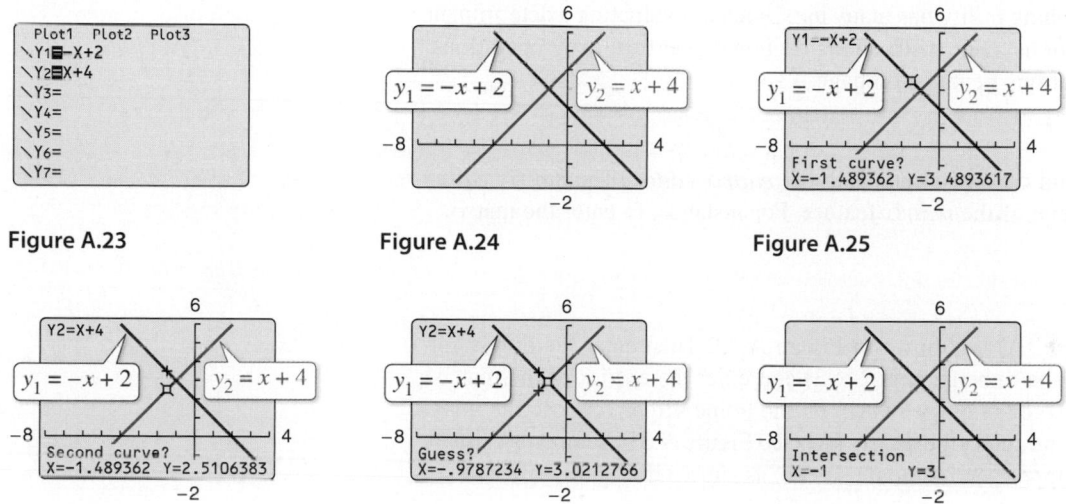

Figure A.23   **Figure A.24**   **Figure A.25**

Figure A.26   **Figure A.27**   **Figure A.28**

List Editor

Most graphing utilities can store data in lists. The *list editor* can be used to create tables and to store statistical data. The *list editor* can be found in the *edit* menu of the *statistics* feature, as shown in Figure A.29. To enter the numbers 1 through 10 in a list, first choose a list (L_1) and then begin entering the data into each row, as shown in Figure A.30.

Figure A.29   **Figure A.30**

You can also attach a formula to a list. For instance, you can multiply each of the data values in L_1 by 3. First, display the *list editor* and move the cursor to the top line.

Then move the cursor onto the list to which you want to attach the formula (L_2). Finally, enter the formula 3*L_1 (see Figure A.31) and then press ENTER. You should obtain the list shown in Figure A.32.

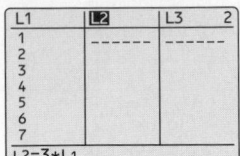

Figure A.31   Figure A.32

Matrix Feature

The *matrix* feature of a graphing utility has many uses, such as evaluating a determinant and performing row operations. (For instructions on how to perform row operations, see Elementary Row Operations Features on page A3.)

Matrix Editor

You can define, display, and edit matrices using the *matrix editor*. The *matrix editor* can be found in the *edit* menu of the *matrix* feature. For instance, to enter the matrix

$$A = \begin{bmatrix} 6 & -3 & 4 \\ 9 & 0 & -1 \end{bmatrix}$$

first choose the matrix name [A], as shown in Figure A.33. Then enter the dimension of the matrix (in this case, the dimension is 2×3) and enter the entries of the matrix, as shown in Figure A.34. To display the matrix on the home screen, choose the *name* menu of the *matrix* feature and select the matrix [A] (see Figure A.35), then press ENTER. The matrix A should now appear on the home screen, as shown in Figure A.36.

Figure A.33   Figure A.34

Figure A.35   Figure A.36

Matrix Operations

Most graphing utilities can perform matrix operations. To find the sum $A + B$ of the matrices shown at the right, first enter the matrices in the *matrix editor* as [A] and [B]. Then find the sum, as shown in Figure A.37. Scalar multiplication can be performed in a similar manner. For instance, you can evaluate $7A$, where A is the matrix at the right, as shown in Figure A.38. To find the product AB of the matrices A and B at the right, first be sure that the product is defined. Because the number of columns of A (2 columns) equals the number of rows of B (2 rows), you can find the product AB, as shown in Figure A.39.

$$A = \begin{bmatrix} -3 & 5 \\ 0 & 4 \end{bmatrix}$$

$$B = \begin{bmatrix} 7 & -2 \\ -1 & 2 \end{bmatrix}$$

Figure A.37

Figure A.38

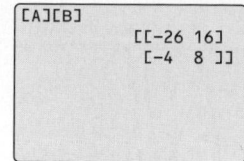

Figure A.39

Inverse Matrix

Some graphing utilities may not have an *inverse matrix* feature. However, you can find the inverse of a square matrix by using the inverse key $\boxed{x^{-1}}$. To find the inverse of the matrix

$$A = \begin{bmatrix} 1 & -2 & 1 \\ -1 & 3 & 0 \\ 2 & 4 & 5 \end{bmatrix}$$

enter the matrix in the *matrix editor* as [A]. Then find the inverse, as shown in Figure A.40.

Figure A.40

Maximum and Minimum Features

The *maximum* and *minimum* features find relative extrema of a function. For instance, the graph of

$$y = x^3 - 3x$$

is shown in Figure A.41. In the figure, the graph appears to have a relative maximum at $x = -1$ and a relative minimum at $x = 1$. To find the exact values of the relative extrema, you can use the *maximum* and *minimum* features found in the *calculate* menu (see Figure A.42). First, to find the relative maximum, choose the *maximum* feature and trace the cursor along the graph to a point left of the maximum and press $\boxed{\text{ENTER}}$ (see Figure A.43). Then trace the cursor along the graph to a point right of the maximum and press $\boxed{\text{ENTER}}$ (see Figure A.44). Note the two arrows near the top of the display marking the left and right bounds, as shown in Figure A.45. Next, trace the cursor along the graph between the two bounds and as close to the maximum as you can (see Figure A.45) and press $\boxed{\text{ENTER}}$. In Figure A.46, you can see that the coordinates of the maximum point are displayed at the bottom of the window. So, the relative maximum occurs at the point $(-1, 2)$.

Figure A.41

Figure A.42

Figure A.43

Figure A.44

Figure A.45

Figure A.46

Figure A.47

You can find the relative minimum in a similar manner. In Figure A.47, you can see that the relative minimum occurs at the point $(1, -2)$.

Mean and Median Features

In real-life applications, you often encounter large data sets and want to calculate statistical values. The *mean* and *median* features calculate the mean and median of a data set. For instance, in a survey, 100 people were asked how much money (in dollars) per week they withdraw from an automatic teller machine (ATM). The results are shown in the table below. The frequency represents the number of responses.

Amount	10	20	30	40	50	60	70	80	90	100
Frequency	3	8	10	19	24	13	13	7	2	1

To find the mean and median of the data set, first enter the data in the *list editor*, as shown in Figure A.48. Enter the amount in L_1 and the frequency in L_2. Then choose the *mean* feature from the *math* menu of the *list* feature, as shown in Figure A.49. When using this feature, you must enter a list and a frequency list (if applicable). In this case, the list is L_1 and the frequency list is L_2. After pressing (ENTER), you should obtain a mean of

    $49.80

as shown in Figure A.50. You can follow the same steps (except choose the *median* feature) to find the median of the data. You should obtain a median of

    $50

as shown in Figure A.51.

Figure A.48

Figure A.50

Figure A.49

Figure A.51

Mode Settings

Mode settings of a graphing utility control how the utility displays and interprets numbers and graphs. The default mode settings are shown in Figure A.52.

Figure A.52

Radian and Degree Modes

The trigonometric functions can be applied to angles measured in either radians or degrees. When your graphing utility is in *radian* mode, it interprets angle values as radians and displays answers in radians. When your graphing utility is in *degree* mode, it interprets angle values as degrees and displays answers in degrees. For instance, to calculate $\sin(\pi/6)$, make sure the calculator is in *radian* mode. You should obtain an answer of 0.5, as shown in Figure A.53. To calculate $\sin 45°$, make sure the calculator is in *degree* mode, as shown in Figure A.54. You should obtain an approximate answer of 0.7071, as shown in Figure A.55. Without changing the mode of the calculator before evaluating $\sin 45°$, you would obtain an answer of approximately 0.8509, which is the sine of 45 radians.

Figure A.53

Figure A.54

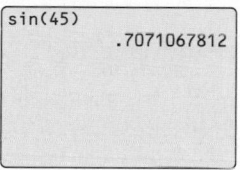

Figure A.55

Function, Parametric, Polar, and Sequence Modes

Most graphing utilities can graph using four different modes.

Function Mode   The *function* mode is used to graph standard algebraic and trigonometric functions. For instance, to graph $y = 2x^2$, use the *function* mode, as shown in Figure A.52. Then enter the equation in the *equation editor*, as shown in Figure A.56. Using a standard viewing window (see Figure A.57), you obtain the graph shown in Figure A.58.

Figure A.56

Figure A.57

Figure A.58

Parametric Mode   To graph parametric equations such as

$$x = t + 1 \quad \text{and} \quad y = t^2$$

use the *parametric* mode, as shown in Figure A.59. Then enter the equations in the *equation editor*, as shown in Figure A.60. Using the viewing window shown in Figure A.61, you obtain the graph shown in Figure A.62.

Figure A.59

Figure A.60

Figure A.61

Figure A.62

Polar Mode   To graph polar equations of the form $r = f(\theta)$, you can use the *polar* mode of a graphing utility. For instance, to graph the polar equation

$$r = 2 \cos \theta$$

use the *polar* mode (and *radian* mode), as shown in Figure A.63. Then enter the equation in the *equation editor*, as shown in Figure A.64. Using the viewing window shown in Figure A.65, you obtain the graph shown in Figure A.66.

Figure A.63

Figure A.64

Figure A.65

Figure A.66

Sequence Mode   To graph the first five terms of a sequence such as

$$a_n = 4n - 5$$

use the *sequence* mode, as shown in Figure A.67. Then enter the sequence in the *equation editor*, as shown in Figure A.68 (assume that n begins with 1). Using the viewing window shown in Figure A.69, you obtain the graph shown in Figure A.70.

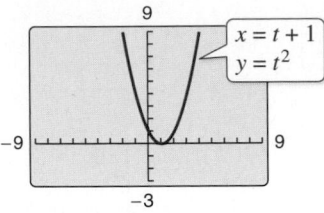

Figure A.67

Figure A.68

Technology Tip

Note that when using the different graphing modes of a graphing utility, the utility uses different variables. When the utility is in *function* mode, it uses the variables x and y. In *parametric* mode, the utility uses the variables x, y, and t. In *polar* mode, the utility uses the variables r and θ. In *sequence* mode, the utility uses the variables u (instead of a) and n.

Figure A.69   **Figure A.70**

Connected and Dot Modes

Graphing utilities use the point-plotting method to graph functions. When a graphing utility is in *connected* mode, the utility connects the points that are plotted. When the utility is in *dot* mode, it does not connect the points that are plotted. For instance, the graph of

$$y = x^3$$

in *connected* mode is shown in Figure A.71. To graph this function using *dot* mode, first change the mode to *dot* mode (see Figure A.72) and then graph the equation, as shown in Figure A.73. As you can see in Figure A.73, the graph is a collection of dots.

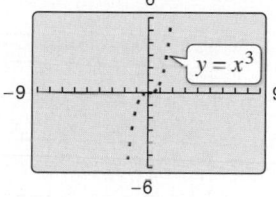

Figure A.71   **Figure A.72**   **Figure A.73**

A problem arises in some graphing utilities when the *connected* mode is used. Graphs with vertical asymptotes, such as rational functions and tangent functions, appear to be connected. For instance, the graph of

$$y = \frac{1}{x + 3}$$

is shown in Figure A.74. Notice how the two portions of the graph appear to be connected with a vertical line at $x = -3$. From your study of rational functions, you know that the graph has a vertical asymptote at $x = -3$ and therefore is undefined when $x = -3$. If your graphing utility draws extraneous vertical lines when graphing functions with vertical asymptotes, you can use the *dot* mode to eliminate the vertical lines, as shown in Figure A.75.

Figure A.74   **Figure A.75**

$_nC_r$ Feature

The $_nC_r$ feature calculates binomial coefficients and the number of combinations of n elements taken r at a time. For instance, to find the number of combinations of eight elements taken five at a time, enter 8 (the n-value) on the home screen and choose the $_nC_r$ feature from the *probability* menu of the *math* feature (see Figure A.76). Next, enter 5 (the r-value) on the home screen and press ENTER. You should obtain 56, as shown in Figure A.77.

Figure A.76   **Figure A.77**

$_nP_r$ Feature

The $_nP_r$ feature calculates the number of permutations of n elements taken r at a time. For instance, to find the number of permutations of six elements taken four at a time, enter 6 (the n-value) on the home screen and choose the $_nP_r$ feature from the *probability* menu of the *math* feature (see Figure A.78). Next, enter 4 (the r-value) on the home screen and press ENTER. You should obtain 360, as shown in Figure A.79.

Figure A.78   **Figure A.79**

One-Variable Statistics Feature

Graphing utilities are useful in calculating statistical values for a set of data. The *one-variable statistics* feature analyzes data with one measured variable. This feature outputs the mean of the data, the sum of the data, the sum of the data squared, the sample standard deviation of the data, the population standard deviation of the data, the number of data points, the minimum data value, the maximum data value, the first quartile of the data, the median of the data, and the third quartile of the data. Consider the following data, which show the hourly earnings (in dollars) of 12 retail sales associates.

8.05, 10.25, 8.45, 9.15, 8.90, 8.20, 9.25, 10.30, 8.60, 9.60, 10.05, 11.35

You can use the *one-variable statistics* feature to determine the mean and standard deviation of the data. First, enter the data in the *list editor*, as shown in Figure A.80. Then choose the *one-variable statistics* feature from the *calculate* menu of the *statistics* feature, as shown in Figure A.81. When using this feature, you must enter a list. In this case, the list is L_1. In Figure A.82, you can see that the mean of the data is

$\bar{x} \approx 9.35$

and the standard deviation of the data is

$\sigma x \approx 0.95$.

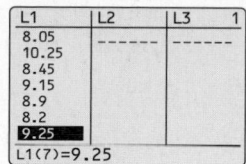

Figure A.80   Figure A.81   Figure A.82

Regression Feature

Throughout the text, you are asked to use the *regression* feature of a graphing utility to find models for sets of data. Most graphing utilities have built-in regression programs for the following.

Regression	*Form of Model*
Linear	$y = ax + b$ or $y = a + bx$
Quadratic	$y = ax^2 + bx + c$
Cubic	$y = ax^3 + bx^2 + cx + d$
Quartic	$y = ax^4 + bx^3 + cx^2 + dx + e$
Logarithmic	$y = a + b \ln x$
Exponential	$y = ab^x$
Power	$y = ax^b$
Logistic	$y = \dfrac{c}{1 + ae^{-bx}}$
Sine	$y = a \sin(bx + c) + d$

For instance, you can find a linear model for the data in the table.

x	y
6	222.8
7	228.7
8	235.0
9	240.3
10	245.0
11	248.2
12	254.4
13	260.2
14	268.3
15	287.0

Enter the data in the *list editor*, as shown in Figure A.83. Note that L_1 contains the x-values, and L_2 contains the y-values. Now choose the *linear regression* feature from the *calculate* menu of the *statistics* feature, as shown in Figure A.84. In Figure A.85, you can see that a linear model for the data is given by

$$y = 6.22x + 183.7.$$

L1	L2	L3	1
6	222.8	------	
7	228.7		
8	235		
9	240.3		
10	245		
11	248.2		
12	254.4		

L1(1)=6

Figure A.83

```
EDIT    CALC    TESTS
1:1-Var Stats
2:2-Var Stats
3:Med-Med
4:LinReg(ax+b)
5:QuadReg
6:CubicReg
7↓QuartReg
```

Figure A.84

```
LinReg
  y=ax+b
  a=6.221212121
  b=183.6672727
  r²=.9508891056
  r=.9751354294
```

Figure A.85

When you use the *regression* feature of a graphing utility, you will notice that the program may also output an "*r*-value." (For some calculators, make sure you select the *diagnostics on* feature before you use the *regression* feature. Otherwise, the calculator will not output an *r*-value.) The *r*-value, or *correlation coefficient,* measures how well the linear model fits the data. The closer the value of $|r|$ is to 1, the better the fit. For the data above,

$$r \approx 0.97514$$

which implies that the model is a good fit for the data.

Row-Echelon and Reduced Row-Echelon Features

Some graphing utilities have features that can automatically transform a matrix to row-echelon form and reduced row-echelon form. These features can be used to check your solutions to systems of equations.

Row-Echelon Feature

Consider the system of equations and the corresponding augmented matrix shown below.

Linear System

$$\begin{cases} 2x + 5y - 3z = 4 \\ 4x + y = 2 \\ -x + 3y - 2z = -1 \end{cases}$$

Augmented Matrix

$$\begin{bmatrix} 2 & 5 & -3 & \vdots & 4 \\ 4 & 1 & 0 & \vdots & 2 \\ -1 & 3 & -2 & \vdots & -1 \end{bmatrix}$$

You can use the *row-echelon* feature of a graphing utility to write the augmented matrix in row-echelon form. First, enter the matrix in the graphing utility using the *matrix editor*, as shown in Figure A.86. Next, choose the *row-echelon* feature from the *math* menu of the *matrix* feature, as shown in Figure A.87. When using this feature, you must enter the name of the matrix. In this case, the name of the matrix is [A]. You should obtain the matrix shown in Figure A.88. You may have to scroll to the right in order to see all the entries of the matrix.

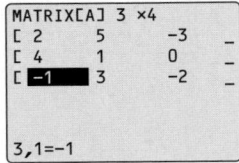

```
MATRIX[A] 3 ×4
[ 2    5    -3   _
[ 4    1    0    _
[ -1   3    -2   _

3,1=-1
```

Figure A.86

```
NAMES   MATH   EDIT
0↑cumSum(
A:ref(
B:rref(
C:rowSwap(
D:row+(
E:*row(
F:*row+(
```

Figure A.87

```
ref([A])
  [[1   .25   0      ...
   [0   1    -.66666...
   [0   0    1       ...
```

Figure A.88

Reduced Row-Echelon Feature

To write the augmented matrix in reduced row-echelon form, follow the same steps used to write a matrix in row-echelon form except choose the *reduced row-echelon* feature, as shown in Figure A.89. You should obtain the matrix shown in Figure A.90. From Figure A.90, you can conclude that the solution to the system is $x = 3$, $y = -10$, and $z = -16$.

Figure A.89   **Figure A.90**

Sequence Feature

The *sequence* feature is used to display the terms of sequences. For instance, to determine the first five terms of the arithmetic sequence

$$a_n = 3n + 5 \qquad \text{Assume } n \text{ begins with 1.}$$

set the graphing utility to *sequence* mode. Then choose the *sequence* feature from the *operations* menu of the *list* feature, as shown in Figure A.91. When using this feature, you must enter the sequence, the variable (in this case n), the beginning value (in this case 1), and the end value (in this case 5). The first five terms of the sequence are 8, 11, 14, 17, and 20, as shown in Figure A.92. You may have to scroll to the right in order to see all the terms of the sequence.

Figure A.91   **Figure A.92**

Shade Feature

Most graphing utilities have a *shade* feature that can be used to graph inequalities. For instance, to graph the inequality

$$y \le 2x - 3$$

first enter the equation $y = 2x - 3$ in the *equation editor*, as shown in Figure A.93. Next, using a standard viewing window (see Figure A.94), graph the equation, as shown in Figure A.95.

Figure A.93   **Figure A.94**   **Figure A.95**

Because the inequality sign is ≤, you want to shade the region below the line $y = 2x - 3$. Choose the *shade* feature from the *draw* feature menu, as shown in Figure A.96. You must enter a lower function and an upper function. In this case, the lower function is -10 (this is the least y-value in the viewing window) and the upper function is Y_1 ($y = 2x - 3$), as shown in Figure A.97. Then press ENTER to obtain the graph shown in Figure A.98.

Figure A.96

Figure A.97

Figure A.98

To graph the inequality

$$y \geq 2x - 3$$

(using a standard viewing window), you would enter the lower function as Y_1 ($y = 2x - 3$) and the upper function as 10 (the greatest y-value in the viewing window).

Statistical Plotting Feature

The *statistical plotting* feature plots data that are stored in lists. Most graphing utilities can display the following types of plots.

Plot Type	Variables
Scatter plot	x-list, y-list
xy line graph	x-list, y-list
Histogram	x-list, frequency
Box-and-whisker plot	x-list, frequency
Normal probability plot	data list, data axis

For instance, use a box-and-whisker plot to represent the following set of data. Then use the graphing utility plot to find the least number, the lower quartile, the median, the upper quartile, and the greatest number.

17, 19, 21, 27, 29, 30, 37, 27, 15, 23, 19, 16

First, use the *list editor* to enter the values in a list, as shown in Figure A.99. Then go to the *statistical plotting editor*. In this editor, you will turn the plot on, select the box-and-whisker plot, select the list you entered in the *list editor*, and enter the frequency of each item in the list, as shown in Figure A.100. Now use the *zoom* feature and choose the *zoom stat* option to set the viewing window and plot the graph, as shown in Figure A.101. Use the *trace* feature to find that the least number is 15, the lower quartile is 18, the median is 22, the upper quartile is 28, and the greatest number is 37.

Figure A.99

Figure A.100

Figure A.101

Sum Feature

The *sum* feature finds the sum of a list of data. For instance, the data below represent a student's quiz scores on 10 quizzes throughout an algebra course.

22, 23, 19, 24, 20, 15, 25, 21, 18, 24

To find the total quiz points the student earned, enter the data in the *list editor*, as shown in Figure A.102. To find the sum, choose the *sum* feature from the *math* menu of the *list* feature, as shown in Figure A.103. You must enter a list. In this case, the list is L_1. You should obtain a sum of 211, as shown in Figure A.104.

Figure A.102

Figure A.103

Figure A.104

Sum Sequence Feature

The *sum* feature and the *sequence* feature can be combined to find the sum of a sequence or series. For instance, to find the sum

$$\sum_{k=0}^{10} 5^{k+1}$$

first choose the *sum* feature from the *math* menu of the *list* feature, as shown in Figure A.105. Then choose the *sequence* feature from the *operations* menu of the *list* feature, as shown in Figure A.106. You must enter an expression for the sequence, a variable, the lower limit of summation, and the upper limit of summation. After pressing (ENTER), you should obtain the sum 61,035,155, as shown in Figure A.107.

Figure A.105

Figure A.106

Figure A.107

Table Feature

Most graphing utilities are capable of displaying a table of values with *x*-values and one or more corresponding *y*-values. These tables can be used to check solutions of an equation and to generate ordered pairs to assist in graphing an equation by hand.

To use the *table* feature, enter an equation in the *equation editor*. The table may have a setup screen, which allows you to select the starting *x*-value and the table step or *x*-increment. You may then have the option of automatically generating values for *x* and *y* or building your own table using the *ask* mode (see Figure A.108).

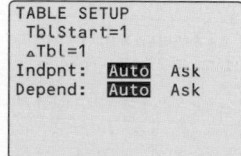

Figure A.108

For instance, enter the equation

$$y = \frac{3x}{x+2}$$

in the *equation editor*, as shown in Figure A.109. In the table setup screen, set the table to start at $x = -4$ and set the table step to 1, as shown in Figure A.110. When you view the table, notice that the first x-value is -4 and that each successive value increases by 1. Also, notice that the Y_1 column gives the resulting y-value for each x-value, as shown in Figure A.111. The table shows that the y-value for $x = -2$ is ERROR. This means that the equation is undefined when $x = -2$.

Figure A.109

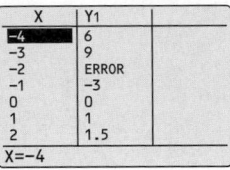

Figure A.110

X	Y1
-4	6
-3	9
-2	ERROR
-1	-3
0	0
1	1
2	1.5

X=-4

Figure A.111

With the same equation in the *equation editor*, set the independent variable in the table to *ask* mode, as shown in Figure A.112. In this mode, you do not need to set the starting x-value or the table step because you are entering any value you choose for x. You may enter any real value for x—integers, fractions, decimals, irrational numbers, and so forth. When you enter

$$x = 1 + \sqrt{3}$$

the graphing utility may rewrite the number as a decimal approximation, as shown in Figure A.113. You can continue to build your own table by entering additional x-values in order to generate y-values, as shown in Figure A.114.

Figure A.112

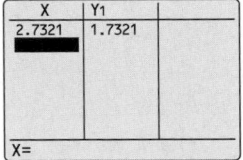

Figure A.113

X	Y1
2.7321	1.7321
-2.5	15
-1.99	-597
-.25	-.4286
.3	.3913
.5	.6
1.6	1.3333

X=1.6

Figure A.114

When you have several equations in the *equation editor*, the table may generate y-values for each equation.

Tangent Feature

Some graphing utilities have the capability of drawing a tangent line to a graph at a given point. For instance, consider the equation

$$y = -x^3 + x + 2.$$

To draw the line tangent to the point $(1, 2)$ on the graph of y, enter the equation in the *equation editor*, as shown in Figure A.115. Using the viewing window shown in Figure A.116, graph the equation, as shown in Figure A.117. Next, choose the *tangent* feature from the *draw* feature menu, as shown in Figure A.118. You can either move the cursor to select a point or enter the x-value at which you want the tangent line to be drawn.

Because you want the tangent line to the point

$(1, 2)$

enter 1 (see Figure A.119) and then press ENTER. The x-value you entered and the equation of the tangent line are displayed at the bottom of the window, as shown in Figure A.120.

Figure A.115

Figure A.116

Figure A.117

Figure A.118

Figure A.119

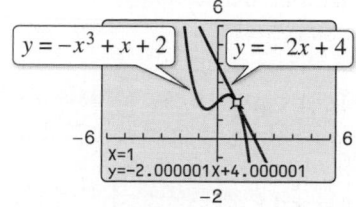

Figure A.120

Trace Feature

For instructions on how to use the *trace* feature, see Zoom and Trace Features on page A23.

Value Feature

The *value* feature finds the value of a function y for a given x-value. To find the value of a function such as

$f(x) = 0.5x^2 - 1.5x$

at $x = 1.8$, first enter the function in the *equation editor* (see Figure A.121) and then graph the function (using a standard viewing window), as shown in Figure A.122. Next, choose the *value* feature from the *calculate* menu, as shown in Figure A.123. You will see "X = " displayed at the bottom of the window. Enter the x-value, in this case $x = 1.8$, as shown in Figure A.124. When entering an x-value, be sure it is between the Xmin and Xmax values you entered for the viewing window. Then press ENTER. In Figure A.125, you can see that when $x = 1.8$,

$y = -1.08$.

Figure A.121

Figure A.122

Figure A.123

Figure A.124

Figure A.125

Viewing Window

A viewing window for a graph is a rectangular portion of the coordinate plane. A viewing window is determined by the following six values (see Figure A.126).

Xmin = the minimum value of x
Xmax = the maximum value of x
Xscl = the number of units per tick mark on the x-axis
Ymin = the minimum value of y
Ymax = the maximum value of y
Yscl = the number of units per tick mark on the y-axis

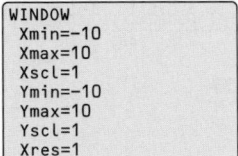

Figure A.126

When you enter these six values in a graphing utility, you are setting the viewing window. On some graphing utilities, there is a seventh value for the viewing window labeled Xres. This sets the pixel resolution (1 through 8). For instance, when

Xres = 1

functions are evaluated and graphed at each pixel on the x-axis. Some graphing utilities have a standard viewing window, as shown in Figure A.127. To initialize the standard viewing window quickly, choose the *standard viewing window* feature from the *zoom* feature menu (see page A23), as shown in Figure A.128.

Figure A.127

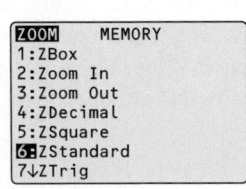

Figure A.128

By choosing different viewing windows for a graph, it is possible to obtain different impressions of the graph's shape. For instance, Figure A.129 shows four different viewing windows for the graph of

$$y = 0.1x^4 - x^3 + 2x^2.$$

Of these viewing windows, the one shown in part (a) is the most complete.

Figure A.129

On most graphing utilities, the display screen is two-thirds as high as it is wide. On such screens, you can obtain a graph with a true geometric perspective by using a square setting—one in which

$$\frac{\text{Ymax} - \text{Ymin}}{\text{Xmax} - \text{Xmin}} = \frac{2}{3}.$$

One such setting is shown in Figure A.130. Notice that the x and y tick marks are equally spaced on a square setting but not on a standard setting (see Figure A.127). To initialize the square viewing window quickly, choose the *square viewing window* feature from the *zoom* feature menu (see page A23), as shown in Figure A.131.

Figure A.130   Figure A.131

To see how the viewing window affects the geometric perspective, graph the semicircles

$$y_1 = \sqrt{9 - x^2}$$

and

$$y_2 = -\sqrt{9 - x^2}$$

using a standard viewing window, as shown in Figure A.132. Notice how the circle appears elliptical rather than circular. Now graph y_1 and y_2 using a square viewing window, as shown in Figure A.133. Notice how the circle appears circular. (Note that when you graph the two semicircles, your graphing utility may not connect them. This is because some graphing utilities are limited in their resolution.)

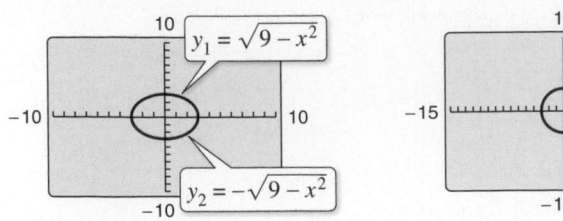

Figure A.132   Figure A.133

Zero or Root Feature

The *zero* or *root* feature finds the real zeros of the various types of functions studied in this text. To find the zeros of a function such as

$$f(x) = 2x^3 - 4x$$

first enter the function in the *equation editor*, as shown in Figure A.134. Now graph the equation (using a standard viewing window), as shown in Figure A.135. From the figure, you can see that the graph of the function crosses the *x*-axis three times, so the function has three real zeros.

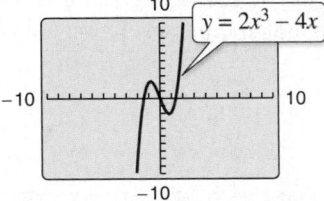

Figure A.134   Figure A.135

To find these zeros, choose the *zero* feature found in the *calculate* menu (see Figure A.136). Next, trace the cursor along the graph to a point left of one of the zeros and press [ENTER] (see Figure A.137). Then trace the cursor along the graph to a point right of the zero and press [ENTER] (see Figure A.138). Note the two arrows near the top of the display marking the left and right bounds, as shown in Figure A.139. Now trace the cursor along the graph between the two bounds and as close to the zero as you can (see Figure A.140) and press [ENTER]. In Figure A.141, you can see that one zero of the function is $x \approx -1.414214$.

Figure A.136   Figure A.137   Figure A.138

Figure A.139   Figure A.140   Figure A.141

Repeat this process to determine that the other two zeros of the function are $x = 0$ (see Figure A.142) and $x \approx 1.414214$ (see Figure A.143).

Figure A.142

Figure A.143

Zoom and Trace Features

The *zoom* feature enables you to adjust the viewing window of a graph quickly (see Figure A.144). For example, the *zoom box* feature allows you to create a new viewing window by drawing a box around any part of the graph.

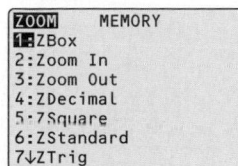

Figure A.144

The *trace* feature moves from point to point along a graph. For instance, enter the equation

$$y = 2x^3 - 3x + 2$$

in the *equation editor* (see Figure A.145) and graph the equation, as shown in Figure A.146. To activate the *trace* feature, press TRACE; then use the arrow keys to move the cursor along the graph. As you trace the graph, the coordinates of each point are displayed, as shown in Figure A.147.

Figure A.145

Figure A.146

Figure A.147

The *trace* feature combined with the *zoom* feature enables you to obtain better and better approximations of desired points on a graph. For instance, you can use the *zoom* feature to approximate the x-intercept of the graph of

$$y = 2x^3 - 3x + 2.$$

From the viewing window shown in Figure A.146, the graph appears to have only one x-intercept. This intercept lies between -2 and -1. To zoom in on the x-intercept, choose the *zoom-in* feature from the *zoom* feature menu, as shown in Figure A.148. Next, trace the cursor to the point you want to zoom in on, in this case the x-intercept (see Figure A.149). Then press ENTER. You should obtain the graph shown in Figure A.150.

Now, using the *trace* feature, you can approximate the *x*-intercept to be

$$x \approx -1.468085$$

as shown in Figure A.151. Use the *zoom-in* feature again to obtain the graph shown in Figure A.152. Using the *trace* feature, you can approximate the *x*-intercept to be

$$x \approx -1.476064$$

as shown in Figure A.153.

Figure A.148

Figure A.149

Figure A.150

Figure A.151

Figure A.152

Figure A.153

Here are some suggestions for using the *zoom* feature.

1. With each successive zoom-in, adjust the *x*-scale so that the viewing window shows at least one tick mark on each side of the *x*-intercept.

2. The error in your approximation will be less than the distance between two scale marks.

3. The *trace* feature can usually be used to add one more decimal place of accuracy without changing the viewing window.

You can adjust the scale in Figure A.153 to obtain a better approximation of the *x*-intercept. Using the suggestions above, change the viewing window settings so that the viewing window shows at least one tick mark on each side of the *x*-intercept, as shown in Figure A.154. From Figure A.154, you can determine that the error in your approximation will be less than 0.001 (the Xscl value). Then, using the *trace* feature, you can improve the approximation, as shown in Figure A.155. To three decimal places, the *x*-intercept is

$$x \approx -1.476.$$

Figure A.154

Figure A.155

Appendix B: Concepts in Statistics

B.1   Representing Data Graphically

Line Plots

Statistics is the branch of mathematics that studies techniques for collecting, organizing, and interpreting data. In this section, you will study several ways to organize data. The first is a **line plot,** which uses a portion of a real number line to order numbers. Line plots are especially useful for ordering small sets of numbers (about 50 or less) by hand.

Many statistical measures can be obtained from a line plot. Two such measures are the *frequency* and *range* of the data. The **frequency** measures the number of times a value occurs in a data set. The **range** is the difference between the greatest and least data values. For example, consider the data values

20,   21,   21,   25,   32.

The frequency of 21 in the data set is 2 because 21 occurs twice. The range is 12 because the difference between the greatest and least data values is $32 - 20 = 12$.

> ### What you should learn
> ▶ Use line plots to order and analyze data.
> ▶ Use histograms to represent frequency distributions.
> ▶ Use bar graphs to represent and analyze data.
> ▶ Use scatter plots to represent and analyze data.
> ▶ Use line graphs to represent and analyze data.
>
> ### Why you should learn it
> Double bar graphs allow you to compare visually two sets of data over time. For example, in Exercise 15 on page A32, you will create a double bar graph showing the total college enrollments for women and men.

EXAMPLE 1   Constructing a Line Plot

The scores from an economics class of 30 students are listed. The scores are for a 100-point exam.   *(Spreadsheet at LarsonPrecalculus.com)*

 93, 70, 76, 67, 86, 93, 82, 78, 83, 86, 64, 78, 76, 66, 83,
83, 96, 74, 69, 76, 64, 74, 79, 76, 88, 76, 81, 82, 74, 70

a. Use a line plot to organize the scores.

b. Which score occurs with the greatest frequency?

c. What is the range of the scores?

Solution

a. Begin by scanning the data to find the least and greatest numbers. For the data, the least number is 64 and the greatest is 96. Next, draw a portion of a real number line that includes the interval $[64, 96]$. To create the line plot, start with the first number, 93, and record a ● above 93 on the number line. Continue recording a ● for each number in the list until you obtain the line plot shown in the figure.

Test scores

b. From the line plot, you can see that 76 occurs with the greatest frequency.

c. Because the range is the difference between the greatest and least data values, the range of scores is

$$96 - 64 = 32.$$

✓ **Checkpoint** ◀))) *Audio-video solution in English & Spanish at LarsonPrecalculus.com.*

Rework Example 1 for the test scores listed.   *(Spreadsheet at LarsonPrecalculus.com)*

 68, 73, 67, 95, 71, 82, 85, 74, 82, 61, 87, 92, 78, 74, 64,
71, 74, 82, 71, 83, 92, 82, 78, 72, 82, 64, 85, 67, 71, 62

Histograms and Frequency Distributions

When you want to organize large sets of data, it is useful to group the data into intervals and plot the frequency of the data in each interval. A **frequency distribution** can be used to construct a **histogram.** A histogram uses a portion of a real number line as its horizontal axis. The bars of a histogram are not separated by spaces.

EXAMPLE 2   Constructing a Histogram

The table at the right shows the percent of the resident population of each state and the District of Columbia who were at least 65 years old in 2012. Construct a frequency distribution and a histogram for the data.   (Source: U.S. Census Bureau)

Solution

To begin constructing a frequency distribution, you must first decide on the number of intervals. There are several ways to group the data. However, because the least number is 8.5 and the greatest is 18.2, it seems that six intervals would be appropriate. The first would be the interval

[8, 10)

the second would be

[10, 12)

and so on. By tallying the data into the six intervals, you obtain the frequency distribution shown below.

Interval	Tally
[8, 10)	II
[10, 12)	IIII
[12, 14)	IIII IIII IIII
[14, 16)	IIII IIII IIII IIII IIII I
[16, 18)	III
[18, 20)	I

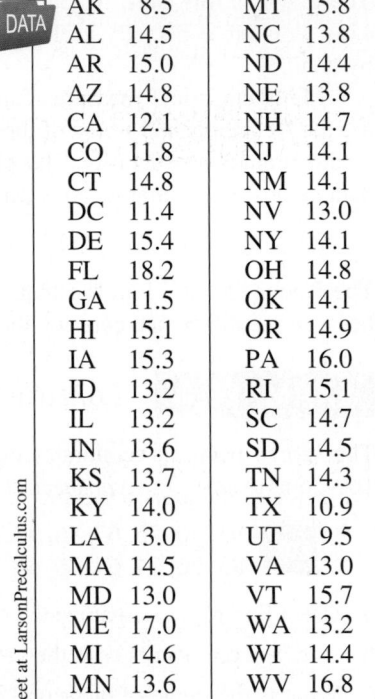

AK	8.5	MT	15.8
AL	14.5	NC	13.8
AR	15.0	ND	14.4
AZ	14.8	NE	13.8
CA	12.1	NH	14.7
CO	11.8	NJ	14.1
CT	14.8	NM	14.1
DC	11.4	NV	13.0
DE	15.4	NY	14.1
FL	18.2	OH	14.8
GA	11.5	OK	14.1
HI	15.1	OR	14.9
IA	15.3	PA	16.0
ID	13.2	RI	15.1
IL	13.2	SC	14.7
IN	13.6	SD	14.5
KS	13.7	TN	14.3
KY	14.0	TX	10.9
LA	13.0	UT	9.5
MA	14.5	VA	13.0
MD	13.0	VT	15.7
ME	17.0	WA	13.2
MI	14.6	WI	14.4
MN	13.6	WV	16.8
MO	14.7	WY	13.0
MS	13.5		

Spreadsheet at LarsonPrecalculus.com

You can construct the histogram by drawing a vertical axis to represent the number of states and a horizontal axis to represent the percent of the population 65 and older. Then, for each interval, draw a vertical bar whose height is the total tally, as shown in Figure B.1. Note that the break in the horizontal axis indicates that the numbers 0 through 7 have been omitted.

Figure B.1

Checkpoint   Audio-video solution in English & Spanish at LarsonPrecalculus.com.

Construct a frequency distribution and a histogram for the data in Example 1.

Bar Graphs

A **bar graph** is similar to a histogram, except that the bars can be either horizontal or vertical, and the labels of the bars are not necessarily numbers. For instance, the labels of the bars can be the months of a year, names of cities, or types of vehicles. Another difference between a bar graph and a histogram is that the bars in a bar graph are usually separated by spaces.

EXAMPLE 3   Constructing a Bar Graph

The table shows the numbers of Wal-Mart stores from 2008 through 2013. Construct a bar graph for the data. What can you conclude?   (Source: Wal-Mart Stores, Inc.)

DATA Year	Number of stores
2008	7,720
2009	8,416
2010	8,970
2011	10,130
2012	10,773
2013	10,942

Spreadsheet at LarsonPrecalculus.com

Solution

To create a bar graph, begin by drawing a vertical axis to represent the number of stores and a horizontal axis to represent the year. The bar graph is shown below.

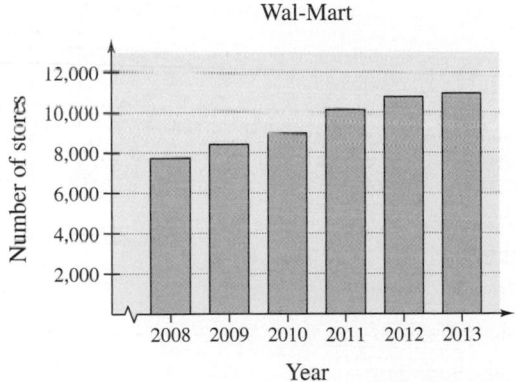

From the graph, you can see that the number of stores has steadily increased from 2008 to 2013.

✔ **Checkpoint** 🔊))) *Audio-video solution in English & Spanish at LarsonPrecalculus.com.*

The table shows the numbers of Dollar General stores from 2008 through 2013. Construct a bar graph for the data. What can you conclude?   (Source: Dollar General Corporation)

DATA Year	Number of stores
2008	8,362
2009	8,828
2010	9,372
2011	9,937
2012	10,506
2013	11,132

Spreadsheet at LarsonPrecalculus.com

EXAMPLE 4   Constructing a Double Bar Graph

The table shows the percents of associate degrees awarded to males and females for selected fields of study in the United States in 2012. Construct a double bar graph for the data.   (Source: U.S. National Center for Education Statistics)

Field of Study	% Female	% Male
Agriculture and Natural Resources	34.8	65.2
Biological and Biomedical Sciences	66.6	33.4
Accounting	75.1	24.9
Business/Commerce	58.6	41.4
Communication/Journalism	53.5	46.5
Education	87.2	12.8
Engineering	13.3	86.7
Family and Consumer Sciences	96.1	3.9
Emergency Medical Technician	29.4	70.6
Legal Professions	86.2	13.8
Mathematics and Statistics	31.3	68.7
Physical Sciences	43.3	56.7
Precision Production	6.1	93.9
Psychology	76.8	23.2
Social Sciences	65.1	34.9

Spreadsheet at LarsonPrecalculus.com

Solution

For the data, a horizontal bar graph seems to be appropriate. This makes it easier to label and read the bars, as shown below.

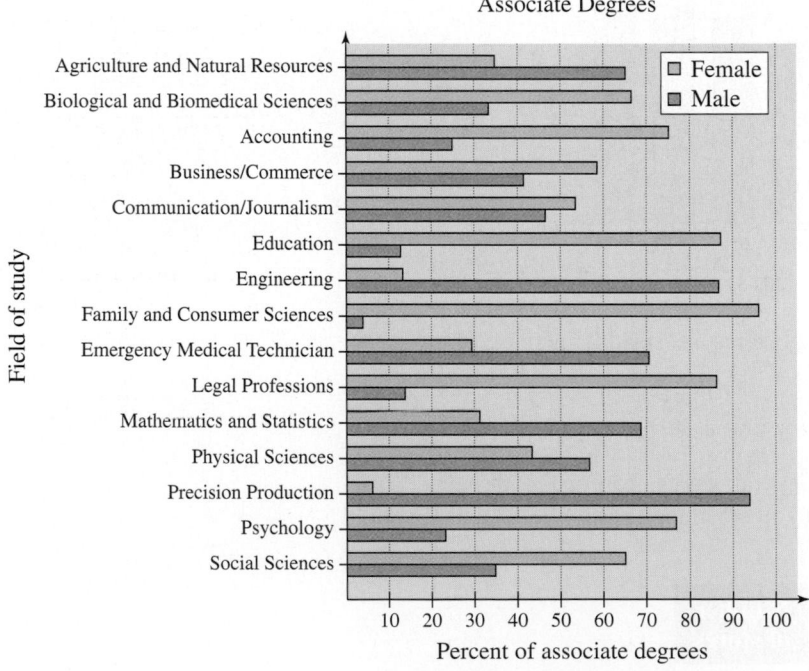

Associate Degrees

Checkpoint   Audio-video solution in English & Spanish at LarsonPrecalculus.com.

Construct a double bar graph for the numbers of Wal-Mart and Dollar General stores in Example 3 and the Checkpoint after Example 3, respectively.

Scatter Plots

Data can be represented graphically by points plotted in a rectangular coordinate system. This type of graph is called a **scatter plot.** (To review the rectangular coordinate system, see Appendix C.1 at this textbook's *Companion Website*.)

EXAMPLE 5   Sketching a Scatter Plot

The numbers of employees E (in thousands) in dentist offices in the United States from 2004 through 2013 are shown in the table, where t represents the year. Sketch a scatter plot of the data by hand.   (Source: U.S. Bureau of Labor Statistics)

Year, t	Employees, E
2004	760
2005	774
2006	786
2007	808
2008	818
2009	818
2010	828
2011	844
2012	854
2013	870

Solution

Before you sketch the scatter plot, it is helpful to represent each pair of values by an ordered pair (t, E) as follows.

$(2004, 760), (2005, 774), (2006, 786), (2007, 808), (2008, 818),$
$(2009, 818), (2010, 828), (2011, 844), (2012, 854), (2013, 870)$

To sketch a scatter plot of the data shown in the table, first draw a vertical axis to represent the number of employees (in thousands) and a horizontal axis to represent the year. Then plot the resulting points, as shown in the figure. Note that the break in the t-axis indicates that the numbers 0 through 2003 have been omitted.

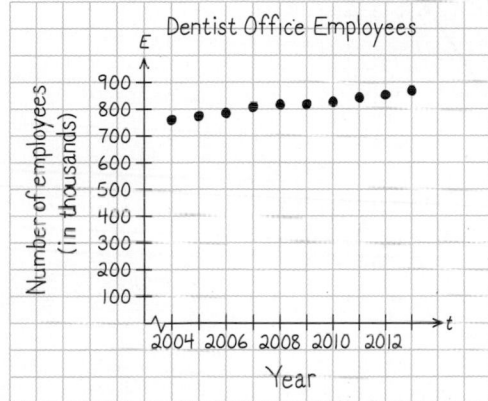

Technology Tip

You can use a graphing utility to graph the scatter plot in Example 5. For instructions on how to use the *list editor* and the *statistical plotting* feature, see Appendix A; for specific keystrokes, go to this textbook's *Companion Website*.

✓ **Checkpoint** 🔊))) *Audio-video solution in English & Spanish at LarsonPrecalculus.com.*

The numbers of employees E (in thousands) in outpatient care centers in the United States from 2004 through 2013 are shown in the table, where t represents the year. Sketch a scatter plot of the data by hand.   (Source: U.S. Bureau of Labor Statistics)

Year, t	Employees, E
2004	451
2005	473
2006	493
2007	512
2008	533
2009	558
2010	600
2011	621
2012	649
2013	682

In Example 5, you could have let $t = 1$ represent the year 2004. In that case, the horizontal axis of the graph would not have been broken, and the tick marks would have been labeled 1 through 10 (instead of 2004 through 2013).

Line Graphs

A **line graph** is similar to a standard coordinate graph. Line graphs are usually used to show trends over periods of time.

EXAMPLE 6   Constructing a Line Graph

The table at the right shows the number of immigrants (in thousands) legally entering the United States for each decade from 1901 through 2010. Construct a line graph for the data. What can you conclude?   (Source: U.S. Department of Homeland Security)

Solution

Begin by drawing a vertical axis to represent the number of immigrants in thousands. Then label the horizontal axis with decades and plot the points shown in the table. Finally, connect the points with line segments, as shown in Figure B.2. From the line graph, you can see that the number of immigrants hit a low point during the depression of the 1930s. Since then, the number has steadily increased.

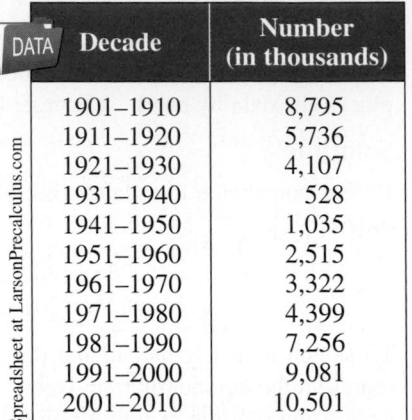

DATA	Decade	Number (in thousands)
	1901–1910	8,795
	1911–1920	5,736
	1921–1930	4,107
	1931–1940	528
	1941–1950	1,035
	1951–1960	2,515
	1961–1970	3,322
	1971–1980	4,399
	1981–1990	7,256
	1991–2000	9,081
	2001–2010	10,501

Spreadsheet at LarsonPrecalculus.com

Figure B.2

You can use a graphing utility to check your sketch, as shown in Figure B.3.

Figure B.3

✓ *Checkpoint* ◀))) *Audio-video solution in English & Spanish at LarsonPrecalculus.com.*

Construct a line graph for the data in Example 3.

Technology Tip

You can use the *statistical plotting* feature of a graphing utility to create different types of graphs, such as line graphs. For instructions on how to use the *statistical plotting* feature, see Appendix A; for specific keystrokes, go to this textbook's *Companion Website*.

B.1   Exercises

See *CalcChat.com* for tutorial help and worked-out solutions to odd-numbered exercises.
For instructions on how to use a graphing utility, see Appendix A.

Vocabulary and Concept Check

In Exercises 1–6, fill in the blank.

1. _____ are useful for ordering small sets of numbers by hand.

2. A _____ uses a portion of a real number line as its horizontal axis, and the bars are not separated by spaces.

3. You can use a _____ to construct a histogram.

4. The bars in a _____ can be either vertical or horizontal.

5. A _____ represents data graphically as points plotted in a rectangular coordinate system.

6. _____ show trends over periods of time.

Procedures and Problem Solving

7. **Economics** The line plot shows a sample of average prices of unleaded regular gasoline in 25 different cities.

(a) What price occurred with the greatest frequency?

(b) What is the range of prices?

8. **Environmental Science** The line plot shows the weights (to the nearest hundred pounds) of municipal waste hauled by a garbage truck in 30 trips to a landfill.

(a) What weight occurred with the greatest frequency?

(b) What is the range of weights?

Education **In Exercises 9 and 10, use the following scores from an algebra class of 30 students. The scores are for one 25-point quiz and one 100-point exam.**

Quiz 20, 15, 14, 20, 16, 19, 10, 21, 24, 15, 15, 14, 15, 21, 19, 15, 20, 18, 18, 22, 18, 16, 18, 19, 21, 19, 16, 20, 14, 12

Exam 77, 100, 77, 70, 83, 89, 87, 85, 81, 84, 81, 78, 89, 78, 88, 85, 90, 92, 75, 81, 85, 100, 98, 81, 78, 75, 85, 89, 82, 75

9. Construct a line plot for the quiz. Which score(s) occurred with the greatest frequency?

10. Construct a line plot for the exam. Which score(s) occurred with the greatest frequency?

11. **Demographics** The list shows the percents of individuals living below the poverty level in the 50 states in 2012. Use a frequency distribution and a histogram to organize the data. *(Spreadsheet at LarsonPrecalculus.com)* (Source: U.S. Census Bureau)

DATA			
AK 10.8	AL 15.8	AR 19.4	AZ 18.1
CA 16.4	CO 12.5	CT 10.2	DE 13.6
FL 15.1	GA 18.3	HI 13.0	IA 10.4
ID 15.1	IL 13.4	IN 15.4	KS 14.2
KY 16.9	LA 21.1	MA 10.9	MD 9.6
ME 13.1	MI 14.3	MN 10.0	MO 15.3
MS 19.7	MT 15.0	NC 16.3	ND 10.7
NE 11.2	NH 7.9	NJ 10.4	NM 21.3
NV 15.6	NY 16.6	OH 15.2	OK 16.0
OR 13.9	PA 13.2	RI 13.5	SC 17.8
SD 13.7	TN 17.4	TX 17.2	UT 11.0
VA 11.0	VT 11.4	WA 12.1	WI 12.2
WV 17.1	WY 10.2		

12. **Education** The list shows the numbers of students enrolled in public schools (in thousands) in the 50 states and the District of Columbia in 2012. Use a frequency distribution and a histogram to organize the data. *(Spreadsheet at LarsonPrecalculus.com)* (Source: National Education Association)

DATA			
AK 128	AL 736	AR 472	AZ 1070
CA 6185	CO 869	CT 550	DC 76
DE 131	FL 2681	GA 1703	HI 177
IA 501	ID 294	IL 2084	IN 1031
KS 486	KY 659	LA 708	MA 954
MD 860	ME 185	MI 1544	MN 843
MO 907	MS 493	MT 143	NC 1488
ND 99	NE 303	NH 189	NJ 1358
NM 334	NV 478	NY 2590	OH 1868
OK 673	OR 564	PA 1739	RI 134
SC 683	SD 127	TN 980	TX 5059
UT 601	VA 1266	VT 82	WA 1053
WI 872	WV 282	WY 91	

13. Meterology The table shows the normal monthly precipitation (in inches) in Seattle, Washington. Construct a bar graph for the data. Write a brief statement regarding the precipitation in Seattle, Washington, throughout the year. (Source: National Oceanic and Atmospheric Administration)

Month	Precipitation
January	5.47
February	3.52
March	3.85
April	2.79
May	2.01
June	1.57
July	0.85
August	0.94
September	1.30
October	3.38
November	5.98
December	6.06

Spreadsheet at LarsonPrecalculus.com

14. Business The table shows the revenues (in billions of dollars) for Costco Wholesale stores in the years from 1997 through 2013. Construct a bar graph for the data. Write a brief statement regarding the revenue of Costco Wholesale stores over time. (Source: Costco Wholesale Corporation)

Year	Revenue (in billions of dollars)
1997	21.874
1998	24.270
1999	27.456
2000	32.164
2001	34.797
2002	38.762
2003	42.546
2004	48.107
2005	52.935
2006	60.151
2007	64.909
2008	72.483
2009	71.449
2010	77.946
2011	88.915
2012	99.137
2013	105.156

Spreadsheet at LarsonPrecalculus.com

15. *Why you should learn it* (p. A25) The table shows the total college enrollments (in thousands) for women and men in the United States from 2005 through 2012. Construct a double bar graph for the data. (Source: U.S. National Center for Education Statistics)

Year	Women (in thousands)	Men (in thousands)
2005	10,032	7,456
2006	10,184	7,575
2007	10,432	7,816
2008	10,914	8,189
2009	11,658	8,770
2010	11,971	9,045
2011	11,968	9,026
2012	11,724	8,919

Spreadsheet at LarsonPrecalculus.com

16. Demographics The table shows the populations (in millions) of the five most populous cities in the United States in 1990 and 2012. Construct a double bar graph for the data. (Source: U.S. Census Bureau)

City	1990 population (in millions)	2012 population (in millions)
New York, NY	7.32	8.34
Los Angeles, CA	3.49	3.86
Chicago, IL	2.78	2.71
Houston, TX	1.63	2.16
Philadelphia, PA	1.59	1.55

Spreadsheet at LarsonPrecalculus.com

17. Accounting The table shows the sales y (in millions of dollars) for Apple Inc. for the years 2000 through 2009. Sketch a scatter plot of the data. (Source: Apple Inc.)

Year	Sales, y (in millions of dollars)
2004	8,279
2005	13,931
2006	19,315
2007	24,006
2008	32,479
2009	36,537
2010	65,255
2011	108,249
2012	156,508
2013	170,910

Spreadsheet at LarsonPrecalculus.com

18. Meteorology   The table shows the lowest temperature on record y (in degrees Fahrenheit) in Flagstaff, Arizona, for each month x, where $x = 1$ represents January. Sketch a scatter plot of the data. (Source: U.S. National Oceanic and Atmospheric Administration)

DATA	Month, x	Temperature, y
	1	-22
	2	-23
	3	-16
	4	-2
	5	14
	6	22
	7	32
	8	24
	9	23
	10	-2
	11	-13
	12	-23

Economics   **In Exercises 19–24, use the line graph, which shows the average prices of a gallon of premium unleaded gasoline from 2005 through 2013.** (Source: U.S. Energy Information Administration)

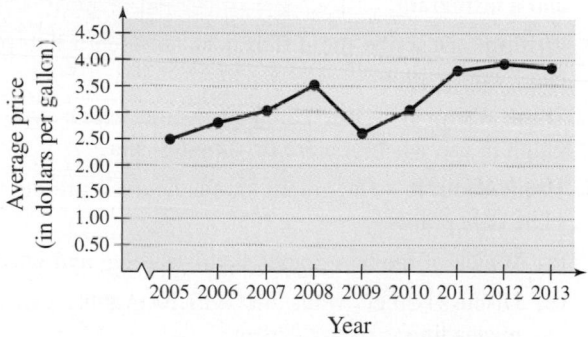

19. Describe the trend in the price of premium unleaded gasoline from 2005 to 2008.

20. Describe the trend in the price of premium unleaded gasoline from 2008 to 2009.

21. Determine when the price of premium unleaded gasoline showed the greatest rate of decrease from one year to the next.

22. Determine when the price of premium unleaded gasoline showed the greatest rate of increase from one year to the next.

23. Approximate the percent decrease in the price per gallon of premium unleaded gasoline from 2008 to 2010.

24. Approximate the percent increase in the price per gallon of premium unleaded gasoline from 2009 to 2013.

25. Human Resources   The table shows the percents of wives in two-income families in the United States who earned more than their husbands from 2000 through 2012. (Source: U.S. Bureau of Labor Statistics)

(a) Construct a line graph for the data.

(b) Write a brief statement describing what the graph reveals.

DATA	Year	Percent
	2000	23.3
	2001	24.1
	2002	25.0
	2003	25.2
	2004	25.3
	2005	25.5
	2006	25.7
	2007	25.9
	2008	26.6
	2009	28.9
	2010	29.2
	2011	28.1
	2012	29.0

26. Economics   The table shows the trade deficits (the differences between imports and exports) of the United States from 1998 through 2013. (Source: U.S. Census Bureau)

(a) Construct a line graph for the data.

(b) Write a brief statement describing what the graph reveals.

DATA	Year	Trade deficit (in billions of dollars)
	1998	230
	1999	329
	2000	436
	2001	412
	2002	468
	2003	532
	2004	655
	2005	772
	2006	828
	2007	809
	2008	816
	2009	504
	2010	635
	2011	725
	2012	731
	2013	689

Education In Exercises 27–30, refer to the scatter plot, which shows the mathematics entrance test scores x and the final examination scores y in an algebra course for a sample of 10 students.

27. Find the entrance test score of any student with a final exam score in the 80s.

28. Find the final exam score of any student with an entrance test score in the 50s.

29. Did the student with the highest entrance test score have the highest final exam score?

30. Does a higher entrance test score necessarily imply a higher final exam score? Explain.

31. **Networking** The list shows the percent of households in each of the 50 states and the District of Columbia with Internet access in 2012. Use a graphing utility to organize the data in the graph of your choice. Explain your choice of graph. *(Spreadsheet at LarsonPrecalculus.com)* (Source: U.S. Census Bureau)

DATA

AK 83.1	AL 72.0	AR 74.8
AZ 73.7	CA 81.3	CO 85.7
CT 84.0	DC 77.5	DE 78.2
FL 81.5	GA 79.2	HI 85.0
IA 80.2	ID 86.8	IL 82.7
IN 77.7	KS 80.7	KY 74.4
LA 67.7	MA 86.0	MD 83.6
ME 84.2	MI 80.8	MN 87.4
MO 75.4	MS 64.8	MT 78.3
NC 77.7	ND 84.0	NE 76.1
NH 87.7	NJ 83.7	NM 73.9
NV 82.8	NY 81.0	OH 75.6
OK 74.8	OR 87.9	PA 80.8
RI 82.2	SC 73.7	SD 78.3
TN 74.3	TX 72.6	UT 85.2
VA 77.2	VT 85.7	WA 85.1
WI 80.7	WV 70.6	WY 82.9

32. **Athletics** The table shows the numbers of participants (in thousands) in high school athletic programs in the United States from 2002 through 2013. Organize the data in an appropriate display. Explain your choice of graph. (Source: National Federation of State High School Associations)

DATA Year	Female athletes (in thousands)	Male athletes (in thousands)
2002	2807	3961
2003	2856	3989
2004	2865	4038
2005	2908	4110
2006	2953	4207
2007	3022	4321
2008	3057	4372
2009	3114	4423
2010	3173	4456
2011	3174	4494
2012	3208	4485
2013	3223	4491

Spreadsheet at LarsonPrecalculus.com

Conclusions

33. **Writing** Describe the differences between a bar graph and a histogram.

34. **Writing** Describe the differences between a line plot and a scatter plot.

35. **Think About It** How can you decide which type of graph to use when you are organizing data?

36. **Think About It** The graphs shown below represent the same data points.

(a) Which of the two graphs is misleading, and why?

(b) Discuss other ways in which graphs can be misleading.

(c) Why would it be beneficial for someone to use a misleading graph?

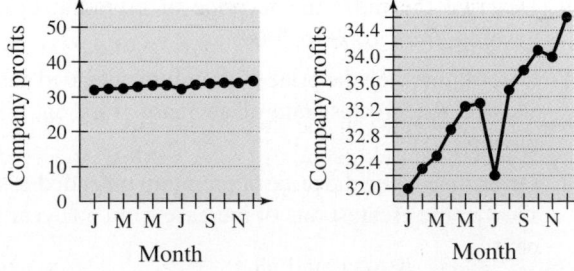

37. **Writing** Name a different type of graph you could use to display the data in the given exercise. Then name a type of graph that you would *not* use to display the data. Explain.

(a) Exercise 11   (b) Exercise 14

B.2 Measures of Central Tendency and Dispersion

Mean, Median, and Mode

In many real-life situations, it is helpful to describe data by a single number that is most representative of the entire collection of numbers. Such a number is called a **measure of central tendency.** The most commonly used measures are as follows.

1. The **mean,** or **average,** of n numbers is the sum of the numbers divided by n.

2. The **median** of n numbers is the middle number when the numbers are written in numerical order. If n is even, then the median is the average of the two middle numbers.

3. The **mode** of n numbers is the number that occurs most frequently. If two numbers tie for most frequent occurrence, then the collection has two modes and is called **bimodal.**

EXAMPLE 1   Comparing Measures of Central Tendency

An analyst states that the average annual income of a company's 25 employees is $60,849. The actual annual incomes of the 25 employees are shown below. What are the mean, median, and mode of the incomes?   *(Spreadsheet at LarsonPrecalculus.com)*

DATA				
$17,305	$478,320	$45,678	$18,980	$17,408
$25,676	$28,906	$12,500	$24,540	$33,450
$12,500	$33,855	$37,450	$20,432	$28,956
$34,983	$36,540	$250,921	$36,853	$16,430
$32,654	$98,213	$48,980	$94,024	$35,671

Solution

The mean of the incomes is

$$\text{Mean} = \frac{17{,}305 + 478{,}320 + 45{,}678 + 18{,}980 + \cdots + 35{,}671}{25}$$

$$= \frac{1{,}521{,}225}{25}$$

$$= \$60{,}849.$$

To find the median, order the incomes as follows.

$12,500	$12,500	$16,430	$17,305	$17,408
$18,980	$20,432	$24,540	$25,676	$28,906
$28,956	$32,654	$33,450	$33,855	$34,983
$35,671	$36,540	$36,853	$37,450	$45,678
$48,980	$94,024	$98,213	$250,921	$478,320

From this list, you can see that the median income is $33,450. You can also see that $12,500 is the only income that occurs more than once. So, the mode is $12,500.

✓ **Checkpoint** ◀))) *Audio-video solution in English & Spanish at LarsonPrecalculus.com.*

Find the mean, median, and mode of the following data set.

68, 73, 67, 95, 71, 82, 85, 74, 82, 61

In Example 1, was the analyst telling the truth about the annual incomes? Technically, the person was telling the truth because the average is (generally) defined to be the mean. However, of the three measures of central tendency—*mean:* $60,849, *median:* $33,450, *mode:* $12,500—it seems clear that the median is most representative. The mean is inflated by the two highest salaries.

Choosing a Measure of Central Tendency

Which of the three measures of central tendency is most representative of a particular data set? The answer depends on the distribution of the data *and* the way in which you plan to use the data.

For instance, in Example 1, the mean salary of $60,849 would not seem very representative to a potential employee (the mean is inflated by the two highest salaries). A better use of the mean is for estimating income tax. For instance, to estimate a 1% income tax for the 25 employees, a tax collector would use 1% of the *mean* annual income of the employees.

EXAMPLE 2   Choosing a Measure of Central Tendency

Which measure of central tendency is most representative of the data given in each frequency distribution?

a.

Number	1	2	3	4	5	6	7	8	9
Frequency	7	20	15	11	8	3	2	0	15

b.

Number	1	2	3	4	5	6	7	8	9
Frequency	9	8	7	6	5	6	7	8	9

c.

Number	1	2	3	4	5	6	7	8	9
Frequency	6	1	2	3	5	5	8	3	0

Solution

a. For this data set, the mean is 4.23, the median is 3, and the mode is 2. Of these, the median or mode is probably the most representative measure.

b. For this data set, the mean and median are each 5, and the modes are 1 and 9 (the distribution is bimodal). Of these, the mean or median is the most representative measure.

c. For this data set, the mean is 4.88, the median is 5, and the mode is 7. Of these, the mean or median is the most representative measure.

 ✓ **Checkpoint** ◀))) *Audio-video solution in English & Spanish at LarsonPrecalculus.com.*

Which measure of central tendency is the most representative of the data shown in each frequency distribution?

a.

Number	1	2	3	4	5	6	7	8	9
Frequency	1	1	1	1	3	1	1	1	1

b.

Number	1	2	3	4	5	6	7	8	9
Frequency	0	3	4	5	5	3	2	1	6

c.

Number	1	2	3	4	5	6	7	8	9
Frequency	4	3	2	1	0	1	2	3	4

d.

Number	1	2	3	4	5	6	7	8	9
Frequency	11	8	3	2	0	15	7	20	15

Technology Tip

Most graphing utilities have *mean* and *median* features that can be used to find the means and medians of data sets. Enter the data from Example 2(a) in the *list editor* of a graphing utility. Then use the *mean* and *median* features to verify the solution to Example 2(a), as shown below.

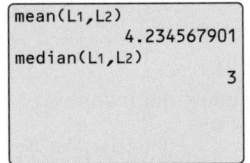

```
mean(L1,L2)
              4.234567901
median(L1,L2)
                        3
```

For instructions on how to use the *list*, *mean*, and *median* features, see Appendix A; for specific keystrokes, go to this textbook's *Companion Website*.

Variance and Standard Deviation

Very different sets of numbers can have the same mean. You will now study two **measures of dispersion,** which give you an idea of how much the numbers in a set differ from the mean of the set. These two measures are called the *variance* of the set and the *standard deviation* of the set.

Definitions of Variance and Standard Deviation

Consider a set of numbers $\{x_1, x_2, \ldots, x_n\}$ with a mean of $\bar{x}$. The **variance** of the set is

$$v = \frac{(x_1 - \bar{x})^2 + (x_2 - \bar{x})^2 + \cdots + (x_n - \bar{x})^2}{n}$$

and the **standard deviation** of the set is $\sigma = \sqrt{v}$ (σ is the lowercase Greek letter sigma).

The standard deviation of a set is a measure of how much a typical number in the set differs from the mean. The greater the standard deviation, the more the numbers in the set vary from the mean. For instance, each of the sets

$$\{5, 5, 5, 5\}, \quad \{4, 4, 6, 6\}, \quad \text{and} \quad \{3, 3, 7, 7\}$$

has a mean of 5. The standard deviations of the sets are 0, 1, and 2, respectively.

$$\sigma_1 = \sqrt{\frac{(5 - 5)^2 + (5 - 5)^2 + (5 - 5)^2 + (5 - 5)^2}{4}} = 0$$

$$\sigma_2 = \sqrt{\frac{(4 - 5)^2 + (4 - 5)^2 + (6 - 5)^2 + (6 - 5)^2}{4}} = 1$$

$$\sigma_3 = \sqrt{\frac{(3 - 5)^2 + (3 - 5)^2 + (7 - 5)^2 + (7 - 5)^2}{4}} = 2$$

EXAMPLE 3   **Estimations of Standard Deviation**

Consider the three frequency distributions represented by the histograms in Figure B.4. Which data set has the least standard deviation? Which has the greatest?

Solution

Of the three data sets, the numbers in data set *A* are grouped most closely to the center and the numbers in data set *C* are the most dispersed. So, data set *A* has the least standard deviation and data set *C* has the greatest standard deviation.

✓ **Checkpoint** ◀))) *Audio-video solution in English & Spanish at LarsonPrecalculus.com.*

Consider the three frequency distributions represented by the histograms shown below. Which data set has the least standard deviation? Which has the greatest?

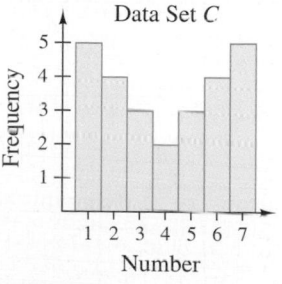

Figure B.4

EXAMPLE 4   Finding a Standard Deviation

Find the standard deviation of each data set shown in Example 3.

Solution

Because of the symmetry of each histogram, you can conclude that each has a mean of

$$\bar{x} = 4.$$

The standard deviation of data set A is

$$\sigma = \sqrt{\frac{(-3)^2 + 2(-2)^2 + 3(-1)^2 + 5(0)^2 + 3(1)^2 + 2(2)^2 + (3)^2}{17}}$$

$$\approx 1.53.$$

The standard deviation of data set B is

$$\sigma = \sqrt{\frac{2(-3)^2 + 2(-2)^2 + 2(-1)^2 + 2(0)^2 + 2(1)^2 + 2(2)^2 + 2(3)^2}{14}}$$

$$= 2.$$

The standard deviation of data set C is

$$\sigma = \sqrt{\frac{5(-3)^2 + 4(-2)^2 + 3(-1)^2 + 2(0)^2 + 3(1)^2 + 4(2)^2 + 5(3)^2}{14}}$$

$$\approx 2.22.$$

These values confirm the results of Example 3. That is, data set A has the least standard deviation and data set C has the greatest.

✓ **Checkpoint**   *Audio-video solution in English & Spanish at LarsonPrecalculus.com.*

Find the standard deviation of each data set shown in the Checkpoint with Example 3.

The following alternative formula provides a more efficient way to compute the standard deviation.

Alternative Formula for Standard Deviation

The standard deviation of $\{x_1, x_2, \ldots, x_n\}$ is given by

$$\sigma = \sqrt{\frac{x_1^2 + x_2^2 + \cdots + x_n^2}{n} - \bar{x}^2}.$$

Because of lengthy computations, this formula is difficult to verify. Conceptually, however, the process is straightforward. It consists of showing that the expressions

$$\sqrt{\frac{(x_1 - \bar{x})^2 + (x_2 - \bar{x})^2 + \cdots + (x_n - \bar{x})^2}{n}}$$

and

$$\sqrt{\frac{x_1^2 + x_2^2 + \cdots + x_n^2}{n} - \bar{x}^2}$$

are equivalent. Try verifying this equivalence for the set $\{x_1, x_2, x_3\}$ with

$$\bar{x} = \frac{x_1 + x_2 + x_3}{3}.$$

Technology Tip

Most graphing utilities have *statistical* features that can be used to find different statistical values of data sets, such as the standard deviation. Enter data set A from Example 3 in the *list editor* of a graphing utility. Then use the *one-variable statistics* feature to verify the solution in Example 4, as shown below.

```
1-Var Stats
 x̄=4
 Σx=68
 Σx2=312
 Sx=1.58113883
 σx=1.533929978
↓n=17
```

In the figure above, the standard deviation is represented as σx, which is about 1.53. For instructions on how to use the *one-variable statistics* feature, see Appendix A; for specific keystrokes, go to this textbook's *Companion Website*.

EXAMPLE 5   Using the Alternative Formula

Use the alternative formula for standard deviation to find the standard deviation of the following set of numbers.

5, 6, 6, 7, 7, 8, 8, 8, 9, 10

Solution

Begin by finding the mean of the set, which is 7.4. So, the standard deviation is

$$\sigma = \sqrt{\frac{5^2 + 2(6^2) + 2(7^2) + 3(8^2) + 9^2 + 10^2}{10} - (7.4)^2}$$

$$= \sqrt{\frac{568}{10} - 54.76}$$

$$\approx 1.43.$$

✓ **Checkpoint** *Audio-video solution in English & Spanish at LarsonPrecalculus.com.*

Use the alternative formula for standard deviation to find the standard deviation of the following set of numbers.

3, 3, 3, 4, 4, 5, 5, 6, 6, 7

A well-known theorem in statistics, called *Chebychev's Theorem*, states that at least

$$1 - \frac{1}{k^2}$$

of the numbers in a distribution must lie within k standard deviations ($k > 1$) of the mean. So, at least $\frac{3}{4}$ or 75% of the numbers in a collection must lie within two standard deviations of the mean, and at least $\frac{8}{9}$ or $88\frac{8}{9}$% of the numbers must lie within three standard deviations of the mean. For most distributions, these percents are low. For instance, in all three distributions shown in Example 3, 100% of the numbers lie within two standard deviations of the mean.

 EXAMPLE 6   Describing a Distribution

The table at the right shows the estimated numbers of registered nurses (in thousands) in each state and the District of Columbia in 2013. Find the mean and standard deviation of the numbers. What percent of the numbers lie within two standard deviations of the mean?   (Source: U.S. Bureau of Labor Statistics)

Solution

Begin by entering the numbers in a graphing utility. Then use the *one-variable statistics* feature to obtain

$$\bar{x} \approx 52.2 \quad \text{and} \quad \sigma \approx 52.0.$$

The interval that contains all numbers that lie within two standard deviations of the mean is

[52.2 − 2(52.0), 52.2 + 2(52.0)]   or   [−51.8, 156.2].

From the table, you can see that all but four of the numbers (about 92%) lie in this interval—all but the numbers that correspond to the numbers of registered nurses in California, Florida, New York, and Texas.

DATA		
AK	6	MT	9
AL	44	NC	88
AR	23	ND	8
AZ	46	NE	20
CA	253	NH	12
CO	42	NJ	75
CT	35	NM	15
DC	11	NV	17
DE	10	NY	170
FL	163	OH	124
GA	66	OK	26
HI	10	OR	28
IA	32	PA	125
ID	12	RI	12
IL	109	SC	42
IN	60	SD	12
KS	27	TN	58
KY	42	TX	190
LA	41	UT	19
MA	79	VA	60
MD	46	VT	7
ME	14	WA	53
MI	92	WI	57
MN	58	WV	18
MO	65	WY	5
MS	28		

Spreadsheet at LarsonPrecalculus.com

✓ **Checkpoint** *Audio-video solution in English & Spanish at LarsonPrecalculus.com.*

In Example 6, what percent of the data lie within one standard deviation of the mean?

Box-and-Whisker Plots

Standard deviation is the measure of dispersion that is associated with the mean. **Quartiles** measure dispersion associated with the median.

Definition of Quartiles

Consider an ordered set of numbers whose median is m. The **lower quartile** is the median of the numbers that occur before m. The **upper quartile** is the median of the numbers that occur after m.

EXAMPLE 7   Finding Quartiles of a Set

Find the lower and upper quartiles for the following data set.

34, 14, 24, 16, 12, 18, 20, 24, 16, 26, 13, 27

Solution

Begin by ordering the set.

12, 13, 14,	16, 16, 18,	20, 24, 24,	26, 27, 34
1st 25%	2nd 25%	3rd 25%	4th 25%

The median of the entire set is 19. The median of the six numbers that are before 19 is 15. So, the lower quartile is 15. The median of the six numbers that are after 19 is 25. So, the upper quartile is 25.

✓ **Checkpoint** *Audio-video solution in English & Spanish at LarsonPrecalculus.com.*

Find the lower and upper quartiles for the following data set.

39, 47, 81, 43, 23, 23, 27, 86, 15, 3, 74, 55

Quartiles are represented graphically by a **box-and-whisker plot,** as shown in Figure B.5. In the plot, notice that five numbers are given: the least number, the lower quartile, the median, the upper quartile, and the greatest number. Also notice that the numbers are spaced proportionally, as though they were on a real number line.

```
     12    15     19        25              34
```

Figure B.5

Technology Tip

You can use a graphing utility to graph the box-and-whisker plot in Figure B.5. After entering the data in the graphing utility's *list editor*, use the *statistical plotting* and *ZoomStat* features to display the box-and-whisker plot, as shown in Figure B.6. For instructions on how to use the *list editor* and *statistical plotting* features, see Appendix A; for specific keystrokes, go to this textbook's *Companion Website*.

Figure B.6

The next example shows how to find quartiles when the number of elements in a set is not divisible by 4.

EXAMPLE 8   Sketching Box-and-Whisker Plots

Sketch a box-and-whisker plot for each data set.

a. 82, 82, 83, 85, 87, 89, 90, 94, 95, 95, 96, 98, 99

b. 11, 13, 13, 15, 17, 17, 20, 24, 24, 27

Solution

a. This set has 13 numbers. The median is 90 (the seventh number). The lower quartile is 84 (the median of the first six numbers). The upper quartile is 95.5 (the median of the last six numbers). See Figure B.7.

82   84   90   95.5   99

Figure B.7

b. This set has 10 numbers. The median is 17 (the average of the fifth and sixth numbers). The lower quartile is 13 (the median of the first five numbers). The upper quartile is 24 (the median of the last five numbers). See Figure B.8.

11   13   17   24   27

Figure B.8

✓ **Checkpoint** 🔊))) *Audio-video solution in English & Spanish at LarsonPrecalculus.com.*

Sketch a box-and-whisker plot for the data set: 19, 22, 38, 44, 50, 54, 56, 62, 67, 79, 81, 85, 93.

B.2   Exercises

Vocabulary and Concept Check

In Exercises 1–4, fill in the blank(s).

1. A single number that is the most representative of a data set is called a _____ of _____ .

2. If two numbers are tied for the most frequent occurrence, then the collection has two _____ and is called _____ .

3. Two measures of dispersion are called the _____ and the _____ of a data set.

4. _____ measure dispersion associated with the median.

Procedures and Problem Solving

Comparing Measures of Central Tendency   In Exercises 5–10, find the mean, median, and mode of the data set.

5. 4, 12, 7, 16, 8, 9, 7, 5

6. 30, 37, 32, 39, 33, 34, 32

7. 4, 12, 7, 32, 8, 9, 7, 5

8. 17, 37, 32, 39, 33, 34, 32

9. 21, 4, 18, 6, 25, 3

10. 2, 10, 19, 3, 7, 5, 3, 10, 31, 11

11. Exploration   Compare your answers in Exercise 5 with those in Exercise 7. Which of the measures of central tendency is sensitive to extreme measurements? Explain your reasoning.

12. Exploration

(a) Add 6 to each number in Exercise 8 and find the mean, median, and mode of the revised data set. How are the measures of central tendency changed?

(b) When a constant k is added to each number in a set of data, how will the measures of central tendency change?

13. Sales   A car rental company kept the following record of the numbers of miles a rental car was driven. What are the mean, median, and mode of the data?

Monday	410	Tuesday	260
Wednesday	320	Thursday	320
Friday	460	Saturday	150

14. Demographics   A study was done on families having six children. The table shows the numbers of families in the study with the indicated numbers of girls. Determine the mean, median, and mode of the data.

Number of girls	0	1	2	3	4	5	6
Frequency	0	24	45	54	50	19	7

Spreadsheet at LarsonPrecalculus.com

15. Athletics   The table shows the bowling scores of a three-member team for a three-game series.

Team member	Game 1	Game 2	Game 3
Jay	181	222	196
Hank	199	195	205
Buck	202	251	235

Spreadsheet at LarsonPrecalculus.com

(a) Find the mean for each team member.

(b) Find the mean of the nine scores.

(c) Find the median of the nine scores.

(d) Which measure of central tendency best describes the nine scores?

16. Sales   The selling prices of 12 new homes built in one subdivision are listed.

$525,000	$375,000	$425,000	$550,000
$385,000	$500,000	$550,000	$425,000
$475,000	$500,000	$350,000	$450,000

(a) Find the mean, mode, and median of the prices.

(b) Which measure of central tendency best describes the prices? Explain.

17. Think About It   Construct a collection of numbers that has the following properties. If this is not possible, explain why.

Mean = 6, median = 4, mode = 4

18. Think About It   Construct a collection of numbers that has the following properties. If this is not possible, explain why.

Mean = 6, median = 6, mode = 4

19. Education   An English professor records the following scores for a 100-point exam.

99, 64, 80, 77, 59, 72, 87, 79, 92, 88, 90, 42, 20, 89, 42, 100, 98, 84, 78, 91

Which measure of central tendency best describes these test scores?

20. Sales   A salesperson sold eight pairs of men's brown dress shoes. The sizes of the eight pairs were

$10\frac{1}{2}$, 8, 12, $10\frac{1}{2}$, 10, $9\frac{1}{2}$, 11, and $10\frac{1}{2}$.

Which measure (or measures) of central tendency best describes (describe) the typical shoe size for these data?

Finding Mean and Standard Deviation   In Exercises 21 and 22, line plots of data sets are given. Determine the mean and standard deviation of each data set.

21. (a)

(b)

(c)

(d)

22. (a)

(b)

(c)

(d)

Finding Mean, Variance, and Standard Deviation   In Exercises 23–30, find the mean ($\bar{x}$), variance (v), and standard deviation (σ) of the data set.

23. 4, 10, 8, 2

24. 3, 15, 6, 9, 2

25. 1, 1, 1, 5, 5, 5

26. 2, 2, 2, 2, 2, 2

27. 0, 1, 1, 2, 2, 2, 3, 3, 4

28. 1, 2, 3, 4, 5, 6, 7

29. 49, 62, 40, 29, 32, 70

30. 1.5, 0.4, 2.1, 0.7, 0.8

Using the Alternative Formula   In Exercises 31–34, use the alternative formula to find the standard deviation of the data set.

31. 2, 4, 6, 6, 13, 5

32. 246, 336, 473, 167, 219, 359

33. 8.1, 6.9, 3.7, 4.2, 6.1

34. 9.0, 7.5, 3.3, 7.4, 6.0

35. Think About It Without calculating the standard deviation, explain why the set {4, 4, 20, 20} has a standard deviation of 8.

36. Think About It When the standard deviation of a set of numbers is 0, what does this imply about the set?

37. Education An instructor adds five points to each student's exam score. Will this change the mean or standard deviation of the exam scores? Explain.

38. Exploration

(a) Multiply each number in Exercise 28 by 3 and find the mean, variance, and standard deviation of the revised data set. Compare these measures with what you found in Exercise 28. How did the measures change?

(b) When each number in a data set is multiplied by a constant k, how will the mean, variance, and standard deviation change?

39. *Why you should learn it* *(p. A35)* The following data represent the average prices of gold (in dollars per ounce) for the years 1990 through 2013. Use a graphing utility to find the mean, variance, and standard deviation of the data. What percent of the data lie within two standard deviations of the mean? (Source: Austin Rare Coins, Inc.)

384,	362,	344,	360,	384,	384,
388,	331,	294,	279,	279,	271,
310,	363,	410,	445,	603,	695,
872,	972,	1225,	1568,	1669,	1531

40. Athletics The total number of points scored by the 437 players who played in the 2013–2014 NBA regular season had a mean and standard deviation of 563 and 468, respectively. Use Chebychev's Theorem to determine the intervals containing at least $\frac{3}{4}$ and at least $\frac{8}{9}$ of the point totals. How do the intervals change when the standard deviation is 225? (Source: National Basketball Association)

Sketching a Box-and-Whisker Plot   In Exercises 41–44, (a) find the lower and upper quartiles of the data and (b) sketch a box-and-whisker plot for the data without using a graphing utility.

41. 23, 15, 14, 23, 13, 14, 13, 20, 12

42. 11, 10, 11, 14, 17, 16, 14, 11, 8, 14, 20

43. 46, 48, 48, 50, 52, 47, 51, 47, 49, 53

44. 25, 20, 22, 28, 24, 28, 25, 19, 27, 29, 28, 21

Creating a Box-and-Whisker Plot   In Exercises 45–48, use a graphing utility to create a box-and-whisker plot for the data.

45. 19, 12, 14, 9, 14, 15, 17, 13, 19, 11, 10, 19

46. 9, 5, 5, 5, 6, 5, 4, 12, 7, 10, 7, 11, 8, 9, 9

47. 20.1, 43.4, 34.9, 23.9, 33.5, 24.1, 22.5, 42.4, 25.7, 17.4, 23.8, 33.3, 17.3, 36.4, 21.8

48. 78.4, 76.3, 107.5, 78.5, 93.2, 90.3, 77.8, 37.1, 97.1, 75.5, 58.8, 65.6

49. Think About It The histograms represent the test scores of two classes of a college course in mathematics. Which histogram has the smaller standard deviation?

50. Manufacturing A company has redesigned a product in an attempt to increase the lifetime of the product. The two sets of data list the lifetimes (in months) of 20 units with the original design and 20 units with the new design. Create a box-and-whisker plot for each set of data, and then comment on the differences between the plots.

Original Design

15.1	78.3	56.3	68.9	30.6
27.2	12.5	42.7	72.7	20.2
53.0	13.5	11.0	18.4	85.2
10.8	38.3	85.1	10.0	12.6

New Design

55.8	71.5	25.6	19.0	23.1
37.2	60.0	35.3	18.9	80.5
46.7	31.1	67.9	23.5	99.5
54.0	23.2	45.5	24.8	87.8

B.3   Least Squares Regression

In many of the examples and exercises in this text, you have been asked to use the *regression* feature of a graphing utility to find mathematical models for sets of data. The *regression* feature of a graphing utility uses the **method of least squares** to find a mathematical model for a set of data. As a measure of how well a model fits a set of data points

$$\{(x_1, y_1), (x_2, y_2), (x_3, y_3), \ldots, (x_n, y_n)\}$$

you can add the squares of the differences between the actual y-values and the values given by the model to obtain the **sum of the squared differences.** For instance, the table shows several values of x and y. The table also shows the values of a linear model $y^* = 0.21x - 2.0$ for each x-value. The sum of the squared differences for the model is 28.0178.

x	70	72	75	76	77	78	80
y	10.9	11.2	11.7	12	12.2	12.3	12.6
y^*	12.70	13.12	13.75	13.96	14.17	14.38	14.80
$(y - y^*)^2$	3.24	3.6864	4.2025	3.8416	3.8809	4.3264	4.84

The model that has the *least* sum of the squared differences is the **least squares regression** line for the data. The least squares regression line for the data in the table is $y = 0.18x - 1.5$. The sum of the squared differences is 0.4032.

To find the least squares regression line $y = ax + b$ for the points $\{(x_1, y_1), (x_2, y_2), (x_3, y_3), \ldots, (x_n, y_n)\}$ algebraically, you need to solve the following system for a and b.

$$\begin{cases} nb + \left(\displaystyle\sum_{i=1}^{n} x_i\right)a = \displaystyle\sum_{i=1}^{n} y_i \\ \left(\displaystyle\sum_{i=1}^{n} x_i\right)b + \left(\displaystyle\sum_{i=1}^{n} x_i^2\right)a = \displaystyle\sum_{i=1}^{n} x_i y_i \end{cases}$$

In the system,

$$\sum_{i=1}^{n} x_i = x_1 + x_2 + \cdots + x_n$$

$$\sum_{i=1}^{n} y_i = y_1 + y_2 + \cdots + y_n$$

$$\sum_{i=1}^{n} x_i^2 = x_1^2 + x_2^2 + \cdots + x_n^2$$

$$\sum_{i=1}^{n} x_i y_i = x_1 y_1 + x_2 y_2 + \cdots + x_n y_n.$$

What you should learn
▶ Use the sum of squared differences to determine a least squares regression line.
▶ Find a least squares regression line for a set of data.
▶ Find a least squares regression parabola for a set of data.

Why you should learn it
The method of least squares provides a way of creating a mathematical model for a set of data, which can then be analyzed.

Technology Tip

Recall from Section 1.7 that when you use the *regression* feature of a graphing utility, the program may output a correlation coefficient, r. When $|r|$ is close to 1, the model is a good fit for the data.

EXAMPLE 1   Finding a Least Squares Regression Line

Find the least squares regression line for $(-3, 0)$, $(-1, 1)$, $(0, 2)$, and $(2, 3)$.

Solution

Begin by constructing a table, as shown below.

x	y	xy	x^2
-3	0	0	9
-1	1	-1	1
0	2	0	0
2	3	6	4
$\sum_{i=1}^{n} x_i = -2$	$\sum_{i=1}^{n} y_i = 6$	$\sum_{i=1}^{n} x_i y_i = 5$	$\sum_{i=1}^{n} x_i^2 = 14$

Applying the system for the least squares regression line with $n = 4$ produces

$$\begin{cases} nb + \left(\sum_{i=1}^{n} x_i\right)a = \sum_{i=1}^{n} y_i \\ \left(\sum_{i=1}^{n} x_i\right)b + \left(\sum_{i=1}^{n} x_i^2\right)a = \sum_{i=1}^{n} x_i y_i \end{cases} \implies \begin{cases} 4b - 2a = 6 \\ -2b + 14a = 5 \end{cases}$$

Solving this system of equations produces $a = \frac{8}{13}$ and $b = \frac{47}{26}$. So, the least squares regression line is $y = \frac{8}{13}x + \frac{47}{26}$, as shown in Figure B.9.

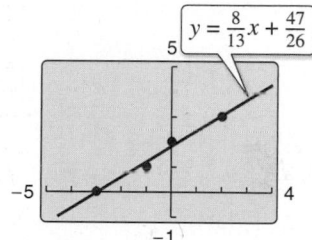

Figure B.9

✓ **Checkpoint**))) *Audio-video solution in English & Spanish at LarsonPrecalculus.com.*

Find the least squares regression line for the points $(-1, -1)$, $(0, 0)$, $(1, 2)$, and $(2, 4)$.

The least squares regression parabola $y = ax^2 + bx + c$ for the points

$$\{(x_1, y_1), (x_2, y_2), (x_3, y_3), \ldots, (x_n, y_n)\}$$

is obtained in a similar manner by solving the following system of three equations in three unknowns for a, b, and c.

$$\begin{cases} nc + \left(\sum_{i=1}^{n} x_i\right)b + \left(\sum_{i=1}^{n} x_i^2\right)a = \sum_{i=1}^{n} y_i \\ \left(\sum_{i=1}^{n} x_i\right)c + \left(\sum_{i=1}^{n} x_i^2\right)b + \left(\sum_{i=1}^{n} x_i^3\right)a = \sum_{i=1}^{n} x_i y_i \\ \left(\sum_{i=1}^{n} x_i^2\right)c + \left(\sum_{i=1}^{n} x_i^3\right)b + \left(\sum_{i=1}^{n} x_i^4\right)a = \sum_{i=1}^{n} x_i^2 y_i \end{cases}$$

B.3   Exercises

Finding a Least Squares Regression Line   In Exercises 1–4, find the least squares regression line for the points. Verify your answer with a graphing utility.

1. $(-4, 1)$, $(-3, 3)$, $(-2, 4)$, $(-1, 6)$

2. $(0, -1)$, $(2, 0)$, $(4, 3)$, $(6, 5)$

3. $(-3, 1)$, $(-1, 2)$, $(1, 2)$, $(4, 3)$

4. $(0, -1)$, $(2, 1)$, $(3, 2)$, $(5, 3)$

Answers to Odd-Numbered Exercises and Tests

Chapter 1

Section 1.1   (page 11)

1. (a) iii   (b) i   (c) v   (d) ii   (e) iv   **3.** parallel

5. 0   **7.** (a) L_2 (b) L_3 (c) L_1 **9.** $\frac{3}{2}$

11.

13. $m = -\frac{5}{2}$

15. m is undefined.

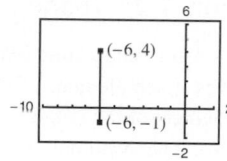

17. $(0, 1), (3, 1), (-1, 1)$ **19.** $(1, 4), (1, 6), (1, 9)$

21. $(-1, -7), (-2, -5), (-5, 1)$

23. $(3, -4), (5, -3), (9, -1)$

25. $y = 3x - 2$ **27.** $y = -\frac{1}{2}x - 2$

29. $x = 6$ **31.** $y = \frac{3}{2}$

33. $y = \frac{1}{30}x + \frac{19}{15}$; about \$1.9 million

35. $m = \frac{2}{3}$; y-intercept: $(0, -3)$; a line that rises from left to right

37. $m = \frac{2}{5}$; y-intercept: $(0, 2)$; a line that rises from left to right

39. Slope is undefined; no y-intercept; a vertical line at $x = -6$

41. $m = 0$; y-intercept: $\left(0, -\frac{2}{3}\right)$; a horizontal line at $y = -\frac{2}{3}$

43. (a) $m = 5$;
y-intercept: $(0, 3)$

(b)

45. (a) Slope is undefined;
there is no y-intercept.

(b)

47. (a) $m = 0$;
y-intercept: $\left(0, -\frac{5}{3}\right)$

(b)

49. $y = 2x - 5$

51. $y = -\frac{3}{5}x + 2$

53. $x + 8 = 0$

55. $y = -\frac{1}{2}x + \frac{3}{2}$

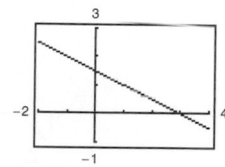

57. $y = -\frac{6}{5}x - \frac{18}{25}$

59. $y = \frac{2}{5}x + \frac{1}{5}$

61.

The first and second graphs do not give an accurate view of the slope. The third graph is best because it uses a square setting.

63. Perpendicular   **65.** Parallel
67. (a) $y = 2x - 3$ (b) $y = -\frac{1}{2}x + 2$
69. (a) $y = -\frac{3}{4}x + \frac{3}{8}$ (b) $y = \frac{4}{3}x + \frac{127}{72}$
71. (a) $y = -\frac{6}{5}x - 6.08$ (b) $y = \frac{5}{6}x + 1.85$
73. (a) $x = 3$ (b) $y = -2$ **75.** (a) $y = 1$ (b) $x = -5$
77. $y = 2x + 1$ **79.** $y = -\frac{1}{2}x + 1$
81. The lines $y = \frac{1}{4}x$ and $y = -4x$ are perpendicular.

83. The lines $y = -\frac{1}{2}x$ and $y = -\frac{1}{2}x + 3$ are parallel. Both are perpendicular to $y = 2x - 4$.

85. 12 ft
87. (a) The greatest increase was from 2010 to 2011, and the greatest decrease was from 2008 to 2009.
(b) $y = 3.559x + 5.309$
(c) There is an increase of about \$3.559 billion per year.
(d) \$65.812 billion; Answers will vary.
89. $V = 125t + 665$ **91.** $V = -2000t + 50,400$
93. (a) $V = 25,000 - 2300t$
(b)

t	0	1	2	3	4
V	25,000	22,700	20,400	18,100	15,800

t	5	6	7	8	9	10
V	13,500	11,200	8900	6600	4300	2000

95. (a) $C = 30.75t + 36,500$ (b) $R = 80t$
(c) $P = 49.25t - 36,500$ (d) $t \approx 741.1$ h
97. (a) Increase of about 1295 students per year
(b) 76,090; 89,040; 95,515
(c) $y = 1295x + 73,500$; where $x = 0$ corresponds to 1994; $m = 1295$; The slope determines the average increase in enrollment.
99. False. The slopes $\left(\frac{2}{7} \text{ and } -\frac{11}{7}\right)$ are not equal.

101.   **103.**

a and b represent the x- and y-intercepts.

a and b represent the x- and y-intercepts.

105. $9x + 2y - 18 = 0$ **107.** $12x + 3y + 2 = 0$
109. a   **111.** c
113. No. Answers will vary. Sample answer: The line $y = 2$ does not have an x-intercept.
115. Yes. Once a parallel line is established to the given line, there are an infinite number of distances away from that line, and thus an infinite number of parallel lines.
117. Yes; $x + 20$ **119.** No   **121.** No
123. $(x - 9)(x + 3)$ **125.** $(2x - 5)(x + 8)$
127. Answers will vary.

Section 1.2   (page 24)

1. domain, range, function   **3.** No   **5.** No
7. Yes. Each element of the domain is assigned to exactly one element of the range.
9. No. The National Football Conference, an element in the domain, is assigned to three elements in the range, the Giants, the Saints, and the Seahawks; The American Football Conference, an element in the domain, is also assigned to three elements in the range, the Patriots, the Ravens, and the Steelers.
11. Yes. Each input value is matched with one output value.
13. No. The inputs 1, 2, and 3 are each matched with two outputs.
15. (a) Function
(b) Not a function because the element 1 in A corresponds to two elements, -2 and 1, in B.
(c) Not a function from A to B. It is a function from B to A.
17. Yes; yes; Each input value (year) is matched with exactly one output value (average price) for both name brand and generic drug prescriptions.
19. Not a function   **21.** Function   **23.** Function
25. Not a function   **27.** Function   **29.** Not a function
31. (a) 7   (b) -11 (c) $3t + 7$
33. (a) 0   (b) -0.75 (c) $x^2 - 10x + 24$
35. (a) 1   (b) 2.5   (c) $3 - 2|x|$
37. (a) Undefined   (b) $-\frac{1}{5}$ (c) $\frac{1}{y^2 + 6y}$
39. (a) 1   (b) -1 (c) $\frac{|t|}{t}$
41. (a) -1 (b) 2   (c) 6   **43.** (a) 6   (b) 3   (c) 10
45. (a) 0   (b) 4   (c) 5
47. $\{(-2, 9), (-1, 4), (0, 1), (1, 0), (2, 1)\}$
49. $\{(-2, 4), (-1, 3), (0, 2), (1, 3), (2, 4)\}$
51.

t	-5	-4	-3	-2	-1
$h(t)$	1	$\frac{1}{2}$	0	$\frac{1}{2}$	1

53. 5   **55.** $\frac{4}{9}$ **57.** All real numbers x
59. All real numbers t except $t = 0$
61. All real numbers x

63. All real numbers x except $x = 0, -2$

65. All real numbers y such that $y > 10$

67.   **69.**

Domain: $[-4, 4]$ Domain: $(-\infty, \infty)$
Range: $[0, 4]$ Range: $[0, \infty)$

71. $A = \dfrac{C^2}{4\pi}$

73. (a) 1024 cm^3

(b)   Yes, it is a function.

(c) $V = x(24 - 2x)^2, 0 < x < 12$

(d)

The function fits the data points; Answers will vary.

75. $A = 2xy = 2x\sqrt{36 - x^2}, 0 < x < 6$

77. (a) $C = 68.75x + 248,000$ (b) $R = 99.99x$

(c) $P = 31.24x - 248,000$

(d) $376,800$; $376,800 profit for 20,000 units

(e) $-248,000$; $248,000 loss for 0 units

79. (a) The independent variable is t and represents the year. The dependent variable is n and represents the numbers of miles traveled.

(b)

t	0	1	2	3	4	5
$n(t)$	3.95	3.96	3.98	3.99	4.00	4.02

t	6	7	8	9	10	11
$n(t)$	4.03	4.04	4.05	4.07	4.08	4.09

(c) The model fits the data well.

(d) Sample answer: No. The function may not accurately model other years.

81. Yes; The ball is 6 feet high when it reaches the other child.

83. $2, c \neq 0$ **85.** $3 + h, h \neq 0$

87. False. The range is $[-1, \infty)$.

89. $f(x) = \sqrt{x} + 2$

Domain: $x \geq 0$
Range: $[2, \infty)$

91. No, f is not the independent variable because the value of f depends on the value of x.

93. $\dfrac{12x + 20}{x + 2}$ **95.** $\dfrac{(x + 6)(x + 10)}{5(x + 3)}, x \neq 0, \dfrac{1}{2}$

Section 1.3   (page 37)

1. decreasing   **3.** $[1, 4]$ **5.** Relative maximum

7. Domain: $(-\infty, \infty)$ **9.** Domain: $[-4, 4]$
Range: $(-\infty, 1]$ Range: $[0, 4]$
$f(0) = 1$ $f(0) = 4$

11.   **13.**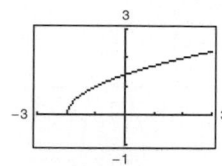

Domain: $(-\infty, \infty)$ Domain: $[-2, \infty)$
Range: $(-\infty, 3]$ Range: $[0, \infty)$

15.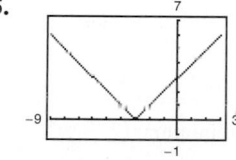

Domain: $(-\infty, \infty)$
Range: $[0, \infty)$

17. (a) $(-\infty, \infty)$ (b) $[-2, \infty)$ (c) $-1, 3$
(d) x-intercepts   (e) -1 (f) y-intercept
(g) $-2; (1, -2)$ (h) $0, (-1, 0)$ (i) 2

19. Function. Graph the given function over the window shown in the figure.

21. Not a function. Solve for y and graph the two resulting functions.

23. Increasing on $(-\infty, \infty)$

25. Increasing on $(-\infty, 0), (2, \infty)$
Decreasing on $(0, 2)$

27. (a) 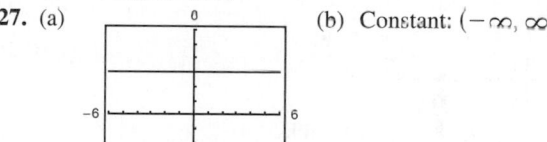   (b) Constant: $(-\infty, \infty)$

29. (a) 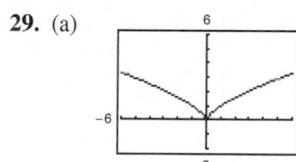   (b) Decreasing on $(-\infty, 0)$
Increasing on $(0, \infty)$

31. (a)   (b) Increasing on $(-2, \infty)$
Decreasing on $(-3, -2)$

33. (a)   (b) Decreasing on $(-\infty, -1)$
Constant on $(-1, 1)$
Increasing on $(1, \infty)$

35.   Relative minimum: $(3, -9)$

37.   Relative minimum: $(-1.70, -16.86)$
Relative maximum: $(1.37, 12.16)$

39.   Relative minimum: $(0.33, -0.38)$

41.   Relative minimum: $(2, -9)$

43.   Relative minimum: $(1, -2)$
Relative maximum: $(-1, 2)$

45.   Relative minimum: $(1, -2)$

47.   **49.**

51.

53.

Domain: $(-\infty, \infty)$
Range: $[0, 2)$
Sawtooth pattern

55.   **57.**

59.   **61.**

63. Even   **65.** Neither

67. Even   **69.** Neither

71. Neither

73. (a) $\left(-\frac{3}{2}, 4\right)$ (b) $\left(-\frac{3}{2}, -4\right)$
75. (a) $(2, -9)$ (b) $(2, 9)$
77. (a) $(-x, -y)$ (b) $(-x, y)$
79. (a)–(c) Neither   **81.** (a)–(c) Odd
83. (a)–(c) Odd   **85.** (a)–(c) Even

87.

$(-\infty, 4]$

89.

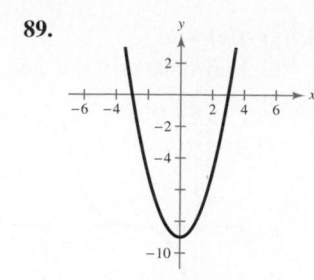

$(-\infty, -3], [3, \infty)$

91. (a) C_2 is the appropriate model. The cost of the first hour is $1.00 and the cost increases $0.50 when the next hour begins, and so on.

(b)

$4.50

93. $h = -x^2 + 4x - 3, 1 \le x \le 3$

95. (a)

(b) Decreasing from 2010 to 2011; increasing from 2011 to 2013

(c) About 480

97. False. Counterexample: $f(x) = \sqrt{1 + x^2}$

99. c   **100.** d   **101.** b   **102.** e   **103.** a   **104.** f

105. No. Each y-value corresponds to two distinct x-values when $y > 0$.

107. Yes

109. (a) Even. g is a reflection in the x-axis.

(b) Even. g is a reflection in the y-axis.

(c) Even. g is a vertical shift downward.

(d) Neither. g is shifted to the left and reflected in the x-axis.

111. Proof

113. Terms: $-2x^2, 11x, 3$; coefficients: $-2, 11$

115. Terms: $\dfrac{x}{3}, -5x^2, x^3$; coefficients: $\dfrac{1}{3}, -5, 1$

117. (a) -17 (b) -17 (c) $-x^2 + 3x + 1$

119. $h + 4, h \ne 0$

Section 1.4 (page 47)

1. Horizontal shifts, vertical shifts, reflections

3. $-f(x), f(-x)$

5.

7.

9.

11.

13.

15.

17.

19. (a)

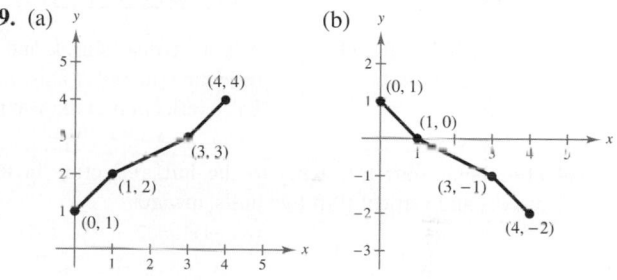

21. (a) (b)

(c) (d)

(e) (f)

(g)

21. The graph of $f(x) = x^2$ should have been shifted one unit to the left instead of one unit to the right.

23. Vertical shift two units upward

25. Horizontal shift four units to the right

27. Vertical shift two units downward

29. Vertical shift of $y = x$; $y = x + 3$

31. Vertical shift of $y = x^2$; $y = x^2 - 3$

33. Reflection in the x-axis and a vertical shift one unit upward of $y = \sqrt{x}$; $y = 1 - \sqrt{x}$

35. Reflection in the x-axis

37. Reflection in the y-axis (identical)

39. Reflection in the x-axis   **41.** Vertical stretch

43. Vertical shrink   **45.** Horizontal shrink

47.   **49.**

g is a horizontal shift and h is a vertical shrink.

g is a vertical shrink and a reflection in the x-axis and h is a reflection in the y-axis.

51. (a) $f(x) = x^2$

(b) Horizontal shift five units to the left, reflection in the x-axis, and vertical shift two units upward

(c) 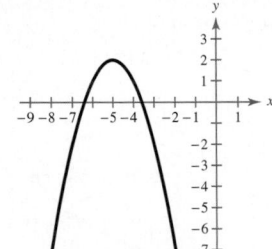   (d) $g(x) = 2 - f(x + 5)$

53. (a) $f(x) = x^2$

(b) Horizontal shift four units to the right, vertical stretch, and vertical shift three units upward

(c) 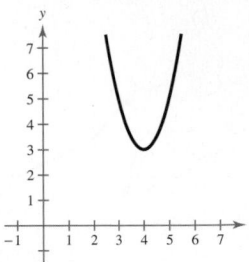   (d) $f(x) = 3 + 2f(x - 4)$

55. (a) $f(x) = x^3$

(b) Horizontal shift two units to the right and vertical shrink

(c)   (d) $g(x) = \frac{1}{3}f(x - 2)$

57. (a) $f(x) = x^3$

(b) Horizontal shift one unit to the right and vertical shift two units upward

(c) 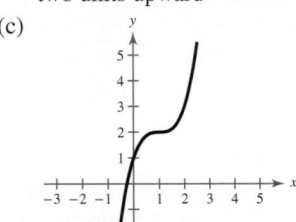   (d) $g(x) = f(x - 1) + 2$

59. (a) $f(x) = \dfrac{1}{x}$

(b) Horizontal shift eight units to the left and vertical shift nine units downward

(c)   (d) $g(x) = f(x + 8) - 9$

61. (a) $f(x) = |x|$

(b) Horizontal shift one unit to the right, reflection in the x-axis, vertical stretch, and vertical shift four units downward

(c)   (d) $g(x) = -2f(x - 1) - 4$

63. (a) $f(x) = \sqrt{x}$

(b) Horizontal shift three units to the left, reflection in the x-axis, vertical shrink, and vertical shift one unit downward

(c)

(d) $g(x) = -\frac{1}{2}f(x + 3) - 1$

65. (a) Horizontal shift 26.17 units to the right, reflection in the x-axis, vertical shrink, and vertical shift 126.5 units upward

(b)

(c) $N(t) = -0.03[(t + 9) - 26.17]^2 + 126.5$

$= -0.03(t - 17.17)^2 + 126.5$

To make a horizontal shift 9 years backward (9 units left), add 9 to t.

67. False. When $f(x) = x^2$, $f(-x) = (-x)^2 = x^2$. Because $f(x) = f(-x)$ in this case, $y = f(-x)$ is not a reflection of $y = f(x)$ across the x-axis in all cases.

69. $x = -2$ and $x = 3$

71. Cannot be determined because it is a vertical shift

73. c   **75.** c   **77.** Answers will vary.

79. (a) The graph of g is a vertical shrink of the graph of f.

(b) The graph of g is a vertical stretch of the graph of f.

81. Neither

83. All real numbers x except $x = 9$

85. All real numbers x such that $-10 \le x \le 10$

Section 1.5 (page 56)

1. addition, subtraction, multiplication, division

3. $g(x)$ **5.** $2x$

7.

9.

11. (a) $2x$ (b) 6 (c) $x^2 - 9$ (d) $\dfrac{x + 3}{x - 3}$

All real numbers x, except $x = 3$

13. (a) $3x^2 - 5x + 6$ (b) $3x^2 + 5x - 6$

(c) $-15x^3 + 18x^2$ (d) $\dfrac{3x^2}{6 - 5x}$

All real numbers x, except $x = \frac{6}{5}$

15. (a) $x^2 + 5 + \sqrt{1 - x}$ (b) $x^2 + 5 - \sqrt{1 - x}$

(c) $(x^2 + 5)\sqrt{1 - x}$ (d) $\dfrac{x^2 + 5}{\sqrt{1 - x}}, x < 1$

17. (a) $\dfrac{x + 1}{x^2}$ (b) $\dfrac{x - 1}{x^2}$ (c) $\dfrac{1}{x^3}$ (d) $x, x \ne 0$

19. 9   **21.** 1   **23.** -280 **25.** $-\frac{24}{7}$

27. $t^2 + t + 1$ **29.** $-125t^3 - 50^2 + 5t + 2$

31. $\dfrac{t^2 - 8t + 15}{t - 6}$

33.

35.

37.

39.

$f(x), 0 \le x \le 2$; $f(x), 0 \le x \le 2$;

$g(x), x > 6$ $f(x), x > 6$

41. (a) $2(x + 4)^2$ (b) $2x^2 + 4$ (c) 32

43. (a) $20 - 3x$ (b) $-3x$ (c) 20

45. (a) All real numbers x such that $x \ge -7$

(b) All real numbers x

(c) All real numbers x such that $x \le -\dfrac{\sqrt{7}}{2}$ or $x \ge \dfrac{\sqrt{7}}{2}$

47. (a) All real numbers x

(b) All real numbers x such that $x \ge 0$

(c) All real numbers x such that $x \ge 0$

49. (a) All real numbers x except $x = 0$

(b) All real numbers x except $x = -3$

(c) All real numbers x except $x = -3$

51. (a) All real numbers x (b) All real numbers x

(c) All real numbers x

53. (a) All real numbers x

(b) All real numbers x except $x = \pm 2$

(c) All real numbers x except $x = \pm 2$

55. (a) $(f \circ g)(x) = \sqrt{x^2 + 4}$

$(g \circ f)(x) = x + 4, x \ge -4$;

Domain of $f \circ g$: all real numbers x

(b)

$f \circ g \ne g \circ f$

57. (a) $(f \circ g)(x) = x; (g \circ f)(x) = x$;

Domain of $f \circ g$: all real numbers x

(b)

$f \circ g = g \circ f$

CHAPTER 1

59. (a) $(f \circ g)(x) = x^4; (g \circ f)(x) = x^4;$
Domain of $f \circ g$: all real numbers x

(b)

$f \circ g = g \circ f$

61. (a) $(f \circ g)(x) = x; (g \circ f)(x) = x$ (b) $x = x$

(c)

x	0	1	2	3
$g(x)$	$-\frac{4}{5}$	$-\frac{3}{5}$	$-\frac{2}{5}$	$-\frac{1}{5}$
$(f \circ g)(x)$	0	1	2	3

x	0	1	2	3
$f(x)$	4	9	14	19
$(g \circ f)(x)$	0	1	2	3

63. (a) $(f \circ g)(x) = \sqrt{x^2 + 1}; (g \circ f)(x) = x + 1, x \geq -6$
(b) $x + 1 \neq \sqrt{x^2 + 1}$

(c)

x	0	1	2	3
$g(x)$	-5	-4	-1	4
$(f \circ g)(x)$	1	$\sqrt{2}$	$\sqrt{5}$	$\sqrt{10}$

x	0	1	2	3
$f(x)$	$\sqrt{6}$	$\sqrt{7}$	$\sqrt{8}$	3
$(g \circ f)(x)$	1	2	3	4

65. (a) $(f \circ g)(x) = |2x^3|; (g \circ f)(x) = 2|x|^3$
(b) $|2x^3| = 2|x|^3$

(c)

x	-2	-1	0	1	2
$g(x)$	-16	-2	0	2	16
$(f \circ g)(x)$	16	2	0	2	16

x	-2	-1	0	1	2
$f(x)$	2	1	0	1	2
$(g \circ f)(x)$	16	2	0	2	16

67. (a) 3   (b) 0   **69.** (a) 2   (b) 4
71. $f(x) = x^2, g(x) = 2x + 1$ **73.** $f(x) = \sqrt[3]{x}, g(x) = x^2 - 4$
75. $f(x) = \frac{1}{x}, g(x) = x + 2$
77. $f(x) = x^2 + 2x, g(x) = x + 4$
79. (a) $T = \frac{3}{4}x + \frac{1}{15}x^2$

(b)

(c) B. For example, $B(60) = 240$, whereas $R(60)$ is only 45.

81. (a) $r(x) = \frac{x}{2}$ (b) $A(r) = \pi r^2$

(c) $(A \circ r)(x) = \pi \left(\frac{x}{2}\right)^2$

$(A \circ r)(x)$ represents the area of the circular base of the tank with radius $x/2$.

83. (a) $T = 1.3t^2 + 72.4t + 1322$

(b)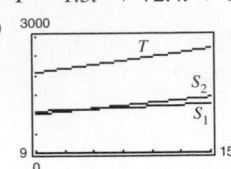

85. (a) $N(T(t))$ or $(N \circ T)(t) = 40t^2 + 590; N(T(t))$ or $(N \circ T)(t)$ represents the number of bacteria after t hours outside the refrigerator.
(b) $(N \circ T)(12) = 6350$; There are 6350 bacteria in a refrigerated food product after 12 hours outside the refrigerator.
(c) About 3.9 h

87. $s(t) = \sqrt{(150 - 450t)^2 + (200 - 450t)^2}$
$= 50\sqrt{162t^2 - 126t + 25}$

89. False. $g(x) = x - 3$

91. a, c   **93.** Odd (Proofs will vary.)

95. (a) $Y = O - 12$; Answers will vary.
(b) Middle child is 7 years old, oldest child is 14 years old.

97. $(0, -5), (1, -5), (2, -7)$

99. $(0, 7), \left(1, 4\sqrt{3}\right), \left(2, \sqrt{45}\right)$

Section 1.6   (page 67)

1. inverse, f^{-1} **3.** $y = x$ **5.** At most once

7. $f^{-1}(x) = \frac{x}{6}$ **9.** $f^{-1}(x) = x - 11$

11. $f^{-1}(x) = 2x + 1$ **13.** $f^{-1}(x) = x^3$

15. c   **16.** b   **17.** a   **18.** d

19. $f(g(x)) = f(\sqrt[3]{x}) = (\sqrt[3]{x})^3 = x$
$g(f(x)) = g(x^3) = \sqrt[3]{x^3} = x$

Reflections in the line $y = x$

21. $f(g(x)) = f(x^2 + 4), x \geq 0$
$= \sqrt{(x^2 + 4) - 4} = x$
$g(f(x)) = g(\sqrt{x - 4})$
$= (\sqrt{x - 4})^2 + 4 = x$

Reflections in the line $y = x$

23. $f(g(x)) = f\left(\sqrt[3]{1-x}\right) = 1 - \left(\sqrt[3]{1-x}\right)^3 = x$
$g(f(x)) = g(1-x^3) = \sqrt[3]{1-(1-x^3)} = x$

Reflections in the line $y = x$

25. (a) $f(g(x)) = f\left(-\dfrac{2x+6}{7}\right)$

$\qquad = \dfrac{-7}{2}\left(-\dfrac{2x+6}{7}\right) - 3 = x$

$\quad g(f(x)) = g\left(-\dfrac{7}{2}x - 3\right)$

$\qquad = -\dfrac{2\left(-\dfrac{7}{2}x - 3\right) + 6}{7} = x$

(b)

(c)

x	0	2	-2	6
$f(x)$	-3	-10	4	-24

x	-3	-10	4	-24
$g(x)$	0	2	6	6

27. (a) $f(g(x)) = f\left(\sqrt[3]{x-5}\right) = \left(\sqrt[3]{x-5}\right)^3 + 5 = x$
$g(f(x)) = g(x^3 + 5) = \sqrt[3]{(x^3 + 5) - 5} = x$

(b)

(c)

x	0	1	-1	-2	4
$f(x)$	5	6	4	-3	69

x	5	6	4	-3	69
$g(x)$	0	1	-1	-2	4

29. (a) $f(g(x)) = f(8 + x^2)$
$\qquad = -\sqrt{(8 + x^2) - 8}$
$\qquad = -\sqrt{x^2} = -(-x) = x, x \le 0$
$\quad g(f(x)) = g\left(-\sqrt{x-8}\right)$
$\qquad = 8 + \left(-\sqrt{x-8}\right)^2$
$\qquad = 8 + (x - 8) = x, x \ge 8$

(b)

(c)

x	8	9	12	15
$f(x)$	0	-1	-2	$-\sqrt{7}$

x	0	-1	-2	$-\sqrt{7}$
$g(x)$	8	9	12	15

31. (a) $f(g(x)) = f\left(\dfrac{x}{2}\right)$

$\qquad = 2\left(\dfrac{x}{2}\right) = x$

$\quad g(f(x)) = g(2x)$

$\qquad = \dfrac{2x}{2} = x$

(b)

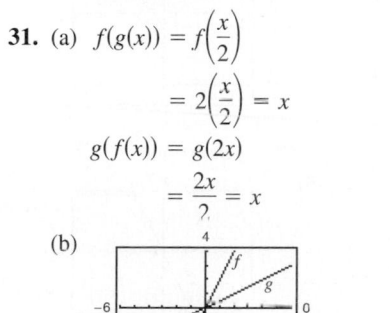

(c)

x	-4	-2	0	2	4
$f(x)$	-8	-4	0	4	8

x	-8	-4	0	4	8
$g(x)$	-4	-2	0	2	4

33. (a) $f(g(x)) = f\left(-\dfrac{5x+1}{x-1}\right)$

$\qquad = \dfrac{\left(-\dfrac{5x+1}{x-1}\right) - 1}{\left(-\dfrac{5x+1}{x-1}\right) + 5} = \dfrac{\dfrac{6x}{x-1}}{\dfrac{6}{x-1}} = x, x \ne 1$

$\quad g(f(x)) = g\left(\dfrac{x-1}{x+5}\right)$

$\qquad = -\dfrac{5\left(\dfrac{x-1}{x+5}\right) + 1}{\left(\dfrac{x-1}{x+5}\right) - 1} = \dfrac{\dfrac{6x}{x+5}}{\dfrac{6}{x+5}} = x, x \ne -5$

(b)

(c)

x	-3	2	-1	0	2	3	4
$f(x)$	-2	-1	$-\frac{1}{2}$	$-\frac{1}{5}$	$\frac{1}{7}$	$\frac{1}{4}$	$\frac{1}{3}$

x	-2	-1	$-\frac{1}{2}$	$-\frac{1}{5}$	$\frac{1}{7}$	$\frac{1}{4}$	$\frac{1}{3}$
$g(x)$	-3	-2	-1	0	2	3	4

35. Yes. No two elements in the domain of f correspond to the same element in the range of f.

37. No. -3 and 0 both correspond to 6, so f is not one-to-one.

39. Not a function   **41.** Function; one-to-one

43. Function; one-to-one

45.

One-to-one

47.

Not one-to-one

49.

Not one-to-one

51.

Not one-to-one

53.

One-to-one

55.

Not one-to-one

57.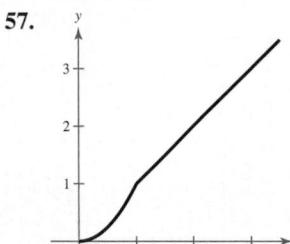

An inverse function exists.

59. Not one-to-one   **61.** $f^{-1}(x) = \dfrac{5x - 4}{3}$

63. Not one-to-one   **65.** $f^{-1}(x) = \sqrt{x} - 3$

67. $f^{-1}(x) = \dfrac{x^2 - 3}{2}, x \geq 0$ **69.** $f^{-1}(x) = 2 - x, x \geq 0$

71. $f^{-1}(x) = \dfrac{x + 9}{4}$

Reflections in the line $y = x$

73. $f^{-1}(x) = \sqrt[5]{x}$

Reflections in the line $y = x$

75. $f^{-1}(x) = -\sqrt[4]{x}$

Reflections in the line $y = x$

77. $f^{-1}(x) = \sqrt{4 - x^2}$, $0 \leq x \leq 2$

The graphs are the same.

79. $f^{-1}(x) = \sqrt[3]{\dfrac{4}{x}}$

Reflections in the line $y = x$

81. $f^{-1}(x) = \sqrt{x} + 2$

Domain of f: all real numbers x such that $x \geq 2$
Range of f: all real numbers y such that $y \geq 0$
Domain of f^{-1}: all real numbers x such that $x \geq 0$
Range of f^{-1}: all real numbers y such that $y \geq 2$

83. $f^{-1}(x) = x - 2$

Domain of f: all real numbers x such that $x \geq -2$
Range of f: all real numbers y such that $y \geq 0$
Domain of f^{-1}: all real numbers x such that $x \geq 0$
Range of f^{-1}: all real numbers y such that $y \geq -2$

85. $f^{-1}(x) = \sqrt{x} - 3$

Domain of f: all real numbers x such that $x \geq -3$
Range of f: all real numbers y such that $y \geq 0$
Domain of f^{-1}: all real numbers x such that $x \geq 0$
Range of f^{-1}: all real numbers y such that $y \geq -3$

87. $f^{-1}(x) = \dfrac{\sqrt{-2(x + 5)}}{2}$

Domain of f: all real numbers x such that $x \geq 0$
Range of f: all real numbers y such that $y \leq -5$
Domain of f^{-1}: all real numbers x such that $x \leq -5$
Range of f^{-1}: all real numbers y such that $y \geq 0$

89. $f^{-1}(x) = x + 3$

Domain of f: all real numbers x such that $x \geq 4$
Range of f: all real numbers y such that $y \geq 1$
Domain of f^{-1}: all real numbers x such that $x \geq 1$
Range of f^{-1}: all real numbers y such that $y \geq 4$

91.

x	-4	-2	2	3
$f^{-1}(x)$	-2	-1	1	3

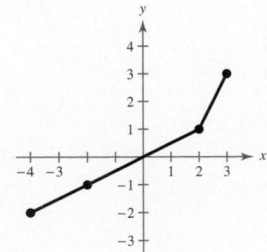

93. 4   **95.** −2   **97.** 0   **99.** 2

101. (a) and (b)

(c) Inverse function because it satisfies the Vertical Line Test.

103. (a) and (b)

(c) Not an inverse function because it does not satisfy the Vertical Line Test.

105. 32   **107.** −168   **109.** $8\sqrt[3]{x} + 24$

111. $\dfrac{x + 1}{2}$ **113.** $\dfrac{x + 1}{2}$

115. (a) f is one-to-one because no two elements in the domain (men's U.S. shoe sizes) correspond to the same element in the range (men's European shoe sizes).

(b) 44   (c) 10   (d) 41   (e) 12

117. (a) 19 9 64 64 4 69 29 4 64 9 104 29 94

(b) $f^{-1}(x) = \dfrac{x - 4}{5}$; What time

119. False. For example, $y = x^2$ is even, but does not have an inverse.

121. This situation could be represented by a one-to-one function. The inverse function would represent the number of miles completed in terms of time in hours.

123. This function could not be represented by a one-to-one function because it oscillates.

125. The graph of f^{-1} is a reflection of the graph of f in the line $y = x$.

127. (a) The function will be one-to-one because no two values of x will produce the same value for $f(x)$.

(b) $f^{-1}(50)$ represents the value of 50 degrees Fahrenheit in degrees Celsius.

129. Constant function   **131.** Proof   **133.** $9x, x \neq 0$

135. $-(x + 6), x \neq 6$ **137.** Not a function   **139.** Function

Section 1.7 (page 76)

1. positive   **3.** Negative correlation

5. (a)

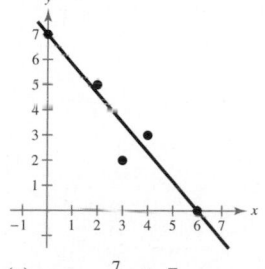

Years of experience

(b) Yes, the data appear somewhat linear. More experience, x, corresponds to higher sales, y.

7. Negative correlation   **9.** No correlation

11. (a) and (b)

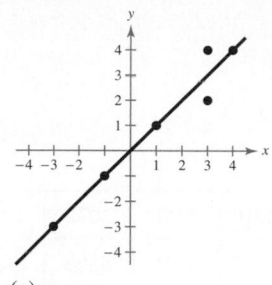

(c) $y = x$

13. (a) and (b)

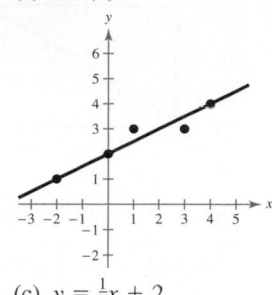

(c) $y = \frac{1}{2}x + 2$

15. (a) and (b)

(c) $y = -\frac{7}{6}x + 7$

17. $y = 0.46x + 1.6$

(a)

(b)

x	−3	−1	0	2	4
Linear equation	0.22	1.14	1.6	2.52	3.44
Given data	0	1	2	3	3

The model fits the data well.

19. (a)

Elongation (in centimeters)

Force (in kilograms)

(b) $d = 0.07F - 0.3$

(c) $d = 0.066F$

(d) 3.63 cm

21. (a) and (c)

(b) $V = 22.8t + 13$

The model fits the data well.

(d) 2015: $355 million; 2020: $469 million; Answers will vary.

(e) 22.8; The slope represents the average annual increase in enterprise values (in millions of dollars).

CHAPTER 1

23. (a) and (c) (b) $P = 37.3t + 8416$

(d)

Year	2008	2009	2010	2011	2012	2013
Actual	8711	8756	8792	8821	8868	8899
Model	8714.4	8751.7	8789	8826.3	8863.6	8900.9

The model fits the data well.

(e) 10,280,800 people; Answers will vary.

25. (a) $45.70x + 108.0$

(b)

(c) The slope represents the increase in sales due to increased advertising.

(d) $176,550

27. (a) $T = -0.015t + 4.79$

$r \approx -0.866$

(b) The negative slope means that the winning times are generally decreasing over time.

(c)

(d)

Year	1956	1960	1964	1968	1972
Actual	4.91	4.84	4.72	4.53	4.32
Model	4.70	4.64	4.58	4.52	4.46

Year	1976	1980	1984	1988	1992
Actual	4.16	4.15	4.12	4.06	4.12
Model	4.40	4.34	4.28	4.22	4.16

Year	1996	2000	2004	2008	2012
Actual	4.12	4.10	4.09	4.05	4.02
Model	4.10	4.04	3.98	3.92	3.86

The model does not fit the data well.

(e) The closer $|r|$ is to 1, the better the model fits the data.

(f) No; The winning times have leveled off in recent years, but the model values continue to decrease to unrealistic times.

29. True. To have positive correlation, the y-values tend to increase as x increases.

31. Answers will vary.

33. (a) 10 (b) $2w^2 + 5w + 7$ **35.** $-\frac{3}{5}$ **37.** $-\frac{1}{4}, \frac{3}{2}$

Review Exercises   (page 82)

1.

$m = 0$

3.

m is undefined.

5.

$m = \frac{3}{7}$

7.

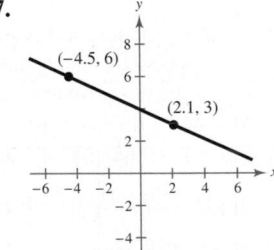

$m = -\frac{5}{11}$

9. (a) $x - 4y - 6 = 0$ (b) $(6, 0), (10, 1), (-2, -2)$

11. (a) $3x + 2y + 10 = 0$ (b) $(4, -11), (2, -8), (-2, -2)$

13. (a) $y - 6 = 0$ (b) $(0, 6), (1, 6), (-1, 6)$

15. (a) $x - 10 = 0$ (b) $(10, 1), (10, 3), (10, -2)$

17. $y = -1$

19. $x = \frac{5}{6}$

21. $y = \frac{2}{7}x + \frac{2}{7}$

23. $y = -\frac{1}{2}x + \frac{1}{2}$

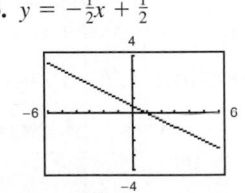

25. $V = 850t + 8250$ **27.** $V = 42.70t + 412$

29. $220,000

31. (a) $y = \frac{5}{4}x - \frac{23}{4}$

(b) $y = -\frac{4}{5}x = \frac{2}{5}$

33. (a) Not a function because element 20 in A corresponds to two elements, 4 and 6, in B.

(b) Function

35. Not a function **37.** Function **39.** Function

41. Not a function

43. (a) 2 (b) 10 (c) $b^6 + 1$ (d) $x^2 - 2x + 2$

45. (a) -3 (b) -1 (c) 2 (d) 6

47. All real numbers x except $x = -2$

49. All real numbers x such that $-5 \leq x \leq 5$.

51. (a) $C = 5.25x + 17,500$ (b) $P = 3.18x - 17,500$

53. $2h + 4x + 3, h \neq 0$

55.

57.

Domain: all real numbers x Domain: $[-3, \infty)$

Range: $(-\infty, 3]$ Range: $[4, \infty)$

59.

61.

Domain: $[-6, 6]$ Domain: all real numbers x

Range: $[0, 6]$ Range: $[2, \infty)$

63. Function. Solve for y and graph the resulting function.

65. Not a function. Solve for y and graph the two resulting functions.

67. (a)

  (b) Increasing on $(-\infty, -1), (1, \infty)$

     Decreasing on $(-1, 1)$

69. (a)

  (b) Increasing on $(6, \infty)$

71. Relative maximum: $(0, 16)$

   Relative minima: $(-2, 0), (2, 0)$

73. Relative minimum: $(0, 3)$

   Relative maximum: $(-2.67, 12.48)$

75.

77.

79. Even   **81.** Even   **83.** Neither   **85.** Odd

87. Rational function $f(x) = \dfrac{1}{x}$

   Horizontal shift three units right

   $g(x) = \dfrac{1}{x - 3}$

89. Quadratic function $f(x) = x^2$

   Vertical shift one unit upward, horizontal shift two units right

   $g(x) = (x - 2)^2 + 1$

91. Absolute value function $f(x) = |x|$

   Vertical shift three units upward

   $g(x) = |x| + 3$

93.

95.

97. (a) Rational function $f(x) = \dfrac{1}{x}$

   (b) Vertical shift six units downward

   (c)

   (d) $h(x) = f(x) - 6$

99. (a) Cubic function $f(x) = x^3$

   (b) Horizontal shift two units right, vertical shift five units upward

   (c)

   (d) $h(x) = f(x - 2) + 5$

101. (a) Square root function $f(x) = \sqrt{x}$

   (b) Reflection in the x-axis, vertical shift six units downward

   (c)

   (d) $h(x) = -f(x) - 6$

CHAPTER 1

103. (a) Absolute value function $f(x) = |x|$
(b) Vertical shift nine units upward, horizontal shrink
(c) 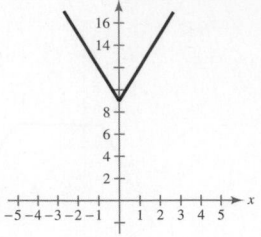 (d) $h(x) = f(3x) + 9$

105. (a) Rational function $f(x) = \dfrac{1}{x}$
(b) Horizontal shift one unit left, reflection in the x-axis, vertical stretch, vertical shift three units downward
(c)   (d) $h(x) = -2f(x + 1) - 3$

107. -7 **109.** -42 **111.** 5 **113.** 17
115. -97 **117.** $f(x) = x^2, g(x) = x + 3$
119. $f(x) = \sqrt{x}, g(x) = 4x + 2$ **121.** $f(x) = \dfrac{4}{x}, g(x) = x + 2$

123.

125. $f^{-1}(x) = \dfrac{x}{6}$ **127.** $f^{-1}(x) = 2x - 6$

129. Answers will vary.
131.   **133.**

One-to-one   Not one-to-one

135. $f^{-1}(x) = 2x + 10$ **137.** $f^{-1}(x) = \sqrt[3]{\dfrac{x + 3}{-5}}$

139. $f^{-1}(x) = x^2 - 10, x \geq 0$
141. $f^{-1}(x) = \sqrt{4x - 4}$ **143.** Negative correlation
145. (a)

(b) Yes. Answers will vary.

147. (a)

(b) Answers will vary.
Sample answer: $s = 10t - 0.4$
(c) $s = 9.7t + 0.4; r \approx 0.99933$
(d) 24.65 m/sec
149. False. The point $(-1, 28)$ does not lie on the graph of the function $g(x) = -(x - 6)^2 - 3$.
151. False. For example, $f(x) = 4 - x = f^{-1}(x)$.

Chapter Test (page 86)

1. (a) $5x + 2y - 8 = 0$ (b) $2x - 5y + 20 = 0$
2. $y = -x + 1$
3. No. To some x there correspond two values of y.
4. (a) -9 (b) 1 (c) $|t - 4| - 15$ **5.** $(-\infty, 3]$
6. $C = 24.60x + 25,000$
$P = 76.9x - 25,000$
7. Odd **8.** Even
9. Increasing: $(-2, 0), (2, \infty)$; Decreasing: $(-\infty, -2), (0, 2)$
10. Increasing: $(-2, 2)$; Constant: $(-\infty, -2), (2, \infty)$
11.

Relative minimum: $(-3.33, -6.52)$
Relative maximum: $(0, 12)$
12.

Relative minimum: $(1.34, 1.10)$
Relative maximum: $(-1.34, 6.90)$
13. (a) Cubic function $f(x) = x^3$
(b) Horizontal shift five units to the right, reflection in the x-axis, vertical stretch, and vertical shift three units upward
(c)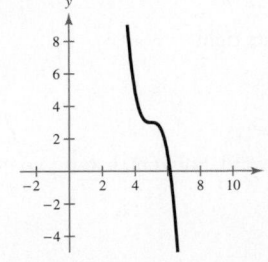

14. (a) Square root function $f(x) = \sqrt{x}$
   (b) Reflection in the y-axis and horizontal shift two units to the left, horizontal shrink
   (c)

15. (a) Absolute value function $f(x) = |x|$
   (b) Reflection in the y-axis (no effect), vertical stretch, and vertical shift seven units downward
   (c)

16. (a) $x^2 - \sqrt{2 - x}, (-\infty, 2]$ (b) $\dfrac{x^2}{\sqrt{2 - x}}, (-\infty, 2)$
   (c) $2 - x, (-\infty, 2]$ (d) $\sqrt{2 - x^2}, \left[-\sqrt{2}, \sqrt{2}\right]$
17. $f^{-1}(x) = \sqrt[3]{x - 8}$ **18.** No inverse
19. $f^{-1}(x) = \left(\frac{8}{3}x\right)^{2/3}, x \geq 0$ **20.** $C = 2.48t + 30.36; 2022$

Chapter 2

Section 2.1   (page 96)

1. nonnegative integer, real   **3.** Yes; $(2, 3)$
5. c   **6.** d   **7.** b   **8.** a
9.   **11.**

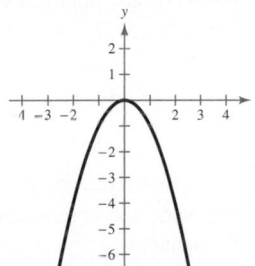

Reflection in the x-axis   Horizontal shift three units to the left

13.   **15.**

     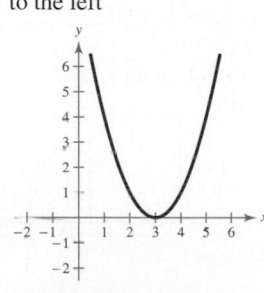

Horizontal shift one unit   Horizontal shift three units
to the left   to the right

17. Parabola opening downward
   Vertex: $(0, 20)$
19. Parabola opening upward   **21.** Parabola opening upward
   Vertex: $(0, -5)$ Vertex: $(-3, -4)$
23. Parabola opening upward   **25.** Parabola opening upward
   Vertex: $(1, 0)$ Vertex: $\left(\frac{1}{2}, 1\right)$
27. Parabola opening downward
   Vertex: $(1, 6)$
29. Parabola opening upward
   Vertex: $\left(\frac{1}{2}, 20\right)$
31. Parabola opening upward   **33.** Parabola opening downward
   Vertex: $(-4, -5)$ Vertex: $(1, 16)$
   x-intercepts: $\left(-4 \pm \sqrt{5}, 0\right)$ x-intercepts: $(-3, 0), (5, 0)$
35. Parabola opening downward
   Vertex: $(4, 1)$
   x-intercepts: $\left(4 \pm \frac{1}{2}\sqrt{2}, 0\right)$
37. $y = -(x + 1)^2 + 4$ **39.** $f(x) = (x + 2)^2 + 5$
41. $y = 4(x - 1)^2 - 2$ **43.** $y = -\frac{104}{125}\left(x - \frac{1}{2}\right)^2 + 1$
45. $(5, 0), (-1, 0)$ **47.** $(-4, 0)$
49.   **51.**

$(0, 0), (4, 0)$ $\left(-\frac{5}{2}, 0\right), (6, 0)$
53.

$(7, 0), (-1, 0)$
55. $f(x) = x^2 - 2x - 3$ **57.** $f(x) = 2x^2 + 7x + 3$
   $g(x) = -x^2 + 2x + 3$ $g(x) = -2x^2 - 7x - 3$
59. $55, 55$ **61.** $12, 6$
63. (a)

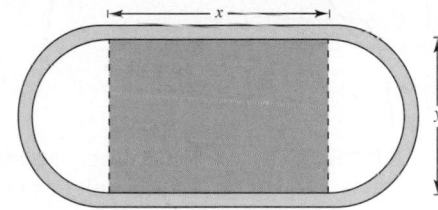

   (b) $r = \dfrac{1}{2}y; \ d = y\pi$ (c) $y = \dfrac{200 - 2x}{\pi}$
   (d) $A - x\left(\dfrac{200 - 2x}{\pi}\right)$
   (e)

   $x = 50 \text{ m}, y = \dfrac{100}{\pi} \text{ m}$

65. (a)   (b) $\frac{3}{2}$ ft

(c) About 104 ft   (d) About 228.6 ft

67. (a) $A = -2x^2 + 112x - 600$ (b) $x = 28$ in.

69. (a)

(b) 1963; 4110 cigarettes

(c) Yes; Consumption began decreasing.

(d) 1057 cigarettes per year; about 3 cigarettes per day

71. True. The vertex is $(0, -1)$ and the parabola opens down.

73. False. The vertex of $f(x)$ is $(-1, 4)$ and the vertex of $g(x)$ is $(-1, -4)$.

75. c, d   **77.** Horizontal shift z units to the right

79. Vertical stretch $(z > 1)$ or shrink $(0 < z < 1)$ and horizontal shift three units to the right

81. $b = \pm 20$ **83.** $b = \pm 8$ **85.** Proof

87. $y = -x^2 + 5x - 4$; Answers will vary.

89. Model (a). The profits are positive and rising.

91. $(4, 2)$ **93.** $(2, 11)$

Section 2.2 (page 109)

1. continuous   **3.** (a) solution   (b) $(x - a)$ (c) $(a, 0)$

5. No   **7.** $f(x_2) > 0$ **9.** f   **10.** h

11. c   **12.** a   **13.** e   **14.** d   **15.** g   **16.** b

17.   **19.**

Horizontal shift three units to the right

Reflection in the x-axis and vertical shift four units upward

21.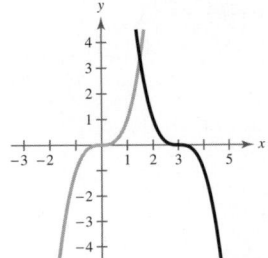

Reflection in the x-axis and horizontal shift three units to the right

23.   **25.**

Yes, because both graphs have the same leading coefficient.

Yes, because both graphs have the same leading coefficient.

27.

No, because the graphs have different leading coefficients.

29. Rises to the left, rises to the right

31. Falls to the left, falls to the right

33. Falls to the left, rises to the right

35. Falls to the left, falls to the right

37. (a) $\left(2 \pm \sqrt{3}, 0\right)$

(b)

(c) $(0.27, 0), (3.73, 0)$; Answers are approximately the same.

39. (a) $(-1, 0), (1, 0)$

(b)

(c) $(-1, 0), (1, 0)$; Answers are the same.

41. (a) $(0, 0), \left(\pm\sqrt{2}, 0\right)$

(b)

(c) $(-1.41, 0), (0, 0), (1.41, 0)$; Answers are approximately the same.

43. (a) $\left(\pm\sqrt{5}, 0\right)$

(b)

(c) $(-2.236, 0), (2.236, 0)$; Answers are approximately the same.

45. (a) $(4, 0), (\pm 5, 0)$

(b)

(c) $(-5, 0), (4, 0), (5, 0)$; Answers are the same.

47. (a) $(0, 0), \left(\frac{5}{2}, 0\right)$ (c) $(0, 0), (2.5, 0)$

(b)

Answers are the same.

49. ± 5 (multiplicity 1)   **51.** 3 (multiplicity 2)

53. $1, -2$ (multiplicity 1)

55. 2 (multiplicity 2), 0 (multiplicity 1)

57. $\dfrac{-5 \pm \sqrt{37}}{2}$ (multiplicity 1)

59.

Zeros: $\pm 1.680, +0.421$

Relative minima: $(\pm 1.225, -3.500)$

Relative maximum: $(0, 1)$

61.

Zero: -1.178

Relative minimum: $(0.324, 5.782)$

Relative maximum: $(-0.324, 6.218)$

63.

Zeros: $-1.618, -0.366, 0.618, 1.366$

Relative minimum: $(0.101, -1.050)$

Relative maxima: $(-1.165, 3.267), (1.064, 1.033)$

65. $f(x) = x^2 - 7x$ **67.** $f(x) = x^3 + 6x^2 + 8x$

69. $f(x) = x^4 - 4x^3 - 9x^2 + 36x$ **71.** $f(x) = x^2 - 2x - 1$

73. $f(x) = x^3 - 6x^2 + 7x + 2$

75. $f(x) = x^3 + 5x^2 + 8x + 4$

77. $f(x) = x^4 + 2x^3 - 23x^2 - 24x + 144$

79. $f(x) = -x^3 - 4x^2 - 5x - 2$

81.   **83.**

$y = -x^3 + 3x - 2$

$y = x^5 - 5x^2 - x + 2$

85. (a) Falls to the left, rises to the right

(b) $(0, 0), (3, 0), (-3, 0)$

(c) and (d)

87. (a) Falls to the left, rises to the right

(b) $(0, 0), (3, 0)$

(c) and (d)

89. (a) Falls to the left, falls to the right

(b) $(\pm 2, 0), \left(\pm \sqrt{5}, 0\right)$

(c) and (d)

91. (a) Falls to the left, rises to the right

(b) $(\pm 3, 0)$

(c) and (d)

93. (a) Falls to the left, falls to the right

(b) $(-2, 0), (2, 0)$

(c) and (d)

CHAPTER 2

95. (a)

$(-1, 0), (1, 2), (2, 3)$

(b) $-0.879, 1.347, 2.532$

97. (a)

$(-2, -1), (0, 1)$

(b) $-1.585, 0.779$

99. (a)

$(-1, 0), (3, 4)$

(b) $-0.578, 3.418$

101.

Two x-intercepts

103.

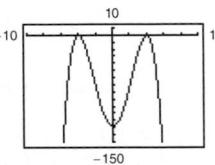

y-axis symmetry
Two x-intercepts

105.

Origin symmetry
Three x-intercepts

107.

Three x-intercepts

109. (a) Answers will vary.

(b) Domain: $0 < x < 18$

(c)

Height, x	Volume, V
1	1156
2	2048
3	2700
4	3136
5	3380
6	3456
7	3388

$5 < x < 7$

(d)

$x = 6$

111. $(200, 160)$

113. (a)

The model fits the data well.

(b)

Answers will vary. Sample answer: You could use the model to estimate production in 2015 because the result is somewhat reasonable, but you would not use the model to estimate the 2020 production because the result is unreasonably high.

(c)

The model fits the data well.

Answers will vary. Sample answer: You could use the model to estimate production in 2015 because the result is somewhat reasonable, but you would not use the model to estimate the 2020 production because the result is unreasonably high.

115. False. The graph will always cross the x-axis.

117. True. The degree is odd and the leading coefficient is -1.

119. False. The graph crosses the x-axis at $x = -3$ and $x = 0$.

121.

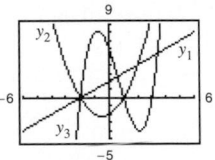

123. 69   **125.** $-\frac{1408}{49} \approx -28.73$ **127.** 109

129. $x > -8$ **131.** $-26 \le x < 7$

Section 2.3   (page 124)

1. $f(x)$ is the dividend, $d(x)$ is the divisor, $q(x)$ is the quotient, and $r(x)$ is the remainder.

3. constant term, leading coefficient   **5.** upper, lower

7. 7   **9.** $(x + 3)(x + 2)$ **11.** $(x + 2)(x + 6)(x - 3)$

13. $x^2 - x - 20 - \dfrac{54}{x - 3}$ **15.** $7x^2 - 14x + 28 - \dfrac{53}{x + 2}$

17. $5x - 1$ **19.** $x - \dfrac{x + 9}{x^2 + 1}$ **21.** $2x - \dfrac{17x - 5}{x^2 - 2x + 1}$

23. $3x^2 - 2x + 5, x \neq 5$ **25.** $6x^2 + 25x + 74 + \dfrac{248}{x - 3}$

27. $9x^2 - 16, x \neq 2$ **29.** $x^2 - 8x + 64, x \neq -8$

31. $4x^2 + 14x - 30, x \neq -\frac{1}{2}$

33.   **35.**

37. $f(x) = (x - 4)(x^2 + 3x - 2) + 3, f(4) = 3$

39. $f(x) = \left(x - \sqrt{2}\right)\left[x^2 + \left(3 + \sqrt{2}\right)x + 3\sqrt{2}\right] - 8,$
$f\left(\sqrt{2}\right) = -8$

41. $f(x) = \left(x - 1 + \sqrt{3}\right)\left[4x^2 - \left(2 + 4\sqrt{3}\right)x - \left(2 + 2\sqrt{3}\right)\right],$
$f\left(1 - \sqrt{3}\right) = 0$

43. (a) -2 (b) 1 (c) $-\frac{1}{4}$ (d) 5

45. (a) -35 (b) -22 (c) -10 (d) -211

47. $(x + 1)(x + 3)(x - 4)$ **49.** $(2x + 3)(x - 3)(x - 7)$
Zeros: $-1, -3, 4$ Zeros: $-\frac{3}{2}, 3, 7$

51. $\left(x - \sqrt{3}\right)\left(x + \sqrt{3}\right)(x + 2)$
Zeros: $\pm\sqrt{3}, -2$

53. (a) Answers will vary.   (b) $(2x - 1), (x - 1)$
(c) $(x + 2)(x - 1)(2x - 1)$ (d) $-2, 1, \frac{1}{2}$

55. (a) Answers will vary.   (b) $(x - 1), (x - 2)$
(c) $(x - 5)(x + 4)(x - 1)(x - 2)$ (d) $-4, 1, 2, 5$

57. (a) Answers will vary.   (b) $(x + 7), (3x - 2)$
(c) $(2x + 1)(3x - 2)(x + 7)$ (d) $-7, -\frac{1}{2}, \frac{2}{3}$

59. $\pm 1, \pm 3; \pm 1, -3$

61. $\pm 1, \pm 3, \pm 5, \pm 9, \pm 15, \pm 45, \pm\frac{1}{2}, \pm\frac{3}{2}, \pm\frac{5}{2}, \pm\frac{9}{2}, \pm\frac{15}{2}, \pm\frac{45}{2}; -1, \frac{3}{2}, 3, 5$

63. 4, 2, or 0 positive real zeros, no negative real zeros

65. 2 or 0 positive real zeros, 1 negative real zero

67. (a) 1 positive real zero, 2 or 0 negative real zeros
(b) $\pm 1, \pm 2, \pm 4$
(c)   (d) $-2, -1, 2$

69. (a) 3 or 1 positive real zero(s), 1 negative real zero
(b) $\pm 1, \pm 2, \pm 4, \pm 8, \pm\frac{1}{2}$
(c)   (d) $-\frac{1}{2}, 1, 2, 4$

71. (a) 2 or 0 positive real zeros, 1 negative real zero
(b) $\pm 1, \pm 3, \pm\frac{1}{2}, \pm\frac{3}{2}, \pm\frac{1}{4}, \pm\frac{3}{4}, \pm\frac{1}{8}, \pm\frac{3}{8}, \pm\frac{1}{16}, \pm\frac{3}{16}, \pm\frac{1}{32}, \pm\frac{3}{32}$
(c)   (d) $-\frac{1}{8}, \frac{3}{4}, 1$

73. Answers will vary; 1.937, 3.705

75. Answers will vary; ± 2 **77.** $\pm 2, \pm\frac{3}{2}$ **79.** $\pm 1, \frac{1}{4}$

81. d   **82.** a   **83.** b   **84.** c

85. $-\frac{1}{2}, 2 \pm \sqrt{3}, 1$ **87.** $-1, \frac{3}{2}, 4 \pm \sqrt{17}$

89. $-3, 0, \dfrac{3 \pm \sqrt{14}}{5}$ **91.** $-1, 2$ **93.** $-6, \frac{1}{2}, 1$

95. $-3, -\frac{3}{2}, \frac{1}{2}, 4$ **97.** $-3, 0, \dfrac{-1 \pm \sqrt{7}}{4}$

99. $-\frac{3}{2}, -\frac{5}{4}, -1, 1, 2$

101. (a) $-2, 0.268, 3.732$ (b) -2
(c) $h(t) = (t + 2)\left(t - 2 + \sqrt{3}\right)\left(t - 2 - \sqrt{3}\right)$

103. (a) $0, 3, 4, -1.414, 1.414$ (b) $0, 3, 4$
(c) $h(x) = x(x - 3)(x - 4)\left(x + \sqrt{2}\right)\left(x - \sqrt{2}\right)$

105. (a)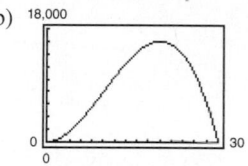

(b) The model fits the data well.
(c) 45.6 subscriptions; Sample answer: No, the number of subscriptions is unlikely to decrease.

107. (a) Answers will vary.
(b)

$20 \times 20 \times 40$

(c) $15, \dfrac{15 \pm 15\sqrt{5}}{2}$;

$\dfrac{15 - 15\sqrt{5}}{2}$ represents a negative volume.

109. False. If $(7x + 4)$ is a factor of f, then $-\frac{4}{7}$ is a zero of f.

111. $-2(x - 1)^2(x + 2)$

113. $-(x - 2)(x + 2)(x + 1)(x - 1)$

115. (a) $x + 1, x \neq 1$ (b) $x^2 + x + 1, x \neq 1$
(c) $x^3 + x^2 + x + 1, x \neq 1$

$\dfrac{x^n - 1}{x - 1} = x^{n-1} + x^{n-2} + \cdots + x^2 + x + 1, x \neq 1$

117. $\pm\dfrac{\sqrt{17}}{2}$ **119.** $-\frac{4}{3}, 5$

Section 2.4 (page 133)

1. (a) ii   (b) iii   (c) i   **3.** $15; 11i$ **5.** $-2 + 4i$

7. $a = -9, b = 4$ **9.** $a = 3, b = 5$ **11.** $4 + 3i$

13. 12 **15.** $1 - 8i$ **17.** -11 **19.** $0.3i$

21. $-3 + 3i$ **23.** $7 + 3i$ **25.** $-14 + 20i$

27. $\frac{19}{6} + \frac{37}{6}i$ **29.** $-4.2 + 7.5i$ **31.** $12 + 20i$

33. $5 + i$ **35.** $-20 + 32i$ **37.** 24 **39.** $-13 + 84i$

41. $80i$ **43.** $6 + 2i; 40$ **45.** $-1 - \sqrt{7}i; 8$

47. $-\sqrt{29}i; 29$ **49.** $9 + \sqrt{6}i; 87$ **51.** $-6i$

53. $\frac{8}{41} + \frac{10}{41}i$ **55.** $\frac{3}{5} + \frac{4}{5}i$ **57.** $-\frac{40}{1681} - \frac{9}{1681}i$

59. $-\frac{1}{2} - \frac{5}{2}i$ **61.** $3\left(\sqrt{2} - \sqrt{6}\right)i$

63. $4 + 2\left(\sqrt{6} - \sqrt{11}\right)i$ **65.** $-2\sqrt{3}$ **67.** -10

69. $-2 - 4\sqrt{6}i$ **71.** $\pm 5i$ **73.** $1 \pm i$ **75.** $-2 \pm \dfrac{i}{2}$

77. $\dfrac{1}{8} \pm \dfrac{\sqrt{11}}{8}i$ **79.** $2 \pm \sqrt{2}i$ **81.** $\dfrac{5}{7} \pm \dfrac{5\sqrt{15}}{7}$

83. $-1 + 6i$ **85.** $-375\sqrt{3}i$ **87.** i

89. (a) $3.12 - 0.97i$ (b) $12.82 + 5.28i$

91. False. Any real number is equal to its conjugate.

93. True. Answers will vary.

95. $\sqrt{-6}\sqrt{-6} = \left(\sqrt{6}i\right)\left(\sqrt{6}i\right) = 6i^2 = -6$

97. $16x^2 - 25$ **99.** $3x^2 + \frac{23}{2}x - 2$

Section 2.5 (page 140)

1. Fundamental Theorem, Algebra   **3.** n linear factors

5. c   **6.** d   **7.**   **8.** a   **9 and 11.** Answers will vary.

13. Zeros: $4, -i, i$. One real zero; they are the same.

15. Zeros: $\sqrt{2}i, \sqrt{2}i, -\sqrt{2}i, -\sqrt{2}i$. No real zeros; they are the same.

17. $2 \pm \sqrt{3}$

$\left(x - 2 - \sqrt{3}\right)\left(x - 2 + \sqrt{3}\right)$

19. $6 \pm \sqrt{10}$

$\left(x - 6 - \sqrt{10}\right)\left(x - 6 + \sqrt{10}\right)$

21. $\pm 5i$

$(x + 5i)(x - 5i)$

23. $\pm\frac{3}{2}, \pm\frac{3}{2}i$

$(2x - 3)(2x + 3)(2x - 3i)(2x + 3i)$

25. $\dfrac{1 \pm \sqrt{223}i}{2}$

$\left(z - \dfrac{1 - \sqrt{223}i}{2}\right)\left(z - \dfrac{1 + \sqrt{223}i}{2}\right)$

27. $\pm i, \pm 3i$

$(x + i)(x - i)(x + 3i)(x - 3i)$

29. $\frac{5}{3}, \pm 4i$

$(3x - 5)(x - 4i)(x + 4i)$

31. $-5, 4 \pm 3i$

$(t + 5)(t - 4 + 3i)(t - 4 - 3i)$

33. $1 \pm \sqrt{5}i, -\frac{1}{5}$

$(5x + 1)\left(x - 1 + \sqrt{5}i\right)\left(x - 1 - \sqrt{5}i\right)$

35. $2, 2, \pm 2i$

$(x - 2)^2(x + 2i)(x - 2i)$

37. (a) $7 \pm \sqrt{3}$ (b) $\left(x - 7 - \sqrt{3}\right)\left(x - 7 + \sqrt{3}\right)$

(c) $\left(7 \pm \sqrt{3}, 0\right)$

39. (a) $\frac{3}{2}, \pm 2i$ (b) $(2x - 3)(x - 2i)(x + 2i)$ (c) $\left(\frac{3}{2}, 0\right)$

41. (a) $-6, 3 \pm 4i$ (b) $(x + 6)(x - 3 - 4i)(x - 3 + 4i)$

(c) $(-6, 0)$

43. (a) $\pm 4i, \pm 3i$ (b) $(x + 4i)(x - 4i)(x + 3i)(x - 3i)$

(c) None

45. $f(x) = x^3 - 5x^2 + x - 5$

47. $f(x) = x^4 - 2x^3 + 5x^2 - 8x + 4$

49. $f(x) = x^4 + 3x^3 - 7x^2 + 15x$

51. (a) $-2(x + 1)(x - 2)(x + i)(x - i)$

(b) $f(x) = -2x^4 + 2x^3 + 2x^2 + 2x + 4$

53. (a) $3(x + 1)\left(x - 2 + \sqrt{5}i\right)\left(x - 2 - \sqrt{5}i\right)$

(b) $3x^3 - 9x^2 + 15x + 27$

55. (a) $(x^2 + 1)(x^2 - 7)$ (b) $(x^2 + 1)\left(x + \sqrt{7}\right)\left(x - \sqrt{7}\right)$

(c) $(x + i)(x - i)\left(x + \sqrt{7}\right)\left(x - \sqrt{7}\right)$

57. (a) $(x^2 - 6)(x^2 - 2x + 3)$

(b) $\left(x + \sqrt{6}\right)\left(x - \sqrt{6}\right)(x^2 - 2x + 3)$

(c) $\left(x + \sqrt{6}\right)\left(x - \sqrt{6}\right)\left(x - 1 - \sqrt{2}i\right)\left(x - 1 + \sqrt{2}i\right)$

59. $-\frac{3}{2}, \pm 5i$ **61.** $-3, 5 \pm 2i$ **63.** $-\frac{2}{3}, 1 \pm \sqrt{3}i$

65. (a) $1.000, 2.000$ (b) $-3 \pm \sqrt{2}i$

67. (a) 0.750 (b) $\dfrac{1}{2} \pm \dfrac{\sqrt{5}}{2}i$

69. No. Setting $h = 50$ and solving the resulting equation yields imaginary roots.

71. False. A third-degree polynomial must have at least one real zero.

73. Answers will vary.

75. Parabola opening upward   **77.** Parabola opening upward

Vertex: $\left(\frac{7}{2}, -\frac{81}{4}\right)$ Vertex: $\left(-\frac{5}{12}, -\frac{169}{24}\right)$

Section 2.6 (page 147)

1. rational functions   **3.** vertical asymptote

5. (a) Domain: all real numbers x except $x = 1$

(b)

x	$f(x)$	x	$f(x)$
0.5	-2	1.5	2
0.9	-10	1.1	10
0.99	-100	1.01	100
0.999	-1000	1.001	1000

x	$f(x)$	x	$f(x)$
5	0.25	-5	$-0.1\overline{6}$
10	$0.\overline{1}$	-10	$-0.\overline{09}$
100	$0.\overline{01}$	-100	$-0.\overline{0099}$
1000	$0.\overline{001}$	-1000	$-0.\overline{000999}$

(c) f approaches $-\infty$ from the left and ∞ from the right of $x = 1$.

7. (a) Domain: all real numbers x except $x = 1$

(b)

x	$f(x)$	x	$f(x)$
0.5	3	1.5	9
0.9	27	1.1	33
0.99	297	1.01	303
0.999	2997	1.001	3003

x	$f(x)$	x	$f(x)$
5	3.75	-5	-2.5
10	$3.\overline{33}$	-10	-2.727
100	$3.\overline{03}$	-100	-2.97
1000	$3.\overline{003}$	-1000	-2.997

(c) f approaches ∞ from both the left and the right of $x = 1$.

9. (a) Domain: all real numbers x except $x = \pm 1$

(b)

x	$f(x)$	x	$f(x)$
0.5	-1	1.5	5.4
0.9	-12.79	1.1	17.29
0.99	-147.8	1.01	152.3
0.999	-1498	1.001	1502.3

x	$f(x)$	x	$f(x)$
5	3.125	-5	3.125
10	$3.\overline{03}$	-10	$3.\overline{03}$
100	$3.\overline{0003}$	-100	$3.\overline{0003}$
1000	3.000003	-1000	3.000003

(c) f approaches ∞ from the left and $-\infty$ from the right of $x = -1$. f approaches $-\infty$ from the left and ∞ from the right of $x = 1$.

11. a   **12.** d   **13.** c   **14.** e   **15.** b   **16.** f

17. Vertical asymptote: $x = 0$
Horizontal asymptote: $y = 0$

19. Vertical asymptotes: $x = -3, 2$
Horizontal asymptote: $y = 2$

21. Vertical asymptote: $x = 2$
Horizontal asymptote: $y = -1$
Hole at $x = 0$

23. Vertical asymptotes: $x = 0, x = -8$
Horizontal asymptote: $y = 1$
No hole

25. (a) Domain: all real numbers x
(b) Continuous
(c) Horizontal asymptote: $y = 5$

27. (a) Domain: all real numbers x except $x = 3$
(b) Not continuous
(c) Vertical asymptote: $x = 3$
Horizontal asymptote: $y = 0$

29. (a) Domain of f: all real numbers x except $x = 4$
Domain of g: all real numbers x
(b) Vertical asymptote: none; Hole in f at $x = 4$

(c)

x	1	2	3	4	5	6	7
$f(x)$	5	6	7	Undef.	9	10	11
$g(x)$	5	6	7	8	9	10	11

(d)

(e) Graphing utilities are limited in their resolution and therefore may not show a hole in a graph.

31. (a) Domain of f: all real numbers x except $x = -1, 3$
Domain of g: all real numbers x except $x = 3$
(b) Vertical asymptote: $x = 3$; Hole in f at $x = -1$

(c)

x	-2	-1	0	1	2	3	4
$f(x)$	$\frac{3}{5}$	Undef.	$\frac{1}{3}$	0	-1	Undef.	3
$g(x)$	$\frac{3}{5}$	$\frac{1}{2}$	$\frac{1}{3}$	0	-1	Undef.	3

(d)

(e) Graphing utilities are limited in their resolution and therefore may not show a hole in a graph.

33. 1; less than; greater than   **35.** 2; greater than; less than

37. ± 3 **39.** -3 **41.** $-4, 5$ **43.** -7

45. (a)

(b) 333 deer, 500 deer, 800 deer

(c) 1500. Because the degrees of the numerator and the denominator are equal, the limiting size is the ratio of the leading coefficients, $60/0.04 = 1500$.

47. (a)

M	200	400	600	800	1000
t	0.472	0.596	0.710	0.817	0.916

M	1200	1400	1600	1800	2000
t	1.009	1.096	1.178	1.255	1.328

The greater the mass, the more time required per oscillation.

(b) $M \approx 1306$ g

49. (a)

(b) \$4411.76; \$25,000; \$225,000
(c) No. The function is undefined at $p = 100$.

51. False. $\dfrac{1}{x^2 + 1}$ has no vertical asymptote.

53. No. If $x = c$ is also a zero in the denominator, then f is undefined at $x = c$.

55.

Both graphs have the same slope.

57. $x - y - 1 = 0$ **59.** $3x - y + 1 = 0$

61. $x + 9 + \dfrac{42}{x - 4}$ **63.** $2x^2 - 9 + \dfrac{34}{x^2 + 5}$

Section 2.7   (page 157)

1. slant, asymptote   **3.** Yes

5.

Reflection in the x-axis, vertical shift two units upward

7.

Horizontal shift three units to the right, vertical shift one unit downward

9.

Vertical shift

11.

Reflection in the x-axis

13.

Vertical shift

15.

Horizontal shift

17.

19.

21.

23.

25.

27.

29.

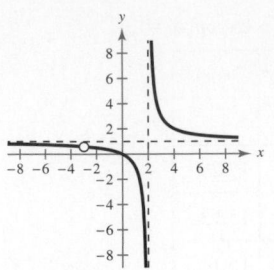

There is a hole at $x = -3$.

31.

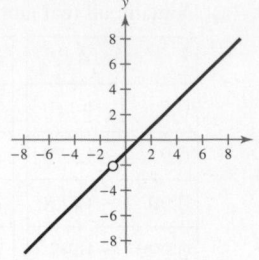

There is a hole at $x = -1$.

33.

Domain: $(-\infty, 1), (1, \infty)$
Vertical asymptote: $x = 1$
Horizontal asymptote: $y = -1$

35.

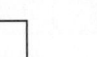

Domain: $(-\infty, 0), (0, \infty)$
Vertical asymptote: $x = 0$
Horizontal asymptote: $y = -3$

37.

Domain: $(-\infty, \infty)$
Horizontal asymptote: $y = 0$

39.

Domain: $(-\infty, -2), (-2, 3), (3, \infty)$
Vertical asymptotes: $x = -2, x = 3$
Horizontal asymptote: $y = 0$

41.

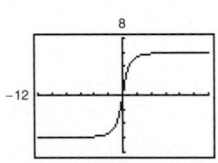

Domain: $(-\infty, 0), (0, \infty)$
Vertical asymptote: $x = 0$
Horizontal asymptote: $y = 0$

43.

There are two horizontal asymptotes, $y = \pm 6$.

45.

There are two horizontal asymptotes, $y = \pm 4$, and one vertical asymptote, $x = -1$.

47.

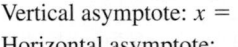

The graph crosses the horizontal asymptote, $y = 4$.

49.   **51.**

53.   **55.**

57. $(-1, 0)$ **59.** $(1, 0), (-1, 0)$

61.   Domain: $(-\infty, -1), (-1, \infty)$
Vertical asymptote: $x = -1$
Slant asymptote: $y = 2x - 1$

63.   Domain: $(-\infty, 0), (0, \infty)$
Vertical asymptote: $x = 0$
Slant asymptote: $y = -x + 3$

65. Vertical asymptotes: $x = \pm 2$; horizontal asymptote: $y = 1$;
slant asymptote: none; holes: none
67. Vertical asymptote: $x = -\frac{3}{2}$; horizontal asymptote: $y = 1$;
slant asymptote: none; hole at $x = 2$
69. Vertical asymptote: $x = -2$; horizontal asymptote: none;
slant asymptote: $y = 2x - 7$; hole at $x = -1$

71.   **73.**

$(-4, 0)$ $(-8, 0)$

75.   **77.**

$(-2, 0), (1, 0)$ $\left(\dfrac{-3 \pm \sqrt{5}}{2}, 0\right)$

79.   **81.**

None $\left(\dfrac{-5 \pm \sqrt{65}}{4}, 0\right)$

83. (a) Answers will vary.   (b) $[0, 950]$
(c)

The concentration increases more slowly; 75%

85. (a) Answers will vary.   **87.**
(b) $(2, \infty)$
(c)

$x \approx 40$

5.9 in $\times$ 11.8 in.

89. (a) $C = 0$. The chemical will eventually dissipate.
(b)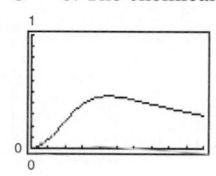

$t \approx 4.5$ h
(c) Before about 2.6 hours and after about 8.3 hours

91. (a) $A = -0.14t + 3.1$

(b) $A = \dfrac{1}{0.035t + 0.253}$

(c) Answers will vary.

93. False. The graph of a rational function is continuous when the
polynomial in the denominator has no real zeros.

95.

The denominator is a factor of the numerator.

97. *Horizontal asymptotes:*

If the degree of the numerator is greater than the degree of the denominator, then there is no horizontal asymptote.

If the degree of the numerator is less than the degree of the denominator, then there is a horizontal asymptote at $y = 0$.

If the degree of the numerator is equal to the degree of the denominator, then there is a horizontal asymptote at the line given by the ratio of the leading coefficients.

Vertical asymptotes:

Set the denominator equal to zero and solve.

Slant asymptotes:

If there is no horizontal asymptote and the degree of the numerator is exactly one greater than the degree of the denominator, then divide the numerator by the denominator. The slant asymptote is the result, not including the remainder.

99. $\dfrac{512}{x^3}$ **101.** 3

103.

Domain: $(-\infty, \infty)$
Range: $\left[\sqrt{6}, \infty\right)$

105.

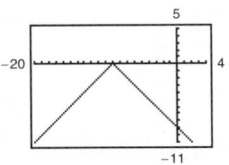

Domain: $(-\infty, \infty)$
Range: $(-\infty, 0]$

107. Answers will vary.

Section 2.8 (page 165)

1. Quadratic   **3.** Quadratic   **5.** Linear   **7.** Neither

9. (a)

(b) Linear

(c) $y = 0.14x + 2.2$

(d)

(e)

x	0	1	2	3	4	5
Actual, y	2.1	2.4	2.5	2.8	2.9	3.0
Model, y	2.2	2.3	2.5	2.6	2.8	2.9

x	6	7	8	9	10
Actual, y	3.0	3.2	3.4	3.5	3.6
Model, y	3.0	3.2	3.3	3.5	3.6

11. (a)

(b) Quadratic   (c) $y = 5.50x^2 - 274.6x + 2822$

(d)

(e)

x	0	5	10	15	20
Actual, y	2795	1590	650	-30	-450
Model, y	2822	1586.5	626	-59.5	-470

x	25	30	35	40
Actual, y	-615	-520	-55	625
Model, y	-605.5	-466	-51.5	638

x	45	50	55
Actual, y	1630	2845	4350
Model, y	1602.5	2842	4356.5

13. (a)

(b) Linear   (c) $y = 2.48x + 1.1$

(d)

(e)

x	1	2	3	4	5
Actual, y	4.0	6.5	8.8	10.6	13.9
Model, y	3.6	6.1	8.5	11.0	13.5

x	6	7	8	9	10
Actual, y	15.0	17.5	20.1	24.0	27.1
Model, y	16.0	18.5	20.9	23.4	25.9

15. (a)

(b) Quadratic   (c) $y = 0.14x^2 - 9.9x + 591$

(d)

(e)

x	0	5	10	15	20	25
Actual, y	587	551	512	478	436	430
Model, y	591	545	506	474	449	431

x	30	35	40	45	50
Actual, y	424	420	423	429	444
Model, y	420	416	419	429	446

17. (a) and (c)

(b) $P = 0.1601t^2 - 2.206t + 7.65$; $r^2 \approx 0.9185$

(d) July   (e) July; They are the same.

19. (a) and (c)

(b) $P = -0.805t^2 + 19.10t - 39.3$

(d) 2017; No, by 2022 the model gives negative values.

21. (a)

(b) $T = 1.23t + 102.4$
$r^2 \approx 0.9468$

(c)

(d) $T = -0.076t^2 + 2.14t + 100.8$
$r^2 \approx 0.9870$

(e)

(f) Quadratic. Its coefficient of
determination is closer to 1.

(g) Linear: 2015
Quadratic: Not possible

23. True. See "Basic Characteristics of Quadratic Functions" on page 91.

25. The model is consistently above the data points.

27. (a) $(f \circ g)(x) = 2x^2 + 5$ (b) $(g \circ f)(x) = 4(x^2 - x + 1)$

29. (a) $(f \circ g)(x) = x$ (b) $(g \circ f)(x) = x$

31. $f^{-1}(x) = \dfrac{x - 5}{2}$ **33.** $f^{-1}(x) = \sqrt{x - 5}$

35. $1 + 3i$; 10   **37.** $5i$; 25

Review Exercises   (page 170)

1.

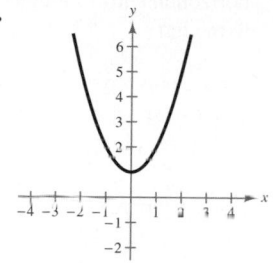

Vertical shift one unit upward

3.

Horizontal shift six units to the right

5.

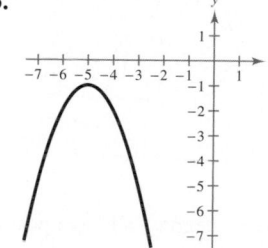

Reflection in the x-axis, horizontal shift five units to the left, vertical shift one unit downward

7. Parabola opening upward
Vertex: $\left(-\frac{3}{2}, 1\right)$

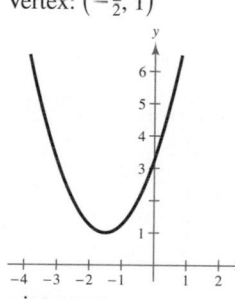

x-intercept: none

9. Parabola opening upward
Vertex: $\left(-\frac{5}{2}, -\frac{41}{12}\right)$

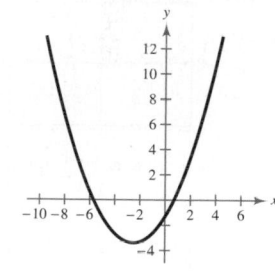

x-intercepts:
$\left(\dfrac{-5 \pm \sqrt{41}}{2}, 0\right)$

11. $f(x) = -(x + 3)^2 + 4$

13. (a) $A = x\left(\dfrac{8 - x}{2}\right)$, $0 < x < 8$

(b)

$x = 4, y = 2$

(c) $A = -\frac{1}{2}(x - 4)^2 + 8$; $x = 4$, $y = 2$; They are the same.

15.

Horizontal shift five units
to the right

17.

Reflection in the x-axis,
horizontal shift four units
to the left

19.

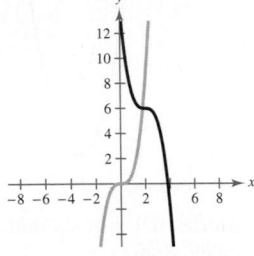

Reflection in the x-axis, horizontal shift two units to the right,
vertical shift six units upward

21.

Yes. Both functions are of the same degree and have positive
leading coefficients.

23. Rises to the left,
rises to the right

25. Falls to the left,
falls to the right

27. (a) $x = -1, 0, 0, 2$

(b)

(c) $x = -1, 0, 0, 2$; They are the same.

29. (a) $t = 0, \pm\sqrt{3}$

(b)

(c) $t = 0, \pm 1.73$; They are the same.

31. (a) $x = -3, -3, 0$

(b)

(c) $x = -3, -3, 0$; They are the same.

33. $f(x) = x^3 - 12x - 16$ **35.** $f(x) = x^3 - 7x^2 + 13x - 3$

37. (a) Rises to the left, rises to the right

(b) $x = -3, -1, 3, 3$

(c) and (d)

39. (a) $(-3, -2), (-1, 0), (0, 1)$ (b) $x = -2.25, -0.56, 0.80$

41. (a) $(-3, -2), (-1, 0), (3, 4)$ (b) $x = -2.98, -0.55, 3.53$

43. $8x + 5 + \dfrac{2}{3x - 2}$ **45.** $x^2 - 2, \ x \neq \pm 1$

47. $5x + 2, \ x \neq \dfrac{3 \pm \sqrt{5}}{2}$ **49.** $3x^2 + 5x + 8 + \dfrac{10}{2x^2 - 1}$

51. $3x^2 + 2x + 20 + \dfrac{58}{x - 4}$

53. $0.25x^3 - 4.5x^2 + 9x - 18 + \dfrac{36}{x + 2}$

55. $6x^3 - 27x, \ x \neq \dfrac{2}{3}$ **57.** (a) -421 (b) -156

59. (a) Answers will vary.   (b) $(x + 1)(x + 7)$

(c) $f(x) = (x - 4)(x + 1)(x + 7)$ (d) $x = 4, -1, -7$

61. (a) Answers will vary.   (b) $(x + 1)(x - 4)$

(c) $f(x) = (x + 2)(x - 3)(x + 1)(x - 4)$

(d) $x = -2, 3, -1, 4$

63. $\pm 1, \pm 3, \pm\frac{3}{2}, \pm\frac{3}{4}, \pm\frac{1}{2}, \pm\frac{1}{4}$

65. 2 or 0 positive real zeros   **67.** Answers will vary.
1 negative real zero $x = \frac{3}{4}$

69. $x = -1, 2, 3$ **71.** $x = -1, \frac{3}{2}, 3, \frac{2}{3}$ **73.** $3 - 4i$

75. $-4 - i$ **77.** $8 + 8i$ **79.** $40 + 65i$

81. $-4 - 46i$ **83.** -80 **85.** $-26 + 7i$ **87.** $3 + 9i$

89. $1 - 6i$ **91.** $\frac{17}{26} + \frac{7}{26}i$ **93.** $x = \pm 4i$

95. $x = -\dfrac{3}{2} \pm \dfrac{\sqrt{15}}{2}i$ **97.** $x = \dfrac{5}{6} \pm \dfrac{\sqrt{47}}{6}i$

99 and 101. Answers will vary.   **103.** $x = 0, -3$

105. $x = 4, \dfrac{3 \pm \sqrt{15}i}{2}$;

$(x - 4)\left(x - \dfrac{3 + \sqrt{15}i}{2}\right)\left(x - \dfrac{3 - \sqrt{15}i}{2}\right)$

107. $x = 2, -\frac{3}{2}, 1 \pm i$;
$(x - 2)(2x + 3)(x - 1 + i)(x - 1 - i)$

109. $x = 0, -1, \pm\sqrt{5}i; \ x^2(x + 1)(x + \sqrt{5}i)(x - \sqrt{5}i)$

111. (a) $x = 2, 1 \pm i$

(b) $(x - 2)(x - 1 - i)(x - 1 + i)$ (c) $(2, 0)$

113. (a) $x = -6, -1, \frac{2}{3}$ (b) $-(x + 1)(x + 6)(3x - 2)$

(c) $(-6, 0), (-1, 0), (\frac{2}{3}, 0)$

115. (a) $\pm 3i, \pm 5i$

(b) $(x - 3i)(x + 3i)(x - 5i)(x + 5i)$ (c) None

117. $f(x) = x^3 - 5x^2 + 9x - 45$

119. $f(x) = x^3 + 6x^2 + 28x + 40$

121. (a) $(x^2 + 9)(x^2 - 2x - 1)$

(b) $(x^2 + 9)\big((x - 1 + \sqrt{2})(x - 1 - \sqrt{2})\big)$

(c) $(x + 3i)(x - 3i)(x - 1 + \sqrt{2})(x - 1 - \sqrt{2})$

123. $x = -3, \pm 2i$

125. (a) Domain: all real numbers x except $x = -3$

(b) Not continuous

(c) Vertical asymptote: $x = -3$

Horizontal asymptote: $y = -1$

127. (a) Domain: all real numbers x except $x = 6, -3$

(b) Not continuous

(c) Vertical asymptotes: $x = 6, x = -3$

Horizontal asymptote: $y = 0$

129. (a) Domain: all real numbers x except $x = 7$

(b) Not continuous

(c) Vertical asymptote: $x = 7$

Horizontal asymptote: $y = -1$

131. (a) Domain: all real numbers x except $x = \pm\dfrac{\sqrt{6}}{2}$

(b) Not continuous

(c) Vertical asymptotes: $x = \pm\dfrac{\sqrt{6}}{2}$

Horizontal asymptote: $y = 2$

133. (a) Domain: all real numbers x except $x = 5, -3$

(b) Not continuous

(c) Vertical asymptote: $x = -3$

Horizontal asymptote: $y = 0$

135. (a) Domain: all real numbers x except $x = -3, 0, 8$

(b) Not continuous

(c) Vertical asymptotes: $x = -3, x = 0, x = 8$

Horizontal asymptote: $y = 0$

137. (a) \$176 million; \$528 million; \$1584 million

(b)

Answers will vary.

(c) No. As $p \to 100$, the cost approaches ∞.

139. Vertical asymptote: $x = -1$

Horizontal asymptote: $y = 1$

Hole at $x = 1$

141. Vertical asymptote: $x = -1$

Slant asymptote: $y = 3x + 2$

143. **145.**

147.   **149.**

151.

153. (a)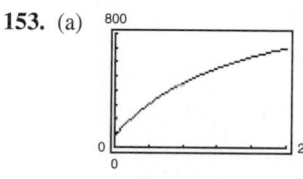

(b) 1,200,000, because N has a horizontal asymptote at $y = 1200$.

304,000; 453,333; 702,222

155. Quadratic   **157.** Linear

159. (a)

(b)

(c) $S = -1.13t^2 + 68.9t + 5926$

$r^2 \approx 0.9695$

(d)

(e) Cubic; The cubic model more closely follows the pattern of the data.

(f) 6511 stations

161. False. For the graph of a rational function to have a slant asymptote, the degree of its numerator must be exactly one more than the degree of its denominator.

163. False. Example: $(1 + 2i) + (1 - 2i) = 2$.

165. Answers will vary.

167. The first step is completed incorrectly: $\sqrt{-4} = 2i \neq 4i$

CHAPTER 2

Chapter Test   (page 175)

1. Vertex: $\left(-\frac{5}{2}, -\frac{1}{4}\right)$
Intercepts: $(0, 6), (-3, 0), (-2, 0)$

2. $y = (x - 3)^2 - 6$

3. 0, multiplicity 1; $\frac{3}{2}$, multiplicity 2

4.

5. $2x + \dfrac{x - 3}{x^2 + 2}$ **6.** $2x^3 + 4x^2 + 3x + 6 + \dfrac{9}{x - 2}$ **7.** 13

8. $\pm 1, \pm 2, \pm 3, \pm 4, \pm 6, \pm 8, \pm 12, \pm 24, \pm\frac{1}{2}, \pm\frac{3}{2}$

$t = -2, \frac{3}{2}$

9. $\pm 1, \pm 2, \pm\frac{1}{3}, \pm\frac{2}{3}$

$\pm 1, -\frac{2}{3}$

10. $x = -1, 4 \pm \sqrt{3}i$
$(x + 1)\left(x - 4 + \sqrt{3}i\right)\left(x - 4 - \sqrt{3}i\right)$

11. $-9 - 18i$ **12.** $6 + \left(2\sqrt{5} + \sqrt{14}\right)i$ **13.** $13 + 4i$

14. $-17 + 14i$ **15.** $5 - 8i$ **16.** $-1 + 2i$

17. $\frac{4}{13} + \frac{7}{13}i$ **18.** $x = \pm 3\sqrt{6}i$ **19.** $x = 1 \pm \sqrt{7}i$

20.

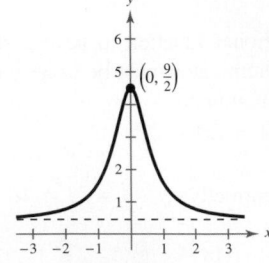

21.

22.

23. (a) and (c)

The model fits the data well.

(b) $A = -11.313t^2 + 241.07t - 585.7$

(d) \$484.9 billion, $-$\$289.5 billion

(e) No. By 2019, the model gives negative values.

Chapter 3

Section 3.1   (page 189)

1. transcendental   **3.** Horizontal shift one unit to the left

5. 4112.033 **7.** 0.006

9.

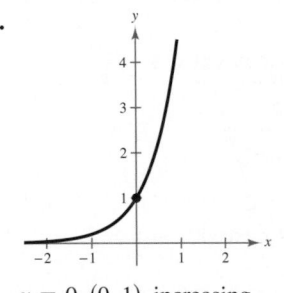

$y = 0$, $(0, 1)$, increasing

11.

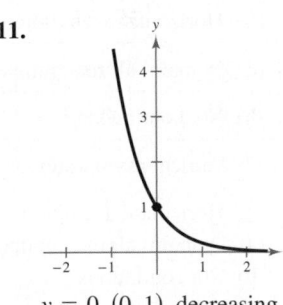

$y = 0$, $(0, 1)$, decreasing

13.

$y = 0$, $(0, 1)$, increasing

15.

$y = 0$, $(0, 1)$, decreasing

17. d   **18.** a   **19.** c   **20.** b

21. Right shift of five units   **23.** Upward shift of five units

25. Left shift of four units
and reflection in the x-axis

27. Right shift of two units
and downward shift of
three units

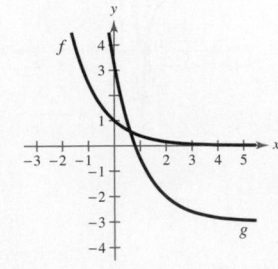

29. Reflection in the y-axis and upward shift of two units

31. (a)

(b) $e^{0.5} \approx 1.6487$

X	Y₁
10	1.6289
100	1.6467
1000	1.6485
10000	1.6487
100000	1.6487
1E6	1.6487

Y₁=1.64872106461

33. 9897.129   **35.** 54.164

37.

x	−2	−1	0	1	2
f(x)	0.16	0.4	1	2.5	6.25

Asymptote: $y = 0$

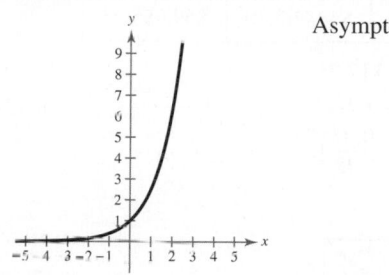

39.

x	−2	−1	0	1	2
f(x)	0.03	0.17	1	6	36

Asymptote: $y = 0$

41.

x	−3	−2	−1	0	1
f(x)	0.33	1	3	9	27

Asymptote: $y = 0$

43.

x	−1	0	1	2	3	4
y	1.04	1.11	1.33	2	4	10

Asymptote: $y = 1$

45.

x	−2	−1	0	1	2
f(x)	7.39	2.72	1	0.37	0.14

Asymptote: $y = 0$

47.

x	−6	−5	−4	−3	−2
f(x)	0.41	1.10	3	8.15	22.17

Asymptote: $y = 0$

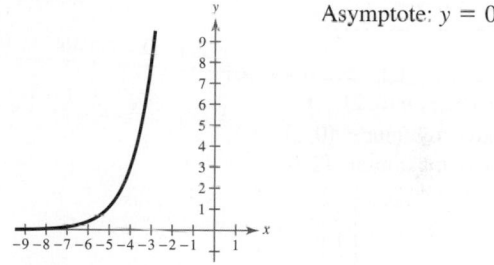

49.

x	3	4	5	6	7
f(x)	2.14	2.37	3	4.72	9.39

Asymptote: $y = 2$

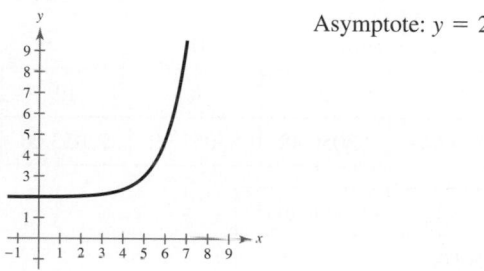

CHAPTER 3

51.

t	-2	-1	0	1	2
$s(t)$	2.54	2.26	2	1.77	1.57

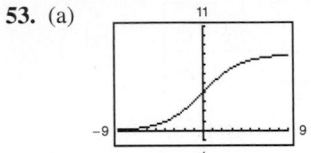

Asymptote: $y = 0$

53. (a)   (b) $y = 0, y = 8$

55. (a)   (b) $y = -3, y = 0, x \approx 3.47$

57. (86.350, 1500)   **59.** $(-8.419, 0.2)$

61. (a)

(b) Decreasing on $(-\infty, 0), (2, \infty)$
Increasing on $(0, 2)$
(c) Relative minimum: $(0, 0)$
Relative maximum: $(2, 0.54)$

63. (a)

(b) Decreasing on $(-\infty, -3)$
Increasing on $(-3, \infty)$
(c) Relative minimum: $(-3, -1.344)$

65.

n	1	2	4	12
A	$3047.49	$3050.48	$3051.99	$3053.00

n	365	Continuous
A	$3053.49	$3053.51

67.

n	1	2	4	12
A	$5477.81	$5520.10	$5541.79	$5556.46

n	365	Continuous
A	$5563.61	$5563.85

69.

t	1	10	20
A	$12,489.73	$17,901.90	$26,706.49

t	30	40	50
A	$39,841.40	$59,436.39	$88,668.67

71.

t	1	10	20
A	$12,427.44	$17,028.81	$24,165.03

t	30	40	50
A	$34,291.81	$48,662.40	$69,055.23

73. $1530.57   **75.** $17,281.77

77. (a) $y_1 = 500(1 + 0.07)^t$

$$y_2 = 500\left(1 + \frac{0.07}{4}\right)^{4t}$$

$$y_3 = 500e^{0.07t}$$

(b) y_3 yields the highest return after 20 years.
$y_2 - y_1 = \$68.36$
$y_3 - y_2 = \$24.40$
$y_3 - y_1 = \$92.76$

79. (a) 10 g   (b) 7.84 g
(c)

81. (a)

(b)

t	20	21	22	23	24	25
P	41.35	41.62	41.89	42.16	42.44	42.71

t	26	27	28	29	30	31
P	42.99	43.27	43.56	43.84	44.13	44.41

t	32	33	34	35	36	37
P	44.70	44.99	45.29	45.58	45.88	46.18

t	38	39	40	41	42	43
P	46.48	46.78	47.09	47.40	47.71	48.02

t	44	45	46	47	48	49
P	48.33	48.64	48.96	49.28	49.60	49.93

t	50	51	52	53	54	55
P	50.25	50.58	50.91	51.24	51.58	51.91

t	56	57	58	59	60
P	52.25	52.59	52.93	53.28	53.63

(c) 2053

83. True. The definition of an exponential function is $f(x) = a^x$, $a > 0, a \neq 1$.

85. d

87.

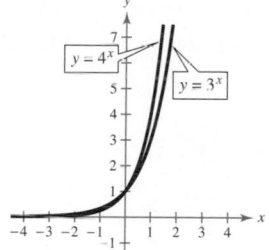

$3^x < 4^x$ when $x > 0$

89. >   **91.** >   **93.** $f^{-1}(x) = \dfrac{x + 7}{5}$

95. $f^{-1}(x) = x^3 - 8$ **97.** Answers will vary.

Section 3.2   (page 199)

1. logarithmic function   **3.** $a^{\log_a x} = x$ **5.** $b = a^c$

7. $4^3 = 64$ **9.** $7^{-2} = \frac{1}{49}$ **11.** $32^{2/5} = 4$

13. $2^{1/2} = \sqrt{2}$ **15.** $\log_5 125 = 3$ **17.** $\log_{81} 3 = \frac{1}{4}$

19. $\log_6 \frac{1}{36} = -2$ **21.** $\log_g 4 = a$ **23.** 4   **25.** -3

27. 2.538   **29.** 7.022   **31.** 9   **33.** 2   **35.** $\frac{1}{10}$

37. $3x$ **39.** -3

41.

43.

45.

Domain: $(-2, \infty)$
Vertical asymptote: $x = -2$
x-intercept: $(-1, 0)$

47.
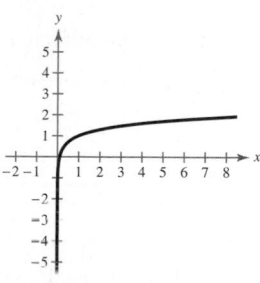

Domain: $(0, \infty)$
Vertical asymptote: $x = 0$
x-intercept: $\left(\frac{1}{10}, 0\right)$

49.
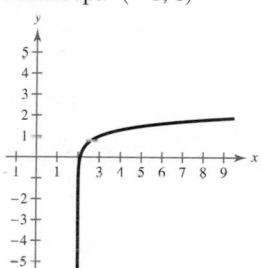

Domain: $(2, \infty)$
Vertical asymptote: $x = 2$
x-intercept: $\left(\frac{21}{10}, 0\right)$

51. b   **52.** c   **53.** d   **54.** a

55. Reflection in the y-axis

57. Reflection in the x-axis, vertical shift four units upward

59. Horizontal shift three units to the right and vertical shift two units downward

61. $e^{1.7917\ldots} = 6$ **63.** $e^1 = e$ **65.** $e^{1/2} = \sqrt{e}$

67. $e^{2.1972\ldots} = 9$ **69.** $\ln 20.0855\ldots = 3$

71. $\ln 3.6692\ldots = 1.3$ **73.** $\ln 1.3956\ldots = \frac{1}{3}$

75. $\ln 4.4816\ldots = \frac{3}{2}$ **77.** 2.398   **79.** 0.693

81. 2   **83.** 1.8   **85.** 0   **87.** 1

89.

91.

Domain: $(1, \infty)$
Vertical asymptote: $x = 1$
x-intercept: $(2, 0)$

Domain: $(-\infty, 0)$
Vertical asymptote: $x = 0$
x-intercept: $(-1, 0)$

93. Horizontal shift eight units to the left

95. Vertical shift five units downward

97. Horizontal shift one unit to the right and vertical shift two units upward

99. (a)   (b) Domain: $(0, \infty)$

(c) Decreasing on $(0, 2)$; increasing on $(2, \infty)$

(d) Relative minimum: $(2, 1.693)$

101. (a)   (b) Domain: $(0, \infty)$

(c) Decreasing on $(2.718, \infty)$; increasing on $(0, 2.718)$

(d) Relative maximum: $(2.718, 5.150)$

103. (a)

(b) Domain: $(-\infty, -2), (1, \infty)$

(c) Decreasing on $(-\infty, -2); (1, \infty)$

(d) No relative maxima or minima

105. (a)

(b) Domain: $(-\infty, 0), (0, \infty)$

(c) Decreasing on $(-\infty, 0)$; increasing on $(0, \infty)$

(d) No relative maxima or minima

107. (a)   (b) Domain: $[1, \infty)$

(c) Increasing on $(1, \infty)$

(d) Relative minimum: $(1, 0)$

109. (a) 80   (b) about 71.89   (c) about 61.65

111. (a)

K	1	2	4	6	8
t	0	19.80	39.61	51.19	59.41

K	10	12
t	65.79	71.00

It takes about 19.80 years for the principal to double.

(b)

113. (a) 30 yr, 10 yr

(b) Total amount: \$323,179.20; interest: \$173,179.20
Total amount: \$199,108.80; interest: \$49,108.80

115. False. Reflect $g(x)$ about the line $y = x$.

117. 2   **119.** $\frac{1}{9}$ **121.** b

123. $\log_a x$ is the inverse of a^x only if $0 < a < 1$ and $a > 1$, so $\log_a x$ is defined only for $0 < a < 1$ and $a > 1$.

125. (a)

(b)

$y_4 = (x - 1) - \frac{1}{2}(x - 1)^2 + \frac{1}{3}(x - 1)^3 - \frac{1}{4}(x - 1)^4$

Answers will vary.

127. (a)

x	1	5	10	10^2
$f(x)$	0	0.32	0.23	0.046

x	10^4	10^6
$f(x)$	0.00092	0.0000138

(b) 0

129. $(x + 3)(x - 1)$ **131.** $(4x + 3)(3x - 1)$

133. $(4x + 5)(4x - 5)$ **135.** $x(2x - 9)(x + 5)$ **137.** 15

139. The graphs do not intersect. No real solution.   **141.** 27.67

Section 3.3   (page 207)

1. change-of-base   **3.** $\log_3 24 = \dfrac{\ln 24}{\ln 3}$

5. (a) $\dfrac{\log_{10} x}{\log_{10} 5}$ (b) $\dfrac{\ln x}{\ln 5}$ **7.** (a) $\dfrac{\log_{10} x}{\log_{10} 6}$ (b) $\dfrac{\ln x}{\ln 6}$

9. (a) $\dfrac{\log_{10} \frac{3}{10}}{\log_{10} a}$ (b) $\dfrac{\ln \frac{3}{10}}{\ln a}$ **11.** (a) $\dfrac{\log_{10} x}{\log_{10} 2.6}$ (b) $\dfrac{\ln x}{\ln 2.6}$

13. 1.771   **15.** -4 **17.** -0.059 **19.** 2.691

21. $\ln 5 + \ln 4$ **23.** $2 \ln 5 - \ln 4$ **25.** 1.0686

27. -0.2294

29.   **31.**

33.   **35.**

37. $\frac{3}{2}$ **39.** $4 + 4\log_2 3$ **41.** $6 + \ln 5$ **43.** $\ln 6 - 2$

45. Answers will vary.   **47.** $1 + \log_{10} x$

49. $\log_{10} t - \log_{10} 8$ **51.** $4\log_8 x$ **53.** $\frac{1}{2}\ln z$

55. $\ln x + \ln y + \ln z$ **57.** $\log_6 a + 3\log_6 b - 2\log_6 c$

59. $\frac{4}{3}\ln x - \frac{1}{3}\ln y$ **61.** $\ln(x+1) + \ln(x-1) - 3\ln x,\ x > 1$

63. $4\log_b x + \frac{1}{2}\log_b y - 5\log_b z$

65. (a)

(b)

x	4	5	6	7	8	9	10
y_1	Error	3.22	4.28	4.99	5.55	6.00	6.40
y_2	Error	3.22	4.28	4.99	5.55	6.00	6.40

(c) $y_1 = y_2$

67. (a)

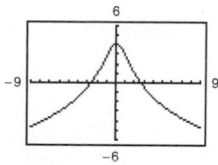

(b)

x	0	3	4	5	6	7	8
y_1	Error	4.39	4.85	5.34	5.78	6.17	6.53
y_2	Error	4.39	4.85	5.34	5.78	6.17	6.53

(c) $y_1 = y_2$

69. $\ln 4x$ **71.** $\log_4 \dfrac{z}{y}$ **73.** $\log_3(x+2)^4$

75. $\ln\left(x\sqrt{x^2+4}\right)$ **77.** $\ln \dfrac{x}{(x+1)^3}$ **79.** $\ln \dfrac{2(x-2)}{y^3}$

81. $\ln \dfrac{x}{(x^2-4)^2}$ **83.** $\ln \sqrt[3]{\dfrac{x(x+3)^2}{x^2-1}}$

85. (a)

(b)

x	-5	-4	-3	-2	-1
y_1	-2.36	-1.51	-0.45	0.94	2.77
y_2	-2.36	-1.51	-0.45	0.94	2.77

x	0	1	2	3	4	5
y_1	4.16	2.77	0.94	-0.45	-1.51	-2.36
y_2	4.16	2.77	0.94	-0.45	-1.51	-2.36

(c) $y_1 = y_2$

87. (a)

(b)

x	-1	0	1	2
y_1	Error	Error	0.35	1.24
y_2	Error	Error	0.35	1.24

x	3	4	5
y_1	1.79	2.19	2.51
y_2	1.79	2.19	2.51

(c) $y_1 = y_2$

89. 2   **91.** 6.8

93. Not possible; -4 is not in the domain of $\log_2 x$.

95. 3   **97.** -4 **99.** 8   **101.** $-\frac{1}{2}$

103. (a)

(b)

x	-5	-4	-3	-2	-1
y_1	3.22	2.77	2.20	1.39	0
y_2	Error	Error	Error	Error	Error

x	0	1	2	3	4	5
y_1	Error	0	1.39	2.20	2.77	3.22
y_2	Error	0	1.39	2.20	2.77	3.22

(c) No. The domains differ.

105. (a)

(b)

x	-4	-3	0	3
y_1	Error	Error	Error	1.61
y_2	2.48	1.61	Error	1.61

x	4	5	6
y_1	2.48	3.04	3.47
y_2	2.48	3.04	3.47

(c) No. The domains differ.

CHAPTER 3

107. (a) $\beta = 120 + 10 \log_{10} I$

(b)

I	10^{-4}	10^{-6}	10^{-8}	10^{-10}	10^{-12}	10^{-14}
β	80	60	40	20	0	-20

109. (a)

(b) $T = 54.4(0.964)^t + 21$

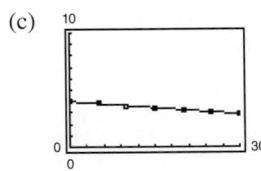

The model fits the data.

(c)

$$\ln(T - 21) = -0.037t + 3.997$$
$$T = e^{(-0.037t + 3.997)} + 21$$

(d)

$$\frac{1}{T - 21} = 0.0012t + 0.0162$$

$$T = \frac{1}{0.0012t + 0.0162} + 21$$

111. True

113. False. $f(\sqrt{x}) = \frac{1}{2}f(x)$

115. True. $\ln x < 0$ when $0 < x < 1$.

117. The error is an improper use of the Quotient Property of logarithms.

$$\ln \frac{x^2}{\sqrt{x^2 + 4}} = \ln x^2 - \ln \sqrt{x^2 + 4} = 2 \ln x - \frac{1}{2} \ln(x^2 + 4)$$

119. $\ln 1 = 0$ $\ln 9 \approx 2.1972$

$\ln 2 \approx 0.6931$ $\ln 10 \approx 2.3025$

$\ln 3 \approx 1.0986$ $\ln 12 \approx 2.4848$

$\ln 4 \approx 1.3862$ $\ln 15 \approx 2.7080$

$\ln 5 \approx 1.6094$ $\ln 16 \approx 2.7724$

$\ln 6 \approx 1.7917$ $\ln 18 \approx 2.8903$

$\ln 8 \approx 2.0793$ $\ln 20 \approx 2.9956$

121. No.

Domain of y_1: $(-\infty, 0), (2, \infty)$

Domain of y_2: $(2, \infty)$

123. $\dfrac{x^3}{64y^4}$, $x \neq 0$ **125.** $\dfrac{3x^4}{2y^3}$, $x \neq 0$

Section 3.4   (page 217)

1. (a) $x = y$ (b) $x = y$ (c) x (d) x **3.** 7

5. Subtract 3 from both sides.   **7.** (a) Yes   (b) No

9. (a) No   (b) Yes   (c) Yes, approximate

11. (a) Yes, approximate   (b) No   (c) Yes

13. (a) Yes   (b) Yes, approximate   (c) No

15.

$\left(\frac{1}{2}, 8\right); \frac{1}{2}$

17.

$(4, 10); 4$

19.

$(243, 20); 243$

21.

$(-4, -3); -4$

23. 2   **25.** -4 **27.** -2 **29.** -4 **31.** $\ln 14$

33. $\log_{10} 36$ **35.** 5   **37.** 5   **39.** e^{-9} **41.** 5

43. $\dfrac{1}{11}$ **45.** $\dfrac{e^5 + 1}{2}$ **47.** x^2 **49.** $x^2 - 3$

51. $2x - 1$ **53.** $-x^2 + 4$ **55.** 0.944   **57.** 2

59. 184.444   **61.** 0.511   **63.** 1.099   **65.** -1.498

67. 6.960   **69.** -277.951 **71.** 1.609   **73.** $-1, 2$

75. 0.586, 3.414   **77.** 1.946   **79.** 183.258

81. (a)

x	0.6	0.7	0.8	0.9	1.0
e^{3x}	6.05	8.17	11.02	14.88	20.09

$(0.8, 0.9)$

(b)

(c) 0.828

83. (a)

x	5	6	7	8	9
$20(100 - e^{x/2})$	1756	1598	1338	908	200

$(8, 9)$

(b)

(c) 8.635

85. 21.330   **87.** 2.720

89.   **91.**

$x = -0.427$ $x = 12.207$

93. 0.050   **95.** 2.042   **97.** $-\frac{1}{2}$ **99.** 4453.242

101. 17.945   **103.** ±9   **105.** 5.389

107. 1.718, -3.718 **109.** 2   **111.** 3   **113.** 180.384

115. (a)

x	2	3	4	5	6
$\ln 2x$	1.39	1.79	2.08	2.30	2.48

(5, 6)

(b)   (c) 5.512

5.512

117. (a)

x	12	13	14	15	16
$6 \log_3(0.5x)$	9.79	10.22	10.63	11.00	11.36

(14, 15)

(b)   (c) 14.988

14.988

119. 1.469, 0.001   **121.** 3.398   **123.** $-1.993, 3.738$

125.   **127.**

(4.585, 7) $(-14.979, 80)$

129.

(663.142, 3.25)

131. $-1, 0$ **133.** 1   **135.** $e^{-1/2} \approx 0.607$

137. $e^{-1} \approx 0.368$ **139.** $\dfrac{\ln y - \ln a}{b}$

141. $b \pm \sqrt{c(\ln y - \ln a)}$ **143.** (a) 9.90 yr   (b) 15.69 yr

145. (a) 27.73 yr   (b) 43.94 yr

147. (a) 93 months   (b) 124 months

149. 2011

151. (a)

(b) $y = 20$. The object's temperature cannot cool below the room's temperature.

(c) 0.81 h   (d) About 1.22 h

153. False; $e^x = 0$ has no solutions.

155. The error is that both sides of the equation should be divided by 2 before taking the natural log of both sides.

$$2e^x = 10$$
$$e^x = 5$$
$$\ln e^x = \ln 5$$
$$x = \ln 5$$

157. (a)

(1.258, 1.258), (14.767, 14.767)

(b) $a = e^{(1/e)} \approx 1.445$ (c) $1 < a < e^{(1/e)}$

159.   **161.**

Section 3.5   (page 228)

1. (a) iv   (b) i   (c) iii   (d) vi   (e) ii   (f) v

3. sigmoidal   **5.** Exponential decay

7. c   **8.** e   **9.** b   **10.** a   **11.** d   **12.** f

Initial Investment	Annual % Rate	Time to Double	Amount After 10 Years
13. $10,000	4%	17.3 yr	$14,918.25
15. $7500	3.30%	21 yr	$10,432.26
17. $5000	1.25%	55.45 yr	$5665.74
19. $63,762.82	4.5%	15.40 yr	$100,000.00

21.

r	2%	4%	6%	8%	10%	12%
t	54.93	27.47	18.31	13.73	10.99	9.16

CHAPTER 3

23.

Continuous compounding

Isotope	Half-Life (years)	Initial Quantity	Amount After 1000 Years
25. ^{226}Ra	1600	10 g	6.48 g
27. ^{231}Pa	32,800	1.53 g	1.5 g
29. ^{241}Am	432.2	26.4 g	5.31 g

31. $y = e^{0.768x}$ **33.** $y = 4e^{-0.2773x}$

35. (a) Increasing. The positive exponent indicates that the model is increasing.
    (b) 97,301 people; 101,171 people; 105,194 people
    (c) 2019

37. (a) 0.0178   (b) About 467,309 people

39. About 15,601 years ago

41. (a) $V = -7160.5t + 39,780$
    (b) $V = 39,780e^{-0.2231t}$
    (c)

    (d) Exponential model
    (e) $0 < t < 2; t \geq 2$

43. (a)

    (b) 100

45. (a) About 203 animals   (b) About 13 mo
    (c)

    The horizontal asymptotes occur at $p = 1000$ and $p = 0$. The asymptote at $p = 1000$ means there will not be more than 1000 animals in the preserve.

47. (a) 10,000,000   (b) 199,526,232   (c) 1,995,262

49. (a) 20 dB   (b) 70 dB   (c) 120 dB

51. 97.49%   **53.** 4.64   **55.** About 31,623 times

57. (a)

    (b) 53.08 yr; yes

59. 3:00 A.M.

61. False. The domain can be all real numbers.

63. No. Any x-value in the Gaussian model will give a positive y-value.

65. Gaussian model   **67.** Exponential growth model

69. a; $(0, -3)$, $\left(\frac{9}{4}, 0\right)$ **71.** d; $(0, 25)$, $\left(\frac{100}{9}, 0\right)$

73. Falls to the left, rises to the right

75. Rises to the left, falls to the right

77. $2x^2 + 3 + \dfrac{3}{x - 4}$ **79.** Answers will vary.

Section 3.6   (page 238)

1. $y = ax^b$ **3.** Scatter plot   **5.** Logarithmic model

7. Quadratic model   **9.** Exponential model

11. Linear model

13.

Logarithmic model

15.

Exponential model

17.

Linear model

19. $y = 4.752(1.2607)^x$; 0.96773

21. $y = 7.707(0.8070)^x$; 0.9448

23. $y = 2.083 + 1.257 \ln x$; 0.98672

25. $y = -4.730 \ln x + 10.353$; 0.9661

27. $y = 1.985x^{0.760}$; 0.99686

29. $y = 16.103x^{-3.174}$; 0.88161

31. (a) Exponential model: $S = 2952.790(1.1203)^t$; 0.9821
Power model: $S = 877.314t^{1.0326}$; 0.9782
(b) Exponential model: Power model:

(c) Exponential model
33. (a) Linear model: $P = 7.57t + 352.7$; $r^2 \approx 0.9786$

(b) Power model: $P = 248.55t^{0.2351}$; $r^2 \approx 0.9438$

(c) Exponential model: $P = 366.630(1.0160)^t$; $r^2 \approx 0.9866$

(d) Logarithmic model: $P = 111.66 \ln t + 168.6$;
$r^2 \approx 0.9289$

(e) The exponential model is the best fit because its
coefficient of determination is closest to 1.
(f)
Linear:

Year	2014	2015	2016	2017	2018
Population (in thousands)	534.4	542.0	549.5	557.1	564.7

Power:

Year	2014	2015	2016	2017	2018
Population (in thousands)	524.7	529.7	534.7	539.4	544.1

Exponential:

Year	2014	2015	2016	2017	2018
Population (in thousands)	536.6	545.2	553.9	562.8	571.8

Logarithmic:

Year	2014	2015	2016	2017	2018
Population (in thousands)	523.5	528.0	532.4	536.6	540.7

(g) and (h) Answers will vary.
35. (a) $S = 3.723(1.1117)^t$
(b) $S = 3.723(e^{0.1059t})$
(c) \$25.05 billion; Answers will vary.
37. (a) $P = \dfrac{88.2676}{1 + 901.9894e^{-0.2560r}}$
(b)

The model fits the data well.
39. True. See page 221.
41. Answers will vary.
43. Slope: $-\frac{2}{5}$; y-intercept: $(0, 2)$

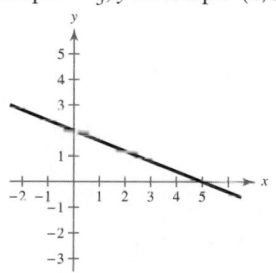

45. Slope: 0.16; y-intercept: $(0, -5)$

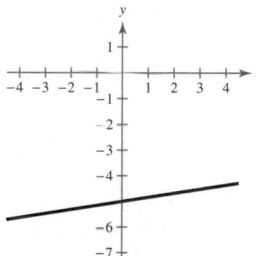

47. $y = -(x + 1)^2 + 2$ **49.** $y = -2(x - 3)^2 + 2$

Review Exercises   (page 244)

1. 10.3254   **3.** 0.0167
5. c   **6.** d   **7.** b   **8.** a

9.

Horizontal asymptote: $y = 0$
y-intercept: $(0, 1)$
Increasing on $(-\infty, \infty)$

11.

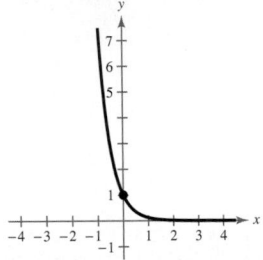

Horizontal asymptote: $y = 0$
y-intercept: $(0, 1)$
Decreasing on $(-\infty, \infty)$

13.

x	0	1	2	3	4
$h(x)$	0.37	1	2.72	7.39	20.09

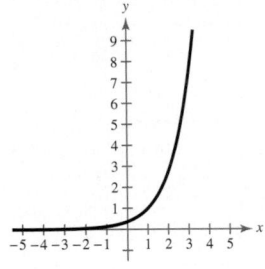

Horizontal asymptote: $y = 0$

15.

x	-2	-1	0	1	2
$h(x)$	2.86	2.63	2	0.28	-4.39

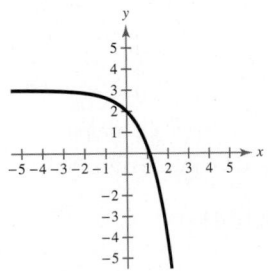

Horizontal asymptote: $y = 3$

17.

x	-1	0	1	2	3	4
$f(x)$	6.59	4	2.43	1.47	0.89	0.54

Horizontal asymptote: $y = 0$

19.

t	1	10	20
A	\$10,832.87	\$22,255.41	\$49,530.32

t	30	40	50
A	\$110,231.76	\$245,325.30	\$545,981.50

21. (a)

(b) \$19,708.80
(c) When it is first sold; yes; Answers will vary.

23. $5^4 = 625$ **25.** $64^{1/6} = 2$ **27.** $\log_4 64 = 3$
29. $\ln 24.532 \ldots = 3.2$ **31.** $\log_{1/2} 8 = -3$
33. 3   **35.** -1
37. Domain: $(0, \infty)$ **39.** Domain: $(1, \infty)$
Vertical asymptote: $x = 0$ Vertical asymptote: $x = 1$
x-intercept: $(10,000, 0)$ x-intercept: $(1.000001, 0)$

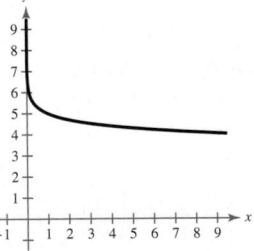

41. 3.068   **43.** 0.896
45.   **47.**

Domain: $(0, \infty)$ Domain: $(0, \infty)$
Vertical asymptote: $x = 0$ Vertical asymptote: $x = 0$
x-intercept: $(0.05, 0)$ x-intercept: $(1, 0)$

49. (a) $0 \le h < 18{,}000$

(b)

Asymptote: $h = 18{,}000$

(c) The time required to increase its altitude further increases.

(d) 5.46 min

51. 1.585   **53.** 1.041

55.

57.

59. 1.13   **61.** 0.41   **63.** $\ln 5 - 2$

65. $2 + \log_{10} 2$ **67.** $1 + 2 \log_5 x$

69. $\log_{10} 5 + \frac{1}{2} \log_{10} y - 2 \log_{10} x$

71. $\ln(x + 3) - \ln x - \ln y$ **73.** $\log_2 9x$

75. $\ln \dfrac{\sqrt{2x - 1}}{(x + 1)^2}$ **77.** $\ln \dfrac{3\sqrt[3]{4 - x^2}}{x}$

79. (a)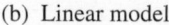

(b)

h	4	6	8	10	12	14
s	38	33	30	27	25	23

(c) The decrease in productivity starts to level off.

81. 4   **83.** -3 **85.** -5 **87.** 4096   **89.** 9

91. e^4 **93.** $e^2 + 1$ **95.** -0.757 **97.** 4.459

99. 1.760   **101.** 3.916   **103.** 1.609, 0.693

105. 200.615   **107.** 36.945   **109.** 53.598

111. 4   **113.** 0.9   **115.** -1 **117.** 0.368

119. 10.05 yr

121. e   **122.** b   **123.** f   **124.** d   **125.** a   **126.** c

127. $k = 0.0184$; 11,645,427

129. (a) 11.08 weeks   (b) 24.16 weeks

131. Logistic model

133. (a) Linear model: $N = 40.4t + 2728$; $r^2 \approx 0.9836$

Exponential model: $N = 2737.170(1.0135)^t$;
$r^2 \approx 0.9832$

Power model: $N = 2688.8t^{0.0645}$; $r^2 \approx 0.8748$

(b) Linear model:

Exponential model:

Power model:

(c) The linear model is the best fit because its coefficient of determination is closest to 1.

(d) 2023–2024

135. True. $e^{x-1} = e^x \cdot e^{-1} = \dfrac{e^x}{e}$ **137.** False. $x > 0$

139. Because $1 < \sqrt{2} < 2$, then $2^1 < 2^{\sqrt{2}} < 2^2$.

Chapter Test   (page 248)

1.

x	-2	-1	0	1	2
$f(x)$	100	10	1	0.1	0.01

Horizontal asymptote: $y = 0$
y-intercept: $(0, 1)$

2.

x	0	2	3	4
$f(x)$	-0.03	-1	-6	-36

Horizontal asymptote: $y = 0$
y-intercept: $\left(0, -\frac{1}{36}\right)$

3.

x	-2	-1	0	1	2
$f(x)$	0.9817	0.8647	0	-6.3891	-53.5982

Horizontal asymptote: $y = 1$
Intercept: $(0, 0)$

4. -0.89 **5.** 9.2 **6.** 2

7.

8.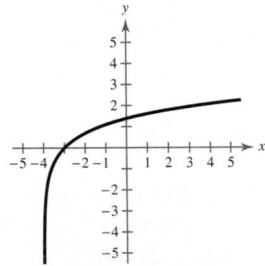

Domain: $(0, \infty)$
Vertical asymptote: $x = 0$
x-intercept: $(10^{-6}, 0)$

Domain: $(-4, \infty)$
Vertical asymptote: $x = -4$
x-intercept: $(-3, 0)$

9.

Domain: $(6, \infty)$
Vertical asymptote: $x = 6$
x-intercept: $(6.37, 0)$

10. 1.945 **11.** -0.286 **12.** 1.674

13. $\log_2 3 + 4 \log_2 a$ **14.** $\ln 5 + \frac{1}{2} \ln x - \ln 6$

15. $\ln x + \frac{1}{2} \ln(x + 1) - \ln 2 - 4$ **16.** $\log_3 13y$

17. $\ln \dfrac{x^4}{y^4}$ **18.** $\ln \dfrac{x(2x - 3)}{x + 2}$ **19.** 4

20. 2.431 **21.** $117{,}649$ **22.** $100{,}004$ **23.** 1.321

24. 1 **25.** 1.597 **26.** 1.649 **27.** 62.34%

28. (a) Logarithmic model: $R = 81.2970 \ln t - 144.646$
Exponential model: $R = 2.006(1.3266)^t$
Power model: $R = 0.099t^{2.5639}$

(b) Logarithmic model:

Exponential model:

Power model:

(c) Exponential model; $\$430.9$ billion

Cumulative Test for Chapters 1–3
(page 249)

1. (a) $y = -x + 3$
(b) Answers will vary. Sample answer: $(0, 3), (1, 2), (2, 1)$

2. (a) $y = -2x$
(b) Answers will vary. Sample answer:
$(0, 0), (1, -2), (2, -4)$

3. (a) $x = \frac{3}{7}$
(b) Answers will vary. Sample answer: $\left(\frac{3}{7}, 0\right), \left(\frac{3}{7}, 1\right), \left(\frac{3}{7}, -3\right)$

4. (a) $\dfrac{5}{3}$ (b) Undefined   (c) $\dfrac{5 + 4s}{3 + 4s}$

5. (a) -32 (b) 4 (c) 20

6. No. It does not pass the Vertical Line Test.

7.

Decreasing on $(-\infty, 5)$
Increasing on $(5, \infty)$

8. (a) Vertical shrink   (b) Vertical shift
(c) Horizontal shift and reflection in the x-axis

9. -53 **10.** $\frac{197}{16}$ **11.** -31 **12.** 42

13. $h^{-1}(x) = \dfrac{x + 2}{5}$

14.

15.

16.

17. $x = -2, \pm 2i$ **18.** -5.151 **19.** $4x + 2 - \dfrac{15}{x + 3}$

20. $2x^2 + 7x + 48 + \dfrac{268}{x - 6}$ **21.** 73

22. Answers will vary. Sample answer: $f(x) = x^4 + x^3 + 18x$

23.   **24.**

 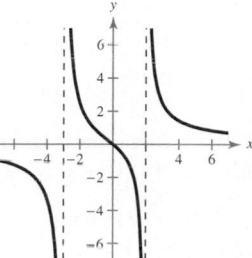

Asymptotes: Asymptotes:
$x = 3, y = 2$ $x = 3, x = 2, y = 0$

25.   **26.**

 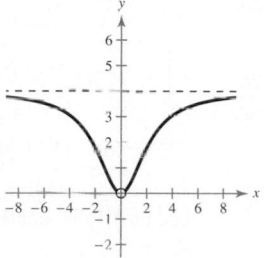

Asymptotes: $x = 2, y = x - 1$ Asymptote: $y = 4$

27. 3.443   **28.** 8772.934   **29.** 0.202   **30.** 51.743

31.   **32.**

33.   **34.**

35. 1.723   **36.** 0.905   **37.** 0.585

38. $\ln(x + 2) + \ln(x - 2) - \ln(x^2 + 1)$

39. $\ln\dfrac{x^2(x + 1)}{x - 1}$ **40.** 1.242   **41.** 6.585   **42.** 12.8

43. 105.966   **44.** 0, 1   **45.** No solution

46. (a) $A = x(273 - x)$

(b) $0 < x < 273$

(c) 76.23 ft $\times$ 196.77 ft

47. (a) Quadratic model:
$S = -1.16963t^2 + 40.2326t + 147.853; r^2 \approx 0.9905$
Exponential model: $S = 229.067(1.0652)^t; \ r^2 \approx 0.9486$
Power model: $S = 160.681t^{0.4294}; r^2 \approx 0.9921$

(b) Quadratic model:

Exponential model:

Power model:

(c) The power model is the best fit because its coefficient of determination is closest to 1.

(d) \$581.603 billion; Answers will vary.

Chapter 4

Section 4.1   (page 261)

1. Trigonometry   **3.** standard position   **5.** radian

7. 180°   **9.** No   **11.** 2

13. (a) Quadrant I   (b) Quadrant III

15. (a) Quadrant IV   (b) Quadrant II

17. (a) Quadrant IV   (b) Quadrant III

19. (a)   (b)

CHAPTER 4

21. (a) (b)

23. (a) 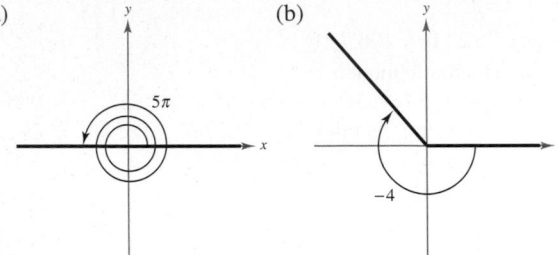 (b)

25. (a) $\dfrac{13\pi}{6}, -\dfrac{11\pi}{6}$ (b) $\dfrac{8\pi}{3}, -\dfrac{4\pi}{3}$

27. (a) $\dfrac{\pi}{4}, -\dfrac{7\pi}{4}$ (b) $\dfrac{28\pi}{15}, -\dfrac{32\pi}{15}$

29. $210°$ **31.** (a) Quadrant I   (b) Quadrant III

33. (a) Quadrant III   (b) Quadrant IV

35. (a) Quadrant II   (b) Quadrant I

37. (a) (b)

39. (a) (b)

41. (a) 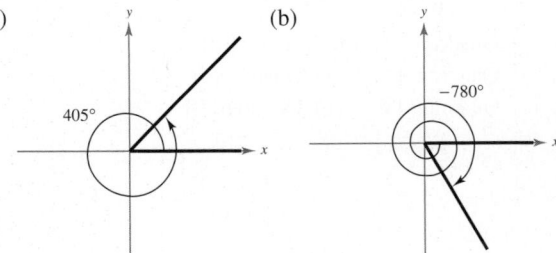 (b)

43. (a) $412°, -308°$ (b) $324°, -396°$

45. (a) $60°, -660°$ (b) $590°, -130°$ **47.** (a) $\dfrac{\pi}{6}$ (b) $\dfrac{5\pi}{6}$

49. (a) $\dfrac{\pi}{10}$ (b) $-\dfrac{4\pi}{3}$ **51.** (a) $270°$ (b) $-210°$

53. (a) $420°$ (b) $-39°$ **55.** 2.007 **57.** -3.776

59. -0.014 **61.** $25.714°$ **63.** $1170°$ **65.** $-114.592°$

67. $64.75°$ **69.** $85.308°$ **71.** $-125.01°$ **73.** $13°\,5'15''$

75. $23°\,1'1''$ **77.** $280°\,36'$ **79.** $-345°\,7'12''$

81. $-20°\,20'24''$ **83.** Complement: $66°$; supplement: $156°$

85. Complement: none; supplement: $13°$

87. Complement: $\dfrac{\pi}{6}$; supplement: $\dfrac{2\pi}{3}$

89. Complement: none; supplement: $\dfrac{\pi}{3}$

91. Complement: none; supplement: none

93. $\dfrac{8}{15}$ rad   **95.** $\dfrac{70}{29}$ rad   **97.** 14π in.   **99.** 18π m

101. About 22.92 ft   **103.** About 34.80 mi

105. About 591.32 mi   **107.** About $4°\,2'33''$

109. About $275.02°$ **111.** About 435.71 km/min

113. (a) 2100π rad/min   (b) About $64{,}324.1$ in./min

115. (a) $\dfrac{1000\pi}{3}$ rad/sec   (b) About 62.83 m/sec

117. False. A radian is larger: 1 rad $\approx 57.3°$.

119. True. The sum of the angles of a triangle must equal

$180° = \pi$ radians, and $\dfrac{2\pi}{3} + \dfrac{\pi}{4} + \dfrac{\pi}{12} = \pi$.

121. $\dfrac{50\pi}{3}$ m^2

123. (a) $A = 0.4r^2, r > 0; s = 0.8r, r > 0$

The area function changes more rapidly for $r > 1$ because it is quadratic and the arc length function is linear.

(b) $A = 50\theta, 0 < \theta < 2\pi; s = 10\theta, 0 < \theta < 2\pi$

125. Answers will vary.

127.   **129.**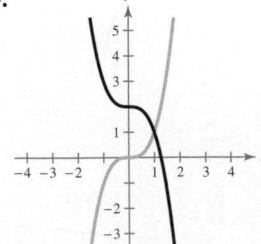

Horizontal shift one unit to the right

Reflection in the x-axis, vertical shift two units upward

131.

Horizontal shift one unit to the left, vertical shift three units downward

Section 4.2   (page 270)

1. unit circle   **3.** odd, even

5. Even: cos, sec; Odd: sin, csc, tan, cot   **7.** 8

9. $\sin \theta = \frac{15}{17}$

$\cos \theta = -\frac{8}{17}$

$\tan \theta = -\frac{15}{8}$

$\csc \theta = \frac{17}{15}$

$\sec \theta = -\frac{17}{8}$

$\cot \theta = -\frac{8}{15}$

11. $\sin \theta = -\frac{5}{13}$

$\cos \theta = -\frac{12}{13}$

$\tan \theta = -\frac{5}{12}$

$\csc \theta = -\frac{13}{5}$

$\sec \theta = \frac{13}{12}$

$\cot \theta = -\frac{12}{5}$

13. $\left(\frac{\sqrt{2}}{2}, \frac{\sqrt{2}}{2}\right)$ **15.** $\left(-\frac{\sqrt{3}}{2}, -\frac{1}{2}\right)$ **17.** $(0, -1)$

19. $\left(\frac{\sqrt{2}}{2}, \frac{\sqrt{2}}{2}\right)$ **21.** $(1, 0)$

23. $\sin \frac{\pi}{4} = \frac{\sqrt{2}}{2}$

$\cos \frac{\pi}{4} = \frac{\sqrt{2}}{2}$

$\tan \frac{\pi}{4} = 1$

25. $\sin\left(-\frac{7\pi}{4}\right) = \frac{\sqrt{2}}{2}$

$\cos\left(-\frac{7\pi}{4}\right) = \frac{\sqrt{2}}{2}$

$\tan\left(-\frac{7\pi}{4}\right) = 1$

27. $\sin \frac{2\pi}{3} = \frac{\sqrt{3}}{2}$

$\cos \frac{2\pi}{3} = -\frac{1}{2}$

$\tan \frac{2\pi}{3} = -\sqrt{3}$

29. $\sin\left(-\frac{\pi}{2}\right) = -1$

$\cos\left(-\frac{\pi}{2}\right) = 0$

$\tan\left(-\frac{\pi}{2}\right)$ is undefined.

31. $\sin\left(-\frac{\pi}{6}\right) = -\frac{1}{2}$

$\cos\left(-\frac{\pi}{6}\right) = \frac{\sqrt{3}}{2}$

$\tan\left(-\frac{\pi}{6}\right) = -\frac{\sqrt{3}}{3}$

33. $\sin \frac{3\pi}{4} = \frac{\sqrt{2}}{2}$

$\cos \frac{3\pi}{4} = -\frac{\sqrt{2}}{2}$

$\tan \frac{3\pi}{4} = -1$

$\csc \frac{3\pi}{4} = \sqrt{2}$

$\sec \frac{3\pi}{4} = -\sqrt{2}$

$\cot \frac{3\pi}{4} = -1$

35. $\sin 2\pi = 0$

$\cos 2\pi = 1$

$\tan 2\pi = 0$

$\csc 2\pi$ is undefined.

$\sec 2\pi = 1$

$\cot 2\pi$ is undefined.

37. $\sin\left(-\frac{4\pi}{3}\right) = \frac{\sqrt{3}}{2}$

$\cos\left(-\frac{4\pi}{3}\right) = -\frac{1}{2}$

$\tan\left(-\frac{4\pi}{3}\right) = -\sqrt{3}$

$\csc\left(-\frac{4\pi}{3}\right) = \frac{2\sqrt{3}}{3}$

$\sec\left(-\frac{4\pi}{3}\right) = -2$

$\cot\left(-\frac{4\pi}{3}\right) = -\frac{\sqrt{3}}{3}$

39. 0   **41.** $-\frac{1}{2}$ **43.** $\frac{\sqrt{3}}{2}$ **45.** $-\frac{\sqrt{2}}{2}$

47. (a) $-\frac{1}{3}$ (b) -3 **49.** (a) $-\frac{1}{5}$ (b) -5

51. (a) $-\frac{4}{5}$ (b) $\frac{5}{4}$ **53.** 0.4339   **55.** 0.8090

57. -5.6713 **59.** -0.1288 **61.** -1.1504

63. -1.1547 **65.** 1.6003   **67.** 1.1319

69. (a) -0.9 (b) -0.4

71. (a) 0.25, 2.89   (b) 1.82, 4.46   **73.** 0.79 amp

75. (a) 0.25 ft   (b) About 0.02 ft   (c) About -0.25 ft

77. False. $\sin(-t) = -\sin t$ means that the function is odd, not that the sine of a negative angle is a negative number.

79. True. $a - 6\pi$ is coterminal with a.

81. It is an odd function.

83. (a) y-axis   (b) $\sin t_1 = \sin(\pi - t_1)$

(c) $\cos(\pi - t_1) = -\cos t_1$

85. (a) $\frac{2}{3}$ (b) $-\frac{2}{3}$ **87.** Answers will vary.

89.

91.

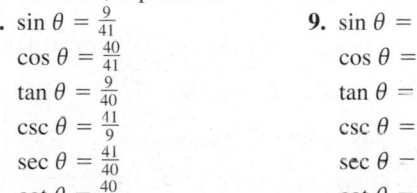

Section 4.3   (page 280)

1. (a) iii   (b) vi   (c) ii   (d) v   (e) i   (f) iv

3. elevation, depression   **5.** 12

7. $\sin \theta = \frac{9}{41}$

$\cos \theta = \frac{40}{41}$

$\tan \theta = \frac{9}{40}$

$\csc \theta = \frac{41}{9}$

$\sec \theta = \frac{41}{40}$

$\cot \theta = \frac{40}{9}$

9. $\sin \theta = \frac{8}{17}$

$\cos \theta = \frac{15}{17}$

$\tan \theta = \frac{8}{15}$

$\csc \theta = \frac{17}{8}$

$\sec \theta = \frac{17}{15}$

$\cot \theta = \frac{15}{8}$

11. $\sin \theta = \frac{3}{5}$

$\cos \theta = \frac{4}{5}$

$\tan \theta = \frac{3}{4}$

$\csc \theta = \frac{5}{3}$

$\sec \theta = \frac{5}{4}$

$\cot \theta = \frac{4}{3}$

The triangles are similar and corresponding sides are proportional.

CHAPTER 4

13. $\cos \theta = \dfrac{\sqrt{11}}{6}$

$\tan \theta = \dfrac{5\sqrt{11}}{11}$

$\csc \theta = \dfrac{6}{5}$

$\sec \theta = \dfrac{6\sqrt{11}}{11}$

$\cot \theta = \dfrac{\sqrt{11}}{5}$

15. $\sin \theta = \dfrac{\sqrt{15}}{4}$

$\cos \theta = \dfrac{1}{4}$

$\tan \theta = \sqrt{15}$

$\csc \theta = \dfrac{4\sqrt{15}}{15}$

$\cot \theta = \dfrac{\sqrt{15}}{15}$

17. $\sin \theta = \dfrac{3\sqrt{10}}{10}$

$\cos \theta = \dfrac{\sqrt{10}}{10}$

$\csc \theta = \dfrac{\sqrt{10}}{3}$

$\sec \theta = \sqrt{10}$

$\cot \theta = \dfrac{1}{3}$

19. $\sin \theta = \dfrac{2\sqrt{13}}{13}$

$\cos \theta = \dfrac{3\sqrt{13}}{13}$

$\tan \theta = \dfrac{2}{3}$

$\sec \theta = \dfrac{\sqrt{13}}{3}$

$\csc \theta = \dfrac{\sqrt{13}}{2}$

21. $\dfrac{\pi}{6}, \dfrac{1}{2}$ **23.** $60°, \sqrt{3}$ **25.** $45°, \dfrac{\pi}{4}$ **27.** $30°, \dfrac{\sqrt{3}}{2}$

29. $45°, \dfrac{\pi}{4}$ **31.** (a) 0.1736   (b) 0.1736

33. (a) 1.3499   (b) 1.3430   **35.** (a) 5.0273   (b) 0.4142

37. $\csc \theta$ **39.** $\cot \theta$ **41.** $\cos \theta$ **43.** $\dfrac{\sin \theta}{\cos \theta}$

45. 1   **47.** $\cos \theta$ **49.** $\cot \theta$ **51.** $\csc \theta$

53. (a) $\sqrt{3}$ (b) $\dfrac{1}{2}$ (c) $\dfrac{\sqrt{3}}{2}$ (d) $\dfrac{\sqrt{3}}{3}$

55. (a) $\dfrac{1}{3}$ (b) $\dfrac{2\sqrt{2}}{3}$ (c) $\dfrac{\sqrt{2}}{4}$ (d) 3

57. (a) $\dfrac{1}{4}$ (b) $\sqrt{17}$ (c) $\dfrac{\sqrt{17}}{4}$ (d) 4

59–65. Answers will vary.

67. (a) $30° = \dfrac{\pi}{6}$ **69.** (a) $60° = \dfrac{\pi}{3}$

(b) $30° = \dfrac{\pi}{6}$ (b) $45° = \dfrac{\pi}{4}$

71. (a) $60° = \dfrac{\pi}{3}$

(b) $45° = \dfrac{\pi}{4}$

73. $y = 35\sqrt{3}, r = 70\sqrt{3}$ **75.** $x = 8, y = 8\sqrt{3}$

77. (a) About 519.33 ft   (b) About 1174.17 ft

(c) About 173.8 ft/min

79. About 160 ft

81. $(x_1, y_1) = (28\sqrt{3}, 28)$

$(x_2, y_2) = (28, 28\sqrt{3})$

83. (a)

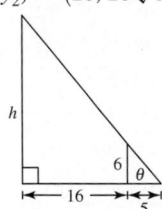

(b) $\tan \theta = \dfrac{h}{21}$

(c) $h = 25.2$ ft

85. True. $\csc x = \dfrac{1}{\sin x}$ **87.** False. $\dfrac{\sqrt{2}}{2} + \dfrac{\sqrt{2}}{2} \neq 1$

89. False. $1.7321 \neq 0.0349$

91. Yes, with the Pythagorean Theorem. Answers will vary.

93. (a)

θ	0°	20°	40°	60°	80°
$\sin \theta$	0	0.3420	0.6428	0.8660	0.9848
$\cos \theta$	1	0.9397	0.7660	0.5	0.1736
$\tan \theta$	0	0.3640	0.8391	1.7321	5.6713

(b) Sine: increasing

Cosine: decreasing

Tangent: increasing

(c) Answers will vary.

95.

x	-1	0	1	2
$f(x)$	-0.05	-1	-20.09	-403.43

Asymptote: $y = 0$

97.

x	-1	0	1	2
$f(x)$	-3.95	-3	16.09	399.43

Asymptote: $y = -4$

99.   **101.**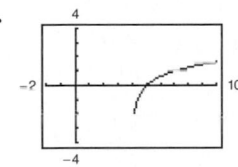

Domain: $(0, \infty)$ Domain: $(4, \infty)$

Vertical asymptote: $x = 0$ Vertical asymptote: $x = 4$

x-intercept: $\left(\frac{1}{3}, 0\right)$ x-intercept: $(5, 0)$

Section 4.4   (page 289)

1. $\dfrac{y}{r}$ **3.** $\dfrac{y}{x}$ **5.** $\cos \theta$ **7.** reference angle   **9.** $0, \pi$

11. (a) $\sin \theta = \frac{3}{5}$ (b) $\sin \theta = -\frac{15}{17}$

$\cos \theta = \frac{4}{5}$ $\cos \theta = -\frac{8}{17}$

$\tan \theta = \frac{3}{4}$ $\tan \theta = \frac{15}{8}$

$\csc \theta = \frac{5}{3}$ $\csc \theta = -\frac{17}{15}$

$\sec \theta = \frac{5}{4}$ $\sec \theta = -\frac{17}{8}$

$\cot \theta = \frac{4}{3}$ $\cot \theta = \frac{8}{15}$

13. (a) $\sin \theta = -\dfrac{1}{2}$ (b) $\sin \theta = \dfrac{\sqrt{2}}{2}$

$\cos \theta = -\dfrac{\sqrt{3}}{2}$ $\cos \theta = -\dfrac{\sqrt{2}}{2}$

$\tan \theta = \dfrac{\sqrt{3}}{3}$ $\tan \theta = -1$

$\csc \theta = -2$ $\csc \theta = \sqrt{2}$

$\sec \theta = -\dfrac{2\sqrt{3}}{3}$ $\sec \theta = -\sqrt{2}$

$\cot \theta = \sqrt{3}$ $\cot \theta = -1$

15. $\sin \theta = \frac{24}{25}$ **17.** $\sin \theta = -\frac{12}{13}$

$\cos \theta = \frac{7}{25}$ $\cos \theta = \frac{5}{13}$

$\tan \theta = \frac{24}{7}$ $\tan \theta = -\frac{12}{5}$

$\csc \theta = \frac{25}{24}$ $\csc \theta = \frac{13}{12}$

$\sec \theta = \frac{25}{7}$ $\sec \theta = \frac{13}{5}$

$\cot \theta = \frac{7}{24}$ $\cot \theta = -\frac{5}{12}$

19. $\sin \theta = \frac{2}{5}$ **21.** $\sin \theta = -\frac{4\sqrt{41}}{41}$

$\cos \theta = -\dfrac{\sqrt{21}}{5}$ $\cos \theta = -\dfrac{5\sqrt{41}}{41}$

$\tan \theta = -\dfrac{2\sqrt{21}}{21}$ $\tan \theta = \dfrac{4}{5}$

$\csc \theta = \dfrac{5}{2}$ $\csc \theta = -\dfrac{\sqrt{41}}{4}$

$\sec \theta = -\dfrac{5\sqrt{21}}{21}$ $\sec \theta = -\dfrac{\sqrt{41}}{5}$

$\cot \theta = -\dfrac{\sqrt{21}}{2}$ $\cot \theta = \dfrac{5}{4}$

23. Quadrant III   **25.** Quadrant I

27. $\sin \theta = \frac{3}{5}$ **29.** $\sin \theta = -\frac{15}{17}$

$\cos \theta = -\frac{4}{5}$ $\cos \theta = \frac{8}{17}$

$\tan \theta = \frac{3}{4}$ $\tan \theta = -\frac{15}{8}$

$\csc \theta = \frac{5}{3}$ $\csc \theta = -\frac{17}{15}$

$\sec \theta = -\frac{5}{4}$ $\sec \theta = \frac{17}{8}$

$\cot \theta = -\frac{4}{3}$ $\cot \theta = -\frac{8}{15}$

31. $\sin \theta = \dfrac{\sqrt{3}}{2}$ **33.** $\sin \theta = 0$

$\cos \theta = -\dfrac{1}{2}$ $\cos \theta = -1$

$\tan \theta = -\sqrt{3}$ $\tan \theta = 0$

$\csc \theta = \dfrac{2\sqrt{3}}{3}$ $\csc \theta$ is undefined.

$\sec \theta = -2$ $\sec \theta = -1$

$\cot \theta = -\dfrac{\sqrt{3}}{3}$ $\cot \theta$ is undefined.

35. $\sin \theta = \dfrac{\sqrt{2}}{2}$ **37.** $\sin \theta = -\dfrac{2\sqrt{5}}{5}$

$\cos \theta = -\dfrac{\sqrt{2}}{2}$ $\cos \theta = -\dfrac{\sqrt{5}}{5}$

$\tan \theta = -1$ $\tan \theta = 2$

$\csc \theta = \sqrt{2}$ $\csc \theta = -\dfrac{\sqrt{5}}{2}$

$\sec \theta = -\sqrt{2}$ $\sec \theta = -\sqrt{5}$

$\cot \theta = -1$ $\cot \theta = \dfrac{1}{2}$

39. -1 **41.** Undefined   **43.** -1 **45.** Undefined

47. $\theta' = 60°$ **49.** $\theta' = 30°$

51. $\theta' = 45°$

53. $\theta' = \dfrac{\pi}{3}$

55. $\theta' = \dfrac{\pi}{6}$

57. $\theta' = \dfrac{\pi}{6}$

59. $\theta' = 28°$

61. $\theta' = 68°$

63. $\theta' = \dfrac{\pi}{5}$

65. $\theta' \approx 1.342$

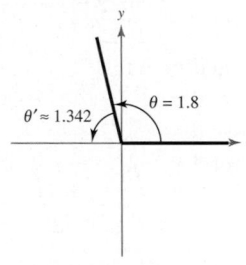

67. $\sin 225° = -\dfrac{\sqrt{2}}{2}$

$\cos 225° = -\dfrac{\sqrt{2}}{2}$

$\tan 225° = 1$

69. $\sin(-750°) = -\dfrac{1}{2}$

$\cos(-750°) = \dfrac{\sqrt{3}}{2}$

$\tan(-750°) = -\dfrac{\sqrt{3}}{3}$

71. $\sin \dfrac{5\pi}{3} = -\dfrac{\sqrt{3}}{2}$

$\cos \dfrac{5\pi}{3} = \dfrac{1}{2}$

$\tan \dfrac{5\pi}{3} = -\sqrt{3}$

73. $\sin\left(-\dfrac{5\pi}{6}\right) = -\dfrac{1}{2}$

$\cos\left(-\dfrac{5\pi}{6}\right) = -\dfrac{\sqrt{3}}{2}$

$\tan\left(-\dfrac{5\pi}{6}\right) = \dfrac{\sqrt{3}}{3}$

75. $\sin \dfrac{11\pi}{4} = \dfrac{\sqrt{2}}{2}$

$\cos \dfrac{11\pi}{4} = -\dfrac{\sqrt{2}}{2}$

$\tan \dfrac{11\pi}{4} = -1$

77. $\sin\left(-\dfrac{17\pi}{6}\right) = -\dfrac{1}{2}$

$\cos\left(-\dfrac{17\pi}{6}\right) = -\dfrac{\sqrt{3}}{2}$

$\tan\left(-\dfrac{17\pi}{6}\right) = \dfrac{\sqrt{3}}{3}$

79. $\dfrac{4}{5}$ **81.** $-\sqrt{3}$ **83.** $\dfrac{\sqrt{65}}{4}$

85. $\cos \theta = \dfrac{\sqrt{21}}{5}$

$\tan \theta = \dfrac{2\sqrt{21}}{21}$

$\csc \theta = \dfrac{5}{2}$

$\sec \theta = \dfrac{5\sqrt{21}}{21}$

$\cot \theta = \dfrac{\sqrt{21}}{2}$

87. $\sin \theta = \dfrac{4\sqrt{17}}{17}$

$\cos \theta = -\dfrac{\sqrt{17}}{17}$

$\csc \theta = \dfrac{\sqrt{17}}{4}$

$\sec \theta = -\sqrt{17}$

$\cot \theta = -\dfrac{1}{4}$

89. $\sin \theta = -\dfrac{2}{3}$

$\cos \theta = \dfrac{\sqrt{5}}{3}$

$\tan \theta = -\dfrac{2\sqrt{5}}{5}$

$\sec \theta = \dfrac{3\sqrt{5}}{5}$

$\cot \theta = -\dfrac{\sqrt{5}}{2}$

91. 0.1736 **93.** -1.7434 **95.** -0.3420

97. -0.1080 **99.** 0.8391 **101.** -2.9238

103. (a) $30° = \dfrac{\pi}{6}, 150° = \dfrac{5\pi}{6}$ (b) $210° = \dfrac{7\pi}{6}, 330° = \dfrac{11\pi}{6}$

105. (a) $60° = \dfrac{\pi}{3}, 120° = \dfrac{2\pi}{3}$ (b) $135° = \dfrac{3\pi}{4}, 315° = \dfrac{7\pi}{4}$

107. (a) $150° = \dfrac{5\pi}{6}, 210° = \dfrac{7\pi}{6}$ (b) $\dfrac{11\pi}{6} = 330°, \dfrac{5\pi}{6} = 150°$

109. (a) $\dfrac{1 + \sqrt{3}}{2}$ (b) $\dfrac{\sqrt{3} - 1}{2}$ (c) $\dfrac{3}{4}$

(d) $\dfrac{\sqrt{3}}{4}$ (e) $\dfrac{\sqrt{3}}{2}$ (f) $\dfrac{\sqrt{3}}{2}$

111. (a) 0 (b) $\sqrt{2}$ (c) $\dfrac{1}{2}$ (d) $-\dfrac{1}{2}$ (e) -1 (f) $\dfrac{\sqrt{2}}{2}$

113. (a) $\dfrac{-1 - \sqrt{3}}{2}$ (b) $\dfrac{1 - \sqrt{3}}{2}$ (c) $\dfrac{3}{4}$ (d) $\dfrac{\sqrt{3}}{4}$

(e) $\dfrac{\sqrt{3}}{2}$ (f) $-\dfrac{\sqrt{3}}{2}$

115. (a) $-\dfrac{1 + \sqrt{3}}{2}$ (b) $\dfrac{1 - \sqrt{3}}{2}$ (c) $\dfrac{3}{4}$ (d) $\dfrac{\sqrt{3}}{4}$

(e) $\dfrac{\sqrt{3}}{2}$ (f) $-\dfrac{\sqrt{3}}{2}$

117. (a) $-\dfrac{1 + \sqrt{3}}{2}$ (b) $\dfrac{-1 + \sqrt{3}}{2}$ (c) $\dfrac{1}{4}$ (d) $\dfrac{\sqrt{3}}{4}$

(e) $\dfrac{\sqrt{3}}{2}$ (f) $-\dfrac{1}{2}$

119. (a) 1 (b) -1 (c) 0 (d) 0 (e) 0 (f) 0

121. (a) -1 (b) 1 (c) 0 (d) 0 (e) 0 (f) 0

123. (a) 60.4°F (b) 92.4°F (c) 76.4°F

125. (a) 12 mi (b) 6 mi (c) 6.93 mi

127. True. $0 < \cos \theta < 1$ in Quadrant I, so

$$\sin \theta < \frac{\sin \theta}{\cos \theta} = \tan \theta.$$

129. False. Sine is positive in Quadrant II.

131.

θ	0°	20°	40°
$\sin \theta$	0	0.3420	0.6428
$\sin(180° - \theta)$	0	0.3420	0.6428

θ	60°	80°
$\sin \theta$	0.8660	0.9848
$\sin(180° - \theta)$	0.8660	0.9848

$\sin \theta = \sin(180° - \theta)$

133. The calculator mode is in degrees instead of radians.

135. 7 **137.** 3.449, -1.449 **139.** 4.908, -5.908

Section 4.5 (page 299)

1. amplitude **3.** $\dfrac{2\pi}{b}$ **5.** 2π

7. It vertically shifts the graph d units.

9. (a) $x = -2\pi, -\pi, 0, \pi, 2\pi$ (b) $y = 0$

(c) Increasing: $\left(-2\pi, -\dfrac{3\pi}{2}\right), \left(-\dfrac{\pi}{2}, \dfrac{\pi}{2}\right), \left(\dfrac{3\pi}{2}, 2\pi\right)$

Decreasing: $\left(-\dfrac{3\pi}{2}, -\dfrac{\pi}{2}\right), \left(\dfrac{\pi}{2}, \dfrac{3\pi}{2}\right)$

(d) Relative maxima: $\left(-\dfrac{3\pi}{2}, 1\right), \left(\dfrac{\pi}{2}, 1\right)$

Relative minima: $\left(-\dfrac{\pi}{2}, -1\right), \left(\dfrac{3\pi}{2}, -1\right)$

11. Period: π **13.** Period: 4π
Amplitude: 3 Amplitude: 5

15. Period: 2 **17.** Period: 2π
Amplitude: $\dfrac{2}{3}$ Amplitude: 2

19. Period: $\dfrac{3\pi}{2}$
Amplitude: $\dfrac{1}{4}$

21. g is a shift of f π units to the right.

23. g is a reflection of f in the x-axis.

25. g is a shift of f three units upward.

27. g is a reflection of f in the y-axis and has five times the amplitude of f.

29. g has twice the amplitude of f.

31. g is a horizontal shift of f π units to the right.

33. **35.**

37.

39. **41.**

43. **45.**

47. **49.**

51. **53.**

55.

57. **59.**
Amplitude: 2 Amplitude: 5
Period: 3 Period: 24

CHAPTER 4

61.

Amplitude: $\dfrac{2}{3}$

Period: 4π

63.

Amplitude: 2

Period: $\dfrac{\pi}{2}$

65.

Amplitude: 1

Period: 1

67.

Amplitude: 5

Period: π

69.

Amplitude: $\dfrac{1}{100}$

Period: $\dfrac{1}{60}$

71. $a = -4, d = 4$

73. $a = -1, d = -3$

75. $a = -3, b = 2, c = 0$

77. $a = 1, b = 1, c = \dfrac{\pi}{4}$

79.

$x = -\dfrac{5\pi}{6}, -\dfrac{\pi}{6}, \dfrac{7\pi}{6}, \dfrac{11\pi}{6}$

81.

80 beats/min

83. (a)

(b) Maximum sales: December
    Minimum sales: June

85. (a)

(b) Minimum height: 5 ft
    Maximum height: 55 ft

87. (a) and (c)

The model fits the data well.

(b) $y = 0.5 \sin(0.210x + 2.830) + 0.5$

(d) About 30 days   (e) About 70.8%

89. True. The period of $\sin x$ is 2π. Adding 2π moves the graph one period to the right.

91. False. The function $y = \tfrac{1}{2} \cos 2x$ has an amplitude that is one-half that of the function $y = \cos x$.

93.

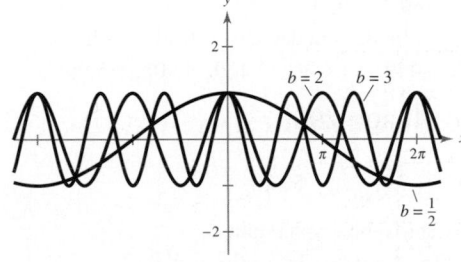

The value of b affects the period of the graph.

$b = \tfrac{1}{2} \rightarrow \tfrac{1}{2}$ cycle

$b = 2 \rightarrow 2$ cycles

$b = 3 \rightarrow 3$ cycles

95. a

97. (a)

Even

(b)

Even

(c)

Odd

99. (a)

x	-1	-0.1	-0.01
$\dfrac{\sin x}{x}$	0.8415	0.9983	1.0000

x	-0.001	0	0.001
$\dfrac{\sin x}{x}$	1.0000	Undefined	1.0000

x	0.01	0.1	1
$\dfrac{\sin x}{x}$	1.0000	0.9983	0.8415

(b)

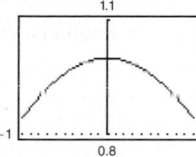

$f \to 1$ as $x \to 0$

(c) The ratio approaches 1 as x approaches 0.

101. (a)

The polynomial function is a good approximation of the sine function when x is close to 0.

(b)

The polynomial function is a good approximation of the cosine function when x is close to 0.

(c) $\sin x \approx x - \dfrac{x^3}{3!} + \dfrac{x^5}{5!} - \dfrac{x^7}{7!}$

$\cos x \approx 1 - \dfrac{x^2}{2!} + \dfrac{x^4}{4!} - \dfrac{x^6}{6!}$

The accuracy increased.

103.

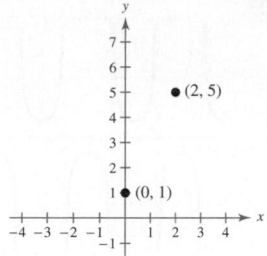

$m = 2$

105. 487.014°   **107.** Answers will vary.

Section 4.6   (page 311)

1. vertical   **3.** tangent, cotangent

5. (a) $x = -2\pi, -\pi, 0, \pi, 2\pi$ (b) $y = 0$

(c) Increasing on $\left(-2\pi, -\dfrac{3\pi}{2}\right), \left(-\dfrac{3\pi}{2}, -\dfrac{\pi}{2}\right), \left(-\dfrac{\pi}{2}, \dfrac{\pi}{2}\right),$
$\left(\dfrac{\pi}{2}, \dfrac{3\pi}{2}\right), \left(\dfrac{3\pi}{2}, 2\pi\right)$

(d) No relative extrema

(e) $x = -\dfrac{3\pi}{2}, -\dfrac{\pi}{2}, \dfrac{\pi}{2}, \dfrac{3\pi}{2}$

7. (a) No x-intercepts   (b) $y = 1$

(c) Increasing on $\left(-2\pi, -\dfrac{3\pi}{2}\right), \left(-\dfrac{3\pi}{2}, -\pi\right), \left(0, \dfrac{\pi}{2}\right), \left(\dfrac{\pi}{2}, \pi\right)$

Decreasing on $\left(-\pi, \dfrac{\pi}{2}\right), \left(\dfrac{\pi}{2}, 0\right), \left(\pi, \dfrac{3\pi}{2}\right), \left(\dfrac{3\pi}{2}, 2\pi\right)$

(d) Relative minima: $(-2\pi, 1), (0, 1), (2\pi, 1)$
Relative maxima: $(-\pi, -1), (\pi, -1)$

(e) $x = -\dfrac{3\pi}{2}, -\dfrac{\pi}{2}, \dfrac{\pi}{2}, \dfrac{3\pi}{2}$

9.

11.

13.

15.

17.

19.

CHAPTER 4

21.   **23.**

25.   **27.**

29.   **31.**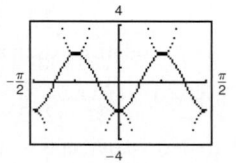

Answers will vary.   Answers will vary.

33.

Answers will vary.

35. $-5.498, -2.356, 0.785, 3.927$

37. $-5.236, -1.047, 1.047, 5.236$

39. $-3.665, -0.524, 2.618, 5.760$

41. Even   **43.** Odd   **45.** Odd

47.   **49.**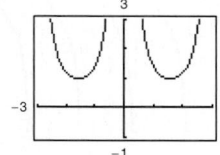

Equivalent   Equivalent

51. d; as x approaches 0, $f(x)$ approaches 0.

52. a; as x approaches 0, $f(x)$ approaches 0.

53. b; as x approaches 0, $g(x)$ approaches 0.

54. c; as x approaches 0, $g(x)$ approaches 0.

55.

$-e^{-x} \le e^{-x} \cos x \le e^{-x}$

Touches $y = \pm e^{-x}$ at $x = n\pi$

Intercepts at $x = \dfrac{\pi}{2} + n\pi$

57.

Touches $y = \pm 2^{-x^2/4}$ at $x = \dfrac{\pi}{2} + n\pi$

Intercepts at $x = n\pi$

59. (a) $f \to -\infty$ (b) $f \to \infty$ (c) $f \to -\infty$ (d) $f \to \infty$

61. (a) $f \to \infty$ (b) $f \to -\infty$ (c) $f \to -\infty$ (d) $f \to \infty$

63. $d = 7 \cot x$

65. (a)

(b) Not periodic and damped; approaches 0 as t increases.

67. (a) Yes. To each t there corresponds one and only one value of y.

(b) 1.3 oscillations/sec   (c) $y = 12(0.221)^t \cos(8.2t)$

(d) $y = 12e^{-1.5t} \cos(8.2t)$

(e)   Answers will vary.

69. True. The sine function is damped.

71. True. $\sec x = \csc\left(x - \dfrac{\pi}{2}\right) = \dfrac{1}{\sin\left(x - \dfrac{\pi}{2}\right)}$

73. (a)

(b) $\left(-1, \tfrac{1}{3}\right)$ (c) $\left(-1, \tfrac{1}{3}\right)$; The intervals are the same.

75. (a)

x	-1	-0.1	-0.01
$\dfrac{\tan x}{x}$	1.5574	1.0033	1.0000

x	-0.001	0	0.001
$\dfrac{\tan x}{x}$	1.0000	Undefined	1.0000

x	0.01	0.1	1
$\dfrac{\tan x}{x}$	1.0000	1.0033	1.5574

(b)

$f \to 1$ as $x \to 0$

(c) The ratio approaches 1 as x approaches 0.

77.

$y = \tan x$ $y = x + \dfrac{2x^3}{3!} + \dfrac{16x^5}{5!}$

The polynomial function is a good approximation of the tangent function when x is close to 0.

79. Distributive Property   81. Additive Identity Property

83. Not one-to-one

85. One-to-one. $f^{-1}(x) = \dfrac{x^2 + 14}{3}, x \geq 0$

87. Domain: all real numbers x
Intercepts: $(-4, 0), (1, 0), (0, -4)$
No asymptotes

89. Domain: all real numbers x
Intercept: $(0, 5)$
Asymptote: $y = 2$

Section 4.7   (page 322)

1. $y = \sin^{-1} x, -1 \leq x \leq 1$ 3. $\sin^{-1} x$ or $\arcsin x$

5. (a) $\dfrac{\pi}{6}$ (b) 0   7. (a) $-\dfrac{\pi}{2}$ (b) 0

9. (a) $\dfrac{\pi}{6}$ (b) Not possible   11. (a) $-\dfrac{\pi}{3}$ (b) $\dfrac{\pi}{6}$

13. (a) Not possible   (b) $-\dfrac{\pi}{6}$

15. (a)

x	-1	-0.8	-0.6	-0.4	-0.2
y	-1.571	-0.927	-0.644	-0.412	-0.201

x	0	0.2	0.4	0.6	0.8	1
y	0	0.201	0.412	0.644	0.927	1.571

(b)

(c)

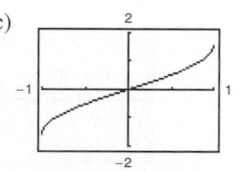

They are the same.

(d) Intercept: $(0, 0)$; symmetric about the origin

17. $\left(-\sqrt{3}, -\dfrac{\pi}{3}\right), \left(-\dfrac{\sqrt{3}}{3}, -\dfrac{\pi}{6}\right), \left(1, \dfrac{\pi}{4}\right)$ 19. 0.47

21. 0.64   23. Not possible   25. 2.69

27. -1.41 29. -0.85 31. 1.29

33.

35.

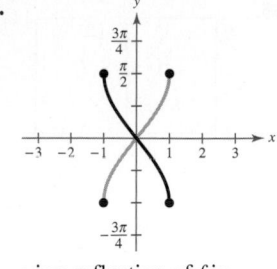

g is a horizontal shift of f three units to the left.

g is a reflection of f in the y-axis.

37.

39.

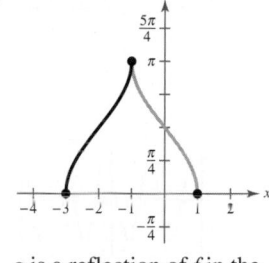

g is a horizontal shift of f π units to the left.

g is a reflection of f in the y-axis and a horizontal shift of f two units to the left.

41.

43.

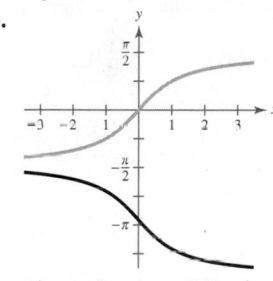

g is a vertical shift of f one unit upward.

g is a reflection of f in the x-axis and a vertical shift of f three units down.

45. $\theta = \arctan \dfrac{x}{8}$ 47. $\theta = \arcsin \dfrac{x + 2}{5}$

49. $\sqrt{4 - x^2}$; $\theta = \arcsin \dfrac{x}{2}, \theta = \arccos \dfrac{\sqrt{4 - x^2}}{2}$,

$\theta = \arctan \dfrac{x}{\sqrt{4 - x^2}}$

51. $\sqrt{x^2 + 2x + 5}$; $\theta = \arcsin \dfrac{x + 1}{\sqrt{x^2 + 2x + 5}}$,

$\theta = \arccos \dfrac{2}{\sqrt{x^2 + 2x + 5}}, \theta = \arctan \dfrac{x + 1}{2}$

53. 0.3   55. Not possible   57. -0.5 59. $-\dfrac{\pi}{6}$

61. $\dfrac{\pi}{2}$ 63. $\dfrac{\pi}{2}$ 65. $\dfrac{4}{5}$ 67. $\dfrac{5}{3}$ 69. $\dfrac{\sqrt{5}}{3}$

71. $-\dfrac{3\sqrt{7}}{7}$ 73. $\dfrac{1}{x}$ 75. $\sqrt{-x^2 - 4x - 3}$

77. $\dfrac{\sqrt{25 - x^2}}{x}$ 79. $\dfrac{\sqrt{x^2 + 7}}{x}$ 81. $\dfrac{14}{\sqrt{x^2 + 196}}$

83. $\dfrac{|x - 1|}{\sqrt{x^2 - 2x + 10}}$

CHAPTER 4

85.

87.

89.

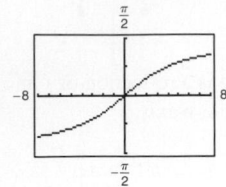

91. $3\sqrt{2} \sin\left(2t + \dfrac{\pi}{4}\right)$

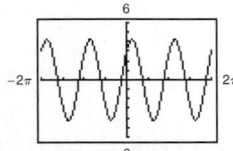

The two forms are equivalent.

93. $\dfrac{\pi}{2}$ **95.** $\dfrac{\pi}{2}$ **97.** π

99. (a)

(b) About 0.574 rad
(c) About 8.08 m

101. (a) $\theta = \arctan\dfrac{6}{x}$ (b) About 0.54 rad, about 1.11 rad

103. False. $5\pi/6$ is not in the range of the arcsine function.

105. False. Inverse trigonometric functions do not have the same relationships that trigonometric functions have.

107.

109.

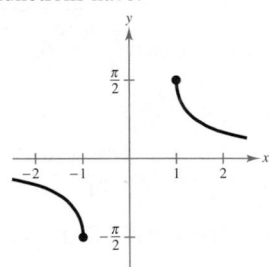

111. $\dfrac{\pi}{4}$ **113.** $\dfrac{5\pi}{6}$ **115 and 117.** Proofs

119. $\dfrac{\sqrt{2}}{2}$ **121.** $\dfrac{\sqrt{3}}{3}$

123. $\cos\theta = \dfrac{\sqrt{11}}{6}$

$\tan\theta = \dfrac{5\sqrt{11}}{11}$

$\csc\theta = \dfrac{6}{5}$

$\sec\theta = \dfrac{6\sqrt{11}}{11}$

$\cot\theta = \dfrac{\sqrt{11}}{5}$

125. $\sin\theta = \dfrac{\sqrt{7}}{4}$

$\tan\theta = \dfrac{\sqrt{7}}{3}$

$\csc\theta = \dfrac{4\sqrt{7}}{7}$

$\sec\theta = \dfrac{4}{3}$

$\cot\theta = \dfrac{3\sqrt{7}}{7}$

Section 4.8   (page 332)

1. harmonic motion   **3.** No
5. $B = 60°$ **7.** $A = 19°$ **9.** $A \approx 26.57°$
  $a \approx 5.77$ $a \approx 4.82$ $B \approx 63.43°$
  $c \approx 11.55$ $c \approx 14.81$ $c \approx 13.42$
11. $A \approx 17.24°$ **13.** $B = 77° \, 45'$
  $B \approx 72.76°$ $a \approx 91.34$
  $b \approx 51.58$ $b \approx 420.70$
15. 5.12 in.   **17.** 24.10 m   **19.** 19.32 ft   **21.** 113.63 ft
23. 2089.99 ft   **25.** 30.00 ft   **27.** 1933.32 ft
29. 3.23 mi   **31.** 75.97°   **33.** 5098.78 ft
35. (a) $h \approx 161.26$ ft

(b)

(c) $d = \dfrac{h}{\tan\theta}$

(d) 914.55; 443.060; 279.31; 192.18; 135.31
(e) No. Answers will vary.
37. (a) $l = \sqrt{h^2 + 28h + 10{,}196}$ (b) $\theta = \arccos\dfrac{100}{l}$

(c) $h \approx 56$ ft
39. (a) 61.82°; 15.64°   (b) 31.10 ft
41. 104.95 nm south, 58.18 nm west   **43.** N 56.31° W
45. (a) N 58° E   (b) 68.82 m   **47.** 78.69°   **49.** 35.26°
51. $y = \sqrt{3}\,r$ **53.** $a \approx 12.2, b \approx 7.0$
55. $d = 8 \sin \pi t$ **57.** $d = 3 \cos \dfrac{4\pi t}{3}$
59. (a) 4   (b) 4   (c) 4   (d) $\dfrac{1}{16}$
61. (a) $\dfrac{1}{16}$ (b) 70   (c) 0   (d) $\dfrac{1}{140}$
63. $\omega = 528\pi$
65. (a)

(b) $\dfrac{\pi}{8}$ sec   (c) $\dfrac{\pi}{32}$ sec

67. (a)

θ	L_1	L_2	$L_1 + L_2$
0.1	$\dfrac{8}{\sin 0.1}$	$\dfrac{6}{\cos 0.1}$	86.16
0.2	$\dfrac{8}{\sin 0.2}$	$\dfrac{6}{\cos 0.2}$	46.39
0.3	$\dfrac{8}{\sin 0.3}$	$\dfrac{6}{\cos 0.3}$	33.35
0.4	$\dfrac{8}{\sin 0.4}$	$\dfrac{6}{\cos 0.4}$	27.06

(b)

θ	L_1	L_2	$L_1 + L_2$
0.5	$\dfrac{8}{\sin 0.5}$	$\dfrac{6}{\cos 0.5}$	23.52
0.6	$\dfrac{8}{\sin 0.6}$	$\dfrac{6}{\cos 0.6}$	21.44
0.7	$\dfrac{8}{\sin 0.7}$	$\dfrac{6}{\cos 0.7}$	20.26
0.8	$\dfrac{8}{\sin 0.8}$	$\dfrac{6}{\cos 0.8}$	19.76

19.76 ft

(c) $L_1 + L_2 = \dfrac{8}{\sin \theta} + \dfrac{6}{\cos \theta}$

(d)

19.73 ft; They are almost identical.

69. (a) and (b)

$S = 3.15 \sin(0.524t + 1.5686) + 4$
The model fits the data well.

(c) 12 mo; Yes, sales of outerwear are seasonal.

(d) Maximum displacement of 3.15 million dollars from the average sales of 4 million dollars.

71. False. Sine or cosine is used to model harmonic motion.

73. S 58° E, N 58° W; Answers will vary.

75. $4x - y + 6 = 0$ **77.** $4x + 5y - 22 = 0$

79. All real numbers x **81.** All real numbers x

83. All real numbers x such that $x > 6$

Review Exercises   (page 340)

1. 1 rad

3. (a) 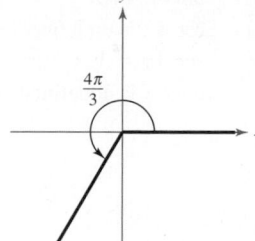   (b) Quadrant III

(c) $\dfrac{10\pi}{3}, -\dfrac{2\pi}{3}$

5. (a)   (b) Quadrant III

(c) $\dfrac{7\pi}{6}, -\dfrac{17\pi}{6}$

7. (a)   (b) Quadrant I

(c) 405°, −315°

9. (a)   (b) Quadrant IV

(c) 315°, −45°

11. −1.571   **13.** 8.343   **15.** 128.571°   **17.** −200.535°

19. 135.279°   **21.** −6.572°   **23.** 135° 17′24″

25. −85° 21′36″   **27.** Complement: $\dfrac{3\pi}{8}$; supplement: $\dfrac{7\pi}{8}$

29. Complement: none; supplement: $\dfrac{3\pi}{10}$

31. Complement: 85°; supplement: 175°

33. Complement: none; supplement: none

35. $\dfrac{6}{5}$ rad   **37.** $\dfrac{46\pi}{3}$ m   **39.** 6000π cm/min

41. $\left(\dfrac{\sqrt{2}}{2}, -\dfrac{\sqrt{2}}{2}\right)$ **43.** $\left(-\dfrac{\sqrt{3}}{2}, \dfrac{1}{2}\right)$

45. $\left(-\dfrac{1}{2}, -\dfrac{\sqrt{3}}{2}\right)$ **47.** $\left(-\dfrac{\sqrt{2}}{2}, \dfrac{\sqrt{2}}{2}\right)$

CHAPTER 4

49. $\sin \dfrac{4\pi}{3} = -\dfrac{\sqrt{3}}{2}$

$\cos \dfrac{4\pi}{3} = -\dfrac{1}{2}$

$\tan \dfrac{4\pi}{3} = \sqrt{3}$

$\csc \dfrac{4\pi}{3} = -\dfrac{2\sqrt{3}}{3}$

$\sec \dfrac{4\pi}{3} = -2$

$\cot \dfrac{4\pi}{3} = \dfrac{\sqrt{3}}{3}$

51. $\sin 4\pi = 0$

$\cos 4\pi = 1$

$\tan 4\pi = 0$

$\csc 4\pi$ is undefined.

$\sec 4\pi = 1$

$\cot 4\pi$ is undefined.

53. $\sin\left(-\dfrac{11\pi}{6}\right) = \dfrac{1}{2}$

$\cos\left(-\dfrac{11\pi}{6}\right) = \dfrac{\sqrt{3}}{2}$

$\tan\left(-\dfrac{11\pi}{6}\right) = \dfrac{\sqrt{3}}{3}$

$\csc\left(-\dfrac{11\pi}{6}\right) = 2$

$\sec\left(-\dfrac{11\pi}{6}\right) = \dfrac{2\sqrt{3}}{3}$

$\cot\left(-\dfrac{11\pi}{6}\right) = \sqrt{3}$

55. $\sin\left(-\dfrac{5\pi}{3}\right) = \dfrac{\sqrt{3}}{2}$

$\cos\left(-\dfrac{5\pi}{3}\right) = \dfrac{1}{2}$

$\tan\left(-\dfrac{5\pi}{3}\right) = \sqrt{3}$

$\csc\left(-\dfrac{5\pi}{3}\right) = \dfrac{2\sqrt{3}}{3}$

$\sec\left(-\dfrac{5\pi}{3}\right) = 2$

$\cot\left(-\dfrac{5\pi}{3}\right) = \dfrac{\sqrt{3}}{3}$

57. 1   **59.** $-\dfrac{1}{2}$ **61.** (a) $-\dfrac{3}{5}$ (b) $-\dfrac{5}{3}$

63. (a) $\dfrac{2}{3}$ (b) $\dfrac{3}{2}$ **65.** 0.5   **67.** -0.8935

69. $\sin \theta = \dfrac{\sqrt{65}}{9}$

$\cos \theta = \dfrac{4}{9}$

$\tan \theta = \dfrac{\sqrt{65}}{4}$

$\csc \theta = \dfrac{9\sqrt{65}}{65}$

$\sec \theta = \dfrac{9}{4}$

$\cot \theta = \dfrac{4\sqrt{65}}{65}$

71. $\sin \theta = \dfrac{5\sqrt{61}}{61}$

$\cos \theta = \dfrac{6\sqrt{61}}{61}$

$\tan \theta = \dfrac{5}{6}$

$\csc \theta = \dfrac{\sqrt{61}}{5}$

$\sec \theta = \dfrac{\sqrt{61}}{6}$

$\cot \theta = \dfrac{6}{5}$

73. $\sin \theta = \dfrac{7}{10}$

$\cos \theta = \dfrac{\sqrt{51}}{10}$

$\tan \theta = \dfrac{7\sqrt{51}}{51}$

$\csc \theta = \dfrac{10}{7}$

$\sec \theta = \dfrac{10\sqrt{51}}{51}$

$\cot \theta = \dfrac{\sqrt{51}}{7}$

75. 75. $\sin \theta = \dfrac{\sqrt{17}}{17}$

$\cos \theta = \dfrac{4\sqrt{17}}{17}$

$\tan \theta = \dfrac{1}{4}$

$\csc \theta = \sqrt{17}$

$\sec \theta = \dfrac{\sqrt{17}}{4}$

$\cot \theta = 4$

77. (a) 0.1045   (b) 0.1045   **79.** (a) 0.7071   (b) 1.4142

81. Answers will vary.   **83.** 235 ft

85. $\sin \theta = \dfrac{4}{5}$

$\cos \theta = \dfrac{3}{5}$

$\tan \theta = \dfrac{4}{3}$

$\csc \theta = \dfrac{5}{4}$

$\sec \theta = \dfrac{5}{3}$

$\cot \theta = \dfrac{3}{4}$

87. 87. $\sin \theta = \dfrac{2\sqrt{53}}{53}$

$\cos \theta = -\dfrac{7\sqrt{53}}{53}$

$\tan \theta = -\dfrac{2}{7}$

$\csc \theta = \dfrac{\sqrt{53}}{2}$

$\sec \theta = -\dfrac{\sqrt{53}}{7}$

$\cot \theta = -\dfrac{7}{2}$

89. $\sin \theta = \dfrac{15\sqrt{481}}{481}$

$\cos \theta = \dfrac{16\sqrt{481}}{481}$

$\tan \theta = \dfrac{15}{16}$

$\csc \theta = \dfrac{\sqrt{481}}{15}$

$\sec \theta = \dfrac{\sqrt{481}}{16}$

$\cot \theta = \dfrac{16}{15}$

91. $\sin \theta = -\dfrac{\sqrt{11}}{6}$

$\cos \theta = \dfrac{5}{6}$

$\tan \theta = -\dfrac{\sqrt{11}}{5}$

$\csc \theta = -\dfrac{6\sqrt{11}}{11}$

$\cot \theta = -\dfrac{5\sqrt{11}}{11}$

93. $\sin \theta = \dfrac{\sqrt{21}}{5}$

$\tan \theta = -\dfrac{\sqrt{21}}{2}$

$\csc \theta = \dfrac{5\sqrt{21}}{21}$

$\sec \theta = -\dfrac{5}{2}$

$\cot \theta = -\dfrac{2\sqrt{21}}{21}$

95. $\theta' = 30°$ **97.** $\theta' = \dfrac{\pi}{4}$

99. $\theta' = 84°$ **101.** $\theta' = \dfrac{\pi}{5}$

103. $\sin 240° = -\dfrac{\sqrt{3}}{2}$

$\cos 240° = -\dfrac{1}{2}$

$\tan 240° = \sqrt{3}$

105. $\sin(-225°) = \dfrac{\sqrt{2}}{2}$

$\cos(-225°) = -\dfrac{\sqrt{2}}{2}$

$\tan(-225°) = -1$

107. $\sin 4\pi = 0$

$\cos 4\pi = 1$

$\tan 4\pi = 0$

109. $\sin\left(-\dfrac{9\pi}{4}\right) = -\dfrac{\sqrt{2}}{2}$

$\cos\left(-\dfrac{9\pi}{4}\right) = \dfrac{\sqrt{2}}{2}$

$\tan\left(-\dfrac{9\pi}{4}\right) = -1$

111. 0.6494   **113.** 3.2361

115.

117.

119. Period: 2; amplitude: 5

121. Period: π; amplitude: 3.4

123.

125.

127.

129.

131.

133.

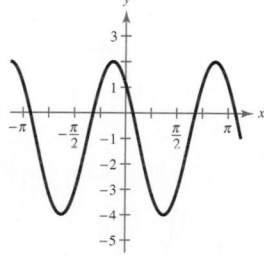

135. $a = 3, b = 2, c = 0$

137. $a = -\dfrac{3}{4}, b = 1, c = \dfrac{\pi}{4}$

Maximum sales: June

Minimum sales: December

139.

141.

143.

145.

147.

149.

151.

153.

155.

Answers will vary.

157.

Answers will vary.

159.

Answers will vary.

161.

Answers will vary.

163.

$-e^x \le e^x \sin 2x \le e^x$

Touches $y = \pm e^x$ at $x = \dfrac{\pi}{4} + \dfrac{n\pi}{2}$

Intercepts at $x = \dfrac{n\pi}{2}$

CHAPTER 4

165.

$-2x \le 2x \cos x \le 2x$

Touches $y = \pm 2x$ at $x = n\pi$

Intercepts at $x = \dfrac{\pi}{2} + n\pi$

167. (a) $-\dfrac{\pi}{6}$ (b) $\dfrac{5\pi}{6}$ **169.** (a) $\dfrac{\pi}{2}$ (b) $-\dfrac{\pi}{4}$

171. 1.14 **173.** -1.22 **175.** 1.52 **177.** 0.68

179. $\theta = \arcsin \dfrac{x}{16}$ **181.** $\dfrac{1}{\sqrt{1-x^2}}$ **183.** $\dfrac{2\sqrt{4-2x^2}}{4-x^2}$

185. 0.071 km   **187.** 9.47 mi   **189.** $d = 3 \cos \dfrac{2\pi t}{15}$

191. False. y is a function but is not one-to-one on $30° \le \theta \le 150°$.

193. False. Sine or cosine is used to model harmonic motion.

195. (a)

s	10	20	30
θ	1.28°	5.12°	11.40°

s	40	50	60
θ	19.72°	29.25°	38.88°

(b) θ is not a linear function of s.

197. (a)

The polynomial function is a good approximation for the arctangent function when x is close to 0.

(b) $\arctan x \approx x - \dfrac{x^3}{3} + \dfrac{x^5}{5} - \dfrac{x^7}{7} + \dfrac{x^9}{9}$

The accuracy of the approximation increases as additional terms are added.

Chapter Test   (page 345)

1. (a)

(b) Answers will vary. Sample answer: $\dfrac{11\pi}{3}, -\dfrac{\pi}{3}$

(c) $300°$

2. $44\frac{4}{9} \approx 44.44$ rad/sec

3. $\sin \theta = \dfrac{4\sqrt{17}}{17}$

$\cos \theta = -\dfrac{\sqrt{17}}{17}$

$\tan \theta = -4$

$\csc \theta = \dfrac{\sqrt{17}}{4}$

$\sec \theta = -\sqrt{17}$

$\cot \theta = -\dfrac{1}{4}$

4. $\sin \theta = \dfrac{7\sqrt{53}}{53}$

$\cos \theta = \dfrac{2\sqrt{53}}{53}$

$\csc \theta = \dfrac{\sqrt{53}}{7}$

$\sec \theta = \dfrac{\sqrt{53}}{2}$

$\cot \theta = \dfrac{2}{7}$

5. $\theta' = 75°$

6. Quadrant III

7. $150°, 210°$ **8.** $1.33, 1.81$

9. $\sin \theta = \dfrac{4}{5}$

$\tan \theta = -\dfrac{4}{3}$

$\csc \theta = \dfrac{5}{4}$

$\sec \theta = -\dfrac{5}{3}$

$\cot \theta = -\dfrac{3}{4}$

10.

11.

12.

13.

14.

15.

16.

Period: 2

17.

Not periodic

18. $a = 2, b = \dfrac{1}{2}, c = -\dfrac{\pi}{4}$ **19.** $\dfrac{\sqrt{5}}{2}$

20.

21.

22.

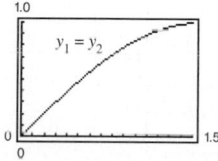

23. $231.34°$

24. $d = -6 \cos \pi t$

Chapter 5

Section 5.1 (page 354)

1. (a) iii (b) i (c) ii **3.** $\sin u$ **5.** $\sec u$

7. $\tan x = \dfrac{\sqrt{3}}{3}$

$\csc x = 2$

$\sec x = \dfrac{2\sqrt{3}}{3}$

$\cot x = \sqrt{3}$

9. $\cos \theta = \dfrac{\sqrt{2}}{2}$

$\tan \theta = -1$

$\csc \theta = -\sqrt{2}$

$\sec \theta = \sqrt{2}$

11. $\sin x = -\dfrac{7}{25}$

$\cos x = -\dfrac{24}{25}$

$\csc x = -\dfrac{25}{7}$

$\cot x = \dfrac{24}{7}$

13. $\cos \phi = -\dfrac{15}{17}$

$\tan \phi = -\dfrac{8}{15}$

$\csc \phi = \dfrac{17}{8}$

$\cot \phi = -\dfrac{15}{8}$

15. $\sin x = \dfrac{2}{3}$

$\cos x = -\dfrac{\sqrt{5}}{3}$

$\csc x = \dfrac{3}{2}$

$\sec x = -\dfrac{3\sqrt{5}}{5}$

$\cot x = -\dfrac{\sqrt{5}}{2}$

17. $\sin \theta = -\dfrac{2\sqrt{5}}{5}$

$\cos \theta = -\dfrac{\sqrt{5}}{5}$

$\csc \theta = -\dfrac{\sqrt{5}}{2}$

$\sec \theta = -\sqrt{5}$

$\cot \theta = \dfrac{1}{2}$

19. $\sin \theta = 0$

$\cos \theta = -1$

$\tan \theta = 0$

$\sec \theta = -1$

$\cot \theta$ is undefined.

21. d **22.** a **23.** b **24.** f **25.** e **26.** c
27. b **28.** c **29.** f **30.** a **31.** e **32.** d
33. $\cos x$ **35.** $\cos^2 \phi$ **37.** $\sec x$ **39.** 1 **41.** $\cot x$

43. $1 + \sin y$ **45.** $\cos^2 x$ **47.** $\cos x + 2$ **49.** $\sec^4 x$
51. $\sin^2 x - \cos^2 x$ **53.** $(\csc x - 1) \cot^2 x$
55. $1 + 2 \sin x \cos x$ **57.** $\cot^2 x$ **59.** $2 \csc^2 x$
61. $-\cot x$ **63.** $2 \sec x$ **65.** $\cos x$
67. $1 + \cos y$ **69.** $3(\sec x + \tan x)$

71.

x	0.2	0.4	0.6	0.8
y_1	0.1987	0.3894	0.5646	0.7174
y_2	0.1987	0.3894	0.5646	0.7174

x	1.0	1.2	1.4
y_1	0.8415	0.9320	0.9854
y_2	0.8415	0.9320	0.9854

73.

x	0.2	0.4	0.6	0.8
y_1	1.2230	1.5085	1.8958	2.4650
y_2	1.2230	1.5085	1.8958	2.4650

x	1.0	1.2	1.4
y_1	3.4082	5.3319	11.6814
y_2	3.4082	5.3319	11.6814

75. $\csc x$ **77.** $\tan x$ **79.** $5 \cos \theta$ **81.** $3 \sec \theta$
83. $7 \cos \theta$ **85.** $3 \sec \theta$ **87.** $\sqrt{2} \cos \theta$ **89.** $27 \sec^3 \theta$

91. $0 \le \theta \le \pi$ **93.** $0 \le \theta < \dfrac{\pi}{2}, \dfrac{3\pi}{2} < \theta < 2\pi$

95. $\ln|\cot \theta|$ **97.** $\ln|\tan x|$ **99.** $\ln|(\cos x)(1 + \sin x)|$
101. (a) and (b) Answers will vary.
103. (a) and (b) Answers will vary. **105.** $\mu = \tan \theta$

107. Answers will vary. **109.** False. $\cos 0 \cdot \sec \dfrac{\pi}{4} \ne 1$

111. 1, 1 **113.** $-\infty, 0$
115. $\cos \theta = \pm\sqrt{1 - \sin^2 \theta}$

$\tan \theta = \pm\dfrac{\sin \theta}{\sqrt{1 - \sin^2 \theta}}$

$\csc \theta = \dfrac{1}{\sin \theta}$

$\sec \theta = \pm\dfrac{1}{\sqrt{1 - \sin^2 \theta}}$

$\cot \theta = \pm\dfrac{\sqrt{1 - \sin^2 \theta}}{\sin \theta}$

The sign depends on the choice of θ.

117. $\dfrac{\sin \theta}{\cos \theta}$ **119.** $\dfrac{x^2 + 6x - 8}{(x + 5)(x - 8)}$ **121.** $\dfrac{-x^3 - 5x^2 + 4x}{(x - 5)(x + 5)}$

123.   **125.**

Section 5.2 (page 362)

1. $\cot u$ **3.** $\tan u$ **5.** $\cos^2 u$ **7.** $\cos u$ **9.** No

11–19. Answers will vary.

21.

x	0.2	0.4	0.6	0.8
y_1	1.0203	1.0857	1.2116	1.4353
y_2	1.0203	1.0857	1.2116	1.4353

x	1.0	1.2	1.4
y_1	1.8508	2.7597	5.8835
y_2	1.8508	2.7597	5.8835

23.

x	0.2	0.4	0.6	0.8
y_1	24.3360	5.5943	2.1366	0.9433
y_2	24.3360	5.5943	2.1366	0.9433

x	1.0	1.2	1.4
y_1	0.4123	0.1511	0.0297
y_2	0.4123	0.1511	0.0297

25.

x	0.2	0.4	0.6	0.8
y_1	4.8348	2.1785	1.2064	0.6767
y_2	4.8348	2.1785	1.2064	0.6767

x	1.0	1.2	1.4
y_1	0.3469	0.1409	0.0293
y_2	0.3469	0.1409	0.0293

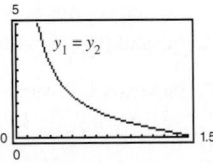

27.

x	0.2	0.4	0.6	0.8
y_1	5.0335	2.5679	1.7710	1.3940
y_2	5.0335	2.5679	1.7710	1.3940

x	1.0	1.2	1.4
y_1	1.1884	1.0729	1.0148
y_2	1.1884	1.0729	1.0148

29.

x	0.2	0.4	0.6	0.8
y_1	5.1359	2.7880	2.1458	2.0009
y_2	5.1359	2.7880	2.1458	2.0009

x	1.0	1.2	1.4
y_1	2.1995	2.9609	5.9704
y_2	2.1995	2.9609	5.9704

31. $\cot(-x) = -\cot(x)$ **33.** $(\tan^2 x)^2$

35–59. Answers will vary.

61.   **63.**

$y = 1$ $\qquad\qquad$ $y = \sin x$

65. Answers will vary. **67.** 1 **69.** 2

71–77. Answers will vary.

79. (a) Answers will vary.

(b)

θ	15°	30°	45°	60°	75°	90°
s	18.66	8.66	5	2.88	1.34	0

(c) Maximum: 15°

Minimum: 90°

(d) Noon

81. False. $\sin^2\left(\dfrac{\pi}{4}\right) + \cos^2\left(\dfrac{\pi}{4}\right) \neq 1 + \tan^2\left(\dfrac{\pi}{4}\right)$

83. (a) Answers will vary.

(b) No. Division by zero.

85. $a \cos \theta$ **87.** $a \sec \theta$ **89.** $\sqrt{\sec^2 x - 1} = |\tan x|; \dfrac{3\pi}{4}$

91. $1 - \cos^2 \theta = \sin^2 \theta; \pi$ **93.** Answers will vary.

95.

x	-4	-2	0	2	3
y	3.0625	3.25	4	7	11

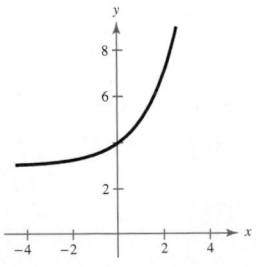

Horizontal asymptote at $y = 3$

97.

x	-3	-2	0	2	4
y	7	3	0	-0.75	-0.9375

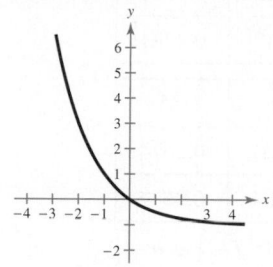

Horizontal asymptote at $y = -1$

Section 5.3   (page 373)

1. general   **3.** No   **5–9.** Answers will vary.
11. $0°, 180°$ **13.** $135°, 225°$ **15.** $45°, 225°$
17. $\dfrac{5\pi}{6}, \dfrac{7\pi}{6}$ **19.** $\dfrac{3\pi}{4}, \dfrac{7\pi}{4}$ **21.** $\dfrac{5\pi}{6}, \dfrac{11\pi}{6}$ **23.** $\dfrac{7\pi}{6}, \dfrac{11\pi}{6}$
25. $\dfrac{\pi}{6}, \dfrac{7\pi}{6}$ **27.** $\dfrac{3\pi}{4}, \dfrac{7\pi}{4}$ **29.** $\dfrac{7\pi}{6} + 2n\pi, \dfrac{11\pi}{6} + 2n\pi$
31. $\dfrac{\pi}{3} + 2n\pi, \dfrac{2\pi}{3} + 2n\pi$ **33.** $\dfrac{\pi}{6} + n\pi, \dfrac{5\pi}{6} + n\pi$
35. $n\pi, \dfrac{3\pi}{2} + 2n\pi$ **37.** $\dfrac{2\pi}{3}, \dfrac{4\pi}{3}$ **39.** $\dfrac{\pi}{4}, \dfrac{3\pi}{4}, \dfrac{5\pi}{4}, \dfrac{7\pi}{4}$
41. $0, \dfrac{\pi}{2}, \pi, \dfrac{3\pi}{2}$ **43.** $\dfrac{\pi}{2}, \dfrac{3\pi}{2}$ **45.** No solution   **47.** $0, \pi$
49. $3.6652, 4.7124, 5.7596$ **51.** $0.8614, 5.4218$
53. 1.5708 **55.** $0.5236, 2.6180$
57. (a)

(b) $\sin 2x = x^2 - 2x$
(c) $(0, 0), (1.7757, -0.3984)$

59. (a)

(b) $\sin^2 x = e^x - 4x$
(c) $(0.3194, 0.0986),$
$(2.2680, 0.5878)$

61. $2\pi + 4n\pi$ **63.** $\dfrac{\pi}{16} + \dfrac{n\pi}{4}$ **65.** $\dfrac{\pi}{12} + \dfrac{n\pi}{2}, \dfrac{5\pi}{12} + \dfrac{n\pi}{2}$
67. $\dfrac{\pi}{2} + 4n\pi, \dfrac{7\pi}{2} + 4n\pi$ **69.** $x = -1, 3$
71. $x = \pm 2$ **73.** $1.1071, 4.2487$ **75.** $0.8603, 3.4256$
77. $0, 2.6779, 3.1416, 5.8195$
79. $0.5236, 0.7297, 2.4119, 2.6180$
81. $\arctan 3 + n\pi, \arctan(-4) + n\pi$
83. $\dfrac{\pi}{4} + n\pi, \arctan 5 + n\pi$ **85.** $\dfrac{5\pi}{3} + 2n\pi, \dfrac{\pi}{3} + 2n\pi$
87. $-1.154, 0.534$ **89.** 1.110

91. (a)

Maxima: $(0.7854, 1), (3.9270, 1)$
Minima: $(2.3562, -1), (5.4978, -1)$
(b) $\dfrac{\pi}{4}, \dfrac{3\pi}{4}, \dfrac{5\pi}{4}, \dfrac{7\pi}{4}$

93. (a)

Maxima: $(1.0472, 1.25), (5.2360, 1.25)$
Minima: $(0, 1), (3.1416, -1), (6.2832, 1)$
(b) $0, \dfrac{\pi}{3}, \pi, \dfrac{5\pi}{3}, 2\pi$

95. (a)

Maximum: $(0.7854, 1.4142)$
Minimum: $(3.9270, -1.4142)$
(b) $\dfrac{\pi}{4}, \dfrac{5\pi}{4}$

97. 1   **99.** May, June, July
101. (a) All real numbers x except $x = 0$
(b) y-axis symmetry; horizontal asymptote: $y = 1$
(c) Oscillates   (d) Infinite number of solutions
(e) Yes. 0.6366
103. 0.04 sec, 0.43 sec, 0.83 sec   **105.** $41.37°, 48.63°$
107. (a)

$x \approx 0.86, A \approx 1.12$
(b) $0.6100 < x < 1.0980$
109. 1
111. False. The range of the sine function does not include 3.4.
113. Answers will vary.   **115.** 2.164 rad
117. -3.763 rad   **119.** Answers will vary.

Section 5.4   (page 381)

1. $\sin u \cos v - \cos u \sin v$ **3.** $\dfrac{\tan u + \tan v}{1 - \tan u \tan v}$
5. $\cos u \cos v + \sin u \sin v$
7. Sample answer: $\sin(135° + 60°)$ **9.** (a) $-\dfrac{1}{2}$ (b) $-\dfrac{3}{2}$
11. (a) -1 (b) $\dfrac{1 + \sqrt{3}}{2}$

13. $\sin 105° = \dfrac{\sqrt{2} + \sqrt{6}}{4}$

$\cos 105° = \dfrac{\sqrt{2} - \sqrt{6}}{4}$

$\tan 105° = -2 - \sqrt{3}$

15. $\sin 195° = \dfrac{\sqrt{2} - \sqrt{6}}{4}$

$\cos 195° = -\dfrac{\sqrt{2} + \sqrt{6}}{4}$

$\tan 195° = 2 - \sqrt{3}$

17. $\sin\left(-\dfrac{11\pi}{12}\right) = \dfrac{\sqrt{2} - \sqrt{6}}{4}$

$\cos\left(-\dfrac{11\pi}{12}\right) = -\dfrac{\sqrt{2} + \sqrt{6}}{4}$

$\tan\left(-\dfrac{11\pi}{12}\right) = 2 - \sqrt{3}$

19. $\sin 285° = -\dfrac{\sqrt{2} + \sqrt{6}}{4}$

$\cos 285° = \dfrac{\sqrt{6} - \sqrt{2}}{4}$

$\tan 285° = -2 - \sqrt{3}$

21. $\sin(-105°) = -\dfrac{\sqrt{2} + \sqrt{6}}{4}$

$\cos(-105°) = \dfrac{\sqrt{2} - \sqrt{6}}{4}$

$\tan(-105°) = 2 + \sqrt{3}$

23. $\sin\dfrac{13\pi}{12} = \dfrac{\sqrt{2} - \sqrt{6}}{4}$

$\cos\dfrac{13\pi}{12} = -\dfrac{\sqrt{2} + \sqrt{6}}{4}$

$\tan\dfrac{13\pi}{12} = 2 - \sqrt{3}$

25. $\sin\left(-\dfrac{7\pi}{12}\right) = -\dfrac{\sqrt{2} + \sqrt{6}}{4}$

$\cos\left(-\dfrac{7\pi}{12}\right) = \dfrac{\sqrt{2} - \sqrt{6}}{4}$

$\tan\left(-\dfrac{7\pi}{12}\right) = 2 + \sqrt{3}$

27. $\sin 50°$ **29.** $\tan 209°$ **31.** $\cos\dfrac{16\pi}{63}$

33. $\sin(3.5x + 1.2y)$ **35.** $\dfrac{\sqrt{3}}{2}$ **37.** $\dfrac{\sqrt{3}}{2}$ **39.** $-\sqrt{3}$

41.

x	0.2	0.4	0.6	0.8
y_1	0.9605	0.8484	0.6812	0.4854
y_2	0.9605	0.8484	0.6812	0.4854

x	1.0	1.2	1.4
y_1	0.2919	0.1313	0.0289
y_2	0.2919	0.1313	0.0289

43. $-\dfrac{63}{65}$ **45.** $\dfrac{56}{65}$ **47.** $\dfrac{4}{3}$ **49.** $\dfrac{44}{125}$ **51.** 1

53. $\dfrac{2x^2 - \sqrt{1 - x^2}}{\sqrt{4x^2 + 1}}$ **55.** 0   **57.** 1   **59.** $\dfrac{24}{25}$

61–67. Answers will vary.   **69.** $\dfrac{\pi}{2}$ **71.** $0, \dfrac{\pi}{3}, \pi, \dfrac{5\pi}{3}$

73. 0.7854, 5.4978   **75.** $\dfrac{\pi}{2}, \pi, \dfrac{3\pi}{2}$ **77.** Answers will vary.

79. False. $\cos(u \pm v) = \cos u \cos v \mp \sin u \sin v$

81. (a) All real numbers h except $h = 0$

(b)

h	0.01	0.02	0.05
$f(h)$	0.4957	0.4913	0.4781
$g(h)$	0.4957	0.4913	0.4781

h	0.1	0.2	0.5
$f(h)$	0.4559	0.4104	0.2674
$g(h)$	0.4559	0.4104	0.2674

(c)

(d) $f \to \frac{1}{2}$ as $h \to 0$

$g \to \frac{1}{2}$ as $h \to 0$

83 and 85. Answers will vary.

87. (a) $\sqrt{2}\sin\left(\theta + \dfrac{\pi}{4}\right)$ (b) $\sqrt{2}\cos\left(\theta - \dfrac{\pi}{4}\right)$

89. (a) $13\sin(3\theta + 0.3948)$ (b) $13\cos(3\theta - 1.1760)$

91. $2\cos\theta$ **93.** $15°$

95. $u + v = w$. Answers will vary.   **97.** $(0, 19), (38, 0)$

99. $(0, 4), (2, 0), (7, 0)$

Section 5.5   (page 390)

1. $\dfrac{1 + \cos 2u}{2}$ **3.** $-2\sin\left(\dfrac{u + v}{2}\right)\sin\left(\dfrac{u - v}{2}\right)$

5. $\tan\dfrac{u}{2}$ **7.** (a) ii   (b) i   (c) iii

9. (a) $\dfrac{3}{5}$ (b) $\dfrac{4}{5}$ (c) $\dfrac{3}{4}$ (d) $\dfrac{24}{25}$

(e) $\dfrac{7}{25}$ (f) $\dfrac{25}{7}$ (g) $\dfrac{25}{24}$ (h) $\dfrac{7}{24}$

11. $0, 1.0472, 3.1416, 5.2360; 0, \dfrac{\pi}{3}, \pi, \dfrac{5\pi}{3}$

13. $0.2618, 1.3090, 3.4034, 4.4506; \dfrac{\pi}{12}, \dfrac{5\pi}{12}, \dfrac{13\pi}{12}, \dfrac{17\pi}{12}$

15. $0, 2.0944, 4.1888; 0, \dfrac{2\pi}{3}, \dfrac{4\pi}{3}$

17. $0, 1.5708, 3.1416, 4.7124; 0, \dfrac{\pi}{2}, \pi, \dfrac{3\pi}{2}$

19. $0.5236, 1.5708, 2.6180, 3.6652, 4.7124, 5.7596;$

$\dfrac{\pi}{6}, \dfrac{\pi}{2}, \dfrac{5\pi}{6}, \dfrac{7\pi}{6}, \dfrac{3\pi}{2}, \dfrac{11\pi}{6}$

21. $\sin 2u = -\dfrac{24}{25}$

$\cos 2u = \dfrac{7}{25}$

$\tan 2u = -\dfrac{24}{7}$

23. $\sin 2u = \dfrac{4}{5}$

$\cos 2u = \dfrac{3}{5}$

$\tan 2u = \dfrac{4}{3}$

25. $\sin 2u = -\dfrac{\sqrt{3}}{2}$

$\cos 2u = -\dfrac{1}{2}$

$\tan 2u = \sqrt{3}$

27. $3\sin 2x$ **29.** $\frac{1}{2}\cos 2x$

31. $\dfrac{1 - \cos 2x}{2}$ **33.** $\dfrac{\cos x + \cos x \cos 2x}{2}$

35. $\frac{1}{8}(3 + 4 \cos 2x + \cos 4x)$

37. $\frac{1}{128}(35 - 48 \cos 2x + 28 \cos 4x - 16 \cos 2x \cos 4x + \cos 8x)$

39. $\frac{1}{32}(2 + \cos 2x - 2 \cos 4x - \cos 6x)$ **41.** $\frac{1}{2}(1 - \cos 4x)$

43. $\frac{1}{2}(1 + \cos x)$ **45.** $\frac{1}{2}(1 - \cos 2x)$

47. $\frac{1}{8}(3 - 4 \cos x + \cos 2x)$

49. (a) $\dfrac{4\sqrt{17}}{17}$ (b) $\dfrac{\sqrt{17}}{17}$ (c) $\dfrac{1}{4}$ (d) $\dfrac{\sqrt{17}}{4}$

  (e) $\sqrt{17}$ (f) 4 (g) $\dfrac{8}{17}$ (h) $\dfrac{2\sqrt{17}}{17}$

51. $\sin 75° = \dfrac{\sqrt{2 + \sqrt{3}}}{2}$ **53.** $\sin 112° \, 30' = \dfrac{\sqrt{2 + \sqrt{2}}}{2}$

  $\cos 75° = \dfrac{\sqrt{2 - \sqrt{3}}}{2}$ $\cos 112° \, 30' = -\dfrac{\sqrt{2 - \sqrt{2}}}{2}$

  $\tan 75° = \sqrt{3} + 2$ $\tan 112° \, 30' = -1 - \sqrt{2}$

55. $\sin \dfrac{\pi}{8} = \dfrac{\sqrt{2 - \sqrt{2}}}{2}$ **57.** $\sin \dfrac{7\pi}{12} = \dfrac{\sqrt{2 + \sqrt{3}}}{2}$

  $\cos \dfrac{\pi}{8} = \dfrac{\sqrt{2 + \sqrt{2}}}{2}$ $\cos \dfrac{7\pi}{12} = -\dfrac{\sqrt{2 - \sqrt{3}}}{2}$

  $\tan \dfrac{\pi}{8} = \sqrt{2} - 1$ $\tan \dfrac{7\pi}{12} = -2 - \sqrt{3}$

59. $\sin \dfrac{u}{2} = \dfrac{3}{5}$ **61.** $\sin \dfrac{u}{2} = \dfrac{\sqrt{50 + 15\sqrt{10}}}{10}$

  $\cos \dfrac{u}{2} = \dfrac{4}{5}$ $\cos \dfrac{u}{2} = -\dfrac{\sqrt{50 - 15\sqrt{10}}}{10}$

  $\tan \dfrac{u}{2} = \dfrac{3}{4}$ $\tan \dfrac{u}{2} = -\sqrt{10} - 3$

63. $\sin \dfrac{u}{2} = \dfrac{3\sqrt{10}}{10}$

  $\cos \dfrac{u}{2} = -\dfrac{\sqrt{10}}{10}$

  $\tan \dfrac{u}{2} = -3$

65. $|\sin 3x|$ **67.** $-|\tan 4x|$ **69.** π **71.** $\dfrac{\pi}{3}, \pi, \dfrac{5\pi}{3}$

73. $5(\cos 60° + \cos 90°)$ **75.** $3\left(\sin \dfrac{2\pi}{3} + \sin 0\right)$

77. $\dfrac{5}{2}(\cos 2\theta - \cos 4\theta)$ **79.** $\frac{1}{2}(\sin 2x + \sin 2y)$

81. $2 \cos 3\theta \sin 2\theta$ **83.** $2 \cos 4x \cos 2x$

85. $2 \cos \alpha \sin \beta$ **87.** $-2 \sin \theta \sin \dfrac{\pi}{2}$ **89.** $\dfrac{\sqrt{6}}{2}$

91. $-\sqrt{2}$ **93.** $0, \dfrac{\pi}{4}, \dfrac{\pi}{2}, \dfrac{3\pi}{4}, \pi, \dfrac{5\pi}{4}, \dfrac{3\pi}{2}, \dfrac{7\pi}{4}$ **95.** $\dfrac{\pi}{6}, \dfrac{5\pi}{6}$

97. $\frac{25}{169}$ **99.** $\frac{4}{13}$ **101–113.** Answers will vary.

115. $2x\sqrt{1 - x^2}$ **117.** $1 - 2x^2$ **119.** $\dfrac{2x}{x^2 + 1}$

121. (a) $x = 0, \dfrac{\pi}{3}, \pi, \dfrac{5\pi}{3}, 2\pi$

  (b) $x = \arccos \dfrac{1 \pm \sqrt{33}}{8}, 2\pi - \arccos \dfrac{1 \pm \sqrt{33}}{8}$

123. $23.85°$ **125.** $x = 2r(1 - \cos \theta)$

127. False. $\sin \dfrac{x}{2} = -\sqrt{\dfrac{1 - \cos x}{2}}$ for $\pi \le \dfrac{x}{2} \le 2\pi$.

129. (a) $f(x) = \dfrac{3}{4} + \dfrac{\cos 4x}{4}$

  (b) Answers will vary.

    Sample answer: $f(x) = \frac{1}{2}(1 + \cos^2 2x)$

  (c)–(e) Answers will vary.

131. (a)   (b) $2\sqrt{10}$ (c) $(2, 3)$

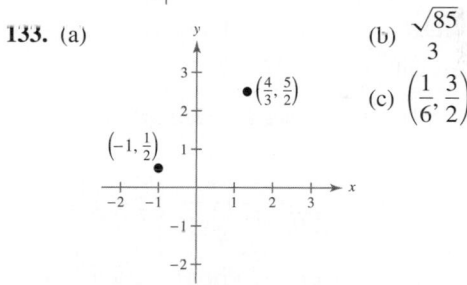

133. (a)   (b) $\dfrac{\sqrt{85}}{3}$ (c) $\left(\dfrac{1}{6}, \dfrac{3}{2}\right)$

135. (a) Complement: $35°$; supplement: $125°$

  (b) Complement: none; supplement: $18°$

137. (a) Complement: $\dfrac{4\pi}{9}$; supplement: $\dfrac{17\pi}{18}$

  (b) Complement: $\dfrac{\pi}{20}$; supplement: $\dfrac{11\pi}{20}$

139. 12.8282 cm

Review Exercises   (page 396)

1. $\sec x$ **3.** $\cos x$ **5.** $|\sin x|$ **7.** $\tan x$ **9.** $\sec x$

11. $\tan x = \dfrac{4}{3}$ **13.** $\cos x = \dfrac{\sqrt{2}}{2}$

  $\csc x = \frac{5}{4}$ $\tan x = -1$

  $\sec x = \frac{5}{3}$ $\csc x = -\sqrt{2}$

  $\cot x = \frac{3}{4}$ $\sec x = \sqrt{2}$

    $\cot x = -1$

15. $\cos^2 x$ **17.** $-\sin \theta$ **19.** 1 **21.** $\csc x$

23. $\sec x + 1$ **25–37.** Answers will vary.

39. $\dfrac{\pi}{6} + 2n\pi, \dfrac{5\pi}{6} + 2n\pi$ **41.** $\dfrac{\pi}{3} + 2n\pi, \dfrac{2\pi}{3} + 2n\pi$

43. $\dfrac{\pi}{3} + n\pi$ **45.** $\dfrac{\pi}{3} + n\pi, \dfrac{2\pi}{3} + n\pi$

47. $\dfrac{\pi}{3} + 2n\pi, \dfrac{\pi}{2} + n\pi, \dfrac{5\pi}{3} + 2n\pi$ **49.** $n\pi$

51. $0, \dfrac{2\pi}{3}, \dfrac{4\pi}{3}$ **53.** $0, \dfrac{\pi}{2}, \pi$ **55.** $\dfrac{\pi}{8}, \dfrac{3\pi}{8}, \dfrac{9\pi}{8}, \dfrac{11\pi}{8}$

57. $\dfrac{\pi}{3}, \dfrac{5\pi}{3}$ **59.** $\dfrac{7\pi}{12} + n\pi, \dfrac{11\pi}{12} + n\pi$ **61.** $\dfrac{\pi}{12} + \dfrac{n\pi}{6}$

63. $n\pi, \arctan 2 + n\pi$

65. $\dfrac{3\pi}{2} + 2n\pi, \arcsin\left(\dfrac{2}{3}\right) + 2n\pi, -\arcsin\left(\dfrac{2}{3}\right) + (2n+1)\pi$

67. $\sin 285° = -\dfrac{\sqrt{2} + \sqrt{6}}{4}$ **69.** $\sin\dfrac{31\pi}{12} = \dfrac{\sqrt{2} + \sqrt{6}}{4}$

$\cos 285° = \dfrac{\sqrt{6} - \sqrt{2}}{4}$ $\cos\dfrac{31\pi}{12} = \dfrac{\sqrt{2} - \sqrt{6}}{4}$

$\tan 285° = -2 - \sqrt{3}$ $\tan\dfrac{31\pi}{12} = -2 - \sqrt{3}$

71. $\sin(-15°)$ **73.** $\tan 75°$ **75.** $-\dfrac{4}{5}$ **77.** $-\dfrac{44}{117}$

79. $\dfrac{3}{5}$ **81–85.** Answers will vary.   **87.** $\dfrac{\pi}{4}, \dfrac{7\pi}{4}$

89. $\sin 2u = \dfrac{20\sqrt{6}}{49}$ **91.** $\sin 2u = -\dfrac{36}{85}$

$\cos 2u = -\dfrac{1}{49}$ $\cos 2u = \dfrac{77}{85}$

$\tan 2u = -20\sqrt{6}$ $\tan 2u = -\dfrac{36}{77}$

93 and 95. Answers will vary.   **97.** $15°, 75°$

99. $\dfrac{1 - \cos 8x}{1 + \cos 8x}$ **101.** $\dfrac{1}{8}(3 + 4\cos 4x + \cos 8x)$

103. $\dfrac{1}{128}(3 - 4\cos 4x + \cos 8x)$

105. $\sin 15° = \dfrac{\sqrt{2 - \sqrt{3}}}{2}$ **107.** $\sin\dfrac{7\pi}{8} = \dfrac{\sqrt{2 - \sqrt{2}}}{2}$

$\cos 15° = \dfrac{\sqrt{2 + \sqrt{3}}}{2}$ $\cos\dfrac{7\pi}{8} = -\dfrac{\sqrt{2 + \sqrt{2}}}{2}$

$\tan 15° = 2 - \sqrt{3}$ $\tan\dfrac{7\pi}{8} = 1 - \sqrt{2}$

109. $\sin\dfrac{u}{2} = \dfrac{2\sqrt{13}}{13}$ **111.** $\sin\dfrac{u}{2} = \dfrac{3\sqrt{14}}{14}$

$\cos\dfrac{u}{2} = \dfrac{3\sqrt{13}}{13}$ $\cos\dfrac{u}{2} = \dfrac{\sqrt{70}}{14}$

$\tan\dfrac{u}{2} = \dfrac{2}{3}$ $\tan\dfrac{u}{2} = \dfrac{3\sqrt{5}}{5}$

113. $-|\cos 4x|$ **115.** $\tan 5x$

117. $V = \sin\dfrac{\theta}{2}\cos\dfrac{\theta}{2}\ \text{m}^3$ **119.** $3\left(\sin\dfrac{\pi}{2} + \sin 0\right)$

121. $\dfrac{1}{2}(\cos\alpha - \cos 9\alpha)$ **123.** $2\cos\left(\dfrac{9\theta}{2}\right)\cos\left(\dfrac{\theta}{2}\right)$

125. $2\cos x\sin\dfrac{\pi}{4}$ **127.** $y = \dfrac{1}{2}\sqrt{10}\sin\left(8t - \arctan\dfrac{1}{3}\right)$

129. $\dfrac{\sqrt{10}}{2}\ \text{ft}$ **131.** False. $\cos\dfrac{\theta}{2} > 0$

133. True. Answers will vary.   **135.** Answers will vary.

137. No. $\sin\theta = \dfrac{1}{2}$ has an infinite number of solutions but is not an identity.

139. $y_3 = y_2 + 1$

Chapter Test   (page 399)

1. $\sin\theta = \dfrac{-3\sqrt{13}}{13}$ **2.** 1   **3.** 1

$\cos\theta = \dfrac{-2\sqrt{13}}{13}$

$\csc\theta = \dfrac{-\sqrt{13}}{3}$

$\sec\theta = \dfrac{-\sqrt{13}}{2}$

$\cot\theta = \dfrac{2}{3}$

4. $\csc\theta\sec\theta$ **5.** $0, \dfrac{\pi}{2} < \theta \le \pi, \dfrac{3\pi}{2} < \theta < 2\pi$

6.

$y_1 = y_2$

7–12. Answers will vary.   **13.** $\dfrac{\sqrt{2} - \sqrt{6}}{4}$

14. $\dfrac{1}{16}\left(\dfrac{10 - 15\cos 2x + 6\cos 4x - \cos 6x}{1 + \cos 2x}\right)$

15. $\tan 2\theta$ **16.** $2(\sin 6\theta + \sin 2\theta)$

17. $-2\sin 2\theta\sin\theta$ **18.** $0, \dfrac{3\pi}{4}, \pi, \dfrac{7\pi}{4}$ **19.** $\dfrac{\pi}{6}, \dfrac{\pi}{2}, \dfrac{5\pi}{6}, \dfrac{3\pi}{2}$

20. $\dfrac{\pi}{6}, \dfrac{5\pi}{6}, \dfrac{7\pi}{6}, \dfrac{11\pi}{6}$ **21.** $\dfrac{\pi}{6}, \dfrac{5\pi}{6}, \dfrac{3\pi}{2}$ **22.** $-2.596, 0, 2.596$

23. $\sin 2u = \dfrac{4}{5}$ **24.** $76.52°$

$\cos 2u = -\dfrac{3}{5}$

$\tan 2u = -\dfrac{4}{3}$

Chapter 6

Section 6.1   (page 410)

1. oblique   **3.** $\dfrac{1}{2}bc\sin A; \dfrac{1}{2}ab\sin C; \dfrac{1}{2}ac\sin B$

5. AAS (or ASA) and SSA

7. $C = 95°, b \approx 24.59$ in., $c \approx 28.29$ in.

9. $C = 120°, a \approx 16.33$ cm, $b \approx 5.98$ cm

11. $C = 74°\ 15', a \approx 6.41$ km, $c \approx 6.26$ km

13. $B \approx 21.55°, C \approx 122.45°, c \approx 11.49$

15. $C = 105°, a \approx 5.94, b \approx 6.65$

17. $B \approx 48.74°, C \approx 21.26°, c \approx 48.23$

19. $B \approx 60.9°, b \approx 19.32, c \approx 6.36$

21. $A = 48°, b \approx 2.29, c \approx 4.73$

23. $B \approx 18°\ 13', C \approx 51°\ 32', c \approx 40.05$

25. No solution   **27.** No solution

29. Two solutions

$B \approx 72.21°, C \approx 49.79°, c \approx 10.27$

$B \approx 107.79°, C \approx 14.21°, c \approx 3.30$

31. Given: $A = 36°$, $a = 5$

  (a) One solution if $b \le 5$ or $b = \dfrac{5}{\sin 36°}$.

  (b) Two solutions if $5 < b < \dfrac{5}{\sin 36°}$.

  (c) No solution if $b > \dfrac{5}{\sin 36°}$.

33. Given: $A = 10°$, $a = 10.8$

  (a) One solution if $b \le 10.8$ or $b = \dfrac{10.8}{\sin 10°}$.

  (b) Two solutions if $10.8 < b < \dfrac{10.8}{\sin 10°}$.

  (c) No solution if $b > \dfrac{10.8}{\sin 10°}$.

35. 28.19 square units   **37.** 20 square units

39. 2888.57 square units   **41.** 24.12 m   **43.** 240.03°

45. (a)

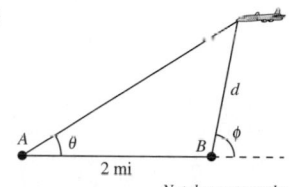

2 mi

Not drawn to scale

  (b) $d = \dfrac{2 \sin \theta}{\sin(\phi - \theta)}$ (c) 3.76 mi

47. $\theta \approx 16.08°$

49. (a) $\alpha \approx 5.36°$

  (b) $\beta = \arcsin\left(\dfrac{d \sin \theta}{58.36}\right)$ (c) $d = \sin(84.64 - \theta)\left[\dfrac{58.36}{\sin \theta}\right]$

  (d)

θ	10°	20°	30°	40°	50°	60°
d	324.08	154.19	95.19	63.80	43.30	28.10

51. False. The triangle cannot be solved if only three angles are known.

53. False. AAS and ASA cases have unique solutions.

55. (a) Answers will vary; Sample answer: $b = 4$

  (b) Answers will vary; Sample answer: $b = 7$

  (c) Answers will vary; Sample answer: $b = 10$

57. $\tan \theta = -\frac{12}{5}$; $\csc \theta = -\frac{13}{12}$; $\sec \theta = \frac{13}{5}$; $\cot \theta = -\frac{5}{12}$

59. $3(\sin 11\theta + \sin 5\theta)$ **61.** $\dfrac{1}{6}\left(\sin \dfrac{11\pi}{6} + \sin \dfrac{3\pi}{2}\right)$

Section 6.2   (page 417)

1. $c^2 = a^2 + b^2 - 2ab \cos C$ **3.** No   **5.** Yes

7. $A \approx 40.80°$, $B \approx 60.61°$, $C \approx 78.59°$

9. $A \approx 49.51°$, $B \approx 55.40°$, $C \approx 75.09°$

11. $A \approx 31.40°$, $C \approx 128.60°$, $b \approx 6.56$ mm

13. $A \approx 30.11°$, $B \approx 43.16°$, $C \approx 106.73°$

15. $A \approx 29.44°$, $C \approx 100.56°$, $a \approx 23.38$

17. $B \approx 27.46°$, $C \approx 32.54°$, $a \approx 11.27$

19. $A \approx 103.52°$, $B \approx 38.24°$, $C \approx 38.24°$

21. $A \approx 154° \, 14'$, $C \approx 17° \, 31'$, $b \approx 8.58$

23. $A \approx 33.80°$, $B \approx 103.20°$, $c \approx 0.54$

	a	b	c	d	θ	ϕ
25.	4	8	11.64	4.96	30°	150°
27.	10	14	20	13.86	68.20°	111.80°
29.	15	16.96	25	20	77.22°	102.78°

31. Law of Cosines; $B \approx 48.57°$, $C \approx 91.43°$, $a \approx 12.86$ m

33. Law of Cosines; $A \approx 102.44°$, $C \approx 37.56°$, $b \approx 5.26$

35. Law of Sines; no solution

37. Law of Sines; $C = 103°$, $a \approx 0.82$, $b \approx 0.71$

39. 104.57   **41.** 19.81   **43.** 0.27   **45.** 0.18

47. 483.40 m   **49.** (a) N 59.7° E   (b) N 72.8° E

51. 72.28°   **53.** 131.12 ft, 118.56 ft   **55.** 9655.79 ft²

57. (a) $49 = 2.25 + x^2 - 3x \cos \theta$

  (b) $x = \frac{1}{2}\left(3 \cos \theta + \sqrt{9 \cos^2 \theta + 187}\right)$

  (c)

       (d) 6 in.

59. True   **61.** Proof

63. To solve the triangle using the Law of Cosines, substitute values into $a^2 = b^2 + c^2 - 2bc \cos A$.

Simplify the equation so that you have a quadratic equation in terms of c. Then, find the two values of c, and find the two triangles that model the given information.

Using the Law of Sines will give the same result as using the Law of Cosines.

Sample answer: An advantage of using the Law of Cosines is that it is easier to choose the correct value to avoid the ambiguous case, but its disadvantage is that there are more computations. The opposite is true for the Law of Sines.

65. $-\dfrac{\pi}{2}$ **67.** $\dfrac{\pi}{6}$

Section 6.3   (page 429)

1. directed line segment   **3.** magnitude

5. standard position   **7.** resultant

9. magnitude and direction   **11.** Answers will vary.

13. $\langle 1, 3 \rangle$, $\|\mathbf{v}\| = \sqrt{10}$ **15.** $\langle -3, 2 \rangle$, $\|\mathbf{v}\| = \sqrt{13}$

17. $\langle 0, 5 \rangle$, $\|\mathbf{v}\| = 5$ **19.** $\langle 8, 6 \rangle$, $\|\mathbf{v}\| = 10$

21. $\langle -3.6, -3.6 \rangle$, $\|\mathbf{v}\| = \dfrac{18}{5}\sqrt{2}$ **23.** $\left\langle \dfrac{7}{6}, \dfrac{9}{5} \right\rangle$, $\|\mathbf{v}\| = \dfrac{\sqrt{4141}}{30}$

25.

27.

CHAPTER 6

29.

31.

33.

35.

37. (a) $\langle 12, 2 \rangle$ (b) $\langle -4, 2 \rangle$

      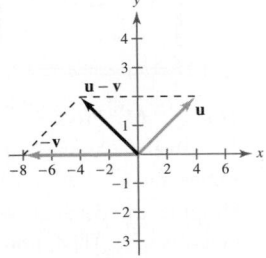

(c) $\langle -16, 4 \rangle$ (d) $\langle 20, 8 \rangle$

39. (a) $\langle -4, -4 \rangle$ (b) $\langle -8, -12 \rangle$

(c) $\langle -18, -28 \rangle$ (d) $\langle -23, -30 \rangle$

41. (a) $3\mathbf{i} - 2\mathbf{j}$ (b) $-\mathbf{i} + 4\mathbf{j}$

(c) $-4\mathbf{i} + 11\mathbf{j}$ (d) $5\mathbf{i} + \frac{5}{2}\mathbf{j}$

      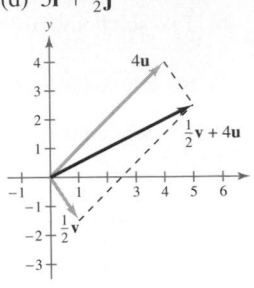

43. $\mathbf{u} + \mathbf{v}$ **45.** $\mathbf{w} - \mathbf{v}$ **47.** $\langle 1, 0 \rangle$

49. $\left\langle -\frac{\sqrt{2}}{2}, \frac{\sqrt{2}}{2} \right\rangle$ **51.** $\left\langle -\frac{24}{25}, -\frac{7}{25} \right\rangle$ **53.** $\frac{4}{5}\mathbf{i} - \frac{3}{5}\mathbf{j}$

55. $\mathbf{j}$ **57.** $\langle -6, 8 \rangle$ **59.** $\left\langle \frac{40\sqrt{61}}{61}, \frac{48\sqrt{61}}{61} \right\rangle$

61. $\frac{21}{5}\mathbf{i} + \frac{28}{5}\mathbf{j}$ **63.** $7\mathbf{i} + 4\mathbf{j}$ **65.** $6\mathbf{i} - 3\mathbf{j}$

67. $\mathbf{v} = \left\langle 3, -\frac{3}{2} \right\rangle$ **69.** $\mathbf{v} = \langle 4, 3 \rangle$

       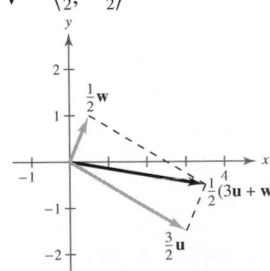

71. $\mathbf{v} = \left\langle \frac{7}{2}, -\frac{1}{2} \right\rangle$

73. $\|\mathbf{v}\| = 5$, $\theta = 60°$

75. $\|\mathbf{v}\| = 3\sqrt{41}$, $\theta \approx 51.34°$

77. $\|\mathbf{v}\| = \sqrt{29}$, $\theta \approx 111.80°$

79. $\mathbf{v} = \langle 3, 0 \rangle$

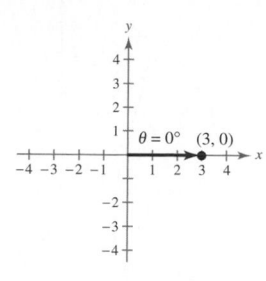

81. $\mathbf{v} = \left\langle -\dfrac{7}{4}, \dfrac{7\sqrt{3}}{4} \right\rangle$

83. $\mathbf{v} = \left\langle -\dfrac{3\sqrt{6}}{2}, \dfrac{3\sqrt{2}}{2} \right\rangle$

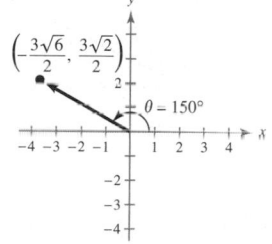

85. $\mathbf{v} = \left\langle \dfrac{\sqrt{10}}{5}, \dfrac{3\sqrt{10}}{5} \right\rangle$

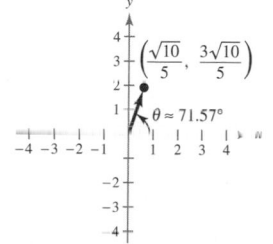

87. $\langle 5, 5 \rangle$ **89.** $\langle -32.84, 31.24 \rangle$ **91.** $90°$

93.

$\|\mathbf{v}\| \approx 647.85,\ \theta \approx 44.11°$

95. $62.72°$

97. Vertical component: about 45.00 ft/sec
Horizontal component: about 53.62 ft/sec

99. 19,785.83 lb and 15,484.09 lb

101. (a) $T = 3000 \sec \theta$; Domain: $0° \leq \theta < 90°$

(b)

θ	10°	20°	30°
T	3046.28	3192.53	3464.10

θ	40°	50°	60°
T	3916.22	4667.17	6000

(c)

(d) The component in the direction of the motion of the barge decreases.

103. (a) 12.10°, 357.85 N

(b) $M = 10\sqrt{660 \cos \theta + 709}$

$\alpha = \arctan \dfrac{15 \sin \theta}{15 \cos \theta + 22}$

(c)

θ	0°	30°	60°	90°
M	370	357.85	322.34	266.27
α	0°	12.10°	23.77°	34.29°

θ	120°	150°	180°
M	194.68	117.23	70
α	41.86°	39.78°	0°

(d)

(e) For increasing θ, the two vectors tend to work against each other, resulting in a decrease in the magnitude of the resultant.

105. N 26.67° E, 130.35 km/h   **107.** True by definition.

109. True. $a = b = 0$

111. (a) 0°   (b) 180°

(c) No. The magnitude is equal to the sum when the angle between the vectors is 0°.

113. Answers will vary.   **115.** Proof

117. $\langle 1, 3 \rangle$ or $\langle -1, -3 \rangle$

119. (a) Vector; Answers will vary.

(b) Scalar; Answers will vary.

(c) Scalar; Answers will vary.

(d) Scalar; Answers will vary.

(e) Scalar; Answers will vary.

(f) Vector; Answers will vary.

121. $\dfrac{3s^3}{10t^4},\ s \neq 0$ **123.** $\dfrac{5}{4a^2},\ b \neq 0$ **125.** 2.47×10^{-1}

127. $n\pi,\ \dfrac{5\pi}{4} + 2n\pi,\ \dfrac{7\pi}{4} + 2n\pi$ **129.** $\dfrac{7\pi}{6} + 2n\pi,\ \dfrac{11\pi}{6} + 2n\pi$

131. $7 \tan \theta$

Section 6.4   (page 440)

1. Yes   **3.** scalar   **5.** $\left(\dfrac{\mathbf{u} \cdot \mathbf{v}}{\|\mathbf{v}\|^2} \right)\mathbf{v}$ **7.** 0   **9.** 14

11. 8, scalar   **13.** -8, scalar   **15.** $\langle -102, -102 \rangle$, vector

17. 13   **19.** $5\sqrt{41}$ **21.** 4   **23.** 90°   **25.** 86.63°

27. 90°   **29.** $\dfrac{5\pi}{12}$

31.

$\theta \approx 4.40°$

33.

$\theta \approx 53.13°$

35. $26.57°, 63.43°, 90°$ **37.** $41.63°, 53.13°, 85.24°$

39. $-162\sqrt{2}$ **41.** -20

43. Orthogonal   **45.** Not orthogonal   **47.** Orthogonal

49. Parallel   **51.** 3 **53.** $\frac{20}{7}$ **55.** 0

57. $\frac{14}{37}\langle 6, 1\rangle,\ u = \left\langle \frac{84}{37}, \frac{14}{37}\right\rangle + \left\langle -\frac{10}{37}, \frac{60}{37}\right\rangle$

59. $\frac{45}{229}\langle 2, 15\rangle,\ \mathbf{u} = \left\langle \frac{90}{229}, \frac{675}{229}\right\rangle + \left\langle -\frac{90}{229}, \frac{12}{229}\right\rangle$ **61. u**   **63. 0**

65. $\langle 3, -1\rangle, \langle -3, 1\rangle$ **67.** $-\frac{3}{4}\mathbf{i} - \frac{1}{2}\mathbf{j}, \frac{3}{4}\mathbf{i} + \frac{1}{2}\mathbf{j}$ **69.** 32

71. (a) $39,761.25$; It is the total dollar amount paid to the employees.

   (b) Multiply **v** by 1.02.

73. (a) Force $= 30,000 \sin d$

   (b)

d	$0°$	$1°$	$2°$	$3°$
Force	0	523.57	1046.98	1570.08

d	$4°$	$5°$	$6°$	$7°$
Force	2092.69	2614.67	3135.85	3656.08

d	$8°$	$9°$	$10°$
Force	4175.19	4693.03	5209.45

   (c) $29,885.84$ lb

75. (a) Work $= 125\sqrt{3}d$

   (b)

d	25	50	100
Work	5412.66	$10,825.32$	$21,650.64$

77. 679.73 ft-lb

79. True. The zero vector is orthogonal to every vector.

81. Orthogonal. $\mathbf{u} \cdot \mathbf{v} = 0$

83. 1. The angle between **u** and itself is 0. Then, using the equation

$$\cos \theta = \frac{\mathbf{u} \cdot \mathbf{u}}{\|\mathbf{u}\|\,\|\mathbf{u}\|}$$

   and substituting 0 for θ, you see that $\cos 0 = 1$.

85. (a) **u** and **v** are parallel.   (b) **u** and **v** are orthogonal.

87 and 89. Proofs

91. g is a horizontal shift of f four units to the right.

93. g is a vertical shift of f six units upward.

95. $15 + 12i$ **97.** 10 **99.** $\frac{47}{26} - \frac{27}{26}i$

Section 6.5   (page 452)

1. absolute value   **3.** nth root

5. The distance from the origin to the point (a, b)

7.

$\sqrt{130}$ 13

11.

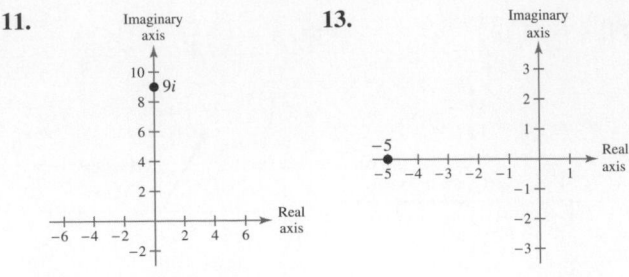

9 5

15. $2\left(\cos\dfrac{\pi}{2} + i\sin\dfrac{\pi}{2}\right)$ **17.** $4(\cos\pi + i\sin\pi)$

19. $3\sqrt{2}\left(\cos\dfrac{5\pi}{4} + i\sin\dfrac{5\pi}{4}\right)$ **21.** $2\left(\cos\dfrac{11\pi}{6} + i\sin\dfrac{11\pi}{6}\right)$

23.

$8\left(\cos\dfrac{3\pi}{2} + i\sin\dfrac{3\pi}{2}\right)$ $5\left(\cos\dfrac{\pi}{2} + i\sin\dfrac{\pi}{2}\right)$

27.

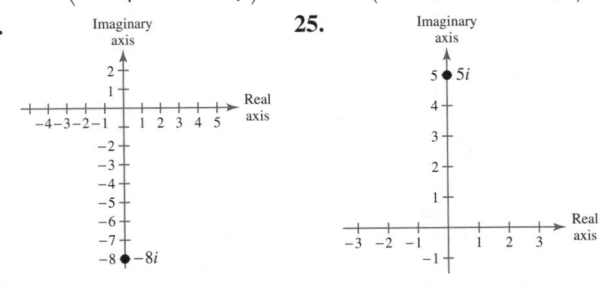

$7\sqrt{2}\left(\cos\dfrac{7\pi}{4} + i\sin\dfrac{7\pi}{4}\right)$ $2\left(\cos\dfrac{\pi}{6} + i\sin\dfrac{\pi}{6}\right)$

31.

$\sqrt{2}\left(\cos\dfrac{\pi}{4} + i\sin\dfrac{\pi}{4}\right)$ $4\left(\cos\dfrac{4\pi}{3} + i\sin\dfrac{4\pi}{3}\right)$

35.

$\sqrt{65}(\cos 2.622 + i\sin 2.622)$ $3(\cos 0 + i\sin 0)$

39.

$$2\sqrt{3}\left(\cos\frac{\pi}{6}+i\sin\frac{\pi}{6}\right)$$

41.

Imaginary axis

$$\sqrt{26}(\cos 4.515 + i\sin 4.515)$$

43.

Imaginary axis

$5-2i$

$$\sqrt{29}(\cos 5.903 + i\sin 5.903)$$

45.

Imaginary axis

$$\sqrt{67}(\cos 5.257 + i\sin 5.257)$$

47.

Imaginary axis

$3+3\sqrt{3}i$

$$3+3\sqrt{3}i$$

49.

$$-\frac{15\sqrt{2}}{8}+\frac{15\sqrt{2}}{8}i$$

51.

Imaginary axis

$-1+\sqrt{3}i$

$$-1+\sqrt{3}i$$

53.

$$\frac{5\sqrt{3}}{4}-\frac{5}{4}i$$

55.

Imaginary axis

$-\sqrt{12}i$

$$-\sqrt{12}i$$

57.

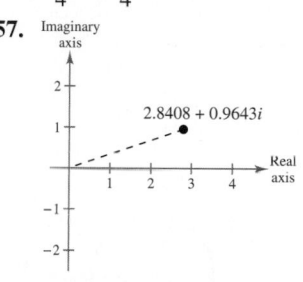

$$2.8408 + 0.9643i$$

59. $-3.8302 + 3.2139i$ **61.** $4.7693 + 7.6324i$

63. $27(\cos 0 + i\sin 0)$ **65.** $6\left(\cos\frac{3\pi}{2}+i\sin\frac{3\pi}{2}\right)$

67. $\frac{10}{9}(\cos 200° + i\sin 200°)$ **69.** $\cos 130° + i\sin 130°$

71. $\cos 30° + i\sin 30°$ **73.** $\frac{5}{4}(\cos\pi + i\sin\pi)$

75. $6(\cos 312° + i\sin 312°)$

77. (a) $2\sqrt{2}\left(\cos\frac{7\pi}{4}+i\sin\frac{7\pi}{4}\right)$ (b) and (c) 4

$\sqrt{2}\left(\cos\frac{\pi}{4}+i\sin\frac{\pi}{4}\right)$

79. (a) $2\sqrt{2}\left(\cos\frac{\pi}{4}+i\sin\frac{\pi}{4}\right)$ (b) and (c) 4

$\sqrt{2}\left(\cos\frac{7\pi}{4}+i\sin\frac{7\pi}{4}\right)$

81. (a) $2\left(\cos\frac{3\pi}{2}+i\sin\frac{3\pi}{2}\right)$ (b) and (c) $2-2i$

$\sqrt{2}\left(\cos\frac{\pi}{4}+i\sin\frac{\pi}{4}\right)$

83. (a) $2\left(\cos\frac{3\pi}{2}+i\sin\frac{3\pi}{2}\right)$ (b) and (c) $-2-2\sqrt{3}i$

$2\left(\cos\frac{11\pi}{6}+i\sin\frac{11\pi}{6}\right)$

85. (a) $2(\cos 0 + i\sin 0)$ (b) and (c) $2-2i$

$\sqrt{2}\left(\cos\frac{7\pi}{4}+i\sin\frac{7\pi}{4}\right)$

87. (a) $5(\cos 0.93 + i\sin 0.93)$

$2\left(\cos\frac{5\pi}{3}+i\sin\frac{5\pi}{3}\right)$

(b) and (c) $\left(\frac{3}{4}-\sqrt{3}\right)+\left(\frac{3\sqrt{3}}{4}+1\right)i$

89. (a) $5(\cos 0 + i\sin 0)$ (b) and (c) $\frac{5}{4}-\frac{5}{4}i$

$2\sqrt{2}\left(\cos\frac{\pi}{4}+i\sin\frac{\pi}{4}\right)$

CHAPTER 6

91. (a) $4\left(\cos\dfrac{\pi}{2} + i \sin\dfrac{\pi}{2}\right)$

$\sqrt{2}\left(\cos\dfrac{3\pi}{4} + i \sin\dfrac{3\pi}{4}\right)$

(b) and (c) $2 - 2i$

93.

The absolute value of each is 1.

95.   **97.**

99.   **101.**

103.   **105.**

107. $-2 + 2i$ **109.** $8i$ **111.** $-32\sqrt{3} - 32i$

113. $\dfrac{125}{2} + \dfrac{125\sqrt{3}}{2}i$ **115.** i **117.** $16{,}384$

119. $2048 + 2048\sqrt{3}i$ **121.** $\dfrac{9\sqrt{2}}{2} + \dfrac{9\sqrt{2}}{2}i$

123. $-597 - 122i$ **125.** $4.5386 - 15.3428i$

127. Answers will vary.   **129.** $1 + i, -1 - i$

131. $-\dfrac{\sqrt{6}}{2} + \dfrac{\sqrt{6}}{2}i, \dfrac{\sqrt{6}}{2} - \dfrac{\sqrt{6}}{2}i$

133. $-1.5538 + 0.6436i, 1.5538 - 0.6436i$

135. $\dfrac{\sqrt{6}}{2} + \dfrac{\sqrt{2}}{2}i, -\dfrac{\sqrt{6}}{2} - \dfrac{\sqrt{2}}{2}i$

137. (a) $\sqrt{5}(\cos 60° + i \sin 60°)$
$\sqrt{5}(\cos 240° + i \sin 240°)$

(b)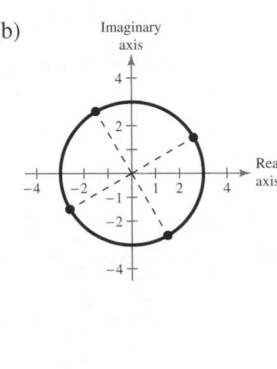

(c) $\dfrac{\sqrt{5}}{2} + \dfrac{\sqrt{15}}{2}i, -\dfrac{\sqrt{5}}{2} - \dfrac{\sqrt{15}}{2}i$

139. (a) $3\left(\cos\dfrac{\pi}{6} + i \sin\dfrac{\pi}{6}\right)$ (b)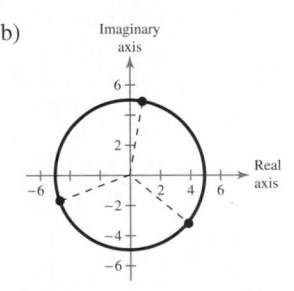

$3\left(\cos\dfrac{2\pi}{3} + i \sin\dfrac{2\pi}{3}\right)$

$3\left(\cos\dfrac{7\pi}{6} + i \sin\dfrac{7\pi}{6}\right)$

$3\left(\cos\dfrac{5\pi}{3} + i \sin\dfrac{5\pi}{3}\right)$

(c) $2.5981 + 1.5i,$
$-1.5 + 2.5981i,$
$-2.5981 - 1.5i,$
$1.5 - 2.5981i$

141. (a) $\sqrt[3]{25}\left(\cos\dfrac{\pi}{2} + i \sin\dfrac{\pi}{2}\right)$ (b)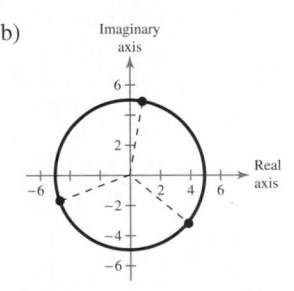

$\sqrt[3]{25}\left(\cos\dfrac{7\pi}{6} + i \sin\dfrac{7\pi}{6}\right)$

$\sqrt[3]{25}\left(\cos\dfrac{11\pi}{6} + i \sin\dfrac{11\pi}{6}\right)$

(c) $2.9240i,$
$-2.5323 - 1.4620i,$
$2.5323 - 1.4620i$

143. (a) $5\left(\cos\dfrac{4\pi}{9} + i \sin\dfrac{4\pi}{9}\right)$ (b)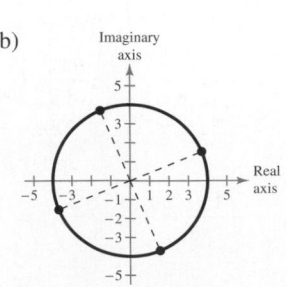

$5\left(\cos\dfrac{10\pi}{9} + i \sin\dfrac{10\pi}{9}\right)$

$5\left(\cos\dfrac{16\pi}{9} + i \sin\dfrac{16\pi}{9}\right)$

(c) $0.8682 + 4.9240i,$
$-4.6985 - 1.7101i,$
$3.8302 - 3.2139i$

145. (a) $4\left(\cos\dfrac{\pi}{8} + i \sin\dfrac{\pi}{8}\right)$ (b)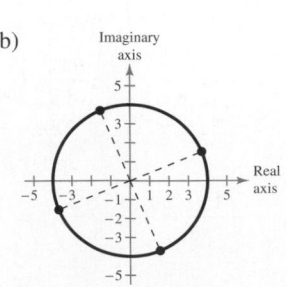

$4\left(\cos\dfrac{5\pi}{8} + i \sin\dfrac{5\pi}{8}\right)$

$4\left(\cos\dfrac{9\pi}{8} + i \sin\dfrac{9\pi}{8}\right)$

$4\left(\cos\dfrac{13\pi}{8} + i \sin\dfrac{13\pi}{8}\right)$

(c) $3.6955 + 1.5307i,$
$-1.5307 + 3.6955i,$
$-3.6955 - 1.5307i,$
$1.5307 - 3.6955i$

147. (a) $\cos 0 + i\sin 0$

$\cos\dfrac{2\pi}{5} + i\sin\dfrac{2\pi}{5}$

$\cos\dfrac{4\pi}{5} + i\sin\dfrac{4\pi}{5}$

$\cos\dfrac{6\pi}{5} + i\sin\dfrac{6\pi}{5}$

$\cos\dfrac{8\pi}{5} + i\sin\dfrac{8\pi}{5}$

(b)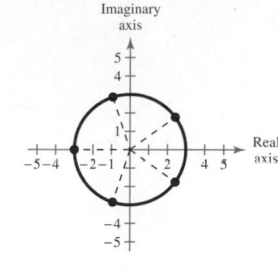

(c) $1, 0.3090 + 0.9511i, -0.8090 + 0.5878i,$
$-0.8090 - 0.5878i, 0.3090 - 0.9511i$

149. (a) $5\left(\cos\dfrac{\pi}{3} + i\sin\dfrac{\pi}{3}\right)$

$5(\cos\pi + i\sin\pi)$

$5\left(\cos\dfrac{5\pi}{3} + i\sin\dfrac{5\pi}{3}\right)$

(c) $\dfrac{5}{2} + \dfrac{5\sqrt{3}}{2}i, -5,$

$\dfrac{5}{2} - \dfrac{5\sqrt{3}}{2}i$

(b)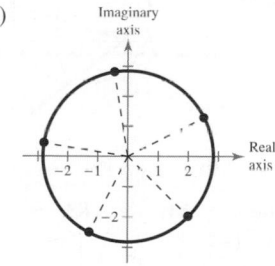

151. (a) $2\sqrt{2}\left(\cos\dfrac{3\pi}{20} + i\sin\dfrac{3\pi}{20}\right)$

$2\sqrt{2}\left(\cos\dfrac{11\pi}{20} + i\sin\dfrac{11\pi}{20}\right)$

$2\sqrt{2}\left(\cos\dfrac{19\pi}{20} + i\sin\dfrac{19\pi}{20}\right)$

$2\sqrt{2}\left(\cos\dfrac{27\pi}{20} + i\sin\dfrac{27\pi}{20}\right)$

$2\sqrt{2}\left(\cos\dfrac{7\pi}{4} + i\sin\dfrac{7\pi}{4}\right)$

(b)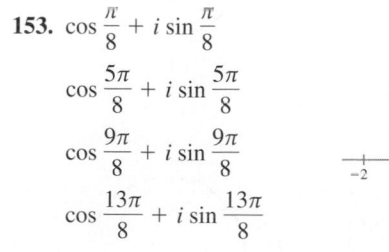

(c) $2.5201 + 1.2841i, -0.4425 + 2.7936i,$
$-2.7936 + 0.4425i, -1.2841 - 2.5201i, 2 - 2i$

153. $\cos\dfrac{\pi}{8} + i\sin\dfrac{\pi}{8}$

$\cos\dfrac{5\pi}{8} + i\sin\dfrac{5\pi}{8}$

$\cos\dfrac{9\pi}{8} + i\sin\dfrac{9\pi}{8}$

$\cos\dfrac{13\pi}{8} + i\sin\dfrac{13\pi}{8}$

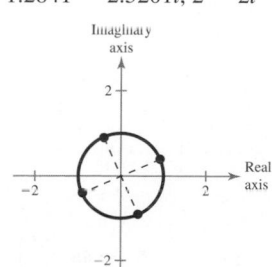

155. $3\left(\cos\dfrac{\pi}{5} + i\sin\dfrac{\pi}{5}\right)$

$3\left(\cos\dfrac{3\pi}{5} + i\sin\dfrac{3\pi}{5}\right)$

$3(\cos\pi + i\sin\pi)$

$3\left(\cos\dfrac{7\pi}{5} + i\sin\dfrac{7\pi}{5}\right)$

$3\left(\cos\dfrac{9\pi}{5} + i\sin\dfrac{9\pi}{5}\right)$

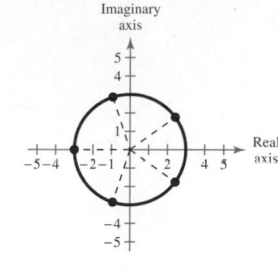

157. $2\left(\cos\dfrac{3\pi}{8} + i\sin\dfrac{3\pi}{8}\right)$

$2\left(\cos\dfrac{7\pi}{8} + i\sin\dfrac{7\pi}{8}\right)$

$2\left(\cos\dfrac{11\pi}{8} + i\sin\dfrac{11\pi}{8}\right)$

$2\left(\cos\dfrac{15\pi}{8} + i\sin\dfrac{15\pi}{8}\right)$

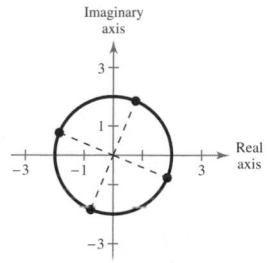

159. $\sqrt[6]{2}\left(\cos\dfrac{7\pi}{12} + i\sin\dfrac{7\pi}{12}\right)$

$\sqrt[6]{2}\left(\cos\dfrac{5\pi}{4} + i\sin\dfrac{5\pi}{4}\right)$

$\sqrt[6]{2}\left(\cos\dfrac{23\pi}{12} + i\sin\dfrac{23\pi}{12}\right)$

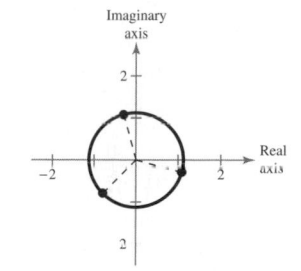

161. $E = 34 + 38i$ **163.** $Z = \dfrac{3}{2} - \dfrac{1}{2}i$ **165.** $I = \dfrac{39}{34} + \dfrac{3}{34}i$

167. True. $\left[\dfrac{1}{2}\left(1 - \sqrt{3}i\right)\right]^9 = -1$

169. True. $z_1 z_2 = r_1 r_2[\cos(\theta_1 + \theta_2) + i\sin(\theta_1 + \theta_2)] = 0$ if and only if $r_1 = 0$ and/or $r_2 = 0$.

171. Answers will vary.   **173.** (a) r^2 (b) $\cos 2\theta + i\sin 2\theta$

175. Answers will vary.

177. Maximum displacement: $16; t = 2$

179. Maximum displacement: $\dfrac{1}{8}; t = \dfrac{1}{24}$

Review Exercises   (page 458)

1. $C = 98°, b \approx 23.13, c \approx 29.90$

3. $A = 66°, b \approx 2.53, c \approx 9.11$

5. $C = 74° \, 15', a \approx 5.84, c \approx 6.48$

7. $B \approx 39.48°, C \approx 65.52°, c \approx 48.24$

9. Two solutions

$A \approx 40.92°, C \approx 114.08°, c \approx 8.64$

$A \approx 139.08°, C \approx 15.92°, c \approx 2.60$

11. 19.06   **13.** 221.34   **15.** 31.01 ft

17. $A \approx 15.29°, B \approx 20.59°, C \approx 144.11°$

19. $B \approx 9.90°, C \approx 20.10°, a \approx 29.09$

21. $A \approx 86.38°, B \approx 28.62°, c \approx 22.70$

23. 4.29 ft, 12.63 ft   **25.** 7.64 square units

27. 511.71 square units   **29.** Answers will vary.

31. $\langle 7, -5\rangle, \|\mathbf{v}\| = \sqrt{74}$ **33.** $\langle 7, -7\rangle, \|\mathbf{v}\| = 7\sqrt{2}$

CHAPTER 6

35. (a) $\langle -4, 3 \rangle$ (b) $\langle 2, -9 \rangle$ (c) $6\mathbf{i} - 3\mathbf{j}$ (d) $20\mathbf{i} + \mathbf{j}$

(c) $\langle -3, -9 \rangle$ (d) $\langle -11, -3 \rangle$ **41.** $\left\langle \frac{10}{3}, 1 \right\rangle$ **43.** $\langle 74, -5 \rangle$

37. (a) $\langle -1, 6 \rangle$ (b) $\langle -9, -2 \rangle$

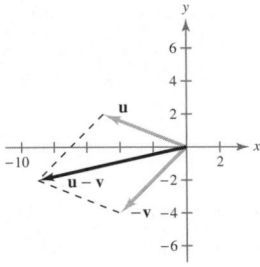

45. $\langle 0, -1 \rangle$ **47.** $\frac{8}{17}\mathbf{i} - \frac{15}{17}\mathbf{j}$ **49.** $9\mathbf{i} - 8\mathbf{j}$

51. $\|\mathbf{v}\| = 7; \theta = 120°$ **53.** $\|\mathbf{v}\| = \sqrt{41}; \theta = 38.7°$

55. $\|\mathbf{v}\| = \sqrt{65}; \theta = 119.7°$

57. 133.92 lb, 5.55° from the 85-lb force **59.** 115.47 lb

61. -17 **63.** 7 **65.** 52, scalar **67.** $\langle 16, 8 \rangle$, vector

69. 2.802 **71.** $\dfrac{11\pi}{12}$

(c) $\langle -15, 6 \rangle$ (d) $\langle -17, 18 \rangle$ **73.** **75.**

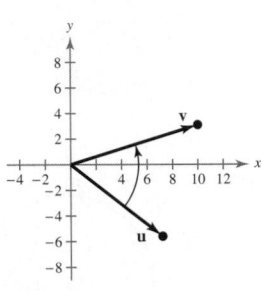

90° 55.098°

77. Orthogonal **79.** Neither **81.** $\frac{1}{2}$ **83.** -1

85. $\frac{13}{17}\langle -4, -1 \rangle, \left\langle -\frac{52}{17}, -\frac{13}{17} \right\rangle + \left\langle -\frac{16}{17}, \frac{64}{17} \right\rangle$

87. $\frac{5}{2}\langle -1, 1 \rangle, \left\langle -\frac{5}{2}, \frac{5}{2} \right\rangle + \left\langle \frac{9}{2}, \frac{9}{2} \right\rangle$ **89.** 72,000 ft-lb

39. (a) $7\mathbf{i} + 2\mathbf{j}$ (b) $-3\mathbf{i} - 4\mathbf{j}$ **91.** **93.**

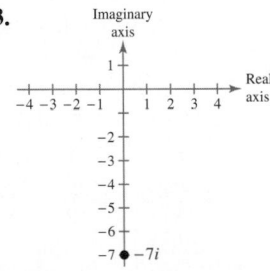

$\sqrt{34}$ 7

95. $4\left(\cos \dfrac{\pi}{2} + i \sin \dfrac{\pi}{2}\right)$ **97.** $2\left(\cos \dfrac{7\pi}{6} + i \sin \dfrac{7\pi}{6}\right)$

99. $10\left(\cos \dfrac{3\pi}{4} + i \sin \dfrac{3\pi}{4}\right)$ **101.** $4(\cos 240° + i \sin 240°)$

103. (a) $2\sqrt{2}\left(\cos \dfrac{7\pi}{4} + i \sin \dfrac{7\pi}{4}\right)$ (b) and (c) 12

$3\sqrt{2}\left(\cos \dfrac{\pi}{4} + i \sin \dfrac{\pi}{4}\right)$

105. (a) $3\sqrt{2}\left(\cos\dfrac{7\pi}{4} + i\sin\dfrac{7\pi}{4}\right)$ (b) and (c) $-\dfrac{3}{2}i$

$2\sqrt{2}\left(\cos\dfrac{\pi}{4} + i\sin\dfrac{\pi}{4}\right)$

107. $\dfrac{625}{2} + \dfrac{625\sqrt{3}}{2}i$ **109.** $2035 - 828i$

111. $\pm(0.3660 + 1.3660i)$ **113.** $\sqrt{2} - \sqrt{2}i, -\sqrt{2} + \sqrt{2}i$

115. (a) $3\left(\cos\dfrac{\pi}{4} + i\sin\dfrac{\pi}{4}\right)$ (b)

$3\left(\cos\dfrac{7\pi}{12} + i\sin\dfrac{7\pi}{12}\right)$

$3\left(\cos\dfrac{11\pi}{12} + i\sin\dfrac{11\pi}{12}\right)$

$3\left(\cos\dfrac{5\pi}{4} + i\sin\dfrac{5\pi}{4}\right)$

$3\left(\cos\dfrac{19\pi}{12} + i\sin\dfrac{19\pi}{12}\right)$

$3\left(\cos\dfrac{23\pi}{12} + i\sin\dfrac{23\pi}{12}\right)$

(c) $2.1213 + 2.1213i, -0.7765 + 2.8978i,$
$-2.8978 + 0.7765i, -2.1213 - 2.1213i,$
$0.7765 - 2.8978i, 2.8978 - 0.7765i$

117. (a) $2(\cos 0 + i\sin 0)$ (b)

$2\left(\cos\dfrac{2\pi}{3} + i\sin\dfrac{2\pi}{3}\right)$

$2\left(\cos\dfrac{4\pi}{3} + i\sin\dfrac{4\pi}{3}\right)$

(c) $2, -1 + \sqrt{3}i,$
$-1 - \sqrt{3}i$

119. $4\left(\cos\dfrac{\pi}{4} + i\sin\dfrac{\pi}{4}\right)$

$4\left(\cos\dfrac{3\pi}{4} + i\sin\dfrac{3\pi}{4}\right)$

$4\left(\cos\dfrac{5\pi}{4} + i\sin\dfrac{5\pi}{4}\right)$

$4\left(\cos\dfrac{7\pi}{4} + i\sin\dfrac{7\pi}{4}\right)$

121. $2\left(\cos\dfrac{\pi}{2} + i\sin\dfrac{\pi}{2}\right)$

$2\left(\cos\dfrac{7\pi}{6} + i\sin\dfrac{7\pi}{6}\right)$

$2\left(\cos\dfrac{11\pi}{6} + i\sin\dfrac{11\pi}{6}\right)$

123. True. $\sin 90°$ is defined in the Law of Sines.

Chapter Test   (page 461)

1. $C = 46°, a \approx 13.07, b \approx 22.03$
2. $A \approx 22.33°, B \approx 49.46°, C \approx 108.21°$
3. $B \approx 40.11°, C \approx 104.89°, a \approx 7.12$
4. $A = 88°, a \approx 29.98, c \approx 27.81$

5. Two solutions
$B \approx 41.10°, C \approx 113.90°, c \approx 38.94$
$B \approx 138.90°, C \approx 16.10°, c \approx 11.81$
6. No solution   **7.** 675 ft   **8.** 2337 m²
9. $\mathbf{w} = \langle 12, 13\rangle, \|\mathbf{w}\| \approx \sqrt{313}$
10. (a) $\langle 1, 8\rangle$ (b) $\langle -19, -22\rangle$ (c) $\langle -51, -44\rangle$
11. (a) $\langle -7, -18\rangle$ (b) $\langle -2, 32\rangle$ (c) $\langle -21, 50\rangle$
12. (a) $13\mathbf{i} + 17\mathbf{j}$ (b) $-17\mathbf{i} - 28\mathbf{j}$ (c) $-19\mathbf{i} - 41\mathbf{j}$
13. (a) $-\mathbf{j}$ (b) $5\mathbf{i} + 9\mathbf{j}$ (c) $14\mathbf{i} + 23\mathbf{j}$
14. $\left\langle\dfrac{24}{25}, -\dfrac{7}{25}\right\rangle$ **15.** $\left\langle\dfrac{18\sqrt{34}}{17}, -\dfrac{30\sqrt{34}}{17}\right\rangle$
16. $\theta \approx 14.87°, 250.15$ lb   **17.** -1 **18.** $105.95°$
19. Yes. $\mathbf{u} \cdot \mathbf{v} = 0$ **20.** $\left\langle\dfrac{185}{26}, \dfrac{37}{26}\right\rangle, \mathbf{u} = \left\langle\dfrac{185}{26}, \dfrac{37}{26}\right\rangle + \left\langle-\dfrac{29}{26}, \dfrac{145}{26}\right\rangle$
21. $z = 6\sqrt{2}\left(\cos\dfrac{3\pi}{4} + i\sin\dfrac{3\pi}{4}\right)$ **22.** $-50 - 50\sqrt{3}i$
23. $-\dfrac{6561}{2} + \dfrac{6561\sqrt{3}}{2}i$ **24.** $5832i$

25. $4\left(\cos\dfrac{\pi}{12} + i\sin\dfrac{\pi}{12}\right)$

$4\left(\cos\dfrac{7\pi}{12} + i\sin\dfrac{7\pi}{12}\right)$

$4\left(\cos\dfrac{13\pi}{12} + i\sin\dfrac{13\pi}{12}\right)$

$4\left(\cos\dfrac{19\pi}{12} + i\sin\dfrac{19\pi}{12}\right)$

26. $5\left(\cos\dfrac{\pi}{8} + i\sin\dfrac{\pi}{8}\right)$

$5\left(\cos\dfrac{5\pi}{8} + i\sin\dfrac{5\pi}{8}\right)$

$5\left(\cos\dfrac{9\pi}{8} + i\sin\dfrac{9\pi}{8}\right)$

$5\left(\cos\dfrac{13\pi}{8} + i\sin\dfrac{13\pi}{8}\right)$

Cumulative Test for Chapters 4–6 (page 462)

1. (a)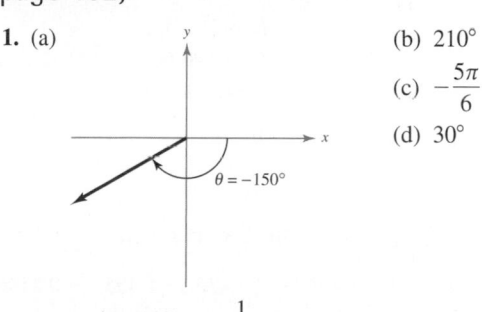

(b) $210°$

(c) $-\dfrac{5\pi}{6}$

(d) $30°$

(e) $\sin(-150°) = -\dfrac{1}{2}$

$\cos(-150°) = -\dfrac{\sqrt{3}}{2}$

$\tan(-150°) = \dfrac{\sqrt{3}}{3}$

$\csc(-150°) = -2$

$\sec(-150°) = -\dfrac{2\sqrt{3}}{3}$

$\cot(-150°) = \sqrt{3}$

2. $146.1°$ **3.** $\cos\theta = \dfrac{20}{29}$

CHAPTER 6

4.   **5.**

6. 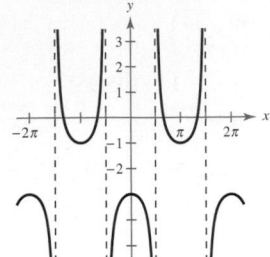   **7.** $a = 3, b = \pi, c = \pi$

8. Not possible   **9.** $\frac{3}{5}$ **10.** $\sqrt{1 - 4x^2}$ **11.** $2 \tan \theta$

12–14. Answers will vary.   **15.** $\dfrac{3\pi}{2} + 2n\pi$

16. $\dfrac{\pi}{6} + n\pi, \dfrac{5\pi}{6} + n\pi$ **17.** $1.7646, 4.5186$

18.   **19.**

$\dfrac{\pi}{3}, \dfrac{5\pi}{3}$ $\dfrac{\pi}{4}, \dfrac{5\pi}{4}$

20. $\dfrac{16}{63}$ **21.** $\dfrac{4}{3}$ **22.** $\dfrac{2\sqrt{5}}{5}$

23. $2 \cos 6x \cos 2x$ **24–27.** Answers will vary.

28. $B \approx 14.89°$ **29.** $B \approx 52.82°$
$\quad\;\; C \approx 119.11°$ $\quad\;\; C \approx 95.18°$
$\quad\;\; c \approx 17.00$ $\quad\;\; a \approx 5.32$

30. $B = 55°$ **31.** $A \approx 26.07°$
$\quad\;\; b \approx 20.14$ $\quad\;\; B \approx 33.33°$
$\quad\;\; c \approx 24.13$ $\quad\;\; C \approx 120.60°$

32. 131.71 in.^{2} **33.** 599.09 m^2 **34.** $3\mathbf{i} + 5\mathbf{j}$

35. $\dfrac{2\sqrt{5}}{5}\mathbf{i} - \dfrac{\sqrt{5}}{5}\mathbf{j}$ **36.** -18 **37.** 1

38. $\left\langle -\frac{1}{13}, -\frac{5}{13} \right\rangle; \mathbf{u} = \left\langle \frac{105}{13}, -\frac{21}{13} \right\rangle + \left\langle -\frac{1}{13}, -\frac{5}{13} \right\rangle$

39. $3\sqrt{2}\left(\cos \dfrac{3\pi}{4} + i \sin \dfrac{3\pi}{4} \right)$ **40.** $-9 + 3\sqrt{3}i$

41. $-12\sqrt{3} + 12i$ **42.** $1.4553 + 0.3436i, -1.4553 - 0.3436i$

43. $1, -\dfrac{1}{2} + \dfrac{\sqrt{3}}{2}i, -\dfrac{1}{2} - \dfrac{\sqrt{3}}{2}i$

44. $6\left(\cos \dfrac{\pi}{4} + i \sin \dfrac{\pi}{4} \right)$ **45.** 5 ft   **46.** $d = 7 \cos \dfrac{\pi}{4}t$

$\quad\;\; 6\left(\cos \dfrac{3\pi}{4} + i \sin \dfrac{3\pi}{4} \right)$

$\quad\;\; 6\left(\cos \dfrac{5\pi}{4} + i \sin \dfrac{5\pi}{4} \right)$

$\quad\;\; 6\left(\cos \dfrac{7\pi}{4} + i \sin \dfrac{7\pi}{4} \right)$

47. $54.34°; 489.45$ km/h   **48.** $80.28°$

Chapter 7

Section 7.1   (page 476)

1. system, equations   **3.** substitution   **5.** Break-even point
7. (a) No   (b) No   (c) No   (d) Yes
9. (a) No   (b) Yes   (c) No   (d) No
11. $(2, 2)$ **13.** $(2, 6), (-1, 3)$
15. $(0, 2), \left(\sqrt{3}, 2 - 3\sqrt{3} \right), \left(-\sqrt{3}, 2 + 3\sqrt{3} \right)$
17. $(4, 4)$ **19.** $(10, -10)$ **21.** $\left(\frac{1}{2}, 3 \right)$
23. $(1, 1)$ **25.** $\left(\frac{20}{3}, \frac{40}{3} \right)$ **27.** No solution
29. \$2000 at 4%, \$16,000 at 2%
31. \$3500 at 5.6%, \$14,500 at 6.8%   **33.** $(-2, 0), (3, 5)$
35. No real solution   **37.** $(0, 0), (1, 1), (-1, -1)$
39. $(-3, 1)$ **41.** $(1, 2)$ **43.** No real solution
45. $(-3, 0), (2, -5)$ **47.** $(4, -0.5)$ **49.** $(8, 3), (3, -2)$
51. $(\pm 1.540, 2.372)$ **53.** $(0, 1)$ **55.** $(2.318, 2.841)$
57. $(2.25, 5.5)$ **59.** $(0, -13), (\pm 12, 5)$ **61.** $(1, 2)$
63. $(-2, 0), \left(\frac{29}{10}, \frac{21}{10} \right)$ **65.** No real solution
67. $(0.25, 1.5)$ **69.** $(0.287, 1.751)$ **71.** $(0, 1), (1, 0)$
73. No real solution

75.   **77.**

$\quad\;\;$ 192 units; \$1,910,400 $\quad\;\;$ 3133 units; \$10,308

79. 6 m $\times$ 9 m

81. (a)

Week	Animated	Horror
1	336	42
2	312	60
3	288	78
4	264	96
5	240	114
6	216	132
7	192	150
8	168	168
9	144	186
10	120	204
11	96	222
12	72	240

(b) and (c) $x = 8$

(d) The answers are the same.
(e) During week 8, the same number of animated and horror films were rented.

83. (a) $C = 9.45x + 16,000$ (b) 344 units
$\quad\quad\;\; R = 55.95x$

85. 8 mi × 12 mi

87. (a) $\begin{cases} x + y = 20{,}000 \\ 0.055x + 0.075y = 1300 \end{cases}$

(b)

(c) $10,000. The solution is (10,000, 10,000).

89. (a)

t	Year	Colorado	Minnesota
13	2013	5265	5417
14	2014	5339	5450
15	2015	5413	5483
16	2016	5487	5516
17	2017	5561	5549
18	2018	5635	5582
19	2019	5709	5615
20	2020	5783	5648

(b) 2017

(c)

(16.71, 5539.34)

(d) (16.71, 5539.34)

(e) At one point in 2016, the populations of Colorado and Minnesota are equal.

91. False. You can solve for either variable before back-substituting.

93. For a linear system, the result will be a contradictory equation such as $0 = N$, where N is a nonzero real number. For a nonlinear system, there may be an equation with imaginary roots.

95. (a) $\begin{cases} 3x + y = 3 \\ 3x + y = 5 \end{cases}$ (b) $\begin{cases} 3x + y = 4 \\ 2x + y = 2 \end{cases}$ (c) $\begin{cases} 6x + 3y = 9 \\ 2x + y = 3 \end{cases}$

97. (a)

(b) There are three points of intersection when b is even.

99. $y = \frac{2}{7}x + \frac{22}{7}$

101. $x = 4$; A vertical line cannot be written in slope-intercept form.

103. Domain: All real numbers x except $x = 6$
Asymptotes: $y = 0, x = 6$

105. Domain: All real numbers x except $x = \pm 4$
Asymptotes: $y = 1, x = \pm 4$

107. Domain: All real numbers x
Asymptote: $y = 0$

Section 7.2   (page 485)

1. method, elimination   **3.** Inconsistent   **5.** Yes

7. (2, 1)   **9.** (1, −1)

11. Inconsistent

13. $\left(2, \frac{1}{2}\right)$ **15.** (3, 4)   **17.** $\left(-3, \frac{3}{2}\right)$ **19.** $\left(\frac{12}{7}, \frac{18}{7}\right)$

21. $\left(\frac{5}{2}, 0\right)$ **23.** Inconsistent   **25.** $\left(\frac{2}{9}, \frac{4}{3}\right)$

27. b; One solution, consistent

28. a; Infinitely many solutions, consistent

29. d; No solutions, inconsistent

30. c; One solution, consistent

31. $\left(\frac{3}{2}, -\frac{1}{2}\right)$ **33.** Inconsistent

35. All points on $6x + 8y - 1 = 0$ **37.** $\left(\frac{7}{2}, -\frac{1}{2}\right)$

39. All points on $-5x + 6y = -3$

41. Inconsistent   **43.** (101, 96)   **45.** (−1, 1)

47.

Consistent; (1, −1)

49.

Consistent; all points on $6x + 3y = -8$

51.

Inconsistent

53.

(3.833, 7)

55.

(6, 5)

57.

(1, −0.667)

59.

(−4, 5)

61. $(4, 1)$ **63.** $(2, -1)$ **65.** $(6, -3)$ **67.** $\left(\frac{49}{4}, \frac{33}{4}\right)$

69. $\begin{cases} \frac{1}{5}x + y = 1 \\ 3x - 2y = 15 \end{cases}$ **71.** $\begin{cases} 2x + \frac{1}{4}y = 4 \\ -4x - 3y = 2 \end{cases}$

73. $(240, 404)$ **75.** $(2{,}000{,}000, 100)$

77. Plane: 550 mi/h, wind: 50 mi/h

79. (a) $\begin{cases} 15A + 12C = 16{,}275 \\ A + C = 1175 \end{cases}$

    (b) $A = 725, C = 450$; Answers will vary.

    (c) $A = 725, C = 450$

81. 9 oranges, 7 grapefruit

83. (a) $S \approx 1761.89$, $t \approx 8.98$; Answers will vary.

    (b) In 2018, both retailers had sales of $1761.89 million.

    (c) The coefficient is the annual increase in sales for each retailer.

    (d) The retailers would never have the same amount of sales for any year.

85. $y = 0.97x + 2.1$ **87.** $y = -0.58x + 5.39$

89. (a) and (b) $y = 14x + 19$

    (c)   (d) 41.4 bushels per acre

91. True. A linear system can have only one solution, no solution, or infinitely many solutions.

93. False. Sometimes you will be able to get only a close approximation.

95. (a) $k = 18$ (b) $k \neq 18$ **97.** $u = 1$; $v = -\tan x$

99. $x \leq -\frac{22}{3}$

101. $-2 < x < 18$

103. $-5 < x < \frac{7}{2}$

105. $\ln 6x$ **107.** $\log_9 \dfrac{12}{x}$ **109.** $\ln \dfrac{x^2}{x + 2}$

111. Answers will vary.

Section 7.3   (page 499)

1. row-echelon   **3.** Gaussian

5. three-dimensional   **7.** Independent

9. (a) No   (b) Yes   (c) No   (d) No

11. (a) No   (b) No   (c) Yes   (d) No

13. $(2, -2, 2)$ **15.** $(3, 10, 2)$ **17.** $\left(\frac{11}{4}, 7, 11\right)$

19. $\begin{cases} x - 2y + 3z = 5 \\ y - 2z = 9 \\ 2x - 3z = 0 \end{cases}$

    It removed the x-term from Equation 2.

21. $(1, 2, 3)$ **23.** $(-4, 8, 5)$ **25.** $(2, -3, -2)$

27. Inconsistent   **29.** $\left(1, -\frac{3}{2}, \frac{1}{2}\right)$ **31.** $(-a + 3, a + 1, a)$

33. Inconsistent   **35.** $(-1, 1, 0)$ **37.** Inconsistent

39. $(2a, 21a - 1, 8a)$ **41.** $(9a, -35a, 67a)$

43. $\begin{cases} x + y + z = 1 \\ 2x + y + z = 4 \\ x + y - 3z = -7 \end{cases}$ **45.** $\begin{cases} x + y + 2z = -10 \\ -x + 12y + 8z = -14 \\ x + 14y - 4z = -6 \end{cases}$

47. $\begin{cases} x - z = 0 \\ -x + y = 4 \end{cases}$

49.   **51.**

Sample answer: $(8, 0, 0)$,   Sample answer: $(4, 0, 0)$,
$(0, 8, 0)$, $(0, 0, 8)$, $(4, 0, 4)$ $(0, 6, 0)$, $(0, 0, 6)$, $(2, 3, 0)$

53. $\dfrac{A}{x} + \dfrac{B}{x - 14}$ **55.** $\dfrac{A}{x} + \dfrac{B}{x^2} + \dfrac{C}{x - 10}$

57. $\dfrac{A}{x - 5} + \dfrac{B}{(x - 5)^2} + \dfrac{C}{(x - 5)^3}$

59. $\dfrac{A}{x} + \dfrac{Bx + C}{x^2 + 1} + \dfrac{Dx + E}{(x^2 + 1)^2}$ **61.** $\dfrac{1}{x} - \dfrac{1}{x + 1}$

63. $\dfrac{3}{2x - 1} - \dfrac{2}{x + 1}$ **65.** $-\dfrac{3}{x} - \dfrac{1}{x + 2} + \dfrac{5}{x - 2}$

67. $\dfrac{3}{x} - \dfrac{1}{x^2} + \dfrac{1}{x + 1}$ **69.** $2x - 7 + \dfrac{17}{x + 2} + \dfrac{1}{x + 1}$

71. $x + 3 + \dfrac{6}{x - 1} + \dfrac{4}{(x - 1)^2} + \dfrac{1}{(x - 1)^3}$

73. $-\dfrac{1}{x - 1} + \dfrac{x + 2}{x^2 - 2}$

75. $\dfrac{3}{x} - \dfrac{2}{x - 4}$

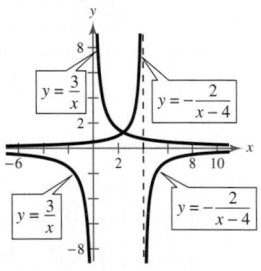

The vertical asymptotes are the same.

77. $s = -16t^2 + 144$ **79.** $s = -16t^2 - 32t + 400$

81. $y = x^2 - 3x$ **83.** $y = -2x^2 - 7x - 4$

85. $x^2 + y^2 - 10x = 0$ **87.** $x^2 + y^2 + 6x - 8y = 0$

89. $20,000 at 4%, $2500 at 6%, and $7500 at 8%

91. $187,500 + s$ in certificates of deposit

    $187,500 - s$ in municipal bonds

    $125,000 - s$ in blue-chip stocks

    s in growth stocks

93. 22 two-point baskets, 13 three-point baskets, 10 free throws

95. $I_1 = 1, I_2 = 2, I_3 = 1$ **97.** $y = -\frac{5}{24}x^2 - \frac{3}{10}x + \frac{41}{6}$

99. $y = x^2 - x$

101. (a) $\begin{cases} 900a + 30b + c = 55 \\ 1600a + 40b + c = 105 \\ 2500a + 50b + c = 188 \end{cases}$

$y = 0.165x^2 - 6.55x + 103$

(b)   (c) 453 ft

103. $\dfrac{60}{100 - p} - \dfrac{60}{100 + p}$

105. False. The leading coefficients are not all 1.

107. The student did not work the problem correctly. Because $\dfrac{x^2 + 1}{x(x - 1)}$ is an improper fraction, the student should have divided before decomposing.

109. No. There are two arithmetic errors. The constant in the second equation should be -11 and the coefficient of z in the third equation should be 2.

111. $\begin{cases} 2x + y - 5z = 3 \\ -4x - 2y + 10z = 7 \end{cases}$

113. $x = 5, y = 5, \lambda = -5$

115. (a) $-4, 0, 3$ **117.** (a) $-4, -\frac{3}{2}, 3$

(b)   (b)

119. $\dfrac{\pi}{6} + n\pi$ **121.** Answers will vary.

Section 7.4   (page 513)

1. matrix   **3.** Gauss-Jordan elimination   **5.** No

7. 1×2 **9.** 3×1 **11.** 2×2

13. $\begin{bmatrix} 4 & -3 & \vdots & -5 \\ -1 & 3 & \vdots & 12 \end{bmatrix}$ 2×3

15. $\begin{bmatrix} 1 & 10 & -2 & \vdots & 2 \\ 5 & -3 & 4 & \vdots & 0 \\ 2 & 1 & 0 & \vdots & 6 \end{bmatrix}$ 3×4

17. $\begin{bmatrix} 7 & -5 & 1 & \vdots & 13 \\ 19 & 0 & -8 & \vdots & 10 \end{bmatrix}$ 2×4

19. $\begin{cases} 3x + 4y = 0 \\ x - y = 7 \end{cases}$

21. $\begin{cases} 12y + 3z = 0 \\ -2x + 18y = 10 \\ x + 7y - 8z = 43 \end{cases}$

23. Multiply R_1 by $-\frac{1}{4}$.   **25.** Add 5 times R_1 to R_3.

27. $\begin{bmatrix} 1 & 4 & 3 \\ 0 & 2 & -1 \end{bmatrix}$

29. $\begin{bmatrix} 1 & 1 & 4 & -1 \\ 0 & 5 & -2 & 6 \\ 0 & 3 & 20 & 4 \end{bmatrix}, \begin{bmatrix} 1 & 1 & 4 & -1 \\ 0 & 1 & -\frac{2}{5} & \frac{6}{5} \\ 0 & 3 & 20 & 4 \end{bmatrix}$

31. (a) i) $\begin{bmatrix} 3 & 0 & \vdots & -6 \\ 6 & -4 & \vdots & -28 \end{bmatrix}$ ii) $\begin{bmatrix} 3 & 0 & \vdots & -6 \\ 0 & -4 & \vdots & -16 \end{bmatrix}$

iii) $\begin{bmatrix} 3 & 0 & \vdots & -6 \\ 0 & 1 & \vdots & 4 \end{bmatrix}$ iv) $\begin{bmatrix} 1 & 0 & \vdots & -2 \\ 0 & 1 & \vdots & 4 \end{bmatrix}$

(b) $x = -2, y = 4$ (c) Answers will vary.

33. i) `row+([A],2,1)→[B]`   ii) `*row+(-2,[B],1,2)→[C]`
`[[3 0 -6 ]`   `[[3 0 -6 ]`
` [6 -4 -28]]`   ` [0 -4 -16]]`

iii) `*row(-1/4,[C],2)→[D]` iv) `*row(1/3,[D],1)→[E]`
`[[3 0 -6]`   `[[1 0 -2]`
` [0 1 4]]`   ` [0 1 4]]`

35. Reduced row-echelon form

37. Not in row-echelon form   **39.** Row-echelon form

41. $\begin{bmatrix} 1 & -3 & 3 \\ 0 & 1 & -2 \end{bmatrix}$ **43.** $\begin{bmatrix} 1 & 2 & -1 & 3 \\ 0 & 1 & -2 & 5 \\ 0 & 0 & 1 & -1 \end{bmatrix}$

45. $\begin{bmatrix} 1 & 0 & 0 \\ 0 & 1 & 0 \\ 0 & 0 & 1 \end{bmatrix}$ **47.** $\begin{bmatrix} 1 & 0 & -\frac{3}{7} & -\frac{8}{7} \\ 0 & 1 & -\frac{12}{7} & \frac{10}{7} \end{bmatrix}$

49. $\begin{cases} x - 2y = 4 \\ y = -3 \end{cases}$

$(-2, -3)$

51. $\begin{cases} x - y + 4z = 0 \\ y - z = 2 \\ z = -2 \end{cases}$

$(8, 0, -2)$

53. $(7, -5)$ **55.** $(-4, -8, 2)$ **57.** $(3, 2)$

59. Inconsistent   **61.** $(-4, -3, 6)$

63. $(3, -2, 5, 0)$ **65.** $(4, -3, 2)$ **67.** Inconsistent

69. $(2a + 1, 3a + 2, a)$ **71.** $(5a + 4, -3a + 2, a)$

73. $(0, -6, 2)$ **75.** $(-5a, a, 3)$ **77.** Yes; $(-1, 1, -3)$

79. No   **81.** $y = x^2 + 2x + 5$ **83.** $y = 2x^2 - x + 1$

85. $f(x) = -9x^2 - 5x + 11$ **87.** $f(x) = x^3 - 2x^2 - 4x + 1$

89. $I_1 = \frac{13}{10}, I_2 = \frac{11}{5}, I_3 = \frac{9}{10}$

91. $\begin{cases} x + 5y + 10z + 20w = 95 \\ x + y + z + w = 26 \\ y - 4z = 0 \\ x - 2y = -1 \end{cases}$

15 \$1 bills, 8 \$5 bills, 2 \$10 bills, 1 \$20 bill

93. $\dfrac{8x^2}{(x - 1)^2(x + 1)} = \dfrac{2}{x + 1} + \dfrac{6}{x - 1} + \dfrac{4}{(x - 1)^2}$

95. (a) $y = 24t^2 + 67t + 1831$

(b)   (c) 2015: \$2766
2020: \$4901
2025: \$8236

(d) Answers will vary.

97. (a) $x_1 = s, x_2 = t, x_3 = 600 - s,$
$x_4 = s - t, x_5 = 500 - t, x_6 = s, x_7 = t$
(b) $x_1 = 0, x_2 = 0, x_3 = 600, x_4 = 0, x_5 = 500,$
$x_6 = 0, x_7 = 0$
(c) $x_1 = 500, x_2 = 100, x_3 = 100, x_4 = 400,$
$x_5 = 400, x_6 = 500, x_7 = 100$

99. True. See Example 7.

101. $\begin{cases} x + y + 7z = -1 \\ x + 2y + 11z = 0 \\ 2x + y + 10z = -3 \end{cases}$
(Answer is not unique.)

103. No; Answers will vary.

105.

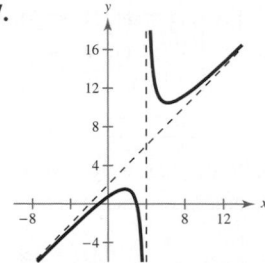

Asymptotes: $x = -1, y = 0$

107.

Asymptotes:
$x = 4, y = x + 2$

Section 7.5 (page 527)

1. equal   **3.** zero, O

5. (a) iii   (b) i   (c) iv   (d) v   (e) ii

7. No, not in general.   **9.** $x = 5, y = -8$

11. $x = -1, y = 4, z = 8$

13. (a) $\begin{bmatrix} 8 & -1 \\ 1 & 7 \end{bmatrix}$ (b) $\begin{bmatrix} 2 & -3 \\ 5 & -5 \end{bmatrix}$
(c) $\begin{bmatrix} 15 & -6 \\ 9 & 3 \end{bmatrix}$ (d) $\begin{bmatrix} 9 & -8 \\ 13 & -9 \end{bmatrix}$

15. (a) $\begin{bmatrix} 9 & 5 \\ 1 & -2 \\ -3 & 15 \end{bmatrix}$ (b) $\begin{bmatrix} 7 & -7 \\ 3 & 8 \\ -5 & -5 \end{bmatrix}$
(c) $\begin{bmatrix} 24 & -3 \\ 6 & 9 \\ -12 & 15 \end{bmatrix}$ (d) $\begin{bmatrix} 22 & -15 \\ 8 & 19 \\ -14 & -5 \end{bmatrix}$

17. (a) $\begin{bmatrix} 5 & 5 & -2 & 4 & 4 \\ -5 & 10 & 0 & -4 & -7 \end{bmatrix}$
(b) $\begin{bmatrix} 3 & 5 & 0 & 2 & 4 \\ 7 & -6 & -4 & 2 & 7 \end{bmatrix}$
(c) $\begin{bmatrix} 12 & 15 & -3 & 9 & 12 \\ 3 & 6 & -6 & -3 & 0 \end{bmatrix}$
(d) $\begin{bmatrix} 10 & 15 & -1 & 7 & 12 \\ 15 & -10 & -10 & 3 & 14 \end{bmatrix}$

19. (a) Not possible   (b) Not possible
(c) $\begin{bmatrix} 18 & 0 & 9 \\ -3 & -12 & 0 \end{bmatrix}$ (d) Not possible

21. $\begin{bmatrix} -8 & -7 \\ 15 & -1 \end{bmatrix}$ **23.** $\begin{bmatrix} -3 & -\frac{1}{3} & 1 \\ -4 & \frac{8}{3} & -5 \end{bmatrix}$

25. $\begin{bmatrix} -17.143 & 2.143 \\ 11.571 & 10.286 \end{bmatrix}$ **27.** $\begin{bmatrix} -16.463 & -33.373 \\ 3.706 & -26.654 \\ 2.167 & 18.382 \end{bmatrix}$

29. $\begin{bmatrix} -\frac{2}{3} & \frac{8}{3} \\ \frac{7}{3} & 0 \\ -3 & -\frac{7}{3} \end{bmatrix}$ **31.** $\begin{bmatrix} 2 & -5 \\ -5 & 0 \\ 5 & 6 \end{bmatrix}$ **33.** $\begin{bmatrix} 11 & 1 \\ -11 & 5 \\ 54 & -6 \end{bmatrix}$

35. Not possible   **37.** $\begin{bmatrix} 2 & 0 & 0 \\ 0 & -1 & 0 \\ 0 & 0 & -\frac{1}{3} \end{bmatrix}$

39. $\begin{bmatrix} 10 & -40 & 20 \\ -6 & 24 & -12 \\ 8 & -32 & 16 \end{bmatrix}$

41. (a) $\begin{bmatrix} 0 & 15 \\ 6 & 12 \end{bmatrix}$ (b) $\begin{bmatrix} -2 & 2 \\ 31 & 14 \end{bmatrix}$ (c) $\begin{bmatrix} 9 & 6 \\ 12 & 12 \end{bmatrix}$

43. (a) $\begin{bmatrix} 0 & -10 \\ 10 & 0 \end{bmatrix}$ (b) $\begin{bmatrix} 0 & -10 \\ 10 & 0 \end{bmatrix}$ (c) $\begin{bmatrix} 8 & -6 \\ 6 & 8 \end{bmatrix}$

45. (a) $\begin{bmatrix} 7 & 7 & 14 \\ 8 & 8 & 16 \\ -1 & -1 & -2 \end{bmatrix}$ (b) $\begin{bmatrix} 13 \end{bmatrix}$ (c) Not possible

47. $\begin{bmatrix} 124 & -70 \\ 228 & 452 \\ 192 & -72 \end{bmatrix}$ **49.** Not possible

51. $\begin{bmatrix} 5 & 8 \\ -4 & -16 \end{bmatrix}$ **53.** $\begin{bmatrix} -4 & 10 \\ 3 & 14 \end{bmatrix}$

55. (a) No   (b) Yes   (c) No   (d) No

57. (a) No   (b) No   (c) No   (d) Yes

59. (a) $\begin{bmatrix} -1 & 1 \\ -2 & 1 \end{bmatrix}\begin{bmatrix} x_1 \\ x_2 \end{bmatrix} = \begin{bmatrix} 4 \\ 0 \end{bmatrix}$ (b) $\begin{bmatrix} 4 \\ 8 \end{bmatrix}$

61. (a) $\begin{bmatrix} -2 & -3 \\ 6 & 1 \end{bmatrix}\begin{bmatrix} x_1 \\ x_2 \end{bmatrix} = \begin{bmatrix} -4 \\ -36 \end{bmatrix}$ (b) $\begin{bmatrix} -7 \\ 6 \end{bmatrix}$

63. (a) $\begin{bmatrix} 1 & -2 & 3 \\ -1 & 3 & -1 \\ 2 & -5 & 5 \end{bmatrix}\begin{bmatrix} x_1 \\ x_2 \\ x_3 \end{bmatrix} = \begin{bmatrix} 9 \\ -6 \\ 17 \end{bmatrix}$ (b) $\begin{bmatrix} 1 \\ -1 \\ 2 \end{bmatrix}$

65. (a) $\begin{bmatrix} 1 & -5 & 2 \\ -3 & 1 & -1 \\ 0 & -2 & 5 \end{bmatrix}\begin{bmatrix} x_1 \\ x_2 \\ x_3 \end{bmatrix} = \begin{bmatrix} -20 \\ 8 \\ -16 \end{bmatrix}$ (b) $\begin{bmatrix} -1 \\ 3 \\ -2 \end{bmatrix}$

67. (a) $\begin{bmatrix} 7 & -2 & 5 \\ -6 & 13 & -8 \\ 16 & 11 & -3 \end{bmatrix}$ (b) $\begin{bmatrix} 7 & -2 & 5 \\ -6 & 13 & -8 \\ 16 & 11 & -3 \end{bmatrix}$
The answers are the same.

69. (a) $\begin{bmatrix} 25 & -34 & 28 \\ -53 & 34 & -7 \\ -76 & 30 & 21 \end{bmatrix}$ (b) $\begin{bmatrix} 25 & -34 & 28 \\ -53 & 34 & -7 \\ -76 & 30 & 21 \end{bmatrix}$
The answers are the same.

71. (a) $\begin{bmatrix} 26 & 11 & 0 \\ 11 & 20 & -3 \\ 11 & 14 & 0 \end{bmatrix}$ (b) $\begin{bmatrix} 26 & 11 & 0 \\ 11 & 20 & -3 \\ 11 & 14 & 0 \end{bmatrix}$
The answers are the same.

73. (a) and (b) $\begin{bmatrix} 3 & -6 & 0 \\ 3 & 3 & 0 \end{bmatrix}$

75. Not possible, undefined   77. Not possible, undefined

79. (a) and (b) $\begin{bmatrix} 5 & 16 & -13 \\ -8 & 5 & 0 \end{bmatrix}$

81. $\begin{bmatrix} -4 & 0 \\ 8 & 2 \end{bmatrix}$ 83. $\begin{bmatrix} 85 & 102 & 51 & 34 \\ 119 & 136 & 170 & 68 \end{bmatrix}$

85. $\begin{bmatrix} 84 & 60 & 30 \\ 42 & 120 & 84 \end{bmatrix}$

87. (a) [\$3.50 \$6.00]
  (b) [\$1037.50 \$1400.00 \$1012.50]
  The entries represent the total profits made at the three outlets.

89. $\begin{bmatrix} \$23.20 & \$20.50 \\ \$38.20 & \$33.80 \\ \$76.90 & \$68.50 \end{bmatrix}$ The entries represent labor costs at the two plants for the three boat sizes.

91. $\begin{bmatrix} 0.40 & 0.15 & 0.15 \\ 0.28 & 0.53 & 0.17 \\ 0.32 & 0.32 & 0.68 \end{bmatrix}$ P^2 represents the proportion of changes in party affiliations after two elections.

93. True. To add two matrices, you add corresponding entries.

95. Not possible   97. 3×2 99. Not possible

101. 2×3 103 and 105. Answers will vary.

107. $AC = BC = \begin{bmatrix} 2 & 3 \\ 2 & 3 \end{bmatrix}, A \neq B$

109. (a) $A^2 = \begin{bmatrix} -1 & 0 \\ 0 & -1 \end{bmatrix}, A^3 = \begin{bmatrix} -i & 0 \\ 0 & -i \end{bmatrix}, A^4 = \begin{bmatrix} 1 & 0 \\ 0 & 1 \end{bmatrix}$
  The entries on the main diagonal are i^2 in A^2, i^3 in A^3, and i^4 in A^4.
  (b) $B^2 = \begin{bmatrix} 1 & 0 \\ 0 & 1 \end{bmatrix}$
  B^2 is the identity matrix.

111. (a) No, because they have different dimensions.
  (b) No, because they have different dimensions.
  (c) Yes, because the number of columns of A is equal to the number of rows of B.

113. $\ln \dfrac{64}{\sqrt[3]{x^2 + 3}}$

Section 7.6   (page 538)

1. inverse   3. No   5–9. Answers will vary.

11. $\begin{bmatrix} \frac{1}{2} & 0 \\ 0 & \frac{1}{3} \end{bmatrix}$ 13. $\begin{bmatrix} -3 & 2 \\ -2 & 1 \end{bmatrix}$

15. Does not exist   17. Does not exist

19. $\begin{bmatrix} 1 & 1 & -1 \\ -3 & 2 & -1 \\ 3 & -3 & 2 \end{bmatrix}$ 21. $\begin{bmatrix} -\frac{3}{2} & \frac{3}{2} & 1 \\ \frac{9}{2} & -\frac{7}{2} & -3 \\ -1 & 1 & 1 \end{bmatrix}$

23. $\begin{bmatrix} -12 & -5 & -9 \\ -4 & -2 & -4 \\ -8 & -4 & -6 \end{bmatrix}$ 25. $\dfrac{5}{11}\begin{bmatrix} 0 & -4 & 2 \\ -22 & 11 & 11 \\ 22 & -6 & -8 \end{bmatrix}$

27. Does not exist   29. Does not exist

31. $\dfrac{1}{59}\begin{bmatrix} 16 & 15 \\ -4 & 70 \end{bmatrix}$ 33. $\begin{bmatrix} \frac{5}{13} & -\frac{3}{13} \\ \frac{1}{13} & \frac{2}{13} \end{bmatrix}$ 35. $k = 0$

37. $(5, 0)$ 39. $(-8, -6)$ 41. $(3, 8, -11)$

43. $(2, 1, 0, 0)$ 45. $(2, -2)$

47. Not possible, because A is not invertible.

49. $(-4, -8)$ 51. $(-1, 3, 2)$

53. $(0.3125t + 0.8125, 1.1875t + 0.6875, t)$

55. $(5, 0, -2, 3)$

57. \$4000 in AAA-rated bonds, \$2000 in A-rated bonds, and \$4000 in B-rated bonds

59. \$30,000 in AAA-rated bonds, \$90,000 in A-rated bonds, and \$180,000 in B-rated bonds

61. $I_1 = \frac{1}{2}$ ampere, $I_2 = 3$ amperes, $I_3 = 3.5$ amperes

63. 100 bags for seedlings, 100 bags for general potting, 100 bags for hardwood plants

65. (a) $\begin{cases} 2.5r + 4l + 2i = 300 \\ -r + 2l + 2i = 0 \\ r + l + i = 120 \end{cases}$
  (b) $\begin{bmatrix} 2.5 & 4 & 2 \\ -1 & 2 & 2 \\ 1 & 1 & 1 \end{bmatrix}\begin{bmatrix} r \\ l \\ i \end{bmatrix} = \begin{bmatrix} 300 \\ 0 \\ 120 \end{bmatrix}$
  (c) 80 roses, 10 lilies, 30 irises

67. True; $AA^{-1} = I = A^{-1}A$.

69. False; Only square matrices are nonsingular.

71. Answers will vary.

73. (a) Answers will vary.
  (b) $A^{-1} = \begin{bmatrix} \frac{1}{a_{11}} & 0 & 0 & 0 & \cdots & 0 \\ 0 & \frac{1}{a_{22}} & 0 & 0 & \cdots & 0 \\ 0 & 0 & \frac{1}{a_{33}} & 0 & \cdots & 0 \\ \vdots & \vdots & \vdots & \vdots & \cdots & \vdots \\ 0 & 0 & 0 & 0 & \cdots & \frac{1}{a_{nn}} \end{bmatrix}$

75. $\ln 3 \approx 1.099$ 77. $\dfrac{e^{12/7}}{3} \approx 1.851$

Section 7.7   (page 545)

1. determinant   3. -5 5. 4   7. 32

9. -24 11. -9 13. 7.76   15. 11.998

17. (a) $M_{11} = -5, M_{12} = 2, M_{21} = 4, M_{22} = 3$
  (b) $C_{11} = -5, C_{12} = -2, C_{21} = -4, C_{22} = 3$

19. (a) $M_{11} = 10, M_{12} = -43, M_{13} = 2, M_{21} = -30,$
    $M_{22} = 17, M_{23} = -6, M_{31} = 54, M_{32} = -53,$
    $M_{33} = -34$
  (b) $C_{11} = 10, C_{12} = 43, C_{13} = 2, C_{21} = 30, C_{22} = 17,$
    $C_{23} = 6, C_{31} = 54, C_{32} = 53, C_{33} = -34$

21. (a) -75 (b) -75 23. (a) 170   (b) 170

25. -58 27. 0   29. -9 31. -168

33. 412   35. -336 37. 566

39. (a) 0   (b) -1 (c) $\begin{bmatrix} -2 & -5 \\ 4 & 10 \end{bmatrix}$
  (d) 0; $|AB| = |A| \cdot |B|$

41. (a) -23 (b) 1 (c) $\begin{bmatrix} -9 & 4 & 1 \\ -5 & -10 & 6 \\ 4 & -1 & -1 \end{bmatrix}$

(d) -23; $|AB| = |A| \cdot |B|$

43. (a) -25 (b) -220 (c) $\begin{bmatrix} -7 & -16 & -1 & -28 \\ -4 & -14 & -11 & 8 \\ 13 & 4 & 4 & -4 \\ -2 & 3 & 2 & 2 \end{bmatrix}$

(d) 5500; $|AB| = |A| \cdot |B|$

45–49. Answers will vary.   **51.** $x = \pm 2$

53. $x = \pm\frac{3}{2}$ **55.** $x = -1, 3$ **57.** $x = -4, -1$

59. $x = 1, \frac{1}{2}$ **61.** $x = 3$ **63.** $8uv - 1$

65. e^{5x} **67.** $1 - \ln x$

69. True. Expansion by cofactors on a row of zeros is zero.

71. Answers will vary. Sample answer:

$$A = \begin{bmatrix} 1 & 0 & -3 \\ 6 & -2 & 7 \\ 9 & 5 & -1 \end{bmatrix}, \quad B = \begin{bmatrix} 3 & 1 & 5 \\ -8 & 1 & 0 \\ -7 & 6 & -2 \end{bmatrix}$$

$|A + B| = -328$, $|A| + |B| = -404$

73. (a) 6 (b) $\begin{bmatrix} \frac{1}{3} & -\frac{1}{3} \\ \frac{1}{3} & \frac{1}{6} \end{bmatrix}$ (c) $\frac{1}{6}$ (d) They are reciprocals.

75. (a) 2 (b) $\begin{bmatrix} -4 & -5 & 1.5 \\ -1 & -1 & 0.5 \\ -1 & -1 & 0 \end{bmatrix}$ (c) $\frac{1}{2}$

(d) They are reciprocals.

77. (a) Columns 2 and 3 are interchanged.

(b) Rows 1 and 3 are interchanged.

79. (a) 3 is factored from the second row.

(b) 2 and 4 are factored from the first and second columns, respectively.

81. (a) 15 (b) -75 (c) -120

The determinant of a triangular matrix is the product of the numbers along the main diagonal.

83. Answers will vary.   **85.** $(2y - 3)^2$ **87.** $(2, -4)$

Section 7.8   (page 556)

1. Cramer's Rule   **3.** $-\frac{1}{2}$ **5.** $\frac{5}{2}$ **7.** $\frac{33}{8}$

9. 24 **11.** $x = 0, -\frac{16}{5}$ **13.** Collinear

15. Not collinear   **17.** $x = 3$ **19.** $(-3, -2)$

21. $(-1, 2)$ **23.** Not possible

25. (a) and (b) $\left(0, -\frac{1}{2}, \frac{1}{2}\right)$

27. (a) $y = 0.143t^2 + 1.417t + 57$

(b)

The model fits the data well.

(c) 110.43 billion

29. (a) $[3 \quad 15], [13 \quad 5], [0 \quad 8], [15 \quad 13], [5 \quad 0], [19 \quad 15],$
$[15 \quad 14]$

(b) $48 \quad 81 \quad 28 \quad 51 \quad 24 \quad 40 \quad 54 \quad 95 \quad 5 \quad 10 \quad 64$
$113 \quad 57 \quad 100$

31. (a) $[3 \quad 1 \quad 12], [12 \quad 0 \quad 13], [5 \quad 0 \quad 20], [15 \quad 13 \quad 15],$
$[18 \quad 18 \quad 15], [23 \quad 0 \quad 0]$

(b) $-68 \quad 21 \quad 35 \quad -66 \quad 14 \quad 39 \quad -115 \quad 35 \quad 60$
$-62 \quad 15 \quad 32 \quad -54 \quad 12 \quad 27 \quad 23 \quad -23 \quad 0$

33. HAPPY NEW YEAR   **35.** CANCEL ORDERS SUE

37. True. Cramer's Rule divides by the determinant.

39. Answers will vary.   **41.** $x + 4y - 19 = 0$

43. $2x - 7y - 27 = 0$

Review Exercises   (page 560)

1. $(1, 1)$ **3.** No solution   **5.** $(0.25, 0.625)$ **7.** $(5, 4)$

9. $(0, 0), (2, 8), (-2, 8)$ **11.** $(2, -0.5)$

13. $(0, 0), (4, -4)$ **15.** $(4, 4)$ **17.** 800 plants

19. 96 m $\times$ 144 m   **21.** $(-8, 1)$ **23.** $\left(\frac{5}{2}, 3\right)$

25. Infinitely many solutions   **27.** $(0, 0)$ **29.** No solution

31.   **33.**

Consistent: $(1.6, -2.4)$ Inconsistent

35.

Consistent; All points on the line $8x - 2y = 10$

37. $\left(\dfrac{500,000}{7}, \dfrac{159}{7}\right)$

39. 218.75 mi/h; 193.75 mi/h   **41.** $(2, -4, -5)$

43. $\left(-\frac{257}{16}, -\frac{5}{16}, \frac{11}{16}\right)$ **45.** $(3a + 4, 2a + 5, a)$

47. $\left(-\frac{19}{6}, \frac{17}{12}, \frac{1}{3}\right)$ **49.** $(a - 4, a - 3, a)$

51.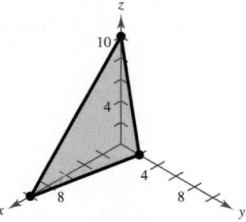

Sample answer: $(10, 0, 0), (0, 2, 0), (0, 0, 10), (2, 1, 3)$

53. $\dfrac{3}{x + 2} - \dfrac{4}{x + 4}$ **55.** $\dfrac{1}{2}\left(\dfrac{3}{x - 3} - \dfrac{3}{x + 3}\right)$

57. $\dfrac{1}{2}\left(\dfrac{3}{x - 1} - \dfrac{x - 3}{x^2 + 1}\right)$ **59.** $y = 2x^2 + x - 5$

61. 4 par-3 holes, 10 par-4 holes, 4 par-5 holes

63. 3×1 **65.** 1×1

67. $\begin{bmatrix} 6 & -7 & \vdots & 11 \\ -2 & 5 & \vdots & -1 \end{bmatrix}$ **69.** $\begin{bmatrix} 3 & -5 & 1 & \vdots & 25 \\ -4 & 0 & -2 & \vdots & -14 \\ 6 & 1 & 0 & \vdots & 15 \end{bmatrix}$

71. $\begin{cases} 5x + y + 7z = -9 \\ 4x + 2y = 10 \\ 9x + 4y + 2z = 3 \end{cases}$ **73.** $\begin{bmatrix} 1 & -\frac{5}{3} & 3 \\ 0 & 1 & \frac{9}{7} \end{bmatrix}$

75. $\begin{bmatrix} 1 & 1 & 1 \\ 0 & 1 & 2 \\ 0 & 0 & 1 \end{bmatrix}$ **77.** $\begin{bmatrix} 1 & 0 \\ 0 & 1 \end{bmatrix}$ **79.** $\begin{bmatrix} 1 & 0 & 0 \\ 0 & 1 & 0 \\ 0 & 0 & 1 \end{bmatrix}$

81. $(10, -12)$ **83.** Inconsistent **85.** $\left(\frac{1}{2}, -\frac{1}{3}, 1\right)$
87. $(3a + 1, -a, a)$ **89.** $(a - 3, -2a, a)$
91. $(2, -3, 3)$ **93.** Inconsistent **95.** $(1, 2, 2)$
97. $(3, 0, -4)$ **99.** Inconsistent
101. $x = 12, y = -7$ **103.** $x = 1, y = 11$
105. (a) $\begin{bmatrix} 17 & -17 \\ 13 & 2 \end{bmatrix}$ (b) $\begin{bmatrix} -3 & 23 \\ -15 & 8 \end{bmatrix}$

(c) $\begin{bmatrix} 14 & 6 \\ -2 & 10 \end{bmatrix}$ (d) $\begin{bmatrix} 37 & -57 \\ 41 & -4 \end{bmatrix}$

107. (a) Not possible (b) Not possible

(c) $\begin{bmatrix} -22 & 32 & 38 \\ -14 & -4 & 2 \end{bmatrix}$ (d) Not possible

109. $\begin{bmatrix} -13 & -8 & 18 \\ 0 & 11 & -19 \end{bmatrix}$ **111.** $\begin{bmatrix} 17 & -39 \\ 37 & 6 \end{bmatrix}$

113. $\begin{bmatrix} 21 & -\frac{45}{4} & -\frac{159}{8} \\ \frac{93}{8} & \frac{327}{8} & \frac{291}{8} \end{bmatrix}$ **115.** $\begin{bmatrix} -4 & -2 \\ \frac{7}{2} & -\frac{17}{2} \\ -\frac{17}{2} & -1 \end{bmatrix}$

117. $\frac{1}{3}\begin{bmatrix} 6 & 2 \\ -4 & 11 \\ 10 & 0 \end{bmatrix}$ **119.** $\begin{bmatrix} 14 & -2 & 8 \\ 14 & -10 & 40 \\ 36 & -12 & 48 \end{bmatrix}$

121. Not possible
123. $\begin{bmatrix} 14 & -22 & 22 \\ 19 & -41 & 80 \\ 42 & -66 & 66 \end{bmatrix}$ **125.** $\begin{bmatrix} 1 & 17 \\ 12 & 36 \end{bmatrix}$

127. (a) $[\$99 \quad \$112]$
(b) $[\$12,400 \quad \$23,080 \quad \$22,820]$
The entries represent the total prices of all tires at each factory.
129. Answers will vary.
131. $\begin{bmatrix} 4 & -5 \\ 5 & -6 \end{bmatrix}$ **133.** $\begin{bmatrix} \frac{1}{2} & -1 & -\frac{1}{2} \\ \frac{1}{2} & -\frac{2}{3} & -\frac{5}{6} \\ 0 & \frac{2}{3} & \frac{1}{3} \end{bmatrix}$ **135.** $\begin{bmatrix} \frac{1}{5} & \frac{1}{5} \\ \frac{1}{10} & -\frac{1}{15} \end{bmatrix}$

137. Does not exist
139. $\begin{bmatrix} -3 & 6 & -5.5 & 3.5 \\ 1 & -2 & 2 & -1 \\ 7 & -15 & 14.5 & -9.5 \\ -1 & 2.5 & -2.5 & 1.5 \end{bmatrix}$ **141.** $\begin{bmatrix} 1 & -1 \\ 4 & -\frac{7}{2} \end{bmatrix}$

143. Does not exist **145.** $\begin{bmatrix} 2 & \frac{20}{3} \\ \frac{1}{10} & \frac{1}{6} \end{bmatrix}$ **147.** $(36, 11)$

149. $(2, -1, -2)$ **151.** Not possible **153.** $(-3, 1)$
155. $(1, 1, -2)$ **157.** -23 **159.** -42 **161.** 550
163. (a) $M_{11} = 4, M_{12} = 7, M_{21} = -1, M_{22} = 2$
(b) $C_{11} = 4, C_{12} = -7, C_{21} = 1, C_{22} = 2$
165. (a) $M_{11} = 30, M_{12} = -12, M_{13} = -21, M_{21} = 20,$
$M_{22} = 19, M_{23} = 22, M_{31} = 5, M_{32} = 2, M_{33} = 19$
(b) $C_{11} = 30, C_{12} = 12, C_{13} = -21, C_{21} = -20,$
$C_{22} = 19, C_{23} = -22, C_{31} = 5, C_{32} = 2, C_{33} = 19$

167. 130 **169.** -24 **171.** -27 **173.** 279
175. 16 **177.** 1.75 **179.** 48 **181.** Not collinear
183. Collinear **185.** $(1, 2)$ **187.** Not possible
189. $(-1, 4, 5)$ **191.** $(0, -2.4, -2.6)$
193. (a) and (b) $\left(\frac{53}{33}, -\frac{17}{33}, \frac{61}{66}\right)$
195. (a) $[12 \quad 15 \quad 15], [11 \quad 0 \quad 15], [21 \quad 20 \quad 0], [2 \quad 5 \quad 12],$
$[15 \quad 23 \quad 0]$
(b) $-21 \quad 6 \quad 0 \quad -68 \quad 8 \quad 45 \quad 102 \quad -42 \quad -60 \quad -53$
$20 \quad 21 \quad 99 \quad -30 \quad -69$
197. I WILL BE BACK
199. THAT IS MY FINAL ANSWER
201. False. The solution may have irrational numbers.
203. Elementary row operations correspond to the operations performed on a system of equations.

Chapter Test (page 566)

1. $(4, -2)$ **2.** $(0, -1), (1, 0), (2, 1)$
3. No solution **4.** $(3, -4)$ **5.** $\left(\frac{7}{13}, -\frac{85}{26}\right)$
6. $(1, 0, -2)$ **7.** $y = -\frac{1}{2}x^2 + x + 6$
8. $\frac{5}{x - 1} + \frac{3}{(x - 1)^2}$ **9.** $\frac{1}{x} + \frac{2}{x^2} - \frac{1}{x^2 + 1}$
10. $(-2a + 1.5, 2a + 1, a)$ **11.** $(5, 2, -6)$
12. (a) $\begin{bmatrix} 1 & 0 & 4 \\ -7 & -6 & -1 \\ 0 & 4 & 0 \end{bmatrix}$ (b) $\begin{bmatrix} 15 & 12 & 12 \\ -12 & -12 & 0 \\ 3 & 6 & 0 \end{bmatrix}$

(c) $\begin{bmatrix} 7 & 6 & 12 \\ -18 & -16 & -2 \\ 1 & 10 & 0 \end{bmatrix}$ (d) $\begin{bmatrix} 36 & 20 & 4 \\ -28 & -24 & -4 \\ 10 & 8 & 2 \end{bmatrix}$

13. $(-2, 3, -1)$ **14.** 67 **15.** -2
16. 30 **17.** $\left(1, -\frac{1}{2}\right)$
18. $x_1 = 700 - s - t, x_2 = 300 - s - t,$
$x_3 = s, x_4 = 100 - t, x_5 = t$

Chapter 8

Section 8.1 (page 577)

1. terms **3.** index, upper limit, lower limit
5. (a) Finite sequence (b) Infinite sequence
7. $-3, -1, 1, 3, 5$ **9.** $3, 9, 27, 81, 243$
11. $-\frac{1}{2}, \frac{1}{4}, -\frac{1}{8}, \frac{1}{16}, -\frac{1}{32}$ **13.** $2, \frac{3}{2}, \frac{4}{3}, \frac{5}{4}, \frac{6}{5}$ **15.** $\frac{1}{2}, \frac{2}{5}, \frac{3}{10}, \frac{4}{17}, \frac{5}{26}$
17. (a) $0, 1, 0, 0.5, 0$ (b) $0, 1, 0, \frac{1}{2}, 0$
19. (a) $0.5, 0.75, 0.875, 0.938, 0.969$ (b) $\frac{1}{2}, \frac{3}{4}, \frac{7}{8}, \frac{15}{16}, \frac{31}{32}$
21. (a) $1, 0.354, 0.192, 0.125, 0.089$ (b) $1, \frac{1}{2^{3/2}}, \frac{1}{3^{3/2}}, \frac{1}{8}, \frac{1}{5^{3/2}}$
23. (a) $-1, 0.25, -0.111, 0.063, -0.04$
(b) $-1, \frac{1}{4}, -\frac{1}{9}, \frac{1}{16}, -\frac{1}{25}$
25. (a) and (b) $3, 15, 35, 63, 99$
27. $9, 15, 21, 27, 33, 39, 45, 51, 57, 63$
29. $3, \frac{5}{2}, \frac{7}{3}, \frac{9}{4}, \frac{11}{5}, \frac{13}{6}, \frac{15}{7}, \frac{17}{8}, \frac{19}{9}, \frac{21}{10}$ **31.** $0, 2, 0, 2, 0, 2, 0, 2, 0, 2$
33. $\frac{100}{101}$ **35.** -73 **37.** $\frac{256}{129}$ **39.** $a_n = 5n - 2$
41. $a_n = 6n + 1$ **43.** $a_n = n^2 - 1$ **45.** $a_n = \frac{n + 1}{n + 2}$

47. $a_n = \dfrac{(-1)^{n+1}}{2^n}$ **49.** $a_n = 1 + \dfrac{1}{n}$

51. $a_n = (-1)^n + 2(1)^n = (-1)^n + 2$ **53.** 28, 24, 20, 16, 12

55. 3, 4, 6, 10, 18   **57.** 1, 3, 4, 7, 11

59. 6, 8, 10, 12, 14; $a_n = 2n + 4$

61. 81, 27, 9, 3, 1; $a_n = \dfrac{243}{3^n}$

63. (a) 1, 1, 0.5, 0.167, 0.042   (b) $1, 1, \frac{1}{2}, \frac{1}{6}, \frac{1}{24}$

65. (a) 0, 0.5, 0.667, 0.375, 0.133   (b) $0, \frac{1}{2}, \frac{2}{3}, \frac{3}{8}, \frac{2}{15}$

67. (a) 1, 0.5, 0.042, 0.001, 2.480×10^{-5}

(b) $1, \frac{1}{2}, \frac{1}{24}, \frac{1}{720}, \frac{1}{40,320}$

69. $\frac{1}{12}$ **71.** 495   **73.** $(n + 3)(n + 2)(n + 1)$

75. $\dfrac{1}{2n(2n + 1)}$ **77.** c   **78.** b   **79.** d   **80.** a

81.

83.

85.
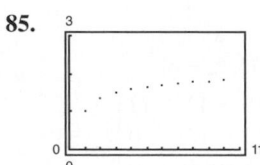

87. 35   **89.** 364   **91.** $\frac{124}{429}$ **93.** 40   **95.** 186

97. 31   **99.** 81   **101.** $0.6\overline{3}$

103. $\displaystyle\sum_{i=1}^{9} \dfrac{1}{3i} \approx 0.94299$ **105.** $\displaystyle\sum_{i=1}^{8}\left[2\left(\dfrac{i}{8}\right) + 3\right] = 33$

107. $\displaystyle\sum_{i=1}^{6}(-1)^i 3^i = 546$ **109.** $\displaystyle\sum_{i=1}^{20}\dfrac{(-1)^{i+1}}{i^2} \approx 0.821$

111. $\displaystyle\sum_{i=1}^{5}\dfrac{2^i - 1}{2^{i+1}} \approx 2.0156$ **113.** $\dfrac{1092}{625}$ **115.** $-\dfrac{3}{2}$

117. (a) $\dfrac{3333}{5000}$ (b) $\dfrac{2}{3}$ **119.** (a) $\dfrac{7777}{10,000}$ (b) $\dfrac{7}{9}$

121. (a) $A_1 = \$5037.50, A_2 = \$5075.28$,
$A_3 = \$5113.35, A_4 = \$5151.70$,
$A_5 = \$5190.33, A_6 = \$5229.26$,
$A_7 = \$5268.48, A_8 = \$5307.99$

(b) \$6741.74

123. (a) $p_0 = 5500, p_n = (0.75)p_{n-1} + 500$

(b) 4625, 3969, 3477, 3108; These values represent the number of trout in the lake for the years 2016 through 2019.

(c) 2000 trout; Answers will vary. Sample answer: As time passes, the population of trout decreases at a decreasing rate. Because the population is growing smaller and still declines 25%, each time 25% is taken from a smaller number there is a smaller decline in the number of trout.

125. True by the Properties of Sums

127. 1, 1, 2, 3, 5, 8, 13, 21, 34, 55, 89, 144;
$1, 2, \frac{3}{2}, \frac{5}{3}, \frac{8}{5}, \frac{13}{8}, \frac{21}{13}, \frac{34}{21}, \frac{55}{34}, \frac{89}{55}$

129. 1, 1, 2, 3, 5

131. $a_{n+1} = \dfrac{1}{2}a_n + \dfrac{\left(1 + \sqrt{5}\right)^n + \left(1 - \sqrt{5}\right)^n}{2^{n+1}}$

$a_{n+2} = \dfrac{3}{2}a_n + \dfrac{\left(1 + \sqrt{5}\right)^n + \left(1 - \sqrt{5}\right)^n}{2^{n+1}}$

133. $x, \dfrac{x^2}{2}, \dfrac{x^3}{6}, \dfrac{x^4}{24}, \dfrac{x^5}{120}$ **135.** $-\dfrac{x^3}{3}, \dfrac{x^5}{5}, -\dfrac{x^7}{7}, \dfrac{x^9}{9}, -\dfrac{x^{11}}{11}$

137. $-\dfrac{x^2}{2}, \dfrac{x^4}{24}, -\dfrac{x^6}{720}, \dfrac{x^8}{40,320}, -\dfrac{x^{10}}{3,628,800}$

139. $-x, \dfrac{x^2}{2}, -\dfrac{x^3}{6}, \dfrac{x^4}{24}, -\dfrac{x^5}{120}$

141. $x + 1, -\dfrac{(x + 1)^2}{2}, \dfrac{(x + 1)^3}{6}, -\dfrac{(x + 1)^4}{24}, \dfrac{(x + 1)^5}{120}$

143. $\dfrac{1}{4}, \dfrac{1}{12}, \dfrac{1}{24}, \dfrac{1}{40}, \dfrac{1}{60}; \dfrac{1}{2} - \dfrac{1}{2n + 2}$

145. $\dfrac{1}{6}, \dfrac{1}{12}, \dfrac{1}{20}, \dfrac{1}{30}, \dfrac{1}{42}; \dfrac{1}{2} - \dfrac{1}{n + 2}$

147. Yes, if there is a finite number of integer terms, you can always find a sum.

149. (a) $\begin{bmatrix} 2 \\ 6 \end{bmatrix}$ (b) $\begin{bmatrix} -10 \\ -15 \end{bmatrix}$ (c) Not possible

(d) Not possible

151. (a) $\begin{bmatrix} -3 & -7 & 4 \\ 4 & 4 & 1 \\ 1 & 4 & 3 \end{bmatrix}$ (b) $\begin{bmatrix} 8 & 17 & -14 \\ -12 & -13 & -9 \\ -3 & -15 & -10 \end{bmatrix}$

(c) $\begin{bmatrix} -2 & 7 & -16 \\ 4 & 42 & 45 \\ 1 & 23 & 48 \end{bmatrix}$ (d) $\begin{bmatrix} 16 & 31 & 42 \\ 10 & 47 & 31 \\ 13 & 22 & 25 \end{bmatrix}$

Section 8.2   (page 586)

1. $a_n = a_1 + (n - 1)d$

3. A sequence is arithmetic when the differences between consecutive terms are the same.

5. Arithmetic sequence, $d = 2$

7. Arithmetic sequence, $d = -\frac{1}{2}$

9. Not an arithmetic sequence

11. 21, 34, 47, 60, 73
Arithmetic sequence, $d = 13$

13. 25, 21, 17, 13, 9
Arithmetic sequence, $d = -4$

15. 3, 6, 11, 20, 37
Not an arithmetic sequence

17. 1, 5, 1, 5, 1
Not an arithmetic sequence

19. $\frac{1}{4}, \frac{1}{4}, \frac{1}{4}, \frac{1}{4}, \frac{1}{4}$
Arithmetic sequence, $d = 0$

21. $a_n = 6n - 5$ **23.** $a_n = -7n + 50$

25. $a_n = -\frac{3}{4}n + \frac{15}{4}$ **27.** $a_n = 9n - 14$

29. $a_n = 103 - 3n$ **31.** 5, 11, 17, 23, 29

33. $-2.6, -2.4, -2.2, -2.0, -1.8$ **35.** $-2, 2, 6, 10, 14$

37. 22.45, 20.725, 19, 17.275, 15.55

39. 15, 19, 23, 27, 31; $d = 4; a_n = 11 + 4n$

41. $\frac{3}{5}, \frac{1}{2}, \frac{2}{5}, \frac{3}{10}, \frac{1}{5}; d = -\frac{1}{10}; a_n = -\frac{1}{10}n + \frac{7}{10}$

43. 59   **45.** -10.2

47.

49. (graph with 2.4 top, 0 left, 11 right, −2.0 bottom)

51. −1, 3, 7, 11, 15, 19, 23, 27, 31, 35

53. 19.25, 18.5, 17.75, 17, 16.25, 15.5, 14.75, 14, 13.25, 12.5

55. 1.55, 1.6, 1.65, 1.7, 1.75, 1.8, 1.85, 1.9, 1.95, 2   **57.** 110

59. −25   **61.** 5050   **63.** −4585   **65.** 620   **67.** 36

69. 4000   **71.** 1275   **73.** 355   **75.** 129,250

77. 440   **79.** 2777.5   **81.** 14,268

83. 405 bricks   **85.** \$200,000

87. (a) $a_n = 0.39x + 1.89$

(b)

Year	2006	2007	2008	2009
Sales (in billions of dollars)	4.23	4.62	5.01	5.40

Year	2010	2011	2012	2013
Sales (in billions of dollars)	5.79	6.18	6.57	6.96

The model fits the data well.

(c) \$44.76 billion   (d) \$69.72 billion; Answers will vary.

89. True. Use the recursion formula, $a_{n+1} = a_n + d$.

91. $x, 3x, 5x, 7x, 9x, 11x, 13x, 15x, 17x, 19x$

93. Given a_1 and a_2, you know that $d = a_2 - a_1$. So, $a_n = a_1 + (n-1)d$.

95. $S_n + 5n$; Answers will vary.

97. Answers will vary. Sample Answer: Gauss saw that the sum of the first and last numbers was 101, the sum of the second and second-last numbers was 101, and so on. Seeing that there were 50 such pairs of numbers, Gauss simply multiplied 50 by 101 to get the summation 5050.

$a_n = (n+1)\left(\dfrac{n}{2}\right)$, where n is the total number of natural numbers.

99. $(1, 5, -1)$ **101.** Answers will vary.

Section 8.3   (page 595)

1. geometric, common   **3.** geometric series   **5.** $|r| < 1$

7. Geometric sequence, $r = 3$

9. Not a geometric sequence

11. Geometric sequence, $r = -\frac{1}{2}$

13. Geometric sequence, $r = 0.1$

15. Not a geometric sequence   **17.** 6, 18, 54, 162, 486

19. $1, \frac{1}{2}, \frac{1}{4}, \frac{1}{8}, \frac{1}{16}$ **21.** $5, -\frac{1}{2}, \frac{1}{20}, -\frac{1}{200}, \frac{1}{2000}$

23. $9, 9e, 9e^2, 9e^3, 9e^4$

25. $64, 32, 16, 8, 4; \ r = \frac{1}{2};$
$a_n = 64\left(\frac{1}{2}\right)^{n-1}$

27. $9, 18, 36, 72, 144; \ r = 2;$
$a_n = 9(2)^{n-1}$

29. $6, -9, \frac{27}{2}, -\frac{81}{4}, \frac{243}{8}; \ r = -\frac{3}{2};$
$a_n = 6\left(-\frac{3}{2}\right)^{n-1}$

31. (a) and (b) 15.227   **33.** (a) 44.949   (b) $\frac{32,768}{729}$

35. (a) and (b) −8192   **37.** (a) and (b) 633.568

39. $a_n = 7(3)^{n-1}$; 45,927   **41.** $a_n = 5(6)^{n-1}$; 50,388,480

43. $\frac{1}{128}$ **45.** $-\frac{2}{9}$

47.

49.

51. $8, 4, 6, 5, \frac{11}{2}$

53.

n	S_n
1	16
2	24
3	28
4	30
5	31
6	31.5
7	31.75
8	31.875
9	31.9375
10	31.96875

55. 511   **57.** 43   **59.** 2700.31   **61.** 6.4

63. 2092.60   **65.** $\displaystyle\sum_{n=1}^{7} 5(3)^{n-1}$ **67.** $\displaystyle\sum_{n=1}^{7} 2\left(-\frac{1}{4}\right)^{n-1}$

69. 50   **71.** $\frac{10}{3}$

73. Series does not have a finite sum because $\left|\frac{7}{3}\right| > 1$.

75. $\frac{1000}{89}$ **77.** $-\frac{30}{19}$ **79.** 27

81. Series does not have a finite sum because $\left|\frac{5}{2}\right| > 1$.

83. $-\frac{49}{9}$ **85.** $\frac{4}{11}$ **87.** $\frac{113}{90}$

89. Geometric; $r = 2$; 262,136

91. Geometric; $r = \frac{1}{3}$; 135   **93.** Arithmetic; $d = 6$; 720

95. Geometric; $r = 0.8$; 28.944   **97.** \$6480.83

99. Answers will vary.

101. (a) \$26,198.27   (b) \$26,263.88

103. (a) \$153,237.86   (b) \$153,657.02   **105.** 126 in.²

107. (a) $T_n = 70(0.8)^n$ (b) 18.4°F; 4.8°F

(c)

3.5 h

109. (a) $S = \displaystyle\sum_{n=0}^{\infty} 4\pi$ (b) $V = \displaystyle\sum_{n=0}^{\infty} \frac{4}{3}\pi\left(\frac{1}{3}\right)^n$

(c) Infinite surface area. Finite volume: 2π cubic units

111. 42 ft   **113.** True. The terms all equal a_1.

115. $3, \dfrac{3x}{2}, \dfrac{3x^2}{4}, \dfrac{3x^3}{8}, \dfrac{3x^4}{16}$ **117.** $100e^{8x}$

119. (a)   (b)

Horizontal asymptote: Horizontal asymptote:
$y = 12$ $y = 10$
Corresponds to the sum   Corresponds to the sum of
of the series   the series.

121. Divide the second term by the first to obtain the common ratio. The nth term is the first term times the common ratio raised to the $(n - 1)$th power.

123. -38 **125.** Answers will vary.

Section 8.4 (page 604)

1. $_nC_r$ or $\binom{n}{r}$ **3.** Binomial Theorem, Pascal's Triangle

5. 21   **7.** 15,504   **9.** 14   **11.** 1   **13.** 210

15. 4950   **17.** 749,398   **19.** 230,300   **21.** 31,125

23. $x^5 + 5x^4 + 10x^3 + 10x^2 + 5x + 1$

25. $a^3 + 9a^2 + 27a + 27$ **27.** $y^3 - 12y^2 + 48y - 64$

29. $x^5 + 5x^4y + 10x^3y^2 + 10x^2y^3 + 5xy^4 + y^5$

31. $32x^5 - 80x^4y + 80x^3y^2 - 40x^2y^3 + 10xy^4 - y^5$

33. $64y^3 - 144y^2 + 108y - 27$

35. $64r^6 - 576r^5s + 2160r^4s^2 - 4320r^3s^3 + 4860r^2s^4$
$\qquad - 2916rs^5 + 729s^6$

37. $x^8 + 8x^6 + 24x^4 + 32x^2 + 16$

39. $-x^{10} + 25x^8 - 250x^6 + 1250x^4 - 3125x^2 + 3125$

41. $x^8 + 4x^6y^2 + 6x^4y^4 + 4x^2y^6 + y^8$

43. $729x^{18} - 1458x^{15}y + 1215x^{12}y^2 - 540x^9y^3 + 135x^6y^4$
$\qquad - 18x^3y^5 + y^6$

45. $\dfrac{1}{x^5} + \dfrac{5y}{x^4} + \dfrac{10y^2}{x^3} + \dfrac{10y^3}{x^2} + \dfrac{5y^4}{x} + y^5$

47. $\dfrac{16}{x^4} - \dfrac{64y}{x^3} + \dfrac{96y^2}{x^2} - \dfrac{64y^3}{x} + 16y^4$

49. $-512x^4 + 576x^3 - 240x^2 + 44x - 3$

51. $3x^5 + 15x^4 + 34x^3 + 42x^2 + 27x + 7$

53. $-4x^6 - 24x^5 - 60x^4 - 83x^3 - 42x^2 - 60x + 20$

55. $61,440x^7$ **57.** $360x^3y^2$ **59.** $1,259,712x^2y^7$

61. $-4,330,260,000x^3y^9$ **63.** $1,732,104$ **65.** 180

67. $-489,888$ **69.** 210   **71.** 35   **73.** 6

75. $3125y^5 + 6250y^4 + 5000y^3 + 2000y^2 + 400y + 32$

77. $32x^5 + 240x^4y + 720x^3y^2 + 1080x^2y^3 + 810xy^4 + 243y^5$

79. $81t^4 - 216t^3v + 216t^2v^2 - 96tv^3 + 16v^4$

81. $27x^{3/2} + 135x + 225\sqrt{x} + 125$

83. $x^2 - 3x^{4/3}y^{1/3} + 3x^{2/3}y^{2/3} - y$

85. $3x^2 + 3xh + h^2, h \neq 0$

87. $6x^5 + 15x^4h + 20x^3h^2 + 15x^2h^3 + 6xh^4 + h^5, h \neq 0$

89. -4 **91.** $161 + 240i$ **93.** $2035 + 828i$

95. $-115 + 236i$ **97.** $-23 + 208\sqrt{3}i$ **99.** 1

101. $-\frac{1}{8}$ **103.** 1.172   **105.** 510,568.785

107.

g is shifted two units to the right of f.
$g(x) = x^4 - 8x^3 + 19x^2 - 12x - 4$

109.

g is shifted five units to the left of f.
$g(x) = -x^3 - 12x^2 - 45x - 54$

111.

$p(x)$ is the expansion of $f(x)$.

113. 0.273   **115.** 0.171

117. (a) $g(t) = 0.005t^2 - 0.27t + 22.5$

119. True. Pascal's Triangle is made up of binomial coefficients.

121. The first and last numbers in each row are 1. Every other number in each row is formed by adding the two numbers immediately above the number.

$\quad$ 1 $\quad$ 8 $\quad$ 28 $\quad$ 56 $\quad$ 70 $\quad$ 56 $\quad$ 28 $\quad$ 8 $\quad$ 1

$\quad$ 1 $\quad$ 9 $\quad$ 36 $\quad$ 84 $\quad$ 126 $\quad$ 126 $\quad$ 84 $\quad$ 36 $\quad$ 9 $\quad$ 1

1 $\quad$ 10 $\quad$ 45 $\quad$ 120 $\quad$ 210 $\quad$ 252 $\quad$ 210 $\quad$ 120 $\quad$ 45 $\quad$ 10 $\quad$ 1

123 and 125. Answers will vary.

127. $5(2x)^4(-3y)^1 = -240x^4y$; Answers will vary.

129. $\begin{bmatrix} -1 & 6 \\ -1 & 5.5 \end{bmatrix}$

Section 8.5 (page 613)

1. Fundamental Counting Principle   **3.** Permutation

5. 8   **7.** 6   **9.** 11   **11.** 3   **13.** 200   **15.** 1024

17. (a) 900   (b) 648   (c) 180

19. 24,000,000   **21.** (a) 100,000   (b) 20,000

23. (a) 10,000   (b) 9000   **25.** (a) 720   (b) 48

27. 120   **29.** 362,880   **31.** 24   **33.** 336   **35.** 720

37. 427,518,000   **39.** 197,149,680   **41.** 11,880

43. 1,092,624

45. ABCD, ABDC, ACBD, ACDB, ADBC, ADCB,
BACD, BADC, CABD, CADB, DABC, DACB,
BCAD, BDAC, CBAD, CDAB, DBAC, DCAB,
BCDA, BDCA, CBDA, CDBA, DBCA, DCBA

47. 420   **49.** 2530   **51.** 10   **53.** 4   **55.** 1
57. 40,920   **59.** 850,668
61. AB, AC, AD, AE, AF, BC, BD, BE, BF, CD, CE, CF, DE, DF, EF
63. 4.42×10^{16} **65.** 5,586,853,480   **67.** 175,223,510
69. 462,000   **71.** 3744   **73.** 5   **75.** 20
77. $n = 5$ or $n = 6$ **79.** $n = 10$ **81.** $n = 3$ **83.** $n = 2$
85. False. Because order does not matter, it is an example of a combination.
87. For some calculators, the answer is too large.
89. $_nP_r$ represents the number of ways to choose and order r elements out of a collection of n elements.
91 and 93. Answers will vary.   **95.** $(-2, -8)$

Section 8.6   (page 622)

1. sample space   **3.** mutually exclusive
5. $0 \le P(E) \le 1$ **7.** $P(E) = 1$
9. $\{(H, 1), (H, 2), (H, 3), (H, 4), (H, 5), (H, 6),$
$(T, 1), (T, 2), (T, 3), (T, 4), (T, 5), (T, 6)\}$
11. $\{$ABC, ACB, BAC, BCA, CAB, CBA$\}$ **13.** $\frac{3}{8}$ **15.** $\frac{7}{8}$
17. $\frac{3}{13}$ **19.** $\frac{3}{26}$ **21.** $\frac{5}{36}$ **23.** $\frac{1}{6}$ **25.** $\frac{3}{100}$ **27.** $\frac{9}{25}$
29. $\frac{1}{5}$ **31.** $\frac{2}{5}$ **33.** 0.25   **35.** $\frac{1}{3}$ **37.** 0.88   **39.** $\frac{7}{20}$
41. $\frac{4}{13}$ **43.** $\frac{2}{13}$ **45.** $\frac{11}{32}$ **47.** $\frac{5}{8}$ **49.** $\frac{3}{32}$ **51.** $\frac{1}{8}$
53. $\frac{27}{1000}$ **55.** $\frac{2}{125}$
57. $P(\{\text{Taylor wins}\}) = \frac{1}{2}$
$P(\{\text{Moore wins}\}) = P(\{\text{Perez wins}\}) = \frac{1}{4}$
59. (a) 24.00 million   (b) 0.317   (c) 0.881   (d) 0.415
61. (a) $\frac{1}{120}$ (b) $\frac{1}{24}$ **63.** (a) $\frac{14}{55}$ (b) $\frac{12}{55}$ (c) $\frac{54}{55}$
65. (a) 0.1024   (b) 0.32   (c) 0.4624
67. (a) $\frac{1}{15,625}$ (b) $\frac{4096}{15,625}$ (c) $\frac{11,529}{15,625}$
69. (a) $\frac{\pi}{4}$ (b) Answers will vary.
71. True. The sum of the probabilities of all outcomes must be 1.
73. (a) As you consider successive people with distinct birthdays, the probabilities must decrease to take into account the birth dates already used. Because the birth dates of people are independent events, multiply the respective probabilities of distinct birthdays.
(b) $\frac{365}{365} \cdot \frac{364}{365} \cdot \frac{363}{365} \cdot \frac{362}{365}$ (c) Answers will vary.
(d) Q_n is the probability that the birthdays are *not* distinct, which is equivalent to at least two people having the same birthday.
(e)

n	10	15	20	23	30	40	50
P_n	0.88	0.75	0.59	0.49	0.29	0.11	0.03
Q_n	0.12	0.25	0.41	0.51	0.71	0.89	0.97

(f) 23; From the table in part (e), $Q_n = 0.51$ when $n = 23$.
75. (a) No. $P(A) + P(B) = 0.76 + 0.58 = 1.34 > 1$. The sum of the probabilities is greater than 1, so A and B cannot be mutually exclusive.
(b) Yes. $A' = 0.24$, $B' = 0.42$, and $A' + B' = 0.66 < 1$, so A' and B' can be mutually exclusive.
(c) $0.76 \le P(A \cup B) \le 1$
77. 70   **79.** 165

Review Exercises   (page 628)

1. $\frac{2}{3}, \frac{4}{5}, \frac{8}{9}, \frac{16}{17}, \frac{32}{33}$ **3.** $a_n = 5n + 2$ **5.** $a_n = \dfrac{2}{2n - 1}$
7. $9, 3, 1, \frac{1}{3}, \frac{1}{9}$ **9.** $\frac{1}{380}$ **11.** $(n + 1)(n)$ **13.** 30
15. $\frac{205}{24}$ **17.** $\sum_{k=1}^{20} \frac{1}{2k} \approx 1.799$ **19.** $\sum_{k=1}^{9} \frac{k}{k + 1} \approx 7.071$
21. (a) $\frac{1111}{1250}$ (b) $\frac{8}{9}$ **23.** (a) 0.0404   (b) $\frac{4}{99}$
25. (a) 3015.00, 3030.08, 3045.23, 3060.45, 3075.75, 3091.13, 3106.59, 3122.12
(b) \$3662.38
27. Arithmetic sequence, $d = -2$
29. Not an arithmetic sequence
31. 3, 7, 11, 15, 19   **33.** 1, 4, 7, 10, 13
35. $35, 32, 29, 26, 23$; $d = -3$; $a_n = 38 - 3n$
37. $a_n = 103 - 3n$; 1600   **39.** 110   **41.** 6375
43. (a) \$57,564   (b) \$277,160
45. Geometric sequence, $r = 2$
47. Not a geometric sequence   **49.** $4, -1, \frac{1}{4}, -\frac{1}{16}, \frac{1}{64}$
51. $9, 6, 4, \frac{8}{3}, \frac{16}{9}$ **53.** $120, 40, \frac{40}{3}, \frac{40}{9}, \frac{40}{27}$; $r = \frac{1}{3}$; $a_n = 120(\frac{1}{3})^{n-1}$
55. (a) $-\frac{1}{2}$ (b) -0.5 **57.** 19,531   **59.** 9831
61. 32   **63.** Not possible because $\left|\frac{3}{2}\right| > 1$.
65. (a) $a_t = 130,000(0.7)^t$ (b) \$21,849.10
67. 45   **69.** 126   **71.** $x^4 + 20x^3 + 150x^2 + 500x + 625$
73. $a^5 - 20a^4b + 160a^3b^2 - 640a^2b^3 + 1280ab^4 - 1024b^5$
75. 21   **77.** 70   **79.** 10
81. (a) 216   (b) 108   (c) 36   **83.** 95,040   **85.** 5040
87. $n = 3$ **89.** 28   **91.** 479,001,600   **93.** $\frac{1}{9}$
95. (a) 0.416   (b) 0.8   (c) 0.074
97. True. $\dfrac{(n + 2)!}{n!} = \dfrac{(n + 2)(n + 1)n!}{n!} = (n + 2)(n + 1)$
99. (a) Each term is obtained by adding the same constant (common difference) to the preceding term.
(b) Each term is obtained by multiplying the same constant (common ratio) by the preceding term.

Chapter Test   (page 631)

1. $3, 2, \frac{4}{3}, \frac{8}{9}, \frac{16}{27}$ **2.** 12, 16, 20, 24, 28
3. $-x, \dfrac{x^2}{2}, -\dfrac{x^3}{3}, \dfrac{x^4}{4}, -\dfrac{x^5}{5}$ **4.** $-x^3, -\dfrac{x^5}{2}, -\dfrac{x^7}{6}, -\dfrac{x^9}{24}, -\dfrac{x^{11}}{120}$
5. 7920   **6.** $\dfrac{1}{n + 1}$ **7.** $2n$ **8.** $a_n = n^2 + 1$
9. $a_n = 5100 - 100n$ **10.** $a_n = 4(\frac{1}{2})^{n-1}$
11. $\sum_{n=1}^{12} \dfrac{2}{3n + 1}$ **12.** $\sum_{n=1}^{\infty} 2(\frac{1}{4})^{n-1}$ **13.** 57.17   **14.** 189
15. $\frac{25}{7}$ **16.** $81a^4 - 540a^3b + 1350a^2b^2 - 1500ab^3 + 625b^4$
17. 84   **18.** 1140   **19.** 328,440   **20.** 72   **21.** $n = 3$
22. 26,000   **23.** 12,650   **24.** $\frac{3}{52}$ **25.** $\frac{1}{924}$
26. (a) $\frac{1}{4}$ (b) $\frac{121}{3600}$ (c) $\frac{1}{60}$

Chapter 9

Section 9.1   (page 643)

1. conic section   **3.** circle, center
5. The standard form of the equation of a circle; (h, k) represents the center of the circle, r represents the radius of the circle.

7. $x^2 + y^2 = 16$ **9.** $(x - 3)^2 + (y - 7)^2 = 53$

11. $(x + 3)^2 + (y + 1)^2 = 10$

13. Center: $(0, 0)$ **15.** Center: $(5, 0)$
Radius: 6   Radius: 3

17. Center: $(-1, -6)$
Radius: $\sqrt{19}$

19. $x^2 + y^2 = 4$ **21.** $x^2 + y^2 = \dfrac{3}{4}$

Center: $(0, 0)$ Center: $(0, 0)$

Radius: 2   Radius: $\dfrac{\sqrt{3}}{2}$

23. $(x - 1)^2 + (y + 3)^2 = 1$ **25.** $\left(x + \frac{3}{2}\right)^2 + (y - 3)^2 = 1$
Center: $(1, -3)$ Center: $\left(-\frac{3}{2}, 3\right)$
Radius: 1   Radius: 1

27. Center: $(0, 0)$ **29.** Center: $(-4, -1)$
Radius: 4   Radius: 3

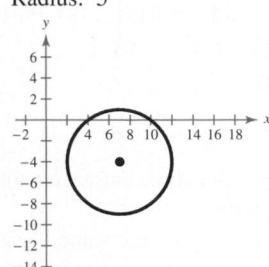

31. Center: $(7, -4)$ **33.** Center: $(-1, 0)$
Radius: 5   Radius: 6

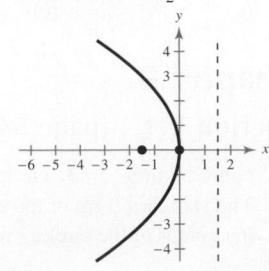

35. x-intercepts: $(-1, 0), (-9, 0)$
y-intercept: $(0, 3)$

37. x-intercepts: $\left(6 \pm \sqrt{7}, 0\right)$
y-intercepts: none

39. x-intercepts: $\left(1 \pm 2\sqrt{7}, 0\right)$
y-intercepts: $(0, 9), (0, -3)$

41. (a) $x^2 + y^2 = 2704$ (b) Yes   (c) 2 mi

43. e   **44.** b   **45.** d   **46.** f   **47.** a   **48.** c

49. $x^2 = \frac{3}{2}y$ **51.** $x^2 = 8y$ **53.** $y^2 = -2x$

55. $x^2 = -16y$ **57.** $y^2 = 8x$ **59.** $y^2 = 3x$

61. Vertex: $(0, 0)$ **63.** Vertex: $(0, 0)$

Focus: $\left(0, \frac{1}{2}\right)$ Focus: $\left(-\frac{3}{2}, 0\right)$

Directrix: $y = -\frac{1}{2}$ Directrix: $x = \frac{3}{2}$

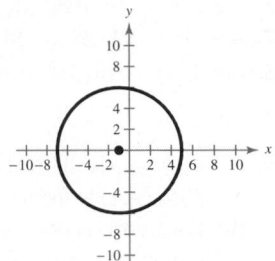

65. Vertex: $(0, 0)$ **67.** Vertex: $(-1, -2)$
Focus: $\left(0, -\frac{3}{2}\right)$ Focus: $(-1, 0)$
Directrix: $y = \frac{3}{2}$ Directrix: $y = -4$

69. Vertex: $\left(-\frac{3}{2}, 2\right)$ **71.** Vertex: $(-2, -3)$
Focus: $\left(-\frac{3}{2}, 3\right)$ Focus: $(-4, -3)$
Directrix: $y = 1$ Directrix: $x = 0$

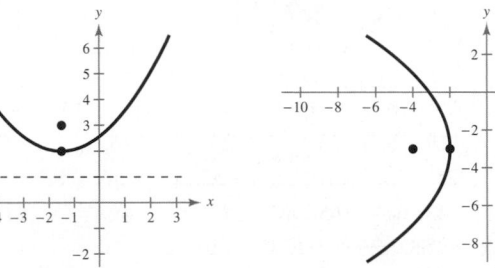

73. Vertex: $(-2, 1)$ **75.** Vertex: $\left(\frac{1}{4}, -\frac{1}{2}\right)$
Focus: $\left(-2, -\frac{1}{2}\right)$ Focus: $\left(0, -\frac{1}{2}\right)$
Directrix: $y = \frac{5}{2}$ Directrix: $x = \frac{1}{2}$

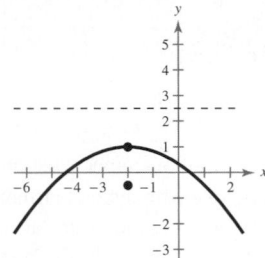

77. Vertex: $(1, 1)$
Focus: $(1, 2)$
Directrix: $y = 0$

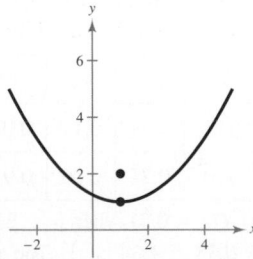

79. $(x - 3)^2 = -(y - 1)$ **81.** $y^2 = 4(x + 4)$

83. $y^2 = 2(x + 2)$ **85.** $(y - 2)^2 = -8(x - 5)$

87. $x^2 = 8(y - 4)$ **89.** $(y - 2)^2 = 8x$

91.

(2, 4)

93. $4x - y - 8 = 0$ **95.** $4y - x + 2 = 0$

97. $x^2 = -4(y - 4)$ **99.** $x^2 = -\frac{25}{4}(y - 48)$

101. (a)   (b) $x^2 = \frac{51,200}{19}y$

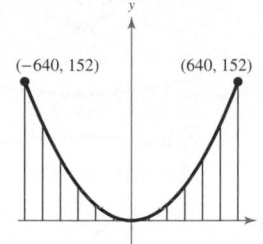

(c)

x	0	200	400	500	600
y	0	14.844	59.375	92.773	133.59

103. (a) $y^2 = 6x$ (b) 2.67 in.

105. (a) $x^2 = -49(y - 100)$ (b) 70 ft   **107.** $y = \frac{3}{4}x - \frac{25}{4}$

109. $y = \frac{\sqrt{2}}{2}x - 3\sqrt{2}$ **111.** $y = -\frac{3}{4}x + 12$

113. False. $x^2 + (y + 5)^2$ represents a circle with its center at $(0, -5)$ and a radius of 5.

115. False. A circle is a conic section.

117. False. A parabola does not touch its directrix.

119.

The intersection results in a point.

121. $y = \sqrt{6(x + 1)} + 3$

123. Minimum: $(0.67, 0.22)$; maximum: $(-0.67, 3.78)$

125. Minimum: $(-0.79, 0.81)$

Section 9.2   (page 653)

1. ellipse, foci   **3.** minor axis   **5.** Vertical   **7.** 4

9. b   **10.** a   **11.** c   **12.** d

13. $\frac{x^2}{4} + \frac{y^2}{16} = 1$ **15.** $\frac{x^2}{9} + \frac{y^2}{5} = 1$ **17.** $\frac{x^2}{24} + \frac{y^2}{49} = 1$

19. $\frac{5x^2}{48} + \frac{y^2}{16} = 1$ **21.** $\frac{(x - 2)^2}{4} + \frac{(y + 1)^2}{1} = 1$

23. $\frac{(x - 4)^2}{16} + \frac{(y - 2)^2}{1} = 1$ **25.** $\frac{x^2}{308} + \frac{(y - 4)^2}{324} = 1$

27. $\frac{(x - 3)^2}{36} + \frac{(y - 2)^2}{32} = 1$

29. Center: $(0, 0)$
Vertices: $(\pm 8, 0)$
Foci: $(\pm \sqrt{55}, 0)$
Eccentricity: $\frac{\sqrt{55}}{8}$

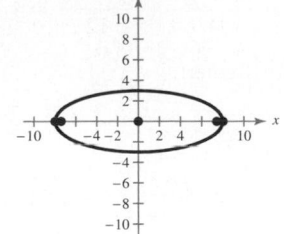

31. Center: $(4, -1)$
Vertices: $(4, 4), (4, -6)$
Foci: $(4, 2), (4, -4)$
Eccentricity: $\frac{3}{5}$

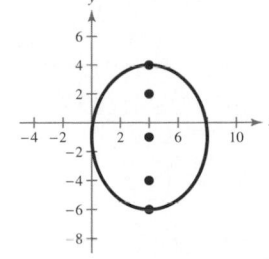

33. Center: $(-5, 1)$
Vertices: $\left(-\frac{7}{2}, 1\right), \left(-\frac{13}{2}, 1\right)$
Foci: $\left(-5 \pm \frac{\sqrt{5}}{2}, 1\right)$
Eccentricity: $\frac{\sqrt{5}}{3}$

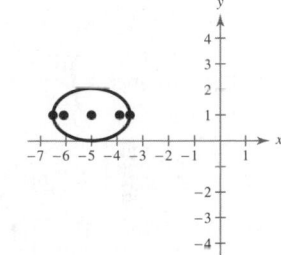

35. (a) $\frac{x^2}{36} + \frac{y^2}{4} = 1$ (c)
(b) Center: $(0, 0)$
Vertices: $(\pm 6, 0)$
Foci: $(\pm 4\sqrt{2}, 0)$
Eccentricity: $\frac{2\sqrt{2}}{3}$

37. (a) $\frac{x^2}{4} + \frac{y^2}{49} = 1$ (c)
(b) Center: $(0, 0)$
Vertices: $(0, \pm 7)$
Foci: $(0, \pm 3\sqrt{5})$
Eccentricity: $\frac{3\sqrt{5}}{7}$

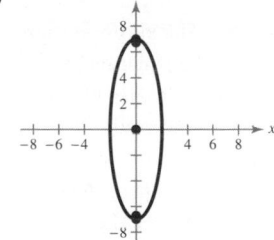

39. (a) $\frac{(x + 2)^2}{4} + \frac{(y - 3)^2}{9} = 1$ (c)
(b) Center: $(-2, 3)$
Vertices: $(-2, 6), (-2, 0)$
Foci: $(-2, 3 \pm \sqrt{5})$
Eccentricity: $\frac{\sqrt{5}}{3}$

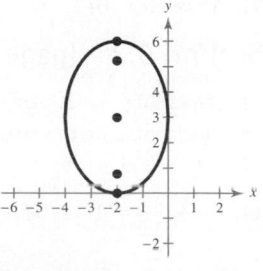

CHAPTER 9

41. (a) $\dfrac{\left(x + \frac{3}{2}\right)^2}{4} + \dfrac{\left(y - \frac{5}{2}\right)^2}{12} = 1$

(b) Center: $\left(-\dfrac{3}{2}, \dfrac{5}{2}\right)$ (c)

Vertices: $\left(-\dfrac{3}{2}, \dfrac{5 \pm 4\sqrt{3}}{2}\right)$

Foci: $\left(-\dfrac{3}{2}, \dfrac{5}{2} \pm 2\sqrt{2}\right)$

Eccentricity: $\dfrac{\sqrt{6}}{3}$

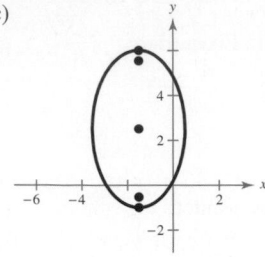

43. (a) $\dfrac{\left(x - \frac{1}{2}\right)^2}{5} + \dfrac{(y + 1)^2}{3} = 1$

(b) Center: $\left(\dfrac{1}{2}, -1\right)$ (c)

Vertices: $\left(\dfrac{1}{2} \pm \sqrt{5}, -1\right)$

Foci: $\left(\dfrac{1}{2} \pm \sqrt{2}, -1\right)$

Eccentricity: $\dfrac{\sqrt{10}}{5}$

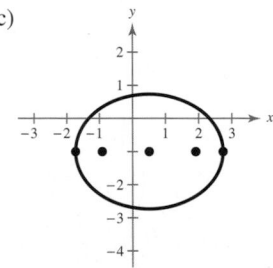

45. $\dfrac{\sqrt{5}}{3}$ **47.** $\dfrac{2\sqrt{2}}{3}$ **49.** $\dfrac{x^2}{25} + \dfrac{y^2}{16} = 1$

51. $\dfrac{(x - 1)^2}{45} + \dfrac{(y - 7)^2}{81} = 1$ **53.** $\dfrac{x^2}{318.09} + \dfrac{y^2}{18.80} = 1$

55. $40\sqrt{33}$ mm ≈ 229.8 mm   **57.** 40 units

59.

61.

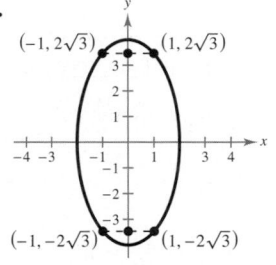

63. True. The ellipse is more elongated when e is close to 1.

65. No. The equation represents an ellipse.

67. Nearly circular because its eccentricity is about 0.055, which is close to zero.

69. (a) $2a$

(b) The sum of the distances from the two fixed points is constant.

71. Proof   **73.** Geometric   **75.** Arithmetic

77. 15.0990

Section 9.3 (page 665)

1. hyperbola   **3.** $Ax^2 + Bxy + Cy^2 + Dx + Ey + F = 0$

5. Horizontal: a, d; vertical: b, c

7. a   **8.** d   **9.** b   **10.** c

11. $\dfrac{y^2}{4} - \dfrac{x^2}{12} = 1$ **13.** $\dfrac{(x - 4)^2}{4} - \dfrac{y^2}{12} = 1$

15. $\dfrac{(y - 5)^2}{16} - \dfrac{(x - 4)^2}{9} = 1$ **17.** $\dfrac{y^2}{9} - \dfrac{4(x - 2)^2}{9} = 1$

19. $\dfrac{(y - 2)^2}{4} - \dfrac{x^2}{4} = 1$

21. Center: $(0, 0)$

Vertices: $(\pm 1, 0)$

Foci: $\left(\pm\sqrt{2}, 0\right)$

Asymptotes: $y = \pm x$

23. Center: $(0, 0)$

Vertices: $(0, \pm 1)$

Foci: $\left(0, \pm\sqrt{17}\right)$

Asymptotes: $y = \pm\frac{1}{4}x$

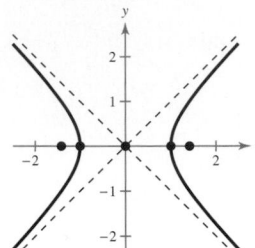

25. Center: $(0, 0)$

Vertices: $(0, \pm 4)$

Foci: $\left(0, \pm 2\sqrt{5}\right)$

Asymptotes: $y = \pm 2x$

27. Center: $(3, 1)$

Vertices: $(0, 1), (6, 1)$

Foci: $\left(3 \pm \sqrt{10}, 1\right)$

Asymptotes:

$y = 1 \pm \frac{1}{3}(x - 3)$

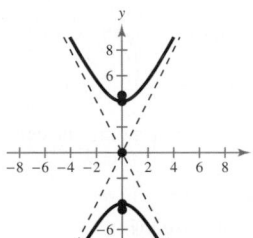

29. Center: $(2, -6)$

Vertices: $(2, -5), (2, -7)$

Foci: $\left(2, -6 \pm \dfrac{\sqrt{17}}{4}\right)$

Asymptotes: $-6 \pm 4(x - 2)$

31. (a) $\dfrac{x^2}{9} - \dfrac{y^2}{4} = 1$ (c)

(b) Center: $(0, 0)$

Vertices: $(\pm 3, 0)$

Foci: $\left(\pm\sqrt{13}, 0\right)$

Asymptotes: $y = \pm\dfrac{2}{3}x$

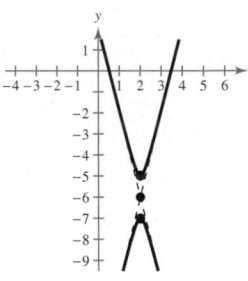

33. (a) $\dfrac{y^2}{4} - \dfrac{x^2}{8} = 1$ (c)

(b) Center: $(0, 0)$

Vertices: $(0, \pm 2)$

Foci: $\left(0, \pm 2\sqrt{3}\right)$

Asymptotes: $y = \pm\dfrac{\sqrt{2}}{2}x$

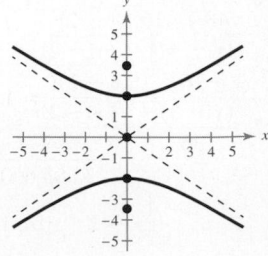

35. (a) $(x - 2)^2 - \dfrac{(y + 3)^2}{9} = 1$

(b) Center: $(2, -3)$

Vertices: $(3, -3), (1, -3)$

Foci: $\left(2 \pm \sqrt{10}, -3\right)$

Asymptotes: $y = -3 \pm 3(x - 2)$

(c)

37. (a) $\dfrac{(x + 4)^2}{7} - \dfrac{y^2}{2} = 1$

(b) Center: $(-4, 0)$

Vertices: $\left(-4 \pm \sqrt{7}, 0\right)$

Foci: $(-7, 0), (-1, 0)$

Asymptotes: $y = \pm\dfrac{\sqrt{14}}{7}(x + 4)$

(c)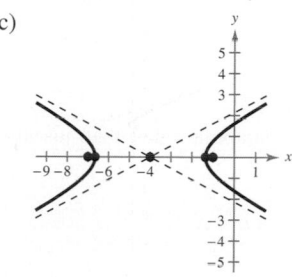

39. (a) $\dfrac{(y + 3)^2}{2} - \dfrac{(x - 1)^2}{18} = 1$

(b) Center: $(1, -3)$

Vertices: $\left(1, -3 \pm \sqrt{2}\right)$

Foci: $\left(1, -3 \pm 2\sqrt{5}\right)$

Asymptotes: $y = -3 \pm \dfrac{1}{3}(x - 1)$

(c)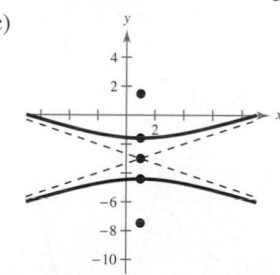

41. $\dfrac{x^2}{1} - \dfrac{y^2}{25} = 1$ **43.** $\dfrac{17y^2}{1024} - \dfrac{17x^2}{64} = 1$

45. $\dfrac{(x - 2)^2}{1} - \dfrac{(y - 2)^2}{1} = 1$ **47.** $\dfrac{(x - 3)^2}{9} - \dfrac{(y - 2)^2}{4} = 1$

49. $\dfrac{(x - 4)^2}{16} - \dfrac{(y - 3)^2}{9} = 1$

51. $\dfrac{x^2}{98,010,000} - \dfrac{y^2}{13,503,600} = 1$

53. (a) $x^2 - \dfrac{y^2}{27} = 1$ (b) 1.89 ft = 22.68 in.

55. $\left(12\sqrt{5} - 12, 0\right) \approx (14.83, 0)$ **57.** Ellipse

59. Hyperbola   **61.** Parabola   **63.** Circle

65. $(3, 0)$ **67.** e   **68.** b   **69.** f

70. a   **71.** d   **72.** c

73. $\dfrac{(y')^2}{2} - \dfrac{(x')^2}{2} = 1$ **75.** $(x')^2 - \dfrac{(y')^2}{1/3} = 1$

   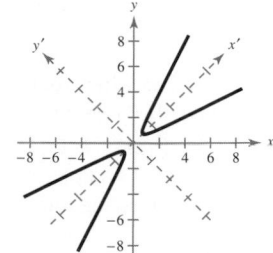

77. $\dfrac{(x')^2}{6} + \dfrac{(y')^2}{3/2} = 1$ **79.** $x' = -(y')^2$

   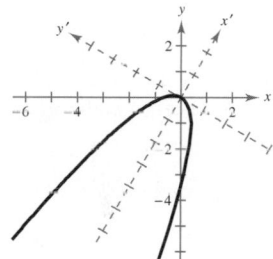

81. $(y')^2 = 4(x' - 1)$

83.   **85.**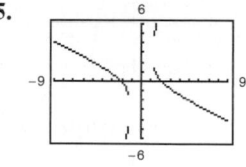

$\theta = 45°;$ $\theta \approx 26.57°;$

Answers will vary.   Answers will vary.

87.   **89.**

CHAPTER 9

91.

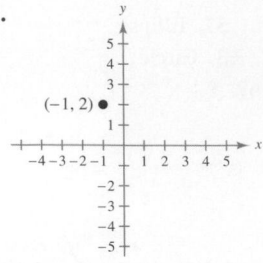

(-1, 2) ●

93. True. For a hyperbola, $c^2 = a^2 + b^2$. The larger the ratio of b to a, the larger the eccentricity of the hyperbola, $e = c/a$.

95. False. If $D = E$ or $D = -E$, the graph is two intersecting lines. For example, the graph of $x^2 - y^2 - 2x + 2y = 0$ is two intersecting lines.

97. False. The constant term F remains the same.

99. The asymptotes pass through the corners of the rectangle.

101. $\dfrac{(x-6)^2}{9} - \dfrac{(y-2)^2}{7} = 1$ **103.** Proof

105. $x^3 + x^2 + 2x - 6$ **107.** $x^2 - 2x + 1 + \dfrac{2}{x+2}$

109. $x(x+4)(x-4)$ **111.** $2x(x-6)^2$

113. $2(2x+3)(4x^2 - 6x + 9)$

115.

117.

119.

121.

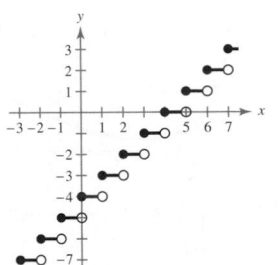

Section 9.4 (page 674)

1. plane curve, parametric equations, parameter

3. Eliminate the parameter.

5. c   **6.** d   **7.** b   **8.** a

9. (a)

t	0	1	2	3	4
x	0	1	$\sqrt{2}$	$\sqrt{3}$	2
y	2	1	0	-1	-2

(b)

The curve starts at $(0, 2)$ and moves along the right half of the parabola.

(c)

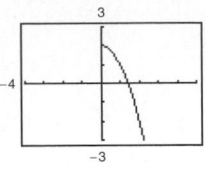

(d) $y = 2 - x^2$

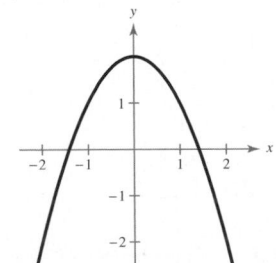

The graph is an entire parabola rather than just the right half.

11. b

13. (a)

(b) $y = -4x$

15. (a)

(b) $y = \dfrac{2}{3}x + 3$

17. (a)

(b) $y = 16x^2$

19. (a)

(b) $y = (x-2)^2$

21. (a)

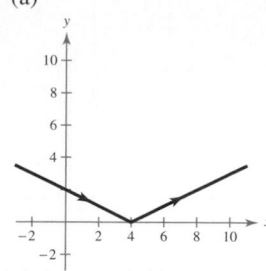

(b) $y = \frac{1}{2}|x - 4|$

23. (a)

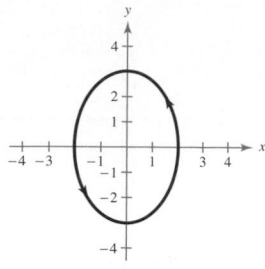

(b) $\dfrac{x^2}{4} + \dfrac{y^2}{9} = 1$

25. (a)

(b) $y = x^{-3}, x > 0$

27. (a)

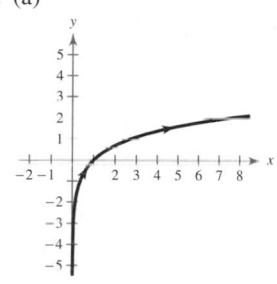

(b) $y = \ln x$

29.

Not a function

31.

Not a function

33.

Function

35. Each curve represents a portion of the line $y = 2x + 1$.

Domain	Orientation
(a) $(-\infty, \infty)$	Left to right
(b) $[-1, 1]$	Depends on θ
(c) $(0, \infty)$	Right to left
(d) $(0, \infty)$	Left to right

37. $y - y_1 = \dfrac{y_2 - y_1}{x_2 - x_1}(x - x_1)$

39. $\dfrac{(x - h)^2}{a^2} + \dfrac{(y - k)^2}{b^2} = 1$

41. $x = 1 + 3t, y = -1 + 9t$

43. $x = 5 \cos \theta, y = 3 \sin \theta$

45. (a) $x = t, y = -2t + 1$ (b) $x = 2 - t, y = 2t - 3$

47. (a) $x = t, y = \dfrac{3}{t}$ (b) $x = 2 - t, y = \dfrac{3}{2 - t}$

49. (a) $x = t, y = 4t^2 + 5$
(b) $x = 2 - t, y = 4t^2 - 16t + 21$

51. (a) $x = t, y = e^{-t}$ (b) $x = 2 - t, y = e^{t-2}$

53.

55.

57.

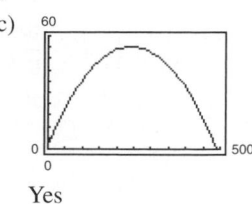

59. b   **60.** c   **61.** d   **62.** a

63. (a) $x = (146.67 \cos \theta)t$
$y = 3 + (146.67 \sin \theta)t - 16t^2$

(b)

(c)

No   Yes

(d) About $19.4°$

65. True. Both sets of parametric equations correspond to $y = x^2 + 1$.

67. False. The set $x = t^2, y = t$ does not correspond to y as a function of x.

69. (a) Counterclockwise   (b) $0 \le \theta < 2\pi$
(c) Answers will vary. Sample answer:
$x = 6 \cos \theta, y = -6 \sin \theta$
(d) The curve begins at the point $(0, 6)$ and is traced in a clockwise direction.

71. Even   **73.** Neither

Section 9.5   (page 681)

1. pole

3. $x = r \cos \theta, y = r \sin \theta$ and $\tan \theta = \dfrac{y}{x}, r^2 = x^2 + y^2$

5. $A; (0, 2)$ **7.** $C; (0, 0)$

9.

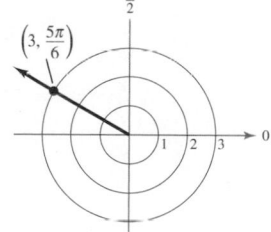

$\left(3, -\dfrac{7\pi}{6}\right), \left(-3, \dfrac{11\pi}{6}\right), \left(-3, -\dfrac{\pi}{6}\right)$

11.

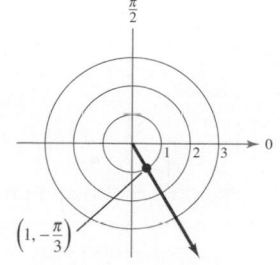

$\left(1, \dfrac{5\pi}{3}\right), \left(-1, \dfrac{2\pi}{3}\right), \left(-1, -\dfrac{4\pi}{3}\right)$

13.

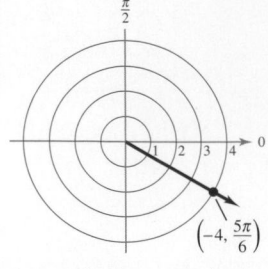

$\left(4, \dfrac{11\pi}{6}\right), \left(-4, -\dfrac{7\pi}{6}\right), \left(4, -\dfrac{\pi}{6}\right)$

15.

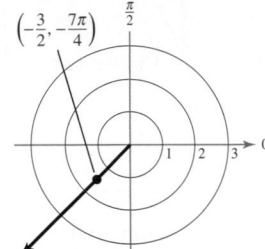

$\left(-\dfrac{3}{2}, \dfrac{\pi}{4}\right), \left(\dfrac{3}{2}, \dfrac{5\pi}{4}\right), \left(\dfrac{3}{2}, -\dfrac{3\pi}{4}\right)$

17.

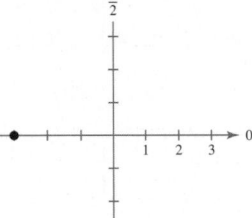

$\left(0, \dfrac{\pi}{2}\right), \left(0, \dfrac{3\pi}{2}\right), \left(0, -\dfrac{3\pi}{2}\right)$

19.

$(-3, 0)$

21.

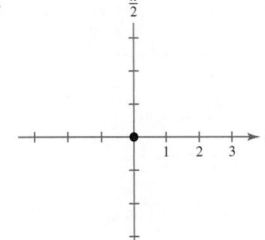

$\left(-\dfrac{\sqrt{2}}{2}, -\dfrac{\sqrt{2}}{2}\right)$

23.

$(0, 0)$

25.

$(0, 5)$

27. $(1.53, 1.29)$ **29.** $(-1.20, -4.34)$

31. $(-1.42, -0.47)$

33.

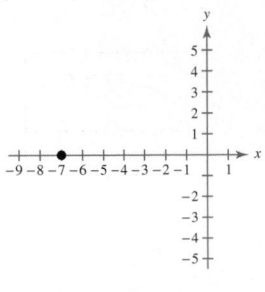

$(7, \pi), (-7, 0)$

35.

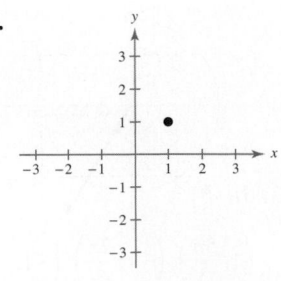

$\left(\sqrt{2}, \dfrac{\pi}{4}\right), \left(-\sqrt{2}, \dfrac{5\pi}{4}\right)$

37.

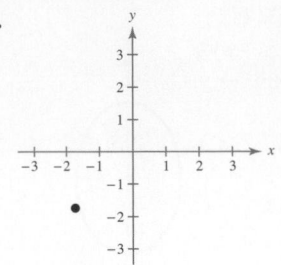

$\left(\sqrt{6}, \dfrac{5\pi}{4}\right), \left(-\sqrt{6}, \dfrac{\pi}{4}\right)$

39.

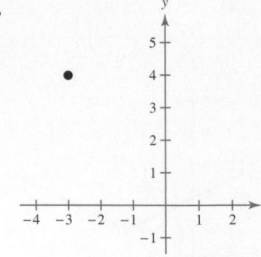

$(5, 2.214), (-5, 5.356)$

41. $(3.61, -0.59)$ **43.** $(2.65, 2.28)$ **45.** $(2.83, 0.49)$

47. $r = 3$ **49.** $\theta = \dfrac{\pi}{4}$ **51.** $r = a \csc \theta$

53. $r = -\dfrac{2}{3 \cos \theta - \sin \theta}$ **55.** $r^2 = 8 \csc 2\theta$

57. $r^2 = 9 \cos 2\theta$ **59.** $r = 6 \cos \theta$ **61.** $r = 2a \cos \theta$

63. $r = \tan^2 \theta \sec \theta$ **65.** $x^2 + y^2 - 4y = 0$

67. $y = -\dfrac{\sqrt{3}}{3}x$ **69.** $x = 0$ **71.** $y = -3$

73. $(x^2 + y^2)^3 = x^2$ **75.** $(x^2 + y^2)^2 = 6x^2y - 2y^3$

77. $y^2 = 2x + 1$ **79.** $4x^2 - 5y^2 = 36y + 36$

81. The graph is a circle centered at the origin with a radius of 6; $x^2 + y^2 = 36$.

83. The graph consists of all points on the line that makes an angle of $\pi/4$ with the positive x-axis; $x - y = 0$.

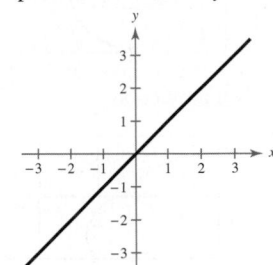

85. The graph is a vertical line through $(3, 0)$; $x - 3 = 0$.

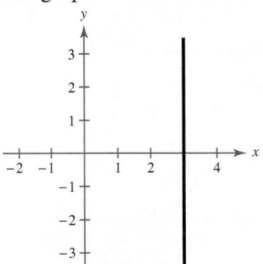

87. (a) $r = 30$

(b) $(30, 5\pi/6)$; 30 represents the distance of the passenger car from the center, and $5\pi/6 = 150°$ represents the angle to which the car has rotated.

(c) $(-25.98, 15)$; The car is about 25.98 feet to the left of the center and 15 feet above the center.

89. True. Because r is a directed distance, (r, θ) can be represented by $(-r, \theta \pm (2n + 1)\pi)$, so $|r| = |-r|$.

91. (a) Answers will vary.

(b) $d = |r_1 - r_2|$; Answers will vary.

(c) $d = \sqrt{r_1^2 + r_2^2}$; Answers will vary.

93. Answers will vary.

95. $(x - h)^2 + (y - k)^2 = h^2 + k^2$; radius $= \sqrt{h^2 + k^2}$;

center: (h, k)

97. $B \approx 14.13°$ **99.** $A \approx 41.86°$

$C \approx 141.87°$ $C \approx 67.14°$

$c \approx 15.18$ $b \approx 29.76$

Section 9.6   (page 689)

1. convex limaçon   **3.** lemniscate

5. When (r, θ) can be replaced with $(r, \pi - \theta)$ or $(-r, -\theta)$ and yield an equivalent equation

7. Rose curve   **9.** Lemniscate

11. c   **12.** d   **13.** a   **14.** c

15. $\theta = \frac{\pi}{2}$, polar axis, pole   **17.** Polar axis

19. $\theta = \frac{\pi}{2}$ **21.** Pole

23.   **25.**

27.   **29.**

31.   **33.**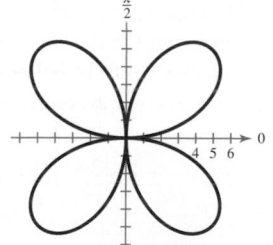

Symmetry: polar axis

Zeros: $\frac{\pi}{6}, \frac{\pi}{2}, \frac{5\pi}{6}$

Symmetry: $\theta = \frac{\pi}{2}$, polar axis, pole

Zeros: $0, \frac{\pi}{2}, \pi, \frac{3\pi}{2}, 2\pi$

35.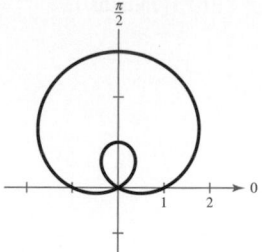

Symmetry: $\theta = \frac{\pi}{2}$

Zeros: $\frac{7\pi}{6}, \frac{11\pi}{6}$

37.   **39.**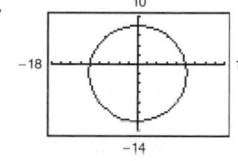

Answers will vary.   Answers will vary.

41.   **43.**

Answers will vary.   Answers will vary.

45.   **47.**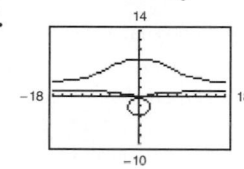

Answers will vary.   Answers will vary.

49.   **51.**

Answers will vary. $0 \le \theta < 2\pi$

53.   **55.**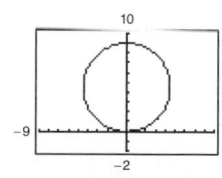

$0 \le \theta < 4\pi$ $0 \le \theta < \pi$

57.   **59.**

CHAPTER 9

61. (a) 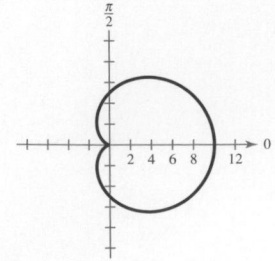   (b) 0 radians

Cardioid

63. True. $n = 5$

65. False. The rose curve $r = a \cos 3\theta$ is not symmetric with respect to the line $\theta = \pi/2$.

67. Answers will vary.

69. (a) $r = 2 - \sin\left(\theta - \dfrac{\pi}{4}\right)$ (b) $r = 2 + \cos \theta$

(c) $r = 2 + \sin \theta$ (d) $r = 2 - \cos \theta$

71. $x = -3, 3$ **73.** $x = \dfrac{13}{5}$

Section 9.7   (page 695)

1. conic   **3.** vertical

5.   **7.**

(a) Parabola   (a) Parabola
(b) Ellipse   (b) Ellipse
(c) Hyperbola   (c) Hyperbola

9. b   **10.** c   **11.** f   **12.** e   **13.** d   **14.** a

15. Parabola   **17.** Hyperbola   **19.** Ellipse

21. Ellipse   **23.** Hyperbola

25. Parabola   **27.** Hyperbola

29. Ellipse   **31.**

33.   **35.**

37. $r = \dfrac{1}{1 - \cos \theta}$ **39.** $r = \dfrac{1}{2 + \sin \theta}$

41. $r = \dfrac{2}{1 + 2 \cos \theta}$ **43.** $r = \dfrac{2}{1 - \sin \theta}$

45. $r = \dfrac{10}{1 - \cos \theta}$ **47.** $r = \dfrac{10}{3 + 2 \cos \theta}$

49. $r = \dfrac{11}{6 - 5 \sin \theta}$ **51.** $r = \dfrac{9}{4 - 5 \sin \theta}$

53. $r = \dfrac{3}{1 - 4 \cos \theta}$ **55.** Answers will vary.

57. $r = \dfrac{9.2930 \times 10^7}{1 - 0.0167 \cos \theta}$ **59.** $r = \dfrac{1.4040 \times 10^8}{1 - 0.0934 \cos \theta}$

Perihelion: Perihelion:
9.1404 × 10⁷ mi   1.2841 × 10⁸ mi
Aphelion: Aphelion:
9.4508 × 10⁷ mi   1.5487 × 10⁸ mi

61. $r = \dfrac{1.0820 \times 10^8}{1 - 0.0068 \cos \theta}$

Perihelion:
1.0747 × 10⁸ km
Aphelion:
1.0895 × 10⁸ km

63. (a) $r_{\text{Neptune}} = \dfrac{4.4977 \times 10^9}{1 - 0.0086 \cos \theta}$

$r_{\text{Pluto}} = \dfrac{5.5404 \times 10^9}{1 - 0.2488 \cos \theta}$

(b) Neptune: Perihelion: 4.4593 × 10⁹ km
         Aphelion: 4.5367 × 10⁹ km
     Pluto: Perihelion: 4.4366 × 10⁹ km
         Aphelion: 7.3754 × 10⁹ km

(c)

(d) Yes; because on average, Pluto is farther from the sun than Neptune.

(e) Using a graphing utility, it would appear that the orbits intersect. No, Pluto and Neptune will never collide because the orbits do not intersect in three-dimensional space.

65. False. The equation can be rewritten as $r = \dfrac{-4/3}{1 + \sin \theta}$.

Because ep is negative, p must be negative, and because p represents the distance between the pole and the directrix, the directrix has to be below the pole.

67. True. The graphs represent the same hyperbola.

69. Answers will vary.

71. $r^2 = \dfrac{24,336}{169 - 25 \cos^2 \theta}$ **73.** $r^2 = \dfrac{400}{25 - 9 \cos^2 \theta}$

75. $r^2 = \dfrac{144}{25 \cos^2 \theta - 16}$ **77.** Circle

79. Answers will vary.   **81.** $-\dfrac{7\sqrt{2}}{10}$ **83.** $\dfrac{7\sqrt{2}}{10}$

Review Exercises   (page 700)

1. Hyperbola   **3.** $x^2 + y^2 = 25$

5. $(x - 2)^2 + (y - 4)^2 = 13$

7. $x^2 + y^2 = 36$
    Center: $(0, 0)$
    Radius: 6

9. $\left(x - \frac{1}{2}\right)^2 + \left(y + \frac{3}{4}\right)^2 = 1$

Center: $\left(\frac{1}{2}, -\frac{3}{4}\right)$

Radius: 1

11.

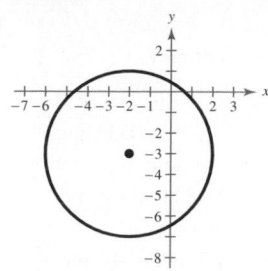

Center: $(-2, -3)$

Radius: 4

13. $\left(0, -4 \pm \sqrt{5}\right)$

15. Vertex: $(0, 0)$

Focus: $(0, -2)$

Directrix: $y = 2$

17. Vertex: $(0, 0)$

Focus: $(-9, 0)$

Directrix: $x = 9$

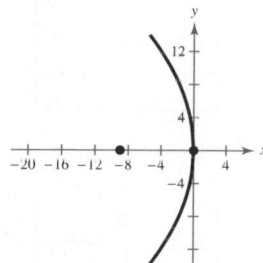

19. $x^2 = 20y$ **21.** $(x + 6)^2 = -9(y - 4)$

23. $2x + y - 2 = 0$ **25.** $8\sqrt{6}$ m

27. Center: $(0, 0)$

Vertices: $(0, \pm 6)$

Foci: $\left(0, \pm\sqrt{11}\right)$

Eccentricity: $\dfrac{\sqrt{11}}{6}$

29. Center: $(3, 2)$

Vertices: $(9, 2), (-3, 2)$

Foci: $\left(3 \pm 4\sqrt{2}, 2\right)$

Eccentricity: $\dfrac{2\sqrt{2}}{3}$

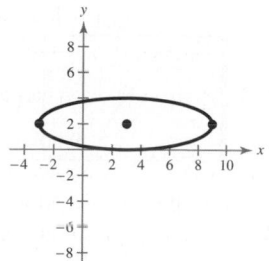

31. (a) $\dfrac{(x - 1)^2}{9} + \dfrac{(y + 4)^2}{16} = 1$

(b) Center: $(1, -4)$ (c)

Vertices: $(1, 0), (1, -8)$

Foci: $\left(1, -4 \pm \sqrt{7}\right)$

Eccentricity: $\dfrac{\sqrt{7}}{4}$

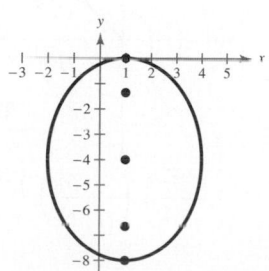

33. (a) $\dfrac{(x + 2)^2}{1/3} + \dfrac{(y - 7)^2}{1/8} = 1$

(b) Center: $(-2, 7)$ (c)

Vertices: $\left(-2 \pm \dfrac{\sqrt{3}}{3}, 7\right)$

Foci: $\left(-2 \pm \dfrac{\sqrt{30}}{12}, 7\right)$

Eccentricity: $\dfrac{\sqrt{10}}{4}$

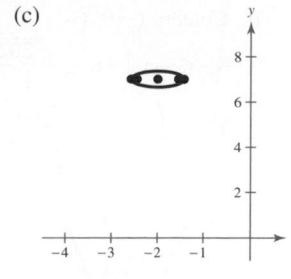

35. $\dfrac{x^2}{25} + \dfrac{y^2}{9} = 1$ **37.** $\dfrac{(x - 2)^2}{25} + \dfrac{y^2}{21} = 1$

39. The foci should be placed 3 feet on either side of the center at the same height as the pillers.

41. $e \approx 0.0539$ **43.** $\dfrac{x^2}{16} - \dfrac{y^2}{20} = 1$

45. $\dfrac{y^2}{16/5} - \dfrac{(x - 3)^2}{4/5} = 1$

47. (a) $\dfrac{y^2}{4} - \dfrac{x^2}{5} = 1$

(b) Center: $(0, 0)$

Vertices: $(0, \pm 2)$

Foci: $(0, \pm 3)$

Eccentricity: $\dfrac{3}{2}$

(c)

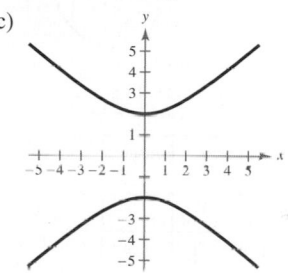

49. (a) $\dfrac{(x - 1)^2}{16} - \dfrac{(y + 1)^2}{9} = 1$

(b) Center: $(1, -1)$

Vertices: $(5, -1), (-3, -1)$

Foci: $(6, -1), (-4, -1)$

Eccentricity: $\dfrac{5}{4}$

(c)

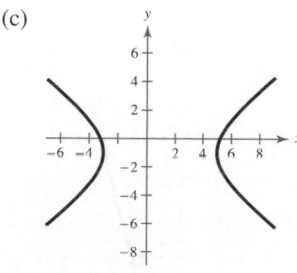

51. (a) $\dfrac{(x+6)^2}{101/2} - \dfrac{(y-1)^2}{202} = 1$

(b) Center: $(-6, 1)$

Vertices: $\left(-6 \pm \dfrac{\sqrt{202}}{2}, 1\right)$

Foci: $\left(-6 \pm \dfrac{\sqrt{1010}}{2}, 1\right)$

Eccentricity: $\sqrt{5}$

(c)

53. About 72 mi

55. Parabola   **57.** Circle

59. $\dfrac{(x')^2}{6} - \dfrac{(y')^2}{6} = 1$ **61.** $\dfrac{(x')^2}{3} + \dfrac{(y')^2}{2} = 1$

    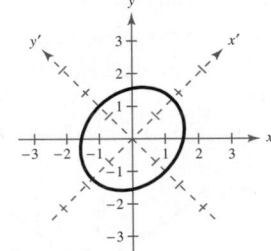

63.

t	-2	-1	0	1	2	3
x	-8	-5	-2	1	4	7
y	15	11	7	3	-1	-5

65.

$y = 2x$

67.

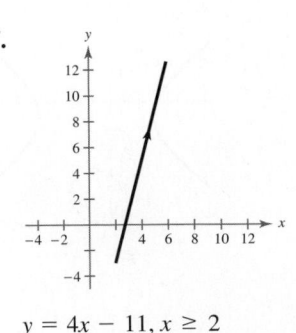

$y = 4x - 11, x \geq 2$

69.

$y = \dfrac{1}{2}x^{2/3}$

71.

Not a function

73.

Function

75.

Function

77.

Function

79.

Function

81.

Not a function

83. (a) $x = t, y = 6t + 2$ (b) $x = 1 - t, y = 8 - 6t$

85. (a) $x = t, y = t^2 + 2$ (b) $x = 1 - t, y = t^2 - 2t + 3$

87. $x = 3, y = t$ **89.** $x = -5t, y = 4 + 3t$

91. $x = \dfrac{v_0 t \sqrt{3}}{2}, y = 7 + \dfrac{v_0 t}{2} - 16t^2$

93.

15.19 ft

95.

$\left(2, -\dfrac{7\pi}{4}\right), \left(-2, \dfrac{5\pi}{4}\right), \left(-2, -\dfrac{3\pi}{4}\right)$

97.

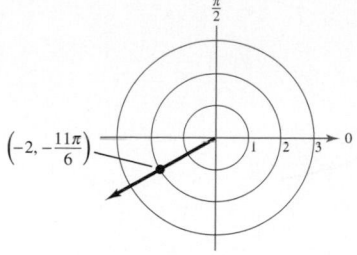

$$\left(-2, \frac{\pi}{6}\right), \left(2, \frac{7\pi}{6}\right), \left(2, -\frac{5\pi}{6}\right)$$

99.

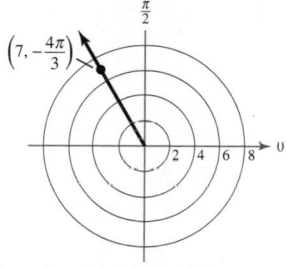

$$\left(7, \frac{2\pi}{3}\right), \left(-7, -\frac{\pi}{3}\right)\left(-7, \frac{5\pi}{3}\right)$$

101.

$(0, 3)$

103.

$(2, -2\sqrt{3})$

105.

$(0, 0)$

107.

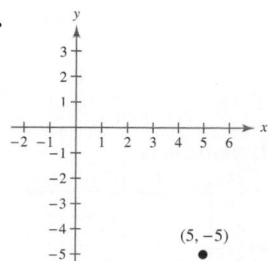

$$\left(-9, \frac{\pi}{2}\right), \left(9, \frac{3\pi}{2}\right)$$

109.

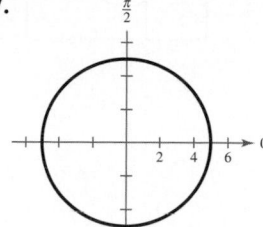

$$\left(-5\sqrt{2}, \frac{3\pi}{4}\right), \left(5\sqrt{2}, \frac{7\pi}{4}\right)$$

111. $r = 9$ **113.** $r = 4 \cos \theta$ **115.** $r^2 = 5 \sec \theta \csc \theta$

117. $r^2 = \dfrac{1}{1 + 3\cos^2 \theta}$ **119.** $x^2 + y^2 = 25$

121. $x^2 + y^2 = 3x$ **123.** $(x^2 + y^2)^2 - x^2 + y^2 = 0$

125. $y = x$

127.

129.

131.

133. Convex limaçon

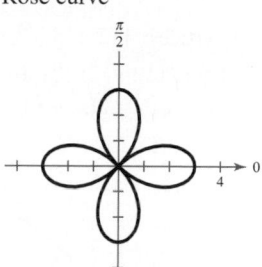

Symmetry: Polar axis

Zeros of r: None

135. Limaçon with inner loop

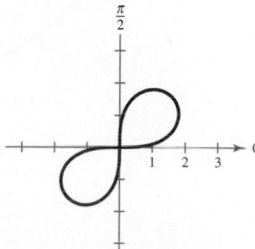

Symmetry: $\theta = \dfrac{\pi}{2}$

Zeros of r: $\theta \approx 0.64, 2.50$

137. Rose curve

Symmetry:
    Pole, polar axis, $\theta = \dfrac{\pi}{2}$

Zeros of r: $\theta = \dfrac{\pi}{4}, \dfrac{3\pi}{4}, \dfrac{5\pi}{4}, \dfrac{7\pi}{4}$

139. Lemniscate

Symmetry: Pole

Zeros of r: $\theta = 0, \dfrac{\pi}{2}$

CHAPTER 9

141. Hyperbola

143. Ellipse

145. Parabola

147. $r = \dfrac{6}{1 - \cos \theta}$ **149.** $r = \dfrac{5}{3 - 2 \sin \theta}$

151. $r = \dfrac{1.512}{1 - 0.093 \cos \theta}$

Perihelion: 1.383 astronomical units

Aphelion: 1.667 astronomical units

153. False. The equation of a hyperbola is a second-degree equation.

155. (a) Vertical translation

(b) Horizontal translation

(c) Reflection in the y-axis

(d) Vertical shrink

157. The orientation would be reversed.

Chapter Test   (page 704)

1.

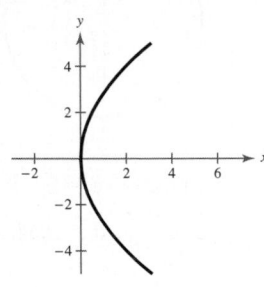

Vertex: $(0, 0)$

Focus: $(2, 0)$

2.

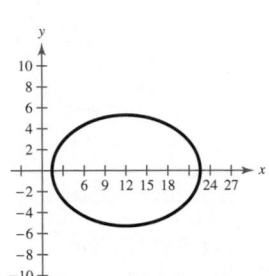

Vertices: $\left(12 \pm 4\sqrt{7}, 0\right)$

Foci: $\left(12 \pm 2\sqrt{21}, 0\right)$

3.

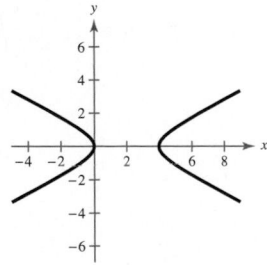

Vertices: $(0, 0), (4, 0)$

Foci: $\left(2 \pm \sqrt{5}, 0\right)$

4. $(y + 2)^2 = 8(x - 6)$

5. $\dfrac{(x + 6)^2}{16} + \dfrac{(y - 3)^2}{49} = 1$ **6.** $\dfrac{y^2}{9} - \dfrac{x^2}{4} = 1$

7.

Answers will vary.

8. (a) $45°$

(b)

9.

$y = 5 - 5x$

10.

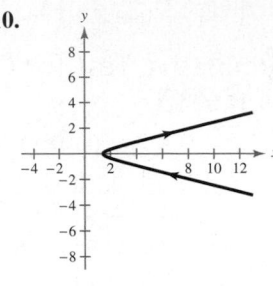

$\dfrac{x^2}{2} - \dfrac{y^2}{1/8} = 1, x \geq \sqrt{2}$

11.

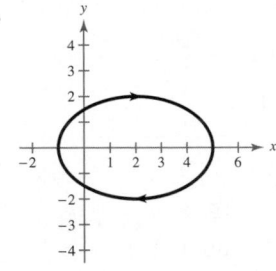

$\dfrac{(x - 2)^2}{9} + \dfrac{y^2}{4} = 1$

12. (a) $x = t, y = -3t + 5$ (b) $x = 2 - t, y = 3t - 1$

13. (a) $x = t, y = \dfrac{8}{t}$ (b) $x = 2 - t, y = \dfrac{8}{2 - t}$

14. (a) $x = t, y = \dfrac{4 - t^2}{2}$ (b) $x = 2 - t, y = \dfrac{4t - t^2}{2}$

15. $\left(\sqrt{3}, -1\right)$

16. Sample answer: $\left(2\sqrt{2}, \dfrac{7\pi}{4}\right); \left(2\sqrt{2}, -\dfrac{\pi}{4}\right), \left(-2\sqrt{2}, \dfrac{3\pi}{4}\right)$

17. $r = 3 \cos \theta$ **18.** $x^2 + (y - 1)^2 = 1$

19. Limaçon with inner loop

20. Parabola

21. Hyperbola

22. $r = a \sin 7\theta, a \neq 0$

23.

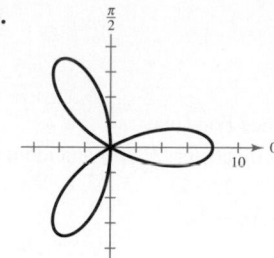

Symmetry: Polar axis

Zeros: $\dfrac{\pi}{6}, \dfrac{\pi}{2}, \dfrac{5\pi}{6}$

24. $r = \dfrac{4}{4 + \sin \theta}$ **25.** $r = \dfrac{10}{4 + 5 \sin \theta}$

Cumulative Test for Chapters 7–9 (page 705)

1. $(4, -3)$ **2.** $(8, 4), (2, -2)$

3. $\left(\dfrac{3}{5}, -4, -\dfrac{1}{5}\right)$ **4.** $(1, 2, 0)$

5. $\begin{bmatrix} -7 & -10 & -16 \\ -6 & 18 & 9 \\ -12 & 16 & 7 \end{bmatrix}$ **6.** $\begin{bmatrix} -18 & 15 & -14 \\ 28 & 11 & 34 \\ -20 & 52 & -1 \end{bmatrix}$

7. $\begin{bmatrix} 3 & -31 & 2 \\ 22 & 18 & 6 \\ 52 & -40 & 14 \end{bmatrix}$ **8.** $\begin{bmatrix} 5 & 36 & 31 \\ -36 & 12 & -36 \\ 16 & 0 & 18 \end{bmatrix}$

9. (a) $\begin{bmatrix} -175 & 37 & -13 \\ 95 & -20 & 7 \\ 14 & -3 & 1 \end{bmatrix}$ (b) 1

10. 22   **11.** (a) $\dfrac{1}{5}, -\dfrac{1}{7}, \dfrac{1}{9}, -\dfrac{1}{11}, \dfrac{1}{13}$ (b) 3, 6, 12, 24, 48

12. 135   **13.** $\dfrac{47}{52}$ **14.** 34.48   **15.** 66.67   **16.** $\dfrac{15}{8}$

17. $-\dfrac{5}{51}$ **18.** $\dfrac{8}{3}$ **19.** (a) 190   (b) 190

20. $x^4 + 12x^3 + 54x^2 + 108x + 81$

21. $32x^5 + 80x^4y^2 + 80x^3y^4 + 40x^2y^6 + 10xy^8 + y^{10}$

22. $x^6 - 12x^5y + 60x^4y^2 - 160x^3y^3 + 240x^2y^4 - 192xy^5 + 64y^6$

23. $6561a^8 - 69,984a^7b + 326,592a^6b^2 - 870,912a^5b^3$
$\qquad + 1,451,520a^4b^4 - 1,548,288a^3b^5 + 1,032,192a^2b^6$
$\qquad - 393,216ab^7 + 65,536b^8$

24. 120   **25.** 90,720   **26.** 420   **27.** 50,400

28. Hyperbola

29. Ellipse

30. Hyperbola

31. Circle

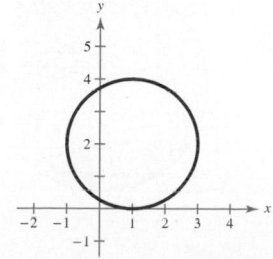

32. $(x - 2)^2 = -\dfrac{4}{3}(y - 3)$

33. $\dfrac{(x - 1)^2}{25} + \dfrac{(y - 4)^2}{4} = 1$ **34.** $\dfrac{(y + 4)^2}{4} - \dfrac{x^2}{16/3} = 1$

35.

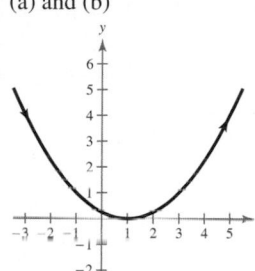

$\theta \approx 37.98°$

36. (a) and (b)

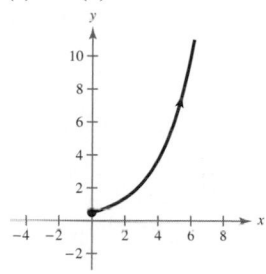

(c) $y = \dfrac{x^2 - 2x + 1}{4}$

37. (a) and (b)

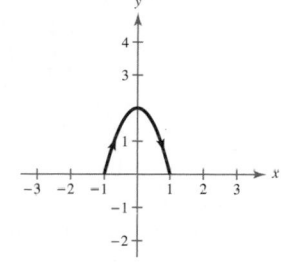

(c) $y = 2 - 2x^2,$
$\quad -1 \le x \le 1$

38. (a) and (b)

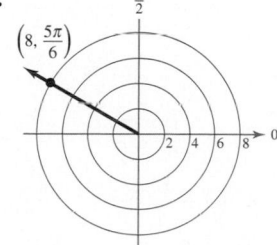

(c) $y = 0.5e^{0.5x}, x \ge 0$

39. (a) $x = t, y = 3t - 2$ (b) $x = 2t, y = 6t - 2$

40. (a) $x = t, y = t^2 - 16$ (b) $x = 2t, y = 4t^2 - 16$

41. (a) $x = t, y = \dfrac{2}{t}$

(b) $x = 2t, y = \dfrac{1}{t}$

42. (a) $x = t, y = \dfrac{e^{2t}}{e^{2t} + 1}$

(b) $x = 2t, y = \dfrac{e^{4t}}{e^{4t} + 1}$

43.

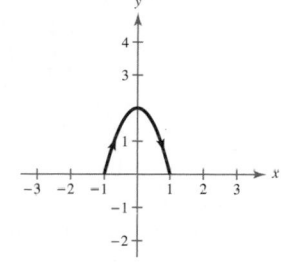

$\left(8, -\dfrac{7\pi}{6}\right), \left(-8, -\dfrac{\pi}{6}\right), \left(-8, \dfrac{11\pi}{6}\right)$

CHAPTER 9

44.

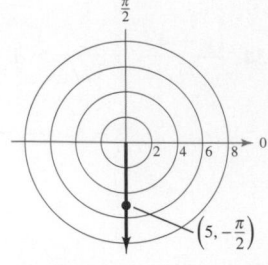

$$\left(5, \frac{3\pi}{2}\right), \left(-5, -\frac{3\pi}{2}\right), \left(-5, \frac{\pi}{2}\right)$$

45.

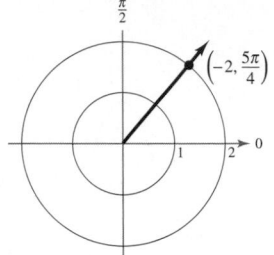

$$\left(-2, -\frac{3\pi}{4}\right), \left(2, -\frac{7\pi}{4}\right), \left(2, \frac{\pi}{4}\right)$$

46.

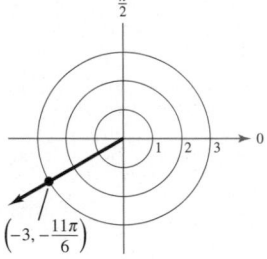

$$\left(-3, \frac{\pi}{6}\right), \left(3, -\frac{5\pi}{6}\right), \left(3, \frac{7\pi}{6}\right)$$

47. $r = -\dfrac{1}{4 \sin \theta + 4 \cos \theta}$ **48.** $(x-2)^2 + y^2 = 4$

49. $\dfrac{\left(x + \frac{10}{9}\right)^2}{\frac{64}{81}} - \dfrac{y^2}{\frac{4}{9}} = 1$

50. Circle   **51.** Convex limaçon

52. Ellipse

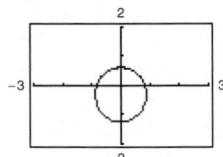

53. \$604,464.70   **54.** $\frac{1}{4}$ **55.** $24\sqrt{2}$ m

Chapter 10

Section 10.1 (page 716)

1. three-dimensional   **3.** Distance Formula
5. surface, space   **7.** A sphere with center (h, k, j) and radius r
9. $A(-2, -1, 4), B(3, -2, 0), C(-2, 2, -3)$
11. $A(2, -1, 4), B(1, 3, -2), C(-3, 0, -2)$
13.   **15.**

17.

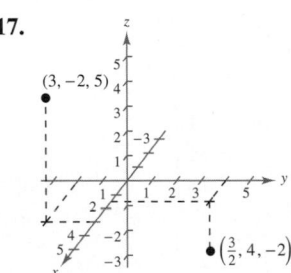

19. $(-3, 3, 5)$ **21.** $(11, 0, 0)$ **23.** $(0, 2, 7)$
25. Octant IV   **27.** Octants I, II, III, and IV
29. Octants II, IV, VI, and VIII   **31.** $3\sqrt{21}$ units
33. $\sqrt{44}$ units   **35.** $\sqrt{154}$ units   **37.** 12 units
39. $2\sqrt{5}, 3, \sqrt{29}$ **41.** $3, 6, 3\sqrt{5}$
43. $6, 6, 2\sqrt{10}$; isosceles triangle
45. $\sqrt{29}, \sqrt{66}, \sqrt{61}$; neither   **47.** $(0, -1, 7)$ **49.** $\left(\frac{3}{2}, \frac{7}{2}, \frac{1}{2}\right)$
51. $\left(\frac{5}{2}, 2, 6\right)$ **53.** $(x-3)^2 + (y-2)^2 + (z-4)^2 = 16$
55. $(x+1)^2 + (y-2)^2 + z^2 = 3$
57. $x^2 + (y-4)^2 + (z-3)^2 = 16$
59. $(x+3)^2 + (y-7)^2 + (z-5)^2 = 25$
61. $\left(x - \frac{3}{2}\right)^2 + y^2 + (z-3)^2 = \frac{45}{4}$
63. Center: $(3, 0, 0)$; radius: 3
65. Center: $(2, -1, 0)$; radius: $\sqrt{5}$
67. Center: $(-2, 0, 4)$; radius: 1
69. Center: $(2, -1, 3)$; radius: 2
71. Center: $(1, -2, 0)$; radius: $\dfrac{\sqrt{21}}{2}$
73. Center: $\left(\frac{1}{2}, 4, -1\right)$; radius: 3
75.

77.

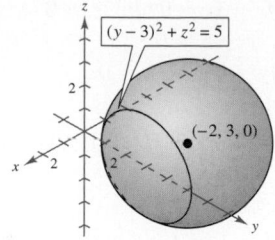

$(y - 3)^2 + z^2 = 5$
$(-2, 3, 0)$

79.

$(1, 0, 2)$

81.

$y^2 + (z - 2)^2 = 3$

83.

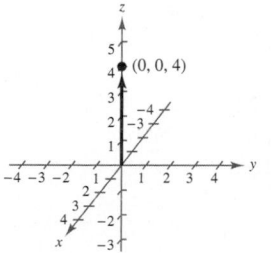

85. $(3, 3, 3)$ **87.** $x^2 + y^2 + z^2 = \dfrac{205^2}{4}$

89. False. z is the directed distance from the xy-plane to P.

91. $0; 0; 0$ **93.** $(x_2, y_2, z_2) = (2x_m - x_1, 2y_m - y_1, 2z_m - z_1)$

95. $v = -\dfrac{3 \pm \sqrt{17}}{2}$ **97.** $x = \dfrac{5 \pm \sqrt{5}}{2}$

99. $y = -\dfrac{1 \pm \sqrt{10}}{2}$ **101.** -7

Section 10.2   (page 724)

1. zero   **3.** parallel   **5.** $\|\mathbf{v}\| = \sqrt{v_1^2 + v_2^2 + v_3^2}$

7. (a) $\langle 0, 0, 4 \rangle$ **9.** (a) $\langle -2, 3, 1 \rangle$

(b)   (b)

$(0, 0, 4)$ $(-2, 3, 1)$

11. (a) $\langle 7, -3, -3 \rangle$ (b) $\sqrt{67}$ (c) $\dfrac{\sqrt{67}}{67}\langle 7, -3, -3 \rangle$

13. (a) $\langle 7, -5, 5 \rangle$ (b) $3\sqrt{11}$ (c) $\dfrac{\sqrt{11}}{33}\langle 7, -5, 5 \rangle$

---

15. (a)

$\langle 2, 2, 6 \rangle$

(b)

$\langle -1, -1, -3 \rangle$

(c)

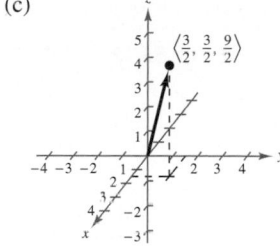

$\left\langle \dfrac{3}{2}, \dfrac{3}{2}, \dfrac{9}{2} \right\rangle$

(d)

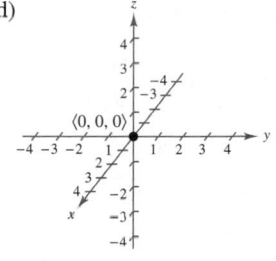

$\langle 0, 0, 0 \rangle$

17. (a)

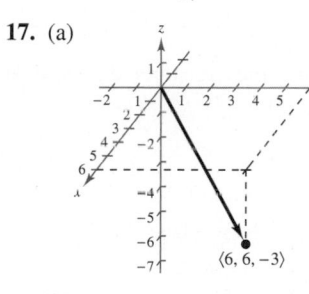

$\langle 6, 6, -3 \rangle$

(b)

$\langle -4, -4, 2 \rangle$

(c)

$\left\langle 5, 5, -\dfrac{5}{2} \right\rangle$

(d)

$\left\langle 3, 3, -\dfrac{3}{2} \right\rangle$

19. $\mathbf{z} = \langle -3, 7, 6 \rangle$ **21.** $\mathbf{z} = \left\langle -\dfrac{5}{2}, 12, \dfrac{15}{2} \right\rangle$

23. $\mathbf{z} = \left\langle \dfrac{1}{2}, 6, \dfrac{3}{2} \right\rangle$ **25.** $9\sqrt{2}$ **27.** $\sqrt{21}$ **29.** $\sqrt{101}$

31. $\sqrt{34}$ **33.** (a) $\dfrac{1}{13}(5\mathbf{i} - 12\mathbf{k})$ (b) $-\dfrac{1}{13}(5\mathbf{i} - 12\mathbf{k})$

35. (a) $\dfrac{\sqrt{74}}{74}(8\mathbf{i} + 3\mathbf{j} - \mathbf{k})$ (b) $-\dfrac{\sqrt{74}}{74}(8\mathbf{i} + 3\mathbf{j} - \mathbf{k})$

37. $\langle -26, 0, 48 \rangle$ **39.** 8.73 **41.** $\langle 0.55, 0.50, -0.67 \rangle$

43. -4 **45.** 0 **47.** $124.45°$ **49.** $109.92°$

51. Parallel   **53.** Neither   **55.** Orthogonal

57. Collinear   **59.** Not collinear

61. Right triangle. Answers will vary.

63. Acute triangle. Answers will vary.

65. $(3, 1, 7)$ **67.** $\left(6, \dfrac{5}{2}, -\dfrac{7}{4} \right)$ **69.** $\pm \dfrac{3\sqrt{14}}{14}$

71. $\langle 0, 2\sqrt{2}, 2\sqrt{2} \rangle$ or $\langle 0, 2\sqrt{2}, -2\sqrt{2} \rangle$ **73.** 2.75 lb

75. True. $\cos^{-1} 0 = 90°$

77. Sphere of radius 4 centered at (x_1, y_1, z_1)

Section 10.3   (page 731)

1. cross product   **3.** $\|\mathbf{u}\| \|\mathbf{v}\| \sin \theta$ **5.** $\langle -1, 0, 2 \rangle$

7. $\langle 1, 1, 1 \rangle$ **9.** $\langle -13, 60, -51 \rangle$ **11.** $-7\mathbf{i} + 13\mathbf{j} + 16\mathbf{k}$

CHAPTER 10

13. $-17\mathbf{i} + \mathbf{j} + 10\mathbf{k}$ **15.** $-\frac{7}{6}\mathbf{i} - \frac{7}{8}\mathbf{j}$ **17.** $\frac{1}{18}\mathbf{i} - \mathbf{j}$

19. $-\mathbf{i} - 2\mathbf{j} - \mathbf{k}$ **21.** $\langle 10, -2, -4 \rangle$

23. $-6\mathbf{i} - 15\mathbf{j} - 6\mathbf{k}$ **25.** $-\frac{1}{4}\mathbf{i} - \frac{7}{10}\mathbf{j} - 2\mathbf{k}$ **27.** 0

29. $21\mathbf{i} - 33\mathbf{j} - 24\mathbf{k}$ **31.** 0 **33.** $\frac{1}{3}\mathbf{i} - \frac{2}{3}\mathbf{j} - \frac{2}{3}\mathbf{k}$

35. $\frac{\sqrt{19}}{19}(\mathbf{i} - 3\mathbf{j} + 3\mathbf{k})$ **37.** $\frac{\sqrt{573}}{573}(-16\mathbf{i} + 11\mathbf{j} + 14\mathbf{k})$

39. $\frac{\sqrt{2}}{2}(\mathbf{i} - \mathbf{j})$ **41.** 1 **43.** $\sqrt{806}$ **45.** 56

47. (a) Answers will vary.   (b) $6\sqrt{10}$

49. $\frac{3\sqrt{13}}{2}$ **51.** $3\sqrt{11}$ **53.** -16 **55.** 2 **57.** 2

59. 12 **61.** 84

63. (a) $T(p) = \frac{p}{2}\cos 40°$

(b)

p	15	20	25	30	35	40	45
T	5.75	7.66	9.58	11.49	13.41	15.32	17.24

65. True. The cost product is defined only for three-dimensional vectors.

67 and 69. Proofs   **71.** $-\frac{1}{2}$

Section 10.4   (page 740)

1. direction   **3.** perpendicular   **5.** yz-plane

7. (a) $x = t, y = 2t, z = 3t$ (b) $x = \frac{y}{2} = \frac{z}{3}$

9. (a) $x = -4, y = 1 + 6t, z = -5t$
   (b) Not possible

11. (a) $x = 3 + 2t, y = 6 - 3t, z = -5 + t$
   (b) $\frac{x-3}{2} = \frac{y-6}{-3} = z + 5$

13. (a) $x = 2 - t, y = 4t, z = 2 - 5t$
   (b) $\frac{x-2}{-1} = \frac{y}{4} = \frac{z-2}{-5}$

15. (a) $x = -3 + 4t, y = 8 - 10t, z = 15 + t$
   (b) $\frac{x+3}{4} = \frac{y-8}{-10} = z - 15$

17. (a) $x = 3 - 4t, y = 1, z = 2 + 3t$
   (b) Not possible

19. (a) $x = -\frac{1}{2} + 3t, y = 2 - 5t, z = \frac{1}{2} - t$
   (b) $\frac{x+\frac{1}{2}}{3} = \frac{y-2}{-5} = \frac{z-\frac{1}{2}}{-1}$

21.

23. $x - 2 = 0$ **25.** $-2x + y - 2z + 10 = 0$

27. $-x - 2y + z + 2 = 0$ **29.** $-3x - 9y + 7z = 0$

31. $6x - 2y - z - 8 = 0$ **33.** $y - 5 = 0$

35. $y - z + 2 = 0$ **37.** $7x + y - 11z - 5 = 0$

39. $x = 2 + 3t, y = 3 + 2t, z = 4 - t$

41. $x = 5, y = -3 + 2t, z = -4 - 6t$

43. $x = -2 - t, y = 7 + 4t, z = 4 + 5t$

45. Orthogonal   **47.** Parallel

49. (a) $28.27°$
   (b) $x = t, y = 5t, z = 3t$

51. (a) $77.83°$
   (b) $x = 1 + 6t, y = t, z = 1 + 7t$

53.   **55.**

57. $\frac{3\sqrt{5}}{5}$ **59.** $\frac{2\sqrt{6}}{3}$ **61.** $88.45°$

63. False. Lines that do not intersect and are not in the same plane may not be parallel.

65. The point and the vector are reversed. The correct answer should be
$$\frac{x-1}{3} = \frac{y-2}{5} = \frac{z-6}{4}.$$

67. Parallel. $\langle 10, -18, 20 \rangle$ is a scalar multiple of $\langle -15, 27, -30 \rangle$.

Review Exercises   (page 744)

1.

3. $(-10, 9, 0)$ **5.** $3\sqrt{6}$ **7.** $\sqrt{29}, \sqrt{38}, \sqrt{67}$

9. $(0, -1, 3)$ **11.** $(1, 1, -9)$

13. $(x - 2)^2 + (y - 3)^2 + (z - 5)^2 = 1$

15. $(x + 4)^2 + y^2 + (z - 1)^2 = \frac{289}{4}$

17. Center: $(2, 3, -1)$; radius: $2\sqrt{2}$

19. (a)

(b)

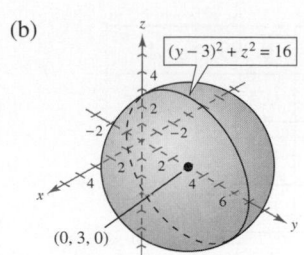

(0, 3, 0)

21. (a) $\langle -5, 7, -1 \rangle$ (b) $5\sqrt{3}$ (c) $\dfrac{\sqrt{3}}{15}\langle -5, 7, -1 \rangle$

23. (a) $\langle -10, 6, 7 \rangle$ (b) $\sqrt{185}$ (c) $\dfrac{\sqrt{185}}{185}\langle -10, 6, 7 \rangle$

25. -9 **27.** -5 **29.** $90°$ **31.** $69.22°$

33. Orthogonal   **35.** Orthogonal

37. Not collinear   **39.** Collinear

41. A: 159.10 lb of tension
B: 115.58 lb of tension
C: 115.58 lb of tension

43. $\langle -2, 24, 6 \rangle$ **45.** $-52\mathbf{i} + 40\mathbf{j} + 11\mathbf{k}$

47. $\dfrac{\sqrt{7602}}{7602}(-71\mathbf{i} - 44\mathbf{j} + 25\mathbf{k})$

49. (a) Answers will vary.   (b) $2\sqrt{43}$ **51.** 75

53. (a) $x = 3 + 6t, y = 11t, z = 2 + 4t$

(b) $\dfrac{x-3}{6} = \dfrac{y}{11} = \dfrac{z-2}{4}$

55. (a) $x = -5t, y = -10 + 2t, z = 3 + 3t$

(b) $\dfrac{x}{-5} = \dfrac{y+10}{2} = \dfrac{z-3}{3}$

57. (a) $x = -1 + 2t, y = 3 - t, z = 5 + 3t$

(b) $\dfrac{x+1}{2} = \dfrac{y-3}{-1} = \dfrac{z-5}{3}$

59. $2x - 8y + 5z - 20 = 0$ **61.** $z - 2 = 0$

63.

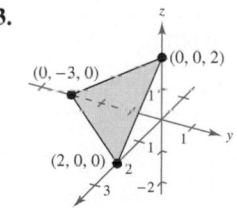

(0, -3, 0)   (0, 0, 2)
(2, 0, 0)

65.

(0, 0, -2)
(3, 0, 0)

67. $\dfrac{\sqrt{110}}{110}$ **69.** $\dfrac{\sqrt{110}}{55}$ **71.** False. $\mathbf{u} \times \mathbf{v} = -(\mathbf{v} \times \mathbf{u})$

73 and 75. Answers will vary.

77. $\mathbf{u} \times \mathbf{v} = (u_2v_3 - u_3v_2)\mathbf{i} - (u_1v_3 - u_3v_1)\mathbf{j} + (u_1v_2 - u_2v_1)\mathbf{k}$

Chapter Test   (page 746)

1.

(5, -2, 3)   (-3, 4, 2)
(2, 1, -1)

2. No. Answers will vary.   **3.** $(7, 1, 2)$

4. $(x - 7)^2 + (y - 1)^2 + (z - 2)^2 = 19$

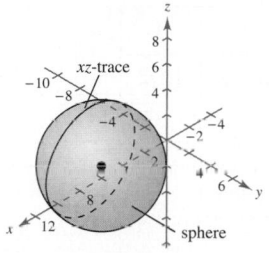

xz-trace

sphere

5. $\langle 2, 5, -10 \rangle; \sqrt{129}$ **6.** $\langle -3, -6, 13 \rangle; \sqrt{214}$

7. $\mathbf{u} = \langle -2, 6, -6 \rangle, \mathbf{v} = \langle -12, 5, -5 \rangle$

8. (a) $\sqrt{194}$ (b) 84   (c) $\langle 0, 62, 62 \rangle$ **9.** $46.23°$

10. Answers will vary. Sample answer:

(a) $x = 8 - 2t, y = -2 + 6t, z = 5 - 6t$

(b) $\dfrac{x-8}{-2} = \dfrac{y+2}{6} = \dfrac{z-5}{-6}$

11. Neither   **12.** Orthogonal   **13.** Parallel

14. Answers will vary; $2\sqrt{230}$

15. $27x + 4y + 32z + 33 = 0$ **16.** 200

17.

10   (0, 0, 9)

(0, 3, 0)
(6, 0, 0)

18.

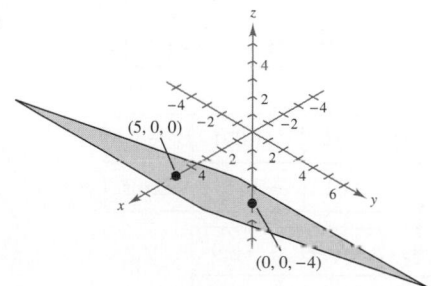

(5, 0, 0)

(0, 0, -4)

19. $\dfrac{4\sqrt{14}}{7}$

CHAPTER 10

Chapter 11

Section 11.1   (page 757)

1. limit   **3.** 3

5. (a)

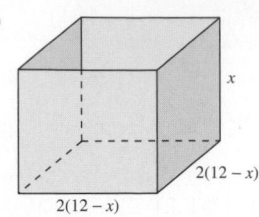

(b) Answers will vary.

(c)

x	3	3.5	3.9	4
V	972	1011.5	1023.5	1024

x	4.1	4.5	5
V	1023.5	1012.5	980

$\lim\limits_{x \to 4} V = 1024$

(d)

7.

x	1.9	1.99	1.999	2
f(x)	13.5	13.95	13.995	14

x	2.001	2.01	2.1
f(x)	14.005	14.05	14.5

14; Yes

9.

x	−1.1	−1.01	−1.001	−1
f(x)	−0.3226	−0.3322	−0.3332	Error

x	−0.999	−0.99	−0.9
f(x)	−0.3334	−0.3344	−0.3448

−0.3333; No

11.

x	−1.1	−1.01	−1.001	−1
f(x)	−2.1	−2.01	−2.001	Error

x	−0.999	−0.99	−0.9
f(x)	−1.999	−1.99	−1.9

−2

13.

x	0.9	0.99	0.999	1
f(x)	0.2564	0.2506	0.2501	Error

x	1.001	1.01	1.1
f(x)	0.2499	0.2494	0.2439

0.25

15.

x	5.9	5.99	5.999	6
f(x)	0.16713	0.16671	0.16667	Error

x	6.001	6.01	6.1
f(x)	0.16666	0.16662	0.16621

$\frac{1}{6}$

17.

x	−4.1	−4.01	−4.001	−4
f(x)	0.4762	0.4975	0.4998	Error

x	−3.999	−3.99	−3.9
f(x)	0.5003	0.5025	0.5263

0.5

19.

x	−0.1	−0.01	−0.001	0
f(x)	0.9983	0.99998	0.9999998	Error

x	0.001	0.01	0.1
f(x)	0.9999998	0.99998	0.9983

1

21.

x	−0.1	−0.01	−0.001	0
f(x)	−0.0997	−0.0100	−0.0010	Error

x	0.001	0.01	0.1
f(x)	0.0010	0.0100	0.0997

0

23.

x	−0.1	−0.01	−0.001	0
f(x)	0.9063	0.9901	0.9990	Error

x	0.001	0.01	0.1
f(x)	1.0010	1.0101	1.1070

1

25.

x	1.9	1.99	1.999	2
f(x)	2.2314	2.0203	2.002	Error

x	2.001	2.01	2.1
f(x)	1.998	1.9803	1.8232

2

27.

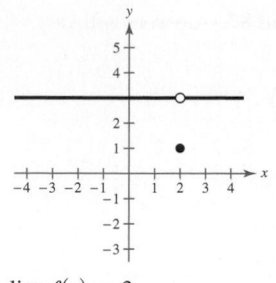

$$\lim_{x \to 2} f(x) = 3$$

29.

$$\lim_{x \to 2} f(x) = 5$$

31.

Limit does not exist.

33. 2

35. Limit does not exist; One-sided limits do not agree.

37. Limit does not exist; One-sided limits do not agree.

39. -1

41. Limit does not exist; Function oscillates between -2 and 2.

43.

No

45.

Yes

47.

No

49.

Yes

51. (a) -16 (b) 12 (c) $\frac{1}{2}$ (d) 2

53. (a) 16 (b) $\frac{3}{8}$ (c) 6 (d) $-\frac{125}{8}$

55. -15 **57.** 7 **59.** -2 **61.** $-\frac{9}{10}$ **63.** $\frac{7}{13}$

65. 1 **67.** $\frac{3}{4}$ **69.** e^3 **71.** 0 **73.** $\frac{\pi}{6}$

75. True. See Condition 1 on page 754.

77. (a) and (b) Answers will vary.

79. (a) No. The function may approach different values from the right and left of 4.

(b) No. The function may approach 4 as x approaches 2, but the function could be undefined at $x = 2$.

81. $-\frac{1}{3}, x \neq 5$ **83.** $\dfrac{5x + 4}{5x + 2}, x \neq \frac{1}{3}$

85. $\dfrac{x^2 - 3x + 9}{x - 2}, x \neq -3$

Section 11.2   (page 767)

1. dividing out technique   **3.** Rationalizing technique

5. (a) 1   (b) 3   (c) 5   (d) -1
    $g_2(x) = -2x + 1$

7. (a) 2   (b) 0   (c) 0   (d) 6
    $g_2(x) = x(x + 1)$

9. $\frac{1}{12}$ **11.** 3   **13.** 4   **15.** 12   **17.** 80   **19.** $\frac{7}{2}$

21. $\frac{1}{3}$ **23.** $\frac{\sqrt{5}}{10}$ **25.** $\frac{1}{4}$ **27.** -1 **29.** $-\frac{1}{16}$

31. 0   **33.** 0   **35.** 0

37.

x	-0.1	-0.01	-0.001	0
$f(x)$	1.813	1.980	1.998	Error

x	0.001	0.01	0.1
$f(x)$	2.002	2.020	2.214

2.000

39.

x	0.9	0.99	0.999	1
$f(x)$	0.9491	0.9949	0.9995	Error

x	1.001	1.01	1.1
$f(x)$	1.0005	1.005	1.0492

1

41.

x	-0.1	-0.01	-0.001	0
$f(x)$	23.59	20.391	20.116	Error

x	0.001	0.01	0.1
$f(x)$	20.055	19.788	17.449

20.090

43.

2.000

45.

1.000

47.

0.333

49.

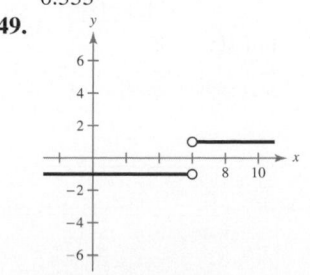

Limit does not exist.

51.

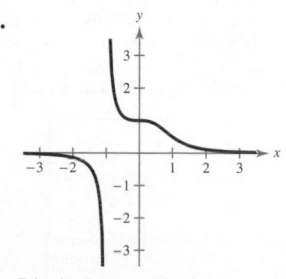

Limit does not exist.

CHAPTER 11

53.

$$\lim_{x \to 2} f(x) = 1$$

55.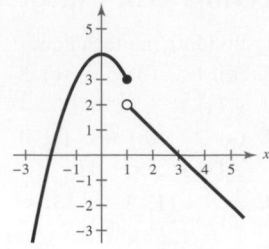

Limit does not exist.

57. (a) and (b) 0.50   (c) $\frac{1}{2}$

59. (a) and (b) -0.13 (c) $-\frac{1}{8}$

61. -32 ft/sec   **63.** Answers will vary.

65. (a)

(b) (i) 2.25; 15 photocopies will cost $2.25.
   (ii) 14.7; 98 photocopies will cost $14.70.
   (iii) 40.5; 405 photocopies will cost $40.50.

(c) Answers will vary. Sample answers:

(i)

x	8.999	9	9.001
$C(x)$	1.7998	1.8	1.35015

(ii)

x	98.999	99	99.001
$C(x)$	14.84985	14.85	9.9001

(iii)

x	998.999	999	999.001
$C(x)$	99.8999	99.9	79.92008

(d) The graph shows that one-sided limits are not equal, which can be seen when the graph "jumps" at $x = 9, 99,$ and $999.$

67. 3   **69.** $\dfrac{1}{2\sqrt{x}}$ **71.** $2x - 3$ **73.** $-\dfrac{1}{(x + 2)^2}$

75. (a) Direct substitution; 0   (b) 1

77.   **79.**

$$\lim_{x \to 0} f(x) = 0$$ $$\lim_{x \to 0} f(x) = 0$$

81.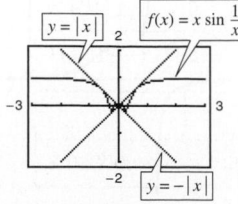

$$\lim_{x \to 0} f(x) = 0$$

83. True. See page 761.   **85 and 87.** Answers will vary.

89. Parabola   **91.** Hyperbola

Section 11.3 (page 777)

1. Calculus   **3.** secant line   **5.** 2   **7.** 0

9. $\frac{1}{2}$ **11.** 2   **13.** -6 **15.** $-\frac{3}{4}$ **17.** $\frac{1}{8}$

19. $m = -2x$; (a) -4 (b) 8

21. $m = -\dfrac{1}{(x + 4)^2}$; (a) $-\dfrac{1}{16}$ (b) $-\dfrac{1}{4}$

23. $m = \dfrac{1}{2\sqrt{x - 3}}$; (a) $\dfrac{1}{2}$ (b) $\dfrac{1}{6}$

25.   **27.**

2          $-\frac{1}{2}$

29. $-\dfrac{1}{3}$ **31.** $4x - 7$ **33.** 0   **35.** $-\dfrac{2}{x^3}$

37. $\dfrac{1}{2\sqrt{x + 4}}$ **39.** $-\dfrac{1}{2(x - 9)^{3/2}}$

41. (a) 4   **43.** (a) 1
   (b) $y = 4x - 5$ (b) $y = x - 2$
   (c)   (c)

45. (a) -3 **47.** (a) $\frac{1}{6}$
   (b) $y = -3x - 10$ (b) $y = \frac{1}{6}x + 2$
   (c)   (c)

49. (a) -1
   (b) $y = -x - 3$
   (c)

51.

x	-2	-1.5	-1	-0.5	0
$f(x)$	2	1.125	0.5	0.125	0
$f'(x)$	-2	-1.5	-1	-0.5	0

x	0.5	1	1.5	2
$f(x)$	0.125	0.5	1.125	2
$f'(x)$	0.5	1	1.5	2

They appear to be the same.

53.

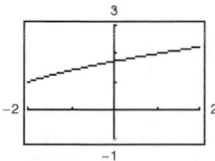

x	-2	-1.5	-1	-0.5	0
$f(x)$	1	1.225	1.414	1.581	1.732
$f'(x)$	0.5	0.408	0.354	0.316	0.289

x	0.5	1	1.5	2
$f(x)$	1.871	2	2.121	2.236
$f'(x)$	0.267	0.25	0.236	0.224

They appear to be the same.

55. $f'(x) = 2x - 4; (2, -1)$

57. $f'(x) = 6x^2 - 8; \left(-\dfrac{2\sqrt{3}}{3}, \dfrac{32\sqrt{3}}{9}\right), \left(\dfrac{2\sqrt{3}}{3}, \dfrac{32\sqrt{3}}{9}\right)$

59. $(-1, -1), (0, 0), (1, -1)$

61. $\left(\dfrac{\pi}{6}, \sqrt{3} + \dfrac{\pi}{6}\right), \left(\dfrac{5\pi}{6}, \dfrac{5\pi}{6} - \sqrt{3}\right)$

63. $(0, 0), (-2, 4e^{-2})$ **65.** $(e^{-1}, -e^{-1})$

67. (a) $y = 0.25t^2 - 3.56t + 20.7$

(b)

2.5; The revenue for eBay, Inc. was increasing by approximately \$2.5 billion per year in 2012.

(c) $y' = 0.5t - 3.56; 2.44$

(d) Answers will vary.

69. (a) $V'(r) = 4\pi r^2$ (b) About 201.06

(c) Cubic inches per inch; The derivative is a formula for rate of change.

71. (a) $s'(t) = -32t + 64$ (b) 16 ft/sec

(c) $t = 2$ sec; Answers will vary.

(d) -96 ft/sec

(e)

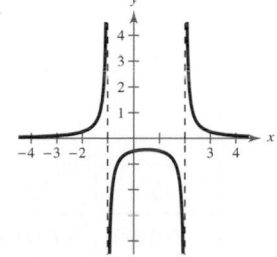

73. True. The graph of the derivative is a line, which is a one-to-one function.

75. (a) Answers will vary.

(b) Use the equation $m = \lim\limits_{h \to 0} \dfrac{f(x + h) - f(x)}{h}$

77. Answers will vary. Sample answer: A sketch of any linear function with positive slope

79.

Section 11.4   (page 786)

1. 5   **3.** converge   **5.** c   **6.** a   **7.** d

8. b   **9.** f   **10.** g   **11.** h   **12.** e

13. 2   **15.** $-\dfrac{9}{4}$ **17.** 2   **19.** -4

21. Limit does not exist.   **23.** $\dfrac{4}{3}$ **25.** 2   **27.** -1

29. 2   **31.** -5

33. (a)

x	10^0	10^1	10^2	10^3
$f(x)$	1	-2.857	-2.062	-2.006

x	10^4	10^5
$f(x)$	-2.00060018	-2.000060002

x	10^6
$f(x)$	-2.000006

-2

(b)

(c) $\lim\limits_{x \to \infty} f(x) = -2$

35. (a)

x	10^0	10^1	10^2	10^3
$f(x)$	Error	-0.7071	-0.07	-0.007

x	10^4	10^5	10^6
$f(x)$	-0.0007	0.00007	-0.000007

0

CHAPTER 11

(b)

(c) $\lim\limits_{x\to\infty} f(x) = 0$

0

37. (a)

x	10^0	10^1	10^2	10^3
$f(x)$	-2	0.97	0.9997	0.999997

x	10^4	10^5	10^6
$f(x)$	0.99999997	0.9999999997	1

1

(b)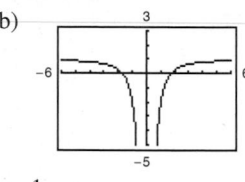

(c) $\lim\limits_{x\to\infty} f(x) = 1$

1

39. (a)

x	10^0	10^1	10^2	10^3
$f(x)$	-0.7321	-0.0995	-0.0100	-0.0010

x	10^4	10^5	10^6
$f(x)$	-1.0×10^{-4}	-1.0×10^{-5}	-1.0×10^{-6}

0

(b)

0

41. (a)

x	10^0	10^1	10^2	10^3
$f(x)$	-0.7082	-0.7454	-0.7495	-0.74995

x	10^4	10^5	10^6
$f(x)$	-0.749995	-0.7499995	-0.7500

-0.75

(b)

-0.75

43. $1, \frac{3}{5}, \frac{2}{5}, \frac{5}{17}, \frac{3}{13}$
Limit: 0

45. $\frac{4}{3}, 2, \frac{16}{7}, \frac{22}{9}, \frac{28}{11}$
Limit: 3

47. $\frac{1}{5}, \frac{1}{2}, \frac{9}{11}, \frac{8}{7}, \frac{25}{17}$
Limit does not exist.

49. $2, 3, 4, 5, 6$
Limit does not exist.

51. $-1, \frac{1}{2}, -\frac{1}{3}, \frac{1}{4}, -\frac{1}{5}$
Limit: 0

53.

n	10^0	10^1	10^2	10^3
a_n	2	1.55	1.505	1.5005

1.5
$\lim\limits_{x\to\infty} a_n = \frac{3}{2}$

55.

n	10^0	10^1	10^2	10^3
a_n	13.33	5.683	5.06683	5.0066683

5
$\lim\limits_{x\to\infty} a_n = 5$

57. (a) $\overline{C}(x) = \dfrac{73x + 25{,}000}{x}$　(b) \$98; \$78

(c) \$73; As the number of MP3 players gets very large, the average cost approaches \$73.

59. (a)

The model fits the data well.

(b) 2013: 1.0914 million
2014: 1.099 million

(c) 0; As time passes, the number of United States ready reserve personnel approaches 0.

(d) Answers will vary.

61. False. $y = \dfrac{x^2}{x + 1}$ does not have a horizontal asymptote.

63. True. See page 784.

65. Answers will vary. Sample answer: Let $f(x) = x^2$ and $g(x) = x^2$. Then $\lim\limits_{x\to\infty} x^2 = \infty$ and $\lim\limits_{x\to\infty} [f(x) - g(x)] = 0$.

67. 　**69.**

Converges to 0　　Diverges

71. The limit is $-\frac{1}{4}$.

73.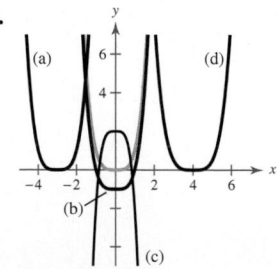

75. 60　**77.** 176

Section 11.5　(page 794)

1. $\dfrac{n(n + 1)}{2}$　**3.** 100 rectangles　**5.** 420　**7.** 44,100

9. 131,980　**11.** 6175

13. (a) $S(n) = \dfrac{n^2 + 2n + 1}{4n^2}$

(b)

n	10^0	10^1	10^2	10^3	10^4
$S(n)$	1	0.3025	0.2550	0.2505	0.2501

(c) $\displaystyle\lim_{n\to\infty} S(n) = \dfrac{1}{4}$

15. (a) $S(n) = \dfrac{2n^2 + 3n + 6}{n^2}$

(b)

n	10^0	10^1	10^2	10^3	10^4
$S(n)$	11	2.36	2.0306	2.003	2.0003

(c) $\displaystyle\lim_{n\to\infty} S(n) = 2$

17. (a) $S(n) = \dfrac{14n^2 + 3n + 1}{6n^3}$

(b)

n	10^0	10^1	10^2	10^3	10^4
$S(n)$	3	0.2385	0.0234	0.0023	0.0002

(c) $\displaystyle\lim_{n\to\infty} S(n) = 0$

19. 14.25   **21.** 1.27

23.

n	4	8	20	50
Approximate area	18	21	22.8	23.52

25.

n	4	8	20	50
Approximate area	3.5156	2.8477	2.4806	2.3409

27.

n	4	8	20	50	100	∞
Area	40	38	36.8	36.32	36.16	36

29.

n	4	8	20	50	100	∞
Area	14.25	14.81	15.13	15.25	15.29	$\frac{46}{3}$

31.

n	4	8	20	50	100	∞
Area	19	18.5	18.2	18.08	18.04	18

33. $\frac{3}{2}$ **35.** 9   **37.** 45   **39.** 12   **41.** $\frac{3}{4}$ **43.** 144

45.

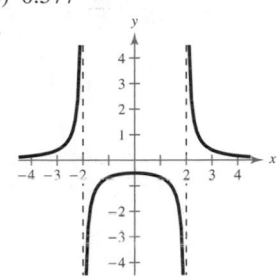

105,208.33 ft²

47. True. See Formula 2 on page 789.

49. Answers will vary.

Review Exercises   (page 798)

1.

x	2.9	2.99	2.999	3
$f(x)$	16.4	16.94	16.994	17

x	3.001	3.01	3.1
$f(x)$	17.006	17.06	17.6

17; Yes

3.

x	-0.1	-0.01	-0.001	0
$f(x)$	0.5017	0.50002	0.5	Error

x	0.001	0.01	0.1
$f(x)$	0.5	0.50002	0.5017

0.5; No

5. 2   **7.** Limit does not exist.

9. (a) 8   (b) 1   (c) 10   (d) $\frac{2}{5}$

11. 5   **13.** $\dfrac{10}{3}$ **15.** -2 **17.** 0   **19.** e **21.** $\dfrac{\pi}{2}$

23. $-\frac{1}{4}$ **25.** $\frac{1}{15}$ **27.** -9 **29.** -1 **31.** $\frac{1}{4}$

33. (a) and (b) 0.17   **35.** Limit does not exist.

37. (a) and (b) 2   **39.** (a) and (b) 0.577

41.

Limit does not exist.

43.

Limit does not exist.

45.

Limit does not exist.

47.

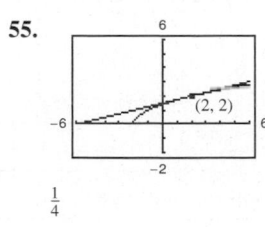

Limit does not exist.

49. $3 - 2x$ **51.** 2

53.

-2

55.

$\frac{1}{4}$

57.

$-\frac{3}{2}$

59. $m = 2x - 4$; (a) 4   (b) -6

61. $m = -\dfrac{4}{(x-6)^2}$; (a) $-\dfrac{4}{9}$ (b) -1

63. $f'(x) = 0$ **65.** $h'(x) = -6$ **67.** $g'(x) = 4x + 1$

69. $f'(t) = \dfrac{1}{2\sqrt{t+5}}$ **71.** $g'(s) = -\dfrac{4}{(s+5)^2}$

73. $g'(x) = -\dfrac{1}{2(x+4)^{3/2}}$

75. (a) 12   (b) $12x - 19$
    (c)

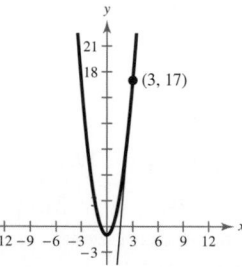

77. (a) 3   (b) $y = 3x - 1$
    (c)

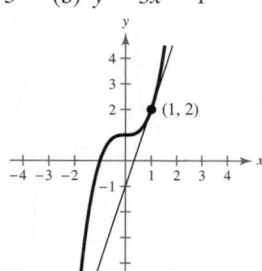

79. 2   **81.** -1 **83.** Limit does not exist.   **85.** 3

87. $-\frac{1}{9}, \frac{1}{14}, \frac{3}{19}, \frac{5}{24}, \frac{7}{29}$ **89.** $-1, \frac{1}{8}, -\frac{1}{27}, \frac{1}{64}, -\frac{1}{125}$
    Limit: $\frac{2}{5}$ Limit: 0

91. $-\frac{1}{2}, -\frac{9}{8}, -\frac{7}{6}, -\frac{37}{32}, -\frac{57}{50}$
    Limit: -1

93. (a) $S(n) = \dfrac{5n^2 + 9n + 4}{6n^2}$

(b)

n	10^0	10^1	10^2	10^3	10^4
$S(n)$	3	0.99	0.8484	0.8348	0.8335

(c) $\dfrac{5}{6}$

95. 6.75

97.

n	4	8	20	50
Approximate area	7.5	6.375	5.74	5.4944

99. 10   **101.** 21   **103.** 68

105. (a) $y = (-3.376 \times 10^{-7})x^3 + (3.753 \times 10^{-4})x^2 - 0.168x + 132$

(b)

(c) 88,700 ft^2

107. True. See page 775.

Chapter Test   (page 801)

1.

-0.75
$\lim\limits_{n \to -2} f(x) = -\frac{3}{4}$

2.

6
$\lim\limits_{x \to 1} f(x) = 6$

3.

Limit does not exist.

4.

1.6667

5.

3.0000

6. (a) $m = 6x - 5$; 7   (b) $m = 6x^2 + 6$; 12

7. $f'(x) = -\frac{2}{5}$ **8.** $f'(x) = 4x + 4$

9. $f'(x) = -\dfrac{1}{(x+1)^2}$ **10.** 0   **11.** -3

12. Limit does not exist.

13. $0, \frac{3}{4}, \frac{14}{19}, \frac{12}{17}, \frac{36}{53}$ **14.** $0, 1, 0, \frac{1}{2}, 0$
    Limit: $\frac{1}{2}$ Limit: 0

15. 12.5   **16.** 12   **17.** $\frac{34}{3}$

18. (a) $y = 8.79x^2 - 6.2x - 0.4$ (b) 81.7 ft/sec

Cumulative Test for Chapters 10 and 11 (page 802)

1. $(-7, 8, 9)$ **2.** $(0, 0, -5)$ **3.** $\sqrt{149}$

4. 3, 4, 5   **5.** $\left(-1, 2, \frac{1}{2}\right)$

6. $(x-2)^2 + (y-2)^2 + (z-4)^2 = 24$

7.

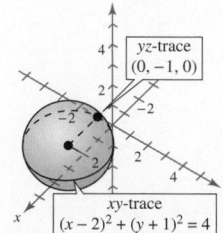

8. $\mathbf{u} \cdot \mathbf{v} = -38$
    $\mathbf{u} \times \mathbf{v} = \langle -18, -6, -14 \rangle$

9. Neither   **10.** Orthogonal   **11.** Parallel   **12.** 12

13. (a) $x = -2 + 7t, y = 3 + 5t, z = 25t$

    (b) $\dfrac{x + 2}{7} = \dfrac{y - 3}{5} = \dfrac{z}{25}$

14. $x = -1 + 2t, y = 2 - 4t, z = t$

15. $75x + 50y - 31z = 0$

16.

17. $\dfrac{\sqrt{30}}{2}$ **18.** 84.26°   **19.** 4   **20.** Limit does not exist.

21. $\dfrac{1}{14}$ **22.** Limit does not exist.   **23.** -1

24. Limit does not exist.   **25.** $-\frac{1}{9}$ **26.** $\frac{1}{8}$ **27.** $\frac{1}{4}$

28. $m = -2x; 4$ **29.** $m = \frac{1}{2}(x + 6)^{-1/2}; \frac{1}{8}$

30. $m = -(x + 3)^{-2}; -\frac{1}{16}$

31. $m = 2x - 1; 1$ **32.** Limit does not exist.   **33.** -8

34. 3   **35.** 0   **36.** 0   **37.** Limit does not exist.

38. $-12,875$ **39.** 8190   **40.** 672,880   **41.** 10.5

42. 8.13   **43.** 2.69   **44.** 1.57   **45.** $\frac{26}{3}$ **46.** 32

47. $\frac{34}{3}$ **48.** $\frac{3}{4}$

Appendix B

Appendix B.1   (page A31)

1. Line plots   **3.** frequency distribution   **5.** scatterplot

7. (a) 3.52   (b) 0.56

9.

15

11. Sample answer:

Interval	Tally
[7, 10)	||
[10, 13)	‖Ht ‖Ht ‖Ht
[13, 16)	‖Ht ‖Ht ‖Ht |||
[16, 19)	‖Ht ‖Ht |
[19, 22)	||||

13.

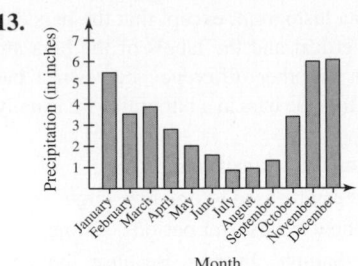

Answers will vary. Sample answer: The amount of precipitation decreases at a fairly constant rate from January to July, and then it starts to increase at a fairly constant rate until December.

15.

17.

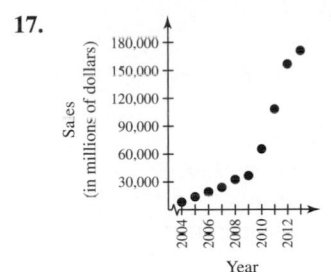

19. The price increased at a fairly constant rate from 2005 to 2008.

21. 2008 to 2009   **23.** About 13%

25.

Answers will vary. Sample answer: As time progresses from 2000 to 2012, the percent of wives who earned more income than their husbands increased at a fairly constant rate.

27. 65   **29.** Yes

31.

Answers will vary. Sample answer: A histogram is best because the data are percents within a year that do not relate to increasing or decreasing behavior.

33. A bar graph is similar to a histogram, except that the bars can be either horizontal or vertical and the labels of the bars are not necessarily numbers. Another difference between a bar graph and a histogram is that the bars in a bar graph are usually separated by spaces.

35. Line plots are useful for ordering small sets.

Histograms or bar graphs can be used to organize larger sets.

Line graphs are used to show trends over periods of time.

37. (a) Answers will vary. Sample answer: Because the data are from a single year and do not relate to increasing or decreasing behavior, a bar graph could be used. Because the data do not need to be shown as trends over time, a line graph would not be used.

(b) Answers will vary. Sample answer: Because the data relate to increasing and decreasing behavior over time, a line graph could be used. Because the data are from separate years, a histogram would not be used.

Appendix B.2   (page A41)

1. measure, central tendency
3. variance, standard deviation
5. Mean: 8.5; median: 7.5; mode: 7
7. Mean: 10.5; median: 7.5; mode: 7
9. Mean: About 12.83; median: 12; mode: none
11. The mean; Answers will vary.
13. Mean: 320; median: 320; mode: 320
15. (a) Jay: 199.67; Hank: 199.67; Buck: 229.33
(b) 209.56   (c) 202   (d) median
17. Answers will vary. Sample answer: $\{4, 4, 10\}$
19. The median
21. (a) $\bar{x} = 12$; $\sigma \approx 2.83$ (b) $\bar{x} = 20$; $\sigma \approx 2.83$
(c) $\bar{x} = 12$; $\sigma \approx 1.41$ (d) $\bar{x} = 9$; $\sigma \approx 1.41$
23. $\bar{x} = 6$, $v = 10$, $\sigma \approx 3.16$ **25.** $\bar{x} = 3$, $v = 4$, $\sigma = 2$
27. $\bar{x} = 2$, $v = \frac{4}{3}$, $\sigma \approx 1.15$ **29.** $\bar{x} = 47$, $v = 226$, $\sigma \approx 15.03$
31. 3.42   **33.** 1.65
35. $\bar{x} = 12$ and $|x_i - 12| = 8$ for all x_i.
37. The mean will increase by 5, but the standard deviation will not change.
39. Mean ≈ 613.46, $v \approx 191{,}651.33$, $\sigma \approx 437.78$; 87.5% of the data lie within two standard deviations of the mean.
41. (a) Upper quartile: 21.5   (b)
    Lower quartile: 13

43. (a) Upper quartile: 51   (b)
    Lower quartile: 47

45.   **47.**

49. a

Appendix B.3   (page A45)

1. $y = 1.6x + 7.5$ **3.** $y = 0.262x + 1.93$

Index of Selected Applications

Biology and Life Sciences

Bacteria count, 55, 58, 223
Calorie burning activities, 530
Calories in food, 487
Concentration of a chemical in the bloodstream, 159
Defoliation from gypsy moth, 237
Dissections, 613
Environment
  carbon monoxide levels, 160
  removal of industrial and municipal pollutants, 146
  spread of a lake contaminant, 58
Forest yield, 219
Fruit flies experiment, 188, 223
Growth, 79, 111, 247
Health
  blood pressure, 301
  lithotripter machine, 654
  respiratory cycle, 301
Heights of men and women, 219
Human memory model, 198, 201, 246
Human range of vision, 149
IQ scores, 230
Population, 70, 98, 222, 229, 239, 597
Potting soil production, 540
Spread of a virus, 226
Surface area of a tumor, 779
Wheat yield, 487
Wildlife
  deer herd population, 148
  elk herd population, 160
  population of fish, 173, 579
Yeast, population of, 230

Business

Advertising and sales, 230
Apartment demand, 14
Break-even analysis, 475, 477, 478, 479, 560
Cost, revenue, and profit, 27
Demand, 246, 488
Depreciation, 230
  of SUV, 244
  of vehicles, 629
Greeting card production, 783
Manufacturing, 530, 563, 598
MP3 player production, 787
Number of stores, Target Corporation, 78
Point of equilibrium for demand and supply, 486, 560
Profits, 58, 83, 141, 598
  Buffalo Wild Wings, 13
  for car stereos, 86
  for fruit crops, 530
Revenues, 98, 99
  from advertising, 111
  Amazon.com, 248

eBay, 778
Expedia and Priceline.com, 479
Netflix, 579
Salaries
  Dallas Cowboys, 12
  New York Yankees, 12
Sales, 58, 82, 441
  Apple, 6
  Coca-Cola Company, 13
  Green Mountain Coffee Roasters, 28
  PetSmart, 587
  Office Depot, 174
  of outerwear, 337
    of snowboards, 301
  Starbucks, 240
  of tablet computers, 149
  Whole Foods Market, 239
Ticket sales, 486

Chemistry and Physics

Astronomy
  Halley's comet, 654, 694
  orbits of comets, 651, 661, 694
  orbits of planets, 652, 696, 701, 703
  path of an asteroid, 703
Atmospheric pressure by altitude, 240
Bicycle pedal force and torque, 732
Braking load, 438, 441, 442, 460
Carbon dating, 224, 230
Chemical reaction, 235
Crankshaft torque, 732
Crystal classification, 718
Depth of the tide, 40, 70
Earthquake intensity, 227, 230, 231, 247, 643
Falling object, 85, 99, 163, 587, 768
Forensics, time of death, 231
Harmonic motion, 271, 272, 301, 313, 330, 331, 336, 337, 344, 345, 375, 382, 398, 455, 463
Hooke's Law, 77
Hyperbolic mirror, 667
Launch of space shuttle, 801
Locating an explosion, 661, 666, 701
Mach number, 393
Meteorology
  precipitation in San Francisco, 165
  temperatures
    Chicago and Quillayute, WA, 302
    Dallas, 771
    Savannah, GA, 291
  thunder location, 666
Path of a ball, 22, 28, 40, 516
Percent of moon's face illuminated, 301
pH level, 231
Planetary motion, 206
Projectile motion, 95, 98, 141, 271, 375, 392, 397, 645, 646, 676, 702

Radioactive decay, 188, 190, 191, 229, 230, 236, 244, 248
Resultant force, 431, 432, 459, 461, 723, 725, 745
Satellite orbit, 654, 697
Sound intensity, 201, 208, 231
Standing wave, 382
Temperature
  conversion, 14, 70
  of a heated object as it cools, 220
  of liquid as it cools, 209, 240
Tension in two cables supporting a load, 431, 432, 459
Thermodynamics of a diesel engine, 503
Tuning fork, 336
Vehicle stopping distance, 57
Velocity, components of, 431, 432
Vertical motion, 498, 501, 779
Work, 439, 442, 460

Construction and Engineering

Architecture
  A-frame cottage, 332
  archway, 645, 700, 701, 706
  church window, 645, 700
  spherical building, 718
Automobile
  braking system, 502
  headlight, 645
Bridge length, 411
Child care safe play areas, 97
Classroom ventilation, 201
Electrical
  circuit, 539
  impedance, 134
  voltage, 455
Exercise facility, 97
Force against a dam, 27
Fuel tank design, 741
Golden Gate Bridge, 645
Ice rink construction, 170
Machine shop calculations, 282, 335
Network analysis
  traffic flow, 566
  water flow, 517
Patio design, 587
Railroad tracks, 393
Road design, 645
Space vehicle communications, 624
Testing a machine part, 85
Water slide, 334

Consumer

ATM codes (PIN), 613
Cellular phone subscriptions, 126
Cost
  of an automobile, 59
  of cable television, 86

of towing a car, 769
Entertainment system, 613, 630
Fruit purchase, 487
Hotel packages, 530
Mortgage, 231, 245
Overnight shipping, 765, 768
Payment methods, 624
Ranking brands, 622

Geometry

Angle
    between two lines, 383
    between two nonvertical lines, 335
    of elevation, 324, 334, 411
Area
    of circular ripples in water, 58
    of an inscribed rectangle, 170, 376
    of a lemniscate loop, 690
    of a parcel of land, 461, 795, 800
    of a rectangular plot of land, 250
Aviation, 333, 344, 345
Flight bearing, 411
Height
    of a balloon, 283
    of a flagpole, 278, 333, 411, 463
    of a mountain, 282, 333
    of a streetlight, 283
Johnstown Inclined Plane, 282
Length
    of a ladder, 336
    of a shadow cast by a gnomon, 364
    of a skateboard ramp, 279
Maximum volume of a box, 26, 111, 127
MP3 player value over time, 82
Page design, 156, 159, 173
Photographing a painting, 324
Sprinkler coverage, 643
Submarine depth, 332
Surface area
    of a honeycomb, 372
    of a sphereflake fractal, 597
Surveying, 335, 418
Volume
    of a balloon, 779
    of a parallelepiped, 730, 732, 745,
        746, 802
    of a sphere, 21
Width of a river, 282, 341, 458

Interest Rate

Annuity, 190, 594, 596, 597
Borrowing, 501, 516
Compound interest, 187, 190, 201, 228,
    229, 244, 576, 579, 628, 629
Doubling an investment, 216, 219, 246
Investment portfolio, 472, 477, 478, 501,
    539, 560, 561
Tripling an investment, 219, 228, 229

Miscellaneous

Auditorium seating, 587

Aviation, 334
Bird bath, 725
Book sales by price, 778
Cell phone usage, 621
Clock design, 666
College survey, 630
Computer paper sales, 516
Cost
    of an oil change, 191
    of seizing illegal drugs, 173
Cryptography, 553-555, 557, 565
Drawing cards, 617, 618, 619, 622, 623,
        624, 631
DVD rentals, 478
Earth's surface, longitude, and latitude, 718
Education
    course schedule, 613, 630
    Penn State enrollment, 14
    reading rate, 247
    scholarship contest, 614
Election probabilities, 623
Electoral votes, 24
Ferris wheel, 301, 682
Fibonacci sequence, 572, 580
Floral design, 540
Game show, 624, 706
Jury selection, 615
License plate numbers, 613, 631
Lock combinations, 608
Lottery, 615
Marine transportation, 333, 334
Miles ran, number of, 70
National Football League, 24
Outdoor movie screen, 334
Panoramic photo, 667
Political party affiliations, 624
Political party analysis using a stochastic
        matrix, 531
Radio station call letters, 614
Rappelling, 332
Recycling costs of a supermarket, 787
Salary, 706, 768
    of an accountant, 629
Seating arrangements, 614
Shoe sizes, 69, 75
Sports
    100-meter dash, 614
    batting order, 614
    figure skating, 263
    golf, 501, 561
    NCAA basketball, 501, 631
    Olympic swimming, 79, 85
Sundial Bridge, 333
Telephone numbers, 608, 613, 630
Television coverage of a parade, 312
Tossing coins, 616, 617, 622
Tossing dice, 616, 618, 622
ZIP codes, 613

Time and Distance

Airplane

ascent, 245, 333
    speed, 484, 486, 560
Angular and linear speed
    of a Blu-ray disc, 264
    of a motorcycle wheel, 263
    of a saw blade, 260, 263
Distance
    to an airplane, 291, 312, 411
    between latitudes, 263
    between pitcher's mound and first
        base, 415
Linear speed
    of a satellite, 263
    of a tire spin balance machine, 264
Locating a fire, 335, 411
Navigation, 415, 428, 432, 459, 463, 666
Rate of descent on a zip line, 282
Speed
    of a bicycle, 264
    of a current, 486

U.S. Demographics

Commercial banks, number of, 219
Condominium sales, 39
Cruise line single beds, 239
Education,
    enrollment, 83
    level of attainment, 624
    number of colleges and
        universities, 618
Employees
    education and health services, 127
    interior design services industry, 22
FM radio stations, 174
Health expenditures, 58
International travelers to U.S., 540
Masters Degrees, 588
Military
    defense expenditures, 175
    ready reserve personnel, 787
Newspaper reading, annual per capita, 166
Population
    California, 40, 191
    Cameron County, TX, 229
    Florida, 565
    New Jersey, 78
    North Carolina, 246
    United States, 71, 73
    Wyoming, 78
Salaries
    college faculty, 628
    financial manager, 788
    public school teachers, 77, 216
SAT exam
    number of students who take, 84, 220
    scores, 225
Smartphone owners, 219
Sports, female participation, 247
Televisions, number in U.S. homes, 167
Unemployed workers, 74, 164, 623
Wireless network subscribers, 77

Index

A

Absolute value
    of a complex number, 443
    function, 2, 19, 41
Acute angle, 255
Addition
    of complex numbers, 129
    of matrices, 519
        properties of, 520
    vector, 422, 719
        parallelogram law for, 422
        properties of, 423
        resultant of, 422
Additive identity
    for a complex number, 129
    for a matrix, 520
Additive inverse for a complex number, 129
Adjacent side of a right triangle, 273
Adjoining matrices, 534
Algebraic
    function, 2, 180
    properties of the cross product, 727, 747
Alternative
    definition of conic, 691
    form of Law of Cosines, 413, 465
    formula for standard deviation, A38
Ambiguous case (SSA), 406
Amplitude of sine and cosine curves, 294
Analytic geometry, solid, 712
Angle(s), 254
    acute, 255
    between two planes, 736
    between two vectors, 435, 467
        in space, 720
    central, 255
    complementary, 258
    conversions between degrees and
        radians, 257
    coterminal, 254
    degree measure of, 257
    of depression, 278
    direction, of a vector, 426
    of elevation, 278
    initial side of, 254
    measure of, 255
    negative, 254
    obtuse, 255
    positive, 254
    radian measure of, 255
    reference, 286
    of repose, 324
    standard position, 254
    supplementary, 258
    terminal side of, 254
    vertex of, 254
Angular speed, 259

Annuity, increasing, 594
Aphelion distance, 651, 696
Apogee, 651
Arc length, 259
Arccosine function, 2, 317, 319
Arcsine function, 2, 315, 317, 319
Arctangent function, 2, 317, 319
Area
    of an oblique triangle, 408
        formula, 416
    of a plane region, 793
    problem, 792
    of a region, 780
    of a triangle
        using a determinant, 548
        Heron's Area Formula, 416, 466
        standard formula, 416
Argument of a complex number, 444
Arithmetic
    combination of functions, 50
    sequence, 581
        common difference of, 581
        nth partial sum of, 584
        nth term of, 582
        recursion formula, 583
        sum of a finite, 584, 633
Ask mode, A17
Associative Property of Addition
    for complex numbers, 130
    for matrices, 520
Associative Property of Multiplication
    for complex numbers, 130
    for matrices, 524
Associative Property of Scalar
    Multiplication for matrices, 520, 524
Astronomical unit, 694
Asymptote(s)
    horizontal, 143
    of a hyperbola, 658
    oblique, 155
    of a rational function, 144
    slant, 155
    vertical, 143
Augmented matrix, 505
Average, A35
    rate of change, 775
Axis (axes)
    conjugate, of a hyperbola, 658
    imaginary, 443
    major, of an ellipse, 647
    minor, of an ellipse, 647
    of a parabola, 90, 639
    polar, 677
    real, 443
    rotation of, 663
    of symmetry, 90
    transverse, of a hyperbola, 656

B

Back-substitution, 471
Bar graph, A27
Base, natural, 184
Basic
    Characteristics of Quadratic
        Functions, 91
    conics, 636
        circle, 636
        ellipse, 636
        hyperbola, 636
        parabola, 636
    limits, 755
Bearings, 328
Bell-shaped curve, 225
Biconditional statement, 88
Bimodal, A35
Binomial, 599
    coefficient, 599
    expanding, 601
    Theorem, 599, 634
Bound
    lower, 122
    upper, 122
Box-and-whisker plot, A40
    lower quartile, A40
    quartiles, A40
    upper quartile, A40
Branches of a hyperbola, 656
Break-even point, 475

C

Calculus, 770
    area of a region, 780
    tangent line, 780
Cardioid, 687
Center
    of a circle, 637
    of an ellipse, 647
    of a hyperbola, 656
Central
    angle of a circle, 255
    tendency, measure of, A35
Certain event, 617
Change
    in x, 772
    in y, 772
Change-of-base formula, 203
Characteristics of a function from
        set A to set B, 16
Chebychev's Theorem, A39
Circle, 637, 687
    arc length of, 259
    central angle of, 255
    classifying, by general equation, 662
    standard form of the equation of, 637
    unit, 265

Circular arc, length of, 259
Classification of conics by general
    equation, 662
Coded row matrices, 553
Coefficient(s)
    binomial, 599
    correlation, 75
    of determination, 164
    matrix, 505, 525
Cofactor(s)
    expanding by, 544
    of a matrix, 543
Cofunction identities, 350
Cofunctions of complementary angles, 275
Collinear points, 549, 722
    test for, 549
Column matrix, 504
Combinations
    of functions, 50
    of n elements taken r at a time, 612
Common
    difference of an arithmetic
        sequence, 581
    logarithmic
        function, 193
        model, 221
    ratio of a geometric sequence, 589
Commonly used functions, 41
Commutative Property of Addition
    for complex numbers, 130
    for matrices, 520
Commutative Property of Multiplication
    for complex numbers, 130
Complement
    of an event, 623
        probability of, 623
Complementary angles, 258
    cofunctions of, 275
Complex conjugates, 131
Complex number(s), 128
    absolute value of, 443
    addition of, 129
    additive identity, 129
    additive inverse, 129
    argument of, 444
    Associative Property of Addition, 130
    Associative Property of
        Multiplication, 130
    Commutative Property of Addition, 130
    Commutative Property of
        Multiplication, 130
    conjugate of, 131
    difference of, 129
    Distributive Property, 130
    division of, 446
    equality of, 128
    imaginary part of, 128
    modulus of, 444
    multiplication of, 446
    nth root of, 449, 450

unity, 451
    polar form of, 444
    powers of, 448
    product of two, 446
    quotient of two, 446
    real part of, 128
    standard form of, 128
    subtraction of, 129
    sum of, 129
    trigonometric form of, 444
Complex plane, 443
    imaginary axis, 443
    real axis, 443
Complex solutions of quadratic equations,
    132
Complex zeros occur in conjugate pairs,
    137
Component form
    of a vector $\mathbf{v}$, 421
    of a vector in space, 719
Components
    vector, 421, 437
        horizontal, 424
        vertical, 424
Composition of functions, 52
Compound interest
    continuously compounded, 186
    formulas for, 186
Conclusion, 87
Condensing logarithmic expressions, 205
Conditional
    equation, 357
    statement, 87
Conditions under which limits do not
        exist, 754
Conic(s) or conic section(s), 636, 691
    alternative definition, 691
    basic, 636
        circle, 636
        ellipse, 636
        hyperbola, 636
        parabola, 636
    classifying, by general equation, 662
    degenerate, 636
        line, 636
        point, 636
        two intersecting lines, 636
    eccentricity of, 691
    locus of, 636
    polar equations of, 691, 709
    rotation of axes, 663, 708
Conjugate, 137
    axis of a hyperbola, 658
    of a complex number, 131, 137
    pairs, 137
        complex zeros occur in, 137
Connected mode, A11
Consistent system of linear equations, 482
Constant
    function, 6, 31, 90, 180

matrix, 525
    spring, 77
Continuous
    compounding, 186
    function, 100, 669
Contradiction, proof by, 567
Contrapositive, 87
Converge, 784
Converse, 87
Conversions between degrees and radians,
    257
Convex limaçon, 687
Coordinate
    axes, reflections in, 44
    conversion, 679
        polar-to-rectangular, 679
        rectangular-to-polar, 679
    planes, 712
        xy-plane, 712
        xz-plane, 712
        yz-plane, 712
    system
        polar, 677
        three-dimensional, 494, 712
        plane, 494
Coordinate(s), polar, 677
Correlation, 72
    coefficient, 75
    negative, 72
    positive, 72
Cosecant function, 2, 266, 273, 307, 310
    of any angle, 284
    graph of, 307, 310
Cosine curve, amplitude of, 294
Cosine function, 2, 266, 273, 293, 310
    of any angle, 284
    common angles, 287
    domain of, 268
    graph of, 296, 310
    inverse, 2, 317, 319
    period of, 295
    range of, 268
    special angles, 275
Cotangent function, 2, 266, 273, 306, 310
    of any angle, 284
    graph of, 306, 310
Coterminal angle, 254
Counterexample, 87
Counting Principle, Fundamental, 608
Cramer's Rule, 550, 551
Cross product
    algebraic properties of, 727, 747
    determinant form of, 726
    geometric properties of, 728, 748
    of two vectors in space, 726
Cryptogram, 553
Cubic function, 2, 41, 101
Cumulative sum feature, A2
Curve
    bell-shaped, 225

logistic, 226
orientation of, 670
plane, 669
rose, 686, 687
sigmoidal, 226
sine, 292
Cycle of a sine curve, 292

D

Damping factor, 309
Data, fitting a line to, 73
Decomposition of $N(x)/D(x)$
    into partial fractions, 495
Decreasing function, 31
Defined, 23
Degenerate conic, 636
line, 636
point, 636
two intersecting lines, 636
Degree, 257
conversion to radians, 257
fractional part of, 258
measure of angles, 257
mode, A9
DeMoivre's Theorem, 448
Denominator, rationalizing, 360
Dependent
system of linear equations, 491
variable, 17, 23
Derivative, 775
Descartes's Rule of Signs, 121
Determinant
area of a triangle using, 548
feature, A2
form of the cross product, 726
of a square matrix, 541, 544
of a 2×2 matrix, 536, 541
Diagonal
matrix, 531, 547
of a polygon, 615
Difference
common, of an arithmetic sequence, 581
of complex numbers, 129
of functions, 50
limit of, 755
quotient, 23, 605, 772
    limit of, 766
of vectors, 422
Dimension of a matrix, 504
Diminishing returns, point of, 111
Dimpled limaçon, 687
Direct substitution to evaluate a limit, 755
Directed line segment, 420
equivalent, 420
initial point of, 420
length of, 420
magnitude of, 420
terminal point of, 420
Direction
angle of a vector, 426
numbers, 733

vector, 733
Directrix of a parabola, 639
Distance
between a point and a plane, 739
Formula, 637
    in space, 713
Distinguishable permutations, 611
Distribution, frequency, A26
Distributive Property
for complex numbers, 130
for matrices, 520
Diverge, 784
Dividing out, technique for evaluating a
    limit, 760
Division
Algorithm, 114
of complex numbers, 446
long, of polynomials, 113
synthetic, 116
Domain
of the cosine function, 268
of a function, 16, 23
implied, 20, 23
of a rational function, 142
of the sine function, 268
Dot mode, A11
Dot product, 434
properties of, 434, 467
of vectors in space, 719
Double subscript notation, 504
Double-angle formulas, 384, 401
Doyle Log Rule, 478
Draw inverse feature, A2

E

e, the number, 184
Eccentricity, 691
of a conic, 691
of an ellipse, 652, 691
of a hyperbola, 660, 691
of a parabola, 691
Elementary function, 2
Elementary row operations, 506
features, A3
for matrices, 506
for systems of equations, 490
Eliminating the parameter, 672
Elimination
Gaussian, 490
    with back-substitution, 510
Gauss-Jordan, 511
method of, 480, 481
Ellipse, 647, 691
center of, 647
classifying, by general equation, 662
eccentricity of, 652, 691
foci of, 647
latus rectum of, 655
major axis of, 647
minor axis of, 647
standard form of the equation of, 648

vertices of, 647
Entry of a matrix, 504
main diagonal, 504
Equal
matrices, 518
vectors, 421
Equality
of complex numbers, 128
of vectors, in space, 719
Equation(s)
circle, standard form, 637
conditional, 357
of conics, polar, 691, 709
ellipse, standard form, 648
exponential, solving, 210
hyperbola, standard form, 656
of a line
    general form of, 8
    point-slope form, 5, 8
    slope-intercept form, 7, 8
    summary of, 8
    two-point form, 5
logarithmic, solving, 210, 213
parabola, standard form, 639, 707
parametric, 669
    of a line in space, 733
of a plane
    general form, 735
    standard form, 735
polar, graph of, 683
polynomial, solution of, 104
position, 498
quadratic type, 368
sphere, standard form, 714
symmetric, of a line in space, 733
system of, 470
three variables, graph of, 494
trigonometric, solving, 365
Equilibrium point, 486
Equivalent directed line segments, 420
Equivalent systems, 481, 490
operations that produce, 490
Euler's Formula, 455
Evaluating trigonometric functions of
    any angle, 287
Even function, 35
trigonometric, 269
Even/odd identities, 350
Event(s), 616
certain, 617
complement of, 623
    probability of, 623
impossible, 617
independent, 621
    probability of, 621
mutually exclusive, 619
probability of, 617
    the union of two, 619
Existence
of an inverse function, 64
of a limit, 764

theorems, 135
Expanding
    a binomial, 601
    by cofactors, 544
    logarithmic expressions, 205
Experiment, 616
    outcomes of, 616
    sample space of, 616
Exponents, 182
    irrational, 180
    properties of, 181
Exponential
    decay model, 221
    equations, solving, 210
    function, 2, 180, 182
        f with base a, 180
        graph of, 181
        natural, 184
    growth model, 221
Exponentiating, 213
Extrema, 104
    maxima, 104
    minima, 104

F

Factor(s)
    damping, 309
    of a polynomial, 104, 138, 177
    prime, 138
        quadratic, 138
    scaling, 294
    Theorem, 117, 176
Factorial, 573
Family of functions, 42
Fibonacci sequence, 572
Finding
    an inverse function, 65
    an inverse matrix, 534
    nth roots of a complex number, 451
Finite
    sequence, 570
    series, 575
Fitting a line to data, 73
Fixed point, 374
Focal chord
    latus rectum, 641
    of a parabola, 641
Focus (foci)
    of an ellipse, 647
    of a hyperbola, 656
    of a parabola, 639
Formula(s)
    area of a triangle, 416
    change-of-base, 203
    for compound interest, 186
    Distance, 637
        in space, 713
    double-angle, 384, 401
    Euler's, 455
    half-angle, 387
    Heron's Area, 416, 466

Midpoint, in space, 713
    power-reducing, 386, 401
    product-to-sum, 388
    radian measure, 259
    recursion, 583
    reduction, 379
    standard deviation, alternative, A38
    sum and difference, 377, 400
    summation, 789
    sum-to-product, 388, 402
Fractal, 597
Fraction(s)
    partial, 495
        decomposition, 495
Fractional parts of degrees
    minute, 258
    second, 258
Frequency, 329, A25
    distribution, A26
Function(s), 2, 6, 16, 23
    absolute value, 2, 19, 41
    algebraic, 2, 180
    arccosine, 2, 317, 319
    arcsine, 2, 315, 317, 319
    arctangent, 2, 317, 319
    arithmetic combinations of, 50
    characteristics of, 16
    combinations of, 50
    common logarithmic, 193
    commonly used, 41
        absolute value, 41
        cubic, 41
        linear, 41
        quadratic, 41
        rational, 41
        square root, 41
    composition of, 52
    constant, 6, 31, 90, 180
    continuous, 100, 669
    cosecant, 2, 266, 273, 284, 307, 310
    cosine, 2, 266, 273, 284, 293, 310
    cotangent, 2, 266, 273, 284, 306, 310
    cubic, 2, 41, 101
    decreasing, 31
    defined, 23
    derivative of, 775
    difference of, 50
    domain of, 16, 23
    elementary, 2
    even, 35
    exponential, 2, 180, 182
    graph of, 29
    greatest integer, 2, 34
    of half-angles, 384
    identity, 6
    implied domain of, 20, 23
    increasing, 31
    input value of, 18, 23
    inverse, 60, 61
        cosine, 2, 317, 319
        existence of, 64

    finding, 65
    sine, 2, 315, 317, 319
    tangent, 2, 317, 319
    trigonometric, 317
    limits of, 755, 756, 804
    linear, 2, 6, 41, 90
    logarithmic, 2, 192, 195
    mode, A9
    of multiple angles, 384
    name of, 18, 23
    natural,
        exponential, 184
        logarithmic, 196
    nonelementary, 2
    notation, 18, 23
    odd, 35
    one-to-one, 64
    output value of, 18, 23
    parent
        absolute value, 2, 19, 41
        cosecant, 2, 307, 310
        cosine, 2, 293, 310
        cotangent, 2, 306, 310
        cubic, 2, 41, 101
        exponential, 2, 182
        greatest integer, 2, 34
        inverse
            cosine, 2, 319
            sine, 2, 319
            tangent, 2, 319
        linear, 2, 6, 41
        logarithmic, 2, 195
        quadratic, 2, 41, 92
        rational, 2, 41, 152
        secant, 2, 307, 310
        sine, 2, 293, 310
        square root, 2, 20, 41
        tangent, 2, 304, 310
    period of, 268
    periodic, 268
    piecewise-defined, 19
    polynomial, 90
    power, 101
    product of, 50
    quadratic, 2, 41, 90, 92
        basic characteristics of, 91
    quotient of, 50
    radical, 20
    range of, 16, 23
    rational, 2, 41, 142, 152
        limits at infinity, 783
    reciprocal, 152
    secant, 2, 266, 273, 284, 307, 310
    sine, 2, 266, 273, 284, 293, 310
    square root, 2, 20, 41
    squaring, 92
    step, 34
    sum of, 50
    summary of terminology, 23
    tangent, 2, 266, 273, 284, 304, 310

test
  even, 36
  odd, 36
transcendental, 2, 180
transformations of, 41
  nonrigid, 46
  rigid, 46
trigonometric, 266, 273, 284
undefined, 23
value of, 18, 23
Vertical Line Test, 30
Fundamental
  Counting Principle, 608
  Theorem of Algebra, 135
  trigonometric identities, 276, 350

G

Gaussian elimination, 490
  with back-substitution, 510
Gaussian model, 221
Gauss-Jordan elimination, 511
General form
  of the equation of a line, 8
  of the equation of a plane, 735
Geometric
  properties of the cross product,
    728, 748
  property of the triple scalar
    product, 730
  sequence, 589
    common ratio of, 589
    nth term of, 590
    sum of a finite, 592, 633
  series, 593
    sum of an infinite, 593
Geometry, solid analytic, 712
Graph
  bar, A27
  of cosecant function, 307, 310
  of cosine function, 296, 310
  of cotangent function, 306, 310
  of an equation in three variables, 494
  of an exponential function, 181
  of a function, 29
  of inverse cosine function, 319
  of an inverse function, 63
  of inverse sine function, 319
  of inverse tangent function, 319
  line, A30
  of a logarithmic function, 194
  of a polar equation, 683
  of a polynomial function,
    x-intercept of, 104
  of a rational function, 151
    guidelines for graphing, 151
  reflecting, 44
  of secant function, 307, 310
  shifting, 42
  of sine function, 296, 310
  slope of, 772
  special polar, 687

  of tangent function, 304, 310
Graphical interpretations of solutions, 482
Graphical method for solving a system of
    equations, 470
Graphing utility
  equation editor, A1
  features
    cumulative sum, A2
    determinant, A2
    draw inverse, A2
    elementary row operations, A3
    intersect, A5
    list, A2
    matrix, A6
    maximum, A7
    mean, A8
    median, A8
    minimum, A7
    $_nC_r$, A12
    $_nP_r$, A12
    one-variable statistics, A12
    reduced row-echelon, A15
    regression, A13
    root, A22
    row addition, A4
    row multiplication and addition, A4
    row swap, A3
    row-echelon, A14
    sequence, A15
    shade, A15
    statistical plotting, A16
    store, A3
    sum, A17
    sum sequence, A17
    table, A17
    tangent, A18
    trace, A19, A23
    value, A19
    zero, A22
    zoom, A23
  inverse matrix, A7
  list editor, A5
  matrix editor, A6
  matrix operations, A6
  mode settings, A9
    ask, A18
    connected, A11
    degree, A9
    dot, A11
    function, A9
    parametric, A9
    polar, A10
    radian, A9
    sequence, A10
  uses of, A1
  viewing window, A20
Greatest integer function, 2, 34
Guidelines
  for graphing rational functions, 151
  for verifying trigonometric
    identities, 357

H

Half-angle
  formulas, 387
  functions of, 384
Harmonic motion, simple, 329, 330
Heron's Area Formula, 416, 466
Histogram, A26
Hooke's Law, 77
Horizontal
  asymptote, 143
    of a rational function, 144
  component of **v**, 424
  line, 8
  Line Test, 64
  shift, 42
  shrink, 46
    of a trigonometric function, 295
  stretch, 46
    of a trigonometric function, 295
  translation of a trigonometric
    function, 296
Human memory model, 198
Hyperbola, 143, 656, 691
  asymptotes of, 658
  branches of, 656
  center of, 656
  classifying, by general equation, 662
  conjugate axis of, 658
  eccentricity of, 660, 691
  foci of, 656
  standard form of the equation of, 656
  transverse axis of, 656
  vertices of, 656
Hypotenuse of a right triangle, 273
Hypothesis, 87

I

i, imaginary unit, 128
Identities
  cofunction, 350
  even/odd, 350
  Pythagorean, 276, 350
    equivalent forms, 359
  quotient, 276, 350
  reciprocal, 276, 350
  trigonometric
    fundamental, 276, 350
    guidelines for verifying, 357
Identity, 357
  function, 6
  matrix of order $n \times n$, 524
If-then form, 87
Imaginary
  axis of the complex plane, 443
  number, 128
    pure, 128
  part of a complex number, 128
  unit i, 128
Implied domain, 20, 23
Impossible event, 617
Improper rational expression, 114

Inconsistent system of linear equations, 482, 510
Increasing
    annuity, 594
    function, 31
Independent
    events, 621
        probability of, 621
    system of linear equations, 491
    variable, 17, 23
Indeterminate form, 761
Index
    of refraction, 399
    of summation, 574
Indirect proof, 567
Induction, mathematical, 634
Inductive, 544
Infinite
    geometric series, 593
        sum of, 593
    sequence, 570
    series, 575
Infinity, limit at, 780, 781
    for rational functions, 783
Initial point, 420
Initial side of an angle, 254
Input, 16, 18
    value of a function, 18, 23
Instantaneous rate of change, 775
Interest
    compound, formulas for, 186
    continuously compounded, 186
Intermediate Value Theorem, 108
Intersect feature, A5
Intersection, points of, 470
Inverse, 87
    cosine function, graph of, 319
    function, 60, 61
        cosine, 2, 317, 319
        existence of, 64
        finding, 65
        graph of, 63
        Horizontal Line Test, 64
        sine, 2, 315, 317, 319
        tangent, 2, 317, 319
    of a matrix, 532
        finding, 534
    matrix with a graphing utility, A7
    multiplicative, of a matrix, 532
    properties
        of logarithms, 193
        of natural logarithms, 196
        of trigonometric functions, 320
    sine function, graph of, 319
    tangent function, graph of, 319
    trigonometric functions, 317
Invertible matrix, 533
Irrational exponents, 180
Irreducible
    over the rationals, 138
    over the reals, 138

K
Kepler's Laws, 694
Key points of the graph of a trigonometric
        function, 292
    intercepts, 292
    maximum points, 292
    minimum points, 292

L
Lagrange multiplier, 503
Latus rectum
    of an ellipse, 655
    of a parabola, 641
Law of Cosines, 413, 465
    alternative form, 413, 465
    standard form, 413, 465
Law of Sines, 404, 464
Law of Tangents, 464
Leading 1, 508
Leading Coefficient Test, 102
Least squares regression, A44
    line, 73, 487
    method of, A44
    parabola, 502
Left Distributive Property for matrices,
        524
Left-handed orientation, 712
Lemniscate, 687
Length
    of a circular arc, 259
    of a directed line segment, 420
    of a vector, 421
        in space, 719
Limaçon, 685, 687
    convex, 687
    dimpled, 687
    with inner loop, 687
Limit(s), 751
    basic, 755
    of a difference, 755
        quotient, 766
    evaluating
        direct substitution, 755
        dividing out technique, 760
        rationalizing technique, 762
    existence of, 764
    indeterminate form, 761
    at infinity, 780, 781
        for rational functions, 783
    from the left, 764
    nonexistence of, 754
    one-sided, 764
    of a polynomial function, 756, 804
    of a power, 755
    of a power function, 804
    of a product, 755
    properties of, 755
    of a quotient, 755
    of a rational function, 756
    from the right, 764
    of a scalar multiple, 755

of a sequence, 784
of a sum, 755
of summation
    lower, 574
    upper, 574
of summations, 789
of a trigonometric function, 755
Line(s)
    general form of the equation of, 8
    graph, A30
    horizontal, 8
    least squares regression, 73
    parallel, 9
    perpendicular, 9
    in the plane, least squares regression, 487
    plot, A25
    point-slope form of the equation of, 5, 8
    secant, 772
    segment, directed, 420
    slope of, 3, 4
    slope-intercept form of the
            equation of, 7, 8
    in space, 733
        parametric equations of, 733
        symmetric equations of, 733
    summary of equations, 8
    tangent, 770, 780
        to a parabola, 641
    two-point form of the equation of, 5
    vertical, 8
Linear
    combination of vectors, 424
    equation
        general form, 8
        point-slope form, 5, 8
        slope-intercept form, 7, 8
        summary of, 8
        two-point form, 5
    Factorization Theorem, 135, 177
    function, 2, 6, 41, 90
    growth, 585
    speed, 259
    system
        consistent, 482
        dependent, 491
        elementary row operations, 490
        inconsistent, 482, 510
        independent, 491
        nonsquare, 493
        number of solutions, 491
        row-echelon form, 489
        square, 493
List
    editor, A5
    feature, A2
Locus, 636
Logarithm(s)
    change-of-base formula, 203
    natural
        properties of, 196, 204, 251
            inverse, 196

one-to-one, 196
power, 204, 251
product, 204, 251
quotient, 204, 251
properties of, 193, 204, 251
inverse, 193
one-to-one, 193
power, 204, 251
product, 204, 251
quotient, 204, 251
Logarithmic
equations, solving, 210, 213
expressions
condensing, 205
expanding, 205
function, 2, 192, 195
with base a, 192
common, 193
graph of, 194
natural, 196
model, 221
common, 221
natural, 221
Logistic
curve, 226
growth model, 221
Long division of polynomials, 113
Lower
bound, 122
limit of summation, 574
quartile, A40
triangular matrix, 547

M
Magnitude
of a directed line segment, 420
of a vector, 421
in space, 719
Main diagonal entries of a square matrix, 504
Major axis of an ellipse, 647
Mathematical
induction, 634
model, 71
Matrix (matrices), 504
addition, 519
properties of, 520
additive identity, 520
adjoining, 534
augmented, 505
coded row, 553
coefficient, 505, 525
cofactor of, 543
column, 504
constant, 525
determinant of, 536, 541, 544
diagonal, 531, 547
dimension of, 504
editor, A6

elementary row operations, 506
entry of, 504
equal, 518
feature, A6
identity, 524
inverse of, 532
finding, 534
invertible, 533
lower triangular, 547
main diagonal entries of, 504
minor of, 543
multiplication, 522
properties of, 524
nonsingular, 533
operations with a graphing utility, A6
reduced row-echelon form, 508
representation of, 518
row, 504
row-echelon form, 508
row-equivalent, 506
scalar identity, 520
scalar multiplication, 519
properties of, 520
singular, 533
square, 504
stochastic, 531
subtraction, 520
triangular, 547
uncoded row, 553
upper triangular, 547
zero, 520
Maximum
feature, A7
relative, 32
value of a quadratic function, 95
Mean, A35
feature, A8
Measure of an angle, 255
degree, 257
radian, 255
Measure of central tendency, A35
average, A35
mean, A35
median, A35
mode, A35
Measures of dispersion, A37
standard deviation, A37
variance, A37
Median, A35
feature, A8
Method
of elimination, 480, 481
of least squares, A44
of substitution, 470
Midpoint Formula in space, 713
Minimum
feature, A7
relative, 32
value of a quadratic function, 95
Minor axis of an ellipse, 647

Minor of a matrix, 543
Minors and cofactors of a square matrix, 543
Minute, fractional part of a degree, 258
Mode, A35
Mode settings, A9
ask, A18
connected, A11
degree, A9
dot, A11
function, A9
parametric, A9
polar, A10
radian, A9
sequence, A10
Modulus of a complex number, 444
Multiple angles, functions of, 384
Multiple, scalar, 422
Multiplication
of complex numbers, 446
of matrices, 522
properties of, 524
scalar
of matrices, 519
of vectors, 422, 719
Multiplicative inverse of a matrix, 532
Multiplicity, 105
Multiplier, Lagrange, 503
Mutually exclusive events, 619

N
n factorial, 573
Name of a function, 18, 23
Natural base, 184
Natural exponential function, 184
Natural logarithm
function, 196
model, 221
properties of, 196, 204, 251
inverse, 196
one-to-one, 196
power, 204, 251
product, 204, 251
quotient, 204, 251
$_nC_r$, feature, A12
Negation, 87
Negative
angle, 254
correlation, 72
number, principal square root of, 132
of a vector, 422
Newton's Law of Cooling, 231, 232
Nonelementary function, 2
Nonexistence of a limit, 754
Nonrigid transformations, 46
Nonsingular matrix, 533
Nonsquare system of linear equations, 493
Normal vector, 735
Normally distributed, 225

Notation
double subscript, 504
function, 18, 23
sigma, 574
standard unit vector, 719
summation, 574
$_nP_r$, feature, A12
nth partial sum, 575, 584
of an arithmetic sequence, 584
nth root(s)
of a complex number, 449, 450
of unity, 451
nth term
of an arithmetic sequence, 582
of a geometric sequence, 590
Number(s)
complex, 128
direction, 733
of equally likely outcomes, 617
imaginary, 128
pure, 128
negative, principal square root of, 132
Number of combinations of n elements
taken r at a time, 612
Number of permutations of n elements,
609
taken r at a time, 610
Number of solutions of a linear system,
491

O

Oblique
asymptote, 155
triangle, 404
area of, 408
formula, 416
Obtuse angle, 255
Octant, 712
Odd/even identities, 350
Odd function, 35
trigonometric, 269
One cycle of a sine curve, 292
One-sided limit, 764
One-to-one
function, 64
property
of logarithms, 193
of natural logarithms, 196
One-variable statistics feature, A12
Opposite side of a right triangle, 273
Ordered triple, 489
Orientation of a curve, 670
Origin
of polar coordinate system, 677
symmetric with respect to, 35
Orthogonal vectors, 436
in space, 720
Outcomes, 616
equally likely, number of, 617
Output, 16, 18
value of a function, 18, 23

P

Parabola, 90, 639, 691
axis of, 90, 639
classifying, by general equation, 662
directrix of, 639
eccentricity of, 691
focal chord of, 641
focus of, 639
latus rectum of, 641
least squares regression, 502
reflective property of, 641
standard form of the equation of,
639, 707
tangent line to, 641
vertex of, 90, 639
Parallel
lines, 9
planes, 736
vectors in space, 721
Parallelogram law for vector addition, 422
Parameter, 669
eliminating, 672
Parametric
equations, 669
of a line in space, 733
mode, A9
Parent function
absolute value, 2, 19, 41
cosecant, 2, 307, 310
cosine, 2, 293, 310
cotangent, 2, 306, 310
cubic, 2, 41, 101
exponential, 2, 182
greatest integer, 2, 34
inverse
cosine, 2, 319
sine, 2, 319
tangent, 2, 319
linear, 2, 6, 41
logarithmic, 2, 195
quadratic, 2, 41, 92
rational, 2, 41, 152
secant, 2, 307, 310
sine, 2, 293, 310
square root, 2, 20, 41
tangent, 2, 304, 310
Partial fraction, 495
decomposition, 495
Partial sum, nth, 575, 584
Pascal's Triangle, 603
Perigee, 651
Perihelion distance, 651, 696
Period
of a function, 268
of sine and cosine functions, 295
Periodic function, 268
Permutation(s), 609
distinguishable, 611
of n elements, 609
taken r at a time, 610

Perpendicular
lines, 9
planes, 736
vectors, 436
Phase shift, 296
Piecewise-defined function, 19
Plane(s)
angle between two, 736
coordinate, 712
curve, 669
orientation of, 670
general form of the equation of, 735
parallel, 736
perpendicular, 736
region, area of, 793
in space, 735
sketching, 738
standard form of the equation of, 735
three-dimensional coordinate
system, 494
trace of, 738
Plot
line, A25
scatter, 71, A29
Point(s)
break-even, 475
collinear, 549, 722
test for, 549
of diminishing returns, 111
equilibrium, 486
fixed, 374
initial, 420
of intersection, 470
terminal, 420
Point-slope form of the equation of a line,
5, 8
Polar
axis, 677
coordinate system, 677
pole (origin) of, 677
coordinates, 677
conversion to rectangular, 679
tests for symmetry in, 684, 685
equation
of conics, 691, 709
graph of, 683
form of a complex number, 444
mode, A10
Pole, 677
Polygon, diagonal of, 615
Polynomial(s)
equation, solution of, 104
factors of, 104, 138, 177
function, 90
Leading Coefficient Test, 102
limit of, 756, 804
real zeros of, 104
of x of degree n, 90
x-intercept of the graph of, 104
zeros of, 104

long division of, 113
prime quadratic factor, 138
synthetic division, 116
Position equation, 498
Positive
angle, 254
correlation, 72
Power
of a complex number, 448
limit of, 755
Power function, 101
limit of, 804
Power property
of logarithms, 204, 251
of natural logarithms, 204, 251
Power-reducing formulas, 386, 401
Prime
factor of a polynomial, 138
quadratic factor, 138
Principal square root of a negative
number, 132
Probability
of a complement, 623
of an event, 617
of independent events, 621
of the union of two events, 619
Product
of functions, 50
limit of, 755
of trigonometric functions, 384
triple scalar, 730
of two complex numbers, 446
Product property
of logarithms, 204, 251
of natural logarithms, 204, 251
Product-to-sum formulas, 388
Projection of a vector, 437
Proof
by contradiction, 567
indirect, 567
without words, 568
Proper rational expression, 114
Properties
of the cross product
algebraic, 727, 747
geometric, 728, 748
of the dot product, 434, 467
of exponents, 181
geometric, of the triple scalar
product, 730
inverse, of trigonometric functions, 320
of limits, 755
of logarithms, 193, 204, 251
inverse, 193
one-to-one, 193
power, 204, 251
product, 204, 251
quotient, 204, 251
of matrix addition and scalar
multiplication, 520

of matrix multiplication, 524
of natural logarithms, 196, 204, 251
inverse, 196
one-to-one, 196
power, 204, 251
product, 204, 251
quotient, 204, 251
reflective, of a parabola, 641
summation, 789
of sums, 574, 632
of vector addition and scalar
multiplication, 423
Pure imaginary number, 128
Pythagorean
identities, 276, 350
equivalent forms, 359
Theorem, 348

Q
Quadratic
equation, complex solutions of, 132
factor, prime, 138
function, 2, 41, 90, 92
basic characteristics of, 91
maximum value, 95
minimum value, 95
standard form of, 93, 95
type equations, 368
Quartiles, A40
lower, A40
upper, A40
Quick tests for symmetry in polar
coordinates, 685
Quotient
difference, 23, 605, 772
limit of, 766
of functions, 50
identities, 276, 350
limit of, 755
property
of logarithms, 204, 251
of natural logarithms, 204, 251
of two complex numbers, 446

R
Radian, 255
conversion to degrees, 257
measure formula, 259
mode, A9
Radical function, 20
Radius, 637
Random selection
with replacement, 607
without replacement, 607
Range, A25
of the cosine function, 268
of a function, 16, 23
of the sine function, 268
Rate of change
average, 775
instantaneous, 775

Rational expression(s)
improper, 114
proper, 114
Rational function, 2, 41, 142, 152
asymptotes of, 144
domain of, 142
graph of, guidelines for graphing, 151
limit of, 756
at infinity, 783
Rational Zero Test, 119
Rationalizing
a denominator, 360
technique for evaluating a limit, 762
Real
axis of the complex plane, 443
part of a complex number, 128
zeros of a polynomial function, 104
Reciprocal
function, 152
identities, 276, 350
Rectangular coordinates, conversion to
polar, 679
Recursion formula, 583
Recursive sequence, 572
Reduced row-echelon
feature, A15
form of a matrix, 508
Reducible over the reals, 138
Reduction formulas, 379
Reference angle, 286
Reflection, 44
of a trigonometric function, 295
Reflective property of a parabola, 641
Refraction, index of, 399
Region, plane, area of, 793
Regression
feature, A13
least squares, A44
line, 73, 487
parabola, 502
Relation, 16
Relative
maximum, 32
minimum, 32
Remainder
using in synthetic division, 118
Theorem, 117, 176
Repeated zero, 105, 135
Representation of matrices, 518
Resultant of vector addition, 422
Right Distributive Property for matrices,
524
Right triangle
adjacent side of, 273
definitions of trigonometric
functions, 273
hypotenuse of, 273
opposite side of, 273
solving, 278
Right-handed
orientation, 712

system, 728
Rigid transformations, 46
Root feature, A22
Root(s) of a complex number, 449, 450
Rose curve, 686, 687
Rotation of axes, 663
  to eliminate an *xy*-term, 663, 708
Row addition and row multiplication and
    addition features, A4
Row-echelon
  feature, A14
  form, 489
    of a matrix, 508
      reduced, 508
Row-equivalent matrices, 506
Row matrix, 504
  coded, 553
  uncoded, 553
Row multiplication feature, A4
Row operations, elementary, 506
Row swap feature, A3

S
Sample space, 616
Scalar, 422, 519
  Identity Property for matrices, 520
  multiple, 422, 519
    limit of, 755
    of a vector in space, 719
  multiplication
    of matrices, 519
      properties of, 520
    of a vector, 422
      properties of, 423
Scaling factor, 294
Scatter plot, 71, A29
Scribner Log Rule, 478
Secant
  function, 2, 266, 273, 307, 310
    of any angle, 284
    graph of, 307, 310
  line, 772
Second, fractional part of a degree, 258
Sequence, 570
  arithmetic, 581
  convergence of, 784
  divergence of, 784
  feature, A15
  Fibonacci, 572
  finite, 570
  geometric, 589
  infinite, 570
  limit of, 784
  mode, A10
  *n*th partial sum of, 575
  recursive, 572
  terms of, 570
Series, 575
  finite, 575
  geometric, 593
  infinite, 575

geometric, 593
Shade feature, A15
Shifting graphs, 42
Shrink
  horizontal, 46
  vertical, 46
Sigma notation, 574
Sigmoidal curve, 226
Simple harmonic motion, 329, 330
  frequency, 329
Sine
  curve, 292
    amplitude of, 294
    one cycle of, 292
  function, 2, 266, 273, 293, 310
    of any angle, 284
    common angles, 287
    domain of, 268
    graph of, 296, 310
    inverse, 2, 315, 317, 319
    period of, 295
    range of, 268
    special angles, 275
Sines, cosines, and tangents of special
    angles, 275
Singular matrix, 533
Sketching planes in space, 738
Slant asymptote, 155
Slope, 3, 733, 772
  of a graph, 772
  of a line, 3, 4
Slope-intercept form of the equation
    of a line, 7, 8
Solid analytic geometry, 712
Solution(s)
  of a linear system, number of, 491
  of a polynomial equation, 104
  of a quadratic equation, complex, 132
  of a system of equations, 470
    graphical interpretations, 482
Solving
  exponential and logarithmic
      equations, 210
  right triangles, 278
  a system of equations, 470
    Cramer's Rule, 550, 551
    Gaussian elimination, 490
      with back-substitution, 510
    Gauss-Jordan elimination, 511
    graphical method, 470
    method of elimination, 480, 481
    method of substitution, 470
  a trigonometric equation, 365
Space
  Distance Formula in, 713
  lines in, 733
  Midpoint Formula in, 713
  planes in, 735
    sketching, 738
  surface in, 715

vector in, 719
Special angles
  cosines of, 275
  sines of, 275
  tangents of, 275
Speed
  angular, 259
  linear, 259
Sphere, 714
  standard form of the equation of, 714
Spring constant, 77
Square matrix, 504
  determinant of, 541, 544
  diagonal, 547
  lower triangular, 547
  main diagonal entries of, 504
  minors and cofactors of, 543
  triangular, 547
  upper triangular, 547
Square root(s)
  function, 2, 20, 41
  of a negative number, 132
    principal, 132
Square system of linear equations, 493
Square of trigonometric functions, 384
Squared differences, sum of, 73, 234, A44
Squaring function, 92
Standard deviation, A37
  alternative formula, A38
Standard form
  of a complex number, 128
  of the equation
    of a circle, 637
    of an ellipse, 648
    of a hyperbola, 656
    of a parabola, 639, 707
    of a plane, 735
    of a sphere, 714
  of Law of Cosines, 413, 465
  of a quadratic function, 93, 95
Standard position
  of an angle, 254
  of a vector, 421
Standard unit vector, 424
  notation in space, 719
Statistical plotting feature, A16
Statistics, A25
Step function, 34
Stochastic matrix, 531
Store feature, A3
Strategies for solving exponential and
    logarithmic equations, 210
Stretch
  horizontal, 46
  vertical, 46
Substitution
  direct, to evaluate a limit, 755
  method of, 470
Subtraction
  of complex numbers, 129

of matrices, 520
Sum(s)
    of complex numbers, 129
    and difference formulas, 377, 400
    feature, A17
    of a finite arithmetic sequence, 584, 633
    of a finite geometric sequence,
        592, 593, 633
    of functions, 50
    of an infinite geometric series, 593
    limit of, 755
    nth partial, 575, 584
    properties of, 574, 632
    sequence feature, A17
    of squared differences, 73, 234, A44
    of vectors, 422
        in space, 719
Summary
    of equations of lines, 8
    of function terminology, 23
Summation
    formulas and properties, 789
    index of, 574
    limit of, 789
    lower limit of, 574
    notation, 574
    upper limit of, 574
Sum-to-product formulas, 388, 402
Supplementary angles, 258
Surface in space, 715
    trace of, 715
Symmetric equations of a line in space, 733
Symmetry
    axis of, of a parabola, 90
    in polar coordinates, tests for, 684, 685
    with respect to the origin, 35
    with respect to the x-axis, 35
    with respect to the y-axis, 35
Synthetic division, 116
    using the remainder in, 118
System of equations, 470
    equivalent, 481, 490
    solution of, 470
    solving, 470
    with a unique solution, 537
System of linear equations
    consistent, 482
    dependent, 491
    elementary row operations, 490
    inconsistent, 482, 510
    independent, 491
    nonsquare, 493
    number of solutions, 491
    row-echelon form, 489
    square, 493

T
Table feature, A17
Tangent
    feature, A18
    function, 2, 266, 273, 304, 310

of any angle, 284
common angles, 287
graph of, 304, 310
inverse, 2, 317, 319
special angles, 275
vertical asymptotes of, 304
line, 770, 780
    to a parabola, 641
Term of a sequence, 570
Terminal
    point, 420
    side of an angle, 254
Test(s)
    for collinear points, 549
    even function, 36
    Horizontal Line, 64
    Leading Coefficient, 102
    odd function, 36
    Rational Zero, 119
    for symmetry, in polar coordinates,
        684, 685
    Vertical Line, 30
Theorem
    of Algebra, Fundamental, 135
    Binomial, 599, 634
    DeMoivre's, 448
    Descartes's Rule of Signs, 121
    existence, 135
    Factor, 117, 176
    Intermediate Value, 108
    Linear Factorization, 135, 177
    Pythagorean, 348
    Remainder, 117, 176
Three-dimensional coordinate system,
    494, 712
    left-handed orientation, 712
    octant, 712
    plane, 494
    right-handed orientation, 712
Trace
    feature, A19, A23
    of a plane, 738
    of a surface, 715
Transcendental function, 2, 180
Transformations of functions, 41
    nonrigid, 46
    rigid, 46
Transverse axis of a hyperbola, 656
Triangle
    area of
        using a determinant, 548
        Heron's Area Formula, 416, 466
        standard formula, 416
    oblique, 404
        area of, 408
Triangular matrix, 547
Trigonometric
    equations, solving, 365
    form of a complex number, 444
        argument of, 444
        modulus of, 444

functions, 266, 273, 284
    of any angle, 284
        evaluating, 287
    cosecant, 2, 266, 273, 284, 307, 310
    cosine, 2, 266, 273, 284, 293, 310
    cotangent, 2, 266, 273, 284, 306, 310
    even, 269
    horizontal
        shrink of, 295
        stretch of, 295
        translation of, 296
    inverse, 317
        properties of, 320
    key points, 292
        intercepts, 292
        maximum points, 292
        minimum points, 292
    limit of, 755
    odd, 269
    product of, 384
    reflection of, 295
    right triangle definitions of, 273
    secant, 2, 266, 273, 284, 307, 310
    sine, 2, 266, 273, 284, 293, 310
    square of, 384
    tangent, 2, 266, 273, 284, 304, 310
    unit circle definitions of, 266
    vertical
        shrink of, 294
        stretch of, 294
        translation of, 297
identities
    cofunction, 350
    even/odd, 350
    fundamental, 276, 350
    guidelines for verifying, 357
    Pythagorean, 276, 350
        equivalent forms, 359
    quotient, 276, 350
    reciprocal, 276, 350
    values of common angles, 287
Trigonometry, 254
Triple scalar product, 730
    geometric property of, 730
Two-point form of the equation of a line, 5

U
Uncoded row matrices, 553
Undefined, 23
Union of two events, probability of, 619
Unit
    circle, 265
        definitions of trigonometric
            functions, 266
    vector, 421
        in the direction of v, 424
        form, 719
        notation, standard, 719
        in space, in the direction of v, 719
        standard, 424
Unity, nth roots of, 451

Upper
  bound, 122
  limit of summation, 574
  and Lower Bound Rules, 122
  quartile, A40
  triangular matrix, 547
Uses of a graphing utility, A1
Using the remainder in synthetic division, 118

V

Value
  feature, A19
  of a function, 18, 23
Variable
  dependent, 17, 23
  independent, 17, 23
Variance, A37
  in sign, 121
Vector(s), 420, 719, 733
  addition of, 422, 719
    properties of, 423
    resultant of, 422
  analysis, 747
  angle between two, 435, 467, 720
  component form of, 421, 719
  components of, 421, 437
  cross product of, 726
  difference of, 422
  directed line segment
      representation, 420
  direction, 733
    angle of, 426
  dot product of, 434, 719
    properties of, 434, 467
  equal, 421, 719
  horizontal component of, 424
  length of, 421, 719
  linear combination of, 424
  magnitude of, 421, 719
  negative of, 422
  normal, 735
  orthogonal, 436, 720
  parallel, 721

parallelogram law, 422
perpendicular, 436
in the plane, 420
projection of, 437
resultant of, 422
scalar multiplication of, 422, 719
  properties of, 423
in space, 719
  addition of, 719
  angle between two, 720
  component form of, 719
  cross product of, 726
  direction, 733
  dot product of, 719
  equal, 719
  length of, 719
  magnitude of, 719
  normal, 735
  orthogonal, 720
  parallel, 721
  scalar multiple of, 719
  standard unit, 719
  sum of, 719
  triple scalar product, 730
  unit, in the direction of **v**, 719
  unit form, 719
  zero, 719
standard position of, 421
sum of, 422, 719
triple scalar product, 730
unit, 421
  in the direction of **v**, 424, 719
  form, 719
  standard, 424, 719
v in the plane, 420
vertical component of, 424
zero, 421, 719
Vertex (vertices)
  of an angle, 254
  of an ellipse, 647
  of a hyperbola, 656
  of a parabola, 90, 639
Vertical
  asymptote, 143

of a rational function, 144
of a tangent function, 304
component of **v**, 424
line, 8
Line Test, 30
shift, 42
shrink, 46
  of a trigonometric function, 294
stretch, 46
  of a trigonometric function, 294
translation of a trigonometric
    function, 297
Viewing window, A20

W

With replacement, 607
Without replacement, 607
Work, 439

X

x, change in, 772
x-axis, symmetric with respect to, 35
x-intercepts, of the graph of a polynomial
    function, 104
xy-plane, 712
xz-plane, 712

Y

y, change in, 772
y-axis, symmetric with respect to, 35
yz-plane, 712

Z

Zero(s)
  feature, A22
  matrix, 520
  multiplicity of, 105
  of a polynomial function, 104
    bounds for, 122
  repeated, 105, 135
  vector, 421
    in space, 719
Zoom feature, A23

Linear Function (*p. 6*)

$$f(x) = x$$

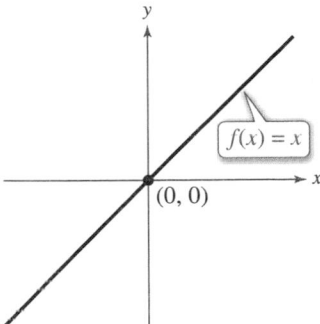

Domain: $(-\infty, \infty)$
Range: $(-\infty, \infty)$
Intercept: $(0, 0)$
Increasing

Absolute Value Function (*p. 19*)

$$f(x) = |x| = \begin{cases} x, & x \geq 0 \\ -x, & x < 0 \end{cases}$$

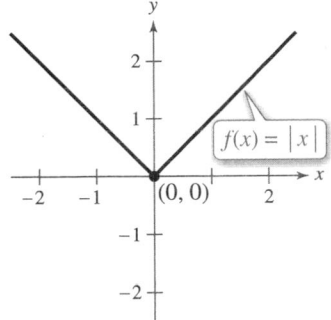

Domain: $(-\infty, \infty)$
Range: $[0, \infty)$
Intercept: $(0, 0)$
Decreasing on $(-\infty, 0)$
Increasing on $(0, \infty)$
Even function
y-axis symmetry

Square Root Function (*p. 20*)

$$f(x) = \sqrt{x}$$

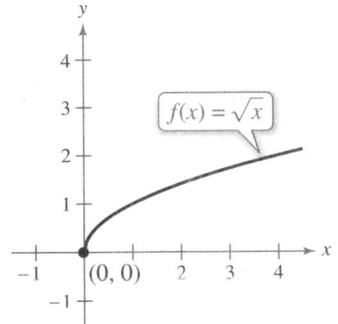

Domain: $[0, \infty)$
Range: $[0, \infty)$
Intercept: $(0, 0)$
Increasing on $(0, \infty)$

Greatest Integer Function (*p. 34*)

$$f(x) = [\![x]\!]$$

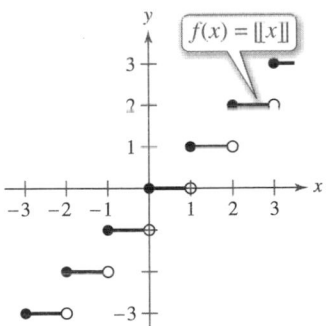

Domain: $(-\infty, \infty)$
Range: the set of integers
x-intercepts: in the interval $[0, 1)$
y-intercept: $(0, 0)$
Constant between each pair of
  consecutive integers
Jumps vertically one unit at
  each integer value

Quadratic Function (*p. 92*)

$$f(x) = x^2$$

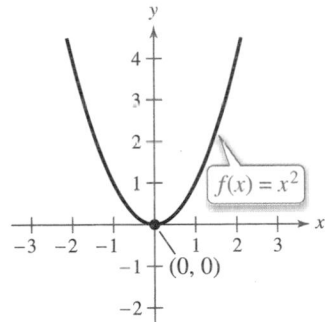

Domain: $(-\infty, \infty)$
Range: $[0, \infty)$
Intercept: $(0, 0)$
Decreasing on $(-\infty, 0)$
Increasing on $(0, \infty)$
Even function
Axis of symmetry: $x = 0$
Relative minimum or vertex: $(0, 0)$

Cubic Function (*p. 101*)

$$f(x) = x^3$$

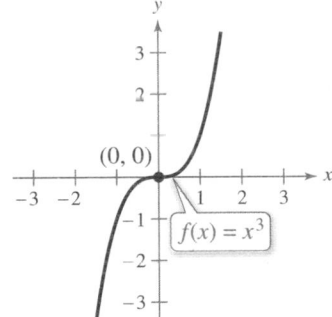

Domain: $(-\infty, \infty)$
Range: $(-\infty, \infty)$
Intercept: $(0, 0)$
Increasing on $(-\infty, \infty)$
Odd function
Origin symmetry

Rational Function (*p. 152*)

$$f(x) = \frac{1}{x}$$

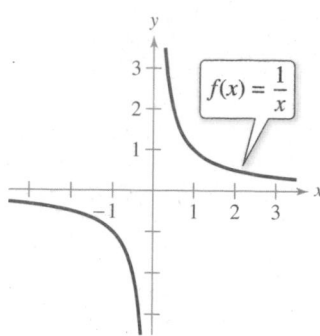

Domain: $(-\infty, 0) \cup (0, \infty)$
Range: $(-\infty, 0) \cup (0, \infty)$
No intercepts
Decreasing on $(-\infty, 0)$ and $(0, \infty)$
Odd function
Origin symmetry
Vertical asymptote: *y*-axis
Horizontal asymptote: *x*-axis

Exponential Function (*p. 182*)

$$f(x) = a^x, a > 1$$

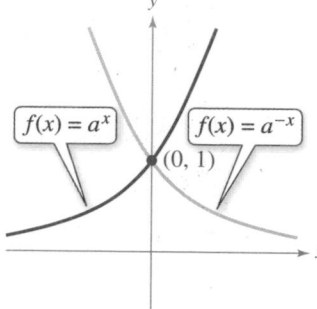

Domain: $(-\infty, \infty)$
Range: $(0, \infty)$
Intercept: $(0, 1)$
Increasing on $(-\infty, \infty)$
   for $f(x) = a^x$
Decreasing on $(-\infty, \infty)$
   for $f(x) = a^{-x}$
x-axis is a horizontal asymptote
Continuous

Logarithmic Function (*p. 195*)

$$f(x) = \log_a x, a > 1$$

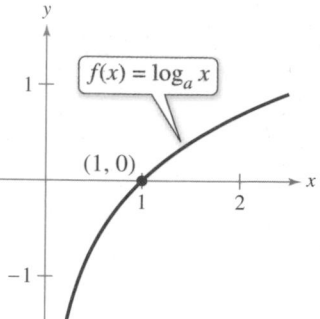

Domain: $(0, \infty)$
Range: $(-\infty, \infty)$
Intercept: $(1, 0)$
Increasing on $(0, \infty)$
y-axis is a vertical asymptote
Continuous
Reflection of graph of $f(x) = a^x$
   in the line $y = x$

Sine Function (*p. 293*)

$$f(x) = \sin x$$

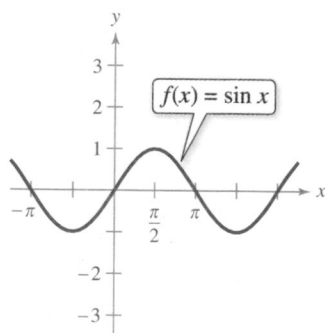

Domain: $(-\infty, \infty)$
Range: $[-1, 1]$
Period: 2π
x-intercepts: $(n\pi, 0)$
y-intercept: $(0, 0)$
Odd function
Origin symmetry

Cosine Function (*p. 293*)

$$f(x) = \cos x$$

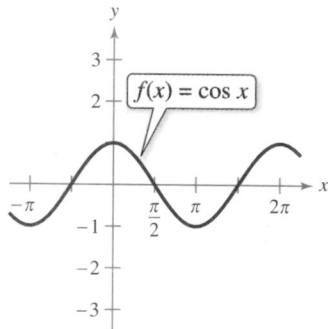

Domain: $(-\infty, \infty)$
Range: $[-1, 1]$
Period: 2π
x-intercepts: $\left(\frac{\pi}{2} + n\pi, 0\right)$
y-intercept: $(0, 1)$
Even function
y-axis symmetry

Tangent Function (*p. 304*)

$$f(x) = \tan x$$

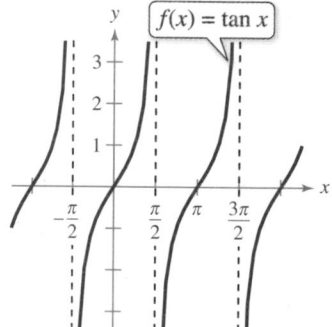

Domain: $x \neq \frac{\pi}{2} + n\pi$
Range: $(-\infty, \infty)$
Period: π
x-intercepts: $(n\pi, 0)$
y-intercept: $(0, 0)$
Vertical asymptotes: $x = \frac{\pi}{2} + n\pi$
Odd function
Origin symmetry